Central and
South-Eastern Europe
2004

Central and
South-Eastern Europe
2004

4th Edition

 **Europa Publications**
Taylor & Francis Group

LONDON AND NEW YORK

Fourth edition 2003

© **Europa Publications 2003**
11 New Fetter Lane, London, EC4P 4EE, United Kingdom
(A member of the Taylor & Francis Group)

ISBN 1-85743-186-3
ISSN 1470-5699

Editor: Imogen Bell

Regional Organizations Editor: Catriona Appeatu Holman

Statistics Editor: Philip McIntyre

Technology Editor: Ian Preston

Assistant Editors: Camilla Chew, Katie Dawson, Anthony Gladman, Dominic Heaney,
Catriona Marcham, James Middleton, Nicholas Walmesley

Contributors: Rebecca Bomford, Simon Chapman, David Lea,
Gareth Wyn Jones

Typeset by Ignition UK and printed by Unwin Brothers Limited
The Gresham Press
Old Woking, Surrey

FOREWORD

In 1990 Europa Publications began work on a book that finally emerged under the title of EASTERN EUROPE AND THE COMMONWEALTH OF INDEPENDENT STATES. At that time both the Soviet and the Yugoslav federations were still in existence and the book was originally intended to cover eight countries; the second edition covered 27. The subsequent divergence in the course of developments in the former USSR and in Central and South-Eastern Europe has increased. The countries of Central Europe and the Balkans are intent on the 'common European home', on the economic and political institutions of the West. The Baltic states of Estonia, Latvia and Lithuania, although once Soviet republics, have developed democratic systems and reformed their economies, reclaiming the independent statehood possessed before the Second World War. Older links and geographical proximity are reasserting themselves in the definition of the region, notably in the case of Greece, which, culturally and historically, is very much at the heart of South-Eastern Europe.

Even since the third edition of this book was published, in 2002, significant developments have taken place in the region. The symbolic announcement, in November 2002, that the North Atlantic Treaty Organization (NATO) intended to admit the former communist states of Bulgaria, Estonia, Latvia, Lithuania, Romania, Slovakia and Slovenia in 2004, was followed in December 2002 by confirmation that the European Union (EU) planned to admit the Czech Republic, Estonia, Hungary, Latvia, Lithuania, Poland, Slovakia and Slovenia in May of the same year. Subsequently, in a separate development, in February 2003 the Federal Republic of Yugoslavia was reconstituted as the new State Union of Serbia and Montenegro.

Part One of this fourth edition of CENTRAL AND SOUTH-EASTERN EUROPE consists of nine articles on different aspects of the region as a whole, ranging from political and economic issues to the environment and social welfare. In Part Two there are chapters on each of the 16 states, including information on the country, its people, its history, its politics and its economy: a geography and map is followed by a chronology and two essays, one a political narrative, the other an examination of the economy, written by leading area specialists. There is a detailed statistical survey, and directory sections, which give data on major companies, other financial and business organizations, state institutions, religion, culture and the media, to list but a few. The section on government provides information on local administration. Each chapter concludes with a bibliography. Part Three is an up-to-date Political Profiles section, including about 125 biographical outlines of men and women prominent in the region. Regional Information (Part Four) provides details of international organizations operating in Central and South-Eastern Europe, as well as research institutes engaged in the study of the region. There is also a select bibliography of periodicals relevant to the area, and a books bibliography.

The Editor is grateful to all the contributors for their articles and help and to the numerous governments and organizations that provided statistical and other information.

August 2003

ACKNOWLEDGEMENTS

The editors gratefully acknowledge the co-operation, interest and advice of all the authors who contributed to this volume. Thanks are due to Prof. Tom Gallagher for his contribution to the Political Profiles. We are also indebted to many organizations connected with the region, particularly the national statistical offices, whose help is greatly appreciated. We owe special thanks to a number of embassies and ministries. In addition, we are grateful to Edward Oliver, who prepared the maps that are included in this volume.

We are most grateful for permission to make extensive use of material from the following sources: the United Nations' *Demographic Yearbook, Statistical Yearbook, Monthly Bulletin of Statistics, International Trade Statistics Yearbook* and *Industrial Commodity Statistics Yearbook*; the United Nations Educational, Scientific and Cultural Organization's *Statistical Yearbook*; the Food and Agriculture Organization of the United Nations' Statistical Database and *Yearbook of Fishery Statistics*; the International Labour Office's Statistical Database and *Yearbook of Labour Statistics*; the World Bank's *World Bank Atlas, Global Development Finance, World Development Report* and *World Development Indicators*; the International Monetary Fund's Statistical Database and *International Financial Statistics* and *Government Finance Statistics Yearbook*; the World Tourism Organization's *Yearbook of Tourism Statistics*; and *The Military Balance 2002–2003*, a publication of the International Institute for Strategic Studies, Arundel House, 13–15 Arundel Street, London WC2R 3DX.

HEALTH AND WELFARE STATISTICS: SOURCES AND DEFINITIONS

Fertility Source: WHO, *The World Health Report* (2002). The number of children that would be born per woman, assuming no female mortality at child-bearing ages and the age-specific fertility rates of a specified country and period.

Under-5 mortality rate Source: UNICEF, *The State of the World's Children* (2003). The ratio of registered deaths of children under 5 years to the total number of registered live births over the same period.

HIV/AIDS Source: UNAIDS. Estimated percentage of adults aged 15 to 49 years living with HIV/AIDS. <indicates 'fewer than'.

Health expenditure Source: WHO, *The World Health Report* (2002).
US $ per head (PPP)
International dollar estimates, derived by dividing local currency units by an estimate of their purchasing-power parity (PPP) compared with the US dollar. PPPs are the rates of currency conversion that equalize the purchasing power of different currencies by eliminating the differences in price levels between countries.
% of GDP
GDP levels for OECD countries follow the most recent UN System of National Accounts. For non-OECD countries a value was estimated by utilizing existing UN, IMF and World Bank data.
Public expenditure
Government health-related outlays plus expenditure by social schemes compulsorily affiliated with a sizeable share of the population, and extrabudgetary funds allocated to health services. Figures include grants or loans provided by international agencies, other national authorities, and sometimes commercial banks.

Access to water and sanitation Source: WHO, *Global Water Supply and Sanitation Assessment* (2000 Report). Defined in terms of the type of technology and levels of service afforded. For water, this includes house connections, public standpipes, boreholes with handpumps, protected dug wells, protected spring and rainwater collection; allowance is also made for other locally defined technologies. 'Access' is broadly defined as the availability of at least 20 litres per person per day from a source within 1 km of the user's dwelling. Sanitation is defined to include connection to a sewer or septic tank system, pour-flush latrine, simple pit or ventilated improved pit latrine, again with allowance for acceptable local technologies. Access to water and sanitation does not imply that the level of service or quality of water is 'adequate' or 'safe'.

Human Development Index (HDI) Source: UNDP, *Human Development Report* (2002). a summary of human development measured by three basic dimensions: prospects for a long and healthy life, measured by life expectancy at birth; knowledge, measured by adult literacy rate (two-thirds' weight) and the combined gross enrolment ratio in primary, secondary and tertiary education (one-third weight); and standard of living, measured by GDP per head (PPP US $). The index value obtained lies between zero and one. A value above 0.8 indicates high human development, between 0.5 and 0.8 medium human development, and below 0.5 low human development. A centralized data source for all three dimensions was not available for all countries. In some cases other data sources were used to calculate a substitute value; however, this was excluded from the ranking. Other countries, including non-UNDP members, were excluded from the HDI altogether. In total, 173 countries were ranked for 2000.

CONTENTS

CONTENTS

PART THREE

Political Profiles of the Region

PART FOUR

Regional Information

THE CONTRIBUTORS

Othon Anastasakis. St Antony's College, University of Oxford.

Susan Baker. Cardiff University.

Richard Ross Berry. University of Glasgow.

George Blazyca. Professor at the University of Paisley.

Vesna Bojičić. London School of Economics and Political Science, University of London.

Michael Bourdeaux. Keston Institute, Oxford.

Keith S. Brown. Watson Institute, Brown University, Providence.

Cathie Carmichael. University of East Anglia.

Richard Clogg. Professor at St Antony's College, University of Oxford.

Richard J. Crampton. Professor at St Edmund Hall, University of Oxford.

Matthew Dunn. Political analyst for Control Risks Group, London.

David A. Dyker. University of Sussex.

Jonathan Eyal. Director of Studies at the Royal United Services Institute for Defence Studies, London.

Tom Gallagher. Professor at University of Bradford.

Kęstutis Girnius. Radio Free Europe/Radio Liberty, Prague.

Andres Kasekamp. Associate Professor at the University of Tartu.

Michael Kaser. Professor at University of Birmingham and St Antony's College, University of Oxford.

J. Michael Lyons. Latvian correspondent for Agence France-Presse.

Jeffrey Miller. University of Delaware, Newark, DE.

Steven Morrison. Freelance writer on Latvian affairs.

Martin Myant. University of Paisley.

David Norris. University of Nottingham.

Peter Palmer. Senior analyst for the International Crisis Group.

László Péter. Emeritus Professor of History, University of London.

Jan Repa. Senior analyst on Poland and Central Europe, BBC World Service.

Andrew Ryder. University of Portsmouth.

Alan Smith. Professor at the School of Slavonic and East European Studies, University of London.

Mladen Staničić. Director of the Institute for International Relations, Zagreb.

Paul Stubbs. Globalism and Social Policy Programme, University of Sheffield, and social development consultant based in Zagreb, Croatia.

Marcus Tanner. Journalist and author.

Miranda Vickers. Political analyst specializing in Albanian affairs.

Heido Vitsur. Economic analyst, and adviser at the Ministry of Economic Affairs of Estonia.

Gordon Wightman. University of Liverpool.

ABBREVIATIONS

Acad.	Academician; Academy
AD	anno domini
Adm.	Admiral
admin.	administration
a.i.	ad interim
AID	(US) Agency for International Development
AIDS	Acquired Immunodeficiency Syndrome
Al.	Aleja (Alley, Avenue)
Alt.	Alternate
AM	Amplitude Modulation
amalg.	amalgamated
approx.	approximately
asscn	association
assoc.	associate
asst	assistant
Aug.	August
auth.	authorized
Ave.	Avenija (Avenue)
Ave	Avenue
b.	born
BC	before Christ
Bd	Board
Bd.	Bulevardi
b/d	barrels per day
Bldg	Building
blk	block
Blvd	Boulevard
br.(s)	branch(es)
Brig.	Brigadier
BSE	bovine spongiform encephalopathy
BSEC	(Organization of the) Black Sea Economic Co-operation
bul.	bulvar (boulevard)
bulv.	bulvarīs (boulevard)
C	Centigrade
c.	circa; child, children
CAP	Common Agricultural Policy
cap.	capital
Capt.	Captain
CBSS	Council of Baltic Sea States
Cdre	Commodore
CEFTA	Central European Free Trade Agreement
CEI	Central European Initiative
Cen.	Central
CEO	Chief Executive Officer
CFE	Conventional Forces in Europe
Chair.	Chairman/woman
c.i.f.	cost, insurance and freight
CIS	Commonwealth of Independent States
C-in-C	Commander-in-Chief
circ.	circulation
cm	centimetre(s)
CMEA	Council for Mutual Economic Assistance
c/o	care of
Co	Company; County
Col	Colonel
Commdr	Commander
Commdt	Commandant
Commr	Commissioner
Corpn	Corporation
CP	Communist Party
CSCE	Conference on Security and Co-operation in Europe
Cttee	Committee
cu	cubic
cwt	hundredweight
d.	daughter(s)
d.d.	dioničko društvo, delniška družba (Joint-Stock Company)
Dec.	December
dep.	deposits
Dept	Department
devt	development
Dir	Director
DM	Deutsche Mark (German mark)

Dr	Doctor
dwt	dead weight tons
E	East; Eastern
EBRD	European Bank for Reconstruction and Development
EC	European Community
ECE	(United Nations) Economic Commission for Europe
ECO	Economic Co-operation Organization
Econ.	Economist; Economics
ECOSOC	(United Nations) Economic and Social Council
ECU	European Currency Unit
edn	edition
EEC	European Economic Community
EFTA	European Free Trade Association
e.g.	exempli gratia (for example)
EIB	European Investment Bank
e-mail	electronic mail
EMU	economic and monetary union
Eng.	Engineer; Engineering
est.	established; estimate; estimated
et al.	et alii (and others)
etc.	et cetera
EU	European Union
excl.	excluding
exec.	executive
F	Fahrenheit
f.	founded
FAO	Food and Agriculture Organization
FDI	foreign direct investment
Feb.	February
FM	frequency modulation
fmrly	formerly
f.o.b.	free on board
Fr	Father
Fri.	Friday
FRY	Federal Republic of Yugoslavia
FYRM	former Yugoslav republic of Macedonia
ft	foot (feet)
g	gram(s)
GATT	General Agreement on Tariffs and Trade
GDP	gross domestic product
GDR	German Democratic Republic
Gen.	General
GNI	gross national income
GNP	gross national product
Gov.	Governor
Govt	Government
grt	gross registered tons
GWh	gigawatt hours
ha	hectares
HE	His (or Her) Eminence; His (or Her) Excellency
HIV	human immunodeficiency virus
hl	hectolitre(s)
HM	His (or Her) Majesty
Hon.	Honorary (or Honourable)
hp	horsepower
HQ	Headquarters
HRH	His (or Her) Royal Highness
IAEA	International Atomic Energy Agency
IBRD	International Bank for Reconstruction and Development (World Bank)
ibid.	ibidem (from the same source)
ICC	International Chamber of Commerce, International Criminal Court
ICFTU	International Confederation of Free Trade Unions
ICRC	International Committee of the Red Cross
ICTY	International Criminal Tribunal for the former Yugoslavia
IDA	International Development Association
i.e.	id est (that is to say)
ILO	International Labour Organization/Office

ABBREVIATIONS

IMF	International Monetary Fund		p.u.	paid up
in (ins)	inch (inches)		publ.	publication; published
Inc, Incorp., Incd	Incorporated		Publr	Publisher
incl.	including		q.v.	quod vide (to which refer)
Ind.	Independent			
INF	Intermediate-range Nuclear Forces		Rd	Road
Ing.	Engineer		reg., regd	register; registered
Insp.	Inspector		reorg.	reorganized
Int.	International		Rep.	Republic; Representative
IRF	International Road Federation		res	reserve(s)
irreg.	irregular		retd	retired
Is	Islands		Rev.	Reverend
			Rm.	Room
Jan.	January			
JNA	Jugoslovenska narodna armija (Yugoslav People's Army)		s.	son(s)
			S	South; Southern; San
Jr	Junior		SAR	Serbian Autonomous Region
Jt	Joint		SDR(s)	Special Drawing Right(s)
			Sec.	Secretary
kg	kilogram(s)		Secr.	Secretariat
KGB	Komitet Gosudarstvennoi Bezopasnosti (Committee for State Security)		sel.	seleniyi (settlement)
			Sen.	Senior
kHz	kilohertz		Sept.	September
km	kilometre(s)		SFRY	Socialist Federal Republic of Yugoslavia
kom.	komnata (room)		Soc.	Society
kv.	kvartira (apartment); kvartal (apartment block)		Sq.	Square
			sq	square (in measurements)
kW	kilowatt(s)		SS	Saints
kWh	kilowatt hours		SSR	Soviet Socialist Republic
			St	Saint; Street
lb	pound(s)		START	Strategic Arms' Reduction Treaty
LCY	League of Communists of Yugoslavia		Str.	Strada (street)
Lt, Lieut	Lieutenant		Sun.	Sunday
Ltd	Limited		Supt	Superintendent
			sv.	svetac (saint)
m	metre(s)			
m.	married; million		tech., techn.	technical
Maj.	Major		tel.	telephone
Man.	Manager; managing		Thurs.	Thursday
mem.	member		Tř	Třída (avenue)
mfrs	manufacturers		Treas.	Treasurer
Mgr	Monseigneur; Monsignor		Tues.	Tuesday
MHz	megahertz		TV	television
Mil.	Military			
mm	millimetre(s)		u.	utca (street)
Mon.	Monday		u/a	unit of account
MP	Member of Parliament		UK	United Kingdom
MSS	Manuscripts		ul.	ulica, ulice (street)
MW	megawatt(s); medium wave		UN	United Nations
MWh	megawatt hour(s)		UNAIDS	United Nations Joint Programme on HIV/AIDS
			UNCTAD	United Nations Conference on Trade and Development
N	North; Northern			
n.a.	not available		UNDP	United Nations Development Programme
nám.	náměstí (square)		UNEP	United Nations Environment Programme
Nat.	National		UNESCO	United Nations Educational, Scientific and Cultural Organization
NATO	North Atlantic Treaty Organization			
NCO	Non-Commissioned Officer		UNHCHR	United Nations High Commissioner for Human Rights
NGO	non-governmental organization			
NMP	net material product		UNHCR	United Nations High Commissioner for Refugees
no.	number			
Nov.	November		UNICEF	United Nations Children's Fund
nr	near		Univ.	University
nrt	net registered tons		UNPA	United Nations Protected Area
			UNPROFOR	United Nations Protection Force in Yugoslavia
Oct.	October		USA	United States of America
OECD	Organisation for Economic Co-operation and Development		USAID	United States Agency for International Development
OIC	Organization of the Islamic Conference		USSR	Union of Soviet Socialist Republics
OPEC	Organization of the Petroleum Exporting Countries			
			VAT	value-added tax
opp.	opposite		Ven.	Venerable
Org.	Organization		VHF	Very High Frequency
OSCE	Organization for Security and Co-operation in Europe		viz.	videlicet (namely)
			vol.(s)	volume(s)
p.	page		W	West; Western
p.a.	per annum		WCL	World Confederation of Labour
Parl.	Parliament(ary)		Wed.	Wednesday
Perm. Rep.	Permanent Representative		WEU	Western European Union
pl.	ploshchad (square)		WFTU	World Federation of Trade Unions
PLC	Public Limited Company		WHO	World Health Organization
POB	Post Office Box		WTO	World Trade Organization
pr.	praspekt (avenue)			
Pres.	President		YPA	Yugoslav People's Army
Prin.	Principal		yr	year
Prof.	Professor			
Pte	Private			

INTERNATIONAL TELEPHONE CODES

To make international calls to telephone and fax numbers listed in *Central and South-Eastern Europe*, dial the international code of the country from which you are calling, followed by the appropriate country code for the organization you wish to call (listed below), followed by the area code (if applicable) and telephone or fax number listed in the entry.

	Country code	+ GMT*
Albania	355	+1
Bosnia and Herzegovina	387	+1
Bulgaria	359	+2
Croatia	385	+1
Czech Republic	420	+1
Estonia	372	+2
Greece	30	+2
Hungary	36	+1
Latvia	371	+2
Lithuania	370	+2

	Country code	+ GMT*
Macedonia, former Yugoslav republic	389	+1
Poland	48	+1
Romania	40	+2
Serbia and Montenegro	381	+1
Slovakia	421	+1
Slovenia	386	+1

* Time difference in hours + Greenwhich Mean Time (GMT). The times listed compare the standard (winter) times. Some countries adopt Summer (Daylight Saving) Times—i.e. + 1 hour—for part of the year.

EXPLANATORY NOTE ON THE DIRECTORY SECTION

The Directory section of each chapter is arranged under the following headings, where they apply:

THE CONSTITUTION

THE GOVERNMENT
    HEAD OF STATE
    CABINET/COUNCIL OF MINISTERS
    MINISTRIES

LEGISLATURE

LOCAL GOVERNMENT

POLITICAL ORGANIZATIONS

DIPLOMATIC REPRESENTATION

JUDICIAL SYSTEM

RELIGION

THE PRESS

PUBLISHERS

BROADCASTING AND COMMUNICATIONS
    TELECOMMUNICATIONS
    RADIO
    TELEVISION

FINANCE
    CENTRAL BANK
    STATE BANKS
    DEVELOPMENT BANKS
    COMMERCIAL BANKS
    FOREIGN BANKS
    STOCK EXCHANGE
    INSURANCE

TRADE AND INDUSTRY
    GOVERNMENT AGENCIES
    DEVELOPMENT ORGANIZATIONS

    CHAMBERS OF COMMERCE
    INDUSTRIAL AND TRADE ASSOCIATIONS
    EMPLOYERS' ASSOCIATIONS
    UTILITIES
    MAJOR COMPANIES
    TRADE UNIONS

TRANSPORT
    RAILWAYS
    ROADS
    INLAND WATERWAYS
    SHIPPING
    CIVIL AVIATION

TOURISM

CULTURE
    NATIONAL ORGANIZATIONS
    CULTURAL HERITAGE
    SPORTING ORGANIZATIONS
    PERFORMING ARTS
    ASSOCIATIONS

EDUCATION
    UNIVERSITIES

SOCIAL WELFARE
    NATIONAL AGENCIES
    HEALTH AND WELFARE ORGANIZATIONS

ENVIRONMENT
    GOVERNMENT ORGANIZATIONS
    ACADEMIC INSTITUTIONS
    NON-GOVERNMENTAL ORGANIZATIONS
    REGIONAL ORGANIZATIONS

DEFENCE

PART ONE

General Survey

CENTRAL AND SOUTH-EASTERN EUROPE: FINALLY UNITED, STILL DIFFERENTIATED

Dr JONATHAN EYAL

More than one decade after the demise of communism in Central and South-Eastern Europe, the main questions facing the region had been answered: Europe and its multilateral institutions—chiefly the European Union (EU) and the North Atlantic Treaty Organization (NATO)—were to embrace nations throughout the region, from the Baltics to the Black Sea. For the first time in Europe's history, therefore, there had been an explicit and very public admission that the economic prosperity, political stability and military security of each nation, however small or large, however well-developed or economically underdeveloped, however 'old' or 'new', however heterogeneous or ethnically homogenous, and however distant from the old centre of Europe's power base, belonged to the same family and was, at least theoretically, entitled to the same level of protection and the same voice in the councils of the continent. None of the problems that will be outlined in this analysis can detract from the sheer magnitude of this achievement. The old psychological barriers that divided the continent had not disappeared, and were unlikely to do so for many years to come. However, at least in practical and legal terms, the problems of, say, Romania deserved as much attention in Western European centres, such as the United Kingdom and France, as did those of Belgium. For the generation born after the end of the 'Cold War' this would seem only natural and logical; for those who lived through the long period of ideological confrontation, the same reality would continue to be regarded as nothing short of a miracle. The fact that this outcome was achieved in small stages, through a mixture of conscious decision and accident, and often against the instincts of a majority of Europe's political leaders, made this development even more remarkable. However, from late 2002 a new reality also became evident: although Central and South-Eastern Europe might be being recognized as an equal part of the continent, the region was reasserting its own identity.

After last-minute debates over the tiniest of economic details, the EU had finally decided on the largest territorial enlargement since its creation. In October 2002 the European Council confirmed that no fewer than eight countries from the former communist eastern part of Europe (the Czech Republic, Estonia, Hungary, Latvia, Lithuania, Poland, Slovakia and Slovenia) were to be invited to join the EU in 2004, and accession negotiations were concluded at the Copenhagen summit, Denmark, in December 2002. Gone were the old ideological dividing lines, which harked back to the Second World War. Gone, too, were the recriminations between the victors and the vanquished in that War. By May 2004, when the enlargement was due to be completed, the EU would have a larger population than the USA and, if all went well, a larger economy as well. It was, without exaggeration, one of the most significant events in Europe's modern history. Yet, the reality remained that no-one knew how the enlargement would work out: it had the potential to make Europe flourish, but it also held the danger of creating massive social and economic problems. It remained an exercise without precedent and, therefore, without any established rules.

The exercise was enormously complex. During the first two decades of its existence, what was to become the EU had comprised just six states (Belgium, France, Germany, Italy, Luxembourg and the Netherlands), which shared more or less the same standards of living, the same traumas of the Second World War and similar political arrangements. In 1973 three additional countries joined, one of them large (the United Kingdom), and two smaller (Denmark and Ireland). Greece became a member in 1981, and Portugal and Spain were admitted in 1986. Austria, Finland and Sweden became members in 1995. In 2004, however, 10 new countries (including Cyprus and Malta) were to enter the Union, in just one stage, adding around 74m. citizens to the EU, thus increasing its population by some 20%. The new members would range from a country the size of Poland, a nation of almost 40m. people, to the Baltic countries (Estonia, Latvia and Lithuania), each with a population of less than 4m. The new members would also be relatively poor; in aggregate terms, their per-head income was just one-third the EU average. They were also fragile democracies: Slovenia, for example, came into existence as an independent state less than 15 years ago; others, like the Baltic countries, had been briefly independent in the first half of the 20th century, only to be absorbed, for decades, into the USSR. Across the region, societies were still recovering from the effects of communist dictatorship.

Western Europe, much wealthier, and with a longer history of independent existence, was asserting, with a sense of self-righteousness, that it remained prepared to pay the price for helping its poorer Eastern brethren to attain its level of economic development. Perhaps, but at least in the short term there was little evidence of magnanimity. Almost one-half of the EU's existing budget was spent on agricultural subsidies. Central and South-Eastern Europe, which had large numbers of poor farmers, hoped to benefit from similar funding, but those countries invited to join the EU had been promised barely one-quarter of these subsidies. The ongoing reform of the Common Agricultural Policy was to be welcomed, but its net effect would not be to increase agricultural subsidies to Central and South-Eastern Europe; instead, it would merely mean a shift in emphasis, and a possible reduction in financial transfers to Western European farmers, who would remain a privileged group. Overall, the entire enlargement project would cost the EU only 0.07% of its existing gross domestic product (GDP). In summary, this was a huge historic project, but not the greatest transfer of resources to poorer countries.

In their defence, Western European leaders emphasized the fact that enlargement did not only consists of subsidies, but involved opening up markets to further trade. Although this was true, it was not at all obvious that new members would benefit rapidly. Economies emerging from communism required an adaptable labour market, incentives for foreign investment and the flexibility to manage their own currencies. However, in order to join the EU, new members had to eliminate many of the incentives that they provided to non-European investors (Poland, for example, reneged on special tax concession promised to car manufacturers in the Republic of Korea), accept new social provisions that would make labour more expensive, and were scheduled to adopt economic and monetary union (EMU), with its own rigid criteria. In essence, the new members were expected to implement an economic regime more suited to mature, developed economies.

Certainly, in the long term, the effects were likely to be hugely beneficial: the political stability associated with membership of the EU would attract foreign investment and stimulate local economies. The question was how long this period of transition would last, and whether it would, in fact, be longer and more arduous inside, rather than outside the EU. The evidence was mixed: the economy of Ireland, in the northern part of Europe, had performed strongly since its accession; Greece, however, on the southern part of the continent, remained the poorest EU member state, despite its positive economic and political progress. The reason for this disparity was the quality of the national administration and, unfortunately, the new countries that were about to join were—with certain exceptions—more likely to reproduce the pattern of Greece than Ireland.

The EU was designed for countries with efficient bureaucracies; the existing body of EU legislation that the new members were required to digest extended to over 50,000 laws and regulations, laid out in 175,000 pages of text, covering everything from the quality of fruit in a market stall, to the system of taxation. The new countries had been negotiating these details with the EU for years, but, at least in the short term, all they had done was to pledge that the laws would be respected. There was considerable doubt that this would be possible; in many of the new member states, bureaucracies remained ineffective, with high levels of corruption.

The EU evidently hoped that, as time went by, such problems would diminish. The complication, however, was that nobody knew how the people of Central and South-Eastern Europe would react to these new opportunities. Instead of waiting for prosperity to arrive in their countries, new nations might well decide to move in search of prosperity. The EU estimated that, when borders were opened for the free movement of people in 2004, only a few million would migrate to the wealthier part of the continent in search of employment. However, demographic projections and patterns of migration were among the least predictable statistics. What could be said with certainty was that millions of Central and South-Eastern Europeans were unemployed, and many more were already working illegally inside the Union. Since Western European nations were barely reproducing themselves, while Central and South-Eastern Europe had both a young population and surplus labour, opening the frontiers made perfect economic sense. The risk was that if large numbers of people began to migrate at the same time, this might fuel prejudice in the West. Yet, without closing the borders again—which was unthinkable—the Union has no other mechanism to stem this human flow.

Of course, the picture was not entirely negative. The aspirant members had only recently escaped from the influence of the USSR, and had no desire to become mere colonies in a new empire. They would demand greater input in the EU, and a more democratic method of reaching decisions. Nor were the new countries particularly interested in ideas, such as those expressed by the French, for the creation of a European army. The EU of the future would be more than merely a free-trade area, but would also be likely to remain something less than a 'superpower'. For Europe's partners around the world, this was just about the best possible outcome.

Thus, the enlargement must be considered to be progress, provided those involved were prepared to admit that what they were undertaking was only the beginning of a long and painful process of accommodation, a gamble that was evidently worth taking, but in which mistakes could still be made. Although a rational approach would have been to debate all these points, the entire process was marked by almost total silence throughout Europe. The political elites in both the aspirant countries and in the 15 existing members states limited themselves to meticulous discussion of agricultural production quotas and subsidies, but barely mentioned their future arrangements, so that the continent's citizens knew very little about the historic dimension of the process.

Economic difficulties were almost certain to dominate events until accession. Uncertainties over timing and terms of entry to EMU were likely to keep Central and South-Eastern European currency and bond markets volatile; the IMF did not expect any former communist states to join the eurozone before 2008. Of course, it was important to recall the legal framework for the operation of the common European currency, the euro. Under the relevant agreements, the Treaty on European Union, or Maastricht Treaty, effective from 1 November 1993, and the subsequent treaties that envisaged the enlargement of the Union, including the key Treaty of Nice, which entered into force on 1 February 2002, the prospective member states would not have the freedom to 'opt out' of any obligations of membership, including that of monetary union. Existing member states, however, such as the United Kingdom, Denmark and Sweden, were permitted to maintain their exclusion from the provisions of monetary union for as long as they wished. The question for the new countries was, therefore, not whether they joined EMU, but when, and under what conditions. The membership negotiations were well-advanced, although details of their entry into the eurozone were not being disclosed. The main reason was not so much to prevent speculation concerning the exchange band by which the new currencies' rates of exchange would be fixed to the euro—although this was crucial to their immediate economic well being, and Hungary had already implemented measures to devalue its currency—but rather more because the Union was divided over the operation of the enlargement of the eurozone, and any precedent created was likely to be adopted permanently by future members. In purely legal terms, each country had to fix its rate of exchange to a reference rate in relation to the euro for a period of no less than two years. Only when this period expired could the country concerned adopt the euro as its national legal tender, while accepting all the obligations of the operation of the currency, including the jurisdiction of the European Central Bank (ECB) in Frankfurt, Germany. Theoretically, it was possible to join the so-called Exchange Rate Mechanism (ERM) as soon as a country had concluded the negotiation and ratification process for entering the EU, which was expected to take place by the end of 2003, at the latest, for all the candidate countries. Under this scenario, therefore, the Central and South-Eastern European applicant states could adopt the European single currency by the time they became full members in 2004. But there were two practical difficulties with this approach. First, the legalities were fairly opaque; it was possible to argue that a country could join the ERM at any stage after it had been promised a date for full EU membership, but it was equally possible to claim that the candidate country could only join the mechanism once it had become a member of the EU. Indeed, a rigid reading of existing EU treaties would point to the second interpretation. According to this, the earliest the countries of the former communist block could actually adopt the euro was towards the end of 2006. Secondly, many candidate countries might prefer to wait a little longer, if only to continue enjoying the flexibility of their currency rates, at a time when their transition from a state-controlled economy had still to be completed. Finally, there was the political question of whether national governments in the region would wish to force the public to assess the benefits of EU membership and membership of the currency union at the same time. In some countries this would not be a problem; in others, it could become a sensitive political issue.

The debate about the merits of each scenario was very much part of the internal political discussions of each candidate state. Supporters of rapid monetary integration argued that euro membership would encourage growth by reducing the cost of financing and servicing debt and by linking economies more effectively, stimulate trade by eliminating exchange-rate risks, and raise wealth by increasing the value of all types of asset. Sceptics predictably argued that the euro criteria would hinder attempts by the former communist countries to close the gap in wealth between them and their richer Western neighbours, demand reforms that were too severe for societies to bear, and involve too hasty a loss of freedom in economic policy-making.

A decision on the parity rate, the fairly rigid rate of exchange by which national currencies were to be locked into the ERM, and the date when ERM entry could take place, was to be taken by the ECB, the central banks of candidate states and political leaders. However, there was a further complication. Under the ERM procedures, the two years' preparation was the minimum required, not the maximum advisable. There was, thus, the possibility that countries might wish to lock their currencies into the ERM, but then take longer than usual to adopt the euro. The ECB had already signalled its desire that some poorer candidates should spend longer than two years in the ERM to allow more time for wage and price levels to move closer to the EU average. The ECB was keen to see evidence of 'real' economic convergence, where faster growth than that recorded in the existing EU member states would raise living standards, as opposed to 'nominal' convergence, where the currency of applicants would appreciate in value, but wealth disparities would remain the same.

Membership of the ERM was supposed to smooth a currency's entry to the euro, and the ECB pledged to intervene to prevent speculators driving a nation's money out of the 30% fluctuation margin (which permitted fluctuations in currencies of 15% in either direction). The candidate countries would also be required to satisfy economic conditions, widely known as the Maastricht criteria, which stipulated that national debt amount to less than 60% of GDP, that the fiscal deficit amount to less than 3% of GDP, and that the annual rate of inflation be no more than 1.5% higher than the average of the three euro-zone members with the lowest rates of inflation. Analysts predicted few problems for most countries in meeting debt criteria, but reducing inflation and public spending was expected to be arduous and politically costly for many euro hopefuls. The ECB said it would not ease entry criteria, although there were some demands for a softer stance on inflation, given the relatively small weight new members would have in the euro-zone economy and the challenges they face in overcoming communist-era economic legacies.

Hungary was the furthest advanced of the candidate countries, at least in terms of mental preparedness for the adoption of the euro. Entry terms and targets were already part of political debate, with the ruling coalition eager to join as soon as possible. Both the Government and the central bank hoped that Hungary could join both the EU and ERM in 2004, and the eurozone in 2006. In Poland, central bankers also desired early euro entry, in order to push down borrowing costs and import currency stability. However, the leftist Government formed in October 2001 had taken a more cautious approach, arguing that the weak economy needed time to return to health and create auspicious conditions for euro entry. Under Polish law, government and central bank decided jointly any changes to the exchange-rate regime. Being so small, the economies of the Baltic region were of less concern.

For the moment, confusion reigned on this topic, as both the EU and the countries of the region attempted to keep the issue fluid and undetermined. A statement was likely to be made by the end of 2003 to confirm that a ruling on entry into the ERM would be made at a later date, probably in the second half of 2005. The question of how long individual countries would spend inside the ERM, whether this would be two years, or

more, would be kept open, with the eventual decision being based on individual circumstances. This had the advantage of maintaining pressure on the new members to put their finances in order, while ensuring the integrity of the euro system. The result would, therefore, be that the earliest appearance of the euro as a national currency in former communist states was likely to be at the end of 2007 or in mid-2008, and the process was not likely to be completed until the end of the decade in the remaining regional member states. The certainty of these countries' membership would, however, provide benefits for their economic activities from as early as 2004.

Bulgaria and Romania were to remain outside the wave of enlargement in 2004. This decision was undoubtedly correct, and actually beneficial to local economies. Because the promise of full membership was enshrined in international treaties, the two Balkan states had the best possible guarantee that if they completed all the accession procedures, they would finally enter. The old problem of offering promises to Balkan states without offering guarantees had, therefore, gone. Indeed, European politicians had been quite explicit in their statements that, if all went well, Bulgaria and Romania would join by 2007. There was a reasonable expectation, therefore, that developments in these two countries would be positive. They continued to encounter huge problems in adapting the EU's *acquis communautaire*, the body of necessary legislation, treaties and case law, but there is little doubt that efforts would be made to reach the target date. A much larger problem hovered over other countries in the Balkans, specifically Albania, Bosnia and Herzegovina, Croatia, the former Yugoslav republic of Macedonia (FYRM), Serbia and Montenegro and the Serbian province of Kosovo, which was effectively a UN protectorate. Here, the EU had explicitly refused to make any promises, and it was difficult to see how EU membership could be offered before the middle of the next decade. Thus, the fact remained that a large part of the Balkans—indeed, the majority of the countries of that region—would remain outside the scope of the EU. The EU was engaged in a major reconstruction effort in the region, and the Balkans were the recipients of much of the EU aid programme. A great deal had been achieved, but the Balkans remained Europe's most problematic area, differentiated in every possible way from the rest of the continent.

The same, in many respects, could be said about another major development, agreement on the further enlargement of NATO, announced at an Alliance summit meeting in Prague, Czech Republic, in November 2002. The Czech Republic, Hungary and Poland had been invited to become members of the Alliance in 1997. The subsequent decision to admit Bulgaria, Estonia, Latvia, Lithuania, Romania, Slovakia and Slovenia from 2004 was remarkable in no less than four respects. First, it represented NATO's largest-scale enlargement since its foundation in the late 1940s. Second, it broke the taboo that countries that had formed part of the USSR proper, such as the Baltic states, should not be included in the Alliance. Furthermore, once the enlargement process was completed, NATO would not only border Russia (apart from in the far north-west, something that would have been unthinkable even one year previously), but would actually isolate the Russian enclave of Kaliningrad altogether. Remarkably, therefore, provisions would have to be put in place to allow the transit of Russian troops through NATO territory. Finally, the most substantial aspect of the enlargement, at least in terms of territory and potential military assets, was taking place in South-Eastern Europe, the most turbulent area of the continent, in which virtually no Western government originally wished to become involved.

It would be harsh to suggest that NATO's enlargement would not have a substantial effect on all of Europe. Indeed, the almost universal rejoicing that greeted the Alliance's decision was the clearest indication of a widespread perception that NATO's arrival in the region would have a profound impact. However, most of the people in the candidate countries, as well as a large proportion of their political class, merely viewed this event in its broad historic terms: as representing the obliteration of old ideological division lines, and as a final 'recompense' for the alleged 'betrayal' of Eastern Europe by the West at the end of the Second World War. This view was not necessarily wrong; after all, an older generation could still recall the time when it became apparent that Central and South-Eastern European nations were destined to become part of the Soviet empire; for the population of the Baltics it had entailed the utter obliteration of their independent existence. Furthermore, all generations shared the view that their countries' social and economic troubles could be ascribed to these Western machinations over half a century before. The fact that NATO no longer claimed to be, and was not, the same alliance of the Cold War years remained utterly immaterial for most ordinary people; they viewed NATO in its original guise, as a military organization created and managed by the USA, a body that, almost by definition, was there to prevent another Russian onslaught. Yet again, the fact that nations continued to adhere to this antiquated view should not be criticized too much. When communism collapsed, the Baltic states were told that it would be decades before they would be allowed to become full members of any military alliance, while the countries of South-Eastern Europe, which were theoretically offered a better prospect of military integration, nevertheless remained mere spectators in the broader security debate that ranged across their continent. The views of all these countries were seldom sought, and even less frequently taken into account. As a result, politicians remained focused on one notion: whether Europe's two chief institutions, NATO and the EU, were prepared to accept them. No serious debate had ever taken place over what these institutions stood for, how they might change as a result of the collapse of communism, or what they had to offer to the region; the entire issue was distilled into a simple question of either full membership or total isolation. The outcome was the worst possible: a lack of understanding about what NATO represented in the post-Cold War period, coupled with uneven military reform throughout the region, and an ever greater determination to become a member of the Alliance at any cost. The idea of a leisurely, organized enlargement—an almost 'scientific' exercise in managing European security—ultimately failed. Furthermore, when the decision to enlarge was taken in Prague, it was the US President, George W. Bush, who travelled to convey the old message that this process was, after all, about the final triumph of the West in the Cold War. In a victory lap, which took him from Vilnius, Lithuania, on the Baltic Sea to Bucharest, Romania, in the Balkans, the speeches of the US President emphasized the countries' liberation from communism and recompense for previous suffering under dictatorship, a reiteration of the points made by his father, George Bush, during his own tenure as US leader more than one decade previously. The political reasons for President Bush's actions were understandable, but the result was the same: a simplistic belief that NATO's enlargement amounted to the last triumph of the USA over the old USSR.

In the years to come, the nations of Central and South-Eastern Europe would discover that, although NATO would provide many advantages, many of these would belong much more to the psychological realm, while the practicalities of regional security remained to be addressed. Nevertheless, the psychological effects of NATO's enlargements remained overwhelmingly beneficial, and were considerable. They can be broadly classified as follows:

Independence becomes immutable. There would no longer be any question that foreign domination over small nations could return;

A diminished 'Balkans complex'. The Balkans had suffered for more than a century from the belief that, whatever they did, the rest of Europe would continue to regard the region in terms of a problem that required a solution, rather than as simply a geographic area that would benefit from incorporation into continent-wide institutions. The fact that, at the height of the West's preoccupation with Yugoslavia during the mid-1990s, NATO rebuffed the membership applications of countries such as Romania and Slovenia was held as further proof of this supposedly unalterable historic fact. The complex was now waning: for the first time since independence, countries in South-Eastern Europe had been invited to become full members of one of the West's most important institutions;

Compensation for slower EU integration. For the Baltic states, NATO membership would nicely complement EU membership, which would be happening at the same time. However, Bulgaria and Romania had long accepted that they would not become full members of the EU in 2004. Although there was no legal correlation between the two institutions, there was a connection in the minds of European citizens; if NATO failed to admit countries such as Bulgaria and Romania, it would have been very difficult for the EU to justify a postponement of the membership claims of both countries at the same time. As matters stood, however, the Bulgarian and Romanian Governments will find it easier to justify their inferior position with regard to the EU accession negotiations to their own national electorates. The postponement of EU membership was more easily digestible when it was accompanied by feverish preparations for membership of NATO;

Greater flexibility for the EU accession process. Indirectly, the EU was likely to gain a great deal from NATO's decision. The fact that the Baltic states were being admitted to NATO eliminated any need for the EU to claim that it was providing military security in the Baltic region. The EU was also awarded some additional flexibility in the Balkans. Bulgaria and Romania had succeeded in their demands to be provided with a 'road map', containing guide-lines, with detailed timetables, relating to their EU accession negotiations, and a guarantee that, if all went well, they would be admitted as full members in 2007. The EU was aware that fulfilment of this guarantee would depend not only on the future performance of Bulgaria and Romania, but also on the impact of large-scale enlargement in 2004 on the Union itself. If NATO failed to invite Bulgaria and Romania, the EU's membership promise to these countries would have carried even less weight. As it was, the EU could not only claim that its pledge to admit Bulgaria and Romania in the future was genuine, but could also derive one further advantage: that of a positive discrimination between the applications of Bulgaria and Romania. Largely for accidental reasons, Bulgaria and Romania had been bracketed together in their EU membership applications, despite the fact that Bulgaria's progress was slightly more promising, and the sheer size of Romania's economy and problems effectively put the country in a separate category. If neither of these Balkan countries was admitted to NATO, any acknowledgement of their differences by the EU would have been likely to be interpreted as an impossible further humiliation for Romania. Instead, the EU had gained some additional room for manoeuvre: although it remained likely that Bulgaria and Romania would enter the EU at the same time, the EU was able to begin implementing a discreet differentiation in the membership applications of the two countries, and would be able to disregard the Romanian outrage that was likely to follow;

Normalized relations in the region. The idea of intra-Balkan co-operation was as old as the region itself and, overall, it remained a myth. All the countries of the region experienced the same economic problems: all had bloated agricultural sectors, a decrepit industrial base, surplus and largely unskilled labour, and an urgent demand for foreign investment. Far from being economically compatible, the countries of South-Eastern Europe remained competitors. Nevertheless, a great deal could be done to simplify border procedures, improve transport infrastructure and co-operate in the fight against organized crime. With NATO's guarantee in place, these tasks could begin to be tackled, although words would continue to speak louder than deeds when it came to Balkan co-operation;

Better relations with the former Yugoslavia. With the exception of Slovenia, none of the republics of the former Yugoslavia was invited to join the Alliance. Indeed, one of the largest, and little-mentioned, disappointments of the 2002 NATO summit was that the Alliance failed to conclude a new partnership agreement with the Federal Republic of Yugoslavia. Nevertheless, the fact that very soon several NATO countries were to border its successor state, Serbia and Montenegro, was likely to have a beneficial effect on all of the former Yugoslav republics. The countries that were to join the Alliance had different views of this Balkan conflict—both Bulgaria and Romania wanted NATO to move away from a narrow fixation on pursuing alleged war criminals and towards a more genuine engagement with the Government of Serbia and Montenegro and the country's military. Furthermore, the Alliance would have to deepen its partnership programmes with the former Yugoslav states. No answers would be provided for Bosnia and Herzegovina and Kosovo, two territories that were likely to remain in abeyance. However, the Alliance's relations with Bosnia and Herzegovina, Croatia and the FYRM, as well as Albania, were certain to receive increased attention;

The virtual disappearance of old territorial disputes. Hidden, informal, but popular resentment at perceived old historic injustices would not evaporate overnight. Nevertheless, NATO membership subtly raised the threshold of acceptability in articulating such demands. This was already clear in Romania. In the preceding decade up to one-fifth of the Romanian electorate had routinely voted for parties which campaigned vigorously against the supposed Hungarian territorial threat to Transylvania, but it could not legitimately be argued that such a threat continued to exist. The fact that Hungary was unable to raise old territorial or ethnic disputes in the process of ratifying NATO's enlargement (if only because the ratification process concerned seven countries, and it was inconceivable that the Hungarian parliament would either single out Romania or block the path of other candidates) provided additional reassurance. Over the previous decade, there had also been quite substantial support in Romania for a potential union with neighbouring Moldova. Certainly, this historically romantic view was already waning before NATO issued its invitation to Romania, but subsequently it became truly moribund: no ordinary Romanian was likely to argue that, in order to keep alive the dream of reunification with Moldova, the country should decline the offer of NATO membership. A similar effect could be observed in Bulgaria, where ideas of a possible historic link with Macedonia were truly dead. Both Estonia and Latvia had their own historic territorial disputes. Once again, any resentment would not disappear overnight, but leaders in those countries would be able to deal with past issues on a more rational basis;

Normal relations with Russia. Paradoxically, precisely because candidate countries viewed NATO's enlargement as Russia's ultimate defeat, once the process of enlargement was completed, this might give them greater flexibility in dealing with their giant eastern neighbour. Indeed, Romania finally signed a friendship and co-operation treaty with Russia in July 2003; since 1992 all attempts to negotiate such a treaty had been blocked by Romanian public opinion, which remained focused on highly emotive historic disputes, such as demands for compensation for Romanian jewels retained by the USSR after the First World War, or demands that Russia officially repudiate the Treaty of Non-aggression with Germany (the Nazi-Soviet Pact) of 1939. In Bulgaria's case the scenario was reversed, but the outcome was likely to be the same. Successive Bulgarian Governments stood accused of co-operating too much with Russia; one of the chief claims of Prime Minister Simeon Saxe-Coburg-Gotha (2001–) was precisely that he would turn Bulgaria's foreign policy away from Russia. Now, this false dichotomy no longer mattered. In the Baltics, too, disputes over the status of ethnic Russians, access to the Russian enclave of Kaliningrad and broader economic co-operation with Russia could be discussed calmly. Furthermore, Russia had shown that it was ready to seize the opportunity. Unlike the situation in 1997, Russian ambassadors throughout Europe did not criticize the Alliance's enlargement decision, but emphasized the possibilities for further co-operation. Russia would not be entirely trusted for decades to come, but its involvement could now be viewed more pragmatically;

Some normality in national politics. One of the defining disputes in internal politics in each candidate country was the claim by various leaders that only they would be able to 'deliver' full NATO membership. On the whole, this debate mirrored the divide between reformed former communists and those who were untainted by association with the past. In Bulgaria the rightist Union of Democratic Forces Government of 1997–2001 had claimed that it would guide the country into NATO, and similar situations prevailed in Romania and in the Baltic states. Ultimately, this left–right divide did not matter. In Romania in 1997 the explicitly anti-communist Government failed to secure admission to NATO, and it was President Ion Iliescu, once the ideology chief of the communist party, who received his country's invitation to join the Alliance. For those who fought against communism for five decades, this might represent the final irony but, seen in a broader context, the effect could be positive. Arid debate about a politicians' past activities would slowly recede, as had been the case in Poland, where it was President Aleksander Kwaśniewski, a former communist, and not Lech Wałęsa, the former Solidarity leader (see the chapter on Poland), who led the country into NATO. Personalities were still likely to dominate local politics, but politicians would no longer be able to claim that they were the West's 'favourites' or that their opponents would not be 'accepted' by the West. In short, politics would slowly begin to resemble that elsewhere in Europe, once the debate moved away from the simple one of being either in or out of Europe's institutions.

No one who had followed regional events, or who had even a superficial familiarity with their history could deny that the advantages are substantial. Yet the reality remained that many of these achievements were confined to a change in mentality and the dissipation of old historic fears; they were important, but they represented only the beginning of the process of reshaping Europe's security map.

A potential source of discomfort in the years to come was the likelihood of corruption scandals relating to arms procurement projects. Defence-equipment contracts, always keenly contested and involving billions of dollars of highly-complex offset production arrangements, were traditional sources of corruption in even the most law-abiding countries. It was therefore possible that when similar contracts were discussed in the accession countries some incidences of corruption might be unavoidable.

Further scandals were possible in an area that had been barely addressed by the latest round of NATO enlargement: that of the security services. Here, the Baltic states were better placed, if only because their security services had been created from scratch after the collapse of the USSR. In the Balkans, however, the problem was acute. Uniquely among former communist countries in Europe, Romania's security services were answerable directly to the President. He not only appointed the heads of the internal and external security services, but also intervened in lower-level personnel promotions and was the recipient of their reports. The military intelligence service was the only security organization under a government department, the Ministry of Defence, but even this ministry was controlled by a close confidant of the President. The Romanian Prime Minister was, therefore, virtually 'blind' when it came to intelligence material; he had no input into even the budgets of the security services. Romania had no fewer than four of these 'special' services, and the battle for control of these bodies had been ongoing since the beginning of the 1990s and had, if anything, worsened as a result of increasing political confrontation between Adrian Năstase, the Prime Minister, and Iliescu. In this respect, at least, the situation in Bulgaria appeared to be better. Although the Bulgarian President had nominal access to these services, they were effectively controlled by the Bulgarian Government, and the country's parliament had a committee that was quite active in such matters. The problem in Bulgaria was that the security services remained full of people educated in Russia, probably the largest concentration anywhere in Europe. The Alliance might claim that Russia had become a trusted partner, but NATO military planners were under no illusion that this 'partnership' with Russia extended to espionage activities. Thus, the Alliance was faced with a choice of working with the Romanian intelligence services—relatively efficient and well-informed, but alleged to be venal and under looser control—or the Bulgarian services, less effective, but under better political control. Unless this problem was resolved, neither country would be in a position to make much impact in the decision-making mechanism at NATO's headquarters.

The politicians in the candidate countries might not yet realize it, but membership of the Alliance would also entail making some difficult choices about their existing constitutional set-up. In many of the candidate countries, the heads of state continued to retain a fair degree of control (and, in Romania, almost full control) over foreign and security policy. Theoretically, this could continue. But, in practice, NATO membership entailed some hasty decision-making, which, in turn, depended on smooth co-ordination between the foreign and defence ministries in each country. Such co-ordination was best accomplished at the prime ministerial level; France, which tried to run foreign and security policy from the presidency and the government at the same time had some awful experiences in NATO. The fact that a similar situation existed in co-ordinating policy towards the EU would increase the impetus for constitutional reform inside the candidate countries. The powers of the head of state had become a contentious issue in all the accession countries, and the debate was likely to intensify in the years to come.

For the moment, however, politicians in Eastern Europe had set their sights on a much narrower objective: the possibility of maximizing the potential of their invitations to join NATO by holding early elections and securing another term in office. Both the Bulgarian and the Romanian Governments were considering the idea, with the Romanians slightly more in favour. Again, the concept sounded beneficial, at least at first sight. Neither Bulgaria nor Romania could offer their electorates great economic progress, but the assumption in both countries was that the euphoria generated by the invitation to join the Alliance would make up for the Government's temporary unpopularity. However, politicians were likely to be disappointed. There was no historic evidence to suggest that NATO membership could be translated into popular votes; indeed, the Czech, Hungarian and Polish Governments all lost power after their countries were invited to join the Alliance in 1997. The Bulgarian and Romanian Governments were likely to discover rapidly that the euphoria generated by NATO would be short-lived. This, in essence, was the verdict over the entire exercise. Psychologically, NATO's expansion into the Baltics and the Balkans remained important: for the first time in centuries, Europe's sensitive flanks had become wholly part of the continent. But the security offered remained conditional, and most of the problems that beset the candidate countries could not be resolved by the Alliance.

However, in a curious way, the two issues of NATO and the EU came into one for Central and South-Eastern Europe over the dispute that dominated events in the region in the first half of 2003: that of the war in Iraq, and its wider ramifications for European–US relations. Indeed, the fiercest intra-European diplomatic battle took place over the position of the 10 former communist countries of Eastern Europe that were candidates for EU membership and soon to become NATO members. It was at times an undignified dispute, but a crucial one, for the outcome of this confrontation would decide the shape not only of Europe's trans-Atlantic relations, but also of the EU.

Surprisingly, given the torrent of diplomatic abuse that they received from the media in many Western European countries, the nations of Central and South-Eastern Europe reacted to the crisis in Iraq in very similar terms to the remainder of Europe. Opinion polls conducted in the former communist east indicated that large majorities of the population were against the war. There was also a high degree of cynicism about the USA's policies in the Middle East. Finally, the idea that the USA was fighting the war in order to control petroleum sources was as prevalent in the east as it was in the western part of the continent. The difference, however, was that politicians in the East were under very little pressure from their electorates to address the issue and, as the dispute developed, both populations and their leaders in the East became much more determined in their support for the USA. The reasons for this change were complicated, but were unlikely to change in the years to come. They can be classified as follows:

History. The people of Central and South-Eastern Europe knew that they were not 'liberated' by the West from Soviet occupation; they liberated themselves. Nevertheless, there was a strong perception throughout the region that Western Europe was a passive observer of this process of liberation, while the USA was its principal driving force. The fact that NATO, a US-led Alliance, was the first European-based organization to admit new members from the East, well before the EU even considered its eastward enlargement, also contributed to this perception. Therefore, those opposing the Iraq war in Central and South-Eastern Europe were unable to turn anti-US sentiment to their advantage, and the leaders of the applicant countries did not have to contend with any organized opposition when they decided to support the USA's position on Iraq;

Immediate instincts. The Iraq debate was launched in Europe immediately after the German parliamentary elections of September 2002, when quite a few German politicians—although not the country's Government—engaged in a more general anti-US rhetoric. Comparisons between Hitler's propaganda techniques and Bush's justifications for the war were received particularly badly in Eastern Europe;

The link between France and Germany in opposition to the war in Iraq. The co-ordination of policy between these two countries, on what was seen as an explicitly anti-US platform, was regarded with dismay throughout the eastern half of the continent. France and Germany, with their recent history of accommodating the USSR during the period of détente, were not remembered fondly;

Legal arguments. Western Europe was primarily interested in the legality of the operation in Iraq, whether force could be used to affect 'regime change' (the removal from power of President Saddam Hussain), and whether a war could be initiated without explicit authorization from the UN Security Council. In Central and South-Eastern Europe, however, this question was largely irrelevant, partly because there was less agonizing over legal niceties, but also because the legal implications that concerned Central and South-Eastern Europe were in the completely different direction. The suggestion that the USA, viewed throughout the region as the ultimate guarantor of their nations' security, could be restricted in what it did by the UN was considered as tantamount to saying that Russia, the old colonial master, should still have a voice in the security of the world—an anathema;

Errors in handling Central and South-Eastern Europe. Instead of trying to dispel its fears, France and Germany did much to further alienate the eastern half of the continent. France and Germany rapidly expressed their fury that the Central and South-Eastern European nations dared to express their support for military action in Iraq before the EU had adopted a common foreign policy. The fact that the EU's lack of a joint policy on Iraq had not prevented other Western European countries, such as Belgium, from expressing their views did not unduly concern the French President, Jacques Chirac, and the German Chancellor, Gerhard Schröder; in early 2003 both indicated that the Central and South-Eastern European states should have followed the lead of Western European nations. Subsequently, ignoring the sensitivities of the East, France and Germany welcomed Russia's President, Vladimir Putin, who rapidly expressed his support for the Franco-German position. The humiliation of the Central and South-Eastern European nations seemed complete when their leaders were undiplomatically advised not to attend an EU summit in February, organized with the aim of reaching a common position on the Iraq crisis, despite the fact that the aspirant states had been invited to attend by Greece, which held the EU Presidency;

NATO drawn into the crisis. Alarm increased in Central and South-Eastern Europe when it became clear that the dispute over Iraq was threatening to paralyse NATO, which Central and South-Eastern Europeans considered essential to their security. The issue appeared minor to those countries (Belgium, France and Germany) that initially opposed proposals, in February 2003, to send air-defence reinforcements to Turkey in the event of a war in Iraq, but matters were interpreted differently in Central and South-Eastern Europe. Turkey had responded by invoking Article 4 of the founding North Atlantic Treaty (the Washington Treaty), which states that NATO members 'will consult together whenever, in the opinion of any of them, the territorial integrity, political independence or security of any of the parties is threatened'. The subsequent argument of those states that had opposed the NATO decision was that Article 4 did not require immediate action, but merely consultation about action, and they claimed to be doing precisely that when they demanded 'further information' before a decision on reinforcing Turkey was taken. However, viewed from the capitals of Central and South-Eastern Europe, the situation was intolerable. Largely for practical and political reasons, in 1997 the decision had been taken to expand NATO, but not to position any permanent bases further east. Indeed, NATO made an explicit statement to that effect at the summit meeting held in Madrid, Spain, in 1997, mainly in order to reassure Russia. Central and South-Eastern Europe was led to understand, however, that should a crisis arise that threatened its security, NATO forces could arrive rapidly to defend its territory. This reassurance was subsequently rehearsed and implemented in various Alliance exercises and contingency plans. However, any such troop reinforcement in Central and South-Eastern Europe depended on the invocation of Article 4 of the North Atlantic Treaty, precisely the article referred to by Turkey during the Iraqi dispute. In many respects, therefore, Article 4 mattered more to the Central and South-Eastern European members and applicant countries of the Alliance than Article 5, which was usually considered NATO's key security guarantee. Thus, any attempt to redefine—as Central and South-Eastern Europe interpreted it—Article 4 was guaranteed to create alarm throughout the region. None the less, there was no evidence to suggest that the countries that had initially opposed the NATO decision on Turkey were aware of the profound significance of their behaviour for Central and South-Eastern Europe.

As each reverse came, the nations of Central and South-Eastern Europe became increasingly determined to support the US position on Iraq, less because the nations of that region were convinced of the merits of US policy in the Middle East, and more because the alternatives presented by the USA's critics in Europe appeared worse. In the short-term, this bitter dispute would have few practical consequences. The treaties for the EU candidate countries were already in place, and the process of admitting them could not realistically be halted. It was inconceivable that any existing EU member state would block the process of enlargement. Nor would the Central and South-Eastern Europeans relish their new-found status as opponents of French and German policies in Europe; Central and South-Eastern Europe depends for much of its trade on the EU as a whole, and on Germany in particular. Nevertheless, the row over Iraq would have profound implications for the future of the entire continent, and some of the opinions formed during this short but intense dispute would linger on for years. The hope throughout Europe was that, as the eastern half rejoined the continent, the distinction between the old 'east' and 'west' would no longer be so relevant. Nevertheless, the dispute over Iraq indicated that, at least in matters of defence, the nations of Central and South-Eastern Europe would remain distinct, more apprehensive about Russia, more emotionally dependent on the USA, and a great deal more suspicious of any European defence efforts, particularly if these were led by either France or Germany. In economic matters, too, the region would remain vulnerable for decades to come. Almost all the developments towards integration that had taken place between mid-2002 and mid-2003 had turned out to be beneficial, but challenges still remained.

CENTRAL AND SOUTH-EASTERN EUROPEAN ECONOMIES

ALAN SMITH

INTRODUCTION: PROGRESS AND PERFORMANCE IN THE TRANSITION TO A MARKET ECONOMY

The transition to a market economy in the former socialist countries of Central and South-Eastern Europe has not been without difficulty, with each of the economies experiencing substantial declines in both output and income in the early 1990s, as the economic institutions and the structure of demand created by the communist economic system collapsed. Nevertheless, by 2003 the majority of the former centrally planned economies in the region had made reasonable progress towards creating the institutions of functioning market economy, while eight of those countries had received invitations to become full members of the European Union (EU) in 2004. Furthermore, each of the economies of the region managed to sustain sound levels of economic growth in 2002, despite the global economic slowdown and the relatively poor economic performance of Germany, which is their major export market. The progress made towards creating the institutions of a functioning market economy varied substantially from country to country in the 1990s, and was also reflected in substantial differences in economic performance. The main consequence was that the gap between the richer and poorer economies in the region, which became apparent in the first half of the 1990s, widened in the second half of the decade. However, by the early 2000s there were some indications that the relative gap in income between the richer economies of Central Europe (the Czech Republic, Hungary, Poland, Slovenia and Slovakia) and the Baltic states (Estonia, Latvia and Lithuania), on the one hand, and the poorer economies of South-Eastern Europe, on the other, might be starting to close. The latter had begun to recover from the economic crises they experienced in the mid- to late 1990s and (with the possible exception of the former Yugoslav republic of Macedonia—FYRM) grew more rapidly in the early 2000s than their northern counterparts. Despite this progress, the gap in economic performance and living standards between the economies to the north and to the south of the region remains substantial, and could widen once the EU enlarges to accept the more prosperous economies of the region. By and large, the economies that were preparing for admission to the EU in 2004 were those that made the most sustained progress towards creating the institutions of a market economy and industrial restructuring in the early years of the transition. This, in turn, created the conditions for more successful economic performance in the second half of the 1990s. Advancement in the creation of the institutions of a market economy and economic recovery also reflected the geopolitical structure of the region and its proximity to the EU. The countries of Central Europe made the greatest progress in transition in the 1990s, were more successful in attracting foreign investment and, in the main, managed to sustain economic growth in the second half of the 1990s. By the end of 2002 each of the Central European economies had surpassed the level of real gross domestic product (GDP) attained in the final years of communism. More importantly, the structure of output in these economies differed substantially from that produced under communism and reflected the demands of consumers far more closely. The Central European economies also made significant progress in reducing the inflationary pressures that were experienced in the early 1990s and had created relatively stable currencies by the end of the decade, which was essential if they were to become full members of the EU in 2004 and were to take on the responsibilities of economic and monetary union. They also succeeded in changing the structure of domestic production, which enabled them to redirect exports, away from the countries of the former USSR and towards the EU member states. The growth in export trade to the EU market was a major factor contributing to economic recovery in Central Europe. Similarly, imports of capital goods from the EU, and investment by multinational corporations based in the EU, was an important factor in stimulating industrial restructuring and the modernization of the capital stock. The economic recovery, after the initial recession in Central Europe, was accompanied by an improvement in living standards and the avoidance of widespread poverty, with the exception of Poland, which continued to experience considerable rural poverty, and some regions of Hungary and Slovakia.

The Baltic states, which had been incorporated into the USSR, were badly affected by the break-up of supply networks and trade relations with other former Soviet republics. This contributed to declines in GDP of over 40% in 1990–93. By the mid-1990s Estonia, Latvia and Lithuania had already made good progress in implementing economic reforms, liberalizing trade, reducing inflation and stabilizing their currencies by utilizing a currency board with a fixed rate of exchange. Progress in macroeconomic stabilization was sustained into the early 2000s, and in early 2002 each of the Baltic states linked their currencies to the common European currency, the euro. Estonia was more successful in attracting foreign direct investment and in redirecting its exports to the EU than Latvia and Lithuania, which had only moderate success in that area. Critically, those economies continued to experience significant levels of poverty, particularly in rural areas, and would need to maintain steady growth for several years in order to reduce the proportion of their population living in poverty. The Russian financial crisis of 1998 (the combined effects of a decline in world petroleum prices, the Asian financial crisis and unsustainable levels of government borrowing to finance budgetary deficits contributed to a devaluation of the rouble in August) presented an obstacle to the Baltics' economic recovery, owing to their continued trade dependence on Russia. However, all of the Baltic states achieved relatively high rates of growth in the early 2000s and staged an economic recovery from 2000, following declines in output in Estonia and Lithuania in 1999. Although in 2002 output in each of these economies lagged substantially behind the nominal levels declared in official statistics in 1989, this production was far more closely targeted towards the demands of consumers.

The creation of the institutions of a functioning market economy and the stimulation of economic recovery proved to be far more difficult in the South-Eastern European economies of Albania, Bulgaria and Romania. Between 1990 and 1993 GDP declined by 40% in Albania and by 25% in Bulgaria and Romania. These economies entered the transition from a far more disadvantageous position and were affected by the disruption to trade flows with Central Europe resulting from wars in the former Yugoslavia and UN sanctions against Yugoslavia (now Serbia and Montenegro). Such obstacles partly accounted for their failure to attract substantial volumes of foreign investment to modernize industry, agriculture and financial institutions. However, the economic problems experienced by these economies also reflected a reluctance by successive governments to subject loss-making industries to financial discipline, to undertake industrial restructuring and to reduce fiscal deficits. Most critically, these economies failed to create functioning financial institutions and capital markets that were capable of both safeguarding household savings and channelling investment towards small businesses. Albania and Bulgaria both experienced major financial crises in 1996 and 1997, which led to the resurgence of inflationary pressures and culminated in the collapse of the existing financial and monetary system and significant decreases in output. However, output in these economies made a substantial recovery between 1998 and 2002, with Albania surpassing the levels of output achieved under communism. In October 2002 the EU recognized that Bulgaria, which had also introduced a currency board, with a fixed rate of exchange with the euro from 2002, had achieved the status of a functioning market economy. Romania experienced continued declines in GDP, industrial output and living standards and the resurgence of open inflation and balance-of-payments problems in 1997–2000, after embarking on a further transition programme under a new administration. However, Romania staged a reasonably sound economic recovery in 2001–02 and had made more solid, if unspectacular, progress in implementing economic reforms. Despite this, in October 2002 the EU concluded in its annual report that Romania did not have a functioning market economy, and consequently did not satisfy the economic criteria for membership of the EU. More seriously, these economies have been affected by a major growth of income inequality and the emergence of poverty on a large scale following the collapse of communism, while corruption remains a major problem throughout the region.

The performance of the economies of the former Yugoslavia was varied in the 1990s. Not surprisingly, output in those states worst affected by war halved in 1990–94. Slovenia, which was largely unaffected by war and was the wealthiest of the former socialist economies, made a sustained economic recovery from 1992. Slovenia remained by far the richest economy in the region, and was invited to become a member of the EU from 2004. Croatia also made relatively rapid progress in reform and experienced sustained growth in the early 2000s. Economic performance in the remaining former Yugoslav economies (Bosnia and Herzegovina, the FYRM and Yugoslavia) was severely affected by the impact of conflict. However, with the exception of the FYRM, where output actually declined in 2001, the former Yugoslav republics sustained relatively rapid economic growth by international standards in 2000–02, and a reduction in inflation, as they recovered from the adverse impact of war in the region. However, each of the economies of the former Yugoslavia, together with Albania, continued to experience substantial trade and current-account deficits, financed by foreign direct investment and aid flows, as they attempted to rebuild their economies.

THE TRANSITION TO A MARKET ECONOMY

Strategies for the Transition

The economic problems inherited from communism varied substantially within the region. However, all countries shared a sufficient number of common features to suggest that they arose from the nature of the communist economic system itself, and could only be overcome by the introduction of a more market-orientated system. There was no historic prece-

dent that directly paralleled the collapse of the communist economic system in Eastern Europe and that could indicate the measures that were required for the transition to a market economy. A set of policies based on the IMF's programmes of economic liberalization and macroeconomic stabilization, known as the 'Washington Consensus', was first adopted in Poland in 1990, and came to be accepted as the basic model for the transition to a market economy. These policies consisted of four interrelated steps: macroeconomic stabilization, internal economic liberalization, the development of a private sector and the liberalization of trade and investment. However, the removal of government controls over internal and external economic activity alone, was not sufficient to build the institutional and productive base for a functioning market economy. Liberalization and stabilization had to be accompanied by positive measures to create the legal framework for a market economy and to create the institutions of a functioning market economy. The latter included systems of government supervision, the creation of sound financial institutions and the enforcement of economic obligations and responsibilities (for example, contract fulfilment, safety regulations, compliance with tax and accountancy regulations) on economic agents, in addition to granting them the freedom to enjoy the rights and privileges that arise from private economic activity. It was also necessary to build mechanisms for enforcing regulations after these had been enacted into law. This, in turn, required the construction of a social and political framework that respected the rule of law. The impetus to maintain and accelerate reforms has been sustained in many economies by the need to satisfy the economic criteria for membership of the EU. This section will examine the major features of the transition to a market economy and will review the progress made by the Central and South-Eastern European economies in such a transition.

Macroeconomic Stabilization

The communist economic system placed major emphasis on central controls over prices as a means of suppressing inflationary pressures. In the majority of communist economies, demand for goods in consumer markets exceeded the total supply of goods, resulting in unsatisfied demand, involuntary savings, queues and shortages. Consequently, macroeconomic stabilization was required to eliminate inflationary pressures and the threat of 'hyperinflation' once central controls on prices had been lifted. This necessitated the replacement of the lax monetary policies pursued in the later stages of the communist era with more restrictive monetary policies. This, in turn, required the implementation of restrictive fiscal policies with limited budget deficits. The majority of transition economies encountered severe difficulties in reducing central-government budget deficits below the targets established in agreements for financial assistance from the IMF in the initial stages of the transition. This was largely a result of the changeover to 'rule-based' tax systems based on profits and income taxes and value-added tax (VAT) in place of the direct expropriation of enterprise profits and payroll taxes that had been major sources of government revenue under communism. It was more difficult to estimate potential revenues from the new taxes, which were also easier to evade, resulting in declining tax returns. At the same time, growing demand for welfare payments, including unemployment benefits, to protect the living standards of those who had been adversely affected by the transition made it difficult to limit government expenditure. Poorly developed capital markets in the majority of Central and South-Eastern European economies also severely limited the government's ability to borrow from the public to finance government deficits during the early stages of the transition.

Each of the Central and South-Eastern European economies experienced an initial sharp increase in consumer prices when price controls were removed. Only Hungary and Czechoslovakia (then a single country) avoided an average annual inflation rate of over 100% between 1990 and 1993. In the mid-1990s each of the economies of the region experienced difficulties in reducing the annual rate of inflation to less than 10%, and Yugoslavia experienced hyperinflationary pressures in 1992–93, owing to the impact of war and UN sanctions. In 1997 Bulgaria also experienced hyperinflation, which resulted in the collapse of both the monetary system and the Government; it was forced to introduce a fixed rate of exchange linked to the German Deutsche Mark, and subsequently linked to the euro in 2002, in order to restore credibility. By 2001–02 each of the economies of the region (except Romania and Yugoslavia) had managed to reduce inflation to less than 10%. In general, those economies that had succeeded in fixing their currencies to the euro (which limited price increases for imported goods) had been the most successful in reducing inflation, although it is debatable whether this policy can be sustained over the long term, particularly in economies that continue to experience above-average levels of inflation.

Internal Liberalization

Internal liberalization involved the removal of the majority of government restrictions on economic activity. The most important of these consisted of the removal of governments' ability to determine wholesale and retail prices and wage rates (although some controls over wage increases were retained to help control inflation). Central controls over prices under communism had contributed to the growth of shortages of specific goods where supply was insufficient to meet demand at state-determined prices. This had contributed to the growth of the 'grey economy' and was a major factor behind the emergence of organized crime groups and corrupt officials who controlled the supply of 'shortage' commodities in exchange for bribes. The need to create a price system that reflects the conditions of supply and demand, both to enable consumers to make choices between different consumer goods based on the real costs of production, and to allow enterprises to respond to patterns of consumer demand, suggests that the process of price liberalization should be undertaken as soon as possible in the transition process. Rapid price liberalization, however, had the potential to create major social problems. The prices of basic staple goods (including housing, food, heating and transport) had been subsidized under communism and an egalitarian wage policy had been pursued as part of a deliberate social strategy. The removal of price controls and the emergence of greater wage differentials as enterprises became more responsive to conditions in labour markets resulted in greater income inequality and the emergence of poverty. Consequently, the creation of a social-welfare system that directed assistance to those in greatest need was an urgent requirement. However, a simple relationship between price liberalization and the growth of income inequality and poverty could not be detected. The countries of Central Europe and the Baltic states, together with Albania and the FYRM, liberalized the majority of prices in the early stages of the transition. In the Baltic states and Poland this was accompanied by growth in income inequality and a major growth in poverty. This was largely avoided in Czechoslovakia (now the Czech Republic and Slovakia) and Hungary. Although Bulgaria and Romania retained some central controls over prices, income inequality widened more sharply in these economies than in Central Europe, while the proportion of the population living in absolute poverty in Romania, Albania and the FYRM exceeded 40% in 2002.

The Development of a Private Sector

Under communism the private sector in the majority of Central and South-Eastern European states had been confined to small family businesses, which faced major restrictions over the forms of activity they could undertake and the number of people they could employ. Virtually all medium and large-scale industrial enterprises, and the majority of small industrial enterprises, were state-owned. Yugoslavia, where small businesses had been allowed to flourish under communism and medium and large-scale industry had been largely controlled by a system of self-management by workers, was an exception. It was considered important to free enterprises from political control and to encourage them to make decisions based on economic criteria. Privatization was also considered to be the best method for creating effective systems of corporate governance and for improving enterprise efficiency. The development of a private sector consisted of two major aspects. First, it involved the removal of restrictions on private-sector activity that would permit the spontaneous development of new private companies (*de novo* firms). Second, it involved the privatization of existing state-owned enterprises and their exposure to competition, with the threat of bankruptcy and closure for enterprises that continued to make losses.

Privatization of State-owned Enterprises

The privatization of existing state-owned enterprises raised major technical issues concerning the identification and evaluation of the enterprises' assets, in addition to issues of efficiency and equity. Consequently, the privatization of medium-sized and large state-owned enterprises could not be implemented widely in the first years of the transition. The first step in the process of privatization was to identify and evaluate an enterprise's assets. A state holding company was then responsible for disposing of the assets, either through direct sales to new owners, or by sales of shares over a period of time. A major problem was that the local populations did not possess sufficient financial resources to permit a system of privatization involving large-scale direct sales of shares in companies to the public. Similarly, the number of domestic private institutions that could take over an enterprise as a going concern was exceedingly small. Consequently, several countries introduced schemes for the mass privatization of state-owned enterprises, which involved the distribution (or sale at a nominal price) of vouchers to the population. These could then be exchanged for shares in companies and financial trusts, which were created to acquire shares in companies. Subsequent tranches of shares in enterprises were sold on the market after the initial distribution of vouchers. It was hoped that these schemes would create widespread ownership of shares and popular support for privatization. However, it had the disadvantage that share ownership in any given company could be widely dispersed, which would make it difficult for the new 'owners' to influence enterprise management. Furthermore, workers and managers often used their vouchers to acquire shares in their own enterprises. In many countries it was also considered necessary to encourage workers to buy shares in their own enterprises, in order to win workers' support for privatization. Consequently, 'insider privatization', in the form of management and employee buy-outs (MEBOs), in which managers and employees held a working majority of shares in the enterprise, became the dominant form of privatization in many countries. This problem was most acute in the countries of the former Yugoslavia, which had a tradition of worker-ownership, and in Romania. In most cases, however, employees acquired a genuine ownership share in the company, which they could dispose of if they wanted, creating the possibility of more widespread ownership in the future. The major exception to the predominant form of 'insider ownership' was direct sales to strategic investors (normally foreign owners) who acquired a majority interest in the company. Direct sales were most important in Estonia and Hungary, where foreign direct investment made a substantial contribution to privatization revenue. This form of privatization accelerated in the late 1990s and early 2000s, and acquired increasing significance in Albania, Bulgaria and Romania, where the process of reform had been less rapid.

Trade Liberalization and the Creation of an Open Economy

During the communist era foreign economic relations were administered by a highly centralized state monopoly in the majority of the countries of the region (with the exception of Yugoslavia). In its strictest form, this meant that enterprises and individuals were not allowed to engage directly in import or export activities, but had to follow orders given by the foreign-trade ministry. Prices in the domestic economies were entirely separated from prices prevailing on the world market and currencies were inconvertible, in the sense that they could not be exchanged for other currencies on demand. The exchange rate of the currency had little economic purpose and existed largely for statistical purposes. Systems of multiple exchange rates existed in areas where exchange rates did influence economic decisions. Enterprises were protected from foreign competition and had little or no incentive to meet the more demanding conditions and quality standards expected in the more competitive Western markets. Foreign investment was confined to joint ventures involving Western and Eastern companies that had very limited powers of independent decision-making.

As a consequence, measures to end the isolation of the former centrally planned economies from world markets, which would expose enterprises to foreign competition and encourage them to seek foreign markets for their products, were considered to be vital components of the transition to a market economy. It was also important to create an environment conducive to foreign investment, as a source of both financial capital and modern technology. In addition, it was hoped that exposure to foreign competition would force enterprises to meet world-market quality standards in order to survive. Although the abolition of the foreign-trade monopoly was an essential part of this process, it was also necessary to create new institutions to promote foreign trade. The first step in the majority of economies was the introduction of 'current-account convertibility'. This enabled enterprises and individuals to exchange the domestic currency into convertible currencies at market-determined exchange rates for the purchase of imports and to convert foreign-exchange earnings from the sale of exports back into the domestic currency. In addition, it encouraged foreign enterprises to invest in the domestic economy, in the knowledge that profits could be repatriated.

The liberalization of foreign trade was closely linked to the question of price liberalization. The relaxation of controls on imports and exports meant that domestic producers and consumers were exposed to world market prices for goods and services. Consequently, domestic prices started to adjust to those prevailing on world markets. As a result, progress in liberalizing the foreign-trade system tended to match that of price liberalization. The economies of Central Europe and the Baltic states liberalized their foreign-trade systems relatively early in the transition. This carried the danger that domestic enterprises were exposed to foreign competition in domestic markets before they had had time to adjust to the stricter conditions required to survive in competitive world markets. By the early 2000s all the economies of the region had introduced current-account convertibility and the majority of Central European economies had begun the process of liberalizing capital flows.

Unemployment, Low Wages and Poverty

The decline in output in the first stage of the transition was accompanied by the growth of recorded, open unemployment.

This was a new phenomenon in Central and South-Eastern Europe and the Baltic states, where industrial workers had been accustomed to job security under central planning. Industrial unemployment arose from two major sources. First, the excessive emphasis on heavy industry in the communist period meant that the collapse of communism resulted in a major decline in demand for industrial products. The newly emerging private sector, particularly in services, simply could not expand quickly enough to absorb labour displaced from industrial enterprises that were no longer viable. Second, widespread overstaffing of industry meant that competitive pressures forced a reduction in the demand for labour within industrial enterprises. In the initial stages of the transition industrial output declined far more sharply than industrial employment, indicating that enterprises that had managed to stay in business (often by obtaining subsidies and 'soft' credits) were not shedding labour and were continuing to employ workers on a short-time basis. Although the pattern of unemployment varied across the region, some broadly common features can be observed. Official statistics (which need to be treated with some caution) indicated that registered unemployment grew steadily throughout the region until the mid-1990s and, despite some reductions in unemployment levels between 1995 and 1998, unemployment began to rise in several economies in 1999 and 2000 and remained high in 2001–02. Only four economies (the Czech Republic, Hungary, Slovenia and Romania) recorded official rates of unemployment of less than 10% in 2001, and Bosnia and Herzegovina, the FYRM and Yugoslavia recorded rates of around 30%, or higher. The remaining economies of the region recorded rates of between 10% and 20%.

The growth of unemployment and low-wage employment was a major factor in the growth of income inequality and poverty across the region, although it was augmented by other factors, including family size (as a result of which a disproportionately high percentage of children in the region lived in poverty). Poverty was also highest in rural areas. In the main, poverty in the region was associated with low levels of education and training and a preponderance of job-specific skills, which drastically reduced the prospects of securing employment at anything higher than moderate wages for relatively low-skilled industrial, clerical and agricultural workers. At the same time, people with the skills that were in high demand and short supply in the new market environment were able to command relatively high wages in the private sector. Absolute poverty was naturally highest in the poorest countries, where low relative wages were most likely to push low-income families below the poverty threshold. Countries that had implemented only partial reforms (for example, Albania, Bulgaria and Romania) tended to have higher levels of income inequality and poverty, although in 2002 poverty remained high (particularly in rural areas) in the Baltic states, Poland and parts of Hungary and Slovakia. The remaining Central European economies avoided widespread poverty. Not surprisingly, poverty was most prevalent in those former Yugoslav republics that have been disrupted by war.

Progress in Implementing Reforms on the Eve of EU Enlargement

On the eve of the planned eastward enlargement of the EU in 2004, it was possible to distinguish between the Central European economies and the Baltic states, which had introduced reforms consistently and credibly and had created the institutions of a functioning market economy, and the South-Eastern European economies, which, in the main, had only introduced partial reforms. The South-Eastern European economies, particularly Bulgaria and Romania, which were less successful in creating the institutions of a market economy in the 1990s were also less successful in attracting foreign direct investment to restructure and modernize industry, while large, obsolete industries were maintained by subsidies and 'soft' credits. At the same time, economies that failed to develop functioning capital markets, which could channel savings to investment, were unable to develop a thriving small-business sector, companies that could both satisfy consumer demand and increase employment prospects for workers made redundant by large enterprises. As a result, these economies encountered capacity constraints when they relaxed macroeconomic policies in the second half of the 1990s, leading to renewed inflation and pressures on the balance of payments, which had to be financed by foreign borrowing. This raises the critical question of whether the 'partial reformers' would make further progress in implementing reforms and would also progress to full membership of the EU, or whether they would retain 'semi-reformed' economies.

ECONOMIC RELATIONS WITH THE EU AND THE REDIRECTION OF TRADE TO WESTERN EUROPE

Relations with the EU and the Question of Enlargement

In 1991–93 Bulgaria, the Czech Republic, Hungary, Poland, Romania and Slovakia concluded association agreements with the European Community (EC—it became known as the EU in November 1993). At a 1993 meeting of EC leaders in Copenhagen, Denmark, it was agreed to extend the prospect of full membership to the associated states provided they met certain economic and political criteria. These included progress towards the creation of a liberal democracy, the establishment of a functioning market economy capable of withstanding competitive pressures and the ability to undertake the commitments of full economic and monetary union. The association agreements and the prospect of full membership were extended to the Baltic states in 1995 and to Slovenia in the following year. In late 1997 the Czech Republic, Estonia, Hungary, Poland and Slovenia, identified by the European Commission of the EU as satisfying the economic and political criteria established at the Copenhagen Summit, were invited to open bilateral negotiations for entry. Slovakia, which was omitted from the first round of negotiations on political grounds, together with the remaining four 'associated states' (Bulgaria, Latvia, Lithuania and Romania), were invited to open entry negotiations at the EU summit in Helsinki, Finland, in December 1999.

In October 2002 the European Commission recommended that eight of the candidate economies in the region (the Czech Republic, Estonia, Hungary, Latvia, Lithuania, Poland, Slovakia and Slovenia), together with Cyprus and Malta, should be invited to complete entry negotiations. The decision was ratified at an EU summit meeting in Copenhagen in December, which extended an invitation for accession in May 2004 to the 10 states. The Commission also recommended that Bulgaria and Romania should be offered an entry date of 2007, and issued a 'road map' for each country, which specified in considerable detail the requirements that each of the countries would be required to meet before accession would be granted. The remaining states in the region had no promise of entry, although Croatia, in particular, could become a potential candidate for accession.

It was apparent that eastward enlargement of the EU would be far more complex than earlier enlargements. This was partly because the difference between per-head incomes in the Central and South-Eastern European economies and the existing members of the EU was far greater than had been the case when Greece, Spain and Portugal were admitted. More importantly, the EU was deepening the process of integration between members and was placing far greater demands on its existing and potential members than had

previously been the case. New members of the EU would be required to participate in the single market, which involved full mobility of labour and capital, and would be expected to prepare for economic and monetary union and, ultimately, membership of the single currency. Although some of the potential new members already had currencies that were linked to the euro by a fixed exchange rate, they would all be required to spend at least two years in the Exchange Rate Mechanism before they could become members of the euro area. Membership of 'euroland' required member countries to reduce inflation to EU levels (in the absence of offsetting increases in productivity) or face severe competitive pressures. In addition, citizens of the new member states would not be granted the facility of automatic free mobility of labour within the EU during a transitional period.

Trade Relations with the EU

The collapse of the Soviet economy and the disruption to trade flows between Eastern Europe in general and the former Soviet republics were important factors in the decline in industrial output and GDP in the early stages of the transition to a market economy. Furthermore the capital stock inherited from communism was targeted towards the low-income Soviet market, not the more sophisticated tastes of western consumers. It therefore became imperative that the Central and South-Eastern European economies should redirect their exports towards markets in Western Europe, and the EU in particular, which, in turn, required imports of capital goods for industrial modernization and restructuring. By 2002 the EU accounted for nearly two-thirds of the exports of Central and South-Eastern European economies, and for approximately 90% of their trade with the industrial West. Although exports from the 10 countries with association agreements with the EU increased more than threefold between 1992 and 2001, EU exports to the associated countries increased more rapidly, resulting in a growing trade deficit.

Deficits in trade with the EU contributed to substantial current-account deficits on the balance of payments, which were experienced by all the countries of the region from the mid-1990s onwards. Current-account deficits remained high in the majority of economies in the early 2000s and averaged the equivalent of just under 5% of GDP in Central Europe (a relatively high figure by international standards) and over 10% of GDP in South-Eastern Europe. Trade deficits in Central Europe partly reflected continued imports of capital goods (machinery and equipment, electronic goods and components, etc.), which were required for the continued modernization of industry and infrastructure. The Czech Republic, Hungary and Poland (together with Estonia, Slovenia and, from 2000, Slovakia) were relatively successful in attracting foreign investment by multinational corporations, which enabled them to finance current-account deficits and contributed to technology transfer. Trade deficits in the South-Eastern European economies, which were far less successful in attracting foreign direct investment and in importing capital goods, partly reflected their dependence on labour-intensive exports and their comparative inability to penetrate EU markets for higher value-added products. Trade deficits in the former Yugoslav republics, which exceeded 20% of GDP, were financed by a combination of foreign direct investment, aid flows and remittances from workers abroad. Critical differences could be observed between the structure of exports in the Central European economies with the EU, on the one hand, and the South-Eastern European economies, on the other. The export structure of the Central European economies to the EU reflected a growing proportion of goods that were based on 'human-capital intensive' methods of production (predominantly consisting of machinery and equipment, sophisticated chemicals, and electronic goods and optical equipment). These were the goods that predominated in intra-EU trade, and indicated that these economies were successfully restructuring industrial output towards goods that were in high demand in EU markets. It also indicated that these economies would be capable of withstanding the competitive pressures they would encounter following their entry into the EU.

However, the structure of exports in the South-Eastern European economies, together with two of the Baltic states (Latvia and Lithuania) remained highly concentrated on labour-intensive goods (predominantly clothing, furniture and footwear, much of which was produced under outward-processing agreements) and resource-intensive goods (ferrous and non-ferrous metals, wood products, etc.). Furthermore, the import structure of these economies reflected a far lower level of capital goods per head, expressed as a proportion of GDP. This indicated that these economies had been relatively less successful than the Central European economies in restructuring industry towards the demands of EU markets. There was also a danger that the long-term competitiveness of these economies would rely heavily on low wage rates relative to both the EU and other competitors outside the EU.

CONCLUSION

By mid-2003 the economies of Central Europe had made significant progress in creating the institutions of a market economy and restructuring their industrial output towards the demands of EU markets. With the exception of Poland, and parts of Hungary and Slovakia, absolute poverty was relatively rare in Central Europe, and income distribution was not excessively unequal. Furthermore, these economies had demonstrated considerable resilience in the deteriorating global economic situation of 2002. Although growth rates declined in Central Europe in that year, they remained sound compared with those of the majority of industrialized economies. Similarly, inflation rates in the accession countries continued to fall and, with the exception of Hungary and Slovenia, were beginning to approach EU levels. However, fiscal deficits, resulting from the pressures to finance investment in education, health and infrastructure, while providing an adequately functioning welfare system, remained high and were partly financed by foreign borrowing. These economies would continue to experience major problems in funding welfare requirements, including provision for ageing populations and continued high levels of unemployment. This indicated the need for measures to deepen financial institutions and to increase private provision for a range of financial services, from insurance to pensions, while concentrating state provision on the poorer sectors of the community and on the provision of education and training. There were also concerns that the increased attractiveness of these economies to foreign investors, resulting from their invitations to join the EU, could result in a destabilizing inflow of speculative capital, which could result in a resurgence of inflationary pressures. Measures to improve corporate governance and to submit enterprise management to genuine external control had also to be accelerated to stimulate greater efficiency. However, the Central European economies were still expected to grow faster than the EU economies in the 2000s, which would help to reduce the income difference between that region and the existing EU member countries. Despite this, it remained unlikely that the per-head incomes of the Central European economies would approach the levels of the poorest Western European countries before the end of the first decade of the 21st century.

The economies of South-Eastern Europe also demonstrated considerable resilience in maintaining relatively high growth rates in 2002. Nevertheless, these economies still face major problems, which could be exacerbated by their exclusion from the next round of EU enlargement. The relatively slow pace of reform and industrial restructuring and modernization in these economies meant that they were still experiencing problems inherited from the communist economic system, in addition to new problems arising from the process of transition. These problems were compounded by the impact of civil conflict in the former Yugoslavia. Industrial modernization had been slow, resulting in difficulties in penetrating EU markets. Exports to the EU remained highly dependent on labour-intensive, low-technology industries, which preserved their competitiveness through low wage rates. These economies had been less successful in attracting foreign direct investment to modernize their economies and there was a danger that multinational corporations might prefer to invest in the economies that were scheduled to enter the EU in 2004, rather than in the more uncertain economies of South-Eastern Europe. Consequently, expectations that they would be able to narrow the technological gap between themselves and the Central European economies through increased foreign investment, were likely to be unfounded. Moreover, these economies faced major social problems, in part resulting from the slow pace of reform. Subsidies to loss-making industries contributed to high fiscal deficits, and the need to curb budgetary deficits to control inflation reduced the amount available to finance a properly functioning welfare system, including unemployment benefits, pensions and child benefits, and contributed to the growth of absolute poverty in the region. It also reduced the amount available to finance urgently required investment in infrastructure, education and training.

The financial systems in many South-Eastern European states lacked transparency and remained subject to greater levels of manipulation for private gain and outright corruption. The continuation of price controls and government and local authority restrictions on legal economic activities in the 1990s stimulated the development of the 'grey' economy. This, in turn, reduced tax revenues and required legal enterprises (including many foreign-owned enterprises) to pay higher tax rates on profits and VAT. These factors greatly impeded the expansion of more dynamic enterprises in the private sector, which created fewer productive employment opportunities for workers displaced from industries for which demand had decreased. At the same time, low unemployment benefits increased the risk to workers moving from secure employment to more uncertain ventures. The lack of opportunities in the private sector, combined with the increased risk, provided workers with an incentive to remain in low-paid jobs with low productivity. This resulted in the preservation of employment in overstaffed state-owned enterprises and companies subject to employee buy-outs and increased political opposition to the threat of unemployment. As a result, workers developed mechanisms for coping with the existing situation by taking additional employment in the 'grey' economy, which had come to represent a major challenge to reform in the region.

BIBLIOGRAPHY

Aslund, A. *Building Capitalism: The Transformation of the Former Soviet Bloc*. Cambridge, Cambridge University Press, 2002.

Barr, N. (Ed.). *Labor Markets and Social Policy in Central and Eastern Europe*. New York, NY, Oxford University Press, 1994.

Courbis, R., and Władysław, W. (Eds). *Central and Eastern Europe on its way to European Union*. Frankfurt, Peter Lang, 2000.

Eatwell, J., Ellman, M., Karlsson, M., Nuti, D. M., and Shapiro, J. *Transformation and Integration*. London, Institute for Public Policy Research, 1995.

Not 'Just Another Accession': The Political Economy of EU Enlargement to the East. London, Institute for Public Policy Research, 1997.

European Bank for Reconstruction and Development. *Transition Report*. London, EBRD, 1994–2002.

European Commission. *The Western Balkans in Transition*. No 1, Brussels, Directorate-General for Economic and Financial Affairs, 2003.

Grabbe, H. *Profiting from EU Enlargement*. London, Centre for European Reform, 2001.

Gros, D., and Steinherr, A. *Winds of Change: Economic Transition in Central and Eastern Europe*. London and New York, NY, Longman, 1995.

Lavigne, M. *The Economics of Transition: From Socialist Economy to Market Economy*. Basingstoke, Palgrave Macmillan, 1999, 2nd edn.

Mayhew, A. *Recreating Europe. The European Union's Policy towards Central and Eastern Europe*. Cambridge, Cambridge University Press, 1998.

Milanovic, B. *Income, Inequality and Poverty during the Transition from Planned to Market Economy*. Washington, DC, World Bank, 1998.

Smith, A. H. *The Return to Europe: The Reintegration of Eastern Europe into the European Economy*. Basingstoke, Palgrave Macmillan, 2000.

SOCIAL POLICY AND WELFARE IN CENTRAL AND SOUTH-EASTERN EUROPE: LEGACIES, TRENDS AND CHOICES

Dr PAUL STUBBS

INTRODUCTION

The countries of Central and South-Eastern Europe vary enormously in their levels of economic and social development. With the exception of Greece, a member of the European Union (EU), all the remaining countries of the region have experienced post-communist transition associated with, often, quite dramatic social effects on people's welfare. In addition, systems of social policy and social welfare, for much of the early transition years 'the most important neglected area of post-communist reform' (Ringold, 1999—see the Bibliography), have also been adapted and changed dramatically in recent years. This chapter seeks to provide a broad overview of the key issues in social policy and welfare for countries in Central and South-Eastern Europe, focusing on the historical legacy; social trends, well-being and human development; the key features of reforms; and continued debates regarding possible welfare futures.

In this chapter, social policy is defined very broadly to refer to 'any policy developed at supranational, state, local or community level which is underpinned by a social vision of society and which, when operationalized, affects the rights or abilities of citizens to meet their livelihood needs' (Overseas Development Agency, 1995). Each country can be said to constitute a 'welfare regime', which refers to the inter-relationship between the state, the market, civil society and households, in terms of developing structures to meet livelihood needs. Often, social policy is discussed in terms of identifiable sub-systems, such as housing, education, health, social security, social services, pensions, and labour and employment policies. Clearly, this essay can only cover some of the most important social-policy themes, issues and debates in broad overview terms.

Throughout the region, average living standards have declined in the last 15 years, and some countries have experienced dramatic increases in unemployment, poverty and inequality. Citizens have been faced with unprecedented economic and social risks and, in some cases, war and large-scale forced migration. The response of countries has been variable, although all have faced the challenge of developing new, mixed models of welfare provision, compatible with a European future and in the context of the pressures of global competitiveness. The need for reform in the context of increased demands, high expectations and decreasing revenues has been felt acutely. Above all, a new balance is being struck between social policy as an element of a more active labour market policy and as a 'safety net' for particularly vulnerable groups.

THE HISTORICAL LEGACY

Some recent authors have stressed the importance of tradition and a long-term perspective, so that it is important to recognize that 'pre-socialist welfare agents, factors and actors had a significant impact on future welfare trends' (Novak, 2001) throughout the region. This notwithstanding, during the socialist period social policy in many countries became an inextricable part of an economic and political system that rejected market mechanisms and political democracy. A broad social contract sought to maintain the system through high levels of state expenditure on universal social welfare, guaranteed full employment, and the comprehensive and largely equitable provision of health, education, housing, child care, cash assistance and social services, some of which were provided in the work-place (Deacon, 2000).

For much of the socialist period, in most of the region, real and significant increases in welfare were obtained for much of the population, particularly in terms of health and education. Spending on social sectors in 'premature welfare states' (Kornai, 1992) was between 15% and 25% of gross domestic product (GDP) in most countries of the region at the time of transition (Ringold, 1999). In contrast, Greece can be seen rather to be a 'delayed welfare state' (Katrogoulas, 1996), with social expenditure increasing from less than 10% of GDP in 1979 to close to the European Community average of 20% in 1989 (Katrogoulas, 1996).

In terms of the balance sheet of social policy under socialism, it must be remembered that many universal services were of poor quality, inefficiently organized and managed, dominated by paternalistic professionals and experts, and unable to respond to the diverse needs of the population. Hence, quality services were often available only to those who could pay and/or who had connections. In addition, the science of defectology, combined with an ideological emphasis on the role of the state, and chronic under-investment in preventive and supportive family services, meant that large numbers of children, particularly those with disabilities, languished in poor quality institutional care, becoming more or less 'a forgotten underclass, who frequently lost all contact with their families' (UNICEF, 1999).

It is also important to remember the 'Yugoslav exception' throughout much of this period, as the country maintained 'very highly developed' social-policy provision, combining 'development with decentralization' (World Bank, 1975). In the former Yugoslavia, unlike much of the region, there was recognition from the late 1950s of the need for professional social-work intervention to solve social problems, and the establishment of university-based, social-work education programmes and a network of public Centres for Social Work (Stubbs, 2001).

In the 1980s increasing strains were felt throughout the region, as economic crises created a situation in which there was 'an egalitarianism of poverty and inefficient provision of services' (Deacon, 2000). Poverty, already found among marginal groups living outside the formal economy, such as the Gypsy (Roma) population, spread to other sectors of the population, including those in work. In Hungary, for example, unofficial figures suggested that 14% of wage-earners were poor in 1987 (Deacon, 2000). Hence, it would be wrong to assume that reform and declining living standards began only in the post-1989 period. Nevertheless, the fact that the post-socialist era coincided with the height of a neo-liberal approach to welfare, in which state expenditure was meant to be curtailed, does set a context for reform, despite the fact that in the early 1990s 'few governments adopted measures to cut social spending' (Ringold, 1999).

WELFARE AND WELL-BEING: THE SOCIAL COSTS OF TRANSITION

The UN Children's Fund (UNICEF) MONEE project (a regional 'monitoring' project for the countries of 'Eastern' Europe and the 12 former Soviet countries of the Commonwealth of Independent States—CIS) is the most reliable source of comparative data on welfare in 27 countries in transition, including 15 of the 16 Central and South-Eastern European countries (with the exception of Greece). The database, notwithstanding data-collection difficulties, makes it possible to trace and compare the economic and social impact of transition between 1989 and 1999. The 2001 report (see the Bibliography) shows a mixed picture for the countries of the region in terms of 20 economic and social indicators. A majority of the 15 countries showed improvements with regard to 12 indicators, mainly relating to health and education (for example, 14 countries recorded increased enrolment in higher education; 13 recorded an increase in female life expectancy; 10 recorded an increase in male life expectancy; and 10 registered an improvement in maternal mortality rates). A majority also showed a deterioration, however, in respect of eight indicators, mainly relating to economic and social issues (for example, all 15 recorded a deterioration in employment ratios; 12 recorded an increased number of placements in infant homes; 12 recorded a decline in GDP per head; and 10 registered a decline in real wages).

By 1999 only three countries in the region—Hungary, Poland and Slovenia—had managed to exceed the level of GDP per head recorded in 1989, while the Czech Republic and Slovakia were approaching the 1989 level. In terms of purchasing-power parity, Slovenian GDP per head exceeded that of Greece. All of the transition countries were ranked higher in terms of their position on the UN Development Programme's (UNDP) Human Development Index (HDI), which measures indicators of health and education as well as income, than in terms of their economic performance alone, suggesting that accumulated social gains had been achieved. HDI rankings ranged from 29th (Slovenia) to 85th (Albania), with GDP figures expressed in terms of purchasing-power parity ranging from 31st (Slovenia) to 101st (Albania). The richer, more developed countries in the region tended to show most improvements on the 20 indicators (Poland improved on 14 indicators; Hungary 14; Croatia 13; Slovenia 13; the Czech Republic 13; and Slovakia 12), with the poorer countries, and the Baltic states (Estonia, Latvia and Lithuania), showing the greatest deterioration (Bulgaria 13; Latvia 12; Romania 11; Estonia 11; Lithuania 10; and Albania nine).

In terms of future policy issues and choices, three broad trends, not made explicit by these figures, are of crucial importance:

Demographic change and increases in dependency ratios. According to UNICEF, between 1989 and 2000 the total child population declined in all of the Central and South-Eastern European transition countries except Albania. The population aged between nought and four years had fallen in all countries, in some cases quite dramatically (by 54% in Latvia; by 48% in Estonia; by 42% in Bulgaria; and by 39% in Bosnia and Herzegovina). As the proportion of children in the population decreased, the proportion of older people increased. The elderly dependency ratio (comparing the proportion of those aged over 60 years with those aged between 18 and 59 years) also increased between 1990 and 1997 in all the transition countries of the region, with the exception of the Czech Republic and Hungary (UNDP, 1999). When these two trends were combined, as in some countries, with large-scale out-migration, particularly of

young, skilled people, a dependency crisis was clearly looming unless action was taken immediately;

Increases in inequality and income poverty. Although not as dramatic as in parts of the CIS, there were significant increases in inequality throughout the region in the 1990s (as measured by the Gini coefficient, which is used to calculate ratios of income equality, and where 0 indicates absolute equality of the population). In some countries the increase was large, so that inequality exceeded the Organisation for Economic Co-operation and Development (OECD) average for developed countries of 0.31 (in Bulgaria the Gini coefficient rose from 0.23 in 1987–89 to 0.33 in 1997–99; in Estonia it increased from 0.28 to 0.36; and in Poland it increased from 0.28 to 0.33—UNICEF, 2001). Combined with a decline in real income, the region also experienced a sharp increase in both absolute and relative income poverty rates. In all the countries of the region, the proportion of children living in poverty was much higher than the figure for the overall population. Using an absolute poverty indicator of US \$4.30 per day, in the late 1990s the proportion of 0–15-year-olds living in poverty was: 93.2% in Albania, 75.7% in Romania, 52.5% in Latvia, 34.7% in Lithuania, 30.7% in Poland, 28.8% in Hungary, and 24.6% in Bulgaria; however, the proportion was only 4.9% in Croatia, 1.9% in the Czech Republic and 0.9% in Slovenia (ibid.);

Children in Institutional Care. Given the legacy of high numbers of children in institutional care, and the fact that concern regarding children in orphanages in Romania was instrumental in framing international responses to children in care throughout Central and South-Eastern Europe, the fact that rates of institutionalization have continued to rise 'contrary to all policy intentions' (UNICEF, 1999) is of immense importance. The number of children in residential care, expressed in terms of the rate per 100,000 of the population aged between 0 and 17 years ranged from 40.0 in Albania (1998) to 169.8 in the former Yugoslav republic of Macedonia (1999) to 1,472.1 in Romania (1997) and to 1,520.8 in Bulgaria (1996). The rates were over 750 per 100,000 in five of the 15 countries, and between 500 and 750 per 100,000 in a further four countries. Even more worryingly, the rate increased during the 1990s in nine countries, sometimes dramatically (it increased by more than 150% in Latvia), including in those countries that already had high rates of institutional care in the 1980s. A similar picture emerged regarding the numbers of children aged between 0 and 3 years in infant homes, with increased rates in 11 countries and declines in just two (figures were unavailable for the remaining two countries). The highest figures, and some of the greatest rates of increase (expressed for 1999, from a base of 100 in 1989) were in Bulgaria (1,280.8 per 100,000, 143.2), Romania (950.7 per 100,000, 155.6) and Latvia (955.9 per 100,000, 179.5) (UNICEF, 2001).

REFORMING SOCIAL POLICY: KEY THEMES

In terms of the reforms that have been implemented or advocated in social policy in Central and South-Eastern Europe, we can focus on five of the most important broad areas:

Pensions

Pensions is, perhaps, the most important and one of the most controversial areas of social-policy reform. Throughout the region, governments inherited a legacy of relatively young retirement ages, and insurance-based, 'pay-as-you-go', single-tier, universal and relatively generous pensions, with many additional benefits included. This system faced enormous pressures in terms of increased demand, decreased contributions as wages and employment declined, erosion of pensions by inflation, and the impact of restructuring-induced early retirement. Nevertheless, in the context of political lobbying and the formation, in some countries, of pensioners' parties, pensions continued to consume the largest share of social spending in the region as a whole, and rose rapidly as a proportion of GDP in some countries. In Croatia, Poland, Slovakia and Slovenia public-pension expenditure amounted to more than 13% of GDP, twice their pre-transition level (World Bank, 2002).

Pensions reform in the region was uneven and quite slow. Most countries raised retirement ages and attempted to limit expenditure, or at least render it more transparent, by tightening the link between contributions and benefits, changing indexation formulae, etc. There was pressure on regional governments from the World Bank, the IMF, and other international organizations to introduce a three-tier pensions policy. According to this approach, the first 'pillar' of the traditional, state-funded pay-as-you-go scheme would be much reduced, and limited to a minimum uniform-rate pension. Pensions would be supplemented by a mandatory second tier of individually accounted, non-solidaristic pension funds, and a voluntary third tier of completely private pension provision. This 'multi-pillar' model was most advanced in Croatia, Hungary and Latvia.

Elsewhere, there was a degree of resistance to this approach and, indeed, a recognition by the World Bank that such reforms involved considerable 'political opposition and administrative weakness' (World Bank, 2002). In particular, the introduction of a multi-pillar system entails high initial fiscal costs and, in the context of a considerable degree of risk and uncertainty regarding the performance of funds, no guarantee of success. In this context, the need for less ideological solutions to the pensions crisis were being considered, tied to notions of basic human security.

Income Maintenance and Poverty Reduction

In the context of a renewed global emphasis on co-ordinated poverty reduction, best exemplified by the UN's Millennium Development Goals (MDGs), which facilitate the measurement of progress in the least-developed countries, there has also been a concomitant acknowledgement that considerable numbers of poverty-affected areas are found in middle-income countries, including the transition countries. Initially, there was considerable concern to target social-security and social-assistance benefits to those most in need, through systems of means-testing and restrictive eligibility criteria. However, there was increasing recognition that such schemes risked a low rate of adoption, owing to factors such as stigma, complexity and the arbitrary discretion of front-line officials (UNDP, 1999). A combination of minimum wages, child benefits, utility and housing subsidies, and schemes to mitigate the effects of loss of income in economic restructuring began to be considered more effective, although the idea of a basic, sustainable, minimum-income guarantee was also advocated, and had been introduced in some countries.

Throughout the region, the drawing up of poverty reduction strategies by governments, in consultation with civil society and international financial organizations, was well under way, involving a degree of long-term social and economic planning, as well as wide-ranging consultations with diverse groups, including those living in poverty and many local non-governmental organizations (NGOs) and community-based organizations. However, balancing the poverty reduction strategy papers' macroeconomic emphasis on privatization, fiscal discipline, reductions in public expenditure, and the economic pricing of services (including utilities), with the importance of maintaining and improving standards of health, education and social-welfare services, remained contentious.

More generally, the importance of linking welfare to work, through various kinds of 'workfare' programmes, appeared to be gaining acceptance throughout the region, with Bulgaria, Hungary and Slovenia, for example, introducing schemes that required certain categories of welfare claimant, usually the longer-term unemployed, to perform some kind of socially useful labour, in return for the continued receipt of social-assistance benefits for themselves and their families. The costs and benefits of different programmes were fiercely contested, not least in terms of whether they targeted already-stigmatized groups, and whether they had any role in retraining and preparing people for meaningful employment.

The challenge of reducing social exclusion and human poverty tended to be tackled through a range of local initiatives, small-scale pilot projects or, in some countries, demand-driven social funds, which were able to encourage and reward social innovation and the direct participation of vulnerable groups and communities. Although this certainly enabled new groups, including local NGOs, to become directly involved in provision, some observers questioned whether the poorest of the poor were able to benefit from such projects and whether it was possible to ensure that the more successful initiatives were 'scaled up' to have an impact at the macro level.

Social Services

There was a considerable focus in parts of the region on policies to reduce the number of people, particularly children, in institutions, to develop a continuum of care resources (including preventive services, day care, and fostering and adoption services), and to transform institutions and improve the quality of care. As already noted, the success of these measures was mixed, in the context of a wider crisis of poverty and insecurity. In addition, there was a mixed picture with respect to external assistance, some of which promoted the construction of new institutional care facilities, and led to increased pressure for the international adoption of very young children, sometimes in contravention of global conventions on inter-country adoptions.

In many countries of the region, social work and social care as professions had been introduced only in the 1990s, so that there was a considerable need for capacity-building, financing, legislation and policy frameworks. In the post-Yugoslav countries, there were ongoing debates about the role and function of a public social-work service. The expansion of non-state provision of social services, through NGOs and the private sector, also led to an increased understanding of the need for a system of quality standards to be introduced. However, as measures were implemented for the greater decentralization of services, issues of inequity between richer and poorer areas became increasingly noticeable. Real partnerships, between the public, private and not-for-profit sectors, were rare outside specific local pilot programmes.

There was also less progress than there could have been in terms of user participation in services and in self-help and community-development initiatives, so that many services may remain paternalistic in form, rather than being client-centred in approach. Moreover, this made responsiveness to new or newly discovered problems, such as drug misuse, child abuse and trafficking, somewhat slow and uneven throughout the region. There were also particular concerns regarding the balance of care and control within the social services, and whether particular groups, such as the Roma, were over-represented within the control system, particularly in the sphere of juvenile justice.

Access to Education

Although the proportion of public expenditure allocated to education was maintained at between 4% and 6% of GDP throughout Central and South-Eastern Europe in 1989–99 (UNICEF, 2001), this was in the context of a smaller total budget. Overall, access to education had fallen, with little improvement in the quality of education offered, and increasing inequities, so that education services contributed less to challenging social exclusion than had been the case in the past. This was particularly pronounced with regard to pre-school provision, which was formerly widespread, free, often provided at the place of work and, fulfilling both child-care and learning functions, was a major factor facilitating the active participation of women in the labour market. Although there had been much-needed innovations in pre-school provision, coverage had declined significantly throughout the region.

Access to free basic education remained high throughout the region, although there was an erosion of teachers' salaries, and a consequent loss of many of the most able and motivated teachers. In addition, there was a decline in general subsidies for transport, school meals and textbooks, so that the cost of sending a child to school had increased overall, with targeted schemes to provide rebates and subsidies for the poorest having only limited success. The educational infrastructure was chronically underfunded, especially in post-conflict areas, and heating costs had increased, so that some schools were forced to close for long periods in the winter. Throughout the region, access to basic education for Roma children remained very limited, although a number of innovative programmes, commencing with pre-school provision, had been developed (Save the Children Fund, 2001).

There was greater diversity in the provision of secondary and higher education and, in both sectors, a greater degree of responsiveness to the demands of a modern labour market, although the dominant approach to teaching and learning remained fact-based in most of the region. There was a need for much greater attention to flexible and distance-based learning, continuing education and the accreditation of prior learning, as well as more work on the comparability and transferability of qualifications. Again, as a mixed model took hold, an increased focus on standards and on quality control would be needed.

Health Services

The decline in real income, combined with the heavy reliance on tertiary health care, meant that health-service reforms were advocated quite early as a necessary response to the dramatic fiscal crisis in the health sector. Throughout the region, there was a gradual adoption of health-insurance schemes, already found in the former Yugoslavia before the transition. However, such schemes found it difficult to provide increased resources in the context of low participation, together with increased labour costs. Hence, a degree of rationing and supplementary charging for particular services and medicines was also introduced. Barriers to the private practise of medicine were removed, although few doctors took advantage of this, other than as a source of additional income. There was, in this sense, a degree of subsidization of private practice from public expenditure.

The importance of greater attention to preventive, community-based, primary health-care services was recognized, and there was a greater degree of responsiveness to, and understanding of, a wider notion of health beyond simply the absence of disease. Nevertheless, there was a real danger that a two-tier health system might emerge in parts of the region, with over-stretched and ineffective basic services for all, and reasonable care available only to those who participated in the formal economy and those who could afford it.

WELFARE FUTURES: DEBATES ON THE POST-COMMUNIST WELFARE REGIME

Going beyond the specifics of the issues discussed above, there was considerable debate on the likely nature of the overall future welfare regime in the countries of Central and South-Eastern Europe. In addition, there was an ongoing debate about the way the role of global and regional agencies might lead to a degree of convergence in welfare systems within the region, and between Central and South-Eastern Europe and the more developed northern and western parts of the continent.

An early study (Deacon *et al*, 1997) pointed to the fact that advice from different international agencies tended to be mixed and to reinforce internal divisions between ministries of finance and ministries of social welfare, in terms of the kind of reform necessary. Although the traditional division between international financial institutions, such as the IMF and the World Bank, on the one hand, and the more socially orientated international organizations, such as the International Labour Organization (ILO), on the other, remained important, there were many changes and a degree of unpredictability in the nature of the reform advice offered. In this context, more traditional, residualist and neo-liberal approaches to social policy advocated by the IMF and the World Bank, with an emphasis on narrowly targeted 'safety net' benefits for the most vulnerable, were no longer presented as the only alternative.

Increasingly, the influence of the EU and the fulfilment of conditions for accession should have a more important affect on welfare regimes in the region. In a sense, however, social conditionalities had been something of a weak link within the accession process, although it was notable that judgements regarding Bulgarian and Romanian alignment to the social *acquis communautaire* (the body of EU legislation, treaties and case law), in terms of issues such as children in institutions and homeless children, were important in justifying the eventual decision not to accept those countries in the initial stage of EU expansion in 2004. Although both the PHARE (named for the original Poland/Hungary Aid for Restructuring of Economies, later expanded to cover other EU candidate countries) and subsequent CARDS (Community Assistance for Reconstruction, Development and Stabilization) programmes were concerned with social-welfare measures, these were not addressed in a coherent or consistent way, and there were real dangers that a two-tier accession process might increase the social disparities between the first group of accession countries and those that joined at a later stage.

Considerable uncertainty remained about the role of the state in the future social policy of Central and South-Eastern Europe, not least in the context of uncertain sovereignty in parts of the region and the existence of what is effectively a UN protectorate in Kosovo (Serbia and Montenegro). The phenomenon of 'state desertion' (UNDP, 1999) could be found in many parts of the region, with processes of privatization, decentralization and the general growth of a 'project and contract' culture. Even more importantly, issues of welfare governance and the need to set clear and measurable policy objectives were relatively underdeveloped, given the wider political uncertainty and the effective marginalization of social-policy issues. Indeed, the absence of clear political debate between social-democratic, liberal and conservative parties over social-policy choices was striking. The future of welfare had, instead, become much more a battle between new 'technocrats' and traditional socialist conservatives.

In the context of declining human security, there was a renewed impetus to construct new forms of universal social policy to meet the needs of diverse populations in a flexible market place and an increasingly informal economy. The focus of a new social compact, which has been suggested, would require provision for a strong role for the state, in partnership with both the non-profit and profit sectors, in which revenue collection by means of taxation would create possibilities for a new system, which would have the virtue of 'achieving transparency, fostering social solidarity, attaining cost-effectiveness administratively, and not undermining work incentives' (UNDP, 1999). In this way, social cohesion could become a defining principle and characteristic of social policy, as countries in Central and South-Eastern Europe seek to tackle growing inequities and challenge the perpetuation of internal and inter-country zones of inclusion and exclusion.

BIBLIOGRAPHY

Deacon, B. 'East European Welfare States: The Impact of the Politics of Globalization', in *Journal of European Social Policy*, Vol. 10, No. 2, May 2000.

Deacon, B., Hulse, M., and Stubbs, P. *Global Social Policy: International Organisations and the Future of Welfare*. London, Sage Publications, 1997.

Katrogoulas, G. 'The South European Welfare Model: The Greek Welfare State in Search of an Identity', in *Journal of European Social Policy*, Vol. 6, No. 1, 1996.

Kornai, J. 'The Post-socialist Transition and the State', in *American Economic Review*, Vol. 82, No. 2, 1992.

Novak, M. 'Reconsidering the Socialist Welfare State Model', in Woodward A., and Kohli, M. (Eds), *Inclusions and Exclusions in European Societies*. London, Routledge, 2001.

Overseas Development Administration (ODA). 'Social Policy Research for Development.' Mimeograph, ODA/ESCOR, 1995.

Ringold, D. 'Social Policy in Postcommunist Europe: Legacies and Transition', in Cook, L. *et al* (Eds). *Left Parties and Social Policy in Post-Communist Europe*. Boulder, CO, Westview Press, 1999.

Save the Children Fund. *Denied a Future? The Right to Education of Roma, Gypsy and Traveller Children in Europe*. London, Save the Children Fund, 2001.

Stubbs, P. *Rights in Crisis and Transition: Developing a Children's Agenda for South Eastern Europe*. Belgrade, South East European Child Rights Network (SEECRAN) and Save the Children Fund, 2001.

UNDP. *Human Development Report for Central and Eastern Europe and the CIS*. New York, NY, UNDP, 1999.

UNICEF. *After the Fall: the Human Impact of Ten Years of Transition*. Florence, UNICEF Innocenti Research Centre, 1999.

A Decade of Transition. Regional Monitoring Report, No 8. Florence, UNICEF Innocenti Research Centre, 2001.

World Bank. *Yugoslavia: Development with Decentralization*. Baltimore, MD, Johns Hopkins University Press, 1975.

A Decade of Transition. Washington, DC, World Bank, 2002.

RELIGION IN CENTRAL AND SOUTH-EASTERN EUROPE

Rev. Canon MICHAEL BOURDEAUX

In every country of the collapsing communist bloc religion played a role. The more strongly it combined with the forces of nationalism, the more decisive was its contribution. There was, nevertheless, enormous variation from country to country, and the points of comparison have become ever fewer since that time. Even where religion had been annihilated from the surface of society, a subliminal desire on the part of people remained: Albania was the prime example, but there is a clear comparison with the People's Republic of China. More tangibly, organized religion provided a secure environment where human rights could be discussed (as in the German Democratic Republic—GDR, or East Germany). In Lithuania and Poland the alliance of religion and nationalism led to a volatile climate in which change became inevitable.

It is often asked why the communist leaders so resolutely selected religion as a prime object of persecution. Ultimately, history showed that they, in their own terms, were 'right' to do so: religious commitment could prompt people to political activity long after the relevant institutions had lost their temporal power. Soviet anti-religious policy originated with Lenin (Vladimir Ilych Ulyanov), whose hostility far surpassed anything to be found in the writings of Karl Marx and Friedrich Engels, the progenitors of communism. In a letter to Maksim Gorkii in 1913, Lenin wrote, 'Every religious idea, every idea of God, even every flirtation with this idea of God, is unutterable vileness'. Starting with his Decree on the Separation of Church and State in January 1918, Lenin proceeded to apply his philosophical thoughts on religion to practical policy. His successor as Soviet leader, Stalin (Iosif Vissarionovich Dzhugashvili) instituted organized and nation-wide persecution of religion (as of all other non-communist institutions), which was so successful on the surface that by the end of the 1930s religion had virtually disappeared from public life and only a handful of open churches remained.

However, the German invasion of the USSR in 1941 caused a volte-face: compromise was necessary in order to reinforce the morale of the country in the face of mortal danger. Clergy who had survived in the prison camps and who were willing to take an oath of allegiance to the Soviet state were allowed, in many instances, to return to their congregations and reopen their churches. The conquest of vast new territories by the Red Army in the last years of the Second World War confronted Soviet anti-religious policy, which had not renounced its ultimate goals, with a dilemma. It was ironic that Stalin, who had achieved so much in his attempted liquidation of the Church one decade previously, should subsequently acquire lands in which Christianity existed in a particularly vigorous form, most notably the Catholic Church, both in its Latin and Byzantine forms, but also Eastern Orthodoxy in Romania and Bulgaria and Lutheranism in East Germany.

Soviet practice was not consistent. In those regions incorporated into the USSR the policy was to reduce religion as quickly as possible to the same status it would have had if they had formed part of the Union from 1917. Thus, Soviet Moldavia (Moldova), western Ukraine, western Belarus and the Baltic republics of Estonia, Latvia and Lithuania were subjected to particularly severe policies. The Baltic states experienced the brutality of mass deportations (already begun on a smaller scale in 1939, when the USSR invaded prior to

the German occupation of 1941). The intention was to remove from society all those with leadership capacity in every field of endeavour. In Lithuania, for example, some 200,000 men, women and children were deported to Siberia, Russia, in the immediate post-War period.

It was clearly impossible to apply measures on anything like this scale to any of the countries that remained outside the USSR. The Soviet authorities established 'puppet' regimes in all those countries, but even in their subjection they had to take account of local religious traditions and popular allegiances. In some instances, existing institutions were simply too strong to be liquidated, so the methods of reducing their influence varied from country to country. However, between 1948 and 1956 it was still possible to speak of a common Soviet-dominated policy towards religion. This changed following the denunciation of Stalin by Nikita Khrushchev (leader of the USSR, 1953–64) in 1956, each regime in the region by this time following its own policies on religion. It is instructive to examine the diversity of the situations by considering each major religion and denomination in turn, rather than using a narrower, geographical basis.

THE ROMAN CATHOLIC CHURCH

Roman Catholics (of both Western, 'Latin', and Eastern, 'Byzantine', Rites) were important in the overturning of communism in Eastern Europe and, indeed, in the eventual downfall of the USSR. It is, therefore, appropriate to begin with a consideration of the role of the Vatican and its many followers in the region.

While Poland clearly offered the foremost bastion of resistance to communism, its much smaller northern neighbour, Lithuania, witnessed events that were, ultimately, lethal to the integrity of the Soviet system. The Roman Catholic Church in Lithuania united a small nation, the very existence of which was threatened by Soviet rule. Even the deportations failed totally to break the resistance of the Church in Lithuania, and there are many examples of its clandestine activities in Siberian labour camps. At home, the diocesan bishops were shot or exiled, but some 600 parish churches managed to keep their doors open. Return from exile following Khrushchev's 'secret speech' of 1956 strengthened ecclesiastical resistance and in the 1970s the vast majority of the clergy secretly united to gather information about the persecution and to convey it to the world outside by means of the clandestine *Chronicle of the Lithuanian Catholic Church*. Mikhail Gorbachev (Soviet leader, 1985–91) failed to realize how powerful were the forces with which he was dealing. *Perestroika*, Gorbachev's policy of 'restructuring' the communist state, allowed a more public expression of repressed nationalist feelings, and the churches became deeply involved as the nation reclaimed its heritage. Events such as the return of the Bishop of Vilnius, Julijonas Steponavičius, following 29 years' exile and house arrest, to reclaim his diocese and his cathedral, led to popular demonstrations, which Gorbachev could neither understand nor counter. The Lithuanian Movement for Reconstruction (Sąjūdis), the popular front political movement, which was solidly in league with the Roman Catholic Church, guided the country towards a declaration of independence in March 1990. Gorbachev declined to negotiate, but the attempted coup against him and the subsequent collapse of the USSR at the end of 1991 resulted in the formal transformation of Lithuania from a constituent republic of the USSR to an independent state, as it had been in the inter-War years. As in Poland, the Church in Lithuania became less politically active thereafter, losing some of its influence in the process. However, the resurgence of the political left did not threaten religious liberty.

From its beginnings it was clear that the Stalinist policy of brutal oppression was destined to fail in Poland, short of a policy of genocide being applied. The country contained the world's most powerful national Roman Catholic Church and, like Lithuania, one of the most homogenous (from the religious point of view) populations on earth. At the end of 1953, the year of Stalin's death, Cardinal Stefan Wyszyński, eight other bishops, 900 priests and some 1,000 lay activists were in prison. Even this total, however, created very little noticeable difference in the numbers of churchgoers and served to strengthen the resolve of the millions who remained at liberty. Upon his release in 1956 Cardinal Wyszyński proclaimed a Novena, a nine-year programme to re-educate the people in the faith, to compensate for the 10 years lost under communist rule. Gradually, but consistently, the Church regained influence, although the state never completely halted its interference in Church affairs.

In October 1978 a conclave of the Roman Catholic Church's College of Cardinals elected Karol Wojtyła of Kraków as the first Slav Pope. Clearly, the Church felt that the greatest spiritual strength could be found where the Church had most fully developed its hidden reserves; what the cardinals did not envisage was that this appointment would contribute to the beginning of a process that would, in little more than one decade, overturn communism. Christians throughout the region, even some Protestant groups in Siberia, were encouraged by this unprecedented event. Wojtyła's first visit to Poland as Pope John Paul II in mid-1979 generated large-scale popular demonstrations. These were followed by widespread labour unrest in 1980 and the foundation of Solidarity (Solidarność), the first anti-communist, and specifically Christian, trade union in the Eastern bloc. Its repression and the imposition of martial law in December 1981 only strengthened the opposition. By April–May 1989 the Church, or, more precisely, its 'political wing', in the form of Solidarity, was powerful enough to bring about a 'round table' conference between the Government and the opposition. This introduced a limited democratic process and the eventual representation of anti-communist forces in government. In August a Roman Catholic Prime Minister, Tadeusz Mazowiecki, was appointed, and in December of the following year a Roman Catholic President, Lech Wałęsa, was elected.

The strength of Roman Catholicism in Poland did not prevent the defeat of Wałęsa in the presidential election of 1995, however. He was succeeded as President by Aleksander Kwaśniewski, the leader of Social Democracy of the Republic of Poland (Socjaldemokracja Rzeczypospolitej Polskiej—SdRP), the successor to the Communist Party. Polish Catholics were, nevertheless, able to continue their moral reconstruction of society. Although traditional morality was not perceived to be as damaged as in other former communist countries, it was felt that there had been some deterioration from 1948 (the controversy over abortion, for example, indicated the conflict between religious and secular values). In an attempt to counter this decline, the Church became involved in an extensive project to rebuild Christian educational and social institutions. Cardinal Józef Glemp, primate after the death of Cardinal Wyszyński in 1981, shunned publicity and resisted the intrusions secularism made into the Church in the 1990s. There were also attempts to bring the Polish Church into line with other aspects of papal policy. Thus, Pope John Paul II urged tolerance of minorities during his visit of June 1991, something which did not, conventionally, form part of Polish Catholic behaviour.

Poland was by no means the only country where the Roman Catholic Church was politically significant. It was prominent, for example, in the abortive counter-revolution in Hungary in 1956. Cardinal József Mindszenty was one of the best known and, from the moral point of view, most vigorously defended of all the hierarchs who suffered under the Stalinist rulers of Eastern Europe. When the Hungarians briefly regained their freedom he was released from prison and his words, broadcast over the radio, became a classic example of Christian defence against communism. Not even subsequent implied criticism nor his removal from office by the Vatican could eradicate his example. He had been, from 1956 to 1974, a refugee in the US legation in Budapest, the Hungarian capital, during which time the Vatican attempted to reach an accord with the Government. The crowds who attended the reinterment of his remains at Esztergom, Hungary, in 1991, demonstrated their undying loyalty. However, unlike Poland, the Roman Catholic Church in Hungary was not monolithic. Although by the third millennium the total population of Hungary was some 10m., of whom an estimated 62% were baptized Roman Catholics, there was much nominalism and the Church received universal support only in some country areas.

As Hungarian society recovered from the repressions that followed the 1956 uprising, criticism of the Church leadership by its followers became more insistent. The Vatican appointed new bishops, after the secular authorities agreed the names, but, as a balance, quietly encouraged 'base communities', which developed into a powerful movement. At its most popular point the movement comprised some 5,000 groups and 100,000 individual members. In the late 1970s and early 1980s the base communities caused tension within the Church as they came into conflict with the bishops; the movement's pacifism and its challenge to communism threatened the hierarchy's relationship with the secular authorities.

No single Christian leader emerged to inspire and lead believers as democracy became more of a possibility. From 1988, however, Roman Catholic bishops became increasingly insistent in their questioning of the politicians. The Prime Minister, Károly Grósz, hearing from Cardinal László Paskai that youth work was increasing, replied: 'We agree that only a Church that is capable of functioning can fruitfully assist the realization of our social objectives'. However, the opportunities for the Church to help any Hungarian government achieve socialist (Marxist) objectives were soon to end. On 23 January 1990 the democratic National Assembly enacted a law guaranteeing complete religious freedom.

For decades the Vatican's *Ostpolitik* (policy towards the East, evolved, controversially, in the hope of safe-guarding the long-term existence of the Church in the East, while making short-term compromises) clearly envisaged that there would be a long period of repression. The appointment of bishops approved by the state, for example, was permitted, in return for the promise of freedom of worship and some rights in education. The abruptness of the collapse of communism found the Church (not only Roman Catholics) in many places considerably less than ready to take best advantage of the new freedoms. Thus, the rebuilding of Roman Catholicism in Hungary during the 1990s occurred at a steady, rather than a rapid, pace.

Christians in the former Czechoslovakia were much more openly engaged in an active struggle for religious freedom. The policy of the regime virtually ensured this, because it remained repressive during the 1970s and 1980s, while in nearby Hungary the Government was gradually relaxing restrictions. After the 'Prague Spring' and the Soviet invasion of 1968, Christian activists, Protestants, as well as Roman

Catholics, were systematically removed from the professions and forced to take menial jobs. They remained in this position until after the events of late 1989, so their reinstatement, sometimes occurring overnight, was all the more striking. In no other new Eastern European democracy was the situation so dramatic, with Václav Havel (President of Czechoslovakia from 1989 and of the Czech Republic in 1993–2003) an obvious example in political life. The churches lost nearly two-thirds of their members under communism, but the remainder (for the Roman Catholics, more than 3m. people) still represented a substantial minority. Gradually, after the trauma of 1968, the churches regained confidence; thus, the human rights movement, Charter 77, contained Christian activists from its foundation.

The Roman Catholic Church, as an international organization, enjoyed the benefits of foreign contacts, stronger and more public even than the external links of the Czechoslovakian Protestants. Perhaps most influential was the way in which the aged Roman Catholic primate, František Tomášek (Archbishop of Prague, 1978–91), became more outspoken and seemingly more resilient with his declining years. He was already in his mid-70s when he became a cardinal in 1976 (the appointment was not announced immediately); he strenuously opposed the 'peace priests' of Pacem in Terris (Peace on Earth), a group which the state had persuaded to endorse its political propaganda. Later, after their decline in influence, his own public statements aimed to incite people to action. Cardinal Tomášek lived to see the fall of communism, retired at the age of 91 and died one year later. His successor, Cardinal Miroslav Vlk, proved to be a strong leader, one who had personally experienced deprivation during the communist era; like many other priests, he was banned from office, and found work as a window-cleaner.

The Roman Catholic Church in Czechoslovakia remained surprisingly silent during the approach to the division of the country into two on 1 January 1993. It was predictable that the Church's role was to be different in the two new states of the Czech Republic and Slovakia. Indeed, religious differences contributed to the dissolution of the federation. The Czech Lands (Bohemia and Moravia) continued to be among the most secularized of the formerly communist territories. Conversely, Slovakia exhibited a traditional piety and Roman Catholicism engaged the loyalty of the majority of the population. Slovakia became one of Europe's most Christian countries, comparable to its northern neighbour, Poland. However, of the Slovak Catholics, a large number in Eastern Slovakia (around Prešov and Košice) were the dispossessed Catholics of the Eastern Rite ('Greek' Catholics, often known as Uniates). Communist policy had outlawed this Church in 1948, with all its property passing to the less numerically significant Orthodox Christians. This political act repeated the fate of the Ukrainian Greek Catholics immediately to the east. Although the Slovak, Eastern Rite faith regained legal status during the 'Prague Spring' of 1968, no property was returned. The collapse of communism, therefore, provided the opportunity for the Eastern Rite Catholics to reclaim their churches and presbyteries from the Orthodox. The Slovak Orthodox were left economically bereft, and additionally burdened by an undeserved moral stigma. The majority, Latin Rite Roman Catholics co-existed in considerable numbers with the Eastern Rite Catholics in eastern Slovakia and dominated the west of the country, so the situation remained unsettled.

The total number of Catholics of the Byzantine and Latin Rites in Romania was approximately 2m. at the end of 2000; Byzantine Rite Catholicism had re-emerged after the collapse of communism, following its abolition and incorporation into the Romanian Orthodox Church in 1948. The leader of the Byzantine Rite in Romania, Alexandru Todea (who died in May 2002, after having been incapacitated through illness for the final 10 years of his life), experienced imprisonment and house arrest for over 40 years, following his secret consecration as a bishop. Upon regaining his freedom after the execution of President Nicolae Ceaușescu at the end of 1989, Todea petitioned unsuccessfully for more than two years for the return of church property from the Orthodox Church. He became a cardinal in 1991. Todea's charitable attitude towards the Orthodox paved the way for the visit to Romania by Pope John Paul II in May 1999, which marked the first visit of a head of the Roman Catholic Church to a principally Orthodox country. Although Latin Rite Catholics (mainly ethnic Hungarians and Germans) also lost their bishops in the communist period, they faced somewhat fewer difficulties in reconstructing their basic administration.

The most impressive instance of Roman Catholic revival in Eastern Europe occurred in Albania. In 1967 the regime led by Enver Hoxha (Albanian leader, 1944–85) went further than any other communist state in banning religious activity completely. Even the People's Republic of China, which provided Albania's ideological model, retained a nominal church leadership during the Cultural Revolution of that time. Figures based on declared religious affiliations dating from 1945 estimated that approximately 70% of the population of 3m. were Muslims, 20% Eastern Orthodox Christian (mostly living in the south, adjacent to Greece) and 10% Roman Catholics (living in the north). The smallest of the main groups, the Roman Catholic Church, was from the late 19th century nevertheless strongly linked with Albanian nationalism. After the 1967 ban every place of worship was closed, many of the buildings destroyed and all the active clergy removed to prison camps. There was, however, evidence of clandestine observance of religious practices, but the authorities continued to campaign relentlessly against religion. Hoxha's regime soon proclaimed nil adherents to religion and even after his death in 1985 the ideological structure of the state seemed to remain intact. However, this ideology was soon to be dramatically overturned.

Albania's imperviousness to the fall of communism in 1989 was only superficial. Beginning in January 1990, riots, increasing in force, took place in the northern city of Shkodër; some of the activists were Roman Catholics. On 8 May the Government announced that the ban on religious propaganda had ended. Acting defensively, the Government permitted public Easter celebrations, with the Roman Catholic service in Tirana, the capital, attended by the best-known Albanian of all, Mother Teresa. In Shkodër the cathedral was reopened. In mid-1991 it was agreed that diplomatic relations should be established with the Holy See. In April 1993 John Paul II made the first-ever papal visit to Albania. All religious institutions having been devastated, no easy forecast was possible in 2003 as to how quickly Roman Catholics, in contrast to Muslims (q.v.), might begin to play a significant role in public life again. Religious education had been entirely neglected and its full reinstatement would take decades. Foreign financial support was made available, some towards the development of (non-indigenous) Protestant institutions. It was external help, however, that enabled the Roman Catholics to re-establish an infrastructure in a very short time.

THE EASTERN ORTHODOX CHURCH

In contrast to the Roman Catholic Church, the Eastern Orthodox Churches, from Byzantine times, adopted a position of political loyalty to the regime in power. The consequence of this for the USSR was that the Russian Orthodox Church never formulated any united policy of opposition to communist atheism and the same applied to the other Orthodox churches of the former communist bloc. Although the Orthodox Church enjoyed influence in many former communist countries, it was spiritually unprepared for the unprecedented opportunities that arose after 1989.

The Romanian Orthodox Church used resurgent nationalism and the opportunity for new freedoms to reinforce its own position in national life. Nevertheless, the Orthodox Church was important in the development of civic consciousness in a country where the suppression of opposition was widespread and effective. The Romanian Orthodox Church had remained the state religion after 1945 and claimed at least 19m. adherents (some 83% of the population). During the communist period hundreds of thousands of lay people and some 1,900 Orthodox priests (including 18 bishops) were imprisoned. Many died, including Nicodim, Patriarch at the time of the communist takeover. The National Resistance Movement continued for years, and any person suspected of aiding it faced immediate arrest. The intimidated remainder co-operated with the communist regime and became politically dependent upon the Moscow Patriarchate. None the less, there were always individuals prepared to voice contrary opinions, and in the mid-1970s a Christian Committee for the Defence of Religious Freedom and Freedom of Conscience emerged, in which Orthodox Christians were allied with Baptists. The state neutralized the Committee by forcing the leading activists to emigrate. During the same period Fr Gheorghe Calciu-Dumitreasa angered the regime and his own hierarchy by teaching courses critical of socialism at the Bucharest Theological Academy. His imprisonment in 1979 caused international protests, as did Nicolae Ceauşescu's later plans to build his palace and to replace old villages with apartment blocks, both of which entailed considerable destruction of church properties. After the collapse of communism, the Archbishop of Timişoara and Caransebeş, Nicolae Corneanu, publicly repented for having been an informer for the Securitate. Patriarch Teoctist himself resigned after the execution of Ceauşescu, owing to his close links with the secular power, but he was soon reinstated by the Holy Synod on account of his veracity and self-judgment. In general, the Romanian Orthodox Church was much more positive in its foreign relations than its Russian counterpart, taking, for example, every opportunity to send its graduates and young priests abroad for further theological study. It remains the most ecumenical of all the Orthodox churches.

In Bulgaria individual churchmen came to prominence in the progress of democratization. The most influential was the Bulgarian Orthodox monk (and former scientist), Hristofor Subev, who established an Independent Association for the Defence of Human Rights in Bulgaria in February 1988. Its membership included representatives of both the Muslim and the Protestant minorities. Persecuted by the state and under pressure from his own Church, Fr Subev nevertheless supported Muslim cultural and religious rights when protests began in May 1989. His imprisonment for some 10 weeks in mid-1989 only strengthened the resolve of his supporters. Previous to this the Bulgarian Orthodox Church (with 2m. active members, out of a population of 9m., and many more baptized, but inactive, members) was among the most passive of all within the communist bloc. It suffered widespread persecution and intimidation during the 1950s, but enjoyed limited benefits as a national church. As an organization it was not critical of the regime and discouraged its priests, like Fr Subev, from being so. In December 1989, however, following agitation supported by other emerging human rights groups, the Independent Association was granted legal status. In July 1990 the Holy Synod of the Bulgarian Orthodox Church made public an act of repentance, in which it declared it was in error to have criticized Fr Subev. In 1992 Subev became involved in a schism in the Bulgarian Church. He and two metropolitans established an alternative Synod, in opposition to Patriarch Maksim, whose election, they claimed, had

been engineered by the communist regime. By 1995 Subev had lost much of his support and emigrated to the USA. The schism long survived all attempts to heal it, but when Pope John Paul II visited Bulgaria in May 2002 he acknowledged Patriarch Maksim as the legitimate leader of the Orthodox Church.

The Serbian Orthodox Church was in a weak position throughout the communist period, but was an opposition element insofar as it represented the national interests of the Serbs. With the collapse of Yugoslavia, the Serbian Church found itself centre-stage in a new, nationalist Serbia; however, for several years before the fall of the Serbian, and later federal, President, Slobodan Milošević, in 2000, it was increasingly critical of his policies.

THE PROTESTANT CHURCHES

Of all the countries of the formerly communist bloc of Eastern Europe and the USSR, only in the former GDR and in Estonia and Latvia were the Protestant Churches the majority religious grouping. A number of Lutheran activists emerged in each of these, stimulating pluralism and hastening the democratic process.

The territory of the GDR was the homeland of Martin Luther and the heartland of the Reformation, but the Evangelical Church in Germany (Evangelische Kirche in Deutschland—EKD), under the communist regime, declined to some 3m. members out of a population of 17m. However, after the Second World War there was no purge of the Church leadership, as occurred elsewhere in the socialist bloc; the clergy never compromised with the political system under duress, nor did their leaders adopt an anti-communist policy, as in Poland. Instead, the leaders of the EKD described themselves as the 'Church in Socialism' and reserved the right to criticize if the regime clearly contradicted Christian morality or opposed the interests of the Church. (In the late 1990s it became apparent from the files of the state security service—Staatssicherheitsdienst or, colloquially, the Stasi—that some clergy had collaborated.) In the 1980s the truce between church and state gradually disintegrated. Young people began to challenge Marxism more openly, and the Church provided protection for them, as those involved in political opposition began to congregate in and around Protestant churches. The state leadership, fearful of adverse opinion, decided it could not expel such people from church premises, treating them as though they had gained the medieval right of sanctuary, despite some opposition. From 1982, in St Nicholas Church in Leipzig, there were weekly prayer services for peace. Increasingly, these accommodated young activists with a political agenda, and in September and early October 1989 some 6,000 people attended the meetings, and three times as many marched around the city at night, chanting slogans. The clergy were powerless to restrain the demonstrations and a violent confrontation appeared inevitable. Yet the Stasi still failed to intervene. Although political events developed separately, resulting in the breaching of the Berlin Wall on 9 November, the important role of the Church was emphasized when four clergy and several Protestants were appointed to the new Government's 23-strong cabinet. The demise of the GDR as an independent state, therefore, concluded one of the most remarkable chapters in 20th-century church history.

In Romania the revolt of workers in Braşov was followed by strong protests from among the ethnic Hungarian minority in Transylvania, eventually leading to the anti-communist revolution of December 1989. László Tőkés was an ethnic Hungarian and an outspoken pastor of the Hungarian Reformed Church. The authorities, with the support of the bishop, attempted to evict him from his parish house in Timişoara. His resistance inspired street protests there, making opposition to the regime public, and stimulated riots elsewhere in the country. After the fall of Ceauşescu, Tőkés became a bishop and enjoyed regional and international authority. However, he continued to be treated as a Hungarian nationalist and was distrusted by the Romanian authorities. Following the general election of November 1996, ethnic Hungarians won significant democratic and linguistic rights, and representation in the new coalition Government. After the collapse of communism the Baptists, for long repressed, made effective use of their new freedom, especially in the sphere of education. In 1994, for example, they established an impressive seminary in Oradea.

In Estonia and Latvia the Lutheran Churches were for many years more passive towards the Soviet regime than the Roman Catholic Church in Lithuania, but in the late 1980s they took an increasingly significant part in the democratic process that led to independence.

JUDAISM

The genocide of Eastern European Jewry under the Nazis during the Second World War had a devastating effect everywhere, except in those parts of the USSR that they did not reach. Nevertheless, popular anti-Semitism persisted in Poland, and research has proven that in one place Poles actively participated in genocide. Jewish spiritual leaders recognized that Romania was the state most hospitable to Jews in Eastern Europe. There were deportations in that part of Transylvania annexed by Hungary, but not in Romania itself, and Jews continued to run a State Jewish Theatre even during the Second World War. Although the Chief Rabbi, Moses Rosen, later helped Romanian Jews to emigrate to Israel, this took place in collaboration with Ceauşescu, who collected considerable sums of money as a result.

ISLAM

In Bulgaria the Muslim minority benefited considerably from the ending of communist rule. Muslims lost virtually all rights under the former regime, even suffering the 'bulgarization' of personal and family names. With the advent of democracy, however, their circumstances improved.

In the Balkans the reasonable relations between Islam and Christianity seriously deteriorated in the post-communist period. Ethnic conflict, rather than religious fanaticism, was at the root of the civil wars in the former Yugoslavia, and both Islam and Christianity became the victims, rather than the instigators, of conflict. Serbian elements destroyed mosques in Bosnia and Herzegovina on a massive scale in the early 1990s, and Muslim Albanians destroyed many Orthodox churches and monasteries in the Serbian province of Kosovo and Metohija in the late 1990s. Further attacks continued into the early 2000s. For a time it seemed that Albania, with its resurgent Islam, professed by the majority of the population by the end of the 20th century, would remain outside the conflict. However, the country became involved in the dispute in Kosovo as a result of the Serbian repression of the ethnic Albanian people there. The ethnic conflicts in the former Yugoslavia left predominantly Muslim areas in Bosnia and Kosovo dependent on UN protection. This conflict extended, for the first time, into the former Yugoslav republic of Macedonia (FYRM) in 2001, when ethnic Albanians were reported to be attempting to establish a 'greater Albania' to incorporate Kosovo and parts of the FYRM into one Islamist state. Religious conflict between Orthodox and Muslims had, therefore, become a small part of a larger picture.

BIBLIOGRAPHY

Beeson, T. *Discretion and Valour: Religious Conditions in Russia and Eastern Europe*. London, Fontana, 1982, revised edn.

Bourdeaux, M. *Land of Crosses: The Struggle for Religious Freedom in Lithuania, 1939–78*. Chulmleigh, Augustine Publishing House, 1979.

Forest, J. *The Resurrection of the Church in Albania*. Geneva, WCC Publications, 2002.

Luxmoore, J., and Babiuch, J. *The Vatican and the Red Flag: the Struggle for the Soul of Eastern Europe*. London, Geoffrey Chapman, 1999.

Michel, P. *Politics and Religion in Eastern Europe*. Cambridge, Polity Press, 1991.

Mojzes, P. *Religious Liberty in Eastern Europe and the USSR: Before and After the Great Transformation*. New York, NY, Colombia University Press, 1992.

Ramet, S. P. *Nihil Obstat: Religion, Politics and Social Change in East-Central Europe and Russia*. Durham, NC, Duke University Press, 1998.

Religion, State and Society: The Keston Journal. Oxford, Keston Institute, quarterly.

Weigel, G. *The Final Revolution*. Oxford, Oxford University Press, 1992.

APPENDIX: THE RELIGIONS OF THE REGION

A brief survey of the main religions, denominations and sects in the region follows.

CHRISTIANITY

The Christian religion is a monotheistic faith, which evolved from Judaism in the first century AD. Christianity is based on a belief in the divinity and teachings of Jesus Christ, the Messiah or Son of God, through whom salvation (life after death) can be obtained. His followers established the institution of a single Church, originally based on the four leading cities of the Roman Empire: Antioch, Alexandria, Rome itself and Constantinople (from AD 330, the capital). Four distinct traditions emerged: the Syrian or Jacobite Church was based on Antioch; the Coptic Church was based on Alexandria; the western, or Latin, Church was based on Rome and became known as the Roman Catholic Church (the Protestants sprang from this tradition too); and the eastern, or Greek, Orthodox Church became centred on Constantinople (this is the tradition of most of the region's Orthodox Churches). Later divisions resulted in the emergence of the Armenian (Gregorian) Church and the Nestorian Church.

The Church also established the Christian era (a calendar of years denoted by *Anno Domini*), a reckoning that is now the most widely-used international system and is in official use throughout Central and South-Eastern Europe. Likewise, it was the Church that preserved the use of the ancient Roman, Julian calendar (used in the Russian Empire until the Revolution). In 1582 a reformed Gregorian calendar (in normal use now) was first introduced, but by Pope Gregory XIII, so its adoption was initially resisted by non-Roman Catholic countries. For religious purposes the Eastern Orthodox Church still uses a version of the old Julian calendar. (Muslims use a lunar calendar, which is about 10 days shorter than the solar calendar of the Gregorian reckoning. Islam dates its years from the *Hijra*—the flight of the Prophet Muhammad from Mecca to Medina. The Jewish calendar is luni-solar and reckons years in the Era of Creation—*Anno Mundi*.)

The Eastern Orthodox Church

In 1054 the split (schism) in the Church that had become established in the old Roman Empire became formal. The bishops of what had been the Latin-speaking West supported the authority of the Pope, the Roman patriarch, and the insertion of the *filioque* clause into the standard confession of faith, the Nicene Creed. (This claimed that the Holy Spirit, a constituent part of the triune deity, was a product of both the Father and the Son—*Logos*—not merely of the Father.) The bishops of the Greek-speaking Eastern Roman Empire, dominated by the Byzantine Patriarch of Constantinople (today still regarded as the Ecumenical Patriarch), rejected this and so formalized a division of Europe into East and West. The Eastern, or Greek, Orthodox Church continued to use the Greek alphabet, but had also added to the success of its missionary work among the 'barbarian' peoples, on the Byzantine borders, by the introduction of the Cyrillic alphabet and a Slavonic liturgy. This powerful formative influence of the Church, particularly on culture, education and national identity, is still most relevant today. The Romanian Orthodox are unique among the Orthodox in the use of the Latin alphabet. The other non-Greek orthodox churches use the Cyrillic alphabet, the invention of which is attributed to the Byzantine missionaries, St Cyril (Constantine) and St Methodius, in the ninth century.

The Eastern Orthodox churches have a membership of some 200m., most of them in South-Eastern Europe and Russia. They are not formally linked save in acknowledging the pre-eminence of the Ecumenical Patriarch (Bartholomeo I of Constantinople and New Rome, since 1991), who convened a meeting of 12 of the highest Eastern Orthodox patriarchs in the Turkish city of İstanbul (formerly Constantinople) during 1992. They met regularly thereafter. There are some Greek Orthodox in southern Albania, who fall under the jurisdiction of the Greek Church, and in 1996 the Estonian Church was placed under the jurisdiction of the Ecumenical Patriarchate, despite the protests of Russia's Moscow Patriarchate, which had been responsible for it since 1940; the Estonian Orthodox Church of the Moscow Patriarchate was officially registered in April 2002. Other strains resulted from the collapse of the authoritarian states, as in Bulgaria, where the fall of communism led to a schism. The main autocephalous (autonomous) Orthodox churches of South-Eastern Europe are in Bulgaria, Romania and Serbia and Montenegro (the Serbian Orthodox Church). The separate existence of the Macedonian Orthodox Church is not acknowledged by the others. All the countries of the region have at least some Orthodox Christians.

The Roman Catholic Church

The western, or Roman Catholic Church, was the Church of Poland and the Baltic peoples, and the peoples of the Central European empires of the Germans, Austrians and Hungarians (though, after the Reformation, a significant number became Protestant). This original divide was important in the disintegration of the former Yugoslavia and the continuing tensions in the area: the Slovenes are Roman Catholic; so too are the Croats, who speak the same language as the Serbs, but write it in the Latin script. The Roman Catholics were distinguished by their use of a liturgy in Latin, which is still referred to as the Latin Rite, although most services are now conducted in the vernacular.

The Latin Rite is not used by the adherents of the 'Greek' Catholic or 'Uniate' Church. This denomination is part of the Roman Catholic Church, but uses the Eastern or 'Byzantine' Rite; their Orthodox predecessors had acknowledged the primacy of the Roman pontiff, the Pope (also the existence of Purgatory, the doctrine of the *filioque* and the use of unleavened bread for communion), but retained their traditional liturgies and ecclesiastical organization. This first occurred in the late 15th century, as an attempt to consolidate Polish (Roman Catholic) power in a traditionally Orthodox area. A similar process took place in Transylvania (Hungary) at the end of the 17th century. Not all Uniates use the Byzantine Rite; there are some from non-Orthodox traditions.

Protestant Churches

In the Reformation period of the 16th and 17th centuries some of the western, or Catholic, Christians protested against the authority of the Roman pontiff, the Pope, and formed separate ('Protestant') sects. Most of these groups relied more on the authority of the Bible and rejected the episcopal organization of the Church (the Lutherans and some others retain bishops in the hierarchy, but often reject the 'apostolic' nature of their authority). The main denominations are: Lutheran Evangelical (who define their faith by the Augsburg Confession of 1530); the more fundamentalist Calvinists and Presbyterians (the Reformed Church of Hungary, etc.); Baptists; Pentecostalists; and Unitarians. There are also communities of Seventh-day Adventists (distinguished among Christians by their observance of the Sabbath on Saturday), Methodists, Mennonites (mainly of German descent, they combine characteristics of the Baptists and the Society of Friends—Quakers) and many others.

Other Christian Churches

The major split in the western Church was the Protestant defection from Rome. However, there were some precursors of this movement in the 15th century, notably the Hussites of Bohemia and Moravia, who adapted the teachings of English Lollardy. Several sects that sprang from the Hussite factions still exist, mainly in the former Czechoslovakia: there are the Hussite Church and the Brethren churches, notably the Moravian Church, which has a significant world-wide presence, owing to its extensive missionary activity. Both the Roman Catholic and the Orthodox Churches lost some members when they underwent reformation. There are Old Catholic communities in many of the countries of the region (formed in the 19th century).

ISLAM

Islam means 'submission' or surrender to God. It is the preferred name for the monotheistic religion founded by Muhammed, the Prophet (AD 570–632), in Arabia. The unparalleled spread of the religion in its first centuries can be attributed to the concept of holy war (*jihad*).

The Five Pillars of the practice of Islam are: the Witness that 'there is no god but God' (*Allah*) and that 'Muhammed is His Prophet'; Prayer, which takes place five times daily and includes prostration in the direction of the holy city of Mecca (Saudi Arabia) and recitation of set verses, and is also performed in congregational worship at a mosque on Fridays, the Muslim holy day; Almsgiving; Fasting, which must take place during the hours of daylight for the whole of the ninth month, Ramadan (some exceptions are allowed); finally, the Pilgrimage (*hajj*) to Mecca, which is incumbent at least once in the lifetime of a Muslim. The heart of Islam is contained in the Koran, which is considered above criticism as the very Word of God as uttered to his Prophet. This authority is supplemented by various traditions (*hadith*). To interpret the application of Islamic law (*shari'a*) into normal activity, four main schools of thought emerged, the main one in the region being the Hanafi. An ideal of the Islamic community (*umma*) is that the brotherhood of Muslims is its basis and that the religion is international and beyond tribal division. However, there has not been an unchallenged Muslim leader since the Prophet, and the last of the caliphs (*khalifas* or 'successors' of Muhammed), who resided in Constantinople, had his office abolished by the Turkish Government in 1924.

There are significant minorities of Turkish Muslims throughout the Balkan countries, and there are small Tatar communities in Poland and Lithuania. In the former communist bloc of Eastern Europe the main Muslim groups are either Albanian or Slavic Muslims, the latter mainly being the Bosnian Muslims (Bosniaks) of Bosnia and Herzegovina, the Sandžak Muslims of Serbia and Montenegro and the Pomaks of Bulgaria.

Sunni Muslims and Other Traditions

Some 80% of the world's Muslims are Sunni, followers of 'the path' or customary way. They acknowledge the first four Caliphs as successors of Muhammed—Abu Bakr, 'Umar (Omar), 'Uthman (Othman) and 'Ali—and follow one of the four main schools of law. Other Muslims differ only in the interpretation of the true tradition (*sunna*). Most of the region's Muslims are Sunni and of the Hanafi sect, but there are also some Sufi Muslims. The Sufis are mystics, found in all branches of Islam since very early in the religion's history. Named for their woollen (*suf*) monastic robes, the Sufis tempered orthodox formalism and deism, with a quest for complete identification with the Supreme Being and annihilation of the self (the existence of the latter is known as polytheism—*shirk*), although this sometimes approached pantheism. They are organized into what are loosely known as 'brotherhoods' (*turuq* or, singular, *tariqa*). In Albania, a Sufi dervish sect, the liberal Bektashis, enjoyed strong support before the suppression of religion and were making a revival during the early 1990s. Founded by Haji Bektash early in the 14th century, the sect flourished in the Balkans under the Ottoman Empire. Bektashi beliefs had a syncretic element, were less strict than those of most Muslims (and included the equal participation of women), were practised in tekkes rather than mosques and taught by priests known as babas.

OTHER RELIGIONS

Judaism is the oldest of the major monotheistic religions, and also advocates a code of morality and civil and religious duties. Its holy book (the Old Testament of the Christian Bible) is supported by traditions, expounded by the rabbis, who are doctors of the law and leaders of the Jewish congregations, which meet in synagogues. There are two main Jewish communities, which observe distinct rituals, but have no doctrinal differences. The predominant European group is the Ashkenazim; the Sephardim of the region are mainly found in the Balkans. Although both Christianity and Islam claim descent from, or to be the fulfilment of, Judaism, the Jews, as a race as well as a religion, have long been the victims of prejudice. Anti-Semitism has a long history in the Christian Church and, in Islam, the more recent, ongoing Arab–Israeli conflict bolstered the prejudice. The Jews are widespread throughout Eastern Europe. Their numbers, however, were seriously reduced during the Second World War, particularly in areas dominated by the Nazis. This holocaust of the Jewish people was the most extreme manifestation of the anti-Semitism that was endemic in Central and South-Eastern Europe. These traditional prejudices were not completely rejected by the communist regimes, but, after the fall of these governments, anti-Semitism re-emerged strongly in some areas, despite the often small number of Jews. Emigration, usually to Israel, also reduced numbers.

There are few Hindus in the region, but missionary work was conducted by one such sect, the Hare Krishna (named for their chant) or Krishna Consciousness. They worship the Hindu pantheon and advocate a harmonious life-style, are vegetarian, and distinguished by the orange robes of their devotees. There are only small groups of Buddhists, mainly converts, in the region.

MINORITIES IN CENTRAL AND SOUTH-EASTERN EUROPE

Prof. TOM GALLAGHER

In the mid-1990s, of the approximately 130m. people living in the former communist states of Central and South-Eastern Europe, almost 15% belonged to national and ethnic minorities. About 30 peoples attempted to co-exist in the wider lands stretching from the Aegean and Black Seas to the Baltic Sea. They practised four principal religions—Roman Catholicism, Orthodoxy, Islam and Protestantism. They spoke numerous languages and used three different alphabets—Cyrillic, Latin and Greek.

National minorities are defined as groupings which, to differing extents, possess a national consciousness, but find themselves dominated by the political agenda of a larger grouping. This larger grouping has a nation-state of its own, in which the influence of the minorities is usually small.

Ethnic minorities do not possess a distinct national outlook of their own, but their culture and customs might place them apart from other groups in society, thus strengthening their identity. Besides groups such as the Jews and the Germans, the largest ethnic minority in Eastern Europe at the beginning of the 21st century was the Gypsies or Roma (the name used hereafter). Approximately 5m. Roma lived in Eastern Europe; their communities ranged in number from 7,000 in Slovenia to over 2m. in Romania. According to one survey conducted in a number of Balkan countries in 1994, prejudice towards the Roma was generally comparable to that felt by the white community towards the black community in the south of the USA, prior to the civil-rights era beginning in 1965. Inadequate education and poor employment prospects, compounded by poverty, low health standards and a shorter-than-average life expectancy placed the Roma at the bottom of the social structure. The fragmentation of the Roma into castes impeded effective political organization and put the community at a disadvantage when dealing with hostile state officials.

National minorities usually claim a national identity different from that of the core ethnic group in the state. It is an identity they wish to preserve and pass on to the next generation. This goal gives rise to different strategies, ranging from statehood to amalgamation of the territories they inhabit with a state dominated by their co-ethnics, to demands for institutions and laws that give official protection and recognition to their identity.

Possession of a distinctive language is at the core of identity for most Central and South-Eastern European minorities. The demand for group rights, to ensure state protection of languages, has been the customary political demand of minorities. Minority parties and pressure groups have campaigned for the public use of minority languages in the courts and the local administration, as well as the right to be schooled in their own language and to enjoy access to own-language radio and television broadcasts.

Most Central and South-Eastern European states possess a dominant national group, which prefers to create a single national identity, even if the state is ethnically mixed. The state-building nationality has usually resisted minority demands for group rights. Before the era of national states, the region was dominated by a series of empires, which usually contained a vast array of peoples. Some 30 different peoples found themselves under the rule of the Hapsburg Austro-Hungarian Empire, the Osmanlı (Ottoman) Turkish Empire, the Romanov Russian and the Hohenzollern German Empire.

Until the 19th century religion was the main focus of group identification for peoples east of the Elbe river, Germany. Unlike Western European rulers, the Eastern dynasties often did not insist that the religion of the court or ruling family be adopted by the population at large. Ethnic groups that shared the religion of the ruling dynasty usually enjoyed privileges and opportunities denied to others. However, the ability of much of the region to escape the wars of religion that periodically convulsed Western Europe between 1530 and 1715 meant that most territories possessed mixed populations, not just in religious, but in linguistic and many other terms as well.

MAJORITIES AND MINORITIES IN CONTESTED LANDS

The multicultural traditions of the Eastern world were undermined by the rise of nationalism after the French Revolution of 1789–95. The idea that a community that felt itself to be a nation was entitled to have a state of its own was attractive to merchants and small, educated groups outside the ruling elite, which felt constrained by imperial rigidities. With varying degrees of success, these nationally-minded groups sought to convince the peasant masses that they should replace a purely local or religious identity with a national one and be prepared to support the break-up of the dynastic empires.

Nationalist intellectuals drew up impressive-sounding claims for territory based on a group having been there first or having already created a viable state in some earlier period before alien rule was imposed. However, with few exceptions, the territory claimed by the embryo nation-states between the Baltic and the Black Seas was occupied by several distinct ethnic groupings. As a result, the independence movement usually involved a struggle, not just with the unpopular dynasty, but between rival ethnic groups. These rival groups often had the same monopolistic approach to a contested territory, an approach regarded as necessary for the success of their state-building programme.

Thus, from about 1848 territorial conflicts ensued, in which groups vying for control of mixed territories were involved. Groups such as the Serbs and the Hungarians were in a strong position, having established states of their own ahead of their later rivals. Nevertheless, early progress in forming nation-states was no guarantee of continued success. The previously ascendant Hungarians and Germans found substantial portions of their populations reduced to minority status because of the way international conflicts before 1945 upset a fragile balance of power. Later still, in the case of the Serbs, intransigence towards other Southern Slavs and the Albanians produced a hostile response, which, by the end of the 1990s, had actually diminished the size of their territory.

The violent collapse of dynastic empires and the tendency of nation-building efforts by successor states to be subverted by invasion, war and revolution, created deep insecurity from 1918. As a result, few ascendant peoples were inclined voluntarily to share power with minorities. The transient nature of boundaries and states increased the predisposition of nationalist elites to impose cultural uniformity when they gained control of territories regarded as part of their natural homelands.

Many new states were created, or existing ones enlarged, following the end of the First World War. In 1918 the US President, Woodrow Wilson (1913–21), singled out national self-determination as the new organizing concept for a Central and South-Eastern Europe shorn of multinational empires. Hitherto ascendant peoples such as the Russians, Germans, Austrians, Hungarians and Turks thus witnessed a contraction of their states. From the Western Slavs the two large states of Czechoslovakia and Poland emerged. A new union of Southern Slav peoples—Yugoslavia—was created. Romania increased its size and population threefold, receiving the territories of Bessarabia, Bucovina, Transylvania, the Banat and Crisana-Maramureş. The Baltic states of Estonia, Latvia and Lithuania were granted independence from Russia, as was Finland.

Building a state identity that included elements of minority culture was usually unwelcome in the highly-charged atmosphere following independence. Instead, exchanges of population, expulsion, or the marginalization of minorities became normal practice in many new states intent on cultural uniformity after 1918. A precedent had been established when Muslim populations were expelled from Serbia, Greece and Bulgaria, following those states' acquisition of independence in the 1870s. The way religion reinforced nationalism made the presence of large numbers of Muslims in avowedly Christian states unacceptable, even if they came from the same southern Slav stock as state-building nations. The same principle was applied in the 1990s, when religious criteria were used to justify the 'ethnic cleansing' of Bosnian Muslims by other Southern Slavs, who claimed to be driven by religious imperatives.

The self-determination concept was applied inconsistently in Eastern Europe after 1918. One-quarter of the population remained ethnic minorities. At the Versailles (France) peace conferences of 1919–20 the territorial map was redrawn by the victorious Entente Powers (France, Russia and the United Kingdom), which insisted that some protection for minorities be incorporated into the peace treaties. In 1920 a League of Nations was established as a regulatory institution, designed, among other things, to safeguard minorities. However, by the mid-1920s the international community was already beginning to conclude that it might be easier to separate peoples rather than keep them together. Before 1918 the Great Powers had already met with stubborn resistance from nationalist elites in Romania, when they tried to protect a large Jewish minority, which was denied full citizenship. In 1923 the League of Nations approved the Treaty of Lausanne, which included a wholesale transfer of population between Greece and Turkey. Over 1.1m. Greeks moved from Turkey to Greece and 380,000 Muslim Turks moved in the opposite direction. This was no voluntary repatriation, however, but two deportations into exile. Nevertheless, the United Kingdom and France increasingly favoured clearing territory between those neighbouring states that could not easily agree on where their boundaries should be fixed. Homogenizing disputed territories such as Macedonia or Transylvania was seen as a step towards peace, however unpalatable.

The League of Nations lost its credibility once its sponsors appeared reluctant to invest the necessary time and energy in the development of a minority-protection framework. Minorities instead preferred to look to co-ethnics in charge of their own state for salvation, or else to powers such as Germany and Italy, which were opposed to the Versailles treaties. During the economic depression of the 1930s ethnic minorities were often victimized and described as 'the enemy within' when ambitious state-building projects ran into difficulties.

Radicalized and embittered, they sometimes combined with external forces to subvert the Versailles order. Between 1938 and 1941 the rise of totalitarian power in the Russian-dominated USSR and in Italy and Germany contributed to the subversion of most of the new states of Central and South-Eastern Europe.

COMMUNISM AND MINORITIES

After 1945 Soviet-led communism triumphed everywhere in Eastern Europe except for Finland and Greece. It promised an end to debilitating inter-ethnic conflicts and dismissed nationalism as the tool of bourgeois forces. There was the expectation that communist modernization would lead to the steady erosion of national differences. However, there was a contrasting response among peoples of the region to the brief success of internationalism on Soviet terms. Not surprisingly, minorities that felt disadvantaged before 1945 showed a relatively high level of support for communism. Nevertheless, minority groups proved an unreliable base of support for a new social system with vaulting ambitions, especially when the majority was historically distrustful of the Russians (as was the case in Romania).

When the USSR relaxed control of its satellites, unpopular elites began to appeal to the national feeling of the majority population wherever this was felt to be expedient. Communism as a doctrine was better suited to ethnic homogenization than to the promotion of ethnic pluralism, so such a development might not have been merely a desperate stratagem by elites seeking popularity. However, access to the ranks of the elite was restricted to certain nationalities at the expense of others, thereby creating unequal opportunities for social advancement. This characterized South-Eastern Europe, in particular, where state-led efforts to assimilate the Hungarian minority in Romanian Transylvania and the Turkish and Slavic Muslim communities in Bulgaria had resumed in the 1960s and 1980s, respectively. Thus, the nationalist variant of Marxism-Leninism seen in Romania under the regime of Nicolae Ceauşescu (1965–89) resulted in furious efforts by a personalist leadership to forge a single national culture and merge diverse populations into one single mass.

An ambitious experiment in federalism occurred in multi-ethnic Yugoslavia after 1945. In order to satisfy the aspirations of the different Southern Slav national communities for autonomy, central power was devolved to six republics and two provinces. Communist decentralization proved to be a formula for internal peace as long as the charismatic leader of its wartime liberation struggle, Josip Broz (Tito), was in charge. The death of Tito in 1980 left a political vacuum in the country that was filled from the late 1980s by the Serbian leader, Slobodan Milošević. Milošević was an unyielding communist, who attempted to recentralize Yugoslavia around Serbia by responding to complaints, from intellectuals in particular, that a strong Yugoslavia had been achieved by weakening Serbia. The new Serbian Constitution of 1990 revoked the autonomous status of the Serbian provinces of Vojvodina and Kosovo. The Hungarian minority in Vojvodina suffered, but far worse was the plight of the ethnic Albanian majority in Kosovo. After 1989 most were dismissed from public employment and the entire economy, along with the education and health systems, was 'serbianized'.

In the 1990s civil wars were fought in Yugoslavia, largely at Milošević's instigation, in which Serb forces initially gained ascendancy, but were eventually forced to surrender territory. As a result, several million Serbs were transformed into minorities as the constituent Yugoslav republics of Slovenia, Croatia, Macedonia and Bosnia and Herzegovina each gained independence. Furthermore, in 1999, following the conflict in Kosovo between North Atlantic Treaty Organization (NATO) forces and the Milošević regime, which arose from the ill-treatment of the majority Albanian population there, the position of the Serb minority deteriorated. Despite efforts by the UN to protect them, many Serbs were persecuted by revenge-seeking Albanians or by those with a political agenda, based on ethnic exclusivism. By the early 2000s the UN was striving to preserve the multicultural character of Kosovo, by offering a role for its Slav and Roma minorities in new governing arrangements, which stopped short of full independence for the territory.

Almost everywhere under communism the emphasis on homogenization, and on internal and external enemies, adversely affected political culture, as did the devaluation of civil society and the emphasis on authoritarian solutions for both large and mundane problems. When majority–minority disputes resurfaced, the lack of a tradition of bargaining or compromise under communism increased the likelihood that such disputes would escalate. In ethnically-mixed communist states such as Yugoslavia and Romania, where chauvinists were influential in the 1980s, politics was increasingly shaped along ethnic lines. As concessions to pluralism were unavoidable at the end of the Cold War, efforts were made to prevent normal electoral competition and a genuine transition to democracy by invoking minorities as a threat to the security, or even to the survival, of the state.

Laying the blame on minorities diverted the attention of voters from political abuses: Romania was not the only country where privatization based on informal mechanisms occurred and a new economic oligarchy sprang up, based around elements of the former communist nomenklatura (party–state apparatus).

INTOLERANCE FROM THE RIGHT AND THE CENTRE

State discrimination against minorities, combining ethnic nationalism with remnants of communist authoritarianism, gave rise to human-rights violations. Nevertheless, minorities also fared badly in a number of states that had acquired statehood by breaking free from communism.

In the Baltic states of Estonia, Latvia, and Lithuania, large Russian minorities suffered as new laws made place of birth and ancestry the qualification for citizenship. Since most ethnic Russians had settled in the Baltic states after independence was lost in 1940, they were not eligible for citizenship and could not vote in elections after 1990. The demographic challenge posed by large Russian-speaking minorities, whose co-ethnics across the border possessed a massive state of their own, explained why the Baltic states courted international disapproval by suspending some conventional human rights.

In Croatia, the loss of territory (subsequently regained) to the Serbs in 1991 resulted in the persecution of the large Serb minority by the nationalist regime of President Franjo Tudjman (1990–99). Serbs in mainly Croat-inhabited areas came under strong pressure to assimilate or leave. In 1995 Croatia recovered the Krajina region, home to 150,000 Serbs, nearly all of whom were driven out or forced to flee.

Minorities could still be threatened in states where a territorial challenge was absent and other indicators suggested that a smooth transition from communism was occurring. In the Czech Republic the Government of Václav Klaus (1992–97) had few of the problems of political legitimacy that prompted contemporaries elsewhere to implement nationalist policies. However, discrimination against the Roma was widespread. The police and judiciary often showed a lenient attitude to their antagonists. In 1993, shortly after the dissolution of Czechoslovakia, human-rights observers complained that a proposed citizenship law was designed to exclude as many Roma as possible.

Post-communist regimes of different complexions could employ a wide range of devices to make minorities feel unwelcome. Citizens' rights could be denied or else made subject to onerous conditions. Minorities could be excluded from the privatization of the state-led economy by various discretionary measures. New constitutions could refrain from acknowledging the existence of ethnic minorities and could even discriminate against them by prohibiting political parties based on ethnic groupings, as in Bulgaria. School textbooks could promote negative images, as in Romania where, until 1997, history books described Hungarians as adversaries of Romanians. Demagogues who incited anti-minority violence could operate with immunity from the law and sometimes with the covert, or real, encouragement of the authorities. Economic pressure could be exerted to induce minorities to leave the territory they inhabited. Finally, attempts could be made by armed groups operating with the approval of the central authorities to drive out and destroy ethnic minorities, as happened in the former Yugoslavia throughout the 1990s, a policy that became known as 'ethnic cleansing'.

The Czech Republic and the Baltic states were to be among the first to benefit from the European Union's (EU) strategy of eastward enlargement, a foreign-policy goal that made those countries more receptive to external pressure to regularize the position of minorities. However, under EU membership minorities in the region might still face hardships.

Greece, a member of the EU (then known as the European Community) from 1981, refused to recognize the existence of ethnic minorities, except for the Muslims of Eastern Thrace, whose fundamental rights were guaranteed by the 1923 Treaty of Lausanne. It therefore refused to recognize the Slavophone (sometimes viewed as ethnic Macedonian) minority in the north of the country. Public use of Macedonian was discouraged and the display of posters in the language prohibited. Many Macedonian speakers who fled Greece during the 1946–49 civil war were banned from returning. Discrimination against the Roma and the large population of Albanian migrant workers was frequently reported. From the late 1990s the Government of Konstantinos Simitis (1996–) sought to improve minority rights, despite the fact that liberal official policies were often frustrated by middle- and lower-ranking officials. However, from 1999 improvements in Greek-Turkish relations at state level lightened the domestic atmosphere. In July 1999 the Greek Minister of Foreign Affairs, Georgios Papandreou, declared that if the small number of ethnic Turks to be found in the Muslim minority were regarded as 'a huge national problem, we will drown in a drop of water'. With the Greek capital, Athens, due to be the site of the 2004 Olympic Games, in May 2003 it was announced that a mosque was to be built in the city, the first to operate in the city since independence was obtained from Ottoman Turkey in 1832.

THE MINORITY RESPONSE

Tactics that minorities normally pursued to promote their goals were:

Participation in state and local elections. This resulted in minority parties being included in Balkan governments when no party enjoyed an overall majority. The mainly Muslim Movement for Rights and Freedoms (MRF) participated in several Bulgarian governments from the early 1990s; various ethnic Albanian parties were represented in the former Yugoslav republic of Macedonia—FYRM's cabinets continuously from 1996; and, in Romania, the Democratic Alliance of Hungarians in Romania (DAHR) provided much-needed stability in the coalition Government of 1996–2000.

Non-violent civil disobedience. This strategy was most widely employed in the province of Kosovo between 1990 and 1998, as a protest by the Albanian community against the systematic discrimination practised by the Serbian authorities. Nevertheless, the ethnic Albanian population in the province maintained the radical aim of secession from the Serbian state.

Seeking support from co-ethnics who predominate in a neighbouring state. Hungarians in Slovakia and Romania looked to Hungary and expected Hungarian governments of whichever political complexion to rally to their defence whenever they faced threats. The so-called 'status' law, passed by the Hungarian legislature in June 2001, provided a range of social and economic concessions, but not permanent residence, to co-ethnics in neighbouring states working temporarily in Hungary. The Government of Viktor Orbán (1998–2002) had feared that the growing domestic labour shortage would impel many economically active ethnic Hungarians, of the 3m. living elsewhere in the region, to move permanently to Hungary, thus annulling the hitherto strong Hungarian cultural presence in Transylvania and Slovakia. However, Romania protested vigorously against the law, which it regarded as a violation of its sovereignty, and which it considered to discriminate against ethnic Romanians; there were also fears in Romania that millions of ethnic Romanians would declare themselves to be Hungarian, in order to avail themselves of the law's economic benefits. Eventually, in December 2001, a compromise was agreed between the two states, although Slovakia continued to protest against the law's provisions. In contrast to Hungary, a poor, unstable country such as Albania found itself unable to protect effectively the interests of Albanians in Kosovo or the FYRM.

Violence. This was very much a last resort. It was less prevalent among minorities in Eastern Europe than in Western Europe. Until the emergence of the Kosovo Liberation Army (KLA) in the late 1990s, following the exhaustion of non-violent strategy in the province, there was no equivalent of the Basque separatist organization, ETA (Euskadi ta Azkatasuna—Basque Homeland and Liberty) in Spain or the pro-independence Provisional IRA (Irish Republican Army) in Northern Ireland (United Kingdom). No tradition of bearing arms existed in most of Central and South-Eastern Europe and, in the past, governments were far more ruthless than their Western counterparts in suppressing minority violence.

Advancing minority claims on a European or world stage. In December 1992 the UN issued a Declaration on the Rights of Persons belonging to National or Ethnic, Religious and Linguistic Minorities. It was the first time that the UN had drawn up a declaration exclusively devoted to minority concerns. The Organization for Security and Co-operation in Europe (OSCE) and the Council of Europe also issued documents containing specific standards regarding the rights of persons belonging to national minorities, to which states must adhere (see below). Both organizations were widely seen as gateways to European and global economic and political integration. Minorities and majorities in the region alike, with the exception of recalcitrant regimes such as that of Milošević in the Federal Republic of Yugoslavia (FRY—now Serbia and Montenegro), felt it in their interests to co-operate with such bodies.

THE INTERNATIONALIZATION OF THE MINORITY QUESTION

By the beginning of the 21st century international constraints on state behaviour towards minorities could be applied in order to prevent an escalation of tension. It was probably no longer true to say that state elites had complete sovereignty over national minorities. The military interventions by NATO in Bosnia and Herzegovina in 1995 and in Kosovo in 1999, in order to curtail Serbian aggression against weaker ethnic groups, might prove to be important benchmarks. In 2001 the EU and NATO had to confront the possibility of civil war in the FYRM, as the Government of Ljubčo Georgievski (1998–2002), effectively controlled by Macedonian nationalists, faced a challenge by ethnic Albanian militants operating across the border, from Kosovo. Despite little prior warning and their heavy engagement in Bosnia and Herzegovina and Kosovo, the two institutions acted speedily to avert full-scale war. Months of intensive diplomacy by the EU culminated in the signature, on 13 August, at Ohrid, of a framework peace agreement, and the dispatch to the FYRM of a 3,500-strong NATO force, the main aim of which was to demilitarize the Albanian insurgents. Despite continuous obstruction by radical members of the FYRM Government, the European Commission urged the adoption of measures that would award the large ethnic Albanian minority, and other significant minorities, a much greater role in decision-making. Amendments to the Constitution in November, and the adoption of a law on local self-government in January 2002, represented important progress towards that objective. In March an amnesty allowing Albanian militants who had renounced violence to avoid criminal charges and to play a role in public life was also approved by the Government. In September Ali Ahmeti, leader of the rebel National Liberation Army during the 2001 Albanian revolt, emerged as a major political figure, when his newly established Democratic Union for Integration (DUI) trounced rival ethnic Albanian parties in the legislative election. The main winner of the election was an alliance led by the Social Democratic Alliance of Macedonia (SDAM), which subsequently formed a coalition Government with Ahmeti's party.

For intervention in an internal conflict to be effective, the EU had to be prepared to commit its resources for a lengthy period, and financial incentives, which translated into improved economic conditions for vulnerable members of the majority group, as well as for the minority, were necessary. Otherwise, the momentum for partnership between two increasingly estranged ethnic groups would be difficult to maintain.

States joining the Council of Europe had to sign the European Convention on the Protection of Human Rights and Fundamental Freedoms, which imposed some limits on national state authority and gave unfairly treated citizens the chance to seek redress from state injustice through a higher transnational jurisdiction. On 10 November 1994 the Council of Europe adopted the Framework Convention for the Protection of National Minorities, which came into force on 1 February 1998. It set out the principles to be respected and implemented by the parties of the Convention in their treatment of minorities. The fact that one of the signatories, Russia, subsequently became involved in a brutal civil war in its autonomous republic of Chechnya from 1999, in which civilians suffered severely, revealed the Convention's limitations. However, the Council of Europe was actively seeking to ensure that it was implemented in other former communist countries, where more effective leverage could be exercised.

In 1991 all OSCE member states signed a declaration specifying that 'issues concerning national minorities, as well as compliance with international obligations and commitments concerning the rights of persons belonging to them, are matters of legitimate international concern and, consequently, do not constitute exclusively an internal affair of a respective state'. There was evidence that intolerant nationalism at state level was being discouraged and ethnic politics advanced, at least in some Central and South-Eastern European countries (Romania, for example). However, the evidence from countries such as Turkey, where the human rights of the Kurdish minority were comprehensively violated in the 1990s, pointed to the limitations of the OSCE declaration.

At the instigation of the Dutch Government, in 1993 the OSCE appointed a High Commissioner on National Minorities, whose role was to identify ethnic tensions between member states and to promote their early resolution. The first High Commissioner, Max van der Stoel, a former Dutch foreign minister, played a sometimes crucial role in interposing between alienated minorities and unreasonable majority governments, often mediating between the two, in a range of Central and South-Eastern European countries. In his mediating work, van der Stoel rejected the scenarios of secession and assimilation. He argued that a national group does not need independence to protect its interests. Nor does a majority have to suppress a minority in order to preserve its security. He supported the concept of the multi-ethnic state in Central and South-Eastern Europe, despite the risk of friction between ethnic groups.

During the first half of the 1990s such views carried little weight even in the OSCE, and the office of the High Commissioner found itself poorly resourced. In Bosnia and Herzegovina, international mediators, such as Lord David Owen (of the United Kingdom) and Thorvald Stoltenberg (of Norway), formulated peace plans based on *de facto* partition and the transfer of minorities from previously mixed areas, in order to create mono-ethnic areas. The General Framework Agreement for Peace in Bosnia and Herzegovina, signed in Dayton, Ohio, in December 1995, despite preserving a single territory, provided, in practice, for the existence of three entities, dominated by rival nationalists, and in control of their own armies and police (see the chapter on Bosnia and Herzegovina in Part Two).

Van der Stoel's demand for methods to be found to accommodate and integrate ethnic diversity into state structures acquired increasing influence from the late 1990s. Instead of managing separation, the UN-appointed High Representative of the International Community in Bosnia and Herzegovina, who was to oversee the implementation of the Dayton peace agreement, attempted to accelerate the return of refugees to their homes, in order to weaken the influence of ethnic intransigents. A much increased rate of repatriation coincided with strong electoral gains in central Bosnia and Herzegovina for parties with a multi-ethnic appeal.

In July 2000 the Constitutional Court of Bosnia and Herzegovina ruled that the entity structures established under the Dayton Accords were unconstitutional, as they failed to provide for equal rights for all ethnic groups. The main objector to this notion was the entity known as the Serb Republic (Republika Srpska), dominated by ethnic Serbs, and from which other ethnic groups had been largely driven before 1995. In April 2002 the High Representative, Wolfgang Petritsch, an Austrian diplomat, was eventually compelled to impose constitutional reforms awarding all Bosnian citizens equal status, after the entities failed to ratify an agreement on the issue, which had been reached in the previous month. The arrival, in May, of a new High Representative, a British former political party leader, Sir Jeremy John Durham (Paddy) Ashdown, coincided with demands by Western donors and global institutions that central government be reinforced at the expense of entities such as the Serb Republic, which had displayed little willingness to make a common state work.

The UN Interim Administration Mission in Kosovo (UNMIK) was also eager to reinforce the multi-ethnic character of the territory, despite its domination, in numerical terms, by ethnic Albanians, who wished to put an end to its technical status as part of the FRY. In May 2001 UNMIK announced a Constitutional Framework for Provisional Self-

Government in Kosovo, according to which minority groups were to hold up to one-quarter of the seats in a new legislative assembly. Roughly one-half of the approximately 170,000 Serb members of the electorate participated in the elections to the Kosovo Assembly, held on 17 November, awarding the Serbian Return (Povratak) coalition 11.0% of the votes cast. Since no ethnic Albanian party held an overall majority, some level of political partnership between the representatives of the two ethnic groups, previously implacable rivals, was expected to be unavoidable, and Michael Steiner, the German diplomat appointed by the UN to oversee the post-war reconstruction of Kosovo in 2002–03, had appeared committed to a permanent multi-ethnic settlement.

In 2000–01 Western efforts to guarantee a future in Kosovo for non-Albanian communities, not only Serbs, but Roma and others, were accompanied by firm action to prevent ethnic Albanians in the adjacent Presovo valley, in southern Serbia, from seceding to join Kosovo, as NATO troops in Kosovo joined forces with the Yugoslav armed forces to defeat armed ethnic Albanian insurgents. In return, the FRY's post-Milošević Government agreed to adopt reforms designed to conciliate the ethnic Albanians and to encourage them to support moderate leaders: the establishment of a multi-ethnic police force; the withdrawal of the army to barracks; increased investment; and measures enabling ethnic Albanians to participate in local government, in proportion to their numbers.

By 2001, therefore, the relevance of the High Commissioner on National Minorities' conflict-prevention approach appeared to have been confirmed, as van der Stoel retired, to be succeeded by Rolf Ekéus (of Sweden) in July.

Non-governmental organizations (NGOs) played sometimes crucial roles in safeguarding minorities. Respected human rights groups such as Amnesty International and Human Rights Watch skilfully petitioned on behalf of minorities and took advantage of the growing willingness of Western governments to make the treatment of minorities an important criterion in their attitude to Eastern European states. External support from the Open Society Fund, part of the Soros Foundation network, also enabled newspapers and other media outlets concerned with overcoming majority–minority divides to continue their work relatively unimpeded. Local initiatives also needed to be documented. Various national Helsinki Committees (named after the Helsinki Final Act of 1975) played invaluable roles in documenting human-rights abuses and briefing international organizations about local developments in the region.

WHY ELITES SHOW RESTRAINT

International intervention to prevent a leader such as Milošević taking drastic action against ethnic minorities, or to prevent the dissolution into civil conflict of a state such as the FYRM, may have succeeded in restraining other leaders in the region with an anti-minority agenda. However, wider factors have also been at work.

In Central and South-Eastern Europe, the communications revolution made the forced assimilation of minorities more difficult to accomplish. Satellite television broadcasting from Hungary and Turkey helped to preserve minority cultures. Some minorities could rely on supportive public opinion in influential states such as Germany, or had influence in the US political establishment if they had a significant diaspora in the USA. During the 1990s the Albanian diaspora in Central European countries proved to be a more effective source of support for the 'parallel state' in Kosovo than the Albanian Government, but radicals among both Albanian and Croatian émigrés had a disruptive effect on politics in their homelands, owing to their readiness to back ethnic extremists with 'greater Albania' and 'greater Croatia' projects.

The growing sophistication of voters was another restraining factor. It gradually became less easy for nomenklatura nationalists to incite the majority against the minority. Leaderships with a record of economic incompetence (true of all former nomenklatura regimes in Central and South-Eastern Europe) found that inflammatory rhetoric usually had diminishing appeal. Voters assessed their intentions far more sceptically and there was a growing awareness that prospects for a peaceful existence and economic improvements were jeopardized by constant references to race and nation.

The rise of new political forces on the left also weakened nomenklatura nationalism. Former communist reformers, keen to integrate their countries with the West, and willing to accept international norms for minorities and for relations with their neighbours, were elected to power in Poland and Hungary in 1993 and 1994, respectively. In Poland, the ruling left increased state protection for the German minority; it knew that a positive attitude from the German Government was required if Poland's bid to join the EU was to advance. Following the overwhelming electoral victory of the Hungarian Socialist Party in 1994, the new administration re-orientated its foreign policy for similar reasons. Its attitude to neighbouring states was no longer determined solely by how its co-ethnics were treated. In treaties with Slovakia (1995) and Romania (1996), Hungary abandoned any claims to territory beyond its frontiers where its co-ethnics were a minority.

Meanwhile, in the late 1990s centrist reformers in the region made important advances, which improved the conditions of national minorities. In 1997, in Bulgaria, the Union of Democratic Forces won an electoral majority and governed for four years. In 1998, following legislative elections in Slovakia, a coalition of centre parties formed an administration, bringing to an end a period of authoritarian rule by the Movement for a Democratic Slovakia. Already, by 1996, the Hungarian minority movement, the DAHR, had been included in the Romanian coalition Government. The desire to be included in Euro-Atlantic integration processes made the incoming reformers far more willing to accept liberal EU norms for minority rights than their predecessors. In late 2000 the return to power of ex-communists, who had previously been committed to ethnic nationalism, created apprehension. However, in January 2002 the Romanian Government of Adrian Năstase (2000–) signed a pact with the DAHR, which agreed to give its support, in return for various measures designed to protect the ethnic Hungarian minority, particularly in the area of local government. In 2001 Romania also adopted a detailed strategy to improve the circumstances of the country's estimated 3m. Roma, working closely with international partners. By this time it was well aware that an outwardly conciliatory approach to minorities was viewed positively by prospective EU and NATO partners; hitherto, they had been unimpressed by Romania's efforts to modernize its administration and break up communist-era economic networks in order to create a public-service orientated bureaucracy and a competitive economy.

The position of minorities in the FRY eased greatly following the removal from power of Milošević in October 2000. The new, moderate coalition Government implemented measures to improve conditions for minorities, such as ethnic Hungarians in Vojvodina and Muslims in the Sandžak region. Greater autonomy was awarded to Vojvodina in January 2002, and the renegotiated state union of Serbia and Montenegro, agreed in mid-March 2002, and which came into effect on 4 February 2003, replacing the FRY, included provisions to defend minority interests.

In Croatia, the death of President Tudjman in December 1999, and the electoral victory of an anti-nationalist coalition in January 2000, improved international relations, as well as the prospects of the Serb minority. The new President, Stipe Mesić, immediately set about improving relations with neighbouring Bosnia and Herzegovina, which his predecessor had sought to partition in collusion with the federal Yugoslav leader, Milošević. President Mesić expressed his support for the return of Serb civilians driven out of the Krajina region in 1995.

SLOW PROGRESS

The reformist-sounding Governments in Serbia, Croatia and the mainly Muslim-populated part of the Bosnian Federation were weak. They presided over shattered economies, which would take decades to restore, irrespective of the level of international assistance. Moreover, citizens were little prepared to make concessions to minorities, when militants from those minorities were held responsible for violent actions; in Croatia and Kosovo, civilian administrators at lower levels were not eager to implement measures that would allow Serbs to return to their homes and gain access to local services.

These reformist Governments had also inherited from their extremist predecessors military, police, security-service and judicial structures that were often hostile to upholding human rights, and in the ranks of which ethnic minorities had little or no presence. The over-sized security establishment in post-war Croatia and Serbia had demonstrated its strength by resisting efforts to reduce its size and, in the case of Serbia, blocking the extradition of certain individuals to the International Criminal Tribunal for the former Yugoslavia (ICTY) in The Hague, Netherlands. None the less, Milošević's extradition, in June 2001, to face the jurisdiction of the ICTY, was an undoubted triumph for the cause of human rights in the region.

The behaviour of parties that claimed to act in defence of ethnic minorities sometimes risked jeopardizing their interests. For the Roma in Romania, there was evidence that the main party claiming their allegiance was sometimes concerned with advancing its personal interests, rather than those of the community at large. The situation was not altogether different in Bulgaria, where the MRF, representing the Turkish Muslim minority, took advantage of the patriarchal and traditional culture, which offered the leadership unconditional loyalty. Nor did the discovery of connections between the MRF leadership and the communist-era security services lessen its hold. In April 2002 the MRF demanded the improved integration of ethnic minorities into the state administration, but there was a danger that the beneficiaries would be the retinue associated with its leadership.

In Romania, the DAHR had elaborate consultative mechanisms, which made it one of the most democratic political organizations in Central and South-Eastern Europe. It prided itself on representing a wide-range of ethnic Hungarians, with common interests. However, strains in the Alliance emerged over the terms of the pact agreed with the ruling Social Democratic Party (SDP), a successor to the former communist party. The protagonists agreed that political engagement with their ethnic Romanian counterparts was vital, but reformers argued that the DAHR had helped the SDP to recover its credibility in the West, by offering it parliamentary support, for far too small a price. As a result of the pact, the DAHR leadership was prepared only to raise issues that would cause minimal disruption for the Government, and the issue of autonomy for the ethnic Hungarian minority had been allowed to slip from the agenda. There were also fears that if the DAHR gained real political power, the oligarchical tendencies to be found in most Romanian formations would soon come to shape its existence. For its part, the SDP allowed the more accommodating DAHR parliamentarians access to business opportunities that, hitherto, had been denied to them, in the hope of triggering divisions within the Alliance's ranks;

although such divisions emerged within the DAHR in early 2003, only a few elected officials left the party.

Thus it was the tactics of minority parties and alliances, as well as the behaviour of state and international bodies, which helped to determine the extent to which minority interests could be advanced in the post-communist era.

CONCLUSION

At the beginning of the 21st century ethnicity remained a major organizing principle in Central and South-Eastern Europe. Minorities were regularly depicted as a threat by nationalist leaderships, right-wing as well as left, which were intent on extending their tenure in office, or on acquiring wealth by shaping the privatization process around nationalist criteria.

Mobilized minorities in states with a tradition of mistreatment were more pragmatic than perhaps might have been expected in the face of such provocation. Group rights remained a significant objective, but the demand was usually for educational and cultural rights, which could ensure the preservation of a minority identity, rather than for secession or territorial autonomy. Demands for autonomy shaped around territory won little support from Western European or global bodies prepared to use their weight to defend submerged communities. These demands brought an unavailing and sometimes violent response from majority state nationalisms.

Groups such as the Roma, which did not develop a national consciousness, had few champions outside the international human-rights community. However, the EU, increasingly aware of the need to challenge the economic and social underdevelopment of the Roma community, urged programmes of affirmative action on applicant states with large Roma communities, and from 2001 began to encourage regional consciousness among different Roma communities by popularizing the concept of the Roma as an international minority.

The future course of majority-minority relations in Eastern Europe might well be decided by two factors. The first is the speed and extent to which the region overcomes chronic economic difficulties associated with moving from a state-led to a market economy. Majorities are less inclined to make concessions to minorities when economic prospects are bleak. Demagogues who insist that minority rights are a violation of national sovereignty will always find a more receptive audience in periods of economic hardship than in times of economic contentment. The second factor is the fate of the European integration process. In May 2004 10 states, all but two of them from Central and South-Eastern Europe, were due to become full members of the EU. The EU placed the defence of democratic rights at the centre of the entry requirements for each candidate country and issued annual reports monitoring progress towards accession, in which state treatment of ethnic minorities was often emphasized. For well over a decade the EU has required part of the funding given to candidate countries to be used to improve the position of minorities, in countries where they constitute a distinct section of the population. The EU has also promoted cross-border integration, which has benefited ethnic communities separated by international frontiers since 1918. The criteria agreed at the Copenhagen summit in Denmark in 1993, setting out the conditions for membership, required states to show 'respect for and protection of minorities'. However, it was notable that this was the only part of the Copenhagen criteria not to be adopted as primary EU law in the subsequent Amsterdam Treaty, agreed in 1997. So, there is a danger that a positive approach towards minorities will be viewed only as a condition for entry, not membership. If some minorities, particularly the Roma, see no improvement in their conditions, there is a possibility that they might emigrate en masse to Western Europe, given the lifting of visa restrictions. In the Balkans, support for EU entry was high, because it was seen as an opportunity to escape economic decline and poverty. Even without a formal date for accession, Bulgaria and Romania were unlikely to lose their commitment to European integration. The position of minorities in both countries, which faced assimilation or expulsion in the last years of communism, had been strengthened, thanks to the orientation of both to the EU and NATO democracies. However, in the Czech Republic and Poland there was some scepticism about the benefits of EU entry, which risked promoting a brand of nationalism that might make the positions of minorities more uncomfortable.

In their negotiations with prospective new members, both the EU and NATO clearly indicated that the resolution of ethnic-minority problems was regarded as a vital precondition for Euro-Atlantic integration in the realms of the economy and security. The civil wars that followed the fragmentation of the former Yugoslavia at the beginning of the decade showed that Europe as a whole had a strong interest in preventing ethnic disputes from escalating into generalized violence. At the beginning of the 21st century a new policy agenda for Eastern Europe was linking a range of tangible benefits to the adoption of policies of co-operation with neighbours and the conciliation of minorities. In July 1999 the adoption, at the instigation of the EU and NATO, of the Stability Pact for South Eastern Europe was an indication of a willingness on the part of the West to integrate the Balkans economically and politically with the rest of the continent. However, such initiatives are likely to prosper only if they are properly funded, coherently organized and based on a long-term approach. It is clear that the national question in Central and South-Eastern Europe will probably only recede from view if the region as a whole is offered the same opportunities and external support that enabled the warring states of Western Europe to put aside their own not inconsiderable differences following the end of the Second World War in 1945.

THE BALTIC SEA REGION

Dr KĘSTUTIS GIRNIUS

The Baltic Sea region, or the Baltic Rim as it is often called, encompasses 10 littoral states: the Nordic countries of Denmark, Finland, Norway and Sweden; the three Baltic states of Estonia, Latvia and Lithuania; and Germany, Poland and the northern regions of Russia—the St Petersburg/Leningrad, Kaliningrad, Kareliya—and, perhaps, in the future, Pskov regions. Because of its links with the Nordic countries, Iceland also participates in most of the political and economic activities of the region. The region has between 50m. and 80m. inhabitants, depending on how broad a swathe of German and Polish territories are included in the calculation. There are 49 cities with at least 100,000 inhabitants, 76 significant ports and a hinterland of almost 230m. people. One of the fastest developing areas of the world, the region's knowledge-intensive sector is flourishing. Finland and Sweden are among the world leaders in information technology, the internet and mobile telecommunications. Yet the region faces special challenges that include harsh climatic conditions, long distances, insufficient transport and border-crossing facilities. The region is marked by deep differences in levels of economic development. The Nordic countries have some of the highest living standards in the world. In 2000 real gross domestic product (GDP) per head in each of those countries was more than US $31,000, well above the European Union (EU) average and about eight times the average for the Baltic states. Although by the early 2000s Poland and the three Baltic states had made substantial progress in modernizing their economies, it will take several decades, at least, before their standard of living approaches that of their northern neighbours. Economic and social conditions in north-west Russia were even worse. In Finland the infant mortality rate was four times lower than in Russia, while male life expectancy in Finland was 74 years, almost 15 years more than in Russia. The southern part of the Baltic Rim region is primarily composed of agricultural lands, and forests and mountains dominate much of the northern areas. The Baltic Sea, the element common to the region, is both an economic lifeline and a source of grave concern, owing to the precarious state of its delicate ecosystem.

RECENT HISTORY

In the 1990s the Baltic Sea region underwent fundamental political and economic change. During the years of the Cold War the Baltic region was dominated by the USSR, which had annexed the three Baltic states in 1940 and later imposed its rule on Eastern Europe, including Poland. Sweden and Finland were officially and officiously neutral, even eschewing membership of the EU (then known as the European Community) as a means of indicating the depth of their non-alignment. Finland, in particular, was extremely careful to ensure that its foreign policy did not transgress the perceived security interests of its mighty eastern neighbour. A North Atlantic Treaty Organization (NATO) and EU presence was felt only in the western approaches of the region. Denmark, Germany and Norway were members of NATO, and the first two also belonged to the EU. However, Denmark was one of NATO's most independent and contentious members, pursuing a more pacific foreign and defence policy than that of its allies.

The political topography of the Baltic Sea region was radically transfigured in the 1990s. Soviet dominance based on

military power yielded to the overwhelming economic superiority of the EU. Although the transformation would not have been possible without the internal reforms introduced by Soviet leader Mikhail Gorbachev in the 1980s, the Baltic Sea states were not merely passive beneficiaries of the process of imperial withdrawal. Even before Gorbachev's assumption of power, the Solidarity (Solidarność) trade-union movement successfully challenged the hegemony of Poland's communist rulers, serving as a model for other Soviet bloc countries. The Baltic states, in particular Lithuania, were the first Soviet republics openly to seek independence, rather than merely greater autonomy within the Soviet state. The Nordic countries, led by Denmark and Iceland, supported the aspirations of the Baltic people for national self-determination more vigorously than most of their Western European counterparts. The bonds of mutual trust and co-operation forged between the Baltic and Nordic states even before the formal resumption of diplomatic ties established the foundations of subsequent co-operation.

By 2006 the Baltic Sea will have become, for all practical purposes, an internal sea within the EU. Finland and Sweden joined the EU in 1995 and pursued more assertive foreign policies, albeit formally retaining their neutrality. The rejection of Soviet tutelage was never more evident than during the civil war in the former Yugoslavia, when the President of Finland, Martti Ahtisaari (1994–2000), played the leading role in the negotiations that led to the Federal Republic of Yugoslavia's (FRY—renamed Serbia and Montenegro in 2003) decision to submit to NATO demands. The Russian envoy, Viktor Chernomyrdin, who accompanied Ahtisaari to the FRY, remained in the background. Poland (together with the Czech Republic and Hungary) joined NATO in March 1999, and in November 2002 Estonia, Latvia and Lithuania were among seven countries that received invitations to join the Alliance, at a NATO summit meeting held in Prague, Czech Republic. Accession was to take place in 2004. All four countries had also successfully completed negotiations for entry into the EU and were due to become members in May 2004. Their entry would serve to increase the influence of the Baltic Sea region in the EU.

Although its influence waned, Russia's involvement in the region did not diminish. The dissolution of the USSR shifted the centre of gravity of Russia's geographical and economic interests to the north and the west, and the Baltic Sea remained a crucial waterway for Russian trade.

SECURITY AND POLITICS

The pace and the scope of the peaceful consolidation of the region following the fall of communism exceeded expectations. German-Polish rapprochement was on the same scale as that of France and Germany following the end of the Second World War. Continued co-operation was a staple of the foreign policy of both countries, and Germany was a forceful advocate of Poland in the latter's efforts to join NATO and the EU. A joint German-Polish-Danish corps was established shortly after Poland joined NATO, and is based in the Polish Baltic city of Szczecin.

Similar progress marked Polish-Lithuanian relations. In the period between the First and Second World Wars the hostility between the two countries was intense enough to thwart all attempts at broader regional co-operation, even in the face of the Nazi menace. In the 1990s the two countries formed wide-ranging institutions to deepen co-operation. Joint councils at presidential, governmental and parliamentary levels were established in 1997, and a joint Lithuanian-Polish peace-keeping battalion, LITPOLBAT, inaugurated in April 1999, formed the basis of military co-operation.

Russia remained a unique case. Vastly diminished in size and population, economically and military weakened, Russia, none the less, remained the region's great power. Maintaining good neighbourly relations with Russia was a primary aim of the other Baltic Rim states. To mark the 10th anniversary of its foundation, in March 2002 the Council of Baltic Sea States (CBSS) held its annual ministerial session in Svetlogorsk, Kaliningrad, followed, in June, by a summit meeting of heads of government in St Petersburg, in a symbolic assertion of its continuing concern with developments in Russia. Co-operation has deepened, as the benefits of good relations, in particular the opportunities for expanded trade and investments, are potentially vast.

Russia was the only country in the region not to seek NATO or EU membership. In principle, Russia welcomed EU enlargement and closer economic links, although some problems arose. Russian governments repeatedly stated that the EU's Schengen Agreement on border controls, which demanded visas for Russian citizens entering EU countries, was an obstacle to travel and European consolidation, as well as a form of discrimination against Russian citizens. However, after intense discussion and EU intervention an agreement was reached, whereby from 1 July 2003 Russia's nationals were able to travel to and from the Kaliningrad region, via Lithuania, with facilitated travel documentation; the issuing procedure for the documentation was simpler and cheaper than that required to obtain a visa. Lithuania retained the right to control the flow of travellers and to deny entry to undesirable persons. Progress was also made towards finding common ground on three more contentious issues, namely, NATO's expansion into the Baltics, Russia's relations with Estonia and Latvia, and the future of Russia's Kaliningrad region.

During the 1990s Russia was vehemently opposed to the Baltic states' membership of NATO. Russian officials at the highest level often reiterated that Baltic entry into the Western military structure constituted a threat to Russian security and that Russia would respond appropriately. Among possible retaliatory measures mentioned were the forward redeployment of Russian military forces, including tactical nuclear weapons. NATO members, and the USA in particular, were equally determined in their rejection of any Russian veto over the Alliance's expansion plans. In a speech in Warsaw, Poland, in June 2001, US President George W. Bush made clear the USA's continued strong support for NATO enlargement. However, Russian opposition to NATO expansion moderated significantly from the latter months of 2001. This may, in part, have been a case of accepting the inevitable, but improved relations between Russia and the USA, particularly after the large-scale suicide attacks on the USA of 11 September 2001, also played a role. The Alliance also embarked on a major effort to give Russia a greater voice in NATO deliberations. The establishment of a new NATO-Russia Council in May 2002 was an important step in this direction.

Although Russia's relations with Lithuania were good, its interaction with Estonia and Latvia was less cordial. The Russian Government frequently accused both countries of violating the human and civil rights of their large ethnic Russian minorities and imposed punitive tariffs on imports from Estonia and Latvia. Although observers from the Council of Europe and the Organization for Security and Co-operation in Europe (OSCE) rejected Russian charges as exaggerated, both countries were urged to make greater efforts to integrate their minorities and address ethnic-minority concerns. An easing of tensions was unlikely in the short term, as Russia would continue to find fault with Estonian, and particularly Latvian, policies, often for domestic political reasons.

The Kaliningrad region is a very special problem and a sensitive issue, not only for the Baltic Sea region, but also for the EU and its relations with Russia. Encompassing an area of 15,100 sq km (5,830 sq miles, or about one-half the size of Belgium) and with an estimated population of 943,200 (at 1 January 2002), this western Russian oblast (region) is separated from the rest of the country by Belarusian, Lithuanian and Polish territory. Kaliningrad is one of the least prosperous regions of Russia, with one of the lowest standards of living. Some 50% of the region's population are estimated to live below the official poverty line, and the real rate of unemployment is estimated to be around 25%. Kaliningrad has been beset by an unattractive investment climate, declining industrial production, massive debts and high levels of corruption, crime, contraband and communicative disease, particularly AIDS and tuberculosis. On the positive side, the number of troops present in the oblast decreased from an estimated 150,000 to as few as 40,000 by the end of the 1990s, thus reducing fears that the region would be transformed into a heavily armed military outpost. However, as Russia's only ice-free port in the Baltic Sea and home to its Baltic Fleet, Kaliningrad retained its military value.

Many major problems remained unresolved. Although Poland and Lithuania, in fulfilment of preconditions for EU membership, were set to impose restrictions on the travel of Russian nationals to Kaliningrad, both countries and the EU as a whole sought to integrate, rather than isolate, the region. The EU indicated its willingness to make substantial investment to ease the economic impact of the imposition of a full visa regime, and stated that it would pay for the preparations required to issue facilitated transit documents, create a control system, etc., and assured Lithuania that it would finance all additional expenses incurred during 2004–06. Poland, and especially Lithuania, developed close ties with Kaliningrad. Lithuania and Russia applied jointly for EU aid for environmental action, the modernization of road links to Vilnius and the construction of gas pipelines through Lithuania and Kaliningrad. By granting the oblast financial and technical assistance and by enmeshing it in a growing network of co-operative ventures, Kaliningrad's neighbours hoped to convince both the local administration and the Russian Government that Kaliningrad's future lay in developing its potential for trade, rather than as a forepost of Russian arms.

INSTITUTIONS OF CO-OPERATION

The EU was the dominant political and economic force in the Baltic Sea region, particularly after the accession, in 1995, of Finland and Sweden. Through its various institutions and member states, primarily the Nordic countries, the EU was influential in helping set the agenda for the whole region. The Nordic states were instrumental in attempts to foster greater integration among the region's states. The project of forging a common regional identity was accompanied by a parallel effort to convince others, including the EU as a whole, of the importance and special features of the region. The process was relatively successful.

The main body for regional co-operation was the CBSS, founded in 1992 under the auspices of the Danish and German Ministers of Foreign Affairs. All the states of the Baltic Sea littoral, represented by their ministers of foreign affairs, as well as the European Commission, were members of the CBSS. The Council promoted regional co-operation, broadened the network of contacts and fostered economic and democratic development. Special programmes were created for fighting organized crime, controlling the spread of communicable diseases, fostering higher education and encouraging sustainable development. Particular attention was placed on problems in the Baltic states and Russia, and on the means for resolving them. The work of the CBSS was supplemented by the Union of Baltic Cities, a network of around 100 cities, founded in 1991. The EU was also instrumental in creating various 'Euroregions', such as 'Baltija', created in February 1998 with the participation of representatives from regions in Denmark, Latvia, Lithuania, Poland and Sweden and from the Kaliningrad region.

Owing to their 1,300-km border with Russia, the EU's only direct geographical link with that country, the Nordic states played the leading role in developing the so-called 'Northern Dimension' of the EU, as well as contributing to the formulation of the EU's common strategy toward Russia, as embodied in a partnership and co-operation agreement, which entered into force on 1 December 1997. The Northern Dimension sought to foster mutual interdependence between EU members and other Baltic Sea region countries, promote economic development and stability, address cross-border issues and implement programmes to reduce divergence among the societies of the region; it specifically avoided addressing military and security issues. Priority was given to efforts to integrate Russia into a common European economic and social area by undertaking projects that dealt with environmental pollution, nuclear risks and cross-border organized crime. For example, there were plans to develop a cross-border information-society model in Kareliya (Karelia) in an attempt to stimulate growth, particularly in the forestry and wood-processing industries, and to bridge the digital divide between the Russian and Finnish sides of the territory. It should be noted that the Northern Dimension was not limited to the Baltic Sea region. Of equal importance was the Barents Sea region, where questions of nuclear safety and pollution in Russia's Kola peninsula were particularly acute. However, despite the Finnish and Swedish presidencies of the EU and the adoption of an Action Plan in June 2000, the Northern Dimension remained a somewhat indefinite process, without specific budgetary appropriation. Environmental and nuclear safety, cross-border facilities and aid to Kaliningrad received substantial funding from EU financial instruments, including PHARE (originally Poland/Hungary Aid for Restructuring of Economies—but later extended to 14 countries), and Technical Assistance to the Commonwealth of Independent States (TACIS) and INTERREG (Inter-regional co-operation) programmes.

Baltic Sea co-operation initiatives received broad financial support from different sources. The Nordic states granted priority to assistance to the Baltic Sea region, as soon as it became apparent that major political changes were imminent there. In 1990–93 the Nordic states contributed about ECU 1,400m. to Poland, the Baltic states and north-west Russia. Subsequently, co-operation with the so-called 'Adjacent Area'—the Baltic states, north-west Russia and the Arctic region—became one of the three pillars of Nordic co-operation, and was one that continued to grow thereafter, receiving an ever larger share of funding. In 1998–99 this pillar was allocated almost one-fifth of the total aggregate Nordic budget. Among the many projects for which funding was provided were training courses for journalists, measures to fight disease and promote public health, internship and youth-exchange programmes. The EU and other international structures also contributed substantially in 1995–99, when overall support to the region amounted to approximately €4,000m.

The predominant role that the Nordic countries played in the Baltic Sea region was not unexpected. Wealthier and more developed than the former Eastern bloc countries, they were also committed to the region as the main area for their diplomatic and economic endeavours. In contrast, Germany and Poland had equal, if not greater, concerns in Central Europe. Moreover, Mecklenberg-Vorpommern, the German state with the longest coastline on the Baltic Sea, was one of Germany's least prosperous and underdeveloped regions.

Even more important was the fact that decades of fruitful regional co-operation contributed to the evolution of a common Nordic identity, based on shared values, experiences and expectations. The Nordic countries had a similar climate, related languages, a venerable tradition of democracy and municipal autonomy, and analogous links between the state and the Protestant churches. The countries enjoyed advanced, mixed economies and a political consensus on funding generous welfare benefits through high taxation. Nordic countries also placed great value on gender equality (they had a far greater proportion of female parliamentarians and ministers than most other Western democracies) and the preservation of the environment.

This common identity formed and, in turn, was formed by two institutions, which served as a framework for their joint endeavours. The Nordic Council, founded in 1952 by Denmark, Iceland, Norway and Sweden (Finland joined in 1955), and composed of parliamentarians nominated by their respective parties, was a forum for co-operation between parliaments and governments, rather than a supranational legislature. From 1971 its work was supplemented by the Nordic Council of Ministers, the composition of which varied depending on the issues being discussed. The Council of Ministers implemented the recommendations of the Nordic Council, reported to the Council on its activities and managed the practical aspects of Nordic co-operation in all policy areas. Both Councils were served by separate secretariats. In 2002 the Council of Ministers' budget amounted to almost US \$100m., with each member country contributing according to its share of the aggregate GDP.

The three Baltic states drew on the Nordic model to establish a similar structure for regional co-operation. The Baltic Assembly, a biannual gathering of parliamentarians, was a consultative and co-ordinating body intended to parallel the work of the Nordic Council. Its first session was held in January 1992. The Baltic Council, founded in the following year by the Assembly, comprised 60 parliamentarians from Estonia, Latvia and Lithuania. Its Council of Ministers, established in 1994, was charged with implementing the recommendations of the Baltic Assembly. In contrast to their Nordic counterparts, these Baltic institutions had symbolic, rather than substantive, importance, and their hortatory and declarative resolutions were usually ignored by their respective governments. Underfunding also limited the structures' effectiveness. Thus, in 1999 the Baltic Assembly had a budget of US \$54,000, while the Council of Ministers had no funding of its own.

The weakness of Baltic institutions reflects the realities of the region's relations. Despite a tendency to conceive the Baltic states as an integral unit, their peoples had fewer linguistic, cultural, religious and historical similarities than their northern neighbours. Disputes concerning the delimitation of sea borders and duties on agricultural products, competition for foreign investment and the Russian transit trade, a perceived lack of solidarity, as well as other factors, adversely affected bilateral links. Relations were cordial, but lacked warmth and deeper commitment. However, simultaneous entry into the EU and NATO was expected to strengthen co-operation.

From 1996 the Nordic Council and the Baltic Assembly met in joint session every two years. In the session held in April 2003 the parliamentarians analyzed means to improve co-operation in fighting organized crime, managing environmental crises and providing better health care. They also discussed the possibility of organizing a joint parliamentary forum of all eight countries once the Baltic states had formally joined the EU in 2004.

The EU and NATO played a decisive role in developing co-operation between the three Baltic states. The degree of their involvement was the best predictor of the likelihood that a particular project would be successful. The EU adopted the function of an external facilitator, or supervisor, fostering mutuality and solving co-ordination problems by providing rules for co-operation and domestic policy-making. The importance that the EU initially placed on co-operation encouraged Baltic governments to implement co-operation schemes, in particular, the removal of barriers to the free exchange of goods and services. However, plans for a customs union faltered, in part because each country was primarily concerned with individually fulfilling the criteria for EU entry, and intra-Baltic trade remained very modest. However, military co-operation under NATO supervision made greater progress. A joint Baltic peace-keeping battalion (BALTBAT) was serving in the Balkans in the early 2000s (although in early 2003 plans were announced for its dissolution), while a naval squadron (BALTRON), an air surveillance network (BALTNET) and a defence college (BALTDEFCOL) were also established.

COMMERCE

The Baltic Sea region has an ancient history of vigorous economic activity. During the most prosperous period of the Hanseatic League in the late Middle Ages, and the subsequent years of Dutch ascendancy, the Baltic Sea was the centre of European trade. Even during the Cold War, commerce in the region never completely halted, even between nations on opposite sides of the political divide. Finland's 'vodka tourism' to Estonia and Russia (in particular, to Leningrad, now St Petersburg) was a case in point.

In the 1990s economic links between the states of the region underwent dramatic expansion and intensification. The impetus in the renewal of commerce was also taken by the Nordic states, which not only extended aid to the Baltic region, but invested heavily in Baltic companies and infrastructure projects. At the end of 1995 four of the largest 10 foreign investors in Lithuania were Scandinavian. The Nordic presence was even greater in Estonia and Latvia. Swedish and Finnish ventures helped to modernize the banking and telecommunications sectors of all three Baltic states. Scandinavian companies purchased shares of breweries and invested in the services sector, particularly hotels, shops and restaurants. Investment took place despite substantial bureaucratic impediments in all three Baltic countries and the lack of visa-free travel. During 1996–2000 Swedish companies were the largest investors in the three Baltic countries, accounting for 37.6% of investment in Estonia, 32.3% in Latvia and 17.3% in Lithuania. Although the Nordic share of Baltic foreign direct investment was substantial, investments in the Baltics constituted a small percentage of total Nordic outward direct investment. Swedish companies were no less active among their Nordic neighbours. Sweden's share of foreign investment in Finland was 50.1%, and it was 32.3% in Norway and 22.7% in Denmark. German investment in the region was, in general, modest, although Germany accounted for some 13% of all investment in Poland. Polish investment in the Baltic states was minimal, even in Lithuania. Latvia was unique in having attracted significant Russian investment. The only Baltic country with a sizeable investment in its Baltic neighbours was Estonia, accounting for about 5% of total foreign direct investment in both Latvia and Lithuania. In turn, Lithuania was the leading foreign investor in Kaliningrad.

Trading patterns among the region's states varied considerably. Germany was by far Poland's most important trading partner. German commercial links with the Nordic countries were limited, as were those of Poland. Intra-Nordic trade was well-developed, but the bulk of Nordic commerce was with other EU countries, particularly Germany and the United Kingdom. The Nordic states accounted for around one-half of Estonia's imports and exports, but less than 25% of Latvia's and Lithuania's, which had a wider range of partners. Because of their still underdeveloped economies and need for capital goods, the three Baltic states and Poland had substantial trade deficits.

Commercial links with Russia developed slowly and, in some cases, even regressed. Because of Russian economic mismanagement and corruption, commercial ties and investment there were seen as excessively hazardous. In the early 1990s the Baltic states were still thoroughly integrated into the Russian economy, which was their major source of raw materials and the primary market for finished goods. However, a radical decoupling occurred during the decade, accelerated by a conscious turn to the West, as well as by fears of economic and, thus, indirectly, political dependence on Russia. The Russian economic crisis of 1998 further exacerbated the situation, as the fourfold decline in the value of the rouble made Baltic and Nordic goods priced in 'hard' currency too expensive for the Russian market.

Nevertheless, Russia remained an alluring target, with a market of almost 150m. inhabitants and seemingly boundless reserves of natural resources. Investment in the exploitation of these resources was crucial not only to the Baltic Sea region, but also to the EU. A 'partnership in energy' between the EU and Russia, formalized at a summit meeting in Paris, France, in 2000, foresaw increased energy deliveries from Russia in exchange for investment and new technologies. In 2000 imported gas accounted for 40% of EU supplies; by 2020 this figure was expected to rise to 70%. In 1999 Russia produced an estimated 591,000m. cu m of natural gas, and its known reserves, primarily in the northern Taiga and the Barents Sea, were substantial. Petroleum, mineral and forest resources were also plentiful. However, Russia, in turn, was dependent on the Baltic Sea countries. In 2000 approximately 40% of its maritime transport was shipped via Baltic Sea ports, and the ports of the Baltic states controlled about 75%–80% of this traffic. Finnish ports shipped another 10% of the tonnage, as did the Russian ports of St Petersburg and Kaliningrad. From 2001 Russia moved aggressively to limit its dependence on the Baltic ports and to acquire influence over the energy sector of the Baltic states. Terminals at Primorsk and Bukhta Batareinaya on the Gulf of Finland were built as part of Russia's Baltic Pipeline System, in order to increase its shipping capacity. Russia's state-controlled petroleum pipeline operator, Transfneft, sharply reduced its petroleum supplies to Latvia in 2002, and they were further reduced in the first half of 2003, prompting speculation that the action was intended to lessen the value of Latvia's Ventspils Nafta oil terminal, prior to the anticipated sale of the remaining state-owned shares in the company. Latvia even appealed to the USA to intervene on its behalf, by asking Russia to restart the flow of petroleum.

ENERGY AND THE ENVIRONMENT

The countries of the region embarked on wide-ranging co-operative ventures in the face of contemporary problems and future challenges. Energy, the environment, economic development, transportation and the fight against organized crime were among the priority areas. Of particular importance was 'Agenda 21 for the Baltic Sea Region', a CBSS initiative begun in October 1996 and officially adopted at the ministerial session of the CBSS held in June 1998. Baltic 21, as the agenda was also known, aimed to develop a plan for sustainable-energy development in the area, based on regional co-operation and emphasizing the importance of ecological issues.

The region was rich in energy resources, both fossil and renewable. The ratio between total reserves and annual production was 12 years for petroleum and 55 years for gas. Electricity production was diversified. Hydroelectric power accounted for 35% of total electricity output, nuclear power for 22%, combined heat and power for 20% and traditional condensing for 23%. Although the energy supply per head in the Baltic Sea region was higher than the world average, it was less than the Organisation for Economic Co-operation and Development (OECD) average, primarily because of the developments in the new democracies. Increased prices for energy, coupled with a decrease in purchasing power, reduced the supply of energy available to inhabitants.

In 2000 there was a surplus power-production capacity in the Baltic Sea region; however, the projected closure of nuclear plants was likely to alter this situation. Moreover, Latvia and the Kaliningrad region, as well as Belarus, were heavily dependent on the import of power. Long-term projects aimed at integrating electricity and gas infrastructures and markets in the region in order to reduce costs, rationalize investments and reduce emissions. Plans were drafted to create a Baltic energy ring encompassing the whole region, and investors were being targeted for the construction of connections between Sweden and Poland, and Norway and Germany. In 2001 Lithuania and Poland signed an accord to build an electrical power bridge between the countries by 2008—a development that would close the gap in the planned energy ring. In March 2003 three electricity companies, Eesti Energia AS (Estonia), Latvenergo (Latvia) and Pohjolan Voima (Finland), signed an agreement on the construction of an underwater power cable between Estonia and Finland, to be known as the Estlink, which was to connect the Finnish grid with the Estonian network, and allow transmission in both directions. The Estlink, which was scheduled to be completed by the end of 2005, would represent the first connection between the power grids of the Baltic states and the Nordic countries.

There were similar plans, albeit less developed, to create a Baltic gas network. The Nordic Gas Grid was considering the construction of a pipeline connection from North Sea gas resources, through Denmark, Finland and Sweden, and a connection to the Russian and Baltic states' gas supply system. A direct connection between the gas infrastructures of Poland and Denmark was planned, as were links between Finland and Estonia, and Lithuania and Poland.

Environmental protection was a long-standing matter for concern in the Baltic Sea region. In 1974 the Nordic states initialled the first regional marine convention, the Convention on the Protection of the Marine Environment of the Baltic Sea Area, and subsequently established the Helsinki Commission (HELCOM) to co-ordinate the work of states, municipalities, industry and agriculture in protecting the ecosystem. Environmental awareness increased in the following decade. The explosion at a nuclear reactor in Chornobyl (Chernobyl), Ukraine, in 1986 (Scandinavian monitors were the first in the West to register the radiation in the atmosphere), epidemics among the seal population and the discovery of toxic algae in the Baltic Sea all disclosed broad ecological vulnerability and interdependence. The Nordic countries sought to transmit their ecological values to the new democracies, offering substantial aid for the construction of waste- and water-management facilities, the reduction of the use of coal and high-sulphur-content fuels. Encouraged by the Nordic countries, the EU has contributed substantial sums of money for environmental protection. In 2000–06 the EU was to contribute annually some €500m. for environmental protection in the Baltic Sea region, as well as north-west Russia. About €200m. were to be used to help decommission the Soviet-style nuclear reactor in Ignalina, in north-east Lithuania.

The collapse of the command economies in Eastern Europe had an important and generally beneficial effect on environmental quality. The restructuring of industry and the closure of many inefficient factories diminished environmental pollution. The dismantling of collective farms reduced the use of fertilizers and the size of pig and cattle herds, which resulted in an improvement in the water quality of the region's rivers, a reduction in the amount of untreated sewage flowing into the Baltic Sea and reduced acidification of soils and waters. Although the nutrient pollution reaching the Sea had decreased by 20%–25%, it continued to exceed its biological capacity, ensuring that the Baltic remained one of the world's most polluted seas. The principal culprit was the city of St Petersburg, which treated only two-thirds of its waste water. The Nordic countries, particularly Finland, mobilized substantial resources to restrict the discharge of sewage and to build new sewage-treatment plants. However, Russian indifference to environmental concerns prevented the implementation of more aggressive programmes.

Measures were taken to conserve terrestrial and marine biodiversity in the Baltic Sea region, to protect at least 10% of each major biotope within the Baltic Sea catchment area, to ensure the survival of species and to minimize the risks involved in the introduction of non-indigenous species. Measures were also adopted to reduce pollution from heavy metals and toxic, persistent organic compounds. From 1987 a 90% reduction of discharges of organo-halogen compounds from the pulp industry was achieved. Although there were no major shipping accidents, the substantial number of petroleum spills, primarily illegal operational discharges, remained a cause for concern. Environmental activists feared that government support for activities related to the import and export of petroleum, in particular the competition for the transport of Russian petroleum, contributed to the growth in the volume of petroleum shipments and, thus, to the number of substandard ships sailing in the Baltic, increasing the chances of a major environmental accident.

PROSPECTS

Despite the general amity in the region, the implementation of some of the co-operative ventures would face difficulties. The Baltic Sea states each had different resources and priorities. The premium that the wealthy Nordic states placed on environmental protection was not region-wide. The Nordic states favoured the total elimination of nuclear reactors by 2030 and at least a 50% decrease in the use of oil shale, coal and lignite, although Finland rebelled in 2002 by approving a plan to build a fifth nuclear power plant, the first such decision by an EU country in more than a decade. In general, the burden of implementation would fall on states that were economically less developed, that had relatively inflexible labour markets and that could least afford higher unemployment. Oil shale was produced in north-east Estonia, coal in Silesia, Poland. The planned closure of the Ignalina nuclear plant led to protests and fears that the huge financial burden of closure would be borne primarily by that country. Miners remained a political force in Poland, and the interests of that sector could not be ignored.

The vast divergence in wealth and resources was another potential source of misunderstanding, if not discord. Despite the mutual benefits of foreign investment, fears that Scandinavians were purchasing local companies with the highest earning potential and, thus, further impoverishing their native countries, caused some resentment in the remainder of the region. The perception that foreign investors were taking advantage of their dominance to extract exorbitant rates fuelled further dissatisfaction. In the late 1990s there were numerous demonstrations in Lithuania protesting the sale, in 1998, of the state telecommunications company, Lietuvos Telekomas, and the subsequent increase in telephone tariffs. In 2001 local Estonian and Lithuanian businessmen sought to prevent the sale of important economic assets to Western investors, arguing that such companies should remain under local control. The aggressive acquisition policies of Russian oil and energy companies also led to resentment and concern in the Baltic states.

Because of general impoverishment in Russia and, to a far lesser degree, in the three Baltic states and Poland, infectious diseases such as tuberculosis, syphilis, jaundice and diphtheria began to re-emerge, and HIV/AIDS had grown to epidemic proportions. In the Kaliningrad region, the HIV infection rate in 2000 was 350 cases per 100,000 inhabitants, while in the three Baltic states the rates of multi-drug-resistant tuberculosis were among the highest in the world. Violent crime, caused in part by alcohol and drug abuse, had increased sharply, and some of it was being exported to the Nordic countries by Baltic organized criminals, as well as by individual, often youthful, offenders. The Finnish police claimed that one-10th of criminals dealing in illegal drugs come from Estonia. Were such trends to continue, the benevolent attitude of the citizens of the Nordic countries to their less-favoured neighbours might well decrease.

Finally, the lethargic pace of EU enlargement and the conditions placed on entry—for example, restrictions on the free movement of labour and limited subsidies for local farmers—had heightened fears that new members were unwelcome and would be treated as inferiors. These concerns were mitigated by the EU's decision to grant membership to Poland and the Baltic states. Russia remained the exception, and the lengthy and, at times, tense discussions concerning transit to and from Kaliningrad reflected its fears that it might be isolated, and its citizens discriminated against. However, the commonality of interests and the habits of dialogue and co-operation among the countries of the Baltic Sea region should ensure that any such disagreements remain those of neighbours with a clear interest in their resolution.

THE FORMER YUGOSLAVIA AFTER MILOŠEVIĆ

Dr OTHON ANASTASAKIS

INTRODUCTION

The assassination in March 2003 of the Serbian Prime Minister, Zoran Djindjić, was a shocking reminder to the international community that the Balkans were still experiencing the delicate and difficult transition to stability, democracy and economic well-being. Although in recent years the Balkans region has ceased to be the 'danger zone' of the 1990s, it remains a very troubled area, where the fear of regression to extremism has not disappeared. In 2003 the regional picture presented some hopeful signs of reform, including the predominance of electoral politics, the deepening of relations with the European Union (EU) and the re-emergence of regional co-operation, on the one hand, and some signs of reverse, including lingering ethnic mistrust, undefined territorial borders and a large informal and criminal sector, on the other. With the signature of the Treaty of Accession in Athens, Greece, on 16 April, by the 15 existing and 10 anticipated members of the EU, the Balkan region was excluded from the 'big bang' enlargement of the Union to the East. The region's integration with the EU still required great effort, hard choices and radical changes on the part of its constituent countries. Despite the planned enlargement and signs of 'Balkan fatigue' on the part of the EU, the latter remains the main external player with an impact in the region. Through its Stabilization and Association process, the Stability Pact for South Eastern Europe, and a more involved Common Foreign and Security Policy (CFSP), the EU is expected to contribute to the reform and the eventual integration of the Balkan countries into Europe. The following chapter will examine recent developments in the region, arguing that while progress made in the years following the collapse of the regime of the former Yugoslav President, Slobodan Milošević, has paved the way for a degree of normalization in the region's political, economic and social affairs, extremist and reactionary forces from the previous decade retain the capacity to obstruct reform and transition in the former Yugoslav region.

TRANSITION IN SERBIA

On 24 September 2000 the Federal Republic of Yugoslavia (FRY) elected Vojislav Koštunica, a candidate supported by a coalition of 18 parties, known as the Democratic Opposition of Serbia (DOS), as its new President, in place of Milošević, in a dramatic electoral procedure, amid popular unrest. In December the Serbian parliamentary elections awarded the DOS a comfortable majority, with 64% of the votes cast, and 176 of the 250 seats in the republican National Assembly, thus further consolidating the victory of the anti-Milošević opposition, which for more than a decade had been unable to unite effectively against Milošević's rule. The downfall of Milošević raised hopes for the future of the region, as Serbia had been regarded as the driving force behind much of the instability in the Balkans. Milošević's removal from power ended Serbia's international isolation, and international support was demonstrated by the lifting of sanctions, initially imposed in 1992. Early membership of the IMF and the World Bank was accompanied by special financial assistance from both the EU and the USA. The FRY became part of the Stability Pact for South Eastern Europe, obtained a seat at the UN, and was readmitted to the Organization for Security and Co-operation in Europe (OSCE). The country restored diplomatic relations with the USA and the countries of Western Europe, normalized relations with neighbouring Bosnia and Herzegovina, Croatia and Albania, and was included in the Stabilization and Association Process of the EU.

Although most of the more visible successes took place at diplomatic level, some successes were recorded in the economic domain. When Koštunica came to power, some 65% of Serbians were officially reported to be living in poverty and nearly 30% were unemployed (although the unofficial figure was far higher). Moreover, the country experienced very high rates of annual inflation, of some 115%, a bankrupt state sector, a huge public deficit, high levels of external debt and a large informal sector. This economic situation was the outcome of years of government mismanagement, economic sanctions imposed from abroad and the costs of successive wars. The economic reform pursued by the new, democratic leadership relied on external support and the policies of the influential economic research institution, G17, which opened in the capital of the FRY, Belgrade, in mid-2001, and which was determined to introduce the necessary market economic changes and to secure the country's reintegration into international financial institutions. The FRY rapidly regained membership of almost all of the most important global financial institutions and re-established economic relations with the majority of countries. The new Government attempted to attract foreign direct investment and to raise money by privatizing state funds. The Governor of the central bank, Mladjan Dinkić (who was, however, removed from the post in July 2003), earned respect for his economic reforms, and enjoyed the confidence of Serbia's financial supporters. He stabilized the Yugoslav dinar, reduced inflation and negotiated the cancellation of some Milošević-era debts. On the whole, the Serbian authorities displayed a determination to undertake some necessary reform and to move towards the rapid reconstruction of the country. They recorded some progress in areas such as the independence of the media and the respect for human rights. However, the sustainability of the transition process was threatened by serious reverses, caused by domestic power struggles, economic hardship, a dominant informal sector, the influential role of the unreformed military and paramilitary forces, and the unclear status of both the Serbian province of Kosovo (Kosovo and Metohija) and the Republic of Montenegro (Serbia's partner in the FRY).

From the beginning of the democratic transition, Serbian politics were permeated by the uneasy partnership between Koštunica and Djindjić over a wide range of issues, such as the pace of reform, corruption and organized crime, and co-operation with the International Criminal Tribunal for the former Yugoslavia (ICTY, based in the Hague, Netherlands). In August 2001 Koštunica's Democratic Party of Serbia (DPS) withdrew from the Serbian Government, and in June 2002 all 45 DPS deputies left the Serbian parliament, the National Assembly, in protest at Djindjić's actions. The Serbian presidential election of October 2002 confirmed Koštunica's popularity, but exposed popular apathy towards electoral politics. Although Koštunica topped the poll, the election was declared invalid, because the rate of participation fell below the 50% threshold required by law; the same scenario was repeated in December.

The troubled politics of Serbia were further shaken in March 2003, when Djindjić was assassinated outside the government building in Belgrade. During the Milošević era,

Djindjić had been one of the most vocal opponents of the ruling regime. He came to international prominence at the end of 1996, when he helped to inspire and co-ordinate nearly three months of mass demonstrations against the attempts of the Milošević administration to annul the victories of the opposition Zajedno (Together) bloc in municipal elections throughout Serbia. Djindjić consequently became Mayor of Belgrade in February 1997, and played a key role in the co-ordinating the opposition that led to the eventual downfall of Milošević in 2000. He was appointed Prime Minister of Serbia in January 2001. As Serbian Prime Minister, Djindjić projected a Western-orientated, 'technocratic' style of leadership, by showing a clear determination for free-market reforms, facilitating Milošević's transferral to the Hague, and acting as an advocate of attempts to combat corruption. However, he was criticized domestically for his opportunistic leadership, as well as for the clandestine agreements and links with informal networks that he used to consolidate his power. In fact, Djindjić inherited from Milošević a legacy of deals and close relationships with the worlds of business, organized crime and the security forces. The authorities were frequently criticized for not tackling the mafia bosses—particularly when the criminal enterprises of such individuals began to resemble more legitimate businesses. Nevertheless, it appeared that the most likely reason for Djindjić's assassination was his determination to push through free-market reforms and to combat more efficiently corruption and organized crime, thus attacking the interests of the powerful Serbian mafias. The Serbian authorities blamed the assassination on the Zemun clan, a crime network linked to a special police unit known as the Red Berets, which was highly active under Milošević. The assassination of Djindjić led the Government to carry out widespread arrests, some of them high profile, under a state of emergency. Serbia's new Prime Minister, Zoran Živković, a popular Mayor of the city of Niš, following the North Atlantic Treaty Organization—NATO's air campaign against the FRY in 1999 (precipitated by the ethnic conflict between the Serbs and Kosovo's predominantly ethnic Albanian population), was largely expected to continue along Djindjić's path; however, his determination remained to be seen.

Co-operation by the federal authorities with the ICTY was a particularly controversial issue affecting relations between the FRY and the international community, on the one hand, and the federal authorities and the Serbian Government, on the other. Within the DOS, opinion was divided between those who openly denounced the ICTY as illegitimate and anti-Serb, and those who claimed that the FRY had an obligation to co-operate with it. The UN Security Council Resolutions 827 and 1034, of 25 May 1993 and 21 December 1995, respectively, explicitly demanded that the FRY and its neighbouring countries co-operated fully with the ICTY. This co-operation was understood to include the arrest and transfer to the ICTY of individuals suspected of war crimes, as well as the granting to the ICTY of access to evidence, documentation and witnesses. As a co-signatory of the General Framework Agreement for Peace in Bosnia and Herzegovina, signed in Dayton, Ohio (USA), in December 1995 (the Dayton accords), Yugoslavia was committed to full co-operation with the ICTY. However, although some positive measures were taken by the new Serbian authorities, including the delivery of Milošević to the ICTY in June 2001, the Federal Government of Yugoslavia did not fully co-operate with the Tribunal, owing to strong resistance from the pro-Milošević Socialist People's Party of Montenegro, unwillingness from inside the Government and resistance from the Yugoslav Army. For his part, Koštunica was also reluctant to co-operate, accusing the ICTY of rewriting history against the Serbs and failing to respect its own statutes. Both the USA and the EU applied significant pressure on the FRY to co-operate with the ICTY, linking co-operation to the release of funds. The handing over of Milošević to the ICTY was the outcome of such pressure—shortly afterwards an international donor conference pledged US $1,280m. to help rebuild the FRY's economy. In March 2002 the USA applied additional pressure to encourage further extraditions, by suspending $40m. in aid. As a result, in April the upper house of the Yugoslav parliament, the Chamber of Republics, passed a draft law, which provided for the extradition of indicted war crime suspects to the ICTY. The list of indicted suspects included, among many others, four senior Serbian officials, comprising Milan Milutinović (who at that time retained the post of Serbian President that he had held since 1997), a former Yugoslav Deputy Prime Minister, Nikola Sainović, the Yugoslav Army's former Chief of Staff, Gen. Dragoljub Ojdanić, and a former republican Minister of Internal Affairs, Vlajko Stojiljković. The last, who had headed the police forces under Milošević, shot himself outside the federal parliament in April 2002, just hours after its members had voted to permit the extradition of suspects to the ICTY. Ojdanić and Sainović surrendered to the Tribunal in late April and early May, respectively. In January 2003, when his term as Serbian President had come to an end, Milutinović also surrendered, pleading not guilty to charges of crimes against humanity. Moreover, the Serb nationalist politician Vojislav Šešelj, well-known for his extreme ethnic rhetoric, surrendered voluntarily to the Tribunal in February. Despite these moves, the international community remained unconvinced that the Serbian authorities were committed to full co-operation, claiming that suspects such as the former Bosnian military leader, Gen. Ratko Mladić, the former President of the Serb Republic of Bosnia and Herzegovina, Radovan Karadžić, and the so-called Vukovar three (former Yugoslav army officers indicted for the massacre in 1991 of some 200 ethnic Croats in Vukovar, in eastern Croatia—Mile Mrksić, Miroslav Radić and Veselin Sljivancanin) were protected by informal networks of highly influential and powerful army personnel and prominent politicians.

THE END OF YUGOSLAVIA

On 4 February 2003 both chambers of the Yugoslav parliament, the Federal Assembly, approved the final dissolution of the Yugoslav federation after 74 years of existence. Its forerunner had been founded after the First World War (1914–18) as the Kingdom of Serbs, Croats and Slovenes, and renamed Yugoslavia in October 1929. A Socialist Republic of Yugoslavia, comprising Serbia, Montenegro, Bosnia and Herzegovina, Croatia, Macedonia and Slovenia, was proclaimed in 1943, and established as the Federative People's Republic of Yugoslavia in 1945. Under authoritarian communist leader Josip Broz (Tito) ethnic tensions were contained. In 1963 the country's name was changed to the Socialist Federal Republic of Yugoslavia (SFRY). After Tito's death in 1980, the federation lasted for over 10 years, but, following the dramatic changes of 1989 across Eastern Europe, the country was torn apart by bloodshed throughout the 1990s. The third Yugoslavia, the FRY, was proclaimed in haste in April 1992, on the assertion that Serbia and Montenegro represented the continuation of the SFRY, from which the other four republics had unilaterally seceded. The Constitution that was drafted replicated features of the former SFRY, with an emphasis on equal representation and consensual decision-making in the federal bodies. However, the FRY never functioned as envisaged by its Constitution, and the federal structures were ignored by both Serbia and Montenegro, and were rapidly dismantled after 1998. Most executive power lay with the two republican governments, rather than at federal level.

In Montenegro a powerful independence movement led by the Montenegrin President, Milo Djukanović (1998–2002), and the Democratic Party of Montenegrin Socialists (DPMS) advocated the right to self-determination and secession. At the same time, the movement experienced strong opposition from an anti-independence movement based mostly among the republic's Serb population. Shortly after the war in Kosovo, in August 1999 the Montenegrin Government presented a plan to redefine the FRY as a confederation of two equal states, with separate monetary systems, separate foreign ministries, and even separate defence systems. In November Montenegro introduced the German Deutsche Mark (DM) as its official currency—jointly with the dinar—and the DM (and subsequently the euro) was later adopted as the republic's sole currency. For their part, the international financial institutions treated the two republics as separate economic units, and foreign aid from the West was directed towards Montenegro, despite sanctions and the isolation of the FRY.

The fall of Milošević reduced secessionist desires in Montenegro, and the population of the republic became more evenly divided over the issue of independence. Similarly, Western sympathy for the independence movement diminished substantially. The debate on constitutional reform was blocked, and any attempt by Koštunica to discuss the constitutional question was impeded by Djukanović and Djindić. In December 2001, under EU pressure, the process of dialogue got under way, focusing on technical and political issues. In March 2002 representatives of the FRY and its two republics announced agreement on a new, looser structure for Yugoslavia, together with a new name for the federation, 'Serbia and Montenegro'. The deal was the result of extensive mediation by the EU and its first High Representative for CFSP, Javier Solana Madariaga (of Spain), owing to fears that a referendum on the issue of independence, initially scheduled for May, would lead to turmoil and conflict within the republic, and generate further secessionist aspirations within Kosovo, the former Yugoslav republic of Macedonia (FYRM) and Bosnia and Herzegovina. Under the terms of the agreement, the two republics were to share common foreign and defence policies, as well as some common federal institutions, but were to maintain separate economic systems, currencies and customs duties. Moreover, Montenegro was offered certain guarantees in the context of the federal structure, in order not to be outvoted on some important issues. The deal enabled the two countries to re-evaluate the arrangement after three years, and stage any move towards independence at that time. The controversy surrounding the agreement led almost immediately to the collapse of the Government in Montenegro, where its supporters came into conflict both with those who felt that it failed to award the republic sufficient independence and with those who thought that it awarded the republic too much. However, the position of parties in favour of the agreement was strengthened following the elections to the Montenegrin Republican Assembly in October. In November Djukanović resigned as republican President in order to assume the more powerful position of Prime Minister. The Constitutional Charter for the new state union was approved in December. As agreed in March, under the Charter the country was to retain a federal presidency and federal defence and foreign ministries, but the two republics were to be semi-independent states, in charge of their own economies. In March 2003 the Assembly of Serbia and Montenegro (the union parliament) elected Svetozvar Marović, a Montenegrin, as the country's first President. Marović was to chair the five-member cabinet—comprising ministries of defence, foreign affairs, both internal and external economic relations, and human and minority rights—and the Supreme Defence Council, the highest military authority. The 126-member Assembly had itself been elected by the parliaments of Serbia and Montenegro (accounting for 91 and 35 seats,

respectively). The new Assembly was expected to pass legislation on a new flag, national symbols and anthem by the end of 2003.

THE INTERNATIONAL PROTECTORATE OF KOSOVO

On 10 June 1999 UN Security Council Resolution 1244, which approved the peace plan for Kosovo, ordered the withdrawal of all Yugoslav military, police and paramilitary forces from the province and authorized the deployment of international and civilian personnel in the region. The international presence was dominated by the NATO-led Kosovo Force (KFOR), responsible for military protection, and the UN Interim Administration Mission in Kosovo (UNMIK), which was responsible for the civilian protection of the area. Kosovo remained an integral part of Yugoslavia, although it was, effectively, an international protectorate. Following the conflict of 1999, the province was affected by incidents of ethnic violence against Kosovar Serbs, and a series of reprisals against the Serbs led to their exodus from Kosovo in large numbers during the months following the peace agreement.

In May 2001 the head of UNMIK, Hans Hækkerup, a Danish former Minister of Defence, promulgated the Constitutional Framework for Provisional Self-Government, which dealt with the way in which Kosovo was to be governed, pending an eventual final settlement on its status. On 17 November elections to the new Kosovo Assembly took place for the first time, with the aim of introducing self-administration for the province and the devolution of power from UNMIK to the local population. The Democratic League of Kosovo (DLK), under its comparatively moderate and pacifist leader, Ibrahim Rugova, won the largest proportion of the votes cast in the parliamentary election, with 45.7%, and secured 47 seats in the 120-seat Assembly. However, the DLK failed to secure an overall majority, and was compelled to seek coalition partners in order to elect a president and form a government. The Democratic Party of Kosovo (DPK), the political successor of the Kosovo Liberation Army (KLA), was second-placed, with 25.7% of the votes cast and 26 seats. A coalition of Serb parties, Return (Povratak), received 11.3% of the votes cast and 22 seats in the Assembly. According to the Constitutional Framework, parliament has the right to choose a president and approve a government with limited powers to run departments such as health, education, transport and culture; however, it does not have the right to declare independence. UNMIK retains control of foreign affairs, monetary policy, justice and public order, and is able to veto any measures that appear to violate UN resolutions on Kosovo. KFOR holds responsibility for defence and security. In March 2002 the new Assembly chose Rugova as the province's first President, ending a three-month impasse caused by the latter's reluctance to appoint a prime minister from the rival DPK. However, in the local elections held in October there was a participation rate of less than 55%, confirming the widespread apathy of the electorate across the region, already witnessed in Serbia.

Overall, after Kosovo became an international protectorate some progress was made towards the restoration of stability in the province and the establishment of a functioning administration. At the same time, there was deep ethnic hatred between the Kosovar Albanians and the Kosovar Serbs and a particularly poor economy, mainly based on international money and remittances from the Albanian diaspora. According to a report published in April 2003 by the human rights organization Amnesty International, Serbs and other ethnic minorities in Kosovo remained at serious risk of death or injury, despite almost four years of peace and the presence of UN and NATO peace-keepers. Resolution 1244 left the issue of the province's final status open, but there were fears among the international community that any attempt to address the issue might lead to further secessionist desires and increase regional instability, particularly taking into account the fact that from 1999 Kosovo was the main source of the extremist tendencies demonstrated in the FYRM and southern Serbia. Michael Steiner, the head of UNMIK from January 2002 until July 2003, called for 'standards before status', with primacy of the rule of law to precede efforts to deal with the difficult question of whether Kosovo should remain part of Serbia. However, the reality on the ground was that the vast majority of the population in Kosovo desired full independence, and would not be willing to form part of Serbia under any circumstances.

THE IMPACT OF DAYTON IN BOSNIA AND HERZEGOVINA

The consequences of the war of 1992–95, which left some 200,000 dead and created about 1.2m. refugees, are still apparent in Bosnia and Herzegovina. The Dayton accords introduced a complex system of governance to a country that was deeply divided and dominated by ethnic intolerance between the three ethnic groups of Serbs, Croats and Bosnian Muslims (Bosniaks). Post-Dayton Bosnia and Herzegovina remained a single state within its existing borders, but reorganized into two entities: the Federation of Bosnia and Herzegovina and the Serb Republic (Republika Srpska), both of which enjoyed a high degree of autonomy and had different constitutional systems; in the Federation authority was exercised at the entity, cantonal, city and municipal levels, whereas in the Serb Republic it was exercised at the entity and municipal levels, with the emphasis on the entity level. Owing to its multiple levels of governance, Bosnia and Herzegovina was a state with 13 constitutions, 13 legislatures, 13 governments and some 200 ministries. Within this decentralized and asymmetric system of governance, the state government and the state rotating presidency had very limited scope and authority over the lower levels of government and very few resources, relying for the most part on transfers from the entities. State responsibilities were limited to the domains of foreign policy, immigration, monetary policy, foreign trade, external debt and inter-entity transport and communications.

In addition, the Dayton accords placed Bosnia and Herzegovina under the status of a protectorate of the international community. The Office of the High Representative acted on behalf of the international community to oversee the implementation of the peace process and the consolidation of new institutions, and to co-ordinate the activities of international organizations. Its powers were overwhelming in both executive and legislative matters, varying from travel documentation and privatization, to the dismissal of politicians of the state and the entities. A NATO-led international armed force was assigned the military aspects of the peace, initially as the Implementation Force (IFOR), a 60,000-strong force with a large US contingent, which was later replaced by a Stabilization Force (SFOR), a 35,000-strong unit; by January 2003 it had been reduced in size, to around 13,000 troops. On the whole, the military aspect of the Dayton accords was regarded as a success, given that there was no resumption of fighting after the war ended in 1995. The international community's presence was overwhelming in many other, civilian sectors, including the Constitutional Court of Bosnia and Herzegovina (to which the President of the European Court of Human Rights appointed three foreign nationals), the Central Bank (the IMF appoints a foreign national as the Bank's Governor), the Human Rights Ombudsman (appointed by the OSCE) and the Human Rights Chamber (eight of its 14 members were foreign nationals, appointed by the Council of Europe). The Office of the UN High Commissioner for Refugees (UNHCR) is the leading agency for all humanitarian operations, and the OSCE organizes and supervises elections and, in some cases, approves candidates.

Bosnia and Herzegovina's progress towards the establishment of a multi-ethnic and democratic country has been slow. Nationalist parties dominated the political scene after the country gained independence, and the Dayton accords did not manage to change that pattern. Following the conclusion of the peace accords, Bosnia and Herzegovina conducted numerous elections, which resulted in the predominance of nationalist parties—the Serbian Democratic Party of Bosnia and Herzegovina (SDP), the Croatian Democratic Union of Bosnia and Herzegovina (CDU—BH) and the Muslim Party of Democratic Action (PDA)—which retained a firm hold on power in their respective regions and entities. The November 2000 elections saw, for the first time, the strengthening of the reformist Alliance for Change, a coalition of political parties, led by the pro-European, moderate, centre-left Social Democratic Party of Bosnia and Herzegovina (SDP BiH). The electoral outcome of 2000 gave rise to hopes that the country was about to enter the path of normalization, state unification and integration with the EU. However, the persistence of ethnic polarization and the highly decentralized structure of the state often impeded effective government and gave the citizens of Bosnia and Herzegovina the impression that the Government was unable to deliver. In the Federation, Croat nationalists attempted to undermine multi-ethnic institutions by blocking government appointments and encouraging Bosnian Croat soldiers to leave the Muslim-dominated Federation Army. In March 2001 a group of parties led by the CDU—BH attempted to declare unilateral autonomy for Croat-inhabited area in Bosnia and Herzegovina, only to be stopped by the High Representative, Wolfgang Petritsch (1999–2002). In the Serb Republic, the SDP was determined to keep the entity as free from Bosnian Croats and Bosniaks as possible. The riots of May 2001, in Banja Luka and Trebinje, at which Bosnian Serbs clashed with police forces, international delegates and Muslim refugees in an attempt to disrupt ceremonies to mark the reconstruction of mosques destroyed during the war, were indicative of the persistence of nationalist-extremist thinking in that part of the country. Opposition to the reintegration of refugees marked not only the mentality of the public, but also the policies of the Serb Republic Government's Ministry of Refugees and Displaced Persons. Moreover, deputies and ministers in the Serb Republic consistently opposed any legislation that might enhance, or even define, the competencies of the state, at the expense of the entity. Petritsch repeatedly warned the SDP that the international community would reduce the disbursement of aid to the entity, unless the party became more co-operative and less obstructive to government policies. His successor as High Representative, Sir Jeremy John Durham (Paddy) Ashdown (2002–) introduced wide-ranging changes to the Constitution of the Serb Republic, which aimed to strengthen state institutions. In April 2003 he removed all references to statehood from the entity's Constitution, ordering that the words 'state', 'independence' and 'sovereignty' be erased. He also abolished the Serb Republic's Supreme Defence Council, accused of profiting from two scandals that involved both the Bosnian Serb military and civilian elites: the first was an illicit business deal, involving the export of arms to Iraq, in violation of international sanctions; the second was an espionage operation allegedly carried out by the Bosnian Serb military against the international organizations involved in implementing the Bosnian peace process.

Throughout the early 2000s some progress was recorded in Bosnia and Herzegovina in respect of the repatriation of refugees, co-operation with the ICTY and diplomatic relations with the country's neighbours. Developments in Croatia and Yugoslavia/Serbia and Montenegro also helped to create a more favourable environment, less conducive to nationalist extremism. Koštunica made an historic visit to Bosnia and Herzegovina in January 2001, one month after the two countries agreed to establish diplomatic relations and normalize bilateral relations. Djindjić travelled to Bosnia and Herzegovina in June of the same year, at the head of a 56-strong delegation of representatives from Serbian companies and banks, with the aim of strengthening economic ties, in the first such visit since the Yugoslav conflicts commenced. In May 2001 the Croatian President, Stjepan (Stipe) Mesić (2000–), an opponent of the 'greater Croatia' policy, also visited Bosnia and Herzegovina, and indicated clearly his lack of support for Bosnian Croat nationalism. In mid-July 2002 members of the Bosnian Presidency met the Presidents of Croatia and the FRY in Sarajevo, in their first trilateral summit meeting since the dissolution of the former Yugoslavia.

Under the Dayton peace agreement, political parties in Bosnia and Herzegovina are obliged to co-operate with the ICTY. The attitude of the Federation of Bosnia and Herzegovina has been more open and co-operative than that of the Serb Republic, although in October 2001 the latter also adopted a law on co-operation with the Tribunal. By mid-2003 the most important indictees, Karadžić and Mladić, had not yet been arrested. A number of other suspects, however, had been arrested, tried or sentenced. In 2001 a former President of the Serb entity, Biljana Plavšić, surrendered to the ICTY, and pleaded innocent to charges of genocide and war crimes; in February 2003, however, she was sentenced to 11 years in prison for crimes against humanity. Meanwhile, in February 2001 the ICTY sentenced three Bosnian Serbs to long terms of imprisonment for the systematic torture and rape of Muslim women in 1992. The verdict marked the first occasion on which the ICTY had identified rape as a crime against humanity. In August 2001 the ICTY found Bosnian Serb Radislav Krstić guilty of genocide for his role in the massacre at Srebreniča in 1995, and sentenced him to 46 years in prison. It was the ICTY's first conviction for genocide, and the harshest sentence passed to date.

Bosnia and Herzegovina recorded high rates of economic growth, mostly sustained by the large influx of external assistance. Despite high growth, however, Bosnia and Herzegovina remained the second poorest country in South-Eastern Europe, with gross domestic product (GDP) per head at one-half the pre-war level, and with an estimated 45%–55% of the population living in poverty. There were regional differences, with the Croat areas enjoying the highest standard of living and the Serb Republic the lowest. The capacity of the state to provide social-welfare payments and services was limited, and was exacerbated by the additional demands placed on the system, as a result of the war, by veterans, families of deceased soldiers and returnees. The need to attract foreign investment was increasing, especially as foreign donor assistance appeared to be gradually diminishing. The investment climate was very difficult, with one of the lowest rankings in Eastern Europe, owing also to the country's complex investment rules and corruption problems. Unemployment stood at around 40%, and the results of a UN study indicated that nearly two-thirds of young people expressed a desire to leave the country permanently. Corruption was particularly acute, as the country's status and inadequate control of borders enabled criminal organizations to develop transit routes for smuggling, illegal immigration and human trafficking. Corruption was also prevalent in everyday life, affecting businesses, public services and day-to-day affairs. Furthermore, there was a weak, fragmented and ill-defined judicial system, which was widely regarded to be neither impartial nor professional. Despite the presence of an international military mission, the illegal trafficking of migrants from the Arab

states and Turkey, via Bosnia and Herzegovina, was a large-scale business, estimated to be worth some US $150m. per year. International agencies claimed that senior government officials were operating in the capital, Sarajevo, and a publication of the UN Mission in Bosnia and Herzegovina (UNMIBH) indicated that the Sarajevo route for illegal migrants heading to the West was particularly popular. The flourishing 'grey' economy, estimated to be equivalent to some 50%–60% of GDP, was indicative of state weakness, the lack of the rule of law, and the inadequate business regulatory framework. The results of the parliamentary elections held in October 2002 saw strong support for nationalist parties in both the national legislature and the legislatures of both entities (the House of Representatives of the Federation and the National Assembly of the Serb Republic). The results were interpreted as the expression by voters of their disillusionment at the failure of the authorities to improve the economy and their overall quality of life. Ashdown acknowledged the need for reform in this deeply divided and traumatized country, and pledged to make the fight against crime and the creation of jobs his main priority. Above all, however, he repeatedly stated that his role in Bosnia and Herzegovina was, ultimately, to make his role unnecessary.

AFTER THE OHRID AGREEMENT IN THE FYRM

With the fragmentation of Yugoslavia, the FYRM was spared inter-ethnic violence, and was considered by the international community to be an 'island' of stability, with the democratic co-existence of different ethnic communities, despite maintaining difficult relations with its neighbours. Even during the war over Kosovo, the FYRM did not become embroiled in the conflict, although it was the country that bore the largest influx of Kosovar Albanian refugees, in its northern territory. In return, the EU signed its first Stabilization and Association Agreement with the FYRM, offering the country the status of a potential candidate for EU membership. However, although the FYRM had managed to avoid engagement in the wider Balkan conflict, the post-war situation in Kosovo took its toll, and the country came close to civil conflict in 2001, one decade after independence. The status of the Albanian minority in the FYRM had been a contentious issue since independence, and ethnic Albanians demanded equal constitutional rights, considering themselves to hold an inferior position to that they had enjoyed in the former Yugoslavia. They claimed that they were treated as second-class citizens, virtually excluded from the Macedonian police force and army, denied state funding for the Albanian-language university in Tetovo, and subject to a Constitution that described the country as the 'national state of the Macedonian people'. Following the end of the conflict in Kosovo in 1999, and the expulsion of Yugoslav authority from the province, extremist Albanian groups from the territories of Kosovo, southern Serbia and the FYRM commenced guerrilla warfare, initially in southern Serbia (the Preševo valley) in early 2000, and from January 2001 in the FYRM itself. The rebels fighting in the northern part of the FYRM, who formed part of the National Liberation Army (NLA), a group that emerged at the beginning of 2001, claimed themselves mainly to be Macedonian-born Albanians. However, it was clear that they included in their ranks many Albanians who had fought with the KLA, and that the group was using Kosovo as a base for supplies and as a 'safe area'.

The conflict prompted an exodus of refugees, and the rebels made some territorial gains. After seven months of clashes between the NLA and Macedonian government forces, intensive negotiations took place in the western town of Ohrid, at which the EU and US envoys brought the two sides progressively closer until, in August 2001, a peace deal was signed, according to which the guerrillas agreed to surrender their arms, in return for improved rights for the ethnic Albanian community. The agreement, which was signed by the President of Macedonia, Boris Trajkovski (1999–), and the leaders of the Slav and the principal ethnic Albanian parties, provided for a significant increase in ethnic Albanian participation in public office, and the extensive use of the Albanian language in public institutions. Subsequently, NATO forces undertook a month-long disarmament mission, Operation Essential Harvest. Based on the provisions of the peace accord, in November the Macedonian legislature, the Assembly (Sobranie), adopted amendments to the Constitution, which were designed to give greater rights to the country's ethnic Albanian population, by recognizing Albanian as a second official language in communities where ethnic Albanians comprised more than 20% of the population, and by providing ethnic Albanians with improved access to public-sector employment and the police force. A law granting an amnesty to ethnic Albanian rebels was subsequently passed in March 2002, as part of the peace deal. In parliamentary elections held in mid-September, Macedonian voters removed the nationalist Prime Minister Ljupčo Georgievski from office, by bringing a 10-party alliance, Together for Macedonia, to power, led by Branko Crvenkovski's Social Democratic Alliance of Macedonia. Six weeks later, despite protests from Macedonian nationalists, the Sobranije approved Crvenkovski's coalition cabinet, to which the Democratic Union for Integration (DUI), established by the former rebel leader Ali Ahmeti, contributed a Deputy Prime Minister and four other ministers.

After the worrying months of the 2001 conflict in the FYRM, a fifth war in the former Yugoslav region appeared to have been averted and some changes were introduced. Local councils were given increased powers, the Albanian language could be used in parliament and identity papers were issued with greater ease. In return, the guerrilla army had disbanded and the Macedonian security forces had returned to almost all of the territory once occupied by the rebels. To consolidate the existing climate of détente, international donors approved a US $515m. package for the reconstruction of the Macedonian economy. However, as in all the Balkan countries, there were worries that such a large sum of money might be mismanaged within the climate of corruption that many observers believed to characterize much of the political elite. Overall, however, the FYRM had avoided large-scale ethnic war, on the model of Bosnia and Herzegovina, owing to the more moderate character of those involved and the rapid reaction of the international community, which applied strong pressure on both sides to end the fighting and to accept the necessary constitutional amendments. None the less, the international community—the OSCE, the EU and NATO forces—remained in the FYRM to prevent incidents that might lead to the beginning of a new ethnic war, thereby creating another semi-protectorate in the former Yugoslav region.

THE EU INFLUENCE

The international factor has had a prominent role in Balkan developments from the beginning of the disintegration of Yugoslavia, through economic aid, political pressure, sanctions, military intervention and even outright government control. In fact, for over a decade the Balkans constituted one of the main preoccupations of the international community, owing to the successive, and massively destructive, wars and the subsequent need for reconstruction and reconciliation. Following the fall of Milošević, international involvement focused on matters such as co-operation with the ICTY, the constitutional relationship between Serbia and Montenegro, the ethnic crisis in the FYRM, and the day-to-day running of Bosnia and Herzegovina and Kosovo. For their part, western Balkan countries felt that the contribution of the international community was indispensable in terms of military and police presence, as well as economic assistance for reconstruction and development. However, the international community seemed to be experiencing 'Balkan fatigue', mainly owing to two factors. First, despite the substantial human and financial resources invested in the Balkans, very little overall progress had actually been achieved. Second, the context of international relations following the suicide attacks on the USA of 11 September 2001 had reshaped global priorities, and diverted attention to other causes and regions of international instability.

Against this changing international background, the role of the EU as a factor for peace, stability and economic development in the region became increasingly important. After a decade of limited and unsuccessful policies, the EU had finally adopted a more consistent and committed approach towards the Balkans by using the following instruments: first, the Stabilization and Association Process, as the main framework for bilateral relations between the countries of the western Balkan region and the EU; second, the Stability Pact for South Eastern Europe, as the main regional framework for co-operation, investment and development; third, financial assistance through a new programme for Assistance and Reconstruction, Development and Stabilization (CARDS—targeting Albania, Bosnia and Herzegovina, Croatia, the FYRM and Serbia and Montenegro), concentrating on the building up and modernization of institutions, the rule of law, respect for minorities and the development of a market economy; and fourth, a more involved CFSP. The last was demonstrated by the commencement of two significant EU operations in the region in 2003. On 1 January the EU initiated its first Police Mission (EUPM) in Bosnia and Herzegovina, taking over policing duties from the UN. Like its predecessor, the EUPM was expected to work alongside the NATO-led SFOR deployed under the Dayton accords, and with a mandate until December 2005. At the end of March 2003 the EU launched its first military mission in the FYRM. Known as Operation Concordia, its 350 troops were expected mainly to patrol the mountainous areas on the FYRM's borders with Albania, Kosovo and Serbia, where many ethnic Albanians live. Both forces represented important milestones in the EU's European Security and Defence Policy, and were expected to add political and military strength to the EU's economic clout. The integration of the Balkan region into the EU is not only a difficult project for the countries in the region—it is also a test of the EU's capacity to contribute to peace, stability and prosperity throughout Europe.

THE MACEDONIAN QUESTION

Dr KEITH BROWN

INTRODUCTION

The 'Macedonian Question' was first posed at the end of the 19th century, and arose out of the meeting of two sets of interests: those of the Great Powers (Austria-Hungary, France, Germany, Italy, Russia and the United Kingdom) pursuing policy in the southern Balkans, and those of the new states formed in the wake of Osmanlı (Ottoman) Turkish retreat from the continent of Europe. These political actors operated in an historical context where self-determination came to be identified as the tool by which borders would be drawn in the aftermath of imperial rule. Even after the First World War (1914–18) the application of this principle posed specific problems in the territory then referred to as Macedonia. Partition, vigorous campaigns of national assimilation in Greece and Serb-led Yugoslavia, and major population movements provided respite, but also contributed to feelings of resentment and expressions of resistance in Macedonia. These provided fertile ground for the principles of international socialism, which were further reinforced during the anti-Fascist war that began in 1941, after the Albanian, Bulgarian, German and Italian occupation of Macedonia. Although by the end of the fighting the region had been repartitioned, Macedonian autonomy within the new Federative People's Republic of Yugoslavia, established in November 1945, satisfied the demands of at least some of the activists who had kept the question alive. During the Cold War, the Yugoslav premier, Josip Broz (Tito), suppressed more radical autonomists and irredentists in the new Macedonian republic, while Bulgaria and Greece resumed assimilationist policies. None the less, organizations of displaced people and nationalist politicians propagated an ideal of Macedonian unity and autonomy.

When the Socialist Federal Republic of Yugoslavia (SFRY—the country had been renamed in April 1963) dissolved in the early 1990s there were various predictions that the Macedonian Question would come into salience again. What quickly became evident, however, was that the period from 1945 had wrought further changes in former Yugoslav, Greek and Bulgarian Macedonia. Separated from each other by national borders, the different populations had been exposed to different kinds of pressure from within the countries of which they were a part. Although it has attracted considerable attention, by the early 21st century the Macedonian Question in Greece and Bulgaria was primarily symbolic. In Yugoslav Macedonia, where a distinctive sense of Macedonian identity was formed, it took a different form, reflecting again the problem of satisfying the principle of self-determination when borders are being redrawn. From 1945 the ethnic Albanian population of the republic and of the neighbouring Serbian province of Kosovo increased in number, as well as in international profile. Following Serbian repression of Kosovar Albanians and the ensuing international military involvement in the region in 1999, the Macedonian Question seemed set to resurface in a new guise.

THE CONCEPTUAL AND GEOPOLITICAL ASPECTS OF THE QUESTION

The Macedonian Question is a particular product of the political project of nationalism. The phrase was coined in the late 19th century, when nationalism was conceived by political philosophers such as John Stuart Mill (1806–73) as synonymous with anti-imperialism and self-government. It was, in other words, seen as a desirable goal and an alternative to the political and economic subjection of one ethnic group by another. Drawing political boundaries around culturally or ethnically homogenous groups, its proponents argued, would reduce internal dissension and also prevent states from intervening in the affairs of their neighbours on the pretext of bringing salvation to an oppressed minority.

The principle of nationality, then, played a part in the creation of the new Balkan states. More significant, however, were political expediency and the shifting balance of power between major states. Russia was a key player in Serbia's early history. Greece's creation after the 1821 Uprising was a product of activism by local people, especially the island populations, and the Greek commercial and intellectual diaspora in Europe, but could not have been achieved without external support, especially from the United Kingdom. Bulgaria owed its creation in 1878 to the Russo–Turkish war of 1877–78, although the other Great Powers reduced the size of what they clearly saw as a Russian vassal state. During the Balkan Wars of 1912–13 the Great Powers intervened again to amend the settlement made between Bulgaria, Greece and Serbia, and to bring into being an Albanian state.

In each case the new state created had a core population, which was considered by nationality—whether judged in linguistic, religious or historical terms—to be homogenous. No such population established itself in Macedonia, where instead, each of the new states claimed unredeemed brethren. Additionally, the major valley routes by which the Balkans can be traversed, either east–west or north–south, ran through Macedonia, which also contained one of the major ports of the region, Thessaloníki, Greece. The territory's resources were evident both to neighbouring states and to their Great Power sponsors. The economic integrity of the region was clear, but the challenge of bringing into being an internally heterogeneous and externally coveted state—in British Prime Minister William Gladstone's often misquoted 1897 phrase, a 'Macedonia for Macedonians'—was too great, either for its own population or for European Great Powers anxious to maintain their relations with existing allies in the region, and concerned by the growing threat of war.

THE OTTOMAN LEGACY AND THE END OF IMPERIAL RULE, 1870–1912

Ottoman administrative procedures were not designed with the future partition of the Empire along national state lines in mind. Indeed, some historians have disputed whether they were designed at all, or merely evolved *ad hoc* to deal with the contingencies and variables posed by a multi-confessional and geographically vast area. The loss of territories in Europe and the fear that internal unrest might provoke further intervention by the other Great Powers, however, clearly did prompt a set of deliberate reforms in the mid-19th century. The so-called *Tanzimat* reforms of the judiciary and civil service in the 1840s and 1850s promised economic modernization and greater equality to all imperial subjects. More critical in Macedonia, however, was an initiative in 1870 that granted self-determination to a people in the religious sphere, but which ultimately led to widespread intercommunal killing among the Christian population of the region.

Turkey in Europe was divided into administrative regions called *vilayets*, each administered from a major city: the area known as Macedonia was divided into the *vilayets* of Salonica (Thessaloníki), Monastir (Bitola) and Usküb (Skopje). Within each the population was mixed and included, as well as a significant urban, Ottoman Turkish-speaking element, speakers of Albanian, Greek, Vlach and Romani, as well as speakers of Slavic dialects on the continuum between Serbian and Bulgarian. Multilingualism was, at least in towns, probably the rule rather than the exception. The Empire did not emphasize linguistic differences, but classified its subjects as members of *millets*, or religious communities, each with a headquarters in Constantinople (now İstanbul, Turkey). *Millets* were not in their origins territorially based: significant numbers of members of the *Rum*, or Greek Orthodox *millet*, could be found in Alexandria (Egypt), Skopje, or Smyrna, as well as in the territories between Ioannina (now Greece), Monastir and Salonica where they were concentrated. The head of the *Rum millet* in Constantinople was the Ecumenical Patriarch.

The *Rum millet* included speakers of Greek, Slav, Albanian and Vlach vernacular languages. In the mid-19th century, however, Greek was the language of worship: although Old Church Slavonic (OCS) had been in common use in the territories of modern Macedonia and Bulgaria until 1767, the church hierarchy in Constantinople, known as the Phanariots, had campaigned to increase the status of Greek as the unique 'truth-language' for communication with God. This status had been transferred into secular realms, so that Greek became the language of upward social mobility within the Empire's Orthodox Christian community in the Balkans. A class hierarchy developed, in which Greek-speaking priests and merchants came to see themselves as culturally superior to others, in particular Slav-speaking villagers in Macedonia and Bulgaria, whom they referred to as Bulgars. Bulgars, in turn, came to view Greeks as spiritual accomplices in their social and economic oppression within the Ottoman Empire.

In the mid-19th century Bulgar resentment of Greek domination simmered and was manifested in demonstrations against Greek clergy, and in the production of bibles in Russian, Old Church Slavonic and the new Bulgarian literary language. In 1870 the Sultan signed a decree, which recognized a new Christian Orthodox religious community, headed by the Exarch, which came to be known as the Exarchate. It was initially authorized only in *vilayets* within modern Bulgaria: it therefore represented a revolutionary advance in the understanding of the *millet*, cementing a connection between religious belief, language (in this case Bulgarian) and territory. The name of the Patriarch was still to be mentioned in services. An additional important clause in the decree, however, was a provision that other areas could come under the religious jurisdiction of the Exarchate, subject to an expression of will to do so by a majority vote among the Christian population. The decree thus explicitly provided for a form of self-determination, and also created a situation that would place supporters of the new Exarchate in direct competition with authorities of the old *Rum millet*, or Patriarchate, for popular support.

The succeeding years, especially after the establishment of Bulgaria in 1878, saw conflict between the two Churches in Macedonia. The Exarchate increasingly promoted Bulgarian national identity and saw support for the Patriarchate by Slav-speaking villagers as a form of national treason. The Patriarchate, on the other hand, declared the new Church and its supporters schismatic. Serbia, whose expansion in other directions had been stymied by Austro-Hungarian pressure, also saw grounds for claims on territory in the Slav-speaking population of Macedonia, and devoted resources to the region. Villages switched allegiances, or were bitterly divided; schools

and churches were built and then closed, or occupied by force by one side or the other; services and lessons were often disrupted. Soon the conflict extended into other spheres. It was further complicated by the creation in 1893 of the Internal Macedonian Revolutionary Organization (IMRO), which was predominantly composed of Orthodox Christians, but whose leaders tried to win support across confessional lines. After IMRO led an abortive uprising in 1903, armed bands supported by Bulgaria, Greece and Serbia increased their activities to try to complete the work begun by their priests and teachers, and instil a national consciousness in the population. In the absence of international support for a new Macedonian state, rival neighbours thus sought to gain control of areas in the disputed region in anticipation of its eventual partition.

WARS AND TREATIES, 1912–19

Macedonia's partition was finally brought about after the Balkan Wars of 1912–13. Recognizing that the Great Powers were at an impasse, and would not sanction further erosion of Ottoman territory, Bulgaria, Greece and Serbia (and Montenegro) put aside their differences and went to war against the Empire. Their arrangements for the consensual division of the Macedonian spoils, however, were disrupted, first by the different speeds at which their armies advanced and, second, by the insistence of the Great Powers on the creation of Albania. On both counts Bulgaria's gains were less than its leaders felt they had earned, and the Bulgarian army made a disastrous surprise attack on its former allies in an attempt to redress the injustice. Soundly defeated, Bulgaria then entered the First World War on the side of the Central Powers, the leaders of which promised restitution. The single-mindedness of Bulgaria in this period was driven by a conviction that the dominant Slavic Christian population of Macedonia, as far south as Kastoria in Greece, as far west as Ohrid, and as far north as Skopje, were truly Bulgarian in the ethnic sense. The presence of around 200,000 refugees from the region in Sofia provided further proof of the population's allegiance, and incentive for such sustained action.

At the Versailles Peace Conference of 1919 in France, however, the Macedonian Question was not addressed. No delegates from Bulgaria were invited. Greece and Serbia, as members of the winning side, enjoyed the support of powerful patrons among the Allies. Thus the borders set after the wars of 1912–13 were largely restored: Bulgaria was stripped of further land, leaving the territory hitherto described as Macedonia divided between Greece, Serb-dominated Yugoslavia and Bulgaria, in a ratio of 5:4:1, respectively. The three parts came to be known correspondingly as Aegean Macedonia, Vardar Macedonia and Pirin Macedonia. Although Italy and the USA reportedly made a proposal for Macedonian autonomy it was ignored, as was a call for a plebiscite in Macedonia, submitted by representatives of the Macedonian emigration in Bulgaria. Although the Conference was built around the principle of self-determination, it became clear to people in Macedonia that this was not equally applied.

DEMOGRAPHICS AND DISSENT, 1920–41

In 1919 the Slavic-speaking population of the three parts of Macedonia remained politically orientated either to Bulgaria or to IMRO, the organization that had orchestrated the uprising in 1903. Some supported both, as the 'annexationists' within IMRO promoted eventual union with Bulgaria. Others favoured the autonomist faction of IMRO, which sought an independent Macedonian state. While they recognized cultural links with Bulgaria, they sought a separate political future. This latter view had particular support in the western area of Macedonia around the cities of Bitola, Resen, Florina and Kastoria, where the uprising of 1903 had been concentrated. It also influenced the significant diaspora of Macedonians in the USA and Canada, which numbered around 40,000 in the 1920s. In 1921 this North American diaspora formed the Macedonian Political Organization to work to promote the cause of Macedonian autonomy in the wider world.

Expressions of Macedonian or Bulgarian sentiments, however, were sources of concern to the Serbian and Greek authorities, which were seeking to consolidate their control over these newly acquired territories. Their methods varied, depending, in part, on the climate of international relations at any given time. Greece, for example, in compliance with directives from the League of Nations (the predecessor of the UN), commissioned schoolbooks in the Slavic dialect (although rendered in the Latin alphabet) for use in Aegean Macedonia. For the most part, however, more direct measures were taken. Serbian colonists, including First World War veterans, were given land in Vardar Macedonia and a strong police presence was maintained. In legislative elections in 1920, despite a low rate of participation, a plurality of Macedonian voters supported the Communist Party of Yugoslavia (CPY), which campaigned against Serb domination in Yugoslavia (the party was subsequently declared illegal). In the 1920s there were two major movements of populations, between Greece and Bulgaria and Turkey, the latter in the wake of the Greek defeat in the Greco–Turkish War of 1921–22. Muslims were sent to Turkey and some Slav speakers sent to Bulgaria, thus reducing the 'non-Greek' population of Aegean Macedonia. At the same time, large numbers of new Greek citizens migrated to the region. The settlement of large numbers of Asia Minor refugees in Aegean Macedonia changed the demographic character of the territory and finally destroyed any hope among Macedonian activists that their maximalist dream, that of an autonomous united Macedonia, could be achieved by means of any plebiscite they might eventually obtain.

In Pirin Macedonia IMRO remained a powerful force, although increasingly riven by factionalism between annexationists and autonomists. The Bulgarian state generally favoured the former, but ignored, for the most part, the internecine violence and the criminal methods IMRO leaders used to raise funds and compete for power. Still hostile towards Yugoslavia and in thrall to a strong Macedonian pressure group in Sofia, Bulgaria also overlooked IMRO's cross-border campaigns of violence in Vardar Macedonia, which sought to disrupt the process of Serbian colonization. Yugoslavia responded by increasing military and police presence throughout the province and along the border in the late 1920s and early 1930s, and seeking alliances with other powers that excluded Bulgaria. As IMRO attacks in Vardar Macedonia became increasingly random, leaving the population to face Serb reprisals, local support waned. This further increased the danger of betrayal for IMRO's bands operating in Vardar Macedonia. Thus, by 1934 IMRO's destructive energies were being largely expended within Bulgaria—the country was diplomatically isolated, its south-west region was not under government control and IMRO's extremists acted without restraint in Sofia. Finally, in May 1934 a military coup led to the destruction of IMRO's power in the country. The organization's last act of vengeance was to supply the assassin who killed King Alexander of Yugoslavia, its sworn enemy, and the French foreign minister in Marseilles, France, in September of that year.

FASCISM VERSUS COMMUNISM, 1941–49, AND TITO'S YUGOSLAVIA

Good will toward IMRO and Bulgaria resurfaced in Vardar and Aegean Macedonia in 1941, when Bulgarian troops sup-

ported Germany's assault on Yugoslavia, and borders were redrawn again. Although Germany retained control of the strategic north–south road and rail corridor that ended in Thessaloníki, and Albania expanded into north-west Vardar Macedonia, much of the territory was reunited under Bulgarian control. Bulgarian troops were initially welcomed by elements of the local population still resentful of Serb and Greek treatment. Outright annexation was not authorized by Germany, but Bulgaria enacted measures that included the imposition of Bulgarian nationality on all residents unless they registered themselves otherwise. The oppressiveness of the occupation and the complicity of former IMRO members served to undermine Vardar Macedonian support for the organization in its previous form. It also decisively reduced fraternal feelings towards Bulgaria. Again, the CPY served as a conduit for anti-occupation sentiments, this time in both Aegean and Vardar Macedonia. However, the power politics of the party's position on the question of Macedonian autonomy diffused its ability to mobilize widespread support. The result was conflict between three or more factions within the Macedonian population. In Aegean Macedonia, for example, some initially supported the royalist resistance to occupation and, subsequently, the post-war Government; others saw the Bulgarian occupiers as liberators, and others again joined the communist partisans, who later fought against the Greek national army and who made the most explicit promises regarding Macedonian autonomy. In Vardar Macedonia there were pro-Serbs and pro-Bulgarians, as well as autonomists and communists. Besides contemporary ideologies, historical grievances and loyalties at the village or family level also played a role, and the result was bitter fighting within communities.

By the end of the Greek Civil War in 1949 the most radical communists and autonomists had been either driven out of Greece or imprisoned. The history of the Civil War remains a sensitive topic in northern Greece. Ironically, after Yugoslavia's expulsion from the Soviet-dominated Cominform (Communist Information Bureau) in 1948, Yugoslav federalists loyal to Tito were forced to eliminate similar elements in Vardar Macedonia. Those who remained loyal to Soviet principles, or who called for an autonomous and united Macedonia, were also silenced. A historical tradition developed in Yugoslav Macedonia, emphasizing the multi-confessional and socialist ideals of 1903 activism. Efforts were made in language and religion to distinguish Macedonian from Bulgarian. Expressions of irredentism from Aegean Macedonian exiles and refugees in Yugoslavia were generally kept in check by Tito's Government and surfaced only when relations between the two countries were tense for other reasons—for example, during the 'Colonels' regime' in Greece in 1967–74. The Aegean Macedonian diaspora elsewhere, however, continued to demand recognition of what they perceived to be Greece's harsh treatment of, and assimilative policies towards, the 'Slavophones' of north-western Greece.

THE MACEDONIAN QUESTION IN THE 1990s

Those who believed that the collapse of federal Yugoslavia in the early 1990s would immediately reignite the Macedonian Question were only partly correct. International fears of possible Macedonian irredentism, none the less, affected the treatment of the former Yugoslav republic of Macedonia—FYRM's petition for recognition, submitted to the Commission of the European Community (EC—known as the European Union, EU, from November 1993) in late 1991. Although the legal commission approved the country's petition, EC recognition was withheld, in part because of objections from Greece. Popular opinion in Greece was mobilized around an argument that the name Macedonia was a vital part of Greek heritage, which included, in particular, the historical figure of

Alexander the Great, and that recognition of a foreign state with that name represented both a usurpation and a potential future threat to the integrity of Greece. Expressions of cultural difference by small numbers of 'Slavo-Macedonians' in Aegean Macedonia, even when they declared political loyalty to Greece, were seen as signs of irredentist activism orchestrated from Skopje. The 1990 electoral success of a new nationalist party in the FYRM, the Internal Macedonian Revolutionary Organization—Democratic Party for Macedonian National Unity (IMRO—DPMNU) also alarmed Greece, despite the fact that the party subsequently left the coalition Government to sit in opposition. A particularly inflammatory issue in the Greek–Macedonian conflict was the FYRM's choice of a flag that carried the Star of Vergina, a device associated with ancient Macedonia. Inter-governmental relations deteriorated, culminating in a Greek-imposed embargo, injurious to both economies, in 1994. In 1995 the FYRM's parliament voted to introduce a less controversial flag, and relations between the two countries improved steadily thereafter. Overseas Macedonian organizations continued to protest against alleged discriminatory Greek policies that prevented former refugees and exiles from returning to Aegean Macedonia. However, by the beginning of the 2000s Greek investment was playing a part in the development both of that region and of the FYRM.

Bulgaria sought to maintain consistently good relations with the FYRM, being the first state to recognize its sovereignty. Initially, however, it did not recognize Macedonian national identity or language as distinct from Bulgarian, thus continuing the policy applied to Pirin Macedonia during the communist regime. This refusal complicated the formalization of agreements between the two countries. Another potentially tense issue was the revival in the 1990s of Pirin Macedonian activism for recognition of its cultural rights. However, the FYRM officially distanced itself from Macedonian political organizations in Bulgaria, and the language issue was resolved in early 1999. The national borders that separated the FYRM from Greece and Bulgaria seemed relatively stable in the early 2000s, as did the Macedonian–Albanian frontier. In all of these states, government and business leaders were actively seeking rapprochement and co-operation.

A majority of the frontiers established in 1919, then, appeared to have acquired general acceptance by the early 21st century. Within the former Yugoslavia, however, the demarcation of new political units proved more contentious. A key issue was the future of the former Yugoslavia's Albanian population. Although more numerous than Macedonians, Yugoslav Albanians were divided between several administrative regions. Social and political connections transcended these divisions, and until 1981 the Yugoslav Albanian community regarded the capital of Kosovo, Priština, as a cultural and educational centre in its struggle for greater political rights, either through the creation of its own republic within Yugoslavia, through autonomy, or through some form of 'greater Albania'.

Repression of nationalist sentiment in Kosovo by the Serbian authorities continued throughout the 1980s and, under Slobodan Milošević, into the 1990s. This prompted the formation of a non-violent resistance movement that established parallel state institutions. Despite winning international approval, this movement did not bring about political change. Its authority was, ultimately, challenged by more militant forces within the ethnic Albanian population, most notoriously the Kosovo Liberation Army (KLA). In turn, repressive measures by Serbian forces increased, which led, finally, to military intervention by the North Atlantic Treaty Organization (NATO) from March 1999, and to large numbers of refugees entering neighbouring Albania and the FYRM. Most

returned within a year, after hostilities ended and a UN protectorate was established in Kosovo.

After the repression of the early 1980s, many politically active Kosovar Albanians had sought refuge in the Republic of Macedonia. This, together with the higher birth rate among Albanians, created fears among the Macedonian population that they would in the future become a minority in what they saw as their own country. Macedonian-Albanian relations became increasingly polarized, and Macedonian governmental measures against Albanian activism at times resembled those of Serbia. A referendum on Macedonian independence held in 1991 was largely boycotted by the Albanian population. Ethnic Albanian resistance to the new state undoubtedly also played a part in delaying international recognition of the FYRM. However, from 1992 ethnic Albanian political parties formed part of every coalition government. They sought to address their constituents' concerns regarding employment, education and language by working mainly within the legal and constitutional system. Frustration with the slow pace of reforms sparked some isolated incidents of protest in the mid-1990s, when ethnic Albanian activists established an illegal university in Tetovo and mounted demonstrations in western Macedonia. Frictions also led to the formation of a more radical party, the Democratic Party of Albanians, which by 1998 had overwhelming support from the Albanian population. In a surprising development, the new party entered a government coalition with IMRO—DPMNU, and the votes it commanded played a particularly significant role in the election of Boris Trajkovski of IMRO—DPMNU as President in the closely fought presidential election of late 1999. Although some Macedonians remained suspicious that this civic participation masked secessionist or autonomist agendas, many observers perceived it as signalling a new Albanian commitment to non-violent methods of political action.

THE NEW MACEDONIAN QUESTION

When Milošević was finally ousted from power in Yugoslavia in October 2000, Macedonia's decade-long struggle for recognition entered its final stage. Since the early 1990s, policy-makers had feared the possibility that violence of the type witnessed in Croatia and Bosnia and Herzegovina might spread into the FYRM. Milošević had always refused to ratify the new Yugoslav–Macedonian border, and Yugoslav army troops had often violated Macedonian territory. Such provocations roused fears that a major regional war could develop on Macedonia's territory, and that Albania, Bulgaria and Greece would quickly become involved in any conflict, as would Turkey. As a preventative measure, UN troops were deployed in the FYRM from 1993 until 1999, and Western powers consistently affirmed support for the maintenance of existing borders. In early 2001, under international pressure, the new Government in the Yugoslav and Serbian capital, Belgrade, signed a treaty fixing the Yugoslav–Macedonian frontier, and seemingly put an end to arguments over the new country's existence.

Independence-seeking Albanians in southern Serbia, Kosovo and Macedonia, however, continued to dispute that Yugoslav administrative boundaries between republics should constitute the frontiers of successor states. The KLA's success in prompting international intervention provided a model for new paramilitary activism among Macedonia's Albanians, led by veterans of the war against Yugoslav forces in Kosovo. The commitment of the former KLA to such new struggles was strengthened by its poor performance in Kosovo's democratic elections in October 2000; its leaders and members came to view the perpetuation of violence and instability as vital for their survival.

Yugoslavia's new commitment to the territorial and political *status quo* posed a threat to the minority among the region's Albanian population who sought to redraw international frontiers along ethnic lines. The early months of 2001 witnessed their response, in the form of a guerrilla campaign in north-western Macedonia. Members of Macedonia's security forces were killed in an apparent attempt to prompt governmental and popular reprisals against the republic's Albanian minority, and thereby polarize Macedonia's population along ethnic lines. At the same time, the self-styled National Liberation Army (NLA) claimed to share the agenda of Albanian political parties that pursue greater rights and representation for Albanians in the FYRM. By mid-2001 Macedonia was in crisis, as its security forces bombarded guerrilla positions in the hills and villages in the north of the country, and civilian unrest increased.

Driven by lessons learned from the experiences of military intervention in Bosnia and Herzegovina and in Kosovo, the international community took a proactive role in Macedonia. Negotiators from the USA and the EU worked intensively to bring representatives of Macedonian and ethnic Albanian political parties together to end the fighting, especially after NLA forces occupied Aracinovo, a suburb of Skopje, in June 2001, and threatened to shell the airport. After extensive negotiations, on 13 August leaders of the FYRM's four largest political parties signed the Ohrid Agreement. Forces provided by NATO oversaw a swift disarmament programme, and constitutional changes projected in the Agreement were rapidly passed through parliament, in the knowledge that international donors would withhold reconstruction assistance until the legislation had been adopted. Tensions diminished, as the international community consistently affirmed its support for the integrity of the country within its existing borders, and the former NLA's leadership pledged to pursue its goals through non-violent means. After a successful showing in the parliamentary elections of September 2002, the Democratic Union for Integration, a new political party formed by NLA members, became part of a new coalition Government.

The Macedonian Question emerged at the end of the 19th century because the region's religious and linguistic diversity seemed bound to prevent the peaceful creation of nation-states, the political frontiers of which would also separate culturally distinct populations. At that time, nation-states were considered to realize the principle of self-determination and to provide the best guarantee of international stability. The 'solution' to the Macedonian Question adopted by neighbouring powers and sanctioned by the international community was expansionist war, partition and vigorous campaigns of expulsion or national assimilation. Only within federal Yugoslavia after the Second World War did Macedonians achieve a measure of self-determination, in a repub-

lican territory within which they constituted a majority, but which remained ethnically heterogeneous. However, the recognition of Macedonian rights generated an awareness of cultural and political disenfranchisement among a growing Albanian population also politicized by close links with the nationalist movement in Kosovo. In Yugoslavia's aftermath, ethnic Albanians in Kosovo and Macedonia appealed to the principles of self-determination and demanded greater control over their future. After years of relatively peaceful activism, extremists turned to violence in both regions and sought international support for their cause. The Macedonian Question thus resurfaced in the 21st century with new actors, engaged in similar projects to those of the early 20th century. Names of territories and peoples, and the status of religious and linguistic communities again drive disputes over present and future state frontiers, and once again, too, Macedonia's inhabitants find themselves confronting solutions forged by powerful outsiders.

BIBLIOGRAPHY

Brown, K. *The Past in Question: Modern Macedonia and the Uncertainties of Nation*. Princeton, NJ, Princeton University Press, 2003.

Danforth, L. *The Macedonian Conflict: Ethnic Nationalism in a Transnational World*. Princeton, NJ, Princeton University Press, 1995.

Karakasidou, A. *Fields of Wheat, Hills of Blood: Passages to Nationhood in Greek Macedonia 1870–1990*. Chicago, IL, University of Chicago Press, 1997.

Kennan, G. F. (Ed.). *The Other Balkan Wars: A Carnegie Endowment Inquiry in Retrospect with a New Introduction and Reflections on the Present Conflict*. Washington, DC, Carnegie Endowment for International Peace, 1993.

Lange-Akhund, N. *The Macedonian Question 1893–1908 in Western Sources*. Boulder, CO, East European Monographs, 1998.

Pettifer, J. (Ed.). *The New Macedonian Question*. New York, NY, St Martin's Press, 1999.

Poulton, H. *Who are the Macedonians?* Indianapolis and Bloomington, IN, Indiana University Press, 1995.

Roudometof, V. (Ed.). *The Macedonian Question: Culture, Historiography, Politics*. Boulder, CO, East European Monographs, 2000.

Shea, J. *Macedonia and Greece: The Struggle to Define a New Balkan Nation*. Jefferson, NC, McFarland, 1997.

Weiner, M. 'The Macedonian Syndrome: An Historical Model of International Relations and Political Development', in *World Politics*, 23 (4), pp. 665–683, 1971.

THE ENVIRONMENTAL DIMENSION OF TRANSITION IN CENTRAL AND SOUTH-EASTERN EUROPE

Dr SUSAN BAKER

DIFFERENTIATING TRANSITION

This chapter explores the environmental dimension of the transition process in Central and South-Eastern Europe. It begins by outlining the principal environmental legacies of communist rule and the new pressures that transition has placed on the environment. It then examines post-1989 strategies to deal with the environment. Here, political and economic reform has shaped the capacity of governments effectively to manage the environment. Reform has also given a new role to economic and social actors in the environmental policy process. Finally, account is taken of the key role that the European Union (EU) has played in influencing environmental policy, not only in those countries targeted for membership of the Union, but across the region as a whole.

An examination of the environmental dimension of transition must take account of the fact that in 2003 countries in the region were still undergoing a process of profound political, economic and social change. Within that context, there was a great deal of variation in the way in which countries were managing the environment. This variation was the result of several factors. First, it arose from differences in levels of industrialization among countries in the region, which, in turn, gave rise to differences in the environmental legacies inherited from the period of communist rule. Second, the role played by environmental groups in mobilizing opposition to the communist regimes also differed, resulting in the environmental movement commanding varying levels of popular respect post-1989. Third, differences in the economic and socio-political experiences of states under communism and in the extent to which the revolutions of 1989 fully ousted the old regimes, were reflected in the subsequent variation in the levels of legitimacy of the new, post-communist governments in the region. Hungary provided an example of a relatively smooth transition to democracy, where the existence of some form of pluralism before the collapse of the old regime allowed stable, democratic practices to develop quickly. In addition, this facilitated the development of environmental non-governmental organizations (NGOs) in the realm of civil society (Rootes, 1996—see the Bibliography).

In contrast, prior to the legislative election of June 2001, Bulgaria provided an example of a country that sought to manage the environment in an unstable transition, with political reform commanding only limited legitimacy, and with continuing attempts by the communist successor party to block reforms of both the system of public administration and local government (Baker and Baumgartl, 1998). Indeed, South-Eastern Europe (comprising, for our purposes, Albania, Bosnia and Herzegovina, Croatia, the former Yugoslav republic of Macedonia—FYRM, and Serbia and Montenegro—including the Serbian province of Kosovo, under UN administration) was less stable than were the 'Visegrad Four' (the Czech Republic, Hungary, Poland and Slovakia), as countries across South-Eastern Europe continued to experience frequent changes of government, low public acceptance of change, continuous support for the communist successor parties and poor commitment to economic and political reform. This region was highly fragmented, and characterized by a complex political, economic and social situation, with a large number of refugees and displaced persons. Political insecurity and weak economies had contributed to a gradual deterioration of the environmental infrastructure, an accumulation of hazardous industrial waste and a growing number of heavily polluted environmental 'hot spots' (Regional Environmental Centre for Central and Eastern Europe—REC, 2003 a). Environmental management was also very difficult when effective state structures were still required and macroeconomic stability had still to be achieved. Romania was also experiencing continued problems, having failed to achieve sufficient macroeconomic stability to launch an effective environmental management programme. In general, there was a highly differentiated response to the environment between, on the one hand, the countries of South-Eastern Europe and, on the other, countries elsewhere in Central Europe, in particular the Visegrad Four. Beyond the general level, however, there were also internal differences, most noticeably within the Visegrad group of countries. The final group of countries covered in this survey are the former Soviet Baltic states of Estonia, Latvia and Lithuania.

MAIN ENVIRONMENTAL PROBLEMS OF THE REGION

Environmental Legacies of Communist Rule

The environment in Central and South-Eastern Europe could be characterized by the sharp contrast between environmental 'hot spots' and large tracts of unspoilt land, often possessing a rich biodiversity (European Environmental Agency—EEA, 1999). This contrast was attributed to the communist system of central planning, which concentrated industrial production (in particular, heavy industry) in a small number of regions, close to cheap, and often dirty, sources of energy. Much of the area between these agglomerations remained relatively untouched (von Homeyer, 2001). As a result, many states gained expertise in nature conservation and forest management. However, in the post-communist period, biodiversity came under threat from the pressures that rapid modernization placed on delicate ecosystems.

Environmental problems inherited from the communist period included poor air and water quality, inadequate waste treatment and disposal (including hazardous and nuclear waste), soil deterioration and contamination of land (including agricultural land and land used for Soviet military installations). Achieving improvements in water quality remained a major challenge. This led the EU's European Commission, for example, to identify its legislation on water quality as investment-intensive directives that would be particularly difficult for pre-accession countries to implement. Waste management also remained a major problem, with most countries lacking a comprehensive waste-management strategy and effective legislation (European Commission, 2002 a), despite the fact that several countries experienced sharp rises in the generation of municipal waste (REC, 2003 a). Countries of South-Eastern Europe, in particular, recorded increased migration from rural to urban areas and an attendant growth in the amount of municipal waste generated. However, while environmental damage was to be found in all parts of Central and South-Eastern Europe, there were variations in the level and type of pollution across the region. High levels of atmospheric pollution were, typically, found close to power stations and areas where heavy industry had been concentrated, most noticeably in the so-called 'black triangle', covering the former Czechoslovakia, Poland and the former German Democratic Republic (the GDR, or East Germany). Other areas of especially high concentrations of pollution included the Black Sea and the Danube river basin. In addition, large cities suffered as a result of air pollution, including from domestic heating systems, especially those that relied on the burning of brown coal (lignite), which produces high emissions of sulphur dioxide (Carter and Turnock, 2002, and EEA, 1995).

After 1989 the collapse of production in many of the large industrial enterprises established under the communist regimes led to some improvement in ambient quality, especially in the environmental 'hot spots', with a particularly noticeable improvement in air quality in the Czech Republic (Carter and Turnock, 2002). Fortunately, there was some evidence to suggest that renewed industrial activity in the post-communist period had not always resulted in a return to the low environmental standards of the past. In Poland, for example, despite the fact that between 1990 and 1996 output in the manufacturing sector increased by 49%, emissions of sulphur dioxide and nitrogen oxide decreased by 18.8% and 1.5%, respectively, and similar emissions from industrial processes were reduced by 26% and 41% (Kramer, 2001). During 1991–2000 emissions of sulphur dioxide decreased by 40%–50% in Bulgaria, Slovenia, Hungary and Poland and by a dramatic 80% in the Czech Republic, Latvia and Lithuania (REC, 2003 a). With regard to carbon emissions, to take another example, between 1980 and 1995 there were quite significant overall and per-head reductions across the region as a whole (Turnock and Carter, 2002).

Industrial restructuring has discouraged waste-production in all sectors, and from 1995 there was a decline in the energy intensity of the economies of the region. However, improvements were still needed, particularly given that even the least energy-intensive economy, Slovenia, continued to use about twice as much energy as the average EU member state (REC, 2003). Gaseous emissions also remained higher per-head than the average for the EU member states, and the coming period was expected to record an increase in pollution emissions from the developing transport sector. All EU candidate countries, for example, registered growth in the number of cars and an rapid increase in road traffic, which resulted in higher emissions of nitrous oxides from this source (REC, 2003).

There were also transboundary pollution problems in the region. Poland suffered transboundary pollution from the former GDR, and Bulgaria's own pollution problems were worsened by emissions from Romanian factories, most notoriously in the town of Ruse (Baker, 1996). Hungary experienced considerable transboundary water pollution and water quality in the Danube, in particular, remained a pressing issue, although air pollution was also a continuing problem.

The threat of transboundary pollution posed by the numerous nuclear power stations in the region was also of concern, particularly to the EU. A 1998 EU-sponsored study of nuclear safety concluded that six reactors were operating at high levels of risk. These included the Kozloduy reactor in Bulgaria, the Ignalina reactor in Lithuania and the Jaslovské-Bohunice reactor in Slovakia. Deep concern was expressed about the Ignalina reactor, which was of the same design, and used the same technology, as the Chornobyl (Chernobyl) reactor in Ukraine (European Commission, 1998), the site of a

serious accident in April 1986. In 2000 Bulgaria agreed to the closure of some of the Kozloduy units, in exchange for a substantial loan from the European Commission to modernize the remainder of the nuclear plant. However, progress in meeting this commitment remained slow and there was little evidence that Bulgaria was either strengthening the capacity of its Nuclear Regulatory Authority or developing alternative energy strategies, required as part of the plans to close down the Kozloduy unites (European Commission, 2002). Lithuania's Ignalina reactor was due to be decommissioned by 2009, and closures were also expected at Slovakia's Jaslovské-Bohunice reactor. Controversy was not limited to ageing and unsafe nuclear reactors; the dispute between the Czech Republic and Austria over the Czech decision to open two Soviet-designed reactors at Temelín, close to the border with Austria, for example, was a case in point. In April 2003 a leak at Hungary's Paks nuclear power plant added this facility to the list of controversial sites in the region (REC, *The Bulletin*, Vol. 12, No. 1, May 2003).

New Environmental Problems

While the collapse in industrial production that followed the disintegration of the old regime brought some environmental relief to the region, particularly in lowering levels of air pollution, there was no simple one-to-one relationship between the end of communist rule and improvements in environmental quality. On the contrary, from 1989 many countries in the region witnessed a shift in the nature of environmental pressure, whereby, unfortunately, a reduction in some traditional sources of environmental pollution combined with the arrival of new environmental pressures. Mention has already been made of the increasing environmental problems associated with consumerism, such as the growth in private ownership of cars, and the generation of municipal waste. Biodiversity was also threatened, both by domestic pressures, including peasants dependent on the produce of their small, restituted farms (Turnock and Carter, 2002), and by the opening of hitherto closed borders to European hunters and rare-bird collectors (REC, *The Bulletin*, Vol. 10, No. 4, Dec. 2001). Funding from the EU for road-development programmes was of particular concern, and is discussed below. Economic reform also led to substantial growth in the number of small and medium-sized enterprises (SMEs), which gave rise to problems associated with environmental monitoring and the safe disposal of waste. In Bulgaria, for example, the proliferation of SMEs had the cumulative effect of increasing severely the problem of waste management. At the same time, most Bulgarian SMEs were reluctant to implement measures to deal with the problem, having neither the resources nor the profit margins to take effective action. Not all environmental problems had their roots in the process of economic reform, however. Political instability, particularly in the Balkans, also contributed to the emergence of new environmental pressures. The wars that followed the disintegration of the former Yugoslavia brought new environmental damage to the Balkans region, including UN reports of the presence of radioactivity, resulting from depleted uranium in ammunition used by NATO during its aerial bombardment of the Yugoslav republic of Serbia in 1999. However, in January 2000 member countries of the Stability Pact for South Eastern Europe launched a Regional Environmental Reconstruction Programme (REReP), following the conflicts in the region (Turnock, 2002). The European Commission was, and remains, a driving force behind this programme. As a platform for regional co-operation, REReP can, it is hoped, contribute to the achievement of stability and security in South-Eastern Europe. The Commission also regarded REReP as a vehicle with which to assist countries adopting the EU's environmental *acquis communautaire*, that is, the body of EU legislation, treaties and case law (see below), and, more generally, to integrate environmental considerations into the regional reconstruction process.

STRATEGIES FOR ENVIRONMENTAL MANAGEMENT IN TRANSITION COUNTRIES

Post-1989, countries in the region adopted three strategies for managing the environment. First, they began a process of environmental 'clean-up', particularly in heavily polluted industrial zones. Second, attention was paid to enhancing the legal, administrative and institutional capacity of the state, in some cases largely driven by the need to adopt the *acquis communautaire*. This did not only allow the state to manage the environment more effectively, but also enabled it to adopt a more pro-active, preventative approach towards pollution. Third, new strategies for regional co-operation were developed, especially among neighbouring states that shared a common ecological feature or resource. In addition to these direct, state-level responses, there was a parallel process of ecological modernization of the economy, including at company level, and within the production process, which shaped how the environment was being managed in transition societies. This process was accompanied by equally profound changes at the societal level, which, in turn, shaped the ways in which environmental concerns were articulated. We first address the direct strategies of the state, before going on to discuss the impact of economic reform and, subsequently, societal changes on the environment dimensions of transition.

Environmental Remediation

In the immediate post-1989 period, environmental 'clean-up' operations in the region were plagued by a number of major obstacles, including the lack of knowledge about polluted sites, lack of expertise in pollution management and site amelioration, and severe resource limitations. The setting of priorities also took some time. Attempts were, nevertheless, made to overcome these obstacles. In Hungary, for example, the Government attempted to implement environmental remediation in relation to the short-term Environmental Action Programme that it adopted in 1991. One of the most pressing problems identified at this stage was the need to tackle contamination in abandoned Soviet barracks and drilling grounds. However, the lack of resources meant that Hungary, like many other countries in the region, encountered difficulties in implementing its plans. The Hungarian National Environmental Programme (1998–2002) again addressed the issue of environmental remediation, prioritizing air pollution for immediate attention, in particular in the capital, Budapest, and in the industrial region of north Transdanubia (Dunántúl—Hungarian Ministry of the Environment, 1998). The cost of such remediation can be very high. In 2001 up to 30% of the environmental budget of the republics of Serbia and Montenegro was spent on the mitigation of environmental hazards in industrial enterprises, the majority of which remained socially owned (REC, 2003 a).

Enhancing Environmental Management Capacity

Most governments in the region tackled the task of enhancing institutional, administrative and legislative capacity for environmental management with a degree of success. Capacity building at the institutional level was evident from the establishment of environmental units within ministries and the setting up of new environmental monitoring bodies and agencies. By 2002 each EU candidate country had established a separate environment ministry, although not all of them had introduced the appropriate administrative infrastructure. Some countries, for example Poland, recorded substantial increases in staffing numbers within the Ministry of the Environment (European Commision, 2002 c). Others streamlined their environment ministries and established parallel regulatory authorities, such as environmental protection

agencies and, in Slovenia, a Nature Conservation Institute (2002), while in the same year a Nature Protection Board was established in Latvia. Many countries also enhanced their environmental monitoring capacity though the provision of resources and monitoring equipment for their regional environmental inspectorates. As was so often the case in the West, too, however, environment ministries remained the weaker partners in government and their capacity to act was further limited by the fragmentation of administrative responsibilities. Typically, they shared responsibility with sector ministries, for example, in relation to water and air quality, biodiversity and waste management. The integration of environmental considerations with other policy areas has not been easy to achieve under these conditions. Nevertheless, capacity enhancement at the ministerial level enabled countries to begin strategic environmental planning. Poland, for example, adopted a national environmental policy in 2001, while the Czech Republic introduced a national strategy for sustainable development in the same year (European Commission, 2002 d).

It was not until 2000 that reviews of the function and organization of environmental ministries began in South-Eastern European countries, following the decision by regional environment ministries to endorse the REReP. Serbia, for example, initiated a complete revision of its body of legislation, including in the environmental sector. Many environmental ministries were integrated with ministries of physical planning or of water in an effort to improve capacity and efficiency. Through EU funding of so called 'Quick Start' REReP projects, in the early 2000s there was a strengthening of environmental institutions, the enactment of new environmental legislation and the development of new policies, as well as new efforts to build and support environmental civil society. Nevertheless, capacity remained low. A 2002 report on environmental enforcement and compliance capacity in South-Eastern Europe identified a depressing list: a lack of human, technical and financial resources; the uncertain position of environmental authorities within governmental structures; insufficient regulatory frameworks; inefficient compliance and enforcement activities; weak permitting systems; non-compliance with multilateral environmental agreements; and a lack of public participation. The lack of legal training among environmental inspectorates was identified as particularly worrying, especially when confronted with major legislative changes and developments (REC, 2002).

In this context, the importance of REReP lies in providing a framework for the donor community to fund specific projects in environmental priority areas. Its Regional Priority Environmental Investment Programme (PEIP) identified institution-building, support to environmental civil society, support to existing environmental regional co-operation mechanisms and cross-border projects, and reduction of environmental health threats as the most urgent investment priorities. The REReP was also successful in stimulating regional co-operation among South-Eastern European countries. Similarly, the so called 'road maps' produced by the European Commission, containing guide-lines with detailed timetables for the candidate countries of Bulgaria and Romania, also provided a framework for the allocation of environmental investment (European Commission, 2002 b).

Among the most perceptible areas of capacity enhancement, at least formally, was at the legislative level. Most Central and South-Eastern countries passed new, framework environmental legislation shortly after the collapse of the old regimes. Examples include the National Environmental Framework Law approved in Hungary in 1992 and the Environmental Protection Act adopted in Bulgaria in 1991. In contrast to the speed of earlier developments, Bulgaria's proposed new Environmental Protection Act, designed to improve compliance with a number of EU directives, was repeatedly delayed, but was eventually adopted in September 2002. Several environmental laws were passed in Poland in 1991 and an Environmental Protection Act was passed in Slovenia in 1993. In South-Eastern Europe the pace of reform was slower, and only from 2001 did new framework legislation begin to be introduced, the standards of which were largely derived from EU directives. Legislative modernization was also evident in South-Eastern Europe, with a move away from sectoral permitting and inspection to a more integrated approach (REC, 2002).

In addition to sector-specific environmental legislation, many countries adopted procedural regulations on environmental impact assessment (EIA), and the Århus Convention on Access to Environmental Information was ratified in several countries in the region, including Hungary, Poland and Slovakia. This participatory approach represented a considerable shift from the technology-driven policy culture that, by and large, characterized environmental management under communist rule. The UN Framework Convention on Climate Change was also ratified by several countries, including Poland, the Czech Republic, Hungary, Estonia, Lithuania and Slovenia, although capacity needs for meeting the requirements of the associated Kyoto Protocol were substantial (REC, 2003 a).

Parallel to these legislative developments, democratic control over the system of public administration was gradually strengthened. The adoption of a Civil Service Act in the Czech Republic and the 2001 Law on Civil Servants in Hungary, for example, provided a legal framework for central public administration, thereby bringing administration acts under the rule of law. However, the implementation of this type of law remained problematic, as demonstrated in the case of Slovakia (European Commission, 2002 a). Similarly, although Bulgaria had adopted a Strategy for Modernization of the State Administration and a National Reform Strategy for the Bulgarian Judicial System, implementation remained slow (European Commission, 2002 b). Administrative capacity was also increased through the enhancement of environmental expertise. This was aided, at least in the early days of transition, by the appointment of many environmental activists to positions of power, including in Bulgaria, where 'green' activists held ministerial-level positions in the first post-communist Government.

There were also reforms at the regional and local levels of government that were important for enhancing environmental-management capacity, including administrative reforms in Poland in 1999. Many environmental problems, especially those relating to pollution, occurred at the local level. Policy implementation, pollution monitoring, as well as waste and refuse collection, typically required direct input from local government. However, decentralization was taking place at different rates across the region. Although most countries had taken steps to devolve environmental responsibility to the regional and local levels and to strengthen subnational administrative capacity in the environmental sector, many, such as Slovenia, were still struggling to put financial-investment plans into operation and to enhance scientific and legal expertise at the local level (European Commission, 2002 a and 2002 e).

Nevertheless, monitoring and enforcement capacity had improved. In Bulgaria, for example, 15 Regional Inspectorates were established under the Ministry of the Environment and Water. However, in Bulgaria, as elsewhere, the fact than an enormous amount of legislation had been rapidly approved by parliament (in Bulgaria, this amounted to over 70 acts and regulations between 1998 and 2002) exposed the system's lack of trained personnel for environmental monitoring, inspections and the dissemination of information. Although the

situation in Bulgaria may appear problematic, the fact that the Environmental Inspection Service of Serbia urgently required basic equipment, such as cars, mobile cellular telephones and computers with printers, indicated even greater capacity problems (REC, 2002).

In short, from 1989 most Central and South-Eastern countries witnessed an increase in the capacity of their governments, whether at the central, regional or local level, to manage the environment (after 1991 for the Baltic states). However, the formal dimensions of reform were more robust than the substantive dimensions of change, and there were noticeable differences between capacity enhancement in the Visegrad countries and those in the Balkans. This gap between the formal and substantive dimensions of change was notable within the system of public administration, which had still to overcome numerous legacies of communist rule, including the lack of accountability and transparency in administrative practice (Baker, 2002). The highly fragmented nature of environmental administration in the Czech Republic, for example, made it difficult to allocate resources efficiently or to demarcate administrative responsibility, and led to ongoing problems of implementation and monitoring (European Commission, 2002 d). A similar problem existed in Lithuania (European Commission, 2002 f).

However, in some countries the problem was of a more political nature. In Bulgaria, for example, a close relationship continued to exist between polluter and regulator, and partisanship, corruption and bureaucratic arbitrariness remained embedded in the political and administrative culture of the state (Baker, 2001). Furthermore, many Balkan states, such as Bulgaria, remained extremely centralized, with weak regional and local governments and underdeveloped interest and pressure groups. Old-style centralized administrations remained dominant in South-Eastern Europe, and regional inspectorates, where they existed, remained directly accountable to central governments. Single-media inspections were common, as were separate permits for different media. Similarly, although Romania had developed a substantial body of new legislation, largely derived from EU law, the capacity of the system of public administration to implement and enforce newly adopted legislation remained extremely weak (European Commission, 2002 b).

Nevertheless, countries in South-Eastern Europe were not alone in experiencing problems with respect to corruption and the reform of their judicial system. In Lithuania, despite the adoption of a National Anti-Corruption Programme and a Law on Corruption Prevention, administrative corruption remained rife (European Commission, 2002 a). A corruption scandal over the abuse of PHARE (originally Poland/Hungary Aid for the Restructuring of Economies—subsequently extended to include eight additional EU candidate countries) funds came to light in Slovakia in 2001, and prompted investigation by the EU's anti-corruption unit, the European Anti-Fraud Office (OLAF). Problems of corruption also marked the political, administrative and business cultures in Poland (European Commission, 2002 a), and Latvia retained major deficiencies in its judicial system, including problems relating to pre-trial detention, the accumulation of unheard court cases and, more seriously, the lack of *de facto* independence of the judiciary (European Commission, 2002 a).

New Structures for Regional Co-operation

In contrast to the almost complete lack of regional co-operation on environmental matters during the period of communist rule, from 1989 several structures to facilitate regional environmental co-operation were developed. The REC, located in Budapest and established in 1990, plays a crucial role in facilitating this co-operation and also acts as the secretariat to the REReP task force.

In the area of water management, much of the drive for regional co-operation has come from the river basin approach contained in the EU Framework Water Directive. This encourages states to develop transboundary management plans for international rivers. In 1991, for example, the international Environmental Programme for the Danube River was launched. In 1994 11 countries, along with the EU, signed the Convention on Co-operation for the Protection and Sustainable Use of the River Danube. A strategic action plan for the Danube basin was subsequently launched, built upon a system of national plans, which were combined with international monitoring. A rapid environmental and health-risk assessment initiative for the Danube was also launched, under the auspices of the REReP, in response to a cyanide spill into the Tisza river in 2000 (REC, 2003). Similarly, structures for regional co-operation were framed within the 1992 Convention for the Prevention of Pollution of the Black Sea and its three protocols (Organisation for Economic Co-operation and Development—OECD, 1996). In 2001 these areas were the focus of new attention from the European Commission, with the establishment of the Danube and Black Sea Region Task Force (DABLAS), which aimed to provide a platform for international co-operation on the 'clean-up' of the Black Sea basin and its tributaries (European Commission, 2001 a). The Environment Programmes for the Danube, the Black Sea and the Caspian Sea formed part of the UN Environment Programme's (UNEP) inter-state environmental action initiative, the Regional Seas Programme.

Other regional co-operative initiatives included: the establishment of a ministerial-level working group between the Visegrad Four in relation to the transboundary impact of environmental catastrophes; the establishment of a Polish-Czech Joint Commission for Environmental Protection, to deal with the Jizerské (Iser) mountain region; and the signing of a ministerial-level environmental agreement between Bulgaria and Romania in relation to the harmonization of environmental legislation (Kramer, 2001). In addition, in December 2001 the Balkan Environmental Regulatory Compliance and Enforcement Network (BERCEN) was established, with the REC acting as its secretariat. BERCEN operates within the framework of the EU's Stabilization and Association Process and the REReP to assist in the enforcement of regulations throughout South-Eastern Europe. Bulgaria and Romania, in the process of accession to the EU, were awarded observer status at BERCEN; BERCEN works closely with its sister networks, the EU's Network for the Implementation and Enforcement of Environmental Law (IMPEL) and that for the Accession Countries (AC-IMPEL). Several other regional networks exist, for example, in relation to the Århus Convention, a South-Eastern European Environmental NGO Network (SEEENN), as well as a waste-management experts network and an advocacy network (REC, 2003 b).

THE DEVELOPMENT OF NEW ENVIRONMENTAL PROPONENTS WITHIN THE ECONOMY AND SOCIETY

Impact of Economic Reform on the Environment

Economic reform was taking place at different speeds across the region, with privatization being a principal element of that reform. In some countries, most noticeably Hungary, privatization took place, by and large, through the sale of state-owned companies to foreign buyers. Where privatization resulted in foreign ownership, many countries, such as Bulgaria, were compelled to clarify their laws and practices on environmental liability. Such purchases also led to the penetration of ecologically progressive foreign firms, leading to the development of environmental proponents in the economic sector. Nevertheless, in many countries in the region, notably in Poland, environmental concerns and liability issues were disregarded, especially in the initial privatization phase. Nevertheless, privatization enabled the industrial sector to engage in environmental investment, particularly in the areas of air and waste-water management. Thus, for example, an increase in industrial investment in environmental protection occurred in both Bulgaria and Hungary (REC, 2003 a). The establishment of public-private partnerships, including both 'build, operate and transfer' as well as 'build, own and operate' schemes, proved particularly popular with respect to waste management and landfill (Slovakia), water and sewage schemes (for example, in the Czech Republic) or municipal water (in Sofia, Bulgaria).

The establishment of functioning markets was also a principal element in the economic-reform process. Marketization was important in so far as environmental policy-making was concerned, because many environmental-policy tools were reliant upon an effective market process. The preparation for EU membership placed emphasis on the more effective use of market-led policy tools. In addition, marketization compelled domestic firms that wished to remain in business to reduce production costs by minimizing the inefficient use of energy and other resources, which had been a prominent feature of production during the period of communist rule.

However, economic reform also proved problematic for the environment, not least because the economic impact of transition did much to displace the centrality accorded to environmental concerns. Furthermore, in many countries, such as Bulgaria, privatization was often in the hands of the old nomenklatura, which had a history of eschewing environmental regulations. This enabled it to rework its old political power into a new economic hegemony and allowed the political 'embeddedness' of institutional governance, production and environmental regulation to endure in the post-communist period (Baker, 2001). Across the region, more generally, the emergence of a class of *nouveau riche* and of organized crime had the potential to threaten the environmental gains won by transition, since, together, these constituted the least public-spirited segments of society. Such groups had demonstrated their preference for private gain over public good, and their continued strength retarded the formation of strong environmental norms in the region.

The Development of Environmental NGOs

Under the communist regimes, the strength of academic ecology, the presence of official conservation cadres and the extent of synergy between official groups and other social movements, including the independent opposition, varied considerably between countries in the region (Tickle and Welsh, 1998). Only in Bulgaria did the *principal* challenge to the old regime take the form of environmental protest, and only there did the environmental movement stimulate the development of a mass movement that proved capable of challenging the communist monopoly of power (Waller and Millard, 1992). The role played by the environmental movement in the collapse of the communist regimes proved important in shaping their strength after 1989. As a result, the ability of the environmental movement to participate in the political developments of the post-communist period varied widely. Existing opportunities also differed, particularly given differences in the substantive nature of the democratic reform process between countries.

Despite these differences, however, from 1989 mass mobilization around environmental issues declined throughout the entire region. There was a marked shift from protest to more modest, and moderate, forms such as lobbying, negotiation and discussion. Environmental concern was increasingly expressed through participation in professional, goal-orientated environmental NGOs (Jancar-Webster, 1998). There was considerable debate about the benefits of this change and of the consequences of the strong influence exercised by foreign groups and funding agencies on environmental NGOs in the region. On the one hand, there was much criticism of the growing dependence of the region's environmental NGOs on foreign aid and support. This resulted, it was claimed, in a shift in priorities, away from domestic concerns, to those most likely to receive such support (Jancar-Webster, 1998). On the other hand, funding of this kind helped to enhance the capacity of environmental NGOs, enabling them to take advantage of the new opportunities that arose as a result of political reforms. There was little doubt, however, that the process of democratization had given a new opportunity for, perhaps even imperative to, environmentalists to engage in more institutional forms of political activity. Examples included the involvement of Bulgarian NGOs in the National Centre for Environment and Sustainable Development (Baker, 2001), subsequently known as the Executive Environment Agency. Similarly, in Poland, there was an institutionalization of consultation between the environment ministry and environmental NGOs (O'Toole and Hanf, 1998). In Hungary, NGOs participated in the creation of a National Development Plan (CEE Bankwatch Network and Friends of the Earth Europe, 2002), and were represented in the Hungarian National Environmental Council; the Czech Republic also provided a good example (CEE Bankwatch Network and Friends of the Earth Europe, 2002). The EU facilitated this process. From 1999 the EU's Directorate-General dealing with the environment held regular meetings with environmental NGOs from the candidate countries, with the REC acting as facilitator for the dialogue. In addition, environmental NGOs were represented on national Instrument for Structural Policies for Pre-Accession (ISPA) environmental monitoring committees in Bulgaria, the Czech Republic, Lithuania and Poland (CEE Bankwatch Network and Friends of the Earth Europe, 2002). In contrast, however, Estonia provided an example of a country where the role of NGOs remained weak (Mardiste, 2001). Despite their role in the policy-making process, however, a report on environmental NGOs in Central and South-Eastern Europe found that, despite foreign funding, the vast majority remained unstable and poor, and rarely co-operated with other NGOs; moreover, over two-thirds were concentrated in only four countries, the Czech Republic, Hungary, Poland and Slovakia (REC, 1997).

The adoption of legislation on EIA also helped to open up the policy process, although there were marked differences in the application of legislation. The Czech Republic was slow to develop EIA legislation and the 1995 amendment to the Bulgarian Environmental Protection Act restricted the participatory opportunities available to environmental NGOs and undermined the spirit of the legislation (Baker, 2001, and CEE Bankwatch Network and Friends of the Earth Europe, 2002). Despite these reverses, however, where participation was evolving, it had strengthened the substantive component of the democratization process, although it should be noted that, in the region as a whole, the process of becoming insiders, or participants, in the policy-making process was uneven.

In sum, it can be argued that, from the end of the communist era, the policy-making process became more open to environmental interests, despite marked differences in practices among countries. This provided new opportunities for environmental groups and strengthened the pressure on governments to integrate environmental considerations into policy-making. When coupled with the trend towards the ecological modernization of the economy, particularly at the micro level, these developments were significant. Their significance lay in contributing to the incorporation of environmental considerations into the normal business of government and to the acceptance of environmental protection as a legitimate task for those charged with the governance of transition.

THE ROLE OF THE EU IN SHAPING ENVIRONMENTAL MANAGEMENT

It was impossible to speak about the environmental dimensions of the transition process without taking into account the role played by international organizations, including the EU, in shaping environmental management in the region.

The Environment for Europe Programme

From 1991 the UN Economic Commission for Europe—ECE's Environment for Europe programme became the main internationally driven, strategic framework guiding environmental policy development in the region (Solcock, 1999). A significant development in this programme occurred at the second Ministerial Conference of regional and OECD environment ministers, held in Lucerne, Switzerland, in 1993, at which an Environmental Action Programme (EAP) for Central and Eastern Europe was launched. The EAP provided a framework for combining national environmental action with international assistance programmes, and placed emphasis on policy reform, institutional strengthening and environmental investment. In addition, it encouraged countries to set priorities for tackling environmental problems and, as a result, country-specific National Environmental Action Plans were launched across the region. These Plans helped countries to prioritize environmental action, which was especially important given the enormity of the environmental tasks that they faced and the limited resources available to undertake them. At the ECE's fifth ministerial Environment for Europe conference, held in Kiev, Ukraine, in May 2003, several legally binding, multilateral environmental agreements were signed, including in relation to the Convention on Environment Impact Assessment in a Transboundary Context (Espoo Convention), and a Convention on Environment Protection and Sustainable Development of the Carpathians was also signed (by the Czech Republic, Hungary, Romania, Serbia and Montenegro, Slovakia and Ukraine), thereby anchoring Eastern European states more tightly into international environmental-management regimes.

Towards EU Membership

Greece, in the early 2000s the region's only EU member, acceded to the Union's predecessor, the European Community, in January 1981. By the mid-1990s, however, 10 countries in the region had signed association agreements with the EU. Under the so-called Copenhagen Criteria, association countries could apply for membership of the EU, provided they met certain economic and political conditions (Mayhew, 1998, and European Commission, 1997). In December 2002 eight candidate countries in the region (as well as the Mediterranean countries of Cyprus and Malta) were formally invited to become members of the EU in May 2004, while Bulgaria and Romania were expected to achieve membership in 2007. In all of the candidate countries, membership of the Union had become the determining factor in shaping environmental policy (Baker and Jehlička, 1998). It should be remembered, however, that there was a substantial group of non-candidate states in the western Balkans and nor were the former communist states outside Central and South-Eastern Europe (that is, the 12 member countries of the Commonwealth of Independent States—CIS) directly involved in the EU enlargement project.

Association agreements were significant for environmental governance in the region in a number of ways. They laid down a set of conditions governing the management of the environment in transition countries. These included stipulations that countries approximate all of their environmental laws to those of the EU—in other words that candidate countries adopt the EU's *acquis communautaire* (Turnock, 2002, provides details of environmental legislative action in candidate countries in 1999–2000). By the end of 2002 the EU had concluded its accession negotiations on environmental issues (chapter 22) with the eight 'first round' accession states, although it had to concede transitional periods for several environmental directives, particularly those identified as investment intensive. Negotiations with Romania and Bulgaria remained open at mid-2003.

Adoption entailed not only the transposition of EU legislation into national legislation, but also its implementation and enforcement. It was also expected that policies, including at the sectoral levels, be guided by the principle of sustainable development and that countries meet certain EU norms and standards regarding the conduct of policy-making and its implementation. Progress in relation to the adoption and subsequent implementation of the EU environmental *acquis* varied across the region, with Poland's achievements, for example, having been identified by the Commission as particularly poor (European Commission, 2001 b). Despite this unevenness, however, preparation for membership strengthened environmental legislation, broadened the range of issues covered by legislation and policy (for example, waste management) and provided a new impetus to achieve more effective policy implementation, which was often only weakly addressed under the old communist system. It also helped to introduce greater transparency to the environmental policy-making process and to facilitate participation, particularly by environmental interests, in policy-making. For its part, from 1999 the Commission held regular dialogues with the principal environmental NGOs from candidate countries. This contributed to the enhancement of the roles of environmental NGOs and, thus, to the evolution of civil society in candidate countries across the region.

The Challenges Ahead

Despite having completed negotiations with the majority of candidate countries on the environmental chapter of the *acquis*, Eastern enlargement nevertheless presented a major challenge for European environmental policy (European Commission, 1998). Lack of administrative and financial resources continued to hamper effective implementation of legislation, and monitoring remained weak. The continued prioritization of economic development over environmental protection was also of concern. In addition, negotiations on the contribution that new member states were to make to the EU's international obligations regarding climate change were expected to be difficult. In their defence, it could be argued that the adoption of the environmental *acquis* was particularly difficult for candidate countries, given that environmental legislation was both expensive and technically complex to implement.

Financing Environmental Protection

Finding new ways to finance environmental management was an essential part of capacity enhancement, especially given the harsh economic conditions that confronted transition states. By and large, public-sector environmental expenditure relied on three major sources of financing: local government revenues; transfers from central budgets; and grants or 'soft' loans from environmental funds. Most countries in the region had established environmental-protection funds, including Hungary (1992) and Bulgaria (1995). In the case of Hungary, funds were drawn largely from environmental-product charges on fuel, with funds being mainly targeted at environmental-protection measures. The introduction of charges and taxes for environmental purposes, and thus the accumulation and allocation of revenues for environmental spending, differentiated the transition economies from those of existing EU

member states. In EU countries, environmental taxes generally represented central budget revenues, with no explicit link to environmental spending priorities. In contrast, environmental funds played an important role in financing environmental investment in Central and South-Eastern Europe. In 2000 in Latvia, for example, environmental funds contributed around 43% of total expenditure, while in Slovenia the figure was 23% (REC, 2003 a). Decentralization contributed to the growing importance of environmental funds. Although state budget transfers to local authorities historically played an important role in financing local authorities, during transition this source of finance was eliminated. Local authorities, therefore, had to turn to other sources, such as environmental funds, or attracting the involvement of the private sector, to finance their expanding environmental responsibilities.

Despite environmental funds, however, many countries in Central and South-Eastern Europe decreased their annual expenditure on the environment during 1996–2000. In Estonia, environmental expenditure declined from the equivalent of 2.2% of gross domestic product (GDP) to 1.2%, while the corresponding decline in the Czech Republic was from 2.3% to 2.0%. In contrast, there was, however, an increase in expenditure in both Bulgaria and Lithuania. Expenditure per head also varied dramatically, reaching €106 per head in the Czech Republic, but only €17 per head in Latvia, with an average expenditure in 2000 of around €50 per head among the candidate countries for EU membership.

Most countries in the region remained dependent upon international assistance to implement environmental investment projects. Throughout 1996–2001, international environmental assistance to the pre-accession countries and to South-Eastern Europe increased. In 2000, in particular, there was an increase in funding provision to South-Eastern Europe, as a result of the introduction of the REReP. At the same time, in the accession countries the launch of the ISPA programme, which provided financing for projects involving environmental and transport infrastructure, contributed to an increase in the level of international financial assistance. The highest levels of environmental lending were provided by the European Investment Bank, the EU's long-term financing institution. The majority of funded projects were linked to urban development, environmental policy and the water sector (REC, 2003 a).

In 2000–06 financial assistance from the European Commission to the candidate countries was to be provided through ISPA, the Special Accession Programme for Agriculture and Rural Development (SAPARD) and PHARE. It was estimated that €3,000m. per year was to be made available during this period (European Commission, 2002). Spending on the environment was expected to account for 8%–9% of expenditure under the existing programme. It should be noted that the accession treaty was to result in the gradual withdrawal of pre-accession funds, with PHARE funding, in particular, expected to be phased out by 2006 (European Commission, 2002 a). Environmental investment was henceforth to be framed within the Priority Environmental Programme for Accession, which was designed by the European Commission to assist countries in prioritizing environmental investment strategies. The Commission's strategic investment plans targeted specific gaps, such as air-pollution projects, directives involving private-sector expenditure, waste management and training for local authorities (European Commission, 2001 c).

The ISPA was the principal means through which the EU provided environmental aid for candidate countries, although it provided funds for both environmental and transport infrastructure developments. In the first two years of the ISPA operation (2000–01), the EU channelled over €1,100m. towards the implementation of Union environmental policy, and largely targeted investment-heavy environmental directives. Nevertheless, ISPA was a weak tool for environmental management. The provision of environmental safeguards in the ISPA tended to be weaker than those of the Cohesion Fund, on which the ISPA was modelled, despite the fact that the Cohesion Fund had itself been subject to severe criticism on environmental grounds. It was also argued that, as the ISPA prioritized road building over environmental protection, the EU was contributing to environmental degradation and to developing a 'car dependent' society in the region (CEE Bankwatch Network and Friends of the Earth Europe, 2000). In addition, transport infrastructure development projects mainly funded the extension into the region of the Trans-European Networks (TENs), which came under severe criticism from environmental groups, although subsequent funding allocations also favoured the development of rail networks.

Similarly, there were fears that the SAPARD would support intensive agricultural methods, which had already resulted in severe loss of habitat in the existing EU member states. The SAPARD's prime objective was to support structural adjustment in the agricultural sector and rural areas, but it also had an environmental component. However, delays, especially the need to establish implementation agencies, meant that by 2003 the Programme was only just beginning to be operationalized. There were fears, nevertheless, that the SAPARD would support industrialized, intensive agriculture, which had been the norm within EU agricultural policy. Together with the negative environmental consequences of such a development, this might exacerbate the existing social problems of rural areas in pre-accession states (CEE Bankwatch Network and Friends of the Earth Europe, 2002).

Launched in 1989, the PHARE programme provided finance to promote economic and political reform in Central and South-Eastern Europe, with an increasing percentage of its annual budget being devoted to institutional capacity-building, including in the environmental arena, through twinning arrangements between administrations and agencies, and the Technical Assistance Information Exchange Office (TAIEX), which was founded in 1995. With the establishment of the ISPA, PHARE resources were reallocated, away from large environmental investment projects towards investment related to the *acquis* and to economic and social cohesion. In the environmental field, PHARE supports three accession-driven initiatives: a sustainable nature-protection project organized through the EuroParcs network of European nature parks; *ad hoc* assistance to prepare for membership of the European Environment Agency, which monitors environmental issues in EU member countries; and the 'black triangle' inventory of non-compliance with EU environmental directives. In 2000 the €6.25m. Regional Environmental Accession Project (REAP) was launched. This major new initiative aimed to enhance implementation capacity through the provision of information and guidance to municipalities, and also aimed to help build information networks with both NGOs and the general public. The PHARE also supports cross-border programmes, including in relation to energy conservation, although infrastructure projects account for many of the programmes sponsored, with co-operation between Bulgaria, Romania and Greece.

On balance, however, the environmental component of the PHARE programme was weak and under-funded, and was strongly criticized for channelling much of its benefits to Western consultants. It was also claimed that PHARE assistance tended to reflect the priorities of donor countries, such as transboundary pollution, providing pressures to displace domestic environmental concerns from the policy agenda of transition states. In addition, it was considered to be biased in favour of large-scale projects, although smaller-scale projects

could have been more efficient in their use of resources and more effective in supporting long-term sustainable regional development (CEE Bankwatch Network and Friends of the Earth Europe, 2002).

In general, EU funding attracted criticism for its support of environmentally damaging projects, such as the Via Baltica motorway project, linking Warsaw, Poland, and Helsinki, Finland, and traversing protected areas in north-eastern Poland (World Wide Fund for Nature—WWF, 2003), and the construction of the Struma motorway, which was to link Greece and Bulgaria, passing along the length of Bulgaria's Kresna gorge, a natural ecosystem identified by the EU-administered Co-ordination of Information on the Environment (CORINE) Biotopes project and a candidate for inclusion in the Natura 2000 network of protected sites. Similarly, the EU-funded D8 motorway, part of a European transport corridor from Berlin, Germany, to İstanbul, Turkey, posed environmental threats, as a section passed through a nature park, a site that was also being prepared for inclusion in the Natura 2000 network. Furthermore, it was argued that, far from encouraging environmental best practice, EU funding favoured remedial solutions, particularly with respect to landfill, rather than preventative measures, such as recycling and waste reduction.

More serious was the argument that EU funding was framed within the context of a deepening asymmetrical relationship between Central and South-Eastern Europe and the EU (Caddy, 1997). This allowed the EU to have a very strong, some would argue undemocratic, influence on how the environment was managed in transition states (Baker, 2002).

Despite their negative consequences, association agreements nevertheless anchored environmental management in many countries in Central and South-Eastern Europe into a trans-national, EU-level legislative, enforcement and monitoring framework. This not only reinforced the position of national environmental policy-makers in several states, but it also allowed them to keep environmental *policy* firmly on the agenda, even when environmental *politics* had sunk beneath a tide of other issues of popular concern (Slocock, 1999).

CONCLUSION

Environmental management in Central and South-Eastern Europe was taking place against a background of profound change, marked by a complex interface between the legacies of the old communist regimes and the new political and economic systems that were being introduced. As far as environmental policy was concerned, this interface was producing a complex picture. On the one hand, there was a great deal of continuity with the past, including in relation to the low priority that was assigned to environmental protection compared to economic development; the limited role played by environmental NGOs in public-policy formation, partly arising from the weaknesses in civil society; and the co-existence of centralized administrative structures alongside closed and highly politicized bureaucratic cultures (Smith and Pickles, 1998), which made it difficult successfully to manage the environment at the sub-national, regional and local levels. On the other hand, there was also much that was new. The region was experiencing new environmental pressures, in particular from the growth in consumerism and EU-funded infrastructure projects. More positively, and chiefly as a result of the democratization of political life, the policy-making process had become more open, at least in a tentative form, to input from environmental interests; economic reform was helping to modernize the economy ecologically, particularly at the micro level; marketization was strengthening the use of a wider range of environmental instruments, in turn leading to more effective policy implementation; and decentralization, when pursued by governments, was enhancing the role of sub-national, regional and local levels of government in environmental management. In addition, environmental management was increasingly being anchored to an EU-level legislative and administrative framework. This placed greater emphasis on pro-active environmental management, more effective policy implementation and greater openness, transparency and accountability in the system of environmental governance than was ever the case under the communist regime.

In short, old environmental problems remained and new ones were arising. However, it was fair to say that transition had witnessed an enhancement of the environmental-management capacity of most states in the region. In addition, new proponents of the environment, from within industry and from across society, had arisen and were, in turn, slowly being drawn into the environmental policy-making process. It should be noted, however, that the transition process was still evolving, and there were marked differences between the responses of countries within the region, especially between the more stable Visegrad countries and those in the Balkans. The overall impact of this unevenness for the environmental prospects of the region as a whole remained uncertain.

BIBLIOGRAPHY

Baker, S. 'The Scope for East–West Co-operation', in Blowers, A., and Glasbergen, P., (Eds). *Environmental Policy in an International Context,* Vol. 3. London, Arnold, 1996.

'Environmental Capacity Building in Bulgaria', in Jänicke, M., and Widner, H., (Eds). *National Environmental Policies: A Comparative Study of Capacity Building*, Vol. 2. Berlin and New York, NY, Springer, 2001.

'Environmental Politics and Transition', in Carter, F. W., and Turnock, D. (Eds). *Environmental Problems of East Central Europe,* 2nd edn. London, Routledge, 2002.

Baker, S., and Baumgartl, B. 'Bulgaria: Managing the Environment in an Unstable Transition', in Baker, S., and Jehlička, P. (Eds). *Dilemmas of Transition: The Environment, Democracy and Economic Reform in East Central Europe.* London, Frank Cass, 1998.

Baker, S., and Jehlička, P. 'Dilemmas of Transition: The Environment, Democracy and Economic Reform in East Central Europe: An Introduction', in *Dilemmas of Transition: The Environment, Democracy and Economic Reform in East Central Europe.* London, Frank Cass, 1998.

Caddy, J. 'Harmonisation and Asymmetry: Environmental Policy Co-ordination between the European Union and Central Europe', in *Journal of European Public Policy*, Vol. 4, No. 3, 1997.

Carter, F. W., and Turnock, D. (Eds). *Environmental Problems of East Central Europe*, 2nd edn. London, Routledge, 2002.

CEE Bankwatch Network and Friends of the Earth Europe. *Billions for Sustainability? The Use of EU Pre-Accession Funds and their Environmental and Social Implications.* Prague and Brussels, CEE Bankwatch Network and Friends of the Earth Europe, 2000.

Billions of Sustainability: Lessons Learned from the Use of Pre-Accession Funds. Prague and Brussels, CEE Bankwatch Network and Friends of the Earth Europe, 2002.

European Commission. *Agenda 2000: For a Stronger and Wider Europe.* Brussels, European Commission, 1997.

Nuclear Safety in Central and Eastern Europe and in the New Independent States. Brussels, European Commission, 1998.

Accession Strategies for Environment: Meeting the Challenge of Enlargement with the Candidate Countries in Central and Eastern Europe. Brussels, European Commission, 1998.

Composite Report from the Commission on Progress Towards Accession by Each of the Candidate Countries. Brussels, European Commission, 1999.

The Enlargement Process and the Three Pre-Accession Instruments: Phare, ISPA, Sapard. Brussels, European Commission, 2002.

Environmental Co-operation in the Danube-Black Sea Region. Brussels, European Commission, 2001 a.

Making a Success of Enlargement: Strategy Paper and Report of the European Commission on the Progress towards Accession by Each of the Candidate Countries. Brussels, European Commission, 2001 b.

The Challenge of Environmental Financing in the Candidate Countries. Brussels, European Commission, 2001 c.

Towards the Enlarged Europe: Strategy Paper and Report. Brussels, European Commission, 2002 a.

Roadmaps for Bulgaria and Romania. Brussels, European Commission, 2002 b.

Regular Report on Poland's Progress towards Accession. Brussels, European Commission, 2002 c.

Regular Report on Czech Republic's Progress towards Accession. Brussels, European Commission, 2002 d.

Regular Report on Slovenia's Progress towards Accession. Brussels, European Commission, 2002 e.

Regular Report on Lithuania's Progress towards Accession. Brussels, European Commission, 2002 f.

European Environment Agency (EEA). *Europe's Environment: The Dobříš Assessment.* Copenhagen, EEA, 1995.

Environment in the European Union at the Turn of the Century. Environmental Assessment Report, No. 2. Copenhagen, EEA, 1999.

Hungarian Ministry of the Environment. *National Environmental Programme of the Republic of Hungary, 1998–2002.* Budapest, Hungarian Ministry of the Environment, 1998.

von Homeyer, I. 'Enlarging EU Environmental Policy', at the Environmental Studies Workshop, Robert Schuman Centre for Advanced Studies, European University Institute, Florence. May 2001.

Jancar-Webster, B. 'Environmental Movement and Social Change in the Transition Countries', in Baker, S., and Jehlička, P. (Eds). *Dilemmas of Transition: The Environment, Democracy and Economic Reform in East Central Europe.* London, Frank Cass, 1998.

Kramer, J. M. 'EU Enlargement and the Environment in Central and Eastern Europe', at the Environmental Studies Workshop, Robert Schuman Centre for Advanced Studies, European University Institute, Florence. May 2001.

Mardiste, P. 'Environmental Consequences of EU Pre-Accession Funds in CEE Region', Environmental Studies Workshop, at the Robert Schuman Centre for Advanced Studies, European University Institute, Florence. May 2001.

Mayhew, A. *Recreating Europe: The European Union's Policy towards Central and Eastern Europe.* Cambridge, Cambridge University Press, 1998.

Organisation for Economic Co-operation and Development (OECD). *Environmental Performance Reviews.* Paris, Centre for Co-operation with the Economies in Transition, OECD, 1996.

O'Toole, L., and Hanf, K. 'Hungary: Political Transformation and Environmental Change', in Baker, S., and Jehlička, P. (Eds). *Dilemmas of Transition: The Environment, Democracy and Economic Reform in East Central Europe.* London, Frank Cass, 1998.

Regional Environmental Centre for Central and Eastern Europe (REC). *Problems, Progress and Possibilities: A Needs Assessment of Environmental NGOs in Central and Eastern Europe*. Szentendre, REC, 1997.

Environmental Enforcement and Compliance in South Eastern Europe. Szentendre, REC, 2002.

Environmental Financing in Central and Eastern Europe 1996–2001. Szentendre, REC, 2003 a.

Highlights of the Regional Environmental Reconstruction Programme. Szentrendre, REC, 2003 b.

Rootes, C. 'Environmental Movements and Green Parties in Western and Eastern Europe', in Redclift, M., and Woodgate, G. (Eds). *International Handbook of Environmental Sociology*. Cheltenham, Edward Elgar, 1996.

Slocock, B. 'Whatever Happened to the Environment: Environmental Issues in the Eastern Enlargement of the European Union', in Henderson, K. (Ed). *Back to Europe: Central and Eastern Europe and the European Union*. London, University College London Press, 1999.

Smith, A., and Pickles, J. 'Introduction: Theorizing Transition and the Political Economy of Transformation', in *Theorizing Transition: The Political Economy of Post-Communist Transformations*. London, Routledge, 1998.

Tickle, A., and Welsh, I. 'Environmental Politics, Civil Society and Post-Communism', in *Environment and Society in Eastern Europe*. Harlow, Longman, 1998.

Turnock, D. 'The Central Importance of the European Union', in Carter, F. W., and Turnock, D. (Eds). *Environmental Problems of East Central Europe*, 2nd edn. London, Routledge, 2002.

Turnock, D., and Carter, F. W. 'Introduction', in Carter, F. W., and Turnock, D. (Eds). *Environmental Problems of East Central Europe*, 2nd edn. London, Routledge, 2002.

Waller, M., and Millard, F. 'Environmental Politics in Eastern Europe', in *Environmental Politics*, Vol. 1, No. 2, 1992.

World Wide Fund for Nature (WWF). *Structural Funds in an Enlarged EU*. Gland, WWF, 2003.

ETHNIC GROUPS

- Albanians
- Baltic
- Bulgarians
- Czechs
- Eastern Slavs
- Finno-Ugrian
- Germans
- Greeks
- Hungarians
- Italians
- Macedonians
- Poles
- Romanians
- Serbo-Croats
- Slovaks
- Slovenes
- Swedes
- Turks

SWEDEN

ESTONIA

RUSSIA

LATVIA

Baltic Sea

LITHUANIA

RUSSIA

BELARUS

GERMANY

POLAND

UKRAINE

CZECH REPUBLIC

SLOVAKIA

MOLDOVA

AUSTRIA

HUNGARY

ROMANIA

SLOVENIA

CROATIA

BOSNIA AND
HERZEGOVINA

YUGOSLAVIA

Black
Sea

Adriatic Sea

BULGARIA

ITALY

MACEDONIA

ALBANIA

GREECE

TURKEY

Ethnic Groups of Central and South-Eastern Europe

PART TWO

Country Surveys

ALBANIA

Geography

PHYSICAL FEATURES

The Republic of Albania (formerly the People's Socialist Republic of Albania) is situated in South-Eastern Europe, on the Balkan Peninsula. It is bordered by Greece, to the south, by the former Yugoslav republic of Macedonia (FYRM), to the east, and by Montenegro to the north, and Serbia (province of Kosovo and Metohija) to the north-east. To the west there is a 420-km (260-mile) coastline along the Adriatic Sea and the Strait of Otranto (parts of the Mediterranean Sea). Albania covers an area of 28,748 sq km (11,100 sq miles).

More than three-quarters of Albania's territory is mountain or hill country and nearly one-half is covered by woodland. The Albanian Alps, characterized by tall forests and alpine pastures, dominate the north of the country and rise to a height of 2,693 m (8,835 ft) at Jezerce. The central mountain region lies between the valley of the River Drin in the north and the central Devoll and lower Osum valleys in the south. It is a less rugged area than the Alps, with wider valleys, dense forests and large lakes such as the Ohrid and Prespa, but it also has high peaks, reaching 2,751 m at Mount Korabi, the highest point in the country. South of the Osum valley the more regular ranges of the southern mountain region continue into northern Greece and extend westwards to the sea. These three mountain areas surround the western coastal lowlands. Communications with the south and east, therefore, are difficult. There are, however, east–west routes along the valleys of the Shkumbin, Devoll and Drin rivers. The western lowlands extend some 200 km from the foothills of the Alps in the north to Vlorë in the south and some 50 km inland. The land is flat and marshy and extensive land reclamation was necessary to allow previously unused areas to be cultivated.

CLIMATE

The climate is Mediterranean throughout much of the country, although winters in the mountain areas are cold, with snow cover lasting several months. Summers are hot and dry, with average July temperatures of 24°–25°C (75°–77°F). During the winter frequent cyclones make the weather unstable, but it remains relatively mild in the plains, with January temperatures averaging 8°C (47°F) in the coastal town of Durrës, and 4°C (39°F) in the more northerly inland city of Shkodër. Average annual rainfall is 1,300 mm, but regional variations are pronounced; in the Alps it is over 2,000 mm, whereas in the valleys of the interior it is only 650–700 mm.

POPULATION

According to the results of the census of 1 April 2001, the total population of Albania was 3,069,275. At the census of April 1989 approximately 98% of the population were ethnic Albanians. Other nationalities included 58,758 Greeks, the majority of whom live in the south, 4,697 Macedonians, small numbers of Bulgarians and Gypsies (Roma) and about 100 Serbs, Croats and Montenegrins. However, all figures for minority groups in Albania were disputed. Some sources asserted that there were several thousand Serbs and Montenegrins in Albania and 55,000–60,000 Macedonians. Greek sources claimed that there were more than 300,000 ethnic

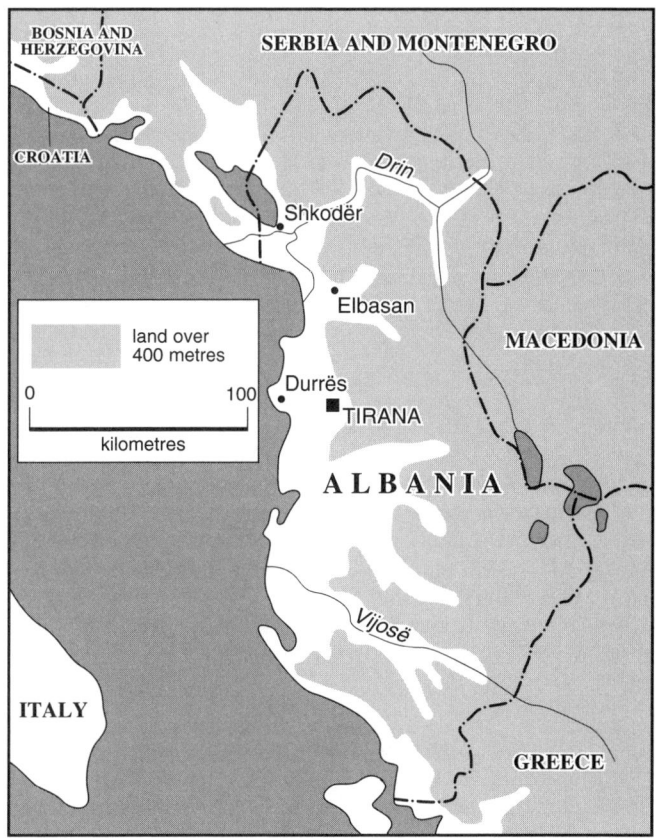

Greeks living in Albania, whereas independent estimates asserted a lower figure of some 100,000–120,000. Western sources also mentioned some 35,000 Vlahs (descendants of the autochthonous Thracians), living in the Korçë region, and more than 5,000 Roma.

The official ban on religious worship, which was in effect between 1967 and 1990, makes it difficult to assess the religious affiliations of the population. According to the religious census of 1945, 72.8% of the population was Muslim, 17.1% Eastern Orthodox and 10.1% Roman Catholic. Of the Muslim population, an estimated 75% were orthodox Sunni Muslims and the remaining 25% were members of the liberal Bektashi sect, a Sufi dervish order. In late 1990 and early 1991 the small community of some 300 Albanian Jews emigrated in its entirety to Israel.

The official language is Albanian, the principal dialects being Gheg (spoken north of the River Shkumbin) and Tosk (in the south). The literary language is a fusion of the two dialects, with the phonetic and morphological structure of Tosk prevailing. Ethnic Greeks continue to use their own language.

The majority of the population live on the coastal plains and nearly one-half of the population lives outside major towns. According to the census of 1 April 2001, the population density (persons per sq km) was 106.8, although that of the lowland plains was much higher. At April 2001 the population density in the coastal province of Lushnjë was 202.0, whereas in the mountain province of Pukë, in the north, it was only 33.3. There are many ethnic Albanians living in other countries, including some 1.7m. in Serbia and Montenegro, mainly in the

Kosovo region of Serbia (Kosovar Albanians), and a further 450,000 in the FYRM. The capital, Tirana (Tiranë), is situated in the centre of the country and had a population of 343,078 at the 2001 census. Other important towns include Durrës (Durazzo), Albania's largest port (99,546), Elbasan, a major industrial centre (87,797), and Shkodër (Scutari—82,455).

Chronology

168 BC: Illyria (which included modern-day Albania) was annexed by the Roman Empire.

AD 395: Following a division of the administration of the Roman Empire, Illyria was ruled by the Eastern Roman ('Byzantine') Emperor in Constantinople (now İstanbul in Turkey).

6th–7th centuries: Slavs invaded the Balkan Peninsula.

11th century: Vlachs (Wallachians) migrated into the territory still occupied by the remnants of the Thracian-Illyrian population.

1385: Osmanlı (Ottoman) Turkish forces reached the Albanian coast.

1443: Gjergj Kastrioti (Skënderbeu or Skenderbeg) led Albanians in a revolt against Ottoman dominance.

1468: Death of Skënderbeu.

1478: The Ottomans established full control over Albania and, under their rule, many Albanians converted to Islam.

1756: Mehemet of Bushan established an independent principality in northern Albania.

1787: Ali Pasha of Tepelenë (Janina) established an independent principality in southern Albania and neighbouring territories.

1822: Ottoman forces overthrew Ali Pasha.

1831: Mustafa Pasha, of the Bushan dynasty, was overthrown.

1878: The Congress of Berlin allotted parts of Albanian territory to Bulgaria, Greece, Montenegro and Serbia. The Albanian League for the Defence of the Rights of the Albanian Nation was established.

1881: The Albanian League was disbanded by the Ottomans.

1910: An uprising against Ottoman rule was suppressed by Turkish forces.

October 1912: The First Balkan War began; Albania was occupied by neighbouring powers.

28 November 1912: A national convention, convened in Vlorë, proclaimed the independence of Albania; Ismail Qemal was appointed President.

July 1913: The London Ambassadors' Conference recognized the principle of Albanian independence, but designated the country a protectorate, under the control of the Great Powers; Kosovo was granted to Serbia; other territories were gained by Greece.

March 1914: Prince William of Wied, who had been appointed ruler of the Albanian protectorate by the Great Powers, arrived in Albania; he left in September, following local opposition to his rule.

August 1914: Italy and Greece occupied southern Albania at the outbreak of the First World War.

April 1915: The secret Treaty of London, providing for the partition of much of Albania between Greece, Italy, Montenegro and Serbia, was signed.

January 1920: The Congress of Lushnjë reaffirmed Albania's independence and appointed a new Government; Tirana (Tiranë) was declared the capital of Albania.

August 1920: Italy agreed to withdraw its forces from Albania and recognize Albanian independence.

December 1920: Albania was admitted to the League of Nations.

10 June 1924: After an armed uprising, a Government headed by Fan Noli came to power.

24 December 1924: The Government of Fan Noli was overthrown by forces led by Ahmet Zogu.

January 1925: The Republic of Albania was proclaimed; Ahmet Zogu was appointed President.

September 1928: A monarchy was established, with Zogu proclaiming himself King Zog I.

April 1939: Italian troops invaded Albania; King Zog was forced into exile. The union of Albania and Italy under the Italian Crown was subsequently proclaimed.

November 1941: The Communist Party of Albania was founded; Enver Hoxha became its first leader.

September 1942: The National Liberation Front, a communist-led resistance organization, was established.

September 1943: Italy surrendered to the Allies; Albania was invaded by Nazi German forces.

1943–44: Fierce fighting occurred between Nazi forces and resistance groups, and also between resistance groups of different political persuasions.

24–28 May 1944: The Congress of Përmet established, as a provisional government, the Anti-Fascist Committee for National Liberation, headed by Enver Hoxha.

29 November 1944: The National Liberation Front proclaimed the liberation of Albania.

2 December 1945: Elections with only communist candidates took place; the communists, as the Democratic Front, won some 90% of the votes cast.

11 January 1946: The People's Republic of Albania was proclaimed; King Zog was declared deposed.

1948: Close relations with Yugoslavia were ended after that country's expulsion from the Communist Information Bureau (Cominform). The Albanian Communist Party was renamed the Party of Labour of Albania (PLA).

1949: Albania joined the Council for Mutual Economic Assistance (CMEA). Koci Xoxe (former Minister of the Interior) and other officials were executed as alleged pro-Yugoslav traitors.

1954: Hoxha resigned as Chairman of the Council of Ministers (head of government), but retained effective power as First Secretary of the PLA. Mehmet Shehu was appointed head of government.

1955: Albania joined the Warsaw Treaty Organization (Warsaw Pact). The Soviet *rapprochement* with Yugoslavia strained Soviet-Albanian relations.

1961: The USSR denounced Albania and severed diplomatic relations after Hoxha announced his support for the Chinese communist leader, Mao Zedong, in his ideological conflict with the USSR.

1962: Albania formally left the CMEA.

1967: Religious worship was outlawed and all mosques and churches were closed.

1968: Albania formally left the Warsaw Pact.

1972: Improved US-Chinese relations were denounced by Albania.

1975: Gen. Beqir Balluku, who had been dismissed as Minister of Defence in 1974, was executed as an alleged pro-Chinese traitor.

1976: A new Constitution was adopted; the country's name was changed to the People's Socialist Republic of Albania.

1978: Albania declared its support for Viet Nam, in its conflict with the People's Republic of China; China suspended all military and economic ties.

December 1981: Mehmet Shehu, the Head of Government, died in a shooting incident. There were subsequent allegations that he had been murdered.

November 1982: Ramiz Alia replaced Haxhi Lleshi as Chairman of the Presidium of the People's Assembly (head of state).

April 1985: Death of Enver Hoxha. He was succeeded as First Secretary of the PLA by Ramiz Alia.

August 1987: In an attempt to improve relations, Greece ended the technical state of war which had existed between it and Albania since 1945.

December 1989: Despite some indication of reform, there were reports of anti-Government demonstrations in the northern town of Shkodër (Scutari) and such activity increased throughout 1990.

May 1990: The People's Assembly adopted measures to liberalize the penal code, to end the ban on religious propaganda and to relax the constitutional prohibition on foreign investment, following economic reforms announced by Alia the previous month.

July 1990: Some 5,000 Albanians were eventually allowed to leave the country after seeking asylum in the embassies of foreign countries. Diplomatic contact was resumed with the USSR.

December 1990: Opposition activists formed, and registered, the Democratic Party of Albania (DPA), while other proposed reforms included guaranteeing multi-party democracy and economic liberalization.

January 1991: Konstantinos Mitsotakis, the Prime Minister of Greece, visited Tirana, in an attempt to quell the exodus of ethnic Greeks from Albania. Later in the month a new Government included more reformists, such as Fatos Nano, an economist.

February 1991: Demonstrations in Tirana and student protests prompted Ramiz Alia to declare presidential rule and appoint a provisional government under Nano.

March 1991: The Italian navy was ordered to prevent any more vessels landing at the Italian port of Brindisi, after some 20,000 Albanians had arrived on ships seized in Albanian ports. Diplomatic relations with the USA were renewed.

31 March 1991: The PLA won over 60% of the votes cast in Albania's first multi-party election since the 1920s.

30 April 1991: Ramiz Alia was elected to the new post of President of the Republic by the People's Assembly, which had renamed the country the Republic of Albania and declared the 1976 Constitution invalid, replacing it, on an interim basis, with a Law on the Major Constitutional Provisions of the People's Assembly of the Republic of Albania.

June 1991: With continuing protests throughout the country and after a general strike, Ylli Bufi became Head of Government; he formed a Government that included the first non-communist ministers since the Second World War. The PLA changed its name to the Socialist Party of Albania (SPA) and elected Nano its leader. Albania was admitted as a member of the Conference on Security and Co-operation in Europe (later Organization for Security and Co-operation in Europe—OSCE).

October 1991: The Assembly voted to recognize the 'Republic of Kosovo' (the predominantly ethnic Albanian area of neighbouring Yugoslavia), after protests at Serbian repression.

December 1991: The Bufi Government finally collapsed when the DPA withdrew from the coalition; Vilson Ahmeti was the new Chairman of the Council of Ministers. There were food riots in various parts of the country and increasing industrial unrest.

February 1992: A new electoral law prevented the Democratic Union of the Greek Minority (OMONIA), which held five seats in the Assembly, from submitting candidates for the general election (the Greek community achieved representation through the Union of Human Rights Party).

22 and 29 March 1992: Elections to the new Assembly were won by the DPA, which obtained 62% of the votes cast in the first round (and 92 of the 140 seats), while the SPA only obtained 26% (and 38 seats).

9 April 1992: Sali Berisha of the DPA was elected President of the Republic by the People's Assembly, following the resignation of Alia some days before. Berisha appointed Aleksander Meksi to lead a new coalition Government.

July 1992: The Albanian Communist Party (founded in 1991) was banned. At local elections the DPA obtained the most votes (43% of the total), but the SPA improved its support, obtaining 41%.

September 1992: There was a split in the DPA, following accusations that the Berisha regime was becoming more right-wing and authoritarian. Former President Alia was arrested and charged with corruption, joining several other prominent members of the old communist regime in detention.

December 1992: Albania became a member of the Organization of the Islamic Conference (OIC).

February 1993: Former premier Ahmeti was placed under house arrest following allegations of corruption; he was sentenced to two years' imprisonment in August.

July 1993: Former premier Nano was charged with misappropriating state funds; he was found guilty in 1994.

6 November 1994: A draft constitution, providing for enhanced powers for the executive, was rejected by 53.9% of participants in a referendum. The same month the Albanian Republican Party (ARP) and a faction of the Social Democratic Party withdrew from the governing coalition.

May 1995: In an effort to restrict the mass migration of Albanians to Italy, the two Governments increased coastal security.

June 1995: The sale of newspapers and magazines in Tirana was to be restricted to government-owned establishments. Ilir Hoxha, the son of Enver Hoxha, was charged with inciting national hatred following the publication of a newspaper interview in which he denounced the DPA (he was later convicted). Such incidents were cited as evidence of growing government intolerance of criticism, even from within the DPA.

7 July 1995: The Government granted an amnesty to former President Alia and some 30 other political prisoners; Albania was accepted as a member of the Council of Europe.

September 1995: The 'Genocide Law', enacted by a small majority, prohibited the appointment of any person who held office during the communist period to the executive, the legislature or the judiciary.

10 February 1996: Former President Alia was detained, pending trial for several charges, among them allegations that he had ordered the killing of those attempting to flee across the border in 1991.

March 1996: Following several years of poor relations between the two countries, President Berisha and the Greek President, Konstantinos Stefanopoulos, signed a Treaty of Mutual Friendship and Co-operation.

26 May 1996: Elections to the People's Assembly, the conduct of which was widely condemned by international observers, were boycotted by the main opposition parties; the DPA, therefore, won 122 out of a total of 140 parliamentary seats.

12 July 1996: A new cabinet, again led by Meksi, was sworn in; it consisted mainly of DPA members, but the ARP, the Christian Democratic Party of Albania and the Union of Social Democrats were also represented.

October 1996: In local government elections, widely regarded to have been conducted fairly, the DPA secured the largest number of votes in 58 of the 64 municipalities and in 267 of the 309 communes.

January 1997: The collapse of several popular 'pyramid' investment schemes, resulting in huge losses of individual savings, prompted violent anti-Government demonstrations.

1 March 1997: President Berisha declared a state of emergency, as anti-Government protests escalated into insurgency and, often supported by rebel troops, opposition groups gained control of several towns.

3 March 1997: The People's Assembly re-elected Berisha, who was unopposed, for a second five-year term in the presidency.

11 March 1997: With the evacuation of foreign nationals and the flight of many Albanians, Berisha appointed Bashkim Fino, a former SPA mayor of Gjirokastër, to lead an interim Government of National Reconciliation, to include representatives of eight opposition parties, in advance of a general election.

11 April 1997: A UN-sanctioned Multinational Protection Force, established to facilitate the distribution of humanitarian assistance, was deployed, principally in government-controlled areas of northern and central Albania.

29 June 1997: The first round of voting in the general election took place. A simultaneous referendum on the restoration of the monarchy resulted in 66.7% of the participating electorate favouring the republic.

6 July 1997: With the second round of voting in the general election, the SPA secured 101 of the 155 seats in the enlarged People's Assembly, with the DPA winning 29 seats; the electoral process was declared satisfactory by the OSCE.

24 July 1997: Rexhep Mejdani, hitherto the Secretary-General of the SPA, was elected President by the People's Assembly. Subsequently, a new Council of Ministers was appointed, comprising representatives of the SPA and its allied parties, with former premier Nano as the Head of Government.

14 August 1997: The operation of the Multinational Protection Force formally ended, as the Government dispatched troops to the south of the country to restore order in areas that were still controlled by insurgents.

September 1997: A parliamentary commission was established to draft a new constitution in accordance with government proposals.

20–21 October 1997: Berisha was re-elected party chairman at the DPA's national conference. Former President Alia and three other senior officials of his administration were acquitted of charges of genocide.

November 1997: Negotiations between Nano and the Yugoslav President, Slobodan Milošević, led to an announcement that relations between the two countries were to be normalized, although Milošević emphasized that the unrest in Kosovo remained an internal issue of the Federal Republic of Yugoslavia (FRY—Serbia and Montenegro).

6 March 1998: Following the use of the security forces by the Serbian authorities against ethnic Albanian villages, huge crowds gathered in protest in Tirana. President Mejdani condemned Serbian action against civilians.

June 1998: Reports indicated that about 20,000 ethnic Albanian refugees had crossed into Albania to escape fighting between Serb forces and Kosovar guerrillas.

21 June 1998: In partial local elections, the conduct of which was declared satisfactory by OSCE observers, an SPA-led electoral coalition, Alliance for the State, achieved a significant victory, winning control of five of the seven municipalities and six of the nine communes where voting took place.

6 July 1998: The People's Assembly approved the final report on the civil unrest of early 1997; it recommended the prosecution of several leading DPA officials, including former President Berisha, for the violation of constitutional provisions and the unlawful use of force. The following day the DPA announced a new, indefinite boycott of parliament.

12 September 1998: Azem Hajdari, a leading DPA official, and his two bodyguards were shot and killed in Tirana; following two days of violent protest; as Berisha alleged government responsibility for the murders, state troops regained control of the capital.

18 September 1998: A parliamentary commission lifted Berisha's immunity from prosecution and Nano stated that Berisha would be charged with an attempted coup.

28 September 1998: Nano resigned as Prime Minister, claiming that a lack of support for him had contributed to the Government's weakness and the collapse of public order. The following day the SPA nominated its Secretary-General, Pandeli Majko, to succeed Nano, who remained Chairman of the SPA.

22 November 1998: In a referendum, 93.1% of the participating electorate voted in favour of the adoption of a new constitution. However, Berisha claimed the referendum was invalid, and urged DPA supporters to protest against the results; additional troops were deployed in Tirana to maintain public order.

28 November 1998: The new Constitution was officially adopted; the DPA announced that it would continue its refusal to recognize the Constitution.

11–12 April 1999: Albanian border villages came under heavy bombardment by Serbian troops fighting the ethnic Albanian Kosovo Liberation Army (KLA), in Kosovo; later in the month Serbian forces advanced into Albanian territory, but were repelled by Albanian forces.

17 July 1999: The DPA voted to end its boycott of the legislature.

1 September 1999: The North Atlantic Treaty Organization (NATO) announced the end of its mission in Albania to help the country cope with the influx of Kosovar Albanians fleeing Serbian military action in the province. The troops were to be replaced by a 2,400-member contingent, to be known as Communications Zone West (COMMZ-W), which would assist international peace-keepers in Kosovo and help to maintain public order in Albania. COMMZ-W was officially dissolved in June 2002, when a NATO headquarters was established in Tirana.

11 October 1999: Nano, who had resigned as SPA Chairman in January, was re-elected to the post, narrowly defeating the Prime Minister, Majko.

26 October 1999: Following his defeat in the party leadership contest, Majko resigned as premier; the Deputy Prime Minister, Ilir Meta, a close ally of Nano, was immediately nominated as Majko's successor. The DPA subsequently announced a boycott of a parliamentary motion to approve the new Council of Ministers formed by Meta, and the staging of protests following the return of Nano to the SPA leadership.

8 November 1999: Despite the DPA's boycott, the People's Assembly formally approved the new Government.

9 December 1999: The Constitutional Court formally abolished the death penalty.

30 June 2000: Following the resignation of Namik Dokle, the SPA elected Gramoz Ruci as Secretary-General.

8 September 2000: Albania became a member of the World Trade Organization.

1 and 15 October 2000: Local government elections took place in two rounds; the SPA won 252 local council seats and the DPA 118. However, many DPA supporters had boycotted the second round of voting, following allegations of widespread electoral irregularities, and the DPA refused to accept the official results.

19 January 2001: Following the election, in September 2000, of Vojislav Koštunica as President of the FRY, Albania and Yugoslavia restored diplomatic relations.

24 June and 8 July 2001: Parliamentary elections took place in two rounds. Further rounds of voting took place in July and early August, following alleged irregularities. According to the final results, the SPA won 73 of the 140 seats in the People's Assembly, while the opposition electoral alliance, the Union for Victory, led by the DPA, secured 46 seats.

7 September 2001: A reorganized Council of Ministers, which was again headed by Ilir Meta, was approved.

29 January 2002: Following continued division within the SPA, Meta tendered his resignation from the office of Prime Minister.

7 February 2002: Pandeli Majko, an associate of Meta and hitherto Minister of Defence, was appointed to the office of Prime Minister for the second time.

22 February 2002: Following negotiations between the two SPA factions, a new Council of Ministers, nominated by Majko, was approved.

24 June 2002: Alfred Moisiu, a retired general who had served under Berisha, was elected to the presidency by 97 of the 140 deputies in the People's Assembly, following lengthy negotiations between the SPA and the DPA.

24 July 2002: At the expiry of Mejdani's term of office, Moisiu was inaugurated as Head of State.

25 July 2002: Majko resigned from the office of Prime Minister, in favour of Nano, after the SPA General Steering Committee decided that the party Chairman should be head of government.

31 July 2002: Nano's new Government, which included Meta as Deputy Prime Minister and Minister of Foreign Affairs, and Majko as Minister of Defence, was approved in the People's Assembly.

31 January 2003: Albania commenced negotiations with the European Union on the signature of a Stabilization and Association Agreement.

18 July 2003: Despite a truce reached between the two SPA factions prior to October local government elections, Meta resigned from his government office, accusing Nano of authoritarianism.

29 July 2003: Nano's nomination of Marko Bello as Minister of Foreign Affairs was rejected in the People's Assembly, owing to the opposition of Meta's faction. It was announced that the deputy minister was provisionally to assume the post.

History

MIRANDA VICKERS

THE ESTABLISHMENT OF THE ALBANIAN STATE

On 28 November 1912, after more than 400 years under Osmanlı (Ottoman) Turkish rule, Albania declared its independence under a provisional Government. International recognition followed at the London Conference of July 1913, which diminished the territory claimed by the Albanian state, granting the region of Kosovo to Serbia and the area known as Chamouria (Northern Epirus) to Greece. During the turmoil of the First World War the armies of the Habsburgs (Austria-Hungary), Greece and Italy, and the forces of Serbia and Montenegro occupied Albanian territory. Italy continued its occupation until 1920, when Albanian independence was re-established.

Until 1924 the country underwent a period of great internal instability, with frequent changes of government. In December of that year Ahmet Zogu, who had previously held office as Minister of Internal Affairs, overthrew the incumbent Government and assumed power. Zogu quickly established an autocratic, centralized state and proclaimed himself King Zog I in 1928. In order to consolidate his regime, Zog accepted substantial financial subsidies from Italy, which resulted in increased political influence until eventually, in 1939, Benito Mussolini, the Italian leader, demanded a formal protectorate over Albania. When Zogu resisted, Italian forces invaded. Albania's ill-equipped army was soon defeated and Zogu fled into exile. Albania and Kosovo were united with Italy for four years, before being occupied by German forces in

1943. The Germans withdrew one year later, allowing the communist-led National Liberation Front (NLF) to take power.

ALBANIA UNDER COMMUNIST RULE

In November 1941, under Yugoslav direction, a unified Albanian Communist Party (ACP) was formed, and in the following year the NLF was established. The victory of the NLF in November 1944 brought to power a provisional government, headed by Enver Hoxha, the leader of the ACP. In December 1945 elections took place, with a single list of communist-sponsored candidates.

After 1945 Albania was dominated by the personality of Hoxha, the chief ideologist of Albanian-style socialism. He was born in Gjirokastër, in southern Albania, in 1908. During the early 1930s he studied and worked in France and Belgium, returning to Albania in 1936, where he became active in the communist movement and was elected leader of the Provisional Committee of the ACP in 1941. Under Hoxha's rule, Albania experienced four distinct phases. During 1944–48 the ACP became virtually a branch of the Yugoslav Communist Party (CPY). Albanian sovereignty effectively disappeared as its dependence on Yugoslavia grew. Had it not been for the rupture of relations between Tito (Josip Broz), the leader of the CPY, and the Soviet leader, Stalin (Iosif V. Dzhugashvili), in 1948, Albania would probably have become the seventh republic of Yugoslavia. During the second phase of Hoxha's rule, from 1948 to 1961, Albania's main international ally was the USSR. Hoxha followed the Stalinist pattern in developing his dictatorship, using widespread purges to eliminate any opposition to the ruling Party of Labour of Albania (PLA—which was reconstituted from the ACP in 1948). While ensuring political orthodoxy, the leadership also continued the transformation of the economy and social system, eliminating private ownership of industry and commerce and forcibly effecting the collectivization of agriculture. Ambitious social-policy schemes improved access to medical and educational facilities, leading to a substantial rise in health and literacy standards.

Soviet-Albanian relations began to deteriorate after Stalin's death in 1953. Nikita Khrushchev's *rapprochement* with Tito in 1955, and the new Soviet leader's denunciation of Stalin the following year, severely strained relations. In 1960 the Albanian leadership openly declared its support for the People's Republic of China in the escalating Sino–Soviet ideological dispute. In response, the USSR severed relations with Albania in 1961. There were further purges as Hoxha attempted to imitate the Chinese 'Cultural Revolution' in his own country. In the relentless pursuit of ideological purism, in 1967 the practice of religion was prohibited, and Albania was proclaimed the world's first atheist state. From the early 1970s relations with China deteriorated. This followed the improvement in Chinese relations with the USA in 1972 and the death of Mao Zedong, the Chinese leader, in 1976. In 1978 the People's Republic of China suspended all economic and military co-operation with Albania, after Albania had declared its support for Viet Nam in the Sino–Vietnamese dispute. During the fourth phase of Hoxha's rule, from 1978 until 1985, Albania's isolationist policies reached their extreme. Internal political orthodoxy was enforced with the utmost vigour. The internal security police, the Sigurimi, prevented the development of any opposition movements within Albania. Meanwhile, Hoxha's collected works consolidated his 'cult of personality'.

THE POST-HOXHA YEARS

Enver Hoxha died in April 1985 and was succeeded as First Secretary of the PLA by Ramiz Alia. Alia had played a significant role in the development of post-1945 Albania, as Secretary for Ideology in the PLA from the 1960s. As First Secretary, Alia adopted a less rigid style than his predecessor and during the late 1980s the Government began to distance itself gradually from the Hoxha legacy. There were cautious attempts at liberalization and decentralization and a far more flexible foreign policy led to improved relations with a number of Western European countries.

Albania's relations with its immediate neighbours, Yugoslavia and Greece, also improved in the 1980s, although alleged ill-treatment of the Albanian community in Yugoslavia and the ethnic Greek minority in Albania at times threatened increased co-operation. Relations with Greece were normalized in 1987, when Greece decided formally to end the technical state of war with Albania, which had been in existence since 1945, and annul Greek territorial claims to 'Northern Epirus' (southern Albania). However, the status of the ethnic Greek minority in southern Albania remained a sensitive issue.

In 1988 Albania participated in the Balkan Conference of Foreign Ministers in Belgrade, Yugoslavia, the first official meeting of all six Balkan states in more than 50 years. By its involvement, Albania reassured its neighbours, particularly Yugoslavia, of the country's willingness to help establish a general framework of co-operation in the region. Yugoslavia was one of Albania's major trading partners, and any ideological differences between them tended to be exaggerated, involving more rhetoric than reality. This was especially so in the case of the Albanian population in the Yugoslav region of Kosovo (officially known as Kosovo and Metohija from September 1991). Although the Albanian leadership often used the situation in Kosovo as a way of deflecting discontent at home, several decades of isolation accentuated the social and psychological differences separating Albanians from Kosovars. The comparatively sophisticated Kosovars are related to Albania's northern Gheg-speaking people; these groups are divided by cultural, linguistic and historical differences from the southern Tosk-speaking Albanians. Although Tosk became the predominant dialect after the Second World War, it did not have the unifying effect anticipated and, with the diffusion of central authority, regionalism again surfaced during the 1990s.

ALBANIA'S 'PERESTROIKA'

Albania embarked on mildly reformist policies, for economic reasons, before the collapse of the communist regimes in Eastern Europe in 1989. In late January 1990 the Ninth Plenum of the Central Committee of the PLA approved a programme of limited reform, which proposed greater decentralization of the economy and some democratic reform in political institutions. Nevertheless, Alia continued to reject the idea of a multi-party system, claiming that such a system was not appropriate for Albania. The pace of reform quickened throughout 1990, following a number of student demonstrations. Enterprises were to be allowed to sell some surplus goods on the open market and Albanians were to be granted passports and the right to travel abroad. The announcement that the practice of religion was no longer an offence led to the gradual reopening of mosques and churches.

Despite increasing liberalization, however, there was further unrest in July 1990, when security forces violently dispersed anti-Government demonstrators in Tirana (Tiranë). In subsequent days several thousand people sought refuge in foreign embassies. The refugee crisis was finally resolved when some 5,000 Albanians were allowed to leave the country, assisted by a multinational relief operation, co-ordinated by the UN. In foreign affairs there were significant changes, as Albania sought to escape its self-imposed isolation. In July the restoration of diplomatic links with the USSR was announced and, following negotiations beginning in August, diplomatic relations with the USA were finally re-established in March 1991. Representatives from the United Kingdom and Albania also met to discuss the restoration of diplomatic relations between the two countries. Albania had always insisted on the return of gold seized by the United Kingdom at the end of the Second World War before diplomatic ties could be resumed. The United Kingdom's claim on this gold was agreed by the International Court of Justice (based in The Hague, Netherlands) as compensation for the sinking, allegedly by Albanian mines, of two British warships in the Corfu Channel in 1946. However, both parties agreed that arguments over the confiscated gold should be postponed until after the resumption of diplomatic ties, which were finally restored in May 1991. The gold, valued at some US \$30m., was eventually returned in February 1996.

THE INTRODUCTION OF A MULTI-PARTY SYSTEM

In early December 1990 student demonstrators in Tirana demanded the introduction of a multi-party system for the elections to the People's Assembly, which were scheduled for February 1991. On 11 December 1990, in response to growing unrest, the Central Committee of the PLA agreed to legalize independent political parties. The establishment of the Democratic Party of Albania (DPA), the first legal opposition party to be formed since before the Second World War, was announced on the following day. The DPA, led by Dr Sali

Berisha, a cardiologist, and Gramoz Pashko, an economist, demanded that Albania agree to the four principles of the Paris Charter, signed in late 1990 by all members of the Conference on Security and Co-operation in Europe (CSCE), which became the Organization for Security and Co-operation in Europe (OSCE) in December 1994: a free-market economy, self-determination, free elections and the right to own private property. The first opposition newspaper, *Rilindja Demokratike (Democratic Revival)*, was published in January 1991. By March the membership of the DPA had risen to some 60,000, compared with the PLA's estimated membership of 130,000.

The announcement of the new party came amid an outbreak of violent unrest in Shkodër (Scutari), following protests at the slow pace of reform. The Government's response was the dismissal of more conservative officials and a cautious but significant renunciation of Stalinism. However, strikes in the mining and public-transport sectors in mid-January 1991 forced the second round of government changes in less than six weeks. Fatos Nano and Shkelqim Çani, both reformist economists, were appointed deputy premiers. Such concessions failed to prevent an increasing number of ethnic Greeks from attempting to leave Albania; by mid-January more than 5,000 had crossed the border into Greece. Konstantinos Mitsotakis, the Greek Prime Minister, urged ethnic Greeks to remain in Albania and keep faith with the reform process, fearing that Greece might be overwhelmed by the flight of a substantial proportion of the ethnic Greek Albanians. (The Greek Government estimated that the community could number 250,000–300,000, any of whom could claim Greek citizenship if they crossed the border, although the Albanian authorities only recognized a minority numbering some 50,000.)

February and March 1991 were a time of political crisis in Albania. The status of Enver Hoxha remained the main focus of the conflict between the youth-led, anti-communist opposition in the towns and the older, conservative communists who controlled the security forces and were stronger in the provinces. In response to the growing unrest, Alia declared presidential rule and announced the formation of a new Government and the establishment of a Presidential Council. In early March a new crisis began, when thousands of ethnic Greek Albanians, mostly unemployed young men, commandeered ships in the port of Durrës (Durazzo) and sailed to the Italian port of Brindisi. The Italian navy was ordered to prevent any more ships from landing, and the Albanian authorities placed Durrës under military rule. In all, more than 20,000 people arrived in Brindisi, some of whom subsequently returned to Albania.

THE 1991 GENERAL ELECTION AND ITS AFTERMATH

Despite the unrest that preceded them, Albania's first multi-party elections for six decades took place peacefully at the end of March 1991. After the establishment of the DPA in December 1990, other smaller parties were registered, including the Albanian Republican Party (ARP), the Agrarian Party (AP), the Ecology Party and the Democratic Union of the Greek Minority (OMONIA). All of these smaller parties nominated candidates for the elections, but the main contenders were the DPA and the PLA. While the PLA offered a gradual transition from Stalinism, the DPA campaign promised a transformation of living standards, to be brought about by membership of the European Community (EC, which became the European Union—EU in November 1993), Western financial aid and jobs in Italian and German factories for the thousands of unemployed. It also advocated privatization of land, a policy that was condemned by the PLA, which claimed it would leave peasants landless.

According to official figures, in the first round of elections on 31 March 1991, almost 97% of the 1.9m. electorate voted, the highest level in any multi-party election in the region. Further rounds of voting took place on 7 and 14 April. Overall, the PLA won a total of 169 of the 250 seats in the People's Assembly, just over the two-thirds' majority (167) required to adopt a new constitution; the DPA won 75 seats and OMONIA won five seats. The opposition secured all the urban constituencies, while the rural areas voted predominantly for the PLA. A crucial factor in the defeat of the DPA was the widespread belief that it would privatize and redistribute land, whereas the PLA had promised to protect the peasantry from privatization. The PLA received more support in the Tosk-dominated south, where communist sympathies were strongest. Most independent Western observers attested to the overall fairness of the election, claiming that fraud and manipulation were minimal, although they admitted that the PLA had close control of electoral monitors in some rural areas and had dominated the media. Opposition protests continued.

The new People's Assembly convened on 10 April 1991 and a draft constitution was presented later that month. However, upon the insistence of the opposition, the People's Assembly instead adopted interim legislation outlining the basic principles of the state and renaming the country the Republic of Albania. Political pluralism was formally established, the right to private property was endorsed and the rights to strike, to demonstrate and to emigrate were guaranteed. The Presidium of the People's Assembly was replaced by an executive head of state, a President who was to be elected by two-thirds of the votes cast in the People's Assembly. On 30 April Ramiz Alia was elected to this post. He then resigned all positions in the PLA, in accordance with the new constitutional provisions that prevented the President from holding office in a political party. In early May the People's Assembly approved a new Government, headed by Fatos Nano, the former deputy premier. All the new ministers were PLA members, but the programme presented to the Assembly by Nano envisaged fundamental reforms in both political and economic affairs, including extensive privatization and a rapid shift to a market-based economy. The new Government, however, had immense problems, and Nano admitted that the economy was in crisis.

THE END OF COMMUNIST RULE

The continuing unrest and the deteriorating economic and political situation in the country forced the resignation of Nano's Government on 4 June 1991. On the following day Ylli Bufi, previously Minister of Food in the outgoing Government, was appointed Chairman of the Council of Ministers (Prime Minister), and a new 'Government of National Stability', with a total of 12 non-communist ministers, was formed. Further changes were evident at the 10th Congress of the PLA, which also took place in June. The PLA was renamed the Socialist Party of Albania (SPA) and the SPA's new manifesto stated that the party would be modern and progressive, committed to democracy, social justice and economic reform. Despite domestic unrest, Albania continued its reintegration into international society. In June it was finally admitted to the CSCE and diplomatic relations were established with the EC. However, armed conflict in Yugoslavia did not encourage any further development of Balkan co-operation. The Albanian Government issued statements containing strong criticism of the policies of the Serbian leadership in Kosovo, and in October the People's Assembly voted to recognize the 'Republic of Kosovo' as a 'sovereign and independent state'.

Towards the end of 1991 there were further strikes, particularly in the fuel-supply industry, and opposition demonstrations were staged in October to demand new elections and the resignation of President Alia. In late November the crisis deepened when Berisha, the Chairman of the DPA, demanded that DPA members resign from the Government, and all seven ministers left the 21-member Council of Ministers. Berisha accused the SPA of deliberately obstructing the reform process in the countryside and instigating increased violent crime and the refugee crisis. However, Pashko, the incumbent Deputy Prime Minister, opposed the dissolution of the Government, arguing that it would lead to anarchy. Nevertheless, on 6 December Bufi and his Government resigned. In an attempt to restore some stability, President Alia appointed a temporary Government, headed by Vilson Ahmeti, until further elections were held in March 1992.

THE BERISHA PRESIDENCY

In the elections of 21 March 1992 the DPA won an overwhelming victory, winning 62% of votes cast in the first round, while support for the SPA fell to just 26%. On 29 March the DPA consolidated its first-round victory, by securing a further 11 seats in areas where a second round of voting was necessary. In total, the DPA received 92 seats in the new legislature, while the SPA obtained only 38; the Social Democratic Party (SDP) won seven seats, the Union of Human Rights Party (UHRP) two seats, and the ARP one seat. The defeat of the SPA finally ended five decades of communist rule, a process completed on 3 April by the resignation of Alia. On 9 April Sali Berisha was elected to the presidency by a large parliamentary majority. Berisha then appointed the new Government, led by Aleksander Meksi, a member of the DPA. In addition to the premiership, the DPA occupied 14 ministries in the new administration, while the SDP and the ARP received one portfolio each; the SPA was not represented.

The new, youthful and inexperienced cabinet encountered a huge range of problems. Industrial and agricultural production had declined disastrously, and there were high levels of unemployment. In addition, the rapid dismantling of the one-party state had led to an erosion of state authority, resulting in a sharp increase in serious crime, which acted as a major deterrent to foreign investment. Following the collapse in agricultural production, Albania's population was almost entirely dependent on foreign food aid, and only 'Operation Pelican', the Italian food-distribution programme, prevented mass starvation. In view of this social and economic hardship, it was not surprising that support for the DPA decreased sharply at local elections in late July 1992. The DPA obtained just 43% of the votes cast, significantly fewer than in the March general election, while the SPA's share of the votes cast rose to 41%. Moreover, in September serious divisions within the DPA culminated in the defection of several leading members of the party to form a new political grouping, the Albanian Democratic Alliance (later the Democratic Alliance Party—DAP). Among them was Gramoz Pashko, who strongly criticized President Berisha's administration for becoming more authoritarian and intolerant, and described the party's programme as 'right-wing extremism'. Moreover, with the arrest of former President Alia in the same month, there were accusations that corruption charges against former communist officials had been brought in an attempt to distract public opinion from social and economic conditions.

President Berisha's foreign policy, which his opponents accused him of conducting largely single-handed, was marked by controversy, particularly concerning Albania's relations with Muslim countries, with the former Yugoslav republic of Macedonia (FYRM) and with Greece. On 2 December 1992, on the initiative of Berisha, Albania became a member of the Organization of the Islamic Conference (OIC). The decision was strongly opposed by the SPA, which was increasingly concerned about greater activity by Muslim organizations in

Albania and relatively large amounts of aid received from Islamist states. Berisha's enthusiasm for the development of close relations with Muslim countries, and above all with Turkey, reflected not only a need for economic assistance, but a desire to gain some measure of support should the conflict in Bosnia and Herzegovina spread south to Kosovo or if Albanian-Greek relations should worsen yet further.

Relations with Greece deteriorated rapidly during 1992 and 1993, owing to the alleged mistreatment of the Greek minority in southern Albania and the influx of Albanian refugees into Greece. In late June 1993 the Albanian authorities expelled Archimandrite Chrysostomos Maidans, a senior Greek Orthodox clergyman, from Albania, accusing him of advocating the secession of southern Albania to Greece. Greece retaliated by deporting some 20,000 Albanian immigrants, a small part of the estimated 150,000 Albanians believed to have entered Greece since 1990, most of them illegally. Although the position of the Greek minority had improved considerably since the 1980s—it enjoyed freedom of religion and had its own Greek-language schools, newspapers, publishing houses and broadcasting facilities—there were continued allegations of ill-treatment of ethnic Greeks by Albanian security forces. There was also strong criticism of the electoral law, which outlawed the Greeks' main party, OMONIA (instead they gained representation through the UHRP). Although there was a variety of opinion in the Greek community, many seemed to favour recognition of a separate 'Epirot' identity, leading to the gradual integration of the south of Albania into the Epirus region of northern Greece.

Albanian-Greek relations continued to deteriorate throughout 1993. The arrests at the end of October of the mayors of two predominantly ethnic Greek villages in southern Albania, Vouliarates and Dervichani, following their hoisting of Greek flags to commemorate the 'Ochi' Day (anniversary of Greece's defiance of Italy's 1940 ultimatum) celebrations of 28 October, caused indignation on the part of the Greek Government and fear among the Greek minority. The protest among ethnic Greeks was a demonstration against the Albanian Government's alleged campaign to de-Hellenize 'Northern Epirus'.

At the beginning of April 1994 the first paramilitary violence broke out, with an attack on an Albanian border unit in the village of Peshkopi near the Greek frontier, in which two guards were killed and three others wounded. A Greek extremist group, known as the Northern Epirus Liberation Front, claimed responsibility for the raid. President Berisha linked the attack to Greece's support for Serbia (Yugoslavia), claiming that it was designed to encourage Serbian aggression in the north of the Balkans and destabilize the south of the region for expansionist reasons. The Greek Government rejected the charges. The following week four leaders of OMONIA were arrested and tried with complicity in the attack. Greece immediately vetoed a proposed loan by the EU to Albania in protest. However, relations with Greece improved considerably thereafter, after the Albanian Government recognized the importance of Albanian workers' remittances from Greece. In March 1996 the Greek President, Konstantinos Stefanopoulos, signed a Treaty of Mutual Friendship and Co-operation with President Berisha.

Despite some improvement in the Albanian economy in 1992–93, President Berisha's administration continued to confront considerable social and economic problems, in addition to the problems caused by the unstable international environment in the Balkans. During 1993 Albanian politics became sharply polarized. The right-wing Balli Kombëtar faction of the DPA accounted for about one-half of all DPA deputies in the People's Assembly by mid-1993, and remained in a position to exert considerable influence on the leadership. The shift to more nationalistic and anti-communist policies by the DPA prompted attempts by the SDP and the Republicans to distance themselves from the DPA, while remaining in the Government.

During 1992–93 Ramiz Alia, Fatos Nano and other former communist leaders were arrested and variously charged with corruption and the misuse of power, thus giving added credence to reports that the right wing of the DPA was gaining influence over President Berisha's administration. The SPA, meanwhile, remained politically isolated and seriously damaged by the continuing arrests and trials of its members for their actions under the communist regime. In April 1994 Nano, the SPA leader, was sentenced to 12 years in prison, after being found guilty of channelling large profits to providers of food aid and of falsifying official documents during his brief term as Prime Minister in 1991. At the beginning of July 1994 the ongoing series of political trials culminated in the sentencing of former President Alia to nine years in prison for abuse of power and violating the rights of citizens. A former premier, Adil Çarçani, was found guilty of similar charges, but his five-year prison term was suspended because of his poor health. These events, however, did little to alleviate the increasingly deep public resentment felt throughout the country at the high level of corruption in public life. In July 1995 Alia was released from prison, along with about 30 other political prisoners, as part of a general amnesty, in a further bid to ensure Albania's admittance to the Council of Europe.

The Constitutional Referendum

Although interim constitutional arrangements had been in place since 1991, work on drafting a new constitution did not begin until mid-1993. The slow progress of the constitutional reform bill was eventually accelerated when it was believed that Albania had a realistic chance of being granted admission to the Council of Europe once an acceptable basic law had been decided upon. Constitutional legislation, however, required a two-thirds' majority in parliament, and the DPA had a majority of only eight. President Berisha attempted to avoid the parliamentary process by personally appointing a Constituent Assembly to draft the new fundamental provisions and by proposing that it be endorsed by a referendum (although only the People's Assembly was empowered to order such a poll). A referendum was arranged following parliamentary rejection of the draft Constitution in October 1994 (partly representing a protest by SDP deputies at the Government's impeding of corruption investigations) and even some DPA deputies abstained. The draft was controversial as a result of the balance of power between executive and legislature. Thus, the President was to be given increased power in official appointments and was to be authorized to halt criminal investigations into corruption. Most opponents were also concerned about assuring the independence of the judiciary. Just before the referendum three judges at the Constitutional Court resigned in protest at the disregard for parliamentary approval of the poll.

The referendum was the first major test of national support for the DPA since its election victory in March 1992, but the final result of the plebiscite, held on 6 November 1994, demonstrated that the majority of voters were firmly opposed to the new Constitution: of the 84.4% of Albania's electorate taking part in the referendum, 53.9% voted against the proposals. The result was not only a vote of 'no confidence' in the DPA Government, but also in the President, and the result seriously weakened Berisha's position. The opposition immediately demanded his resignation and that the general election, scheduled for April 1996, be brought forward. Dhimitër Anagnosti, the Minister of Culture, Youth and Sport, resigned in protest at President Berisha's refusal to relinquish his post, and the dismissal and subsequent replacement of nine out of the 19 members of the Cabinet followed. Berisha's beleaguered administration lost the last of its coalition support as

the ARP withdrew from the Government, claiming that the DPA was incapable of fighting corruption. Berisha also lost some nationalist support, when four ethnic Greek political activists, arrested in April, were released by the High Court at the beginning of February 1995.

THE 1996 GENERAL ELECTION AND ITS AFTERMATH

Prior to the general election, scheduled for early 1996, the DPA devised a number of new and radical laws, with the apparent motive of ensuring the party a second victory. The first, the so-called 'Genocide Law', which was narrowly approved by the People's Assembly at the end of September 1995, prohibited anyone who had occupied a position of power before 31 March 1991 (that is, under the communist regime) from holding parliamentary, judicial or governmental office until 2002. This legislation provided the basis for a further enactment, the 'Verification Law', which was designed to assess the suitability of election candidates through a government-appointed Commission on the Scrutiny of Political Figures. The opposition, however, maintained that there was no need for such laws, because Articles 73 and 74 of the existing penal code allowed for the arrest and prosecution of those who held high office under the old regime. By the time of the 1996 general election, the Genocide Law had effectively banned a total of 136 candidates, including not only the leaders of the two main opposition parties, Skënder Gjinushi of the SDP and Fatos Nano of the SPA, but also more than one-quarter of the incumbent SPA deputies, through accusations of collaboration with the former regime on the basis of still-classified secret-police files. Communist and anti-communist factions made mutual allegations relating to before the Second World War. In February 1996 Alia was arrested under the legislation; he was acquitted in October 1997.

However, the Genocide Law appeared to have been drafted with the aim of isolating the SPA by destroying the smaller opposition parties, thereby preventing the formation of a strong opposition coalition. The DPA also began scrutinizing the existing electoral law, under which 4% of votes cast ensured legislative representation. The ruling party made an unsuccessful attempt to raise the minimum to 10%, provoking harsh criticism from the EU and the USA. In a further move to ensure its majority in the new People's Assembly, by means of a new electoral law, the DPA managed to increase the number of directly elected legislative seats from 100 to 115, thus minimizing the chances of the smaller parties gaining representation. In addition, observers were deeply concerned about the alleged widespread intimidation of supporters of the opposition, with many journalists forced to leave the country, fearful of arrest. Opposition leaders stressed the importance of monitoring any attempt to adjust the existing electoral law, which all opposition parties considered to be fair. The 1992 electoral law had been drafted after a six-month study of the laws of such differing countries as Bulgaria, Germany, Hungary and the United Kingdom, and was deemed appropriate for smaller parties, providing a balance between the majority ('first-past-the-post') system and the proportional system.

At the beginning of October 1995 the SPA initiated its parliamentary election campaign, which was aimed at attracting the votes of those disaffected with the DPA. However, despite efforts to project itself as a highly organized and united party, the SPA was affected by deep division, which was publicly exploited by the powerful DPA media organs. Following the 1992 elections, two distinct factions had emerged within the SPA: the traditional and conservative communists; and a younger, more liberal element, known as Eurosocialists. With its leader, Nano, still in prison, the SPA failed in its attempts to limit the divisions and in March 1996 the Albanian New Socialist Party was created by members of the Eurosocialist faction.

As the elections approached there were widespread allegations of intimidation by the police and secret service, mainly of members of the SPA and the DAP. Opposition parties were also banned from holding rallies in town centres. The first round of voting, on 26 May 1996, was boycotted by all but one opposition party, in protest at these irregularities. The DPA consequently won a total of 95 of the 115 directly elected seats and 67.8% of the popular vote. In a series of 'run-off' elections, held on 2 June, the party acquired further seats, raising its total to more than the two-thirds' majority required to pass constitutional laws. The conduct of the general election was widely claimed to have been fraudulent, and was condemned by representatives of the international community, including the OSCE. There were further protests at the violent dispersal of an SPA rally in late May. In response to international pressure, President Berisha agreed to conduct an investigation into the behaviour of the police at the rally and to organize further elections in the 17 constituencies where alleged manipulation of the result had been most serious. With the majority of the opposition continuing to boycott the voting, however, on 16 June the DPA was opposed by only a few minority right-wing parties, and won every seat, securing an overall 122 of the total 140 seats. Of the few remaining seats, the SPA won 10, the ARP and the UHRP each acquired three, and the National Front two. The new People's Assembly convened on 1 July 1996, amid Western concern that four years of relative political stability and economic progress in Albania were coming to an end.

The 'Pyramid' Banking Crisis and Civil Unrest

In January 1997 the collapse of several popular, 'pyramid' investment schemes (which had claimed to offer high rates of interest), resulting in huge losses to individual savers, prompted violent anti-Government demonstrations, particularly in Tirana and the southern town of Vlorë. It was widely believed that members of the Government were associated with the 'pyramid' banking schemes, which allegedly had been used to finance illegal activities. The People's Assembly adopted legislation prohibiting the schemes and granted President Berisha emergency powers to restore order. Many protesters were arrested and some killed in ensuing violent clashes between security forces and demonstrators, who continued to demand the President's resignation and state reimbursement for their financial losses. Nevertheless, on 3 March Berisha was re-elected, unopposed, by the legislature for a second five-year term; the SPA continued to boycott the People's Assembly, after having refused to recognize the results of the 1996 general election.

Exacerbated by the financial crisis, an escalation in hostilities between insurgents and government forces in the south of the country prompted President Berisha to declare a national state of emergency at the beginning of March 1997. New regulations empowered troops to shoot demonstrators and imposed total official censorship. Insurgent groups gained control of the southern towns of Vlorë, Sarandë and Gjirokastër, as large numbers of government forces defected to the rebels. With opposition to the regime steadily increasing, particularly in the south, a former SPA mayor of Gjirokastër, Bashkim Fino, was appointed Prime Minister. Berisha subsequently approved the formation of a Government of National Reconciliation, which included representatives of eight opposition parties. Despite these concessions, the insurgency continued, reaching the northern town of Tropojë and Tirana, where the rebels seized the airport. Many prisoners, including Nano and Alia, were released; Nano was subsequently granted an official pardon by Berisha. Western European and US nationals were evacuated and thousands of

Albanians fled to Italy, amid extreme hardship and fears that the fighting would escalate into widespread civil conflict.

By late March 1997 it was reported that government forces had regained control of Tirana and the north was largely held by paramilitary units loyal to President Berisha. The south of the country was controlled by anti-Government groups, and the Government of National Reconciliation requested foreign military assistance in the restoration of civil order. In late March the new premier, Fino, attended a meeting of EU foreign ministers in Rome, Italy, to appeal for the establishment of a multinational force to supervise humanitarian aid distribution in Albania. Fino also initiated discussions with rebel leaders, although Berisha refused to support negotiations with the insurgents. A 5,915-member Multinational Protection Force for Albania, sanctioned by the UN Security Council, began to arrive in mid-April and was deployed in government-controlled regions of northern and central Albania.

At the beginning of April 1997 the SPA ended its boycott of the People's Assembly, which subsequently voted to end press restrictions that had been imposed under the state of emergency, and also introduced legislation to regulate 'pyramid' investment schemes. It was agreed that further elections would take place by the end of June, but there was disagreement over the number of parliamentary deputies who would be elected by proportional representation. In May DPA-sponsored legislation on a new electoral system was approved, despite a further boycott by SPA deputies. Under the system, the number of deputies in the People's Assembly was to be increased from 140 to 155, of whom 115 were to be directly elected and the remainder elected on the basis of proportional representation. The SPA and its allied parties (the AP, the DAP, the SDP and the UHRP) agreed to participate in the elections only after President Berisha complied to a stipulation that an electoral commission be appointed by the interim Government of National Reconciliation; the establishment of the new, 17-member body, chaired by a member of the DPA, was announced later in May.

THE 1997 GENERAL ELECTION

After a campaign disrupted by a number of violent incidents, including bomb explosions in Tirana and the attempted assassination of President Berisha at a rally near Durrës, the first and second rounds of voting in the general election took place on 29 June and 6 July 1997, respectively. Later in July the Central Electoral Commission announced that the SPA had secured 101 of the 155 seats in the enlarged People's Assembly, with the DPA winning 29 seats. The SPA and its allied parties had thereby received the two-thirds' majority needed for the approval of constitutional amendments. The electoral process was declared satisfactory by OSCE observers. A referendum on the restoration of the monarchy, conducted at the same time as the first round of voting, resulted in 66.7% of votes in favour of retaining the republic.

On 24 July 1997, following the resignation of the widely discredited Berisha, Dr Rexhep Mejdani, the Secretary-General of the SPA, was elected President by the People's Assembly. A new Council of Ministers was appointed, comprising representatives of the SPA and its allies, with former premier Nano as the head of government and Fino as his deputy. It was quickly apparent that the administration would operate differently to its predecessor. Nano's Government would be based on an executive premiership, with President Mejdani in primarily an honorary role. Mejdani was a moderate politician who had never been a member of the ACP under Enver Hoxha, unlike Nano and Berisha. He was appointed to the Presidential Council under Alia in 1991, shortly before the collapse of the communist regime. The new Government submitted a programme for the restoration of civil order and economic reconstruction, which was supported in the People's Assembly.

By the end of August 1997 the Multinational Protection Force had departed and government troops had restored some order in the south of the country. Foreign advisers returned to Albania to assist the Government in the reorganization of the military and security forces. In early September a parliamentary commission was established to draft a new constitution, in accordance with amendments proposed by the Government. However, relations between the SPA and the DPA continued to deteriorate. In October Berisha was re-elected Chairman of the DPA.

Apart from Albania's serious economic problems, as well as continuing DPA-incited agitation, increasing tension in the Yugoslav province of Kosovo once again threatened to destabilize the Balkan region. In November 1997, following negotiations between Prime Minister Nano and Slobodan Milošević, the President of the Federal Republic of Yugoslavia (FRY), it was announced that relations between the two countries were to be normalized, although Milošević emphasized that the situation in Kosovo remained an internal issue. However, an intensification of Serbian activity against the ethnic Albanian majority in Kosovo in early 1998 led to repeated denunciations of Serbian actions by the Albanian Government. In March huge crowds gathered in Tirana to denounce Serbian aggression in Kosovo, and President Mejdani alleged that Serbia was guilty of 'brutal violence' against ethnic Albanian civilians. In April border clashes between Yugoslav troops and smugglers transporting weapons from Albania to separatist guerrillas in Kosovo strengthened fears that the crisis there could lead to a conflict that would extend beyond the FRY's borders. The Albanian Minister of Foreign Affairs, Paskal Milo, denied the claims of the Serbian Government that the Albanian administration was covertly assisting the smuggling of weapons from northern Albania into Kosovo. By June about 20,000 ethnic Albanian refugees had crossed into Albania to escape the fighting between Yugoslav forces and Kosovar guerrillas. The Government accused the Serbian administration of a deliberate strategy of forced expulsions and appealed to Western officials for military intervention to halt what it characterized as a genocidal campaign.

Meanwhile, the Nano Government was also dealing with continued civil unrest within Albania. On 22 February 1998, in the worst outbreak of violence in the country since the anarchy of March 1997, rioters and rebel police units took control of the northern town of Shkodër (traditionally a stronghold of DPA and monarchist support), after looting and burning banks, shops and civic buildings. Two days later security forces regained control of the town, but Berisha accused the Government of violating the law and urged Albanians to widen their protests and demand new elections, despite the requests of European leaders to halt opposition agitation. Relations between the Government and the opposition deteriorated significantly over the next few months.

The partial local elections of 21 June 1998, conducted in seven municipalities and nine communes, were contested by broad electoral pacts led by the principal parties. The elections, the conduct of which was declared satisfactory by OSCE observers, resulted in a significant victory for the Alliance for the State grouping, comprising the governing SPA, the DAP, the SDP, the AP, the UHRP and the National Unity Party. The other coalition, the Union for Democracy, consisted of the DPA, the Christian Democratic Party, the Democratic Unity Party, the Legality Movement Party and the Union of Social Democrats. On 6 July the People's Assembly approved the final report of the parliamentary commission established to investigate the civil unrest of January–March 1997. The report recommended that the state bring prosecutions against several leading DPA officials, including former President Berisha, for the violation of constitutional provisions and the unlawful use of force against protesters. Berisha resisted requests for his resignation from members of his own party and the DPA subsequently announced a further boycott of parliament.

On 12 September 1998 Azem Hajdari, a popular politician and one of Berisha's chief deputies in the DPA, was shot dead, along with his two bodyguards, outside the party headquarters in Tirana. Berisha publicly blamed Nano and the SPA for the killing and demanded the Government's resignation. On the following day several thousand supporters of Berisha were involved in violent protests, during which they attacked the parliament building and the Prime Minister's offices, seized control of the state television and radio centre and captured at least four army tanks. After two days of lawlessness on the streets of the capital, which also witnessed widespread looting and vandalism, police units loyal to the Government recaptured the buildings occupied by Berisha's followers, after clashes in which three rebels were killed and 14 wounded, according to official sources. Nano accused Berisha and his associates of a deliberate attempt to stage a coup and asserted that they would be tried and sentenced accordingly.

On 28 September 1998 Nano resigned from the premiership, claiming that his position had become untenable, owing to the constant pressure being applied by his political enemies and the absence of support from within the Government. In his address to President Mejdani, Nano declared that he took responsibility for the breakdown of public order and hoped that his resignation would permit the Government and the opposition to adopt more constructive approaches. The following day SPA deputies voted to nominate the Secretary-General of the party, Pandeli Majko, as the new Prime Minister. Majko formed a new Government in early October.

The new Constitution, which was narrowly adopted by a referendum on 22 November 1998, produced a weak victory for the Government, and consequently there were some tentative grounds for optimism regarding Albania's internal politics. The overall security situation, however, remained very poor. This was especially apparent in the north of the country, where Kosovo Liberation Army (KLA) militia had established their bases and were constantly crossing the border with Yugoslavia. The Albanian Government was extremely anxious to avoid any confrontation with the large number of Serbian troops stationed at the other side of the border, yet in the interests of national solidarity, the Albanian authorities were obliged to ignore the activities of the Kosovar insurgents in Albania.

In March 1999 large numbers of Kosovar refugees arrived in northern Albania, following efforts by the Serb military to suppress KLA operations in the province. On 24 March NATO launched an air offensive against Yugoslavia, following the failure of President Milošević to comply with demands to withdraw Serbian forces from Kosovo. By April the refugee crisis worsened, with almost 500,000 Kosovar Albanians crossing the border into Albania. The country was subsequently turned into a key logistics centre for NATO troops, who were deployed in northern Albania to assist in the huge humanitarian relief effort. In June the NATO bombardment ended and KFOR troops were deployed in Kosovo, enabling the gradual repatriation of refugees. NATO subsequently reduced its contingent in Albania to around 8,000 troops.

During the second half of 1999 the perpetually volatile nature of Albanian politics was further polarized by the defeat of moderate elements in the two main political parties. In October the opposition DPA re-elected Sali Berisha as its leader, in a reverse for moderates within the party, led by the party's deputy leader, Genc Pollo, who wished to see a freer exchange of ideas in the party and more liberal policies. In the same month Fatos Nano returned to power by narrowly defeating Majko for the post of leader of the SPA. Majko was forced to resign and his 30 year-old deputy, Illir Meta, was chosen as a compromise candidate in order to avert a potential rebellion that threatened to split the ruling party. The following month, the DPA leadership criticized moderate deputies, who ignored party orders by attending the vote of confidence in the new socialist Government. In response, Pollo, who had been expelled from the DPA's National Council, accused Berisha of corruption as the moderates announced the formation of the Democratic Alternative within the party, in an attempt to gain more party support by challenging the dominant position of Berisha.

While national reconciliation within Albania was making slow progress, the concept of regenerating links between the nation as a whole was gathering momentum. Albania hoped to provide a national support mechanism for all the ethnic Albanians in the southern Balkans. In the aftermath of the Kosovo crisis, Albania had become a base for instigating pan-Albanian initiatives on social, cultural, economic and political grounds. As a result, the 'National Question' regarding the future status of Albanians living outside Albania continued to dominate Albanian foreign policy.

THE OCTOBER 2000 LOCAL ELECTIONS

There was a heavily polarized political scene prior to the local elections on 1 and 15 October 2000, which represented the first test of popular support for the SPA-led Government since it came to power in 1997. After losing power, former President Sali Berisha and the main opposition DPA leadership had refused to accept the legitimacy of the socialist-led coalition. Consequently, the DPA continued to undermine the Government and to disrupt the political process in general. The DPA urged its members to boycott the local elections, and demanded that detailed amendments be made to the draft electoral code, together with changes to the Central Electoral Commission. Following the decisive victory of the SPA, the DPA denounced the results as fraudulent, citing the manipulation of voters' lists. Representatives of Albania's ethnic Greek minority also claimed violations in electoral procedures, particularly in the southern, predominantly ethnic Greek district of Himara. Nevertheless, although the OSCE declared that some serious irregularities had occurred, the fraud was not considered sufficiently significant to influence the overall result. Relations with the Greek minority were becoming increasingly sensitive, however. OMONIA accused the Government of marginalizing minority demands over land ownership, disregarding the quota for minority representation in police and army structures, and stalling the return of Christian Orthodox monasteries to religious institutions. Meanwhile, many Albanians accused representatives of the Greek minority of gathering funds from Greek nationalist lobbies to Hellenize the southern coast of Albania. Both the Albanian and Greek Governments, however, recognized the importance of maintaining good bilateral relations. Greece no longer threatened to deport Albanian workers, the expulsion of whom would seriously harm both countries' economies: Greece would lose indispensable cheap labour, and Albania would lose the workers' valuable remittances. Therefore, following a meeting in Athens, Greece, in December 2000, Albania agreed to accelerate the passing of legislation covering Greek minority rights, while Greece pledged to continue to provide comprehensive assistance to Albania in several fields.

In contrast to the situation in 1998, the main threat to the stability of Albania by the early 2000s came from forces outside the country—from the Albanian-inhabited territories of the former Yugoslavia, and internationally-based organized crime. From the end of the 1990s the Government had continued to consolidate public order throughout the country.

None the less, Albania became a major transit centre for the trafficking of drugs and illegal immigrants into Western Europe. By 2001 the main priority was no longer that of trying to eliminate criminal individuals or gangs, as had been the previous focus of police activity. Instead, the biggest challenge for the security forces was posed by organized crime, which had grown steadily more sophisticated, as it consolidated links between Albanian diaspora clans, and the wider world of organized crime. Such crime proved more difficult to solve because the hierarchy of these criminal networks were largely based outside Albania.

In January 2001 Albania re-established diplomatic relations with Yugoslavia, which were severed in March 1999, following Albania's support for the NATO bombing campaign against Yugoslavia. The resumption of diplomatic ties followed the ousting of President Slobodan Milošević and the inauguration of the new Government of President Vojislav Koštunica in the FRY in late 2000. However, with the status of Kosovo still unresolved, Albania faced the prospect of renewed fighting on its borders with the countries of the former Yugoslavia. In February 2001 Albania's relations with the FYRM became strained after fighting broke out between ethnic Albanian rebels and Macedonian troops. The Albanian Government immediately distanced itself from the insurgents by declaring a policy of 'zero tolerance' towards anyone caught supplying weapons to the Macedonian Albanians. Checkpoints were subsequently set up on all roads leading to Macedonia. Albania was concerned at a possible weakening in international support should it be seen to be taking no action to avert the crisis. In view of the clashes following soon after a further attack by ethnic Albanian rebels against Serbian forces in the Preševo Valley area of southern Serbia, the Albanian authorities were anxious to demonstrate their opposition to the concept of a 'greater Albania'.

THE 2001 GENERAL ELECTION

In February 2001 a reformist faction within the DPA announced the formation of a new political association, known as the New Democratic Party (NDP), headed by Pollo. The new party aimed to gain support from right-wing elements, which had recently become alienated from the DPA, owing to its anti-progressive stance and Berisha's rigid authoritarianism. In April a number of opposition parties, led by the DPA, established an electoral alliance, known as the Union for Victory, in preparation for the forthcoming legislative elections.

The first ballot of the elections to the People's Assembly was held on 24 June 2001, and further rounds of voting were conducted throughout July. In August it was finally announced that the SPA had won a decisive victory, securing 73 seats in the 140-member legislature, while the Union for Victory coalition had obtained 46 seats. The SPA consequently retained a sufficient majority to form a new government and, crucially, with the support of allied parties, to elect a new president in 2002, when Mejdani's term of office expired. (Berisha, however, rejected the election results, and announced that the Union for Victory would boycott the People's Assembly.) International observers declared the elections to be the most free and fair to be conducted in Albania, although concerns remained regarding isolated electoral irregularities. Overall, however, the elections were judged to have been relatively orderly and peaceful. Meta was returned to the office of Prime Minister and a reorganized Council of Ministers was approved on 7 September.

Political Discord

In early 2002 severe division developed within the SPA between supporters of Meta and Nano. Nano accused Meta's Government of corruption, forcing the resignation of four SPA ministers, and on 29 January Meta tendered his resignation, after failing to resolve four months of bitter dispute within the SPA, and in a perceived effort to prevent the party from dividing. Majko, an ally of Meta and hitherto the Minister of Defence, became the new Prime Minister. Following negotiations between the two SPA factions, a new transitional Council of Ministers, in which posts were divided between supporters of Nano and Meta, was established. Deputies from the DPA-led Union for Victory decided to resume participation in the People's Assembly, thereby ending a five-month boycott of the legislature.

Meanwhile, as the expiry of Mejdani's term of office approached, it became apparent that Nano (who had announced his intention of contesting the presidency) would be unable to secure majority support in the People's Assembly, owing to strong opposition from Berisha. Following prolonged negotiations between the SPA and the DPA, the parties agreed to nominate Alfred Moisiu, a retired general who had served in the Berisha administration. He was elected by 97 of the 140 deputies in the People's Assembly on 24 June, and was inaugurated on 24 July (when Mejdani's tenure officially expired). On the following day Majko resigned as Prime Minister, after the SPA General Steering Committee decided that the party's Chairman should head the administration. A new Government, led by Nano, was approved at the end of the month, with Majko returning to his former position as Minister of Defence.

In late June 2002 the claimant to the throne and son of King Zog, Leka Zogu, returned to Albania from exile, following a vote in the People's Assembly. (He had previously returned to Albania in 1997, but had lost a referendum on the restoration of the monarchy and, following ensuing violent protests in which three people were killed, had left Albania before he could be detained by the police.) He was granted an official pardon by President Mejdani in early 2002. Despite his stated wish for a further referendum on the restoration of the monarchy, public opinion appeared to be largely indifferent to his presence in the country.

Albania's key foreign policy goal remains achieving the country's integration into the EU and NATO. Preliminary negotiations with the EU on the signature of a Stabilization and Association Agreement officially commenced in January 2003. The Albanian Government endeavoured to remain as neutral as possible regarding the ethnic conflicts in Kosovo, southern Serbia and the FYRM, and has established normal relations with neighbouring Slavic countries. Prior to a NATO summit meeting in Prague, Czech Republic, in November 2002, the Presidents of Albania, Croatia and the FYRM agreed to adopt a common strategy for integration. Although those countries were not among the seven candidate nations invited at the summit to engage in accession discussions, NATO officials indicated that Albania's proposed entry would be considered in the future, subject to the implementation of further democratic and military reforms. In May 2003 Nano signed a bilateral agreement with the US Government concerning the new International Criminal Court, prompting criticism from the EU, which urged the People's Assembly not to ratify the accord. During a visit to Albania in early June, the US Secretary of Defense, Donald Rumsfeld, expressed gratitude for the support of the Albanian Government (which had contributed 75 troops) for US-led military operations in Iraq. Under a bilateral co-operation plan, the USA was to increase its military presence in Albania (where a NATO headquarters had been established in June 2002). Also in 2003 negotiations between the Governments of Albania and Greece were expected to result in an agreement, whereby ethnic Greek Albanians would be granted dual citizenship.

Although the current political climate is calmer and stability has been restored to most of the country, severe social and economic problems remain, which if left unresolved could result in further political insecurity. Albania's institutions are weakened by endemic corruption and an inefficient public administration, which is greatly impeding the country's reform process. Other major difficulties include an increase in organized crime, a weak judiciary, high unemployment, low production, severe environmental problems, and an ongoing energy crisis.

The Economy

Prof. MICHAEL KASER

Albania's continuing state of poverty contrasts with the country's estimated reserves of extractable minerals, worth some US $50,000m., and onshore petroleum reserves, worth some $40,000m. (in addition to offshore deposits, including natural gas, which were as yet unmeasured). Albania has the world's fourth-largest chromite (chromium ore) reserves and substantial deposits of copper, iron-nickel, manganese and bauxite. There are also deposits of phosphate, calcium, kaolin, barytes, gypsum, magnesite and olivinite, and of high-quality building materials (dolomite, marble, granite, alabaster, limestone and sand). Natural-resource exports continue to offer the best long-term prospects, conditional on domestic and foreign capital investment, but, in the short term, the low cost of labour had been exploited by a substantial 'outward processing trade', manufacturing goods (mainly clothing and leatherwear) from contractors' own materials. Such trade accounted for more than two-thirds of total exports in 2002, when the value of total exports amounted to $330m., and imports to $1,485m. The largest offset to the trade deficit of $1,155m. was remittances from Albanians living abroad (some 15% of the population had left Albania since the relaxation, in 1990, of an absolute ban on emigration), which were

$543m. in 2001 and $549m. in 2002, covering about 50% of the trade deficit. The contribution of foreign direct investment declined markedly to $156m. (about 10%) in 2002, compared with $204m. in 2001. Official transfers were steady at $115m. in 2002, compared with $125m. in 2001. These and other inflows led to a rise in gross international reserves (from $737m. in 2001 to $809m. in 2002), equivalent to 4.7 months and 4.5 months of imports of goods and services, respectively. External confidence to lend to Albania was boosted by the IMF's approval of a three-year Poverty Reduction and Growth Facility (PRGF) in mid-2002, requiring the imposition of a strict programme of monetary stabilization, privatization and institutional reform.

Albania's underdevelopment was largely attributable to the policy, under the dictatorship of Enver Hoxha (from 1943), of economic isolationism and a more rigidly centralized administration than in other European communist states, with fixed prices, state or co-operative ownership of all means of production and the planned determination of output. The prohibition of even small-scale private crafts or farming and of all private trading was matched by total state control of investment and foreign trade, and the prohibition of migration.

After Hoxha's death in 1985, in a vain attempt to modernize the underdeveloped economy, the leadership relaxed a few controls, but without changing its ideological basis. Although the elections of March–April 1991 still gave a majority to the government party (which shortly afterwards reconstituted itself as the Socialist Party of Albania—SPA), a new opposition group, the Democratic Party of Albania (DPA), secured enough support to be admitted into a 'Government of National Solidarity'. Short-lived as the coalition was, it launched general economic liberalization and a depoliticization of state institutions. Following the victory of the DPA in the elections of March 1992, the new administration introduced policies designed to produce a radical transformation of the economic system, including large-scale privatization and the introduction of a market economy. Such policies, although necessary, remained fraught with difficulties, as both industrial and agricultural production had declined sharply, and the economy had become dependent on external assistance. A recovery in production began in 1993, mainly as agriculture emerged from the chaos of decollectivization: real GDP in 1996 was already 85% of that of 1989. If the substantial 'unofficial economy' could be taken into account, the pre-1989 level might well have been reached. The process of decontrol had, however, been too rapid: while some 75% of officially measured GDP was generated in the private sector, the legal and regulatory framework remained primitive. The laws on banking and on deposit-taking went little further than generalities on mutual contract, and advantage was taken by purveyors of unsound 'pyramid' schemes (in which early depositors were paid excessive returns from the funds of later depositors), which either had to find high-yielding investments or be revealed as fraudulent. As schemes ceased payment of either interest or capital, violent protests enveloped one-third of the country in early 1997—the southern, SPA-supporting zone—and forced the DPA Government, support for which had always been concentrated in the north, to bring forward legislative elections to mid-1997. Following these elections, in June, the incoming SPA-led coalition Government, in accordance with Albania's agreement with the IMF, undertook measures to reverse a 7% decline in GDP and to reduce the annual average rate of inflation. Growth in GDP was 8.0% in 1998 (one of the highest levels in Europe), and remained at 7.8% in 2000, but declined to an estimated 4.7% in 2002 (principally owing to political dissension, continuing energy shortages and severe flooding in that year). Annual average inflation, after reaching a rate of 32.1% in 1997, declined to a negligible level in 2000, but registered a 5.6% rise in 2002. Following long-standing political tension, a new SPA-led Government was installed in July 2002 (the third since elections in June 2001); nevertheless, continuing weakness of governance was deemed to pose a risk to the pace of reform (see below). Negotiations with the European Union (EU) on a Stabilization and Association Agreement officially commenced at the end of January 2003.

THE ALBANIAN ECONOMY UNDER COMMUNISM

Before the Second World War Albania was a largely agricultural country, but had begun to industrialize with mainly Italian capital, especially during its occupation by the Axis Powers (1939–43). With little war damage to repair, and Europe lacking the primary products it could supply, Albania's economic prospects could have been promising. Taking sole power, initially under Yugoslav suzerainty, the Albanian Communist Party (ACP) excluded any role for foreign capital or for domestic entrepreneurs by comprehensive nationalization, by the state monopolization of foreign trade and, later, by collectivization. Having transferred its political allegiance to the USSR when the Yugoslav leader, Tito (Josip Broz), defied the Soviet leader, Stalin (Iosif V. Dzhugashvili), in 1947, the

ruling party (redesignating itself the Party of Labour of Albania—PLA) gained external resources from the USSR and markets among its Eastern European allies. By the time Enver Hoxha engineered another change of protector, to the People's Republic of China in 1960, the official estimates of net material product (NMP—a concept excluding most services counted in Western product definitions) gave mining and industry a 57.1% share, compared with 9.8% in 1938. New industrial enterprises included hydroelectric power-stations, mineral-processing plants and industrial ventures associated with forestry and agriculture. However, the increase in industrial production in the 1950s was not matched by a corresponding improvement in agricultural production.

The withdrawal of Soviet assistance to Albania in 1961 disrupted the third Five-Year Plan (1961–65), in which the planned growth rate for agriculture was greater than that envisaged for industry, but the ensuing fourth Five-Year Plan (1966–70) could count on substantial aid and technical expertise from the People's Republic of China. Living standards remained extremely low by Western standards, a position reinforced during Albania's 'Cultural Revolution' in the 1960s (a conscious imitation of the policies initiated in the People's Republic of China), when attempts were made to minimize differentials between occupations and between manual and non-manual workers. During the 1970s measures continued to narrow income differentials, so that rewards and a privileged life-style could be the arbitrary gift of party functionaries. The guarded fences surrounding prison-labour camps and the zone of Tirana (Tiranë) occupied by the political élite (known as the 'Block') symbolized the economic deprivation and privilege of what was judged to be the most repressive regime in Europe. There was limited progress in the introduction of modern technology: Albania's first television station was opened in 1971, and every village had at least one telephone by 1973.

Albania ceased to publish credible statistics in the 1980s and it was clear that the 1976 constitutional prohibition on accepting loans and credits from foreign sources severely constrained economic growth and served to keep foreign trade at the barter stage. The ban saved Albania from the convertible-currency indebtedness that plagued other communist countries, but also deprived it of any gain from foreign trade. The ending of all economic agreements with the People's Republic of China, which until 1978 accounted for about one-half of all Albania's external commerce, also had serious consequences for Albania's international trade.

During the 1980s growth rates steadily declined: the UN Economic Commission for Europe estimated real GDP growth at only 1.5% in 1980–90. Over the same period, the population increased at an average annual rate of 2.1% (the highest rate in Europe), indicating a decline in GDP per head. In November 1986, at the Ninth Congress of the PLA, Ramiz Alia, the successor of Hoxha, admitted that economic performance during the seventh Five-Year Plan had been much poorer than expected, but the minor reforms he introduced proved to be ineffective.

The high rate of population growth, encouraged by the communist regime, itself caused part of the problem. The population increased from 1.2m. in 1950 to 3.3m. in 1990. Almost two-thirds of the population was under the age of 26 and the annual addition to the labour force was around 40,000. With the end of the planned economy, state enterprises no longer had guaranteed suppliers and customers and, with the end of repression, the prison camps were opened and residence restrictions lifted. Consequently, unemployment increased rapidly and was registered at 25% of the labour force in 1993. However, it subsequently declined, owing to mass emigration (the 2002 population was 3.1m.) and the resumption of growth in industry and services. In 1997 the average rate of unemployment was 14.9% of the domestic labour force. After reaching an average of 18.0% in 1999, the unemployment rate declined to 16.8% in 2000, and to 15.8% in 2002.

AGRICULTURE

Agriculture remains the principal sector of the Albanian economy. Agriculture (including forestry and fishing) employed 48% of the population and contributed 40% of GDP in 1990, but, owing to absolute declines in the contributions of industry and of transport, its share was as high as 54% in 1998. Subsequently growth in other branches was more dynamic and by 2002 its share had declined to an estimated 33.2% of GDP. (Growth in the agricultural sector in 2002 was 2.1%, compared with a projected rate of 3%). In 1990 (the final year of the state control of land) the total area of arable land was 704,000 ha (almost 1.75m. acres), nearly twice the 391,000 ha in use in 1950. This increase had been achieved largely through terracing, irrigation, drainage and desalination projects carried out in the 1960s and 1970s. There was considerable investment in afforestation and the construction of reservoirs and irrigation canals. In 1987 some 57% of agricultural land was irrigated, compared with only 10% of a much smaller area of land in agricultural use in 1938. Farm work in that period was highly labour intensive, virtually unaided by machinery, to a degree that justified the regime being labelled 'Muscular Socialism'. However, little but ownership changed in the decade following the system's collapse. A 1999 government survey of 466,766 agricultural units showed that 42% worked with human or animal power alone and 49% failed to purchase either arable or animal products. No other European rural economy demonstrated such little use of mechanical power or such high food self-reliance. The same survey recorded 1.93m. ha of registrable land, of which 839,000 ha was agricultural.

Peasant landholdings had been merged into collective and state farms in the 1950s and early 1960s, and by 1967 collectivization was claimed to be complete. The Hoxha Government forced farm co-operatives into total subordination to the authorities (the 'co-operatives of a higher type' differed little from outright state farms), with the result that there were only 420 farms in the entire country (according to 1983 figures). Together with small personal allotments granted to collective farm workers and state property, these constituted the sole legal form of agricultural landholding. Better crop yields were obtained on peasants' private allotments, which, until 1990, were not permitted to exceed 200 sq m and any surplus of which could not be privately sold.

The most harmful of the PLA's agrarian measures was a campaign to herd livestock held on private plots on to collective farms. Farmers reacted to this directive by slaughtering thousands of animals, with dramatic effects on the supply of meat and dairy products. It was not until July 1990, when various reversals of the policies of the Hoxha period began, that farmers were allowed to rear cattle on their own plots; co-operatives were required to transfer some of their stock to members for this purpose. It was also recommended that co-operatives in hilly or mountainous regions grant each of their members 2,000 sq m of land, in addition to their private plots; co-operative members in lowland areas were permitted to increase their existing landholdings up to a maximum of 2,000 sq m. In a further relaxation by the regime, in July 1990 private markets were authorized, where farmers were permitted to set their own prices. The distribution of the land and assets of co-operative and state farms was one of the main elements in the programme of the DPA, the PLA's main contender in the general election of March 1991. When the PLA won overwhelmingly, most collective-farm members unilaterally claimed plots of land, generally on the basis of pre-

collectivization holdings, but often demolished buildings constructed by the state or the collective on the land; some 750 village schools and many health centres were destroyed. The coalition Government, the first to include non-communists, which took office in June, ceded to pressure and adopted legislation that formally allowed private usufruct of land, including rights of inheritance.

However, uncertainty persisted on eventual ownership of land and farmers were reluctant to sow crops on land that might be taken from them in the future. A lack of fertilizers, insecticides and spare parts for largely obsolete machinery contributed to a crisis by 1992, when the urban population, and even part of the rural population, became dependent on international food aid for survival.

By the end of 1993 some 92% of agricultural land had been distributed to private farmers, and the first positive results of privatization were evident. Production of dairy and meat products rose, as a result of private farmers herding sheep, goats and cattle more efficiently than under the collective system. However, production requiring use of machinery or fertilizers was slower to recover: the size of the average landholding was reduced to 1.5 ha, distributed among 3.3 separate plots of land, by the dissolution of collective farms. According to the 1999 survey, the average holding was 4.1 ha, of which 1.8 ha was arable land. Whereas in the 1970s and 1980s Albania was self-sufficient in wheat, production decreased as a result of decollectivization, and in 1992 only 252,000 metric tons were produced, approximately 400,000 tons below of domestic requirements. Wheat production was then fostered by the creation of farmers' associations, in which private farmers joined with neighbouring landholders to form groups averaging about 40 ha. Wheat and spelt production declined to 272,000 tons in 1999 (compared with 395,000 tons in 1998), increasing to 341,100 tons in 2000, before declining to 282,200 tons in 2001. In 2001 the maize crop was 198,300 tons, potatoes 163,700 tons and other vegetables 650,000 tons. As transport and wholesaling were re-established, export crops (in particular, olives, oranges and tobacco) regained importance. After reaching 11.0% of total exports in 1997, the share of food (including vegetables), beverage and tobacco exports declined and was 8.4% of the total in 2001.

Agrarian reform was completed by two laws of July 1995. The first transformed titles to usage into property titles, thereby allowing a market in agricultural land. The second permitted foreign companies or individuals to buy land if they combined this with an investment equivalent to three times the purchase price. Land commissions were slow to ratify titles to agricultural land, however, and land sales were initially limited because such sales could take place only when all the land in a village area had been registered in title. The land-registration programme, funded by the US Government's foreign aid organization, the Agency for International Development (USAID), was accelerated in 1998 as a condition of the IMF's credit programme, and by the end of 2000 98% of agricultural land had been distributed to lawful owners and titles had been issued with respect to 96%. The final stages of the process were not, however, expected to be completed until 2004.

INDUSTRY

Whereas the serious problems of transition in agriculture were overcome relatively rapidly, collapse was virtually complete in industry. The gross value of mining and manufacturing, in real terms, was only 18% of the 1989 level in 1996, but had reached 31% of that level in 2002. In that year industry accounted for 12.8% of GDP, compared with some 16.9% in 1990. The GDP of the industrial sector increased by 5.0% in 2000 and by 6.5% in 2001. In 2002 industry recorded the lowest growth level of 2.0%, compared with a projected rate of 5.0%, owing, in part, to severe energy shortages.

Manufacturing

Before the recession of the first half of the 1990s, the five largest industrial sectors, measured by the value of output, were food processing, textiles and garment making, engineering, mining and construction materials. In pursuance of self-sufficiency, in the 1960s Albania had begun developing a manufacturing base for consumer goods, providing 85% of domestic requirements of foodstuffs, textiles and clothing by 1987. The production of chemicals was developed to provide inputs to agriculture. The growth of engineering was needed to supply spare parts for foreign-made machines installed from many sources as Albania's alliance orientation shifted (production of spare parts increased by more than 25 times between 1960 and 1984). However, demand for these products decreased as soon as import and foreign-exchange controls were relaxed in 1992, with previously suppressed retail demand overwhelmingly favouring imports. The influx of money in 1999 to help the country deal with refugees from Kosovo, as well as expenditure on humanitarian and military accounts, stimulated the production of consumer goods, but a more fundamental factor in continuing expansion was the 'outward processing trade' (involving the production for re-export of semi-finished or finished articles, mostly clothing and footwear, using materials imported by foreign customers). Such trade accounted for over two-thirds of exports in 2001.

Energy

The communist regime had made Albania not only self-sufficient in energy but a net exporter, largely owing to the development of hydroelectric power stations. A vast mobilization of forced labour raised huge earth dams to create hydroelectric stations, such as the Vau i Dejes (250,000 kW) and the Fierzë (500,000 kW) plants. Albania's largest power station was a 600,000-kW plant at Koman, on the River Drin. However, the reliance on hydroelectricity left Albania vulnerable to the effects of prolonged drought, with severe supply shortages occurring from mid-2000. Despite government-subsidized imports equivalent to domestic generation, power outages have been regularly imposed. Annual generation fell from a peak of 5,396,000 kWh in 1999 to 3,684,000 kWh in 2001, covering only one-third of normal consumption. International donors made aid to the State Electricity Corporation of Albania (Korporata Elektroenergjetike Shqiptare—KESH) conditional on extensive reorganization (and eventual privatization). In 1999 the electricity corporations of Albania, Bulgaria and the former Yugoslav republic of Macedonia (FYRM) established a consortium to link their grids in order to distribute their peak loads, but privatization and the contribution of foreign capital and technology was accepted by the authorities as essential. The Government introduced in 2002 a two-year action plan (initially developed at the end of 2000, in consultation with the World Bank) to end the illegal use of electricity, improve the financial situation of KESH, reduce excessive demand and budgetary subsidies by the end of 2004, and increase generating capacity. However, delays in meeting targets for electricity-sector reform were reported from May 2002, owing principally to the non-payment of arrears to KESH by water companies. The action plan was to be further updated in 2003–04, with further measures to improve bill collection and reduce losses. Electricity prices were to be increased in January 2003, with further increases based on a report financed by the World Bank, accompanied by measures to alleviate effects on poor households. The installation of electricity meters to reduce excessive demand was to be completed by the end of 2004.

In 1999 Albania linked its gas distribution network with those of Greece and the FYRM and, in the longer-term,

planned to reinstate the natural gas industry by supplying gas to Italy. The connecting pipeline was to run under the Adriatic Sea, from Brindisi, Italy, to Vlorë, Albania. Extraction of natural gas in Albania began during the German occupation in 1943. In pursuit of self-sufficiency in energy, Albania's communist regime raised natural gas output to an annual average of 600m. cu m in the late 1980s. However, output fell to 141m. cu m in 1991, dropping to 23m. cu m in 1996 and declining even further, to 10m. cu m in 2001.

In 1970 crude petroleum production was at a record 1.5m. metric tons, but during the 1980s output steadily declined, as extraction encountered increasing technical difficulties, reaching 1.1m. tons in 1990, just 585,000 tons in 1992 and 329,000 tons in 2001. The effects of previous isolation from Western technology and catastrophic environmental damage became revealed. Foreign investment became essential for revival and environmental restoration. However, offshore exploration proved disappointing, and foreign investment became focused onshore. In 1997 Premier Oil of the United Kingdom and Preussag of Germany had formed a joint venture with the then state-owned Albpetrol, to invest US $247m. in the existing Patos deposit and in a new zone at Marinez, which was expected to produce some 2.5m. tons annually. In 2000 Occidental Petroleum (USA), in a joint undertaking with Forest Oil (USA) and Lundin Oil (Sweden), began drilling a $15m. well near Berat. Foreign investment in such projects and in buying and developing the constituent parts of Albpetrol was expected to guarantee output (including offshore) of 2.5m. tons by 2016. Construction of a pipeline to transport Caspian Sea crude from the Bulgarian port of Bourgas, across the FYRM, to Vlorë, was judged to be feasible, at a cost of $1,000m. and a throughput of 750,000 barrels per day, but the Bulgarian Government suspended the project in 2001, in favour of a pipeline to the Greek port of Alexandropoulos.

Albania was largely self-sufficient in coal, but the coal produced was mostly low-quality lignite (brown coal of a particularly low calorific value) from small deposits scattered throughout Albania. Hence, some 300,000 metric tons of coking coal were imported annually, mainly from Greece and Bulgaria. Output declined from 1,086,000 tons in 1991 to 113,000 tons in 1996, after which production was steadily diminished until the closure of coal mining in 2001.

Metals

The communist-period exploitation of Albania's rich endowment of mineral resources, notably chromite, ferro-nickel and copper, was effected by low-paid, often forced, labour working under conditions injurious to health and safety and with primitive equipment and techniques. None of this could be tolerated in a democracy with trade unions and a market economy. A strike in the chromite mines of April 1991 was a symbolic turning point in the development of the mining sector. Whereas 1.2m. metric tons of chromium ore had been produced in 1989, and 587,000 tons in 1991, only 17,000 tons were extracted in 2001. Output of copper ore had also decreased significantly, from some 1m. tons in 1989 and 561,000 tons in 1991, to just 34,000 tons in 1999, when the mines were closed. Concessions granted to foreign corporations for the mining of chromite, ferro-chrome, copper and steel were regenerating these industries, but nickel- and iron-ore mining had not yet attracted new investment.

INFRASTRUCTURE AND SERVICES

While Hoxha's Albania was emulating Mao's China, it probably had a higher proportion of its work-force engaged in infrastructure construction than any other country. Labour conditions reverted to normal after 1990: employment in construction quickly halved (from 99,000 in 1990 to 43,000 in 1993) and the then substantial building-materials industry succumbed to Italian imports. In 1994 240,000 metric tons of cement was produced, but only 30,000 tons was produced in 2001; compared with the 90,000 tons of bricks and 3m. tiles produced in 1992, none were produced in 2001. Construction generated 10.3% of GDP in 2001. In contrast to an earlier infrastructure boom, under Italian occupation in 1939–43, when road-building was the focus, investment in the communist period went mainly to industry, agriculture and defence. Some 180,000 concrete bunkers were built in the coastal plains and the frontier mountains to repel supposed capitalist invaders. By 2000, of an estimated 18,000 km of roads, only 3,220 km were paved main roads; in that year some 39% of the total network was paved. Some 400 villages and many more hamlets and farmsteads were inaccessible by motor vehicle for at least part of the year. In the absence of an extensive rail network, roads continued to carry most of the country's freight. Traffic grew considerably once the private ownership of cars was legalized in 1991, but bicycles and draught animals were still common a decade later. Among many projects of the EU's Transport Corridor Europe–Central Asia (TRACECA) programme was Corridor VIII, a west–east highway from the port of Durrës to the FYRM and the Black Sea, and Corridor X, running north–south from Hani i Hotit on the Monetenegrin border to Tri Urat on the Greek frontier. The 1999 conflict in Kosovo had demonstrated the inadequacies of the north–south routes within the country. To secure its communications and logistics in Kosovo, troops from the North Atlantic Treaty Organization (NATO) reconstructed the road from Durrës to Kukës, which was rehabilitated to the border with US funds. The World Bank, the European Investment Bank and the EU undertook in October 2001 to continue to finance Albanian road reconstruction and extension. A new road tax, introduced in August 2002, was to contribute to financing additional road construction.

Apart from a small mining line, Albania's first railway was constructed in 1947–48 and linked Durrës with Tirana. With lines north–south (Han i Hotit to Vlorë) and west–east (from Durrës to Podgradec on Lake Ohrid), the system aggregated 720 km by 1994. The connection with the European railway network via Han i Hotit, which had been built in 1986, but remained unused, was reopened for passengers and freight in early 2002 and renovated in March 2003. In December 1997 a bilateral accord was reached for an eventual extension of the railway from Pogradec to connect with the Greek railhead at Florina. The system was, however, in such poor condition that in 1998 the Government considered closing it altogether. None the less, in July 1999 it accepted a report stating that US $247m. was needed for the complete rehabilitation of the system ($5m. of which was needed for the construction of a line into the FYRM). In early 2001 the Islamic Development Bank provided a concessional loan of $3.7m. for the reconstruction of the line between Durrës and Vlorë. Albanian Railways transported 2.7m. passengers and 19m. ton-km of freight in 2001.

Until the Kosovo conflict of 1999 Albania had only one civilian airport, at Rinas, near Tirana, which was handling as few as 80 passengers a day in 1990. Work to invest in its modernization, to meet international safety standards, was briefly suspended during the 1997 insurgency. Progress was slow until the airport became a NATO base during its air offensive against the FRY from March 1999, when it was also required for the transportation of humanitarian aid and the evacuation of Kosovar refugees. Improvements were made at Rinas and small airports were built at Kukës and Korcë. Since 1999 a US firm, Evergreen, has provided civilian helicopter services within Albania and domestic services include a new civil and military airport at Pish Poro, near Vlorë. Albania participates in a regional agreement with the FYRM and Greece for the harmonization of radar and air-traffic control

systems. Under the Government's investment programme for 2002, US $12m. was allocated for the rehabilitation of ports and Rinas airport.

Ferry services link Durrës with the Italian ports of Ancona, Bari and Trieste, Sarandë with the Greek island of Corfu and Vlorë with the Italian ports of Bari and Brindisi. A series of foreign credits resulted in the complete rehabilitation of the port of Durrës, and the previously insignificant ports of Sarandë and Shëngjin were expanded. A regular lake service joins Ohrid in the FYRM with Pogradec. Overall, transportation generated 10.1% of GDP in 2001.

The need to remedy the inadequacy of telecommunications in Albania made this sector a priority in the SPA Government's privatization programme in 1998. In 1995 there had been only 1.2 telephone lines per 100 inhabitants (compared with 49.4 per 100 in Greece), which rose to 6.3 by 2001. In 2000 Albanian Mobile Communications was sold to a Greek/Norwegian consortium and a second mobile telephony licence was sold to a British/Greek consortium in 2001, when there were 11.1 mobile telephones per 100 inhabitants. Preparations for the privatization of the fixed-line operator, Albanian Telecom, were completed in September 2002 and sale to a strategic investor was to be undertaken when international market conditions were judged suitable. The postponement of privatization for other state-controlled services, in view of markets, was also applied to the Insurance Institute of Albania (INSIG), but in February 2003 the IMF urged the Government to sell the Savings Bank, to improve competition in the banking sector, with emphasis on credit provision for private firms, and to strengthen implementation of the Money Laundering Law. Much, however, had already been done to convert financial services from the 'monobank', which had been a feature of Albanian central planning, in the wake of the collapse of the 'pyramid' schemes and the subsequent civil unrest. In 1996 and early 1997 a significant amount of money was withdrawn (US $1,200m., the equivalent of 60% of GDP) from households into the accounts of the 'pyramid' deposit-takers. Following the bankruptcy of the 'pyramid' investment schemes, their enforced liquidation was effected by international accountants under government supervision. In March 2002 the rates at which depositors would be reimbursed were published. Those who had invested in the largest would only be repaid 10% of lost capital, although depositors of some of the smaller schemes would receive 50% and, in one case, 78%.

In 1997 a World Bank mission, invited by the incoming SPA administration, recommended the liquidation of one of the state-owned commercial banks, the Rural Commercial Bank, and the privatization of two others, the National Commercial Bank (implemented in 2000) and the Savings Bank (see above). Of 13 private commercial banks licensed by 2002, four were Greek-owned. Under the terms of the Privatization Law of 1991, Albania's retailing and other small businesses were almost all privatized by the end of 1992 and, by a Law on the Privatization of State-Owned Housing of 1992, dwellings were transferred to private ownership, mostly to occupiers. Overall, 42.3% of GDP was generated by services in 2001.

TOURISM

Tourism in Albania was not encouraged under isolationist communism, for fear of contact between Albanians and 'alien ideological influences', but from 1989 the industry was viewed as an important potential source of foreign earnings. A 1994 Law on Investments in Priority Tourism Development Zones approved a long-term scheme delineated by external consultants. Although this was initiated (hotel accommodation was enlarged and improved in Tirana), some projects were hindered by corruption, and development was postponed by the destruction of a number of transport facilities and of accommodation during the 1997 insurgency. The problems of the sector were compounded by the need to repair environmental damage, such as the concrete bunkers littering the landscape, the raw sewage in Albania's rivers and the marshland polluted by petroleum products. Brigandage added to the inadequacy of roads, public transport, petrol stations and local hotels to inhibit touring. The influx of foreign military, press and humanitarian personnel during the Kosovo conflict of 1999 significantly increased the supply of hotels and private accommodation, and restaurants and bars. With greater assurance of personal security in travel around the country, in August the Interministerial Council on Tourism Development Policies, chaired by the Deputy Prime Minister, began co-ordinating a US $258m. private-sector investment programme for the development of tourism in the coastal areas of Durrës, Golem and Sarandë. Tourism receipts totalled $446m. in 2001, compared with just $27m. in 1997. According to the World Tourism Organization, total arrivals (including same-day visitors) increased from 317,149 in 2000 to 342,908 in 2001.

ECONOMIC REFORM AND STABILIZATION

The economic disorder and recession of 1991 resulted in a sharp decline in tax revenues, but commitment to a very large public sector continued: central and local government expenditure was equivalent to 62% of GDP and the deficit to 31% of GDP. Although the monetization of the deficit and the liberalization of the price controls of the communist period resulted in inflation, it was lower than in most post-communist economies. The reduction of the government deficit, an agreement between the Government and trade unions to index-link increases in public-sector wages, and a tighter control over the money supply brought the annual rate of consumer-price inflation down to 8% in 1995, the second lowest of any post-communist state. The Bank of Albania had to exercise control over the money supply as the economy moved from communist-era reliance on cash transactions in the household sector and bookkeeping transfers in the enterprise sector. Between December 1992 and December 1996 the ratio of reserve money (notes, coins and deposits at the Bank of Albania) to total money declined from 71% to 40%, and the ratio declined further, to 27%, by December 2002. The supply interruptions that resulted from the civil disruption of 1997 refuelled inflation that year to 32.1%. Stabilization under an IMF programme moderated it to 20.9% in 1998, to a negligible 0.4% in 1999 and to zero in 2000. Inflation resumed, but at acceptable rates, in 2001 at 3.2% and at an estimated 5.6% in 2002, with the IMF urging the Government to remain within the range of 2%–4%.

The transition from an exclusively state-controlled economy to a market system was promoted early by small-scale denationalization and the promotion of small business. A scheme to privatize the 950 medium-sized and larger state-owned enterprises (which employed some 160,000 people) was approved in 1995. Citizens were to receive vouchers entitling them to buy shares, or to deposit them with investment funds for such purchases. According to the theory that the older people were, the more consumption they had forgone in order for the communist state to have made the investments creating the assets to be privatized, the value of a voucher increased according to the age of its recipient. An Enterprise Restructuring Agency (financed by the World Bank) was responsible for restructuring the worst-performing enterprises, at least to some degree, before disposal. Some 50 firms were initially sold by the National Agency for Privatization, but when the new administration took over in mid-1997 it accelerated sales, aiming at major strategic investors, but honouring vouchers (within a maximum of 20% of the equity in any one privatized firm). By 2001, with over 75% of GDP generated in the private sector and the disposal of viable

small and medium-sized enterprises largely completed, the sale began of the remaining state-owned large enterprises, including Albpetrol (oil extraction, refining and distribution), Albbaker (copper), Albchrome, INSIG, Albanian Telecom and KESH. Structural reforms slowed from mid-2001, with delays in the privatization programme, owing to political instability, together with the weakened international market (see above). The 2002 budget was amended in May to accommodate shortfalls in privatization receipts. Reforms were accelerated prior to meetings with the IMF and World Bank in mid-2002, with the adoption of new bankruptcy legislation, a deposit insurance scheme and a privatization law for INSIG.

Under the central economy all taxation was paid by state and co-operative enterprises to the exclusion of any personal income tax. The lifting of restraints on private enterprise and privatization of state firms had hence to be accompanied by fiscal reform, from 1991 a personal income tax, property and profits taxes and customs duties, and from 1995 a value-added tax (VAT). In 2002 the central government tax structure included a personal income tax (progressive after exempt income from 5% to 25%), small business tax (4% after a fixed-fee threshold), corporation tax (25%), VAT (20%), excise duty (on tobacco, alcoholic and soft drinks, coffee and petroleum products), customs duties (zero to 15%) and solidarity tax (a fixed fee per legal entity); local authorities levy a property tax. Central and local tax revenue as a share of GDP was, at 15.6% in 2001, the third-lowest among transition states (after civil war, the shares in Georgia and Tajikistan were lower), and fell far short of expenditure, totalling 31.5% of GDP. The shortfall was met by social security premiums (3.8% of GDP), revenue from the Bank of Albania and budgetary institutions (3.5%), privatization sales (2.1%), domestic borrowing (2.6%) and foreign loans and grants (3.9%).

The low share of tax revenue in GDP was principally a consequence of the magnitude of the unofficial economy, which was tentatively estimated at one-third of officially measured GDP, together with unmeasured activities equal to another 50% of GDP. Concealment of so much from the authorities required pervasive corruption, and Transparency International (based in Berlin, Germany) ranked Albania as 81st on its corruption index of 102 countries surveyed—the most corrupt transition country was Azerbaijan, ranked 95th, and the best Slovenia, at 27th. There were only two countries (Azerbaijan and Tajikistan) that ranked lower than Albania among the transition economies in the 2002 index of commercial legal and regulatory processes compiled by the European Bank for Reconstruction and Development.

UNEMPLOYMENT AND SOCIAL SECURITY

Until 1991 the existence of unemployment was not officially admitted, yet absenteeism and underemployment were widespread. High unemployment emerged in 1992 (when it constituted 27.9% of the labour force), especially among young people, and prompted mass emigration, mostly to Greece and Italy. Unemployment declined until 1996 (when the end-year rate was 9.6%), but rose after the disruptions of the following year, to reach 18.4% at the end of 1999. There was much concealed unemployment in rural areas after the dissolution of the collective and state farms (private farmers numbered 761,000). The SPA-led coalition Government made unemployment one of its priorities, and a job-creation scheme had somewhat reduced the rate of unemployment to 15.8% by 2002.

The state insurance scheme for unemployment, maternity, sickness and retirement benefits was funded by state-employer contributions in the communist period. After the reforms of the early 1990s the employers' premium was initially high (32.5% of gross wages, subject to upper and lower limits), but by 2002 was moderated to 30.7%; employee contributions declined from 10.0% of wages (within corresponding limits) to 9.5%. Health-care insurance was funded by premiums of 1.7% of gross wages, paid by both employers and employees. A one-year maximum for unemployment benefit was introduced and means-testing was applied to social assistance. The dismantling of the collective-farm system and the closure of prison camps resulted in an influx of some 0.5m. people into urban areas, and unregulated 'shanty' settlements became a major cause of concern, especially as water and sewage services in those areas were generally inadequate. Homelessness became a problem in the early 1990s owing to internal migration and return from abroad (Greece and Italy expelled many illegal immigrants), and worsened in 1997 when thousands of families sold their dwellings, newly acquired under privatization, for cash to invest in the 'pyramid' schemes, which they lost until partial reimbursements were made in 2002. Edi Rama, hitherto Minister of Culture, Youth and Sports, who was elected Mayor of Tirana in the local elections held in October 2000, initiated a major rehabilitation programme for the capital; population growth, from 250,000 to some 750,000 in 11 years, had resulted in the unregulated dramatic increase of shanties and kiosks, and to gross inadequacies of water, sewage and other municipal services. Rama's Tirana project supported greater transparency for service provision and for citizens' complaints and requirements. SPA victories in over 250 towns and communes, most taken from the DPA, attracted central government funding for many other local regeneration projects.

According to the Government's National Strategy for Socio-Economic Development (NSEED), one-fourth of the Albanian population subsists in extreme poverty. Poverty is higher in the rural zones, which had 66% more poor people than in Tirana and 50% more than in the other urban areas. Consistent with implementation of the NSEED, in June 2002 the IMF renewed a PRGF and the World Bank a Poverty Reduction Support Credit. Under NSEED objectives, the percentage of the population living in poverty (subsisting on US $2 per day) was to be reduced from 25% in 2002, to 20% in 2006, and to 13% in 2015. The percentage of the population living in extreme poverty (less than $1 per day) was to be reduced from 5% in 2002, to 3%–4% in the medium term, and was to be completely eradicated by 2015.

The national health service was reformed in 1998, allowing modest charges for some services. By 2015 the NSEED aimed to reduce the under-five mortality rate and the general death rate for AIDS and malaria by two-thirds, and reduce the number of people without access to a safe supply of drinking water by one-half. Education has remained free but, as for health care, much was provided in dilapidated facilities and quality primary education was not available throughout the country. The Ministry of Education and Science was to complete the formulation of the national education strategy in the 2003–06 period, with the support of the World Bank. Long-term objectives were to include all children in quality basic education, and to increase the secondary enrolment rate to 90% by 2015.

EXTERNAL ECONOMIC RELATIONS

Despite its isolationist economic policy, Albania maintained trade links with about 50 countries in the 1980s, although at a low level. While the value of exports remained fairly constant throughout the 1980s, the value of imports rose by 51% in 1980–90. Machinery and equipment continued to form the largest proportion of imports (31.0% in 1990), followed by fuels, metals and minerals (24.5%), agricultural raw materials (including unprocessed foodstuffs—15.7%), processed foodstuffs (10.1%), chemical products (9.3%) and consumer goods (8.4%).

Until 1989 more than one-half of all trade went to member countries of the Council for Mutual Economic Assistance (CMEA), but the collapse of the CMEA and Albania's need for more consumer goods and higher-quality equipment led to a reorientation of trade towards the EU member countries, chiefly Greece and Italy. The collapse in Albanian industrial production from 1991 led to a decline in exports, which that year reached only 60% of the value of imports (compared to 94% in 1987), beginning a series of structural trade deficits, which continued throughout the decade: from US $254m. in 1991, the annual deficit on merchandise trade rose to $1,155.1m. in 2002. During that decade Albania was dependent upon economic aid from Western countries and emigrants' remittances; the latter reached a maximum level of $425m. in 1996 (partly for investment in the 'pyramid' schemes), subsequently fell, but had recovered to $549m. in 2002. Foreign direct investment reached a peak in 1996 ($97m.), peaked again at $204m. in 2001, but was $156m. in 2002.

After 1992 there were virtually no quantitative restrictions on imports and very few on exports: in 2002 Albania rated a very liberal one (out of 10) on the IMF's trade restrictiveness index. Some protection was afforded domestic products by conventional tariffs, but these had to be reduced from January 2001, as a result of Albania's membership of the World Trade Organization (WTO) the previous year. In 2002 the combined average tariff was 8.7%. As part of the EU's Stability Pact for South Eastern Europe, a Steering Committee was established in early 2001 with the European Commission to plan negotiations on a Stabilization and Association Agreement, with the prospect of eventual membership for Albania. In October 2002, following the installation of a new Government in July, the EU invited Albania to commence negotiations; discussions on the Agreement were finally initiated at the end of January 2003. (A decline in the level of trade between Albania and the EU member countries was reported in mid-2003, however.) Albania has signed Free Trade Agreements with Bosnia and Herzegovina, Bulgaria, Croatia and the FYRM, in an effort to stimulate regional trade relations. In 2001 the principal exports were manufactures, mostly textiles, clothing and footwear (69.5%). Some three-quarters of imports comprised merchandise for further processing, and machinery and transport equipment accounted for 18.4% of imports in 2001. In 2001 Italy was both the principal market for exports (accounting for 71.1% of total exports) and the principal source of imports (33.3%).

The prohibition in the 1976 Constitution of acceptance of credits from non-socialist states was annulled in 1990 and the Government subsequently borrowed extensively to pay for increased imports. By 1995, unable to service the foreign debt, Albania rescheduled US $500m. of its external medium-term debt and managed to clear most of its short-term bank debt. By September 2002 Albanian entities had gross assets of $353m. in Western banks reporting to the Bank for International Settlements (some $100m. being the product of legal and illegal capital 'flight'), compared with debts of $192m. At the end of 2002 total external debt stood at $1,154m., most of which was owed to multilateral creditors; this amount was modest in relation to GDP (24.7% in 2002), but high with respect to exports of goods and services (140.2%).

The lek replaced the Albanian gold franc in 1946 and was once redenominated (one new lek replacing 10 old lekë in 1965). The exchange rate was kept artificially at about five lekë to one US dollar during the communist period, but increased to almost nine lekë to the dollar during 1990, the last year of communist rule. Full current-account convertibility was applied in 1992 and after an early devaluation the lek appreciated during the 1994–95 economic recovery. The civil disruption of 1997 weakened the currency considerably, but it gained in value as order was restored and normal trade resumed. By the end of May 2003, at 118 lekë to the US dollar, the lek had appreciated in real terms by 22% since the end of 1995. In view of international reserves being equivalent to 4.5 months of imports of goods and services, improved political stability and the avoidance of recession in the EU, the IMF's revised targets of 6% annual average real GDP growth for 2003–05 appeared achievable.

Statistical Survey

Sources (unless otherwise indicated): Institute of Statistics (Instituti i Statistikës), POB 8194, Tirana; tel. (4) 222411; fax (4) 228300; e-mail root@instat .gov.al; internet www.instat.gov.al; Bank of Albania (Banka e Shqipërisë), Sheshi Skënderbeu 1, Tirana; tel. (4) 222752; fax (4) 223558; e-mail public@ bankofalbania.org; internet www.bankofalbania.org.

Area and Population

AREA, POPULATION AND DENSITY

Area (sq km)	
Land	27,398
Inland water	1,350
Total	28,748*
Population (census results)	
2 April 1989	3,182,417
1 April 2001	
Males	1,530,443
Females.	1,538,832
Total	3,069,275
Population (UN estimates at mid-year)†	
1999	3,131,000
2000	3,134,000
2001	3,145,000
Density (per sq km) at 1 April 2001	106.8

* 11,100 sq miles.

† Figures not revised to take account of 2001 census.

Source: UN, World *Population Prospects: The 2000 Revision*.

Ethnic Groups (census of 2 April 1989): Albanian 3,117,601; Greek 58,758; Macedonian 4,697; Montenegrin, Serb, Croat, etc. 100; others 1,261.

DISTRICTS
(census of 1 April 2001)

District (Rreth)	Area (sq km)	Population	Density (per sq km)	Capital
Berat	939	127,837	136.1	Berat
Bulqizë	469	42,968	91.6	Bulqizë
Delvinë	348	10,765	30.9	Delvinë
Devoll	429	34,641	80.8	Bilisht
Dibër	1,088	85,699	78.7	Peshkopi
Durrës	433	181,662	419.6	Durrës
Elbasan. . . .	1,372	221,635	161.5	Elbasan
Fier	785	199,082	253.5	Fier
Gjirokastër . . .	1,137	54,647	48.0	Gjirokastër
Gramsh	695	35,750	51.5	Gramsh
Has	393	19,660	50.0	Krumë
Kavajë	414	78,179	188.7	Kavajë
Kolonjë	805	17,161	21.3	Ersekë
Korçë	1,752	142,909	81.6	Korçë
Krujë	333	63,517	190.8	Krujë
Kuçovë	84	35,338	420.2	Kuçovë
Kukës	938	63,786	68.0	Kukës
Kurbin	273	54,392	199.0	Laç
Lezhë	479	67,734	141.3	Lezhë
Librazhd	1,023	72,387	70.7	Librazhd
Lushnjë. . . .	712	143,933	202.0	Lushnjë
Malësi e Madhe .	555	36,692	66.2	Koplik
Mallakastër . . .	393	39,529	100.6	Ballsh
Mat	1,029	61,187	59.5	Burrel
Mirditë	867	37,056	42.7	Rrëshen
Peqin	109	32,964	303.3	Peqin
Përmet	930	25,780	27.7	Përmet
Pogradec	725	70,471	97.2	Pogradec
Pukë	1,034	34,386	33.3	Pukë
Sarandë. . . .	749	35,089	46.9	Sarandë
Shkodër. . . .	1,973	185,395	94.0	Shkodër
Skrapar. . . .	775	29,845	38.5	Çorovodë
Tepelenë	817	32,404	39.6	Tepelenë
Tiranë	1,238	519,720	419.6	Tiranë
Tropojë	1,043	27,947	26.8	Bajram Curri
Vlorë	1,609	147,128	91.4	Vlorë
Total	28,748	3,069,275	106.8	

PRINCIPAL TOWNS
(population at 2001 census, preliminary results)

Tiranë (Tirana, the capital)	343,078	Korçë (Koritsa) . .	55,130
Durrës (Durazzo) .	99,546	Berat	40,112
Elbasan . . .	87,797	Lushnjë	32,580
Shkodër (Scutari) .	82,455	Kavajë.	24,817
Vlorë (Vlonë or Valona)	77,691	Pogradec	23,843
Fier	56,297	Gjirokastër . . .	20,630

BIRTHS, MARRIAGES AND DEATHS*

	Registered live births		Registered marriages		Registered deaths	
	Number	Rate (per 1,000)	Number	Rate (per 1,000)	Number	Rate (per 1,000)
1994	72,179	22.5	27,895	8.7	18,342	5.7
1995	72,081	22.2	26,989	8.3	18,060	5.6
1996	68,358	20.8	27,690	8.4	17,600	5.4
1997	61,739	18.6	24,122	7.3	18,237	5.5
1998	60,139	17.9	27,871	8.3	18,250	5.4
1999	57,948	17.2	27,254	8.1	16,720	5.0
2000	50,077	14.7	25,820	7.6	16,421	4.8
2001	52,715	15.4	25,717	8.4	15,813	4.6

* Rates are based on official population projections for 1 January each year, and have not been revised to take account of the results of the census of 1 April 2001.

Expectation of life (WHO estimates, years at birth): 69.5 (males 66.3; females 73.2) in 2001 (Source: WHO, *World Health Report*).

ECONOMICALLY ACTIVE POPULATION
('000, end of period)

	1999	2000	2001
Agriculture, hunting, forestry and fishing	768	767	767
Mining and quarrying	16	9	8
Manufacturing	53	34	32
Electricity, gas and water	13	15	16
Construction	11	13	13
Wholesale and retail trade	29	49	46
Hotels and restaurants	14	19	9
Transport, storage and communications	32	26	24
Education	48	47	51
Health	26	23	26
Other activities	55	66	71
Total employed	1,065	1,068	1,063
Registered unemployed	240	215	181
Total labour force	1,305	1,283	1,244
Males	791	754	730
Females	514	529	514

Health and Welfare

KEY INDICATORS

Total fertility rate (children per woman, 2001)	2.4
Under-5 mortality rate (per 1,000 live births, 2001)	30
HIV/AIDS (% of persons aged 15–49, 1999)	<0.01
Physicians (per 1,000 head, 1998)	1.29
Hospital beds (per 1,000 head, 1995)	3.19
Health expenditure (2000): US $ per head (PPP)	129
Health expenditure (2000): % of GDP	3.4
Health expenditure (2000): public (% of total)	62.1
Human Development Index (2000): ranking	92
Human Development Index (2000): value	0.733

For sources and definitions, see explanatory note on p. vi.

Agriculture

PRINCIPAL CROPS
('000 metric tons)

	1999	2000	2001
Wheat and spelt	272.0	341.1	282.2
Barley	2.9	1.8	3.0
Maize	206.0	205.7	198.3
Rye	3.4	1.5	3.7
Oats	13.2	15.7	15.3
Sorghum*	14.5	14.7	14.7
Potatoes	161.9	161.0	163.7
Sugar beet	39.9	42.0	38.5
Dry beans	26.0	25.2	22.1
Tree-nuts*	3.0	3.0	3.0
Olives	42.0	36.2	39.6
Sunflower seed	2.7	2.9	2.7
Tomatoes	160.0	162.0	170.9
Other vegetables*	250.0	250.0	250.0
Oranges	2.2	2.2*	2.2*
Apples	11.8	12.0	15.8
Pears	2.4	2.8	3.5
Cherries	4.5	5.0	6.8
Peaches and nectarines	2.0	2.0	6.1
Plums	12.1	12.1	17.0
Grapes	70.4	79.3	85.1
Watermelons	220.0	250.0	277.0
Figs	12.1	13.1	22.8
Tobacco (leaves)	7.3	6.2	4.1

* FAO estimate(s).

Source: FAO.

LIVESTOCK
('000 head, year ending September)

	1999	2000	2001
Horses*	65	65	65
Mules*	25	25	25
Asses*	113	113	113
Cattle	720	728	708
Pigs	81	103	103
Sheep	1,941	1,939	1,906
Goats	1,120	1,106	1,027
Chickens	4,010	4,087	4,285

* FAO estimates.

Source: FAO.

LIVESTOCK PRODUCTS
('000 metric tons)

	1999	2000	2001
Beef and veal*	33.7	35.9	35.3
Mutton and lamb	11.7*	12.3*	12.3†
Goat meat	6.4*	7.2*	7.2
Pig meat	6.2*	6.8*	7.5†
Poultry meat	5.0	4.0	4.0
Cows' milk	761.0	807.0	840.0
Sheep's milk	73.0	70.0	72.0
Goats' milk	73.0†	71.0	72.0
Cheese	11.4†	10.7	10.3
Butter†	1.6	1.7	1.7
Hen eggs	20.2	21.0	24.0
Wool: greasy	3.0	3.4	3.3
Cattle hides†	7.0	7.5	7.9
Sheep and lamb skins†	3.2	3.4	3.4
Goat and kid skins†	1.6	1.8	1.8

* Unofficial figure(s).
† FAO estimate(s).

Source: FAO.

Forestry

ROUNDWOOD REMOVALS
('000 cubic metres, excl. bark)

	1999	2000	2001
Sawlogs, veneer logs and logs for sleepers	39	119	131
Pulpwood	3	4*	4*
Other industrial wood . . .	14	—	—
Fuel wood	174	324	324†
Total	230	447	459

* Unofficial figure.
† FAO estimate.

Source: FAO.

SAWNWOOD PRODUCTION
('000 cubic metres, incl. railway sleepers)

	1998	1999	2000
Coniferous (softwood) . . .	9	15	47
Broadleaved (hardwood). . .	19	20	43
Total	28	35	90

2001: Figures assumed to be unchanged from 2000.

Source: FAO.

Fishing

(metric tons, live weight)

	1998	1999	2000
Capture	2,683	2,745	3,320
Common carp	230	216	230
Silver carp	104	130	140
Other cyprinids	229	227	300
Salmonoids	102	104	110
European hake.	340	341	330
Bogue	220	220	220
Surmullets	143	145	140
Mullets	136	140	150
Jack and horse mackerels . .	85	92	90
Rays, stingrays and mantas . .	86	78	85
Common squids	93	93	90
Common octopus	93	90	85
Aquaculture	124	310	307
Mediterranean mussel . . .	100	200	200
Total catch	2,807	3,055	3,627

Note: Figures exclude Sardinia coral (metric tons): 0.5 in 1998; 0.9 in 1999; 1.0 in 2000.

Source: FAO, *Yearbook of Fishery Statistics.*

Mining

('000 metric tons, unless otherwise indicated)

	1998	1999	2000
Lignite (brown coal)	49	33	21
Crude petroleum	365	323	314
Natural gas (million cu metres) .	17	14	11
Copper (metric tons)*	3,200	900	900
Chromium ore (gross weight) . .	150	79	57

* Figures refer to estimated metal content.

Sources: IMF, *Albania: Selected Issues and Statistical Appendix* (July 2001), and US Geological Survey.

Industry

SELECTED PRODUCTS
('000 metric tons, unless otherwise indicated)

	1997	1998	1999
Wheat flour	68	83	n.a.
Wine ('000 hectolitres)	—	—	7
Cigarettes (million)	414	764	63
Veneer sheets ('000 cubic metres)*	10	10	10
Plywood ('000 cubic metres) . .	6	6	3
Mechanical wood pulp	2	2	—
Chemical wood pulp	14	14	14
Paper and paperboard*	44	44	8
Phosphatic fertilizers†	27	26	n.a.
Soap	2	2	n.a.
Motor spirit (petrol)	74	21	20
Kerosene	57	2	1
Gas-diesel (distillate fuel) oil . .	107	91	65
Residual fuel oils	39	39‡	n.a.
Petroleum bitumen (asphalt)‡ . .	14	14	n.a.
Cement	100	84	107
Ferro-chromium	31	30	28
Crude steel	22	22	16
Copper (unrefined)	0.9	2.3	0.9
Electric energy (million kWh) . .	5,681	5,068	5,396

2000 ('000 metric tons, unless otherwise indicated): Wine ('000 hectolitres) 5; Cigarettes (million) 62; Veneer sheets ('000 cubic metres) 37; Motor spirit 24; Kerosene 2; Gas-diesel oil 72; Cement 180; Ferro-chromium 9; Crude steel 65; Electric energy (million kWh) 4,737.

* FAO estimate(s).
† Production in terms of phosphoric acid.
‡ Provisional or estimated production.

Sources: UN, *Industrial Commodity Statistics Yearbook*, and IMF, *Albania: Selected Issues and Statistical Appendix* (July 2001).

Finance

CURRENCY AND EXCHANGE RATES

Monetary Units
    100 qindarka (qintars) = 1 new lek.

Sterling, Dollar and Euro Equivalents (30 May 2003)
    £1 sterling = 195.0 lekë;
    US $1 = 118.4 lekë;
    €1 = 139.9 lekë;
    1,000 lekë = £5.128 = $8.448 = €7.146.

Average Exchange Rate (lekë per US $)
    2000   143.71
    2001   143.48
    2002   140.15

STATE BUDGET
(million lekë)

Revenue*	1999	2000	2001
Counterpart sales revenue . . .	155	—	—
Tax revenue	83,530	104,098	114,294
Turnover tax/value-added tax	29,794	38,107	41,149
Taxes on income and profits . .	10,331	14,346	18,521
Social security contributions . .	18,157	20,053	22,506
Import duties and export taxes	11,450	13,548	12,795
Excise taxes	6,961	9,153	9,544
Other revenue	24,124	16,490	21,190
Profit transfer from Bank of Albania	17,591	10,225	10,912
Income from budgetary institutions	5,352	4,841	5,569
Total	107,809	120,588	135,484

Expenditure	1999	2000	2001
Current expenditure	131,545	134,361	142,653
Wages	24,208	25,820	32,940
Social security contributions . .	6,976	7,420	8,268
Interest	34,938	29,572	23,620
Operational and maintenance .	19,499	19,294	15,741
Subsidies	2,706	5,247	7,778
Social security	34,437	37,402	43,502
Unemployment insurance . .	1,450	1,919	1,881
Social assistance	6,360	6,661	6,938
Capital expenditure (investment)	34,127	35,062	43,397
Total	165,672	169,423	186,050

* Excluding privatization receipts (million lekë): 906 in 1999; 8,975 in 2000; 12,686 in 2001.

Source: IMF, *Albania: Selected Issues and Statistical Appendix* (March 2003).

INTERNATIONAL RESERVES
(US $ million at 31 December)

	2000	2001	2002
Gold*	30.40	30.70	27.68
IMF special drawing rights . . .	76.00	81.52	81.60
Reserve position in IMF	4.37	4.22	4.56
Foreign exchange	535.27	654.17	752.62
Total	646.05	770.60	866.46

* Valued at market-related prices.
Source: IMF, *International Financial Statistics*.

MONEY SUPPLY
(million lekë at 31 December)

	2000	2001	2002
Currency outside banks	99,236	119,084	130,775
Demand deposits at deposit money banks	24,805	23,945	21,900
Total money	124,041	143,028	152,675

Source: IMF, *International Financial Statistics*.

COST OF LIVING
(Consumer Price Index; base: December 1993 = 100)

	1999	2000	2001
Food, beverages and tobacco . .	210.9	206.2	213.1
Clothing and footwear . . .	208.0	202.6	192.1
Rent, water, fuel and power . .	416.3	487.3	524.1
Fuel and power	759.5	876.4	936.1
Household goods and maintenance	151.3	137.6	134.2
Transport and communications .	225.6	233.2	235.5
Recreation, education and culture .	150.2	137.4	132.7
All items (incl. others) . . .	218.3	218.3	225.2

NATIONAL ACCOUNTS
(million lekë at current prices)

Expenditure on the Gross Domestic Product

	1998	1999	2000
Final consumption expenditure .	464,767	481,444	494,385
Households	424,205	437,333	446,875
Non-profit institutions serving households	340	408	490
General government	40,222	43,703	47,020
Gross fixed capital formation . .	57,770	81,590	110,417
Changes in inventories . . .	−368	2,163	61,865
Total domestic expenditure . .	522,169	565,197	666,667
Exports of goods and services . .	45,585	74,858	101,100
Less Imports of goods and services	142,398	151,445	216,485
GDP in market prices . . .	425,356	488,611	551,282

Gross Domestic Product by Economic Activity

	1998	1999	2000
Agriculture, hunting and forestry .	116,442	125,838	138,598
Industry	43,424	50,282	57,611
Mining and quarrying . . .	2,758	3,634	4,083
Manufacturing	40,666	46,648	53,528
Construction	15,484	21,601	29,885
Wholesale and retail trade, hotels and restaurants	80,366	102,442	105,132
Transport	33,490	39,407	39,154
Post and communications . . .	5,440	8,897	9,761
Other services	105,747	114,056	131,426
Sub-total	400,393	462,523	511,567
Less Financial intermediation services indirectly measured . .	20,731	21,424	18,508
Gross value added in basic prices	379,662	441,099	493,060
Taxes on products	48,059	49,578	63,086
Less Subsidies on products . . .	2,365	2,066	4,864
GDP in market prices . . .	425,356	488,610	551,281

BALANCE OF PAYMENTS
(US $ million)

	2000	2001	2002
Exports of goods f.o.b.	255.7	304.5	330.2
Imports of goods f.o.b.	−1,070.0	−1,331.6	−1,485.4
Trade balance	−814.3	−1,027.1	−1,155.1
Exports of services	447.8	534.3	585.0
Imports of services	−429.3	−444.1	−590.2
Balance on goods and services	−795.8	−936.9	−1,160.3
Other income received	115.9	162.5	148.3
Other income paid	−9.3	−13.5	−20.6
Balance on goods, services and income	−689.2	−787.9	−1,032.6
Current transfers received . .	629.0	647.5	683.7
Current transfers paid	−96.1	−76.9	−58.6
Current balance	−156.3	−217.3	−407.5
Capital account (net)	78.0	117.7	121.2
Direct investment from abroad .	143.0	207.3	135.0
Portfolio investment assets . . .	−25.0	−23.5	−36.8
Other investment assets . . .	−40.2	−197.2	−2.7
Other investment liabilities . .	110.6	123.4	118.0
Net errors and omissions . . .	9.8	136.3	108.5
Overall balance	119.9	146.7	35.6

Source: IMF, *International Financial Statistics*.

External Trade

PRINCIPAL COMMODITIES
(US $ million)

Imports c.i.f.	1999	2000	2001
Live animals and animal products	41.4	30.3	28.9
Vegetable products	85.9	90.7	101.9
Prepared foodstuffs; beverages spirits and vinegar; tobacco and manufactured substitutes . .	108.8	97.6	108.2
Mineral products	81.3	141.7	184.6
Products of chemical or allied industries	51.4	60.4	71.9
Textiles and textile articles . .	118.1	128.5	138.6
Footwear, headgear, umbrellas walking-sticks, whips, etc.; prepared feathers; artificial flowers; articles of human hair .	34.8	27.7	47.4
Articles of stone, plaster, cement asbestos, mica, etc.; ceramic products; glass and glassware .	30.1	41.9	49.6
Base metals and articles thereof	75.8	83.8	118.2
Machinery and mechanical appliances; electrical equipment; sound and television apparatus .	108.9	148.9	246.5
Vehicles, aircraft, vessels and associated transport equipment	70.6	80.1	70.9
Total (incl. others)	943.0	1,079.3	1,337.5

Exports f.o.b.	1999	2000	2001
Vegetable products	12.6	12.1	11.4
Prepared foodstuffs; beverages spirits and vinegar; tobacco and manufactured substitutes . .	12.7	13.7	14.1
Mineral products	17.5	7.4	5.9
Raw hides and skins, leather furskins and articles thereof; saddlery and harness; travel goods, handbags, etc. . . .	7.0	8.3	10.9
Textiles and textile articles . .	98.3	108.7	113.8
Footwear, headgear, umbrellas walking-sticks, whips, etc.; prepared feathers; artificial flowers; articles of human hair .	67.9	69.0	87.1
Base metals and articles thereof .	14.6	21.5	24.4
Machinery and mechanical appliances; electrical equipment; sound and television receivers .	12.4	4.4	7.1
Total (incl. others)	274.4	255.9	304.6

PRINCIPAL TRADING PARTNERS
(US $ million*)

Imports c.i.f.	1999	2000	2001
Austria	17	15	16
Belgium	10	6	9
Bulgaria	27	27	29
Croatia	8	13	18
Finland	2	7	26
France (incl. Monaco)	12	16	11
Germany	52	54	64
Greece	265	305	383
Italy	354	399	446
Macedonia, former Yugoslav republic	17	24	17
Netherlands	10	8	9
Romania	6	6	13
Slovenia	17	20	27
Spain	14	11	15
Turkey	52	59	82
United Kingdom	10	8	45
Total (incl. others)	943	1,079	1,338

Exports f.o.b.	1999	2000	2001
Austria	6	2	1
Denmark	3	3	1
Germany	17	17	17
Greece	40	31	40
Italy	184	182	217
Macedonia, former Yugoslav republic	4	2	5
Turkey	1	2	3
Yugoslavia	3	7	9
Total (incl. others)	274	256	305

* Imports by country of origin; exports by country of destination.

Transport

RAILWAYS
(traffic)

	1999	2000	2001
Passengers carried ('000) . . .	2,270	2,381	2,676
Passenger-km (million)	121	125	138
Freight carried ('000 metric tons) .	361	412	258
Freight ton-km (million) . . .	27	28	19

ROAD TRAFFIC
(motor vehicles in use at 31 December)

	1999	2000	2001
Passenger cars	92,252	114,532	133,533
Buses and coaches	12,306	16,806	20,813
Lorries and vans	35,266	43,301	49,600
Road tractors	1,860	2,274	2,721
Motorcycles and mopeds . . .	3,214	3,808	3,447

SHIPPING

Merchant Fleet
(registered at 31 December)

	1999	2000	2001
Number of vessels	33	34	33
Displacement ('000 gross registered tons)	21.4	23.9	25.2

Source: Lloyd's Register-Fairplay, *World Fleet Statistics*.

International Sea-borne Freight Traffic
('000 metric tons)

	1998	1999	2000
Goods loaded	108	120	132
Goods unloaded	1,536	2,040	2,424

2001 ('000 metric tons): Goods loaded 13.2 (Source: UN, *Monthly Bulletin of Statistics*).

CIVIL AVIATION
(traffic on scheduled services)

	1997	1998	1999
Passengers carried ('000) . . .	55	21	20
Passenger-km (million)	35	7	7
Total ton-km (million)	3	1	1

Source: UN, *Statistical Yearbook*.

Tourism

FOREIGN TOURIST ARRIVALS BY COUNTRY OF ORIGIN*

	1999	2000	2001
Germany	11,761	11,978	13,255
Greece	13,717	28,374	28,022
Italy	41,067	40,734	46,715
Macedonia, former Yugoslav republic	63,498	72,646	68,755
Turkey	8,226	8,889	9,446
United Kingdom	4,653	10,676	15,572
USA	10,087	12,695	12,234
Yugoslavia	155,914	93,297	109,042
Total (incl. others)	358,481	317,149	342,908

* Figures refer to arrivals at frontiers of visitors from abroad and include same-day visitors.

Tourism receipts (US $ million): 27 in 1997; 54 in 1998; 211 in 1999; 255 in 2000; 446 in 2001.

Sources: Bank of Albania; World Tourism Organization, *Yearbook of Tourism Statistics*; World Bank, *World Development Indicators*.

Communications Media

	1999	2000	2001
Television receivers ('000 in use)	455	480	n.a.
Telephones ('000 main lines in use)	140.4	152.7	197.5
Facsimile machines ('000 in use)	18.3	n.a.	n.a.
Mobile cellular telephones ('000 subscribers)	11.0	29.8	350.0
Personal computers ('000 in use)	20	25	30
Internet users ('000)	2.5	3.5	10.0

Radio receivers ('000 in use): 810 in 1997.

Book production (1991): 381 titles (including 18 pamphlets).

Daily newspapers (1996): 5; Average circulation ('000 copies) 116.

Sources: UN, *Statistical Yearbook*; UNESCO, *Statistical Yearbook*; International Telecommunication Union.

Education

(2001/02)

	Students		
	Males	Females	Total
Pre-primary	n.a.	n.a.	78,473
Primary	272,370	250,883	523,253
Secondary:			
General	48,972	51,110	100,082
Vocational	12,691	5,804	18,495
Higher*	16,036	26,124	42,160
Universities, etc.	15,953	25,713	41,666
Other	83	411	494

* Figures include those enrolled at distance-learning institutions.

Institutions: *Pre-primary:* 2,670 in 1995/96; *Primary:* 1,782 in 1994/95; *Secondary (General):* 162 in 1990; *Secondary (Vocational):* 259 in 1990; *Higher (Universities, etc.):* 8 in 1993/94; *Higher (Other):* 2 in 1993/94.

Teachers: *Pre-primary:* 4,416 in 1995/96; *Primary:* 31,369 in 1995/96; *Secondary (General):* 4,147 in 1995/96; *Secondary (Vocational):* 2,174 in 1995/96; *Higher (Universities, etc.):* 2,304 in 1996/97; *Higher (Other):* 44 in 1996/97.

Sources: Ministry of Education, Tirana, and UNESCO, *Statistical Yearbook*.

Adult literacy rate (UNESCO estimates): 84.7% (males 92.1%; females 77.0%) in 2000 (Source: UN Development Programme, *Human Development Report*).

Directory

The Constitution

In October 1998 the People's Assembly approved a new Constitution, which had been drafted by a parliamentary commission. The Constitution was endorsed at a national referendum on 22 November, and was officially adopted on 28 November.

GENERAL PROVISIONS

Albania is a parliamentary republic. The Republic of Albania is a unitary state, with a system of government based on the separation and balancing of legislative, executive and judicial powers. Sovereignty is exercised by the people through their elected representatives. The Republic of Albania recognizes and protects the national rights of people who live outside the country's borders. Political parties are created freely, and are required to conform with democratic principles. The Republic of Albania does not have an official religion, and guarantees equality of religious communities. The economic system of the Republic of Albania is based on a market economy, and on freedom of economic activity, as well as on private and public property. The armed forces ensure the independence of the country, and protect its territorial integrity and constitutional order. Local government in the Republic of Albania is exercised according to the principle of decentralization of public power. The fundamental political, economic and social rights and freedoms of Albanian citizens are guaranteed under the Constitution.

LEGISLATURE

The People's Assembly comprises at least 140 deputies, and is elected for a term of four years. One hundred deputies are elected directly in single-member constituencies, while parties receiving more than 3% of votes cast nationally are allocated further deputies in proportion to the number of votes won. The Council of Ministers,

every deputy and 20,000 voters each have the right to propose legislation. The People's Assembly makes decisions by a majority of votes, when more than one-half of the deputies are present. The 25-member Council of the Assembly is elected by the members of the People's Assembly at the beginning of the first session. The Council of the Assembly reviews preliminary draft laws, and gives opinions on specific issues.

PRESIDENT

The President of the Republic is the Head of State and represents the unity of the people. A candidate for President is proposed to the People's Assembly by a group of not less than 20 deputies. The President is elected by secret ballot by a majority of three-fifths of the members of the People's Assembly for a term of five years.

COUNCIL OF MINISTERS

The Council of Ministers comprises the Prime Minister, Deputy Prime Minister and ministers. The President of the Republic nominates as Prime Minister the candidate presented by the party or coalition of parties that has the majority of seats in the People's Assembly. The Prime Minister, within 40 days of his appointment, forms a Council of Ministers, which is presented for approval to the People's Assembly.

LOCAL GOVERNMENT

The units of local government are communes, municipalities, and regions. The representative organs of the basic units of local government are councils, which are elected by general direct elections for a period of three years. The executive organ of a municipality or commune is the Chairman. The Council of Ministers appoints a Prefect in every region as its representative.

JUDICIARY

Judicial power is exercised by the High Court, as well as by the Courts of Appeal and the Courts of First Instance. The Chairman and members of the High Court are appointed by the President of the Republic, with the approval of the People's Assembly, for a term of seven years. Other judges are appointed by the President upon the proposal of a High Council of Justice. The High Council of Justice comprises the Chairman of the High Court, the Minister of Justice, three members elected by the People's Assembly for a term of five years, and nine judges who are elected by a national judicial conference. The Constitutional Court arbitrates on constitutional issues, and determines the conformity of proposed legislation with the Constitution. The Constitutional Court comprises nine members, who are appointed by the President, with the approval of the People's Assembly, for a term of nine years.

The Government

HEAD OF STATE

President of the Republic: ALFRED MOISIU (elected 24 June 2002; took office 24 July 2002).

COUNCIL OF MINISTERS
(July 2003)

Prime Minister: FATOS NANO.

Deputy Prime Minister and Minister for Integration: ERMELINDA MEKSI.

Minister of Foreign Affairs: LUAN HAJDARAGA (acting).

Minister of Defence: PANDELI MAJKO.

Minister of Public Order: LUAN RAMA.

Minister of Justice: SPIRO PEÇI.

Minister of Transport and Telecommunications: SPARTAK POÇI.

Minister of Finance: KASTRIOT ISLAMI.

Minister of Education and Science: LUAN MEMUSHI.

Minister of Culture, Youth and Sports: ARTA DADE.

Minister of Local Government and Decentralization: BEN BLUSHI.

Minister of the Environment: LUFTER XHUVELI.

Minister of Agriculture: AGRON DUKA.

Minister of Economic Co-operation and Trade: ARBEN MALAJ.

Minister of Health: MUSTAFA XHANI.

Minister of Industry and Energy: VIKTOR DODA.

Minister of Labour and Social Affairs: VALENTINA LESKAJ.

Minister of Territory Adjustment and Tourism: BESNIK DERIVISHI.

Minister of State, responsible for Anti-corruption: BLENDI KLOSI.

MINISTRIES

Office of the Prime Minister: Bulevardi Dëshmorët e Kombit, Tirana; tel. (4) 229980; fax (4) 256267; e-mail haxhinastom@interalb.net.

Ministry of Agriculture: Bulevardi Dëshmorët e Kombit, Tirana; tel. (4) 232796; fax (4) 227924; e-mail personel@icc.al.eu.org; internet www.dfishery.gov.al.

Ministry of Culture, Youth and Sports: Ministria e Kulturës, Bulevardi Dëshmorët e Kombit, Tirana; tel. (4) 223474; fax (4) 232488; e-mail kabkult@mkrs.gov.al; internet www.mkrs.gov.al.

Ministry of Defence: Ministria e Mbrojtjes, Bulevardi Dëshmorët e Kombit, Tirana; tel. (4) 222103; fax (4) 228325; e-mail info@mod.gov.al; internet www.mod.gov.al.

Ministry of Economic Co-operation and Trade: Tirana; tel. (4) 234668; fax (4) 234658; internet www.mbet.gov.al.

Ministry of Education and Science: Ministria e Arsimit dhe Shkences, Rruga Durrësit 23, Tirana; tel. (4) 226307; fax (4) 232002; e-mail rspahia@mash.gov.al; internet www.mash.gov.al; f. 1912.

Ministry of the Environment: Rruga Durrësit 27, Tirana; tel. (4) 270630; fax (4) 270627.

Ministry of Finance: Ministria e Financave, Bulevardi Dëshmorët e Kombit, Tirana; tel. (4) 226001; fax (4) 226111; e-mail secretary.minister@minfin.gov.al; internet www.minfin.gov.al.

Ministry of Foreign Affairs: Ministria e Punëve të Jashtme, Bulevardi Zhan D'Ark 6, Tirana; tel. (4) 229521; fax (4) 362084; e-mail dshtypi@abissnet.com.al; internet www.mfa.gov.al.

Ministry of Health: Ministria e Shendetesisë, Tirana; tel. and fax (4) 264632.

Ministry of Industry and Energy: Bulevardi Dëshmorët e Kombit, Tirana; tel. (4) 227617; fax (4) 234052; e-mail dpzh@abissnet.com.al; internet www.mepp.gov.al.

Ministry for Integration: Tirana.

Ministry of Justice: Ministria e Drejtësise, Bulevardi Dëshmorët e Kombit, Tirana; tel. (4) 224041; fax (4) 228359; e-mail ministidre@albaniaonline.net.

Ministry of Labour and Social Affairs: Ministria e Punës dhe Ndihmës Sociale, Rruga e Kavajes, Tirana; tel. (4) 240412; fax (4) 227779; e-mail molsa@icc-al.org; internet www.molsa.gov.al.

Ministry of Local Government and Decentralization: Bulevardi Dëshmorët e Kombit, Tirana; tel. (4) 233538.

Ministry of Public Order: Bulevardi Dëshmorët e Kombit, Tirana; tel. and fax (4) 224364.

Ministry of Territory Adjustment and Tourism: Bulevardi Dëshmorët e Kombit, Tirana; tel. and fax (4) 227879; e-mail militar@albaniaonline.net.

Ministry of Transport and Telecommunications: Sheshi Skënderbej, Tirana; tel. (4) 234674; fax (4) 232389; e-mail cajuph@yahoo.com; internet www.mtrans.gov.al.

Legislature

KUVENDI POPULLOR
(People's Assembly)

Tirana; e-mail mmyftiu@parliament.tirana.al; internet www.parlament.al.

President (Speaker): SERVET PELLUMBI.

Deputy President: MAKBULE CECO.

General Election, 24 June and 8 July 2001

Party	% of votes	Seats
Socialist Party of Albania	41.5	73
Union for Victory*	36.8	46
Democratic Alternative	5.1	6
Social Democratic Party of Albania . . .	3.6	4
Union for Human Rights Party	2.6	3
Agrarian Party	2.6	3
Democratic Alliance Party	2.5	3
Independents	—	2
Others	5.3	—
Total	100.0	140

* Alliance comprising the Democratic Party of Albania, the Legality Movement, the Liberal Party, the National Front and the Republican Party.

Local Government

For the purposes of local government, Albania is divided into 12 prefectures, 36 districts, 65 municipalities and 305 communes. Each level of local government is independent from the others. Prefectures are administered by a representative of the Government, the Prefect, nominated by the Council of Ministers. Districts, municipalities and communes are administered by elected Councils. The chief official of a district or commune, the Chairman, is elected by the councillors. Mayors are directly elected by the people. On 27 May 1998 Albania became a signatory of the European Charter of Self-Government; subsequently, the Ministry of Local Government began to draft revised laws, in order to reform local government in accordance with the Charter. Partial local elections were held on 21 June. Further elections were held on 1 and 15 October 2000, following the preparation of a new voters' register, with assistance from the UN Development Programme. The Socialist Party of Albania (SPA) won the first round of voting, with some 43% of the votes cast, while the Democratic Party of Albania (DPA) received 34% of the votes. A second round was held for a number of mayoralities and local government councils where no candidate had obtained an overall majority in the first round of voting. Final, official results indicated that the SPA had secured 252 seats on local government councils, while the DPA had won 118.

Mayor of Tirana: EDI RAMA (SPA).

PREFECTURES

Berat: tel. (62) 34141; Prefect PELIVAN SHATRI.

Dibër: Prefect HAJREDIN TAHIRI.

Durrës: tel. (52) 23459; Prefect PETRIT AJAZI.

Elbasan: tel. (545) 2138; Prefect D. HUSHI.

Fier: tel. (642) 2187; Prefect P. ARAPI.

Gjirokastër: tel. (526) 3434; Prefect S. MANTHO.

Korçë: tel. (824) 3064; Prefect B. ALICKOLLI.

Kukës: tel. (242) 3701; Prefect QEMAL ELEZI.

Lezhë: tel. (382) 23719; Prefect GJERGJI LEQEJZA.

Shkodër: tel. (224) 2338; Prefect GJOK JAKU.

Tirana: tel. (4) 240865; Prefect ARTAN NELAJ.

Vlorë: tel. (63) 23447; Prefect TARE HAMO.

Political Organizations

Agrarian Party (AP) (Partia Agrar Shqiptare): Rruga Budi 6, Tirana; tel. and fax (4) 227481; f. 1991; Chair. LUFTER XHUVELI.

Albanian Civil Party: Tirana; f. 1998; Chair. ROLAND VELKO; Sec. ETLEVA GJERMENI.

Albanian Communist Party: Tirana; f. 1991; granted legal recognition 1998; Chair. HYSNI MILLOSHI.

Albanian Conservative Party (Partia Konservatore Shqiptare): Tirana; Chair. ARMANDO RUCO.

Albanian Ecological Party (Partia Ekologjike Shqiptare): Rruga Aleksander Moissi 26, POB 135, Tirana; tel. (4) 222503; fax (4) 234413; f. 1991; environmental political party; Chair. Dr NAMIK VEHBI, FADILE HOTI.

Albanian Green Party (Partia e Blertë Shqiptare): POB 749, Tirana; tel. and fax (4) 233309; f. 1991; campaigns on environmental issues; Chair. NEVRUZ MALUKA; Sec. SHYQRI KONDI.

Albanian Helsinki Forum (Forum Shqiptar i Helsinkit): Tirana; f. 1990; mem. International Federation of Helsinki; Chair. Prof. ARBEN PUTO.

Albanian National Democratic Party (Partia Nacional Demokratike): Tirana; f. 1991; Chair. FATMIR ÇEKANI.

Albanian Nationalist Party: Tirana; f. 1993.

Albanian New Socialist Party: Tirana; f. 1996 by former mems of the SPA.

Albanian Republican Party (ARP) (Partia Republikane Shqiptare—PRS): Tirana; f. 1991; Gen. Council of 54 mems, Steering Commission of 21 mems; Chair. SABRI GODO; Vice-Chair. FATMIR MEDIU; Sec. CERCIZ MINGOMATAS.

Albanian Women's Federation (Forum i Grus Shqiptare): Tirana; tel. (4) 228309; f. 1991; independent organization uniting women from various religious and cultural backgrounds; Chair. DIANA ÇULI.

Albanian Workers' Movement Party (Partia Levizja e Punëtóreve Shqiptare): Tirana; f. 2000; Chair. SOKOL QENDRO.

Çamëria Political and Patriotic Association (Shoqata Politike-Patriotike Çamëria): Tirana; supports the rights of the Çam minority (an Albanian people) in northern Greece; f. 1991; Chair. Dr ABAZ DOJAKA.

Christian Democratic Party of Albania (CDPA): Rruga Dëshmorët e 4 Shkurtit, Tirana; tel. (4) 2240574; fax (4) 2233024; e-mail zbushati@libero.it; f. 1991; Pres. ZEF BUSHATI; Gen.-Sec. SHPRESA PROSEKU.

Democratic Alliance Party (DAP): Tirana; internet www.aleanca .org; f. 1992 by former members of the DPA; Chair. NERITAN ÇEKA; Sec.-Gen. EDMOND DRAGOTI.

Democratic Alternative: Tirana; f. 1999 by breakaway faction of reformist members of the Democratic Party of Albania; Leader GENC POLLO.

Democratic Party of Albania (DPA) (Partia Demokratike e Shqipërisë—PDSH): Rruga Punetoret e Rilindjes; Tirana; tel. (4) 228091; fax (4) 223525; e-mail profsberisha@albaniaonline.net; internet www.albania.co.uk/dp; f. 1990; committed to centre-right democratic ideals and market economics; contested the legislative elections of June–July 2001 as part of the Union for Victory alliance; Chair. Prof. Dr SALI BERISHA; Sec.-Gen. DASHAMIR SHEHI BLERINA GJOKA.

Democratic Party of the Right: Tirana; Leader PETRIT KALAKULA.

Democratic Prosperity Party (Partia e Prosperitetit Demokratik): Tirana; f. 1991; Chair. YZEIR FETAHU.

Democratic Union of the Greek Minority (OMONIA) (Bashkimia Demokratik i Minoritet Grek): Tirana; f. 1991; Chair. JORGO LABOVITJADHI.

Democratic Unity Party (Partia e Bashkimit Demokratik): Tirana; Chair. XHEVDET LIBOHOVA.

Independent Party (Partia Indipendente): Tirana; f. 1991; Chair. EDMOND GJOKRUSHI.

Legality Movement (Partia Lëvizja e Legalitetit): Tirana; f. 1992; monarchist; contested the legislative elections of June–July 2001 as part of the Union for Victory alliance; Chair. GURI DUROLLARI.

Liberal Party (Partia Liberale): Tirana; f. 1991; contested the legislative elections of June–July 2001 as part of the Union for Victory alliance; Chair. VALTER FILE.

Movement for Democracy (Levizja per Democraci): Tirana; f. 1997 by former mems of the DPA; Leader DASHAMIR SHEHI.

National Committee of the War Veterans of the Anti-Fascist National Liberation War of the Albanian People (Komiteti Kombëtar i Veteranëve të Luftës Antifashiste Nacional Çlirimtare të Popullit Shqiptar): Rruga Dëshmorët e 4 Shkurtit, Tirana; f. 1957; Chair. PIRRO DODBIBA; Gen. Sec. QAMIL PODA.

National Front (Balli Kombëtar): c/o Kuvendi Popullor, Tirana; e-mail ilirians@hotmail.com; contested the legislative elections of June–July 2001 as part of the Union for Victory alliance; Chair. EKREM SPAHIA.

National Progress Party (Partia e Perparimit Kombëtar): Tirana; f. 1991; Chair. MYRTO XHAFERRI.

National Unity Party (Partia e Unitetit Kombëtar): Rruga Alqi Kondi, Tirana; tel. (4) 227498; fax (4) 223929; f. 1991; Chair. of Steering Cttee IDAJET BEQIRI.

New Democratic Party: Tirana; f. Feb. 2001 by former members of the DPA; Leader GENC POLLO.

New Party of Labour: Tirana; f. 1998; left-wing; defines itself as successor to the former communist Party of Labour of Albania.

People's Party (Partia Popullore): Tirana; f. 1991; aims to eradicate communism; Chair. BASHKIM DRIZA.

Republican Party (Partia Republika e Shqipërisë): Tirana; contested the legislative elections of June–July 2001 as part of the Union for Victory alliance; Chair. FATMIR MEDIU.

Right National Party: Tirana; f. 1998 by a breakaway faction of the National Front; Leader HYSEN SELFO.

Social Democratic Party of Albania (SDP) (Partia Social Demokratike e Shqipërisë—PSDS): Rruga Asim Vokshi 26, Tirana; tel. (4) 226540; fax (4) 227485; f. 1991; advocates gradual economic reforms and social justice; 100-member National Managing Council; Chair. SKENDER GJINUSHI; Gen. Sec. ENGJËLL BEJTAJ.

Social Justice Party (Partia e Drejtësise Shoqërore): Tirana.

Social Labour Party of Albania (Partia Socialpunëtórë Shqipërisë): Burrel; f. 1992; Pres. RAMADAN NDREKA.

Socialist Party of Albania (SPA) (Partia Socialiste e Shqipërisë—PSS): Tirana; tel. (4) 227409; fax (4) 227417; f. 1941 as Albanian Communist Party, renamed Party of Labour of Albania PLA in 1948, adopted present name in 1991; now rejects Marxism-Leninism and claims commitment to democratic socialism and a market economy; Managing Cttee of 81 mems, headed by Presidency of 15 mems; Chair. FATOS NANO; Sec.-Gen. GRAMOZ RUCI; 110,000 mems.

Union for Human Rights Party (UHRP) (Partia për Mbrojtjen e të Drejtat e Njeriut—PBDNj): Tirana; f. 1992; represents the Greek and Macedonian minorities; Chair. VASIL MELO; Sec.-Gen. THOMA MICO.

Union of Social Democrats (USD): Tirana; f. 1995; breakaway faction of the SDP; Leader TEODOR LACO.

Diplomatic Representation

EMBASSIES IN ALBANIA

Austria: Rruga Frederik Shiroka, Tirana; tel. (4) 233157; fax (4) 233140; e-mail tirana-ob@bmaa.gv.al; Ambassador HORST-DIETER RENNAU.

Bulgaria: Rruga Skënderbeu 12, Tirana; tel. (4) 233155; fax (4) 232272; Ambassador BOBI NIKOLOV BOBEV.

Canada: Rruga Brigada e Tete, Pall. 2, POB 47, Tirana; tel. (4) 257274; fax (4) 257273; e-mail canadalb@canada.gov.al; Ambassador STEPHEN MORAN.

China, People's Republic: Rruga Skënderbeu 57, Tirana; tel. (4) 232385; fax (4) 233159; e-mail chem@adanet.com.al; Ambassador TIAN CHANGCHUN.

Croatia: Rruga Abdyl Frashëri, Tirana; tel. (4) 228390; fax (4) 230578; Ambassador JOSIP JURAS.

Czech Republic: Rruga Skënderbeu 4, Tirana; tel. (4) 234004; fax (4) 232159; e-mail tirana@embassy.mzv.cz; Chargé d'affaires a.i. MIROSLAV ŠINDELÁŘ.

Denmark: Rruga Nikolla Tupe 1, POB 1743, Tirana; tel. (4) 257422; fax (4) 257420; e-mail tiaamb@um.dk; internet www.um.dk; Chargé d'affaires FINN THEILGAARD.

Egypt: Rruga Skënderbeu 43, Tirana; tel. (4) 233022; fax (4) 232295; Ambassador ATTIA QARAM.

France: Rruga Skënderbeu 14, Tirana; tel. (4) 234250; fax (4) 233763; e-mail ambcrtir@mail.adanet.com.al; Ambassador MICHEL MENACHEMOFF.

Germany: Rruga Skënderbeu 8, Tirana; tel. (4) 274505; fax (4) 233497; e-mail german.embassy@icc.al.eu.org; Ambassador HELMUTH SCHRÖDER.

Greece: Rruga Frederik Shiroka 3, Tirana; tel. (4) 234290; fax (4) 234443; e-mail grconstir@albnet.net; Ambassador DIMITRIS ILIOLOPOULOS.

Holy See: Rruga e Durrësit 13, POB 8355, Tirana; tel. (4) 233516; fax (4) 232001; e-mail nunap-al@icc-al.org; Apostolic Nuncio Most Rev. GIOVANNI BULAITIS (Titular Archbishop of Narona).

Hungary: Rruga Skënderbeu 16, Tirana; tel. (4) 232238; fax (4) 233211; Ambassador SÁNDOR MESZAROS.

Iran: Rruga Mustafa Matohiti 20, Tirana; tel. (4) 227869; fax (4) 230409; Ambassador MOHAMMAD KAZEM BIGDELI SOLTANI.

Italy: Rruga Lek Dukagjini, Tirana; tel. (4) 234045; fax (4) 234276; e-mail ambittia@icc.al.eu.org; internet www.ambitalia-tirana.com; Ambassador ATTILIO MASSIMO IANNUCCI.

Libya: Rruga Dëshmorët e 4 Shkurtit 48, Tirana; tel. (4) 228101; fax (4) 232098; Bureau Chief YOUSSEF ELTAEF SASSI.

Macedonia, former Yugoslav republic: Rruga Lek Dukagjini, Vila 2; tel. (4) 233036; fax (4) 232514; Ambassador ELEONORA KARANFILOVSKA.

Netherlands: Rruga e Vilave Gjermane 8, POB 1735, Tirana; tel. (4) 375111; fax (4) 375982; Ambassador FREDERIK LODEWIJK.

Norway: Rruga Dëshmorët e 4 Shkurtit 7/1; tel. and fax (4) 257035; Chargé d'affaires TOBIAS FRAMBE SVENNINGSEN.

Poland: Rruga e Durrësit 123, Tirana; tel. (4) 234190; fax (4) 233464; Ambassador ARTUR TOMASZEWSKI.

Romania: Rruga Themistokli, Gjermeni 2, Tirana; tel. (4) 256071; fax (4) 256072; e-mail roemb@adanet.co.al; Ambassador CONSTANTIN EREMIA.

Russia: Rruga Asim Zeneli 5, Tirana; tel. (4) 256040; fax (4) 256046; Ambassador VLADIMIR N. TOKIN.

Saudi Arabia: Bulevardi Dëshmorët e Kombit; tel. (4) 248307; fax (4) 229982; Chargé d'affaires MOHAMMED LABANI.

Serbia and Montenegro: Tirana; Ambassador CAFO KAPETANOVIĆ.

Switzerland: Rruga e Elbasanit 81, Tirana; tel. (4) 234890; fax (4) 234889; e-mail swissemb@adanet.com.al; Ambassador FRANCIS COUSIN.

Turkey: Rruga Konferenca e Kavajes 31, Tirana; tel. (4) 233399; fax (4) 232719; e-mail turkemb@interalb.al; Ambassador MEHMET MURAT OĞUZ.

United Kingdom: Rruga Skënderbeu 12, Tirana; tel. (4) 234973; fax (4) 247697; Ambassador DAVID LANDSMAN.

USA: Rruga Labinoti 103, Tirana; tel. (4) 247285; fax (4) 232222; e-mail wm_tirana@pd.state.gov; internet www.usemb-tirana.rpo.al; Ambassador JAMES FRANKLIN JEFFREY.

Judicial System

The judicial structure comprises the High Court, the Courts of Appeal and the Courts of First Instance. The Chairman and members of the High Court are appointed by the President of the Republic, with the approval of the legislature, for a term of seven years. Other judges are appointed by the President upon the proposal of a High Council of Justice. The High Council of Justice comprises the Chairman of the High Court, the Minister of Justice, three members elected by the legislature for a term of five years, and nine judges of all levels who are elected by a national judicial conference. The Constitutional Court arbitrates on constitutional issues, and determines, *inter alia*, the conformity of proposed legis-

lation with the Constitution. It is empowered to prohibit the activities of political organizations on constitutional grounds, and also formulates legislation regarding the election of the President of the Republic. The Constitutional Court comprises nine members, who are appointed by the President, with the approval of the legislature, for a term of nine years.

Supreme Court (Gjykata e Larte): Tirana; e-mail supremecourt@albaniaonline.net; internet www.gjykataelarte.gov.al; Chief Justice THIMJO KONDI.

Constitutional Court: e-mail kujtim.osmani@gjk.gov.al; internet www.gjk.gov.al; Chair. Dr FEHMI ABDIU.

Religion

All religious institutions were closed by the Government in 1967 and the practice of religion was prohibited. In May 1990, however, the prohibition on religious activities was revoked, religious services were permitted and, from 1991, mosques and churches began to be reopened. Under the Constitution of November 1998, Albania is a secular state, which observes freedom of religious belief. On the basis of declared affiliation in 1945, it is estimated that some 70% of the population are of Muslim background (mainly Sunni or adherents of the liberal Bektashi order), 20% Eastern Orthodox Christian (mainly in the south) and some 10% Roman Catholic Christian (mainly in the north).

ISLAM

Albanian Islamic Community (Bashkesia Islame e Shqipërisë): Rruga Puntoret e Rilindjes, Tirana; e-mail icalb@yahoo.com; f. 1991; Chair. HAFIZ H. SABRI KOÇI; Grand Mufti of Albania HAFIZ SELIM STAFA.

Bektashi Sect

World Council of Elders of the Bektashis: Tirana; f. 1991; Chair. RESHAT BABA BARDHI.

CHRISTIANITY

The Eastern Orthodox Church

Orthodox Autocephalous Church of Albania (Kisha Orthodhokse Autoqefale të Shqipërisë): Rruga Kavaja 151, Tirana; tel. (4) 234117; fax (4) 232109; e-mail orthchal@ocual.tirana.al; the Albanian Orthodox Church was proclaimed autocephalous at the Congress of Berat in 1922, its status was approved in 1929 and it was recognized by the Ecumenical Patriarchate in Istanbul (Constantinople), Turkey, in 1936; Archbishop ANASTAS JANNOULATOS.

The Roman Catholic Church

Many Roman Catholic churches have been reopened since 1990, and in September 1991 diplomatic relations were restored with the Holy See. Albania comprises two archdioceses, four dioceses and one apostolic administration. At 31 December 2001 there were an estimated 495,085 adherents in the country, representing about 13.4% of the total population.

Bishops' Conference: Conferenza Episcopale dell'Albania, Rruga Don Bosco, Tirana; tel. and fax (4) 247159; e-mail cealbania@albnet.net; Pres. Most Rev. ANGELO MASSAFRA (Metropolitan Archbishop of Shkodër).

Archbishop of Durrës-Tirana: Most Rev. RROK K. MIRDITA, Arqipeshkvia, Bulevard Zhan d'Ark, Tirana; tel. (4) 232082; fax (4) 230727; e-mail arq@icc.al.org.

Archbishop of Shkodër: Most Rev. ANGELO MASSAFRA, Kryeipeshkëvi, Sheshi Gijon Pali II, Shkodër; tel. (22) 42744; fax (22) 43673.

The Press

Until 1991 the Press was controlled by the Party of Labour of Albania, now the Socialist Party of Albania (SPA), and adhered to a strongly Marxist-Leninist line. From 1991 many new periodicals and newspapers were established by the newly emerging independent political organizations. In 2000 there were some 12 daily newspapers and 18 principal weekly periodicals in publication. The total daily circulation of all newspapers declined to less than 50,000 in 2000, compared with 65,000 in 1999.

PRINCIPAL DAILIES

Albania: POB 749, Tirana; tel. and fax (4) 233309; f. 1991; weekly; organ of the Albanian Green Party; environmental issues.

Albanian Daily News: Rruga Hile Mosi, 5, Tirana; tel. and fax (4) 227639; e-mail adn@icc.al.eu.org; internet www.albaniannews.com; f. 1995; weekly; English-language newspaper; Editor ARBEN LESKAJ.

Ekonomia: Bulevardi Zhan D'Ark, Tirana; tel. (4) 250766; fax (4) 250767; e-mail gazekonomia@albaniaonline.com.

Gazeta Shqiptare: Rruga e Dibres 370, Tirana; tel. (4) 262646; fax (4) 263885; e-mail gazesh@katamail.com.

Koha Jonë (Our Time): Sami Frasheri, Pallatet e Aviacionit, Tirana; tel. (4) 247004; fax (4) 247005; e-mail kohajone@albnet.net; internet www.kohajone.com; f. 1991; independent; Editor-in-Chief KICO BLUSHI; circ. 400,000.

Republika: Sami Frasheri, Pallatet e Aviacionit, Tirana; tel. and fax (4) 25988; e-mail republika@albaniaonline.net; internet www.pages.albaniaonline.net/republika; organ of the Republican Party; Editor-in-Chief YLLI RAKIPI.

Rilindja Demokratike (Democratic Revival): Rruga Punetoret e Rindjes 16, Tirana; tel. (4) 229609; fax (4) 242329; e-mail gazetard@albaniaonline.net; internet www.rilindjademokratike.com; f. 1991; organ of the DPA; Editor-in-Chief LORENC LIGORI; circ. 50,000.

Shekulli: Rruga Don Bosko, Vilat e Reja, Tirana; tel. (4) 251425; fax (4) 251424; e-mail webmaster@shekulli.com.al; internet www.shekulli.com.al; independent; Editor-in-Chief ZAMIR ALUSHI.

Tema: Rruga Xhorxhi Martini 10; tel. (4) 251069; fax (4) 251073; e-mail tema@albaniaonline.net.

Zëri i Popullit (The Voice of the People): Bulevardi Zhan D'Ark, Tirana; tel. (4) 222192; fax (4) 227813; e-mail zeri@zeripopullit.com; internet www.zeripopullit.com; f. 1942; daily, except Mon.; organ of the SPA; Editor-in-Chief ERION BRACE; circ. 105,000.

PERIODICALS

Agrovizion: Rruga d'Istria, Tirana; tel. (4) 226147; f. 1992; 2 a week; agricultural economic policies, new technology in farming, advice for farmers; circ. 3,000.

Albanian Observer: Rruga Perlat Rexhepi Pall. 9, Shkurtit 1, Tirana; tel. and fax (4) 227419.

Bashkimi Kombëtar: Bulevardi Zhan D'Ark, Tirana; tel. (4) 228110; f. 1943; Editor-in-Chief QEMAL SAKAJEVA; circ. 30,000.

Blic: Rruga Fortuzi 44, Tirana; tel. (4) 234319; e-mail blici@juno.com; weekly; politics, information and culture; Editor ILIR YZEIRI.

Ditet Tona: Rruga Margaret Tutulani, Pall. 23, Shkurtit 1, Tirana; tel. (4) 230585.

Drita (The Light): Rruga Konferenca e Pezës 4, Tirana; tel. (4) 227036; f. 1960; weekly; publ. by Union of Writers and Artists of Albania; Editor-in-Chief BRISEIDA MEMA; circ. 31,000.

Fatosi (The Valiant): Tirana; tel. (4) 223024; f. 1959; fortnightly; literary and artistic magazine for children; Editor-in-Chief XHEVAT BEQARAJ; circ. 21,200.

Hosteni (The Goad): Tirana; f. 1945; fortnightly; political review of humour and satire; publ. by the Union of Journalists; Editor-in-Chief NIKO NIKOLLA.

The Hour of Albania: Rruga Dëshmorët e 4 Shkurtit, Tirana; tel. (4) 242042; fax (4) 234024; weekly; organ of the Christian Democratic Party of Albania; Editor-in-Chief Dr FAIK LAMA; circ. 3,000.

Identity: Rruga Daut Boriçi 874, Shköder; tel. (22) 41229; e-mail irsh@albnet.net.

Intervista: Rruga e Dibres 133, Tirana; tel. (4) 233164.

Klan: Rruga Myslym Shyri 8/1, Tirana; tel. (4) 240304; fax (4) 234424; e-mail klan@albnet.net.

Kombi (The Nation): Rruga Alqi Kondi, Tirana; tel. (4) 227498; fax (4) 229329; f. 1991; 2 a week; organ of the Party of National Unity; circ. 15,000.

Mbrojtja (The Defence): Bulevardi Dëshmorët e Kombit, Tirana; tel. (4) 226701; fax (4) 225726; e-mail tanct@al.pims.org; f. 1931; every 2 months; publ. by the Ministry of Defence; Editor-in-Chief ELMAZ LECI; circ. 1,500.

Official Gazette of the Republic of Albania: Kuvendi Popullore, Tirana; tel. (4) 228668; fax (4) 227949; f. 1945; occasional government review.

Pasqyra (The Mirror): Bulevardi Zogu I, Pall. A. Kelmendi, Tirana; tel. (4) 222956; fax (4) 229169; e-mail marketingu@pasqyra.com; internet www.pasqyra.com; f. 1991 to replace *Puna* (*Labour*); f. 1945; weekly; organ of the Confederation of Albanian Trade Unions; Editor-in-Chief XHAFER SHATRI.

Progresi (Progress): Rruga Budi 6, Tirana; tel. (4) 227481; fax (4) 227481; f. 1991; 2 a week; organ of the Agrarian Party.

Revista Pedagogjike: Naim Frashëri St 37, Tirana; fax (4) 256441; f. 1945; quarterly; organ of the Institute of Pedagogical Studies;

educational development, psychology, didactic; Editor BUJAR BASKA; circ. 4,000.

Shëndeti (Health): M. Duri 2, Tirana; tel. (4) 227803; fax (4) 227803; f. 1949; monthly; publ. by the National Directorate of Health Education; issues of health and welfare, personal health care; Editors-in-Chief KORNELIA GJATA, AGIM XHUMARI.

Shqiptarja e Re (The New Albanian Woman): Tirana; f. 1943; monthly; political and socio-cultural review; Editor-in-Chief VALENTINA LESKAJ.

Sindikalisti (Trade Unionists): Tirana; f. 1991; newspaper; organ of the Union of Independent Trade Unions of Albania; Editor-in-Chief VANGJEL KOZMAI.

Spektër (The Spectre): Tirana; e-mail redaksia@spekter.com.al; internet www.spekter.com.al; f. 1991; illustrated independent monthly; in Albanian and Italian.

Sporti Shqiptar: Rruga e Kavajës 23, Sheshi Ataturk, 2908 Tirana; tel. and fax (4) 220237; f. 1935; 3 a week; Editor BESNIK DIZDARI; circ. 10,000.

Tregtia e Jashtme Popullore (Albanian Foreign Trade): Rruga Konferenca e Pezës 6, Tirana; tel. (4) 222934; f. 1961; 6 a year; in English and French; organ of the Albanian Chamber of Commerce; Editor AGIM KORBI.

Tribuna e Gazetarit (The Journalist's Tribune): Tirana; 6 a year; publ. by the Union of Journalists of Albania; Editor NAZMI QAMILI.

Ushtria (Army): Bulevardi Dëshmorët e Kombit, Tirana; tel. (4) 224350; fax (4) 225726; f. 1945; weekly; publ. by the Ministry of Defence; Editor-in-Chief BARDHYL GOSNISHTI; circ. 3,200.

NEWS AGENCIES

Albanian Independent News Agency: Rruga 4 Dëshmorët 80, Tirana; tel. (4) 241727; fax (4) 233866.

Albanian Telegraphic Agency (ATA): Bulevardi Zhan D'Ark 23, Tirana; tel. (4) 222929; fax (4) 234230; e-mail hola@ata.tirana.al; internet www.ata-al.net; f. 1929; domestic and foreign news; brs in provincial towns and in Kosovo, Serbia and Montenegro; Dir-Gen. FRROK CUPI.

Enter: Shetitorja Dëshmorët e Kombit, Tirana; tel. (4) 240129; fax (4) 235916; internet www.Albania.co.uk/enter.

Foreign Bureau

Xinhua (New China) News Agency (People's Republic of China): Rruga Zef Jubani 3, Apt 903, Tirana; tel. (4) 233139; fax (4) 248019; e-mail xinhua-tirana@china.com; Bureau Chief LI JIYU.

PRESS ASSOCIATIONS

Albanian Media Institute: Rruga Gjin Bue Shpata 8, Tirana; tel. and fax (4) 229800; e-mail info@institutemedia.org.

Union of Journalists of Albania (Bashkimi i Gazetarëve të Shqipërisë): Tirana; tel. (4) 228020; f. 1949; Chair. MARASH HAJATI; Sec.-Gen. YMER MINXHOZI.

Publishers

Agjensia Qëndrore e Tregtimit të Librit Artistik dhe Shkencor (Central Agency of the Artistic and Scientific Book Trade): Tirana; tel. and fax (4) 227246.

Botime të Akademisë së Shkencave të RSH: Tirana; publishing house of the Albanian Academy of Sciences.

Botime të Universitetit Bujqësor te Tiranës: Kamzë, Tirana; publishing house of the Agricultural University of Tirana.

Botime të Shtëpisë Botuese 8 Nëntori: Tirana; tel. (4) 228064; f. 1972; books on Albania and other countries, political and social sciences, translations of Albanian works into foreign languages, technical and scientific books, illustrated albums, etc.; Dir XHEMAL DINI.

Dituria Publishing House: Rruga Dervish Hima 32, Tirana; tel. and fax (4) 225882; f. 1991; dictionaries, calendars, encyclopedias, social sciences, biographies, fiction and non-fiction; Gen. Dir PETRIT YMERI.

Drejtoria e Informacionit Agro-Ushqimor (Agriculture and Food Information Directory): Rruga S. Kosturi, Tirana; tel. (4) 226147; f. 1970; publishes various agricultural periodicals; Gen. Dir Prof. AGO NEZHA.

Fan Noli: Tirana; tel. (4) 242739; f. 1991; Albanian and foreign literature.

Shtëpia Botuese e Librit Shkollor: Tirana; tel. (4) 222331; f. 1967; educational books; Dir SHPËTIM BOZDO.

Shtëpia Botuese 'Libri Universitar': Rruga Dora d'Istria, Tirana; tel. (4) 225659; fax (4) 229268; f. 1988; publishes university textbooks on science, medicine, engineering, geography, history, literature, foreign languages, economics, etc.; Dir Mustafa Fezga.

Shtëpia Botuese e Lidhjes së Shkrimtarëve: Konferenca e Pezës 4, Tirana; tel. (4) 222691; fax (4) 225912; f. 1990; artistic and documentary literature; Dir Zija Çela.

Shtëpia Botuese Naim Frashëri: Tirana; tel. (4) 227906; f. 1947; fiction, poetry, drama, criticism, children's literature, translations; Dir Gaqo Bushaka.

Broadcasting and Communications

TELECOMMUNICATIONS

State Department of Posts and Telecommunications: Rruga Myslym Shyri 42, Tirana; tel. (4) 227204; fax (4) 233772; e-mail kote@dshpt.tirana.al; Gen. Dir Hydajet Kopani; Man. Dir Frederik Kote.

Albanian Mobile Communications (AMC): Rruga Gjergi Legisi, Laprake, Tirana; tel. (4) 234915; fax (4) 235157; e-mail agreva@amc.al; f. 1996; fmrly state-owned, bought by a Greek/Norwegian consortium in 2000; operates mobile-telephone network; Man. Dir Stefanos Oktapodas.

Albanian Telecom (Telekomi Shqiptar): Rruga Myslym Shyri 42, Tirana; tel. (4) 232169; fax (4) 233323; e-mail infocenter@atnet.com.al; internet www.atnet.com.al; scheduled for privatization in 2003; Dir-Gen. Dhimitraq Rafti.

BROADCASTING

In 1991 state broadcasting was removed from political control and made subordinate to the Parliamentary Commission for the Media. By the end of 2000 the National Council of Radio and Television had licensed two national television stations, 45 local television stations, one national radio station and 31 local radio stations.

Regulatory Authority

National Council of Radio and Television (NCRT): Rruga Abdi Toptani, Tirana; tel. (4) 233326; fax (4) 226287; e-mail scela@kkrt.gov.al; internet www.kkrt.gov.al; f. 1998; Chair. Sefedin Cela.

Radio

Radio Televizioni Shqiptare: Rruga Ismail Qemali 11, Tirana; tel. (4) 228310; fax (4) 227745; e-mail dushiulp@yahoo.com; internet www.rtsh.sil.al; f. 1938 as Radio Tirana; two channels of domestic services (19 and five hours daily) and a third channel covering international broadcasting (two services in Albanian and seven in foreign languages); Chair. Kastrist Causbi; Dir-Gen. Eduard Mazi; Dir of Radio Martin Leka.

Kontakt Radio: Rruga Muhamet Gjollesha, Kati i9, Tirana; tel. (4) 249474; fax (4) 257602; e-mail radiokontakt@albaniaonline.net; internet www.radiokontakt.com; independent radio station; commenced broadcasts Oct. 1997; Dir Agron Bala.

Radio Klan: Rruga Myslim Shyri 8/1, Tirana; tel. (4) 240304; e-mail klan@albnet.net.

Top Albania Radio: International Centre of Culture, Bulevardi Dëshmorët e Kombit, Tirana; tel. (4) 247492; fax (4) 247493; e-mail topalbaniaradio@albaniaonline.net; internet www.pages.albania online.net/topalbaniaradio.

Television

Radio Televizioni Shqiptare: Rruga Ismail Qemali 11, Tirana; tel. (4) 256056; fax (4) 256058; f. 1960; broadcasts range of television programmes; Chair. Kastrist Causbi; Dir-Gen. Eduard Mazi; Dir of Television Vena Isak.

Alba Television: International Centre of Culture, Bulevardi Dëshmorët e Kombit, Tirana; tel. and fax (4) 234142; e-mail albatv@albaniaonline.net; internet www.pages.albaniaonline.net/albatv; private television station; Dir Paulin Shkjezi.

Shijak TV: Rruga Kavajes, Sheshi Ataturk, Tirana; tel. and fax (4) 247135; e-mail shijaktv01@albaniaonline.net; internet www.shijaktv.com; Pres. Gëzim Ismaili.

Teutar Televizion: Tirana; e-mail teutartv@albaniaonline.net; internet www.teutartv.com.

Finance

(cap. = capital; dep. = deposits; res = reserves; m. = million; brs = branches; amounts in lekë, unless otherwise stated)

BANKING

Central Bank

Bank of Albania (Banka e Shqipërisë): Sheshi Skënderbeu 1, Tirana; tel. (4) 222752; fax (4) 223558; e-mail public@bankofalbania.org; internet www.bankofalbania.org; f. 1992; cap. 750m., res 11,395m., dep. 41,491m. (Dec. 2001); Gov. Shkëlqim Cani; 5 brs.

State Bank

Savings Bank of Albania: Rruga Dëshmorët e 4 Shkurtit 6, Tirana; tel. (4) 224972; fax (4) 223587; e-mail info@bkursimeve.com.al; internet www.bkursimeve.com.al; f. 1991; state-owned, scheduled for privatization in Dec. 2003; cap. 700m., res 2,109m., dep. 147,300m. (Dec. 2001); Gen. Man. Ardian Kamberi; 37 brs.

Other Banks

American Bank of Albania (Banka Amerikanë e Shqipërisë): Rruga Ismail Qemali 27, POB 8319, Tirana; tel. (4) 248753; fax (4) 248762; e-mail americanbank@ambankalb.com; internet www.albambank.com; f. 1998; owned by Albanian-American Enterprise Fund USA; cap. US $5.1m.; Chair. Michael Granoff; Pres. and Chief Exec. Lorenzo Roncari.

Arab-Albanian Islamic Bank: Dëshmorët e Kombit 8, POB 128, Tirana; tel. (4) 227408; fax (4) 228460; e-mail aaib@albaniaonline.net; f. 1994; joint venture; cap. US $10.0m., res $1.1m., dep. $7.1m. (2001); Chair. Solaiman Elkhereiji; Gen. Dir Waheed Alaui.

Fefad Bank: Rruga Ami Frasheri, POB 2395, Tirana; tel. (4) 220774; fax (4) 233481; e-mail fefad@icc.al.eu.org; internet www.fefadbank.com; f. 1996 as Foundation for Enterprise Finance and Development; name changed 1999; cap. 700.0m., res 56.7m., dep. 7,352.2m. (Dec. 2002); Gen. Man. Emmanuel Decamps; 9 brs.

Italian-Albanian Bank (Banka Italo Shqiptare): Rruga e Barrikadave, Tirana; tel. (4) 235693; fax (4) 235700; e-mail biatia@adanet.com.al; f. 1993; cap. US $15.5m., res $0.9m., dep. $99.9m.; Pres. Edmond Leka; Chair. Giovanni Bogani.

National Commercial Bank of Albania: Bulevardi Zhan D'Ark, Tirana; tel. (4) 250955; fax (4) 250960; e-mail bkt@albmail.com; internet www.come.to.ncba; f. 1993; following merger of National Bank of Albania and Commercial Bank of Albania; privatized in 2000; cap. US $10.0m., res $2.8m., dep. $207.8m. (Dec. 2001); Chair. Ilhan Nebioglu; 30 brs.

Tirana Bank SA: Bulevardi Zogu I 55/1, Tirana; tel. (4) 233441; fax (4) 247140; e-mail tiranabank@icc.al.eu.org; f. 1996; cap. 1,040.5m., res 118.9m., dep. 17,127.7m. (Dec. 2001); Chair. Stavros Lekakos.

INSURANCE

Agjensia Shqiptare e Garancisë (ASHG): Rruga Ismail Qemali 34, Tirana; tel. (4) 247048; fax (4) 247047; e-mail aga@aga-al.com; internet www.aga-al.com.

Insurance Institute of Albania (Instituti i Sigurimeve të Shqipërisë): Bulevardi Marcel Cachin, Tirana; tel. (4) 234170; fax (4) 223838; e-mail info@insig.com.al; internet www.insig.com.al; f. 1991; all types of insurance; Gen. Dir Qemal Disha; 12 brs.

Sigal: Bulevardi Dëshmorët e Kombit, Pall. i Diplomatëve 57, Tirana; tel. and fax (4) 250220; e-mail info@sigal.com.al; internet www.albanianinsurance.com.

STOCK EXCHANGE

Tirana Stock Exchange: Sheshi Skënderbeu 1, Tirana; tel. (4) 235568; fax (4) 223558; e-mail emeka@bankofalbania.org; internet www.asc.gov.al/tiranastock.html; f. 1996; Gen. Dir Elvin Meka (acting).

Trade and Industry

PRIVATIZATION AGENCY

National Agency for Privatization (NAP): Tirana; tel. and fax (4) 227933; govt agency under the control of the Council of Ministers; prepares and proposes the legal framework concerning privatization procedures and implementation; Dir Niko Glozheni.

SUPERVISORY ORGANIZATIONS

Albanian Securities Commission (ASC): Bulevardi Dëshmorët e Kombit, Tirana; tel. and fax (4) 228260; e-mail asc@albaniaonline .net; internet www.asc.gov.al; Chair. ELISABETA GTONI.

Albkontroll: Rruga Skënderbeu 45, Durrës; tel. (52) 23377; fax (52) 22791; f. 1962; brs throughout Albania; independent control body for inspection of goods for import and export, means of transport, etc.; Gen. Man. DILAVER MEZINI; 15 brs.

State Supreme Audit Control: Region Eurosai, Tirana; tel. and fax (4) 232491; e-mail klsh@albaniaonline.net; internet www.pages .albanianonline.net/klsh.

DEVELOPMENT ORGANIZATIONS

Albanian Centre for Economic Research: Rruga Frasheri 24, POB 2934, Tirana; tel. and fax (4) 225021; e-mail zefi@qske.tirana .al; internet www.arc.online.bq/ngos/albanian/acer.html; Pres. ZEF PREÇI.

Albanian Centre for Foreign Investment Promotion: Bulevardi Zhan D'Ark, Tirana; tel. (4) 228439; internet www.ipanet.net.

Albanian Development Fund: Rruga Durrësi, Tirana; tel. and fax (4) 2234885; e-mail eneida@a-d-f.org; Exec. Dir MAKS MITROJORGJI.

Albanian Economy Development Agency (AEDA): Bulevardi Zhan D'Ark, Tirana; tel. (4) 230133; fax (4) 228439; e-mail xhepa@ cpfi.tirana.al; internet www.aeda.gov.al; f. 1993; govt agency to promote foreign investment in Albania and to provide practical support to foreign investors; publishes Ekonomia; Chair. SELAMI XHEPA.

Business in Albania: Lagja Luigi Gurakuqi, Palliti 73, Elbasen; tel. and fax (54) 58994; e-mail gmaksuti@yahoo.com; provision of information on commerce and business in Albania; market research; Pres. TOM LODGE.

Enterprise Restructuring Agency (Agjensia e Ristrukturimit te Ndermarrjeve): Rruga e Durrësit 83, Tirana; tel. (4) 227878; fax (4) 225730; govt agency established to assist state-owned enterprises to become privately owned by offering enterprise sector surveys, strategic plans and consultations; provides technical assistance; Dir ADRIATIK BANKJA.

Foreign Investors' Association of Albania: Tirana Business Centre, Suite 20, Bulevardi Zogu I-re, Tirana; tel. (4) 256296; fax (4) 256291; e-mail fiaalb@hotmail.com; internet www.fiaalbania.org.

International Research And Exchange Board: Rruga Him Kolli 45, Tirana; tel. (4) 247543; fax (4) 247544; e-mail promedia@irex .tirana.al; internet www.irex.org.

Trade and Investment Promotion Support: Bulevardi Zhan D'Ark, Tirana; tel. and fax (4) 262067; e-mail besnik@tips.tirana.al; internet www.tips.eu.org/albania.

CHAMBERS OF COMMERCE

Union of Chambers of Commerce and Industry of Albania: Rruga Kavajes 6, Tirana; tel. and fax (4) 222934; f. 1958; Pres. ANTON LEKA.

Durrës Chamber of Commerce: Durrës; f. 1988; promotes trade with southern Italy.

Gjirokastër Chamber of Commerce: Gjirokastër; f. 1988; promotes trade with Greek border area.

Korçë Chamber of Commerce and Industry: Bulevardi Republika, Korçë; tel. and fax (82) 42457; e-mail dhtiko@icc.al.eu.org; internet www.albchamber.org; f. 1995.

Shkodër Chamber of Commerce: Shkodër; promotes trade with Yugoslav border area.

Tirana Chamber of Commerce and Industry: Rruga Kavajes 6, Tirana; tel. (4) 232448; fax (4) 229779; e-mail ccitr@abissnet.com.al; internet www.cci.gov.al; f. 1926; Chair. LUAN BREGASI.

There are also chambers of commerce in Kukës, Peshkopi, Pogradec, Sarandë and Vlorë.

UTILITIES

Electricity

State Electricity Corporation of Albania (Korporata Elektroenergjetike Shqiptare—KESH): Biloky 'Vasil Shanto', Tirana; tel. (4) 228434; fax (4) 232046; e-mail kesh@icc.al.eu.org; state corpn for the generation, transmission, distribution and export of electrical energy; govt-controlled; scheduled for reorganization in 2003, prior to transfer to private ownership; Chair. BASHKIM QATIPI; Gen. Dir Dr NAKO HOBDARI.

MAJOR COMPANIES

Prior to 1990 foreign trade was a state monopoly in Albania, and was conducted solely through foreign-trade organizations. By 2001 over 75% of gross domestic product was generated in the private sector, and the divestment of viable small and medium-sized enterprises had been largely completed.

Agroeksport SHPK: Rruga 4 Shkurti 6, Tirana; tel. (4) 229788; fax (4) 223871; fmrly foreign trade org.; exports of pharmaceuticals, trade in food and groceries, and import of consumer goods; Man. Dir PERPARIM RAMA.

Albanian Petroleum Corpn (Albpetrol): Rruga Fier, Tirana; tel. and fax (4) 256506; privatized in 2001; Chair. Dr FOTAQ DIAMANTI; Gen. Dir GJERGJ KERRI.

Albbaker: Blloku Vasil Shanto, Institut te Kemise, Tirana; tel. (4) 225190; fax (4) 242736; f. 1992 to aid the reorganization, restoration and development of Albania's copper industry; managed by Metals Research Group of the USA from May 2000.

Albchrome: Bulquza; state-owned mining and smelting group; scheduled for privatization; Gen. Dir RAMADAN DISHA.

Apolon-5 SHPK: Rruga Kongresi i Manastirit 20, Tirana; tel. and fax (4) 223862; e-mail bekjo@albaniaonline.net; production and sale of alcoholic beverages and tobacco; Pres. MIRUSH BEJKO.

Arteksportimport: Rruga 4 Shkurti 6, Tirana; tel. (4) 226417; fax (4) 225578; f. 1989; fmrly foreign trade org.; imports and exports handicrafts, light industrial products, clothing, food, and raw materials for the chemical and textiles industries; Gen. Dir TEFIK KOKONA; 70 employees.

Bora Chemical Plant (ND Kimike Bora): Rruga 5 Maji, Tirana; tel. and fax (4) 232522; produces and sells chemicals and ferrous metals.

Botimpex: Rruga Naim Frasheri P 84; tel. and fax (4) 226886; e-mail botimpex@albaniaonline.net; internet www.botimpex.com; Dir Dr ESTREF BEGA.

Dibërimpeks: Peshkopi; f. 1990; former regional foreign trade org.; handles border trade with Yugoslavia and the former Yugoslav republic of Macedonia; minerals and agricultural products.

Durrësimpeks: Rruga Skënderbeu 177, Durrës; tel. (52) 22199; f. 1988; former regional foreign trade org.; handles border trade with southern Italy (Puglia); industrial and agricultural goods; Dir TAQO KOSTA.

Elbasan Steel Works: Kombinati Siderurgjik, Elbasan; tel. (54) 56500; fax (54) 57844; owned by Kurum Demir (Turkey); Gen. Dir BÜLENT SARAGÜL.

Gjirokastërimpeks: Rruga Kombëtare 55, Gjirokastër; tel. (526) 707; f. 1988; former regional foreign trade org.; handles border trade with Greece; industrial and agricultural goods.

INCAT (Albania): Lagia 1, Rruga Qemal Stafa, Durrës; tel. and fax (52) 23855; owned by INCAT Group (Channel Islands); civil engineering, constructs oilfields, pipelines, water and sewage treatment facilities, and related equipment; Gen. Man. SIMONA BRACI.

Industrialimpeks: Rruga 4 Shkurti 6, Tirana; tel. (4) 226123; fmrly foreign trade org.; exports copper wires, furniture, kitchenware, paper, timber, wooden articles, cement, etc.; imports fabrics, cement, chemicals, paper, cardboard, school and office items, etc.; Gen. Man. FARUK BOROVA.

Karajani SHPK: Rruga Seit Toptani 2, Tirana; tel. (4) 223972; processes and recycles metals; Gen. Dir THANAS KARAJANI.

Kukësimpeks: Kukës; former regional foreign trade org.; handles trade with Serbia and Montenegro and the former Yugoslav republic of Macedonia; Dir ASIM BARUTI.

Lushnje Plastic Plant: Lushnje; tel. (4) 234607; fax (4) 222387; f. 1976; manufactures plastic goods; 520 employees.

Mak Albania: Sheshi Italia, Tirana; tel. (4) 227606; fax (4) 227803; e-mail makal-ao@icc.eu.al.ork; internet www.makalbania.com; f. 1994; owned by Kharafi Group (Kuwait); construction of tourist facilities and hospitals; Pres. NASSER AL-KHARIFI.

Makinaimpeks: Rruga 4 Shkurti 6, Tirana; tel. (4) 223267; fax (4) 227903; f. 1958; fmrly foreign trade org.; imports vehicles, factory installations, machinery and parts; exports explosives; Gen. Man. AFRIM BALLKA; 70 employees.

Mandimpeks: Rruga Lek Dukagjini, Tirana; tel. (4) 234508; fmrly foreign trade org.; imports metals, concrete, paints and design materials; exports cement, marble and ceramics.

Minergoimpeks: Rruga Marsel Kashen 86, Tirana; tel. (4) 223961; fax (4) 234073; f. 1990; fmrly foreign trade org.; exports products of the mining, metallurgical and petroleum industries; imports machinery and equipment, lubricating oils and raw materials; Gen. Dir QAZIM WAZIMI.

Transalbania: Rruga Deshmorët e 4 Shkurti 6, Tirana; tel. (4) 229727; fax (4) 227605; e-mail tiabo@kuna.geis.com; f. 1960; fmrly foreign trade org.; transport and forwarding of foreign trade goods by sea, road and rail; agents in Durrës, Vlorë and at Albanian border crossings; Gen. Man. Andon Hila.

Uzina Dinamo (Dinamo Factory): Rruga Ferrit Xhajko, Tirana; tel. and fax (4) 262401; produces ferrous metals and mining equipment, metal components and storage tanks; Gen. Dir Ditbardh Pelinku.

Uzina Elektromekanike (Electromechanical Plant): Rruga Durresi, Tirana; tel. (4) 226644; fax (4) 227656; produces electrical transformer equipment; Dir Hakim Viluku.

Vloraimpeks: Vlorë; former regional foreign trade org.; handles trade and economic co-operation with southern Italy; industrial and agricultural goods.

TRADE UNIONS

Until 1991 independent trade-union activities were prohibited, the official trade unions being represented in every work and production centre. During 1991, however, independent unions were established. The most important of these was the Union of Independent Trade Unions of Albania. Other unions were established for workers in various sectors of the economy.

Confederation of Albanian Trade Unions (Konfederata e Sindikatave të Shqipërisë—KSSh): Bulevardi Zogu I, Pall. A. Kelmendi, Tirana; tel. (4) 222956; fax (4) 229169; e-mail kssh@icc.al.eu.org; f. 1991 to replace the official Central Council of Albanian Trade Unions; f. 1945; includes 13 trade union federations representing workers in different sectors of the economy; Chair. of Man. Council Kastriot Muço.

Union of Independent Trade Unions of Albania (Bashkimi i Sindikatave të Pavarura të Shqipërisë—BSPSh): Tirana; f. 1991; Chair. (vacant).

Other Trade Unions

Agricultural Trade Union Federation (Federata Sindikale e Bujqesise): Tirana; f. 1991; Leaders Alfred Gjomo, Nazmi Qoku.

Free and Independent Miners' Union (Sindikata e Lire dhe e Pavarur e Minatoreve): Tirana; f. 1991; Chair. Gezim Kalaja.

Trade Union Federation of Employees and Pensioners of Albania: Bulevardi Dëshmorët e Kombit; tel. (4) 229169; Chair. Petraq Tapia.

Union of Oil Industry Workers: Tirana; seceded from the Confederation of Albanian Trade Unions in 1991; represents workers in the petroleum and natural gas industry; Chair. Menpor Xhemali.

Transport

RAILWAYS

In 1994 there were approximately 720 km of railway track, with lines linking Tirana–Vlorë–Durrës, Durrës–Kavajë–Rrogozhinë–Elbasan–Librazhd–Prenjas–Pogradec, Rrogozhinë–Lushnjë–Fier–Ballsh, Milot–Rrëshen, Vlorë–Laç–Lezhë–Shkodër and Selenicë–Vlorë. There are also standard-gauge lines between Fier and Selenicë and between Fier and Vlorë. In 2000 projects were under way to rehabilitate the Rrogozhinë–Vlorë and Fier–Ballsh railway lines. The 50-km international freight link between Shkodër and Podgorica, Montenegro (Serbia and Montenegro), reopened in 2003, after a 10-year suspension of service.

Albanian Railways: Rruga Skënderbeg, Durrës; tel. and fax (52) 22037; internet www.pages.albaniaonline.net/hsh; Dir-Gen. L. Burnaci.

ROADS

In 2000 the road network comprised an estimated 18,000 km of classified roads, including 3,220 km of main roads and 4,600 km of secondary roads; 39% of the total network was paved. All regions are linked by the road network, but many roads in mountainous districts are unsuitable for motor transport. A three-year public investment plan, which was initiated in 1995, included substantial funds for the rehabilitation of the road network; the principal projects were the creation of east–west (Durrës–Kapshtice) and north–south highways. In 2000 investment projects concentrated on rehabilitating the north–south corridor, in an effort to encourage more goods' transport between Italy and Croatia. In December 2002 a 23.5 km road, linking Greece with southern Albania, was opened.

SHIPPING

At December 2001 Albania's merchant fleet had 33 vessels, with a total displacement of 25,170 grt. The chief ports are those in Durrës, Vlorë, Sarandë and Shëngjin. In 1996 the port of Himare, which was closed in 1991, was reopened. Ferry services have been established between Durrës and three Italian ports (Trieste, Bari and Ancona) and between Sarandë and the Greek island of Corfu. Services also connect Vlorë with the Italian ports of Bari and Brindisi. A new ferry terminal, financed by the EU, was under construction at Durrës in 2000. Furthermore, the World Bank and Italy's OPEC Fund were financing a US \$23m. project to improve existing port facilities.

Adetare Shipping Agency Ltd: Durrës; tel. (52) 23883; fax (52) 23666.

Albanian State Shipping Enterprise: Durrës; tel. (52) 22233; fax (52) 229111.

CIVIL AVIATION

There is a small international airport at Rinas, 25 km from Tirana. Reconstruction of the airport was undertaken in the late 1990s. On average, 900,000 metric tons of goods were carried by air each year. A civil and military airport was constructed at Pish Poro, 29 km from Vlorë, under an agreement between the Ministries of Defence of Albania and Italy. The Government planned to increase the capacity of the international airport from an estimated 500,000 passengers in 2002 to 1m. by 2010.

General Directorate of Civil Aviation: Rruga e Kavajes, Perballe Xhamise, POB 205, Tirana; tel. and fax (4) 223969; e-mail dpac2@albanet.net.

Ada Air: Rruga Kemal Stafa 262, Tirana; tel. (4) 256111; fax (4) 226245; e-mail contact@adaair.com; internet www.adaair.com; f. 1991; operates passenger and cargo flights to Greece, Italy, Serbia and Montenegro and Switzerland; Pres. Marsel Skendo; Gen. Dir Ilir Zeka.

Albanian Airlines SHPK: Rruga Mine Peza 2, Tirana; tel. and fax (4) 228461; e-mail tiadplvasita@msmail.com; f. 1992 as Albanian Airlines, a jt venture between the Albanian state-owned air agency, Albtransport, and the Austrian airline, Tyrolean Airways; acquired in 1995 by the Kuwaiti co, Aviation World Mak, and assumed present name; scheduled services to Germany, Italy and Turkey; Pres. Fikry Abdul Wahhab; Man. Dir Ashraf Hashem.

Tourism

In 2001 there were some 342,908 international tourist arrivals. In that year receipts from tourism totalled US \$446m., compared with \$211m. in 1999. The main tourist centres include Tirana, Durrës, Sarandë, Shkodër and Pogradec. The Roman amphitheatre at Durrës is one of the largest in Europe. The ancient towns of Apollonia and Butrint are important archaeological sites, and there are many other towns of historic interest. However, expansion of the tourist industry has been limited by the inadequacy of Albania's infrastructure and a lack of foreign investment in the development of new facilities. Regional instability, particularly during the NATO air offensive against Yugoslavia in early 1999, also inhibited tourist activity.

Albturist: Bulevardi Dëshmorët e Kombit, Hotel Dhajti, Tirana; tel. (4) 251849; fax (4) 234359; e-mail albturist.t.a.@albnet.net; brs in main towns and all tourist centres;28 hotels throughout the country; Dir-Gen. Besnik Pellumbi.

Committee for Development and Tourism: Bulevardi Dëshmorët e Kombit 8, Tirana; tel. (4) 258323; fax (4) 258322; e-mail arskenderi@albaniaonline.com; govt body.

Culture

The Butrinti National Park, near Saranda, in southern Albania, was established by the Government under the Law for the Protection of Cultural Property in 1999. The Park and the archaeological site at the ancient town of Butrint have been designated a World Heritage Site by the UN Educational, Scientific and Cultural Organization (UNESCO). In 2001 there were 22 national museums (13 of which were located in the capital), a national gallery of art, and two national theatres.

NATIONAL ORGANIZATIONS

Albanian Committee for Cultural Relations with Foreign Countries (Komiteti Shqiptar për Marrëdhënie Kulturore me Botën e Jashtme): Tirana; tel. (4) 223338; fax (4) 223791; attached to the Ministry of Foreign Affairs; manages cultural relations with over 40 countries; Chair. Jorgo Melika.

Ministry of Culture, Youth and Sports: see section on The Government (Ministries).

CULTURAL HERITAGE

Institute of Archaeology (Instituti Arkeologjisë): Bulevardi Dëshmorët e Kombit, Tirana; tel. (4) 226541; fax (4) 240712; e-mail instark@albmail.com; f. 1976; attached to Acad. of Sciences; responsible for research on Albania's archaeological sites and for the **National Museum of Archaeology**; publ. *Iliria* (*Illyria*, 2 a year, in Albanian and French); Dir Prof. Dr MUZAFER KORKUTI; Curator of Museum Dr ILIR GJIPALI.

Institute of Cultural Monuments (Instituti i Monumenteve të Kulturës): Alqi Kondi 7, Tirana; tel. (4) 227511; fax (4) 228512; f. 1965; research and restoration of ancient and medieval architecture, cultural buildings and artistic monuments; library of 7,100 vols; publ. *Monuments*, 2 a year; Dir VALTER SHTYLLA.

Institute of Folk Culture (Instituti i Kulturës Popullore): Rruga Kont Urani 3, Tirana; tel. (4) 222323; fax (4) 223818; f. 1979; attached to Acad. of Sciences; study of Albanian folklore and ethnography; includes historical archive of recordings and collection of instruments; publs *Etnografia Shqiptare* (*Albanian Ethnography*), *Kultura Popullore* (*Popular Culture*), *Ceshtje te Folklorit Shqiptare* (*Question of Albanian Folklore*); Dir AGRON XHAGOLLI.

Institute of History (Instituti i Historisë): Rruga Naim Frashëri, Tirana; tel. and fax (4) 225869; f. 1972; attached to Acad. of Sciences; library of 52,000 vols, 10,000 periodicals; publ. Studime Historike (Study of History, annually); Dir KASEM BIÇOKU.

National Centre of Folk Activities (Qendra Kombetare e Veprimtarive Folklorike): Rruga Muhamet Gjollesha, Tirana; tel. (4) 225068; Dir ERMIR DIZDARI.

National Gallery of Arts: Bulevardi Dëshmorët e Kombit, Tirana; tel. and fax (4) 233975; e-mail masgal@icc.al.eu.org; 4,132 paintings by over 500 artists; produces magazine *pamorART* every three months; Dir GËZIM QËNDRO.

National Historical Museum: Skenderbe Sq., Tirana; tel. and fax (4) 228389; f. 1981; Illyrian and Graeco-Roman artefacts; history of Albania since Roman times; Dir VILSON KURI.

National Inventory Centre for Culture Properties (Qendra Kombëtare e Inventarizimit te Veprave te Artit): Rruga Muhamet Gjollesha, Tirana; tel. (4) 226903; Dir KOÇO GJIPALI.

National Library: Sheshi Skenderbej, Tirana; tel. and fax (4) 223843; e-mail plasari@natlib.tirana.al; f. 1922; 1m. vols; 431,696 items on Albanology and Balkanology; publ. *National Bibliography of Albanian Periodicals* (monthly); Dir AUREL PLASARI.

SPORTING ORGANIZATIONS

Albanian Confederation of Sports (Konfederata Shumësportëshe Shqiptare): Rruga Dervish Hima 31, Tirana; tel. (4) 228599; Dean HYSEN DOMI.

Albanian Confederation of Football (Konfederata Shqiptare e Futbollit): Rruga Dervish Hima 31, Tirana; tel. (4) 227877; Pres. MIÇO PAPADHOPULI.

Centre of Sports' Scientific Research (Qendra e Kërkimore Shkencore e Sportit): Tirana; tel. (4) 248397; Dir BASHKIM MILO.

National Olympic Committee of the Republic of Albania: Rruga Dervish Hima 31, Tirana; tel. (4) 240602; fax (4) 240565; e-mail koksh@albaniaonline.net; internet www.albaniaonline.net/koksh; Pres. Prof. HYSEN DOMI; Sec.-Gen. STAVRI BELLO.

Sports Promotion and Organization Department (Drejtoria e Promocionit të Sportit): Tirana; tel. (4) 228923; attached to the Ministry of Culture, Youth and Sports; Dir LEONIDHA TOSKA.

Technical Department of Sports (Drejtoria Teknike e Sportit): Tirana; tel. (4) 228923; attached to the Ministry of Culture, Youth and Sports; Dir ARTAN SHYTI.

PERFORMING ARTS

Ensemble of Folk Songs and Dances: Tirana; tel. (4) 227701; f. 1957; Dir RIZO HAJRO.

National Opera and Ballet Theatre and Folk Music Ensemble (Teatri i Operes e i Baletit dhe Ansambli Popular): Palace of Culture, Sheshi Skënderbeu, Tirana; tel. (4) 227471; fax (4) 225856; f. 1953; opera, ballet and folk-music; 34 shows in 2001; Gen. Dir ZANA ÇELA; Man. MANJOLA SEFERI.

National Theatre: Tirana; tel. (4) 223022; fax (4) 228933; 44 shows in 2001; Dir XHEVDET FERRI.

Film Studio

New Albania Film Studio (Shqipëria e Re): Tirana; tel. (4) 232733; f. 1952; produces 40 documentaries and 12–15 feature films annually; Dir TEODOR LACO.

ASSOCIATION

Union of Writers and Artists of Albania (Lidhja e Shkrimtarëve dhe e Artistëve të Shqipërisë): Rruga Konferenca e Pezës 4, Tirana; tel. (4) 229689; f. 1957; 26 brs throughout the country; 1,750 mems; Pres. DRITËRO AGOLLI.

Education

Education in Albania for children between the ages of six and 14 years is free and compulsory at primary and secondary level; students in higher education pay a fee related to the family income. Children between the ages of three and six years may attend nursery school (kopshte). Approximately 43.4% of children aged three to six years (boys 41.9%; girls 44.9%) attended pre-primary education in 1999/2000. Children between the ages of six and 14 years must attend an 'eight-year school'. In 2000 there were some 1,500 primary schools, which were attended by children aged between six and 10 years, and 1,700 secondary schools, providing education for children between the ages of 11 and 14 years. High schools in Albania are attended by students aged between 14 and 18 years. In 2000/01 97.6% of children in the relevant age-group (boys 97.7%; girls 97.4%) were enrolled at primary schools, while 72.9% of children in the appropriate age-group (boys 72.9%; girls 75.0%) attended secondary schools. In 2000 there were eight universities and two institutes of higher education in Albania. In 2001/02 some 42,160 students were enrolled in tertiary education.

The principal objective of the Ministry of Education and Science in 2002 was to make available quality basic education to all children; to this end, the enrolment rate of primary education was to be increased to 100% and that of secondary education to 90% by 2015, while the average duration of school attendance was to be extended to 13.5 years. Financial support was to be provided to facilitate the participation of children from poor areas. In 2002 investment in education increased by 12.2%. On a national level, 47.8% of school facilities required rehabilitation. Expenditure on education in 2002 was equivalent to some 11% of total public expenditure and 3.4% of GDP.

UNIVERSITIES

Agricultural University of Tirana (Universiteti Bujqësor i Tiranës): Kaméz, Tirana; tel. (4) 228296; fax (4) 227804; tel. (4) 353873; fax (4) 353874; e-mail ubtsekhet@abissnet.com.al; f. 1991 to replace the Higher Institute of Agriculture; 170 teachers, 2,552 students; Rector Prof. VELESIN PEÇULI; Vice-Rector Prof. BIZENE BIJO.

Fan S. Noli University: Rruga Gjergj Kastrioti, Korçë; tel. and fax (824) 2230; f. 1971 as the Higher Agricultural Institute; adopted present name 1992; 71 teachers, 2,132 students; Rector Asst Prof. Dr GJERGJI PENDAVINJI; Vice-Rector Dr ROBERT DAMO.

Luigj Gurakuji University of Shkodër: Bulevardi Prilli 2, Shkodër; tel. and fax (22) 43747; e-mail rektori@unishk.tirana.al; f. 1991 to replace the Luigj Gurakuji Higher Institute of Education; f. 1957; 6 faculties, 140 teachers, 2,050 students; Rector Prof. MAHIR HOTI; Vice-Rector Asst Prof. Dr ARTAN HAXHI.

University of New York: Rruga Komuna e Parasit, Tirana; tel. and fax (4) 273056; e-mail rector@unyf.edu.al.

University of Tirana (Universiteti i Tiranës): Bulevardi Deshmorët e Kombit, Tirana; tel. (4) 228402; fax (4) 223981; e-mail rectorut@albaniaonline.net; f. 1957; in 1991 the name was changed from the Enver Hoxha University of Tirana; 7 faculties, 750 teachers, 8,755 full-time students, 4,900 part-time students; brs in Berat, Elbasan, Korçë, Shkodër; Rector Dr SEZAI ROKAJ; Vice-Rector Dr FLORESHA DADO.

Social Welfare

The state funds a basic range of medical services for the whole population. However, the quality of health care declined considerably during the early 1990s. In 1993 the number of hospitals totalled 40, compared with 160 in 1990, and in 1995 there were 319 beds available for every 100,000 persons. In 1998 there were 129 physicians and 380 nurses per 100,000 of the population. In 1996 women were entitled to 180–360 days of maternity leave, receiving 80% of their salary. There was a non-contributory state social-insurance system for all workers, with 70%–100% of salary being paid during sick leave. In 1991 a system of social-security payments for the unemployed was introduced; previously the existence of unemployment was not officially acknowledged. A pension system provided for the old and disabled. At this time men retired between the ages of 55 and 65, and women between 50 and 60. Retirement pensions represented 70% of the average monthly salary. In mid-1993 social assistance became the responsibility of municipalities and communes. Of total current expenditure in the 2001 state budget, 43,502m. lekë (23.4%) was for social security, 1,881m. lekë (1.0%) for unemployment insurance, and 6,938m. lekë (3.7%) for social assistance. The budgets for 2001 and 2002 envisaged government spending on health equivalent to some 3.1% of GDP.

NATIONAL AGENCIES

Ministry of Health: see section on The Government (Ministries) incl.

National Directorate for Health Education: M. Duri 2, Tirana; tel. (4) 227106; fulfils educational role in preventative health.

Ministry of Labour and Social Affairs: see section on The Government (Ministries).

HEALTH AND WELFARE ORGANIZATIONS

Albanian Civil Society Foundation: Rruga Asim Vokshi 137, Tirana; tel. (4) 238056; e-mail postmaster@acsf.tirana.al; internet www.inet.uni-c.dk/~dialogue/acsf.htm; Dir ELVIS TOÇI.

Albanian Human Rights Group: Rruga M. Shyri 44, Tirana; tel. (4) 251995; e-mail info@ahrg.org; Dir ELSA BALLAURI.

Albanian Red Cross (Kryqi i Kuq Shqiptar): Sheshi Karl Topia, Rruga Muhamet Gjollesha, Tirana; f. 1921; Pres. Prof. Dr SHYQYRI SUBASHI; Sec.-Gen. Dr PANDORA KETRI.

Forum for the Protection of Human Rights (Forumi per Mbrojtjen e të Drejtave të Njeriut dhe Lirive Themelore): Tirana; f. 1990; provides humanitarian assistance to former political prisoners; Chair. Prof. ARBEN PUTO.

Open Society Foundation (Albania): Rruga Pjeter Bogdani, Pall. 23/1, Tirana; tel. (4) 234621; fax (4) 235855; e-mail webmaster@soros.al; internet www.soros.al.

The Environment

The Ecology Party (Albanian Green Party), founded in 1991, was the first unofficial response to environmental problems in Albania. Albania did not have the same concentration of heavy industries as some parts of Eastern Europe, but, nevertheless, there was serious pollution from coal-fired power stations and obsolete factories. By the end of the 1990s the situation had failed to improve: there was widespread pollution of the country's land and rivers, largely owing to the inadequate measures employed in the disposal of raw sewage and of industrial and domestic waste. A report by the Institute of Statistics, published in mid-2001, reported that nine species of mammal and 58 species of flora in Albania were threatened with extinction, owing to environmental damage.

GOVERNMENT ORGANIZATIONS

Ministry of the Environment: see section on The Government (Ministries).

Committee for Environmental Protection: Bulevardi Bajram Curri, Tirana; tel. and fax (4) 227907; f. 1991; the highest environmental body in Albania, responsible for all relevant issues; Chair. Dr LIRIM SELFO; Vice-Chair. GANI DELIU.

Environment and Health (Mjedisi dhe Shendeti): Dept of Primary Health Care, Tirana; tel. and fax (4) 264671; f. 1997; task group responsible for preparing an action plan for environment and health in Albania; management of environmental issues relevant to health, including air and water quality and waste management; Dir of Primary Health Care TATJANA HARITO.

State Sanitary Inspectorate: Tirana; tel. (4) 228303; fax (4) 234632; responsible for environmental health, pollution monitoring, research.

Permanent Commission of the People's Assembly on Health, Protection of the Environment, and Public Services: Kryesisa e Kuvendi Popullor, Tirana; tel. (4) 232602; fax (4) 227949; f. 1997; analyses health and environmental issues, organizes projects, and provides information; Chair. Dr NEXHAT KALAJ; Vice-Chair. Prof LEKË GJIHAURI.

The Ministries of Health and of Agriculture are also involved in matters affecting the environment.

ACADEMIC INSTITUTES

Academy of Sciences (Akademia Shkencave): Sheshi Fan S. Noli, Tirana; tel. (4) 250368; fax (4) 227476; e-mail esulstar@akad.edu.al; f. 1972; research in social and natural-technique sciences, 13 scientific institutions and centres; publs *Studia Albanica* (2 a year), *Gjuha jonë* (quarterly); Pres. SHABAN DEMIRAJ.

Institute of Hydrometeorology (Instituti Hidrometeorologjik): Rruga e Durrësit 219, Tirana; tel. (4) 222439; fax (4) 223518; e-mail mitots@yahoo.com; f. 1962; responsible for monitoring the quality of surface waters and the atmosphere; publs meteorological and hydrological bulletins, *Studime Meteorologjike dhe HidrologjikeMeteorological and Hydrological Studies*; Dir MITOT SANXHOKU.

Agricultural Research Institute (Instituti i Kërkimeve Bujqësore): Lushnjë; tel. (824) 2194; f. 1952; studies include agricultural pollution control, and cultivating new varieties of bread, wheat, cotton, sunflower seed and dry bean; library of 8,000 vols; Dir VLADIMIR MALO.

Agricultural University of Tirana (Universiteti Bujqësor i Tiranës): see section on Education (Universities).

Faculty of Natural Sciences, University of Tirana (Fakulteti i Shkencave Natyrore, Universiteti i Tiranës): Bulevardi Dëshmorët e Kombit, Tirana; tel. and fax (4) 227669; e-mail lpuka@fshn.tirana.al; f. 1957; Dean of Faculty of Natural Sciences Prof. Dr LLUKAN PUKA.

NON-GOVERNMENTAL ORGANIZATIONS

Albanian Ecological Club-International Friends of Nature (Klubi Ekologjik Shqiptar-Miqte Nderkombetar te Natyres): Rruga Todi Shkurti, Shkurti 4, Apt 32, Tirana; tel. and fax (4) 273148; e-mail eco-club@san.com.al; f. 1992; environmental education, publications, films and information, seminars, conferences and training, protection of rare and endemic plant species; Pres. ALI ELTARI; 29 brs.

Albanian Ecological Party (Partia Ekologjike Shqiptare): see section on Political Organizations.

Albanian Ecologist Tourism Association: Rruga Bardhyl 87/11; tel. (4) 228746; fax (4) 27815.

Albanian Green Party (Partia e Blertë Shqiptare): see section on Political Organizations.

Association for the Protection and Preservation of the Natural Environment in Albania (Shoqata e Ruajtjes dhe e Mbrojtjes Natyror ne Shqiperi): Bulevardi Zogu I 97/5, Tirana; tel. and fax (4) 249571; e-mail ppnea@albmail.com; f. 1991; Head DHURATA BOZO.

Organization for the Protection and Preservation of the Natural Environment in Albania (Ruajtja dhe Mbrojtja e Mjedisit Natyror ne Shqiperi): Shkurti 4, Apt 25, Tirana; tel. and fax (4) 227048; f. 1991; active in the protection of Albania's forests and the botanical gardens of Tirana; Head LEKË GJIKMURI; Deputy Head ALGI ÇULLAJ; Sec. DHURATA FRASHËRI.

Defence

In 2002 the armed forces were undergoing a programme of reorganization, with assistance from the US and European Governments. In August of that year the army numbered about 20,000, the air force 4,500 and the navy 2,500. Paramilitary forces consisted of an internal security force, based in Tirana, and units in major towns, as well as an estimated 500 border police. Military service is compulsory and lasts for 12 months. From September 1999 a 2,400-member contingent, known as Communications Zone West (COMMZ-W), was deployed in Albania to maintain civil order and to support NATO forces in neighbouring Kosovo and Metohija (see chapter on Serbia and Montenegro). In June 2002 COMMZ-W was offically dissolved, when a NATO headquarters was established at Tirana. The budget for 2002 allocated some 6,300m. lekë to defence.

Commander-in-Chief: President of the Republic.

Chief of the General Staff: Maj.-Gen. PELLUB QAZIMI.

Bibliography

Biberaj, E. *Albania and China: A Study of an Unequal Alliance*. Boulder, CO, Westview Press, 1986.

Albania in Transition: the Rocky Road to Democracy (Nations of the Modern World Series). Boulder, CO, Westview Press, 1999.

Carver, R. *The Accursed Mountains*. London, John Murray, 1998.

Costa, N. *Albania: A European Enigma*. Boulder, CO, East European Monographs, 1995.

Durham, E. *High Albania*. London, Phoenix Press, 2001.

Elsie, R. *A Dictionary of Albanian Religion, Mythology and Folk Culture*. New York, NY, New York University Press, 2000.

Fischer, B. J. *Albania at War 1939–45*. London, C. Hurst, 1999.

Fleming, K. E. *The Muslim Bonaparte*. Princeton, NJ, Princeton University Press, 1999.

Giaffo, L. *Albania: Eye of the Balkan Vortex*. Philadelphia, PA, Xlibris Corpn, 2001.

Albania: Wellspring of Antiquity. Philadelphia, PA, Xlibris Corpn, 2002.

Griffith, W. E. *Albania and the Sino–Soviet Rift*. Cambridge, MA, MIT Press, 1963.

Hall, D. *Albania and the Albanians*. London, Pinter, 1994.

Halliday, J. (Ed.) *The Artful Albanian: Memoirs of Enver Hoxha*. London, Chatto & Windus, 1987.

Hibbert, R. *Albania's National Liberation Struggle*. London, Pinter, 1991.

Human Rights Watch. *Albania: Post Communist*. Helsinki, Human Rights Watch, 1995.

Kaser, M. *Albania under and after Enver Hoxha, East European Economies, Vol. 3* Washington, DC, USGPO (Joint Economic Committee of the US Congress), 1986.

Kola, P. *The Myth of Greater Albania*. New York, NY, New York University Press, 2003.

Logoreci, A. *The Albanians: Europe's Forgotten Survivors*. Boulder, CO, Westview Press, 1977.

Marmallaku, R. *Albania and the Albanians*. London, C. Hurst, 1975.

Pano, N. C. *The People's Republic of Albania*. Baltimore, MD, Johns Hopkins Press, 1968.

Pipa, A. *Albanian Stalinism* (East European Monographs). New York, NY, Columbia University Press, 1990.

Prifti, P. *Socialist Albania since 1944*. Cambridge, MA, MIT Press, 1978.

Pritchett Post, S. E. *Women in Modern Albania*. Jefferson, NC, MacFarland and Co, 1998.

Saltmarshe, D. *Identity in a Post-Communist Balkan State: an Albanian Village Study*. Aldershot, Ashgate, 2001.

Schwandner-Sievers, S., and Fischer, B. J. (Eds). *Albanian Identities: Myth and History*. Bloomington, IN, Indiana University Press, 2002.

Senechal, M. *Long Life to Your Children: a Portrait of High Albania*. Boston, MA, University of Massachusetts Press, 1997.

Skendi, S. *The Albanian National Awakening, 1878–1912*. Princeton, NJ, Princeton University Press, 1967.

Vickers, M. *The Albanians: A Modern History*. London, Tauris, 1995.

Vickers, M., and Pettifer, J. *Albania: From Anarchy to a Balkan Identity*. London, C. Hurst, 1997.

Winnifrith, T. J. *Badlands-Borderland: a History of Southern Albania/Northern Epirus*. London, Duckworth Publishers, 2003.

World Council of Churches. *The Resurrection of the Church in Albania*. Geneva, World Council of Churches, 2002.

BOSNIA AND HERZEGOVINA

Geography

PHYSICAL FEATURES

Bosnia and Herzegovina is a mountainous territory with only about 20 km (12 miles) of coastline, which is of little maritime significance. Roughly triangular in shape, the country juts into Croatia, which forms its western border (running from north-west to south-east, along the Dinaric Alps) and its northern border. The rest of its borders are with Serbia and Montenegro: Serbia lies to the east (there is a short border with the Serbian territory of the Vojvodina in the north-east) and Montenegro to the south-east. The total area of the country, formerly part of the Yugoslav federation, is 51,129 sq km (19,741 sq miles).

The ancient province of Bosnia is roughly the territory bounded by the Sava, Drina and Una rivers. Along the Sava, which forms the northern border, there are fertile lowlands. The chief town, and the country's capital, is Sarajevo, which is in the south, near the head-waters of the River Bosna (from which the province acquired its name). The smaller province of Herzegovina (only 18.0% of the total area) occupies the south of the country, with the Dalmatian coastal strip, Croatia, to the south-west and Montenegro to the south-east. Its chief town is Mostar. Most of Herzegovina is mountainous and unfertile, but there are fruitful valleys.

Under the terms of the General Framework Agreement for Peace in Bosnia and Herzegovina, agreed at Dayton, Ohio, the USA, on 21 November 1995, the legal continuity of the state of Bosnia and Herzegovina within its existing borders was recognized. However, it was also agreed that the state comprised two entities: the Federation of Bosnia and Herzegovina (itself a union of the Muslim-led Government of the old Republic of Bosnia and Herzegovina with the 'Croat Republic of Herzeg-Bosna'); and the Serb Republic of Bosnia and Herzegovina. The Federation occupied the west and centre of the country, its territory tapering north-eastwards, with a road linking it to the eastern enclave of Goražde. The Serb Republic comprised the remaining 49% of the country, its territory concentrated along the eastern border and in the north of the country, around Banja Luka.

CLIMATE

The largely mountainous territory of Bosnia and Herzegovina has a continental climate, although this is moderated with proximity to the coast. The hinterland of the Dalmatian coast (Croatia) and the territory around Bosnia and Herzegovina's small coastal town of Neum has a Mediterranean climate.

POPULATION

The population, according to the census of 1991, totalled 4,377,033, with a density of 85.6 per sq km. At mid-2002, according to UN estimates, the total population numbered 4,126,000, and the population density was 80.7 per sq km. No single ethnic group constituted an overall majority in Bosnia and Herzegovina. The Bosnian Muslims (Bosniaks) are a Serbo-Croat-speaking people, originally Roman Catholic, who adopted Islam during the Ottoman occupation. In 1971 they were accorded separate status as a Yugoslav national unit

(the term 'Muslim' not only included the Bosnian Muslims, however, but other Slav Muslims in the former Yugoslavia) and they were the largest single group in Bosnia and Herzegovina. In 1991 they comprised 43.7% of the total population. The Serbs accounted for 31.4% of the population and the Croats 17.3%. Religious affiliation is roughly equated with ethnicity. Most of the Bosniaks are Sunni, although a few are members of a Dervish order, introduced in 1974. The Croats are Roman Catholic, while the Serbs and Montenegrins adhere to the Eastern Orthodox Church. The principal language is Serbo-Croat; the Muslims use the Latin script, like the Croats, and the Serbs use the Cyrillic.

Sarajevo is the country's largest city. It is the capital of the country and of the Federation. An outer suburb of the city, Pale, is part of the Serb Republic and the seat of its parliament until 1998, when the country's second city, Banja Luka, became the capital of the Serb Republic. Mostar is an ethnically mixed city, but the chief town in the main area of Croat settlement. Two other important towns in Federation territory are Tuzla in the north-east and Bihać in the north-west. Other towns of strategic significance include Goražde, Mrkonjič Grad (to the south of Banja Luka—territory around here was ceded by Croat forces to the Serb Republic under the Dayton accord) and Brčko. This last town, north of Tuzla and on the Croatian border, formerly under Serb control, became a neutral district under joint authority in March 2000. It stands at the narrowest point of the so-called Posavina 'corridor', a vital Serb link running westwards along the valley of the Sava. It is flanked by Federation territory, because the Croat-dominated enclave of Orašje lies to the north.

Chronology

168 BC: Illyria (which included Bosnia and Herzegovina and other former Yugoslav territories) was annexed by the Roman Empire.

AD 395: Following a division of the administration of the Roman Empire, Illyria was ruled by the Eastern Roman ('Byzantine') Emperor in Constantinople (İstanbul, now in Turkey); this marked the beginning of the history of Bosnia and Herzegovina as a region on the borders of Western and Eastern Europe.

5th century: Southern Slav peoples began to move from the north into Illyria and the Balkans.

7th–8th centuries: Western Christian missionaries, from Aquileia (Trieste, now in Italy) and Salzburg (now in Austria), were active among the Croats and the Slovenes, respectively, introducing the Latin script and a Western cultural orientation.

863: The missionary activity of the Byzantine brothers, SS Constantine (Cyril) and Methodius, led to the conversion of the Serbs (including the ancestors of the Bosnians) and the Bulgars to Eastern Orthodox Christianity; a Slavonic liturgy was introduced with a written language, in the Cyrillic script.

11th century: Emergence of the Serb principality of Rama, the original Bosnian state, although it soon fell under the influence of the Catholic Croat kingdom.

1102: Croatia's personal union with Hungary effectively linked it to the Hungarian Crown.

1180–1204: The local ruler (ban) under the Hungarian Crown, Kulin, despite the disapproval of the Catholic authorities, was tolerant of the emergence of a local Christian heresy, sometimes equated with the dualism of the Bogomils; this was widely adopted by the local élite of a territory strongly disputed for by not only the Hungarians, but also the Serbs, Byzantines and Venetians.

1187: The Emperor in Constantinople acknowledged Serbian independence and Hungarian conquests in Croatia and Bosnia, but authority in the area remained uncertain. By the middle of the next century the local élite enjoyed sufficient independence from the Catholic and Orthodox powers that the heretical Bosnian Church (*ecclesia Sclavoniae*) was virtually a state religion.

1322–53: Reign of Stjepan II Kotromanić, who established a powerful Bosnian state, nominally subject to Hungary.

1346: Coronation of Uroš IV (Stefan Dušan of Raška, who reigned 1331–55) as Tsar (King) of the Serbs and Greeks, at Skopje; his empire incorporated the territory subsequently known as Herzegovina.

1377: Stjepan Trvtko I (1353–91) proclaimed himself Tsar of the Bosnians and Serbs, renouncing Hungarian overlordship; his kingdom secured control of much of the Adriatic coast.

1389: The Turkish Ottoman Empire destroyed the Serbian nobility at a battle on the plain of Kosovo Polje.

1448: Herzegovina became a border duchy of Austria (herceg means duke), as the Habsburgs attempted to improve the security of the Serbian princes and the Bosnian kingdom against the encroaching Ottomans.

1463: The Ottomans finally ended Bosnian independence.

1483: The province of Herzegovina was annexed to the Ottoman Empire.

1624: After some 150 years of Ottoman rule and the often political conversion of the Slav élite, two-thirds of the population of the provinces of Bosnia and Herzegovina were officially reckoned to be Muslim.

July 1878: At the Congress of Berlin, the Habsburg Empire of Austria-Hungary (already having regained Croatia) secured administration rights in Bosnia and Herzegovina; the Bosnian élite's National Muslim Organization (later the Yugoslav Muslim Organization), which sought to protect the Muslim community against competing Croat and Serb claims, was tolerated, but had less influence under the Habsburgs.

5 October 1908: Austria-Hungary formally annexed Bosnia and Herzegovina, despite international objections, following the 'Young Turk' uprising in the Ottoman Empire, which led to disturbances in the Balkans; the Habsburg ally, Germany, prevented war against Serbia.

1910: The secret 'Greater Serb' society, Union or Death (the 'Black Hand'), was founded by Col Dimitrijević-Apis.

28 June 1914: The heir to the Habsburg throne, Archduke Francis Ferdinand, and his wife were assassinated in Sarajevo, by a Bosnian student acting for the Serb Black Hand group.

28 July 1914: Austria-Hungary declared war on Serbia, which started the First World War between the Central Powers, of Austria-Hungary and Germany, and the Entente Powers, of France, Russia, Serbia and the United Kingdom.

July 1917: Serbia and the other Southern Slavs (excluding the Bulgarians) declared their intention to form a unitary state, under the Serbian monarchy.

29 October 1918: Following the defeat and dissolution of the Danubian Monarchy, the Southern Slav (Yugoslav) peoples separated from the Austro-Hungarian system of states (a Southern Slav republic was established on 15 October); Dalmatia, Croatia and Slavonia, Bosnia and Herzegovina, parts of Carinthia, Carniola and the Banat were, subsequently, ceded formally to the new state.

4 December 1918: Proclamation of the Kingdom of Serbs, Croats and Slovenes (Kingdom of Yugoslavia from 1929), which united Serbia and Montenegro with the former Habsburg lands.

1937: Tito (Josip Broz) became General Secretary of the Communist Party of Yugoslavia (later the League of Communists of Yugoslavia—LCY), which was to become the main partner in the Partisan (National Liberation Army) resistance to invasion during the Second World War.

10 April 1941: Following the German-Italian invasion and partition of Yugoslavia, an Independent State of Croatia (including Bosnia and Herzegovina) was proclaimed, with the Italian, Duke Aimone of Spoleto (Split), as King, and a Government under Ante Pavelić, leader of the Fascist Ustaša (Rebel) movement.

29 November 1943: In the Bosnian town of Jajce, following fierce resistance and civil conflict with the Serb royalist Četniks (Yugoslav Army of the Fatherland) and with the Ustaša regime, Gen. (later Marshal) Tito's Partisans proclaimed their own government for liberated areas (including much of eastern Bosnia).

29 November 1945: Following elections for a Provisional Assembly, the Federative People's Republic of Yugoslavia was proclaimed, with Tito as Prime Minister.

January 1946: A Soviet-style Constitution, establishing a federation of six republics, of which one was Bosnia and Herzegovina, and two autonomous regions, was adopted. The communist regime subsequently banned the 'Young Muslims' organization, which sought to champion the rights of Muslims, but was condemned as a terrorist group.

April 1963: A new Constitution changed the country's name to the Socialist Federal Republic of Yugoslavia (SFRY).

1971: The Slav Muslims (mainly the Bosnian Muslims or Bosniaks) achieved recognition as a distinct ethnic group and the status of one of the six 'nations of Yugoslavia'. Greater autonomy was granted to the federal units and the system of collective leadership and the regular rotation of posts was adopted in the federation and in the administration of Bosnia and Herzegovina.

February 1974: A new federal Constitution was adopted.

4 May 1980: Tito died; his responsibilities were transferred to the collective federal State Presidency and to the Presidium of the LCY.

18 November 1990: Elections to the collective State Presidency of Bosnia and Herzegovina were held (the three nationalist parties—representing the main Bosnian Muslim, Serb and Croat ethnic groups—secured all seven seats); the first round of voting for the new, bicameral Assembly also took place (the second round was on 2 December).

9 December 1990: The final round of voting for the Assembly took place; of the 240 seats, the predominantly Muslim Party of Democratic Action (PDA) won 86, the Serb Democratic Party (SDP) 72 and the Croatian Democratic Union of Bosnia and Herzegovina (CDU—BH) 44.

20 December 1990: The three main parties, all nationalist groups, announced their coalition agreement: Dr Alija Izetbegović, the leader of the PDA, was to be President of the republican State Presidency; Jure Pelivan of the CDU—BH, the premier; and Momčilo Krajišnik of the SDP, President of the Assembly.

26 April 1991: Serb-dominated districts in the north-west of Bosnia and Herzegovina unilaterally announced the formation of the 'Municipal Community of Bosanska (Bosnian) Krajina'; the move was repudiated by the republican authorities, who feared a link with the Serb 'Krajina' territory in Croatia.

15 May 1991: The 'Serbian bloc' (the representatives of Serbia, Kosovo and Metohija, Vojvodina and Montenegro) on the federal State Presidency prevented the accession, as its first non-communist President, of Stipe Mesić of Croatia, effectively depriving Yugoslavia of a head of state.

30 June 1991: A European Community (EC, known as the European Union—EU—from November 1993) mediating team secured agreement to a cease-fire in Slovenia and Croatia (both of which had declared their independence six days previously), with the threat of EC sanctions, and the immediate proclamation of Stipe Mesić as President of the federal State Presidency; there was to be a three-month moratorium on further implementation of the Croatian and Slovenian declarations of dissociation.

September 1991: Despite EC efforts to negotiate peace, fighting continued in Croatia. Meanwhile, in Bosnia and Herzegovina various groups of Serb-dominated municipalities formed four 'Serb Autonomous Regions' (SARs) and ethnic tensions resulted in shooting incidents along the borders with Croatia and Montenegro—prompting a declaration of neutrality by the State Presidency in the following month.

15 October 1991: The Assembly declared the sovereignty of Bosnia and Herzegovina; this resolution was rejected by the SARs, which declared themselves subject only to the federation.

24 October 1991: The Serb deputies of the republican Assembly announced the formation of an 'Assembly of the Serb Nation of Bosnia and Herzegovina' (Serb Assembly).

9–10 November 1991: A referendum organized by the Serb Assembly was reported to have indicated overwhelming support for remaining in a common Serb state.

February 1992: Following an agreement in the previous month, a UN Protection Force (UNPROFOR) was established by the Security Council; it was based in Sarajevo and its peace-keeping role in Croatia was extended to Bosnia and Herzegovina later in the year.

29 February–1 March 1992: In a referendum, boycotted by the Serb community, 99.4% of those voting (comprising 63% of the electorate) supported full independence. The country was declared independent and renamed the Republic of Bosnia and Herzegovina.

27 March 1992: The formation of the 'Serb Republic of Bosnia and Herzegovina' was announced, to be headed by the leader of the SDP, Dr Radovan Karadžić.

7 April 1992: Two days after the beginning of the siege of Sarajevo by Serb forces, Bosnia and Herzegovina's independence was formally recognized by the EC countries and the USA.

19 May 1992: The Yugoslav People's Army (YPA) announced the withdrawal of its troops from Bosnia and Herzegovina.

22 May 1992: Bosnia and Herzegovina was accepted as a member of the UN.

7 July 1992: The formation of the 'Croat Union of Herzeg-Bosna' was announced; led by Mate Boban, it claimed about 30% of the territory of Bosnia and Herzegovina.

26–27 August 1992: The London Conference was held in the United Kingdom, co-chaired by mediators from the UN (Cyrus Vance, former US Secretary of State) and the EC (Lord Owen, former British Secretary of State for Foreign and Commonwealth Affairs); a peace plan was announced in October, in Geneva, Switzerland.

December 1992: Following allegations of 'ethnic cleansing' and organized rape, the UN Human Rights Commission condemned the Serbs as largely responsible for violations of human rights in the country. Later in the month the UN Security Council demanded access to all Serb detention centres.

22 February 1993: The UN Security Council decided to prosecute war criminals by establishing an International Criminal Tribunal for the former Yugoslavia (ICTY), based in The Hague, the Netherlands.

May 1993: The Serb Assembly at Pale decisively rejected the Vance-Owen Plan. France, Russia, Spain, the United Kingdom and the USA proposed the formation of six 'safe areas' for the Bosniaks—effective from 22 July.

July 1993: Representatives of the three sides in the conflict reached a constitutional agreement in Geneva, whereby the country would become the 'Union of Republics of Bosnia and Herzegovina'—a loose confederation of three ethnically based states.

27 August 1993: During a session of the State Presidency, the Croat Prime Minister, Mile Akmadžić, was dismissed, in a sign of growing tensions between the Muslims and the Croats. He was to be succeeded by a Muslim, Haris Silajdžić.

28 August 1993: An assembly met in Grude and officially proclaimed the 'Croat Republic of Herzeg-Bosna'; the deputies accepted the Geneva Plan on condition that the other two sides in the conflict also accepted it. On the same day the Serb Assembly voted in favour of the Plan.

31 August 1993: At a session of the Bosnia and Herzegovina Assembly the Geneva Plan was rejected in its existing form, but deputies agreed that it should be a basis for further peace negotiations.

27 September 1993: In Velika Kladusa, one of the chief towns of the district of Bihać, the 'Autonomous Province of Western Bosnia' was established; a Muslim member of the State Presidency, Fikret Abdić, was elected President by its 'Constituent Assembly'; a state of martial law was imposed by Izetbegović on the whole of 'Western Bosnia'.

28 September 1993: The majority of delegates at a 'Bosnian Convention' voted in favour of accepting the Geneva Plan, but only if the territories captured from the Bosnian Muslims (or, as the Convention favoured, Bosniaks) were returned.

October 1993: The Muslim Democratic Party was established in Velika Kladusa; Abdić was named Chairman. There was fighting between forces loyal to Izetbegović and those supporting Abdić.

5 February 1994: The shelling of a Sarajevo market-place by Serb forces, causing many casualties, provoked the UN to threaten military intervention; this led to a cease-fire around Sarajevo, particularly following a Russian diplomatic initiative.

8 February 1994: Boban resigned as President of Herzeg-Bosna, to be replaced by a Presidential Council.

25 March 1994: The premier of the Serb Republic, Vladimir Lukić, resigned.

31 March 1994: A Constituent Assembly of mainly Bosniak and Croat deputies declared the formation of the Federation of Bosnia and Herzegovina, in accordance with a US-brokered plan to end almost one year of fighting between Croat and government forces.

10 April 1994: The UN ordered the first North Atlantic Treaty Organization (NATO) air-strike against Serb ground forces, which were attacking Goražde; earlier in the year similar threats had improved the situation in Sarajevo (both towns were 'safe areas').

May 1994: Zubak was elected President of the new Federation, Ejup Ganić (a Bosniak and deputy leader of the State Presidency) Vice-President and Silajdžić Prime Minister; the following month a joint Government was elected.

July 1994: A plan presented by the 'Contact Group' (consisting of France, Germany, Russia, the United Kingdom and the USA), which granted 51% of Bosnian territory to the Federation, and 49% to the Bosnian Serbs, was accepted by Izetbegović and President Tudjman of Croatia.

August 1994: NATO air-strikes against the Bosnian Serbs resumed, following Serb attacks against UN forces and the renewed bombardment of Sarajevo. The Serbian President, Slobodan Milošević, the most powerful figure in the FRY leadership, formally severed relations with the Bosnian Serbs. Government troops defeated Abdić's forces in Bihać; thousands of rebel troops and civilians, including Abdić, escaped to Serb-held territory in Croatia.

1 September 1994: The Bosnian Serb Assembly unanimously approved the result of a referendum in which 96% of participants voted against the Contact Group Plan.

3 October 1994: In order to secure the relaxation of all remaining sanctions (some had been lifted the previous month) and to force the Bosnian Serbs to accept the peace plan, the FRY closed its border with Serb-occupied Bosnia and Herzegovina to all but humanitarian supplies.

31 December 1994: The mediation of a former US President, Jimmy Carter, resulted in the acceptance by both sides of a revised version of the Contact Group Plan (providing for possible confederal links between the Bosnian Serbs and the FRY) and a four-month cease-fire agreement was signed, with effect from the next day.

February 1995: Against a background of increasing violation of the cease-fire, the Bosnian Serbs and the Croatian Serbs established a joint Supreme Defence Council and guaranteed mutual military assistance.

March 1995: A formal military alliance was announced between the Croatian, Bosnian Croat and Bosnian government forces, and military action against the Serbs intensified.

April 1995: At a meeting in Bonn, Germany, the Bosnian Croats and the Muslim-dominated Bosnian Government agreed to unite their police forces, local governments and, eventually, their armed forces. A Russian plan for FRY recognition of Bosnia and Herzegovina failed.

May 1995: Heavy shelling of Sarajevo by the Serbs provoked the UN to request air-strikes by NATO forces, carried out on Serb ammunitions depots. Relations between the Serb forces and UNPROFOR continued to deteriorate and a large number of peace-keepers were taken hostage, prompting the UN to create, in the following month, a 10,000-strong 'rapid reaction force', to provide the peace-keepers with added protection.

July 1995: The Serbs captured the 'safe area' of Srebreniča and then, despite punitive NATO air-strikes, the 'safe area' of Žepa.

4 August 1995: The Croatian army began a major offensive that routed the Krajina Serbs, thereby causing a massive influx of refugees into Bosnian Serb territory and depriving the Serb Republic of vital military and strategic support.

6–7 August 1995: The siege of Bihać, which was begun on 20 July by the Bosnian Serbs, the Krajina Serbs and Bosniak supporters of Abdić, was effectively ended by Bosnian government and Croatian troops.

9 August 1995: The US Assistant Secretary of State, Richard Holbrooke, proposed a peace plan based on earlier proposals by the Contact Group, but acknowledging the Serb possession of Srebrenica and Žepa.

30 August 1995: Two days after a mortar attack in central Sarajevo (presumed to be the work of the Serbs), which left 41 civilians dead and over 80 wounded, a series of devastating NATO air- and artillery-strikes (known as 'Operation Deliberate Force') began against Serb positions across the country; this continued despite Russian objections.

8 September 1995: At a meeting in Geneva, which was chaired by the Contact Group, the foreign ministers of Bosnia and Herzegovina, Croatia and the FRY (acting for the Bosnian Serbs) agreed the basic principles for a peace accord (including recognition that Bosnia and Herzegovina should comprise two existing 'entities'—the Federation and the Serb Republic—and that the country should be divided between them, with 51% for the Federation).

11 September 1995: Joint Bosnian government and Croatian forces began an assault on Serb-held territory in western and central Bosnia.

20 September 1995: The Bosnian Serbs completed the withdrawal of heavy weapons from around Sarajevo.

26 September 1995: In New York, USA, the foreign ministers of Bosnia and Herzegovina, Croatia and the FRY agreed the basic principles of an elected national parliament and presidency, with the Bosnian Serbs guaranteed representation by one-third of both bodies.

12 October 1995: A 60-day cease-fire, agreed under US pressure, came into force. Despite the truce, forces on both sides continued attempts to gain more territory before a final peace settlement.

1 November 1995: The 'Peace Proximity Talks' began at the Wright-Patterson Air Force Base near Dayton, Ohio, the USA, under the aegis of the Contact Group.

21 November 1995: At Dayton leaders of the Federation of Bosnia and Herzegovina, Croatia and the FRY initialled a General Framework Agreement for Peace in Bosnia and Herzegovina; this, with its attached accords, provided for the division of the country between the Federation (51%) and the Serb Republic (49%); the city of Sarajevo was to have special status.

14 December 1995: The Dayton accords were formally signed in Paris, France.

18 December 1995: The Serb Republic's parliament elected Rajko Kasagić as premier in a new Government.

20 December 1995: According to the terms of the Dayton accords, the mandate of the 60,000-strong NATO-controlled Implementation Force (IFOR) began, and the formal transfer of power from UNPROFOR took place.

21 December 1995: Bosnia and Herzegovina became a member of the IMF.

12 January 1996: Silajdžić resigned as premier and formed a new Party for Bosnia and Herzegovina.

30 January 1996: The republican Assembly elected a new Government for the Republic of Bosnia and Herzegovina, to be chaired by Hasan Muratović. The following day Izudin Kapetanović was confirmed as head of a new federal Government by the Constituent Assembly of the Federation.

19 March 1996: With the final suburb of Sarajevo, Grbavica, coming under the control of the federal police, the Bosnian capital was reunified; much of its Bosnian Serb population, however, had fled the city for Serb-held areas.

15 May 1996: Karadžić dismissed Kasagič, the moderate premier of the Bosnian Serbs and their main contact with the international community, and replaced him with the more extreme Gojko Klicković.

18 May 1996: Karadžić deputized one of the Vice-Presidents, Biljana Plavšić, to execute most of his presidential functions, including dealings with the international community.

30 June 1996: Controversial local elections were finally held in Mostar; List for a United Mostar, a Bosniak electoral alliance that included the PDA, won some 47.4% of the votes and the CDU—BH 44.6%. The Croat representatives refused to accept the results or to attend the new city assembly until August, when a compromise was agreed.

19 July 1996: Under considerable pressure from the international community, Karadžić agreed formally to resign his posts of President of the Serb Republic and leader of the SDP. Plavšić became acting President.

14 September 1996: The Organization for Security and Co-operation in Europe (OSCE) organized elections to the state Presidency and the federal legislature, to the presidency and legislature of the Serb Republic, and to the legislature and cantonal authorities of the Bosnian Federation. Izetbegović was elected Chairman of the Presidency, while the PDA won the majority of seats in the Federation's section of the national House of Representatives and in the Federation's own legislature. Similarly, the SDP obtained a majority in the Serb section of the House of Representatives and in the Serb National Assembly; Plavšić was elected President of the Serb Republic, with some 59% of the votes cast.

30 September 1996: One day after their inauguration the three members of the Presidency of Bosnia and Herzegovina, Izetbegović, Zubak and Krajišnik, convened for the first time, in a meeting organized by the High Representative of the International Community, Carl Bildt, who was responsible for implementing the Dayton accords.

1 October 1996: The UN Security Council resolved finally to end sanctions (suspended at the end of 1995) against the Serb Republic and the FRY.

3 October 1996: Full diplomatic relations between Bosnia and Herzegovina and the FRY were agreed, following mediation by the French President, Jacques Chirac: the FRY agreed to respect the territorial integrity of Bosnia and Herzegovina; and Bosnia and Herzegovina recognized the FRY as the successor state of the former Yugoslavia.

5 October 1996: The inaugural session of the state Presidency was held in Sarajevo; Krajišnik refused to attend, however, claiming his life would be at risk in the city. The inaugural session of the republican Assembly was postponed, owing to a boycott by Serb deputies.

8 November 1996: President Plavšić dismissed Gen. Ratko Mladić as commander of the Serb armed forces, replacing him with Maj.-Gen. Pero Colić; it was not until 28 November, however, that Mladić, who was wanted for the investigation of war crimes, agreed to relinquish his post.

27 November 1996: A new Serb Government was appointed, again headed by Klicković.

17 December 1996: The Government of the Republic of Bosnia and Herzegovina formally transferred its remaining functions to the Federation and, therefore, officially ceased to exist; it was also announced that the Croat polity of Herzeg-Bosna no longer existed.

18 December 1996: Edhem Bičakčić replaced Kapetanović as Prime Minister of the Federation.

20 December 1996: The successor to IFOR, known as the Stabilization Force (SFOR), formally began operations in the country. SFOR was about one-half the size of IFOR and had a mandate of 18 months, subsequently extended.

3 January 1997: The inaugural session of the Bosnia and Herzegovina Assembly was finally held; it approved the Council of Ministers nominated by the Co-Prime Ministers, Silajdžić of the Party for Bosnia and Herzegovina and Boro Bosić of the SDP, who had been appointed by the state Presidency in the previous month—each of the Bosnian ethnic groups held an equal number of offices in the new cabinet.

28 February 1997: The Governments of the Serb Republic and the FRY signed an agreement to foster mutual economic co-operation and to collaborate on regional security; the Serb Republic's legislature ratified the agreement in March, despite opposition from President Plavšić and from some Bosniak and Bosnian Croat leaders.

30–31 May 1997: A conference of the Peace Implementation Council met in Sintra, Portugal: Carlos Westendorp, a Spanish former Minister of Foreign Affairs, was appointed the new High Representative; NATO officials stipulated deadlines for the approval by the entities of a number of laws on property, passports and citizenship; a new list of ambassadors was demanded, to better reflect the ethnic diversity of the country.

3 July 1997: Supported by the UN and the OSCE, President Plavšić dissolved parliament and announced that elections were to be held in early September; the decision was opposed by the legislature and, following the Constitutional Court's ruling in August that Plavšić's decision was illegal, it voted to disregard future decrees by the Bosnian Serb President.

9 July 1997: The EU announced the suspension of aid to the Serb Republic owing to its failure to extradite suspected war criminals to the ICTY.

13–14 September 1997: Local elections in both entities, originally scheduled for September 1996, finally took place, observed by the OSCE; of the 91 parties that contested the elections, the three main nationalist groups, the PDA, the CDU and the SDP, received the vast majority of the votes cast.

22–23 November 1997: In elections to the Serb Republic's National Assembly, the SDP won the largest number of seats (24 of a total of 70), but had a reduced representation in parliament, and the Coalition for a Single and Democratic Bosnia, an alliance including the PDA and the Party for Bosnia and Herzegovina, obtained 16 seats, while President

Plavšić's recently formed Serb National Alliance and the Serb Radical Party each secured 15 seats.

27 December 1997: At the inaugural session of the National Assembly, the Serb President, Plavšić, nominated an independent, Mladen Ivanić, as premier; following objections by the SDP, Ivanić proposed an inter-party agreement on an interim 'government of national unity', until new elections.

18 January 1998: Following the failure of Ivanić's all-party negotiations, a moderate, Milorad Dodik, won sufficient parliamentary support to form a new Bosnian Serb Government; he announced his intention to govern in adherence to the terms of the Dayton accords.

31 January 1998: Following the swearing in of the new cabinet, the Bosnian Serb Assembly voted to relocate the Republic's capital from Pale to Banja Luka.

15 February 1998: Two Bosnian Serbs became the first indicted war crimes suspects to surrender voluntarily to the ICTY.

1 April 1998: Following a devaluation of the Yugoslav dinar, the Serb Republic declared Germany's Deutsche Mark (DM) to be its official currency.

20 June 1998: As agreed in February, SFOR's new mandate, which stated that a multinational specialized unit would remain in the region indefinitely and that six-monthly reviews would take place, was enforced.

22 June 1998: A new national currency, the convertible mark, was introduced; it was to be 'pegged' to the DM and was valid for 18 months.

12–13 September 1998: Elections to the Bosnian collective Presidency and national legislature, the Federation's House of Representatives, and the Serb Republic's Presidency and National Assembly took place. Izetbegović was re-elected to the state Presidency, and Zivko Radišić, a moderate representative of the Serbs, and Ante Jelavić, a nationalist Croat, were elected for the first time; Radišić was inaugurated as Chairman of the state Presidency for an eight-month term. The national legislature and Federation's House of Representatives continued to be dominated by nationalist parties: a PDA-led alliance obtained 14 of the 42 seats in the Bosnian House of Representatives and 68 of the 140 seats in the Federation House of Representatives. In the election to the Bosnian Serb Presidency, the Chairman of the Serb Radical Party (SRP), Nikola Poplasen, defeated the Western-backed Plavšić. The SDP retained the largest number of seats (19 out of 83) in the National Assembly of the Serb Republic, although the moderate parties maintained significant representation.

12 December 1998: Ganić was re-elected President of the Federation of Bosnia and Herzegovina and a new Federation Council of Ministers was established.

5 March 1999: Following his attempt to dismiss Dodik from the post of Prime Minister of the Serb Republic, President Poplasen was removed from office on the grounds that he had exceeded his authority; Mirko Sarović, hitherto Vice-President, provisionally assumed the presidential role.

7 March 1999: International arbitrators in Vienna, Austria, ruled that Serb control of Brčko would end, and that the town would henceforth be governed jointly by the Serb Republic and the Federation, under international supervision; in mid-April a new municipal government, comprising Serbs, Muslims and Croats was elected in the town.

15 June 1999: Jelavić replaced Radišić as Chairman of the state Presidency.

18 June 1999: The UN Security Council voted to extend the mandate of SFOR and the principally civilian security force, the UN Mission in Bosnia and Herzegovina (UNMIBH), for a further 12 months; at the same time, NATO announced a reduction in the SFOR contingent, to approximately 16,500 troops.

August 1999: Wolfgang Petritsch, hitherto Austrian ambassador to the FRY, succeeded Westendorp as High Representative of the international community in Bosnia and Herzegovina.

1 October 1999: Petritsch prohibited Poplasen and a further two SRP officials from contesting forthcoming local elections, on the grounds that they had consistently obstructed the implementation of the Dayton peace agreement.

December 1999: Ivo Andrić-Luzanski, hitherto the Federation Vice-President, assumed the Federation Presidency, in accordance with the one-year rotational mandate stipulated in the Constitution.

9 February 2000: Legislation allowing for the restructuring of the state Presidency was agreed, following the Constitutional Court's decision, in the previous month, that certain tenets of the Presidency were unconstitutional; henceforth, the collective Presidency would consist of two Ministers of State and a Chairman, which would rotate between Muslim, Serb and Croat representatives every eight months.

11 February 2000: Haris Siladžić, the Bosniak co-premier of the national Council of Ministers, resigned his post in protest at the Government's perceived failure to ensure the safe return of refugees.

14 February 2000: Alija Izetbegović took over from Ante Jelavić as Chairman of the state Presidency.

19 February 2000: The Socialist Party of the Bosnian Serb Republic (SPRS) withdrew from the ruling Accord Coalition following disagreement with Dodik and the other coalition partners; the Bosnian Serb premier's refusal to reinstate the former SPRS Deputy Prime Minister, Tihomir Gligorić, who had been dismissed in the previous month, resulted in the resignation, two days later, of the four other SPRS ministers.

8 March 2000: Following the completion of demilitarization in the disputed northern town of Brčko, an Interim District Government was officially inaugurated; the new structure, which was announced by the international supervisor for Brčko, Robert Farrand, was to consist of four Serbs, four Bosniaks and one Croat member, and was to be headed by Sinisa Kisić, hitherto mayor of Brčko.

21 March 2000: Robert Farrand appointed the 29 deputies that would comprise the transitional assembly of Brčko; the legislature, the mandate of which would last until district elections were held, consisted of 13 Serb, nine Bosniak and seven Croat representatives.

3 April 2000: The former joint President of the Presidency and a close ally of Karadžić, Momčilo Krajišnik, was arrested in Pale by SFOR troops and extradited to the ICTY in the Netherlands to answer charges of war crimes.

8 April 2000: Local elections were held; according to results released by the OSCE, the SDP secured a majority in 49 of the country's 145 municipalities, mainly in the Bosnian Serb Republic. The CDU—BH won control of 25 councils and the PDA secured control of 23 municipalities, mainly in the Federation. The moderate, multi-ethnic Social Democratic Party (SDP BiH) made significant electoral gains, however, winning control of 15 municipalities in the Federation (compared to one in the previous ballot) and achieving representation in 98 municipalities, including 26 in the Serb Republic.

3 May 2000: The Stara Gradiska–Bosanska Gradiska international border crossing between Bosnia and Herzegovina and Croatia was reopened, facilitating the return of displaced persons and contributing to better transport connections and stronger trade relations between the two countries.

24 May 2000: The PDA-led Federation Government survived a vote of 'no confidence' in the House of Representatives, proposed by the SDP BiH. Ganić was expelled from the PDA, owing to his failure to comply with the party's decision that he resign as Federation Vice-President.

22 June 2000: The new republican Government of Spasoje Tusevljak (who had been elected Chairman of the Council of Ministers earlier in the month) was approved in the House of Representatives.

7 September 2000: The Bosnian Serb National Assembly endorsed a motion of 'no confidence' in the Government of Milorad Dodik, proposed by the SDP. However, four days later the Bosnian Serb Government challenged the legitimacy of the motion and referred the matter to the Constitutional Court, stating that it would remain in office until the legislative elections scheduled for November.

14 October 2000: Izetbegović resigned from the collective Presidency on grounds of age (although he retained his post as PDA leader). Halid Genjac of the PDA replaced him as the Bosniak member of the Presidency on an acting basis, while the Serbian representative, Zivko Radišić, became Chairman.

11 November 2000: Elections to the national House of Representatives, the legislatures of both entities and the presidency of the Serb Republic took place. Mirko Sarović and Dragan Cavić were elected as President and Vice-President, respectively, of the Serb Republic; the SDP won 36% of the votes (31 seats) to the Serb Republic National Assembly. The Party of Democratic Action (PDA) won 27% of the votes (38 seats) in the elections to the Federation House of Representatives, while the SDP BiH won 26% (37 seats), the CDU—BH 18% (25 seats) and the Party for Bosnia and Herzegovina 15% (21 seats). In elections to the national House of Representatives the SDP BiH won 19% of the votes (nine seats), the PDA 18% (eight seats), the SDP 18% (six seats), and the Party for Bosnia and Herzegovina and CDU—BH 11% (five seats) each.

20 December 2000: Mladen Ivanić was designated by Sarović as Prime Minister of the Serb Republic.

10 January 2001: The former Bosnian Serb President, Biljana Plavšić, who had been indicted in April 2000, surrendered to the ICTY, but denied accusations of major involvement in the organization of a campaign of genocide and deportation against Muslims and Croats between July 1991 and December 1992.

12 January 2001: Ivanić formed the Serb Republic's first multi-ethnic Council of Ministers. Following international concern over the inclusion of several SDP members, Ivanić replaced the new Minister of Trade and Tourism, a prominent SDP member.

7 February 2001: The national Parliamentary Assembly rejected the designated Prime Minister, Martin Raguz of the CDU—BH. A newly-formed coalition, the Alliance for Change, comprising the SDP BiH and nine other non-nationalist parties, held 17 of the 42 seats in the House of Representatives, in addition to 69 seats in the federal legislature.

22 February 2001: An SDP BiH member, Bozidar Matić, nominated a new national Council of Ministers, which was approved by the House of Representatives.

23 February 2001: Three Bosnian Serbs were convicted by the ICTY of the systematic rape and enslavement of Muslim women in the town of Foca in 1992; they received a combined sentence of 60 years. Three days later a Bosnian Croat official, Dario Kordić, was convicted of authorizing murders and war crimes against Bosnian Muslims in 1993–94; he was sentenced to 25 years' imprisonment.

4 March 2001: A grouping of parties, led by the CDU—BH, known as the self-styled Croat People's Assembly (CPA), announced self-government in three Croat-majority cantons.

7 March 2001: Jelavić was dismissed from the collective state Presidency by Petritsch, following the declaration by the CPA of its intention to create a separate Croat state.

12 March 2001: The Federation legislature endorsed the nomination of Alija Behmen of the SDP BiH as Prime Minister and a new Government, comprising representatives of the Alliance for Change, was approved.

28 March 2001: The House of Representatives voted in favour of appointing Jozo Križanović of the SDP BiH as the new Croat member of the collective Presidency. Beriz Belkić of the Party for Bosnia and Herzegovina replaced Halid Genjac.

14 June 2001: Križanović officially assumed the chairmanship of the collective Presidency for a period of eight months. (Beriz Belkić was to replace him after this period).

22 June 2001: Bozidar Matić resigned from the chairmanship of the national Council of Ministers, in response to the rejection of legislation providing for the country's admission to the EU.

18 July 2001: Zlatko Lagumdzija, hitherto Minister of Foreign Affairs, was appointed Prime Minister by the Bosnian legislature, following the resignation of Matić.

25 September 2001: Gen. Sefer Halilović, a former Chief of Staff of the Bosnian army and hitherto a Federation minister, surrendered to the ICTY, after being indicted on charges related to the killing of Croatian civilians in 1993.

2 October 2001: Legislation, providing for full co-operation with the ICTY, was finally adopted by the Serb Republic National Assembly. Security forces were henceforth required to pursue actively war crimes suspects who remained at large (notably Gen. Ratko Mladić and Radovan Karadžić).

15 March 2002: Dragen Mikerević was appointed to the rotating chairmanship of the national Council of Ministers.

27 March 2002: The leading Bosnian political parties, under pressure from Petritsch, reached agreement on the adoption of constitutional reforms. The reforms, which ensured the representation of the three constituent peoples (Serb, Croat and Bosniak) at all levels of government, were officially adopted on 19 April. Petritsch amended the electoral law accordingly, and elections were scheduled for 5 October.

16 April 2002: The Dutch Government resigned, after a report by the Netherlands Institute for War Documentation emphasized the failure of Dutch peace-keeping troops to prevent the massacre at Srebreniča in 1995.

24 April 2002: Bosnia and Herzegovina became a member of the Council of Europe.

24 May 2002: Petritsch issued a ruling, providing for the adoption of judiciary reforms, which would ensure the independent appointment of judges and prosecutors.

27 May 2002: Petritsch named the first seven judges to a new Bosnian state court, representing the establishment of the first state-level judiciary apparatus since the signature of the Dayton accords. On the same day Sir Jeremy John Durham (Paddy) Ashdown, a British politician, officially replaced Petritsch as High Representative.

14 June 2002: Ashdown dismissed the Federation Deputy Prime Minister and Minister of Finance, Nikola Grabovac. On the same day the Serb Republic Minister of Finance, Milenko Vracar, tendered his resignation, following pressure from Ashdown (who had criticized malpractice in the customs agencies of both entities).

30 June 2002: The USA vetoed a further extension of the mandate of the UNMIBH, after failing to secure immunity from prosecution in the new International Criminal Court for US peace-keeping troops. A compromise agreement was subsequently reached with the US Government, and the UN Security Council extended the mandate of the UNMIBH until the end of 2002, when the contingent was to be transferred to the control of the EU.

15 July 2002: The members of the Bosnian Presidency met with the Presidents of Croatia and the FRY in Sarajevo (the first trilateral summit meeting since the dissolution of the former Yugoslavia). The leaders of the three countries agreed to strengthen co-operation.

5 October 2002 : Elections were conducted to legislatures at national and entity level, and to the state and Serb Republic presidencies. The Chairman of the PDA, Sulejman Tihić, was elected the Bosniak member of the collective Presidency, with 37.3% of the votes cast, while Dragan Čović of the CDU—BH (61.5%) became the Croat member and Mirko Sarović of the SDP (35.5%) the Serb member. Dragan Čavić secured the Serb Republic presidency, with 40.1% of the votes. The PDA became the strongest single party in the 42-member national House of Representatives, with 10 seats, and also secured the highest number of seats (32) in the 98-member federal House of Representatives. In the elections to the 83-member Serb Republic National Assembly, the SDP won 26 seats.

29 October 2002: The Serb Republic Minister of Defence and the Chief of the General Staff of the Army both resigned, following the discovery that a state-owned aviation company had exported military equipment to Iraq, in contravention of a UN embargo.

29 November 2002: The former leader of a Serbian para-military group was sentenced to 20 years' imprisonment at the ICTY for atrocities perpetrated against Bosnian Muslims in 1992–94.

1 January 2003: Following the official expiry of the mandate of UNMIBH, the UN transferred responsibility for reorganizing and training the country's security forces to an EU Police Mission.

13 January 2003: A new all-Bosnian Government, headed by Adnan Terzić of the PDA, was formed.

17 January 2003: The Serb Republic National Assembly approved the nomination of Dragan Mikerević of the Party of

Democratic Progress as Prime Minister, and a new Government for the entity, which comprised eight Serbian, five Bosniak and three Croatian representatives.

27 January 2003: The Federation House of Representatives elected Niko Lozancić of the CDU—BH to the entity's presidency, and, for the first time, a Bosniak and a Serb as joint Vice-Presidents. The State Court of Bosnia and Herzegovina officially commenced operations.

14 February 2003: A new Federation Government, headed by Ahmet Hadžipašić, was established.

20 February 2003: The newly appointed Serb Republic Minister of Finance resigned his portfolio, following allegations of malpractice.

27 February 2003: Biljana Plavšić, who had previously agreed to plead guilty at the ICTY to one charge of crimes against humanity, was sentenced to 11 years' imprisonment.

2 April 2003: Mirko Sarović resigned from the collective Presidency, after being implicated in the illicit exports to Iraq and alleged espionage activities by the Serb Republic military. One week later Borislav Paravac, also a member of the SDP, was nominated by the national legislature to replace Sarović. Also on 2 April Ashdown removed all references of statehood from the entity's Constitution, and abolished the Serb Republic Supreme Military Council.

7 July 2003: Ashdown suspended the financial accounts of 14 Bosnian Serbs who were suspected of being connected with war crime suspects, including the relatives of Karadžić.

11 July 2003: Mikerević attended a ceremony commemorating the massacre of some 7,000 Muslims by Serb forces at Srebrenica in 1995 (the first time that an important Serb Republic official had observed the anniversary).

31 July 2003: A former mayor of Prijedor, Milomir Stakić, was sentenced to life imprisonment by the ICTY (the first time that the Tribunal had imposed such a verdict) for leading a campaign to remove non-Serb civilians from the region during the Bosnian conflict.

History

PETER PALMER

The territory that constitutes modern Bosnia and Herzegovina was settled by Slavs in the sixth and seventh centuries AD. Having been under notional, and occasionally real, Eastern Roman ('Byzantine') authority during the early Middle Ages, the original Bosnian principality, Rama, experienced periods of rule by Serbs and, subsequently, Croats during the 10th and 11th centuries. At the beginning of the 12th century the rule of the Hungarian Crown extended to Croatia and much of Bosnia. By the late 12th century, however, under the local ruler, Kulin (1180–1204), Bosnia was effectively independent of Hungarian rule. Kulin's realm covered areas in the centre and north-east of present Bosnia. Politically and culturally connected with Croatia and Hungary by the 12th century, Bosnia's western links could also be attributed to the fact that it came under the authority of Roman Catholic bishops. Further south, however, the area of Hum (modern Herzegovina) was largely Eastern Orthodox and linked with Serbia.

Persistent Hungarian pressure in the 13th century was influenced by ecclesiastical politics, as the papacy encouraged Hungary to eradicate heresy in Bosnia. The 'Church of Bosnia' probably developed as a result of isolation and neglect by the dominant Christian denominations. In the 14th century Bosnia was, for a time, a major regional power; by the reign of King Stjepan Tvrtko I (1353–91) it extended over most of the present Bosnia and Herzegovina, much of Dalmatia and parts of Montenegro and south-west Serbia. Following Tvrtko's death, Bosnia was beset by rivalries among competing nobles, who often sought support from Hungary or, by the early 15th century, from the Ottoman Turks, whose armies had in the 1430s occupied much of Bosnia's territory. In an attempt to win support against the Turks, Tvrtko's successor, Stjepan Tomač, agreed to eliminate the Bosnian Church, already weakened by prolonged Franciscan proselytism. However, his appeals were to no avail, and in 1463 the Turkish conquest of Bosnia was completed. Meanwhile, the powerful ruler of Hum, Stjepan Vukić, had adopted the title of duke (herceg in Serbo-Croat, hence the name Herzegovina) in 1448. A 'rump' Herzegovina maintained some independence from the Turks until the early 1480s.

OTTOMAN AND HABSBURG RULE

Under Ottoman rule there followed a period of slow but steady islamization, so that by the late 16th or early 17th century Muslims constituted a majority in Bosnia. While the advantages to be gained from conversion to Islam under Ottoman rule presented a principal reason for this, the relative lack of a strong Christian Church organization in a region that had long been the scene of ecclesiastical competition was also a major factor. Another important demographic change lay in the large-scale migration by Orthodox Serbs and Vlachs (who were eventually assimilated by their Serb co-religionists) to regions of northern Bosnia, which had been depopulated by warfare. The Eastern Orthodox Church became a powerful institution under the *millet* system, which categorized people according to religion and gave religious leaders considerable responsibility for the secular affairs of their congregations.

Consequently, the ethnic and religious profile of Bosnia was substantially altered during the Ottoman period, which also saw the creation in 1580 of a specifically Bosnian entity, covering all of present Bosnia and parts of Serbia and Croatia. During the 17th century Bosnia was severely strained by frequent wars with the Habsburgs and with Venice. The most serious of these was the war of 1683–99, when Habsburg armies expelled the Turks from Hungarian lands and made incursions into the Balkans. The 18th century was also unsettled, with numerous revolts, often involving protests by local Muslims against taxes, which were required to finance the repeated wars. Mostar was a particular centre of unrest, while Sarajevo managed to assert a significant measure of autonomy.

During the 19th century there were concerted efforts by Ottoman rulers to reform their declining Empire, to raise the efficiency of its army and administration and to impose their authority on powerful regional rulers. Their efforts met with strong resistance from the conservative Bosnian Muslim élite. There were frequent and often violent protests among the peasantry, usually originating in economic hardship. Although there was initially little evidence of serious religious antagonism, this started to change after the middle of the century, especially as a result of Muslim resentment at foreign sponsorship of Christian institutions in Bosnia and Herzegovina (Russia favoured the Orthodox Serbs and Austria-Hungary the Roman Catholic Croats).

The Bosnian crisis of 1875–78 began in Herzegovina, following agrarian discontent. Encouraged by Serb nationalists, it spread, and the terrorization of Christian peasants in both Bosnia and Bulgaria internationalized the conflict. In 1877 Russia intervened to help Serbia, which had declared war on the Ottoman Empire in 1876, inflicting a heavy defeat on the Turks. However, the concern on the part of the other Great Powers of Europe at Russian influence in the region resulted in the Congress of Berlin of 1878, at which Bosnia and Herzegovina was mandated to the control of Habsburg Austria-Hungary.

Under Austro-Hungarian rule, control over Bosnia and Herzegovina was the responsibility of the imperial finance ministry in Vienna, Austria. A particularly sensitive issue at this time was that of national identity. Benjamin Kallay (Austro-Hungarian finance minister from 1882 to 1903) sought to isolate Bosnia and Herzegovina from Serb and Croat nationalism, and to establish a unifying Bosnian identity, according to which there would be no Serbs or Croats, just Orthodox, Roman Catholic and Muslim Bosnians. The idea found some support among leading Sarajevan Muslims. Such isolation was impossible, however, as the idea of both Serb and Croat identity was already well established in Bosnia and Herzegovina by the mid-19th century. Both sought to claim the Muslims as their own, regarding them as Serbs or Croats who had been denationalized by the alien occupier. However,

most Muslims rejected advances from either side, or tried to balance their competing interests. Some conservative elements claimed that by becoming Muslim they had given up nation for faith, arguing that Islam was incompatible with notions of nationhood. Although any sense of identity in this period was principally religious, in Muslim moves to organize, in order to protect their interests under the rule of the infidel, lay the seeds of the idea of a Muslim, or Bosniak, nation in Bosnia and Herzegovina.

Relations between Austria-Hungary and Serbia deteriorated, following a coup in Belgrade (Serbia) in 1903, which brought to power a Government much more assertive of Serbian interests. The Austro-Hungarian authorities had a well-founded fear that the Serbs of Bosnia and Herzegovina, much the largest single group there at that time, would ally themselves with neighbouring Serbia. When, in 1908, Austria-Hungary formally annexed Bosnia and Herzegovina, Serbia was resentful. Nationalist organizations spread their activities throughout Bosnia and Herzegovina. The First Balkan War of 1912, when Serbia expanded its territory twofold, at the expense of Turkey, caused further strain, as excitement among Serbs, and many Yugoslav-orientated Croats, resulted in the suppression of Serb organizations in Bosnia and Herzegovina. The culmination of this tension was the assassination in Sarajevo of Archduke Franz Ferdinand, the Habsburg heir, by Gavril Princip, a young Serb nationalist and professed Yugoslav, on 28 June 1914. Austria-Hungary used this as a pretext to attack Serbia, thus beginning the First World War.

BOSNIA AND HERZEGOVINA IN YUGOSLAVIA

The Kingdom of Serbs, Croats and Slovenes (known as Yugoslavia from 1929) was proclaimed on 1 December 1918. In practical political terms it was largely dominated by Serbs from the pre-war Kingdom of Serbia. As they were not in a majority, the Serbs sought allies, and the Bosnian Muslim leaders, through their party, the Yugoslav Muslim Organization, managed to gain concessions and limited influence by coming to terms with the Serbian leaders. However, the failure of the country's two largest ethnic groups, the Serbs and Croats, to become reconciled, caused difficulties in the new state, which, in 1929, King Aleksandar I sought to resolve by proclaiming a royal dictatorship. He reorganized the Kingdom into nine provinces (banovine). Much to the disappointment of the Muslims, Bosnia and Herzegovina was partitioned, with sections of its territory attached to banovine in neighbouring Serbia, Montenegro and Croatia. In 1939, in an attempt to appease the Croats, the Regent, Prince Pavle (Paul—who was ruling on behalf of the young King Petar II, following the assassination of Aleksandar I in 1934) agreed to the creation of a united Croatian banovina, which included large parts of western Herzegovina and central Bosnia. Still worse for the Muslims, this appeared to imply that the banovine to the east of Croatia, including most of Bosnia and Herzegovina, were Serbian, so that Bosnia and Herzegovina would simply be divided between its neighbours.

The Second World War forestalled any such development, as Bosnia and Herzegovina was incorporated into the Nazi 'puppet' Independent State of Croatia (Nezavisna Država Hrvatska—NDH). Inter-communal tensions and violence were not new to Bosnia and Herzegovina, but the German imposition of the genocidal Ustaša regime on the NDH gave rise to unprecedented brutality. The Croat Ustaše, sometimes joined by Muslims, indiscriminately murdered a great number of Serbs, and Serbs retaliated in kind. From this civil war the communist-dominated Partisan movement, led by Josip Broz (Tito), emerged victorious. With their pan-Yugoslav ideology, seeking to appeal to all the nations of Yugoslavia in their quest for power, the communists after the war reinstated a united Bosnia and Herzegovina as one of the constituent republics of Yugoslavia. The communists thus sought to limit Serbian power within the federation and avoid a return to Serbian hegemony, but also to defuse Serb-Croat rivalry over Bosnia and Herzegovina. In 1968, taking effect from the 1971 census, Bosnia's Muslims were recognized as one of the constituent 'nations' of Yugoslavia.

THE DISINTEGRATION OF YUGOSLAVIA AND WAR IN BOSNIA AND HERZEGOVINA

Under communism, Bosnia and Herzegovina experienced one of the most repressive regimes in Yugoslavia, since its rulers perceived repression as the only safe solution to the potential pressures in that multi-ethnic, multi-confessional republic. As communist rule disintegrated in Yugoslavia, a vigorous reassertion of Serb and Croat nationalism forced Bosnia and Herzegovina's Muslims (Bosnian Muslims, or Bosniaks) to assert their identity. Although the largest ethnic group in Bosnia and Herzegovina (comprising some 43.7% of the population), they were not in an overall majority, and were still at risk from the competing Serb and Croat claims to Bosnian territory.

In Bosnia and Herzegovina's first free elections, in November 1990, ethnically based parties representing the three constituent peoples emerged victorious. They formed an uneasy coalition, with the leader of the main Bosniak party, the Party of Democratic Action (PDA), Alija Izetbegović, as President of the State Presidency. Fearing that the Bosniaks would be caught between their more powerful neighbours, and their interests ignored, Izetbegović tried to maintain good relations with both Serbs and Croats, to seek a compromise that would leave both the Yugoslav federation and Bosnia and Herzegovina intact. For the Bosniaks, the federal Yugoslav state allowed them to assert their identity in their own mother republic, within a wider union, in which Serbs and Croats were linked to their co-nationals in Serbia and Croatia.

With the recognition by the European Community (EC—known as the European Union, EU, from November 1993) of Slovenia and Croatia as independent states in January 1992, Bosnia and Herzegovina was set on a course to war. The Croats and Bosniaks of Bosnia and Herzegovina would not consent to live in a 'rump' Yugoslavia dominated by Serbia, and the Bosnian Serbs would not live in a sovereign Bosnia and Herzegovina dominated by Bosniaks. The Serbs voted in a referendum in November 1991 to remain with Serbia if Bosnia and Herzegovina sought independence. They had armed themselves and counted on the support of Serbia and the remnants of the Yugoslav People's Army (YPA). For the Bosniaks, secession meant war at a great military disadvantage. The EC had promised that if a referendum opted for independence, Bosnia and Herzegovina would be recognized as such. On 29 February–1 March 1992 a referendum was duly held, producing a considerable majority in favour of independence, as most Serbs predictably boycotted it. Bosnian independence was recognized in April, but the Bosnian Serbs, having declared their own 'Serb Republic of Bosnia and Herzegovina' on 27 March, had already opted for war.

The war was characterized by atrocities on the part of Serb forces, in particular, which, through an organized campaign of 'ethnic cleansing' removed the non-Serb population from large regions of the country. A similar strategy, on a smaller scale, was also employed by Bosnian Croat and occasionally Bosniak forces. With their extensive military superiority, the Serbs besieged several Bosnian government-controlled towns, including Sarajevo.

Bosnia's state institutions maintained their support for a continuing, multi-ethnic, unitary state, but were, in effect, dominated by Bosniaks. The Croats were nominally allied with the Bosniaks, but the Presidents of Serbia and Croatia,

Slobodan Milošević and Franjo Tudjman, had secretly reached a deal on a Serb–Croat division of Bosnia and Herzegovina. In July 1992 the Bosnian Croats established their own state (the 'Croat Union of Herzeg-Bosna'), centred on the Croat heartlands of Western Herzegovina and central Bosnia. Croats and Bosniaks were in conflict from late 1992 until the beginning of 1994, when the USA mediated a peace agreement, resulting in the formation of a Federation of Bosnia and Herzegovina on 31 March 1994, on territory controlled by the Bosniaks and Croats. The alliance was unstable and, in practice, the parallel institutions of Herzeg-Bosna and the Bosniak-dominated Republic continued to operate for a considerable time.

A series of international attempts to halt or alleviate the impact of the war included the stationing of UN troops in the country, a 'no-fly' or exclusion zone in Bosnian airspace (enforced for the UN by the North Atlantic Treaty Organization—NATO), a large-scale aid effort and, in July 1993, the declaration of UN 'safe areas' in six Bosniak-held towns. On the diplomatic front, a plan presented in early 1993 by the EC representative, Lord (David) Owen (a former British Foreign Secretary), and Cyrus Vance (a former US Secretary of State), acting for the UN, envisaged the division of the country into 10 autonomous units: three Serb, three Bosniak, three Croat and a joint capital in Sarajevo. The Croats and Bosniaks agreed to the plan, but, despite intense pressure from Milošević, who was anxious to secure the removal of sanctions imposed by the UN on the Federal Republic of Yugoslavia (FRY, comprising Serbia and Montenegro), it was rejected by the Bosnian Serb Assembly in May 1993. A new plan, presented by the 'Contact Group' (France, Germany, Russia, the United Kingdom and the USA) in June 1994, was based on a territorial division between the Federation (which would receive 51% of Bosnian territory) and the Serb Republic (allocated 49%). However, the Serbs (who held some 70% of the country at that time) also rejected this plan.

The split between Milošević and the Bosnian Serbs was to prove vital to further attempts to reach peace, as Milošević withdrew support for their war efforts, and the balance of military strength shifted towards the Croatian army. The USA assumed control of the peace negotiations, taking a much more robust stand towards the conflict than the hitherto ineffectual EU. Following the fall of two UN-protected 'safe areas', Srebreniča and Žepa, to the Serbs in July, NATO (acting for the UN) responded swiftly to a suspected Serb mortar attack on Sarajevo on 28 August, with air and artillery attacks on Serb positions and installations.

Bosnian Croat and government forces, supported by the Croatian army, took advantage of the NATO attacks on the Bosnian Serbs to launch their own offensives, which resulted in a division of territory more closely resembling that envisaged in the Contact Group plan. Milošević finally forced the still recalcitrant Bosnian Serbs to accept a peace settlement to be negotiated on their behalf by the FRY. A cease-fire was implemented, and in November 1995 a peace agreement was negotiated at Dayton, Ohio, the USA.

PEACE AND AN INTERNATIONAL PROTECTORATE

According to the terms of the General Framework Agreement for Peace in Bosnia and Herzegovina and its attached subsidiary accords, Bosnia and Herzegovina remained a single state within its internationally recognized borders, and comprised two entities, the Federation and the Serb Republic, to which considerable powers were devolved. Within the Federation powers were devolved to its 10 constituent cantons. Central institutions included a joint presidency, comprising Bosniak, Serb and Croat representatives, a parliament, a constitutional court and a central bank. Individuals indicted for war crimes were banned from political office.

Implementation of the Dayton accords has been uneven. The military separation of the warring parties, supervised by the NATO-led Implementation Force (IFOR), and the territorial exchanges stipulated in the Dayton accords proceeded rapidly in late 1995 and early 1996. However, progress on the political front was slower. The frustration of international efforts, led by an international High Representative, to establish the institutions of a functioning state prompted the international community in Bosnia and Herzegovina increasingly to assume the attributes of an international protectorate. In December 1997 the Peace Implementation Council, comprising states involved in the Bosnian peace process, decided to extend the High Representative's powers to allow him to impose decisions when government leaders were unable to reach agreement, and to remove obstructive officials.

The international community's hopes that elections would produce institutions with a democratic mandate, capable of reintegrating the multi-ethnic state were repeatedly disappointed, confirming the high levels of support for narrowly nationalist parties representing the three main ethnic groups, the PDA, the Serb Democratic Party (SDP) and the Croatian Democratic Union of Bosnia and Herzegovina (CDU—BH). The first post-war elections for institutions at state and entity level in September 1996 were held in deeply unsatisfactory conditions, without freedom of movement and with the main ethnic parties controlling most of the media. The elections resulted in overwhelming victories for the three nationalist parties.

The nationalist parties persistently thwarted efforts to reconstruct a reintegrated, functioning state. The priority for all organizations was to preserve their dominance in their own ethnic regions, and they demonstrated no real commitment to the reintegration of the country. The greater powers granted to his office in 1997 enabled the High Representative, Carlos Westendorp (a former Spanish Minister of Foreign Affairs), to resolve the impasse in several areas, including citizenship and common passports, common vehicle licence plates, a new flag and the design of the new common currency. Wolfgang Petritsch (a former Austrian ambassador to the FRY), who succeeded Westendorp in August 1999, continued to make frequent use of these enhanced powers.

Although much progress was made in a number of areas, the basic difficulty of establishing an effective Bosnian administration remained unresolved. The High Representative's frequent use of his powers enabled the establishment of the country's institutional framework to be advanced, but it failed to contribute to the reconstruction of a self-sustaining, democratic Bosnian state, which could at some point function without the need for international supervision. The efforts of the international community to impose its vision of an integrated state were constantly undermined by the nationalist parties, with their powers of patronage, control of the economy and links with organized crime.

The international community repeatedly attempted to exploit divisions in the CDU—BH, in the hope of bringing more compromising elected authorities to power. Thus, following a split in the organization in 1998, the international community made efforts to consolidate the position of the more moderate New Croat Initiative (NCI), which was formed by the Croat member of the state Presidency, Krešimir Zubak. However, despite international efforts to make the campaign for the September 1998 elections fairer, and thereby to increase the NCI's chances, the party was overwhelmingly defeated by the CDU—BH. Divisions among the nationalist leaders of the Serb Republic were also exploited in order to promote a more moderate option. In 1997 the President of the Serb Republic, Biljana Plavšić, encountered opposition from the wartime Bosnian Serb leader, Radovan Karadžić, and

other SDP leaders, including Momčilo Krajišnik, a former Serb member of the joint Presidency, over her objections to corruption among prominent party officials. Although the indicted Karadžić had relinquished the Serb Republic presidency to Plavšić (who had not yet been indicted by the International Criminal Tribunal for the former Yugoslavia—ICTY, based in the Hague, the Netherlands) in July 1996, he continued to exercise power unofficially. The international community's support, especially that of the reduced Stabilization Force (SFOR—which had superseded IFOR in December 1996), enabled Plavšić to gain control of much of the Serb Republic in 1997. For her part, Plavšić adopted a more moderate, compromising stance. The international community's approach initially appeared successful and, following Plavšić's expulsion from the SDP in July 1997, support for the party declined in legislative elections held in the Serb Republic in November. Plavšić appointed Milorad Dodik of the small Party of Independent Social Democrats (PISD), who was a long-standing opponent of the SDP's nationalist policies, as Prime Minister in January 1998.

However, international hopes were to be disappointed in the Serb Republic in the September 1998 elections, in which support for 'hardline' nationalists remained strong. In the election to the presidency of the Serb Republic, Plavšić was defeated by Nikola Poplasen, the leader of the extreme nationalist Serb Radical Party (SRP). With international support, Dodik remained Prime Minister, and in March 1999 Westendorp removed Poplasen, who had openly opposed refugee return and expressed hopes for the Serb Republic's eventual union with the FRY, from office. Anxious to avoid a return to an extremist leadership in the Serb Republic, the international community was reluctant to undermine Dodik. Therefore, only limited demands were placed on the Bosnian Serb premier by the international community, and progress towards further implementation of the peace accord under his leadership was modest.

Although granted high priority in the Dayton accords, the return of refugees was initially often regarded as being in conflict with the maintenance of the fragile security, and was thus limited. However, as the security situation improved, the international community was more active in pressurizing local authorities to allow refugees to return and taking measures to ensure the property rights of returnees. Consequently, from 2000 a sharp increase in numbers of refugees returning to regions in which their ethnic group represented a minority was reported. The pursuit of indicted war crimes suspects and their extradition to the ICTY was also uneven. In particular, IFOR and SFOR were much criticized for failing to arrest key war crimes suspects, such as Karadžić and the Bosnian Serb military leader, Ratko Mladić. Notable among Bosnian Serb suspects who were arrested by NATO troops and transferred to the ICTY, however, was Krajišnik, in April 2000.

PROGRESS TOWARDS NATIONAL REINTEGRATION

After the repeated impediments to efforts of the international community to reconstruct Bosnia as a functioning state, a number of combined factors in 2000 raised hopes that a transitional point might have been reached. Following the defeat of the Croatian Democratic Union in legislative and presidential elections in Croatia in January and February 2000, the CDU—BH no longer received support from the Croatian Government for its extremist nationalist policies. Political changes in Serbia following the fall of Milošević in October produced varied results with regard to the FRY's relationship with Bosnia and Herzegovina. While efforts were made to normalize relations between the two countries, the new Yugoslav President, Vojislav Koštunica, appeared to endorse the nationalist SDP in the campaign prior to elections in Bosnia and Herzegovina in November 2000. In a public address in 2002, Koštunica provoked protests by asserting that the Bosnian Serb Republic was part of a Serb state, but temporarily separated. Nevertheless, the end of the Milošević regime undoubtedly contributed to an overall much more favourable regional environment for the advancement of the international community's agenda in Bosnia and Herzegovina.

Optimism among the international community was raised by the apparent rise to power of the non-ethnically based Social Democratic Party of Bosnia and Herzegovina (SDP BiH) in elections in 2000. Following successes at local elections in April, and in legislative elections in November, the SDP BiH emerged as the party with the largest representation in the Bosnian House of Representatives. Encouraged by the international community, the SDP BiH formed the 10-party Alliance for Change coalition, which established a Government in February 2001. Concerted efforts from the PDA, the SDP and the CDU—BH to prevent the Alliance from securing a majority in the legislature demonstrated the extent to which the interests of the three main nationalist parties, despite having been bitter wartime enemies, now coincided.

The period both before and after the November 2000 elections was distinguished by increasing confrontation between the CDU—BH and the international community. This development was prompted by a highly significant decision by the Constitutional Court in July 2000 that all three of Bosnia and Herzegovina's peoples should be constituent throughout the entire country. This ruling had implications for the ethnic basis of the country, in which, under the Dayton agreement, the Serb Republic was perceived to be the homeland of the Serbs in Bosnia, and the Federation that of the Bosniaks and Croats. It strengthened the position of those urging that the central authorities be granted greater powers, and that the entities be gradually marginalized within a unified Bosnian state, in which all its citizens would enjoy equal rights. As such, the ruling represented a major challenge for the nationalist parties.

Following the court's decision, the legislation under which the November 2000 legislative elections were to be contested was amended to reflect the ruling. The CDU—BH objected to a new provision whereby non-Croats would be able to participate in the election by the Federation legislature of Croat representatives to the Bosnian upper chamber, the House of Peoples. CDU—BH leaders scheduled a referendum for the day of the elections to demonstrate Croat support for a Declaration on the Rights and Position of the Croat People. The CDU—BH's strategy of encouraging a general perception that Croats in Bosnia and Herzegovina were under threat proved profitable in the November elections, and the party's support was maintained. However, as a result of the considerable losses by the PDA to the SDP BiH, the Alliance for Change was able to form a Federation Government in March 2001 that excluded both the CDU—BH and the PDA.

The exclusion of the CDU—BH from the Bosnian and Federation Governments prompted the party leadership to increase its demands in the dispute with the international community. A Croat People's Assembly (CPA), established by the CDU—BH in March 2001, declared its intention to assume control of all civil administration functions in Croat-held regions, as well as over the Croat component of the Federation army. Many Croat members of the armed forces, as well as police, customs officials and others, declared their loyalty to the new autonomous power structures. Petritsch responded with resolution, removing Jelavić from the state presidency and the leadership of the CDU—BH, as well as replacing several other senior prominent CDU—BH members. In April officials of the Office of the High Representative seized bank branches across the Croat-held west of the country, notably the Hercegovačka Banka branch in Mostar,

which controlled financial operations on behalf of the Croat parallel structures. Faced with such international resolution, the CDU—BH insurrection petered out, and in May and June its deputies ended their boycott of the national legislature. The party made efforts to maintain pressure on the international community, and in July announced that it envisaged conducting a referendum on a third, Croat entity. However, Jelavić acknowledged that Croat self-rule had not been a success, and in November CDU—BH deputies ended their boycott of the Federation House of Representatives.

In the Serb Republic the results of the November 2000 elections were disappointing for the international community, as support for the SDP recovered, partly benefiting from the votes of followers of the SRP, which had been prohibited from participating. The SDP candidate, Mirko Šarović, won the Serb Republic Presidency, and the SDP emerged as the strongest party in the Serb Republic National Assembly. Despite SDP protestations that it had reformed and that it would respect the Dayton accords, the USA, in particular, insisted that continued aid to the Serb Republic was conditional on the SDP's exclusion from the Serb Republic Government. In January 2001 the leader of the newly formed Party of Democratic Progress (PDP), Mladen Ivanić, formed a Government with the support, among others, of the SDP. Although Ivanić avoided the appointment of ministers with open SDP affiliation, in an effort to placate the international community, SDP members commanded considerable influence in government organs and state-owned companies. The SDP persistently obstructed the achievement of the aims of the international community.

The main focus of the Alliance for Change was to implement reforms which, in accordance with the July 2000 Constitutional Court decision, would strengthen the authority and effectiveness of central, state bodies and protect the equality of all citizens throughout the country, regardless of ethnicity. An early reverse was the failure of the Alliance's proposal that the post of national Prime Minister should cease to be rotated every eight months among the three constituent ethnic groups, and instead be a four-year office. As well as being opposed by the CDU—BH and the SDP, the proposal was also opposed by the Alliance's coalition partners from the Serb Republic at state level (Ivanić's PDP and the Party of Independent Social Democrats), and was withdrawn in July 2001.

Another difficult issue confronting the Alliance for Change administration concerned new election legislation. As the Organization for Security and Co-operation in Europe (OSCE) prepared to transfer responsibility for organizing elections to the Bosnian authorities, the necessity of adopting new legislation became urgent. Some parties in the Alliance hoped to introduce legislation, which, in accordance with the July 2000 Constitutional Court ruling, would aim to prevent the customary practice of voting according to ethnic group. However, as with the proposals on the rotation principle, these hopes also encountered strong opposition. Finally, in August 2001 an election law was adopted, which, in the most significant respects, failed to meet the demands of the integrationist parties.

Progress towards greater national reintegration was achieved in April 2002, with the imposition by Petritsch of constitutional amendments prior to elections in October, in accordance with the July 2000 Constitutional Court decision. The amendments were designed to ensure that all Bosnians, regardless of ethnicity, would be represented at all levels of government and public administration in both entities. For example, in the Serb Republic only eight of 16 government ministers were henceforth to be Serbs, and the administration was to include five Bosniak and three Croat representatives. Petritsch also amended the electoral law in accordance with the revised Constitutions of the two entities. On 27 May 2002

Petritsch was replaced as High Representative by Sir Jeremy (Paddy) Ashdown, a former prominent British politician.

The hopes of the international community, following the November 2000 elections, for a new era of co-operation with moderate Bosnian authorities suffered a reverse in the elections of 5 October 2002 (which were conducted to the national presidency, the presidency of the Serb Republic, and the national and entity legislatures). The Alliance for Change had already been divided by serious disagreement for several months, with key members of the coalition, the NCI and the Party for Bosnia and Herzegovina, objecting to what they regarded as the dominance of the SDP BiH. The Alliance came under particular strain in June of that year, when Ashdown removed from office the Federation Deputy Prime Minister and Minister of Finance, Nikola Grabovac, who was also the deputy leader of the NCI, following a scandal in the customs administration. Zubak responded by declaring that the NCI would not participate in any future Alliance government after new elections. Relations between the Party for Bosnia and Herzegovina and the SDP BiH further deteriorated, after Nijaz Duraković, a former Bosnian communist leader and founder of the SDP BiH, who remained a prominent figure in the organization, agreed to head the Party for Bosnia and Herzegovina's list of candidates in the October 2002 elections for the national Parliamentary Assembly. This development confirmed the intention of the Party for Bosnia and Herzegovina to challenge the SDP BiH in the forthcoming elections. The SDP BiH emerged from the elections with the greatest loss of support, while the PDA reclaimed its position as the dominant party among the Bosniak community. Once again, the three posts of the collective Presidency were secured by representatives of the three main nationalist parties, Mirko Sarović of the SDP, Dragan Čović of the CDU—BH and Sulejman Tihić of the PDA. However, the results did not reflect a general resurgence of nationalist appeal. Rather, a notable feature of the elections was a very low rate of participation by the electorate, reflecting widespread popular disaffection with politics and a loss of faith in all of the parties on offer. Despite its non-ethnic profile, the SDP BiH's support was derived principally from Bosniak voters, many of whom, having failed to vote for the PDA in November 2000, had by October 2002 become alienated from the Alliance's perceived failure to produce tangible improvements, and either abstained from voting or returned to the PDA. The SDP and the CDU—BH had not secured similar success among the Serb and Croat communities, respectively, and had not suffered the same kind of defeat as the PDA in 2000. In 2002 they remained much the most important parties among their respective communities, although, as a result of the low participation rate, their level of support actually declined. Also encouraging for the international community were the significant gains secured by the moderate PISD in the Serb Republic.

New Governments were formed at national and entity level by February 2003, after protracted inter-party discussions. The three victorious nationalist parties, the PDA, CDU—BH and SDP, unable to establish administrations without the support of other parties, were joined by the Party for Bosnia and Herzegovina and the PDP. In the Federation, the Party for Bosnia and Herzegovina was divided over whether to join forces with the PDA and the CDU—BH. The Federation Government, led by Ahmet Hadžipašić of the PDA and including members of the Party for Bosnia and Herzegovina, was finally established in February 2003. In the Serb Republic, Dragan Čavić of the SDP was installed as President on 28 November 2002. The PISD demanded the formation of a pro-reform government, but the PDP instead decided to continue its co-operation with the SDP. In January 2003 Dragan Mikerević of the PDP was officially appointed Prime

Minister of the Serb Republic, and a new Government (which, under the new constitutional arrangements to ensure equal ethnic representation, included members of the SDP and the PDA) was established in the entity. Corruption scandals continued to prove troublesome to the authorities, particularly in the Serb Republic. There had been tensions between the PDP and the SDP over investigations of prominent SDP members, following allegations of customs malpractice, which emerged in June 2002, prompting the removal of the Serb Republic Minister of Finance, Milenko Vracar, and his Federation counterpart. In January 2003 allegations of fraud involving the privatization of a bank forced the resignation of his successor, Simeun Vilendecić. In February further allegations of corruption in the Serb Republic electricity company, which had suffered major losses, prompted Ashdown to dismiss its management. In April Sarović was forced to resign from the collective Presidency, having been implicated in a report confirming that a Serb Republic aviation company had been exporting military equipment to Iraq, in contravention of UN sanctions. The election by the Serb Republic legislature of Borislav Paravac to replace Sarović prompted concerns, owing to his wartime record as a 'hardline' SDP representative. One of Ashdown's main priorities was to strengthen the central Bosnian authorities. In December 2002, despite fierce opposition from parties in the Serb Republic, he imposed legislation on the entity's Council of Ministers in order to make that body more of an executive authority for the state. Another priority, given particular urgency by the discovered illicit exports to Iraq, was the necessity of reforming the defence industry, including bringing it under central control. This was also identified as a requirement for Bosnia to be permitted to join NATO's 'Partnership for Peace' programme (also strongly opposed by the Serb Republic). In April 2003, following revelations that the Serb Republic military had been spying on international agencies, Ashdown announced the removal of all mentions of statehood from the Serb Republic Constitution and abolition of the entity's Supreme Defence Council.

Meanwhile, following the transfer of Milošević to the ICTY in June 2001, pressure on the Serb Republic to comply with the indictments issued by the Tribunal increased. However, legislation on co-operation with the ICTY, adopted by the Serb Republic National Assembly in October, had produced few tangible results. Repeated attempts by SFOR troops to capture Karadžić proved unsuccessful, while Mladić was believed to have taken refuge in Serbia. In February 2003 Plavšić, who had surrendered to the ICTY in January 2001, was sentenced to 11 years' imprisonment, having pleaded guilty to one charge of crimes against humanity. Her transfer to a Swedish prison in June 2003, at the request of the ICTY, prompted domestic concern that she might serve only part of her sentence. Also in June a former Bosnian Serb prison guard pleaded guilty to one charge of crimes against humanity at the ICTY.

The persistent frustration of international efforts to transform Bosnia and Herzegovina into a stable, functioning state, respecting the equal rights of all its citizens, regardless of ethnicity, has prompted many international commentators to question whether the two-entity Dayton framework itself might be unfeasible in the long term. The constitutional amendments imposed in April 2002, followed by the measures taken by Ashdown to strengthen the central authorities, represented an attempt to construct a stable, functioning state within the basic terms of the Dayton agreement. Ashdown was especially keen to promote Bosnia and Herzegovina's integration with EU member states. The prospect of eventual EU membership is regarded as a crucial incentive for the Bosnian authorities to co-operate in constructing functioning state structures. The involvement of the EU in Bosnia has increased. At the end of 2002 the mandate of the UN

Mission in Bosnia and Herzegovina, established in 1995, officially expired, and the UN transferred responsibility for supervising and retraining the country's security forces to an EU Police Mission. It was envisaged that an EU force might also eventually replace SFOR; in June 2003 the 90 Russian troops belonging to the contingent withdrew from the country.

The Economy

Dr VESNA BOJIČIĆ

During the communist period the economy of Bosnia and Herzegovina was dominated by industry and mining, which accounted for 51% of gross domestic product (GDP) and almost 50% of total employment. The greater part of output was concentrated in traditional, heavy industry, which provided raw and semi-processed materials for manufacturing industries predominantly located in more developed parts of the former Socialist Federal Republic of Yugoslavia (SFRY— of which Bosnia and Herzegovina was one of six republics). As a result, Bosnia and Herzegovina was highly integrated into the former SFRY's economy, and consequently suffered disproportionately when the country disintegrated in 1990. Economic deterioration was further exacerbated by the 1992–95 conflict, which caused massive material damage and human suffering. Production was virtually suspended, and by the end of the conflict in 1995, GDP had declined by more than two-thirds, compared with 1991 (the largest output contraction of any former communist country during transitional recession). In per-head terms, GDP declined to some US $500, from about $1,900 prior to the conflict. Killings and the exodus of refugees reduced the population by more than 1m.; almost 60% of the country's population was displaced by 1996. The rate of unemployment at the end of 1995 was estimated at 70%–80%. Large-scale damage was inflicted on all aspects of infrastructure, which had already been in a fairly neglected state owing to the years of economic crisis that preceded the war. Extensive reconstruction of housing and commercial dwellings, schools and hospitals was necessary.

The conflict also halted market-orientated economic reforms, which had commenced much earlier in the SFRY than in other former communist countries. By the end of the 1980s some prices had been liberalized, the privatization of enterprises had started and the role of central planning had been reduced. Following the dissolution of SFRY in 1991, each of the successor states of the country, including Bosnia and Herzegovina, has followed its distinctive programme of reforms with varying success, depending on individual circumstances. The administrative and governance framework of Bosnia and Herzegovina disintegrated during the conflict, and three separate economic and political administrations controlled by its three main ethnic groups were established in the territories where each represented a majority. Different economic legislation and practices were in place in each of these entities, including different currencies: Croatian kuna in the Croat-dominated parts of Bosnia and Herzegovina; the Yugoslav dinar in the Serb-dominated regions; and the Bosnian dinar in areas with a Muslim majority. The German Deutsche Mark (DM) was universally accepted throughout the country. Fiscal policies and management were implemented by separate authorities. The majority Bosnian Croat and Bosnian Serb territories were effectively integrated into Croatia and Serbia, respectively. This proved to be one of the principal obstacles to the advancement of economic reforms, which were promoted under the internationally-sponsored programme in the aftermath of the conflict.

POST-WAR RECONSTRUCTION

As part of the peace agreement for Bosnia and Herzegovina, the international community agreed a reconstruction programme, which was to create the basic preconditions for sustained economic growth for a period of three to four years. The programme identified national reconstruction, the creation of institutions for the macroeconomic management of the country and the initiation of transitional reforms as the three main priorities. The amount of international assistance required to support the programme was estimated at US $5,100m., which was to be co-ordinated by the World Bank and the European Union (EU). In 1996 the focus of international assistance was on the repair and reconstruction of infrastructure as a precondition for the revival of production and trade, as well as the restoration of basic public services to the general population. A number of emergency reconstruction schemes contributed to the resumption of a regular supply of electricity and water throughout most of the country, to the reparation of roads and rail networks, and to the restoration of basic health, education and housing services. With the exception of telecommunications, the emphasis was to repair the damage and restore services to their pre-war level. In the telecommunications sector, the programme co-ordinated by the European Bank for Reconstruction and Development (EBRD) aimed to improve the quality of service compared to that prior to the conflict.

The physical reconstruction of infrastructure proceeded without major difficulties. The accompanying policy reforms, designed to provide for a more efficient utilization of infrastructure divided along ethnic lines, were, however, obstructed by the local authorities. This prompted the Peace Implementation Council (the main body overseeing the implementation of the peace agreement) to grant the High Representative the powers to impose legislation obstructed by local authorities. From the end of 1997, when these new powers of the High Representative entered into effect, the emphasis of the internationally-sponsored programme shifted towards institution building. Under the Dayton agreement, Bosnia and Herzegovina's central state was attributed a minimum of economic competencies; instead, economic powers were vested in entities. Strengthening integrative elements entailed in the new Bosnian Constitution has proved to be the most difficult task for the international community in the country. With regard to infrastructure, by the end of 2002, under concerted pressure from the international agencies involved in the programme, progress was made, both at state level and within the Federation, in overcoming the legacy of three separate utility systems. In 2001 supervision of the telecommunications sector was placed under the new Communications Regulatory Agency and preparations for its privatization began. Progress was also achieved in negotiations with Croatia over the resumption of railway traffic along Bosnia and Herzegovina's principal north–south railway line and in 2000, after a period of more than seven years, commercial and passenger traffic resumed. Reforms in the railway sector were scheduled for 2003, in accordance with the Constitution, which stipulated the establishment of a single public company from three state-owned railway companies. Substantial progress was made in the rehabilitation of housing, although at the end of 2002 a significant proportion remained in need of reconstruction and repair. Comparatively, a much smaller proportion of the overall reconstruction funds was allocated to the rehabilitation of production (18% of the Priority Reconstruction Programme), compared with expenditure on infrastructure. The emphasis was on assisting the reparation of war damage and providing working capital, primarily in the private sector. Such aid helped a number of small and medium-sized companies to become active again. Various micro-credit schemes provided initial capital for new businesses. Bosnia and Herzegovina's principal state-owned enterprises, which dominated its pre-war economy, largely failed to receive reconstruction assistance, as a result of the internationally supported economic concept that privatization was essential to the reconstruction framework. Even in incidences where infrastructural damage was minimal, it proved extremely difficult, or impossible, for these enterprises to resume production, owing to lack of finance, loss of markets and absence of managerial skills. Agriculture and the food industry, which were devastated during the conflict, also received substantial aid. Programmes were introduced to help farmers rebuild herds and crops, and many food-processing capacities were restored or newly built through donor-finance credit schemes. New strategies for the development of agriculture, harmonized under the UN's Food and Agriculture Organization (FAO), were initiated.

ECONOMIC REFORM

In June 1997 the Parliamentary Assembly of Bosnia and Herzegovina adopted the 'Quick Start Package' of basic economic laws at state level. This was at the initiative of the international community, which aimed to expedite the process of creating the basic conditions necessary for macroeconomic management of the country, hitherto absent owing to the extensive powers assigned to the entities. The package included legislation on establishing a central bank and on foreign debt, foreign trade, customs tariffs, customs policy and the budget. The programme was supported by an IMF stand-by arrangement of US $82m.; the loan was subsequently augmented to $130m. and extended until May 2001.

One of the significant early achievements of the 'Quick Start Package' legislation was the establishment of the Central Bank of Bosnia and Herzegovina, which commenced operations in August 1997. Its main aim was to supervise the introduction of a common currency, and to maintain the currency-board system on which it was based. Bosnia and Herzegovina's new national currency, the convertible mark (konvertibilna marka—KM), was introduced in June 1998, gradually replacing other currencies in circulation at that time. The DM, which was the only universally accepted currency throughout Bosnia and Herzegovina, remained in circulation until the end of 2001. The major factor contributing to the successful introduction of the new currency was its stability, achieved through the strict implementation of the currency-board rules. The KM was fixed to the DM until January 2002, when the DM was replaced by the common European currency, the euro.

Another important early success of the Quick Start Package legislation was the agreement on the budgets of the entities and the state, which was reached in 1997. The Constitution agreed as part of the peace settlement placed fiscal sovereignty entirely with the entities, leaving the central state minimal financial power. The agreement provided for the system of automatic transfers of the entity contributions to the state budget (which was financed one-third from the Serb Republic and two-thirds from the Federation). Overall, however, the reform process moved slowly and sporadically. Political communication between the two entities only commenced in mid-1998, following the election of a more moderate Government in the Serb Republic in 1997. This made the passage of legislation somewhat easier, in view of the insistence of the international community on the conditionality of its financial assistance, but its implementation remained difficult and sometimes subject to delays. For example, although the unified foreign-trade regime and common customs tariff was agreed in March 1998, it only entered into effect in March 1999, after the free-trade agreements with Croatia and the Federal Republic of Yugoslavia (FRY, comprising Serbia and Montenegro) were terminated and an agreement between the entities was reached on additional import duties. Previously, goods entering from Croatia and the FRY were tax-free, except for a 1% administrative tax, and each entity applied its own excise duties. On the one hand, such a situation deprived the budgets of the two entities of significant customs revenues; on the other, it created ample opportunities for tax fraud, given the different tariffs in the two entities. The new trade agreements with Croatia and the FRY only entered into force in January 2001 and February 2002, respectively.

The two-year election cycle also contributed to slow progress in reforms. By 2002 the legislation on foreign debt, customs tariffs and foreign investments had been adopted, of which some (such as the foreign investment law) had to be imposed by the High Representative. In 1999 the reform of the payment system commenced as part of the rehabilitation of the financial system of Bosnia and Herzegovina. It was also essential for the efficient functioning of the currency-board regime supporting the new national currency. The payment bureaux had been retained from the command economy, allowing full control of payment transactions and providing channels for diverting public funds. Moreover, they were depriving the financial system of much-needed liquidity and were detrimental to the banking sector. The capability of payment bureaux to create credit presented a direct threat to the currency board. In early 2001 the payment bureaux were closed and replaced by a commercial-bank clearing system, while the Central Bank assumed responsibility for high-risk transactions. After some initial difficulties, the banks managed to provide an adequate payment-transactions clearing service.

Banking reform commenced in 1998 and proceeded in conjunction with the reform of the payment system. Bosnia and Herzegovina inherited a weak banking sector dominated by state-owned banks, which suffered from bad loan portfolios and poor banking practices. In 1995 state-owned banks controlled some 90% of banking assets. Although the number of private banks increased dramatically during and after the conflict, they were generally small in terms of capital and the operations involved, engaging mostly in foreign-currency transactions. As a result, the banking sector remained weak and incapable of supporting larger investment projects. In 1997 negative bank capital in the Federation amounted to US $2,000m. As part of the reform, entity banking agencies were established with the responsibility of supervising the banks and promoting the reforms. The first signs of progress were apparent in 2001, when in the Federation, for the first time since 1995, the banking sector demonstrated a profit. By the end of 2001 the number of banks, particularly in the Federation, declined (to about 50 in the Federation and 19 in the Serb Republic), as a result of dual and mutually-connected processes, an increase in the minimum capital requirement and a number of bank mergers as part of the consolidation of the banking system. The minimum capital requirement was increased from some KM 5m. to KM 7.5m. in 2001, and to some KM 15m. by April 2003. By the end of 2002 a total of 44 banks operated in Bosnia and Herzegovina. Despite this, the banks remained small in size and with an unfavourable structure of deposits. In 2002 there were some signs of long-term deposits increasing their share, especially in the Federation, and of increased credit activity (domestic lending dominates bank loan portfolios). Bank privatization, which proceeded much more successfully in the Federation than in the Serb Republic, contributed to the consolidation of the banking sector; by the end of 2002 private ownership accounted for about 80% of total capital in Bosnia and Herzegovina, compared with 1995, when the banking sector was 90% state-owned. Some 10 foreign banks were operating in the Federation in 2002. The establishment of deposit insurance agencies in both entities represented progress towards the revival of public confidence in the banking sector (reinforced by the stable currency and low inflation), which was reflected in the gradual, although in terms of volume modest, increase in savings. The conversion of household foreign-currency holdings into euros at the end of 2001 stimulated savings, which was, in turn, reflected in a significant expansion of credit activity in 2002. Lending to private enterprises also accelerated, but remained far below the economy's need for capital; poor provision of financial services continued to restrict the country's development, particularly the establishment of new business.

The reform of the pension system and labour market were similarly slow and required intervention by the High Representative. Bosnia and Herzegovina inherited a generous entitlement system from the SFRY, which was inconsistent with its fiscal capacity. As a result, no comprehensive social policy existed and large arrears were accumulating within the system in both entities. The IMF insisted that new legislation on pensions and disability be adopted, under which pensions and disability allowances would be paid according to the amount of revenues collected. The approval of the legislation on pensions and disability in the Federation, where two separate pensions systems operated, encountered opposition from local parties, necessitating its imposition by the High Representative in November 2000. The legislation entered into force on 1 January 2001, but the new system experienced serious difficulties, as a result of obstruction to revenue collection. In time, pensions were paid more regularly, although the amounts involved were significantly reduced. The two Federation pension funds merged in 2002 and the reforms progressed towards the harmonization of entity pension legislation. The reform of disability benefits remained contentious but was considered necessary for consolidating public finance.

Labour-market reform commenced in the second half of 2000. These measures were designed to eliminate the socialist-era practices, which involved over-generous entitlements, inhibiting growth in the labour market, and aggravating the development of the private sector. Restrictive labour-market legislation was an important factor that contributed to low worker and job mobility. Modern labour legislation was introduced in both entities, and the revised unemployment insurance programme, introduced in 2000, provided income compensation to the unemployed. The reform encountered considerable resistance, from local political structures, as well as from trade unions. The role of the High Representative in implementing the economic-reform programme remained essential; in December 2000 he imposed extensive legislation and legal amendments, which were designed to maintain the momentum of economic reforms threatened by political disagreement. These included legislation on pension and disability allowance, and amendments to the law on privatization, income taxation and the payment system. The emphasis of reforms in 2001 gradually shifted to the harmonization of the legislation between the two entities and the creation of a single market. Some of these reforms were included in an EU action plan, agreed in March 2000, which identified the 18 most important measures for the advancement of Bosnia and Herzegovina's relations with the EU. The

'roadmap', which recommended the removal of all barriers to inter-entity trade, was declared to be completed at the beginning of 2003, thereby permitting progression to the feasibility study for the Stabilization and Association Agreement. In 2002 a number of measures were taken towards improving the business environment of Bosnia and Herzegovina, which was identified as containing some of the most egregious barriers to business development.

Economic Policy

Following a period of 'hyperinflation' at the beginning of the conflict, the local authorities of Bosnia and Herzegovina tried to stabilize the economy. In the Muslim-controlled territories a new currency (the Bosnian dinar, fixed to the DM) was introduced in 1994, resulting in the stabilization of the economy in 1995–96. In the Croat-controlled territories the stabilization programme was launched in 1993, so that by 1995 inflation was brought under control. In the Serb Republic, fiscal restraint, in response to the sanctions by Serbia, also eased inflationary pressures. In the post-war period macroeconomic stabilization remained the main objective of the Government's economic policy, closely monitored by the IMF and other international institutions assisting Bosnia and Herzegovina's economic recovery. The principal means to this end was the stable currency, achieved by strict adherence to the currency-board regulations and the inflow of international assistance. The currency board prohibited the Government from borrowing from the banking sector (a regulation that was enforced following the introduction of the KM). The KM, which was made fully convertible, remained stable, its rate reflecting fluctuations of the DM, and subsequently the euro, against other currencies. The Government's fiscal policy was largely prudent, based on the conditions of the IMF's stand-by arrangement (a further such arrangement was agreed in August 2002). The fiscal deficit was not high, but accumulation of arrears was widespread at all levels of government, and external budgetary support continued to supplement the lack of funds. Public-sector financial reform, designed to balance public revenue and expenditure, featured prominently in the reform agenda supported by the IMF and the World Bank, and gathered momentum in 2001. Both entities made efforts to increase revenue by improvement in collection of taxes, and to restrain expenditure, which was difficult in a post-war environment with large claims on the Government. A programme to rationalize the armed forces as a means of reducing disproportionately high military expenditure was undertaken in 2002, when some 10,000 members of the armed forces in the Federation and about 6,000 in the Serb Republic were demobilized, in order to ease demand on the budget.

Privatization in Bosnia and Herzegovina, which commenced in 1999, proceeded much more slowly than anticipated. Although privatization models differed slightly in the two entities, the main feature in both was mass privatization. The Government issued vouchers to citizens in compensation for war-related debts, such as unpaid wages, pensions and lost foreign-currency savings. Furthermore, in the Federation all citizens of more than 18 years of age were entitled to a general certificate, valued at KM 1,900, augmented by an amount corresponding to the number of years in employment. Mass privatization was designed to remove state-owned enterprises from the public sector rapidly, while the sale of tender was to be the principal means of attracting strategic investors and fresh capital.

From the outset the privatization programme was impeded by technical difficulties, lack of public interest, unresolved land property issues, lack of attractive enterprises and, above all, political interference. Tender sales were temporarily suspended in the Federation in April 2000, owing to non-transparent practices and, after changes demanded by the international community had been adopted, resumed in October. Henceforth, tender privatization of some 86 strategic companies was to be assisted by the Advisory Group for Privatization, comprising the World Bank, the US Government Agency for International Development (USAID) and the EU. The first tender sale took place in mid-2001, but the overall process continued to be slow, owing to the lack of information on enterprise performance and non-transparent bidding practices. Political obstructions also contributed to the delay of tender privatization. By the end of 2002 some 70% of small enterprises in the Federation and 50% in the Serb Republic had been sold. Of the total 1,064 large enterprises in the Federation (excluding the so-called 'strategic companies'), 25% were privatized, while the comparable proportion in the Serb Republic was 40%. Only seven strategic enterprises in the Federation and four in the Serb Republic had been sold by the end of 2002, prompting government measures designed to improve the efficiency of privatization agencies. The aim of the government action was to grant privatization agencies more responsibility and greater decision-making powers to allow for improved flexibility in cancelling liabilities and engaging in pre-privatization restructuring.

ECONOMIC PERFORMANCE

Bosnia and Herzegovina's economy grew strongly, following the end of the conflict in 1995. The reconstruction programme, which during 1996–2000 provided an average annual inflow of US $1,000m. in donor assistance, stimulated strong economic recovery. In 1996, the first year of the programme's implementation, annual GDP increased by more than 50%, although primarily from very low levels. Strong growth, led by reconstruction-related activities, continued until 2000, although at rapidly decelerating rates. Real GDP growth had slowed to about 4% by 2002, when GDP per head remained at just more than 50% of its pre-war level. Growth continued to be based on externally funded public investment and on public consumption. Exports grew strongly, but unsteadily, and from a very low base, consequently not contributing significantly to growth levels. A significant feature of post-conflict recovery was a large 'grey' economy (the parallel, semi-legal sector), which was believed to amount to 55%–66% of GDP.

Economic recovery was strong in the Federation, but weaker and unsteady in the Serb Republic. The main reason for this was that the Federation initially received most of the reconstruction funds, while aid was mainly withheld from the Serb Republic until 1998, owing to its policy of non-co-operation with the international agencies engaged in the reconstruction programme in Bosnia and Herzegovina. Following the election of a moderate Government in November 1997, the attitude of international donors towards assisting the Serb Republic (which had begun to affect adversely progress in the overall reconstruction effort) became more favourable. Its economic performance remained irregular, owing to its close links with the FRY, which until 2001 suffered severe economic instability. Slow progress in the implementation of reforms and an overall decline in reconstruction aid resulted in a sharp deceleration in economic activity in the Serb Republic in 2001–02. High agricultural production in 2002 contributed to offsetting the recessionary effect.

The structure of Bosnia and Herzegovina's economy changed significantly as a consequence of war and the nature of post-war recovery. A process of de-industrialization was set in motion, with industry (including mining) and utilities accounting for approximately 32% of GDP in 2001. This occurred despite strong growth in industrial output throughout the post-1995 period in Bosnia and Herzegovina, particularly in the Federation, where industrial output increased by 35.7% in 1997 and by 23.8% in 1998. By 2001, however, rates of growth declined sharply; compared with the previous year, industrial output increased by 12.2% in the Federation, but declined by 17.8% in the Serb Republic. This trend continued in 2002, when industrial output increased by 9.2% in the Federation, and declined by 2.5% in Serb Republic.

The deceleration in industrial growth partly represented a return to more sustainable rates of growth, and partly an absence of a large-scale industrial revival. National industrial output at the end of 2002 was just more than one-third of its 1991 level. Industrial recovery in the country was mainly concentrated in sectors, such as electricity generation, power transmission and distribution, and coal extraction; consequently, any fluctuation in these sectors significantly affected overall industrial performance. Recovery of manufacturing, which gathered momentum during 1999–2001, continued in 2002, increasing by 13.2% in the Federation. There too, the recovery remained concentrated in a small number of industries, such as base metals and metal-processing, foodstuffs, wood-processing and textiles. In most of these industries only one or two companies were active. Prior to the conflict, about 50% of industrial output and employment in Bosnia and Herzegovina had been generated by several large enterprises in the energy and raw-materials producing sectors, and in the electrical engineering, textiles, leather and footwear industries. Some of those enterprises were particularly affected by the conflict and the disintegration of the SFRY. Most enterprises remained state-owned (35% of all businesses were privately owned at the beginning of 2000), and thus outside the scope of the reconstruction programme, which was primarily orientated towards supporting small and medium-scale, private-sector activities. In 2002 the recovery in industrial output continued to benefit only a few industries, such as food and beverages, other non-metallic minerals, chemicals and metal manufacturing.

The internationally-funded reconstruction programme provided strong impetus to construction activity. The greater part of the programme consisted of the repair of infrastructure and housing. This growth, however, was uneven, owing to the changing dynamics of the international donors' aid. In mid-1998 annual growth rates reached 40%–60%, but declined thereafter and stagnated in 2001, compared with the previous year, reflecting a gradual reduction in reconstruction-related activities. Construction output demonstrated a further recovery in 2002, most of which was attributed to the increase in new construction, indicating a decline in reconstruction work. A similar pattern was also recorded in the Serb Republic. Construction, particularly civil engineering, was well developed in Bosnia and Herzegovina before the war and was an important earner of foreign currency. In 1999 the first larger contracts abroad were signed in the Middle East and Africa; in 2002 the value of work contracted abroad amounted to US $54m. in the Federation.

Trade grew strongly in Bosnia and Herzegovina in 1995–2002, as obstacles to the free movement of goods and people gradually diminished, and accounted for about 16% of GDP in 2002. In 1997 progress was made in integrating the three separate payment systems within the country, thus enabling the clearing of payment transactions within the Federation and between the two entities. Inter-entity trade increased in 1998, and continued to grow strongly, with Federation sales to the Serb Republic surpassing by several-fold the value of goods purchased from the Serb Republic. In 1998–2002 Federation exports to the Serb Republic mainly comprised miscellaneous and electrical products; food accounted for most of the Federation's purchases from the Serb Republic. An increase in retail sales was fuelled by strong growth in wages, together with the spending of international personnel stationed in Bosnia and Herzegovina and remittances from Bosnian nationals abroad.

In 2000 agriculture (including hunting, forestry and fishing) accounted for some 8.8% and some 23.9% of GDP in the Federation and the Serb Republic, respectively. It was estimated that agricultural GDP in the Serb Republic, where most of the country's arable land was situated, declined by 39.5% in 1995. The agricultural sector of the Federation demonstrated a more modest decline, of 1.1%, in the same year. Revival of the agricultural sector remained subdued in the immediate post-war period, despite international assistance. However, agricultural output improved thereafter, increasing by 27.3% in 1996 and by 25.2% in 1997 in the Serb Republic, and by 5.9% and by 0.5% in 1996 and 1997, respectively, in the Federation. Following a sharp decline in output, caused by drought, in 2000, agricultural production recovered in 2001–02. Disputed land ownership was one of the main factors impeding the development of the agricultural sector.

A large number of mines remaining from the war also presented an obstacle in recovering land for production. The normalization of the supply of goods, stabilization of currency and the authorities' tight fiscal policy brought consumer prices under control. Following the introduction of the KM in 1998, prices started to fall, particularly in the Federation, where disinflation was recorded by 1999. A 1.9% rise in consumer prices in the Federation in 2000, partially resulting from the secondary effect of an increase in the prices of petroleum and food, was followed by a 1.5% rise in 2001. The rate of inflation in the Federation declined by 0.2% in 2002. In the Serb Republic consumer prices began to converge with those in the Federation; in 2002 inflation in the Serb Republic declined to 1.9%, compared with 14.1% in 1999.

UNEMPLOYMENT AND WAGES

Strong post-war growth in Bosnia and Herzegovina failed to generate sufficient new employment. The number of officially employed increased very slowly, with the result that in 2002 it exceeded its 1997 level by just more than 10%. The number of registered unemployment grew steadily over the same period. In 2000–02 the trends in employment and unemployment began to diverge, with the former declining and the latter rising. This was the period in which reconstruction-related activity subsided. The unemployment rate, based on official statistics, was estimated at about 40% in early 2002, and was believed to be slightly higher in the Serb Republic than in the Federation. The actual employment situation at that time proved difficult to ascertain, owing to the large numbers working in the informal economy. Informal employment was estimated at 32% in the Federation and 41% in the Serb Republic. The situation was further complicated by the practice of most enterprises of retaining a 'waiting list' of workers who were without jobs, but officially in employment. In parallel to changes in the size of the sectors, the structure of official employment shifted away from manufacturing and towards services. The share of employment in manufacturing contracted in absolute terms, and in 2002 amounted to just less than one-half of its 1991 level.

Most new jobs created from 1996 were in the services sector, particularly in public administration. By 2000 the number of employed in the public-administration sector in the Federation surpassed its pre-war level, reflecting the oversized government sector created by the new constitutional structure detailed in the Dayton agreement. Employment in the agricultural sector helped to reduce somewhat the rate of unemployment in the Serb Republic. In the absence of a wide-scale recovery, high unemployment was likely to remain a problem, with intensifying pressure on enterprises to restructure, and more refugees returning to the country. Further pressure resulted from a demilitarization programme, which commenced in 2001, with some 13,000 former members of the armed forces seeking employment in the Federation alone. In

early 2001 the new central state Government took action to lower wage contributions, in an attempt to facilitate new employment as part of wider labour-market reforms.

Wages, both in nominal and real terms, increased strongly throughout the post-war period, although at a decelerating pace from 1999. This was in contrast to both the employment dynamics and economic performance, thereby demonstrating the rigidity of Bosnia and Herzegovina's labour market. Growth in wages surpassed real GDP growth for most of the period. The high wages received by the employees of the international organizations based in the country exerted some pressure on local wages. Wages in the Federation remained higher than in the Serb Republic, although the differential began to narrow sharply in 1999. At the end of 2002 the average net nominal wage reached KM 484 in the Federation, and KM 347 in the Serb Republic. Wages were paid irregularly, particularly in the Serb Republic. In 2002 there were indications that unsuitable skills had been developed, a tendency that would further contribute to the continuing high level of unemployment.

GOVERNMENT FINANCE

A weak fiscal position was one of the main features of Bosnia and Herzegovina's macroeconomic situation. The post-war recovery was accompanied by a high level of public spending, made possible by financial support from donors, estimated at about 40% of total public expenditure in 1997–99. Locally generated revenue covered recurrent social expenditure and defence spending, with capital expenditure funded by donors. General government expenditure amounted to 64.5% in 1998, but declined to 56.2% of GDP in 2002. At the same time tax reductions and the decline in international financial support contributed to a slight decrease in revenue, which fell from 56.7% of GDP to 52.2% in 2002. As a result, Bosnia and Herzegovina recorded budgetary deficits each year from 1997. The international community made fiscal consolidation one of the main conditions for its continuing financial support. The emphasis was on reductions in expenditure, in view of the country's precarious situation and its weak fiscal capacity (but these were accompanied by efforts to reform tax system and improve tax collection). One of the major problems was the high level of military expenditure, which in 2001 (after several reductions) amounted to 25% and 8% of total expenditure in the Federation and the Serb Republic, respectively. The central government deficit (on a commitment basis) reached some 13% of GDP in 2001. The budgets of the two entities required rebalancing both in 2000 and 2001 (twice in the Federation in 2000), as well as (in the case of the Serb Republic) emergency funding. In 2001 the state budget was rebalanced, owing to higher than expected expenditure on the foreign service and state border security. The consolidated budget deficit was gradually reduced from 5.1% of GDP in 1998 to 4.4% in 2002.

The international community continued to promote measures that were designed to provide for the fiscal sustainability of Bosnia and Herzegovina. Some of these measures necessitated major reforms of tax and expenditure policies. Such efforts were successful, with, for example, the promulgation of state-level legislation on customs and tariffs at the beginning of 1998. The legislation represented major progress towards recovering custom revenue, which accounted for most of the revenue of the entity Governments, and which was undermined by the previous custom laws and procedures of the two entities. The reform of public finances was supported by the World Bank's Public Finance Structural Reform project, which became operational in 1998. However, in early 2000 a serious deterioration in the fiscal situation, resulting from higher than projected expenditure on refugees, wages, transfers to pension funds, and increased foreign-debt service (owing to the depreciation of the KM against the US dollar), indicated that progress in public-finance reform was necessary.

Accumulated arrears reached 4% of GDP in 2000. The reduction and restructuring of public expenditure represented the main feature of public-finance reform undertaken by the new entity Governments, which were installed in early 2001. The new administrations succeeded in ending the accumulation of arrears, and paid some pension arrears. Military expenditure was reduced in the Federation, with the implementation of a large demobilization programme. In an effort to increase revenue, reform of sales tax was completed in 2001, thus reducing the incentives and opportunities for tax evasion. Customs and tax-administration reform was also advanced, with the aim of improving tax collection. Despite all these measures, the deceleration in growth and continued tax evasion resulted in a revenue shortfall in 2001. This coincided with the increasing significance of the state institutions, necessitating additional funding; state-budget expenditure increased to about 3% of GDP in 2001. In 2002 some progress was made in reducing fiscal imbalances, as a result of stronger economic performance, improved tax administration and tightened control on spending. The funding of the central state institutions proved to be a problem, in view of the limited fiscal powers assigned to the state and an increasing range of competencies it assumed in the course of the post-war development of Bosnia and Herzegovina. By the end of 2001 it was evident that the development of a more secure system of state funding was required, and various options, including the introduction of state-level value-added tax (VAT), were considered. In an attempt to improve budget management and transparency, a Ministry of the Treasury was established at state level in 2000 and treasury systems were introduced in both entities in January 2002. Progress was made in discussions on the introduction of the state-level VAT, to which the Serb Republic Government was initially strongly opposed.

FOREIGN TRADE

Economic recovery from the mid-1990s was accompanied by strong growth in imports related to the projects financed under the reconstruction programme. Exports began to increase in 1998, although from a very low base, growing strongly in 2000. In 2001–02, however, exports contracted; export trade totalled some US $1,114.2m. in 2002. Exports were concentrated in a small number of raw materials and intermediate goods, such as base metals, wood, and leather products. Strong growth in imports, stimulated by a massive reconstruction effort, continued, with the value of imports totalling $4,513.5m. in 2002, resulting in an increased trade deficit of $3,399.3m. Bosnia and Herzegovina's principal market was the EU member countries, accounting for 48% of the Federation's exports in 2001 and 38% of the Serb Republic's exports in 2000. Italy was the Federation's largest export market from 1998, but in 2002 was exceeded in value by Germany, which accounted for 15.2% of Federation exports in that year. The FRY (known as Serbia and Montenegro from February 2003) was the Serb Republic's main trading partner, contributing 25.6% of exports in 2002. Bosnia and Herzegovina was granted free access to the EU market for most commodities in 2000, but failed to benefit from it fully, owing to the absence of the state-level institutions assuring compliance with the standards and certificates required by the EU. The markets of the successor states of the SFRY continued to represent an increasingly important proportion of Bosnia and Herzegovina's foreign trade, accounting for some 36% of exports in 2001. Croatia remained the state's main trading partner, accounting for 14.9% of exports and 16.3% of imports in 2002. Bosnia and Herzegovina has benefited from new trade agreements with both Croatia and Serbia, signed in 2000 and 2001, respectively.

The large trade deficit was the main contributory factor to the high deficit on the current account of the balance of payments, which was estimated at more than US $2,106m. in 2002. Although there was a surplus on other components of the current account, it was, nevertheless, insufficient to reduce significantly the effect of a large trade deficit. The deficit was financed by foreign aid, local spending by foreigners and remittances. Bosnia and Herzegovina's foreign-trade performance prompted further concern from the international agencies assisting the process of economic reform, when levels of foreign assistance began to decline in 2001 and the foreign-trade gap widened further. There was no indication that local economic performance had improved sufficiently to offset the declining inflow of foreign assistance, which threatened to undermine macroeconomic stability.

FOREIGN INVESTMENT

During 1996–99 the inflow of foreign direct investment was very limited. Political risks, lack of attractive business opportunities and complex legislation, in conjunction with the small size of Bosnia and Herzegovina's market, acted as strong deterrents to potential investors. Foreign direct investment stock was estimated at KM 835.4m. in 1998–2001. The inflow of foreign direct investment recovered somewhat in 2000–01 as privatization progressed, particularly in the banking sector, where by 2002 more than 50% of capital was foreign-owned. In 2002 foreign direct investment totalled US $240m. and was one of the lowest in South-Eastern Europe. 'Greenfield' investment remained minimal and was mainly concentrated in the retail trade sector. Individual investment was typically small, the single largest being the Kuwaiti Investment Authority's purchase of shares in an iron and steel mill at Zenica. Croatia and Slovenia were principal investors, while there was also some German, Italian, Yugoslav, French and Turkish investment. Austria was by far the largest investor in the banking sector.

In 1997–98, with the assistance of the World Bank and the EU, two investment guarantee schemes intended to encourage private capital flows were established. As the international assistance began to decline, attracting larger inflows of foreign direct investment became increasingly important in the Government's programme. Until then, the authorities postponed adoption of the necessary legislation. A state-level law on foreign investment was adopted in 1998, but the adoption of the new Federation law on foreign investment was delayed. The World Bank Foreign Investment Advisory Service found the laws contained numerous barriers to investment, which required the Government subsequently to formulate an action plan to address the objections to the foreign investment law. The Foreign Investment Promotion Agency was established in 1999, but suffered from understaffing and insufficient finance. It was estimated that Bosnia and Herzegovina would need an average annual inflow of US $200m. during 2001–04 to sustain growth and remain on schedule with debt repayment.

FOREIGN DEBT

Bosnia and Herzegovina inherited considerable foreign debt from the former Yugoslavia. In 1995 Bosnia and Herzegovina's total external debt amounted to US $3,200m., of which $1,900m. was in arrears. Following the clearance of outstanding arrears to the IMF and the World Bank, the country commenced negotiations with other creditors. In December 1997 an agreement with the 'London Club' of international creditors was reached, resulting in an 85.8% debt reduction. An agreement with the 'Paris Club' of creditors to cancel 67%

of debt followed in October 1998. By the end of 2001 total external debt amounted to $2,226m., of which much was owed to multilaterals, principally the World Bank and the IMF. Most of the new debt acquired since 1995 was on concessional terms, thus making the debt burden fairly moderate (the debt to GDP ratio was about 52% in 2002 and debt-servicing as a share of the value of exports amounted to some 19.1%). Nevertheless, debt-servicing remained a source of concern.

The new Law on External Debt was adopted in 1997, which made the servicing of the foreign debt the responsibility of the central Government, with entities providing the revenue for it. After initial problems in 1998, when the Serb Republic failed to provide its share of revenue, the mechanism providing an automatic transfer of the funds from the entities was agreed.

PROSPECTS

The immediate recovery from severe contraction caused by the war was strong, but in 1995–2002 Bosnia and Herzegovina made only initial progress in establishing institutions to enable its economic self-sustainability. Widespread and sustained revival of economic activity was difficult in the opaque business environment and weak-performing nascent institu-

tions. In conjunction with these constraints, substantial international assistance in the initial stage of post-war reconstruction resulted in the development of an aid-dependent pattern of development with weak export performance and low job generation. Poverty in the country increased to some 19% of the population in 2002. As a result of a particular post-war pattern of development, Bosnia and Herzegovina was encumbered with both fiscal and current-account deficits. Poor enterprise performance constrained fiscal capacity, which remained weak, presenting a serious threat to maintaining macroeconomic stability, which is essential for continuing with the next phase of structural reforms. Weak export performance, in the absence of substantial foreign inflows, could undermine the currency board underpinning the stability of Bosnia and Herzegovina's currency, as well as constrain foreign debt-servicing. The country's capacity for borrowing at commercial terms is weak, indicating that international assistance will remain essential for many years. The greatest risk to Bosnia and Herzegovina's economic prospects is presented by the political developments in the country, in particular the commitment of its political leadership to proceed with essential reforms, which would bring a change in enterprise business attitudes and investment behaviour, favouring long-term growth.

Statistical Survey

Source (unless otherwise stated): Agencija za statistiku Bosne i Hercegovine, 71000 Sarajevo; tel. and fax (33) 2206222; e-mail bhas@bih.net.ba; internet www.bhas.ba.

Area and Population

AREA, POPULATION AND DENSITY

Area (sq km)	51,129*
Population (census results)	
31 March 1981	4,124,008
31 March 1991	
Males	2,183,795
Females.	2,193,238
Total	4,377,033
Population (UN estimates at mid-year)†	
2000	3,977,000
2001	4,067,000
2002	4,126,000
Density (per sq km) at mid-2002	80.7

* 19,741 sq miles.
† Source: UN, *World Population Prospects: The 2000 Revision.*

PRINCIPAL ETHNIC GROUPS
(1991 census, provisional)

	Number	% of total population
Muslims	1,905,829	43.7
Serbs	1,369,258	31.4
Croats	755,892	17.3
'Yugoslavs'	239,845	5.5
Total (incl. others)	4,364,574	100.0

PRINCIPAL TOWNS
(population at 1991 census)

Sarajevo (capital) .	416,497	Bihać	45,995
Banja Luka . . .	143,079	Brčko	41,405
Zenica	96,027	Bijeljina	37,216
Tuzla	83,770	Prijedor	34,613
Mostar.	75,865		

Source: Thomas Brinkhoff, *City Population* (internet www.citypopulation.de).

BIRTHS AND DEATHS
(UN estimates, annual averages)

	1985–90	1990–95	1995–2000
Birth rate (per 1,000)	17.1	12.9	10.5
Death rate (per 1,000)	7.1	7.1	7.4

Sources: UN, *World Population Prospects: The 2001 Revision* and *World Population Prospects: The 2002 Revision.*

Expectation of life (WHO estimates, years at birth): 72.8 (males 69.3; females 76.4) in 2001 (Source: WHO, *World Health Report*).

EMPLOYMENT
(Federation of Bosnia and Herzegovina, average for December)

	1997	1998	1999
Activities of the material sphere . . .	173,857	204,117	217,000
Non-material services	113,723	131,945	127,345
Total	287,580	336,062	344,345

Source: IMF, *Bosnia and Herzegovina: Selected Issues and Statistical Appendix* (June 2000).

Total employed (Federation of Bosnia and Herzegovina, at 31 December): 412,305 in 2000; 405,689 in 2001; 390,201 in 2002.

Total employed (Republika Srpska, at 31 December): 228,834 in 2000; 219,954 in 2001; 234,713 in 2002.

Unemployed (Federation of Bosnia and Herzegovina, persons registered at 31 December): 261,773 in 2000, 269,004 in 2001; 290,715 in 2002.

Unemployed (Republika Srpska, persons registered at 31 December): 153,264 in 2000; 147,749 in 2001; 144,790 in 2001.

Source: Central Bank of Bosnia and Herzegovina.

Health and Welfare

KEY INDICATORS

Total fertility rate (children per woman, 2001)	1.3
Under-5 mortality rate (per 1,000 live births, 2001) . . .	18
HIV/AIDS (% of persons aged 15–49, 1999)	0.10
Physicians (per 1,000 head, 1998)	1.43
Hospital beds (per 1,000 head, 1995)	1.84
Health expenditure (2000): US $ per head (PPP) . . .	319
Health expenditure (2000): % of GDP	4.5
Health expenditure (2000): public (% of total)	69.0

For sources and definitions, see explanatory note on p. vi.

Agriculture

PRINCIPAL CROPS
('000 metric tons)

	1999	2000	2001
Wheat	257.8*	338.5*	269.5
Barley	56.3*	53.1*	64.6
Maize	984.1*	474.9*	510.2
Rye	9.0*	11.7*	13.9
Oats	61.7*	56.9*	45.7
Potatoes	437.8*	282.8*	185.1
Dry beans	14.1*	5.8*	7.1
Soybeans (Soya beans)	8.7*	4.0*	3.6
Cabbages	111.6*	68.5*	68.4
Tomatoes	36.9*	29.6*	23.3
Chillies and green peppers . . .	36.9*	37.0†	37.0†
Dry onions	36.6*	21.6*	23.4
Garlic	8.5*	4.0*	7.4
Carrots	14.5*	5.6*	10.2
Other vegetables†	458.8	504.7	510.8
Grapes	12.7*	13.2*	13.3†
Apples	25.9*	14.4*	14.4
Pears	10.6*	9.0†	8.1
Plums	27.0*	26.8*	26.8
Tobacco (leaves)	4.1*	3.3*	3.4

* Unofficial figure.
† FAO estimate(s).

Source: FAO.

LIVESTOCK
('000 head, year ending September)

	1999	2000	2001
Horses	20*	18†	18*
Cattle	443†	462†	440*
Pigs*	350	355	330
Sheep	633†	662†	640*
Chickens	1,100*	1,000*	4,740†
Ducks*	120	120	120
Geese*	150	150	150
Turkeys*	120	120	120

* FAO estimate(s).
† Unofficial figure.

Source: FAO.

LIVESTOCK PRODUCTS
('000 metric tons)

	1999	2000	2001
Beef and veal	12.4*	12.5†	13.0†
Mutton and lamb	2.7*	2.7	2.7*
Pig meat*	11.7	5.0	6.0
Poultry meat	8.9*	8.4	8.4*
Cows' milk	569.4†	540.0*	460.0*
Sheep's milk	7.6†	7.1†	7.0*
Cheese	11.0*	8.7†	8.5*
Hen eggs*	15.0	15.2	15.1
Cattle and buffalo hides* . . .	2.4	2.4	2.4

* FAO estimate(s).
† Unofficial figure.

Source: FAO.

Forestry

ROUNDWOOD REMOVALS
('000 cubic metres, excluding bark)

	1999*	2000	2001
Sawlogs, veneer logs and logs for sleepers	2,800	2,875	2,531
Pulpwood	130	158	141
Other industrial wood	290	299	286
Fuel wood	910	950	860
Total	4,130	4,282	3,818

* Unofficial figures.

Source: FAO.

SAWNWOOD PRODUCTION
(FAO estimates, '000 cubic metres, including railway sleepers)

	1999	2000	2001
Coniferous (softwood)	80	50	60
Broadleaved (hardwood) . . .	250	270	250
Total	330	320	310

Source: FAO.

Fishing

(FAO estimates, metric tons, live weight)

	1998	1999	2000
Total catch (capture, freshwater fish)	2,500	2,500	2,500

Source: FAO, *Yearbook of Fishery Statistics*.

Mining

('000 metric tons)

	1998	1999	2000
Lignite and brown coal	1,764	1,800*	1,800*
Iron ore: gross weight*	100	100	100
Iron ore: metal content*	35	35	36
Bauxite*	75	75	75
Kaolin (crude)*	3	3	3
Ceramic clay (crude)*	20	20	20
Barite (Barytes) concentrate* . . .	2	2	2
Salt (unrefined)*	50	50	50
Gypsum (crude)*	30	30	30

* Estimated production.

Source: US Geological Survey.

Industry

SELECTED PRODUCTS
('000 metric tons, unless otherwise indicated)

	1990
Electric energy (million kWh).	14,632
Crude steel	1,421
Aluminium	89
Machines.	16
Tractors (number)	34,000
Lorries (number)	16,000
Motor cars (number)	38,000
Cement	797
Paper and paperboard	281
Television receivers (number).	21,000

Electric energy (million kWh): 2,461 in 1997; 2,538 in 1998; 2,615 in 1999 (Source: UN, *Industrial Commodity Statistics Yearbook*).

Mineral manufactures (estimates, '000 metric tons): Crude steel 115 in 1996, 110 per year in 1997–2000; Aluminium (primary and secondary) 15 per year in 1996–2000; Cement 150 in 1996, 200 in 1997, 300 per year in 1998–2000 (Source: US Geological Survey).

Finance

CURRENCY AND EXCHANGE RATES

Monetary Units
100 pfeninga = 1 konvertibilna marka (KM or convertible marka).

Sterling, Dollar and Euro Equivalents (30 May 2003)
£1 sterling = KM 3.8095;
US $1 = KM 2.3121;
€1 = KM 1.9558;
KM 100 = £26.25 = $43.25 = €51.13.

Average Exchange Rate (KM per US $)
2000	2.1244
2001	2.1872
2002	2.0796

Note: The new Bosnia and Herzegovina dinar (BHD) was introduced in August 1994, with an official value fixed at 100 BHD = 1 Deutsche Mark (DM). The DM, the Croatian kuna and the Yugoslav dinar also circulated within Bosnia and Herzegovina. On 22 June 1998 the BHD was replaced by the KM, equivalent to 100 of the former units. The KM was thus at par with the DM. From the introduction of the euro, on 1 January 1999, the German currency had a fixed exchange rate of €1 = DM 1.95583.

BUDGET
(KM million*)

Revenue†	1999	2000	2001
Tax revenue	3,660.9	4,094.8	4,209.2
Indirect taxes	1,474.6	1,554.6	1,470.3
Trade taxes.	491.6	599.0	840.0
Direct taxes	336.1	415.3	362.4
Social security contributions.	1,358.7	1,526.0	1,536.5
Other revenue (incl. grants)	470.7	355.1	446.7
Total	**4,131.6**	**4,449.9**	**4,655.9**

Expenditure	1999	2000	2001
Interest payments	103.1	131.2	129.3
Subsidies and transfers to non-public agents‡	1,631.2	1,918.9	2,011.1
Other current expenditure	2,530.5	2,567.6	2,571.6
Investment expenditure.	1,505.5	1,340.8	1,235.4
Total	**5,770.3**	**5,958.5**	**5,947.4**

* Figures represent a consolidation of the budgetary accounts of the central Government and the authorities in the Federation of Bosnia and Herzegovina and (except for local and district administration) the Serb Republic.
† Excluding grants (KM million): 1,143.4 in 1999; 939.8 in 2000; 777.3 in 2001.
‡ Excluding transfers by Federation Cantons.

Source: IMF, *Bosnia and Herzegovina: First Review Under the Stand-By Arrangement and Request for Waiver of Performance Criteria* (January 2003).

INTERNATIONAL RESERVES
(US $ million at 31 December)

	2000	2001	2002
IMF special drawing rights .	10.7	6.1	3.1
Foreign exchange	485.9	1,215.1	1,318.2
Total	**496.6**	**1,221.2**	**1,321.4**

Source: IMF, *International Financial Statistics*.

MONEY SUPPLY
(KM million at 31 December)

	2000	2001	2002
Currency outside banks	652	1,674	1,734
Demand deposits at banks	733	957	1,221
Total money (incl. others)	**1,471**	**2,790**	**3,154**

Source: IMF, *International Financial Statisitics*.

COST OF LIVING
(Retail Price Index; base: December 1995 = 100)

Federation

	1999	2000	2001
All items	123.5	125.8	127.7

Republika Srpska

	1999	2000	2001
All items	84.0	96.3	104.2

Source: IMF, *Bosnia and Herzegovina: Statistical Appendix* (March 2002).

NATIONAL ACCOUNTS

Expenditure on the Gross Domestic Product
(US $ million at current prices)

	1996	1997	1998
Government final consumption expenditure	3,237	3,589	3,914
Private final consumption expenditure			
Increase in stocks	1,124	1,438	1,481
Gross fixed capital formation.			
Total domestic expenditure	**4,361**	**5,027**	**5,396**
Exports of goods and services	658	1,002	1,367
Less Imports of goods and services	−2,278	−2,606	−2,864
GDP in purchasers' values	**2,741**	**3,423**	**3,899**

Source: IMF, *Bosnia and Herzegovina: Selected Issues and Statistical Appendix* (June 2000).

Gross Domestic Product by Economic Activity
(KM million at current prices)

	2000	2001
Agriculture, hunting and forestry.	1,061.4	1,112.6
Fishing	2.6	1.6
Mining and quarrying	182.2	172.7
Manufacturing	1,014.0	1,073.5
Electricity, gas and water	630.1	691.7
Construction	463.8	439.3
Wholesale and retail trade.	789.7	995.7
Hotels and restaurants.	188.9	202.9
Transport and communications	804.3	947.7
Financial intermediation	323.6	329.6
Real estate and business services. . . .	197.2	199.9
Public administration and defence . . .	1,147.3	1,265.3
Education	501.9	523.5
Health and social welfare	450.5	455.4
Other personal services	177.9	190.7
Sub-total	7,935.4	8,602.1
Less Imputed bank service charges	212.5	236.5
GDP at basic prices	7,723.0	8,365.5
Taxes, less subsidies, on products	1,888.2	2,114.4
GDP in purchasers' values	9,611.2	10,480.0

GDP (US $ million): 4,536 in 2000; 4,795 in 2001 (Source: Central Bank of Bosnia and Herzegovina, *Annual Report 2002*).

BALANCE OF PAYMENTS
(estimates, US $ million)

	2000	2001	2002
Exports of goods f.o.b.	1,172.8	1,136.5	1,114.2
Imports of goods f.o.b.	−3,793.2	−4,047.3	−4,513.5
Trade balance	−2,620.4	−2,910.8	−3,399.3
Exports of services	291.6	300.4	301.0
Imports of services	−189.1	−191.2	−235.5
Balance on goods and services .	−2,518.0	−2,801.5	−3,333.8
Other income received	391.8	396.1	340.0
Other income paid	−76.7	−77.3	−83.2
Balance on goods, services and income	−2,202.8	−2,482.7	−3,077.0
Current transfers received . .	1,013.7	987.7	999.0
Current transfers paid . . .	−2.8	−3.5	−27.9
Current balance	−1,191.9	−1,498.5	−2,106.0
Capital account (net)	406.0	386.7	381.9
Direct investment from abroad. .	146.0	125.3	283.8
Other investment assets . . .	389.4	1,264.5	813.1
Other investment liabilities . .	203.4	131.7	285.5
Net errors and omissions . . .	15.8	245.7	112.7
Overall balance	−31.4	655.3	−228.9

Source: IMF, *International Financial Statistics*.

External Trade

SELECTED COMMODITIES
(US $ million*)

Imports	1996	1997
Electric power	19.7	39.6
Fabricated metal products	33.9	22.9
Electrical machinery and equipment	5.1	28.7
Wood and paper products	11.5	29.9
Foodstuffs	39.9	50.2
Total (incl. others)	1,172.6	1,225.0

Exports	1996	1997
Electric power	0.3	5.7
Iron and steel	7.0	12.4
Fabricated metal products	4.5	5.3
Transport equipment	6.5	3.4
Electrical machinery and equipment	0.3	4.6
Wood and paper products	18.2	18.1
Textile products	2.1	0.8
Total (incl. others)	57.8	87.3

* Figures are provisional and refer only to the Federation of Bosnia and Herzegovina (the Bosniak- and Croat-majority areas, excluding the Serb Republic).

1999 (Federation and Serb Republic, KM million): Total imports 6,047; Total exports 1,375 (Source: Office of the High Representative).

PRINCIPAL TRADING PARTNERS
(KM '000)

Imports	2000	2001	2002
Austria.	368,070	397,479	463,792
Croatia.	953,158	1,104,538	1,330,043
France	132,462	94,051	134,568
Germany	805,186	735,596	998,530
Hungary	307,711	405,272	491,428
Italy	704,214	957,233	789,765
Slovenia	998,717	917,001	906,329
Switzerland	138,114	206,462	148,998
Yugoslavia	439,282	521,050	697,798
Total (incl. others)	6,582,609	7,331,430	8,168,125

Exports	2000	2001	2002
Austria.	91,115	80,546	83,644
Croatia.	161,771	234,006	313,265
Germany	188,870	326,918	262,699
Hungary	7,053	9,485	12,932
Italy	480,865	515,136	248,885
Slovenia	110,018	170,476	174,258
Switzerland	284,336	228,650	229,992
Yugoslavia	444,282	456,833	421,059
Total (incl. others)	2,264,921	1,267,873	2,099,204

Source: Central Bank of Bosnia and Herzegovina, *Annual Report 2000, 2001* and *2002*.

Transport

RAILWAYS
(traffic)

	1998	1999	2000
Passenger-km ('000):			
Federation	5,118	9,386	9,320
Republika Srpska	52,000	41,000	38,000
Freight ton-km ('000):			
Federation	73,115	114,839	140,000
Republika Srpska	12,292	31,000	83,000

Source: IMF, *Bosnia and Herzegovina: Statistical Appendix* (March 2002).

Tourism

FOREIGN TOURIST ARRIVALS BY COUNTRY OF ORIGIN
('000)*

Country of Origin	1999	2000	2001
Austria.	3	3	3
Croatia.	24	28	19
Czech Republic	1	3	3
France .	3	3	3
Germany .	7	7	7
Italy .	6	7	6
Slovenia .	8	9	9
Turkey .	3	3	2
United Kingdom .	4	3	3
USA	7	8	7
Yugoslavia	4	5	6
Total (incl. others) .	89	108	90

* Figures refer to arrivals at frontiers by visitors from abroad, and include same-day visitors.
Source: World Tourism Organization, *Yearbook of Tourism Statistics*.

Tourism receipts (US $ million): 21 in 1998; 21 in 1999; 17 (estimate) in 2000 (Source: World Tourism Organization).

Communications Media

	1999	2000	2001
Telephones ('000 main lines in use)	367.9	407.6	450.1
Mobile cellular telephones ('000 subscribers).	52.6	219.7	233.3
Internet users ('000) .	7.0	n.a.	45.0

Daily newspapers (government-controlled areas only): 2 (average circulation 520,000 copies) in 1995; 3 in 1996.
Non-daily newspapers (1992): 22 (average circulation 2,508,000 copies).
1997: Radio receivers ('000 in use) 940; Television receivers ('000 in use) 900.
Sources: UN, *Statistical Yearbook*; UNESCO, *Statistical Yearbook*, International Telecommunication Union.

Education

(1997/98)

	Institutions	Teachers	Students
Primary* .	955	11,331	260,407
Secondary .	184	6,065	97,303
Higher .	55	2,833	34,477

* 1996/97 figures.

Source: US Information Service, Sarajevo.

Directory

The Constitution*

The Constitution of Bosnia and Herzegovina was Annexe 4 to the General Framework Agreement for Peace in Bosnia and Herzegovina, signed in Paris, France, on 14 December 1995. These peace accords were negotiated at Dayton, Ohio, the USA, in November and became the Elysées or Paris Treaty in December. Annexe 4 took effect as a constitutional act upon signature, superseding and amending the Constitution of the Republic of Bosnia and Herzegovina.

The previous organic law, an amended version of the 1974 Constitution of the then Socialist Republic of Bosnia and Herzegovina (part of the Socialist Federal Republic of Yugoslavia—the name was changed to the Republic of Bosnia and Herzegovina upon the declaration of independence following a referendum on 29 February–1 March 1992), provided for a collective State Presidency, a Government headed by a Prime Minister and a bicameral Assembly.

The institutions of the Republic continued to function until the firm establishment of the bodies provided for by the Federation of Bosnia and Herzegovina, which was formed on 31 March 1994. This was an association of the Muslim- or Bosniak-led Republic and the Croat Republic of Herzeg-Bosna. The federal Constitution provided for a balance of powers between Bosniak and Croat elements in a Federation divided into cantons. The federal Government was to be responsible for defence, foreign and economic affairs, and its head, the Prime Minister, was to have a greater executive role than the President. These two posts were to rotate between the two ethnic groups.

According to the General Framework Agreement, the Federation was one of the two constituent 'entities' of the new union of Bosnia and Herzegovina, together with the Serb Republic (Republika Srpska) of Bosnia and Herzegovina. The Serb Republic was proclaimed by the Serb deputies of the old Bosnian Assembly on 27 March 1992. Its Constitution provided for an executive President (with two Vice-Presidents), a Government headed by a Prime Minister and a unicameral National Assembly. Under the terms of the General Framework Agreement, known as the Dayton accords (after the US town where the treaty was negotiated in November 1995), the two Entities were to exist under their current Constitutions, which were to be amended to conform with the peace agreement.

The Dayton accords included 12 annexes on: the military aspects of the peace settlement (including the establishment of an international Implementation Force—IFOR, superseded by a Stabilization Force—SFOR in 1996); regional stabilization; inter-entity boundaries; elections; arbitration; human rights; refugees and displaced persons; a Commission to Preserve National Monuments; Bosnia and Herzegovina public corporations (specifically a Transportation Corporation); civilian implementation (including the office of a High Representative of the International Community); and an international police task force. One of the annexes was the Constitution of Bosnia and Herzegovina, summarized below, and it was signed by representatives of the Republic, the Federation and the Serb Republic.

CONSTITUTION OF BOSNIA AND HERZEGOVINA

The Preamble declares the basic, democratic principles of the country and its conformity with the principles of international law. The Bosniaks, Croats and Serbs are declared to be the constituent peoples (along with Others) of Bosnia and Herzegovina.

Article I affirms the continuation of Bosnia and Herzegovina with the Republic of Bosnia and Herzegovina, within its existing international boundaries, but with its internal structure modified. Bosnia and Herzegovina is a democratic state, consisting of two Entities, the Federation of Bosnia and Herzegovina and the Serb Republic. The capital of the country is Sarajevo and the symbols are to be determined by the legislature. Citizenship is to exist both for Bosnia and Herzegovina and for the Entities.

Article II guarantees human rights and fundamental freedoms, and makes specific mention of the Human Rights Commission to be established under Annexe 6 of the General Framework Agreement. The provisions of a number of international agreements are assured and co-operation and access for the international war-crimes tribunal specified. The provisions of this Article, according to Article X, are incapable of diminution or elimination by any amendment to the Constitution.

The responsibilities of and relations between the Entities and the institutions of Bosnia and Herzegovina are dealt with in Article III. The institutions of Bosnia and Herzegovina are responsible for foreign policy (including trade and customs), overall financial policy, immigration and refugee issues, international and inter-entity law enforcement, common and international communications facilities, inter-entity transportation and air-traffic control. Any governmental functions or powers not reserved to the institutions of Bosnia and Herzegovina by this Constitution are reserved to the Entities, unless additional responsibilities are agreed between the Entities or as provided for in the General Framework Agreement (Annexes 5–8). The Entities may establish special, parallel relations with neighbouring states, provided this is consistent with the sovereignty and territorial integrity of Bosnia and Herzegovina. The Constitution of

Bosnia and Herzegovina has primacy over any inconsistent constitutional or legal provisions of the Entities.

The Parliamentary Assembly

Bosnia and Herzegovina has a bicameral legislature, known as the Parliamentary Assembly. It consists of a House of Peoples and a House of Representatives. The House of Peoples comprises 15 Members, five each from the Bosniaks, the Croats and the Serbs, who are elected for a term of four years. The Bosniak and Croat Delegates are selected by, respectively, the Bosniak and Croat Delegates to the House of Representatives of the Federation, and the Serb Delegates by the National Assembly of the Serb Republic.

The House of Representatives consists of 42 Members, of whom two-thirds are directly elected from the territory of the Federation and one-third from the territory of the Serb Republic. Deputies are elected for a term of four years.

The Parliamentary Assembly convenes in Sarajevo and each chamber rotates its chair between three members, one from each of the constituent peoples. The Parliamentary Assembly is responsible for: necessary legislation under the Constitution or to implement Presidency decisions; determining a budget for the institutions of Bosnia and Herzegovina; and deciding whether to ratify treaties.

The Presidency

Article V concerns the state Presidency of Bosnia and Herzegovina. The head of state consists of three Members: one Bosniak and one Croat, each directly elected from the Federation; and one Serb, directly elected from the Serb Republic. Members are elected for a term of four years and are restricted to two consecutive terms. Chairmanship of the Presidency is rotated between the Members every eight months. A Presidency decision, if declared to be destructive of a vital interest of an Entity, can be vetoed by a two-thirds' majority in the relevant body: the National Assembly of the Serb Republic if the declaration was made by the Serb Member; or by the Bosniak or Croat Delegates in the Federation House of Peoples if the declaration was made by, respectively, the Bosniak or Croat Members of the Presidency. The Presidency is responsible for the foreign policy and international relations of Bosnia and Herzegovina. It is required to execute the decisions of the Parliamentary Assembly and to propose an annual central budget to that body, upon the recommendation of the Council of Ministers.

The Chair of the Council of Ministers is nominated by the Presidency and confirmed in office by the House of Representatives. The post of Chair rotates between Bosniak, Croat and Serb representatives every eight months. Each appointed Chair of the Council of Ministers is to be from a different constituent people to the Chair of the Presidency. In addition, the Chair holds one of the six ministerial posts in the Council of Ministers. Other Ministers and Deputy Ministers are nominated by the Chair of the Council of Ministers, and also approved by the House of Representatives. The Council of Ministers is responsible for carrying out the policies and decisions of Bosnia and Herzegovina and reporting to the Parliamentary Assembly. There are also guarantees that no more than two-thirds of Ministers be from the territory of the Federation, and Deputy Ministers are to be from a different constituent people to their Minister.

Each Member of the Presidency has, *ex officio*, civilian command authority over armed forces. Each Member is a member of a Standing Committee on Military Matters, appointed by the Presidency and responsible for co-ordinating the activities of armed forces in the country. The inviolability of each Entity to any armed force of the other is assured.

Other Institutions and Provisions

Article VI is on the Constitutional Court, which is to have nine members, four selected by the House of Representatives of the Federation and two by the National Assembly of the Serb Republic. The three remaining judges, at least initially, are to be selected by the President of the European Court of Human Rights. The first judges will have a term of office of five years; thereafter judges will usually serve until they are 70 years of age (unless they retire or are removed by the consensus of the other judges). The Constitutional Court of Bosnia and Herzegovina is to uphold the Constitution, to resolve the jurisdictions of the institutions of Bosnia and Herzegovina and the Entities, to ensure consistency with the Constitution and to guarantee the legal sovereignty and territorial integrity of the country. Its decisions are final and binding.

The Central Bank of Bosnia and Herzegovina is the sole authority for issuing currency and for monetary policy in Bosnia and Herzegovina. For the first six years of the Constitution, however, it is not authorized to extend credit by creating money; moreover, during this period the first Governing Body will consist of a Governor, appointed by the International Monetary Fund, and three members appointed by the Presidency (a Bosniak and a Croat, sharing one vote, from the Federation, and one from the Serb Republic). The Governor, who may not be a citizen of Bosnia and Herzegovina or any neighbouring state, will have a deciding vote. Thereafter, the Governing Body

shall consist of five members, appointed by the Presidency for a term of six years, with a Governor selected by them from among their number.

Article VIII concerns the finances of Bosnia and Herzegovina and its institutions. Article IX concerns general provisions, notably forbidding anyone convicted or indicted by the International Criminal Tribunal for the former Yugoslavia from standing for or holding public office in Bosnia and Herzegovina. These provisions also guarantee the need for all public appointments to be generally representative of the peoples of Bosnia and Herzegovina. Amendments to the Constitution need a two-thirds majority of those present and voting in the House of Representatives. The penultimate Article XI is on transitional arrangements provided for in an annexe to the Constitution.

* At the instigation of the High Representative, constitutional reforms were agreed by the leading political parties, and were officially adopted in both entities on 19 April 2002, thereby amending the terms of the General Framework Agreement. Under the new reforms, the Serbian, Croat and Bosniak languages received equal status in both entities, and the three principal constituent peoples and other minorities were ensured representation in government institutions throughout the country. The electoral law was amended accordingly.

The Government
(July 2003)

HIGH REPRESENTATIVE OF THE INTERNATIONAL COMMUNITY IN BOSNIA AND HERZEGOVINA

Under the terms of the treaty and annexes of the General Framework Agreement for Peace in Bosnia and Herzegovina, signed in December 1995, the international community, as authorized by the UN Security Council, was to designate a civilian representative to oversee the implementation of the peace accords and the establishment of the institutions of the new order in Bosnia and Herzegovina.

High Representative: Sir JEREMY JOHN DURHAM (PADDY) ASHDOWN, 71000 Sarajevo, Emerika Bluma 1; tel. (33) 283500; fax (33) 283501; internet www.ohr.int.

BOSNIA AND HERZEGOVINA

Presidency

The Dayton accords, which were signed into treaty in December 1995, provide for a three-member Presidency for the state, comprising one Bosniak (Muslim), one Croat and one Serb. The Presidency has responsibility for governing Bosnia and Herzegovina at the state level. The Presidency was subsequently reconstituted to comprise a Chairman and a further two members, with the post of Chairman rotating every eight months between Bosniak, Croat and Serb representatives. The Presidency nominates a Prime Minister (subject to the approval of the legislature), who appoints a Council of Ministers.

Chairman of the Presidency: DRAGAN ČOVIĆ (Croatian Democratic Union of Bosnia and Herzegovina).

Member of the Presidency: SULEJMAN TIHIĆ (Party of Democratic Action).

Member of the Presidency: BORISLAV PARAVAC (Serbian Democratic Party of Bosnia and Herzegovina).

Council of Ministers
(July 2003)

A coalition of the Party of Democratic Action (PDA), the Party of Democratic Progress (PDP), the Croatian Democratic Union of Bosnia and Herzegovina (CDU), the Party for Bosnia and Herzegovina, and the Serbian Democratic Party (SDP).

Prime Minister and Minister of European Integration: ADNAN TERZIĆ (PDA).

Minister of Foreign Affairs: MLADEN IVANIĆ (PDP).

Minister of Security: BARISA COLAK (CDU).

Minister of Civil Affairs: SAFET HALILOVIĆ (Party for Bosnia and Herzegovina).

Minister of Foreign Trade and Economic Relations: MILA GADZIĆ (CDU).

Minister of Human Rights and Refugees: MIRSAD KEBO (PDA).

Minister of Finance and the Treasury of the Institutions of Bosnia and Herzegovina: LJERKA MARIČT (CDU).

Minister of Transportation and Communications: BRANKO DOKIĆ (PDP).

Ministries

Office of the Presidency: 71000 Sarajevo, Musala 5; tel. (33) 664941; fax (33) 472491.

Office of the Prime Minister: 71000 Sarajevo, Vojvode Putnika 3; tel. (33) 664941; fax (33) 443446.

Ministry of Civil Affairs: 71000 Sarajevo, Vojvodc Putnika 3; tel. (33) 786822; fax (33) 786944.

Ministry of European Integration: 71000 Sarajevo, trg Bosne i Hercegovine; tel. and fax (33) 264330.

Ministry of Finance and the Treasury of the Institutions of Bosnia and Herzegovina: 71000 Sarajevo, trg Bosne i Hercegovine 1; tel. (33) 205345; fax (33) 471822.

Ministry of Foreign Affairs: 71000 Sarajevo, Musala 2; tel. (33) 663813; fax (33) 472188; e-mail info@mvp.gov.ba; internet www.mvp .gov.ba.

Ministry of Foreign Trade and Economic Relations: 71000 Sarajevo, trg Oktobra bb; tel. (33) 445750; fax (33) 655060.

Ministry of Human Rights and Refugees: 71000 Sarajevo, trg Bosne i Hercegovine 1; tel. (33) 471630; fax (33) 206140.

Ministry of Security: Sarajevo.

Ministry of Transportation and Communications: Sarajevo.

Presidency and Legislature

PRESIDENCY OF BOSNIA AND HERZEGOVINA

Election, 5 October 2002

	Votes	% of votes
Bosniak Candidates		
Sulejman Tihić (Party of Democratic Action)	192,661	37.29
Haris Silajdžić (Party for Bosnia and Herzegovina)	179,726	34.79
Alija Behmen (Social Democratic Party of Bosnia and Herzegovina)	90,434	17.51
Fikret Abdić (Democratic People's Union)	21,164	4.10
Others	32,625	6.31
Croat Candidates		
Dragan Covic (Croatian Democratic Union of Bosnia and Herzegovina/Croatian Christian Democratic Union)	114,606	61.52
Mladen Ivanković-Lijanović (Economic Bloc HDU-For Progress)	32,411	17.40
Mijo Anić (New Croatian Initiative)	16,345	8.77
Stjepan Kljuić (Republican Party)	9,413	5.05
Others	13,516	7.26
Serb Candidates		
Mirko Sarović (Serbian Democratic Party of Bosnia and Herzegovina)	180,212	35.52
Nebojsa Radmanović (Party of Independent Social Democrats)	101,119	19.93
Ognjen Tadić (Serb Radical Party of the Serb Republic)	44,262	8.72
Desnica Radivojević (Party of Democratic Action)	41,667	8.21
Ranko Bakić (Party of the Social Democratic Centre)	41,228	8.13
Mirko Banjac (Alliance of National Renesans)	23,238	4.58
Grahovac Mladen (Social and Democratic Party of Bosnia and Herzegovina)	22,852	4.50
Dragutin Ilić (Socialist Party of the Serb Republic)	18,533	3.65
Milorad Djokić (Democratic National Alliance)	16,129	3.18
Others	18,174	3.58

PARLIAMENTARY ASSEMBLY

The General Framework Agreement, signed in December 1995, provided for a Parliamentary Assembly of Bosnia and Herzegovina, comprising two chambers, the House of Peoples and the House of Representatives. The House of Representatives has 42 deputies, of whom 28 are directly elected from the Federation and 14 from the Serb Republic for a two-year term.

Dom Naroda
(House of Peoples)

There are 15 deputies in the House of Peoples, of whom 10 are elected by the Federation legislature and five by the Serb Republic legislature.

Speaker: VELIMIR JUKIĆ.

Zastupnièki dom
(House of Representatives)

Speaker: SEFIĆ DZAFEROVIĆ.

General Election, 5 October 2002

Party	% of votes	Seats
Party of Democratic Action	21.9	10
Serbian Democratic Party of Bosnia and Herzegovina	14.0	5
Party for Bosnia and Herzegovina	10.5	6
Social Democratic Party of Bosnia and Herzegovina	10.4	4
Party of Independent Social Democrats	9.8	3
Croatian Democratic Community/Croatian Christian Democratic Union—Bosnia and Herzegovina	9.5	5
Party of Democratic Progress of the Serb Republic	4.6	2
Socialist Party of the Serb Republic	1.9	1
Bosnian Party	1.5	1
Others	15.9	5
Total	100.0	42

Local Government

Bosnia and Herzegovina was comprised of two Entities, the Federation of Bosnia and Herzegovina and the Serb Republic of Bosnia and Herzegovina. The Federation was divided into 10 cantons, each headed by a Župan or governor (for details, see the section on The Entities—Federation of Bosnia and Herzegovina, Local Government). There were 145 municipalities in the country. Local elections were held in both Entities on 8 April 2000.

Interim District Government of Brčko

On 8 March 2000, following completion of a demilitarization process, the north-eastern Bosnian town of Brčko was established as a neutral district and placed under joint Serb, Croat and Muslim authority, bringing to an end sole Serb control of the area. An Interim District Government was appointed by the International Supervisor for Brčko, comprising four Serb members, four Bosniak members and one Croat member. SINISA KISIĆ, the mayor of Brčko, was appointed Prime Minister of the transitional government. In the same month the transitional district assembly, consisting of 13 Serb, nine Muslim and seven Croat deputies, was also appointed. The legislature's mandate was to last until elections were held. MIRSAD DJAPO was appointed President of the legislature.

Political Organizations

Association of the Democratic Initiative of Sarajevo Serbs (Udruženje demokratske inicijative Srba iz Sarajeva): Sarajevo; f. 1996 to affirm and protect the rights of Serbs in Muslim-held Sarajevo; Chair. MAKSIM STANISIĆ.

Bosnia and Herzegovina Democratic Alternative: Sarajevo; f. 1990; Chair. MUHAMED CENGIĆ.

Bosnian Party (Bosanska Stranka): Tuzla, Stari Grad 9; tel. and fax (35) 251035; e-mail boss.bh@delta.com.ba; Chair. MIRNES AJANOVIĆ.

Bosnian Rights Party of Bosnia and Herzegovina (Bosanska Stranka Prava Bosne i Hercegovine—BSP BiH): Sarajevo.

Civic Democratic Party (Gradjanska Demokratska Stranka): Sarajevo, Maršala Tita 9A; tel. (33) 666621; fax (33) 213435; Chair. IBRAHIM SPAHIĆ.

Croatian Christian Democratic Union—Bosnia and Herzegovina (Hrvatska Kršćanska Demokratska Unija—Bosne i Hercegovine): 80240 Tomislavgrad; tel. and fax (80) 52051; e-mail bihdem@ posluh.hr; internet www.posluh.hr; Pres. ANTE PASALIĆ.

Croatian Democratic Community: f. May 2002 by mems of the CDU—BH; Leader BARISA COLAK.

Croatian Democratic Union of Bosnia and Herzegovina (CDU—BH) (Hrvatska Demokratska Zajednica Bosne i Hercegovine—HDZ BiH): 71000 Sarajevo, Titova 16; tel. (33) 471213; internet www.hdzbih.org; f. 1990; affiliate of the CDU in Croatia; adopted new party statute July 2000; Croat nationalist party; Chair. ANTE JELAVIĆ; Gen.-Sec. MARKO TOKIĆ.

Croatian Peasants' Party (Hrvatska Seljacka Stranka): Sarajevo, Radićeva 4; tel. and fax (33) 441987; affiliated to Croatian Peasants' Party in Croatia; Chair. ILIJA SIMIĆ.

Croatian Rights Party (Hrvatska Stranka Prava): Ljubuški, Fra Petra Bakule 2; tel. and fax (36) 834917; contested 1996 elections; nationalist; Pres. ZDRAVKO HRSTIĆ.

Democratic National Alliance: Banja Luka; tel. (51) 215542; fax (51) 216951; internet www.dnsrs.org; f. 2000 by fmr mems of the Serb National Alliance (q.v.); Chair. Dr DRAGAN KOSTIĆ.

Democratic Party for Banja Luka and Krajina: Banja Luka; f. 1997 by fmr mems of Serb Radical Party of the Serb Republic (q.v.); Chair. NIKOLA SPIRIĆ.

Democratic Party of Pensioners of Bosnia and Herzegovina (Demokratska Stranka Penzionera BiH): Tuzla, 8 Basanske 51; tel. (61) 151390; e-mail dsp.bih@bih.net.ba; Pres. ALOJZ KNEZOVIĆ.

Democratic Party of the Serb Republic (Demokratska Stranka Republike Srpske): Banja Luka.

Democratic Patriotic Bloc of the Serb Republic (Demokratski Patriotski Blok Republike Srpske): contested 1996 elections; Chair. PREDRAG RADIĆ.

Democratic People's League (Demokratski Narodni Savez).

Democratic People's Union (Narodna Demokratska Zajednica—NDZ): Velika Kladuša, D. Pucara Starog 23; tel. and fax (77) 770407; e-mail dnzbih@bih.net.ba; f. 1996; Chair. FIKRET ABDIĆ.

Democratic Socialist Party: Bijeljina; f. 2000 by fmr mems of Socialist Party of the Serb Republic (q.v.); Pres. NEBOJSA RADMANOVIĆ.

Eastern Bosnian Muslim Party (Istočnobosanska Muslimanska Stranka): Sarajevo; f. 1997; Chair. IBRAN MUSTAFIĆ.

Homeland Party: Banja Luka; f. 1996 by fmr members of Serb Democratic Union—Homeland Front; nationalist; Chair. PREDRAG RASIĆ.

Liberal Democratic Party (LDP) (Liberalna Demokratska Stranka): Sarajevo, Maršala Tita 9A; tel. (33) 664540; e-mail liberali@bih.net.ba; f. 2000 by merger of Liberal Party of Bosnia and Herzegovina and the Liberal Bosniak Organization; Chair. RASIM KADIĆ.

Liberal Social Party of Bosnia and Herzegovina (Liberalna Socijalna Partija—LSP): Sarajevo; f. 1998; centre party; Chair. HIDAJET REPOVAC; Deputy Chair. JADRANKA MIKIĆ, NAMIK TERZIMEHEC, VINKO CURO.

Muslim Democratic Alliance (Muslimanski Demokratski Savez—MDS): Bihać; f. 1994; seeks to promote equality between the ethnic groups of Bosnia and Herzegovina.

New Croatian Initiative (Nova Hrvatska Inicijativa): Sarajevo, Sime Milutinovića 2/II; tel. (33) 214602; fax (33) 214603; e-mail nhi@nhi.ba; f. 1998 by fmr mems of the Croatian Democratic Union of Bosnia and Herzegovina (q.v.); Chair. KREŠIMIR ZUBAK.

New Radical Party: member of the People's Alliance for Peace and Progress electoral coalition; Chair. GORAN ZMIJANAĆ.

Party for Bosnia and Herzegovina: Sarajevo, Maršala Tita 7A; tel. and fax (33) 214417; e-mail zabih@zabih.ba; f. 1996; integrationist; member of the Coalition for a Single and Democratic Bosnia electoral alliance; Pres. Dr SAFET HALILOVIĆ.

Party of Democratic Action (PDA) (Stranka Demokratske Akcije—SDA): 71000 Sarajevo, Mehmeda Spahe 14; tel. (33) 667274; fax (33) 650429; e-mail sda@bih.net.ba; internet www.sda.ba; f. 1990; leading Muslim nationalist party; member of the Coalition for a Unified and Democratic Bosnia electoral alliance; Chair. SULEJMAN TIHIĆ; Sec.-Gen. MIRSAD CEMAN.

Party of Democratic Development: Bijeljina; f. 2001; Chair. RADOVAN SIMIĆ.

Party of Democratic Progress (PDP): Banja Luka; Chair. MLADEN IVANIĆ.

Party of Economic Prosperity (Stranka Privednog Prosperita—SPP): Zenica; f. 1996; Chair. PANE SKRBIĆ; Sec.-Gen. SAFET REDZEPAGIĆ.

Party of Independent Social Democrats (PISD) (Stranka Nezavisnih Socijaldemokrata—SNSD): 78000 Banja Luka, Petra Kočića 5; tel. (51) 318492; fax (51) 318495; e-mail snsd@snsd.org; internet www.snsd.org; Chair. MILORAD DODIK; Sec.-Gen. SLAVKO MITROVIĆ.

Party of Independent Social Democrats of the Serb Republic: f. 1999; breakaway faction of the Party of Independent Social Democrats; Leader BRANE MILJUS.

Party of Serb Unity (Stranka Srpskog Jedinstva): Bijeljina; extreme nationalist; Chair. (vacant).

Patriotic Party of Bosnia and Herzegovina (Patriotska Stranka BiH): Sarajevo, Hakije Kulenovića 9; tel. and fax (33) 216881; Pres. SEFER HALILOVIĆ.

Pensioners' Party of the Bosnia and Herzegovina Federation (Stranka Penzionera Federacije BiH).

Pensioners' Party of the Serb Republic (Penzionerska Stranka Republike Srpske).

People's Party of the Serb Republic (Narodna Stranka Republicka Srpska): Leader MILAN TRBOJEVIĆ.

Radical Party of the Serb Republic (Radikalna Stranka Republika Srpska).

Republican Party (Republikanska Stranka BiH): Sarajevo, Antuna Hangija 35; tel. and fax (33) 834917; e-mail republ94@bih.net.ba; integrationist; Chair. STJEPAN KLJUIĆ.

Serbian Civic Council: Sarajevo; anti-nationalist; org. of Serbs in the Federation of Bosnia and Herzegovina; Chair. Dr MIRKO PEJANOVIĆ.

Serbian Democratic Party of Bosnia and Herzegovina (SDP) (Srpska Demokratska Stranka Bosne i Hercegovine—SDS BiH): c/o Pale, National Assembly of the Serb Republic; f. 1990; allied to SDP of Croatia; Serb nationalist party; member of the Serb Coalition of the Serb Republic electoral alliance; Chair. DRAGAN KALINIĆ.

Serb Democratic Union—Homeland Front: nationalist; Pres. BOŽIDAR BOJANIĆ.

Serb National Alliance (SNA) (Srpski Narodni Savez—SNS): Banja Luka; f. 1997; Leader SVETOZAR RADIVOJEVIĆ.

Serb Patriotic Party (Srpska Patriotska Stranka): contested 1996 elections; Chair. STOJAN ZUPLJANIN; Vice-Chair. PETAR DJAKOVIĆ.

Serb Party of Krajina (Srpska Stranka Krajina—SSK): Banja Luka; f. 1996; regional party in favour of the creation of clear borders between nations; Pres. PREDRAG LAZAREVIĆ; Chair. of Exec. Cttee DJORDJE UMICEVIĆ.

Serb Radical Party of the Serb Republic (Srpska Radikalna Stranka Srpske Republike—SRS SR): internet www.srpskastrars.org; br. of SRS in Serbia; member of the Serb Coalition of the Serb Republic; Chair. RADISLAV KANJERIĆ; Chair. of Exec. Bd MIRKO BLAGOJEVIĆ; Gen. Sec. OGNJEN TADIĆ.

Social Alliance: c/o 71000 Sarajevo, trg Dure Pucara bb; fmr communist mass organization; allies of Social Democratic Party; left-wing.

Social Democratic Party of Bosnia and Herzegovina (Socijaldemokratska Partija BiH—SDP BiH): 71000 Sarajevo, Branislava Durdeva 8; tel. (33) 203667; fax (33) 210942; e-mail sdp@sdpbih-centar.com; internet www.sdpbih-centar.com; f. 1908; merged with Social Democrats of Bosnia and Herzegovina; Chair. Dr ZLATKO LAGUMDŽIJA; Sec.-Gen. KARLO FILIPOVIĆ.

Social Liberal Party: Banja Luka; reintegrationist; member of the People's Alliance for Peace and Progress electoral coalition; merged with the Party of Independent Social Democrats in Dec. 1999; Chair. MIODRAG ZIVANOVIĆ; Gen. Sec. MILAN TUKIĆ.

Socialist Party of the Serb Republic (Socijalistička partija za Republiku Srpsku—SPRS): Kralja Petra 1 Karadorćevića 103/1; tel. and fax (51) 231643; e-mail sprs@inecco.net; f. 1993; br. of the Socialist Party of Serbia; Chair. ZIVKO RADIŠIĆ; Sec.-Gen. ŽELJKO MIRJANIĆ; 40,000 mems.

Youth Party of Bosnia and Herzegovina: Sarajevo; tel. (51) 370255; e-mail contact@strankamladih.org; Chair MILAN BASTINAC.

Yugoslav Left of the Serb Republic: Bijeljina; f. 1996; branch of pro-communist party based in Belgrade (Serbia and Montenegro); Pres. MILORAD IVOSEVIĆ.

Diplomatic Representation

EMBASSIES IN BOSNIA AND HERZEGOVINA

Austria: 71000 Sarajevo, Džidžikovac 7; tel. (33) 279400; fax (33) 668339; Ambassador GERHARD JANDL.

Belgium: Sarajevo, Abdesthana 4; tel. (33) 233772; fax (33) 233774; Ambassador ROBERT DEVRIESE.

Bulgaria: Sarajevo, Trampina 14/11; tel. (33) 668191; fax (33) 668182; Ambassador GEORGI DOJCEV JURUKOV.

Canada: Sarajevo, Logavina 7; tel. (33) 447900; fax (33) 447901; Ambassador SHELLEY WHITING.

China, People's Republic: Sarajevo, Braće Begića 17; tel. (33) 215102; fax (33) 215108; Ambassador Li Shuyuan.

Croatia: 71000 Sarajevo, Mehmeda Spahe 20; tel. (33) 444330; fax (33) 472434; Ambassador Dr Josip Vrbošić.

Czech Republic: 71000 Sarajevo, Potoklinica 6; tel. (33) 447525; fax (33) 447526; Ambassador Jiří Kudéla.

Denmark: 71000 Sarajevo, Splitska 9; tel. (33) 665901; fax (33) 665902; e-mail danamb@bih.net.ba; Ambassador Johannes Dahl-Hansen.

Egypt: Sarajevo, Nurudina Gackića 58; tel. (33) 666498; fax (33) 666499; e-mail eg.em.so@bih.net.ba; Ambassador Dr Salah Riyad el Ashry.

France: 71000 Sarajevo, Kapetanović Ljubušaka 18; tel. (33) 668149; fax (33) 668103; e-mail france-1@bih.net.ba; internet www.ambafrance.com.ba; Ambassador Bernard Bajolet.

Germany: 71000 Sarajevo, ul. Buka 11-13; tel. (33) 275000; fax (33) 652978; e-mail debosara@bih.net.ba; Ambassador Hans Jochen Peters.

Greece: Sarajevo, Obala Maka Dizdara I; tel. (33) 203516; fax (33) 203512; e-mail greekemb@bih.net.ba; Ambassador Mihail Koukakis.

Holy See: Pehlivanuša 9, 71000 Sarajevo, Nadbiskupa Josipa Stadlera 5; tel. (33) 207847; fax (33) 207863; e-mail nunbosnia@lsinter.net; Apostolic Nuncio Mgr Giuseppe Leanza.

Hungary: 71000 Sarajevo, Satvetbega Basagića 58/A; tel. (33) 238512; fax (33) 218685; e-mail hungcons@bih.net.ba; Ambassador István Várga.

Iran: 71000 Sarajevo, Obala Maka Dizdara 6; tel. (33) 650210; fax (33) 663910; e-mail iries1@bih.net.ba; Ambassador Seyed Homayoun Amir Khalili.

Italy: 71000 Sarajevo, Čekaluša 39; tel. (33) 218022; fax (33) 659368; e-mail ambsara@bih.net.ba; Ambassador Saba D'Elia.

Japan: Sarajevo, Mula Mustafe Baseskije 2; tel. (33) 209580; fax (33) 209583; Chargé d'affaires a.i. Mitsunori Namba.

Libya: 71000 Sarajevo, Tahtali sokak 17; tel. (33) 657534; fax (33) 663620; Head of People's Bureau Ibrahim Ali Tagiuri.

Macedonia, former Yugoslav republic: 71000 Sarajevo, Emerika Bluma 23; tel. and fax (33) 206004; Chargé d'affaires a.i. Stojan Rumenovski.

Malaysia: 71000 Sarajevo, Trnovska 6; tel. (33) 201578; fax (33) 667713; e-mail malsrjevo@bih.net.ba; Ambassador Zakaria bin Sulong.

Malta: 71000 Sarajevo, Mula Mustafe Baseskije 12; tel. and fax (33) 668632; e-mail lor.tac@tiscalinet.it; Ambassador Dr Lorenzo Tacchella.

Netherlands: 71000 Sarajevo, Obala Kulina Bana 4/2; tel. (33) 668422; fax (33) 668423; e-mail nlgovsar@bih.net.ba; internet www.netherlandsembassy.ba; Ambassador Robert Bosscher.

Norway: 71000 Sarajevo, Ferhadija 20; tel. (33) 666373; fax (33) 666505; e-mail emb.sarajevo@mfa.no; Ambassador Henrik Ofstad.

Pakistan: 71000 Sarajevo, Emerika Bluma 17; tel. (33) 211836; fax (33) 211837; e-mail parep@bih.net.ba; Ambassador Tariq Azizuddin.

Poland: 71000 Sarajevo, Emerika Bluma 27; tel. (33) 201142; fax (33) 233796; Ambassador Dr Leszek Hensel.

Romania: 71000 Sarajevo, Tahtali sokak 13–15; tel. (33) 207447; fax (33) 668940; e-mail rumunska@bih.net.ba; Ambassador Petre Catrinciuc.

Russia: 71000 Sarajevo, Urjan Dedina 93–95; tel. (33) 668147; fax (33) 668148; Ambassador Alexander S. Grishchenko.

Saudi Arabia: 71000 Sarajevo, Koševo 44; tel. (33) 211861; fax (33) 211744; Ambassador Fahd bin Abdul-Muhsin al-Zeida.

Serbia and Montenegro: 71000 Sarajevo, Obala Maka Dizdara 3a; tel. (33) 260080; fax (33) 221469; e-mail yugoamba@bih.net.ba; Ambassador Stanimir Vukičević.

Slovenia: 71000 Sarajevo, Bendbaša 7; tel. (33) 271260; fax (33) 271270; Chargé d'affaires a.i. Vojko Kuzman.

Spain: 71000 Sarajevo, Čekaluša 16; tel. (33) 278560; fax (33) 208758; Ambassador Rafael Valle Garagorri.

Sweden: 71000 Sarajevo, Ferhadija 20; tel. (33) 276030; fax (33) 276060; e-mail ambassaden.sarajevo@foreign.ministry.se; Ambassador Andreas Möllander.

Switzerland: 71000 Sarajevo, Josipa Štadlera 15; tel. (33) 275850; fax (33) 665246; e-mail swissemb@bih.net.ba; Ambassador Heidi Tagliavini.

Turkey: 71000 Sarajevo, Hamdije Kreševljakovića 5; tel. and fax (33) 472437; e-mail turksa@bih.net.ba; Ambassador Sina Baydur.

United Kingdom: 71000 Sarajevo, Tina Ujevića 8; tel. (33) 444429; fax (33) 666131; e-mail britemb@bih.net.ba; internet www.britishembassy.ba; Ambassador Ian Cameron Cliff.

USA: 71000 Sarajevo, Alipašina 43; tel. (33) 659969; fax (33) 445700; internet www.usis.com.ba; Ambassador Clifford Bond.

Judicial System

The Constitutional Court of Bosnia and Herzegovina has three international judges (selected by the President of the European Court of Human Rights) and six national judges (of whom four are elected by the House of Representatives of the Federation and two by the National Assembly of the Serb Republic). The Constitutional Court has competence regarding constitutional matters in both entities, but there are separate judicial systems in the Bosnian Federation and the Serb Republic. The judicial system of each entity comprises a Constitutional Court, a Supreme Court and local district courts. The State Court of Bosnia and Herzegovina, which was officially inaugurated on 27 January 2003, represents the country's highest judicial organ. The eight judges of the Court were appointed by the Bosnian High Representative.

State Court of Bosnia and Herzegovina: Sarajevo; inaugurated 27 Jan. 2003; state-level court and highest judicial organ; comprises eight judges and four prosecutors; Pres. Martin Raguz.

Constitutional Court of the Republic of Bosnia and Herzegovina: 71000 Sarajevo, Reisa Dzemaludina Causevića 6/III; tel. (33) 251210; fax (33) 663784; e-mail info@ccbh.ba; internet www.ccbh.ba; nine mems; elected for a five-year term; Pres. Dusan Kalember.

Constitutional Court of the Serb Republic: Banja Luka; internet www.ustavnisud.org; eight mems; Pres. Rajko Kuzmanović; Sec. Miodrag Simović.

Supreme Court of the Federation of Bosnia and Herzegovina: 71000 Sarajevo, Valtera Perića 15; tel. (33) 664754; Pres. Venceslav Ilić.

Supreme Court of the Serb Republic: Banja Luka; Pres. Jovo Rosić.

Office of the Federal Prosecutor: 71000 Sarajevo, Valtera Perića 11; tel. (33) 214990; internet www.tuzilastvo-rs.org; Federal Prosecutor Suljo Babić.

Religion

Bosnia and Herzegovina has a diversity of religious allegiances. Just over one-half of the inhabitants are nominally Christian, but these are divided between the Serbian Orthodox Church and the Roman Catholic Church. The dominant single religion is Islam. The Reis-ul-ulema, the head of the Muslims in the territory comprising the former Yugoslavia, is resident in Sarajevo. Most of the Muslims are ethnic Muslims or Bosniaks (Slavs who converted to Islam under the Ottomans). There are, however, some ethnic Albanian and Turkish Muslims. Virtually all are adherents of the Sunni persuasion. There is a small Jewish community; since 1966, however, there has been no rabbi in the community. In June 1997 an agreement to establish an inter-religious council was signed by the leaders of the Roman Catholic, Serbian Orthodox, Jewish and Islamic communities.

ISLAM

Islamic Community of the Sarajevo Region: 71000 Sarajevo; Pres. of Massahat Salih Efendija Colaković; Mufti of Bosnia and Herzegovina Hadži Mustafa Tirić; Reis-ul-ulema Mustafa Efendi Cerić.

CHRISTIANITY

The Serbian Orthodox Church

Metropolitan of Dabrobosna: Nicolaj, c/o Serbian Patriarchate, 11001 Belgrade, Kralja Petra 5, POB 182, Yugoslavia.

The Roman Catholic Church

For ecclesiastical purposes, Bosnia and Herzegovina comprises one archdiocese and three dioceses. At 31 December 2001 adherents of the Roman Catholic Church represented about 15.6% of the total population.

Bishops' Conference
(Biskupska Konferencija Bosne i Hercegovine)
Nadbiskupski Ordinarijat, 71000 Sarajevo, Kaptol 7; tel. (33) 664784; fax (33) 472178.

f. 1995; Pres. Rt Rev. FRANJO KOMARICA (Bishop of Banja Luka).

Archbishop of Vrhbosna-Sarajevo: Cardinal VINKO PULJIĆ, Nad-biskupski Ordinarijat Vrhbosanski, 71000 Sarajevo, Kaptol 7; tel. (33) 472430; fax (33) 472429.

JUDAISM

Jewish Community of the Sarajevo Region: 71000 Sarajevo, Hamdije Kreševljekoviće 59; tel. (33) 663472; fax (33) 663473; e-mail la-bene@open.net.ba; internet www.soros.org.ba; Pres. JAKOB FINCI.

The Press

In 2000 five daily newspapers (with a total circulation of about 100,000 copies per day) and six principal weekly, or bi-weekly, newspapers were published.

PRINCIPAL DAILIES

Dnevni Avaz: 71000 Sarajevo; e-mail redakacija@avaz.ba; internet www.avaz.ba.

Glas Srpski: Banja Luka; Serb Republic government newspaper; Editor-in-Chief TOMO MARIĆ; Deputy Editor-in-Chief NIKOLA GUZIJAN.

Nezavisne novine (The Independent): 51000 Banja Luka, Kra-jiskih brigada 8; tel. (51) 213515; fax (51) 213341; e-mail nnovine@blic.net; f. 1995; Editor-in-Chief ŽELJKO KOPANJA.

Oslobodjenje (Liberation): 71000 Sarajevo, Džemala Bijedića 185; tel. (33) 454144; fax (33) 460982; e-mail info@obodjenje.net; internet www.oslobodjenje.com.ba; f. 1943; morning; Editor MEHMED HAL-ILOVIĆ; circ. 56,000.

Večernje novine: 71000 Sarajevo, Pruščakova St 13; tel. (33) 664874; fax (33) 664875; f. 1964; special edition published daily in Serb Republic; privatized in May 2000; Editor-in-Chief AHMED BOSNIĆ; Dir IRFAN LJEVAKOVIĆ; circ. 15,000.

WEEKLY NEWSPAPERS

Glas Srpski: Banja Luka; Serb Republic government newspaper; Editor-in-Chief TOMO MARIĆ; Deputy Editor-in-Chief NIKOLA GUZIJAN.

Hrvatska Rijec: 71000 Sarajevo; e-mail h_rijec@bih.net.ba; internet www.hrvatska-rijec.com; Croat weekly.

Ljiljan: 71000 Sarajevo, Sime Milutinovica Sarajlije 12; tel. (33) 664895; fax (33) 664697; e-mail ljiljan@bih.net.ba; internet www .nippljiljan.com; official newspaper of the PDA; Chair. MENSUR BRDAR; Editor-in-Chief DŽEMALUDIN LATIĆ.

Slobodna Bosna: 71000 Sarajevo, Muhameda Kantardžića 3; tel. (33) 444041; fax (33) 444895; e-mail slobo-bosna@zamir-sa.ztn.atc .org; Editor SENAD AVDIĆ.

PERIODICALS

Alternativa: Doboj; f. 1996; every two weeks; Editor-in-Chief PAVLE STANISIĆ; Deputy Editor-in-Chief ŽIVKO SAVKOVIĆ; Dir SLOBODAN BABIĆ; circ. 5,000.

Dani: 71000 Sarajevo, Skenderija 31A; e-mail bhdani@bih.net.ba; internet www.bhdani.com; independent; political and cultural; 4 a week; Editor-in-Chief SENAD PECANIN.

Reporter: 78000 Banja Luka, Grčka 20; tel. (51) 221220; fax (51) 221228; e-mail rep@inecco.net; internet www.reportermagazin.com; f. 1996; independent; Editor PERICA VUCINIĆ.

Svijet: Sarajevo; illustrated; weekly; Editor-in-Chief JELA JEVRE-MOVIĆ; circ. 115,000.

Zadrugar: Sarajevo, Omladinska 1; f. 1945; weekly; journal for farmers; Editor-in-Chief FADIL ADEMOVIĆ; circ. 34,000.

NEWS AGENCIES

Alternativna Informativna Mreza (AIM) (Alternative Infor-mation Network): Sarajevo; exchange of information between inde-pendent media in the former Yugoslavia; non-commercial and dependent on financial support from abroad.

BH Press: 71000 Sarajevo, Branilaca grada 21/II; tel. (33) 663389; e-mail bhpress@bih.net.ba; internet www.bihpress.com; state news agency.

HABENA: 88000 Mostar, Kralja Tvrtka 9; tel. (36) 319222; fax (36) 319422; e-mail habena@habena.ba; f. 1993; Bosnian Croat news agency; Man. MARKO DRAGIĆ; Editor-in-Chief ZDRAVKO NIKIĆ.

Novinska Agencija Bosne i Hercegovine: 71000 Sarajevo, Bra-nilaca grada 21; tel. (33) 445336; fax (33) 445312; e-mail bhpres@bih .net.ba; internet www.bihpress.ba.

ONASA (Oslobodjenje News Agency): Sarajevo, Hasana Kikića 3; tel. (33) 276580; fax (33) 276599; e-mail onasa@onasa.com.ba; internet www.onasa.com.ba; f. 1994; Gen. Man. MEHMED HUSIĆ.

SNRA: Banja Luka; Bosnian Serb news agency; Man. Dir DRAGAN DAVIDOVIĆ.

Publishers

Novi Glas: 78000 Banja Luka, Borisa Kidriča 1; tel. (51) 12766; fax (51) 12758; general literature; Dir MIODRAG ŽIVANOVIĆ.

Public Company for Newspaper Publication Organization, Official Gazette of Bosnia and Herzegovina: Sarajevo, Magri-bija 3; tel. (33) 663470; e-mail slist@bih.net.ba; internet www.sllist .ba; publishes legislation for official newspapers, and books and other material from the field of newspaper-publication activities.

Student's Printing House of the University of Sarajevo: Sar-ajevo, Obala Kulina Bana 7; tel. and fax (33) 526138; university textbooks; Dir EMIR KADRIĆ; Chief Editor DRAGAN S. MARKOVIĆ.

Svjetlost: 71000 Sarajevo, Petra Preradovića 3; tel. (33) 212144; fax (33) 272352; f. 1945; textbooks and literature; Dir SAVO ZIROJEVIĆ.

Veselin Masleša (Sarajevo Publishing): 71000 Sarajevo, Obala Kulina Bana 4; tel. (33) 521476; fax (33) 272369; f. 1950; school and university textbooks, general literature; Dir RADOSLAV MIJATOVIĆ.

PUBLISHERS' ASSOCIATION

Association of Publishers and Booksellers of Bosnia and Herzegovina: 71000 Sarajevo, M. Tita brigade 9A; tel. and fax (33) 207945; Pres. IBRAHIM SPAHIĆ; Gen. Sec. DRAGAN S. MARKOVIĆ.

Broadcasting and Communications

TELECOMMUNICATIONS

HPT Mostar: 88000 Mostar, Kneza Branimira; tel. and fax (36) 395555; internet www.hpt-mostar.ba; scheduled for privatization in 2002; Dir of Man. Bd FARUK KUCIĆ.

Bosnia-Herzegovina Post: 71000 Sarajevo, Obala Kulina bana 8; tel. (33) 252606; fax (33) 252711; internet www.bhp.ba; f. 1992; Gen. Dir KASIM DZAJIĆ.

Telekom Srpske: Banja Luka, Kralja Petra I, Karadjordjevica 61A; tel. (51) 211150; fax (51) 240101; e-mail ts.office@telekom-rs.com; Deputy Dir-Gen. MILE BAJALICA.

BROADCASTING

In the late 1990s broadcasting in Bosnia and Herzegovina was largely controlled by the three nationalist parties: the Party of Democratic Action (PDA); the Croatian Democratic Union of Bosnia and Herzegovina (CDU—BH); and the Serbian Democratic Party (SDP). There were, however, a number of locally based independent radio and television stations. In May 1996 two such organizations, NTV Zetel and ITV Hayat (both television companies), had created, with the Mostar and Tuzla branches of Radio-Televizija Bosne i Hercegovine, the TVIN-TV International Network. This was to be open to media and correspondents from the Bosniak-Croat Feder-ation and the Serb Republic, in accordance with the aims of the Dayton accords.

Regulatory Authority

At the decision of the High Representative for Bosnia and Herzego-vina, the Communication Regulatory Authority was established in 2001 through the merger of the former Independent Media Com-mission, which had regulated the broadcasting sector, and the Telecommunication Regulatory Agency, responsible for telecommu-nications. The new regulatory body was to have jurisdiction over both broadcasting and telecommunications as an independent state agency.

Communication Regulatory Agency (CRA): Sarajevo, Vilsonovo setaliste 10; tel. (33) 250600; fax (33) 713080; e-mail info@cra.ba; internet www.cra.ba; f. 2001.

Radio

Croat Radio Herzeg-Bosna: Mostar; Dir TOMISLAV MAZALO; Editor-in-Chief IVAN KRISTIĆ.

Pan Radio: Bijegina, Brace Subotića 3; tel. and fax (55) 402661; e-mail panorama@bn.rstel.net.

Radio Fern: 71000 Sarajevo, Mula Mustafe Baseskije 6; tel. (33) 668052; e-mail radio.fern@ekis.com.ba.

Radio Kameleon: 75000 Tuzla, Milana Jovanovića 6; tel. and fax (35) 250055; e-mail kameleon@kameleon.ba; internet www.kameleon.ba; f. 1992; independent radio station; Gen. Dir ZLATKO BERBIĆ.

Radio Q: 71300 Visoko, ul. Hazima Dedića 13; tel. and fax (32) 735280; e-mail radioq@radioq.co.ba; internet www.radioq.co.ba.

Radio-Televizija (RTV) Bosne i Hercegovine: 71000 Sarajevo, Bulevar Meše Selimovića 12; tel. (33) 455124; fax (33) 455104; f. 1945; 4 radio programmes; broadcasts in Serbo-Croat; Dir-Gen. JOHN SHEARER; Dir of Radio NADJA PAŠIĆ; Editor-in-Chief ESAD CEROVIĆ.

Radio-Televizija Republika Srpska (RTRS): Banja Luka; Editor-in-Chief DRAGOLJUB MILANOVIĆ.

Radio ZID: Sarajevo; f. Dec. 1992; commenced broadcasts March 1993; independent radio station; cultural and educative programmes; Chair. ZDRAVKO GREBO; Editor-in-Chief VLADO AZINOVIĆ.

Serb Radio Banja Luka: Banja Luka; f. 1997 as independent radio station following breakaway from Serb Radio and Television (q.v.); eight-mem. editorial council; Chair. RADOMIR NESKOVIĆ.

Studio 99: Sarajevo; f. 1991; independent radio station; broadcast political information during the civil conflict; Editor-in-Chief ADIL KULENOVIĆ; Editor of Programmes ZORAN ILIĆ.

Television

Alternativna Televizija Informisanje: 78000 Banja Luka, Karadjordjeva 2; tel. and fax (51) 311904; e-mail atv@inecco.net; Dir NATASA TESANOVIĆ.

Independent TV Tuzla: Tuzla; f. 1991 by a group of journalists; promotes the values of democratic society.

Independent TV Zetel: Stara carsija bb, 72000 Zenica; tel. (32) 410552; fax (32) 417317; e-mail zetel@bih.net.ba; f. 1992; transmits 13 hours per day to Zenica and surrounding area; cultural, political, educative and sports programmes; Dir ZELJKO LINCNER; Editor TAIB BAJARAMOVIĆ.

ITV Hayat: Sarajevo; e-mail itvhayat@bih.net.ba; internet www.ntvhayat.com; Muslim influences; broadcasts 18 hours daily; Dir and Editor-in-Chief ELVIR SVRAKIĆ.

Konjic Radio-TV: Konjic; fmrly a public-service station, sold in April 2000; Owners ERMIN MUSTAFIC, ENES RATKUSIĆ.

Open Broadcast Network: 71000 Sarajevo, Bulevar Mese Selimovića 18; tel. (33) 460550; fax (33) 460547.

Radio-Televizija (RTV) Bosne i Hercegovine: 71000 Sarajevo, Bulevar Meše Selimovića 12; tel. (33) 652333; fax (33) 461569; e-mail radio@rtvbih.ba; internet www.rtvbih.ba; f. 1969; 2 TV programmes; incorporated new channel (BHTV 1) in 2002; Dir-Gen. JOHN SHEARER; Dir of TV AMILA OMERSOFTIĆ; Editor-in-Chief ESAD CEROVIĆ.

Radio-Televizija Republika Srpska (RTRS): Banja Luka; Editor-in-Chief DRAGOLJUB MILANOVIĆ.

Finance

(d.d. = dioničko društvo (joint-stock company); cap. = capital; res = reserves; dep. = deposits; m. = million; amounts in konvertibilna marka (KM or convertible marka) unless otherwise stated; brs = branches)

BANKING

In 2001 there were some 69 banks operating in Bosnia and Herzegovina, of which 50 were in the Federation and 19 in the Serb Republic. The total number of banks in operation had declined to 44 by the end of 2002.

Central Bank

Central Bank of Bosnia and Herzegovina: 71000 Sarajevo, 25 Maršala Tita; tel. (33) 664548; fax (33) 201517; e-mail contact@cbbh.gov.ba; internet www.cbbh.gov.ba; replaced the National Bank of the Federation of Bosnia and Herzegovina, and the National Bank of the Republika Srpska, which ceased monetary operations in Aug. 1997; cap. 25.0m., res 96.5m., dep. 785.6m. (2001); Gov. PETER NICHOLL.

Selected Banks

Balkan Investment Bank a.d.: 78000 Banja Luka, Krajških Brigada 2; tel. (51) 216285; fax (51) 211445; e-mail contact@balkaninvestment.com; internet www.balkaninvestment.com; f. 2000; cap. 5m., dep. 8.7m. (Dec. 2000); Chair. VALDAS VARANAVICIUS.

Bobar Banka a.d.: 76300 Bijeljina, Filipa Višnjica 211; tel. (55) 211153; fax (55) 401863; e-mail bobarbank@rstel.net; internet www.bobar.com; f. 1998; cap. 10.0m., res 0.1m., dep. 4.0m. (2001); Gen. Man. DRAGAN RADUMILO.

Central Profit Banka d.d. Sarajevo: Sarajeva, Zelenih Beretki 24; tel. (33) 663307; fax (33) 238340; e-mail international@cpb.ba; internet www.cpb.ba; f. 1919; cap. 10.7m., res 4.1m., dep. 261.6m. (2001); Gen. Man. FEHIM F. KAPIDŽIĆ; 13 brs.

Ekvator Banka a.d.: 78000 Banja Luka, POB 59, Marije Bursac 2; tel. and fax (51) 211885; e-mail ekvator@inecco.net; internet www.ekvator.com; f. 1996; cap. and res 6.3m., dep. 8.1m. (1999); Pres. DJORDJE DAVIDOVIĆ.

Federation Investment Bank: 71000 Sarajevo, Igmanska 1; tel. (33) 277900; fax (33) 668952; e-mail info@ibf-bih.com; internet www.ibf-bih.com; total assets 130.4m. (2000); Gen. Man. ASIM OMANIĆ.

Hercegovačka Banka d.d. Mostar: 88000 Mostar, Kneza Domagoja b.b.; tel. (36) 320555; fax (36) 324771; e-mail herbank@hercegovacka-banka.com; internet www.hercegovacka-banka.com; f. 1997; cap. 15.6m., res 0.6m., dep. 103.9m. (1999); Chair. FRANKA EREŠ.

Investiciono-Komercijalna Banka d.d., Zenica: 72000 Zenica, POB 62, trg Samoupravljača 1; tel. (32) 401804; fax (32) 417022; e-mail ikbsejo@ikbze.com.ba; internet www.ikbze.com.ba; f. 1990; cap. 10.7m., res 7.0m., dep. 76.4m. (Dec. 2000); Gen. Man. UZEIR FETIĆ.

Nova Banka a.d., Bijeljina: Bijeljina, ul. Svetog Save br. 46; tel. (55) 401409; fax (55) 401410; e-mail office@novabanka.com; internet www.novabanka.com; f. 1992 as Export Banka a.d. Bijeljina; name changed 1999; cap. 10.9m., res 2.0m., dep. 42.9m. (2001); Pres. MIHAJLO VIDIĆ; Chair. DJURO STANOJEVIĆ.

Privredna Banka a.d. Doboj: 74000 Doboj, Svetog Save 1; tel. (53) 241657; fax (53) 241662; e-mail pbaddo@inecco.net; f. 1992; cap. 11.4m., res 2.6m., dep. 5.5m. (2001); Pres. RADMILA STOJNIĆ; Chair. MIODRAG KUDIĆ.

Privredna Banka Gradiška d.d.: Gradiška, Vidovdanska bb; tel. (51) 813333; fax (51) 813205; e-mail pbgrad@pbanka-gradiska.com; internet www.pbanka-gradisko.com; f. 1953, registered as independent bank since 1992; privatization commenced in early 2001; cap. 8.1m., res 2.1m., dep. 55.0m. (Dec. 1999); Pres. MIRA STRAZIVUK.

Privredna Banka Sarajevo a.d.: Pale, ul. Srpskih Ratnika br. 14; tel. (33) 664852; fax (33) 663807; f. 1970 by merger of five banks; Man. Dir MOMČILO MANDIĆ.

Privredna Banka Sarajevo d.d., Sarajevo: 71000 Sarajevo, Alipašina 6; tel. (33) 209804; fax (33) 210360; e-mail pbscba22@bih.net.ba; f. 1971; cap. 19.1m., res 9.1m., dep. 45.0m. (Dec. 1999); Chair. ALIJA ČELIKOVI; 10 brs.

Raiffeisen Bank HPB Mostar: 88000 Mostar, Kneza Domagoja b.b.; tel. (36) 398301; fax (36) 317010; e-mail hpb_hb@int.tel.hr; f. 1994 as Hrvatska Postanska Banka d.d. Mostar; name changed 2001; cap. 10.0m., res 0.3m., dep. 41.0m. (2000); Pres. MICHAEL MÜLLER.

Turkish Ziraat Bank Bosnia d.d.: 71000 Sarajevo, Ferhadija 295; tel. (33) 230619; fax (33) 441902; e-mail ziraat@bih.net.ba; internet www.ziraatbosnia.com; f. 1996; cap. 25.0m., res 7.8m., dep. 30.8m. (Dec. 2001); Chair. SUPHI KABADAYL.

Tuzlanska Banka d.d. Tuzla: 75000 Tuzla, Maršala Tita 34; tel. (35) 259259; fax (35) 250596; e-mail tuzbank@bih.net.ba; internet www.tuzbank.ba; f. 1990; cap. 12.0m., res 12.5m., dep. 144.5m. (2001); Pres. MUHAMED HAJDARBEGOVIĆ; Chair. NUSRET SOFTIĆ.

Union Banka d.d. Sarajevo: 71000 Sarajevo, Dubrovačka 6; tel. (33) 664470; fax (33) 219201; e-mail unionban@bih.net.ba; f. 1955; cap. 34.3m., res 16.4m., dep. 71.0m. (2001); Gen. Man. SULEJMAN HODŽIĆ.

VB Banka a.d. Banja Luka: 78000 Banja Luka, Milana Tepica 4; tel. (51) 221610; fax (51) 221623; e-mail info@vbbanka.com; internet www.vbbanka.com; f. 1998; cap. 13.0m., res 0.2m., dep. 32.0m. (2001); Gen. Man. RADOVAN BAJIĆ.

Volksbank BH d.d.: 71000 Sarajevo, Fra Andjela Zvizdovića 1; tel. (33) 483265; fax (33) 263832; e-mail info@volksbank.ba; internet www.volksbank.ba; cap. 10.0m., dep. 25.0m. (2000); Gen. Man. Dr PETER SETZER.

Zagrebačka Banka BH d.d.: 88000 Mostar, Kardinala Štepinca b.b.; tel. (36) 312121; fax (36) 312129; e-mail zababh@zaba.hr; internet www.zaba.ba; f. 1992 as Hrvatska Banka d.d. Mostar; name changed 2000; cap. 34.2m., res 8.1m., dep. 499.1m. (Dec. 2001); Pres. DAMIR ODAK; Gen. Man. BERISLAV KUTLE.

Banking Agencies

Agency for Banking of the Federation of Bosnia and Herzegovina (Agencija za Bankarstvo Federacije Bosne i Hercegovine): 71000 Sarajevo; f. 1996; Dir ZLATKO BARŠ.

Banking Agency of Republika Srpska: Banja Luka, Marije Bursac 4; tel. (58) 218111; fax (58) 216675.

STOCK EXCHANGE

Sarajevo Stock Exchange: 71000 Sarajevo, Zvizdovića br 1; tel. (33) 251462; fax (33) 251478; e-mail uprava@sase.ba; internet www.sase.ba; f. April 2002; Dir AKIF SERDAREVIĆ.

Trade and Industry

GOVERNMENT AGENCIES

Foreign Investment Promotion Agency: 71000 Sarajevo, Branilaca Sarajeva 21; tel. (33) 278000; fax (33) 278081; e-mail fipa@fipa.gov.ba; internet www.fipa.gov.ba; f. July 1999; provides services to foreign investors; Gen. Dir MIRZA HAJRIĆ.

Privatization Agency of the Federation of Bosnia and Herzegovina: Sarajevo, Alipašina 41; tel. (33) 212884; fax (33) 212883; e-mail apfbih@bih.net.ba; internet www.apf.com.ba; Dir ADNAD MUJAGIĆ.

Republika Srpska Directorate for Privatization: 51000 Banja Luka, Mladena Stoganovića 4; tel. (51) 308311; fax (51) 311245; e-mail dip@inecco.net; internet www.rsprivatizacija.com; Dir BORISLAV OBRADOVIĆ.

Republika Srpska Securities Commission: 78000 Banja Luka, Vuka Karadžića 6; tel. (51) 218361; fax (51) 218362; e-mail kontakt@khov-rs.org; internet www.khov-rs.org; Pres. BRANKA BODROŽA.

Securities Commission of the Federation of Bosnia and Herzegovina: 71000 Sarajevo, Ćemaluša 9; tel. (33) 665897; fax (33) 211655; e-mail komvp@bih.net.ba; internet www.komvp.gov.ba; f. 1999; Pres. EDIB BASIĆ.

DEVELOPMENT ORGANIZATIONS

Bosnia and Herzegovina Local Economic Development Agency: Travnik, Zenjak 21B; tel. (32) 511877; fax (32) 818495; e-mail lebeda@bih.net.ba; internet www.ilsleda.com.

Directorate for the Reconstruction and Development of Sarajevo: Sarajevo, Hamdije Kresevljakovice 19; tel. (33) 650563; fax (33) 470887.

Federal Development Planning Institute: Sarajevo, Alipašina 41; tel. (33) 667272; fax (33) 212625; e-mail fzzprfbh@bih.net.ba; internet www.fzzpr.gov.ba; Dir Prof. NESET MUMINAGIĆ.

CHAMBERS OF COMMERCE

Chamber of Economy of Bosnia and Herzegovina: 71000 Sarajevo, Branislava Durdeva 10; tel. (33) 663631; fax (33) 663632; e-mail cis@komorabih.com; internet www.komorabih.com; Pres. MAHIR HADŽIAHMETOVIĆ.

Chamber of Economy of the Federation of Bosnia and Herzegovina: 71000 Sarajevo, Branislava Durdeva 10; tel. (33) 663370; fax (33) 663635; internet www.kfbih.com; Pres. AVDO RAPA.

Chamber of Commerce of the Republika Srpska: 78000 Banja Luka, Dure Daničića 1/II; tel. (51) 310908; fax (51) 303273; internet www.pkrs.inecco.net.

Chamber of Economy of Sarajevo Canton: 71000 Sarajevo, Hamdije Kreševljakovića 3; tel. and fax (33) 664597; e-mail webmaster@pksa.com.ba; internet www.pksa.com.ba; Pres. KEMAL GREBO.

MAJOR ENTERPRISES AND COMPANIES

At the end of 2000 approximately 35% of companies were privately owned.

Agrokomerc d.d.: Velika Kladusa, trg Ahmeta Mržljaka; tel. (37) 75553; fax (37) 77997; f. 1965; farming and production of foodstuffs; Dir ŠEFIK ŠTULAMOVIĆ; 2,000 employees.

ALHOS Export-Import: 71000 Sarajevo, Tesanjska 24A; tel. (33) 39481; fax (33) 215999; clothing manufacturer; Dir of Manufacture KEMAL HUJIĆ; 1,400 employees.

Aluminij: 88000 Mostar, 25 Novembra bb; tel. (36) 411333; fax (36) 33951; produces alumina, etc.; Gen. Man. MIJO BRAJKOVIĆ; 4,500 employees.

Bosnaputevi: 71000 Sarajevo, Pehlavanuša 3/3; tel. (51) 212140; fax (51) 212830; e-mail info@blbanka.com; internet www.blbanka.com; Dir MOMČILO POPARIĆ; 300 employees.

Bratstvo: 72290 Pućarevo, Borisa Kidrića 1; tel. (32) 791022; fax (32) 791018; manufactures parts for and assembles automobiles and tractors; Gen. Dir JOZO KRIŽANOVIĆ; 11,000 employees.

Energoinvest: 71000 Sarajevo, Hamdije Cemerlica; tel. (33) 610355; fax (33) 656756; e-mail generalmanager@energoinvest.com; internet www.tradepoint.ba; production, design and development of power systems; scheduled for privatization in 2001; Man. Dir NEDŽAD BRANKOVIĆ; 47,000 employees.

Energopetrol: 71000 Sarajevo, Maršala Tita 36; tel. (33) 664132; fax (33) 663992; f. 1951; subsidiary of Energoinvest; concerned with petroleum research, production and sale of petroleum products; Dir NAMUK BUSATLIĆ; 150 employees.

Famos Holding d.d.: 71000 Sarajevo, Envera Šehovića 54; tel. (33) 230797; fax (33) 657382; e-mail famosh@bih.net.ba; f. 1950; manufactures motor vehicles and components; Gen. Dir SAFET DAUT; 2,500 employees.

Feroelektro: 71000 Sarajevo, Maršala Tita 28; tel. (33) 664439; fax (33) 663946; f. 1947; 60.7% state-owned; import and export of goods and services; Gen. Dir SALKO SELIMOVIĆ; 259 employees.

Krajinametal d.d.: 37000 Bihač, Jablanska b.b.; tel. (37) 331198; fax (37) 331197; e-mail kraji@bih.net.ba; internet www.krajinametal.com; f. 1969; 60% state-owned; Pres. SENAD FELIĆ.

Krivaja Industrijsko Preduzece d.d.: 72220 Zavidovici, Radnička 1; tel. (32) 871220; fax (32) 874874; e-mail krivajaz@bih.net.ba; internet www.krivaja.com.ba; f. 1884; timber industry, construction industry and metals industry; Gen. Dir HIMZO HUSIĆ; 4,000 employees.

Lijanovici d.o.o.: Visoka glavica b.b., Široki Brijeg; tel. (39) 384102; fax (39) 384134; e-mail slavo.ivanovic@lijanovici.com; internet www.lijanovici.com; Pres. SLAVO IVANKOVIĆ.

Lukavać Coke and Chemical Combine (Koksno-Hemijski Kombinat d.d.): 75300 Lukavać, Zeljeznicka 1; tel. (35) 567473; fax (35) 281390; e-mail fuad_amra@bih.net.ba; production of coke, bitumen and chemicals; 2,000 employees.

Natron d.d.: 74250 Maglaj, Lijesnica b.b.; tel. (32) 603672; fax (32) 603788; e-mail natrondd@pksa.co.ba; f. 1956; 70% govt-owned; manufacturer of paper; Gen. Dir Dr SALIM IBRAHIMFENDIČ; 1,950 employees.

RMK Zenica: 72000 Zenica, Kučukovići 2; tel. (32) 410293; fax (32) 412273; e-mail rmkprom@bih.net.ba; internet www.rmkprom.com; f. 1977; international and domestic trade; Gen. Man. MUNIB HUSEJNAGIĆ.

Ro Rafinerija Ulja, Modrica: 74480 Modrica, Vjekoslava Bakulica 49; tel. (53) 880160; fax (53) 882541; production of base oils, paraffin waxes, special mineral oils, etc.; Gen. Man. STEVO DOKIĆ; 930 employees.

Sodaso: 75000 Tuzla, Slatina br. 2; tel. (35) 212444; fax (35) 821398; f. 1970; salt and mineral products; detergents, shampoos, cosmetics; Gen. Dir Dr IZUDIN KEŠETOVIĆ; 4,100 employees.

Unis: 71000 Sarajevo, Ismeta Mujezinovica 24; tel. (33) 664192; fax (33) 664193; a variety of businesses, incl. cars and motor accessories; Gen. Man. SACIR BOSKAJLO; 1,450 employees.

UTILITIES

Electricity

Elektroprivreda of Bosnia and Herzegovina Ltd: 88000 Mostar, ul. Mile Budaka 106a; tel. and fax (36) 310847; fax (36) 317157; e-mail ephzhb@tel.net.ba; internet www.ephzhb.com; generation, transmission and distribution of electric energy; Dir-Gen. MATAN ŽARIĆ.

Gas

Bosnia and Herzegovina Gas (BH—Gas): 71000 Sarajevo, Hamdije Cemerlića 2; tel. (33) 279000; fax (33) 231621; e-mail development@bh-gas.ba; internet www.bh-gas.ba; f. 1997; Man. Dir HUSO HADŽIDEDIĆ.

TRADE UNIONS

Independent Union of Professional Journalists: Obala Kulina Bana, 2/III Sarajevo; tel. (33) 670813; fax (33) 534495; e-mail nupnbih@bih.net.ba; f. 1994; Pres. MEHMED HUSIĆ.

Trade Unions of Bosnia and Herzegovina: Sarajevo, Obala Kulina Bana 1; tel. (33) 664872.

Trade Unions of Republika Srpska: Banja Luka, Srpska 32; tel. (51) 310711; fax (51) 304241.

Transport

RAILWAYS

At the beginning of the 1990s the railway system consisted of some 1,030 km of track, of which 75% was electrified. Much of the system was damaged or destroyed during the civil war, but in July 1996 the Sarajevo–Mostar service was restored and in 1997 the Tuzla–Doboj service reopened. The Tuzla–Brčko service resumed in 2002. Following the outbreak of hostilities, the state railway company was divided into three regional state-owned companies: the Bosnia and Herzegovina Railway Company (ZBH), based in Sarajevo; the Herzeg-Bosnia Railway Company (ZHB), based in the Croat-majority part of the Federation; and the Serb Republic Railway and Transport Company (ZTP), based in Banja Luka. In 1998 an overarching organization, the Bosnia and Herzegovina Railways Public Corpn, was established. Further reforms were anticipated in 2003. In March 2000 the Presidents of Bosnia and Herzegovina and Croatia signed an agreement to recommence railway traffic between the two countries. By the end of that year post-war reconstruction assistance had resulted in the restoration of about 85% of track; however, regular train services between the Federation and the Serb Republic remained suspended.

ROADS

The transport infrastructure in Bosnia and Herzegovina was badly damaged during the civil war of 1992–95. Some 35% of the country's roads and 40% of its bridges were affected by the conflict. A new Transportation Corporation was established (with its headquarters in Sarajevo), under the terms of the Dayton accords, in order to organize and operate roads, ports and railways on the territory of the two entities. The agreement also provided for the construction of a new road linking the Goražde enclave, in the east of Bosnia and Herzegovina, with the rest of the Federation. There were 21,846 km of roads in Bosnia and Herzegovina in 2001, of which 14,020 km were paved. In 1997 an internationally-funded project to rehabilitate and rebuild the road network in the Serb Republic commenced. In June 2000 the Governments of Bosnia and Herzegovina and Croatia signed an accord on the construction of the Ploče–Budapest corridor, linking the Croatian seaport with the Hungarian capital through Bosnian territory.

c/o Federation Ministry of Transport and Communications: 71000 Sarajevo, Alipašina 41; tel. (33) 668907; fax (33) 667866; internet www.fmpik.gov.ba.

Republic Directorate for Roads: Banja Luka, Vase Pelagica 10; tel. (51) 309061; fax (51) 308316; Dir NEMANJA VASIĆ.

CIVIL AVIATION

The country has an international airport at Sarajevo, and three smaller civil airports, at Tuzla, Banja Luka and Mostar. Civil aviation was severely disrupted by the 1992–95 civil war. Commercial flights resumed to Sarajevo in August 1996, to Banja Luka in November 1997 and to Mostar in July 1998. In June 1997 it was announced that a new airport at Dubrave, near Tuzla, was to be built.

Department of Civil Aviation of Bosnia and Herzegovina: 33000 Sarajevo, Envera Sehovića 2; tel. (33) 653016; fax (33) 653008; e-mail bhdca@bhdca.gov.ba; internet www.bhdca.gov.ba.

Air Bosna: 71000 Sarajevo, Cemalasa 6; tel. (33) 667953; fax (33) 650974; e-mail marketing@airbosna.ba; internet www.airbosna.ba; f. 1994; 51% state-owned; regular services to Croatia, Germany, Slovenia, Sweden, Turkey and Serbia and Montenegro; Man. Dir OMER KULIĆ.

Air Srpska: 78000 Banja Luka, Veselina Maslese 28; tel. (51) 212806; fax (51) 211348; f. 1999; flights from Banja Luka airport to Yugoslavia and Switzerland.

Mast Air: 78000 Banja Luka; tel. (51) 304551; flights from Tuzla airport to Hungary, Italy, Slovenia and Turkey.

RS Airlines: Pale; f. 1997; flights from Banja Luka airport to Bulgaria, Greece, Hungary, Romania, Serbia and Montenegro and Russia; Dir JOVAN TINTOR.

Tourism

Following the adverse affects of the civil conflict of 1992–95, the tourism sector recovered rapidly. Tourist arrivals increased from 89,000 in 1999 to an estimated 110,000 in 2000, when receipts from tourism were estimated at US $17m. However, arrivals declined to some 90,000 in 2001.

Culture

Severe damage was done to many of the cultural monuments of Bosnia and Herzegovina during the civil war of 1992–95. Fighting caused much damage, such as to the Stari Most (the famous 16th-century bridge at Mostar, destroyed in early November 1993), but there was also deliberate damage by militias against the cultural heritage of other ethnic groups, notably the widespread destruction of mosques in Serb-held areas and the National Library in Sarajevo. Under the terms of the Dayton accords (Annexe 8 to the General Framework Agreement for Peace in Bosnia and Herzegovina) a five-member Commission to Preserve National Monuments, based in Sarajevo, was to be established. The Director-General of UNESCO was to appoint the first Chairman and one other member of the Commission. Following the ratification of an annexe to an agreement on special relations between the Federation of Bosnia and Herzegovina and Croatia in March 2000, the two territories began to co-operate on matters of tourism, science, technology and university education. By the beginning of the 2000s there was some renovation of museums in Bosnia and Herzegovina.

NATIONAL ORGANIZATIONS

Commission to Preserve National Monuments: c/o High Representative of the International Community, 71000 Sarajevo, trg. Djece Sarajeva bb; tel. (33) 447275; fax (33) 447420.

Institute for the Protection of the Cultural, Historical and Natural Heritage of Bosnia and Herzegovina (Zavod za Zaštitu Kulturno, Historijskog i Prirodnog Naslijedja BiH): 71000 Sarajevo, Alekse Šantića 8/II; tel. and fax (33) 663299; Dir Prof. MUHAMED HAMIDOVIĆ.

Institute for the Protection of the Cultural, Historical and Natural Heritage of the Canton of Sarajevo (Kantonalni Zavod a Zaštitut Kulturni, Historisjkog i Prirodnog Naslijedja Sarajevo): Sarajevo, Kaptol 16; tel. (33) 260980; fax (33) 663298; e-mail heritsa@bih.net.ba; f. 1965; library of 15,000 vols; Dir Valida Čelić Ćemerlić.

Ministry of Culture and Sport: see section on The Entities (Federation of Bosnia and Herzegovina, The Government—Ministries).

Ministry of Education and Culture of the Serb Republic: see section on The Entities (Serb Republic, The Government—Ministries).

CULTURAL HERITAGE

Art Gallery of Bosnia and Herzegovina (Umjetnička galerija Bosne i Hercegovine): 71000 Sarajevo, JNA 38; tel. (33) 667532; fax (33) 664162; e-mail ugbih@bih.net.ba; f. 1946; collections of modern art; library of 3,000 vols; Dir Prof. SEID HASANEFENDIĆ.

Museum of Bosanska Krajina (Muzej Bosanske Krajine): 78000 Banja Luka, V. Karadžića bb; tel. (51) 35486; f. 1930; regional museum for north-west Bosnia; depts of archaeology, history, ethnography, national revolution, workers' movement; library of 9,500 vols; Dir AHMET ČEJVAN.

Museum of the Serb Republic (Muzej Republike Srpske): 78000 Banja Luka, Djure Daničića 1; tel. (51) 305290; fax (51) 47318; f. 1930; history, archaeology and ethnography; 5,500 vols; Dir Dr VASO POPOVIĆ.

National Museum of Bosnia and Herzegovina (Zemaljski Muzej Bosne i Hercegovine): 71000 Sarajevo, Zmaja od Bosne 3; tel. and fax (33) 668025; e-mail z.muzej@bih.net.ba; internet www.zemaljskimuzej.ba; f. 1888; museology, scientific research, education, comprises the departments of archaeology, ethnology, natural history and a library; Dir DJENANA BUTUROVIĆ.

National and University Library of Bosnia and Herzegovina (Narodna i univerzitetska biblioteka Bosne i Hercegovine): 71000 Sarajevo, Zmaja od Bosna 83; f. 1945; 3m. vols; copyright and deposit library; library building and collection severely damaged in Aug. 1992; Head Dr ENES KUJUNDŽIĆ.

National and University Library of the Serb Republic: 78000 Banja Luka, Jevrejska 30; tel. (51) 215894; e-mail nubrs@urc.bl.ac.yu; internet www.nubrs.rs.ba.

SPORTING ORGANIZATIONS

Olympic Committee of Bosnia and Herzegovina: 71000 Sarajevo, Maršala Tita 9, A/I; tel. (33) 663513; fax (33) 663410; e-mail okbih@bih.net.ba; internet www.okbih.ba; f. 1992; Pres. BOGIĆ BOGIĆEVIĆ; Gen. Sec. SEJDALIJA MUSTAFIĆ.

Union of Organizations for Physical Culture (Savez Organizacija Fizičke Kulture): 71000 Sarajevo, Mahmuta Baštlije 2.

PERFORMING ARTS

55 Chamber Theatre: 71000 Sarajevo, Maršala Tita 56/II; tel. and fax (33) 471184; e-mail kamerni@lsinter.net; internet www .kamerniteatar55.ba; Dir ZLATKO TOPČIĆ.

National Theatre (Narodno Pozoriste): 71000 Sarajevo, Obala Kulina Bana 9; tel. (33) 518795; fax (33) 445138; e-mail nps@utic.net .ba; Ballet and Opera Dir TEODOR ROMANIĆ.

Obala Open Theatre: 71000 Sarajevo, Obala Kulina Bana 13; tel. and fax (33) 536825.

Youth Theatre: Sarajevo, Kulovića 8; tel. (33) 442572.

Music

Sarajevo Philharmonic Orchestra (Sarajevska Filharmonija): 71000 Sarajevo, Obala Kulina Bana 9; tel. (33) 666519; fax (33) 666521; e-mail dusanka@bih.net.ba; f. 1923; Man. and Artistic Dir EMIR NUHANOVIĆ.

Symphony Orchestra RTV Sarajevo (Simfonijski Orkestra RTV Sarajevo): 71000 Sarajevo, VI Proleterske brigade 4; tel. (33) 461101; Chief Conductor JULIO MARIĆ.

ASSOCIATIONS

Association of Musicians (Udruženje Muzičkih Umjetnika): Muzička akademija, 71000 Sarajevo, Stadlera 1; tel. and fax (33) 444896; Pres. Prof. FARUK SIJARIĆ.

Society of Music Lovers and Young Musicians (Musička Omladina): Muzička akademija, 71000 Sarajevo, Mis Irbina 10; tel. and fax (33) 665713; e-mail muzomlsa@soros.org.ba; internet www .muzomlsa/~soros.org.ba; f. 1958; organizes concerts, lectures, theatre events, exhibitions, film shows; 40,000 mems; library of 1,000 vols, record library of 1,000 items; Pres. REŠAD ARNAUTOVIĆ; Sec. SLAVICA ŠPOLJARIĆ.

Education

Primary education in Bosnia and Herzegovina was free and compulsory for all children aged between seven and 15 years. Various types of secondary education were available to those who qualified; vocational and technical schools were the most popular, but children could also attend a general secondary school (gymnasium), an art school, an apprentice school or a teacher-training school. In 1996/97 some 260,407 pupils were enrolled in 955 primary schools. Some 97,303 pupils attended 184 secondary schools in 1997/98. In 2001 about 57,800 students were enrolled at the country's four principal universities. In the Federation, 256,169 students were enrolled in primary education, 111,444 in secondary education and 48,866 in higher-education institutions in 2001.

UNIVERSITIES

University of Banja Luka (Univerzitet u Banoj Luci): 78000 Banja Luka, trg Srpskih vladara 2; tel. (51) 312112; fax (51) 317057; e-mail uni-bl@bl.ac.yu; internet www.urc.bl.ac.yu; f. 1975; state control; 12 faculties, 1 academy; 520 teachers, 14,500 students; Rector Prof. Dr DRAGOLJUB MIRJANIĆ.

University of Mostar (Sveučilište u Mostaru): 88000 Mostar, trg Hrvatskih velikana 1; tel. (36) 310778; fax (36) 320885; internet www.unist.hr/hum; f. 1977, adopted new name 1992; 7 faculties, 5 institutes; 215 teachers, 3,500 students; Rector Prof. Dr ZDENKO KORDIĆ.

University of Sarajevo (Univerzitet u Sarajevu): 71000 Sarajevo, Obala Kulina bana 7/II; tel. (33) 663392; fax (33) 663393; e-mail rektorat@unsa.ba; internet www.unsa.ba; f. 1949; 26 faculties, 4 institutes; 1,450 teachers, 34,800 students; Rector Prof. Dr BORIS TIHI.

University of Tuzla (Univerzitet u Tuzli): 75000 Tuzla, M. Fizovića-Fiska 6, POB 528; tel. (35) 252061; fax (35) 251405; e-mail unitz@untz.ba; f. 1976; 8 faculties; 425 teachers, 5,000 students; Rector Prof. Dr SADIK LATIFAGIĆ.

Social Welfare

Health care in Bosnia and Herzegovina is state-administered and free of charge. Following the end of the civil conflict in December 1995, budgetary funds allocated to the health service were used principally for emergency relief and humanitarian aid. In 1998 there were 143 physicians, 452 nurses, 19 dentists and 11 pharmacists per 100,000 people. Social-fund expenditure was estimated at 29.4% of total spending by the central Government in 1999. Economic and social reconstruction continued to be supported by international aid.

NATIONAL AGENCIES

Ministry of Human Rights and Refugees: see section on The Government (Ministries).

Ministry of Displaced Person and Refugees: see section on The Entities (Federation of Bosnia and Herzegovina, The Government—Ministries).

Ministry of Health: see section on The Entities (Federation of Bosnia and Herzegovina, The Government—Ministries).

Ministry of Issues of War Veterans and the Disabled: see section on The Entities (Federation of Bosnia and Herzegovina, The Government—Ministries).

Ministry of Labour and Social Policy: see section on The Entities (Federation of Bosnia and Herzegovina, The Government—Ministries).

Ministry of Health and Social Welfare of the Serb Republic: see section on The Entities (Serb Republic, The Government—Ministries).

Ministry of Refugees and Displaced Persons of the Serb Republic: see section on The Entities (Serb Republic, The Government—Ministries).

Ministry of War Veterans and Labour Affairs of the Serb Republic: see section on The Entities (Serb Republic, The Government—Ministries).

NON-GOVERNMENTAL ORGANIZATIONS

Bosnian Committee for Help: 75000 Tuzla, Djura Djakovica 5; tel. (56) 281607; fax (56) 252448; e-mail bospo@bih.net.ba; internet www.swwb.org; Man. NEJIRA NELIĆ.

Open Society Fund of Bosnia and Herzegovina: Sarajevo, Dženetića Čikma 2; tel. (33) 444488; e-mail osf@soros.org.ba; internet www.soros.org.ba; f. 1993; Dir DOBRILA GOVEDARICA.

Project Enterprise of Bosnia and Herzegovina (PRIZMA): 88104 Mostar, Marsala Tita 56; tel. (36) 552682; fax (36) 555151; e-mail info@prizma.ba; internet www.prizma.ba; Dir MAJA GIZOLIĆ.

The Environment

Most environmental activity by research bodies and the 'Green' movement took place at the federal level when the country was a constituent part of the Yugoslav federation. Such activity at a local level became irrelevant and ineffective during the period of civil war. The war caused immense environmental damage such as soil destruction. Another consequence was the dissemination of almost 3m. landmines. Following the signing of the 1995 Dayton accords, which placed the responsibility of the environment on the two entities, progress was very slow. In 1999 the Environmental Steering Committee was established, with the aim of co-ordinating activities between the two entities.

GOVERNMENT ORGANIZATIONS

Ministry of Urban Planning and the Environment: see section on The Entities (Federation of Bosnia and Herzegovina, The Government—Ministries).

Ministry of Urban Planning, Housing and the Environment: see section on The Entities (Serb Republic of Bosnia and Herzegovina, The Government—Ministries).

ACADEMIC INSTITUTES

Centre for Ecology and Natural Resources: 71000 Sarajevo, Zmaja od Bosne 35; tel. (33) 649196; fax (33) 649342; e-mail sdug@ usa.net; internet www.cepres.pmf.unsa.ba; Contact Prof. Dr SULEJMAN REDŽIĆ.

Hydro-Engineering Institute: 71000 Sarajevo, Stjepana Tomića 1; tel. (33) 212466; fax (33) 207949; e-mail heis@heis.com.ba; internet www.heis.com.ba; f. 1954; responsibilities incl. water and air pollution; Contact Prof. Dr TARIK KUPUSOVIĆ.

Institute for Agropedology: 71000 Sarajevo, Dolina 6; tel. (33) 221780; fax (33) 268261; e-mail zapsa@pksa.com.ba; concentrates on soil contamination; Contact Prof. Dr HUSNIJA RESULOVIĆ.

Meteorological Institute: 71000 Sarajevo, Bardakičije 12; tel. (33) 663508; fax (33) 524040; e-mail martin_tais@hotmail.com; Contact TAIS MARTIN.

NON-GOVERNMENTAL ORGANIZATIONS

Bosnian Environmental Technologies Association (BETA): 71000 Sarajevo, Stjepana Tomića 1; tel. and fax (33) 200226; e-mail mjuric@utic.net.ba; Contact Prof. ESMA VELAGIĆ-HABUL.

Centre for Ecology and Natural Resources: 71000 Sarajevo, Zmaja od Bosne 35; tel. (33) 649196; fax (33) 649342; e-mail sdug@usa.net; internet www.cepres.pmf.unsa.ba; Contact Prof. Sulejman Redžić.

Centre for the Environmentally Sustainable Development of Bosnia and Herzegovina (Centar za Okolišno Odiženi Razvoj Bih): 71000 Sarajevo, Stjepana Tomica 1; tel. and fax (33) 207949; e-mail coorsa@bih.met.ba; internet www.coorsa.ba; Chair. Prof. Tarik Kupusović.

Croatian Eco Association Buna (Hrvatska ekološka udruga Buna): 88000 Mostar, Buna bb; tel. (36) 480038; fax (36) 480380; Contact Damir Brljević.

EKOBiH (Society for Environment, Protection and Improvement of Bosnia and Herzegovina): 71000 Sarajevo, Stari Grad, Patke bb; tel. (33) 232634; fax (33) 441040; Contact Faik Kulović.

EKOS Ecological Society (Ekolŏsko društvo RS 'EKOS'): 78000 Banja Luka, Stepe Stepanovića 75; tel. (51) 61392; fax (51) 63024; Contact Prof. Dr Branislav Nedović.

Foundation for Sustainable Development, Stimulation and Quality of Life (Fond Eko): 71000 Sarajevo, Branilaca Sarajeva 47, ul. Rudarska 72; tel. and fax (33) 211354; e-mail fondeko@bih.net.ba; Contact Prof. Dr Dubravka Šoljan.

Green Eco-Movement (Ekološki pokret Zeleni): 77240 Bosanska Krupa, Reis-ul. Dž. Čauševića bb; tel. (77) 472844; fax (77) 471072; Contact Zajnil Palić.

Defence

At August 2002 the two entities of Bosnia and Herzegovina maintained separate armed forces: at that time the Serb Republic had an army of about 6,600 and the Federation an army (comprising the former Croatian Defence Council—HVO—and Bosniak forces) of more than 13,200. Under the terms of the Dayton agreement of 1995, the size of the armed forces of the two entities was restricted. In April 2003 the High Representative of Bosnia and Herzegovina announced further restructuring of the armed forces, prior to the country's admission to the North Atlantic Treaty Organization (NATO).

On 20 December 1995 the UN Protection Force, which had some 25,000 troops deployed in Bosnia and Herzegovina, formally transferred its powers to a new international force, the 60,000-strong Implementation Force (IFOR), which was under the command of NATO. IFOR was granted wide-ranging powers to oversee the implementation of the General Framework Agreement for Peace in Bosnia and Herzegovina. On 20 December 1996 IFOR was superseded by a Stabilization Force (SFOR), which initially comprised about 32,000 troops. In February 1998 NATO agreed to extend SFOR's mandate indefinitely. Following restructuring, the number of troops in SFOR deployed in Bosnia and Herzegovina numbered about 12,000 in early 2003. In March the authorities of Bosnia and Herzegovina invited the European Union (EU) to undertake its police mission. At the end of 2002 the mandate of the UN Mission in Bosnia and Herzegovina, established in 1995, was officially completed, and a European Union Police Mission (EUPM) commenced operations on 1 January 2003. The EUPM, which comprised 512 police-officers, supported by 50 civilian monitors and 300 local staff, was to supervise the reorganization and training of the country's security forces. It was envisaged that SFOR would also be replaced with a EU operation. (In July 2003, however, SFOR's mandate was extended for a further year.)

Chief of the General Staff: Chairman of the Presidency of Bosnia and Herzegovina.

Commander of the Army of the Federation of Bosnia and Herzegovina: Lt-Gen. Atif Dudaković.

Chief of the General Staff of the Army of the Serb Republic: Maj.-Gen. Cvjetko Savić.

Stabilization Force (SFOR)

Commander: Lt-Gen. William E. Ward.

SFOR Headquarters: 71000 Sarajevo, Butmir Camp; tel. (33) 495000; fax (33) 447604; e-mail cpic_online@sfor.nato.int.

THE ENTITIES OF BOSNIA AND HERZEGOVINA

Under the new Constitution, which was Annexe 4 to the General Framework Agreement for Peace in Bosnia and Herzegovina, signed on 14 December 1995, the Republic of Bosnia and Herzegovina comprised two constituent 'entities', the Federation of Bosnia and Herzegovina and the Serb Republic of Bosnia and Herzegovina.

FEDERATION OF BOSNIA AND HERZEGOVINA

Introduction

The Federation of Bosnia and Herzegovina occupies the west and centre of Bosnia and Herzegovina, its territory tapering north-eastwards, with a road linking it to the eastern enclave of Goražde. It comprises 51% of the country, some 26,076 sq km (10,068 sq miles).

In March 1992, following the outbreak of civil war in Yugoslavia, a sovereign Republic of Bosnia and Herzegovina was proclaimed. The Serb deputies of the republican legislature withdrew and, aided by the Yugoslav People's Army, established a 'Serb Republic' on much of the territory of Bosnia and Herzegovina. The republican institutions were left to the Bosnian Muslim (Bosniak) and Croat members, dominated by the Bosniaks. Therefore, in July the formation of the 'Croat Union of Herzeg-Bosna', which was to be centred on Mostar, was announced, to be led by the Herzegovinian Croat, Mate Boban. On 28 August 1993 this 'Union' was declared the 'Croat Republic of Herzeg-Bosna' by a Bosnian Croat assembly in Grude. With Croat territories in virtual union with Croatia and Serb forces controlling most of the remaining territory of Bosnia and Herzegovina, the Bosniak-dominated Government of the Republic was reluctant to accept any peace plans. The Croat moves contributed to tension in the republican institutions and, on the ground, fighting between government and Croat forces (the Croat Defence Council—HVO, Hrvatsko Vijece Obrane).

In September 1993 an 'Autonomous Province of Western Bosnia' was proclaimed in the Muslim enclave of Bihać, and Fikret Abdić, a Bosniak member of the republican State Presidency, was elected its President. Abdić dissolved the municipal assembly of Velika Kladusa and declared that elections were to be held for a new constituent body. Alija Izetbegović, head of the State Presidency, declared a state of martial law in the area. On 3 October the first skirmishes were reported between forces loyal to the Government and those supporting Abdić in Velika Kladusa.

On 1 March 1994, despite almost one year of fierce fighting between Croat and government forces in central Bosnia, delegates of the 'Croat Republic of Herzeg-Bosna' and of the mainly Bosniak Government, meeting in Washington, DC, the USA, agreed to establish a Croat-Bosniak federation in a confederal association with Croatia. On 18 March the leader of the Bosnian Croats, Kresimir Zubak (who had succeeded Mate Boban), and the Bosnian Prime Minister, Haris Silajdžić, signed an agreement on the creation of a Federation of Bosnia and Herzegovina, with power shared equally between Muslims and Croats. The Federation came into being on 31 March.

Under the federal Constitution, which was finalized in March 1994, the Federation was to consist of cantons ruled by a strong federal Government, which was to be responsible for defence, foreign affairs and the economy. Greater executive power was to be vested in the office of the Prime Minister than that of the President and both posts were to rotate annually between members of the Muslim and Croat ethnic groups. Until the full implementation of the Federation and the holding of elections, Izetbegović was to remain President of the collective State Presidency and the emerging federal institutions were to operate in parallel with those of the old Republic. In May it was announced that the existing republican Bosnian Assembly would act in a dual capacity as the federal legislature until such time as its dissolution. In late May the Constituent Assembly of the Federation held its inaugural meeting, at which it elected Zubak to the post of President of the Federation. Ejup Ganić,

who was concurrently Vice-President of the collective State Presidency of the Republic of Bosnia and Herzegovina, was elected Vice-President and Haris Silajdžić was appointed federal Prime Minister. In late June a joint Government of the Republic of Bosnia and Herzegovina and of the Federation was formed.

In August and September 1994 tensions increased between the Bosniaks and Croats over the establishment of the Federation. In a meeting in mid-September in Zagreb, Croatia, between Izetbegović and the Croatian President, Franjo Tudjman, it was agreed that interim municipal governments should be established by 30 September and cantonal authorities by 31 October. It was also agreed that a joint command of the Bosnian government army and Bosnian Croat army should be instituted as soon as possible. On 8 April 1995 an agreement was signed between the Federation's President, Zubak, and its Vice-President, Ganić, aimed at accelerating the establishment of federal institutions. The inaugural session of the Federation's Constituent Assembly duly took place in Novi Travnik on 4 May, during which the Bonn Agreement on the implementation of federal principles was unanimously adopted.

In early September 1995 major progress in the peace process was made when, in a meeting chaired by the 'Contact Group' of Western countries, representatives from Bosnia and Herzegovina, Croatia and the Bosnian Serbs signed an agreement determining the basic principles of an accord. Under this agreement the Federation would be granted 51% of Bosnia and Herzegovina, while the Bosnian Serbs would be apportioned 49%. Bosnia and Herzegovina would continue to exist within its present borders but would be composed of two entities, the Federation and a Serb Republic. It was agreed that the Federation would control two-thirds of the republican legislature and that Bosniaks and Croats would comprise two-thirds of a collective national presidency. These accords formed the basis of a comprehensive peace agreement, the General Framework for Peace in Bosnia and Herzegovina, initialled by the Bosnian, Croatian and Yugoslav leaders in Dayton, Ohio, the USA, on 21 November.

Under the terms of the Dayton accords Sarajevo was to have a special status as a united city within the Federation, with Serb-held suburbs of the capital transferred to federal control. Goražde was to remain under the control of the Federation and was to be linked to Sarajevo via a Federation-administered land corridor. Earlier in November 1995 Presidents Izetbegović and Tudjman had signed an accord aimed at reinforcing the 1994 Federation agreement, which included a provision for the unification of the divided city of Mostar as the eventual federal capital and seat of the federal presidency.

On 31 January 1996, following the resignation of Silajdžić in protest at what he believed to be the dominance of the Muslim Party of Democratic Action (PDA) in the Federation, Izudin Kapetanović was appointed premier of a new federal Government. By early April the strengthening of the federal institutions was continuing apace, with the establishment of a customs union linking the two sides of the Federation. Agreements were also reached on a single federal budget and a unitary banking system and, in May, on the earlier proposed merger of Croat and Bosniak armed formations. Nevertheless, Croat–Muslim tensions still delayed federal integration. Particular conflict was centred around Mostar, where Bosnian Croats had announced a new government of 'Herzeg-Bosna' in mid-June, in defiance of federal agreements. Municipal elections there at the end of the month, however, brought victory for the PDA. Bosnian Croat leaders agreed to dissolve 'Herzeg-Bosna' in mid-August, but the dissolution was in name only.

On 14 September 1996 elections to the Federation's legislature were held. As expected, the PDA and the Croatian Democratic Union of Bosnia and Herzegovina (CDU—BH) won the majority of seats in the federal House of Representatives. Nevertheless, a Bosniak and Croat social-democratic alliance, the Joint List of Bosnia and Herzegovina, and the Party for Bosnia and Herzegovina, led by Silajdžić, also secured a significant number of seats. On 17 December the republican Government formally transferred its remaining functions to the Federation. On the same day the Bosnian Croats announced that 'Herzeg-Bosna' had ceased to exist. One week later the new federal legislature elected Edhem Bičkčić as federal premier. Zubak (concurrently the Croat member of the state Presidency of the union of Bosnia and Herzegovina) remained as President until March 1997, when he was replaced by Vladimir Soljić. Soljić, in turn, was succeeded in the presidency by Ganić, hitherto Vice-President, in December.

New elections to the federal legislature were held on 12–13 September 1998. The Coalition for a Single and Democratic Bosnia and Herzegovina, led by the PDA, won the largest number of seats (68), while the CDU—BH gained the second largest number, 28. The former communists, now reconstituted as the Social Democratic Party, won 19 seats. In early December the new Federation Parliament re-elected Ganić as President, while Ivo Andrić-Luzanski became Vice-President. At the same time, a new Federation cabinet, nominated by Bičakčić, was appointed. One year later, in accordance with the Constitution, Andrić-Luzanski succeeded Ganić as President.

Progress in the Federation of Bosnia and Herzegovina was restricted by significant problems in the late 1990s. The establishment of federal institutions was slow. The Bosnian Croats, in particular, continued to impede the integration process by demanding the division of mixed federal cantons. Despite federal provisions, parallel authorities still operated in Croat- and Bosniak-controlled municipalities. In Mostar the process of establishing a city administration, including a joint police force, continued slowly; in January 1998 a Bosniak mayor and a Croat deputy were appointed. Nevertheless, no real integration of the Muslim east bank and the Croat west bank of Mostar had been achieved. In general, although agreements were in place providing for joint federal institutions, in reality, separate Muslim and Croat bodies remained in operation. However, the establishment in March 2000 of the north-eastern town of Brčko as a neutral district under joint Bosniak, Croat and Serb control was seen by the Federation's leaders as an example for the rest of Bosnia and Herzegovina.

In April 2000, following his party's poor performance in the local elections, the PDA Deputy Chairman, Ganić, resigned his party posts, following a vote of 'no confidence' from the PDA board. He refused, however, to resign as Vice-President of the Federation and was subsequently expelled from the party. In May Bičakčić survived a vote of 'no confidence' in the House of Representatives.

In elections to the federal House of Representatives, which took place on 11 November 2000, the PDA, with 27% of the votes cast, won 38 seats, while the reconstituted Social Democratic Party of Bosnia and Herzegovina (SDP BiH) secured 37 seats, the CDU—BH 25 seats and the Party for Bosnia and Herzegovina 21 seats. In December the CDU—BH and a further six Croat parties threatened to withdraw from Federation government institutions, after members of the Alliance for Change (a parliamentary coalition led by the SDP BiH) were elected Speaker and Deputy Speaker of the federal House of Representatives. In March 2001, after the CDU—BH candidate for the Bosnian premiership, Martin Raguz, was rejected, the Croat People's Assembly (CPA—Hrvatska Narodni Skupština—HNS), a grouping of parties led by the CDU—BH, declared self-government in three Croat-majority cantons, and voted to establish autonomous power structures. Petritsch subsequently dismissed Ante Jelavić, the leader of the CDU—BH, from the collective state Presidency. Many Croat members of the armed forces and local officials declared support for the CPA, which announced that it intended to secede from the Federation (in violation of the Dayton agreement). Following negotiations with the federal authorities and international community officials, however, the HNS agreed to end its boycott of government institutions.

In late September 2001 Gen. Sefer Halilović, a former Chief of Staff of the Bosnian army and the hitherto Federation Minister of Social Welfare and Refugees, surrendered to the ICTY. Halilović (who was the most senior Muslim official to be indicted by the Tribunal) pleaded not guilty to charges relating to the killing of 62 Croatian citizens by troops under his command in 1993. Following the terrorist attacks on the USA on 11 September 2001, SFOR took measures to investigate suspected supporters of the Saudi Arabian-born Islamist leader held responsible, Osama bin Laden. In early October the Federation Minister of the Interior, Mohammed Besić, was forced to resign, after media ridicule of his statement that supporters of bin Laden's al-Qa'ida (Base) organization were planning to take refuge in Bosnia and Herzegovina. (He was replaced by Ramo Masleša in December.)

In June 2002 Sir Jeremy John Durham (Paddy) Ashdown, who officially replaced Petritsch as High Representative on 27 May, dismissed the Federation Deputy Prime Minister and Minister of Finance, Nikola Grabovac, following allegations of official malpractice. At the legislative elections, conducted at national and entity level on 5 October, the PDA secured the highest number of seats (32) in the federal House of Representatives (which had been reduced in size from 140 to 98 seats); an alliance of the CDU—BH and Croatian Christian Democratic Union won 16 seats, the SDP BiH 15 seats and the Party for Bosnia and Herzegovina 15 seats. On 27 January 2003 the House of Representatives elected Niko Lozancić, a member of the CDU—BH, to the presidency, and under reforms to the entity's system of government, introduced in April 2002, a Bosniak and a Serb as joint Vice-Presidents (the first time that a Serb had been elected to public office in the Federation). In mid-February the legislature elected Ahmet Hadžipašić of the PDA (a Bosniak) to the office of Prime Minister, and a Croat and a Serb as Deputy Prime Ministers. The 16-member Government, which was subsequently established, comprised six members of the PDA, five of the CDU—BH, and five of the Party for Bosnia and Herzegovina (eight Bosniaks, five Croats and three Serbs).

Directory

The Government

President: NIKO LOZANCIĆ (Croatian Democratic Community).

Vice-Presidents: SAHBAZ DZIKANOVIĆ (Party for Bosnia and Herzegovina), DEZNICA RADIVOJEVIĆ (Party of Democratic Action).

Ministers
(July 2003)

Prime Minister: Dr AHMET HADŽIPAŠIĆ.

Deputy Prime Minister and Minister of Finance: DRAGAN VRANKIĆ.

Deputy Prime Minister and Minister of Culture and Sports: GAVRILO GRAHOVAC.

Minister of Defence: MIROSLAV NIKOLIĆ.

Minister of Internal Affairs: MEVLUDIN HALILOVIĆ.

Minister of Justice: BORJANA KRIŠTO.

Minister of Energy, Mining and Industry: Dr IZET ŽIGIĆ.

Minister of Transport and Communications: NEDŽAC BRANKOVIĆ.

Minister of Labour and Social Policy: RADOVAN VIGNJEVIĆ.

Minister of Displaced Persons and Refugees: EDIN MUŠIĆ.

Minister of Issues of War Veterans and the Disabled: IBRAHIM NADAREVIĆ.

Minister of Health: TOMO LUČIĆ.

Minister of Education and Science: Dr ZIJAD PAŠIĆ.

Minister of Trade: MAID LJUBOVIĆ.

Minister of Urban Planning and the Environment: RAMIZ MEHMEDAGIĆ.

Minister of Agriculture, Water Management and Forestry: MARINKO BOŽIĆ.

Minister of Development, Entrepreneurship and Crafts: MLADEN ČABRILO.

Ministries

Office of the President: 71000 Sarajevo; tel. and fax (33) 472618.

Office of the Prime Minister: 71000 Sarajevo, Alipašina 41; tel. (33) 663649; fax (33) 444718; e-mail ebicakcic@fbihvlada.gov.ba.

Ministry of Agriculture, Water Management and Forestry: 71000 Sarajevo, Hamdije Kresevljakovica 3/III; tel. (33) 443338; fax (33) 663659; e-mail fmpvs@bih.net.ba.

Ministry of Defence: 71000 Sarajevo, Hamdije Kresevljakovica 98; tel. (33) 664926; fax (33) 663785; e-mail cabmod@bih.net.ba.

Ministry of Displaced Persons and Refugees: 71000 Sarajevo, Alipašina 41/II; tel. (33) 663977; e-mail povratak@bih.net.ba.

Ministry of Education and Science: 71000 Sarajevo, Obala Maka Dizdara 2; tel. (33) 663691; fax (33) 664381; e-mail fmonks@bih.net.ba.

Ministry of Energy, Mining and Industry: 71000 Sarajevo, Alipašina 41; tel. (33) 663779; fax (33) 642064; e-mail fmeri-mo@bih.net.ba.

Ministry of Finance: 71000 Sarajevo, Mehmeda Spahe 5; tel. (33) 2034117; fax (33) 203152; e-mail dcovic@fbihvlada.gov.ba; internet www.fmf.gov.ba.

Ministry of Health: 71000 Sarajevo, Titova 9; tel. and fax (33) 664245; e-mail moh@bih.net.ba.

Ministry of Internal Affairs: 71000 Sarajevo, Mehmeda Spahe 7; tel. (33) 667246; fax (33) 472976; internet www.fmup.ba.

Ministry of Issues of War Veterans and the Disabled: 71000 Sarajevo, Alipašina 41; tel. (33) 212932; fax (33) 209333; e-mail fpurisevic@fbihvlada.gov.ba.

Ministry of Justice: 71000 Sarajevo, Valtera Perica 15; tel. and fax (33) 213151; e-mail zeljas@pris.gov.ba.

Ministry of Trade: Mostar, Kneza Domagoja 12; tel. (36) 310148; fax (36) 318684.

Ministry of Transport and Communications: 71000 Sarajevo, Alipašina 41; tel. (33) 668907; fax (33) 667866; internet www.fmpik.gov.ba.

Ministry of Urban Planning and the Environment: 71000 Sarajevo, Maršala Tita 9A; tel. and fax tel. and fax (33) 473124; e-mail fmpuio@fbihvlada.gov.ba.

Legislature

ZASTUPNIÈKI DOM FEDERACIJE
(House of the Representatives of the Federation)
Speaker: SEFIĆ DZAFEROVIĆ.

Election, 5 October 2002

Party	Votes	% of votes	Seats
Party of Democratic Action . . .	234,923	32.7	32
Croatian Democratic Community/Croatian Christian Democratic Union—Bosnia and Herzegovina	113,197	15.8	16
Social Democratic Party of Bosnia and Herzegovina	111,668	15.6	15
Party for Bosnia and Herzegovina	109,843	15.3	15
Bosnian Party	20,188	2.8	3
Pensioners' Party of Bosnia and Herzegovina	16,583	2.3	2
Democratic People's Union . . .	16,363	2.3	2
Economic Bloc HDU-For Progress	14,130	2.0	2
New Croatian Initiative	13,967	2.0	2
Others	67,230	9.2	9
Total	**718,092**	**100.0**	**98**

Local Government

For administrative purposes, The Federation was divided into 10 cantons, each headed by a Župan, or Governor. Each assembly elects a President, who serves a term of two years. The President of each canton nominates a Government and judges to the cantonal courts.

On 13–14 September 1997, following a 12-month delay owing to alleged irregularities in voter registration, cantonal elections were held in the Federation. Further local elections were held on 9 April 2000. Elections to the cantonal assemblies took place on 5 October 2002. The Party of Democratic Action secured the highest number of votes in six of the 10 assemblies, while an alliance led by the Croatian Democratic Union of Bosnia and Herzegovina secured control of the remaining four.

Central Bosnia: Travnik; tel. (30) 711903; Župan NEDŽAD HADŽIĆ; Prime Minister UZEIR MLIVO.

Neretva: Mostar; tel. (36) 551052; Župan DRAGAN VRANKIĆ; Prime Minister MIROSLAV CORIĆ.

Podrinje: Župan SALEM HALILOVIĆ; Prime Minister SALKO OBHODJAS.

Posavina: Orašje; tel. (86) 712160; Župan MIJO MATANOVIĆ; Prime Minister IVO VICENTIĆ.

Sarajevo: Sarajevo, ul. Reisa Džemaludina Čauševića br.1; tel. (33) 663845; fax (33) 471268; e-mail premijer@ks.gov.ba; internet www.ks.gov.ba; Župan VLADO REGUZ; Prime Minister DENIS ZVIZDIĆ.

Tuzla: 75000 Tuzla, Slatina 2; tel. (35) 282291; fax (35) 232978; internet www.vladatk.kim.ba; Župan SELIM BEŠLAGIĆ; Prime Minister BAJAZIT JASAREVIĆ.

Una-Sana: Bihać; tel. (37) 520098; Župan MIRSAD SAHINOVIĆ; Prime Minister ATIF HODZIĆ.

West Bosnia: 80101 Livno, Stjepana II Kotromanića b.b.; tel. and fax (34) 200904; internet www.hbzup.com; Župan DRAGAN BAGARIĆ; Prime Minister ANTE OMAZIĆ.

West Herzegovina: Široki Brijeg; tel. (88) 310060; Župan VINKO ZORIĆ; Prime Minister ANDJELKO MIKULIĆ.

Zenica-Doboj: Zenica, Kučukovići 2; tel. (32) 414165; fax (32) 417019; Župan MUGDIN HERCEG; Prime Minister VAHID HECO.

THE SERB REPUBLIC
(REPUBLIKA SRPSKA)

Introduction

The Serb Republic of Bosnia and Herzegovina occupies the territory along the northern and eastern borders of the Republic of Bosnia and Herzegovina. In the north it borders Croatia and, to the east, Serbia and Montenegro. It comprises 49% of the country, some 25,023 sq km (9,973 sq miles).

On 15 October 1991, against a background of the dissolution of the Socialist Federal Republic of Yugoslavia, the Assembly of Bosnia and Herzegovina declared the sovereignty of Bosnia and Herzegovina. Rightly considering this to be a precursor to a declaration of Bosnian independence, and wishing to remain part of a Serbian-dominated Yugoslavia, the newly formed 'Serb Autonomous Regions' (SARs), of Eastern and Old Herzegovina, Bosanska Krajina, Romanija and Northern Bosnia, declared themselves subject only to the federation. On 24 October Serb deputies in the republican legislature formed a parliament, the 'Assembly of the Serb Nation', based in Pale. This Assembly claimed overwhelming support among the Serb community for remaining in a common Serb state. Following the proclamation of an independent Republic of Bosnia and Herzegovina on 1

March 1992, a 'Serb Republic of Bosnia and Herzegovina' was declared on 27 March. The 'Serb Republic', which comprised Serb-held areas of Bosnia, including the SARs, was led by the head of the Serb Democratic Party of Bosnia and Herzegovina, Dr Radovan Karadžić. It was immediately declared illegal by the President of the State Presidency of the Republic of Bosnia and Herzegovina, Dr Alija Izetbegović, the Bosnian Muslim (Bosniak) leader.

Following more than one year of fighting in Bosnia and Herzegovina, during which time the UN had identified Serb forces as being largely responsible for 'ethnic cleansing' and other atrocities in Muslim- and Croat-dominated areas of the country, a peace plan was proposed by the international community, but was rejected by the Serb Assembly in May 1993.

By 1994 the 'Serb Republic' had become increasingly isolated internationally, following condemnation of their forces' attacks on UN-declared 'safe areas'. Nevertheless, a new peace plan presented in June by the 'Contact Group' of Western countries, which proposed a Serb Republic occupying 49% of Bosnia and Herzegovina, was rejected by the Serbs (who controlled about 70% of the country at this time). In August the Serb Republic's main ally, Serbian President Slobodan Milošević, was forced formally to sever relations with the Bosnian Serbs, in an attempt to secure the lifting of sanctions against the Federal Republic of Yugoslavia (FRY).

Serbia continued clandestinely to aid the Bosnian Serb war effort, however, until mid-1995, when President Milošević withdrew support from the Serb Republic, in protest at its continued refusal to accept the peace plan. This, combined with North Atlantic Treaty Organization (NATO) air attacks, allowed government and Croat forces to recapture territory in September. Having lost so much land the 'Serb Republic' had less to lose by acquiescing to Contact Group negotiations. Represented by delegates from the FRY, the 'Serb Republic' participated in the negotiations in Dayton, Ohio, the USA, which resulted in the signing of the General Framework Agreement for Peace in Bosnia and Herzegovina in December. According to the treaty, the Serb Republic was to constitute one of the two territorial entities comprising Bosnia and Herzegovina, with 49% of the country's area. It was to retain its own executive presidency, government and parliament, known as the National Assembly. It was forced to cede Sarajevo to federal control.

In December 1995 the Serb Republic's legislature elected Rajko Kasagić, a moderate, head of a new Government. The new premier did much to improve relations with the international community. However, in May 1996 the entity President, Karadžić, who was suspected of war crimes, replaced Kasagić with the less compromising Gojko Kličković. Karadžić subsequently promoted a Vice-President, Biljana Plavšić, to deal with most of his presidential tasks. Following international pressure (the Dayton accords prohibited indicted war criminals from holding public office), Karadžić resigned his post in July and Plavšić became acting President. She was confirmed in this post in September, after presidential and legislative elections. Nevertheless, Karadžić continued to wield power unofficially and during 1997 a power struggle developed between the former Bosnian Serb President and the incumbent, following the latter's attempts to reduce corruption among the higher echelons of the Bosnian Serb leadership. In doing so President Plavšić alienated other Serb Democratic Party (SDP) leaders, including Momčilo Krajišnik, Serb member of the Bosnian joint Presidency. Her dismissal of the commander of the Serb armed forces, Gen. Ratko Mladić, also indicted for war crimes, in November 1996 had led to clashes between their supporters. Mladić finally agreed to surrender his position at the end of November.

Although President Plavšić was not a moderate, she increasingly found herself relying on the moderate opponents of the SDP leadership. This support was also important in securing international aid. Assisted by UN troops in the region, Plavšić and her supporters secured control of most of the north-west half of the Serb Republic during 1997. However, at the same time she faced increasing opposition from the Bosnian Serb legislature. Her dismissal of the Minister of Internal Affairs in June was opposed by the Assembly. In the following month, supported by the UN and the Organization for Security and Co-operation in Europe, Plavšić dissolved the legislature and announced that elections would be held at the beginning of September. Her action was denounced by the Prime Minister, Kličković, and several resolutions designed to undermine the President were passed by the National Assembly. In August the legislature voted to disregard future decrees by Plavšić and appointed an alternative interior minister to the President's choice. A constitutional crisis was averted in September, when agreement was reached between the National Assembly and the presidential team for legislative elections to be held in November. It was also agreed that radio and television would be broadcast on alternate days from Pale and Banja Luka. A difference in editorial policy had arisen between the two stations, which supported, respectively, the National Assembly and President Plavšić. In October UN troops seized television transmitters allegedly being used for propaganda purposes by Karadžić's supporters. The action was condemned by SDP leaders, including Krajišnik, who was a member of the station's management board.

Elections to the Bosnian Serb National Assembly were held on 22–23 November 1997. Although the SDP retained the largest number of seats, their majority was reduced. The Coalition for a Single and Democratic Bosnia and Herzegovina obtained 16 seats and the Serb National Alliance (SNA), formed by Plavšić following her expulsion from the SDP in July, won 15 seats, as did the nationalist Serb Radical Party. The SDP were unable to form a government, even with the support of the Serb Radical Party. Following the failure of all-party negotiations to form an interim 'government of national unity', in January 1998 Milorad Dodik, a moderate, was approved by the legislature as Prime Minister. He proceeded to form a coalition Government, which relied on the Bosniak Party of Democratic Action (Coalition for a Single and Democratic Bosnia and Herzegovina) for support. At the end of the month the National Assembly voted in favour of relocating the Serb Republic's capital to Banja Luka, from Pale, where Karadžić continued to be based. This symbolic move, as well as Dodik's pledge to adhere to the Dayton accords, did much to improve the Serb Republic's international standing.

Elections to the Bosnian Serb legislature and presidency were held on 12–13 September 1998. Although Plavšić was expected to retain the presidency, Nikola Poplasen, the candidate of the nationalist Serb Coalition of the Serb Republic (which comprised Poplasen's Serb Radical Party of the Serb Republic—SRP and Karadžić's SDP) obtained the majority of votes in the presidential election. Furthermore, in legislative elections, the SDP became the largest single party in the National Assembly, winning 19 of the 83 seats. The Coalition for a Single and Democratic Bosnia and Herzegovina secured 15 seats, while the moderate SNA failed to consolidate its parliamentary representation, reducing its number of seats from 15 to 12, although the Accord Coalition, of which the SNA was a member, held a total of 32 seats. It was clear that the nationalists retained much support in the Serb Republic, despite clear discouragement from the international community. At his inauguration Poplasen pledged to abide by the terms of the Dayton agreement.

In January 1999, following the continued failure of the National Assembly to agree on a new government, Poplasen nominated Branje Miljus, a member of the Party of Independent Social Democrats, as Prime Minister. His nomination was rejected by the legislature, however, which supported the incumbent premier, Dodik, leader of the Party of Independent Social Democrats. Miljus was expelled from the party and subsequently formed the breakaway Party of Independent Social Democrats of the Serb Republic. In March Poplasen proposed a motion in the legislature in an attempt to instigate the dismissal of Dodik. As a result, the High Representative of the International Community in Bosnia and Herzegovina, Carlos Westendorp, announced Poplasen's removal from office, on the grounds that he had exceeded his authority. Although the National Assembly initially opposed Westendorp's decision, it subsequently withdrew its opposition, and Vice-President Mirko Sarović temporarily assumed the presidential office. However, in early February 2000 Sarović returned to his vice-presidential duties, once it became clear that he did not have the approval of the Office of the High Representative. In the same month it was announced that the post of President of the Serb Republic of Bosnia and Herzegovina would remain vacant until the next elections, scheduled to be held in November 2000. In October 1999 the High Representative again intervened in the Serb Republic politics, when Westendorp's successor, Wolfgang Petritsch, prohibited Poplasen and two other SRP officials from standing as candidates in the forthcoming local elections, on the grounds that they had obstructed the implementation of the Dayton accords.

In February 2000 the Socialist Party of the Bosnian Serb Republic (SPRS), led by Zivko Radišić, withdrew from the ruling Accord Coalition, following disagreement over Prime Minister

Dodik's policies. Despite efforts by colleagues to convince SPRS ministers to remain in the coalition, all but four ministers resigned their government positions. The four who remained were expelled from the party and, following Dodik's refusal to reinstate the dismissed SPRS deputy premier, Tihomir Gligorić, they too resigned from the Government. In the following month the former SPRS member, Nebojsa Radmanović, established the breakaway Democratic Socialist Party (DSP). By mid-April one-third of the municipal board of the SPRS had joined the DSP, which was based in Banja Luka. In May the DSP joined the Accord Coalition.

In May 2000 most of the leadership of the SNA, including Plavšić, tendered their resignations, following disagreements with the party's main committee. In early June Plavšić was replaced by Dragan Kostić. She immediately declared her intention to establish a breakaway faction. However, Kostić's election was later declared invalid and he and his supporters established their own party, the Democratic National Alliance. A new main committee of the SNA was elected in mid-June. Plavšić remained party leader.

In July 2000 Dodik announced his candidacy in the election to the Serb Republic presidency, scheduled to take place in November. In September the National Assembly of the Serb Republic adopted a motion, proposed by the SDP, expressing 'no confidence' in Dodik's administration. However, the Government submitted a legal challenge at the entity's Constitutional Court and announced that it would remain in office, pending the forthcoming legislative elections. Elections to the Serb Republic presidency and legislature took place on 11 November. The SDP secured 31 of the 83 seats in the National Assembly, while the SPRS and the Party of Democratic Progress of the Serb Republic (PDP) each received 11 seats. Mirko Sarović, the SDP candidate who had reportedly received the support of Karadžić, was elected with some 49.8% of votes cast to the presidency, defeating Dodik. The SDP subsequently announced that it was to establish a parliamentary coalition with the PDP, the SPRS and the Party of Democratic Action, thereby securing a majority in the National Assembly. In December Sarović designated Mladen Ivanić, a member of the PDP, as Prime Minister of the Serb Republic. In January 2001 Ivanić formed the Republic's first multi-ethnic Council of Ministers. However, the inclusion in the Council of Ministers of several SDP representatives proved controversial, following warnings by the US Government that it might suspend financial aid to the Serb Republic if the SDP entered the Government. Ivanić subsequently requested that government members suspend party activities, and replaced the newly-appointed Minister of Trade and Tourism (a prominent SDP member), in an attempt to address international concerns over SDP representation in the Government.

In January 2001 Plavšić surrendered to the ICTY, following her indictment in April 2000. She subsequently pleaded not guilty to charges that she, and other Serb officials, had planned a campaign of genocide and deportation against the Muslim and Croat inhabitants of Bosnia and Herzegovina from July 1991 to December 1992. In July 2001 the Serb Republic Government adopted draft legislation, providing for full co-operation with the ICTY. (The new legislation, which required the Serb Republic security forces actively to pursue and extradite war crimes suspects, was finally adopted by the National Assembly in early October.) At the beginning of August a former officer in the Serb security forces was sentenced to 10 years' imprisonment by the ICTY, after pleading guilty to participation in the killing and torture of Muslims and Croats in 1992–93. On 2 August 2001 a former senior Serb army officer, Radislav Krstić, received a term of imprisonment of 46 years for his involvement in the massacre at Srebreniča in 1995. Although the Tribunal succeeded in gaining a conviction on charges of genocide for the first time, the sentence was criticized as inadequate by relatives of those killed. In the same month three former Muslim army officers, who had been secretly indicted for crimes committed against Croats in central Bosnia in 1993, were arrested and extradited to the ICTY. At the end of August 2001 the ICTY provisionally released Plavšić (who was then the only woman in detention at the Hague), pending her trial. In early 2002 repeated attempts by SFOR troops to locate and arrest Karadžić proved unsuccessful. In March the SDP formally removed Karadžić from the leadership of the party, replacing him with Dragan Kalinić.

In June 2002 the Serb Republic Minister of Finance, Milenko Vracar, tendered his resignation, following pressure from the new High Representative, Sir Jeremy John Durham (Paddy) Ashdown, who had criticized malpractice in the customs agencies of both entities. In July the Minister of Defence, Slobodan Bilić, was obliged to resign from the Government, following his defection from the SPRS to the People's Party of the Serb Republic. Presidential and legislative elections were conducted in the Serb Republic on 5 October. The leader of the SDP, Dragan Čavić, secured the presidency, with 40.1% of the votes cast. The SDP also won the highest number of seats (26) in the 83-member National Assembly, while the Party of Independent Social Democrats obtained 19 seats. Cavić was inaugurated as President of the Serb Republic on 28 November. On 7 December Cavić nominated Dragan Mikerević of the PDP, hitherto the national Prime Minister and Minister of European Integration, as Prime Minister. The National Assembly approved Mikerević's nomination as Prime Minister, and a new Government for the entity, which (under constitutional amendments, adopted in April, to ensure equal rights for the three ethnic communities) comprised eight Serbian, five Bosniak and three Croatian representatives. At the end of October both the Serb Republic Minister of Defence and the Chief of the General Staff of the Army resigned, after it emerged that a state-owned aviation company had exported military equipment to Iraq, in contravention of a UN armaments embargo.

In mid-February 2003 the newly appointed Serb Republic Minister of Finance resigned his portfolio, following allegations of malpractice against him. Later in February Ashdown dismissed the management of the entity's electricity company, which had suffered substantial losses, owing, in part, to corrupt practices. On 2 April Mirko Sarović (who on 5 October 2002 had been elected as the Serb member of the collective presidency), tendered his resignation, after being implicated in the illicit exports to Iraq and alleged espionage activities by the Serb Republic military. Ashdown removed all references of statehood from the entity's Constitution, and abolished the Serb Republic Supreme Military Council. Borislav Paravac, also a member of the SDP, was nominated by the national legislature to replace Sarović.

On 27 February 2003 Biljana Plavšić, who had previously agreed to plead guilty at the ICTY to one charge of crimes against humanity, was sentenced to 11 years' imprisonment. (In June it was announced that, at the request of the ICTY, Plavšić was to be transferred to a Swedish prison.) Meanwhile, Ashdown criticized the continued failure of efforts by SFOR troops to locate and arrest Gen. Ratko Mladić and Karadžić. In early July Ashdown announced that the Office of the High Representative had frozen the bank accounts of 14 Bosnian Serbs who were suspected of supporting war crime suspects, including the relatives of Karadžić.

Directory

The Government

President: Dragan Čavić (Serbian Democratic Party).
Vice-President: Adil Osmanović (Party of Democratic Action).
Vice-President: Ivan Tomljenović (Serbian Democratic Party).

Ministers
(July 2003)

Prime Minister: Dragan Mikerević.

Minister of the Interior: Dzoran Djerić.

Minister of Justice: Saud Filipović.

Minister of Education and Culture: Dr Gojko Savanović.

Minister of Finance: Simeun Vilendecić.

Minister of Defence: Milovan Stanković.

Minister of Administration and Local Government: Slaven Pekić.

Minister of Science and Technology: Dr Dzemal Konolić.

Minister of Health and Social Welfare: Dr Marin Kvaternik.

Minister of the Economy, Energy and Development: Milan Bogicević.

Minister of Agriculture, Water Resources and Forestry: Rodoljub Trkulja.

Minister of Transport and Communications: Dragan Solaja.

Minister of Trade and Tourism: Boris Gaspar.

Minister of Urban Planning, Housing and the Environment: Mensur Sehagić.

Minister of War Veterans and Labour Affairs: Mico Micić.

Minister of Foreign Economic Relations and Co-ordination: Omer Branković.

Minister of Refugees and Displaced Persons: Jasmin Samardzić.

Ministries

Office of the Prime Minister: 78000 Banja Luka; tel. (51) 331333; fax (51) 331332; e-mail kabinet@vladars.net.

Ministry of Administration and Local Government: 51000 Banja Luka, Vuka Karadžica 4; tel. (51) 331680; fax (51) 331681; e-mail muls@muls.vladars.net.

Ministry of Agriculture, Water Resources and Forestry: 76300 Bijelina, Milosa Obilica 51; tel. (55) 471412; fax (55) 472353; e-mail mps@mps.vladars.net.

Ministry of Defence: 51000 Banja Luka, Bana Lazarevica; tel. (51) 218823; fax (51) 300243; e-mail mo@mo.vladars.net.

Ministry of the Economy, Energy and Mining: 51000 Banja Luka, Vuka Karadžica; tel. (51) 331710; fax (51) 331702; e-mail mer@mer.vladars.net.

Ministry of Education and Culture: 51000 Banja Luka, Vuka Karadžica 4; tel. (51) 331422; fax (51) 331423; e-mail mp@mp.vladars.net.

Ministry of Finance: 51000 Banja Luka, Vuka Karadžica 4; tel. (51) 331350; fax (51) 331351; e-mail mf@mf.vladars.net.

Ministry of Foreign Economic Relations: 51000 Banja Luka, Vuka Karadžica 4; tel. (51) 331430; fax (51) 331436; e-mail e-mail meoi@meoi.vladars.net; internet www.vladars.net.

Ministry of Health and Social Welfare: 51000 Banja Luka, Zdrave Korde 8; tel. (51) 331600; fax (51) 331601; e-mail mzsz@mzsz.vladars.net.

Ministry of the Interior: 78000 Banja Luka, Jug Bogdana 108; tel. (51) 331100; e-mail mup@mup.vladars.net.

Ministry of Justice: 51000 Banja Luka, Vuka Karadžica 4; tel. (51) 331582; fax (51) 331593; e-mail mpr@mpr.vladars.net.

Ministry of Refugees and Displaced Persons: 51000 Banja Luka, Vuka Karadžica 4; tel. (51) 331470; fax (51) 331471; e-mail mirl@mirl.vladars.net.

Ministry of Science and Technology: 51000 Banja Luka, Vuka Karadžica 4; tel. (51) 331542; fax (51) 331548; e-mail mnk@mnk.vladars.net.

Ministry of Trade and Tourism: 51000 Banja Luka, Vuka Karadžica 4; tel. (51) 331523; fax (51) 331499; e-mail mtt@mtt.vladars.net.

Ministry of Transport and Communications: 51000 Banja Luka, Vuka Karadžica 4; tel. (51) 331611; fax (51) 331612; e-mail msv@msv.vladars.net.

Ministry of Urban Planning, Housing and the Environment: 51000 Banja Luka, trg Srpskih Junaka 4; tel. (51) 215511; fax (51) 215548; e-mail mgr@mgr.vladars.net.

Ministry of War Veterans and Labour Affairs: 51000 Banja Luka, Vuka Karadžica 4; tel. (51) 331651; fax (51) 331652; e-mail mpb@mpb.vladars.net.

PRESIDENCY OF THE SERB REPUBLIC (REPUBLIKA SRPSKA)

Election, 5 October 2002

Candidate	Votes	% of votes
Dragan Čavić (Serbian Democratic Party) .	183,121	35.9
Milan Jelić (Party of Independent Social Democrats)	112,612	22.1
Dragan Mikerivić (Party of Democratic Progress of the Serb Republic) . . .	39,978	7.8
Adil Osmanović (Party of Democratic Action)	34,129	6.7
Petar Cokić (Socialist Party of the Serb Republic)	27,137	5.3
Others	113,286	22.2
Total	510,263	100.0

NARODNA SKUPŠTINA REPUBLIKA SRPSKA
(National Assembly of the Serb Republic)

Speaker: Dragan Kalinić.

Election, 5 October 2002

Party	Votes	% of votes	Seats*
Serbian Democratic Party of Bosnia and Herzegovina	159,164	31.2	26
Party of Independent Social Democrats.	111,226	21.8	19
Party of Democratic Progress of the Serb Republic	54,756	10.7	9
Party of Democratic Action . .	36,212	7.1	6
Serbian Radical Party of the Serb Republic	22,396	4.4	4
Socialist Party of the Serb Republic	21,502	4.2	3
Democratic People's League	29,375	4.0	3
Party for Bosnia and Herzegovina	18,624	3.7	4
Social Democratic Party of Bosnia and Herzegovina	17,227	3.4	3
Others	39,895	6.5	6
Total	510,377	100.0	83

* About three-quarters of deputies are elected in multi-seat constituencies, with the remainder selected through compensatory lists.

Local Government

The Serb Republic was divided into 61 municipalities. At local elections, which took place on 8 April 2000, the Serb Democratic Party won control of most of the municipalities in the Serb Republic. Each municipality elects a Governing Council for a period of two years, and judges to the municipal courts. Municipal elections were scheduled to take place in October 2004.

Bibliography

Andjelić, N. *Bosnia-Herzegovina: the End of a Legacy.* London, Frank Cass, 2003.

Andrić, I. *The Bridge over the Drina.* London, Harvill, 1994.

Bell, M. *In Harm's Way: Reflections of a War-Zone Thug,* 2nd Edn. London, Penguin, 1996.

Black, E., and Bell-Fialkoff, A. *Bosnia: Fractured Region (World in Conflict).* Minneapolis, MN, Lerner Publications, 2003.

Bose, S. *Bosnia after Dayton.* London, C. Hurst, 2002.

Burg, S. L. and Shoup, P. S. *The War in Bosnia-Herzegovina: Ethnic Conflict and International Intervention.* Armank, NY, M. E. Sharpe, 2000.

Campbell, D. *National Deconstruction: Violence, Identity and Justice in Bosnia.* Minneapolis, University of Minnesota Press, MN, 1998.

Cigar, N. *Genocide in Bosnia.* College Station, TX, Texas A & M University Press, 1995.

Cothran, H. *War-Torn Bosnia (History Firsthand).* Westport, CT, Greenhaven Press, 2002.

Daalder, I. H. *Getting to Dayton: The Making of America's Bosnia Policy.* Washington, DC, Brookings Institution Press, 2000.

The Dayton Peace Accords: General Framework Agreement for Peace in Bosnia and Herzegovina. Washington, DC, US Department of State (Office of Public Communications, Bureau of Public Affairs), 1995.

Donia, R., and Fine, J. V. A., Jr. *Bosnia and Hercegovina: A Tradition Betrayed.* New York, NY, Columbia University Press, 1994.

Fratkin, L., and Gjelten, T. *Sarajevo Self-Portrait: The View from Inside.* New York, NY, Umbrage Editions, 2000.

Friedman, F. *The Bosnian Muslims.* Boulder, CO, Westview Press, 1996.

Bosnia: a Polity on the Brink (Postcommunist States and Nations). London, Routledge, 2002.

Gjelten, T. *Sarajevo Daily.* New York, NY, HarperCollins, 1995.

Glenny, M. *The Fall of Yugoslavia.* 3rd edn. London, Penguin, 1996.

Izetbegović, A. *Izetbegović of Bosnia and Herzegovina: Notes from Prison, 1983–1988*. Westport, CT, Praeger, 2002.

Lovrenović, I. *Bosnia: A Cultural History*. New York, NY, New York University Press, 2001.

Magas, B. and Zanić, I. (Eds). *The War in Croatia and Bosnia-Herzegovina 1991–95*. London, Bosnian Institute, 2001.

Mahmutcehajić, R. *The Denial of Bosnia (Post-Communist Cultural Studies)*. University Park, PA, Pennsylvania State University Press, 2000.

   Sarajevo Essays: Politics, Ideology and Tradition. New York, NY, New York University Press, 2003.

Malcolm, N. *Bosnia: A Short History*. London, Macmillan, 1994.

Mazower, M. *The War in Bosnia: An Analysis*. London, Action for Bosnia, 1992.

Moody, C. J. *Cast Down the Waters: A Bosnia in Flames*. Eastman, GA, GoldenIsle Publishers, 2000.

Noel, M. *Bosnia*. London, Pan Macmillan, 2002.

O'Ballance, E. *Civil War in Bosnia, 1992–94*. London, Macmillan, 1995.

O'Shea, B. *Crisis at Bihac- Bosnia's Bloody Battlefield*. Gloucestershire, Sutton Publishing Ltd, 1998.

Rakić, S. *Serbian Icons from Bosnia-Herzegovina*. New York, NY, A. Pankovich Publishers, 2000.

Rieff, D. *Slaughterhouse: Bosnia and the Failure of the West*. New York, NY, Simon and Schuster, 1995.

Rohde, D. *Endgame: The Betrayal and Fall of Srebrenica, Europe's Worst Massacre since World War II*. Boulder, CO, Westview Press, 1998.

Sells, M. *The Bridge Betrayed: Religion and Genocide in Bosnia (Comparative Studies in Religion and Society, Vol. 11)*. Berkeley, CA, University of California Press, 1996.

Shatzmiller, M. (Ed.). *Islam and Bosnia: Conflict Resolution and Foreign Policy in Multi-Ethnic States*. Montréal, QC, McGill-Queens University Press, 2002.

Sobel, R. *International Public Opinion and the Bosnia Crisis*. Lanham, MD, Lexington Books, 2003.

Sudetić, C. *Blood and Vengeance: One Family's Story of the War in Bosnia*. New York, NY, Penguin, 1999.

Tanović-Miller, N. *Testimony of a Bosnian (Eastern European Series, 14)*. College Station, TX, Texas A & M University Press, 2001.

Tvrtković, P. *Bosnia-Hercegovina: Back to the Future*. London, Paul Tvrtković, 1993.

Wentz, L. (Ed.) *Lessons from Bosnia: the IFOR Experience*. Portland, OR, University Press of the Pacific, 2002.

Wiebes, C. *Intelligence and the War in Bosnia 1992–1995*. London, Lit Verlag, 2003.

Woolf, A. *Assassination in Sarajevo (Days that Shook the World)*. London, Hodder & Stoughton, 2002.

BULGARIA

Geography

PHYSICAL FEATURES

The Republic of Bulgaria lies in South-Eastern Europe, on the east of the Balkan Peninsula. The country is bordered by Romania to the north, by Serbia to the north-west and by the former Yugoslav republic of Macedonia (FYRM) to the south-west, by Greece to the south and by Turkey to the south-east. The country has an eastern coastline along the Black Sea. Its total area is 110,994 sq km (42,855 sq miles).

Central Bulgaria is traversed from west to east by the Balkan Mountains (Stara Planina), which separate the Danubian plains in the north from the Thracian plains of Eastern Rumelia in the south-east. The Rhodope Mountains (Rhodopi Planina) occupy south-west Bulgaria and form the borders with Greece and the FYRM. The mountain of Musala (Riladağ, in Turkish, and also once known as Stalin Peak) is located in this range, to the south of Sofia, and is Bulgaria's highest point, rising to 2,925 m (9,596 ft). The Sofia depression, in the west of the country, is hill country, separating the Balkan Mountains from the southern mountains. This area is the main centre of population and communications. The general elevation slopes down from the west towards the Black Sea, and some two-thirds of Bulgaria is less than 500 m above sea level. The River Danube (Dunav) forms most of the length of Bulgaria's northern border, with the exception of the area between the town of Silistra (where the Danube flows northwards) and the Black Sea (that is, as far east as the Dobrudzha). The fertile Bulgarian plateau, between the Danubian border and the Balkan Mountains, averages some 100 km in width and is traversed by several tributaries of the Danube, the major one being the Iskur. The main rivers running south of the Balkan watershed are the Struma and the Maritza, which flow into the Aegean Sea (part of the Mediterranean Sea). The broad Maritza valley, which leads on to the Thracian plains, is one of the principal agricultural areas of the country.

CLIMATE

The climate is continental, with hot summers and cold winters. In the south the climate is moderated by the influence of the Mediterranean Sea, with both warmer and wetter winters. Winters on the Black Sea coast are also slightly milder, although north-easterly winds can bring very cold weather. The mean temperatures in Sofia range between 21°C (69°F) in July and –2°C (28°F) in January. Varna, on the Black Sea, has comparative mean temperatures ranging between 23°C (74°F) and 1°C (34°F). The mean annual rainfall in Sofia is 635 mm (25 in) and in Varna 485 mm (19 in).

POPULATION

The Bulgars are a Finno-Ugrian people, whose ancestors crossed the Danube in the seventh century AD and merged with the Slavonic population. In 2001, according to the official census results, 83.5% of the total population were ethnic Bulgarians, 9.5% ethnic Turks and 4.6% Gypsies (Roma). There were also small communities of Macedonians, Karakachani (Vlahs or Vlachs—who speak a language related to Romanian), Albanians, Sarakatsani (a Greek people), Armenians, Russians and other nationalities. Bulgarian, the official language, is one of the Southern Slavonic tongues, closely related to Serbo-Croat and also to Russian, and is written in the Cyrillic alphabet. Minority languages include Turkish, Macedonian (a Slavonic dialect) and Romany. Most of the population are Christian and adhere to the Bulgarian Orthodox Church (some 80%), although there are small communities of Roman Catholics (including Uniates), Armenian Orthodox and Protestants. Of the 9% of the population who are estimated to profess Islam, most are ethnic Turks, although some are ethnic Bulgarians, known as Pomaks, who account for some 3% of the population. Most of the Roma are Muslim. There is also a small Jewish community.

The total population of the country, according to official estimates, was 7,845,499 at 31 December 2002, with a population density of 70.7 per sq km. Sofia, the capital, which is located in the central western part of Bulgaria, is the largest city, with a population of 1,096,389 at the 2001 census. Other important cities include Plovdiv (340,638), in central Bulgaria, and Varna (314,539) on the Black Sea coast.

Chronology

865: The Khan of the Bulgars, Boris (852–89), converted to Eastern Orthodox Christianity, following the missionary activity of the Eastern Roman ('Byzantine') brothers, SS Constantine (Cyril) and Methodius, 'the Apostles of the Slavs'.

893–927: Reign of Simeon, first Tsar (Caesar) of the Bulgars, who failed in his ambition to take Constantinople (İstanbul, now in Turkey) and the Byzantine throne, but established a powerful empire and instituted the Bulgarian Church as the first new autocephalous Orthodox church.

971: Annexation of eastern Bulgaria as a Byzantine province.

1014: The Bulgar ruler, Samuel, was defeated at the battle of Balathista by the Emperor Basil II ('the Slayer of the Bulgars'), who subsequently designated western Bulgaria a Byzantine province.

1187: Following a decline in Byzantine power the Emperor in Constantinople recognized the establishment of the second Bulgarian Empire, under the Asen dynasty.

1330: The Bulgars were defeated by Serbian forces at the battle of Küstendil (Velbuzhde).

1396: Bulgaria became a province of the Turkish Ottoman Empire.

1870: Establishment of an autocephalous Exarchate of the Bulgarian Orthodox Church (not recognized by Constantinople until 1945).

1876: Violent suppression of Bulgarian uprisings by the Ottomans.

1877: Russia declared war on the Turks in support of the Orthodox, Slav subjects of the Ottoman Empire.

1878: The Ottomans recognized an autonomous principality of Bulgaria, at the Congress of Berlin; Eastern Rumelia and Macedonia remained under Turkish rule.

1879: The First Grand National Assembly of Bulgaria, meeting in the town of Turnovo (now Veliko, 'Grand', Turnovo), adopted a liberal constitution (the 'Turnovo Constitution') and invited the nephew of the Russian tsarina, Alexander (Aleksandur) von Battenburg, of the House of Hesse-Darmstadt, to become the ruling prince.

1885: Eastern Rumelia was annexed by Bulgaria. Serbian forces were defeated at the battle of Slivnitsa.

1887: Election of Ferdinand of Saxe-Coburg as Prince of Bulgaria, following the abdication of Aleksandur.

2 August 1903: Bulgarians in Pirin Macedonia took part in the Ilinden uprising—a revolt against the Ottoman authorities organized by the Internal Macedonian Revolutionary Organization (IMRO). The revolt was suppressed.

October 1908: Upheavals in the Ottoman Empire included the proclamation of Tsar (King) Ferdinand I of an independent Bulgarian kingdom.

August 1913: The Peace of Bucharest concluded the Second Balkan War: Bulgaria lost Macedonia and the Dobrudzha.

12 October 1915: Bulgaria declared war on Serbia, thus entering the First World War on the side of the Central Powers of Germany, Austria-Hungary and the Turkish Empire, under the Osmanlı (Ottoman) dynasty.

29 September 1918: Bulgaria surrendered unconditionally to the Entente Powers, with the consequent abdication of Ferdinand I and the accession of Boris III.

29 November 1919: The Treaty of Neuilly was signed: Bulgaria was forced to cede its Thracian territories and Mediterranean coast to Greece; it also ceded territory on its western frontier to Yugoslavia (then known as the Kingdom of Serbs, Croats and Slovenes); and returned the Dobrudzha (which it had regained by the Peace of Bucharest of May 1918) to Romania.

1923: A *putsch* by army officers resulted in the suppression of the Peasants Party and the Communist Party.

19 May 1934: A coup by two nationalist organizations, Zveno and the Association of the Officers of the Reserve, led to the establishment of the authoritarian regime of Col Kimon Georghiev.

January 1935: Col Georghiev resigned; authoritarian rule was continued by Boris III.

30 August 1940: The second Arbitration Award of Vienna restored Southern Dobrudzha to Bulgaria (confirmed in 1947).

1 March 1941: Bulgaria signed a pact with the Axis Powers of Germany and Italy and, following the commencement of war in the Balkans, gained western Macedonia from Yugoslavia.

August 1943: Death of Boris III; a regency was established for the young Tsar, Simeon II.

5 September 1944: The USSR declared war on Bulgaria.

8 September 1944: Bulgaria declared war on Germany.

9 September 1944: Following a coup by the Fatherland Front, a left-wing alliance dominated by the Bulgarian Communist Party (BCP), the Soviet army occupied Bulgaria.

28 October 1944: An armistice was signed with the Allies.

August 1945: The Agrarian and Social Democratic Parties left the Front and the Government.

15 September 1946: Tsar Simeon II was formally deposed and a Republic was declared, following a referendum.

November 1946: Georgi Dimitrov, First Secretary of the BCP, became Chairman of the Council of Ministers (Prime Minister).

22 February 1947: A peace treaty was signed with the Allies.

December 1947: A new Constitution abolished all opposition parties and established a system based on the Soviet model. Bulgaria became a People's Republic.

March 1949: Dimitrov was replaced as Chairman of the Council of Ministers by Vasil Kolarov.

July 1949: Vulko Chervenkov became leader of the BCP, following Dimitrov's death, and Chairman of the Council of Ministers from February 1950.

March 1954: Todor Zhivkov became leader of the BCP.

April 1956: Anton Yugov replaced Chervenkov as Chairman of the Council of Ministers.

November 1962: Zhivkov replaced Yugov as Chairman of the Council of Ministers.

1965: An army coup attempt was discovered and suppressed, enabling Zhivkov to consolidate his position.

16 May 1971: A new Constitution was adopted, following a referendum; the Constitution established the Council of State as the supreme executive and legislative body. Zhivkov relinquished his former government posts to become President of the Council of State (head of state) and was succeeded as Prime Minister by Stanko Todorov.

June 1981: Following elections to the National Assembly, Grisha Filipov became Chairman of the Council of Ministers.

December 1985: On the occasion of a national census the Government was accused of trying forcibly to assimilate the ethnic Turkish population ('Bulgarian Muslims'), through a 'regenerative programme'.

20 March 1986: Filipov was replaced as Prime Minister by Georgi Atanasov.

July 1987: Zhivkov promised liberalization and pluralism in government in his so-called 'July Concept'.

March 1988: Candidates other than those nominated by the BCP were permitted to stand in local elections, although in July a number of prominent proponents of reform were dismissed from office.

22 August 1989: The Turkish Government closed the border with Bulgaria, some 310,000 refugees having fled the programme of assimilation and the violent suppression of protests.

10 November 1989: Zhivkov was forced to resign his post as General Secretary of the BCP, following demonstrations against him, and was replaced by the Minister of Foreign Affairs, Petar Mladenov. One week later Mladenov was elected by the National Assembly to succeed Zhivkov as President of the Council of State. The Government announced the dissolution of the secret police.

December 1989: Following a strike by Podkrepa (Support), the independent trade union movement, the Government agreed to begin negotiations about 'round-table' meetings between the BCP, the Bulgarian Agrarian People's Union (BAPU) and the Union of Democratic Forces (UDF—a recently established alliance of opposition groups). The Government approved measures to end discrimination against the Muslim minority.

January 1990: The National Assembly revoked the leading role of the BCP.

February 1990: Aleksandur Lilov replaced Mladenov as head of the Supreme Council of the BCP. Atanasov resigned as Prime Minister and was replaced by Andrei Lukanov, who headed a Government comprising only members of the BCP. Later, the official trade union congress completed its renunciation of any party or state affiliations and changed its name to the Confederation of Independent Trade Unions in Bulgaria (CITUB).

3 April 1990: Mladenov was elected to the new post of President of the country by the National Assembly. The BCP changed its name to the Bulgarian Socialist Party (BSP).

17 June 1990: The second round of voting in elections to a constituent Grand National Assembly (GNA) took place, amid widespread allegations of electoral irregularities. However, the BSP received 211 seats out of a total of 400, the UDF 144 and the Muslim Movement for Rights and Freedoms (MRF) won 23.

July 1990: Mladenov announced his resignation as President, following a series of protests and strikes. The GNA convened in Veliko Turnovo, but the BSP soon lost its majority as the reformist Alternative Socialist Party faction left the party (joining the UDF in October).

1 August 1990: Zheliu Zhelev, hitherto leader of the UDF, was eventually elected President of the country by the GNA. President Zhelev proposed that Lukanov form a new Government, although the UDF refused to join a coalition with the BSP.

September 1990: Bulgaria was elected to membership of the IMF.

November 1990: Despite some reforms, including renaming the country the Republic of Bulgaria, there were increasing protests at the lack of progress in the GNA on a new constitution. A general strike prompted the resignation of Lukanov once there was agreement on a multi-party administration under a non-party premier (later decided to be Dimitur Popov).

14 December 1990: The major political groups signed the Agreement Guaranteeing the Peaceful Transition to a Democratic Society, which committed support to the Popov Government, the drafting of a new constitution, the introduction of a market economy and general elections to be held in 1991.

May 1991: A group of 39 UDF deputies withdrew from the GNA session, protesting at its delays (lack of progress on constitutional issues had provoked violent demonstrations in March); this boycott was resolved, but marked the beginning of a split in the UDF and its constituent parties.

12 July 1991: The GNA finally ratified the Constitution, which was signed by 309 of the 400 deputies and came into effect on 13 July.

13 October 1991: Despite internal divisions, in the elections to the National Assembly the UDF emerged as the largest party, obtaining 110 seats. The UDF nominated the leader of the Green Party, Filip Dimitrov, as Prime Minister.

19 January 1992: Zheliu Zhelev won the presidential election with 53% of the votes cast, having been forced into a second round of voting by the BSP-backed candidate, Vulko Vulkanov.

30 August 1992: President Zhelev, speaking on television, strongly criticized Dimitrov and his cabinet.

December 1992: Lyuben Berov was eventually nominated for the post of Prime Minister (Dimitrov had lost a vote of censure in October) by the MRF; he was subsequently elected by the National Assembly to head a cabinet largely without party affiliation (with the parliamentary support of the MRF, the BSP and a faction of the UDF). Berov resigned in September 1994, after failing to negotiate a reduction in Bulgaria's foreign debt.

October 1994: The BSP and the UDF refused to form a government, so President Zhelev dissolved parliament and appointed Reneta Indzhova to head an interim Government.

18 December 1994: In the general election the BSP, led by Zhan Videnov, secured an outright majority in the National Assembly, receiving 52.1% of the votes cast. Videnov was appointed Prime Minister of a new Government at the end of January 1995.

1 February 1995: A 'Europe Agreement' between Bulgaria and the European Union (EU) came into force; the following year Bulgaria officially applied for membership.

May 1996: Escalating problems in the banking sector and a steadily deteriorating currency culminated in a financial crisis, with a massive withdrawal of funds and a series of measures that failed to improve government finances or to halt the devaluation of the lev.

2 June 1996: In US-style primary elections for a presidential candidate for a united opposition, President Zhelev was defeated by Petar Stoyanov of the UDF, who obtained 66% of the votes.

2 October 1996: The former Prime Minister, Andrei Lukanov (who had remained an influential member of the BSP and critic of the Videnov regime), was assassinated.

3 November 1996: In the second round of voting in the presidential election, Stoyanov was elected to the presidency, with 59.7% of the votes cast.

December 1996: Following increasing dissatisfaction within his own party and demonstrations by the UDF, Videnov offered his resignation as Prime Minister and party leader.

January 1997: The BSP designated the Minister of the Interior, Nikolai Dobrev, as Prime Minister, but, following an increase in demonstrations by the UDF, President Zhelev revoked Dobrev's mandate. On 19 January Stoyanov was inaugurated as President, and he again invited the BSP to form an administration.

February 1997: The UDF rejected the proposed Government under Dobrev; amid fears of civil conflict, Dobrev resigned and President Stoyanov nominated the Mayor of Sofia, Stefan Sofianski, as Prime Minister; he formed an interim Council of Ministers and the National Assembly was dissolved on 19 February.

March 1997: The interim Government announced that the former Prime Minister, Videnov, and other members of his regime were to be charged with criminal negligence, over the severe economic hardship that resulted from his policies.

19 April 1997: In elections to the National Assembly the UDF secured 52.6% of the votes cast and 137 seats, while the BSP, which contested the elections in the Democratic Left alliance, obtained 22.1% of the votes and 58 seats; the Alliance for National Salvation, a coalition dominated by the MRF, won 19 seats; the newly established Euro-Left obtained 14 seats; and the Bulgarian Business Bloc (BBB) secured 12 seats.

8 May 1997: A formal political consensus was adopted by the National Assembly, on economic reform, on the restoration of agricultural land to its rightful, pre-communist ownership and on entry to the EU and to the North Atlantic Treaty Organization (NATO).

21 May 1997: The National Assembly elected Ivan Kostov of the UDF as Prime Minister.

1 July 1997: As stipulated by the IMF, a currency board was introduced to halt the continuing economic decline.

December 1998: Following the Constitutional Court's ruling that the communist confiscation of property was illegal, former Tsar Simeon II—Simeon Saxe-Coburg Gotha (Saxe-Coburgotski) returned to Bulgaria from his home in Spain, after 52 years in exile.

5 May 1999: Despite public opposition, which had increased after a misdirected missile damaged a suburb of Sofia in the previous month, the legislature approved the Government's decision to grant NATO use of its airspace in its bombardment against the Federal Republic of Yugoslavia, in return for security guarantees.

5 July 1999: The lev was redenominated, in order to ease the worsening financial situation, one new lev being equal to 1,000 old leva.

16 and 23 October 1999: In municipal elections the UDF won the largest number of votes cast (31.3%), narrowly defeating the BSP, which obtained 29.4% of the ballot.

28 March 2000: Negotiations for Bulgaria's entry into the EU opened in Brussels, Belgium.

28 April 2001: The Supreme Court of Appeal upheld a ruling of the City Court of Sofia that the National Movement, founded on 6 April, could not legally register to participate in the forthcoming legislative election as its leader, Simeon Saxe-Coburg Gotha, did not fulfil all the requisite eligibility criteria. The National Movement subsequently announced the formation of an alliance with two smaller, registered parties, forming the National Movement Simeon II (NMSII), led by Vesela Draganova, in order to take part in the election.

17 June 2001: In the general election a decisive victory was won by the NMSII, with 42.7% of the votes cast and 120 of the 240 seats in the National Assembly, while the incumbent UDF obtained 18.2% of the votes and the Coalition for Bulgaria (an alliance dominated by the BSP) secured 17.1%. The only other party to receive the 4% of votes required for representation in parliament was the Movement for Rights and Freedoms (MRF), with 7.5%.

24 July 2001: Saxe-Coburg Gotha was sworn in as Prime Minister of a coalition Government comprising the NMSII, the MRF and the BSP.

18 November 2001: In the second round of voting in the presidential election, contested by Georgi Parvanov and Stoyanov, Parvanov emerged the victor, with 54.1% of the votes cast.

15 December 2001: Sergey Stanishev replaced Parvanov as Chairman of the BSP.

19 January 2002: Parvanov was sworn in as the country's President.

13 February 2002: Saxe-Coburg Gotha's Government survived a vote of 'no confidence' proposed by the UDF, with 134 of the 184 votes cast in the National Assembly.

6 April 2002: The NMSII was finally registered as a party, and Saxe-Coburg Gotha was elected as its Chairman.

31 October 2002: Kostadin Paskalev resigned as Deputy Prime Minister and Minister of Regional Development and Public Works, reportedly following a dispute over the 2003 budget and restrictions on reform.

21 November 2002: At a NATO summit meeting, held in Prague, Czech Republic, Bulgaria was one of seven countries to be formally invited to accede to the Alliance in 2004.

29 November 2002: The Government survived two votes of 'no confidence', initiated by the UDF and the Coalition for Bulgaria, after it had signed an agreement with the EU bringing forward the proposed date for the decommissioning of two reactors at the Kozloduy nuclear power plant; the Supreme Administrative Court subsequently ruled the agreement to be invalid, since it had been signed without the approval of the National Assembly.

17 April 2003: The Constitutional Court ruled that amendments to the privatization bill (passed in January), which had enabled the Government to exempt certain deals from judicial scrutiny, were unconstitutional.

29 May 2003: Saxe-Coburg Gotha's Government survived a further vote of 'no confidence' in the National Assembly, initiated by the UDF, and supported by the Coalition for Bulgaria.

2 July 2003: The National Assembly approved draft electoral legislation, introducing a mixed system of voting, whereby one-half of parliament's 240 members were to be elected by majority vote in their constituencies, and the remainder by a system of proportional representation from a national list. A revised version of the draft legislation was to be introduced following municipal elections, expected to be held in October.

16 July 2003: Saxe-Coburg Gotha implemented a government reshuffle.

History

Prof. RICHARD J. CRAMPTON

BULGARIA BEFORE 10 NOVEMBER 1989

The Bulgarians established their first state in 681 AD and became part of the Eastern or Orthodox Christian community in the ninth century. They fell under the domination of Byzantium in the 11th century and were incorporated into the Osmanlı (Ottoman) Empire in the late 14th century. The modern Bulgarian state was not created until 1878. It was a constitutional monarchy in which the prince (known after 1908 as the Tsar or King) dominated foreign policy. Expansion into areas that were regarded as ethnically Bulgarian, chiefly Macedonia, was the ultimate aim of Bulgarian foreign policy and determined Bulgaria's alignment with Germany in both World Wars, with a view to occupation as a reward. In 1944 the Red Army entered Bulgaria and did much to help the communists entrench themselves. In 1947 the young Tsar Simeon II went into exile and at the end of that year a new constitution gave the Bulgarian Communist Party (BCP) full control of the country. In 1954 Todor Zhivkov became leader of the party. His rule was marked by an unwavering conformity to the Soviet pattern of development: industrialization, collectivization and urbanization. By 1989 his regime was experiencing severe economic problems and attempts to 'bulgarize' the ethnic Turkish minority (accounting for about 9% of the population) led to internal disquiet and international condemnation. Zhivkov was removed by a coup within the BCP on 10 November 1989. He was replaced by Petar Mladenov.

THE ERA OF TRANSITION: CHANGES IN FORM BUT NOT IN STRUCTURE

The fall of Zhivkov was followed by the formation of opposition political parties, 15 of which established the Union of Democratic Forces (UDF). On 29 December 1989 all anti-Turkish legislation was revoked. In early 1990 the UDF and the BCP began a series of 'round-table' discussions, aimed at dismantling the one-party system and introducing a multi-party system. The BCP reformed itself, shed most of its totalitarian features and changed its name to the Bulgarian Socialist Party (BSP). Elections took place on 10 and 17 June for a Grand National Assembly (GNA), which was twice the size of an ordinary assembly. The BSP held an absolute majority (211 of the 400 seats); the UDF obtained 144 seats and the Movement for Rights and Freedoms (MRF), which was primarily concerned with protecting the interests of the ethnic Turkish population, secured 23 seats.

The first task of the GNA was to elect a new president, Mladenov having resigned in July 1990, following the revelation of taped evidence, in which he appeared to advocate the use of force against demonstrators in December 1989. After several attempts, the leader of the UDF, Zheliu Zhelev, was duly elected on 1 August 1990. Some weeks later Andrei Lukanov of the BSP formed a one-party Government. However, economic hardship caused by the collapse of the Council for Mutual Economic Assistance (CMEA, or COMECON), Bulgaria's main trading outlet, and the observance of sanctions against Iraq (which deprived Bulgaria of 600,000 metric tons of crude petroleum, due in repayment of Iraqi debt), together with suspicion that the electoral process had not been entirely fair, caused demonstrations and strikes, which forced Lukanov from office at the end of November.

The new premier, Dimitur Popov, confirmed by the GNA on 7 December 1990, was a non-party lawyer. His appointment did much to calm the political atmosphere, and on 14 December the major political groupings signed the Agreement Guaranteeing the Peaceful Transition to a Democratic Society. The new administration's main tasks were to devise a new constitution and to enact the necessary legislation for the creation of a market economy. Accordingly, interest rates were raised and, on 1 February 1991, price controls abolished. A further important enactment was a law of 1 March, by which land could be decollectivized and returned to its previous owners. This process of land privatization was slow and exceedingly contentious. Popov's economic reforms produced little real change and there was equally slow progress towards constitutional reform. A series of procedural delays and disputes delayed the introduction of the new Constitution until 13 July.

New elections were held on 13 October 1991. The UDF emerged as the largest party in the National Assembly, with 110 seats. The BSP retained 106 seats, while the MRF, which was the only other party to exceed the 4% threshold necessary for representation, held 24. The UDF faction chose the leader of the Green Party, Filip Dimitrov, as Prime Minister. In January 1992 Zhelev won the first-ever direct presidential election in Bulgaria.

THE DIMITROV GOVERNMENT

Under the Dimitrov administration closer links were established with Western Europe. In May 1992 Bulgaria was admitted to the Council of Europe and by December it had signed an association agreement with the European Community (EC, known as the European Union—EU from November 1993). The agreement was ratified and came into force in February 1995.

Inevitably, Dimitrov's Government was greatly challenged by the problems that emerged following the disintegration of Yugoslavia. In January 1992 Bulgaria became the first country to recognize Macedonia (eventually recognized by the UN as the former Yugoslav republic of Macedonia—the FYRM), although the Government specified that while it recognized a separate Macedonian state, it did not acknowledge the existence of a separate Macedonian nation.

At home, Dimitrov's cabinet addressed the problem of economic reform and restructuring. In 1992 legislation was passed that encouraged and facilitated foreign investment, reformed the banking system, and restored to its previous owners some of the property confiscated under communist rule. The Dimitrov Government, however, displayed an alarming capacity to alienate its natural supporters. These included the pro-UDF Podkrepa (Support) trade union, which was angered by the rapidly widening discrepancy between wages and prices, and even President Zhelev. Dimitrov was also losing the support of the MRF, as the recent economic changes had caused great hardship in Turkish areas, and prompted protests by ethnic Turks that the land privatization programme discriminated against them. On 28 October the MRF aligned with the BSP to pass a successful vote of censure against the Government.

THE BEROV GOVERNMENT

Dimitrov's successor was not elected until December 1992. Lyuben Berov, an economic historian and a former adviser to President Zhelev, headed a cabinet comprising mainly non-party technocrats, and his support in the National Assembly was based on a combination of the MRF, the majority of the BSP and a schismatic section of the UDF, which, by March 1993, had come together as the New Union for Democracy (NUD).

The advent of the NUD considerably enhanced the chances of survival for the Berov Government. This embittered the UDF, which intensified its criticism of the Government and of the President who had allowed it to be formed. The UDF claimed that the cabinet was attempting to reintroduce socialism, a claim seen to be justified by government interference in the media and the reinstatement of some dismissed former communists.

In its 'Plan of Action', announced in February 1993, the Berov Government confirmed that it would follow the economic policies of its predecessor. A number of important Western firms entered into joint ventures with Bulgarian concerns and in mid-1993 Bulgaria was granted 'most favoured nation' status by the US Congress. This, in addition to the signing of a free-trade agreement with the European Free Trade Association (EFTA), greatly improved trading prospects, despite the delay of the EC in ratifying the Association Agreement of December 1992.

Bulgaria's most serious economic problem was the servicing of its foreign debt. In November 1993 its request for a 50% reduction in its US $10,000m. debt to the 'London Club' of international creditors was unexpectedly granted. Economic difficulties remained, however. Bulgaria remained steadfast in its application of sanctions against the 'rump' Yugoslav state, even after the imposition of stricter sanctions in May caused severe disruption to Bulgaria's trade, by closing its main access route to Central Europe and the West. The total losses to the Bulgarian economy, between 1 January and 30 June 1993, according to Bulgarian estimates, amounted to $1,300m.

In the course of 1994 this problem led to agreements on the rescheduling of Bulgaria's debts. In June Berov also succeeded in enacting privatization legislation. The legislative proposal that evoked the most public interest, however, was that of reforming the judiciary, its main provision being that senior legal officers must have a service record of at least five years. This, in effect, restricted the upper ranks of the judiciary to communist-appointed officials.

Despite the agreements on debt rescheduling and the privatization law, there was very little progress towards fundamental economic reform. Economic and social indicators worsened: inflation was to average 121.9% for the year; unemployment, even by official estimates, reached 20% of the workforce; the introduction of a value-added tax (VAT) in April 1994 resulted in an increase in tax levels; and, to defend the currency, interest rates were increased from 27% to 72%. The resulting social tensions were most starkly demonstrated on 4 May, when 800,000 workers affiliated to the Confederation of Independent Trade Unions in Bulgaria (CITUB) participated in industrial action, intended to serve as a warning to the Government.

A further social concern was the rise in crime. This was a phenomenon common to all the post-communist states of Eastern Europe, but in Bulgaria the situation was complicated by the imposition of sanctions on the former Yugoslavia. Huge fortunes could be made through illicit trading over the border and the organized gangs that did so were widely believed to have collaborators within the administration and the police. Economic stagnation, social tensions and public concerns over crime and political corruption finally prompted Berov to resign on 2 September 1994. An interim Government under Reneta Indzhova, the former head of the Privatization Agency, was formed, and a general election was scheduled for 18 December.

THE GOVERNMENT OF THE BSP

The general election of December 1994 resulted in a major victory for the BSP, which obtained 125 seats in the Assembly, compared with the UDF's 69 seats, and the MRF's 15. There were two new parties in the Assembly: the Popular Union (PU), with 18 seats, and the Bulgarian Business Bloc (BBB), with 13. In January 1995 the BSP leader, Zhan Videnov, formed a new administration, which included some members of the Bulgarian Agrarian National Union and a representative of the environmental pressure group, Ecoglasnost.

Videnov's absolute majority led many to hope that, free from concerns about his support in the Assembly, he would concentrate on government rather than politics. These hopes were disappointed. Firstly, Videnov's support in the National Assembly was more apparent than real, a fact that exposed him to undue influence from some extra-parliamentary elements. Most serious were growing suspicions of links between the Government, the BSP and a number of large commercial conglomerates, which had emerged after the fall of totalitarianism and the connections of which with organized crime were the subject of much speculation.

In July 1995 President Zhelev suggested that the BSP was incapable of economic reform because it was 'genetically connected' with criminal circles, which were determined to prevent the break-up of the old controlled economy, from which they were making huge profits. In October of the following year the conglomerates were to be suspected of complicity in the murder of former premier, Andrei Lukanov, who was reported to be about to expose the links the conglomerates had with the BSP establishment.

The conjoined issues of the economy and organized crime soon resulted in the most serious crisis experienced since the collapse of the totalitarian regime. The first warning came in December 1995, when the Minister of Finance admitted that the budgetary deficit for that year would be 17% higher than expected. Inflation too, appeared likely to increase. The problem with the budget meant that repayment of foreign debt became more difficult, which, in turn, increased the pressure on the lev, the national currency. To contain this problem, interest rates were raised in February 1996 from 8% to 42%. However, it was a crisis within the banking system that initiated the most severe economic effects. In February

the Bank for Agricultural Credit (Vitosha—BZK) failed and had to be taken over by the central bank, the Bulgarian National Bank (BNB). Despite efforts to stabilize the lev, its value against the US dollar began to decline sharply, and at the end of February President Zhelev expressed his fear that the inadequacies of the banking system were 'plundering' the nation.

The situation was so grave that the Governor of the BNB said that, without external help, Bulgaria would be unable to meet its foreign-debt obligations. In mid-March 1996, with a critical need to find extra revenue, the Government announced the sale of a number of state enterprises, including a 25%–30% share in the national telecommunications company and the sale of the Sodi works in Devnya, one of the world's largest producers of calcinated soda. These measures had little effect. By the end of April the lev had lost 20% of its value, compared with the beginning of the year, and in mid-May its value was 70% lower.

On 16 May 1996 came 'Black Friday'. Two banks had to be placed under the special supervision of the BNB. Depositors, fearful that their savings were in danger, attempted immediately to withdraw their funds and translate them into goods or dependable currencies. The Government responded by announcing that it would close 64 loss-making enterprises and a further 70 would be 'isolated', that is, denied further subsidies. Other measures intended to reduce the budgetary deficit included the raising of the rate of VAT from 18% to 22%, a 5% levy on imports, and very large increases in fuel and public utility costs. However, these extreme measures failed to contain the crisis. The currency continued to lose value and in late 1996 the IMF declared that it would offer no further assistance to the country unless Bulgaria introduced a currency board (which assumes responsibility for monetary supervision from the central bank, including regulation of the exchange rate) and allowed the IMF some authority over the BNB. The Videnov Government refused this concession and continued to introduce a series of structural changes, all considered overdue, and none of which either contained the worsening crisis or placated the IMF. At the end of the year the exchange rate of the lev was approximately 500 per US dollar, inflation was at around 300% and government finances were in severe disarray. The ensuing social hardship was extreme. The Government also had to deal with the problem of a grain shortage, caused, in part, by the continuing uncertainties surrounding land ownership, but also by a number of ill-advised or illegal grain exports, all of which were profitable to the conglomerates that organized them.

The political consequences of the economic catastrophe soon became evident through large-scale public protests. The public also used the presidential elections of 3 November 1996 to express its displeasure. The candidate of the UDF, Petar Stoyanov, obtained 59.7% of the votes cast in the second round 'run-off' against the BSP candidate, Ivan Mazarov, whose party obtained barely one-half of the proportion of votes it had secured in the parliamentary elections of December 1994. Videnov survived a vote of censure at a meeting of the BSP Supreme Council on 12 November 1996, but his reputation was damaged by the economic disaster and by allegations of links with one of the conglomerates. His position was critically undermined when 19 senior BSP figures circulated an open letter to party members demanding his resignation as party leader. In late December he resigned from that post and from the premiership.

The departure of Videnov once again raised hopes that real change might be imminent. However, the election of Georgi Parvanov as party leader and, on 8 January 1997, of the Minister of the Interior, Nikolai Dobrev, as Prime Minister showed that there was little likelihood of such change. There were immediate protests (some of which resulted in violence and were severely suppressed) demanding early general elections. Initially, Dobrev insisted on his party's right to form a new government, but pressure from Stoyanov, who took office as President on 19 January, and the threat of widespread industrial action forced him to relinquish his mandate. On 4 February he resigned as Prime Minister and announced that a general election would take place in April. A 'caretaker' administration was formed under the Mayor of Sofia, Stefan Sofianski. In the election of 19 April the BSP was resoundingly defeated. The UDF obtained 137 seats in parliament, with the Democratic Left, a coalition dominated by the BSP, securing only 58 seats. The UDF leader, Ivan Kostov, formed a new Government in the following month.

THE KOSTOV GOVERNMENT

The Government of Ivan Kostov was the first in the history of post-totalitarian Bulgaria to run its full constitutional course of four years. Kostov's first priority was to remedy the deteriorating economic situation. There seemed a real danger that Bulgaria would default on its foreign-debt payments, although the departure of Dobrev eased the situation, as the IMF was prepared to extend further lending if the new administration promised to introduce a currency board, to which Kostov agreed. The board began its operations in July 1997 and, with the exchange rate of the lev linked to that of the Deutsche Mark, the German currency, and the board refusing to increase the money supply unless the national reserves warranted it, stability began to return to the economic sector.

The other main objectives of the new Government were to ensure that reforms were justly and evenly administered; to accelerate the restoration of land to its former owners and to encourage agricultural production; to oppose organized crime and corruption; to publish the files of the former secret police, in order to prevent the blackmail of public figures; to strengthen Bulgaria's links with the EU; and to join the North Atlantic Treaty Organization (NATO). Some progress was subsequently made in the implementation of this programme. Police files were made open to inspection and in November 1997 the Restitution Law provided for the return of all property confiscated by former communist regimes. In foreign affairs, the Government relaxed the policy of closeness with Russia, which the BSP administration had, in general, sought to revive, although this did not prevent the conclusion, in April 1998, of a vital agreement on the supply of Russian gas to Bulgaria. Relations with the FYRM continued to improve; in February 1999 Kostov and his Macedonian counterpart, Ljubčo Georgievski, signed a declaration pledging that neither country had a territorial claim on the other. Furthermore, in March 2000 the long-standing disagreement with Romania on the location of a second bridge over the River Danube (Dunav) was resolved, with the economically confident Bulgaria agreeing to meet all construction costs, estimated at almost US $180m. In external affairs, Bulgaria's support for NATO's aerial bombardment of the Federal Republic of Yugoslavia in 1999 earned the country credit with Western Governments, although it was less favourably received by the Bulgarian population.

The desire to become part of the EU remained the sovereign goal of Bulgarian foreign policy. Bulgaria had been placed on the list of applicants invited to begin membership talks at a meeting of EU leaders in Helsinki, Finland, in December 1999, and negotiations on accession began in Brussels, Belgium, in March 2000. Progress towards the harmonization of Bulgarian legislation with that of the EU was achieved, and in February 2001 Prime Minister Kostov declared Bulgaria to be second only to Hungary in this respect. Bulgarians gained great satisfaction from an EU decision in March to abolish the visa requirement for Bulgarians entering EU member states. Meanwhile, the entire Balkan region was threatened by the potential destabilization of the FYRM. Many Bulgarians had personal links with Macedonia, causing the issue to become highly emotive. The Kostov Government, despite sending arms to the FYRM, was insistent that it wished to continue Bulgaria's policy of preserving order and security in the Balkan region. The continuation of such a policy was necessary for further progress to be made in the critical accession negotiations with the EU, and in March 2001 the EU Commissioner in charge of enlargement, Günther Verheugen, observed that Bulgaria needed to represent 'an anchor of stability in a strategically very important region'.

By mid-2000 the Kostov Government had restored and preserved economic stability, while reform, although still slow, was, at last, progressing. In January 2001 a report by the Organisation for Economic Co-operation and Development (OECD) praised reforms made in the agricultural sector. However, a number of domestic problems remained. The rate of unemployment continued to be high, and reached 18.4% in February 2001, while prices continued to increase at a greater rate than most fixed incomes. The former state airline, Balkan Bulgarian Airlines (BalkanAir), in which, after its majority privatization in 1999, the Israeli Zeevi Group was the largest shareholder, was declared bankrupt. There was also concern over crime rates and corruption remained a problem, despite measures taken by the Kostov regime.

THE RETURN OF THE TSAR

Concern over the continuing price increases and even greater concern over crime and corruption doomed the Kostov Government and, consequently, the UDF. The BSP, still tainted by the failures of 1996–97, was hardly more popular. Thus, in one of the most extraordinary tranformations in modern history, in 2001 the electorate turned instead to former Tsar Simeon II, Simeon Saxe-Coburg Gotha (Saxe-Coburgotski). Saxe-Coburg Gotha was barred from standing for the presidency by a regulation that required all candidates for that office to have been resident in Bulgaria for five years prior to the election, so he chose instead to enter the parliamentary contest. He returned to Bulgaria, and in early April established the National Movement Simeon II (NMSII). Saxe-Coburg Gotha, or 'the King' as he was still referred to by many in Bulgaria, rapidly attracted support from all sections of the electorate, and in the legislative election of 17 June 2001 the NMSII won 120 seats, exactly one-half the total number in the National Assembly. This victory owed something to Saxe-Coburg Gotha's proven business acumen, his links with influential institutions and individuals outside Bulgaria, and his personal charm. His overwhelming advantage, however, was that he had no connection with either of the two predominant political parties and, above all, he was entirely free from any taint of corruption. On 24 July Saxe-Coburg Gotha became Prime Minister, at the head of a governmental alliance of the NMSII and the MRF, although the Government also included two BSP members. The most notable feature of the new administration was the appointment of a number of young, Western-trained businessmen to economic posts in the cabinet.

The NMSII had pledged to improve living standards within 800 days of taking office, by eliminating corruption and freeing business from bureaucratic interference and restrictive taxation. The Government's economic programme consisted of tax reductions to encourage investment and the establishment of a state fund to provide loans for small businesses. Fuel prices were to rise significantly, but minimum wages in the public sector were increased by 17% in October 2001. Economic reform under the NMSII administration was slow, but steady. This was recognized by the international financial agencies, which granted a number of loans to Bulgaria from July 2001, and in 2002 the country's credit rating was upgraded five times. Macroeconomic progress, however, incurred a social cost, as prices, especially those in the energy sector, continued to increase. All important aspects of government policy, both domestic and external, were conditioned by the Government's principal foreign-policy objective of accession to both NATO and the EU. Success in the former was achieved in November 2002, at a NATO summit held in Prague, Czech Republic, when Bulgaria was one of seven states invited to join the Alliance in 2004. Significant progress towards the latter objective was also recorded at an EU summit in Copenhagen, Denmark, in December, when, although Bulgaria was not judged ready for accession in 2004, it was announced that both Bulgaria and Romania were expected to join the Union in 2007.

Preparations for membership of NATO, the more easily achievable goal, had been thorough. In 2002 the Minister of Foreign Affairs, Solomon Pasi, launched what he termed a 'spring offensive', in order to promote the country's readiness for accession. An important feature of this campaign was a restructuring of the military establishment, to bring it into greater conformity with NATO practices. 'Plan 2004', approved by the National Assembly in April, envisaged a reduction in the size of the armed forces from 65,000 to 45,000, a review of military hardware and the transfer of control of the National Protection Service and the National Intelligence Service to the Council of Ministers. A commitment to the destruction of all former Soviet missiles on Bulgarian territory was fulfilled in October. Bulgaria also enhanced its candidature by remaining steadfastly pro-USA, not only during the US-led military operation in Afghanistan in late 2001, initiated in response to the suicide attacks against the USA of 11 September, but also during the subsequent crisis in Iraq, despite attracting strong criticism from France (which opposed military action in Iraq) in early 2003. During the military operation in Afghanistan, the Bulgarian Government offered the USA the use of refuelling facilities at the Sarafovo airbase near Burgas and in 2003 US refuelling aircraft again made use of the base, prompting protests from local people and some disquiet on the part of the BSP. There were subsequent plans to dispatch a small anti-nuclear-, anti-biological-, and anti-chemical-warfare unit to Iraq.

The Government's determination to attain membership of the EU was emphasized by the fact that the first foreign visit made by the new Prime Minister was to the EU headquarters in Brussels. By the end of 2002 Bulgaria had reached agreement on 21 of the 30 chapters of the *acquis communautaire*, that is, the body of EU treaties, legislation and case law required in order to qualify for membership. The most controversial of these related to the energy sector, owing to doubts over the safety of the Kozloduy Nuclear Power-Station, a major provider of Bulgarian electricity. The complex consisted of six reactors, the first two of which were decommisioned at the end of 2002, in agreement with the EU, in return for US $400m. in compensation. The EU also insisted, however, that the third and fourth reactors should be closed, with a similar sum to be paid in compensation. In mid-November 2002 the Government eventually agreed to decommission the reactors by 2006, but provoked considerable protest, partly owing to fears of further increases in electricity prices. Opposition parties also questioned the legality of the Government's decision, a view that was upheld by the Supreme Administrative Court, which ruled in early January 2003 that only the National Assembly was empowered to make a decision on the closure of the reactors.

Privatization was an integral part of the Government's economic-reform programme, and two major privatization agreements were reached in 2002, on the divestment of the state tobacco group, Bulgartabac, and the Bulgarian Telecommunications Company (BTC). However, both agreements were annulled by the Supreme Administrative Court following complaints of irregularities in the privatization processes. The case of Bulgartabac was particularly sensitive, as the MRF, the junior member of the ruling coalition, was anxious to ensure that privatization would not inflict too much harm on the nation's tobacco growers (most of whom are ethnic Turks), and there was a more general fear of massive unemployment among the estimated 460,000 people who depended on the tobacco industry for their livelihoods. Another potential problem related to the fact that at least one of the consortiums bidding for Bulgartabac included among its leadership a Russian expelled from Bulgaria in August 2000, who was thought to have connections with illegal organizations. The Court's intervention in privatization of Bulgartabac and BTC prompted the Government to introduce, in January 2003, legislation depriving the judiciary of the power to veto privatization projects. Following the enactment of this law, privatization deals for both Bulgartabac and BTC were signed, although BSP deputies continued to contest the legality of the new regulations. In mid-April the Constitutional Court upheld its contention that certain clauses of the act were unconstitutional.

The controversy over both the Kozloduy plant and the privatization law placed strain on relations between the Prime Minister and the President, Georgi Parvanov. Parvanov had been elected in November 2001, and he took office in January 2002. A former Chairman of the BSP, he made it clear that as President he would attempt to defend the social well-being of the nation and its citizens. He was also determined to resist measures designed to further the EU accession process which, he believed, could adversely affect the interests of the country and the living conditions of its citizens. Since the collapse of communism, Bulgaria had experienced rule by its two principal political parties, a number of non-party administrations and a returned monarch, brought to power by a populist campaign. It had twice experienced civil unrest, driving the incumbent administration from power. Simultaneously, economic reform, dictated to a large extent by external factors, had caused severe internal social suffering. Yet the democratic process survived, the media was unrestricted and individual liberties were, by and large, respected. Admission to NATO would be an acknowledgement of this political stability. The advances made towards EU membership were slow and painful, but steady. Important obstacles remained, and judicial, as well as economic, restructuring was essential. Bulgaria, like other countries in the region, had been criticized for the conditions of its Roma minority, although it received little commendation for the efforts it had made to improve the provision of education in the Turkish language for the ethnic Turkish minority. In the immediate political future, further tensions between the Prime Minister and the President were likely, but the experience of recent history suggested that such tensions could be resolved successfully within the constitutional framework.

The Economy

Prof. JEFFREY MILLER

OVERVIEW

Prior to the introduction of the communist regime, Bulgaria's had been an agricultural economy. During the communist period, along with other socialist economies, Bulgaria embarked on a major industrialization programme, which led to significant demographic shifts, as people moved from rural areas to the cities. Bulgaria had a large foreign-trade sector, and much of its trade was conducted with member countries of the Council for Mutual Economic Assistance (CMEA, or Comecon); given the poor quality of Bulgarian exports, most of its remaining markets were developing countries. During the 1980s lower growth rates led to economic reforms and extensive foreign borrowing.

Upon the fall of the communist Government of Todor Zhivkov in late 1989, several features of the inherited economic system made the transition to a market economy especially difficult. The country was fully integrated into the CMEA trading system, and had even developed certain specializations, such as high-technology goods to serve the Soviet bloc. In 1989 about 80% of exports and 70% of imports were with CMEA countries; this was a far larger proportion than in other Central and South-Eastern European countries. (For example, only 35% of Polish exports and 32% of Polish imports were with CMEA countries.) Therefore, when the CMEA system collapsed, Bulgaria had great difficulty finding other markets and had limited business contacts in those markets.

Furthermore, because Bulgaria is a resource-poor country, it is very dependent on imports of raw materials for its manufacturing industries, and, in particular, energy. During the communist period it had relied on energy imports from the USSR at subsidized prices. Bulgaria continued to rely heavily on Russian natural gas imports, but they were subsequently imported at world prices, which made the economy vulnerable to sharp fluctuations in global energy prices.

Unfolding international events also had a negative effect on the economy. The dissolution of Yugoslavia and the crisis in the Persian (Arabian) gulf in 1990–91 created problems in export markets. Arab countries, including Iraq and Kuwait, had been important markets for Bulgarian goods exports, particularly in the construction sector, and in 1990 the repayment by Iraq of foreign debt worth some US $2,000m. was halted.

Another area of weakness as the transition began was Bulgaria's own substantial levels of foreign debt. By 1989 Bulgaria's foreign debt amounted to US $9,200m. (In 1990 gross domestic product—GDP—was $6,900m.) In March 1990 a unilateral moratorium was declared, which effectively suspended Western commercial credits until agreement was reached with the 'London Club' of international creditors in November 1993, according to which the remaining London Club debt was to be fully collateralized by bonds. Although the agreement greatly reduced and extended the country's foreign-debt repayments, overall its commitments remained quite onerous and played a significant role in creating the currency crisis of 1996 (see below).

In 1990 economic reformers faced a daunting task, but with the help of the IMF a stabilization plan was devised. The plan demanded price liberalization, a unified, 'floating' exchange rate, tight limits on government expenditure, significant increases in nominal interest rates and controls on bank credit. In accordance with the programme, a form of 'shock therapy' was instituted in February 1991, as many controlled prices were liberalized. Prices consequently increased dramatically, and the annual rate of consumer-price inflation was 338% in 1991. However, goods began to reappear in the stores and progress was made towards the creation of a market economy.

Political instability and corruption impeded the implementation of many other reforms as output declined sharply during the early 1990s. Restructuring efforts floundered as successive governments were reluctant to deny credit to hard-pressed state enterprises, fearing that further redundancies would compound the already rising level of unemployment. Restitution of agricultural land and urban construction began, but the privatization of large state enterprises stalled. A 'black' market, or unofficial economy, flourished, as an embargo on trade with, or through, the Federal Republic of Yugoslavia (FRY—Serbia and Montenegro) was imposed by the UN in 1992.

These problems finally resulted in a severe financial crisis in 1996. Many banks failed, the national currency, the lev, depreciated sharply, output declined precipitously and inflation reached 'hyperinflationary' levels in February 1997. In January demonstrations led to the resignation of the Government headed by Nikolai Dobrev of the Bulgarian Socialist Party (BSP). An interim Government was appointed and a general election took place in April. In order to restore stability, the IMF took the unusual measure of negotiating with an interim government, and a currency board was installed with IMF support in July. The board linked the exchange rate of the lev to that of the German currency, the Deutsche Mark (and subsequently the common European currency, the euro).

The creation of a currency board, which placed severe limitations on economic policy-makers, stabilized the economy and created an environment for much-needed structural reform. From 1998 the economy began to register growth, albeit slowly. Average annual rates of inflation in the years immediately following were less than 20%. Privatization programmes moved forward, and enterprise restructuring was finally under way.

However, many Bulgarians remained disappointed in the progress made by the economy during the transition period. This was reflected in the demographic statistics: between the censuses of 1985 and 2001, the population declined from approximately 9m. to about 8m. people. It was estimated that about two-thirds of this decline was attributable to migration, with many young adults seeking improved employment opportunities abroad.

In March 2000 negotiations on Bulgaria's accession to the European Union (EU) commenced. Although Bulgaria did not expect to be among the candidate countries invited to join in the first round of enlargement in 2004, eventual accession had become an economic goal, and the *acquis communautaire*, the agreement between members of the EU, an important model for guiding economic reform. Formal recognition by the EU in 2002 that Bulgaria was a functioning market economy brought Bulgaria closer to fulfilling its objective of joining the EU by 2007.

MACROECONOMIC PERFORMANCE AND FOREIGN TRADE FLOWS

Although the period of transition was difficult for all the countries of Central and South-Eastern Europe, the macroeconomic performance of the Bulgarian economy was among the weakest. Output declined dramatically, both immediately after the transition began and during the financial crisis of 1996–97. Following the first period of decline, in 1993 output was only 80% of its 1990 level. The second decline in 1996–97 caused a further deterioration, and in 1997 output was 70% of its pre-transition level. With the establishment of a currency board in mid-1997, the economy began to recover, but initially at a slower rate than might have been hoped, especially given the severity of the earlier declines. Still this was impressive, given the impact of the Russian financial crisis of 1998, the fighting in the Serbian province of Kosovo and Metohija in 1999, and the conflict in the former Yugoslav republic of Macedonia (FYRM) in 2001. In 2002 output increased by 4.8%, its fifth year of expansion. Although GDP remained below the level achieved before the transition began, GDP per head (in euros), given the sharp drop in population, was close to the level recorded in 1990.

Before the establishment of the currency board, inflation was also a serious problem. After prices were liberalized in February 1991, the rate of inflation stood at more than 300%. However, the inflation rate was under 100% in 1992 and 1993, although it surged to 120% in 1994, when the nominal value of the lev declined significantly. There was a marked improvement in 1995, but the financial crisis began in 1996 and inflation consequently rose dramatically. Prices increased by more than two-fold during February 1997, but once it became clear that a currency board was to be established, inflation declined to a much more reasonable level. By 1998 the rate of annual inflation was 22.3%, and subsequently remained relatively low (declining to 2.6% in 1999), despite increases in world petroleum prices and domestic price adjustments, which were necessary in order to bring previously controlled energy prices closer to global levels.

Bulgaria is a small country: in 2002 total GDP amounted to some US $15,700m. The foreign trade sector was important, and in 2002 the value of exports totalled $5,600m. (equivalent to some 36% of GDP) and imports were worth some $7,800m. (about 50% of GDP). Over time, trade with the former USSR had declined and that with the EU had increased—in 2002 over 55% of Bulgaria's exports went to the EU, and fewer than 5% to the countries of the former USSR.

Within the EU, Italy, accounting for 15.3% of Bulgaria's exports in 2002, had become the country's largest export market. This reflected, in part, the shift towards exports of clothing and footwear, which accounted for around 20% of Bulgaria's exports in 2002. Outside the EU, Turkey, accounting for 9.3% in 2002, had also become an important export market. With regard to imports, the situation was considerably different, since Bulgaria remained very dependent on Russia for energy supplies; in 2002 14.7% of imports came from Russia. However, the EU supplied around 50% of imported goods, with Germany accounting for the largest proportion, 14.3%. Bulgaria imported a very small percentage of goods from its neighbours. Greece was its largest neighbouring trading partner, providing 6.0% of imports in 2002, followed by Turkey (accounting for 5.0%) and Romania (2.0%). Trade with other Balkan countries was minimal, accounting for some 1% of imports.

Although it was too early to make a firm judgment, in 2002 Bulgaria appeared to have made significant progress in relation to one potentially serious macroeconomic problem. After the establishment of the currency board, the current-account deficit became progressively worse, reaching 6.4% of GDP in 2001, while the deficit on the balance of trade (which includes exports and imports of goods and services) was even higher, at 10.8% of GDP. In 2002 the current-account deficit declined to 4.2% of GDP, and the balance of trade to 7.8% of GDP, despite an appreciating currency. Low inflation in 2002, and the fact

that the lev was fixed to the euro, the currency of its major export market, reduced the impact of the appreciation.

The current-account deficits were financed by a significant increase in foreign investment in Bulgaria. Throughout 1998 foreign investment was very low. Total foreign investment in 1992–98 amounted to just US $1,800m., or about $225 per person. There were several contributing factors. Firstly, there was the moratorium on debt payments, which was finally lifted in 1994, once negotiations with the London Club had been concluded. Secondly, foreign investors were discouraged by the high levels of political and economic instability. Between 1991 and 1997 there were seven governments (two of which were interim administrations), resulting in many changes to commercial law. This factor, together with high levels of inflation and declining output, did not create a positive environment for foreign investors.

From the time of the currency board's establishment in 1997, conflicting forces affected the foreign investment climate. The internal economic and political climate improved, and not only did the economy stabilize, but growing confidence in the fixed rate of exchange reduced the risk for foreign investors. However, the international climate deteriorated. The Russian financial crisis resulted in reduced international investor interest in the region, and events in Kosovo and the FYRM reinforced the perception that the Balkans was a high-risk, unstable region. None the less, foreign investment continued to increase, albeit at a slower rate than that directed at several other Central and South-Eastern countries, and such investment totalled US $2,600m. during 1999–2001. This increase reflected, in part, the efforts of the Government of Ivan Kostov (1997–2001) to privatize large firms and to sell them to foreign buyers. For example, one-quarter of this foreign investment targeted the financial sector, in which there was a strong impetus to privatize the banking system through sales to foreign banks. Although some smaller-scale divestments continued under the Government of Simeon Saxe-Coburg Gotha (2001–), the inflow of foreign investment from privatization declined to just $155m. in 2001–02.

Foreign investors in Bulgaria came from a diverse range of countries. Notable among them was investment from Cyprus (accounting for 10% of the total in 1996–2002), representing investment in the banking sector; Italy (12%), demonstrating its role as a major trading partner; Belgium (11%), reflecting the purchase of Sodi Devnya (now known as Solvay Sodi), a major soda ash producer; Greece (10%) and Austria (10%). US investment, although much smaller-scale (6%), included investment by American Standard (air-conditioning, vehicle-control systems and domestic plumbing), which exported throughout the region from its Bulgarian plant.

PRIVATIZATION AND STRUCTURAL CHANGE

Structural change proceeded very slowly. Early privatization was focused on the return of agricultural land and the restitution of urban buildings to their former owners. The restitution of agricultural land was much more problematic than originally anticipated. Small plots were returned to the families of the original owners. (It was estimated that 3m.–5m. people would become land-owners once the restitution process was finally completed.) However, the small plots proved inefficient and delays in land titling and land markets made it more difficult to consolidate production units. Animal herds declined when farmers received animals before they obtained the land to support them.

Despite these problems, and the sharp decline in agricultural production, agriculture remained an important sector, and was relatively large compared with other countries in Central and South-Eastern Europe, contributing some 13.7% of GDP, and engaging 26.3% of the employed labour force, in 2001. (In that year industry contributed 28.4% of GDP, and provided 27.6% of employment, while the services sector contributed 57.9% of GDP, and employed 46.0% of the employed labour force, with tourism providing an increasingly significant contribution.) Only in Poland and Romania were a higher percentage of the work-force employed in agriculture. Unusually, the agricultural work-force actually increased in size during the post-communist period. The sector also contributed substantially to export trade (accounting for some 16% at the beginning of the 2000s), although it had declined in importance since the early 1990s, when agricultural exports represented 20%–25% of total exports. The major agricultural exports were wine, tobacco, and fresh and processed fruit and vegetables, and most were exported to the countries of the former USSR.

For much of the 1990s food-processing and marketing was highly regulated. Food was produced on private farms, processed in state-owned enterprises and sold in private retail markets. The goal of government policy was to provide inexpensive food to the urban population through price controls and import and export licenses. After 1996 many of these controls were abandoned, and intervention in agricultural markets was reasonably limited, especially in comparison to other Central and South-Eastern European countries. The major exception was tobacco, where processing and marketing was still managed by the state-owned holding company, Bulgartabac, the planned privatization of which was proving to be controversial in 2002–03.

In contrast to restitution in agriculture, restitution of urban property proved more successful, and provided an avenue for the expansion of small retail and wholesale businesses. This was particularly important in the early years of transition, when many entrepreneurs wanted to start small businesses. Obtaining larger tracts of land for industrial projects remained a problem, however, and improving these markets was a primary government objective.

The privatization of large-scale enterprises proved to be a much more politically sensitive issue than restitution. It was estimated that only 5%–7% of state-enterprise assets were privatized between 1992 and 1997, and there was little restructuring of state enterprises during that period. Managerial turnover was high, as managerial positions were often linked to the political situation, and governments changed several times during the early transition period. Short tenures, however, encouraged the practice of acquiring control of companies simply in order to sell off their assets. When the Government made a more concerted effort to privatize large state-owned enterprises through cash sales, the bid prices were very low, partly because there had been so little investment in these enterprises and they had already been divested of their existing assets.

In January 1995 a BSP Government, led by Zhan Videnov, came to power and initiated a mass privatization programme. The programme was modelled on the Czech example, according to which citizens paid a small fee for vouchers, which could be used to bid for shares in state-owned enterprises in national auctions. The first phase of this plan was completed in June 1997, just as the financial crisis was ending and the currency board was being established. About one-quarter of Bulgaria's state-owned enterprises were partially privatized in this way. Although this represented less than one-sixth of the estimated assets of the state-enterprise sector, the mass privatization scheme privatized twice as many assets as had been previously privatized through other methods.

The original mass privatization programme demanded a second phase, similar to the first, but the Kostov Government, which came to power in May 1997, was opposed to it, and elected to implement an alternative approach, ultimately a failure in terms of additional privatization. Instead, the major

privatization trend involved management-employee dispossessions and cash privatization schemes. Many of the large enterprises sold for cash went to foreign buyers. By the end of 2002 it was estimated that about 75% of the economy was under private ownership. Only a few major privatization projects remained, the most important of which were the planned divestments of Bulgartabac and the Bulgarian Telecommunications Company (BTC). Attempts to privatize these two companies were subject to numerous delays, as intervention by the courts created additional obstacles (see History).

The first phase of the mass privatization programme provided a strong impetus for the development of the Bulgarian Stock Exchange. However, trading on the exchange was limited, and many companies that were part of the privatization programme were soon unavailable for trading. Very little capital was raised on that market, so it was not a significant source of investment funds. The privatization scheme also spurred the development of mutual funds. Most of these became holding companies and exercised ownership control, together with the State, which retained substantial holdings in many of the companies that were part of the programme.

BANKING AND FINANCIAL SECTOR DEVELOPMENT

Under the system of central planning, the Bulgarian banking system operated under a state-operated central bank. This bank combined issue and credit functions, and implemented the 'cash and credit plan', which formed part of the general economic plan. The bank, the Bulgarian National Bank (BNB), was under the direct control of the Government. In addition to the BNB, there were only two other banking institutions, each with strictly limited functions. The State Savings Bank was the only financial institution permitted to hold the accounts of individuals, and it continued to hold the largest consumer deposit base. The Bulgarian Foreign Trade Bank, later known as Bulbank, handled all foreign-exchange operations. Bulbank was privatized in 2000, and DSK Bank plc (as the State Savings Bank had been renamed) in 2003.

When the transition began, rapid changes in banking institutions were undertaken as Bulgaria moved swiftly to transform the banking structure to a two-tier system designed to support a market economy. Although new banking institutions were created rapidly, fashioning well-functioning financial institutions proved to be a much more formidable task. Many newly formed commercial banks were poorly capitalized with bad 'loans'; these were not true loans to state enterprises, but nominal loans made under the centrally planned system. As economic conditions deteriorated and state enterprises suffered, more loans were extended, and the volume of unrecoverable loans expanded dramatically.

Attempts by the Government to manage these problems, by recapitalizing the banks through the substitution of government debt for unrecoverable loans, largely failed. Government debt increased dramatically and the accounts did not improve, as commercial banks continued to disburse additional lending. With so much credit pouring into state enterprises, there was little incentive to restructure and the real sector of the economy also suffered.

Weaknesses in both government and bank balance sheets led to the financial crisis of 1996–97. Several banks, holding about one-third of bank assets, collapsed. The public, having lost money in failing banks, withdrew its deposits from the banking system and deposits returned only very slowly. The financial crisis, and the establishment of the currency board in 1997, represented a turning point for the banking system and for the economy. Under the currency-board system, the central bank had no discretion to conduct monetary policy and could not lend money either to the government or to the banks (except in extreme circumstances). Once the currency board was established, the growth rate of the money supply slowed significantly, and commercial bank balances improved. The flow of easy credit to the real sector ceased. Indeed, after the establishment of the currency board, it was very difficult for firms to obtain credit, which also halted the free flow of money to the enterprise sector. Enterprises were forced to restructure or fail. With the restructuring of enterprises, the unemployment rate increased, from 11% in 1995 to 19% in 2001, but it declined to 16% in 2002, as the economy expanded.

In an attempt at reform, almost the entire banking system had been sold to foreign banks, and credit conditions eased. Banks, which had purchased foreign securities during the early currency-board period, had begun to repatriate this money and make more loans to businesses in Bulgaria. This aided the expansion of the economy and helped to finance the current-account deficits, as other sources of financing declined. Since other non-bank financial institutions were still in the early stages of development, the banks remained the most important source for financing investment.

PROSPECTS

After 1997 the economy registered consistent growth and inflation was brought under control, indicating that progress had been made. Admission to NATO from 2004, formal recognition by the EU that Bulgaria had a functioning market economy, five years of expansion, and a growth performance in 2002 that was among the best in Europe attested to the positive developments in the economy. None the less, important challenges remained, and the financial resources to meet those challenges were limited.

Bulgaria remained a relatively poor country; GDP per head was among the lowest in the EU applicant countries, and rates of poverty were among the worst. An important economic objective was EU membership, and Bulgaria understood that major institutional reforms had to be undertaken if the country was to achieve this goal. Progress had been made in two important areas that had major budgetary consequences for the Government: the financing of medical care and pension reform. The Government had reduced taxation without causing serious budgetary consequences, but improving revenue collection had been a challenge.

The energy sector also required restructuring. Energy consumption was high at the beginning of the transition period, reflecting the underpricing of energy under the centrally planned system, and continued to be significantly higher than in countries such as the Czech Republic, Hungary, Poland and Romania. Bulgaria remained extremely dependent on external sources of supply and, in addition, there was considerable pressure from the EU to close the Kozloduy Nuclear Power-Station, which supplied a large proportion of Bulgaria's electric power, and from the populace to halt the increase in prices.

Four key forces would determine the future direction of the economy: the currency board, the desire for accession to the EU, the IMF (which supported the currency board) and popular discontent with the status quo. The currency board had been a force for economic stability, but it also imposed severe constraints on macroeconomic policy options. Furthermore, currency boards can fail, as was demonstrated in Argentina at the beginning of 2002; however, they can also provide an opportunity for reform if a country takes advantage of the situation, and Bulgaria hoped to have sufficient opportunity to implement the reforms necessary for EU membership. By mid-2002 many reforms had already been carried out; the economy had stabilized, levels of foreign debt had been reduced, and government budgets were reasonably balanced (as had not been the case in Argentina).

The currency board was not the answer to all Bulgaria's problems. The current account maintained a deficit that had to be financed; one possible scenario was that the deficit could be financed by foreign investment. If such investment supported further growth and enhanced future exports, the deficits would eventually decrease. However, if new funds were not forthcoming, under a currency-board arrangement the money supply would contract and growth would slow, without continued funding of the deficits.

Under either scenario, government programmes to improve economic productivity were required to improve welfare provision and encourage exports. This necessitated further economic restructuring, greater investment (including foreign investment) and reform of the civil service. The Government could provide assistance, by reducing corruption and providing a legal and regulatory environment that promoted competitive market activities. The goal of EU membership is an important force for change in that direction. Laws and regulations were being rewritten and institutions were being restructured to meet the requirements for accession.

The IMF programme in Bulgaria also exerted enormous influence over economic developments. With its large foreign debt, Bulgaria needed IMF support, not only to obtain lending from the IMF itself, but also to provide a signal to the capital markets. Without IMF support Bulgaria could not access capital markets, and it was this access that had enabled the country to restructure its debt in 2002. External debt had been reduced to approximately 70% of GDP (from over 100% in 1997), with prospects for further reductions in the near future. The IMF had also applied pressure to the Government to keep the state budget under control. In late 2001, for example, the new Government of Saxe-Coburg Gotha came under pressure to amend a proposed economic programme that would have created much larger government deficits.

Despite many positive signs that the economy was growing and that economic restructuring was finally taking place, there was general despair about the state of the economy and disappointment in the Government. For many Bulgarians, the existing economic situation was not favourable. Output remained substantially below 1990 levels, unemployment was high, and widening disparities in incomes created even greater hardship for many people. Moreover, it was a problem that was not likely to be resolved in the short term. Economies grow slowly, and it would take several additional years of significant growth until even the 1990 output levels were reached. Ironically, as the economy improved and the foreign-debt problem was resolved, the influence of the IMF was likely to wane and the threat of larger budget deficits to increase. This would be especially true as fresh legislative elections approached. While staying the course and continuing to implement market reforms might be the most advisable long-term strategy, it might prove to be increasingly difficult politically.

Statistical Survey

Sources (unless otherwise indicated): National Statistical Institute, 1038 Sofia, P. Volov St 2; tel. (2) 985-77-00; fax (2) 985-76-40; e-mail info@nsi.bg; internet www.nsi.bg; Bulgarian National Bank, 1000 Sofia, Blvd Aleksandur Battenberg 1; tel. (2) 914-51-203; fax (2) 980-24-25; e-mail press–office@bnbank.org; internet www.bnb.bg; Center for Economic Development, 1408 Sofia, j. k. Ivan Vazov, Balsha 1, Bl. 9; tel. (2) 953-42-04; e-mail stat@ced.bg; internet www.stat.bg.

Area and Population

AREA, POPULATION AND DENSITY

Area (sq km)*	110,994†
Population (census results)	
4 December 1992.	8,487,317
1 March 2001	
Males	3,888,440
Females.	4,085,231
Total	7,973,671
Population (official estimates at 31 December)	
2001	7,891,095
2002	7,845,499
Density (per sq km) at 31 December 2002	70.7

* Including territorial waters of frontier rivers (261.4 sq km).
† 42,855 sq miles.

ETHNIC GROUPS
(2001 census)

	Number	%
Bulgarian.	6,660,682	83.53
Turkish	757,781	9.50
Gypsy	365,797	4.59
Others.	121,773	1.53
Unknown	67,640	0.85
Total	7,973,673	100.00

ADMINISTRATIVE REGIONS
(2001 census)

	Area (sq km)	Population	Density (per sq km)
Sofia (town)*	1,310.8	1,173,811	895.5
Burgas (Bourgas)	14,724.3	802,932	54.5
Khaskovo	13,824.1	816,874	59.1
Lovech	15,150.0	924,505	61.0
Montana†	10,606.8	559,449	52.7
Plovdiv	13,585.4	1,175,628	86.5
Ruse (Roussé)	10,842.5	702,292	64.8
Sofia (region)*	19,021.1	930,958	48.9
Varna	11,928.6	887,222	74.4
Total	110,993.6	7,973,671	71.8

* The city of Sofia, the national capital, has separate regional status. The area and population of the capital region are not included in the neighbouring Sofia region.
† Formerly Mikhailovgrad.

PRINCIPAL TOWNS
(population at 2001 census)

Sofia (capital)	. .	1,096,389	Dobrich*	100,379
Plovdiv	.	340,638	Shumen	89,054
Varna	.	314,539	Pernik	86,133
Burgas (Bourgas)	.	193,316	Yambol	82,924
Ruse (Roussé) .	.	162,128	Khaskovo	80,870
Stara Zagora . .	.	143,989	Pazardzhik . . .	79,476
Pleven	.	122,149	Blagoevgrad . . .	71,361
Sliven	.	100,695		

* Dobrich was renamed Tolbukhin in 1949, but its former name was restored in 1990.

BIRTHS, MARRIAGES AND DEATHS

	Registered live births		Registered marriages*		Registered deaths	
	Number	Rate (per 1,000)	Number	Rate (per 1,000)	Number	Rate (per 1,000)
1994 . .	79,442	9.4	37,910	4.5	111,787	13.2
1995 . .	71,967	8.6	36,795	4.4	114,670	13.6
1996 . .	72,188	8.6	n.a.	4.3	117,056	14.0
1997 . .	64,125	7.7	34,772	4.2	121,861	14.7
1998 . .	65,361	7.9	35,591	4.3	118,190	14.3
1999 . .	72,291	8.8	35,540	4.3	111,786	13.6
2000 . .	73,679	9.0	n.a.	4.3	115,087	14.1
2001 . .	68,180	8.7	n.a.	4.0	112,368	14.3

* Including marriages of Bulgarian nationals outside the country, but excluding those of aliens in Bulgaria.

Source: partly UN, *Population and Vital Statistics* and *Monthly Bulletin of Statistics*.

Expectation of life (WHO estimates, years at birth): 71.5 (males 68.4; females 74.8) in 2001 (Source: WHO, *World Health Report*).

EMPLOYMENT
(annual averages, excluding armed forces)

	1999	2000	2001
Agriculture, hunting, forestry and fishing	818,195	781,566	774,080
Mining and quarrying . . .	47,941	40,684	35,521
Manufacturing	662,963	615,691	591,843
Electricity, gas and water supply	57,860	59,710	58,632
Construction	123,736	127,554	126,967
Wholesale and retail trade; repair of motor vehicles, motorcycles and personal and household goods	337,696	352,383	355,189
Hotels and restaurants . . .	68,200	85,059	94,484
Transport and communications	232,857	219,453	214,195
Financial intermediation . . .	35,799	32,791	34,344
Real estate, renting and business activities	95,188	121,035	131,825
Public administration; compulsory social security	91,744	91,700	96,869
Education	231,977	218,302	203,972
Health and social work . . .	165,096	148,250	138,325
Other community, social and personal service activities . .	102,661	85,930	84,046
Total employees	3,071,913	2,980,108	2,940,292

Unemployment (persons registered at 31 December): 610,551 in 1999; 682,792 in 2000; 662,260 in 2001.

Health and Welfare

KEY INDICATORS

Total fertility rate (children per woman, 2001).	1.1
Under-5 mortality rate (per 1,000 live births, 2001) . .	16
HIV/AIDS (% of persons aged 15–49, 2001)	<0.10
Physicians (per 1,000 head, 1998)	3.45
Hospital beds (per 1,000 head, 1997)	8.6
Health expenditure (2000): US $ per head (PPP) . . .	198
Health expenditure (2000): % of GDP	3.9
Health expenditure (2000): public (% of total) . . .	77.6
Access to water (% of persons, 2000).	100
Access to sanitation (% of persons, 2000)	100
Human Development Index (2000): ranking	62
Human Development Index (2000): value	0.779

For sources and definitions, see explanatory note on p. vi.

Agriculture

PRINCIPAL CROPS
('000 metric tons)

	1998	1999	2000
Wheat	3,203.4	2,637.0	2,775.0
Rice (paddy)	10.3	7.0	10.0
Barley	717.1	652.0	676.0
Maize	1,303.4	1,719.0	818.0
Rye.	26.6	30.0*	20.0*
Oats	63.7	52.0*	49.0*
Other cereals	20.3	34.8*	15.0*
Potatoes	478.3	566.0	398.0
Sugar beet.	61.7	53.0	23.0
Dry beans	23.5	24.0	9.0
Groundnuts (in shell) . . .	9.7	10.0	8.0
Sunflower seed	524.2	606.0	423.0
Cabbages	142.9	154.0	151.2*
Asparagus.	12.5	12.7*	13.2*
Tomatoes	490.2	446.0	410.0
Pumpkins, squash and gourds	47.0	45.0†	45.0†
Cucumbers and gherkins . .	193.3	171.0	131.0
Aubergines (Eggplants) . . .	32.8	33.0*	34.7*
Chillies and green peppers . .	242.3	202.0	190.0
Dry onions	107.1	104.0	68.0
Garlic	28.2	28.7*	29.8*
Green beans	17.2	17.5*	18.2*
Carrots	23.3	26.7*	24.6*
Other vegetables	122.2	121.9*	129.0†
Apples	129.1	92.0	89.0
Pears	20.2	18.6	20.0†
Apricots	9.1	10.9	13.0*
Cherries	33.5	32.0	28.0
Peaches and nectarines . .	42.0	39.0	42.0
Plums	61.8	66.0	62.0
Strawberries	7.8	10.0	9.0
Grapes.	396.3	400.6	416.5
Watermelons	288.2	384.0	233.0
Other fruit	28.0	28.4	43.2*
Tobacco (leaves)	38.7	34.5	6.7*

* Unofficial figure.
† FAO estimate.
Source: FAO.

LIVESTOCK
('000 head at 1 January each year)

	1999	2000	2001
Horses	133	141	140
Asses	221	208	196
Cattle	671	682	640
Pigs	1,721	1,512	1,144
Sheep	2,774	2,549	2,286
Goats	1,048	1,046	970
Poultry.	15,686†	14,963†	16,035*
Rabbits	466	431	550*

* FAO estimate.
† Unofficial figure.
Source: FAO.

LIVESTOCK PRODUCTS
('000 metric tons)

	1998	1999	2000
Beef and veal	55.0*	63.4*	66.6†
Mutton and lamb.	45.7*	50.0*	45.8†
Goat meat.	7.3†	7.0*	7.3†
Pig meat	248.1	267.1	243.0*
Poultry meat	105.1	106.0	100.0*
Rabbit meat	5	5	5†
Cows' milk	1,327.0	1,388.8	1,389.8
Buffaloes' milk	11.3	11.3	11.5*
Sheeps' milk	109.3	106.2	105.0*
Goats' milk	190.7	200.0	200.0*
Cheese.	71.6	56.1	48.3
Butter	1.7	1.3	1.6
Hen eggs	90.5	88.3	92.4
Other poultry eggs	5.1	5.2	2.0†
Honey	5.5	5.7	5.7†
Wool: greasy	8	8	8†
Wool: scoured	3.8*	3.8*	3.7†
Sheepskins†	18	18	16
Goatskins†	2.5	2.5	2.5
Cattle and buffalo hides† . . .	9.0	8.5	9.0

* Unofficial figure.
† FAO estimate(s).
Source: FAO.

Forestry

ROUNDWOOD REMOVALS
('000 cubic metres, excl. bark)

	1999	2000	2001
Sawlogs, veneer logs and logs for sleepers	2,218	1,626	1,292
Pulpwood	939	957*	971*
Other industrial wood*	94	94	94
Fuel wood	1,101	2,107	1,635
Total	**4,352**	**4,784**	**3,992**

* FAO estimate(s).
Source: FAO.

SAWNWOOD PRODUCTION
('000 cubic metres, incl. sleepers)

	1998*	1999	2000
Coniferous (softwood)	186	290	258
Broadleaved (hardwood). . . .	67	35	54
Total	**253**	**325**	**312**

* FAO estimates.
Source: FAO.

Fishing
('000 metric tons, live weight)

	1998	1999	2000
Capture	10.8	10.6	7.0
Silver carp	0.6	0.5	0.0
Other cyprinids	1.3	1.5	0.5
Gobies	0.4	0.4	0.1
European sprat	3.3	3.6	1.7
Sea snails	4.3	3.8	3.8
Aquaculture	4.3	7.8	3.6
Common carp	1.5	2.9	1.3
Grass carp	0.2	0.9	0.7
Other cyprinids	1.5	1.0	0.9
Wels (som) catfish	0.2	1.4	0.1
Rainbow trout	0.6	0.4	0.4
Total catch	**15.0**	**18.3**	**10.6**

Source: FAO, *Yearbook of Fishery Statistics*.

Mining

('000 metric tons, unless otherwise indicated)

	1998	1999	2000
Anthracite.	16	17	18*
Other hard coal	105	106	100*
Lignite.	27,435	22,696	23,765*
Other brown coal.	3,692	3,074	3,211*
Crude petroleum.	32	39	41*
Natural gas (million cu metres)	33	27	15*
Iron ore: gross weight	895	699	559
Iron ore: metal content	250*	223	178
Copper concentrate†	88	96	92*
Lead concentrate†	24.2*	17.0*	10.5
Zinc concentrate* †	17.0	10.2	9.4
Manganese ore†	17*	—	—
Silver (metric tons)†	68	59	60*
Gold (kilograms)‡	1,253	2,743	2,347
Bentonite.	176	232	296
Kaolin (washed)*.	150	140	15
Barite (Barytes)*.	100	120	120
Salt (unrefined)	2,400	1,300	1,700
Gypsum and anhydrite (crude).	184	149	170

* Estimated production.
† Figures relate to the metal content of ores and concentrates.
‡ Figures relate to metal production.

Source: US Geological Survey.

Industry

SELECTED PRODUCTS

('000 metric tons, unless otherwise indicated)

	1999	2000	2001
Flour.	607	590	600
Refined sugar	250	216	182
Wine ('000 hectolitres).	1,714	1,833	810
Beer ('000 hectolitres).	4,045	4,048	4,570
Cigarettes and cigars (metric tons)	25,715	26,700*	26,600*
Cotton yarn (metric tons)[1]	19,800	19,100	15,700
Woven cotton fabrics ('000 metres)[2]	52,000	49,800	47,600
Flax and hemp yarn (metric tons)	300	n.a.	n.a.
Wool yarn (metric tons)[1]	3,400	3,900	3,700
Woven woollen fabrics ('000 metres)[2]	4,800	4,700	7,300
Woven fabrics of man-made fibres ('000 metres)[3]	11,900	13,400	14,500
Leather footwear ('000 pairs).	4,591 }	5,700	2,800
Rubber footwear ('000 pairs).	812 }		
Chemical wood pulp	74.2	77.2	72.6
Paper and paperboard.	125.7	136.0	65.1
Sulphuric acid (100%).	456	641	620
Nitrogenous fertilizers[4]	272	395	318
Phosphate fertilizers[4]	51.9	83.0	88.6
Clay building bricks (million)	259	166	149
Cement	2,060	2,209	2,088
Pig-iron and ferro-alloys	1,140	n.a	n.a.
Crude steel	1,846	n.a.	n.a
Refined copper—unwrought (metric tons)	27,200	34,000	41,000
Refined lead—unwrought (metric tons)	83,300	80,600	81,800
Zinc—unwrought (metric tons)	71,400	76,600	86,700
Metal-working lathes (number)	1,611	1,563	1,698
Fork-lift trucks (number)[5]	1,448	1,200*	1,100*
Refrigerators—household (number)	44,200	17,900	n.a.
Television receivers (number)	2,400	n.a.	n.a.
Construction: dwellings completed (number)[6]	9,824	8,795	5,937
Electric energy (million kWh)	38,248	40,925	43,849

[1] Pure and mixed yarn. Figures for wool include yarn of man-made staple.
[2] Pure and mixed fabrics, after undergoing finishing processes.
[3] Finished fabrics, including fabrics of natural silk.
[4] Figures for nitrogenous fertilizers are in terms of nitrogen, and for phosphate fertilizers in terms of phosphoric acid. Data for nitrogenous fertilizers include urea.
[5] Including hoisting gears.
[6] Including restorations and conversions.
* Figures are rounded.

Finance

CURRENCY AND EXCHANGE RATES

Monetary Units
100 stotinki (singular: stotinka) = 1 new lev (plural: leva).

Sterling, Dollar and Euro Equivalents (30 May 2003)
£1 sterling = 2.7258 new leva;
US $1 = 1.6544 new leva;
€1 = 1.9558 new leva;
100 new leva = £36.69= $60.44 = €51.13.

Average Exchange Rate (new leva per US$)
2000   2.1233
2001   2.1847
2002   2.0770

Note: On 5 July 1999 a new lev, equivalent to 1,000 old leva, was introduced. In January 1999 the value of the old lev had been linked to the German currency, the Deutsche Mark (DM), when an official exchange rate of DM1 = 1,000 old leva was established. The new lev was thus at par with the DM. From the establishment of the euro, on 1 January 1999, the German currency had a fixed exchange rate of €1 = 1.95583. Some of the figures in this Survey are still in terms of old leva.

STATE BUDGET

(million new leva)*

Revenue†	1999	2000	2001
Taxation	6,143.6	7,140.7	7,495.5
Taxes on income, profits, etc.	1,029.0	1,044.6	1,277.0
Social security contributions.	1,883.2	2,241.8	2,310.3
From employers.	1,506.9	1,427.7	1,439.5
Domestic taxes on goods and services	2,633.7	3,529.8	3,603.7
Sales, turnover or value-added taxes	1,926.9	2,359.0	2,454.4
Excises	691.2	1,131.3	1,106.7
Taxes on international trade and transactions	258.4	220.7	195.4
Import duties	258.3	220.6	195.4
Other current revenue	1,738.0	1,872.2	2,310.3
Entrepreneurial and property income	271.5	480.1	973.0
Administrative fees and charges, non-industrial and incidental sales	689.1	730.6	836.7
Fines and forfeits	424.0	353.1	271.4
Contributions to government employee pension and welfare funds	248.5	227.1	187.6
Capital revenue	124.1	111.6	68.5
Total revenue	**8,005.7**	**9,124.5**	**9,874.3**

Expenditure‡	1999	2000	2001
General public services	729.3	731.8	673.0
Defence	681.3	644.3	622.2
Public order and safety	532.8	509.2	553.9
Education	347.9	425.7	456.1
Health	409.9	524.1	984.9
Social security and welfare	2,689.1	3,461.4	3,622.1
Housing and community amenities	108.8	134.0	192.8
Recreational, cultural and religious affairs and services	141.6	153.5	143.3
Economic affairs and services	816.8	914.8	1,157.3
Fuel and energy	189.3	103.6	95.7
Agriculture, forestry, fishing and hunting	147.9	165.3	202.3
Transport and communications	327.4	515.9	489.9
Other purposes	1,665.3	1,945.9	1,806.9
Total expenditure	**8,122.7**	**9,444.8**	**10,212.6**
Current§	7,243.5	8,436.9	9,136.4
Capital.	879.2	1,007.9	1,076.2

* Figures refer to the consolidated accounts of the central Government (including social security funds and other extrabudgetary units).
† Excluding grants received (million new leva): 214.2 in 1999; 215.4 in 2000; 394.0 in 2001.
‡ Excluding lending minus repayments (million new leva): −251.5 in 1999; −259.6 in 2000; −500.2 in 2001.
§ Including interest payments (million new leva): 892.6 in 1999; 1,067.0 in 2000; 1,095.6 in 2001.

Source: IMF, *Government Finance Statistics Yearbook*.

INTERNATIONAL RESERVES
(US $ million at 31 December)

	2000	2001	2002
Gold*	305.3	289.6	340.0
IMF special drawing rights . .	84.6	2.3	0.7
Reserve position in IMF . . .	42.7	41.2	44.6
Foreign exchange	3,027.6	3,247.3	4,361.8
Total	3,460.2	3,580.4	4,747.1

* Valued at market-related prices.

Source: IMF, *International Financial Statistics*.

MONEY SUPPLY
(million new leva at 31 December)

	2000	2001	2002
Currency outside banks	2,374.1	3,081.0	3,334.9
Demand deposits at deposit money banks	1,323.1	1,655.4	2,086.5
Total money	3,976.3	4,883.8	5,542.7

Source: IMF, *International Financial Statistics*.

COST OF LIVING
(Consumer Price Index; base: 1995=100)

	1998	1999	2000
Food	2,962.4	2,724.3	3,003.5
Fuel and light	4,494.2	5,415.4	6,411.8
Clothing	4,938.6	5,956.6	6,922.4
Rent	3,227.1	3,243.3	4,489.9
All items (incl. others)	3,046.4	3,124.8	3,447.1

Source: ILO.

All items (base: 1995=100): 3,700.8 in 2001; 3,915.9 in 2002 (Source: IMF, *International Financial Statistics*).

NATIONAL ACCOUNTS
(million new leva at current prices)

Expenditure on the Gross Domestic Product

	1999	2000	2001
Final consumption expenditure .	20,901	23,291	25,825
Households	16,870	18,396	20,479
Non-profit institutions serving households	94	110	135
General government . . .	1,827	2,182	2,306
Gross capital formation . . .	4,262	4,894	6,035
Gross fixed capital formation .	3,600	4,206	5,260
Changes in inventories . . . } Acquisitions, less disposals, of valuables . . . . . . }	662	688	775
Total domestic expenditure .	25,163	28,185	31,860
Exports of goods and services .	10,601	14,902	16,494
Less Imports of goods and services	11,974	16,334	18,712
Statistical discrepancy . . .	—	—	−24
GDP in market prices . . .	23,790	26,753	29,618

Gross Domestic Product by Economic Activity

	1999	2000	2001
Agriculture	3,370	3,231	3,511
Forestry	88	70	68
Mining	403	386	380
Manufacturing	3,582	4,213	4,592
Electricity, gas and water . . .	918	1,216	1,323
Construction	1,069	1,087	1,162
Trade	1,656	1,952	2,204
Transport	1,316	1,656	1,898
Communications	801	1,061	1,472
Financial services	602	706	790
Other services	7,400	8,119	8,804
Gross value added in basic prices	21,205	23,697	26,204
Less Financial intermediation services indirectly measured . .	−360	−476	−475
Taxes on products	2,686	3,311	3,694
Import duties	259	221	195
GDP in market prices . . .	23,790	26,753	29,618

BALANCE OF PAYMENTS
(US $ million)

	1999	2000	2001
Exports of goods f.o.b.	4,006.4	4,824.6	5,106.8
Imports of goods f.o.b.	−5,087.4	−6,000.1	−6,682.4
Trade balance	−1,081.0	−1,175.5	−1,575.6
Exports of services	1,786.3	2,175.3	2,419.2
Imports of services	−1,471.1	−1,669.4	−1,879.2
Balance on goods and services	−765.8	−669.6	−1,035.6
Other income received . . .	265.5	322.9	351.6
Other income paid	−484.2	−644.2	−693.4
Balances on goods, services and income	−984.5	−990.9	−1,377.4
Current transfers received . .	328.7	354.1	588.5
Current transfers paid	−28.9	−64.4	−100.1
Current balance	−684.7	−701.2	−889.0
Capital account (net)	−2.4	25.0	—
Direct investment abroad . .	−16.8	1.9	−9.8
Direct investment from abroad .	806.1	1,001.5	691.9
Portfolio investment assets . .	−207.5	−62.0	−40.2
Portfolio investment liabilities .	8.0	−114.9	105.1
Financial derivatives liabilities .	—	−1.8	17.5
Other investment assets . . .	16.6	−136.6	349.2
Other investment liabilities . .	171.0	195.2	−19.0
Net errors and omissions . . .	6.1	−70.1	167.6
Overall balance	96.4	137.0	373.3

Source: IMF, *International Financial Statistics*.

External Trade

PRINCIPAL COMMODITIES
(US $ million)

Imports c.i.f.	1999	2000	2001*
Mineral products	1,454.6	2,044.5	1,926.8
Ores, slag and ash	168.0	216.0	247.7
Mineral fuels, mineral oils and products of their distillation	1,189.0	1,741.2	1,604.6
Products of chemical or allied industries; plastics, rubber and articles thereof	676.8	731.6	878.6
Plastics and articles thereof	159.3	195.6	230.5
Base metals and articles thereof	290.8	391.7	426.6
Nuclear reactors, boilers machinery and mechanical appliances; parts thereof	718.8	734.3	756.7
Electrical machinery, equipment and parts; sound and television apparatus, parts and accessories	375.1	365.9	568.7
Vehicles other than railway or tramway rolling-stock, and parts and accessories	457.3	454.5	580.7
Total (incl. others)	5,515.1	6,507.1	7,240.1

Exports f.o.b.	1999	2000	2001*
Mineral products	466.4	814.8	777.6
Mineral fuels, mineral oils and products of their distillation	358.3	711.0	690.2
Products of chemical or allied industries; plastics, rubber and articles thereof	496.5	628.6	629.5
Knitted or crocheted clothing and accessories	219.3	289.5	362.4
Non-knitted clothing and accessories	357.4	410.5	545.6
Footwear, gaiters, etc., and parts	111.9	118.0	159.9
Base metals and articles thereof	652.8	1,000.2	915.0
Iron and steel	263.8	387.7	352.4
Copper and articles thereof	170.5	354.3	299.7
Nuclear reactors, boilers machinery and mechanical appliances; parts thereof	264.6	274.2	319.3
Electrical machinery, equipment and parts; sound and television apparatus, parts and accessories	126.9	156.6	196.3
Total (incl. others)	4,006.4	4,824.6	5,106.5

* Figures are provisional.

PRINCIPAL TRADING PARTNERS
(US $ million*)

Imports c.i.f.	2000	2001	2002
Austria	145.2	144.5	163.9
Belgium	85.7	107.3	109.9
Czech Republic	118.2	116.3	121.5
France	316.4	437.9	441.1
Germany	902.6	1,109.4	1,117.5
Greece	317.9	411.6	469.8
Italy	549.6	695.9	883.4
Japan	62.6	76.8	87.4
Netherlands	109.4	132.5	157.6
Poland	89.5	106.8	98.7
Romania	230.8	172.3	158.4
Russia	1,582.4	1,452.7	1,145.8
Spain	98.1	120.3	152.0
Switzerland	82.4	84.7	98.8
Turkey	214.4	273.3	386.5
Ukraine	182.4	234.9	239.5
United Kingdom	138.6	180.6	204.3
USA	190.7	190.8	169.6
Total (incl. others)	6,507.1	7,260.8	7,806.1

Exports f.o.b.	2000	2001	2002
Austria	68.3	85.1	95.3
Belgium	301.7	249.5	274.9
France	231.2	286.4	299.0
Georgia	58.1	53.6	n.a.
Germany	437.0	487.7	539.3
Greece	377.0	448.6	515.6
Italy	687.7	766.3	854.5
Macedonia, former Yugoslav republic	110.3	112.5	124.7
Netherlands	86.1	80.0	100.5
Poland	27.6	34.8	40.7
Romania	86.7	129.1	158.0
Russia	118.7	119.5	90.7
Slovenia	27.3	19.4	24.4
Spain	101.3	168.0	183.2
Switzerland	47.2	58.4	94.3
Turkey	492.8	412.8	516.1
Ukraine	59.6	61.8	52.5
United Kingdom	114.4	134.9	161.7
USA	189.5	284.7	253.6
Yugoslavia, Federal Republic	374.7	212.8	171.3
Total (incl. others)	4,824.6	5,112.9	5,578.1

* Imports by country of purchase; exports by country of sale.

Transport

RAILWAYS
(traffic)

	1999	2000	2001
Passengers carried ('000)	53,112	50,029	41,817
Passenger-kilometres (million)	3,819	3,472	2,990
Freight carried ('000 metric tons)	21,090	21,082	19,285
Freight net ton-kilometres (million)	5,297	5,538	4,904

ROAD TRAFFIC
(motor vehicles in use at 31 December)

	1998	1999	2000
Passenger cars	1,809,350	1,908,392	1,908,392
Buses and coaches	41,487	41,971	41,971
Lorries and vans	220,948	230,131	271,463
Motorcycles and mopeds	515,701	519,212	519,212

Source: International Road Federation, *World Road Statistics*.

INLAND WATERWAYS
(traffic)

	1999	2000	2001
Passengers carried ('000)	121	76	67
Passenger-kilometres (million)	12	1	n.a.
Freight carried ('000 metric tons)	1,469	1,846	1,300
Freight ton-kilometres (million)	320	397	365

SHIPPING

Merchant Fleet
(registered at 31 December)

	1999	2000	2001
Number of vessels	173	164	172
Total displacement ('000 grt)	1,035.8	989.6	955.3

Source: Lloyd's Register-Fairplay, *World Fleet Statistics*.

Sea-borne Traffic
(international and coastal)

	1997	1998	1999
Passengers carried ('000) . . .	21	7	n.a.
Freight ('000 metric tons) . . .	19,623	16,446	16,822

2000: Freight carried ('000 metric tons) 18,619; Freight ton-kilometres (million) 74,391.

2001: Freight carried ('000 metric tons) 16,737; Freight ton-kilometres (million) 67,551.

CIVIL AVIATION
(traffic)

	1998	1999	2000
Passengers carried ('000) . . .	1,458	1,354	1,261
Passenger-kilometres (million) . .	3,311	2,680	2,257
Freight carried ('000 metric tons) .	38	30	22
Freight ton-kilometres (million) .	101	63	46

Tourism

ARRIVALS OF FOREIGN VISITORS

Country of origin	2000	2001	2002
Austria.	8,382	27,253	24,358
Belgium	17,499	24,946	29,076
Czech Republic	28,992	36,986	48,485
Denmark	15,035	19,372	31,628
Finland	19,275	29,178	38,108
France	21,416	27,305	30,983
Germany	263,034	374,323	480,460
Greece	321,651	344,677	391,386
Israel	30,910	50,368	64,064
Macedonia, former Yugoslav republic*	658,395	643,106	621,875
Poland	18,968	31,492	48,738
Romania*	203,974	227,286	92,826
Russia	105,622	130,886	99,389
Slovakia	18,739	30,999	42,452
Sweden	39,998	48,070	54,898
Turkey	95,567	44,243	29,645*
Ukraine	59,279	70,168	39,426
United Kingdom	51,973	69,202	110,902
USA	20,969	25,560	25,417
Yugoslavia, Federal Republic* .	218,394	359,467	534,816
Total (incl. others)	2,354,052	2,775,717	2,992,590

* Includes 'shuttle traders'.

Source: Ministry of the Economy, Sofia.

Receipts from tourism (US $ million): 966 in 1998; 932 in 1999; 1,074 in 2000 (Sources: World Bank and Bulgarian National Bank).

Communications Media

	1999	2000	2001
Television receivers ('000 in use)	3,550	3,692	n.a.
Telephones ('000 main lines in use)	2,833.4	2,881.8	2,913.9
Mobile cellular telephones ('000 subscribers)	350	738	1,550
Personal computers ('000 in use)	220	361	n.a.
Internet users ('000)	235	430	605
Book production:*			
titles	4,971	5,027	4,984
copies ('000)	10,400	9,400	6,600
Newspapers:			
titles	545	545	465
total circulation ('000 copies). .	397,300	442,600	372,600
Magazines:†			
titles	581	647	678
total circulation ('000 copies). .	11,800	19,100	16,700

* Including pamphlets.
† Including bulletins.

Facsimile machines (number in use): 15,000 in 1995 (estimate).

Sources: partly UN, *Statistical Yearbook*, UNESCO, *Statistical Yearbook*, and International Telecommunication Union.

Education

(2001/02)

	Institutions	Teachers	Students
Kindergartens	3,242	18,637	199,206
General schools	2,812	63,261	839,518
Special	136	2,333	15,631
Vocational technical	3	36	1,962
Secondary vocational	112	2,664	39,365
Technical colleges and schools of arts	376	15,222	145,697
Semi-higher institutes*	48	2,342	16,646
Higher educational	42	21,546	211,748†

* Including technical, teacher-training, communications and librarians' institutes.
† Including post-graduate students.

Adult literacy rate (UNESCO estimates): 98.4% (males 97.9%; females 99.0%) in 2000 (Source: UN Development Programme, *Human Development Report*).

Directory

The Constitution

The Constitution of the Republic of Bulgaria, summarized below, took effect upon its promulgation, on 13 July 1991, following its enactment on the previous day.

FUNDAMENTAL PRINCIPLES

Chapter One declares that the Republic of Bulgaria is to have a parliamentary form of government, with all state power derived from the people. The rule of law and the life, dignity and freedom of the individual are guaranteed. The Constitution is the supreme law; the power of the State is shared between the legislature, the executive and the judiciary. The Constitution upholds principles such as political and religious freedom (although no party may be formed on separatist, ethnic or religious lines), free economic initiative and respect for international law.

FUNDAMENTAL RIGHTS AND OBLIGATIONS OF CITIZENS

Chapter Two establishes the basic provisions for Bulgarian citizenship and fundamental human rights, such as the rights of privacy and movement, the freedoms of expression, assembly and association, and the enfranchisement of Bulgarian citizens aged over 18 years. The Constitution commits the State to the provision of basic social welfare and education and to the encouragement of culture, science and the health of the population. The study and use of the Bulgarian language is required. Other obligations of the citizenry include military service and the payment of taxes.

THE NATIONAL ASSEMBLY

The National Assembly is the legislature of Bulgaria and exercises parliamentary control over the country. It consists of 240 members, elected for a four-year term. Only Bulgarian citizens aged over 21 years (who do not hold a state post or another citizenship and are not under judicial interdiction or in prison) are eligible for election to parliament. A member of the National Assembly ceases to serve as a deputy while holding ministerial office. The National Assembly is a permanently acting body, which is free to determine its own recesses and elects its own Chairman and Deputy Chairmen. The Chairman represents and convenes the National Assembly, organizes its proceedings, attests its enactments and promulgates its resolutions.

The National Assembly may function when more than one-half of its members are present, and may pass legislation and other acts by a majority of more than one-half of the members present, except where a qualified majority is required by the Constitution. Ministers are free to, and can be obliged to, attend parliamentary sessions. The most important functions of the legislature are: the enactment of laws; the approval of the state budget; the scheduling of presidential elections; the election and dismissal of the Chairman of the Council of Ministers (Prime Minister) and of other members of the Council of Ministers; the declaration of war or conclusion of peace; the foreign deployment of troops; and the ratification of any fundamental international instruments to which the Republic of Bulgaria has agreed. The laws and resolutions of the National Assembly are binding on all state bodies and citizens. All enactments must be promulgated in the official gazette, *Durzhaven Vestnik*, within 15 days of their passage through the legislature.

THE PRESIDENT OF THE REPUBLIC

Chapter Four concerns the Head of State, the President of the Republic of Bulgaria, who is assisted by a Vice-President. The President and Vice-President are elected jointly, directly by the voters, for a period of five years. A candidate must be eligible for election to the National Assembly, but also aged over 40 years and a resident of the country for the five years previous to the election. To be elected, a candidate must receive more than one-half of the valid votes cast, in an election in which more than one-half of the eligible electorate participate. If necessary, a second ballot must then be conducted, contested by the two candidates who received the most votes. The one who receives more votes becomes President. The President and Vice-President may hold the same office for only two terms and, during this time, may not engage in any unsuitable or potentially compromising activities. If the President resigns, is incapacitated, impeached or dies, the Vice-President carries out the presidential duties. If neither official can perform their duties, the Chairman of the National Assembly assumes the prerogatives of the Presidency, until new elections take place.

The President's main responsibilities include the scheduling of elections and referendums, the conclusion of international treaties and the promulgation of laws. The President is responsible for appointing a Prime Minister-designate (priority must be given to the leaders of the two largest parties represented in the National Assembly), who must then attempt to form a government.

The President is Supreme Commander-in-Chief of the Armed Forces of the Republic of Bulgaria and presides over the Consultative National Security Council. The President has certain emergency powers, usually subject to the later approval of the National Assembly. Many of the President's actions must be approved by the Chairman of the Council of Ministers. The President may return legislation to the National Assembly for further consideration, but can be overruled.

THE COUNCIL OF MINISTERS

The principal organ of executive government is the Council of Ministers, which supervises the implementation of state policy and the state budget, the administration of the country and the Armed Forces, and the maintenance of law and order. The Council of Ministers is headed and co-ordinated by the Chairman (Prime Minister), who is responsible for the overall policy of government. The Council of Ministers, which also includes Deputy Chairmen and Ministers, must resign upon the death of the Chairman or if the National Assembly votes in favour of a motion of no confidence in the Council or in the Chairman.

JUDICIAL POWER

The judicial branch of government is independent. All judicial power is exercised in the name of the people. Individuals and legal entities are guaranteed basic rights, such as the right to contest administrative acts and the right to legal counsel. One of the principal organs is the Supreme Court of Cassation, which exercises supreme judicial responsibility for the precise and equal application of the law by all courts. The Supreme Administrative Court rules on all challenges to the legality of acts of any organ of government. The Chief Prosecutor supervises all other prosecutors and ensures that the law is observed, by initiating court actions and ensuring the enforcement of penalties, etc.

The Supreme Judicial Council is responsible for appointments within the ranks of the justices, prosecutors and investigating magistrates, and recommends to the President of the Republic the appointment or dismissal of the Chairmen of the two Supreme Courts and of the Chief Prosecutor (they are each appointed for a single, seven-year term). These last three officials are, *ex officio*, members of the Supreme Judicial Council, together with 22 others, who must be practising lawyers of high integrity and at least 15 years of professional experience. These members are elected for a term of five years, 11 of them by the National Assembly and 11 by bodies of the judiciary. The Supreme Judicial Council is chaired by the Minister of Justice, who is not entitled to vote.

LOCAL SELF-GOVERNMENT AND LOCAL ADMINISTRATION

Chapter Seven provides for the division of Bulgaria into regions and municipalities. Municipalities are the basic administrative territorial unit at which local self-government is practised; their principal organ is the municipal council, which is elected directly by the population for a term of four years. The council elects the mayor, who is the principal organ of executive power. Bulgaria is also divided into regions. Regional government, which is entrusted to regional governors (appointed by the Council of Ministers) and administrations, is responsible for regional policy, the implementation of state policy at a local level and the harmonization of local and national interests.

THE CONSTITUTIONAL COURT

The Constitutional Court consists of 12 justices, four of whom are elected by the National Assembly, four appointed by the President of the Republic and four elected by the justices of the two Supreme Courts. Candidates must have the same eligibility as for membership of the Supreme Judicial Council. They serve a single term of nine years, but a part of the membership changes every three years. A chairman is elected by a secret ballot of the members.

The Constitutional Court provides binding interpretations of the Constitution. It rules on the constitutionality of: laws and decrees; competence suits between organs of government; international agreements; national and presidential elections; and impeachments. A ruling of the Court requires a majority of more than one-half of the votes of all the justices.

CONSTITUTIONAL AMENDMENTS AND THE ADOPTION OF A NEW CONSTITUTION

Chapter Nine provides for constitutional changes. Except for those provisions reserved to the competence of a Grand National Assembly (see below), the National Assembly is empowered to amend the Constitution with a majority of three-quarters of all its Members, in three ballots on three different days. Amendments must be proposed by one-quarter of the parliamentary membership or by the President. In some cases, a majority of two-thirds of all the Members of the National Assembly will suffice.

Grand National Assembly

A Grand National Assembly consists of 400 members, elected by the generally established procedure. It alone is empowered to adopt a new constitution, to sanction territorial changes to the Republic of Bulgaria, to resolve on any changes in the form of state structure or form of government, and to enact amendments to certain parts of the existing Constitution (concerning the direct application of the Constitution, the domestic application of international agreements, the irrevocable nature of fundamental civil rights and of certain basic individual rights even in times of emergency or war, and amendments to Chapter Nine itself).

Any bill requiring the convening of a Grand National Assembly must be introduced by the President of the Republic or by one-third of the members of the National Assembly. A decision to hold elections for a Grand National Assembly must be supported by two-thirds of the members of the National Assembly. Enactments of the Grand National Assembly require a majority of two-thirds of the votes of all the members, in three ballots on three different days. A Grand National Assembly may resolve only on the proposals for which it was elected, whereupon its prerogatives normally expire.

The Government

HEAD OF STATE

President: GEORGI PARVANOV (elected 18 November 2001; inaugurated 19 January 2002; took office 22 January 2002).

COUNCIL OF MINISTERS
(July 2003)

A coalition of the National Movement Simeon II (NMSII), the Movement for Rights and Freedoms (MRF), and the Bulgarian Socialist Party (BSP).

Prime Minister: SIMEON SAXE-COBURG GOTHA (NMSII).

Deputy Prime Minister: PLAMEN PANAYOTOV (NMSII).

Deputy Prime Minister and Minister of the Economy: LIDIYA SHOULEVA (NMSII).

Deputy Prime Minister and Minister of Transport and Communications: NIKOLAI VASSILEV (NMSII).

Minister of Defence: NIKOLAI AVRAMOV SVINAROV (NMSII).

Minister of Foreign Affairs: SOLOMON ISAK PASI (NMSII).

Minister of Finance: MILEN EMILOV VELCHEV (NMSII).

Minister of the Interior: GEORGI PETROV PETKANOV (NMSII).

Minister of Justice: ANTON ILIEV STANKOV (NMSII).

Minister of Education and Science: IGOR DAMYANOV (NMSII).

Minister of European Affairs: MEGLENA KUNEVA (NMSII).

Minister of Agriculture and Forestry: MEKHMED MEKHMED DIKME (MRF).

Minister of Regional Development and Public Works: VALENTIN IVANOV TSEROVSKI (NMSII).

Minister of Labour and Social Policy: HRISTINA HRISTOVA (NMSII).

Minister of Health: SLAVCHO BOGOEV (NMSII).

Minister of Culture: BOZHIDAR ZAFIROV ABRASHEV (NMSII).

Minister of the Environment and Water: DOLORES BORISOVA ARSENOVA (NMSII).

Minister of Energy and Energy Resources: MILKO KOVACHEV (NMSII).

Minister of State Administration: DIMITAR GEORGIEV KALCHEV (BSP).

Minister of Youth and Sport: VASSIL MINCHEV IVANOV (NMSII).

Minister without Portfolio: FILIZ HYUSMENOVA (MRF).

MINISTRIES

Office of the President: 1123 Sofia, Blvd Dondukov 2; tel. (2) 923-93-33; e-mail press@president.bg; internet www.president.bg.

Council of Ministers: 1000 Sofia, Blvd Dondukov 1; tel. (2) 940-27-70; fax (2) 980-20-56; e-mail iprd@government.bg; internet www.government.bg.

Ministry of Agriculture and Forestry: 1040 Sofia, Blvd Botev 55; tel. (2) 980-99-27; fax (2) 980-62-56; internet www.mzgar.government.bg.

Ministry of Culture: 1040 Sofia, Blvd A. Stamboliyski 17; tel. (2) 980-53-84; fax (2) 981-81-45; e-mail press.culture@bta.bg; internet www.culture.government.bg.

Ministry of Defence: 1000 Sofia, Aksakov St 1; tel. (2) 987-95-62; fax (2) 87-32-28; internet www.md.government.bg.

Ministry of the Economy: 1000 Sofia, Slavyanska St 8; tel. (2) 988-55-32; fax (2) 980-26-90; e-mail s.bozukova@mi.government.bg; internet www.mi.government.bg.

Ministry of Education and Science: 1540 Sofia, A. Stamboliyski 18; tel. (2) 84-87-44; fax (2) 988-26-93; e-mail press_mon@minedu.government.bg; internet www.minedu.government.bg.

Ministry of Energy and Energy Resources: 1040 Sofia, Triadica St 8; tel. and fax (2) 987-84-25; e-mail pressall@doe.bg; internet www.doe.bg/cgi-bin/i.pl.

Ministry of the Environment and Water: 1000 Sofia, William Gladstone St 67; tel. (2) 940-62-31; fax (2) 988-59-13; internet www.moew.govrn.bg.

Ministry of European Affairs: 1040 Sofia, Al. Zhendov St 1; tel. (2) 971-32-12; fax (2) 971-29-06; e-mail mkuneva@mfa.government.bg; internet www.evroportal.bg.

Ministry of Finance: 1000 Sofia, Rakovski St 102; tel. (2) 985-920-20; fax (2) 87-05-81; e-mail feedback@minfin.government.bg; internet www.minfin.government.bg.

Ministry of Foreign Affairs: 1113 Sofia, Al. Zhendov St 2; tel. (2) 73-79-97; fax (2) 70-30-41; internet www.mfa.government.bg.

Ministry of Health: 1000 Sofia, Blvd Sveta Nedelya 5; tel. (2) 930-011-07; fax (2) 981-26-39; e-mail press@mh.government.bg; internet www.mh.government.bg.

Ministry of the Interior: 1000 Sofia, Shesti Septemvri St 29; tel. (2) 982-20-14; fax (2) 982-20-47; e-mail spvo@mvr.bg; internet www.mvr.bg.

Ministry of Justice: 1040 Sofia, Slavyanska St 1; tel. (2) 988-48-23; fax (2) 981-91-57; e-mail pr@mjeli.government.bg; internet www.mjeli.government.bg.

Ministry of Labour and Social Policy: 1051 Sofia, Triaditza St 2; tel. (2) 87-33-94; fax (2) 986-13-18; e-mail mlsp@mlsp.government.bg; internet www.mlsp.government.bg.

Ministry of Regional Development and Public Works: Sofia, Kirili Metodi 17–19; tel. (2) 988-29-54; fax (2) 987-58-56; e-mail press@mrrb.government.bg; internet www.mrrb.government.bg.

Ministry of State Administration: 1594 Sofia, Blvd Dondukov 1; tel. (2) 940-27-17; fax (2) 940-21-70; e-mail k.zdravskovska@government.bg.

Ministry of Transport and Communications: 1000 Sofia, Levski St 9; tel. (2) 940-95-00; fax (2) 987-18-05; e-mail vluleva@mtc.government.bg; internet www.mtc.government.bg.

Ministry of Youth and Sport: Sofia.

President and Legislature

PRESIDENT

Presidential Election, First Ballot, 11 November 2001

Candidates	% of votes
Georgi Parvanov (Coalition for Bulgaria)	36.4
Petar Stoyanov (Independent)	34.9
Bogomil Bonev (Civic Party for Bulgaria)	19.3
Reneta Indzhova (Democratic Alliance)	4.9
Others	4.5
Total	100.0

Second Ballot, 18 November 2001

Candidates	% of votes
Georgi Parvanov	54.1
Petar Stoyanov	45.9
Total	100.0

NARODNO SOBRANIYE
(National Assembly)

National Assembly: 1000 Sofia, Blvd Narodno Sobraniye 3; tel. (2) 980-85-01; fax (2) 981-01-81; e-mail infocenter@nt52.parliament.bg; internet www.parliament.bg.

Chairman: OGNYAN GERDZHIKOV.

General Election, 17 June 2001

Parties	% of votes	Seats
National Movement Simeon II*	42.73	120
Union of Democratic Forces	18.17	51
Coalition for Bulgaria†	17.14	48
Movement for Rights and Freedoms	7.45	21
Gergyovden Movement—Inner Macedonian Revolutionary Organization	3.63	—
Others	10.88	—
Total	100.00	240

* The National Movement contested the election in alliance (as the National Movement Simeon II) with the Party of Bulgarian Women and Oborishte Party for National Revival, in order to be permitted legally to register.
† The Bulgarian Socialist Party contested the election in alliance, as part of the Coalition for Bulgaria, comprising 15 left and left-of-centre parties.

Local Government

The 1991 Constitution provided for the division of Bulgaria into municipalities and regions. These were partially re-organized in 1994. There are 259 municipalities, each with a municipal council, elected for a period of four years. Municipal elections were held in October 1999, in 255 municipalities, and elections were held in four municipalities in April 2002. In mid-1998 the number of regions was increased from nine to 28. The Governors of the regions are appointed by the Council of Ministers.

Sofia City People's Council: 1000 Sofia, Alabin St 22; tel. (2) 986-09-47; fax (2) 988-47-94; Gov. ROSEN ZLATANOV VLADIMIROV.

Blagoevgrad Region People's Council: Blagoevgrad, Blvd G. Izmirliev 9; tel. (73) 844-80; fax (73) 814-03; e-mail bl-obl@avala.bg; Gov. ANTON VELIMIROV BRICHKOV.

Burgas Region People's Council: Burgas, Tsar Petar St 1; tel. (56) 84-26-01; fax (56) 84-25-62; e-mail upravitel@bsregion.org; Gov. IVAN VITANOV.

Dobrich Region People's Council: 9300 Dobrich, Blvd Nezavisimost 5; tel. and fax (58) 273-79; e-mail pressdob@netplusdb.bg; Gov. IVAN DIMITROV IVANOV.

Gabrovo Region People's Council: Gabrovo, Blvd Vazrazhdane 5; tel. and fax (66) 330-01; e-mail governor@gb.government.bg; Gov. TSVETAN MARINOV NANOV.

Haskovo Region People's Council: Haskovo, Blvd Svoboda 5; tel. (38) 248-72; fax (38) 600-91; e-mail reghas@haskovo.spnet.net; Gov. GEORGI MILANOV ZARCHEV.

Kardjali Region People's Council: 6600 Kardjali, Blvd Bulgaria 41; tel. (361) 217-58; fax (361) 217-62; e-mail obl.adm.kj@infotel.bg; Gov. KALIN TODOROV PRIMOV.

Kjustendil Region People's Council: 2500 Kjustendil, Blvd Velbuzhd 1; tel. (78) 510-05; fax (87) 510-04; e-mail oblast.kn@infotel.bg; Gov. Dr LYUDMIL STOYANOV.

Lovech Region People's Council: 5500 Lovech, Targovska St 43; tel. (68) 221-80; fax (68) 227-79; e-mail governorlv@lv.bia-bg.com; Gov. MARIAN PENCHEV BALEV.

Montana Region People's Council: 3400 Montana, Blvd Zheravitsa 1; tel. (96) 210-46; fax (96) 30-07-00; e-mail oblastmont@net-surf.net; Gov. MARIAN GEORGIEV SVETANOV.

Pazardjik Region People's Council: 4400 Pazardjik, Ekzarh Iosif St 2; tel. (34) 44-34-48; fax (34) 44-23-38; e-mail secretary@pz-oblast.cybcom.net; Gov. IVAN VASILEV DIMITROV.

Pernik Region People's Council: Pernik, Blvd Ivan Rilski 1B; tel. (76) 64-99-13; fax (76) 60-47-55; e-mail reg_pk.pr@pernik.spnet.net; Gov. DIMITR KOLEV.

Pleven Region People's Council: Pleven, Blvd Vzrazhdane 1, 4th floor; tel. (64) 80-10-73; fax (64) 80-10-72; e-mail jivanova@el-soft.com; Gov. NIKOLAI NIKOLOV MARINOV.

Plovdiv Region People's Council: Plovdiv, N. Moshanov Pl. 1; tel. (32) 60-55-11; fax (32) 62-57-19; Gov. GOKA BOGDANOV PETROV.

Razgrad Region People's Council: Razgrad, Beli Lom Blvd 37A; tel. (84) 30-62-25; fax (84) 30-62-03; e-mail gov_rz@mbox.infotel.bg; Gov. SULEIMAN BEKHCHET.

Ruse Region People's Council: Ruse, Blvd Svoboda 6; tel. (82) 81-22-23; fax (82) 23-56-70; internet www.ruse.bg/index.shtml; Gov. RUMEN YANUAROV.

Shumen Region People's Council: Shumen, Blvd Slavianski 30; tel. (54) 699-85; fax (54) 635-62; e-mail oblast@iservice.bg; Gov. NORA CHALUKOVA-SIMEONOVA.

Silistra Region People's Council: Silistra, Dobrudzha St 29; tel. (86) 82-09-00; fax (86) 82-08-00; e-mail oblast-s@mbox.infotel.bg; Gov. PETKO DRAGANOV DOBREV.

Sliven Region People's Council: 8800 Sliven, Dimitar Dobrovich St 3; tel. (44) 370-90; fax (44) 370-90; e-mail governments@regionsliven.com; Gov. IVAN BLAGOEV BLAGOEV.

Smolyan Region People's Council: 4700 Smolyan, Blvd Bulgaria 14; tel. (301) 628-92; fax (301) 623-33; e-mail obl_adm_sm@bsbg.net; Gov. DIMITR KOSTADINOV PALAGACHEV.

Sofia Region People's Council: 1000 Sofia, Blvd Vitosha 6; tel. (2) 988-38-03; fax (2) 988-34-84; e-mail sofoblast@government.bg; Gov. ROSEN VLADIMIROV.

Stara Zagora Region People's Council: Stara Zagora, Tsar Simeon Veliki St 108; tel. (42) 267-26; fax (42) 60-06-40; e-mail oblastsz@sz.bia-bg.com; Gov. MARIA NEIKOVA.

Targovishte Region People's Council: 7700 Targovishte, Stefan Karadja St 2; tel. (601) 623-58; fax (601) 642-28; e-mail oblast@tg.bia-bg.com; Gov. IBRAHIM KERIM BEKHCHET.

Varna Region People's Council: 9000 Varna, Preslav St 26; tel. (52) 60-06-17; fax (52) 60-21-20; e-mail oblasten_upravitel@oa.vn.government.bg; internet district.varna-bg.com; Gov. YANI DIMITROV YANEV.

Veliko Turnovo People's Council: Veliko Turnovo, Blvd Tsentr 2; tel. (62) 60-08-34; fax (62) 60-04-64; e-mail turnovo-dc@mbox.digsys.bg; Gov. KRASIMIR GENCHEV GENCHEV.

Vidin Region People's Council: Vidin, Dunavska St 6; tel. (94) 451-42; fax (94) 476-14; e-mail obl-vidin@mbox.digsys.bg; Gov. MARTIN NIKOLOV DONCHEV.

Vratsa Region People's Council: Vratsa, Blvd Demokratsia 1; tel. (92) 610-46; fax (92) 611-59; e-mail obl-vr@isv.net; Gov. LACHEZAR OCENOV BORISOV.

Yambol Region People's Council: Yambol, George Papazov St 18; tel. (46) 627-44; fax (46) 622-77; e-mail yambol@digicom.bg; internet yambol.government.bg; Gov. MINCHO SPASSOV.

Political Organizations

There are over 80 registered political parties in Bulgaria, many of them incorporated into electoral alliances. The most significant political forces are listed below:

Aleksandur Stamboliyski Bulgarian Agrarian People's Union (Bulgarski Zemedelski Naroden Sayuz 'Aleksandur Stamboliyski'): Sofia.

Bulgarian Communist Party (Bulgarska Komunisticheska Partiya): 1404 Sofia, Blvd P. J. Todorov, Bl. 5B; tel. and fax (2) 59-16-73; e-mail spasov@internet-bg.net; re-formed in 1990; First Sec. of the Central Cttee VLADIMIR SPASOV.

Bulgarian Socialist Party (BSP) (Bulgarska Sotsialisticheska Partiya): Sofia, Positano St 20; POB 382; tel. (2) 981-57-08; fax (2) 981-17-88; e-mail bsp@bsp.bg; internet www.bsp.bg; f. 1891 as the Bulgarian Social Democratic Party (BSDP); renamed the Bulgarian Communist Party (BCP) in 1919; renamed as above in 1990; 320,000 mems (Jan. 1996); Chair. SERGEY STANISHEV.

Christian Republican Party: Sofia; f. 1989; Chair. KONSTANTIN ADZHAROV.

Civic Party for Bulgaria: Sofia; f. 2000; centre-right; also known as Citizens' Party for Bulgaria; Chair. BOGOMIL BONEV.

Coalition for Bulgaria: Sofia; f. by the Bulgarian Socialist Party (q.v.) to contest the legislative election of June 2001; alliance of 15 left and left-of-centre parties.

Confederation—Kingdom Bulgaria (Tsarstvo Bulgaria): 7000 Ruse, Vassil Kolarov 45; tel. (82) 299-64; f. 1990; monarchist; Chair. GEORGI BAKARDZHIEV.

Conservative Union—EKIP: Sofia; f. 2001 by members of the Union of Democratic Forces, who supported Simeon Saxe-Coburg Gotha; Chair. CHRISTO BISEROV.

Democratic Alliance/Democratic Alternative for the Republic (DAR): Sofia; left-of-centre coalition; Co-Chair. RENETA INDZHOVA, Dr KONSTANTIN TRENCHEV.

Democratic Party of Justice: Sofia; f. 1994; ethnic Turkish group; fmrly part of the Movement for Rights and Freedoms; Chair. NEDIM GENDZHEV.

Fatherland Party of Labour: 1000 Sofia, Slavyanska St 3, Hotel Slavyanska Beseda; tel. (2) 65-83-10; nationalist; Chair. RUMEN POPOV.

Fatherland Union: Sofia, Blvd Vitosha 18; tel. (2) 88-12-21; f. 1942 as the Fatherland Front (a mass organization unifying the BAPU, the BCP—now the BSP—and social organizations); named as above when restructured in 1990; a socio-political organization of independents and individuals belonging to different political parties; Chair. GINYO GANEV.

Free Radical Democratic Party: Sofia.

Georgi Ganchev Bloc: 1000 Sofia, Shipka 13; tel. (2) 44-61-28; f. 2000 as a successor to the Bulgarian Business Bloc; Leader GEORGI GANCHEV; Chair. DOBRI DOBREV.

Gergyovden Movement (St George's Day Political Movement): Sofia, Blvd G. M. Dimitrov 16; tel. (2) 965-16-74; fax (2) 965-16-79; e-mail g-day@gergiovden.com; internet www.gergiovden.com; contested the legislative election of June 2001 in alliance with the Inner Macedonian Revolutionary Organization; Pres. ORLIN CHOCHOV.

Green Party: 1000 Sofia, Lavele St 30; tel. (2) 987-69-24; fax (2) 987-85-38; e-mail green@mail.bol.bg; internet www.greenparty.bg; f. 1989; Chair. ALEKSANDUR KARAKACHANOV.

Inner Macedonian Revolutionary Organization (IMRO): 1301 Sofia, Pirotska St 5; tel. (2) 980-25-82; fax (2) 980-25-83; e-mail vmro@vmro.org; internet www.vmro.org; f. 1893; contested the legislative election of June 2001 in alliance with the Gergyovden Movement; Chair. KRASSIMIR KARAKACHANOV.

Liberal Congress Party: Sofia; f. 1989 as the Bulgarian Socialist Party, renamed Bulgarian Social Democratic Party (non-Marxist) in 1990 and as above in 1991; membership of the Union of Democratic Forces suspended 1993; c. 20,000 mems; Chair. YANKO N. YANKOV.

Liberal Democratic Alternative: 1000 Sofia, Triaditsa St 4; tel. and fax (2) 986-37-14; e-mail lda@bulgarianspace.com; internet www.bulgarianspace.com/lda/; f. 1997; Leader ZHELIU ZHELEV.

Movement for Rights and Freedoms (MRF) (Dvizhenie za Prava i Svobodi—DPS): Sofia, Blvd Aleksandur Stamboliyski 45A; tel. (2) 988-18-23; internet www.dps.bg; f. 1990; represents the Muslim minority in Bulgaria; 95,000 mems (1991); Pres. AHMED DOGAN.

National Movement Simeon II (NMSII): 1000 Sofia, Vrabtcha St 23; tel. (2) 980-38-09; e-mail ndsv@ndsv.bg; internet www.ndsv.bg; April 2001 by supporters of the former monarch; contested the legislative election of 17 June in coalition with the Party of Bulgarian Women and the Oborishte Party for National Revival; registered as a political party in April 2002; Chair. SIMEON SAXE-COBURG GOTHA.

National Movement for Rights and Freedoms: f. 1999; breakaway faction of the MRF; Leader GYUNER TAHIR.

New Choice Liberal Alliance: f. 1994 by a former faction of the Union of Democratic Forces; Co-Chair. DIMITUR LUDZHEV, IVAN PUSHKAROV.

New Union for Democracy (NUD): Sofia; f. 1993; fmrly section of the Union of Democratic Forces.

Party of Free Democrats (Centre): 6000 Stara Zagora; tel. (42) 2-70-42; f. 1989; Chair. Asst Prof. CHRISTO SANTULOV.

Union of Democratic Forces (UDF) (Sayuz na Demokratichnite Sili—SDS): 1000 Sofia, Blvd Rakovski 134; tel. (2) 93-06-132; fax (2) 981-05-22; e-mail pr@sds.bg; internet www.sds.bg; Pres. IVAN KOSTOV; Chair. NADEZHDA MIHAILOVA; f. 1989 as an alliance that included the following parties, organizations and movements; plans for its reconstitution as a single, centre-right Christian Democratic Party were announced in 2001.

> **Bulgarian Agrarian People's Union—'Nikola Petkov'** (Bulgarski Zemedelski Naroden Sayuz—'Nikola Petkov'): Sofia; tel. (2) 87-80-81; fax (2) 981-09-49; f. 1899; Leader GEORGI PINCHEV.

> **Bulgarian Democratic Forum:** 1000 Sofia, Blvd Dondukov 9, 2nd Floor; tel. (2) 980-31-42; internet bdf.hit.bg; Chair. MURAVEI RADEV.

> **Bulgarian Social Democratic Party (United—BSDP):** 1504 Sofia, Ekzarkh Yosif St 37; tel. (2) 80-15-84; fax (2) 73-24-76; e-mail president@bsdp.net; internet www.bsdp.net; f. 1891; re-established 1989; Pres. GEORGI ANASTASOV.

> **Christian Democratic Union:** Sofia; Chair. JULIUS PAVLOV.

> **Christian 'Salvation' Union:** Sofia; Chair. Bishop CHRISTOFOR SAHEV.

> **Citizens' Initiative Movement:** Sofia; tel. (2) 39-01-93; Chair. TODOR GAGALOV.

> **Democratic Party in Bulgaria:** 1000 Sofia, POB 216, Vrabcha St 10, 1st Floor; tel. (2) 981-03-40; internet dpb.search.bg; reformed 1990; Chair. ALEKSANDUR PRAMATARSKI.

> **Democratic Party 1896:** f. 1994 by a former faction of the Democratic Party; Chair. STEFAN RAYCHEVSKI.

> **Federation of Democracy Clubs:** Sofia; f. 1988 as Club for the Support of Glasnost and Perestroika; merged with other groups, as above in 1990; Chair. YORDAN VASSILEV.

> **Federation of Independent Student Committees:** Sofia; Leader ANDREI NENOV.

> **New Social Democratic Party:** Sofia; tel. (2) 44-99-47; f. 1990; membership of UDF suspended 1991, resumed 1993; Chair. Dr VASSIL MIKHAILOV.

> **New United Labour Bloc:** f. 1997; Chair. KRUSTYU PETKOV.

> **Radical Democratic Party:** 1220 Sofia, Blvd Rogen 101; tel. (2) 936-04-76; fax (2) 936-02-06; e-mail kvelev@online.bg; Chair. KIRIL VELEV.

> **Republican Party:** 1000 Sofia, POB 787, Christo Belchev St 1, 3rd Floor; tel. (2) 986-35-72; fax (2) 986-67-22; e-mail republican_party_bg@hotmail.com; f. 1990; Chair. LENKO RUSSANOV.

> **United Christian Democratic Centre:** Sofia; tel. (2) 80-04-09.

Union of Free Democrats: Sofia; f. 2001 as a breakaway faction of the Union of Democratic Forces; Leader STEFAN SOFIANSKI.

The Independent Association for Human Rights in Bulgaria (Leader STEFAN VALKOV), the Union of Victims of Repression (Leader IVAN NEVROKOPSKY) and the Union of Non-Party Members (Leader BOYAN VELKOV) all enjoyed observer status in the UDF.

Diplomatic Representation

EMBASSIES IN BULGARIA

Afghanistan: 1618 Sofia, Ovcha Kupel, Boryana St 61, Bl. 216A; tel. (2) 55-61-96; fax (2) 955-99-76.

Albania: Sofia, Krakra St 10; tel. (2) 946-12-22; fax (2) 943-30-69; Ambassador KOCO KOTE.

Algeria: Sofia, Slavyanska St 16; tel. (2) 980-22-50; Ambassador ZINE EL-ABIDINE HACHICHI.

Argentina: Sofia, POB 635, Dragan Tsankov 36, 2nd Floor; tel. (2) 971-25-39; fax (2) 71-61-30-28; Ambassador ARTURO HOTTON RISLER.

Armenia: 1606 Sofia, 20 April St 11, 11th Floor; tel. and fax (2) 52-60-46; e-mail armembsof@sof.omega.bg; Ambassador SEVDA SEVAN.

Austria: 1000 Sofia, Shipka St 4; tel. (2) 980-35-72; fax (2) 987-22-60; e-mail obsofia@online.bg; Ambassador Dr GEORG POTYKA.

Belarus: 1113 Sofia, Charles Darwin St 6; tel. and fax (2) 973-31-00; e-mail embassyblr@omega.bg; Ambassador ALYAKSANDR PETROV.

Belgium: 1164 Sofia, Velchova Zavera St 1; tel. (2) 988-72-90; fax (2) 963-36-38; e-mail ambabel@einet.bg; Ambassador EDMOND DE WILDE.

Brazil: 1113 Sofia, Frédéric Joliot Curie St 19, Bl. 156/1; tel. (2) 72-35-27; fax (2) 971-28-18; e-mail sofbrem@main.infotel.bg; Ambassador CARLOS ALBERTO PESSÔA PARDELLAS.

Cambodia: Sofia, Mladost 1, Blvd S. Allende, Res. 2; tel. (2) 75-71-35; fax (2) 75-40-09; Ambassador BO RASSI.

China, People's Republic: 1113 Sofia, Aleksandur von Humboldt St 7; tel. (2) 973-39-10; fax (2) 971–10–81; internet www .chinaembassy.bg; Ambassador XIE HANGSHENG.

Croatia: 1504 Sofia, Veliko Turnovo St 32; tel. (2) 943-32-55; fax (2) 946-13-55; e-mail dkp_rh@infotel.bg; internet www.infotel.bg/croembassy; Ambassador TONCI STANIČIĆ.

Cuba: 1113 Sofia, Konstantin Shtarkelov St 1; tel. (2) 72-09-96; fax (2) 72-04-60; e-mail consulcuba@mbox.digsys.bg; Ambassador LUIS FELIPE VÁZQUEZ.

Cyprus: Sofia, G. Gagarin St, Bl. 154A, Flat 2; tel. (2) 971-22-41; fax (2) 971-37-70; e-mail cyembsof@fintech.bg; Chargé d'affaires PHILIPPOS KRITIOTIS.

Czech Republic: 1000 Sofia, Yanko Sakazov St 9; tel. (2) 946-11-10; fax (2) 946-18-00; e-mail sofia@embassy.mzv.cz; Ambassador PETR DOKLÁDAL.

Denmark: 1000 Sofia, Blvd Dondukov 54, POB 1393; tel. (2) 980-08-30; fax (2) 980-08-31; e-mail sofambu@um.dk; Ambassador CHRISTIAN FABER-ROD.

Egypt: 1000 Sofia, Shesti Septemvri St 5; tel. (2) 87-02-15; fax (2) 980-12-63; Ambassador MAY ABOUL-DAHAB.

Finland: 1504 Sofia, Krakra St 16, Flat 4; tel. (2) 942-49-10; fax (2) 942-49-11; e-mail finembassy@online.bg; Ambassador TAISTO TOLVANEN.

France: 1054 Sofia, Oborishte St 27–29; tel. (2) 965-11-00; fax (2) 965-11-20; internet www.ambafrance-bg.org; Ambassador JEAN-LOUP KUHN-DELFORGE.

Germany: 1113 Sofia, Frédéric Joliot Curie St 25, POB 869; tel. (2) 91-83-80; fax (2) 963-16-58; e-mail gemb@vilmat.com; internet www .german-embassy.bg; Ambassador (vacant).

Greece: 1504 Sofia, San Stefano St 33; tel. (2) 946-10-27; fax (2) 946-12-49; e-mail sofia@greekembassy.bg; internet www.greekembassy .bg; Ambassador PROKOPIOUS MANDZURANIS.

Holy See: 1000 Sofia, 11 August 6, POB 9; tel. (2) 981-17-43; fax (2) 981-61-95; e-mail nuntius@mbox.digsys.bg; Apostolic Nuncio (VACANT).

Hungary: Sofia, Shesti Septemvri St 57; tel. (2) 963-04-60; fax (2) 963-21-10; Ambassador BÉLA KOLOZSI.

India: Sofia, Blvd Patriiarkh Evtimii 31; tel. (2) 981-17-02; fax (2) 981-41-24; e-mail india@inet.bg; Ambassador DINKAR KHULLAR.

Indonesia: 1700 Sofia, Blvd Simeonovsko Shosse 53; tel. (2) 962-52-40; fax (2) 962-58-42; e-mail indosof@geobiz.net; Ambassador ANAK AGUNG GDE RAKA.

Iran: Sofia, Blvd Vassil Levski 77; tel. (2) 44-10-13; Ambassador FEREIDUN HAKBIN.

Iraq: 1113 Sofia, Anton Chekhov St 21; tel. (2) 973-33-48; fax (2) 971-11-91; e-mail iraqiyah@asico.net.

Israel: Sofia, Blvd Bulgaria 1, NDK Administration Bldg, 7th Floor; tel. (2) 951-50-29; fax (2) 952-11-01; e-mail sofia@israel.net; Ambassador EMANUEL ZISMAN.

Italy: Sofia, Shipka St 2; tel. (2) 980-45-07; fax (2) 980-37-17; e-mail italdiplsofia@online.bg; Ambassador ALESSANDRO GRAFFINI.

Japan: Sofia, Lyulyakova Gradina St 14; tel. (2) 971-27-08; fax (2) 971-10-95; Ambassador YASUYOSHI ICHIHASHI.

Korea, Democratic People's Republic: Sofia, Mladost 1, Blvd S. Allende, Res. 4; tel. (2) 77-53-48; Ambassador KIM HA-DONG.

Korea, Republic: 1414 Sofia, Blvd Bulgaria 1, National Palace of Culture; tel. (2) 650-162; Ambassador PILL-JOO SUNG.

Kuwait: 1700 Sofia, Blvd Simeonovsko Shosse, Res. 15; tel. (2) 962-51-30; e-mail kwtemsf@omega.bg; Ambassador MUHAMMAD A. AL-AWADHI.

Lebanon: 1113 Sofia, Frédéric Joliot Curie St 19; tel. (2) 971-31-69; fax (2) 973-32-56; e-mail amliban@bgnet.bg; Ambassador HUSSEIN MOUSSAWI.

Libya: 1784 Sofia, Blvd Andrei Sakharov 1; tel. (2) 974-35-56; fax (2) 974-32-73; Secretary of People's Bureau FARAG GIBRIL.

Macedonia, former Yugoslav republic: 1113 Sofia, Frédéric Joliot Curie St 17, Bl. 2, Floor 1, Suite 1; Ambassador LJUBISA GEORGIEVSKI.

Moldova: 1000 Sofia, Blvd Patriiarkh Evtimii 17; tel. (2) 981-73-70; fax (2) 981-85-53; e-mail moldova@www1.infotel.bg; Ambassador VASILE STURZA.

Mongolia: 1113 Sofia, Frédéric Joliot Curie St 52; tel. (2) 65-84-03; fax (2) 963-07-45; e-mail mongemb@mbox.infotel.bg.

Morocco: Sofia, Blvd Evlogui Georgiev 129; tel. (2) 44-27-94; fax (2) 946-10-43; e-mail sifmasof@bulnet.bg; Ambassador ABDESSELAM ALEM.

Netherlands: 1126 Sofia, Galichitsa St 38; tel. (2) 962-57-90; fax (2) 962-59-88; e-mail info@netherlandsembassy.bg; internet www .netherlandsembassy.bg; Ambassador H. J. C. M. VAN LYNDEN.

Nicaragua: Sofia, Mladost 1, Blvd Allende, Res. 1; tel. (2) 75-41-57; Ambassador UMBERTO CARIÓN.

Peru: 1113 Sofia, POB 514, Frédéric Joliot Curie St 17, Bl. 2, 2nd Floor; tel. (2) 971-37-08; fax (2) 973-33-46; e-mail peru@mail.bol.bg; Chargé d'affaires JULIO VEGA ERAUSQUÍN.

Poland: Sofia, Khan Krum St 46; tel. (2) 987-26-10; fax (2) 987-29-39; e-mail polamba@internet-bg.net; Ambassador JAROSŁAW LINDEN-BERG.

Portugal: 1124 Sofia, Ivatz Voivoda St 6; tel. (2) 943-36-67; fax (2) 943-30-89; e-mail embport@online.bg; Ambassador PAULO TIAGO GERÓNIMO DA SILVA.

Romania: Sofia, Sitniakovo St 4; tel. (2) 971-28-58; fax (2) 973-34-12; e-mail ambsofro@exco.net; Ambassador CONSTANTIN GRIGORIE.

Russia: Sofia, Blvd Dragan Tsankov 28; tel. (2) 963-44-58; fax (2) 963-41-03; e-mail consulate@datacom.bg; Ambassador VLADIMIR TITOV.

Serbia and Montenegro: Sofia, Veliko Turnovo St 3; tel. (2) 946-16-33; fax (2) 946-10-59; e-mail yembisof@tradenel.net; Ambassador CEDOMIR RADOJKOVIĆ.

Slovakia: 1504 Sofia, Blvd Janko Sakazov 9; tel. (2) 943-32-81; fax (2) 943-38-37; e-mail svkemba@tba.bg; Ambassador JÁN KOVÁČ.

Spain: Sofia, Sheinovo St 27, Ap. P. K. 381; tel. (2) 943-30-32; fax (2) 946-12-01; e-mail embespbg@mail.mae.es; Ambassador JOSÉ CORDERCH.

Sweden: Sofia, Alfred Nobel St 4; POB 620; tel. (2) 971-24-31; fax (2) 973-37-95; e-mail sweembg@einet.bg; Ambassador STEN ASK.

Switzerland: 1504 Sofia, Shipka St 33; tel. (2) 946-01-97; fax (2) 946-11-86; Ambassador PIERRE LUCIRI.

Syria: Sofia; tel. (2) 944-15-85; Chargé d'affaires SADDIK SADDIKNI.

Turkey: 1000 Sofia, Blvd Vassil Levski 80; tel. (2) 987-14-64; fax (2) 981-93-58; e-mail turkel@techno-link.com; Ambassador HAYDAR BERK.

Ukraine: 1618 Sofia, Ovcha Kupel, Boriana St 29; tel. (2) 955–94-78; e-mail puvrb@mail.bol.bg; internet www.ukramb.bol.bg; Ambassador VYACHESLAV POKHVALSKYI.

United Kingdom: 1000 Sofia, Moskovska St 9; tel. (2) 980-12-20; fax (2) 980-12-29; e-mail britembsof@mbox.cit.bg; internet www .british-embassy.bg; Ambassador IAN SOUTAR.

USA: 1000 Sofia, Suborna St 1; tel. (2) 980-52-41; fax (2) 981-89-77; e-mail irc@usembassy.bg; internet www.usembassy.bg; Ambassador JAMES W. PARDEW.

Uruguay: Sofia, Tsar Ivan Asen II St 91; POB 213; tel. (2) 943-45-45; fax (2) 943-40-40; e-mail urubulg@mbox.digsys.bg; Ambassador OLGA BARBAROV.

Venezuela: 1504 Sofia, Tulovo St 1, Flat 2; tel. (2) 943-30-61; fax (2) 943-30-10; e-mail embavenez@mbox.digsys.bg; internet www .embavenez-sofia.bgi; Ambassador GERARDO E. WILLS.

Viet Nam: 1113 Sofia, Jetvarka St 1; tel. (2) 963-26-09; fax (2) 963-36-58; e-mail dsqvietnam@sf.icn.bg; Ambassador NGUYEN VAN DAC.

Yemen: Sofia, Blvd S. Allende, Res. 3; tel. (2) 75-61-63; Ambassador ALI MUNASSAR MUHAMMAD.

Judicial System

The 1991 Constitution provided for justice to be administered by the Supreme Court of Cassation, the Supreme Administrative Court, courts of appeal, courts of assizes, military courts and district courts. The main legal officials are the justices, or judges, of the higher courts, the prosecutors and investigating magistrates. The judicial system is independent, most appointments being made or recommended by the Supreme Judicial Council. The Ministry of Justice coordinates the administration of the judicial system and the prisons. There is also the Constitutional Court, which is the final arbiter of constitutional issues. Under transitional arrangements attached to the 1991 Constitution, the existing Supreme Court of Bulgaria was to exercise the prerogatives of the two new Supreme Courts until the new judicial system was enacted and established.

Supreme Court of Cassation: 1000 Sofia, Blvd Vitosha 2, Sudebna Palata; tel. (2) 987-76-98; fax (2) 88-39-85; Pres. IVAN GRIGOROV.

Supreme Administrative Court: Sofia, Blvd A. Stamboliyski 18; tel. (2) 981-30-42; fax (2) 981-87-51; internet www.sac.government .bg; Pres. (vacant).

Constitutional Court: 1594 Sofia, Blvd Dondukov 1; tel. (2) 987-50-08; fax (2) 987-19-86; e-mail s.petrova@constcourt.government .bg; internet www.constcourt.bg; Chair. LAZAR GRUEV; Sec.-Gen. KIRIL A. MANOV.

Supreme Judicial Council: Sofia; tel. (2) 981-79-74; Head ANTON ILIEV STANKOV (Minister of Justice).

Ministry of Justice: see The Government (Ministries).

Office of the Prosecutor-General: 1040 Sofia, Blvd Vitosha 2; tel. and fax (2) 988-52-13; Prosecutor-General NIKOLA FILTCHEV; Deputy Prosecutor-General CHRISTO MANCHEV.

Religion

Most of the population profess Christianity, the main denomination being the Bulgarian Orthodox Church, with a membership of more than 80% of the population. The 1991 Constitution guarantees freedom of religion, although Eastern Orthodox Christianity is declared to be the 'traditional religion in Bulgaria'. In accordance with the 1949 Bulgarian Law on Religious Faith, all new religious denominations must be registered by a governmental board before being allowed to operate freely. There is a significant Muslim minority (some 9% of the population), most of whom are ethnic Turks, although there are some ethnic Bulgarian Muslims, known as Pomaks. There is a small Jewish community.

Directorate of Religious Affairs: 1000 Sofia, Blvd Dondukov 1; tel. and fax (2) 988-04-88; a dept of the Council of Ministers; conducts relations between govt and religious organizations; Chair. Dr IVAN ZHELEV DIMITROV.

CHRISTIANITY

In 1992 a schism occurred in the Bulgarian Orthodox Church, although this was resolved in October 1998.

Bulgarian Orthodox Church: 1090 Sofia, Oborishte St 4, Synod Palace; tel. (2) 87-56-11; fax (2) 89-76-00; f. 865; autocephalous Exarchate 1870 (recognized 1945); administered by the Bulgarian Patriarchy; 11 dioceses in Bulgaria and two dioceses abroad (Diocese of North and South America and Australia, and Diocese of West Europe), each under a Metropolitan; Chair. of the Bulgarian Patriarchy His Holiness Patriarch MAKSIM.

Armenian Apostolic Orthodox Church: Sofia 1080, Nishka St 31; tel. (2) 88-02-08; 20,000 adherents (1996); Bishop DIRAYR MARDIKIYAN; administered by (resident in Bucharest, Romania); Chair. of the Diocesan Council in Bulgaria OWANES KIRAZIAN.

The Roman Catholic Church

The Latin (Western) Rite, which is organized in two dioceses, had some 80,000 adherents at 31 December 2001. The Byzantine-Slav (Eastern) Rite is organized in one diocese. All three dioceses are directly responsible to the Holy See.

Bishops' Conference (Mejduritualna Episcopska Konferenzia vâv Bâlgaria): 1606 Sofia, Lulin Planina 5; tel. (2) 953-04-06; fax (2) 952-61-86; e-mail cproykov@technolink.bg; Pres. CHRISTO NIKOLOV PROYKOV (Titular Bishop of Briula).

Western Rite

Bishop of Nicopolis: Petko Jordanov Christov, 7000 Ruse, Ivan Vazov St 26A; tel. (82) 22-52-45; fax (82) 82-28-81; e-mail dio_nicop@ elits.rousse.bg; 30,000 adherents (2002).

Diocese of Sofia and Plovdiv: Georgi Ivanov Jovčev (Apostolic Administrator), 4000 Plovdiv, Blvd Maria Luisa 3; tel. (32) 62-20-42; fax (32) 62-15-22; e-mail lubovenkov@hotmail.com; 35,000 adherents (2002).

Eastern Rite

Apostolic Exarch of Sofia: Christo Nikolov Proykov (Titular Bishop of Briula), 1606 Sofia, Lulin Planina 5; tel. (2) 953-04-06; fax (2) 952-61-86; e-mail cproykov@technolink.bg; 15,000 adherents (2002).

The Protestant Churches

Bulgarian Church of God: Sofia 1408, Petko Karavelov St 1; tel. (2) 65-75-52; fax (2) 51-91-31; 30,000 adherents (1992); Head Pastor Pavel Ignatov.

Bulgarian Evangelical Church of God: Plovdiv, Velbudge St 71; tel. (32) 43-72-92; 300 adherents (1992); Head Pastor Blagoi Isev.

Bulgarian Evangelical Methodist Episcopal Church: 1000 Sofia, Rakovski St 86; tel. (2) 981-37-83; fax (2) 980-94-83; e-mail umc-supint@mbox.digsys.bg; 2,000 adherents (2000); Gen. Superintendent Rev. Bedros G. Altunian.

Church of Jesus Christ of Latter-day Saints in Bulgaria: Sofia, Drugba estate, Bl. 82/B/6, Flat 54; tel. (2) 74-08-06; f. 1991; 64 adherents (1992); Pres. Ventseslav Lazarov.

Open Biblical Confraternity: 9300 Dobrich, General Kolev St 8; f. 1991; Head Pastor Antonia Popova.

Union of the Churches of the Seventh-day Adventists: Sofia, Solunska St 10; tel. (2) 88-12-18; fax (2) 980-17-09; e-mail sda.bg@ sbline.net; 6,700 adherents (1997); Head Pastor Agop Tachmissjan.

Union of Evangelical Baptist Churches: 1303 Sofia, Ossogovo St 63; tel. and fax (2) 931-06-82; 4,000 adherents (1999); Pres. Dr Theodor Angelov.

Union of Evangelical Congregational Churches: Sofia, Solunska St 49; tel. (2) 980-56-85; fax (2) 980-69-02; e-mail sescbg@ yahoo.com; f. 1888; 4,000 adherents (1998); Head Pastor Rev. Dr Christo Kulichev.

Union of Evangelical Pentecostal Churches: 1557 Sofia, Bacho Kiro St 21; tel. (2) 83-51-69; f. 1928; 30,000 adherents (1991); Head Pastor Viktor Virchev.

Universal White Fraternity: 1612 Sofia, Balshik St 8B, Flat 27; tel. (2) 54-69-43; f. 1900; unifies the principles of Christianity with the arts and sciences; more than 6,000 adherents (1994); Chair. Dr Iliyan Stratev.

ISLAM

Supreme Muslim Theological Council: Sofia, Bratya Miladinovi St 27; tel. (2) 87-73-20; fax (2) 39-00-23; adherents estimated at 9% of the actively religious population, with an estimated 708 acting regional imams; Chair. Hadzhi Nedim Gendzhev; Chief Mufti of the Muslims in Bulgaria Hadzhibasri Hadzhisharif.

JUDAISM

Central Jewish Theological Council: 1000 Sofia, Ekzarkh Yosif St 16; tel. (2) 83-12-73; fax (2) 83-50-85; 5,000 adherents (1992); Head Yossif Levi.

The Press

PRINCIPAL DAILIES

24 Chasa (24 Hours): 1504 Sofia, Blvd Tzarigradsko 47; tel. (2) 44-19-45; fax (2) 433-93-39; f. 1991; privately owned; Editor-in-Chief Valeri Naidenov; circ. 330,000.

Bulgarska Armiya (Bulgarian Army): 1080 Sofia, Ivan Vasov St 12, POB 629; tel. (2) 87-47-93; fax (2) 987-91-26; f. 1944 as *Narodna Armiya*, name changed 1991; organ of the Ministry of Defence; Editor-in-Chief Col Vladi Vladkov; circ. 30,000.

Chernomorsky Far (Black Sea Lighthouse): 8000 Burgas, Milin Kamak St 9; tel. (56) 422-48; fax (56) 401-78; f. 1958; independent regional from 1988; Editorial Dir Georgi Ingilisov; circ. 37,000.

Duma (Word): Sofia, Positano St 20; Sofia, POB 382; tel. (2) 980-12-91; fax (2) 980-52-91; e-mail bsp@mail.bol.bg; internet www.bsp.bg/ media-en/index.html; f. 1990 as an organ of the Bulgarian Socialist

Party; resumed publication in Oct. 2001; Editor-in-Chief Vyacheslav Tunev.

Kontinent: 1000 Sofia, Blvd Tzarigradsko 47A; tel. (2) 943-44-46; fax (2) 44-19-04; e-mail kont@bgnet.bg; internet www.tetracom.com/ kontinent; f. 1992; independent; Editor-in-Chief Boiko Pangelov; circ. 12,000.

Maritza: 4000 Plovdiv, Blvd Christo Botev 27A; tel. (32) 60-34-50; fax (32) 60-34-22; e-mail mpolit@maritsa.com; internet www.digsys .bg/bgnews/maritsa; f. 1991; Editor-in-Chief Anton Bayev; circ. 30,000.

Narodno Delo (People's Cause): 9000 Varna, Blvd Christo Botev 3; tel. (52) 23-10-71; fax (52) 23-90-67; f. 1944; 6 a week; regional independent; business, politics and sport; Editor-in-Chief Dimitur Krasimirov; circ. 56,000.

Noshten Trud (Night Labour): 1000 Sofia, Blvd Dondukov 52; tel. and fax (2) 87-70-63; f. 1992; 5 a week; Editor-in-Chief Plamen Kamenov; circ. 332,000.

Nov Glas (New Voice): 5500 Lovech, G. Dimitrov St 24, 3rd Floor; tel. (68) 2-22-42; f. 1988; regional independent; Editor-in-Chief Venetsii Georgiev.

Novinar: 1505 Sofia, Oborishte St 44; tel. (2) 43-55-22; fax (2) 943-45-32; e-mail novinar@novinar.net; internet www.novinar.org; f. 1992; Editor-in-Chief Dr Stoyko Tonev; circ. 45,000 (1997).

Otechestven Vestnik (Fatherland Newspaper): Sofia; tel. (2) 43-431; f. 1942 as *Otechestven Front*; published by the journalists' co-operative 'Okchestvo'; Editor-in-Chief Konstance Anschva; total circ. 16,000.

Pari (Money): 1504 Sofia, Blvd Tzarigradsko 47A; POB 46; tel. (2) 943-36-46; fax (2) 943-31-88; e-mail office@pari.bg; internet www .pari.bg; f. 1991; 5 a week; financial and economic news online; in Bulgarian and English; Editor-in-Chief Stefan Nedelchev; circ. 10,000.

Podkrepa (Support): 1000 Sofia, Ekzarkh Yosif St 37; tel. (2) 83-12-27; fax (2) 46-73-74; f. 1991; organ of the Podkrepa (Support) Trade Union Confederation; Editor-in-Chief (vacant); circ. 18,000.

Shipka: Khaskovo; tel. (38) 12-52-52; fax (38) 3-76-28; f. 1988; independent regional newspaper; Editor-in-Chief Dimitur Dobrev; circ. 25,000.

Sport: 1000 Sofia, Vassil Levski Stadium, Sektor V; Sofia, POB 88; tel. (2) 88-03-43; fax (2) 88-36-28; f. 1927; Editor-in-Chief Ivan Nankov; circ. 80,000.

Standart News Daily: 1784 Sofia, Blvd Tzarigradsko 113A; tel. (2) 975-36-88; fax (2) 76-28-77; e-mail root@standartnews.com; internet www.standartnews.com; f. 1992; Editor-in-Chief Yuly Moskov; circ. 110,000.

Trud (Labour): 1000 Sofia, Blvd Dondukov 52; tel. (2) 987-98-05; fax (2) 80-11-40; f. 1923; organ of the Confederation of Independent Trade Unions in Bulgaria; Editor-in-Chief Tosho Toshev; circ. 200,000.

Vecherni Novini (Evening News): Sofia; f. 1951; independent newspaper; centre-left; publ. by the Vest Publishing House; Dir Georgi Ganchev; Editor-in-Chief Lyubomir Kolarov; circ. 35,000.

Vselena (Universe): Montana; tel. (96) 2-25-06; fmrly *Delo*; Editor-in-Chief Boyan Mladenov.

Zemedelsko Zname (Agrarian Banner): Sofia; tel. (2) 87-38-51; f. 1902; organ of the Aleksandur Stamboliyski Bulgarian Agrarian People's Union; Editor Iliya Danov.

Zemya (Earth): Sofia, 11 August St 18; tel. (2) 88-50-33; fax (2) 83-52-77; f. 1951 as *Kooperativno Selo*; renamed 1990; fmrly an organ of the Ministry of Agriculture; Editor-in-Chief Kosta Andreev; circ. 53,000.

PRINCIPAL PERIODICALS

168 Chasa (168 Hours): 1504 Sofia, Blvd Tzarigradsko 47; tel. (2) 433-92-88; fax (2) 433-93-15; f. 1990; weekly; business, politics, entertainment; Editor-in-Chief Vaselka Valileva; circ. 93,000.

166 Politzeiski Vesti (166 Police News): 1680 Sofia, J. K. Belite Brezi, Solun St, Bl. 25 and 26, Ground Floor; tel. (2) 82-30-30; fax (2) 82-30-28; f. 1945; fmrly *Naroden Strazh*; weekly; criminology and public security; Editor-in-Chief Petar Vitanov; circ. 22,000.

Pro i Anti: 1000 Sofia, POB 1078; tel. (2) 66-18-75; fax (2) 963-42-36; e-mail anti_bg@yahoo.co.uk; internet www.pro-anti.net; f. 1991; weekly; Editor-in-Chief Vasil Stanilov; circ. 7,000.

Avto-moto Svyat (Automobile World): 1000 Sofia, Sveta Sofia St 6, POB 1348; tel. and fax (2) 88-08-08; f. 1957; monthly; illustrated publication on cars and motor sports; Editor-in-Chief Ilja Seliktar; circ. 33,600.

Az Buki (Alphabet): 1113 Sofia, Blvd Tzarigradsko 125; tel. (2) 71-65-73; f. 1991; weekly; education and culture; for schools; sponsored by the Ministry of Education and Science; Editor-in-Chief MILENA STRAKOVA; circ. 11,800.

Bulgarski Biznes (Bulgarian Business): 1505 Sofia, Oborishte St 44, POB 15; tel. (2) 46-70-23; fax (2) 44-63-61; weekly; organ of National Union of Employers; Editor-in-Chief DETELIN SERTOV; circ. 10,000–15,000.

Bulgarski Fermer (Bulgarian Farmer): 1797 Sofia, Blvd Dr G. M. Dimitrov 89; tel. (2) 71-04-48; fax (2) 73-10-08; f. 1990; weekly; Editor-in-Chief VASSIL ASPARUHOV; circ. 20,000.

Computer: 1504 Sofia, Panayot Volov St 11; tel. and fax (2) 943-41-28; e-mail office@newteck.bg; internet www.newteck.bg; f. 1991; monthly; information technology; Editor-in-Chief PETAR PETROV; circ. 7,000.

Computer World: 1421 Sofia, Blvd Hr. Smirnenski 1, Bl. B, Flat 1111; tel. (2) 963-20-17; fax (2) 963-28-41; internet www.eunet.bg/idg/; f. 1991; weekly; US-Bulgarian joint venture; information technology; Editor-in-Chief TATIANA HINOVA; circ. 7,000.

Domashen Maistor (Household Manager): Sofia; tel. (2) 87-09-14; f. 1991; monthly; magazine for household repairs; Editor-in-Chief GEORGI BALANSKI; circ. 12,000.

Durzhaven Vestnik (State Gazette): 1169 Sofia, Blvd Aleksandur Battenberg 1; tel. (2) 986-10-76; e-mail dv@nt52.parliament.bg; f. 1879; 2 a week; official organ of the National Assembly; 2 bulletins of parliamentary proceedings and the publication in which all legislation is promulgated; Editor-in-Chief IVAN GAJDARSKI; circ. 42,000.

Ekho (Echo): 1000 Sofia, Vassil Levski St 75; tel. (2) 87-54-41; f. 1957; weekly; organ of the Bulgarian Tourist Union; tourism publication; Editor-in-Chief LUBOMIR GLIGOROV; circ. 7,000.

Emigrant: Sofia; tel. (2) 87-23-08; fax (2) 87-46-17; f. 1991; (to replace *Kontakti*); weekly; magazine for Bulgarians living abroad; Editor-in-Chief MANOL MANOV; circ. 20,000.

Film: 1184 Sofia, Blvd Tzarigradsko 113A, Rodina Co; tel. (2) 76-15-02; fax (2) 77-02-27; e-mail film@online.bg; f. 1993; monthly; Editor DIMA DIMOVA; circ. 11,000.

Futbol (Football): 1000 Sofia, Blvd Bulgaria 1, Vassil Levski Stadium; tel. (2) 87-19-51; fax (2) 65-72-57; f. 1988; weekly; independent soccer publication; Editor-in-Chief IVAN CHOMAKOV; circ. 132,500.

Ikonomicheski Zhivot (Economic Life): 1000 Sofia, Alabin St 33; tel. (2) 87-95-06; fax (2) 87-65-60; e-mail ikonzhiv@dir.bg; f. 1970; weekly; independent; marketing and finance; Editor-in-Chief VASIL ALEKSIEV; circ. 21,000.

Kapital: 1000 Sofia, Ivan Vazov St 9; tel. (2) 981-58-16; fax (2) 87-69-07; f. 1993; weekly; also online; Man. Editor FILIP HARMANDJIEV; circ. 30,000 (1999).

Komunistichesko Delo (Communist Cause): Sofia; tel. (2) 59-16-73; organ of the Bulgarian Communist Party; Editor-in-Chief VLADIMIR SPASSOV.

Krile (Wings): 1784 Sofia, POB 11; tel. (2) 974-51-26; fax (2) 974-51-25; e-mail kaloian_1999@yahoo.com; f. 1911; fmrly *Kam Nebeto*, renamed 1991; monthly; official organ; civil and military aviation; Pres. and Editor-in-Chief ROSSEN KALUDOV PANTCHELIEV; circ. 20,000.

Kultura (Culture): 1040 Sofia, Blvd Aleksandur Battenberg 4; tel. (2) 988-33-22; fax (2) 980-04-95; e-mail kultura@online.bg; internet www.online.bg/kultura; f. 1957; weekly; issue of the Culture Space Foundation; arts, publicity and cultural affairs; Editor-in-Chief KOPRINKA CHERVENKOVA; circ. 5,000.

Kurier 5 (Courier 5): 1000 Sofia, Blvd Tzarigradsko 47; tel. (2) 46-30-26; f. 1991; weekdays; advertising newspaper; Editor-in-Chief STEPAN ERAMIAN; circ. 30,000.

Liberalen Kongres (Liberal Congress): Sofia; tel. (2) 39-00-18; fax (2) 68-77-14; f. 1990; weekly; organ of the Liberal Congress Party; Editor-in-Chief ROSSEN ELEZOV; circ. 12,000.

LIK: Sofia, Blvd Tzarigradsko 49; weekly; publication of the Bulgarian Telegraph Agency; literature, art and culture; Editor-in-Chief SIRMA VELEVA; circ. 19,000.

Literaturen Forum (Literary Forum): 1000 Sofia, Blvd Aleksandur Battenberg 4; tel. (2) 88-10-69; fax (2) 88-10-69; f. 1990; weekly; independent; Editor-in-Chief ATANAS SVILENOV; circ. 5,300.

Makedonia (Macedonia): 1301 Sofia, Pirotska St 5; tel. (2) 80-05-32; fax 87-46-64; e-mail mpress@virbus.bg; f. 1990; weekly; organ of the Inner Macedonian Revolutionary Organization IMRO —Union of Macedonian Societies; Editor-in-Chief DINKO DRAGANOV; circ. 22,000.

Missul (Thought): 1000 Sofia, Pozitano St 20, POB 382; tel. (2) 85-141; f. 1990; weekly; organ of the Marxist Alternative Movement; politics, culture; Editor-in-Chief GEORGI SVEZHIN; circ. 15,000.

Napravi Sam (Do It Yourself): 1504 Sofia, Panayot Volov St 11; tel. and fax (2) 943-41-28; e-mail newteck@einet.bg; internet www.newteck.bg; f. 1981; monthly; Editor-in-Chief GEORGI BALANSKI; circ. 8,000.

Nie Zhenite (We the Women): Sofia; tel. (2) 52-31-98; f. 1990; weekly; organ of the Democratic Union of Women; Editor-in-Chief EVGINIA KIRANOVA; circ. 176,600.

Nov Den (New Day): 1000 Sofia, Lege St 5; tel. (2) 77-39-82; e-mail ivan_kalchev@yahoo.com; f. 1991; weekly; organ of the Union of Free Democrats; Editor-in-Chief IVAN KALCHEV; circ. 25,000.

Novo Vreme (New Time): Sofia, Positano St 20; Sofia, POB 382; tel. (2) 980-12-91; fax (2) 980-52-91; e-mail bsp@mail.bol.bg; internet www.bsp.bg/media-en/nv.html; monthly; organ of the Bulgarian Socialist Party.

Paraleli: 1040 Sofia, Blvd Tzarigradsko 49; tel. (2) 87-40-35; f. 1964; weekly; illustrated publication of the Bulgarian Telegraph Agency; Editor-in-Chief KRASSIMIR DRUMEV; circ. 50,000.

Pardon: 1504 Sofia, Blvd Tzarigradsko 47; tel. (2) 43-431; f. 1991; weekly; satirical publication; Editor-in-Chief CHAVDAR SHINOV; circ. 8,560.

PC Magazine Bulgaria: 1000 Sofia, Blvd Vassil Levski 3, Saga Technology; f. 1993; monthly; Chief Exec. ANNA BAKALOVA; circ. 12,000.

Pogled (Review): 1090 Sofia, Blvd Slaveikov 11; tel. (2) 87-70-97; fax (2) 65-80-23; f. 1930; weekly; organ of the Union of Bulgarian Journalists; Editor-in-Chief DAMYAN OBRECHKOV; circ. 47,300.

Prava i Svobodi (Rights and Freedoms): Sofia; tel. (2) 46-72-12; fax (2) 46-73-35; f. 1990; weekly; organ of the Movement for Rights and Freedoms; politics, culture; Editor-in-Chief (vacant); circ. 7,500.

Progres (Progress): 1000 Sofia, Gurko St 16; tel. (2) 89-06-24; fax (2) 89-59-98; f. 1894; fmrly *Tekhnichesko Delo*; weekly; organ of the Federation of Scientific and Technical Societies in Bulgaria; Editor-in-Chief PETKO TOMOV; circ. 35,000.

Starshel (Hornet): Sofia; tel. and fax (2) 70-85-54; f. 1946; weekly; humour and satire; Editor-in-Chief KRASTYN KRASTEV; circ. 45,200.

Start: 1000 Sofia, Vassil Levski Stadium, POB 797; tel. (2) 980-25-17; fax (2) 981-29-42; f. 1971; weekly; sports, illustrated; Editor-in-Chief NIKOLAY RANGELOV; circ. 21,300.

Televiziya i Radio (Television and Radio): 1756 Sofia, Bulgarska Natsionalna Televiziya, Blvd Tzarigradsko 111; tel. (2) 70-01-88; fax (2) 974-36-93; e-mail petmar@mail.techno-link.com; f. 1964; weekly; broadcast listings; Editor-in-Chief LUBOMIR YANKOV; circ. 30,000 (1999).

Tsarkoven Vestnik (Church Newspaper): 1000 Sofia, Oborishte St 4; tel. (2) 87-56-11; f. 1900; weekly; organ of the Bulgarian Orthodox Church; Editor-in-Chief DIMITUR KIROV; circ. 4,000.

Uchitelsko Delo (Teachers' Cause): Sofia; tel. and fax (2) 70-00-12; internet udelo.edubg.info; f. 1905; weekly; organ of the Union of Bulgarian Teachers; Editor-in-Chief MARGARITA CHOLAKOVA; circ. 12,000.

Vek 21 (21st Century): 1000 Sofia, Kaloyan St 10; tel. (2) 46-54-23; fax (2) 46-61-23; f. 1990; weekly; organ of the Radical Democratic Party; liberal politics and culture; Editor-in-Chief ALEKSANDUR YORDANOV; circ. 5,900.

Zdrave (Health): Sofia; tel. (2) 44-30-26; f. 1955; monthly; published by Bulgarian Red Cross; Editor-in-Chief YAKOV YANAKIEV; circ. 55,000.

Zhenata Dnes (Women Today): 1000 Sofia, Blvd Narodno Sobraniye 12; tel. (2) 89-16-00; f. 1946; monthly; organ of Zhenata Dnes Ltd; Editor-in-Chief BOTIO ANGELOV; circ. 50,000.

Zname (Banner): 1184 Sofia, Blvd Kniyas Korsakov 34; tel. (2) 80-01-83; f. 1894; publ. until 1934 and 1945–49, resumed publication 1990; weekly; Editor-in-Chief BOGDAN MORFOV; circ. 20,000.

NEWS AGENCIES

Bulgarska Telegrafna Agentsia (BTA) (Bulgarian Telegraph Agency): 1024 Sofia, Blvd Tzarigradsko 49; tel. (2) 92-62-42; fax (2) 986-22-89; e-mail bta@bta.bg; internet www.bta.bg; f. 1898; official news agency; domestic, Balkan and international news in Bulgarian and English; also economic and sports news; publishes weekly surveys of science and technology, international affairs, literature and art; Gen. Dir MAKSIM MINCHEV.

Bulnet: 1000 Sofia, Rakovski St 127; tel. (2) 987-11-22; fax (2) 980-30-71; e-mail support@bulnet.bg; f. 1994; provides online access, internet services, communications software, hardware and consultancy; photo service; Exec. Dir INA STOIANOVA.

LEFF Information Service: 1000 Sofia, Rakovski St 127; tel. (2) 87-11-22; fax (2) 81-34-42; e-mail leffnews@bulnet.bg; private and independent news agency via internet; publishes daily economic and current affairs newsletters; Pres. BORIS BASMADJIYEV.

Sofia-Press Agency: 1040 Sofia, Slavyanska St 29; tel. (2) 88-58-31; fax (2) 88-34-55; internet sun.iecs.bas.bg/press; f. 1967 by the Union of Bulgarian Writers, the Union of Bulgarian Journalists, the Union of Bulgarian Artists and the Union of Bulgarian Composers; publishes socio-political and scientific literature, fiction, children's and tourist literature, publications on the arts, a newspaper, magazines and bulletins in foreign languages; also operates.

Sofia-Press Info: tel. (2) 87-66-80; Pres. ALEKSANDUR NIKOLOV; which provides up-to-date information on Bulgaria, in print and for broadcast; Dir-Gen. KOLIO GEORGIEV.

Foreign Bureaux

Agence France-Presse (AFP): 1504 Sofia, Blvd Yanko Sakazov 19; tel. (2) 944-10-78; fax (2) 46-34-63; e-mail afpsofia@afp.com.

Agencia EFE Spain: Sofia; tel. (2) 87-29-63; Correspondent SAMUEL FRANCÉS.

Ceska kancelar (CTK) (Czech Republic): Sofia; tel. (2) 70-91-36; Correspondent VĚRA IVANOVIČOVÁ.

Deutsche Presse-Agentur (dpa) (Germany): Sofia; tel. (2) 72-02-02; Correspondent ELENA LALOVA.

Informatsionnoye Telegrafnoye Agentstvo Rossii—Telegrafnoye Agentstvo Suverennykh Stran (ITAR—TASS) (Russia): 1000 Sofia, A. Gendov St 1, Flat 29; tel. (2) 87-38-03; Correspondent ALEKSANDR STEPANENKO.

Magyar Távirati Iroda (MTI) (Hungary): Sofia, Frédéric Joliot Curie St 15, Bl. 156/3, Flat 28; tel. (2) 70-18-12; Correspondent TIVADAR KELLER.

Novinska Agencija Tanjug (Yugoslavia): 1000 Sofia, L. Koshut St 33; tel. (2) 71-90-57; Correspondent PERO RAKOSEVIĆ.

Polska Agencja Prasowa (PAP) (Poland): Sofia; tel. (2) 44-14-39; Correspondent BOGDAN KORNEJUCK.

Prensa Latina (Cuba): Sofia; tel. (2) 71-91-90; Correspondent SUSANA UGARTE SOLER.

Reuters (United Kingdom): 1000 Sofia, Ivan Vazov St 16; tel. (2) 911-88; fax (2) 980-91-31; e-mail sofia.newsroom@reuters.com; Correspondent THALIA GRIFFITHS.

Rossiyskoye Informatsionnoye Agentstvo—Novosti (RIA—Novosti) (Russia): Sofia; Bureau Man. YEVGENII VOROBYOV.

United Press International (UPI) (USA): Sofia; tel. (2) 62-24-65; Correspondent GUILLERMO ANGELOV.

Xinhua (New China) News Agency (People's Republic of China): Sofia; tel. (2) 88-49-41; Correspondent U. SIZIUN.

The following agencies are also represented: SANA (Syria) and Associated Press (USA).

PRESS ASSOCIATIONS

Union of Bulgarian Journalists: 1000 Sofia, Ekzarkh Yosif St 37; tel. (2) 83-19-95; fax (2) 83-54-84; f. 1944; Pres. CHAVDAR TONCHEV; 5,500 mems.

Publishers

Darzhavno Izdatelstvo 'Christo G. Danov' ('Christo G. Danov' State Publishing House): 4005 Plovdiv, Stoyan Chalakov St 1; tel. (32) 23-12-01; fax (32) 26-05-60; f. 1855; fiction, poetry, literary criticism; Dir NACHO CHRISTOSKOV.

Darzhavno Izdatelstvo 'Tekhnika': 1000 Sofia, Blvd Slaveikov 1; tel. (2) 87-12-83; fax (2) 87-49-06; f. 1958; textbooks for technical and higher education and technical literature; Dir NINA DENEVA.

Darzhavno Izdatelstvo 'Zemizdat': 1504 Sofia, Blvd Tzarigradsko 47; tel. (2) 44-18-29; f. 1949; specializes in works on agriculture, shooting, fishing, forestry, livestock-breeding, environmental studies and popular scientific literature and textbooks; Dir PETAR ANGELOV.

Galaktika: 9000 Varna, Blvd Nezavissimost 6; tel. (52) 24-11-56; fax (52) 23-47-50; f. 1960; science fiction, economics, Bulgarian and foreign literature; Dir ASSYA KADREVA.

Izdatelstvo na Bulgarskata Akademiya na Naukite 'Marin Drinov': 1113 Sofia, Acad. Georgi Bonchev St, Bl. 6; tel. (2) 72-09-22; fax (2) 70-40-54; f. 1869; scientific works and periodicals of the Bulgarian Academy of Sciences; Dir TODOR RANGELOV.

Izdatelstvo 'Bulgarski Houdozhnik': 1504 Sofia, Shipka St 6; tel. (2) 46-72-85; fax (2) 946-02-12; e-mail filchev@mail.orbitel.bg; f. 1952; art books, children's books; Dir BOUYAN FILCHEV.

Izdatelstvo 'Bulgarsky Pisatel': Sofia, Shesti Septemvri St 35; tel. (2) 87-58-73; fax (2) 87-24-95; publishing house of the Union of Bulgarian Writers; Bulgarian fiction and poetry, criticism; Dir GERTCHO ATANASOV.

Izdatelstvo 'Christo Botev': Sofia; tel. (2) 44-14-08; f. 1944; fmrly the Publishing House of the Bulgarian Communist Party, renamed as above 1990; Dir IVAN DINKOV.

Izdatelstvo 'Medizina i Fizkultura': 1080 Sofia, Blvd Slaveikov 11; tel. (2) 987-13-09; fax (2) 987-99-75; e-mail medpubl@netplus.bg; f. 1948; medicine, physical culture and tourism; Dir PETKO PETKOV.

Izdatelstvo na Ministerstvo na Otbranta (Ministry of Defence Publishing House): 1000 Sofia, Ivan Vazov St 12; tel. (2) 88-44-31; fax (2) 88-15-68; Head Maj. BOYAN SULTANOV.

Izdatelstvo Mladezh, (Youth Publishing House): Sofia; tel. (2) 88-21-37; fax (2) 87-61-35; f. 1945; art, history, original and translated fiction, political science and sociology; Gen. Dir STANIMIR ILCHEV.

Izdatelstvo 'Profizdat' (Publishing House of the Central Council of Bulgarian Trade Unions): Sofia; specialized literature and fiction; Dir STOYAN POPOV.

Izdatelstvo 'Prosveta' AS: 1184 Sofia, Blvd Tzarigradsko 117; tel. (2) 76-11-82; fax (2) 76-44-51; e-mail prosveta@tradel.net; internet www.prosveta.net; f. 1945; educational publishing house; Pres. JOANA TOMOVA; Dir YONKO YONCHEV.

Naouka i Izkoustvo Ltd: 1000 Sofia, Slaveikov Sq. 11; tel. (2) 987-47-90; fax (2) 987-24-96; e-mail nauk_izk@sigma-bg.com; f. 1948; general publishers; Man. LORETA PUSHKAROVA.

'Narodna Kultura' Publishers: 1000 Sofia, Angel Kanchev St 1; POB 421; tel. (2) 987-80-63; e-mail nauk-izk@sigma-bg.com; f. 1944; general; Dir PETAR MANOLOV.

Reporter Ltd Publishing Co: 1184 Sofia, Blvd Tzarigradsko 113; tel. (2) 76-90-28; fax (2) 71-83-77; e-mail reporter@techno-link.com; f. 1990; private publishers of fiction and documentary literature.

Sinodalno Izdatelstvo: Sofia, Oborishte St 4; tel. (2) 87-56-11; religious publishing house; Dir ANGEL VELITEHKOV.

STATE ORGANIZATION

Jusautor: Sofia; tel. (2) 87-28-71; fax (2) 87-37-40; state organization of the Council of Ministers; Bulgarian copyright agency; represents Bulgarian authors of literary, scientific, dramatic and musical works, and deals with the granting of options, authorization for translations, and drawing up of contracts for the use of works by foreign publishers and producers; Dir-Gen. YANA MARKOVA.

PUBLISHERS' ASSOCIATION

Bulgarian Book Publishers' Association: 1000 Sofia, Blvd Slaveikov 11; POB 1046; tel. and fax (2) 986-79-70; e-mail bba@otel.net; internet www.bba-bg.org; f. 1994; Exec. Dir MADLENA ROMANOVA; Chair. RAYMOND WAGENSTEIN.

WRITERS' UNION

Union of Bulgarian Writers: Sofia, Blvd Slaveikov 2; tel. (2) 88-06-85; fax (2) 87-47-57; f. 1913; Chair. NIKOLAI HAITOV; 495 mems.

Broadcasting and Communications

TELECOMMUNICATIONS

At 31 December 2000 12% of the telephone network was digitized. In 2001 there were 2.9m. main telephone lines in use, and a total of 1.6m. subscribers to mobile cellular telephone services.

Committee of Posts and Telecommunications: 1000 Sofia, Gourko St 6; POB 1352; tel. (2) 981-29-49; fax (2) 980-61-05; internet www.cpt.bg; supervises and regulates the post and telecommunications systems; Pres. ANTONI SLAVINSKI.

Bulgarian Telecommunications Company (BTC): 1606 Sofia, Blvd Totleben 8; tel. (2) 88-94-38; fax (2) 87-58-85; e-mail central.office@btc.bg; internet www.btc.bg; provides telecommunications and information services; Chair. RALITZA MARINOVA; Exec. Dirs IVAN SPASSOV, BOYKO DIMITRACHKOV; 23,000 employees.

Mobikom (Radiotelecommunication Company Mobikom): 1000 Sofia, POB 101; tel. (2) 974-40-27; fax (2) 960-56-13; internet www.mobikom.com; f. 1992; 49% owned by Cable and Wireless (USA), 39% owned by Bulgarian Telecommunications Co; Man. Dir JOHN MUNNERY.

MobilTel EAD: 1408 Sofia, Balsha St 3, Bl. 8; tel. (88) 50-00-31; fax (88) 50-00-32; e-mail pr@mobiltel.bg; internet www.mobiltel.bg; f. 1994 as a private joint-stock co; provides mobile telecommunications services.

BROADCASTING

National Radio and Television Council: 1504 Sofia, San Stefano St 29; tel. (2) 46-81; internet www.bild.net/nsrt; Dir IVAN BORISLAVOV.

Radio

Bulgarsko Nationalno Radio: 1040 Sofia, Blvd Dragan Tzankov 4; tel. (2) 963-43-30; fax (2) 963-44-98; e-mail bgintrel@nationalradio .bg; internet www.nationalradio.bg; f. 1929; two Home Service programmes; local stations at Blagoevgrad, Plovdiv, Shumen, Stara Zagora and Varna. The Foreign Service broadcasts in Bulgarian, Turkish, Greek, Serbo-Croat, French, German, English, Russian, Spanish and Albanian; Dir-Gen. POLYA STANCHEVA.

Radio Alma Mater: 1000 Sofia, Moskovska St 49; tel. (2) 986-16-07; fax (2) 930-84-80; f. 1993; cable radio service introduced by Sofia Univ.; from July 1998 24-hour broadcasting at 87.7 MHz in Sofia; culture and science programmes; Editor-in-Chief DILIANA KIRKOVSKA.

Television

Balkan News Corporation: Sofia; daily news transmission of commercial news, family entertainment and locally-produced programmes, on bTV channel; Chief Exec. MARTY POMPADUR.

Bulgarska Natsionalna Televiziya: 1504 Sofia, San Stefano St 29; tel. (2) 44-63-29; fax (2) 946-12-10; internet www.bnt.bg; f. 1959; daily transmission of programmes on Channel 1 and Efir 2 and on the satellite channel—TV Bulgaria; Dir-Gen. KIRIL GOTSEV; 3,000 employees.

Nova Televiziya: 1000 Sofia, Blvd Sveta Nedelya 16; tel. (2) 80-50-25; fax (2) 87-02-98; f. 1994; first private television channel in Bulgaria; commercial news and entertainment.

Finance

(cap. = capital; dep. = deposits; res = reserves; m. = million; amounts in new leva, unless otherwise indicated)

BANKING

By late 1991 the transition to a two-tier banking sector had been achieved. In late 1992 21 commercial banks merged to form the United Bulgarian Bank, which opened in 1993. In early 1993 two new banks emerged, Commercial Bank Expressbank (formed from the merger of 12 banks) and Hebrosbank (a merger of eight banks). In 1996 14 banks, including five state-owned banks, collapsed. In October 1997 state-owned banks accounted for 73% of the total. A currency board was established in July 1997. By early 2003 34 commercial bank were in operation in Bulgaria (of which six were branches of foreign banks). The country's remaining state-owned bank, DSK Bank plc, was privatized in 2003.

Currency Board

Currency Board of the Republic of Bulgaria: Sofia; f. 1997; monetary supervision; Head MARTIN ZAIMOV.

Central Bank

Bulgarian National Bank (Bulgarska Narodna Banka): 1000 Sofia, Blvd Aleksandur Battenberg 1; tel. (2) 914-51-203; fax (2) 980-24-25; e-mail press_office@bnbank.org; internet www.bnb.bg; f. 1879; bank of issue; cap. 20m., res 1,353.6m., dep. 780.7m. (Dec. 2001); Gov. SVETOSLAV GAVRIYSKI (acting); 6 brs; 1,000 employees.

State Savings Bank

DSK Bank plc: 1040 Sofia, Moskovska St 19; tel. (2) 985-57-220; fax (2) 980-64-77; e-mail office@dskbank.bg; internet www.dskbank.bg; f. 1951 as State Savings Bank; name changed as above in 1998; provides general retail banking services throughout the country; wholly divested to National Savings and Commercial Bank—OTP Bank (Hungary) in May 2003; cap. 70.0m., res 113.6m., dep. 1,316.5m. (Dec. 2001); Chair. KRASSIMIR ANGARSKI; 126 brs.

Commercial Banks

BNP-Paribas (Bulgaria) AD: 1000 Sofia, Blvd Tsar Osvoboditel 2; POB 11; tel. (2) 921-86-40; fax (2) 921-86-95; e-mail bulgaria_bnpparibas@bnpparibas.com; f. 1994; fmrly BNP-Dresdner Bank; name changed as above in 2001; 20% owned by the European Bank for Reconstruction and Development; cap. 36.0m., res 13.8m., dep. 220.2m. (Dec. 2001); Chief Exec. ULLRICH GUENTER SCHUBERT.

Bulbank AD: 1000 Sofia, Blvd Sveta Nedelya 7; tel. (2) 923-21-11; fax (2) 988-46-36; e-mail info@sof.bulbank.bg; internet www .bulbank.bg; f. 1964 as the Bulgarian Foreign Trade Bank; name changed in 1994; privatized in 2000; 85.2% owned by UniCredito

Italiano SpA (Italy); cap. 166.4m., res 50.0m., dep. 2,114.9m. (Dec. 2001); Chair. and Chief Exec. LEVON HAMPARTZOUMIAN; 98 brs.

Bulgarian-American Credit Bank AD: 1504 Sofia, Shipka St 3; tel. (2) 965-83-45; fax (2) 944-50-10; e-mail bacb@baefinvest.com; f. 1996; cap. US $8.9m., dep. $6.6m.; Chief Exec. FRANK BAUER.

Bulgarian Post Bank JSC: 1414 Sofia, Bulgaria Sq. 1; tel. (2) 963-20-96; fax (2) 963-04-82; e-mail intldiv@postbank.bg; internet www .postbank.bg; f. 1991; privatized in 1999; cap. 56,697m., res 15,219m., dep. 576,903m. (Dec. 2002); Chair. and Chief Exec. PANAIOTIS VARELAS; 112 brs and offices.

CB Unionbank Ltd: 1606 Sofia, Damyan Gruev St 10–12; tel. (2) 915-33-33; fax (2) 980-20-04; e-mail mainmail@unionbank.bg; internet www.unionbank.bg; f. 1992; cap. 15,412m., res 14,470m., dep. 83,004m. (Dec. 2002); Chair. and Exec. Dir DORCHO DIMITROV ILCHEV; 10 brs.

Central Co-operative Bank plc: 1000 Sofia, G. S. Rakovski St 103; tel. (2) 926-62-37; fax (2) 987-19-48; e-mail falev@ccbank.bg; internet www.ccbank.bg; f. 1991; cap. 16.2m., res 10.9m., dep. 170.7m. (Dec. 2001); Chair. ALEKSANDUR VODENICHAROV; 33 brs.

Commercial Bank Biochim: 1026 Sofia, Ivan Vazov St 1; tel. (2) 926-92-10; fax (2) 926-94-40; e-mail info@biochim.com; internet www.biochim.com; f. 1987; scheduled for privatization; cap. 28.8m., res 27.4m., dep. 534.7m. (2001); Chair. RUMEN BEREMSKI; Exec. Dirs NIKOLAI KAVARDJIKLIEV, EMILIA PALIBACHIYSKA; 40 brs.

Commercial Bank Bulgaria Invest AD: 1202 Sofia, Blvd Maria Louiza 65; tel. (2) 980-52-00; fax (2) 981-93-07; e-mail admin@bank .allianz.bg; internet www.allianz.bg; f. 1989 as Yambol Commercial Bank; cap. 27.8m., dep. 155.2m. (Dec. 2001); Chair. DIMITAR ZHELEV.

Corporate Commercial Bank AD: 1000 Sofia, Graf Ignatiev St 10; POB 632; tel. (2) 980-93-62; fax (2) 980-89-48; e-mail corpbank@ corpbank.bg; internet www.corpbank.bg; f. 1989 as BSFK Bulgarsovinvest; cap. 10.0m., res 1.3m., dep. 50.1m. (Dec. 2001); Chair. TZVETAN VASSILEV.

Demirbank (Bulgaria) AD: 1000 Sofia, Blvd Tsar Osvoboditel 8; tel. (2) 989-44-44; fax (2) 989-48-48; e-mail info@demirbank.bg; internet www.demirbank.bg; f. 1999; cap. 15.0m., dep. 55.0m. (Dec. 2002); Chief Exec. HALUK KURCER; Sr Man. SINAN KIRCALI MARIN SHOSHKOV.

EIBANK AD: 1000 Sofia, Saborna St 11A; tel. (2) 985-00-240; fax (2) 981-25-26; e-mail info@hq.eibank.bg; internet www.eibank.bg; f. 1994 as Bulgarian Russian Investment Bank; known as Bribank AD in 1999–2000; cap. 20.0m., res 8.0m., dep. 219.9m. (Dec. 2001); Chair. VASSIL SIMOV; 10 brs.

Eurobank plc: 1407 Sofia, Blvd Cherni Vrach 43; tel. (2) 62-33-66; fax (2) 68-10-86; e-mail eurobank@eurobank.bg; internet www .eurobank.bg; f. 1993 as Commercial Bank Mollov Ltd; cap. 39.6m., dep. 112.2m. (Dec. 2001); Chair. EMIL ANGELOV.

First East International Bank: 1504 Sofia, Blvd Vassil Levski 106, POB 256; tel. (2) 946-16-82; fax (2) 946-16-83; e-mail correbanking@feibbank.com; internet www.feibbank.com; f. 1989 as Trade Bank Kremikovzi, name changed in 1991; cap. 20.1m., res 4.9m., dep. 54.0m. (Dec. 2001); Pres. ANNA SABEVA; 29 brs.

First Investment Bank Ltd: 1000 Sofia, St Karadja St 10; tel. (2) 910-01-00; fax (2) 980-50-33; e-mail fib@fibank.bg; internet www .fibank.bg; f. 1993; cap. 60.2m., dep. 342.2m. (2001); Exec. Dirs MAJA GEORGIEVA, MATTHEW MATTEEV; Chair. of Supervisory Bd GEORGI DIMITROV MUTAFCHIEV; 29 brs.

Hebrosbank: 4018 Plovdiv, Blvd Tsar Boris III Obedinitel 37; tel. (32) 90-26-68; fax (32) 62-39-64; e-mail hebros@hebros.bg; internet www.hebros.bg; f. 1993 following merger of eight banks; commercial, investment, corporate and retail banking; cap. res 80.0m., dep. 320.8m. (Dec. 2001); Chair. and Chief Exec. GAUTAM VIR; 59 brs.

HVB Bank Bulgaria EAD: 1000 Sofia, Rakovski St 90; tel. (2) 932-01-00; fax (2) 980-53-13; e-mail vladimir_babursky@bg .hypovereinsbank.com; f. 1987 as Bayerisch-Bulgarische Handelsbank GmbH; name changed to Hypovereinsbank Bulgaria GmbH in 1998, and as above in 2002; cap. 10.2m., res 0.3m., dep. 83.9m. (Dec. 2000); Gen. Man. LUDMIL GATCHEV.

Municipal Bank plc: 1000 Sofia, 6 Vrabcha St; tel. (2) 930-01-85; fax (2) 981-51-47; f. 1996 as Sofia Municipal Bank Plc; name changed Jan. 1998; cap. 25.0m., res 8.1m., dep. 227.7m. (Dec. 2001); Chief Exec. VANYA GEORGIEVA VASSILEVA; 15 brs.

Neftinvestbank plc: 1000 Sofia, 155 Rakovski St; POB 1138; tel. (2) 981-69-38; fax (2) 980-77-22; e-mail office@nib.bg; internet www .nib.bg; f. 1994 as International Orthodox Bank 'St Nikola'; cap. 84.8m., dep. 47.8m. (Dec. 2001); Chair. PETIA IVANOVA BARAKOVA-SLAVOVA; 9 brs.

Raiffeisenbank (Bulgaria) AD: 1504 Sofia, Gogol St 18–20; tel. (2) 919-85-101; fax (2) 943-45-28; e-mail ibgamts@rbb-sofia.raiffeisen

.at; internet www.rbb.bg; f. 1994; cap. 16.7m., res 14.4m., dep. 390.1m. (Dec. 2001); Chair. JOHANN JONACH.

Roseximbank plc: 1000 Sofia, Blvd Dondukov 4–6; tel. (2) 930-71-36; fax (2) 980-26-23; e-mail info@roseximbank.bg; internet www.roseximbank.bg; f. 1994; cap. 51.1m., dep. 233.4m. (Dec. 2001); Chair. DIANA MLADENOVA; Chief Exec. Dir VLADIMIR VLADIMIROV.

SG Expressbank AD: 9000 Varna, Blvd Vl. Varnenchik 92; tel. (52) 66-04-80; fax (52) 60-13-24; e-mail office@expressbank.bg; internet www.expressbank.bg; f. 1987 as Transport Bank, name changed following merger of 12 banks in 1993; privatized in 1999; 97.95% owned by Société Générale (France); cap. 28.5m., res 37.4m., dep. 483.8m. (Dec. 2001); Chief Exec. SANDY GILLIO; 23 brs; 900 employees.

Teximbank: 1202 Sofia, Blvd Maria Louiz 107, Serdika Municipality; tel. (2) 31-40-38; fax (2) 931-12-07; e-mail texim@omega.bg; f. 1992; private entrepreneurial bank; cap. 10,000m. old leva, res 982,500m. old leva, dep. 2,869.1m. old leva (Dec. 1998); Pres. MARIA VIDOLOVA.

United Bulgarian Bank AD: 1040 Sofia, Sveta Sofia St 5; tel. (2) 98-54-00; fax (2) 988-08-22; e-mail info@sof.ubb.bg; internet www.ubb.bg; f. 1993 following a merger of 22 commercial banks; universal commercial bank; privatized in 1999; 89.9% owned by National Bank of Greece SA; cap. 76.0m., res 33.7m., dep. 1,266.0m. (Dec. 2001); Chief Exec. STILIAN VATEV; 57 brs.

STOCK EXCHANGE

Bulgarian Stock Exchange: 1040 Sofia, Blvd Makedonia 1; tel. (2) 986-59-15; fax (2) 986-58-63; e-mail bsemail@online; internet www.online.bg/bs; Chair. GEORGI PROHASKI; Chief Exec. APOSTOL APOSTOLOV.

INSURANCE

In 1947 all insurance firms were nationalized, and reorganized into a single state insurance company. In 1989 private insurance companies began to reappear.

General Insurance Plc (DZI): 1000 Sofia, Georgi Benkovski St 3; tel. (2) 981-57-99; fax (2) 987-45-33; e-mail general.ins@dzi.bg; internet www.dzi.bg; f. 1946; all areas of insurance; privatization approved in Aug. 2002; Chair. DANCHO DANCHEV; 27 agencies, 101 brs.

Bulstrad Insurance and Reinsurance: 1000 Sofia, Blvd Pozitano 5, POB 627; tel. (2) 985-66-100; fax (2) 985-66-103; f. 1961; all classes of insurance and reinsurance; Chief Exec. RUMEN YANCHEV.

Trade and Industry

GOVERNMENT AGENCIES

Privatization Agency: 1000 Sofia, Aksakov St 29; tel. (2) 897-75-79; fax (2) 981-62-01; e-mail bgpriv@priv.government.bg; internet www.priv.government.bg; f. 1992; organizes the privatization of state-owned enterprises; Exec. Dir ILYA VASSILEV VASSILEV.

INTERNATIONAL FREE-TRADE ZONES

Burgas Free-Trade Zone: 8000 Burgas, Trapezitza St 5, POB 154; tel. (56) 84-20-47; fax (56) 84-15-62; e-mail freezone@bse.bg; internet www.freetradezone-bourgas.com; f. 1989; Exec. Dirs ANGELIN POPOV, KRASIMIR GRUDOV.

Dobrotitza Free-Trade Zone: 4649 Kranevo, Dobrich District.

Dragoman Free-Trade Zone: 2210 Dragoman; tel. (9971) 72-20-14.

Plovdiv Free-Trade Zone: 4003 Plovdiv, Vassil Levski St 242A; POB 75; tel. (32) 90-62-33; fax (32) 96-08-33; e-mail frzone@plovdiv.techno-link.com; internet www.freezone-plovdiv.com; f. 1990; Exec. Dir ALEKSANDUR NIKOLOV.

Ruse International Free-Trade Zone: 7000 Ruse, Knyazheska St 5, POB 107; tel. (82) 27-22-47; fax (82) 27-00-84; e-mail trade@freezone-rousse.bg; internet www.freezone-rousse.bg; f. 1988; Gen. Man. YORDAN KAZAKOV.

Svilengrad Free-Trade Zone: 6500 Svilengrad; tel. (359) 379-74-45; fax (359) 379-75-41; e-mail sbz@svilengrad.com; internet www.svilengrad.com/sbz; f. 1990; Exec. Dir DIMO HARAKCHIEV.

Vidin Free-Trade Zone: 3700 Vidin; tel. (94) 228-37; fax (94) 309-47; f. 1988; Gen. Man. K. MARINOV.

CHAMBER OF COMMERCE

Bulgarian Chamber of Commerce and Industry (BCCI): 1058 Sofia, Parchevich St 42; tel. (2) 987-26-31; fax (2) 987-32-09; e-mail bcci@bcci.bg; internet www.bcci.bg; f. 1895; promotes economic relations and business contacts between Bulgarian and foreign cos and

orgs; organizes participation in international fairs and exhibitions; publishes economic publs in Bulgarian and foreign languages; organizes foreign trade advertising and publicity; provides legal and economic consultations, etc.; registers all Bulgarian cos trading internationally (more than 40,000 at the end of 2000); Pres. BOJIDAR BOJINOV; 28 regional chambers.

EMPLOYERS' ASSOCIATIONS

Bulgarian Industrial Association (BIA): 1000 Sofia, Alabin St 16–20; tel. (2) 932-09-11; fax (2) 987-26-04; e-mail office@bia-bg.com; internet www.bia-bg.com; f. 1980; assists Bulgarian economic enterprises with promotion and foreign contacts; economic analysis; legal and arbitration services; intellectual property protection; training and qualification; Chair. and Exec. Pres. BOJIDAR DANEV.

Employers Association of Bulgaria (EABG): 1202 Sofia, Industrialna St 11; tel. (2) 917-88-68; fax (2) 917-88-61; e-mail headoffice@eabg.org; internet www.eabg.org; f. 2000; Chair. VASSIL VASSILEV; Gen. Sec. YEVGENII IVANOV.

National Union of Employers: 1505 Sofia, Oborishte St 44, POB 15; f. 1989; federation of businessmen in Bulgaria.

Union of Private Owners in Bulgaria: Sofia; f. 1990; Chair. DIMITUR TODOROV.

Vuzrazhdane Union of Bulgarian Private Manufacturers: 1618 Sofia, Blvd Todor Kableshkov 2; tel. (2) 55-00-16; Chair. DRAGOMIR GUSHTEROV.

UTILITIES

Electricity

Central Laboratory of Solar Energy and New Energy Sources: 1784 Sofia, Blvd Tzarigradsko 72; tel. and fax (2) 75-40-16; e-mail solar@phys.bas.bg; research into alternative energy production; Dir Assoc. Prof. PETKO VITANOV.

National Electricity Company EAD (Natsionalna Elektricheska Kompania): 1040 Sofia, Veslets St 5; tel. (2) 986-56-06; fax (2) 980-12-43; e-mail nek@nek.bg; internet www.nek.bg; f. 1991; wholly state-owned, scheduled for privatization; national transmission company responsible for all thermal, nuclear and hydroelectric electricity production from 14 plants; Chair. of Bd ANGEL MINEV; Exec. Dir VASIL ANASTASOV.

State Agency on the Peaceful Use of Nuclear Energy: 1574 Sofia, Blvd Shipchenski Prokhod 69; tel. (2) 72-02-17; fax (2) 70-21-43; f. 1957; Chair. TINKO GANCHEV (acting).

Gas

Bulgargaz EAD: 1336 Sofia, Filipovsko Ch. 66, Zh. K. Lyulin, POB 3; tel. (2) 98-42-51; fax (2) 92-50-41; e-mail bgaz.hq@bulgargaz.com; internet www.bulgargaz.com; f. 1973; renamed 1990; state-owned; import, transmission, distribution, storage and transit of natural gas; Chair. GATI AL-JEBOURI; Chief Exec. KIRIL GEORGIEV GEGOV.

Topenergy Joint-Stock Co: Sofia; f. 1995; owned by Gazprom of Russia; responsible for supply of Russian natural gas to Bulgaria; Chair. BOGDAN BUDZULIAK; Dir SERGEI PASHIN.

MAJOR COMPANIES

Until 1989 foreign trade was a state monopoly in Bulgaria, and was conducted through foreign-trade organizations and various state enterprises and corporations. In 1989 legislation was enacted, introducing the *firma* (company) as a basic structural unit of the economy. The Bulgarian economy was subsequently opened to foreign investment. In 1991 further legislation provided for the transfer of state enterprises to the private sector. By the end of 2002 approximately 75% of companies were privately owned.

Agromashinaimpex: 1330 Sofia, Blvd Vaskresenie 1; tel. (2) 22-37-58; fax (2) 20-91-29; e-mail ami@mbox.digsys.bg; f. 1965; state-owned co; import and export of agricultural machinery; Exec. Dir S. DIMITROV; 455 employees.

Agropolychim JSC: 9164 Devnya, Industrial Zone; tel. (51) 9-29-44; e-mail postmaster@agropolychim.bg; produces nitrogen and phosphoric fertilizers; CEO IVAN DIAKOV; 2,122 employees.

Albena Style EAD: 9300 Dobrich, Blvd 25 Septemvri 55; tel. (58) 265-54; fax (58) 242-34; e-mail office@albenastyle.netplusdb.bg; internet www.netplusdb.bg/albenastyle/; f. 1961; manufactures and exports clothing; Man. NIKOLAI MITEV; 1,570 employees.

Alen Mak Perfumery and Cosmetics AD: 4003 Plovdiv, Vassil Levski St 148; tel. (32) 95-41-01; fax (32) 95-33-66; e-mail foreign@alenmak.bg; internet www.bpg.bg/alenmak; f. 1892; produces and exports personal care, cosmetic and perfumery products; owned by Bulgarian Pharmaceutical Group Ltd; Gen. Dir ANTONIA HEKIMOVA; Chief Exec. STEFAN PAPALEZOV; 1,150 employees.

Assenova Krepost: 4230 Assenovgrad, Ivan Vazov St 2; tel. (33) 12-23-20; fax (33) 12-79-45; e-mail askr@mbox.digsys.bg; manufactures packaging and polymer materials; Chair. CHRISTO KINTEV; 1,605 employees.

Balkancarpodem (Balkancar Holding Co): 1040 Sofia, Blvd Kliment Ohridsky 18; tel. (2) 91-967; fax (2) 975-39-89; e-mail office@balkancar.netplus.bg; internet www.bia-bg.com/balkancar; f. 1983; import and export of cranes and lifting equipment; Pres. TOMA TRAYANOV; 4,724 employees.

Balkanpharma Holding AD: 1000 Sofia, Blvd Maria Louisa 2, Business Centre Tzum; tel. (2) 932-15-00; fax (2) 981-54-45; e-mail sales@balkanpharma.com; internet www.balkanpharma.com; f. 1999; pharmaceuticals; 100% owned by Pharmaco (Iceland); subsidiaries include Balkanpharma-Dupnitsa AD (2,500 employees), Balkanpharma-Razgrad AD (1,620 employees), Balkanpharma-Troyan AD (650 employees); Chief Exec. KRISTJAN SVERRISSON; 4,500 employees.

Belopal: 9150 Beloslav, Industrial Zone; tel. (5152) 24-10; fax (5152) 33-80; e-mail belopal@binco.com; f. 1893; manufactures glassware and porcelain; Exec. Dir ILYA ZHONZHOROV; 2,400 employees.

Berg Montana Fittings: 3400 Montana, Industrial Zone; tel. (96) 284-92; fax (96) 210-23; f. 1962; manufactures and produces cast iron; Gen. Man. VESSELIN PARVANOU ANGELOU; 1,180 employees.

Blagoevgrad BT: 2800 Blagoevgrad, Pokrovnishko St 1; tel. (7) 32-39-67; tobacco producers; Chief Exec. DIMITAR DIMITROV; 1,345 employees.

Bulgarski Morski Flot Co: see section on Transport (Shipping and Inland Waterways).

Bulgartabac Holding Group: 1000 Sofia, Graf Ignatiev St 62; tel. (2) 987-52-11; fax (2) 987-88-20; e-mail info@bulgartabac.bg; internet www.bulgartabac.bg; scheduled for privatization; covers manufacture, import and export of raw and manufactured tobacco; Chair. ROUMEN POROJANOV; Man. Dir GEORGI KOSTOV; 18,176 employees.

Central Co-operative Union (CCU): 1000 Sofia, Rakovskiy St 99; tel. (2) 981-78-06; fax (2) 981-73-66; f. 1947; agricultural production; purchase of agricultural products; retail of food, etc.; Pres. PANTCHO IVANOV; 37,000 employees.

Chimco AD: 3037 Vratza, Mezdra Rd; tel. (92) 6-10-71; fax (92) 6-11-18; e-mail info@chimco.bg; internet www.chimco.bg; f. 1967; producer of nitrogen fertilizers; privatized in 1999; 57% of shares owned by IBE Trans (USA); Chair. and Chief Exec. VALENTIN DIMITROV; 1,400 employees.

Chimimport AD: 1080 Sofia, Stefan Karadja St 2; tel. (2) 980-16-11; fax (2) 981-61-91; e-mail info@chimimport.bg; internet www.chimimport.bg; f. 1947; import and export of pharmaceuticals, chemicals, petrochemicals, fertilizers, etc.; Gen. Dir BELO BELOV.

Electroimpex: 1040 Sofia, G. Washington St 17; tel. (2) 989-55-56; fax (2) 980-02-72; e-mail elimpex@mb.bia-bg.com; internet www.electroimpex.bg; f. 1960; engineering, installation, maintenance, import/export of electrical tools and equipment; Exec. Dir ALEKSANDUR VAKLINOV; 180 employees.

Elma EAD: 5600 Troyan, Industrial Zone; tel. (670) 22-780; fax (670) 22-350; f. 1989; manufactures electric motors and generators; Man. Dir PENCHO KALEV ADARSKIY; 2,210 employees.

Eltos: 5500 Lovech, Kubrat St 9; tel. (68) 2-35-50; fax (68) 2-00-69; production of electrical tools; f. 1989; Man. NIKOLAI ATANASOV KALBOV; 1,788 employees.

Glavbolgarstroy (GBS): 1619 Sofia, Damyanitza St 3–5; tel. (2) 915-17-03; fax (2) 957-10-88; e-mail marketing@gbs-bg.com; internet www.gbs-bg.com; f. 1969; domestic and overseas design, construction and civil-engineering contractor; privatized in 1997; subsidiary: Glavbolgarstroy Engineering AD (150 employees); Pres. SIMEON PESHOV; Chief Exec. EVGENNI MARINOV; 6,500 employees.

Hemus: 1000 Sofia, Benkovsky St 14; tel. (2) 987-05-05; fax (2) 981-33-41; e-mail hemusb&p@bitex.com; f. 1965; import and export of books, periodicals, numismatic items, art products, musical instruments, gramophone records and CDs, cinematographic equipment, film and photo consumables and souvenirs; consigned paper warehouse; Exec. Dir ASSEN PEINERDJIEV; 60 employees.

Hraninvest-Hranmashkomplekt: 6000 Stara Zagora, Blvd Patriarch Evtimi 23; tel. (42) 60-06-03; fax (42) 60-06-13; e-mail hihmkt@sz.inetg.bg; joint stock company; manufactures food-processing machinery; Man. Dir A. ANGELOV; 3,080 employees.

Incoms-Telecom Holding: 1309 Sofia, Kukush St 1; tel. (2) 23-11-60; fax (2) 23-01-07; e-mail incoms@mail.orbitel.bg; internet www.incoms-telecom.com; f. 1991; export and import of radioelectronic equipment and technology for the communications industry; Exec. Dir VALERI LAZAROV TAKOV.

Industrialengineering: 1000 Sofia, Tri Ushi St 1; tel. (2) 980-08-99; fax (2) 980-09-01; state-owned co; general engineering and contracting; Gen. Man. STEFAN STOJANOV.

Petar Karaminchev PLC: 7005 Ruse, Blvd Lipnik 73; tel. (82) 84-53-46; fax (82) 84-57-27; e-mail office@pkar.bg; internet www.pkar.bg; f. 1928; manufacture of floorings, synthetic leather, PVC goods, etc.; Man. Dir VALENTIN MADJAROV; 650 employees.

KCM SA: 4009 Plovdiv, Assenovgradsko St; tel. (32) 62-35-77; fax (32) 62-35-70; e-mail nd200@kcm.bg; internet www.kcm.bg; non-ferrous metalworks; Exec. Dir Dr N. DOBREV; 2,085 employees.

Koraboimpex Group PLC: 9000 Varna, Blvd Osmi Primorski Polk 128; tel. (52) 30-18-64; fax (52) 30-18-38; e-mail koraboimpex@net.bg; f. 1965; holding company of Koraboimpex group of companies; import and export of ships, marine and port equipment; engineering; industrial and financial broking services; Chair. NIKOLAI PARASHKEVOV.

Kozloduy Nuclear Power-Station: nuclear power producer; fmrly part of National Electric Company; privatized in 2000; two of the power station's six reactors were closed at the end of 2002, and an additional two were to be decommissioned at a later date; Chair. ANTON IVANOV; Exec. Dir and Chair. YORDAN YORDANOV.

Kremikovtzi Co: 1870 Sofia, Botunetz Complex; tel. (2) 935-21-02; fax (2) 987-98-06; e-mail info@kremiokovtzi.com; internet www.kremikovtzi.com; f. 1963; privatized 1999; manufacture of coke, ferrous metals, steel cast and rolled iron; Chair. and Chief Exec. VALENTIN ZAHARIEV; 8,000 employees.

Kvartz Co: 8800 Sliven, Industrialen Complex; tel. (44) 2-32-63; fax (44) 8-06-91; e-mail quartz@sl.bia-bg.com; f. 1933; produces household and medical glassware, and crystal goods; Man. PETKO IVANOV CHENKOV; 1,251 employees.

Lukoil Neftochim Bourgas AD: 8104 Bourgas, Industrial Zone; tel. (56) 89-82-01; fax (56) 89-82-00; e-mail iskra@lukoil.bg; internet www.lukoil.bg; privatized in 1999; 58% owned by Lukoil (Russia); refinery and petrochemical plant; Gen. Man. Lukoil Bulgaria VALENTIN ZLATEV; Chief Exec. Lukoil Neftochim Bourgas IGOR KUZMIN; 8,500 employees.

Machinoexport: 1616 Sofia, Belovodski Pat. 15–17; tel. (2) 917-03-57; fax (2) 981-77-37; e-mail machinoexport@techno-link.com; f. 1962; import and export of machine tools, wood-working machines, hydraulic and pneumatic components, tools and spare parts; Exec. Dir P. MADJOUKOV.

Metalni Konstruktsii: 1606 Sofia, Kamen Andreev St 24; tel. (2) 987-38-87; fax (2) 987-57-59; production and installation of metal structures; Pres. BOYIDAR VLACHOV; Man. Dir NIKOLA IKONOMOV; 3,200 employees.

Mono Bobov Dol AD (Bobov Dol Mines): 2670 Bobov Dol, Sofia; tel. (70) 122-10; fax (70) 12-51-33; f. 1992; coal and liquid gas; Dir VENTSISLAV TODOROV; 7,200 employees.

Neochim EAD: 6403 Dimitrovgrad; tel. (391) 652-05; fax (391) 605-55; e-mail neochim@neochim.bg; internet www.neochim.bg; f. 1951; 24% state-owned, 39% owned by Evrofert SA, 12% owned by Karimex Chemicals International SA (Lebanon); produces organic and inorganic chemicals, including ammonium nitrate fertilizer; 1,500 employees.

Petrol AD: Sofia, Blvd Cherni Vrix 43; tel. (2) 969-02-26; fax (2) 969-02-10; e-mail office@petrol.bg; internet www.petrol.bg; f. 1992; production, import and export of petroleum and products; Chair. of Bd IVAN IVANOV; 3,300 employees.

Pharmachim Holding: 1220 Sofia, Iliensko St 16; tel. (2) 936-03-61; fax (2) 936-03-68; e-mail pharma.e@ttm.com; internet clients.ttm.bg/pharm; f. 1965; state-owned co; import and export of pharmaceutical products; Pres. ASEN BORISOV STOYANOV; 11,000 employees.

Plama Pleven Oils: 5800 Pleven, Industrial Zone; tel. (64) 239-55; fax (64) 383-22; f. 1969; declared insolvent 1998; petroleum products; Pres. NIKOLA PUKALSKIY; 2,100 employees.

Plovdiska Conserva Ltd: 4003 Plovdiv, D. Stambolov St 2; tel. (32) 55-31-72; fax (32) 55-37-71; e-mail villy@mail.techno-link.com; f. 1947; fruit and vegetable processing; Dir BORIS KALIBATZEV; 1,458 employees.

Raznoiznos: 1202 Sofia, Maria Luiza Blvd 95; tel. (2) 931-13-87; fax (2) 931-14-55; e-mail razoiznos@mbox.cit.bg; internet www.bcci.bg/clients/raznoiznos; f. 1947; export and import of industrial and craftsmen's products, glassware, kitchen utensils, carpets, orthopaedic and optical products, etc.; Exec. Dir DIMITRI PAMPOULOV.

Rudmetal AD: 1000 Sofia, Dobrudzha St 1; tel. (2) 980-16-85; fax (2) 980-45-04; e-mail deliradev@rudmetal.bg; internet www.rudmetal.bg; f. 1952; export and import of ferrous and non-ferrous metals and products, lead zinc, copper, pure lead, coal, etc.; Gen. Dir EMIL DELIRADEV; 100 employees.

Sopharma JSC: 1220 Sofia, Iliensko St 16; tel. (2) 936-10-01; fax (2) 936-02-86; e-mail mail@sopharma.bg; internet www.sopharma.bg; f. 1933; 86.76% owned by Elfarm AD; chemical and pharmaceutical products; research and development; Exec. Dir OGNIAN DONEV; 1,629 employees (2000).

Solvay Sodi AD: 9160 Devnya, Industrial Zone; tel. (52) 68-58-92; fax (5) 68-50-06; internet www.solvay.com; f. 1954; 67% owned by Solvay SA (Belgium); manufactures calcinated soda ash and bicarbonate; Exec. Dirs IVAN BOTCHOUKOV, PAUL JACQUELOT; 1,100 employees.

Somat: 1138 Sofia, Gorublyane; tel. (2) 974-38-31; fax (2) 975-33-09; f. 1960; cargo transport; owned by the Ministry of Transport; Chair. NIKOLAI GANCHEV; 6,600 employees.

Stomana Industry AD: 2304 Pernik, Vladaysko Vostanie St 3; tel. (76) 68-11-11; fax (76) 68-19-50; e-mail markt@stomana.bg; internet www.stomana.bg; f. 1953; steel products; Exec. Dir VALENTIN CANKOV BAKALOV; 5,800 employees.

Technoimpex: 1000 Sofia, Tsar Kaloyan St 8; POB 932; tel. (2) 988-15-71; fax (2) 988-34-15; e-mail tehimpex@main.infotel.bg; internet www.infotel.bg/~tehimpex; f. 1965; provides scientific and technological assistance abroad in the fields of industry, architecture, construction, engineering, transport and communications, and education; representation of foreign companies; barter; import, export and re-export; specific commercial operations; leasing, etc.; Dir-Gen. KORNELIA PETROVA; 48 employees.

Technoimportexport PLC: 1040 Sofia, Frédéric Joliot Curie St 20; tel. (2) 963-00-40; fax (2) 963-12-35; e-mail office@tiexport.com; f. 1986; operates in all fields of engineering; import and export of power generating equipment, etc.; Exec. Dir GRETA DONCHEVA; 170 employees.

Toplivo AD: 1000 Sofia, Solunska St 2; tel. (2) 987-76-55; fax (2) 988-55-78; e-mail toplivo.ad@mbox.cit.bg; internet www.toplivo.bg; coal mining; Chief Exec. OGNIAN NIKOLOV; 1,500 employees.

Toplofikazia-Sofia EAD (Sofia District Heating Co.): 1680 Sofia, Yastrebets St 23; tel. (2) 958-22-44; fax (2) 958-22-43; e-mail toplo@bonmar.bg; internet www.toplofikacia-sofia.bg; f. 1957; generates electricity and heat, provides maintenance services; Chair. VALENTIN DIMITROV; 2,470 employees.

Transimpex JSC: 1606 Sofia, Blvd Skobelev 65; tel. (2) 952-58-00; fax (2) 952-23-25; e-mail trimp@transimpex.bg; internet www.transimpex.bg; f. 1967; state-owned; 5 brs; general trading; ship suppliers; manning of sea-going vessels; duty-free operations; hotels and restaurants; engineering and consulting; import and export of railway equipment, wagons, locomotives, boats and shipping parts; Chair. ANTONI NAOUMOV; Exec. Dir DRAGOMIR NEDELCHOV; 450 employees.

Union Miniere Pirdop Copper: 2070 Pirdop, Industrial Zone; tel. (7) 18-58-51; metalworks; Chief Execs P. ROMBAUT, A. ALEXANDROV; 2,750 employees.

Vidachim AD: 3704 Vidin, Southern Industrial Zone; tel. (94) 23-262; fax (94) 23-054; f. 1970; manufactures tyres, yarns and fibres; Chair. MIRCHO KAMENOV; 6,000 employees.

Yukos Petroleum Bulgaria: 9000 Varna, Musala St 9; tel. (52) 60-26-95; petroleum and gas production; Chief Exec. MIHAIL SABEV; 250 employees.

Zaharni Zavodi (Sugar Plants Ltd): tel. (618) 41-46; fax (618) 4-17-09; f. 1913; produces refined sugar and sugar products; Man. RUMEN MIHAILOV IVANOV; 1,614 employees.

ZMM Inc.: 1220 Sofia, Iliensko St 8; tel. (2) 3-8-49-60; fax (2) 936-03-57; manufacture of machines for metal- and woodwork; Man. TODOR IVANOV STANKOV; 700 employees.

CO-OPERATIVE

Central Union of Workers' Productive Co-operatives: 1000 Sofia, Blvd Dondukov 11; POB 55; tel. (2) 80-39-38; fax (2) 87-03-20; f. 1988; over-arching organization of 164 workers' productive co-operatives; Pres. STILIAN BALASSOPOULOV; 60,000 mems.

TRADE UNIONS

Confederation of Independent Trade Unions in Bulgaria (CITUB): 1040 Sofia, Blvd Makedonia 1; tel. (2) 917-04-79; fax (2) 988-59-69; f. 1904; name changed from Bulgarian Professional Union and independence declared from all parties and state structures in 1990; in 1998 remained the main trade-union organization; approx. 75 mem. federations and four associate mems (principal mems listed below); Chair. Prof. Dr KRUSTYU PETKOV; Sec. MILADIN STOYNOV; some 3m. mems.

Edinstvo (Unity) People's Trade Union: 1000 Sofia, Moskovska St 5; tel. (2) 87-96-40; f. 1990; co-operative federation of Clubs, based on professional interests, grouped into 84 asscns, 2 prof. asscns and 14 regional groups; Chair. OGNYAN BONEV; 384,000 mems.

Podkrepa (Support) Trade Union Confederation: 1000 Sofia, Angel Kanchev St 2; tel. (2) 981-45-51; fax (2) 981-29-28; e-mail koseva@bulinfo.net; f. 1989 as the first opposition trade union (affiliated to the Union of Democratic Forces); 35 regional and 27 branch union orgs; Chair. DIMITAR MANOLOV; Gen. Sec. PETAR GANCHEV; 155,000 mems (2000).

Principal CITUB Trade Unions

Federation of Independent Agricultural Trade Unions: 1606 Sofia, Dimo Hadzhidimov St 29; tel. (2) 52-15-40; Pres. LYUBEN KHARALAMPIEV; 44,600 mems (mid-1994).

Federation of Independent Trade Unions of Construction Workers: Sofia; tel. (2) 80-16-003; Chair. NIKOLAI RASHKOV; 220,000 mems.

Federation of the Independent Trade Unions of Employees of the State and Social Organizations: 1000 Sofia; tel. (2) 87-98-52; Chair. PETAR SUCHKOV; 144,900 mems.

Federation of Independent Mining Trade Unions: 1233 Sofia, 32 Veania St; tel. (2) 931-07-00; fax (2) 931-00-50; f. 1992; Pres. PENCHO TOKMAKCHIEV; 20,000 mems.

Federation of Light Industry Trade Unions: 1040 Sofia, Blvd Makedonia 1; tel. (2) 88-15-70; fax (2) 88-15-20; Chair. IORDAN VASSILEV IVANOV; 64,320 mems (1997).

Federation of Metallurgical Trade Unions: Sofia; tel. (2) 88-48-21; fax (2) 88-27-10; f. 1992; Pres. VASSIL YANACHKOV; 20,000 mems.

Federation of Trade Unions in the Chemical Industry: 1040 Sofia, Blvd Makedonia 1; tel. (2) 87-39-07; Pres. LYUBEN MAKOV; 60,000 mems (mid-1993).

Federation of Trade Union Organizations in the Forestry and Woodworking Industries: 1606 Sofia, Vladayska St 29; tel. (2) 52-31-21; fax (2) 51-73-97; Pres. PETER IVANOV ABRACHEV; 16,570 mems (mid-1999).

Federation of Trade Unions of Health Services: 1202 Sofia, Blvd Maria Louisa 45; tel. (2) 988-20-97; fax (2) 83-18-14; e-mail fsz-citub@mail.orbitel.bg; f. 1990; Pres. Dr IVAN KOKALOV; 24,065 mems (2000).

Independent Trade Union Federation of the Co-operatives: 1000 Sofia, Rakovski St 99; tel. (2) 87-36-74; Chair. NIKOLAI NIKOLOV; 96,000 mems.

Independent Trade Union Federation for Trade, Co-operatives, Services and Tourism: 1000 Sofia, 6 Septemvri St 4; tel. (2) 88-02-51; Chair. PETAR TSEKOV; 212,221 mems.

Independent Trade Union of Food Industry Workers: 1606 Sofia, Dimo Hadzhidimov St 29; tel. (2) 52-30-72; fax (2) 52-16-70; Pres. SLAVCHO PETROV; 53,000 mems (mid-1994).

National Federation of Energy Workers: 1040 Sofia, Blvd Makedonia 1; tel. (2) 88-48-22; f. 1927; Pres. BOJIL PETROV; 15,000 mems.

National Trade Union Federation 'Metal-elektro': 1040 Sofia, Blvd Makedonia 1; POB 543; tel. (2) 987-48-06; fax (2) 987-75-38; e-mail nsf-me@netbg.com; Pres. ASSEN ASSENOV; 40,000 mems (1999).

Trade Union of Bulgarian Teachers: 1000 Sofia, Gen. Parensov St 11; tel. (2) 987-78-18; fax (2) 988-17-94; e-mail seb@internet-bg.net; internet sbu.internet-bg.net; f. 1905; Pres. IANKA TANEVA; 186,153 mems.

Union of Transport Workers: 1233 Sofia, Blvd Maria Louisa 106; tel. (2) 31-51-24; fax (2) 31-71-24; f. 1911; Pres. IORDANKA MILANOVA RADEVA; 18,000 mems (Dec. 2001).

Other Principal Trade Unions

Bulgarian Military Legion 'G. S. Rakovski': Sofia; tel. (2) 87-72-96; Chair. DOICHIN BOYADZHIEV.

Construction, Industry and Water Supply Federation 'Podkrepa': 1000 Sofia, Uzundjovska St 12; tel. (2) 987-96-70; fax (2) 98-87-38; e-mail fciw@mail.techno-link.com; Pres. IOANIS PARTENIOTIS; 15,000 mems (2000).

Podkrepa National Union of Petrochemical Workers: 8000 Burgas, Neftohim EAD; tel. (56) 80-09-01; fax (56) 80-12-89.

Podkrepa Professional Trade Union for Chemistry, Geology and Metallurgy Workers: 1000 Sofia, Angel Kanchev St 2; Chair. LACHEZAR MINKOV (acting); 15,000 mems.

Podkrepa Professional Trade Union for Doctors and Medical Personnel: 1000 Sofia, Angel Kanchev St 2; Chair. Dr K. KRASTEV; 20,000 mems.

Podkrepa Union of Journalists: 1000 Sofia, Angel Kanchev St 2; tel. (2) 87-21-98.

Union of Architects in Bulgaria: 1504 Sofia, Krakra St 11; tel. (2) 46-31-09; fax (2) 946-08-00; e-mail sab@bguet.bg; internet www.bulgarianarchitects.org; f. 1893; Chair. TANKO SERAFIMOV.

Union of Bulgarian Lawyers: 1000 Sofia, Treti April St 7; tel. (2) 87-58-59; Chair. PETAR KORNAZHEV.

Transport

Ministry of Transport and Communications: 1000 Sofia, Levski St 9; tel. and fax (2) 988-53-29; directs the state rail, road, water and air transport organizations.

Despred International Freight Forwarders JSC: 1202 Sofia, Vesletz St 284; tel. (2) 931-39-56; fax (2) 983-14-84; e-mail info@despred.com; internet www.despred.com; f. 1947; Exec. Dir STOJAN INDJEV.

RAILWAYS

In 2001 there were 4,320 km of track in Bulgaria, of which 65.9% were electrified. The international and domestic rail networks are centred on Sofia. Construction of a 52-km underground railway system for Sofia commenced in 1979; the first section, comprising 6.1 km, was opened in January 1998. There were also 159 km of operational tram lines and 626 km of trolleybus routes in 2001.

Bulgarian State Railways (BDZ): 1080 Sofia, Ivan Vazov St 3; tel. (2) 987-30-45; fax (2) 987-71-51; e-mail bdzboev@bg400.bg; internet www.bdz.bg; f. 1888; owns and controls all freight and passenger railway transport; manufactures railway coaches and equipment; Pres. KRASSIMIRA MARTINOVA; Exec. Dir GEORGI NESHEV; 18,554 employees.

ROADS

There were 37,286 km of roads in Bulgaria in 2000, of which 3,011 km were principal roads; 94% of the network was paved. Two important international motorways traverse the country and a major motorway runs from Sofia to the coast.

Road Executive Agency: 1606 Sofia, Blvd Makedonia 3; tel. (2) 952-17-68; fax (2) 951-54-22; e-mail pdikovsky@rea.bg; f. 1952; develops, manages and maintains the national road network; provides conditions for the realization of state road policy; Dir-Gen. PAVEL DIKOVSKY.

SHIPPING AND INLAND WATERWAYS

The Danube (Dunav) River is the main waterway, with Ruse and Lom the two main ports. There are external services from Black Sea ports (the largest being Varna and Burgas) to the former USSR, the Mediterranean and Western Europe. The port of Tsarevo was opened to international shipping in 1995. In September 1998 it was announced that the port of Burgas was to be modernized, with financial assistance from the Japanese Government. In 2001 the European Commission provided €22m. for the restoration of navigation along the Danube, which had been blocked for two years, following the aerial bombardment of the Federal Republic of Yugoslavia (now Serbia and Montenegro) by NATO forces in 1999.

Bulgarian River Shipping Company: 7000 Ruse, Blvd Otets Paisi 2; tel. (82) 82-20-81; fax (82) 82-21-30; e-mail main@brp.bg; internet www.brp.bg; f. 1935; shipment of cargo and passengers on the Danube; storage, handling and forwarding of cargo; scheduled for privatization; Chair. STEFAN ZAGOROV; Gen. Dir VRANGEL NIKIFOROV; 1,100 employees.

Bulgarski Morski Flot Co: 9000 Varna, Panaguirishte St 17; tel. (52) 22-63-16; fax (52) 22-53-94; organization of sea and river transport; carriage of goods and passengers on waterways; controls all aspects of shipping and shipbuilding; research, design and personnel training; Dir-Gen. ATANAS YONKOV.

Burgas Port Authority: 8000 Burgas, Aleksandur Battenberg St 1; tel. (56) 84-04-93; fax (56) 84-01-56; e-mail ivanov@port-burgas.com; internet www.port-burgas.com; Chief Exec. GEORGE DERELIEV.

Lom Port Authority: 3600 Lom, Pristanishtna St 21; tel. (971) 422-08; fax (971) 269-31; e-mail port@lom-bg.com; internet port.lom-bg.com.

Navigation Maritime Bulgare Ltd (Navibulgar): 9000 Varna, Blvd Primorski 1; tel. (52) 63-31-00; fax (52) 63-30-33; e-mail office@navbul.com; internet www.navbul.com; f. 1892; scheduled for privatization; major enterprise in Bulgaria employed in sea transport and ship repair; owns 93 tankers, bulk carriers and container, ferry, cargo and passenger vessels with a capacity of 1.8m. dwt (2002); also owns Varna shipyard; Dir-Gen. Capt. IVAN BORISSOV; 5,000 employees.

Varna Port Authority: Varna; tel. (52) 69-25-08; fax (52) 63-29-53; e-mail tihomir@port-varna.bg; internet port-varna.bg; Dir DANAIL PAPAZOV.

CIVIL AVIATION

There are three international airports in Bulgaria; at Sofia, Varna and Burgas, and seven other airports for domestic services. Construction work to modernize Sofia Airport was initiated in the mid-1990s.

Air Sofia: 1000 Sofia, Blvd Patriiarkh Evtimii 64; tel. (2) 981-09-25; fax (2) 980-29-07; internet www.airsofia.com; f. 1992; international charter flights; Pres. LILIAN TODOROV; Man. Dir GEORGI IVANOV.

Air Via Bulgarian Airways (Via): Sofia, Blvd Dimitros 54; tel. (2) 971-28-69; fax (2) 973-34-54; f. 1990; began services in 1997; first private charter airline, internal charter services to Burgas, Plovdiv and Varna; Man. Dir MIKHAIL DONSKY.

Balkan Air Tour: 1540 Sofia, Sofia Airport; tel. (2) 98-44-89; fax (2) 79-12-06; e-mail balkan@balkanairlines.bg; f. 1991 as a tour operator owned by Sofia Airport; transformed into a state-owned national carrier in 2002, as the successor to the bankrupt co Balkan Bulgarian Airlines (Balkanair); scheduled for privatization; passenger and cargo services.

Heli Air Services: 1540 Sofia, Sofia Airport North; tel. (2) 79-50-36; fax (2) 71-75-26; e-mail heliair@intech.bg; f. 1991; Exec. Dir GEORGI SPASSOV.

Hemus Airlines: 1540 Sofia, Sofia Airport; tel. (2) 70-20-76; fax (2) 79-63-80; internet www.geocities.com/CapeCanaveral/3514/hemus.html; f. 1991; 66% state-owned; Man. Dir DIMITAR PAVLOV.

Tourism

Bulgaria's tourist attractions include the resorts on the Black Sea coast, mountain scenery and historic centres. Under the communist regime most visitors to Bulgaria were from former Eastern bloc countries, or in transit to or from Turkey. Following the end of communist rule, fewer Eastern Europeans holidayed within Eastern Europe, and there was, overall, a severe reduction in the numbers of tourists staying at Black Sea resorts. The European Community (now the European Union) granted aid for developing tourism in 1993–95. In 1997 the tourism authorities promoted the creation of a national system of tourist offices, to be managed by local governments. In 2002 there were 2,992,590 foreign visitor arrivals. Tourism receipts totalled US $1,074m. in 2000 and an estimated $1,350m. in 2002, compared with $496m. in 1997.

Bulgarian Tourist Chamber: 1000 Sofia, Sveta Sofia St 8; tel. (2) 987-40-59; fax (2) 986-51-33; e-mail btch_tz@yahoo.com; internet www.btch.org; f. 1991; assists tourism enterprises, provides training, and co-ordinates non-governmental organizations; Chair. TSVETAN TONCHEV.

Balkantourist: 1040 Sofia, Blvd Vitosha 1; tel. (2) 980-23-24; fax (2) 981-01-14; e-mail sofia.agency@balkantourist.bg; internet www.balkantourist.bg; f. 1948; Bulgaria's first privatized travel company; leading tour operator and travel agent; Chair. and Man. Dir VLADIMIR ANGELOU.

Culture

NATIONAL ORGANIZATIONS

Ministry of Culture: see section on The Government (Ministries).

National Commission for UNESCO: 1000 Sofia, Rokovski St 96B; tel. (2) 87-54-49; Vice-Chair. LYUBOMIR DRAMALIEV.

CULTURAL HERITAGE

Amateur Artists' Centre: Sofia; tel. (2) 80-11-30; Man. PETAR GRIGOROV.

National Academy of Arts: 1040 Sofia, Shipka St 1; tel. (2) 88-17-01; fax (2) 87-33-28; internet www.art.acad.bg/art/index-e.html; f. 1896; 131 teachers, 828 students; Rector Prof. O. SHOSHEV.

National Archaeological Museum: 1000 Sofia, Saborna St 2; tel. and fax (2) 88-24-06; f. 1892; attached to the Bulgarian Academy of Sciences; Dir Y. IURUKOVA.

National Art Gallery: 1000 Sofia, Blvd Aleksandur Battenberg 1; tel. and fax (2) 980-00-71; e-mail nag@intech.bg; f. 1948; modern and contemporary Bulgarian art, br. in Aleksandur Nevski Cathedral—icons and ecclesiastical art; Dir Dr ROUJA MARINSKA.

National Gallery of Applied and Decorative Arts: 1000 Sofia, Vassil Levski 56; tel. and fax (2) 65-41-72; f. 1976; Dir ZDRAVKO MAVRODIEV.

National Museum of Ecclesiastical History and Archaeology: 1000 Sofia, Blvd Sveta Nedelya 19; tel. (2) 89-01-15; Dir N. KHADZHIEV.

National Museum of History: 1000 Sofia, Blvd Vitosha 2; tel. (2) 980-22-58; fax (2) 980-42-60; e-mail info@historymuseum.org; internet www.historymuseum.org; f. 1973; Bulgarian history from pre-history until the 20th century; over 500,000 exhibits; Dir ILYA PROKOPOV.

National Museum of Literature: 1000 Sofia, G. Rakovski St 138; tel. (2) 988-24-93; Dir J. KAMENOV.

'Pancho Vladigerov' State Academy of Music: 1504 Sofia, E. Georgiev 94; tel. (2) 47-01-81; fax (2) 46-36-77; e-mail kissip@bgcict.acad.bg; internet www.bulgarianspace.com/musicacademy; f. 1921; 220 teachers, 995 students; Rector Prof. GEORGUI KOSTOV.

SS Cyril and Methodius National Library: 1504 Sofia, Blvd Vassil Levski 88; tel. (2) 88-28-11; fax (2) 43-54-95; e-mail nbkm@bgcict.acad.bg; f. 1878; largest public scientific library in Bulgaria; publs 17 information periodicals; Dir Dr KIRIL TOPALOV.

SPORTING ORGANIZATIONS

Bulgarian Sports Union: 1040 Sofia, Blvd Vassil Levski 75; tel. (2) 86-52-22; fax (2) 87-96-70; fmrly Bulgarian Union of Physical Culture and Sports; public non-governmental sports organization; organizes early sport training and contests for children, youth, élite and professional athletes; Chair. TZVETAN TZVETANOV.

Bulgarian Workers' Sports Federation: 1040 Sofia, Blvd Makedonia 1; tel. (2) 917-04-61; fax (2) 987-41-42; e-mail knsb@knsb-bg.org; f. 1993; fmrly Federation of Physical Culture and Sports; trade union; Pres. SVETLOZAR SAVEV PETKOV.

Olympic Committee of the Republic of Bulgaria: 1000 Sofia, Angel Kanchev St 4; tel. (2) 980-42-97; fax (2) 987-03-79; e-mail info@bgolympic.org; internet www.bgolympic.org; f. 1923; recognized 1924; Chair. Prof. IVAN BORISSOV SLAVKOV; Gen. Sec. Prof. BELTCHO IVANOV.

PERFORMING ARTS

Theatre

Aleko Konstantinov State Satirical Theatre: 1000 Sofia, Stefan Karadzha St 5; tel. (2) 88-54-24; Dir PLAMEN MARKOV.

Central Puppet Theatre: 1000 Sofia, Gurko St 14; tel. and fax (2) 987-72-88; e-mail theatre@netel.bg; internet www.geocities.com/bulunima/central.htm; f. 1946; Man. KIRIAKOS ARGIROPULOS.

Ivan Vazov National Theatre: 1000 Sofia, Levski St 5; tel. (2) 987-78-00; fax (2) 987-70-66; e-mail ntvazov@roys.net; Dir ALEXANDER MORFOV.

N. O. Massalitinov Drama Theatre Plovdiv: 4000 Plovdiv, Niyaz Aleksandur I 38; tel. (32) 63-23-45; e-mail drama@plovdiv.ttn.bg; internet puldin.ttn.bg/theatre_plovdiv; f. 1881; Dir BOGOMIL STOILOV.

Salza i Smyakh (Tears and Laughter) Drama Theatre: 1000 Sofia, Slavyanska St 5; tel. (2) 87-33-89; Dir PETAR MARINKOV.

Sofia Drama Theatre: 1000 Sofia, Blvd A. Vl. Zaimov 23; tel. (2) 45-35-12; Dir VILLY TSANKOV.

Opera Houses

Sofia National Opera and Ballet: 1000 Sofia, Blvd Dondukov 30; tel. (2) 988-58-69; fax (2) 987-79-98; e-mail sfopera@geobiz.net; internet www.geobiz.com/sfopera; Dir Assoc. Prof. CHRISTINA ANGELAKOVA.

National Opera in Burgas: 8000 Burgas; tel. (56) 4-30-57; Dir IVAN VULPE.

National Opera in Varna: 9000 Varna, Blvd Nezavisimost 1; tel. (52) 60-20-86; fax (52) 60-20-88; e-mail opera-varna@mbox.actbg.bg; internet www.operavarna.bg; f. 1947; Dir CHRISTO IGNATOV.

ASSOCIATIONS

Asabay: Silistra; f. 1993; non-political org.; traces and preserves documents relating to the fate of the Crimean Tatars, restores Tatar folklore and publishes newspaper *Ushun*; Chair. Exec. Council ZIYA SELYAMED.

Bulgarian PEN Centre: 1040 Sofia, Angel Kanchev St 5; tel. (2) 87-47-11; affiliated to international writers' org.; Chair. BOGOMIL NOVEV.

Independent Federation of the Bulgarian Circus Community: 1000 Sofia, Iskar St 11; tel. (2) 83-29-22; trade union; mem. of CITUB (see section on Trade and Industry); Chair. CH. CHOHADZHIEV; 480 mems.

International Charity Foundation for the Development of Islamic Culture: 1000 Sofia, Blvd Ruski 8; tel. (2) 87-38-16; Chair. NEDIM HAAFUZ.

Podkrepa Trade Union Confederation: see Trade and Industry there are Podkrepa Professional Trade Unions for: Actors (160

mems); Artists (Chair. NIKOLAI RANOV 250 mems); Culture (150 mems); Journalists (Chair. BOYAN DASKALOV 400 mems); Musicians (1,500 mems); the Preservation of Cultural and Historical Heritage (400 mems).

Union of Bulgarian Actors (UBA): 1000 Sofia, Blvd Narodno Sabranie 12; tel. (2) 987-07-25; fax (2) 988-11-78; e-mail ubasab@abv.bg; f. 1919; trade union; mem. of CITUB (see section on Trade and Industry) and the International Federation of Actors; Chair. STEFAN ILIEV; 1,200 mems.

Union of Bulgarian Artists: 1504 Sofia, Shipka St 6; tel. (2) 944-61-15; fax (2) 946-02-12; f. 1893; Chair. Prof. CHRISTO HARALAMPIEV.

Union of Bulgarian Composers: 1000 Sofia, Ivan Vazov St 2; tel. (2) 988-15-60; fax (2) 987-43-78; e-mail ubc@mail.bol.bg; f. 1947; Chair. Prof. LAZAR NIKOLOV.

Union of Bulgarian Film-Makers: 1504 Sofia, Blvd Dondukov 67; tel. and fax (2) 946-10-69; e-mail sbfd@bitex.com; f. 1934; Publ. *Kino* (6 a year); Chair. P. A. VASSEV.

Union of Bulgarian Journalists: see section on The Press (Press Associations).

Union of Bulgarian Musicians: 1000 Sofia, Alabin St 52; tel. (2) 87-73-32; f. 1965; Chair. Prof. G. ROBEV.

Union of Bulgarian Writers: see section on Publishers (Writers' Union).

Education

Education is free and compulsory at primary and secondary level (seven to 16 years of age); higher education is also supported by the State, although private schools do exist. Children between the ages of three and six years may attend kindergartens. In 2001/02 there were 199,206 pupils in pre-primary education. Education from the age of six upwards is organized into a 12-year model of schooling, introduced in 1998; this is divided into three stages: primary, presecondary and secondary. In 2001/02 there were 839,518 students in general schools. There are two types of secondary schools: secondary vocational-technical schools (*gymnasiums*), which train executive cadres; and technical colleges (*tekhnikums*), which provide specialized training in areas such as industry, agriculture, transport, trade and public health. In addition, there are professional colleges, which offer two-year vocational courses on the completion of secondary education. Education is administered by the Ministry of Education and Science, in conjunction with the organs of local government. In 1997 97.9% of the relevant age group were enrolled in primary schools, compared with 77.6% in secondary education.

During the mid-1990s the higher education system was extensively reorganized, with a degree system introduced and many foundations renamed. In mid-1999 tuition fees for university students were introduced. In 1999/2000 there were 211,748 students enrolled at institutes of higher education. In 2001 government expenditure on education was 456.1m. new leva, representing 4.5% of total expenditure by the central Government.

UNIVERSITIES

St Clement of Ohrid University of Sofia (Sofiiski Universitet 'Sveti Kliment Ohridski'): 1504 Sofia, Blvd Tsar Osvoboditel 15; tel. (2) 930-82-00; fax (2) 946-02-55; e-mail rector@uni-sofia.bg; internet www.uni-sofia.bg; f. 1904; state-controlled; 15 faculties, 1,608 teachers, 25,454 students; Rector Prof. BOYAN BIOLTCHEV.

St Cyril and St Methodius University of Veliko Turnovo (Velikoturnovski Universitet 'Sv. sv. Kiril i Metodij'): 5003 Veliko Turnovo, T. Turnovski St 2; tel. (62) 62-01-89; fax (62) 62-80-23; e-mail mbox@uni-vt.bg; internet www.uni-vt.bg; f. 1971; 7 faculties, 916 teachers, 9,971 students ; Rector Prof. IVAN HARALAMPIEV.

University of Forestry—Sofia: 1756 Sofia, Blvd Kl. Ohridski 10; tel. (2) 62-30-59; fax (2) 62-28-30; internet www.ltu.acad.bg; f. 1925; 5 faculties, 226 teachers, 3,250 students; Rector Prof. Dr DIMITUR KOLAROV.

University of National and World Economics: 1156 Sofia, Studentski grad. Christo Botev; tel. (2) 962-39-03; fax (2) 68-90-29; e-mail secretary@unwe.acad.bg; internet www.unwe.acad.bg; f. 1990 as a university (formerly Karl Marx Higher Institute of Economics); f. 1920; 7 faculties, 525 teachers, 27,600 students; Rector Prof. KAMEN MIRKOVICH.

University of Plovdiv 'Paisii Hilendarski' (Plovdivski Universitet 'Paisii Hilendarski'): 4000 Plovdiv, Tsar Assen 24; tel. (32) 63-14-53; fax (32) 63-50-49; e-mail pduniv@pu.acad.bg; internet www.uni-plovdiv.bg; f. 1961; 9 faculties, 800 teachers, 15,000 students; Rector Prof. OGNIAN SAPAREV.

Social Welfare

From 1951 the state provided all medical services and treatment free. In post-communist Bulgaria this health service was retained and doctors' salaries increased, but private medical provision was also encouraged (private medical and dentistry practices were banned between 1972 and November 1989). A health insurance system for primary care commenced operations in July 2000, and more than 16,000 medical specialists were transferred from the state-financed to the commercial sector. All primary-care facilities and hospitals were transformed into commercial partnerships, as a precursor to privatization. A restructuring of the emergency care system was also completed in that year. In 1999 there were 27,940 doctors and 4,684 dentists. In the same year there were 276 hospital establishments, with 62,404 hospital beds, and 38,712 beds in 3,890 sanatoriums and other institutions. The Ministry of Health is responsible for the health service, with the assistance of local government and the Bulgarian Red Cross. In October 1993 a bill on health insurance was passed by the Council of Ministers. The bill was founded on the principles of compulsory insurance for all citizens, competition between those providing medical care, universal access to medical services and the autonomy of the National Health Insurance Fund (this fund was to be raised from a variety of sources and managed by a national insurance institute).

Other social benefits, such as unemployment and pension payments, were also retained. Owing to the high level of unemployment in the early and mid-1990s, the Government adopted a bill on social security provision during unemployment. The bill provided for the establishment of an independent Occupational Training and Unemployment Fund and regulated relations between the state, the individual and the employer in cases of unemployment. Bulgarian workers receive compensation during sick leave, full paid maternity leave before and after childbirth and non-contributory pensions (this last provision was considered likely to be adjusted). The retirement age was 60 years for men and 55 years for women, although many employees were entitled to early retirement. State social insurance is directed by the Department of Public Insurance and the Directorate of Pensions. Government expenditure on health was 984.9m. new leva in 2001 (9.6% of total government expenditure) and expenditure on social security and welfare was 3,622.1m. leva (35.5% of total expenditure). In 1999 Bulgaria initiated social and health-care reforms, including reform of the pension system. In 2001 Pension Fund expenditure was projected at 2,600m. leva. According to government estimates there were 2,370,938 pensioners at the beginning of 2001.

NATIONAL AGENCIES

Ministry of Health: see section on The Government (Ministries).

Ministry of Labour and Social Policy: see section on The Government (Ministries).

Department of Public Insurance: Sofia.

National Council for Employment and Occupational Training: Sofia; co-ordinates employment programmes and measures.

National Health Insurance Fund: 1407 Sofia, Krichim St 1; tel. (2) 965-91-57; fax (2) 965-91-52; e-mail clients@nhif.bg; internet www.nhif.bg; Chair. KIRIL ANANIEV.

National Social Security Institute (NSSI): 1303 Sofia, Blvd Stambolijski 62–64; tel. (2) 926-16-00; fax (2) 926-16-66; e-mail noi@nssi.bg; internet www.noi.bg; f. 1951.

> **Directorate of Pensions:** responsible for the administration of pensions and the establishment of a pensions fund; 27 regional brs; Gen. Man. NIKOLOV.

State Agency for Child Protection: 1051 Sofia, Triaditza St 2; e-mail sacp@sacp.government.bg; internet www.sacp.government.bg; Chair. SHIRIN MESTAN.

Agency for International Aid (AIA): 1000 Sofia, Vrabcha St 1; tel. (2) 981-10-85; fax (2) 988-15-51; e-mail aia@omega.bg; state institution created for the purpose of receiving, storing, distributing and monitoring the use of humanitarian aid donated by foreign states, organizations and citizens; Dir Dr VLADIMIR ABADJIEV.

HEALTH AND WELFARE ORGANIZATIONS

Bulgarian National Committee for UNICEF: 1606 Sofia, Blvd Pentcho Slaveykov 18; tel. and fax (2) 951-54-04; e-mail unicefbg@techno-link.com; Chair. Minister of Health, SLAVCHO BOGOEV.

Bulgarian Red Cross: 1000 Sofia, James Bawcher St 76; tel. (2) 943-45-02; fax (2) 943-42-37; e-mail secretariat@redcross.bg; f. 1878; Pres. STOYAN SAEV.

Commission of Human Rights: 1000 Sofia, Narodno Blvd Sabranie 12; tel. (2) 986-27-72; fax (2) 87-88-59; Chair. KONSTANTIN TELLALOV.

Foundation Against Cancer: 1000 Sofia, Blvd Sveta Nedelya 5; Chair. Minister of Health, SLAVCHO BOGOEV.

Union of the Blind: 1000 Sofia, Naytcho Tzanov St 172; tel. (2) 22-01-49; fax (2) 22-00-18; e-mail skarlatov@ssb.sofianet.net; f. 1921; social support of the blind; Chair. IVAN KRUMOV.

Union of the Deaf: 1000 Sofia, Denkoglu St 12–14; tel. (2) 981-98-07; fax (2) 980-16-96; Chair. VASSIL PANEV.

The Environment

Environmental concerns prompted the formation of one of the first opposition groups to the communist regime: Ecoglasnost and the Independent Committee for the Protection of the Environment (or Ruse Committee) began the Green Movement in 1989. There are estimated to be some 20 environmental groups in Bulgaria. The Bulgarian Government is a member of the Danube Commission (based in Hungary), the Joint Danube Fishery Commission (Slovakia) and the International Union for the Conservation of Nature and Natural Reserves (IUCN—Gland, Switzerland). During the 1990s Bulgaria improved environmental co-operation with Romania and other Black Sea nations. One of the main international concerns was the Kozloduy nuclear power station on the River Danube, which provided up to one-half of the country's electricity. In April 2000 Bulgaria was granted an European Union (EU) loan of €212.5m. to modernize the plant. In order to comply with conditions for EU membership, Bulgaria closed two of the Kozloduy nuclear power installation's six reactors at the end of 2002. There was some controversy over terms for the closure of two additional reactors; however, they were not expected to be decommissioned before 2006. Bulgaria was to be granted financial assistance from the EU for restructuring the energy sector and upgrading the two remaining nuclear reactors. The country also required considerable resources to repair environmental damage created by its heavy industries. In late 1999 a cyanide spill in the Danube was a cause for major environmental concern, and in 2002 the World Bank granted Bulgaria a US $7.5m. loan for the protection of the environment around the Danube. Bulgaria, which was expected to become a member of the EU in 2007, joined the EU's Environment Agency at the beginning of 2002.

GOVERNMENT ORGANIZATIONS

Ministry of the Environment and Water: see section on The Government (Ministries).

Committee on the Use of Atomic Energy for Peaceful Purposes: 1574 Sofia, Blvd Shipchenski Prokhod 69; tel. (2) 940-68-00; fax (2) 940-69-19; e-mail mail@bnsa.bas.bg; internet www.bnsa.bas.bg; f. 1957; Chair. Prof. EMIL IVANOV VAPIREV.

Executive Environment Agency: Sofia, Blvd Tsar Boriss III 136; POB 251; tel. (2) 55-85-68; e-mail cds@nfp-bg.eionet.eu.int; co-ordinates research, analysis, environmental protection programmes and national standards; Dir Assoc. Prof. IVAN PEYTCHEV.

The Ministry of Agriculture and Forestry and the Ministry of Energy and Energy Resources are also concerned with environmental matters.

ACADEMIC INSTITUTES

Bulgarian Academy of Sciences: 1040 Sofia, 15 Noemvri 1; tel. (2) 989-84-46; fax (2) 986-25-23; e-mail president@eagle.cu.bas.bg; internet www.bas.bg; f. 1869; Pres. Prof. IVAN YUKHNOVSKI.

> **Forestry Research Institute:** 1756 Sofia, Blvd St Kl. Ohridski 132; tel. (2) 962-04-42; fax (2) 962-04-47; e-mail forestin@bulnet.bg; internet www.bulnet.com/forestin; f. 1928; studies the structure and functioning of forest ecosystems, etc.; Dir Prof. Dr IVAN RAEV.

> **Institute of Botany:** 1113 Sofia, Acad. Georgi Bonchev St 23; tel. (2) 72-09-51; fax (2) 71-90-32; e-mail botinst@bio.bas.bg; internet www.bio.bas.bg/botany; f. 1889; plant taxonomy, monitoring and conservation of rare and threatened plant species; assessment of plant resources; palaeobotany; Dir Prof. Dr EMANEL PALAMAREV.

> **Central Laboratory of General Ecology:** 1113 Sofia, Gagarin St 2; tel. (2) 73-61-37; fax (2) 70-54-98; e-mail ecolab@ecolab.bas.bg; internet www.ecolab.bas.bg; f. 1956; research in the fields of ecology and environmental impact assessment; Dir Assoc. Prof. Dr GEORGI HIEBAUM.

> **Institute of Oceanology** (Institut po okeanologiya): 9000 Varna, Kv. Asparuhovo St 40; POB 152; tel. (52) 77-20-38; fax (52) 77-42-56; e-mail office@io.bas.bg; f. 1973; marine geology, physical ocean-

ography, chemistry, biology and ecology, coastal management, underwater technology; Dir Dr Christo Slabakov.

Institute of Water Problems: 1113 Sofia, Acad. Georgi Bonchev St 1; tel. (2) 72-25-72; fax (2) 72-25-77; e-mail santur@bgcict.acad.bg; internet www.iwp.bas.bg; f. 1963; research in the field of rational planning, construction and operation of water resource systems, rehabilitation and maintenance of inland waters; Dir Prof. Ohanes Santurjian.

Institute of Zoology: 1000 Sofia, Blvd Tsar Osvoboditel 1; tel. (2) 988-31-63; fax 988-28-97; e-mail zoology@bulinfo.net; f. 1889; publication of four journals: *Acta Zool, Bulgarica, Fauna of Bulgaria, Catalogi Faunæ Bulgaricæ* and *Birdbanding*; biological monitoring and preparation of the *Red Data* series on animal and bird life in Bulgaria; morphology, taxonomy, ecology and study of the evolution of Bulgarian and Palaearctic fauna; experimental zoology and protozoology; Dir Prof. Dr Vassil Grigorov Golemansky.

National Centre of Hygiene, Medical Ecology and Nutrition: 1431 Sofia, Blvd Dimitur Nestorov 15; tel. (2) 958-18-94; fax (2) 958-12-77; e-mail nch@aster.net; fmrly Inst. of Hygiene and Occupational Health; assesses the impact of environmental damage and pollution on the health of the population; Dir Assoc. Prof. Nikolai Rizov.

National Institute of Meteorology and Hydrology: 1784 Sofia, Tsarigradsko shosse 66; tel. (2) 975-39-96; fax (2) 988-44-94; e-mail office@meteo.bg; internet www.meteo.bg; monitors air, soil and water pollution and radioactivity; Dir Assoc. Prof. K. Tsankov.

N. Pushkarov Research Institute of Soil Science and Agroecology: 1080 Sofia, Bankya shosse 7; tel. (2) 924-61-41; fax (2) 924-89-37; f. 1947; monitors the pollution of soils and underground waters; Dir Assoc. Prof. V. Valev.

NON-GOVERNMENTAL ORGANIZATIONS

Association of Bulgarian Ecologists (ABECOL): 1000 Sofia, Slaveykov Pl. 7; tel. (2) 981-72-22; fax (2) 988-53-49; f. 1990; research and education into all aspects of ecological science; Pres. Prof. Dr Simeon Nedialkov.

Association Ecoforum: 1113 Sofia, Gagarin St 2; tel. (2) 70-53-79; fax (2) 955-10-67; org. of scientists, businessmen and public workers committed to promoting sustainable development and conservation, particularly in the transition to a market economy; Gen. Sec. Assoc. Prof. Pavel Georgiev.

Bulgarian Society for the Conservation of the Rhodope Mts: 4850 Chepelare, Sportna St 13; tel. and fax (3051) 39-71; e-mail bsc_rhodope_m@dir.bg; f. 1990; union committed to the conservation of the natural and cultural heritage of the Rhodope Mountains; promotion of eco-tourism; Chair. Elena Simeonova Stankova.

Bulgarian Society for the Protection of Birds (BSPB) (Birdlife Bulgaria): 1111 Sofia, Yavorov Complex 71, Entrance 4, 1st Floor; POB 50; tel. (2) 970-75-79; fax (2) 972-26-40; e-mail bspb_hq@bspb .org; internet bspb.novhost.com; f. 1988; independent ornithological asscn; research programmes; field projects; management of species populations, reserves; public awareness campaigns; Pres. Bozhidar Ivanov; Exec. Dir Boris Barov; over 1,600 mems.

Bulgarian Society of Natural Research: 1421 Sofia, Blvd Dragan Tsankov 8, POB 1136; tel. (2) 966-65-94; f. 1896; scientific and educational society of natural scientists; promotes the study and conservation of the environment; over 20 regional brs and five scientific sections, incl. one on ecology; Chair. Prof. Dr Vassil Golemanski; over 1,500 mems.

Chernomorski Ekologichen Informatsionen Tsentar (Black Sea Environmental Information Centre): 9002 Varna, Bratya Miladnovi St 68g, Apt 23; tel. (52) 23-09-57; e-mail banchev@ms3.tu-varna .acad.bg.

Ecoforum for Peace: 1431 Sofia, Dimitur Nestorov St 15; tel. (2) 959-61-23; fax (2) 959-91-26; f. 1986; internat. movement for world peace and environmental protection; 15 brs in other countries; secretariat in Bulgaria; Gen. Sec. Vasselin Heykov.

ECOS Foundation: 1000 Sofia, Blvd Aleksandur Stamboliyski 2a, 6th Floor; tel. (2) 714-33-71; fax (2) 987-24-00; educational foundation, promotes ecological awareness; Dir-Gen. Ognian Champoev.

Green Party: see section on Political Organizations.

Green Society Foundation: 1000 Sofia; tel. and fax (2) 987-24-21; f. 1991; co-operates in projects and campaigns with other groups; operates seven environmental programmes; Pres. Assoc. Prof. Petar Gulubov; Exec. Dir Radiana Stanoeva.

National Ecological Club: 1113 Sofia, Akad. G. Bonchev St, Bl. 29a; tel. (2) 970-52-25; independent public org.; promotes conservation; provides ecological education; committed to the conservation of nature; Principal Officer Vassil Sgurev.

National Movement of Ecoglasnost: 1000 Sofia, POB 548, Blvd Dondukov 9, 4th Floor, Rm 45; tel. (2) 986-22-21; fax (2) 988-15-30; e-mail ekogl@bulnet.bg; officially in 1989; campaigns against nuclear power and pollution; promotes environmental protection and sustainable development; Pres. Ivan Sungarsky; Sec. Hachadur Chuldjian.

Priroden Fond (Wilderness Fund): 1000 Sofia, Serdika St 26; tel. (2) 988-09-14; fax (2) 983-92-94; e-mail wild_fund@mbox.cit.bg; internet wf-bg.org; f. 1999; attached to the Institute of Ecology; assesses the best places to establish reserves for the protection of the natural environment; Chair. Jeko Spirodonov.

Union for Nature Protection: 1040 Sofia, Blvd Vitosha 18; tel. (2) 983-26-72; f. 1928 as Union for Native Nature Protection; restructured 1991; independent public org.; local brs and internat. contacts; Chair. Assoc. Prof. Dr Svetoslav Gerasimov.

Defence

In August 2002 the total strength of the armed forces was 68,450 (including an estimated 49,000 conscripts). This comprised an army of 31,050, an air force of 17,780, a navy of an estimated 4,370, and 15,250 centrally controlled staff and Ministry of Defence staff. Paramilitary forces included an estimated 12,000 border troops (commanded by the Ministry of the Interior), 18,000 railway and construction troops and 4,000 security police. In 1999 plans were announced to reduce the armed forces to number 45,000 by 2004. In 2000 compulsory military service for all males was reduced to nine months. The 2002 state budget allocated 828m. new leva to defence. Bulgaria joined the North Atlantic Treaty Organization's (NATO) 'Partnership for Peace' programme of military co-operation in 1994. In November 2002 the country was invited to become a full member of NATO from 2004.

Commander-in-Chief: President of the Republic.

Chief of the General Staff: Gen. Nikola Kolev.

Security Council of the Republic of Bulgaria: Sofia; national security activities; Chair. Simeon Saxe-Coburg Gotha (Prime Minister).

Bibliography

Bell, J. D. (Ed.). *The Bulgarian Communist Party from Blagoev to Zhivkov.* Stanford, CA, Hoover Institution Press, 1986.

Bulgaria in Transition, Eastern Europe After Communism. Boulder, CO, Westview Press, 1998.

Crampton, R. J. *Bulgaria 1878–1918: A History.* Boulder, CO, Eastern European Quarterly (distributed by Columbia University Press), 1983.

A Short History of Modern Bulgaria. Cambridge, Cambridge University Press, 1987.

A Concise History of Bulgaria. Cambridge, Cambridge University Press, 1997.

Dimitrov, V. *Bulgaria: The Uneven Transition.* London, Routledge, 2003.

Gavrilova, R. *Bulgarian Urban Culture in Eighteenth and Nineteenth Centuries.* Susquehanna, NY, Susquehanna University Press, 1999.

Gehrmann, U. *Bulgariens Weg zur neuen Identität: Rückblicke und Aussichten einer unvollendeten 'Preustroystvo' auf dem Balkan.* Cologne, Bundesinstitut für ostwissenchaftliche und internationale Studien, 1993.

Giatzidis, E. *An Introduction to Post-Communist Bulgaria: Political, Economic and Social Transformation.* Manchester, Manchester University Press, 2002.

Grothusen, K. D. (Ed.). *Bulgarien: Südosteuropa Handbuch, Band VI.* Göttingen, Vandenhoeck und Ruprecht, 1990.

Jones, D. C., and Miller, J. (Eds) *The Bulgarian Economy: Lessons from Reform During Early Transition.* Aldershot, Ashgate, 1997.

Lampe, J. R. *The Bulgarian Economy in the Twentieth Century.* London, Croom Helm, 1986.

Lang, D. M. *The Bulgarians from Pagan Times to the Ottoman Empire.* London, Thames and Hudson, 1976.

Melone, A. P. *Creating Parliamentary Government: The Transition to Democracy in Bulgaria.* Columbus, OH, Ohio University Press, 1998.

Miller, L. M. *Bulgaria during the Second World War.* Stanford, CA, Stanford University Press, 1975.

Perry, D. *Stefan Stambolov and the Emergence of Modern Bulgaria, 1870–1895.* Durham, NC, Duke University Press, 1993.

Schönfelder, B. (Ed). *Problems of Privatization in Bulgaria.* Südosteuropa Aktuell Vol. 24, Munich, Südosteuropa-Gesellschaft, 1997.

Tzvetkov, P. S. *A History of the Balkans: A Regional Overview from a Bulgarian Perspective,* Vols 1 and 2. Lampeter, Edwin Mellen Press, 1993.

Zloch-Christy, I. *Bulgaria in a Time of Change: Economic and Political Dimensions.* Aldershot, Avebury, 1996.

CROATIA

Geography

PHYSICAL FEATURES

The Republic of Croatia (formerly a constituent partner in the Socialist Federal Republic of Yugoslavia) has a long western coastline on the Adriatic Sea. It is bordered by Slovenia to the north-west, Hungary to the north-east and the Vojvodina area of Serbia (Serbia and Montenegro) to the east. Bosnia and Herzegovina abuts into Croatia, forming a southern border along the Sava river, and an eastern one inland from the Dalmatian coast which stretches southwards. At the southern tip of this narrowing stretch of Croatia, beyond a short coastal strip of Bosnia and Herzegovina, is the territory of Dubrovnik (once known as Ragusa), which has a short border with Montenegro.

Croatia, which has a total area of 56,542 sq km (21,831 sq miles), consists of two principal parts: there is a long coastal region, narrowing as it goes south, extending from the Istrian peninsula, down the Dalmatian coast to the area of the former city state of Dubrovnik; the north of this coastal region is attached, by a relatively narrow bridge of territory, to eastern Croatia, which extends inland. Beyond the 'waist' attaching it to the coast, the country widens out into Croatia proper, beyond the mountains, and stretches eastwards. Slovenia juts into this 'waist' from the north-west and Bosnia from the south-east. To the north-east of the waist of the country lies the capital, Zagreb (Agram), in the heart of old Croatia. Eastwards is the fertile, petroleum-rich territory of Slavonia, an ancient province that lies on the plains between the Drava and the Sava rivers. Western or coastal Croatia is defined by the mountains running parallel to the littoral, which is fringed with more than 1,100 islets and islands.

CLIMATE

The climate in Croatia is Mediterranean on the coast and continental inland. The highlands have a colder climate with heavy snow in winter, but in summer it can be very hot. Temperatures inland average 10°C (50°F), while on the coast the mean temperature is 15°C (59°F). Rainfall is fairly constant throughout the year, although summer is the wettest season in the north of the country. The average annual rainfall is 890 mm (35 in) in Zagreb.

POPULATION

According to the results of the census of 31 March 2001, the population totalled 4,381,000, giving a density of 77.5 per

sq km. At the 2001 census, ethnic Croats comprised 89.6% of Croatia's total population, while there was a Serb minority of 4.5%, concentrated mainly along the border with Bosnia and Herzegovina. (The Habsburgs settled many Serbs along the frontier with its Muslim rival, the Ottoman Empire, in an area known as the Krajina, the borderlands.) Both peoples speak versions of Serbo-Croat (or Croato-Serb), but the largely Roman Catholic Croats use the Latin script and the Eastern Orthodox Serbs use the Cyrillic script. The Roman Catholic Church is the largest religious denomination. Since 1991 the Croatians have rejected the 1954 Novi Sad Agreement, and claim the distinctness of a Croatian language. The capital, Zagreb, was the largest city in the country (with a population of 691,724, according to the results of the 2001 census). The most populous towns of the coast were Split (Spalato—175,140), in the central coastal area, and Rijeka (Fiume—143,800), in the north. The main town of Slavonia, Osijek, in the east of the country had a population of 90,411 in 2001.

Chronology

168 BC: Illyria (which included modern-day Croatia) was annexed by the Roman Empire.

AD 395: Following a division of the administration of the Roman Empire, Illyria was ruled by the Eastern Roman ('Byzantine') Emperor in Constantinople (İstanbul, now in Turkey).

5th century: Southern Slav peoples began to move from Pannonia into Illyria and the Balkans.

7th–8th centuries: Western Christian missionaries from Aquileia (Trieste) were active among the Croats, introducing the Latin script and a Western cultural orientation.

812: By the Treaty of Aix-la-Chapelle (Aachen), the Byzantine Emperor, Michael I, acknowledged the Frankish (German) ruler, Charles ('the Great'—Charlemagne), as Emperor in the West; Byzantine suzerainty over Istria and Dalmatia was confirmed and German influence to the north of the Croats was established.

1076: Coronation, by the Pope (the leader of the Roman Church), of Dimitar Zvonimir, who had rejected Eastern, Byzantine overlordship of the Croatian kingdom established in the 10th century.

1082: Venice was granted trading privileges in the Eastern Empire, securing its independence and growing influence along the formerly Byzantine Dalmatian coast.

1102: Croatia's personal union with Hungary (under the *Pacta Conventa*) linked it to the Hungarian Crown, together with parts of Dalmatia.

1187: The Emperor in Constantinople acknowledged Hungarian conquests in Croatia and Bosnia.

1490: Death of the Hungarian King, Matthias I Corvinus, who had secured modern Croatia and the Vojvodina (Slavonia and the Banat) for Hungary and, temporarily, conquered the Habsburg lands.

1526: Louis II and the Hungarian forces were destroyed by the Ottomans at the Battle of Mohács; the Hungarian Crown was claimed as a hereditary possession of the House of Habsburg, but the kingdom itself was subsequently partitioned between the Habsburgs (northern Croatia) and the Ottomans (southern Croatia and Slavonia).

1718: The Peace of Passarowitz confirmed the Habsburg liberation of Hungary, including Croatia and Slavonia; the Ottomans ceded the Banat and northern Serbia (but the latter was held only until 1739).

1815: The Congress of Vienna confirmed Austrian rule over Istria and Dalmatia, which were formerly Venetian.

1848: At a time of revolution in Habsburg and other territories, the Croatian assembly, in Agram (Zagreb), was forced to end consideration of a Southern Slav (Yugoslav) state.

1868: Croatia, united with Slavonia, was granted autonomy by Hungary, which, since the *Ausgleich* or Compromise of the previous year, was now a partner in the Habsburg 'Dual Monarchy'.

1881: Final abolition of the 'Military Frontier' or Vojna Krajina, in which, since the 17th century, the Habsburgs had allowed some autonomy to Serb settlers defending the borders against the Ottomans in Bosnia. (Austria-Hungary had secured administration rights in Bosnia and Herzegovina in 1878.).

1903: Accession of Petar I Karadjordjević, leader of the Radical party, to the throne of Serbia; he was anti-Habsburg and encouraged the Southern Slav movement ('Yugoslavism'), the champion of which in Croatia-Slavonia was Bishop Josip Strossmayer.

28 June 1914: The heir to the Habsburg throne, Archduke Francis Ferdinand, and his wife were assassinated in Sarajevo (Bosnia and Herzegovina).

28 July 1914: Austria-Hungary declared war on Serbia, which started the First World War between the Central Powers, of Austria-Hungary and Germany, and the Entente Powers, of France, Russia, Serbia and the United Kingdom.

July 1917: Representatives of the Croats, Serbia and the other Southern Slavs (excluding the Bulgarians) declared their intention to form a unitary state, under the Serbian monarchy.

29 October 1918: Following the defeat and dissolution of the Danubian Monarchy, the Southern Slav peoples separated from the Austro-Hungarian system of states (a Southern Slav republic was established on 15 October); Dalmatia, Croatia-Slavonia, Bosnia and Herzegovina, parts of Carinthia, Carniola and the Banat were, subsequently, ceded formally to the new state.

4 December 1918: Proclamation of the Kingdom of Serbs, Croats and Slovenes, which united the former Habsburg lands with Serbia and Montenegro.

August 1921: Prince Aleksandar, Regent of Serbia since 1914 and of the new Kingdom since its formation, became King, upon the ratification of the 'Vidovdan' (St Vitus Day) Constitution.

August 1928: A separatist Croatian assembly convened in Zagreb.

3 October 1929: Following the imposition by King Aleksandar of a royal dictatorship, the country was formally named Yugoslavia.

1931: The dictatorship was suspended by the introduction of a new Constitution, although this did not prevent Croat unrest and the rise of the Fascist Ustaša (Rebel) movement.

October 1934: King Aleksandar I of Yugoslavia was assassinated in France by Croatian extremists; his brother, Prince Paul, became Regent, on behalf of the young King Petar II.

1937: Tito (Josip Broz) became General Secretary of the Communist Party of Yugoslavia (CPY), which was to become the main partner in the Partisan (National Liberation Army) resistance to the German invasion.

March 1941: A *coup d'état* installed King Petar II, who reversed previous policies and aligned himself with the Allied Powers of the Second World War.

9 April 1941: An Independent State of Croatia (Nczavisna Država Hrvatska) was established, following the invasion of Yugoslavia by German and Italian forces; the State included much of Bosnia and Herzegovina, while the rest of Yugoslavia was dismembered by Albania, Bulgaria, Germany, Hungary and Italy (the last annexing some of the Dalmatian coast); the Italian, Duke Aimone of Spoleto, was King of Croatia, with an Ustaša Government under Ante Pavelić.

29 November 1943: Proclamation of a government for 'liberated' areas by the Partisans, following a savage resistance struggle and civil war with the Ustaša regime and the royalist Četniks (Yugoslav Army of the Fatherland) of western Serbia; Tito's leadership was subsequently acknowledged by the Allies and the royal Government-in-Exile.

1944: King Petar II was declared deposed.

29 November 1945: Following elections for a Provisional Assembly, the Federative People's Republic of Yugoslavia was proclaimed, with Tito as Prime Minister.

January 1946: A Soviet-style Constitution was adopted, establishing a federation of six republics, one of which was Croatia (including Dalmatia and Slavonia).

1954: Istria was partitioned between Italy, which gained the city of Trieste, and Yugoslavia (mostly becoming part of Croatia, but the north going to Slovenia—denying Croatia a border with Italy). The so-called Novi Sad Agreement proclaimed Serbo-Croat to be one language with two scripts.

1966: Reformists, who had already achieved some economic liberalization, secured the fall of Vice-President Aleksandar Ranković, the head of the secret police and an advocate of strong central government.

July 1971: Following the granting of the rights of autonomy to the federal units, Tito introduced a system of collective leadership and the regular rotation of posts.

December 1971: The reformist Croatian leadership was forced to resign following criticism from Tito; the suppression of the Croatian 'mass movement', or *Maspok*, and a purge of liberals throughout Yugoslavia followed.

1974: A new Constitution came into force, aimed at containing nationalist tendencies, particularly within Croatia.

4 May 1980: Tito died; his responsibilities were transferred to the collective State Presidency of the federation and to the Presidium of the League of Communists of Yugoslavia (LCY).

March 1989: Against a background of increasing tension in the Serbian province of Kosovo and declining economic conditions, a new Federal Government, under Ante Marković, was appointed.

22 April 1990: The first-round elections to the three chambers of the Croatian Assembly (for a maximum of 356 seats) were held.

6–7 May 1990: A second round of voting took place; in the final results, the nationalist opposition party, the Croatian Democratic Union (CDU), secured 205 of the eventual 351 seats in the Assembly.

30 May 1990: The Assembly elected Franjo Tudjman, leader of the CDU, as President of the State Presidency of Croatia; Stjepan ('Stipe') Mesić was elected President of the Executive Council (premier).

25 July 1990: The Croatian Assembly approved constitutional changes, including: the removal of the word 'Socialist' from the Republic's title; the redesignation of the republican Executive Council as a 'Government'; the replacement of the republican State Presidency with a President and six Vice-Presidents; and the downgrading of the use of the Cyrillic alphabet. The leaders of the Serb minority in Croatia, who had formed a 'Serb National Council', denounced the amendments and demanded a referendum on immediate cultural autonomy.

August 1990: The Assembly dismissed Croatia's member of the federal State Presidency, a communist, and nominated their premier, Mesić, instead (endorsed by the Federal Assembly on 19 October); Josip Manolić was elected premier.

1 October 1990: The Serb National Council, after announcing its referendum results, proclaimed autonomy for the Serb-dominated Krajina areas of Croatia (the 'Serb Autonomous Region—SAR of Krajina', which was based in Knin).

November 1990: The Assembly placed the Territorial Defence Force under republican control.

21 December 1990: The Croatian Assembly (Sabor) promulgated a new Constitution, which proclaimed the Republic's full sovereignty and its right to secede from Yugoslavia.

20 January 1991: Croatia and Slovenia concluded a mutual defence pact, amid rising tension between the republican authorities and the Yugoslav People's Army (YPA).

25 January 1991: The YPA agreed to end its state of alert and the Croatians agreed to demobilize, if not disband, all paramilitary groups. However, 10 days later, the YPA ordered the arrest of Croatia's Minister of Defence on sedition charges.

21 February 1991: Croatia asserted the primacy of its Constitution and laws over those of the federation and declared its conditions for participation in a confederation of sovereign states.

28 February 1991: The self-proclaimed SAR of Krajina declared its separation from Croatia and its desire to unite with Serbia (on 16 March it formally resolved on its adherence to the Yugoslav federation).

11 April 1991: Croatia established an army, the Croatian National Guard Corps (to replace the Territorial Defence Force), after increasing anxieties about the intentions of the YPA following clashes between it and Croatian forces.

30 April 1991: The SAR of Krajina's self-proclaimed government or executive council announced the formation of a Krajina Assembly.

19 May 1991: In a referendum in Croatia, some 94% of participants voted in favour of an independent republic (possibly as part of a confederation of sovereign states).

29 May 1991: The SAR of Krajina announced that its basic statute was a constitutional law; its Assembly appointed a Government led by Milan Babić.

25 June 1991: The Sabor declared the independence and sovereignty of the republic, beginning the process of 'dissociation' from the federation at the same time as Slovenia. Two days later the union of the two Krajinas was announced: the SAR in Croatia; and Bosanska (Bosnian) Krajina in Bosnia and Herzegovina.

30 June 1991: Following fighting, mainly in Slovenia, a cease-fire was secured; one condition was implemented forthwith—the proclamation of Stipe Mesić as President of the federal State Presidency; it was subsequently agreed that Croatia and Slovenia should have a three-month moratorium on further implementation of their declarations of dissociation.

18 July 1991: In Croatia, as fighting continued to escalate, Josip Manolić was appointed the head of a new war cabinet or state council, being replaced as premier (Prime Minister) by his deputy, Franjo Greguric.

1 August 1991: Tudjman reorganized the Croatian Government, forming an administration of 'democratic unity', with 16 of the 27 posts being filled by opposition parties.

13 August 1991: An SAR of Western Slavonia was declared; later that month the SAR of Slavonia, Baranja and Western Srem (Eastern Slavonia) also proclaimed its autonomy.

25 September 1991: The UN Security Council unanimously ordered an arms embargo on Yugoslavia. In the SAR of Slavonia, Baranja and Western Srem, its 'Grand National Assembly' enacted a constitutional law.

8 October 1991: The Sabor declared all federal laws null and void, the European Community (EC—now the European Union, EU) moratorium on the Croatian and Slovenian processes of dissociation having expired the previous day. Later in the month the SARs of Krajina and Bosanska Krajina announced their unification, subsequently being joined by the SAR of Slavonia, Baranja and Western Srem; Babić, leader of the Knin regime, was authorized to represent the areas at a peace conference for Yugoslavia in the Hague, the Netherlands.

October 1991: The siege of Dubrovnik by the YPA began (it did not end until 28 May 1992).

18 November 1991: The town of Vukovar, on the Danube (Dunav) river, was captured by Serb forces.

19 November 1991: Croatians were ordered to leave all federal offices and subsequently to serve only the Croatian state.

5 December 1991: Stipe Mesić resigned as President of the Yugoslav federation; two weeks later the federal Prime Minister, Ante Marković, also left office. In the same month the 'Republic of Serb Krajina' (RSK) was proclaimed, formed by the union of the three SARs.

23 December 1991: A Croatian dinar was introduced.

2 January 1992: The UN negotiated a cease-fire between the Croatian National Guard and the YPA.

15 January 1992: An independent Republic of Croatia was recognized by the EC.

February 1992: The UN Protection Force in Yugoslavia (UNPROFOR) was deployed in Croatia to supervise the withdrawal of the YPA and the demilitarization of Serb-held enclaves.

May 1992: Croatia was formally admitted to the UN. The Croatian People's Party left the coalition Government, over a law that gave special rights to Serbs residing in areas with a Serb majority. The YPA began to withdraw from Croatia.

June 1992: Following attacks by Croatian forces on several Serb areas, a UN Security Council resolution demanded the immediate withdrawal by Croats to the positions they had held before 21 June.

2 August 1992: Parliamentary and presidential elections were held; Tudjman, one of eight candidates, was re-elected President (winning 56% of the votes cast), and the ruling CDU obtained 85 of the 138 seats in the new Chamber of Representatives, the lower house of the Sabor. The new Government, headed by Hrvoje Šarinić, took office on 8 September.

26 August 1992: Following the failure of the peace negotiations in The Hague in 1991, the London Conference opened in the United Kingdom; it was decided that a permanent conference would be established in Geneva, Switzerland.

22 January 1993: In an effort to win control of the Maslenica bridge Croatian troops breached UNPROFOR peace-keeping lines and began an offensive in Serb-held Krajina.

7 February 1993: In elections to the Chamber of Municipalities, the upper house of the Sabor, the CDU won a majority (37 seats out of 67).

29 March 1993: The Šarinić Government resigned under pressure; President Tudjman appointed Nikica Valentić as Prime Minister.

14 July 1993: Serb paramilitary forces began to reoccupy the regions of Karlovac and Zemunik, in response to the continued presence of Croatian troops in the Maslenica area.

15–16 July 1993: The so-called Erdut Agreement, negotiated by the UN, was signed by the Serbian and Croatian Presidents. On 13 August, however, the Agreement was declared null and void by the Croatian Minister of Foreign Affairs, Mate Granić.

4 October 1993: UN Security Council Resolution 871 required the extension of UNPROFOR's mandate; it also demanded the disarming of Serb paramilitary groups and the transferral of all 'pink zones' (areas with majority Serb populations lying outside the official UN Protected Areas—UNPAs) to Croatian control; eight days later the Krajina Serb Assembly voted to reject the resolution and ordered the mobilization of all conscripts.

23 January 1994: Milan Martić was elected President of the RSK, beating his rival, Milan Babić, in a second round of voting.

30 March 1994: Following the expiry of a three-month cease-fire the rebel Serbs and the Croatian Government signed a new agreement, which provided for the creation of a 'buffer zone' between the two front lines, to be monitored by UNPROFOR.

5 April 1994: Josip Manolić, the President of the Chamber of Municipalities, and Stipe Mesić, the President of the Chamber of Representatives, left the CDU in protest at President Tudjman's anti-Muslim stance. They founded a new party, the Croatian Independent Democrats, later in the month, with Mesić as Chairman.

30 May 1994: A new currency, the kuna, was introduced.

October 1994: A negotiating forum, the Zagreb Group or 'Z4', was created with the aim of finding a solution to the conflict in the RSK; the Group comprised two EU representatives, and the US and Russian ambassadors to Croatia. In December the Zagreb Group secured the agreement of the Croatian Government and the RSK to the re-establishment of basic infrastructural links between the Krajina and the rest of Croatia.

8 February 1995: In an attempt to force President Tudjman to reverse his decision, made in the previous month, to expel UN troops, the RSK parliament voted to suspend implementation of the enclave's economic agreement with Croatia. Also in February the RSK agreed a military alliance with the Bosnian Serbs.

12 March 1995: President Tudjman agreed to a continued UN presence in Croatia, but only of a smaller force (known as the UN Confidence Restoration Operation—UNCRO). In the same month a formal military alliance between Croatia, the Bosnian Croats and the Bosnian Government was announced.

13 April 1995: Bosnian Serb artillery began an assault on Dubrovnik and its airport, in which one person was killed.

1–2 May 1995: Croatian government troops reoccupied the territory of Western Slavonia (despite its status as a UNPA), forcing many Serbs to flee the area. The Serbs retaliated with attacks on Karlovac and Sisak. A UN-brokered cease-fire was agreed the following day.

4–8 August 1995: In a major offensive, Croatian government forces seized Knin and gained control of most of the Krajina; some 150,000 Croatian Serb refugees fled to Serb-held areas in Bosnia and Herzegovina and Yugoslavia. Of the former RSK territories, only Eastern Slavonia remained under Serb control, effectively reinforced by the presence of Yugoslav troops on its border.

September 1995: A new electoral law reduced from 13 to three the number of parliamentary seats allocated to the Serb minority, while a further 12 seats were granted to Croatian *émigrés*; amendments to the law on minorities further reduced the rights of the Krajina Serbs.

3 October 1995: After heavy fighting in Eastern Slavonia an 11-point agreement was signed by Croatian government officials and Serb leaders; this agreement provided for a 'transitional period' during which the enclave would be demilitarized.

29 October 1995: At a general election the CDU won 45 out of 80 elected seats in the Chamber of Representatives and 37 out of 63 seats in the Chamber of Municipalities. A new Government was subsequently appointed, headed by the former Minister of the Economy, Zlatko Mateša.

12 November 1995: The Basic Agreement on the Region of Eastern Slavonia, Baranja and Western Sirmium was signed at Erdut. The accord provided for the reintegration of Eastern Slavonia into Croatia, under UN supervision.

15 January 1996: On the same day that UNCRO's mandate expired, the UN Security Council established the UN Transitional Administration for Eastern Slavonia, Baranja and Western Sirmium (UNTAES), to supervise the region's demilitarization and reintegration over a period of two years.

1 May 1996: The Croatian Government dissolved the opposition-led Zagreb City Assembly and appointed a Government Commissioner in its place.

21 May 1996: Following the full deployment of UNTAES a 30-day period of demilitarization began in Eastern Slavonia.

1 July 1996: Transitional police forces, under the command of Petar Djukić, assumed control of Eastern Slavonia.

23 August 1996: An agreement on mutual recognition, signed by the foreign ministers of Croatia and the Federal Republic of Yugoslavia (FRY), formally ended five years of hostility between the two countries.

16 October 1996: The Council of Europe agreed to accept Croatia's application for membership, following its Government's pledge to ratify the European Convention on Human Rights within one year of admission.

January 1997: The Croatian Government announced a Memorandum on the Completion of the Peaceful Reintegration of Eastern Slavonia, which attempted to appease the largely Serb population there by offering new voting rights and senior posts in the enclave's government, as well as making military service optional.

1 April 1997: In a referendum in Eastern Slavonia 99.5% of the participating electorate voted in favour of the enclave remaining a single administration under Serb control after its return to Croatia.

13 April 1997: In elections to the upper house the CDU secured 42 of the 63 elective seats, while the Croatian Peasants' Party obtained nine, the Croatian Social-Liberal Party (CSLP) six and the Social Democratic Party (SDP) four; the remaining two seats were won by the IDA. In simultaneously held local elections in Eastern Slavonia, in which some 85% of the voting population participated, the Independent Democratic Serb Party, led by Vojislav Stanimirović, secured control of 11 of the 28 contested municipalities.

15 June 1997: Despite reports that he was seriously ill, Franjo Tudjman was re-elected to the presidency, with 61.4% of the votes cast. Although the Organization for Security and Co-operation in Europe (OSCE) alleged that the elections had not been carried out fairly, the Constitutional Court endorsed the results later in the month.

1 July 1997: International institutions suspended financial aid to Croatia in protest at the lack of progress in the resettlement of refugees in Eastern Slavonia, as well as the Government's failure to comply with extradition orders by the International Criminal Tribunal for the former Yugoslavia (ICTY) in The Hague on those suspected of war crimes.

10 October 1997: The IMF approved the resumption of aid to Croatia following the surrender of 10 Bosnian Croat war crimes suspects to the ICTY.

21 November 1997: The Chamber of Representatives approved constitutional changes, proposed by President Tudjman and already endorsed by the upper house earlier in the month, which, notably, prohibited the re-establishment of a union of Yugoslav states.

13 January 1998: The UN Security Council voted to extend the mandate of the UN Mission of Observers in Prevlaka (UNMOP), deployed in the peninsula since February 1996, until 15 July (the mandate was subsequently extended further).

15 January 1998: The Croatian Government formally resumed control of Eastern Slavonia following the expiry of the mandate of UNTAES in the Serb-dominated enclave.

12 February 1998: Following international criticism, the Government annulled a decree, issued the previous month, which had effectively allowed the eviction of Serbs from their homes in Eastern Slavonia by permitting the mainly Croat former occupants to reclaim state-owned apartments left during the Serb–Croat conflict.

31 March 1998: The Government proposed the legal provisions under which Serb refugees could return to Croatia; the plan was immediately criticized by the OSCE, which maintained that the right to return to one's country was inalienable and could not be dependent on the fulfilment of other conditions.

8 May 1998: The 'Article 11' Commission, which was established by the international community to oversee the reintegration of Eastern Slavonia into Croatia, declared that sanctions would be imposed on Croatia if the Government failed to allow the free return of displaced persons.

14 May 1998: The Government announced a relaxation of the conditions of the Serb refugees' return, which it claimed was a compromise between the demands of the international community and the national interests of Croatia.

23 June 1998: A draft agreement on the status of the disputed area of Prevlaka was presented to the UN Security Council; the plan proposed the establishment of a joint Croatian-Yugoslav Commission to demarcate borders, around which there would be a five-year demilitarization zone.

26 June 1998: The Chamber of Representatives voted to adopt the Government's Programme for the Return and Accommodation of Displaced Persons, Refugees and Exiled Persons, which contained the Programme for the Return, a document that met with the approval of the international community.

19 September 1998: In a meeting in Zagreb the Minister of Foreign Affairs, Mate Granić, and the US ambassador to Croatia, William Montgomery, agreed to establish Croatian-US working groups to implement the Dayton peace accords and to accelerate Croatia's inclusion in the 'Partnership for Peace' programme of the North Atlantic Treaty Organization (NATO).

18 May 1999: An OSCE report severely criticized Croatia's progress in implementing its international commitments.

7 July 1999: Croatia and Bosnia and Herzegovina agreed on a common border.

9 August 1999: Following his indictment by the ICTY, Vinko Martinović was extradited to the Hague to answer charges of crimes committed during the Croatian–Muslim conflict in 1993–94. However, Croatia's reluctance to extradite Mladen Naletilić, indicted on similar charges, invoked severe international criticism.

1 November 1999: President Tudjman underwent emergency medical treatment after becoming seriously ill.

26 November 1999: The Sabor declared President Tudjman to be 'temporarily incapacitated' and provisionally transferred the powers of Head of State to the parliamentary Speaker, Vlatko Pavletić, who postponed the forthcoming parliamentary elections, due to be held on 22 December, to 3 January 2000. Six principal opposition parties, the 'Opposition Six', signed an agreement on the establishment of a coalition Government in the event of winning the elections.

10 December 1999: President Tudjman died. His funeral, three days later, was attended by large crowds. However, President Süleyman Demirel of Turkey was the only international head of state to attend the occasion.

3 January 2000: Elections to the Chamber of Representatives were held. A coalition comprising the SDP, the CSLP and two regional groups won the largest share (47.0%) of the votes cast and 71 of the 152 legislative seats; the ruling CDU obtained 30.5% of the votes cast and 40 seats, and the alliance of the other four main opposition parties, together with the Croatian Social Democrats' Action, won 15.9% of the ballot and 25 seats.

14 January 2000: In what was considered to be the first significant international judgment on 'ethnic cleansing' in Croatia, the ICTY found five Bosnian Croats guilty of crimes against more than 100 Muslims in 1993; Vladimir Santić received the most severe sentence, of 25 years' imprisonment.

24 January 2000: Voting in the first round of the presidential elections took place; opposition candidate Stipe Mesić obtained 41.1% of the votes cast, compared with Dražen Budiša, the CSLP leader, who attracted 27.7%, and the CDU's Mate Granić, who won 22.5% of the ballot. As no candidate received more than 50% of the votes cast, a second ballot between the two leading candidates was to take place.

27 January 2000: The SDP leader, Ivica Račan, was formally appointed Prime Minister; he immediately announced the establishment of a new coalition Government, comprising members of the Opposition Six.

2 February 2000: Zlatko Tomcić, leader of the Croatian Peasants' Party, was elected President of the Sabor and acting head of state.

7 February 2000: In the second round of the presidential election, Mesić defeated Budiša, winning 56.1% of the votes cast, compared with the latter's 43.9%. Mesić was sworn in as President on 18 February.

2 March 2000: Mate Granić announced his decision to leave the CDU and establish the Democratic Centre, a pro-European party of the moderate centre, with Vesna Skare-Ozbolt.

3 March 2000: After being found guilty of war crimes, Tihomir Blaskić was sentenced to 45 years' imprisonment by the ICTY, the harshest sentence meted out by the Tribunal thus far.

9 March 2000: The Minister of Foreign Affairs of Croatia, Tonino Picula, and the Prime Minister of the Bosnian Serb Republic, Milorad Dodik, signed a joint statement on the return of refugees and displaced persons. The two ministers agreed to submit legislation to their respective parliaments regarding the return of refugees to areas controlled by other ethnic groups and, in the mean time, allowed 2,000 refugees to return to their homes within three months.

21 March 2000: The indicted war criminal, Mladen Naletilić ('Tuta'), was extradited to the ICTY to face charges.

31 March 2000: The Croatian Government established a council for co-operation with the ICTY, which was to be attended by a deputy premier and the foreign minister; on 14 April the Sabor approved a Declaration of Co-operation between Croatia and the ICTY.

7 May 2000: Municipal elections were held in Zagreb. The SDP—Croatian Pensioners' Party coalition obtained the largest share of the votes cast (21%) and 15 of the 50 councillor seats, the CPP won 19% of the votes cast, and the CSLP and the CDU secured 15% and 12%, respectively, of the ballot. The newly formed Democratic Centre won 7% of the votes cast and the Croatian Peasants' Party received 2% of the votes. The low rate of voter participation (33.7%) was attributed to the frequency of elections.

19 May 2000: Eleven of the 22 people indicted for genocide and war crimes against civilians during the siege and fall of Vukovar in 1991 were found guilty by the ICTY. The longest sentence meted out was 20 years' imprisonment.

25 May 2000: Croatia officially joined NATO's Partnership for Peace programme. Five days later Croatia was granted associate membership of NATO's Parliamentary Assembly.

28 August 2000: Milan Levar, an important witness in the ICTY's investigation into atrocities allegedly committed by Croatian forces in 1991, was killed in an explosion at his home; in subsequent months the frequency of arrests of those suspected of involvement in war crimes increased.

29 September 2000: A number of senior military figures, including seven generals, were ordered to retire after they published a letter critical of the Government's policy of co-operation with the ICTY.

October 2000: Transcripts of recordings of conversations held by Tudjman during his time in office began to be released; the recordings were held to support allegations of corruption on the part of Tudjman, his family and his associates. In December Tudjman's family began legal proceedings to prevent the release of any further transcripts or recordings.

9 November 2000: The Sabor adopted amendments to the Constitution, transferring the power to appoint the government from the President of the Republic to the Sabor and restricting the powers of the Chamber of Counties in the legislative process. The restrictions on the role of the presidency displeased Mesić and the amendments were only approved following protracted discussions between the President and the Government.

30 November 2000: Croatia became a member of the World Trade Organization.

21 December 2000: It was confirmed that the army Chief of the General Staff, Col-Gen. Petar Stipetić, had been summoned to appear before the ICTY as a possible suspect. Stipetić had previously been summoned to the Tribunal as a witness.

15 February 2001: In a rally organized by Tudjman's followers, 100,000 nationalists protested in Split against government attempts to arrest Gen. Mirko Norac, who was suspected of involvement in the murder of more than 40 Serb civilians in 1991. Eight days later Gen. Norac surrendered to a district court and was remanded in custody.

26 February 2001: A Croatian military Commander, Mario Cerkez, was convicted by the ICTY on numerous counts of murder and other war crimes committed against Bosnian Muslims between 1993 and 1994; he received a 15-year sentence.

28 March 2001: The legislature approved constitutional amendments, providing for the abolition of the opposition-controlled upper house, the Chamber of Counties.

20 May 2001: At local government elections the SDP won control of 14 of the 21 County Assemblies, while the CDU secured only four.

7 June 2001: Fikret Abdić, a former Bosnian presidential candidate and a Croatian citizen, was arrested in Rijecka on war crimes charges. His trial commenced in Karlovac in the following month, and he was sentenced to 20 years' imprisonment in July 2002.

8 July 2001: Four ministers belonging to the CSLP resigned, following the decision of the Government to extradite two major war crimes suspects to the ICTY.

5 December 2001: The Croatian legislature ratified the signature of a Stabilization and Association Agreement with the EU.

27 February 2002: Three CSLP representatives (including a Deputy Prime Minister) were removed from the Government by Dražen Budiša (who had been re-elected to the party leadership); the remaining three CSLP ministers resigned in protest at the decision.

15 March 2002: Following lengthy discussions between the coalition parties in the Government, a reorganization, in which Budiša became First Deputy Prime Minister, was agreed.

10 April 2002: The Ministers of Foreign Affairs of Croatia and the FRY, Picula and Goran Svilanović, agreed to designate the boundary between Croatia and Montenegro (FRY) as the state border of the disputed Prevlaka region, in the first formal bilateral accord on Prevlaka to be reached since the dissolution of the Yugoslav federation.

21 May 2002: Milan Martić, the former President of the RSK, pleaded innocent at his trial on war crimes charges.

3 July 2002: Budiša finally withdrew the CSLP from the government coalition, after an agreement on joint ownership of the Krško nuclear power installation in Slovenia was ratified in the Sabor, despite the opposition of 17 of the 23 CSLP deputies. He threatened to expel the six dissident CSLP deputies from the party.

5 July 2002: Račan submitted his resignation to Mesić, following the collapse of his administration.

10 July 2002: Račan was returned to the office of Prime Minister, after his nomination by Mesić was supported by 84 deputies in the Sabor; under the terms of the Constitution, he was to form a new administration (without the participation of the CSLP) within a period of 30 days.

15 July 2002: The Presidents of Croatia and the FRY met members of the Bosnian Presidency in Sarajevo (the first trilateral summit meeting since the dissolution of the former

Yugoslavia). The leaders of the three countries agreed to strengthen co-operation.

28 July 2002: Račan and the leaders of the other political parties belonging to the ruling coalition reached agreement on a new Council of Ministers, which was approved by the Sabor at the end of that month.

17 September 2002: The ICTY issued an indictment against Gen. Janko Bobetko, the army Chief of Staff in 1991–95, for his alleged involvement in war crimes against Serbs. Račan refused for the first time to co-operate with the Tribunal, on the grounds that Bobetko was unfit to be extradited, owing to ill health. (Bobetko died in April 2003.).

15 December 2002: The mandate of UNMOP officially ended, after the Governments of Croatia and the FRY signed a provisional agreement on the Prevlaka peninsula. Under the accord, the peninsula was to remain demilitarized, and joint maritime patrols were to be introduced.

21 February 2003: Croatia submitted a formal application for membership of the EU.

23 March 2003: A former army commander, Gen. Mirko Novac, was sentenced by a Croatian court to 12 years' imprisonment for his involvement in war crimes perpetrated against ethnic Serbs in 1991.

2 April 2003: The Sabor approved amendments to electoral legislation, which included an increase to eight in the number of legislative seats allocated to members of ethnic minorities.

History

MARCUS TANNER

The Croats began migrating into the Balkan Peninsula from the fifth century, following the collapse of the Roman Empire, from a region that is now Belarus and Ukraine. The word Croat (Hrvat) points to an Iranian (Persian) or Ostrogothic origin, but the Croats were a Slavic tribe by the time they settled in the old Roman province of Dalmatia and in the Pannonian hinterland. By about 800 they had organized themselves into several dukedoms and accepted Christianity. Unlike their Serb neighbours, the Croats looked to Rome rather than Constantinople (Byzantium) for their faith, a decision of immense significance for their future cultural and political development. The various Croat entities were united into one unit under Tomislav, who ruled a large area covering most of modern Croatia and Bosnia and Herzegovina in about 910–29, and was crowned Croatia's first king, according to legend, in 925.

The Croatian kingdom was unable to maintain its independence. After King Dimitar Zvonimir died without an heir in 1089, neighbouring Hungary invaded and the country remained a separate, junior kingdom within Hungary until 1525. After the last Hungarian king was killed in battle against the Ottoman Turks at Mohacs in 1526 the Hungarian-Croatian crown passed to the Habsburgs. Union with Austria did not halt the advance of the Ottomans, who by the end of the 16th century had seized most of Croatia, except for a small area around the city of Zagreb. This remnant of Croatia preserved its separate status within the Habsburg Empire. However, the Habsburgs placed Croatian territory along the Ottoman border under military jurisdiction. This Croatian 'Military Frontier' (Vojna Krajina) was governed without reference to the Croatian parliament, the Sabor. The Habsburgs encouraged immigration into the Krajina of Vlahs, Serbs and other Orthodox refugees from the Ottoman Empire, permanently altering Croatia's ethnic and religious composition.

The Austrian campaigns of the 1680s and 1690s liberated Croatia from Turkish rule. However, most of the new land was assigned to the Vojna Krajina, a decision that created tension between the Croat noble class and the Habsburgs. In the late 18th century Hungarian nationalists began to demand greater control over Croatia. This pressure stimulated the rise of a Slav national consciousness among the Croats. The Croat national revival gained momentum in the aftermath of Hungary's revolt in 1848, when the Croats fought against Hungary on the side of the Habsburgs. The national movement in Croatia was confused. Some sought a common Slav front with the Serbs against the Hungarians, and called themselves Illyrians ('Yugoslav' or Southern Slav). Their leader in the mid- to late 19th century was the bishop of Djakovo, Juraj Strossmayer. Opposition to the Illyrians was led by Ante Starcević and his Party of Rights. Starcević and his followers took a stand on the historic rights of the Croat kingdom and looked to an independent Croatia, not a joint Croat-Serb state.

THE YUGOSLAV PERIOD

The collapse of the Habsburg Empire at the end of the First World War posed a threat to Croatia, as Italy sought the support of the Entente Powers (France, Russia, Serbia and the United Kingdom) for the annexation of Dalmatia, while Serbia sought guarantees that it would gain Bosnia and parts of Slavonia. To deflect the partition of Croat lands among several powers, a group of Croat intellectuals established a 'Yugoslav Committee' to negotiate the union of all Croat, Serb and Slovene lands in one state. The establishment in 1918 of the Kingdom of Serbs, Croats and Slovenes, which later became Yugoslavia, was marred by misunderstandings. The Croats believed they had been promised a federal state. The Serbs treated the union as an annexation and, in 1921, forced through a constitution centralizing power in Belgrade, the Serbian capital, and abolishing Croatia as a historic unit.

Yugoslav politics between the First and Second World Wars was dominated by the struggle between the dominant Serbs and the Croats over the question of Croatian autonomy. The struggle reached its height in 1928 when the Croats' popular leader, Stjepan Radić, was assassinated in the parliament building in Belgrade by a pro-government deputy. King Aleksandar I used this murder as a pretext to establish a royal dictatorship in January 1929. The imposition of the dictatorship resulted in the flight of extreme Croat nationalists and the formation in exile of a radical, militant Croat nationalist movement, the Ustaša (Rebel). Led by a former Zagreb lawyer, Ante Pavelić, the Ustaša assassinated Aleksandar in Marseilles, France, in 1934.

The new Regent, Prince Pavle, acting for the teenage King Petar II, resolved to appease Croat grievances and a *sporazum* (agreement) granting Croatia autonomy was signed shortly before the outbreak of the Second World War. However, in March 1941 the Regent was overthrown by a military *putsch*, after acceding to German demands to join a German-Italian military pact. The coup was followed by German invasion on 6 April. German military intervention led to the establishment, three days later, of a Fascist, Ustaša-run Independent

State of Croatia (Nezavisna Država Hrvatska). The new State was granted extensive territories by the Axis Powers, covering most of Croatia and Bosnia and Herzegovina. The large Serb minority staged an uprising against the newly independent Croatia. The Ustaša also confronted an insurrection by communist Partisans (National Liberation Army), led by the Croat head of the Communist Party of Yugoslavia (CPY), Tito (Josip Broz). The revolts were partly a response to the Ustaša's Nazi-inspired pogroms against Croatia's Serbs, Jews and Gypsies (Roma). These led to the virtual extermination of the Bosnian and Croatian Jewish communities, and to the deaths of thousands of Serbs. The exact death toll among the Serbs in Croatia's most notorious concentration camp, at Jasenovać, south of Zagreb, was to cause bitter controversy after the Second World War.

By 1944 Tito's communist Partisans had displaced the royalist Serbs, known as Četniks (Yugoslav Army of the Fatherland), as the main resistance force in Croatia. Tito entered Belgrade in November 1944 and in May 1945 Pavelić fled to Argentina. As a result, Croatia became one of the six constituent republics that made up post-war Yugoslavia. The new communist regime was ruthless when dealing with its political opponents. After the Četnik leader, Draza Mihajlović, was captured in eastern Bosnia in 1946, then tried and executed as a traitor, the regime turned its attention to its most influential opponent in Croatia—the Roman Catholic Church. The Archbishop of Zagreb, Alojzije Stepinać, was arrested in September 1946 on charges of collaboration with the Pavelić regime and sentenced to 16 years' imprisonment. He was released under house arrest in 1951 and died, still under house arrest, 11 years later (he was beatified by Pope John Paul II in October 1998).

Tito's break with Stalin's (Iosif V. Dzhugashvili) USSR in 1948 did not immediately ease the climate of repression in Yugoslavia. Liberalization came only after the removal from power in 1966 of Tito's Serb Vice-President and presumed successor, Aleksandar Ranković. The relaxation led to the growth of a reform movement within the Croatian communist party known as the 'Croatian Spring'. Led by Savka Dabčević-Kucar and Miko Tripalo, part of the younger generation of communists, the movement pushed for greater cultural, fiscal and political autonomy for the Yugoslav republics. The movement received strong support from the previously hostile or apolitical mass of the population in Croatia. As the Croatian Spring leaders organized larger rallies throughout Croatia, and their demands became more strident, Tito turned against them. In December 1971 Tito demanded the resignations of Dabčević-Kucar and Tripalo. Their removal was followed by a purge of nationalists in the Croatian communist party, the media and the university.

The subjugation of the Croatian Spring diminished the legitimacy of the League of Communists of Yugoslavia (LCY—as the CPY had been renamed in 1952) in the eyes of the Croats and, ultimately, helped to discredit the very notion of Yugoslavia among its former supporters. An entire generation was forced into early retirement. Others, such as Croatia's future President, Franjo Tudjman, received jail sentences for publicly complaining about the CPY's regime to foreign journalists. For the remainder of Tito's life, repression of so-called nationalists was mitigated by relative prosperity, sustained by huge Western loans, and by constitutional changes that seemed to concede to some of the Croatian Spring's demands. A new Constitution in 1974 gave more power to the six constituent republics and to Serbia's two autonomous provinces, Kosovo and Vojvodina.

THE DISINTEGRATION OF YUGOSLAVIA

Tito's death in May 1980 was followed by a smooth transition of power to a collective head of state. However, by the early 1980s Yugoslavia was experiencing a severe economic crisis in the aftermath of the international petroleum crisis of the mid-1970s. As Western loans were suspended and the country confronted rampant inflation, the republics began to disagree publicly over economic strategy. Croatia and Slovenia, the most economically advanced republics, argued for fiscal restraint, reductions in subsidies to industry and a decrease in the large military budget. The Serbs, who dominated the YPA, argued for a large military budget and centralized economic management.

Yugoslavia's economic woes precipitated an increase in ethnic tension, especially in the Serbian province of Kosovo, where the ethnic Albanian majority wanted their region upgraded to the status of a republic. By the mid-1980s the Kosovo issue dominated Serbian politics and was posing enormous strain on the federation. Serbian frustration over Kosovo led directly to the fall of the Serbian communist leader Ivan Stambolić in September 1987 and to the ascendancy of Slobodan Milošević, an uncompromising Serb nationalist. Milošević's appeal to previously submerged Serb national grievances provoked a counter-movement among Croats and Slovenes. The communist leaders of Croatia and Slovenia distanced themselves from Serbia and announced that multiparty elections would be held in both republics in early 1990. The Croatian League of Communists, led by Ivica Račan from December 1989, was confident that its resistance to Milošević and to Serb nationalism would ensure victory in the election of 22 April 1990. Instead, Račan was defeated by the Croatian Democratic Union (CDU), led by the Croatian Spring veteran, Franjo Tudjman. The reasons for Tudjman's popularity were obvious. He had been imprisoned twice after 1971 for publicly criticizing repression in Croatia and as an old partisan soldier—he had resigned with the rank of general in 1961—he had a clear authority. Tudjman also received support from the Croatian diaspora, remittances from which increased the CDU's funds.

CIVIL WAR

Following the CDU's election victory, after a second round of voting on 6–7 May 1990, Tudjman was elected President by Croatia's first multi-party parliament since the Second World War. The CDU's victory was mitigated by the success in the Krajina of a Serb nationalist party, led by a psychiatrist from Knin, Dr Jovan Rašković. The Serb Democratic Party rapidly established itself as the uncompromising voice of the Croatian Serbs, who comprised about 12% of the Croatian population, and countered President Tudjman's demand for greater Croatian independence with a demand for autonomy in Croatia for majority-Serb districts. The Serb Democratic Party also cultivated close links with Milošević.

Despite threats from the Serb Democratic Party, a proposed new constitution in June 1990 demoted the Serbs from one of two 'constituent nations' in Croatia to a minority. The Krajina Serbs retaliated on 17 August, by seizing control of the northern Dalmatian town of Knin. President Tudjman attempted to restore control by sending police helicopters, which the Yugoslav air force threatened to shoot down. The Serb Democratic Party proclaimed a 'Serb Autonomous Region (SAR) of Krajina' on 1 October. Within weeks the Croatian Serbs had seized control of the northern Dalmatian municipalities of Obrovac, Benkovac, Donji Lapac, and Korenica. The Serb Democratic Party was well equipped and it was generally accepted that the YPA was supplying arms to the Croatian Serbs. By October 1991 the Serbs had established two more SARs, in Eastern Slavonia and Western Slavonia.

The Serb campaigns in Croatia, which soon moved well outside the boundaries of the territory's 12 Serb-majority municipalities, prompted Croatia and Slovenia to secede from

Yugoslavia, and on 19 May 1991 Croatia held a referendum in which an overwhelming majority voted in favour of independence. On 25 June the legislatures of both Slovenia and Croatia declared their countries' independence.

Slovenia's independence provoked a 10-day war with the YPA in which the Slovenes soon gained the advantage. Crucially, Serbia endorsed Slovenian independence in order to concentrate on Croatia. At an international conference on the Croatian island of Brioni on 7 July 1991, diplomats from the European Community (EC, known as the European Union—EU from November 1993) brokered an agreement on the withdrawal of the YPA in Slovenia. Fighting in the Krajina then escalated, with the YPA offering increasingly open support to the Croatian Serbs.

The six months between the Brioni summit and the UN-negotiated cease-fire in early January 1992 were marked by intense fighting between the Croatians and the joint forces of the Krajina and the YPA. The Serb forces gained control of almost one-third of Croatian territory. Both sides invested particular importance in seizing the eastern town of Vukovar, in Eastern Slavonia, which, for Croatia, became a symbol of the country's independence struggle. Vukovar finally fell to Serb forces on 18 November 1991. By December, when the Serb offensive appeared to be losing momentum, both sides accepted an offer of mediation by the UN envoy, Cyrus Vance, a former US Secretary of State, which led to the cease-fire agreement of 2 January 1992.

The cease-fire coincided with Croatia's success in gaining international recognition. Despite British and French opposition, Germany insisted on recognizing the two secessionist Yugoslav republics. In order to avoid a public rift between member states, the EC announced unanimous recognition of Croatia and Slovenia on 15 January 1992. The cease-fire agreement signed that month was a compromise. It involved the withdrawal of the YPA from Croatia, including the 'Republic of Serb Krajina' (RSK). The agreement also allowed for the installation of a 15,000-strong UN Protection Force (UNPROFOR) in the RSK and its environs. The RSK was designated a UN Protected Area (UNPA). The cease-fire agreement did not address the question of sovereignty over the RSK, nor the matter of the return of hundreds of thousands of Croat and Serb refugees. Nor were the RSK's forces disarmed. As a result, Croatian opinion shifted rapidly against UNPROFOR in 1992.

Croatia's growing military strength, as well as the lack of progress in peace negotiations, led Tudjman (who had been re-elected President in August 1992, in direct elections) to launch an offensive against the RSK on 22 January 1993. The Croatian army captured Zemunik airport and the vital Maslenica road bridge, which linked southern Dalmatia with the rest of the country. The UN Security Council condemned the action, but Croatia escaped the imposition of sanctions.

Croatia was criticized more for its involvement in the internal ethnic conflict in neighbouring Bosnia and Herzegovina. The republic seceded from Yugoslavia in March 1992, and was immediately overwhelmed by a tripartite struggle between the republic's Serb, Croat and Muslim communities. While the YPA aided a Bosnian Serb campaign to overrun 60% of the republic's territory, President Tudjman encouraged Bosnian Croats to declare their own mini-state, the 'Croat Union of Herzeg-Bosna', in July 1992. However, confronted with a growing threat of international sanctions at the end of 1993 and an ultimatum to withdraw regular forces from Bosnia in February 1994, the President retreated. In late February Croatia endorsed a union of Croat- and Muslim-held territory in a Federation, in exchange for greater US support for the recovery of Serb-held territory in Croatia. This strategy proved more effective. At the end of April 1995 the re-equipped and strengthened Croatian army attacked the

weakest point in the RSK, an exposed Serb-held triangle of land in central Slavonia. 'Operation Flash' (Bljesak) was a complete success. The enclave, although a UNPA, fell in a matter of hours.

In July 1995, under the leadership of Radovan Karadžić and his military commander, Gen. Ratko Mladić, Bosnian Serbs commenced an offensive against Žepa, Srebreniča and Goražde, three UN-protected Bosniak enclaves in Serb-held eastern Bosnia. After the capture of Srebreniča on 11 July, when an estimated 8,000 of Srebreniča's male population were killed, and of Žepa later in the month, Mladić turned his attention to the much larger enclave of Bihać, in north-western Bosnia. The threat to this strategic city prompted the Bosnian Government of Alija Izetbegović to appeal publicly to Croatia for military assistance, an appeal endorsed by the USA. Almost immediately, a Bosnian Croat offensive, supported by the Croatian army, attacked the overstretched Bosnian Serb forces in north-western Bosnia.

President Tudjman ordered an attack on the RSK on 4 August 1995. 'Operation Storm' (Oluja) was a rapid success. The RSK army, although large in number (40,000 men), was demoralized by the confidence of the Croats and feared correctly that Milošević had lost interest in their fate. On 5 August the Croatian army entered the Krajina capital of Knin, having suffered few casualties. Three days later Operation Storm was complete and Croatia was in control of the whole of the RSK, with the exception of Eastern Slavonia (or Slavonia, Baranja and Western Srem), the strip of land along the Danube. About 180,000 Serbs, almost the entire civilian population, fled east into Serb-held Bosnia and towards Serbia.

The defeat of Serb forces in the RSK and in western Bosnia and Herzegovina was followed, on 28 August 1995, by a suspected Serb mortar attack on a Sarajevo market-place, which killed 41 civilians. The bombing provoked a series of air and artillery strikes by the North Atlantic Treaty Organization (NATO), known as 'Operation Deliberate Force', against Serb military targets. Bosniak and Bosnian Croat forces captured much Serb-held territory in western Bosnia throughout September and October. These reversals opened the way for talks between representatives of Bosnia and Herzegovina, Croatia and the 'rump' Yugoslavia (the Federal Republic of Yugoslavia—FRY, comprising Montenegro and Serbia) at the Wright-Patterson Air Force Base near Dayton, Ohio, the USA, in November 1995, which led to the end of the war in Bosnia and Herzegovina. The General Framework Agreement for Peace in Bosnia and Herzegovina also resulted in the total normalization of relations between Croatia and Yugoslavia. The part of the peace accords applying to Croatia, the Basic Agreement on the Region of Eastern Slavonia, Baranja and Western Srem, was signed at Erdut in mid-November. The Basic Agreement was to restore to Croatia the last remnant of the RSK (Eastern Slavonia). There was to be a gradual transfer of power, under the supervision of the UN Transitional Administration for Eastern Slavonia (UNTAES). UNTAES was formally established on 15 January 1996 and completed the transfer of power in the region to the Croatian authorities exactly two years later.

DOMESTIC POLITICS UNDER FRANJO TUDJMAN

The war strengthened an authoritarian tendency in President Tudjman's Government. Under the Constitution, the President enjoyed enormous power, appointing the Prime Minister and commanding the armed forces. As the conflict with the Serbs intensified, opposition to President Tudjman was increasingly identified in the government media as virtual treason. The opposition alleged that the privatization of state enterprises was increasingly being used to enrich the President's family and his political supporters. In local elections in

March 1996 disenchantment with the CDU was reflected in the defeat of the ruling party in Zagreb. Significantly, President Tudjman used his presidential powers to prevent the confirmation of an opposition mayor in the capital, dissolved the City Assembly and appointed a Government Commissioner instead.

Despite these arbitrary actions, Tudjman faced no real opposition in the presidential elections of mid-June 1997. The failure of the opposition parties to unite enabled President Tudjman to be re-elected with 61% of the votes cast. The election was judged free but not fair by international monitors, given the Government's overwhelming control of the media and its strong support among the Bosnian Croats, who, although citizens of a neighbouring state, were permitted to vote.

The strength of President Tudjman's hold on power was confirmed by the results of elections to Croatia's upper house (the Chamber of Counties) earlier in 1997, in which the CDU increased its representation from 37 to 42 of the 63 elective seats. President Tudjman's success was attributed once more to his party's strict control of the national media. Overt pressure was brought to bear on dissenting newspapers, such as the Split-based *Feral Tribune*. Some journalists were prosecuted under wide-ranging laws forbidding 'defamation' of the President. Another factor was the continued weakness of the main opposition parties.

President Tudjman's authoritarian politics confounded Croatia's attempts to join international institutions and under his rule Croatia was barred from applying for EU membership. Croatia's integration into the international community was also impeded by the unresolved conflict over the rights of Croatian Serb refugees. About 180,000 ethnic Serbs fled Croatia in 1995, and the EU and other international bodies felt strongly that they should be allowed to return freely. By 1998 only a few thousand had returned. A second, serious source of discord was provided by the Croatian Government's refusal to hand over all the Croats named as suspects by the International Criminal Tribunal for the former Yugoslavia (ICTY), based in The Hague, Netherlands. President Tudjman consented to the handover of Bosnian Croat suspects but, in October 1999, he declared that he would not allow regular Croatian army leaders accused of complicity in attacks on Serb civilians in the 1995 Operation Storm to be extradited to the Netherlands.

CROATIA AFTER TUDJMAN

Following a long illness, which was concealed from the public, President Tudjman died on 11 December 1999. Only one foreign Head of State, Süleyman Demirel of Turkey, attended his funeral, an indication of the international community's disapproval of his government. Although 100,000 Croats demonstrated their respects to the late President, the public rejected his political legacy in the parliamentary elections that followed on 3 January 2000. For the first time following independence in 1992, the CDU lost its parliamentary majority, winning only 45 seats and 31% of the ballot, compared with a coalition led by the Social Democratic Party (SDP—formerly the League of Communists) and the Croatian Social-Liberal Party (CSLP), which won a total of 68 seats (47% of the votes cast) in the 151-seat Chamber of Representatives. The Croatian Peasants' Party secured 16 seats and the remaining seats were won by smaller parties. The opposition's electoral victory resulted in the appointment as Prime Minister, on 27 January, of Ivica Račan, the head of the SDP and last communist leader of Croatia. The new premier declared that his priority would be to rebuild the economy, which had suffered as a consequence of war damage, international isolation, corruption, the economic collapse of neighbouring Yugoslavia and the decline of the once vital tourist industry.

Račan announced his intention to reduce the state budget and offer economic incentives to investors. He also pledged to revoke the previous Government's legislation restricting media freedom.

The opposition victory in the legislative elections was repeated in the results of the presidential elections, the first round of which was held on 24 January 2000. The CDU's candidate, Mate Granić, the former Deputy Prime Minister and Minister of Foreign Affairs, was defeated by Stipe Mesić, the last President of the former Yugoslavia and independent Croatia's first Prime Minister, who was the candidate of the Croatian Peasants' Party, the Liberal Party, the Croatian People's Party and the Istrian Democratic Assembly. In the first round of voting, Mesić obtained 41% of the votes, compared with the 28% won by the SDP and CSLP candidate, Dražen Budiša. Granić came third, with almost 23% of the ballot. As none of the candidates obtained more than 50% of the votes, a second round was held on 7 February. Mesić won this ballot convincingly, securing 56% of the votes. He was sworn into office on 18 February.

The new President, who had resigned from the CDU in 1994 in protest at Tudjman's authoritarianism, declared his intention to bring Croatia closer to Europe, co-operate more closely with the ICTY, cease all interference in Bosnia and Herzegovina and reduce the powers of the presidency. The EU demonstrated its approval of the election of Mesić by announcing that initial negotiations on Croatian membership of the 15-nation body were to commence.

THE RAČAN GOVERNMENT

The first two years of the tenure of the new, centre-left Government, headed by Račan, produced varied results. The Government's willingness to co-operate with international agencies on refugee returns and suspected war criminals greatly improved the prospects for integration into Western European financial and political institutions, and in October 2001 Croatia signed a Stabilization and Association Agreement with the EU, with the aim of promoting economic and trade relations, and ultimately gaining membership of the organization.

In defiance of nationalist opinion, the Government ceased to support separatist agitation among ethnic Croats in neighbouring Bosnia and Herzegovina. The Government ended obvious interference in the media, particularly regarding the news content of the state television. The process of refugee returns was also conducted more satisfactorily. While most exiled Croatian Serbs remained in the FRY, internationally supervised returns of several thousand Serbs proceeded, encountering little protest. The country's last remaining frontier dispute with the FRY Government, over the Prevlaka peninsula, near Dubrovnik, was resolved peacefully in April 2002.

While these measures gained approval from the international community, they failed to increase the domestic popularity of the Government. The initial enthusiasm that followed the fall of the CDU was replaced by increasing resentment at the administration's failure to address the stagnant economy. Neither Račan nor Mesić had economic experience, and Račan appeared more concerned with preserving the unstable coalition than in arresting the economic decline that had commenced in 1997. The Government resisted IMF pressure to close loss-making enterprises, owing to concern that such measures might threaten up to one-half of the country's businesses, prompting mass unemployment and social unrest, which would be exploited by the nationalist right-wing element.

Tudjman's CDU was left in disorder by his death and the exposure of the former Government's extensive corruption. It was prevented from attacking the Government effectively by an ongoing power struggle between the party leader, Ivo Sanader, and Tudjman's former close associate, Ivic Pasalić, who represented the extreme-right element. Despite Sanader's re-election to the party leadership in April 2002, this division within the CDU appeared likely to continue.

Weakened by its internal conflict, the CDU failed to rally public opinion, even over the Government's unpopular decision to allow ICTY officials to investigate suspected war crimes committed against Serbs inside Croatia during the 1991–95 war (in particular, in the July 1995 Operation Storm). A series of large demonstrations followed the 45-year sentence of imprisonment imposed on the Bosnian Croat Commander, Tihomir Blaskić, in March 2000, for his involvement in the massacre of Muslims in central Bosnia and Herzegovina in 1993. The indictments of three Croatian generals, Mirko Norac, Ante Gotovina and Rahim Ademi, provided a further major source of discontent for nationalists, who staged mass protests at the Government's perceived disowning of the 'Homeland War' against the Serbs. The decision of the Government in July 2001 to extradite Ademi and Gotovina to the ICTY resulted in prolonged instability within the ruling coalition. Ademi surrendered to the Tribunal later that month, while Gotovina remained in hiding.

In early February 2002 Budiša (who had expressed open antagonism to Račan) was re-elected to the presidency of the CSLP and in early July he withdrew the CSLP from the governing coalition. Račan subsequently submitted his resignation, following the collapse of his administration. Nevertheless, he was returned to the office of Prime Minister, after his nomination by Mesić was supported by 84 deputies in the Sabor. He formed a new Government (without the participation of the CSLP) in late July, thereby allowing the continued implementation of reforms. By mid-2003, however, it was reported that the electorate was becoming increasingly disillusioned with Račan's centre-left Government.

EUROPEAN INTEGRATION

In 2002 government stability was adversely affected by a further extradition order, served in September against Gen. Janko Bobetko, the 83-year-old former army Chief of Staff and popular war veteran, over alleged crimes committed against ethnic Serbs near Gospic in 1993. As the oldest and most senior Croat to be indicted, the issue of Bobetko's extradition was particularly sensitive and Bobetko's refusal to surrender voluntarily to the ICTY presented the Government with a dilemma, which it resolved by insisting that Bobetko was unfit to travel to The Hague, on grounds of ill health. In April 2003 the ICTY suspended the extradition order, after physicians confirmed Bobetko's ill health, and he died later that month. Nevertheless, despite the fierce controversy provoked by the case, the nationalist right-wing element presented less of a threat to the Government than before, and having served one-half of its mandate, Račan's administration showed no sign of losing the reform initiative. It benefited considerably from a significant economic recovery, based on the vigorous revival of the crucial tourist sector.

Despite the Government's progress in implementing democratic reforms, ICTY cases still had the power to polarize public opinion to a dangerous extent, and the authorities' ambivalent stance towards co-operation with the Tribunal continued to attract criticism from the EU. The related issue of the Serb minority also remained highly contentious; the first post-war census merely attracted more attention to the issue by revealing that the Serb proportion of the population had declined from 12% in 1991 to 5% in 2001, thereby inadvertently confirming Serb claims that they were victims of 'ethnic cleansing'. Nevertheless, the policy of *rapprochement* with Croatia's neighbours and with the EU continued to gather momentum and the first (highly symbolic) summit of former Yugoslav Heads of State was convened in Sarajevo in July 2002. In February 2003, meanwhile, Croatia formally presented its request for admission to the EU at a summit meeting in Athens, Greece. The EU commended the Government's ambitious efforts to promote legal and economic harmonization with EU standards under the Stabilization and Association Agreement, although diplomats predicted that the organization would await the outcome of the next Croatian elections before officially signalling consent to the country's accession, in case the nationalist right-wing parties were returned to power. However, at a summit meeting of EU Heads of State, held in Thessaloníki, Greece, in June, officials indicated that it would be very likely that Croatia, together with Bulgaria and Romania, would be invited to join the EU in 2007, as envisaged by the Croatian Government.

The Economy

Dr MLADEN STANIČIĆ

INTRODUCTION

The Croatian economy, while still part of the Yugoslav economy, was partially affected by international development. Structural changes and business standards prevailing on the world market were to some extent operative on the domestic market. The parallel development of a Soviet-type economy of accelerated industrialization, on the one hand, and the partial acceptance of international business standards, on the other, resulted in an economy that was better prepared for market transformation and adaptation to the structural changes in the world economy than the economies of other post-communist states. Croatia has production capacity, trained personnel and experience in dealing with international business partners, as well as well-developed economic relations with all segments of the world market. In addition, its geographical position as a transport route is a great asset. It has acquired experience in development, in the export of services and in agriculture, and has a deep-rooted Central European entrepreneurial spirit. This fact made it easier for Croatia to withstand the disintegration of the state (the former Yugoslavia), of which it was one of the federal units, and to bear the associated economic burden. Although it was more developed than the other federal units (with the exception of Slovenia) and, therefore, naturally strove to achieve greater economic independence, it had a market in the less-developed Yugoslav republics and had become accustomed to standards that were lower than those required on the markets of developed countries. After the collapse of communism and the disintegration of the former Yugoslavia, Croatia lost the Yugoslav market, as well as the markets of

Eastern Europe, which are still undergoing a difficult transition, as well as, to a certain extent, the markets of the developing countries in which Croatian companies used to be present, as part of the broader economic policy of the Yugoslav state.

ECONOMIC PERFORMANCE

In 1993 the Croatian Government launched a heterodox macroeconomic stabilization programme, which stabilized the exchange rate and brought down inflation. This macroeconomic environment helped to attract large capital inflows and contributed to strong economic growth between 1994 and 1997. However, as economic activity slowed in 1998 and became negative in 1999, it became clear that growth during this period was not based on a firm foundation, owing to at least two reasons. Firstly, reform of public finances, including addressing the structural problems of the banking and enterprise sectors, had been inadequate. Secondly, and possibly most importantly, growth was based largely on reconstruction efforts and domestic consumption, rather than on investment that would have enhanced the country's competitiveness. Croatia's recent, and still structurally unsatisfactory, growth and weak export performance signals the need for deeper reform.

However, owing to an improved external environment and increased tourism activity, together with rising domestic consumption, based on growing liquidity in the banking industry, gross domestic product (GDP) resumed growth in 2000, increasing by 3.7% in 2000, by 4.5% in 2001 and by as much as 5.2% in 2002 (one of the highest levels of growth recorded among the transition countries). Expanding domestic demand was the major driving force, especially in 2002, with investment and private consumption increasing by 9.4% and 6.0%, respectively. Growth in industrial production was 5.5% in 2002, while retail sales increased by 13.5% and construction increased by 12.5% during the first 11 months of the year. A very high rate of growth was also recorded in the financial sector, with intensive credit activity throughout 2002. The annual increase in loans to individuals exceeded 30%, while the growth of credits to companies exceeded 20%. However, with the exception of industry, other sectors do not directly affect export growth, and are therefore regarded as factors of development only to a limited extent. At the end of 2002 the trade deficit was higher than the overall level of Croatian exports: the total value of commodity exports amounted to US $4,995m., while the visible trade deficit rose to $5,279m.

The rate of inflation was 2.2% at the end of 2002, with commodity prices increasing by 0.6%, and the cost of services increasing by 7.9%. However, a further positive tendency was a decline in services costs towards the end of the year, additional evidence that competition had a positive effect on prices. The Croatian inflation rate is about the same as the European average. Wages rose by 2.9%, in real terms, during the first 11 months of 2002, with the average monthly wage amounting to about $500. Compared with the results of economic activity overall, the increase in wages, in real terms, was considerably lower, but was, however, accompanied by a dramatic expansion in credit. Unemployment began to decline in the second half of 2002, and the rate of unemployment was 21.5% by the end of the year. In 2002 the average number of unemployed totalled 389,741, a 2.5% increase compared with the previous year. A slight increase in the number of unemployed was recorded in January 2003, compared with December 2002, but this figure actually represented an exceptionally sharp decline of 10.7%, year-on-year. In January 2002 the total number of unemployed was 411,115, while in January 2003 official statistics indicated that 367,118 people were seeking employment in Croatia. Another indication of positive trends in employment was the fact that in January 2003 the number of newly registered unemployed was considerably lower than the number of people who found employment. Employment Bureau records demonstrated that in that month 37.4% fewer new people had registered as unemployed, than had registered in the same period in the previous year.

FOREIGN TRADE

In 2002 foreign trade in Croatia generated one of its largest trade deficits, of US $5,279.3m. Total exports were valued at $4,994.6m., while the value of imports amounted to $10,273.9m.; imports increased by 16.0% in that year, and import trade increased, year-on-year, by more than 20% in December. Structural changes in the Croatian economy consequently demanded increased exports. Indeed, exports of goods increased by 5.0% in 2002. However, since goods exports accounted for less than 50% of the structure of total exports, its growth could not have a strong effect on overall export developments. If international trade is observed in terms of 69 standard groups of products, Croatia exports more than it imports in the following 10 areas, thereby achieving a trade surplus: fish and fish products, sugar, tobacco, raw materials, cork and wood, cellulose and paper waste, metal ore and metal waste, fertilizers, clothes and footwear, and communications and ship-building. In contrast, the largest single contributor to the trade deficit was imports of motor cars, accounting for $1,500m., or 12.2% more than in 2001 (a record year for car imports). Imports of motor cars account for around one-10th of total imports. Evidently, the extraordinary growth in credit has stimulated a huge increase in domestic consumption, which is directly linked to the increasing number of imported cars.

Traditionally, Croatia's exports to the countries of the European Union (EU) were the most significant, accounting for about 53% of total export trade. However, exports to EU countries declined by 3.6% in 2002, primarily owing to a decline of 15% in exports to Germany, which has traditionally been one of Croatia's three most significant trading partners. In the same year exports to Italy declined by more than 5%. However, a 28% increase in exports to Austria helped to stabilize export figures relating to EU countries, as did dramatically increased exports to Greece, of about 166%. Outside the EU, Central European Free Trade Association (CEFTA) countries purchased a significant proportion of exports, accounting for over 12%, and a further 22% went to other European developing countries. While exports to the EU declined, exports to the CEFTA countries were maintained at an even level; exports to the countries of the former USSR and the former Yugoslavia increased by 6%. Owing to an extraordinary increase in exports to Bosnia and Herzegovina, of more than 17%, that country became Croatia's second largest trading partner and, at the same time, the country with which Croatia maintained the largest trade surplus, of more than US $400m. The country's fourth largest trading partner was Slovenia, with a trade surplus of more than $500m., while the total decline in exports to that country was 6%. Among other countries, an increase in export trade with Yugoslavia (now Serbia and Montenegro) of 8% was significant, as was as a 36% increase in exports to Hungary. The largest trade deficit was recorded in trade with Germany (amounting to about $1,500m.), followed by Italy (about $900m.) and Russia (about $800m.). Increased exports were closely related to developments in the process of restructuring Croatian industry.

FOREIGN DEBT

By the end of December 2002 Croatia's foreign debt reached US $15,200m., mounting by 36% in that year alone. Moreover, in the first months of 2003 foreign debt exceeded an estimated $16,000m., which forced the central bank to impose restrictions on credit facilities. Statistics indicated that foreign debt accounted for about 60% of GDP, and analysts advised caution with regard to the rate and size of further debts. This unfavourable picture was somewhat mitigated by the fact that part of the debt accumulated in 2002 could be attributed to exchange-rate differentials. Foreign debt is expressed in terms of the US dollar, which had weakened considerably in relation to the common European currency, the euro, and about 70% of Croatia's external debt is denominated in euros. In other words, any decline in the value of the dollar augments the nominal sum of the foreign debt, since more dollars have to be set aside for every euro. As for the structure of foreign debt, the state continues to represent the largest debtor, accounting for about 42%, overall. As to what extent foreign debt of this size represents a threat to the macroeconomic stability and international liquidity of Croatia, many analysts consider the situation to be alarming, and such growth in foreign debt to be highly undesirable in the long term. Some observers believe that the foreign-debt trend should follow the rate of GDP growth. Although there is no strict set point at which external debt becomes a threat to a country's economy, it is generally accepted that the size and character of the foreign debt should be measured against three major indicators: the share of foreign debt in GDP, the share of foreign debt in total exports of goods and services, and the share of repayments of capital and interest in total exports of goods and services. The experiences of countries that have encountered problems in repaying external debt have indicated that the critical point is reached when the share of foreign debt amounts to about 200% of the total value of exports of goods and services. In 2002 foreign debt was equivalent to about 60% of GDP, that is, somewhat more than 130% of the value of exports of goods and services, considerably more than in previous years. In countries that have had difficulties in repaying debt the share of foreign debt has amounted to more than 230% of the value of exports, while the transition countries of Central and South-Eastern Europe have accrued external debt amounting to roughly the same value as their total exports. Evidently, with regard to the foreign debt to exports ratio, Croatia was in the second group, with neighbouring transition countries. A short-term indicator of the viability of external debt is measured by comparing the cost of making repayments of capital and interest with the total value of exports of goods and services; the critical point is reached when the former is equivalent to 25% of the total, a situation that was almost recorded in 2002, and which again placed Croatia towards the bottom of the list of transition countries. Indebtedness requires careful monitoring, accompanied by the careful analytical examination of each debt incurred by an economy. At a time of very low interest rates and the appreciation of the US dollar, each new debt should be subjected to close scrutiny. Croatia should be particularly careful when it comes to financing transport infrastructure, because the rate of debt must be harmonized with the period of repayment. At 2003 repayments were not a great problem. Croatia's international liquidity was safe, and the foreign-currency reserves of the central bank were at record levels. However, analysts warned that the time had come to insist that Croatia strive for lower deficits and higher shares of 'in-house' funds to finance public needs, with no major foreign debt.

FINANCIAL-SECTOR REFORM

Consolidation of the banking system was continuing, and the confidence of banks and depositors appeared to be returning. The financial performance of banks, as well as the quality of loan portfolios, was improving. The lending activities of banks to enterprises and households were also growing. Following privatization, foreign-owned banks accounted for more than 80% of Croatia's total banking assets. New legislation affecting the central bank, which provided for greater independence, was adopted in April 2001, mandating the National Bank of Croatia to place strong emphasis on price stability. From October of that year commercial banks had the right to handle payment orders directly, a function that was previously reserved for the State Bureau of Payment Transactions.

The environment in Croatia remains difficult for domestic and foreign investment. While the legal framework is largely in place, its proper enforcement is problematic, because of the weaknesses of the judiciary. This applies in particular to bankruptcy law and proceedings. Inaccurate and incomplete cadastral and land registry records create uncertainty with regard to property rights. In addition to these legal issues, investors also encounter significant and numerous bureaucratic hurdles. As a result, the overall situation is discouraging for foreign investors and inhibits growth by domestic investors.

The range of available financial products is slowly being modernized. However, long-term finance remains scarce, reflecting the problem of providing collateral for financing purposes. The financial sector, in general, remains under-developed, essentially restricted to banking products, and with only a limited number of listed companies. However, measures have been taken to unite the Croatian and Slovenian capital markets, and the introduction of a 'three-pillar' pension system is expected to lead to an evolution of capital markets.

The tax base of Croatia's budget has been expanded over the years. Since its introduction in 1998, value-added tax has been the single most important source of revenue, accounting for more than 50% of the total. However, the overall tax burden borne by the private sector is one of the highest in the region, and is likely to have driven a substantial proportion of illicit economic activity into that sphere and to have reduced profitability in the formal sector. With revenue-raising capacities limited, much of the adjustment will have to be made on the expenditure side, including improvements to the effectiveness of budgetary management.

In general, progress with structural reforms has been slow in recent years, reflecting the fragile government coalition and public opposition to a number of unpopular measures. Progress has been achieved in rationalizing social transfers and implementing the second pillar of the pension system, initiating fiscal decentralization, and introducing a single treasury. However, reforms have taken place more slowly than in other areas, such as privatization, education and health. By mid-2003 labour-market reform, aimed at increased flexibility, had not yet been adopted. In addition, the enforcement of existing legislation often remains a challenge, owing either to delays in the adoption of the necessary implementing regulations or to weak administrative capacity. More generally, Croatia needs to pay special attention to strengthening its public administration, with a view to ensuring that the relevant ministries and other public authorities are in a position to implement fully the numerous legislative reforms to which Croatia has committed itself.

PROSPECTS FOR EU ACCESSION

In February 2003 Croatia submitted an application for full EU membership, on the basis of Article 49 of the 1992 Treaty on European Union (commonly known as the Maastricht Treaty, after the town in the Netherlands where it was signed). The Council of the EU formally accepted the application, which enabled the usual formal accession procedure to commence. The Croatian application was also based on its membership of the Stabilization and Association Process, which was initiated by the EU for those countries not covered by Europe Agreements (Albania, Bosnia and Herzegovina, Croatia, the former Yugoslav republic of Macedonia—FYRM, and Yugoslavia/Serbia and Montenegro). The Process is realized through Stabilization and Association Agreements (SAAs), which have important implications for international trade and investment. A proper understanding of the provisions of the agreement and their impact on the economy was very important, in order to introduce measures that would help maximize the benefits and accept the costs of closer integration into the EU. Following accession to the World Trade Organization (WTO) in November 2000, the Croatian Government negotiated an SAA with the EU, signing it in October 2001. The SAA strengthened the position of Croatia as a potential candidate for EU membership through an 'evolutive clause' contained in the political preamble (provided that the SAA was successfully implemented) and, moreover, created a framework likely to benefit overall economic growth. Therefore, the SAA should be regarded as a means for Croatia to be integrated into the emerging pan-European free-trade area, resulting in a significant removal of trade barriers between all the countries that are gaining associate membership status. It should be regarded as a process of transformation from small, closed, national economies to countries integrated across a wide area, permitting the free movement of goods, services and investment.

Pending the entry into force of the SAA, an Interim Agreement covering trade and trade-related matters applied provisionally from 1 January 2002, and entered into force on 1 March. Trade in textiles products was also governed by a separate agreement, which applied from 1 January 2001. In order to complete the contractual trade regime, a wine protocol to the Interim Agreement and to the SAA was signed in December, and came into force on 1 January 2002. This protocol established reciprocal concessions for wine exports and defined the rules for the protection of denominations of wines and spirits.

According to a March 2003 report of the European Commission, Croatia has the capacity to implement the obligations included in the framework of the SAA and Interim Agreement. The implementation of the first tranche of trade concessions, from 1 January 2002, had not caused problems. The Government is actively working on the development of legislative harmonization strategies and has begun gradual implementation in the field of trade-related legislation. A long-term commitment to this demanding process is required.

Croatia has begun to establish the necessary inter-ministerial co-ordination mechanisms. The capacity of the Ministry for European Integration, the co-ordinator of the SAA and Interim Agreement implementation process, has been substantially reinforced. Efforts need to be made to create and strengthen administrative capacity in all the government bodies that will be involved in the process of harmonization with European legislation and practices, beginning with areas where contractual obligations already exist. In order to be better prepared for the next round of negotiations, Croatia established an inter-ministerial co-ordination team.

This process should have a significant impact on the Croatian economy, since many of Croatia's major trading partners are EU member states (for example, Italy, Germany and Austria). Croatia's exports to the EU remain the highest in the region, which makes Croatia by far the most significant beneficiary of EU trade liberalization. However, as already mentioned, the trade balance remained heavily negative, owing to the substantial reduction in Croatia's overall export level following its loss of international competitiveness, essentially as a result of higher wage growth than productivity growth, delayed enterprise restructuring, and 'insider' privatization. The trend appeared to be improving slowly, however. Moreover, in a European Commission report on the feasibility of the SAA negotiations it was emphasized that, apart from political improvements, measures taken in the economy were encouraging, and the problems the Croatian economy has to address could be solved through a comprehensive programme of economic reform, adopted by the Croatian Government.

Industrial products represent the greater part of Croatian trade. The main exports are textiles, chemicals and shipbuilding, while the main imports include machinery and electrical equipment. Agricultural products remain uncompetitive on European markets, with a trade balance largely positive for the EU. The sector represented about 10% of Croatia's total import trade (of which 42% came from EU member states), and 14% of total exports (of which 10% was directed to EU markets). Since this sector was previously subject to high protection, it is claimed to be the most sensitive to trade liberalization. The country's absence from the process of European integration was among the most important reasons for the stagnation of Croatian exports. Although analysis of the possible effects of liberalization is hindered by many overlapping developments, a very simplified analysis has shown that the static short-term impact (increase of trade) resulting from the SAA may range between 2.2% and 3.7% for exports and between 5.7% and 9.4% for imports. Within six years the effect may be significantly more dramatic, with external trade potentially increasing by between 30% and 90%, and averaging about 55.5%.

From the point of view of the economy as a whole, the net effect of trade liberalization should be positive. However, some sectors may experience especially high rates of import growth and could experience severe problems when encountering stringent competition. Generally, sectors that may be severely affected are those that are highly protected, and/or not engaged in foreign trade, as well as those that cannot be competitive based on relative factor endowments. The protected sectors (textiles, footwear, beverages, tobacco, petroleum, metal products, construction materials and wood products) may experience increased imports, owing to the elimination of the existing rather high tariffs. Some sectors are also likely to register significant export growth. If Croatia follows the experience of the most successful accession countries, the leading sectors may be those that require technology and skilled personnel, such as vehicles, electrical machinery and equipment, and mineral and metal products, while labour-intensive activities may lose their share. Although it is impossible to predict accurately, following the experience of the most successful accession countries, which have all recorded a significant increase in the contribution of the EU to total exports, it is a reasonable assumption that, as a consequence of the SAA, the contribution of EU member states to total Croatian exports of goods and services may increase to some 65%–70%.

Statistical Survey

Source (unless otherwise stated): Central Bureau of Statistics of the Republic of Croatia, 10000 Zagreb, Ilica 3; tel. (1) 4806111; fax (1) 4806148; e-mail stat.info@dzs.hr; internet www.dzs.hr.

Area and Population

AREA, POPULATION AND DENSITY

Area (sq km)	56,542*
Population (census results)	
31 March 1991	4,784,265
31 March 2001†	
Males	2,135,900
Females.	2,301,560
Total	4,437,460
Population (official estimates at mid-year)	
1999	4,554,000
2000	4,381,000
2001	4,437,000
Density (per sq km) at 31 March 2001	78.5

* 21,831 sq miles.
† Data are not directly comparable to those from the 1981 and 1991 censuses, owing to a change in the definition used to calculate total population.

POPULATION BY ETHNIC GROUP
(census of 31 March 2001)

	Number ('000)	%
Croat	3,977.2	89.6
Serb	201.6	4.5
Muslim	20.8	0.5
Italian.	19.6	0.4
Hungarian	16.6	0.4
Albanian	15.1	0.3
Slovenian	13.2	0.3
Czech	10.5	0.2
Gypsy	9.5	0.2
Montenegrin	4.9	0.1
Slovak	4.7	0.1
Macedonian	4.3	0.1
Others*	139.5	3.3
Total	**4,437.5**	**100.0**

* Including other groups, ethnically non-declared persons and unknown ethnicity.

COUNTIES
(census of 31 March 2001)

Županije (County)	Area (sq km)	Population	Density (per sq km)
Zagreb	3,078	309,696	100.6
Krapina and Zagorje . . .	1,230	142,432	115.8
Sisak and Moslavina . . .	4,448	185,387	41.7
Karlovac	3,622	141,787	39.1
Varaždin	1,260	184,769	146.6
Koprivnica and Križevci . .	1,734	124,467	71.8
Bjelovar and Bilogora . .	2,638	133,084	50.4
Primorje and Gorski Kotar .	3,590	305,505	85.1
Lika and Senj	5,350	53,677	10.0
Virovitica and Podravina . .	2,021	93,389	46.2
Požega and Slavonia . . .	1,821	85,831	47.1
Slavonski Brod and Posavina	2,027	176,765	87.2
Zadar	3,643	162,045	44.5
Osijek and Baranja . . .	4,149	330,506	79.7
Šibenik and Knin . . .	2,994	112,891	37.7
Vukovar and Srem (Sirmium)	2,448	204,768	83.6
Split and Dalmatia . . .	4,524	463,676	102.5
Istria	2,813	206,344	73.4
Dubrovnik and Neretva . .	1,782	122,870	67.0
Meimurje	730	118,426	162.2
City of Zagreb	640	779,145	1,217.4
Total	**56,542**	**4,437,460**	**78.5**

PRINCIPAL TOWNS
(population at 2001 census)

Zagreb (capital) . .	691,724	Šibenik	37,060
Split	175,140	Sisak	36,785
Rijeka	143,800	Velika Gorica. . .	33,339
Osijek	90,411	Vinkovci	33,239
Zadar	69,556	Dubrovnik . . .	30,436
Slavonski Brod. . .	58,642	Vukovar	30,126
Pula	58,594	Bjelovar	27,783
Karlovac . . .	49,082	Koprivnica . . .	24,809
Sesvete	44,914	Požega	20,943
Varaždin	41,434	Dakovo	20,912

BIRTHS, MARRIAGES AND DEATHS

	Registered live births		Registered marriages		Registered deaths	
	Number	Rate (per 1,000)	Number	Rate (per 1,000)	Number	Rate (per 1,000)
1994 . .	48,584	10.9	23,966	5.3	49,482	11.1
1995 . .	50,182	11.2	24,385	5.1	50,536	11.3
1996 . .	53,811	12.0	24,596	5.5	50,636	11.3
1997 . .	55,501	12.1	24,517	5.4	51,964	11.4
1998 . .	47,068	10.5	24,243	5.4	52,311	11.6
1999 . .	45,179	9.9	23,778	5.2	51,953	11.4
2000* . .	43,746	10.0	22,017	5.0	50,246	11.5
2001* . .	40,993	9.2	22,076	5.0	49,552	11.2

* Rates in 2000 and 2001 are calculated on the basis of the March 2001 census total of persons usually resident. Figures for earlier years were based on estimates of *de jure* population (permanent residents).

Expectation of life (WHO estimates, years at birth): 72.9 (males 68.9; females 77.1) in 2001 (Source: WHO, *World Health Report*).

EMPLOYMENT
(annual averages, '000 persons)

	2000	2001	2002
Agriculture, hunting and forestry	115.1	107.4	101.3
Fishing	3.6	3.8	4.2
Mining and quarrying	8.2	7.7	7.0
Manufacturing	288.9	287.0	285.1
Electricity, gas and water supply	27.4	27.7	27.1
Construction	88.7	90.2	98.3
Wholesale and retail trade; repair of motor vehicles, motorcycles and personal and household goods	198.3	205.8	213.9
Hotels and restaurants	75.0	76.4	77.4
Transport, storage and communications	96.5	96.8	96.2
Financial intermediation . . .	30.3	29.8	30.3
Real estate, renting and business activities	66.3	69.6	71.8
Public administration and defence; compulsory social security . .	122.4	121.3	118.2
Education	82.5	83.8	85.3
Health and social work	82.1	82.4	82.6
Other community, social and personal service activities . .	42.4	44.0	46.9
Private households with employed persons	10.0	11.4	10.6
Total employed (incl. others) . .	**1,341.0**	**1,348.3**	**1,359.0**
Registered unemployed	357.9	380.2	389.7
Total labour force	**1,698.9**	**1,728.5**	**1,748.7**

Health and Welfare

KEY INDICATORS

Total fertility rate (children per woman, 2001)	1.7
Under-5 mortality rate (per 1,000 live births, 2001) . . .	8
HIV/AIDS (% of persons aged 15–49, 2001)	<0.10
Physicians (per 1,000 head, 1998)	2.29
Hospital beds (per 1,000 head, 1994)	5.91
Health expenditure (2000): US $ per head (PPP)	638
Health expenditure (2000): % of GDP	8.6
Health expenditure (2000): public (% of total)	84.6
Human Development Index (2000): ranking	48
Human Development Index (2000): value	0.809

For sources and definitions, see explanatory note on p. vi.

Agriculture

PRINCIPAL CROPS
('000 metric tons)

	1999	2000	2001
Wheat	558.2	1,032.1	965.2
Barley	124.9	151.4	161.5
Maize	2,135.5	1,526.2	2,211.6
Rye	6.2	7.3	8.7
Oats	56.8	51.1	47.6
Potatoes	728.6	553.7	463.7
Sugar beet	1,114.0	482.2	964.9
Dry beans	22.3	9.9	16.5
Soybeans (Soya beans) . . .	115.9	65.3	91.9
Sunflower seed	72.4	54.0	43.0
Rapeseed	32.6	29.4	22.5
Cabbages	144.0	112.0	123.7
Tomatoes	70.8	69.6	73.9
Cucumbers and gherkins . . .	37.9	28.0	36.0
Dry onions	55.6	44.8	58.1
Garlic	10.3	8.1	9.9
Carrots	29.9	24.2	28.2
Apples	66.8	81.3	32.5
Pears	10.0	10.1	6.7
Peaches and nectarines . . .	10.2	9.3	9.0
Plums	38.0	39.9	39.6
Grapes	394.1	353.5	359.0
Watermelons and melons . . .	53.4	50.1	50.0
Tobacco (leaves)	10.1	9.7	10.5

Source: FAO.

LIVESTOCK
('000 head at 31 December)

	2000	2001	2002
Horses	11	10	8
Cattle	427	438	417
Pigs	1,233	1,234	1,286
Sheep	528	539	580
Goats	80	93	96
Poultry	11,256	11,747	11,665

Source: FAO.

LIVESTOCK PRODUCTS
('000 metric tons)

	1999	2000	2001
Beef and veal	19	19	16
Mutton and lamb	2	2	1
Pigmeat	64	52	33
Poultry meat	32	40	49
Cows' milk	622	606	654
Butter	2	2	3
Cheese (all kinds)	19	21	23
Hen eggs	49	47	47
Honey	1	2	2

Source: FAO.

Forestry

ROUNDWOOD REMOVALS
('000 cubic metres)

	1999	2000	2001
Sawlogs and veneer logs . . .	1,915	1,976	1,938
Pulpwood	311	551	561
Other industrial wood	166	166*	222
Fuel wood	1,094	976	747
Total	**3,486**	**3,669**	**3,468**

* FAO estimate.

Source: FAO.

SAWNWOOD PRODUCTION
('000 cubic metres)

	1999	2000	2001
Coniferous (softwood)	166	95	118
Broadleaved (hardwood) . . .	519	547	516
Total	**685**	**642**	**634**

Source: FAO.

Fishing

('000 metric tons, live weight)

	1999	2000	2001
Freshwater fishes	3.3	3.4	4.4
Marine fishes	19.3	21.6	20.5
Crustaceans and molluscs . . .	2.5	2.7	5.2
Total catch	**25.1**	**27.7**	**30.1**

Mining

('000 metric tons, unless otherwise indicated)

	1999	2000	2001
Coal	15	n.a.	n.a.
Crude petroleum	1,292	1,214	1,121
Natural gas (million cu m) . . .	1,567	1,768	2,009
Bentonite	8.4	10.0	10.6
Ceramic clay	6.0	5.0	32.6
Salt (unrefined)	18.4	33.7	n.a.
Gypsum (crude)	188.0	150.8	130.9

Source: partly US Geological Survey.

Industry

SELECTED PRODUCTS
('000 metric tons, unless otherwise indicated)

	2000	2001	2002
Beer ('000 hectolitres) . . .	3,847	3,799	3,624
Spirits ('000 hectolitres). . . .	177	163	151
Cigarettes (million)	13,692	14,716	n.a.
Cotton fabrics and blankets ('000 sq metres)	13,873	14,059	14,083
Household linen ('000 sq metres) .	7,229	6,502	n.a.
Ready-to-wear clothing ('000 sq metres)	24,397	24,468	19,591
Leather footwear ('000 pairs) . .	5,430	6,167	5,135
Paper and cardboard	228	234	n.a.
Cardboard packaging	174	184	198
Motor spirit (petrol)	1,333	1,250	n.a.
Gas oil (distillate fuels)	1,050	1,036	n.a.
Compound fertilizers	492	407	469
Synthetic materials and resin . .	57	64	65
Cement	2,852	3,246	3,378
Tractors (number)	1,751	2,386	n.a.
Tankers ('000 gross registered tons)	144	225	368
Cargo ships ('000 gross registered tons)	147	224	126
Chairs ('000)	1,502	1,834	2,051
Electric energy (million kWh) . .	10,293	12,674	12,724

Finance

CURRENCY AND EXCHANGE RATES

Monetary Unit
100 lipa = 1 kuna.

Sterling, Dollar and Euro Equivalents (30 May 2003)
£1 sterling = 10.494 kuna;
US $1 = 6.369 kuna;
€1 = 7.529 kuna;
1,000 kuna = £95.30 = $157.01= €132.82.

Average Exchange Rate (kuna per US $)
2000   8.277
2001   8.340
2002   7.869

Note: The Croatian dinar was introduced on 23 December 1991, replacing (and initially at par with) the Yugoslav dinar. On 30 May 1994 the kuna, equivalent to 1,000 dinars, was introduced.

STATE BUDGET
(million kuna)

Revenue	2000	2001*	2002*†
Tax revenue	39,939.0	47,274.0	67,517.3
Taxes on personal income . .	4,094.6	3,404.4	3,567.4
Taxes on corporate income . .	1,673.8	1,987.2	2,035.1
General sales, turnover or value-added taxes	21,978.4	22,882.3	24,512.2
Excises	7,572.1	7,224.4	7,481.7
Excises on petroleum products	4,632.8	4,194.3	3,429.4
Excises on tobacco products .	2,073.7	2,094.7	2,700.0
Customs duties	3,896.5	4,229.9	3,928.2
Other current revenue	1,595.9	1,632.3	2,479.6
Capital revenue	3,100.7	4,597.3	221.0
Proceeds of privatization . . .	2,867.0	4,241.0	—
Total	44,635.7	53,503.6	70,217.9

Expenditure‡	2000	2001*	2002*†
General public services	2,933.2	2,978.3	3,040.9
Defence	5,479.5	4,338.6	4,354.7
Public order and safety	5,185.3	4,761.2	4,890.7
Education	6,576.0	6,581.9	6,194.7
Health	332.4	270.3	10,790.5
Social security and welfare . . .	14,947.3	25,153.7	32,339.3
Housing and community amenities	1,803.3	1,677.0	1,055.3
Recreational, cultural and religious affairs	904.1	955.7	963.3
Fuel and energy	0.3	7.7	8.7
Agriculture, forestry and fisheries	1,723.8	1,641.6	1,879.4
Mining and mineral resources manufacturing and construction	624.1	466.4	437.8
Transport and communications. .	4,953.2	3,113.1	1,356.7
Other economic affairs and services	813.2	832.2	876.8
Other purposes	3,291.8	3,945.6	4,665.7
Total	49,567.5	56,723.3	72,854.4

* From July 2001 includes social security funds, but excludes revenue and expenditure from Croatian Roads Company and Croatian Motorways.
† Projected figures.
‡ Excluding lending minus repayments (million kuna): 1,176.1 in 2000; 1,089.5 in 2001; 1,579.7 in 2002 (projected figure).

Source: Ministry of Finance, Zagreb.

INTERNATIONAL RESERVES
(US $ million at 31 December)

	2000	2001	2002
IMF special drawing rights . . .	147.2	107.4	1.5
Reserve position in IMF. . . .	0.2	0.2	0.2
Foreign exchange.	3,376.9	4,595.6	5,883.2
Total	3,524.4	4,703.2	5,884.9

Source: IMF, *International Financial Statistics*.

MONEY SUPPLY
(million kuna at 31 December)

	2000	2001	2002
Currency outside banks	6,636.7	8,507.4	9,680.9
Demand deposits at deposit money banks	11,386.0	15,180.6	21,166.2
Total (incl. others)	18,030.2	23,703.6	30,866.3

Source: IMF, *International Financial Statistics*.

COST OF LIVING
(Consumer price index; base: 1990 = 100)

	1999	2000	2001
Food	62,359.2	62,608.6	63,923.4
Fuel and light	58,798.1	64,677.9	72,698.0
Clothing (incl. footwear). . . .	69,816.8	74,424.7	77,104.0
Housing	56,473.4	60,426.5	64,293.8
All items (incl. others)	67,259.0	70,823.7	74,223.2

Source: ILO.

2002 (base: 2001 = 100): Food 100.3; Clothing (incl. footwear) 103.0; Housing 101.3; All items (incl. others) 101.9.

NATIONAL ACCOUNTS

Gross Domestic Product by Economic Activity
(million kuna at current prices)

	1998	1999	2000
Agriculture, hunting and forestry	10,661.6 }	11,366	12,387
Fishing	238.9 }		
Mining and quarrying. . . .	642.5 }		
Manufacturing	24,661.2 }	30,871	35,174
Electricity, gas and water supply	3,770.4 }		
Construction	7,732.1	7,957	7,648
Wholesale and retail trade; repair of motor vehicles, motorcycles and personal and household goods	13,787.8	14,328	16,401
Hotels and restaurants . . .	3,581.2	3,452	4,232
Transport, storage and communications	9,777.2	10,507	12,596
Financial intermediation . . .	4,901.7 }	17,396	18,502
Real estate, renting and business activities	11,485.8 }		
Public administration and defence; compulsory social security	11,684.0 }		
Education	4,944.7 }		
Health and social work . . .	5,702.4 }	27,070	29,540
Other community, social and personal service activities . .	2,685.3 }		
Private households with employed persons	36.6 }		
Sub-total	116,293.4	122,947	136,480
Less Financial intermediation services indirectly measured .	5,232.4	5,603	6,037
GDP at basic prices . . .	111,061.0	117,344	130,443
Taxes, *less* subsidies, on products	26,542.7	25,356	27,068
GDP in purchasers' values .	137,603.7	142,700	157,511

BALANCE OF PAYMENTS
(US $ million)

	2000	2001	2002
Exports of goods f.o.b.	4,567.2	4,758.7	4,994.6
Imports of goods f.o.b.	−7,770.9	−8,860.0	−10,273.9
Trade balance	−3,203.8	−4,101.3	−5,279.3
Exports of services	4,095.9	4,875.5	5,550.4
Imports of services	−1,828.0	−1,948.5	−2,432.2
Balance on goods and services	−935.9	−1,174.3	−2,161.1
Other income received	345.8	418.9	461.1
Other income paid	−752.5	−935.3	−939.7
Balance on goods, services and income	−1,342.6	−1,690.8	−2,639.6
Current transfers received . . .	1,101.0	1,174.5	1,357.4
Current transfers paid	−217.8	−208.8	−264.3
Current balance	−459.4	−725.1	−1,546.5
Capital account (net)	20.9	133.0	24.0
Direct investment abroad . . .	−3.9	−154.6	−94.6
Direct investment from abroad. .	1,088.7	1,561.3	980.5
Portfolio investment assets . . .	−22.7	−129.3	−634.6
Portfolio investment liabilities . .	730.3	730.0	418.3
Other investment assets . . .	−844.5	396.6	471.0
Other investment liabilities . .	981.5	124.5	2,370.2
Net errors and omissions . . .	−880.1	−594.3	−1,290.9
Overall balance	610.7	1,342.1	697.2

Source: IMF, *International Financial Statistics*.

External Trade

PRINCIPAL COMMODITIES
(distribution by SITC, US $ million)

Imports c.i.f.	1999	2000	2001
Food and live animals . . .	560.3	556.1	691.1
Mineral fuels, lubricants, etc. .	859.3	1,144.5	1,175.6
Petroleum and petroleum products	673.1	856.8	836.6
Chemicals and related products	939.8	1,004.8	1,038.5
Basic manufactures	1,251.8	1,390.1	1,786.9
Textile yarn, fabrics, etc. . . .	160.2	249.2	355.8
Iron and steel.	211.0	243.8	315.8
Machinery and transport equipment.	2,732.5	2,568.3	3,102.7
Machinery specialized for particular industries	257.1	250.5	236.5
General industrial machinery equipment and parts . . .	372.8	302.6	398.2
Telecommunications and sound equipment	155.3	209.5	297.5
Electrical machinery, apparatus etc. (excl. telecommunications and sound equipment) . . .	338.8	326.0	427.5
Road vehicles and parts* . . .	815.7	857.0	943.0
Other transport equipment and parts*	482.9	342.4	260.0
Miscellaneous manufactured articles.	923.7	946.9	1,042.9
Clothing and accessories (excl. footwear)	212.8	278.5	258.0
Total (incl. others)	7,798.6	7,886.5	9,147.1

Exports f.o.b.	1999	2000	2001
Food and live animals . . .	290.5	273.3	322.5
Crude materials (inedible) except fuels	243.0	251.3	241.4
Cork and wood	164.2	160.1	148.0
Mineral fuels, lubricants, etc. .	338.3	485.8	476.6
Petroleum and petroleum products	287.0	381.9	346.0
Chemicals and related products	515.0	553.8	494.3
Medicinal and pharmaceutical products.	169.1	189.0	173.8
Plastics in primary forms . . .	135.5	122.4	102.1
Basic manufactures	572.2	669.2	663.7
Non-metallic mineral manufactures	152.7	169.0	183.0
Machinery and transport equipment.	1,261.9	1,195.0	1,367.9
Electrical machinery, apparatus etc. (excl. telecommunications and sound equipment) . . .	230.4	215.1	243.7
Transport equipment and parts (excl. road vehicles)*	712.8	632.2	719.8
Miscellaneous manufactured articles.	966.1	887.2	968.2
Clothing and accessories (excl. footwear)	525.2	469.2	491.8
Footwear	173.8	156.8	165.5
Total (incl. others)	4,302.5	4,431.6	4,665.9

* Data on parts exclude tyres, engines and electrical parts.

PRINCIPAL TRADING PARTNERS
(US $ million)

Imports c.i.f.	1999	2000	2001
Austria .	557.6	528.7	631.2
Belgium* .	114.2	115.0	128.3
Bosnia and Herzegovina	116.8	81.6	126.7
China, People's Republic	75.6	87.3	144.3
Czech Republic	148.4	179.2	209.3
France .	392.5	436.4	397.6
Germany	1,441.0	1,297.7	1,583.2
Hungary	174.1	183.8	238.0
Iraq	15.4	101.4	73.1
Italy	1,240.1	1,310.7	1,656.9
Japan .	137.9	135.2	145.8
Korea, Republic	79.5	71.8	69.1
Libya	26.4	99.7	74.5
Netherlands	141.8	129.8	164.0
Russia .	668.1	672.0	654.1
Slovenia	616.2	626.6	711.7
Spain .	82.6	101.2	127.0
Sweden	115.7	111.6	110.4
Switzerland† .	157.9	150.7	149.9
United Kingdom .	186.9	179.7	226.1
USA‡ .	240.9	239.0	297.0
Total (incl. others) .	7,798.6	7,886.5	9,147.1

Exports f.o.b.	1999	2000	2001
Austria .	276.0	292.4	267.9
Bosnia and Herzegovina	545.7	494.8	560.6
Cayman Islands .	—	—	70.1
Cyprus .	84.5	1.0	9.3
France .	108.2	125.9	163.1
Germany	676.1	631.8	689.6
Greece .	33.9	89.3	24.0
Hungary	39.6	60.0	56.9
Italy	774.7	989.0	1,105.4
Liberia .	169.1	223.5	138.1
Macedonia, former Yugoslav republic .	64.1	59.0	52.5
Malta .	99.4	48.1	55.6
Netherlands .	49.9	49.9	46.7
Norway .	113.1	4.5	6.3
Poland .	39.6	22.4	20.0
Russia .	70.8	56.6	83.5
Slovenia	454.2	480.0	426.4
United Kingdom .	79.9	76.2	67.3
USA‡ .	86.5	90.0	107.4
Yugoslavia .	27.3	107.2	149.2
Total (incl. others) .	4,302.5	4,431.6	4,665.9

* Including trade with Luxembourg.
† Including trade with Liechtenstein.
‡ Including trade with Puerto Rico.

Transport

RAILWAYS
(traffic)

	2000	2001	2002*
Passenger journeys ('000) . .	34,937	36,964	36,239
Passenger-kilometres (million) .	1,252	1,241	1,195
Freight carried ('000 metric tons) .	10,059	10,807	10,654
Freight net ton-km (million) . .	1,788	2,074	2,206

* Provisional data.

ROAD TRAFFIC
(registered motor vehicles at 31 December)

	2000	2001	2002*
Passenger cars .	1,124,825	1,195,450	1,244,252
Buses .	4,660	4,770	4,792
Registered goods vehicles . .	113,134	119,899	128,955
Motorcycles and mopeds . . .	65,292	73,766	n.a.

* Provisional data.

INLAND WATERWAYS
(vessels and traffic)

	1999	2000	2001
Tugs .	27	32	32
Motor barges .	3	3	4
Barges .	95	100	95
Goods unloaded (million metric tons) .	1	1	1

SHIPPING

Merchant Fleet
(registered at 31 December)

	1999	2000	2001
Number of vessels	257	246	243
Total displacement ('000 grt) . .	868.9	734.3	775.2

Source: Lloyd's Register-Fairplay, *World Fleet Statistics*.

International Sea-borne Freight Traffic

	1999	2000	2001
Vessels entered (million grt) . .	20.8	24.8	30.6
Goods loaded ('000 metric tons) .	3,728	5,471	5,847
Goods unloaded ('000 metric tons)	6,739	6,877	6,815
Goods in transit ('000 metric tons)	2,680	1,809	3,794

CIVIL AVIATION

	1999	2000	2001
Kilometres flown ('000)	11,434	12,178	13,225
Passengers carried ('000) . . .	926	1,072	1,245
Passenger-kilometres (million) . .	643	763	922
Freight carried (metric tons) . .	4,858	5,697	6,007
Ton-kilometres ('000)	3,219	3,775	3,997

Tourism

FOREIGN TOURIST ARRIVALS BY COUNTRY OF ORIGIN
('000)

	2000	2001	2002
Austria .	640	687	690
Bosnia and Herzegovina . .	182	172	173
Czech Republic	711	742	698
Germany .	1,048	1,300	1,482
Hungary .	250	280	318
Italy .	1,011	1,060	1,099
Poland .	285	392	358
Slovakia .	188	203	191
Slovenia .	849	877	870
Total (incl. others)	5,832	6,544	6,944

Nautical tourists ('000): 376 in 1999; 517 in 2000; 580 in 2001.

Receipts from tourism (US $ million): 2,493 in 1999; 2,758 in 2000.

Communications Media

	2000	2001	2002
Radio licences ('000)	1,120	1,150	n.a.
Television licences ('000) . . .	1,093	1,080	n.a.
Telephone licences ('000) . . .	1,646	1,783	1,879
Mobile cellular telephones ('000 subscribers)*	1,033.0	1,755.0	2,278.0
Personal computers ('000 in use)*	361	400	760
Internet users ('000)*	250	n.a.	789
Book production (titles)	2,969	3,832	n.a.
Daily newspapers (number). . .	14	14	n.a.

* Source: International Telecommunication Union.

Facsimile machines (number in use): 50,237 in 1997 (Source: UN, *Statistical Yearbook*).

Non-daily newspapers (1996): 767; Average circulation 584,000.

Other periodicals (1990): Number 352; Average circulation 6,357,000 (Source: UNESCO, *Statistical Yearbook*).

Education

(2002/03)

	Institutions	Teachers	Students
Pre-primary	1,067	6,783	89,107
Basic schools	2,139	27,905	495,702
Secondary schools	650	19,733	196,147
Higher education*†	102	7,622	111,782

* Including post-graduate students.
† Data for 2001/02.

Adult literacy rate (UNESCO estimates): 98.3% (Males 99.3%; Females 97.3%) in 2000 (Source: UN Development Programme, *Human Development Report*).

Directory

The Constitution

The Constitution of the Republic of Croatia was promulgated on 21 December 1990. Croatia issued a declaration of dissociation from the Socialist Federal Republic of Yugoslavia in June 1991, and formal independence was proclaimed on 8 October. Constitutional amendments, which were adopted in November 1997, included a prohibition on the re-establishment of a union of Yugoslav states.

The following is a summary of the main provisions of the Constitution:

GENERAL PROVISIONS

The Republic of Croatia is a democratic, constitutional state where power belongs to the people and is exercised directly and through the elected representatives of popular sovereignty.

The Republic of Croatia is an integral state, while its sovereignty is inalienable, indivisible and non-transferable. State power in the Republic of Croatia is divided into legislative, executive and judicial power.

All citizens of the Republic of Croatia over the age of 18 years have the right to vote and to be candidates for election to public office. The right to vote is realized through direct elections, by secret ballot. Citizens of the Republic living outside its borders have the right to vote in elections for the Assembly and the President of the Republic.

In a state of war or when there is a direct threat to the independence and unity of the Republic, as well as in the case of serious natural disasters, some freedoms and rights that are guaranteed by the Constitution may be restricted. This is decided by the Assembly of the Republic of Croatia by a two-thirds' majority of its deputies and, if the Assembly cannot be convened, by the President of the Republic.

BASIC RIGHTS

The following rights are guaranteed and protected in the Republic: the right to life (the death sentence has been abolished), fundamental freedoms and privacy, equality before the law, the right to be presumed innocent until proven guilty and the principle of legality, the right to receive legal aid, the right to freedom of movement and residence, the right to seek asylum, inviolability of the home, freedom and secrecy of correspondence, safety and secrecy of personal data, freedom of thought and expression of opinion, freedom of conscience and religion (all religious communities are equal before the law and are separated from the State), the right of assembly and peaceful association, the right of ownership, entrepreneurship and free trade (monopolies are forbidden), the right to work and freedom of labour, the right to a nationality, the right to strike, and the right to a healthy environment.

Members of all peoples and minorities in the Republic enjoy equal rights. They are guaranteed the freedom to express their nationality, to use their language and alphabet and to enjoy cultural autonomy.

GOVERNMENT

Legislature*

Legislative power resides with the unicameral Assembly (Sabor), which comprises the 151-member Chamber of Representatives (Zastupnički dom). The Assembly decides on the adoption and amendment of the Constitution, approves laws, adopts the state budgets, decides on war and peace, decides on the alteration of the borders of the Republic, calls referendums, supervises the work of the Government and other public officials responsible to the Assembly, in accordance with the Constitution and the law, and deals with other matters determined by the Constitution.

Members of the Assembly are elected by universal, direct and secret ballot for a term of four years, and their term is not mandatory. The Assembly may be dissolved, with the approval of the majority of all the deputies. The Assembly has the power to appoint and dismiss the Prime Minister and (upon his recommendation) the ministers.

President of the Republic

The President of the Republic is the Head of State of Croatia. The President represents the country at home and abroad and is responsible for ensuring respect for the Constitution, guaranteeing the existence and unity of the Republic and the regular functioning of state power. The President is elected directly for a term of five years.

The President is the Supreme Commander of the Armed Forces of the Republic of Croatia. In the event of war or immediate danger, the President issues decrees having the force of law. The President may convene a meeting of the Government and place on its agenda items that, in his opinion, should be discussed. The President attends the Government's meetings and presides over them.

Ministers

Executive power in the Republic resides with the President, the Prime Minister and the Ministers. The Government of the Republic consists of the Ministers and the Prime Minister. The Government issues decrees, proposes laws and the budget, and implements laws and regulations that have been adopted by the Assembly. In its work, the Government is responsible to the President of the Republic and the Assembly.

JUDICATURE

Judicial power is vested in the courts and is autonomous and independent. The courts issue judgments on the basis of the Constitution and the law. The Supreme Court is the highest court and is responsible for the uniform implementation of laws and equal rights of citizens. Judges and state public prosecutors are appointed and relieved of duty by the Judicial Council of the Republic, which is elected, from among distinguished lawyers, by the Assembly for a term of eight years.

* The Chamber of Counties, the upper chamber of the, hitherto, bicameral legislature, was abolished by a constitutional amendment adopted in March 2001.

The Government

HEAD OF STATE

President of the Republic: STIPE MESIĆ (elected 7 February 2000; inaugurated 18 February).

Office of the President: 10000 Zagreb, Banski Dvori.

GOVERNMENT
(July 2003)

A coalition of the Social Democratic Party (SDP), the Croatian People's Party (CPP), the Liberal Party (LP) and the Croatian Peasants' Party.

Prime Minister: IVICA RAČAN (SDP).

First Deputy Prime Minister: ANTE SIMONIĆ (Croatian Peasants' Party).

Deputy Prime Minister: GORAN GRANIĆ (Ind.).

Deputy Prime Minister, in charge of the Economy: SLAVKO LINIĆ (SDP).

Deputy Prime Minister, in charge of Social Affairs, and Minister of Defence: ŽELIJKA ANTUNOVIĆ (SDP).

Minister of Finance: MATO CRKVENAC (SDP).

Minister of the Interior: ŠIME LUČIN (SDP).

Minister of Foreign Affairs: TONINO PICULA (SDP).

Minister of Public Works, Reconstruction and Construction: RADIMIR ČAČIĆ (CPP).

Minister of the Economy: LJUBO JURČIĆ (SDP).

Minister of Croatian Homeland War Defenders: IVICA PANČIĆ (SDP).

Minister of Agriculture and Forestry: BOŽIDAR PANKRETIĆ (Croatian Peasants' Party).

Minister of Maritime Affairs, Transport and Telecommunications: ROLAND ŽUVANIĆ (SDP).

Minister of Justice, Administration and Local Self-Government: INGRID ANTIČEVIĆ-MARINOVIĆ (SDP).

Minister of Environmental Protection and Physical Planning: BOŽO KOVAČEVIĆ (LP).

Minister of Education and Sport: VLADIMIR STRUGAR (Croatian Peasants' Party).

Minister of Labour and Social Welfare: DAVORKO VIDOVIĆ (SDP).

Minister of Tourism: PAVE ŽUPAN RUSKOVIĆ (Ind.).

Minister of Health: ANDRO VLAHUŠIĆ (SDP).

Minister of Science and Technology: GVOZDEN FLEGO (SDP).

Minister of Culture: ANTUN VUJIĆ (SDP).

Minister of European Integration: NEVEN MIMICA (SDP).

Minister of Trades, Small and Medium Businesses: ŽELJKO PECEK (SDP).

Minister without Portfolio, in the Office of the Prime Minister: GORDANA SOBOL (SDP).

MINISTRIES

Office of the Prime Minister: Govt of the Republic of Croatia, 10000 Zagreb, trg sv. Marka 2; tel. (1) 4569201; fax (1) 432041.

Ministry of Agriculture and Forestry: 10000 Zagreb, Ave. Vukovar 78; tel. (1) 6133444; fax (1) 442070; internet www.mps.hr.

Ministry of Croatian Homeland War Defenders: Park Stara Trešnjevka 4, Zagreb; tel. (1) 3657800; fax (1) 3657852; e-mail pommin4@mhbdr.tel.hr.

Ministry of Culture: 10000 Zagreb, trg Burze 6; tel. (1) 4569000; fax (1) 410487; internet www.mini-kulture.hr.

Ministry of Defence: 10000 Zagreb, trg kralja Petra Krešimira IV 1; tel. (1) 4567111; e-mail infor@morh.hr; internet www.morh.hr.

Ministry of the Economy: 10000 Zagreb, trg sv. Marka 2; tel. (1) 4569207; fax (1) 4550606; e-mail info@mingo.hr; internet www.mingo.hr.

Ministry of Education and Sport: 10000 Zagreb, trg Hevatskih Velikana 6; tel. (1) 4569009; fax (1) 4569087; e-mail office@mips.hr; internet www.mips.hr.

Ministry of Environmental Protection and Physical Planning: 10000 Zagreb, Republike Austrije 20; tel. (1) 3782444; fax (1) 3772822; e-mail kabinet.ministra@zg.tel.hr; internet www.mzopu.hr.

Ministry of European Integration: 10000 Zagreb, ul. grada Vukovara 62; tel. (1) 4569335; fax (1) 6303182; e-mail info@mei.hr; internet www.mei.hr.

Ministry of Finance: 10000 Zagreb, ul. Katančićeva 5; tel. (1) 4591333; fax (1) 4922583; e-mail kabinet@mfin.hr; internet www.mfin.hr.

Ministry of Foreign Affairs: 10000 Zagreb, trg Nikole Šubića Zrinskog 7–8; tel. (1) 4569964; fax (1) 4569977; e-mail mvp@mvp.hr; internet www.mvp.hr.

Ministry of Health: 10000 Zagreb, ul. Baruna Tranka 6; tel. (1) 431068; fax (1) 431067; internet www.tel.hr/mzrh.

Ministry of the Interior: 10000 Zagreb, Savska cesta 39; tel. (1) 6122129; fax (1) 6122299; e-mail webinfo@vlada.hr; internet www.vlada.hr.

Ministry of Justice, Administration and Local Self-Government: 10000 Zagreb, Savska cesta 41; tel. (1) 535935; fax (1) 536321.

Ministry of Labour and Social Welfare: 10000 Zagreb, Prisavlje 14; tel. (1) 6169111; fax (1) 6169206; e-mail info@mrss.hr; internet www.mrss.hr.

Ministry of Maritime Affairs, Transport and Telecommunications: 10000 Zagreb, Prisavlje 14; tel. (1) 6169100; fax (1) 6196519; internet www.pomorstvo.hr.

Ministry of Public Works, Reconstruction and Construction: Zagreb, Savska cesta 41/12; tel. (1) 6176011; fax (1) 6176161; e-mail mpu@mpu.hr.

Ministry of Tourism: 10000 Zagreb, Ave. Vukovar 78; tel. (1) 6106300; fax (1) 6109300; e-mail ministarstvo.turizma@mint.hr; internet www.mint.hr.

Ministry of Trades, Small and Medium Businesses: 10000 Zagreb, Ksaver 200; tel. (1) 4698300; fax (1) 4698310; e-mail momsp@momsp.hr; internet www.momsp.hr.

President and Legislature

PRESIDENT

Presidential Election, First Ballot, 24 January 2000

	Votes	% of votes
Stipe Mesić*	1,100,671	41.11
Dražen Budiša†	741,837	27.71
Dr Mate Granić (Croatian Democratic Union)	601,588	22.47
Slaven Letica (Independent)	110,782	4.14
Ante Djapić (Croatian Party of Rights)	49,288	1.84
Ante Ledić (Independent)	22,875	0.85
Tomislav Mercep (Croatian People's Party)	22,672	0.85
Ante Prkacin (New Croatia)	7,401	0.28
Dr Zvonimir Šeparović (Independent)	7,235	0.27
Total	2,664,349‡	100.00

* Candidate of the Croatian Peasants' Party, the Liberal Party, the Croatian People's Party and the Istrian Democratic Assembly.
† Candidate of the Social Democratic Party and the Croatian Social-Liberal Party.
‡ Excluding 13,212 invalid votes (0.49% of the total votes).

Presidential Election, Second Ballot, 7 February 2000*

	% of votes
Stipe Mesić†	56.21
Dražen Budiša‡	43.79
Total	100.00

* Preliminary results.
† Candidate of the Croatian Peasants' Party, the Liberal Party, the Croatian People's Party and the Istrian Democratic Assembly.
‡ Candidate of the Social Democratic Party and the Croatian Social-Liberal Party.

SABOR
(Assembly)

President: ZLATKO TOMČIĆ, 10000 Zagreb, trg sv. Marka 617; tel. (1) 4569222; fax (1) 276483.

Vice-Presidents: MATO ARLOVIĆ, ZDRAVKO TOMAC, BALTAZAR JALSOVEC, VLATKO PAVLETIĆ, IVIĆ PASALIĆ.

Zastupnički dom
(Chamber of Representatives)

Election, 3 January 2000

	% of votes	Seats
Social Democratic Party		44
Croatian Social-Liberal Party	47.0	24
Primorian-Goranian Union		2
Slavonian-Baranian Croatian Party . .		1
Croatian Democratic Union	30.5	45
Croatian Peasants' Party		16
Istrian Democratic Assembly		4
Liberal Party	15.9	2
Croatian People's Party		2
Croatian Social Democrats' Action . .		1
Croatian Party of Rights	3.3	5
Others	3.3	1
Total	**100.0**	**151**

Local Government

Legislation passed in November 1992 provided for the division of Croatia, for electoral purposes, into 21 counties or communes (Županije), including the City of Zagreb. Each county has a local assembly (Županijska skupština) consisting of 40 councillors, with the exception of Zagreb City, which has 60 councillors. The head of the county administration is the known as the Župan. On 1 May 1996, one month after nation-wide local elections, in which opposition parties in Zagreb City had won 64% of the votes, President Franjo Tudjman dissolved the Zagreb City Assembly and replaced it with a Government Commissioner. Primorje and Gorski Kotar County Assembly was also disbanded; both measures were declared illegal by the Constitutional Court on 10 May. Further elections to the Zagreb City Assembly took place on 7 May 2000. At further local government elections, which took place on 20 May 2001, the Social Democratic Party won control of 16 of the 21 County Assemblies, and the Croatian Democratic Union (CDU) four. Elections were held in Dubrovnik and Neretva in September, in which the CDU secured 10 of the 25 seats in the local government.

Zagreb County (I): 10000 Zagreb, Vukovarska 72, Županija Zagrebačka; tel. (1) 6345000; fax (1) 6345209; e-mail zagzup.kabinet@zg.tel.hr; internet www.members.tripod.com; Župan STJEPAN KOŽIĆ.

Krapina and Zagorje County (II): 49000 Krapina, Magistratska 3, Županija Krapinsko–Zagorska; tel. (49) 329212; fax (49) 329211; internet www.zagorje.com; Župan ŽELIMIR HITREC.

Sisak and Moslavina County (III): 44000 Sisak, ul. S. I. A. Radića 36, Županija Sisačko–Moslavačka; tel. (44) 522777; fax (44) 524158; Župan DJURO BRODARAC.

Karlovac County (IV): 47000 Karlovac, ul. A. Vranyczanyja 2, Karlovačka Županija; tel. (47) 666111; fax (47) 666261; e-mail zupan@karlovacka-zupanija.hr; internet www.karlovacka-zupanija.hr; Župan VLADO JELKOVAC.

Varaždin County (V): 42000 Varaždin, Kratka 1, Županija Varaždinska; tel. (42) 12377; fax (42) 45866; Župan MARIJAN MLINARIĆ.

Koprivnica and Križevci County (VI): 43000 Koprivnica, ul. A. Nemčića 5, Županija Koprivničko–Križevačka; tel. (48) 658111; fax (48) 622584; internet www.hrvatska.com/zupanija-kc; Župan NIKOLA GREGUR.

Bjelovar and Bilogora County (VII): 43000 Bjelovar, Dr Ante Starčevića 8, Županija Bjelovarsko–Bilogorska; tel. (43) 244892; fax (43) 244450; internet www.hinet.hr/bbz; Župan DAMIR BAJS.

Primorje and Gorski Kotar County (VII): 51000 Rijeka, Adamićeva 10, Županija Primorsko–Goranska; tel. (51) 226222; fax (51) 212948; internet www.kvarner.hr; Župan ZLATKO KOMADINA.

Lika and Senj County (IX): 53000 Gospić, ul. Budačka 55, Županija Ličko–Senjska; tel. (53) 572811; fax (53) 572100; internet www.licko-senjska.com; Župan ANTE FRKOVIĆ.

Virovitica and Podravina County (X): 33000 Virovitica, trg Ljudevila Patačića 1, Županija Virovitičko–Podravska; tel. (46) 725144; fax (46) 725305; e-mail zu-viroviticko-podravska-tajnistvo@vt.tel.hr; internet www.viroviticko-podravska-zupanija.hr; Župan IVAN HORVAT.

Požega and Slavonia County (XI): 34000 Požega, Županiska 7–9, Županija Požeško–Slavonska; tel. (34) 272355; fax (34) 272843; Župan ANTO BAGARIĆ.

Slavonski Brod and Posavina County (XII): 35000 Slavonski Brod, Kralja Petra Krešimira IV 1, Županija Brodsko–Posavska; tel.

(35) 447411; fax (35) 445903; internet www.tel.hr/zubrps; Župan MATO DORIĆ.

Zadar County (XIII): 23000 Zadar, Božidara Petranovića 8, Županija Zadarsko; tel. (23) 315142; fax (23) 312578; internet www.zadar.hr; Župan ŠIME PRTENJAČA.

Osijek and Baranja County (XIV): 31000 Osijek, trg Ante Starčevića 2, Županija Osječko–Baranjska; tel. (31) 221500; fax (31) 203191; internet www.jwarehr.com/osbarzup; Župan ZDRAVKO BOSANČIĆ.

Šibenik and Knin County (XV): 22000 Šibenik, trg Pavla Šubića 1, 2, Županija Šibenska-Kninska; tel. (22) 22633; fax (22) 28966; internet www.sibenik-knin.com; Župan GORDON BARAKA.

Vukovar and Sirmium County (XVI): 32100 Vinkovci, Glagoljaška 27/II, Županija Vukovarsko–Srijemska; tel. (32) 331211; fax (32) 331981; Župan NIKOLA SAFER.

Split and Dalmatia County (XVII): 21000 Split, Vukovarska 1, Županija Splitsko–Dalmatinska; tel. (21) 341644; fax (21) 45164; Župan BRANIMIR LUKŠIĆ.

Istria County (XVIII): 52000 Pazin, Dršćevka 1, Županija Istarska; tel. (52) 621822; fax (52) 212416; internet www.istra.com; Župan IVAN JAKOVČIĆ.

Dubrovnik and Neretva County (XIX): 20000 Dubrovnik, Pred Dvorom 1, Županija Dubrovačko–Neretvanska; tel. (20) 351402; fax (20) 321059; e-mail 20/n-tajnistvo@du.tel.hr; Župan IVAN ŠPRLJE.

Meimurje County (XX): 40000 Čakovec, Rudeva Boškovića 2, Županija Meimurska; tel. (40) 374111; fax (40) 391005; e-mail zupanija-medijimurska.hr; internet www.zupanija-medjimurska.hr; Župan BRANKO LEVAČIĆ.

City of Zagreb (XXI): 10000 Zagreb, Skupština–Županija Grad Zagreb; tel. (1) 511141; fax (1) 511546; Mayor VLASTA PAVIĆ.

THE DANUBE REGION

On 15 January 1998 the Serb-dominated region of what was part of the 'Republic of Serb Krajina', Slavonia, Baranja and Western Srem (Eastern Slavonia), was formally reconstituted into Croatia. This was in accordance with the provisions of the Basic Agreement on the Region of Eastern Slavonia, Baranja and Western Sirmium, signed by representatives of the Croatian Government and the Serb community in Eastern Slavonia in November 1995. Under the terms of this Agreement, a UN Transitional Administration for Eastern Slavonia, Baranja and Western Sirmium (UNTAES) had been established to supervise the region's demilitarization and reintegration into Croatia. The mandate of UNTAES expired on 14 January 1998 and the Danube Region, as the area was thenceforth known, once more became an integral part of Croatia. The counties of Osijek and Baranja and Vukovar and Srem (see above) made up the Županije of the region. The Serb officials and politicians remained associated in a Serb Council of Counties. An OSCE monitoring mission remained in the region.

Serb Council of Counties: Osijek; Leader VOJISLAV STANIMIROVIĆ.

Political Organizations

Alternative for Rijeka (Alternativa za Rijeka): Rijeka, Trpimirova 2/10; tel. (51) 610726; e-mail azra_sna@hotmail.com; internet www.azra.2ya.com; Pres. GORANA TUŠKAN.

Christian People's Party (CPP) (Kršćanska Narodna Stranka—KNS): 10000 Zagreb, Degenova 7; tel. (1) 427258; fax (1) 273595; Pres. ZDRAVKO MRŠIĆ.

Croatian Bloc-Movement for a Modern Croatia: f. 2002; Chair. IVIC PASALIĆ.

Croatian Christian Democratic Union (CCDU) (Hrvatska Kršćanska Demokratska Unija—HKDU): 10000 Zagreb; tel. (1) 327233; fax (1) 325190; e-mail bihdem@posluh.hr; internet www.posluh.hr; Pres. MIJO IVANČIĆ.

Croatian Democratic Centre (Demokratski Centar): 10000 Zagreb; internet www.demokratski-centar.hr; f. March 2000 by a breakaway faction of the Croatian Democratic Union; pro-European, moderate; Pres. MATE GRANIĆ.

Croatian Democratic Party (CDP) (Hrvatska Demokratska Stranka—HDS): 10000 Zagreb; tel. (1) 431837; Pres. MARKO VESELICA.

Croatian Democratic Republican Party: f. Oct. 2000 by merger of Croatian Spring, National Democratic Party and Croatian Peasants' National Party; Leader JOSKO KOVAC.

Croatian Democratic Union (CDU) (Hrvatska Demokratska Zajednica—HDZ): 10000 Zagreb, trg hrvatskih velikana 4; tel. (1) 4553000; fax (1) 4552600; e-mail hdz@hdz.hr; internet www.hdz.hr;

f. 1989; Christian Democrat; Chair. Ivo SANADER; Sec.-Gen. Joso SKARA.

Croatian Independent Democrats (CID) (Hrvatski Nezavisni Demokrati—HND): 10000 Zagreb; f. 1994 by a faction from the CDU; Chair. JOSIP MANOLIĆ.

Croatian Liberation Movement (Hrvatski Oslobodilački Pokret): 10000 Zagreb, Šenoina 27; fax (1) 4923035; e-mail ndh@hop.hr; internet www.hop.hr.

Croatian Muslim Democratic Party (CMDP) (Hrvatska Muslimanska Demokratska Stranka—HMDS): 10000 Zagreb; tel. (1) 421562.

Croatian Party of Rights (CPR) (Hrvatska Stranka Prava—HSP): 10000 Zagreb, ul. Šenoina 13; tel. and fax (1) 4839938; e-mail hsp1861@hsp1861.hr; internet www.hsp.hr; f. 1861; re-established 1990; right-wing, nationalist; armed br. was the Croatian Defence Asscn or Hrvatske Obrambene Snage (HOS); Pres. ANTE DJAPIĆ.

Croatian Party of Slavonia and Baranja (CPSB) (Slavonsko–Baranjska Hrvatska Stranka—SBHS): Osijek.

Croatian Peasants' Party (Hrvatska Seljačka Stranka—HSS): 10000 Zagreb, ul. Kralja Zvonimira 17; tel. and fax (1) 4553624; e-mail hss-sredisnjica@hss.hr; internet www.hss.hr; Pres. ZLATKO TOMČIĆ.

Croatian Peasants' Party Trogir (Hrvatska Seljačka Stranka—gradska organizacija Trogir): Trogir, ul. Blaža Jurjeva Trogiranina 4; tel. (21) 882449; fax (21) 884868; e-mail hss-trogir@inet.hr; internet www.hss-trogir.com; Pres. MILIVOJ ŠPIKA.

Croatian Pensioners' Party: 10000 Zagreb; contested local elections in 2000 in a coalition with the SDP.

Croatian People's Party (CPP) (Hrvatska Narodna Stranka—HNS): 10000 Zagreb, Tomićeva 2; tel. (1) 4877000; fax (1) 4877009; e-mail webmaster@hns.hr; internet www.hns.hr; Pres. VESNA PUSIĆ.

Croatian Republican Community (CRC) (Hrvatska Republikanska Zajednica—HRZ): 10000 Zagreb, Nalješkovićeva 11; tel. and fax (1) 4666740; e-mail hrz@zg.tel.hr; internet www.hrz.hr; Pres. BORKO JURIN.

Croatian Republicans' Party (Hrvatski Republikanci): 10000 Zagreb, trg bana Josipa Jelačića 1/III; tel. (1) 4812353; fax (1) 4811685; e-mail republikanci@zg.tel.hr; internet www.republikanci .hr; Pres. TOMISLAV BOGDANIĆ.

Croatian Social Democrats' Action (Akcija socijaldemokrata Hrvatska—ASH): Zagreb.

Croatian Social-Liberal Party (CSLP) (Hrvatska Socijalno-Liberalna Stranka—HSLS): 10000 Zagreb, trg N. Š. Zrinskog 17; tel. (1) 4810401; fax (1) 4810404; e-mail hsls@hsls.hr; internet www.hsls .hr; f. 1989; Pres. DRAŽEN BUDIŠA.

Dalmatian Action (DA) (Dalmatinska Akcija): 21000 Split, ul. bana Jelačića 4/I; tel. (21) 344322; f. 1990; Pres. Dr MIRA LJUBIĆ-LORGER.

Independent Democratic Serb Party (Samostalne Demokratska Srpska Stranka—SDSS): 32000 Vukovar, Radnički dom 1–3; tel. and fax (32) 665116; f. 1997 by Serbs in Eastern Slavonia; Pres. Dr VOJISLAV STANIMIROVIĆ.

Istrian Democratic Assembly (IDA) (Istarski Demokratski Sabor—IDS): Pula, Splitska 3; tel. (52) 223316; fax (52) 213702; e-mail ids-ddi@pu.tel.hr; internet www.ids-ddi.com; Pres. IVAN JAKOVČIĆ.

Istrian People's Party (IPP) (Istarska Pučka Stranka—IPS): Pula, trg revolucije 3; tel. (52) 23863; fax (52) 23832; Pres. JOSIP FABRIS.

Liberal Party (Liberalna Stranka): 10000 Zagreb; e-mail liberali@ bbm.hr; internet www.liberali.hr; f. 1998 by a breakaway faction of the Croatian Social-Liberal Party; Pres. IVO BANAC.

New Croatia: Zagreb; Pres. ANTE PRKACIN.

Party of Serbs: 10000 Zagreb; f. 1993 by mems of Serb cultural asscn Prosveta (Enlightenment) and Serb Democratic Forum; promotes liberal, democratic values; Leader MILORAD PUPOVAĆ.

Primorian-Goranian Union (Primorski-Goranski Savez): Zagreb; regionalist.

Programme for Croatian Identity and Prosperity: f. Nov. 2000 by former supporters of Pres. Dr Franjo Tudjman; Leader MIROSLAV TUDJMAN.

Rijeka Democratic Alliance (RDA) (Riječki Demokratski Savez—RDS): 51000 Rijeka, Žrtava fašizma 29; tel. (51) 423713; Pres. NIKOLA IVANIŠ; Sec. FRANJO BUTORAC.

Serb People's Party (SPP) (Srpska Narodna Stranka—SNS): 10000 Zagreb, trg Mažuranića 3; tel. and fax (1) 451090; promotes cultural and individual rights for ethnic Serbs in Croatia; 4,500–5,000 mems; Pres. MILAN DUKIĆ.

Slavonian-Baranian Croatian Party (Slavonsko-baranjska hrvatska stranka): Zagreb; internet www.osijek-online.com.

Social Democratic Party (SDP) (Socijaldemokratska Partija Hrvatske—SPH): 10000 Zagreb, trg Iblerov 9; tel. (1) 4552658; fax (1) 4552842; e-mail sdp@sdp.tel.hr; internet www.sdp.hr; fmrly the ruling League of Communists of Croatia (Party of Democratic Reform), renamed as above in 1993; 20,000 mems; Chair. IVICA RAČAN.

Social Democratic Union of Croatia (SDUC) (Socijalno Demokratska Unija Hrvatske—SDUH): 10000 Zagreb, Tratinska 27; tel. and fax (1) 394055; f. 1992; Pres. VLADIMIR BEBIĆ.

Social Democrats of Croatia: 10000 Zagreb, Gunduliaeva 21A/III; tel. (1) 4854261; fax (1) 485428; e-mail ash@hinet.hr; internet www .hinet.hr/ash.

Socialist Party of Croatia (SPC) (Socijalistička Stranka Hrvatske—SSH): 10000 Zagreb, Prisavlje 14; tel. (1) 517835; fax (1) 510235; Pres. ŽELJKO MAŽAR.

Socialist Workers' Party of Croatia (SRPH) (Socijalističke Radničke Partije Hrvatskih): 10000 Zagreb; tel. (1) 483958; e-mail srp@ srp.hr; internet www.srp.hr; f. 1997; Leader STIPE SUVAR.

Zagreb Party (ZP) (Zagreb Stranka—ZS): Zagreb; f. April 2001; aimed to focus on local government issues; Leader MATE MESTROVIĆ.

Diplomatic Representation

EMBASSIES IN CROATIA

Albania: 10000 Zagreb, Jurišićeva 2A; tel. (1) 4810679; fax (1) 4810682; e-mail veleposlanstvo-albanije@zg.tel.hr; Ambassador ARBEN CICI.

Australia: 10000 Zagreb, Nova Ves 11; tel. (1) 4891200; fax (1) 4836606; internet www.auembassy.hr; Ambassador FRANCES NEIL.

Austria: 10000 Zagreb, Jabukovać 39; tel. (1) 4834457; fax (1) 4834461; e-mail austrijsko-veleposlanstvo@alf.tel.hr; internet www .atembassy.hr; Ambassador HANS KNITEL.

Belgium: 10000 Zagreb, Pantovčak 125; tel. (1) 4578901; fax (1) 4578902; Ambassador LUC LIEBAUT.

Bosnia and Herzegovina: 10001 Zagreb, Torbarova 9; tel. (1) 4683761; fax (1) 4683764; e-mail ambasada-bh-zg@zg.tel.hr; Ambassador ZLATKO DIŽDAREVIĆ.

Bulgaria: 10000 Zagreb, Novi Goljak 25; tel. (1) 4823336; fax (1) 4823338; e-mail veleposlanstvo-bugarske1@zg.hinet.hr; Ambassador VICTOR VALKOV.

Canada: 10000 Zagreb, Prilaz Gjure Deželića; tel. (1) 4881200; fax (1) 4881230; e-mail zagreb@dfait-maeci.gc.ca; Ambassador DENNIS A. SNIDER.

Chile: 10000 Zagreb, Smičiklasova 23/II; tel. (1) 4611958; internet www.clembassy.hr; Ambassador JORGE DOPOUY GREZ.

China, People's Republic: 10000 Zagreb, Mlinovi 132; tel. (1) 4637011; fax (1) 4637012; e-mail chnemb@zg.tel.hr; Ambassador ZHI ZHAOLIN.

Czech Republic: 10000 Zagreb, Savska cesta 41; tel. (1) 6177239; fax (1) 6176630; Ambassador PETR BURIANEK.

Egypt: 10000 Zagreb, Tuškanac 58A; tel. (1) 4834272; fax (1) 4834247; Ambassador HELMY BEDEIER.

Finland: 10000 Zagreb, Berislavićeva 2/II; tel. (1) 4811662; fax (1) 4819946; internet www.finembassy.hr; Ambassador ILPO MANNINEN.

France: 10000 Zagreb, Schlosserove stube 5; tel. (1) 4818110; fax (1) 4557765; e-mail presse@ambafrance.hr; internet www.ambafrance .hr; Ambassador FRANCIS BELLANGER.

Germany: 10000 Zagreb, ul. grada Vukovara 64; tel. (1) 6158100; fax (1) 6158103; internet www.deutschebotschaft-zagreb.hr; Ambassador GERHARDT WEISS.

Greece: 10000 Zagreb, Opatička 12; tel. (1) 4810444; fax (1) 4810419; internet www.grembassy.hr; Ambassador CHRISTIAN GEORGES-STAVROS VASSILOPOULOS.

Guinea-Bissau: 10000 Zagreb, Jurjevska 51; tel. (1) 4863500; fax (1) 4663502; Chargé d'affaires a.i. DESIDERIUS OSTROGONAC DA COSTA.

Holy See: 10000 Zagreb, Ksaverska cesta bb 10A; tel. (1) 4673996; fax (1) 4673997; e-mail apostolska.nuncijatura.rh@inet.hr; Apostolic Delegate Most Rev. GIULIO EINAUDI (Titular Archbishop of Villamagna in Tripolitania).

Hungary: 10000 Zagreb, Pantovcak 255–257A; tel. (1) 4890900; fax (1) 4579301; e-mail hungemb-tajnica@hungemb.tel.hr; internet www.hungemb.hr; Ambassador (vacant).

India: 10000 Zagreb, ul. Boškovićeva 7A; tel. (1) 4873240; fax (1) 4817907; e-mail embassy.india@zg.tel.hr; Ambassador KAILASHA LAL AGRAWAL.

Iran: 10000 Zagreb, Pantovčak 125C; tel. (1) 4578981; fax (1) 4578987; Ambassador JAFAR SHAMSIAN.

Italy: 10000 Zagreb, Medulićeva 22; tel. (1) 4846386; fax (1) 4846384; e-mail veleposlanstvo_italije@zg.tel.hr; Ambassador FABIO PIGLIAPOCO.

Japan: 10000 Zagreb, Ksaver 211; tel. (1) 4677755; fax (1) 4677766; Ambassador KANAME IKEDA.

Macedonia, former Yugoslav republic: 10000 Zagreb, Petrinjska 29/I; tel. (1) 4922903; fax (1) 4922902; e-mail amb.makedonije.zgb@zg.tel.hr; Ambassador SERVET AVZIU.

Malaysia: 10000 Zagreb, Slavujevac 4A; tel. (1) 4834346; fax (1) 4834348; Ambassador MOHAMAD BIN SANI.

Netherlands: 10000 Zagreb, Medvešćak 56; tel. (1) 4684880; fax (1) 4684582; e-mail nlgovzag@zg.tel.hr; internet www.netherlandsembassy.hr; Ambassador LIONEL S. VEER.

Norway: 10000 Zagreb, Petrinjska 9; tel. (1) 4922829; fax (1) 4922828; Ambassador KNUT TORAASEN.

Poland: 10000 Zagreb, Krležin Gvozd 3; tel. (1) 4899444; fax (1) 4834576; Ambassador JERZY CHMIELEWSKI.

Portugal: 10000 Zagreb, trg ban J. Jelačića 5/II; tel. (1) 4882210; fax (1) 4920663; Ambassador ANA BARATA.

Romania: 10000 Zagreb, Srebrnjak 150A; tel. (1) 2430137; Ambassador MIHAIL DINUCU.

Russia: 10000 Zagreb, Bosanska 44; tel. (1) 3755038; fax (1) 3755040; e-mail veleposlanstvo-ruske-federacije@zg.tel.hr; Ambassador EDUARD LEONIDOVICH KUZMIN.

Serbia and Montenegro: 10000 Zagreb, Mesićeva 19; tel. (1) 4680552; fax (1) 4680770; e-mail ambasada-sav-rep-jugoslavije@zg.tel.hr; Ambassador MILAN SIMURDIĆ.

Slovakia: 10000 Zagreb, Prilaz Djure Deželića 10; tel. (1) 4848941; fax (1) 4848942; e-mail velep-rep-slovacke-u-rh@zg.tel.hr; Ambassador JÁN PETRÍK.

Slovenia: 10000 Zagreb, Savska cesta 41/II; tel. (1) 6311000; fax (1) 6177236; Ambassador PETER ANDREJ BEKEŠ.

Spain: 10000 Zagreb, Medulićeva 5; tel. (1) 4848603; fax (1) 4848605; Ambassador SEBASTIAN DE ERICE GOMEZ-ACEBO.

Sweden: 10000 Zagreb, Frankopanska 22; tel. (1) 4849322; fax (1) 4849244; e-mail swedish.embassy@zg.tel.hr; Ambassador STURE THEOLIN.

Switzerland: 10000 Zagreb, Bogovićeva 3; tel. (1) 4810891; fax (1) 4810890; e-mail swiemzag@zg.tel.hr; Ambassador PAUL WIDMER.

Turkey: 10000 Zagreb, Masarykova 3/II; tel. (1) 4855200; fax (1) 4855606; e-mail turembzag@zg.tel.hr; Ambassador UFUK TEVFIK OKYAYUZ.

Ukraine: 10000 Zagreb, Voćarska 52; tel. (1) 4616296; fax (1) 4633726; internet www.ukrembassy.hinet.hr; Ambassador VIKTOR A. KYRYK.

United Kingdom: 10000 Zagreb, Vlaska 121; tel. (1) 4555310; fax (1) 4551685; e-mail british-embassy@zg.tel.hr; Ambassador NICHOLAS JARROLD.

USA: 10000 Zagreb, Andrije Hebranga 2; tel. (1) 4555500; fax (1) 4558585; internet www.usembassy.hr; Ambassador RALPH FRANK.

Judicial System

The judicial system of Croatia is administered by the Ministry of Justice. The Constitutional Court consists of 11 judges, elected by the Assembly for a period of eight years. The Supreme Court is the highest judicial body in the country, comprising 26 judges, also elected for a period of eight years.

Public Prosecutor: (vacant).

Ombudsman: 10000 Zagreb, Opatička 4; tel. (1) 4814893.

Constitutional Court of Croatia: 10000 Zagreb, Marka trg 4; tel. (1) 4851276; fax (1) 4550908; internet www.usud.hr; Pres. SMILJO SOKOL.

Supreme Court: 10000 Zagreb, trg Nikole Zrinskog 3; tel. (1) 4810036; fax (1) 4810035; e-mail jsrh@jsrh.hr; Pres. IVICA CRNIĆ.

Office of the Public Prosecutor: 10000 Zagreb, ul. Vinogradska 25; tel. (1) 3712700; fax (1) 3769302; e-mail dorh@zg.hinet.hr.

Religion

Most of the population are Christian, the largest denomination being the Roman Catholic Church, of which most ethnic Croats are adherents. The Archbishop of Zagreb is the most senior Roman Catholic prelate in Croatia. The Croatian Old Catholic Church does not acknowledge the authority of Rome or the papal reforms of the 19th century. There is a significant Serbian Orthodox minority. According to the 1991 census, 76.5% of the population of Croatia were Roman Catholics, 11.1% were Serbian Orthodox, 1.2% Muslims and there were small communities of Protestants and Jews.

CHRISTIANITY

The Roman Catholic Church

For ecclesiastical purposes, Croatia comprises four archdioceses (including one, Zadar, directly responsible to the Holy See) and 11 dioceses (including one for Catholics of the Byzantine rite). At 31 December 2001 there were an estimated 3.8m. adherents.

Latin Rite

Bishops' Conference
10000 Zagreb, Kaptol 22; tel. (1) 4811893; fax (1) 4811894; e-mail tanjnistvo@hbk.hr.
f. 1993; Pres. Mgr JOSIP BOZANIĆ (Archbishop of Zagreb).

Archbishop of Rijeka: Dr IVAN DEVČIĆ, Nadbiskupski Ordinarijat, 51000 Rijeka, Slaviše Vajnera Čiče 2; tel. (51) 337999; fax (51) 215287; e-mail rijecka-nadbiskupija@ri.hinet.hr.

Archbishop of Split-Makarska: MARIN BARIŠIĆ, 21001 Split, pp 328, ul. Zrinjsko-Frankopanska 14; tel. (21) 319523; fax (21) 319522; e-mail marin.barisic@hbk.hr.

Archbishop of Zadar: IVAN PRENDJA, Nadbiskupski Ordinarijat, 23000 Zadar, trg Zeleni 1; tel. (23) 315712; fax (23) 316299; e-mail nadbiskupija.zadarska@zd.te.hr.

Archbishop of Zagreb: JOSIP BOZANIĆ, 10001 Zagreb, pp 553, Kaptol 31; tel. (1) 4894802; fax (1) 4816094; e-mail uzgnadb@zg.hinet.hr.

Byzantine Rite

Bishop of Križevci: SLAVOMIR MIKLOVŠ, Ordinarijat Križevačke Eparhije, 10000 Zagreb, Kaptol 20; tel. (1) 270767; 48,975 adherents (1993).

Old Catholic Church

Croatian Catholic Church: Hrvatska Katolička Crkva Ordinariat, 10000 Zagreb, ul. Kneza Branimira 11; tel. (1) 4841361; f. 894; re-established 1923; Archbishop MIHOVIL DUBRAVČIĆ.

Serbian Orthodox Church

Metropolitan of Zagreb and Ljubljana: Bishop JOVAN, Srpska Biskupija, 10000 Zagreb.

The Press

PRINCIPAL DAILIES

Osijek

Glas Slavonije: 31000 Osijek, Hrvatske Republike 20; tel. (31) 223200; fax (31) 223203; e-mail glas@glas-slavonije.tel.hr; internet www.glas-slavonije.hr; morning; independent; Editor SANJA MARKETIĆ; circ. 25,000.

Pula

Glas Istre: 52100 Pula, Riva 10; tel. (52) 212969; fax (52) 211434; morning; Dir ŽELJKO ŽMAK; circ. 20,000.

Rijeka

Novi List: 51000 Rijeka, POB 130, Zvonimirova 20A; tel. (51) 32122; fax (51) 213654; morning; Editor VELJKO VICEVIĆ; circ. 60,000.

La Voce del Popolo: 51000 Rijeka, Zvonimirova 20A; tel. (51) 211154; fax (51) 213528; e-mail lavoce@edit.hr; f. 1944; morning; Italian; Editor RODOLFO SEGNAN; circ. 4,000.

Split

Nedjeljna Dalmacija: 21000 Split, Gundulićeva 23; tel. (21) 362821; fax (21) 362526; f. 1972; weekly; politics and culture; Editor DRAŽEN GUDIĆ; circ. 45,000.

Slobodna Dalmacija: 21000 Split, ul. Hrvatske mornarice 4; tel. (21) 513888; fax (21) 551220; internet www.slobodnadalmacija.com; morning; Editor Josip Jović; circ. 102,000.

Zagreb

Nedjeljna Dalmacija: 10000 Zagreb, Ilica 24/II; tel. (1) 433716; fax (1) 433916; f. 1972; weekly; politics and culture; Editor-in-Chief Dubravko Grakalić; circ. 45,000.

Novi Vjesnik: 10000 Zagreb, Slavonska Ave. 4; tel. (1) 333333; fax (1) 341650; f. 1940; morning; Editor Radovan Stipetić; circ. 45,000.

Sportske novosti: 10000 Zagreb, Slavonska Ave. 4; tel. (1) 341920; fax (1) 341950; morning; Editor Darko Tironi; circ. 55,000.

Večernji list: 10000 Zagreb, Slavonska Ave. 4; tel. (1) 6500600; fax (1) 6500679; e-mail vecernji@vecernji.net.tel.hr; internet www .vecernji-list.hr; evening; Editor Ružica Cigler; circ. 200,000.

Vjesnik: 10000 Zagreb, Slavonska Ave. 4, POB 104; tel. (1) 342760; fax (1) 341602; internet www.vjesnik.com; morning; Editor Igor Mandić; circ. 50,000.

PERIODICALS

Arena: 10000 Zagreb, Slavonska Ave. 4; tel. (1) 6162795; fax (1) 6161572; e-mail arena@eph.hr; f. 1957; illustrated weekly; Editor Mladen Gerovac; circ. 135,000.

Feral Tribune: 21000 Split; e-mail webmaster@feral.hr; internet www.feral-tribune.com; weekly; satirical; Editor Viktor Ivancić.

Glasnik: 10000 Zagreb, trg hrvatskih velikana 4; tel. (1) 453000; fax (1) 453752; fortnightly; Editor Zdravko Gavran; circ. 9,000.

Globus: 10000 Zagreb, Slavonska Ave. 4; tel. (1) 6162057; fax (1) 6162058; e-mail globus@eph.hr; f. 1990; political weekly; Editor Mirko Galić; circ. 110,000.

Gloria: 10000 Zagreb, Slavonska Ave. 4; tel. (1) 6161288; fax (1) 6182042; e-mail gloria@eph.hr; weekly; Editor Dubravka Tomeković-Aralica; circ. 110,000.

Informator: 10000 Zagreb, Zelinska 3; tel. (1) 6111500; fax (1) 6111446; e-mail informator@informator.hr; internet www .informator.hr; f. 1952; economic and legal matters; Dir Dr Faruk Redžepagić.

Mila: 10000 Zagreb, Slavonska Ave. 4; tel. (1) 6161982; fax (1) 6162021; e-mail mila@eph.hr; weekly; Editor Zoja Padovan; circ. 110,000.

Nacionalni Oglasnik: 10000 Zagreb, Slavonska Ave. 4; tel. (1) 6162061; fax (1) 6161541; weekly; Editor Ivo Pukanić; circ. 55,000.

OK: Croatia: 10000 Zagreb, Slavonska Ave. 4; tel. (1) 6162127; fax (1) 6162125; e-mail ok@eph.hr; f. 1989; illustrated monthly; Editor Neven Kepeski; circ. 55,000.

Privredni vjesnik: 10000 Zagreb, Kačićeva 9a; tel. (1) 422182; fax (1) 422100; f. 1953; weekly; economic; Man. Ante Gavranović; Editor-in-Chief Franjo Žilić; circ. 10,000.

Republika: 10000 Zagreb, trg bana Josipa Jelačića; tel. (1) 274211; fax (1) 434790; f. 1945; monthly; published by Društvo hrvatskih književnika; literary review; Editor-in-Chief Velimir Visković.

Studio: 10000 Zagreb, Slavonska Ave. 4; tel. (1) 6162085; fax (1) 6162031; e-mail studio@eph.hr; f. 1964; illustrated weekly; Editor Robert Naprta; circ. 45,000.

Vikend: 10000 Zagreb, Slavonska Ave. 4; tel. and fax (1) 6162064; 2 a week; Editor Josip Mušnjak; circ. 50,000.

NEWS AGENCIES

HINA News Agency: 10000 Zagreb, trg Marulidev 16; tel. (1) 4808700; fax (1) 4808820; e-mail newsline@hina.hr; internet www .hina.hr; f. 1990; Man. Mirko Bolfek.

IKA (Catholic Information Agency): 10000 Zagreb, Kaptol 4; tel. (1) 4814951; fax (1) 4814957; e-mail ika-zg@zg.tel.hr; internet www.ika .hr; Man. Editor Anton Šuljić.

Publishers

AGM Publisher: 10000 Zagreb, Mihanovićeva 28; tel. (1) 4856307; fax (1) 4856316; Croatian and foreign literature, arts, economics, science; Gen. Dir Bože Čović.

Algoritam: 10000 Zagreb, Gajeva 12; tel. (1) 4803333; fax (1) 271541; e-mail mm@algoritam.hr; international bestsellers; Pres. Neven Antičević.

August Cesarec: 10000 Zagreb, Prilaz Gjure Deželića 57; tel. (1) 171071; fax (1) 573695; Croatian and foreign literature.

Books Trade and Services (BTS) Knjiga Trgovina: 10000 Zagreb, Donji prečac 19; tel. (1) 2421754; fax (1) 2421831; e-mail info@btsltd.com; internet www.btsltd.com; imports and exports publications; Gen. Man. Branko Vuković.

Ceres: 10000 Zagreb, Tomašićeva 13; tel. (1) 4558501; fax (1) 4550387; e-mail ceres@zg.tel.hr; internet www.ceres.hr; poetry, fiction, and philosophical and scientific writings; Gen. Dir Dragutin Dumančić.

Erasmus Publishing: 10000 Zagreb, Rakušina 4; tel. and fax (1) 433114; Croatian literature; Gen. Dir Srećko Lipovčan.

Europa Press: 10000 Zagreb, Slavonska Ave. 4; tel. (1) 6190011; fax (1) 6190033; Dir Marjan Jurleka.

Hena Com: 10000 Zagreb, Horvaćanska 65; tel. and fax (1) 3750206; e-mail hena-com@hena-com.hr; internet www.hena-com.hr; childrens' books; Gen. Man. Uzeir Husković.

Hrvatska Akademija Znanosti i Umjetnosti: 10000 Zagreb, trg Zrinski 11; tel. (1) 4819983; fax (1) 4819979; e-mail kabpred@ mahazu.hazu.hr; f. 1861; publishing dept of the Croatian Academy of Sciences and Arts; Pres. Dr Ivo Padovan.

Izvori: 10000 Zagreb, Trnjanska 64; tel. and fax (1) 6112576; e-mail izvori@iname.com; internet www.bakal.hr/izvori; scientific journalism, literature, comic books.

Kršćanska Sadašnjost: 10001 Zagreb, trg Marulićev 14, POB 434; tel. (1) 4828219; fax (1) 4828227; e-mail ks@zg.tel.hr; internet www .ks.hr; theological publications.

Leksikografski zavod 'Miroslav Krleža' (Miroslav Krleža Lexicographic Institute): 10000 Zagreb, Frankopanska 26; tel. (1) 4800333; fax (1) 4800399; f. 1951; encyclopedias, bibliographies and dictionaries; Pres. Dalibor Brozović.

Masmedia: 10000 Zagreb, ul. baruna Trenka 13; tel. (1) 4577400; fax (1) 4577769; e-mail masmedia@zg.tel.hr; business and professional literature; Gen. Dir Stjepan Andrašić.

Matica Hrvatska (Matrix Croatica): 10000 Zagreb, trg Strossmayerov 2; tel. (1) 4819310; fax (1) 4819319; arts and science; Pres. Prof. Josip Bratulić.

Mladost: 10000 Zagreb, Ilica 30; tel. (1) 453222; fax (1) 434878; f. 1947; fiction, science, art, children's books; Gen. Dir Branko Vuković.

Mosta: 10000 Zagreb, Majevička 12a; tel. (1) 325196; fax (1) 327898; popular fiction; Gen. Dir Nladimir Vučur.

Mozaik Knjiga: 10000 Zagreb, Tomićeva 5a; tel. (1) 425011; fax (1) 431291; educational books; Gen. Dir Nives Tomašević.

Nakladni zavod Matice hrvatske: 10000 Zagreb, ul. Matice hrvatske 2; tel. (1) 4812422; fax (1) 4819317; e-mail nzm@zg.tel.hr; f. 1960; fiction, popular science, politics, economics, sociology, history; Dir Niko Vidović.

Naprijed: 10000 Zagreb, POB 1029, trg bana Jelacica 17; tel. (1) 432026; fax (1) 426897; e-mail naklada-napried@zg.tel.hr; f. 1946; philosophy, psychology, religion, sociology, medicine, dictionaries, children's books, art, politics, economics, tourist guides; Dir Zdenko Ljevak.

Naša Djeca: 10000 Zagreb, Gundulićeva 40; tel. (1) 4856046; fax (1) 4856613; e-mail nasa-djeca@zg.tel.hr; picture books, postcards, etc.; Dir Prof. Drago Kozina.

Nip Školske Novine: 10000 Zagreb, Hebranga 40; tel. (1) 4855709; fax (1) 4855712; education, religion, poetry, textbooks; Gen. Man. Ivan Rodić.

Sims: 10000 Zagreb, Ive Tijardovića 4; tel. (1) 3880500; fax (1) 3880731; e-mail info@sims-hr.com; internet www.simshr.com; exports Croatian and foreign language books; Gen. Man. Ivan Matijević.

Školska Knjiga: 10001 Zagreb, POB 1039, Masarykova 28; tel. (1) 420784; fax (1) 430260; e-mail skolska@skolskaknjiga.hr; education, textbooks, art; Dir Dr Dragomir Maderić.

Tehnička Knjiga: 10000 Zagreb, Jurišićeva 10; tel. (1) 278172; fax (1) 423611; f. 1947; technical literature, popular science, reference books; Gen. Man. Zvonimir Vistrička.

Verbum: 21000 Split, Kraj zlatnih vrata 1; tel. and fax (21) 356770; e-mail verbum@st.tel.hr; religion, philosophy and humanism; Gen. Man. Miro Radalj.

Znanje: 10000 Zagreb, Zvonimirova 17; tel. (1) 4556000; fax (1) 4553652; e-mail znanje@zg.tel.hr; f. 1946; popular science, agriculture, fiction, poetry, essays; Pres. Žarko Šepetavić; Dir Branko Jazbec.

PUBLISHERS' ASSOCIATION

Croatian Publishers' and Authors' Business Union (Poslovna Zajednica Izdavača i Knjižara Hrvatske): 10000 Zagreb, Klaićeva 7; fax (1) 171624.

Broadcasting and Communications

TELECOMMUNICATIONS

Croatian Telecommunications (Hrvatski Telekomunikacije—HT): 10000 Zagreb, Jurišićeva 13; tel. (1) 435435; fax (1) 429000; internet www.ht.hr/index.shtml; f. 1987; 51% owned by Deutsche Telekom (Germany); Pres. IVICA MUDRINIĆ.

BROADCASTING

Radio

Croatian Radio: 10000 Zagreb, HRT House, Dezmanova 6; tel. (1) 4807199; fax (1) 4807190; e-mail medjunrodni_hr@hrt.hr; internet www.hrt.hr; f. 1926; 3 radio stations; 8 regional stations (Sljeme, Osijek, Pula, Rijeka, Split, Zadar, Dubrovnik and Knin); broadcasts in Serbo-Croat, English and Spanish; Dir IVANKA LUCEV.

Radio 101: Zagreb; independent radio station; Editor-in-Chief ZRINKA VRABEC-MOJZES.

Radio Baranja: Beli Manastir; independent radio station; Dir KAROLJ JANESI.

Vaš Otvoreni Radio: 10000 Zagreb, Radnička cesta 27; tel. (1) 6154805; fax (1) 6154802; broadcasts nation-wide.

Television

Croatian Television: 10000 Zagreb, HRT House, Prisavlje 3; tel. (1) 6342634; fax (1) 6343712; e-mail program@hrt.hr; internet www.hrt.hr; f. 1956; 3 channels; broadcasts in Serbo-Croat; Head of TV MIRKO GALIĆ; Editor-in-Chief JASNA ULAGA VALIĆ.

Finance

(A new currency, the kuna (equivalent to 1,000 Croatian dinars), was introduced on 30 May 1994. (d.d. = dioničko društvo (joint-stock company); cap. = capital; res = reserves; dep. = deposits; m. = million; amounts in kuna, unless otherwise indicated; HRD = Croatian dinars; brs = branches))

BANKING

Central Bank

National Bank of Croatia: 10000 Zagreb, trg hrvatskih velikana 3; tel. (1) 4564555; fax (1) 4550726; e-mail webmaster@hnb.hr; internet www.hnb.hr; in 1991 it assumed the responsibilities of a central bank empowered as the republic's bank of issue; cap. 2,500.0m., res 3,311.7m., dep. 28,321.5m. (Dec. 2001); Gov. ŽELJKO ROHATINSKI.

Selected Banks

Croatia Banka d.d.: 10000 Zagreb, Kvaternikov trg 9; tel. (1) 2391111; fax (1) 2332470; e-mail marketing@crbanka.tel.hr; internet www.croatiabanka.hr; f. 1989; cap. 204.6m., res 75.3m., dep. 994.8m. (Dec. 2001); Chair. NIKOLA ŠEREMET; 29 brs.

Croatian Bank for Reconstruction and Development (Hrvatska Banka za Obnovu i Razvoj—HBOR): 10000 Zagreb, Strossmayerov trg 9; tel. (1) 4591696; fax (1) 4591689; e-mail dstimac@hbor.hr; internet www.hbor.hr; f. 1995; cap. 2,972.0m., res 1.1m., dep. 282.2m. (Dec. 2001); Pres. ANTON KOVAČEV.

Dresdner Bank d.d.: 10000 Zagreb, Gajeva 1; tel. (1) 4866777; fax (1) 4866779; e-mail contact.croatia@dresdner-bank.com; internet www.dresdner-bank.hr; f. 1997; cap. 100.0m., res 5.0m., dep. 507.2m. (Dec. 2001); Pres. Dr HANS-JOACHIM GERSMANN.

Dubrovačka Banka d.d., Dubrovnik (Bank of Dubrovnik): 20000 Dubrovnik, put Republike 9; tel. (20) 356333; fax (20) 356778; e-mail dubank@dubank.hr; internet www.dubank.hr; f. 1955; controlled by Dalmatinska Banka d.d. from Feb. 2002; cap. 185.0m., res 73.2m., dep. 2,516.9m. (Dec. 2001); Pres. VLAHO ŠUTIĆ.

Erste and Steiermärkische Bank d.d.: 10000 Zagreb, Varšavska 3–5; tel. (1) 4561999; fax (1) 4561900; e-mail esb@esb.hr; internet www.esb.hr; f. Sept. 2000 by merger of Bjelovarska Banka d.d., Cakoveka Banka d.d. and Trgovačka Banka d.d.; cap. 271.9m., res 149.5m., dep. 2,936.0m. (Dec. 2001); Chair. REINHARD ORTNER.

Hrvatska Poštanska Banka d.d.: 10000 Zagreb, Jurišićeva 4; tel. (1) 4804400; fax (1) 4810773; internet www.hpb.hr; f. 1991; cap. 584.8m., res 157.9m., dep. 1,990.1m. (Dec. 2001); Chair. JOSIP SLADE.

Hypo Alpe-Adria-Bank d.d.: 10000 Zagreb, Koturaška 47; tel. (1) 6103666; fax (1) 6103555; e-mail hypo@hypo.hr; internet www.hypo.hr; f. 1996; cap. 280.4m., res 26.2m., dep. 4,158.9m. (Dec. 2001); Chair. MAG GUENTER STRIEDINGER.

Istarska Kreditna Banka Umag d.d.: 52470 Umag, Ernesta Miloša 1; tel. (52) 702300; fax (52) 741275; e-mail marketing@ikb.hr; internet www.ikb.hr; f. 1956; commercial and joint-stock bank; controlled by Dalmatinska Banka d.d.; cap. 64.9m., res 46.3m., dep. 961.5m. (Dec. 2001); Chair. MIRO DODIĆ; 16 brs.

Karlovačka Banka d.d: 47000 Karlovac, Ivana Gorana Kovačića 1; tel. (47) 611540; fax (47) 614206; e-mail karlovacka.banka@hinet.hr; internet www.kaba.hr; f. 1955; cap. 57.4m., res 11.1m., dep. 730.6m. (2001); Pres. SANDA CVITESIĆ.

Kreditna Banka Zagreb d.d.: 10000 Zagreb, ul. grada Vukovara 74; tel. (1) 6167333; fax (1) 6116466; e-mail kbz-uprava@kbz.hr; internet www.kbz.hr/kbz; f. 1994; cap. 132.0m., res 24.1m., dep. 452.0m. (Dec. 2001); Pres. RUDO MIKULIĆ.

Medimurska Banka d.d., Čakovec: 40000 Čakovec, Valenta Morandinija 37; tel. (40) 370676; fax (40) 370505; e-mail info@mb.hr; internet www.mb.hr; f. 1954; cap. 127.9m., res 20.3m., dep. 1,074.4m. (Dec. 2000); Pres. MLADENA GOMBAR.

Nova Kreditna Banka Maribor d.d.: 2505 Maribor, Vita Kraigherja 4; tel. (2) 2292290; fax (2) 2524371; e-mail info@nkbm.si; internet www.nkbm.si; f. 1955 as Komunalna Banka Maribor; cap. 5,600m., res 33,859m., dep. 365,924m. (Dec. 2001); Pres. CRTOMIR MESARIĆ.

Privredna Banka Zagreb d.d.: 10000 Zagreb, POB 1032, Račkoga 6; tel. (1) 4723344; fax (1) 4723131; e-mail pbz@pbz.hr; internet www.pbz.hr; f. 1966; commercial bank; cap. 1,666m., res 368m., dep. 16,254m. (Dec. 2000); Chief Exec. BOZO PRKA; 28 brs.

Raiffeisenbank Austria d.d.: 10000 Zagreb, POB 651, ul. Petrinjska 59; tel. (1) 4566466; fax (1) 4811624; e-mail rba@rba.tel.hr; internet www.rba.hr; cap. 240.0m., res 24.8m., dep. 6,386.5m. (Dec. 2001); Chair. ZDENKO ADROVIĆ.

Riadria Banka d.d.: 51000 Rijeka, Dure Šporera 3; tel. (51) 3567777; fax (51) 211095; e-mail riadra-banka@ri.tel.hr; internet www.riab.hr; f. 1992; cap. 165.8m., res 20.4m., dep. 1,390.1m. (Dec. 2001); Pres. and CEO VESNA BADURINA.

Riječka Banka d.d.: 51000 Rijeka, POB 300, trg Jadranski 3A; tel. (51) 208211; fax (51) 330525; e-mail drazen.kurpisl@rbri.tel.hr; internet www.rbri.hr; f. 1954 as Komunalna banka i štedionica, renamed 1967; acquired by Erste Bank (Austria) in April 2002; cap. 503.3m., res 102.3m., dep. 7,910.4m. (Dec. 2001); Pres. CHRISTIAN CORETH; 15 brs.

Slavonska Banka d.d., Osijek (Bank of Slavonia): 31000 Osijek, POB 108, Kapucinska 29; tel. (31) 231231; fax (31) 201039; e-mail slbo@slbo.hr; internet www.slbo.hr; f. 1989; cap. 75.0m., res 165.0m., dep. 1,183.6m. (Dec. 2000); Pres. IVAN MIHALJEVIĆ; 9 brs.

Splitska Banka d.d. Split: 21000 Split, Boškovića 16; tel. (21) 312560; fax (21) 312586; e-mail info@splitskabanka.hr; internet www.splitskabanka.hr; f. 1966; cap. 363.5m., res 134.0m., dep. 6,989.8m. (Dec. 2001); Pres. ANTON KNETT.

Varaždinska Banka d.d.: 42000 Varaždin, POB 95, trg Kapucinski 5; tel. (42) 400000; fax (42) 400742; internet www.banka.hr; f. 1869; adopted current name 1981; cap. 164.7m., res 288.5m., dep. 2,711.1m. (Dec. 2001); Pres. MATO LUKINIĆ; 17 brs.

Volksbank d.d.: 10000 Zagreb, Varšavska 9; tel. (1) 4801300; fax (1) 4801365; e-mail info@volksbank.tel.hr; internet www.volksbank.hr; f. 1997; cap. 70.2m., res 10.6m., dep. 694.0m. (Dec. 2001); Chair. HEINRICH ANGELIDES.

Zagrebačka Banka Zagreb d.d. (Bank of Zagreb): 10000 Zagreb, Paromlinska 2; tel. (1) 6104000; fax (1) 6110555; e-mail zaba@zaba.hr; internet www.zaba.hr; f. 1913; cap. 1,096m., res 724m., dep. 37,903m. (Dec. 2001); Chair. FRANJO LUKOVIĆ; 150 brs.

Bankers' Organization

Croatian Banking Association: 10000 Zagreb, Centar Kaptol, Nova Ves 17; tel. (1) 4860080; fax (1) 4860081; e-mail info@hub.hr; internet www.hub.hr; Man. Dir Dr ZORAN BOHACEK.

STOCK EXCHANGE

Zagreb Stock Exchange: 10000 Zagreb, Ksaver 208; tel. (1) 428455; fax (1) 420293; e-mail zeljko.kardum@zse.hr; internet www.zse.hr; f. 1990; Gen. Man. MARINKO PAPUGA.

INSURANCE

Croatia Osiguranje: 35000 Slavonski Brod, Matije Gupca 29; tel. and fax (35) 214131; e-mail info@festung.hr; internet www.festung.hr; f. 1884; state-owned; scheduled for privatization in 2002.

Merkur Osiguranje: 10000 Zagreb, ul. grada Vukovara 237; tel. (1) 6308333; fax (1) 6157130; internet www.merkur.hr.

Trade and Industry

GOVERNMENT AGENCY

Croatian Investment Promotion Agency: 10000 Zagreb, World Trade Center Bldg, Ave. Dubrovnik 15; tel. (1) 6555333; fax (1) 6554563; e-mail hapu@zg.tel.hr; internet www.tel.hr.

Croatian Privatization Fund: 10000 Zagreb, Ivana Lučića 6; tel. (1) 4569111; fax (1) 4596294; e-mail hfp@hfp.hr; internet www.hfp.hr; f. 1994 by merger of the Croatian Fund for Development and the Restructuring and Development Agency; Chair. HRVOJE VOJKOVIĆ.

CHAMBERS OF COMMERCE

Croatian Chamber of Economy (Hrvatska Gospodarska Komora): 10000 Zagreb, trg Rooseveltov 2; tel. (1) 4561555; fax (1) 4828380; e-mail hgk@alf.hr; internet www.hgk.hr; Pres. NADAN VIDO-ŠEVIĆ.

Zagreb Chamber of Commerce: 10000 Zagreb, Draškovićeva 45; tel. (1) 4606777; fax (1) 4606813; e-mail hgk-zagreb@hgk.hr; internet www.hgk.hr; f. 1852.

UTILITIES

Electricity

HEP—Hrvatska Elektroprivreda d.d.: 10000 Zagreb, Ave. Vukovar 37; tel. (1) 6322111; fax (1) 6170430; e-mail ivo.covic@hep.hr; internet www.hep.hr; f. 1990; production and distribution of electricity; scheduled for privatization in 2002; Dir IVO COVIĆ.

Gas

Gradska Plinara: 10000 Zagreb, Radnička 1; tel. (1) 6302333; fax (1) 6184653; f. 1862; municipal and regional distribution of natural gas; Dir IVAN VULAS.

INA—Naftaplin: 10020 Zagreb, Većeslava Holjevca 10; tel. (1) 6450000; fax (1) 6452100; internet www.ina.hr; subsidiary of Industrija Nafte d.d.; exploration of petroleum, natural-gas and geothermal energy; agreement on purchase of 25% of shares by the Hungarian Oil and Gas Co Ltd signed in July 2003; Chair. TOMISLAV DRAGICEVIĆ.

Water

Hrvatske Vode: 10000 Zagreb, Vukovara 220; tel. (1) 6307333; fax (1) 6151388; e-mail du.vode@zg.hinet.hr; internet www.voda.hr; f. 1995; state water management organization; Dir ŠTEPAN ŠTURLAN.

MAJOR ENTERPRISES AND COMPANIES

Agrokor d.d.: 10000 Zagreb, trg Dražena Petrovića 3; tel. (1) 4894111; fax (1) 4894080; e-mail agrokor@agrokor.tel.hr; internet www.agrokor.hr; f. 1989; production of flowers, cereals, cattle feed, comestibles and wood products; Pres. IVICA TODORIĆ; 134 employees.

Belišće d.d.: 54551 Belišće, trg Ante Starčevića 1; tel. (31) 663116; fax (31) 663562; f. 1884; manufacture of pulp; Man. Dir JOSIP LULIĆ; 3,255 employees.

Belupo d.o.o.: 43300 Koprivnica, Delekovečka cesta bb; tel. (48) 622910; fax (48) 622996; e-mail belupo@belupo.hr; internet www.belupo.hr; f. 1971; manufacture and sale of pharmaceutical and veterinary products; Man. Dir NIKOLA FELAK; 805 employees.

Bilokalnik Industrija Papirne Ambalze d.o.o: 43300 Koprivnica, Pavelinska bb; tel. (48) 647555; fax (48) 647498; e-mail ipau.bilokalnik@bilokalnik.tel.hr; internet www.bilokalnik.tel.hr; f. 1991; cardboard packaging; Man. Dir JURAJ ŠPANIČEK; 934 employees.

Brodogradilište 'Viktor Lenać' (Victor Lenać Shipyard): 51001 Rijeka, POB 210, Martinšćica bb; tel. (51) 216255; fax (51) 217033; e-mail viktor.nagt@ri.tel.hr; internet www.zse.hr/listed1/vlenac.html; f. 1947; private ownership; builds, repairs and services ships; Pres. GIANCARLO ZACCHELLO; 541 employees.

Brodomerkur d.d.: 21000 Split, Poljička cesta 35; tel. (21) 301330; fax (21) 460824; e-mail brodomerkur@st.tel.hr; internet www.brodomerkur.com; f. 1946; import and export of goods; Pres. ANTE LETICA; 785 employees.

Brodosplit–Brodogradilište (Split Shipyard): 21000 Split, put Supavla 21; tel. (21) 345955; fax (21) 589269; e-mail ivp@brodosplit.hb.hr; internet www.brodosplit.hb.hr; f. 1922; design, manufacture and repair of vessels; Gen. Man. VINKO ROSIĆ; 3,400 employees.

Crosco d.o.o. (Crosco Integrated Drilling and Well Service Co Ltd): 10000 Zagre, ul. grada Vukovara 18; tel. (1) 3652333; fax (1) 3096448; e-mail marketing.crosco@crosco.tel.hr; internet www.crosco.com; f. 1997; state-owned; Pres. MARIN KOCEIĆ; 2,500 employees.

Dalekovod d.d. production: 10040 Velika Gorica, Vukomericka bb; tel. (1) 6228111; fax (1) 6221199; e-mail product.dal@dalekovod.hr; internet www.dalekovod.hr; f. 1949; hardware fittings for overhead transmission lines; Gen. Man. LUKA MILIČIC; 1,384 employees.

Dalmacijacement d.d.: 21212 Kaštel Sućurac, cesta bb; tel. (21) 211466; fax (21) 211255; f. 1861; production of cement; partially privatized in 1998; Man. Dir VINKO JANJAK; 1,400 employees.

Diona d.d.: 10000 Zagreb, Donje Svetice 127; tel. (1) 2394777; fax (1) 2394704; e-mail diona@diona.hr; internet www.diona.hr; f. 1960; retail sale in non-specialized stores, predominantly selling food, beverages and tobacco; operation of supermarkets; Man. Dir DJURO HORVAT; 2,324 employees.

ECS-Eurocomputer Systems: 10000 Zagreb, Maksimirska 120; tel. (1) 2236344; fax (1) 2303374; e-mail delimir.purgar@ecs.hr; internet www.ecs.hr.

Elcon d.d.: 41247 Ziatar Bistrica, ul. Josep Kras 3; tel. (49) 463222; fax (49) 463020; e-mail uprava@elcon-dd.hr; f. 1971; automobile wholesalers; Pres. STJEPAN MUHEK; 880 employees.

Elektrokontakt: 10000 Zagreb, Radnička bb 11; tel. (1) 2330866; fax (1) 220847; e-mail ekz-informatika@ekz.tel.hr; manufacturers of electrical equipment; Man. Dir VLADIMIR FERDELJI; 1,545 employees.

Elektroprojekt: 10000 Zagreb, Alexandera von Humboldta 4; tel. (1) 6307777; fax (1) 6152686; e-mail ured.gd@elektroprojekt.tel.hr; internet www.elektroprojekt.hr; construction; Dir KRUNO GALIĆ.

Elka d.d.: 10000 Zagreb, Žitnjak bb; tel. (1) 2404200; fax (1) 2404898; e-mail elka-marketing@elka.hr; internet www.elka.hr; f. 1927; manufacture of insulated wire and cable; partially privatized in 1998; Chair. MARJAN PEJEIĆ; 999 employees.

Ericsson Nikola Tesla: 10000 Zagreb, Krapinska 45; tel. (1) 354055; fax (1) 328540; e-mail etkpeos@etk.ericsson.se; internet www.etk.ericsson.se; f. 1995; development, design, manufacture and installation of telecommunications systems and equipment; Pres. PER OLOV SJÖSTEDT; 1,850 employees.

Exportdrvo d.d.: 10000 Zagreb, Maruličev trg 18; tel. (1) 4560222; fax (1) 4829942; e-mail exportdrvo@exportdrvo.hr; internet www.exportdrvo.hr; production of timber, wood products and paper; Man. Dir MARKO ŽUPAN.

Finvest Corp d.d.: 51306 Cabar, Ivana Gorana Kovačica 24; tel. (51) 821007; fax (51) 821225; f. 1993; production of industrial gases and of wooden products; Man. Dir MARIJAN FILIPOVIĆ; 900 employees.

Heruc d.d.: 10000 Zagreb, Petračićeva 4; tel. (1) 393377; fax (1) 393380; f. 1950; textile manufacturers, road-freight operators, hotel operators; Man. Dir DRAGUTIN BIONDIĆ; 1,185 employees.

Hrvatske Šume d.o.o.: 10000 Zagreb, Ljudevita F. Vukotinovića 2; tel. (1) 4804111; fax (1) 4804101; internet www.hrsume.hr; f. 1990; forestry and logging; Dir IVAN TARNAJ; 10,164 employees.

Industrija Nafte d.d.: 10000 Zagreb, Ave. Veceslava Holjevca 10; tel. (1) 6450000; fax (1) 6505110; internet www.ina.hr; f. 1963; production and refining of petroleum; Chair. Dr TOMISLAV DRAGIĆEVIĆ; 13,600 employees.

Industogradnja d.d.: 10000 Zagreb, Savska cesta 66; tel. (1) 6176211; fax (1) 6176386; e-mail davorin.tepes@industrogradnja.tel.hr; internet www.industrogradnja.tel.hr; f. 1980; construction, engineering; Dir MATO ČOP; 4,931 employees.

Jelen d.d.: 42300 Čakovec, Zagrebačka 93; tel. (40) 384311; fax (40) 384318; e-mail jelen@jelen.com; internet www.jelen.com; f. 1959; manufacturers of footwear and leather products; Dir IVAN KUSTER; 920 employees.

Kamensko d.d.: 10000 Zagreb, Reljkovićeva 8; tel. (1) 3778822; fax (1) 578607; f. 1949; manufacture and sale of clothes and other merchandise; Man. Dir KARLO PAVIČIĆ; 2,074 employees.

Karlovačka Industrija Obuce d.o.o.: 47000 Karlovac, Marmontova Aleja 6; tel. (47) 331699; fax (47) 335330; f. 1991; shoe manufacturers and retailers; Chair. WALTER WOLF; 364 employees.

Končar-Elektroindustrija d.d. (Končar Industrial Group): 10000 Zagreb, Fallerovo šetalište 22; e-mail koncarhead@koncar1.tel.hr; internet www.koncar.hr; manufacture and sale of industrial equipment; Chair. NEVEN MIMIĆA; 4,000 employees.

Konzum d.d.: 10000 Zagreb, M. Ćavića 1A; tel. (1) 2482000; fax (1) 2482010; f. 1949; general merchandise manufacturers and retailers; Man. Dir ANTE PAIC-MAJDIĆ; 2,291 employees.

Kraš: 10000 Zagreb, Maksimirska 130; tel. (1) 2396111; fax (1) 222084; e-mail info@kras.hr; internet www.kras.hr; f. 1911; processing and manufacture of confectionery products; partially privatized in 1998; Man. Dir BORIS MARCAĆ; 2,014 employees.

Lura d.d.: 10000 Zagreb, ul. grada Vukovara 271/11; tel. (1) 6169700; fax (1) 6040565; e-mail lurainfo@lura.hr; internet www.luragroup.hr; production and export of dairy products and fruit juices; Chair. LUKA RAJIĆ; 1,600 employees.

Medimurška Trikotaža Čakovec—MTČ d.d.: 40000 Čakovec, Matice Hrvatske 10; tel. (40) 810055; fax (40) 815916; f. 1946; manufacture of clothing; Dir ALOJZ HUDIČEK; 530 employees.

Montmontaža d.d.: 10000 Zagreb, Rakitnica 2; tel. (1) 6168700; fax (1) 6168731; e-mail montmontaz@cro-mont.tel.hr; f. 1950; construction of plants, industries and power-stations; Pres. NIKOLA LISICAR; 3,700 employees.

Oriolik d.d.: 43000 Oriovac, Mate Grabica 11–13; tel. (55) 431000; fax (55) 431215; internet www.oriolik.hr; f. 1959; furniture-maker; Man. Dir STJEPAN PLSONIĆ; 900 employees.

Pamucna Industrija Duga Resa d.d.: 47250 Duga Resa, ul. Josefa Jeruzalema 8; tel. (47) 841423; fax (47) 841421; e-mail pamucna@ka.tel.hr; internet www.miltonia.com/pamucna; f. 1884; clothing manufacturers; Man. Dir ANTON GRGURIĆ; 1,250 employees.

Petrokemija d.d.: 44320 Kutina, Aleja Vukovar 4; tel. (44) 647122; fax (44) 680882; e-mail uprava@petrokemija.tel.hr; internet www .petrokemija.tel.hr; Man. Dir JOSIP JAGUŠT; 3,085 employees.

Pik Vrbovec—Mesna Industrija d.d.: 10340 Vrbovec, Zagrebačka 148; tel. (1) 894777; fax (1) 891863; internet www.pik-vrbovec.hr; f. 1962; produces meat and meat products; Dir RADKO DOMINIKOVIĆ; 1,790 employees.

Pliva d.d.: 10000 Zagreb, ul. grada Vukovara 49; tel. (1) 6120999; fax (1) 6111011; internet www.pliva.hr; f. 1921; partially privatized in 1996; manufacture of pharmaceuticals, animal-health and agrochemical products, foodstuffs and cosmetic and hygiene products; Chair. ŽELKO ČOVIĆ; 6,035 employees.

Podravka d.d.: 48001 Koprivnica, Ante Starčevića 32; tel. (48) 621027; fax (48) 622518; e-mail podravka@podravka.hr; internet www.podravka.com; f. 1947; manufacture of food products and pharmaceuticals; partially privatized in 1998; Pres. DARKO MARINAČ; 6,834 employees.

Pomgrad d.d.: 21000 Split, ul. Ivana Gundulica 25; tel. (21) 341288; fax (21) 349061; e-mail mladen.skomrlj@pomgrad.hr; f. 1947; civil engineering; Man. Dir MLADEN SKOMRLJ; 1,078 employees.

Tempo d.d.: 10000 Zagreb, Boškovićeva 5; tel. (1) 4873337; fax (1) 4873197; e-mail tempo@zg.tel.hr; internet www.tel.hr; construction and sale of housing; Gen. Dir ZVONIMIR POGAČIĆ; 1,000 employees.

Tep d.d.: 10000 Zagreb, Medarska 69; tel. (1) 3782222; fax (1) 156539; e-mail tep@zg.tel.hr; f. 1949; manufacturers of electrical lighting and heating devices; Pres. MARIJAN RAJIĆ; 580 employees.

Top d.d.: 41431 Samobor, Kerestinečka cesta 57; tel. (1) 871801; fax (1) 871031; f. 1922; aluminium production; Man. Dir MIROSLAVA KOLIĆ; 963 employees.

Tvin d.d.: 43400 Virovitica, Zbora Narodne Garde 6; tel. (33) 742219; fax (33) 742211; e-mail tvin1@vt.tel.hr; internet www.tel.hr/tvin; f. 1913; furniture makers; Man. Dir IVAN SLAMIĆ; 1,248 employees.

Tvornica Duhana Zagreb d.d.: 10000 Zagreb, bb Jagićeva; tel. (1) 571064; fax (1) 3771359; f. 1817; cigarette and tobacco manufacturers; Man. Dir MILAN REBAĆ; 2,500 employees.

(Tvornica Željezničkih Vozila) GREDELJ d.o.o. (TŽV): 10000 Zagreb, Trnjanska 1; tel. (1) 6134622; fax (1) 6110121; e-mail gredelj@tzv-gredelj.hr; internet www.tzv-gredelj.hr; f. 1894; manufacture and maintenance of railway and tramway locomotives and rolling stocks; Dir DAMIR ŠTEFAN; 1,780 employees.

Uljanik Brodogradilište d.d.: 52100 Pula, Flaciusova 1; tel. (52) 214110; fax (52) 211563; e-mail rudjero.batelic@uljanik.tel.hr; internet www.shipyard.uljanik.hr; f. 1856; shipbuilding and repairs; Dir KARLO RADOLOVIĆ; 2,076 employees.

Vesna Modna Zenska Konfekcija d.d.: 10000 Zagreb, Nova cesta 57; tel. (1) 561271; fax (1) 321889; f. 1954; clothes and textiles manufacturers; Man. Dir MIJO PETRICEK; 800 employees.

Viadukt: 10000 Zagreb, Kranjčevićeva 2; tel. (1) 3668284; fax (1) 3668305; e-mail info@viadukt.com; internet www.viadukt.com; f. 1947; civil engineering; Dir DURO DEKANOVIĆ; 1,600 employees.

Zadranka d.d.: 23000 Zadar, Uvala Bregdetti 23; tel. (23) 312112; fax (23) 436200; f. 1946; general wholesalers; Man. Dir ANTE MARASOVIĆ; 711 employees.

Zeljezara Sisak (Sisak Steelworks): 44010 Sisak, Božidara Adžije 19; tel. (44) 565202; fax (44) 565090; e-mail svetozar.krotin@zs-nova .hr; internet www.tel.hr/zlisisak; f. 1938; manufacture of seamless and welded pipes and tubes; metal products; Man. Dir STJEPAN PAULIN; 1,730 employees.

TRADE UNIONS

Confederation of Independent Trade Unions of Croatia: 10000 Zagreb; f. 1990; 40,000 mems; Pres. DAVOR JURIĆ.

Croatian Co-operate Union: 1000 Zagreb, Amruševa 8; tel. (1) 4922935; fax (1) 4922936; e-mail predsjednik@hzs.hr.

Croatian Employers Association: 1000 Zagreb, Pavla Hatza 12; tel. (1) 4897555; fax (1) 4897556; e-mail hup@hup.hr; internet www .hup.hr; Gen. Dir ŽELJKO IVANČEVIĆ.

Union of Autonomous Trade Unions of Croatia: 10000 Zagreb, trg kralja Petra Krešimira 2; tel. (1) 4655013; fax (1) 4655040; e-mail sssh@sssh.hr; internet www.sssh.hr; f. 1990; 26 branch unions with some 500,000 mems; Pres. DAVOR JURIĆ.

Workers' Trade Union Association of Croatia: 1000 Zagreb, Ilića Kralja Držislava 4/1; tel. (1) 4612896; fax (1) 4612896; e-mail ursh@inet.hr; internet www.ursh.hr.

Transport

RAILWAYS

In 2001 there were an estimated 2,726 km of railway lines in Croatia, and 36% of the rail network was electrified in 1995. In mid-1996 railway links between Croatia and Serbia, via Eastern Slavonia, were reopened. In May 2000 the Government announced plans for the modernization of railroad linking Rijeka and Budapest, Hungary.

Croatian Railways Ltd (Hrvatske Željeznice p.o.): 10000 Zagreb, Mihanovićeva 12; tel. (1) 4577111; fax (1) 4577730; f. 1990 as Hrvatsko Željezničko poduzeće, renamed 1992; state-owned; public railway transport, construction, modernization and maintenance of railway vehicles; Pres. DAVOR ŠTERN; Gen. Dir DRAGUTIN ŠUBAT.

ROADS

The Road Fund is responsible for the planning, construction, maintenance and rehabilitation of all interurban roads in Croatia. In 2001 there were an estimated 28,275 km of roads in Croatia, of which 429 km were motorways; there were 7,427 km of main roads and 10,499 km of secondary roads in 2000. A project to construct a 75 km motorway linking Dragonje, near the Slovenian border, with Pula in southern Istria was completed in the late 1990s. In October 2001 the European Bank for Reconstruction and Development (EBRD) pledged some US $80m. to Croatia for the construction of a Rijecka–Zagreb highway; the road was due for completion in 2004. In June 2000 Croatia and Bosnia and Herzegovina signed a statement on the construction of the Ploče–Budapest transport corridor, to link Croatia with Hungary, via Bosnia and Herzegovina. The construction of this 'C5' corridor was to end the isolation of Croatia's southern areas and ensure the optimal use of Ploče's port capacity. More than 130 km of new and rehabilitated highway, connecting the northern borders of the country with the south, were opened in mid-2003. Further sections, including 338 km of road connecting Zagreb with Split, were scheduled for completion by mid-2005.

Croatian Roads Authority (Hrvatske Ceste): 10000 Zagreb, Vončinina 3; tel. (1) 445422; fax (1) 445215; f. 1991; state-owned; maintenance, construction and reconstruction of public roads; Pres. J. ZAVOREO; Man. Dir ALEKSANDAR ČAKLOVIĆ.

SHIPPING

Atlantska Plovidba d.d.: 20000 Dubrovnik, od sv. Mihajla 1; tel. (20) 412666; fax (20) 20384; f. 1974; Dir ANTE JERKOVIĆ.

Croatia Line: 51000 Rijeka, POB 379, Riva 18; tel. (51) 205111; fax (51) 335811; e-mail erc.hr@croatialine.com; internet www .croatialine.com; f. 1986; cargo and passenger services; chartering and tramp service; Gen. Man. DARIO VUKIĆ; 368 employees.

Jadrolinija (Adriatic Shipping Line): 51000 Rijeka, Riva 16; tel. (51) 666111; fax (51) 213116; e-mail jadrolinija@jadrolinija.hr; internet www.jadrolinija.hr; f. 1872; regular passenger and car-ferry services between Italian, Greek and Croatian ports; Pres. SLAVKO LONČAR.

Jadroplov: 21000 Split, Obala kneza Branimira 16; tel. (21) 302666; fax (21) 342198; f. 1984; fleet of 17 vessels and 1,500 containers engaged in linear and tramp service; Gen. Man. NIKŠA GIOVANELLI.

Slobodna Plovidba: 22000 Šibenik, Drage 2; tel. (22) 23755; fax (22) 27860; f. 1976; transport of goods by sea; tourism services; Dir VITOMIR JURAGA.

Tankerska Plovidba d.d.: 23000 Zadar, Božidara Petranovića 4; tel. (23) 202202; fax (23) 202375; internet www.tankerska.hr; f. 1976; Dir STANKO BANIĆ; 1,283 employees.

CIVIL AVIATION

There are 10 international airports in Croatia.

Croatia Airlines: 10000 Zagreb, Savska 41; tel. (1) 6160066; fax (1)

6176845; e-mail pr@ctn.tel.hr; internet www.croatiaairlines.com; f. 1989 as Zagreb Airlines; name changed 1990; operates domestic services and 16 international routes to European destinations; Pres. IVAN MIŠETIĆ.

Tourism

The attractive Adriatic coast and the country's 1,185 islands made Croatia a very popular tourist destination before the 1990s. However, the civil conflict of the early 1990s greatly reduced tourist activity in the country. The industry showed signs of recovery after 1992, with foreign tourist arrivals reaching some 4.1m. in 1998. Revenue generated by tourism in 1998 reached US $2,733m. In 1999, however, foreign tourist arrivals declined to 3.8m., owing to the conflict in Kosovo, the Federal Republic of Yugoslavia, in March–June. In that year income from tourism declined to $2,493m. In 2000 foreign tourist arrivals recovered to 5.8m. and revenue from tourism to $2,758m., and the number of foreign tourist arrivals increased further, to 6.5m. in 2001 and to 6.9m. in 2002.

Croatian National Tourist Board: 10000 Zagreb, Ilica 1A; tel. (1) 4556455; fax (1) 4816757; e-mail info@htz.hr; internet www.htz.hr/text_e/htz.htm.

Generalturist: 10000 Zagreb, Praška 5; tel. (1) 4805555; fax (1) 4810420; e-mail generalturist@generalturist.com; f. 1923; renamed 1963; 17 brs.

Jadran-Turist d.d.: 55210 Rovinj, V. Nazora 6; tel. (52) 800300; fax (52) 800376; e-mail jadrantur-rovinj@pu.tel.hr; internet www.istra.com/rovinj/jadranturist; f. 1954; Dir IVAN SORIĆ.

Culture

Armed hostilities between Serbs and Croats during the 1991–95 civil war caused extensive damage to Croatia's cultural heritage, most notably to the medieval quarter of Dubrovnik. The UN Educational, Scientific and Cultural Organization (UNESCO) announced a programme for the restoration of the heritage institutions of Dubrovnik, which was ongoing in 2003.

NATIONAL ORGANIZATIONS

Ministry of Culture: see section on The Government (Ministries).

State Directorate for the Protection of Cultural and Natural Heritage: 10000 Zagreb, Ilica 44; tel. (1) 431150; fax (1) 431515; f. 1910; Dir MIHO MILJANIĆ.

Regional Institute for the Preservation of Historical Monuments: 21000 Split, Porinova 2; tel. (21) 305444; fax (21) 305418; Dir Dr JOŠKO BELAMARIĆ.

CULTURAL HERITAGE

Archaeological Museum of Split (Arheološki muzej u Splitu): 21000 Split, Zrinjsko–Frankopanska 25; tel. (21) 44574; fax (21) 44685; e-mail arheoloski-muzej-st@st.tel.hr; f. 1820; Dir Prof. EMILIO MARIN.

City Museum of Zagreb (Muzej grada Zagreba): 10000 Zagreb, Opatička 20–22; tel. and fax (1) 4851359; e-mail muzej-grada-zagreba@mgz.tel.hr; f. 1907; Dir Prof. VINKO IVIĆ.

Croatian Academy of Sciences and Arts: 10000 Zagreb, Zrinski trg 11; tel. (1) 4872902; fax (1) 4819979; e-mail kabpred@hazu.hr; internet www.hazu.hr; Pres. IVO PADOVAN; Sec.-Gen. ANDRIJA KAŠTELAN.

Croatian National History Museum: 10000 Zagreb, Demetrova 1; tel. (1) 4851700; fax (1) 4851644; e-mail hpm@hpm.hr; internet www.hp.hr; Dir NIKOLA TVRTKOVIĆ.

Croatian State Archives (Hrvatski državni arhiv): 10000 Zagreb, Marulićev trg 21; tel. (1) 4829244; fax (1) 4829000; e-mail hda@arhiv.hr; f. 1643; documents dating from the 10th century, concerning the history of Croatia; Croatian film archives; library of 160,000 vols, collection of microfilms and photographs; Dir JOSIP KOLANOVIĆ.

Fine Arts Archives: 10000 Zagreb, Demetrova 18; tel. (1) 4851880; e-mail arlikum@hazu.hr; internet www.mahazu.hazu.hr; Dir Prof. VELIMIR NEIDHARDT.

Gallery of Modern Art (Moderna Galerija): 10000 Zagreb, Andrije Hebranga 1; tel. and fax (1) 433802; f. 1905; 19th- and 20th-century Croatian arts; collections of painting, sculpture and graphic arts; Dir Prof. IGOR ZIDIĆ.

Historical Museum of Croatia (Hrvatski povijesni muzej): 10000 Zagreb, Matoševa 9; tel. (1) 4851900; fax (1) 4851909; e-mail hismus@zg.tel.hr; f. 1846; Dir Prof. ANKICA PANDŽIĆ.

Museum of Contemporary Art (Muzej suvremene umjetnosti): 10000 Zagreb, Habdelićeva 2; tel. (1) 4851930; fax (1) 4851931; e-mail msu@msu.hr; internet www.msu.hr; f. 1954; fmrly Zagreb City Galleries; controls: Gallery of Contemporary Art; Benko Horvat Collection (antique and Renaissance art); Dir SNJEŽANA PINTARIĆ.

Museum of Modern Art (Moderna Galerija Rijeka): 51000 Rijeka, Dolac 1/II; tel. (51) 334280; fax (51) 330982; e-mail moderna-galerija-rijeka@ri.tel.hr; internet www.mgr.hr; f. 1948; national and international collection, international exhibition of drawings, Biennale of Young Mediterranean Artists; Dir DUJMOVIĆ KOSOVAC.

Strossmayer Gallery of Old Masters (Strossmayerova galerija starih majstora): 10000 Zagreb, trg Nikole Šubića Zrinskog 11; tel. (1) 4895115; fax (1) 4819979; e-mail sgallery@hazu.hr; internet www.mdc.hr/strossmayer; f. 1884; 14th to 19th centuries; Dir DURO VANDURA; 4,000 vols.

Zagreb Archaeological Museum (Arheološki muzej u Zagrebu): 10000 Zagreb, trg Nikole Šubića Zrinskog 19; tel. (1) 4873102; fax (1) 427724; e-mail amz@zg.tel.hr; internet www.arheoloski.hr; f. 1846; archaeological finds from neolithic times to the 13th century, chiefly from Croatia; Egyptian collection and Liber Linteus Zagrebiensis; Dir Prof. ANTE RENDIĆ-MIOČEVIĆ.

SPORTING ORGANIZATION

Croatian Olympic Committee: 10000 Zagreb, trg sportova 11; tel. (1) 3659666; fax (1) 3659600; e-mail hoo@hoo.tel.hr; internet www.hoo.tel.hr; f. 1991; Pres. ANTUN VRDOLJAC; Gen. Sec. SLAVKO PODGORELEC.

PERFORMING ARTS

Theatre

In 2001 there were 48 theatres in Croatia, 10 of which were children's theatres.

Croatian National Theatre (Hrvatsko narodno kazalište): 10000 Zagreb, trg Maršala Tita 15; tel. (1) 449311; e-mail hnk@zg.hinet.hr; internet www.hnk.hr; Dir GEORGIJ PARO.

> **Croatian National Theatre—Ivan Zajc** (Hrvatsko narodno kazalište 'Ivan Zajc'): 51000 Rijeka, Aldo Negri 1/I; tel. (51) 424679.

> **Croatian National Theatre—Osijek** (Hrvatsko narodno kazalište—Osijek): 31000 Osijek, Županijska 9; tel. (31) 220700; fax (31) 220734; e-mail hnkos@os.hinet.hr; Dir ŽELJKO ČAGALJ.

> **Croatian National Theatre—Split** (Hrvatsko narodno kazalište—Split): 21000 Split, trg Gaje Bulata 1; tel. (21) 585999; internet www.hnk-split.hr.

> **Komedija—Zagreb Municipal Theatre of Comedy:** 10000 Zagreb, Kaptol 9; tel. (1) 4813200; fax (1) 4812179; e-mail komedija@komedija.hr; internet www.komedija.hr; Editor NIKO PAVLOVI.

> **Theatre Etcetera:** 10000 Zagreb, Savska cesta 25; tel. (1) 4593610; fax (1) 4843492; e-mail dlukic@sczg.hr; performing arts, workshops, literary evenings; Man. and Artistic Dir DARKO LUKIĆ.

Music

In 2001 there were six professional orchestras in Croatia, and one professional choir.

Dubrovnik Symphony Orchestra (Dubrovački simfonijski orkestar): 50000 Dubrovnik, Ante Starčevića 29; tel. (20) 417101; fax (20) 417060; f. 1925; Chief Conductor IVAN DRAŽINIĆ.

Zagreb Concert Management (Koncertna direkcija Zagreb): 10000 Zagreb, Trnjanska bb; tel. (1) 539995; impresarios and concert promoters; Dir MIROSLAV POLJANEC.

Zagreb Philharmonic Orchestra (Zagrebačka filharmonija): 10000 Zagreb, Kneza Mislava 18; tel. (1) 4611809; fax (1) 4611807; e-mail zgfilhar@open.hr; internet www.open.hr/com/zg-fh; f. 1871; Permanent Guest Conductors NICHOLAS MILTON, PAVLE DEŠPALJ; Conductor Laureate MILAN HORVAT.

ASSOCIATIONS

Croatian Association of Orchestral and Chamber Musicians: 10000 Zagreb, Ilica 42; tel. and fax (1) 4847570; e-mail huoku@huoku.hr; internet www.huoku.hr; f. 1955.

Croatian Library Association: 10000 Zagreb, Hrvatske bratske zajednice bb; tel. (1) 6164111; fax (1) 6164186; e-mail hkd@nsk.hr; internet www.srce.hr/hkd; f. 1940; Pres. DUBRAVKA STANŠIN-ROŠIĆ.

Croatian Museum Association (Hrvatsko Muzejsko Društvo): 10000 Zagreb, Habdelićeva 2; tel. (1) 4851808; fax (1) 4851977; e-mail msu@msu.tel.hr; f. 1945; Pres. NADA VRKLJAN-KRŽIĆ.

Croatian Musicians' Union: 10000 Agreb, Poljička 31; tel. (1) 6190057; fax (1) 6190058; e-mail hgu@hgu.hr; internet www.hgu.hr.

Museum Documentation Centre: 10000 Zagreb, Mesnička 5; tel. (1) 432936; fax (1) 430851; e-mail info@museum.mdc.hr; internet www.museum.mdc.hr.

Education

Pre-school education, for children aged from three to six years, is free of charge. Education is officially compulsory for eight years, between seven and 15 years of age. Primary education, which is free, begins at the age of seven and lasts for four years. Primary enrolment in 1998 was equivalent to 77% of children in the appropriate age group. Secondary school education is available free (although there are private schools in Croatia) and lasts for up to eight years. There are grammar schools, technical schools and mixed-curriculum schools at secondary level. Enrolment at secondary schools in 1997 was equivalent to 82% of the relevant age group (boys 81%, girls 83%). A total of 111,782 students were enrolled in 102 higher education institutions in 2001/02. There were four universities (in Zagreb, Rijeka, Osijek and Split). In 2002 projected state budget expenditure on education was 6,194.7m. kuna (8.5% of total spending).

Ministry of Education and Sport: see section on The Government (Ministries).

UNIVERSITIES

Josip Juraj Strossmayer University of Osijek (Sveučilište Josipa Jurja Strossmayera u Osijeku): 31000 Osijek, trg sv. Trojstva 3; tel. (31) 224102; fax (31) 207015; e-mail rektorat@dora.unios.hr; internet www.rektorat.unios.hr; f. 1975; language of instruction: Croat; 9 faculties, 1 teachers' school of professional higher education, 1 dept; 494 teachers, 9,531 students; Rector GORDANA KRALIK.

University of Rijeka (Sveučilište u Rijeci): 51000 Rijeka, trg braće Mažuranića 10; tel. (51) 218288; fax (51) 216671; e-mail ured@uniri.hr; internet www.uniri.hr; f. 1973; language of instruction: Croatian (and some courses in Italian); 10 faculties, 3 teachers' schools, 1 dept; 899 teachers; 15,582 students; Rector Prof. DANIEL RUKAVINA.

University of Split (Sveučilište u Splitu): 21000 Split, Livanjska 5; tel. (21) 558200; fax (21) 355163; e-mail rektorat.office@unist.hr; internet www.unist.hr; f. 1974; language of instruction: Croat; 10 faculties, 2 teachers' schools, 1 academy, 1 dept; 697 teachers; 10,000 students; Rector Prof. Dr IVO BABIĆ.

University of Zagreb (Sveučilište u Zagrebu): 10000 Zagreb, trg Maršala Tita 14, POB 815; tel. (1) 4564111; fax (1) 420388; e-mail rektorat@rektor.unizg.hr; internet www.unizg.hr; f. 1669; language of instruction: Croat; 28 faculties, 3 academies, 1 teachers' school; 4,800 teachers; 53,000 students; Rector Prof. JASNA HELENA MENCER.

Social Welfare

Health care in Croatia is available to all citizens, free of charge. The effects of the civil conflict in Croatia, particularly the number of refugees, placed considerable pressure on the social-welfare system in the 1990s. Most government spending on social services is disbursed through extrabudgetary social funds (the Pension Fund, the Health Fund, the Employment Fund and the Child Benefit Fund). From January 1999 the retirement age rose by five years, to 65 years for men and 60 years for women. In January 2000, in an attempt to reduce government expenditure on pensions, the Government introduced a private pension scheme.

In 1998 there were some 229 physicians, 474 nurses and 66 dentists for every 100,000 inhabitants in the country. Of total projected expenditure by the central Government in 2002, 10,790.5m. kuna (14.8%) was allocated to health, and a further 32,339.3m. kuna (44.4%) to social security and welfare.

NATIONAL AGENCIES

Ministry of Health: see section on The Government (Ministries).

Ministry of Labour and Social Welfare: see section on The Government (Ministries).

Croatian Institute for Health Insurance: 10000 Zagreb, Magaretska 3; tel. (1) 4806340; fax (1) 4806325; e-mail webmaster@hzzo-net.hr; internet www.hzzo-net.hr; Gen. Man. ZDRAVKO LONČAREC.

Fund for Workers' Pensions and Disability Insurance: 10000 Zagreb, Mihanovićeva 3; tel. (1) 4595400; fax (1) 4595054.

NON-GOVERNMENTAL ORGANIZATIONS

Institute for Medicinal Research and Occupational Health: 10000 Zagreb, Ksaverska cesta 2, POB 291; tel. (1) 420412; fax (1) 420398; e-mail uprava@imi.hr.

Open Society Institute: 10000 Zagreb, Ilica 73; tel. (1) 4855576; fax (1) 4856459; e-mail office@soros.hr; internet www.soros.hr; f. 1992; programmes promoting open society in Croatia, in particular in law, culture, education, media, economy, science, public health, women's issues and non-governmental organizations.

Women's Infoteka (Ženska Infoteka): 10000 Zagreb, Varšavska 16; tel. (1) 4830557; fax (1) 4830552; e-mail zinfo@zamir.net; feminist non-governmental organization.

The Environment

GOVERNMENT ORGANIZATIONS

Ministry of Environmental Protection and Physical Planning: see section on The Government (Ministries).

APO Ltd.: 10000 Zagreb, Savska cesta 41/IV; tel. (1) 6176736; fax (1) 6176734; e-mail apo@apo.tel.hr; internet www.apo.hr; f. 1991; provides consulting services and engineering activities relating to environmental protection; Dir DAMIR SUBAŠIĆ.

Committee for Physical Planning and Environmental Protection: 10000 Zagreb, trg sv. Marka 6, Sabor; tel. (1) 4569417; fax (1) 6303514; internet www.sabor.hr/rad_tijel.htm; Chair. ZLATKO KRAMARIĆ.

Meteorological and Hydrological Service of Croatia: 10000 Zagreb, Grič 3; tel. (1) 4565693; fax (1) 4851901; e-mail dhmz@cirus.dhz.hr; internet www.tel.hr/dhmz; Dir MLADEN MATVIJEV.

State Directorate for Water: 10000 Zagreb, ul. grada Vukovara 220; tel. (1) 6307344; fax (1) 6151821; e-mail natasa.benic@zg.tel.hr; Dir ZORISLAV BALIĆ.

ACADEMIC INSTITUTES

Agricultural Institute Osijek (Poljoprivredni Institut Osijek): 31000 Osijek, Južno predgrade 17; tel. (31) 503310; fax (31) 503404; Dir JOSIP KOVAČEVIĆ.

Croatian Society of Natural Sciences, Section for the Protection of Nature (Hrvatsko Prirodoslovno Društvo): 10000 Zagreb, Ilica 16/III; tel. and fax (1) 4812408; e-mail periodicumbiologorum@public.srce.hr; f. 1885; Pres. Prof. Dr VELIMIR PRAVDIĆ; Sec. Dr LIDIA ŠUMAN.

Forest Research Institute (Šumarski Institut): 10450 Jastrebarsko, Cvjetno naselje 41; tel. (1) 6281492; fax (1) 6273035; e-mail josog@jaska.sumins.hr; Dir JOSO GRAČAN.

Hrvoje Požar Energy Institute (Energetski Institut Hrvoje Požar): 10000 Zagreb, ul. grada Vukovara 37; tel. (1) 6118400; fax (1) 6118401; e-mail eihp@eihp.hr; Dir GORAN GRANIĆ.

Institute of Adriatic Crops and Karst Reclamation (Institut za jadranske kulture i melioraciju krša): 21000 Split, Put Duilova 11; tel. (21) 316458; fax (21) 316584; e-mail slavko@krs.hr; internet www.krs.hr; Dir PETAR MALEŠ.

Institute of Oceanography and Fisheries (Institut za oceanografiju i ribarstvo): 21000 Split, Šetalište I. Meštrovića 63; tel. (21) 358688; fax (21) 358650; Dir IVONA MARASOVIĆ.

Ruder Bošković Institute, Centre for Marine and Environmental Research (Institut Ruder Bošković, Zavod za istraživanje mora i okoliša): 10002 Zagreb, Bijenička cesta 54, POB 180; tel. (1) 4561111; fax (1) 4680084; e-mail cosovic@rudjer.irb.hr; internet www.irb.hr; f. 1950; concentrates on environmental concerns in the Adriatic Sea and freshwater systems of Croatia; Dir Dr STJEPAN MARČELJA.

NON-GOVERNMENTAL ORGANIZATIONS

BIOS Association for Protection and Preservation of the Adriatic (Udruga za zaštitu i očuvanje jadranskog podmorja 'BIOS'): 21000 Split, Marmontova 1; tel. and fax (21) 591156; e-mail ante.zuljevic@jadran.izor.hr; Sec. ANTE ŽULJEVIĆ.

Caput Insulae Eco Centre—Beli (Eko Centar Caput Insulae—Beli): 51000 Rijeka, E. Jardasa 35; tel. and fax (51) 621877; e-mail orlov-let@ri.tel.hr; Pres. GORAN SUŠIĆ.

Croatian Environmental Education Centre (Hrvatski Centar 'Znanje za okoliš'): 10000 Zagreb, ul. grada Vukovara 68; tel. (1) 6111110; fax (1) 6191804; e-mail vladimir.lay@zg.tel.hr; Pres. VELIMIR PRAVDIĆ.

Croatian Geological Society (Hrvatsko geološko društvo): 10000 Zagreb, Sachsova bb; tel. (1) 4592942; fax (1) 4592224; Sec. ŽELJKO KRUŠLIN.

Croatian Solar Energy Association (Hrvatsko Udruženje za Sunčew Energiju): 51000 Rijeka, ul. Vukovarska 58; tel. and fax (51) 675801; e-mail huse@riteh.hr; education, research and congresses; Pres. Prof. BERNARD FRANKOVIĆ.

Drop of Life Ecological Association (Ekološka udruga 'Kap Života'): 53000 Gospić, ul. dr. Ante Sarčevića bb; tel. (53) 560450; fax (53) 560451; e-mail kap_zivota@hotmail.com; Pres. IVANA SVETIĆ.

Eko-Liburnia: 51000 Rijeka, Jelačićev trg 1/III; tel. and fax (51) 331184; e-mail eko-liburnia@ri.tel.hr; internet www.eko-liburnia .hr/eko; Pres. RANKO TADIĆ.

Eko Rijeka Ecological Association (Ekološka udruga 'Eko Rijeka'): 51222 Bakar, Primorje 39; tel. (51) 761315; fax (51) 761137; e-mail nadja-mifka.profozic@public.srce.hr; Pres. RATKO PROFOZIĆ.

Eurocoast—Croatian Association (Eurocoast—Hrvatska udruga): 10000 Zagreb, Rooseveltov trg 6; tel. 4877748; fax (1) 4826260; e-mail antonieta.pozar-domac@zg.tel.hr; promotes scientific and technical collaboration at state and international levels, education and conservation of coastal regions; Pres. Prof. ANTONIETA POŽAR-DOMAC.

Franjo Koščec Ecological Association (Ekološka udruga 'Franjo Koščec'): 42000 Varaždin, Augusta Šenoe 10A; tel. (42) 320357; Pres. DORA RADOSAVLJEVIĆ.

Green Action (Zelena Akcija): 10000 Zagreb, POB 952, Frankopanska 1; tel. and fax (1) 4813096; e-mail zelena-akcija@zg.tel.hr; internet www.zelena-akcija.hr; f. 1990; local, national and international environmental issues, sustainable development; Pres. TONI VIDAN.

Larus—Association for Sustainable Development and Protection of Marine and Coastal Areas (Larus—Udruga za održivi razvoj i zaštitu mora i priobalja): 52440 Poreč, Massa Lombarda 14; tel. (52) 453395; fax (52) 434765; e-mail vladimir.sladonja@pu.tel.hr; Pres. BARBARA MARTINČIĆ.

Moslavina Green Movement (Zeleni Moslavine): 44320 Kutina, A. Hebranga 8/III; tel. and fax (44) 637087; e-mail marijana_petir@yahoo.com; Pres. MARIJANA PETIR.

Natura Society for Nature Protection of Croatia (Društvo za zaštitu prirode Hrvatske 'Natura'): 10000 Zagreb, Čavalski put 4; tel. (1) 4851700; fax (1) 4851644; e-mail drasko.holcer@hpm.hr; Pres. DRAŠKO HOLCER.

Nobilis Environmental Protection Organization (Zaštitarsko ekološka organizacija Nobilis): 40000 Čakovec, Šenkovec Vrtna 1; tel. and fax (40) 343646; e-mail sinisa.golub@yahoo.com; Pres. SINIŠA GOLUB.

Ombla Ecological Association (Ekološka udruga 'Ombla'): 20000 Dubrovnik, Mokošica—Marina Kneževića 6; tel. (20) 453850; fax (20) 432524; Co-ordinator JADRANKA ŠIMUNOVIĆ.

Road Environmental Communication Society ('Put'—Društvo za komuniciranje ambijenta): 52220 Labin, G. Martinuzzi 2A; tel. and fax (52) 856721; e-mail dag-tours@pu.tel.hr; Pres. LORI LUKETA DAGOSTIN.

Society for the Protection of Birds and of Nature Conservatio (Hrvatsko Društvo za Zastitu Ptica i Prirode): 10000 Zagreb, Ilirski trg 9; tel. and fax (1) 3895445; e-mail jasmina@hazu.hr; Pres. JASMINA MUŽINIĆ.

SUN Environmental Association (Udruga za zaštitu okoliša 'Sunce'): 21000 Split, Bana Jelačića 4/II, Rm. 7; tel. and fax (21) 360779; e-mail sunce_split@hotmail.com; internet www.st.carnet .hr/sunce.

SVANIMIR—Croatian Association for the Protection of Natural, Cultural and Historical Heritage (Hrvatsko udruženje za zaštitu prirodnog i kulturno-povijesnog nasljeda 'Svanimir'): 10000 Zagreb, Ilirski trg 9; tel. (1) 4851322; e-mail vtutis@mahazu.hazu .hr; Pres. VESNA TUTIŠ.

Defence

Military service in Croatia is compulsory for men and lasts for a period of 10 months. In August 2002 the estimated total strength of the Croatian Armed Forces was 51,000 (including an army of 45,000, a navy of 3,000 and an air force of 3,000). The number of reservists totalled 140,000. In addition, there were 10,000 armed military police. The mandate of the UN Mission of Observers in Prevlaka, deployed in Croatia from 1996, officially ended in December 2002. Projected expenditure on defence by the central Government totalled an estimated 4,354.7m. kuna (6.0% of total spending) in 2002.

Supreme Commander of the Armed Forces: President of the Republic.

Commander of the Army: Gen. MARIJAN MAREKOVIĆ.

Chief of the General Staff: Maj.-Gen. JOSIP LUCIĆ.

Bibliography

Bartlett, W. *Croatia: Between Europe and the Balkans.* London, Routledge, 2002.

Croatia: a Crossroads Between East and West (Postcommunist States and Nations). London, Routledge, 2002.

Bilandzić, D., et al. *Croatia between War and Independence.* Zagreb, University of Zagreb and OKC Zagreb, 1991.

Goldstein, I. *Croatia: A History.* London, C. Hurst, 1999.

Head, L. *Dancing in the Dark: the Nature of Escape and Evasion in Croatia During the Second World War.* Lincoln, NE, Writers Club Press, 2002.

Kerrigan, J., and Novick, W. *Healing the Heart of Croatia.* Costa Mesa, CA, Paulist Press, 1998.

Magas, B. (Ed.). *The War in Croatia and Bosnia-Herzegovina, 1991–1995.* London, Frank Cass, 2002.

Malesević, S. *Ideology, Legitimacy and the New State: Yugoslavia, Serbia and Croatia (Cass Series-Nationalism and Ethnicity, 4).* London, Frank Cass, 2002.

Malović, S., and Selnow, G. *The People, Press and Politics of Croatia.* Westport, CT, Praeger, 2001.

Miksić, B. *American Dream: A Guy from Croatia.* St Paul, MN, Cortec Corpn, 2002.

Radovinović, R., and Naprijed, N. *Croatian Adriatic.* Cincinnati, OH, Seven Hills Book Distributors, 1999.

Staničić, M. et al. *Croatia on its Way Towards the EU.* Baden Baden, Nomos Verlaggesellschaft, 2002.

Tanner, M. *Croatia.* 2nd edn, Yale, CT, Yale University Press, 2001.

Tudjman, F., Tuman F., and Mijatović, K. *Horrors of War: Historical Reality and Philosophy.* New York, NY, M. Evans and Co, 1997.

Violich, F. *The Bridge to Dalmatia: A Search for the Meaning of Place.* Baltimore, MD, Johns Hopkins University Press, 1998.

THE CZECH REPUBLIC

Geography

PHYSICAL FEATURES

The Czech Republic is a land-locked state located in Central Europe, covering an area of 78,866 sq km (30,450 sq miles). It comprises the lands of Bohemia and Moravia (the latter also includes part of the historic region known as Silesia, most of which is now in Poland). The country is bordered by Poland to the north, Slovakia (which together with the Czech Republic formed Czechoslovakia between 1918 and 1992) to the east, Germany to the west and Austria to the south.

Bohemia, the westernmost of the Czech Lands, covers the region drained by the upper Labe (Elbe) and its tributary, the Vltava (Moldau), on which the capital, Prague (Praha), stands. This region is a plateau (average height 500 m), bordered to the north-west and south-west by low ranges of mountains (the Krušné Hory, or Erzgebirge, and the Český Les, or Böhmerwald, respectively), which form a natural frontier with Germany. The Krkonoše Hory (Riesengebirge) range, the highest of the Sudetic (Sudeten) mountains, marks the border with Poland, rising to 1,603 m (5,259 ft) at Mount Sněžka. Several important rivers, including the Vltava and the Ohře, rise in the south-western hill country and flow north into the Labe, and hence into the North Sea. Moravia, in the east of the country, is a mainly lowland region, which has traditionally been a crossing point between Poland and south Central Europe. It is drained by the Dyje and Morava rivers; the latter forms part of the border with Slovakia and flows south to join the Danube (Dunaj) on the borders of Slovakia and Austria. Eastern Moravia is more rugged and mountainous, with the Little and White Carpathian Mountains forming the rest of the border with Slovakia.

CLIMATE

The climate is typically continental, with cold, dry winters and hot, humid summers. The average July temperature in Prague is 19°C (66°F) and the average January temperature is –1°C (30°F). Prague receives an average annual rainfall of 485 mm, which often falls as snow in winter months. There is little climatic variation throughout the country.

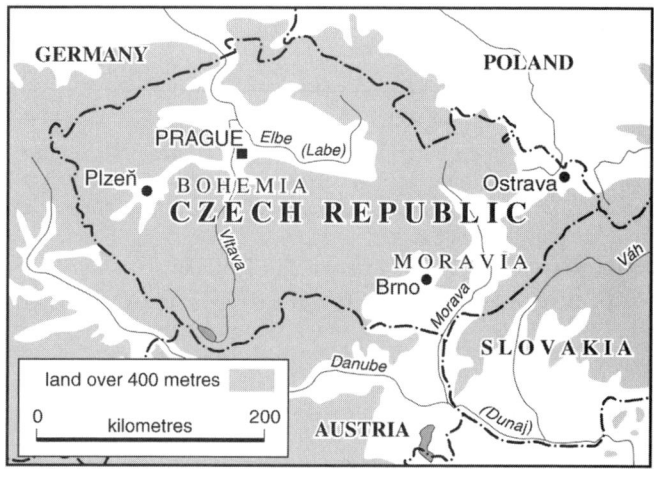

POPULATION

At the census of March 2001 the population of the Czech Republic was 10,292,933. Of this total, 90.1% of the population were Czechs (Bohemians), 3.6% Moravians and 1.8% Slovaks; there were also small communities of Poles, Germans, Ukrainians, Vietnamese, Russians, Hungarians, Roma (Gypsies) and Silesians. The official language is Czech, a member of the Western Slavonic group of languages. Members of ethnic minorities continued to use their own languages. The major religion was Christianity. At the census of March 2001 some 27% of the population professed to be adherents of the Roman Catholic Church. About 60% of the population declared themselves to have no religious beliefs.

According to official estimates, at December 2002 the population totalled 10,203,269, giving a density of 129.4 per sq km. The capital city is Prague. It is situated in central Bohemia and had an estimated population of 1,161,938 at the end of December 2002. Other important towns were Brno (population 370,505), the administrative capital of Moravia, and Ostrava (314,102), also situated in Moravia.

Chronology

5th–7th centuries: Slavic tribes migrated to central Europe from the eastern plains.

830: The establishment of the Great Moravian Empire, which comprised Bohemia, Moravia and Slovakia.

907: Following the Battle of Bratislava (Pressburg), the Great Moravian Empire was overthrown and the Kingdom of Bohemia was established.

1041: Bohemia became a fief of the Holy Roman Empire, after the subjugation of Prince Bretislav of Bohemia, by the forces of Henry III, the German Emperor.

1310: After a four-year struggle over the succession, the Bohemian nobles granted the throne to John of Luxembourg, thus ending the Přemyslid dynasty in Bohemia.

1346–78: The reign of Charles I of Bohemia (Charles IV as Holy Roman Emperor), who encouraged the cultural and commercial development of the Czech Lands.

1419: Following the martyrdom of Jan Hus (1415), the leader of a reformist religious movement centred in Prague, his followers, the Hussites, rebelled against German rule after the first 'Defenestration of Prague'.

1420–33: The Hussite Wars were fought, in which forces loyal to the Holy Roman Empire attempted to suppress the Hussite rebellion.

1526: Czech nobles elected the Habsburg Archduke Ferdinand I to the throne.

1620: After a two-year rebellion, which began with the Second Defenestration of Prague, Czech troops were defeated at the Battle of the White Mountain.

1781–85: Serfdom was abolished in the Czech Lands.

1848: An unsuccessful uprising against the Habsburgs took place in Prague.

30 May 1918: The Pittsburgh Agreement, which provided for the creation of a common Czech-Slovak state, was signed between Slovak and Czech exiles in the USA.

28 October 1918: The Republic of Czechoslovakia was proclaimed; Tomáš Garrigue Masaryk was elected President.

28 June 1919: The Treaty of Versailles provided international recognition to the Czechoslovak state and confirmed its frontiers.

November 1935: Masaryk resigned as President; he was succeeded by Edvard Beneš.

29 September 1938: The Munich Conference took place in Germany between the leaders of France, Germany, Italy and the United Kingdom; an agreement was signed, which permitted the cession of the Czechoslovak territories known as Sudetenland to Germany.

5 October 1938: Beneš resigned as President.

15–16 March 1939: Adolf Hitler, the German leader, invaded the Czech Lands: Bohemia and Moravia became a German Protectorate; Slovakia was proclaimed an independent state, under the pro-Fascist leadership of Mgr Jozef Tiso.

3 April 1945: Beneš and his Government-in-exile returned to Czechoslovakia.

9 May 1945: Soviet troops entered Prague.

16 May 1946: National elections took place; the Czechoslovak Communist Party (CPCz) won 38% of the votes cast; Klement Gottwald, leader of the CPCz, was appointed Prime Minister.

25 February 1948: The communists seized power, following the resignation of 12 non-communist ministers.

9 May 1948: A new Constitution was approved, which declared Czechoslovakia a 'people's democracy'.

30 May 1948: Elections took place, with only communist-approved candidates nominated.

June 1948: Beneš resigned, after refusing to sign the new Constitution.

December 1952: Rudolf Slánský, former Secretary-General of the CPCz, and other prominent communists were executed after 'show trials'.

March 1953: Klement Gottwald died. Antonín Novotný was appointed First Secretary of the CPCz; Antonín Zápotocký became President; Viliám Široký was appointed Prime Minister.

1957: First Secretary of the CPCz, Antonín Novotný, replaced Zápotocký as President.

July 1960: A new Constitution was enacted; Czechoslovakia was renamed the Czechoslovak Socialist Republic.

1963: Prime Minister Široký was replaced by Jozef Lenárt, who launched the mildly reformist New Economic Model. Rudolf Slánský and other communists who had been purged in the 1950s were rehabilitated.

October 1967: A student rally was violently dispersed by police.

5 January 1968: Antonín Novotný resigned as First Secretary of the CPCz; he was replaced by Alexander Dubček, leader of the Communist Party of Slovakia (CPS).

March 1968: Censorship of the press was ended.

April 1968: The Central Committee of the CPCz adopted an Action Programme, which proposed constitutional and economic reforms. Gen. Ludvík Svoboda was appointed President. Oldřich Černík was appointed Prime Minister.

3 August 1968: Representatives of the communist parties of member countries of the Warsaw Pact (except Romania) met in Bratislava, Slovakia, to discuss Czechoslovakia's 'Prague Spring' reforms.

20–21 August 1968: Warsaw Pact troops invaded Czechoslovakia; Dubček and other government and party leaders were abducted to the Soviet and Russian capital, Moscow.

1 January 1969: A federal system of government was introduced.

16 January 1969: A student, Jan Palach, immolated himself and died, in protest at the ending of reforms.

17 April 1969: Gustáv Husák replaced Dubček as First Secretary of the CPCz.

January 1970: Černík was dismissed as Prime Minister.

11 December 1973: A treaty, signed between the Federal Republic of Germany ('West' Germany) and Czechoslovakia, normalized relations between the two countries and formally annulled the 1938 Munich Agreement.

May 1975: Svoboda resigned as President and was replaced by Husák.

1 January 1977: A group of dissidents, including Václav Havel, the playwright, published the 'Charter 77' manifesto, which demanded an end to the abuse of civil and political rights.

December 1987: Miloš Jakeš replaced Gustáv Husák as General Secretary of the CPCz.

21 August 1988: Large anti-Government demonstrations took place in Prague, on the 20th anniversary of the 1968 Soviet invasion; further demonstrations took place on the same day in the following year.

10 October 1988: Lubomír Štrougal resigned as federal Prime Minister; he was replaced by Ladislav Adamec.

16 January 1989: A large demonstration took place to mark the 20th anniversary of the suicide of Jan Palach; Václav Havel and 13 other dissidents were arrested (international protests later secured Havel's release).

1 May 1989: The traditional May Day rally was disrupted when police dispersed demonstrators protesting against human-rights violations.

28 October 1989: Anti-Government demonstrations took place, on the 71st anniversary of the establishment of a Czechoslovak state.

17 November 1989: Students participating in an officially sanctioned demonstration were attacked by riot police; 140 people were injured. Later some 300 opposition activists from various non-communist organizations united to form Civic Forum, a broad anti-Government coalition (in Slovakia, its counterpart was known as Public Against Violence—PAV).

21 November 1989: Adamec began discussions with Civic Forum.

24 November 1989: With protests and strikes continuing to take place, Miloš Jakeš, General Secretary of the CPCz, and all other members of the Presidium of the Central Committee and the Secretariat of the CPCz, resigned; Karel Urbanek was elected leader of the CPCz. Alexander Dubček returned to Prague and spoke to a large crowd in Wenceslas Square.

28 November 1989: Civic Forum was officially registered as a legal organization.

29 November 1989: The Federal Assembly abolished the CPCz's constitutional monopoly of power.

7 December 1989: Adamec resigned as Prime Minister; he was replaced by Marián Čalfa.

10 December 1989: Čalfa announced a new federal Government, with a majority of non-communist members. Husák resigned as President.

28 December 1989: Dubček was elected Chairman of the Federal Assembly. The following day it elected Václav Havel President of Czechoslovakia.

1 February 1990: The abolition of the StB (Státni bezpeč-nost—the secret police) was announced.

6 February 1990: Petr Pithart was appointed Prime Minister of the Czech Republic.

7 February 1990: The National Front, the communists' political organization, was disbanded.

27–28 March 1990: The Federal Assembly approved new laws guaranteeing freedom of association and freedom of the press, and allowing exiles to reclaim their citizenship.

29 March 1990: The name of the country was changed to the Czech and Slovak Federative Republic.

27 May 1990: Václav Klaus, federal Minister of Finance, announced a reform-orientated budget.

June 1990: Elections to the Federal Assembly took place; Civic Forum (in Bohemia and Moravia) and PAV (in Slovakia) won an overall majority. A coalition Government was formed, with participation from all major parties, except the CPCz.

5 July 1990: Havel was re-elected as President for a transitional two-year period.

12 December 1990: The Federal Assembly approved constitutional legislation delimiting the powers of the federal, Czech and Slovak governments.

23 February 1991: Civic Forum was formally disbanded; its members formed two new political parties, the conservative Civic Democratic Party (CDP) and the liberal Civic Movement.

26 February 1991: Legislation allowing privatization of state-owned enterprises was approved.

2 March 1991: Thousands of people took part in demonstrations in Moravia, demanding autonomous status for their region.

10–14 March 1991: There were large demonstrations in Slovakia, in favour of independence for the republic; President Havel was attacked by crowds when he visited Bratislava.

27 April 1991: The Civic Movement officially constituted itself as an independent political party.

13 June 1991: The first phase of the 'large privatization' programme began, with the sale of 50 state-owned enterprises to Western companies.

21 June 1991: The withdrawal of Soviet forces, which had been stationed in Czechoslovakia since 1968, was completed.

1 July 1991: Leaders of the member countries of the Warsaw Pact met in Prague to complete the dissolution of the organization, by formally ending the work of its Political Consultative Committee.

5–6 June 1992: At federal and republican legislative elections there were strong performances by the Movement for a Democratic Slovakia (MDS) and other parties favouring separation between the Czech Lands and Slovakia. However, the pro-federal CDP became the single largest party; the successors to the communists (Left Bloc in the Czech Lands, Party of the Democratic Left in Slovakia) came third and fourth. Negotiations commenced between the CDP and the MDS to form a federal government. Meanwhile Vladimír Mečiar was appointed Slovak Prime Minister.

July 1992: A transitional federal Government was appointed, dominated by members of the CDP and the MDS, with Jan Stráský of the CDP as Prime Minister. Czech politicians accepted that total separation of the Czech Lands and Slovakia was preferable to the compromise measures proposed. Václav Klaus was appointed Prime Minister of the new Czech Government. Three rounds of voting in the Federal Assembly failed to elect a new president, with the MDS and the Slovak National Party blocking the re-election of Havel, who duly resigned.

26 October 1992: A Customs Union treaty and other accords were agreed between the Czech and Slovak Governments.

25 November 1992: The Federal Assembly adopted legislation enabling the constitutional disbanding of the federation, with the assets divided 2:1 in the Czech Republic's favour, in accordance with the balance of population.

December 1992: A treaty of good neighbourliness, friendly relations and co-operation was signed between the two republics, followed by the exchange of diplomatic relations. A new Constitution of the Czech Republic was adopted; the Czech National Council became the Chamber of Deputies (lower house), retaining the existing 200 members, while a Senate (upper house) was to be elected at a later date. Czechoslovakia, Hungary and Poland signed an agreement with the European Community (EC, known as the European Union—EU from November 1993) granting them associate member status.

1 January 1993: Separation of the Czech Republic and Slovakia took effect.

26 January 1993: Havel was elected President of the Czech Republic.

February 1993: Separate Czech and Slovak currencies (both called the koruna) were introduced.

June 1993: Parliament voted to establish a Constitutional Court and a Supreme Control Office (an independent body to audit government finances). At the congress of the Communist Party of Bohemia and Moravia (CPBM), neo-Stalinists were expelled and reformists left to form a new party, the Party of the Democratic Left.

July 1993: The former Czechoslovak communist regime was declared illegitimate and criminal. Border controls were introduced on the Czech–Slovak frontier to stem the flow of 'third-party' refugees, mainly heading for Germany; Slovak citizens, however, were to be unaffected.

March 1994: The Czech Republic joined the North Atlantic Treaty Organization's (NATO) 'Partnership for Peace' programme of military co-operation.

September 1994: A law introduced new qualifications, of two years' established residence and five years without any criminal record, for nationality and associated rights and benefits.

1 October 1995: An act to make the koruna widely convertible came into effect.

28 November 1995: The Czech Republic became the first former communist country to join the Organisation for Economic Co-operation and Development (OECD).

January 1996: The Ministers of the Interior of the Czech Republic and Slovakia approved a treaty to finalize the Czech–Slovak border (following opposition among citizens to be transferred to Slovak jurisdiction, the Chamber of Deputies rejected the treaty in April). The Prime Minister, Klaus, submitted the Czech Republic's application to join the EU.

31 May–1 June 1996: In the Czech Republic's first general election as an independent state the CDP-led government alliance won 99 seats—CDP 68, Christian Democratic Union—Czechoslovak People's Party (CDU—CPP) 18, Civic Democratic Alliance (CDA) 13—two seats short of an overall majority; the opposition Czech Social Democratic Party (CSDP) won 61 seats, the CPBM 22 and the Association for the Republic—Republican Party of Czechoslovakia (AFR—RPC) 18.

27 June 1996: Klaus was reappointed Prime Minister of a minority coalition Government, which included the CDP, the CDU—CPP and the CDA; Miloš Zeman, the leader of the CSDP, was appointed Chairman (speaker) of the Chamber of Deputies.

15–16 November 1996: Only 30% of the electorate voted in the delayed Senate elections; after a second round on 22–23 November the CDP had 32 of the 81 seats and the CSDP 25.

August 1997: Hundreds of Gypsies (Roma) sought asylum in Canada and the United Kingdom, claiming persecution, and drawing international attention to allegations of institutional racism in the Czech Republic; the status of the Roma minority remained a significant political issue in the early 2000s.

30 November 1997: The Prime Minister, Klaus, and the Government resigned, after the withdrawal of the CDU—CPP and the CDA from the coalition, following allegations of corruption against the CDP.

17 December 1997: Jozef Tošovský, hitherto Governor of the central bank, was appointed Prime Minister, to head a 'care-taker', largely non-political administration, supported by the old coalition, in advance of an early general election.

8 January 1998: Ivan Pilip, the finance minister, resigned from the CDP, after Klaus declared that CDP members serving in the interim Government did not have party authorization; subsequently, the other three CDP ministers also resigned from the party.

18 January 1998: A new party, the Freedom Union (FU), was established by 30 of the 69 CDP deputies; Jan Ruml was elected leader.

20 January 1998: Havel was re-elected President for a second five-year term.

15 April 1998: The Chamber of Deputies approved Czech membership of NATO.

19–20 June 1998: In the general election the CSDP obtained 32.3% of the votes cast and 74 seats in the 200-seat Chamber of Deputies; the CDP obtained 27.7% of the votes and 63 seats; the other parties to secure representation in parliament were the CPBM (24 seats), the CDU—CPP (20) and the FU (19).

17 July 1998: Zeman was appointed Prime Minister of a minority CSDP Government supported by the CDP, which had failed to negotiate a coalition with the CDU—CPP and the FU.

16 March 1999: The Czech Republic was granted full membership of NATO, along with Hungary and Poland.

17 November 1999: At demonstrations to mark the 10th anniversary of the collapse of communism protesters urged several senior political figures to allow younger politicians to succeed them; a further demonstration held in Prague in early December attracted some 50,000 people.

January 2000: The CDP reaffirmed its agreement to maintain the minority CSDP Government, on the condition that the premier reorganize the Council of Ministers and propose measures of electoral reform. Four ministers were consequently replaced in April.

24 May 2000: Miloš Zeman, the Prime Minister, and his Slovak counterpart, Mikuláš Dzurinda, signed a declaration resolving property disputes arising from the distribution of the assets of the Czechoslovak state upon its dissolution at the end of 1992.

25 May 2000: The Chamber of Deputies endorsed a series of amendments to electoral legislation, increasing the number of electoral districts in the Czech Republic from eight to 35, establishing a single round of voting in elections to the Chamber of Deputies and increasing the minimum percentage of votes cast required for coalitions to gain parliamentary representation. In January 2001, however, an appeal by President Havel and a number of senators against the former provision was upheld by the Constitutional Court.

8 June 2000: Libor Novák, the former Deputy Chairman of the CDP, was acquitted of tax offences with regard to party funds, an issue which forced the resignation of the CDP Government in November 1997.

9 August 2000: A constitutional amendment was introduced that would allow Czech soldiers to serve as peace-keepers abroad, and allow the deployment of foreign troops in the Czech Republic for up to 60 days without approval by the legislature. The amendment was aimed at meeting the country's NATO obligations.

October 2000: The first reactor became operational at the Temelín nuclear power station in southern Bohemia, straining relations with Austria, which had concerns as to the plant's safety and objected to the presence of such a facility some 60 km (35 miles) from its frontier.

30 November 2000: Tošovský, who had returned to his position as Governor of the central bank after the end of his period of office as Prime Minister, resigned from the post. President Havel appointed Zdeněk Tůma, hitherto a Vice-Governor of the bank, to replace Tošovský. The appointment was widely criticized, as new legislation was to come into effect in December transferring the right to nominate the Governor to the Prime Minister.

11 January 2001: Jiří Hodac, thought to have sympathies with the CDP, resigned as Director-General of the state television company, following the occupation of the station buildings by staff and demonstrations by an estimated 100,000 people in central Prague against his appointment in late December.

7 April 2001: The ruling CSDP elected Vladimír Špidla as its leader, replacing Miloš Zeman, who was to remain Prime Minister until the legislative elections, due to take place in June 2002.

3 December 2001: The trial of Jaromír Obzina, a former Minister of the Interior, and four other former government officials, all charged with abuses of power and intimidation of dissidents, began in Prague.

10 December 2001: EU officials announced that they were satisfied with the energy component of the Czech Republic's membership bid, providing outstanding safety recommendations for the Temelín power station were implemented before the end of accession negotiations.

1 February 2002: The so-called Quad Alliance of the CDU—CPP, the CDA, the FU and the Democratic Union was dissolved; all except the CDA later reformed as the Coalition.

24 April 2002: The Chamber of Deputies unanimously approved a resolution stipulating the inviolability of the so-called Beneš Decrees, which had provided for the expulsion of ethnic Germans from the Sudetenland in 1945, in response to right-wing demands for their abolition from Austria, Germany and Hungary.

22 May 2002: A former Minister of Finance, Ivo Svoboda (1998–99), was arraigned on charges of embezzlement relating to his time in office.

14–15 June 2002: The CSDP was the most successful party at elections to the lower house (with 30.2% of the votes cast); a low rate of participation by the electorate appeared to confirm suggestions of widespread popular disenchantment with the political establishment.

17 June 2002: President Havel invited CSDP leader Vladimír Špidla to commence negotiations to form a new government.

4 July 2002: Hana Marvanova resigned as leader of the FU (one of the constituent parties of the Coalition), claiming that the party was making unreasonable concessions to the CSDP in negotiations to formulate a political agenda for the future coalition government.

9 July 2002: A formal agreement establishing terms of coalition government was signed by the leaders of the CSDP and the Coalition.

15 July 2002: A new, 17-member coalition Government, headed by Špidla, was officially appointed by President Havel.

12 August 2002: A state of emergency was declared in Prague and several other regions of the country, following severe flooding, in which 17 people were killed and some 220,000 residents were evacuated from the capital. Subsequent discussions in the legislature concerning the introduction of tax increases to fund reconstruction work threatened to divide the governing coalition.

23 September 2002: The former Prime Minister, Jozef Lenárt, and former leader of the CPCz, Miloš Jakeš, were acquitted of charges of collaborating with the Warsaw Pact troops that invaded Czechoslovakia in August 1968.

25–26 October and 1–2 November 2002: Elections to 27 of the 81 seats in the Senate took place, at which the representation of the governing coalition parties decreased to a total of 34 seats, while CDP seats increased from 22 to 26 seats.

13 December 2002: The Czech Republic, together with nine other countries, was formally invited to become a full member of the EU from 1 May 2004.

28 February 2003: Following several unsuccessful rounds of voting in the presidential elections, Václav Klaus (who had resigned the chairmanship of the CDP) was finally elected President, defeating the ruling coalition candidate, Jan Sokol, with 142 of the 281 votes cast in both chambers.

7 March 2003: Klaus was inaugurated as President.

11 March 2003: Špidla requested a parliamentary vote of confidence, which he won by a single vote.

14 March 2003: Špidla dismissed the Minister of Industry and Trade, Jiří Rusnok, for failing to support the candidate of the CSDP in the presidential election.

20 March 2003: The Government published a list of some 75,000 informers who had denounced friends and colleagues to the communist regime. The list revealed that one in 130 Czechs had worked for the secret police.

29 May 2003: The Minister of Defence, Jaroslav Tvrdík, resigned in protest at reductions in military expenditure under the Government's public-finance reform.

4 June 2003: Draft legislation, providing for direct presidential elections, was approved by the Government. The bill required further approval by both chambers of the legislature.

13–14 June 2003: At a referendum on the Czech Republic's accession to the EU, in which 55% of eligible voters participated, some 77% indicated their support for joining the organization.

History

Dr GORDON WIGHTMAN

INTRODUCTION

On 1 January 1993 Czechoslovakia separated into independent Czech and Slovak Republics. This was a considerable disappointment to those Czechs who had believed in the desirability and viability of the common state they had established with the Slovaks only 74 years earlier, in 1918. Czechoslovakia had been one of the new states to emerge at the end of the First World War, following the collapse of the Austro-Hungarian Empire of the Habsburgs. It was not, however, the first Czech state in the region. The Czech kingdom of Bohemia and Moravia had been a major political and cultural power in Central Europe in the medieval period. The first university in Central Europe was established in its capital, Prague, in 1348, by Charles I of Bohemia, who was crowned Holy Roman Emperor seven years later (as Charles IV). In the early 15th century the Hussite movement (named after Jan Hus, Rector of Charles University, who was burned at the stake in 1415) established the Czech kingdom as a Protestant power. However, the Czechs were defeated by the Austrians at the Battle of the White Mountain in 1620. Despite this defeat and their subsequent incorporation into the Habsburg Empire and enforced conversion to Roman Catholicism, the Protestant legacy was to play an important part in the search for a Czech national identity in the 19th century.

Before the First World War most Czechs envisaged satisfaction of their nationalist aspirations within a reformed Habsburg Empire. By 1914, however, that had come to seem unlikely and, increasingly, Czechs began to think in terms of national independence. In 1915 the formation, in Paris, France, of a Czech National Council by Prof. Tomáš Masaryk signalled the start of a political and diplomatic campaign for independence, which eventually incorporated the Czechs' closest Slav neighbours, the Slovaks. Masaryk was aided by the Czech sociologist, Dr Edvard Beneš, and the Slovak army officer, Maj. Milan Rostislav Štefánik. However, the success of the campaign owed as much to the part played by ordinary Czechs and Slovaks, exiles or prisoners of war in France, Italy and Russia, who volunteered to serve in the military units that were formed in those countries to fight on the side of the Allied Powers. The formation in Russia of a 50,000-strong Czechoslovak Legion, which Masaryk hoped, following the Russian withdrawal from the war in March 1918, to transfer to the Western Front, became a vital source of positive publicity. Its eventual involvement in armed conflict with the Bolshevik Red Army, despite Masaryk's injunction that it should avoid intervention in Russian affairs, brought the force international sympathy and enhanced the Czech and Slovak case for independence with Western governments.

THE CZECHOSLOVAK FIRST REPUBLIC, 1918–38

Czechoslovakia was the only country in Eastern Europe where parliamentary democracy survived intact for almost all of the period between the First and Second World Wars. Much of the credit for this success can be attributed to the influence of its first two Presidents, Masaryk (1918–35) and Beneš (1935–38 and 1945–48). Democracy was maintained despite defects in the constitutional system. Ethnic diversity weakened a party system that was also highly fragmented by economic and social divisions. The system produced coalition governments of relatively short duration, which failed to provide lasting political stability. A more serious threat to the security of the country, however, was the growing disaffection felt by two of the three major ethnic groups, the Slovaks and the Germans.

Slovak disaffection with the pre-1938 Czechoslovak state stemmed, in part, from the predominant role played by Czechs in the country's political and economic life. It was aggravated by official attempts to propagate the concept, unacceptable to many Slovaks, of a single Czechoslovak nation, of which Czechs and Slovaks were said to be two distinct, but closely related, branches.

The establishment of Czechoslovakia as a unitary state was one source of Slovak discontentment during the 1920s and 1930s. However, it was the dissatisfaction of the German minority that proved fatal to Czechoslovak democracy and to the survival of the country. Although many of the German inhabitants had come to terms with the Czechoslovak state and some German political parties participated in government, the rise of Nazism encouraged the emergence of an extreme German nationalism. The Sudeten German Party, led by Konrad Henlein, attracted some 67% of the votes cast by Germans in the 1935 parliamentary elections. The problem might have been successfully contained had not France and the United Kingdom consented, in the Munich Agreement of 29 September 1938, to Germany's annexation of Czechoslovakia's border regions (the Sudetenland—mainly inhabited by members of the German minority). Less than one week later, on 5 October, Beneš resigned as President, only three years after his election to that post. He left a country that had not only lost territory, but also its strategic defences. Six months later, on 15 March 1939, Nazi armed forces entered Prague and established a German Protectorate of Bohemia and Moravia. In Slovakia, which had been granted self-government in late 1938, a separate Slovak state was formed, ruled by the 'puppet' regime of Jozef Tiso.

CZECHOSLOVAKIA AFTER 1945

Beneš spent the Second World War campaigning for the restoration of Czechoslovakia, within its pre-1938 frontiers; six years later, in May 1945, he was able to return to Prague as President. Nevertheless, Czechoslovakia was by then a very different country. As Beneš had anticipated, the USSR's influence was very much greater than it had been before the War, and not only because Czechoslovakia by that time had a common border with the Soviet state (following the Soviet annexation of Sub-Carpathian Ruthenia from Czechoslovakia—now in Ukraine). The liberation of most of its territory by the Red Army and the tendency to favour left-wing parties in much of Europe at that time also increased support for its protégé, the Communist Party of Czechoslovakia (CPCz). Within one year of the War's end, the problem of the German minority was resolved by its deportation. Also, attempts were made, albeit with grudging acquiescence from Beneš, to satisfy Slovak demands for greater autonomy, through the establishment in Bratislava of a legislature (the Slovak National Council) and an executive Board of Commissioners.

Recognition that the proliferation of political parties in the pre-war First Republic had been a major source of political instability led President Beneš to favour a reduction in the number of parties that would be permitted after 1945. It was a policy, however, that contributed to the curtailment, rather than the strengthening, of parliamentary democracy. It was achieved largely through the prohibition not only of parties that had collaborated with the Nazis, but the proscription of the Agrarian Party, electorally the most popular of pre-war Czech parties.

The first parliamentary elections since the Second World War, which took place in May 1946, demonstrated a marked increase in support for the CPCz, particularly in the Czech Lands, where it attracted over 40% of the votes cast. (In Slovakia the CPCz obtained 30%.) The CPCz formed the largest group in the new Constituent National Assembly, with 114 of the 300 seats. Of the three other parties that nominated candidates in Czech constituencies, the moderate Czechoslovak Socialist Party won 55 seats, the Roman Catholic-orientated Czechoslovak People's Party 46 and the centre-left Czechoslovak Social Democrats 37. The remaining seats went

to three parties standing only in Slovakia: the Democratic Party, which won 62% of the popular vote there and was allocated 43 seats in the Assembly, and the Labour Party and the Freedom Party, which won two and three seats, respectively.

The success of the CPCz, which had never attracted more than 13% of the votes cast before 1939, reflected a number of factors. The party's patriotic stance in the late 1930s and its association with the USSR, which had liberated most of Czechoslovakia from German occupation, contributed to its appeal. Also, its acceptance by Beneš and its participation in the Provisional Government that had governed the country prior to the general election conferred a legitimacy and respectability that it had lacked previously. Moreover, its leaders' avowed commitment to 'a specific Czechoslovak road to socialism' implied that the CPCz would remain faithful to the country's democratic and parliamentary traditions. However, that commitment to democracy proved short-lived. After two years of an all-party coalition Government, the CPCz leader and Prime Minister, Klement Gottwald, took the opportunity provided by the resignation of 12 non-communist ministers to seize power by ostensibly constitutional means. On 25 February 1948 President Beneš was forced to agree to the appointment of a new Government, which was dominated by communists. Thereafter, events moved quickly. On 9 May parliament approved a new Constitution, which declared Czechoslovakia 'a people's democracy'. On 30 May new elections were held to the National Assembly, but with a single list of candidates. This allowed some representation of non-communist parties, but those parties were already under the control of communist sympathizers. On 2 June, following his refusal to ratify the new Constitution, Beneš resigned from the presidency and, 12 days later, Gottwald succeeded him in that office.

In the years that followed, political repression was directed not only at the communists' opponents, including representatives of the Roman Catholic Church and leading figures in other parties, but also at members of the CPCz, in a series of 'show trials', which were among the most severe in Eastern Europe. They reached their most extreme in November 1952, when 14 senior party and government officials, including Rudolf Slánský, a former Secretary-General of the CPCz, were found guilty on charges of conspiracy against the state. Eleven of them, including Slánský, were subsequently executed. By the time of Gottwald's death, on 14 March 1953, only one week after the death of Stalin (Iosif V. Dzhugashvili), the Soviet leader, Czechoslovakia had abandoned any pretence at divergence from the ideology of the Soviet regime introduced since 1948. The continuation of uncompromising policies was demonstrated by the brutal suppression, in June 1953, of workers' demonstrations in Plzeň (Pilsen) and other Czech towns. The workers were protesting against price rises and a currency reform that depleted the value of savings. Furthermore, political trials continued, notably those of alleged 'Slovak nationalists', in 1954, which led to the imprisonment of a number of leading Slovak communists. Among them was Gustáv Husák, who was later to become General Secretary of the CPCz and President of Czechoslovakia.

It was not until the early 1960s that the changes introduced by the post-Stalinist leadership in the USSR had any real effect in Czechoslovakia. One decade after Stalin's death Antonín Novotný, who had become First Secretary of the CPCz in September 1953 and Czechoslovak President in 1957, finally recognized that the country had suffered from the same Stalinist 'personality cult' as its neighbours. In the years that followed, support for economic and political reform grew within the CPCz. On 5 January 1968 Novotný, who was seen as an obstacle to radical change, was persuaded to resign as CPCz leader and was replaced by Alexander Dubček, until then leader of the Communist Party of Slovakia, part of the CPCz. Dubček immediately embarked on a programme of radical political and economic reforms, thus beginning a short period of political tolerance, which came to be known as the 'Prague Spring'.

THE 1968 'PRAGUE SPRING' AND ITS AFTERMATH

The reforms agreed by the new Dubček leadership envisaged the combination of a socialist economy, albeit one in which market mechanisms would have a role to play, with a democratization of the political system. In addition, greater freedom of expression was to be permitted, a greater degree of separation between party and state was anticipated and a federal system of government was to be introduced. However, the proposals were seen by the Soviet leadership as a threat to the political stability of other countries in Eastern Europe and, therefore, to the security interests of the USSR. On the night of 20–21 August 1968 troops from the other Warsaw Treaty Organization, or Warsaw Pact, states (except Romania), led by Soviet forces, invaded Czechoslovakia. The Soviet leadership's original intention of replacing Dubček with more orthodox communists, however, failed, owing to popular resistance and the refusal of Ludvík Svoboda (who had replaced Novotný as President in April) to accept pro-Soviet nominees. Nevertheless, the invasion ended the Prague Spring reforms and, eight months later, on 17 April 1969, the USSR was able to force Dubček's resignation as party leader.

Of the 1968 reforms, only one survived: the federal system, which had been introduced on 1 January 1969. Separate Czech and Slovak Republics were established, within a Czechoslovak federation; a Czech National Council and a Czech administration were created (to parallel those established in Slovakia in 1945); and the former National Assembly was transformed into a bicameral Federal Assembly. However, failure to federalize the CPCz and increasing centralization during the 1970s rendered the changes ineffective as a means of granting the Slovaks the greater autonomy that they sought.

Under Gustáv Husák, Dubček's successor as party leader, Czechoslovakia reverted to a model of socialism more acceptable to the Soviet leadership. Between 1969 and 1971 the CPCz lost one-quarter of its members, as proponents of reform left or were expelled. Reformers were also dismissed from influential posts in other institutions and organizations. Newspapers, journals and organizations such as the Writers' Union and the Youth Union, which opposed the new course, were closed and opposition of any kind suppressed. It was only in the latter half of the 1970s that a durable dissident movement began to emerge, with the appearance of Charter 77 and the Committee for the Defence of the Rights of the Unjustly Persecuted (VONS). Their focus on civil and political rights, which the communist regime ostensibly recognized, and pursuit of their objectives in ways which were, in theory at least, permitted by the Constitution, seemed to promise greater prospects for survival than outright opposition. Although neither Charter 77 nor VONS can be said to have had a direct impact on the regime, they did make a positive contribution in a number of ways. VONS, which dealt with wrongful arrests, became a valuable source of information about civil-rights abuses in Czechoslovakia. Charter 77 preserved the democratic values that had been revived during the Prague Spring and publicized the continuing struggle for civil and political rights. However, perhaps the principal strength of both movements was in uniting people from diverse sections of the political spectrum, including former communists, liberal democrats and members of the Christian opposition. They established a sense of community, co-operation and trust, which was to bear fruit in November 1989, when the communists' power was finally challenged.

THE END OF COMMUNIST RULE

Throughout the 1970s and 1980s it was clear that change in Czechoslovakia would not come about without change first in the USSR. Yet, even Mikhail Gorbachev's election as General Secretary of the Communist Party of the Soviet Union in March 1985, and his pursuit of radical reform, had little immediate effect in Czechoslovakia. In December 1987 Husák gave up his post as leader of the CPCz (while retaining the presidency, to which he had been elected in 1975), but his successor was Miloš Jakeš, the man who had been responsible for the purge of the CPCz in 1970. The continuing repressive character of the regime was evident in its generally harsh response to the public protests against its policies, which became a more common event from 1988 onwards. Changing attitudes among the public were increasingly evident. A greater readiness on the part of those outside traditional dissident groups to demonstrate their support for radical changes was shown on 21 August 1988, when several thousand protesters demonstrated in Wenceslas Square, in Prague. A similar protest took place on 28 October, the 70th anniversary of the foundation of Czechoslovakia. On 10 December, UN Human Rights' Day, the authorities for once agreed to allow an unofficial meeting, which was to be addressed by the playwright and leading figure in Charter 77 and VONS, Václav Havel.

A still more serious challenge to the authorities came in early 1989, when demonstrations took place on 15–20 January, to commemorate the suicide of Jan Palach 20 years earlier. Palach had burnt himself to death in protest at the concessions made by the Dubček leadership to the USSR's demands for the ending of the 1968 reforms. The crowds were brutally dispersed by police, leading dissidents who had been involved in the demonstrations were arrested (including Havel, who was sentenced to nine months' imprisonment) and restrictive legislation was introduced, in an attempt to prevent further protests. None of these measures, however, had much effect. Pro-democracy demonstrations took place again, on 1 May, 21 August and 28 October. Furthermore, the police brutality in January had provoked a written protest to Ladislav Adamec, the federal Prime Minister, from Cardinal František Tomášek, the Roman Catholic Archbishop of Prague. A petition, signed by more than 2,000 people, condemned the police attacks on the demonstrators and demanded the release of those who had been arrested. In June another petition, entitled 'A Few Sentences', was published. Among other things, it demanded greater political freedom, the release of political prisoners and an end to censorship and to the suppression of independent initiatives.

The growing public assertiveness was encouraged by events beyond Czechoslovakia's frontiers. The appointment of a non-communist Prime Minister in Poland in August 1989 and the opening of the Berlin Wall (which divided the city between an eastern German Democratic Republic and a western Federal Republic of Germany) in early November were clear signals to Czechs and Slovaks that the Soviet administration would no longer oppose radical change in the countries of the Eastern European bloc. The event that was to stimulate sufficiently widespread protests to displace the communist regime came on 17 November, when student participants in an officially sanctioned march in Prague, to mark the anniversary of the Nazis' execution of Czech students 50 years earlier, were brutally attacked by special police units. Following week-long demonstrations, which spread throughout the country, the entire CPCz leadership resigned on 24 November. The Prime Minister, Adamec, attempted to negotiate with representatives of the opposition, which had quickly established two new political movements, Civic Forum in the Czech Republic and Public Against Violence (PAV) in Slovakia, to co-ordinate all democratic forces. Adamec's hopes of forming a transitional administration including CPCz representatives proved futile and he resigned in early December. On 10 December the 'Government of National Understanding' took office, with Marián Čalfa (formerly Adamec's deputy) as Prime Minister. The communists were allocated only a minority of places. The clearest indication that communist rule had ended in Czechoslovakia came three weeks later, on 29 December, when Václav Havel was elected President of Czechoslovakia.

RETURN TO PARLIAMENTARY DEMOCRACY

Confirmation of the communists' defeat came in June 1990, when the first genuinely free general election since the Second World War was held in Czechoslovakia. The results indicated overwhelming support for parliamentary democracy, with a rate of voter participation of 96.4%, and the CPCz winning just 13% of the votes cast. In the Czech Republic Civic Forum attracted one-half of the votes cast, securing a majority in the Czech legislature (127 of the 200 seats) and a majority of Czech seats in both houses of the Federal Assembly.

Although the rejection of communism was clear, the future direction of policy was less certain. Both Czechs and Slovaks had indicated they favoured the re-establishment of a pluralist democracy but, during the two years before the second parliamentary elections, which were fixed for mid-1992, sharp differences emerged over a range of fundamental policies. Two issues in particular were to demonstrate divergence between the two federal partners: economic policy and the character of the state.

Well before the 1992 elections it had become clear that it would be difficult to reconcile the Slovak desire for greater autonomy, albeit within a 'common state', and for greater state intervention in the economy, with the Czech insistence on a strong federal government and a radical shift to a market economy. By the time of the June 1992 elections Civic Forum and PAV had both disappeared. In the Czech Republic the more right-wing of the successor parties, the Civic Democratic Party (CDP), led by Václav Klaus, the outgoing federal finance minister and protagonist of a free-market economy, emerged as the strongest party. The victory in Slovakia of the Movement for a Democratic Slovakia, which favoured much greater devolution of power than was acceptable to the victorious Czech parties, created an impasse in the Federal Assembly, where the balance of forces provided little prospect of a viable government. Thus, in the next six months agreement was reached to bring the common state to an end and, on 1 January 1993, independent Czech and Slovak Republics came into being. In the Czech Republic a centre-right coalition, led by Klaus, remained in office for a full four-year term. The new Government was committed to the introduction of a market economy, the strengthening of parliamentary democracy and the negotiation of the Czech Republic's entry into the North Atlantic Treaty Organization (NATO) and the European Community (known as the European Union—EU from November 1993).

Disagreements within the coalition, which comprised Klaus' CDP, the much smaller Civic Democratic Alliance (CDA) and the Christian Democratic Union—Czechoslovak People's Party (CDU—CPP), were relatively minor and did not undermine its cohesion. It was not until the June 1996 elections to the Chamber of Deputies (Poslanecká sněmovna—previously the Czech National Council, since separation and independence the lower house of the Czech parliament—although an upper house was not created until November 1996), when the coalition lost its parliamentary majority, that serious doubts arose about its survival. Whereas the three coalition parties had held 105 of the 200 seats in the outgoing Chamber of Deputies, they won only a combined 99 seats in 1996, despite increasing their overall share of the vote by about 2%. The reason for this anomaly

was a technical one. Their majority in 1992 had, in part, been the consequence of the large number of votes given to parties that failed to achieve the 5% share necessary for parliamentary representation. As a consequence, successful parties were accorded a higher number of seats than was merited by their share of the poll. In 1996 the number of such 'wasted' votes was halved, largely to the benefit of the Czechoslovak Social Democratic Party (CSDP), which quadrupled its share of the vote to 26%, winning 61 seats, as it consolidated the support of the democratic left.

The CSDP agreed to give tacit support to a minority Government, with Klaus continuing as Prime Minister. In return, the governing coalition elected the CSDP leader, Miloš Zeman, as Chairman (speaker) of the Chamber of Deputies. That this Government survived for only 18 months was not owing to its numerical weakness, however, but rather was the consequence of tensions between the coalition parties and more fundamental disagreements within the CDP. The resignation of Jozef Zieleniec from his position as Minister for Foreign Relations and Deputy Chairman of the CDP in October 1997 was the first clear indication of problems within the party's leadership. Subsequently, it was revealed that in 1995 the CDP had accepted a campaign donation from a Czech businessman who had later bid successfully in a privatization tender for a steelworks; Klaus denied knowledge of the ostensibly foreign sponsor's identity, but Zieleniec claimed to have informed the Prime Minister prior to the 1996 general election. Further accusations of financial irregularities against the CDP followed, including the alleged existence of a Swiss bank account for party funds. On 30 November 1997 Klaus and his Government resigned, following the withdrawal of the CDA and the CDU—CPP from the coalition. The re-election of Klaus as Chairman of the CDP in December led important figures within the party, including the former interior minister, Jan Ruml, to defect and form a new centre-right party called the Freedom Union (FU).

In mid-December 1997 Jozef Tošovský, hitherto Governor of the central bank, was appointed as an independent Prime Minister and given the task of forming an interim government. The new Government was appointed the following month and included seven non-political ministers, as well as several from each of the parties of the former governing coalition, though the four CDP ministers defected to the FU in February 1998, after a dispute with Klaus over their participation in Tošovský's Government. The interim Government did much to restore stability, but the early parliamentary elections of 19–20 June appeared to achieve little by way of a long-term resolution of the political uncertainties. The three centre-right parties, the CDP, the CDU—CPP and the FU, won 102 of the 200 seats, but the bitter disputes between them made agreement on forming a coalition impossible. Moreover, since the CSDP emerged as the largest single party, with 74 seats (13 more than in 1996), Havel, who had been re-elected President earlier in the year, invited their leader, Zeman, to try to form a government. Unwilling to attempt a coalition with the communists (who won 24 seats) and himself unable to reach agreement with the CDU—CPP and the FU, Zeman arranged with Klaus that a minority CSDP administration would not be voted out of office by the CDP. In return, Klaus was elected Chairman of the Chamber of Deputies and a number of other CDP deputies gained other important parliamentary posts.

In 1998 the CSDP increased its share of the votes cast to 32.3%, but just as many voters (over 40%) remained committed to centre-right parties as in 1992 and 1996. However, deteriorating economic performance, characterized by rates of unemployment unprecedented in the Czech Republic, occasioned a decrease in the party's popularity in 1999 and 2000. Opinion polls demonstrated a resurgence in support for the communists, who were frequently the second most popular party, although this revival seemed more likely to represent the electorate's disaffection with the CSDP Government in the middle of its term of office than a genuine return to the far left.

In March 1999 the Czech Republic formally acceded to membership of NATO, along with Hungary and Poland, the first three former communist countries in Europe to be accepted into the Organization. Admission to NATO had been the primary focus of successive Czech Governments' foreign policies, despite opposition from certain factions within the country and from its easterly neighbours. The expanded Organization's first military intervention, the aerial attacks on the Federal Republic of Yugoslavia (FRY), began later that month. The Czech Government was initially criticized from within the country for both a perceived ambivalence towards NATO's objectives in the FRY and excessive support for NATO. In April Zeman advocated a negotiated solution to the conflict and warned that the NATO action might strengthen the position of the President of the FRY, Slobodan Milošević. Operational support for the NATO action was slower in being granted than in other countries of the region, although later in April the Government permitted NATO aircraft to fly in Czech air-space and ground transport to cross Czech territory.

Throughout the 1990s admission to the EU was considered crucial to the future development of the nation by most Czech political figures. In 1998 it was announced that the Czech Republic would be one of the countries in the 'first wave' of enlargement, and formal negotiations regarding the Republic's accession to the EU began. The date established by the Czech negotiators as a target for Czech accession, 1 January 2003, was widely regarded to be somewhat optimistic, given the numerous technical issues that needed to be resolved and continuing uncertainty in existing member countries over the eastward expansion of the EU. Nevertheless, by mid-2002 the prospect of Czech accession by 2004 seemed more likely as negotiations proceeded and domestic legislation was increasingly adjusted to correspond to that of EU member states. Meanwhile, by mid-1999 there were further indications of increasing disenchantment with both the CSDP and the general political situation. In July a number of public figures, many of whom were former associates of President Havel, issued an appeal under the title 'Impuls 99'. The declaration was more a criticism of the current political establishment than a direct challenge to it. It sought to counter popular alienation from democratic politics by encouraging wider participation in political life and the development of a more active civil society, rather than through direct pursuit of political power. The group included Tomáš Halík, a Roman Catholic priest and professor of sociology, who was widely regarded as a potential successor to Havel upon the latter's completion of his second term as President in 2003 (indeed Havel had himself spoken favourably of Halík's potential as a presidential candidate).

The clearest demonstration of public disillusionment with party politics was provided by the CDP's August 1999 defeat in a by-election for a seat in the Senate (Senat) which, it had been assumed, it would easily win. The ballot was won by an independent candidate, Václav Fischer, who based his electoral campaign on his non-involvement with any political party and on the contrast between his record of probity in business and the numerous allegations of corruption against members of the parliamentary parties. Following his election, Fischer gained in popularity throughout the country and in May 2000 an opinion poll revealed him to be the political figure seen by Czechs as of most benefit to the country. On 17 November 1999, the 10th anniversary of the 'velvet revolution' that ended communist rule, a statement entitled 'Děkujeme, Odejděte' (Thank You, Now Leave) was issued by a number of former student leaders who had participated in those events. They argued that, in order to revive popular interest in the political process, leading figures of the 1990s, including Klaus and Zeman, should accept that they could no longer contribute further to the country's political transition, and withdraw from political life in favour of a younger generation. The movement that grew from this statement gained the support of many Czechs, attracting an estimated 50,000 people to a rally in Prague in early December, by which time 150,000 signatures of support had been obtained.

These apparent challenges had little effect on the policies of the two principal parties. In January 2000 the CDP renewed its agreement to sustain the minority CSDP Government; consequently, that administration remained in power until the next general election in June 2002. Nevertheless, neither party was happy with the situation and looked for ways to create more stable government in future. An attempt was made by the CSDP and the CDP to force through changes to the electoral law, which were designed to reduce the number of parties elected to the Chamber of Deputies and ensure their dominance of the Czech political scene. The amendments were approved by that body in May 2000, overturning a presidential veto. They were thwarted only after President Havel appealed to the Constitutional Court, which ruled that they were in breach of a provision in the Constitution that the Chamber of Deputies be elected by a system of proportional representation.

Popular dissatisfaction with the CSDP Government was made clear in November 2000, when elections were held to one-third of the seats in the Senate and to the regional assemblies of 14 new, higher self-governing units (regions), which were to replace the 73 districts hitherto in place. The CSDP performed badly in both elections; in the election to the Senate, it won only one of the 26 seats contested. The CDP did somewhat better, winning eight seats. However, the election proved a greater success for the so-called Quad Coalition (an informal, right-of-centre alliance, embracing the CDU—CPP, the FU, the CDA and the small Democratic Union). The alliance won 16 seats, resulting in an increase in total representation to 39 of the 81 seats in the Senate, making it the strongest grouping in the upper house. In the election to the regional assemblies, the CSDP was the fourth-placed party (even the communists achieved greater success). In seven of the 14 new assemblies control was secured by the CDP, while another six were won by the Quad Coalition. The Communist Party of Bohemia and Moravia secured the 14th region, based in the north Bohemian town of Ústí nad Labem.

These reverses notwithstanding, the CSDP's popularity seemed to increase in the first months of 2001. This improvement in popularity was achieved despite, or possibly because of, Prime Minister Zeman's resignation, in April, as leader of the party and his replacement as leader by Vladimír Špidla, who had been Deputy Prime Minister and Minister of Labour and Social Affairs since 1998. Although Zeman was to continue to lead the Government until the parliamentary elections scheduled for June 2002, Špidla was regarded not only as a more reassuring figure than the polemical Zeman, but also as a politician capable of leading the party to renewed success in future elections.

Popular disillusionment with party politics in the Czech Republic was reflected in the low rate of voter participation at the general election held on 14–15 June 2002, which, at 58%, was well below the level of participation achieved in 1998, when three-quarters of the electorate had gone to the polls. Although popular alienation from the two largest parties, the CSDP and the CDP, appeared to be largely responsible for the increase in voter apathy, the collapse of the Quad Coalition, owing to inter-party disagreement, in early 2002 was also believed to have contributed to the low participation rate. Although the remaining parties—the CDU—CPP, the FU and the Democratic Union—reformed in what was then called simply the Coalition, confidence in this third political force as a potential challenger to the traditionally dominant parties had been significantly undermined.

The results of the elections—held under a new, 'compromise' electoral system, which divided the country into 15 constituencies, and which Havel had decided not to oppose because of the imminence of the elections—were considered a victory for the CSDP, although its share of the vote declined slightly (to 30.2%, equivalent to 70 of the 200 seats in the lower house) compared with the 1998 poll. The elections were a considerable disappointment for the CDP, which came second with 24.5% of the votes, more than 3% less than in 1998. The biggest surprise of the elections, however, was the success of the communists in increasing their share of the votes by more than 7%, to 18.5%, leaving the Coalition, with 14.3%, in fourth place. The communists' success was all the more remarkable because its support had increased, in absolute terms, despite the lower rate of participation by the electorate.

Although the CSDP and the CDP remained the major forces in Czech politics following the elections, they had failed to move the country towards the two-party system both had appeared to be promoting during the previous parliament. The bilateral agreements that had kept the minority CSDP Government in power throughout that period were obviated for the future. On 17 June 2002 President Havel invited Špidla to begin negotiations to form a new government. Despite the resignation of Hana Marvanova from the leadership of the FU (citing incompatible political agendas) during these negotiations, on 9 July a formal agreement establishing the terms of coalition government between the CSDP and the parties of the Coalition was signed by the party leaders. A new, 17-member coalition Government headed by Špidla was officially appointed by Havel on 15 July.

The 2002 elections were, in a number of ways, a significant turning point in Czech politics. For the first time in over a decade, overall support for parties of the centre-right dropped to below 40% of the votes. The formation of the new coalition Government demonstrated that the CSDP, under Špidla, was at last an acceptable partner to smaller parties on the right, which had been unwilling to work with it so closely in the past. However, that was not the only striking change on the political scene. Zeman's departure from both the CSDP leadership and the premiership, and Klaus's resignation as leader of the CDP, after its electoral defeat, appeared to represent the end of an era dominated by figures who emerged to the forefront of political life at the time of the 'velvet revolution'. The expiry in early 2003 of Havel's second, and final, term as the country's President also created an impression of generational change.

In practice, however, neither Klaus nor Zeman proved ready to leave the political stage for good. In fact, both were focused on the presidency, vacated by Havel on 2 February 2003. Zeman's entry into the presidential contest proved futile and, moreover, divided the CSDP. His failure owed as much to opposition by his party's leader, as to his unacceptability to other members of the Chamber of Deputies; Špidla can only have regarded Zeman's elevation as a potential threat to his power and authority. Nor was Klaus's election a foregone conclusion. It took nine attempts to meet the rather complex conditions for electing a president before he eventually secured election on 28 February.

The long, protracted process that preceded Klaus's election persuaded many sceptics in the Czech Republic that the country should join neighbouring states in moving to a system of popular election to the presidency, rather than election by the legislature. None the less, whatever doubts parliamentarians had about Klaus's suitability for the post, he had the advantage over other contenders of an international reputation, as well as extensive political experience and undoubted intellectual abilities. In that respect, he could prove as successful a President as his immediate predecessor.

It was, nevertheless, something of a paradox that the Czech Republic's best known 'Eurosceptic' was elected President less than four months before the country held a referendum on its accession to the EU, to which it had been invited to accede from May 2004. However, at the referendum, which took place on 13–14 June 2003, and in which only 55% of the electorate participated, more than 77% of votes were cast in support of the country's membership of the Union.

The Economy

Dr MARTIN MYANT

INTRODUCTION

The territory of the existing Czech Republic experienced industrialization in the late 19th and early 20th centuries, making it the centre for coal, steel and textiles in the old Habsburg Empire. In the inter-war period the economic structure of the then Czechoslovakia was close to that of advanced countries of the time, with 45% of the active population employed in mining and manufacturing, and per-head national income estimated at about 75% of the level achieved in France. This economic strength, together with the absence of serious destruction during the Second World War, gave Czechoslovakia a special position within the emerging Soviet bloc.

During the early 1950s the economy was reorientated towards the export of heavy machinery and armaments to Czechoslovakia's new allies in the East. Exports to the planned economies rose, representing 71% of the total in 1951–55 (a figure that remained fairly stable until the 1980s), while the contribution of machinery to total exports increased from 20% in 1948 to 42% in 1953. Throughout the 1950s growth was reasonably rapid (national income increased by 150% in Czechoslovakia, and by 138% in the already more developed Czech part between 1948 and 1962), owing to high investment and the ease of selling to the East. However, the light industrial sector and more sophisticated consumer goods, such as motorcycles and cars, were unable to compete in Western Europe. As a result, exports to market economies, which remained essential for many of the economy's import needs, could only be maintained by selling at low prices and by switching to selling semi-manufactures, such as steel and cement, and raw materials. Thus, incorporation into the Soviet bloc led to isolation from contact with the most advanced economies and, consequently, a widening technological gap. Difficulties with the export trade contributed to a sharp decline in growth in the early 1960s, stimulating pressure for economic reform and the search for a new economic orientation.

The attempted reform and Warsaw Pact invasion of 1968 (see History) reinforced Czechoslovakia's incorporation into the Soviet bloc. Although the economic system did not fully return to the centralized model of the 1950s, talk of comprehensive reform was, from then on, taboo, and closer contacts with the West were discouraged. Nevertheless, the economy continued to expand in the early 1970s, with annual rates of growth of more than 5% from 1970 to 1975, owing to cheap petroleum from the USSR and to the economy's ability to reorientate towards the mass production of consumer goods, again largely for export to the East. From 1976, however, the economy suffered insidious stagnation, and low levels of competitiveness on international markets led to an increase in the contribution of planned economies to exports, reaching 77% by 1985. Central planning was still able to ensure full employment and price stability, but it lacked the adaptability and dynamism to guarantee rising living standards and to give access to the range of new consumer goods available in Western Europe. This failure was particularly striking in a country that had taken pride in being part of the developed world from the beginning of the century. Czechoslovak gross domestic product (GDP) per head was around 50%–55% of the level of advanced market economies in Western Europe.

ECONOMIC POLICY

Liberalization

Czechoslovakia began the transition to a market economy from a relatively strong position. Its hard-currency debt was a manageable US $7,900m. The country was even a net creditor, although loans to a number of underdeveloped and Eastern bloc countries were unlikely to be repaid. It had a history of price stability and had not suffered from the chronic shortages of basic consumer goods experienced in other countries; there was no inflationary legacy from past forced savings. Nevertheless, despite some exaggerated hopes about the country's economic performance, industrial productivity was about one-third the average level for members of the European Community (known as the European Union—EU from November 1993). Although enterprises producing modern manufactured goods were soon to prove incapable of competing in an open economy, the country's excellent location in Central Europe appeared advantageous for rapid integration into the international economy.

There were debates about the pace and sequencing of reform measures. Disagreement centred on the extent and speed of price and import liberalization, and on the extent and method of privatization. The first issue was resolved, in practice, in January 1991. Prices were freed for goods covering over 80% of consumer spending: basics such as rent and electricity remained government-controlled. Extensive import liberalization was accompanied by a 53% devaluation of the currency and the abolition of the old system of multiple exchange rates. The immediate result was a short period of sharp inflationary increases; consumer-price inflation reached 56.5% in the Czech Republic as a whole in 1991, but was largely concentrated in the first two months of the year. It was quickly brought under control by a very tight monetary policy and by strict controls on wage increases, which were relaxed by 1992. Inflation then averaged 10% from 1992 to 1998, largely driven in the later years by increases in the remaining government-controlled prices, dropping to an average rate of 4.3% over the 1999–2001 period and 0.6% in 2002. In 1991, however, the effect of inflation—as it could not be matched by wage increases—was to reduce real earnings by 26%, and real domestic consumer spending declined by 26.5%. The liberalization of imports also began to reorientate some consumer demand to foreign goods, such as second-hand cars. The inevitable result was a decline in domestic industrial output.

This decline was exacerbated by a simultaneous collapse in demand from Eastern bloc countries with the disintegration of the trading system of the Council for Mutual Economic Assistance. As a result of these factors there was a decline in Czech GDP in 1991 of 11.6% and a further decline of 0.5% in 1992.

Privatization

Debates over privatization centred on the relative merits of the use of vouchers to distribute shares among the population, compared with direct sales to foreign companies, or restructuring under state ownership. The last of these methods was favoured for a time for a few sectors, such as steel and energy, but very little was done, and the preference shifted to the two other methods. These laid the basis for a very rapid transfer of state assets to private ownership. The contribution of the private sector to GDP, calculated rather optimistically to include organizations with only a partial private share, was reported to be 75% by 1996, when the Ministry of Privatization was dissolved, its tasks allegedly completed. Such claims, and the success in controlling inflation at a reasonable level by Central European standards, stimulated international confidence in the Czech Republic, which was accepted as the first transition economy into the Organisation for Economic Co-operation and Development (OECD) in November 1995. They also stimulated confidence domestically that the transition was progressing well, and full convertibility of the currency on the current account, in line with Article VIII of the IMF's Articles of Agreement (see Regional Organizations in Part Four), was introduced in October of that year.

The biggest early sale to a foreign company was that, in 1991, of a controlling stake in the ŠKODA car manufacturer to Volkswagen of Germany. This led to a steady increase in car output from 180,000 in 1989, a level that had been reached in the mid-1970s, to 460,886 by 2001. Some 82% of cars were exported, accounting for about 10% of total exports. Volkswagen also introduced modernization, often by encouraging further inward investment to the components industry, which contributed another 6% of total exports by 2001. However, there were disagreements with the Czech Government, when Volkswagen reduced some initial investment plans, and there were persistent suspicions of the motives of inward investors among many Czech politicians. The sale of enterprises to multinational companies, therefore, remained limited to a few branches of manufacturing.

Privatization to domestic owners was generally preferred. In the absence of substantial savings, this had to proceed either by vouchers or by credit. Despite some political doubts, the voucher method was used in two phases for 35% of the property offered for privatization, between 1992 and 1995. All citizens could buy voucher books for a nominal sum and exchange the voucher points for shares in firms through a complex bidding process. Some 77% of the adult population took part in the first phase of privatization, and 74% in the second. However, 70% of shares were accumulated by privatization investment funds, to which individuals entrusted their voucher points; large banks controlled the majority of these funds, but they played a relatively minor role in corporate governance. Voucher privatization left firms broadly under the control of emerging managements, and rarely introduced external expertise or new sources of finance for investment. Many firms that experienced this form of privatization were either unable to win the struggle for survival after the loss of demand in 1991, or did so on the basis of bank credits that they were later unable to repay.

Privatization by credit was increasingly favoured, particularly after the completion of the two phases of voucher privatization. This, together with sales to foreign companies, accounted for much of the property privatized by the end of 1997. There had also been some free transfer of property, mostly to local government bodies, but a large amount remained under state ownership. Privatization by sale enabled the Government to ensure that firms had powerful owners, but it also left those owners heavily in debt. By 1999 the Government had concluded that firms privatized by voucher or credit schemes had performed worse than those left under state ownership, and much worse than those sold to foreign companies. Unable to repay their debts, many companies were on the brink of bankruptcy.

RENEWED GROWTH

The resumption of economic growth was slightly delayed by the cost of the break-up of Czechoslovakia, but GDP subsequently increased rapidly, reaching a peak rate of 6.5% in 1995. There were three sources of renewed growth. The first, and most permanent source, was expansion based on inward investment, at first in the motor industry, but subsequently in electrical consumer goods and electronics, as the country's location in Central Europe attracted multinational companies. The second source was a very rapid expansion of new, small businesses, especially in the services sector. Self-employment increased, to account for 7.5% of the total employed labour force in 1995. This was partly a unique occurrence, rather than a sustainable expansion, as it filled a vacuum left by the under-development of services under central planning, when self-employment was unknown. Moreover, much of the early expansion was based on credit, and by the mid-1990s banks became more cautious, as too many debtors began to default on their repayments.

The third source was the reorientation of the export trade from East to West. The developed market economies accounted for 57% of exports in 1993, rising steadily to account for 75% in 2001. With this came a change in product types. Metal goods declined from 63.7% of Czechoslovak exports in 1989, to 34% of Czech exports in 1994—for machinery and transport equipment the decline was from 38% to 26%—as the share of raw materials and semi-manufactures increased. Competition in markets for these products depended on price rather than product quality, and Czech labour costs were approximately 40% of the average EU level. Later in the decade the trend was reversed, as inward investment laid the basis for exports of more sophisticated products: machinery and transport equipment accounted for 50% of exports in 2002. However, it was more basic products that first enabled exports to expand into advanced market economies, a form of growth that had limits. Profitability was low, on account of competition from other low wage areas, and exports had to be restrained to counter the threat of restrictions from the EU when domestic industries, such as steel and textiles, in EU member states complained of the 'dumping' of low-cost products.

INSTABILITY AND DECLINE

Economic growth peaked in 1995. The deceleration over the following two years was primarily the result of the exhaustion of two of the growth sources outlined above, and partly the failure of domestically-owned industries to compete both in domestic and in export markets. As a result, consumption spending, the leading factor in GDP growth, was increasingly directed to imported consumer goods. The deficit on the current account of the balance of payments increased steadily, reaching 7.4% of GDP in 1996 and 8.3% in the first quarter of 1997. This was considered a dangerously high level for any country, but had been masked for some time by an inflow of capital.

Some of this capital was stable, long-term investment by multinational companies, but larger shares were taken by portfolio investment (foreign investment companies buying shares that had previously been exchanged for vouchers) and, above all, by short- and long-term bank credits, which were highly unstable. Suggestions of imminent devaluation and a critical report from the IMF led to a sharp reduction in lending by foreign banks and to speculation against the Czech currency.

In April and May 1997 the Government was compelled to implement emergency measures to reduce the level of demand so as to reduce imports and restore equilibrium on the current account. Budget spending was reduced, in real terms, by 2.6% between 1996 and 1998, with public-sector pay affected particularly severely. Restrictive monetary measures also led banks to reassess their lending strategies, and two of the largest banks had effectively halted lending by the end of 1997. Many companies were almost unaffected—some sectors made little use of credit, while solid monopolies, like electricity, were able to borrow from foreign banks—but some large firms in engineering, chemicals and heavy industry were very seriously affected.

The combined effect of lower demand and restricted credit, together with continuing difficulties in competing with imported goods, led to declines in real GDP of 1.2% and 0.4% in 1998 and 1999, respectively. The following two years saw renewed growth, with the most dynamic element being the newly created branches of multinational companies. From 1998, policies were developed to attract inward investment to 'greenfield' sites, replacing the *laissez-faire* approach of the previous years.

REVIVAL OF ENTERPRISES AND BANKS

However, the Government faced two lasting areas of difficulty. The first was in major manufacturing enterprises, several of which were refused credit even to continue existing levels of production. The Government tried to find a systematic solution. In October 1999 it established the Revitalization Agency as an independent body, which, by means of debt-equity swaps, took control of a small number of large firms. They were then mostly sold to foreign companies after substantial reductions in scale. The impact was limited by the finance available. Only eight companies were involved and finding satisfactory foreign purchasers proved difficult and time-consuming. A solution was still needed for much more of Czech industry. Emergency, short-term solutions were found for some key enterprises, with the Government guaranteeing credits for continued production only. A new Czech Consolidation Agency was formed in September 2001 out of the former Consolidation Bank, a state body that had handled enterprises' bad debts. It inherited substantial shareholdings in many firms, but lacked the resources or the expertise to play a major role in their restructuring.

The second difficulty was in the banking sector, the core of which was represented by four large banks, inherited from the period of central planning. Three had been partially privatized in the first phase of voucher distribution, but had been pressured by the Government into supporting its strategy of rapid transformation. This meant giving credits to newly emerging small businesses that could offer no collateral, giving loans for privatization, and helping to finance firms undergoing voucher privatization that were often already experiencing financial difficulties. By the mid-1990s the banks were growing wary of lending to the domestic economy, but some of their attempts to diversify into foreign operations proved even riskier.

During 1998 and 1999 it became clear that these banks were bearing an unacceptable burden of risky credits that might never be repaid, surpassing 40% of total credits in at least one case. The Government's solution was to devise rescue packages that could enable the banks to continue operating, but this was made conditional on changes to management and the re-establishment of full state majority control. It then sought speedy privatization by sale to a reputable foreign bank. Three were sold to foreign banks, and one faced collapse and was brought under state control in June 2000, and quickly sold to another Czech bank, by then under Belgian ownership. The favourable terms of the sale meant that much of its bad debt and share ownership ended up with the Czech Consolidation Agency. Thus, in both large-scale industry and in banking, the effort to privatize into Czech ownership proved expensive and was finally partially reversed, with the temporary restoration of state ownership, followed by sale to foreign companies. The 'costs of transformation' appear in the state budget as losses for the Consolidation Agency, equivalent in 2002 to about 4% of GDP. Part may be recovered from proceeds from privatization, including lucrative shares in the telecommunications and electricity sectors.

AGRICULTURE

The usual division into primary, secondary and tertiary sectors displayed a rapid transformation in the Czech economy. The primary sector, including agriculture and the extraction of raw materials, underwent a sharp decline, from accounting for 15.3% of employment in 1989 to 5.5% of the labour force at the time of the March 2001 national census. Before 1989, agriculture had been based on co-operatives, accounting for 79% of the sectoral labour force, with state farms accounting for the remaining 21%. Together they ensured net self-sufficiency in food production. In 1990–91 the sector was adversely affected by the removal of price subsidies on basic foods and, subsequently, by full price liberalization. Later in the decade, particularly as conditions for progression towards EU accession necessitated greater openness to agricultural imports, food imports increased to cover 40% of consumption. Agriculture as a whole suffered a reduction in relative income, from 9% above the average for the economy as a whole in 1989, to 23% below the average in 2001, together with the dramatic decline in employment. Output over the same period declined by 27.5%, but much of this was owing to the cessation of inefficient production on less productive land. Thus, labour productivity improved by 136%, a considerably greater increase than that in other major sectors.

The reorganization of the agricultural sector was a source of continuing controversy. The 1,749 co-operatives inherited from the past often included profitable ancillary activities, which either ceased or were continued by new, independent private businesses. Much of agriculture remained collectivized, although by 2001 the giant state farms and co-operatives had been divided into 5,492 businesses of various legal forms.

Laws passed in 1991 and 1992 gave co-operative members the right to reclaim the land that they had owned before the establishment of co-operatives in the 1950s. The number of independent farmers slowly increased to exceed 101,394 in 2001, representing some 57% of the total sectoral labour force. Others were to be allowed to claim financial compensation, although this was an unpopular measure with much of the farming community, as most co-operative members had owned no land, while the former landowners, or their heirs, often had no continuing links to agriculture. The issue of payment remained unresolved, partly because co-operatives lacked the financial means to honour the law.

INDUSTRY

The secondary sector, including manufacturing industry and construction, but excluding the extraction of raw materials, also witnessed a decline in its contribution to total employment, from 42.7% of the total in 1989, to 36.5% of the total labour force at the time of the March 2001 national census. Construction was transformed from a sector based on large firms, serving major housing-construction projects that had largely come to a halt in the 1990s, to one with a predominance of small enterprises and self-employed craftsmen working on smaller-scale construction projects. Its fortunes largely followed those of the rest of the economy.

Czech statistics for sectoral GDP tend to group extractive and manufacturing industries together. Total industrial output declined by 31.7% between 1990 and 1993. Recovery was also slow, with a peak growth rate of 4.4% in 1997. A decline of 2.6% in 1999 was followed by renewed vigorous growth, reaching 6.5% in 2001. Overall, industrial output in 2001 was 14% below its 1990 level. These figures masked a shifting structure, with markedly different levels of performance for different branches. Decline in output was most consistent in textiles and garments and leather and footwear, which decreased by 51% and 84%, respectively, between 1990 and 2001. The share of these branches in total industrial output also declined, from 7.0% and 2.3%, respectively, to 4.0% and 0.5%.

By way of contrast, the transport-equipment branch, including the ŠKODA car manufacturer, but also the deeply troubled Czech-owned manufacturers of goods vehicles and railway locomotives, for which demand had almost disappeared after 1991, registered a decline of only 5% over the same period. There was a clear recovery in the production of electrical and optical instruments, with growth resuming in 1994, leading to an overall expansion in output of 90.8% between 1990 and 2001, and an increase in share of output from 4.6% to 8.8%. The recovery resulted from inward investment by multinational companies, after demand for domestically-manufactured consumer electronics had collapsed in the early part of the decade.

Real wages in industry declined by 25% in 1991, but steadily recovered thereafter, exceeding their 1990 level in 1996 and reaching a figure 16% above that level in 2001. There were some changes in the branch structure of pay, but they were small: the dominant tendency was for wages to move up in line with a 'going rate' established by union bargaining and reflecting expectations of inflation. Employment declined steadily, but initially less quickly than the decline in output. By 2001 employment was 25% below the 1990 level, with slightly larger reductions in declining branches.

The willingness of management structures to concede wage increases above the level of productivity growth meant that wage costs were an increasing burden on enterprises facing difficulties. Light industry, with declining sales and rising wages, was the most severely affected, while some of the large engineering firms suffered more seriously from reduction in credit provisions at the end of the 1990s. However, branches of multinational companies faced no such constraints. By 2000, following steady growth in the preceding years, companies under foreign control accounted for 21.5% of industrial employment and 33.4% of value added, indicating a level of productivity 24% below that of the remaining state-owned companies and 81% above that of private Czech-owned firms.

SERVICES

The proportion of employment accounted for by the tertiary sector increased from 42.8% in 1989 to 57.9% at the time of the March 2001 national census. This included an enormous diversity of occupations, including transport, trade and repair, and health and education. Employment declined in transport and communications, health, education and a variety of other public services, but increased by 90% in the field of public administration and social security, as the performance of such functions proved to be more, rather than less, demanding in a market economy. In the same period, employment increased by 24% in the field of trade and repair, and by 81% in hotels and catering, although it was declining slightly by 1999. Both areas were dominated by new, small businesses, although the latter years of the decade witnessed increased investment by large, foreign companies. Growth in these two branches of the services sector partly reflected a 'catching up' process, as they were grossly under-developed under central planning, and partly reflected new demand from increased tourism. Spending by foreign visitors increased from 0.4% of GDP for the whole of Czechoslovakia in 1989, to 5.5% of Czech GDP in 2001.

Growth in new, small businesses was associated with a widening income disparity. The extent of pay differentiation among employees changed little from 1989, although the ordering of different occupations showed marked shifts. The main increase in inequality was in earnings from independent business activity. Small businesses also helped to halt rising unemployment. This reached 4.1% in December 1991 and then declined, only to surpass that level in 1997, and stabilize at 8.9% in 2001, following the deceleration in job creation in the services sector and the continuing decline in employment in industry and agriculture. Unemployment was highest in old mining areas that were unattractive to tourism and to inward investment by multinationals, and that lacked traditions of entrepreneurial activities. Even in most rural areas, the sharp decline in agricultural employment was balanced for a time by growth in new employment opportunities.

Financial services registered a growth in employment of 216% between 1990 and 1999, before declining slightly. This was based on large banks and insurance companies, which hired new employees to cope with the increased demand for transactions in a market economy and for more varied forms of deposit. There was also an increase in the personal-savings rate, from 3.2% of disposable consumer incomes in 1989 to 7.3% in 2001. Much work was routine, and the end of the decade witnessed some decline in banking employment as simpler tasks were computerized. Relative pay in the finance sector increased from 2% above the average in 1990 to 99% above the average in 2000. The sector was almost entirely internally-orientated, and neither finance nor other business services developed into activities that could attract foreign-currency earnings.

PROSPECTS

The future of the economy depended on its integration into the EU from 2004, support for which was confirmed at a referendum held in June 2003. By 2002 some costs were already being encountered in the limited scope to restrict imports; this applied particularly to agriculture. The clearest tangible benefit was an acceleration of inward investment by multinational companies, which was dependent on the expectation of unrestricted access to the entire EU market. Foreign direct investment reached US $8,400m. in 2002, equivalent to 12.7% of GDP. However, around one-half of this comprised privatization payments in the transport and telecommunications sectors. A much smaller part was made up of genuinely new 'greenfield' investment by multinational companies in the export-orientated manufacturing fields of electronics and motor vehicles.

Accession to the EU will bring the further benefit of aid, through various Union programmes. 'Pre-accession' assistance had already enabled Czech agencies to gain experience of EU practices. Full membership will bring help primarily to projects supporting business development, environmental improvements and the transport infrastructure. This could contribute an additional 2% to GDP, but that will depend on the ability of actors in the Czech economy to formulate convincing plans. The intention is that resources should then be used to bring further benefits by improving the economy's level of competitiveness. Ultimately, accession to the EU implies becoming a member of the European Monetary System (EMS). That prospect is complicated by the growing budget deficit, equivalent to 4.6% of GDP in 2002; to conform with EMS rules the maximum level should be 3.0%. The problem stems partly from an ageing population, alongside generous retirement provisions, and partly from the bill for the 'costs of transformation'. The first of these is likely to cause an escalating deficit and a resulting increase in public-sector debt, from 22.6% of GDP in 2002 to over 40% by the end of the decade. That is an acceptable figure by international standards, but pressure can be expected from international agencies to ensure the stabilization of budget deficits at a level that adheres to EMS rules. Although this issue will have to be resolved, there is little danger of an immediate economic crisis. Unlike the situation in 1997, the current-account deficit remains manageable, and is more than balanced by the inflow of capital. This is predominantly in the form of direct investment, rather than short-term funds that can be withdrawn quickly. The prospect is, therefore, for steady growth, albeit not sufficiently rapid to approach the average level of GDP per head recorded in the EU.

Statistical Survey

Source: mainly Czech Statistical Office, Sokolovská 142, 186 04 Prague 8; tel. (2) 66042451; fax (2) 66310429; e-mail bondyova@gw.czso.cz; internet www .czso.cz.

Area and Population

AREA, POPULATION AND DENSITY

Area (sq km)	78,866*
Population (census results)	
3 March 1991	10,302,215
1 March 2001	
Males	5,019,381
Females	5,273,552
Total	10,292,933
Population (official estimates at 31 December)	
2000	10,266,546
2001	10,206,436
2002	10,203,269
Density (per sq km) at 31 December 2002	129.4

* 30,450 sq miles.

POPULATION BY NATIONALITY*
(census of 1 March 2001)

	Number	%
Czech (Bohemian)	9,270,615	90.1
Moravian	373,294	3.6
Slovak	183,749	1.8
Polish	50,971	0.5
German	38,321	0.4
Roma (Gypsy)	11,716	0.1
Silesian	11,248	0.1
Others and unknown	353,019	3.4
Total	**10,292,933**	**100.0**

* Preliminary figures.

REGIONS
(31 December 2002)

	Area (sq km)	Population	Density (per sq km)
Praha (Prague, capital) . .	496	1,161,938	2,343
Středočeský.	11,014	1,128,674	102
Jihočeský	10,056	625,097	62
Plzeňský	7,560	549,374	73
Karlovarský	3,315	304,220	92
Ústecký.	5,335	819,712	154
Liberecký	3,163	427,321	135
Královéhradecký . . .	4,757	548,437	115
Pardubický.	4,519	506,534	112
Vysočina	6,925	517,630	75
Jihomoravský	7,067	1,121,792	159
Olomoucký	5,139	636,750	124
Zlínský	3,965	593,130	150
Moravskoslezský . . .	5,555	1,262,660	227
Total	78,866	10,203,269	129

PRINCIPAL TOWNS
(population at 31 December 2002)

Praha (Prague, the capital) . . .	1,161,938	Pardubice. . . .	89,725
Brno	370,505	Havířov	85,271
Ostrava	314,102	Zlín	79,841
Plzeň (Pilsen). . .	163,791	Kladno	70,328
Olomouc . . .	101,624	Most	68,028
Liberec . . .	97,677	Karviná . . .	64,146
České Budějovice (Budweis) . . .	95,986	Opava	60,731
Hradec Králové . .	95,755	Frýdek-Místek . .	60,603
Ústí nad Labem . .	94,544		

BIRTHS, MARRIAGES AND DEATHS

	Registered live births		Registered marriages		Registered deaths	
	Number	Rate (per 1,000)	Number	Rate (per 1,000)	Number	Rate (per 1,000)
1994 . .	106,579	10.3	58,440	5.7	117,373	11.4
1995 . .	96,097	9.3	54,956	5.3	117,913	11.4
1996 . .	90,446	8.8	53,896	5.2	112,782	10.9
1997 . .	90,657	8.8	57,804	5.6	112,744	10.9
1998 . .	90,535	8.8	55,027	5.3	109,527	10.6
1999 . .	89,471	8.7	53,523	5.2	109,768	10.7
2000 . .	90,910	8.8	55,321	5.4	109,001	10.6
2001 . .	90,715	8.9	52,374	5.1	107,755	10.5

Expectation of life (WHO estimates, years at birth): 75.4 (males 71.9; females 78.8) in 2001 (Source: WHO, *World Health Report*).

ECONOMICALLY ACTIVE POPULATION
(persons aged 15 years and over)

	1999	2000	2001*
Agriculture, hunting, forestry and fishing	234,439	212,498	200,882
Mining and quarrying . . .	64,604	58,687	57,074
Manufacturing	1,390,997	1,377,416	1,393,941
Electricity, gas and water . . .	77,278	73,617	70,257
Construction	402,380	392,032	370,958
Trade, restaurants and hotels .	861,420	891,472	901,299
Transport, storage and communications	350,251	344,410	348,458
Finance, insurance, real estate and business activities	489,292	501,982	516,937
Public administration, defence and compulsory social security . .	178,309	186,771	189,144
Education	300,721	297,558	296,291
Health and social welfare . .	265,506	264,819	268,255
Other community, social and personal services	145,021	150,195	152,818
Total	4,760,218	4,751,457	4,766,314

* Estimates.

Health and Welfare

KEY INDICATORS

Total fertility rate (children per woman, 2001)	1.2
Under-5 mortality rate (per 1,000 live births, 2001) . . .	5
HIV/AIDS (% of persons aged 15–49, 2001)	<0.10
Physicians (per 1,000 head, 1998)	3.03
Hospital beds (per 1,000 head, 1999)	8.7
Health expenditure (2000): US $ per head (PPP) . . .	1,031
Health expenditure (2000): % of GDP	7.2
Health expenditure (2000): public (% of total)	91.4
Human Development Index (2000): ranking.	33
Human Development Index (2000): value	0.849

For sources and definitions, see explanatory note on p. vi.

Agriculture

PRINCIPAL CROPS
('000 metric tons)

	1999	2000	2001
Wheat	4,028	4,084	4,476
Barley	2,137	1,629	1,966
Maize	261	304	409
Rye*	202	150	149
Oats	179	136	136
Potatoes	1,407	1,476	1,131
Sugar beet.	2,691	2,809	3,259
Dry peas	105	75	83
Rapeseed	931	844	973
Cabbages	133	134	104
Tomatoes	34	31	25
Cauliflowers	34	29	23
Cucumbers and gherkins . .	52	41	35
Dry onions	99	76	84
Carrots	79	59	52
Apples	264	339	221
Pears	23	25	16
Peaches	7	11	5
Plums	21	18	23
Grapes.	67	67	68
Hops	6	5	7

* Including mixed crops of wheat and rye.

LIVESTOCK
('000 head at 1 March)

	1999	2000	2001
Horses	24	26	27
Cattle	1,574	1,582	1,466
Pigs	3,688	3,594	3,348
Sheep	84	90	97
Goats	32	28	26
Chickens	17,505	18,767	21,785
Ducks	446	451	279
Geese	132	127	28
Turkeys	669	723	887

LIVESTOCK PRODUCTS
('000 metric tons)

	1999	2000	2001
Beef and veal	120.7	107.4	126.1
Pig meat	451.6	416.6	474.8
Poultry meat	200.7	215.0	235.7
Milk	2,834.6	2,805.1	2,797.0
Cheese	138.2	142.3	139.8
Hen eggs	202.9	188.0	183.3

Source: FAO.

Forestry

LOGGING

('000 cubic metres)

	1999	2000	2001
Coniferous (softwood)	12,422	12,851	12,680
Broadleaved (hardwood). . . .	1,781	1,590	1,694
Total	14,203	14,441	14,374

Fishing*

(metric tons)

	1999	2000	2001
Common carp.	19,454	20,664	20,981
Others	3,511	3,465	3,763
Total catch	22,965	24,129	24,744

* Figures refer only to fish caught by the Fishing Association (formerly State Fisheries) and members of the Czech and Moravian Fishing Union.

Mining

('000 metric tons)

	1999	2000	2001
Hard coal	14,342	14,855	15,138
Brown coal and lignite	44,790	50,307	50,968
Crude petroleum*	176	n.a.	n.a.
Kaolin	1,049	1,242	1,140

* Source: US Geological Survey.

Industry

SELECTED PRODUCTS

('000 metric tons, unless otherwise indicated)

	1999	2000	2001
Wheat flour and meal	713	803	783
Refined sugar.	420	367	482
Wine ('000 hectolitres)	561	538	605
Beer ('000 hectolitres)	17,946	17,796	17,734
Cotton yarn (metric tons) . . .	56,118	58,871	65,124
Woven cotton fabrics ('000 metres)	265,461	226,088	231,917
Woollen fabrics ('000 metres) . .	17,445	14,297	13,517
Linen fabrics ('000 metres) . .	18,727	19,780	16,377
Paper and paperboard	185	170	183
Footwear ('000 pairs)	4,645	3,398	2,937
Nitrogenous fertilizers*	220	257	262
Soap	27	37	38
Motor spirit (petrol)	954	1,033	1,104
Gas-diesel (distillate fuel) oil . .	2,172	2,125	2,250
Residual fuel oils.	1,128	911	773
Coke	3,332	3,411	3,522
Cement	4,241	4,093	3,591
Pig-iron†	4,022	4,621	n.a.
Crude steel†	5,613	5,700	n.a.
Trucks (number)	23,113	23,641	4,701
Motorcycles and mopeds (number).	4,814	6,389	10,602
Bicycles (number)	181,988	229,377	236,574
Electric energy (million kWh) . .	64,692	73,466	74,647

* Production in terms of nitrogen.
† Source: US Geological Survey.

Finance

CURRENCY AND EXCHANGE RATES

Monetary Units

100 haléřů (singular: haléř—heller) = 1 Czech koruna (Czech crown or Kč.; plural: koruny).

Sterling, Dollar and Euro Equivalents (30 May 2003)

£1 sterling =40.36 koruny
US $1 = 24.50 koruny
€1 = 28.96 koruny
1,000 koruny = £24.78 = $40.82 = €34.53.

Average Exchange Rate (koruny per US $)
2000   38.598
2001   38.035
2002   32.739

Note: In February 1993 the Czech Republic introduced its own currency, the Czech koruna, to replace (at par) the Czechoslovak koruna.

BUDGET

('000 million koruny, including local authorities)

Revenue	2000	2001*	2002†
Current revenue	770.3	840.4	880.1
Taxation	721.1	782.0	822.2
Personal income tax . . .	98.3	104.4	117.2
Corporate profits tax . . .	75.8	92.0	81.1
Value-added tax. . . .	145.9	150.9	160.5
Excises	70.9	76.3	82.4
Social security contributions .	287.4	318.9	338.1
Other tax revenue . . .	29.2	29.5	32.9
Other current revenue . . .	49.2	58.4	57.9
Capital revenue	9.5	9.7	15.4
Total revenue ‡.	779.8	850.1	895.5

Expenditure	2000	2001*	2002†
Current expenditure.	751.7	843.1	971.4
Goods and services	171.0	175.0	206.7
Wages and salaries	70.3	76.3	73.8
Other goods and services . .	100.6	98.8	132.9
Interest payments	21.2	21.8	25.1
Subsidies and other current			
transfers	559.6	646.3	739.6
Subsidies	157.7	209.5	276.5
Transfers.	401.8	436.8	463.1
To households and non-profit			
institutions	399.1	433.6	459.1
Social benefits	270.8	288.8	305.6
Capital expenditure	116.2	120.8	131.3
Acquisition of fixed capital assets	72.8	75.0	74.1
Capital transfers	39.3	41.7	57.2
Total expenditure §	867.9	963.9	1,102.7

* Preliminary figures.
† Projected figures.
‡ Excluding grants received ('000 million koruny): 1.2 in 2000; 2.8 in 2001 (preliminary figure).
§ Excluding lending minus repayments ('000 million koruny): −24.9 in 2000; −58.8 in 2001; −243.3 in 2002.

Source: IMF, Czech Republic: *Selected Issues and Statistical Appendix* (August 2002).

INTERNATIONAL RESERVES

(US $ million at 31 December)

	2000	2001	2002
Gold*	22	23	28
IMF special drawing rights . . .	—	1	5
Reserve position in IMF. . . .	3	151	236
Foreign exchange.	13,016	14,189	23,315
Total	13,041	14,364	23,584

* National valuation.

Source: IMF, *International Financial Statistics*.

MONEY SUPPLY
('000 million koruny at 31 December)

	2000	2001	2002
Currency outside banks	171.82	180.38	197.81
Demand deposits at deposit money banks	326.53	402.50	626.31
Total money (incl. others). . .	498.96	583.55	827.04

Source: IMF, *International Financial Statistics.*

COST OF LIVING
(Consumer Price Index; base: 1994 = 100)

	1999	2000	2001
Food, beverages and tobacco . .	127.5	129.0	133.1
Clothing and footwear	140.8	138.0	135.8
Housing, water, fuel and light . .	208.2	225.6	247.9
Furnishings, household equipment and maintenance	125.3	126.0	126.3
All items (incl. others)	145.6	151.3	158.4

NATIONAL ACCOUNTS
('000 million koruny at current prices)

Expenditure on the Gross Domestic Product

	2000	2001	2002
Government final consumption expenditure.	388.3	436.0	487.1
Private final consumption expenditure.	1,074.1	1,155.6	1,200.6
Increase in stocks	27.2	39.0	41.2
Gross fixed capital formation . .	561.5	603.3	599.3
Total domestic expenditure. .	2,051.1	2,233.9	2,328.2
Exports of goods and services . .	1,385.9	1,539.3	1,483.0
Less Imports of goods and services	1,452.2	1,598.0	1,535.6
GDP in purchasers' values (market prices)	1,984.8	2,175.2	2,275.6
GDP at constant 1995 prices .	1,467.3	1,512.6	1,542.2

Source: IMF, *International Financial Statistics.*

Gross Domestic Product by Economic Activity*

	2000	2001	2002
Agriculture, hunting, forestry and fishing	79.1	86.9	77.1
Mining and quarrying. . . .	25.3	27.3	25.5
Manufacturing	495.9	548.0	563.1
Electricity, gas and water . .	72.5	79.8	83.0
Construction	130.9	134.7	138.6
Wholesale and retail trade . .	262.3	295.6	311.1
Restaurants and hotels . . .	41.6	43.0	43.3
Transport, storage and communications	149.5	169.1	189.2
Financial intermediation . . .	83.0	73.2	85.6
Real estate, renting and business activities	223.2	240.2	264.8
Other services	277.0	303.5	326.9
Sub-total	1,840.3	2,001.3	2,108.2
Less Financial intermediation services indirectly measured .	69.7	49.5	60.5
Gross value added in basic prices	1,770.6	1,951.7	2,048.3
Taxes on products	239.9	246.8	254.3
Less Subsidies on products . .	25.5	23.3	27.0
GDP in market prices . .	1,984.8	2,175.2	2,275.6

* Totals may not be equal to the sum of components, owing to rounding.

BALANCE OF PAYMENTS
(US $ million)

	1999	2000	2001
Exports of goods f.o.b.	26,259	29,019	33,404
Imports of goods f.o.b.	−28,161	−32,115	−36,482
Trade balance	−1,902	−3,095	−3,078
Exports of services	7,049	6,840	7,092
Imports of services	−5,850	−5,436	−5,568
Balance on goods and services.	−704	−1,692	−1,554
Other income received	1,859	1,952	2,170
Other income paid	−3,209	−3,323	−3,710
Balance on goods, services and income	−2,053	−3,063	−3,094
Current transfers received . .	1,310	948	959
Current transfers paid . . .	−722	−575	−489
Current balance	−1,466	−2,690	−2,624
Capital account (net)	−2	−5	−9
Direct investment abroad . . .	−90	−43	−95
Direct investment from abroad. .	6,313	4,987	4,924
Portfolio investment assets . . .	−1,882	−2,236	125
Portfolio investment liabilities .	500	482	798
Financial derivatives assets . .	—	−129	−254
Financial derivatives liabilities .	—	89	168
Other investment assets . . .	−2,688	984	−1,271
Other investment liabilities . .	928	−300	−337
Net errors and omissions . .	27	−297	362
Overall balance	1,639	844	1,787

Source: IMF, *International Financial Statistics.*

External Trade

COMMODITY GROUPS
(distribution by SITC, million koruny)

Imports f.o.b.	2000	2001	2002
Food and live animals	50,199	53,670	54,273
Beverages and tobacco	7,386	7,283	6,600
Crude materials (inedible) except fuels	39,381	40,045	38,192
Mineral fuels, lubricants, etc. . .	119,936	125,774	100,534
Chemicals and related products .	139,101	151,098	148,480
Basic manufactures	257,870	280,317	273,018
Machinery and transport equipment	496,704	585,345	561,916
Miscellaneous manufactured articles	128,288	139,916	140,026
Total (incl. others)	1,241,924	1,386,938	1,326,339

Exports f.o.b.	2000	2001	2002
Food and live animals	32,998	34,416	31,099
Beverages and tobacco	8,396	8,743	8,547
Crude materials (inedible) except fuels	39,565	38,603	34,765
Mineral fuels, lubricants, etc. . .	34,245	38,151	35,951
Chemicals and related products .	79,597	81,684	74,625
Basic manufactures	285,140	309,141	294,056
Machinery and transport equipment	498,402	601,427	620,713
Miscellaneous manufactured articles	140,486	154,890	149,242
Total (incl. others)	1,121,099	1,269,749	1,251,884

PRINCIPAL TRADING PARTNERS
(million koruny)

Imports f.o.b.	2000	2001	2002
Austria.	61,332	63,296	57,539
China, People's Republic	26,813	40,596	61,639
France.	61,643	66,516	63,550
Germany	400,549	456,491	430,675
Hungary	19,895	24,025	26,037
Italy	64,198	72,841	71,594
Japan	23,760	25,670	27,484
Netherlands	29,018	32,777	31,261
Poland	44,332	52,015	53,179
Russia	80,237	75,966	60,120
Slovakia	74,583	74,569	69,229
Switzerland	19,268	21,897	20,832
United Kingdom	51,342	55,388	41,587
USA	54,829	55,196	43,419
Total (incl. others)	1,241,924	1,386,938	1,326,339

Exports f.o.b.	2000	2001	2002
Austria.	66,956	73,075	69,248
France.	45,085	54,396	58,301
Germany	453,525	484,424	456,669
Hungary	21,010	23,988	30,293
Italy	42,389	51,495	50,774
Netherlands	25,781	35,394	48,714
Poland	60,902	65,788	59,248
Russia	14,915	18,535	16,884
Slovakia	86,070	101,926	96,706
Switzerland	14,934	17,478	19,534
United Kingdom	48,099	69,359	72,056
USA	31,608	38,016	35,613
Total (incl. others)	1,121,099	1,269,749	1,251,884

Transport

RAILWAYS
(traffic)

	2000	2001	2002
Passenger-km (million)	7,266	7,262	6,562
Freight net ton-km (million)	18,183	17,365	16,130

ROAD TRAFFIC
(motor vehicles in use at 31 December)

	1999	2000	2001
Passenger cars*	3,439,745	3,438,870	3,529,791
Buses and coaches	18,981	18,259	18,384
Commercial vehicles.	268,259	275,617	296,412
Special-purpose commercial vehicles .	85,726	70,838	67,106
Motorcycles	799,647	748,140	755,482

* Including vans.

INLAND WATERWAYS
(freight carried, '000 metric tons)

	1999	2000	2001
Imports	574	482	420
Exports	721	621	432
Internal	407	635	584
Total (incl. others)	1,877	1,906	1,594

AIR TRANSPORT

	1999	2000	2001
Kilometres flown ('000)	52,743	61,434	63,949
Passengers carried ('000)	2,904	3,484	3,946
Freight carried (metric tons)	17,359	18,950	16,079
Passenger-km ('000)	4,353,602	5,864,666	6,398,920
Freight ton-km ('000)	30,326	37,786	29,209

Tourism

FOREIGN TOURIST ARRIVALS*

Country of origin	2000	2001	2002
Austria.	137,787	163,748	180,676
Denmark	161,593	137,927	96,501
France .	151,989	187,118	185,192
Germany	1,493,958	1,551,353	1,394,581
Israel	189,876	n.a.	105,281
Italy	234,905	309,517	253,992
Netherlands	266,094	270,930	190,887
Poland .	296,456	369,883	318,272
Russia	102,936	n.a.	105,549
Slovakia	134,095	209,348	211,274
Spain	129,413	156,568	139,985
Sweden	101,792	n.a.	71,526
United Kingdom	246,974	278,818	286,746
USA	224,418	218,139	187,837
Total (incl. others)	4,666,305	5,193,973	4,579,015

* Figures refer to visitors staying for at least one night at registered accommodation facilities.

Receipts from tourism (US $ million): 3,718.8 in 1998; 3,034.7 in 1999; 2,982.0 in 2000.

Communications Media

	1999	2000	2001
Radio receivers ('000 subscribers) .	3,201.9	2,867.8	2,832.3
Television receivers ('000 subscribers).	3,438.3	3,288.7	3,209.5
Telephones ('000 main lines in public networks)	5,750.7	8,217.7	10,808.0
Mobile cellular telephones ('000 subscribers)*	1,944.6	4,346.0	6,947.2
Personal computers ('000 in use)* .	1,100	1,250	1,500
Internet users ('000)*	700	1,000	1,500
Book production (titles) .	12,551	11,965	14,321
Daily newspapers (number).	n.a.	103	105
Other periodicals (number).	3,686	3,192	3,364

* Source: International Telecommunication Union.

2002: Mobile cellular telephones ('000) 8,610.2.

Education

(2001/02)

	Institutions	Teachers	Students
Pre-primary	5,642	23,345	276,438
Basic:			
primary	} 4,263	67,594	1,027,827
lower secondary			
Upper secondary:			
general	346	11,665	136,729
technical	804	19,581	210,387
vocational.	565	10,669	184,174
Tertiary:			
higher professional schools	164	2,738	26,670
universities	24	13,322	200,450

Directory

Note: All telephone lines in the Czech Republic were renumbered on 21–22 September 2002, becoming standardized at nine digits. Fourteen new nodal telephone areas (NTAs—to correspond to the 14 new administrative regions scheduled for the end of 2002 were introduced at the same time, replacing the 159 existing area codes.

The Constitution

The following is a summary of the main provisions of the Constitution of the Czech Republic, which was adopted on 16 December 1992 and entered into force on 1 January 1993:

GENERAL PROVISIONS

The Czech Republic is a sovereign, unified and democratic law-abiding state, founded on the respect for the rights and freedoms of the individual and citizen. All state power belongs to the people, who exercise this power through the intermediary of legislative, executive and judicial bodies. The fundamental rights and freedoms of the people are under the protection of the judiciary.

The political system is founded on the free and voluntary operation of political parties respecting fundamental democratic principles and rejecting force as a means to assert their interests. Political decisions derive from the will of the majority, expressed through the free ballot. Minorities are protected in decision-making by the majority.

The territory of the Czech Republic encompasses an indivisible whole, whose state border may be changed only by constitutional law. Procedures covering the acquisition and loss of Czech citizenship are determined by law. No one may be deprived of his or her citizenship against his or her will.

GOVERNMENT

Legislative Power

Legislative power in the Czech Republic is vested in two chambers, the Chamber of Deputies and the Senate. The Chamber of Deputies has 200 members, elected for a term of four years. The Senate has 81 members, elected for a term of six years. Every two years one-third of the senators are elected. Both chambers elect their respective Chairman and Deputy Chairmen from among their members. Members of both chambers of the legislature are elected on the basis of universal, equal and direct suffrage by secret ballot. All citizens of 18 years and over are eligible to vote.

The legislature enacts the Constitution and laws; approves the state budget and the state final account; and approves the electoral law and international agreements. It elects the President of the Republic (at a joint session of both chambers), supervises the activities of the Government, and decides upon the declaration of war.

President of the Republic

The President of the Republic is Head of State. He/she is elected for a term of five years by a joint session of both chambers of the legislature. The President may not be elected for more than two consecutive terms.

The President appoints, dismisses and accepts the resignation of the Prime Minister and other members of the Government, dismisses the Government and accepts its resignation; convenes sessions of the Chamber of Deputies; may dissolve the Chamber of Deputies; names the judges of the Constitutional Court, its Chairman and Deputy Chairmen; appoints the Chairman and Deputy Chairmen of the Supreme Court; has the right to return adopted constitutional laws to the legislature; initials laws; and appoints members of the Council of the Czech National Bank. The President also represents the State in external affairs; is the Supreme Commander of the Armed Forces; receives heads of diplomatic missions; calls elections to the Chamber of Deputies and to the Senate; and has the right to grant amnesty.

Council of Ministers

The Council of Ministers is the highest organ of executive power. It is composed of the Prime Minister, the Deputy Prime Ministers and Ministers. It is answerable to the Chamber of Deputies. The President of the Republic appoints the Prime Minister, on whose recommendation he/she appoints the remaining members of the Council of Ministers and entrusts them with directing the ministries or other offices.

JUDICIAL SYSTEM

Judicial power is exercised on behalf of the Republic by independent courts. Judges are independent in the exercise of their function. The judiciary consists of the Supreme Court, the Supreme Administrative Court, high, regional and district courts.

The Constitutional Court is a judicial body protecting constitutionality. It consists of 15 judges appointed for a 10-year term by the President of the Republic with the consent of the Senate.

The Government

HEAD OF STATE

President: Václav Klaus (elected 28 February 2003; inaugurated 7 March 2003).

COUNCIL OF MINISTERS
(August 2003)

A coalition Government of the Czech Social Democratic Party (CSDP) and the Coalition, comprising the Christian Democratic Union—Czechoslovak People's Party (CDU—CPP) and the Freedom Union—Democratic Union (FU—DU).

Prime Minister: Vladimír Špidla (CSDP).

Deputy Prime Minister and Minister of the Interior: Stanislav Gross (CSDP).

Deputy Prime Minister and Minister of Justice: (vacant).

Deputy Prime Minister and Minister of Foreign Affairs: Cyril Svoboda (CDU—CPP).

Deputy Prime Minister: Petr Mareš (FU—DU).

Minister of Defence: Miroslav Kostelka (CSDP).

Minister of Industry and Trade: Milan Urban (CSDP).

Minister of Agriculture: Jaroslav Palas (CSDP).

Minister of the Environment: Libor Ambrozek (CDU—CPP).

Minister of Finance: Bohuslav Sobotka (CSDP).

Minister of Health: Marie Součková (CSDP).

Minister of Education, Youth and Sport: Petra Buzková (CSDP).

Minister of Transport: Milan Šimonovský (CDU—CPP).

Minister of Labour and Social Affairs: Zdeněk Škromach (CSDP).

Minister of Culture: Pavel Dostál (CSDP).

Minister of Regional Development: Pavel Němec (FU—DU).

Minister of Information: Vladimír Mlynar (FU—DU).

MINISTRIES

Office of the Government of the Czech Republic: nábř. E. Beneše 4, 118 01 Prague 1; tel. 224002111; fax 224810231; e-mail www@vlada.cz; internet www.vlada.cz.

Ministry of Agriculture: Těšnov 17, 117 05 Prague 1; tel. 22181111; fax 224810478; e-mail vicenova@mze.cz; internet www.mze.cz.

Ministry of Culture: Milady Horákové 139, 160 41 Prague 6; tel. 257085294; fax 224324282; e-mail minkult@mkcr.cz; internet www.mkcr.cz.

Ministry of Defence: Tychonova 1, 160 01 Prague 6; tel. 220201111; fax 220212359; e-mail press.service@army.cz; internet www.army.cz.

Ministry of Education, Youth and Sport: Karmelitská 8, 118 12 Prague 1; tel. 257193111; fax 257193397; e-mail cink@msmt.cz; internet www.msmt.cz.

Ministry of the Environment: Vršovická 65, 100 10 Prague 10; tel. 267121111; fax 267310308; e-mail info@env.cz; internet www.env.cz.

Ministry of Finance: Lětenská 15, 118 00 Prague 1; tel. 257041111; fax 257042788; e-mail podatelna@mfcr.cz; internet www.mfcr.cz.

Ministry of Foreign Affairs: Loretánské nám. 5, 118 00 Prague 1; tel. 224181111; fax 224182044; e-mail info@mzv.cz; internet www.mzv.cz.

Ministry of Health: Palackého nám. 4, POB 81, 128 01 Prague 2; tel. 224971111; fax 224972111; e-mail mzcr@mzcr.cz; internet www.mzcr.cz.

Ministry for Industry and Trade: Na Františku 32, 110 15 Prague 1; tel. 224851111; fax 224811089; e-mail mpo@mpo.cz; internet www.mpo.cz.

Ministry of Information: Havelkova 2, 130 00 Prague 3; tel. 221008111; fax 222721745; e-mail posta@micr.cz; internet www .micr.cz.

Ministry of the Interior: Nad štolou 3, 170 34 Prague 7; tel. 261432972; fax 261433552; e-mail public@mvcr.cz; internet www .mvcr.cz.

Ministry of Justice: Vyšehradská 16, 128 10 Prague 2; tel. 2219977111; fax 224919927; e-mail msp@msp.justice.cz; internet www.justice.cz.

Ministry of Labour and Social Affairs: Na poříčním právu 1, 128 01 Prague 2; tel. 224918391; fax 221922664; e-mail webmaster@ mpsv.cz; internet www.mpsv.cz.

Ministry for Regional Development: Staroměstské nám. 6, 110 15 Prague 1; tel. 224861111; fax 224861333; e-mail posta@mmr.cz; internet www.mmr.cz.

Ministry of Transport: nábř. L. Svobody 12, 110 15 Prague 1; tel. 251411111; fax 251431184; e-mail posta@mdcr.cz; internet www .mdcr.cz.

Legislature

The Czech Constitution, which was adopted in December 1992, provided for the creation of a bicameral legislature as the highest organ of state authority in the Czech Republic (which was established as an independent state on 1 January 1993, following the dissolution of the Czech and Slovak Federative Republic). The lower house, the Chamber of Deputies, retained the structure of the Czech National Council (the former republican legislature). The upper chamber, or Senate, was first elected in November 1996.

CHAMBER OF DEPUTIES
(Poslanecká sněmovna)

Chairman: LUBOMÍR ZAORALEK.

General election, 14–15 June 2002

Party	% of votes	Seats
Czech Social Democratic Party	30.2	70
Civic Democratic Party	24.5	58
Communist Party of Bohemia and Moravia .	18.5	41
Coalition*	14.3	31
Green Party	2.4	—
Others	10.1	—
Total	**100.0**	**200**

* An informal electoral alliance of the Christian Democratic Union— Czechoslovak People's Party and the Freedom Union—Democratic Union.

SENATE
(Senát)

Chairman: PETR PITHART.

Party	Seats after elections*	
	Nov. 2000	Oct.–Nov. 2002
Civic Democratic Party	22	26
Christian Democratic Union— Czechoslovak People's Party† . . .	21	16
Freedom Union—Democratic Union† .	18	15
Czech Social Democratic Party . .	15	11
Communist Party of Bohemia and Moravia	3	3
Others	—	8
Independents	2	2
Total	**81**	**81**

* One-third of the 81 seats are renewable every two years.
† Contested the 2000 and 2002 elections as an informal electoral alliance (in 2000 together with the Civil Democratic Alliance).

Local Government

The Constitution of the Czech Republic requires that the country should be divided into several new territorial and administrative regions. After some delay, in 1997 parliament approved the Government's plan to create 14 self-governing units (regions). In November 2000 elections were held to the regional assemblies of the new regions, which were to replace the 73 districts (*okres*) hitherto in place. The new regions were as follows: Hlavní město Praha (Prague); Středočeský; Jihočeský; Plzeňský; Karlovarský; Ústecký; Liberecký; Královéhradecký; Pardubický; Vysočina; Jihomoravský; Olomoucký; Zlínský; and Moravskoslezský. According to legislation passed by the Chamber of Deputies in March 2000, the elected regional assemblies were to be empowered to elect and dismiss the region's governor and council and to subsidize municipalities.

Local elections took place on 1–2 November 2002, in which the Civic Democratic Party (CDP) won the largest proportion of the votes cast (25.2%).

Institute for Local Administration: Dlážděná 6, 110 00 Prague 1; e-mail dotazy@institutpraha.cz.

Political Organizations

Alternative 2000 (Alternativa 2000): POB 154, 718 00 Ostrava 18; e-mail kvazar@telecom.cz; f. 1998.

Association for the Republic—Republican Party of Czechoslovakia (Sdružení pro republiku–Republikánská strana Československa): Gerstnerova 5, 170 00 Prague 7; tel. 220571450; fax 220570075; f. 1989; extreme right-wing; Chair. MIROSLAV SLÁDEK; Vice-Chair. MARTIN SMETANA.

Christian Democratic Union—Czechoslovak People's Party (CDU—CPP) (Křesťanská a demokratická uniei—Československá strana lidová): Karlovo náměstí 5, 12 801 Prague 2; tel. 224923874; fax 224917630; e-mail info@kdu.cz; internet www.kdu.cz; f. 1992; Chair. CYRIL SVOBODA.

Civic Democratic Alliance (CDA) (Občanská demokratická aliance): Štefánikova 21, 150 00 Prague 5; tel. 257329855; fax 257327072; e-mail usek@oda.cz; internet www.oda.cz; f. 1991 as a formal political party, following a split in Civic Forum (f. 1989); fmrly an informal group within Civic Forum; conservative; Chair. DANIEL KROUPA.

Civic Democratic Party (CDP) (Občanská demokratická strana): Sněmovní 3, 110 00 Prague 1; tel. 23114809; fax 224510731; e-mail info@ods.cz; internet www.ods.cz; f. 1991 following a split in Civic Forum (f. 1989); merged with Christian Democratic Party in 1996; liberal-conservative; c. 17,000 mems (March 1998); Chair. MIREK TOPOLANEK.

Communist Party of Bohemia and Moravia (Komunistická strana Čech a Moravy): Politických vězňů 9, 110 00 Prague 1; tel. 222897428; fax 222897449; e-mail leftnews@kscm.cz; internet www .kscm.cz; f. 1991 as a result of the reorganization of the fmr Communist Party of Czechoslovakia; c. 130,000 mems; Leader MIROSLAV GREBENÍČEK.

Communist Party of Czechoslovakia: f. 1995 as Party of Czechoslovak Communists renamed as above 1999; 19,980 mems; Sec.- Gen. MIROSLAV STEPAN.

Conservative Consensus Party (Strana konzervativní smlouvy): Čímská 26, 120 00 Prague 2; tel. 2250223; fax 2259424; e-mail skos@ skos.cz; internet www.skos.cz; f. 1998 by fmr mems of right-wing faction in CDA.

Countryside Party: f. 1996 to promote interests of rural areas; c. 3,000 mems; Chair. JAN VELEBA.

Czech Right (Česká pravice): Pod Dívínem 34, 150 00 Prague 5; e-mail cp-praha@ceskapravice.cz; internet www.ceskapravice.cz; f. 1994; conservative.

Czech Social Democratic Party (CSDP) (Česká strana sociálně demokratická): Lidový dům, Hybernská 7, 110 00 Prague 1; tel. and fax 224219911; e-mail info@socdem.cz; internet www.cssd.cz; f. 1878; prohibited 1948; re-established 1989; formerly the Czechoslovak Social Democratic Party; Chair. Ing. VLADIMÍR ŠPIDLA.

Democratic Left (Strana demokratická levice): Čitná 49, 110 00 Prague 1; tel. 224221313; fax 224221506; Chair. JOSEF MEÉL.

Democratic Socialist Party (Strana demokratického socialismu): e-mail mailto:secret@sds.cz; f. 1997 by merger of Left Bloc and Party of the Democratic Left; c. 9,000 mems; Chair. MARIE STIBOROVA.

European Democrats (ED): Prague; f. July 2002 by breakaway mems of Civic Democratic Party; Chair. JAN KASL.

Free Democrats—Liberal National Social Party (Svobodní demokraté—Liberální strana národně sociální): Republiky nám. 7, 111 49 Prague 1; tel. 224223443; fax 221618554; e-mail sdlsns@ mbox.vol.cz; f. 1995 by merger of Free Democrats (fmrly Civic Movement) and Liberal National Social Party (fmrly Czechoslovak Socialist Party); Chair. JIŘÍ DIENSTBIER.

Freedom Union—Democratic Union (FU—DU) (Unie svobody—Demokratická unie): Legerova 72, 120 00 Prague 2; tel. 224221291; fax 224221215; e-mail info@unie.cz; internet www.unie .cz; Freedom Union; f. 1998 following a split in the Civic Democratic Party; merged with Democratic Union in 2001; Leader PETR MARES.

Green Party (Strana zelených): Murmanská 13, Prague 10; tel. and fax 2736580; f. 1989; Chair. EMIL ZEMAN.

Moravian Democratic Party: Starobrněnská 20, 60200 Brno; tel. 542215290; e-mail modestr@seznam.cz; internet www.mujweb.cz/ www/modestr; f. 1997 by merger of Bohemian-Moravian Union of the Centre and Moravian National Party; Chair. IVAN DRIMAL.

Union for Europe (Unie pro Evropu): Plzeň; f. 2000; c. 6,000 mems.

Workers' Party: Prague; f. Jan. 2003; Chair. JIŘÍ STEPANEK.

Diplomatic Representation

EMBASSIES IN THE CZECH REPUBLIC

Afghanistan: Na Kazance 7/634, 170 00 Prague 7; tel. 28544228; fax 28542009; Ambassador AZIZOLLAH KARZAI.

Albania: Pod kaštany 22, 160 00 Prague 6; tel. 233370594; fax 233377232; e-mail alembprg@mbox.vol.cz; Ambassador PIRO MILKANI.

Algeria: V tišině 10/483, POB 204, 160 41 Prague 6; tel. 233371142; fax 233371147; internet www.algeria.cz; Ambassador ABDERRAHMANE MEZIANE-CHERIF.

Argentina: Panska 6, 110 00 Prague 1; tel. 224212448; fax 222241246; e-mail embar@iol.cz; Ambassador JUAN EDUARDO FLEMING.

Austria: Viktora Huga 10, 151 15 Prague 5; tel. 257090511; fax 257316045; e-mail austrianembassy@vol.cz; internet www.austria .cz; Ambassador KLAUS DAUBLEBSKY.

Belarus: Sádky 626, 171 00 Prague 7; tel. 26888216; fax 26888217.

Belgium: Valdštejnská 6, 118 01 Prague 1; tel. 257533524; fax 257320753; e-mail prague@diplobel.org; Ambassador BERNARD PIERRE.

Brazil: Sušická 12, POB 79, 160 41 Prague 6; tel. 224324965; fax 224312901; e-mail chebrem@mbox.vol.cz; Ambassador FRANCISCO DE PAULA DE ALMEIDA N. JUNQUEIRA.

Bulgaria: Krakovská 6, 110 00 Prague 1; tel. 222211259; fax 222211728; e-mail bulvelv@mbox.vol.cz; Ambassador MARTIN TOMOV.

Canada: Mickiewiczova 6, 125 33 Prague 6; tel. 272101800; fax 272101890; e-mail prague@dfait-maeci.gc.ca; internet www .dfait-maeci.gc.ca; Ambassador BRUCE JUTZI.

Chile: U Vorlíků 4/623, 160 00 Prague 6; tel. 224315064; fax 224316069; e-mail echilecz@mbox.vol.cz; internet www.eol.cz/chile; Ambassador RICARDO CONCHA GAZMURI.

China, People's Republic: Pelléova 22, 160 00 Prague 6; tel. 224311323; fax 224319888; e-mail tecoprag@mbox.vol.cz; Ambassador ROY Y. Y. WU.

Colombia: Washingtonova 25, 110 00 Prague 1; tel. 221674200; fax 224225538; e-mail emcol@mbox.vol.cz; Ambassador MARÍA MERCEDES RENGIFO DE DUQUE.

Congo, Democratic Republic: Kolínská 13, 130 00 Prague 3; tel. and fax 271730212; Ambassador GOMEZ NDUBA KIMBAYA.

Croatia: V Průhledu 9, 162 00 Prague 6; tel. 233355695; fax 23123464; e-mail velrhprag@vol.cz; Ambassador ZORAN PIČULJAN.

Cuba: Sibiřské nám. 1, 160 00 Prague 6; tel. 224311253; fax 23121029; Ambassador DAVID PAULOVICH ESCALONA.

Cyprus: Sibiřské nám. 6, 160 00 Prague 6; tel. 224316833; fax 224317529; e-mail cyprusembass@mbox.vol.cz; Ambassador CHRISTOPHOROS YIANGOU.

Denmark: Maltézské nám. 5, POB 25, 118 01 Prague 1; tel. 257531600; fax 257531410; e-mail danemb@terminal.cz; internet www.denmark.cz; Ambassador JØRGEN RUD HANSEN BØJER.

Egypt: Pelléova 14, 160 00 Prague 6; tel. 224311506; fax 224311157; e-mail embassyegypt@iol.cz; Ambassador ABDEL RAHMAN MOHAMED MOUSSA.

Estonia: Na Kampě 1, 118 00 Prague 1; tel. 257530512; fax 257530513; e-mail sekretar@estemb.cz; Ambassador MART LAANEMÄE.

Finland: Hellichova 1, Chotkův palác, 118 00 Prague 1; tel. 257007130; fax 257007132; e-mail sanomat.pra@formin.fi; Ambassador RISTO RÄNNALI.

France: Velkopřevorské nám. 2, POB 102, 118 01 Prague 1; tel. 257532756; fax 257532757; e-mail ambafrcz@vol.cz; internet www .france.cz; Ambassador PHILIPPE COSTE.

Germany: Vlašská 19, POB 88, 118 01 Prague 1; tel. 257113111; fax 257534056; e-mail d_botschaft@volny.cz; internet www .german-embassy.cz; Ambassador Dr MICHAEL LIBAL.

Ghana: V tišině 4, 160 00 Prague 6; tel. 233377236; fax 233375647; e-mail ghanaemb@mbox.vol.cz; Chargé d'affaires a.i. EDWIN NII ADJEI.

Greece: Helenska 2, 120 00 Prague 2; tel. 222250943; fax 222253686; Ambassador ELEFTHERIOS KARAYANNIS.

Holy See: Voršilská 12, 110 00 Prague 1; tel. 224999811; fax 224999833; e-mail nunciatgc@mbox.vol.cz; Apostolic Nuncio Most Rev. ERWIN JOSEF ENDER (Titular Archbishop of Germania di Numidia).

Hungary: Českomalínská 20, 160 00 Prague 6; tel. 233324454; fax 233322104; e-mail huembprg@vol.cz; Ambassador KRISTÓF JÁNOS FORRAI.

India: Valdštejnská 6, 118 00 Prague 1; tel. 257533490; fax 257533378; e-mail indembprague@bohem-net.cz; Ambassador Dr S. JAISHANKAR.

Indonesia: Nad Buď'ánkami II/7, 150 21 Prague 5; tel. 257214388; fax 257212105; e-mail informace@indoneske-velvyslanectvi.cz; internet www.indoneske-velvyslanectvi.cz; Ambassador SOENARTO SOEDARNO.

Iran: Na Zátorce 18, 160 00 Prague 6; tel. 220570454; fax 233380255; Chargé d'affaires MOHSEN SHARIF KHODAEI.

Ireland: Tržiště 13, 118 00 Prague 1; tel. 257530061; fax 257531387; e-mail hibernia@terminal.cz; Ambassador JOE HAYES.

Israel: Badeniho 2, 170 06 Prague 7; tel. 233325109; fax 233320092; e-mail israemba@bohem-net.cz; Ambassador ARTHUR AVNON.

Italy: Nerudova 20, 118 00 Prague 1; tel. 233080111; fax 257531522; e-mail italemba@mbox.vol.cz; internet www.italianembassy.cz; Ambassador GIORGIO RADICATI.

Japan: Maltézské nám. 6, 118 01 Prague 1; tel. 257533546; fax 257532377; Ambassador KOICHI TAKAHASHI.

Kazakhstan: Fetrovská 15, 160 00 Prague 6; tel. 23114596; fax 23112124; e-mail kzembas@bon.cz; Ambassador TULEUTAI SULEIMENOV.

Korea, Democratic People's Republic: Na Zátorce 6, 160 00 Prague 6; tel. 224320783; fax 224318817; Chargé d'affaires a.i. KIM SUNG NAM.

Korea, Republic: Slavíčkova 5, 160 00 Prague 6; tel. 2234090411; fax 2234090450; Ambassador LEE JOON-HEE.

Kuwait: Na Zátorce 26, 160 00 Prague 6; tel. 2205707813; fax 220570787; Ambassador KHALED MUTLAQ ZAYED AL-DUWAILAH.

Latvia: Hradešínská 3, POB 54, 101 00 Prague 10; tel. 224252454; fax 224255099; Ambassador IVETA SULCA.

Lebanon: Masarykovo nábřeží 14, 110 00 Prague 1; tel. 224930495; fax 224919088; e-mail ZOUHEIR KAZZAZ.

Libya: Na baště sv. Jiří 7, 160 00 Prague 6; tel. 233324160; fax 233322173; Chargé d'affaires a.i. IBRAHIM H. JABAH.

Lithuania: Pod Klikovkou 1916/2, 150 00 Prague 5; tel. 257210122; fax 257210124; e-mail ltembcz@mbox.vol.cz; internet www .ltembassycz.urrn.lt; Ambassador VYGINTAS GRINIS.

Mexico: Nad Kazankou 8, 171 00 Prague 7; tel. 28555554; fax 28550477; e-mail embamex@rep-checa.cz; Ambassador FEDERICO SALAS LOFTE.

Mongolia: Na Marně 5, 160 00 Prague 6; tel. 224311198; fax 224314827; e-mail monemb@bohem-net.cz; Ambassador ODONBAATAR SHIJEEKHUU.

Morocco: Ke starému Bubenči 4, 160 00 Prague 6; tel. 233320267; fax 233322634; Ambassador ABDESSELEM OUAZZANI.

Netherlands: Gotthardská 6/27, 160 00 Prague 6; tel. 224312190; fax 224312160; e-mail nlgovpra@mail.ti.cz; internet www .netherlandsembassy.cz; Ambassador IDA L. VAN VELDHUIZEN.

Nigeria: Před bateriemi 18, POB 27, 162 01 Prague 6; tel. 224312065; fax 224312072; e-mail embassy@nigeria.cz; Ambassador JULIE JOKE AYORINDE.

Norway: Na Ořechovce 69, 162 00 Prague 6; tel. 23111411; fax 23123797; e-mail noramb@noramb.cz; Ambassador LASSE SEIM.

Peru: Muchova 9, 160 00 Prague 6; tel. 224316210; fax 224314749; e-mail emba.peru@worldonline.cz; Ambassador RAÚL PATIÑO-ALVÍSTUR.

Philippines: Senovazne namesti 8, 110 00 Prague 1; tel. 224216397; fax 224216390; e-mail praguepe@phembassy.cz; Ambassador CARMELITA RODRÍGUEZ SALAS.

Poland: Valdštejnská 8, 118 01 Prague 1; tel. 257530388; fax 257530135; e-mail ambrpczechy@mbox.vol.cz; internet www.ambpol.cz; Ambassador ANDRZEJ KRAWCZYK.

Portugal: Kinských nám. 7, 150 00 Prague 5; tel. 257311230; fax 257311234; e-mail embport@mbox.vol.cz; Ambassador ANA MARTINHO.

Romania: Nerudova 5, POB 87, 118 01 Prague 1; tel. 257534210; fax 257531017; e-mail embrprg@mbox.vol.cz; Ambassador GHEORGHE TINCA.

Russia: Pod kaštany 1, 160 00 Prague 6; tel. 233374100; fax 233377235; e-mail rusembassy@cdnet.org; Ambassador IGOR SERGEJEVICH SAVOLSKII.

Serbia and Montenegro: Mostecká 15, 118 00 Prague 1; tel. 257532075; fax 257533948; Ambassador ALEKSANDAR ILIĆ.

Slovakia: Pod hradbami 1, 160 00 Prague 6; tel. 233321442; fax 233324289; e-mail skembassy@pha.inecnet.cz; Ambassador LADISLAV BALLEK.

Slovenia: Pod hradbami 15, 160 41 Prague 6; tel. 233081211; fax 224314106; Ambassador DAMJAN PRELOVŠEK.

South Africa: Ruská 65, POB 133, 100 00 Prague 10; tel. 267311114; fax 267311395; e-mail saprague@terminal.cz; Ambassador NOEL NOA LEHOKO.

Spain: Pevnostní 9, 162 00 Prague 6; tel. 224311222; fax 233341770; e-mail embpraha@gts.cz; Ambassador CABANAS ANSORENA.

Sweden: Úvoz 13-Hradčany, POB 35, 160 12 Prague 612; tel. 220313200; fax 220313240; e-mail ambassaden.prag@foreign.ministry.se; Ambassador HARALD FÄLTH.

Switzerland: Pevnostní 7, POB 84, 162 01 Prague 6; tel. 220400611; fax 224311312; e-mail vertretung@pra.rep.admin.ch; Ambassador HANSRUDOLF HOFFMAN.

Syria: Pod kaštany 16, 160 00 Prague 6; tel. 224310952; fax 224317911; Chargé d'affaires a.i. HAYSSAM MASHFEJ.

Thailand: Romaina Rollanda 3, 160 00 Prague 6; tel. 220571435; fax 220570049; e-mail thai@thaiemb.cz; internet www.thaiemb.cz; Ambassador TAMNU TANGKANASING.

Tunisia: Nad Kostelem 8, 147 00 Prague 4; tel. 244460652; fax 244460825; e-mail atprague@vol.cz; Ambassador MONCEF LARBI.

Turkey: Pevnostní 3, 162 00 Prague 616; tel. 224311402; fax 224311279; Ambassador SABRI CENK DUATEPE.

Ukraine: Charlese de Gaulla 29, 160 00 Prague 6; tel. 233342000; fax 233344366; e-mail kosak@mbox.vol.cz; internet www.ukrembassy.cz; Ambassador SERHII USTYCH.

United Kingdom: Thunovská 14, 118 00 Prague 1; tel. 257530278; fax 257530285; e-mail info@britain.cz; internet www.britain.cz; Ambassador ANNE PRINGLE.

USA: Tržiště 15, 118 01 Prague 1; tel. 257530663; fax 257530583; internet www.usembassy.cz; Ambassador CRAIG ROBERTS STAPLETON.

Uruguay: Muchova 9, 160 00 Prague 6; tel. 224314755; fax 224313780; e-mail urupra@urupra.cz; Ambassador Dr PEDRO VIDAL SALABERRY.

Venezuela: Jánský vršek 2/350, 118 00 Prague 1; tel. 257532211; fax 257531376; e-mail embaven@mbox.vol.cz; internet www.vol.cz/embavenezuela; Ambassador ORLANDO SUÁREZ GALEANO.

Viet Nam: Plzeňská 214, 150 00 Prague 5; tel. 257211540; fax 257211792; Ambassador DOAN THANG.

Yemen: Pod hradbami 5, 160 00 Prague 6; tel. 23111598; fax 23112204; Ambassador ALI ABDULLAH ABO-LOHOM.

Judicial System

The judicial system comprises the Supreme Court, the Supreme Administrative Court, chief, regional and district courts. There is also a 15-member Constitutional Court.

Supreme Court: Buresova 20, 657 37 Brno; tel. 541213293; fax 541212917; e-mail sekretariat@nsoud.cz; internet www.nsoud.cz; Chair. IVA BROZOVA.

Office of the Attorney-General: Jezuitska 4, 660 55 Brno; tel. 542512111; fax 542219621; Attorney-Gen. MARIE BENESOVA.

Constitutional Court: Joštova 8, 660 83 Brno; tel. 542161111; fax 542218326; e-mail ivan@concourt.cz; internet www.concourt.cz; Chair. ZDENĚK KESSLER; Dep. Chair. MILOŠ HOLEČEK.

Religion

The principal religion in the Czech Republic is Christianity. The largest denomination in 2001 was the Roman Catholic Church. According to the results of the March 2001 national census, about 60% of the population profess no religious belief.

CHRISTIANITY

Ecumenical Council of Churches in the Czech Republic (Ekumenická rada církví v České republice): Donská 5/370, 101 00 Prague 10; tel. and fax 271742326; e-mail ekumrada@iol.cz; internet www.ecumenicalcouncil.cz; f. 1955; 11 mem. churches; Pres. Bishop VLADISLAV VOLNÝ; Gen. Sec. JITKA KRAUSOVÁ.

The Roman Catholic Church

Latin Rite

The Czech Republic comprises two archdioceses and six dioceses. According to the results of the March 2001 national census, there were 2,740,780 adherents in the Czech Republic, equivalent to some 27% of the total population. The Roman Catholic Church estimated a total of 3,813,475 adherents in the country at 31 December 2001.

Czech Bishops' Conference (Česká biskupská konference): Thákurova 3, 160 00 Prague 6; tel. 220181421; fax 224310144; e-mail cbk2@ktf.cuni.cz; f. 1990; Pres. Most Rev. JAN GRAUBNER (Archbishop of Oloumouc).

Archbishop of Olomouc: Most Rev. JAN GRAUBNER, Wurmova 9, POB 193, 771 01 Olomouc; tel. 585500401; fax 585224840; e-mail gatnarp@arcibol.cz; internet www.ado.cz.

Archbishop of Prague: Cardinal Dr MILOSLAV VLK, Hradčanské nám. 16, 119 02 Prague 1; tel. 220392123; fax 220514647; e-mail kancler@arcibiskpraha.cz.

Byzantine Rite

Apostolic Exarch in the Czech Republic: Rt Rev. IVAN LJAVINEC (Titular Bishop of Acalissus,), Haštalské nám. 4, 110 00 Prague 1; tel. and fax 22312817; e-mail exarchat@volny.cz; 250,000 adherents (Dec. 2000).

The Eastern Orthodox Church

Orthodox Church (Pravoslavná církev): V jámě 6, 111 21 Prague 1; divided into two eparchies: Prague and Olomouc; Head of the Orthodox Church, Metropolitan of Prague and of all Czechoslovakia His Holiness Patriarch DOROTEJ.

Protestant Churches

Baptist Union in the Czech Republic: Na Topolce 14, 140 00 Prague 4; tel. and fax 241434256; e-mail czechbaptist@iol.cz; f. 1994; 2,395 mems; Pres. Rev. MILOŠ SOLA; Sec. Rev. JAN TITERA.

Brethren Church: Soukenická 15, 110 00 Prague 1; tel. and fax 22318131; e-mail pavel.cerny@cb.cz; internet www.cbchurch.cz; f. 1880; 8,331 mems, 46 churches; Pres. PAVEL ČERNÝ; Sec. KAREL FOJTÍK.

Christian Corps: nám. Konečného 5, 602 00 Brno; tel. (5) 756365; 3,200 mems; 123 brs; Rep. Ing. PETR ZEMAN.

Evangelical Church of Czech Brethren (Presbyterian): Jungmannova 9, 111 21 Prague 1; tel. 224999211; fax 224999219; e-mail srcce@srcce.cz; f. 1781; united since 1918; activities extend over Bohemia, Moravia and Silesia; 138,616 adherents (1997) and 264 parishes (1995); Pres. Rev. PAVEL SMETANA; Synodal Curator Dr LYDIE ROSKOVCOVÁ.

Silesian Evangelical Church of the Augsburg Confession in the Czech Republic (Silesian Lutheran Church): Na nivách 7, 737 01 Český Těšín; tel. 558731804; fax 558731815; e-mail sceav@sceav.cz; internet www.sceav.cz; founded in the 16th century during the Lutheran Reformation, reorganized in 1948; 40,000 mems; Bishop VLADISLAV VOLNÝ.

United Methodist Church: Ječná 19, 120 00 Prague 2; tel. 2290623; fax 2290167; e-mail ecmradacz@mbox.vol.cz; 1,890 mems; 17 parishes; Supt JOSEF ČERVEŇÁK.

Unity of Brethren (Moravian Church): Kollárova 456, 509 01 Nová Paka; tel. and fax 493721258; e-mail jbmb@iol.cz; internet www.moravian.cz; f. 1457; 2,447 mems; 21 parishes; Pres. Rev. JAROSLAV PLEVA.

Other Christian Churches

Apostolic Church in the Czech Republic: V Zídkách 402, 280 02 Kolín; tel. 321720457; fax 321727668; e-mail hqbishopac@clever.cz; f. 1989; 4,277 mems; Bishop RUDOLF BUBIK.

Church of the Seventh-day Adventists: Zálesí 50, 142 00 Prague 4; tel. 24723745; fax 244471863; e-mail unie@casd.cz; internet www.casd.cz; f. 1919; 10,000 mems; 183 churches; Pres. KAREL NOWAK.

Czechoslovak Hussite Church: Wuchterlova 5, 166 26 Prague 6; tel. 220398111; fax 224320308; f. 1920; 101,000 mems; six dioceses, divided into 301 parishes; Bishop-Patriarch Dr JAN SCHWARZ.

Old Catholic Church: Na Baterinch 27, 162 00 Prague 6; tel. and fax 224319528; e-mail stkat@comp.cz; 4,000 mems, 12 parishes; Bishop Mgr DUŠAN HEJBAL.

JUDAISM

Federation of Jewish Communities in the Czech Republic (Federace židovských obcí v České republice): Maiselova 18, 110 01 Prague 1; tel. 224811090; fax 224810912; e-mail fedzid@vol.cz; 3,000 mems; Pres. Dr JAN MUNK; Chief Rabbi KAROL SIDON.

The Press

PRINCIPAL DAILIES

Brno

Brněnský večerník (Brno Evening Paper): Jakubské nám. 7, 658 44 Brno; tel. 542321227; fax 545215150; f. 1968; Editor-in-Chief PETR HOSKOVEC; circ. 16,000.

Rovnost (Equality): M. Horákové 9, 658 22 Brno; tel. 545321121; fax 545212873; f. 1885; morning; Editor-in-Chief LUBOMÍR SELINGER; circ. 62,000.

České Budějovice

Jihočeské listy (South Bohemia Paper): Vrbenská 23, 370 45 České Budějovice; tel. 7312682; f. 1991; morning; Editor-in-Chief VLADIMÍR MAJER; circ. 53,000.

Hradec Králové

Hradecké noviny (Hradec News): Škroupova 695, 501 72 Hradec Králové; tel. 495613511; fax 495615681; Editor-in-Chief JAROMÍR FRIDRICH; circ. 30,000.

Karlovy Vary

Karlovarské noviny (Karlovy Vary News): třída TGM 32, 360 21 Karlovy Vary; tel. 353224496; fax 353225115; f. 1991; Editor-in-Chief JIŘÍ LINHART; circ. 15,000.

Ostrava

Moravskoslezský den (Moravia-Silesia Daily): Novinářská 7, 700 00 Ostrava 1; tel. 5955134; fax 5957021; f. 1991; Editor-in-Chief VLADIMÍR VAVRDA; circ. 130,000.

Svoboda (Freedom): Mlýnská 10, 701 11 Ostrava; tel. 592472311; fax 592472312; f. 1991; morning; Editor-in-Chief JOSEF LYS; circ. 100,000.

Pardubice

Pardubické noviny (Pardubice News): Tříd Míru 60, 530 02 Pardubice; tel. 46517366; fax 46517156; f. 1991; Editor-in-Chief ROMAN MARČÁK; circ. 15,000.

Plzeň

Plzeňský deník (Plzeň Daily): Husova 15, 304 83 Plzeň; tel. 37551111; fax 37551234; f. 1991; (fmrly *Pravda*, f. 1919); Editor-in-Chief JAN PERTL; circ. 50,000.

Prague

Hospodářské noviny (Economic News): Dobrovského 25, 170 55 Prague 7; tel. 233071111; fax 233072307; e-mail data@hn.economia.cz; internet www.ihned.cz; f. 1957; morning; Editor-in-Chief PETR ŠTĚPÁNEK; circ. 97,000 (1999).

Lidové noviny (People's News): Pobřežni 20/224, 186 21 Prague 8; tel. 267098700; fax 267098799; e-mail inzerce@lidovky.cz; internet www.lidovenoviny.cz; f. 1893, re-established 1988; morning; Editor-in-Chief PAVEL ŠAFR; circ. 83,728.

Mladá fronta Dnes (Youth Front Today): Senovážná 4, 110 00 Prague 1; tel. 222062111; fax 222062229; e-mail mfdnes@mafra.cz; f. 1990; morning; independent; Editor-in-Chief PETR ŠABATA; circ. 350,000.

Právo (Right): Slezská 13, 120 00 Prague 2; tel. 221001111; fax 221001361; e-mail redakce@pravo.cz; internet www.pravo.cz; f. 1920 as *Rudé právo*: name changed as above 1995; morning; Editor-in-Chief ZDENĚK PORYBNÝ; circ. 250,000.

Slovo (Word): Václavské nám. 36, 112 12 Prague 1; tel. 224227258; fax 224229477; f. 1945; Editor-in-Chief LIBOR ŠEVČÍK; circ. 95,000.

Večerník Praha (Evening Prague): Na Florenci 19, 111 21 Prague 1; tel. 224227625; fax 22327361; f. 1991; (fmrly *Ve černí Praha*, f. 1955); evening; Editor-in-Chief IVAN ČERVENKA; circ. 130,000.

Ústí nad Labem

Severočeský deník (North Bohemia Daily): Ústí nad Labem; tel. 475220525; fax 475220587; f. 1920; Editor-in-Chief MARIE SRPOVÁ; circ. 95,000.

PRINCIPAL PERIODICALS

Czech Language

100+1 ZZ: Karlovo nám. 5, 120 00 Prague 2; tel. (2) 293291; fax (2) 299824; f. 1964; fortnightly foreign press digest; Editor-in-Chief VÁCLAV DUŠEK; circ. 85,000.

Amatérske Radio: Radnická 2, 150 00 Prague 5; tel. 257317311; e-mail a-radio@mbok.inet.cz; internet www.aradio.cz; amateur radio technology and popular electronics; circ. 25,000 (2000).

Ateliér (Studio): Masarykovo nábř. 250, 110 00 Prague 1; tel. and fax 221732338; e-mail atelier.art@volny.cz; f. 1988; visual arts; fortnightly; Editor-in-Chief BLANKA POLÁKOVÁ.

Auto Tip: Střelnična 1680/8, 182 21 Prague 8; tel. 266193173; fax 266193172; e-mail v.kodym@axelspringer.cz; f. 1990; fortnightly for motorists; Editor-in-Chief VÍTĚZSLAV KODYM; circ. 60,000.

Českomoravský profit (Czech–Moravia Profit): Domažlická 3, 130 00 Prague 3; tel. (2) 277084; fax (2) 278514; weekly; Editor-in-Chief JAN BALTUS.

Divadelní noviny (Theatre News): c/o Divadelní ústav, Celetná 17, 110 00 Prague 1; tel. and fax (2) 2315912; e-mail divadelni.noviny@czech-theatre.cz; internet www.divadlo.cz/noviny; fortnightly; Editor-in-Chief JAN KOLÁŘ.

Ekonom (Economist): Dobrovského 25, 170 55 Prague 7; tel. 233071301; fax 233072002; e-mail ekonom@economia.cz; weekly; Editor-in-Chief BAYNEK FIALA.

Katolický týdeník (Catholic Weekly): Londýnská 44, 120 00 Prague 2; tel. 224250385; fax 224257041; e-mail tydenik@mbox.vol.cz; f. 1989; weekly; Editor-in-Chief NORBERT BADAL; circ. 70,000.

Květy (Flowers): Na Florenci 3, 117 14 Prague 1; tel. and fax 224219549; f. 1834; illustrated family weekly; Editor-in-Chief JINDŘICH MAŘAN; circ. 320,000.

Mladý svět (Young World): Na Poříčí 30, 112 86 Prague 1; tel. 224229087; fax 224210211; f. 1956; illustrated weekly; Editor-in-Chief OLGA DOUBRAVOVÁ; circ. 110,000.

PC World: Seydlerova 2451, 155 00 Prague; tel. 257088111; fax (2) 6520812; e-mail pcworld@idg.cz; internet www.idg.cz; monthly; Editor JAROSLAV VYDRA; circ. 28,000 (1997).

Reflex: Jeseniova 51, 130 00 Prague 3; tel. 267097542; fax 261216239; f. 1990; social weekly; Editor-in-Chief PETR BÍLEK; circ. 220,000.

Respekt: Sokolská 66, 120 00 Prague 2; tel. 224941962; fax 224941965; e-mail redakce@respekt.cz; f. 1990; political weekly; Editor-in-Chief PETER HOLUB; circ. 30,000.

Romano Hangos (Romany Voice): f. 1999; fortnightly; Editor-in-Chief KAREL HOLOMEK.

Romano Kurko (Romany Week): Černovické nábř. 7, 618 00 Brno; tel. and fax (5) 330785; f. 1991; weekly; in Czech with Romany vocabulary; Dir M. SMOLEŇ; circ. 8,000.

Sondy (Soundings): W. Churchilla 2, 130 00 Prague 3; tel. 224462328; fax 224462313; f. 1990; weekly; Editor-in-Chief JANA KAŠPAROVÁ; circ. 40,000.

Týdeník Rozhlas (Radio Weekly): Na Florenci 3, 112 86 Prague 1; tel. and fax (2) 2323261; f. 1923; Editor-in-Chief AGÁTA PILÁTOVÁ; circ. 170,000.

Vesmír (Universe): Národní 3, 111 42 Prague 1; tel. 224229181; fax 224240513; e-mail vesmir@mbox.cesnet.cz; f. 1871; monthly; popular science magazine; Editor IVAN M. HAVEL; circ. 8,000–10,000.

Vlasta: Žitná 18, 120 00 Prague 2; tel. (2) 298641; fax (2) 294535; f. 1947; weekly; illustrated magazine for women; Editor-in-Chief MARIE FORMÁČKOVÁ; circ. 380,000.

Výběr: K. Rotunde 89/4, 120 00 Prague 2; tel. 224232429; fax 224233283; internet www.vyber.cz; f. 1993; monthly; general interest; Editor-in-Chief VERONIKA MAXOVA; circ. 180,000 (1998).

Zahrádkář (Gardener): Prague; tel. (2) 766346; fax (2) 768042; monthly; Editor-in-Chief ANTONÍN DOLEJŠÍ; circ. 200,000.

Zora: Krakovská 21, 115 17 Prague 1; tel. 224228126; fax 224228120; f. 1917; every two months; for the visually handicapped; Editor-in-Chief Jiří Reichel.

Other Languages

Amaro Lav (Our Word): Černovické nábř. 7, 618 00 Brno; tel. and fax (5) 330785; f. 1990; monthly; in Romany and Czech; Dir M. Smoleň; circ. 3,000.

Czech Business and Trade: V jirchářích 8, 110 00 Prague 1; tel. 224912185; fax 224912355; e-mail journal@ppagency.cz; internet www.ppagency.cz; f. 1960; monthly; publ. in English, German, Spanish, Russian and French; Editor-in-Chief Dr Pavla Podskalská; circ. 15,000.

Prager Wochenblatt (Prague Weekly): Vítkovická 373, 199 00 Prague 9; tel. (2) 6282029; weekly; politics, culture, economy; in German; Editor-in-Chief Felix Seebauer; circ. 30,000.

Prague Post: Štěpánská 20 Prague 1; tel. 296334400; fax 296334450; e-mail office@praguepost.cz; internet www.praguepost.cz; f. 1991; political, economic and cultural weekly in English; Editor-in-Chief Alan Levy; circ. 15,000.

Prognosis: Prague; tel. (2) 3167007; fax (2) 368139; f. 1991; political, economic and cultural fortnightly in English; Editor-in-Chief Ben Sullivan; circ. 10,000.

NEWS AGENCIES

Česká tisková kancelář (ČTK) (Czech News Agency): Opletalova 5–7, 111 44 Prague 1; tel. 222098111; fax 224220553; e-mail ctk@mail.ctk.cz; internet www.ctk.cz; f. Nov. 1992, assuming control of all property and activities (in the Czech Lands) of the former Czechoslovak News Agency; news and photo-exchange service with all international and many national news agencies; maintains network of foreign correspondents; Czech and English general and economic news service; publishes daily bulletins in English; Gen. Dir Dr Milan Stibral.

Foreign Bureaux

Agence France-Presse (AFP): Ječná 15, 120 00 Prague 2; tel. 224921155; fax 224919155; e-mail afp@mbox.vol.cz; Bureau Chief René Pascal Biagi.

Agencia EFE (Spain): Uhrineveska 65, 100 00 Prague 1; tel. 271735816; fax 274782319; e-mail efe@iol.cz; internet www.efe.es; Bureau Chief Miguel Fernández.

Agenzia Nazionale Stampa Associata (ANSA) (Italy): Prague; tel. and fax 224222793.

Allgemeiner Deutscher Nachrichtendienst (ADN) (Germany): Milevská 835, 140 00 Prague 4; tel. (2) 6921911; fax (2) 6921627; Bureau Chief Steffi Gensicke.

Associated Press (AP) (USA): Prague; tel. 224224346; fax 224227445; Correspondent Ondřej Hejma.

Deutsche Presse-Agentur (dpa) (Germany): Petrské nám. 1, 110 00 Prague 1; tel. 224810290; fax 222315196; Bureau Chief Wolfgang Jung.

Informatsionnoye Telegrafnoye Agentstvo Rossii—Telegrafnoye Agentstvo Suverennykh Stran (ITAR—TASS) (Russia): Pevnostní 5, 162 00 Prague 6; tel. (2) 328307; fax (2) 327527; Bureau Chief Aleksandr Yakovlev.

Magyar Távirati Iroda (MTI) (Hungary): Prague; tel. and fax 266710131; Bureau Chief György Harsányi.

Novinska Agencija Tanjug (Yugoslavia): Prague; tel. (2) 2674401; Correspondent Branko Stošić.

Polska Agencja Prasowa (PAP) (Poland): Petrské nám. 1, 110 00 Prague 1; tel. and fax 224812205; Correspondent Zbygniew Krzystynjak.

Rossiiskoye Informatsionnoye Agentstvo—Novosti (RIA—Novosti) (Russia): Italská 36, 130 00 Prague 3; tel. 222253088; fax 222253084; e-mail riapraha@bohem-net.cz; Bureau Chief Valerij Enin.

Tlačová agentúra Slovenskej republiky (TASR) (Slovakia): Šmeralova 7, 170 00 Prague 7; tel. 233372617; fax 233379663; e-mail bkopcak@iol.cz; internet www.tasr.sk; Correspondent Bohdan Kopčák.

Xinhua (New China) News Agency (People's Republic of China): Pelléova 22, 169 00 Prague 6; tel. and fax 224311325; Correspondent San Xi-You.

Syndicate of Journalists of the Czech Republic: Pařížská 9, 116 30 Prague 1; tel. (2) 2325109; fax (2) 2327782; e-mail sncr@mbox.vol.cz; f. 1877; reorganized in 1990; 5,000 mems; Chair. Irena Válová.

Publishers

Academia: Legerova 61, 120 00 Prague 2; tel. 224942584; fax 224941982; f. 1953; scientific books, periodicals; Dir Alexander Tomský.

AkcentiBlok: Rooseveltova 4, 657 00 Brno; tel. and fax 542214516; f. 1957; regional literature, fiction, general; Dir Jaroslav Novák.

Albatros: Truhlářská 9, 110 01 Prague 1; tel. 224810704; fax 224810850; internet www.albatros.cz; f. 1949; literature for children and young people; Dir Martin Slavík.

Kalich, nakladatelství a knihkupectví, s.r.o.: Jungmannova 9, 111 00 Prague 1; tel. 224947505; fax 224947504; e-mail kalichknih@volny.cz; internet www.kalich.evangnet.cz; f. 1920; Dirs Michal Plzák, Markéta Langouá.

Kruh (Circle): Dlouhá 108, 500 21 Hradec Králové; tel. 49522076; f. 1966; regional literature, fiction and general; Dir Dr Jan Dvořák.

Melantrich: Václavské nám. 36, 112 12 Prague 1; tel. 222093215; fax 224213176; f. 1919; general, fiction, humanities, newspapers and magazines; Dir Milan Horský.

Mladá fronta (Young Front): Mezi Vodami 1952/9, 143 00 Prague 4; tel. 225276282; fax 225276278; e-mail prodej@mf.cz; f. 1945; fiction, history, poetry, popular science, magazines; Dir Martina Hartova; Editor-in-Chief Vlastimil Fiala.

Nakladatelství dopravy a spojů (Transport and Communications): Hybernská 5, 115 78 Prague 1; tel. (2) 2365774; fax (2) 2356772; Dir Ing. Alois Houdek.

Nakladatelství Svoboda (Freedom): Na Florenci 3, POB 704, 113 03 Prague 1; tel. 224224705; fax 224226026; f. 1945 as the publishing house of the Communist Party; restructured in 1992–94 as a limited company; in voluntary liquidation since Sept. 1997; politics, history, philosophy, fiction, general; Dir Stefan Szeryński.

Odeon: Prague; tel. 224225248; fax 224225262; f. 1953; literature, poetry, fiction (classical and modern), literary theory, art books, reproductions; Dir Miluše Slapničková.

Olympia: Klimentská 1, 110 15 Prague 1; tel. 224810146; fax 22315192; e-mail olympia@mbox.vol.cz; f. 1954; sports, tourism, encyclopaedias, fiction, illustrated books; Dir Ing. Karel Zelníček.

Panton: Radlická 99, 150 00 Prague 5; tel. and fax (2) 548627; f. 1958; publishing house of the Czech Musical Fund; books on music, sheet music, records; Dir Karel Černý.

Práce (Labour): Václavské nám. 17, 112 58 Prague 1; tel. 224009100; fax (2) 2320989; f. 1945; trade-union movement, fiction, general, periodicals; Dir Jana Schmidtová.

Rapid, a.s.: 28. října 13, 112 79 Prague 1; tel. 224195111; fax 22327520; advertising; Dir-Gen. Čestmír Čejka.

Severočeské nakladatelství (North Bohemian Publishing House): Ústí nad Labem; tel. 4728581; regional literature, fiction and general; Dir Jiří Švejda.

Státní pedagogické nakladatelství: Ostrovní 30, 113 01 Prague 1; tel. and fax 224912206; f. 1775; state publishing house; school and university textbooks, dictionaries, literature; Dir Milan Kovář.

Vyšehrad: Bartolomějská 9, 110 00 Prague 1; tel. (2) 2326851; fax (2) 268390; e-mail vysehrad@login.cz; f. 1934; religion, philosophy, history, fiction; Dir Pravomil Novák; Chief Editor Vlasta Hesounová.

Association of Czech Booksellers and Publishers: Jana Masaryka 56, 120 00 Prague 2; tel. 290030150; fax 222513198; e-mail sckn@mbox.vol.cz; internet www.sckn.cz; f. 1879; Chair. Jaroslav Císař.

Society of Writers (Obec spisovatelů): POB 669, 111 21 Prague 1; tel. and fax 222220106; e-mail obecspis@volny.cz; f. 1989; 700 mems; Dir Antonín Jelínek.

Broadcasting and Communications

TELECOMMUNICATIONS

Český Telecom: Olšanská 5, 130 34 Prague 3; tel. 840114114; fax 266316666; e-mail jindrich.trpisovsky@ct.cz; internet www.telecom .cz; fmrly SPT Telecom, renamed 2000; partially privatized 1995; 51% stat-owned, 27%-owned by Dutch/Swiss consortium; further privatization pending in 2003; monopoly operator of long-distance and international services; Chair. of Bd and CEO ONDREJ FELIX.

EuroTel: Sokolovská 225, POB 49, 190 00 Prague 9; tel. 267011111; fax 267011101; internet www.eurotel.cz; f. 1991; mobile telephone communications; launched GSM service July 1996; owned by SPT Telecom (51%) and West Atlantic (49%—consortium of US West and Bell Atlantic); Chief Exec. and Man. Dir EDWARD KINGMAN.

Český Mobil: Prague; 51% owned by Telesystem International Wireless (Canada); awarded licence to operate mobile telephone network in October 1999; Dir-Gen. ALEXANDER TOLSLTOY.

České Radiokomunikace, a.s.: U nákladového nádraži 4, 130 00 Prague 3; tel. 267005111; fax 271774885; e-mail info@cra.cz; internet www.cra.cz; f. 1994; privatized 2000; Dir-Gen. MIROSLAV ČURÍN.

Contactel: Vinohradská 174, 130 19 Prague 3; tel. 233011111; fax 233011112; e-mail press@contact.cz; internet www.contactel.cz; f. 1999; owned by České Radiokomunikace, a.s. (50%) and Tele Danmark A/S (50%); internet, data and voice services; Chief Exec. MICHAL ČUPA.

RadioMobil, a.s.: Londýnská 5759, 120 00, Prague 2; owned by České Radiokomunikace, a.s. (51%) and an international consortium, C-Mobil (49%); awarded 20-year licence to operate mobile telephone network in April 1996; launched GSM service Sept. 1996; Man. Dir KLAUS TEBBE.

RADIO

The national networks include Radio Prague (medium wave and VHF), Radio Vltava (VHF from Prague—programmes on Czech and world culture), Radio Regina (medium and VHF—programme of regional studios), and Interprogramme (medium and VHF—for foreign visitors to the Czech Republic, in English, German and French).

Local stations broadcast from Prague (Central Bohemian Studio), Brno, České Budějovice, Hradec Králové, Ostrava, Plzeň, Ústí nad Labem and other towns. By August 1993 44 private stations had been licensed, 37 of which were in operation (14 in Prague).

Český rozhlas (Czech Radio): Vinohradská 12, 120 99 Prague 2; tel. 221551111; fax 224222223; e-mail press@cro.cz; internet www .rozlas.cz; 4 nation-wide stations; Dir-Gen. VÁCLAV KASÍK.

Country Radio: Zenklová 34, 180 00 Prague 8; tel. 25102411; fax 251024224; e-mail country@ecn.cz; internet www.ecn.cz/country; commercial station; Man. Dir ZDENĚK PETERA.

Evropa 2: Nádraží 56, 150 05 Prague 5; tel. 257001808; fax 257001807; e-mail info@evropa2.cz; internet www.evropa2.cz; commercial station; Pres. MICHAEL FLEISCHMANN.

Frekvence 1: Nádraží 56, 150 05 Prague 5; tel. 257001900; fax 257314186; e-mail info@frekvence1.cz; internet www.frekvence1.cz; commercial station; Pres. MICHAEL FLEISCHMANN.

Radio Alfa: Na Poříčí 12, 110 00 Prague 1; tel. 224872822; fax 224872823; commercial station; Man. Dir V. KASÍK.

Radio FM Plus: POB 40, 320 90 Plzeň; tel. 37276666; fax 377422221; e-mail info@fmplus.cz; internet www.fmplus.cz; commercial station; Dir ZBYNĚK SUCHÝ.

Radio Free Europe/Radio Liberty: Vinohradská 1, 110 00 Prague 1; fax 221123420; internet www.rferl.org; broadcasts in 23 languages.

TELEVISION

In 2000 there were five main television stations: the two state-run channels, ČT1 and ČT2, reached 98% and 71% of the population, respectively, while two private commercial stations, Nova TV and Prima TV, were received by 99% and approximately 50%, respectively. TV3, which began broadcasting in May 2000, was initially received by some 30% of the population and aimed to reach 45% by the end of that year.

Česká televize (Czech Television): Kavčí hory, 140 70 Prague 4; tel. 261131111; fax 26927202; e-mail jakub.puchalsky@czech-tv.cz; internet www.czech-tv.cz; f. 1992; state-owned; two channels; studios in Prague, Brno and Ostrava; Dir JIŘÍ JANEČEK.

Nova TV: Vladislavova 20, 113 13 Prague 1; tel. 221100111; fax 221100565; f. 1994, through a joint venture with Central European Media Enterprises (CME—of the USA) as the Czech Republic's first independent commercial station; CME lost control of the station in 1999.

Prima TV: Na žertvách 24, 180 00 Prague 8; tel. 266100111; fax 266100201; e-mail kvizova@prima-televize.cz; internet www .prima-televize.cz; f. 1993; Gen. Dir KATEŘINA FRIČOVÁ.

TV3: Prague; e-mail info@tv3.cz; internet www.tv3.cz; f. 2000; independent commercial station; Dir JAN OBERMAN.

Finance

(cap. = capital; res = reserves; dep. = deposits; m. = million; brs = branches; amounts in Czech koruny)

BANKING

With the establishment of independent Czech and Slovak Republics on 1 January 1993, the State Bank of Czechoslovakia was divided and its functions were transferred to the newly-created Czech National Bank and National Bank of Slovakia. The Czech National Bank is independent of the Government.

At 31 March 2003 there were 37 banks operating in the Czech Republic, 11 of which were majority owned by Czech investors.

Central Bank

Czech National Bank (Česká národní banka): Na Příkopě 28, 115 03 Prague 1; tel. 224411111; fax 224413708; e-mail alice.frisaufova@ cnb.cz; internet www.cnb.cz; f. 1993; bank of issue, the central authority of the Czech Republic in the monetary sphere, legislation and foreign exchange permission; central bank for directing and securing monetary policy, supervision of activities of other banks and savings banks; cap. 1,400m., res 4,229m., dep. 351,906m. (Dec. 2001); Gov. ZDENĚK TŮMA; 7 brs.

Commercial Banks

Banka Haná, a.s.: Prikop 8, POB 58, 602 00 Brno; tel. 542219549; fax 545215969; internet www.bhan.cz; f. 1990; cap. 5,101.2m., res 3,177.9m., dep. 17,506.7m. (Dec. 1998); banking licence surrendered in Dec. 2000; Chair. STANSLAV ZALMANEK; 2 brs.

Česká exportní banka as: Vodičkova 34, 111 221 Prague 1; e-mail ceb@ceb.cz; internet www.ceb.cz; f. 1994; cap. 1,650.0m., res 299.0m., dep. 21,196.54m. (Dec. 2001); Chair. LADISLAV ZELINKA.

Česká konsolidační agentura: Janovského 438/2, 170 06 Prague 7; tel. 220141111; fax 233370033; e-mail kobp@ms.aned.cz; internet www.kopb.cz; f. 1991; fmrly Konsolidační banka Praha, s.p.ú.; current name adopted in Sept. 2001 following surrender of banking licence; cap. 5,950m., res 942.9m., dep. 106,661.5m. (Dec. 1998); Chair. KAMIL ZIEGLER.

Československá obchodní banka, a.s. (CSOB) (Czechoslovak Commercial Bank): Na Příkopě 14, 115 20 Prague 1; tel. 224111111; fax 224225049; e-mail webmaster@csob.cz; internet www.csob.cz; f. 1965; 66% state holding purchased by KBC Bank (Belgium) May 1999; commercial and foreign-trade transactions; cap. 5,105m., res 19,592m., dep. 506,930m. (Dec. 2001); Chair. and Gen. Man. PAVEL KAVÁNEK; 34 brs.

Investiční a Poštovní banka, a.s.: Senovážné nám. 32, POB 819, 114 03 Prague 1; tel. 222041111; fax 224244035; e-mail info@ ipb.cz; internet www.ipb.cz; f. 1990; 36% state holding purchased by Nomura (Japan) March 1998; placed under central-bank administration and subsequently transferred to ownership of CSOB in June 2000; cap. 13,383m., res 1,755m., dep. 231,135m. (Dec. 1998); Chair. and Gen. Man. JAN KLACEK; 157 brs.

Komerční banka, a.s.: Na Příkopě 33, POB 839, 114 07 Prague 1; tel. 222432111; fax 224243020; e-mail mojebanka@koba.cz; internet www.koba.cz; f. 1990; 49% state-owned; agreement to sell 60% state holding to Société Générale (France) reached in June 2001; cap. 19,005m., res 5,922m., dep. 381,113m. (Dec. 2001); Chair. and Chief Exec. ALEXIS RAYMOND JUAN; 354 brs.

Volksbank CZ, a.s.: M-Palác Herspická 5, POB 226, 658 26 Brno; tel. 543525111; fax 543525555; e-mail mail@volksbank.cz; internet www.volksbank.cz; cap. 650.0m., res 27.1m., dep. 10,546.9m. (Dec. 2001); Chair. JOHANN LURF.

Foreign and Joint-Venture Banks

Citibank, a.s.: Evropská 178, 166 40 Prague 6; tel. 233061111; fax 233061617; internet www.citibank.com/czech; f. 1991; wholly-owned subsidiary of Citibank Overseas Investment Corpn (Delaware, USA); cap. 2,425.0m., res 2,821m., dep. 41,091.8m. (Dec. 2000); Chair. ATIF BAJWA; 6 brs.

Crédit Lyonnais Bank Praha, a.s.: Ovocný trh 8, 117 19 Prague 1; tel. 222076111; fax 222076119; e-mail crlytre@mbox.vol.cz; internet www.clbp.cz; wholly-owned subsidiary of Crédit Lyonnais

Global Banking, Paris; cap. 500m., res 270.9m., dep. 16,252.4m. (Dec. 2000); Chair. and Gen. Man. CHRISTIAN RAMANOEL.

Dresdner Bank (CZ), a.s.: Vítězná 1, POB 229, 150 00 Prague 5; tel. 257006111; fax 257006200; internet www.bnp-dresdner-bank.cz; f. 1991; ownership: Banque Nationale de Paris (50%), Dresdner Bank (50%); cap. 1,000m., res 250.9m., dep. 19,500.1m. (Dec. 2001); Chair. MARKUA HERMANN.

GE Capital bank, a.s.: Vyskočilova 1422, BB Centrum, 140 28 Prague 4; tel. 224441111; fax 224441500; e-mail tomas.rajbr@gecapital.com; internet www.gecb.cz; f. 1998, from purchase of Agrobanka Praha, a.s.; wholly-owned by GE Capital International Holdings Corpn, Wilmington; cap. 500.0m., res 6,404.3m., dep. 68,751.7m. (Dec. 2001); Chair. PETR ŠMÍDA; 192 brs.

HypoVereinsbank CZ, a.s.: Namesti republiky 3a, POB 70, 110 00 Prague 1; tel. 221112111; fax 221112132; internet www.hvb.cz; f. 1999 by merger of HYPO-BANK CZ and Vereinsbank CZ; merged with Bank Austria Creditanstalt Czech Republic in Oct. 2001; cap. 5,047.0m., res 4,122.6m., dep. 129,234.7m. (Dec. 2001); Exec. Mems of Bd HANS-PETER HORSTER, Dr KAREL KRATINA, HARTMUT HAGEMANN.

Interbanka, a.s.: Václavské nám. 40, 110 00 Prague 1; tel. 224406111; fax 224215591; e-mail info@interbanka.cz; internet www.interbanka.cz; f. 1991; cap. 1,708.7m., res 22.2m., dep. 1,849.7m. (Dec. 2000); Chair. and Chief Exec. MANFRED JÜRGEN BAUMANN.

Raiffeisenbank, as: Vodičkova 38, 111 21 Prague 1; tel. 224231270; fax 224231278; e-mail raiffeisenbank@rb.cz; internet www.rb.cz; f. 1993; cap. 1,500.0m., res 38.5m., dep. 55,398.0m. (Dec. 2001); Chair. and Gen. Man. Ing. KAMIL ZIEGLER.

Živnostenská banka, a.s.: Na Příkopě 20, POB 421, 113 80 Prague 1; tel. 224121111; fax 224125555; e-mail info@zivnobanka.cz; internet www.zivnobanka.cz; f. 1868; cap. 1,360.4m., res 1,120.7m., dep. 56,878.3m. (Dec. 2001); Vice-Chair. of Bd JOSEF PITRA; 8 brs.

Savings Bank

Czech Savings Bank (Česká spořitelna, a.s.): Na Prikope 29, POB 838, 113 98 Prague 1; tel. 261073492; fax 261073006; e-mail csas@csas.cz; internet www.csas.cz; f. 1825; 52% holding purchased by Erste Bank AG (Austria) in February 2000; absorbed Erste Bank Sparkassen (ČR), a.s., in October 2000; accepts deposits and issues loans; total assets 491,605m., dep. 430,382m. (Dec. 2001); Chair. and Chief Exec. JOHN JAMES STACK; 684 brs.

Bankers' Organization

Association of Banks, Prague: Vodičkova 30, 110 00 Prague 1; tel. 224225926; fax 224225957; e-mail bank.asociace@mbox.vol.cz; Pres. JIŘÍ KUNERT; Vice-Pres. PAVEL KAVÁNEK.

STOCK EXCHANGE

Prague Stock Exchange (Burza cenných papírů Praha, a.s.): Rybná 14, 110 05 Prague 1; tel. 221831111; fax 221833040; e-mail info@pse.cz; internet www.pse.cz; f. 1992; Chair. GEORGE JEDLICKA; Vice-Chair. DUSAN BARAN.

Regulatory Authority

Czech Securities Commission: Prague; f. 1998; Chair. FRANTIŠEK JAKUB.

INSURANCE

Czech Co-operative Insurance Company (Kooperativa, a.s., pojišťovna, a.s.): Templová 747, 110 01 Prague 1; tel. 221000111; fax 22322562; e-mail info@koop.cz; internet www.koop.cz; f. 1993; Chair. and Gen. Man. Ing. VLADIMÍR MRÁZ.

Czech Insurance and Reinsurance Corporation (Česká Pojišťovna, a.s.): Spálená 16, 113 04 Prague 1; tel. 224051111; fax 224052200; e-mail murban@cpoj.cz; internet www.cpoj.cz; f. 1827; many home brs and some agencies abroad; issues life, accident, fire, aviation, industrial and marine policies, all classes of reinsurance; Lloyd's agency; Chair. of Bd IVAN KOČÁRNÍK; Gen. Man. LADISLAV BARTONÍČEK.

ČS Zivnostenská pojišťovna, a.s.: Smilova 547, 530 02 Pardubice; tel. (40) 6051111; fax (40) 6051380; e-mail zivpo@zivpo.cz; internet www.zivpo.cz; f. 1992; Chair. and Gen. Dir Ing. JAROSLAV KLAPAL.

Trade and Industry

GOVERNMENT AGENCIES

Czech Trade Promotion Agency (Česká agentura na podporu obchodu): Vittrichova 21, POB 76, 128 01 Prague 2; tel. 224907500; fax 224907503; e-mail info@czechtrade.cz; internet www.czechtrade.cz; Gen. Dir MARTIN TLAPA.

Česká agentura pro zahraniční investice (CzechInvest): Štěpánská 15, 120 00 Prague 2; tel. 296342500; fax 296342502; e-mail marketing@czechinvest.org; internet www.czechinvest.org; f. 1992; foreign investment agency; Chief Exec. Ing. MARTIN JAHN.

National Property Fund: Rašínovo nábřeží 42, 128 00 Prague 2; tel. 224991285; fax 222718211; e-mail predseda@fnm.cz; internet www.fnm.cz; responsible for state property and state-owned companies in the period up to their privatization; Chair. JAN JUCHELKA.

CHAMBER OF COMMERCE

Economic Chamber of the Czech Republic (Hospodářská komora České republiky): Argentinská 38, 170 05 Prague 7; tel. 266794939; fax (2) 875438; f. 1850; has almost 20,000 members (trading corporations, industrial enterprises, banks and private enterprises); Chair. Dr ZDENĚK SOMR.

EMPLOYERS' ORGANIZATIONS

Association of Entrepreneurs of the Czech Republic (Sdružení podnikatelů České republiky): Škrétova 6/44, 120 59 Prague 2; tel. and fax 224230572; Chair. RUDOLF BARÁNEK.

Confederation of Industry of the Czech Republic (Svaz průmyslu a dopravy České republiky): Mikulandská 7, 113 61 Prague 1; tel. 224915679; fax 224919311; e-mail spcr@spcr.cz; internet www.spcr.cz; f. 1990; Dir-Gen. ZDENĚK LIŠKA.

UTILITIES

Electricity

Central Bohemian Electricity Distribution Company (Středočeská Energetická—STE a.s.): Vinohradská 325/8, 120 21 Prague 2; tel. 222031111; fax 222032555; e-mail inbox@ste.cz; internet www.ste.cz; f. 1994; Chair. and Gen. Man. JAROSLAV HÁBA.

České Energeticke Zavody (ČEZ): Hlavni Sprava, Jungmannova 29, 111 48 Prague 1; tel. 224081111; fax 224082440; e-mail info@hs.cez.cs; internet www.cez.cz; 68% state-owned; production co; Gen. Man. JAROSLAV MÍL; 7,600 employees.

Dukovany Nuclear Power Plant ČEZ, a.s.: 675 50 Dukovany; tel. 568811111; fax 568866360; e-mail sedlaj2.edu@mail.cez.cz; Dir JOSEF SEDLAK.

East Bohemian Electricity Company (Východočeská Energetika—VCE): Sladovského 215, 501 03 Hradec Králové; tel. 4955841111; fax 49530150; f. 1994; Chair. and Chief Exec. PETR ZEMAN; 2,094 employees.

Moravskoslezské Teplárny, a.s.: Října 152 28; 709 74 Ostrava; tel. 596609111; fax 596609158; f. 1992; Gen. Man. JAROSLAV VESELSKÝ.

North Bohemian Electricity (Severočeská Energetika—SČE a.s.): Teplická 8, 405 49 Děčín IV; tel. 412571111; fax 412572977; e-mail info@sce.cz; internet www.sce.cz; f. 1994; Chair. JIŘÍ ŠTASTNÝ.

North Moravian Electricity (Severomoravská Energetika—SME a.s.): 28 Října 152, 709 02 Ostrava; tel. 596671111; fax 596673284; internet www.sme.cz; distribution co; Dir-Gen. TOMÁŠ HÜNER.

Opatovice Electricity (Elektrarny Opatovice a.s.): Pardubice 0, 532 13 Opatovice nad Labem; tel. 466841111; fax 466536010; f. 1905; generation and distribution co; 48% owned by National Power (United Kingdom); Chair. and Man. Dir ARNOŠT POUL.

Prazská Energetika, a.s.: Na Hroudé 4, 100 05 Prague 10; tel. 267051111; fax 267310817; internet www.pre.cz; distribution; Chair. and Gen. Man. Ing DRAHOMÍR RUTA.

Prazská Teplárenská, a.s.: Partyzanska 7, 170 00 Prague 7; tel. 266751111; fax (2) 876328; e-mail ptas@ptas.cz; internet www.ptas.cz; f. 1992; electricity supply; Chair. of Bd and Gen. Man. Ing. LUBOS PAVLAS.

South Bohemian Electricity (Jihočeská Energetika—JČE a.s.): Lannova 16, 370 49 České Budějovice; tel. 387312682; fax 386359803; e-mail info@jce.cz; internet www.jce.cz; majority-owned by Bayernwerk (Germany) and Raiffesenlandesbank (Austria); Pres. and Dir JAN ŠPIKA.

South Moravian Electricity (Jihomoravska Energetika—JME): Lidicka 36, POB 344, 659 44 Brno; tel. 545141111; fax 545142551;

e-mail jme@jme.cz; internet www.jme.cz; f. 1994; Man. Dir ZDENĚK MACHALA.

State Office for Nuclear Safety (Státní úřad pro jadernou bezpečnost): Senovážné nám. 9, 110 00 Prague 1; tel. 221624111; fax 221624396; internet www.sujb.cz; state supervision of nuclear safety, co-ordination of international relations in the sphere of nuclear safety; Chair. DANA DRÁBOVÁ.

Gas

North Moravian Gas (Severomoravsjká Plynárenská—SMP): Plynární 6, POB 72/73, 702 00 Ostrava; tel. 596102525; fax 596113985; e-mail sek.gr@smpas.cz; internet www.smpas.cz; f. 1994; distribution co; Chair. of Bd KAREL MAZAL.

South Moravian Gas Company (Jihomoravská plynárenská—JMP a.s.): Plynárenská 1, 657 02 Brno; tel. 545548111; fax (5) 578571; e-mail jmpas@jmpas.cz; internet www.jmpas.cz; distribution co; Chair. JÖRG SCHELER.

Transgas/Český Plynárensky Podnik: Limuzská 12, 100 98 Prague 10; tel. 270771111; fax 270776965; e-mail info@transgas.cz; internet www.transgas,cz; f. 1971; sale of majority stake to RWE Energie AG (Germany) approved in May 2002; import and distribution co; Chief Exec. TOMÁŠ TICHÝ.

Water

Prazske Vodovody a Kanalizace a.s.: Narodni 13, 112 65 Prague; tel. 257320132; fax 257535011; e-mail info@pvk.cz; internet www .pvk.cz; f. 1998; water supply and sewerage co; privatized in 2000.

MAJOR COMPANIES

ABB Energeticke Systemy, s.r.o.: Olomoucka 7/9, 656 66 Brno; tel. (5) 5141111; fax 545213007; f. 1993; production of power-plant and electricity-generation equipment; Pres. and Chief Exec. DAN TOK; 3,034 employees.

Adamovske Strojirny, a.s.: Mírová 2, 679 04 Adamov; tel. (506) 511111; fax (506) 951121; e-mail adastpro@adast.cz; f. 1992; production of printing equipment; country's eighth largest exporter; Chair. of Bd JOSEF BUZEK; 2,082 employees.

AERO Holding: Beranových 130, 199 04 Prague 9; tel. 266310727; fax (2) 886581; f. 1918; holding group for 10 aeronautical cos; Gen. Dir FRANTIŠEK PETRASEK; 15,000 employees.

Letecké Závody—L.Z.— a.s. (Aeronautical Industries): Letecká 1177, 686 04 Kunovice; tel. (632) 816110; fax (632) 816112; e-mail let@let.cz; internet www.let.cz; f. 2001; manufacture of aircraft and components for aircraft and automotive industries; Pres. LIBOR SOSKA; 1,107 employees.

Aliachem, a.s.: Division Synthesia, 532 17 Pardubice; tel. (40) 6821111; fax (40) 6821020; e-mail synthesia@synthesia.cz; internet www.synthesia.cz; f. 1920; production of chemicals, organic intermediates, industrial fertilizers, plant protection agents, plastic nitrocellulose, cellulose derivatives, explosives and pharmaceuticals; Gen. Dir MARTIN BOROVIČKA; 3,800 employees.

AssiDomän Sepap, a.s.: Litoměřická 272, 411 08 Štětí; tel. 411801111; fax 411802255; e-mail sepap@asdo.cz; internet www .asdo.se; f. 1949; pulp, paper and paper products; 97% owned by forestry group AssiDomän (Sweden); Gen. Man. TOMÁŠ ŠABATKA; 1,185 employees.

Ateso, a.s.: B. Nemcové nám. 1, 466 90 Jablonec nad Nisou; tel. (428) 352111; fax (428) 352407; e-mail obc@ateso.cz; internet www .ateso.cz; f. 1952; manufacture of road-vehicle and aircraft parts; Gen. Man. RUDOLF HIPPMAN; 1,293 employees.

AVX Czech Republic Spol, s.r.o.: Dvorakova 328, 563 01 Lanskroun; tel. (467) 558111; fax (467) 523010; e-mail company@avx.cz; internet www.avxcorp.com; f. 1992; owned by AVX Ltd (United Kingdom); manufacture of capacitors; Gen. Man. Ing. JIŘÍ SKALA; 4,500 employees.

Barum Continental Spol s.r.o.: Objízdná 1628, 765 31 Otrokovice; tel. (67) 7511111; fax (67) 7512075; e-mail info@barum.cz; internet www.barum.cz; manufacture of tyres and rubber products; f. 1993; Pres. and Man. Dir PAVEL PRAVEC; 4,152 employees.

Benar, a.s.: Ceskolipská 224, 407 22 Benesov nad Ploucini; tel. 412586241; fax 412945435; internet www.benar.cz; f. 1956; production of cotton fabrics and clothes; Gen. Dir Ing. MILOS VOJTECH; 1,200 employees.

Brano, a.s.: Opavská, 747 43 Hradec nad Moravicí; tel. (653) 632111; fax (653) 783181; e-mail info@brano.cz; internet www.brano .cz; f. 1862; manufacture of door systems, lifting and hydraulic equipment and machinery; Chair. and Chief Exec. PAVEL JUŘÍČEK; 1,100 employees.

Čechofracht: Na Příkopě 8, 111 83 Prague 1; tel. 224198111; fax 224198416; e-mail mailbox@cechofracht.cz; internet www

.cechofracht.cz; f. 1949; foreign trade corpn; shipping and international forwarding joint-stock co; Gen. Dir Ing. LEŠEK WRONKA; 750 employees.

ČEPRO a.s.: Spálená 5, 111 21 Prague 5; tel. 224913059; fax 224910373; internet www.ceproas.cz; f. 1994; trade in petroleum products; Pres. and Chair. ZDENEK SEDMIK; 1,200 employees.

Česká Gumárenska Spolenčost (ČGS): Pod Višňovkou 21, POB 58, 142 00 Prague 4; tel. 261386801; fax 261386802; internet www .cgs.cz; f. 1991; production of rubber and tyres; Chair. and Chief Exec. JAROSLAV ČECHURA; 6,512 employees.

Česká Zbrojovka, a.s.: Svatopluka Čecha 1283, 688 27 Uherský Brod 1; tel. (633) 651111; fax (633) 633665; e-mail general@czub.cz; internet www.czub.cz; manufacture and sale of small arms; Pres. JIŘÍ MARTINEC; 3,000 employees.

Českomoravské Doly a.s.: Vita Nejedlého 1575, 272 61 Kladno; tel. 312893111; fax 312628782; e-mail sprava@cmd.cz; internet www .cmd.cz; f. 1993; anthracite mining; Chair. VIKTOR KOLÁČEK; 7,400 employees.

Chemapol Group, a.s.: Kodaňská 46, 100 10 Prague 10; tel. 267151111; fax 267311262; e-mail sekret@group.chemapol.cz; f. 1948; foreign trade corpn; imports and exports chemical and pharmaceutical products, petroleum and other raw materials; Chair. and Man. Dir VÁCLAV JUNEK.

Chlumčanské Keramické Závody, a.s.: 33431 Chlumčany; tel. (19) 7811111; fax (19) 7973173; e-mail info@lbpl.cz; internet www .chkz.cz; f. 1992; manufacture of ceramic tiles; Chair. and Gen. Dir Ing. LADISLAV SKLADÝ; 1,121, employees.

ČKD Blansko, a.s.: Gellhornova 1, 678 18 Blansko; tel. (506) 401111; fax (506) 417126; e-mail ckdblansko@ckdblansko.cz; internet www.ckdblansko.cz; f. 1698; heavy engineering, incl. water turbines, hydrotechnical equipment, vertical lathes, pipeline closures; Man. Dir Ing. LADISLAV ŠTÉGNER; 830 employees.

ČKD Praha Holding a.s.: Freyova 27, 190 02 Prague 9; tel. 266032000; fax 266310834; e-mail vladimir.zizka@holding.ckd.cz; parent company of ČKD industrial group, which comprises two core businesses: passenger rail transport vehicles and turn-key power and utilities projects; Chair. and Man. Dir JIŘÍ MAROUŠEK; 13,800 employees.

ČKD Pragoimex: Českomoravská 19, 190 05 Prague 9; tel. 266039131; fax 266312334; e-mail ckdpragoimex@mbox.vol.cz; f. 1991; foreign trade corpn; refurbishment of rail vehicles, import and export of machinery, passenger cars, spare parts; Gen. Dir KAREL HALA.

COLORLAK: Tovární 1076, 686 02 Staré Město; tel. (632) 527111; fax (632) 541538; e-mail info@colorlak.cz; internet www.colorlak.cz; f. 1925; production of paints and lacquers; Gen. Dir JIŘÍ KOUTNY; 450 employees.

Crystalex, a.s.: Egermannova 634, 473 13 Novy Bor; tel. (424) 741111; fax (424) 32250; e-mail or@crystalex.cz; glassware, including lead crystal; Gen. Dir Ing. RADEK ZAMRZLA; 4,202 employees.

DESTA Děčín, a.s.: Ústecká 20, 405 02 Děčín 5; tel. 412510177; fax 412510216; internet www.desta.cz; f. 1910; manufactures transport equipment, incl. fork-lift trucks; Pres. and Man. Dir Ing. MIROSLAV GRÉGR; 2,700 employees.

Deza, a.s.: Masarykova 753, 757 28 Valasske Mezirici; tel. (651) 691111; fax (651) 611546; e-mail info@deza.cz; internet www.deza .cz; f. 1892; manufacture of chemicals; Chief Exec. ZBYNEK PRUŠA; 1,122 employees.

Diamo State Enterprise: 471 27 Straz pod Ralskem; tel. (425) 851338; fax (425) 85145656; e-mail diamo@diamo.cz; f. 1946; uranium mining, engineering and underground construction; Pres. JAROSLAV MAKOVICKA; 4,716 employees.

Eltodo EG, Co Inc.: Novodvorská 1010/14, 142 00 Prague 4; tel. 261341111; fax 261710669; e-mail eltodo@eltodo.cz; internet www .eltodo.cz; f. 31 Dec. 2001; through merger of Eltodo, a.s. and Energovod, a.s.; lighting, traffic-monitoring and signalling equipment; design and construction of high-voltage electrical-generation and distribution equipment; Chair. of Bd LIBOR HÁJEK; 1,007 employees.

Fatra: 763 61 Napajedla; tel. (67) 7501111; fax (67) 7505555; internet www.fatra.cz; f. 1935; division of Aliachem, j.s.; manufactures plastic products, incl. PVC floorings, conveyor belts, insulating and packaging foils; Gen. Dir JAROSLAV TOUFAR; 1,577 employees.

Ferona, a.s.: Havličkova 11, 111 82 Prague 1; tel. 224812250; fax 224812721; internet www.ferona.cz; f. 1992; metallurgical products; Chair. and Man. Dir JIŘÍ HYPŠ; 2,650 employees.

Glassexport Co Ltd: tř. 1. máje 52, 461 74 Liberec; tel. 485235111; fax 485100214; e-mail inform@falco.vslib.cz; foreign trade corpn; export and import of glassware; Gen. Dir Josef Molata.

Glaverbel Czech, a.s.: Sklářská 450, 416 74 Teplice; tel. 417341111; fax 41727777; internet www.glaverbel-czech.com; f. 1991 as Glavunion, a.s.; subsidiary of Asahi Glass Co (Japan); glass and glass products; Chief Exec. Arthur Ulens; 2,515 employees.

Gumotex, a.s.: Mládežnická 3A, 690 75 Břeclav; tel. (627) 314111; fax (627) 322909; e-mail info@gumotex.cz; internet www.gumotex .cz; f. 1950; manufacture of foam and protective fabrics, automotive accessories and inflatable products; Man. Dir Ing. Jiří Kalužík; 1,550 employees.

Hutní Montáze Ostrava, a.s.: Hrušková 20, 702 28 Ostrava 1; tel. (69) 6204111; fax (69) 6216504; e-mail sekg.pr@hutni-montaze.cz; internet www.hutni-montaze.cz; f. 1953; privatized 1998; construction of steel structures and installations; Pres. Ladislav Kratochvíl; 1,923 employees.

Hybler s.r.o.: Barlnárŝká 137, 513 01 Semily; tel. (431) 621200; fax (431) 621202; e-mail hybler@hybler.cz; internet www.hybler.cz; f. 1995; manufacture of cotton textiles and cotton products; Gen. Dir Michael Záverka; 1,000 employees.

Imex: Karlovo nám. 31, 120 00 Prague 2; tel. 224908111; fax 224708301; f. 1969; foreign trade corpn; imports and exports consumer goods; Pres. František Pivoda.

Interkontakt Group, a.s.: Pod Pekárnami 245, 190 00 Prague 9; tel. 266032244; fax 266032134; f. 1991; wholesale and retail of foodstuffs, toiletries, household products and electrical goods; Chair. Jan Tlačbaba; 8,100 employees.

Inzenyrske a prumyslové stavby-IPS, a.s.: Kubánské nám. 11, 100 05 Prague 10; tel. 267095351; fax 267310644; e-mail dir@ips.cz; internet www.ips.cz; f. 1953; construction; Chair. and Man. Dir Zdenek Burda; 4,329 employees.

Jablonex, a.s.: Palackého 3145/41, 466 37 Jablonec nad Nisou; tel. (428) 350111; fax (428) 317191; e-mail sales@jablonex.cz.cz; internet www.jablonex.cz; f. 1952; foreign trade corpn; imports and exports fashion jewellery and decorations; Gen. Dir Otakar Havel.

Jäkl Karviná, a.s.: Rudé armády 471, 733 23 Karviná; tel. (69) 6391111; fax (69) 6391392; e-mail jakl@jakl.cz; internet www.jakl .cz; f. 1993; manufacture of steel tubes; Chair. and Gen. Man. Ing. Vlastislav Sehnal; 1,300 employees.

Jihomoravské dřevařské závody: Drážní 7, 627 00 Brno; tel. 542212008; fax 542212219; internet www.jmdz.cz; f. 1994; timber and timber products; Chair. Karel Hruda; 1,100 employees.

Juta, a.s.: Dukelská 417, 544 15 Dvur Králové nad Labem; tel. (437) 829500; fax (437) 820268; e-mail juta@juta.cz; internet www.juta.cz; manufacture of fabrics and textiles; Chair. of Bd Ing. Jiří Hlavatý; 2,000 employees.

Karel Dvořák: Čelkovice 208, 390 01 Tábor; tel. (361) 282681; fax (361) 282682; e-mail dvorakta@mbox.vol.cz; f. 1990; construction and retail developments; Man. Karel Dvořák; 1,300 employees.

Karosa, a.s.: Dobrovského 74, 566 03 Vysoké Myto; tel. (468) 551111; fax (468) 552869; e-mail karosa@hrk.pvtnet.cz; manufacture of commercial road vehicles; Chair. and Man. Dir Rudolf Černý; 1,735 employees.

Kaucuk: 278 52 Kralupy nad Vltavou; tel. (205) 711111; fax (205) 23566; e-mail kaukuk@kaukuk.cz; internet www.kaukuk.cz; f. 1958; produces rubber, polystyrene and petroleum products; Chair. Radomír Věk; 1,779 employees.

Keramika Horni Briza a.s.: 330 12 Horni Briza; tel. (19) 7802531; fax (19) 7955081; e-mail fichtll@hob.cz; internet www.hob.cz; f. 1882; ceramic tiles and industrial ceramic products; Gen. Dir Jaroslav Široky; 2,030 employees.

Koli Holding, a.s.: Klapálka 519, 549 01 Nový Mesto nad Metují; tel. (441) 71114; fax (441) 71508; e-mail koli@mm.cesnet.cz; internet www.lik.cesnet.cz; f. 1992; ready-prepared meals, baby food, and sauces; Chair. and Gen. Dir Petr Maur; 1,200 employees.

Koospol Ltd: Evropská 178, 160 67 Prague 6; tel. 23362061; fax 23165234; f. 1946; foreign trade corpn; imports and exports foodstuffs; Chair. Ing. Oldřich Perutka.

Kovosvit, a.s.: Tomáse Bati nám. 419, 391 02 Sezimovo–Ústí; tel. (361) 411111; fax (361) 276372; e-mail mas@kovosit.cz; internet www.kovosit.cz; f. 1939; manufacture of machine-tools drills; Gen. Dir Jiří Konůpek; 1,622 employees.

Králodvorské Zelezárny, a.s.: Berouna 1, 267 01 Králův Dvůr; tel. (311) 62201; fax (311) 1662999; e-mail kz.general@oha.pvnet.cz; internet www.kzas.cz; iron and steel; Man. Dir Miroslav Krebec; 1,500 employees.

Kras-Haka Brno, a.s.: Belidla 6, 603 71 Brno; tel. 543123111; fax 543210288; e-mail kras-haka@kras-haka.cz; internet www .kras-haka.cz; f. 1949; manufacture of clothes and uniforms; 1,577 employees.

Krkonosske Papirny, a.s.: Nadrazni 266, 543 71 Hostinné; tel. (438) 501111; fax (438) 501155; e-mail krpa@krpa.cz; internet www .krpa.cz; f. 1992; paper and paper products; Man. Dir Jaroslav Jiříčka; 710 employees.

Ligna: Vodičkova 41, 112 09 Prague 1; tel. 224151111; fax 224947535; e-mail ligna@ligna.cz; internet www.ligna.cz; foreign trade corpn; imports and exports timber, wood products, musical instruments and paper; Gen. Dir Ing. Miroslav Mrna.

Lovochemie, a.s.: Terenzínská 57, 410 17 Lovosice; tel. (419) 56111; fax 419562090; e-mail info@lovochemie.cz; f. 1903; produces industrial fertilizers, viscose rayon cord, abrasive materials for toothpastes, concrete paving stones; Man. Dir Luděk Peleška; 1,700 employees.

Magneton, a.s.: Hulínská 4, 767 53 Kroměříz; tel. (634) 592400; fax (634) 592400; e-mail marketing@magneton.cz; internet www .magneton.cz; f. 1926; manufactures motor-vehicle engine components; Pres. and Man. Dir Petr Peštuka; 1,300 employees.

Meopta Přerov, a.s.: Kabelíkova 1, 750 58 Přerov; tel. (641) 241111; fax (641) 204732; e-mail meopta@meopta.com; internet www.meopta.com; f. 1991; manufacture of optical equipment; Gen. Man. Vladimír Chlup; 1,360 employees.

Metalimpex, a.s.: Štěpánská 34, 112 17 Prague 1; tel. 224492111; fax 22320630; f. 1949; foreign trade corpn; imports and exports nonferrous and precious metals, electrical power, gas and solid fuels; Chair. and Man. Dir Petr Paukner.

Metra Blansko, a.s.: Hybesova 53, 678 23 Blansko; tel. (506) 822; fax (506) 4578; e-mail metra@metra.cz; internet www.metra.cz; f. 1911; manufacture of electronic measuring instruments and recording devices; Gen. Dir Jaroslav Šejnoha; 2,150 employees.

Mileta, a.s.: Husova 1599, 508 14 Hořice v Podkrkonoší; tel. (435) 644111; fax (435) 621066; e-mail mileta@mileta.cz; f. 1992; manufactures towels and linen; Pres. Elard Marwin Maron; 1,662 employees.

Mitas, a.s.: Švehlova 1900, 106 25 Prague 10; tel. 267111330; fax 272658306; e-mail marie.svobodova@mitas.cgs.cz; internet www.cgs .cz; f. 1934; manufacture of tyres and rubber products; Chief Exec. Jaroslav Čechura; 1,900 employees.

Mora Moravia, a.s.: Nádražni 50, 783 66 Hlubočky; tel. (68) 5061111; fax (68) 5351220; internet www.mora.cz; f. 1825; sheet metal, domestic appliances; Gen. Man. Vojtěch Vlček; 3,000 employees.

Moravské Naftové Doly, a.s.: Uprkova 6, 695 30 Hodonín; tel. (628) 315111; fax (628) 21455; e-mail director@mnd.cz; internet www.mnd.cz; f. 1992; petroleum and gas exploration and production; Man. Dir Ing. Stanislav Benada; 1,250 employees.

Moravskoslezské Dřevžské Závody Šumperk, a.s.: Hlavni třída 5, 787 84 Šumperk; tel. (649) 212401; fax (649) 215986; f. 1991; manufacture of wooden buildings and related products; Chair. of Bd Jiří Šula; 2,100 employees.

Motokov, a.s.: nábř strži 63, 140 62 Prague 4; tel. 261141111; fax 261211307; e-mail mtk@motokov.cz; internet www.motokov.cz; f. 1951; foreign trade corpn; imports and exports vehicles, agricultural machinery and light engineering products; Chair. and Gen. Dir Ing. René Kraus.

Motorpal, a.s.: Strojirenska 9, 587 22 Jihlava; tel. (66) 7131111; fax (66) 7132272; e-mail motorpal@motorpal.cz; internet www.motorpal .cz; f. 1946; manufacture of diesel engines and fuel-injection systems; Man. Dir Ing. Jaroslav Nechvatal; 2,500 employees.

Nová Huť, a.s.: Vratimovská 689, 707 02 Ostrava-Kunčice; tel. (69) 5681111; fax (69) 5682686; e-mail webmaster@novahut.cz; internet www.novahut.cz; f. 1951; manufacture of metallurgical products; Gen. Dir Ing. František Chowaniec; 12,261 employees.

Omnipol: Nekázanka 11, 112 21 Prague 1; tel. 224011111; fax 224012241; e-mail omnipol@gts.cz; internet www.omnipol.cz; foreign trade corpn; import and export of sports and civil aircraft; Chair. and Gen. Man. Michal Hon.

Ostravsko-Karvinske Doly-OKD, a.s.: Prokešovo nám. 6, 728 30 Ostrava 1; tel. (69) 6261111; fax (69) 6118890; e-mail dzida@okd.cz; internet www.okd.cz; f. 1991; mining, energy distribution and wholesale of fuels and related products; Pres. and Gen. Dir Ing. Ivan Dzida; 29,000 employees.

Otavan Trebon, a.s.: Nádražni 641, 379 20 Třeboň; tel. (333) 751911; fax (333) 721542; e-mail luboms@otavan.cz; internet www .otavan.cz; f. 1991; manufacture of clothing; 2,100 employees.

Plzeňský Prazdroj a.s.: Prazdroje 7, 304 97 Plzeň 3; tel. (19) 7061111; fax (19) 7062230; e-mail marketing.dept@pilsner-urquell

.com; internet www.pilsner-urquell.com; f. 1842; brewing; Chair. VÁCLAV BERKA; 2,811 employees.

Pragoexport, a.s.: Antal Staška 34, 146 01 Prague 4; tel. 261041111; fax 261042204; e-mail marketing@pragoexport.cz; internet pragoexport.webpark.cz; f. 1948; foreign trade corpn; imports and exports consumer goods; Gen. Dir Ing. PAVEL MAJOR.

Preciosa Lustry, a.s.: 471 14 Kamenicky Senov; tel. (424) 713111; fax (424) 92739; e-mail sales@lustry.preciosa.cz; internet www .lustry.preciosa.cz; f. 1950; light fittings; Pres. Ing. KARL LUDVÍK.

PSP Přerovské strojírny, a.s.: Kojetínská 53, 750 53 Přerov; tel. (641) 231111; fax (641) 204979; e-mail name@holdingpsp.cz; internet www.holdingpsp.cz; f. 1948; produces machinery and equipment for the construction industry; Gen. Dir RICHARD BENÝŠEK; 3,700 employees.

PVT, a.s.: Kovanecká 30, 190 00 Prague 9; tel. 266198111; fax (2) 6849313; e-mail obch@pha.pvt.cz; internet www.pvt.cz; f. 1991; data processing and computer networks; Chair. and Chief Exec. Ing. JIŘÍ FABIÁN; 2,228 employees.

Setuza, a.s.: Žukovova 100, 401 29 Ústi nad Labem; tel. 475291111; fax 475293899; internet www.setuza.cz; f. 1992; production of oils, fats, soaps and detergents; Man. Dir PETR VOBORNÍK; 1,500 employees.

Siemens, s.r.o.: Evropská 33A, 160 00 Prague 6; tel. 233031111; fax 233031112; e-mail hotmail@rg.siemens.cz; internet www.siemens .cz; sale of electrical and electronic equipment; Gen. Dir PAVEL KAFKA; 1,007 employees.

Sigma Group, a.s.: Jana Sigmunda, 783 50 Lutín; tel. (68) 5651111; fax (68) 5221353; e-mail sigmaspc@mbox.vol.cz; production and sale of pumps and pumping equipment, casting of iron and non-ferrous metals, manufacture of tools, consulting services; Man. Dir Ing. MILAN ŠIMONOVSKÝ; 2,500 employees.

Sklárny Kavalier, a.s.: Sklarská 359, 285 96 Sazava; tel. 328400111; fax 328491426; e-mail marketing@kavalier.cz; internet www.kavalier.cz; f. 1837; manufacture of domestic and industrial glassware; Man. Dir LUMÍR GAWLAS; 1,900 employees.

ŠKODA, a.s.: Tylova 57, 316 00 Plzeň; tel. (19) 7711111; fax (19) 7221985; e-mail info@skoda.cz; internet www.skoda.cz; parent co. of numerous engineering, manufacturing and wholesaling concerns; Chair. and Man. Dir LUBOMÍR SOUDEK; 18,622 employeees.

ŠKODA Energo s.r.o.: Cesky bratrí nám; tel. (19) 7075000; fax (19) 7074910; e-mail energo-obchod@ego.ln.skoda.cz; f. 1998; manufactures power generation and transmission machinery; Gen. Dir J. STARÝ; 3,850 employees.

ŠKODA JS a.s.: Orlík 266, 316 06 Plzeň; tel. (19) 7042942; fax (19) 7524755; e-mail info@jad.ln.skoda.cz; internet www.skoda.cz/eng/podnik_index.htm; f. 1993; design and manufacture of machinery for chemical, petrochemical and nuclear industries, aerospace, healthcare and shipbuilding equipment, repairs and servicing; Chair. and Chief Exec. VÁCLAV LOBOVSKÝ; 1,415 employees.

ŠKODA Mnichovo Hradiště, a.s.: Tř. Víte Nejedlého 101, 295 23 Mnichovo Hradiště; tel. 329776471; fax 329771021; e-mail ouskodamh@iol.cz; internet www.liaz-mh.cz; f. 1998; fmrly ŠKODA Liaz, a.s.; manufacture of heavy motor vehicles; Gen. Man. Ing. JIŘÍ MIKULEC; 3,448 employees.

ŠKODA Praha, a.s.: Milady Horákové 109, 160 41 Prague 6; tel. 224396003; fax 224396428; e-mail ou@skodanet.cz; internet www .skodanet.cz; f. 1953; construction, civil engineering and manufacture of industrial machinery; Chair. and Chief Exec. STANISLAV SVOBODA; 2,169 employees.

ŠKODA Steel: Tylova 57, 316 00 Plzeň; tel. (19) 7732096; fax (19) 7734436; e-mail steel-export@kov.ln.skoda.cz; f. 1993; steel factories and works, and steel products; Man. Dir VLADIMÍR RADA; 1,930 employees.

ŠKODA TS: tel. (19) 7735167; fax (19) 7736454; e-mail mdolezal@tst.ln.skoda.cz; internet www.skoda.cz/companies/ts; f. 1993; manufacture of machine tools and other industrial machinery; Man. Dir Ing. MIROSLAV DOLEZAL; 855 employees.

ŠKODA automobilová a.s.: Václava Klementa 869, 293 60 Mladá Boleslav; tel. 326831150; fax 326721328; internet www.skoda-auto .com; f. 1991; wholly owned by Volkswagen AG (Germany); manufacture of passenger cars and car components; Chair. VRATISLAV KULHÁNEK; 22,322 employees.

Škodaexport Co Ltd: Opletalova 41, 113 32 Prague 1; tel. 221004111; fax 224228951; e-mail kontakt@skodaexport.cz; internet www.skodaexport.cz; f. 1966; foreign trade corpn; exports and imports power engineering and metallurgical plants, engineering works, electrical locomotives and trolleybuses, tobacco machines, pipelines; Pres. OLDRICH PERUTKA.

SKOFIN s.r.o.: Pekařska 6, 155 00 Prague 1; tel. 224992111; fax 224992561; e-mail marketing@skofin.cz; internet www.skofin.cz; f.

1992; motor vehicle leasing service; Man. Dirs VRATISLAV VÁLEK, TOMÁŠ HLAVÁČ; 170 employees.

Slévána Zetor, a.s.: Trnkova 111, 632 00 Brno; tel. and fax 544210280; e-mail info@slevzet.cz; internet www.slevzet.cz; f. 1946 as Zetor, a.s.; current name adopted in 1998; metal foundry products; Dir Ivo STACHOVEČ.

Slezan Frýdek-Místek, a.s.: Na Příkope 1221, 738 15 Fr&ycarondek-Místek; tel. (658) 610111; fax (658) 623538; e-mail slezan@slezan.cz; manufacture of cotton and fabrics; Gen. Man. IVAN KRUPNÍK; 2,670 employees.

Sokolovská Uhelná, a.s.: Staré nám. 69, 356 00 Sokolov; tel. (168) 621012; fax (168) 621038; e-mail mail@suas.cz; internet www.suas .cz; f. 1994; mining, petroleum, gas, and chemical production, power generation; Chair. JAN STEISS; 7,097 employees.

Spolek pro Chemickou a Hutní Výrobu, a.s. (United Chemical and Metallurgical Works, Ltd): Revoluční 86, 400 32 Ústí nad Labem; tel. 475261111; fax 475210289; e-mail rytir@spolchemie.cz; internet www.spochemie.cz; produces chemicals and related products; Gen. Dir ČENEK KYSIKA; 1,500 employees.

Stavby silnic a Železnic, a.s.: třída Národní 10, 113 19 Prague 1; tel. 224952020; fax 224933551; e-mail provoz@ssz.cz; internet www .ssz.cz; f. 1951; construction of roads, railways, bridges and utility lines; Chair. and Gen. Man. BOŘIVOJ KAČENA; 2,700 employees.

Strojexport, a.s.: : Václavské nám. 56, POB 662, 113 26 Prague 1; tel. 224031111; fax 222211138; e-mail odd.41@strojexport.anet.cz; f. 1953; foreign trade corpn; imports and exports machines and machinery equipment, civil engineering works; Chair. LUDĚK VINŠ.

Strojimport Joint-Stock Company: U Nákladového nádraží 6, 130 86 Prague 3; tel. 222863111; fax 222863333; e-mail marketing@strojimport.cz; internet www.strojimport.cz; f. 1953; foreign trade corpn; imports and exports machine tools, tools and gauges, and industrial plants; Pres. IVAN ČAPEK; 97 employees.

Tamda, a.s.: Hudcova 72, 621 00 Brno; tel. 541518111; fax 541518541; f. 1992; wholesale of pharmaceutical products; Chair. and Man. Dir DUŠAND NOVOTNÝ; 366 employees.

Tatra, a.s.: Štefánikova 1163, 742 21 Kopřivnice; tel. (656) 721156; fax (656) 721148; e-mail tatra@tatra.cz; internet www.tatra.cz; f. 1850; sale of 92% stake to SDC International (USA) approved in Nov. 2001; manufacture and assembly of motor vehicles; built Central Europe's first automobile in 1897; Pres. and Chief Exec. PETER A. URBAN; 2,800 employees.

Technoexport: Václavské nám. 1, 113 34 Prague 1; tel. 224471111; fax 224224158; e-mail info@technoexport.cz; internet www .technoexport.cz; f. 1953; foreign trade corpn; imports and exports machines and equipment for chemical, petrochemical, rubber, food and mechanical engineering industries; Pres. JOSEF CÍLEK.

Textilana, a.s.: Jablonecká 36, 461 09 Liberec; tel. 485396111; fax 485100515; e-mail marketing@textilana.cz; internet www.textilana .cz; f. 1807; manufacture of textiles; Pres. and Man. Dir Ing. STANISLAV NOSEK; 2,666 employees.

Tiba, a.s.: Dobrovskeho 338, Dvur Kralove nad Labem; tel. (437) 800111; fax (437) 800501; e-mail info@tiba.cz; internet www.tiba.cz; f. 1993; manufacture of cotton fabrics and clothing; Chair. and Man. Dir STANISLAV SEDLÁČEK; 2,220 employees.

Ton, a.s.: Thoneta 148, 768 61 Bystrice pod Hostynem; tel. (635) 325111; fax (635) 378259; e-mail ton@brn.pvtnet.cz; f. 1994; production of wooden furniture; Gen. Dir Ing. PETR JOSINEK; 2,209 employees.

Třinecké Železárny a.s.: Przymslová 1000, 739 70 Třinec; tel. (659) 411111; fax (659) 331831; e-mail department@trz.cz; internet www.trz.cz; f. 1839; privatized in 1996; rolled metal and metal products; Chair. and Chief Exec. JIŘÍ CIENCIALA; 8,113 employees.

Unex, a.s.: Brníčko 1032, 783 93 Uničov; tel. (643) 471111; fax (643) 472001; e-mail lubomir.pokorny@unex.cz; internet www.unex.cz; f. 1950; manufacture of construction machinery and equipment; Chief Exec. LUBOMÍR POKORNY; 2,600 employees.

Unipetrol, a.s.: Trojská 13, 182 00 Prague 8; tel. 284012111; fax 26881516; e-mail name@unipetrol.cz; internet www.unipetrol.cz; f. 1995; chemical and petroleum industries; Chair. and Chief Exec. PAVEL ŠVARC; 7,756 employees.

Česka Rafinérská, a.s.: Záluzí 1, 436 70 Litvinov; tel. 356161111; fax 356165086; e-mail info@crc.cz; internet www.crc .cz; f. 1995; refining of crude oil, and production and sale of petroleum products; Chair. and Man. Dir Ing. IVAN OTTIS; 1,219 employees.

Chemopetrol, a.s.: Zaluzi 1, 436 70 Litvinov; tel. 356161111; fax (35) 28917; internet www.chemopetrol.cz; f. 1996; manufactures chemical products, including plastics, fertilizers and nitrogen compounds, and sewage-treatment products; Chair. of Bd PAVEL ŠVARC; 3,283 employees.

Vertex, a.s.: Sokolovská 106, 570 21 Litomysl; tel. (464) 651111; fax (464) 612769; e-mail obchod@vertex.cz; internet www.vertex.cz; f. 1950; manufacture of glass fibre products; Chair. of Bd Bořivoj Frýbert; 1,646 employees.

Vítkovice, a.s.: Ruská 101, 703 00 Ostrava 6; tel. (69) 2921401; fax (69) 2921406; e-mail trade@vitkovice.cz; internet www.vitkovice.cz; f. 1828; iron and steel, engineering; Exec. Dir Václav Pastrňak; 17,500 employees.

ŽĎAS, a.s.: Strojírenská 6, 591 71 Žďár nad Sázavou; tel. (616) 641111; fax (616) 642882; e-mail zdas@zdas.cz; internet www.zdas.cz; f. 1951; produces plant and equipment for the iron and steel industry; Chair. of Bd Otakar Jurečka; 3,500 employees.

ZDB, a.s.: Bezručova 300, 735 93 Bohumín; tel. (69) 6081111; fax (69) 6082820; e-mail secretariat@zdb.cz; internet www.zdb.cz; f. 1993; manufacture of steel products; Gen. Man. Jiří Maléř; 5,564 employees.

Zelezarny Hradek, a.s.: Nova Hut 204, 338 42 Hradek; tel. (181) 765111; fax (181) 723895; internet www.zhr.cz; produces high-grade steel bars and tubes; Gen. Dir Vladimír Vejkovsky; 2,450 employees.

ZS Brno, a.s.: Burešova 17, 660 02 Brno; tel. 541571111; fax 541212166; e-mail stefl@zsbrno.cz; internet www.zsbrno.cz; f. 1992; building, contracting and civil engineering; Gen. Man. Ing. Michal Štefl; 2,311 employees.

ZVVZ a.s.: Sažinova 888, 399 25 Milevsko; tel. (368) 551111; fax (368) 521163; e-mail zvvzas@zvvz.cz; internet www.zvvz.cz; f. 1948; environmental protection equipment, container manufacture, ventilation equipment; Gen. Man. Stanislav Kázacký; 1,350 employees.

TRADE UNIONS

Czech-Moravian Confederation of Trade Unions (Českomoravská konfederace odborových svazů): W. Churchilla nám. 2, 113 59 Prague 3; tel. 224461111; fax 222718994; f. 1990; 30 affiliated unions (1999); Pres. Richard Falbr.

Affiliated unions include the following:

Czech-Moravian Trade Union of Workers in Education (Českomoravský odborový svaz školství): W. Churchilla nám. 2, 113 59 Prague 3; tel. 222721721; fax 222722685; e-mail cmos .skolstvi@cmkos.cz; internet www.skolskeodbory.cz; Pres. Jaroslav Rössler; 80,000 mems.

Trade Union of the Health Service and Social Care of the Czech Republic (Odborový svaz zdravotnictví a sociální péče ČR): Koněvova 54, 130 00 Prague 3; tel. 222714629; fax 222718211; e-mail osz_cr@cmkos.cz; internet www.osz.cmkos.cz; Pres. Jiří Schlanger; 65,000 mems.

Trade Union of Workers in Textile, Clothing and Leather Industry of Bohemia and Moravia (Odborový svaz pracovníků textilního, oděvního a kožedělného průmyslu Čech a Moravy): W. Churchilla nám. 2, 113 59 Prague 3; tel. 224222123; fax (2) 273589; Pres. Karel Nocotny; 79,600 mems.

Trade Union of Workers in Woodworking Industry, Forestry and Management of Water Supplies in the Czech Republic (Odborový svaz pracovníků dřevozpracujícího odvětví, lesního a vodního hospodářství v České republice): W. Churchilla nám. 2, 113 59 Prague 3; tel. 224462659; fax 222716373; e-mail kyncl.rudolf@cmkos.cz; Pres. Rudolf Kyncl; 43,000 mems.

TU UNIOS: W. Churchilla nám. 2, 113 59 Prague 3; tel. 224463172; fax 224463185; f. 1994 to succeed Czech-Moravian Trade Union of Workers in Services (f. 1990); Pres. Karel Sladkovský; 38,000 mems.

Transport

RAILWAYS

In 1998 the total length of the Czech railway network was 9,430 km.

České dráhy (Czech Railways): nábř. L. Svobody 1222/12, 110 15 Prague 1; tel. 251431111; fax 224812569; e-mail infoservis@gr.cdrail .cz; internet www.cdrail.cz; f. 1993 as successor to Czechoslovak State Railways; Gen. Dir Ing. Dalibor Zelený.

Prague Metropolitan Railway: Dopravní podnik hlavního města Prahy, a.s.-Metro, o.z., Sliačská 1, 141 41 Prague 4; tel. 271763657; fax 2764762; e-mail pavlicar@dp-praha.cz; the Prague underground railway opened in 1974, and in 1998 50 km were operational; 50 stations; Chair. M. Hejl; Gen. Dir (vacant).

ROADS

In 2000 there were an estimated 55,408 km of roads in the Czech Republic, including 499 km of motorways.

INLAND WATERWAYS

The total length of navigable waterways in the Czech Republic is 663.6 km. The Elbe (Labe) and its tributary, the Vltava, connect the Czech Republic with the North Sea via the port of Hamburg (Germany). The Oder provides a connection with the Baltic Sea and the port of Szczecin (Poland). The Czech Republic's river ports are Prague Holešovice, Prague Radotín, Kolín, Mělník, Ústí nad Labem and Děčín, on the Vltava and Elbe.

Czechoslovak Elbe Navigation Ltd (Československá plavba labská, a.s.): K. Čapka 1, 405 91 Děčín; tel. 412561111; fax 412510140; f. 1922; river transport of goods to Germany, Poland, the Netherlands, Belgium, Luxembourg, France and Switzerland; Man. Dir Karel Horyna.

SHIPPING

Since August 1997 no ships have operated under the Czech flag. All Czech-owned ships operate under the Maltese and Cypriot flags.

Czech Ocean Shipping, Joint-Stock Company (Česká námořní plavba, akciová společnost): Počernická 168, 100 99 Prague 10; tel. (2) 778941; fax (2) 773962; e-mail coscompu@login.cz; internet www .cos.cz; f. 1959; six ships totalling 199,331 dwt; Man. Dir Capt. Pavel Trnka.

CIVIL AVIATION

There are main civil airports at Prague (Ruzyně), Brno, Karlovy Vary and Ostrava, operated by the Czech Airport Administration. The opening of a new terminal at Ruzyně in November 1997 increased the airport's capacity from 2.3m. passengers to 4.8m.

Air Ostrava: Ostrava International Airport, 742 51 Mosnov; tel. (69) 6659401; fax (69) 6659402; e-mail air.ostrava@ova.prtnet.cz; internet www.airostrava.cz; f. 1994; services to international, regional and domestic destinations; Pres. Milan Rousar; Man. Dir Pavel Hradec.

ČSA (České aerolinie, a.s.) (Czech Airlines): Ruzyně Airport, 160 08 Prague 6; tel. 220111111; fax 220562266; e-mail info@uit.csa.cz; internet www.csa.cz; f. 1923; external services to most European capitals, the Near, Middle and Far East, North Africa and North America; scheduled for privatization; Pres. Miroslav Kula.

Tourism

The Czech Republic has magnificent scenery, with summer and winter sports facilities. Prague, Kutna Hora, Olomouc, Český Krumlov and Telč are among the best known of the historic towns, and there are famous castles and cathedrals and numerous resorts, as well as spas with natural mineral springs at Karlovy Vary (Carlsbad) and Mariánské Lázně (Marienbad). Registered accommodation establishments recorded some 5.2m. stays of at least one night by foreigners in 2001. In the following year a total of almost 4.6m. tourist arrivals were recorded. In 2000 tourism receipts totalled US $2,982.0m.

Czech Tourist Authority: Vinohradská 46, POB 32, 120 41 Prague 2; tel. 222515078; fax 224257145; e-mail kejvalova@cccr-cta.cz; internet www.visitczech.cz; f. 1993; Dir Karel Nejdl.

Čedok Travel Corpn: Na Příkopě 18, 111 35 Prague 1; tel. 224197111; fax (2) 2321656; internet www.cedok.cz; f. 1920; 80 domestic travel offices; eight branches throughout Europe; Pres. Čestmír Sajda.

Culture

NATIONAL ORGANIZATIONS

Ministry of Culture (Ministerstvo kultury): see section on The Government (Ministries).

Czech Commission for Co-operation with UNESCO (Česká komise pro spolupráci s UNESCO): Toskán, Hradčanské nám. 5, 118 00 Prague 1; tel. 224182258; fax 224182808; e-mail unescocz@mbox .vol.cz; Chair. Jaroslava Moserova; Sec.-Gen. Karel Komarek.

Czech National Heritage Chamber: Prague; f. 1993; asscn for organizations concerned with the preservation of national monuments; Chair. Karel Liska.

Information and Consultation Centre for Local Culture (Informační a poradenské středisko pro místní kulturu): Vinohrady, Blanická 4, 120 21 Prague 2; tel. (2) 250161; fax (2) 258434; f. 1906; Dir Jiří Valenta.

CULTURAL HERITAGE

Aleš South Bohemian Gallery (Alšova jihočeská galerie): 373 41 Hluboká nad. Vltavou; tel. 387967041; fax 387965436; e-mail ajghluboka@volny.cz; f. 1953; 13th- to 20th-century Czech art, 16th–18th-century European art, 20th-century Czech and world ceramics; library of 12,300 vols; Dir Dr HYNEK RULÍŠEK.

Archaeological Institute AS CR, Prague (Archeologická ústav AC ČR, Praha): Letenská 4, 118 01 Prague 1; tel. 257533782; fax 257532288; e-mail arupraha@arup.cas.cz; internet www.arup.cas.cz; f. 1919; attached to the Academy of Sciences of the Czech Republic; library of 63,000 vols; Dir LUBOŠ JIRÁŇ.

Czech Museum of Fine Arts (České muzeum výtvarných umění): Husova 19/21, 110 01 Prague 1; tel. 222220218; fax 222221190; e-mail muzeum@cmvu.cz; internet cmvu.cz; f. 1963; temporary exhibitions of modern and contemporary art; Dir Dr IVAN NEUMANN.

Czech National Library (Národní knihovna České Republiky): Klementinum 190, 110 01 Prague 1; tel. 221663111; fax 221663261; e-mail public.ur@nkp.cz; internet www.nkp.cz; f. 1781; 6m. vols; national literature collection; national bibliography; Dir Dr VOJTĚCH BALÍK.

Historical Museum (Historické muzeum): Václavské nám. 68, 115 79 Prague 1; tel. 224497111; fax 224226488; e-mail nm@nm.cz; materials relating to Czech history, ethnography; prehistoric and classical archaeology; numismatics; Dir Dr EDUARD ŠIMEK.

Jewish Museum in Prague (Židovské muzeum v Praze): U staré školy 1, 110 00 Prague 1; tel. 224819456; fax 224819458; e-mail office@jewishmuseum.cz; internet www.jewishmuseum.cz; f. 1906; liturgical objects, textiles, paintings, synagogues, medieval Jewish cemetery; library of ancient books, archives of Bohemian and Moravian Jewish communities; Dir Dr LEO PAVLÁT.

Moravian Gallery in Brno (Moravská galerie v Brno): Husova 18, 662 26 Brno; tel. 542215753; fax 542215758; e-mail m-gal@moravska-galerie.cz; internet www.moravska-galerie.cz; f. 1873; mostly European fine and applied arts of all periods; library of 110,000 vols; Dir Dr KALIOPI CHAMONIKOLA.

Moravian Library (Moravská zemská knihovna): Kounicova 65A, 601 87 Brno; tel. 541646101; fax 541646100; e-mail mzk@mzk.cz; internet www.mzk.cz; f. 1808; 3.5m. vols; 4,300 periodicals; second largest library in the Czech Republic; specializes in social sciences, medicines, and technical literature, also has historical collection; Dir Dr JAROMÍR KUBÍČEK.

Municipal Library of Prague (Mestská knihovna v Praze): Mariánské nám. 1, 115 72 Prague 1; tel. 222113555; fax 222113305; e-mail informace@mlp.cz; internet www.mlp.cz; f. 1891; 2.2m. vols; Dir ANNA BIMKOVÁ.

Museum of Czech Music (Muzeum české hudby): Novotného lávka 1, 110 00 Prague 1; tel. and fax 224229075; f. 1976; musical scores and other documents, exhibitions on composers and collections of musical instruments; Dir Dr MARKÉTA HALLOVÁ.

Museum of Decorative Arts (Uměleckoprůmyslové muzeum v Praze): ul. 17 Llistopadu 2, 110 01 Prague 1; tel. 251093111; fax 224811666; e-mail upm.direct@volny.cz; f. 1885; has special collection of glass; library of 150,000 vols; Dir Dr HELENA KOENIGSMARKOVÁ.

National Gallery in Prague (Národní galerie v Praze): Hradčanské nám. 15, 119 04 Prague 1; tel. 22329331; fax 22324641; internet www.czech.cz/ng; f. 1796; art of all periods; library of 71,000 vols; Dir Mgr MARTIN ZLATOHLÁVEK.

National Museum (Národní muzeum): Václavské nám. 68, 115 79 Prague 1; tel. 224497111; fax 224226488; e-mail nm@nm.cz; internet www.nm.cz; f. 1818; Dir Dr MICHAL LUKEŠ.

National Museum Library (Knihovna Národního muzea): Václavské nám. 68, 115 79 Prague 1; tel. 224497111; fax 224226488; e-mail helga.turkova@nm.cz; internet www.nm.cz; f. 1818; c. 3.6m. vols; humanities and natural science; Dir Dr HELGA TURKOVÁ.

West Bohemian Gallery in Plzeň (Západočeská galerie v Plzni): Pražská 13, 301 14 Plzeň; tel. (19) 377223759; fax (19) 377322970; e-mail info@spc-galerie.cz; internet www.spc-galerie.cz; f. 1954; Czech art from 14th century to the present; Dir Dr JANA POTUŽÁKOVÁ.

SPORTING ORGANIZATION

Czech Olympic Committee (Český olympijský výbor): Benesovská 6, 110 00 Prague 10; tel. 271734734; fax 271731318; e-mail info@olympic.cz; Pres. Dr MILAN JIRASEK; Gen. Sec. VLADIMÍR DOSTÁL.

PERFORMING ARTS

Czech Philharmonic Orchestra (Česka filharmonie): Alšovo nábřeží 12, 110 01 Prague 1; tel. 224893111; fax 222314110; e-mail cfekon@mbox.vol.cz; internet www.czechphilharmonic.cz; f. 1896; Chief Conductor VLADIMÍR ASHKENAZY; Dir VÁCLAV RIEDLBAUCH.

Minor Theatre: Senovážné nám. 28, 113 58 Prague 1; e-mail minor@ms.easynet.cz; f. 1949; puppet performances for children and adults; Dir KAREL MAKONJ.

National Theatre (Národní divadlo): Ostrovní 1, 112 30 Prague; tel. 224914204; fax 224911530; e-mail ntprague@ntprague.anet.cz; internet www.narodni-divadlo.cz; opera, ballet, drama; Dir JIŘÍ SRSTKA.

Prague Spring International Music Festival (Pražské jaro): Hellichova 18, 110 00 Prague 1; tel. 257312547; fax 257313725; e-mail info@festival.cz; internet www.festival.cz; Dir ROMAN BELOR.

State Opera—Prague: Legerova 75, 110 00 Prague 1; tel. 224227693; fax 224229437.

Theatre of the Estates (Stavovské divadlo): Ovocný tř. 1, 110 00 Prague 1; tel. 224228503.

Theatre Institute (Divadelní ústav): Celetná 17, 110 00 Prague 1; tel. 224809111; fax 224811452; e-mail divadelni.ustav@divadlo.cz; internet www.czech-theatre.cz; f. 1956; research and documentation on historical and contemporary Czech drama, opera and ballet; Dir ONDŘEJ ČERNÝ.

ASSOCIATIONS

Association of Musicians and Musicologists (Asociace hudebních umělců a vědců): Maltézské nám. 1, 118 00 Prague 1; tel. (2) 533661; fax (2) 539062; f. 1990; Pres. Mgr LUBOŠ SLUKÁ; Exec. Sec. MARCELA POSEJPALOVÁ.

Association of Theatre Designers (Asociace scénografu): c/o Labyrint, Štefánikova 57, 150 43 Prague 5; tel. and fax (2) 544541.

Czech Association of Museums and Galleries (AMG) (Asociace muzeí a galerií): Jindřišská 901/5, 110 00 Prague 1; tel. 224210037; fax 224210047; e-mail amg@vol.cz; internet www.cz-museums.cz; Dir Dr JAN DOLÁK.

Czech Centre for International PEN: Two Bears House, 28 Říjen 9, 110 00 Prague 1; tel. 224234343; fax 224221926; f. 1924; 217 mems; Pres. JIŘÍ STRÁNSKÝ; Int. Sec. LIBUŠE LUDVÍKOVÁ.

Czech Film and Television Association (Český filmový a televizni svaz—FITES): Pod nuselskými schody 3, 120 00 Prague 2; tel. (2) 6910310; fax (2) 6911375; f. 1966; 760 mems; Pres. MARTIN SKYBA.

Czech Literature Fund (Český literární fond): Pod nuselskými schody 3, 128 00 Prague 2; tel. (2) 6911908.

Czech Music Information Centre: Besední 3, 118 00 Prague 1; tel. 257312422; fax 257317424; e-mail his@vol.cz; f. 1964; information service, promotion and documentation of contemporary music, publications; Dir MIROSLAV PUDLÁK.

Czech Music Society (Česká hudební společnost): Radlická 99, 150 00 Prague 5; tel. and fax 251552453; internet www.nipax.cz/chr/main.html; f. 1934; 4,500 mems; Pres. MÍLA SMETÁČKOVÁ; Sec.-Gen. EVA ŠTRAUSOVÁ.

Institute of Czech Literature AS CR (Ústav pro českou literaturu AV ČR): Na Florenci 3/1420, 110 15 Prague 1; tel. (2) 22828111; fax (2) 24818437; e-mail ucl@cas.cz; internet www.ucl.cas.cz; f. 1947; attached to the Academy of Sciences; library of 150,000 vols; Dir Dr PAVEL JANOUŠEK.

Literary Society (Literárnevedná společnost): Valentinská 1, 110 00 Prague 1; tel. (2) 2320167; f. 1934; 285 mems; Pres. SLAVOMÍR WOLLMAN.

Moravian Society of History and Literature (Matice moravská): A. Nováka 1, 602 00 Brno; tel. 541121372; fax 541121406; e-mail stouraco@phil.muni.cz; f. 1849; 560 mems; Pres. Prof. JAN JANÁK.

Society of Czech Architects (Obec architektů): Letenská 5, 118 00 Prague 1; tel. 257535025; fax 257535033; e-mail obecarch@volny.cz; internet www.architekt.cz; f. 1990; 1,200 mems; Pres. JIŘÍ MOJŽÍŠ.

Society of Czech Writers (Obec spisovatelů): POB 669, 111 21 Prague 1; tel. and fax (2) 22220106; f. 1989; 710 mems; Dir ANTONÍN JELÍNEK.

Theatre Association (Divadelní obec): c/o Labyrint, Štefánikova 57, 150 43 Prague 5; tel. and fax (2) 544541.

Union of Czech Dramatic Artists (Svaz českých dramatických umělců): Pod Nuselskými schody 3, 120 00 Prague 2; tel. (2) 250682; f. 1978; 3,100 mems; Pres. KÁKOŠ.

Visual Artists Association (Unie výtvarných umělců): Masarykovo nábřeží 250, 110 00 Prague 1; tel. (2) 292215; fax (2) 292442; f. 1990; 3,000 mems; Pres. JAROSLAV ZAPLETAL; Sec.-Gen. VÍT WEBER.

Education

Some 90% of children between the ages of three and six attend kindergarten (mateřská škola). In April 2002 the Government approved a proposal to introduce a pre-school programme for Roma (Gypsy) children. Education is compulsory between the ages of six and 15 years, when children attend basic school (základní škola). Most children continue their studies after basic school, either at a secondary grammar school, a secondary vocational school or a secondary technical school. In all three types of institution students follow three- to four-year courses. There are also apprentice-training centres, at which courses last from two to four years, which prepare young people for workers' professions. In 1990 the establishment of private and religious schools was legalized, and many, particularly at upper secondary level, were established. In 2001/02 1,027,827 children attended basic schools and 531,290 the different types of secondary school; there were 227,120 students in higher education. Fees for higher education were introduced from September 1994. In 1999 budgetary expenditure on education was 66,576m. koruny (some 9.9% of total spending).

UNIVERSITIES

Brno University of Technology (Vysoké učení technické v Brně): Antoninska 1A, 601 90 Brno; tel. 541145111; fax 541211309; e-mail vavrin@ro.vutbr.cz; internet www.vutbr.cz; f. 1899; 9 faculties; 1,051 teachers;14,720 students; Rector Prof. Ing. PETR VAVŘÍN.

Brno University of Veterinary and Pharmaceutical Sciences (Veterinární a farmaceutická univerzita Brno): Palackého 1–3, 612 42 Brno; tel. 541562002; fax 549250478; e-mail rektor@vfu.cz; internet www.vfu.cz; f. 1918; 3 faculties; 186 teachers; 1,499 students; Rector Prof. Dr VÁCLAV SUCHÝ.

Charles University (Univerzita Karlova): Ovocný; tř. 5, 116 36 Prague; tel. 224491111; fax 224210695; e-mail uk@cuni.cz; internet www.cuni.cz; f. 1348; 16 faculties; 3,206 teachers; 27,569 students; Rector Prof. Ing. IVAN WILHELM.

Czech Technical University of Prague (České vysoké učení technické v Praze): Zikova 4, 166 36 Prague 6-Dejvice; tel. 224353488; fax 224310783; e-mail zuna@vc.cvut.cz; internet www .cvut.cz; f. 1707; 6 faculties; 1,350 teachers; 17,700 students; Rector Prof. Ing. PETR ZUNA.

Czech University of Agriculture, Prague (Českákola zemědělská univerzita v Praze): Suchdol, Kamýcká 129, 165 21 Prague 6; tel. 224381111; fax 220920431; e-mail webmaster@czu.cz; internet www.czu.cz; f. 1906; 4 faculties, 1 institute; 415 teachers; 7,006 students; Rector Prof. Ing. JOSEF KOZÁK.

Institute of Chemical Technology, Prague (Vysoká škola chemicko-technologická v Praze): Technická 5, 166 28 Prague 6; tel. 224351111; fax 224311082; e-mail lea.knoblochova@vscht.cz; internet www.vscht.cz; f. 1807; 4 faculties; 360 teachers; 2,700 students; Rector Prof. VLASTIMIL RŮŽIČKA.

Masaryk University (Masarykova Univerzita): Žerotínovo nám. 9, 601 77 Brno; tel. 542128111; fax 542128300; e-mail info@muni.cz; internet www.muni.cz; f. 1919; 9 faculties; 2,253 teachers; 21,565 students; Rector Prof. Dr JIŘÍ ZLATUŠKA.

Mendel University of Agriculture and Forestry, Brno (Mendlovakola zemědělská a lesnická univerzita v Brně): Zemědělská 1, 615 00 Brno; tel. 545131111; fax 545211128; e-mail webmaster@mendelu.cz; internet www.mendelu.cz; f. 1919; 4 faculties; 350 teachers; 4,587 full-time and 423 part-time students; Rector STANISLAV PROCHÁZKA.

Palacký University, Olomouc (Univerzita Palackého v Olomouci): KříŽkovského 8, 771 47 Olomouc; tel. 585231455; fax 585222731; e-mail hrbek@risc.upol.cz; internet www.upol.cz; f. 1573; reopened 1946; 7 faculties, 960 teachers, 12,000 students; Rector Prof. Dr JANA MAČÁKOVÁ.

Prague University of Economics (Vysoká škola ekonomická v Praze): W. Churchilla nám. 4, 130 67 Prague 3; tel. 224095111; fax 224220657; e-mail postmaster@vse.cz; internet www.vse.cz; f. 1953; 6 faculties; 13,380 students; Rector Prof. JAROSLAVA DURČÁKOVÁ.

Technical University of Liberec (Technická univerzita v Liberci): Hálkova 6, 461 17 Liberec; tel. 485351111; fax 485105882; internet www.vslib.cz; f. 1953; 6 faculties; 574 teachers; 6,009 students; Rector Prof. DAVID LUKÁŠ.

Technical University of Ostrava (Vysoká škola báňská—technická univerzita Ostrava): tř. 17 listopadu 15, 708 33 Ostrava 4; tel. (69) 6991111; fax (69) 6918507; e-mail vaclav.roubicek@vsb.cz; internet www.vsb.cz; f. 1716; 6 faculties; 779 teachers; 12,700 students; Rector Prof. Ing. VÁCLAV ROUBÍČEK.

University of Pardubice (Univerzita Pardubice): Studentská 95, 532 10 Pardubice; tel. (40) 6036111; fax (40) 6036361; e-mail promotion@upce.cz; internet www.upce.cz; f. 1950; renamed 1994; 3 faculties; 1 institute; 370 teachers; 4,030 students; Rector Dr Ing. MIROSLAV LUDWIG.

University of South Bohemia in České Budějovice (Jihočeská Univerzita v Českých Budějovicích): Branišovská 31, 370 05 České Budějovice; tel. and fax 385300348; e-mail rektorat@jcu.cz; internet www.jcu.cz; f. 1991; 5 faculties; 418 teachers; 5,500 students; Rector Prof. Ing. FRANTIŠEK STŘELEČEK.

University of West Bohemia (Zápdočeská Univerzita): Univerzitní 8, 306 14 Plzeň; tel. (19) 7491111; fax (19) 279222; e-mail zahranici@rek.zcu.cz; internet www.zcu.cz; f. 1949; 7 faculties; teachers 732; students 11,278; Rector Prof. Z. VOSTRACKÝ.

Social Welfare

A single and universal social-security system was established in Czechoslovakia after the Second World War. Protection of health was stipulated by law, and medical care, treatment, medicines, etc. were, in most cases, available free of charge to the entire Czechoslovak population.

In 1991 a new system of social security was introduced. The Government planned to guarantee a minimum level of social welfare to all citizens, in an attempt to mitigate the expected consequences of radical economic reform. In addition, benefit was made available to unemployed workers for a maximum period of 12 (later reduced to six) months, and mandatory redundancy payments, equivalent to two months' wages, were introduced. At the end of 1991 a General Health Insurance Fund was established; this introduced an element of consumer choice of health-care provider, while providers were themselves allowed to compete for patients. Later, other health-insurance funds were allowed to compete for patients' payroll contributions. By early 1996 there were 28 such funds, although the Minister of Health proposed that this number should be reduced to 18. Following the dissolution of Czechoslovakia in January 1993 the Czech Government permitted the privatization of some hospitals; 11 such privatizations had been approved by September 1994. In that year combined pensions, sickness, health-insurance fund and unemployment taxes amounted to 12.75% of wages for the employee and 35.75% for the employer.

In 1998 there were 303 physicians, 886 nurses and 62 dentists per 100,000 inhabitants. In 1999 there were 87 hospital beds per 10,000 inhabitants. Health-care expenditure in 1999 was 117,031m. koruny (some 17.5% of total budgetary spending), while expenditure on social security and welfare totalled 248,723m. koruny (37.1%). A new pensions insurance law came into effect in 1996, which was gradually to increase the retirement age for men to 62 years (from 60 years) and for women to 57 years–61 years (from 54 years–57 years, depending on the number of children borne) by 2007.

GOVERNMENT AGENCIES

Ministry of Labour and Social Affairs (Ministerstvo práce a sociálních věcí České Republiky): see section on The Government (Ministries).

Board of Representatives from the Organizations of Disabled People: Na Topolce 1A, 140 00 Prague 4; tel. and fax 261211588; Chair. Ing. PAVEL DUŠEK.

Czech Social Security Administration (Česká správa sociálního zabezpečení): Křížová 25, 150 00 Prague 5; tel. (2) 541141; Dir Dr LADISLAV ANTOŠIK.

Government Board for People with Disabilities: Nabř. Dr Beneše 4, 118 01 Prague 1; tel. 224002218; fax 224002207; e-mail hruby@vlada.cz; internet www.vlada.cz; Exec. Dir Dr Ing. JAROSLAV HRUBÝ.

Parliamentary Social Affairs and Health Committee: Sněmovní 4, 118 26 Prague 1; tel. (2) 530418; fax (2) 531211; committee of the Chamber of Deputies; Chair. Dr MARTYN SYKA.

HEALTH AND WELFARE ORGANIZATIONS

Association of Disabled People in the Czech Republic: Karlínské nám. 12, 186 03 Prague 8; tel. (2) 2310177; fax 224816835.

Czech Red Cross: Thunovska 18, 118 04 Prague; tel. 251104111; fax 257532113; e-mail cck.zahranicni@iol.cz; Pres. Dr ZDENKO VIK; Sec.-Gen. Dr JIŘÍ PROCHAZKA.

The Environment

Environmental issues caused some of the first expressions of opposition to the communist regime and remained important throughout the 1990s. Of particular concern is the region of Northern Bohemia, where sulphur-dioxide emissions from coal-fired power-stations have caused serious air pollution. According to official figures,

Czechoslovakia produced more air pollutants per head of population than any other European country. In the 1990s some 80% of pine trees over 60 years old had suffered moderate to severe damage. There were also concerns about waste streams entering the River Labe (Elbe), which flows into Germany and is used as a drinking-water source in that country. New environmental regulations were introduced in the Czech Republic, based on the 'polluter-pays' principle. There were plans to reduce pollution by substituting gas for coal in power generation. The opening of the Temelín nuclear power station in October 2000 caused controversy, and caused relations with neighbouring Austria to become strained. Waste-water treatment facilities were being improved, and in 1994 the State Environmental Fund spent US $77m. on 84 new plants. By 1998 the Czech Republic had such plants in practically all communities over 10,000 people, but the European Union (EU) demanded they be built in all towns with more than 5,000 inhabitants. In addition, gas emissions from industrial sources continued to cause massive deforestation and soil degradation in Northern Bohemia. In late 1998 the Organisation for Economic Co-operation and Development released a report criticizing the rate at which new environmental legislation was being enacted. The process accelerated during 1999, although certain criticisms remained. In June 1998 the Ministry of the Environment estimated that an investment of $15,000m. was required if the country was to meet the environmental standards required for membership of the EU; in May 2000 the Ministry acknowledged that this sum was insufficient. In June 2003 a new, seven-year environmental remediation programme was approved by the Government.

GOVERNMENT ORGANIZATIONS

Ministry of the Environment: see section on The Government (Ministries).

Agency for Nature Conservation and Landscape Protection of the Czech Republic (Agentura ochrany přírody a krajiny ČR—AOPK ČR): Kališnická 4–6, POB 85, 130 23 Prague 3; tel. 26970013; fax (2) 6970012; e-mail aopk@nature.cz; internet www.nature.cz; fmrly Český ústav ochrany přírody ČÚOP; scientific research; nature conservation; landscape protection; data management; international co-operation; environmental education; remote sensing; Dep. Dir Dr JAN PLESNÍK.

Central Office for State Nature Conservation (Ustredie státnej ochrany prírody): Leninova 11, 031 01 Liptovský Mikulás; tel. (2) 24177; conservation strategies; environmental management and planning; database; protection of endangered animal and plant species; management and planning of protected areas; environmental statistics; resource, impact and damage assessments; promotion of environmental law; resource management; Dir ANTON LUCIN-KIEWICZ.

Czech Environmental Inspectorate (CEI) (Česká inspkece životního prostředí—ČIŽP): Na Břehu 267, 190 00 Prague; tel. 283891564; fax 283892662; e-mail public@czip.cz; internet www.cizp.cz.

Czech Environmental Institute (Český ekologický ústav): Kodaňská 10, 100 10 Prague 10; tel. 267225226; fax 271742306; e-mail info@ceu.cz; internet www.ceu.cz; f. 1992; Dir Dr JOSEF SEJÁK.

Krkonose National Park Administration (Správa Krkonošského národního parku): Dobrovského 3, 543 11 Vrchlabí; tel. (438) 456311; fax (438) 422095; e-mail posta@krnap.cz; internet www.krnap.cz; f. 1963; affiliated to the Ministry of Environment; conservation of the fauna, flora, soils and landscape of the National Park; forest management; monitoring traffic and construction; education and research; Dir JIŘÍ NOVÁK.

State Institute for the Protection of Monuments (Státní ústav památkové péče): Valdštejnské nám. 3, 118 01 Prague; tel. 257010111; fax (2) 535496.

ACADEMIC INSTITUTES

Academy of Sciences of the Czech Republic (Akademie věd České Republicky): Národní tř. 3, 111 42 Prague 1; tel. 224229610; fax 224240512; e-mail president@kav.cas.cz; internet www.cas.cz; f. 1993; Pres. Dr HELENA ILLNEROVÁ.

Institute of Atmospheric Physics: Boční II–1401, 141 31 Prague 4; tel. 272764336; fax 272763745; e-mail ufa@ufa.cas.cz; internet www.ufa.cas.cz; f. 1961; monitors atmospheric pollution, research in meteorology, climatology, ionospheric and magnetospheric physics; Dir Dr JAN LAŠTOVIČKA.

Institute of Chemical Process Fundamentals: Rozvojová 135, 165 02 Prague 6 Suchdol; tel. 224311498; fax (2) 342073; e-mail postmaster@icpf.cas.cz; internet www.icpf.cas.cz; f. 1960; fundamental research in chemical, biochemical, catalytic and environmental engineering; internationally supported projects include polymer-supported ligands for ecological problems, a new refining scheme and catalysis for the production of environmentally friendly diesel fuels, fuel reactivity and release of pollutants, and studies of atmospheric chemistry and air pollution; Dir JIŘÍ DRAHOŠ.

Institute of Experimental Botany: Rozvojová 135, 165 02 Prague 6; tel. 220390453; fax 220390456; e-mail machackova@ueb.cas.cz; f. 1962; plant physiology, genetics, pathology and biotechnology; Dir Dr IVANA MACHÁČKOVÁ.

Institute of Industrial Landscape Ecology: Chittussiho 10, 710 00 Ostrava 2; tel. (69) 213249; fax (69) 222828; e-mail skacel@osu.cz; promotes the application of ecology to planning industrial land use.

Institute of Landscape Ecology: Květná 8, 603 65 Brno; tel. 543321306; fax 543321346; f. 1954; promotes the application of ecology to planning land use; Dir MILAN PEŇÁZ.

Charles University Environment Centre: Univerzita Karlova v Praze, U. Kříže 8, 158 00 Prague 5; tel. 251080202; fax (2) 5610441; e-mail czp@czp.cuni.cz; internet www.czp.cuni.cz; Dir Dr BEDŘICH MOLDAN.

Dřípatka Centre for Ecological Education: Rumpálova 402, 383 01 Prachatice; tel. and fax (338) 23091; f. 1967; workshops and courses on nature conservation, excursions to National Parks, owns land with field station and nature trails; Principal Officer HELENA KLIMEŠOVÁ.

Prague Institute for the Environment (Ústav pro životní prostředí—pobočka Praha): U Michelského lesa 366, 140 00 Prague 4; tel. (2) 2195; fax (2) 496619.

NON-GOVERNMENTAL ORGANIZATIONS

Brontosaurus Movement (Hnuti brontosaurus): Bubenská 6, 170 00 Prague 7; tel. and fax 266710245; voluntary youth environmental movement in Bohemia and Moravia; environmental education and campaigning; conservation work; Principal Officer HELENA IZBICKÁ.

Czech Environmental Management Centre: Jevanská 12, 100 31 Prague 10; tel. 274784447; fax 274775869; e-mail cemc@cemc.cz; Exec. Dir JIŘÍ ŠTUDEMT.

Czech Society for the Environment (Česká spolecnost pro zivotní prostredí): Novotneho pavka 5, 116 68 Prague 1; tel. 221082631; fax 221082365; Principal Officer Ing. VLADIMÍR PRCHLK.

Czech Union for Nature Conservation (Česky svaz ochráncu přírody—ČSOP): Uruguayská 7, 120 00 Prague 2; tel. 222516115; fax 222511496; e-mail csop@ecn.cz; f. 1979; independent asscn of conservation groups; campaigns on protected areas, national parks, nature reserves, endangered animal and plant species, wildlife habitats, resource protection, forest management, pollution, waste disposal, protected monuments, and enforcement and promotion of environmental law; environmental education and training; Pres. Dr PETR DOLEJSKÝ.

EcoTerra o.p.s.: Ostrovni 5, 110 00 Prague 1; tel. and fax 224932971; e-mail ecoterra@telecom.cz; f. 1991; promotes participation in rural activities; Dir BOHUSLAV BLAZEK.

Environmental Law Service (Ekologicky právní servis—EPS): Bubenská 6, 170 00 Prague 7; tel. and fax (2) 8023355; e-mail jiri.dusik@ecn.gn.apc.org.

Environmental Partnership for Central Europe (Nadace partnerstvi): Panska 9, 602 00 Brno; tel. 542218350; fax 542221744; e-mail pship@ecn.cz; f. 1991; Dir MIROSLAV KUNDRATA.

Friends of the Earth (FoE) Czech Republic (Hnuti duha): Bratislavska 31, 602 00 Brno; tel. 545214431; fax 545214429; e-mail org.hduha@ecn.cz; internet www.duhafoe.cz; national office of Friends of the Earth— FoE International (Netherlands).

Green Party: see section on Political Organizations.

Greenpeace Czech Republic: Českomalínská 27, 160 00 Prague 6; tel. 224319667; fax (2) 3112289; e-mail greenpeace@ecn.cz; the national office of Greenpeace International (Netherlands).

Defence

At the end of 1992 the Czech Republic assumed responsibility for 100,000 of the remaining 150,000 Czechoslovak military personnel. In March 1999 the Czech Republic acceded to full membership of the North Atlantic Treaty Organization. In August 2002 the total armed forces numbered 49,450 (including 25,000 conscripts); the Army numbered 36,370 (15,500 conscripts) and the Air Force 11,300 (8,500 conscripts). In addition there were an estimated 4,000 border guards and 1,600 internal security forces. In June 1993 a further reduction in the length of service for conscripted troops was instituted, from 18 months to 12 months, following an earlier reduction in 1990 from two years, when an alternative of 27 months of non-military duty was also introduced. Service with the reserve lasts until 60 years of age. In April 2000 the Ministry of Defence announced that a review would be undertaken to investigate the viability of the abolition of military service and the creation of a professional army. The esti-

mated budget allocated to the Czech armed forces in 2002 was 48,000m. koruny.

Commander-in-Chief: President of the Republic.

Chief of Staff of the Army: Maj.-Gen. PAVEL STEFKA.

Bibliography

Adam, J. *Social Costs of Transformation to a Market Economy in Post-Socialist Countries: the Case of Poland, the Czech Republic and Hungary*. New York, NY, St Martin's Press, 2000.

Bradley, J. F. N. *Post-Communist Czechoslovakia*. New York, NY, Columbia University Press, 2002.

Dedek, O. (Ed.). *The Break-Up Of Czechoslovakia: An In-Depth Economic Analysis*. Milton Keynes, Avebury, 1996.

Fawn, R. *Czech Republic*. Reading, Harwood Academic, 2000.

Havel, V. *The Art of the Impossible: Politics as Morality and Practice. Speeches and Writings, 1990–96*. New York, NY, Knopf, 1997.

Hochman, J. *Historical Dictionary of the Czech State*. Langham, MD, Scarecrow Press, 1998.

Holy, L. *The Little Czech and the Great Czech Nation: National Identity and the Post-Communist Social Transformation*. Cambridge, Cambridge University Press, 1996.

Innes, A. *Czechoslovakia: The Short Goodbye*. New Haven, CT, and London, Yale University Press, 2001.

Janos, A. C. *Czechoslovakia and Yugoslavia: Ethnic Conflict and the Dissolution of Multinational States*. Sacramento, CA, University of California International, 1997.

Lieval, H. J. *Languages of Community: the Jewish Experience in the Czech Lands*. Berkeley, CA, University of California Press, 2000.

King, J. *Budweisers into Czechs and Germans: A Local History of Bohemian Politics, 1848–1948*. Princeton, NJ, Princeton University Press, 2002.

Korbel, J. *Twentieth Century Czechoslovakia: The Meaning of Her History*. New York, NY, Columbia University Press, 1977.

Kraus, M., and Stanger, A. (Eds). *Irreconcilable Differences: Explaining Czechoslovakia's Dissolution*. Lanham, MD, Rowman and Littlefield, 2000.

Kusin, V. P. *From Dubček to Charter 77: A Study of 'Normalization' in Czechoslovakia, 1968–1978*. Edinburgh, Q Press, 1979.

The Intellectual Origins of the Prague Spring. Cambridge, Cambridge University Press, 1971.

Leff, C. S. *The Czech and Slovak Republics: Nation Versus State*. Boulder, CO, Westview Press, 1996.

Lukes, I. *Czechoslovakia between Stalin and Hitler: the Diplomacy of Edvard Beneš in the 1930s*. New York, NY, Oxford University Press Inc., 1996.

Mamatey, V. S., and Luža, R. (Eds). *A History of the Czechoslovak Republic, 1918–1948*. Princeton, NJ, Princeton University Press, 1973.

Musil, J. (Ed.). *The End of Czechoslovakia*. Budapest, Central University Press, 1995.

Myant, M. *The Czechoslovak Economy*. Cambridge, Cambridge University Press, 1989.

Myant, M. *The Rise and Fall of Czech Capitalism: Economic Development in the Czech Republic since 1989*. Cheltenham, Edward Elgar, 2003.

OECD Country Reports, *Czech Republic*. Paris, annual.

Olivová, V. *The Doomed Democracy: Czechoslovakia in a Disrupted Europe, 1914–1938*. London, Sidgwick and Jackson, 1972.

Paul, D. W. *Czechoslovakia: Profile of a Socialist Republic at the Crossroads of Europe*. Boulder, CO, Westview Press, 1981.

Potucek, M. *Not Only the Market: The Role of the Market, Government and Civic Sector in Postcommunist Societies*. New York, NY, and Budapest, Central European University Press, 1999.

Pynsent, R. B. *Questions of Identity: Czech and Slovak Ideas of Nationality and Personality*. Budapest, Central European University Press, 1995.

Sayer, D. *The Coasts of Bohemia: A Czech History*. Princeton, NJ, Princeton University Press, 1998.

Schutte, C. *Privatization and Corporate Control in the Czech Republic*. Cheltenham, Edward Elgar, 2000.

Seton-Watson, R. W. *A History of the Czechs and Slovaks*. North Haven, CT, Shoe String Press, 1965.

Shepherd, R. H. E. *Czechoslovakia: The Velvet Revolution and Beyond*. New York, NY, St Martin's Press, 2000.

Simmons, M. *The Reluctant President: A Political Life of Vaclav Havel*. London, Methuen, 1991.

Skilling, G. H. *Charter 77 and Human Rights in Czechoslovakia*. London, Allen and Unwin, 1981.

Czechoslovakia's Interrupted Revolution. Princeton, NJ, Princeton University Press, 1976.

Skilling, G. H., and Wilson, P. (Eds). *Civic Freedom in Central Europe: Voices from Czechoslovakia*. London, Macmillan, 1991.

Stein, E. *Czecho/Slovakia: Ethnic Conflict, Constitutional Fissure, Negotiated Breakup*. Ann Arbor, MI, University of Michigan Press, 1997.

Svejnar, J. (Ed.) *The Czech Republic and Economic Transition in Eastern Europe*. San Diego, CA, Academic Press, 1995.

Taborsky, E. *Communism in Czechoslovakia, 1948–1960*. Princeton, NJ, Princeton University Press, 1961.

Tampke, J. *Czech–German Relations and the Politics of Central Europe: From Bohemia to the EU*. London, Palgrave Macmillan, 2002.

Teich, M. *Bohemia in History*. Cambridge, Cambridge University Press, 1999.

Ulč, O. *Politics in Czechoslovakia*. San Fransisco, CA, W. H. Freeman, 1974.

Vondorova, J., et al. *The Prague Spring, 1968*. New York, NY, and Budapest, Central European University Press, 1998.

Wheaton, B., and Kavan, Z. *The Velvet Revolution: Czechoslovakia 1988–1991*. Boulder, CO, Westview Press, 1992.

Wightman, G. 'The Collapse of Communist Rule in Czechoslovakia and the July 1990 Parliamentary Elections', in *Parliamentary Affairs*, Vol. 44, No. 1 (January 1991).

Williams, K. *The Prague Spring and its Aftermath: Czechoslovak Politics 1968–1970*. Cambridge, Cambridge University Press, 1997.

Wolchik, S. L. *Czechoslovakia in Transition: Politics, Economics and Society*. New York, NY, Continuum International Publishing, 1991.

Zeman, Z., and Klimek, A. *The Life of Edvard Beneš, 1884–1948: Czechoslovakia in Peace and War*. Oxford, Clarendon Press, 1997.

ESTONIA

Geography

PHYSICAL FEATURES

The Republic of Estonia is situated in north-eastern Europe. It is bordered to the south by Latvia and to the east by Russia. Its northern coastline is on the Gulf of Finland and its territory includes over 1,520 islands, mainly off its western coastline in the Gulf of Rīga and the Baltic Sea. The country covers an area of 45,227 sq km (17,462 sq miles). Before 1945, when a small amount of territory south of Lake Pihkva (Pskov) was ceded to the Russian Federation, Estonia covered an area of 47,548 sq km.

Estonia is situated on the north-western edge of the Great Russian Plain. The land is mainly flat, with some undulating terrain in the south. Forests cover almost one-half of the territory (48% in 1993, according to the UN's Food and Agriculture Organization). Rivers, the largest of which is the Narva, are mainly short and carry low volumes of water. There are many marshes and bogs, and more than 1,500 lakes, of which the largest are the Estonian parts of the Peipsi (Chudskoye) and Pihkva (Pskov) lakes, on the eastern border with Russia. The largest of the country's many islands are Saaremaa and Hiiumaa, in the Gulf of Rīga.

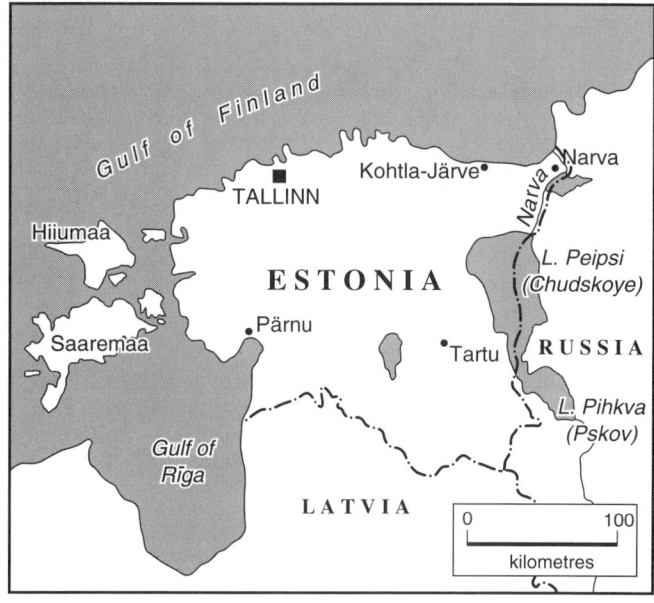

CLIMATE

The climate is influenced by the country's position between the Eurasian land mass and the Baltic and North Atlantic seas. The mean January temperature in Tallinn is −0.9°C (30.4°F); in July the mean temperature is 20.0°C (68.0°F). Average annual precipitation is 568 mm.

POPULATION

The total population declined from 1,565,662 at the 1989 census, to 1,370,052 at the census of March 2000. According to official estimates, the population numbered 1,356,045 at 1 January 2003, giving a population density of 30.0 per sq km. At 1 January 2000 an estimated 65.3% of the population were Estonians, 28.1% Russians, 2.5% Ukrainians, 1.5% Belarusians and 0.9% Finns. Other nationalities included Tatars (3,232), Latvians (2,638), Jews (2,275), Poles (2,290) and Lithuanians (2,188). In 1989 Estonian replaced Russian as the official state language, prompting protests by ethnic Russian residents, 85% of whom did not speak Estonian. Estonian is a member of the Baltic-Finnic group of the Finno-Ugric languages and is written in the Latin script. It is closely related to Finnish. Most of the population are adherents of the Christian religion. By tradition, Estonians belong to the Evangelical Lutheran Church, and the Russian Orthodox Church and smaller Protestant sects are also represented in the country.

The capital is Tallinn, which is situated in the north of the country, on the Gulf of Finland. Excluding the suburbs, it had an estimated population of 398,434 at 1 January 2002. Other important towns include the university town of Tartu (formerly Dorpat—101,140), the Russian-dominated industrial towns of Narva (68,117) and Kohtla-Järve (47,106) in the north-east of Estonia, and Pärnu on the western coast (45,040).

Chronology

c. 3,000 BC: Finno-Ugric peoples, the ancestors of the Estonians, first began to migrate from eastern Europe to the north-east coast of the Baltic Sea.

AD 1219: Valdemar II of Denmark and the German Sword Brethren, a crusading order, conquered Estonia.

1346: The Danes sold their share of Estonian territory to the Livonian Order of Teutonic Knights (an alliance of the Sword Brethren and the German Order of Teutonic Knights).

1524–39: The State of Teutonic Knights renounced religious allegiance to Rome and converted to Lutheranism.

1561: In the secularization and partition of the State of Teutonic Knights, Estonia (now northern Estonia) became part of Sweden. Livonia (now Latvia and southern Estonia) was placed under Polish rule, as part of the Lithuanian-Polish Duchy of Courland (Kurland).

1595: Sweden's right to Narva and Estonia was recognized by the Peace of Teusin, signed by Sweden and the Russian Empire, although Sweden did not assume full control of Estonia until 1607.

1629: Sweden gained the territory of Livonia by the Armistice of Altmark, after the Swedish–Polish Wars.

1721: The Treaty of Nystad, between Russia and Sweden, ended the Great Northern War and brought Estonia and Livonia under Russian rule.

1816–19: Serfdom was abolished in Estonia.

November 1905: Following a revolution in Russia the previous month, an increase in Estonian nationalist feeling resulted in a demand for autonomy by the all-Estonian Assembly; the uprising was eventually suppressed.

1 August 1914: Russia entered the First World War against the Empires of Austria-Hungary, Germany and the Ottomans (the Central Powers).

2 March (New Style 15 March) 1917: Abdication of the last Tsar, Nicholas II, after demonstrations and strikes in Petrograd (St Petersburg); a Provisional Government, led by Prince Lvov, took power.

30 March (12 April) 1917: The Provisional Government granted Estonia its autonomy.

24 February (Old Style 11 February) 1918: The independent Republic of Estonia was declared; Konstantin Päts led a Provisional Government, although this was not recognized by the German occupiers.

3 March 1918: The Bolsheviks, in control of the Government of Russia, signed the Treaty of Brest-Litovsk with Germany, thereby ceding large areas of western territory, including Estonia, to Germany.

November 1918: Following Germany's surrender, the Provisional Government assumed control in Estonia.

2 February 1920: The Treaty of Tartu (Dorpat) ended hostilities between Estonia and Soviet Russia; the Soviet Government recognized Estonian independence and renounced any claims on its territory. In August a parliamentary Constitution was introduced.

January 1921: Estonia was recognized as an independent state and admitted to the League of Nations.

1924: An attempt by communists to seize power in Estonia failed.

1933: The increasing influence of the right-wing War of Independence Veterans' League, or movement of freedom fighters, forced the introduction of a constitutional system with an executive presidency.

12 March 1934: The parliamentary system in Estonia was replaced by a period of dictatorship, after premier Päts seized control in a bloodless coup and curbed the influence of the right.

April 1938: Following the adoption of a new Constitution, which provided for a presidential system of government and a bicameral parliament, Päts was elected President.

23 August 1939: The Treaty of Non-Aggression (the Nazi-Soviet Pact) was concluded by Joachim von Ribbentrop and Vyacheslav Molotov, the foreign ministers of Germany and the USSR, respectively; the 'Secret Protocols' to this Pact provided for the annexation of Estonia and Latvia by the USSR.

June 1940: The Baltic states (Estonia, Latvia and Lithuania) and Bessarabia were occupied by the USSR; the Estonian Government resigned and was replaced by a Soviet-appointed administration, led by Johannes Vares-Barbarus.

21 July 1940: The new Estonian parliament (consisting entirely of members sympathetic to the Soviet regime) proclaimed the Estonian Soviet Socialist Republic.

6 August 1940: Estonia was admitted to the USSR as a constituent Union Republic of the federation.

June 1941: More than 10,000 Estonians were deported to Siberia by the Soviet authorities; deportations continued until the death of Stalin (Iosif V. Dzhugashvili) in 1953.

July 1941: German forces entered Estonia, having invaded the USSR the previous month.

September 1944: Despite expelling all German troops from Estonia, the Soviet regime endured a series of armed attacks by the so-called 'forest brethren' (*metsavennad*), a pro-independence guerrilla movement, which continued its campaign until 1955.

1947–March 1949: Collectivization, and continuing mass deportations, occurred in Estonia.

October 1980: The brutal suppression of a protest by schoolchildren at the 'russification' of Estonia prompted a critical 'Letter of the Forty' from prominent intellectuals to the authorities.

23 August 1987: A crowd of 2,000 demonstrators commemorated the anniversary of the Molotov-Ribbentrop Pact; soon afterwards, an Estonian Group for the Publication of the Molotov-Ribbentrop Pact was established, becoming the Estonian National Independence Party (ENIP) in 1988.

13 April 1988: The Estonian Popular Front (EPF) was formed; mass demonstrations against the Soviet regime were organized by the EPF throughout July and August.

16 June 1988: Vaino Väljas replaced Karl Vaino (leader of Estonia since 1978) as First Secretary of the Communist Party of Estonia (CPE). In the following month Intermovement, a political group intended to counteract the influence of the increasingly popular opposition, was formed.

16 November 1988: The Estonian Supreme Soviet declared the sovereignty of the Republic. The declaration, which included the right to annul all-Union legislation, was declared unconstitutional by the USSR's Supreme Soviet, but was affirmed by the Estonian Supreme Soviet the following month.

18 January 1989: Estonian was adopted as the state language and the tricolour of independent Estonia was reinstated as the official flag.

March 1989: In elections to the all-Union Congress of People's Deputies, the EPF won 27 of the 36 Estonian seats, while Intermovement won five. The ENIP refused to participate in the elections and proposed a rival parliament, the 'Congress of Estonia', to be elected only by citizens of pre-1940 Estonia and their descendants.

May 1989: Estonia declared its economic independence from the all-Union authorities; this decision was ratified by the Supreme Soviet of the USSR in November.

August 1989: A new electoral law, increasing the residency requirements for voters and candidates, was strenuously opposed (mainly by ethnic Russians); the legislation was eventually suspended.

November 1989: The Estonian Supreme Soviet voted to annul the 1940 decision to join the USSR.

22 February 1990: The Estonian legislature approved a declaration demanding immediate negotiations with the all-Union Supreme Soviet on the restoration of independence. The following day the legal pre-eminence of the communists was abolished.

11–12 March 1990: The Congress of Estonia, to which elections had been held in late February and early March, convened and declared itself the constitutional representative of the Estonian people.

18 March 1990: In elections to the Estonian Supreme Soviet, the EPF won 43 of the 105 contested seats; other pro-independence groups obtained 35 seats, with the remainder secured by the Intermovement group. At the first session of the new legislature, Arnold Rüütel, previously Chairman of the Presidium of the Supreme Soviet, was elected Chairman.

30 March 1990: The Supreme Soviet declared a transitional period towards independence; at the same time, the validity of Soviet power in Estonia was denied.

3 April 1990: Edgar Savisaar, leader of the EPF, was elected Prime Minister by the Supreme Soviet (Supreme Council).

8 May 1990: The first five articles of the 1938 Constitution were reinstated; the formal name of independent Estonia, the Republic of Estonia, was restored, as well as the state emblems, the flag and the anthem. The following week the Soviet President annulled Estonia's declaration of independence and some 2,000 protesters against the declaration attempted to occupy the parliament building.

3 March 1991: In a referendum, 77.8% of the participants (comprising 82.9% of the registered electorate) voted in favour of independence.

17 March 1991: Of the 225,000 Slavs in north-eastern Estonia who participated in the all-Union referendum, approximately 95% voted in favour of keeping the USSR as a 'renewed federation'.

19 August 1991: At the same time as an attempted coup in Moscow (Russia—the Soviet capital), Gen. Fedor Kuzmin, Commander of the Soviet Baltic Military District, declared that he was assuming control of Estonia.

20 August 1991: Military vehicles entered Tallinn; at a session of the Estonian Supreme Council full and immediate independence was declared.

21 August 1991: Soviet troops occupied the television station in Tallinn, but, in Moscow, the *coup d'état* collapsed.

22 August 1991: Among measures against those who had allegedly supported the coup, the Estonian Government banned the all-Union Communist Party, Intermovement and the United Council of Work Collectives.

6 September 1991: The newly formed State Council of the USSR recognized Estonia's independence.

17 September 1991: Estonia was admitted to the UN.

9 October 1991: The USSR (which was finally to be dissolved in December) established diplomatic relations with Estonia.

6 November 1991: A new citizenship law stated that only persons who had been citizens of Estonia prior to 1940, and their descendants, were eligible to vote.

30 January 1992: Edgar Savisaar resigned as Prime Minister and was replaced by Tiit Vähi.

20 June 1992: The Estonian crown or kroon replaced the rouble as sole legal tender.

3 July 1992: Following approval by 91% of the electorate in a referendum in late June, a new Constitution came into force, providing for a 101-member parliament, the Riigikogu (State Assembly), and a presidency with limited powers.

20 September 1992: In legislative elections the largest number of seats (29) was won by the Pro Patria (Fatherland) Union (in Estonian, Isamaaliit). No presidential candidate secured an absolute majority.

5 October 1992: Lennart Meri was elected President by the Riigikogu. President Meri appointed a coalition Government under Mart Laar of the Pro Patria (Fatherland) Union.

14 May 1993: Notwithstanding opposition from the Russian Government, Estonia was admitted to the Council of Europe.

June 1993: Despite significant protests by ethnic Russians against the citizenship laws, all non-Estonians were required to apply for citizenship or for a residence permit by 1 January 1996 (provoking further tensions with Russia). In January 1995 the residency requirement was extended to five years.

13 November 1993: Members of the EPF agreed to disband the organization.

February 1994: Estonia was admitted to the North Atlantic Treaty Organization's (NATO) 'Partnership for Peace' programme of military co-operation.

29 August 1994: The last former Soviet troops were finally withdrawn from Estonia.

26 September 1994: With the coalition weakening, following a revelation that he had contravened an agreement with the IMF, Laar was forced to resign as Prime Minister.

27 October 1994: Andres Tarand of the Moderates' Party was appointed Prime Minister for the coalition.

5 March 1995: In legislative elections an alliance of the Estonian Coalition Party (ECP) and the Rural Union won the largest number of seats (41) in the Riigikogu; a coalition of the Estonian Reform Party (ERP) and liberal groups obtained 19 seats, followed by the Estonian Centre Party with 16 seats. Six seats were secured by the Our Home is Estonia pact, an alliance representing the Russian-speaking minority.

23 March 1995: Tiit Vähi, leader of the ECP, was asked to form a Government by President Meri and, on 31 March, the newly appointed Prime Minister agreed a coalition with the Rural Union and the Estonian Centre Party.

17 April 1995: A new Council of Ministers was appointed; the former premier and the leader of the Estonian Centre Party, Edgar Savisaar, was appointed Deputy Prime Minister and Minister of the Interior.

10 October 1995: Following Savisaar's dismissal from the cabinet, after revelations that he had secretly recorded political negotiations in March, and the effective collapse of the coalition, Vähi and the rest of the Council of Ministers resigned.

3 November 1995: Vähi, who had been reappointed premier, succeeded in forming a new coalition of his ECP and the Rural Union with the ERP.

15 November 1995: The European Parliament ratified Estonia's associate membership of the European Union (EU).

26–27 August 1996: After three rounds of voting in the Riigikogu, neither Meri nor Rüütel obtained sufficient votes to be elected to the presidency. A larger electoral college continued the presidential election. None of the five candidates in the first round achieved an overall majority; the second-round candidates were once again Meri and Rüütel, with Meri finally being re-elected in September.

November 1996: Estonia agreed to omit consideration of the 1920 Treaty of Tartu from an agreement demarcating the Russian–Estonian border; the Government had previously insisted that Russia recognize the Treaty as the basis of relations between the two countries.

22 November 1996: The six ERP ministers resigned, after a co-operation agreement was signed by the ECP and the Estonian Centre Party, without informing the ERP; this initiated the collapse of the ruling coalition.

1 December 1996: A minority Government, still headed by Vähi and supported by the ECP, the Rural Union and independent members, was finally appointed.

25 February 1997: Vähi resigned, following a series of allegations, which he continued to deny, concerning abuse of office. Mart Siimann, the leader of the ECP, was appointed Prime Minister two days later.

14 March 1997: The ECP, the Rural Union and some independents again formed a minority Government.

13 December 1997: Estonia was invited to be one of the six countries to be considered for the next phase of EU enlargement; negotiations began on 31 March 1998.

13 March 1998: The Riigikogu voted to abolish the death penalty.

8 December 1998: The Riigikogu approved amendments to the citizenship law, providing for the naturalization of the children of ethnic Russians and other minorities resident in Estonia for at least five years. The amendments came into effect on 12 July 1999.

15 December 1998: Despite opposition from the Organization for Security and Co-operation in Europe (OSCE), the Riigikogu approved legislation requiring elected officials to demonstrate sufficient command of Estonian to be able to participate in basic bureaucratic procedures of office. The legislation, which came into force in May 1999, was also condemned by the Russian Government.

7 March 1999: In legislative elections the Estonian Centre Party won the largest number of seats (28) in the Riigikogu; the ERP and Pro Patria (Fatherland) Union won 18 seats each, the Moderates' Party (in alliance with the People's Party) obtained 17 seats, followed by the Estonian Country People's Party (seven) and the United People's Party of Estonia (six).

25 March 1999: A centre-right coalition Government was formed by the ERP, Pro Patria (Fatherland) Union and the Moderates' Party, each taking five ministerial posts; the leader of the Pro Patria (Fatherland) Union, Mart Laar, was appointed Prime Minister.

17 October 1999: In local elections, a coalition of the Pro Patria (Fatherland) Union and the Moderates' Party gained control of 13 of Estonia's 15 counties.

13 November 1999: Estonia became a member of the World Trade Organization.

9 February 2001: Estonia and the Federal Republic of Yugoslavia established diplomatic relations.

February 2001: Laar was the subject of an inquiry into an incident in 1999 in which he and other officials were alleged to have taken aim at a picture of the Estonian Centre Party leader, Edgar Savisaar, during an informal shooting practice. A subsequent vote of 'no confidence' was defeated by eight votes.

21 September 2001: Arnold Rüütel was elected President by an electoral college, in a second round of voting, after the Riigikogu failed three times to elect a candidate in presidential elections held on 27–28 August. Rüütel was inaugurated on 8 October.

19 December 2001: Mart Laar announced that he and his Government were to resign on 8 January 2002, owing to tensions within the coalition.

31 December 2001: The OSCE terminated its mission to the country upon the expiry of its mandate (prompting Russian objections), after the language law was further amended (initial modifications had been made in April 2000, following a statement by the OSCE High Commissioner on National Minorities) to remove the stipulation that electoral candidates be proficient in Estonian.

22 January 2002: Following the resignation of Laar's Government on 8 January, Siim Kallas, the Chairman of the ERP, was approved to head a new coalition Government, comprising the ERP and the Estonian Centre Party.

20 October 2002: Local elections took place. Parties represented in the national Government won the most votes, although the rightist Union for the Republic Res Publica also received strong support.

21 Novermber 2002: At a NATO summit meeting, held in Prague, Czech Republic, Estonia was one of seven countries formally invited to join the Alliance in 2004.

13 December 2002: Estonia, together with nine other countries, received a formal invitation to become a member of the EU from 1 May 2004.

25 February 2003: The Riigikogu approved the first amendment to the country's Constitution since its adoption, extending the term of local councils from three years to four.

2 March 2003: In legislative elections, the Estonian Centre Party won 25.4% of the votes cast and 28 seats in the Riigikogu, while the Union for the Republic Res Publica received 24.6% of the votes (and 28 seats). The rate of participation by the electorate was some 58.2%.

9 April 2003: After Edgar Savisaar refused Rüütel's invitation to form a Government, Juhan Parts, the leader of the Union for the Republic Res Publica, was nominated to head a new administration. His coalition Government, which also comprised the ERP and the Estonian People's Union, was approved one week later.

8 July 2003: The Council of Ministers supported proposals to introduce new legislation permitting the country's president to be directly elected by popular vote.

14 September 2003: A national referendum on the country's proposed admission to the EU was scheduled to be held.

History

ANDRES KASEKAMP

EARLY HISTORY

The Estonians were subjugated by the German crusading order, the Sword Brethren, and the Danes in the 13th century. In the 16th century the Lutheran reformation and internal divisions fatally weakened German colonial rule and laid the region open for covetous neighbours. A series of protracted wars beginning in 1558, and involving the Swedes, Danes, Russians and Poles, left most of the north-eastern Baltic area under Swedish rule from 1629. Although Estonia and the northern half of Livonia, the territory inhabited by the Estonians, were conquered by Russia in 1710, the Baltic German land-owning nobility retained their political, social and economic hegemony under the Russian Empire. The Estonian peasants were emancipated from serfdom in 1816–19. However, it was only as a result of the series of agrarian reforms that began in 1849 and continued into the 1860s that a native Estonian property-owning class came into existence. This development laid the basis for an Estonian cultural revival, some of the most significant events of which were the publication of a national epic, *Kalevipoeg*, in 1857, and a nation-wide song festival in 1869. Demands for national autonomy were first made during the failed Russian revolution of 1905.

INDEPENDENT ESTONIA

The unexpected collapse of both the Russian and German empires in 1917–18 provided the nations of the eastern Baltic with the opportunity to establish their own sovereign states. After the overthrow of the Russian Tsar, Nicholas (Nikolai) II, in March 1917, Estonia became a single, autonomous administrative unit for the first time. Estonians elected an assembly (Maanõukogu), which vied for control with the Bolshevik-dominated soviets (councils). The Bolshevik seizure of power, which resulted in civil war throughout Russia, and the threat of German military occupation impelled Estonian national leaders to act. The Estonian Salvation Committee, appointed by the Maanõukogu, and comprising the major political parties, declared independence on 24 February 1918. As the Bolsheviks abandoned Estonia, German forces advanced, although after Germany's capitulation to the Entente powers (of France and the United Kingdom) in November, the Estonian Provisional Government, headed by Konstantin Päts, re-established control. Independence, however, was secured only after Estonian forces repelled an invasion by the Bolshevik Red Army. A peace accord with Soviet Russia, the Treaty of Tartu (Dorpat), was signed on 2 February 1920, under which Russia recognized Estonian independence in perpetuity. International recognition came in the following year, with Estonia's admittance to the League of Nations in September 1921.

Two noteworthy achievements of the Republic of Estonia were the land reform of 1919, which expropriated the large estates of the ethnic German 'Baltic barons' and distributed the land among the peasants, and the 1925 law on cultural autonomy for ethnic minorities, generally recognized as one of the most liberal provisions regarding minorities in the world at the time. For most of its existence between the First and Second World Wars the country was a liberal democracy, but from 1934–40 it came under moderate authoritarian rule. The 1920 Constitution concentrated power in the legislature, the State Assembly (Riigikogu), at the expense of the relatively weak executive (Riigivanem). In 1933 a right-wing, populist movement, the War of Independence Veterans' League, succeeded in attaining popular support in a referendum for amendment of the Constitution to introduce a strong presidency. In order to prevent a potential electoral victory of the radical right, on 12 March 1934 the premier and acting President, Konstantin Päts, and Gen. Johan Laidoner imposed martial law and suspended the Riigikogu. In 1938 Päts legitimized his rule by introducing a new Constitution, which provided for a presidential system of government, with a bicameral legislature. In April he was elected President. Although the Päts regime restricted civil liberties and established corporatist institutions, it allowed limited pluralism and enjoyed substantial popular support, especially in rural areas.

SOVIET OCCUPATION

Following the Treaty of Non-Aggression (the Nazi-Soviet Pact) of 23 August 1939, which divided Eastern Europe into spheres of influence, Estonia was confronted with a Soviet ultimatum to conclude a Treaty of Mutual Assistance. Estonia complied on 28 September and was forced to grant the USSR military bases on its territory. The sudden resettlement to Germany of virtually the entire Baltic German community in the final months of 1939 ominously hinted at what lay ahead. On 16 June 1940, while the German army conquered France, the USSR issued another ultimatum demanding the formation of a pro-Soviet government and the entry of the Red Army into the country. The Estonian Government capitulated to these demands. A pro-Soviet Government under Johannes Vares-Barbarus, chosen by Stalin's (Iosif V. Dzhugashvili) special emissary, Andrei Zhdanov, was installed, single-party elections were held, and on 6 August Estonia was formally incorporated into the USSR as a Union Republic.

The new regime proceeded with the rapid sovietization of political, cultural and economic life in Estonia. Leading members of religious, military, educational, political and administrative institutions were arrested and deported, with a significant number executed. The era of Soviet 'terror' was interrupted by German occupation from 1941 to 1944. During the Second World War the Soviet and German armies in turn mobilized Estonian men into their ranks. An Estonian provisional Government sought to restore independence in September 1944, as the German forces retreated, but was immediately suppressed by the advancing Red Army. The Soviet reoccupation was resisted into the early 1950s by small bands of pro-independence guerrillas known as the 'forest brethren' (*metsavennad*). Approximately 70,000 Estonians fled the country to avoid the returning Red Army.

To administer the country, the Soviets installed russified Estonians from the USSR to head the Communist Party of Estonia (CPE) and other important state institutions. Collectivization of agriculture was carried out in 1947–49, accompanied by the deportation of over 20,000 people, most of whom were women and children. Perhaps the most lasting consequence of Soviet rule was a drastic demographic shift: at the end of the Second World War over 90% of the population were ethnically Estonian, but by 1989 the Estonian proportion of the population had decreased to 61.5%. Estonia's high standard of living, compared with the rest of the USSR, and the Soviet policy of developing heavy industry, particularly in north-eastern Estonia, contributed to a massive influx of Russians and other Slavs. To Estonians this seemed to be part of an intentional policy of assimilation. Thus, concern for ethnic survival was one of the primary factors in the drive for independence in the late 1980s.

RESTORATION OF INDEPENDENCE

The policies of *glasnost* (openness) and *perestroika* (restructuring) advocated by the last Soviet leader, Mikhail Gorbachev, from the mid-1980s, were seized upon by Estonians to challenge the Soviet system. The first mass protests arose in early 1987 against a planned phosphate mining project, which would have devastated the environment. This led, in September, to a proposal by four Estonian economists for economic self-management, the first republican attempt to gain more autonomy from the all-Union authorities. At the Plenary Conference of the Creative Unions, held in April 1988, the nation's intellectual élite directly criticized the leadership of the CPE. The pro-reformist Estonian Popular Front (EPF) was established on 13 April, an initiative soon imitated in other Soviet republics.

Most important in undermining the legitimacy of Soviet rule was the recovery of historical memory. This movement was led by the Estonian Heritage Society, which began to restore independence-era monuments that had been removed by the Soviet authorities. The Society also organized a campaign to publish the 'Secret Protocols' of the Nazi-Soviet Pact. The critical moment of national self-assertion, known as the 'singing revolution', occurred in mid-1988, a period of mass protest gatherings at the song festival grounds, where the national tricolour was openly displayed. On 16 June the CPE First Secretary, Karl Vaino, was replaced by a Gorbachev protégé, Vaino Väljas, the first native Estonian to lead the CPE since the 1940s. Responding to pressure from the EPF, the Estonian Supreme Soviet adopted a declaration of sovereignty on 16 November 1988, an act soon followed by other Union Republics. On 18 January 1989 Estonian was made the state language. The EPF developed close links with popular fronts in the remaining Baltic republics of Latvia and Lithuania. This co-operation was most spectacularly illustrated by the human chain formed from Tallinn to Vilnius, Lithuania, on 23 August, to protest against the Nazi-Soviet Pact on its 50th anniversary.

The EPF's strategy of reform from within the system was challenged by a 'grass-roots' movement, known as the Citizens' Committees, which sought to restore the independent republic that had existed between the First and Second World Wars, on the basis of legal continuity. The Committees circumvented the 'illegal' institutional structures of the Soviet republic by successfully registering the great majority of Estonian citizens (according to pre-1940 criteria) and holding elections on 24 February 1990 to a Congress of Estonia, which claimed to represent the will of the Estonian citizenry. The impact of the Congress, however, was lessened by the victory of the EPF in elections to the Estonian Supreme Soviet, held on 18 March. Edgar Savisaar, the leader of the EPF, was elected Chairman of the Council of Ministers (Prime Minister) in early April.

On 30 March 1990 the Estonian Supreme Council (as the Supreme Soviet had been renamed) declared a period of transition to independence. The Estonian Government began to create new state institutions, such as border guards and the Bank of Estonia. In May Gorbachev declared measures towards independence null, following the restoration of independent Estonia's name, flag and anthem. However, in the midst of the Soviet military intervention in Lithuania, a republic with similar secessionist ambitions, in January 1991, Boris Yeltsin, the Chairman of the Russian Supreme Soviet, signed an agreement recognizing Estonian sovereignty. A referendum on independence was held on 3 March, with almost 78% of participants responding favourably. Estonia refused to participate in a referendum on the future of the USSR, which took place in the same month.

On 20 August 1991, in response to the attempted *putsch* in the Russian and Soviet capital, Moscow, the Estonian Supreme Council declared immediate independence. Soviet troops seized the television tower outside Tallinn, but withdrew as the coup failed. The new Soviet State Council recognized Estonian independence on 6 September, and on 17 September Estonia was admitted to the UN.

DOMESTIC POLITICS

A deterioration in the economic situation, caused by the collapse of the Soviet system, resulted in Savisaar's resignation on 30 January 1992. He was replaced by Tiit Vähi, the former Minister of Transport, who formed a technocratic, transitional cabinet. The new Government's main achievement was the introduction, against prevailing Western advice, of a convertible Estonian currency, the kroon (crown), which was 'pegged' to the German currency, the Deutsche Mark. This measure, the first by a former Soviet republic, laid the basis for Estonia's economic recovery.

A Constituent Assembly, with delegates provided by both the Supreme Council and the Congress of Estonia, produced a Constitution, which, after approval in a referendum, came into force on 3 July 1992. The Constitution provided for a 101-member parliament, the Riigikogu, and a presidency with limited powers. In the first legislative elections, held on 20 September, the Pro Patria (Fatherland) Union (Isamaaliit), led by an historian, Mart Laar, obtained the largest number of seats, and formed a coalition Government with the Estonian National Independence Party (ENIP) and the Moderates' Party in the following month. In the direct presidential election, held simultaneously, Arnold Rüütel, previously Chairman (speaker) of the Supreme Council, won 42% of the votes cast, but not the required absolute majority. In a second round of voting, contested by the two leading candidates, the Riigikogu elected the former foreign minister, Lennart Meri, to the presidency. The centre-right Government possessed few links with the past: several ministers were under 35 years of age, including Laar, and three were émigrés.

Laar's Government embarked on a radical policy of transition to a free-market economic system, which won plaudits from the IMF, but angered farmers and pensioners. Following a series of scandals and defections from his own party, Laar was forced to resign on 26 October 1994, and was replaced in the following month by his Minister of the Environment, Andres Tarand, a member of the Moderates' Party. The composition of the cabinet remained basically unaltered and the Tarand Government continued the policies of its predecessor.

The second post-independence elections were held on 5 March 1995. The largest number of seats in the legislature (41 of the total of 101) was won by an alliance of former premier Vähi's Estonian Coalition Party (ECP–Koonderakond) and the Rural Union, comprising various agrarian parties and led by Rüütel. A coalition of the newly established Estonian Reform Party (ERP) and liberal parties won 19 seats and the Estonian Centre Party 16 seats.

On 23 March 1995 Vähi was invited to form a Government, which was supported by the Rural Union and the Estonian Centre Party, headed by another former Prime Minister, Savisaar, who was appointed Deputy Prime Minister and Minister of the Interior. The coalition, however, lasted only until early October, when it was discovered that Savisaar had secretly recorded conversations with other politicians. The Government resigned, but Vähi formed a new coalition, which was announced on 3 November. The new ECP/Rural Union administration included the pro-business ERP, led by Siim Kallas, the former President (governor) of the Bank of Estonia.

Presidential elections were held in August 1996. Once again the incumbent, Meri, defeated Rüütel, after a larger electoral college was convened, comprising the 101 deputies and 273 local government representatives. The six ERP members of the Government withdrew in November 1996, after a co-operation agreement was signed between the ECP and the Estonian Centre Party, without their knowledge. Vähi formed a new Government in December, but was forced to resign in February 1997 owing to a series of allegations of abuse of office. A new Government was formed by former broadcaster Mart Siimann, also of the ECP. Siimann's minority Government managed to survive until legislative elections were held on 7 March 1999.

The Estonian Centre Party won the largest number of seats (28), but was unable to form a majority coalition, and Laar and his Pro Patria (Fatherland) Union subsequently formed a centre-right coalition Government with the ERP and the social-democratic Moderates' Party. The Laar Government strove to complete infrastructural privatization, with the two principal sectors being those of energy and railways. However, complex privatization deals were mismanaged, resulting in public outcry and the erosion of the Government's popularity. The Laar Government was irreparably damaged by the outcome of the presidential election of August–September 2001, in which two of the governing parties, the Pro Patria Union and the ERP, each believed that they possessed the strongest candidate. Their failure to support a compromise candidate eventually led to the unexpected victory of the perennial runner-up, Rüütel, who had been widely discounted as a relic of the past. The triumph of Rüütel, a former rector of the country's agricultural academy, was also attributed, in part, to the support of rural delegates in the electoral college that was convened on 21 September. The governing coalition subsequently began to weaken, and on 8 January 2002 Laar resigned, claiming that he had been betrayed by the ERP, which had ousted the Pro Patria Union from the Tallinn City Government, and formed an alliance with the rival Estonian Centre Party.

A new governing coalition was formed on 22 January 2002 by the pro-business ERP and the populist Estonian Centre Party. The new Government was headed by the ERP's Siim Kallas, Minister of Finance in the Laar Government, although the Estonian Centre Party held eight of the cabinet's 14 portfolios. To general surprise, this coalition of ideological opposites was remarkably cohesive. In the legislative elections of 2 March 2003 both the governing parties not only maintained their popularity, but even slightly increased their share of the votes. This was unprecedented, as in previous elections voters had always tended to penalize the parties in power at that time. The election campaign had been fought over the question of whether to introduce a progressive income tax, or to lower the existing uniform tax rate, and on increasing financial support for young mothers. Although Savisaar's Estonian Centre Party won the most votes (25.4%), a new, right-wing party, Union for the Republic Res Publica, received an equal number of seats (28) in the Riigikogu. Res Publica championed law and order and the fight against corruption, but also internal party democracy and transparency. Its leader, Juhan Parts, a former state auditor, was sworn in as Prime Minister on 10 April, leading a coalition that included the ERP and the Estonian People's Union, which represented the rural population. The Parts cabinet was widely regarded as exceptionally young and inexperienced, even by Estonian standards. Overall, however, all eight Governments to hold office since 1992 have demonstrated strong continuity in their commitment to a liberal market economy, European integration, and their approach to the Russian minority issue.

INTEGRATION OF ETHNIC MINORITIES

The most problematic social and political issue, and the one that received the most international attention, was the status of the Russian-speaking minority. Estonian legislation was based on the principle that Estonia was not a newly created state, but a restored state that was illegally occupied from 1940. Thus, the citizenship law of November 1991 follows the principle of legal continuity; that is, all those who were citizens of Estonia prior to the Soviet annexation in 1940, and their descendants, were automatically citizens of the restored republic. As citizenship was not ethnically based, this included Russians who were citizens of the pre-Second World War state and their descendants. However, the overwhelming majority of Russians arrived in Estonia only after the Second World War and had to apply to be naturalized. Initially, the requirements were two years' residency, plus a one-year waiting period and an elementary knowledge of the Estonian language (1,500 words). Many non-Estonians, however, proved unable or unwilling to take the language test (pensioners were exempted). Consequently, a substantial number of residents opted instead to take Russian citizenship. For those who do not apply for citizenship, the Estonian Government issues an aliens' passport that serves as an international travel document.

Predictions of ethnic unrest and the possible rise of a secessionist movement in the predominantly Russian northeastern region of the country did not come to pass during the 1990s, and the situation remained remarkably calm. Although the Russian Government repeatedly accused Estonia of systematic discrimination and the violation of the human rights of ethnic Russians in Estonia, international organizations such as the Council of Europe and the Organization for Security and Co-operation in Europe (OSCE) found no evidence to justify such claims. Nevertheless, the OSCE and the European Union (EU) urged Estonia to relax its citizenship and language legislation and to be more accommodating towards the non-Estonian minority. In particular, the substantial number of stateless persons—those who had chosen neither Estonian nor Russian citizenship—remained a concern.

Several important steps were taken to encourage the integration of the Russian-speaking minority into Estonian society. The State Integration Programme was adopted by the Government in 2000, temporary residence permits were replaced by permanent residence permits for non-citizens and stateless persons, and changes were made to language legislation, relaxing requirements for the use of Estonian in the private sector. By the end of 2001 Estonia had fulfilled all the recommendations of the OSCE regarding the rights of ethnic minorities. The final measure was the amendment of the electoral law to allow candidates who did not know the state language to stand for election. The progress made in addressing the concerns of the Russian-speaking minority

was demonstrated by the closure of the OSCE mission in Estonia at the end of 2001, upon the fulfilment of its mandate.

FOREIGN POLICY

The primary concern of Estonian foreign policy from 1991 to 1994 was the removal of former Soviet (mainly Russian) troops from Estonian territory. The troops' withdrawal was completed in August 1994, after Estonia agreed to give social and civil guarantees to retired Soviet military personnel residing in Estonia. The military withdrawal did not, however, lead to a relaxation of tensions between the two neighbours. Russia expressed disapproval of Estonia's insistence on attempting to gain membership of the North Atlantic Treaty Organization (NATO), of the status of ethnic Russians in Estonia, and of the Estonian Apostolic Orthodox Church's return to the jurisdiction of the Constantinople Patriarchate (based in İstanbul, Turkey), independent of the Moscow Patriarchate. Estonians, in turn, were alarmed by what was perceived as neo-imperialist rhetoric in Russian politics and Russia's refusal to acknowledge that the incorporation of Estonia into the USSR in 1940 had been carried out against the will of the Estonian population.

A further obstacle to improved relations between the two countries was a border dispute regarding land awarded to Estonia in 1920, by the Treaty of Tartu, but annexed by Russia in 1945. In 1995 Estonia renounced its territorial claims, in the hope that Russia would reciprocate by recognizing the validity of the 1920 Treaty, which would amount to an acknowledgement that the Soviet occupation of 1940 was illegal. Agreement was reached in 1999 and the text of the border treaty was initialled by the countries' respective foreign ministers, but the Russian Government did not submit the Treaty to the Duma for ratification. It appeared that the Russian side hoped that by keeping the issue unresolved it could hinder Estonia's progress towards NATO membership. While bilateral relations have not notably improved, the Russian President, Vladimir Putin, nevertheless softened his country's opposition to Baltic membership of NATO in the wake of the suicide attacks on the USA on 11 September 2001.

A central feature of Estonian foreign policy was close co-operation with Latvia and Lithuania. The major forum for this co-operation was the Baltic Assembly, a consultative body consisting of the parliamentary deputies of all three countries, established in late 1991. Co-operation with Nordic countries, particularly Finland and Sweden, also played a crucial role in Estonia's successful transition to a free-market democracy. From 1992 an institutional framework for co-operation was provided by the Council of Baltic Sea States. Increasingly, high-level political meetings took place using a 'five plus three' format; that is, the Nordic states (Denmark, Finland, Norway, Sweden—and Iceland) and the Baltic states, together. The Nordic countries were the most significant investors in the region and championed the interests of the Baltic states in international organizations. Estonia had a special relationship with Finland, not only because the Finnish capital, Helsinki, is a mere 85 km (52.7 miles) from Tallinn, and Finland was Estonia's biggest trading partner, but also because of their linguistic kinship and close cultural ties.

Estonia's primary foreign policy goal was to integrate quickly into European and trans-Atlantic institutions. The first step was admission to the Council of Europe in May 1993. However, the main focus of Estonian efforts was membership of the EU and NATO. Estonia applied for EU membership in 1995. Owing to its more rapid economic reforms, in December 1997 Estonia was the only Baltic state among six countries invited to commence EU membership negotiations in 1998. Although this initially led to some concern about the future of Baltic solidarity, it provided a tremendous boost to Estonia's image internationally. Paradoxically, of the candidate countries, opinion polls consistently showed the Estonian population to be the most sceptical about the benefits of accession to the EU, although the principal political parties were unanimous in their support for membership. Thus, there was a clear divergence between the political elite and the general public, which was also common in many EU member states.

Estonia's strategy in the EU membership negotiations was to strive to fulfil all the necessary criteria and to implement fully the EU's *acquis communautaire* (the body of EU legislation, treaties and case law) in the least possible time, without presenting any awkward problems. In December 2002 accession negotiations were successfully completed at an EU summit meeting in Copenhagen, Denmark. On 16 April 2003 Estonia signed the Treaty of Accession in Athens, Greece. If the population approved EU membership in a referendum, scheduled to be held on 14 September, Estonia (together with nine other countries, including Latvia and Lithuania) was to join the EU on 1 May 2004.

Membership of the NATO defence Alliance was considered the only possible guarantee of Estonian security. The idea of neutrality, which was proposed in the early 1990s, was firmly rejected, as leaving Estonia in too ambiguous a position.

Estonia joined NATO's 'Partnership for Peace' programme in 1994. The Baltic states petitioned hard for NATO membership and struggled to overcome Western apprehension that enlargement to include them could prompt a negative Russian reaction. Estonia had striven to demonstrate that a small country could contribute to the Alliance, particularly through the efforts of its peace-keeping troops, which served in Bosnia and Herzegovina, the Serbian province of Kosovo (the Federal Republic of Yugoslavia—now Serbia and Montenegro), Afghanistan and Iraq. Co-operation with Latvia and Lithuania in forming a joint infantry battalion, naval squadron, air surveillance system and staff college also served to demonstrate preparedness for membership of the Alliance. The Laar Government steadily increased the defence budget, until defence expenditure finally reached 2% of gross domestic product (GDP) by 2002, in line with NATO standards. The new Government elected in 2003 pledged to maintain this level. Estonian efforts were rewarded at a NATO summit, held in Prague, Czech Republic, in November 2002, when the country was formally invited to join the Organization. On 26 March 2003 the protocols of accession were signed in Brussels, Belgium and, after ratification by the existing NATO member states, Estonia was expected to become a full member in 2004.

The Economy

HEIDO VITSUR

Revised for this edition by the Editorial Staff

OVERVIEW

At the beginning of the 19th century the Estonian population was almost fully literate and Estonia, being located in close proximity to St Petersburg, the capital of the Russian Empire, belonged to one of its most developed regions. From the end of the century many large, industrial enterprises were established in Estonia, in the textiles, machine-building, and pulp and paper industries, the output of which supplied the Russian market and was protected by high rates of taxation. Just prior to the First World War (1914–18) three ship-building plants were constructed in Tallinn, the Estonian capital, in order to help restore the Russian navy, following its destruction in the Russo–Japanese War of 1904–05. However, after the First World War, the Russian Revolution of 1917 and the establishment of the independent Estonian state in 1920, industrial capabilities had become either damaged or redundant in a country with a population of only 1m., which concentrated on the small, local market, and which found it difficult to find buyers for its products on the world market.

Between the First and Second World Wars agricultural production increased significantly, but progress in the manufacturing sector remained moderate, with the most important contributors being the food-producing industry, the pulp and paper industry and the timber and textiles industries. Any industrial developments were foreshortened, however, when Estonia was incorporated into the USSR in 1940, and a market economy, based on private ownership, was replaced by state or collective property and centralized planning.

Agriculture preserved its strong position in the Estonian economy throughout the Soviet era, especially in dairy-cattle and pig-breeding, the productivity of which was the highest in the USSR. After the Second World War (1939–45) the industrial sector (including energy) began to play a vital role in shaping the economy. In 1939 56% of the rural population were engaged in agriculture, although by 1989 this figure had declined to 28%, and the agricultural labour force consisted predominantly of older people. The share of agriculture in the

state economy decreased correspondingly, and agricultural production represented one-fifth of that of industry at that time.

During the entire Soviet period, the industrial sector remained inefficient, and caused environmental damage; Estonia also proved unable to compete on international markets, owing to the inferior quality and outmoded design of the products produced. In general, raw materials were supplied by the USSR, and the output re-exported. The republic mainly specialized in producing consumer goods; its level of technological development proved satisfactory to the Soviet market and, as a result, a stable level of demand for Estonian goods was sustained. Consequently, Estonia attained the highest rates of labour productivity and living standards in the USSR.

The need for a fundamental reorganization of the Estonian economy emerged as a result of the disintegration of the USSR and its planned economy; the majority of existing large enterprises collapsed just months after Estonia obtained independence in September 1991, as the country lost its former markets. Estonia, therefore, began to pursue the reforms necessary to achieve a market economy, although, in fact, some of the preparations had already been made. In 1987 a proposal for economic independence had been advanced and, during the subsequent two years, a complete programme of economic reforms was elaborated. That programme envisaged the economic independence of Estonia, the rejection of a planned economy and the introduction of market economy principles, independent taxation, and budgetary and monetary policy. Questions regarding ownership reform were barely addressed, however, owing to both political and social limitations.

By the time Estonia obtained independence, therefore, almost all prices had been liberalized and the Soviet tax system transformed. The turnover tax, which was based on fixed prices, was replaced with a value-added tax (VAT) and excises, and the enterprise tax was succeeded by an income tax on enterprises. The Estonian budget was fully separated from that of the USSR, and privatization was undertaken.

Estonia also developed its historically close contacts with Finland, based on the proximity of the two countries and their related languages, and many joint ventures were established in the second half of the 1980s. By 1991 there were 161 joint ventures, of which approximately one-third were in the manufacturing sector. To a considerable extent these joint ventures represented the instrument that helped Estonia to reorientate its trade from East to West. In one year alone, exports to Western Europe countries by such joint ventures increased five-fold, and contributed 43.6% of total exports to the West. However, the success of joint ventures only served to emphasize the overall weakness of trade contacts and the uncompetitiveness of other enterprises, as joint ventures owned only 1.3% of the total assets of Estonian industrial enterprises.

The fact that Estonia had initiated reforms and gained the support of the population prior to the collapse of the USSR gave the country a considerable advantage by the time it secured independence, in comparison with other former Soviet republics. It made possible the implementation of more radical reforms that facilitated, in turn, Estonia's position as the only post-Soviet republic to qualify, in 1998, as a member of the first group of European Union (EU) candidate countries. By 1996 privatization had advanced considerably in the trade and services sectors, and more than 90% of industrial enterprises had been fully privatized. The Government began to divest its large-scale enterprises by means of internationally announced tenders. The privatization of infrastructure was launched in 1997; the national telecommunications operator, Eesti Telekom, was privatized in 1999. Privatization of the railways, however, proved to be a more complicated process than had been anticipated, as did land reform. Land reform had, initially, been postponed for technical reasons, such as the lack of topographical maps, but was, subsequently, largely influenced by restitution and legal proceedings regarding the existing utilization of land. In April 2001 agreement was finally reached on the privatization of a 66% stake in Estonian Railways (Eesti Raudtee), the national rail company. The former state-owned housing fund was privatized under a voucher scheme, and by 2001 95.5% of the living space provided by the housing fund was under private ownership. Between 1996 and 2001 Estonia made thorough preparations for the sale of the Narva Power Plants (Narva Elektrijaamad) to private investors. However, at the end of 2001 the deal collapsed, as the anticipated buyer was unable to obtain the required lending, of US $200m., for the renovation of the Power Plants, without the participation of the Estonian state in the loan process, which was precluded under the terms of the sales contract.

The economic decline that accompanied the establishment of independence began in 1991, and it was estimated that gross national product (GNP) per head declined, in real terms, at an average annual rate of 4.3% between 1989 and 1995. Price liberalization, the rupture of economic contacts with Russia, and the reorientation of foreign trade to the West all contributed to the decline and the accompanying rise in prices. By the end of 1992 the rate of consumer-price inflation had risen 11-fold since 1989, and stood at 1,069%. However, following monetary reform in 1992 this process slowed and the rate of inflation was 90% at 1 January 1994; by 1999 the average annual rate of inflation had declined to just 3.3%, although it increased slightly to 4.0% in 2000 and 5.8% in 2001, owing to the rise in global petroleum prices and increased electricity prices in 2001. In 2002 consumer prices increased by just 3.5%.

Gross domestic product (GDP) increased consistently from 1995 (the greatest increase, of 10.6%, occurring in 1997), until 1999, when the previous year's economic crisis in Russia caused a 1.1% decline in real GDP. However, by the second half of the year the Estonian economy had recovered somewhat, and in 2000 GDP growth reached 6.9%. The decline in the global economy in 2001 did not have a significant impact on economic development in Estonia, and economic growth of 6.5% was recorded in that year; in 2002 GDP increased by 6.0%.

INDUSTRY

In the Soviet period industry dominated the economy, representing approximately two-thirds of national domestic product (NDP—according to Soviet methods of calculation); in the years following independence, however, the role of industry consistently declined (although this pattern was also influenced by changes in the international environment and greater openness in the country's economy). The decline in industrial output began to reverse in 1995, as the sector adapted to its altered circumstances, and production increased by 2%–3%, annually, in 1995 and 1996, and in 1997 growth in industrial production reached its highest level of 16%. Although this progress was temporarily halted as a result of the financial crisis in Russia, with industrial growth increasing by just 1.8% in 1998, and registering a decline of 7.6% in 1999, in 2000 Estonian industry began to overcome this decline, registering sectoral GDP growth of 3.3%. In 2001 industrial production registered continued growth, of 3.2%, and growth was especially strong in the manufacturing industries. Sales of industrial output increased by 7.7%, in real terms. The contraction of the world economy affected mainly those companies that were sub-contractors to international enterprises; such sales declined by some 7%.

The contribution of industry (including mining, manufacturing, energy and construction) to GDP declined from 1994, and it was replaced by services as the dominant economic sector. In 2002 industry (including mining and quarrying, manufacturing, power and construction) contributed 29.3% of GDP, while the services sector accounted for 65.3% of GDP. Of all areas of activity, manufacturing was the most significant contributor to GDP in 2002 (18.6%), followed by transport, storage and communications (15.5%), wholesale and retail trade (14.3%) and real estate, renting and business activities (11.5%)—thus, services accounted for three of the four principal economic activities. The economic development of the industrial sector, as with much of the economy, mainly relied on foreign investment.

Different areas of manufacturing were variously affected by the liberalization of foreign trade and the collapse of the Russian market; for example, the food industry, which traditionally represented the leading industrial sector, in terms of production, faced the challenge of penetrating the highly protected international markets, and the electronics and machinery-building sectors also suffered. Conversely, a number of enterprises in the timber (and consequently furniture) and metals industries flourished at this time. Despite the difficulties that it faced, the food industry remained dominant, typically accounting for approximately 25% of total industrial output, followed by the metal-processing and timber industries. Production of energy, light industry, chemicals and construction materials were also significant.

Electrical-energy production and oil-shale mining for fuelling power plants declined by about one-half from Soviet times, although Estonia was still estimated to account for some 84% of oil-shale production world-wide. The decline in the production of electrical energy was largely attributable to reduced exports, decreased industrial and agricultural production, and the implementation of energy-saving technologies. Estonia is entirely self-sufficient in electric energy (producing 5.1 MWh per inhabitant), and also exports to neighbouring countries. In February 2001 an agreement was signed between Belarus, Estonia, Latvia, Lithuania and Russia regarding the parallel operation of their energy systems, in order to ensure a reliable supply of electrical energy.

AGRICULTURE

In principle, ownership reform and the transformation of agriculture were completed by 1996, owing to Estonia's initiation of reforms some years before independence. In 1989 only 326 large socialist enterprises existed in the agricultural sector, but by the beginning of 1991, prior to independence, there were more than 2,000 private farms. In 1992–96, as part of the process of economic reform, the former large, socialist enterprises were privatized, and 45,000 farms and 500 co-operatives were established in their place. These became the main producers of agricultural output and co-operatives continued to play a role in grain production alone, where they accounted for one-half of all grain produced. The state retained only those farms that were attached to schools of agriculture or to scientific enterprises. The principal crops produced in Estonia are grain, potatoes and cabbages.

Agricultural production declined from approximately 10% of total output following independence to some 3% in 2000. In 1990 there was a national herd of more than 570,000 cows; this had decreased to 280,884 by the agricultural census of mid-2001. Similarly, the number of pigs declined from 960,000 to 329,785 over the same period, and this trend characterized much of the agricultural sector. In 1992 agricultural exports were almost twice the level of imports, but by 1999 this situation had completely reversed. This rapid agricultural decline was caused not only by the collapse of traditional markets, but also by the fact that, in pursuit of free trade, Estonia no longer supported the market with protective tariffs and quotas for imports, or state export subsidies. Agricultural performance improved in 2001. The market for milk products and meat products expanded, and their production increased by 9%–10%. In addition, farmers also began to receive agricultural allowances from the EU under its Special Accession Programme for Agriculture and Rural Development (SAPARD).

FOREIGN TRADE AND PAYMENTS

As a small country, Estonia sought to integrate into the global economy. In the years following independence Estonia implemented an extensively liberalized economic policy, but failed to establish any protective taxes or quotas, or to implement any other such safe-guards permitted by the World Trade Organization (WTO). However, Estonia undertook limited tariff implementation in 2000, in order to comply with the expectations of the EU. Estonia has concluded free-trade agreements with all its principal trading partners, with the exception of Russia, which give its partners access to the Estonian market; it has also concluded bilateral free-trade agreements with Latvia and Lithuania.

Foreign trade increased dramatically in the years that followed the implementation of monetary reform. Exports increased seven-fold between 1992 and 1999, and imports increased 11-fold over the same period. In 2001 the expansion in foreign trade slowed, although turnover increased by more than 5%. In 1992 the country's trade balance recorded a small deficit, of US $90.4m., but this increased thereafter, reaching its maximum level of $1,124.3m., or 26% of GDP, in 1997. The strongly negative foreign-trade balance was not necessarily of detriment to the economy, however, as the deficit was caused, to a considerable extent, by flows of foreign investment into the economy.

Following independence the geography, as well as the structure, of foreign trade altered significantly. Before independ-ence more than 90% of exports had supplied the Soviet market, and no more than 2% had supplied the West. By the end of the 1990s, however, the situation had reversed. After the Russian financial crisis of 1998, Finland and Sweden became the main destination countries for Estonian exports, purchasing 24.8% and 15.3%, respectively, in 2002. The EU as a whole was consistently Estonia's major trading partner; exports to EU member countries accounted for 68% of total exports in 2002, which was a reduction of 5%, compared with 2000. The role of the members of the Commonwealth of Independent States (CIS—comprising the countries of the former USSR, with the exception of the three Baltic states) as destination countries had declined in importance, accounting for some 4%–5% of export trade. At the same time, trade with other countries increased rapidly. Latvia was Estonia's fourth largest export market.

A similar change occurred in the geographical distribution of imports. Estonia latterly imported mainly raw materials and fuels from its former trading partners in the CIS, which accounted for around 16% of total imports by the end of the 1990s and for 10% in 2002. Finland, Estonia's principal trading partner, supplied 17.2% of total imports in 2002, followed by Germany (11.2%), Sweden (9.5%) and Russia (7.4%). From 2001 the People's Republic of China also became a major source of imports, supplying 7.4% in that year.

In 2002 the principal exports were machinery and electrical goods (accounting for 24.8% of export revenue), timber products (15.1%) and textiles (12.1%). The main imports in that year were machinery and electrical goods (accounting for 29.7% of import revenue), transport vehicles (10.8%), agricultural products and food (9.7%), base metals (8.9%) and textiles (8.2%).

In 1992 Estonia became a member of both the IMF and the World Bank. It also joined the European Bank for Reconstruction and Development (EBRD) in the same year. In addition, Estonia is a member of the Council of Baltic Sea States (CBSS). In July 1996 CBSS member states agreed a programme of co-operation, designed to encourage economic development and integration. In July 1999 the premiers of the three Baltic states agreed on the establishment of a Baltic Common Economic Area, and in January 1998 the Presidents of those countries had signed a US-Baltic Charter of Partnership, to develop closer political and economic links with the USA. Estonia became a member of the WTO in November 1999.

The trade balance, as well as the deficit on the balance of payments, derived mainly from inflows of foreign investment for the modernization of the economy and the implementation of structural changes, which did not cause debts. As a result of the persistent foreign-trade deficit and high domestic demand, the current account of the balance of payments was strongly negative, and had been for most of the years following independence. However, this negative balance increased to 12.3% of GDP in 2002, its highest ever level, causing widespread concern.

MONETARY AND FISCAL POLICY

The aim of the monetary reform conducted in 1992 was to provide free convertibility of the Estonian kroon, which replaced the Soviet/Russian rouble from June of that year, as well as to ensure international confidence in the new national currency. It was, therefore, decided to establish the new monetary system on the principles of a currency board, which required Estonia to support all the currency in circulation with convertible 'hard' currency reserves in deposit in the central bank.

Estonia fixed its national currency to the German currency, the Deutsche Mark (DM—and subsequently, from 1 January 1999, to the common European currency, the euro), which provided the kroon with greater stability. The establishment of a non-traditional monetary system could be explained by the fact that it was more important for a small country with an open economy to maintain stable currency exchange rates than stable prices. This also meant that Estonia could not use monetary policy as an instrument of short-term economic policy. The fixing of the national currency to the DM proved prudent, as the majority of Estonia's trading partners, including Germany, subsequently participated in the EU's programme of economic and monetary union, and the associated creation of the 'euro zone'. This protected the Estonian economy from the risks that affected those countries that fixed their currencies to the US dollar.

In addition to the establishment of the currency-board system, confidence in the kroon was maintained through strict fiscal policy. In the years following independence, Estonia succeeded in avoiding significant borrowing. Therefore, levels of public-sector foreign debt remained low, equivalent to less than 3% of GDP in 2001. However, the Government often failed to balance the general government budget. Estonia was characterized by a conservative budgetary policy and, as a rule, the Government succeeded in avoiding a serious budgetary deficit. In 1995–98 the public-sector budgetary deficit was equivalent to only 0.2%–0.3% of GDP. However, the budgetary deficit was adversely affected by the failure of both the Government and parliament to forecast the economic impact of the Russian financial crisis of 1998, partly owing to their preoccupation with the forthcoming parliamentary elections. The centre-right Government of Mart Laar, elected in March 1999, approved additional budgetary proposals, thereby reducing the overall deficit to 4.7% of GDP. In 2000 the budgetary deficit was equivalent to less than 1% of GDP. The state budgetary deficits recorded in 1999 and 2000 did not cause increases in the national debt, as the Government used assets received from the privatization of Eesti Telekom to compensate. In 2001, for the first time in many years, the Government succeeded in balancing public-sector revenue and expenditure, and ended the fiscal year with a budgetary surplus of some 668.5m. kroons. Following the receipt of revenues higher than those forecast, the Government introduced two supplementary budgets in 2002, against the advice of both the central bank and the IMF. A further such budget had been adopted by mid-2003. The 2003 budget was the first to anticipate a deficit since independence. Concerns about the Government's policy centred on the country's large current-account deficit, which investors had tolerated while the budget maintained a sufficient surplus to be able to sustain it.

WAGES AND EMPLOYMENT

Economic chaos and the severe increase in prices accompanying the collapse of the USSR caused a dramatic decline in the Estonian population's living standards. The decline in the purchasing power of earnings was characterized by the fact that in 1992 the average wage rose five-fold, while prices rose by some 11-fold in the same year. The real value of savings and pensions decreased in line with the increases in inflation rates. By the beginning of 2000, however, the average wage had increased over seven-fold, in nominal terms, compared with June 1992, and prices had increased only five-fold, which meant that purchasing power had increased by more than 150% over that period. In 2002 the average wage increased, in real terms, by 8.1%, owing to exceptionally low inflation and the rapid increase of gross earnings.

In Estonia there were 660,000 economically active persons in 2000, of whom about 90,000 (approximately 14%) were unemployed. This was the highest level of unemployment recorded in the decade following independence and contrasted significantly with the situation in 1990, when there was,

officially, no unemployment in Estonia. Unemployment as a social phenomenon occurred after the collapse of the Soviet economy and was accompanied by industrial restructuring. The first competent and comparable data regarding unemployment was collected in 1994, when the rate of unemployment, measured according to International Labour Organization criteria, was recorded at 7.6%. Unemployment increased to 9.7% in 1996, and remained at around the same level until the Russian financial crisis of 1998, the impact of which resulted in an increase in the unemployment rate at the beginning of 1999, when it reached 14%. The unemployment rate declined in 2001, when the average annual rate was 12.6%, and declined further in 2002, to 10.3%.

PROSPECTS

The decade following independence demonstrated the sensitivity of the small, open Estonian economy to external impact and to fluctuations in the global economy. This period also showed the flexibility of the economy in withstanding the financial crisis that emerged in East Asian markets in 1997 and to recover swiftly from the reverses caused by the subsequent Russian crisis. The adaptability of the Estonian economy was confirmed in 2001, when economic growth barely slowed, despite the unstable global economic situation. GDP growth slowed slightly in 2002, in comparison with the high rates maintained in 2001, but continued to compare favourably with the world economy.

Estonian GDP was forecast to maintain an average annual growth rate of 4%–6% throughout the first decade of the 2000s. In 2001 GDP per head was expected to amount to 50% of average per-head GDP in the countries of the EU (at 2000 GDP per head amounted to one-third of the average EU level). Although preparations for accession to the EU, and accession itself, which was expected to take place in May 2004, would have to be accompanied by strong growth in investment (of some 25%–28% of GDP per year), this was not expected dramatically to influence job creation or productivity. The greater proportion of investment was to be directed towards the implementation of environmental requirements.

Services costs for electricity, water-supply and sewage systems, and waste utilization were expected to increase by approximately one-third. This would result in a continued increase in prices, which would, therefore, necessitate a greater increase in productivity, while simultaneously adversely affecting the labour market situation.

The greatest obstacle to an increased pace of development, however, was considered to be that of institutional weakness, which hampered the implementation of measures favouring entrepreneurship and the establishment of a sound, effective tax system. According to ratings of international economic competitiveness, Estonia occupied one of the best positions among the transition countries, and could compete with several of the industrialized member countries of the Organisation for Economic Co-operation and Development. This greatly enhanced the likelihood of increased inflows of investment into the country.

It seemed that the macroeconomic, as well as the political, environment would remain favourable, with low rates of inflation and taxes, healthy economic growth, increased foreign trade and relatively stable government. The main threat to the long-term stability of the economy was the demographic situation and the unfavourable ratio of the employed population to pensioners. In 2000 there were 1.6 workers per pensioner, but, as a result of a declining birth rate, the proportion of employed persons to pensioners appeared likely to worsen each year. Thus, the country was unable to rely on a constant source of labour, and the pensions system appeared likely to come under increased strain in the future, despite the implementation of reforms.

Statistical Survey

Source (unless otherwise stated): Statistical Office of Estonia (Statiskaamet), Endla 15, Tallinn 0100; tel. 625-9202; fax 625-9370; e-mail stat@stat.ee; internet www.stat.ee.

Area and Population

AREA, POPULATION AND DENSITY

Area (sq km)	45,227*
Population (census results)†	
12 January 1989	1,565,662
31 March 2000	
Males	631,851
Females	738,201
Total	1,370,052
Population (official estimates at 1 January)†	
2001	1,366,959
2002	1,361,242
2003	1,356,045
Density (per sq km) at 1 January 2003	30.0

* 17,462 sq miles.

† Figures refer to permanent inhabitants. The *de facto* total was 1,572,916 at the 1989 census and 1,356,931 at the 2000 census.

POPULATION BY NATIONALITY
(estimated permanent inhabitants at 1 January 2000)*

	Number	%
Estonian	939,310	65.3
Russian	403,925	28.1
Ukrainian	36,467	2.5
Belarusian	21,125	1.5
Finnish	12,762	0.9
Tatar	3,232	0.2
Latvian	2,638	0.2
Jewish	2,275	0.2
Polish	2,290	0.2
Lithuanian	2,188	0.2
German	1,228	0.1
Others	11,757	0.8
Total	1,439,197	100.0

* Based on the results of 1989 census and official estimates 1990–99.

POPULATION BY ADMINISTRATIVE COUNTY
(1 January 2003)

Harjumaa . . .	522,252	Pärnumaa . . .		90,127
Hiiumaa . . .	10,348	Raplamaa . . .		37,270
Ida-Virumaa . .	176,181	Saaremaa . . .		35,584
Jõgevamaa . .	37,886	Tartumaa . . .		148,992
Järvamaa . .	38,408	Valgamaa . . .		35,242
Läänemaa . . .	28,232	Viljandimaa . . .		57,148
Lääne-Virumaa . .	67,052	Võrumaa . . .		39,202
Põlvamaa . . .	32,121	**Total**		1,356,045

PRINCIPAL TOWNS
(estimated population, excluding suburbs, at 1 January 2002)

Tallinn (capital) . .	398,434	Kohtla-Järve . . .		47,106
Tartu	101,140	Pärnu		45,040
Narva	68,117	Viljandi		20,608

BIRTHS, MARRIAGES AND DEATHS*

	Registered live births		Registered marriages		Registered deaths	
	Number	Rate (per 1,000)	Number	Rate (per 1,000)	Number	Rate (per 1,000)
1995 . .	13,509	9.4	7,006	4.8	20,828	14.5
1996 . .	13,242	9.3	5,517	3.9	19,020	13.4
1997 . .	12,577	8.9	5,589	3.9	18,572	13.2
1998 . .	12,167	8.7	5,430	3.9	19,445	14.0
1999 . .	12,425	9.0	5,590	4.1	18,447	13.4
2000 . .	13,067	9.5	5,485	4.0	18,403	13.4
2001 . .	12,632	9.3	5,647	4.1	18,516	13.6
2002 . .	13,001	9.6	5,853	4.3	18,355	13.5

* Revised figures, based on the results of the 1989 and 2000 population censuses.

Expectation of life (WHO estimates, years at birth): 71.2 (males 65.7; females 76.5) in 2001 (Source: WHO, *World Health Report*).

EMPLOYMENT
(labour force sample surveys, annual averages, '000 persons aged 15–74 years, excl. armed forces)

	2000	2001	2002
Agriculture, hunting and forestry	38.3	37.3	38.8
Fishing	2.9	2.7	1.9
Mining and quarrying	7.2	5.8	5.7
Manufacturing	129.2	134.1	128.2
Electricity, gas and water supply	14.7	11.4	10.5
Construction	39.7	39.3	38.9
Wholesale and retail trade . . .	79.3	83.6	86.3
Hotels and restaurants . . .	19.9	17.4	17.9
Transport, storage and communications	56.9	53.7	54.5
Financial intermediation . . .	7.7	7.2	7.9
Real estate, renting and business activities	40.0	38.2	44.3
Public administration and defence; compulsory social security . .	34.1	34.8	33.2
Education	44.6	51.0	55.6
Health and social work	28.5	30.9	31.6
Activities not adequately defined	29.6	30.4	30.1
Total employed	572.5	577.7	585.5

Unemployed (annual averages, '000 persons aged 15–74): 89.9 in 2000; 83.1 in 2001; 67.2 in 2002.

Health and Welfare

KEY INDICATORS

Total fertility rate (children per woman, 2001)	1.2
Under-5 mortality rate (per 1,000 live births, 2001) . . .	12
HIV/AIDS (% of persons aged 15–49, 2001)	1.00
Physicians (per 1,000 head, 1998)	2.97
Hospital beds (per 1,000 head, 1997)	7.4
Health expenditure (2000): US $ per head (PPP)	556
Health expenditure (2000): % of GDP	6.1
Health expenditure (2000): public (% of total)	76.7
Human Development Index (2000): ranking	42
Human Development Index (2000): value	0.826

For sources and definitions, see explanatory note on p. vi.

Agriculture

PRINCIPAL CROPS
('000 metric tons)

	1999	2000	2001
Wheat	88.4	146.8	133.0
Barley	186.4	347.5	270.0
Rye	38.8	60.8	42.9
Oats	70.8	117.1	91.4
Other cereals	17.3	24.4	103.4
Potatoes	403.7	471.7	343.1
Dry peas	2.2	5.3	5.0
Rapeseed	29.8	38.8	41.3
Cabbages	18.9	21.5	16.7
Cucumbers and gherkins	6.1	5.6	11.5
Carrots	6.7	8.8	11.6
Other vegetables	17.1*	12.2†	9.4
Apples	11.4	18.5	15.1
Other fruits*	6.2	9.5	13.3

* FAO estimate(s).
† Unofficial figure.

Source: FAO.

LIVESTOCK
('000 head, year ending September)

	1999	2000	2001
Cattle	308	267	253
Pigs	326	286	300
Sheep	29	28	29
Chickens	2,636	2,462	2,366
Ducks	20*	20†	20†
Geese	8*	8†	8†
Turkeys	20*	20†	20†
Rabbits	20	21	55*

* Unofficial figure.
† FAO estimate.

Source: FAO.

LIVESTOCK PRODUCTS
('000 metric tons, unless otherwise indicated)

	1999	2000	2001
Beef and veal	21.7	15.4	14.2
Pig meat	31.3	30.3	33.6
Poultry meat	7.7	7.3	9.2
Cows' milk	625.5	628.9	683.2
Butter	10.9	8.7	6.9
Cheese	21.4	16.0	17.1
Hen eggs	17.2	16.5	18.1
Honey (metric tons)	336	334	291

Source: FAO.

Forestry

ROUNDWOOD REMOVALS
('000 cubic metres, excl. bark)

	1999	2000	2001
Sawlogs, veneer logs and logs for sleepers	2,200	2,850	3,260
Pulpwood	3,350	3,800	3,910
Other industrial wood	350	620	1,150
Fuel wood	804	1,640	1,880
Total	6,704	8,910	10,200

Source: FAO.

SAWNWOOD PRODUCTION
('000 cubic metres, incl. railway sleepers)

	1999	2000	2001
Coniferous (softwood)	1,100	1,346	1,536
Broadleaved (hardwood)	100	90	134
Total	1,200	1,436	1,670

Source: FAO.

Fishing

('000 metric tons, live weight)

	1998	1999	2000
Capture	118.7	111.8	113.1
Blue whiting	6.3	0	—
Atlantic redfishes	4.0	2.1	8.7
Atlantic herring	42.7	44.0	41.7
European sprat	32.2	36.4	41.4
Chub mackerel	7.2	3.4	—
Atlantic mackerel	7.4	3.6	2.7
Northern prawn	7.2	12.4	12.8
Aquaculture	0.3	0.2	0.2
Total catch	119.0	112.0	113.4

Source: FAO, *Yearbook of Fishery Statistics*.

Mining

('000 metric tons)

	1998	1999	2000
Oil-shale	12,463	10,685	11,726
Peat	365	1,299	586

Source: US Geological Survey.

Industry

SELECTED PRODUCTS
('000 metric tons, unless otherwise indicated)

	1999	2000	2001
Distilled spirits ('000 hectolitres)	66	86	115
Wine ('000 hectolitres)	24	33	30
Beer ('000 hectolitres)	957	950	1,015
Soft drinks ('000 hectolitres)	824	699	721
Woven cotton fabric ('000 sq metres)	95	121	121
Linen fabric ('000 sq metres)	3,910	n.a.	n.a.
Carpets ('000 sq metres)	1,352	1,866	2,069
Footwear ('000 pairs)	1,347	1,443	1,345
Plywood ('000 cubic metres)	17	18	29
Particle board ('000 cubic metres)	147.8	175.8	185.9
Fibreboard (million sq metres)	17.0	17.7	17.3
Chemical wood pulp	49.5	54.4	51.7
Paper	47.9	52.4	53.3
Nitrogenous fertilizers*	41	38	39
Building bricks (million)	17	17	20
Cement	358	329	405
Electric energy (million kWh)	8,268	8,513	8,483

* In terms of nitrogen.

Electric energy (million kWh): 8,527 in 2002.

Finance

CURRENCY AND EXCHANGE RATES

Monetary Units

100 cents = 1 kroon

Sterling, Dollar and Euro Equivalents (30 May 2003)

£1 sterling = 21.79 kroons;
US $1 = 13.23 kroons;
€1 = 13.64 kroons;
1,000 kroons = £45.89 = $75.61 = €63.96.

Average Exchange Rate (kroons per US $)

2000	16.969
2001	17.564
2002	16.612

Note: In June 1992 Estonia reintroduced its national currency, the kroon, replacing the rouble of the former USSR, initially at a rate of one kroon per 10 roubles.

BUDGET

(million kroons)*

Revenue†	2000	2001	2002‡
Tax revenue	29,392.7	32,022.5	37,172.8
Taxes on income, profits and			
capital gains	7,448.9	7,847.4	9,154.4
Individual	6,594.4	7,099.1	7,806.4
Corporate.	854.5	748.3	1,348.0
Social security contributions .	10,167.1	11,529.9	12,759.8
Domestic taxes on goods and			
services	11,106.7	12,220.5	14,347.1
General sales, turnover or			
value-added taxes . . .	8,156.2	8,642.5	10,172.0
Excises	2,819.2	3,434.1	3,937.5
Other current revenue . . .	3,402.3	4,266.4	4,900.5
Entrepreneurial and property			
income	1,090.7	1,526.9	n.a.
Administrative fees and charges,			
non-industrial and incidental			
sales	1,127.6	1,225.3	n.a.
Capital revenue	468.2	834.0	n.a.
Sales of land and intangible			
assets	150.4	169.1	n.a.
Total	32,795.0	36,288.9	42,073.3

Expenditure§	2000	2001	2002‡
Current expenditure. . . .	30,954.7	33,205.5	37,415.0
Expenditure on goods and			
services	17,790.2	18,748.1	20,628.3
Wages and salaries . . .	5,332.3	5,606.1	6,313.7
Interest payments	294.5	286.1	267.1
Subsidies and other current			
transfers	12,870.0	14,171.3	16,519.6
Subsidies	681.5	805.0	1,137.7
Transfers to non-profit			
institutions	2,482.2	3,298.0	3,540.9
Transfers to households . .	9,667.3	10,678.6	11,791.2
Capital expenditure	2,736.3	3,315.7	4,219.0
Acquisition of fixed assets . .	2,630.9	3,189.6	3,979.9
Total	33,664.9	36,521.2	41,634.0

* Figures represent a consolidation of the operations of the Government, comprising all central and local government accounts.
† Excluding grants received (million kroons): 267.2 in 2000; 629.5 in 2001; 712.8 in 2002.
‡ Preliminary data.
§ Excluding lending minus repayments (million kroons): −26.1 in 2000; −271.3 in 2001; −131.7 in 2002.

INTERNATIONAL RESERVES

(US $ million at 31 December)

	2000	2001	2002
Gold*	2.25	2.29	2.83
IMF special drawing rights . . .	0.02	0.03	0.07
Reserve position in IMF. . . .	0.01	0.01	0.01
Foreign exchange.	920.62	820.20	1,000.30
Total	922.90	822.53	1,003.21

* National valuation.

Source: IMF, *International Financial Statistics*.

MONEY SUPPLY

(million kroons at 31 December)

	2000	2001	2002
Currency outside banks . . .	6,201.3	6,951.9	6,994.9
Demand deposits at banks . .	14,456.8	17,967.9	20,225.5
Total money (incl. others) . .	20,884.1	24,948.2	27,274.5

Source: IMF, *International Financial Statistics*.

COST OF LIVING

(Consumer Price Index; base: 1997 = 100)

	1999	2000	2001
Food (incl. beverages)	100.9	103.4	111.9
Alcohol and tobacco	119.8	123.8	127.3
Clothing (incl. footwear). . . .	119.8	123.9	128.6
Housing	120.5	123.8	135.9
All items (incl. others)	111.8	116.3	123.0

All items (base: 1995 = 100): 158.2 in 2000; 167.3 in 2001; 173.3 in 2002 (Source: IMF, *International Financial Statistics*).

NATIONAL ACCOUNTS

(million kroons at current prices)

Expenditure on the Gross Domestic Product

	2000	2001	2002
Final consumption expenditure . .	67,588.7	74,312.9	83,177.0
Households	48,584.4	53,795.3	60,810.1
Non-profit institutions serving			
households	633.0	908.2	1,055.9
General government	18,371.3	19,609.4	21,311.0
Gross capital formation	24,253.0	28,248.42	33,929.8
Gross fixed capital formation. . .	22,193.2	25,912.6	30,815.1
Changes in inventories . . . }			
Acquisitions, less disposals, of }	2,059.8	2,335.8	3,114.7
valuables . . . . . . }			
Total domestic expenditure . . .	91,841.7	102,561.3	117,106.8
Exports of goods and services f.o.b. . .	81,831.7	87,533.6	90,930.4
Less Imports of goods and services			
f.o.b.	85,400.7	91,157.3	101,060.6
Statistical discrepancy	−894.2	−1,043.1	1,047.0
GDP in market prices	87,378.5	97,894.5	108,023.6
GDP at constant 2000 prices . .	87,378.5	93,021.1	98,586.7

Gross Domestic Product by Economic Activity

	2000	2001	2002
Agriculture and hunting	2,682.8	2,976.0	2,957.0
Forestry	1,888.2	1,778.8	1,990.1
Fishing	217.2	204.2	206.9
Mining and quarrying	864.8	891.8	986.7
Manufacturing	14,092.9	16,137.9	17,929.9
Electricity, gas and water supply .	2,586.5	2,756.1	2,981.7
Construction	4,762.1	5,406.8	6,312.6
Wholesale and retail trade; repair of motor vehicles, motorcycles and personal and household goods	10,830.7	12,227.6	13,801.8
Hotels and restaurants	1,182.4	1,341.4	1,525.8
Transport, storage and communications	12,693.6	14,410.3	14,937.6
Financial intermediation	3,234.0	3,606.0	4,327.1
Real estate, renting and business activities	8,587.0	10,201.3	10,901.3
Public administration and defence; compulsory social security	3,678.5	3,864.2	4,363.1
Education	4,412.1	4,754.1	5,234.2
Health and social work . . .	2,820.9	3,022.4	3,179.1
Other community, social and personal service activities . . .	3,611.4	4,170.7	4,561.0
Sub-total	78,145.1	87,749.6	96,195.9
Less Financial intermediation services indirectly measured	1,249.9	1,450.4	1,632.2
Gross value added in basic prices	76,895.2	86,299.2	94,563.7
Taxes on products . . . . } *Less* Subsidies on products . . }	10,483.2	11,595.3	13,459.9
GDP in market prices	87,378.4	97,894.5	108,023.6

BALANCE OF PAYMENTS
(US $ million)

	1999	2000	2001
Exports of goods f.o.b. . . .	2,453.1	3,311.4	3,338.1
Imports of goods f.o.b. . . .	−3,330.6	−4,079.5	−4,125.0
Trade balance	−877.5	−768.1	−786.9
Exports of services	1,489.7	1,499.0	1,642.8
Imports of services	−917.6	−936.3	−1,064.9
Balance on goods and services .	−305.4	−205.4	−209.0
Other income received . . .	133.8	117.6	170.6
Other income paid	−235.5	−321.7	−451.8
Balance on goods, services and income	−407.1	−409.6	−490.1
Current transfers received . . .	153.7	144.7	180.4
Current transfers paid	−41.2	−29.1	−29.3
Current balance	−294.6	−294.0	−339.0
Capital account (net) . . .	1.2	16.5	5.1
Direct investment abroad . .	−82.9	−63.4	−199.6
Direct investment from abroad . .	305.2	387.3	539.4
Portfolio investment assets . . .	−132.3	39.8	13.1
Portfolio investment liabilities . .	153.3	75.6	83.0
Financial derivatives assets .	—	−4.7	−0.1
Financial derivatives liabilities .	—	5.4	−2.0
Other investment assets . .	−110.3	−177.1	−297.7
Other investment liabilities . .	285.2	143.8	170.5
Net errors and omissions . . .	−5.4	−1.6	−12.8
Overall balance	119.3	127.6	−40.3

Source: IMF, *International Financial Statistics*.

External Trade

PRINCIPAL COMMODITIES
(million kroons)

Imports c.i.f.	1999	2000	2001
Prepared foodstuffs; beverages spirits and vinegar; tobacco and manufactured substitutes . .	2,715.7	3,009.0	3,368.3
Mineral products	3,044.0	4,416.3	4,616.9
Mineral fuels, mineral oils and products of their distillation; bituminous substances, etc. .	2,846.0	4,239.5	4,389.1
Products of chemical or allied industries	3,985.9	4,791.6	5,273.6
Plastics, rubber and articles thereof	2,456.7	3,258.0	3,586.1
Plastics and articles thereof . .	1,989.7	2,675.4	2,941.8
Paper-making material; paper and paperboard and articles thereof .	1,586.3	2,174.2	2,213.1
Textiles and textile articles . . .	4,493.9	5,416.3	5,962.2
Base metals and articles of base metal	4,121.3	5,867.8	6,087.8
Iron and steel	1,586.7	2,521.6	2,149.3
Machinery and mechanical appliances; electrical equipment; sound and television apparatus .	15,474.3	27,788.5	25,134.4
Nuclear reactors, boilers machinery and mechanical appliances; parts thereof . .	5,069.9	6,426.2	7,180.6
Vehicles, aircraft, vessels and associated transport equipment	3,852.5	4,997.7	6,686.5
Vehicles other than railway or tramway rolling-stock, and parts and accessories . . .	3,405.1	4,570.3	5,952.9
Total (incl. others)	50,452.1	72,717.2	75,074.6

Exports f.o.b.	1999	2000	2001
Live animals and animal products	1,389.4	1,967.9	2,423.1
Prepared foodstuffs; beverages spirits and vinegar; tobacco and manufactured substitutes . .	989.1	857.2	1,801.3
Products of chemical or allied industries	1,431.1	1,997.9	2,477.9
Wood and articles thereof; wood charcoal	6,612.3	7,201.4	7,642.0
Textiles and textile articles . . .	4,929.9	6,094.6	6,633.7
Knitted and non-knitted clothing and accessories	2,944.2	3,338.0	3,622.1
Base metals and articles of base metal	2,722.0	3,828.7	3,974.5
Articles of iron or steel . .	1,301.9	1,545.4	1,984.4
Machinery and mechanical appliances; electrical equipment; sound and television apparatus .	8,522.2	20,182.2	19,121.3
Nuclear reactors, boilers machinery and mechanical appliances; parts thereof . .	1,356.4	1,879.2	2,042.9
Electrical machinery equipment and parts; sound and television apparatus parts and accessories	7,165.8	18,302.9	17,078.4
Vehicles, aircraft, vessels and associated transport equipment .	1,061.7	1,383.6	1,860.5
Miscellaneous manufactured articles	2,757.0	3,578.6	4,665.8
Furniture; bedding, mattresses cushions, etc.; lamps and lighting fittings; prefabricated buildings	2,515.8	3,196.7	4,212.5
Total (incl. others)	35,408.9	53,892.4	57,829.9

PRINCIPAL TRADING PARTNERS
(million kroons)

Imports c.i.f.	1999	2000	2001
Belarus	346.3	569.9	824.4
Belgium	883.2	1,218.1	1,430.3
China, People's Repub.	650.5	2,560.5	6,543.5
Czech Republic	379.2	686.4	894.8
Denmark	1,409.9	1,796.8	1,893.9
Finland	13,077.8	19,809.7	13,550.4
France	1,153.1	1,533.5	1,837.2
Germany	5,247.4	6,841.7	8,224.4
Hungary	335.0	205.4	778.0
Ireland	330.0	389.5	761.7
Italy	1,790.9	2,062.7	2,478.0
Japan	2,709.9	4,371.1	3,340.8
Latvia	1,192.4	1,856.7	1,681.4
Lithuania	903.0	1,184.5	1,950.8
Netherlands	1,308.2	1,524.6	1,851.2
Norway	522.1	981.2	801.4
Poland	1,048.8	1,313.8	1,691.9
Russia	4,043.7	6,123.9	6,097.2
Sweden	5,402.2	7,110.2	6,917.9
Switzerland	574.2	578.0	699.2
Ukraine	494.0	572.0	765.1
United Kingdom	1,293.4	1,650.5	1,772.6
USA	1,415.5	1,586.1	1,713.6
Total (incl. others)	50,452.1	72,217.2	75,074.6

Exports f.o.b.	1999	2000	2001
Belgium	416.4	479.9	387.2
Denmark	1,668.5	1,849.8	2,029.5
Finland	8,254.2	17,431.2	19,575.7
France	501.4	728.3	628.4
Germany	2,998.0	4,579.3	4,005.1
Italy	396.2	536.8	564.3
Latvia	2,936.9	3,789.5	4,014.4
Lithuania	1,200.9	1,511.1	1,732.1
Netherlands	913.9	1,324.0	1,601.8
Norway	915.2	1,267.7	1,617.6
Russia	1,187.0	1,278.1	1,593.9
Sweden	8,039.5	11,050.1	8,096.2
Ukraine	673.2	640.3	828.5
United Kingdom	1,993.7	2,351.5	2,434.4
USA	679.5	721.5	1,057.8
Total (incl. others)	35,408.9	53,892.4	57,829.9

Transport

DOMESTIC PASSENGER TRAFFIC
(million passenger-kilometres)

	2000	2001	2002
Railway traffic	263	183	177
Road traffic (bus traffic)	2,630	2,461	2,330
Sea traffic	455	376	420
Air traffic	303	310	355
Total public transport	3,651	3,330	3,282

DOMESTIC FREIGHT TRAFFIC
(million ton-kilometres)

	2000	2001	2002
Railway traffic	8,102	8,557	9,697
Road traffic	3,932	4,677	4,387
Sea traffic	4,304	2,943	1,958
Air traffic	5	4	5
Total public transport	16,343	16,181	16,047

ROAD TRAFFIC
('000 motor vehicles in use at 31 December)

	2000	2001	2002
Passenger cars	463.9	407.3	400.7
Buses and coaches	6.1	5.5	5.3
Lorries and vans	82.1	80.5	80.2
Motor cycles	6.7	6.8	7.3

SHIPPING

Merchant Fleet
(registered at 31 December)

	1999	2000	2001
Number of vessels	219	209	191
Total displacement (grt)	452,648	379,110	346.6

Source: Lloyd's Register-Fairplay, *World Fleet Statistics*.

International Sea-borne Freight Traffic
('000 metric tons)

	2000	2001	2002
Goods loaded	36,037	37,435	41,835
Goods unloaded	4,513	4,084	5,439

CIVIL AVIATION
(traffic on scheduled services)

	1996	1997	1998
Kilometres flown (million)	4	5	6
Passengers carried ('000)	149	231	297
Passenger-km (million)	114	147	177
Total ton-km (million)	11	14	17

Source: UN, *Statistical Yearbook*.

2000: Passengers carried 332,900; Freight carried (incl. mail) 5,700 metric tons; Passenger-km 302.5m.

2001: Passengers carried 362,300; Freight carried (incl. mail) 7,800 metric tons; Passenger-km 310.0m.

2002: Passengers carried 433,300; Freight carried (incl. mail) 5,900 metric tons; Passenger-km 354.06m.

Tourism

FOREIGN TOURIST ARRIVALS BY COUNTRY OF ORIGIN

	1999	2000	2001
Finland	1,199,584	1,198,887	1,058,386
Germany	n.a.	22,825	26,903
Sweden	33,148	39,267	17,664
USA	32,065	43,522	54,138
Total (incl. others)	1,350,366	1,369,159	1,231,620

Receipts from tourism (US $ million): 560 in 1999; 505 in 2000 (Source: World Bank).

Communications Media

	2000	2001	2002
Television receivers ('000 in use)	850	n.a.	n.a.
Telephones ('000 main lines in use)	523	504	475
Mobile cellular telephones ('000 subscribers).	557	651	881
Personal computers ('000 in use)	220	250	285
Internet users ('000) .	367	430	560
Book production: titles .	3,466	3,506	3,458
Book production: copies ('000) . .	5,931	5,456	5,362
Daily newspapers: number . .	16.	14	13
Non-daily newspapers: number .	93	95	114
Other periodicals: number . . .	956	1,088	1,143
Other periodicals: average annual circulation ('000 copies) . . .	19,843	20,378	21,782

1996: Radio receivers in use 221,000.

Sources: partly UN, *Statistical Yearbook* and International Telecommunication Union.

Education

(2001/02)

	Institutions	Teachers	Students
Pre-primary	624	8,070*	49,900
Primary	372	⎫	108,600
General secondary	236	17,986	99,000
Special.	46	⎭	5,800†
Vocational and professional .	80	1,779†	29,813†
Universities, etc.	33	3,052‡	52,786†

* Figure refers to 1997/98. Including staff in child care and pre-school institutions. (Source: UNESCO, *Statistical Yearbook*).
† Including students enrolled in evening and correspondence courses.
‡ Figure refers to 1996/97.
§ Figures refer to 2000/01.

Adult literacy rate (UNESCO estimates): 99.8% in 1995 (Source: UN Development Programme, *Human Development Report*).

Directory

The Constitution

A new Constitution, based on that of 1938, was adopted by a referendum held on 28 June 1992. It took effect on 3 July. The following is a summary of its main provisions.

FUNDAMENTAL RIGHTS, LIBERTIES AND DUTIES

Every child with one parent who is an Estonian citizen has the right, by birth, to Estonian citizenship. Anyone who, as a minor, lost his or her Estonian citizenship has the right to have his or her citizenship restored. The rights, liberties and duties of all persons, as listed in the Constitution, are equal for Estonian citizens as well as for citizens of foreign states and stateless persons who are present in Estonia.

All persons are equal before the law. No one may be discriminated against on the basis of nationality, race, colour, sex, language, origin, creed, political or other persuasions. Everyone has the right to the protection of the state and the law. Guaranteeing rights and liberties is the responsibility of the legislative, executive and judicial powers, as well as of local government. Everyone has the right to appeal to a court of law if his or her rights or liberties have been violated.

The state organizes vocational education and assists in finding work for persons seeking employment. Working conditions are under state supervision. Employers and employees may freely join unions and associations. Estonian citizens have the right to engage in commercial activities and to form profit-making associations. The property rights of everyone are inviolable. All persons legally present in Estonia have the right to freedom of movement and choice of abode. Everyone has the right to leave Estonia.

Everyone has the right to health care and to education. Education is compulsory for school-age children. Everyone has the right to instruction in Estonian.

The official language of state and local government authorities is Estonian. In localities where the language of the majority of the population is other than Estonian, local government authorities may use the language of the majority of the permanent residents of that locality for internal communication.

THE PEOPLE

The people exercise their supreme power through citizens who have the right to vote by: i) electing the Riigikogu (legislature); ii) participating in referendums. The right to vote belongs to every Estonian citizen who has attained the age of 18 years.

THE RIIGIKOGU

Legislative power rests with the Riigikogu (State Assembly). It comprises 101 members, elected every four years in free elections on the principle of proportionality. Every citizen entitled to vote who has attained 21 years of age may stand as a candidate for the Riigikogu.

The Riigikogu adopts laws and resolutions; decides on the holding of referendums; elects the President of the Republic; ratifies or rejects foreign treaties; authorizes the candidate for Prime Minister to form the Council of Ministers; adopts the national budget and approves the report on its execution; may declare a state of emergency, or, on the proposal of the President, declare a state of war, order mobilization and demobilization.

The Riigikogu elects from among its members a Chairman (Speaker) and two Deputy Chairmen to direct its work.

THE PRESIDENT

The President of the Republic is the Head of State of Estonia. The President represents Estonia in international relations; appoints and recalls, on the proposal of the Government, diplomatic representatives of Estonia and accepts letters of credence of diplomatic representatives accredited to Estonia; declares regular (and early) elections to the Riigikogu; initiates amendments to the Constitution; nominates the candidate for the post of Prime Minister; and is the Supreme Commander of Estonia's armed forces.

The President is elected by secret ballot of the Riigikogu for a term of five years. No person may be elected to the office for more than two consecutive terms. Any Estonian citizen by birth, who is at least 40 years of age, may stand as a candidate for President.

Should the President not be elected after three rounds of voting, the Speaker of the Riigikogu convenes, within one month, an Electoral Body to elect the President.

THE GOVERNMENT

Executive power is held by the Government of the Republic (Council of Ministers). The Government implements national, domestic and foreign policies; directs and co-ordinates the work of government institutions; organizes the implementation of legislation, the resolutions of the Riigikogu, and the edicts of the President; submits draft legislation to the Riigikogu, as well as foreign treaties; prepares a draft of the national budget and presents it to the Riigikogu; administers the implementation of the national budget; and organizes relations with foreign states.

The Government comprises the Prime Minister and Ministers. The President of the Republic nominates a candidate for Prime Minister, who is charged with forming a new government.

JUDICIAL SYSTEM

Justice is administered solely by the courts. They are independent in their work and administer justice in accordance with the Constitution and laws. The court system is comprised of rural and city, as well as administrative, courts (first level); district courts (second level); and the Supreme Court of the Republic of Estonia (the highest court in the land).

The Government

HEAD OF STATE

President: Arnold Rüütel (elected 21 September 2001; inaugurated 8 October).

COUNCIL OF MINISTERS
(July 2003)

A coalition of the Union for the Republic Res Publica, the Estonian Reform Party (ERP) and the Estonian People's Union.

Prime Minister: JUHAN PARTS (Res Publica).

Minister of Internal Affairs: MARGUS LEIVO (Estonian People's Union).

Minister of Foreign Affairs: KRISTIINA OJULAND (ERP).

Minister of Justice: KEN-MARTI VAHER (Res Publica).

Minister of Economic Affairs and Communications: MEELIS ATONEN (ERP).

Minister of Finance: TÕNIS PALTS (Res Publica).

Minister of the Environment: VILLU REILJAN (Estonian People's Union).

Minister of Culture: URMAS PAET (ERP).

Minister of Education and Science: TOIVO MAIMETS (Res Publica).

Minister of Agriculture: TIIT TAMMSAAR (Estonian People's Union).

Minister of Social Affairs: MARKO POMERANTS (Res Publica).

Minister of Defence: MARGUS HANSON (ERP).

Minister of Population and Ethnic Affairs: PAUL-EERIK RUMMO (Estonian People's Union).

Minister of Regional Affairs: JAAN ÕUNAPUU (Estonian People's Union).

MINISTRIES

Office of the Prime Minister: Rahukohtu 3, Tallinn 15161; tel. 631-6701; fax 631-6704; e-mail peaminister@rk.ee; internet www .riik.ee/primeminister/.

Ministry of Agriculture: Lai 39/41, Tallinn 15056; tel. 625-6101; fax 625-6200; e-mail pm@agri.ee; internet www.agri.ee.

Ministry of Culture: Suur Karja 23, Tallinn 15076; tel. 628-2222; fax 628-2200; e-mail info@kul.ee; internet www.kul.ee.

Ministry of Defence: Sakala 1, Tallinn 10141; tel. 640-6012; fax 640-6001; e-mail info@kmin.ee; internet www.mod.gov.ee.

Ministry of Economic Affairs and Communications: Harju 11, Tallinn 15072; tel. 625-6342; fax 631-3660; e-mail info@mkm.ee; internet www.mkm.ee.

Ministry of Education and Science: Munga 18, Tartu 50088; tel. 735-0222; fax 735-0250; e-mail hm@hm.ee; internet www.hm.ee.

Ministry of the Environment: Toompuiestee 24, Tallinn 15172; tel. 626-2800; fax 626-2801; e-mail min@ekm.envir.ee; internet www .envir.ee.

Ministry of Finance: Suur-Ameerika 1, Tallinn 15006; tel. 611-3558; fax 696-6810; e-mail info@fin.ee; internet www.fin.ee.

Ministry of Foreign Affairs: Islandi Väljak 1, Tallinn 15049; tel. 631-7000; fax 631-7099; e-mail vminfo@vm.ee; internet www.vm.ee.

Ministry of Internal Affairs: Pikk 61, Tallinn 15065; tel. 612-5001; fax 612-5087; e-mail sisemin@sisemin.gov.ee; internet www .sisemin.gov.ee.

Ministry of Justice: Tõnismägi 5A, Tallinn 15191; tel. 620-8100; fax 620-8109; e-mail sekretar@just.ee; internet www.just.ee.

Ministry of Population and Ethnic Affairs: Tallinn.

Ministry of Regional Affairs: Tallinn.

Ministry of Social Affairs: Gonsiori 29, Tallinn 15191; tel. 626-9700; fax 626-9802; e-mail smin@sm.ee; internet www.sm.ee.

President and Legislature

PRESIDENT

A presidential election was held on 27–28 August 2001 in the Riigikogu. The first round was contested by Andres Tarand and Peeter Kreitzberg, neither of whom achieved the necessary two-thirds' majority (68 votes). Tarand was subsequently replaced by Peeter Tulviste; Peeter Kreitzberg retained his candidacy. However, neither candidate secured the requisite majority after two further rounds of voting. A larger electoral college, comprising the 101 parliamentary deputies and 266 representatives from local government, was convened on 21 September. Four candidates contested the first round of the election and, as no candidate achieved the necessary 185 votes, the leading two candidates, Toomas Savi and Arnold Rüütel, proceeded to the second round of voting. The election was won by Arnold Rüütel, with 186 votes.

Election, 21 September 2001

Candidate	First round votes*	Second round votes†
Arnold Rüütel	114	186
Toomas Savi	90	155
Peeter Tulviste	89	—
Peeter Kreitzberg	72	—

* There was one abstention and one elector was absent.
† There were 23 abstentions and two invalid votes, with one elector absent.

RIIGIKOGU
(State Assembly)

Riigikogu: Lossi plats 1a, Tallinn 15165; tel. 631-6331; fax 631-6334; e-mail riigikogu@riigikogu.ee; internet www.riigikogu.ee.

Speaker: ENE ERGMA.

Deputy Speakers: TOOMAS SAVI, PEETER KREITZBERG.

General Election, 2 March 2003

Parties	% of votes	Seats
Estonian Centre Party	25.4	28
Union for the Republic Res Publica	24.6	28
Estonian Reform Party	17.7	19
Estonian People's Union	13.0	13
Pro Patria (Fatherland) Union	7.3	7
People's Party Moderates	7.0	6
Others	5.0	0
Total	**100.0**	**101**

Local Government

For administrative purposes, Estonia is divided into 15 counties (maakonds) and six cities. Each maakond is presided over by a county government (headed by a governor) and a county council. The counties are subdivided into 247 rural municipalities (vald) and towns (linn). There are also city councils and city governments, with each of the latter headed by a mayor. Local authority elections were held on 20 October 2002. In 2003 there were plans to reform the system of regional administration, and reduce the number of local government units through voluntary mergers.

Association of Estonian Cities: Varna-Viru 12, Tallinn 0001; tel. 694-3411; fax 694-3425; e-mail inga@ell.ee; internet www.ell.ee; Exec. Dir AIN KALMARU.

Harju County Government: Harju Maavalitsus, Roosikrantsi 12, Tallinn 15077; tel. 611-8701; fax 611-8602; e-mail maavalitsus@ harju.ee; internet www.harju.ee; Gov. ORM VALTSON.

Hiiu County Government: Hiiu Maavalitsus, Leigri 5, Kärdla 92401; tel. (46) 31-129; fax (46) 31-089; e-mail mv@mv.hiiumaa.ee; internet www.mv.hiiumaa.ee; Gov. HANNES MAASEL.

Ida-Viru County Government: Ida-Viru Maavalitsus, Keskväl-jaku 1, Jõhvi 41594; tel. (33) 21-201; fax (33) 21-240; e-mail ivmv@ ivmv.ee; internet www.ivmv.ee; Gov. LEO RAIDMA (acting).

Järva County Government: Järva Maavalitsus, Rüütli 25, Paide 72713; tel. (38) 59-601; fax (38) 50-519; e-mail jmv@jarvamv.ee; internet www.jarvamv.ee; Gov. TÄHVE MILT.

Jõgeva County Government: Jõgeva Maavalitsus, Suur 3, Jõgeva 48306; tel. (77) 66-301; fax (77) 66-322; e-mail margus@jogevamv.ee; internet www.jogevamv.ee/maavalitsus; Gov. MARGUS ORO.

Lääne County Government: Lääne Maavalitsus, Lahe 8, Haap-salu 90503; tel. (47) 25-600; fax (47) 26-601; e-mail info@lmv.ee; internet www.lmv.ee; Gov. JANNUS SAHK.

Lääne-Viru County Government: Lääne-Viru Maavalitsus, Kreutzvaldi 5, Rakvere 44314; tel. (32) 58-001; fax (32) 58-003; e-mail marko@l-virumv.ee; internet www.l-virumv.ee; Gov. MARKO POMERANTS.

Pärnu County Government: Pärnu Maavalitsus, Akadeemia 2, Pärnu 80088; tel. (44) 79-733; fax (44) 79-735; e-mail toomas .kivimagi@mv.parnu.ee; internet www.mv.parnu.ee; Gov. TOOMAS KIVIMÄGI.

Põlva County Government: Põlvamaa Maavalitsus, Kesk 20, Põlva 63308; tel. (79) 94-238; fax (79) 94-128; e-mail mv@polvamaa .ee; internet www.polvamaa.ee; Gov. KOIT NOOK.

Rapla County Government: Rapla Maavalitsus, Tallinn mnt. 14, Rapla 79513; tel. (48) 55-951; fax (48) 55-672; e-mail maavanem@raplamv.ee; internet www.raplamv.ee/mv; Gov. KALLE TALVISTE.

Saare County Government: Saare Maavalitsus, Lossi 1, Kuressaare 93816; tel. (45) 20-501; fax (45) 20-503; e-mail maavanem@saare.ee; internet www.saare.ee; Gov. HANS TEIV.

Tartu County Government: Tartu Maavalitsus, Riia 15, Tartu 51010; tel. (7) 305-200; fax (7) 305-201; e-mail mv@tartumaa.ee; internet www.tartumaa.ee; Gov. EHA PÄRN (acting).

Valga County Government: Valga Maavalitsus, Kesk 12, Valga 68203; tel. (76) 66-111; fax (76) 66-157; e-mail info@valgamv.ee; internet www.valgamv.ee; Gov. GEORG TRAŠANOV (acting).

Viljandi County Government: Viljandi Maavalitsus, Vabaduse plats 2, Viljandi 71020; tel. (43) 30-400; fax (43) 30-404; e-mail maaval@viljandimaa.ee; internet mv.viljandimaa.ee; Gov. KALLE KÜTTIS.

Võru County Government: Võru Maavalitsus, Jüri 12, Võru 65620; tel. (78) 68-301; fax (78) 68-302; e-mail maavanem@mv.werro.ee; internet www.werro.ee/mv; Gov. MAIT KLAASEN.

Kohtla-Järve City Government: Kohtla-Järve Linnavalitsus, Keskallee 19, Kohtla-Järve 30395; tel. (33) 78-500; fax (33) 78-503; e-mail kjlv@estpak.ee; internet www.kjlv.ee; Mayor HANTS HINT.

Narva City Government: Narva Linnavalitsus, Peetri plats 5, Narva 20308; tel. (35) 99-001; fax (35) 99-010; e-mail narvalv@narva.ee; internet www.narva.ee; Mayor TARMO TAMMISTE.

Pärnu City Government: Pärnu Linnavalitsus, Uus 4, Pärnu 80098; tel. (44) 31-405; fax (44) 31-019; internet www.parnu.ee; Mayor MART ALLIKU.

Sillamäe City Government: Sillamäe Linnavalitsus, Kesk 27, Sillamäe 40231; tel. (39) 25-700; fax (39) 25-701; e-mail linnavalitsus@sillamaelv.ee; internet www.sillamaelv.ee; Mayor AIN KIVIORG.

Tallinn City Government: Tallinn Linnavalitsus, Vabaduse 7, Tallinn 15199; tel. (2) 640-4141; fax 640-4327; e-mail foreign@tallinnlv.ee; internet www.tallinn.ee; Mayor EDGAR SAVISAAR.

Tartu City Government: Tartu Linnavalitsus, Raekoda, Tartu 51003; tel. (7) 361-111; fax (7) 361-106; e-mail lv@raad.tartu.ee; internet www.tartu.ee; Mayor ANDRUS ANSIP.

Political Organizations

Democrats–Estonian Democratic Party: Ahdri 6 307, Tallinn 10151; tel. 625-9890; fax 625-9810; e-mail demokraatlik.partei@mail.ee; internet www.demokraadid.ee; former Estonian Blue Party; Chair. JAAN LAAS.

Estonian Centre Party (Eesti Keskerakond): Toom-Rüütli 3/5, Tallinn 10130 POB 3737, Tallinn 0090; tel. 627-3460; fax 627-3461; e-mail keskerakond@keskerakond.ee; internet www.keskerakond.ee; absorbed the Estonian Green Party in mid-1998; f. 1991; Chair. EDGAR SAVISAAR; 5,000 mems.

Estonian Christian People's Party (Eesti Kristlik Rahvapartei): Narva mnt. 51, Tallinn 10152; tel. 504-5760; fax 678-2311; e-mail ekrp@ekrp.ee; internet www.ekrp.ee; f. 1998; Chair. ALDO VINKEL.

Estonian Conservative Party: Järva 19, Pärnu 80023; tel. 561-6207; fax (2) 422-969; e-mail konservatiivid@hot.ee; internet www.hot.ee/konservatiivid; Leader ANDRO ROOS.

Estonian Independence Party: opposes European Union (EU) membership; planned merger with the National Conservative Party-Farmers' Assembly; Chair. VELLO LEITO; 1,047 mems (2002).

Estonian People's Union (Eestimaa Rahvaliit): Marja 4D, Tallinn 10617; tel. 611-2909; fax 611-2908; e-mail erl@erl.ee; internet www.erl.ee; f. 2000 by merger of the Estonian Pensioners' and Families' Party and the Estonian Rural People's Union; merged with the New Estonia Party in Jan. 2003; right-wing; Hon. Chair. ARNOLD RÜÜTEL; Chair. VILLU REILJAN; 8,800 mems.

Estonian Reform Party (ERP) (Eesti Reformierakond): Tõnismagi 3A–15, Tallinn 0001; tel. 640-8740; fax 640-8741; e-mail info@reform.ee; internet www.reform.ee; f. 1994; liberal; Gen. Sec. HEIKI KRANICH; Chair. SIIM KALLAS.

Estonian Social-Democratic Labour Party (Eesti Sotsiaaldemokraatlik Tööpartei): Rävala puiestee 8, POB 4102, Tallinn 10143; tel. 661-2406; fax 661-2402; e-mail esdtp@solo.ee; internet www.esdtp.ee; f. 1920 as the Communist Party of Estonia; renamed Estonian Democratic Labour Party in 1992 and as above in 1997; left-wing; Chair. TIIT TOOMSALU; Dep. Chair. ENDEL PAAP; 1,250 mems (2003).

Estonian United People's Party (Eestimaa Ühendatud Rahvapartei): Estonia pst. 3/5, Tallinn 10143; tel. 645-5335; fax 645-5336;

e-mail eurp@eurp.ee; internet www.eurp.ee; f. 1994; represents the Russian-speaking minority in Estonia; Chair. VIKTOR ANDREYEV.

Farmers' Union (Põllumeeste Kogu): POB 543, Tallinn 0010; tel. (2) 437-733; f. 1992; Chair. ELDUR PARDER.

Moderates' Women's Assembly (Mõõdukad Naiskogu): Tallinn; e-mail moodukad@datanet.ee; f. 1996 to encourage women to take part in politics; Pres. HELJO PIKHOF.

National Conservative Party-Farmers' Assembly: Tallinn; f. 2002 by former mems of the Pro Patria (Fatherland) Union; Chair. MART HELME; approx. 1,700 mems (2002).

People's Party Moderates (Mõõdukad): Vana–Viru 4, Tallinn 10111 POB 3437, Tallinn 19090; tel. 641-2227; fax 644-4605; e-mail kirjad@moodukad.ee; internet www.moodukad.ee; f. 1999 by merger of the People's Party and the Moderates' Party; social-democratic party; Chair. IVARI PADAR; Sec.-Gen. TONU KOIV.

Progressive Party (Arengupartei): Tallinn; e-mail arengupartei@online.ee; internet www.arengupartei.ee; f. 1996 following a split in the Estonian Centre Party; Chair. ANDRA VEIDEMANN; Sec.-Gen. TOIVO KEVA; 1,300 mems.

Pro Patria (Fatherland) Union (Isamaaliit): Wismari 11, Tallinn 10136; tel. 669-1070; fax 660-1071; e-mail info@isamaaliit.ee; internet www.isamaaliit.ee; f. 1995 by merger of the National Fatherland Party Isamaa; f. 1992; and the Estonian National Independence Party; right-wing party; f. 1988; Chair. TUNNE KELAM; Sec.-Gen. TARMO LOODUS; 2,900 mems.

Republican Party (Vabariiklik Partei): Kuperjanovi 56-5, Tartu 50409; tel. 521-4512; e-mail leping.vp@mail.ee; internet www.vabariiklikpartei.ee; f. 1999; Chair. KRISTJAN-OLARI LEPING.

Russian Democratic Movement: Tallinn; tel. (2) 440-421; fax (2) 441-237; f. 1991 to promote domestic peace and mutual understanding between Estonians and Russians living in Estonia.

Russian Party in Estonia: Tallinn; f. 1994; merged with the Russian People's Party of Estonia in early 1996; represents the Russian-speaking minority in Estonia; opposed to North Atlantic Treaty Organization (NATO) membership; absorbed the Estonian Unity Party, the Russian-Baltic Party and the Russian Unity Party in Dec. 2002; Chair. STANISLAV CHEREPANOV.

Union for the Republic Res Publica: Hobujaama 12/Narva mnt. 9E, Tallinn 10151; tel. (2) 610-9244; fax (2) 610-9243; e-mail respublica@respublica.ee; internet www.respublica.ee; f. 2001; right-wing; Chair. JUHAN PARTS; 2,500 mems.

Diplomatic Representation

EMBASSIES IN ESTONIA

Austria: Vambola 6, Tallinn 14114; tel. 627-8740; fax 631-4365; e-mail embassy@austrianembassy.ee; internet www.austrianembassy.ee; Ambassador Dr JAKUB FORST-BATTAGLIA.

Belarus: Magdaleena 3, Section B, Tallinn 11312; tel. and fax 655-8001; Gen. Consul PETR KRECHKO.

Canada: Toom-Kooli 13, Tallinn 10130; tel. 627-3311; fax 627-3310; e-mail tallinn@canada.ee; internet www.canada.ee; Ambassador ROBERT ANDRIGO.

China, People's Republic: Narva mnt. 98, Tallinn 15009; tel. 601-5830; fax 601-5833; e-mail office@chinaembassy.ee; internet www.chinaembassy.ee; Ambassador CONG JUN.

Czech Republic: Roosikrantsi 11, Tallinn 10119; tel. 627-4400; fax 631-4716; e-mail embassy.mzv.cz; internet www.mfa.cz/tallinn; Ambassador VLADISLAV LABUDEK.

Denmark: Wismari 5, Tallinn 15047; tel. 630-6400; fax 630-6421; e-mail tllamb@um.dk; internet www.denmark.ee; Ambassador JØRGEN MUNK RASMUSSEN.

Finland: Kohtu 4, Tallinn 15180; tel. 610-3200; fax 610-3281; e-mail info@datanet.ee; internet www.finemb.ee; Ambassador JAAKKO BLOMBERG.

France: Toom-Kuninga 20, Tallinn 15185; tel. 631-1492; fax 631-1385; e-mail france@datanet-ee.org; internet www.ambafrance-ee.org; Ambassador CHANTAL DE GHAISNE DE BOURMONT.

Germany: Toom-Kuninga 11, Tallinn 15048; tel. 627-5300; fax 627-5304; e-mail deutschland@online.ee; internet www.germany.ee; Ambassador JÜRGEN DRÖGE.

Hungary: Narva mnt. 122, Tallinn 10127; tel. 605-1880; fax 605-4088; e-mail huembtal@mfa.neti.ee; Ambassador LÁSZLÓ NIKICSER.

Ireland: Demini Bldg, Virui/Vene 2, 2nd Floor, Tallinn 10123; tel. 681-1888; fax 681-1889; e-mail embassytallinn@eircom.net; Ambassador SEAN FARRELL.

Italy: Vene 2, 3rd Floor, Tallinn 10123; tel. 627-6160; fax 631-1370; e-mail italemb1@online.ee; internet www.italembtallinn.ee; Ambassador Ruggero Vozzi.

Japan: Harju 6, Tallinn 10130; tel. 631-0531; fax 631-0533; e-mail jaapansk@online.ee; Chargé d'affaires a.i. Keiichi Hasegawa.

Latvia: Tõnismägi 10, Tallinn 10119; tel. 646-1313; fax 631-1366; Ambassador Edgars Skuja.

Lithuania: Uus tn. 15, Tallinn 15070; tel. 631-4030; fax 641-2013; e-mail amber@anet.ee; internet www.hot.ee/lietambasada; Ambassador Antanas Vinkus.

Netherlands: Harju 6, Tallin 10130; tel. 631-0580; fax 631-0583; e-mail neth.gov@delfi.ee; internet www.netherlandsembassy.ee; Ambassador Joanna M. P. F. van Vliet.

Norway: Harju 6, Tallinn 15054; tel. 627-1000; fax 627-1001; e-mail emb.tallinn@mfa.no; Ambassador Per K. Pedersen.

Poland: Pärnu mnt. 8, Tallinn 10503; tel. 627-8206; fax 644-5221; e-mail ambrptal@netexpress.ee; internet www.poola.ee; Ambassador Wojciech Wróblewski.

Russia: Pikk 19, Tallinn 10133; tel. 646-4175; fax 646-4178; e-mail vensaat@online.ee; internet www.estonia.mid.ru; Ambassador Konstantin Provalov.

Sweden: Pikk 28, Tallinn 15055; tel. 640-5600; fax 640-5695; e-mail swedemb@estpak.ee; internet www.sweden.ee; Ambassador Elisabet Borsiin Bonnier.

Turkey: Narva mnt. 30, Tallinn 10152; tel. 627-2880; fax 627-2885; e-mail tallinn.be@mfa.gov.tr; Ambassador Ömer Altug.

Ukraine: Lahe 6, Tallinn 15170; tel. 601-5815; fax 601-5816; e-mail embukr@eol.ee; internet www.uninet.ee/~embukra; Ambassador Mykola Makarevych.

United Kingdom: Wismari 6, Tallinn 10136; tel. 667-4700; fax 667-4755; e-mail information@britishembassy.ee; internet www.britishembassy.ee; Ambassador Sarah Squire.

USA: Kentmanni 20, Tallinn 15099; tel. 668-8100; fax 668-8134; e-mail tallinn@usemb.ee; internet www.usemb.ee; Ambassador Joseph M. DeThomas.

Judicial System

Supreme Court of the Republic of Estonia
Lossi 17, Tartu 50093; tel. (7) 309-002; fax (7) 309-003; e-mail nc@nc.ee; internet www.nc.ee.

Chief Justice and Chairman of the Constitutional Review Chamber: Uno Lõhmus.

Chairman of the Civil Chamber: Jaano Odar.

Chairman of the Criminal Chamber: Jüri Ilvest.

Chairman of the Administrative Law Chamber: Tõnu Anton.

Legal Chancellor's Office: Tõnismägi 16, Tallinn 15193; tel. 693-8400; fax 693-8401; e-mail info@lc.gov.ee; internet www.oiguskantsler.ee; f. 1993; reviews general application of legislative and executive powers and of local governments for conformity with the constitution, supervises activities of state agencies in guaranteeing constitutional rights and freedoms; Legal Chancellor Allar Jõks.

Public Prosecutor's Office: Wismari 7, Tallinn 15188; tel. 631-3002; fax 645-1475; e-mail info@prokuratuur.ee; internet www.prokuratuur.ee; **State Prosecutor-Gen.:** Raivo Sepp.

Religion

CHRISTIANITY

Protestant Churches

Consistory of the Estonian Evangelical Lutheran Church of Estonia: Kiriku plats 3, Tallinn 10130; tel. 627-7350; fax 627-7352; e-mail konsistoorium@eelk.ee; internet www.eelk.ee; Archbishop Jaan Kiivit.

Estonian Conference of Seventh-day Adventists: Lille 18, Tartu 51010; tel. (7) 343-211; fax (7) 343-389; e-mail office@advent.ee; internet www.advent.ee; f. 1917; Chair. Ülo Pärna.

Union of Evangelical Christian and Baptist Churches of Estonia: Pargi 9, Tallinn 11620; tel. 670-0698; fax 650-6008; e-mail eekbl@ekklesia.ee; internet www.ekklesia.ee; Pres. Helari Puu.

United Methodist Church in Estonia: Apteegi 3, Tallinn 10146; tel. (2) 445-447; fax 631-3482; e-mail keskus@emk.edu.ee; internet www.metodistikirik.ee; f. 1907; Superintendent Olav Pärnamets.

The Eastern Orthodox Church
Between 1923 and 1940 the Estonian Apostolic Orthodox Church (EAOC) was subordinate to the Constantinople Ecumenical Patriarchate (based in İstanbul, Turkey). Following the Soviet occupation of Estonia in 1940, the EAOC was banned and its churches and communities were placed under the jurisdiction of the Moscow Patriarchate. The leaders of the EAOC went into exile in Stockholm, Sweden. After the restoration of Estonian independence, in 1993 Estonia recognized the EAOC as the legal successor of the Orthodox Church in operation before the Second World War, and in February 1996 the Constantinople Patriarchate restored the EAOC to its jurisdiction. The Estonian Orthodox Church of the Moscow Patriarchate was officially registered in April 2002.

Estonian Apostolic Orthodox Church (EAOC): Tallinn; Chair. of Synod Nikolai Suuresoot; 59 congregations.

Estonian Orthodox Church of Moscow Patriarchate (EOCMP): Pikk 64/4, Tallinn 10133; tel. 641-1301; fax 641-1302; Archbishop Kornelius; 32 congregations.

The Roman Catholic Church
At 31 December 2001 there were an estimated 5,745 Roman Catholic adherents in Estonia.

Office of the Apostolic Administrator: Jaan Poska 47, Tallinn 10150; tel. 601-3079; fax 601-3190; e-mail admapost@online.ee; Apostolic Administrator Most Rev. Most Rev. Peter Stephan Zurbriggen (Titular Archbishop of Glastonia (Glastonbury), Apostolic Nuncio to Lithuania, Estonia and Latvia (resident in Vilnius, Lithuania)).

Roman Catholic Parish of St Peter and St Paul in Tallinn: Vene 18, Tallinn 0001; tel. 644-6367; fax 644-4678; Parish Priest Fr Zbigniew Piłat.

Tallinn Parish of the Ukrainian Catholic (Uniate) Church: Võrgu 13–6, Tallinn; tel. 632-4306; Chair. of Bd Anatolii Lyutyuk.

ISLAM

Estonian Islamic Congregation: Sütiste 52–76, Tallinn 0034; tel. (2) 522-403; f. 1928; Chair. of Bd Timur Seifullen.

JUDAISM

Hineirry Jewish Progressive Community of Narva: Pk 955, Narva 5; tel. (35) 426-26; Chair. of Bd Aleksandr Spivak.

Jewish Community of Estonia: Karu 16, Tallinn; POB 3576, Tallinn 10507; tel. and fax 662-3034; e-mail community@jewish.ee; internet www.jewish.ee; Chair. Cilja Laud.

Jewish Progressive Community in Tallinn: POB 200, Tallinn; Chair. of Bd David Slomka.

The Press

In 2001 there were 14 officially registered daily newspapers and 95 non-daily newspapers published in Estonia. In that year 10 daily newspapers and 80 non-daily newspapers were published in Estonian. In 2001 1,088 periodicals were published, 881 of which were published in Estonian.

PRINCIPAL NEWSPAPERS
In Estonian except where otherwise stated.

Äripäev (Business Daily): Pärnu mnt. 105, Tallinn 19094; tel. 667-0222; fax 667-0165; e-mail mbp@mbp.ee; internet www.mbp.ee; f. 1989; five days a week; business and finance; Editor-in-Chief Igor Rõtov; circ. 17,200.

Den za Dujan (Day After Day): Pärnu mnt. 130, Tallinn 11313; tel. 678-8288; fax 678-8290; e-mail ambre@dd.ee; internet www.dd.ee; f. 1991; weekly; in Russian; Editor-in-Chief Jana Litvinova; circ. 20,000.

Eesti Ekspress (Estonian Express): Narva mnt. 11e, Tallinn 10151; tel. 669-8080; fax 669-8154; e-mail ekspress@ekspress.ee; internet www.ekspress.ee; f. 1989; weekly; Editor-in-Chief Aavo Kokk; circ. 49,300.

Eesti Kirik (Estonian Church): Ülikooli, Tartu 51003; tel. (7) 431-437; fax (7) 433-243; f. 1923; weekly; Editor-in-Chief Sirje Semm; circ. 2,100.

Eesti Päevaleht (Estonian Daily): Pärnu mnt. 67a, POB 433, Tallinn 10151; tel. 614-4498; fax 614-4334; e-mail mail@epl.ee;

internet www.epl.ee; f. 1905; daily; Editor-in-Chief PRIIT HÕBEMÄGI; circ. 37,000.

Estonija: Madala 16, Tallinn 10315; tel. 665-1100; fax 665-1111; e-mail vestimg@teleport.ee; internet www.vesti.ee; f. 1940; five days a week in Russian (with Estonian edn Mon.); Editor-in-Chief PAVEL IVANOV; circ. 6,100.

Maaleht (Country News): Toompuiestee 16, Tallinn 10137; tel. 661-3718; fax 662-2292; e-mail ml@maaleht.ee; internet www.maaleht .ee; f. 1987; weekly; problems and aspects of politics, culture, agriculture and country life; Editor-in-Chief SULEV VALNER; circ. 42,000.

ME: POB 120, Kentmanni 18, Tallinn 10502; tel. 628-6123; fax 646-1623; e-mail moles@infonet.ee; three days a week; in Russian; Editor-in-Chief ARKADII PRISJAZHNÕI; circ. 5,100.

Meie Meel (Our Mind): POB 104, Tallinn 0090; tel. (2) 681-253; fax 646-1625; e-mail meiemeel@zzz.ee; f. 1991; weekly; youth paper; Editor-in-Chief MARE VETEMAA; circ. 20,700.

Postimees (Postman): Maakri 23A, Tallinn 10145; tel. 666-2302; fax 666-2301; e-mail erik.roose@postimees.ee; internet www.postimees .ee; f. 1857; daily; Editor-in-Chief URMAS KLAAS; circ. 60,200.

Sirp: POB 388, Tallinn 10503; tel. 640-5770; fax 640-5771; e-mail sirp@sirp.ee; internet www.sirp.ee; f. 1940; weekly; cultural; Editor-in-Chief MIHKEL MUTT; circ. 3,500.

SL Õhtuleht (Evening Gazette): Narva mnt. 13, POB 106, Tallinn 10501; tel. 614-4805; fax 614-4001; e-mail priit@sloleht.ee; internet www.sloleht.ee; f. 2000 by merger of Õhtuleht and Sõnumileht newspapers; daily; Editor-in-Chief VÄINO KOORBERG; circ. 67,200.

PRINCIPAL PERIODICALS

Akadeemia: Ülikooli 21, Tartu 51007; tel. (7) 423-050; fax (7) 423-146; e-mail akadeemia@akad.ee; internet www.akad.ee; f. 1989; monthly; journal of the Union of Writers; Editor-in-Chief TOOMAS KIHO; circ. 2,500.

Eesti Arst (Estonian Physician): Pepleri 32, Tartu 51010; tel. and fax (7) 427-825; e-mail ea@gennet.ee; internet www.eestiarst.ee; f. 1922; monthly; Editor-in-Chief VÄINO SINISALU; circ. 3,500.

Eesti Loodus (Estonian Nature): Veski 4, POB 110, Tartu 50002; tel. (7) 421-186; fax (7) 421-143; e-mail toimetus@el.loodus.ee; internet www.loodus.ee/el; f. 1933; monthly; popular science; illustrated; Editor-in-Chief TOOMAS KUKK; circ. 5,200.

Eesti Naine (Estonian Woman): Maakri 23A, Tallinn 10145; tel. 666-2627; fax 666-2557; e-mail katrin.streimann@kirjastus.ee; internet www.kirjastus.ee/eestinaine; f. 1924; monthly; Editor-in-Chief KATRIN STREIMANN; circ. 24,000.

Hea Laps (Good Kid): Harju 1, Tallinn 10146; tel. 631-4428; monthly; for children; Editor-in-Chief LEELO TUNGAL.

Horisont (Horizon): Narva mnt. 5, Tallinn 0117; tel. 661-6163; fax 641-8033; e-mail horisont@horisont.ee; f. 1967; 6 a year; popular scientific; Editor-in-Chief INDREK ROHTMETS; circ. 3,000.

Keel ja Kirjandus (Language and Literature): Roosikrantsi 6, Tallinn 10119; tel. 644-9228; fax 644-1800; e-mail kk@eki.ee; f. 1958; monthly; joint edition of the Academy of Sciences and the Union of Writers; Editor-in-Chief MART MERI; circ. 1,100.

Kodukiri (Your Home): Maakri 23A, Tallinn 10145; tel. 666-2550; fax 666-2558; e-mail velve.saar@kirjastus.ee; f. 1992; monthly; Editor-in-Chief KATRIN KUUSEMÄE; circ. 50,000.

Linguistica Uralica: Roosikrantsi 6, Tallinn 10119; tel. 644-0745; e-mail lu@eki.ee; internet www.gaid.gi.ee/eap/l.-u.htm; f. 1965; Editor-in-Chief VÄINO KLAUS; circ. 400.

Looming (Creation): Harju 1, Tallinn 10146; tel. (2) 627-6420; e-mail looming@hot.ee; f. 1923; journal of the Union of Writers; fiction, poetry, literary criticism; Editor-in-Chief UDO UIBO; circ. 1,800.

Loomingu Raamatukogu (Library of Creativity): Harju 1, Tallinn 10146; tel. 627-6425; e-mail loominguraamatukogu@hot.ee; f. 1957; journal of the Union of Writers; poetry, fiction and non-fiction by Estonian and foreign authors; Editor-in-Chief TOOMAS HAUG; circ. 1,600.

Maakodu (Country Home): Toompuiestee 16, Tallinn 10137; tel. 660-5306; fax 662-2292; e-mail meelim@maaleht.ee; internet www .maaleht.ee; f. 1989; monthly; Editor-in-Chief MEELI MÜÜRIPEAL; circ. 12,000.

Maamajandus (Country Economy): Toompuiestee 16, Tallinn 10137; tel. 660-5305; fax 662-2292; e-mail ylo@maaleht.ee; internet www.maaleht.ee; f. 2000; monthly; Editor-in-Chief ÜLO KALM; circ. 2,000.

Oil Shale: Estonia pst. 7, Tallinn 10143; tel. 646-7512; fax 646-6026; e-mail aili@kirj.ee; internet www.kirj.ee/oilshale; f. 1984; quarterly; geology, chemistry, mining, oil-shale industry; Editor-in-Chief JÜRI KANN; circ. 350.

Põllumajandus (Agriculture): Lai 39, Tallinn 0001; tel. 641-1161; f. 1932; monthly; Editor-in-Chief ARVO SIRENDI; circ. 1,000.

Täheke (Little Star): Pärnu mnt. 67A, Tallinn 10134; tel. 646-3697; e-mail tell@tallpost.ee; f. 1960; monthly; illustrated; for 6–10-year-olds; Editor-in-Chief ELJU SILD; circ. 3,500.

Teater, Muusika, Kino (Theatre, Music, Cinema): POB 3200, Narva mnt. 5, Tallinn 10117; tel. 660-1828; fax (2) 660-1887; e-mail tmk@estpak.ee; f. 1982; monthly; Editor-in-Chief JÜRI AARMA; circ. 1,500.

Vikerkaar (Rainbow): Voorimehe 9, Tallinn 10146; tel. 646-4059; fax (2) 442-484; e-mail vikerkaar@teleport.ee; f. 1986; monthly; fiction, poetry, critical works; in Estonian and Russian; Editor-in-Chief MÄRT VÄLJATAGA; circ. 1,500.

NEWS AGENCY

BNS (Baltic News Service): Pärnu mnt. 105, Tallinn 15043; tel. 610-8800; fax 610-8811; e-mail bns@bns.ee; internet www.bns.ee; f. 1990; Chief Exec. GEORGE SHABAD.

PRESS ORGANIZATIONS

Estonian Journalists' Union: Gonsiori 21-409, Tallinn 10147; tel. 646-3699; fax 646-3672; e-mail eal@eal.ee; internet www.eal.ee; f. 1919; Chair. ALLAN ALAKÜLA.

Estonian Newspaper Association (Eesti Ajalehtede Liit): Pärnu mnt. 67A, Tallinn 10134; tel. 646-1005; fax 631-1210; e-mail eall@ eall.ee; internet www.eall.ee; f. 1990; 39 mem.; newspapers; Chair. IGOR RÕTOV.

Estonian Press Council (Avaliku Sõna Nõukogu): Gonsiori 21, Tallinn 15020; tel. and fax 646-3699; e-mail asn@asn.org.ee; internet www.asn.org.ee; Chair. URMAS LOIT.

Publishers

Eesti Raamat (Estonian Book): Laki 26, Tallinn 12915; tel. and fax 658-7889; e-mail georg.grynberg@mail.ee; f. 1940; fiction; Dir ANNE-ASTRI KASK.

Estonian Encyclopaedia Publishers Ltd: Narva mnt. 4, Tallinn 10117; tel. 699-9620; fax 699-9621; e-mail encyclo@ene.ee; internet www.ene.ee; f. 1991; Man. Dir ANTO RAUKAS.

Huma: Vene 14, Tallinn 10123; tel. and fax 644-0955; e-mail huma@ online.ee; fiction, non-fiction, children's books, art, calendars; Dir LIIVI KESKPAIK.

Ilmamaa: Vanemuise 19, Tartu 51014; tel. (7) 427-290; fax (7) 427-320; e-mail ilmamaa@ilmamaa.ee; internet www.ilmamaa.ee; general fiction, philosophy, cultural history, electronic publishing; Dir MART JAGOMÄGI.

Koolibri: Pärnu mnt. 10, Tallinn 10148; tel. 644-5223; fax 644-6813; e-mail koolibri@koolibri.ee; internet www.koolibri.ee; f. 1991; textbooks, dictionaries, children's books; Dir ANTS LANG.

Kunst (Fine Art): Lai 34, Tallinn 10133; POB 105, Tallinn 10502; tel. 641-1764; fax 641-1762; e-mail kunst.lai@mail.ee; internet www .kirjastused.com/kunst/; f. 1957; fine arts, fiction, tourism, history, biographies; Dir SIRJE HELME.

Kupar: Pärnu mnt. 67A, Tallinn 10134; tel. 628-6174; fax 646-2076; e-mail kupar@netexpress.ee; f. 1987; contemporary fiction; Dir IVO SANDRE.

Logos: Toompuiestee 23, Tallinn 10137; tel. and fax 661-3712; e-mail logos@logos.ee; internet www.logos.ee; f. 1991; religious publications; Chair. INGMAR KURG.

Monokkel: POB 311, Tallinn 10503; tel. 501-6307; fax 656-9176; f. 1988; history, fiction; Dir ANTS ÕÕBIK.

Olion: Laki 26, Tallinn 12915; tel. 655-0175; fax 655-0173; e-mail olion@hot.ee; internet www.kirjastused.com/olion/; f. 1989; politics, reference, history, biographies, children's books; Dir HÜLLE UNT.

Õllu: Harju 1, Tallinn 10146; tel. 652-2038; fiction; Chair. of Bd HEINO KIIK.

Olympia: Pikk 2, Tallinn 10123; tel. 644-2549; fax 661-2853; e-mail olympia@online.ee; sports; Editor-in-Chief PAAVO KIVINE.

Perioodika (Periodicals): Voorimehe 9, Tallinn 10146; POB 3648, Tallinn 10507; tel. 644-1252; fax 644-2484; f. 1964; newspapers, guidebooks, periodicals, fiction, children's books in foreign languages; Dir UNO SILLAJÕE.

Publishing House ILO: Madara 14, Tallinn 10612; tel. 661-0553; fax 661-0556; e-mail ilo@ilo.ee; internet www.ilo.ee; dictionaries, encyclopaedias, business, management and law; Dir SILVI-AIRE VILLO.

Tartu University Press: Tiigi 78, Tartu 50410; tel. (7) 375-961; fax (7) 375-944; e-mail tyk@psych.ut.ee; internet www.psych.ut.ee/tup; f. 1958; science, textbooks, etc; Chair. VAIKO TIGANE.

Tiritamm: Laki 26, Tallinn 12915; tel. and fax 656-3570; e-mail tiritamm@hot.ee; internet www.kirjastused.com/tiritamm/; f. 1991; children's books; Dir SIRJE SAIMRE.

Valgus Publishers: Tulika 19, Tallinn 10613; tel. 650-5025; fax 650-5104; e-mail info@kirjastusvalgus.ee; internet www .kirjastusvalgus.ee; f. 1965; scientific literature, resource materials and textbooks; Man. Dir MARIKA TAMM.

PUBLISHERS' ASSOCIATION

Estonian Publishers' Association: Laki 17, Tallinn 0006; POB 3366, Tallinn 0090; tel. 650-5592; fax 650-5590; f. 1991; unites 31 publishing houses; Chair. of Bd TÕNU KOGER.

Broadcasting and Communications

TELECOMMUNICATIONS

Regulatory Authorities

Broadcasting Council: Gonsiori 21, Tallinn 15020; tel. 611-4305; fax 611-4457; e-mail rhn@er.ee.

National Communications Board: Ädala 4D, Tallinn 10614; tel. 693-1154; fax 693-1155; e-mail postbox@sa.ee; internet www.sa.ee; Dir JÜRI JÕEMA.

Major Provider

Eesti Telekom AS (Estonian Telecom Ltd): Roosikrantsi 2, Tallinn 10119; tel. 631-1212; fax 631-1224; e-mail mailbox@telekom.ee; internet www.telekom.ee; f. 1992 as Eesti Telefon (subsequently a subsidiary, renamed Elion in 2003); privatized in 1999; holding co operating national telecommunications system; Dir-Gen. TOOMAS SOMERA; Chief Exec. JAAN MÄNNIK.

Eesti Mobiltelefon AS (EMT): Lasnamäe 64, Tallinn 19095; tel. 639-7111; fax 611-1897; e-mail emt@emt.ee; internet www.emt.ee; f. 1991; owned by Eesti Telekom AS; Pres. PEEP AAVIKSOO.

BROADCASTING

Radio

In 2002 there were 26 private radio broadcasters operating in Estonia (one with an international broadcasting licence, 15 with regional licences and 10 with local licences), in addition to the public broadcaster, Eesti Raadio (Estonian Radio).

Eesti Raadio (Estonian Radio): Gonsiori 21, Tallinn 15020; tel. 611-4115; fax 611-4457; e-mail raadio@er.ee; internet www.er.ee; f. 1926; five 24-hour channels (three in Estonian, one in Russian and one in English, French and German); external service in English; Chair. and Dir-Gen. AIN SAARNA.

Raadio Elmaar: Õpetaja 9A, Tartu 51003; tel. (7) 427-927; fax (7) 742-044; owned by AS Radio Elmaar; Dir JAAN HABICHT.

Raadio Kuku: Narva mnt. 63, Tallinn 20606; tel. 630-7660; fax 601-5759; internet www.kuku.ee; owned by AS Trio LSL; Chair. of Council REIN LANG.

Raadio Sky Plus: Pärnu mnt. 139C, Tallinn 11317; tel. 678-8777; fax 678-8710; e-mail sky@sky.ee; internet www.skyplus.fm; owned by Taevaraadio AS; Chief Exec. ILMAR KOMPUS.

Raadio Uuno: Narva mnt. 63, Tallinn 20606; tel. 630-7660; fax 601-5759; internet www.uuno.ee; owned by AS Trio LSL; Chair. of Council REIN LANG.

Star FM: Peterburi tee 81, Tallinn 11415; tel. 622-0288; fax 622-0294; internet www.starfm.ee; owned by AS Mediainvest Holding; Chair. SVEN NUTMANN.

Tartu Pereraadio Ühing (Tartu Family Radio Corpn): Annemõisa 8, Tartu 50718; tel. and fax (7) 488-458; e-mail tartu@pereraadio.ee; internet www.pereraadio.ee; f. 1994; Christian radio broadcasting; Pres. JOEL LUHAMETS; Exec. Dir PAAVO PIHLAK.

Television

There are three national commercial television stations and one public broadcaster in Estonia. In addition, five cable television licences have been issued. The commercial stations are:

Eesti Televisioon (Estonian Television): Faehlmanni 12, Tallinn 15029; tel. 628-4113; fax 628-4155; e-mail etv@etv.ee; internet www

.etv.ee; f. 1955; state-owned; one channel; programmes in Estonian and Russian; Chair. ILMAR RAAG.

Kanal 2 (Channel 2): Maakri 23A, Tallinn 10145; tel. 666-2450; fax 666-2451; e-mail info@kanal2.ee; internet www.kanal2.ee; f. 1993; commercial station; owned by AS Kanal 2; Chair. HANS ERIK MATRE.

TV3: Peterburgi tee 81, Tallinn 11415; tel. 622-0200; fax 622-0201; e-mail tv3@tv3.ee; internet www.tv3.ee; f. 1996; owned by AS TV3; Exec. Dir TOOMAS VARA.

Broadcasting Association

Association of Estonian Broadcasters (AEB): Ülemiste tee 3A, Tallinn 11415; tel. and fax 606-1701; e-mail erl@online.ee; internet www.ringhliit.ee; 19 mems.

Finance

(cap. = capital; res = reserves; dep. = deposits; m. = million; brs = branches; amounts in kroons, unless otherwise stated)

BANKING

The bank of Estonia was re-established in 1990, as was a private banking system. During a crisis in the financial sector in 1992 a number of weaker banks collapsed and others merged. New legislation was subsequently enacted to strengthen the sector, with increased supervision. A currency board became responsible for monetary supervision in 1992.

Central Bank

Bank of Estonia (Eesti Pank): Estonia pst. 13, Tallinn 15095; tel. 668-0719; fax 668-0836; e-mail info@epbe.ee; internet www.ee/epbe; f. 1918; re-established 1990; central bank of Estonia; bank of issue; cap. and res 2,356.2m., dep. 3,873.5m. (Dec. 2001); Pres. VAHUR KRAFT.

Commercial Banks

Estonian Credit Bank (Eesti Krediidipank): Narva mnt. 4, Tallinn 15014; tel. 669-0900; fax 661-6037; e-mail krediidipank@ekp.ee; internet www.krediidipank.ee; f. 1992; cap. 85.6m., res 20.9m., dep. 777.1m. (Dec. 2001); Pres. REIN OTSASON; Chair. of Bd ANDRUS KLUGE; 12 brs.

Hansapank: Liivalaia 8, Tallinn 15040; tel. 613-1310; fax 613-1410; e-mail hansa@hansa.ee; internet www.hansa.ee; f. 1991; cap. 50.4m., res 201.6m., dep.1,958.8m. (Dec. 2001); merged with Estonian Savings Bank (Eesti Hoiupank) in 1998; Chair. of Bd INDREK NEIVELT; 103 brs.

Sampo Bank: Narva mnt. 11, POB 19, Tallinn 15015; tel. 630-2100; fax 630-2200; e-mail info@sampopank.ee; internet www.sampo.ee; f. 1992 as Estonian Forexbank; merged with Estonian Investment Bank in 1998 to form Optiva Bank; name changed as above in 2000; wholly owned by Sampo Plc; cap. 323.1m., res 17.1m., dep. 4,446.6m. (Dec. 2001); Chair. HÄRMO VÄRK; 7 brs.

Tallinn Business Bank Ltd (Tallinna Äripanga AS): Estonia pst. 3–5, Tallinn 15097; tel. 668-8000; fax 668-8001; e-mail info@tbb.ee; internet www.tbb.ee; f. 1991; cap. 76.8m., res 9.5m., dep. 445.0m. (Dec. 2001); Chair. of Bd VALERI HARITONOV.

Union Bank of Estonia (Eesti Ühispank): Tornimäe 2, Tallinn 15010; tel. 665-5100; fax 665-5102; e-mail postkast@eyp.ee; internet www.eyp.ee; f. 1992; cap. 665.6m., res 1,271.1m., dep. 14,638.2m. (Dec. 2001); merged with North Estonia Bank in Jan. 1997 and with Tallinna Pank in July 1998; Pres. AIN HANSCHMIDT; 90 brs.

Foreign Bank

Nordea Bank Estonia (Finland): Hobujaama 4, Tallinn 15068; tel. 628-3200; fax 628-3201; e-mail tallinn@nordea.com; internet www .nordea.ee; f. 1995 as Merita Bank Ltd; name changed in 1999; owned by Nordea AB (Finland).

Banking Association

Estonian Banking Association (Eesti Pangaliit): Ahtri 12, Tallinn 10151; tel. 611-6567; fax 611-6568; e-mail post@pangaliit.ee; internet www.pangaliit.ee; f. 1992; Chair. HÄRMO VÄRK; Man. Dir VIKTOR HÜTT.

STOCK EXCHANGE

Tallinn Stock Exchange: Pärnu mnt. 12, Tallinn 10148; tel. 640-8840; fax 640-8801; e-mail hex@hex.ee; internet www.hex.ee; f. 1995; strategically owned by the HEX stock exchange (Finland) from April 2001; Chair. GERT TIIVAS.

ESTONIA

INSURANCE

At the end of 2002 there were 13 insurance organizations operating in Estonia.

Estonian Financial Supervisory Authority: Sakala 4, Tallinn 15030; tel. 668-0500; fax 668-0501; e-mail info@fi.ee; internet www.fi.ee; f. 1993; Chair. of Bd ANDRES TRINK.

Non-life companies comprise ERGO Kindlustus Ltd, Inges Kindlustus Ltd, If Eesti Kindlustus Ltd, Nordea Kindlustus Eesti Ltd, Salva Kindlustus Ltd, Seesam Rahvusvaheline Kindlustus Ltd and Zürich Kindlustuse Eesti Ltd.

Life companies comprise ERGO Elukindlustus Ltd, Hansapanga Kindlustus Ltd, Sampo Elukindlustus Ltd, Seesam Elukindlustus Ltd and Ühispanga Elukindlustuse Ltd.

Trade and Industry

GOVERNMENT AGENCIES

Consumer Protection Board: Kiriku 4, Tallinn 15071; tel. 620-1700; fax 620-1701; e-mail info@consumer.ee; internet www.consumer.ee; f. 1994; Dir-Gen. HELLE ARUNIIT.

Enterprise Estonia: Roosikrantsi 11, Tallinn 10119; tel. 627-9279; fax 627-9427; e-mail info@eia.ee; internet www.eia.ee; Chair. URMAS VAHUR.

Estonian Centre for Standardization: Aru 10, Tallinn 10317; tel. 605-5050; fax 605-5070; e-mail info@evs.ee; internet www.evs.ee; Man. Dir SVEN KASEMAA.

Estonian Competition Board: Kohtu 8, Tallinn 15184; tel. 611-3942; fax 611-3943; e-mail compet@konkurentsiamet.ee; internet www.konkurentsiamet.ee; Dir-Gen. PEETER TAMMISTU.

Estonian Grain Board: Hobujaama 1, Tallinn 0001; tel. (2) 432-815; fax 641-9075; Dir-Gen. AGO SOOTS.

Estonian Investment Agency: Roosikrantsi 11, Tallinn 10119; tel. 627-9420; fax 627-9427; e-mail info@eas.ee; internet www.investinestonia.com; Dir ANDRUS VIIRG.

Estonian Privatization Agency (Eesti Erastamisagentuur): Rävala 6, Tallinn 0105; tel. 630-5600; fax 630-5699; e-mail eea@eea.ee; internet www.eea.ee; Dir-Gen. VÄINO SARNET.

Estonian Trade Council: Liimi 1-503, Tallinn 10621; tel. 656-3299; fax 656-3923; e-mail etc@etc.ee; internet www.etc.ee; f. 1991; Chair. of Bd TAMBET MADE; Dir AARE PUUR.

Estonian Trade Promotion Agency: Roosikrantsi 11, Tallinn 10119; tel. 627-9440; fax 627-9427; e-mail trade@eas.ee; internet www.export.ee; f. 1997.

CHAMBERS OF COMMERCE

Estonian Chamber of Agriculture and Commerce: Vilmsi 53B, Tallinn 10147; tel. 600-9349; fax 600-9350; e-mail info@epkk.ee; internet www.epkk.ee; Chair. ALAR OPPAR.

Estonian Chamber of Commerce and Industry (ECCI): Toom-Kooli 17, Tallinn 10130; tel. 646-0244; fax 646-0245; e-mail koda@koda.ee; internet www.koda.ee; f. 1925; Pres. TOOMAS LUMAN; Gen. Dir SIIM RAIE.

INDUSTRIAL AND TRADE ASSOCIATIONS

Association of Construction Material Producers of Estonia (Eesti Ehitusmaterjalide Tootjate Liit): Kiriku 6, Tallinn 10130; tel. 620-1918; fax 648-9062; e-mail eetl@hot.ee; internet www.hot.ee/eetl; Pres. TOOMAS VAINOLA.

Association of Estonian Electrotechnical and Electronic Industry: Pirita 20, Tallinn 0001; tel. (2) 238-981; fax (2) 237-827; Pres. GUNNAR TOOMSOO.

Association of Estonian Food Industry: Gonsiori 29, Tallinn 10147; tel. 648-6073; fax 631-2718; e-mail info@toiduliit.ee; internet www.toiduliit.ee; f. 1993; Man. Dir HELVE REMMEL.

Association of Estonian International Road Carriers (Eesti Rahvusvaheliste Autovedajate Assotsiatsioon): Narva mnt. 91, Tallinn 10127; tel. 627-3740; fax 627-3741; e-mail info@eraa.ee; internet www.eraa.ee; Sec.-Gen. TOLVO KULDKEPP.

Association of Estonian Local Industry: Tallinn; tel. (2) 422-367; fax (2) 424-962; Chair. HEINO VASAR.

Estimpex Foreign Trade Association: Uus 32/34, Tallinn 0101; tel. (2) 601-462; fax (2) 602-184; import and export of household fixtures, foodstuffs, souvenirs and oil-based products; Gen. Dir OSVALD KALDRE.

Estonian Agricultural Producers Central Union (Eestimaa Pollumajandustootjate Keskliit): Lai 39/41, Tallinn 10133; tel. and fax 641-1113; e-mail epk.epk@mail.ee; Chair. of Bd VIKTOR SARTAKOV.

Estonian Asphalt Pavement Association (Eesti Asfaldiliit): Parnu 24, Tallinn 10141; tel. 611-9365; fax 611-9360; f. 1991; co-ordinates Estonian asphalt paving and mixing companies; Chair. of Bd ALEKSANDER KALDAS.

Estonian Association of Construction Entrepreneurs (Eesti Ehitusettevõtjate Liit): Kiriku 6, Tallinn 10130; tel. and fax 641-0071; e-mail eeel@eeel.ee; internet www.hot.ee/eeel; Man. Dir ILMAR LINK.

Estonian Association of Fisheries: Gonsiori 29-502, Tallinn 10147; tel. 648-4537; fax 641-9006; e-mail kalaliit@online.ee; Chair. JAAN JALAKAS; Man. Dir VALDUR NOORMÄGI.

Estonian Association of Small and Medium-sized Enterprises (EVEA): Pronksi 3, Tallinn 10124; tel. 640-3935; fax 631-2451; e-mail sme@evea.ee; internet www.evea.ee; f. 1988; Pres. RIIVO SINIJÄRV; Man. Dir MARGIT KALLASTE.

Estonian Business Association: Liivalaia 9, 10118 Tallinn; tel. 646-2030; fax 646-2031; e-mail easa@esea.ee; internet www.esea.ee; f. 1996; Pres. URMAS SOORUMAA; Man. Dir JAAK SAARNIIT.

Estonian Clothing and Textile Association (Eesti Rõivaja Tekstiililiit): Tartu mnt. 63, Tallinn 10115; tel. 611-5567; fax 611-5568; e-mail ertl@online.ee; internet www.online.ee/~ertl; Chair. MADIS VÕÕRAS.

Estonian Dairy Association (Eesti Piimaliit): Vilmsi 53, Tallinn 10147; tel. 600-9357; fax 600-9355; e-mail eestipl@online.ee; Chair. of Bd ENN SOKK; Man. Dir REIN REISSON.

Estonian Forest Industries Federation (Eesti Metsatööstuse Liit): Marja 9, Tallinn 10617; tel. 656-7643; fax 656-7644; e-mail info@emtl.ee; internet www.forestindustries.ee; Man. Dir ANDRES TALLIJÄRV.

Estonian Gas Association (Eesti Gaasiliit): Liivalaia 9, Tallinn 0001; tel. 646-1571; fax 631-4340; Chair. of Bd ANDRES SAAR.

Estonian Hotel and Restaurant Association (Easti Hotellide ja Restoranide Liit): Kiriku 6, Tallinn 10130; tel. 641-1428; fax 641-1425; e-mail info@ehrl.ee; Chair. of Bd TARMO SUMBERG.

Estonian Meat Association (Eesti Lihaliit): Lai 39/41, Tallinn 10133; tel. 641-1179; fax 641-1035; e-mail lihaliit@hot.ee; f. 1989; 18 mem. companies (2002); Chair. of Bd AIGAR PINDMAA; Man. Dir PEETER GRIGORJEV.

Estonian Oil Association (Eesti Õliühing): Kiriku 6, Tallinn 10130; tel. 620-1930; fax 620-1935; e-mail maimu@oilunion.ee; internet www.oilunion.ee; f. 1993; represents more than 70% of the fuel market; Chair. RAIVO VARE.

Estonian Society of Merchants: Kiriku 6, Tallinn 10130; tel. 620-1914; fax 620-1935; e-mail info@kaupmeesteliit.ee; internet www.kaupmeesteliit.ee; Chair. of Bd PEETER RAUDSEPP; Man. Dir MARIKA MERILAI.

Estonian Woodworking Federation: Pärnu mnt. 158B, Tallinn 11317; tel. 655-8525; fax 655-8524; e-mail info@furnitureindustry.ee; internet www.furnitureindustry.ee; Chair. AIN SAARMANN; Man. Dir MÄRT RAHAMÄGI.

ETK Managers' Club: Narva mnt. 7, Tallinn 10117; tel. 630-2324; fax 630-2333; f. 1991; Pres. GEORG ILVEST.

Federation of the Estonian Chemical Industry: Kiriku 6, Tallinn 10130; tel. and fax 648-9004; e-mail info@keemia.ee; internet www.keemia.ee; f. 1991; 32 mem. enterprises; Chair. ILMAR VESIALIIK; Man. Dir HALLAR MEIBAUM.

Federation of the Estonian Engineering Industry: Mustamäe 4, Tallinn 10621; tel. 611-5893; fax 656-6640; e-mail eml@ltnet.ee; f. 1991; 80 mem. enterprises; Chair. of Bd MIKHEL PIKNER.

Union of Estonian Automobile Enterprises (Eesti Autoettevõtete Liit): Magasini 31, Tallinn 10138; tel. 643-9476; fax 644-3345; e-mail al@autoettevoteliit.ee; Pres. MATI MÄGI.

Union of Estonian Breweries (Eesti Õlletootjate Liit): Tähtvere 58/62, Tartu 2400; tel. (7) 434-330; fax (7) 431-193; Chair. of Bd MADIS PADDAR.

Union of Estonian Paper Manufacturers (Eesti Paberitööstuse Liit): Tööstuse 19, Kohila 3420; tel. (48) 33-564; fax (48) 32-132; e-mail kohilapv@netexpress.ee; Chair. of Bd HENNO PAVELSON.

Union of Estonian Wine Producers (Eesti Veinitootjate Liit): Karksi, Karksi vald, Vilijandi mk. 69104; tel. and fax (43) 54-022; e-mail veinilitt@hot.ee; Chair. of Bd JÜRI KERT.

EMPLOYERS' ORGANIZATION

Estonian Employers' Confederation (Eesti Tööandjate Keskliit): Kiriku 6, Tallinn 10130; tel. 699-9301; fax 699-9310; e-mail ettk@

ettk.ee; internet www.ettk.ee; f. 1991 as Confederation of Estonian Industry; Chair. of Bd MEELIS VIRKEBAU; Man. Dir TIIT LAJA.

UTILITIES

Electricity

Eesti Energia AS (Estonian Energy Ltd): Laki 24, Tallinn 12915; tel. 715-2222; fax 715-2200; e-mail info@energia.ee; internet www .energia.ee; f. 1939; producer, transmitter and distributor of thermal and electric energy; manufacture of electric motors; electrical engineering; Chair. GUNNAR OKK; 8,000 employees.

Gas

Eesti Gaas AS (Estonian Gas Association): Liivalaia 9, Tallinn 10118; tel. 630-3003; fax 631-3884; e-mail info@gaas.ee; internet www.gaas.ee; f. 1993; purchases and transports natural gas; constructs pipelines; calibrates gas meters; Chair. AARNE SAAR; 255 employees.

Water

Tallinn Water Ltd (AS Tallinna Vesi): Ädala 10, POB 174, Tallinn 10502; tel. 626-2200; fax 626-2300; e-mail tvesi@tvesi.ee; internet www.tallvesi.ee; f. 1997; supply and treatment of water; collection and treatment of waste water; 50.4% owned by British International Water UU; Chair. BOB GALLIENE; Dir-Gen. ENNO PERE; 685 employees.

MAJOR COMPANIES

Ahtme Building Materials Plant: Ahtme, Kohtla-Järve 2020; tel. (33) 22-405; concrete, lime and gypsum building components; Man. Dir ALEKSANDR VOROBYOV.

Alexela Oil AS: Kadaka tee 84C , Tallinn; tel. (7) 650-8509; e-mail secretar@alexela.ee; internet www.alexela.ee; f. 1991; fuel wholesaler and retailer, and provider of chemical-terminal service; Man. Dir HEITI HÄÄL; Chair. of Bd JUHAN KOLK.

Baltex 2000: Kopli 35, Tallinn 10502; tel. 612-9202; fax 612-9302; e-mail baltex2000@baltex2000.ee; internet www.baltex2000.ee; f. 1899; cotton yarns and fabrics, and non-woven materials; owned by the Tolaram Group (Singapore); Chief Exec. K. S. TRIPATHI.

Balti Es As: Linda 2, Narva 20309; tel. (35) 69-675; fax (35) 69-636; e-mail nzrko@balties.ee; internet www.balties.ee; f. 1947; manufacture of mechanical parts for the food, paper, textile and woodworking industries, and sea-freight containers; owned by A.P. Møller/Maersk Group (Denmark); Pres. RAIVO LATTIK; Gen. Dir VLADIMIR NAZARENKO; 720 employees.

Baltika AS: Veerenni 24, Tallinn 10135; tel. 630-2731; fax 630-2814; e-mail baltika@baltika.ee; internet www.baltika.ee; f. 1928; manufactures clothing; Chair. MEELIS MILDER; 1,500 employees.

Desintegraator Tootmise Ltd: Peterburi 71, Tallinn 11415; tel. 620-5000; fax 620-5001; e-mail desi@desi.ee; internet www.desi.ee; f. 1974; design and production of disintegrators and associated machinery; manufacture of emulsifying equipment; metal-working; Pres. JAAN KÄBIN; Gen. Dir LEHO KIVIMA; 40 employees.

Eesti Coca-Cola Joogid AS (Coca-Cola Beverages Estonia): Kadaka 76B, Tallinn 19088; tel. 650-3100; fax 650-3199; e-mail usein@eur.ko.com; f. 1992; Gen. Dir TOOMAS WESTERBERG.

Eesti Fosforiit: Fosforiidi 4, Maardu 74114; tel. 600-6150; fax (2) 233-130; phosphorite mining; production of phosphorous and mixed fertilizers; Man. Dir ANDRES JÄRV.

Eesti Kütus: Nafta 1, Tallinn 0103; tel. (2) 426-000; fax (2) 431-473; petrol retail and maintenance of fuel terminals; Man. Dir TOOMAS SAKS.

Eesti Põlevkivi (Estonian Oil-Shale Stock Company): Jaama 10, Jõhvi 41533, Ida-Viru; tel. (33) 64-801; fax (33) 64-803; e-mail ep@ep .ee; internet www.ep.ee; f. 1945; oil-shale mining and refining; has six subsidiaries; owned by Eesti Energia AS; Chair. of Bd MATI JOSTOV; 4,913 employees.

Eesti Talleks AS: Mustamäe 4, Tallinn 10621; tel. 656-4000; fax 656-4022; e-mail talleks@ltnet.ee; f. 1992; produces mechanical equipment and cast-iron goods, provides catering services, operates supermarket chain, provides security services, and distributes fuel; Chair. ANDRES SARRI; 800 employees.

Ek: Mustamäe 4, Tallinn 10621; tel. 656-4195; fax 656-4199; petrol and petroleum products; Man. Dir HENN PÄRN.

Eksi: Tallinn; tel. (2) 435-846; fax (2) 422-049; copper and aluminium wires and cables; Man. Dir VALERII MALYSHKO.

Elcoteq Tallinn AS: Peterburi 67A, Tallinn 11415; tel. 606-5100; fax 606-5200; e-mail regina.kolts@elcoteq.com; internet www .elcoteq.com; f. 1993; owned by Elcoteq Network Corpn (Finland); electronic components; Dir ILMAR PETERSEN; 2,000 employees.

Esoil: imports and distributes petroleum products.

ESS Group Ltd/Falck Baltics: Tammsaare 25, Tallinn 11314; tel. 651-1700; e-mail grupp@ess.ee; internet www.ess.ee; f. 1991; security, protection and surveillance services and emergency medical services; Pres. URMAS SÕÕRUMA; 4,000 employees.

Estar Oü: Narva mnt. 7A, Tallinn 10117; tel. 661-6217; fax 661-6221; f. 1989; production of textiles, clothing, leather goods, footwear and floor coverings; Pres. JÜRI KRAFT; Dir ENNO HOMMUK; 29,000 employees.

Estel Pluss AS: Telliskivi 60A, Tallinn 10412; tel. 672-9700; fax 672-9701; e-mail estel@estel.ee; internet www.estel.ee; f. 1994; development, manufacture, installation and service of semiconductors and converters; Chair. SERGEI FROLOV.

Estonian Fishing Co (Ookean State Stock Corpn): Paljassaare 28, Tallinn 0025; tel. (2) 471-421; fax (2) 498-190; f. 1992; production and export of processed, canned and frozen fish, seafood and related products; Gen. Dir HIINN NOOR; 2,300 employees.

Flora Kommerts AS: Tulika 19, Tallinn 10613; tel. 650-5000; fax 650-5010; e-mail info@flora.ee; internet www.flora.ee; f. 1889; detergents, candles and repair materials; subsidiaries in real estate and the retail of consumables; Man. ELMAR KRUŠMA; 280 employees.

Horizon Pulp and Paper: Anija 10, Kehra 74305; tel. 608-5007; fax 608-5756; e-mail horizonip@infonet.ee; internet www.horizon.ee; f. 1938; 82.5% owned by the Tolaram Group (Singapore), 17.5% owned by the World Bank; produces pulp and paper; Chief Exec. AVINASH TANEJA; Man. Dir SONNY N. K. ASWANI; 579 employees.

Kalev AS: Pärnu mnt 139, Tallinn 11317; tel. 628-3710; fax 628-3725; e-mail kalev@kalev.ee; internet www.kalev.ee; f. 1806; confectionery; Man. Dir OLIVER KRUUDA; 950 employees.

Krenholm Holding (Kreenholmi Valduse AS): Joala 20, Narva 20103; tel. (35) 65-636; fax (35) 65-963; e-mail holding@krenholm.ee; internet www.krenholm.ee; f. 1857; owned by Borås Wäfveri AB (Sweden); cotton textile production; Pres. MEELIS VIRKEBAU; 4,9009 employees.

Kunda Nordic Cement AS: Jaama 2, Kunda 44106; tel. (32) 29-900; fax (32) 620-9651; e-mail knc@knc.ee; internet www.knc.ee; f. 1992; owned by Heidelberg Cement Gp (Germany); building-materials production; Dir JAN OWREN; 640 employees.

Kuusalu Tehas: Kuusalu 29, Kuusalu 74601; tel. (2) 772-795; fax (2) 772-740; e-mail kuusalu@koda.ee; f. 1951; privatized 1994; renovates car engines; produces metal constructions, installations and machinery; involved in timber production; Man. HEINO VELDI; 70 employees.

Liviko AS: Masina 11, Tallinn 10144; tel. 667-8000; fax 667-8002; e-mail liviko@liviko.ee; internet www.liviko.ee; f. 1898; distillery; Chair. UDO THEMAS.

Masinaehituse AS: Mustamäe 5, Tallinn 10616; tel. 625-9400; fax 625-9449; e-mail ilmarine@ilmarine.ee; f. 1859; formerly Ilmarine AS; manufacture of equipment for industrial boilers; household goods; Chair. and Gen. Man. TOOMAS TALVING; 380 employees.

Microlink AS: Pärnu mnt 158, Tallinn 11317; tel. 650–1700; fax 650–4987; e-mail info@microlink.ee; internet www.microlink.ee; f. 1991; subsidiaries Microlink Systems, Microlink Data and Microlink ServIT merged in 2003; provides information technology services and solutions; Chief Exec. PEETER PRIISALM; 175 employees.

Narva Elektrijaamad (Narva Power Plants): Sepa 4, Narva 20306; tel. (35) 66-100; fax (35) 66-200; e-mail nej@nj.energia.ee; formerly Eesti Elektrijaam; owned by Eesti Energia AS; operates largest oil-shale-fired power plants in the world and operates the oil-shale mining industry; Gen. Dir REIN TALUMAA; 1,829 employees.

Nitrofert JSC: Järveküla 1, Kohtla-Järve 30197; tel. (33) 78-310; fax (33) 78-490; e-mail info@nitrofert.ee; internet www.nitrofert.ee; f. 1993; nitrogen-fertilizer production; processing natural gas into ammonia; Chair. VADIM MURAVIEV; Gen. Dir ALEKSEI NIKOLAEV; 480 employees.

Norma: Laki 14, Tallinn 10621; tel. 650-0444; fax 656-3134; e-mail norma@norma.ee; f. 1891; production of seat-belts and other parts for cars; Pres. and Chief Exec. PEEP SIIMON; 755 employees.

Rakvere Lihakombinaat AS (Rakvere Meat Processing Company Ltd): Roodevälja Küla, Sömeru vald 44305; tel. (32) 29-221; fax (32) 29-300; e-mail rlk@rlk.ee; internet www.rlk.ee; f. 1890; meat-processing company; Pres. TOOMAS KÕUHKNA; Man. Dir PEETER MASPANOV; 850 employees.

Tallegg AS: Saha 18 Loo, Harju mk 74201; tel. (6) 107-012; fax (6) 107-060; e-mail tallegg@tallegg.ee; internet www.tallegg.ee; f. 1993; production of poultry products; Chair. ANTS KÄSPER; 800 employees.

Tallinn Masinatehase AS (Tallinn Engineering Plant Ltd): Kopli 68, Tallinn 10412; tel. 644-1176; fax 644-4621; e-mail avo@infonet .ee; internet www.infonet.ee/avo; f. 1865; manufactures air heaters and coolers and metal castings; Gen. Dir IGOR TIMOFEEV; 450 employees.

Tallinn Pulp and Paper Mill: Masina 20, Tallinn 0104; tel. (2) 430-596; fax 631-2472; f. 1994; produces pulp and paper products; Man. Dir VILLI LIIBERT; 120 employees.

Tamsalu Terko AS: Tööstuse 15, Tamsalu 46107; tel. (32) 30-583; fax (32) 30-090; e-mail terkotms@estpak.ee; f. 1963; manufactures agricultural products and breeds animals; Dir AADU JAANSOO; 400 employees.

TeaSpon: Türi 4, Tallinn 11313; tel. 655-8119; fax 655-8005; e-mail teaspon@online.ee; internet www.koda.ee/teaspon; f. 1959; manufactures textiles for the home; Man. TOOM GUSTEL.

Terg LLC-Metalwork: Aiandi 21, Haabneeme, Harju 74001; tel. and fax 600-8970; e-mail terg@solo.ee; internet www.terg.net; constructs and installs pre-fabricated steel-frame buildings and other metal structures; Man. MARTIN MAIDLA; 70 employees.

Tootsi Turvas Ltd: Tööstuse 1, Tootsi, Pärnu maakond 87501; tel. (44) 71-530; fax (44) 71-540; e-mail info@tootsiturvas.ee; internet www.tootsiturvas.ee; f. 1937; production of peat, peat briquettes and other peat products; Man. Dir KAI MÄELEHT; 410 employees.

Vasar: Vana-Narva 1, Mardu 74 114; tel. (6) 379–221; fax (6) 379-219; e-mail vasar@vasar.ee; internet www.vasar.ee; zinc and aluminium alloy casting; Gen. Man. MARGUS REBANE.

VGT Ltd: Kreutzwaldi 59, Võru 65607; tel. (78) 21-521; fax (78) 21-651; e-mail vgt@estpak.ee; f. 1959; produces monitoring and control equipment; Man. Dir EINAR KUUSE; 180 employees.

Viru Keemia Grupp AS: Järveküla 14, Kohtla Järve 30328; tel. (33) 24-200; fax (33) 75-044; e-mail info@vkg.ee; internet www.vkg.ee; f. 1924; formerly Kiviter AS; manufacture of chemicals and fertilizers; refines and processes oil-shale and electrode coke; owns eight subsidiaries; Chair. JANEK PARKMAN.

Viisnurk AS: Suur-Jõe 48, Pärnu 80042; tel. (44) 78-323; fax (44) 78-320; e-mail mail@viisnurk.ee; internet www.viisnurk.ee; f. 1945; manufacture of wooden products, furniture and sports equipment; Pres. MEELIS KUKK; 750 employees.

Volta Electromechanics Ltd (Elektrimasinaehituse AS): Tööstuse 47, Tallinn 10416; tel. (6) 120–600; fax (6) 120–660; e-mail volta@volta.ee; internet www.volta.ee; f. 1899; formerly Ravor Investeeringute AS; production of motors, electric radiators, generators and transformers; Chair. of Bd AIVAR REIVIK.

TRADE UNIONS

Association of Estonian Chemical Industry Workers' Trade Unions: Kohtla-Järve; tel. (33) 478-28; fax (33) 457-98; f. 1990; Chair. MIHKEL ISKÜL.

Association of Estonian Radio and Electronics Industry Workers' Trade Unions: Rävala 4, Tallinn 0100; tel. (2) 432-318; Chair. LYUBOV SEROVA.

Confederation of Estonian Employee Unions (TeenistujateAmetiliitude Keskorganisatsioon): Gonsiori 21, Tallinn 10147; tel. 641-9800; e-mail talo@online.ee; internet www.talo.ee; f. 1992; comprises 12 member unions; Chair. TOIVO ROOSIMAA.

Confederation of Estonian Food and Landworkers' Unions: 32 Raua Str, Tallinn 10152; tel. and fax 641-0249; e-mail aare .etmk@mail.ee; f. 1989; Chair. AARE-LEMBIT NEEVE.

Confederation of Estonian Trade Unions (Eesti Ametiühingute Keskliit): Pärnu mnt 41A , Tallinn 10119; tel. 641-2800; fax 641-2802; e-mail eakl@eakl.ee; internet www.eakl.ee; f. 1990; Chair. KADI PARNITS.

Estonian Communication Workers' Trade Union (Eesti Sidetöötajate Ametiühingute Liit—ESAL): Masti 2/5, Tallinn 11911; tel. 601-1124; e-mail esal@uninet.ee; internet www.esal.org.ee; Chair. ÕIE VÄLJAS.

Estonian Light Industry Workers' Trade Union: Rävala 4, Tallinn 0100; tel. and fax (2) 431-640; Chair. EVI JAAGURA.

Estonian Transportation and Roadworkers' Union (Eesti Transpordi-ja Teetöötajate Ametiühing—ETTA): Kalju 7–1, Tallinn 10414; tel. 641-3131; fax 641-3129; e-mail etta@etta.ee; internet www.etta.ee; Chair. PEEP PETERSON.

Society of Estonian Economy Workers' Trade Unions: Rävala 4, Tallinn 10143; tel. and fax 661-2414; e-mail emal@online.ee.

Trade Union of Oil-Shale Industry Workers (Põlevkivitootjate Ametiühingu Liit): Jaama 10, Jõhvi 415033; tel. (33) 64-821; fax (33) 64-810; e-mail eptal@ep.ee; Chair. MAIDO AGUR.

Transport

RAILWAYS

In 2002 there were 963 km of railway track in use, of which 131 km were electrified. Main lines link Tallinn with Narva and St Petersburg (Russia), Tartu and Pskov (Russia), Tartu and Valga (Latvia), and Pärnu and Rīga (Latvia). In December 2001 the World Bank disbursed a loan of 870m. kroons to Estonian Railways for the upgrading of engines and infrastructural repairs.

Estonian Railway Administration: Lastekodu 31, Tallinn 10113; tel. 605-7401; fax 605-7410; e-mail raudteeamet@rdtamet.ee; internet www.rdtamet.ee; f. 1999; Dir-Gen. OLEG EPNER.

Estonian Railways Ltd (AS Eesti Raudtee): Pikk 36, Tallinn 15073; tel. 615-8610; fax 615-8710; e-mail raudtee@evr.ee; internet www.evr.ee; f. 1918; privatized in 2001; freight carriers; Chair. and Man. Dir HERBERT PAYNE; 4,000 employees.

ROADS

In 2002 Estonia had a total road network of 51,410 km, of which 1,455 km were main roads, 12,442 km were secondary roads, 2,496 were basic roads and 34,975 km were local roads. The motorway network totalled 87 km in 1999. In 2000 there were plans to construct an international motorway, to be known as the Via Baltica, between Tallinn and Warsaw, Poland. The project was to be partly funded by the EU. In 2000 51.5% of the total road network was asphalted.

Estonian Road Administration: Pärnu Road 24, Tallinn 10141; tel. 611-9300; fax 611-9360; e-mail estroad@mnt.ee; internet www .mnt.ee; f. 1990; Gen. Dir RIHO SÕRMUS; 15 county offices.

INLAND WATERWAYS

In 2002 there were 320 km of navigable inland waterways.

SHIPPING

Tallinn is the main port for freight transportation. There are regular passenger services between Tallinn and Helsinki, Finland. A service between Tallinn and Stockholm, Sweden, was inaugurated in 1991.

Estonian Maritime Administration (EMA) (Veeteede Amet): Valge 4, Tallinn 114113; tel. 620-5500; fax 620-5506; e-mail eva@vta .ee; internet www.vta.ee; f. 1990; government organization; administers and implements state maritime safety policies, ship-control, pilot, lighthouse and hydrography services; Gen. Dir ANDRUS MAIDE; 375 employees.

Shipowning Company

Estonian Shipping Company Ltd (ESCO) (AS Eesti Merelaevandus): Sadama 4, Tallinn 10111; tel. 640-9500; fax 640-9595; e-mail online@eml.ee; internet www.eml.ee; f. 1940; owned by Tschudi and Eitzen (Norway); liner services, ship chartering and cargo shipping; Chair. of Supervisory Bd OLEV SCHULTS; Man. Dir TOM STAGE PETERSEN; 500 employees.

Shipowners' Association

Estonian Shipowners' Association (Eesti Laevaomanike Liit): Luise 1A, Tallinn 10142; tel. and fax 646-0109; e-mail reeder@ teleport.ee; Pres. REIN MERISALU.

Port Authority

Port of Tallinn: Sadama 25, Tallinn 15051; tel. 631-8002; fax 631-8166; e-mail portoftallinn@portoftallinn.com; internet www .portoftallinn.ee; f. 1991; Chair. of Bd RIHO RASMANN; Harbour Master E. HUNT; 990 employees.

CIVIL AVIATION

Estonia has air links with several major cities in the former USSR, including Moscow and St Petersburg (Russia), Kiev (Ukraine), Minsk (Belarus), Rīga (Latvia) and Vilnius (Lithuania), and with several western European destinations.

Estonian Civil Aviation Administration: Rävala pst. 8, Tallinn 10143; tel. 694-9666; fax 694-9667; e-mail info@ecaa.ee; internet www.ecaa.ee; f. 1990; Dir-Gen. TIIT SOORM (acting).

Elk Airways (Estonian Aviation Company Ltd): Eesti Vabariik, Majaka 26, Tallinn 11416; tel. 638-0972; fax 638-0975; e-mail elk@ infonet.ee; internet www.elk.ee; f. 1992; international and domestic passenger and cargo flights to Europe and the CIS; Man. Dir VLADIMIR SLONTCHEVSH.

Estonian Air: Lennujaama 13, Tallinn 11101; tel. 640-1101; fax 601-6092; e-mail ov@estonian-air.ee; internet www.estonian-air.ee; f. 1991; passenger and cargo flights to Europe, the CIS and North Africa; Pres. and Chair. of Bd ERKI URVA.

Tourism

Estonia has a wide range of attractions for tourists, including the historic towns of Tallinn and Tartu, extensive nature reserves and coastal resorts. In 1990 the National Tourism Board was established to develop facilities for tourism in Estonia. In 2001 there were 1,231,620 visitors to Estonia, with Finland the main source of tourists.

Estonian Association of Travel Agents (Eesti Turismifirmade Liit): Kiriku 6, Tallinn 10130; tel. 631-3013; fax 631-3622; e-mail info@etfl.ee; internet www.etfl.ee; f. 1990; Pres. DAISY JÄRVA.

Estonian Marine Tourism Association: Regati pst. 1, 6K, Tallinn 11911; tel. 639-8933; fax 639-8899; e-mail helle.hallika@mail.ee; f. 1990; Man. Dir HELLE HALLIKA.

Estonian Tourist Board: Roosikrantsi 11, Tallinn 10119; tel. 627-9770; fax 627-9777; e-mail info@visitestonia.com; internet www.visitestonia.com; f. 1990; Dir RIINA LÕHMUS.

Culture

NATIONAL ORGANIZATIONS

Ministry of Culture: see section on The Government (Ministries).

Cultural Endowment of Estonia: Suur-Karja 23, Tallinn 10148; tel. 644–6922; fax 631–4085; e-mail kulka@kulka.ee; internet www.kulka.ee; distributes grants derived from state budgetary taxes; comprises eight endowments: literature, music, fine and applied art, dramatic art, architecture, audio-visual art, folk culture, physical fitness and sport; Chair. Minister of Culture URMAS PAET.

Estonian National Commission for UNESCO: Suur-Karja 23, Tallinn 10148; tel. 644-1431; fax 631-3757; e-mail unesco@unesco.estnet.ee; Sec.-Gen. DORIS KAREVA.

National Heritage Board: Uus 18, Tallinn 10111; tel. 640-3050; fax 640-3060; e-mail info@muinas.ee; f. 1993; Dir-Gen. Dr ANNELI RANDLA.

National Language Inspection: Endla 4, Tallinn 10142; tel. 626-3346; fax 660-9883; e-mail ilmar.tomusk@keeleinsp.ee; f. 1990; fmrly Dept of Language; govt agency established to promote use of Estonian language; Dir-Gen. ILMAR TOMUSK.

CULTURAL HERITAGE

In 2001 there were 182 museums and 578 libraries in Estonia.

Centre for Contemporary Arts: Vabaduse 6, Tallinn 10146; tel. 631-4050; fax 631-4049; e-mail post@skkke.ee; internet www.cca.ee; f. 1992; information centre, including multi–media library and database; organizes and promotes international exhibitions and events, publishes material.

Estonian Academic Library: Rävala 10, Tallinn 15042; tel. 665-9401; fax 665-9400; e-mail ear@ear.ee; internet www.ear.ee; f. 1946; Dir ANNE VALMAS.

Estonian Film Foundation (Eesti Filmi Sihtasutus—EFS): Vana-Viru 3, Tallinn 10111; tel. 627-6060; fax 627-6061; e-mail film@efsa.ee; internet www.efsa.ee; f. 1997 by the Government as a private legal body; primary film-financing institution in Estonia; Man. Dir MARTIN AADAMSOO.

Estonian Historical Archives (Ajalooarhiv): Liivi 4, Tartu 50409; tel. (7) 387-501; fax (7) 387-510; e-mail ajalooarhiiv@ra.ee; internet www.eha.ee; f. 1921; approx. 2m. records; unit of the Estonian National Archives (q.v.); Dir INDREK KUUBEN.

Estonian History Museum: Pikk 17, Tallinn 0001; tel. 641-1630; fax 244-3446; e-mail post.eam@tallinn.astronet.ee; internet www.eam.ee; f. 1842; collects, preserves and researches Estonian historical material; holds lectures and conferences; Dir TOOMAS TAMLA.

Estonian Literary Museum: Vanemuise 42, Tartu 51003; tel. (7) 420-155; fax (7) 420-426; e-mail kirmus@kirmus.ee; internet www.kirmus.ee; f. 1909; comprises three archives: the Archival Library and bibliography dept; the Estonian Archives of Cultural History; and the Estonian Folklore Archives; Dir K. ARU.

Estonian Museum of Art: The Knighthood House, Kiriku 1, Tallinn 10130; tel. 644-9340; fax 644-2094; e-mail muuseum@ekm.ee; internet www.ekm.ee; f. 1919; Dir MARIKA VALK.

Estonian National Archives: Liivi 4, Tallinn 50409; tel. (2) 387-500; fax 387-510; e-mail rahvusarhiiv@ra.ee; internet www.ra.ee; f. 1921; Dir AIMAR ALTOSAAR.

Estonian National Museum: Veski 32, Tartu 51014; tel. (7) 421-279; fax (7) 422-254; e-mail erm@erm.ee; internet www.erm.ee; f. 1909; history of the Estonian and other Finno-Ugric peoples; Dir JAANUS PLAAT.

Estonian Natural History Museum (Loodusmuuseum): Lai 29A, Tallinn 10133; tel. and fax 641-1738; e-mail muuseum@online.ee; internet www.loodusmuuseum.ee; over 300,000 items.

Estonian Open-Air Museum: Vabaõhumuuseumi 12, Tallinn 13521; tel. 654-9117; fax 654-9127; e-mail evm@evm.ee; internet www.evm.ee; f. 1957; museum of vernacular architecture; Dir MERIKE LANG.

Estonian Theatre and Music Museum: Müürivahe 12, Tallinn 0001; tel. (2) 644–2132; internet veeb.tallinn.ee/teatrijamuusikamuuseum; f. 1924; Dir ARVO SAAR.

National Library of Estonia: Tõnismägi 2, Tallinn 15189; tel. 631-1411; fax 631-1410; e-mail nlib@nlib.ee; internet www.nlib.ee; f. 1918; collects printed matter in Estonian and about Estonia; compiles national bibliography; provides research, information, exhibition and education services to the Riigikogu and public; 3.4m. items; Dir-Gen. TIIU VALM.

Niguliste Museum and Concert Hall: Niguliste 3, Tallinn; tel. 644-9911; medieval art collection.

SPORTING ORGANIZATIONS

Estonian Athletic Association (Eesti Kergejõustikuliit): Regati pst. 1, Tallinn 11911; tel. 639-8668; fax 639-8667; e-mail ekjl@spin.ee; internet www.sport.ee/ekjl.

Estonian Central Sports Union: Regati 1, Tallinn 0019; tel. 639-8650; fax 639-8653; f. 1922; Chair. ANDRES LIPSTOK; Sec.-Gen. TOOMAS TÕNISE.

Estonian Olympic Committee: Regati 1, Tallinn 11911; tel. 639-8081; fax 639-8773; e-mail eok@eok.ee; internet www.eok.ee; f. 1923; readmitted to International Olympic Movement 1991; Pres. MART SIIMANN; Sec.-Gen. TOOMAS TÕNISE.

Estonian Ministry of Culture Sports Department: Suur–Karja 23, Tallinn 15076; tel. 628-2206; fax 628-2325; e-mail henn@kul.ee; internet www.kul.ee; f. 1991 as the Estonian State Sports Dept, present name adopted in 1996; govt agency; attached to Ministry of Culture; Gen. Dir MATI MARK.

PERFORMING ARTS

In 2002 there were 11 state and town theatres and a further eight small theatres in Estonia.

Eesti Kontsert: Estonia 4, Tallinn 10148; tel. 614-7700; fax 614-7709; e-mail eesti.kontsert@concert.ee; internet www.concert.ee; largest institution to organize concerts and manage musical events; Dir AIVAR MÄE.

Estonian Drama Theatre: Parnü mnt 5, Tallinn 10148; tel. 644-3378; fax 644-0503; e-mail draama@draamateater.ee; internet www.draamateater.ee; f. 1920; Artistic Dir PRIIT PEDAJAS.

Estonian National Opera: Estonia pst 4, Tallinn 10148; tel. 626-0260; fax 626-0246; e-mail info@opera.ee; internet www.opera.ee; Gen. Man. PAUL HIMMA.

Estonian National Symphony Orchestra (Eesti Riiklik Sümfooniaorkester): Estonia pst. 4, Tallinn 10148; tel. 614-7787; fax 631-3133; e-mail erso@erso.ee; internet www.erso.ee; Gen. Man. ANDRES SIITAN.

Estonian Puppet Theatre: Lai 1, Tallinn 10133; tel. 667-9500; fax 667-9501; e-mail info@nukuteater.ee; internet www.nukuteater.ee; f. 1952; Man. Dir MEELIS PAI.

Pärnu Theatre Endla: Keskväljak 1, Pärnu 80010; tel. (44) 20-650; fax (44) 20-652; e-mail teater@endla.ee; internet www.endla.ee; f. 1911; Chief Man. AIN ROOST.

Rakvere Theatre: Kreutzvaldi 2A, Rakvere 44314; tel. (32) 95-451; fax (32) 95–441; e-mail rakvereteater@rakvereteater.ee; internet www.rakvereteater.ee; f. 1940; Exec. Dir INDREK SAAR.

Russian Drama Theatre: Vabaduse 5, Tallinn 10141; tel. and fax 644-3810; e-mail grdt@hot.ee; internet www.grdt.ee; f. 1948; Artistic Dir EDUARD TOMAN.

Tallinn City Theatre: Lai 23, Tallinn 10133; tel. (6) 650-801; fax (6) 650-802; e-mail linnateater@linnateater.ee; internet www.linnateater.ee; f. 1965; repertory theatre; fmrly Estonian Youth Theatre; Chief Man. RAIVO PÕLDMAA.

Vanalinnastuudio Theatre: Sakala 3, Tallinn 10141; tel. (2) 668-781; fax (2) 660-4506; e-mail vanalinnastuudio@vanalinnastuudio.ee; internet www.vanalinnastuudio.ee; Gen. Man. ROMAN BASKIN.

Vanemuine Theatre: Vanemuise 6, Tartu 51003; tel. (7) 427-876; fax (7) 441-065; e-mail teater@vanemuine.ee; internet www.vanemuine.ee; f. 1870; Chief Man. JAAK VILLER.

Viljandi Ugala Theatre: Vaksali 7, 2900 Viljandi; tel. and fax (43) 33-718; e-mail teater@ugala.ee; internet www.ugala.ee; Chief Man. JAAK ALLIK.

Von Krahl Theatre: Rataskaevu 10, Tallinn 10123; tel. 626-9090; fax 626-9099; e-mail krahl@online.ee; internet www.vonkrahl.ee; f. 1992; contemporary performing arts; Man. Dir PRIIT RAUD; Artistic Dir PEETER JALAKAS.

ASSOCIATIONS

Association of Estonian Broadcasters (Eesti Ringhäälingute Liit): Ülemiste tee 3A, Tallinn 11415; tel. and fax 606-1701; e-mail erl@delfi.ee; internet www.ringhliit.ee; f. 1992; 19 mem. orgs; Man. Dir URMAS LOIT.

Association of Estonian Museums: Kiriku Plats 1, Tallinn 0001; tel. (2) 449-340; fax 631-3486; e-mail muuseum@kul.ee; Chair. MARIKA VALK.

International Amateur Theatre Association (IATA): Vene 6, Tallinn 10123; tel. 641-8405; fax 641-8406; Pres. JACQUES LEMAIRE.

Estonian Artists' Association: Vabaduse väljak 6, Tallinn 10146; tel. (2) 627-3630; fax 627-3631; e-mail ekl@eaa.ee; internet www.eaa .ee; f. 1943; protects the rights of artists, supports artistic projects; Chair. JAAN ELKEN.

Estonian Authors' Society: Lille 13, Tallinn 10614; tel. 668-4370; fax 668-4361; e-mail eau@eau.org; internet www.eauthors.ee; Man. Dir KALEV RATTUS.

Estonian Choral Society: Suur-Karja 23, Tallinn 10148; tel. and fax 644-1849; e-mail kooriyhing@kul.ee; internet www.kooriyhing .ee; f. 1922; Chair. AARNE SALUVEER.

Estonian Composers' Union: Lauteri 7C, Tallinn 0001; tel. and fax (2) 645-4068; e-mail heliloojate.liit@mail.ee; internet www.ehl .kul.ee; Chair. LEPO SUMERA.

Estonian Cultural Foundation: Olevimägi 14, Tallinn 0001; tel. 641-1242; fax 641-1220; f. 1987; Chair. SIRJE ENDRE.

Estonian Film-Makers' Union: Uus 3, Tallinn 10111; tel. 646-4164; fax (2) 646-4068; e-mail kinoliit@online.ee; f. 1962; Chair. HANNES LINTROP.

Estonian Handicraft Union: Kuninga 1, Tallinn 0001; tel. 631-4076; Chair. LIIVI SOOVA.

Estonian Heritage Society: POB 3141, Tallinn 10505; tel. 641-1287; f. 1987; collects Estonian memoirs and documents and restores monuments and buildings; Chair. PRIIT HERODES.

Estonian Librarians' Association: Tõnismägi 2, Tallinn 10122; tel. 662-0388; fax 630-7429; e-mail ela@nlib.ee; f. 1923; Pres. KRISTA TALVI.

Estonian Museum Society (Eesti Muuseumiühing): Narva mnt. 23, Tartu 51009; tel. (7) 461-900; internet www.emy.kul.ee.

Estonian National Culture Foundation: Weizenbergi 20A–13, Tallinn 10150; tel. 601-3428; fax 601-3429; e-mail post@erkf.ee; internet www.erkf.ee; f. 1991; Chair. ERI KLAS.

Estonian National Folklore Council (CIOFF—Estonia): Suur-Karja 23, Tallinn 10148; tel. and fax 644-2927; e-mail anne.ojalo@ kul.ee; internet www.folk.kul.ee; f. 1992; aims to develop national and international co-operation in the field of folklore; Sec.-Gen. ANNE OJALO.

Estonian Theatre Union: Uus 5, Tallinn 0001; tel. (2) 441-519; fax (2) 443-584; f. 1945; Chair. TÕNU TEPANDI.

Estonian Writers' Union: Harju 1, Tallinn 10146; tel. 627-6411; fax 627-6400; e-mail ekl@ekl.ee; internet www.ekl.ee; f. 1922; Chair. MATI SIRKEL.

International Council of Monuments and Sites—Estonian National Committee (ICOMOS Eesti Rahvuskomitee): Pikk 46, Tallinn 10505; tel. and fax (2) 641-1287; f. 1993; organizes conferences and heritage days; Pres. JAAN TAMM.

International Council of Museums—Estonian Committee (ICOM Eesti Rahvuskomitee): Pikk 17, Tallinn 10505; tel. 641-1630; fax (2) 601-275.

International Music Council of UNESCO—Estonian Music Council: Suur-Karja 23, Tallinn 0009; tel. and fax 644-9931; e-mail emn@kul.ee; f. 1993; Pres. Prof. PEEP LASSMANN; Sec.-Gen. KADRI RUUDI.

International PEN—Estonian Centre (PEN Rahvusvahelise Klubi Eesti Keskus): POB 66, Tallinn 0001; tel. and fax (2) 446-832.

Mother Tongue Society: Roosikrantsi 6, Tallinn 10119; tel. 644-9331; fax 644-1800; e-mail es@eki.ee; f. 1920; promotes use of Estonian; Chair. Prof. MATI ERELT.

Society of Estonian Regional Studies: Estonia 7, Tallinn 0101; tel. (2) 440-475; f. 1990; Chair. VELLO LÕUGAS.

Union of Estonian Architects: Lai 29, Tallinn 10133; tel. and fax 641-1737; e-mail ealiit@online.ee; internet www.arhitektuur.ee/eal; f. 1921; Chair. TÕNU LAIGU.

Education

The Estonian education system consists of pre-school, primary, secondary, vocational and higher education. There are also 46 special schools, some providing education for disabled pupils, and others giving specialized instruction in music, art and sport. Compulsory education begins at the age of seven and lasts for nine years. The language of instruction at all levels is either Estonian or Russian. In 2000/01 an estimated 59,400 pupils (28% of all school-children) attended Russian-language basic and secondary schools and 5,877 students of higher education institutions (11.6% of the total) received tuition in Russian. Of 685 basic and secondary schools, 566 provided instruction in Estonian, 100 in Russian and 19 in both languages. Estonian was to be the language of instruction in all secondary schools by 2007/08. In 1999 total enrolment at primary schools was equivalent to 96.6% of the relevant age-group, and at secondary level 77.2%. In tertiary education, total enrolment was equivalent to 53.7%. In 2001/02 higher education was provided at 33 institutes of higher education, including universities and academies of agriculture, art, education and music. There were 52,786 students enrolled in higher education in that year. Central government expenditure on education totalled 2,875.5m. kroons in 1999. In the same year, local government expenditure on education amounted to 2,791.2m. kroons. Total public-sector expenditure on education in that year was equivalent to an estimated 7% of GDP.

UNIVERSITIES

Estonian Agricultural University: Kreutzwaldi 64, Tartu 51014; tel. (7) 422-066; fax (7) 466-104; e-mail info@eau.ee; internet www .eau.ee; f. 1951; 6 faculties; 333 teachers; 2,227 students; Rector HENN ELMET.

Tallinn Technical University: Ehitajate 5, Tallinn 19086; tel. 620-2002; fax 620-2020; e-mail teab@edu.ttu.ee; internet www.ttu .ee; f. 1918; languages of instruction: Estonian and Russian; 8 faculties; 486 teachers; 9,428 students; Rector Prof. ANDRES KEE-VALLIK.

University of Tartu: Ülikooli 18, Tartu 50090; tel. (7) 375-100; fax (7) 375-440; e-mail proffice@ut.ee; internet www.ut.ee; f. 1632; languages of instruction: Estonian, Russian and English; 11 faculties; 867 teachers; 15,350 students; Rector Prof. JAAK AAVIKSOO.

Social Welfare

Prior to 1940 health care in Estonia was provided by both state and private facilities. A comprehensive state-funded health system was introduced under Soviet rule; this was restructured in the early 1990s. Social security is administered by the state, while social assistance and social services are the responsibility of local governments. The system of social security comprises pensions insurance (introduced in 1993), health insurance (1991), family benefits (1994), unemployment benefits (1995) and funeral grants (1993). The Ministry of Social Affairs is responsible for administration and policy development in the areas of social security and social assistance, while pensions insurance, family benefits and funeral grants are administered by the National Social Insurance Board. The Estonian Health Insurance Fund administers health insurance, and the National Labour Market Board is responsible for unemployment benefits. In 1994 a minimum income was guaranteed to Estonian families. Under the social-assistance programme, subsistence cash benefits are subject to 'means-testing'. In 1999 there were 31 physicians, 78 hospitals and 72 hospital beds per 10,000 inhabitants. In 2001 there was a total of 152 social-welfare institutions in Estonia. In that year the official retirement age was increased by one year, to 63 years for men and 58 years for women; the average old-age pension amounted to 1,832 kroons per month in early 2003. At 1 January 2003 there were some 296,836 old-age pensioners. The rate of infant mortality was 12 per 1,000 live births in 2001. In 1998 central government expenditure on health amounted to 3,948.6m. kroons, equivalent to 16.4% of central government spending. In the same year, local government expenditure on health totalled 108.7m. kroons, which represented 1.7% of total local government spending.

NATIONAL AGENCIES

Ministry of Social Affairs: see section on The Government (Ministries).

Estonian Labour Market Board: Luha 16, Tallinn 10142; tel. 625-7700; fax 625-7702; e-mail tta@tta.ee; internet www.tta.ee; Dir MATI ILISSON.

Estonian National Social Insurance Board: Lembitu 12, Tallinn 15092; tel. 640-8120; fax 640-8155; e-mail ska@ensib.ee; internet www.ensib.ee; Dir KÜLLI PEDAK.

Estonian Health Insurance Fund (Eesti Haigekassa): Lembitu 10, Tallinn 10114; tel. 620-8430; fax 620-8449; e-mail info@haigekassa.ee; internet www.haigekassa.ee; Chair. HANNES DANILOV.

HEALTH AND WELFARE ORGANIZATIONS

Estonian Children's Fund (SA Eesti Lastefond): Lai 31/Suurtüki 1, Tallinn 10133; tel. (2) 641-1188; fax 641-1189; e-mail lastefond@elf.ee; internet www.elf.ee; f. 1988; Chair. REIN AGUR.

Estonian Pensioners' Union: POB 3665, Tallinn 0090; tel. 646-6423; f. 1990; Chair. OLEG BUROV.

Estonian Red Cross: Lai 17, Tallinn 0001; tel. 641-1125; fax 641-1641; f. 1919; Chair. HILLAR KALDA; Sec.-Gen. RIINA KABI.

Estonian Union for Child Welfare: Endla 6–18, Tallinn 10142; tel. 631-1128; fax 631-1735; e-mail eucw@ngo.ee; internet www.lastekaitseliit.ee.

Union of Estonian Societies of the Disabled: Tatari 14, Tallinn 0001; tel. (2) 442-804; f. 1989; Chair. MIHKEL AITSAM.

The Environment

In early 1996 Estonia and Russia signed an environmental-protection agreement. In 1998 the high level of pollution produced in the industrialized north-east of the country remained a problem. Estonia had, however, improved its treatment of sewerage and drinking water. The Government planned to implement a 10-year programme of environmental management, to meet European Union standards.

In mid-2003 it was reported that the over-exploitation of Estonia's peat deposits risked leading to the destruction of the habitats of a number of rare wildlife species, including the European brown bear, the wolf and the great grey owl.

GOVERNMENT ORGANIZATIONS

Ministry of the Environment: see section on The Government (Ministries).

Environmental Inspectorate: Marja 4D, Tallinn 10617; tel. 656-6720; fax 656-7599; e-mail kersti@klab.envir.ee.

Estonian Meteorological and Hydrological Institute (EMHI): Rävala 8, Tallinn 10143; tel. 646-1563; fax 646-1277; e-mail emhi@emhi.ee; internet www.emhi.ee.

Centre of Forest Protection and Silviculture (Metsakaitse-ja Metsauuenduskeskus): Rõõmu 2, Tartu 51013; tel. (7) 339-464; e-mail mmk@metsad.ee; internet www.metsad.ee; f. 1996; Dir KALLE KAROLES.

Geological Survey of Estonia: Kadaka 82, Tallinn 12618; tel. 672-0094; fax 672-0091; e-mail egk@egk.ee; internet www.egk.ee; mineral resources and groundwater research and geological mapping; Dir VELLO KLEIN.

ACADEMIC INSTITUTES

Environmental Protection Institute: Akadeemia 4, Tartu 51003; tel. and fax (7) 427-432; e-mail tiit@envinst.ee; internet www.envinst.ee; f. 1993; independent scientific and teaching institute of the Estonian Agricultural University; Dir TIIT LEPASAAR.

Estonian Academy of Sciences: Kohtu 6, Tallinn 10130; tel. (2) 644-2129; fax (2) 645-1805; e-mail foreign@akadeemia.ee; internet www.akadeemia.ee; f. 1938; Pres. J. ENGELBRECHT.

Commission for Nature Conservation: Riia 181, Tartu 51014; tel. (7) 421-288; fax (7) 378-013; e-mail tartes@zbi.ee; internet www.zbi.ee/talkk; f. 1955; Chair. Dr URMAS TARTES.

Estonian Environmental Information Centre: Mustamäe 33, Tallinn 10616; tel. 673-7577; fax 656-4071; e-mail info@ic.envir.ee; internet www.envir.ee/itk; f. 1993; Dir LEO SAARE.

Estonian Environmental Institute (Eesti Keskkonnainstituut): Tatari 23/25, Tallinn 10116; tel. 660-4909; fax 660-4908; e-mail ekki@ekki.ee; internet www.ekki.ee.

Estonian Environmental Research Centre: Marja 4D, Tallinn 10617; tel. 611-2900; fax 611-2901; e-mail keskus@klab.envir.ee; internet www.envir.ee/eerc; specializes in chemical analysis in the field of environmental protection; Man. Dir ENN OTSA.

Estonian Institute of Agrarian Economics: Teaduse 1, Saku Sjk., Harjumaa 75501; tel. 672-8630; fax 672-8600; e-mail msepp@online.ee; f. 1994; Dir MATI SEPP.

Estonian Marine Institute (Eesti Mereinstituut): Viljandi mnt 18B, Tallinn 11216; tel. 628-1569; fax 628-1563; internet www.sea.ee; affiliated to the University of Tartu; Dir Prof. TOOMAS SAAT.

Estonian Research Institute of Agriculture : Teaduse 13, Saku 75501, Harjumaa ; tel. 671-1542; fax 671-1540; e-mail anne.toru@mail.ee; internet www.eria.ee; f. 1994; Dir ARVI KALLAS.

Estonian Research Institute of Forestry and Nature Conservation: Rõõmu 2, Tartu 2400; tel. (7) 436-375; fax (7) 436-381; f. 1969; conducts research in forestry, forest management and nature conservation; Dir Dr KALLE KAROLES.

Institute of Botany and Ecology of the University of Tartu: Lai 40, Tartu 51005; tel. and fax (7) 376-222; internet moritz.botany.ut.ee; Chair. Prof. MARTIN ZOBEL.

Institute of Ecology: Kevade 2, Tallinn 10137; tel. 662-1853; fax 662-2283; e-mail eco@eco.edu.ee; internet www.eco.edu.ee; f. 1992; attached to the Tallinn Pedagogical University; research, environmental forecasting and assessment; Dir Prof. Dr JAAN-MATI PUNNING.

Institute of Zoology and Botany: c/o Estonian Agricultural University, Riia 181, Tartu 51014; tel. (7) 428-021; fax (7) 383-013; e-mail zbi@zbi.ee; internet www.zbi.ee; f. 1946; research in microevolution, speciation, population dynamics and ecology; Dir URMAS TARTES.

International Centre for Environmental Biology: Klostrimetsa 44/52, Tallinn 0019; tel. (2) 239-001; fax (2) 238-468; Dir J. MARTIN.

International Laboratory for Plant and Pollution Research: Kloostrimetsa 44, Tallinn 0019; tel. (2) 239-001; fax (2) 238-684; Dir JÜRI MARTIN.

NON-GOVERNMENTAL ORGANIZATIONS

Centre for Ecological Engineering (Tartu Koinsenerikeskus): Viljandi mnt 28, Tartu 2400; tel. (7) 428-254; fax (7) 442-084; e-mail ceet@ceet.tertu.ee; Exec. Dir VALDO KUUSEMETS.

Estonian Environmental Boards' Association (Eesti Keskkonnaametite Liit): Leola 15A, Viljandi 2900; tel. (43) 54-211; fax (43) 53-039; Contact VEIKO KUNBERG.

Estonian Fund for Nature (Eestiamaa Looduse Fond—ELF): Riia 185A, POB 245, Tartu 2400; tel. (7) 428-443; fax (7) 428-166; e-mail elf@elfond.tartu.ee; internet www.elfond.ee; f. 1991; advocates protection of biodiversity and use of sustainable natural resources; Exec. Dir ROBERT OETSEN; Pres. FRED JÜSSI.

Estonian Greens (Eesti Rohelised): POB 1521, Tallin 10402; tel. and fax 641-3402; e-mail roheline@online.ee; f. 1988; political party campaigning on environmental, social and economic issues; Vice-Chair. VALDUR LAHTVEE.

Estonian Society for Nature Conservation: Koidu 80, Tallinn 10139; tel. and fax 684-1584; e-mail nature@hot.ee; f. 1966; organizes courses in landscape management and planning; provides environmental education; Chair. JUHAN TELGMAA.

Friends of the Earth—Estonia (Eesti Roheline Liikumine): POB 318, Tartu 50002; tel. (7) 422-532; fax (7) 422-084; e-mail info@roheline.ee; internet www.roheline.ee; f. 1988.

Society of Environmental Education (MTÜ Keskkonnahariduse Selts): Pargi 22–2, Elva 61503; e-mail info@khs.ee; internet www.khs.ee; Chair. MARKO VALKER.

Union of Protected Areas of Estonia (Eesti Kaitsealade Liit—EKAL): Pk. 30, Viitna 45202; tel. and fax (32) 458-361; e-mail ekal@neti.ee; internet www.ekal.org.ee; f. 1991; Chair. RUUBEN POST; Sec. TEET KOITJÄRV.

Virumaa Foundation: 1 Keskvaljaku, Jõhvi 2045; tel. (33) 22-350; fax (33) 70-009; raises funds for environmental purposes; supports scientific studies; Chair. RAIVO MURD; Dir MART MARITIS.

REGIONAL ORGANIZATION

Association of Baltic National Parks (ABNP) (Balti Rahvusparkide Assotsiatsioon): Secretariat, Lääne-Virumaa, 2128 Viitna; tel. (32) 44-675; fax (32) 44-575; e-mail ekal@estpak.ee; internet www.estpak.ee/~ekal/; f. 1931; Sec. TEET KOITJÄRV.

Defence

Prior to the dissolution of the USSR Estonia did not possess its own armed forces. In April 1992, however, a Ministry of Defence was established and an independent army formed. In August 2002 total armed forces numbered 5,510 (army 2,550, navy 440, air force 220, plus some 2,300 centrally controlled staff). There was also a reserve militia of some 24,000. A paramilitary border guard, consisting of 2,600 troops, was under the command of the Minister of Internal Affairs. In July 2000 military service was reduced from 12 months to eight months. In 1998 the Baltic states agreed to establish a joint airspace observation system (BALTNET), a defence college and a peace-keeping battalion (BALTBAT). A Baltic naval unit (BALTRON) was established in mid-1998. Budgetary expenditure on defence was 1,651m. kroons in 2001. Estonia had increased its defence expenditure, in line with North Atlantic Treaty Organization (NATO) requirements that countries aspiring to membership should assign at least 2.0% of annual GDP to defence. In 2001 the Government approved the foundation of a rapid-reaction unit (ESTBAT) to take part in NATO operations. In November 2002 Estonia was invited to become a full member of NATO in 2004.

Supreme Commander of the Armed Forces: President of the Republic.

Chief of Staff of the Defence Forces: Col ALAR LANEMAN.

Chief of Staff of the Land Forces: Lt-Col PEETER HOPPE.

Commander of the Navy: Sr-Lt AHTI PIIRIMÄGI.

Bibliography

Eilart, J. *The Country and the People*. Tallinn, Eesti Raamat, 1973.

Gerner, K., and Hedlund, S. *The Baltic States and the End of the Soviet Empire*. London, Routledge, 1993.

Hansson, A. *Transforming an Economy while Building a Nation: The Case of Estonia*. Stockholm, Stockholm Institute of East European Economics, 1992.

Hiden, J., and Salmon, P. *The Baltic Nations and Europe: Estonia, Latvia and Lithuania in the Twentieth Century*. London, Longman, 1991.

Kasekamp, A. *The Radical Right in Interwar Estonia* (Studies in Russian and East European History and Society). Basingstoke, Palgrave, 2000.

Koll, A. *Economic Nationalism and Industrial Growth State and Industry in Estonia 1934–39*. Stockholm, Almquist and Wiksell, 1998.

Laar, M. *War in the Woods: Estonia's Struggle for Survival 1944–56*. Washington, DC, Compass Press, 1992.

Lieven, A. *The Baltic Revolution: Estonia, Latvia, Lithuania and the Path to Independence*. New Haven, CT, Yale University Press, 1993.

Mägi, A. *Eesti Rahva Ajaraamat*. Tallinn, Koolibri, 1993.

Misiunas, R., and Taagepera, R. *The Baltic States: Years of Dependence, 1940–1990*. Berkeley, CA, University of California Press, 1993.

Paalberg, H. *Economy, Industry and Agriculture*. Tallinn, Eesti Raamat, 1973.

Parming, T., and Jarvesoo, E. *A Case Study of a Soviet Republic: The Estonian SSR*. Boulder, CO, Westview Press, 1980.

Raun, T. *Estonia and the Estonians*. Stanford, CA, Hoover Institution Press, 1991.

Smith, D. *Estonia: Independence and European Integration*. London, Harwood Academic Publishers, 2002.

Smith, G. (Ed.). *The Baltic States: The National Self-Determination of Estonia, Latvia and Lithuania*, 2nd edn. London, Macmillan, 1996.

Taagapera, R. *Estonia: Return to Independence*. Boulder, CO, Westview Press, 1992.

Vahtre, S. *Eesti Ajalugu*. Tallinn, Olion, 1994.

Various. 'Visions and Policies 1987–93: Estonia's Path to Independence and Beyond', in *Nationalities Papers*, Vol. 23, No. 1 (Special Topics Issue). 1995.

von Rauch, G. *The Baltic States: The Years of Independence, 1917–1940*. London, C. Hurst, 1974.

GREECE

Geography

PHYSICAL FEATURES

The Hellenic Republic lies in south-eastern Europe, on the northern shores of the eastern Mediterranean Sea. Its territory comprises the southern Balkan peninsula (itself including a peninsula, the Peloponnese, connected to the rest of continental Greece by the Isthmus of Corinth), a narrow strip of land on the northern coast of the Aegean Sea and more than 1,400 islands, the largest of which is Crete (Kríti). It is bordered by Albania to the north-west, the former Yugoslav republic of Macedonia and Bulgaria to the north, and Turkey to the north-east. The principal island groups are the Ionians in the west and the Cyclades and Dodecanese in the Aegean Sea to the east. Greece's total area is 131,957 sq km (50,949 sq miles).

Most of continental Greece and many of the islands are mountainous, with much of the land above 1,500 m (4,921 ft). The Pindos Mountains run from north to south along the peninsula, and continue into the Peloponnese and Crete. The Rhodope mountains lie in the northern regions of Macedonia and Thrace and form a natural barrier between Greece and its northern neighbours. The highest point is Mount Olympus, near the eastern coast of the peninsula, at 2,911 m (9,551 ft). The only significant lowlands are in the river valleys and between the mountains and the coast. The principal rivers are the Akhelóös (draining into the Ionian Sea in the west) and the Piniós and Aliákmon, which drain into the Aegean Sea.

CLIMATE

Southern Greece and the islands have a Mediterranean climate, with hot, dry summers and mild, damp winters. Northern regions experience continental influences and are cooler, especially in mountain areas, where snow is common in winter. The hottest month in Athens (Athínai), the capital, is July, with a daily average temperature of 28°C (82°F); the coldest month is January, with a daily average of 9°C (48°F). The west of the country is the wettest area. Average annual rainfall in Athens, in the east of continental Greece, is 414 mm (16.3 ins).

POPULATION

Between the censuses of March 1991 and March 2001 the population increased at an annual average rate of 0.7%. At 1 January 2003, according to official estimates, there was a population of 11,018,400, giving a population density of 83.5

per sq km. Almost all the population are ethnic Greeks; there are small Turkish and Albanian minorities and some Slavophones. Greece has experienced a high degree of internal migration, from the rural areas to the towns and from the mountain areas to the coasts and plains. In 1999 some 60% of the population were resident in urban areas.

Almost all the population speaks modern Greek, of which there are two forms: the formal version, Katharevoussa, which is now little used, and the vernacular language, Demotiki, which is spoken by nearly all and is now used in education and in literature.

The established church is the Eastern Orthodox Church, of which nearly 97% of the population are adherents—there are small communities of Roman Catholics and Muslims.

The capital is Athens, which had a population of 745,514 at the 2001 census, although the Greater Athens area (including the port city of Piraeus, or in Greek, Piraiévs) had a population of more than 3.5m. at that time. Other major cities include Thessaloníki (Salonika, 363,987 inhabitants in 2001), Piraeus (175,697), Patras (163,446) and Iráklion (Heraklion, the principal town of Crete, with 137,711 inhabitants).

Chronology

c. 1500 BC: The early Greeks migrated to the Balkan peninsula from north of the River Danube, displacing the Minoan civilization which had spread from Crete (Kríti) to the southern coast of modern Greece; they established independent states and colonized the coastal regions of the Mediterranean.

1000 BC: Foundation of the Greek state of Sparta, a military society which eventually dominated the southern Peloponnese.

776 BC: The first pan-Hellenic games were held; athletes from all over the Aegean competed; the event is often cited as the first indication of a Greek national consciousness.

7th–6th centuries BC: The city state of Athens (Athínai) developed the traditions of democracy.

490 BC: Persian forces (which had already subjugated the Greek states of Asia Minor) landed at Marathon in Greece and were eventually defeated by the Athenians.

480–479 BC: The Persians again invaded Greece; they advanced on Athens and burned down the city, but were eventually defeated at the Battle of Plataea.

431–421 BC: The first Peloponnesian War was fought between Athens and Sparta.

413–404 BC: The second Peloponnesian War ended with the defeat of Athens.

359 BC: Philip II acceded to the throne in Macedon; Philip's military campaigns in Greece ended the independence of the city states.

336 BC: Accession of Philip II's son, Alexander III ('the Great'), who consolidated his father's position in Greece and then proceeded to invade and conquer the Persian Empire, spreading Hellenic civilization as far as Egypt and the borders of India; Alexander died in 323.

176 BC: With the collapse of the Antigonid dynasty's power outside Macedon proper, the Greek states proclaimed their independence with Roman patronage.

168 BC: Macedon was finally conquered by Rome, and Greece effectively came under imperial rule.

AD 330: The Roman Emperor, Constantine ('the Great'), renamed the city of Byzantium Constantinople (now İstanbul, Turkey) and declared it his capital, the 'New Rome'; it was to become the Christian, Greek-speaking capital of an Empire that continued strong in the East.

395: Following the death of Theodosius I ('the Great'), who had made Christianity the official religion of the Empire and prohibited the worship of the pagan gods, the Empire was finally divided into East ('Byzantine') and West.

6th–7th centuries: Slavs invaded the Balkan peninsula.

895: Conversion of the Bulgars by Orthodox missionaries from the Byzantine stronghold of Thessaloníki (Salonica), SS Constantine (Cyril) and Methodius; their provision of a script and Slavonic liturgy secured the adherence of many Slav tribes to the Eastern Church.

1054: The 'Great Schism' effectively formalized the division of the Church into Catholic West (led by the Roman patriarch, the Pope) and Orthodox East (led by the Patriarch of Constantinople), reflecting the old political division of the Empire and the cultural difference it was based on (Latin cultural domination in Italy and the West, Greek in the East).

1196: The Normans invaded Greece; the Venetians agreed to help the Greeks defend themselves in return for the use of Byzantine trade routes.

1204: The Fourth Crusade arrived in Constantinople and created the so-called 'Latin Empire of Constantinople', dividing the Byzantine Empire into feudal states, ruled mostly by Frankish dynasties.

1259: The Byzantine Emperor Michael VIII captured the Peloponnese from its Frankish rulers; his forces liberated Constantinople in 1261.

1453: Ottoman troops captured Constantinople, thus formally ending the Roman Empire in the East and beginning the period of Muslim rule in Greece—within the Ottoman Empire, Orthodox Christians were to be grouped in the *Rum millet*, headed by the Ecumenical Patriarch in Constantinople.

1571: At the Battle of Lepanto, off the northern coast of the Peloponnese, the Venetians and Spanish defeated the Ottoman navy, ending Turkish naval dominance of the Mediterranean.

1687: Corinth and Athens were captured by Venetian forces.

1767: The Orthodox hierarchy in Constantinople, known as the Phanariots, succeeded in making Greek the pre-eminent Orthodox language of the Empire by displacing Old Church Slavonic from liturgical use.

1770: A nationalist rebellion in the Peloponnese, supported by Orthodox Russia, was defeated; unrest on the island of Crete was suppressed.

1786: Ottoman forces defeated a Russian-inspired rebellion in Epirus.

1814: Three Greeks resident in Odessa (then Russia, now Ukraine) founded a movement in support of Greek independence, the Philiki Etairia (Friendly Society); branches of the organization were established throughout Greece, meeting in secret.

1820: Ali Pasha, the Ottoman governor of Ioannina, began a rebellion against central rule.

25 March 1821: The Greek flag was raised at a monastery in the Peloponnese, beginning the War of Independence.

1821–22: Ottoman forces suppressed a rebellion on the island of Crete, which supported union with an independent Greek state.

13 January 1822: The independence movement having captured much territory, including Athens, Greek independence was proclaimed at Epidaurus.

1824–27: Internal differences within the independence movement meant the imperial forces were able to regain large portions of the territory they had lost, including Athens.

April 1827: Ioannis Kapodistrias was elected President of Greece.

20 October 1827: The Great Powers of France, Russia and the United Kingdom, eager to reduce Ottoman strength in Europe, joined the conflict in support of Greek independence and defeated the Ottoman fleet at Navarino.

1828: French forces having expelled Egyptian forces from Greece, Russia declared war on the Ottoman Empire; the Russians gained an advantage on several fronts and the following year the Ottomans were forced to negotiate a peace.

16 September 1829: By the Treaty of Adrianople, which concluded the war between Russia and the Ottomans, the latter recognized Greek autonomy; Greece henceforth considered itself independent, although its independence was not internationally recognized until the signing of the Protocol of London in 1830.

1831: Kapodistrias was assassinated and the Powers created a hereditary monarchy; in 1833 the Bavarian Prince Otto accepted the throne and moved the capital (hitherto at Nafplion) to Athens.

1832: The Ottoman Empire formally recognized the independence of Greece.

1843: Otto convened a National Assembly, which drafted a Constitution providing for a bicameral parliament.

1862: King Otto was deposed by the military and replaced by the Danish Prince William, who assumed the style of King George I.

1864: The United Kingdom officially ceded the Ionian Islands (a British protectorate since 1815) to Greece; a new Constitution, reducing the powers of the monarchy, was enacted.

1866: A further uprising in Crete saw many Ottoman casualties, but was eventually suppressed.

1870: In the Ottoman Empire, the Orthodox *millet* was divided by decree, with a Slavophone Exarchate separated from the Greek Patriarchate, laying the foundations for Bulgarian–Greek rivalry in the Balkans. (Bulgarian autonomy was recognized in 1878.).

1881: The Great Powers forced the Ottomans to cede Thessaly and a part of southern Epirus to Greece.

1897: Greece's plans to annex Crete resulted in the 'Thirty Day War' with the Ottomans; Greece was defeated and withdrew from the island; according to the terms of a peace settlement, the Ottomans also withdrew and Crete became an international protectorate, but under King George I.

1905: The president of Crete's autonomous assembly, Eleftherios Venizelos, declared the island to be in union with Greece.

1910: Following a *coup d'état* by the military in the previous year, Venizelos was elected Prime Minister of Greece.

30 May 1913: The Treaty of London concluded the First Balkan War, in which a league of Bulgaria, Greece, Montenegro and Serbia succeeded in removing the Turks from the bulk of their European possessions; Greece expanded north and throughout the Aegean islands, and Crete was united with the Kingdom.

August 1913: The Treaty of Bucharest concluded the Second Balkan War; Bulgaria lost Macedonia, which was divided between Serbia and Greece.

October 1916: Owing to a difference in opinion about Greece's alignment in the First World War—Venizelos supported the Entente Powers, of France, Russia, Serbia and the United Kingdom, whereas King Konstantinos (Constantine) I (who had succeeded to the throne in 1913) imposed a policy of neutrality—Venizelos established a rival Government in Thessaloníki.

June 1917: France and the United Kingdom ousted the King and imposed Venizelos as Prime Minister of the whole of Greece.

29 November 1919: The Treaty of Neuilly ceded Bulgarian territory to Greece; the Allied Powers had also granted Greece permission to occupy the predominantly Greek region of Smyrna (now İzmir, Turkey) on the coast of Asia Minor.

1920: Venizelos was defeated in legislative elections; a new, royalist administration restored the monarchy's power.

1922: Turkish nationalists drove back Greek forces, which had advanced far into Anatolia, forcing them to evacuate Smyrna; thousands of refugees fled to Greece, and aspirations for a 'greater Greece', perhaps including even Constantinople, were ended.

1923: The Treaty of Lausanne ordered the exchange of religious minorities in Greece and Turkey; Muslims resident in Greece resettled in Turkey, and more than 1m. Christians from Asia Minor moved to Greece.

1924: The monarchy was abolished when King Konstantinos I was asked to abdicate by the military.

1928: Venizelos was reappointed Prime Minister.

1935: Following an attempted *coup d'état*, a plebiscite (now considered to have been manipulated) resulted in the restoration of the monarchy and the accession of King George II. Venizelos fled to France (where he died in 1936).

April 1936: King George II appointed Gen. Ioannis Metaxas as Prime Minister, resulting in the organization of industrial action by the Communist Party of Greece (CPG).

4 August 1936: Metaxas persuaded the King to impose what became known as the 'Regime of the Fourth of August 1936', in which significant constitutional clauses were suspended; the legislature was dissolved.

28 October 1940: Italy's leader, Benito Mussolini, demanded that Italian forces occupying Albania be permitted to pass through Greece; Metaxas refused this demand, resulting in an invasion of Italian forces from Albania.

April 1941: Germany invaded Greece, which became subject to Bulgarian, German and Italian occupation; the King and his ministers fled into exile in London, United Kingdom, and then Cairo, Egypt, but enjoyed little support among the various resistance groups.

October 1944: Greek and British forces succeeded in liberating Greece from occupation; an agreement between the British and Soviet leaderships ensured that post-war Greece would not be part of the communist 'sphere of influence'.

December 1944: Communist resistance groups launched an armed insurgency against the Government of Georgios Papandreou; fighting continued until early 1945, when a peace agreement was reached, the terms of which included the holding of elections.

1946: A general election in March resulted in an overwhelming victory for royalist parties. A referendum confirmed support for the restoration of the monarchy. Communist groups formed a Democratic Army, the confrontations of which with the official Greek army escalated into civil war.

1949: The communist forces were defeated and the civil war ended.

1952: A new Constitution was enacted, providing for a parliamentary democracy, with a monarch as head of state. The Greek Rally, led by Field Marshal Alexandros Papagos, won a decisive victory in the general election.

1953: Greece, Turkey and Yugoslavia signed a treaty of friendship.

1955: Papagos died in office and was succeeded by Konstantinos Karamanlis. The new premier dissolved the Greek Rally and founded the National Radical Union (NRU—Ethniki Rizospastiki Enosis). Women were given the right to vote.

1956: The NRU won an absolute majority of parliamentary seats in the general election; Karamanlis was reappointed Prime Minister.

May 1958: Following legislative elections the NRU increased its representation in the Vouli (Parliament).

1961: The NRU won absolute majorities of votes and parliamentary seats in the general election; the Centre Union (Enosis Kentrou) was founded by Georgios Papandreou.

1963: Karamanlis resigned; in the resultant general election the Centre Union won the greatest number of seats, although it failed to gain an absolute majority.

1964: King Konstantinos II acceded to the throne on the death of his father, King Paul (who had succeeded George II in 1947). In further legislative elections, the Centre Union won an absolute majority of parliamentary seats.

21 April 1967: A group of army officers seized power and imposed military rule; political leaders were arrested and the general election, scheduled for May, was postponed indefinitely.

13 December 1967: Col Georgios Papadopoulos, who had emerged as the most powerful figure in the 'regime of the Colonels', became Prime Minister; he assumed the foreign affairs portfolio in January 1970 and became Regent in March 1972.

1 June 1973: Following a failed naval mutiny, allegedly inspired by King Konstantinos, the monarchy was abolished and Greece declared a republic, with Papadopoulos assuming the presidency in the following month.

November 1973: Amid increasing public disenchantment with the military regime, unrest among students at the National Polytechnic was violently suppressed by the army; Papadopoulos was ousted in an internal military coup led by the head of the military police, Brig.-Gen. Demetrios Ioannidis; Lt-Gen. Phaedon Ghizikis was appointed President, and a largely civilian cabinet, led by Adamantios Androutsopoulos, was installed; however, effective power remained with Ioannidis.

July 1974: Following an unsuccessful attempt to depose the President of Cyprus, Archbishop Makarios, and the subsequent failure to prevent the Turkish invasion and occupation of northern Cyprus, the Androutsopoulos Government collapsed; the military regime was unable to retain power and Karamanlis was asked to return from exile to form a Government of National Salvation.

November 1974: Karamanlis' new party, New Democracy (Nea Demokratia—ND) won an absolute majority of parliamentary seats at the general election.

December 1974: A proposal to restore the monarchy was defeated in a plebiscite. Michael Stassinopoulos, head of the Council of State, was appointed President.

11 June 1975: A new Constitution was enacted, providing for a parliamentary republic with certain executive powers vested in the presidency; Konstantinos Tsatsos replaced Stassinopoulos as President. In the same month Greece submitted a formal application for membership of the European Community (EC, now European Union—EU).

November 1977: ND was returned to power, albeit with a reduced majority, following legislative elections; the Panhellenic Socialist Movement (usually known by its Greek acronym, PASOK—Panellinion Socialistikon Kinema), led by Andreas Papandreou, became the second-largest party in the Vouli.

May 1980: Karamanlis was elected President; Georgios Rallis succeeded him as premier and ND leader.

1 January 1981: Greece formally acceded to membership of the EC.

October 1981: In a general election, PASOK obtained an absolute majority in the Vouli; Papandreou subsequently formed Greece's first socialist Government.

March 1985: Karamanlis resigned in protest at government plans to amend the Constitution to reduce presidential powers; Christos Sartzetakis was appointed head of state.

June 1985: PASOK retained the largest number of seats (161) in elections to the 300-member Vouli.

August 1985: Greece and Albania reopened their common frontier, closed since 1940; Greece renounced its claim to the Albanian region of Northern Epirus, which contained a sizeable minority of ethnic Greeks.

March 1986: Despite opposition, the Vouli approved constitutional amendments which transferred many of the President's executive powers to the legislature.

August 1987: The Greek Government proclaimed that it no longer considered the country to be at war with Albania, a state which had persisted since the Second World War.

January 1988: Greece and Turkey signed a 'no-war' agreement in Davos, Switzerland, after a decade of increasing tensions, which had brought the countries close to open conflict in March of the previous year.

November 1988: Several prominent members of the PASOK Government resigned after being implicated in a major financial scandal involving alleged embezzlement from the Bank of Crete.

June 1989: ND won the greatest number of seats in parliamentary elections, but failed to gain an overall majority, leading to the formation of a non-political, interim Government, headed by Tzannis Tzannetakis, which announced its intention to implement a *katharsis*, or a campaign of purification, of Greek politics.

November 1989: No party gained a majority at further legislative elections; another coalition administration was formed, led this time by Xenofon Zolotas; however, this Government collapsed in February 1990 and a non-political cabinet was reinstated until a further ballot could be held.

April 1990: ND secured a one-seat majority in another round of elections, and was thus able to form a single-party Government, led by Konstantinos Mitsotakis. In the following month Karamanlis returned to the presidency.

April 1992: Mitsotakis assumed responsibility for the foreign affairs portfolio in order to co-ordinate his Government's opposition to attempts by the former Yugoslav republic of Macedonia to gain international recognition, owing to fears of territorial claims on the Greek province of the same name. In March 1993 the Government accepted a UN proposal that the title 'the former Yugoslav republic of Macedonia' (FYRM) be used temporarily, and that negotiations be pursued on a permanent name acceptable to both sides.

October 1993: The loss of the ND's narrow majority in September, following the defection of several deputies, precipitated a general election; PASOK won the largest number of seats and formed a Government, led once again by Papandreou—who had been acquitted of all charges relating to the Bank of Crete financial scandal in January 1992.

February 1994: The PASOK Government implemented what was effectively a trade embargo, preventing the transport of any goods, other than humanitarian aid, into the FYRM via the Greek port of Thessaloníki. The international community condemned the initiative.

10 March 1995: Konstantinos Stefanopoulos, leader of the small Party of Democratic Renewal (Komma Dimokratikis Ananeosis), was elected President by the legislature.

October 1995: Relations between Greece and the FYRM were normalized, following the implementation of agreements on access to Thessaloníki and alterations to the FYRM's flag.

15 January 1996: Andreas Papandreou resigned as Prime Minister, owing to ill health (he died in June); he was succeeded by Konstantinos (Costas) Simitis.

31 January 1996: In spite of considerable domestic opposition, Prime Minister Simitis complied with a US petition to withdraw Greek military vessels from the area surrounding Imia (Kardak), a small group of uninhabited islands in the Aegean Sea, following Turkish attempts to claim sovereignty of them.

22 September 1996: PASOK, led by Simitis, won 162 seats in the legislative election, having obtained 41.5% of the votes cast; ND won 38.2% of the votes and 108 seats. A Government, similar in composition to the previous one, was subsequently formed.

July 1997: Direct talks held in Madrid, Spain, between Simitis and the Turkish President, Süleyman Demirel, led to the so-called Madrid Declaration, in which the two countries pledged not to use violence or the threat of violence to resolve bilateral disputes; nevertheless, relations between the two countries remained strained.

27 May 1998: A widely observed general strike was held throughout the country, in protest at the Government's privatization plans and the continuing implementation of austerity measures; industrial action continued throughout 1998 and 1999.

18 February 1999: Several members of the cabinet, including the Minister of Foreign Affairs, Theodoros Pangalos, resigned after it emerged that Abdullah Öcalan, leader of a proscribed Kurdish movement which sought secession from Turkey and who was sought there on terrorist charges, had been given refuge at the Greek embassy in Kenya.

17 August 1999: Following a severe earthquake in northwestern Turkey, Greece provided financial and material assistance and renounced its veto on EU financial aid to that country; Turkey reciprocated in the following month when an earthquake in Athens left more than 60,000 people homeless.

20 November 1999: A visit by US President Bill Clinton prompted a series of public protests against the USA's principal role in air-strikes against the Federal Republic of Yugoslavia by forces of the North Atlantic Treaty Organization (NATO) earlier in the year.

10–11 December 1999: At the EU summit meeting in Helsinki, Finland, Greece withdrew its objection to Turkey's candidacy for EU membership.

20 January 2000: Georgios Papandreou became the first Greek Minister of Foreign Affairs to visit Turkey since 1962; the two countries agreed to hold direct talks on their military presence in the Aegean region and signed a number of economic co-operation agreements.

9 February 2000: President Stefanopoulos became the first incumbent Greek head of state to be re-elected to the post, by 269 of the 300 parliamentary deputies.

9 April 2000: In the legislative elections, PASOK, again led by Simitis, won 43.8% of the votes cast and 158 parliamentary seats, narrowly defeating ND, which obtained 42.7% of the votes and 125 seats; the CPG won 5.2% of the ballot and 11 seats, and the Coalition of the Left and Progress secured 3.2% and six seats; three days later Simitis formed a new Government, the principal portfolios remaining with their previous incumbents.

19 June 2000: Greece received a formal invitation to join Stage Three of the EU's programme of Economic and Monetary Union (EMU), from 1 January 2001.

4 May 2001: At the invitation of the Greek Government, the head of the Roman Catholic Church, Pope John Paul II, began the first papal visit to Greece in more than 1,000 years; he had been invited by the Government, but his welcome by the Orthodox clergy was grudging until the pontiff issued an apology for any past transgressions by Roman Catholics against the Orthodox.

23 October 2001: The Minister of National Defence, Apostolos-Athanassios (Akis) Tsohatzopoulos, was transferred to the post of Minister of Development in a reorganization of the Cabinet; earlier in the month Tsohatzopoulos, a frequent critic of Simitis' efforts to introduce unpopular structural reforms, had unsuccessfully challenged the Prime Minister for the leadership of PASOK.

8 November 2001: After months of tension over the issue, the Greek Minister of Foreign Affairs, Georgios Papandreou, and his Turkish counterpart, İsmail Cem, signed an agreement allowing Greece to repatriate illegal Turkish immigrants.

1 January 2002: Notes and coins of the single European currency, the euro, entered circulation; the drachma, Europe's oldest currency, ceased to be legal tender on 28 February.

July 2002: Greek police made the first arrests of suspected members of the clandestine November 17 organization, responsible for more than 20 political assassinations since 1975.

28 November 2002: The European Court of Human Rights ordered the Greek state to pay deposed King Konstantinos some €12m. to compensate for the confiscation of property following the abolition of the monarchy in 1973.

1–2 February 2003: Police arrested three people allegedly linked to the Revolutionary People's Struggle (ELA), a radical leftist group blamed for 200 bombings and two political assasinations between 1975 and its disbandment in 1995. Most notable among the detainees was Angeletos Kanas, Mayor of the Aegean island of Kimolos, who was accused of being principally responsible for producing bombs used by the organization; Kanas insisted that the charges had been fabricated.

3 March 2003: The trial commenced of 19 suspected members of November 17. The two principal defendants were accused of carrying out more than 1,000 criminal acts, including murder, terrorism and bank robbery.

19–21 June 2003: Greece, which had assumed the six-month Presidency of the EU in January, hosted a European Council meeting near Thessaloníki, which was followed by a summit meeting with the leaders of five western Balkan countries.

3 July 2003: Following a decision by Simitis that members of the PASOK executive bureau should not simultaneously hold positions in the Cabinet, PASOK elected a new executive bureau; Michalis Chrisochoidhis, hitherto Minister of Public Order, replaced Costas Laliotis as Secretary-General. A minor government reshuffle subsequently took place.

History
Prof. RICHARD CLOGG

INDEPENDENCE

In 1830 the Greeks became the first of the subject peoples of the Ottoman Empire to acquire the status of a sovereign state, following the success of the revolt against Ottoman rule that had begun in 1821. The protecting Powers of the new state, France, Russia and the United Kingdom, insisted that Greece become an hereditary monarchy and chose as the country's king Otto, a 17-year-old prince of the Bavarian Wittelsbach dynasty. A Constitution, democratic by the standards of the time, was adopted in 1843, following a *coup d'état*, the first in a series of military interventions that punctuated Greek political life in the 19th and 20th centuries.

Greece's fragile democratic institutions, which had been imported from Western Europe rather than evolving organically, proved in practice easy to subvert. Otto was deposed by the military in 1862, to be replaced by King George I of the Danish Glucksburg dynasty, who ruled between 1863 and 1913. Government in the early years of George's reign was characterized by a series of fluid coalitions, although these were superseded during the last quarter of the 19th century by the emergence of a two-party political system.

The Greece of 1830 contained within its borders scarcely one-third of the Greek inhabitants of the Ottoman Empire. As a consequence, the foreign policy (and, indeed, much of the domestic politics) of the new state was dominated by the irredentist vision of the 'Great Idea', the project of incorporating all areas of compact Greek settlement in the Near and Middle East within the bounds of a Greek kingdom, which would have as its capital Constantinople (now İstanbul, Turkey), once the centre of the Eastern Roman ('Byzantine') Empire.

With the support of the European powers that had helped establish the new state, Greece was subsequently able to expand its territory. The Ionian Islands, a British protectorate since 1815, were ceded to Greece in 1864, and the powers forced the Ottomans to cede the agricultural province of Thessaly and a small part of Epirus in 1881. However, the war with the Ottoman Empire in 1897, occasioned by continual unrest on Crete (Kríti) in favour of union with the Greek kingdom, resulted in a rapid and humiliating defeat. The clear lesson of the so-called 'Thirty Day War' was that, without allies, Greek attempts at territorial expansion by military means were doomed to failure.

THE BALKAN WARS

Greece's fortunes improved when, following a coup in 1909, Eleftherios Venizelos came to power in the following year. Venizelos, a native of Crete, was a fervent believer in territorial expansion and in Greece's 'civilizing mission' in the Near and Middle East. When Bulgaria, Montenegro and Serbia sought to exploit Italy's attack on the Ottoman Empire in 1911, Greece could scarcely stand aloof, although, in contrast to the other Balkan states, its *irredenta* were widely scattered throughout the region. In October 1912 Greece attacked the Ottoman Empire, in concert with its Balkan allies, the Great Powers declining to involve themselves in the conflict. Greek forces took Thessaloníki (Salonika) in November and Ioannina, the capital of Epirus, in February 1913. Crete was formally united with the Kingdom, and the remaining islands of the Aegean under Ottoman rule were overrun. Tensions between Greece, Bulgaria and Serbia over territorial claims to Macedonia ensured that the alliance was difficult to maintain, however, and in the brief Second Balkan War of June–July 1913 Greece and Serbia divided up Macedonia at the expense of Bulgaria.

As a result of the Balkan Wars, Greece's territory and population increased by some 70%, although by no means all the inhabitants of the newly acquired territories were ethnic Greeks. Under Venizelos' charismatic leadership the 'Great Idea' appeared to be within Greece's grasp. Over the course of the next decade, however, the vision of a 'Greater Greece' supplanting a declining Ottoman Empire was to collapse.

THE FIRST WORLD WAR

During the First World War Greece was to be divided into two hostile camps—Venizelist champions of a 'Greater Greece' and the supporters of King Konstantinos (Constantine) I, who had acceded to the throne in 1913. The royalists were opposed to further expansionism, advocating a 'small but honourable' Greece. The cause of the 'National Schism' lay in disputes over Greece's alignment in the First World War. Venizelos was an enthusiastic supporter of the Entente Powers (France, Russia and the United Kingdom), while the King and his supporters advocated neutrality. Relations between the King and Venizelos deteriorated to the extent that in October 1916 the latter established a rival Government in Thessaloníki, the Greek inhabitants of which looked upon Venizelos as their liberator, as did most of those in 'New Greece' (the territories acquired in the course of the Balkan Wars).

In June 1917 France and the United Kingdom ousted King Constantine and imposed Venizelos as Prime Minister of the whole of Greece. Venizelos brought Greece into the war as an ally of the Triple Entente. At the Versailles peace conference, convened in France in 1919, therefore, he sought to reap the reward for his support of the Allied cause.

THE 'CATASTROPHE'

In 1919 Greece was permitted by the victorious Allies to occupy a large area in western Asia Minor with a substantial Greek population. The Allies soon withdrew their support for the occupation, however, and it proved to be the catalyst for the Turkish nationalist movement led by Mustafa Kemal (later named Atatürk). In 1920 Greek forces made gains in Asia Minor against those of the new Turkish Nationalist Government, but subsequent declarations of Allied neutrality

weakened the Greek position and encouraged the Nationalists' resurgence.

Isolated internationally, Greece's military position steadily worsened. It was defeated at the Sakarya river in August 1921, and the Nationalist Government gained further international recognition. In August–September 1922 Greek armies suffered a series of heavy defeats; the city of Smyrna (İzmir, in Asia Minor), which had a significant non-Muslim population, was partially destroyed by fire and reoccupied by Turkish forces, while tens of thousands of refugees fled to Greece. The 'Catastrophe', as it became known in Greece, ended all aspirations to the 'Great Idea'. At the ensuing Lausanne peace conference in Switzerland, a compulsory exchange of populations was agreed between Greece and the newly established Republic of Turkey. The arrival of more than 1m. refugees in a country with a population of some 5.5m. placed significant strains on the country's infrastructure. Although the refugees initially encountered prejudice, their resettlement was successfully accomplished—indeed, their arrival occasioned a period of growth in the economy.

POLITICAL INSTABILITY

Throughout the next decade the refugees and the army acted as arbiters of Greece's turbulent political life. The monarchy was abolished and a republic declared in 1924. Venizelos returned to power in 1928, achieving a remarkable *rapprochement* with his erstwhile enemy, Kemal, albeit at the price of abandoning claims for compensation for the property the Asia Minor refugees had been forced to leave behind. However, the economy was severely affected by the world economic crisis of the early 1930s, and this led to a return of political instability. An attempt on Venizelos' life in 1933, and unsuccessful coups in that year and in 1935, contributed to a return to the polarization of the 'National Schism'.

The attempted coup of 1935 prepared the ground for a plebiscite (the integrity of which was persistently questioned) approving the restoration of the monarchy. Upon his accession, King George II called a general election, although this proved indecisive—with neither of the two main parliamentary groupings, the Venizelists and the Royalists, able to form a government. The hitherto insignificant Communist Party of Greece (CPG—Kommunistiko Komma Ellados) held the balance of power. The ensuing political impasse enabled Gen. Ioannis Metaxas, the leader of a small right-wing party, to prevail on King George to allow him to establish what came to be known as the 'Regime of the Fourth of August 1936'. Metaxas' rule became highly personal—key articles of the Constitution were suspended, and parliament, the Vouli, was not to meet again until 1946. Supported by both the army and the King, Metaxas remained in power until his death in January 1941. Although manifesting some of the external characteristics of contemporary right-wing European regimes, Metaxas' policies were neither aggressive towards Greece's neighbours nor racist. Moreover, far from seeking alliances with the Germany of Adolf Hitler or the Italy of Benito Mussolini, Metaxas strongly upheld Greece's traditional British connection in matters of foreign policy.

THE SECOND WORLD WAR

At the outbreak of the Second World War in September 1939, Metaxas, while not hiding his sympathy for the United Kingdom, strove for Greek neutrality. However, Mussolini, seeking to emulate Hitler's military successes, subjected Greece to increasing pressure, which culminated on 28 October 1940 in a humiliating ultimatum. Metaxas rejected this, whereupon the Italians invaded Greece from Albania, although Greek forces rapidly repelled the attack and occupied a substantial area of southern Albania. Nevertheless,

Greece's armed forces, supported by a small British expeditionary force, could offer little more than a token resistance when Germany invaded Greece in April 1941, and Greece was subject to a tripartite German, Italian and Bulgarian occupation. The requisitioning of food stocks caused a devastating famine and 'hyperinflation', while virtually the entire Jewish population of the country, mostly resident in Thessaloníki, was deported to concentration camps.

From the beginning of the occupation, resistance groups came into existence: almost all opposed the return of King George, who had left the country with his Government and part of the armed forces at the time of the invasion. The Government-in-exile, based initially in London, United Kingdom, and then in Cairo, Egypt, had little influence over events in Greece. The resistance groups, with the assistance of a British military mission, achieved some success in attacking lines of communication and harassing the occupying forces. Nevertheless, Greece during the Second World War (as during the First) was a divided society. Growing tension between the communist and non-communist resistance groups escalated during 1943–44 into open conflict. Only the support of the British authorities, increasingly alarmed at the prospect of a communist post-war Greece, prevented the communists from establishing a complete monopoly of the resistance. It was fear of communist dominance that impelled the British Prime Minister, Winston Churchill, to negotiate the 'percentages' agreement with the Soviet leader, Stalin (Iosif V. Dzhugashvili), in October 1944. This agreement, which determined the relative influences of the USSR and the United Kingdom in individual countries in post-war Europe, ensured British hegemony over Greece—regarded as vital to the United Kingdom's post-war interests—in return for Soviet preponderance in Bulgaria and Romania.

Respecting the spirit of this agreement, Stalin offered no support to the communists when, in December 1944, they launched an armed insurgency against the Government of Georgios Papandreou (which had been installed in Greece on the withdrawal of the Germans in October 1944) and the British forces dispatched to Greece in his support. Only after intense fighting was an agreement reached in February 1945, whereby the communist forces agreed to disarm in return for elections and a plebiscite on the monarchy.

CIVIL WAR AND THE RESTORATION OF DEMOCRACY

A general election held in March 1946, with the extreme left abstaining, resulted in a decisive victory for the royalist right. Shortly afterwards a plebiscite approved the restoration of the monarchy. Political stability could not be established, however, and the country slid inexorably towards civil war. The communists established the Democratic Army in October 1946, and in December of the following year a Provisional Democratic Government, which held power in those areas of mountain Greece under communist control, was established. The aid that the Greek communists received from the newly established communist regimes to the country's north was more than matched by the military and economic aid that flowed into the country as a result of US foreign policy. This helped to ensure the eventual defeat of the Democratic Army in mid-1949.

The occupation and ensuing civil war had devastating consequences for the economy, and contributed to the migration from the countryside to the cities which has been such a characteristic feature of post-war Greece. Emigration proved to be both popular and advantageous to the country's economy. It was estimated that during the 1950s and 1960s some 12% of the population emigrated, principally to Australia, Canada and the Federal Republic of Germany (West Germany).

By the early 1950s the foundations were being laid for the remarkable economic and social progress achieved by Greece during the post-war period, although early post-civil war governments maintained some of the more draconian legislation enacted during the civil conflict. By the early 1960s there were signs that the electorate (enlarged to include women in 1955) wanted change, greater liberalization and an end to the monopoly of political power effectively enjoyed by the right.

Such aspirations were embodied in the decisive victory secured by Georgios Papandreou's Centre Union (Enosis Kentrou) party in the general election of 1964. However, the promise of reform and renewal was not borne out. The question of the administration of Cyprus had returned to prominence. In 1960, following a guerrilla campaign against British colonial rule to secure *Enosis* (the union of the island with Greece), Cyprus had been granted not union, but independence. The elaborate constitutional arrangements to share power between the Greek majority and the 18% Turkish minority on the island soon failed.

THE REGIME OF THE COLONELS

Against this background a group of middle-ranking army officers, imbued with the anti-communist mentality of the civil war period, seized power on 21 April 1967, declaring that they had intervened to save the nation from an imminent communist bid for power—although no evidence for this was ever offered. The 'regime of the Colonels', which ruled Greece between 1967 and 1974, was by turns brutal, incompetent and absurd. Its grip on power was strengthened following the failure of a counter-coup led by the young King Konstantinos II (who had succeeded his father, King Paul, in 1964). Power began to be concentrated in the hands of Col Georgios Papadopoulos, who became Prime Minister in December 1967 and Regent in March 1972.

In June 1973, following an unsuccessful naval mutiny, Greece was declared a republic and Papadopoulos, following an election in which he was the sole candidate, became President for an eight-year term. His plans for a 'guided' democracy, however, were thwarted by student protests. In November the student occupation of the National Polytechnic in Athens was violently suppressed, and Papadopoulos was overthrown in a coup led by Brig.-Gen. Dimitrios Ioannidis, the head of the military police. Papadopoulos was replaced as President by Lt-Gen. Phaedon Ghizikis, and a mainly civilian Government, led by Adamantios Androutsopoulos, was installed, although effective power was held by Ioannidis and a small group of military officers. In July 1974 the regime attempted a coup against President Makarios (Archbishop Makarios III) of Cyprus. Makarios retained power, and the attempted coup, together with a dispute with Turkey over petroleum exploration rights in the Aegean Sea, prompted the Turkish occupation of some 37% of the land area of Cyprus. Ioannidis attempted to mobilize Greece for war, but his efforts proved chaotic, and after more than seven years the military regime, with few supporters at home and isolated abroad, collapsed.

KARAMANLIS AND PAPANDREOU

Konstantinos Karamanlis, who had been Prime Minister (with two brief interruptions) from 1955 to 1963, was invited by President Ghizikis to return from his self-imposed exile in France and form a civilian Government of National Salvation. The new Government's priorities were to ensure the return of the military to the barracks, to restore democracy and to defuse the crisis in relations with Turkey occasioned by the Cyprus imbroglio. After removing restrictions on the press and on political parties (including the CPG), Karamanlis moved swiftly to legitimize his power in a general election held in November 1974. His conservative New Democracy (Nea Dimokratia—ND) party secured 54% of the votes cast and 220 of the 300 parliamentary seats. The Centre Union won 20% of the votes cast and 60 seats, the Panhellenic Socialist Movement (Panellinion Socialistikon Kinima—PASOK), founded by Andreas Papandreou, 14% and 12 seats, and the United Left 9% and eight seats. A referendum on the future of monarchy, held the following month, resulted in a 69% vote against the return of King Konstantinos II as a constitutional monarch. In 1975 a new republican Constitution was adopted, providing for a parliamentary democracy while reserving considerable powers to the presidency.

In the general election held in November 1977 ND was re-elected, although PASOK almost doubled its share of the ballot to 25%, displacing the Centre Union as the official opposition. It was clear that the moderate conservatism of Karamanlis, whose primary energies had been focused on bringing about accelerated Greek membership of the European Community (EC, now European Union—EU), an objective that was achieved in 1980, was losing support to Papandreou's nationalism and populism—with its strident opposition to the North Atlantic Treaty Organization (NATO), to the US military presence in Europe, and to the EC. In 1980 Karamanlis was elected to the presidency, his place as Prime Minister and leader of ND being taken by Georgios Rallis.

Rallis proved even less capable than his predecessor of offering a challenge to the increasingly popular Papandreou. PASOK, with its all-encompassing slogan of change, achieved an absolute majority at the general election held in October 1981, winning 172 seats in the Vouli, with a 48% share of the votes cast. Commitments made in opposition to leave NATO and the EC did not materialize, nor did promises of a radical reorientation of domestic policy. However, a number of significant (if low-cost) reforms were introduced in matters of family law and a number of liberalizing measures enacted.

In March 1985 Prime Minister Papandreou proposed amendments to the 1975 Constitution to reduce the powers of the President. Karamanlis resigned in protest, and the Vouli elected Papandreou's own candidate, Christos Sartzetakis, to the presidency. At the general election, held in June, PASOK was re-elected with a slightly reduced share of the votes cast (46%, equating to 161 legislative seats). During his second term of office Papandreou was obliged to introduce an unpopular programme of economic austerity, in part to offset the effects of the spending policies of his first administration.

Throughout the 1980s there were periodic confrontations between Greece and Turkey, the most serious of which, in March 1987, concerned petroleum-prospecting rights in disputed areas of the Aegean Sea and threatened outright war between the two countries. Following the 'no-war' agreement signed in Davos, Switzerland, in January 1988, there was a short-lived improvement in relations between the two countries.

FURTHER POLITICAL INSTABILITY

The unpopularity of the austerity measures and a series of financial scandals, which reached the highest levels of government, as well as highly publicized irregularities in Papandreou's private life and serious ill health, all contributed to the premier's fall from power. At the general election of June 1989 ND won the largest proportion of the votes cast (44%), and secured 145 parliamentary seats, as opposed to PASOK's 125 (with 39%). The Coalition of the Left and Progress (Synaspismos, formed by the CPG and the Greek Left Party—Elleniki Aristera) won 28 seats and thus held the balance of power. After the failure of both the larger parties to form a coalition government, this new alliance was asked by the President to seek a coalition agreement. The result was an

unprecedented ND-Coalition of the Left and Progress administration, led by Tzannis Tzannetakis of ND. The incoming coalition announced its intention to govern for only three months, during which time its priority was to be to bring to justice those political figures implicated in the banking, armaments and financial scandals that had arisen under the previous Government.

A further general election duly took place in November 1989, following the resignation of the interim administration. ND increased its share of the votes cast to 46% and won a further three seats, while PASOK's share increased to 41%, despite the scandals that continued to surround the party. ND remained three seats short of an overall majority; thus, to avoid the prospect of three elections in less than a year, complex negotiations resulted in agreement to form an all-party 'ecumenical' Government under a non-political figure, Xenophon Zolotas. However, the Zolotas Government collapsed in February 1990, and a general election was held in April. ND won 47% of the votes cast, taking exactly one-half of the 300 total seats in parliament. With the support of Konstantinos Stefanopoulos, a minor party's sole member of the Vouli who later reverted to membership of ND, the ND leader, Konstantinos Mitsotakis, was able to form a single-party Government. Karamanlis returned to the presidency in May.

On taking office in April 1990, Mitsotakis introduced an austerity programme and embarked on a series of privatizations aimed at reducing the size of the state-controlled sector of the economy. At the same time, a number of trials arising from scandals affecting the last PASOK Government began. In January 1992 former premier Papandreou was acquitted of all charges of financial misconduct while in office.

Meanwhile, important changes were taking place on Greece's borders. Following the disintegration of the Socialist Federal Republic of Yugoslavia at the beginning of the 1990s, the republic of Macedonia emerged to independent statehood. As a consequence of strong Greek objections, the new state continued to be known officially as the former Yugoslav republic of Macedonia (FYRM). The simultaneous collapse of communism in Albania gave rise to concerns over the 100,000-strong ethnic Greek minority in that country and their possible illegal immigration to Greece. There was also a significant influx of ethnic Greeks from the former USSR, an unusual development in a country that had traditionally experienced emigration.

THE RETURN OF PASOK

In September 1993 ND lost its effective majority when four deputies defected to a newly established party. In the resultant general election, held in October 1993, PASOK obtained 46.9% of the votes cast and 170 parliamentary seats. ND won 39.3% of the votes and 111 seats. Despite deteriorating health, Papandreou was returned to power, with a popular mandate only marginally smaller than that secured in his great triumph of 1981. The growing influence within PASOK of Papandreou's third wife, Dimitra Liani, was formalized when she was placed in charge of the Prime Minister's private office. Relations with Albania and the FYRM remained poor and, as civil war convulsed the former Yugoslavia, the Greeks were out of step with their EU partners in manifesting sympathy for the Serbs, their Orthodox co-religionists.

Although Papandreou had been a harsh critic of Mitsotakis' austerity programme while in opposition, during his third term as premier he instigated measures to reduce Greece's indebtedness, to curtail public-sector deficits and to control the rate of inflation. However, his growing frailty resulted in the increasing concentration of power in the hands of his wife and a small group of advisers. The situation became still more urgent in November 1995 when Papandreou was admitted to hospital, seriously ill with pneumonia. His immediate prime ministerial duties were assumed by the Minister of the Interior and former Secretary-General of PASOK, Apostolos-Athanassios (Akis) Tsohatzopoulos, but for seven weeks Greece was effectively without a head of government as Papandreou clung to life and power. In January 1996 he was finally prevailed upon to resign as Prime Minister. He was succeeded by Konstantinos (Costas) Simitis, a leading modernizer within PASOK, after a closely fought contest with Tsohatzopoulos, the most prominent figure on the populist wing of the party.

AFTER PAPANDREOU

Scarcely had Simitis taken office as Prime Minister in early 1996 than Greek–Turkish relations reached their lowest point since the Turkish invasion of Cyprus in 1974. A dispute over sovereignty of the uninhabited rocky islets of Imia (Kardak), situated between the Greek island of Kalymnos and the Turkish mainland, exacerbated by inflammatory press coverage in both countries, brought the two countries to the brink of war, averted only through the exertion of strong pressure from the USA. The perceived military threat from Turkey led to the announcement of a 10-year, US $16,800m. armaments programme.

Despite distancing himself from the populism of Papandreou, Simitis was able to lead PASOK to outright victory in the general election held in September 1996, at which the party secured 41.5% of the votes cast and 162 of the 300 seats in the Vouli. ND, by this time led by Miltiades Evert, obtained 38.2% of the votes cast and won 108 seats. The CPG secured 11 seats, the broadly 'Euro-communist' Coalition of the Left and Progress (from which the conservative faction of the CPG had withdrawn in 1991, leaving the remaining factions and parties to merge into a single party in 1992) secured 10 seats, and the Democratic Social Movement, a left-wing party of former PASOK members, nine.

On his reappointment as premier Simitis emphasized that his primary objective was to secure Greek membership of Stage Three of the EU's programme of Economic and Monetary Union (EMU) by January 2001, two years after 11 of its European partners had begun to introduce the new single European currency, the euro. The measures of economic retrenchment demanded by this target met with strong opposition from farmers and the powerful public-sector trade unions.

While relations with Albania and the FYRM improved, Greece's relationship with Turkey remained uneasy—despite a pledge, signed by the two countries in mid-1997, not to resort to violence when resolving bilateral disputes. In February 1999 a major crisis was precipitated by Greece's protection of Abdullah Öcalan, the leader of the proscribed Kurdistan Workers' Party, who was wanted in Turkey on a number of charges of terrorist activity. Although the Greek Government had made it clear that it was not prepared to offer asylum to Öcalan, he was admitted into Greece and subsequently given asylum in the Greek embassy in Kenya before his capture by Turkish agents. The Öcalan affair led to the resignation of the Minister of Foreign Affairs, Theodoros Pangalos, and of the Ministers of the Interior, Public Administration and Decentralization and of Public Order. Relations between the two countries continued to be strained, but the new Minister of Foreign Affairs, Georgios Papandreou (the son of Andreas) swiftly indicated that he was not going to emulate his predecessor's confrontational style. Moreover, there was a marked improvement in relations (at least at the level of rhetoric) following the earthquakes that afflicted both countries in August–September 1999, when rescue teams were sent by each country to the aid of victims in the other. A further improvement was marked by the fact that Greece's acceptance of carefully phrased conditions allowed Turkey to be formally admitted as a candidate for EU membership at the union's summit meeting held in Helsinki, Finland, in December of that year.

INTO THE 21ST CENTURY

In February 2000 Konstantinos Stefanopoulos, who had originally been elected President in March 1995, was re-elected to the post for a second term, with the support of both the main parties. Also in February 2000 Prime Minister Simitis announced that a general election would be held on 9 April. This was somewhat earlier than required by the Constitution, because of the need to secure a fresh mandate for his Government's overriding objective—entry into EMU at the beginning of 2001. In March 2000 Greece made a formal application to become the 12th member of EMU. (Entry into EMU was duly achieved in January 2001, with parity being fixed at 340.75 drachmae to the euro.) The strategy of orchestrating an early election proved to be a risky one, for PASOK secured only a very narrow victory over ND, in terms of the popular vote: 43.8% to 42.7%. The electoral system, however, resulted in a clear majority in the Vouli for PASOK, with 158 seats to 125 for ND, in a 300-seat chamber. The CPG won 11 seats, and the left-wing Coalition of the Left and Progress won six seats. PASOK's third successive victory was unprecedented in the country's electoral history.

The sinking in September 2000 of the *Express Samina* ferry off the island of Paros, with the death of 79 passengers, drew attention to the poor condition of many of the ships used on the profitable island ferry services, and provided a reminder of the infrastructural problems that remained to be addressed in Greece. However, the opening of the new, and much admired, Athens airport at Spata in March 2001 alleviated some concerns that Greece was unable to complete large-scale infrastructural projects successfully. In the course of 2002 the Government's attention was increasingly focused on ensuring that the infrastructural arrangements were in place for the Olympic Games, due to be held in Athens in 2004. Major projects included the development of an archaeological park adjacent to the Acropolis and the building of a new museum to house the 'Elgin Marbles' (sculptures and fragments chiefly removed from the site in the early 19th century and currently held in the United Kingdom by the British Museum, return of which has been the subject of a vigorous, although hitherto fruitless, Greek campaign). On a number of occasions the International Olympic Committee (IOC) expressed concern at delays in the construction of facilities and in making improvements to Athens' notoriously poor communications.

In mid-2001 Archbishop Christodoulos of Athens, the Orthodox primate of Greece, orchestrated mass rallies in Athens to protest against the PASOK Government's decision to remove religious affiliation from identity cards. This was a move welcomed by members of Greece's small religious and ethnic minorities and was intended to bring Greek practice into line with that of its EU partners. Despite his unsuccessful campaign, Christodoulos maintained his high profile on the domestic political scene. In a further twist to Greece's Byzantine ecclesiastical politics, in January 2003 police were called in to evict, at the behest of the Ecumenical Patriarch, the monks of Esphigmenou Monastery on Mount Athos. They had refused to accept his authority and were opposed to any *rapprochement* with Rome. However, the visit of Pope John Paul II, the leader of the Roman Catholic Church, to Athens in May 2001 did not arouse the level of opposition that had been expected. In the course of the visit, the Pope tried to assuage Orthodox sensitivities by apologizing for the wrongdoings of Western Christians in dealings with the East, notably for the sack of Constantinople after the diversion of the Fourth Crusade in 1204.

Simitis reshuffled the Cabinet in October 2001. Tsohatzo-poulos—a frequent critic of Simitis' efforts to introduce unpopular structural reforms, who had unsuccessfully challenged the Prime Minister for the PASOK leadership at the party congress earlier that month—was transferred to the post of Minister of Development. He was replaced as Minister of National Defence by Ioannis Papantoniou. Nikolaos (Nikos) Christodoulakis, who had previously held the development portfolio, succeeded Papantoniou as Minister of the National Economy and of Finance, while Dimitris Reppas, hitherto Minister of Press and Media, was accorded responsibility for Labour and Social Affairs.

A significant landmark was the abandonment in early 2002 of Europe's oldest currency, the drachma, with the introduction of euro notes and coins. The introduction of the new European currency, which entered circulation on 1 January, proceeded with relatively little disruption, although the austerity measures necessitated by Greece's entry into EMU provoked considerable unrest in the country's work-force and disquiet on the populist wing of the ruling PASOK, as did attempts to reform the country's complex and costly system of pensions provision. A series of strikes by public-sector workers resulted in the abandonment of proposals to raise the age of retirement.

The opposition ND made some gains in local elections held in October 2002, but not on a scale to pose a potentially serious threat to PASOK. The most significant of these gains led to the election of Dora Bakoyanni, the widow of a victim of November 17 and the daughter of former ND leader Konstantinos Mitsotakis, as Mayor of Athens; she was the first woman to hold the post. Another woman with notable family political connections, Fofi Gennimata, a PASOK member and the daughter of a deceased PASOK minister, Giorgos Gennimatas, was, at the age of 37, elected to the 'superprefecture' of Athens-Piraeus.

In November 2002 the European Court of Human Rights ordered the Greek state to compensate former King Konstantinos, deposed in 1973, for the confiscation of royal properties in Greece. However, the compensation awarded, of €12m., rather than the €320m. claimed by the former King, was far below the market value of the properties concerned. Meanwhile, in another court case that attracted much publicity, in April 2002 14 foreign (mainly British) aircraft enthusiasts had been convicted of esionage activities; eight were awarded prison sentences. The case attracted much adverse publicity in the United Kingdom, but in November the convictions were quashed by an appeals court.

Meanwhile, at the level of rhetoric and gesture, 'earthquake diplomacy' with Turkey had continued into the 2000s. In January 2000 Georgios Papandreou made the first official visit to Turkey by a Greek Minister of Foreign Affairs for 38 years. Shortly afterwards, his Turkish counterpart, İsmail Cem, declared that more had been done to promote good relations between Greece and Turkey during the previous six months than throughout the preceding 40 years. A number of initiatives were taken to further co-operation over non-contentious issues such as combating drugs-trafficking and terrorism, in the promotion of tourism and in economic and technological matters. In April 2001 both countries announced significant reductions in weapons procurement programmes, a move initiated by Greece, which allocated a greater proportion of gross domestic product to defence than any other NATO country.

However, on the major substantive issues of dispute between Greece and Turkey, such as Cyprus and the Aegean territorial claims, there was little progress. In December 2000, for instance, the Turkish Prime Minister, Mesut Yılmaz, warned Greece not to expect 'unilateral concessions by Turkey on Cyprus'. Furthermore, in May 2001 Cem warned

that there would be 'no limits' to Turkey's response were Cyprus to be admitted to the EU as a full member prior to a political settlement. Meanwhile, in June 2000 Greek military aircraft temporarily based in Turkey were withdrawn from a NATO exercise, amid much acrimony, when the Turkish Government insisted that they could not fly over the Greek islands of Ikaria and Lemnos. These had been demilitarized under the terms of the Lausanne treaty of 1923, a provision that Greece maintained the Montreux Convention of 1936 had overridden. In November 2001 the Greek and Turkish Ministers of Foreign Affairs signed an agreement permitting Greece to return illegal immigrants (of whom there were large numbers) to Turkey.

In the latter part of 2000 Greece gave overt support to forces in the Yugoslav republic of Serbia, which were seeking the overthrow of the federal President, Slobodan Milošević. Following his arrest on charges of war crimes (q.v.), in early 2002, Greece agreed to provide UN war crimes investigators with records of transactions from bank accounts suspected of being connected with the regime. This marked a significant shift in official Greek policy—in the 1990s successive Greek governments had afforded a degree of comfort, if not aid, to the Milošević regime.

In January 2003 Greece assumed the Presidency of the EU for a six-month period. The Greek Presidency was inevitably overshadowed by the US-led military operation to bring about 'regime change' (the removal from power of President Saddam Hussain) in Iraq and the diplomatic manoeuvrings that preceded it, and Greek attempts to promote a united European stance over the conflict predictably met with little success. In Greece opposition to the war was manifested by large-scale popular demonstrations. In mid-April, in a ceremony at the foot of the Acropolis, the Treaty of Accession was signed by 10 countries that were due to become members of the EU in 2004, among them Cyprus, the membership of which the Greek Government had strongly supported. However, the collapse in negotiations towards a final peace agreement in Cyprus in March meant that only the Greek Cypriot part of the island was to accede to the EU, and threatened to damage Greece's much-improved relations with Turkey.

None the less, in late May 2003 the Minister of Foreign Affairs, Georgios Papandreou, met the Turkish Minister of Foreign Affairs (and Deputy Prime Minister), Abdullah Gül, and a three-point package of 'confidence-building measures' was announced; the measures were to include exchanges of high-ranking military staff, academic co-operation and medical assistance.

SECURITY CONCERNS AND NOVEMBER 17

Shortly after the 2000 elections, a report by the US Department of State categorized Greece as the 'weakest link' in counter-terrorist efforts in Europe and revealed that US spending on security for its diplomats in Athens was greater than in any other capital city in the world. This provoked an angry reaction from the Greek Government. In June, however, the Marxist-Leninist and strongly nationalist November 17 Revolutionary Organization shot dead the British defence attaché, Brig. Stephen Saunders, in what was claimed to be retaliation for the role played by the United Kingdom in leading NATO bombing attacks on Serbia earlier in the year. No progress was made at this time in tracing the killers, and in January 2001 November 17 was believed to be responsible for a bomb attack in which an ND deputy who had been an outspoken critic of terrorism was wounded. The failure of the authorities to apprehend members of November 17 raised questions regarding Greece's ability to ensure security at the Olympic Games in 2004. This was exacerbated by criticism of the pace of preparations for the Games by the IOC, as well as by a number of prominent resignations from the organizing committee.

After the suicide attacks on the USA in September 2001, attributed to the militant Islamist al-Qa'ida (Base) organization of Osama bin Laden, and in view of the failure of the authorities to apprehend November 17 militants, concern was again expressed about security arrangements in connection with the Olympic Games. However, in July 2002, under considerable international pressure for a demonstrable effort to act against the organization in advance of the Olympic Games, Greek police, in collaboration with US and British authorities, achieved the first significant breakthrough in investigations into the activities of November 17, which for 27 years had, with seeming impunity, murdered politicians, businessmen and diplomats (23 in total). As a result of an inves-

tigation into Savvas Xeros, a painter of icons who was seriously injured at the end of June, when a bomb he was carrying exploded accidentally, by early August 15 suspected members of November 17 were in custody, among them Alexandros Giotopoulos, claimed by Greek police to be the 'ideological leader' of the organization. In September another prominent member of the group, Dimitris Koufodinas, gave himself up to police. The arrests aroused significant media interest, and the trial of Giotopoulos, Koufodinas and 17 others commenced in early March 2003. The apparent neutralization of November 17 lifted the shadow of possible domestic terrorist violence during the Olympic Games, although fears continued to be expressed that the Games might afford a target for terrorists linked to al-Qa'ida.

The Economy
MATTHEW DUNN

INTRODUCTION

Despite being accepted into the European Community (EC, now European Union—EU) in 1981, Greece's economic performance was poor throughout the 1980s and early 1990s. The average annual rate of price inflation was 17.4% in 1984–93, while the economy recorded little or no growth and the national currency, the drachma, underwent a long-term decline on the foreign-exchange markets. There were several reasons for these problems. First, the excessively large public sector dominated the economy, raising questions as to the efficiency of the management and work-force of many of the largest Greek firms, which consequently had little prospect of competing effectively in the European market. In addition, many state enterprises remained untouched by structural changes as the Government continued to support loss-making firms in declining industries. Second, Greece had one of the largest informal economies in the developed world—as much as 50% of economic activity reportedly taking place outside official markets and going unrecorded in national income accounts. Finally, weak political leadership contributed to economic uncertainty and served only to maintain the status quo for much of this period.

Both the 1985–89 Panhellenic Socialist Movement (Panellinion Socialistikon Kinima—PASOK) Government and the 1989–93 New Democracy (Nea Dimokratia—ND) Government implemented fiscal austerity plans and appealed to the EU for financial aid in an attempt to counter high inflation, increasing public debt and widening deficits on the current account of the balance of payments. However, although Greece received substantial transfers from the EU during this period, neither Government succeeded in significantly increasing tax revenues and both provoked industrial unrest and voter disenchantment with their attempts to limit public expenditure. Meanwhile, the rate of inflation remained high and the balance of payments remained chronically in deficit. In October 1993 this pattern of ineffectual economic governance looked set to continue with the reappointment as Prime Minister of the veteran PASOK politician Andreas Papandreou, following the resignation of the ND Government after it lost its narrow parliamentary majority.

CONVERGENCE PROGRAMME

From 1994, however, Greece began to experience a gradual reversal in its economic fortunes. In 1994 the EU agreed a revised economic reform programme with the PASOK Government, aimed at enabling Greece to satisfy the convergence criteria for participation in Stage Three of the EU's programme of Economic and Monetary Union (EMU), established in the 1992 Treaty on European Union (commonly known as the Maastricht Treaty, after the town in the Netherlands where it was signed) in 2001. This obliged the Government to implement a further fiscal austerity programme, which included reductions in public expenditure, restrictions on public-sector wage increases and an attempt to increase revenues by setting a minimum level of income tax payable by all employees, regardless of earnings. Such measures yielded results relatively quickly; in April 1995 the annual rate of inflation was less than 10% for the first time since 1973, albeit at the expense of provoking strikes by public-sector workers, seamen and shopkeepers. This gradual progress towards economic stabilization was aided by the discovery, in late 1995, that the economy ministry had omitted three years' worth of earnings from state pension funds in its annual accounting processes. The US $2,170m. involved assisted the Government in achieving its budget deficit target.

Papandreou's resignation in January 1996 led to the appointment of the former industry minister, Konstantinos (Costas) Simitis, as Prime Minister. Simitis went on to win an absolute majority of parliamentary seats in the general election held in September. His administration's first full term in office was characterized by its focus on pushing Greece's economy towards the EMU convergence criteria. This drive for convergence included negotiating substantial payments from the EU to fund spending on infrastructure and job-creation schemes, granting independence to the Bank of Greece (the central bank) in 1997, in order to ensure that Greece's monetary policy was seen as credible rather than vulnerable to political interference, and reducing indirect taxes on fuel in order to assuage inflationary pressures caused by fluctuations in world petroleum prices. Meanwhile, the Bank of Greece maintained interest rates at around 12% in order to lower the rate of inflation, imposed penalties on commercial banks that exceeded limits on lending, in order to control monetary growth, and oversaw the entry of the drachma into the EU's Exchange Rate Mechanism (ERM) in March 1998.

This mix of fiscal and monetary policy achieved notable success in stabilizing the economy by 2000, when a narrow election victory returned the Simitis Government to power for a second term. The economy grew by an average of 2.8% per year in 1994–99 and recorded real growth in gross domestic product (GDP) of 4.1% in 2000, despite the disruption to economic activity caused by the military action in the Federal Republic of Yugoslavia (FRY) in the previous year. Throughout this period consumer price inflation declined steadily, from an annual rate of 10.9% in 1994 to 2.6% in 1999. In the 12-month EU reference period from April 1999 to March 2000 Greece achieved an inflation rate of 2.0% (by the EU Harmonized Index of Consumer Prices—HICP—measure) and thus satisfied the requirements for EMU entry. Therefore, as Greece had satisfied most of the 'Maastricht' criteria, in June 2000 the European Commission extended a formal invitation to Greece despite the country's wide deficit on the current account of the balance of payments and the high level of government debt relative to GDP. This marked the successful completion of the six-year convergence programme.

In the first three months of 2000 short-term interest rates were on average 540 basis points (5.4 percentage points) above the equivalent 'euro-zone' rates, as the Government used a tight monetary policy to keep inflation under control. Once the EU accepted Greece's application to join EMU, the Government then repeatedly reduced interest rates in order to converge with the main refinancing rate of the European Central Bank (ECB), 4.75%, on entry into EMU on 1 January 2001. This relaxation of monetary policy allowed Greece to enjoy continued strong economic performance in 2001: real GDP increased by 4.1% over the year, despite the negative impact of the economic slowdown in the USA and in Greece's major EU trading partners in the last six months of the year. The economic situation remained relatively positive in 2002: GDP increased in real terms by 4.0%, and in nominal terms, GDP was US $134,075m. at market exchange rates in 2002, while GDP per head was $12,650. In 2002 GDP per head in Greece was 69% of the EU average. However, although the rate of economic growth in Greece was significantly above the average growth of 2.1% recorded in the euro zone in 2002, inflation was also significantly higher than the ECB target rate of 2.0%. Consumer-price inflation in Greece reached 3.6% in 2002, up from 3.4% in 2001, largely because of the increase in petroleum prices over the year. The small size of the Greek economy compared with the rest of the euro zone meant that the country's economic situation had little impact on the ECB's policy agenda. Therefore, despite the relatively high level of inflation in Greece, the ECB maintained its key interest rate at 3.25% for most of 2002, before reducing rates to 2.75% in December 2002, in an attempt to stimulate growth in Germany and other countries experiencing decelerating rates of growth.

PRIVATIZATION

The public sector traditionally played a strong role in the Greek economy—in 1998 an estimated 45% of all recorded economic activity took place in the public sector. This factor was at least partly responsible for Greece's poor economic performance in the 1980s and early 1990s—weak management and militant trade unions characterized state-owned enterprises. However, in the mid-1990s the Government began selling stakes in certain state-owned enterprises, as part of its aim to achieve structural reforms and to reduce the government debt by realizing some of its assets.

The pace of the privatization programme was relatively slow in its early years, as Simitis and other reformists in the PASOK administration were concerned not to anger tradition-alists and trade union members on the left wing of the party. Consequently, the Government maintained the constitutional bar on the sale of greater than a 49% equity stake in state-owned enterprises, generally offering holdings in these enterprises to individual private investors rather than foreign strategic investors who might seek to create a majority holding in the long term. This model of privatization occasioned a significant increase in the value of companies quoted on the Athens Stock Exchange in 1998–99, as large numbers of people entered the equity market for the first time. However, it also meant that in many cases pre-existing management structures remained in place, as there was no intervention from strategic investors seeking to reduce costs and to improve working practices. State enterprises partially privatized in this way included Organismos Telepikoinonion tis Elladas (OTE—Hellenic Telecommunications), the Ionian and Popular Bank of Greece, Hellenic Petroleum, Elefsis Shipyards and the national network of duty-free shops at airports and ports. Despite a failed first attempt to attract foreign investors in 1994, the partial privatization of OTE, in particular, was successful—the company was able to benefit from the expansion in the telecommunications sector and developed a strong mobile telephones business. OTE also expanded into other markets in South-Eastern Europe: in 1998 it acquired 35% of Romtelecom, the Romanian state telecommunications operator, later increasing its stake to over 53% in 2002 and also acquiring stakes in telecommunications operators in Bulgaria and the former Yugoslav republic of Macedonia (FYRM).

In September 2000 the Government accelerated the privatization programme by introducing legislation allowing private investors to acquire up to 66% of shares in newly privatized companies rather than limiting private ownership to 49% as before. Privatization arrangements conducted in 2000–02 included the acquisition by Ferrostahl-HDW of Germany of a strategic stake in Hellenic Shipyards in October 2001; an initial public offering of 15% of total equity in the Public Power Corporation (DEH) in December 2001; the sale of a further 67% stake in the partly privatized Hellenic Industrial Development Bank in June 2002 and the sale of a further 8% in OTE in 2002, so that the state retained only 33% of the equity in the company. However, several privatizations proved problematic. Notably, two separate and protracted attempts to sell off the loss-making state airline Olympic Airways collapsed in February 2002 and January 2003, when in each case prospective bidders withdrew. In April 2003 the European Commission began legal proceedings against Olympic Airways, claiming that the airline should repay subsidies worth US $185m. to the Greek Government as this represented illegal state aid. If Olympic Airways lost the case it could be forced into bankruptcy by 2004. In another failed privatization, LUKoil of Russia won the right to buy a 23% stake in Hellenic Petroleum, but subsequently withdrew, after failing to agree on terms with the Government.

GOVERNMENT FINANCES

In the early 1990s the Government was burdened with a massive public debt caused by the large and inefficient public sector and rapidly increasing debt-service payments, as interest rates averaged around 28%. Therefore, one of the main elements of the country's attempts to qualify for entry into EMU was a concerted effort to eliminate the budget deficit and reduce the government debt. One of the ways in which this was achieved was by widening the tax base. Tax evasion was traditionally commonplace in Greece: it was independently estimated that as recently as the early 1990s many people were paying as little as 5% tax on their personal income. During the course of the late 1990s the Government implemented a new computer system in order to restrict tax evasion and benefit frauds by creating electronic records of individuals' employment history. This led to an increase in tax revenues of at least 5% per year during 1997–2000.

While the state thus enjoyed a significant increase in revenue from taxation and privatizations, it also sought to limit increases in public expenditure. In 1998, for example, the Government implemented a 2.5% limit on nominal wage increases for all public-sector workers; this limit was then reduced to 2.0% in 1999. The Government also restricted spending on other areas, for example, health and education, prompting criticism that it pursued economic goals at the expense of social welfare. The effects of this restrictive fiscal policy were, nevertheless, clear. In 1993 the Government operated a primary deficit (the difference between government expenditure and revenue excluding interest payments on public debt) equivalent to 1.0% of GDP, while the total budget deficit was equal to 13.0% of GDP; in 2000, by contrast, the Government ran a primary surplus equivalent to 5.8% of GDP and a budget deficit equal to just 1.0% of GDP. This satisfied the Maastricht convergence requirement that countries seeking membership of EMU must have a budget deficit not exceeding 3.0% of GDP. In 2001 the Government first reported a budget surplus equivalent to 0.1% of GDP, but later revised this, to report a deficit of 1.2% of GDP after Eurostat (the EU's statistical office) ordered that certain additional items, such as subsidies to state-owned enterprises, should be listed as expenditure. In 2002 the budget deficit remained relatively unchanged, at 1.1% of GDP, which was worse than initially forecast by the Government but significantly better than the deficits reported by other EU states such as Portugal, France and Germany in 2002, equivalent to more than 3.0% of GDP.

The Simitis Government had enjoyed only modest success in reducing the public debt. In 2002 the general government debt was equivalent to 105.3% of GDP, compared with 111.6% in 1993. The Government's assertion that the outstanding public debt would be equivalent to its target of 60% of GDP by 2010 therefore appeared overly optimistic. Problems associated with the privatization strategy were partly responsible for the relatively slow progress in reducing the debt, since the Government often assumed debts from companies undergoing restructuring prior to privatization in order to make them more attractive to private investors. Since 1999, however, the privatization programme has allowed tangible improvements in the public debt position: the Government raised an estimated US $2,600m. (1.9% of GDP) from the sale of state-owned assets in 2002. Despite the fact that Greece's public debt is expected to remain well above the target level of 60% of GDP set out by the Maastricht criteria, this should not prove a major problem over the next few years. Once Greece became a member of EMU, or the euro zone, it benefited from lower interest payments on its public debt, as it enjoyed comparatively low euro-zone interest rates. In 1999, prior to EMU entry, average interest rates in Greece were some 10%; consequently debt-service payments were high (equivalent to 9% of GDP) in comparison with those of the 11 countries of the euro zone (which averaged 4% of GDP), where interest rates stood at about 3.0%. In 2000–02 Greece's relatively strong economic performance reduced the cost of borrowing by the Government; the yield paid on three-year government bonds declined from 5.99% in 2000 to 4.06% at the end of 2002.

EMPLOYMENT AND UNEMPLOYMENT

There was a significant increase in unemployment in the mid-1990s—the number of people registered as unemployed rose from 301,000 (7.7% of the labour force) in 1992 to 446,400 (10.3% of the labour force) in 1996. This increase was caused largely by the Europe-wide economic recession in the first part of the decade. The Greek economy contracted by 1.6% in 1993,

and private investment decreased between 1992 and 1994. This led to redundancies throughout the economy, although sectors already weakened by structural change, such as textiles, manufacturing and mining, were particularly badly affected. Between 1996 and 2002 the rate of unemployment remained relatively stable, at around 10%, with a level of 9.6% reported in 2002. However, the Government expressed concern that among those aged 16–25 years unemployment had reached 29% in 1999. In line with other European governments, in 1998–99 the PASOK administration announced incentives for companies to create jobs for young people—for example, a 50% reduction in employers' social security contributions for new employees.

As mentioned above, national and industry-wide agreements moderated demands for wage increases in the late 1990s. Nevertheless, employees enjoyed average real wage increases of about 3% each year in 1995–2000, after experiencing several years of declining real wage rates, caused by high rates of price inflation and weak economic performance, in the early 1990s. Real wages continued to increase in 2002, as a national wage agreement allowed most employees a minimum increase of 5.4%, well above the rate of inflation. Meanwhile, productivity growth in 2002 was 3.5%, meaning that, in real terms, unit labour costs incurred by employers declined by 0.5% in 2002.

SECTORAL DEVELOPMENT

As in other developed countries, the services sector was the fastest growing element of the Greek economy in the late 1990s. In 2002 agriculture contributed less than 10% of GDP, compared with some 20% for industry (including mining, manufacturing, power and construction) and almost 70% for service industries, the output of which increased by an estimated 5% in 2002. In that year service industries employed 61.7% of the employed labour force, while industry engaged 22.5%. Banking experienced particularly strong growth in the late 1990s, partly as a result of consolidation within the sector, such as the acquisition of Ionian Bank by Alpha Credit Bank in 1999 and EFG Eurobank's purchase of a majority holding in Ergobank. Commercial banks also diversified into new business areas, such as the provision of unit and investment trusts and insurance products, partly in response to the increase in consumer interest in the Athens Stock Exchange in 1997–2000; however, the value of the stock exchange's index declined dramatically between September 2000 and April 2003, forcing many retail investors to retreat from equities, and reducing revenues for banks and stockbrokers. Banks had, however, benefited from the huge rise in demand for consumer credit: in 2002 the market for credit cards alone expanded by more than 30%. The telecommunications sector also performed strongly from the late 1990s, as demand for internet access and for mobile telecommunications increased strongly. In July 2001 the Government raised US $435m. by auctioning third generation mobile telecommunications licences to the incumbent operators Panafon Hellenic Telecom, Stet Hellas and COSMOTE. Construction and tourism also recorded strong performances in the late 1990s, the former sector accounting for an estimated 9.0% of GDP in 1998. The announcement in 1997 that the 2004 Olympic Games were to take place in Athens, along with continued government expenditure on infrastructure projects such as the new Spata airport for Athens (opened in March 2001), led the construction industry to register growth of 8% in 2002; moreover, there were expectations that as a result of the Olympic Games and a number of projects to improve transport infrastructure, construction would account for 12% of GDP by 2004. Meanwhile, revenues from tourism recorded only limited growth in 2001, and declined by 6% in 2002, to $9,800m. This was primarily the result of the negative economic impact of the suicide attacks against the USA on 11 September 2001, and the onset of US-led military action in Iraq in 2003, particularly in terms of deterring US tourists from cruise travel in the eastern Mediterranean.

While service industries showed relatively strong growth in the late 1990s, many traditional manufacturing sectors experienced sharp declines during the same period. For example, the clothing and footwear sector declined by 12.8% in 1998 alone, as companies found themselves unable to compete with strong competition from Eastern Europe and South-East Asia. The clothing sector declined by a further 2% in 2002, as more companies outsourced their manufacturing operations to countries in the Balkans to take advantage of cheaper labour costs. Meanwhile, although the shipping industry performed strongly, other heavy industries, such as cement manufacture and mining, remained stagnant—the cement company AGET Heracles recorded several years of losses and was eventually sold by the Italian Calcestruzzi consortium to Blue Circle International of the United Kingdom in late 1999. Blue Circle, and with it AGET Heracles, subsequently became part of the Lafarge Group (France) in 2001. Meanwhile, difficulties encountered by TVX Gold of Canada in exploiting its collection of assets purchased in 1995 drew attention to regulatory problems in the mining sector. TVX Gold experienced a series of legal challenges from environmentalists and local government officials against its operations in Greece. The company declared *force majeure* on three separate occasions in 2001–03 in response to legal action related to its Stratoni mine, and in March 2002 announced plans to write down the value of its US $250m. investment in the Olympias gold mine project after the highest court in Greece declared its mining permits to be invalid. However, there was an increase in growth in the energy sector from 1998, as the natural gas network came on stream. The Public Gas Corporation (DEPA) began receiving liquefied natural gas (LNG) shipments from Algeria in November 1999, and in 2002 DEPA began negotiations with Boru Hatları ile Petrol Taşıma AŞ (BOTAŞ) of Turkey and Edison, SPA of Italy regarding the possible construction of new pipelines to transport gas to Greece. Other cross-border developments contributing to growth in the energy sector included Hellenic Petroleum's completion in 2002 of a pipeline to transport oil from Thessaloníki to its Okta refinery, near Skopje, the FYRM, and its plans to extend this pipeline from Skopje into the province of Kosovo, Serbia and Montenegro. Finally, in May 2003 Greece signed a memorandum of understanding with Bulgaria and Russia to allow work to begin on a pipeline to transport Russian oil from Burgas, on the Black Sea coast of Bulgaria, to Alexandroupolis.

FOREIGN INVESTMENT

Foreign investment in Greece has remained relatively limited in comparison with other EU countries. Many companies were deterred from investing by the potential problems associated with operating in the country. These included allegations of corruption among public officials, legal challenges from domestic competitors or local interest groups and the sporadic small-scale bomb attacks on foreign companies' offices in Athens and Thessaloníki attributed to extreme left-wing terrorist groups. Nevertheless, many firms operated successfully in Greece—the total stock of foreign investment was estimated at around US $6,500m. in 2001. Major investors included consumer goods companies, such as the US Procter & Gamble, the British-Dutch Unilever and Amstel-Heineken of the Netherlands; petroleum companies, such as BP (United Kingdom-USA) and Royal Dutch Shell (United Kingdom-Netherlands); and banks, such as Crédit Agricole of France. In a significant development, in 2003 the US soft-drinks manufacturer Coca-Cola announced that it was to move its corporate headquarters for Southern Europe and the Middle East from Bahrain to Athens. Net foreign direct investment in 2002 was estimated at $600m., as overseas investment by Greek companies partly offset inward direct investment by foreign companies. Meanwhile, inward portfolio investment was equivalent to $11,115m. in 2002, an increase of 18% compared with the previous year.

FOREIGN TRADE

Greece has traditionally operated a substantial trade deficit, owing to net imports of goods, particularly oil and other energy products, vehicles and other manufactured goods. In 2002 Greece recorded a deficit of US $10,405m. on the current account of the balance of payments. According to official trade statistics, merchandise imports were valued at $31,320m. at market exchange rates, with substantial imports in the following sectors: machinery and vehicles (28% of total imports), chemicals (12%) and petroleum, gas and other energy products (10%). Merchandise exports were valued at $9,868m. in 2002, with textiles (17%), clothing (18%), food and drink (17%) and metals (7%) representing the strongest export sectors. The trade deficit increased over the course of 2002, largely because the country's position as a net importer of petroleum meant that the value of imports increased. Meanwhile, the poor economic environment elsewhere in the EU meant that there was almost no growth in sectors that traditionally provide 'invisible' export earnings—such as tourism and airline travel.

Between 1994 and 2001 the economy received annual net transfers from the EU equivalent to 4% of GDP. These payments will continue until at least 2006, as in 2002 the EU began making a new round of net transfers to Greece under the Community Support Framework Stage Three (CSF III) programme. These were expected to be valued at US $50,000m. between 2002 and 2006, with funds destined for agriculture, infrastructure and the training of employees. Meanwhile, Greece also benefited from net capital inflows between 1997 and 2000, as foreign investors took advantage of high interest rates in Greece, while interest rates declined steadily elsewhere in the EU in preparation for Stage Three of EMU. Greece's strict monetary policy contributed to the gradual erosion of the competitiveness of Greek exports after 1994, however. Although high interest rates supported the Bank of Greece's policy of effectively 'pegging' the drachma to the euro, the country's relatively high rates of inflation led to an increase in the price of Greek goods compared with those produced elsewhere in the EU and, consequently, a gradual appreciation in the real exchange rate.

In 2002–03 the appreciation of the euro against other major currencies, such as the US dollar and the British pound sterling, reduced the competitiveness of exports from the EU, although this had only a limited impact on Greece, as its main trading partners were traditionally the larger economies of the EU. In 2001 Italy supplied 15.6% of all imports to Greece, followed by Germany (15.0%) and France (9.2%). In terms of exports, in 2001 15.9% of all exports from Greece went to Germany, 13.5% to Italy and 6.4% to the United Kingdom. This close relationship with other EU economies resulted partly from their geographical proximity and the fact that they all enjoyed free-trade status within the EU customs union. Foreign trade with countries elsewhere in South-Eastern Europe was relatively limited throughout the most of the 1990s. Ethnic conflicts within the former Yugoslavia led to collapses in economic demand and severe restrictions on trade throughout the Balkan region, while generally poor political relations with Turkey restricted trade with Greece's largest neighbour. However, this situation began to change as a result of a series of positive political developments from 1999.

Following the end of the Kosovo conflict, Greek companies such as OTE also developed a strong presence in Yugoslavia (now Serbia and Montenegro) and other Balkan countries. As an example of this expansion, in early 2003 Hellenic Petroleum bought a 54% majority stake in the state-owned Montenegrin petroleum company, Jugopetrol, for US $68m. Estimates produced by the EU showed that Greece had become the largest investor in the FYRM, with OTE owning controlling stakes in both of the FYRM's mobile telecommunications operators. Meanwhile, the rapid improvement in relations between the Greek and Turkish Governments in late 1999 was facilitated by mutual emergency co-operation following the earthquakes in İzmit, Turkey, in August and in Athens in September (see History). This was a factor contributing to Greece's endorsement of Turkey's application for EU candidate status at the organization's summit meeting in Helsinki, Finland, in December 1999 and to the signature of a series of bilateral accords on trade and economic co-operation in 2000–01. In 2000 an international consortium composed of Exxon-Mobil of the USA, Vama of Turkey and Copelouzos began work on building a natural gas power station in Komotiní to supply electricity to Turkey. This went some way towards removing obstacles to trade with Turkey, which represented a potentially significant export market for Greece, and an increase in bilateral trade was expected in the early years of the 21st century, particularly as Turkey moved closer towards obtaining EU membership.

EXCHANGE RATES

The Greek currency, the drachma, was traditionally weak, its performance in the 1980s and early 1990s characterized by frequent declines in value relative to the US dollar and the German Deutsche Mark. In 1994, following the start of the Government's drive to achieve entry into EMU, the Bank of Greece, under Governor Lukas Papademos, initiated a 'hard drachma' policy, aimed at stabilizing exchange rates. This was achieved by maintaining strict monetary policies, in particular high interest rates, and by intervening when necessary to support the drachma on the foreign-exchange markets. This policy achieved its principal goal of eliminating the wide fluctuations in value of the drachma. Following a devaluation of 12.3% relative to the 'basket' of other EU currencies in March 1998 and a government commitment to continued structural reform, Greece entered the ERM later that month. The drachma entered at a central parity with the European Currency Unit (ECU) of 357:1, around which it was allowed to fluctuate by up to 15%.

As forecast by the convergence programme, the EU ruled in 1998 that Greece had not satisfied the Maastricht convergence criteria and the drachma did not enter Stage Three of EMU in January 1999. Instead the drachma entered a second group of ERM members, known as ERM-2, at a revised central parity with the new euro of 353:1, in order to continue the process of convergence in advance of Greece's entry into EMU in January 2001. Greece's high interest rates and the weak performance of the euro relative to the US dollar and the pound sterling meant that the drachma traded well above its central parity throughout 1999. As a result, in January 2000 the Bank of Greece and the ECB revised the central parity upward to 340:1. This revaluation also reflected the determination of both the Government and the Bank of Greece that the country should enter EMU at a strong exchange rate, in order to ensure that the rate of inflation remained low in the long term, even if this resulted in a further decline in export competitiveness. Greece entered EMU in January 2001, and—along with the other 11 participating members—carried out a successful changeover process in the first two months of 2002 to introduce the euro as the sole legal currency. The country experienced significantly lower interest rates after

monetary policy passed from the Bank of Greece to the ECB, while commercial banks enjoyed increased liquidity as the Government reduced required reserve holdings at the Bank of Greece from 12% of total assets to 2%, in compliance with ECB regulations. These changes in the monetary environment caused growth in money demand: lending to consumers increased at an annual rate of 30% in both 2001 and 2002. However, consumer price inflation remained relatively stable at around 3.5%, and the euro's relatively strong performance in 2002–03 against the US dollar and the pound sterling, in particular, helped to reduce inflationary pressures in Greece and the rest of the euro zone.

OUTLOOK

The PASOK Governments led by Konstantinos Simitis achieved the criteria required for membership of EMU and thus for long-term economic stability. It was anticipated that Greece would in subsequent years enjoy low interest rates and low inflation, creating positive conditions for further domestic economic growth in comparison to the more volatile business environments experienced until the mid-1990s. Meanwhile, improvements in diplomatic relations with the country's close neighbours were also expected to allow Greek companies to expand further into developing markets such as Bulgaria, Romania, Turkey and Serbia and Montenegro. These positive factors were likely to assist Greece in recording further robust economic growth, well in excess of the growth of larger EU member states such as Germany, which were expected to record only modest growth.

However, the economic situation was not entirely positive. First, Greece's heavy dependence on trade with other EU states meant that continued slow rates of growth in Germany, France and Italy in 2003–04 might impede export performance and therefore limit economic growth. Second, continued growth remained to an extent contingent on the success of the Government's programme to reform the economy through the continuation of the privatization process, the liberalization of labour markets and reduced government expenditure. Regarding privatization, opposition from the employees of state-owned enterprises towards any new management, along with investors' limited appetite for new share offerings after three years of falling equity markets, meant that further delays to the planned divestment of key enterprises, such as Olympic Airways and Hellenic Petroleum, appeared likely in 2003–05. Any such delays would damage the Government's attempts to reduce its outstanding public debt and transform inefficient state-owned enterprises into private companies capable of competing against foreign rivals.

Similar delays appeared likely in the long-awaited reforms to the labour market and to the state pensions system, largely because Prime Minister Simitis and his PASOK Government were expected to encounter entrenched resistance from both left-wing PASOK politicians and the centre-right ND opposition to the implementation of further economic reform programmes. Indeed, there was speculation that any major economic reform would be delayed until after the parliamentary elections scheduled to take place by April 2004, as the PASOK Government would instead need to concentrate on other pressing issues, such as the need to complete preparations for the 2004 Olympic Games and attempts to resolve political divisions in Cyprus. Any such delays were likely to have a significant negative impact on the fiscal situation in Greece: the Organisation for Economic Co-operation and Development (OECD) warned that Greece would incur unsustainable budget deficits by 2010 if the Government's existing welfare transfers continued, particularly as the ratio of employed workers to pensioners claiming benefits was expected to decline dramatically and, therefore, put pressure on the 'pay-as-you-go' pension system. Pressure on the Government's finances would be exacerbated by the entry of new member states into the EU from 2004. After CSF III transfers to Greece come to an end in 2006, it appears that Greece will no longer be assured of receiving financial transfers from the EU, as funds are likely to be diverted to poor regions of new member states throughout Central and South-Eastern Europe. This could be significant, as transfers from the EU

are expected to account for up to one-third of all economic growth recorded by Greece in 2002–06. Therefore, once EU transfers are removed, the rate of economic growth in Greece might slow by at least one percentage point each year, undermining the Government's long-term plans to achieve the same level of economic prosperity enjoyed by more developed EU member states.

Statistical Survey

Source (unless otherwise stated): National Statistical Service of Greece, Odos Lykourgou 14–16, 101 66 Athens; tel. (1) 03289530; fax (1) 03241102; e-mail info@statistics.gr; internet www.statistics.gr.

Area and Population

AREA, POPULATION AND DENSITY

Area (sq km)	131,957*
Population (census results)†	
17 March 1991	10,259,900
March 2001	
Males	5,426,446
Females.	5,537,574
Total	10,964,020
Population (official estimates at 1 January)	
2002	10,988,000
2003	11,018,400
Density (per sq km) at 1 January 2003	83.5

* 50,949 sq miles.
† Including armed forces stationed abroad, but excluding foreign forces stationed in Greece.

PRINCIPAL TOWNS
(population at 2001 census)

Athinai (Athens, the capital)	745,514	Larissa	126,076
Thessaloníki (Salonika) . . .	363,987	Volos	82,439
Piraeus	175,697	Kavala. . . .	63,293
Patras	163,446	Serres	56,145
Iráklion	137,711	Canea	53,373

Source: Thomas Brinkhoff, *City Population* (internet www.citypopulation.de).

BIRTHS, MARRIAGES AND DEATHS

	Registered live births Number	Rate (per 1,000)	Registered marriages Number	Rate (per 1,000)	Registered deaths Number	Rate (per 1,000)
1992 . .	104,081	10.1	48,631	4.7	98,231	9.5
1993 . .	101,799	9.8	62,195	6.0	97,419	9.4
1994 . .	103,763	9.9	56,813	5.4	97,807	9.4
1995 . .	101,495	9.7	63,987	6.1	100,158	9.6
1996 . .	100,718	9.6	45,408	4.3	100,740	9.6
1997 . .	102,038	9.7	60,535	5.8	99,738	9.5
1998 . .	100,894	9.6	55,489	5.5	102,668	9.8
1999 . .	100,643	9.6	61,165	5.8	103,304	9.8

2000 (provisional): Registered live births 117,140; Registered deaths 105,439 (Source: UN, *Demographic Yearbook* and *Vital Statistics and Population Report*).

Expectation of life (WHO estimates, years at birth): 78.1 (males 75.5; females 80.8) in 2001 (Source: WHO, *World Health Report*).

ECONOMICALLY ACTIVE POPULATION
(sample surveys, '000 persons aged 15 years and over, April–June)*

	1999	2000	2001
Agriculture, hunting and forestry .	657.4	659.5	615.7
Fishing	11.7	11.2	11.3
Mining and quarrying	18.6	16.5	17.8
Manufacturing	568.8	557.0	557.4
Electricity, gas and water supply .	40.9	38.1	34.3
Construction	273.3	276.6	284.8
Wholesale and retail trade; repair of motor vehicles, motorcycles and personal and household goods	673.8	677.9	673.2
Hotels and restaurants	252.8	252.7	255.0
Transport, storage and communications	248.2	251.4	250.0
Financial intermediation . . .	93.7	107.7	108.0
Real estate, renting and business activities	199.0	195.5	213.0
Public administration and defence; compulsory social security . .	277.5	293.1	290.3
Education	244.2	242.1	251.1
Health and social work	186.3	183.7	177.8
Other community, social and personal service activities . .	141.1	128.4	126.8
Private households with employed persons	51.5	54.7	51.1
Extra-territorial organizations and bodies	1.0	0.2	n.a.
Total employed	3,939.8	3,946.3	3,917.5
Unemployed	523.4	491.1	444.7
Total labour force	4,463.2	4,437.4	4,362.2
Males	2,668.3	2,650.7	2,606.6
Females	1,794.9	1,786.7	1,755.7

2002: Agriculture, hunting, forestry and fishing 623.8; Mining and quarrying 18.9; Manufacturing 540.8; Electricity, gas and water 33.7; Construction and public works 293.9; Trade, restaurants and hotels 947.3; Transport, storage and communications 243.5; Banking, insurance and management of real estate 324.3; Other services 922.7; *Total employed* 3,948.9; Unemployed 420.1; *Total labour force* 4,369.0.

* Including members of the regular armed forces, but excluding persons on compulsory military service.

Source: ILO.

Health and Welfare

KEY INDICATORS

Total fertility rate (children per woman, 2001)	1.3
Under-5 mortality rate (per 1,000 live births, 2001) . . .	5
HIV/AIDS (% of persons aged 15–49, 2001)	0.17
Physicians (per 1,000 head, 1995)	3.92
Hospital beds (per 1,000 head, 1997)	5
Health expenditure (2000): US $ per head (PPP)	1,390
Health expenditure (2000): % of GDP	8.3
Health expenditure (2000): public (% of total)	55.5
Human Development Index (2000): ranking	24
Human Development Index (2000): value	0.885

For sources and definitions, see explanatory note on p. vi.

Agriculture

PRINCIPAL CROPS
('000 metric tons)

	1999	2000	2001
Wheat	2,064.0	2,183.4	2,084.4
Rice (paddy)	161.4	147.5	150.5
Barley	320.0	302.9	274.1
Maize	1,949.9	2,037.5	2,034.8
Rye	35.8	32.0	33.1
Oats	85.9	86.4	81.5
Potatoes	866.7	883.3	936.7
Sugar beet	2,388.8	3,033.2	2,882.4
Dry beans	25.0	23.6	23.0
Other pulses*	3.5	3.5	3.5
Almonds	46.3	47.2	55.3
Olives	2,196.6	2,273.8	2,249.4
Sunflower seed	55.5	35.0	22.8
Cabbages	203.0	200.0	200.0
Tomatoes	2,098.4	2,057.2	1,819.9
Cucumbers and gherkins	152.6	160.9	160.0*
Aubergines	75.0	76.0	75.0*
Chillies and green peppers	102.3	103.7	100.0*
Dry onions	193.0	189.5	208.0
Watermelons	684.7	662.8	644.2
Cantaloupes and other melons	160.0	164.1	165.0*
Grapes*	1,200.0	1,200.0	1,200.0
Apples	318.2	285.0	243.2
Pears	74.0	96.5	85.3
Peaches and nectarines	884.2	920.3	927.1
Oranges	1,117.8	1,068.4	1,022.3
Tangerines, mandarins, clementines and satsumas	92.6	84.0	107.5
Lemons and limes	182.0	172.8	174.3
Apricots	85.3	82.0	68.5
Tobacco (leaves)	139.8	136.6	136.5
Cotton (lint)†	384.0	443.0	455.6

* FAO estimate(s).
† Unofficial figures.

Source: FAO.

LIVESTOCK
('000 head, year ending 30 September)

	1999	2000	2001
Horses	31	33*	33*
Mules	35	35*	35*
Asses	73	72*	72*
Cattle	583	590	585†
Pigs	933	906	936
Sheep	8,930	8,732	9,269
Goats	5,520	5,293	5,180
Chickens	28,453	28,500*	28,000*

* FAO estimate.
† Unofficial figure.

Source: FAO.

LIVESTOCK PRODUCTS
('000 metric tons)

	1999	2000	2001
Beef and veal	66.6	65.7	59.9
Mutton and lamb*	79.5	77.5	78.0
Goat meat*	47.0	47.5	44.1
Pig meat	138.3	143.1	136.6
Horse meat†	2.7	2.7	2.7
Poultry meat	153.4	154.2	154.2†
Other meat†	7.0	7.0	7.0
Cows' milk	777.0	789.0*	815.0*
Sheep's milk	654.0	700.0*	670.0*
Goats' milk*	450.0	450.0	435.0
Cheese	242.4	233.3	233.7
Butter	4.4	3.6	2.8
Poultry eggs	119.1	116.6	106.4
Honey	14.2	13.7	14.0
Wool: greasy	9.8	9.5	9.6†
Wool: scoured	5.7	5.8	5.8†

— *continued*	1999	2000	2001
Cattle hides†	12.7	12.5	12.6
Sheepskins†	16.8	16.8	16.8
Goatskins†	10.2	10.1	9.5

* Unofficial figure(s).
† FAO estimate(s).

Source: FAO.

Forestry

ROUNDWOOD REMOVALS
('000 cubic metres, excl. bark)

	1998	1999	2000
Sawlogs, veneer logs and logs for sleepers	360	696	683
Pulpwood	135	115	113
Fuel wood	1,197	1,403	1,375
Total	1,692	2,214	2,171

Source: FAO.

2001 (FAO estimates): Production assumed to be unchanged from 2000.

SAWNWOOD PRODUCTION
('000 cubic metres, incl. railway sleepers)

	1998	1999	2000
Coniferous (softwood)	85	87	85
Broadleaved (hardwood)	52	53	52
Total	137	140	137

Source: FAO.

2001 (FAO estimates): Production assumed to be unchanged from 2000.

Fishing

('000 metric tons, live weight)

	1998	1999	2000
Capture	108.6	118.8	99.3
Freshwater fishes	3.7	2.8	2.9
Mediterranean horse mackerel	4.4	3.5	3.9
European pilchard (sardine)	17.7	15.2	16.0
European anchovy	17.1	16.5	9.9
Mediterranean mussel	6.4	15.9	0.5
Aquaculture	59.9	79.3	79.9
Barramundi (giant sea perch)	18.5	23.9	26.7
Dorada	22.0	32.8	38.5
Mediterranean mussel	14.5	16.9	9.8
Total catch	188.2	216.0	179.2

Note: Figures exclude aquatic plants and aquatic mammals.

Source: FAO, *Yearbook of Fishery Statistics*.

Mining

('000 metric tons, unless otherwise indicated)

	1999	2000	2001*
Lignite	61,861	65,000*	60,000
Crude petroleum ('000 barrels)	1,200*	2,093	2,000
Iron ore*†	600	575	575
Bauxite	1,883	1,991	1,990
Zinc concentrates	19.6	16.9	20.0
Lead concentrates	22.0	18.2	27.7
Silver ore (metric tons)†	45.8	37.1	36.0
Magnesite	495	500*	500
Salt (unrefined)	176	180	180
Bentonite	1,050	1,150*	1,150
Kaolin*	65	65	65
Gypsum	687	750*	700
Marble ('000 cu m)	178	200*	200
Natural gas ('000 barrels)*	350	350	350

* Estimate(s).
† Figures refer to the metal content of ores and concentrates.

Source: US Geological Survey.

Industry

SELECTED PRODUCTS
('000 metric tons, unless otherwise indicated)

	1996	1997	1998
Edible fats.	44	n.a.	n.a.
Olive oil (crude)	433	457	435
Raw sugar.	288	396	220
Wine ('000 hectolitres)	1,783	1,455	1,456
Beer ('000 hectolitres)	3,766	3,950	3,886
Cigarettes (million)	38,268	36,909	21,427
Cotton yarn	223.9	222.4	109.7
Woven cotton fabrics—pure and mixed (metric tons)	n.a.	n.a.	6,000
Wool yarn (metric tons)	13,900	12,800	4,900
Woven woollen fabrics—pure and mixed (metric tons)	1,322	1,670	792
Yarn of artificial material (metric tons)	9,500	n.a.	11,400
Fabrics of artificial fibres (metric tons)	11,513	n.a.	n.a.
Footwear—excl. rubber and plastic ('000 pairs)	6,769	6,202	5,716
Rubber and plastic footwear ('000 pairs)	3,294	n.a.	n.a.
Paper and paperboard	340	n.a.	n.a.
Sulphuric acid	1,544	1,655	814
Hydrochloric acid (21° Bé)	90.6	66.7	53.1
Nitric acid (54% or 36.3° Bé)	462	n.a.	n.a.
Polyvinyl chloride	94.8	105.9	108.3
Liquefied petroleum gas	555	561	650*
Naphthas	977	970	932*
Motor spirit (petrol)	3,383	3,607	3,671*
Jet fuels	1,942	1,949	1,934*
Distillate fuel oils	4,760	5,144	5,544*
Residual fuel oils	7,424	7,149	6,959*
Cement	13,391	13,660	14,207
Crude steel (incl. alloys)	852	1,020	1,104
Aluminium (unwrought)	141.3	132.0	160.6
Electric energy (million kWh)	n.a.	39,236	41,834

* Estimate.

1999 ('000 metric tons, unless otherwise indicated): Olive oil (crude) 436; Raw sugar 252; Crude steel (incl. alloys) 960; Aluminium (unwrought) 160.8; Electric energy 44,777 million kWh.

Source: mainly UN, *Industrial Commodity Statistics Yearbook*.

Finance

CURRENCY AND EXCHANGE RATES

Monetary Units
100 cent = 1 euro (€)

Sterling, Dollar and Euro Equivalents (30 May 2003)
£1 sterling = 1.394 euros;
US $1 = 0.8459 euros;
100 euros = £71.75 = $118.22.

Average Exchange Rate (euros per US $)
2000   1.0854
2001   1.1175
2002   1.0626

Note: The national currency was formerly the drachma. Greece became a member of the euro area on 1 January 2001, after which a fixed exchange rate of €1 = 340.75 drachmae was in operation. Euro notes and coins were introduced on 1 January 2002. The euro and local currency circulated alongside each other until 28 February, after which the euro became the sole legal tender. Some of the figures in this Survey are still in terms of drachmae.

BUDGET
('000 million drachmae)*

Revenue	1998	1999	2000†
Ordinary budget	9,498.4	10,592.9	11,650.0
Tax revenue	8,839.7	9,897.3	10,890.2
Direct taxes	3,591.3	4,043.5	4,527.0
Personal income tax	1,587.0	1,825.3	1,780.0
Corporate income tax	1,018.3	1,136.7	1,550.0
Indirect taxes	5,248.2	5,853.8	6,363.2
Consumption taxes	1,856.1	1,909.0	1,895.0
Transaction taxes	3,251.0	3,778.6	4,276.0
Value-added tax	2,723.3	2,987.5	3,380.0
Stamp duty	292.5	288.9	301.0
Non-tax revenue	658.7	695.6	759.8
Capital receipts	378.2	400.9	442.0
Investment budget	914.0	1,010.0	1,200.0
Receipts from European Union	891.0	977.0	1,130.0
SAGAP‡	793.0	806.0	895.0
Total	11,205.4	12,408.9	13,745.0

Expenditure	1998	1999†	2000†
Defence	1,018	1,053	1,186
Education	1,217	1,402	1,440
Health, social welfare and insurance	2,229	2,194	2,424
Agriculture	1,242	1,256	1,416
Interest payments§	3,024	3,123	3,165
Other purposes	4,602	5,304	5,779
Total §	13,331	14,332	15,410
Ordinary budget	10,661	11,276	11,995
Investment budget	1,877	2,250	2,520
SAGAP‡	793	806	895

* Figures refer to the budgetary transactions of the central Government, excluding the operations of social security funds and public entities (such as hospitals, educational institutions and government agencies) with individual budgets.
† Provisional.
‡ Special Account for Guarantees of Agricultural Products.
§ Excluding capitalized interest ('000 million drachmae): 27 in 1998.

Source: IMF, *Greece: Selected Issues and Statistical Appendix* (April 2001).

INTERNATIONAL RESERVES
(US $ million at 31 December)*

	2000	2001	2002
Gold†	753.2	1,090.0	1,349.0
IMF special drawing rights	12.0	9.7	15.1
Reserve position in IMF	296.8	357.3	438.4
Foreign exchange	13,115.5	4,787.0	7,629.0
Total	14,177.5	6,243.0	9,431.5

* Figures exclude deposits made with the European Monetary Institute.
† Gold reserves are valued at market-related prices.

Source: IMF, *International Financial Statistics*.

MONEY SUPPLY
('000 million drachmae at 31 December)

	2000	2001*	2002*
Currency in circulation	3,097.3	8,708	9,208†
Demand deposits at banking institutions	4,348.3	15,930	15,106
Total money	7,445.5	24,720	24,314

* Figures in terms of million euros.
† Currency put into circulation by the Bank of Greece was 9,984 million euros.

Source: IMF, *International Financial Statistics*.

COST OF LIVING
(Consumer Price Index; base: 1990 = 100)

	1999	2000	2001
Food	211.6	215.6	226.6
Fuel and light	153.6	173.8	174.1
Clothing	228.6	233.4	241.2
Rent	318.4	330.8	343.9
All items (incl. others) . . .	234.9	242.4	250.7

Source: ILO.

NATIONAL ACCOUNTS
('000 million euros at current prices)*

Expenditure on the Gross Domestic Product

	1998	1999	2000
Final consumption expenditure .	92.0	96.8	103.6
Households	75.6	79.4	84.5
Non-profit institutions serving households	0.3	0.3	0.3
General government . . .	16.2	17.1	18.8
Gross capital formation . . .	22.6	24.2	27.6
Gross fixed capital formation .	22.3	24.5	27.5
Changes in inventories . .	0.2	−0.3	0.0
Total domestic expenditure .	114.6	121.0	131.2
Exports of goods and services . .	21.0	23.2	30.4
Less Imports of goods and services	29.8	31.5	40.0
GDP in market prices . . .	105.8	112.7	121.5

Gross Domestic Product by Economic Activity

	1998	1999	2000
Agriculture, hunting, forestry and fishing	7.9	8.0	8.1
Mining and quarrying	0.6	0.6	0.7
Manufacturing	11.4	11.3	12.3
Electricity, gas and water . . .	2.0	2.1	2.0
Construction	6.9	7.6	7.6
Wholesale and retail trade . . .	13.2	14.0	16.0
Hotels and restaurants . . .	7.4	7.5	7.8
Transport, storage and communication	6.5	7.6	9.4
Financial intermediation† . .	4.8	5.6	6.0
Real estate, renting and business activities	16.7	17.4	18.8
Public administration and defence	6.7	7.2	7.8
Education	4.6	5.0	5.4
Health and social work	5.3	5.6	5.6
Other services	2.5	2.7	2.8
Private households with employed persons	0.3	0.4	0.4
Sub-total	96.8	102.6	110.7
Less Financial intermediation services indirectly measured	3.3	3.8	4.5
Gross value added in basic prices	93.5	98.8	106.2
Indirect taxes, *less* subsidies . .	12.3	14.0	15.5
GDP in market prices . . .	105.8	112.7	121.5

* Totals may not be equal to the sum of components, owing to rounding.
† Including imputed rents of owner-occupied dwellings.
Source: UN, *National Accounts Statistics*.

2001 ('000 million euros): GDP in market prices 130.9 (Source: IMF, *International Financial Statistics*).

2002 ('000 million euros): GDP in market prices 141.1 (Source: IMF, *International Financial Statistics*).

GDP at constant 1995 prices ('000 million euros): 98.5 in 2001; 102.4 in 2002 (Source: IMF, *International Financial Statistics*).

BALANCE OF PAYMENTS
(US $ million)

	2000	2001	2002
Exports of goods f.o.b.	10,202	10,615	9,868
Imports of goods f.o.b.	−30,440	−29,702	−31,320
Trade balance	−20,239	−19,087	−21,452
Exports of services	19,239	19,456	20,223
Imports of services	−11,286	−11,589	−10,677
Balance on goods and services	−12,286	−11,220	−11,906
Other income received . . .	2,807	1,885	1,530
Other income paid	−3,692	−3,652	−3,487
Balance on goods, services and income	−13,171	−12,987	−13,863
Current transfers received . .	4,116	4,592	4,901
Current transfers paid . . .	−764	−1,005	−1,443
Current balance	−9,820	−9,400	−10,405
Capital account (net)	2,112	2,153	1,522
Direct investment abroad . . .	−2,099	−611	−669
Direct investment from abroad .	1,083	1,585	53
Portfolio investment assets . .	−1,184	−474	−1,893
Portfolio investment liabilities .	9,262	9,012	12,315
Financial derivatives liabilities .	348	74	−176
Other investment assets . .	6,970	−1,539	−6,953
Other investment liabilities . .	−3,551	−7,511	8,896
Net errors and omissions . . .	−550	1,011	−828
Overall balance	2,573	−5,699	1,863

Sources: IMF, *International Financial Statistics*, and Bank of Greece.

External Trade

PRINCIPAL COMMODITIES
(US $ million)

Imports c.i.f.	1998	1999	2000
Food and live animals . . .	3,302.0	2,852.9	2,727.4
Meat and meat preparations . .	856.7	721.3	685.0
Crude materials (inedible) except fuels	883.9	673.5	707.0
Mineral fuels, lubricants, etc.	2,229.4	1,541.6	4,013.2
Petroleum, petroleum products, etc.	2,062.8	1,407.5	3,739.9
Crude petroleum oils, etc. . .	1,705.3	944.8	3,015.0
Chemicals and related products	3,643.1	3,235.3	3,414.9
Medicinal and pharmaceutical products	1,080.3	1,060.2	1,133.2
Medicaments (incl. veterinary medicaments)	890.5	910.4	974.7
Basic manufactures . . .	5,217.6	4,262.9	4,566.0
Textile yarn, fabrics, etc. . .	1,143.2	942.0	859.2
Iron and steel	894.3	672.8	838.9
Machinery and transport equipment	10,479.6	9,954.4	10,195.6
Machinery specialized for particular industries . . .	1,033.2	882.4	676.4
General industrial machinery equipment and parts . . .	1,198.5	1,198.4	1,177.8
Telecommunications and sound equipment	1,278.3	1,120.8	1,293.4
Other electrical machinery apparatus, etc.	1,263.0	1,045.2	1,101.4
Road vehicles and parts* . .	2,641.6	3,076.2	2,841.6
Passenger motor cars (excl. buses)	1,570.2	1,926.6	1,886.1
Other transport equipment* . .	1,936.0	1,495.2	1,820.8
Ships, boats and floating structures	1,132.1	674.8	1,568.3
Miscellaneous manufactured articles	3,616.6	3,254.9	3,386.4
Clothing and accessories (excl. footwear)	1,054.7	931.1	1,005.3
Total (incl. others)	30,266.7	26,570.2	29,816.0

* Excluding tyres, engines and electrical parts.

Exports f.o.b.	1998	1999	2000
Food and live animals . . .	2,000.9	1,676.5	1,596.3
Vegetables and fruit	1,295.2	1,018.7	999.2
Fresh or dried fruit and nuts (excl. oil nuts)	492.8	428.5	417.5
Preserved fruit and fruit preparations	349.8	253.0	292.7
Beverages and tobacco . .	596.5	615.3	513.5
Tobacco and manufactures . . .	447.2	494.3	393.6
Unmanufactured tobacco (incl. refuse)	333.6	357.5	264.0
Crude materials (inedible) except fuels	573.5	607.5	594.8
Textile fibres and waste . .	263.2	353.0	313.1
Cotton	253.1	345.5	305.0
Raw cotton (excl. linters) . .	230.4	328.8	289.4
Mineral fuels, lubricants, etc. .	736.5	1,024.6	1,611.8
Petroleum, petroleum products, etc.	707.3	995.8	1,527.7
Refined petroleum products . .	605.2	851.5	1,373.6
Animal and vegetable oils, fats and waxes	357.7	476.0	247.0
Fixed vegetable oils and fats .	353.9	470.5	243.4
Soft fixed vegetable oils . .	352.2	469.7	241.8
Olive oil	315.1	451.0	226.5
Chemicals and related products	666.4	693.8	837.9
Basic manufactures . . .	2,301.5	1,910.6	1,965.7
Textile yarn, fabrics, etc. . .	536.9	411.2	406.7
Non-metallic mineral manufactures	410.4	319.8	328.4
Lime, cement, etc.	303.8	244.5	246.3
Non-ferrous metals	615.1	581.1	640.0
Aluminium	457.5	430.3	455.3
Worked aluminium and aluminium alloys . . .	351.7	327.1	367.9
Machinery and transport equipment	1,173.8	1,024.7	1,314.9
Electrical machinery, apparatus etc.	319.5	291.0	328.6
Miscellaneous manufactured articles	2,293.8	1,947.6	1,937.1
Clothing and accessories (excl. footwear)	1,820.7	1,504.9	1,405.3
Total (incl. others)	10,867.8	10,149.8	10,964.5

Source: UN, *International Trade Statistics Yearbook*.

PRINCIPAL TRADING PARTNERS
(US $ million)*

Imports c.i.f.	1998	1999	2000
Austria	299.2	249.2	249.4
Belgium-Luxembourg . . .	1,036.4	n.a.	n.a.
Bulgaria	394.9	351.1	398.8
China, People's Republic . .	591.8	545.8	699.4
Denmark	425.1	337.9	305.1
Egypt	400.8	188.9	142.9
Finland	349.9	351.3	452.3
France (incl. Monaco) . . .	2,595.4	2,289.8	2,153.4
Germany	4,505.4	3,896.9	3,812.9
Iran	616.4	394.1	1,166.1
Italy	4,824.0	4,007.1	3,855.6
Japan	992.0	1,144.3	1,179.0
Korea, Republic	949.0	732.2	1,110.8
Netherlands	1,874.7	1,655.7	1,734.8
Russia	494.1	504.4	1,094.5
Saudi Arabia	462.4	290.1	949.1
Spain	1,071.4	914.1	1,018.0
Sweden	607.6	490.0	550.0
Switzerland	478.2	513.1	413.3
Turkey	369.7	366.5	396.1
United Kingdom	1,926.8	1,602.6	1,482.5
USA	1,397.9	1,473.2	1,022.5
Total (incl. others)	30,266.7	26,570.2	29,816.0

Exports f.o.b.	1998	1999	2000
Albania	194.4	222.1	248.8
Austria	129.5	105.6	91.6
Belgium-Luxembourg . . .	176.1	n.a.	n.a.
Bulgaria	442.5	447.4	450.5
Cyprus	416.7	414.8	509.4
Egypt	114.8	86.9	109.7
France (incl. Monaco) . . .	504.8	410.4	374.1
Germany	1,994.1	1,552.9	1,345.7
Israel	124.4	115.8	185.6
Italy	1,293.2	1,278.5	1,011.1
Lebanon	114.0	104.7	145.3
Macedonia, former Yugoslav republic	269.3	428.3	470.8
Malta	104.9	112.1	136.4
Netherlands	329.8	291.7	316.8
Romania	203.0	212.7	384.3
Russia	269.1	245.7	249.2
Spain	276.5	317.9	334.7
Sweden	147.6	113.9	136.1
Turkey	346.1	335.3	550.3
Ukraine	84.6	44.6	42.1
United Kingdom	756.2	635.9	691.8
USA	516.1	594.4	638.2
Yugoslavia	187.2	112.7	131.4
Total (incl. others)	10,867.8	10,149.8	10,964.5

* Imports by country of first consignment; exports by country of consumption.

Source: UN, *International Trade Statistics Yearbook*.

Transport

RAILWAYS
(estimated traffic)

	1996	1997	1998
Passenger-kilometres (million) . .	1,752	1,783	1,559
Net ton-kilometres (million) . .	350	330	399

2000 (million): Passenger-kilometres 1,583; Net ton-kilometres 350.

ROAD TRAFFIC
(motor vehicles in use at 31 December)

	1999	2000	2001*
Passenger cars	2,928,881	3,195,065	3,423,704
Buses and coaches . . .	26,769	27,037	27,115
Lorries and vans	1,023,987	1,057,422	1,085,811
Motorcycles	710,755	781,361	853,366

* Estimates.

SHIPPING

Merchant fleet
(registered at 31 December)

	1999	2000	2001
Number of vessels	1,491	1,529	1,529
Total displacement ('000 grt) . .	24,833.3	26,401.7	28,678.2

Source: Lloyd's Register-Fairplay, *World Fleet Statistics*.

International Sea-borne Freight Traffic
('000 metric tons)

	1998	1999	2000
Goods loaded	19,356	20,748	21,384
Goods unloaded	38,700	40,332	40,164

Source: UN, *Monthly Bulletin of Statistics*.

CIVIL AVIATION
(domestic and foreign flights of Olympic Airways)

	1996	1997	1998
Kilometres flown ('000) . . .	65,847	68,415	67,606
Passenger-kilometres ('000). . .	8,533,168	9,260,651	8,561,153
Freight ton-kilometres ('000) . .	118,738	129,100	112,615
Mail ton-kilometres ('000) . . .	12,669	14,662	20,265

1999 ('000): Kilometres flown 75,000; Passenger-kilometres 8,306,000 (Source: UN, *Statistical Yearbook*).

Tourism

TOURISTS BY COUNTRY OF ORIGIN
(foreign citizens, excl. cruise passengers)

Country	1998	1999	2000
Austria.	450,195	501,602	474,996
Belgium-Luxembourg . . .	273,674	332,913	331,942
Denmark	292,532	336,248	338,603
France	486,201	545,981	602,353
Germany	2,136,515	2,450,137	2,395,185
Italy	659,688	745,915	823,245
Netherlands	548,339	616,807	655,285
Norway	226,282	269,419	314,224
Sweden	467,617	468,793	485,749
Switzerland	289,387	308,138	322,575
United Kingdom	2,044,243	2,433,033	2,772,256
USA	219,362	229,314	218,731
Yugoslavia	226,282	269,419	158,670
Total (incl. others)	10,916,046	12,164,088	13,095,545

2001: 14,033,378 tourist arrivals.

Receipts (US $ million): 6,188 in 1998; 8,783 in 1999; 9,221 in 2000.

Source: World Tourism Organization, *Yearbook of Tourism Statistics*.

Communications Media

	1999	2000	2001
Telephone ('000 main lines in use)	5,610.9	5,659.3	5,607.7
Mobile cellular telephones ('000 subscribers).	3,904.0	5,932.0	7,962.0
Personal computers ('000 in use)	750.0	750.0	860.0
Internet users ('000)	705.8	1,000.0	1,400.0

2002: Mobile cellular telephones ('000 subscribers) 9,240.0, Internet users ('000) 2,000.0.

Radio receivers ('000 in use): 5,020 in 1997.

Television receivers ('000 in use): 5,100 in 1999.

Facsimile machines ('000 in use, estimate): 40,000 in 1996.

Daily newspapers (1997): Number 207; Average circulation ('000 copies) 1,389.

Books (titles published): 4,225 in 1996.

Sources: UN, *Statistical Yearbook*, UNESCO, *Statistical Yearbook*, and International Telecommunication Union.

Education

(2001/02, unless otherwise indicated)

	Institutions	Teachers	Students
Pre-primary.	5,694*	n.a.	144,055
Primary.	6,074	49,842	647,041
Secondary: General	3,244	54,123	589,669
Secondary: Technical, vocational and ecclesiastical†	669	15,270	157,217
Higher: Universities†	18	10,149	148,772
Higher: Technical, vocational and ecclesiastical†	74	8,902	91,564

* In addition there were 10,211 kindergardens.
† Figures for 2000/01.

Adult literacy rate (UNESCO estimates): 97.2% (males 98.5%; females 96.0%) in 2000 (Source: UN Development Programme, *Human Development Report*).

Directory

The Constitution

A new Constitution for the Hellenic Republic came into force on 11 June 1975. The main provisions of this Constitution, as subsequently amended, are summarized below.

Greece shall be a parliamentary democracy with a President as Head of State. All powers are derived from the people and exist for the benefit of the people. The established religion is that of The Eastern Orthodox Church of Christ.

EXECUTIVE AND LEGISLATIVE

The President

In March 1986 a series of amendments to the Constitution was approved by a majority vote of Parliament, which relieved the President of his executive power and transferred such power to the legislature, thus confining the Head of State to a largely ceremonial role.

The President is elected by Parliament for a period of five years. The re-election of the same person shall be permitted only once. The President represents the State in relations with other nations, is Supreme Commander of the armed forces and may declare war and conclude treaties. The President shall appoint the Prime Minister and, on the Prime Minister's recommendation, the other members of the Government. The President shall convoke Parliament once every year and in extraordinary session whenever he deems it reasonable. In exceptional circumstances the President may preside over the Cabinet, convene the Council of the Republic, and suspend Parliament for a period not exceeding 30 days. In accordance with the amendment of March 1986, the President was deprived of the right to dismiss the Prime Minister, his power to call a referendum was limited, and the right to declare a state of emergency was trans-

ferred to Parliament. The President can now dissolve Parliament only if the resignation of two Governments in quick succession demonstrates the absence of political stability. If no party has a majority in Parliament, the President must offer an opportunity to form a government to the leader of each of the four biggest parties in turn, strictly following the order of their parliamentary strengths. If no party leader is able to form a government, the President may try to assemble an all-party government; failing that, the President must appoint a caretaker cabinet, led by a senior judge, to hold office until a fresh election takes place. The Constitution continues to reserve a substantial moderating role for the President, however, in that he retains the right to object to legislation and may request Parliament to reconsider it or to approve it with an enlarged majority.

The Government

The Government consists of the Cabinet which comprises the Prime Minister and Ministers. The Government determines and directs the general policy of the State in accordance with the Constitution and the laws. The Cabinet must enjoy the confidence of Parliament and may be removed by a vote of no confidence. The Prime Minister is to be the leader of the party with an absolute majority in Parliament, or, if no such party exists, the leader of the party with a relative majority.

The Council of the Republic

The Council of the Republic shall be composed of all former democratic Presidents, the Prime Minister, the leader of the Opposition and the parliamentary Prime Ministers of governments which have enjoyed the confidence of Parliament, presided over by the President. It shall meet when the largest parties are unable to form a government with the confidence of Parliament and may empower the President to appoint a Prime Minister who may or may not be a member of Parliament. The Council may also authorize the President to dissolve Parliament.

Parliament

Parliament is to be unicameral and composed of not fewer than 200 and not more than 300 deputies elected by direct, universal and secret ballot for a term of four years. Parliament shall elect its own President, or Speaker. It must meet once a year for a regular session of at least five months. Bills passed by Parliament must be ratified by the President and the President's veto can be nullified by an absolute majority of the total number of deputies. Parliament may impeach the President by a motion signed by one-third and passed by two-thirds of the total number of deputies. Parliament is also empowered to impeach present or former members of the Government. In these cases the defendant shall be brought before an *ad hoc* tribunal presided over by the President of the Supreme Court and composed of 12 judges. Certain legislative work, as specified in the Constitution, must be passed by Parliament in plenum, and Parliament cannot make a decision without an absolute majority of the members present, which under no circumstances shall be less than one-quarter of the total number of deputies. The Constitution provides for certain legislative powers to be exercised by not more than two Parliamentary Departments. Parliament may revise the Constitution in accordance with the procedure laid down in the Constitution.

THE JUDICIAL AUTHORITY

Justice is to be administered by courts of regular judges, who enjoy personal and functional independence. The President, after consultations with a judicial council, shall appoint the judges for life. The judges are subject only to the Constitution and the laws. Courts are divided into administrative, civil and penal and shall be organized by virtue of special laws. They must not apply laws which are contrary to the Constitution. The final jurisdiction in matters of judicial review rests with a Special Supreme Tribunal.

Certain laws, passed before the implementation of this Constitution and deemed not contrary to it, are to remain in force. Other specified laws, even if contrary to the Constitution, are to remain in force until repealed by further legislation.

INDIVIDUAL AND SPECIAL RIGHTS

All citizens are equal under the Constitution and before the law, having the same rights and obligations. No titles of nobility or distinction are to be conferred or recognized. All persons are to enjoy full protection of life, honour and freedom, irrespective of nationality, race, creed or political allegiance. Retrospective legislation is prohibited and no citizen may be punished without due process of law. Freedom of speech, of the Press, of association and of religion are guaranteed under the Constitution. All persons have the right to a free education, which the state has the duty to provide. Work is a right and all workers, irrespective of sex or other distinction, are entitled to equal remuneration for rendering services of equal value. The right of peaceful assembly, the right of a person to property and the freedom to form political parties are guaranteed under the Constitution. The exercise of the right to vote by all citizens over 18 years of age is obligatory. No person may exercise his rights and liberties contrary to the Constitution.

MOUNT ATHOS

The district of Mount Athos shall, in accordance with its ancient privileged status, be a self-governing part of the Greek State and its sovereignty shall remain unaffected.

The Government

HEAD OF STATE

President: KONSTANTINOS STEFANOPOULOS (took office 10 March 1995; re-elected 9 February 2000).

THE CABINET
(July 2003)

Prime Minister: KONSTANTINOS (COSTAS) SIMITIS.

Minister of State: ALEKOS AKRIVAKIS.

Minister of the Economy and Finance: NIKOLAOS (NIKOS) CHRISTODOULAKIS.

Minister of Foreign Affairs: GEORGIOS PAPANDREOU.

Minister of National Defence: IOANNIS PAPANTONIOU.

Minister of the Interior, Public Administration and Decentralization: KONSTANTINOS SKANDALIDIS.

Minister of Development: APOSTOLOS-ATHANASSIOS (AKIS) TSOHATZOPOULOS.

Minister of the Environment, Physical Planning and Public Works: VASILIKI (VASSO) PAPANDREOU.

Minister of Education and Religious Affairs: PETROS EPHTHIMIOU.

Minister of Labour and Social Affairs: DIMITRIS REPPAS.

Minister of Health and Welfare: COSTAS STEFANIS.

Minister of Agriculture: GEORGIOS DRYS.

Minister of Justice: PHILIPPOS PETSALNIKOS.

Minister of Culture: EVANGELOS VENIZELOS.

Minister of Transport and Communications: CHRISTOS VERELIS.

Minister of Public Order: GEORGIOS FLORIDIS.

Minister of Merchant Marine: GEORGIOS PASCHALIDIS.

Minister of Press and Mass Media: CHRISTOS PROTOPAPAS.

Minister of Macedonia and Thrace: HARIS KASTANIDIS.

Minister of the Aegean: NIKOLAOS SIFOUNAKIS.

MINISTRIES

Office of the President: Odos Vas. Georgiou 7, 106 74 Athens; tel. (21) 07283111; fax (21) 07248938.

Office of the Prime Minister: Maximos Mansion, Herodou Atticou 19, 106 74 Athens; tel. (21) 03385242; fax (21) 07241776; e-mail mail@primeminister.gr; internet www.primeminister.gr.

Ministry of the Aegean: Filellinon 9, 105 57 Athens; tel. (21) 03311714; fax (21) 03227544; e-mail athens1@ypai.gr; internet www.ypai.gr.

Ministry of Agriculture: Odos Acharnon 5, 104 32 Athens; tel. (21) 02124000; fax (21) 05240475; e-mail webmaster@minagric.gr; internet www.minagric.gr.

Ministry of Culture: Odos Bouboulinas 20–22, 106 82 Athens; tel. (21) 08201648; fax (21) 08201435; e-mail minister@culture.gr; internet www.culture.gr.

Ministry of Development: Odos Mihalakopoulou 80, 101 92 Athens; tel. (21) 07482770; fax (21) 07788279; internet www.ypan.gr.

Ministry of the Economy and Finance: Odos Nikis 5–7, 101 80 Athens; tel. (21) 03332000; internet www.ypetho.gr.

Ministry of Education and Religious Affairs: Odos Metropoleos 15, 101 85 Athens; tel. (21) 03230461; fax (21) 03248264; e-mail webmaster@ypepth.gr; internet www.ypepth.gr.

Ministry of the Environment, Physical Planning and Public Works: Odos Amaliados 17, 115 23 Athens; tel. (21) 06415700; fax (21) 06432589; e-mail minister@minenv.gr; internet www.minenv.gr.

Ministry of Foreign Affairs: Odos Akadimias 1, 106 71 Athens; tel. (21) 03681000; fax (21) 03624195; e-mail mfa@mfa.gr; internet www.mfa.gr.

Ministry of Health and Welfare: Odos Aristotelous 17, 104 33 Athens; tel. (21) 05232820; fax (21) 05231707; e-mail info@ypyp.gr; internet www.ypyp.gr.

Ministry of the Interior, Public Administration and Decentralization: Odos Stadiou 27, 101 83 Athens; tel. (21) 03223521; fax (21) 03240631; e-mail info@ypes.gr; internet www.ypes.gr.

Ministry of Justice: Odos Mesogeion 96, 115 27 Athens; tel. (21) 07711019; fax (21) 07759879; e-mail minjust@otenet.gr; internet www.ministryofjustice.gr.

Ministry of Labour and Social Affairs: Odos Pireos 40, 104 37 Athens; tel. (21) 05295000; fax (21) 05249805; e-mail postmaster@www.labor-ministry.gr; internet www.ypergka.gr.

Ministry of Macedonia and Thrace: Administration Bldg, 541 23 Thessaloníki; tel. (231) 0264321; fax (231) 0263332; e-mail webmaster@mathra.gr; internet www.mathra.gr.

Ministry of Merchant Marine: Odos Gregoriou Lambraki 150, Piraeus; tel. (21) 04121211; fax (21) 04134286; e-mail dopy_g@mail.yen.gr; internet www.yen.gr.

Ministry of National Defence: Mesogion 151, 155 00 Xolargos; tel. (21) 06876789; fax (21) 06876789; e-mail minister@mod.gr; internet www.mod.gr.

Ministry of Press and Mass Media: Odos Zalokosta 10, 101 63 Athens; tel. (21) 03630911; fax (21) 03609682; e-mail press01@otenet.gr; internet www.minpress.gr.

Ministry of Public Order: P. Khanellopoulou 4, 101 77 Athens; tel. (21) 06977000; fax (21) 06921675; e-mail ydt@otenet.gr; internet www.ydt.gr.

Ministry of Transport and Communications: Odos Xenofontos 13, 101 91 Athens; tel. (21) 03251211; fax (21) 03239039; e-mail comm@yme.gr; internet www.yme.gr.

Legislature

VOULI

Parliament

Parliament Bldg, Syntagma Sq., 101 80 Athens; tel. (21) 03288434; fax (21) 03310013; e-mail infopar@parliament.gr; internet www.parliament.gr.

President of the Vouli: APOSTOLOS KAKLAMANIS.

General Election, 9 April 2000

Parties	Seats	% of votes
Panhellenic Socialist Movement (PASOK)	158	43.8
New Democracy (ND)	125	42.7
Communist Party (KKE)	11	5.2
Coalition of the Left and Progress . . .	6	3.2
Democratic Social Movement (DHKKI). .	—	2.7
Others	—	2.4
Total	300	100.0

Local Government

Greece comprises 13 regions, each administered by a Secretary-General, appointed by central government. Each region is responsible for the administration of the other tiers of local government within its territory. The regions are further divided into 54 administrative divisions (nomoi). The nomoi are administered by a prefect, appointed by central government, whose role is to ensure the financial, social and cultural development of the area and to oversee projects involving more than one municipality or community. There are 900 municipalities, each of which has an elected Council and a mayor (dimarkos), and 133 communities, with a communal council and a president. Responsibilities of municipalities and communities include the local environment, basic education, culture and public health, where such issues fall entirely within their territory. In 1997 the Government initiated a five-year programme of reorganization of municipal government in Greece. Municipal elections were last held in October 2002. The region of Mount Athos has self-governing status within the Republic.

Central Union of Municipalities and Communities of Greece (KEDKE): Genadiou 8 and Akadimias 65, 106 78 Athens; tel. (21) 03899600; fax (1) (21) 03302044; e-mail info@kedke.gr; internet www.kedke.gr; Pres. PARIS KOUKOULOPOULOS.

Eastern Macedonia and Thrace (1): G. Kakoulidou 1, 691 00 Komotini; tel. (252) 1081830; fax (253) 1028997; e-mail remth@remth.gr; internet www.remth.gr; Sec.-Gen. ARIS PAPADOPOULOS.

Central Macedonia (2): T. Oikonomidi and K. Rossidou 11, 540 08 Thessaloníki; tel. (231) 0422591; fax (231) 0422590; e-mail root@rcm.gr; internet www.rcm.gr; Sec.-Gen. VASSILIS VALASSOPOULOS.

Western Macedonia (3): Kitrio Pneymatiko Kentro, 501 00 Kozani; tel. (246) 1032633; fax (246) 1032633; Sec.-Gen. ARISTIDIS PAPADOPOULOS.

Epirus (4): Epirou 20, 453 33 Ioannina; tel. (265) 1072164; fax (265) 1031224; e-mail ggphp@otenet.gr; internet www.regionofepirus.gr; Sec.-Gen. ELIAS LIAKOPOULOS.

Thessaly (5): Sokratous 111, 413 36 Larissa; tel. (241) 0552749; fax (241) 0552651; internet www.thessalia.gr; Sec.-Gen. IOANNIS KARATZIOTIS.

Ionian Islands (6): Ethniki Paleokastritsas Alykes Potamou, 491 00 Corfu; tel. (2661) 045245; fax (2661) 044424; Sec.-Gen. ANASTASSIA KANELOPOULOU.

Western Greece (7): Nea Ethniki Odos Athinon–Patron 28, 264 41 Patras; tel. (261) 0453347; fax (261) 0452176; e-mail dytikiellada@mou.gr; internet www.dytikiellada.gr; Sec.-Gen. NIKOLAOS BELIVANIS.

Continental Greece (8): Ypsilanti 1, 351 00 Lamia; tel. (231) 32422; fax (231) 39622; e-mail stereaellada@mou.gr; internet www.stereaellada.gr; Sec.-Gen. VASSILIOS EXARCHOS.

Attica (9): Evangelistrias 2, 105 63 Athens; tel. (21) 03252362; Sec.-Gen. MICHALIS KYRIAKIDIS.

Peloponnese (10): Terma Erythrou Stavrou, 221 00 Tripoli; tel. (2071) 237952; fax (2071) 232383; Sec.-Gen. ANTONIOS MATSIGOS.

Northern Aegean (11): 8 Noembrios 57, 811 00 Mytilni; tel. (0251) 028935; fax (0251) 027601; internet www.northaegean.gr; Sec.-Gen. MARIA SKEMBERI.

Southern Aegean (12): Eptanissou 35, 841 00 Syros; tel. (2281) 087000; fax (2281) 088896; Sec.-Gen. PANAGIOTIS SALTOUROS.

Crete (13): Platia Kountourioti, 712 023 Heraklion; tel. (281) 0346333; fax (281) 0244520; internet www.crete-region.gr; Sec.-Gen. ATHANASIOS KAROUNTSOS.

Athens City Council (Dimos Athineon): Liosion 22, 104 58 Athens; tel. (21) 05242111; fax (210) 5246943; internet www.cityofathens.gr.

Thessaloníki City Council (Dimos Thessaloniki): El. Venizelou 45, 546 31 Thessaloníki; tel. (231) 0238321; fax (231) 0284434; e-mail municipality@thessalonikicity.gr; internet www.thessalonikicity.gr.

Holy Superintendency of Mount Athos: Áyion Óros, Aktí, Khalkidhiki, Macedonia.

Political Organizations

Coalition of the Left and Progress (Synaspismos): Pl. Eleftherias 1, 105 53 Athens; tel. (21) 03378400; fax (21) 03217003; e-mail intrelations@syn.gr; internet www.syn.gr; f. 1989 as an alliance of the nine political groups comprising the Greek Left Party and the Communist Party of Greece ('of the Exterior'); in 1991 the conservative faction of the Communist Party withdrew from the alliance; however, the Coalition continued to command considerable support from the large reformist faction of the KKE; transformed into a single party in 1992; Pres. NIKOS KONSTANTOPOULOS.

Communist Party of Greece (KKE) (Kommunistiko Komma Ellados): Leoforos Irakliou 145, Perissos, 142 31 Athens; tel. (21) 02592111; fax (21) 02592286; e-mail cpg@kke.gr; internet www.kke.gr; f. 1918; banned 1947, reappeared 1974; Gen. Sec. ALEKA PAPARIGA.

Democratic Social Movement (DIKKI): Odos Halkokondili 9, 106 77 Athens; tel. (21) 03829051; fax (21) 03839047; e-mail dikki@otenet.gr; internet www.dikki.gr; f. 1995; leftist party; opposes further integration with the EU; Leader DIMITRIS TSOVOLAS.

Democratic Socialist Party (KODISO): Odos Mavromichali 9, 106 79 Athens; tel. (21) 03602716; fax (21) 03625901; f. 1979 by former EDIK deputies; favours membership of the EU and political wing of NATO, decentralization and a mixed economy; Pres. CH. PROTOPAPAS.

Greek National Political Union (EPEN): Athens; tel. (21) 03643760; fax (21) 08943100; f. 1984; right-wing; Leader CHRYSSANTHOS DIMITRIADIS.

Hellenic Liberal Party: Athens; tel. (21) 03606111; f. 1910; aims to revive political heritage of fmr Prime Minister, Eleftherios Venizelos; 6,500 mems; Pres. NIKITAS VENIZELOS.

Liberal Party: Athens; internet www.liberals.gr; f. 1999; Founder STEFANOS MANOS.

New Democracy Party (ND) (Nea Dimokratia): Odos Rigillis 18, 106 74 Athens; tel. (21) 07290071; fax (21) 07214327; e-mail ir@nd.gr; internet www.nd.gr; f. 1974 by Konstantinos Karamanlis; a broadly-based centre-right party which advocates social reform in the framework of a liberal economy; supports European integration and enlargement; led and completed Greece's accession into the EU; Pres. Dr KONSTANTINOS AL. KARAMANLIS; Dir-Gen. IOANNIS VARTHOLOMEOS.

Panhellenic Socialist Movement (PASOK) (Panellinion Socialistikon Kinima): Odos Charilaou Trikoupi 50, Athens; tel. (21) 03232049; e-mail pasok@pasok.gr; internet www.pasok.gr; f. 1974; incorporates Democratic Defence and Panhellenic Liberation Movement resistance organizations; supports social welfare, decentralization and self-management; aims at a Mediterranean socialist development through international co-operation; 500 local organizations, 30,000 mems; Leader KONSTANTINOS (COSTAS) SIMITIS; Sec.-Gen. MICHALIS CHIRISOCHOIDHIS.

Political Spring (POLAN) (Politiki Anixi): Patision 67, 104 34 Athens; tel. (21) 08228301; fax (21) 08210531; e-mail anixi@otenet.gr; internet www.politikianixi.gr; f. 1993; centre-right; Leader ANTONIS C. SAMARAS.

Union of Democratic Centre Party (EDIK) (Enossi Dimokratikou Kentrou): Odos Charilaou Trikoupi 18, 106 79 Athens; tel. (21) 03609711; fax (21) 03612792; e-mail edik@edik.gr; internet www.edik.gr; f. 1974; democratic socialist party, merging Centre Union (f. 1961 by Georgios Papandreou) and New Political Forces (f. 1974 by

Prof. Ioannis Pesmazoglou and Prof. G. A. Mangakis); favours a united Europe; Chair. Prof. NEOKLIS SARRIS.

Other parties include the People's Militant Unity Party (f. 1985 by PASOK splinter group), the Progressive Party (f. 1979, right-wing), the (Maoist) Revolutionary Communist Party of Greece (EKKE), the Panhellenic Unaligned Party of Equality (PAKI, f. 1988; Leader KHARALAMBOS ALOMA TAMONTSIDES), Olympianism Party (pacifist, Leader GIORGIOS ZOE), and the left-wing United Socialist Alliance of Greece (ESPE, f. 1984).

Dissident organizations include the left-wing November 17 Revolutionary Organization (f. 1975; opposed to Western capitalism and the continuing existence of US military bases in Greece), the 1 May Revolutionary Organization, People's Revolutionary Solidarity, the Anti-State Struggle group, the Christos Tsoutsouvis Revolutionary Organization, the Revolutionary Praxis, Fighting Guerilla Faction and Autonomous Cells of Rebel Action.

Diplomatic Representation

EMBASSIES IN GREECE

Albania: Odos Karachristou 1, Kolonaki, 115 21 Athens; tel. (21) 07234412; fax (21) 07231972; Ambassador BASHKIM ZENELI.

Algeria: Leoforos Vassileos Konstantinou 14, 116 35 Athens; tel. (21) 07264191; fax (21) 07018681; e-mail ambdzath@otenet.gr; Ambassador KAMEL HOUHOU.

Argentina: Leoforos Vassilissis Sofias 59, 115 21 Athens; tel. (21) 07224753; fax (21) 07227568; e-mail egrecmrs@compulink.gr; Ambassador RAUL ALBERTO RICARDES.

Armenia: Leoforos Sygrou 159, 171 21 Athens; tel. (21) 09345727; fax (21) 09352187; e-mail armenia@hol.gr; Ambassador VAHRAN KAZGOIAN.

Australia: Odos Dimitriou Soutsou 37/Odos Tsoha 24, 115 21 Athens; tel. (21) 06447303; e-mail ausembgr@hol.gr; internet www.ausemb.gr; Ambassador STUART HUME.

Austria: Leoforos Alexandras 26, 106 83 Athens; tel. (21) 08257230; fax (21) 08219823; e-mail austria@ath.forthnet.gr; Ambassador Dr RENÉ POLLITZER.

Belgium: Odos Sekeri 3, 106 71 Athens; tel. (21) 03617886; fax (21) 03604289; e-mail athens@diplobel.org; Ambassador CLAUDE RIJMENANS.

Bosnia and Herzegovina: Hatzikosta 3, 115 21 Athens; tel. (21) 06411375; fax (21) 06423154; Ambassador SRDJAN LJUBOJEVIĆ.

Brazil: Plateia Philikis Etairias 14, 106 73 Athens; tel. (21) 07213039; fax (21) 07244731; Ambassador ALCIDES DA COSTA GUIMARĀES FILHO.

Bulgaria: Odos Stratigou Kallari 33A, Palaio Psychiko, 154 52 Athens; tel. (21) 06478105; fax (21) 06478130; Ambassador STEFAN STOYANOV.

Canada: Odos Ioannou Ghennadiou 4, 115 21 Athens; tel. (21) 07273400; fax (21) 07273480; e-mail athns@dfait-maeci.gc.ca; internet www.dfait-maeci.gc.ca/canadaeuropa/greece; Ambassador PHILIP SOMERVILLE.

Chile: Leoforos Vasilissis Sofias 25, 106 74 Athens; tel. (21) 07252574; fax (21) 07252536; e-mail embachilegr@ath.forthnet.gr; Ambassador MARCIA COVARRUBIAS.

China, People's Republic: Odos Krinon 2A, Paleo Psychiko, 154 52 Athens; tel. (21) 06723282; fax (21) 06723819; e-mail embchina@otenet.gr; Ambassador TANG ZHENQI.

Colombia: Vrasida 3, 115 28 Athens; tel. (21) 07236848; fax (21) 07246270; Ambassador ENRIQUE GAVIRIA-LIEVANO.

Congo, Democratic Republic: Athens; tel. (21) 06847013; Ambassador BOMOLO LOKOKA.

Croatia: Tzavela 4, Neo Psychiko, 154 51 Athens; tel. (21) 06777059; fax (21) 06711208; e-mail croatemb@hol.gr; Ambassador DANIEL BUČAN.

Cuba: Odos Sofokleou 5, Filothei, 152 37 Athens; tel. (21) 06842807; fax (21) 06849590; Ambassador ANA MARÍA GONZÁLEZ SUÁREZ.

Cyprus: Odos Herodotou 16, 106 75 Athens; tel. (21) 07232727; fax (21) 04536373; e-mail cyempkl@hol.gr; Ambassador KHARALAMBOS CHRISTOFOROU.

Czech Republic: Odos Georgiou Seferis 6, Palaio Psychiko, 154 52 Athens; tel. (21) 06713755; fax (21) 06710675; e-mail athens@embassy.mzv.cz; Ambassador JANA BOULENOVA.

Denmark: Leoforos Vassilissis Sofias 11, 106 71 Athens; tel. (21) 03608315; fax (21) 03636163; e-mail athamb@athamb.um.dk; internet www.denmark.gr; Ambassador HANS GRUNNET.

Egypt: Leoforos Vassilissis Sofias 3, 106 71 Athens; tel. (21) 03618612; fax (21) 03603538; e-mail emthens@hol.gr; Ambassador Dr MAGDA SHAHIN.

Estonia: Patriarchou Ioakeim 48, 106 76 Athens; tel. (21) 07229803; fax (21) 07229804; e-mail estemb@otenet.gr; Ambassador ANDRES UNGA.

Finland: Odos Eratosthenous 1, 116 35 Athens; tel. (21) 07010444; fax (21) 07515064; e-mail sanomat.ate@formin.fi; internet www.finland.gr; Ambassador TAPANI BROTHERUS.

France: Leoforos Vassilissis Sofias 7, 106 71 Athens; tel. (21) 03391000; fax (21) 03391009; e-mail ambafran@hol.gr; internet www.ambafrance-gr.org; Ambassador JEAN-MAURICE RIPERT.

Georgia: Odos Agiou Dimitriou 24, 154 52 Paleo Psihio, Athens; tel. (21) 06716737; fax (21) 06716722; e-mail embassygeo@hol.gr; Ambassador ZVIAD CHUMBURIDZE.

Germany: Odos Karaoli and Dimitriou 3, 106 75 Athens; tel. (21) 07285111; fax (21) 07251205; e-mail info@germanembassy.gr; internet www.germanembassy.gr; Ambassador ALBERT SPIEGEL.

Holy See: POB 65075, Odos Mavili 2, Palaio Psychiko, 154 52 Athens; tel. (21) 06722728; fax (21) 06742849; e-mail nunate@mail.otenet.gr; Apostolic Nuncio Most Rev. PAUL FOUAD TABET (Titular Archbishop of Sinna).

Honduras: Leoforos Kifissias 74, 115 26 Athens; tel. (21) 06982021; fax (21) 06982080; e-mail hondugre@otenet.gr; Chargé d'affaires a.i. TEODOLINDA BANEGAS DE MAKRIS.

Hungary: Odos Kalvou 16, Palaio Psychiko, 154 52 Athens; tel. (21) 06725337; fax (21) 06740890; e-mail huembath@otenet.gr; Ambassador CSABA KOROSI.

India: Odos Kleanthous 3, 106 74 Athens; tel. (21) 07216227; fax (21) 07211252; e-mail indembassy@ath.forthnet.gr; Ambassador G. S. BEDI.

Indonesia: Odos Papanastasidu 55, Palaio Psychiko, 154 52 Athens; tel. (21) 06712737; fax (21) 06756955; Ambassador FRANCISCO LOPEZ DA CRUZ.

Iran: Odos Kalari 16, Palaio Psychiko, 154 52 Athens; tel. (21) 06471436; fax (21) 06477945; e-mail irembatn@compulik.gr; Ambassador MUHAMMAD TAGHI MOAYYED.

Iraq: Odos Mazaraki 4, Palaio Psychiko, Athens; tel. (21) 06715012; Ambassador FAROUKH AL-FIDYAN (pending new appointment).

Ireland: Leoforos Vassileos 7, Konstantinou, Athens; tel. (21) 07232771; fax (21) 07240217; Ambassador MARGARET HENNESSY.

Israel: Odos Marathonodromou 1, Palaio Psychiko, 154 52 Athens; tel. (21) 06719530; fax (21) 06479510; Ambassador RAM IVIRAM.

Italy: Odos Sekeri 2, 106 74 Athens; tel. (21) 03617260; fax (21) 03617330; e-mail ambaten@hol.gr; internet www.italianembassy.gr; Ambassador AGOSTINO MATHIS.

Japan: 21st Floor, Athens A Tower, Leoforos Messoghion 2–4, Pirgas Athinon, 115 27 Athens; tel. (21) 07758101; fax (21) 07758206; internet www.gr.emb-japan.go.jp; Ambassador TOSHIO MOCHIZUKI.

Jordan: Odos Panagi Zervou 30, Palaio Psychiko, 154 10 Athens; tel. (21) 06474161; fax (21) 06470578; Ambassador AMJAD MAJALI.

Korea, Republic: Odos Eratosthenous 1, 116 35 Athens; tel. (21) 07012122; Ambassador TAE KYU HAN.

Kuwait: Odos Marathonodromou 27, Palaio Psychiko, 154 52 Athens; tel. (21) 06473593; fax (21) 06875875; Ambassador ALI FAHED AZ-ZAID.

Latvia: Odos Irodotou 9, Kolonaki, 106 74 Athens; tel. (21) 07294483; fax (21) 07294479; e-mail latvia@otenet.gr; Ambassador MARTINS LACIS.

Lebanon: 6, Odos Maritou 25, Palaio Psychiko, 154 52 Athens; tel. (21) 06755873; fax (21) 06755612; e-mail grlibemb@otenet.gr; Ambassador WILLIAM HABIB.

Libya: Odos Vironos 13, Palaio Psychiko, 154 52 Athens; tel. (21) 06472120; Secretary of the People's Bureau AYAD M. TAYARI.

Malta: Leoforos Vassilissis Sofias 63, 115 21 Athens; tel. (21) 07258153; fax (21) 07258152; Ambassador EVARIST SALIBA.

Mexico: Plateia Philikis Etairias 14, 106 73 Athens; tel. (21) 07294780; fax (21) 07294783; e-mail embgrecia@sre.gob.mx; Chargé d'affaires a.i. LUIS ALBERTO BARRERO-STAHL.

Morocco: Odos Mousson 14, Palaio Psychiko, 154 52 Athens; tel. (21) 06744209; fax (21) 06749480; Ambassador MUHAMMAD LOFTI AOUAD.

Netherlands: Leoforos Vassileos Konstantinou 5–7, 106 74 Athens; tel. (21) 07239701; fax (21) 07248900; e-mail ath@minbuza.gr; internet www.dutchembassy.gr; Ambassador P. R. BROUWER.

New Zealand: Leoforos Kifissias 268, 152 32 Halandri, Athens; tel. (21) 06874700; fax (21) 06874444; e-mail costas.cotsilinis@gr.pwcglobal.com; Ambassador PETER BENNETT.

Nicaragua: Leoforos Syggrou 206, Athens; tel. (21) 09585064.

Nigeria: Odos Iakinthon 50, Palaio Psychiko, Athens; tel. (21) 06718007; fax (21) 06718008; Ambassador FRANKLIN NCHITA OGBUEWU.

Norway: Leoforos Vassilissis Sofias 23, 106 74 Athens; tel. (21) 07246173; fax (21) 07244989; e-mail norwemba@netplan.gr; Ambassador FINN FOSTERVELL.

Pakistan: Odos Loukianou 6, Kolonaki, 106 75 Athens; tel. (21) 07290122; fax (21) 07257641; e-mail info@pak-embassy.gr; internet www.pak-embassy.gr; Ambassador JAVED HAFIZ.

Panama: Akti Miaoyli 23, Athens; tel. (21) 04133180.

Paraguay: Odos Alopekis 2, 106 75 Athens; tel. (21) 07210669.

Peru: Semitelou 2, 115 28, Athens; tel. (21) 07792761; fax (21) 07792905; e-mail lepruate@compulink.gr; Ambassador BERTHA VEGA PÉREZ.

Philippines: Xenophodos 9, Athens; tel. (21) 03241615; Ambassador LOURDES G. MORALES.

Poland: Odos Chryssanthemon 22, Palaio Psychiko, 154 52 Athens; tel. (21) 06778260; fax (21) 06718394; e-mail atenyamb@internet.gr; internet www.poland-embassy.gr; Ambassador GRZEGORZ DZIEMIDO-WICZ.

Portugal: Leoforos Vassilissis Sofias 23, 106 74 Athens; tel. (21) 07290096; fax (21) 07245122; e-mail embportg@otenet.gr; Ambassador ANTÓNIO SYDER SANTIAGO.

Romania: Odos Emmanuel Benaki 7, Palaio Psychiko, Athens; tel. (21) 06728875; fax (21) 06728883; e-mail roumaniaembassy@ath.forthnet.gr; Ambassador CAIUS TRÁIAN DRAGOMIR.

Russia: Odos Nikiforou Litra 28, Palaio Psychiko, 154 52 Athens; tel. (21) 06725235; fax (21) 06479708; Ambassador MIKHAIL BOCHAR-NIKOV.

Saudi Arabia: Odos Marathonodromou 71, Palaio Psychiko, 154 52 Athens; tel. (21) 06716911; Ambassador Sheikh ABDULLAH ABD AR-RAHMAN AL-MALHOOQ.

Serbia and Montenegro: Leoforos Vassilissis Sofias 106, Athens; tel. (21) 07774344; Ambassador DUSAN BATAKOVIĆ.

Slovakia: Odos Georgiou Seferis 4, Palaio Psychiko, 154 52 Athens; tel. (21) 06776757; fax (21) 06776760; e-mail zuateny@compulink.gr.

South Africa: Leoforos Kifissias 60, 151 25 Athens; tel. (21) 06106645; fax (21) 06106640; e-mail embassy@southafrica.gr; internet www.southafrica.gr; Ambassador JANNIE MOMBERG.

Spain: Odos D. Areapagitou 21, 117 42 Athens; tel. (21) 09213123; fax (21) 09214264; e-mail emb-esp@otenet.gr; Ambassador JAVIER JIMÉNEZ-UGARTE.

Sweden: Leoforos Vassileos Konstantinou 7, 106 74 Athens; tel. (21) 07290421; fax (21) 07229953; e-mail ambassaden.athens@foreign.ministry.se; Ambassador BJÖRN ELMÉR.

Switzerland: Odos Iassiou 2, 115 21 Athens; tel. (21) 07230364; fax (21) 07299471; e-mail vertretung@ath.rep.admin.ch; Ambassador MARIA LUISA CARONI.

Syria: Odos Marathonodromou 79, Palaio Psychiko, Athens; tel. (21) 06725577; Ambassador SHAHIN FARAH.

Thailand: Odos Taigetou 23, Palaio Psychiko, 154 52 Athens; tel. (21) 06717969; fax (21) 06479508; Ambassador PRECHA PITISANT.

Tunisia: Odos Anthéon 2, Palaio Psychiko, 154 52 Athens; tel. (21) 06717590; fax (21) 06713432; e-mail tunisie@otenet.gr; Ambassador MUHAMMAD BACHROUCH.

Turkey: Odos Vassileos Gheorghiou B 8, 106 74 Athens; tel. (21) 07245915; fax (21) 07229597; e-mail turkembgr@hol.gr; Ambassador YIGIT ALPOGAN.

Ukraine: Odos Stefanu Delta 2–4, 152 37 Athens; tel. (21) 06718957; fax (21) 06855363; e-mail ukrembas@otenet.gr; Ambassador VIKTOR KALNYK.

United Kingdom: Odos Ploutarchou 1, 106 75 Athens; tel. (21) 07272600; fax (21) 07272734; e-mail britania@hol.gr; internet www.british-embassy.gr; Ambassador DAVID MADDEN.

USA: Leoforos Vassilissis Sofias 91, 106 60 Athens; tel. (21) 07212951; fax (21) 07226724; e-mail usembassy@usembassy.gr; internet www.usembassy.gr; Ambassador THOMAS J. MILLER.

Uruguay: Odos Likavitou I G, 106 72 Athens; tel. (21) 03613549; Ambassador ULYSSES PEREIRA REVERBEL.

Venezuela: Leoforos Vassilissis, Sophias 112, Athens; tel. (21) 07708769; Ambassador LISAN STREDEL BALLIACHE.

Judicial System

The Constitution of 1975 provided for the establishment of a Special Supreme Tribunal. Other provisions in the Constitution provided for a reorganization of parts of the judicial system to be accomplished through legislation.

SUPREME ADMINISTRATIVE COURTS

Special Supreme Tribunal: Odos Patision 30, Athens; has final jurisdiction in matters of constitutionality.

Council of State

Odos Panepistimiou 47, 105 64 Athens; tel. (21) 03710098; fax (21) 03710097; e-mail s-epikc@otenet.gr.

Has appellate powers over acts of the administration and final rulings of administrative courts; has power to rule upon matters of judicial review of laws.

President: CHRISTOS G. YERARIS.

SUPREME JUDICIAL COURT

Supreme Civil and Penal Court

Leoforos Alexandros 121, 115 22 Athens; tel. (21) 06411506; fax (21) 06433799; e-mail areios@otenet.gr.

Supreme court in the State, having also appellate powers; consists of six sections, four Civil and two Penal, and adjudicates in quorum.

President: STEPHANOS MATHIAS.

COURTS OF APPEAL

There are 12 Courts of Appeal with jurisdiction in cases of Civil and Penal Law of second degree, and, in exceptional penal cases, of first degree.

COURTS OF FIRST INSTANCE

There are 59 Courts of First Instance with jurisdiction in cases of first degree, and in exceptional cases, of second degree. They function both as Courts of First Instance and as Criminal Courts. For serious crimes the Criminal Courts function with a jury.

In towns where Courts of First Instance sit there are also Juvenile Courts. Commercial Tribunals do not function in Greece, and all commercial cases are tried by ordinary courts of law. There are, however, Tax Courts in some towns.

OTHER COURTS

There are 360 Courts of the Justice of Peace throughout the country. There are 48 Magistrates' Courts (or simple Police Courts).

In all the above courts, except those of the Justice of Peace, there are District Attorneys. In Courts of the Justice of Peace the duties of District Attorney are performed by the Public Prosecutor.

Religion

CHRISTIANITY

The Eastern Orthodox Church

The Orthodox Church of Greece

Odos Ioannou Gennadiou 14, 115 21 Athens; tel. (21) 07218381; internet www.ecclesia.gr.

f. 1850; 78 dioceses, 8,335 priests, 84 bishops, 9,025,000 adherents (1985)

The Greek branch of the Holy Eastern Orthodox Church is the officially established religion of the country, to which nearly 97% of the population profess adherence. The administrative body of the Church is the Holy Synod of 12 members, elected by the bishops of the Hierarchy.

Primate of Greece: Archbishop of Athens CHRISTODOULOS.

Within the Greek State there is also the semi-autonomous Church of Crete, composed of seven Metropolitans and the Holy Archbishopric of Crete. The Church is administered by a Synod consisting of the seven Metropolitans under the Presidency of the Archbishop; it is under the spiritual jurisdiction of the Ecumenical Patriarchate of Constantinople (based in İstanbul, Turkey), which also maintains a degree of administrative control.

Archbishop of Crete: Archbishop TIMOTHEOS (whose See is in Heraklion).

There are also four Metropolitan Sees of the Dodecanese, which are spiritually and administratively dependent on the Ecumenical Patriarchate and, finally, the peninsula of Athos, which constitutes the region of the Holy Mountain (Mount Athos) and comprises 20 monasteries. These are dependent on the Ecumenical Patriarchate of Constantinople, but are autonomous and are safeguarded constitutionally.

The Roman Catholic Church

Latin Rite

Greece comprises four archdioceses (including two directly responsible to the Holy See), four dioceses and one Apostolic Vicariate. At 31 December 2001 there were an estimated 44,807 adherents in the country.

Bishop's Conference: Conferentia Episcopalis Graeciae, Odos Homirou 9, 106 72 Athens; tel. (21) 03624311; fax (21) 03618632; f. 1967; Pres. Most Rev. NIKOLAOS FÓSKOLOS (Archbishop of Athens).

Archdiocese of Athens: Archbishopric, Odos Homirou 9, 106 72 Athens; tel. (21) 03624311; fax (21) 03618632; Archbishop Most Rev. NIKOLAOS FÓSKOLOS.

Archdiocese of Rhodes: Archbishopric, Odos I. Dragoumi 5A, 851 00 Rhodes; tel. (2241) 021845; fax (2241) 026688; Apostolic Administrator Most Rev. NIKOLAOS FÓSKOLOS (Archbishop of Athens).

Metropolitan Archdiocese of Corfu, Zante and Cefalonia: Archbishopric, Montzenikhov 3, 491 00 Kerkyra; tel. and fax (2661) 030277; Archbishop Most Rev. ANTONIOS VARTHALITIS.

Metropolitan Archdiocese of Naxos, Andros, Tinos and Mykonos: Archbishopric, 842 00 Tinos; tel. (2283) 022382; fax (2283) 024769; e-mail karcntam@thn.forthnet.gr; also responsible for the suffragan dioceses of Candia, Chios, Santorini, Syros and Milos; Archbishop Most Rev. NIKOLAOS PRINTESIS.

Apostolic Vicariate of Salonika (Thessaloníki): Leoforos Vassilissis Olgas 120B, 546 45 Thessaloníki; tel. (231) 0835780; fax (2661) 031675; Apostolic Administrator Archbishop Most Rev. of Corfu, Zante and Cefalonia ANTONIOS VARTHALITIS.

Byzantine Rite

Apostolic Exarchate for the Byzantine Rite in Greece: Odos Akarnon 246, 112 53 Athens; tel. (21) 08670170; fax (21) 08677039; e-mail grcathex@hol.gr; 3 parishes (Athens and Jannitsa, Macedonia); 7 secular priests, 2,300 adherents (31 Dec. 2001); Exarch Apostolic Rt Rev. ANARGHYROS PRINTESIS (Titular Bishop of Gratianopolis).

Armenian Rite

Exarchate for the Armenian Catholics in Greece: Odos René Piot 2, 117 44 Athens; tel. (21) 09014089; fax (21) 09012109; 550 adherents (31 Dec. 1999); Exarch Archpriest NICHAN KARAKEHEYAN.

Protestant Church

Greek Evangelical Church (Reformed): Odos Markon Botsari 24, 117 41 Athens; tel. (21) 09222684; e-mail info@gec.gr; internet www.gec.gr; f. 1858; comprises 32 organized churches; 5,000 adherents (1996); Moderator Rev. MELETIS MELETIADIS.

ISLAM

The law provides as religious head of the Muslims a Chief Mufti; the Muslims in Greece possess a number of mosques and schools.

JUDAISM

The Jewish population of Greece, estimated in 1943 at 75,000 people, was severely reduced as a result of the German occupation. In 1994 there were about 5,000 Jews in Greece.

Central Board of the Jewish Communities of Greece: Odos Voulis 36, 105 57 Athens; tel. (21) 03244315; fax (21) 03313852; e-mail info@kis.gr; internet www.kis.gr; f. 1945; officially recognized representative body of the communities of Greece; Pres. MOSES KONSTANTINIS.

Jewish Community of Athens: Odos Melidoni 8, 105 53 Athens; tel. (21) 03252823; fax (21) 03220761; e-mail isrkath@hellasnet.gr; Rabbi JACOB D. ARAR.

Jewish Community of Larissa: Odos Kentavrou 27, Larissa; tel. (241) 0220762; Rabbi ELIE SABETAI.

Jewish Community of Thessaloníki: Odos Tsimiski 24, 546 24 Thessaloníki; tel. (231) 0275701; e-mail jct1@compulink.gr; internet www.jct.gr; Pres. DAVID SALTIEL; Rabbi URI BUSKILLA.

The Press

PRINCIPAL DAILY NEWSPAPERS

Morning papers are not published on Mondays, nor afternoon papers on Sundays. Afternoon papers are more popular than morning ones. In 1997 there were 122 daily newspaper titles.

Athens

Apogevmatini (The Afternoon): Odos Phidiou 12, 106 78 Athens; tel. (21) 06430011; fax (21) 03609876; e-mail apo@apogevmatini.gr; internet www.apogevmatini.gr; f. 1956; independent; Publr GEORGIOS HATZIKONSTANTINOU; Editor P. KARAYANNIS; circ. 30,000.

Athens Daily Post: Odos Stadiou 57, Athens; tel. (21) 03249504; f. 1952; morning; English; Owner G. SKOURAS.

Athens News: Odos Christou Lada 3, 102 37 Athens; tel. (21) 03333555; fax (21) 03231384; e-mail athnews@dolnet.gr; internet www.athensnews.gr; f. 1952; morning; English; Publr CHRISTOS D. LAMBRAKIS; Editor JOHN PSAROPOULOS; circ. 10,000.

Athlitiki Icho (Athletics Echo): Konstantinoupelos 161, 104 41 Athens; tel. (21) 05232201; fax (21) 05232433; e-mail text@athlitiki-iho.gr; f. 1945; morning; Publr and Dir KLEOMANLIS GEORGALAS; Editor DEMOSTHENES CHRISTOU; circ. 40,000.

Avgi (Dawn): Odos Ag. Konstantiou 12, 104 31 Athens; tel. (21) 05231831; fax (21) 05231830; e-mail editors@avgi.gr; internet www.avgi.gr; f. 1952; morning; independent newspaper of the left; Publr and Dir D. ALEKSOPOULOS; Editor NIKOS PHILES; circ. 5,400.

Avriani (Tomorrow): Odos Dimitros 11, 177 78 Athens; tel. (21) 03424090; fax (21) 03452190; f. 1980; evening; Publr GEORGE KOURIS; circ. 51,317.

Dimokratikos Logos (Democratic Speech): Odos Dimitros 11, 177 78 Athens; tel. (21) 03424023; fax (21) 03452190; f. 1986; morning; Dir and Editor KOSTAS GERONIKOLOS; circ. 7,183.

Eleftherotypia (Press Freedom): Odos Minoou 10–16, 117 43 Athens; tel. (21) 09296001; fax (21) 09028311; internet www.enet.gr; f. 1974; evening; Publr CHR. TEGOPOULOS; Dir S. FYNDANIDIS; circ. 115,000.

Estia (Vesta): Odos Anthimou Gazi 7, 105 61 Athens; tel. (21) 03230650; fax (21) 03243071; e-mail estianews@otenet.gr; f. 1894; afternoon; Publr and Dir KOINONIA ASTIKOU DIKAIOU; Editor E. PETROU; circ. 60,000.

Ethnos (Nation): Odos Benaki 152, Metamorfosi Chalandriou, 152 35 Athens; tel. (21) 06580640; fax (21) 06396515; internet www.ethnos.gr; f. 1981; evening; Publr GEORGE BOBOLAS; Dir TH. KALOUDIS; circ. 84,735.

Express: Odos Halandriou 39, Paradissos Amaroussiou, 151 25 Athens; tel. (21) 06850200; fax (21) 06852202; internet express.gr; f. 1963; morning; financial; Publr Hellenews Publications; Editor D. G. KALOFOLIAS; circ. 28,000.

Filathlos: Odos Dimitros 31, 177 78 Athens; tel. (21) 03486000; fax (21) 03486450; e-mail info@filathlos.gr; internet www.filathlos.gr; f. 1982; morning; sports; Publr and Dir NICK KARAGIANNIDIS; Editor G. KOLOKOTRONIS; circ. 40,000.

Imerissia (Daily): Odos Benaki & Ag. Nektariou, Metamorfosi Chalandriou, 152 35 Athens; tel. (21) 06061729; fax (21) 06016563; e-mail imerissia@pegasus.gr; f. 1947; morning; financial; Publr PETROS ANTONIADIS; Editor ANTONIS DALIPIS; circ. 26,000.

Kathimerini (Every Day): Ethnarchou Makariou 185–47 & Odos Falireos 2, Athens; tel. (21) 04808000; fax (21) 04808000; e-mail kathi-editor@ekathimerini.com; internet www.kathimerini.gr; f. 1919; morning; Conservative; English edition published with *International Herald Tribune*; Publr THEMISTODIS ALAFOUZOS; Editor CH. PANAGOPOULOS; circ. 34,085.

Kerdos (Profit): Leoforos Kifissias 178, Halandri, 152 31 Athens; tel. (21) 06747881; fax (21) 06747893; e-mail mail@kerdos.gr; internet www.kerdos.gr; f. 1985; morning; financial; Publr and Dir VASILIS VALAMVANOS; Editor VASILIS STEFANAKADIS; circ. 18,000.

Naftemporiki (Daily Journal): Odos Lenorman 205, 104 42 Athens; tel. (21) 05198000; fax (21) 05146013; e-mail info@naftemporiki.gr; internet www.naftemporiki.gr; f. 1924; morning; non-political journal of finance, commerce and shipping; Publr M. ATHANASSIADIS; Editor D. KEFALAKOS; circ. 35,000.

Ora Gia Spor (Time for Sport): Ioannou Metaxa 8, 173 43 Athens; tel. (21) 09251200; fax (21) 09761211; f. 1991; sport; Publr K. SEMPOU; Editor D. AVOURIS.

Rizospastis (Radical): Lefkis 134, Perissos, 145 65 Athens; tel. (21) 06297000; fax (21) 06297999; e-mail mailbox@rizospastis.gr; internet www.rizospastis.gr; f. 1974; morning; Dir D. KOUTSOUMPAS; Editor T. TSIGGAS; circ. 28,740.

Ta Nea (News): Odos Christou Lada 3, 102 37 Athens; tel. (21) 03333555; fax (21) 03228797; e-mail tanea@dolnet.gr; internet ta-nea.dolnet.gr; f. 1944; liberal; evening; Publr L. KARAPANAYIOTIS; Editor HLIAS MATSIKAS; circ. 135,000.

Vradyni (Evening Press): L. Ionias 166, 111 44 Athens; tel. (21) 02113600; fax (21) 02113648; e-mail vradyni@otenet.gr; f. 1923; evening; right-wing; Publr CHRISTINA K. MITSI; Editor PANOS TSIROS; circ. 71,914.

Patras

Peloponnesos: Maizonos 206, 262 22 Patras; tel. (261) 0312530; fax (261) 0312535; internet www.peloponnisos.com.gr; f. 1886; independent conservative; Publr and Editor S. Doukas; circ. 7,000.

Thessaloníki

Ellinikos Vorras (Greek North): Odos Grammou-Vitsi 19, 551 34 Thessaloníki; tel. (231) 0416621; f. 1935; morning; Publr Tessa Levantis; Dir N. Mergios; circ. 14,467.

Thessaloníki: Odos Monastiriou 85, 546 27 Thessaloníki; tel. (231) 0521621; f. 1963; evening; Propr Publishing Co of Northern Greece SA; Dir Lazaros Hadjinakos; Editor Katerina Vellidi; circ. 36,040.

SELECTED PERIODICALS

Agora (Market): Leoforos Kifissias 178, Halandri, 151 31 Athens; tel. (21) 06473384; fax (21) 06477893; e-mail agora@kerdos.gr; internet www.kerdos.gr/agora; f. 1987; fortnightly; politics, finance; Dir Ant. Kefalas; circ. 20,000.

Aktines: Odos Karytsi 14, 105 61 Athens; tel. (21) 03235023; f. 1938; monthly; current affairs, science, philosophy, arts; aims to promote a Christian civilization; Publr Christian Union; circ. 10,000.

Athèmes: Athens; monthly; French; cultural; Chief Editor Emmanuel Adely; circ. 5,000.

The Athenian: Athens; tel. (21) 03222802; fax (21) 03223052; e-mail the-athenian@hol.gr; internet www.hol.gr; f. 1974; monthly; English; Publr Konstantinos Gerou; Editor Joanna Stavropoulos; circ. 14,000.

Auto Express: Odos Halandriou 39, Halandri, 152 32 Athens; tel. (21) 06816906; fax (21) 06825858; Dir D. Kalofolias; circ. 18,828.

Computer Gia Olous (Computers for All): Leoforos Syngrou 44, 117 42 Kallithea, Athens; tel. (21) 09238672; fax (21) 09216847; internet www.cgomag.gr; monthly; Editor George Christopoulos.

Deltion Diikiseos Epichiriseon Euro-Unial (Business Administration Bulletin Euro-Unial): Odos Rhigillis 26, 106 74 Athens; tel. (21) 07235736; fax (21) 07240000; e-mail busadmibul@otenet.gr; monthly; Editor I. Papamichalakis; circ. 26,000.

Demosiografiki (Journalism): Procopiou 7–9, 171 24 Athens; tel. (21) 09731338; e-mail harrynic@yahoo.com; f. 1987; quarterly; Dir John Menoúnos; circ. 4,000.

Ekonomicos Tachydromos (Financial Courier): Odos Christou Lada 3, 102 37 Athens; tel. (21) 03333630; fax (21) 03238740; e-mail oikonomikos@dolnet.gr; internet oikonomikos.dolnet.gr; f. 1926; weekly; illustrated magazine; Man. Dir Dennis Antypas; circ. 23,000.

Elle: Odos Kleisthenous 213, 153 44 Athens; tel. (21) 06062531; fax (21) 06062648; e-mail magelle@compulink.gr; f. 1988; monthly; women's magazine; Editor Flora Tzimaka; circ. 57,120 (1997).

Epiloghi: Odos Stadiou 4, 105 64 Athens; tel. (21) 03238427; fax (21) 03235160; e-mail epilogi@mail.hol.gr; f. 1962; weekly; economics; Editor George Malouhos.

Greece's Weekly for Business and Finance: Odos Fokiodos 10, 115 26 Athens; tel. (21) 07707280; weekly; English; finance; Dir V. Koronakis.

Gynaika (Women): Odos Fragoklissias 7, Marousi, 151 25 Athens; tel. (21) 06199149; fax (21) 06104707; f. 1950; monthly; fashion, beauty, cookery, social problems, news; Publr Christos Terzopoulos; circ. 45,000.

Hellenews: Odos Halandriou 39, Marousi, 151 25 Athens; tel. (21) 06199400; fax (21) 06199421; e-mail alexm@express.kapatel.gr; weekly; English; finance and business; Publr Hellenews Publications; Editor J. M. Germanos.

Idaniko Spiti (Ideal Home): Odos St Nectarios, 152 35 Athens; tel. (1) 06061777; fax (1) 06011044; e-mail pa@pegasus.gr; internet www.idanikospiti.gr; f. 1990; monthly; interior decoration; Editor Petros Antoniadis; circ. 60,000 (2002).

Klik: Odos Fragoklisias 7, 151 25 Athens; tel. (21) 06897945; fax (21) 06899153; internet www.klik.gr; f. 1987; monthly; popular music, media and fashion; Editor Petros Costopoulos.

Marie Claire: Odos Stadiou 24, 105 64 Athens; tel. (21) 03333654; fax (21) 03227770; e-mail marieclaire@dolnet.gr; monthly; women's magazine.

Men: Odos Fragoklisias 7, 151 25 Athens; tel. (21) 06826680; fax (21) 06824730; e-mail mensynt@dolnet.gr; internet www.men.gr; six a year; men's fashion and general interest.

Oikonomiki Viomichaniki Epitheorissis (Industrial Review): Odos Zalokosta 4, 106 71 Athens; tel. (21) 03626360; fax (21) 03626388; e-mail editor@oikonomiki.gr; internet www.oikonomiki.gr; f. 1934; monthly; industrial and economic review; Publr A. C. Vovolini-Laskaridis; Editor D. Karamanos; circ. 25,000.

48 Ores (48 Hours): Leoforos Alexandras 19, 114 73 Athens; tel. (21) 06430313; fax (21) 06461361; weekly; Dir and Editor Sp. Karatzaferis; circ. 9,127.

Pantheon: Odos Christou Lada 3, 102 37 Athens; tel. (21) 03230221; fax (21) 03228797; every two weeks; Publr and Dir N. Theofanides; circ. 23,041.

Politika Themata: Odos Ypsilantou 25, 106 75 Athens; tel. (21) 07218421; weekly; Publr J. Chorn; Dir C. Kyrkos; circ. 2,544.

Pontiki (Mouse): Odos Massalias 10, 106 81 Athens; tel. (21) 03609531; weekly; humour; Dir and Editor K. Papaioannou.

Ptisi (Flight and Space): Odos Helioupoleos 2–4, 172 37 Athens; tel. (21) 09792500; fax (21) 09792528; e-mail ptisi@techlink.gr; internet www.ptisi.gr; f. 1975; monthly; Editor Costas Cavathas; circ. 68,000 (1997).

Radiotileorassi (Radio-TV): Odos Mourouzi 16, 106 74 Athens; tel. (21) 07224811; weekly; circ. 134,626.

Technika Chronika (Technical Times): Odos Karageorgi Servias 4, 105 62 Athens; tel. (21) 03234751; f. 1952; monthly; general edition on technical and economic subjects; Editor D. Rokos; circ. 12,000.

Tilerama: Odos Voukourestiou 18, 106 71 Athens; tel. (21) 03607160; fax (21) 03607032; f. 1977; weekly; radio and television; circ. 189,406.

To Vima (Tribune): Odos Christou Lada 3, 102 37 Athens; tel. (21) 03333103; fax (21) 03239097; e-mail tovima@dolnet.gr; internet tovima.dolnet.gr; f. 1922; weekly; liberal; Dir and Editor Stavros R. Psycharis; circ. 250,000.

La Tribune héllenique: Athens; every two months; French; politics, economics; Dir Theodore Benakis; circ. 3,000.

NEWS AGENCIES

Athens News Agency (ANA): Odos Tsoha 36, 115 21 Athens; tel. (21) 06400560; fax (21) 06400581; e-mail ape@ana.gr; internet www.ana.gr; f. 1895; correspondents in leading capitals of the world and towns throughout Greece; Man. Dir Nikolas Voulelis; Gen. Dir Andreas Christodoulides.

Foreign Bureaux

Agence France-Presse (AFP): Odos Millioni 5, 106 73 Athens; tel. (21) 03633646; fax (21) 03614457; e-mail athensbureau@afp.com; Bureau Chief Jean-Pierre Altier.

Agencia EFE: Athens; tel. (21) 03635826; Bureau Chief D. María-Luisa Rubio; Correspondent Juan José Fernández Elorriaga.

Agenzia Nazionale Stampa Associata (ANSA): Odos Kanari 9, 106 71 Athens; tel. (21) 03605285; fax (21) 03635367; Correspondent Francesco Indraccolo.

Associated Press (AP): Leoforos Amalias 52, 105 52 Athens; tel. (21) 03310802; fax (21) 03310804.

Deutsche Presse-Agentur (dpa): Miniati 1, 116 36 Athens; tel. (21) 09247774; fax (21) 09222185; Correspondent Hildegard Hülsenbeck.

Dow Jones Newswire: Odos Philellinon 34, 105 58 Athens; tel. (21) 03312881; fax (21) 03313180.

ITAR—TASS (Information Telegraphic Agency of Russia): Odos Gizi 39, Palaio Psychiko, 15 452 Athens; tel. and fax (21) 06713069; Bureau Chief Vladimir V. Malyshev.

Reuters Hellas SA: 1 Kolokotroni & Stadiou, 105 62 Athens; tel. (21) 03311800; fax (21) 03311830; e-mail athens.newsroom@reuters.com; fax www.reuters.gr; Man. Dir William Cairley.

Rossiiskoye Informatsionnoye Agentstvo—Novosti (RIA—Novosti): Odos Irodotou 9, 138 Athens; tel. (21) 07291016; Bureau Chief Boris Korolyov; Correspondent J. Kurizin.

Xinhua (New China) News Agency: Odos Amarilidos 19, Palaio Psychiko, Athens; tel. (21) 06724997; Bureau Chief Xie Chenghao.

PRESS ASSOCIATIONS

Enosis Antapokriton Xenou Tipou (Foreign Press Association of Greece): Odos Akademias 23, 106 71 Athens; tel. (21) 03637318; fax (21) 03605035.

Enosis Syntakton Imerission Ephimeridon Athinon (Journalists' Union of Athens Daily Newspapers): Odos Akademias 20, 106 71 Athens; tel. (21) 03632601; fax (21) 03632608; e-mail info@esiea.gr; internet www.esiea.gr; f. 1914; Pres. Fani Petralia; Gen. Sec. Anastasia Daoudaki; 1,400 mems.

Enosis Syntakton Periodikou Tipou (Journalists' Union of the Periodical Press): Odos Valaoritou 9, 106 71 Athens; tel. (21) 03633427; fax (21) 03638627; e-mail espt@otenet.gr; Pres. ATHENESE PAPANDROPOULOS; 650 mems.

Publishers

Agkyra Publications: Leoforos Kifisou 85, Egaleo, 122 41 Athens; tel. (21) 03455276; fax (21) 03474732; f. 1890; general; Man. Dir DIMITRIOS PAPADIMITRIOU.

Akritas: Odos Efessou 24, 171 21 Athens; tel. (21) 09334554; fax (21) 09311436; e-mail akritaspublications@ath.forthnet.gr; f. 1979; history, spirituality, children's books.

D. I. Arsenidis & Co: Odos Akademias 57, 106 79 Athens; tel. (21) 03629538; fax (21) 03618707; biography, literature, children's books, history, philosophy, social sciences; Man. Dir JOHN ARSENIDIS.

Boukoumanis Editions: Odos Mavromichali 1, 106 79 Athens; tel. (21) 03618502; fax (21) 03630669; f. 1967; history, politics, sociology, psychology, belles-lettres, educational, arts, children's books, ecology; Man. ELIAS BOUKOUMANIS.

Dorikos Publishing House: Odos Charalabou Sotiriou 9–11, 114 72 Athens; tel. (21) 06454726; fax (21) 03301866; f. 1958; literature, fiction, history, politics; Editor ROUSSOS VRANAS.

Ekdotike Athenon SA: Odos Academias 34, 106 72 Athens; tel. (21) 03608911; fax (21) 03606157; e-mail ekdath@aias.gr; internet www.addgr.com/comp/ekdotiki; f. 1961; history, archaeology, art; Pres. GEORGE A. CHRISTOPOULOS.

G. C. Eleftheroudakis SA: Odos Panepistimiou 17, 105 64 Athens; tel. (21) 03314180; fax (21) 03239821; e-mail elebooks@netor.gr; internet www.books.gr; f. 1915; general, technical and scientific; Man. Dir VIRGINIA ELEFTHEROUDAKIS-GREGOU.

Exandas Publrs: Odos Didotou 57, 106 81 Athens; tel. (21) 03804885; fax (21) 03813065; e-mail info@exandasbooks.gr; internet www.exandasbooks.gr; f. 1974; fiction, literature, social sciences; Pres. MAGDA N. KOTZIA.

Govostis Publishing SA: Zoodohou Pigis 21, 106 81 Athens; tel. (21) 03815433; fax (21) 03816661; e-mail cotsos@compulink.gr; f. 1926; arts, fiction, politics; Pres. COSTAS GOVOSTIS.

Denise Harvey: Katounia, 340 05 Limni, Evia; tel. and fax (2227) 031154; e-mail denise@teledomenet.gr; f. 1972; modern Greek literature and poetry, belles-lettres, theology, translations, selected general list (English and Greek); Man. Dir DENISE HARVEY.

Hestia-I.D. Kollaros & Co SA: Odos Solonos 60, 106 72 Athens; tel. (21) 03615077; fax (21) 03606759; f. 1885; literature, history, politics, architecture, philosophy, travel, religion, psychology, textbooks, general; Gen. Dir MARINA KARAITIDIS.

Kastaniotis Editions SA: Odos Zalogou 11, 106 78 Athens; tel. (21) 03301208; fax (21) 03822530; e-mail info@kastaniotis.com; internet www.kastaniotis.com; f. 1969; fiction and non-fiction, including arts, social sciences and psychology, children's books; Man. Dir ATHANASIOS KASTANIOTIS.

Kritiki Publishing: Odos Koletti 25, 106 77 Athens; tel. (21) 03803730; fax (21) 03803740; e-mail biblia@kritiki.gr; internet www.kritiki.gr; f. 1987; economics, politics, literature, philosophy, business/management, popular science; Pres. THEMIS MINOGLOU.

Kronos: Odos Egnatia 33, 546 26 Thessaloníki; tel. (231) 0532077; fax (231) 0538158; Dir TH. GIOTAS.

Lambrakis Press SA: Odos Christou Lada 3, 102 37 Athens; tel. (21) 03333555; fax (21) 03228797; internet www.dolnet.gr; newspapers and magazines; 18 titles.

Livani Publishing Org.: Odos Solonos 98, 106 80 Athens; tel. (21) 03661200; fax (21) 03617791; e-mail rights@livanis.gr; internet www.livanis.gr; f. 1972; general; Publr A. A. LIVANI.

Minoas SA: Odos Posseidonos 1, 141 21 N. Iraklio, Athens; tel. (21) 02711222; fax (21) 02711056; e-mail info@minoas.gr; internet www.minoas.gr; f. 1952; fiction, art, history; Man. Dir IOANNIS KONSTANTAROPOULOS.

Odos Panos: Odos Didotou 39, 106 08 Athens; tel. and fax (21) 03616782; internet www.odospanos-cigaret.gr; poetry, drama, biography.

Papazissis Publishers: Nikitara 2, 106 78 Athens; tel. (21) 03822496; fax (21) 03809150; e-mail papazisi@otenet.gr; internet www.papzisi.gr; f. 1929; economics, politics, law, history, school books; Man. Dir VICTOR PAPAZISSIS.

Patakis Publications: Odos Valtetsiou 14, 106 80 Athens; tel. (21) 03638362; fax (21) 03628950; internet www.patakis.gr; f. 1974; art, reference, literature, educational, philosophy, psychology, sociology, religion, music, children's books, educational toys, CD-Rom and audiobooks; Pres. STEFANOS PATAKIS.

Pontiki Publications SA: Odos Massalias 10, 106 80 Athens; tel. (21) 03609531; fax (21) 03645406; f. 1979; govt, history, political science; Man. Dir KOSTAS TABANIS.

John Sideris: Odos Stadiou 44, 105 64 Athens; tel. (21) 03229638; fax (21) 03245052; f. 1898; school textbooks, general; Man. J. SIDERIS.

J. G. Vassiliou: Odos Hippokratous 15, 106 79 Athens; tel. (21) 03623382; fax (21) 03623580; f. 1913; fiction, history, philosophy, dictionaries and children's books; Pres. J. VASSILIOU.

Government Publishing House

Government Printing House: Odos Kapodistriou 34, 104 32 Athens; tel. (21) 05248320.

PUBLISHERS' FEDERATIONS

Hellenic Federation of Publishers and Booksellers: Odos Themistokleus 73, 106 83 Athens; tel. (21) 03300924; fax (21) 03301617; e-mail poev@otenet.gr; f. 1961; Pres. GEORGE DARDANOS; Gen. Sec. TITOS MYLONOPOULOS.

Publishers' and Booksellers' Association of Athens: Odos Themistokleus 73, 106 83 Athens; tel. (21) 03303268; fax (21) 03823222; e-mail seva@otenet.gr; Pres. ELENI KANAKI; Sec. STELIOS ELLINIADIS.

Broadcasting and Communications

TELECOMMUNICATIONS

National Telecommunications Commission (NTC): Leoforos Kifissias 60, 151 25 Athens; tel. (21) 06151000; fax (21) 06805049; e-mail info@eet.gr; internet www.eet.gr; regulatory body; Chair. EMMANOUIL GIACOUMAKIS.

Organismos Telepikoinonion tis Elladas SA (OTE) (Hellenic Telecommunications Organization): Leoforos Kifissias 99, 151 24 Maroussi, Athens; tel. (21) 08827015; fax (21) 06115825; e-mail ote@ote.gr; internet www.ote.gr; f. 1949; owned 42% by the Government, 58% by public shareholders; 6m. lines in service; Man. Dir and Pres. LEFTERIS ANTONACOPOULOS.

COSMOTE: Leoforos Kifissias 44, 151 25 Athens; tel. (21) 06177700; fax (21) 06177594; e-mail customercare@cosmote.gr; internet www.cosmote.gr; f. 1998; 59% owned by OTE, 9%-owned by Telenor (Norway), 7% owned by WR Com (based in Cyprus); mobile services; Man. Dir EVANGELOS MARTIGOPOULOS.

Maritel: Odos Egaleo 8, 185 45 Piraeus; tel. (21) 04599500; fax (21) 04599600; e-mail maritel@maritel.gr; internet www.maritel.gr; OTE subsidiary; marine telecommunications; Chair. THEODOROS VENIAMIS; Man. Dir MICHALIS MICHAELIDES.

Telestet Hellas SA: Leoforos Alex. Papagoy 8, 157 71 Athens; tel. (21) 07772033; e-mail po@telestet.gr; internet www.telestet.gr; 75%-owned by STET International; mobile network; Man. Dir GIACINTO CICCHESE.

Vodafone Panafon: Leoforos Messoghion 2, 115 27 Athens; tel. (21) 07483601; e-mail webmaster@panafon.gr; internet www.vodafone.gr; 55%-owned by Vodafone Europe Holdings BV (United Kingdom); mobile telecommunications; Chair. SOKRATES KOKKALIS; Chief Exec. GEORGE KORONIAS.

RADIO

Elliniki Radiophonia Tileorassi (ERT, SA) (Greek Radio-Television): Leoforos Messoghion 432, 153 42 Athens; tel. (21) 06066835; fax (21) 06009325; e-mail president@ert.gr; internet www.ert.gr; state-controlled since 1938; Chair. and Man. Dir A. STAGKOS.

Elliniki Radiophonia (ERA) (Greek Radio): POB 60019, Leoforos Messoghion 432, 153 42 Aghia Paraskevi, Athens; tel. (1) 06066815; fax (1) 06009425; e-mail ijanetakos@ert.gr; internet www.ert.gr/radio; Dir IOANNIS TZANNETAKOS.

Macedonia Radio Station: Odos Angelaki 2, 546 21 Thessaloníki; tel. (231) 0299400; fax (231) 0299451; e-mail info@ert3.gr; internet www.ert3.gr.

TELEVISION

A television network of 17 transmitters is in operation. The State's monopoly of television broadcasting ended in 1990, and by 1998 there were 17 private broadcasters.

State stations

Elliniki Radiophonia Tileorassi (ERT, SA) (Greek Radio-Television): see Radio.

Elliniki Tileorassi 1 (ET1) (Greek Television 1): Leoforos Messoghion 136, 115 27 Athens; tel. (21) 07758824; fax (21) 07797776; e-mail kalavanos@ert.gr; internet www.ert.gr/et1; Dir-Gen. KONSTANTINOS ALAVANOS.

ET2: Leoforos Messoghion 136, 115 25 Athens; tel. (21) 07701911; fax (21) 07797776; Dir-Gen. PANAYOTIS PANAYOTOU.

ET3: Aggelaki 2, 546 21 Thessaloníki; tel. (231) 0299610; fax (231) 0299655; e-mail pr@ert3.gr; internet www.ert.gr/et3; Dir-Gen. DEMETRIS KATSANTONIS.

Private stations

Antenna TV: Leoforos Kifissias 10–12, 151 25 Maroussi, Athens; tel. (21) 0688600; fax (21) 06834349; e-mail webmaster@antenna.gr; internet www.antenna.gr; Chair. M. X. KYRIAKOU.

Channel Seven-X: Leoforos Kifissias 64, 151 25 Maroussi, Athens; tel. (21) 06897600; fax (21) 06897608.

City Channel: Leoforos Kastoni 14, 41223 Larissa; tel. (241) 232839; fax (241) 232013.

Mega Channel: Leoforos Messoghion 117, 115 26 Athens; tel. (21) 06903000; fax (21) 06983600; e-mail ngeorgiou@megatv.com; internet www.megatv.com; f. 1989; Man. Dir ELIAS TSIGAS.

Neo Kanali SA: Pireos 9—11, 105 52 Athens; tel. (21) 05238230; fax (21) 05247325.

Serres TV: Nigritis 27, 62124 Serres.

Skai TV: Phalereos & Ethnarchou 2, Macaroiu, N. Phaliro.

Star Channel: Odos Thermopylon 87, 351 00 Lamia; tel. (2231) 046725; fax (2231) 038903; e-mail starch@lam.forthnet.gr; f. 1988; Pres. VASILEIOS CHEIMONIDIS.

Tele City: Praxitelous 58, 17674 Athens; tel. (21) 09429222; fax (21) 09413589.

Teletora: Lycabetous 17, 10672 Athens; tel. (21) 03617285; fax (21) 03638712.

Traki TV: Central Square, 67100 Xanthi; tel. (2541) 020670; fax (2541) 027368.

TRT: Odos Zachou 5, 38333 Volos; tel. (2421) 0288013; fax (2421) 036888.

TV Macedonia: Nea Egnatia 222, 54642 Thessaloníki; tel. (231) 0850512; fax (231) 0850513.

TV Plus: Athens; tel. (21) 09028707; fax (21) 09028310.

TV-100: Odos Aggelaki 16, 54621 Thessaloníki; tel. (231) 0265828; fax (231) 0267532.

Finance

(cap. = capital; p.u. = paid up; res = reserves; dep. = deposits; dre = drachmae; m. = million; br. = branch)

BANKING

Central Bank

Bank of Greece: Leoforos E. Venizelos 21, 102 50 Athens; tel. (21) 03201111; fax (21) 03232239; e-mail secretariat@bankofgreece.gr; internet www.bankofgreece.gr; f. 1927; state bank of issue; cap. €49.8m., res €2,137.3m., dep. €11,346.5m. (Dec. 2001); Gov. NIKOS GARGANOS; 27 brs.

Commercial Banks

Agricultural Bank of Greece SA: Odos Panepistimiou 23, 105 64 Athens; tel. (21) 03298911; fax (21) 03298754; e-mail ategt@ate.gr; internet www.ate.gr; f. 1929; state-owned; mainly provides banking services to rural and semi-rural regions; cap. €1,649.3m., res €61.4m., dep. €13,960.3m. (Dec. 2001); Pres. PETROS LAMBROU; 437 brs.

Alpha Bank AE: Stadiou 40, 102 52 Athens; tel. (21) 03260000; fax (21) 03265438; e-mail secretariat@alpha.gr; internet www.alpha.gr; f. 1879, renamed 2000; cap. drc 259,240.2m., res dre 439,592.5m., dep. dre 8,495,035.7m. (Dec. 2001); Chair. and Gen. Man. IOANNIS S. COSTOPOULOS; 423 brs.

Aspis Bank: Odos Othonosm 4, Syntagma, 105 57 Athens; tel. (21) 03364000; fax (21) 03221409; internet www.aspisbank.gr; f. 1992; cap. €76.0m., res €26.6m., dep. €918.7m (Dec. 2001); Pres., Chair. and Man. Dir KONSTANTINOS KARATZAS.

Bank of Attica SA: Odos Omirou 23, 106 72 Athens; tel. (21) 03646910; fax (21) 03646115; e-mail attiki3@netor.gr; internet www.bankofattica.gr; f. 1925; affiliated to the Commercial Bank of Greece; cap. dre 4,742.1m., res dre 44,838.0m., dep. dre 357,962.3m. (Dec. 2000); Chair. and Man. Dir KONSTANTINOS STAMOULIS; 50 brs.

Commercial Bank of Greece SA: Odos Sophokleous 11, 102 35 Athens; tel. (21) 03284000; fax (21) 03253746; e-mail pubrel@combank.gr; internet www.combank.gr; f. 1907; cap. dre 145,588.5m., res dre 540,670.5m., dep. dre 5,205,005.5m. (Dec. 2001); Chair. and CEO IOANNIS STOURNARAS; Vice-Chair. and Gen. Man. GEORGE MICHELIS; 373 brs.

EFG Eurobank Ergasias SA: Odos Othonos 8, 105 57 Athens; tel. (21) 03337000; fax (21) 03337256; internet www.eurobank.gr; f. 1990 as Euromerchant Bank SA (Eurobank), renamed EFG Eurobank in 1997, and as above in 2000; merged with Bank of Athens and Bank of Crete in 1999, with Ergobank in 2000, and with Telesis Investment Bank in 2002; cap. dre 283,661m., res dre 401,409m., dep. dre 5,574,259m. (Dec. 2001); Pres. X. NIKITAS; Man. Dir NIKOLAS NANOPOULOS; 330 brs.

Egnatia Bank SA: Odos Danaidon 4, 546 26 Thessaloníki; tel. (231) 0598600; fax (231) 0598675; e-mail becker@egnatiabank.gr; internet www.egnatiabank.gr; f. 1991; merged with Bank of Central Greece in 1999; cap. dre 38,013.5m., res dre 44,326.5m., dep. dre 628,560.1m. (Dec. 2001); Pres. and Chair. VASSILLIS THEOCHARAKIS; Man. Dir VASSILLIS KELTSOPOULOS; 61 brs.

General Bank of Greece SA: Odos Messogion 109–111, 115 26 Athens; tel. (21) 06975457; fax (21) 06975910; e-mail intdiv@geniki.gr; internet www.geniki.gr; f. 1937 as Bank of the Army Share Fund, renamed General Hellenic Bank in 1966, and as above in 1998; cap. dre 48,030.3m, res dre 25,022.3m., dep. dre 758,376.6m. (Dec. 2001); Chair. and Man. Dir ANTONIS HASIOTIS; Gen. Man. JOHN TSAMOURGELIS; 103 brs.

Investment Bank of Greece SA: Leoforus Kifissias 24B, 151 25 Athens; tel. (21) 08171810; fax (21) 09281800; internet www.ibog.gr; f. 2000; total assets dre 40,109.8m. (Feb. 2001); Pres. ANASTASIOS TZAVELLAS; Man. Dir DIMITRIS S. PAPADOPOULOS.

Laiki Bank Hellas SA: Odos Panepistimiou 16, 106 72 Athens; tel. (21) 03550000; fax (21) 03243141; e-mail cm_lbh@otenet.gr; internet www.laiki.gr; f. 1992 as European Popular Bank, renamed as above in 2000; cap. dre 15,250m., res dre 14,610.4m., dep. dre 431,851.8m. (Dec. 2001); Chair. and Pres. KIKIS LAZARIDES; Man. Dir RENA ROUVITHA-PANOU; 31 brs.

Marfin Bank: Leoforos Kifissias 24, 151 25 Athens; tel. (21) 0817000; fax (21) 08170101; e-mail mail@marfinbank.gr; internet www.marfinbank.gr; f. 1981 as Banque Franco-Hellenique de Commerce International et Maritime SA, renamed Credit Lyonnais Grèce 1994, renamed Piraeus Prime Bank 1998 and as above 2002; cap. €23.2m., res €2.6m., dep. €44.2m. (Dec. 2001); Pres. and Chair. MANOLIS XANTHAKIS; Man. Dir ANDREAS VGENOPOULOS; 4 brs.

National Bank of Greece SA (NBG): Odos Aeolou 86, 102 32 Athens; tel. (21) 03441000; fax (21) 03346550; internet www.nbg.gr; f. 1841; state-controlled, but operates independently of the Government; cap. dre 349,732.9m., res dre 358,763.0m., dep. dre 14,985,516.6m. (Dec. 2001); Gov. THEODOROS B. KARATZAS; 594 brs.

Piraeus Bank SA: Leoforos Amalias 20 & Odos Souri 5, 105 57 Athens; tel. (21) 03335000; fax (21) 03335080; e-mail investor-relations@piraeusbank.gr; internet www.piraeusbank.gr; f. 1916; merged with Macedonia Thrace Bank and Xiosbank in June 2000; cap. €548.3m., res dre €304.3m., dep. €10,598.4m. (Dec. 2001); Chair. M. SALLAS; Exec. Vice-Chair. I. GEORGANAS; 200 brs.

Development Banks

Hellenic Industrial Development Bank SA: Leoforos Syngrou 87, 117 45 Kallithea, Athens; tel. (21) 09242900; fax (21) 09241513; e-mail news@etba.gr; internet www.etba.gr/etba/etbag.html; f. 1964; limited liability banking company; the major Greek institution in the field of industrial investment; cap. dre 245,890.0m., res dre 44,424.3m., dep. dre 502,897.6m. (Dec. 1996); Chair. and Gov. GEORGE KASMAS; 11 brs.

National Investment Bank for Industrial Development SA: Leoforos Amalias 12–14, 105 57 Athens; tel. (21) 03242651; fax (21) 03296211; e-mail public@eteba.gr; internet www.eteba.gr; f. 1963; cap. dre 8,971.8m., res dre 51,740.9m., dep. dre 354,932.3m. (Dec. 2000); long-term loans, equity participation, promotion of co-operation between Greek and foreign enterprises; Chair. THEODORE KARATZAS; Man. Dir DEMETRIOS GOUMAS; 1 br.

STOCK EXCHANGE

Athens Stock Exchange: Odos Sophokleous 10, 105 59 Athens; tel. (21) 03211301; fax (21) 03213938; e-mail webmaster@ase.gr; internet www.ase.gr; f. 1876; Pres. PANAYOTIS ALEXAKIS; Vice-Pres. THEODOROS PANTOLAKIS.

PRINCIPAL INSURANCE COMPANIES

Agrotiki Hellenic Insurance Co: Leoforos Syngrou 163, 171 21 Kallithea, Athens; tel. (21) 9379100; fax (21) 09358924; e-mail info@agroins.com; internet www.agroins.com; Gen. Man. Tr. Lisimachou.

Alpha Insurance: Odos Michalakopoulou 48, 115 28 Athens; tel. (21) 07268000; fax (21) 07268810; e-mail info@alpha-insurance.gr; internet www.alpha-insurance.gr; f. 1999; by merger; Chair. Photis P. Costopoulos; Man. Dir D. Paleologos; Gen. Man. John L. Galanopoulou.

Aspis Pronia General Insurance SA: Leoforos Kifissias 62, 151 25 Maroussi, Athens; tel. (21) 06198960; fax (21) 06198974; e-mail info@aspis.gr; internet www.aspis.gr; f. 1941; Pres. and Chief Exec. Paul Psomiades.

Atlantiki Enosis: Odos Messoghion 71 & Ilidos 36, 115 26 Athens; tel. (21) 07799211; fax (21) 07794446; e-mail atlantiki@atlantiki.gr; internet www.atlanticunion.gr; f. 1970; Pres. Sarandos Stasinopoulos; Man. Dir Notis Lapatas.

Commercial Value SA: Leoforos Kifissias 250–254, 152 31 Athens; tel. (21) 06742411; fax (21) 06741826; e-mail united@atheneos.com; internet www.commercialvalue.gr; f. 2002 by merger; fmrly United Insurance Co SA; Pres. D. Daskalopoulos; Man. Dir P. Atheneos.

Dynamis SA: Leoforos Syngrou 106, 117 41 Kallithea, Athens; tel. (21) 09227255; fax (21) 09237768; e-mail genka@asfgenka.gr; f. 1977; Man. Dir Nikolas Stamatopoulos.

Egnatia Co: Odos Fragon 1, 546 26 Thessaloníki; tel. (231) 0523325; fax (231) 0523555; Rep. P. Migas.

Emporiki Life: Odos Korai 6, 105 64 Athens; tel. (21) 03282346; fax (21) 03282441; e-mail mzanatta@emporikilife.gr; f. 1940; Chair. Dimitris Frangetis; Exec. Dir Michael Zanatta.

Ethniki Hellenic General Insurance Co SA: Odos Karageorgi Servias 8, 102 10 Athens; tel. (21) 03299000; fax (21) 03236101; e-mail ethniki@ethniki-asfalistiki.gr; internet www.ethniki-asfalistiki.gr; f. 1891; Gen. Man. C. Philipou.

Galaxias Insurance Co: Leoforos Syngrou 40–42, 117 42 Kallithea, Athens; tel. (21) 09241082; fax (21) 09241698; f. 1967; Gen. Man. K. Anagnostakis.

Gothaer Hellas SA: Odos Michalakopoulou 174, 115 27 Athens; tel. (21) 07750801; fax (21) 07757094; Gen. Man. S. Galanis.

Hellas Insurance Co SA: Leoforos Kifissias 119, 151 24 Marousi, Athens; tel. (21) 08127600; fax (21) 08027189; e-mail nick.nardis@aig.com; internet www.aig-greece.gr; f. 1973; Gen. Man. N. Nardis.

Hellenic Reliance General Insurances SA: Leoforos Kifissias 304, 152 32 Halandri, Athens; tel. (21) 06843733; fax (21) 06843734; f. 1990; Man. Dir S. F. Triantafyllakis.

Hellenobretanniki General Insurances SA: Leoforos Messogion 2–4, 115 27 Athens; tel. (21) 07755301; fax (21) 07714768; f. 1988.

Helvetia General Insurance Co: Leoforos Kifissias 124, 115 26 Athens; tel. (21) 06980840; fax (21) 06923446; f. 1943; Gen. Man. J. Delendas.

Horizon General Insurance Co SA: Leoforos Amalias 26A, 105 57 Athens; tel. (21) 03227932; fax (21) 03225540; e-mail horizon@hol.gr; f. 1965; Gen. Mans Theodore Achis, Chr. Achis.

Hydrogios: Odos Solonos 137, 176 75 Athens; tel. (21) 09401300; fax (21) 09407072; Gen. Man. A. Kaskarelis.

Ikonomiki: Odos Kapodistriou 38, 104 32 Athens; tel. (21) 05243374; fax (21) 05234962; f. 1968; Gen. Man. D. Nikolaidis.

Imperial Hellas SA: Leoforos Syngrou 253, 171 22 N. Smirni, Athens; tel. (21) 09426352; fax (21) 09426202; e-mail imperiasf@hol.gr; internet www.imperial.gr; f. 1971; Gen. Man. G. Tzanis.

Interamerican Hellenic Life Insurance Co SA: Interamerican Plaza, Leoforos Kifissias 117, 151 80 Maroussi, Athens; tel. (21) 06191111; fax (21) 06191877; e-mail moisssim@interamerican.gr; internet www.interamerican.gr; f. 1971; 79.38% owned by Eureko, a Netherlands-based insurance group; Pres. and Man. Dir Dimitri Kontominas.

Interamerican Health Assistance Insurance Co SA: Interamerican Plaza, Leoforos Kifissias 117, 151 80 Maroussi, Athens; tel. (21) 06192222; fax (21) 08020410; e-mail health@interamerican.gr; internet www.interamerican.gr; Man. Dir A. Papagiannopoulos.

Interamerican Property and Casualty Insurance Co SA: Interamerican Plaza, Leoforos Kifissias 117, 151 80 Maroussi, Athens; tel. (21) 06191111; fax (21) 06191872; e-mail custserv@interamerican.gr; internet www.interamerican.gr; f. 1974; Man. Dir C. Bertsias.

Interamerican Road Assistance Insurance Co SA: Leoforos Syngrou 350, 176 74 Kallithea, Athens; tel. (21) 09304080; fax (21) 09304083; e-mail intauto@compulink.gr; internet www.interamerican.gr; Man. Dir G. Souvagis.

Kykladiki Insurance Co SA: Leoforos Syngrou 80–88, 117 41 Kallithea, Athens; tel. (21) 09247664; fax (21) 09247344; f. 1919; Gen. Man. Pan. Katsikostas.

Phoenix-General Insurance Co of Greece SA: Odos Omirou 2, 105 64 Athens; tel. (21) 03295111; fax (21) 03239135; e-mail phoenix@phoenix.gr; internet www.phoenix.gr; f. 1928; general insurance; Rep. G. Kotsalos.

Poseidon SA: Odos Karaiskou 163, 185 35 Piraeus; tel. (21) 04522685; fax (21) 04184337; e-mail poseidon@otenet.gr; f. 1972; Gen. Man. Thanos J. Melakopides.

Sideris Insurance Co SA: Odos Lekka 3–5, 105 63 Athens; tel. (21) 03224484; e-mail siderisa@acci.gr; fax (21) 03231066; Dir G. Sideris.

Syneteristiki General Insurance Co: Leoforos Syngrou 367, 175 64 Kallithea, Athens; tel. (21) 09491280; fax (21) 09403148; e-mail syne-ins@hol.gr; Gen. Man. D. Zorbas.

Victoria General Insurance Co SA: Odos Tsimiski 21, 546 22 Thessaloníki; tel. (231) 0371100; fax (231) 0371392; e-mail victoria@victoria.gr; internet www.victoria.gr; f. 1972; Man. Dir G. Andoniadis.

A large number of foreign insurance companies also operate in Greece.

Insurance Association

Association of Insurance Companies: Odos Xenophontos 10, 105 57 Athens; tel. (21) 03334100; fax (21) 03334149; e-mail info@eaee.gr; internet www.eaee.gr; 114 mems, of which 32 are foreign insurance companies operating in Greece; Gen. Man. Margarita Antonaki.

Trade and Industry

GOVERNMENT AGENCY

Organismos Anasinkrotiseos Epicheiriseon (Industrial Reconstruction Organization): Athens; f. 1982; reconstruction and sale of Greek businesses under state receivership.

CHAMBERS OF COMMERCE

Athens Chamber of Commerce and Industry: Odos Akademias 7, 106 71 Athens; tel. (21) 03625342; fax (21) 03618810; e-mail info@acci.gr; internet www.acci.gr; f. 1919; Pres. John Kocpralos; Sec.-Gen. Dracoulis Foundoukakos; 70,000 mems.

Athens Chamber of Small and Medium-sized Industries: Odos Akademias 18, 106 71 Athens; tel. (21) 03680700; fax (21) 03614726; e-mail info@acsmi.gr; internet www.acsmi.gr; f. 1940; Pres. D. Charisis; Sec.-Gen. Ath. Pavlou; c. 60,000 mems.

Handicraft Chamber of Piraeus: Odos Karaiscou 111, 185 32 Piraeus; tel. (21) 04110443; fax (21) 04179495; e-mail info@bep.gr; internet www.bep.gr; f. 1925; Pres. Konstantinos Moscholios; Sec.-Gen. Pantelis Antoniadis; 18,500 mems.

Piraeus Chamber of Commerce and Industry: Odos Loudovikou 1, 185 31 Piraeus; tel. (21) 4177241; fax (21) 4178680; f. 1919; Pres. George Kassimatis; Sec.-Gen. Konstantinos Sarantopoulos.

Thessaloníki Chamber of Commerce and Industry: Odos Tsimiski 29, 546 24 Thessaloníki; tel. (231) 0224438; fax (231) 0230237; f. 1919; Pres. Pantelis Konstantinidis; Sec.-Gen. Emmanuel Vlachoyannis; 14,500 mems.

INDUSTRIAL AND TRADE ASSOCIATIONS

Federation of Greek Industries (SEV): Odos Xenophontos 5, 105 57 Athens; tel. (21) 03237325; fax (21) 03222929; e-mail main@fgi.org.gr; internet www.fgi.org.gr; f. 1907; Chair. Eleftherios Antonakopoulos; 950 mems.

Federation of Industries of Northern Greece: Morihovou 1, 7th Floor, 546 35 Thessaloníki; tel. (231) 0539817; fax (231) 0546244; e-mail secretariat@sbbe.gr; internet www.sbbe.gr; f. 1915; Pres. Simeonidis Dimitrios.

Hellenic Cotton Board: Leoforos Syngrou 150, 176 71 Kallithea, Athens; tel. (21) 09225011; fax (21) 09249656; f. 1931; state organization; Pres. P. K. Mylonas.

Hellenic Organization of Small and Medium-sized Industries and Handicrafts (EOMMEX): Odos Xenias 16, 115 28 Athens; tel. (21) 07491100; fax (21) 07491146; e-mail interel@eommex.gr; internet www.eommex.gr; Pres. George Frantzeskakis.

UTILITIES

Electricity

Public Power Corpn (DEH): Odos Xalkokondyli 30, 104 32 Athens; tel. (21) 05230301; fax (21) 05238445; e-mail info@dei.gr; internet www.dei.gr; f. 1950; 84% state-owned, generating capacity 12,069 MW (June 2003); generation, transmission and distribution of electricity in Greece; Chair. D. PAPOULIAS; Chief Exec. and Man. Dir S. NEZIS.

Gas

Public Gas Corpn (DEPA): Leoforos Messoghian 207, 115 25 Athens; tel. (21) 06793500; fax (21) 06749504; e-mail info@depa.gr; internet www.depa.gr; f. 1988; 35% owned by Hellenic Petroleum SA, 65% state-owned; undergoing privatization; began gas imports 1997, initially for industrial use; Man. Dir ARISTEIDIS VAKIRLIS.

Water

In 1980 a law was passed under which Municipal Enterprises for Water Supply and Sewerage (DEYA) were created to manage drinking water and sewerage throughout Greece. Since then some 90 DEYA have been established.

The Hellenic Union of Municipal Enterprises for Water Supply and Sewerage (EDEYA): Odos Anthimou Gaza 3, 4122 22 Larissa; internet www.edeya.gr; f. 1989; 67 mems; co-ordinates activities of DEYA and represents them to the Government.

MAJOR COMPANIES

A feature of the Greek economy was traditionally its large state-owned sector. However, the Governments of Konstantinos Simitis accelerated the process of privatization from 1996.

AGET Heracles General Cement Co SA: Sof. Venizelou 49–51, POB 3500, 102 10 Athens; tel. (21) 02898111; fax (21) 02819406; e-mail info@aget.gr; internet www.aget.gr; f. 1911; cement production; parent company Blue Circle Industries (United Kingdom) bought by the Lafarge Group (France) in 2001; Chair. JEAN-CHARLES BLATZ; Man. Dir ALBERT CORCOS; 1,600 employees.

Aluminium de Grèce SA: Sekeri 1, 106 71 Athens; tel. (21) 03693000; fax (21) 03693615; internet www.alhellas.pechiney.com; f. 1960; production of alumina and aluminium; Chair. J. STRATOS; Chief Exec. JACQUES GANI; 1,250 employees.

Athenian Brewery SA: Kifissou 102, 122 41 Aigaleo; tel. (21) 05384911; fax (21) 05384221; e-mail info@beerexports.gr; internet www.beerexports.gr; f. 1962; production and trading of alcoholic and non-alcoholic beverages; Man. Dir M. TANES; 1,400 employees.

Athens Papermill SA: Odos Chartergaton 1, 118 55 Athens; tel. (21) 03426501; fax (21) 03474628; e-mail info@apm.boltongroup.gr; f. 1957; manufacture of paper, pulp, board, plastic packaging and related products; bought by the Bolton Group (Netherlands) in 1999; Man. Dir A. A. GEORGITSIS; 1,600 employees.

Coca-Cola Hellenic Bottling Co: Odos Fragoklissias 9, 151 25 Athens; tel. (21) 06183100; fax (21) 06183274; e-mail investor .relations@cchbc.com; internet www.coca-colahbc.com; f. 2000 by merger of Coca-Cola Beverages and the Hellenic Bottling Co SA; 36% owned by Leventis (Cyprus), 24% owned by Coca-Cola Co (USA); world's second largest bottler of Coca Cola beverages; Man. Dir IRIAL FINLAN; 35,000 employees.

Delta Dairy SA: Kerkyras 3, 177 78 Tavros; tel. (21) 03494000; fax (21) 03494040; internet www.delta.gr; f. 1952; food and beverage processing; Man. Dir D. DASKOPOULOS; 1,150 employees.

EKO-ELDA ABEE: Athens Tower, Odos Messoghion 2, 115 27 Athens; tel. (21) 07705401; fax (21) 07705847; e-mail webmaster@ eko.gr; internet www.eko.gr; f. 1988 as EKO, following the Government's purchase of Esso Pappas (a subsidiary of ESSO Petroleum); name changed in 1997; fuels and lubricants, bottled gases; petroleum production; state-owned; Man. Dir M. GEORGANTOPOULOS; 600 employees.

Elefsis Shipyards Ltd: 192 00 Elefsis; tel. (21) 05535111; fax (21) 05546016; e-mail cm@mail.elefsis-shipyards.gr; internet www .elefsis-shipyards.gr; partially state-owned.

Elval Hellenic Aluminium Industry SA: Athinon–Lamias National Rd, Km 57, 320 11 Oinofyta; tel. (2262) 031503; fax (2262) 031347; internet www.elval.gr; f. 1977; aluminium processing; Gen. Man. N. KOUDANIS; 650 employees.

Fage Dairy Industry SA: Ermou 35, 144 52 Metamorfossi; tel. (21) 02892555; fax (21) 02828386; e-mail info@fage.gr; internet www .fage.gr; f. 1926; food and beverage production; Man. Dir K. FILPPOU; 1,300 employees.

Halyvourgiki Inc: Dragatsaniou 8, 105 59 Athens; tel. (21) 03243411; fax (21) 03301965; e-mail halyv@hol.gr; f. 1948; ferrous metal processing; Pres. and Gen. Man. P. TZAVELAS; 450 employees.

Hellenic Aerospace Industry Ltd: POB 23, 320 09 Schimatari; tel. (2262) 052000; fax (2262) 052170; e-mail info@haicorp.com; internet www.haicorp.com; f. 1976; manufacture and assembly of aircraft and engine parts, electronic and communications equipment and weapons components; Chair., Man. Dir and CEO G. GOULIOS; 3,000 employees.

Hellenic Arms Industry SA: Leoforos Ilioupoleos 1, 172 36 Hymettus, Athens; tel. (21) 09790900; fax (21) 09790800; e-mail info@ebo.gr; internet www.ebo.gr; f. 1977; manufacture of weapons, explosives and other military material; Man. Dir A. BARAKOS; 1,300 employees.

Hellenic Petroleum SA: 17km Athens-Corinth National Rd, 193 00 Aspropyrgos, Athens; tel. (21) 05533000; fax (21) 05539298; internet www.hellenic-petroleum.gr; partially state-owned; petroleum exploration and production; Chair. GEORGE MORAITIS; Man. Dir ATHAMASSIOS KARACHALIOS; 2,936 employees.

Hellenic Sugar Industry SA: Mitropoleos 34, 541 10 Thessaloníki; tel. (231) 0269555; fax (231) 0228221; internet www.ebz.gr; f. 1960; import, processing and refining of sugar and sugar products; Gen. Man. CH. STAMTSIS; 1,300 employees.

Intracom SA: Leoforos Markopoulou, Km 19.5, 190 02 Paiania, Athens; tel. (21) 06679000; fax (21) 06679001; e-mail info@intracom .internet www.intracom.gr; f. 1974; manufacture and servicing of electronic and communications equipment; Man. Dir SOCRATES KOKKALIS; 4,000 employees.

Lavipharm SA: Odos Agia Marina, POB 59, 190 02 Paiania; tel. (21) 06691151; fax (21) 06691159; e-mail comm@lavipharm.gr; internet www.lavipharm.gr; f. 1911; manufacture, import, trade and distribution of pharmaceuticals and cosmetics; Chair. and Chief Exec. A. LAVIDAS; 900 employees.

Michailides, A., Leaf Tobacco SA: Iatrou Gougoussi 37, 564 30 Stavropouli; tel. (231) 0606204; fax (231) 0651877; e-mail tobacco@ michailides.com; internet www.michailides.com; f. 1886; import, processing and trade of tobacco and tobacco products; Man. Dir A. MICHAILIDES.

Papastratos Cigarette Mfg Co SA: K. Mavromichali and Gravias, 185 45 Piraeus; tel. (21) 04120941; fax (21) 04112303; internet www .papastratos.gr; f. 1931; manufacture and trade of tobacco products; Chair. and Chief Exec. CH. KOMNINOS; 983 employees.

Petrola Hellas SA: Elefsina-Elefsina, POB 20, 192 00 Athens; tel. (21) 05536000; fax (21) 05548509; e-mail info@petrola.gr; internet www.petrola.gr; f. 1969; petroleum refining, distribution of petroleum products; Man. Dir E. STATHIS; 550 employees.

Titan Cement Co SA: Halkidos 22A, 111 43 Athens; tel. (21) 02591111; fax (1) 02591205; e-mail smx@titan.gr; internet www .titan.gr; f. 1911; production of cement and plaster; Man. Dir D. PAPALEXOPOULOS; 1,400 employees.

Ylikon AE: Kefisias 58, 151 25 Marousi; tel. (21) 06197410; fax (21) 06197415; e-mail cvi@hol.gr; internet www.ylikon.gr; manufactures metal components for industrial use.

TRADE UNIONS

There are about 5,000 registered trade unions, grouped together in 82 federations and 86 workers' centres, which are affiliated to the Greek General Confederation of Labour.

Greek General Confederation of Labour (GSEE): Odos Patission 69, Athens; tel. (21) 08834611; fax (21) 08229802; e-mail info@ gsee.gr; internet www.gsee.gr; f. 1918; Pres. CHRISTOS PROTOPAPAS; Gen. Sec. IOANNIS THEONAS; 700,000 mems.

Pan-Hellenic Federation of Seamen's Unions (PNO): Livanos Bldg, Akti Miaouli 47–49, 185 36 Piraeus; tel. (21) 04292960; fax (21) 04293040; f. 1920; confederation of 14 marine unions; Pres. IOANNIS CHELAS; Gen. Sec. JOHN HALAS.

Transport

RAILWAYS

A five-year programme to upgrade the Greek rail network was initiated in 1996, supported by 350m. drachmae from EU structural funds. The major undertaking was to electrify the 500-km Athens–Thessaloníki line and to extend services to the Bulgarian border. Construction of a 26.3 km electrified extension to the Athens–Piraeus line, in order to provide a three-line urban railway system for Athens, designated Metro Line 1, was completed in 2000. Metro Lines 2 and 3, each measuring some 9 km, were scheduled to open prior to the holding of the Olympic Games in 2004.

Attiko Metro SA: Mesogion Ave 191–93, 115 25 Athens; tel. (21) 06792399; fax (21) 06726126; e-mail info@ametro.gr; internet www

.ametro.gr; f. 1999; planning, design, construction and operation of Metro Lines 2 and 3; Chair. IOANNIS CHRISSIKOPOULOS.

Ilektriki Sidirodromi Athinon–Pireos (ISAP) (Athens–Piraeus Electric Railways): Odos Athinas 67, 105 52 Athens; tel. (21) 03248311; fax (21) 03223935; internet www.isap.gr; state-owned; 25.6 km of electrified track; Chair. GEORGE PAPAVASSILIOU; Man. Dir DIONISSIOS RAPPOS.

Organismos Sidirodromon Ellados (OSE) (Hellenic Railways Organization Ltd): Odos Karolou 1–3, 104 37 Athens; tel. (21) 05248395; fax (21) 05243290; internet www.ose.gr; f. 1971; state railways; total length of track: 2,474 km; Chair. CHR. PAPAGEORGIOU; Dir-Gen. A. LAZARIS.

ROADS

In 1999 there were an estimated 117,000 km of roads in Greece. Of this total, an estimated 9,100 km were main roads, and 470 km were motorways. Major new roads under construction in early 2003 included a 65 km ring road for Athens, and the 680 km Egnatia highway, extending from the Adriatic coast to the Turkish border; 288 km of the latter road was already in use, with a further 67 km due to be opened to traffic in 2003.

INLAND WATERWAYS

There are no navigable rivers in Greece.

Corinth Canal: built 1893; over six km long, links the Corinthian and Saronic Gulfs; shortens the journey from the Adriatic to the Piraeus by 325 km; spanned by three single-span bridges, two for road and one for rail; can be used by ships of a maximum draught of 22 ft and width of 60 ft; managed since June 2001 by Sea Containers Group (United Kingdom).

SHIPPING

In 2001 the Greek merchant fleet totalled 1,529 vessels, amounting to 28,678,240 grt. Greece controls one of the largest merchant fleets in the world. The principal ports are Piraeus, Patras and Thessaloníki.

Union of Greek Shipowners: Akti Miaouli 85, 185 38 Piraeus; f. 1916; Pres. NICOS EFTHYMIOU.

Port Authorities

Port of Patras: Patras Port Authority, Central Port Office, Patras; tel. (261) 0316400; fax (261) 0327136; internet www.patrasport.gr; Pres. GEORGE LAZARIS; Harbour Master Capt. NIKOLAS RAFAILOVITS.

Piraeus Port Authority: Piraeus Port Authority, Akti Miaouli 10, 185 35 Piraeus; tel. (21) 04520911; fax (21) 04286843; e-mail olpdsx@otenet.gr; internet www.olp.gr; Pres. SOTIRIS THEOFANIS; Man. Dir HARILAOS PSARAFTIS; Harbour Master Capt. EMMANUEL PELOPONNESIOS.

Port of Thessaloníki: Thessaloníki Port Authority, POB 10467, 541 10 Thessaloníki; tel. (231) 0593129; fax (231) 0510500; e-mail secretariat@thpa.gr; internet www.thpa.gr; Man. Dir SOTIRIS I. GENITSARIS.

Among the largest shipping companies are:

Anangel Shipping Enterprises SA: Akti Miaouli, POB 80004, 185 10 Piraeus; tel. (21) 04224500; fax (21) 04224819; Man. Dir J. PLATSIDAKIS.

Attika Shipping Co: Odos Voucourestion 16, 10671 Athens; tel. (21) 03609631; fax (21) 03601439; Dir G. PRIOVOLOS.

Bilinder Marine Corpn SA: Odos Igias 1–3 and Akti Themistokleos, 185 36 Piraeus; tel. (21) 04287300; fax (21) 04287355; Gen. Man. V. ARMOGENI.

Ceres Hellenic Shipping Enterprises Ltd: Akti Miaouli 69, 185 37 Piraeus; tel. (21) 04591000; fax (21) 04283552; e-mail chse@ceres.gr; internet www.ceres.gr; Dir, Marine Operations NIKOLAOS E. LIVANOS.

Chandris (Hellas) Inc: POB 80067, Akti Miaouli 95, 185 38 Piraeus; tel. (21) 04290300; fax (21) 04290256; e-mail chandris@19080845.multimessage.com; Man. Dirs A. C. PIPERAS, M. G. SKORDIAS.

Costamare Shipping Co SA: Odos Zephyrou 60 and Leoforos Syngrou, 175 64 Kallithea, Athens; tel. (21) 09390000; fax (21) 09409051; Pres. Capt. V. C. KONSTANTAKOPOULOS; Man. Dir Capt. G. SARDIS.

European Navigation Inc: Odos Artemissiou 2 and Fleming Sq., 166 75 Athens; tel. (21) 08981581; fax (21) 08946777; Dir P. KARNESSIS.

Glafki (Hellas) Maritime Co: Odos Mitropoleos 3, 105 57 Athens; tel. (21) 03244991; fax (21) 03228944; Dirs M. FRAGOULIS, G. PANAGIOTOU.

Golden Union Shipping Co SA: Odos Aegales 8, 185 45 Piraeus; tel. (21) 04061000; fax (21) 04061166; e-mail gusc@goldenunion.gr; Man. Dir THEODORE VENIAMIS.

M. Koutlakis and Co Ltd: Makras Stoas 5, 185 31 Piraeus; tel. (21) 04129428; fax (21) 04178755; Dir M. KOUTLAKIS.

Laskaridis Shipping Co Ltd: Odos Chimaras 5, 151 25 Maroussi, Athens; tel. (21) 06899090; fax (21) 06806762; e-mail athens@laskship.cc.cwmail.com; Man. Dirs P. C. LASKARIDIS, A. C. LASKARIDIS.

Marmaras Navigation Ltd: Odos Filellinon 4–6, Okeanion Bldg, 185 36 Piraeus; tel. (21) 04294226; fax (21) 04294304; Dir D. DIAMANTIDES.

Minoan Lines Shipping SA: Odos 25 August 17, 712 02 Iraklion; tel. (281) 0399800; fax (281) 0330308; e-mail info@minoan.gr; internet www.minoan.gr; Pres. KONSTANTINOS KLIRONOMAS.

Naftomar Shipping and Trading Co Ltd: Leoforos Alkyonidon 243, 166 73 Voula; tel. (21) 08914200; fax (21) 08914235; e-mail naftomar@naftomar.gr; internet www.naftomar.gr; Man. Dir RIAD ZEIN.

Strintzis Lines Maritime S.A.: Odos Akti Possidonos 26, 185 31 Piraeus; tel. (21) 04225000; fax (21) 04225265; internet www.strintzis.gr; Man. Dir G. STRINTZIS.

Thenamaris (Ships Management) Inc: Odos Athinas 16 & Odos Vorreou, Kavouri, 166 71 Athens; tel. (21) 08969111; fax (21) 08969653; e-mail thena@thenamaris.gr; internet www.thenamaris.gr; Dir K. MARTINOS.

Tsakos Shipping and Trading SA: Macedonia House, Leoforos Syngrou 367, POB 79141, 175 02 Athens; tel. (21) 09380700; fax (21) 09480710; e-mail mail@tsakoshellas.gr; Dirs P. N. TSAKOS, E. SAROGLOU.

United Shipping and Trading Co of Greece SA: Odos Iassonos 6, 185 37 Piraeus; tel. (21) 04283660; fax (21) 04283630; Dir CH. TSAKOS.

Varnima Corporation International SA: Odos Irodou Attikou 12A, 151 24 Maroussi, Athens; tel. (21) 08093000; fax (21) 08093222; e-mail john_k@attglobal.net; Gen. Man. S. V. SPANOUDAKIS.

CIVIL AVIATION

There are international airports at Athens, Thessaloníki, Alexandroupolis, Corfu, Lesbos, Andravida, Rhodes, Kos and Heraklion/Crete, and 24 domestic airports (of which 13 are authorized to receive international flights). A new international airport called Eleftherios Venizelos, at Spata, some 25 km east of Athens, was opened in March 2001. The airport was expected to have a handling capacity of 16m. passengers per year.

Aegean Airlines: Leoforos Vouliagmenis 572, 164 51 Athens; tel. (21) 09988350; fax (21) 09957598; internet www.aegeanair.com; f. 1987 as Aegean Aviation, name changed as above in 1999, merged with Cronus Airlines in 2001; domestic and international services; Pres. and Chief Exec. THEODOROS VASSILAKIS.

Olympic Airways SA: Leoforos Syngrou 96–100, 117 41 Kallithea, Athens; tel. (21) 09269111; fax (21) 09267154; e-mail olyair10@otenet.gr; internet www.olympic-airways.gr; f. 1957; state-owned; domestic services linking principal cities and islands in Greece, and international services to Singapore, Thailand, South Africa and the USA, and throughout Europe and the Middle East; Chair. and Chief Exec. DIONYSIOS KALOFONOS.

Olympic Aviation: Leoforos Syngrou 96–100, 117 41 Kallithea, Athens; tel. (1) 09269111; fax (1) 09884059; wholly owned subsidiary of Olympic Airways; independent operator of scheduled domestic and regional services; Chair. STERGIOS PAPAPIS; Chief Exec. PETROS STEFANOU.

Tourism

The sunny climate, the natural beauty of the country and its great history and traditions attract tourists to Greece. There are numerous islands and many sites of archaeological interest. The number of tourists visiting Greece increased from 1m. in 1968 to 14m. in 2001. Receipts from tourism, which totalled US $120m. in 1968, reached $9,800m. in 2002. More visitors were expected to be attracted to Greece in 2004, when the country was to host the Olympic Games.

Ellinikos Organismos Tourismou (EOT) (Greek National Tourist Organization): Odos Tsoha 7, 115 21 Athens; tel. (21) 08707000; e-mail info@gnto.gr; internet www.gnto.gr; Pres. IOANNIS STEFANIDES; Vice-Pres. IOANNIS ROUBATIS.

Culture

NATIONAL ORGANIZATION

Ministry of Culture: see section on The Government (Ministries).

CULTURAL HERITAGE

Acropolis Museum: Athens; tel. (21) 03214172; fax (21) 09239023; contains sculptures from the monuments of the Acropolis and from excavations of the site; includes a collection of pediments and metopes from the Parthenon, and sections of the Parthenon frieze.

Greek Film Archives: Kanari 1, 106 71 Athens; tel. (21) 03612046; fax (21) 03628468; Dir THEODOROS ADAMOPOULOS.

Greek Folk Art Museum: Kydathinaion 17, 105 58 Athens; tel. (21) 03229031; fax (21) 03226979; e-mail melt@melt.culture.gr; Dir ELENI ROMAIOU-KARASTAMATI.

Museum of Greek Popular Instruments: Diogenous 1, 105 56 Athens; tel. (21) 03254119; fax (21) 03250198; e-mail ival@atlas.uoa .gr; Dir LAMBROS LIAVAS.

Patras International Festival: POB 1184, 261 10 Patras; tel. (261) 0336390; Artistic Dir ALEXANDROS MYRAT.

Thessaloníki Festival: Gorgous 11, 546 34 Thessaloníki; tel. (231) 0212001; fax (231) 0213888.

Thessaloníki Film Festival: Olympion Cinema, Aristotelous 10, 546 23 Thessaloníki; tel. (231) 0378400; fax (231) 0285759; e-mail info@filmfestival.gr; internet www.filmfestival.gr; Dir MICHEL DEMO-POULOS.

SPORTING ORGANIZATION

Hellenic Olympic Association: Ave Dimitriou Vikelas 52, Halandri, 152 33 Athens; tel. (21) 06878888; fax (21) 06878940; e-mail eoa@ath.forthnet.gr; internet www.hoc.gr; f. 1894; Pres. LAMBIS W. NIKOLAU; Sec.-Gen. DIMITRIS DIATHESSOPOULOS.

PERFORMING ARTS

Athens State Orchestra: Vas. Gerorgiou 17–19, 106 75 Athens; tel. (21) 07257601; fax (21) 07257600; Artistic Dir ARIS GAROUFALIS.

Ballet of the Greek National Opera: Odos Ch. Trikoupi 18, 106 79 Athens; tel. (21) 03600180; fax (21) 03648903; e-mail protocol@els .culture.gr; internet www.nationalopera.gr.

Chamber Opera of Thessaloníki: National Theatre of Northern Greece, Odos Ethnikis Amynis 2, 546 21 Thessaloníki; tel. (231) 0223646(; fax (231) 0223646; e-mail opera@ntng.gr; internet www .ntng.gr.

Dance Theatre of Thessaloníki: National Theatre of Northern Greece, Odos Ethnikis Amynis 2, 546 21 Thessaloníki; tel. (231) 0253397; e-mail dance@ntng.gr; internet www.ntng.gr; Artistic Dir ANASTASIA THEOPHANIDOU.

Greek National Opera: Charilaou Trikoupi 18, 106 79 Athens; tel. (21) 03600180; fax (21) 03648309; e-mail info@nationalopera.gr; internet www.nationalopera.gr; Artistic Dir LUKAS KARYTINOS.

National Conservatory: Maizonos 8 and Mayer 18, 104 38 Athens; tel. (21) 05233175; fax (21) 05245291; e-mail ethnodio@otenet.gr; Artistic Dir PERIKLES KOUKOS.

National Theatre: Agiou Konstantinou 22–24, 104 37 Athens; tel. (21) 05288100; fax (21) 05233371; e-mail protocol@eth.culture.gr; internet www.n-t.gr; Artistic Dir NIKOS KOURKOULOS.

State Orchestra of Hellenic Music: Spyr. Trikoupi 56–58, 114 73 Athens; tel. (21) 08253448; fax (21) 08253451; e-mail koem1@ sparknet.gr; Artistic Dir STAVROS XARCHAKOS.

State Conservatory of Thessaloníki: Leontos Sofou 16 and Frangon 15, 546 25 Thessaloníki; tel. (231) 0510551; fax (231) 0522158; Artistic Dir VICTORIA VICTORATOU.

State School of Dance: Omirou 57, 106 72 Athens; tel. (21) 03612263; fax (21) 03624357; e-mail sdsc@otonet.gr; Dir PAULINA VEREMI.

State Theatre of Northern Greece: Odos Ethnikis Amynis 2, 546 21 Thessaloníki; tel. (231) 0270889; fax (231) 0223447; e-mail info@ ntng.gr; internet www.ntng.gr; Artistic Dir VICTOR ARDITTI.

Thessaloníki State Orchestra: Kolokotroni 21, Lazaristes Monastery, 564 30 Thessaloníki; tel. (231) 0589156; fax (231) 0604854; e-mail info@koth.gr; internet www.koth.gr; Artistic Dir KAROLOS TRIKOLIDIS.

ASSOCIATIONS

Athens Concert Hall Organization: Vas. Sofias and Kokkali 1, 115 21 Athens; tel. (21) 07282000; fax (21) 070290174; internet www .megaron.gr; Artistic Dir N. MANOLOPOULOS.

Centre of Byzantine Arts: Odos Hydras 5, 521 00 Kastoria; tel. (24) 06722312; fax (24) 06722451; Dir ATHANASIOS CHATZIZAMANIS.

Centre for Mediterranean Architecture: Hgoumenou Gabriel 34, 731 34 Chania; tel. (28) 02140101; fax (28) 02127184; Dir DEMETRIS ANTONAKAKIS.

Centre for the Study of Traditional Pottery: Melidoni 4–6, 105 53 Athens; tel. (21) 03318491; fax (21) 03318490; e-mail kmnk@ath .forthnet.gr; f. 1987; Dir BETTY PSAROPOULOU.

Ethnographic Institute of Southern Europe: Meg. Alexandrou 107, 531 00 Florina; tel. (2385) 028400; fax (2385) 023775.

European Cultural Centre of Delphi: Frynichou 9, 105 58 Athens; tel. (21) 03312781; fax (21) 03312786; e-mail epked@culture .gr; Dir VASILIS KARASMANIS.

Hellenic Association for the Preservation and Spread of Tradition: Mantzagriotaki 38, 176 72 Kallithea; tel. (21) 09593884; fax (21) 09599508.

Hellenic Intellectual Property Organization: Metsovou 5, 106 82 Athens; tel. (21) 08253715; fax (21) 08253732; Dir DIONYSIA KALLINIKOU.

Hellenika Educational and Cultural Society: Kiphisodotou 15–17, 118 52 Athens; tel. (21) 03471278.

B. Papantoniou Peloponnese Folklore Foundation: Vas. Alexandrou 1, 211 00 Nauplion; tel. (2752) 028379; fax (2752) 027960; e-mail pff@otenet.gr; internet www.pli.gr; Dir IOANNA PAPANTONIOU.

Thessaloníki Concert Hall Organization: Odos Martiou 25 & Paralia, 546 46 Thessaloníki; tel. (231) 0895800; fax (231) 0895954; e-mail ommth@compulink.gr.

Eleni Tsaouli Association for Greek Folklore Dances: Tsami Karatasou 39, 117 42 Athens; tel. (21) 03250389.

Education

Education is available free of charge at all levels and is compulsory between the ages of six and 15 years. Primary education begins at the age of six and lasts for six years. Secondary education, beginning at the age of 12, is generally for six years and is divided into two equal cycles. In 2001 the total enrolment at primary and secondary schools was equivalent to 99% of the school-age population. Primary enrolment in that year included 97% of children in the relevant age-group (males 97%; females 97%), and the comparable ratio at secondary schools was 87% (males 86%; females 89%). In 2001 an equivalent 63% of the relevant age-group was enrolled in tertiary education (males 60%; females 66%). There are 18 universities. In 2000 projected budgetary expenditure on education was 1,140,000m. drachmae (9.3% of total expenditure).

UNIVERSITIES

Aristotle University of Thessaloníki (Aristotelio Panepistimio Thessalonikis): University Campus, 540 06 Thessaloníki; tel. (231) 0996703; fax (231) 0206138; internet www.auth.gr; f. 1925; 10 faculties; 5 independent departments; 2,491 teachers; 72,000 students; Rector Prof. M. PAPADOPOULOS.

'Democritus' University of Thrace (Demokritio Panepistimio Thrakis): Demokritos Str. 17, 691 00 Komotini; tel. (2531) 039000; fax (2531) 039081; e-mail intrela@duth.gr; internet www.duth.gr; f. 1973; 2 faculties; 18 departments; 381 teachers; 12,466 students; Rector K. SIMOPOULOS.

National and Capodistrian University of Athens (Athinisin Ethnikon Kai Kapodistiakon Panepistimion): Odos Panepistimiou 30, 106 79 Athens; tel. (21) 03614301; fax (21) 03602145; internet www.uoa.gr; f. 1837; 5 faculties; 5 independent faculties; 1,709 teachers; 45,000 students; Rector Prof. PETROS A. GAMTOS.

National Technical University of Athens (Ethniko Metsovio Polytechneio): Polytechnioupoli, Zografou, 157 80 Athens; tel. (21) 07721000; fax (21) 07722048; internet www.ntua.gr; f. 1836; 9 faculties; 33 departments; 566 teachers; 8,269 students; Rector Prof. THEMISTOCLES XANTHOPOULOS.

Technical University of Crete: Agiou Markou St, 731 32 Chania; tel. (2821) 028404; fax (2821) 028418; e-mail phillis@dpem.tuc.gr; internet www.tuc.gr; f. 1977; 5 departments; 150 teachers; 2,500 students; Rector IANNIS A. PHILLIS.

University of the Aegean: Xarilaou Trikoupi kai Faonos. 811 00 Mytilene; tel. (251) 036001; fax (251) 036199; internet www.aegean

.gr; f. 1984; 17 departments; 375 teachers; 7,904 students; Rector Prof. THEMISTOCLES D. LEKKAS.

University of Crete: 741 00 Rethymnon; tel. (831) 77900; fax (831) 77909; e-mail rectsecr@cc.uch.gr; internet www.uch.gr; f. 1973; 5 schools; 400 teachers; 6,618 students; Rector Prof. CHRISTOS NIKO-LAOU.

University of Ioannina: University Campus, 451 10 Ioannina; tel. (2651) 042915; fax (2651) 044112; e-mail intlrel@cc.uoi.gr; internet www.uoi.gr; f. 1964 as a dept of the Aristotle University of Thessaloníki; established as an independent university 1970; 6 schools (and 2 independent depts); 384 teachers; 9,063 students; Rector Prof. CH. MASSALAS.

University of Macedonia: Egnatia 156, POB 1591, 540 06 Thessaloníki; tel. (231) 00844825; fax (231) 00844536; e-mail pubrel@uom.gr; internet www.uom.gr; f. 1957 as Graduate Industrial School of Thessaloníki; 8 departments; 111 teachers; 8,000 students; Rector Prof. GEORGE TSIOTRAS.

University of Patras: 265 00 Patras; tel. (261) 0997608; fax (261) 0991711; e-mail rectorate@upatras.gr; internet www.upatras.gr; f. 1964; 4 schools; 770 teachers; 18,900 students; Rector Prof. NIKOLAOS ZOUMBOS.

COLLEGES OF UNIVERSITY STANDING

Athens School of Fine Art (Anotati Scholi Kalon Technon): Odos Patission 42, 106 82 Athens; tel. (21) 03816930; fax (21) 03816926; e-mail nzamanis@asfa.gr; internet www.asfa.gr; f. 1837; 38 teachers; 783 students; Rector IANNIS PAPADAKIS.

Deree College of the American College of Greece: 6 Gravias St, Aghia Paraskevi, 153 42 Athens; tel. (21) 06009800; fax (21) 06009811; e-mail acg@hol.gr; internet www.acg.edu; f. 1875; undergraduate division of the American College of Greece; 321 teachers; 6,760 students; Pres JOHN S. BAILEY.

Athens Agricultural University (Geoponiko Panepistimio Athinon): Iera Odos 75, 118 55 Athens; tel. (21) 05294802; fax (21) 03460885; e-mail r@aua.gr; internet www.aua.gr; f. 1920; Rector Prof. S. KYRITSIS.

Athens University of Economics and Business (Ikonomiko Panepistimio Athinon): Odos Patission 76, 104 34 Athens; tel. (21) 08237361; fax (21) 08228419; internet www.aueb.gr; f. 1920; 118 professors, 11,800 students; Rector Prof. ANDREAS KINTIS.

University of Piraeus (Panepistimio Pireos): Karaoli and Dimitrou St, 185 34 Piraeus; tel. (21) 04120751; fax (21) 04179064; internet www.unipi.gr; f. 1938; 90 teachers, 11,400 students; Rector T. GAMALETSOS.

'Panteois' University of Social and Political Sciences: Leoforos Syngrou 136, 176 71 Kallithea, Athens; tel. (21) 09220100; fax (21) 09223690; internet www.panteion.gr; f. 1930; 7,500 students; Rector D. CONSTAS.

Social Welfare

Of total projected expenditure by the central Government in 2000, some 2,424,000m. drachmae was allocated to health, social welfare and insurance. This represented some 15.7% of total projected government expenditure. There is a state social insurance scheme for wage-earners, while voluntary or staff insurances provide for salaried staff. Every citizen is entitled to an old-age pension; a full pension is payable after having paid 35 years' social security contributions or upon reaching a certain age, depending on the number of days' contributions paid; the latest retirement age for those entitled to a full pension is 65 for men and 62 for women. The scheme also provides for sickness benefit and health care.

In 1996 Greece had 356 hospital establishments, and in 2000 there were 490 hospital beds and 440 physicians per 100,000 inhabitants. Provision of medical services in the more remote areas of Greece, particularly in the islands, has historically been poorer than in the major towns and cities, owing to the long distances between settlements and the necessity for sea travel.

NATIONAL AGENCIES

Ministry of Health and Welfare: see section on The Government (Ministries).

Ministry of Labour and Social Affairs: see section on The Government (Ministries).

General Directorate of Working Conditions and Health: Pireos 40. 101 82 Athens; tel. (21) 03214327; fax (21) 03214294; internet www.osh.gr; a division of the Ministry of Labour and Social Affairs; oversees health and safety regulations in the workplace.

Social Security Institute (IKA): Ag. Konstantinou 8, 102 41, Athens; tel. (21) 05234211; internet www.ika.gr; administers the pensions, health care and social security systems for some 5.6m. people.

Organization Against Drugs—OKANA: Aristotelous 19, 104 33 Athens; tel. (21) 08253756; fax (21) 08253760; e-mail okana@otenet .gr; internet www.okana.gr.

HEALTH AND WELFARE ORGANIZATIONS

Disabled Hellas: 3 Septevriou 30, 546 36 Thessaloníki; tel. (231) 0211915; fax (231) 0968178; e-mail info@disabled.gr; internet www .disabled.gr; information and support for Greeks with disabilities; Principal Officer NIKOS VOULGAROPOULOS.

Hellenic Cancer Society (Ellinki Antikarkiniki Etairia): An. Tsoha 18–20, 115 21 Athens; tel. (21) 06456713; fax (21) 06410011; e-mail hellas-cancer@ath.forthnet.gr; internet www .cancer-society.gr; f. 1958.

Hellenic Heart Foundation (Elliniko Idrywa Kardiologias—ELIKAR): Vas. Sofias 133, 115 21 Athens; tel. (21) 06401477; fax (21) 06401478; e-mail elikar@aias.gr; internet www.elikar.gr; f. 1991.

Hellenic Red Cross: Lycavittou 1, 106 72 Athens; tel. (21) 03621681; fax (21) 03615606; e-mail ir@redcross.gr; internet www .redcross.gr; f. 1877; Pres Dr ANDREAS MARTINIS; Sec.-Gen. ELLI DIMITRIOU.

Hellenic Society for Disabled Children: Kononos 16, 116 34 Athens; tel. (21) 07251121; fax (21) 07228380; e-mail elepap@hol.gr; internet www.elepap.gr; f. 1937; Pres. MARY CARELLA-DIAMANTO-POULOS; Sec.-Gen. RANYA KONTOYANNIS.

Panhellenic Association of the Blind: Veranzerou 31, 104 32 Athens; tel. (21) 05228333; fax (21) 05222112; e-mail pab@otenet.gr; internet www.pst.gr; f. 1932; Chair. ILIAS MARGIOLAS.

The Environment

The increase in the number of tourists visiting Greece from the 1960s resulted in construction and industrial activity taking place in many previously undeveloped areas of the country, including numerous islands. The resultant environmental concerns led to an increase in the strength of the environmental movement in Greece. The preservation of sites of archaeological interest was another major environmental issue.

GOVERNMENT ORGANIZATION

Ministry of the Environment, Physical Planning and Public Works: See section on The Government (Ministries).

ACADEMIC INSTITUTES

Kentron Erevnis Phissikistis Atmospheras kai Climatologias, Akadimia Athinon (Research Centre for Atmospheric Physics and Climatology, Academy of Athens): Odos Panepistimiou 28, Athens; f. 1977; Dir C. REPAPIS.

National Centre for Marine Research: Aghios Kosmas, Hellinikon, 166 04 Athens; tel. (21) 09820214; fax (21) 09833095; e-mail rpsill@ncmr.gr; internet www.ncmr.gr; f. 1965; marine science, including studies in physical oceanography, biological ocenaography, chemical oceanography, marine geology and geophysics, inland waters, fisheries and aquaculture; Pres. and Dir Prof. G. CHRONIS.

NON-GOVERNMENTAL ORGANIZATIONS

European Study Centre for Development and the Environment (EKAPEM): c/o M. G. Tsaltas, Stakion St, 166 72 Athens; tel. (21) 08970036; scientific research; development projects; environmental protection; Pres. TSALTAS GRIGORIS.

Greenpeace Greece: Zoodochou Pigis 52C, 106 81 Athens; tel. (21) 03840774; fax (21) 03804008; e-mail infogr@diala.greenpeace.gr; internet www.greenpeace.gr; national office of Greenpeace International.

Hellenic Society for the Protection of the Environment and Cultural Heritage (Elliniki Etairia): Tripodon St 28, 105 58 Athens; tel. (21) 03225245; fax (21) 03225240; e-mail elet@ellinikietairia.gr; internet www.ellinikietairia.gr; awareness-raising; environmental protection; lobbying government on environmental legislation; Pres. Dr MICHAEL J. SCOULLOS.

Hellenic Society for the Protection of Nature (HSBN): Nikis St 20, 105 57 Athens; tel. (21) 03224944; fax (21) 03225285; e-mail hspn@hol.gr; internet www.eepf.gr; environmental education programmes; conservation of wild flora and fauna, forests, protected areas, coasts and sea, wetland ecosystems and national parks; Sec.-Gen. MAKIS APERGHIS; Programs Co-ordinator ALIKI VAVOURI.

Mediterranean Centre for the Environment (CME): Polynikous 2, 174 55 Alimos; tel. (21) 09887630; fax (21) 09887565; e-mail medcenv@hellasnet.gr; increases public awareness of environmental problems; promotes sustainable tourism; Man. ISABELLE BOUCHY.

Sea Turtle Protection Society of Greece—STPS/Archelon: Solomou 57, 10 432 Athens; tel. and fax (21) 05231342; e-mail stps@archelon.gr; internet www.archelon.gr; f. 1983; monitoring and management of sea turtle nesting areas and habitats; environmental education; operates the Sea Turtle Rescue Centre; Prin. Officers DIMITRIOS MARGARITOULIS, DIMITRIOS DIMOPOULOS.

World Wide Fund for Nature—WWF Greece: Filellinon St 26, 105 58 Athens; tel. (21) 03314893; fax (21) 03247578; e-mail webmaster@wwf.gr; internet www.wwf.gr; national affiliate organization of the World Wide Fund for Nature—WWF International; Pres. THYMIO PAPAYANNIS.

Defence

In August 2002 the armed forces numbered 177,600, of whom 98,321 were conscripts, and consisted of an army of 114,000 (including a national guard of 34,000), a navy of 19,000 and an air force of 33,000; in addition, there was a coast guard and customs force of 4,000. Military service lasts up to 16 months in the Army and up to 19 months in the Air Force and Navy. Service with the reserve lasts until 50 years of age; in August 2002 the reserve was estimated at 291,000. Since 1978 women have been entitled to volunteer for 30–50 days' basic military training and additional specialized training; in 1998 a law was enacted providing for the conscription of women for four days a year to assist in the defence of the country's borders. The Greek defence budget for 2002 was €3,400m. The USA maintains two military bases in Greece; in August 2002 there were 290 military personnel stationed at these sites.

Supreme Commander of the Armed Forces: President KONSTANTINOS STEFANOPOULOS.

Chief of the General Staff of the Hellenic National Defence: Gen. GEORGE ANTONAKOPOULOS.

Chief of the General Staff of the Hellenic Army: Lt-Gen. PANAGIOTIS HARVALAS.

Chief of the General Staff of the Hellenic Navy: Vice-Adm. GEORGE THEODOROULAKIS.

Chief of the General Staff of the Hellenic Air Force: Lt-Gen. PANAGIOTIS PAPANIKOLOAU.

Bibliography

Allison, G. T., and Nicolaidis, K. (Eds). *The Greek Paradox: Promise Vs Performance* (CSIA Studies in International Security). Cambridge, MA, MIT Press, 1997.

Brewer, D. *The Flame of Freedom: The Greek War of Independence, 1821–1833*. London, John Murray, 2001.

Burn, A. R. *The Penguin History of Greece*. Harmondsworth, Penguin, 1990.

Carabott, P. (Ed.). *Greek Society in the Making, 1863–1913: Realities, Symbols and Visions*. Aldershot, Variorum, 1998.

Clogg, R. *A Concise History of Greece*. Cambridge, Cambridge University Press, 1992.

   Greece in the 1980s. London, Macmillan, 1983.

   The Greek Diaspora in the Twentieth Century. New York, NY, St Martin's Press, 1999.

   Parties and Elections in Greece. London, C. Hurst, 1988.

   A Short History of Modern Greece, 2nd edn. Cambridge, Cambridge University Press, 1986.

   (Ed.) *The Populist Decade: Greece 1981–1991*. London, Macmillan, 1993.

Close, D. H. *The Origins of the Greek Civil War*. Harlow, Addison Wesley Longman, 1995.

Constas, D., and Stavrou, T. G. (Eds). *Greece Prepares for the Twenty First Century*. Baltimore, MD, Johns Hopkins University Press, 1995.

Danforth, L. M. *The Macedonian Conflict: Ethnic Nationalism in a Transnational World*. Princeton, NJ, Princeton University Press, 1995.

Featherstone, K., and Ifantis, K. (Eds). *Greece in a Changing Europe: Between European Integration and Balkan Disintegration*. Manchester, Manchester University Press, 1996.

Featherstone, K., and Katsoudas, D. (Eds). *Political Change in Greece: Before and After the Colonels*. London, Croom Helm, 1987.

Fleming, K. E. *The Muslim Bonaparte: Diplomacy and Orientalism in Ali Pasha's Greece*. Princeton, NJ, Princeton University Press, 1999.

Freris, A. F. *The Greek Economy in the Twentieth Century*. London, Croom Helm, 1986.

Gerolymatos, A., Iatrides, J. O., and Chircop, A. E. (Eds). *The Aegean Sea After the Cold War: Security and Law of the Sea Issues*. New York, NY, St Martin's Press, 2000.

Gourgouris, S. *Dream Nation: Enlightenment, Colonization, and the Institution of Modern Greece*. Palo Alto, CA, Stanford University Press, 1996.

Housepian Dobkin, M. *Smyrna 1922: The Destruction of a City*. London, Faber & Faber, 1972.

Iatrides, J. O., and Wrigley, L. (Eds). *Greece at the Crossroads, The Civil War and Its Legacy*. University Park, PA, Pennsylvania State University Press, 1995.

Jouganatos, G. A. *The Development of the Greek Economy, 1950–1991*. Westport, CT, Greenwood, 1992.

Karakasidou, A. M. *Fields of Wheat, Hills of Blood: Passages to Nationhood in Greek Macedonia, 1870–1900*. Chicago, IL, University of Chicago Press, 1997.

Kassimeris, G. *Europe's Last Red Terrorists: The Revolutionary Organisation November 17*. London, C. Hurst, 2001.

van der Kiste, J. *Kings of the Hellenes: The Greek Kings 1863–1974*. Stroud, Sutton Publishing, 1999.

Koliopoulos, J. S., and Veremis, T. M. *Greece: The Modern Sequel*. London, C. Hurst, 2002.

Lavdas, K. A. *The Europeanization of Greece: Interest Politics and the Crises of integration*. New York, NY, St Martin's Press, 1998.

Llewellyn-Smith, M. *Ionian Vision: Greece in Asia Minor 1919–1922*. Ann Arbor, MI, University of Michigan Press, 1998.

Lock, P. *The Franks in the Aegean, 1204–1500*. Harlow, Addison Wesley Longman, 1995.

Lykogiannis, A. *Britain and the Greek Economic Crisis 1944–1947: From Liberation to the Truman Doctrine*. Columbia, University of Missouri Press, 2002.

Mackridge, P., and Yannakakis, E. (Eds). *Ourselves and Others: The Development of a Greek Macedonian Cultural Identity Since 1912*. Oxford, Berg, 1997.

Mazower, M. *Inside Hitler's Greece: The Experience of Occupation 1941–44*. New Haven, CT, Yale University Press, 1995.

OECD Country Report. *Greece*. Paris, annual.

Pagoulatos, G. *Greece's New Political Economy: State, Finance and Growth from Postwar to EMU* (St Antony's Series). Basingstoke, Palgrave Macmillan, 2003.

Peckham, R. S. *National Histories, Natural States*. London, I. B. Tauris, 2001.

Pirounakis, N. G. *The Greek Economy: Past, Present and Future*. New York, NY, St Martin's Press, 1997.

Ricks, D., and Magdalino, P. (Eds). *Byzantium and the Modern Greek Identity*. Aldershot, Ashgate Publishing, 1998.

Runciman, S. *The Fall of Constantinople, 1453*. Cambridge, Cambridge University Press, 1991.

Tsaliki, P. V. *The Greek Economy*. New York, NY, Praeger 1991.

Tziamperis, A. *Greece, European Political Co-operation and the Macedonian Question*. Aldershot, Ashgate Publishing, 2000.

Vatikiotis, P. J. *Popular Autocracy in Greece 1936–41: A Political Biography of General Ioannis Metaxas*. London, Frank Cass, 1998.

Veremis, T. *The Military in Greek Politics: From Independence to Democracy*. Montreal, Black Rose Books, 1997.

Veremis, T., and Dragoumis, M. *Greece* (World Bibliographical Series). Oxford, Clio Press, 1998.

Woodhouse, C. M. *The Struggle for Greece 1941–49*. Woodstock, NY, Beekman, 1977.

   Modern Greece: A Short History. London, Faber & Faber, 2000.

Yannopoulos, G. N. *Greece and the EEC: Integration and Convergence*. London, Macmillan, 1987.

HUNGARY

Geography

PHYSICAL FEATURES

The Republic of Hungary is a land-locked country in central Europe. It is bordered by Austria to the west, Slovakia to the north and has a short border with Ukraine in the north-east. Romania lies to the east and Hungary's southern border is with Slovenia, Croatia, and Serbia and Montenegro (the province of Vojvodina in Serbia). Hungary has a total area of 93,030 sq km (35,919 sq miles), although its territory was much reduced upon the dissolution of the Habsburg Empire.

The River Danube (Duna) forms Hungary's north-western border with Slovakia and then flows south through Budapest, bisecting the country, which is mostly low-lying and much of it prone to flooding. East of the Danube is the Pannonian or Great Hungarian Plain (Nagyalföld), which is also drained by the Tisza, the longest tributary of the Danube. To the west of the Danube the country is hillier, with a spur of the Alps traversing the region from the south-west to the north-east (the Bakony, Vertes and Philis ranges). South-east of these mountains lie Lake Balaton, the largest lake in Central Europe, and the downlands of Transdanubia (Dunántúl). In the north-west of Hungary, between the mountains and the Danube, are the Little Hungarian Plains (Kisalföld). Only some 2% of the total land area of the country is over 400 m, the highest mountain being Kékestetö, at 1,014 m (3,327 ft), in the Matra range. The Matras lie east of the Danube, along Hungary's northern border, and are foothills of the Carpathian Mountains.

CLIMATE

Hungary has a continental climate, with hot summers and cold winters. In winter the Danube can freeze over for long periods and, in settled weather, fog is frequent. The mean temperatures in Budapest are a maximum of 22°C (71°F) in July and a minimum of –1°C (30°F) in January. Most rainfall is in the spring and early summer, when there are often heavy downpours; in Budapest the annual average is 610 mm. There is little regional variation in the weather.

POPULATION

The Hungarians (Magyars) are a Turkic or Finno-Ugrian people who settled on the Hungarian plains in the seventh century AD. There are still large numbers of ethnic Hungarians outside the borders of the modern state, particularly in

areas that once formed part of the old kingdom, such as north-west Romania (Transylvania), southern Slovakia and Serbia and Montenegro (Vojvodina). In 1984, it was estimated, ethnic Hungarians accounted for 92% of the total population of Hungary. In 1998, however, official figures put the number of ethnic Hungarians at 89.9% of the total population, Romany (Gypsy) people at 4%, Germans at over 2% of the population, Serbs at 2%, Slovaks at 0.8% and Romanians at about 0.7%. The official language is Hungarian (Magyar), but the various nationalities also speak their own languages. The predominant religion is Christianity, the largest denomination being the Roman Catholic Church (an estimated 61% of the population), followed by Calvinists (20%) and Lutherans (5%). There are also small groups of Eastern Orthodox Christians, Jews and Muslims.

The capital of Hungary is Budapest, in the north of the country. The city is located on the Danube, the ancient capital of Buda on the hillier western bank and the commercial centre of Pest on the eastern bank, with a resident population of 1,739,569 at 1 January 2002. Other major towns include Debrecen (206,564), Miskolc (182,408) and Szeged (163,699) east of the Danube, and Pécs (159,794) to the west. In 1998, it was estimated, some 63% of the population lived in urban areas, compared to 35% in 1945. The total resident population was 10,197,119 at the census of 1 February 2001. At December 2002, according to official estimates, the population numbered 10,142,000, giving a population density of 109.0 per sq km.

Chronology

896: The Magyars, under the leadership of Árpád (896–907), migrated to the Hungarian plains.

1000: The coronation of St Stephen I (997–1038), with a crown sent by the Pope, established Hungary as a western Christian kingdom.

1458–90: Reign of Matthias I Corvinus, who prevailed against the rival claims to the throne by the House of Habsburg, extended Hungarian hegemony and moved his capital to Vienna (now in Austria).

1526: The Hungarian army was destroyed by the forces of the Ottoman Empire at the battle of Mohács; with the death of

Louis II, the Habsburgs inherited Hungary's Crown of St Stephen.

1541: Hungary was partitioned between the Habsburgs and the Ottomans.

1687: The Diet of Pressburg (Bratislava) declared the Hungarian Crown to be a hereditary possession of the Austrian House of Habsburg.

1699: The Ottomans ceded Hungary (including Transylvania and Slavonia) to its conqueror, the Habsburg Holy Roman Emperor.

1711: The Peace of Szatmár confirmed the rights of the Hungarian nobility to self-government.

6 August 1806: Francis II, under pressure from Napoleon I of France, dissolved the Holy Roman Empire of the German Nation and reigned henceforth as Francis I, having assumed the imperial title for Austria in 1804.

1848: Hungary under Louis Kossuth established a national government, but, in December, refused to recognize the new Emperor, Francis Joseph I.

1849: Imperial armies regained control of Hungary.

1867: The Compromise (*Ausgleich*) of 1867 reorganized the Habsburg Empire as the Dual Monarchy of Austria (Cisleithania) and Hungary (Transleithania); Emperor Francis Joseph I was crowned as King of Hungary.

28 June 1914: The assassination of the heir to the Dual Monarchy, Archduke Francis Ferdinand, in Sarajevo (Bosnia and Herzegovina) led to the beginning of the First World War.

21 November 1916: Death of Francis Joseph I and the accession of his grand-nephew, Charles I, as King of Hungary.

4 October 1918: Austria-Hungary accepted the same armistice conditions as Germany (to take effect on 4 November).

31 October 1918: Count Mihály Károlyi, who had established a national council six days earlier, was appointed premier by Charles I.

16 November 1918: Hungary was declared a republic.

24 November 1918: The Hungarian Communist Party was established by Béla Kun.

11 January 1919: Károlyi became President of the republic.

21 March 1919: Károlyi resigned in protest at the Allies' territorial demands; Kun formed a coalition Government of communists and social democrats.

August 1919: A Romanian counter-offensive, following Hungarian incursions into Slovakia and Transylvania, resulted in the flight of Kun and the occupation of Budapest.

March 1920: The National Council restored the monarchy and elected Adm. Miklós Horthy de Nagybánya as Regent.

4 June 1920: Signature of the Treaty of Trianon concluding peace at the end of the First World War: Hungary ceded Slovakia and Carpatho-Ukraine (Sub-Carpathian Ruthenia) to Czechoslovakia, Transylvania to Romania, the Banat to Romania and Yugoslavia, Croatia-Slavonia to Yugoslavia and the Burgenland to Austria; the consequent desire of the Hungarians to revise the borders resulted in close relations with Germany.

February 1939: Hungary joined Germany and Italy in the Anti-Comintern Pact.

26 June 1941: Hungary entered the Second World War on the side of Germany by the declaration of war on the USSR.

19 March 1944: German troops occupied Hungary.

15 October 1944: Regent Horthy secretly concluded an armistice with the USSR, but was forced to rescind it and was then arrested and replaced by the Fascist, Ferenc Szálasi.

20 January 1945: A provisional government signed an armistice with the USSR and agreed to the Hungarian borders of 1937 (as established at Trianon).

November 1945: Following a general election, the Smallholders Party, the largest party, formed a coalition Government with the communists.

August 1947: The communists became the largest single party in the general election.

June 1948: The Communist Party merged with the Social Democratic Party to form the Hungarian Workers' Party (HWP).

May 1949: The Hungarian People's Front for Independence (dominated by the HWP) presented a single list of candidates.

August 1949: A People's Republic was established.

1953: Imre Nagy became Prime Minister.

April 1955: Nagy was forced to resign by Mátyás Rákosi, the First Secretary of the HWP, and was expelled from the Party.

July 1956: Rákosi was forced to resign and was replaced by Ernő Gerő.

23 October 1956: Demonstrations and rioting broke out in Budapest against the communist Government.

24 October 1956: Soviet tanks were sent in to quell the rioting.

25 October 1956: The communist Government was replaced by a reformist regime headed by Imre Nagy; Soviet forces withdrew.

3 November 1956: Nagy established an all-party coalition Government, having already renounced membership of the Warsaw Pact.

4 November 1956: Some 200,000 Soviet troops invaded the country; Nagy was overthrown and János Kádár was installed by the USSR as the new premier in an all-communist Government and leader of the newly formed Hungarian Socialist Workers' Party (HSWP).

16 June 1958: Nagy and four associates were executed for their part in the 1956 uprising.

1 January 1968: The New Economic Mechanism, which combined central-planning and market instruments, was introduced.

June 1985: The legislative elections permitted voters a wider choice of candidates under the terms of a new electoral law.

October 1986: A group of academics, supported by Imre Pózsgay and other reformers in the HSWP, drew up a paper, 'Change and Reform', which heralded the breakdown in consensus both inside and outside the party.

June 1987: Károly Grósz was appointed Chairman of the Council of Ministers; he introduced some reforms aimed at alleviating the economic problems of the country.

15 March 1988: Some 10,000 people marched through Budapest, on the 140th anniversary of the 1848 uprising against Austrian rule, demanding the introduction of genuine reforms.

April 1988: Four reformers within the HSWP were expelled from the party for demanding radical political and economic reform. A radical youth group formed an opposition party, the Federation of Young Democrats (FYD).

May 1988: At a special ideological conference of the HSWP János Kádár was replaced as General Secretary of the Central Committee by Károly Grósz; Kádár also lost his membership of the Politburo. Various opposition groups formed the Network of Free Initiatives—subsequently renamed the Alliance of Free Democrats (AFD).

June 1988: Some 50,000 people demonstrated in Budapest against the Romanian Government's proposed destruction of 7,000 villages, including 1,500 ethnic Hungarian villages.

July 1988: The Central Committee of the HSWP approved an austere economic reform programme, which would lead to a reduction in subsidies, a devaluation of the forint and a rapid rise in unemployment.

21 November 1988: Miklós Németh replaced Grósz as Chairman of the Council of Ministers.

20 December 1988: The National Assembly voted to allow the right to demonstrate and the establishment of independent political organizations.

February 1989: The HSWP agreed to the establishment of a multi-party system; its Central Committee agreed to abandon the clause in the Constitution guaranteeing the HSWP's leading role in society.

15 March 1989: Some 100,000 people took part in an anti-Government demonstration in Budapest.

May 1989: The Chairman of the Council of Ministers, Németh, reorganized his cabinet and declared that it would, henceforth, be answerable to the National Assembly before the HSWP; Kádár was relieved of his post as Chairman of the HSWP. 'Round table' negotiations between the HSWP and various opposition groups began.

16 June 1989: Following the rehabilitation of Imre Nagy, he was reburied with four associates at a state funeral in Budapest, which was attended by 300,000 people.

23 July 1989: An opposition deputy was elected to the National Assembly, in a by-election, for the first time since 1947 (by September there were seven opposition deputies, who then formed a parliamentary group).

10 September 1989: The border with Austria was opened, allowing the exodus of thousands of East Germans seeking to emigrate to the West.

18 September 1989: Against a background of continuing demonstrations and industrial unrest, during round table negotiations it was decided that the Constitution and electoral law be modified and that the Presidential Council be dissolved.

7–8 October 1989: The HSWP voted to dissolve itself and reconstitute as the Hungarian Socialist Party (HSP); Rezső Nyers was elected Chairman of the new party.

18 October 1989: Mátyás Szűrös was elected to the newly created post of President of the Republic, in an acting capacity.

23 October 1989: Following the enactment of radical constitutional amendments, the country was renamed the Republic of Hungary.

12 March 1990: Following an agreement with the USSR, the withdrawal of Soviet troops began (completed by June 1991).

March–April 1990: After two rounds of voting in the general election, the Hungarian Democratic Forum (HDF) won 165 of the 386 seats in the National Assembly, while the AFD obtained 92, the Independent Smallholders' Party (ISP) 43 and the HSP only 33. The HDF agreed a coalition Government with the ISP, the Christian Democratic People's Party (CDPP) and independents.

2 May 1990: Árpád Göncz (AFD) was elected interim President and speaker of the National Assembly (and was supported by the HDF in the presidential election); the following day József Antall (HDF) was appointed Chairman of the Council of Ministers.

June 1990: Trading resumed on the Budapest Stock Exchange after a 42-year break. Hungary began a process of disengagement from the activities of the Warsaw Pact.

3 August 1990: Göncz was elected President of the Republic by the National Assembly.

October 1990: The Government offered all state industries for sale; later in the month price rises had to be limited in order to end the disruptions and protests throughout the country.

February 1992: József Torgyán, the leader of the ISP, announced his party's departure from the government coalition; however, only 13 ISP deputies followed his lead.

June 1993: After having been expelled from the HDF at the beginning of the month, the right-wing István Csurka formed his own party, the Hungarian Justice and Life Party (HJLP).

12 December 1993: The Prime Minister, Antall, died; Péter Boros, hitherto the interior minister, succeeded him as premier.

1 February 1994: Hungary's associate membership of the European Union (EU, as the EC was known from November 1993) came into effect.

May 1994: The general election was decided in two rounds of voting; the HSP obtained a clear parliamentary majority, winning a total of 209 out of 386 seats; the AFD won 70 seats; the HDF 37; and the ISP (renamed the Independent Smallholders' and Peasants' Party—ISPP) 26. The CDPP and the FYD won 22 and 20 seats, respectively. The HSP and the AFD subsequently signed a coalition agreement, which installed Gyula Horn of the HSP as Prime Minister.

March 1995: An austerity programme was announced by the Government, which included drastic reductions in government spending and a 9% devaluation of the forint. Later, despite nationalist opposition in Hungary, a Treaty of Friendship and Co-operation was signed between Hungary and Slovakia, which guaranteed the rights of ethnic minorities in the two countries and recognized the inviolability of their joint border (it came into effect in May 1996).

19 June 1995: President Göncz was re-elected by an overwhelming majority in the National Assembly.

16 September 1996: Hungary and Romania signed a Treaty of Understanding, Co-operation and Good-Neighbourliness, according to which Hungary renounced any claim on Transylvania and Romania agreed to guarantee rights to its ethnic Hungarian minority.

25 September 1997: The International Court of Justice (ICJ—based in The Hague, Netherlands) concluded that both Hungary and Slovakia had contravened international law by their actions in the joint Gabčikovo-Nagymaros hydroelectric scheme: Hungary for having breached the terms of the agreement, by withdrawing from the project in May 1989 (owing to environmental concerns), and Slovakia for having decided, in July 1991, to proceed unilaterally with work to re-route the River Danube.

30 March 1998: Hungary began negotiations on accession to the EU, in the first phase of the EU's eastward enlargement.

10 and 24 May 1998: The general election was decided in two rounds of voting. The second round of voting in the general election, in which 57% of the electorate took part, resulted in the Federation of Young Democrats—Hungarian Civic Party (FYD—HCP, as the FYD had been known since April 1995) obtaining a total of 147 of the 386 seats, the HSP winning 134 seats, the ISPP 48 seats, and the AFD 24 seats. The HDF and the HJLP won 18 and 14 seats, respectively.

June 1998: The FYD—HCP, the ISPP and the HDF signed a coalition agreement; the leader of the FYD—HCP, Viktor Orbán, was appointed Prime Minister.

18 October 1998: In municipal elections, the government coalition received 39.6% of votes cast, while the HSP and AFD won 35.1% of the votes.

12 March 1999: Following approval by an overwhelming majority in the National Assembly in the previous month, Hungary officially became a full member of the North Atlantic Treaty Organization (NATO).

May 1999: Hungary allowed NATO use of its air space and military bases to facilitate NATO's aerial bombardment of the neighbouring Federal Republic of Yugoslavia (FRY); however, there were widespread fears that the Government's co-operation with NATO would lead to reprisals against the ethnic Hungarian population in the Serbian province of Vojvodina.

5–6 June 2000: In the presidential election the sole candidate, Ferenc Mádl, obtained 251 out of a possible 386 votes in the National Assembly; as he failed to win the requisite 258 votes, a second round of voting was held the next day. However, after this ballot too proved inconclusive, a third round of voting took place, in which Mádl secured the presidency.

4 August 2000: Mádl took office as President of the Republic.

March 2001: Zsigmond Járai took over as Governor of the Hungarian National Bank, upon the departure of György Surányi.

6 May 2001: The Independent Smallholders' and Civic Party (ISCP—as the ISPP was known by this time), at a convention in Budapest, elected Zsolt Lányi as President, and expelled rival leader József Torgyán from the party's parliamentary faction. However, a simultaneous party convention in Cegléd retained Torgyán as leader, thereby creating a split between the ISCP parliamentary faction and the wider party. Torgyán was finally removed from the chairmanship of the ISCP in May 2002, and expelled from the party in November.

19 June 2001: The legislature passed the 'Status' or 'Benefit' Law. The bill, which came into effect on 1 January 2002, and which granted ethnic Hungarians living in neighbouring states education, employment and other rights in Hungary (but not permanent residence), prompted protests from Romania and Slovakia that the law discriminated against their non-ethnic Hungarian populations, and constituted a violation of sovereignty.

24 December 2001: Orbán and his Romanian counterpart, Adrian Năstase, signed a memorandum of understanding, according to which the short-term employment rights offered to ethnic Hungarians under the legislation adopted in June were to be extended to all Romanian citizens.

7 and 21 April 2002: After two rounds of voting in the legislative elections, the FYD—HCP-HDF secured 48.7% of the votes cast. However, a left-wing coalition of the HSP (with 46.1% of the votes) and the AFD (5.2%) was able to secure an overall majority and form a new Government. Péter Medgyessy of the HSP was sworn in as Prime Minister on 27 May.

19 June 2002: Following media allegations, Prime Minister Medgyessy admitted that he had served as a counter-intelli-gence officer at the Ministry of Finance in 1977–82, but denied having been an 'informant'; the AFD subsequently retracted its threat to withdraw from the governing coalition.

3 July 2002: The FYD—HCP leader, Zoltán Pokorni, who had been deeply critical of Medgyessy, resigned from his party and parliamentary posts after it emerged that his father had worked as a police informer during the communist era.

20 October 2002: The governing coalition consolidated its position, securing some 48% of the votes cast in the local elections.

13 December 2002: Following the conclusion of negotiations with the EU, Hungary was one of 10 countries formally invited to join the Union in May 2004.

1 March 2003: Repeat elections were held to the National Autonomous Authority of the Romany Minority (elections held in January had been declared invalid). The leftist Democratic Roma Coalition secured 49 of the 53 available seats, defeating the Lungo Drom Alliance.

12 April 2003: In a national referendum on EU membership, some 84% of votes were cast in favour of accession. Four days later the Government signed the Treaty of Accession in Athens, Greece.

23 June 2003: The National Assembly approved amendments to the controversial Benefit Law, deleting a reference to the unity of the Hungarian nation and altering the terms for receipt of financial assistance. However, the Slovakian Prime Minister, Mikuláš Dzurinda, denounced the amended legislation as unacceptable and asserted that the implementation of any provision interpreted as threatening Slovakia's territorial integrity would be blocked.

19 July 2003: The Hungarian Minister of Foreign Affairs, Lázsló Kovács, reached agreement with his Slovakian counterpart, Eduard Kukan, on a potential solution to the dispute over the implementation of the Status Law; a similar agreement had been reached with the Romanian Minister of Foreign Affairs, Mircea Geoană, on the previous day.

History
Prof. LÁSZLÓ PÉTER

INTRODUCTION

The Kingdom of Hungary was founded by Stephen I, who was crowned in AD 1000 and canonized in 1083. The kingdom occupied a territory some three times the size of the present-day Republic of Hungary. In 1526 the King of Hungary, Louis II, was killed by the Ottoman Turks at the Battle of Mohács, and the Kingdom was, in 1541, partitioned among the Ottoman Empire, the Habsburgs and the principality of Transylvania. In the late 17th century the Habsburg Emperor, Leopold I, expelled the Turks from Hungary and occupied Transylvania, reuniting it with the Hungarian Crown. Hungary had a substantial degree of autonomy, particularly after 1867, when it became Austria's partner in the Austro-Hungarian Monarchy.

After the collapse of Austria-Hungary in 1918, Hungary became an independent state. However, under the terms of the Treaty of Trianon of 1920, Hungary lost two-thirds of its pre-1918 territories and three-fifths of its population. More than 3m. Hungarians were left in the neighbouring states of Austria, Czechoslovakia, Romania and Yugoslavia. The dismemberment of Hungary had a powerful impact on domestic politics in the years between the First and Second World Wars. The major parties advocated border revisions to recover Hungary's former lands, policies in which the western powers had no interests. As a consequence, Hungary resorted to the support of the Axis Powers and fought against the Allies during the Second World War. The boundaries established by the Treaty of Trianon were confirmed by the Paris Peace Treaty in 1947. From that time Hungary abandoned the aspiration to revise its frontiers.

After 1918 Hungary had a turbulent history. In March 1919 Count Mihály Károlyi's Republic was replaced by Béla Kun's communist dictatorship, which, in turn, was ousted from power by the Romanian army in August. After its withdrawal the National Army, led by Adm. Miklós Horthy de Nagybánya, took over before the old legal order was restored. The National Assembly elected Horthy to be temporary head of state as Regent (kormányzó) in March 1920 and he remained in office until October 1944, when the German army deposed him, after his failed attempt to move Hungary over to the side of the Allies. The Nazi 'puppet' government of Ferenc Szálasi was short-lived, and in late 1944 Hungary was occupied by the Soviet army.

THE COMMUNIST TAKE-OVER AND THE REVOLUTION OF 1956

Communist rule was gradually imposed on the country. Between 1945 and 1947 Hungary was governed by a coalition consisting both of communists and of representatives from the democratic parties. At elections held in November 1945 the communists won only 70 of the 409 seats in parliament, while the Smallholders' Party won 245 seats. However, the communists controlled the Ministry of the Interior and had the active support of the occupying Soviet army. With these advantages, they reduced the influence of the other parties by intimidating their leaders and infiltrating their organizations. The takeover was complete by the end of 1948, by which time the communists had merged with the Social Democrats to form the Hungarian Workers' Party (HWP).

Under its communist leader, Mátyás Rákosi, Hungary was transformed into a model Soviet satellite. The communists destroyed established European institutions like the market system, private ownership and the rule of law. They abolished personal, civil and political rights, destroyed the autonomy of churches and cultural values. They carried out forced industrialization and collectivization and tolerated no political opposition to the regime, either real or imagined. The Department for the Defence of the State (ÁVH) interned hundreds of thousands of people in labour camps. Police terror and 'conception trials' were complemented by ideological terror and party purges.

Following the death of Stalin (Iosif V. Dzhugashvili) in 1953, Rákosi and his associates were reprimanded by the new Soviet leaders for their mistakes and for the 'personality cult' they had introduced. The 'new course' was launched, promising higher living standards, and in June Rákosi was replaced as Prime Minister by Imre Nagy, who had opposed forced collectivization. Rákosi, however, remained First Secretary of the HWP. In March 1955 he secured Soviet support for the replacement of the popular Nagy with András Hegedüs, a close ally of Rákosi. However, in July 1956 he was dismissed as party leader by Khrushchev, the new leader of the Communist Party of the USSR, even though he was succeeded by another Stalinist, Ernő Gerő. By now the intelligentsia was in ferment and the party divided between the Stalinists and Nagy's supporters.

The mood of uncertainty and tension brought about by these changes contributed to the 1956 Revolution. On 23 October the demonstration in the Hungarian capital, Budapest, to reinstate Nagy, introduce reforms and end Soviet domination led to a spontaneous uprising, which swiftly spread to other parts of the country. The Soviet military intervened without success. The Stalinists were ousted. A reformist Government, led by Imre Nagy, was installed, and János Kádár took over as leader of the HWP. Workers' councils were established everywhere by revolutionary committees, the multi-party system was restored and the Government decided to leave the Warsaw Pact by a declaration of neutrality. On 4 November, however, Soviet troops reoccupied Budapest and, after bitter fighting, overthrew the Nagy Government.

KÁDÁR'S 'NEW MODEL' AND ITS FAILURE

After supporting Nagy and the revolution Kádár turned to support the Soviet occupiers. He returned to Budapest with Soviet tanks on 7 November 1956 as Secretary of the renamed Hungarian Socialist Workers' Party (HSWP). Under his leadership, all remaining traces of opposition to the regime were ruthlessly erased. Some 20,000 participants in the Revolution were arrested, of whom 2,000, including Nagy, were subsequently executed in June 1958. Opponents of the regime were deported to the USSR, the precise number still unknown. A workers' militia was established and the collectivization of agriculture was enforced.

In his first years as premier Kádár, having no social support, depended on the former Stalinists as much as on the reformers. By 1961 he felt in a sufficiently strong position to exclude the former group (although Rákosi's group was for-

mally purged only in August 1962). Kádár initiated a new conciliatory policy in December 1961, with the slogan 'he who is not against us is with us'. The regime was willing to enlist non-HSWP specialists into the bureaucracy and to allow a wider debate within the HSWP itself over policy. Police surveillance became less obtrusive. 'Class aliens' who had been forced to take menial jobs were readmitted to public life. This *ralliement* was accompanied by a reassessment of economic objectives, with Kádár endeavouring to remove political dissatisfaction by satisfying economic needs. After five years of debate, the New Economic Mechanism (NEM) was introduced in 1968, under the direction of Rezső Nyers. The NEM partially freed enterprises and collectives from the tutelage of central planning and devolved initiative from the ministries to managers and farming co-operatives. At the same time, policy reorientated the economy from heavy industry towards an expanding consumer sector.

Agriculture benefited most from the NEM, but industrial production and living standards also improved. The international petroleum crises caused the economy to falter in the 1970s, resulting in high inflation, declining output and a growing trade deficit. In 1974 Nyers was dismissed from the HSWP leadership and the NEM was modified. Between 1979 and 1984 Hungarians suffered a real decline in wages of 10%, and many were forced to seek second and third jobs. The Government then attempted to remedy economic deterioration by negotiating loans from international sources. Servicing the consequent debt became Hungary's central problem from 1978. The increase in alcoholism, petty corruption, crime and suicide at this time was widely considered to be a consequence of the country's economic malaise.

Within the HSWP itself there were growing doubts about the way the Government was managing the economy. By 1986, under pressure from economists and the group of reformers led by Imre Pozsgay, the leadership tacitly accepted that wide-ranging reforms were necessary. A change in the electoral law and the 1985 parliamentary election results, whereby 10% of the seats went to independent (non-HSWP) candidates, were indicators of future events. Political transformation began in earnest in September 1987 when reform of parliament led to freer debate. The first of several revisions of the Constitution also occurred. The power of the Presidential Council to issue ordinances was curtailed and, correspondingly, legislation by parliament suddenly increased. The decisive change, however, came much later when the Government became answerable to parliament for its policies rather than to the HSWP. In order for that to happen the party-state had to be dismantled.

TRANSITION TO LIBERAL DEMOCRACY

There were two critical factors of this transformation. The first was the change in Soviet policy when the reformer Mikhail Gorbachev took over leadership in 1985. It soon became clear that the Soviet authorities would not use force to halt major reforms during a political crisis taking place in the satellites. The second factor was the growth of extra-party movements in the relatively tolerant atmosphere of the Kádár regime and their informal contacts with frustrated reformers inside the Party. The extra-party movement evolved into disparate groups: the 'democratic opposition', comprising formerly Marxist intellectuals from Budapest, which focused on civil rights issues in their independent *samizdat* publications, *Beszélö* and *Hirmondó*; and populists and traditionalists, who addressed national issues such as the low birth rate and the position of Hungarian minorities in neighbouring countries. There were also religious groups and a strong environmental movement, which opposed the construction of a dam on the Danube.

However, the HSWP was not yet ready for the demand for political pluralism that soon appeared. In June 1987 Kádár replaced the long-serving Prime Minister György Lázár with the young 'technocrat' (specialist without party affiliation) Károly Grósz to pursue economic reform without, however, breaking the HSWP's monopoly of power. From late 1986, after Gorbachev had begun the policy of *perestroika* (restructuring), the reform wing of the HSWP became increasingly forthright in its criticism of government policy. The Patriotic People's Front, hitherto an overarching organization for elections, headed by Pozsgay, sponsored a discussion paper, worked out by experts and entitled 'Change and Reform', which combined economic reform with a move to a multi-party system. Pozsgay attended the second populist conference at Lakitelek in September 1987. Under his protection, populists and Christian-national groups established the Hungarian Democratic Forum (HDF), which later became a political party. The democratic opposition (or the 'urbanists') likewise became formally organized in early 1988 and later took the name of the Alliance of Free Democrats (AFD). The Fidesz, or the Federation of Young Democrats (FYD), was formed in April by law students who tried to bridge the divide between the 'populists' and the 'urbanists', although initially they were much closer to the latter group.

In May 1988, under pressure from the reform HSWP, with strong encouragement from the USSR and the organized opposition, a newly elected Central Committee of the HSWP dismissed most of the Politbureau. Kádár was ousted as General Secretary and given instead the new honorary title of 'President'. Grósz succeeded him as party leader. The reformers continued to install their supporters in the HSWP and in the ministries, and in November Grósz was replaced as premier by a leading reformer, Miklós Németh. Once established, the new Government sought to introduce constitutional reform. Ten parliamentary committees, dominated by reformers, were created, with instructions to prepare legislation permitting freedom of association and assembly, the establishment of an independent judiciary and the nomination of parliamentary deputies by non-party organizations. At the same time, an historical commission was established to investigate and report on the uprising of 1956. There was a relaxation of censorship laws; parties and independent trade unions with the right to strike were allowed to be formed. In addition, the Government accepted liberty of conscience as an individual right and introduced a liberal law on Church-State relations.

In 1989 the political landscape changed dramatically. In February the HSWP's historical commission published its report, which concluded that in 1956 a popular uprising (*népfelkelés*), rather than a counter-revolution, had taken place. Imre Nagy was rehabilitated by the HSWP in May; his reburial on 16 June, along with four associates, in the Rákoskeresztúr cemetery was attended by 300,000 people. In the same month, the party's Central Committee agreed to support the transition to a multi-party democracy. Nevertheless, at this stage both the membership and the reforming leadership believed that the HSWP would survive as the dominant force in Hungarian politics. Neither side of the opposition was, however, prepared to make that compromise. Agreement became politically possible when the Pozsgay-led reform communists abandoned the HSWP's claim to a 'leading role' and were prepared to compete for political power on equal terms with the opponents of the Communist system. The mechanism for the process of reform was the 'Oppositional Round Table Conference', which worked out the proposals on the basis of common consent in mid-1989. Without this, the opposition could not have compelled the Government to accept the more radical reforms in the so-called 'triangular negotiations', held from June to September between representatives of the Government, which was no longer under party control, social organizations (still largely communist) and opposition groups.

The outcome of these negotiations was the legislative enactment of a new political system. Hungary ceased to be a People's Republic and the red star was removed from public buildings. Formally, the new laws revised the 1949 Constitution, although in actual fact on 23 October 1989, the anniversary of the revolution of 1956, a new Constitution was enacted and the country became a republic. A President was to replace the Presidential Council and the authority of parliament, which passed 58 laws in 1989, was restored. The Constitutional Court became fundamental to Hungary's new liberal democratic system. It maintained the constitutionality, albeit in relative discomfit, of the Government, the President and parliament. The 'judicial activism' of the court (praised by liberal jurists abroad) under the presidency of László Sólyom turned this institution into the guardian of the 'invisible constitution'. Its rulings were accepted and respected by the other institutions.

In November 1989 the two large opposition parties, the HDF and the AFD, found themselves in disagreement over the election of the President. A referendum showed majority support against a directly elected President (had the result been reversed, Pozsgay would have certainly secured the position). The President was later elected by the new parliament. In preparation for the first free elections after 45 years, the HSWP, anxious to display its democratic credentials, renamed the party as the Hungarian Socialist Party (HSP). It dissolved the Workers' Militia and promised to return party property and assets to the state, but the popularity of the reform communists was on the wane.

THE ANTALL COALITION GOVERNMENT

In preparation for the first free election in 45 years, in late 1989 the two principal contenders for power out of some 50 groupings were the AFD and the HDF. The programmes of most parties were broadly similar. They espoused the principles of genuine multi-party democracy, the restoration of a market economy and a 'return to Europe'. The AFD laid greater stress, however, on individual rights and endorsed a programme of rapid transition to a market economy. By contrast, the HDF espoused a more gradualist approach to the economy and emphasized national values. It ceased to be an overarching movement for disparate groups and became a conservative, Christian party. The Christian Democratic People's Party (CDPP) and the Independent Smallholders' Party (ISP) both broadly shared the same political outlook as the HDF. The AFD, conversely, established close links with the FYD.

Parliamentary elections were held on 25 March 1990. A second round of voting took place on 8 April in those constituencies where no candidate had won an overall majority. Out of 386 seats in the new National Assembly, 176 were filled by direct elections in constituencies and 152 from 20 regional party lists. The remaining 58 seats were allocated to parties in accordance with a procedure designed to compensate for the inequities of the 'first-past-the-post' system used in the constituencies. The HDF obtained 165 parliamentary seats, the AFD 92, the ISP 43, the HSP 33 and the FYD and CDPP 21 each. Eleven independent and joint-party candidates were also elected.

The strength of the HDF vote allowed it to form a ruling coalition with the ISP and the CDPP. This conservative coalition controlled 229 seats in the parliament, giving it a comfortable working majority as far as ordinary legislation was concerned. The new coalition Government was sworn in on 23 May 1990, under the premiership of József Antall, an historian who had been imprisoned for re-establishing the ISP during the 1956 revolution, and who inherited from his father, a high civil servant of the *ancien regime*, an unusually strong sense of public duty. The foreign minister was Géza Jeszenszky, another historian, who had excellent connections in the USA and United Kingdom. Of the 16 other cabinet posts, four were given to the ISP, one to the CDPP and three to technocrats. Unprecedented in the region, Hungary's new Government contained no former communist.

A two-thirds' majority in the National Assembly was required to make any constitutional changes, or to approve the budget or even some primary legislation. On forming a Government, Antall reached agreement with the opposition to reduce the remit of the 'two-thirds' rule in order that his coalition's legislative programme would not be impeded. In return, the Government agreed to support the opposition's presidential candidate. In August 1990 Árpád Göncz, a leading AFD writer who had been imprisoned following the 1956 revolution, was elected by parliament to be President for a five-year term. He was duly re-elected for a second term in 1995.

The most urgent task facing the new Government was to transform the command economy into a 'social market' system based on private ownership and enterprise. Prime Minister Antall initially hoped that the transition could be accomplished at reasonable speed and without serious disruption to the social fabric of the country. Living standards in Hungary were falling, but were still better than in most other former Soviet satellites. However, with hindsight the two aims, rapid transformation and social stability, were incompatible. In May 1990 Hungary had the highest per-head foreign debt in Europe, its budgetary deficit and trade imbalance were growing, inflation was running at 30% and one-third of the population already lived under subsistence level. The Government preferred social stability to rapid economic change. The pace of privatization was reduced so as to forestall strikes and a worsening of unemployment, with the administration retaining a strongly *dirigiste* approach towards the economy. Although this gradualist policy was rewarded with high levels of foreign direct investment, deterioration of the current-account and budget deficits, and continuing evidence of economic stagnation, obliged a change of course in 1993.

Following the appointment of Iván Szabó as finance minister at the beginning of 1993, a new round of privatization commenced. The forint was devalued and a strict monetarist course was adopted by the National Bank of Hungary, which seriously reduced the education and social welfare budgets. Although this remedy won the approval of Hungary's international creditors and led to a return to real growth in gross domestic product (GDP) by 1994, the social costs were severe. High interest rates, unemployment amounting to 12% of the work-force, and the conspicuous consumption of the new class of entrepreneurs engendered popular anxiety and dissatisfaction. A survey published at the beginning of 1994 showed that one-half of the population believed that life had been better under the communists' rule. On the positive side, social and political stability were preserved and for years Hungary attracted one-half of all foreign investment in the region (although a Government that was seen as handing over a large part of the country's 'assets' to foreign capitalists was not popular).

Although not successful in turning the economy around, the Antall Government gained popularity by pursuing a foreign policy that was firmly pro-European. Its aim was to attract Western investment and to speed Hungary's accession to the European Community (EC, known as the European Union—EU from November 1993). In October 1990 Hungary became a member of the Council of Europe and in December 1991 an associate member of the EC. This realignment followed the collapse of the economic and military organizations of the former Soviet bloc and the withdrawal of Soviet troops from

Hungary by mid-1991. The Government signed military and economic co-operation agreements with most of its immediate neighbours, including Romania and Ukraine. Hungary, along with Poland and Czechoslovakia (now the Czech and Slovak Republics), was a founder member of the 'Visegrad Group', which was dedicated to democratic reform and economic co-operation leading to a free-trade zone.

Hungary had conflicts with its neighbours over their Hungarian minorities. The Trianon Treaty (which transferred one-third of Hungarians to other states) was still seen by most Hungarians as a national catastrophe. Since the Second World War, Hungary consistently renounced its earlier policy of demanding frontier revisions. However, there was considerable public disquiet concerning the fate of Hungarian minorities remaining in Slovakia and the regions of Transylvania (Romania) and Vojvodina (Federal Republic of Yugoslavia—FRY, now Serbia and Montenegro). The Hungarian public expected the Government to assist the minorities in securing their cultural rights and self-government. After the anti-Hungarian pogrom in Turgu Mureş, Romania, in March 1990, relations between the two countries faltered, but subsequently improved. Hungary's relations with Croatia and Slovenia remained amicable. Hungarian-Slovakian relations temporarily deteriorated during the premiership of Vladimír Mečiar and relations with Ukraine improved after the two countries signed a state treaty in 1993. Relations with the FRY, however, were tense following the outbreak of civil war in Yugoslavia in 1991.

Prime Minister Antall's party was fraught with problems. His liberal conservative policies were challenged by István Csurka, one of six 'deputy leaders', in a controversial populist manifesto in August 1992. Csurka even demanded the resignation of Antall (who was suffering from Hodgkins disease). Fearful of dividing the party, the HDF leadership was slow to repudiate Csurka. Csurka subsequently formed a right-wing faction and was eventually expelled from the party in June 1993, whereupon he established his own party, the Hungarian Justice and Life Party (HJLP). On 12 December Antall died, leaving behind a firmly established liberal democratic system based on the rule of law. Péter Boros, the interior minister, succeeded Antall as Prime Minister. Since he had only recently joined the HDF, the offices of Prime Minister and Chairman of the party were separated, thereby weakening the party organization in the period preceding the 1994 election.

Factionalism was not limited to the leading party in Government. Its coalition partners, the CDPP and ISP, also demonstrated debilitating rifts between moderates and radicals. The opposition AFD suffered divisions quite early on and the FYD lost much support, after having held a leading place in the opinion polls for much of 1993. These internal rifts were beneficial to the HSP, which was cautiously biding its time for the elections, to be held in May 1994.

THE RISE OF THE SOCIALISTS

As in most other countries of the region, the socialists in Hungary benefited from the mistakes of their opponents, as well as from the unavoidable miseries that the economic transition inflicted on the population. In its 1994 election campaign the HSP skilfully exploited popular discontent and nostalgia for the communist past and, to begin with, promised an immediate rise in living standards for almost all sections of the population. Rapidly, however, its campaign was taken over by economists, notably László Békési, Minister of Finance in the Németh Government, who committed the party to the continued expansion of the private sector and to the principles of the market economy. The party's 'traditional left' was kept firmly in the background. Even the leaders' communist past was used to its advantage: by emphasizing its expertise and experience in Government, the HSP drew attention to the lack of experience of the HDF. Indeed, the issue that dominated the election campaign in 1994 was the competence of the incumbent Government. The HSP succeeded in presenting itself as a party of pragmatists; according to the party's leader, Gyula Horn, a former communist foreign minister, the popularity of the HSP rested on the fact that it was free from 'ideological limitations'.

The HDF and its partners led a lacklustre campaign from the beginning of 1994. Instead of confronting the HSP on policy issues, they emphasized their Christian national outlook and their European policy. This did not appeal to an electorate whose living standards had been deteriorating for years. In addition, they drew repeated attention to the communist background of their opponents. Horn's role in the militia after the revolution of 1956 was subjected to prolonged criticism. Nevertheless, the coalition campaign was tainted with allegations of corruption. Furthermore, the HDF-led Government's decision to dismiss radio and state TV chiefs, after accusing them of anti-Government bias, prompted criticism and resulted in the failure to secure parliamentary approval of their successors' appointments. The 'media war' intensified after the Government authorized the dismissal of a large number of media journalists.

The general election of May 1994 resulted in a spectacular victory for the HSP. With 209 out of 386 parliamentary seats, it obtained an outright majority. The HDF's parliamentary representation fell from 165 seats to 37, the AFD's from 92 to 70, and the ISP's (renamed the Independent Smallholders' and Peasants' Party—ISPP) from 43 to 26. The FYD retained 20 seats. The results reflected the superiority of the HSP's campaign and, to a greater extent, its extensive party organization in the country. The size of the HSP's victory was influenced by the electoral system, which, by its complicated method of allocating votes to seats, exaggerated the margin of success.

THE HORN COALITION GOVERNMENT

Gyula Horn, a cautious leader, notwithstanding the overall socialist parliamentary majority, invited the AFD, the second largest party in parliament, to form a left-of-centre coalition Government with the HSP, which assumed office in June 1994. In exchange for its support, the AFD secured three cabinet posts, including that of Deputy Prime Minister, a position filled by Gábor Kuncze. The pact enabled Horn to strengthen the moderate faction against the HSP's 'traditionalists'. Nevertheless, the new Government stalled the privatization programme and allowed the budgetary deficit to grow, an example of profligacy endemic in any government in Hungary. The Minister of Finance, László Békesi, was overruled by the cabinet on austerity measures and resigned in January 1995. His successor, Lajos Bokros, was forced to reduce welfare benefits, limit wage increases in the still-large public sector, drastically increase utility charges and progressively devalue the forint. Bokros' remedies were applauded by the IMF, but dismayed the population, as well as the left-wingers of the HSP. The Government's resolve to carry out the reforms weakened and Bokros also resigned. He was succeeded, in February 1996, by Péter Medgyessy, who had a greater reputation for compromise and consensus-seeking.

The Horn coalition gained from the opposition's disarray following its electoral defeat. József Torgyán's opposition ISPP benefited from the unpopularity of the Government; opinion polls reflected the substantial appeal of their populist rhetoric. However, the rest of the opposition was reluctant to co-operate with Torgyán. The HDF, in order to compete with the ISPP, moved to the right. In March 1996, after much internal wrangling, the HDF finally divided into a right-wing party and a moderate, conservative party, known as the Hungarian Democratic People's Party (HDPP). The FYD

renamed itself the Federation of Young Democrats—Hungarian Civic Party (FYD—HCP) and, under Viktor Orbán's leadership, gradually moved from the centre-left to the centre-right, without as yet having an impact on the public.

The HSP-led Government continued the foreign policy of its predecessor. Foreign minister László Kovács worked towards Hungary's early admission into the EU and the North Atlantic Treaty Organization (NATO). In March 1996 Hungary was granted full membership of the Organisation for Economic Co-operation and Development (OECD). The opening of US and NATO bases in southern Hungary in 1996, to enforce the peace settlement in the former Yugoslavia, gave Hungary the benefits of NATO security without the costs of formal membership. In July 1997 Hungary was invited to enter into discussions regarding its application for membership of NATO, and in November the country's accession was approved by 85% of votes cast in a national referendum. Negotiations with the EU officials over Hungary's membership began in March 1998. The Government was very cooperative in the removal of obstacles in order to ensure early entry.

Like its predecessors, the Government's policy towards Hungary's neighbours created conflicts and accommodation. Although a bilateral treaty with Slovakia was signed in March 1995, its ratification was delayed on account of differing interpretations of its provisions for the protection of national minorities. Nevertheless, the treaty came into effect in May 1996. Relations with Slovakia were further strained in September 1997 when premier Horn rejected Slovak Prime Minister Vladimír Mečiar's 'repatriation programme' for the two countries' ethnic communities. Hungarian-Romanian relations suffered over Romanian legislation concerning minorities. A treaty was agreed between the two countries in September 1996, guaranteeing the inviolability of the joint border and the rights of ethnic minorities. The Hungarian opposition, however, criticized the treaty for its failure to secure Hungarian autonomy. Military agreements between the two countries in February 1997 and in 1998 helped to consolidate relations, a crucial development as both countries aspired to membership of the EU.

The Horn-led coalition disappointed the public. Privatization and structural reforms (in banking for instance) eventually produced signs of economic improvement, but did not benefit enough people. Moreover, the privatization produced more than one corruption scandal. The most notorious of these led to the dismissal of the minister for privatization, Tamás Suchman, as well as the board of the Hungarian Privatization and State Holdings Company (ÁPV Rt) in late 1996. In early 1997 a parliamentary committee found the Government responsible for the irregularities in ÁPV Rt's finances. Horn was personally embarrassed by the findings of another committee in September. An investigation into the past of senior politicians revealed that he had served with a paramilitary force that restored communist power following the 1956 revolution. Horn rejected the committee's demands that he should resign the premiership. Meanwhile, the centre-right opposition parties began to co-operate and Viktor Orbán, the young and dynamic leader of the FYD—HCP, emerged as the dominant personality among the opposition forces.

THE ORBÁN COALITION GOVERNMENT

In May 1998, for the third time since 1989, the electorate voted in an entirely new political regime. In the first round of the general election on 10 May, the HSP obtained some 32% of the votes cast, compared with the FYD—HCP, which secured 28% of the votes cast. In the second round of voting, however, on 24 May, the FYD—HCP obtained 38% of the aggregate vote and became, by a narrow margin, the largest party in the

National Assembly, with 147 seats (out of 386). The HSP won 134 seats, the ISPP 48, the AFD 24, the HDF 18 and the HJLP 14 seats. In June Orbán's FYD—HCP formed a coalition Government with the Torgyán-led ISPP and the HDF. János Martonyi became foreign minister and Torgyán accepted the agriculture portfolio. Orbán pledged that his Government would fight corruption to strengthen law and order, and would continue his predecessors' foreign policy, especially with respect to EU membership. However, it also intended to strengthen existing economic and political relations with Russia.

As with its two predecessors, the Government of Viktor Orbán was assured success in the field of European integration. In March 1999 Hungary became a full member of NATO, together with the Czech Republic and Poland, after Russian objections were overruled. This closed a chapter in Hungary's efforts to attain security in post-communist Europe. Membership, however, incurred obligations to participate in NATO's military action in the FRY in 1999, as well as to modernize Hungary's severely outdated defence force. Furthermore, the embargo on trade with the FRY seriously damaged the Hungarian economy.

Negotiations on Hungary's full EU membership were already under way in mid-1998. Like its socialist predecessor, the new Government hoped that by seeking less assistance and fewer temporary exemptions from EU rules, the EU would, in turn, be flexible. Others in the new coalition criticized the previous Government for yielding too much to the EU's demands and pledged to defend Hungarian interests in the negotiations. In actual fact, agreement had already been reached on many subjects, although some difficult issues had yet to be addressed. Officially, the Government hoped to be ready for EU accession by the end of 2002. Privately, however, the process was expected to last longer, owing to problems among existing EU members. Nevertheless, Hungary was expected to be included in the next round of EU expansion.

Like its predecessors, the new Government encountered regional conflicts over its policy supporting the cultural demands of the Hungarian minorities. The issue in Slovakia centred on the new language law there; furthermore, no settlement had yet been reached between the two countries over the construction of a second dam on the Danube. In Romania, conflict centred on the restoration of the Hungarian University in Cluj. The accidental poisoning of the Tisza and the Danube Rivers by mineral waste from Baia Mare in Romania in February 2000 created a further source of political tension. In the neighbouring Serbian province of Vojvodina, with its large ethnic Hungarian minority, the issue was self-government for the minorities, an aspiration fraught with potential conflict.

The Government was helped by an upturn in the economy, which had already begun under the previous administration. GDP growth reached nearly 5% in 1998 and this high level was subsequently maintained. In March 1999, responding to public demands to combat organized crime, a growing problem throughout the 1990s, the National Assembly passed the new Criminal Code, which established harsher penalties for a large number of crimes. Nevertheless, neither the much-needed law and order measures nor the slow improvement in the economy increased the Government's popularity.

An important source of conflict between the centre-right ruling coalition and the opposition was the antagonism between the central Government and the AFD-controlled municipal government of Budapest, headed by Gábor Demszky, firmly endorsed in office in the October 1998 elections by a 58% majority. The municipal council was angered by the Government's refusal to input the resources necessary to renew the capital's infrastructure and, in particular, its decision to cancel an underground rail project. Orbán and

Demszky even disagreed on where to build the National Theatre. Hungary's young Prime Minister was accused by the opposition parties of pugnacity and of moving closer to the far-right HJLP, led by Csurka. Orbán and his supporters wholly rejected all of these charges. They, in turn, bitterly complained about the media's anti-government bias, an oft-repeated complaint by administrations. In October 1999 President Göncz entreated both sides to return to more civilized dialogue.

On 1 January 2000 Hungary celebrated its millenary. A law commemorated the event, and the crown of St Stephen was solemnly transferred to parliament. The celebration was only a partial success, as not all Hungarians considered the crown as a potent symbol of national identity. In early May all political parties, with the exception of the HJLP, agreed to support Ferenc Mádl, a former minister and well-respected university professor, as the sole candidate in the presidential elections to be held in June. Despite the consensus, however, Mádl failed to secure the requisite two-thirds' majority in the National Assembly ballot. Eventually, in a third round of voting on 6 June, in which only a simple majority was required, Mádl was elected to the presidency. He took office on 4 August. The new President declared that his priorities would be Hungary's entry into the EU and continuing stability in South-Eastern Europe, particularly in the Balkans. However, that it took three parliamentary ballots to elect an unopposed candidate underlined the divisive nature of Hungarian politics.

Protracted disputes about media bias continued between the Government and the opposition, with the former insisting that the media, instead of being dominated by the left, should be politically 'balanced', and the latter retorting that the Government's domination of the media was already overwhelming. There was significant inter-party conflict as well, the issues being personal rather than political. After the 1998 electoral defeat of the HSP, László Kovács, the former Minister of Foreign Affairs, replaced Gyula Horn as leader; Kovács overcame a somewhat desultory leadership challenge from Miklós Németh, the former Prime Minister, at the party Congress in November 2000. Meanwhile, in a major upheaval, Gábor Demszky, the popular Mayor of Budapest, took over the leadership of the AFD from Bálint Magyar in December. Corruption charges against József Torgyán plunged the Independent Smallholders' and Civic Party (ISCP—as the ISPP was known by this time) into protracted crisis, and led to Torgyán's resignation as Minister of Agriculture and Rural Development in February 2001. He was subsequently forced to fight for survival, as the leader of a divided party. However, the crisis in the ISCP did not affect Orbán's centre-right coalition Government, and his party's earlier shift in policy was formally recognized in September 2000 when the FYD—HCP left the world-wide federation of liberal parties, Liberal International, joining the association of conservative and Christian-Democrat parties, the European Democratic Union, in January 2001.

Meanwhile, although poverty remained widespread, and the balance-of-payments situation and the budgetary deficit worsened, the economy showed some signs of improvement; inflation reached single figures in 2000, GDP growth was over 5%, Hungary's international creditworthiness improved, and unemployment had declined, while earnings crept upwards. Moreover, significant progress was made in Hungary's negotiations on EU membership. However, political developments did not match the country's improved economic position and its prospects of early access to full membership of the EU. The vilification of the Government by the opposition, and vice versa, the continuing 'media war' and the feared popularity of Csurka's far-right HJLP kept politics adversarial, and damaged Hungary's international reputation. Conflict also developed between Hungary and two of its neighbours, Romania and Slovakia, when in June 2001 the National Assembly passed a law (with a 92% majority) on Hungarians living in neighbouring countries, which came into force on 1 January 2002.

As was the case in other countries of the region, the Constitution stipulated that Hungary bore some responsibility for the fate of Hungarians living outside its borders, and should, therefore, promote and foster relations. Consequently, Hungary passed a law to implement this constitutional provision. The 'Benefit' Law applied to Hungarians (with nationality defined primarily by personal declaration) living in neighbouring countries, with the exception of Austria. Those who qualified could acquire a 'Certificate of Hungarian Nationality', entitling the holder to economic and cultural benefits. Although Croatia, Slovenia, Ukraine, and the FRY raised no objections to the law, the Governments of Romania and Slovakia lodged complaints at the EU and elsewhere, protesting that the new law served nationalist aims, and Romania asked the EU to determine whether the law was compatible with international law. It emerged from a report issued by the European Commission for Democracy through Law (the Venice Commission) in late October 2001 that the new legislation did not contain any provisions that other states both inside and outside the EU (including Romania and Slovakia) did not provide for their co-nationals. However, the Commission concluded that satisfactory arrangements should be reached between all parties on a bilateral basis.

THE MEDGYESSY COALITION GOVERNMENT

Domestic political activity increased from late 2001, in preparation for the general election due to take place in April 2002. Reflecting the sharp division between left and right, Hungary had moved towards what was, essentially, a two-party system, in which Prime Minister Orbán's FYD—HCP, which formed a conservative coalition with the HDF in September 2001, was challenged by the HSP, led by László Kovács, and its potential ally, the AFD. The incumbent Government based its campaign on its economic achievements, and adopted an uncompromising nationalist stance. Meanwhile, the HSP selected Péter Medgyessy as its candidate for the premiership, and drew attention to the poverty of the elderly and of the underdeveloped regions, while attacking Orbán's perceived arrogance. Following the first round of voting, on 7 April 2002, at which the rate of participation by the electorate was 70% (the highest recorded in Hungary), the HSP unexpectedly established a lead. On a party-list basis the HSP obtained 42.0% of the votes cast, the FYD—HCP secured 41.1% of the votes and the AFD 5.6%. The other parties, including Csurka's far-right HJLP, failed to exceed the 5% threshold required to enter the National Assembly. After the second round of voting, on 21 April, at which the participation rate was 73%, the FYD—HCP-HDF had secured 48.7% of the votes, and a total of 188 seats in the National Assembly. However, the HSP, with 46.1% of the votes and 178 seats, formed a coalition with the AFD (5.2% and 20 seats), as it had in May 1994, to secure an overall majority. The electorate in Budapest and in many of the less-developed eastern regions voted against the incumbent Government, while its main support came from the prosperous western regions; Orbán's principal error had been his failure to attract support from the political centre, the support of which is decisive in a two-party political system. Medgyessy's new, left-wing coalition Government was approved by the National Assembly on 27 May 2002.

The Government consolidated its position at the municipal elections held in October 2002, at which the left won the majority of the votes cast in most counties and towns; Gábor Demszky of the AFD won a fourth term as Mayor of Budapest.

Meanwhile, there was a slow improvement in the country's economic position, with an increase in GDP of over 3% in 2002, which, although lower than in previous years, also helped the Government's prospects. However, a 20% increase in the value of the forint against the common European currency, the euro, reduced Hungary's competitiveness and overspending had steadily augmented the budgetary deficit. Corruption, too, remained a serious problem in Hungary, as in other Central European countries. Despite anti-corruption legislation, the customs services, the health service and the traffic police were among the worst offenders, and there remained a lack of transparency in the financing of political party campaigns and a failure to open certain infrastructure projects to competitive tender.

Public disputes between the Government and the opposition had become wide-ranging. The right wing, in particular former premier Orbán, had failed to learn from its electoral defeat. Rather than re-orientating itself towards the political centre, it adopted a populist position, even in relation to foreign policy, where previously near consensus had existed between the left and right.

The Medgyessy Government was obliged to attempt to renegotiate certain provisions of the Benefit Law (see above) with Romania and Slovakia. Medgyessy, like his predecessor, was able to form a working agreement with Romania, but had more difficulty with the Slovakian Government, which argued that the law was discriminatory and conferred extraterritorial rights on the Hungarian authorities. The Council of Europe considered proposed revisions to the law to be satisfactory, objecting only to the concept of a 'cultural nation', which could be interpreted as implying that Hungary questioned existing borders. Co-operation had consequently faltered among the four 'Visegrad' countries (the Czech Republic, Hungary, Poland and Slovakia), and it was questioned whether the group would retain much relevance following the planned accession of its members to the EU in 2004. None the less, in July 2003 it was reported that a potential solution to the dispute over the Benefit Law had been agreed with the Romanian and Slovakian Governments.

In early 2003 the planned US-led military action to bring about 'regime change' in Iraq (by removing from power President Saddam Hussein) had a significant impact on the Hungarian public, 70% of whom were estimated to be opposed to a war. Prime Minister Medgyessy, however, was one of eight European leaders to sign a statement supporting the US-led coalition in its policy regarding Iraq, consequently attracting criticism from the French President, Jacques Chirac. Nevertheless, Hungary's contribution to the eventual war was extremely limited. At Taszár, in southern Hungary, the USA was training a number of Iraqi volunteers to administer post-war Iraq, and Hungary pledged 300 troops to assist in peace-keeping activities once the main military operation had been completed.

In mid-December 2002, after agreement had been reached with the EU on outstanding matters of contention (in particular, Hungary had negotiated preferential terms on agricultural subsidies for farmers), the country was one of 10 to be formally invited to join the EU in May 2004, at a summit meeting held in Copenhagen, Denmark. On 12 April 2003 Hungary was the first of the former Soviet satellite countries to hold a referendum on membership. Although only 45.6% of the electorate participated in the plebiscite (partly owing to a lack of informative discussion on the issue), nearly 84% of the votes cast were in support of the country's proposed accession; moreover, all the significant political parties, churches and trade unions were in favour of membership. The Treaty of Accession was signed by the Government on 16 April, in Athens, Greece, signalling the fulfillment of a long-term foreign-policy objective.

The Economy

RICHARD ROSS BERRY

INTRODUCTION

The development of the Hungarian economy during the communist period, focusing as it did on the development of heavy industry, paid little attention to the limits imposed by the country's natural assets. Although up to 70% of Hungary's total area of 93,030 sq km (35,919 sq miles) could be used for agricultural purposes, the country possessed few raw materials in any sizeable quantities. Coal reserves, at 4,500m. metric tons, varied in quality and were often difficult to extract. There were deposits of crude petroleum and natural gas, but imports satisfied the vast bulk of demand for these commodities. However, Hungary did possess up to 12% of the world's total reserves of bauxite. There were also quantities of manganese ore and uranium. In general, the country had a low resource base and compensated for this by engaging actively in international trade. In the post-communist era Hungary has encouraged foreign direct investment (FDI) in order to overcome its low resource base and the legacy of the socialist mode of development.

REFORM AND TRANSITION

Hungary was one of the few socialist countries where significant reforms were enacted under the old regime. The use of market mechanisms, in particular, a reduction in the use of planned indicators and the implementation of a more rational price mechanism, was adopted in Hungary in 1968, with the promulgation of the New Economic Mechanism (NEM) under the communist Government of János Kádár. The last communist administration (1987–89) introduced legislation, such as a Companies Act in 1988, which effectively initiated the privatization process. There were also major advances in the creation of a two-tier banking system and in the extension of foreign trade rights.

However, the real changes came in the 1990s with the adoption of a series of measures aimed at instituting a market economy. In the early 1990s Hungary was criticized for not having utilized a 'shock therapy' method of transition—that is, the introduction of a complete set of radical reforms containing the by now classic elements of transition economics: macroeconomic stabilization; control of public finances; extensive new legislation designed to promote the private sector; liberalization of foreign-trade activities; and moves towards currency convertibility. However, all of these elements of the transition process could be found in the various stabilization packages adopted by successive governments. This was achieved despite the poor economic legacy inherited by the new democratic Government.

At the 1990 general election a coalition Government, led by the Hungarian Democratic Forum (HDF), came to power and inherited an economy with high levels of external debt and an antiquated industrial structure. In early 1991 the Government introduced a four-year economic programme based on the acceleration of privatization, controlling inflation and making preparations for the convertibility of the forint. The most important feature of the programme was its target of a minimum 65% contribution of the private sector to gross domestic product (GDP) by 1995. At the time of the programme's initiation, state-controlled or -owned enterprises in Hungary contributed up to 85% of GDP, compared with 15% in most Organisation for Economic Co-operation and Development (OECD) countries. The programme also involved moves towards limited or internal convertibility designed to promote

FDI and to use the exchange rate as an anchor for the domestic economy. This 'Stabilization and Convertibility Plan' long survived its author, the independent finance minister, Mihály Kupa. Indeed, the success of the programme, and its consequent social effects, probably contributed to the political fortunes of finance ministers (seven in 1990–98) and governments (four in the same period) in Hungary.

Under the coalition Government of 1990–94 real GDP fell by 17% and unemployment rose from nil to 12%. The inflation rate dropped below 20% only once after 1990 and even then it was to a relatively high figure of 18% in 1994. There were serious conflicts within the HDF and between the HDF and its coalition allies, centred on repeated attempts to reduce the state budgetary deficit as a percentage of GDP. These factors ensured that the coalition Government was not likely to survive a further election. By the time of the 1994 general election the Government had implemented legislation designed radically to transform the Hungarian economy, although the social consequences of transition placed it in a vulnerable position. However, the implementation of new market-orientated business legislation, including the establishment of a stock exchange and new securities and investment legislation, greatly contributed to the creation of a new market economy.

The general election of 1994 produced a victory for the Hungarian Socialist Party (HSP), which formed a coalition Government with the Alliance of Free Democrats (AFD), even though the socialists had won an overall majority. The HSP's election campaign had guaranteed social provision for those worst affected by the economic transition and promised measures to combat unemployment and to promote economic growth. It was necessary for the HSP Government to continue redefining the role of the state within a market framework. Controlling the budget deficit has been one of the most difficult tasks for any Hungarian government and election commitments either to maintain or increase public spending have been one of the key features of economic policy since the collapse of the old regime. Early in 1995 the socialist-led administration encountered a financial crisis, which led to the introduction of a harsh new stabilization programme, the main aim of which was to reduce overall government expenditure. This led to a reduction in state-based employment, an increase in social-insurance contributions and reduced expenditure on health care. Means-testing was introduced to determine eligibility for social benefits. In addition, in a bid to resolve the external crisis, the forint was devalued by 9% and an import surcharge of 8% was introduced for a short period.

Although the stabilization programme succeeded in reducing both state and internal debt, progress was at the expense of improvements in the standard of living and in real wages. Undoubtedly, the measures contributed greatly to the defeat of the Government in the 1998 legislative elections. The Federation of Young Democrats—Hungarian Civic Party (FYD—HCP) won 147 seats in the election and signed a coalition agreement with the Independent Smallholders' and Peasants' Party (ISPP) and the HDF. However, the change of government did not signal a major shift in economic policy. The new Government still had to become accustomed to controlling state expenditure and addressing complex issues such as health care and the costs of the state pension fund. Moreover, the nature of the coalition, in which the agrarian party shared power, gave rise to quarrels over expenditure on agriculture and on rural areas.

The election of a new socialist administration in 2002 was preceded by campaign commitments to increase public-sector salaries and welfare spending, although the methods for achieving this were not explained. These policies, introduced as part of the new Government's policy of change and improvement within 100 days, were likely to increase the budgetary deficit to between 5.5% and 6.0% of GDP. The second such '100 days' programme, which provided support for agricultural debt, regional development and social security, was likely to increase the 2003 deficit to almost 8% of GDP. Thus, the Government's target of a budgetary deficit of no more than 3% of GDP by 2006 appeared optimistic, and had the potential to cause problems in its relationship with the European Union (EU—see below), which was attempting to obtain assurances from the new coalition members that they would limit fiscal expenditure, in order to control budgetary deficits. However, the Government's strategy was evidently popular with the electorate, as its election by a narrow margin in the legislative election of April 2002 was followed by overwhelming support in the municipal elections of October.

The adoption of market-based measures initially resulted in massive declines in GDP, but from the mid-1990s GDP began to increase. Growth reached 4.6% in 1996, and was estimated at 4.4% in 1997 and at 4.6% in 1998. A figure of 4.5% was recorded in 1999, with an increase to 5.2% in 2000. A lower growth rate, of 3.8%, in 2001 was followed by a figure of 3.2% in 2002, and a predicted figure of, at best, 4.2% in 2003. Growth was fuelled by public and private consumption, and there were fears that government subsidies could lead to a rise in inflation, forcing the National Bank of Hungary into an even more restricted monetary position. The problem with estimating growth was compounded by slow growth in the international economy: the rate of real GDP growth in the EU amounted to only 0.9% in 2002, and was likely to be no more than 1.7% in 2003. Germany, which accounts for over one-third of Hungarian exports, was likely to experience even lower rates of growth in the subsequent two years, which would have further impact on the small Hungarian economy.

For most of the 1990s the annual rate of inflation reached over 25%. This rate subsequently improved, however, and in 1997 the rate of annual inflation was 18.3%, declining to 14.3% in 1998 and to 10.0% in 1999. Government predictions of reducing the annual rate of inflation to 5% proved unfounded; high petroleum and food prices in 2000 resulted in an annual inflation rate of 9.8%. Inflation was 9.2% in 2001, partly owing to public-sector wage increases, up 21% in nominal terms in that year. This high figure stemmed from the reluctance of all political parties to address the issue of public-sector pay prior to the general election of April 2002. In addition, increases in the minimum wage and additional government spending were expected to fuel further inflation. The rate was 5.5% in 2002, and a rate of 4.5% was expected in 2003. Much depended on the Government's stated plans to tackle the budgetary deficit in the following two to three years.

By 2001 there were strong positive tendencies, as the success of the services sector, including telecommunications, banking and tourism, had reorientated Hungary from its former dependency on industry, towards a more modern outlook, matching the pattern of many OECD countries. In 2001 industry, including construction, although still important, accounted for only 33.4% of GDP, compared with some 45% in 1990. Growth in the services sector, notably in transport, communications, and hotels and catering, overtook that of industry. Industrial production increased by 4.1% in 2001, although the rate of growth declined to approximately 2% in 2002, and was not expected to increase substantially in 2003.

The construction industry recorded higher growth rates in 2002, largely owing to publicly funded projects, but this was unlikely to be sustainable in the long term. Growth in the services sector was likely to remain steady at 3.5%–4.0%. One of the more notable features of Hungarian business was the fact that the 100 most successful companies accounted for some 85% of GDP: Magyar Olaj és Gázipari Rt (MOL—the Hungarian Oil and Gas Company) was at the top of this list, closely followed by the Matáv Hungarian Telecommunications Company. Electronics firms, together with machine-manufacturing and pharmaceuticals, dominated the remainder of the largest enterprises on the list.

For much of the 1990s growth was fuelled by the performance of multinational companies; these accounted for 40% of industrial production and 20% of employment, and generated two-thirds of exports. Moreover, many domestic companies were dependent on trade with these companies. In an attempt to increase the performance of domestic companies, the FYD—HCP-led Government introduced the so-called Széchenyi plan in 2000. This plan targeted several priority areas for economic expansion: small businesses; road construction; housing; regional development; tourism; and research and development. The broad aim was to utilize existing resources—only 50,000m. forint of additional spending had been allocated in funds. Many of the provisions in the plan were subsequently supplemented by the new Government's expenditure plans; moreover, regional development is an important component of the relationship with the EU (see below).

GOVERNMENT FINANCES

In the 1990s, in common with other Central and Eastern European countries, there was a radical transformation in the ownership base of the Hungarian economy. Privatization and the growth of new small and medium-sized businesses brought about a transition from state to private ownership. The economic role of the state was, by 2000, largely confined to regulation through monetary and fiscal policy. This change in the state's economic role was exemplified by the new relationship between the Government and the central bank. During the communist period, despite some changes in commercial bank legislation, the National Bank of Hungary remained the Government's bank, printing money to fuel the burgeoning public-sector deficit. By the late 1990s it was, effectively, independent, with government borrowing strictly limited, under the control of György Surýani, who completed his second and final term as President of the bank in March 2001.

From 1 January 1997 the Government had to pay market rates for borrowing from the central bank. This was accompanied by the selling of state interests in other financial institutions, such as banking and insurance companies, again mostly with the aid of FDI. By 2000 state ownership of the banking system was less than 20%, the lowest in the region. Restrictions in the bankruptcy law of 1998 forced businesses to maintain financial discipline.

As noted, controlling the budgetary deficit has been one of the hardest tasks for the various governments in post-communist Hungary. This factor has been compounded by demographics: Hungary has a population of around 10.2m., of whom some 568,000 are aged at least 75 years. If the fact that some 2m. citizens are aged 60 years or more is taken into account, it can be seen that pension costs represent a significant financial burden. In view of this, and the fact that growth rates have remained consistently below the predicted levels, there is not likely to be any significant reduction in the budgetary deficit for some time to come.

PRIVATIZATION

Successive governments sought to ensure the full privatization of the economy. Hungary rejected the more popular forms of privatization scheme and instead relied mainly on direct sales of state assets. In many respects this process was undertaken by encouraging FDI. The process was more transparent than that in the Czech Republic, Poland and Slovakia. Consequently, Hungary avoided the rise of financial intermediaries and disguised government ownership. The scale of privatization, furthermore, was greater since, from 1995, it included the widespread sale of banking interests, public utilities and telecommunications. In 2000 99% of Hungary's almost 3,000 media outlets were owned privately, with the majority of owners belonging to Western media groups. This contributed greatly to government revenues. Net income from the privatization agencies in 1990–98 amounted to over 1,500,000m. forint. In March 1995 the Government overhauled the mechanisms controlling privatization. The new privatization law resulted in the amalgamation of the State Property Agency and the State Holding Company into the Hungarian Privatization and State Holding Company (ÁPV Rt). At mid-2002 ÁPV Rt retained assets worth some 600,000m. forint. However, with more than 80% of GDP accounted for by privately owned enterprises, Hungary was leading the economies of Central Europe in this respect.

EMPLOYMENT AND UNEMPLOYMENT

Throughout its recent history the Hungarian economy has been characterized by rapid and concentrated industrial development. In 1990 Hungary had almost 6,889 industrial enterprises, 770 of which had a work-force of over 300. The decline in production of large-scale enterprises entailed a reduction in the number of employees, a process exacerbated as the decade progressed by privatization and government austerity. One of the most notable features of the transition was the reduction in importance of this once highly influential sector. By 2001 industry, including construction, accounted for only 34.2% of employment. The economy, instead, was benefiting from the fast-growing international services sector, the most prosperous area of which was telecommunications. Management-consultancy firms were the second fastest-growing services sector. Employment in the services sector increased more rapidly than did industrial employment, and in 2002 the services sector employed 59.6% of the active labour force, and contributed 62.4% of GDP.

In 1999 the average rate of unemployment was 7.0% of the labour force. This figure represented a slight decrease compared with the previous year (7.8%), and a significant improvement compared with the jobless rate of the early 1990s, of about 12%. In 2000 the rate of unemployment declined to 6.4% (262,500), and total employment increased by 1.0%. Further improvements were evident in 2001, when the average rate of unemployment declined to 5.7% (232,900), a figure that increased slightly, to 5.9%, in 2002. Almost 50% of unemployed persons were classified as long-term jobless, that is, unemployed for one year or more; the longer-term unemployed tended to comprise the older section of the work-force; however, there was evidence that school-leavers increased difficulties, as employers feared the costs of making more experienced workers redundant. Hungary faced a shortage of skilled labour, particularly in the newer industries, such as information technology.

The overall unemployment figures masked considerable regional disparities, with the rate of unemployment in the capital, Budapest, falling to 2.6% in 2000, while unemployment rates of over 12% were registered in northern Hungary; central Hungary and Transdanubia accounted for over 50% of GDP. The Government of 1994–98 sought to combat the disparities in unemployment and income between the east and west of the country by establishing the Széchenyi plan on national development (see above), based on a public-private partnership to develop a more modern, technology-based economy in underdeveloped regions. EU figures show that while per-head national income in Budapest was 76% that of the EU, this declined to just 32% in the northern, older industrial regions. One of the more encouraging signs for the Government was the fact that, by the beginning of the 2000s, the number of firms employing 50 people or fewer generated 45% of GDP, and employed 70% of the work-force. Moreover, compared to many OECD countries, credit to the corporate sector, at 27% of GDP, was rather low, indicating that there was room for expansion in that sector. However, this would depend on a reduction in interest rates, which were not expected to decline significantly.

AGRICULTURE

One of the most significant features of the transition was the decline in importance of agriculture as a major employer. In 1998 agriculture (including forestry and fishing) employed about 7.5% of the labour force. By mid-2000 it was estimated that only 3% of Hungarians earned their living directly from the sector, with another 5% working on a part-time basis. The sector contributed only 4.2% of GDP in 2002, and agricultural exports accounted for about 10% of overall export trade in the late 1990s, compared with over 20% in the early 1990s. The privatization of land and the dismantling of the old state and collective system encouraged many foreign investors, particularly in the canning and processing sectors. Despite the fact that successive governments continued to offer producer subsidy equivalent (PSE), these remained well below the levels of support offered to EU farmers as part of that organization's Common Agricultural Policy (CAP). In April 2000 the Government signed an agro-trade agreement with the EU that either reduced or abolished subsidies and tariffs on two-thirds of Hungary's agricultural exports to the EU. Although the question of agriculture was likely to continue to cause difficulties in relations with the EU, this agreement was a positive development. A drought in the summer of 2000, and severe flooding in 2002, had a severe impact on a sector that had shown strong growth in the intervening year. Livestock is particularly important to Hungarian agriculture, accounting for 50% of all output. Despite the disestablishment of collective farms, the predominant form of ownership remained co-operative.

The Central European Free Trade Agreement (CEFTA, created in 1992—see below) aided trade in agricultural products, which increased more rapidly than trade in industrial items. In 1996 CEFTA decided to apply a 'zero' tariff rate to more than one-half of all agricultural products. However, in 1999 serious trade disputes arose within CEFTA between Hungary and Poland with respect to agricultural trade. This led to the withdrawal of preferential trade measures and the imposition of tariffs. The Budapest summit of October 1999 went some way to resolving this disagreement, but the dispute was an indication of the sensitive nature of trade in this area, and was also an area of considerable tension with the EU. The debate over agriculture has tended to ebb and flow depending on the political climate: the ISPP, later the Independent Smallholders' and Civic Party (ISCP), which formed part of the 1990–94 and 1994–98 Governments was no longer in power, but support for the sector continued to form part of the new Government's programme. Moreover, the role of agriculture was an integral part of accession negotiations with the EU and the complex future of the CAP.

FOREIGN TRADE

The collapse of the communist trading system—the Council for Mutual Economic Assistance (CMEA or Comecon)—in 1990 necessitated a change in trade policy. New legislation guaranteed extensive trading rights to economic agents and the resultant measures ensured an end to the complex system of state regulation and licensing. For its part, the European Community (EC)/EU extended the Generalized System of Preferences (GSP—the preferential treatment granted to some exports of certain non-member states) to the countries of the region, which allowed increased market access for goods from these countries. Hungary had the most open and transparent trade regime in the region. With more than 90% of exports liberalized, the Government had not resorted to currency manipulation and tariff barriers. In the 1990s the most important development in Hungary's external economic relations was its westward reorientation.

The reorientation of Hungarian foreign trade was made possible by the signing, in December 1991, of an Association Agreement with the EC. Czechoslovakia and Poland signed similar agreements at the same time. In early 1998 Hungary entered into negotiations with the EU with the aim of eventual membership, although the process proved difficult and lengthy. Hungary's Association Agreement with the EU was concluded on an asymmetrical basis: the EU agreed to reduce barriers to trade with Hungary at a greater rate than that initially demanded by EU countries. Despite the asymmetrical nature of the Association Agreements, all of the transition countries continued to record a deficit in external trade, particularly with the countries of the EU. This called into question the possibility of early entry into the organization. Nevertheless, the EU rated Hungary highly in four important areas: the creation of a functioning market economy; the ability to withstand EU competition; legal reform; and reform of the administrative and judicial systems. By the end of 2002 Hungary had closed 26 of the 29 negotiable chapters of the *acquis communautaire* (the body of EU legislation and treaties). The remaining chapters focused on competition, the budget and institutions. The competition chapter remained particularly contentious as it would affect Hungary's generous provisions for corporate investors. The budgetary chapter centred on the CAP and the acceptance of spending limits on structural funds for new members (limited to €23,000m. per year for 2004–06). This meant substantially less funds than were made available to Ireland, Greece or Spain on their accession. In addition, the fact that the amendment of the CAP was subject to a 10-year induction period angered Hungarian farmers (see below). Despite FYD—HCP objections to the financial provisions of EU membership, on 12 April 2003 the Hungarian electorate voted to accept the terms of accession. Over 83% of the votes were cast in favour of EU membership, albeit with a rate of participation of just 48% (unlike the situation in Poland, there was no requirement that the rate of participation be over 50%). Hungary, together with nine other accession states, was expected to join the EU on 1 May 2004.

The most contentious trade issues between Central European countries and the EU were those of increased provision for market access for textiles and agricultural products. Despite attempts to reform the CAP, the system was not conducive to greater market access from the countries of Central Europe. In 2001 the EU proposed that new members be made liable to a 10-year transition period, prior to becoming eligible for support under the CAP scheme. In the mean time, after admission to the EU, farmers were to receive annual funding equivalent to 25% of the full CAP subsidy. It was further proposed that new members be made to wait for a period of at least three years before being awarded regional funding; this provoked widespread outrage in the region.

In December 1992 CEFTA was created by the countries of the so-called Visegrad Group (comprising the Czech Republic, Hungary, Poland and Slovakia), and the Agreement came into effect in March 1993. The main objective was the establishment of a free-trade area in the region by 1 January 2001. Industrial goods were subject to the reduction of barriers, beginning with a 10% reduction in January 1995, followed by subsequent reductions of 15% annually until 2001. There was to be a 20%–50% reduction in tariff barriers on agricultural produce in 1993–98. The initial results of CEFTA showed an increase in intra-regional trade, which had declined to 4%–5% of total trade in 1990, after the introduction of hard-currency payments. However, trade between members rarely exceeded 7% of the overall external trade of any one country. Slovenia, Romania and Bulgaria subsequently joined CEFTA in 1996–98.

In March 1993 the Government signed a free-trade agreement with the European Free Trade Association (EFTA), which came into effect on 1 July. This accelerated the process of trade liberalization within Europe, as did EC measures of that year. By the beginning of 1998 barriers to trade in industrial goods had been removed, although, as noted, questions remained over access for textile goods and agricultural produce.

The main characteristic of Hungarian foreign trade from the mid-1990s was the persistence of a trade deficit, and there was some cause for concern over the increase in consumer imports. In 1997 and 1998 there were deficits on the balance of trade of US $1,962m. and $2,354m., respectively; in 1999 and 2000 the trade deficits amounted to $2,189m. and $1,760m., and there was a deficit of $2,018m. in 2001. The deficit was $2,119m. in 2002.

In 2000 export trade witnessed strong growth, increasing by 17.8% in comparison with 1999, to US $25,747m. However, the value of imports also increased, to $27,506m. In the same year there was a considerable increase in the import of industrial machinery and transport equipment required for restructuring projects, which contributed to the continuing trade deficit. In 1991 this category had accounted for about 30% of total imports; in 2000 such imports accounted for 51.5% of the total. Imports of manufactured goods, according to the Standard Industrial Trade Classification (SITC), accounted for a further 26.4% of imports. By 2002 there were signs of deceleration, as growth in major markets declined and began to affect Hungary, with evidence of an increasing deficit on the current account, which threatened to reach $3,100m. in 2003, and $2,500m. in 2004.

Research carried out in the late 1990s demonstrated that, of the transition economies, Hungary was alone in increasing the share of manufactured goods in its export structure, and machinery and transport equipment and other manufactures accounted for 82.3% of exports in 2000. In 2001 food, beverages and tobacco as well as fuels and electrical energy witnessed strong growth, of some 18%, but in 2002 a downturn negatively affected the fuel and electrical energy sectors. However, continued growth was registered in the export of manufactured goods, which increased by 13%, and in the export of machinery and transport equipment, which increased by 8.8%. It is notable that some 80% of Hungarian exports were produced by companies with a form of foreign involvement. The continued strong growth in machine imports could be interpreted as a sign that the Hungarian economy was continuing to modernize, although there were complaints that some investors were simply using Hungary as an assembly centre. However, this was countered by the strong growth in the automobile sector, where Audi (Germany), Ford (USA), General Motors-Opel (USA/Germany) and Suzuki (Japan) made major investments, totalling US $1,400m. There was considerable controversy over the export of goods from free-trade zones, which granted companies exemptions from customs duties and indirect taxes. Such exports accounted for some 44% of total exports. Despite the fact that Hungary was one of the most open economies in the region—there was tariff harmonization with the EU in industrial goods—these benefits were likely to come under increasing challenge from the Union. This issue had also arisen with respect to agricultural subsidies, which led to Hungary's withdrawal from the 'Cairns group' of agricultural exporting countries. The situation was resolved by the intervention of the World Trade Organization, which brokered a deal to allow subsidies to be retained. However, given the disputes over the CAP this was an issue over which it would be difficult to reach a final agreement.

In 2001 total trade with the countries of the EU accounted for 74.3% of exports and 57.8% of imports. Although there was a decline in imports from the EU in that year, it was compensated by increases from other areas, most notably with respect to petroleum and gas imports from Russia. Italy overtook Austria to become Hungary's second largest source of imports in 2001, providing 7.9% in that year, compared with the 7.4% of imports provided by Austria. However, these figures were small compared with trade with Germany, which accounted for 35.6% of exports and 24.9% of imports in 2001. Hungary remained vulnerable to a downturn in EU growth rates: reduced rates of growth across the EU would adversely affect the domestic economy. As mentioned above, in 2002 the EU registered growth of only 0.9%, and this was expected to rise to a mere 1.7% in 2003.

EXCHANGE-RATE POLICY

The introduction of limited convertibility of the national currency was a central feature of Hungary's initial reform measures of 1990. The forint was made convertible for trade purposes, enabling companies to gain access to foreign capital and foreign investors to convert their locally made profits into hard currency (that is, internationally traded currencies). The exchange rate was determined against a 'basket' of currencies, and was adjusted at intervals by the National Bank. However, the continuing high rates of inflation meant that periodic devaluation was not sufficient to compensate, resulting in an over-valued currency. Following the 1994 general election, the new HSP Government changed the exchange-rate regime from a 'pegged' system, with periodic devaluation, to a 'crawling-peg' system, with a possible devaluation rate of 1.95% per month. In January 1996 the forint became convertible for current financial transactions: Hungarian citizens could, thereafter, use forint bank cards and savings deposits. This was clearly part of the attempt to follow the example of the Czech Republic and join the OECD—to which Hungary was granted membership in March. Following the introduction of a new exchange-rate regime in 1995, Hungary at last established an effective mechanism for linking the domestic to the international economy, taking into account the higher rates of domestic inflation. From January 2000 the forint's exchange rate was determined against the common European currency, the euro. The Government subsequently introduced an exchange-rate system based on periodic intervention by the National Bank. The exchange-rate bands on either side of the euro rose from 2.25% to 15.0%. In effect, this meant that the currency was appreciating, but the government view was that, in the longer term, such a system would help to control inflation (imports would become more expensive, affecting consumer demand). In the early 2000s the Hungarian National Bank pursued a cautious monetary policy, which in effect meant that the forint remained at the high end of the exchange-rate band. The reduction in capital inflows and the widening of the current-account deficit meant that the forint was expected to appreciate, in nominal terms, by 4% in 2003

and by 3% in 2004. In 2002 the reduction in investment income resulted in substantial net outflows, and led the Government to undertake a new Eurobond issue, of US $200m., in early 2003. Hungary planned to join the 'euro zone' by 2008, but this would depend on adhering to targets pertaining to interest rates and the budgetary deficit. The main objective was to avoid entering the new monetary system fixed at too high a rate.

FOREIGN DEBT

In 1990 Hungary had the highest level of debt per head in the region. Total foreign debt in that year amounted to some US $23,000m., a figure, which, owing to interest payments, rose thereafter. By the end of 1995 the country's gross foreign debt, mostly contracted under the communist regime, stood at an estimated $31,248m., and the cost of debt-servicing was equivalent to 39.1% of the value of exports of goods and services. The prompt repayment of external commitments and the additional payments made in the second half of the 1990s meant that by the end of 2000 Hungary's total foreign debt had decreased to $29,415m., of which $14,251m. was long-term public debt; the cost of debt-servicing was equivalent to 24.4% of the value of exports. By 2001 the debt burden amounted to $30,289m., and annual repayments were equivalent to 37.2% of export earnings. However, as the economy grew, the ratio of debt to GDP declined. Servicing the debt will have to come from increased growth in the domestic economy as the strategy of using dwindling privatization receipts comes to an end. Further funds may be available from foreign investment.

FOREIGN INVESTMENT

Hungary sought to accelerate its development by encouraging foreign investment. Considerable tax incentives were available for potential investors, including 130 customs-free zones. FDI amounted to US $20,000m. in 2000, putting Hungary in first place in terms of per-head figures in the region (although Poland's FDI total was higher, at some $30,000m., that country is four times the size of Hungary). In March 2000 the US telecommunications company Motorola announced plans to invest in Hungary and, at the end of May, the Republic of China (Taiwan) declared its intention to invest a further $8m. In June the Japanese car-part manufacturer Musashi Seimitsu Industry announced its decision to provide funds of $20m. for a 'greenfield' project at Ercsi, south of Budapest. According to the Ministry of Economic Affairs, total FDI exceeded $21,000m.; total FDI in Central Europe amounted to $130,000m. To put the figures into perspective, the entire region accounted for only 3% of total world investment. EU investors accounted for 60% of total investment (Germany, Austria and the Netherlands were the biggest investor countries), with the USA accounting for 16%. FDI in Hungary was equivalent to one-third of GDP, compared to 26% in the Czech Republic and 15% in Poland.

Much of this FDI was targeted at the customs-free zones promoted by the Government: more than 100 companies based their operations in these areas. These zones accounted for 43% of all Hungarian exports in 2000, and with regard to machinery and equipment, this percentage rose to over 90%. Hungary's 10 most successful exporters operated in eight industrial customs-free zones: these 10 alone accounted for 30% of all Hungarian exports. Some 58% of the industrial customs-free zones were located in western Hungary, and 17% in Budapest. The Government offered increased subsidies to investors willing to establish operations in the depressed east of the country, in a bid to stimulate regional development and to reduce income disparities. However, the very existence of such zones is a major problem in respect of EU membership, as the EU does not allow such preferential treatment.

CONCLUSION

It was generally acknowledged by OECD, EU and UN sources that Hungary was in the vanguard of the transition countries, and Hungary had made significant progress in adopting the *acquis communautaire* of the EU. During the 1990s the country underwent a remarkable transformation, with the state divesting itself of ownership of the major sectors of the economy. By the end of the decade the private sector accounted for the main part of national production. The social costs of transition, however, were high, and had major electoral consequences. Although the large budgetary deficit and the level of external debt were areas of concern, measures were taken to bring these under control. The high levels of foreign investment and the negotiations regarding the country's membership of the EU were an indication of international, as well as European, confidence in the Hungarian economy.

Statistical Survey

Source (unless otherwise stated): Központi Statisztikai Hivatal (Hungarian Central Statistical Office), 1525 Budapest, Keleti Károly u. 5–7; tel. (1) 345-6136; fax (1) 345-6378; e-mail erzsebet.veto@office.ksh.hu; internet www.ksh.hu.

Area and Population

AREA, POPULATION AND DENSITY

Area (sq km)	93,030*
Population (census results)	
1 January 1990	10,374,823
1 February 2001	
Males	4,863,610
Females.	5,333,509
Total	10,197,119
Population (official estimates at 30 December)†	
2001	10,175,000
2002	10,142,000
Density (per sq km) at 30 December 2002	109.0

* 35,919 sq miles.
† Figures are rounded.

Languages (2001 census): Magyar (Hungarian) 98.6%; German 0.3%; Slovak 0.1%; Romany 0.5%; Croatian 0.1%; Ukrainian 0.1%; Others 0.2%.

ADMINISTRATIVE DIVISIONS
(2001 census)

	Area (sq km)	Population	Density (per sq km)	County town (with population)*
Counties:				
Bács-Kiskun . .	8,445	546,753	64.7	Kecskemét (105,464)
Baranya . .	4,430	408,019	92.1	Pécs (158,607)
Békés . . .	5,631	397,074	70.5	Békéscsaba (63,958)
Borsod-Abaúj-				
Zemplén .	7,247	745,154	102.8	Miskolc (173,629)
Csongrád . .	4,263	433,388	101.7	Szeged (159,133)
Fejér . . .	4,359	434,547	99.7	Székesfehérvár (105,293)
Győr-Moson-				
Sopron . .	4,089	434,956	106.4	Győr (127,275)
Hajdú-Bihar .	6,211	553,043	89.0	Debrecen (205,032)
Heves . . .	3,637	325,673	89.5	Eger (57,891)
Jász- Nagykun-				
Szolnok . .	5,582	415,819	74.5	Szolnok (76,875)
Komárom-				
Esztergom .	2,265	316,780	139.9	Tatabánya (72,054)
Nógrád. . .	2,544	220,576	86.7	Salgótarján (44,404)
Pest . . .	6,393	1,080,759	169.1	Budapest†(1,838,753)
Somogy . .	6,036	335,463	55.6	Kaposvár (66,826)
Szabolcs-				
Szatmár-Bereg.	5,937	582,795	98.2	Nyíregyháza (112,882)
Tolna . . .	3,703	250,062	67.5	Szekszárd (35,358)
Vas. . . .	3,337	268,653	80.5	Szombathely (82,074)
Veszprém . .	4,613	374,346	81.2	Veszprém (62,631)
Zala . . .	3,784	298,056	78.8	Zalaegerszeg (61,033)
Capital city				
Budapest† . .	525	1,775,203	3,381.3	—
Total. . . .	93,030	10,197,119	109.6	—

* At 1 January 1999.
† Budapest has separate County status. The area and population of the city are not included in the larger County (Pest) which it administers.

PRINCIPAL TOWNS
(population at 1 January 2002)

Budapest (capital) .	1,739,569	Nyíregyháza . . .	117,002
Debrecen	206,564	Kecskemét . . .	107,267
Miskolc	182,408	Székesfehérvár . .	104,059
Szeged.	163,699	Szombathely . . .	81,228*
Pécs	159,794	Szolnok	75,962*
Győr	129,287	Tatabánya . . .	71,701*

* 1 January 2000.

Source: Statistics Finland.

BIRTHS, MARRIAGES AND DEATHS

	Registered live births Number	Rate (per 1,000)	Registered marriages Number	Rate (per 1,000)	Registered deaths Number	Rate (per 1,000)
1994 . .	115,598	11.3	54,114	5.3	146,889	14.3
1995 . .	112,054	11.0	53,463	5.2	145,431	14.2
1996 . .	105,272	10.3	48,930	4.8	143,130	14.0
1997 . .	100,350	9.9	46,905	4.6	139,434	13.7
1998 . .	97,301	9.6	44,915	4.4	140,870	13.9
1999 . .	94,645	9.4	45,465	4.5	143,210	14.2
2000 . .	97,597	9.6	48,110	4.7	135,601	13.3
2001 . .	97,047	9.5	43,583	4.3	132,183	13.0
2002 . .	96,804	9.5	46,008	4.5	132,833	13.1

Expectation of Life (WHO estimates, years at birth): 71.7 (males 67.3; females 76.1) in 2001 (Source: WHO, *World Health Report*).

ECONOMICALLY ACTIVE POPULATION
(labour force surveys, '000 persons aged 15 years to 74 years)

	1999	2000	2001
Agriculture, hunting, forestry and fishing	270.4	251.7	239.4
Mining and quarrying	24.4	19.2	13.0
Manufacturing	928.9	931.3	955.8
Electricity, gas and water supply .	89.8	80.1	79.5
Construction	253.0	267.8	272.7
Wholesale and retail trade; repair of motor vehicles, motorcycles and personal and household goods	517.5	540.9	548.4
Hotels and restaurants	133.2	133.3	143.0
Transport, storage and communications	308.3	311.8	310.9
Financial intermediation . . .	80.9	83.7	78.9
Real estate, renting and business activities	183.9	204.6	219.6
Public administration and defence; compulsory social security . .	301.9	299.0	289.6
Education	306.9	317.8	309.8
Health and social work . . .	239.2	241.7	234.9
Other community, social and personal service activities . .	169.8	162.7	160.3
Private household with employed persons	2.0	1.9	2.5
Extra-territorial organizations and bodies	1.4	1.6	1.2
Total employed *	3,811.4	3,849.1	3,859.5
Unemployed	284.7	262.5	232.9
Total labour force	4,096.2	4,111.6	4,092.4
Males	2,273.8	2,281.9	2,273.3
Females	1,822.4	1,829.7	1,819.1

* Excluding persons on child-care leave.

Source: ILO.

2002 (labour force surveys, '000 persons aged 15 years to 74 years): Total employed (excl. persons on child-care leave) 3,870.6; Unemployed 238.8; Total labour force 4,109.4.

Health and Welfare

KEY INDICATORS

Total fertility rate (children per woman, 2001)	1.3
Under-5 mortality rate (per 1,000 live births, 2001) . . .	9
HIV/AIDS (% of persons aged 15–49, 2001)	0.06
Physicians (per 1,000 head, 1998)	3.57
Hospital beds (per 1,000 head, 1999)	8.2
Health expenditure (2000): US $ per head (PPP) . . .	846
Health expenditure (2000): % of GDP	6.8
Health expenditure (2000): public (% of total) . . .	75.7
Access to water (% of persons, 2000)	99
Access to sanitation (% of persons, 2000)	99
Human Development Index (2000): ranking	35
Human Development Index (2000): value	0.835

For sources and definitions, see explanatory note on p. vi.

Agriculture

PRINCIPAL CROPS
('000 metric tons)

	1999	2000	2001
Wheat	2,639.1	3,692.5	5,196.8
Barley	1,042.1	900.5	1,299.1
Maize	7,149.3	4,984.3	7,857.7
Rye	80.3	86.5	121.1
Oats	180.4	97.5	149.7
Triticale (wheat-rye hybrid) . .	253.8	235.6	393.9
Potatoes	1,198.7	863.5	908.4
Sugar beet	2,933.5	1,976.2	2,903.0
Dry beans	107.9	47.6	n.a.
Soybeans (Soya beans)	77.5	30.8	41.5
Sunflower seed	792.9	483.6	632.3
Rapeseed	327.9	179.3	205.1
Cabbages	192.1	130.1	161.3
Tomatoes	301.5	203.4	235.8
Cucumbers and gherkins . . .	125.8	102.7	98.6
Chillies and green peppers . . .	171.2	134.2	134.8
Dry onions	149.5	114.7	174.3
Green peas	163.0	153.3	283.1
Carrots	117.2	89.3	99.3
Green corn	255.7	291.2	415.6
Other vegetables*	386.9	160.6	315.5
Peaches and nectarines	71.0	64.1	56.7
Plums	97.8	91.3	89.8
Grapes	570.3	684.0	811.4
Watermelons	124.9	133.4	130.2
Pimento	33.1	40.0	59.7
Apples	444.5	694.6	605.4
Tobacco (leaves)	15.7	10.5	8.9

* Unofficial figures.

Source: FAO.

LIVESTOCK
('000 head, year ending September)

	1999	2000	2001
Cattle	873	857	805
Pigs	5,479	5,335	4,834
Sheep	909	934	1,129
Goats	149	87	90
Horses	70	70*	75
Chickens	30,557	25,890	30,716
Ducks	2,378	2,269	1,480
Geese	1,074	1,226	1,470
Turkeys	1,986	1,859	3,300

* FAO estimate.

Source: FAO.

LIVESTOCK PRODUCTS
('000 metric tons)

	1999	2000	2001
Beef and veal	51.0	49.4†	47.0*
Mutton and lamb	3.6	2.8*	3.5*
Pig meat	625.9	622.0	587.0†
Poultry meat	399.4	461.4	495.1
Rabbit meat	9.1†	8.8†	9.0*
Cows' milk	2,106.6	2,145.0	2,142.9
Sheep's milk	31.0	33.3	41.5
Goats' milk	4.2	10.8	11.2
Butter	16.6	12.0	13.6
Cheese	91.8	95.6	108.4
Hen eggs	177.2	176.2	182.1
Other poultry eggs	3.4	3.2	3.5
Honey	16.0	15.2	11.3
Wool: greasy	3.4	3.4	3.9
Wool: scoured	1.3†	1.3†	2.3
Cattle hides (fresh)*	3.1	3.0	3.2†

* FAO estimate(s).
† Unofficial figure.

Source: FAO.

Forestry

ROUNDWOOD REMOVALS
('000 cu metres, excl. bark)

	1999*	2000	2001
Sawlogs, veneer logs and logs for sleepers	1,445	1,380	1,430
Pulpwood	515	612	594
Other industrial wood . . .	1,340	1,314	1,468
Fuel wood	2,475	2,597	2,319
Total	5,775	5,903	5,811

* Unofficial figures.

Source: FAO.

SAWNWOOD PRODUCTION
('000 cu metres, incl. railway sleepers)

	1999	2000	2001
Coniferous (softwood)	98	77	75
Broadleaved (hardwood). . . .	210	214	144
Total	308	291	219

Source: FAO.

Fishing

(metric tons, live weight)

	1998	1999	2000
Capture	7,265	7,514	7,101
Common carp	3,373	3,279	3,212
Silver carp	731	676	365
Other cyprinids	1,895	1,666	1,710
Aquaculture	10,222	11,947	12,886
Common carp	7,069	8,158	8,656
Silver carp	1,943	1,882	1,640
Total catch	17,487	19,461	19,987

Source: FAO, *Yearbook of Fishery Statistics*.

Mining

('000 metric tons, unless otherwise indicated)

	1997	1998	1999
Hard coal	924	877	738
Brown coal	6,552	6,004	6,110
Lignite.	8,089	7,610	7,696
Crude petroleum	1,360	1,258	1,243
Bauxite	743	909	935
Natural gas (million cu metres) .	4,689	4,340	3,693

2000 ('000 metric tons): Bauxite 1,047 (Source: US Geological Survey).

Industry

SELECTED PRODUCTS
('000 metric tons, unless otherwise indicated)

	1997	1998	1999
Crude steel	1,819	1,940	1,920
Cement	2,811	2,999	2,980
Nitrogenous fertilizers*	262.1	224.9	188.0
Refined sugar	487.2	439.4	438.3
Buses (number)	1,951	1,232	706
Leather footwear ('000 pairs) .	11,868	11,649	12,639
Electric power (million kWh) .	35,305	37,023	36,968
Television receivers ('000)† . .	963	1,703	2,521
Radio receivers ('000) . . .	528	2,328	2,700

* Production in terms of nitrogen.
† Including video monitors and video projectors.

Finance

CURRENCY AND EXCHANGE RATES

Monetary Units
100 fillér = 1 forint.

Sterling, Dollar and Euro Equivalents (30 May 2003)
£1 sterling = 347.30 forint;
US $1 = 210.79 forint;
€1 = 249.19 forint;
1,000 forint = £2.879 = $4.744 = €4.013.

Average Exchange Rate (forint per US dollar)
2000   282.179
2001   286.490
2002   257.887

BUDGET
('000 million forint)*

Revenue†	1998	1999	2000
Tax revenue	3,221.8	3,857.1	4,227.3
Taxes on income, profits and capital gains	694.8	840.6	988.4
Individual	477.5	578.1	695.7
Corporate.	217.3	262.5	292.7
Social security contributions . .	1,069.0	1,323.9	1,288.0
Domestic taxes on goods and services	1,241.2	1,460.9	1,710.6
General sales, turnover or value-added taxes . . .	796.9	941.8	1,153.7
Excises	320.6	463.7	505.9
Import duties	131.6	141.1	137.7
Other current revenue . . .	438.1	522.1	508.8
Entrepreneurial and property income	150.4	174.6	164.2
Administrative fees and charges, non-industrial and incidental sales	168.5	154.7	207.7
Capital revenue	26.3	23.3	26.5
Total	3,686.2	4,402.5	4,762.6

Expenditure‡	1998	1999	2000
General public services	237.6	240.3	387.3
Defence	102.1	102.1	142.6
Public order and safety . . .	169.6	169.6	198.2
Education	381.2	381.2	256.2
Health	265.4	265.3	321.6
Social security and welfare . . .	1,331.1	1,331.4	1,703.3
Housing and community amenities	68.9	68.9	81.8
Recreational, cultural and religious affairs and services	79.5	79.5	99.5
Economic affairs and services . .	558.3	449.4	717.5
Agriculture, forestry, fishing and hunting	157.0	157.0	178.5
Transport and communications .	184.6	112.0	242.0
Other purposes	1,329.7	1,802.3	1,375.6
Interest payments	779.0	843.9	788.0
Total	4,523.2	4,890.1	5,283.6
Current	4,111.2	4,476.2	4,631.3
Capital.	412.0	413.9	652.3

* Figures refer to the consolidated operations of the central Government, comprising the State Budget, the Pension Fund, the Health Insurance Fund and six extrabudgetary funds.
† Excluding grants received ('000 million forint): 78.6 in 1998; −33.9 in 1999; 19.4 in 2000.
‡ Excluding lending minus repayments ('000 million forint): −106.2 in 1998; −98.0 in 1999; −36.9 in 2000.

Source: partly IMF, *Government Finance Statistics Yearbook*.

INTERNATIONAL RESERVES
(US $ million at 31 December)

	2000	2001	2002
Gold*	28	28	35
IMF special drawing rights . . .	12	21	33
Reserve position in IMF	263	405	595
Foreign exchange	10,915	10,302	9,721
Total	11,218	10,755	10,384

* National valuation.

Source: IMF, *International Financial Statistics*.

MONEY SUPPLY
('000 million forint at 31 December)

	2000	2001	2002
Currency outside banks	883.9	1,037.6	1,181.8
Demand deposits at commercial and savings banks	1,494.3	1,738.3	2,121.0
Total money (incl. others) . .	2,378.4	2,775.9	3,302.9

Source: IMF, *International Financial Statistics*.

COST OF LIVING
(Consumer Price Index; base: 1990 = 100)

	1999	2000	2001
Food	493.7	539.1	613.5
Fuel and light	1,160.0	1,265.6	1,396.0
Clothing and footwear	497.7	526.6	554.5
Rent	510.6	592.8	695.9
All items (incl. others)	569.5	625.3	682.8

Source: ILO.

NATIONAL ACCOUNTS
('000 million forint at current prices)

Expenditure on the Gross Domestic Product

	2000	2001	2002
Government final consumption expenditure	1,273.4	1,509.5	2,039.7
Private final consumption expenditure*	8,342.1	9,534.2	11,234.4
Increase in stocks*	884.9	521.7	296.3
Gross fixed capital formation . .	3,179.8	3,508.4	3,786.4
Total domestic expenditure . .	13,680.2	15,073.8	17,356.8
Exports of goods and services . .	9,863.1	11,041.6	10,944.7
Less Imports of goods and services	10,371.0	11,265.8	11,321.4
GDP in purchasers' values . .	13,172.3	14,849.6	16,980.1
GDP at constant 1998 prices .	11,053.8	11,475.6	n.a.

* Includes non-profit institutions serving households.

Source: IMF, *International Financial Statistics*.

Gross Domestic Product by Economic Activity

	1998	1999	2000
Agriculture, hunting, forestry and fishing	491.5	483.5	472.3
Mining and quarrying	28.1	28.4	30.9
Manufacturing	2,135.3	2,340.2	2,876.3
Electricity, gas and water supply .	341.9	389.2	430.3
Construction	405.8	463.8	520.0
Wholesale and retail trade; repair of motor vehicles, motorcycles and personal and household goods	1,028.6	1,097.5	1,227.0
Hotels and restaurants	158.1	178.1	201.3
Transport, storage and communications	875.1	1,018.4	1,096.3
Financial intermediation	367.7	394.5	455.1
Real estate, renting and business activities	1,332.4	1,603.9	1,888.6
Public administration and defence; compulsory social security . .	638.7	723.4	816.7
Education	411.1	478.0	535.3
Health and social work . . .	393.1	446.1	521.9
Other community, social and personal service activities . .	266.0	328.0	342.4
Sub-total	8,873.5	9,973.0	11,414.4
Less Financial intermediation services indirectly measured . .	245.1	283.8	301.3
Gross value added in basic prices	8,628.4	9,689.2	11,113.1
Taxes *less* subsidies on products .	1,459.1	1,704.3	1,962.1
GDP in market prices . . .	10,087.4	11,393.5	13,075.2

Source: UN, *National Accounts Statistics*.

BALANCE OF PAYMENTS
(US $ million)

	2000	2001	2002
Exports of goods f.o.b.	25,747	28,071	34,792
Imports of goods f.o.b.	−27,506	−30,089	−36,911
Trade balance	−1,760	−2,018	−2,119
Exports of services	6,251	7,707	7,807
Imports of services	−4,476	−5,544	−7,193
Balance on goods and services	15	146	−1,506
Other income received	942	1,111	1,215
Other income paid	−2,516	−2,599	−2,801
Balance on goods, services and income	−1,559	−1,342	−3,092
Current transfers received . . .	520	589	1,001
Current transfers paid	−289	−344	−554
Current balance	−1,328	−1,097	−2,645
Capital account (net)	270	317	179
Direct investment abroad . . .	−532	−337	−264
Direct investment from abroad . .	1,646	2,440	854
Portfolio investment assets . . .	−309	−149	−47
Portfolio investment liabilities . .	−187	1,526	1,838
Financial derivatives assets . .	753	579	1,917
Financial derivatives liabilities .	−692	−457	−2,123
Other investment assets . . .	−1,014	−3,430	−1,574
Other investment liabilities . .	2,555	446	−473
Net errors and omissions . . .	−109	79	546
Overall balance	1,052	−84	−1,792

Source: IMF, *International Financial Statistics*.

External Trade

Note: Beginning in 1997, Hungary's customs territory includes the country's industrial free zones.

PRINCIPAL COMMODITIES
(distribution by SITC, million forint)

Imports c.i.f.	1998	1999	2000
Food and live animals . . .	183,608	176,710	228,688
Mineral fuels, lubricants, etc. . .	361,302	406,814	759,982
Petroleum, petroleum products, etc. .	161,338	213,229	400,907
Gas (natural and manufactured) .	159,902	145,290	293,329
Chemicals and related products	565,446	633,457	800,169
Basic manufactures . . .	1,056,034	1,179,487	1,499,000
Textile yarn, fabrics, etc. . . .	250,717	271,797	304,477
Machinery and transport equipment.	2,566,694	3,334,386	4,666,921
Power-generating machinery and equipment	355,915	403,973	509,379
Machinery specialized for particular industries	179,789	204,644	239,950
General industrial machinery equipment and parts . .	320,716	411,089	480,545
Office machines and automatic data-processing machines . .	319,846	443,359	640,189
Telecommunications and sound equipment	336,457	406,616	588,020
Other electrical machinery apparatus, etc.	600,755	820,947	1,448,297
Road vehicles and parts (excl. tyres, engines and electrical parts) . .	385,384	572,179	665,365
Miscellaneous manufactured articles	593,037	740,751	890,388
Total (incl. others)	5,511,511	6,645,562	9,064,022

Exports f.o.b.	1998	1999	2000
Food and live animals . . .	470,124	437,320	517,196
Chemicals and related products	346,986	365,629	527,262
Basic manufactures	613,358	680,487	853,605
Machinery and transport equipment.	2,564,268	3,401,417	4,765,001
Power-generating machinery and equipment	601,241	689,036	795,897
Office machines and automatic data-processing machines . .	522,323	794,017	1,102,489
Telecommunications and sound equipment	371,889	471,385	857,673
Other electrical machinery apparatus, etc.	533,377	654,676	941,702
Road vehicles and parts (excl. tyres, engines and electrical parts) . .	302,915	535,343	697,584
Miscellaneous manufactured articles.	649,656	768,553	915,262
Clothing and accessories (excl. footwear)	273,871	311,368	345,223
Total (incl. others)	4,934,502	5,938,525	7,942,804

PRINCIPAL TRADING PARTNERS
(US $ million)*

Imports c.i.f.	1999	2000	2001
Austria.	2,502.7	2,366.0	2,487.8
Belgium and Luxembourg . . .	752.9	751.8	791.6
China, People's Republic . .	610.2	n.a.	n.a.
Czech Republic	529.6	646.2	714.8
Finland	317.6	372.7	353.6
France	1,313.2	1,400.5	1,578.5
Germany	8,188.8	8,213.0	8,393.1
Italy	2,158.8	2,407.2	2,647.4
Japan	1,148.2	n.a.	n.a.
Korea, Republic	355.5	n.a.	n.a.
Netherlands	703.3	708.4	699.4
Poland	587.0	605.2	777.0
Romania	n.a.	328.6	362.0
Russia	1,631.1	2,588.6	2,369.3
Singapore	399.9	n.a.	n.a.
Slovakia	474.7	574.9	602.6
Spain	468.6	572.8	616.6
Sweden	317.9	368.8	348.3
Switzerland and Liechtenstein .	426.0	n.a.	n.a.
United Kingdom	853.0	1,017.1	992.7
USA	504.1	569.1	n.a.
Total (incl. others)	28,008.2	32,079.5	33,681.9

Exports f.o.b.	1999	2000	2001
Austria.	2,399.4	2,442.5	2,416.8
Belgium and Luxembourg . . .	760.0	886.6	1,014.3
Czech Republic	370.0	465.3	553.4
France	1,123.1	1,470.2	1,817.8
Germany	9,600.1	10,471.3	10,859.5
Ireland.	250.6	250.7	329.5
Italy	1,476.9	1,654.4	1,905.2
Netherlands	1,296.5	1,522.4	1,402.2
Poland	519.4	605.2	609.4
Romania	467.6	574.2	764.2
Russia	356.2	455.4	472.3
Slovakia	279.0	288.5	411.5
Slovenia	266.9	279.7	308.4
Spain	406.6	522.5	629.4
Switzerland and Liechtenstein . .	304.3	n.a.	n.a.
United Kingdom	1,119.8	1,156.3	1,314.4
USA	1,892.6	2,715.2	n.a.
Total (incl. others)	25,012.5	28,091.9	30,497.8

* Imports by country of origin; exports by country of destination.
Source: partly Ministry of Economic Affairs, Budapest.

Transport

RAILWAYS
(traffic)

	1998	1999	2000
Passengers carried (million) . .	157.0	156.8	156.4
Passenger-kilometres (million). .	8,884	9,514	9,789
Net ton-kilometres (million) . .	8,150	7,734	7,842

2001: 7,731 net ton-kilometres (million).

ROAD TRAFFIC
(motor vehicles in use at 31 December)

	1997	1998	1999
Passenger cars	2,297,115	2,365,000	2,400,000
Buses and coaches	18,616	19,386	19,100
Lorries and vans	315,242	325,300	324,000
Motorcycles and mopeds . . .	137,983	137,983	137,000

Source: IRF, *World Road Statistics*.

2001: Public road motor vehicle stock ('000) 2,974.

SHIPPING

Merchant Fleet
(registered at 31 December)

	2000	2001	2002
Number of vessels	1	1	1
Total displacement (grt). . . .	2,317	1,901	3,784

Source: Lloyd's Register-Fairplay, *World Fleet Statistics*.

Inland Waterways
(traffic)

	1998	1999	2000
Freight carried ('000 metric tons) .	2,108	2,074	2,390
Freight ton-km (million) . . .	2,482	1,644	1,561

CIVIL AVIATION
(traffic)

	1998	1999	2000
Passengers carried	2,188,000	2,352,000	2,476,000
Passenger-km ('000)	3,038,000	3,513,000	3,539,000
Cargo carried: metric tons . .	15,000	16,000	31,000
Cargo ton-km	42,100,000	55,500,000	68,000,000

Tourism

TOURISTS BY COUNTRY OF ORIGIN
('000 arrivals, including visitors in transit)

	1999	2000	2001
Austria.	5,532	5,139	4,790
Bulgaria	354	395	535
Czech Republic and Slovakia . .	4,619	4,273	4,336
Germany	3,206	2,949	2,726
Poland	460	643	767
Romania	3,581	4,661	4,861
Russia	106	125	93
Total (incl. others)	28,803	31,141	30,679

2002: 31,739,000 arrivals.

Tourist receipts (US $ million): 2,504 in 1998; 2,203 in 1999; 3,434 in 2000.

Communications Media

	1998	1999	2000
Radio receivers ('000 in use) . .	7,245	7,231	n.a.
Television receivers ('000 in use) .	4,377	4,519	4,451
Telephones ('000 main lines in use)	3,423.0	3,725.8	3,479.0
Facsimile machines ('000 in use)	180	n.a.	n.a.
Mobile cellular telephones ('000 subscribers).	1,070.2	1,628.2	3,000.4
Personal computers ('000 in use) .	400	750	870
Internet users ('000)	660	600	715
Book production: titles . . .	10,626	9,731	8,986
Book production:copies . . .	47,046	44,652	35,246
Daily newspapers	33	n.a.	n.a.
Average daily circulation . . .	1,846,000	n.a.	n.a.

2001: Telephones ('000 main lines in use) 3,260; Mobile cellular telephones ('000 subscribers) 4,968; Personal computers ('000 in use) 1,000; Internet users ('000) 1,480; Book production (titles) 8,837, (copies) 32,615.

2002: Telephones ('000 main lines in use) 3,666; Mobile cellular telephones ('000 subscribers) 6,562; Personal computers ('000 in use) 1,100; Internet users ('000) 1,600.

Sources: partly UNESCO, *Statistical Yearbook*, and International Telecommunication Union.

Education

(1999/2000, estimates, unless otherwise indicated)

	Institutions	Teachers	Students Males	Students Females	Students Total
Pre-primary . .	4,643	31,409	188,565	177,139	365,704
Primary . . .	3,696	82,829	491,101	469,500	960,601
Secondary: general . . .	1,533	14,155	57,641	87,569	145,210
Secondary: teacher training* . .	n.a.	n.a.	159	1,045	1,104
Secondary: vocational . .	990	26,512	195,268	162,035	357,303
Higher: universities etc.	30	12,804	53,520†	52,761†	88,479
Higher: other .	59	8,338	23,167†	33,716†	83,037

* Estimated figures for full-time teacher training.
† 1998/99 figure.

Adult literacy rate (UNESCO estimates): 99.3% (males 99.7%; females 99.5%) in 2000 (Source: UN Development Programme, *Human Development Report*).

Directory

The Constitution

A new Constitution was introduced on 18 August 1949, and the Hungarian People's Republic was established two days later. The Constitution was amended in April 1972 and December 1983. Further, radical amendments were made in October 1989. Shortly afterwards, the Republic of Hungary was proclaimed.

The following is a summary of the main provisions of the Constitution, as amended in October 1989.

GENERAL PROVISIONS

The Republic of Hungary is an independent, democratic constitutional state in which the values of civil democracy and democratic socialism prevail in equal measures. All power belongs to the people, which they exercise directly and through the elected representatives of popular sovereignty.

Political parties may, under observance of the Constitution, be freely formed and may freely operate in Hungary. Parties may not directly exercise public power. No party has the right to guide any state body. Trade unions and other organizations for the representa-

tion of interests safeguard and represent the interests of employees, members of co-operatives and entrepreneurs.

The State safeguards the people's freedom, the independence and territorial integrity of the country as well as the frontiers thereof, as established by international treaties. The Republic of Hungary rejects war as a means of settling disputes between nations and refrains from applying force against the independence or territorial integrity of other states, and from threats of violence.

The Hungarian legal system adopts the universally accepted rules of international law. The order of legislation is regulated by an Act of constitutional force.

The economy of Hungary is a market economy, availing itself also of the advantages of planning, with public and private ownership enjoying equal right and protection. Hungary recognizes and supports the right of undertaking and free competition, limitable only by an Act of constitutional force. State-owned enterprises and organs pursuing economic activities manage their affairs independently, in accordance with the mode and responsibility as provided by law.

The Republic of Hungary protects the institutions of marriage and the family. It provides for the indigent through extensive social measures, and recognizes and enforces the right of each citizen to a healthy environment.

GOVERNMENT

National Assembly

The highest organ of state authority in the Republic of Hungary is the National Assembly, which exercises all the rights deriving from the sovereignty of the people and determines the organization, direction and conditions of government. The National Assembly enacts the Constitution and laws, determines the state budget, decides the socio-economic plan, elects the President of the Republic and the Council of Ministers, directs the activities of ministries, decides upon declaring war and concluding peace and exercises the prerogative of amnesty.

The National Assembly is elected for a term of four years and members enjoy immunity from arrest and prosecution without parliamentary consent. It meets at least twice a year and is convened by the President of the Republic or by a written demand of the Council of Ministers or of one-fifth of the Assembly's members. It elects a President, Deputy Presidents and Recorders from among its own members, and it lays down its own rules of procedure and agenda. As a general rule, the sessions of the National Assembly are held in public.

The National Assembly has the right of legislation which can be initiated by the President of the Republic, the Council of Ministers or any committee or member of the National Assembly. Decisions are valid only if at least half of the members are present, and they require a simple majority. Constitutional changes require a two-thirds' majority. Acts of the National Assembly are signed by the President of the Republic.

The National Assembly may pronounce its dissolution before the expiry of its term, and in the event of an emergency may prolong its mandate or may be reconvened after dissolution. A new National Assembly must be elected within three months of dissolution and convened within one month of polling day.

Members of the National Assembly are elected on the basis of universal, equal and direct suffrage by secret ballot, and they are accountable to their constituents, who may recall them. All citizens of 18 years and over have the right to vote, with the exception of those who are unsound of mind, and those who are deprived of their civil rights by a court of law.

President of the Republic

The President of the Republic is the Head of State of Hungary. He/she embodies the unity of the nation and supervises the democratic operation of the mechanism of State. The President is also the Commander-in-Chief of the Armed Forces. The President is elected by the National Assembly for a period of five years, and may be re-elected for a second term. Any citizen of Hungary qualified to vote, who has reached 35 years of age before the day of election, may be elected President.

The President may issue the writ for general or local elections, convene the National Assembly, initiate legislation, hold plebiscites, direct local government, conclude international treaties, appoint diplomatic representatives, ratify international treaties, appoint higher civil servants and officers of the armed forces, award orders and titles, and exercise the prerogative of mercy.

Council of Ministers

The highest organ of state administration is the Council of Ministers, responsible to the National Assembly and consisting of the Prime Minister and other Ministers who are elected by the National Assembly on the recommendation of the President of the Republic. The Council of Ministers directs the work of the ministries (listed in a special enactment) and ensures the enforcement of laws and the fulfilment of economic plans; it may issue decrees and annul or modify measures taken by any central or local organ of government.

Local Administration

The local organs of state power are the county, town, borough and town precinct councils, whose members are elected for a term of four years by the voters in each area. Local councils direct economic, social and cultural activities in their area, prepare local economic plans and budgets and supervise their fulfilment, enforce laws, supervise subordinate organs, maintain public order, protect public property and individual rights, and direct local economic enterprises. They may issue regulations and annul or modify those of subordinate councils. Local Councils are administered by an Executive Committee elected by and responsible to them.

JUDICATURE

Justice is administered by the Supreme Court of the Republic of Hungary, county and district courts. The Supreme Court exercises the right of supervising in principle the judicial activities and practice of all other courts.

All judicial offices are filled by election; Supreme Court, county and district court judges are all elected for an indefinite period; the President of the Supreme Court is elected by the National Assembly. All court hearings are public unless otherwise prescribed by law, and those accused are guaranteed the right of defence. An accused person must be considered innocent until proved guilty.

Public Prosecutor

The function of the Chief Public Prosecutor is to supervise the observance of the law. He is elected by the National Assembly, to whom he is responsible. The organization of public prosecution is under the control of the Chief Public Prosecutor, who appoints the public prosecutors.

RIGHTS AND DUTIES OF CITIZENS

The Republic of Hungary guarantees for its citizens the right to work and to remuneration, the right of rest and recreation, the right to care in old age, sickness or disability, the right to education, and equality before the law; women enjoy equal rights with men. Discrimination on grounds of sex, religion or nationality is a punishable offence. The State also ensures freedom of conscience, religious worship, speech, the press and assembly. The right of workers to organize themselves is stressed. The freedom of the individual, and the privacy of the home and of correspondence are inviolable. Freedom for creative work in the sciences and the arts is guaranteed.

The basic freedoms of all workers are guaranteed and foreign citizens enjoy the right of asylum.

Military service (with or without arms) and the defence of their country are the duties of all citizens.

The Government

HEAD OF STATE

President of the Republic: FERENC MÁDL (elected 6 June 2000; took office 4 August 2000).

COUNCIL OF MINISTERS
(July 2003)

A coalition of the Hungarian Socialist Party (HSP) and the Alliance of Free Democrats (AFD).

Prime Minister: PÉTER MEDGYESSY (HSP).

Minister of Foreign Affairs: LÁZSLÓ KOVÁCS (HSP).

Minister of Defence: FERENC JUHÁSZ (HSP).

Minister of Finance: CSABA LÁSZLÓ (Ind.).

Minister of Economy and Transport: ISTVÁN CSILLAG (AFD).

Minister of Home Affairs: MÓNIKA LAMPERTH (HSP).

Minister of Agriculture and Rural Development: IMRE NÉMETH (HSP).

Minister of Health, Social and Family Affairs: JUDIT CSEHÁK (HSP).

Minister of Justice: PÉTER BÁRÁNDY (Ind.).

Minister of Labour and Employment: SÁNDOR BURÁNY (HSP).

Minister of Environmental Protection and Water Management: MIKLOS PERSANYI (AFD).

Minister of Information Technology and Telecommunications: KÁLMÁN KOVÁCS (AFD).

Minister of Cultural Heritage: ISTVÁN HILLER (HSP).

Minister of Education: BÁLINT MAGYAR (AFD).

Minister of Children, Youth and Sports: FERENC GYURCSANY (HSP).

Minister without Portfolio (attached to the Office of the Prime Minister): PÉTER KISS (HSP).

Minister without Portfolio (responsible for the Co-ordination of EU Integration): ENDRE JUHASZ.

Minister without Portfolio (responsible for Equal Opportunities): KATALIN LEVAL.

MINISTRIES

Office of the President: 1055 Budapest, Kossuth Lajos tér 3–5; tel. (1) 441-4103.

Office of the Prime Minister: 1055 Budapest, Kossuth Lajos tér 1–3; tel. (1) 441-4000; fax (1) 268-3050; internet www.kancellaria.gov.hu.

Ministry of Agriculture and Rural Development: 1055 Budapest, Kossuth Lajos tér 11; tel. (1) 301-4000; fax (1) 301-0408; internet www.fvm.hu.

Ministry of Children, Youth and Sports: 1054 Budapest, Hold u. 1; tel. (1) 311-9080; fax (1) 269-0188; internet www.ism.hu/start .htm.

Ministry of Cultural Heritage: 1077 Budapest, Wesselényi u. 20–22; tel. (1) 484-7100; fax (1) 484-7172; internet www.nkom.hu.

Ministry of Defence: 1055 Budapest, Balaton u. 7–11; tel. (1) 236-5111; fax (1) 311-0182; internet www.honvedelem.hu.

Ministry of Economy and Transport: 1055 Budapest, Honvéd u. 13–15; tel. (1) 302-2355; fax (1) 374-2700; internet www.gm.hu.

Ministry of Education: 1055 Budapest, Szalay u. 10–14; tel. (1) 302-0600; fax (1) 302-2002; internet www.om.hu.

Ministry of Environmental Protection and Water Management: 1011 Budapest, POB 351, Fő u. 44–50; tel. (1) 457-3300; fax (1) 201-2846; e-mail kozonsir@mail.ktm.hu; internet www.ktm.hu.

Ministry of Finance: 1051 Budapest, József Nádor tér 2–4; tel. (1) 318-2066; fax (1) 318-2570; internet www.p-m.hu.

Ministry of Foreign Affairs: 1027 Budapest, Bem rkp. 47; tel. (1) 458-1000; fax (1) 212-5981; internet www.mfa.gov.hu.

Ministry of Health, Social and Family Affairs: Budapest; internet www.eum.hu.

Ministry of Home Affairs: 1051 Budapest, József Attila u. 2–4; tel. (1) 331-3700; fax (1) 118-2870; internet www.b-m.hu.

Ministry of Information Technology and Telecommunications: Budapest.

Ministry of Justice: 1055 Budapest, Kossuth Lajos tér 4; tel. (1) 441-3003; internet www.im.hu.

Ministry of Labour and Employment: Budapest.

Legislature

ORSZÁGGYÜLÉS
(National Assembly)

National Assembly
1055 Budapest, Kossuth Lajos tér 1–3; 1357 Budapest, POB 2; tel. (1) 441-4000; fax (1) 441-5000; internet www.mkogy.hu.

President of the National Assembly: KATALIN SZILI.

Deputy Presidents: IBOLYA DAVID, LÁSZLÓ MANOUR, PÉTER HARRACH, JÓZSEF SZAJER, FERENC WEKLER.

General election, 7 and 21 April 2002

Parties	% of votes	Seats
Federation of Young Democrats— Hungarian Civic Party-Hungarian Democratic Forum (FYD—HCP-HDF) .	48.70	188
Hungarian Socialist Party (HSP) . . .	46.11	178
Alliance of Free Democrats (AFD) . . .	5.18	20
Total	100.00	386

Local Government

In 1990 the National Assembly ratified a law providing for the right of citizens to participate extensively in the government of their local communities, the object being to broaden social co-operation and to prevent local politics becoming the monopoly of élite groups. Hungary is divided into 19 counties (megyei). There are, in addition, 168 town authorities (városi), of which 22 larger towns or cities with populations over 50,000 claim separate county status. Larger towns are subdivided into districts; for example, Budapest (with a population almost nine times that of Debrecen, Hungary's second biggest town) is divided into 23 districts, which send delegates to the General Assembly of the capital. In rural areas villages and large villages (with populations over 5,000) have their own representative bodies. Elections are held every four years for the county, town, district and precinct councils, or general assemblies, of which the president heads the local government. However, provisions exist for each representative body to hold a public meeting at least once a year, and for referendums to be held on significant local issues. Minimum levels of participation in elections are set, below which a result is invalidated. There is effectively no hierarchical control over local government in Hungary, each tier being regarded as equal and independent. However, the National Assembly may dissolve a local government if it is operating in contravention of the Constitution, and after consultation with the Constitutional Court. Local government decisions may be revised only by the Constitutional Court, or, in cases of illegality, by the courts. Local authorities are free to co-operate in their own representative associations. In April 1995 a 53-member National Autonomous Authority of the Romany Minority was elected and empowered to administer funds disbursed by the central Government. New elections to the National Autonomous Authority took place in January 1999 and March 2003 (elections held in January were declared invalid). Local elections were held in Hungary in October 1998 and in October 2002.

Hungarian National Association of Local Authorities (Települési Önkormányzatok Országos Szövetsége—TÖOSZ)/ **Association of Local Governments and Representatives (MÖSZ):** 1067 Budapest, Eötvös u. 10; tel. (1) 322-3843; fax (1) 322-7407; e-mail toosz@toosz.hu; internet www.toosz.hu; f. 1989; Gen. Sec. GÁBOR ZONGORI.

National Autonomous Authority of the Romany Minority (Magyarországi Románok Országos Szövetsége): 5700 Gyula, Vár u. 16; Pres. ORBÁN KOLOMPAR.

COUNTIES

Bács-Kiskun: 6000 Kecskemét, Deák Ferenc tér 3; tel. (76) 487-387; fax (76) 573-801; e-mail bkmoh.hu; internet www.bkmoh.hu; Pres. of Gen. Assembly Dr LÁSZLÓ BALOGH.

Baranya: 7621 Pécs, Széchenyi tér 9; tel. (72) 500-400; fax (72) 500-469; e-mail kekes.elnok.bmo@ph.pecs.hu; internet www.bmonk.pecs .hu; Pres. of Gen. Assembly Dr FERENC KÉKES.

Békés: 5600 Békéscsaba, Derkovits sor. 2; tel. (66) 441-156; fax (66) 441-609; e-mail info@bekesmegye.hu; internet www.bekesmegye .hu; Pres. of Gen. Assembly ZOLTÁN VARGA.

Borsod-Abaúj-Zemplén: 3541 Miskolc, Városház tér 1; tel. (46) 323-600; fax (46) 320-601; e-mail elnok@baz.hu; internet www.olh .hu/borsod; Pres. of Gen. Assembly Dr FERENC ÓDOR.

Csongrád: 6741 Szeged, Rákóczi tér 1; tel. (62) 566-000; fax (62) 420-637; e-mail hivatal@csongrad-megye.hu; internet www .csongrad-megye.hu; Pres. of Gen. Assembly Dr JÓZSEF FRANK.

Fejér: 8000 Székesfehérvár, Szent István tér 9; tel. (22) 312-360; fax (22) 314-465; e-mail lferto@fejer.hu; internet www.fejer.hu; Pres. of Gen. Assembly GÁBOR SZABÓ.

Győr-Moson-Sopron: 9021 Győr, Árpád u. 32; tel. (96) 522-222; fax (96) 522-219; e-mail info@gymsmo.hu; internet www.gymsmo.hu; Pres. of Gen. Assembly Dr IMRE SZAKÁCS.

Hajdú-Bihar: 4024 Debrecen, Piac u. 54; tel. (52) 447-255; fax (52) 507-511; e-mail ladanyine@hbmo.hm; internet www.hbmo.hu; Pres. of Gen. Assembly LÉVAI KATALIN JUHÁSZNÉ.

Heves: 3300 Eger, Kossuth L. u. 9; tel. (36) 410-011; fax (36) 411-106; e-mail hmoh@agria.hu; internet www.hevesmegye.hu; Pres. of Gen. Assembly TAMÁS SÓS.

Jász-Nagykun-Szolnok: 5000 Szolnok, Kossuth Lajos. u. 2; tel. (56) 505-330; fax (56) 374-424; e-mail jnszm.elnok@jnszm.hu; internet www.jnszm.hu; Pres. of Gen. Assembly ISTVÁN TOKÁR.

Komárom-Esztergom: 2801 Tatabánya, Fő tér 4; tel. (34) 517-120; fax (34) 311-690; e-mail dunaeuro@matavnet.hu; Pres. of Gen. Assembly MÓZES LÁZÁR.

Nógrád: 3100 Salgótarján, Rákóczi u. 36; tel. (32) 310-161; fax (32) 311-790; e-mail svecz@nograd.hu; internet www.nograd.hu; Pres. of Gen. Assembly DÓRA OTTÓ.

Pest: 1052 Budapest, Városház u. 7; 1364 Budapest, POB 112; tel. (1) 317-6172; fax (1) 317-4295; e-mail pestmegye@pestmegye.hu; internet www.pestmegye.hu; Pres. of Gen. Assembly IMRE SZABÓ.

Somogy: 7400 Kaposvár, Csokonai Vitéz M. u. 3; tel. (82) 313-615; fax (82) 312-634; e-mail elnok@som-onkorm.hu; internet www .somogy.hu; Pres. of Gen. Assembly Dr ISTVÁN GYENESEI.

Szabolcs-Szatmár-Bereg: 4400 Nyíregyháza, Hősök tér 5; tel. (42) 599-599; fax (42) 599-512; e-mail elnok@wall.szabinet.hu; internet www.wall.szabinet.hu; Pres. of Gen. Assembly Dr LÁSZLÓ HELMECZY.

Tolna: 7100 Szekszárd, Szent István tér 11–13; 7101 Szekszárd, Pf. 82; tel. (74) 510-295; fax (74) 510-296; e-mail elnok@tolnamegye.hu; internet www.tolnamegye.hu; Pres. of Gen. Assembly TAMÁS KOLTAI.

Vas: 9700 Szombathely, Berzsenyi D. tér 1; tel. (94) 515-700; fax (94) 515-717; e-mail info@vasmegye.hu; internet www.vasmegye.hu; Pres. of Gen. Assembly PÉTER MARKÓ.

Veszprém: 8200 Veszprém, Megyeház tér 1; tel. (88) 545-000; fax (88) 545-012; internet www.vpmegye.hu; Pres. of Gen. Assembly CSABA KUTI.

Zala: 8900 Zalaegerszeg, Kosztolányi D. u. 10; tel. (92) 311-021; fax (92) 323-600; e-mail zmok@zal.kozig.b-m.hu; internet www .zalamegye.hu; Pres. of Gen. Assembly Dr FERENC KISS.

Budapest

Budapest Metropolitan Area Chief Mayor's Office: 1052 Budapest, Városház u. 9–11; tel. (1) 327-1000; fax (1) 318-9894; e-mail demskyg@budapest.hu; internet www.budapest.hu; Mayor GÁBOR DEMSZKY.

Political Organizations

Agrarian Association (Agrárszövetség): Budapest; Chair. TAMÁS NAGY.

Alliance of Free Democrats (AFD) (Szabad Demokraták Szövetsége—SzDSz): 1143 Budapest, Gizella u. 36; tel. (1) 223-2050; fax (1) 221-0579; e-mail zsolt.udvarvolgyi@szdsz.hu; internet www .szdsz.hu; f. 1988; 19,000 mems (2000); Chair. GÁBOR KUNCZE.

Centrum Party: Budapest; tel. (1) 301-5040; fax (1) 301-5048; e-mail centruminfo@axelero.hu; internet www.centrum-part.hu; f. 2001; electoral coalition of the Hungarian Democratic People's Party, the Christian Democratic People's Party, the Third Side for Hungary Association (HOME) and the Green Democrats Party; Chair. MIHÁLY KUPA.

Christian Democratic People's Party (CDPP) (Kereszténydemokrata Néppárt—KDNP): 1126 Budapest, Nagy Jenő u. 5; tel. (1) 175-0333; fax (1) 155-5772; e-mail kulugy@kdnp.hu; internet www .kdnp.hu; re-formed 1989; formed an electoral alliance, the Centrum Party (q.v.), to contest the 2002 legislative election; Chair. TIDAVAR BARTÓK.

Democratic Roma Coalition: ethnic Roma party; left-wing.

Entrepreneurs' Party: Budapest; was to support the Centrum Party in the 2002 legislative election; Chair. JÓSZEF TACAKS.

Federation of Young Democrats—Hungarian Civic Alliance (FYD—HCA) (Magyar Polgári Szövetség—FIDESZ—MPSZ): 1062 Budapest, Lendvay u. 28; tel. (1) 269-5353; fax (1) 269-5343; e-mail fidesz@fidesz.hu; internet www.fidesz.hu; f. 1988 as the Federation of Young Democrats; renamed April 1995; re-formed as an alliance in 2003, with a new charter; 10,000 mems; Chair. VIKTOR ORBÁN.

Green Party of Hungary: Budapest; f. 1989; Chair. ZOLTÁN MEDVECZKY.

Hungarian Christian Democratic Federation (MKDSZ): f. 1997 by breakaway members of the Christian Democratic People's Party; allied to the Federation of Young Democrats—Hungarian Civic Alliance; Chair. LÁSZLÓ SURJAN.

Hungarian Civic Co-operation Association (Magyar Polgari Egyuettmuekoedes Egyesuelet): Budapest; f. 1996; Chair. GYÖRGY GRANASZTOI; Gen. Sec. ZOLTÁN VESZELOVSZKI.

Hungarian Democratic Forum (HDF) (Magyar Demokrata Fórum—MDF): 1026 Budapest, Szilágyi Erszébet fasor 73; 1539 Budapest, POB 579; tel. (1) 212-2828; fax (1) 225-2290; internet www.mdf.hu; f. 1987; centre-right; formed an alliance with the Federation of Young Democrats—Hungarian Civic Party to contest the general election of 2002; 25,000 mems (2001); Chair. Dr IBOLYA DÁVID.

Hungarian Democratic People's Party (HDPP) (Magyar Demokrata Néppárt—MDN): Budapest; f. 1996 by former mems of the Hungarian Democratic Forum; moderate; formed an electoral alliance, the Centrum Party (q.v.), to contest the 2002 legislative election; Chair. ERZSÉBET PUSZTAI.

Hungarian Justice and Life Party (HJLP) (Magyar Igazság és Élet Párt—MIEP): 1085 Budapest, Rökk Szilárd u. 19; tel. and fax (1) 3171-2692; internet www.miep.hu; f. 1993; Chair. ISTVÁN CSURKA.

Hungarian National Front (Magyar Nemzeti Front): f. 2003 by former members of the Hungarian Justice and Life Party; Chair. ERNO ROZGONYI (acting).

Hungarian Social Democratic Party (HSDP) (Magyarországi Szocialdemokrata Párt—MSzDP): Budapest; tel. and fax (1) 342-3547; f. 1890; absorbed by Communist Party in 1948; revived 1988; affiliated with the Social Democratic Youth Movement; 3,000 mems (Dec. 1997); Chair. MÁTYÁS SZŰRÖS.

Hungarian Socialist Party (HSP) (Magyar Szocialista Párt—MSzP): 1081 Budapest, Köztársaság tér 26; tel. (1) 210-0046; fax (1) 210-0081; internet www.mszp.hu; f. 1989 to replace the Hungarian Socialist Workers' Party; 40,000 mems (Dec. 1999); Chair. LÁSZLÓ KOVÁCS.

Hungarian Workers' Party (HWP) (Magyar Munkáspárt—MMP): 1082 Budapest, Baross u. 61; tel. (1) 334-2721; fax (1) 313-5423; e-mail mpzoo@matavnet.hu; internet www.munkaspart.hu; f.

1956 as Hungarian Socialist Workers' Party; dissolved and replaced by Hungarian Socialist Party (see above) in 1989; re-formed in 1989 as Hungarian Socialist Workers' Party, name changed as above 1992; approx. 30,000 mems (Oct. 1992); Pres. Dr GYULA THÜRMER.

Independent Smallholders' and Civic Party (ISCP) (Független Kisgazda-, Földmunkás- és Polgári Párt—FKgP): 1056 Budapest, Belgrád rkp. 24; tel. and fax (1) 3181824; internet www.fkgp.hu; f. 1988 as the Independent Smallholders' Party, name subsequently changed to the Independent Smallholders' and Peasants' Party; 60,000 mems; Chair. Dr MIKLOS RETI.

Lungo Drom Alliance: 5000 Szolnok, Szapáry u. 19; tel. (56) 420-110; ethnic Roma party; right-wing; Leader FLORIAN FARKAS.

New Left Alliance: Budapest; f. 2001; formed from eight left-wing organizations; agreed to form an electoral coalition with the Romany Co-operation Party of Hungary to contest the 2002 general election; Pres. LÁSZLÓ SCHILLER.

Peace Party of Hungarian Gypsies (Magyar Ciganyok Bekepartja): Budapest; f. 1993; Leader ALBERT HORVÁTH.

Smallholder Alliance—Party of the Smallholder Federation: Budapest; f. 2002 by former mems of the ISCP; conservative; Chair. SANDOR CSEH.

United Historic Smallholders' Party (UHSP) (Egyesült Kisgazdapárt—Történelmi Tagozat—EKgP–TT): Budapest; f. 1992 as the 'Historical Section' of the Independent Smallholders' Party (now the ISCP); renamed 1993; Gen. Sec. ANTAL BELAFI.

Diplomatic Representation

EMBASSIES IN HUNGARY

Albania: 1026 Budapest, Gábor Áron u. 55; tel. (1) 326-8905; fax (1) 326-8904; Ambassador ISUF BASHKURTI.

Algeria: 1121 Budapest, Zugligeti u. 27; tel. (1) 200-6860; fax (1) 200-6781; Ambassador BACHIR ROUIS.

Argentina: 1023 Budapest, Vérhalom u. 12–16, II, 3A; tel. (1) 326-0492; fax (1) 326-0494; Ambassador GUILLERMO JORGE McGOUGH.

Australia: 1126 Budapest, Királyhágó tér 8–9; tel. (1) 457-9777; fax (1) 201-9792; e-mail ausembbp@mail.datanet.hu; internet www .australia.hu; Ambassador LEO CRUISE.

Austria: 1068 Budapest, Benczúr u. 16; tel. (1) 351-6700; fax (1) 352-8795; e-mail budapest@austroamb.hu; Ambassador Dr ERICH KUSSBACH.

Belgium: 1015 Budapest, Toldy Ferenc u. 13; tel. (1) 201-1571; fax (1) 375-1566; e-mail ambabel.budapest@mail.datanet.hu; Ambassador MICHEL CARLIER.

Belarus: 1126 Budapest, Agárdi u. 3B; tel. (1) 214-0553; fax (1) 214-0554; e-mail hungary@belembassy.org; Ambassador ANDREI YEUDACHENKA.

Bosnia and Herzegovina: 1026 Budapest, Pasaréti u. 48; tel. (1) 212-0106; fax (1) 212-0109.

Brazil: 1062 Budapest, Délibáb u. 30; tel. (1) 351-0060; fax (1) 351-0066; e-mail hunbrem@ind.eunet.hu; Ambassador LUCIANO OZORIO ROSA.

Bulgaria: 1062 Budapest, Andrássy u. 115; tel. (1) 322-0824; fax (1) 322-5215; e-mail bgembhu@ibm.net; Ambassador CHRISTO HALATCHEV.

Cambodia: Budapest; tel. (1) 155-1128; fax (1) 155-1128; Ambassador UNG SEAN.

Canada: 1121 Budapest, Budakeszi u. 32; tel. (1) 392-3360; fax (1) 392-3390; internet www.kanada.hu; Ambassador RONALD R. HALPIN (designate).

Chile: 1023 Budapest, Vérhalom u. 12–16, III, 35; tel. (1) 212-0061; fax (1) 212-0059; e-mail echilehu@pronet.hu; internet www.chile.hu; Ambassador CELSO ENRIQUE MORENO LAVAL.

China, People's Republic: 1068 Budapest, Benczúr u. 17; tel. (1) 332-4872; fax 322-9067; e-mail knnk@mail.matav.hu; Ambassador ZHAO XIDI.

Colombia: 1025 Budapest, Józsefhegyi u. 28-30 G-6; tel. (1) 325-7617; fax (1) 325-7618; e-mail embajada.budapest@colombia.hu; Ambassador BELARMINO PINILLA.

Costa Rica: Budapest; tel. (1) 1851-431; Ambassador JORGE EDOARDO VILLAFRANCA NÚÑEZ.

Croatia: 1065 Budapest, Munkácsy Mihály u. 15; tel. (1) 269-5657; fax (1) 354-1319; e-mail hrvhu1@mail.euroweb.hu; Ambassador Dr STANKO NICK.

Cuba: 1025 Budapest, Józsefhegyi u. 28–30, II, 6u.; tel. (1) 200-8916; fax (1) 200-8045; e-mail embacuba.bud@mail.matav.hu; Ambassador CARLOS TREJO SOSA.

Cyprus: 1051 Budapest, Dorottya u. 3, III, 2–3u.; tel. (1) 266-1330; fax (1) 266-0538.

Czech Republic: 1064 Budapest, Rózsa u. 61; tel. (1) 351-0539; fax (1) 351-9189; e-mail budapest@embassy.mzv.cz; Ambassador RUDOLF JINDRÁK.

Denmark: 1122 Budapest, Határőr u. 37; tel. (1) 355-7320; fax (1) 375-3803; Ambassador CLAUS JUUL NEILSON.

Ecuador: 1021 Budapest, Budakeszi u. 55D, P8, V/1; tel. (1) 200-8918; fax (1) 200-8682; e-mail mecuahun@hu.inter.net; Ambassador RAÚL MANTILLA-LARREA.

Egypt: 1016 Budapest, Bérc u. 16; tel. (1) 381-0475; fax (1) 381-0571; e-mail ambegp@pronet.hu; internet ceg.uiuc.edu/~haggag/embassy.html; Ambassador MUHAMMAD EL-SAYED ABBAS.

Estonia: 1062 Budapest, Lendvay u. 12, Fsz. 3; tel. (1) 312-4725; fax (1) 302-6527; e-mail lluht@estemb.hu; Ambassador TOIVO TASA.

Finland: 1118 Budapest, Kelenhegyi u. 16A; tel. (1) 279-2500; fax (1) 385-0843; e-mail sanomat.bud@formin.fi; Ambassador PEKKA KUJA-SALO.

France: 1062 Budapest, Lendvay u. 27; tel. (1) 332-4980; fax (1) 311-8291; e-mail ambasfn-presse@matavnet.hu; internet www.ambafrance.hu; Ambassador DOMINIQUE DE COMBLES DE NAYVES.

Germany: 1014 Budapest, Úri u. 64–66u.; tel. and fax (1) 488-3505; e-mail info@deutschebotschaft-budapest.hu; internet www.deutschebotschaft-budapest.hu; Ambassador URSULA SEILER-ALBRING.

Greece: 1063 Budapest, Szegfű u. 3; tel. (1) 413-2600; fax (1) 342-1934; e-mail greekemb@mail.matav.hu; Ambassador NIKOLAOS KALANTZIANOS.

Holy See: 1126 Budapest, Gyimes u. 1–3; tel. (1) 355-8979; fax (1) 355-6987; e-mail nuntbud@communio.hcbc.hu; Apostolic Nuncio Most Rev. KARL-JOSEF RAUBER (Titular Archbishop of Iubaltiana).

India: 1025 Budapest, Búzavirág u. 14; tel. (1) 325-7742; fax (1) 325-7745; e-mail chancery@indemb.datanet.hu; internet www.indianembassy.hu; Ambassador MANBIR SINGH.

Indonesia: 1068 Budapest, Városligeti fasor 26; tel. (1) 342-8508; fax (1) 322-8669; e-mail kbribud@mail.datanet.hu; internet www.indonesia.hu; Ambassador HASSAN ABDULDJALIL.

Iran: 1143 Budapest, Stefánia u. 97; tel. (1) 460-9260; fax (1) 460-9430; e-mail embiran@pronet.hu; Ambassador ABULFAZ RAHNAMA HEZAVEI.

Ireland: 1944 Budapest, Bank Center Gránit Torony, VII; tel. (1) 302-9600; fax (1) 302-9599; e-mail iremb@elender.hu; Ambassador JIM FLAVIN.

Israel: 1026 Budapest, Fullánk u. 8; tel. (1) 200-0781; fax (1) 200-0783; e-mail budapest@israel.org; Ambassador JUDITH VARNAI SHORER.

Italy: 1143 Budapest, Stefánia u. 95; tel. (1) 343-6065; fax (1) 343-6058; e-mail ambital@pronet.hu; internet www.ambitalia.hu; Ambassador GIOVAN BATTISTA VERDERAME.

Japan: 1125 Budapest, Zalai u. 7; tel. (1) 275-1275; fax (1) 275-1281; internet www.japan-embassy.hu; Ambassador YOSHITOMO TANAKA.

Kazakhstan: 1025 Budapest, II ker., Kapy u. 59; tel. (1) 275-1300; fax (1) 275-2092; e-mail kazak@euroweb.hu; Ambassador SAGYNBEK TURSUNOV.

Korea, Republic: 1062 Budapest, Andrássy u. 109; tel. (1) 351-1179; fax (1) 351-1182; e-mail koremb@mail.matav.hu; Ambassador CHO KYU-HYUNG.

Lebanon: 1112 Budapest, Sasadi u. 160; tel. (1) 249-0900; fax (1) 249-0901.

Libya: 1143 Budapest, Stefánia u. 111; tel. (1) 343-6076; fax (1) 343-1583; Head of People's Bureau OMAR MUFTAH DALLAL.

Macedonia, former Yugoslav republic: 1022 Budapest, Felső Zölmádli u. 120; tel. and fax (1) 315-1921.

Malaysia: 1022 Budapest, Tapolcsányi u. 18; tel. (1) 326-8312; fax (1) 326-8413; e-mail wbdpest@mail.matav.hu.

Mexico: 1023 Budapest, Vérhalom u. 12–16, III, 31–33; tel. (1) 326-0447; fax (1) 326-0485; Ambassador JOSÉ LUIS MARTÍNEZ Y H.

Moldova: 1111 Budapest, Budafoki u. 9–11; tel. (1) 209-1191; fax (1) 209-1195.

Mongolia: 1022 Budapest II, k. Bogár u. 14/C; tel. (1) 212-4579; fax (1) 212-5731; e-mail mnk@mail.matavnet.hu; Ambassador DERGEL-DALIYN DZAMBADZANCAN.

Morocco: 1026 Budapest, Törökvész Lejtő 12A; tel. (1) 200-7855; fax (1) 275-1437; e-mail sifamabudap@attglobal.net; Ambassador SAAD BADDOU.

Netherlands: 1022 Budapest, Füge u. 5–7, 2 District; 1388 Budapest, POB 56; tel. (1) 336-6300; fax (1) 326-5978; e-mail nlbdpez@nextra.hu; internet www.netherlandsembassy.hu; Ambassador F. P. R. VAN NOUHUYS.

New Zealand: Budapest; tel. (1) 131-2144; fax (1) 131-0593; Chargé d'affaires TAMÁS TAKATSY.

Nigeria: 1022 Budapest, Árvácska u. 6; tel. (1) 212-2021; fax (1) 212-2025; e-mail nigeria@matavnet.hu; internet www.nigerianembassy.hu; Ambassador: Chief ABAYOMI AKINTOLA.

Norway: 1015 Budapest, Ostrom u. 13, POB 32; tel. (1) 212-9400; fax (1) 212-9410; e-mail norwegian.embassy@pronet.hu; internet www.norvegia.hu; Ambassador JAN G. JØLLE.

Pakistan: 1125 Budapest, Adonis u. 3A; tel. (1) 355-8017; fax (1) 375-1402; e-mail pakemb@mail.matav.hu.

Panama: 1118 Budapest, Iglói u. 6/B2; tel. and fax (1) 466-9817; e-mail embpanbu@freemail.c3.hu.

Peru: 1025 Budapest, Józsefhegyi u. 28–30, F/2; tel. (1) 335-4019; fax (1) 355-1019; e-mail leprubda@mail.datanet.hu; Ambassador BERTHA VEGA PÉREZ.

Philippines: 1026 Budapest, Gábor Áron u. 58; tel. (1) 200-5523; fax (1) 200-5528; e-mail phbuda@mail.datanet.hu; Ambassador ALEJANDRO DEL ROSARIO.

Poland: 1068 Budapest, Városligeti fasor 16; tel. (1) 342-5566; fax (1) 351-1722; e-mail amb.bud@ind.eunet.hu; Ambassador GRZEGORZ LUBCZYK.

Portugal: 1024 Budapest, Romer Flóris u. 58; tel. (1) 316-2645; fax (1) 316-2642; e-mail embport@mail.matav.hu; Ambassador JOÃO CARLOS BESSA PINTO VERSTEEG.

Romania: 1146 Budapest, Thököly u. 72; tel. (1) 352-0271; fax (1) 343-6035; e-mail roembbud@mail.datanet.hu; Ambassador CALIN FABIAN.

Russia: 1062 Budapest, Bajza u. 35; tel. (1) 302-5230; fax (1) 353-4164; Ambassador VALERY MUSATOV.

Serbia and Montenegro: 1068 Budapest, Dózsa György u. 92B; tel. (1) 322-9838; fax (1) 322-1438; e-mail ambjubo@mail.datanet.hu; Chargé d'affaires BRANISAL NOVAKOVIĆ.

Slovakia: 1143 Budapest, Stefánia u. 22-24; tel. (1) 460-9010; fax (1) 460-9020; e-mail slovakem@matavnet.hu; Chargé d'affaires JURAJ PALACKA.

Slovenia: 1025 Budapest, Cseppkö u. 68; tel. (1) 438-5600; fax (1) 325-9187; Ambassador IDA MOČIVNIK.

South Africa: 1026 Budapest, Gárdonyi Géza út. 17; tel. (1) 392-0999; fax (1) 200-7277; e-mail saemb@elender.hu; internet www.sa-embassy.hu; Ambassador DRIES VENTER.

Spain: 1067 Budapest, Eötvös u. 11B; tel. (1) 342-9992; fax (1) 351-0572; Ambassador FERNANDO PERPIÑÁ-ROBERT.

Sweden: 1146 Budapest, Ajtósi Dürer sor 27A; tel. (1) 460-6020; fax (1) 460-6021; e-mail ambassaden.budapest@foreign.ministry.se; Ambassador STEFFAN CARLSSON.

Switzerland: 1143 Budapest, Stefánia u. 107; tel. (1) 460-7040; fax (1) 343-9492; e-mail vertretung@bud.rep.admin.ch; internet www.swissembassy.hu; Ambassador RUDOLF WEIERSMUELLER.

Syria: 1026 Budapest, Harangvirág u. 3; tel. (1) 200-8046; fax (1) 200-8048; Ambassador (vacant).

Thailand: 1025 Budapest, Verecke u. 79; tel. (1) 438-4020; fax (1) 438-4023; e-mail thaiemba@mail.datanet.hu; Ambassador CHALERMPOM AKE-URU.

Tunisia: 1021 Budapest, Budakeszi u. 55D; tel. (1) 200-8929; fax (1) 200-8931; e-mail ambtunb@mail.matav.hu; Chargé d'affaires ABDELWAHEB BOUZOUITA.

Turkey: 1062 Budapest, Andrássy u. 123; tel. (1) 344-5025; fax (1) 344-5143; e-mail budapest@turkisembassy.hu; Ambassador AYDAN KARAHAN.

Ukraine: 1143 Budapest, Stefania u. 77; tel. (1) 422-4122; fax (1) 220-9873; e-mail ukran.kovetseg@mail.datanet.hu; Ambassador Dr VASYL V. DURDYNETS.

United Kingdom: 1051 Budapest, Harmincad u. 6; tel. (1) 266-2888; fax (1) 266-0907; e-mail info@britemb.hu; internet www.britishembassy.hu; Ambassador JOHN NICHOLS (designate).

USA: 1054 Budapest, Szabadság tér 12; tel. (1) 475-4400; fax (1) 475-4764; internet www.usis.hu; Ambassador GEORGE H. WALKER (designate).

Uruguay: 1023 Budapest 2, Vérhalom u. 12–16, I, 3; tel. and fax (1) 326-0459; e-mail urupest@euroweb.hu; Ambassador Homero Diego Martínez Lawlor.

Venezuela: 1023 Budapest, Vérhalom u. 12–16, I, 14; tel. (1) 326-0460; fax (1) 326-0450; e-mail venhu@ibm.net; Ambassador Jorge A. González.

Viet Nam: 1068 Budapest 2, Benczúr u. 18; tel. (1) 342-5583; fax (1) 325-8798; Ambassador Dao Thi Tam.

Yemen: 1025 Budapest, Józsefhegyi u. 28-30, D/6; tel. (1) 212-3991; fax (1) 212-3883; e-mail al-yemen.al-saida@matavnet.hu; Ambassador (vacant).

Judicial System

The system of court procedure in Hungary is based on an Act that came into effect in 1953 and has since been updated frequently. The system of jurisdiction is based on the local courts (district courts in Budapest, city courts in other cities), labour courts, county courts (or the Metropolitan Court) and the Supreme Court. In the legal remedy system of two instances, appeals against the decisions of city and district courts can be lodged with the competent county court and the Metropolitan Court of Budapest respectively. Against the judgment of first instance of the latter, appeal is to be lodged with the Supreme Court. The Chief Public Prosecutor and the President of the Supreme Court have the right to submit a protest on legal grounds against the final judgment of any court.

By virtue of the 1973 Act, effective from 1974 and modified in 1979, the procedure in criminal cases is differentiated for criminal offences and for criminal acts. In the first instance, criminal cases are tried, depending on their character, by a professional judge; where justified by the magnitude of the criminal act, by a council composed of three members, a professional judge and two lay assessors, while in major cases the court consists of five members, two professional judges and three lay assessors. In the Supreme Court, second instance cases are tried only by professional judges. The President of the Supreme Court is elected by the National Assembly. Judges are appointed by the President of the Republic for an indefinite period. Assessors are elected by the local municipal councils.

In the interest of ensuring legality and a uniform application of the law, the Supreme Court exercises a principled guidance over the jurisdiction of courts. In the Republic of Hungary judges are independent and subject only to the Law and other legal regulations.

The Minister of Justice supervises the general activities of courts. the Chief Public Prosecutor is elected by the National Assembly. The Chief Public Prosecutor and the Prosecutor's Office provide for the consistent prosecution of all acts violating or endangering the legal order of society, the safety and independence of the state, and for the protection of citizens.

The Prosecutors of the independent prosecuting organization exert supervision over the legality of investigations and the implementation of punishments, and assist with specific means in ensuring that legal regulations should be observed by state, economic and other organs and citizens, and they support the legality of court procedures and decisions.

President of the Supreme Court: Zoltán Lomnici.

Chief Public Prosecutor: Péter Polt.

Constitutional Court: 1015 Budapest, Donáti u. 35-45; tel. (1) 488-3100; fax (1) 212-1170; internet www.mkab.hu; Pres. Andras Hollo.

Religion

CHRISTIANITY

Ecumenical Council of Churches in Hungary (Magyarországi Egyházak Ökumenikus Tanácsa): 1026 Budapest, Bimbó u. 127; tel. (1) 394-4847; fax (1) 394-1210; e-mail oikoumene@lutheran.hu; internet oikoumene.lutheran.hu; f. 1943; member churches: Baptist, Bulgarian Orthodox, Evangelical Lutheran, Hungarian Orthodox, Methodist, Reformed Church, Romanian Orthodox and Serbian Orthodox; Pres. Bishop Dr Mihály Márkus; Gen. Sec. Dr Tibor Görög.

The Roman Catholic Church

Hungary comprises four archdioceses, nine dioceses (including one for Catholics of the Byzantine rite) and one territorial abbacy (directly responsible to the Holy See). At 31 December 2001 the Church had 6,241,180 adherents in Hungary.

Bishops' Conference: Magyar Katolikus Püspöki Konferencia, 1071 Budapest, Városligeti fasor 45; tel. (1) 342-6959; fax (1) 342-

6957; e-mail pkt@katolikus.hu; f. 1969; Pres. Dr István Seregély (Archbishop of Eger).

Latin Rite

Archbishop of Eger: Dr István Seregély, 3301 Eger, Széchenyi u. 1, POB 80; tel. (36) 313-259; fax (36) 320-508; e-mail egersek@ektf.hu.

Archbishop of Esztergom-Budapest: Cardinal Dr Péter Erdő (Primate of Hungary), 1014 Budapest, Uri u. 62; tel. (1) 202-5611; fax (1) 202-5458.

Archbishop of Kalocsa-Kecskemét: Dr Balázs Bábel, 6301 Kalocsa, POB 29, Szentháromság tér 1; tel. (78) 462-166; fax (78) 462-130; e-mail kalocsa@hcbc.hu.

Archbishop of Veszprém: Dr Gyula Márfi, 8200 Veszprém, Vár u. 16-18; tel. (88) 426-088; fax (88) 426-287; e-mail veszprem@communio.hcbc.hu.

Byzantine Rite

Bishop of Hajdúdorog: Szilárd Keresztes, 4401 Nyiregyháza, Bethlen u. 5, POB 60; tel. (42) 317-397; fax (42) 314-734; 253,000 adherents (Dec. 1999); the Bishop is also Apostolic Administrator of the Apostolic Exarchate of Miskolc, with an estimated 25,000 Catholics of the Byzantine rite (Dec. 1999).

Protestant Churches

Baptist Union of Hungary (Magyarországi Baptista Egyház): 1068 Budapest, Benczur u. 31; tel. (1) 343-0618; fax (1) 352-9707; e-mail baptist.convention@mail.datanet.hu; f. 1846; 11,500 mems; Pres. Rev. Kálmán Mészáros; Gen.-Sec. Rev. Kornél Mészáros.

Evangelical Lutheran Church in Hungary (Magyarországi Evangélikus Egyház): 1085 Budapest, Üllöi u. 24; tel. (1) 317-5567; fax (1) 317-0872; e-mail orszagos@lutheran.hu; 430,000 mems (1992); Presiding Bishop Imre Szebik; Dir Károly Hafenscher.

Hungarian Methodist Church (Magyarországi Metodista Egyház): 1032 Budapest, Kiscelli u. 73; tel. (1) 250-1536; fax (1) 250-1849; e-mail kiscelli@axelero.hu; Superintendent István Csernák.

Reformed Church in Hungary—Presbyterian (Magyarországi Református Egyház): 1146 Budapest, Abonyi u. 21; tel. (1) 343-7870; e-mail rch@mail.elender.hu; 2m. mems (1987); 1,306 churches; Pres. of Gen. Synod Bishop Dr Gusztáv Bölcskei.

Unitarian Church in Hungary (Magyarországi Unitárius Egyház): 1055 Budapest V, Nagy Ignác u. 4; tel. (1) 111-2801; Bishop Rev. Martin Bencze.

The Eastern Orthodox Church

Hungarian Orthodox Church (Magyar Orthodox Egyház): 1052 Budapest, Petőfi tér 2.1.2.; tel. (1) 318-4813; Archbishop Pavel Ponomarjov.

Romanian Orthodox Church in Hungary (Magyarországi Román Ortodox Egyház): 5700 Gyula, Sz. Miklos park 2; tel. and fax (66) 361-281; f. 1997; monastic community; Bishop Sofronie Drincec.

Serbian Orthodox Diocese (Szerb Görögkeleti Egyházmegye): 2000 Szentendre, POB 22; Bishop Dr Danilo Kristic.

The Russian (6,000 mems) and Bulgarian Orthodox Churches are also represented.

BUDDHISM

Hungarian Buddhist Mission (Magyarországi Buddhista Misszió): 1386 Budapest, Postafiók 952; tel. (36) 138-52098; e-mail amm@dakiniland.net; internet www.dharma.hu; Rep. Dr Lajos Pressing.

Hungarian Zen Buddhist Community (Magyarországi Csan Buddhista Közösség): Budapest; Leader Fárad Lotfi.

ISLAM

There are about 3,000 Muslims in Hungary.

Hungarian Islamic Community (Magyar Iszlám Közösség): Budapest; tel. (1) 177-7602; Leader Dr Balázs Mihá"lffy.

JUDAISM

The Jewish community in Hungary is estimated to number between 100,000 and 120,000 people. Some 80% of Hungary's Jewish community resides in Budapest.

Federation of Jewish Communities in Hungary (Magyarországi Zsidó Hitközségek Szövetsége): 1075 Budapest, Sip u. 12, Budapesti Zsidó Hitközség (Jewish Community of Budapest); tel. (1) 342-1335; fax (1) 342-1790; e-mail bzsh@mail.matav.hu; 80,000 mems; 40 active synagogues; Orthodox and Conservative; Pres. Andras Heisler; Chief Rabbi of Hungary Dr Péter Kardos.

The Press

In 1998 there were 33 dailies, with an average daily circulation of 1,846,000. Budapest dailies circulate nationally. The most popular are: *Népszabadság*, *Nemzeti Sport* and *Népszava*. *Népszabadság*, the most important daily, was formerly the central organ of the Hungarian Socialist Workers' Party, but is now independent. Most daily newspapers were partially foreign-owned.

PRINCIPAL DAILIES

Békéscsaba

Békés Megyei Hírlap (Békés County News): 5601 Békéscsaba, Munkácsy u. 4; tel. (66) 446-242; fax (66) 441-020; internet www .bmhirlap.hu; f. 1945; Editor-in-Chief ZOLTÁN ÁRPÁSI; circ. 49,000.

Budapest

Blikk: Budapest; f. 1994; colour tabloid.

Magyar Hirlap (Hungarian Journal): 1087 Budapest, Kerepesi u. 29B; tel. (1) 210-0050; fax (1) 210-3737; internet www.magyarhirlap .hu; f. 1968; 100% foreign-owned; Editor-in-Chief MÁTYÁS VINCE; circ. 75,000.

Magyar Nemzet (Hungarian Nation): Budapest; tel. (1) 141-4320; internet www.magyarnemzet.com; 45% foreign-owned; Editor-in-Chief GÁBOR LISZKAY; circ. 100,000.

Mai Nap (Today): 1145 Budapest, Szugló u. 14; tel. (1) 470-1382; fax (1) 470-1351; e-mail info@mainap.hu; f. 1988; Editor-in-Chief FERENC KÖSZEGI; circ.100,000.

Metro: 1106 Budapest, Fehér u. 10, 21-es épület; tel. (1) 431-6464; fax (1) 431-6465; e-mail szerk@metro.hu; internet www.metro.hu; Editor IZBÉKI GÁBOR.

NAPI Gazdaság (World Economy): 1135 Budapest, Csata u. 32; tel. (1) 350-4349; fax (1) 350-1117; e-mail napi@mail.eleuder.hu; internet www.napi.hu; Editor-in-Chief ADÁM DANKÓ; circ. 16,000.

Nemzeti Sport (National Sport): 1141 Budapest, Szugló u. 83-85; tel. (1) 460-2600; fax (1) 460-2612; Editor-in-Chief TAMÁS SZEKERES; circ. 140,000.

Népszabadság (People's Freedom): 1960 Budapest, Bécsi u. 122-124; tel. (1) 436-4500; fax (1) 387-8699; e-mail eotvosp@ nepszabadsag.hu; internet www.nepszabadsag.hu; f. 1942; independent; Editor-in-Chief PÁL EÖTVÖS; circ. 200,000.

Népszava (Voice of the People): 1022 Budapest, Törökvész u. 30A; tel. (1) 202-7788; fax (1) 202-7798; e-mail online@nepszava.hu; internet www.nepszava.hu; f. 1873; Editor ANDRÁS KERESZTY; circ. 120,000.

Pest Megyei Hirlap (Pest County Journal): Budapest; tel. (1) 138-2399; Editor-in-Chief Dr ANDRÁS BÁRD; circ. 43,000.

Pesti Hirlap (Pest Journal): 1051 Budapest, Október 6 u. 8; tel. (1) 117-6162; fax (1) 117-6029; f. 1993; Editor-in-Chief ANDRÁS BENCSIK; circ. 50,000.

Üzlet (Business): Budapest; tel. (1) 111-8260; Editor-in-Chief IVÁN ÉRSEK.

Debrecen

Hajdú-Bihari Napló (Hajdú-Bihar Diary): 4024 Debrecen, Dósa nádor tér 10; tel. (52) 413-395; fax (52) 412-326; e-mail naplo@iscomp .hu; internet www.naplo.hu; f. 1944; Editor-in-Chief ZSOLT PORCSIN; circ. 60,000.

Dunaújváros

A Hirlap (The Journal): 2400 Dunaújváros, Városháza tér 1; tel. (25) 16-010; Editor-in-Chief CSABA D. KISS.

Eger

Heves Megyei Hirlap (Heves County Journal): 3301 Eger, Barkóczy u. 7; tel. (36) 13-644; e-mail hmhirlap@axels.hu; internet www .agria.hu/hmhirlap; Editor-in-Chief LEVENTE KAPOSI; circ. 33,000.

Győr

Kisalföld: 9021 Győr, Újlak u. 4/a; tel. (96) 504-444; fax (96) 504-414; e-mail kisalfoldmail.matav.hu; internet www.kisalfold.hu; Editor-in-Chief NYERGES CSABA.

Kaposvár

Somogyi Hirlap (Somogy Journal): 7401 Kaposvár, Latinca Sándor u. 2A; tel. (82) 11-644; internet www.somogyihirlap.hu; Editor-in-Chief Dr IMRE KERCZA; circ. 59,000.

Kecskemét

Petőfi Népe: 6000 Kecskemét, Szabadság tér 1A; tel. (76) 481-391; internet www.petofinepe.hu; Editor-in-Chief Dr DÁNIEL LOVAS; circ. 60,000.

Miskolc

Déli Hirlap (Midday Journal): 3527 Miskolc, Bajcsy-Zsilinszky u. 15; tel. (46) 42-694; Editor-in-Chief DEZSŐ BEKES; circ. 20,000.

Észak-Magyarország (Northern Hungary): 3527 Miskolc, Bajcsy-Zsilinszky u. 15; tel. (46) 341-888; internet www.eszak.hu/eszako.2; Editor-in-Chief LÁSZLÓ GÖRÖMBÖLYI; circ. 45,000.

Nyíregyháza

Kelet-Magyarország (Eastern Hungary): 4401 Nyíregyháza, Zrínyi u. 3–5; tel. (42) 11-277; Editor-in-Chief Dr SÁNDOR ANGYAL; circ. 80,000.

Pécs

Új Dunántúli Napló: 7601 Pécs, Hunyadi u. 11; tel. (72) 15-000; internet 195.184.19.151/index.php3; Editor-in-Chief JENŐ LOMBOSI; circ. 84,000.

Salgótarján

Új Nógrád (New Nógrád): 3100 Salgótarján, Palócz Imre tér 4; tel. (32) 10-589; Editor-in-Chief LÁSZLÓ SULYOK; circ. 23,000.

Szeged

Délvilág (Southern World): 6740 Szeged, Tanácsköztársaság u. 10; tel. (62) 14-911; internet www.delvilag.hu; Editor-in-Chief ISTVÁN NIKOLÉNYI; circ. 20,000.

Délmagyarország (Southern Hungary): 6740 Szeged, Stefánia 10; tel. (62) 481-281; internet www.delmagyar.szeged.hu; Editor-in-Chief IMRE DLUSZTUS; circ. 70,000.

Székesfehérvár

Fejér Megyei Hirlap (Fejér County Journal): 8003 Székesfehérvár, Honvéd u. 8; tel. (22) 12-450; Editor-in-Chief JÁNOS Á. SZABÓ; circ. 52,000.

Szekszárd

Tolna Megyei Népújság (Tolna News): 7100 Szekszárd, Liszt Ferenc tér 3; tel. (74) 16-211; Editor-in-Chief GYÖRGYNÉ KAMARÁS; circ. 32,000.

Szolnok

Új Néplap (New People's Paper): 5001 Szolnok, Kossuth tér 1, I. Irodaház; tel. (56) 42-211; internet www.ujneplap.hu; Editor-in-Chief JÓZSEF HAJNAL; circ. 46,000.

Szombathely

Vas Népe (Vas People): 9700 Szombathely, Berzsenyi tér 2; tel. (94) 12-393; Editor-in-Chief SÁNDOR LENGYEL; circ. 65,000.

Tatabánya

24 Óra (24 Hours): 2800 Tatabánya, Fö tér 4; tel. (34) 514-012; fax (34) 514-011; e-mail szerk.kom@axels.hu; internet www.24ora.hu; Editor-in-Chief FERENC SZTRAPÁK; circ. 23,000.

Veszprém

Napló (Diary): 8201 Veszprém, Szabadság tér 15; tel. (80) 27-444; Editor-in-Chief ELEMÉR BALOGH; circ. 58,000.

Zalaegerszeg

Zalai Hirlap (Zala Journal): 8901 Zalaegerszeg, Ady Endre u. 62; tel. (92) 12-575; Editor-in-Chief JÓZSEF TARSOLY; circ. 71,000.

WEEKLIES

Élet és Irodalom (Life and Literature): 1089 Budapest, Rezsö tér 15; tel. (1) 210-2157; fax (1) 269-9241; e-mail es@es.hu; internet www.es.hu; f. 1957; literary and political; Editor ZOLTÁN KOVÁCS; circ. 16,000.

Élet és Tudomány (Life and Science): 1088 Budapest, Bródy Sándor u 16; tel. and fax (1) 138-2472; f. 1946; popular science; Editor-in-Chief Dr HERCZEG JÁNOS; circ. 20,000.

Evangélikus Élet (Evangelical Life): 1085 Budapest, Üllői u. 24; tel. and fax (1) 117-1108; f. 1933; Evangelical–Lutheran Church newspaper; Editor MIHÁLY TÓTH-SZÖLLŐS; circ. 12,000.

Heti Világgazdaság (World Economy Weekly): 1124 Budapest, Németvölgy u. 62-64; tel. (1) 3555-411; fax (1) 3555-693; internet www.hvg.hu; f. 1979; Editor-in-Chief IVÁN LIPOVECZ; circ. 141,000.

Képes Újság (Illustrated News): 1085 Budapest, Gyulai Pál u. 14; tel. (1) 113-7660; f. 1960; Editor MIHÁLY KOVÁCS; circ. 400,000.

Ludas Matyi: Budapest; tel. (1) 133-5718; satirical; Editor JÓZSEF ÁRKUS; circ. 352,000.

L'udové Noviny (People's News): 1065 Budapest, Nagymező u. 49; tel. (1) 131-9184; in Slovak, for Slovaks in Hungary; Editor PÁL KONDÁCS; circ. 1,700.

Magyar Mezőgazdaság (Hungarian Agriculture): 1355 Budapest, Kossuth Lajos tér 11; tel. (1) 112-2433; f. 1946; Editor-in-Chief Dr KÁROLY FEHÉR; circ. 24,000.

Magyar Nők Lapja (Hungarian Women's Journal): 1022 Budapest, Törökvész u. 30A; tel. (1) 212-4020; fax (1) 326-8264; e-mail noklapja@noklapja.ekh.hu; f. 1949; Editor-in-Chief LILI ZÉTÉNYI; circ. 550,000.

Magyarország (Hungary): Budapest; tel. (1) 138-4644; f. 1964; news magazine; Editor DÉNES GYAPAY; circ. 200,000.

Narodne Novine (People's News): 1396 Budapest, POB 495; tel. (1) 112-4869; f. 1945 for Yugoslavs in Hungary; in Serbo-Croat and Slovene; Chief Editor MARKO MARKOVIĆ; circ. 2,800.

Neue Zeitung (New Paper): 1391 Budapest, Lendvay u. 22, POB 224; tel. (1) 302-6877; e-mail neueztg@mail.elender.hu; f. 1957 for Germans in Hungary; Editor JOHANN SCHUTH; circ. 4,500.

Rádió és Televízióújság (Radio and TV News): 1801 Budapest; tel. (1) 138-8114; fax (1) 138-7349; f. 1924; Editor MÁRTA BÓDAY; circ. 300,000.

Reform: Budapest; tel. and fax (1) 122-4240; f. 1988; popular tabloid; 50% foreign-owned; Editor PÉTER TŐKE; circ. 300,000.

Reformátusok Lapja: 1395 Budapest, POB 424; tel. (1) 117-6809; fax (1) 117-8386; f. 1957; Reformed Church paper for the laity; Editor-in-Chief and Publr ATTILA P. KOMLÓS; circ. 30,000.

Szabad Föld (Free Earth): 1087 Budapest, Könyves Kálmán krt 76; tel. and fax (1) 133-6794; f. 1945; Editor GYULA ECK; circ. 720,000.

Szövetkezet (Co-operative): 1054 Budapest, Szabadság tér 14; tel. (1) 131-3132; National Council of Hungarian Consumer Co-operative Societies; Editor-in-Chief ATTILA KOVÁCS; circ. 85,000.

Tallózó: 1133 Budapest, Visegrádi u. 110-112; tel. and fax (1) 149-8707; f. 1989; news digest; Editor-in-Chief GYÖRGY ANDAI; circ. 35,000.

Tőzsde Kurir (Hungarian Stock Market Courier): Budapest; tel. (1) 122-3273; fax (1) 142-8356; business; Editor-in-Chief ISTVÁN GÁBOR BENEDEK.

Új Ember (New Man): 1053 Budapest, Kossuth Lajos u. 1; tel. (1) 117-3661; fax (1) 117-3471; f. 1945; religious weekly; Editor LÁSZLÓ RÓNAY; circ. 70,000.

OTHER PERIODICALS
(Published monthly unless otherwise indicated)

Állami Gazdaság (State Farming): General Direction of State Farming, Budapest; tel. (1) 112-4617; fax (1) 111-4877; f. 1946; Editor P. GÖRGÉNYI.

Beszeloe (The Speaker): 1364 Budapest, POB 143; tel. and fax (1) 302-1271; e-mail beszelo@mailc3.hu; culture and criticism; Editor-in-Chief ILONA KISS.

Business Partner Hungary: 1081 Budapest, Csokonai u. 3; tel. (1) 303-9586; fax (1) 303-9582; e-mail nemeth@kopdat.hu; internet www.kopdat.hu; f. 1986; every two months; English and German; economic journal published by Economic, Research Marketing and Computing Co Ltd (KOPINT-DATORG); Head of Dept ILONA NÉMETH.

Egyházi Krónika (Church Chronicle): 1052 Budapest, Petőfi tér 2.1.2; tel. and fax (1) 318-4813; f. 1952; every two months; Eastern Orthodox Church journal; Editor Archpriest Dr FERIZ BERKI.

Elektrotechnika (Electrical Engineering): 1055 Budapest, Kossuth Lajos tér 6–8; tel. (1) 353-0117; fax (1) 353-4069; e-mail lernyei .mee@mtesz.hu; f. 1908; organ of Electrotechnical Association; Editor Dr JÁNOS BENCZE; circ. 6,500.

Élelmezési Ipar (Food Industry): 1372 Budapest, POB 433; tel. (1) 214-6691; fax (1) 214-6692; e-mail mail.mete@mtesz.hu; internet www.mtesz.hu; f. 1947; Scientific Society for Food Industry; Editor Dr ISTVÁN TÓTH-ZSIGA.

Energia és Atomtechnika (Energy and Nuclear Technology): 1055 Budapest, Kossuth Lajos tér 6–8; tel. (1) 153-2751; fax (1) 156-1215; f. 1947; every two months; Scientific Society for Energy Economy; Editor-in-Chief Dr G. BŐKI.

Energiagazdálkodás (Energy Economy): 1055 Budapest, Kossuth Lajos tér 6; tel. (1) 153-2751; fax (1) 153-3894; Scientific Society for Energetics; Editor Dr ANDOR ANESINI.

Ezermester (The Handyman): Budapest; tel. (1) 132-1987; f. 1957; do-it-yourself magazine; Editor JÓZSEF PERÉNYI; circ. 50,000.

Gép (Machinery): 1027 Budapest, Fő u. 68; tel. (1) 135-4175; fax (1) 153-0818; f. 1949; Scientific Society of Mechanical Engineering; Editor Dr KORNÉL LEHOFER.

Hungarian Travel Magazine: Budapest, Múzeum u. 11; tel. (1) 138-4643; quarterly in English and German; illustrated journal of the Tourist Board for visitors to Hungary; Man. Editor JÚLIA SZ. NAGY.

Ipar-Gazdaság (Industrial Economy): 1371 Budapest, POB 433; tel. (1) 202-1083; f. 1948; Editor Dr TAMÁS MÉSZÁROS; circ. 4,000.

Jogtudományi Közlöny (Law Gazette): 1535 Budapest, POB 773; 1015 Budapest, Dónáti u. 35-45; tel. (1) 355-0330; fax (1) 355-0441; e-mail jogtud@mkab.hu; f. 1866; legal and administrative sciences; Editor-in-Chief Dr IMRE VÖRÖS; circ. 1,000.

Kortárs (Contemporary): 1426 Budapest, POB 108; tel. (1) 342-1168; e-mail kortars@elender.hu; internet www.elender.hu/kortars; f. 1957; literary gazette; Editor-in-Chief IMRE KIS PINTÉR; circ. 5,000.

Közgazdasági Szemle (Economic Review): 1112 Budapest, Budaörsi u. 43–45; tel. (1) 315-3165; fax (1) 315-3166; internet www .kozgazdasagiszemle.hu; f. 1954; published by Cttee for Economic Sciences of Hungarian Academy of Sciences; Editor KATALIN SZABÓ; circ. 3,000.

Made in Hungary: 1426 Budapest, POB 3; economics and business magazine published in English by Hungarian News Agency (MTI); Editor GYÖRGY BLASITS.

Magyar Hirek (Hungarian News): Budapest; tel. (1) 122-5616; fax (1) 122-2421; every 2 weeks; illustrated magazine primarily for Hungarians living abroad; Editor GYÖRGY HALÁSZ; circ. 70,000.

Magyar Jog (Hungarian Law): 1054 Budapest, Szemere u. 10; tel. (1) 311-4880; fax (1) 311-4013; f. 1953; law; Editor-in-Chief Dr JÁNOS NÉMETH; circ. 2,200.

Magyar Közlöny (Official Gazette): Budapest; tel. (1) 112-1236; Editor Dr ELEMÉR KISS; circ. 90,000.

Magyar Tudomány (Hungarian Science): Hungarian Academy of Sciences, 1051 Budapest, Nádor u. 7; tel. and fax (1) 317-9524; e-mail matud@hefka.iif.hu; internet www.matud.hu; f. 1846; monthly; multidisciplinary science review; Editors VILMOS CSÁNYI, ZSUZSA SZENTGYÖRGYI.

Pedagógusok Lapja (Teachers' Review): 1068 Budapest, Városligeti fasor 10; tel. (1) 322-8464; e-mail psz-seh@mail.matav.hu; internet www.deltasoft.hu/pszseh; f. 1945; published by the Hungarian Union of Teachers; Editor-in-Chief ÁROK ANTAL; circ. 10,000.

Református Egyház (Reformed Church): 1146 Budapest, Abonyi u. 21; tel. (1) 343-7870; f. 1949; official journal of the Hungarian Reformed Church; Editor-in-Chief LAJOS TÓTH; circ. 1,300.

Statisztikai Szemle (Statistical Review): 1525 Budapest, POB 51; tel. (1) 487-4343; fax (1) 487-4344; e-mail statszemle@ksh.gov.hu; internet www.ksh.hu/statszml; f. 1923; Editor-in-Chief Dr LÁSZLÓ HUNYADI; circ. 800.

Technika (Technology): 1027 Budapest, Fö u. 68; tel. (1) 201-7083; fax (1) 201-8564; f. 1957; official journal of the Hungarian Academy of Engineering; monthly in Hungarian, annually in English, German and Russian; Editor-in-Chief MARGIT WELLEK; circ. 15,000.

Turizmus (Tourism): 1088 Budapest, Múzeum u. 11; tel. (1) 266-5853; fax (1) 338-4293; e-mail turizmus@mail.matav.hu; Editor ZSOLT SZEBENI; circ. 8,000.

Új Élet (New Life): 1075 Budapest, Síp u. 12; tel. (1) 322-2829; every 2 weeks; for Hungarian Jews; Editor Dr PÉTER KARDOS; circ. 5,000.

Új Technika (New Technology): Budapest; tel. (1) 155-7122; f. 1967; popular industrial quarterly; circ. 35,000.

Vigilia: 1364 Budapest, POB 48; tel. (1) 317-7246; fax (1) 317-7682; e-mail vigilia@hcbc.hu; internet www.hcbc.hu/vigilia; f. 1935; Catholic; Editor LÁSZLÓ LUKÁCS; circ. 4,000.

NEWS AGENCIES

HT Press News Agency: 1149 Budapest, Angol u. 22; tel. and fax (1) 363-1472.

Hungarian News Agency Co (Magyar Távirati Iroda Rt—MTI): 1016 Budapest, Naphegy tér 8; tel. (1) 375-6722; fax (1) 375-3973; internet www.mti.hu; f. 1880; 19 brs in Hungary; 14 bureaux abroad; Pres. MATYAS VINCE.

Foreign Bureaux

Agence France-Presse (AFP): 1016 Budapest, Naphegy u. 29; tel. (1) 356-8416; fax (1) 201-9161; e-mail afpbud@elender.hu; Correspondent ESZTER SZÁMADÓ.

Agenzia Nazionale Stampa Associata (ANSA) (Italy): 1054 Budapest, Vadász u. 31; tel. (1) 332-3555; fax (1) 332-3556; Bureau Chief GAETANO ALIMENTI.

Associated Press (AP) (USA): Budapest; tel. (1) 156-9129; Correspondent ALEX BANDY.

Informatsionnoye Telegrafnoye Agentstvo Rossii—Telegrafnoye Agentstvo Suverennykh Stran (ITAR—TASS) (Russia): 1023 Budapest, Vérhalom u. 12–16; Correspondent YEVGENII POPOV.

Reuters (United Kingdom): 1088 Budapest, Rákóczi u. 1–3, East-West Business Centre; tel. (1) 266-2410; fax (1) 266-2030; internet www.reuters.hu; Chief Correspondent MITYA NEW.

Rossiyskoye Informatsionnoye Agentstvo—Novosti (RIA—Novosti) (Russia): Budapest; tel. (1) 132-0594; fax (1) 142-3325; Bureau Chief A. POPOV.

Tlačová agentúra Slovenskej republiky (TASR) (Slovakia): Budapest; tel. and fax (1) 135-1843; Bureau Chief PETER KLENKO.

Xinhua (New China) News Agency (People's Republic of China): Budapest; tel. (1) 176-7548; fax (1) 176-2571; Chief Correspondent ZHOU DONGYAO.

PRESS ASSOCIATIONS

Hungarian Newspaper Publishers' Association: 1034 Budapest, Bécsi üt 122-124; tel. (1) 368-8674; fax (1) 388-6707; e-mail mle .peto@mail.matav.hu; f. 1990; Gen. Sec. JÁNOS PETŐ; 40 mems.

National Association of Hungarian Journalists (Magyar Újságírók Országos Szövetsége—MUOSZ): 1062 Budapest, Andrássy u. 101; tel. (1) 322-1699; fax (1) 322-1881; f. 1896; Gen. Sec. GÁBOR BENCSIK; 7,000 mems.

Publishers

PRINCIPAL PUBLISHING HOUSES

Akadémiai Kiadó: 1117 Budapest, Prielle Kornélia u. 4; tel. (1) 464-8200; fax (1) 464-8201; e-mail custservice@akkrt.hu; internet www.akkrt.hu; f. 1828; humanities, social, natural and technical sciences, dictionaries, textbooks and periodicals; Hungarian and English; Man. Dir BUCSI SZABÓ ZSOLT.

Corvina Kiadó Kft.: 1051 Budapest, Vörösmarty tér 1; tel. (1) 318-4347; fax (1) 318-4410; e-mail corvina@mail.matav.hu; f. 1955; Hungarian works translated into foreign languages, art and educational books, fiction and non-fiction, tourist guides, cookery books and musicology; Man. Dir ISTVÁN BART.

EMB Music Publisher Ltd: Budapest, V. Vörösmarty t. 1; tel. (1) 483-3100; fax (1) 483-3101; e-mail musicpubl@emb.hu; internet www.emb.hu; f. 1950; music publishing and books on musical subjects; Dir ISTVÁN HOMOLYA.

Európa Könyvkiadó: 1055 Budapest, Kossuth Lajos tér 13–15; tel. (1) 131-2700; fax (1) 131-4162; f. 1945; world literature translated into Hungarian; Man. LEVENTE OSZTOVITS.

Gondolat Könyvkiadó Vállalat: Budapest; tel. (1) 138-3358; fax (1) 138-4540; f. 1957; popular scientific publications on natural and social sciences, art, encyclopaedic handbooks; Dir GYÖRGY FEHÉR.

Helikon Kiadó: 1053 Budapest, Papnövelde u. 8; tel. (1) 117-4865; fax (1) 117-4865; bibliophile books; Dir KATALIN BERGER.

Képzőművészeti Kiadó: Budapest; tel. (1) 251-1527; fax (1) 251-1527; fine arts; Man. Dr ZOLTÁN KEMENCZEI.

Kossuth Kiadó Rt.: 1043 Budapest, Csányi László u. 36; tel. (1) 370-0607; fax (1) 370-0602; e-mail rt@kossuted.hu; f. 1944; social sciences, educational and philosophy publications, information technology books; Man. ANDRÁS SÁNDOR KOCSIS.

Közgazdasági és Jogi Könyvkiadó Rt: Budapest; tel. (1) 112-6430; fax (1) 111-3210; f. 1955; business, economics, law, sociology, psychology, tax, politics, education, dictionaries; Man. Dir DAVID G. YOUNG.

Magvető Könyvkiadó: 1806 Budapest, POB 123; tel. (1) 235-5032; e-mail magveto@lira.hu; f. 1955; literature; Dir GÉZA MORCSÁNYI.

Medicina Könyvkiadó Rt: 1054 Budapest, Zoltan u. 8; tel. (1) 112-2650; fax (1) 112-2450; f. 1957; books on medicine, sport, tourism; Dir BORBÁLA FARKASVÖLGYI.

Mezőgazda Kiadó: 1165 Budapest, Koronafürt u. 44; tel. (1) 407-6575; fax (1) 407-7571; ecology, natural sciences, environmental protection, food industry; Man. Dr LAJOS LELKES.

Móra Ferenc Ifjúsági Kiadó Rt.: 1134 Budapest, Váci u. 19; tel. (1) 320-4740; fax (1) 320-5382; e-mail mora_kiado@elender.hu; f. 1950; youth and children's books; Man. Dr JÁNOS CS. TÓTH.

Műszaki Könyvkiadó: 1033 Budapest III, Szentendre u. 89–93; tel. (1) 437-2405; fax (1) 437-2404; e-mail lakatosz@muszakikiado .hu; internet www.muszakikiado.hu; f. 1955; scientific and technical, vocational and general text books; Man. SÁNDOR BÉRCZI.

Nemzeti Tankönyvkiadó Rt. (National Textbook Publishing House): 1143 Budapest, Szobránc u. 6-8; tel. (1) 460-1800; fax (1) 460-1869; e-mail public@ntk.hu; internet www.ntk.hu; f. 1949; school and university textbooks, pedagogical literature and language books; Gen. Man. JÓZSEF PÁLFI.

Népszava Lapés Könyvkiadó Vállalat: Budapest; tel. (1) 122-4810; National Confederation of Hungarian Trade Unions; Man. Dr JENŐ KISS.

Statiqum Kiadó és Nyomda Kft: 1033 Budapest, Kaszásdülő u. 2; tel. (1) 250-0311; fax (1) 168-8635; f. 1991; publications on statistics, system-management and computer science; Dir BENEDEK BELECZ.

Szépirodalmi Könyvkiadó: Budapest; tel. (1) 122-1285; f. 1950; modern and classical Magyar literature; Man. SÁNDOR Z. SZALAI.

Zrinyi Kiadó: 1087 Budapest, Kerepesi u. 29B; tel. (1) 133-9165; military literature; Man. MÁTÉ ESZES.

PUBLISHERS' ASSOCIATION

Hungarian Publishers' and Booksellers' Association (Magyar Könyvkiadók és Könyvterjesztők Egyesülése): Budapest; tel. (1) 343-2540; fax (1) 343-2541; e-mail mkke@mkke.hu; f. 1795; most leading Hungarian publishers are members of the Association; Pres. ISTVÁN BART; Sec.-Gen. PÉTER ZENTAI.

WRITERS' UNION

Association of Hungarian Writers (Magyar Írószövetség): 1062 Budapest, Bajza u. 18; tel. (1) 322-8840; f. 1945; Pres. BÉLA POMOGÁTS.

Broadcasting and Communications

TELECOMMUNICATIONS

Matáv Hungarian Telecommunications Co: 1541 Budapest, Krisztina krt 6–8; tel. (1) 458-0000; fax (1) 458-7176; e-mail investor .relations@ln.matav.hu; internet www.matav.hu; f. 1991; 60% owned by Deutsche Telekom AG (Germany); telecommunications service provider; Chief Exec. ELEK STRAUB; 16,034 employees.

Pannon GSM Rt: 2040 Budaörs, Baross u. 165; tel. (1) 464-6000; fax (1) 464-6100; internet www.pgsm.hu; f. 1993; 100% owned by Telenor (Norway); mobile telecommunications; Chair. KLAUS HOLGAARD RASMUSSEN (designate).

Westel Rt: 1117 Budapest, Kaposvár u. 5-7; tel. (1) 265-9210; fax (1) 204-4128; e-mail customer_service@westel.hu; internet www.westel .hu; mobile telecommunications and internet service provider; Chief Exec. ANDRÁS SUGÁR.

BROADCASTING

Hungarian National Radio and Television Board (Országos Rádió és Televízió Testület—ORTT): 1088 Budapest, Reviczky u. 5; tel. (1) 429-8600; fax (1) 267-2612; e-mail ehorvath@ortt.hu; internet www.ortt.hu; Dir ISTVÁN HAJDU.

RADIO

Hungarian Radio (Magyar Rádió): 1800 Budapest, Bródy Sándor u. 5–7; tel. (1) 328-8388; fax (1) 328-7004; internet www.radio.hu; f. 1924; stations: Radio Kossuth, Radio Petőfi, Radio Bartók (mainly classical music); 8 regional studios; external broadcasts in English, German, Hungarian, Romanian, Russian, Slovak and Serbo-Croat; Pres. KATALIN KONDOR.

Antenna Hungária Magyar Msorszóró És, Rádióhírközlési Rt: 1119 Budapest, Petzvál József u 31–33; tel. (1) 203-6060; fax (1) 203-6093; internet www.ahrt.hu; f. 1989; radio and television broadcasting; Chief Exec. ISTVÁN MÁTÉ; 1,290 employees.

Radio C: 1086 Budapest, Teleki tér. 7; tel. (1) 459-0095; fax (1) 459-0094; internet www.radioc.hu; f. 2001; Roma radio station; news and cultural programming suspended in April 2003 owing to lack of funds; Man. GYÖRGY KERENYI.

Radio Danubius: f. 1986; privatized 1998; broadcasts news, music and information in Hungarian 24 hours a day; transmitting stations in Budapest, Lake Balaton region, Sopron, Szeged and Debrecen; Dir JÓZSEF LÁSZLÓ.

TELEVISION

Hungarian Television (Magyar Televízió): 1810 Budapest, Szabadság tér 17; tel. (1) 353-3200; fax (1) 373-4133; e-mail mtvintrel@intrel.mtv.hu; internet www.mtv.hu; f. 1957; first channel, MTV 1, terrestrial, broadcasts 19 hours a day and the second channel, MTV 2, satellite, 24 hours a day, colour transmissions; 100 high-capacity relay stations; Pres. IMRE RAGÁTS.

Antenna Hungária Magyar Msorszóró És, Rádióhírközlési Rt: 1119 Budapest, Petzvál József u 31–33; tel. (1) 203-6060; fax (1) 203-6093; internet www.ahrt.hu; f. 1989; radio and television broadcasting; Chief Exec. ISTVÁN MÁTÉ; 1,290 employees.

Finance

(cap. = capital; res = reserves; dep. = deposits; m. = million; amounts in forint unless otherwise stated)

Under economic reforms, introduced in 1987, three banks were established to assume the commercial banking activities of the National Bank of Hungary: the Hungarian Credit Bank, the Commercial and Credit Bank and the Budapest Bank. The already existing Hungarian Foreign Trade Bank and the National Savings and Commercial Bank also became fully chartered financial institutions. At the end of 1998 28 of Hungary's 36 commercial banks were foreign- or jointly-owned, and there were an additional seven specialized financial institutions. There were also 241 savings co-operatives. By 2001 there were a total of 42 commercial banks in operation in Hungary.

Responsibility for bank supervision is divided between the National Bank of Hungary and the State Banking Supervision Agency. Under legislation introduced in January 1997, the supervisory responsibilities of the National Bank were restricted to areas relating to the operation of monetary policy and the foreign-exchange system.

BANKING

Central Bank

National Bank of Hungary (Magyar Nemzeti Bank): 1850 Budapest, Szabadság tér 8–9; tel. (1) 269-4760; fax (1) 332-3913; internet www.mnb.hu; f. 1924; bank of issue; conducts international transactions; supervises banking system; cap. 10,000m., res 30,862m., dep. 2,202,879m. (Dec. 2001); Pres. ZSIGMOND JÁRAI; 23 brs.

Commercial Banks

Bank of Hungarian Savings Co-operatives Ltd (Magyar Takarékszövetkezeti Bank Rt): 1122 Budapest, Pethényi köz 10; 1525 Budapest, POB 775; tel. (1) 202-3777; fax (1) 355-9082; e-mail info@tbank.hu; internet www.takarekbank.hu; f. 1989; cap. 2,040.8m., res 3,517.1m., dep. 104,465.4m. (Dec. 2000); Pres. PETER DIECKMANN; Gen. Man. PÉTER CSICSÁKY.

BNP Paribas Bank (Hungaria) RT: 1055 Budapest, Honvéd u. 20; tel. (1) 374-6300; fax (1) 269-3967; e-mail info.hu@bnpparibas.com; f. 1991; wholly owned by BNP Paribas (France); cap. 3,500m., res 2,329m., dep. 58,153m. (Dec. 1999); Chair. JACQUES DE LAROSIÈRE; Gen. Man. LÁSZLÓ HAÁS.

Budapest Bank RT: 11138 Budapest, POB 1852, Váci u. 202; tel. (1) 328-1700; fax (1) 269-2417; e-mail info@bbrt.hu; internet www.budapestbank.hu; f. 1987; cap. 19,350m., res 5,768m., dep. 270,902m. (Dec. 2000); 99.25% owned by GE Capital International Financing Corpn (USA); Chief Exec. RICHARD PELLY; 56 brs.

Central-European International Bank Ltd (CIB): 1537 Budapest, Medve u. 4–14, POB 394; tel. (1) 212-1330; fax (1) 212-4200; e-mail cib@cib.hu; internet www.cib.hu; f. 1979; 100% owned by IntesaBci Holding International SA (Luxembourg); merged with CIB Hungária Bank Rt in 1998; cap. 23,500m., res 15,800m., dep. 545,873m. (Dec. 2001); Chair. Dr GYÖRGY SURÁNYI; Dir-Gen. and Chief Exec. ADÁM FARKAS.

Citibank RT: 1051 Budapest, Szabadság tér 7, Bank Center, Citibank Tower; 1367 Budapest, POB 123; tel. (1) 374-5000; fax (1) 374-5100; internet www.citibank.hu; f. 1986; merged with Europai Kereskedelmi Bank RT in 1999; cap. 13,005m., res 3,997m., dep. 241,252m. (Dec. 2001); Chief Exec. and Gen. Man. MARK T. ROBINSON.

Commerzbank (Budapest) RT: 1054 Budapest, Széchenyi rkp. 8; 1254 Budapest, POB 1070; tel. (1) 374-8100; fax (1) 269-4530; e-mail commerzbank@commerzbank.hu; internet www.commerzbank.hu; f. 1993; cap. 2,466.9m., res 6,206.0m., dep. 110, 208.3m. (Dec. 1999);

Pres. and Chair. of Sup. Bd ANDREAS DE MAIZIÈRE; Chair., Chief Exec. and Man. Dir MARTIN FISCHEDICK.

Erste Bank Hungary RT: 1054 Budapest, Hold u. 16; tel. (1) 373-2400; fax (1) 373-2499; internet www.erstebank.hu; f. 1987 as Mezobank RT; present name adopted 1998; cap. 11,210m., res 1,392m., dep. 244,280m. (Dec. 2001); Chair. REINHARD ORTNER; Chief Exec. PÉTER KISBENEDEK; 72 brs.

General Banking and Trust Co. Ltd (Altalános Értékforgalmi Bank RT): 1055 Budapest, Markó u. 9; tel. (1) 269-1473; fax (1) 269-1442; e-mail esebok@gbt.hu; internet www.gbt.hu; f. 1922; 25.5% owned by Gazprombank (Russia); cap. US $76.9m., res –$19.3m., dep. $916.3m. (Dec. 2001); Chair. and Chief Exec. MEGDET RAKHIMKULOV; 11 brs.

Hungarian Development Bank (MFB) Ltd (Magyar Fejlesztési Bank RT): 1051 Budapest, Nádor u. 31; tel. (1) 428-1400; fax (1) 428-1490; e-mail bank@mfb.hu; internet www.mfb.hu; f. 1991 as an investment company; authorized as a bank 1993; cap. 72,270m. (Dec. 2001), res 22,358.6m., dep. 93,388.0m. (Dec. 2000); Chair. of Bd GYÖRGY ZDEBORSKY.

Hungarian Foreign Trade Bank Ltd (Magyar Külkereskedelmi Bank RT): 1056 Budapest, V. Váci u. 38; tel. (1) 269-0922; fax (1) 269-0959; e-mail exterbank@mkb.hu; internet www.mkb.hu; f. 1950; commercial banking; 89.3% owned by Bayerische Landesbank (Germany); cap. 11,520m., res 69,326m., dep. 786,106m. (Dec. 2001); Chair. and Chief Exec. TAMÁS ERDEI; 29 brs.

HVB Bank Hungary RT: 1054 Budapest, Akadémia u. 17; 1363 Budapest, POB 58; tel. (1) 369-0812; fax (1) 353-4959; internet www.hvb.hu; f. 2001 by merger of Bank Austria Creditanstalt Hungary RT and Hypovereinsbank Hungary RT; 100% owned by Bank Austria Creditanstalt AG; cap. 24,118m., res 12,089m., dep. 451,919m. (Dec. 2001); Chief Exec. Dr MATTHIAS KUNSCH.

ING Bank RT: 1061 Budapest, Andrássy u. 9; tel. (1) 235-8700; fax (1) 322-2288; internet www.ing.hu; f. 1992 as NMB Bank; present name adopted 1996; 100% owned by ING Bank NV (Netherlands); cap. 15,758m., res 5,281m., dep. 134,648m. (Dec. 1999); Man. Dir RANDOLPH S. KOPPA.

Inter-Európa Bank RT: 1054 Budapest, Szabadság tér 15, POB 65; tel. (1) 373-6000; fax (1) 269-2526; e-mail ieb@ieb.hu; internet www.ieb.hu; f. 1981 as INTERINVEST; cap. 6,934m., res 2,498m., dep. 115,519m. (Dec. 2001); Chair. FERENC BARTHA; Man. Dir EZIO SALVAI; 20 brs.

Kereskedelmi és Hitelbank RT (K&H Bank RT): 1051 Budapest, Vigadó tér 1; tel. (1) 328-9000; fax (1) 328-9696; e-mail khbinfo@khb.hu; internet www.khb.hu; f. 1987; merged with Kvantum Investment Bank in 1998, merged with ABN Amro (Magyar) Bank RT in 2001; 59.1% owned by KBC Bank NV (Belgium), 40.2% owned by ABN Amro Bank NV (Netherlands); cap. 34,089m., dep. 444,565m. (Dec. 2001); Chair. Dr ISTVÁN SZALKAI; Chief Exec. ÁGNES BÁBA (acting); 176 brs.

Konzumbank RT: 1054 Budapest, Tüköry u. 4, POB 300; tel. (1) 374-7300; fax (1) 374-7355; e-mail info@konzumbank.hu; internet www.konzumbank.hu; f. 1986; 85.7% owned by Hungarian Development Bank (MFB) Ltd; cap. 5,231m., res –735m., dep. 74,084m. (Dec. 2001); Chair. GYULA GAÁL; Chief Exec. TIBOR FERENCI.

National Savings and Commercial Bank Ltd—OTP Bank (Országos Takarékpénztár és Kereskedelmi Bank RT): 1051 Budapest, Nádor u. 16; tel. (1) 353-1444; fax (1) 312-6858; e-mail otpbank@otpbank.hu; internet www.otpbank.hu; f. 1949; savings deposits, credits, foreign transactions; privatized in 1996; cap. 28,000m., res 98,335m., dep. 1,709,380m. (Dec. 2000); Chair. and Chief Exec. Dr SÁNDOR CSÁNYI; 424 brs.

Postbank and Savings Bank Corporation—Postabank (Postabank és Takarékpénztár RTt): 1132 Budapest, Váci u. 48; tel. (1) 318-0855; fax (1) 317-1369; e-mail info@postabank.hu; internet www.postabank.hu; f. 1988; 96.8% owned by Hungarian Post; cap. 20,021m., res 20,467m., dep. 272,597m. (Dec. 2000); Chair. JÚLIA KIRÁLY; Chief Exec. BÉLA SINGLOVICS; 71 brs.

Raiffeisen Bank RT: 1054 Budapest, Akademia u. 6, POB 173; tel. (1) 484-4400; fax (1) 484-4444; e-mail info@raiffeisen.hu; internet www.raiffeisen.hu; f. 1986 as Unicbank RT; present name adopted 1999; 96.8% owned by Raiffeisen Group (Austria); cap. 21,891m., res 9,688m., dep. 293,219m. (Dec. 2001); Pres. Dr HERBERT STEPIC; Man. Dir Dr PÉTER FELCSUTI; 41 brs.

Westdeutsche Landesbank (Hungaria) RT: 1075 Budapest, Madách Imre ut. 13–14; tel. (1) 268-1680; fax (1) 268-1933; e-mail public@westlb.hu; internet www.westlb.de; f. 1985; present name adopted 1993; cap. 4,485.8m., res 2,487.7m., dep. 79,353.3m. (Dec. 2001); Chair. and Dir-Gen. JÜRGEN PHILIPPER; Dir-Gen. GEZA EGYED.

Specialized Financial Institutions

Hungarian Export-Import Bank Ltd—EXIMBANK (Magyar Export-Import Bank RT): 1065 Budapest, Nagymezö u. 46-48; tel. (1) 374-9100; fax (1) 269-4476; e-mail eximh@eximbank.hu; internet www.eximbank.hu; cap. 10,100m., res 1,789m., dep. 100,598m. (Dec. 2001); Chief Exec. Dr FRIGYES BÁNKI.

Merkantil Bank Ltd: 1051 Budapest, József Attila u. 24; tel. (1) 429-7600; fax (1) 429-7601; e-mail molnar.andrasne@mail.merkantil.hu; internet www.merkantil.hu; f. 1988; affiliated to National Savings and Commercial Bank Ltd—OTP Bank; automobile financing transactions; cap. 1,100m.; Chair. and Chief Exec. ADÁM KOLOSSVÁRY.

Opel Bank Hungary RT: 1027 Budapest, Kapás u. 11-15; tel. (1) 457-9110; Gen. Man. JARI ARJAVALTA.

Porsche Bank Hungaria RT.: 1139 Budapest, Váci ut. 85; tel. (1) 465-4700; fax (1) 465-4775; e-mail info@porschebank.hu; internet www.porschebank.hu; Pres. PÁL ANTALL.

Rákóczi Regional Development Bank Ltd (Rákóczi Regionális Fejlesztési Bank RT): 3530 Miskolc, Mindszent tér 1; tel. (46) 510-300; fax (46) 510-396; e-mail central@rakoczibank.hu; f. 1992; Gen. Man. KORNÉL KOSZTICZA.

Other Financial Institution

Central Corporation of Banking Companies (Pénzintézeti Központ): 1093 Budapest, Lónyay u. 38; tel. (1) 117-1255; fax (1) 215-9963; f. 1916; banking, property, rights and interests, deposits, securities, and foreign exchange management; cap. 11,127m., res 3,548m., dep. 12,289m.; Chair. and Chief Exec. PÉTER KIRÁLY; 3 brs.

STOCK EXCHANGE

Budapest Stock Exchange (Budapesti Értéktőzsde): 1052 Budapest, Deák Ferenc u. 5; tel. (1) 429-6700; fax (1) 429-6800; e-mail info@bse.hu; internet www.bse.hu; Pres. GYÖRGY JAKITSKY.

COMMODITY EXCHANGE

Budapest Commodity Exchange (Budapesti Árutőzsde): 1134 Budapest, Róbert Károly krt 61–65; tel. (1) 465-6979; fax (1) 465-6981; e-mail bce@bce-bat.com; internet www.bce-bat.com; Chair. ATTILA KOVÁCS.

INSURANCE

In July 1986 the state insurance enterprise was divided into two companies, one of which retained the name of the former Állami Biztosító. By 1995 13 insurance companies had been established.

AB-AEGON Általános Biztosító RT: 1091 Budapest, u. Üllői 1; tel. (1) 218-1866; fax (1) 217-7065; internet www.aegon.hu; f. 1949 as Állami Biztosító, reorganized 1986, present name since 1992; handles pensions, life and property insurance, insurance of agricultural plants, co-operatives, foreign insurance, etc.; Gen. Man. Dr GÁBOR KEPECS; 4,000 employees.

Garancia Insurance Company (Garancia Biztosító RT): 1054 Budapest, Vadász u. 12; tel. (1) 269-2533; fax (1) 269-2549; f. 1988; cap. 4,050m.; Gen. Man. and Chief Exec. Dr ZOLTÁN NAGY; 25 brs.

Hungária Insurance Company (Hungária Biztosító RT): 1054 Budapest, Bajcsy u. 52; tel. (1) 301-6565; fax (1) 301-6100; f. 1986; handles international insurance, industrial and commercial insurance and motor-car, marine, life, household, accident and liability insurance; cap. 4,266m.; Chair. and Chief Exec. Dr MIHÁLY PATAI.

QBE Atlasz Insurance Company (QBE Atlasz Biztosító RT): 1143 Budapest, Stefánia ùt 51; tel. (1) 460-1400; fax (1) 460-1499; e-mail qbe-atlasz@atlasz.hu; internet www.qbeatlasz.hu; f. 1988; cap. 1,000m.; Gen. Man. DORON GROSSMAN.

Trade and Industry

GOVERNMENT AGENCY

Hungarian Privatization and State Holding Company (ÁPV Rt): 1133 Budapest, Pozsonyi u. 56; tel. (1) 237-4400; fax (1) 237-4100; e-mail apvrt@apvrt.hu; internet www.apvrt.hu; f. 1995 by merger of the State Property Agency and the State Holding Company; Chair. CSABA FARAGÓ.

NATIONAL CHAMBERS OF COMMERCE AND AGRICULTURE

Hungarian Chamber of Agriculture (Magyar Agrárkamara): 1119 Budapest, Etele ut. 57; tel. (1) 371-5517; fax (1) 371-5510; e-mail agota@kozpont.agrarkamara.hu; internet www.agrarkamara.hu; Pres. MIKLÓS CSIKAI.

Hungarian Chamber of Commerce and Industry (Magyar Kereskedelmi és Iparkamara): 1372 Budapest V, POB 452; tel. (1) 474-5141; fax (1) 250-5138; e-mail mkik@mkik.hu; f. 1850; central organization of the 23 Hungarian county chambers of commerce and industry; based on a system of voluntary membership; over 46,000 mems.; Pres. Dr LÁSZLÓ PARRAGH; Sec.-Gen. PÉTER DUNAI.

REGIONAL CHAMBERS OF COMMERCE

Bács-Kiskun County Chamber of Commerce: 6000 Kecskemét, Árpád krt 4, POB 228; tel. (76) 501-500; fax (76) 501-538; e-mail bkmkik@mail.datanet.hu; internet www.iparkamara.hu; f. 1994; Chair. JÓZSEF GAÁL; Sec. LÁSZLÓ LEITNER.

Békés County Chamber of Commerce and Industry: 5600 Békéscsaba, Penza ltp. 5; tel. (66) 451-775; fax (66) 324-976; e-mail bmkik@elender.hu; internet www.bmkik.ini.hu; Chair. TAMÁS HÓDSÁGI; Sec. ZSOLT TÓTH.

Borsod-Abaúj-Zemplén County Chamber of Commerce and Industry (Borsod-Abaúj-Zemplén Kereskedelmi és Iparkamara): 3525 Miskolc, Szentpáli u. 1; tel. (46) 328-539; fax (46) 328-722; e-mail bokik@mail.bokik.hu; internet www.bokik.hu; f. 1990; membership of 1,100 cos; Pres. TAMÁS BIHALL; Sec. ANNA BAÁN-SZILÁGYI.

Budapest Chamber of Industry and Commerce (Budapesti Kereskedelmi és Iparkamara): 1016 Budapest, Krisztina krt 99; tel. (1) 488-2173; fax (1) 488-2180; e-mail nemzetkozi@bkik.hu; internet www.bkik.hu; f. 1850; Chair. LÁSZLÓ KOJI; Sec.-Gen. CSABA BAZSC.

Csongrád County Chamber of Commerce and Industry: 6721 Szeged, Tisza L. krt 2–4; tel. (62) 423-451; fax (62) 426-149; e-mail info@csmkik.hu; internet www.csmkik.hu; Chair. ISTVÁN SZERI; Sec. LAJOS HORVÁTH.

Fejér County Chamber of Commerce and Industry (Fejér Megyei Kereskedelmi és Iparkamara): 8000 Székesfehérvár, Hosszúsétatér 4–6; POB 357; tel. (22) 510-310; fax (22) 510-312; e-mail fmkik@mail.fmkik.hu; internet www.fmkik.hu; Chair. JENŐ RADETZKY; Sec.-Gen. Dr ÉVA SIPOS.

Gyôr-Moson-Sopron County Chamber of Commerce and Industry: 9001 Gyôr, Szent István u. 10/A; POB 673; tel. (96) 520-200; fax (96) 520-291; e-mail kamara@gymskik.hu; internet www.gymskik.gyor.hu; Chair. TOTH BALÁSZ; Sec. ATTILA NAGY.

Hajdú-Bihar County Chamber of Commerce and Industry: 4025 Debrecen, Petőfi tér 10; tel. (52) 500-721; fax (52) 500-720; internet www.hbkik.hu; Chair. FERENC MIKLÓSSY; Sec. Dr EVA SKULTÉTI.

Heves County Chamber of Commerce and Industry: 3300 Eger, Telekessy út. 2; tel. (36) 429-612; fax (36) 312-989; internet hkik.hu; Chair. LEVENTE NAGY; Sec.-Gen. GÁBOR FÜLÖP.

Jász-Nagykun-Szolnok County Chamber of Commerce and Industry: 5000 Szolnok, Verseghy Park 8; tel. (56) 510-610; fax (56) 370-005; e-mail kamara@jnszmkik.hu; internet www.jnszmkik.hu; Chair. Dr ANDRÁS SZIRÁKI; Sec. Dr ZOLTÁN PINTÉR.

Komárom-Esztergom County Chamber of Commerce and Industry: 2800 Tatabánya, Előd vezér u. 17; tel. and fax (34) 316-259; Chair. Dr ISTVÁN HORVÁTH; Sec. ZOLTÁN BÁTOR.

Nógrád County Chamber of Commerce and Industry: 3100 Salgótarján, Alkotmàny u. 9A; tel. (32) 520-860; fax (32) 520-862; e-mail nkik@nkik.hu; internet www.ccinograd.com; Chair. ERZSÉBET FODORNÉ KOVÁCS; Sec. Dr ERZSÉBET KURUCZ BERENTE.

Pécs-Baranya County Chamber of Commerce and Industry: 7625 Pécs, Dr Majorossy I. u. 36; tel. (72) 507-149; fax (72) 507-152; e-mail pbkik@pbkik.hu; internet www.pbkik.hu; Chair. GYULA HIGI; Sec. TAMÁS SÍKFÓI.

Pest County Chamber of Commerce and Industry (Pest Megyei Kereskedelmi és Iparkamara): 1056 Budapest, Vàci u. 40; tel. (1) 317-7666; fax (1) 317-7755; e-mail titkarsag@pmkik.hu; internet www.pmkik.hu; Chair. Dr ZOLTÁN VERECZKEY; Sec.-Gen. Dr LAJOS KUPCSOK.

Somogy Chamber of Commerce and Industry (Somogyi Kereskedelmi és Iparkamara): 7400 Kaposvár, Anna u. 6; tel. (82) 501-000; fax (82) 501-046; e-mail skik@skik.hu; internet www.skik.hu; Chair. JÓZSEF VARGA; Dep. Pres. LAJOS HORVÁTH.

Szabolcs-Szatmár-Bereg County Chamber of Commerce and Industry: 4400 Nyíregyháza, Széchenyi u. 2; tel. (42) 416-074; fax (42) 311-750; Chair. Dr JÁNOS VERES; Sec. NAGY KATALIN VARGA.

Tolna County Chamber of Commerce and Industry: 7100 Szekszárd, Arany J. u. 23–25; tel. (74) 411-661; fax (74) 411-456; e-mail kamara@tmkik.hu; internet www.tmkik.hu; Chair. Dr SÁNDOR FISCHER; Sec. ZSOLT BERÉTI.

Vas County Chamber of Commerce and Industry (Vas Megyei Kereskedelmi és Iparkamara): 9700 Szombathely, Honvéd tér 2; tel. (94) 312-356; fax (94) 316-936; e-mail vmkik@vmkik.hu; internet www.vmkik.hu; Chair. VINCE KOVÁCS; Sec.-Gen. SÁNDOR KISS.

Veszprém County Chamber of Commerce and Industry: 8200 Veszprém, Budapest u. 3; tel. (88) 429-008; fax (88) 412-150; e-mail vkik@veszpremikamara.hu; internet www.veszpremikamara.com; Chair. KÁROLY HENGER; Dir TAMÁS CSABAI.

Zala County Chamber of Commerce and Industry (Zalai Kereskedelmi és Iparkamara): 8900 Zalaegerszeg, Petőfi u. 24; tel. (92) 550-510; fax (92) 550-525; e-mail zmkik@zmkik.hu; internet www .zmkik.hu; Chair. IMRE FARKAS; Sec.-Gen. ISTVÁN TÓTH.

INDUSTRIAL AND TRADE ASSOCIATIONS

HUNICOOP Foreign Trade Company Ltd for Industrial Co-operation: 1036 Budapest, Lajos u. 80; 1367 Budapest 5, POB 111; tel. (1) 250-8117; fax (1) 250-8121; e-mail hunicoop@matavnet.hu; agency for foreign companies in Hungary, export and import; Dir GÁBOR TOMBÁCZ.

Hungarian Industrial Association (Magyar Iparszövetség—OKISz): 1146 Budapest, Thököly u. 58–60; tel. (1) 343-5570; fax (1) 343-5521; e-mail okisz@okiszinfo.hu; internet www.okiszinfo.hu; safeguards interests of over 2,000 member enterprises (all private); Pres. LÁSZLÓ HÖRÖMPÖLY.

National Co-operative Council (Országos Szövetkezeti Tanács——OSzT): 1054 Budapest, Szabadság tér 14; tel. (1) 312-7467; fax (1) 311-3647; f. 1968; Pres. TAMÁS FARKAS; Sec. Dr JÓZSEF PÁL.

National Federation of Agricultural Co-operators and Producers (Mezőgazdasági Szövetkezők és Termelők Országos Szövetsege—MOSZ): 1054 Budapest, Akadémia u. 1–3; tel. and fax (1) 353-2552; e-mail mosz@mail.tvnet.hu; internet www.msztorz.hu; f. 1990; frmly Termelő szövetkezetek Országos Tanácsa TOT (National Council of Agricultural Co-operatives); Pres. TAMÁS NAGY; Sec.-Gen. GÁBOR HORVÁTH; est. 1,300 mem. orgs.

National Federation of Consumer Co-operatives (Általános Fogyasztási Szövetkezetek Országos Szövetsége—ÁFEOSz): 1054 Budapest, Szabadság tér 14; tel. (1) 153-4222; fax (1) 111-3647; safeguards interests of Hungarian consumer co-operative societies; organizes co-operative wholesale activities; Pres. Dr PÁL BARTUS; 800,000 mems.

UTILITIES

Hungarian Energy Office: 1081 Budapest, Köztársaság tér 7; tel. (1) 317-4089; fax (1) 317-1330; e-mail hivatal.energia@eh.ikm .x400gw.itb.hu; f. 1994; regulation and supervision of activities performed by gas and electricity companies, price regulation and protection of consumer interest; Pres. GYÖRGY HATVANI.

Electricity

AES-Tisza Erőmű Kft (AES-Tisza Power Plant Company): 3581 Tiszaújváros Pf 53; tel. (49) 547-333; fax (49) 341-756; internet www .aes.hu; f. 1992; re-founded 1999; owned by AES Corpn (USA); electricity generation and merchandising; Chair. ALLAN B. DWYER; 544 employees.

Budapest Electricity Plc (Budapesti Elektromos Művek Rt, ELMŰ Rt): 1132 Budapest, Váci u. 72–74; tel. (1) 238-1000; fax (1) 238-2822; e-mail elmu@elmu.hu; internet www.elmu.hu; f. 1949; transmission and distribution of electricity; Chair. of Supervisory Bd Dr KLAUS BUSSFELD; 3,371 employees.

Dédász Rt (South Transdanubian Electricity Distribution): 7626 Pécs, Rákóczi, u. 73B; tel. (72) 441-022; fax (72) 445-633; internet www.dedasz.hu; Chair. ZOLTÁN PALUSKA.

Démász Rt (South Hungarian Power Supply Plc): 6720 Szeged, Klauzál tér 9; tel. (62) 476-576; fax (62) 482-500; internet www .demasz.hu; f. 1951; distributes electricity to South-Eastern Hungary; Chair. of Bd Dr DANIEL DUMONT; 1,864 employees.

Dunamenti Power Plant Rt: 2440 Százhalombatta, Erőmű u. 2; tel. (23) 354-161; fax (23) 354-381; electricity generation; Chair. TIBOR KUHL.

Édász Rt (North-Transdanubian Electricity Supply Co): 9027 Győr, Kandó Kálmán u. 11–13; tel. (96) 521-000; fax (96) 521-888; e-mail webmaster@edasz.hu; internet www.edasz.hu; f. 1951; generates and supplies electricity; Chair. BÉLA KÜNSZLER; 2,272 employees.

Émász Rt (North Hungarian Electricity Supply Co Ltd): 3525 Miskolc, Dózsa Gy, u. 13; tel. (46) 411-875; fax (46) 411-871; internet www.emasz.hu.

Hungarian Power Companies Ltd (Magyar Villamos Művek Rt——MVM Rt): 1255 Budapest, POB 77; 1011 Budapest, Vám u. 5–7; tel. (1) 224-6200; fax (1) 202-1246; e-mail mvm@mvm.hu; internet www.mvm.hu; Hungarian national electricity wholesaler and power-system controller; all 6 distributors and 6 (of 8) power-plant companies privatized in 1995–97; Chair. GYULA LENGYEL.

Mátrai Erőmű Részvénytársaság (Mátra Power Plant Rt): 3272 Visonta, Erőmű u. 11; tel. (37) 328-001; fax (37) 328-036; internet www.mert.hu; electricity generation; Chair. JÓSZEF VALASKA; 3,645 employees.

National Power Grid Company Ltd: 1054 Budapest, Szabadsajto u. 5.

Paks Nuclear Plant Ltd (Paksi Atomeromu v Pav): 7031 Paks, POB 71; tel. (75) 508-833; fax (75) 506-662; internet www.npp.hu; f. 1992; electrical energy production; Plant Man. SÁNDOR NAGY; 2,800 employees.

Tiszántúli Áramszolgáltató Részvénytársaság—Titász (East Hungarian Electricity Supply Co): 4024 Debrecen, Kossuth Lajos u. 4; tel. (52) 410-011; fax (52) 414-031; internet www.titasz.hu; Chair. FRANZ ERÉNYI.

Vértesi Erőmű Részvénytársaság (Vértes Power Plant Rt): 2840 Oroszlány, Pf. 23; tel. (34) 360-255; fax (34) 360-882; e-mail vert@ vert.hu; internet www.vert.hu; electricity and heat generation; Chair. KÁROLY TAKÁCS; 5,438 employees.

Gas

Budapest Gas Works (Főgáz) Rt: 1081 Budapest, Köztársaság tér 20; tel. (1) 477-1111; fax (1) 477-1277; internet www.fogaz.hu; f. 1856; gas distribution; Chair. DEZSŐ VASANITS.

Degaz—Delalfoldi Gázszolgáltató Részvénytársaság: 6724 Szeged, Pulcz u. 44; tel. (62) 472-572; fax (63) 324-943; e-mail ugyfel@degas.hu; internet www.degas.hu; public gas supply and services; 1,327 employees.

Hungarian Oil and Gas Company Ltd (MOL) (Magyar Olaj és Gázipari Rt): 1117 Budapest, Október huszonharmadika u. 18; tel. (1) 209-0000; fax (1) 209-0005; e-mail webmaster@mol.hu; internet www.mol.hu; f. 1991 by merger of part of the National Oil and Gas Trust and a technical development co; privatized in 1995, with the state retaining a 25% stake; petroleum and gas exploration, processing, transportation and distribution; 12,000 employees; Chair. and Chief Exec. ZSOLT HERNÁDI.

Tigáz—Tiszántúli Gázszolgáltató Részvénytársaság: 4200 Hajdúszoboszló, Rákóczi u. 184; tel. (52) 558-100; fax (52) 361-149; e-mail titkarsaga@tigaz.hu; internet www.hungas.hu/tagok/tigaz .html; f. 1950; 40% owned by Italgas Gruppo (Italy); gas distribution; Chair. MARINO BIAGIO; 3,324 employees.

MAJOR COMPANIES

Hungary's foreign-trade organizations were modernized throughout the 1980s. New regulations, introduced in 1988, permitted all business organizations to export products and to conduct business with foreign partners without the involvement of specialized traders. By the early 1990s more than 90% of all import activities had been liberalized and no special licences were required for foreign trading. Many of the country's enterprises underwent privatization in the early 1990s: by the end of 1994 a total of 1,204 companies, out of the 1,848 managed by the SPA, had been converted into joint-stock companies. By the end of 1999 there was a high level of foreign investment which contributed to the development of export sectors and modern management techniques. By May 2000 over 80% of the economy was privately-owned.

Agrikon Engineering Co: 6000 Kecskemét, Kulso-Szegedi u. 136; tel. (76) 482-269; fax (76) 481-602; e-mail agrikon.sam@mail.datanet .hu; internet www.agrikon.hu; the group comprises Agrikon Silo and Technical Works Ltd, Kecskemét and Budapest; Agrikon Cabin and Agrotechnical Works Ltd, Kiskunmajsa and Kiskőrös; Agrikon Metalindustrial Ltd, Kerekegyháza; and the Foreign Trade Management company Agrikon SAM Ltd; engineering and servicing for agricultural and food-processing machines and storage facilities; Man. Dir PÁL HUGYECZ; 300 employees.

Alcoa-Köfém Kft: 8000 Székesfehérvári, Verseci u. 1–15; tel. (22) 531-200; fax (22) 312-491; internet www.alcoa-kofem.hu; f. 1941; manufacture of aluminium products and semiproducts, truck bodies and automotive assemblies; Gen. Man. PHIL COLLINS; 1,950 employees.

Audi Hungária Motor Kft: 9027 Győr, Reptéri u. 5475; tel. (96) 501-205; fax (96) 501-210; internet www.audi.hu; f. 1993; automobile manufacturer; owned by Audi (Germany); Man. Dir JÜRGEN LUNEMANN; 5,000 employees.

BHG Elektromechanika Kft: 1519 Budapest, POB 336; Sopron u. 190; tel. (1) 204-5710; fax (1) 204-5715; e-mail bhgkft:axelero.hu; internet www.bhg.hu; also BHG Hiradástechnikai Rt; production of telecommunications equipment; Gen. Dir LÁSZLÓ MIKICS.

Biogal Gyógyszergyár Rt: 4042 Debrecen, Pallagi út 13; tel. (52) 311-868; fax (52) 418-752; internet www.kszgysz.hu/biogal.htm; f. 1951; manufacture and trade in pharmaceutical products; Man. Dir Dr SÁNDOR ARANY; 1,025 employees.

BorsodChem Rt: 3702 Kazincbarcika, Bólyai tér 1, POB 208; tel. (48) 511-211; fax (48) 511-511; e-mail bcrt@borsodchem.hu; internet www.borsodchem.hu; f. 1949; country's second largest producer of plastic raw materials; Chair. LÁSZLÓ F. KOVÁCS; 4,108 employees.

BVM Épelem Elöregyártó és Szolgáltató Kft: 1117 Budapest, Budafoki u. 215; tel. (1) 205-6151; fax (1) 205-6155; e-mail bvmepelem@mail.datanet.hu; internet www.construnet.hu/bvm; f. 1963; manufactures and exports concrete and reinforced concrete structures; Man. Dir JÁNOS PÁLINKÁS; 145 employees.

Chemol International Kereskedelmi Rt: 1134 Budapest, Robert Károly krt 61–65, POB 696; tel. (1) 465-6600; fax (1) 465-6700; f. 1949; export, import and domestic distribution of organic and inorganic chemicals, agrochemicals, plastics; 78% owned by Great Lakes Chemical Corpn (USA); Man. Dir BERNARD SUTCH; 130 employees.

Chinoin Pharmaceutical and Chemical Works Co Ltd: 1045 Budapest, Tó u. 1–5; tel. (1) 369-0900; fax (1) 369-0293; f. 1910; pharmaceutical and chemical works; mem. of Sanofi-Synthelabo (France); Man. Dir PHILLIPPE BESSE; 1,600 employees.

Csépeli Fémmű Rt (Csepel Foundry): 1211 Budapest, Gyepsor u. 1; tel. (1) 276-0456; fax (1) 276-6260; e-mail ubpmarket:intranet.hu; f. 1976; production of copper, nickel, iron and steel castings; Pres. ENDRE SZŰCS; 1,100 employees.

Dalmandi Mezgazdasági Rt: 7211 Dalmand, Felszabadulás u. 42; tel. (74) 439-103; fax (74) 439-808; f. 1949; agricultural co; Gen. Man. Dr JÓZSEF WILHELM; 1,246 employees.

Dunaferr Dunai Vasmű Részvénytársaság (Dunaferr Danube Ironworks Co. Ltd): 2400 Dunaújváros, POB 110, Vasmű tér 1–3; tel. (25) 584-000; fax (25) 584-001; e-mail dunaferr@dunaferr.hu; internet www.dunaferr.hu; f. 1990; manages and operates the assets of Dunaferr Company Group: Dunaferr Co Ltd; production of steel structures for buildings, road balustrade systems, engineering, scaffolding, etc.; Pres. PÉTER HÓNIG; 587 employees.

Egis Gyógyszergyár Rt (Egis Pharmaceuticals Co): 1106 Budapest, Kereszturi u. 30–38; POB 100, 1475 Budapest 10; tel. (1) 265-5555; fax (1) 265-5529; e-mail mailbox@egis.hu; internet www.egis.hu; f. 1913; major pharmaceuticals co; 50.9% stake owned by ATP Servier (France); Gen. Dir ISTVÁN ORBÁN; 2,600 employees.

Elektroimpex Trade: 1051 Budapest, Nádor u. 11; tel. (1) 353-2533; fax (1) 131-0526; f. 1949; export and import of telecommunications and precision articles; 100 employees.

Elektrolux Lehel Kft: 5100 Jászberény, Fémnyomó u. 1; tel. (57) 415-999; fax (57) 416-207; f. 1952; owned by Electrolux AB (Sweden); production of household appliances; Chief Exec. JÁNOS TAKÁCS; 3,8600 employees.

ERBE Power Engineering and Consulting Ltd: 1519 Budapest, POB 469; tel. (1) 204-4200; fax (1) 204-4198; e-mail erbe.energetika@mail.datanet.hu; internet www.erbe.hu; f. 1950; Hungarian Power Companies Ltd (Magyar Villamos Művek Részvénytársaság); power plant investment, design and construction company; Man. Dir ANTAL VAVRIK; 160 employees.

Flextronics International Kft: 9600 Sárvár, Ikervari út 42; tel. (95) 533-000; fax (84) 533-020; e-mail veronika.nemeth@hu.flextronics.com; internet www.flextronics.com/contacts/globallocations/hungarypark.asp; comprises plants in Nyíregyháza, Sárvár, Tab and Zalaegerszeg; engineering and manufacturing of household appliances.

FMV: 1475 Budapest, POB 215, Fehér út 10; tel. (1) 260-9060; fax (1) 262-7931; e-mail fmvrt@mail.matav.hu; f. 1952; production of antennae, telecommunications lines and fibre-optic networks; 480 employees.

Folk-art Trading Co: 1052 Budapest, Régiposta u. 12; tel. (1) 266-5334; fax (1) 266-1489; f. 1948; wholesale, retail and export sale of folk art, handicrafts and confectionery; Dir JUDIT LENDVAI; 105 employees.

Fotex Rt: 1126 Budapest, Nagy Jenő u. 12; tel. (1) 202-2400; fax (1) 202-2451; e-mail fotexrt@elender.hu; internet www.fotex.hu; f. 1984; Zürich Investment Kft; retail and wholesale of household goods, photographic and optical equipment, appliances, cosmetics and pharmaceutical products; Gen. Man. Dr LAJOS CSEPI; 4,000 employees.

Gábor Áron Works: 1087 Budapest, Asztalos Sándor u. 9–12; tel. (1) 133-7970; fax (1) 313-9843; f. 1981; domestic and kitchen appliances; Dir SÁNDOR ANTAL; 170 employees.

Gamma Technical Corpn: 1519 Budapest, POB 330; 1119 Budapest, Petzvál J. u.56; tel. (1) 208-5771; fax (1) 205-5778; e-mail gamma@gammatech.hu; internet www.gammatech.hu; f. 1920; nuclear medical instrumentation, environmental protection and industrial measurement and control; Gen. Man. ATTILA ZSITNONOI; 220 employees.

Ganz Bridge, Crane and Steel Structure Manufacturing Co: 1443 Budapest, POB 136; 1089 Budapest, Golgota u. 6; tel. (1) 459-

6300; fax (1) 313-0847; e-mail ganzacel@ganz.hu; internet www.ganz.hu; Gen. Dir Dr PÉTER DOBROVITS; 700 employees.

Ganz Danubius Kereskedelmi Kft (Danubius Trading Co Ltd): 1138 Budapest, Váci u. 184; tel. (1) 350-5570; fax (1) 329-8041; e-mail gdtco@hu.inter.net; internet www.ganztrading.hu; f. 1988; design and construction of harbour equipment, ships, floating cranes, yachts and watersport equipment, steel constructions, modernization of industrial boilers, export of agricultural products and import of heavy fuel oil; Man. Dir LAJOS MOLNAR; 55 employees.

Ganz Kapcsoló—és Készülékgyártó Kft. (Ganz KK Ltd): 1087 Budapest, Vajda P. u. 12; tel. (1) 210-1177; fax (1) 313-4624; e-mail palinkasl@ganzkk.hu; internet www.ganzkk.hu; f. 1919; low-voltage switchgear and apparatus production for industrial use; Gen. Man. PÉTER SIMÁNDI; 380 employees.

Ganz Transelektro Electric Co Ltd: 1061 Budapest, Király u. 16; tel. (1) 483-6600; fax (1) 266-6832; e-mail info@gaztrans.hu; internet www.gaztrans.hu; f. 1878; electric power generators, transformers, switchgear, electrical vehicles; Man. Dir GYÖRGY RÉTFALVI; 1,855 employees.

GE Hungary Rt: 1340 Budapest, Váci u. 77; tel. (1) 399-1100; fax (1) 369-1672; internet www.ge.com/hu; f. 1949; GE (USA); represents and manages GE business interests in Hungary, including four manufacturing operations; Chief Exec. CRAIG ARNOLD; 12,000 employees.

Globus Konzervipari Rt (Globus Canning Industry Plc): 1106 Budapest, Maglódi u. 47; tel. (1) 432-1600; fax (1) 260-8745; e-mail marketing.globus@globus.hu; internet www.globus.hu; f. 1950; manufacture of meat, vegetable, fruit and sauce products; Pres. ESZTÉR ISTVÁN.

Graphisoft R&D Rt: 1031 Budapest, Záhony u. 7 (Graphisoft Park 1); tel. (1) 437-3000; fax (1) 437-3099; e-mail mail@graphisoft.hu; internet www.graphisoft.com; f. 1982; leading computer-aided design software developer for building design and architectural management; partly owned by CSK and Nippon Investment and Finance (Japan); Pres. and Chief Exec. GÁBOR BOJÁR; 300 employees.

Hajdú-Bét Rt: 4030 Debrecen, Diószegi u. 1–3; tel. (52) 506-425; fax (52) 416-007; e-mail almasisz@hajdubet.hu; internet www.valdor.hu; food, agriculture and trade; Chair. ATTILA BOROS; 4,000 employees.

Hajdú Hajdúsági Piarművek Rt: 4243 Debrecen, Téglás, Pf 1; tel. (52) 315-601; fax (52) 384-706; e-mail hajdu@mail.matav.net; f. 1952; manufactures electrical components, spin dryers and washing machines; Pres. SÁNDOR KOMOR; 1,100 employees.

Hungalu Kereskedelmi Kft (Hungalu Trading Ltd): 1388 Budapest, POB 63; 1106 Budapest, Keresztúri út 39–41; tel. (1) 262-6444; fax (1) 262-8676; f. 1957; wholesale trade in semi-finished and finished aluminium products; Gen. Dir GÁBOR RÓNA; 40 employees.

Hungarocoop Co: 1054 Budapest, Szabadsag tér 14; tel. (1) 153-1711; fax (1) 153-3318; f. 1968; import and export of consumer goods; Pres. ARPAD SCHAFFER; 60 employees.

Hungarofilm: 1065 Budapest, Bajcsy-Zsilinszky u. 7; tel. (1) 267-3026; fax (1) 267-3140; e-mail info@hungarofilm.hu; f. 1952; film production and distribution; Gen. Dir CSABA BERECZKI.

Hungarofruct Co-operative Society: 1063 Budapest, Munkacsy M. u. 19/b; tel. (1) 331-7120; fax (1) 332-1378; f. 1953; export of fresh, dehydrated and quick-frozen fruit and vegetables; Gen. Man. GYÖRGY TÁBORI; 260 employees.

Hungaropharma Rt: 1061 Budapest, Kiraly u. 12; tel. (1) 268-0510; fax (1) 268-1030; e-mail hph@hungaropharma.hu; internet www.hungaropharma.hu; f. 1949; pharmaceutical trading co; Man. Dir FERENC SZABÓ; 900 employees.

Hungarotabak-Tobaccoland Tobacco Trade Rt: 1097 Budapest, Gyáli u. 33; tel. (1) 347-2800; fax (1) 347-2892; f. 1980; wholesale trade in tobacco, tobacco products and gifts and novelties; Chief Exec. MAXIMILIAN SCHLEDERER.

Hungarotex: 1804 Budapest, POB 100; tel. (1) 117-4555; fax (1) 117-3410; f. 1953; export and import of textiles, garments, foodstuffs, etc.; Dir FUZES ELEKNE.

HUNGEXPO Co Ltd: 1437 Budapest, POB 801; tel. (1) 263-6155; fax (1) 263-6098; e-mail info@hungexpo.hu; internet www.hungexpo.hu; f. 1968; organizes trade fairs and exhibitions, provides advertising and direct marketing services, represents foreign trade fair companies; Man. Dir MARIA VISY.

ICN Hungary Co Ltd: 1025 Budapest, Csatárka u. 82-84; tel. (1) 345-5900; fax (1) 345-5918; e-mail info@icnpharm.hu; internet www.icnpharm.hu; f. 1927; owned by ICN Pharmaceuticals Inc. (USA); fmrly Alkaloida Chemical Co Ltd; production and marketing of pharmaceuticals; Chair. MILAN PANIĆ; Gen. Man. PETAR MILANKOVIĆ; 175 employees.

Ikarus Jármügyartó Rt (Ikarus Vehicle Manufacturing Co Ltd): 1165 Budapest, Margit u. 114; tel. (1) 469-6109; fax (1) 469-6170; e-mail ikarus@ikarus.hu; internet www.ikarus.hu; f. 1895; construction and export of buses in complete state or in sets for assembly; Pres. GÁBOR SZÉLES; Chief Exec. ZSOLT SZÉKELY; 3,000 employees.

Interco-operation Marketing and Distribution Co Ltd : 1601 Budapest, POB 18; 1158 Budapest, Késmárk u. 11–13; tel. (1) 416-0351; fax (1) 417-3059; e-mail belsoepiteszet@icmdrt.hu; f. 1968; Getz Bros & Co, Inc. (USA); markets and distributes agricultural, chemical, consumer and industrial products; Gen. Dir LÁSZLÓ CSISZÁR.

KGyV Metallurgical Engineering Corpn: 1138 Budapest, Révész st. 9; tel. (1) 140-3342; fax (1) 120-2101; f. 1951; manufacture of industrial furnaces and steel structures; Gen. Man. ANDRÁS BUDAI.

Kite Rt: 4181 Nádudvar, Bem József u. 1; tel. (54) 480-401; fax (54) 480-331; e-mail info@kite.hu; internet www.kite.hu; f. 1991; Chair. CSABA BALOGH; 600 employees.

Konsumex Trading Co: 1146 Budapest, Hermina u. 17; 1441 Budapest, POB 58; tel. (1) 471-9170; fax (1) 471-9159; f. 1959; consumer goods, household articles, etc.; Gen. Man. Dr FORRAI ZOLTÁN; 176 employees.

Kopint-Datorg Economic Research Marketing and Computing Co Ltd: 1081 Budapest, POB 139, Csokonai u. 3; tel. (1) 303-4444; fax (1) 303-1000; e-mail info@kopdat.hu; internet www.kopdat .hu; f. 1964; business information office, economic research, information and marketing services, data processing, publishing; Gen. Dir PÉTER KRATOCHWILL; 180 employees.

Kunplast—Karsai Rt: 6100 Kiskunfélegyeháza, Szegedi u. 66; tel. (76) 562-300; fax (76) 562-350; e-mail kunplast@mail.matav.hu; f. 1961; production of plastic automotive and electrical components; Pres. ÁGNES FAJÓ; 500 employees.

Laboratoriumi Muszergyar Rt: 1450 Budapest, POB 33; tel. (1) 215-9708; fax (1) 215-0309; f. 1989; scientific instruments, laboratory equipment and engineering; Gen. Dir KÁROLY VARGA; 165 employees.

Lampart Rt: 1475 Budapest, POB 41; tel. (1) 432-6200; fax (1) 261-3440; e-mail lampart@lampart.hu; internet www.lampart.hu; f. 1883; glass-lined and glass-enamelled processing equipment, steel constructions; Gen. Dir IMRE DOBAI; 130 employees.

Lear Automotive (EEDS) Hungary Rt: 2100 Gödöllő, Haraszti u. 4; tel. (28) 520-314; fax (28) 520-166; textiles industry; Chair. LÁSZLÓ STEINER; 3,400 employees.

Licencia Kereskedelmi Kft: 1368 Budapest, POB 207; tel. (1) 317-1055; fax (1) 317-2834; e-mail licencia@win.hu; internet www .licencia.hu; f. 1989; export and import of foodstuffs, garment accessories, plastic and metal products; Gen. Dir FERENC GEBAUER; 10 employees.

MAGNEZITIPAR Rt: 1475 Budapest, POB 11; tel. (1) 260-5700; fax (1) 262-3068; f. 1894; production of refractory bricks and mortar; Dir GYÖRGY PERSAY; 260 employees.

Magyar Aszfalt Kft: 1135 Budapest, Szeged u. 35–37; tel. (1) 270-8368; fax (1) 270-8344; f. 1989; construction; Chair. JÓSZEF APPELSHOFER; 1,500 employees.

Magyar Suzuki Rt: 2500 Esztergom, Schweidel J. u. 52; tel. (33) 414-311; fax (33) 412-014; internet www.suzuki.hu; f. 1991; owned by Suzuki (Japan); vehicle manufacturing; Chair. TAKASHI NAKAYAMA; 1,600 employees.

Masped First Hungarian General Forwarding Co Ltd: 1139 Budapest, Váci u. 85; tel. (1) 452-8100; fax (1) 452-8400; e-mail maspedrt@masped.hu; internet www.masped.hu; international forwarding and carriage, custom services, warehousing, logistic services; Chair. ISTVÁN KAUTZ; 289 employees.

Mechaniki Müvek: 1518 Budapest, POB 64; tel. (1) 227-3819; fax (1) 227-3801; f. 1936; electrical equipment; Man. Dir KAROLY KASZA; 498 employees.

Medicor Rt: 1135 Debrecen, Tahi u. 53–59; tel. (52) 346-093; fax (52) 315-541; e-mail holding@medicor.hu; internet www.medicor.hu; comprises five cos; Chief Exec. Dr PÉTER GÁBOR; 580 employees.

Medimpex: 1808 Budapest, Lehel u. 11; tel. (1) 288-1400; fax (1) 360-6558; e-mail medimpex@medimpex.hu; internet www .medimpex.hu; f. 1949; export and import of pharmaceutical and biological products, laboratory chemicals; trade and consultation agency; trade in medical devices and services, and healthcare products; Chief Exec. KÁROLY GYŐRFI; 65 employees.

Mertcontrol Quality Control Co Ltd: 1095 Budapest, Kvassay J. u. 1/C; tel. (1) 455-9048; fax (1) 455-8092; e-mail sales@mertcontrol .hu; internet www.mertcontrol.hu; f. 1951; quality control and management, and inspection and laboratory testing; Man. Dir LÁSZLÓ DIOSZEGHY.

Metrimpex Kereskedelmi, Szolgaltato es Befekteto Rt: 1025 Budapest, Szepvolgyi u. 52; tel. (1) 267-5600; fax (1) 267-5657; f. 1956; export and import of electronic, nuclear and other instruments and equipment; 160 employees.

Mogürt Trading Co: 1391 Budapest, Veres Palne u. 1; tel. (1) 118-4133; fax (1) 118-8895; f. 1946; foreign trade in motor vehicles and components, agricultural products and equipment; Gen. Man. TIBOR CSAJBI; 600 employees.

Moltrade-Mineralimpex Trade Rt: 1068 Budapest, Benczur u. 13; tel. (1) 462-5300; fax (1) 462-5400; e-mail mail@moltrade.hu; crude petroleum products; Chief Exec. GYULA KAJÁRI; 70 employees.

MOM: 1525 Budapest, POB 52; tel. (1) 156-4122; f. 1876; laboratory and optical instruments; Man. Dir JÓZSEF SEBESFI.

Ofotért: 1135 Budapest, Reítter Ferenc u. 45–49; tel. (1) 120-3669; fax (1) 149-7760; f. 1949; import and distribution of optical and photographic articles; Man. Dir Dr FERENC GREGORITS; 1,388 employees.

OMKER: 1089 Budapest, Rezso u. 5–7; tel. (1) 210-0605; fax (1) 210-0634; f. 1950; medical instruments and pharmaceuticals; Gen. Dir BÉLA DÁVID; 150 employees.

OMV Hungária Kft: 1134 Budapest, Róbert Károly korut. 64–66; tel. (1) 452-7100; fax (1) 452-7102; Chair. JÜRGEN HAAS.

Opel: 9970 Szentgotthárd, Füzesi u. 15; tel. (94) 551-000; fax (94) 551-048; internet www.opel.hu; engineering; Plant Dir RUDOLF HAMP.

Patria Nyomda: 1088 Budapest, Szentiralyi u. 47; tel. (1) 134-0186; fax (1) 114-0876; office stationery; Gen. Man. LAJOS FÜLAKI; 796 employees.

Pharmavit: 2122 Veresegyhaz, Levai u. 5; tel. (27) 38-6890; fax (27) 38-5980; f. 1988; manufacture of pharmaceutical products; owned by Bristol-Myers Squibb (USA); Chief Exec. IMRE SOMODY.

Philatelia Hungarica Ltd: 1675 Budapest, POB 28; tel. (1) 292-0425; fax (1) 291-3278; e-mail philhun@axelero.hu; internet www .philhun-estore.hu; f. 1950; stamps; wholesale only; Gen. Man. ISTVÁN ZALAVÁRI; 90 employees.

Philips Hungary Kft: 1119 Budapest, Fehérvári u. 84A; tel. (1) 382-1700; fax (1) 382-1800; internet www.philips.hu; electronics; owned by Royal Philips Electronics (Netherlands); Chair. WILLEM J. VAN DER VEGT; 9,500 employees.

Phoenix Pharma Rt: 2151 Fót, Keleti Márton, u. 19; tel. (27) 363-063; fax (27) 358-484; internet www.phoenix.hu; f. 1950; pharmaceutical trade; Chair. GABRIELLA DUHA; 410 employees.

Phylaxia-Sanofi: 1107 Budapest, Szállás u. 5; tel. (1) 157-5311; fax (1) 127-4617; f. 1991; vaccines, veterinary products, medicines; Chair. M. GYORGY; 183 employees.

Pick Szeged Co: 6725 Szeged, Szabadkai u. 18; tel. (62) 567-000; fax (62) 567-313; e-mail pbox@pick.hu; internet www.pick.hu; f. 1869; meat-processing; Man. Dir VILMOS BIHARI.

Porsche Hungária Kft: 1139 Budapest, Fáy u. 27; tel. (1) 451-5100; fax (1) 350-1500; internet www.porsche.hu; vehicle trade; owned by Porsche (Germany); Chair. JÓZSEF SZÓRÁD.

RÁBA Rt: 9027 Györ, Budai u. 1–5; tel. (96) 622-000; fax (96) 622-053; e-mail raba@raba.hu; internet www.raba.hu; f. 1896; produces commercial vehicles, diesel engines, agricultural tractors, axles, self-propelled bus chassis; Chief Exec. LÁSZLÓ STEINER; 6,400 employees.

Richter Gedeon Vegyészeti Gyár Rt: 1475 Budapest, Gyömrői u. 19–21, POB 27; tel. (1) 431-4000; fax (1) 260-6650; e-mail posta@ richter.hu; internet www.richter.hu; f. 1901; pharmaceuticals co; partially privatized in 1994; Man. Dir ERIK BOGSCH; 4,600 employees.

Samsung Electronics Hungarian Rt: 1039 Budapest, Csalogány u. 30; tel. (1) 453-1100; fax (1) 453-1101; e-mail info@samsung.hu; internet www.samsung.hu; electronics and trade; owned by Samsung (Republic of Korea); Chair. CHO KYU-DAM.

Sasad: 1112 Budapest, Budaörsi ut 1289; tel. (1) 246-2801; fax (1) 246-2806; property development and projects for commercial, residential and storage purposes; Gen. Man. IMRE RÉTHY.

Shell Hungary Rt: 1036 Budapest, Lajos u. 48–66; tel. (1) 436-3200; fax (1) 436-3399; internet www2.shell.com/home/ Framework?siteId=hu-hu; oil and gas; owned by Royal Dutch Shell (Netherlands-UK); Chair. ISTVÁN KAPITÁNY; 182 employees.

Siemens Regional Company: 1154 Budapest, Gizella u. 51–57; tel. (1) 471-1000; fax (1) 471-2602; internet www.siemens.hu; electronics manufacturing; owned by Siemens (Germany); Chair. PÉTER HETÉNYI; 1,271 employees.

Somogyi Erdö és Fafeldolgozo Gazdaság (Somogy Forestry and Timber Company): 7400 Kaposvár, Bajcsy-Zs, u. 21; tel. (82) 505-

100; fax (82) 505-133; f. 1970; wood and wood products, hunting services; Gen. Dir Jószef Bóna; 1,200 employees.

Taurus Rubber Co: 1087 Budapest, Kerepesi u. 17; tel. (1) 459-2600; fax (1) 459-2602; e-mail vszlaby@hungary.net; f. 1882; rubber manufacturing and trading; Pres. Manuel Weiller; 2,500 employees.

Technoimpex: 1056 Budapest, Dorottya u. 6; tel. (1) 266-0988; fax (1) 266-6418; international trading house specializing in commodities, metals, petroleum products; organizes barter deals, co-operation, leasing and joint ventures; Chair. István Mátyás; 800 employees.

Temaforg: 1115 Budapest, Bartók Béla u. 152; tel. (1) 127-7880; fax (1) 157-4224; textile and synthetic wastes, industrial wipers, geo-textiles for agriculture, road and railway construction; Dir-Gen. Andor Schneider.

Terta, Telefongyár: 1956 Budapest, POB 16; tel. (1) 252-6949; fax (1) 252-9161; f. 1876; telecommunications and data teleprocessing systems.

Tesco Co Ltd: 1367 Budapest, POB 5/101; tel. (1) 311-0850; fax (1) 331-4703; e-mail tesco@mail.matav.hu; f. 1962; organization for international technical and scientific co-operation; export and import of technical services world-wide; Gen. Man. László Pados; 106 employees.

Tesco Glóbál Áruházak Rt: 9023 Győr, Herman Ottó, u. 22A; tel. (96) 504-166; fax (96) 507-218; e-mail kennedy_paul@hu.tesco-europe.com; trading; Chair. Paul Kennedy; 4,085 employees.

Tisza Vegyi Kombinát (TVK) Rt: 3581 Tiszaújváros, Ipartelep Pf. 10u.; tel. (49) 322-222; fax (49) 321-322; e-mail bki@tvk.hu; internet www.tvk.hu; production and processing of plastics; Chief Exec. Miklós Várhegyi; 3,500 employees.

Transelektro Co Ltd: 1051 Budapest, Nador Str. 13; tel. (1) 269-2155; fax (1) 153-0162; f. 1956; main contractor in power generation, transmission and distribution projects; general trading activities; consultancy, etc.; Dir-Gen. Péter Székely; 240 employees.

UKM Rekard KFT: 9027 Győr, Kandó Kálmán u. 5–7; tel. (96) 311-353; fax (96) 313-559; f. 1993; manufacture of farm equipment; Pres. Jochen Radke; 230 employees.

Uvaterv Engineering Consultants Ltd: 1117 Budapest, Dombóvári u. 17–19; tel. (1) 371-4001; fax (1) 204-2969; e-mail uvatervl@mail.datanet.hu; internet www.uvaterv.hu; f. 1948; engineering and consultancy services, building contracting; Pres. and Dir-Gen. Gyula Bretz; Dep. Dir-Gen. Frigyes Kovácsházy; 210 employees.

Vetőmag '95 Ltd: 1077 Budapest, Rottenbiller u. 33; tel. (1) 462-5070; fax (1) 462-5080; e-mail vetomag95@matavnet.hu; f. 1995; seed production, sale of agricultural products; Chief Exec. Dr András Szemők.

Videoton Holding Ltd: 8000 Székesfehérváar, Berényi u. 100; tel. (22) 533-000; fax (22) 533-109; internet www.videoton.hu; f. 1938; consumer electronics, computer technology; Pres. Gabor Szeles; 9,000 employees.

YUGANSKORINNEFTEGAZ Electronic Co Ltd: 1475 Budapest, POB 84; tel. (1) 262-5000; fax (1) 260-6520; f. 1993; televisions, audio and video recorders, satellite receivers, digital microwave and other electrical goods; Gen. Dir Tamás Venekei.

Zalahűs: 8900 Zalaegerszeg, Balatoni u.; tel. (92) 312-200; fax (92) 311-206; meat-processing factory; Man. Dir Imre Farkas; 1,050 employees.

Zoltek Rt: 2537 Nyergesújfalu, Varga József tér 1; tel. (33) 455-244; fax (33) 455-541; f. 1941; production of chemical fibres; 1,400 employees.

TRADE UNIONS

Since 1988, and particularly after the restructuring of the former Central Council of Hungarian Trade Unions (SzOT) as the National Confederation of Hungarian Trade Unions (MSzOSz) in 1990, several new union federations have been created. Several unions are affiliated to more than one federation, and others are completely independent. In May 2000 a trade-unions co-operation council was established.

Trade Union Federations

Association of Hungarian Free Trade Unions (Magyar Szabad Szakszervezetek Szövetsége): Budapest; f. 1994; 200,000 mems.

Autonomous Trade Union Confederation (Autonóm Szakszervezetek Svövetsége): 1068 Budapest, Benczúr u. 45; tel. (1) 342-1776; Pres. Lajos Főcze.

Democratic Confederation of Free Trade Unions (Független Szakszervezetek Demokratikus Ligája—FSzDL): 1068 Budapest, Benczúr u. 41; tel. (1) 321-5262; fax (1) 321-5405; e-mail info@liganet.hu; f. 1988; Pres. István Gaskó; 98,000 mems.

Principal affiliated unions include:

Democratic Trade Union of Scientific Workers (Tudományos Dolgozók Demokratikus Szakszervezete—TDDSz): 1068 Budapest, Városligeti fasor 38; tel. (1) 142-8438; f. 1988; Chair. Pál Forgacs.

Federation of Unions of Intellectual Workers (Értelmiségi Szakszervezeti Tömörülés—ÉSzT): 1068 Budapest, Városligeti fasor 10; tel. (1) 122-8456; Pres. Dr László Kis; Gen. Sec. Dr Gábor Bánk.

Forum for the Co-operation of Trade Unions (Szakszervezetek Együttműködési Fóruma—SzEF): 1068 Budapest VIII, Puskin u. 4; tel. (1) 138-2651; fax (1) 118-7360; f. 1990; Pres. Dr Endre Szabó.

Principal affiliated unions include:

Federation of Hungarian Public Service Employees' Unions (Közszolgálati Szakszervezetek Szövetsége): 1081 Budapest, Kiss Jozsef u. 8 II em; tel. (1) 313-5436; fax (1) 133-7223; f. 1945; Pres. Péter Michalko; Vice-Pres. Dr Judit Bárdos, Dr Csilla Novák.

National Confederation of Hungarian Trade Unions (Magyar Szakszervezetek Országos Szövetsége—MSzOSz): Budapest; tel. (1) 352-1815; fax (1) 342-1799; f. 1898; reorganized 1990; Pres. Dr László Sándor; Dep. Pres. Ferenc Rabi; 405,000 mems in 41 mem. orgs.

Principal affiliated unions include:

Commercial Employees' Trade Union (Kereskedelmi Alkalmazottak Szakszervezete): 1066 Budapest, Jókai u. 6; tel. (1) 331-8970; fax (1) 332-3382; e-mail saling@axelero.hu; f. 1900; Pres. Dr József Sáling; 80,000 mems.

Federation of Agricultural, Forestry and Water Supply Workers' Unions (Mezőgazdasági, Erdészeti és Vizügyi Dolgozók Szakszervezeti Szövetsége—MEDOSZ): 1066 Budapest, Jókai u. 2; tel. (1) 301-9050; fax (1) 331-4568; e-mail medosz.net@matavnet.hu; f. 1906; Gen. Sec. Dr András Bereczky; 16,086 mems.

Federation of Chemical Workers' Unions of Hungary, Confederation Founding Section (Magyar Vegyipari Dolgozók Szakszervezeti Szövetsége, össz-szövetségi alapító tagozata): Budapest; tel. (1) 342-1778; fax (1) 342-9975; Gen. Sec. György Pasztérnák; 12,000 mems.

Federation of Communal Service Workers' Unions (Kommunális Dalgozók Szakszervezete): 1068 Budapest, Benczur u. 43; tel. (1) 111-6950; Gen. Sec. Zsolt Pék; 28,000 mems.

Federation of Hungarian Artworkers' Unions (Müvészeti Szakszervezetek Szövetsége): 1068 Budapest, Városligeti fasor 38; tel. (1) 342-8927; fax (1) 342-8372; e-mail eji@mail.datanet.hu; f. 1957; Pres. László Gyimesi; 32,000 mems.

Federation of Hungarian Metalworkers' Unions (Vasass Szakszervezeti Szövetség): 1086 Budapest, Magdolna u. 5–7; tel. (1) 210-0130; fax (1) 210-01167; e-mail vasasszaksz@mail.datanet.hu; f. 1877; Pres. Károly Szőke; 53,000 mems.

Federation of Local Industry and Municipal Workers' Unions (Helyiipari és Városgazdasági Dolgozók Szövetségének): 1068 Budapest, Benczúr u. 43; tel. (1) 311-6950; f. 1952; Pres. Józsefné Svever; Gen. Sec. Pál Bakányi; 281,073 mems.

Federation of Municipal Industries and Service Workers' Unions (Települési Ipari és Szolgáltatási Dolgozók Szakszervezete): 1068 Budapest, Benczur u. 43; tel. (1) 111-6950; Gen. Sec. Zoltán Szikszai; 20,000 mems.

Federation of Postal and Telecommunications Workers' Unions (Postai és Hirközlési Dolgozók Szakszervezeti Szövetsége): 1146 Budapest, Cházár András u. 13; tel. (1) 142-8777; fax (1) 121-4018; f. 1945; Pres. Enikő Heszky-Gricser; 69,900 mems.

Federation of Transport Workers' Unions (Közlekedési Dolgozók Szakszervezeteinek Szövetségé): 1081 Budapest, Köztársaság tér 3; tel. (1) 113-9046; f. 1898; Pres. István Trenka; 8,000 mems.

Hungarian Federation of Food Industry Workers' Unions (Magyar Élelmezésipari Dolgozók Szakszervezeteinek Szövetsége): 1068 Budapest, Városligeti fasor 44; tel. (1) 122-5880; fax (1) 142-8568; f. 1905; Pres. Gyula Sóki; Gen. Sec. Béla Vanek; 226,243 mems.

Hungarian Graphical Workers' Union (Nyomdaipari Dolgozók Szakszervezete): 1085 Budapest, Kölcsey u. 2; tel. (1) 266-0065; fax (1) 266-0028; f. 1862; Pres. András Bársony; Vice-Pres János Aczél, Emil Szelei; 17,000 mems.

Hungarian Union of Teachers (Magyar Pedagógusok Szakszervezete): 1068 Budapest, Városligeti fasor 10; tel. (1) 122-8456; fax (1) 142-8122; f. 1945; Gen. Sec. Istvánné Szöllősi; 200,000 mems.

Hungarian Union of Textile Workers (Magyar Textilipari Dolgozók Szakszervezete): 1068 Budapest, Rippl-Rónai u. 2; tel. (1) 428-196; fax (1) 122-5414; f. 1905; Pres. (vacant); Gen. Sec. TAMÁS KELETI; 70,241 mems.

Union of Health Service Workers (Egészségügyben Dolgozók Szakszervezeteinek Szövetsége): 1051 Budapest, Nádor u. 32, POB 36; tel. (1) 110-645; f. 1945; Pres. Dr ZOLTÁN SZABÓ; Gen. Sec. Dr PÁLNÉ KÁLLAY; 280,536 mems.

Union of Leather Industry Workers (Bőripari Dolgozók Szakszervezete): 1062 Budapest, Bajza u. 24; tel. (1) 342-9970; f. 1868; Gen. Sec. TAMÁS LAJTOS; 12,000 mems.

Union of Clothing Workers (Ruházatipari Dolgozók Szakszervezete): 1077 Budapest, Almássy tér 2; tel. (1) 342-3702; fax (1) 122-6717; f. 1892; Gen. Sec. TAMÁS WITTICH; 22,000 mems.

Workers Unions of Mining and Energy (Bánya—és Energiaipari Dolgozók Szakszervezete): 1068 Budapest, Városligeti fasor 46–48; tel. (1) 322-1226; fax (1) 342-1942; e-mail bdsz@banyasz.hu; f. 1913; Pres. FERENC RABI; Vice-Pres. Dr JÁNOS HORN; 80,000 mems.

Transport

RAILWAYS

In 2001 the rail network in Hungary amounted to a length of 7,897 km. Some 156.4m. passengers were carried in 2000. There is an underground railway in Budapest, which had a network of three lines, totalling 33 km in 2002; a fourth line was also planned. Since 1996 PHARE, the European Union's (EU) programme for the economic reconstruction of Eastern Europe, has financed a number of modernization projects of the rail network. In 2000 the EU pledged an annual contribution of almost €50m. to fund vital railway and road infrastructure projects.

Budapest Transport Company (BKV) Rt: 1072 Budapest, Akácfa u. 15; tel. (1) 461-6500; fax (1) 461-6557; internet www.bkv.hu; operates metro system, suburban railway network, trams, trolley buses, and conventional buses; served 1,428m. passengers in 2000; Chair. BOTOND ABA; 12,681 employees.

Hungarian State Railways Ltd (Magyar Államvasutak—MÁV): 1940 Budapest, Andrássy u. 73–75; tel. (1) 322-0660; fax (1) 342-8596; internet www.mav.hu; f. 1868; transformed into joint-stock co in 1993; total network 7,785 km, including 2,628 km of electrified lines (2000); Chief Exec. ZOLTÁN MÁNDOKI; Gen. Dir MÁRTON KUKELY; 55,046 employess.

Railway of Győr–Sopron–Ebenfurth (Győr–Sopron–Ebenfurti-Vasút—GySEV/ROeEE): 1011 Budapest, Szilágyi Dezső tér 1; internet www.gysev.hu; Hungarian-Austrian-owned railway; 162 km in Hungary, 65 km in Austria, all electrified; transport of passengers and goods; Dir-Gen. Dr LÁSZLÓ FEHÉRVÁRI.

ROADS

In 2001 there were 448 km of motorways and 30,322 km of national public roads. There are extensive long-distance bus services. Road passenger and freight transport is provided by the state-owned Volán companies and by individual operators. There were plans to extend the road from Budapest to Vienna, Austria; however, owing to the lack of funds, this and a 10-year plan to extend connections to Croatia, Romania and Ukraine, were delayed. The European Union's annual contribution of almost €50m., from 2000, was to fund vital projects. In 2003 a road development programme was approved, for the construction of 420 km of roads, including 326 km of motorways and 94 km of high-speed roads by the beginning of 2007, at a cost of 1,100m. forint (the programme was to be partly funded by loans from the European Bank for Reconstruction and Development and the European Investment Bank). The central budget for 2003 allocated 79,400m. forint for road development.

Hungarocamion: 1442 Budapest, POB 108; tel. (1) 257-3600; fax (1) 256-6755; international road freight transport company; 17 offices in Europe and the Middle East; fleet of 1,100 units for general and specialized cargo; Gen. Man. GABRIELLA SZAKÁL; 3,800 employees.

Centre of Volán Enterprises (Volán Vállalatok Központja): 1391 Budapest, Erzsébet krt 96, POB 221; tel. (1) 112-4290; centre of 25 Volán enterprises for inland and international road freight and passenger transport, forwarding, tourism; fleet of 17,000 lorries, incl. special tankers for fuel, refrigerators, trailers, 8,000 buses for regular passenger transport; 3 affiliates, offices and joint-ventures in Europe; Head ELEMÉR SASLICS.

SHIPPING AND INLAND WATERWAYS

Hungarian Shipping Co (MAHART—Magyar Hajózási Rt): 1366 Budapest, POB 58; 1052 Budapest, Apáozai Cs. J, u. 11; tel. (1) 484-

6421; fax (1) 484-6422; e-mail freeport@mahart.hu; internet www.freeport.hu; f. 1895; transportation of goods on the Rhine–Main–Danube waterway; carries passenger traffic on the Danube; operates port activities at Budapest Csepel National and Free Port (port agency service, loading, storage, handling goods); management of multi-modal and combined transport (cargo booking, oversized goods, chartering); ship-building and ship-repair services; Dir-Gen. Capt. LÁSZLÓ SOMLÓVÁRI.

MAFRACHT International Shipping, Forwarding and Agency Ltd Co: 1364 Budapest 4, POB 105; tel. (1) 266-1208; fax (1) 266-1329; shipping agency.

CIVIL AVIATION

The Ferihegy international airport is 16 km from the centre of Budapest. Ferihegy-2 opened in 1985. In 1999 a new passenger terminal opened. Balatonkiliti airport, near Siófok in western Hungary, reopened to international traffic in 1989. Public internal air services resumed in 1993, after an interval of 20 years, between Budapest and Nyíregyháza, Debrecen, Szeged, Pécs, Szombathely and Győr.

Civil Aviation Authority (Polgári Légiközlekedésigyi Hatóság): Budapest; tel. (1) 296-9502; fax (1) 296-8808; e-mail info@caa.hu; internet www.caa.hu; controls civil aviation; Dir-Gen. ZOLTÁN ANTAL.

Hungarocontrol (Hungarian Air Navigation Services): 1185 Budapest, POB 80, Igló st. 33–35;; tel. (1) 296-9098; fax (1) 296-9026; e-mail info@hungarocontrol.hu; internet www.hungarocontrol.hu; f. 2002; state-owned; operation of air traffic control in Hungary; Dir ISTVÁN MUDRA; 700 employees.

Hungarian Airlines (Magyar Légiközlekedési Részvénytársaság—MALÉV Rt): 1051 Budapest, Roosevelt tér 2, POB 122; tel. (1) 235-3535; fax (1) 266-2685; internet www.malev.hu; f. 1946; regular services from Budapest to Europe, North Africa, North America, Asia and the Middle East; Pres. FERENC SZARVAS; Chief Exec. FERENC KOVÁCS.

LinAir Hungarian Regional Airlines: 1675 Budapest, POB 53; tel. (1) 296-7092; fax (1) 296-7891; e-mail info@linair.hu; internet www.linair.hu; f. 1994; regional carrier; Man. Dir TAMÁS KOVÁCS.

Tourism

Tourism has developed rapidly and is an important source of foreign exchange. Lake Balaton is the main holiday centre for boating, bathing and fishing. Hungary's cities have great historical and recreational attractions, and the annual Budapest Spring Festival is held in March. Budapest has numerous swimming pools watered by thermal springs, which are equipped with modern physiotherapy facilities. Revenue from tourism in 2000 totalled US $3,434m. compared with $2,203m. in 1999. There were 31.7m. foreign visitors in 2002.

Association of Hungarian Travel Agencies: 1364 Budapest, POB 267; tel. and fax (1) 318-4977; e-mail muisz@mail.selectrade.hu; internet www.miwo.hu/partner/muisz; f. 1973; Pres. GABRIELLA MOLNÁR; Gen.-Sec. CSABO CSÓK.

Hungarian Travel Agency (Idegenforgalmi, Beszerzési, Utazási és Szállitási Rt—IBUSZ): 1364 Budapest, Ferenciek tér 5; tel. (1) 118-6866; fax (1) 117-7723; f. 1902; has 118 brs throughout Hungary; Gen. Man. Dr ERIKA SZEMENKÁR.

Tourinform: 1052 Budapest, Sütő u. 2; tel. (1) 317-9800; fax (1) 317-9656; e-mail tourinform@mail.hungarytourism.hu; internet www.hungarytourism.hu.

Tourism Office of Budapest: 1364 Budapest, POB 215; tel. (1) 266-0479; fax (1) 266-7477; e-mail info@budapestinfo.hu; internet www.budapestinfo.hu; Dir LÁSZLÓ FEKETE.

Culture

NATIONAL ORGANIZATIONS

Ministry of Cultural Heritage: see section on The Government (Ministries).

Directorate of Cultural Heritage: Budapest, Magyar u. 40; tel. (1) 327-7701; internet www.koi.hu; Dir Dr DÉNES JANKOVICH-BÉSÁN.

Directorate of Cultural Institutes: 1077 Budapest, Nagydiófa u. 11; tel. (1) 484-7100; Gen. Dir GÉZA ENTZ.

National Cultural Fund: 1062 Budapest, Bajza u. 32; tel. (1) 352-7230; fax (1) 352-7230; e-mail info@nka.hu; internet www.nka.hu; Dir PÁL PERLIK.

Central European Institute: Budapest; f. 2000; represents cultural assets of Central Europe, provides information on cultural events in the region, organizes cultural programmes on a regional scale.

Hungarian Institute of Culture (Magyar Művelődési Intézet): 1011 Budapest, Corvin tér 8; tel. (1) 355-6561; fax (1) 201-5764; e-mail mmi@mmi.hu; internet www.mmi.hu/org/mmint; f. 1951; centre for education, cultural activities, amateur artistic and leisure pursuits, community development; Dir ANDRÁS FÖLDIÁK.

CULTURAL HERITAGE

Budapest History Museum (Budapesti Történeti Múzeum): 1014 Budapest, Szent György tér 2; tel. (1) 225-7810; fax (1) 225-7818; e-mail btm@mail.btm.hu; f. 1887; archaeology and history of Budapest from prehistory to modern times; fine arts; administers Kiscelli Museum and Municipal Picture Gallery; Dir-Gen. Dr SÁNDOR BODÓ.

Hungarian National Archives: 1014 Budapest, Bécsi kapu tér 2–4; tel. (1) 356-5811; e-mail info@natarch.hu; internet www.natarch.hu; Gen. Dir LAJOS GECSÉNYI.

Hungarian National Gallery (Magyar Nemzeti Galéria): 1250 Budapest, Budavári Palota, POB 31; tel. (1) 375-7533; fax (1) 375-8898; e-mail mng@mng.hu; internet www.mng.hu; f. 1957; collections include Hungarian art from 11th to 20th centuries; Dir Dr LÓRÁND BERECZKY.

Hungarian National Museum (Magyar Nemzeti Múzeum): 1088 Budapest, Múzeum krt 14–16; tel. (1) 338-2122; fax (1) 317-7806; e-mail hnm@hnm.hu; internet www.hnm.hu; f. 1802; history, archaeology, numismatics; library of 76,000 vols; Dir-Gen. Dr TIBOR KOVACS.

Ludwig Museum of Contemporary Arts: 1014 Budapest, Szent György tér 2, Royal Palace, Bldg A; tel. (1) 375-7533; fax (1) 212-2534; e-mail info@ludwigmuseum.hu; internet www.ludwigmuseum.hu; f. 1991; Dir KATALIN NÉRAY.

Museum of Applied Arts (Iparművészeti Múzeum): 1091 Budapest, Üllői u. 33–37; tel. (1) 217-5222; fax (1) 217-5838; internet www.imm.hu; f. 1872; European and Hungarian decorative arts; three component museums: Ferenc Hopp Museum of Eastern Asiatic Arts, Ráth György Múzeum and Castle Museum of Nagytétény; library and publishes catalogues; Gen. Dir Dr ZSUZSA LOVAG.

Museum of Fine Arts (Szépművészeti Múzeum): 1146 Budapest, Dózsa György u. 41; tel. (1) 469-7100; fax (1) 469-7171; internet www2.szepmuveszeti.hu; f. 1896; opened 1906; collections include Egyptian and Greco-Roman antiquities, European old masters and 19th–20th century paintings, sculptures, drawings and engravings; library of 150,000 vols; Dir Dr MIKLÓS MOJZER.

National Széchényi Library (Országos Széchényi Könyvtár): 1827 Budapest, Budavári Palota F-épület; tel. (1) 224-3700; fax (1) 202-0804; internet www.oszk.hu; f. 1802; 2.6m. books and periodicals, 4.6m. manuscripts, maps, prints, microfilms, etc.; Dir-Gen. ISTVÁN MONOK.

Office for Heritage Protection: 1014 Budapest, Táncsics M. u. 1; tel. (1) 225-4880; e-mail omh17@mail.datanet.hu; f. 1961; organizes exhibitions for museums; handles international transportation of art for museums; experimental, documentary and advisory centre for conservational and museological education, and heritage protection; Pres. ZOLTÁN CSELOVSZKI.

SPORTING ORGANIZATIONS

National Office for Physical Education and Sport (Országos Testnevélsi és Sporthivatal—OTSH): 1054 Budapest, Hold u. 1; tel. (1) 111-9080; fax (1) 153-2950; dept of the Ministry of Education and of National Cultural Heritage; Pres. REZSŐ GALLOV.

Hungarian Olympic Committee: 1118 Budapest, Balogh Tihamer u. 4; tel. (1) 353-0530; fax (1) 353-0199; e-mail zsn@olympic-hun.org; f. 1895; Pres. PAL SCHMITT; Gen. Sec. Dr TAMÁS AJAN.

PERFORMING ARTS

Hungarian State Opera House (Magyar Állami Operaház): 1061 Budapest, Andrássy u. 22; tel. (1) 332-7913; fax (1) 332-7331; e-mail info@opera.hu; internet www.opera.hu; f. 1884.

Central European Dance Theatre (Közép-Európa Táncszínház): Bethlen Gábor tér 3; tel. and fax (1) 342-7163; e-mail cedt@matavnet.hu.

Erkel Theatre: 1081 Budapest, Köztársaság tér 30; tel. (1) 313-7832; internet www.jegymester.hu/erkel_szinhaz; opera and ballet; Dir MIKLÓS SZINETÁR.

Hungarian Dance Academy: 1061 Budapest, Andrássy u. 25; tel. (1) 267-8646; fax (1) 268-0828; e-mail info@mtf.hu; internet www.mtf.hu; f. 1950; 65 teachers; 152 students; Gen. Dir IMRE DÓZSA.

Hungarian National Philharmonic Orchestra and Choir: 1051 Budapest, Vörösmarty tér 1; POB 49; tel. (1) 429-1090; fax (1) 411-6699; e-mail info@filharmonikusok.hu; internet www.hunphilharmonic.org.hu; Dir GÉZA KOVÁCS.

Hungarian Theatre Pest: 1076 Budapest, Hevesi Sándor tér 4; tel. (1) 341-3849; Chief Dir ISTVÁN IGLÓDI.

Liszt Ferenc Academy of Music: 1061 Budapest, POB 26, Liszt Ferenc tér 8; tel. (1) 321-4406; fax (1) 321-4097; e-mail kutis@elender.hu; internet zeneakademia.hu; f. 1875; 352 teachers; 906 students; Rector SÁNDOR FALVAI.

National Dance Theatre: 1011 Budapest, Corvin tér 8; tel. (1) 201-4407; fax (1) 201-5128; Man. Dir JOLÁN TÖRÖK.

National Theatre: 1062 Budapest, Délibáb u. 19; tel. (1) 322-0635; Dir PÉTER HUSZTI.

Film Studio

MAFILM—Magyar Filmgyarto Vállalat: 1145 Budapest, Rona u. 174; tel. (1) 251-5666; fax (1) 251-2896; e-mail mafilm@mafilm.hu; internet www.mafilm.hu; films, videos, advertisements, management of actors; Gen. Dir LÁSZLÓ VINCZE.

ASSOCIATIONS

Association of Hungarian Theatres (Magyar Szinházművésti Szövetség): 1068 Budapest, Városligeti fasor 38; tel. and fax (1) 342-0146; Mems of Man. Bd ANDRÁS BÁLINT, IMRE KERÉNYI, TAMÁS KOLTAI, GÁBOR MÁTÉ, PÉTER VALLÓ; Man. Sec. MÁRTA VAJDA.

Federation of Hungarian Film Artists (Magyar Filmművészek Szövetsége): 1068 Budapest, Városligeti fasor 38; tel. and fax (1) 342-4760; e-mail filmszovetseg@axelero.hu.

Federation of Hungarian Fine and Applied Artists (Magyar Képzőművészek és Iparművészek Szövetsége): Budapest; Pres. Dr LAJOS NÉMETH.

Hungarian Arts Festivals Federation: Budapest, POB 80, V. Vörösmarty tér 1; tel. (1) 318-8165; e-mail office@artsfestivals.hu; internet www.artsfestivals.hu; f. 1990; 40 mem. festivals.

Hungarian Centre of the International Theatre Institute: 1013 Budapest, Krisztina krt 57; tel. (1) 225-0874; fax (1) 212-5247; e-mail mail@itihun.hu; internet www.itihun.hu.

L'udovit Stur Cultural and Educational Centre: Bank; f. 1996; cultural asscn for the Slovak minority.

Education

In 2000 government spending on all levels of education amounted to 256,200m. forint, equivalent to 4.8% of total public expenditure. Pre-primary education in Hungary is not compulsory, but most children between the ages of three and six years attend kindergartens (óvodák). Children under the age of three years attend crèches (bölcsődék). Education is compulsory for children between the ages of six and 16 years, although most continue their schooling beyond that age. Children attend a basic or primary school (általános iskola) until they are 14, studying general subjects together with some practical training; special provision is made in basic schools for talented children, particularly those with notable ability in languages. In 2000 98% of children of the relevant age-group attended primary schools.

Secondary education starts at the age of 14 years, and secondary enrolment included 97% of children in the relevant age-group in 2000. There are three principal types of secondary school: the gymnasium (gimnázium) provides a four-year course of mainly academic studies, although some vocational training is included in the curriculum; the vocational school (szakközépiskola) curriculum provides full vocational training, together with general education; and the apprentice training school (szakmunkásképző intézetek), which are attached to factories, agricultural co-operatives, etc., and provide training leading to full trade qualifications, with general education having a less prominent role. In addition, there are special schools both for children with physical and/or learning difficulties, and for the particularly gifted. Educational reform aimed at revising the curricula and the method of assessing pupils was taking place, and in southern Hungary bilingual schools were established to promote the languages of national minorities. In 1999–2000 the system of higher education underwent a major transformation, as a result of which, from 1 January 2000, there were 30 state-run universities and colleges, 26 church universities and colleges and six colleges run by various foundations. In 2000 an estimated 25% of the relevant age-group continued into tertiary education.

STATE UNIVERSITIES

Budapest University of Economic Sciences and Public Administration (Budapesti Közgazdaságtudományi és Államigazgatási Egyetem): 1093 Budapest IX, Fővám tér 8; tel. (1) 217-6740; fax (1) 217-6714; internet www.bkae.hu; f. 1948; 4 faculties; 677 teachers; 11,779 students; Rector Dr ATTILA CHIKÁN.

Budapest University of Technology and Economics: 1111 Budapest, Müegyetem rkp 3–9; tel. (1) 463-1111; fax (1) 463-1110; e-mail gyorgyi@rektori.bme.hu; internet www.bme.hu; f. 1782; 8 faculties; 1,123 teachers; 12,950 students; Rector Prof. Dr ÁKOS DETREKŐI.

Eötvös Loránd University (Eötvös Loránd Tudományegyetem): 1056 Budapest, Egyetem tér 1–3; tel. (1) 267-0820; fax (1) 266-9786; e-mail webmaster@elte.hu; internet www.elte.hu; f. 1635; 6 faculties; 1,901 teachers; 24,427 students; Rector Dr ISTVÁN KLINGHAMMER.

Semmelweis University (Semmelweis Orvostudományi Egyetem): 1085 Budapest, Üllői u. 26; tel. (1) 317-2400; fax (1) 317-2220; internet www.sote.hu; f. 1769 as Medical Faculty of University of Nagyszombat, attained university status 1951; 6 faculties; 1,233 teachers; 7,638 students; Rector Prof. Dr LÁSZLÓ ROMICS.

Szent István University: 2103 Gödöllő, Páter K. u. 1; tel. (28) 522-082; fax (28) 410-804; e-mail palfalvy@gikk.szie.hu; internet www .sziu.hu; f. 1787; 10 faculties; 1,079 teachers; 23,704 students; Rector Dr PÉTER SZENDRŐ.

University Medical School of Debrecen (Debreceni Orvostudományi Egyetem): 4032 Debrecen, Egyetem tér 1; tel. (52) 512-900; fax (52) 416-490; internet www.dote.hu; f. 1918 as Faculty of Medicine of István Tirza University, attained university status 1951; 8 faculties; 1925 teachers; 19,189 students; Rector Dr LÁSZLÓ FÉSÜS.

University of Debrecen (Debreceni Egyetem): 4010 Debrecen, Egyetem tér 1; tel. (52) 512-693; fax (52) 310-007; e-mail internationaloffice@admin.unideb.hu; internet www.unideb.hu; f. 1912; fmrly Lajos Kossuth University; 8 faculties; 8 institutes; 1,721 teachers; 21,724 students; Rector Prof. JÁNOS NAGY.

University of Kaposvár: 7401 Kaposvár, Guba Sándor u. 40; tel. (82) 412-613; fax (82) 320-175; 2 faculties; 150 teachers; 2,643 students; Rector Dr PÉTER HORN.

University of Miskolc (Miskolci Egyetem): 3515 Miskolc, Egyetemváros; tel. (46) 565-111; fax (46) 565-014; e-mail stbes@gold .uni-miskolc.hu; internet www.uni-miskolc.hu; f. 1735 in Selmecbánya; moved to Sopron in 1919 and to Miskolc in 1949; 6 faculties in Miskolc, 1 faculty in Sárospatak, Music School, Research Institute of Applied Chemistry; 927 teachers; 12,580 students; Rector Prof. Dr LAJOS BESENYEI.

University of Pécs: 7633 Pécs, Szántó K. János u. 1/B; tel. (72) 501-507; fax (72) 501-508; e-mail rector@rektori.pte.hu; internet www .pte.hu; originally f. 1367; 9 faculties; 1,658 teachers; 27,013 students; Rector Dr JÓZSEF TÓTH.

University of Szeged (Szegedi Tudományegyetem): 6720 Szeged, Dugonics tér 13; tel. (62) 544-001; fax (62) 420-412; e-mail rekthiv@ rekt.u-szeged.hu; internet www.u-szeged.hu; f. 1872; refounded 1921 as Medical Faculty of Szeged University, attained university status 1951, re-inaugurated 2000, incorporating the former József Attila University; languages of instruction: Hungarian and English; 11 faculties; 2,326 teachers; 21,379 students; Rector Prof. Dr REZSŐ MÉSZÁROS.

University of Veszprém (Veszprémi Egyetem): 8201 Veszprém, Egyetem u. 10; tel. (88) 422-022; fax (88) 423-866; internet www.vein .hu; f. 1949; 3 faculties; 409 teachers; 6,318 students; Rector Prof. I. GYŐRI.

University of West Hungary (Nyugat-Magyarországi Egyetem): 9400 Sopron, Bajcsy-Zsilinszky u. 4; tel. (99) 518-100; fax (99) 311-103; e-mail rectoro@nyme.hu; internet www.nyme.hu; f. 1753 as the University of Sopron; renamed in 2000 following merger with Agricultural Faculty of Mosonmagyaróvár (f. 1918), Ápáczai Csere János Teacher Training College (f. 1778), and Benedek Elek College of Pedagogy (f. 1959); 7 faculties; 445 teachers; 10,106 students; Rector Dr JÓZSEF KOLOSZÁR.

Zrínyi Miklós University of National Defence: 1101 Budapest, Hungária krt 9-11; tel. (1) 432-9000; fax (1) 432-9012; internet www .zmne.hu; 3 faculties; 395 teachers; 3,300 students; Rector Dr MIKLÓS SZABÓ.

PRIVATE UNIVERSITY

Central European University: 1051 Budapest, Nádor u. 9; tel. (1) 327-3000; fax (1) 327-3007; e-mail external@ceu.hu; internet www .ceu.hu; f. 1990; originally in Prague (Czech Republic); funded by the Soros Foundation; language of instruction: English; 45 teachers; 450 students; colleges in Prague and Warsaw (Poland); Pres. and Rector Prof. ALFRED C. STEPAN; Sec.-Gen. Dr ANNE LONSDALE.

Social Welfare

Hungary's national insurance scheme is based largely on non-state contributions. Employees contribute 4% of their gross earnings as a health-care contribution and 6% to the pension fund, while employers usually pay 19% of the employees' salaries towards health insurance and 24.5% into the pension fund. The Health Insurance Act, passed in July 1992, made health insurance obligatory. In February 1996 the deficit of the Health Insurance Fund was some 20,000m. forint.

The implementation of the five-day working week was completed by 1985. There is a guaranteed minimum wage, and employment is non-discriminatory. The minimum monthly wage was increased to 50,000 forint (some US $178) in 2001, and the Medgyessy Government, which took office in May 2002, planned to introduce a minimum wage of some 100,000 forint per month for university graduates. Men are usually entitled to receive retirement pensions at the age of 60, and women at 55, drawing between 33% and 75% of their earnings, according to length of service. In 1998 the Government introduced comprehensive pension reforms, supported by the World Bank, whereby employees would be legally obliged to pay 25% of pension contributions to private pension schemes. In 2001 the average monthly pension stood at 38,374 forint, representing an increase of 6.5% compared with the previous year, and equivalent to 59.1% of average net earnings.

Unemployment benefit was introduced in January 1989. However, owing to conditions applied concerning former employment history, and general lack of government funding, in 1996 only 34% of unemployed people in Hungary actually received unemployment benefit, while 42% received welfare payments and 24% no financial aid at all. Sickness benefits are provided by social insurance: employees are usually entitled to sick pay for one year, or for two years in cases of tuberculosis, occupational disease or industrial accident. Most medical consultation and treatment is free, although there are charges towards the cost of medicines and medical appliances. Social insurance also covers maternity benefits (women are entitled to 24 weeks' maternity leave on full pay), invalidity pensions, widows' pensions and orphans allowances. In March 1996 a Labour Market Council was introduced, following the merger of four employment funds. The Council was allocated 100,000m. forint to spend on support of the unemployed and job-creation schemes. A further organization, the Board of Public Works, was created the following month.

In 1999 there were 362 physicians per 100,000 of the population, and in 2001 there were an estimated 80,223 hospital beds (equivalent to 788 per 100,000). The rate of infant mortality was 9 per 1,000 live births in 2001. In 2000 total government expenditure on health was 321,600m. forint (equivalent to 6.1% of total expenditure), and about 1,703,300m forint (32.2%) was spent on social security and welfare.

In June 2000 the first Romany communications resource centre opened in Tatabanya. The centre aimed to provide information regarding jobs and training for the Romany minority in the town, to assist in handling official matters, and to offer toys and distractions for children.

NATIONAL AGENCIES

Ministry of Health, Social and Family Affairs: see section on The Government (Ministries).

Board of Public Works (Koezmunkatanacs): Budapest; f. 1996.

International Alarm Centre: 1134 Budapest, Róbert Károly krt 77; tel. (1) 350-6931; fax (1) 350-6830; f. 1992; provides 24-hour international transportation and medical assistance; Dir Dr SZABÓ KATALIN.

Labour Market Council (Munkaeroepiaci Tanacs): Budapest; f. 1996.

National Ambulance and Emergency Service (Országos Mentöszolgálat): 1134 Budapest, Róbert Károly krt 77; tel. (1) 350-3737; fax (1) 239-7848; internet www.mentok.hu; f. 1948; responsible for ground and air rescue, first aid and transportation; Dir Dr GÁBOR GÖBL.

National Health Insurance Fund (Országos Egészségbiztosítási Pénztár): 1139 Budapest, Váci út 73/a; 1565 Budapest, POB 18; tel. (1) 350-1636; fax (1) 359-6654; e-mail oepweb@oep.hu; internet www .ocp.hu; f. 1992; operates the health-insurance system, participates in the preparation of laws concerning health insurance; assesses, controls and finances the payment of benefits; Dir-Gen. Dr ZSUZSANNA MATEJKA.

HEALTH AND WELFARE ORGANIZATIONS

Against Cancer, for the Future of the People Foundation ('A Rák Ellen, az Emberért, a Holnapért' Társadalmi Alapítvány): 1122 Budapest 1122, Ráth György u. 7–9.

Heart Sounds Foundation ('Szól a Szív' Alapítvány): 1146 Budapest, Ajtósi Dürer sor 39; organization for the aid of blind children.

Heart and Vascular Diseases Foundation (Szív- és Érbetegekért Alapítvány).

Hungarian Red Cross (Magyar Vöröskereszt): 1051 Budapest, Arany János u. 31; Pres. Dr LÁSZLÓ ANDICS; Sec.-Gen. Dr GYÖRGY RÓZSA.

LARES Foundation (LARES Alapítvány): Budapest, Károly krt 2; organization of family-help and self-help groups.

National Institute for Health Promotion (Nemzeti Egészségfejlesztési Intézet): 1062 Budapest, Andrássy u. 82; tel. (1) 332-7380; fax (1) 331-6112; f. 1990; policy planning, monitoring, evaluation and support in health promotion; Dir Dr ANNA M. OLASZY.

Péter Cerny Foundation for Curing Sick Babies (Péter Cerny Alapítvány a Beteg Koraszülöttek Gyógyításáért): 1083 Budapest, Bókay J u. 53u.; tel. and fax (1) 323-3005; e-mail info@cerny.hu; internet www.cerny.hu; f. 1988; Pres. PAUL F. FEKETE.

Semmelweis Foundation for the Development of Orthopaedics in Hungary (Semmelweis Alapítvány a Magyarországi Ortopédia Fejlesztéséért): 1083 Budapest, Karolina u. 27; tel. (1) 466-6059; fax (1) 466-8747; e-mail titkarsag@orto.sote.hu; f. 1988; support of healing and prevention of invalidity; Pres. of the Bd Prof. T. VIZKELETY.

SOS Foundation (SOS Alapítvány): Budapest; organization for the promotion of the welfare of physically-handicapped people.

The Environment

The high sulphur-dioxide emissions and the high levels of hazardous waste production in Hungary, characteristic of the communist-run economies of Central and Eastern Europe, became an important political issue in the 1990s. Opposition to the Danube Dam project, at Gabčíkovo-Nagymarós, produced an organized environmental movement in Hungary, as well as opposition to the communist regime. Following Hungary's withdrawal from the project, the country's relations with Slovakia, which continued with the construction of the hydroelectric plant, deteriorated and the dispute was referred to the International Court of Justice (ICJ—based in the Netherlands) in April 1993. In September 1997 the ICJ ruled that both Hungary and Slovakia had contravened international law and both countries were required to pay compensation for damages incurred. The Hungarian Government is a member of the Danube Commission (Slovakia) and the IUCN (Gland, Switzerland). To meet European Union (EU) requirements, the Government estimated that it needed to invest US $4,000m. in the environment sector. As well as allocating funds from its budget ($11.3m. in 1998), the state receives contributions from the EU's Central Environment Fund. Approximately $109m. were received from the Fund in 1998.

In February 2000 a mineral waste leak from the Romanian gold mine, Baia Mare, led to the accidental poisoning of the Danube and Tisza Rivers. The waste, consisting of cyanide, lead and zinc, killed aquatic life in the Tisza, formerly one of the region's cleanest rivers. By April over 1,200 metric tons of fish had died. The EU pledged about €70m. towards a rehabilitation programme. Hungarian companies and foreign governments also provided financial assistance. In May restoration of aquatic life commenced, and progressed rapidly.

GOVERNMENT ORGANIZATIONS

Ministry of the Environmental Protection and Water Management: see section on The Government (Ministries).

Institute for Environmental Management (Környezetgazdálkodási Intézet): 1369 Budapest, POB 352; tel. (1) 374-3500; fax (1) 311-5826; e-mail kozpont.kgi@ktm.x400gw.itb.hu; promotes and sustains sound environmental management; houses the INFOTERRA national focal point, which disseminates environmental information, provides an environmental information service and manages the National Professional Library of Environmental Protection and Water Management; Dir E. ISTV.

National Committee for the Protection of Clean Air (National Planning Office): 1370 Budapest, POB 613.

National Environmental Protection Authority (Környezetvédelmi Főfelügyelőség): 1011 Budapest, Fő u. 44–50, POB 351; tel. (1) 201-1725; fax (1) 201-4282; f. 1991; inspectorate for waste management and control of noise, air and water pollution; Principal Officers R. REINIGER, P. VARGA, É. LUCZ.

National Inspectorate for Environment and Nature Protection (Környezet és Természetvédelmi Fofelügyeloség): 1011 Budapest, Fő u 44–50; 1384 Budapest, POB 756; tel. (1) 457-3545; fax (1) 201-4282; e-mail bacso.laszlone@ktmdom2.ktm.hu; internet www

.ktm.hu/intez/fofel; f. 1991; inspectorate for waste management and control of noise, air and water pollution; co-ordinates 12 regional environmental inspectorates and nine national park directorates; Dir-Gen. Dr KATALIN UGHY.

ACADEMIC INSTITUTES

Hungarian Academy of Sciences (Magyar Tudományos Akadémia): 1051 Budapest, Roosevelt tér 9; tel. (1) 338-2344; fax (1) 332-8943; e-mail lilla@office.mta.hu; internet www.mta.hu; f. 1825; 11 sections; attached research institutes; 192 honorary mems, 240 mems, 79 corresponding mems, 121 external mems; Pres. FERENC GLATZ; Gen. Sec. NORBERT KROO.

Ecological and Botanical Research Institute of the Hungarian Academy of Sciences (Magyar Tudományos Akadémia Ökológiai és Botanikai Kutatóintézete): 2163 Vácrátót, Alkotmány u 2-4; tel. (28) 360-122; fax (28) 360-110; e-mail pali@botanika.botanika.hu; internet www.botanika.hu/botkert/english; f. 1952; theoretical and experimental research in terrestrial ecology and hydrobiology monitoring biodiversity; 130 mems; Dir Dr ATTILA BORHIDI.

Forest Research Institute (Erdeszeti Tudomanyos Intezet): 1023 Budapest, Frankel Leo u. 42–44; tel. (1) 438-5870; fax (1) 326-1639; e-mail h9439fuh@ella.hu; f. 1949; general research in forestry and environmental matters; Dir-Gen. Dr ERNO FUHRER.

Hungarian Forestry Association (Országos Erdészeti Egyesület): 1027 Budapest, Fő u. 68; tel. (1) 201-6293; fax (1) 201-7737; e-mail oee@mtesz.hu; internet larix.efe.hu/oee/index.html; f. 1866; forestry, forest industries, environmental protection; 5,000 mems; Pres. JÓZSEF KÁLDY.

NON-GOVERNMENTAL ORGANIZATIONS

Alba Kör Erőszakmentes Bèkemozgalom (Alba Circle, Non-Violent Peace Movement in Hungary): 1461 Budapest, V Vadász u 29, POB 653; tel. (1) 303-7235; fax (1) 302-3148; e-mail siktoma@freemailhu; internet www.albakor.hu; f. 1998; includes a Green Group for the protection of the environment against military and civilian damage.

BirdLife Hungary (Magyar Madártani és Természetvédelmi Egyesület): 1121 Budapest, Költö u. 21; tel. and fax (1) 275-6247; e-mail mme@mme.hu; internet www.mme.nature.hu; f. 1974; nature conservation and bird protection; 6,000 mems; Man. Dir JÓZSEF FIDLÓCZKY.

BOCS Foundation: 8003 Székesfehérvár, POB 7; tel. and fax (22) 501-844; e-mail bocs@c3.hu; internet www.bocs.hu; f. 1989; promotes ecology, peace and sustainable development; Pres. GYULA SIMONYI; Sec. ISTVÁN DŐRY.

Clean Air Action Group (Levegő Munkacsoport): 1465 Budapest, POB 1676; tel. (1) 209-3822; fax (1) 365-0438; e-mail levego@levego.hu; internet www.levego.hu; f. 1988; association of 57 environmental NGOs; environmental protection in relation to transport and energy issues, green economics, public awareness raising activities, research, advocacy; Pres. ANDRÁS LUKÁCS; Chair. of Cttee of Experts Dr DEZSŐ RADÓ.

East European Environmental Research Unit—ISTER: 1054 Budapest, Vadász u 29; tel. and fax (1) 153-0100; e-mail vamaa@vargham.zpok.hu; research, advisory work and publications concerning environmental protection; Pres. JÁNOS VARGHA; Chief Exec. GYÖRGY DROPPA.

Ecoservice Foundation, Environmental Counselling Service (Ökoszolgálat Alapítvány, Környezetvédelmi Tanácsadó Szolgálat): 1054 Budapest, Vadász u 29; tel. (1) 311-7855; fax (1) 302-3148; e-mail okosz@okoszolgalat.hu; internet www.okoszolgalat.hu; f. 1990; information service, database of environmental organizations, publications and courses; Head ANDREA HÁGEN.

ELTE Nature Conservation Club (Egyetemes Létezés Természetvédelmi Egyesület): 1054 Budapest, Vadász u 29; 1115 Budapest, Sárbogárdi u. 11; tel. and fax (1) 111-7855; e-mail etkpop@zpok.hu; internet www.etk.hu; f. 1983; educational and conservation projects; Chair. VERONIKA MÓRA; Sec. ERNESE BALOGH.

Environmental Management and Law Association (EMLA): 1082 Budapest, Állöi u. 66/b VI/4; tel. (1) 303-5504; fax (1) 333-2931; e-mail emla@emla.zpok.hu; Contact KISS CSABA.

Friends of the Earth Hungary (Magyar Természetvédők Szövetsége): 1091 Budapest, Ulloi U 91/B III/21; 1450 Budapest, POB 123; tel. and fax (1) 216-7297; e-mail mtvsz@elender.hu; internet www.mtvsz.hu; f. 1989; promotes exchange of information, co-operation and joint programmes with other organizations; environmental policy development; creates public awareness of environmental issues; 76 member groups; Pres. ERZSÉBET SCHMUCK.

Green Heart Youth Movement for Nature Conservation: 2013 Pomáz, Mátyás Király u 2; tel. and fax (26) 325-957; e-mail zoldsziv@freemail.hu; internet www.c3.hu/~zsiv; natural and environmental education; conservation of environmental resources; water quality monitoring on the Danube and Tisza rivers in five countries; 15,000 mems in 16 countries; Pres. ANIKÓ ORGOVÁNYI.

Green Party of Hungary: see section on Political Organizations.

Hungarian Friends of Nature Alliance: 1065 Budapest, Bajcsy-Zsilinszky u. 31, I/3; 1396 Budapest, POB 483; tel. (1) 111-2467; fax (1) 153-1930; e-mail nagyand@okopr.zpok.hu; Contact LÁSZLÓ KALMÁR.

Hungarian National Society of Conservationists (Magyar Természetvédők Szovetsége): 1091 Budapest, Üllői u. 91/b.; tel. and fax (1) 216-7297; e-mail mtvsz@elender.hu; organization of local conservation and environmental groups and regional and national societies; provides members with technical assistance; develops and implements environmental projects at local, national and international levels; raises public awareness and disseminates information on sustainable development; lobbying of politicians; Pres. Dr ERZSÉBET SCHMUCK.

Independent Ecological Centre (Független Ökológiai Központ Alapítvány): 1035 Budapest, Miklós tér 1; tel. (1) 368-6229; fax (1) 250-1456; e-mail office@foek.hu; internet www.foek.hu; Dir Dr VIDA GÁBOR.

Reflex Environmental Protection Society (Reflex Környezetvédő Egyesület): 9024 Győr, Bartók Béla u 7; tel. (96) 316-192; fax (96) 310-988; e-mail reflex@c3.hu; internet www.reflex.gyor.hu; f. 1987; renewable energy, energy efficiency consultancy, environmental law and legal consultancy, nature conservation, environmental conflict resolution, solid waste management and recycling, environmental planning; Pres. JÓZSEF LAJTMANN.

Water Resources Research Centre (Vízgazdálkodási Tudományos Kutató Rt—VITUKI): 1095 Budapest, Kvassay Jenő u. 1; 1453 Budapest, POB 27; tel. (1) 215-6140; fax (1) 216-1514; e-mail vitukirt@vituki.hu; internet www.datanet.hu/hydroinfo/vituki; f. 1952; three institutes, provides research, consulting and engineering services, including water quality surveys, formulation of monitoring strategies, and pollutant-sampling programmes; Dir-Gen. P. BAKONYI.

REGIONAL ORGANIZATIONS

Danube Commission: 1068 Budapest, Benczúr u. 25; tel. (1) 352-1835; fax (1) 352-1839; internet www.dunacom.org; f. 1949; approves projects for river maintenance; also responsible for navigation

issues; mems: Austria, Bulgaria, Croatia, Germany, Hungary, Moldova, Romania, Russia, Serbia and Montenegro, Slovakia, Ukraine; Pres. Dr HELLMUTH STRASSER (Austria); Dir-Gen. of Secr. Capt. DANAIL NEDIALKOV (Bulgaria).

Environmental Partnership for Central Europe (Ökotárs Alapítvány): 1117 Budapest, Móricz Zsigmond ksrtér 15, I/1; 1519 Budapest, POB 411; tel. (1) 466-8866; fax (1) 181-3393; e-mail info@okotars.hu; internet www.okotars.hu; f. 1991; provides small grants and technical and organizational assistance to non-governmental orgs and local authorities in Hungary and other Central European countries; part of a network of similar orgs in the Czech Republic, Poland and Slovakia; Country Dir ZSUZSA FOLTÁNYI.

Regional Environmental Centre for Central and Eastern Europe: 2000 Szentendre, Ady Endre u. 9–11; tel. (26) 504-000; fax (26) 311-294; e-mail info@rec.org; internet www.rec.org; f. 1996; promotes environmental awareness in 15 countries in Central and Eastern Europe.

Defence

Military service in Hungary begins at the age of 18 years and was reduced from nine months to six months in 2001. In August 2002 Hungary's regular armed forces numbered 33,400, of which 22,900 were conscripts. The Land Forces had 23,600 forces and the Air Force 7,700 (there were also 2,100 centrally controlled personnel). Paramilitary forces comprised 12,000 border guards, as well as 2,000 members of the internal security forces. Hungary, formerly part of the communist bloc of states, was prominent in advocating the dissolution of the military association dominated by the USSR. The Warsaw Pact (f. 1955) was finally dissolved in 1991, in which year the last Soviet troops left Hungary. In March 1999 Hungary became a member of the North Atlantic Treaty Organization (NATO). In June 2000 legislation on the reform of the armed forces, including the reduction of the size of the force and the improvement of military technology over three stages by 2010, was adopted. Hungary's defence expenditure was an estimated 265,000m. forint in 2001. The Government planned to increase its defence expenditure, to reach the NATO average of 2% of GDP by 2006.

Commander-in-Chief of the Armed Forces: President of the Republic.

Chief of the Defence Staff: Maj.-Gen. ZOLTÁN SZENES.

Bibliography

Ágh, A. 'The Hungarian Party System' in *Budapest Papers on Democratic Transition*, No. 51. 1993.

Andor, L. *Hungary on the Road to the European Union: Transition in Blue*. Westport, CT, Praeger, 2000.

Andorka, R. *et al* (Eds). *A Society Transformed*. Budapest, Central European University Press, 1999.

Antal-Mokos, Z. *Privatization, Politics, and Economic Performance in Hungary*. Cambridge, Cambridge University Press, 1998.

Batt, J. *Economic Reform and Political Change in Eastern Europe: a Comparison of the Czechoslovak and Hungarian Experiences*. Basingstoke, Macmillan, 1988.

Bekes, C., Byrne, M., and Rainer, J. (Eds). *The 1956 Hungarian Revolution: A History in Documents*. Budapest, Central European University Press, 2002.

Berend, I., and Ránki, G. (Eds). *The Hungarian Economy in the 20th Century*. London, Croom Helm, 1985.

Berend, I. *The Hungarian Economic Reforms 1953–1988*. Cambridge, Cambridge University Press, 1990.

Bozóki, A., Körösény, A., and Schöpflin, G. (Eds). *Post-Communist Transition*. London, Pinter Publishers, 1992.

Brada, J. C., and Dobozi, I. (Eds). *The Hungarian Economy in the 1980s: Reforming the System and Adjusting to External Shocks* (Industrial Development and the Social Fabric Series, Vol. 9). London, JAI Press, 1988.

Braham, R. L., and Miller, S. (Eds). *The Nazis' Last Victims: The Holocaust in Hungary*. Detroit, MI, Wayne State University Press, 2002 (2nd edition).

Congdon, L. *Seeing Red: Hungarian Intellectuals in Exile and the Challenge of Communism*. DeKalb, IL, Northern Illinois University Press, 2001.

Csaba, L. *Eastern Europe in the World Economy*. Budapest, 1990.

Eby, C. D. *Hungary at War: Civilians and Soldiers in World War II*. University Park, PA, Pennsylvania University Press, 1998.

Engel, P. *The Realm of St Steven: a History of Medieval Hungary*. London, I. B. Tauris and Co, 2001.

Gati, C. *Hungary and the Soviet Bloc*. Durham, NC, Duke University Press, 1986.

Hahn, C. M. (Ed.). *Market Economy and Civil Society in Hungary*. Ilford, Frank Cass, 1990.

Haney, L. A. *Inventing the Needy: Gender and the Politics of Welfare in Hungary*. Berkeley, CA, University of California Press, 2002.

Heinrich, H.-G. *Hungary: Politics, Economics and Society* (Marxist Regimes Series). Boulder, CO, Lynne Rienner, 1986.

Hoensch, J. K. *A History of Modern Hungary 1867–1994*. 2nd edn, Harlow, Longman, 1996.

János, A. *The Politics of Backwardness in Hungary 1825–1945*. Princeton, NJ, Princeton University Press, 1982.

Király, B. K. *Basic History of Modern Hungary: 1867–1999*. Malabar, FL, Krieger Publishing, 2001.

Kontler, L. *Millennium in Central Europe, A History of Hungary*. Budapest, Atlantisz, 1999.

Kornai, J. *The Road to a Free Economy*. London and New York, NY, W. W. Norton, 1990.

Körösényi, A. *Government and Politics in Hungary*. Budapest, Central European University Press, 1999.

Kocsis, K., and Kocsisne Hodosi, E. *Ethnic Geography of the Hungarian Minorities in the Carpathian Basin*. Toronto, Matthias Corvinus, 1998.

Koves, A. *Central and East European Economies in Transition*. Boulder, CO, and Oxford, 1990.

Kovrig, B. *Communism in Hungary: From Kun to Kádár*. Stanford, CA, Hoover Institution Press, 1979.

Kürti, L. *The Remote Borderland: Transylvania in the Hungarian Imagination.* Albany, NY, State University of New York Press, 2001.

Lendvai, P. *The Hungarians: A Thousand Years of Victory in Defeat.* London, C. Hurst and Co, 2003.

Liptak, B. G. *A Testament of Revolution.* Texas, TX, Texas A&M University Press, 2001.

Litván, G. (Ed.). *The Hungarian Revolution of 1956: Reform, Revolt and Repression 1953–1956.* Harlow, Longman, 1996.

Lomax, B. *Hungary 1956.* London, Allison and Busby, 1976.

Macartney, C. A. *October the Fifteenth: A History of Modern Hungary, 1929–45,* 2 Vols. Edinburgh, Edinburgh University Press, 1956–57.

   Hungary: A Short History. Edinburgh, Edinburgh University Press, 1962.

Meusberger, P., and Jöns, H. (Eds). *Transformations in Hungary: Essays in Economy and Society.* New York, NY, Physica-Verlag, 2001.

Miller, S. (Ed.). *The Nazis' Last Victims: The Holocaust in Hungary.* Detroit, MI, Wayne State University Press, 1998.

Molnar, M. *From Béla Kun to János Kádár: Seventy Years of Communism.* Oxford, Berg Publishing Ltd, 1990.

   A Concise History of Hungary. Cambridge, Cambridge University Press, 2001.

Révész, G. *Perestroika in Eastern Europe: Hungary's Economic Transformation, 1945–1988.* Boulder, CO, Westview Press, 1990.

Richet, X. *The Hungarian Model: Planning and Market in a Socialist Economy.* Cambridge, Cambridge University Press, 1989.

Roman, E. *Hungary and the Victor Powers, 1945–1950.* London, Macmillan, 1996.

Romsics, I., and Király, B. K. *Geopolitics in the Danube Region: Hungarian Reconciliation Efforts, 1848–1998.* Budapest, Central European University Press, 1998.

Schöpflin, G., and Poulton, H. *Romania's Ethnic Hungarians.* London, Minority Rights Group Report, 1990.

Shawcross, N. *Crime and Compromise: János Kádár and the Politics of Hungary Since the Revolution.* London, Weidenfeld and Nicolson, 1974.

Sugar, P. (Ed.). *A History of Hungary.* London, I. B. Tauris and Co, 1994.

Swain, N. *Hungary: The Rise and Fall of Feasible Socialism.* London, Verso, 1992.

Székely, I. P., and Newbery, D. M. G. (Eds) *Hungary: An Economy In Transition.* Cambridge, Cambridge University Press (Centre for Economic Policy Research), 1992.

Tökés, R. L. *Hungary's Negotiated Revolution: Economic Reform, Social Change, and Political Succession, 1957–1990.* Cambridge, Cambridge University Press, 1996.

Vali, F. *Rift and Reform in Hungary*: Nationalism versus Communism. Cambridge, MA, Harvard University Press, 1961.

Vass, L. 'Changes in Hungary's Governmental System and the Problems of Analysis' in *Budapest Papers on Democratic Transition,* No. 59. 1993.

Also see the Select Bibliography in Part Four.

LATVIA

Geography

PHYSICAL FEATURES

The Republic of Latvia (formerly the Soviet Socialist Republic of Latvia, a constituent partner in the USSR) is situated in north-eastern Europe, on the east coast of the Baltic Sea. It is bounded by Estonia to the north and by Lithuania to the south and south-west. To the east there is a frontier with Russia and, to the south-east, with Belarus. Latvia covers an area of 64,589 sq km (24,938 sq miles). The present territory is essentially that of the pre-1940 Republic, with the exception of the area around Pytalovo (formerly Jaunlatgale), which was transferred to the Russian Federation in 1945.

The country is divided into the Coastal Lowlands and three main inland regions: Western Latvia, Central Latvia and Eastern Latvia. The Coastal Lowlands comprise the low-lying littoral of the Baltic Sea and the Gulf of Rīga, along which there are several natural harbours. Western Latvia is also largely flat terrain, interrupted only by the undulating relief of the Western Kursa Upland. Central Latvia offers more varied terrain, ranging from the Zemgale plain in the south-west, part of which is below sea-level, to the Vidzeme Upland, a region of uneven relief, which includes the highest point in Latvia (Gaizinkalns, which stands at a height of 312 m or 1,030 ft). Eastern Latvia is dominated by the Latgale Upland, which extends to the south-eastern border with Belarus, and includes more than 1,000 lakes. Although there are more than 12,000 rivers in the country, the only major waterways are the Daugava (Dvina), which flows through the centre of the country and empties into the Gulf of Rīga, and the Gauja, which rises in the Vidzeme Upland.

CLIMATE

Owing to the influence of maritime factors, the climate is relatively temperate but changeable. Average temperatures in January range from –2.8°C (26.6°F) in the western, coastal town of Liepāja, to –6.6°C (20.1°F) in the inland town of Daugavpils. Mean temperatures for July range from 16.7°C (62.1°F) in Liepāja to 17.6°C (63.7°F) in Daugavpils. Average annual precipitation in Rīga is 617 mm (24 ins).

POPULATION

According to the results of the census of 31 March 2000, 57.7% of the population were ethnic Latvians, 29.6% Russians, 4.1% Belarusians, 2.7% Ukrainians and 2.5% Poles. Other ethnic groups include Lithuanians, Jews, Roma (Gypsies), Estonians and Germans. The proportion of ethnic Latvians increased slightly after the restoration of independence in 1991, but in

2000 was still far from the levels of the pre-Soviet period; in 1935 75.5% of the population were ethnic Latvians. There were significant communities of Latvians in other countries, notably in the USA. The proportion of the population living in rural areas declined from 68.2% in 1935 to 28.9% in 1989 (according to the World Bank, it was 27% in 1995). Population distribution was quite uneven, with almost 50% of the population living in the region around Rīga. The average population density (persons per sq km) was 35.8 at the beginning of 2003, but was far lower in parts of Western Latvia.

Latvian replaced Russian as the official language of the republic in 1988, when it was still part of the USSR. It is an Indo-European language, a member of the Baltic group, and is written in the Latin script. At the census of 1989 22.3% of ethnic Russians claimed fluency in Latvian; however, by the census of 2000 this figure had increased to 52.3%. Approximately one-third of the population are Russian-speakers. The major religion is Christianity: most ethnic Latvians are traditionally Lutheran, although smaller Protestant sects have a considerable following among the younger generation, and the Roman Catholic Church is also represented. Adherents of the Eastern Orthodox Church in Latvia are mostly ethnic Russians.

The capital is Rīga, which is an important port, situated near the mouth of the River Daugava. Rīga had an estimated population of 739,232 on 1 January 2003. Other important cities included Daugavpils (112,609), Liepāja (86,983) and Jelgava (65,754).

Chronology

c. 2,000 BC: The Balts, the ancestors of the Latvians (Letts), settled on the southern and south-eastern shores of the Baltic Sea.

AD 1201: Albert von Appeldern, the German Bishop of Livonia, founded the city of Rīga and established the crusading order of Sword Brethren.

1209: The German crusading order of the Teutonic Knights invaded Jersika, a town in southern Latvia controlled by a

native ruler, Visvaldis, following his marriage to a pagan Lithuanian princess.

1290: The Teutonic Knights completed their conquest of Latvia with the capture of the kingdom of Zemgale. Latvia and Estonia were subsequently ruled by the Livonian Order of Teutonic Knights (formed in 1237 by an alliance of the German Order of Teutonic Knights and the Sword Brethren) under the name of Livonia.

1494: Serfdom was introduced in Livonia.

1524–34: Livonia renounced religious adherence to Rome and converted to Lutheranism.

1558: Ivan IV (the 'Terrible') of the Russian state of Muscovy attacked Livonia in an attempt to conquer part of the Baltic coast; his move instigated the Livonian War, which continued until 1582.

1561: The Livonian State of Teutonic Knights finally ceased to exist: northern Estonia fell under Swedish control, while the rest came under Polish-Lithuanian rule, with the kingdoms of Kurzeme and Zemgale becoming part of the autonomous Duchy of Courland (Kurland).

1629: Sweden conquered the Livonian territories of Poland.

1721: The Treaty of Nystad, concluded by Russia and Sweden, ended the Great Northern War and brought Estonia and much of Livonia under Russian rule.

1772: At the First Partition of Poland, Latgale, an eastern region of Livonia, was incorporated into the Russian Empire, as part of the Russian province of Vitebsk (now in Belarus).

1795: At the Third Partition of Poland the remainder of the Duchy of Courland became part of the Russian Empire.

1817–19: Serfdom was abolished in Latvia.

1901: The Latvian Social Democratic Party was established, which advocated greater territorial autonomy for Latvia.

October 1905: Two Latvian deputies were elected to the Duma (parliament), which was established in the tsarist capital of St Petersburg.

18 November 1917: A first National Council was elected in Valka, northern Latvia, at a meeting of the Rīga Democratic Bloc; the Council expressed its intention to establish Latvia as an independent sovereign state.

3 March 1918: Treaty of Brest-Litovsk: the Bolsheviks ceded large areas of western territory to Germany, including the Baltic regions.

18 November 1918: An independent Republic of Latvia was declared and a provisional administration, under the premiership of Kārlis Ulmanis, was formed.

3 January 1919: The Soviet Red Army captured Rīga, forcing the Provisional Government to flee to Kurzeme.

May 1919: With the aid of German troops, Latvian forces expelled the Red Army from Rīga.

8 July 1919: The Provisional Government returned to the capital and the Latvian National Council reconvened.

January 1920: The last Soviet troops were finally expelled from Latvia.

1 February 1920: The Latvian and Soviet Governments signed an armistice.

1 May 1920: At the first session of the Constituent Assembly (elections to which were held in the previous month) Jānis Čakste was elected President of the Assembly and of the Republic of Latvia.

11 August 1920: A Latvian-Soviet peace agreement, the Treaty of Rīga, was signed.

7 November 1922: Following the promulgation of a new Constitution, the first session of the new Saeima (Parliament) opened.

16 September 1923: The Saeima passed the Agrarian Reform Bill, initiating land reform in favour of the peasants.

May 1934: Ulmanis carried out a *coup d'état* and established a presidential dictatorship.

1936: Ulmanis became President of Latvia.

23 August 1939: The Treaty of Non-Aggression (the Nazi-Soviet Pact) was signed by the USSR and Germany; it included the 'Secret Protocols', which sanctioned the Soviet annexation of Latvia (as well as Eastern Poland, Estonia, Lithuania and Bessarabia).

17 June 1940: Red Army troops occupied Latvia. A pro-Soviet administration, headed by Augusts Kirhenšteins, was installed.

21 July 1940: The new parliament proclaimed the Latvian Soviet Socialist Republic (SSR) and requested to be admitted to the Soviet federation. The Latvian SSR was incorporated into the USSR on 5 August.

13–14 June 1941: The mass deportation of some 33,000 Latvians over a period of several months culminated in the expulsion from Rīga of 15,000 inhabitants overnight.

1 July 1941: German troops, which had invaded the USSR the previous week, reached Rīga.

13 October 1944: The Soviet army recaptured the Latvian capital and Courland.

24–27 March 1949: In a resumption of the process of Sovietization, some 70,000 Latvians, mainly inhabitants of rural areas, were deported.

1952: The process of collectivization was completed.

1959: In purges of members of the Communist Party of Latvia (CPL) accused of Latvian nationalism, Jānis Kalnērziņš, First Secretary of the CPL since 1940, was dismissed and replaced by Arvīds Pelše.

1966: Augusts Voss succeeded Pelše as First Secretary and continued repressive policies of russification.

1984: Boris Pugo became First Secretary of the CPL. The Environmental Protection Club was established to protest against environmental damage.

July 1986: Under the more tolerant regime of the new Soviet leader, Mikhail Gorbachev, Helsinki-86 was established in Liepāja; the group aimed to monitor observance of the human rights provisions of the Helsinki Final Act of 1975.

14 June 1987: A mass demonstration was organized by Helsinki-86 to mark the 1941 deportation of thousands of Latvian citizens. A further demonstration was held on 23 August to commemorate the signing of the Nazi-Soviet Pact.

June 1988: A resolution was adopted by Latvia's cultural unions demanding that Latvian become the official language, that the Secret Protocols of the Nazi-Soviet Pact of 1939 be published and that ecological damage be repaired.

September 1988: Jan Vigris replaced the conservative Pugo as First Secretary of the CPL.

29 September 1988: Latvian became the state language and the former Latvian flag and national anthem were declared no longer illegal (they were restored to official use in February 1990).

October 1988: The Latvian Popular Front (LPF) was formed by representatives of the opposition and radicals from the CPL; the new group resolved to seek sovereignty for Latvia within a renewed Soviet federation.

February 1989: The Latvian National Independence Movement (LNIM), which advocated full independence, held its first congress.

26 March 1989: In the elections to the all-Union Congress of People's Deputies, candidates supported by the LPF won 26 of the 34 seats contested.

28 July 1989: A declaration of sovereignty and economic independence was adopted by the Latvian Supreme Soviet (legislature).

December 1989: Candidates supported by the LPF won some 75% of the seats in local elections.

January 1990: The Latvian Supreme Soviet voted to end the communist monopoly of power.

15 February 1990: The Latvian Supreme Soviet condemned the 1940 request for admission to the USSR.

March–April 1990: In elections to the Latvian Supreme Soviet (subsequently renamed the Supreme Council), candidates endorsed by the LPF won 131 of the 201 seats contested; the CPL (including an anti-independence faction, Interfront) won some 59 seats and independent candidates obtained 11 seats.

30 April–1 May 1990: A rival parliament, the Congress of Latvia, the members of which were elected only by citizens of pre-1940 Latvia and their descendants, convened; the Congress announced that Latvia was an occupied country and demanded full independence and the withdrawal of Soviet troops.

3 May 1990: Anatolijs Gorbunovs was elected Chairman of the Supreme Council, the republican head of state.

4 May 1990: The Supreme Council declared Latvia's incorporation into the USSR unlawful and announced the beginning of a transitional period towards full independence; Ivars Godmanis was elected premier of a new administration dominated by the LPF.

14 May 1990: A decree issued by President Gorbachev of the USSR annulled the declaration of independence of 4 May.

2 January 1991: Special units of the Soviet Ministry of Internal Affairs, which, the Latvian Government claimed, had been responsible for a series of explosions in Rīga in December, occupied the Rīga Press House.

20 January 1991: The 'Committee of Public Salvation', led by the First Secretary of the CPL, Alfrēds Rubiks, claimed authority in Latvia; his coup attempt eventually failed.

3 March 1991: In a referendum 73.7% of participants voted in favour of Latvian independence.

21 August 1991: Following the attempted *coup d'état* in Moscow (Russia—the Soviet capital), an emergency session of the Supreme Council was convened; the Council declared full independence and pronounced that the *putschist* State Committee for the State of Emergency was unconstitutional.

23 August 1991: Rubiks was arrested and the Communist Party of the Soviet Union (CPSU) was banned in Latvia. In July 1995 Rubiks was sentenced to eight year's imprisonment; however, he was released in November 1997.

6 September 1991: Latvia's independence was formally recognized by the State Council of the USSR.

17 September 1991: Latvia was admitted to the UN.

15 October 1991: Legislation on citizenship was adopted by the Supreme Council; the law stipulated that all residents who were not citizens of pre-1940 Latvia or their descendants must apply for naturalization.

May 1992: The Latvian rouble was introduced for a transitional period until the country adopted its own currency, the lats (LVL), introduced as the only legal tender in Latvia on 18 October 1993.

5–6 June 1993: Elections were held to the new legislature (Saeima): Latvian Way, a political movement formed in February, won 36 of the 100 seats contested and formed a moderate right-wing coalition with the Latvian Farmers' Union (LFU), which won 12 seats. Later, Anatolijs Gorbunovs was elected Chairman and the Saeima voted to restore the Constitution of 1922. The new Government, headed by Valdis Birkavs, was approved by the Saeima on 21 July.

8 July 1993: Guntis Ulmanis of the LFU was inaugurated as President of Latvia, following three rounds of voting in the Saeima.

March 1994: The USA mediated an agreement on the withdrawal of Russian (former Soviet) troops from Latvia, according to which Russia was allowed use of the Skrunda base for a further four years, but all other troops were to leave by 31 August.

11 July 1994: The LFU withdrew from the ruling coalition, following disagreements over economic and agricultural policy, precipitating the Government's resignation.

22 July 1994: The Saeima removed the quota on the naturalization of non-ethnic Latvian residents.

15 September 1994: A new Government, again consisting mainly of Latvian Way members, assumed office, led by Māris Gailis.

February 1995: Latvia was admitted to the Council of Europe.

30 September–October 1995: In a general election nine parties and coalitions obtained representation in the Saeima: the newly established Democratic Party Saimnieks (The Master—DPS) won the largest number of seats (18), followed by Latvian Way (17).

October 1995: Latvia submitted a formal application for full membership of the European Union (EU).

December 1995: The Saeima finally approved the formation of a new Cabinet of Ministers, consisting of members of most of the major parties, excluding the extreme right-wing People's Movement for Latvia (PML—Zigerists' Party), which had obtained 16 seats; the coalition's Prime Minister was Andris Šķēle, who was without party affiliation.

18 June 1996: The Saeima re-elected Ulmanis as President.

12 July 1996: The dispute between Latvia and Estonia over fishing rights in the Gulf of Rīga was settled after the Governments concerned signed an agreement on the demarcation of their maritime borders.

January 1997: Šķēle resigned as premier, following criticism from President Ulmanis over a ministerial appointment; he was later reinstated and a new Cabinet formed on 13 February.

25 July 1997: Šķēle announced the resignation of the Government, because of problems in the coalition; President Ulmanis invited Guntars Krasts, the outgoing Minister of the Economy and a member of the alliance of the Conservative Union 'For Fatherland and Freedom'/Latvian National Independence Movement ('TB'/LNNK), to form a new administration.

7 August 1997: The Saeima approved Krasts' proposal for a coalition of the largest political factions: the 'TB'/LNNK, the DPS, Latvian Way, the LFU and the Christian Democratic Union of Latvia.

October 1997: Latvia and Russia agreed a treaty settling their common border.

16 January 1998: Latvia, Lithuania and Estonia signed a US-Baltic Charter of Partnership with the USA (the first meeting of the Partnership Commission was held on 8 July).

3 April 1998: Atis Sausnitis, the Minister of the Economy, was dismissed, after he published a report on the probable impact of Russian sanctions, should relations continue to deteriorate. All of the ministers from his party, the DPS, resigned five days later.

30 April 1998: The Saeima approved a new coalition Government, comprising members of the LFU, the Latvian Way, and an alliance of the Latvian National Reform Party and the Latvian Green Party.

22 June 1998: In compliance with advice from the Organization for Security and Co-operation in Europe (OSCE), the Saeima approved amendments to the citizenship law, easing requirements for nationalization. These amendments were deemed inadequate by the Russian Government, however, and the 'TB'/LNNK collected enough signatures to force a referendum on the subject. This was held on 3 October, when 52.5% of votes cast approved the changes.

26 June 1998: Despite Saeima opposition, the Government voted to abolish the death penalty.

3 October 1998: At legislative elections the People's Party, led by the former Prime Minister, Škēle, was the most successful, obtaining 24 seats, followed by the Latvian Way with 21 seats, the 'TB'/LNNK with 17 seats and the New Party with eight seats.

26 October 1998: The final citizenship law was formally promulgated, but, together with the later proposal of new legislation promoting the Latvian language in education and broadcasting, provoked some protest.

26 November 1998: A government coalition, headed by the former transport minister, Vilis Krištopans, and comprising the Latvian Way, the 'TB'/LNNK and the New Party, was formed. The Latvian Social Democratic Alliance joined the coalition in February 1999.

10 February 1999: Latvia became a full member of the World Trade Organization (WTO).

17 June 1999: Vaira Vīķe-Freiberga was elected as President, following seven rounds of voting in the Saeima. She took office on 8 July.

5 July 1999: Krištopans announced his Government's resignation, following internal disagreements within the Latvian Way. President Vīķe-Freiberga asked Škēle to form a new coalition Government comprising the People's Party, the 'TB'/LNNK and the Latvian Way.

22 October 1999: Russia abandoned the last military post in the Baltic states, the Skrunda radar station.

9 December 1999: A revised version of controversial language legislation was passed, which allowed Russian to be spoken, while preserving and strengthening the Latvian language; the revision was nevertheless condemned by the Russian Government. The law came into effect on 1 September 2000.

10–11 December 1999: At the EU Heads of State and Government summit meeting in Helsinki, Finland, it was agreed that accession talks with six countries, including Latvia, would begin; formal negotiations commenced in February 2000.

12 April 2000: Škēle resigned as premier following the withdrawal of the Latvian Way from the coalition, after a dispute over privatization.

25 April 2000: President Vīķe-Freiberga invited the former Mayor of Rīga, Andris Bērziņš (of the Latvian Way), to form a new administration. A coalition Government of the People's Party, the 'TB'/LNNK, the Latvian Way and the New Party was subsequently formed. The New Party (re-formed as the New Christian Party and the New Faction) left the Government in February 2001.

1 August 2000: The prosecutor investigating allegations of paedophilia implicating the former premier, Škēle, announced that no evidence had been found to support the allegations and the case would not proceed. Similar announcements had been made with regard to the Minister of Justice and former premier, Valdis Birkavs, and the Director-General of the State Revenue Service, Andrejs Sonciks, the previous day.

11 March 2001: Local elections took place. In Rīga the left-wing Latvian Social Democratic Workers' Party won the largest number of seats on the City Council, with 14, securing 23.4% of the votes cast. The results indicated reduced support for conservative, pro-EU parties, such as the People's Party (which won six seats) and the Latvian Way (five seats). Gundars Bojārs of the Latvia Social Democratic Workers' Party was elected Mayor of Rīga.

31 December 2001: The OSCE terminated its mission to Latvia upon the expiry of its mandate, although Russia maintained that insufficient measures had been taken to protect the rights of Latvia's ethnic Russian minority.

9 May 2002: The Saeima voted to abolish the controversial requirement that electoral candidates be fluent in the Latvian language. However, legislation had been approved on 30 April strengthening the status of Latvian as the official procedural language in the legislature and local government councils.

2 October 2002: The Minister of the Interior, Mareks Segliņš, was dismissed, after allegedly using his office to harrass political opponents.

5 October 2002: Legislative elections were held. Einārs Repše's New Era won 23.9% of the votes cast, securing 26 seats in the Saeima; the leftist, pro-Russian, three-party electoral bloc For Human Rights in a United Latvia obtained 18.9% of the votes (25 seats), and the People's Party received 16.7% (20 seats). Other parties to achieve representation in the Saeima were the Greens' and Farmers' Union (12 seats), the LPP (10 seats) and the 'TB'/LNNK (seven); the Latvian Way failed to secure the 5% of the votes required to obtain a seat in the Saeima. The rate of participation by the electorate was some 72.5%.

7 November 2002: The Saimea approved a new Government, led by Repše; New Era assumed nine posts in the Cabinet of Ministers, the LPP took responsibility for four, the Greens' and Farmers' Union took three portfolios (as well as the position of parliamentary Chairman), and the 'TB'/LNNK controlled two ministries; a new post of Deputy Prime Minister was established, to which Ainārs Šlesers was appointed.

21 November 2002: At a NATO summit meeting, held in Prague, Czech Republic, Latvia was invited to become a full member of the Organization in 2004.

13 December 2002: Latvia, together with nine other countries, was formally invited to become a full member of the EU from 1 May 2004.

7 January 2003: The Cabinet of Ministers approved measures to increase ministers' salaries three-fold, with the reported aim of discouraging corruption.

7 June 2003: The Latvian Socialist Party withdrew from the For Human Rights in a United Latvia alliance, effectively signalling the end of the coalition. The National Harmony Party had withdrawn from the alliance in February.

12 June 2003: Repše survived a motion of 'no confidence' in the Saeima, by 55 votes to 27. The motion had been brought by the People's Party.

20 June 2003: At an extraordinary session of the Saeima, President Vīķe-Freiberga was re-elected unopposed, by 88 votes to six. She was sworn in for a second term on 8 July.

20 September 2003: A referendum to seek support for Latvia's accession to the EU was scheduled to take place.

History

STEVEN MORRISON

Based on an original article by J. MICHAEL LYONS

EARLY HISTORY

Seven times smaller than the Mediterranean, the Baltic Sea has been a subject of much less fascination among Europeans. Used by the Vikings, members of the Hanseatic League and the Russians, the Baltic region was critical to the development of northern Europe. Any country situated on its shores was an economic linchpin in the region.

The first of the Baltic tribes arrived in the east coast region of the Baltic Sea in around 1000 BC, when the Selonians, Semigallians, Couronians and Latgallians and the Livs, a Finno-Ugric tribe, formed a culture and rudimentary system of government. However, the natural evolution of the region was interrupted by aggression from feudal Germany early in the 13th century, when the Order of the Teutonic Knights, which had already marched through Prussia to the west, turned its attention to the Baltic region. In 1201 Rīga, on the Daugava River, was established as the regional trade and governmental centre. The Germans, whose conquest of Latvia was completed by 1290, were the first of many empires to envelop what is present-day Latvia, before any sort of native political system could take root; something that would not happen until the era of modern nationalism.

In the early 1700s Russia turned its attention to the Baltic states. The Treaty of Nystad brought much of the region under Russian control. Despite both a process of industrialization and an accompanying increase in population, Latvia remained very much under Russian control, with little land or wealth in the hands of native Latvians. Feelings of nationalism among the new Latvian intelligentsia, known as the 'First Great Awakening', emerged in Latvia in the mid-19th century and gave rise to demands for Latvian independence. This intelligentsia represented a small minority of a populace that, for the most part, supported an autonomous Latvia within a greater Russia. In time, however, the presence of an autocratic Russian Empire and pockets of German land barons clinging to power in the countryside caused the large population of city workers and landless farmers to begin to contemplate independence and self-determination.

INDEPENDENCE

By 1901 this discontentment was consolidated by the establishment of the Latvian Social Democratic Party, which led a revolt that coincided with the disorder that swept across the Russian Empire in 1905. Troops loyal to Tsar Nicholas II soon crushed the insurrection, executing thousands and sending many more into exile in Siberia. Nevertheless, in 1917 revolution again arose in the Russian Empire as the Bolsheviks seized control in Moscow. The revolution spread to Latvia, where a provisional national Government, formed in November, was taken over by the Bolsheviks. The Soviet 'Izkolat' Government remained in power until November 1918, when the Latvian National Council was formed and, for the first time in the Latvian history, a free and independent state was declared. Within one month, however, the newly installed Soviet Government reclaimed power in Latvia, established the Constitution of the Latvian Soviet Socialist Republic and began to liquidate private land ownership and nationalize industry and banks. Latvian forces, with the help of German troops, succeeded in repelling the Soviet Red Army by early 1920. In January the Latvian Soviet Government was dissolved, and on 11 August Latvia and Soviet Russia signed a peace treaty, in which the latter renounced all claims to Latvian territory.

On 22 September 1921 Latvia, a newly formed, independent country, was admitted to the League of Nations. In November of the following year a Constitution, declaring Latvia to be a democratic, parliamentary republic, was approved by the Saeima (Parliament). The new and inexperienced Government, headed by Prime Minister Karlis Ulmanis, was faced with the difficult task of governing a country devastated by war; the population had decreased by 28%, industrial output had declined by 83% after withstanding the advances and retreats of a series of armies, and few children received a formal education. The Government initiated a series of successful land reforms that distributed farm land appropriated from mostly Baltic Germans to the nearly 70% of the population that were farmers, reducing the once sprawling manorial estates to farms that averaged 55 acres (22 ha). These reforms led to increases in production, and made Latvia a major European supply centre for dairy products and pork. The Government made progress in other areas, too, introducing a national currency, and making education compulsory. In addition, it passed legislation that provided for proportional representation for minorities in the Saeima, as well as cultural and educational autonomy.

Democracy and, thus, the enviable minority-rights system, experienced a reverse in the mid- to late 1930s, after Ulmanis, in May 1934, dissolved the Saeima, declared a state of emergency, briefly imprisoned many of his political opponents and two years later named himself President. Some justified these measures as necessary to prevent destabilization and anarchy arising from conflicts between local Fascist and socialist parties. In his time as Prime Minister and President, Ulmanis instituted a policy of 'Latvianization' that limited minority representation in the legislature and in education, which, in turn, undermined Latvia's enviable system of cultural autonomy. Despite his corporatist regime, Ulmanis did not institute a one-party system or rewrite the Constitution. There was little outright opposition to his style of government, and he lifted the state of emergency in 1938, although he never permitted real democracy again. His administration lasted until the outbreak of the Second World War in 1939, when Germany and Russia again decided Latvia's fate.

OCCUPATION

In August 1939 Latvia's short-term future was determined without its knowledge by the signing by Nazi Germany and the USSR of the Treaty of Non-Aggression, or the Molotov-Ribbentrop Pact, which included the 'Secret Protocols' dividing Eastern Europe between the two states. The Baltic states, including Latvia, fell under impending Soviet rule. Later that year Latvia was forced to sign a 'mutual assistance treaty' with the USSR, which allowed the latter to build military bases in Latvia, making the country, in essence, a Soviet province.

The systematic take-over of Latvia began in June 1940 when the Soviet Government demanded the introduction of a pro-Soviet regime and allowed a further increase in the number of Soviet troops on Latvian soil. On 17 June a full-scale Soviet occupation began. Three days later senior Latvian politicians were deported or imprisoned and the pro-Soviet Latvian People's Government, led by Augusts Kirhen-šteins, was formed. (Ulmanis was imprisoned in the USSR and died there two years later.) A Soviet-sponsored list of candidates, the only candidates allowed to participate, won a hastily assembled parliamentary election; the new legislature abolished the 1922 Constitution and voted to join the USSR. On 21 July 1940 the Latvian Soviet Socialist Republic was formed and, with Soviet leader Joseph Stalin (Iosif V. Dzhugashvili) in charge, a series of atrocities against Latvians and other residents of Latvia, including ethnic Russians, began, which the Latvian people would later call the 'Year of Horror'. The Soviet Government began to eliminate all traces of Latvia's period of independence, removing many of its leading scholars and writers from the newly reformed school curriculum, seizing the national press, banning books and closing churches. The most brutal form of social control, and a method carried out widely after Stalin gained control of the USSR, was deportation and murder; between mid-1940 and mid-1941, before Nazi Germany invaded Latvia, it was estimated that 9% of the country's native population was deported or killed, in an attempt to eliminate resistance to Soviet rule. Many Latvians fled the Soviet purges, which culminated on 13–14 June 1941, when the Narodny Komitet Vnutrennikh Del (NKVD—People's Committee of Internal Affairs), the forerunner to the Komitet Gosudarstvennoi Bezopasnosti (KGB-Committee of State Security) executed or deported an estimated 34,250 Latvians, Russians, and members of other nationalities in Latvia. Two weeks later German troops reached Rīga and defeated the Red Army.

The German occupation, however, proved to be far from benevolent. The Nazi authorities kept secret their long-term plan of mass deportation, immigration and denationalization and began to conscript Latvians into the Nazi army, many of whom fought willingly for the Nazis, who were perceived as liberators from Soviet tyranny. At least 50,000 Latvians died, were wounded or went missing in action while fighting the Soviets. However, many more people in Latvia were killed by order of the Germans, as the Nazis soon began to scour the Baltic states for communists and members of the Jewish population. In 1939 Latvia's Jewish population was estimated at 93,000. As many as 5,000 were deported during the Stalinist purges of 1941 and about 18,000 were drafted into the Red Army or executed. An estimated 30,000 Jews were killed in the early months of German occupation; a further 30,000–40,000 were congregated into ghettos. As the war progressed, the German armies began clearing the ghettos, sending many to five concentration camps scattered throughout Latvia. Many joined thousands of Russian, Poles and Belarusians at the camp in Salaspils, where an estimated 100,000 people were killed. Of the estimated 70,000 Jews left in Latvia following the Soviet army's retreat, only about 4,000 survived. After Soviet forces reoccupied Latvia, official policy prohibited discussion of the Holocaust, which ensured that many Latvians ignored the Nazi atrocities, and the culpability of native Latvians in the killing of Jews was still subject to debate at the beginning of the 21st century.

By 1944 the German army, plagued by manpower shortages and an advancing Soviet army, began retreating from the Baltic states. Rīga was recaptured by the Red Army in October 1944 and the Soviets regained power in most of Latvia. The Latvians' worst fears of the return of the Soviets were not at first realized. Private farming continued and the Soviets allowed the use of some national symbols. However, the deportations soon began as the Soviet secret police began to target alleged Nazi sympathizers and intellectuals. Between 1945 and 1949 as many as 100,000 were believed to be sent to labour camps in Siberia. The deportations continued in earnest throughout the 1950s, when roughly 20% of Latvia's population were either killed, deported, or fled.

To compensate for the human losses and to help fulfil the plan of building Latvia into an important cog in the Soviet industrial machine, tens of thousands of migrant workers were brought to Latvia from Russia, Ukraine and Belarus to build and work in factories. As a consequence, the populations of Latvia's cities and towns increased exponentially. In 1940 35% of Latvia's population lived in cities and towns; by the mid-1950s that number had surpassed 50%. Meanwhile, the ethnic Latvian population decreased in proportion to other groups. In 1945 an estimated 83% of the country's population was ethnically Latvian; by 1950 the figure had dropped to 63% and, according to the results of the 2000 census, it was 58% in that year.

The Soviet authorities chose Latvia as a centre for light manufacturing, including textiles and food production, and also steel manufacturing. Private farms were seized by the state and collectivized into models of communism, with the collective revenue being channelled to the Russian and Soviet capital, Moscow. By 1952 this process of collectivization was complete. As part of its 'Sovietization', a great emphasis was placed on education, in order to inculcate Latvians with the propaganda of Soviet culture, which resulted in the reshaping of Baltic history. Learning Russian was compulsory, and the remaining writers and artists were organized into nationalized unions.

Despite the repression, Latvia progressed under Soviet rule: according to government figures, literacy reached nearly 100%; higher education was made more readily available; medical care was free; and agricultural and industrial production increased dramatically in the wake of declines before and during the war. Throughout the early 1950s life in Latvia continued amid arrests, deportations, or the constant threat of deportation. In March 1953, following the death of Stalin and the appointment as Soviet leader of Nikita Kruschev, conditions began to improve.

During this period the Latvian Deputy Chairman of the Council of Ministers, Eduards Berklavs, a young native communist, attempted to stem the spread of Sovietization by replacing Russian bureaucrats and 'Latvianizing' the local Communist Party. However, by 1959 the Russian branch of the Communist Party of Latvia, and indeed Kruschev himself, grew tired of the attempted reforms. Berklavs and other leaders in the local Communist Party were accused of 'bourgeois nationalism' and were dismissed. A period of neo-Stalinism began in the early 1960s. Industrial production was increased forcibly—between 1960 and 1965 100,000 workers, most of them immigrants, joined Latvia's industrial ranks, to create the largest industrial work-force in the Baltic region. Although these factors helped to increase production, they also exacerbated social and ecological problems.

TOWARDS INDEPENDENCE

By the 1980s bitterness among Latvians towards the Soviet regime had begun to transform into a unified increase in nationalism; this coincided with the appointment, in 1985, of the new Soviet leader, Mikhail Gorbachev, whose programme of *perestroika* (restructuring) would foment revolution in Latvia. In June 1987 the first protest in Latvia since the Second World War took place in Rīga, to commemorate the 1941 deportations. More protests followed the introduction of the policy of *glasnost* (openness) that Gorbachev felt was necessary to save the USSR.

In mid-1988 underground dissidents and would-be reformers emerged at meetings of creative unions. This led to the formation, in October, of the Latvian Popular Front (LPF). Members of the Latvian Writers' Union made public the existence of the hitherto unknown 'Secret Protocols' of the

Molotov-Ribbentrop Pact of 1939; soon afterwards, the maroon and white flag of independent Latvia, which had been outlawed for decades, began to emerge at public gatherings. The LPF quickly became the embodiment of nationalism's rebirth, attracting widespread support. LPF-endorsed candidates dominated Latvia's delegation to the all-Union Congress of People's Deputies in March 1989 and, one year later, LPF candidates won control of the Latvian Supreme Soviet (which was subsequently renamed the Supreme Council). Peaceful protests continued in Latvia, while the Soviet authorities remained muted, although the expectation of independence was growing throughout the empire. Despite the fact that many Russian residents of Latvia supported independence, the high proportion of ethnic Russians occupying senior government posts slowed progress towards it.

In January 1991 Soviet troops moved into Rīga to find thousands of Latvians manning barricades around the country's parliament building. Soviet Ministry of the Interior, or OMON, troops attacked the interior ministry building and met with fierce opposition. Five Latvians died before the Soviet troops retreated. In early March a referendum on Latvian independence yielded an almost 74% vote in favour. Following the failure in mid-August of a coup by 'hard-liners' in Moscow, the Latvian Supreme Council declared the country to be independent. On 6 September the USSR recognized Latvia's independence.

POST-SOVIET LATVIA

Although Latvia experienced periods of instability in the years immediately following independence, including seven changes of prime minister in six years, fears that Russia would attempt to subvert attempts at democracy proved to be largely unfounded, although attempts were made by Russia to undermine Latvia's moral claim to legitimate independence by alleging human rights violations.

In June 1993, following elections to the Saeima, a coalition Government of the centre-right Latvian Way party and the Latvian Farmers' Union (LFU) was appointed, under the leadership of the Latvian Way's Valdis Birkavs. In the following month the new legislature elected Guntis Ulmanis of the LFU to be the country's first freely chosen President since his great-uncle, Karlis Ulmanis, during Latvia's first period of independence 70 years earlier. (He was re-elected for a second term in June 1996.) In September of the following year, following the Latvian Way's resignation from the Government, a new coalition administration, again led by a Latvian Way member, Maris Gailis, was appointed.

In late September and early October 1995 legislative elections were held, the results of which were inconclusive. The largest number of seats (18) was won by the newly established Democratic Party Saimnieks (The Master—DPS). The Latvian Way's share of seats fell from 36 to 17 and the anti-Russian party, the Latvian National Independence Movement (LNNK), funded by an ethnic German, Joachim Zigerist, obtained 16 seats. Negotiations over the composition of a new Government continued until December, when Andris Šķēle, an independent, was appointed Prime Minister of a broad coalition. Throughout 1996 there were internal disagreements, owing to the fragmented nature of the Government, culminating, in January 1997, with Šķēle's resignation. However, he was reappointed by President Ulmanis, and in February a new, largely unaltered cabinet was appointed. Nevertheless, in July the Government resigned, following a series of corruption scandals, and this time Ulmanis appointed Guntars Krasts, a member of the Conservative Union 'For Fatherland and Freedom'/LNNK ('TB'/LNNK—formed by the merger of the Union 'For Fatherland and Freedom' and the Latvian National Independence Movement) as the new premier.

In early 1998 Prime Minister Krasts survived a vote of 'no confidence' in the legislature, following the withdrawal from the Government of all DPS ministers. In October a general election was held; the recently formed People's Party obtained the largest number of seats (24), followed by the Latvian Way with 21 seats and the 'TB'/LNNK with 17 seats. In November, following several weeks of negotiations, a three-party coalition Government led by the Latvian Way's Vilis Krištopans was appointed. The ruling coalition lasted until July 1999, when Krištopans announced its resignation, in protest against the signing of a co-operation accord between the 'TB'/LNNK, one of the members of the coalition, and the opposition People's Party. The newly elected President, Vaira Vīķe-Freiberga, appointed Šķēle to lead a new administration, comprising members of his People's Party, the 'TB'/LNNK and the Latvian Way. This Government lasted until April 2000, when Šķēle resigned, following a vote of 'no confidence', which resulted from his earlier dismissal of the Minister of the Economy, Vladimirs Makarovs.

In late 1999 and early 2000 a parliamentary commission set up to investigate a paedophilia scandal within the Government criticized the Prosecutor-General's handling of the affair. In February 2000 it emerged that Prime Minister Šķēle, Minister of Justice (and former premier) Birkavs, as well as other senior state officials, had been mentioned by witnesses in the affair. By August, however, all charges had been dropped owing to a lack of evidence, and Janis Adamsons, the Chairman of the parliamentary commission, was accused of libel. In September the Saeima voted not to remove Adamsons' parliamentary immunity, thereby preventing his prosecution.

After Skele left office, the Latvian Way's Andris Bērziņš was invited to form a government. A coalition comprising members of that party, the People's Party, and the New Party was approved by the Saeima on 5 May. The 'TB'/LNNK joined shortly afterwards, and in February 2001 the New Party (re-formed as two parties, the New Christian Party and the New Faction), left the coalition Government, following the expulsion of four members for voting in favour of tax legislation that was supported by the opposition. Bērziņš continued to hold the position of Prime Minister, making his the longest-serving Government in Latvia since the restoration of independence, and suggesting that government stability in the state had greatly increased.

In 2000 left-wing political parties also began to attract popular support, demanding a boycott of controversial language legislation, which came into effect at the beginning of September. In January 2001 the campaign for municipal elections began, resulting in a left-wing victory. In Rīga the Latvian Social Democratic Workers' Party won 23.4% of the votes cast, and 14 of the 60 seats on the City Council. The party's Gundars Bojars was elected Chairman of the Council (Mayor) by a left-wing alliance, ousting Andris Argalis of the 'TB'/LNNK. The pro-Russian bloc, For Human Rights in a United Latvia, won 13 seats, and mainstream parties, namely the 'TB'/LNNK, the People's Party, and the Latvian Way, received a total of 23 seats. The social democrats also took control of the Daugavpils municipal Government, but were unable to unseat Aivars Lembergs in Ventspils.

In August 2001 the Governor of the Bank of Latvia, Einars Repše, announced his intention to form a new political party. Although criticized in political circles for his proposed method of fundraising, he was held largely responsible for Latvia's economic stability by the wider public. By November the policy objectives of Repše's party, New Era, were still largely unknown, but it rapidly attracted widespread popular support. At the end of that month Repše resigned the governorship of the central bank, in order to dedicate his time to politics. In the same month President Vīķe-Freiberga proposed changing the Constitution to provide for a popularly elected president, rather than one nominated and confirmed by the Saeima. However, it was unlikely that the legislature would be prepared to relinquish its powers of confirmation.

In 2002–03 corruption was a major problem in Latvia. In various scandals, the activities of high-ranking police-officers and tax officials were called into question, three ministers were dismissed, and Bērziņš was criticized in the media over allegations of conflict of interest. Although a Corruption Prevention Bureau was established in 2002, it was itself criticized in the media over allegations of bribe-taking. While many of these accusations must be false, the European Union (EU) and the North Atlantic Treaty Organization (NATO) had expressed serious concern over the level of corruption in Latvia.

At the parliamentary elections, held on 5 October 2002, the Latvian Way, which had been in government since independence, was ousted from the Saeima, failing to obtain the requisite 5% of the votes cast to secure representation. Repše's New Era capitalized on popular disillusionment with the Government (which some 92% of Latvians believed to be corrupt) through a campaign based on Repše's personal reputation as a proponent of transparency and accountability; the party won 23.9% of the votes cast and became the largest party in the Saeima, with 26 seats. For Human Rights in a United Latvia continued its popular growth, obtaining the second-highest number of seats (25). Andris Šķēle's People's Party was third-placed, with 20 seats (and suffered another reverse when Šķēle resigned the party leadership in November). Other parties to achieve representation in the Saeima were the Greens' and Farmers' Union (12 seats), the First Party of Latvia (LPP—10) and the 'TB'/LNNK (seven). The Social Democratic Workers' Party performed poorly nationally, despite its recent successes, owing to internal conflict and factionalization. Repše pledged not to work with any parties represented in the previous Government, and subsequently formed a coalition with the LPP, the 'TB'/LNNK and the anti-EU Greens' and Farmers' Union. However, given differences among coalition members over the speed of reform, the Government was widely regarded as unstable and, according to some Latvian political analysts, might be the shortest-lived Government in Latvia's post-Soviet history.

Presidential elections in the Saeima were held on 20 June 2003, in which Viķe-Freiberga was the only candidate. She was duly re-elected by 88 votes to six, and her new term of office began on 8 July.

Meanwhile, from late 2000 Latvia experienced a rise in extremist activity. In August 2000 two bombs exploded in Rīga, killing one person, and in November a bomb exploded in the office of a regional journal. A hitherto unknown group, the Latvian National Liberation Movement, apparently seeking to liberate Latvia from exploitative companies, claimed responsibility for the first two bombings. In the same month three members of the Russia-based 'National Bolsheviks' occupied a Rīga church tower, armed with a replica hand-grenade, and demanded the release of their compatriots held in police custody; they were convicted of terrorism in May 2001, and given sentences of between five and 15 years. Many observers criticized the severity of the verdict, particularly since members of a right-wing Latvian group, who had received sentences of between one and three years for attempting to destroy a Soviet monument in Rīga, had been released from prison in January, after having served less than one year of their sentences. However, in October the convicts' sentences were reduced to between one month and six years.

Following the suicide attacks of 11 September 2001 on the US cities of New York and Washington, DC, Latvia took its own measures to combat international terrorism, establishing a special task force on 25 September. In the aftermath of the attacks, Russia named Latvia, along with Afghanistan and Turkey, as a country that supported rebels in the separatist Russian republic of Chechnya. Subsequently, however, Russia's anti-Latvian rhetoric subsided, as it has accepted progress towards NATO's enlargement to the east, partly owing to Russian President Vladimir Putin's improved relations with the USA and the US President, George W. Bush; in an apparent change of policy, Russia declared that Latvia had the right to decide for itself whether to accede to the Organization.

In early 2003 Latvia was one of several Central and South-Eastern European EU candidate countries to express support for the US-led military campaign to remove from power the regime of President Saddam Hussain in Iraq. However, the French President, Jacques Chirac, who opposed military action in Iraq, warned that those countries' support could adversely affect their applications for membership of the EU. Latvia and Lithuania nevertheless reiterated their support for the action, and urged reconciliation between the opposing EU states and the USA. With the apparent conclusion of military operations in Iraq in mid-2003, however, this issue should cease to be contentious.

LATVIAN-RUSSIAN RELATIONS

In April 1994, following several years of discussion, Russian President Boris Yeltsin and President Ulmanis signed an agreement on the complete withdrawal of Russian troops from Latvian soil by the end of August, bringing a resolution to an issue that had impeded bilateral relations following Latvian independence. However, Latvian-Russian relations subsequently centred on the treatment of ethnic Russians in Latvia, the majority of whom were required to apply for citizenship following the restoration of the 1922 Constitution in 1993. Automatic citizenship was only given to Latvians and their descendants who had lived in Latvia before the Soviet invasion of 1940. According to a citizenship law adopted by the Saeima in June 1994, the many ethnic Russians, Ukrainians and Belarusians who came to the country as part of the Soviet industrialization programme were denied citizenship until they could fulfil certain criteria. These included a minimum 10 years' residence in Latvia, a knowledge of the Latvian language and its history, and an oath of allegiance to the republic. The stipulations met with disapproval from Russia and international bodies, including the Organization for Security and Co-operation in Europe (OSCE) and the EU. Particular criticism was levelled at the 'windows' system, whereby citizenship would only be granted to members of certain age groups. The EU linked Latvia's membership prospects to the improved treatment of its non-Latvian population. By June 1996 about 3,700 people had taken the language test, of whom only 2,100 had passed. In the late 1990s it was estimated that about 30% of Latvia's residents were considered 'non-citizens'. They held alien passports, were denied voting rights and often experienced employment discrimination. In Rīga fewer than 40% of residents were ethnic Latvians, and in the country's second-largest city, Daugavpils, the figure was less than 20%.

In June 1998 the legislature approved amendments to the citizenship law, as recommended by the OSCE, which relaxed citizenship requirements for non-ethnic Latvians. However, the changes were deemed to be insufficient by the Russian Government. Nationalist groups succeeded in forcing a referendum on the subject, held in early October, in which 52.5% of the votes were cast in favour of the amendments. Furthermore, in July 1999 the Saeima adopted legislation that required all business and all state and municipal events to be conducted in Latvian. This measure provoked widespread international condemnation and the Council of Europe ruled that the law was incompatible with the European Commission on Human Rights. President Viķe-Freiberga vetoed the legislation. Amended language legislation was eventually approved in December, on the eve of the EU's Helsinki summit (Finland), at which Latvian accession was to be discussed. Russia continued to claim that the law was discriminatory, and the OSCE recommended changes to the law, which Latvia subsequently adopted. The law came into force at the beginning of September 2000, amid left-wing protests. The USA subsequently expressed satisfaction with the law and in November the Council of Baltic Sea States noted Latvia's progress on human rights.

The following year was significant for the further development of human rights in Latvia. In January 2001 the Parliamentary Assembly of the Council of Europe ended its monitoring of Latvia, thus recognizing the country's human rights achievements, including integration policies for non-citizens. In February the Secretary-General of the Council, Walter Schwimmer, welcomed Latvia's adoption of the Expanded Programme for Integration of Society, which was intended to accelerate the naturalization process for non-citizens. To further promote citizenship, in May the Latvian Naturalization Board agreed to work with the UN, the OSCE and the Ministry of Justice on an advertising campaign, which was intended to promote citizenship. The following month, naturalization fees were reduced and the language test procedure was simplified. In December, given Latvia's progress in language education, democracy, naturalization and social integration, the OSCE decided to discontinue its monitoring mission to Latvia. Finally, in May 2002 the Saeima amended the electoral law to abolish the stipulation that candidates should be fluent in the Latvian language. However, at the end of April legislation had been approved that strengthened the status of Latvian as the official procedural language in the legislature and in local government councils. The closure, in March, of the two most popular, predominantly Russian-language radio stations in Latvia, ostensibly for violation of copyright and of a law that requires at least 75% of broadcasting in any 24-hour period to be in the Latvian language, had also attracted accusations of discrimination.

Latvian-Russian relations remained strained in 2000–02. In February 2000 former President Yeltsin refused an award in recognition of his assistance in Latvia's independence process. The Russian Government continued to criticize Latvia's treatment of its ethnic Russian minority, but it also began to condemn what it perceived to be an anti-Soviet bias in Latvia's pursuit of war criminals during the Nazi and Soviet occupations, centred on the Latvian former Nazi, Konrads Kalejs, the anti-Nazi resistance fighter, Vasilii Kononov, and Soviet secret police-officer Mikhail Farbtukh. The pressure on Latvia to pursue war criminals may have been expected to subside somewhat following Kalejs' death in November 2001, and the death of another suspected Nazi war criminal, Karlis Ozols, in April 2002; in March, however, a Latvian court ruled that, despite his failing health, Farbtukh was to remain in confinement. The trial of Nikolai Larionov, a Stalin-era security official, opened in September, only to be adjourned immediately, owing to his ill health. The retrial of Kononov was ongoing in early 2003.

In early May 2000 President Viķe-Freiberga claimed that Russia was trying to provoke tensions between the Baltic states, and further controversy arose in June, when Russia demanded that the Baltic states support its development of an anti-ballistic missile system, a move which would militarize the region. Russia did, however, offer assistance in minesweeping activities in the Baltic Sea, and assisted in the investigation of the August bomb attacks in Rīga. Both sides continued to express their desire for improved relations, which was reflected in 2001 in negotiations on co-operation and the development of tourism. In February an impromptu

meeting in Austria between Vika-Freiberga and the Russian President, Vladimir Putin, appeared to signal an improvement in relations. Soon afterwards, however, Putin described the conversation an 'act of will' on his part, and later in the year compared the conditions of the ethnic Russian minority in Latvia to those of the ethnic Albanian minority in the former Yugoslav republic of Macedonia (FYRM—see the chapter on that country).

The Russian enclave of Kaliningrad was another source of tension. In January 2001 there were unsubstantiated reports that Russia had transferred nuclear weaponry to the enclave. Latvia's consequent revocation, in April, of free visas for Russians travelling through Latvia to Kaliningrad, and Russia's subsequent rerouting of passenger trains through Belarus revealed continued tensions. In the same month Russia presented Lithuania with its requirements for transit to and from Kaliningrad through that country. In June 2002 Latvia imposed a transit visa requirement for all foreigners travelling through the country by rail. Russia, which condemned the measure as antagonistic, argued that it had been implemented without sufficient notice. The introduction of transit visas was, however, supported by the EU, out of its concern to impose tighter border controls. This issue remained to be solved to the satisfaction of the EU, Latvia and Russia, the latter being concerned about maintaining ties with Kaliningrad after Baltic accession to the EU.

Despite tensions between Russia and Latvia, efforts towards the integration of the Russian minority had accelerated. Amendments to electoral legislation had made it easier for Russian-speaking candidates to stand for office, and the requirements for citizenship had been eased. The naturalization process, furthermore, was to be accelerated, possibly in response to the strong performance of For Human Rights in a United Latvia in the legislative elections of October 2002. Nils Muižnieks, a former human rights campaigner, was appointed to the newly created post of Minister of Special Assignment on Social Integration in November. He aimed to renew dialogue between the Government and minorities, and to work to ratify the Council of Europe's Framework Convention for the Protection of National Minorities, a piece of legislation which was opposed by Latvian nationalists and which, if enacted, would necessitate the amendment of many laws in Latvia.

THE EU AND NATO

Shortly after regaining independence, the Baltic states began to institute the necessary reforms to secure full membership of the EU. Latvia, Lithuania and Estonia agreed from the outset to co-operate in their progress towards accession; this partnership became strained, however, in 1995, when the EU identified Estonia as a 'fast track' candidate for accession, and Estonia decided that it would proceed with EU membership regardless of the status of Latvia and Lithuania. Nevertheless, in December 2002 all three Baltic states received simultaneous invitations to join the EU on 1 May 2004 (along with seven other countries).

Latvia had accomplished much over its 11 years of independence. To its development of a market economy and the ability to withstand competitive pressures, as well as its civil, commercial, governmental and judicial reforms, was added an agreement with the EU that demanded further reform of the agricultural sector and food-processing industry. In addition, it still remained for Latvia further to reform the judiciary and various state institutions, to reduce corruption, to adopt the EU's anti-discrimination standards, and to amend some legislation to conform with EU requirements. The incumbent Government wholeheartedly supported EU accession, and would continue work toward this objective. One major aim would be to ensure the support of more than 50% of the voters participating in a referendum on EU membership, scheduled to be held on 20 September 2003; in February opinion polls suggested that popular support for accession to the EU, which had been increasing gradually in recent years, was 52.3%.

Latvia's progress towards NATO membership proceeded alongside that towards membership of the EU. On 21 November 2002 Latvia was invited to join NATO at a summit meeting of the Organization held in Prague, Czech Republic. Latvia had implemented some tough reforms to secure membership: the Saeima approved a budget for 2003 that included a 22% increase in defence spending, so that expenditure conformed, for the first time, to the 2% of gross domestic product (GDP) required by NATO. In addition, the Saeima

had passed constitutional amendments in 2002, removing the stipulation that candidates for national and local office should speak Latvian at a high level of proficiency, thereby meeting NATO recommendations. Moreover, both Latvia and NATO had worked to reduce Russian anxieties over NATO enlargement (see above). Although there had been disagreement between NATO members over the US-led military action in Iraq, and concerns among the aspirant members over the interpretation of the North Atlantic Treaty and the guarantees that NATO would offer to new member states, membership of the Alliance from 2004 remained their best assurance of security.

The Economy

STEVEN MORRISON

Arguably, 2002 was the most important year for the Latvian economy since the country regained independence in 1991. Latvia's unwavering policy of securing membership of the European Union (EU), adopted in 1991, and aimed for in its subsequent legislative reform, treatment of the Russian minority and reorganization of civil society, was rewarded in December 2002 with an invitation to join the Union on 1 May 2004. While the member states declared, through this invitation, their confidence in the viability of the economy of Latvia (and of the nine other states invited simultaneously) there was still work to be done. The chief and perennial issue remained agriculture, one of the unresolved chapters of the *acquis communautaire* (the body of EU legislation and case law that candidate countries had to adopt prior to accession to the EU). Latvian concerns regarding post-accession farming subsidies and quotas, however, had been addressed, with the EU-sceptic political party, the Greens' and Farmers' Union, putting up little resistance to subsidy and quota agreements. Corruption in government remained a serious problem, with Latvia ranked highly in terms of corruption by the organization Transparency International, while 92% of the Latvian populace believed government to be corrupt. None the less, the Prime Minister elected in 2002, Einars Repše (the popular former Governor of the Bank of Latvia) promised to combat corruption; a Corruption Prevention Bureau also opened in that year. Tied to the issue of corruption was that of the judiciary. The EU stated in 2001 that 'judges are under-qualified and overworked, and computers are still not available in all courts'; thus the independence, efficiency and quality of the judicial system was adversely affected. The final major issue concerned support for EU accession among the general population. A referendum was to take place on 20 September 2003, at which more than 50% of voters had to approve accession in order for Latvia to join the EU. Support for accession had been increasing steadily, and a government-sponsored media campaign in favour of accession was expected to do much to convince voters. Furthermore, political parties in the Saeima (Parliament) on both the left and right supported accession, as did the popular President, Vaira Vīķe-Freiberga.

While problems existed in the above areas, as well as those relating to the treatment of the Russian minority in the workplace, administrative capacity, the environment and education, the EU had decided that Latvia was ready to accede for three reasons: its economic performance had improved in a challenging international economic environment, reforms in the country had been accelerated and macroeconomic stability had been achieved. Assuming Latvia continued to address the

issues already mentioned and maintain a prudent fiscal policy, assisted by post-accession aid packages, the EU believed that the country would become a productive member of the Union in the future. For Latvia, it was a chance to rejoin 'Europe' after more than 60 years of isolation, and to benefit both economically and psychologically from such a move.

AGRICULTURE

Immediately after the collapse of the USSR, and the regaining of independence in 1991, the fiscal importance of Latvia's agricultural sector plummeted. The deconstruction of state collective farms, with the reassignment of thousands of small-holdings to their pre-Second World War owners, and the loss of the Soviet market forced agriculture's share of gross domestic product (GDP) down from 17.6% in 1992 to 4.7% in 2002. An extensive drought in 1994, the Latvian banking crisis of 1995, an outbreak of swine fever in 1996 and the Russian economic crisis of 1998 all contributed further to the decline of Latvia's agriculture. Despite revived markets in the Commonwealth of Independent States (CIS) in 2000 and a subsequent upturn in Latvian agriculture, notable gains were prevented by Latvia's failure to find EU markets, owing to its hygiene standards falling below those of the EU. Thus, by 2001 foodstuffs composed only around 6% of Latvia's principal exports.

Although agriculture has been replaced by the services sector in terms of economic importance, it was nevertheless at the centre of accession negotiations with the EU in 2002. It was the most delicate part of the discussions for all 10 invitees, in which both parties had an important stake. For Latvia, its agriculture is a deep-rooted cultural symbol; any perceived interference by the EU would remind many Latvians of the 'Russification' programmes of the USSR. Furthermore, despite its small contribution to GDP, agriculture did provide 1.6% of the 3.8% increase in GDP recorded in the first quarter of 2002, and 0.8% of the 4.9% increase recorded in the second quarter. Figures for 2003 suggested a similar small increase. For the EU, enlargement meant potentially vast increases in farming subsidies. The Common Agricultural Policy (CAP) already composed half of the EU budget, and enlargement promised a 42% increase in EU land under cultivation, and a 120% increase in the number of EU farmers. Furthermore, Germany, the Netherlands, Sweden and the United Kingdom were attempting to reduce the EU budget by decreasing allocations from the CAP.

In January 2002 the EU published its proposals for agricultural subsidies to the new members upon accession. Under the proposals, in the first year of membership new members would receive direct subsidies amounting to 25% of those allocated to existing members. In each subsequent year the amounts were to increase by 5%, to 2007, and then 10%, until the new members achieved parity with existing members in 2013. Latvia and other candidate countries were dissatisfied with the proposals, however, arguing that they would place Latvian farmers at a disadvantage, and that they undermined the EU's principal of equality. The EU responded by stating that new members' agricultural revenues would increase by an average of 123% under the proposals.

A further disappointment was found in EU quotas for Latvian farmers, published in June 2002. These quotas were formulated using figures based on the sector's output in the late 1990s, when the Russian economic crisis of 1998 had reduced Latvia's capacity. Thus, the EU would allow Latvia to produce 480,000 metric tons of dairy products per year, when, in fact, the country had produced 846,000 tons in 2001 and 812,000 tons in 2002. In the second half of 2002 Latvia campaigned for a quota of 1.2m. tons. In September Franz Fischler, the EU Commissioner for Agriculture, made a trip to the Baltics to discuss this issue, and Viķe-Freiberga travelled to France, where she obtained a promise from French President Jacques Chirac to re-examine the quotas for dairy products, sugar beet and grains. If this debate was not resolved, enlargement could be delayed for many years. Since the EU had voted to invite Latvia to join, however, the initiative lay with Latvia, where the situation was just as tenuous: in September Viķe-Freiberga stated that failure to change the quotas could result in a 'no' vote at the accession referendum.

Although accession was assured if the population voted for it, Latvia had still to bring its veterinary controls and the security of its animal feed to EU standards. To obtain a vote in favour of accession, the Government had to convince Latvians that joining the EU was in their best interests. This might be difficult in terms of agriculture, since EU accession will lead to the consolidation of land-holdings, forcing many small and medium-sized farms out of business. Ultimately, Latvian agriculture will have to be satisfied with playing a supporting role in the economy, despite Latvians' memories of its centrality both domestically and in Europe between the two World Wars. However, EU subsidies and markets, while hindering the relative competitive ability of Latvian goods, should bring increased revenues to the sector.

INDUSTRY

Given the small size of the Latvian economy, its industry has always relied on external markets for its prosperity. As a Soviet Republic, Latvia became a centre of industry, holding a near-monopoly among the Baltic republics on finished goods. On the eve of the fall of the USSR manufacturing contributed 34.5% of Latvia's GDP, and construction 9.7%. With independence came the loss of supplies and markets, the reorientation of the Latvian economy toward the West, privatization and the free market. In addition, the services sector was nurtured and heavy industry reduced. As a result, in 2002 manufacturing composed 14.8% of GDP, and construction 6.1%.

Despite the fact that Latvian industry has lost much of its presence in the economy, it remains influential owing to a successful privatization programme, private investment and the establishment of links with Western markets and investors. Indeed, just as the USSR relied on Latvia for many of its finished products, so Western countries—most from the EU—placed production facilities and affiliates in Latvia and the rest of Eastern Europe, motivated by Latvia's skilled labour force, lower salaries relative to the companies' countries of origin, pro-European climate and geographical proximity. There was, however, some fear in the West of higher

unemployment, especially given the potential increase in the relocation of production if Latvia joined the EU in 2004 as expected. These fears of a sudden flight of manufacturing to the east seem unfounded, however, since liberal policies have brought foreign companies into Latvia since 1992. In addition, although analysts stated that the EU candidate countries in Central and South-Eastern Europe could still be considered as the places of optimal production, some economists believed that the influx of Western companies had peaked. Finally, as the new EU nations begin to experience increases in salaries, they can expect Western companies to relocate once again, perhaps to the People's Republic of China and South-East Asia. This was not to say that Latvian industry would experience a bleak future. On the contrary, an increase in industrial production was expected to accompany Latvia's accession to the EU, largely owing to the influence of EU markets on the economy.

Despite the EU's economic woes, and predictions of resulting sluggish growth in Latvian industry, three realities bode well for the sector: an increase in the manufacture of electrical machinery, accounting for a small, but high value-added sector of industry; the spread of Latvia's export base into new markets in the EU, assisted by the strength of the euro against the lats; and Latvia's ability to expand production at short notice all suggest that Latvia is, indeed, poised to see a more robust industrial sector appear. Industrial production increased by 5.8% in 2002, and the initial figures for 2003 suggested further cause for optimism. In February 2003 industrial production increased by 9.7%, the largest increase in the sector's recent history.

In the final analysis, Latvia's industrial sector seemed to be growing gradually, having experienced accelerated growth in 2002, and was poised to record a further acceleration in 2003. It was unclear how EU accession would affect the sector, but predictions anticipated positive changes. If Latvia can continue to attract foreign investment, while gradually increasing salaries, as well as develop its own industry, especially in high value-added sub-sectors such as electrical machinery, it should be able to achieve long-term sectoral stability, growth and prosperity.

SERVICES

Under the USSR Latvia's services sector was underdeveloped, accounting for just 31.9% of GDP in 1990. Independence the following year was a positive development. As industry lost its pre-eminent place in the economy the services sector took over, contributing 70.6% of GDP in 2002. With the continued development of tourism and private domestic and foreign investment—all activities largely ignored by the Soviet authorities—the sector stands to contribute even more to GDP in the future. The work-force has kept up with the changes and is poised for more. While in 1991 26% of employment was in services, by 2002 this figure had reached 58.5%, and with a lack of natural resources, the push toward a technologically advanced economy, and the younger generation's interest in knowledge-based careers such as information technology and business, it is clear that Latvia's future lies in services.

The privatization of large national concerns was also an issue affecting sectoral prosperity. Representing the remains of a successful privatization programme that saw over 40 companies divested by 1998, increased the domestic retail investor base, and made the transition to a free market economy relatively smoothly, three major companies had still to be fully privatized (the telecommunications company SAI Lattelekom, the energy company Latvenergo, and the Latvian Savings Bank). The members of the incumbent coalition Government had agreed that Latvenergo would remain state-owned during its term of office.

Latvia has, for centuries, been a conduit for the east–west and, to a lesser extent north–south, transshipment of goods. For the services sector to thrive as it has, it requires a vibrant transshipment sub-sector. Although it remains strong, the sector was affected in 2002 by a number of adverse factors, relating in particular to the transportation of crude petroleum, which could also have implications in the medium and long term. None the less, in 2002 the transshipment industry accounted for some 15% of GDP.

TRANSPORT

Since 1991 Russia has often taken an antagonistic stance towards Latvia. When the Baltic ports began to charge Russia for their services (Russia had had free access to them since the 18th century) Russia responded with threats to assail the legitimacy of Latvia's position on the Baltic coast and as a conduit for east–west trade. Until December 2001 Russia's threats remained unrealized. However, following the opening of the Russian port at Primorsk in that month, cargo shipments to Latvia began to be adversely affected.

In response to the Primorsk threat, in late 2002 the petroleum transportation company Ventspils Nafta offered lower transit tariffs to Transneft, a Russian petroleum company, in exchange for the transportation of a higher volume of petroleum to the port of Ventspils, which had decreased from 14.9m. metric tons in 2001 to only 7.4m. tons in 2002. Instead, however, Transneft began a three-month boycott of Ventspils in early January 2003, citing higher prices as the cause. Favouring Primorsk and Tallinn, Estonia, the boycott was the first strike against Ventspils in what had been called 'a new maritime battle', in which Lithuania's new Butingue offshore petroleum-processing terminal and, possibly, the Russian enclave of Kaliningrad, might also play a part. Latvia secured pledges of assistance from both the EU and the USA, following a visit by Viķe-Freiberga to Washington, DC, USA, in February. Moreover, Russian petroleum groups and those from other ex-Soviet republics also opposed the boycott, claiming that it would hinder their export business.

With only port business affected by Primorsk and the boycott of Ventspils, freight turnover by rail remained steady in 2001–02, with traffic increasing from 37,884,000 metric tons in 2001 to 40,100,000 tons in 2002. The figures for January and February 2003 suggested a very sizable increase compared with 2002. Given Latvia's impending EU accession, EU funding procured in February 2002 for railway upgrades, and the Russian economic recovery, there is little reason to be concerned about the future of the Latvian rail system.

In sum, Latvia's transport industry is healthy and prepared to grow. The only uncertain factor is that of petroleum transports from Russia, the outcome of which is of great importance to the economy. EU accession will probably reduce competition between Latvia and its Baltic neighbours. It is, furthermore, difficult to envisage Kaliningrad as a 'bridge with the enlarged EU', as Russia would like. The main issue, then, is Primorsk and the port at St Petersburg. Clearly, many in Russia would prefer to use Ventspils for its ice-free conditions, security and favourable geographical position. If their desires are given expression, if Russia softens its stance against Latvia, or if Russian companies such as Transneft and Yukos obtain a stake in Ventspils Nafta, Latvia should not experience a substantial decline in petroleum shipments in the long term.

ENERGY

Independence forced Latvia into a precarious position regarding its energy supply. With the exception of peat and timber, Latvia had no significant domestic energy resources, and as part of the USSR received almost all of its imported energy in 1990 (93% of its total usage) from other Soviet republics. With the fall of communism and the advent in Russia of market capitalism, Russian energy companies began to demand 'hard' currency, which Latvia lacked, at world market prices. As a result, local consumers became indebted to local utility companies, which in turn became indebted to their Russian suppliers. Debts on natural gas purchases from the state-controlled Russian gas monopoly, Gazprom, reached US $12.6m. in 1996; the problem continues into the 2000s as Latvia remains reliant on Russia for more than 75% of its energy.

Latvian—and Baltic—energy is not, however, without hope. With the reopening in August 2001 of the Kegums hydro-electric power plant, and other progress in the sector, Latvia was able in that year to produce about 25% of the energy it required, compared with just 7% in 1990. Although its energy efficiency was still only 50% of the EU average, modernization of equipment made the domestic energy industry more effective. Furthermore, in June 2002 the European Investment Bank agreed to an €80m. loan for the modernization of Latvenergo, which provides two-thirds of Latvia's electricity needs. This loan was to be disbursed over a period of 15 years.

With Latvia's turn towards the West and forthcoming EU accession, its energy policy was largely based on independence from Russia. Out of this policy there emerged in 1998–99 discussions on a co-operative Baltic energy strategy. The proposed energy ring, which received more attention in 2002, would facilitate shipments of Norwegian petroleum and gas to the Baltics, sales of Baltic power to Finland and Sweden, and the interconnectivity of the energy markets. In April a Latvian company performed a test of the Baltic, western Belarusian and Kaliningrad energy grids and found that they could function independently of Russia's north-west energy system. Following Latvia's accession to the EU this grid was to be used to connect the region to Western power suppliers. In August Poland and the three Baltic States agreed to co-operate more closely on energy projects, anticipating EU accession and the inclusion of Scandinavia and Russia. It is, in fact, important to involve Russia, as it will remain a force in the regional energy sector for years to come. For its part, Russia had shown interest in recent years in providing US $1,000m. for the construction of petroleum and gas pipelines through Latvia to Estonia and Finland, although political and financial obstacles remained to be overcome.

Further potential relief from reliance on Russia came in the form of the discovery of possible petroleum reserves under the Baltic Sea. Border disputes with Lithuania had prevented exploration since 1995, but with these disputes mostly solved Latvia opened up a tender in April 2001 for exploration and exploitation rights. A joint Norwegian-US venture, TGS Nopec, bought non-exclusive rights in April 2002, and was expected to begin prospecting for the 250m. metric tons of petroleum believed to lie under Latvian waters. Depending on the rate of extraction, Latvia stood to gain between 2% and 12% of all revenues produced.

EU accession should greatly affect Latvia's energy sector. As with agriculture, negotiations regarding energy were some of the most difficult to conclude, as the sector required major reforms. Latvian energy companies were wary of the increased competition that would result from accession to the EU. This competition could, however, bring lower prices and greater independence from Russia.

Latvia's energy sector can give cause for optimism. Continued discussion of a Baltic energy ring, co-operation with Poland and the other Baltic countries, an energy grid proven to function independently from Russia, and EU accession all bode well for the long-term future of Latvian energy supplies. Possible petroleum reserves and a new nuclear power plant would, if realized, bring positive and immediate changes.

Norwegian and Polish natural gas supplies could bring some relief, as well. Furthermore, if Latvia can continue developing its own energy industry, and if Russian supplies remain stable, the energy sector should continue to provide adequate, if not exceptional, service.

TRADE

With a small domestic market and few natural resources, Latvia has always had to think internationally as regards its trade. Given, furthermore, its geographical position between Western Europe and Russia, it has also had to negotiate between two very different economic systems, each of which progresses at its own pace. By the early 2000s Latvia was in a tenuous yet promising position, having been invited to join the EU, and yet occupying an unusual role among the accession countries for its knowledge of Russia and its strong contacts both there and in the CIS. The global economic downturn of 2002 revealed, furthermore, that Latvia could withstand such crises well, in part by reorientating its trade towards the east or west, depending on demand.

EU accession prospects had already positively affected Latvia's trade. Consumer confidence seemed to have increased, based on sales figures for the end of 2002. The lats was also stronger in 2002, fuelling imports, which increased from 1,933.9m. LVL in 2000 to 2,201.6m. LVL in 2001 and to 2,497.4m. LVL in 2002. Furthermore, according to the UN, Latvia's approaching EU membership had encouraged greater foreign direct investment (FDI), which helped the Latvian economy to improve despite the global economic recession.

Latvia's trade with its eastern neighbour, Russia, has been precarious since regaining independence. In 1991 the USSR took 96.8% of Latvia's exports and provided 87.2% of its imports; in 2002 Russia took just 5.9% of Latvia's exports and provided 8.8% of its imports. Furthermore, Russian actions, such as the construction of the port at Primorsk and plans for a further port at Ust-Luga, intended to avoid cargo shipments through Latvia, together with the boycott of petroleum transshipments through Latvian pipelines, rendered trade relations even more tenuous. However, from 2000 trade between Russia and the EU states had increased by €10,000m. annually, from €65,000m. in 2000 to €85,000m. in 2002. Upon the accession of the 10 new members, this increase would only be reinforced, and benefits to the Latvian economy should follow. For example, exports to the CIS from Latvia increased from 98.3m. LVL in 2000 to 140.6m. LVL in 2002. This increase was, in part, a result of the reorientation of Latvian trade eastward, in response to the Russian economic recovery and the concurrent downturn in the EU economy. This trend may continue, as GDP growth in Russia was forecast at 4.0% in 2003 and 4.2% in 2004, while growth in the EU was forecast to reach a more modest 1.6% in 2003 and 2.2% in 2004. Imports from the CIS, while remaining steady at 327.5m. LVL in 2000–02, appeared likely to increase in 2003.

The future of Latvian trade would be profoundly affected by EU accession. Some analysts predicted a boost to new members' economic competitiveness, owing to anticipated increased trade with Russia and improvements in productivity. Strengthened investment protection should also lead to more FDI. It was predicted that the opening to competition of markets, especially those of water, energy, transport and telecommunications, would have a positive impact on access to these markets for new EU members. If Latvia continues its campaign for CIS markets, while maintaining and strengthening its presence in Western Europe and Scandinavia, and if it develops its own industries to reduce the trade deficit (which reached 1,088.6m. LVL in 2002, compared with 802.6m. LVL in 2000) future Latvian trade should be more stable, profitable and sustainable.

FINANCE

Before independence Latvia was a net contributor to the Soviet budget, owing largely to its industrial base and the transshipment of goods. Independence, however, brought the removal of subsidies, increased energy prices, rising social outlays and revolutionary changes in the market environment. As a result, Latvia experienced a budget deficit and high inflation. Government measures to control the increase in consumer prices reduced inflation from around 1,000% in 1992 to 1.9% in 2002; the deficit, however, remained high (146.4m. LVL in 2002, compared with 86.4m. LVL in 1994), despite the reductions in spending that resulted from the 1995 banking crisis.

Since independence some very positive changes have occurred in the Latvian economy. The national currency, the lats, was successfully reintroduced, the banking sector was reformed after the 1995 crisis, the privatization programme led to reduced spending, increased domestic output and foreign investment and, finally, as evidence of its progress, in 2002 Latvia received invitations to join both the EU and the North Atlantic Treaty Organization (NATO).

With this in mind, Latvia was expected to maintain an expansionary fiscal policy, while keeping the budget deficit at or below the EU-mandated maximum of 3% of GDP. Prioritizing budget expenditure, improving the tax administration and reducing the number of corporate-tax exemptions should help offset increased expenditure resulting from the introduction of an increased minimum wage; an increase in defence spending, to the equivalent of 2% of GDP (to conform with NATO standards); the introduction of provisions to absorb EU agricultural and fisheries funding; and the cost of a government-sponsored media campaign to convince voters of the benefits of EU accession. There were signs that this path was viable: in 2002 tax revenue increased, owing to improved tax-collection methods and a greater willingness to pay, while increased expenditure on defence and the raised minimum wage had not adversely affected forecasts.

According to the Ministry of Finance, EU accession could mean as much as €142m. in aid during Latvia's first year of membership, with €118m. of Latvian funds going to the EU. EU aid had already helped to mitigate the impact of reduced transit revenues in 2002 and 2003. The argument over payments and who will, in the end, be a net contributor to whose economy has been a central question of the 'eurosceptics' in all accession countries. It is likely, in any event, that EU accession will be a shock to Latvia's economy. The President of the European Central Bank warned of the inflationary pressures resulting from EU-targeted structural reforms, and suggested a medium-term policy aimed at price stability.

The lats, well managed by the Bank of Latvia since its reintroduction in 1993, will eventually be replaced by the euro. Fixed to the IMF's Special Drawing Right in 1994, the lats would, upon EU accession, begin to 'float' relative to the euro. For a period of two years (as mandated by the EU), the lats was to be 'pegged' to the euro, during which time Latvia would have to meet stringent inflation and deficit criteria. The EU recommended that Latvia, during this time, concentrate on macroeconomic balance, and the European Central Bank warned of disruptive shocks on adoption of the euro, and suggested a flexible fiscal policy.

It is difficult to predict the effect that EU membership will have on Latvia. It is clear, however, that Latvia has prepared well for entrance: its long term goals of liberalization, stabilization and privatization, completed in the 1990s, have led, along with a relatively stable international economy, to consistently good performance in the early years of the 21st century. Consumer prices have been kept in check, while growth exceeded Russian, EU and world averages in 2000–02. Budget revenues reached 1,895.2m. LVL in 2002, compared with 1,623m. LVL in 2000, with figures for early 2003 suggesting a further increase. Exchange rates against the euro remained stable, and the banking sector experienced increased lending at a low and stable interest rate, and a benign macroeconomic environment. Although increased lending may generate sectoral risks, its existing performance was good and the outlook remained positive. Falling interest rates, however, may encourage foreign depositories to withdraw funds, which contribute 35% to the sector's balance sheet.

Latvia's budget deficit remained a cause for concern, having increased from 120.7m. LVL in 2000 to 146.4m. LVL in 2002, mainly owing to increased expenditure. This situation could improve in 2003, however, as figures for the first two months of the year suggested that expenditure would remain static, with increased revenues compared with 2002.

EMPLOYMENT

The collapse of the USSR led to a major shift in employment from manufacturing to service-orientated industries, which, while addressing needs and being necessary for European integration, caused difficulties in the Latvian employment sector. Since independence, service and commercial centres such as Rīga and Ventspils have tended to maintain unemployment rates of less than 5%, while rural areas have, with the decline in agricultural productivity, experienced much higher rates. Latgale, the easternmost region of Latvia, recorded rates of unemployment of between 20% and 40%, making it one of the poorest regions in the countries negotiating to join the EU. Restructuring of the agricultural sector under the EU would require retraining and education for the rural populace, who often had outdated and overspecialized skills, acquired under the Soviet system. A lack of retraining programmes contributed to Latvia's high unemployment rate, which was 7.8% in 2002—11.6% if unregistered unemployment was taken into account, which, given the short duration and low level of unemployment benefits conferred upon registration, was probably a more accurate figure. It is hoped that such retraining programmes, for which the Government had begun to provide increased funding, will prepare workers for the new service-orientated economy and reduce regional disparities by increasing the flexibility of the labour market.

Poverty is another problem in Latvia: the proportion of the population living in poverty increased from 15.1% in 1995 to 20.3% in 2001. In 2002 the World Health Organization (WHO) concluded a study that used levels of infection with tuberculosis ('a classic disease of poverty') to determine the economic state of countries. According to the WHO, Latvia, Estonia and Russia were severely affected by poverty, mostly in rural areas. Residents of these areas hoped that EU funding would address problems in the countryside.

None the less, wages, although a legitimate cause for complaint, had improved in recent years. Rising rapidly on strong domestic demand, the structural imbalance of the labour market, and concentration of investment in Rīga, the average nominal wage rose by 6.5% in 2001 (or by 3.5%, in real terms). The nominal wage increased by 8.4% in 2002. An increase in the minimum wage was introduced in January 2003, and a further increase was scheduled to be implemented at the beginning of 2004. Given the concomitant increase in labour productivity, high wages had not yet affected Latvia's external competitiveness; however, this was possible, given the likelihood of a deceleration in productivity in 2002. At present wage growth and steady employment had increased private consumption, but had not yet caused high inflation. The inflation rate actually declined in 2002, owing to lower prices for services. The rate of consumer-price inflation was predicted to remain at around 2.2% throughout 2004, while the average rate of registered unemployment was expected to remain at 7.6%–7.7%.

Emigration and the natural decline of the population is cause for concern. Deaths exceeded births by around 12,000 annually, and as a result of net migration over 6,000 people left Latvia each year. Given Latvia's forecasted economic growth, unemployment may be reduced, but labour shortages may also follow, leading to lower productivity and the need for immigration. Indeed, possible migration, to and from Latvia, was a concern of many as Latvia looked toward EU membership.

A concern of Western Europe and Latvia alike was that upon accession Latvia would suffer from so-called 'brain drain', as its best workers moved to the West. Studies indicated, however, that EU accession was actually likely to reduce the rate of emigration, owing to increased economic opportunities domestically. Moreover, existing EU member states have the right to restrict immigration from newly acceded members for a period of five years, and this restriction could be extended for a further two years if a serious disruption to the labour market could be demonstrated. Latvia, in turn, would receive similar rights of restriction. At 2003 Denmark, Greece, Ireland, the Netherlands, Sweden and the United Kingdom had pledged not to apply restrictions. Austria and Germany, which share borders with five accession states, led the drive for restrictions and were expected to apply them.

Another concern regarding EU accession is the extent to which it will affect employment levels and wages. According to some estimates, the increase in imports of EU products to Central Europe led to a loss of some 5m. jobs in 1995–2001. However, some analysts foresee the creation of hundreds of thousands of new jobs, increased wages and a reduction in poverty for new members upon accession. Furthermore, the EU has argued that even without subsidies, Latvian farmers' incomes would increase by 59% upon accession; with the promised subsidies (see Agriculture), this increase would be even more significant. Although the effect that EU accession would have on unemployment and wages remained unclear, the stated objectives of the Union were heartening: according to the Athens declaration, signed in Greece by all existing and acceding members in April 2003, the countries pledged to commit themselves to 'a dynamic and knowledge-based European economy, open to all, focused on sustainable growth and full employment'. The European Commission suggested that new members reduce unemployment by increasing employment in services and skilled sectors and reducing reliance on agricultural and traditional industrial sectors—exactly what Latvia had been doing since regaining independence.

CONCLUSION

A short but vitally important period in the economy of Latvia came to an end in December 2002, with its invitation to join the EU. Providing a policy goal and a framework for legislative, business, administrative and social reforms, the invitation closed an 11-year chapter in Latvia's history that was characterized by its turn away from Russia and towards the West, a wrenching shift from the Soviet command economy to the Western free market model—with the requisite privatization, liberalization and stabilization goals—and upheavals in civil society, from shifts in employment patterns to lowered wages and social services. Since 1991, Latvia has had to adopt new legislation, implement language and citizenship rules for its Russian-speaking minority and meet the requirements of the EU in every area of the economy, government and civil society.

The positive effects of the economic reform programme were seen by 1994, as Latvia introduced a consistently stable national currency, began to undertake privatization, and instituted a free market in most areas of life. Although the 1995 banking crisis revealed abuses in the sector that affected the entire economy and engendered mistrust among the populace, it emerged reformed and stabilized, and government spending became more responsible. The Russian economic crisis of 1998 was a blow to Latvia, restricting its GDP growth to just 1.1% in 1999. The economy rapidly recovered, however, suggesting Latvia's flexibility in facing international reverses. Strong growth, despite the 2002 global economic downturn, further demonstrated this resilience. Latvia's treatment of the Russian minority was also an issue that threatened exclusion from the EU. By 2001, however, its laws had been revised to conform, for the most part, with EU and Organization for Security and Co-operation in Europe (OSCE) requirements, although discrimination against the Russian minority still persisted in society, mostly in the work-place.

Although Latvia's achievements earned it an invitation to join the EU, Latvia has not completed its reforms. Corruption in government was a major concern of the EU and NATO, as was the related issue of the poor quality of the judiciary. The agricultural sector remained problematical; debates between Latvia and the EU over the issue could jeopardize a positive vote at the referendum on accession to the EU to be held in September 2003. To counter this, the Government had allocated funds for a pro-EU media campaign. If Latvia did accede, as was expected, there were concerns about the potential migration of skilled workers. A more tangible problem existed in the Russian port at Primorsk, and in moves by Russia to circumvent Latvia's transshipment corridors. Unemployment and poverty also remained problems. In contrast to the EU's objective of full employment, Latvia was experiencing alarming differences in regional employment rates and high levels of poverty. A negative birth rate and net emigration may decrease unemployment, but will also lead to reduced production, at a time when EU and NATO accession is forcing an expansionary fiscal policy. Finally, EU accession will bring unpredictable, and perhaps radical, changes across the Latvian economy. Latvia should, however, be ready to make a relatively smooth transition to EU membership. Latvia's economy has grown consistently and strongly since 2000 and should continue to do so. Although it would take at least a decade for the standard of living in Latvia to approach that of Western Europe, Latvia's progress to the institutions of Western Europe and greater prosperity seemed secure.

Statistical Survey

Source (unless otherwise stated): Central Statistical Bureau of Latvia, Lāčplēša iela 1, Rīga 1301; tel. 736-6850; fax 783-0137; e-mail csb@csb.lv; internet www.csb.lv.

Area and Population

AREA, POPULATION AND DENSITY

Area (sq km)	64,589*
Population (census results)†	
12 January 1989	2,666,567
31 March 2000	
Males	1,094,964
Females	1,282,419
Total	2,377,383
Population (official estimates at 1 January)	
2001	2,364,254
2002	2,345,768
2003	2,311,480
Density (per sq km) at 1 January 2003	35.8

* 24,938 sq miles.
† Figure refers to the resident population.

POPULATION BY ETHNIC GROUP
(permanent inhabitants)

	1989 census		2000 census	
	Number	%	Number	%
Latvian	1,387,757	52.0	1,370,703	57.7
Russian	905,515	34.0	703,243	29.6
Belarusian	119,702	4.5	97,150	4.1
Ukrainian	92,101	3.5	63,644	2.7
Polish	60,416	2.3	59,505	2.5
Lithuanian	34,630	1.3	33,430	1.4
Jewish	22,897	0.9	10,385	0.4
Total (incl. others)	2,666,567	100.0	2,377,383	100.0

PRINCIPAL TOWNS
(population at 1 January 2003)

Rīga (Riga, the capital) . . .	739,232	Jūrmala	55,156
Daugavpils . . .	112,609	Ventspils	44,010
Liepāja . . .	86,983	Rēzekne	37,777
Jelgava . . .	65,754		

BIRTHS, MARRIAGES AND DEATHS

	Registered live births		Registered marriages		Registered deaths	
	Number	Rate (per 1,000)	Number	Rate (per 1,000)	Number	Rate (per 1,000)
1995 . . .	21,595	8.7	11,072	4.5	38,931	15.7
1996 . . .	19,782	8.1	9,634	3.9	34,320	14.0
1997 . . .	18,830	7.7	9,680	4.0	33,533	13.8
1998 . . .	18,410	7.6	9,641	4.0	34,200	14.2
1999 . . .	19,396	8.1	9,399	3.9	32,844	13.7
2000 . . .	20,248	8.5	9,211	3.9	32,205	13.6
2001 . . .	19,664	8.3	9,258	3.9	32,991	14.0
2002 . . .	20,044	8.6	9,738	4.2	32,498	13.9

Expectation of life (WHO estimates, years at birth): 70.7 (males 65.2; females 76.0) in 2001 (Source: WHO, *World Health Report*).

IMMIGRATION AND EMIGRATION

	1999	2000	2001
Immigrants	1,813	1,627	1,443
Emigrants	5,898	7,131	6,602

EMPLOYMENT
(annual averages, '000 persons)

	2000	2001	2002
Agriculture, hunting and forestry	134	143	147
Fishing	2	2	6
Mining and quarrying	2	1	3
Manufacturing	170	156	167
Electricity, gas and water	12	19	22
Construction	56	68	60
Wholesale and retail trade; repair of motor vehicles, motorcycles and personal and household goods	145	160	148
Hotels and restaurants	22	22	24
Transport, storage and communications	79	78	86
Financial intermediation	12	14	13
Real estate, renting and business activities	45	41	39
Public administration and defence, compulsory social security	71	68	68
Education	87	88	88
Health and social work	48	50	60
Other community, social and personal service activities	44	49	53
Total	**941**	**962**	**989**
Males	n.a.	n.a.	505
Females	n.a.	n.a.	484

Registered unemployed (annual averages, '000 persons): 101.2 in 2000; 93.3 in 2001; 93.6 in 2002.

Health and Welfare

KEY INDICATORS

Total fertility rate (children per woman, 2001)	1.1
Under-5 mortality rate (per 1,000 live births, 2001)	21
HIV/AIDS (% of persons aged 15–49, 2001)	0.40
Physicians (per 1,000 head, 1998)	2.82
Hospital beds (per 1,000 head, 1996)	10.3
Health expenditure (2000): US $ per head (PPP)	398
Health expenditure (2000): % of GDP	5.9
Health expenditure (2000): public (% of total)	60.0
Human Development Index (2000): ranking	53
Human Development Index (2000): value	0.800

For sources and definitions, see explanatory note on p. vi.

Agriculture

PRINCIPAL CROPS
('000 metric tons)

	1999	2000	2001
Wheat	351.9	427.4	451.7
Barley	232.6	261.1	231.1
Rye	88.7	110.7	107.2
Oats	66.1	79.6	82.4
Triticale (wheat-rye hybrid)	11.9	13.5	28.9
Other cereals*	32.4	45.4	46.7
Potatoes	795.5	747.1	615.3
Sugar beet	451.5	407.7	491.2
Dry peas	2.2	3.0	2.6
Other pulses	3.2	1.1	1.4
Rapeseed	8.4	10.0	13.0
Cabbages	65.3	50.4	61.8
Cucumbers and gherkins	10.4	10.4	17.4*
Dry onions	5.5	8.3	7.1
Carrots	20.9	21.1	42.8
Other vegetables*	27.8	15.7	35.6
Apples	34.1	35.4	36.1
Currants	4.4	3.4	4.1
Cranberries	3*	8	8†

* Unofficial figure(s).
† FAO estimate.

Source: FAO.

LIVESTOCK
('000 head at 1 January)

	1999	2000	2001
Cattle	434	378	367
Pigs	421	405	394
Sheep	27	27	29
Goats	10	8	10
Horses	19	19	20
Poultry	3,209	3,237	3,105

Source: FAO.

LIVESTOCK PRODUCTS
('000 metric tons, unless otherwise indicated)

	1999	2000	2001
Beef and veal	20.5	22.4	19.0
Pig meat	34.6	31.5	31.6
Chicken meat	6.3	7.2	8.9
Cows' milk	797.0	823.0	845.6
Cheese	11.2	11.1	13.2
Butter	7.4	7.2	7.1
Hen eggs	23.2*	24.4*	27.1
Cattle hides†	2.8	3.5	2.7
Sheepskins†	9.4	13.9	12.6

* Unofficial figure.
† FAO estimates.

Source: FAO.

Forestry

ROUNDWOOD REMOVALS
('000 cubic metres, excl. bark)

	1999	2000	2001
Sawlogs, veneer logs and logs for sleepers	6,882	8,642	7,359
Pulpwood	2,200	3,517	3,330
Other industrial wood	2,436*	465	572
Fuel wood	2,490	1,680	1,580
Total	**14,008**	**14,304**	**12,841**

* FAO estimate.

Source: FAO.

SAWNWOOD PRODUCTION
('000 cubic metres, incl. railway sleepers)

	1999	2000	2001
Coniferous (softwood)	3,047	3,320	3,195
Broadleaved (hardwood)	593	580	645
Total	**3,640**	**3,900**	**3,840**

Source: FAO.

Fishing

('000 metric tons, live weight)

	1998	1999	2000
Capture	102.3	125.4	136.4
Atlantic cod	7.8	6.9	6.3
Jack and horse mackerels	8.7	14.3	22.6
Atlantic herring	24.4	27.2	26.8
Sardinellas	6.1	15.0	7.9
European sprat	44.9	42.8	46.2
Chub mackerel	2.6	3.1	7.2
European anchovy	2.0	4.9	10.1
Aquaculture	0.4	0.5	0.3
Total catch	**102.8**	**125.9**	**136.7**

Source: FAO, *Yearbook of Fishery Statistics*.

2001 ('000 metric tons, live weight): Total catch, excluding aquaculture 125.4.

Mining

('000 metric tons)

	1997	1998	1999
Peat	554.7	171.7	956.4
for fuel	362.1	45.6	315.4
for agriculture	163.9	111.1	567.1
Gypsum	116.9	119.1	96.6
Limestone	372.7	363.3	436.8

Peat for fuel ('000 metric tons): 61.8 in 2000; 68.3 in 2001.

Peat for agriculture ('000 metric tons): 323.6 in 2000; 430.8 in 2001.

2002 ('000 metric tons, selected enterprises): Peat for fuel 114.2; Peat for agriculture 575.4.

Industry

SELECTED PRODUCTS

('000 metric tons, unless otherwise indicated)

	1997	1998	1999*
Sausages	32.2	33.1	26.4
Preserved fish	89.9	76.6	62.8
Whole milk	61.2	67.3	14.6†
Yoghurt	5.0	4.8	4.4
Ice-cream	6.2	4.7	9.8†
Preserved milk	15.1	17.5	6.1
Chocolate and sugar confectionery containing cocoa	10.1	7.1	10.8
Mayonnaise	5.5	4.4	4.5
Refined sugar	88.5	85.6	66.5
Beer ('000 hectolitres) . . .	714.9	721.0	953.2
Cigarettes (million) . . .	1,775	2,018	1,916
Woven cotton fabrics (million sq metres)	3.1	7.4	11.8
Linen fabrics (million sq metres) .	0.6	0.4	3.7
Leather footwear ('000 pairs) .	577	620	350
Rubber footwear ('000 pairs) . .	499	605	186
Plywood ('000 cu metres) . .	121.4	150.5	202.8
Paper	4.4	3.8	2.4
Synthetic resins	31.4	39.6	25.9
Cement	246	366	301
Crude steel	465.0	471.0	483.7
Washing machines ('000) . .	3.0	1.5	—
Chain drives	6.3‡	6.6‡	3.6
Milking machines ('000) . . .	0.1	0.3	0.3
Radio receivers ('000) . . .	9.9	2.3	1.7
Buses (number)	102	—	—
Electric energy (million kWh) . .	4,503	5,797	4,101

* From 1999 data on industrial production are compiled according to EU classification methods.
† Million litres.
‡ Million metres.

2000 ('000 metric tons, unless otherwise indicated): Sausages 28.3; Preserved fish 72.4; Whole milk 14.5; Yoghurt 5.5; Ice-cream 9.3; Mayonnaise 6.8; Beer ('000 hectolitres) 945.1; Woven cotton fabrics (million sq metres) 13.0; Leather footwear ('000 pairs) 288; Plywood (million cu metres) 245.5; Electric energy (million kWh) 4,134.

2001 ('000 metric tons, unless otherwise indicated): Sausages 28.6; Preserved fish 92.8; Whole milk 22.7; Yoghurt 5.4; Ice-cream 10.0; Mayonnaise 6.4; Beer ('000 hectolitres) 996.6; Woven cotton fabrics (million sq metres) 15.1; Leather footwear ('000 pairs) 282; Plywood (million cu metres) 266.9; Electric energy (million kWh) 4,287.

2002 (selected enterprises, '000 metric tons, unless otherwise indicated): Sausages 27.5; Preserved fish 97.5; Whole milk 17.5; Yoghurt 5.4; Ice-cream 12.6; Mayonnaise 5.4; Beer ('000 hectolitres) 1,179.0; Woven cotton fabrics (million sq metres) 18.7; Leather footwear ('000 pairs) 325; Plywood (million cu metres) 410.7; Electric energy (million kWh) 3,885.

Finance

CURRENCY AND EXCHANGE RATES

Monetary Units
100 santimi = 1 lats (LVL).

Sterling, Dollar and Euro Equivalents (30 May 2003)
£1 sterling = 93.0 santimi;
US $1 = 56.5 santimi;
€1 = 66.7 santimi;
100 LVL = £107.42 = $176.99 = €149.72.

Average Exchange Rate (LVL per US $)
2000   0.607
2001   0.628
2002   0.618

Note: Between March and June 1993 Latvia reintroduced its national currency, the lats, replacing the Latvian rouble (Latvijas rublis), at a conversion rate of 1 lats = 200 Latvian roubles. The Latvian rouble had been introduced in May 1992, replacing (and initially at par with) the Russian (formerly Soviet) rouble.

BUDGET

(million LVL*)

Revenue†	1999	2000	2001
Tax revenue	1,072.9	1,096.9	1,156.5
Taxes on income, profits and capital gains	161.0	147.9	178.2
Individual	68.8	74.2	79.8
Corporate	92.2	73.7	98.4
Social security contributions . .	411.3	424.5	439.2
Domestic taxes on goods and services	483.8	509.9	524.2
General sales, turnover or value-added taxes . . .	316.2	337.9	350.6
Excises	155.1	164.0	161.0
Import duties	16.1	14.4	15.3
Other current revenue	147.9	141.6	87.2
Administrative fees and charges, non-industrial and incidental sales	99.4	95.9	39.2
Capital revenue	12.0	0.4	0.5
Total	**1,232.8**	**1,238.9**	**1,244.1**

Expenditure‡	1999	2000	2001
General public services	77.0	74.7	77.4
Defence	34.5	36.6	43.4
Public order and safety	99.3	93.6	97.7
Education	66.9	77.1	87.8
Health	150.8	146.4	154.4
Social security and welfare . . .	591.4	577.4	570.6
Housing and community amenities .	12.2	18.9	16.8
Recreational, cultural and religious affairs and services . . .	25.5	29.1	25.6
Economic affairs and services . .	190.8	165.1	161.5
Agriculture, forestry, fishing and hunting	76.7	62.4	61.3
Transport and communications	90.6	77.8	75.6
Other purposes	131.6	152.2	164.7
Interest payments	28.0	45.2	48.6
Total	**1,379.9**	**1,371.1**	**1,399.8**
Current	1,267.7	1,275.7	1,310.2
Capital	112.2	95.4	89.7

* Figures refer to the consolidated accounts of the central Government, comprising the operations of the general budget, the Social Security Fund, the State Property Privatization Fund and other extrabudgetary special funds. In 1997 there were changes to education and health functions within the components of central Government and between the Government and local authorities.
† Excluding grants received (million LVL): 16.7 in 1999; 25.9 in 2000; 96.8 in 2001. Data on grants provided through some foreign assistance programmes are not included.
‡ Excluding lending minus repayments (million LVL): 3.3 in 1999; 5.4 in 2000; 5.7 in 2001.

Source: IMF, *Government Finance Statistics Yearbook*.

INTERNATIONAL RESERVES
(US $ million at 31 December)

	2000	2001	2002
Gold*	68.38	69.66	85.90
IMF special drawing rights . . .	0.01	0.09	0.07
Reserve position in IMF. . . .	0.07	0.07	0.08
Foreign exchange.	850.83	1,148.59	1,241.27
Total	919.29	1,218.40	1,327.32

* Valued at market prices.

Source: IMF, *International Financial Statistics*.

MONEY SUPPLY
(million LVL at 31 December)

	2000	2001	2002
Currency outside banks	427.66	485.19	543.13
Demand deposits at banking institutions	332.97	374.97	501.36
Total money (incl. others) . . .	764.57	863.59	1,047.50

Source: IMF, *International Financial Statistics*.

COST OF LIVING
(Consumer price index; base: 1993 = 100)

	2000	2001	2002
Food and non-alcoholic beverages	180.0	188.7	195.2
Fuel and light	202.8	206.0	206.5
Clothing (incl. footwear). . .	301.0	303.6	301.1
Rent	470.4	482.9	485.2
All items (incl. others)	238.2	244.2	248.9

NATIONAL ACCOUNTS
(million LVL at current prices)

Expenditure on the Gross Domestic Product

	2000	2001	2002
Government final consumption expenditure.	857.0	928.9	1,038.0
Private final consumption expenditure.	2,693.5	2,988.9	3,259.3
Increase in stocks	22.5	135.0	112.8
Gross fixed capital formation . .	1,151.5	1,297.5	1,335.6
Total domestic expenditure. .	4,724.5	5,350.3	5,745.7
Exports of goods and services . .	1,983.8	2,138.3	2,361.5
Less Imports of goods and services	2,360.0	2,676.0	2,912.5
GDP in purchasers' values . .	4,348.3	4,812.6	5,194.7
GDP at constant 2000 prices .	4,348.3	4,693.4	4,978.1

Gross Domestic Product by Economic Activity

	2000	2001	2002
Agriculture and hunting . . .	108.5	126.2	133.2
Forestry, logging and related services	62.8	66.2	72.2
Fishing	15.1	13.3	11.2
Mining and quarrying	5.2	6.0	6.9
Manufacturing	560.9	633.6	686.1
Electricity, gas and water supply .	147.7	159.7	167.2
Construction	258.0	259.9	283.1
Wholesale and retail trade; repair of motor vehicles, motorcycles and personal and household goods	688.5	790.4	920.5
Hotels and restaurants	47.1	54.8	56.3
Transport, storage and communications	590.9	661.3	672.6
Financial intermediation . . .	206.1	204.6	211.3
Real estate, renting and business activities	397.6	478.8	513.3
Public administration and defence; compulsory social security . .	253.9	279.0	303.7
Education	206.5	223.2	249.0
Health and social work	119.6	129.7	136.7
Other community, social and personal service activities . .	165.3	178.8	197.9
GDP at basic prices	3,833.7	4,265.5	4,621.2
Taxes *less* subsidies on products	514.6	547.1	573.5
GDP in purchasers' values . .	4,348.3	4,812.6	5,194.7

BALANCE OF PAYMENTS
(US $ million)

	1999	2000	2001
Exports of goods f.o.b.	1,889.1	2,058.1	2,215.9
Imports of goods f.o.b.	−2,916.1	−3,116.3	−3,566.4
Trade balance	−1,027.0	−1,058.2	−1,350.5
Exports of services	1,024.2	1,212.1	1,188.8
Imports of services	−688.5	−770.1	−692.7
Balance on goods and services	−691.3	−616.2	−854.4
Other income received	157.8	215.2	278.2
Other income paid	−213.6	−190.9	−233.9
Balance on goods, services and income	−747.1	−591.9	−810.1
Current transfers received . . .	113.8	202.8	221.4
Current transfers paid	−21.0	−105.4	−142.9
Current balance	−654.3	−494.5	−731.6
Capital account (net)	12.6	29.6	44.7
Direct investment abroad . . .	−17.0	−9.4	−12.4
Direct investment from abroad. .	347.6	410.0	163.9
Portfolio investment assets . . .	57.9	−346.4	−57.1
Portfolio investment liabilities . .	215.4	25.1	184.1
Financial derivatives assets . .	—	2.2	3.4
Financial derivatives liabilities .	—	−0.3	−2.6
Other investment assets . . .	−214.1	−360.5	−66.8
Other investment liabilities . .	378.6	773.3	741.4
Net errors and omissions . . .	38.3	−26.2	47.4
Overall balance	165.0	2.9	314.3

Source: Bank of Latvia.

External Trade

PRINCIPAL COMMODITIES
(million LVL)

Imports c.i.f.	2000	2001	2002
Vegetable products	77.1	73.4	82.2
Prepared foodstuffs; beverages spirits and vinegar; tobacco and manufactured substitutes . .	115.2	135.6	165.3
Mineral products	249.4	245.1	243.2
Products of chemical or allied industries	205.5	230.4	261.1
Plastics, rubber and articles thereof	89.0	104.2	124.0
Paper-making material; paper and paperboard and articles thereof	82.4	92.0	107.7
Textiles and textile articles . . .	147.8	163.4	171.5
Base metals and articles thereof .	162.7	182.4	210.8
Machinery and mechanical appliances; electrical equipment; sound and television apparatus .	400.8	465.0	530.8
Vehicles, aircraft, vessels and associated transport equipment	150.2	206.6	244.5
Total (incl. others)	1,933.9	2,201.6	2,497.4

Exports f.o.b.	2000	2001	2002
Prepared foodstuffs; beverages spirits and vinegar; tobacco and manufactured substitutes . .	40.1	72.5	100.8
Mineral products	30.7	21.2	24.1
Products of chemical or allied industries	72.0	79.5	81.5
Wood, cork and articles thereof; wood charcoal; manufactures of straw, esparto, etc.	423.3	427.3	472.8
Textiles and textile articles . . .	158.7	177.5	180.1
Base metals and artices thereof . .	151.2	159.8	185.4
Machinery and mechanical appliances; electrical equipment; sound and television apparatus .	62.2	80.0	91.0
Miscellaneous manufactured articles	60.4	71.2	83.0
Total (incl. others)	1,131.3	1,256.4	1,408.8

PRINCIPAL TRADING PARTNERS
(million LVL)*

Imports c.i.f.	2000	2001	2002
Austria.	20.7	25.3	34.8
Belarus	66.5	85.3	68.2
Belgium	34.6	40.4	48.9
Czech Republic	24.3	31.2	34.4
Denmark	69.8	81.9	84.8
Estonia	120.5	139.1	153.9
Finland	167.1	176.5	200.2
France	58.7	53.3	65.4
Germany	302.6	374.9	429.5
Italy	70.5	90.6	104.4
Lithuania	146.4	186.4	245.8
Netherlands	66.6	71.5	84.4
Norway	21.6	27.7	31.4
Poland	91.9	110.2	125.8
Russia	224.5	202.2	218.8
Sweden	130.4	143.1	159.5
Switzerland	34.0	38.3	47.8
Ukraine	26.0	31.2	34.0
United Kingdom	51.3	53.1	57.9
USA	38.4	40.6	39.3
Total (incl. others)	1,933.9	2,201.6	2,497.4

Exports f.o.b.	2000	2001	2002
Belarus	13.7	22.5	21.2
Belgium	14.7	15.9	15.3
Denmark	65.9	72.6	80.4
Estonia	60.1	72.1	84.5
Finland	21.7	28.7	32.8
France	20.4	24.3	28.7
Germany	194.3	209.5	218.3
Italy	17.4	23.0	30.4
Lithuania	85.7	102.0	117.7
Netherlands	45.1	46.3	53.8
Poland	18.2	24.1	22.0
Russia	47.3	73.5	82.5
Sweden	122.5	120.1	148.6
Ukraine	26.8	20.9	25.8
United Kingdom	196.5	196.8	205.4
USA	37.7	32.6	59.6
Total (incl. others)	1,131.3	1,256.4	1,408.8

* Imports by country of origin; exports by country of destination.

Transport

RAILWAYS
(traffic)*

	2000	2001	2002
Passenger journeys (million) . .	18.2	20.1	22.0
Passenger-kilometres (million) .	715	706	744
Freight transported (million metric tons)	36.4	37.9	40.1
Freight ton-kilometres (million) .	13,310	14,179	15,020

* Data relating to passengers include railway personnel, and data on freight include passengers' baggage, parcel post and mail.

ROAD TRAFFIC
(motor vehicles in use at 31 December)

	2000	2001	2002
Passenger cars	556,771	586,209	619,081
Buses and coaches	11,501	11,294	11,164
Lorries and vans	97,081	99,708	102,734
Motorcycles and mopeds . . .	20,732	21,366	22,157

SHIPPING

Merchant Fleet
(registered at 31 December)

	2000	2001	2002
Number of vessels	163	160	158
Total displacement ('000 grt) . .	97.9	68.3	88.7

Source: Lloyd's Register-Fairplay, *World Fleet Statistics*.

International Sea-borne Freight Traffic
('000 metric tons)

	2000	2001	2002
Goods loaded	49,276	54,372	48,735
Goods unloaded	2,567	2,546	3,420

CIVIL AVIATION
(traffic)

	2000	2001	2002
Passengers carried ('000) . . .	271.0	298.7	325.9
Passenger-kilometres (million) . .	288.8	276.0	338.1
Cargo ton-kilometres ('000) . . .	6,645	6,544	10,491

Tourism

FOREIGN TOURIST ARRIVALS*

Country of residence	2000	2001	2002
Belarus	6,918	7,806	8,364
Denmark	10,212	11,307	10,202
Estonia	23,840	31,272	35,187
Finland	41,561	50,455	55,702
Germany	31,679	47,674	48,544
Lithuania	19,484	23,949	28,382
Norway	8,859	10,386	11,516
Russia	21,755	28,690	36,403
Sweden	22,408	19,363	20,735
United Kingdom	14,644	15,889	15,657
USA	9,965	11,425	12,805
Total (incl. others)	268,083	322,916	360,927

* Figures refer to arrivals at accommodation establishments. Including excursionists, the total number of visitor arrivals (in '000) was: 1,914 in 2000; 2,039 in 2001; 2,273 in 2002.

Tourism receipts (US $ million): 131 in 2000; 120 in 2001; 161 in 2002.

Communications Media

	2000	2001	2002
Telephones ('000 main lines in use)*	735	722	701
Mobile cellular telephones (subscribers)	401,263	625,197	n.a.
Personal computers ('000 in use)	340	360	n.a.
Internet users ('000)	150	170	n.a.
Book production: titles	2,546	2,530	2,326
Book production: copies ('000)	7,033	6,181	4,599
Daily newspapers: number	9	9	8
Daily newspapers: average circulation ('000 copies)	196	212	183
Non-daily newspapers: number	218	213	211
Non-daily newspapers: average circulation ('000 copies)	1,885	2,041	2,112
Other periodicals: number	325	355	365
Other periodicals: average circulation ('000 copies)	1,856	1,952	1,952

* At 31 December.

Radio receivers ('000 in use): 1,760 in 1997.

Television receivers ('000 in use): 1,220 in 1997.

Facsimile machines (number in use): 900 in 1996.

Sources: mostly UNESCO, *Statistical Yearbook*; UN, *Statistical Yearbook* and International Telecommunication Union.

Education

(2002/03)

	Institutions	Students
Schools*	953	315,448
Latvian	683	199,211
Russian	158	81,715
Latvian-Russian†	105	33,125
Polish	5	1,003
Ukrainian	1	307
Belarusian	1	87
Vocational schools	124	46,533
Higher education institutions	37	118,944
Special schools (for the physically and mentally handicapped)	64	10,055

* Including primary (Grades 1–4), basic schools (Grades 1–9) and secondary schools (Grades 1–12).
† Mixed schools with two languages of instruction.

Teachers: Pre-primary 1,178; Primary (including basic schools) 9,252; Secondary 16,495; Special schools 1,837; Vocational 5,639.

Adult literacy rate (UNESCO estimates): 99.8% (males 99.8%; females 99.8%) in 2000 (Source: UN Development Programme, *Human Development Report*).

Directory

The Constitution

The Constitution of the Republic of Latvia, which had been adopted on 15 February 1922, was annulled at the time of the Soviet annexation in 1940. Latvia became a Union Republic of the USSR and a new Soviet-style Constitution became the legal basis for the governmental system of the republic. The constitutional authority for Latvian membership of the USSR, the Resolution on Latvian Entry into the USSR of 21 July 1940, was declared null and void on 4 May 1990. In the same declaration the Latvian Supreme Council announced the restoration of Articles 1, 2 and 3 of the 1922 Constitution, which describe Latvia as an independent and sovereign state, and Article 6, which states that the legislature (the Saeima) is elected by universal, equal, direct and secret vote, on the basis of proportional representation. On 6 July 1993 the 1922 Constitution was fully restored by the Saeima, following its election on 5 and 6 June. A summary of the Constitution's main provisions (including amendments adopted since its restoration) is given below.

BASIC PROVISIONS

Latvia is an independent, democratic republic, in which the sovereign power of the State belongs to the people. The territory of the Republic of Latvia comprises the provinces of Vidzeme, Latgale, Kurzeme and Zemgale, within the boundaries stipulated by international treaties.

THE SAEIMA

The Saeima (Parliament) comprises 100 representatives of the people and, according to a constitutional amendment adopted in December 1997, is elected by universal, equal, direct and secret vote, on the basis of proportional representation, for a period of four years. All Latvian citizens who have attained 18 years of age are entitled to vote and are eligible for election to the Saeima.

The Saeima elects a Board, which consists of the Chairperson, two Deputies, and Secretaries. The Board convenes the sessions of the Saeima and decrees regular and extraordinary sittings. The sessions of the Saeima are public (sittings in camera are held only by special request).

The right of legislation belongs to both the Saeima and the people. Draft laws may be presented to the Saeima by the President of the Republic, the Cabinet of Ministers, the Committees of the Saeima, no fewer than five members of the Saeima, or, in special cases, by one-tenth of the electorate. Before the commencement of each financial year, the Saeima approves the state budget, the draft of which is submitted by the Cabinet of Ministers. The Saeima decides on the strength of the armed forces during peacetime. The ratification of the Saeima is indispensable to all international agreements dealing with issues resolved by legislation.

THE PRESIDENT OF THE REPUBLIC

According to a constitutional amendment adopted by the Saeima in December 1997, the President of the Republic is elected by a secret ballot of the Saeima for a period of four years. A majority of no fewer than 51 votes is required for his/her election. No person of less than 40 years of age may be elected President of the Republic. The office of President is not compatible with any other office, and the President may serve for no longer than two consecutive terms.

The President represents the State in an international capacity; he/she appoints Latvian representatives abroad, and receives representatives of foreign states accredited to Latvia; implements the decisions of the Saeima concerning the ratification of international treaties; is Head of the Armed Forces; appoints a Commander-in-Chief in time of war; and has the power to declare war on the basis of a decision of the Saeima.

The President has the right to pardon criminals serving penal sentences; to convene extraordinary meetings of the Cabinet of Ministers for the discussion of an agenda prepared by him/her, and to preside over such meetings; and to propose the dissolution of the Saeima. The President may be held criminally accountable if the Saeima sanctions thus with a majority vote of no fewer than two-thirds of its members.

THE CABINET OF MINISTERS

The Cabinet comprises the Prime Minister and the ministers nominated by him/her. This task is entrusted to the Prime Minister by the President of the Republic. All state administrative institutions are subordinate to the Cabinet, which, in turn, is accountable to the Saeima. If the Saeima adopts a vote expressing 'no confidence' in the Prime Minister, the entire Cabinet must resign. The Cabinet discusses all draft laws presented by the ministries as well as issues concerning the activities of the ministries. If the State is threatened by foreign invasion or if events endangering the existing order of the State arise, the Cabinet has the right to proclaim a state of emergency.

THE JUDICIARY

All citizens are equal before the law and the courts. Judges are independent and bound only by law. The appointment of judges is confirmed by the Saeima. Judges may be dismissed from office against their will only by a decision of the Supreme Court. The retiring age for judges is stipulated by law. Judgement may be passed solely by institutions that have been so empowered by law and in such a manner as specified by law. A Constitutional Court was established in 1996 to examine the legality of legislation.

The Government

HEAD OF STATE

President: VAIRA VIĶE-FREIBERGA (inaugurated 8 July 1999; re-elected 20 June 2003; inaugurated 8 July 2003).

CABINET OF MINISTERS
(July 2003)

A coalition of New Era, the First Party of Latvia (LPP), the Greens' and Farmers' Union (Latvian Green Party/LFU) and the Conservative Union 'For Fatherland and Freedom'/LNNK.

Prime Minister: EINARS REPŠE (New Era).

Deputy Prime Minister: AINĀRS ŠLESERS (LPP).

Minister of Defence: ĢIRTS VALDIS KRISTOVSKIS (Conservative Union/LNNK).

Minister of Foreign Affairs: SANDRA KALNIETE (New Era).

Minister of Finance: VALDIS DOMBROVSKIS (New Era).

Minister of the Economy: JURIS LUJĀNS (LPP).

Minister of the Interior: MĀRIS GULBIS (New Era).

Minister of Education and Science: KĀRLIS ŠADURSKIS (New Era).

Minister of Agriculture: MĀRTIŅŠ ROZE (Latvian Green Party/LFU).

Minister of Culture: INGUNA RĪBENA (New Era).

Minister of Welfare: DAGNIJA STAĶE (Latvian Green Party/LFU).

Minister of Transport: ROBERTS ZĪLE (Conservative Union/LNNK).

Minister of Justice: AIVARS AKSENOKS (New Era).

Minister of the Environment: RAIMONDS VĒJONIS (Latvian Green Party/LFU).

Minister of Health: INGRĪDA CIRCENE (New Era).

Minister of Regional Development and Local Governments: IVARS GATERS (New Era).

Minister of Special Assignment on Children and Family Affairs: AINARS BAŠTIKS (LPP).

Minister of Special Assignment on Social Integration: NILS MUIŽNIEKS (LPP).

MINISTRIES

Chancery of the President: Pils lauk. 3, Rīga 1900; tel. 737-7548; fax 709-2106; e-mail chancery@president.lv; internet www.president.lv.

Office of the Cabinet of Ministers: Brīvības bulv. 36, Rīga 1520; tel. 708-2800; fax 728-0469; e-mail pasts@mk.gov.lv; internet www.mk.gov.lv/lv.

Ministry of Agriculture: Republikas lauk. 2, Rīga 1981; tel. 702-7107; fax 702-7250; internet www.zm.gov.lv.

Ministry of Culture: K. Valdemāra iela 11A, Rīga 1364; tel. 722-4772; fax 722-4916; e-mail culture@com.latnet.lv; internet www.culture.lv.

Ministry of Defence: K. Valdemāra iela 10–12, Rīga 1473; tel. 721-0124; fax 721-2307; e-mail kanceleja@mod.lv; internet www.mod.lv.

Ministry of the Economy: Brīvības iela 55, Rīga 1010; tel. 701-3101; fax 728-0882; e-mail em@lem.gov.lv; internet www.lem.gov.lv.

Ministry of Education and Science: Vaļņu iela 2, Rīga 1098; tel. 722-2415; fax 721-3992; e-mail izm@izm.gov.lv; internet www.izm.gov.lv.

Ministry of the Environment: Peldu iela 25, Rīga 1494; tel. 702-6400; fax 782-0442; e-mail pasts@vidm.gov.lv; internet www.varam.gov.lv.

Ministry of Finance: Smilšu iela 1, Rīga 1050; tel. 722-6672; fax 709-5503; internet www.fm.gov.lv.

Ministry of Foreign Affairs: Brīvības bulv. 36, Rīga 1395; tel. 701-6210; fax 782-8121; e-mail info@mfa.gov.lv; internet www.am.gov.lv.

Ministry of Health: Brīvības bulv. 36, Rīga 1520.

Ministry of the Interior: Raiņa bulv. 6, Rīga 1050; tel. 721-9210; fax 722-8283; e-mail pc@iem.gov.lv; internet www.iem.gov.lv.

Ministry of Justice: Brīvības bulv. 36, Rīga 1536; tel. 708-8220; fax 728-5575; e-mail info@tm.gov.lv; internet www.jm.gov.lv.

Ministry of Regional Development and Local Governments: Rīga.

Ministry of Social Integration: Brīvības bulv. 36, Rīga 1520.

Ministry of Transport: Gogoļa iela 3, Rīga 1743; tel. 722-6922; fax 721-7180; e-mail satmin@sam.gov.lv; internet www.sam.gov.lv.

Ministry of Welfare: Skolas iela 28, Rīga 1331; tel. 702-1600; fax 727-6445; internet www.lm.gov.lv.

Legislature

SAEIMA

Parliament

Jekaba iela 11, Rīga 1811; tel. 708-7111; fax 708-7100; e-mail web@saeima.lv; internet www.saeima.lv.

Chairman: INGRIDA UDRE.

Deputy Chairmen: ERIKS JEKABSONS, JĀNIS STRAUME.

General Election, 5 October 2002

Parties and coalitions	% of votes	Seats
New Era	23.93	26
For Human Rights in a United Latvia*	18.94	25
People's Party	16.71	20
First Party of Latvia†	9.58	10
Greens' and Farmers' Union	9.46	12
Conservative Union 'For Fatherland and Freedom'/LNNK	5.39	7
Others	15.99	—
Total	100.00	100

* An electoral bloc composed of the Latvian Socialist Party and the National Harmony Party.

† Including the Christian Democratic Union of Latvia.

‡ Comprising the Latvian Green Party and the Latvian Farmers' Union.

Local Government

For administrative purposes, Latvia is divided into 26 districts and seven towns. The towns are Rīga (the capital), Daugavpils, Jelgava, Jūrmala, Liepāja, Rēzekne and Ventspils. Local elections were held in March 2001.

Ministry of Regional Development and Local Governments: Rīga.

Union of Local and Regional Governments of Latvia: Mazá Pils iela 1, Rīga 1050; tel. 722–6536; fax 721-2241; e-mail lps@lps.lv; internet www.lps.lv; Sec.-Gen. LIGITA ZAČESTA.

DISTRICT ADMINISTRATIONS

Rīgas: K. Valdemāra iela 3, Rīga 1539; tel. 732-0680; fax 722-0785; Chair. of Council GUNDARS BOJĀRS.

Aizkraukles: Lāčplēša iela 1A, Aizkraukle 5101; tel. 512-2750; fax 518-1326; e-mail dome@aizkraukle.apollo.lv; Chair. of Council VILNIS PLŪME.

Alūksnes: Dārza iela 11, Alūksne 4301; tel. 432-4292; fax 438-1150; Chair. of Council GUNTĀRS BĒRZIŅŠ.

Balvu: Sporta iela 1A, Balvi 4501; tel. 452-2830; fax 452-2242; e-mail vilis@apollo.lv; internet www.balvi.lv/dome; f. 1928; Chair. of Council JĀNIS TRUPAVNIEKS.

Bauskas: Uzvaras iela 6, Bauska 3901; tel. 392-2085; fax 392-2832; e-mail dome@bauska.lv; internet www.bauska.lv; Chair. of Council ĀRIJA GAILE.

Cēsu: Raunas iela 4, Cēsis 4101; tel. and fax 412-4571; e-mail gita@dome.apollo.lv; Chair. of Council GINTS ŠĶENDERS.

Daugavpils: Kr. Valdemāra iela 1, Daugavpils 5400; tel. 542-2331; fax 542-1941; e-mail admin@daugavpils.lv; Chair. of Council RIHARDS EIGIMS.

Dobeles: Brīvības iela 17, Dobele 3701; tel. 372-2009; fax 372-2463; e-mail dome@dobele.lv; Chair. of Council ANDRIS ELKSNĪTIS.

Gulbenes: Ābeļu iela 2, Gulbene 4401; tel. 442-3194; fax 447-1311; e-mail dome_gulbene@apollo.lv; Chair. of Council NIKOLAJ STEPANOVS.

Jēkabpils: Brīvības iela 120A, Jēkabpils 5201; tel. 523-2335; fax 523-5333; e-mail jdome@mail.zednet.lv; Chair. of Council LEONĪDS SALCEVIČS.

Jelgavas: Lielā iela 11, Jelgava 3001; tel. 300-5531; fax 302-9059; e-mail dome@dome.jelgava.lv; internet www.jelgava.lv; Chair. of Council ANDRIS RAVINS.

Jūrmalas: Jomas iela 1/5, Jūrmala 2015; tel. 709-3800; fax 776-2288; e-mail info@jpd.gov.lv; Chair. of Council DAINIS URBANOVIČS.

Krāslavas: Rīgas iela 51, Krāslava 5601; tel. and fax 568-1311; e-mail kate@krsdome.apollo.lv; Chair. of Council JĀNIS TRAĆUMS.

Kuldīgas: Baznīcas iela 1, Kuldīga 3301; tel. 332-2469; fax 334-1422; e-mail dome@kuldiga.lv; internet www.kuldiga.lv; Chair. of Council EDGARS ZALĀNS.

Liepājas: Rožu iela 6, Liepāja 3401; tel. 342-2331; fax 342-3391; e-mail info@dome.liepaja.lv; Chair. of Council VALENTĪNA LAZOVSKA.

Limbažu: Baumaņu Kārla 1, Limbaži 4001; tel. 407-0855; fax 407-0857; Chair. of Council OJĀRS PURIŅŠ.

Ludzas: Raiņa iela 16, Ludza 5701; tel. and fax 572-3630; Chair. of Council OJĀRS STARZDS.

Madonas: Saieta laukumā 1, Madona 4801; tel. and fax 482-2430; e-mail maddome@kvarcs.lv; Chair. of Council ANDREJS CELAPĪTERS.

Ogres: Brīvības iela 48, Ogre 5001; tel. 507-1160; fax 507-1161; e-mail ogredome@o.i.c.lv; Chair. of Council VITA PŪKE.

Preiļu: Tirgus laukums 1, Preiļi 5301; tel. 532-2144; fax 532-2766; e-mail dome@preili.lv; Chair. of Council JĀZEPS ŠNEPSTS.

Rēzeknes: Atbrīvošanas alejā 93, Rēzekne 4601; tel. 462-2337; fax 462-2338; e-mail jurists@rpd.apollo.lv; Chair. of Council JURIS ZAČESTS.

Saldus: Avotu iela 12, Saldus 3801; tel. 382-2556; fax 353-8024; e-mail gita@sld.lv; Chair. of Council AIDIS HERINGS.

Talsu: Kareivju iela 7, Talsi 3201; tel. 322-2046; fax 328-1512; e-mail kanceleja@talsu_dome.apollo.lv; Chair. of Council AIVARS LĀCARUS.

Tukuma: Pils iela 18, Tukums 3101; tel. and fax 312-2707; e-mail dome@tukums.lv; Chair. of Council JURIS ŠULCS.

Valkas: Seminara iela 29, Valka 4701; tel. 472-2203; fax 478-1107; e-mail dome@valka.apollo.lv; Chair. of Council VENTS ARMANDS KRAUKLIS.

Valmieras: Lacplesa iela 2, Valmiera 4201; tel. and fax 423-2447; e-mail dome@valmiera.gov.lv; Chair. of Council MĀRIS KUČINSKIS.

Ventspils: Jūras iela 36, Ventspils 3601; tel. 360-1100; fax 360-1118; e-mail dome@ventspils.gov.lv; Chair. of Council AIVARS LEMBERGS.

Political Organizations

There were some 40 political organizations registered in Latvia in 2001; among the most influential were:

Christian Democratic Union of Latvia (CDUL) (Latvijas Kristīgi Demokrātiskā savienība): Jēkaba iela 26, Rīga 1811; tel. 732-3534; fax 783-0333; internet www.kds.lv; f. 1991; Chair. JURIS KOKINS; 600 mems.

Conservative Union 'For Fatherland and Freedom'/LNNK (Aprienība 'Tēvzemei un Brīvībai'/LNNK): Kalēju iela 10, Rīga 1050; tel. 708-7273; fax 708-7268; e-mail agulbe@saeima.lv; internet www.tb.lv; f. 1997; as a result of a merger between the Union 'For Fatherland and Freedom' and the Latvian National Independence Conservative Movement; conservative; Chair. JĀNIS STRAUME; Vice-Chair. VLADIMIRS MAKAROVS.

First Party of Latvia (LPP) (Latvijas Pirmā Partija): Rīga; f. 2002; absorbed New Christian Party in 2003; Christian, centrist; Chair. ERIKS JEKABSONS.

For Latvia's Freedom: Rīga; pro-European Union; forms part of the Centre alliance; Chair. ODISEJS KOSTANDA.

Helsinki-86: A. Čaka iela 28–19, Rīga 1011; tel. 728-0272; as human rights protection group; political status awarded in 1998.

Labour Party: f. 1996; advocates programme for the renewal and restructuring of industry; part of the Centre alliance; Chair. AIVARS KREITUSS.

Latvian Democratic Party: M. Monētu iela 3, Rīga 1050; tel. 728-7739; fax 728-8211; e-mail ldp@ldp.lv; internet www.ldp.lv; f. 1995; fmrly Democratic Party Saimnieks (the Master), name changed 1999; part of the Centre alliance; Chair. ANDRIS AMERIKS; 900 mems.

Latvian Farmers' Union (LFU) (Latvijas Zemnieku savienība): Republikas lauk. 2, Rīga 1010; tel. 702-7163; fax 702-7467; e-mail lzs@delfi.lv; internet www.lzs.lv; f. 1917; re-est. 1990; merged with Political Asscn of Economists 1996; rural, centrist; forms part of the governing Greens' and Farmers' Union; Chair. AUGUSTS BRIGMANIS; 2,850 mems.

Latvian Freedom Party: Rīga; f. 2002; social-liberal; Founder ZIEDONIS CEVERS.

Latvian Green Party (Latvijas Zaļā partija): Kalnciema iela 30, Rīga 1046; tel. 761-4272; fax 761-4927; e-mail lzp@zp.lv; internet www.zp.lv; f. 1990; environmental political party; forms part of the governing Greens' and Famers' Union; Chair. INGRIDA UDRE.

Latvian National Democratic Party (LNDP): Rīga; f. 2000; joined by the unregistered Russian National Unity Party in 2002; Leader YEVGENIY OSIPOV; 1,650 mems.

Latvian Social Democratic Welfare Party: Rīga; f. 1999; against Latvian membership of NATO; Chair. JURIS ZURAVLOVS.

Latvian Social Democratic Workers' Party (Latvijas Sociāldemokrātiskā strādnieku partija—LSDSP): Ranka dambis 1, Rīga 1048; tel. 761-4099; fax 761-4600; e-mail lsdsp@lis.lv; internet www.lsdsp.lv; f. 1999; as a result of a merger with the Latvian Social Democratic Union; Chair. DAINIS IVANS.

Latvian Socialist Party (Latvijas Sociālistiskā Partija): Burtnieku iela 23; tel. and fax 755-5535; internet www.vide.lv/lsp; f.

1994; withdrew from the For Human Rights in a United Latvia bloc in June 2003; Chair. ALFRĒDS RUBIKS.

Latvian United Republican Party: Rīga; f. 2001; Chair. AINARS STRAKIS.

Latvian Way (Latvijas ceļš): Jaunu iela 25/29, Rīga 1050; tel. 728-5539; fax 782-1121; e-mail lc@lc.lv; internet www.lc.lv; f. 1993; unites prominent political figures from Latvia and abroad; Chair. JĀNIS NAGLIS; Dep. Chair. IVĀRS GODMANIS; 900 mems.

National Harmony Party (Tautas Saskanas Partija): Elizabetes iela 23A/15, Rīga 101; tel. 750-8552; fax 728-1619; e-mail tsp@latnet .lv; internet www.tsp.lv; f. 1993; advocates the rapid integration of non-citizens into Latvian society; withdrew from the For Human Rights in a United Latvia bloc in Feb. 2003; Chair. JĀNIS JURKĀNS; Dep. Chair. JĀNIS URBANOVICS.

New Era (Jaunais laiks): Jēkaba Kazarmās, Torna iela 4–3B, Rīga 1050; tel. 720-5472; fax 720-5473; e-mail birojs@jaunaislaiks.lv; internet www.jaunaislaiks.lv; f. 2002; right-wing; Chair. EINĀRS REPŠE.

New Faction: Rīga; f. 2001 by former members of the New Party; Chair. INGRĪDA UDRE; Dep. Chair. IMANTS STIRANS.

Our Latvia (Musu Latvija): Rīga; e-mail mz@parks.lv; internet home.parks.lv/mz; f. 2001; liberal, centrist party; advocates membership of the European Union; Chair. DAINIS TURLAIS.

People's Party (Tautas partija): Dzirnavu iela 68, Rīga; tel. 728-6441; fax 728-6405; e-mail koord1@tautas.lv; internet www .tautaspartija.lv; f. 1998; Chair. ATIS SLAKTERIS; Vice-Chair. JĀNIS LAGZDINS.

Progressive Centre Party: f. 2002; supports President Viķe-Freiberga; Chair. INTA STAMGUTE.

Social Justice and Equal Rights Movement: f. 1996; against membership of the European Union and NATO, and supports the granting of citizenship to all permanent residents of Latvia; also know as the Equality Movement; member of the For Human Rights in a United Latvia alliance; Chair. TATJANA ZDANOKA; 224 mems.

Union of Social Democrats (SDS): Rīga; f. 2002; centre-left; splinter group from Latvian Social Democratic Workers' Party; Chair. EGILS BALDZĒNS; 958 mems.

Diplomatic Representation

EMBASSIES IN LATVIA

Austria: Elizabetes iela 21A, 4th Floor, Apt 11, Rīga 1010; tel. 721-6125; fax 721-4401; Ambassador Dr WOLFGANG JILLY.

Belarus: Jēzusbaznīcas iela 12, Rīga 1050; tel. 722-2560; fax 732-2891; e-mail latvia@belembassy.org; Ambassador VADIM LAMKAU.

Canada: Doma lauk. 4, Rīga 1977; tel. 722-6315; fax 783-0140; e-mail riga@dfait-maeci.gc.ca; internet www.dfait-maeci.gc.ca/dfait/ missions/baltics; Ambassador ROBERT ANDRIGO.

China, People's Republic: Ganību dambis 5, Rīga 1045; tel. 735-7023; fax 735-7025; Ambassador WANG KAIWEN.

Czech Republic: Elizabetes iela 29A, Rīga 1010; tel. 721-7814; fax 721-7821; e-mail zuczriga@parks.lv; internet www.mfa.cz/riga; Chargé d'affaires a.i. IVO LOSMAN.

Denmark: L. Pils iela 11, Rīga 1863; tel. 722-6210; fax 722-9218; e-mail rixamb@um.dk; internet www.denmark.lv; Ambassador OLE HARALD LISBORG.

Estonia: Skolas iela 13, Rīga 1010; tel. 781-2020; fax 781-2029; e-mail embassy.riga@mfa.ee; Ambassador TOOMAS LUKK.

Finland: Kalpaka bulv. 1, Rīga 1605; tel. 707-8800; fax 707-8814; e-mail sanomat.rii@formin.fi; internet www.finland.lv; Ambassador KIRSTI ESKELINEN-LIUKKONEN.

France: Raiņa bulv. 9, Rīga 1050; tel. 703-6600; fax 703-6615; e-mail webmastre.ambafrance-lv@diplomatie.gouv.fr; internet www .ambafrance-lv.org; Ambassador MICHEL FOUCHER.

Germany: Raiņa blvd 13, Rīga 1050; POB 183, 1047 Rīga; tel. 722-9096; fax 782-0223; e-mail mailbox@deutschebotschaft-riga.lv; internet www.deutschebotschaft-riga.lv; Ambassador ECKHART HEROLD.

Israel: Elizabetes iela 2, 3rd Floor, Rīga 1340; tel. 732-0739; fax 783-0170; e-mail press@rig.mfa.gov.il; Ambassador AVRAHAM BENJAMIN.

Italy: Teātra iela 9, 3rd/4th Floors, Rīga 1050; tel. 721-6069; fax 721-6084; e-mail ambitalia.riga@apollo.lv; internet www.ambitalia .apollo.lv; Ambassador MAURIZIO LO RE.

Japan: Kr. Valdemara iela 21, Rīga 1010; tel. 781-2001; fax 781-2004; Chargés d'affaires a.i. TORU NAGATSUKA, HIROSHI OKADA.

Lithuania: Rupniecibas iela 24, Rīga 1010; tel. 732-1519; fax 732-1589; e-mail lt@apollo.lv; Ambassador PETRAS VAITIEKŪNAS.

Netherlands: Torņu iela 4, Jēkaba Kazarmas 1A, Rīga 1050; tel. 732-6147; fax 732-6151; e-mail nlgovrig@mailbox.riga.lv; internet www.netherlandsembassy.lv; Ambassador NICOLAAS BEETS.

Norway: Zirgu iela 14, POB 1173, Rīga 1050; tel. 781-4100; fax 781-4108; e-mail emb.riga@mfa.no; Ambassador JAN WESSEL HEG.

Poland: Mednieku iela 6B, Rīga 1010; tel. 703-1500; fax 703-1549; e-mail ambpol@apollo.lv; Ambassador TADEUSZ FISZBACH.

Russia: Antonijas iela 2, Rīga 1010; tel. 733-2151; fax 783-0209; e-mail rusembas@junik.lv; internet www.latvia.mid.ru; Ambassador IGOR STUDENNIKOV.

Slovakia: Smilšu iela 8, Rīga 1050; tel. 781-4280; fax 781-4290; e-mail embassy@slovakia.lv; Ambassador JOSEF DRAVECKÝ.

Sweden: A. Pumpura iela 8, Rīga 1010; tel. 733-8770; fax 782-8031; e-mail ambassaden.riga@foreign.ministry.se; internet www .swedenemb.lv; Ambassador TOMAS BERTELMAN.

Switzerland: Elizabetes iela 2, 3rd Floor, Rīga 1340; tel. 733-8351; fax 733-8354; e-mail vertretung@rig.rep.admin.ch; internet www .eda.admin.ch/riga; Ambassador WILLY HOLD.

Ukraine: Kalpaka bulv. 3, Rīga 1010; tel. 724-3082; fax 732-5583; e-mail uaemb@neonet.lv; Ambassador VIKTOR MYKHAYLOVSKIY.

United Kingdom: J. Alunāna iela 5, Rīga 1010; tel. 777-4700; fax 777-4707; e-mail british.embassy@apollo.lv; internet www.britain .lv; Ambassador ANDREW TESORIERE.

USA: Raiņa bulv. 7, Rīga 1510; tel. 703-6200; fax 782-0047; e-mail pas@usembassy.lv; internet www.usembassy.lv; Ambassador BRIAN E. CARLSON.

Uzbekistan: Elizabetes iela 11, 2nd Floor, Rīga 1010; tel. 732-2424; fax 732-2306; e-mail posoluz@apollo.lv; Ambassador KOBILJON S. NAZAROV.

Judicial System

Constitutional Court

J. Alunāna iela 1, Rīga 1010; tel. 722-1412; fax 722-0572; e-mail aivars.e@satv.tiesa.gov.lv; internet www.satv.tiesa.gov.lv.

f. 1996 to rule on constitutionality of legislation; comprises seven judges, appointed by the Saeima for a term of 10 years.

Chairman: AIVARS ENDZIŅŠ.

Deputy Chairman: ROMĀNS APSĪTIS.

Supreme Court: Brīvības bulv. 36, Rīga 1050; tel. 702-0350; fax 702-0351.

Chairman: ANDRIS GUĻĀNS.

Office of the Prosecutor-General: Kalpaka bulv. 6, Rīga 1801; tel. 704-4400; fax 704-4449; e-mail gen@lrp.gov.lv; **Prosecutor-General:** JĀNIS MAIZITIS.

Religion

From the 16th century the traditional religion of the Latvians was Lutheran Christian. Russian Orthodoxy was the religion of most of the Slav immigrants. After 1940, when Latvia was annexed by the USSR, many places of religious worship were closed and clergymen were imprisoned or exiled. In the late 1980s there was some improvement in the official attitude to religious affairs. Following the restoration of independence in 1991, religious organizations regained their legal rights, as well as property that had been confiscated during the Soviet occupation. Since 1988 many new religious organizations have been officially registered in Latvia, and at 1 July 2000 the statutes of 1,095 religious organizations were registered. The total number of congregations was 1,072, of which 308 were Lutheran, 250 Roman Catholic, 118 Pentecostal, 117 Orthodox, 85 Baptists, 66 Old Believers (Orthodox), 45 Adventist, 11 Methodist, seven Hebrew and six Muslim.

Association for Freedom of Religion (AFFOR): Ganībudambis 3–2, Rīga 1045; e-mail ringolds.balodis@apollo.lv; f. 1999 to protect religious freedom in Latvia; Vice-Pres. SINTIJA BALODE.

Board of Religious Affairs: Pils lauk. 4, Rīga 1050; tel. 722-0585; e-mail ringolds.balodis@apollo.lv; f. 2000; govt agency, attached to the Ministry of Justice; Principal Dr RINGOLDS BALODIS.

CHRISTIANITY

Protestant Churches

Consistory of the Evangelical Lutheran Church of Latvia: M. Pils iela 4, Rīga 1050; tel. 722-6057; fax 782-0041; e-mail konsistorija@parks.lv; internet www.lutheran.lv; f. 1922; Archbishop Jānis Vanags.

Latvian Conference of Seventh-day Adventists in Latvia: Baznīcas iela 12A, Rīga 1010; tel. and fax 724-0013; e-mail viesturs@baznica.lv; internet www.adventistu.baznica.lv; f. 1920; Pres. of Council Viesturs Reķis.

Union of Baptist Churches in Latvia: Lāčplēša iela 37, Rīga 1011; tel. 722-3379; fax 722-2651; e-mail ildzjur@latnet.lv; f. 1860; Bishop Andrejs Šterns; Gen. Sec. Ilmārs Hiršs.

Union of Latvian Pentecostal Congregations: Laimas iela 14, Jelgava 3000; tel. 302-5011; f. 1989; Bishop Jānis Ozolinkevičs.

United Methodist Church in Latvia: Klaipēdas iela 56, Liepāja 3401; tel. 343-2161; fax 346-9848; re-est. 1991; Supt Ārijs Vīksna.

The Roman Catholic Church

Latvia comprises one archdiocese and three dioceses. At 31 December 2001 there were an estimated 415,271 adherents in the country (equivalent to an estimated 17% of the population).

Bishops' Conference
(Conferentia Episcopalis Lettoniae)

M. Pils iela 2A, Rīga 1050; tel. 722-7266; fax 722-0775.

Pres. Cardinal Jānis Pujats.

Archbishop of Rīga: Cardinal Jānis Pujats, Metropolijas Kurija, M. Pils iela 2A, Rīga 1050; tel. 722-7266; fax 722-0775; internet www.catholic.lv.

The Orthodox Church

Although the Orthodox Church of Latvia has close ties with the Moscow Patriarchate, it has administrative independence. The spiritual head of the Orthodox Church is elected by its Saeima (or assembly).

Synod of the Orthodox Church of Latvia: M. Pils iela 14, Rīga 1050; tel. 722-4345; f. 1850; mems are mostly ethnic Slavs; Bishop Aleksandrs Kudrjašov.

Latvian Old Believer Pomor Church: Krasta iela 73, Rīga 1003; tel. 711-3083; fax 714-4513; e-mail oldbel@junik.lv; f. 1760; Head of Central Council Ivans Mizoļubovs (Fr Ioann).

JUDAISM

Hebrew Religious Community of Rīga: Peitavas iela 6/8, Rīga 1050; tel. 722-4549; f. 1764; Rabbi Natan Barkan.

OTHER RELIGIOUS GROUPS

Dievturu sadraudze: Rīga; community celebrating the ancient Latvian animist religion; Leader Jānis Siliņš.

International Society for Krishna Consciousness: K. Barona iela 56, Rīga 1011; tel. 227-2490; e-mail padasevanam@mail.delfi.lv; internet www.gauranga.lv; Co-ordinator Harijis Sauss.

The Press

The joint-stock company Preses nams (Press House—q.v.) is the leading publisher of newspapers and magazines in Latvia. In 2002 there were eight daily newspapers, with an average circulation of 183,000. In addition, 211 non-daily newspapers and 365 other periodicals were published in Latvia.

The publications listed below are in Latvian, unless otherwise indicated.

DAILIES

Diena (Day): Mūkusalas iela 41, Rīga 1004; tel. 706-3100; fax 706-3190; e-mail diena@diena.lv; internet www.diena.lv; f. 1990; Latvian; social and political issues; Editor-in-Chief Sarmīte Ēlerte; circ. 62,000.

Neatkarīgā Rita Avize (Independent Morning Paper): Balasta dambis 3, Rīga 1081; tel. 706-2462; fax 706-2465; e-mail redakcija@nra.lv; internet www.nra.lv; f. 1990; Editor-in-Chief Aldis Bērziņš; circ. 40,000.

Rīgas Balss (Voice of Rīga): Balasta dambis 3, Rīga 1081; tel. 706-4420; fax 706-2400; e-mail lita@rb.lv; f. 1957; city evening newspaper; Latvian and Russian; Editor-in-Chief Anita Daukste; circ. 56,800 (Mon.–Thurs.), 69,570 (Fri.).

Sports: Balasta dambis 3, Rīga 1081; tel. 246-4117; fax 786-0000; f. 1955; Editor Dace Millere; circ. 7,800.

Vakara Ziņas (Evening News): Rīga; tel. 261-7595; fax 261-2383; f. 1993; Editor-in-Chief Ainis Saulītis; circ. 53,000.

WEEKLIES

The Baltic Times: Skunu iela 16, Rīga 1050; tel. 722-4073; fax 722-6041; e-mail editorial@baltictimes.com; internet www.baltictimes.com; f. 1996; news from Estonia, Latvia and Lithuania; English; Man. Dir Raisa Roldugina; Editor-in-Chief Ilze Arklina; circ. 12,000.

Dienas Bizness (Daily Business): a/k 2, Balasta dambis 3, POB 2, Rīga 1081; tel. 706-2622; fax 706-2309; e-mail nberch@db.lv; internet www.db.lv; f. 1992; Editor-in-Chief Juris Paiders; circ. 17,000.

Ieva: Balasta dambis 3, Rīga 1081; tel. 246-3667; fax 246-1438; e-mail santa@santa.lv; f. 1997; weekly; illustrated journal for women; Latvian; Editor-in-Chief Inga Gorbunova; circ. 76,000.

Izglītība un Kultūra (Education and Culture): Torna iela 11, Rīga 1050; tel. 722-8013; fax 722-5632; f. 1948; Editor Andra Mangale; circ. 6,000.

Latvijas Vēstnesis (Latvian Herald): Brūninieku iela 36-2, Rīga 1001; tel. 229-8833; fax 229-9410; e-mail editor@mail.lv-laiks.lv; internet www.lv-laiks.lv; f. 1993; official newspaper of the Republic of Latvia; Editor-in-Chief Oskars Gerts; circ. 5,200.

Lauku Avīze (Country Newspaper): Dzirnavu iela 21, Rīga 1010; tel. 709-6600; fax 709-6645; e-mail redakcija@laukuavize.lv; f. 1988; three a week; popular agriculture, politics and sport; Editor-in-Chief Viesturs Serdāns; circ. 75,000.

PRINCIPAL PERIODICALS

Daugava: Balasta dambis 3, Rīga 1081; tel. 728-0290; e-mail ravdin@mailbox.riga.lv; f. 1977; 6 a year; literary journal; Latvian; Editor-in-Chief Zhanna Ezit; circ. 500.

Karogs (Banner): Kurša iela 24, Rīga 1006; tel. 755-4145; f. 1940; literary monthly; Editor-in-Chief Māra Zālīte; circ. 2,000.

Klubs: Balasta dambis 3, Rīga 1081; tel. 246-5534; fax 246-5450; e-mail santa@parks.lv; internet www.klubs.lv; f. 1994; monthly; illustrated journal for men; Latvian; Editor-in-Chief Ainārs Ērglis; circ. 20,000.

Liesma (Flame): Balasta dambis 3, Rīga 1081; tel. 246-6480; f. 1958; monthly; for young people; Editor-in-Chief Dainis Caune; circ. 20,000.

Mans Mazais: Balasta dambis 3, Rīga 1081; tel. 762-8274; fax 246-5450; e-mail mansmazais@santa.lv; f. 1994; monthly; illustrated journal for young parents; Latvian; Editor-in-Chief Vita Beļauniece; circ. 20,000.

Mūsmājas (Our Home): Meža iela 4, Rīga 1048; tel. 761-5812; fax 786-0002; e-mail dadzis@latnet.lv; f. 1993; monthly; illustrated magazine for housewives; Latvian; Editor-in-Chief Ilze Strautiņa; circ. 50,000.

Rīgas Laiks (Rīga Times): Lāčplēša iela 25, Rīga 1011; tel. 728-7922; fax 783-0542; e-mail pasts@rigaslaiks.lv; internet www.rigaslaiks.lv; f. 1993; monthly; Editor-in-Chief Inese Zandere; circ 10,000.

Santa: Balasta dambis 3, POB 32, Rīga 1081; tel. 762-8274; fax 246-5450; e-mail santa@santa.lv; f. 1991; monthly; illustrated journal for women; Latvian; Editor-in-Chief Santa Ancha; circ. 42,000.

NEWS AGENCIES

Baltic News Service: Baznīcas iela 8, Rīga 1010; tel. 708-8600; fax 708-8601; e-mail bns@rb.bns.lv; internet bnsnews.bns.lv; f. 1990; news from Latvia, Lithuania, Estonia and the CIS; in English, Russian and the Baltic languages; Dir Liga Mengelsona.

LETA (Latvian News Agency): Palasta iela 10, Rīga 1502; tel. 722-2509; fax 722-3850; e-mail leta.marketing@leta.lv; internet www.leta.lv; f. 1919; independent news agency; Chair. Mārtiņš Barkāns.

Foreign Bureau

Reuters (United Kingdom): Kaļķu iela 15, Rīga 1050; tel. 722-2079; fax 724-3139; e-mail reuters@reuters.lv; Bureau Chief Alan Crosby.

PRESS ASSOCIATIONS

Latvian Journalists' Union (Latvijas Žurnālistu savienība): Marstaļu iela 2, Rīga 1050; tel. 721-1433; fax 782-0233; f. 1992; 700 mems; Pres. Ligita Azovska.

Directory

Publishers

Avots (Spring): Aspazijas bulv. 24, Rīga 1050; tel. 721-1394; fax 722-5824; f. 1980; fiction, dictionaries, crafts, hobbies, art, agriculture, law, reference books, etc.; Pres. JĀNIS LEJA.

Elpa (Breath): Doma lauk. 1, Rīga 1914; tel. 721-1776; fax 750-3326; f. 1990; books and newspapers; Pres. MAIRITA SOLIMA.

Jumava: Dzirnavu iela 73, Rīga 1011; tel. and fax 728-0314; e-mail jumava@parks.lv; internet www.jumava.lv; f. 1994; translations, dictionaries, fiction, etc.; Pres. JURIS VISOCKIS.

Kontinents: Elijas iela 17, Rīga 1050; tel. 720-4130; fax 720-4133; e-mail kontinent@parks.lv; internet www.kontinent.lv; f. 1991.

Latvijas Enciklopēdija (Latvian Encyclopaedia Publishers): Rīga; tel. 722-0150; fax 782-0113; f. 1963; encyclopaedias, dictionaries, reference books; Dir VIKTORS TĒRAUDS.

Nordik: Daugavgrīvas 36–9, Rīga 1007; tel. 760-2672; fax 760-2818; e-mail nordik@nordik.lv; internet www.nordik.lv; sister co, Tapals, at same address; Dir JĀNIS JUŠKA.

Preses nams (Press House): Balasta dambis 3, Rīga 1081; tel. 246-5732; internet www.presesnams.lv; f. 1990; printing, publishing and property management; publishes five newspapers, magazines, encyclopaedias, scientific and field literature; controlling interest owned by Ventspils Nafta (q.v.); Dir EGONS LAPIŅŠ.

Jāņa sēta: Elizabetes iela 83–85, Rīga 1050; tel. 709-2290; fax 709-2292; e-mail janaseta@janaseta.lv; internet www.janaseta.lv; f. 1991; the Jāņa sēta cartographers became a separate co in 1999; travel and culinary books; Dir AIVARS ZVIRBULIS.

Smaile (Peak): Brīvības iela 104, Rīga 1001; tel. 731-5137; f. 1999; fiction, poetry, fine arts; Dir ANDREJS BRIMERBERGS.

Sprīdītis: Kalēju iela 51, Rīga 1050; tel. 728-6516; fax 728-6818; f. 1989; books for children and young people; Dir ANDREJS RIJNIEKS.

Zinātne (Science): Akadēmijas lauk. 1, Rīga 1050; tel. 721-2797; fax 722-7825; e-mail zinatne@navigator.lv; f. 1951; non-fiction, text books, dictionaries, reference books; Dir IEVA JANSONE.

ZVAIGZNE ABC Ltd (Star): K. Valdemāra iela 6, Rīga 1010; tel. 732-4518; fax 750-8798; e-mail info@zvaigzne.lv; internet www.zvaigzne.lv; f. 1966; privately owned since 1993; educational literature, manuals, dictionaries, non-fiction for children and adults, fiction; Pres. VIJA KILBLOKA; 173 employees.

PUBLISHERS' ASSOCIATIONS

Latvian Publishers' Association (Latvijas Grāmatizdevēju asociācija): K. Barona iela 36–4, Rīga 1011; tel. 728-2392; fax 728-0549; e-mail lga@gramatizdeveji.lv; internet www.gramatizdeveji.delfi.lv; f. 1993; 47 mems; Pres. ANITA ROŽKALNE.

Latvian Press Publishers' Association: Balasta dambis 3, Rīga 1081; tel. and fax 732-2489; e-mail epia@age.lv; f. 1993; 33 mems; Pres. AIVARS RUDZINSKIS.

WRITERS' UNION

Latvian Writers' Union (Latvijas Rakstnieku savienība): Kuršu iela 24, Rīga 1426; tel. 755-5180; fax 755-4034; 291 mems; Chair. VALDIS RŪMNIEKS.

Broadcasting and Communications

TELECOMMUNICATIONS

In 2002 there were 701,000 main telephone lines in use; 52% of lines were digital in 2000. The Government was preparing legislation to abolish SIA Lattelekom's monopoly by 2002.

Regulatory Organizations

Department of Communications (Ministry of Transport): Gogoļa iela 3, Rīga 1190; tel. 724-2321; fax 782-0636; e-mail diana.ainep@sam.gov.lv; f. 1991; Dir INĀRA RUDAKA.

Telecommunications Tariff Council: Meistaru iela 10, Rīga 1050; tel. 721-3109; fax 782-0519; Chair. RAIMONDS JONITIS.

Major Service Providers

Latvian Mobile Telephone (Latvijas Mobilais telefons): Unijas iela 39, POB 116, Rīga 1039; tel. 777-3200; fax 753-5353; e-mail inform@lmt.lv; internet www.lmt.lv; f. 1992; partly owned by Telia (Sweden) and Sonera (Finland); Gen. Man. JURIS BINDE; 150 employees.

Radiokom: Elizabetes iela 45–47, Rīga 1010; Dir JANA BALODE.

SIA Lattelekom: Vaļņu iela 30, Rīga 1050; tel. 705-5222; fax 705-5001; e-mail gstrautma@exchange.telekom.lv; internet www.cwcee.co.uk; f. 1992; partially privatized; 44% owned by Sonera; Pres. GUNDARS STRAUTMANIS; 6,500 employees.

Tele2: Kurzemes pr. 3, Rīga 1067; tel. 706-0069; fax 706-0176; internet www.tele2.lv; f. 1991; owned by Tele2 AB (Sweden); name changed from Baltkom GSM in 2001; Pres. BILL BUTLER; 110 employees.

Telecommunication Association of Latvia: Rm 702, Academic lauk. 1, Rīga 1050; tel. 722-6962; e-mail kaiva@mail.lv; Pres. PĒTERIS ŠMIDRE.

BROADCASTING

Amendments to the broadcasting law approved in October 1998 required greater use of the Latvian language in all programmes. Foreign programmes were restricted to 25% of daily broadcast time.

Regulatory Organization

National Broadcasting Council of Latvia: Smilšu iela 1–3, Rīga 1939; tel. 722-1848; fax 722-0448; e-mail tvcounc@mailbox.riga.lv; internet www.nrtp.lv; f. 1992; defends social interests and maintains free accessibility to information; Chair. OJĀRS RUBENIS.

Radio

Latvijas Radio (Latvian Radio): Doma lauk. 8, Rīga 1505; tel. 720-6722; fax 720-6709; internet www.radio.org.lv; f. 1925; state-operated service; broadcasts in Latvian, Russian and English; Dir-Gen. DZINTRIS KOLĀTS.

Alise Plus: Raiņa iela 28, Daugavpils 5403; e-mail alise_plus@daugavpils.apollo.lv; 24-hour transmissions in Russian and Latvian.

European Hit Radio: Elijas iela 17, Rīga 1050; tel. 957-5757; fax 720-4407; e-mail radio@superfm.lv; internet www.europeanhitradio.com; f. 1994; 24-hour transmissions in Latvian, Russian, Estonian, Lithuanian and English; Pres. UGIS POLIS; Dir RICHARD ZAKSS.

Latvijas Kristīgais Radio: Lāčplēša iela 37, Rīga 1011; tel. 721-3704; fax 782-0633; e-mail lkz@am.lv; 24-hour transmissions in Latvian and Russian.

Radio Ef-Ei: Atbrīvošanas aleja 98, Rēzekne 4600; e-mail efei@mailbox.riga.lv; 24-hour transmissions in Russian and Latvian.

Radio Imanta: Tērbatas iela 1, Valmiera 4201; tel. 422-4070; fax 423-1200; e-mail radio@valmiera.lanet.lv; 24-hour transmissions in Russian and Latvian; Chief Editor ANDRIS STRAUME.

Radio Mazsalaca: Avotu iela 13, Mazsalaca 4215; 15 hours daily in Latvian.

Radio Merkūrijs: Bērzpils iela 2A, Balvi 4501; e-mail merkurijs@ridzene.lv; 24-hour transmissions in Latvian and Russian.

Radio Mix FM: L. Nometņu iela 62, Rīga 1002; 24-hour transmissions in Russian.

Radio Rīgai: Televīzijas centrs, Zaķusalas krastmala 3, Rīga 1509; 24-hour transmissions in Latvian.

Radio Saules Iela: Saules iela 8A, Cēsis 4100; 24-hour transmissions in Latvian.

Radio Sigulda: L. Paegles iela 3, Sigulda 2150; 24-hour transmissions in Latvian.

Radio SWH: Skanstes iela 13, Rīga 1013; internet www.radio.swh.lv.

Radio Trīs: Vaļņu iela 5, Cēsis 4101; tel. 412-4566; fax 412-7041; e-mail radio@radio3.lv; internet www.radio3.lv; f. 1994; 24-hour transmissions in Latvian; Dir EGILS VISKRINTS.

Radio Zemgale: Grāfa laukums 6, Lecava 3913; e-mail rz@apollo.lv; internet www.radiozemgalei.lv; f. 2000; 24 hours daily in Latvian; Dir DACE DUBKEVIČA.

Television

Latvijas Televīzija (Latvian Television): Zaķusalas krastmala 3, Rīga 1509; tel. 720-0314; fax 720-0025; e-mail ltv@ltv.lv; internet www.ltv.lv; f. 1954; state-operated service; two channels in Latvian (Channel II also includes programmes in Russian, Polish, Ukrainian, German, English and French); Dir ULDIS GRAVA.

LNT (Latvian Independent Television): Elijas iela 17, Rīga 1050; tel. 707-0200; fax 782-1128; e-mail lnt@lnt.lv; internet www.lnt.lv; f. 1996; entertainment programming, news reports; Dir-Gen. ANDREJS ĒĶIS.

Finance

(cap. = capital; res = reserves; dep. = deposits; m. = million; brs = branches; amounts in LVL)

BANKING

Following the restoration of independence in 1991, the country's central bank, the Bank of Latvia (originally founded in 1922), was re-established, and commercial banks began to proliferate. By late 1993, owing to the country's liberal regulatory system, there were 63 commercial banks operating in Latvia. In the following year the Government began to reorganize the sector, revoking the licences of 11 of the smaller and weaker banks, and declaring a further six insolvent. However, such measures were not sufficient to prevent a crisis in the banking sector in 1995, and further closures, including that of the country's largest commercial bank, Banka Baltija, ensued. The crisis was contained by early 1996. At the end of 2002 there were 22 banks in operation.

Central Bank

Bank of Latvia (Latvijas Banka): K. Valdemāra iela 2A, Rīga 1050; tel. 702-2300; fax 702-2420; e-mail info@bank.lv; internet www.bank.lv; f. 1922; cap. 10.1m., res 64.8m., dep. 211.8m. (Dec. 2001); Gov. and Chair. of Bd ILMĀRS RIMŠĒVIČS.

Commercial Banks

Aizkraukles Banka: Elizabetes iela 23, Rīga 1010; tel. 777-5555; e-mail bank@ab.lv; internet www.ab.lv; f. 1993; cap. 51,541.0 (1997); Chair. of Bd ALEKSANDRS BERGMANIS.

A/S Vereinsbank Rīga: Elizabetes iela 63, Rīga 1050; tel. 708-5500; fax 708-5507; e-mail info@vereinsbank.lv; internet www.vereinsbank.lv; f. 1997; 100% owned by Vereins- und Westbank AG (Germany); cap. 13.9m., res. –0.4m., dep. 68.0m. (Dec. 2001); Pres. THOMAS SCHÜTZE.

Baltic Transit Bank (Baltijas Tranzītu Banka): 13. Janvāra iela 3, Rīga 1050; tel. 702-4747; fax 721-1985; e-mail btb@btb.lv; internet www.btb.lv; f. 1992; joint-stock commercial bank; merged with Rīgas Naftas un Kimijas Banka in 1999; cap. 8.6m., res –1.0m., dep. 101.0m. (Dec. 2001); Pres. and Chair. of Bd EDGARS DUBRA; 30 brs.

Business Bank of Latvia (Latvijas Biznesa Banka): 3 Antonijas iela, Rīga 1010; tel. 777–5800; fax 777–5849; e-mail pstbox@lbb.lv; internet www.lbb.lv; f. 1992; 99.72% owned by Moscow Municipal Bank—Bank of Moscow (Russian Federation); cap. 3.0m., res 0.1m., dep 5.1m. (Dec. 2001); Chair. and Pres. GEORGIJS DRAGILEVS.

Credit Bank of Latvia (Latvijas Kredītbanka): Antonilas iela 7, Rīga 1920; tel. 722-6631; fax 782-1094; f. 1992; cap. 3.5m.; Pres. JĀNIS SILPINS; 3 brs.

Economic Commercial Bank of Latvia—Lateko (Latvijas Ekonomiskā Komercbanka): E. Birznieka-Upiša iela 21, Rīga 1011; tel. 704-1100; fax 704-1111; e-mail latbk@lateko.lv; internet www.lateko.lv; f. 1992; cap 5.0m., res 0.0m., dep. 104.0m. (Dec. 2001); Pres. OSKARS GULĀNS.

Hansabanka: Kaļķu iela 26, Rīga 1050; tel. 702-4444; fax 702-4400; e-mail info@hansabanka.lv; internet www.hansabanka.lv; f. 1992; present name since 1999; merged with Latvijas Zemes banka 1999; merged with Ventspils ABB 2000; cap. 40.0m., res 2.3m., dep. 459.9m. (Dec. 2001); Chair. of Bd INGRIDA BLUMA.

Industrial Bank of Latvia (Latvijas Industriālā banka—Lainbanka): Rīga; tel. 721-6529; fax 722-1135; f. 1991; cap. 9,905.5 (1997); Pres. VILIS DAMBIŅŠ.

Land Bank of Latvia (Latvijas Zemes banka): Republic lauk. 2, Rīga 1924; tel. 702-9883; fax 721-1995; e-mail lzbint@mail.bkc.lv; f. 1989; cap. 6.0m., res 0.2m., dep. 36.5m. (Dec. 1997); Chair. of Bd and Chief Exec. ANDRIS RUSELIS; 16 brs.

JSC Latvian Trade Bank (Latvijas Tirdzniecibas Banka): Trijadibas iela 4, Rīga 1048; tel. 761-1818; fax 786-0077; e-mail ltb@ltblv.com; internet www.ltblv.com; f. 1991; 99.4% owned by Latvian Investment Gp ApS (Denmark); cap. 3.0m., res 0.0m., dep. 85.6m. (Dec. 2001); Pres. and Chair. ARMANDS SHTEINBERGS; Vice-Chair. DZINTARS PELCBERGS.

Māras banka: Lāčplēša iela, Rīga 1011; tel. 728–6661; fax 728–2788; e-mail info@marasbanka.lv; internet www.marasbanka.lv; f. 1997; privately owned; mortgage banking; cap. 3.5m., res 0.9m., dep. 12.4m. (Dec. 2001); Chair. of Exec. Bd and Pres. NIKOLAJS SIGURDS BULMANIS; Dir-Gen. JNGA GULBE.

Merita Nordbanken Latvia: Kaļķu iela 15, Rīga 1050; tel. 709-6200; fax 782-0325; e-mail mnb@meritanordbanken.lv; internet www.meritanordbanken.lv; f. 1992; cap. 5.3m., res. 0.7m., dep. 30.3m. (Dec. 1998); Pres. and Chief Exec. AIVARS JURCĀNS.

Mortgage and Land Bank of Latvia (Latvijas Hipoteku un Zemes Banka): Doma lauk. 4, Rīga 1977; tel. 722-2945; fax 782-0143; e-mail banka@hipo.lv; internet www.hipo.lv; f. 1993; cap. 7.7m., res 1.5m., dep. 92.8m. (Dec. 2001); Pres. and Chair. of Bd INESIS FEIFERIS; 32 brs.

Multibanka: Elizabetes iela 57, Rīga 1772; tel. 728-9546; fax 782-8232; e-mail info@multibanka.com; internet www.multibanka.lv; f. 1994; cap. 4.3m., res –0.1m., dep. 69.2m. (Dec. 2001); Pres., Chair. and Chief Exec. SVETLANA DZENE.

Ogre Commercial Bank (Ogres Komercbank): 36 Brīvības iela, Ogre 5001; f. 1993; cap. 3.3m., res 0.1m., dep. 102.2m. (Dec. 2001); Pres. and Chair. VOLDEMARS EIHE.

Parex Bank (Parekss Banka): Smilšu iela 3, Rīga 1522; tel. 701-0000; fax 701-0001; e-mail inquiry@parex.lv; internet www.parex.lv; f. 1992; 50.93% owned by Europe Holding Ltd; cap. 30.0m., res – 0.2m., dep. 592.5m. (Dec. 2001); Pres. VALERY KARGIN; Chair. VICTOR KRASOVITSKY; 5 brs.

Pirmā Banka JSC (First Bank): Smilšu iela 6, Rīga 1803; tel. 701-5204; fax 732-3449; e-mail office@pirmabanka.lv; internet www.pirmabanka.lv; f. 1989; fmrly Rīgas Komercbanka PLC; operations suspended in March 1999; re-opened as Pirmā Latvijas Komercbanka in Oct. 1999; name changed as above in June 2001; 98.8% owned by Norddeutsche Landesbank Girozentrale (Germany); cap. 20.2m., res 1.4m., dep. 70.7m. (Dec. 2001); Pres. and Chair. of Bd JÜRGEN MACHALETT; 10 brs.

Rietmu Bank: Brīvības iela 54, Rīga 1011; tel. 702-5555; fax 702-5588; e-mail info@rietumu.lv; internet www.rietumu.lv; f. 1992; cap. 17.4m., res 0.02m., dep. 96.6m. (Dec. 1999); merged with Saules Banka in July 2001; Pres. and Chief Exec. MICHAEL J. BOURKE.

Trust Commercial Bank (Trasta komercbanka): Miesnieku iela 9, Rīga 1050; tel. 702-7777; fax 702-7700; e-mail info@tkb.lv; internet www.tkb.lv; f. 1989; present name adopted 1996; cap. 3.6m., res – 0.4m., dep. 15,3m. (Dec. 2001); Pres. GUNDARS GRIEZE.

Unibank (Latvijas Unibanka): L. Pils iela 23, Rīga 1050; tel. 721-2808; fax 721-5335; e-mail public.relations@unibanka.lv; internet www.unibanka.lv; f. 1993; 98.2% of shares acquired by Skandinaviska Enskilda Banken (Sweden) in Nov. 2000; cap. and res 56.3m., dep. 332.3m. (May 2002); 68 brs.

Savings Bank

JSC Latvian Savings Bank (Latvijas Krājbanka): Palasta iela 1, Rīga 1954; tel. 709-2001; fax 721-2083; e-mail info@lkb.lv; internet www.krajbanka.lv; f. 1924 as Post Office Savings Bank, name changed as above 1998; 32.1% state-owned; cap. and res 10.0m., dep. 147.7m. (June 2002); Pres. and Chair. of Bd ZIGURDS JEROMANOVS; 14 brs.

Regulatory Authority

Financial and Capital Markets Commission: Kungu iela 1, Rīga 1050; tel. 702-2267; fax 702-2117; e-mail fk@fk.lv; internet www.fk.lv; f. 2000; Chair. ULDIS CERPS.

Banking Association

Association of Latvian Commercial Banks: Pērses iela 9–11, Rīga 1011; tel. 728-4528; fax 782-8170; e-mail bankas@latnet.lv; f. 1992; 21 mems; Pres. TEODORS TVERIJONS.

INSURANCE

At the end of 1999 there were 27 insurance companies in Latvia.

Balta Insurance Company Ltd: Vaļņu iela 1, Rīga 1050; tel. 722-9660; fax 782-1014; e-mail balta@balta.lv; automobile, property, freight, travel, agricultural insurance; Pres. ANDRIS LAIZĀNS.

Balva: K. Valdemāra iela 36, Rīga 1010; tel. 750-6955; fax 750-6956; e-mail balva@balva.lv; internet www.balva.lv; f. 1992; non-life insurance; Pres. VASILY RAGOZIN.

JSIC ERGO Latvija: Unijas iela 45, Rīga 1035; tel. 784-0101; fax 784-0102; e-mail info@ergo.lv; bought by Alte Leipziger (Germany) in 2000; all types of risk insurance; Pres. of Bd ILMARS VEIDE.

Estora Reinsurance Co: Elizabetes iela 14, Rīga 1010; tel. 733-3335; fax 733-3898; e-mail estora@estora.com; internet www.estora.com; f. 1992; reinsurance; Dir-Gen. JERGENIJS TOLOČKOVS.

Ezerzeme: Raiņa iela 28, Daugavpils 5403; tel. 542-2555; fax 542-2177; f. 1992; state, private firm, personal property, long- and short-term life, life, domestic animals, accident, freight, travel, funeral insurance; Chair. of Bd PĒTERIS SAVOSTJANOVS.

Helga Joint Stock Insurance Company: Elizabetes iela 20, Rīga 1050; tel. 7243-074; fax 7243-067; e-mail helga@parks.lv.

Latva: Vaļņu iela 1, Rīga 1912; tel. 721-2341; fax 721-0134; e-mail latva@latva.lv; f. 1940; state insurance co; accident, passenger, child and adult life insurance; Chair. MARGARITA PABĒRZA.

Rīga Insurance Company: Grēcinieku iela 22–24, Rīga 1050; tel. 721-1764; fax 722-3437; general liability, professional liability,

health, motor, natural disasters, fire, freight insurance; Pres. AIVARS
BERGERS.

Union Unlimited: tel. 221-3150; fax 222-5397; travel, property,
athletes', freight, state, co-operative, joint-stock, credit, medical,
accident insurance; Chair. of Bd AIVARS SALIŅŠ.

COMMODITY AND STOCK EXCHANGES

Latgale Exchange (Latgales birža): Sakņu iela 29, Daugavpils
5403; tel. 542-6044; fax 542-6351; f. 1992; Gen. Dir ANATOLII BOTUSH-
ANSKII.

Latvian Universal Exchange (Latvijas Universālā birža): Rīga;
tel. 721-2559; fax 722-4515; f. 1991; Pres. JĀNIS VALTERS.

Rīga Stock Exchange (Rīgas Fondu birža): Doma lauk. 6, Rīga
1885; tel. 721-2431; fax 722-9411; e-mail rfb@rfb.lv; internet www
.rfb.lv; f. 1993; Pres. GUNTARS KOKOREVICS.

Trade and Industry

GOVERNMENT AGENCY

Latvian Privatization Agency: K. Valdemāra iela 31, Rīga 1010;
tel. 702-1358; fax 783-0363; e-mail lpa@mail.bkc.lv; internet www
.lpa.bkc.lv; f. 1994; Dir-Gen. ARNIS OZOLNIEKS.

DEVELOPMENT ORGANIZATIONS

Interlatvija: Kalpaka bulv. 1, Rīga 1010; tel. 733-3602; f. 1987;
seeks to promote exports, imports and the establishment of joint
ventures; Dir-Gen. MĀRIS FORSTS.

Latvian Development Agency: Pērses iela 2, Rīga 1442; tel. 703-
9400; fax 703-9401; e-mail invest@lda.gov.lv; internet www.lda.gov
.lv; f. 1993; foreign investment and export promotion; Dir-Gen. MĀRIS
ELERTS.

CHAMBER OF COMMERCE

Latvian Chamber of Commerce and Industry (Latvijas Tirdz-
niecības un rūpniecības kamera): K. Valdemāra iela 35, Rīga; tel.
722-5595; fax 782-0092; e-mail info@chamber.lv; internet www
.chamber.lv; f. 1934; re-est. 1990; mem. of International Chamber of
Commerce, Baltic Chambers of Commerce Association, Euro-
chamber; Pres. VIKTORS KULBERGS; Dir-Gen. VOLDEMARS GAVARS.

INDUSTRIAL AND TRADE ASSOCIATIONS

Latvian Association of Business Consultants: Pērses iela 2–
408, Rīga 1011; tel. and fax 722-7623; e-mail lbka@lbka.lv; f. 1995;
Man. Dir DAINIS LOCANS.

Latvian Export Association (Latvijas Exksporta Asociācija): Valmieras iela 41, Rm 11, Rīga; tel. and fax 770-1213; Pres. IVAR
STRAUTINSH.

Latvian Small Business Association: Akas iela 5–7, Rīga 1010;
tel. and fax 727-9808; e-mail info@lbka.lv; f. 1996; Chair. DAINIS
LOCANS.

UTILITIES

Regulatory Authority

Energy Regulation Council: Brīvības bulv. 55, Rīga 1010; tel.
701-3291; fax 731-2763; e-mail regulators@erp.riga.lv; internet
www.erp.riga.lv; f. 1996; operated under auspices of Department of
Energy at Ministry of the Economy; Chair. J. DAUSKANS.

Electricity

Major suppliers include:

Augstsprieguma tikls: Jatnieku iela 95, Daugavpils 5410.

Austrumu Electricity: A. Pumpura iela 5, Daugavpils 5404.

Centralie elektriskie tikli: Stopinu pagasts, Lici 2118.

Dienvidu Electricity Network: Elektribas iela 10, Jelgava 3001.

Latvenergo: Pulkveža brieža 12, Rīga 1230; tel. 732-8309; e-mail
webadm@energo.lv; internet www.energo.lv; state-owned producer
and distributor; Pres. KĀRLIS MIĶELSONS; 7,127 employees.

Northern-eastern Electricity Network (LATVENERGO): Mednieku 3, Aizkraukle 5101; tel. 518-1530; fax 518-1539.

Rigas elektrotikls: Pernavas iela 19, Rīga 1012.

Vangazu elektrikis: Gaujas iela 24, Vangazi 2136; tel. and fax 299-
5535.

Vats: Talsu iela 84, Ventspils 3602.

Western Electricity Network: Rīga iela 56, Liepāja 3401; tel. 342-
3532; fax 342-3105.

Ziemelu Electricity Network: Raiņa iela 14, Valmiera 4201.

Gas

Major suppliers include:

Aga: Katrinas iela 5, Rīga 1045.

Elme L: Aplokciema iela 3, Rīga 1034.

Energija-G: Maskavas iela 85, Rīga 1003.

Gazes transports: Bikernieku iela 111, Rīga 1079.

Katlinieks: Lugazu iela 14, Rīga 1045.

Lanteks: Pernavas iela 42-3, Rīga 1009.

Latvian Gas (Latvijas gaze): A. Briana iela 6, Rīga 1001; tel. 736-
9132; fax 782-1406; e-mail latvijas_gaze@lg.lv; internet www.lg.lv;
partially privatized in 2000–01; 8% state-owned; Chair. MĀRIS
GAILIS; 2,817 employees.

Latvijas Propāna Gāze: Kurzemes prospekts 19, Rīga 1067; tel.
741-3709; fax 741-3712; e-mail lpg@lsg.lv; internet www.lsg.lv; f.
2000; purchase, sale and shipment of liquefied petroleum gas.

Remifa: Abolu iela 3, Rīga 1058.

Rīgas gaze: Vagornu iela 20, Rīga 1009.

SIIL: Pushkina iela 3, Rīga 1050.

Saullekts: Virsu iela 11, Rīga 1035.

VITEG: Bruņinieku iela 108, Rīga 1009.

Vitne: Maskavas iela 457, Rīga 1063.

Water

Major suppliers include:

Aizkraukles udens: Tornu iela 1, Aizkraukle 5101.

A/S Madonas udens: Raiņa iela 54, Madona 4801; tel. 480-7071;
fax 486-0106; e-mail udens@kvarcs.lv.

Bauskas udenssaimnieciba: Birzu iela 8a, Bauska 3901; tel. 396-
0565; fax 396-0566; e-mail baude@apollo.lv.

Buvenergo: Stabu iela 58, Rīga 1011.

Daugavpils Water (Municipal Ltd): Udensvada iela 3, Daugavpils 5403.

JS & J Udenmeistars: Ramulu iela 1, Rīga 1005.

Liepajas udens: K. Valdemāra iela 12, Liepāja 3401; tel. 541-1416;
fax 541-0769; e-mail dmeu@dpu.lv.

Rīgas udens (Rīga Water): Basteja bulv. l, k. 5, Rīga 1495; tel. 708-
8555; fax 722-2660; e-mail office@ru.lv; internet www.rw.lv; water
supply and sewage treatment.

Udens inzinieri: Gānibu dambis 26–601, Rīga 1005.

Udensvada un Kanalizacijas saimnieciba: Udensvada iela 4,
Jelgava 3001.

MAJOR COMPANIES

The privatization process commenced in 1994, but proceeded slowly.
In 1996 all enterprises were transferred to the Latvian Privatization
Agency, and 95% of former state-owned enterprises had been
divested by mid-1998.

Bolderāja AS: Guberņciema iela 7, Rīga 1016; tel. 743-0147; fax
743-0176; e-mail office@bolderaja.lv; internet www.bolderaja.lv;
manufactures hardboard and chipboard products; Pres. JURIS ČAK-
STIŅŠ; 550 employees.

Brivais Vilnis: Ostas iela 1, Salacgriva 4033; tel. 400-0210; fax 407-
1331; e-mail brivais_vilnis@am.lv; internet www.vide.lv/
brivaisvilnis; f. 1949; became a joint-stock co in 1992; produces
canned fish; provides port services; Pres. LIGONIS KRUMINŠ; Dirs
GUNTIS BERGS, GUNTI LAME; 610 employees.

Dailrade Handicrafts and Souvenir Production Association:
Čiekurkalna iela 11, 1 Gara linia, Rīga 1026; tel. 236-7625; fax 782-
8450; f. 1966; manufactures handicraft products and souvenirs;
Pres. and Chair. RAITIS REZAIS; 8,000 employees.

Dati Grupa: Skanstes iela 13, Rīga 1013; tel. 706-7777; fax 782-
1457; e-mail market@dati.lv; internet www.dati.lv; f. 1995; information and telecommunication systems; Pres. VALDIS LOKENBAHS; 500
employees.

Dauer Joint-Stock Co: Valkas iela 2, Daugavpils 5417; tel. 543-
6443; fax 543-0203; e-mail dauer@mbox.latg.lv; f. 1949; manufactures and exports electrical tools; Pres. RICHARDS GERTS; 1,100
employees.

Daugavpils Pievadkežu Rūpnica AS (Daugavpils Drive Chain
Factory): Višku iela 17, Daugavpils 5410; tel. 544-6666; fax 544-
5101; e-mail matosov@dpr.dpunet.lv; internet www.dpr.lv; f. 1949;

Joint-stock co; manufactures roll-drive chains, double-lined plate chains for motorcycles, bicycles and industrial use; Pres. GEORGIY SOROKIN; 990 employees.

Dinaz Joint-Stock Co: Jelgavas iela 2A, Daugavpils 5400; tel. 543-9536; fax 545-3336; wholesale and retail trade in petroleum products; Dir-Gen. NIKOLAJS JERMOLAJEVS.

Grindeks PAS (Grindeks Public Joint-Stock Co): Krustpils iela 53, Rīga 1057; tel. 713-9458; fax 713-8683; e-mail grindeks@grindeks.lv; internet www.grindeks.lv; f. 1991; produces, distributes and sells pharmaceutical products and diagnostic kits; Chair. and Dir-Gen. PĒTERIS STUPANS; 688 employees.

Hanzas Maiznicas AS: Mukusalas iela 51, Rīga 1004; tel. 762-7220; fax 722-7530; e-mail hmmarket@elva.org.lv; private co; produces bread, baked goods and confectionery; Dir SARMITE TIEBE; 1,000 employees.

Jelgavas Cukurfabrika: Cukura iela 22, Jelgava 3002; tel. 302-3885; fax 308-3031; e-mail info@jcf.lv; internet www.jcf.lv; f. 1926; sugar factory, food-processing; Pres. HARI VEDERIS; 515 employees.

Jelgavas Masinbuves Rupnica (Jelgava Engineering Co): Kr. Barona iela 40, Jelgava 3001; tel. 302-2994; fax 302-6214; e-mail masinbuv@apollo.lv; internet www.jmr.lv; joint-stock co; produces components for heavy machinery, shipping containers and semi-trailers; Pres. PĒTERIS BILA; 530 employees.

Juglas Manufaktura Joint-Stock Co: Markaines iela 10, Rīga 1024; tel. 752-1255; fax 752–0097; e-mail jugla@mailbox.riga.lv; f. 1993; private co; manufactures cotton yarns and raw cotton fabrics; Pres. and CEO ALEKSANDRS VAINSTEINS; 720 employees.

Jūraslīcis AS: Lašu iela 11, Jūrmala 2010; tel. 775-2340; fax 775-2815; e-mail contact@juraslicis.lv; internet www.juraslicis.lv; f. 1947; became joint-stock co in 1992; manufactures canned fish products; Chair. and Dir-Gen. ILGONIS BUMBURS; 1,500 employees.

Kaija AS: Atlantijas iela 15, Rīga 1015; tel. 702-9282; fax 702-9205; e-mail kaija@kaija.lv; internet www.kaija.lv; f. 1882; became joint-stock co in 1992; produces canned, smoked and salted fish; Pres. and Chair. IMANTS KALNIŅŠ; 772 employees.

Kolka: Caka 114, Rīga 1012; tel. 227-4481; fax 227-8129; f. 1993; joint-stock co; produces frozen, smoked and canned fish; Pres. ROKISLAVS ZUBKOVS; 500 employees.

Laima Joint-Stock Co: Sporta iela 2, Rīga 1145; tel. 733-4278; fax 708-0302; e-mail laima@laima.lv; internet www.laima.lv; f. 1870; became joint-stock co in 1993; produces cocoa, chocolate confectionery and chocolate drinks; Dir-Gen. IVARS KALVIŠĶIS; 770 employees.

Latvijas Finieris: Bauskas iela 59, Rīga 1004; tel. 762-7850; fax 782-0112; e-mail market@finieris.lv; internet www.finieris.lv; manufactures plywood, sawn timber, furniture, veneer, etc.; Dir-Gen. JURIS BIKIS; 2,000 employees.

Latvia Garment Joint-Stock Co: Zilupes iela 7, Rīga 1019; tel. 714-5034; fax 711-2208; f. 1959; became joint-stock co in 1991; manufactures clothing; Pres. PĒTERIS ŅEFEDOVS; 3,000 employees.

Lauma Joint-Stock Co: Ziemelu iela 19, Liepāja 3417; tel. 344-1091; fax 348-6214; e-mail lauma@lauma.lv; internet www.lauma.lv; f. 1971; manufactures lace and other fabrics, including medical bandages; Pres. ZIGRĪDA RUSINA; 1,200 employees.

Liepājas Metalurgs: Brīvības iela 93, Liepāja 3401; tel. 345-5959; fax 345-5947; e-mail lm@metalurgs.lv; internet www.metalurgs.lv; f. 1882; steel wire, rolled low-carbon steel bars, iron castings; Exec. Dir L. PTICHKIN; Pres. KIROVS LIPMANS; 2,600 employees.

Lokomotīve AS: Marijas iela 1, Daugavpils 5400; tel. 540-4420; fax 540-4421; f. 1998; repairs engines; undergoing privatization; Pres. EMILS BUSS; 3,000 employees.

Nelss Limited Co: Elizabetes iela 2A, Rīga 1340; tel. 732-1045; fax 783-0184; f. 1993; woodworking and export of wooden products; Chair. ANDRIS HISTORS; 600 employees.

New Rosme: Hanzas iela 18, Rīga 1045; tel. 783-0219; fax 783-0314; lingerie production; Dir ANNA ROMAŠENOKA; 600 employees.

Ogre Joint-Stock Co: Rīgas iela 98, Ogre 5001; tel. 500-3405; fax 500-3630; e-mail ogre@jsc-ogre.lv; f. 1969; became joint-stock co in 1997; produces wool yarn, knitted products and fabrics; Chair. VASILYS MELNIKS; 3,000 employees.

Olaines Kīmiski Farmaceitiskā Rūpnīca: Rūpnīcu iela 5, Rīga 2114; tel. 701-3700; fax 701-3777; e-mail olainfarm@mail.eunet.lv; internet www.olainfarm.lv; f. 1972; became joint-stock co in 1994; manufactures biologically active compounds; Chair. VALERIY MALIGIN; 600 employees.

Preses Nams: Balasta Dambis 3, Rīga 1081; tel. 246-9246; fax 246-5624; prints newspapers, journals, books, and other stationery products; Pres. KAZIMIRS DUNDURS; 550 employees.

RAF Joint Stock Co: Aviacijas iela 18, Jelgava 3001; tel. 302-0243; fax 302-9224; f. 1957; became joint-stock co in 1990; produces minibuses, ambulances and goods vehicles; Dir-Gen. NIKOLAI IVANOVICH SAMODUROV; 2,500 employees.

Rebir Joint-Stock Co: Viļkas iela 4, Rēekne 4600; tel. 463-2185; fax 463-3405; e-mail rebir@rebir.lv; f. 1971; manufactures electric tools and plastic goods; Pres. JĀNIS ZUDĀNS; 2,000 employees.

Rhodia Industrial Yarns Ltd: Višku iela 21, Daugavpils 5410; tel. 540-2112; fax 540-2120; internet www.rhodia-iy.com; f. 1991 as Dauteks Joint-Stock Co; manufactures textiles and fabric; Dir STEFAN BALLOK; 3,000 employees.

Rīgas Autoelektroaparātu Rūpnīca Joint-Stock Co (Riga Autoelectrical Plant): Klijānu iela 2/14, Rīga 1013; tel. 737-8670; fax 737-2581; e-mail rar@mail.bkc.lv; f. 1946; produces accessories and apparatus for vehicles; Dir ALFRĒDS AUZIŅŠ; 900 employees.

Rīgas Elektromašīnbūes Rūpnīca (Rīga Electrical Engineering Works): Ganību dambis 31, Rīga 1005; tel. 738-1193; fax 733-4133; f. 1946; produces electrical equipment sets, motors, generators, washing-machines and dryers; Pres. JĀNIS ČAKSTIŅŠ; 800 employees.

Rīgas Miesniks Joint-Stock Co: Atlasa iela 7, Rīga 1026; tel. 736-8643; fax 733-9180; f. 1992; produces tinned meat; Dir-Gen. ANDRIS NIKITINS; 1,100 employees.

Rīgas Piena Kombināts Joint-Stock Co: Bauskas iela 180, Rīga 1004; tel. 706-6888; fax 786-0037; e-mail rpk@avelat.lv; internet www.piens.biz.lv; f. 1991; produces dairy products, cheese, butter, ice-cream; Pres. MARĢERS RĀVA; 650 employees.

Rīgas Piensaimnieks AS: Valmieras iela 2, Rīga 1009; tel. 731-1947; fax 782-8335; e-mail rpiens@com.latnet.lv; private co; produces dairy products, cheese, butter, ice-cream; Dir-Gen. ARVIDS USCA; 500 employees.

Rīgas Siltums AS: Cesu iela 3A; Rīga 1012; tel. 701-7300; fax 701-7363; e-mail siltums@rs.lv; internet www.rs.lv; f. 1996; heating and ventilation equipment and distribution; Chair. ARIS ŽIGURS; 2,186 employees.

Rīgas Vagonu Rūpnīca (Rīga Carriage Plant): Brīvības iela 201, Rīga 1039; tel. 227-5327; fax 782-8396; e-mail root@rvr.mrk.neonet.riga.lv; f. 1895; manufactures electrical and diesel trains, rolling stock and auxiliary equipment; Pres. JĀNIS ANDERSONS; 3,000 employees.

Rojas Zivju Konservu Rūpnīca: Selgas iela 1, Roja, Talsu rajons 3264; tel. 326-9103; fax 326-9834; manufactures tinned and frozen fish, provides harbour services; Chair. IVARS AMOLIŅŠ; 575 employees.

Tolaram Fibres: Višku iela 21, Daugavpils 5410; tel. 542-3197; fax 544-1061; f. 1991; frmly Dauteks; bought by French company Rhodia in May 2000; textiles production; 4,000 employees.

Tramvaju Trolejbusu Parvalde (Tram and Trolleybus Transport Co): Brīvības iela 191, Rīga 1012; tel. 737-8392; fax 754-1748; e-mail ttp@mail.junik.lv; f. 1882; Chief Exec. ALEXANDRS ZALITIS; 3,890 employees.

Valmieras Stikla Šķiedra AS (Valmiera Glass Fibre JSC): Cempu iela 13, Valmiera 4201; tel. 428-1221; fax 934-8837; e-mail glassfibre@vss.lv; internet www.vss.lv; f. 1963; produces glass fibre products; Pres. INĀRS POĻAKS; 1,145 employees.

VEF Komutacijas Tehnikas Rupnica Joint Stock Co: Brīvības iela 214, Rīga 1039; tel. 755-2013; fax 782-8073; f. 1919; produces telecommunication equipment and components; one of six independent VEF Cos, the others producing precision tools, mechanical devices, printed circuit boards, etc.; Pres. EDVINS LAUCIS; 2,000 employees.

Ventamonjaks AS: Dzintaru iela 66, Ventspils 3602; tel. 366-3195; fax 368-0105; e-mail office@ventamonjaks.lv; internet www.ventamonjaks.lv; transhipment of liquid chemicals; Pres. KRISTS SKUJA; 600 employees.

Ventspils Nafta: Talsu iela 75, Ventspils 3600; tel. 366-0490; fax 362-4341; e-mail office@vnafta.lv; internet www.vnafta.lv; f. 1991; export and import of petroleum and petroleum products; Chair. IGORS SKOKS; 827 employees.

Vide Infra Grupa: Brivibas iela 224, Rīga 1039; tel. 784-0060; fax 784-0061; e-mail info@videinfra.com; internet www.videinfra.lv; f. 1998; re-organized as an independent co in 2000; privately-owned; information technology and website design; Dir ANTON SULSKY.

TRADE UNIONS

Free Trade Union Confederation of Latvia (LBAS): Bruņinieku iela 29–31, Rīga 1001; tel. 727-0351; fax 727-6649; e-mail intern@latnet.lv; internet www.lbas.lv; f. 1990; Pres. JURIS RADZEVICS.

Transport

RAILWAYS

In 2000 there were 2,298 km of railways on the territory of Latvia. In 2002 Latvian railways carried 22.0m. passengers and 40.1m. metric tons of freight.

Latvian Railway (Latvijas Dzelzceļš): Gogoļa iela 3, Rīga 1547; tel. 583-4940; fax 782-0231; e-mail info@ldz.lv; internet www.ldz.lv; f. 1993; state joint-stock co; Dir-Gen. ANDRIS ZORGEVICS.

ROADS

In 2000 Latvia's total road network was 73,202 km, of which 7,011 km were main roads. In 2002 there were 619,081 passenger cars, 102,734 goods vehicles and 11,164 buses and coaches in use.

Latvian Road Administration: Gogoļa iela 3, Rīga 1050; tel. 702-1868; fax 702-8304; e-mail lad@lad.lv; internet www.lad.lv; Dir TĀLIS STRAUME.

SHIPPING

At 31 December 2001 the Latvian-registered merchant fleet numbered 160 vessels, with a combined total displacement of 68,253 grt. In 2002 some 48.7m. metric tons of freight were transported through the three main and seven smaller Latvian ports (Ventspils—accounting for 37.9m. metric tons in 2001, Rīga—14.9m. in 2001, and Liepāja (which was used as a Russian naval port until its conversion into a trade port in the early 1990s). Ventspils is particularly important for the shipping of petroleum and fuel exports (27.3m. metric tons in 1998) and is included in a special economic zone; Rīga and Ventspils operate in a free port regime.

Maritime Department: Gogoļa iela 3, Rīga 1743; tel. 702-8198; fax 733-1406; e-mail krastins@sam.gov.lv; internet www.sam.gov.lv; Dir AIGARS KRASTIŅŠ.

Port Authorities

Liepāja Port Authority: Liepāja Special Economic Zone, Feniksa iela 4, Liepāja 3401; tel. 342-7605; fax 348-0252; e-mail authority@lsez.lv; internet www.lsez.lv; Man. Dir AIVARS BOJA.

Rīga Commercial Port: Eksporta iela 15, Rīga 1227; tel. 732-9224; fax 783-0215; e-mail rto@mail.bkc.lv; internet www.rto.lv; Pres. AIVARS TAURINS.

Rīga Fishing Seaport: Atlantijas iela 27, Rīga 1020; tel. 235-1514; fax 235-3168; Dir G. SHEVCHUK.

Rīga Port Authority: Eksporta iela 6, Rīga 1010; tel. 703-0800; fax 783-0051; e-mail rop@mail.rop.lv; internet www.rop.lv; f. 1992; Chief Exec. LEONIDS LOGINOVS.

Ventspils Free Port Authority: Jāņa iela 19, Ventspils 3601; tel. 362-2586; fax 362-1297; e-mail vbparvalde@apollo.lv; internet www.ventspils.lv; f. 1991; Chief Exec. IMANTS SARMULIS.

Ventspils Commercial Port Authority: Dzintaru iela 22, Ventspils 3602; tel. 362-2821; fax 366-8870; e-mail vcp@vcp.lv; Pres. VALERIY PASHUTA.

Shipping Companies

Latvian Shipping Co (LASCO) (Latvijas Kugniecība): Basteja bulv. 2, Rīga 1807; tel. 702-0111; fax 782-8106; e-mail lsc@lsc.riga.lv; internet www.latshipcom.lv; f. 1991; tanker, reefer, LPG and dry cargo transportation; partially privatized in 2002; Pres. ANDRIS KLAVIŅŠ.

Rīga Shipping Co: Balasta dambis 9, Rīga 1048; tel. 760-1133; fax 786-0243; e-mail riga@shipping.lv; internet www.rigashipping.lv; f. 1994; complete technical management of ships including crewing; Dir MIKS ĒKBAUMS.

CIVIL AVIATION

There are two international airports, at Rīga and at Jelgava (southwest of Rīga). The Department of Aviation of the Ministry of Transport co-ordinates the financing of air transport in Latvia, and the Civil Aviation Administration supervises the operation and safety of flights.

Civil Aviation Administration of Latvia: Rīga Airport, Rīga 1053; tel. 720-7307; fax 720-7417; internet www.caa.lv; Dir-Gen. MĀRIS GORODCOVS.

Department of Aviation: Gogoļa iela 3, Rīga 1743; tel. 702-8209; fax 721-7180; Dir ARNIS MUIŽNIEKS.

AirBaltic Corpn AS: Rīga Airport, Rīga 1053; tel. 720-7069; fax 720-7369; e-mail info@airbaltic.lv; internet www.airbaltic.lv; f. 1995; 52.58% govt-controlled; operates services to Scandinavia, the Baltic states and Western Europe; Pres. and Chief Exec. BERTOLT FLICK.

Baltic Express Line: Dzirnavu iela 100, Rīga 1010; tel. 728-1037; fax 728-4806; e-mail bel@binet.lv; internet www.binet.lv/home/bel/english; f. 1993; flights to Bulgaria, Egypt, Greece, Spain and Turkey; Pres. BORIS BELOUSSOV; Dir VALERIY LITAVAR.

A/C Inversija: Rīga Airport, Rīga 1053; tel. 720-7095; fax 720-7476; f. 1988; cargo service; operates routes to destinations in Europe and the Far East; Dir-Gen. SEFIM BROOK.

RAF-AVIA: Duntes iela 34, Rīga 1005; tel. 732-4661; fax 733-9045; e-mail rafaviation@hotmail.com; internet www.rafavia.com; f. 1991; scheduled and charter flights; Pres. JURIJS HMELEVSKII.

Transeast Airlines: Rīga International Airport, Rīga 1053; tel. 720-7771; fax 720-7772; e-mail tea@mail.junik.lv; internet www.junik.lv/~tea/; f. 1992; scheduled services between Rīga and Denmark and Sweden; Man. Dir SERGEY AVVAKUMOVS.

Tourism

Among Latvia's principal tourist attractions are the historic centre of Rīga, with its medieval and art nouveau buildings, the extensive beaches of the Baltic coastline, and Gauja National Park, which stretches east of the historic town of Sigulda for nearly 100 km along the Gauja river. Sigulda also offers winter sports facilities. Revenue from tourism in 2000 was some US $131m.; however, revenue declined to some $120m. in 2001, before increasing to $161m. in 2002. Foreign tourist arrivals in 2002 numbered 360,927, of whom 15.4% were from Finland, 13.4% from Germany, 10.1% from Russia and 9.7% from Estonia.

Latvia Tours: Kaļķu iela 8, Rīga 1050; tel. 708-5001; fax 782-0020; e-mail hq@latviatours.lv; internet www.latviatours.lv; Dir GUNDEGA ZELTIŅA.

Latvian Tourism Development Agency: Pils lauk. 4, Rīga 1050; tel. and fax 722-9945; e-mail tda@latviatourism.lv; internet www.latviatourism.lv; f. 1993; Dir AIVARS KALNINSCARON.

Culture

NATIONAL ORGANIZATIONS

Ministry of Culture: see section on The Government (Ministries).

State Inspectorate for Heritage Protection: M. Pils iela 19, Rīga 1050; tel. 722-9272; fax 722-8808; e-mail vkpai@latnet.lv; internet www.km.gov.lv/vkpai/; f. 1989; implements state control on the preservation of cultural monuments; issues licences and grants for conservation, restoration and repair of monuments; Dir JURIS DAMBIS.

CULTURAL HERITAGE

Bibliography Institute of the National Library: Anglikāņu iela 5, Rīga 1816; tel. 722-5135; fax 722-4587; e-mail anitag@lbi.lnb.lv; internet www.lnb.lv; f. 1989; research and compilation of a national bibliography, in co-operation with IFLA and UNESCO; analysis of publishing activities; Dir ANITA GOLDBERGA.

City of Rīga History and Maritime Museum: Palasta iela 4, Rīga 1050; tel. 721-1358; fax 721-0226; internet vip.latnet.lv/LMA/museums/Riga; f. 1773; Dir KLĀRA RADZIŅA.

General Directorate of Latvian State Archives: Šķūņu iela 11, Rīga 1050; POB 1454; tel. 721-2539; fax 722-5564; e-mail direkcija@arhivi.lv; internet www.arhivi.lv; f. 1991; manages the state archives; Dir-Gen. VALDIS ŠTĀLS.

Latvian Academic Library: Rūpniecības iela 10, Rīga 1235; tel. 710-6206; fax 710-6202; e-mail acadlib@lib.acadlib.lv; f. 1524; 3.1m. vols; special collection of Latvian literature; Dir VENTA KOCERE.

Latvian National Library: K. Barona iela 14, Rīga 1423; tel. 728-9874; fax 728-0851; e-mail lnb@lbi.lnb.lv; internet vip.latnet.lv/LNB/; f. 1919; over 5m. vols; Dir ANDRIS VILKS.

Latvian War Museum: Smilsu iela 20, Riga 1868; internet www.karamuzejs.lv; f. 1919; Dir AIJA FLEIJA.

Library of the University of Latvia: Kalpaka bulv. 4, Rīga 1820; tel. and fax 722-3984; e-mail lulib@lub.lv; internet www.lub.lv; f. 1862; 2m. vols; Dir GUNARS MANGULIS.

Museum of Decorative Applied Art: Skārņu iela 10–20, Rīga 1050; tel. 722-2235; f. 1989; over 10,000 exhibits; Head ALĪDA KRĒSLIŅA.

Museum of Foreign Art: M. Pils iela 3, Rīga 1050; tel. 722-6467; fax 722-8776; e-mail arzemju.mm@apollo.lv; f. 1773; library of 17,300 vols; 18,800 exhibits; Dir DAIGA UPENIECE.

Museum of the History of Latvia: Pils laukums 3, Rīga 1050; tel. 722-3004; fax 722-0586; e-mail museum@history-museum.lv; f. 1869; materials on archaeology, history, ethnography, numismatics; Dir ARNIS RADIŅŠ.

Museum of Literature, Theatre and Music: Pils iela 2, Rīga 1050; tel. and fax 721-6425; e-mail pumpurs@acad.latnet.lv; f. 1925; over 550,000 exhibits; materials on Latvian literature, theatre, music, folk art and cinema; Dir IVARS ZUKULIS.

Open-Air Museum of Ethnography: Brīvības bulv. 440, Rīga 1056; tel. 799-4510; fax 799-4178; f. 1924; Dir JURIS INDĀNS.

Paul Stradin Museum for the History of Medicine: Antonijas iela 1, Rīga 1060; tel. 722-2914; fax 721-1323; e-mail museum1@apollo.lv; f. 1957; 192,038 exhibits; Dir Dr KĀRLIS ĒRIKS ARONS.

Rundāle Palace Museum: Pilsrundāle, Rundāles pagasts, Bauskas raj., 3921; tel. 396-2274; fax 392-2274; e-mail rmp@eila.lv; internet www.rpm.apollo.lv; f. 1972; Latvian ancient art; Dir IMANTS LANCMANIS.

State Museum of Art: K. Valdemāra iela 10A, Rīga 1342; tel. 732-5021; fax 722-0714; e-mail vmm@latnet.lv; internet www.vmm.lv; f. 1905; 15,000 exhibits from the late 18th century until the first half of the 20th century; Dir MĀRA LĀCE.

> **Arsenāls Exhibition Hall:** Torņa iela 1, Rīga 1050; tel. 721-3695; fax 722-9570; e-mail sundari@latnet.lv; internet www.vmm.lv; f. 1988; contemporary art collection from the second half of the 20th century; over 15,000 exhibits; Head of Collections NATALIE SUYUNSHALIEVA.

SPORTING ORGANIZATIONS

Latvian Academy of Sport Education: Brīvības bulv. 333, Rīga 1006; tel. 754-3433; fax 754-3480; e-mail rector@lspa.lanet.lv; educational and training establishment; 1,200 students; Rector Prof. ULDIS GRĀVĪTIS.

Latvian Olympic Committee: Elizabetes iela 49, Rīga 1010; tel. 728-2461; fax 728-2123; e-mail lok@apollo.lv; internet www.lov.lv; f. 1922; readmitted to the Olympic Movement 1991; Pres. VILNIS BALTIŅŠ; Sec.-Gen. ALDONS VRUBLEVSKIS.

Latvian Sports Department: Tērbatas iela 4, Rīga 1011; tel. 728-4206; fax 728-4412; e-mail lsp@acad.latnet.lv; govt dept; Dir EINARS FOGELIS.

PERFORMING ARTS

Art Theatre (Dailes teātris): Brīvības bulv. 75, Rīga 1147; tel. 227-0424; fax 727-1736; f. 1920; Dir BĒRTULIS PIZIČS.

Kabata (Pocket) Independent Theatre: Peldu iela 19, Rīga 1050; tel. 721-2943; fax 721-1341; f. 1987; Man. Dir KĀRLIS RINGS.

Latvian Circus: Merķeļa iela 4, Rīga 1050; tel. and fax 721-3479; f. 1888; Chief Dir GUNĀRS KATKEVIČS.

Latvian National Opera: Aspazijas iela 3, Rīga 1050; tel. 707-3715; fax 722-8930; e-mail info@opera.lv; internet www.opera.lv; f. 1919; Gen. Dir ANDREJS ŽAGARS.

Latvian National Symphony Orchestra: Amatu iela 6, Rīga 1664; tel. 722-9537; fax 722-4850; e-mail lnso@mail.bkc.lv; internet www.music.lv/orchestra/; f. 1926; Man. Dir ILONA BREĢE.

Latvian National Theatre: Kronvalda bulv. 2, Rīga 1829; tel. 732-2828; fax 732-3002; f. 1919; Dir MĀRIS JAUNOZOLS.

New Rīga Theatre: Lāčplēša iela 25, Rīga 1050; tel. 728-3323; fax 728-2945; internet www.jrt.lv/; f. 1992; Dir ALVIS HERMANIS.

New Theatre Institute of Latvia: Merkela 13–426, Rīga 1050; tel. 721-2622; fax 721-2471; e-mail jti@latnet.lv; internet www.vip.lv/jti; f. 1998; Homo Novus theatre festival; Dir BAIBA TJARVE.

Rīga Russian Drama Theatre: Kaļķu iela 16, Rīga 1050; tel. 722-4660; fax 722-9692; e-mail art@trd.riga.lv; f. 1883; Man. EDUARD TSECHOVAL.

State Puppet Theatre of Latvia: K. Barona iela 16/18, Rīga 1050; tel. and fax 728-1022; fax 728-5418; e-mail info@puppet.lv; internet www.puppet.lv; f. 1945; Dir VIJA BLUZMA (acting).

Valmiera Drama Theatre: Lāčplēša iela 4, Valmiera 4200; tel. and fax (42) 07-297; e-mail vdd@e-apollo.lv; f. 1919; Dir PĒTERIS SŪCIS.

ASSOCIATIONS

Artists' Union of Latvia: K. 11 Novembra iela 35, Rīga 1050; tel. 722-8497; fax 722-6066; e-mail lms@re-lab.net; internet www.gallery.lv/Latart; f. 1941; Chair. EGILS ROZENBERGS.

Association of Latvian Academic Libraries (ALAL): Šķūņu iela 17, Rīga 1974; tel. 703-9221; e-mail lataba@rgsl.edu.lv; internet www.acadlib.lv/lataba; f. 1994; Pres. LIGITA VASERMANE; 19 mems.

Designers' Union of Latvia: Ģertrūdes iela 5A, Rīga 1010; tel. and fax 731-3316; e-mail lds@mailbox.riga.lv; f. 1988; Chair. INGRĪDA LAUCE.

Journalists' Union of Latvia: Mārstaļu iela 2, Rīga 1050; tel. 721-1433; fax 782-0233; e-mail reiteras@zn.apollo.lv; f. 1992; Chair. LIGITA AZOVSKA.

Latvian Arts Education Centre: Raiņa iela 23/2, Rīga 1050; tel. 722-1762; fax 722-4495; e-mail vkc@km.gov.lv; Deputy Head JĀNIS PORIETIS.

Latvian Association of Architects: Torņa iela 11, Rīga 1050; tel. 721-2802; fax 722-3902; e-mail latarch@lat.net; f. 1924; Chair. JURIS POGA.

Latvian Composers' Union: K. 11 novembra iela 35, Rīga 1050; tel. 721-4353; f. 1944; Chair. LEONS AMOLIŅŠ.

Latvian Culture Foundation: Basteja bulv. 12, Rīga 1665; tel. 722-7230; fax 721-2545; e-mail peterisb@parks.lv; internet www.lkf.lv; f. 1992; promotes Latvian culture, provides scholarships for cultural studies; Chair. PĒTERIS BANKOVSKIS.

Latvian Film-makers' Union: Elizabetes iela 49, Rīga 1010; tel. 728-8536; fax 724-0543; f. 1958; also represents cinematographers; Chair. IEVA ROMANOVA.

Latvian Museum Association: Brīvības iela 38, Rīga 1050; tel. 728-9767; fax 722-7335; e-mail muzasoc@acad.latnet.lv; internet www.muzeji.lv; f. 1992; Chair. AIJA FLEIJA.

Latvian Theatre Union: Dzirnavu iela 135, Rīga 1050; tel. and fax 728-7895; f. 1944; Chair. ARTŪRS ĒĶIS.

National Centre for Cinema: Elizabetes iela 49, Rīga 1010; tel. 750-5085; fax 750-5077; e-mail nfc@nfc.gov.lv; Dir BRUNO AŠČUKS.

Photo Artists Union of Latvia: Mārstaļu iela 6, Rīga 1050; tel. 721-0327; fax 736-9794; e-mail latv.photo@apollo.lv; internet www.foto.lv; Pres. AIVARS ĀĶIS.

State Authority on Museums: Kaļķu iela 11A, Rīga 1050; tel. 750-3871; fax 722-8083; e-mail janis.garjans@km.gov.lv; Head JĀNIS GARJANS.

State Folk Art Centre: Pils Laukums 4, Rīga 1050; tel. 722-8985; fax 722-7405; e-mail pasts@tmc.gov.lv; internet www.folklora.lv; Head JĀNIS KURPNIEKS.

Writers' Union of Latvia: Kuršu iela 24, Rīga 1424; tel. 755-5180; fax 755-4034; f. 1940; Chair. VALDIS RŪMNIEKS.

Education

Primary education in Latvia begins at seven years of age and lasts for four years. Secondary education, beginning at the age of 11, comprises a first cycle of five years and a second of three years. The first nine years of education are officially compulsory. In 1998 primary enrolment included 94% of children in the relevant age-group. The comparable ratio for secondary education was 83%. After the adoption of Latvian as the state language in 1988 (replacing Russian), the teaching of Latvian became a compulsory part of the curriculum for all pupils. In 2000/01 71% of school-age pupils were taught in Latvian-language schools, and 17% in Russian-language schools; 12% were taught in schools offering instruction in both Latvian and Russian.

In 1990/91 the first schools for educating the less numerous ethnic minorities opened. In 2002/03 there were five Polish schools (with a total of 1,003 pupils), one Ukrainian school (307 pupils) and one Belarusian school (87 pupils). Latvian was due to become the main language of instruction in all secondary schools from September 2004; however, 40% of teaching in schools for ethnic minorities would be permitted to take place in other languages. In 2002/03 higher education was offered at 37 institutions, with a total enrolment of 118,944 students. In 2001 government expenditure on education amounted to 87.8m. LVL (representing 6.3% of total budgetary expenditure).

UNIVERSITIES

Daugavpils Pedagogical University: Vienības iela 13, Daugavpils 5400; tel. 542-2180; fax 542-2922; e-mail dau@dau.lv; internet www.dau.lv; 6 faculties; Rector JĀNIS POKULIS.

Latvian University of Agriculture: Liela iela 2, Jelgava 3001; f. 1939; renamed 1991; 9 faculties; 468 teachers; Rector PĒTERIS BUSMANIS.

Rīga Technical University: Kaļķu iela 1, Rīga 1658; tel. 708-9300; fax 782-0094; e-mail rtu@adm.rtu.lv; internet www.rtu.lv; f. 1862; eight faculties; 1,400 teachers; 14,600 students; Rector Prof. IVARS KNĒTS.

University of Latvia: Raiņa bulv. 19, Rīga 1586; tel. 703-4444; fax 703–4513; e-mail alina@lanet.lv; internet www.lu.lv; f. 1919; languages of instruction: Latvian and English; 13 faculties; 885 teachers; 9,670 students; Rector Prof. Dr IVARS LĀCIS.

Vidzeme University College: Cesu iela 4, Valmiera; tel. 420-7230; fax 420-7229; e-mail info@va.lv; internet www.va.lv; Rector PĒTERIS CIMDIŅŠ.

Social Welfare

In 1995 seven laws relating to social-security reform were passed by the Saeima. These covered areas such as state pensions, unemployment and disability insurance, sickness and maternity benefits, social assistance and social-insurance tax. The pension law provided for the gradual introduction of a 'multi-pillar' pension system, which took effect in 1998. At the end of 2002, according to official figures, 89,735 Latvians were registered as unemployed, and 496,900 people were in receipt of old-age pensions; in that year the average monthly pension amounted to 62.1 LVL. The minimum monthly wage was increased to 70 LVL in 2003, and was to be further increased to 80 LVL from 1 January 2004. In 2001 total budgetary expenditure on social security and welfare was some 570.6m. LVL, equivalent to 40.8% of total spending.

Reform of the health-care system began in 1998. In 2002 there were 2.9 physicians and 7.8 hospital beds per 1,000 persons. According to the UN Development Programme, the rate of infant mortality was 21 per 1,000 live births in 2001. In 2001 government expenditure on health care totalled some 154.4m. LVL, equivalent to 11.0% of total spending.

NATIONAL AGENCIES

Ministry of Health: see section on The Government (Ministries).

Ministry of Welfare: see section on The Government (Ministries).

Central Agency of National Obligatory Health Insurance: Baznīcas iela 25, Rīga 1010; tel. 704-3700; fax 704-3701; Dir INĀRA BLUĶE.

State Centre of Children's Rights: Brīvības iela 85, Rīga 1001; tel. 731-5700; fax 731-4914; e-mail centrs@vbtac.lv; internet www .vbtac.lv; Dir INETE IELĪITE.

State Employment Service: K. Valdemāra iela 38, Rīga 1010; tel. 702-1706; fax 727-0253; e-mail nvd@nvd.gov.lv; internet www.nvd .gov.lv; f. 1991; Dir ALVIS VĪTOLS.

State Labour Inspectorate: K. Valdemāra iela 38, Rīga 1010; tel. 702-1702; fax 702-1569; Dir JĀNIS BĒRZIŅŠ.

State Social Assistance Fund: Ojāra Vācieša iela 4, Rīga 1004; tel. 761-5659; fax 750-0120; e-mail spf@spf.gov.lv; internet www.spf .lv; Dir OLGA DZENE.

State Social Insurance Agency: Lāčplēša iela 70A, Rīga 1011; tel. 728-6616; fax 728-6717; Dir INESE ŠMITIŅA.

HEALTH AND WELFARE ORGANIZATIONS

Disabled People's Union of Latvia: Raunas iela 64, Rīga 1039; tel. 751-5856; fax 751-5855; e-mail steks99@inbox.lv; Chair. LILITA LAUBE.

Latvian Association of the Deaf: Elvīras iela 19, Rīga 1083; tel. 747-0595; fax 747-0444; e-mail lns@lns.lv; internet www.lns.lv; f. 1920; Pres. ARNOLDS PAVLIŅŠ.

Latvian Children's Fund: Brīvības bulv. 310–75, Rīga 1006; tel. 754-2072; fax 754-1814; e-mail bernufonds@mail.lv; f. 1989; independent, non-profit organization; assists deprived children; Pres. ANDRIS BĒRZIŅŠ.

Latvian Federation of Pensioners: Bruņinieku iela 29/31 306, Rīga 1001; tel. and fax 727-6789; f. 1992; Chair. JĀNIS PORIETIS.

Latvian Red Cross Society: Skolas iela 1, Rīga 1010; tel. and fax 227-5635; f. 1918; Pres. ULDIS LAUCIS.

Latvian Society of the Blind: Pāles iela 14/1, Rīga 1024; tel. and fax 753-2607; e-mail lnbcv@e-apollo.lv; f. 1926; Chair. JĀNIS POLIS.

Pakāpieni Mission: Ventas iela 1A, Jūrmala 2015; tel. 776-7456; fax 776-1317; aid for one-parent and poor families; Pres. VILJAMS ŠULCS.

The Environment

The emission of untreated sewage and industrial waste into the Daugava (Dvina) river, the high levels of harmful effluent from industrial plants and the degradation of agricultural soil and other land were among the major concerns of environmental groups, which

began to emerge from the 1980s. During the early 1990s Latvia joined other countries with a Baltic coastline in a number of initiatives to limit environmental damage to the Sea; in the late 1990s a State Programme for Marine Monitoring was established. In mid-1998 concerns were raised over potential pollution from the construction of a petroleum refinery at Butinge (Lithuania), a site close to the Latvian border. In August 2001 it was reported that environmental expenditure in Latvia amounted to some 7.4m. LVL in 2000. Latvia, which was due to become a member of the EU in 2004, became a member of the EU's Environment Agency from the beginning of 2002.

GOVERNMENT ORGANIZATIONS

Ministry of the Environment: see section on The Government (Ministries).

Dabas Aizsardzibas Pārvalde (Nature Protection Board): Eksporta iela 5, Rīga 1010 ; tel. 750-9545; fax 750-9544; e-mail dap@ dap.gov.lv; internet www.dap.gov.lv; f. 2002; Dir ROLANDS AUZIŅŠ.

Latvijas Vides Agentūra (Latvian Environment Agency—LEA): Straumes iela 2, Jurmala 2015; tel. 781-1492; fax 781-1494; e-mail vdc@vdc.lv; internet www.vdc.lv; f. 1989; co-ordinates the activities of laboratories collecting data on environmental pollution and control of natural resources; Dir Dr ILZE KIRSTUKA.

Ziemeļvidzemes Biosfēras Rezervāts (North Vidzeme Biosphere Reserve): Rigas iela 10A,Salacgrīva 4033; tel. 407-1408; fax 407-1407; e-mail biosfera@biosfera.gov.lv; internet www.biosfera.gov.lv; f. 1997; a specially protected territory of international importance of 4,500 sq km of land and 165.7 sq km of marine area; Dir SANDRA BĒRZIŅA.

ACADEMIC INSTITUTES

Latvijas Zinātņu Akadēmija (Latvian Academy of Sciences): Akadēmijas laukums 1, Rīga 1524; tel. 722-5361; fax 782-1153; e-mail lza@ac.lza.lv; internet www.lza.lv; several institutes involved in environmental research; Pres. JĀNIS STRADINS.

> **Nuclear Research Centre:** Miera iela 31, Salaspils, Rīgas rajons 2169; tel. 790-1210; fax 790-1212; e-mail alap@latnet.lv; Dir ANTONS LAPENAS.

NON-GOVERNMENTAL ORGANIZATIONS

Baltic Environmental Forum: Peldu iela 26/28, Rm 505, Rīga 1050; tel. 721-4477; fax 721-4448; e-mail bef@latnet.lv; internet www.bef.lv; f. 1995; Project Man. HEIDRUNN FAMMLER.

Environmental Protection Club (Vides aizsardzibas klubs): Audēju 7/9, Rīga 1050; tel. 722-6042; fax 721-3697; e-mail vak@com .latnet.lv; f. 1984; active environmental group; Pres. ARVĪDS ULME.

Latvian Fund for Nature (Latvijas Dabas fonds): Kronvalda bulv 4, Rīga 1010; tel. 703-4894; fax 783-0291; e-mail inga@lanet.lv; internet www.daba.lu.lv/ldf; f. 1990; Chief Exec. MĀRIS KREILIS.

Latvian Green Party (Latvijas Zaļā partija): see section on Political Organizations.

World Wide Fund for Nature—WWF Latvia (WWF Latvijas birojs): Elizabetes iela 8–4, Rīga 1010; tel. 750-5640; fax 750-5651; e-mail wwf@org.latnet.lv; internet www.wwf.lv; national affiliate organization of WWF International; Chief Exec. UGIS ROTBERGS.

Defence

Until it became independent in August 1991, Latvia had no armed forces of its own; in November a Ministry of Defence was established. Latvia's National Armed Forces totalled 5,500 in August 2002, comprising an army of 4,300 (including 1,022 conscripts), a navy of 930 (including 290 conscripts and a coast guard of 250) and an air force of 270. In addition, there was a paramilitary force of 3,200, which was entirely comprised of a border guard, supervised by the Ministry of the Interior. Reserve forces in the national guard numbered 14,050. Military service is compulsory from 19 years of age and lasts for 12 months, or three months for university graduates; farmers and the self-employed may serve their 12-month military service over a period of three years.

During 1997 and 1998 a number of treaties and agreements relating to defence were signed. Together with Estonia and Lithuania, Latvia agreed to establish a joint airspace observation system (BALTNET), a defence college (BALTDEFCOL) and a peace-keeping battalion (BALTBAT). A Baltic naval unit (BALTRON) was established in mid-1998. The Latvian Government announced the creation of a military police force and the transformation of the border guard to a professional body (although this was delayed, owing to a lack of funds). In January 1998 it was announced that a 742-strong professional military unit (the Latvian Battalion—LATBAT) was to be created over the following four years.

Expenditure on defence totalled 43.4m. LVL in 2001, equivalent to 1.0% of GDP and 3.1% of expenditure. The budget for 2002 allocated annual expenditure of 69.0m. LVL on defence.

In November 2002 Latvia was invited to become a member of the North Atlantic Treaty Organization (NATO) from 2004. In order to achieve this, the Saeima approved a budget for 2003 that increased Latvia's defence budget to the 2% of gross domestic product (GDP) required to conform to NATO standards.

Commander of the National Armed Forces: Rear-Adm. GAIDIS ANDREJS ZEIBOTS.

Chief of the General Staff: Col KARLIS KRESLINS.

Commander of the Air Force: Col VITALIJS VIESINS.

Commander of the Navy: Capt. ILMARS LESINSKIS.

Bibliography

Dreifelds, J. *Latvia in Transition.* Cambridge, Cambridge University Press, 1996.

Eglitis, D. S. *Imagining the Nation: History, Modernity and Revolution in Latvia (Post–Communist Cultural Studies Series).* University Park, PA, Penn State University Press, 2002.

Ezergailis, A. *The 1917 Revolution in Latvia.* New York, NY, Columbia University Press, 1974.

The Holocaust in Latvia. Rīga, Historical Institute of Latvia, 1996.

Jubulis, M. A. *Nationalism and Democratic Transition: The Politics of Citizenship and Language in Post-Soviet Latvia.* Lanham, MD, University Press of Amer, 2001.

Kondratev, M. (Ed.). *Latvia: A Path Chosen Twice.* Moscow, Novosti, 1987.

Latvia: An Economic Profile. Washington, DC, Document Expediting (DOCEX) Project, 1992.

Latvia: An Economic Profile for the Foreign Investor. Rīga, Ministry of Economic Reforms, 1993.

Moshes, A. *Overcoming Unfriendly Stability: Russian-Latvian Relations at the End of 1990s.* Helsinki, Ulkopoliittinen instituuti, 1999.

Neimanis, A. *Gender and Human Development in Latvia.* New York, NY, United Nations Development Programme, 1999.

Nissinen, M. *Latvia's Transition to a Market Economy: Political Determinants of Economic Reform Policy (Studies in Russia and East Europe).* Basingstoke, Palgrave, 1998.

Penikis, J., and Penikis, A. *Latvia.* New York, NY, Westview, 1997.

Penikis, J. *Latvia: Independence Renewed.* London, HarperCollins, 2000.

Plakans, A. *The Latvians: A Short History.* Stanford, CA, Hoover Institution Press, 1995.

Historical Dictionary of Latvia (European Historical Dictionaries). Lanham, MD, Scarecrow Press, 1997.

Sinka, J. *Latvia and Latvians.* London, Central Board Daugavas Vanagi, 1988.

Terterov, M. (Ed.). *Doing Business with Latvia (Global Market Briefings).* London, Kogan Page, 2003.

See also the Select Bibliography in Part Four.

LITHUANIA

Geography

PHYSICAL FEATURES

The Republic of Lithuania, formerly the Lithuanian Soviet Socialist Republic (a constituent member of the USSR), is situated on the eastern shore of the Baltic Sea, in north-eastern Europe. It is bounded by Latvia to the north, Belarus to the south-east, Poland to the south-west and by the territory of Russia around Kaliningrad (formerly Königsberg) to the west. It covers an area of 65,301 sq km (25,213 sq miles).

The low-lying littoral along the Baltic coastline, known as the Pajūrio Lowland, extends some 15–20 km from the sea. To the east of the coastal plain lies the Žemaičių Upland, which rises to a height of 234 m (772 ft) at Medvėgalis. The Upland is separated from the Baltic Highlands of the south and east by a long plain across the central regions, called the Middle Lowland. The highest point in Lithuania is at Juozapinė Hill (294 m), in the east of the country. There is a dense network of waterways, the main river being the Nemunas (Neman), which flows from the south to the north and empties into the Baltic Sea. There are also many lakes concentrated in the northern regions of the Baltic Highlands.

CLIMATE

Lithuania's maritime position moderates an otherwise continental-type climate. Temperatures range from an average in January of –4.9°C (23.2°F) to a July mean of 17.0°C (62.6°F). The level of precipitation varies considerably from region to region. In the far west average annual precipitation is 700 mm–850 mm (28 ins–33 ins), while in the central plain it is about 600 mm.

POPULATION

At the census of 6 April 2001 the population was 3,483,972. According to official estimates, the population numbered 3,462,600 at 1 January 2003, giving a population density of 53.0 per sq km. Of the total population in 2001, 83.5% were Lithuanians, 6.7% Poles and 6.3% Russians. Other ethnic groups included Belarusians (1.2%) and Ukrainians (0.7%). There were also Jewish, German and Tatar, Latvian, Gypsy

(Roma) and Armenian minorities. In 1988 Lithuanian, a Baltic tongue which uses the Latin alphabet, replaced Russian as the official state language. The predominant religion in Lithuania is Christianity. Most ethnic Lithuanians are Roman Catholics by belief or tradition (79.0% of the population at the census of 2001), but there are small communities of Lutherans (0.6%) and Reformists (0.2%). Adherents of Russian Orthodoxy (4.1% of the population at the census of 2001) are almost exclusively ethnic Slavs, and there are also small numbers of Lithuanian Old Believers (0.8%). Most Tatars retain an adherence to Islam.

The capital of Lithuania is Vilnius, which is situated in the south-east of the country and was part of Poland until 1939 (when it was known as Wilno). At the 2001 census it had a population of 542,287. Other important towns include Kaunas (Kovno—378,943), situated on the upper reaches of the Nemunas river and the capital in the 1920s and 1930s; Klaipėda (Memel—192,954), which is Lithuania's principal port; and Šiauliai (133,883) and Panevėžys (119,749), in the north of the country.

Chronology

1231: Mindouh (Mindaugas), a regional chieftain, united Lithuanian tribes by founding the Grand Duchy of Lithuania (Litva) and Rus (many of the ruling class were Orthodox Slavs).

1386: The personal union between Lithuania and Poland was achieved by the marriage of the Lithuanian Grand Duke Jahaila (Jagiełło, baptized Władysław in 1386) and the Polish Queen Jadwiga (Hedwig). The following year Lithuania officially adopted Christianity.

1392–1430: Vytautas (Witold) the Great expanded Lithuanian power further east and towards the Black Sea, despite the Tatar victory at Vorskla in 1399.

1569: Lithuania (which included much of modern Belarus and, since the 15th century, the Samogitian lowlands of western Lithuania) surrendered its separate status by the Union of Lublin; the new Polish-Lithuanian Commonwealth

was created to counter the threat from Sweden, the Russian state of Muscovy and the Turkish Ottoman Empire.

1795: At the Third Partition of Poland Lithuania was annexed by the Russian Empire.

1863: Following the additional rural hardships consequent to the emancipation of 1861, there was a revolt by the Lithuanian peasantry which was savagely repressed. A policy of russification was then instituted, although a strong nationalist movement emerged in the later decades of the century.

1915: Lithuania was occupied by German troops, following the outbreak of the First World War.

September 1917: A Lithuanian Conference was convened; the Conference adopted a resolution demanding the independence of the Lithuanian state and elected a Council of Lithuania, headed by Antanas Smetona.

16 February 1918: Lithuania's independence was formally declared by the Council of Lithuania. The declaration was contrary to the wishes of the German authorities, which had allowed the formation of the Council because they expected it to generate popular support for Germany's occupation of Lithuania.

1919: Lithuanian troops defended Lithuania's territory against invasion by Bolshevik, German and 'White' Russian forces.

April 1920: Elections were held to the Constituent Assembly.

12 July 1920: Lithuania's independence was recognized by Soviet Russia in the Treaty of Moscow.

9 October 1920: The Polish army captured Vilnius (Wilno) and its surrounding area. Poland did, however, subsequently recognize the independent state of Lithuania, with its capital at Kaunas.

1 August 1922: Lithuania's first Constitution was adopted, which declared Lithuania to be a parliamentary democracy.

1923: Lithuania occupied the former German territory of Klaipėda (Memel), which was under the jurisdiction of the League of Nations.

17 December 1926: Following the victory of the left wing in the May elections, Antanas Smetona, the leader of the Nationalist Party and former Chairman of the Council of Lithuania, seized power in a military coup and established authoritarian rule.

1938: Diplomatic relations with Poland were restored.

23 August 1939: In the 'Secret Protocols' to the Nazi-Soviet Pact (Treaty of Non-Aggression) Lithuania was assigned to Germany.

28 September 1939: The Treaty on Friendship and Existing Borders, agreed between Germany and the USSR, permitted the USSR to occupy Lithuania.

10 October 1939: Lithuania was compelled to sign a Treaty of Mutual Assistance with the USSR; the Treaty forced Lithuania to accept the stationing of 20,000 Soviet troops on its territory, in return for which Vilnius (previously controlled by Poland) was returned. The city subsequently became Lithuania's capital.

15 June 1940: The Soviet Red Army invaded Lithuania; Smetona fled the country and a 'puppet' Government was formed.

3 August 1940: Lithuania was formally incorporated into the USSR.

June 1941: Some 20,000 Lithuanians were deported to Siberia, Russia, shortly before the German invasion of the USSR and occupation of Lithuania, during which some 210,000 people were killed.

1944: With the defeat of Nazi Germany, Lithuania was recaptured by the Red Army. The collectivization of agriculture and a further series of deportations commenced. Organized partisan resistance to Soviet rule occurred throughout the country until 1952.

May 1972: Anti-communist demonstrations took place in Kaunas.

August 1987: Dissident groups demonstrated on the anniversary of the signing of the Nazi-Soviet Pact.

February 1988: The security services prevented a celebration marking the 70th anniversary of Lithuanian independence.

3 June 1988: The Lithuanian Movement for Reconstruction (Sąjūdis) was formed by a group of intellectuals and writers.

August 1988: Aleksandr Yakovlev, a political ally of Mikhail Gorbachev (who had become the Soviet leader in 1985), visited Lithuania; his failure to condemn the actions of Sąjūdis served to strengthen the movement's position.

23 August 1988: At a mass rally in Vilnius the leaders of Sąjūdis denounced the Nazi-Soviet Pact and declared that the USSR had illegally occupied Lithuania.

October 1988: The First Secretary of the Communist Party of Lithuania (CPL), Ringaudas Songaila, was dismissed from his post and succeeded by Algirdas Brazauskas.

November 1988: As one of a number of concessions to Lithuanian nationalism, the Lithuanian Supreme Soviet recognized Lithuanian as the state language.

March 1989: In the elections to the all-Union Congress of People's Deputies Sąjūdis won 36 out of a total of 42 contested seats in Lithuania.

18 May 1989: The Lithuanian Supreme Soviet approved a declaration of Lithuanian sovereignty, which asserted the supremacy of Lithuania's laws over all-Union legislation.

20 December 1989: At a CPL Congress the Party declared its independence from the Communist Party of the Soviet Union (CPSU) and its support for multi-party democracy and independent statehood.

24 February 1990: Sąjūdis won an overall majority of seats in the elections to the Lithuanian Supreme Soviet.

11 March 1990: The Supreme Soviet (renamed the Supreme Council) declared the restoration of Lithuanian independence, the first of the Soviet republics to make such a declaration; on the same day it elected Vytautas Landsbergis, the leader of Sąjūdis, as its Chairman (*de facto* head of state). The legislature also restored the pre-1940 name of 'Republic of Lithuania', and suspended the USSR Constitution on Lithuanian territory.

17 March 1990: Kazimiera Prunskienė was appointed Prime Minister of Lithuania, the first female premier of any of the Soviet territories.

April 1990: The USSR imposed an economic embargo on Lithuania, in retaliation for its declaration of independence; Soviet forces had also occupied CPL buildings in Vilnius and taken control of newsprint presses.

30 June 1990: Lithuania agreed to a six-month moratorium on independence. Discussions began in August, but were ended shortly afterwards by the Soviet Government.

January 1991: Prunskienė resigned as Prime Minister, following disagreements with Landsbergis on economic and foreign policy; she was replaced by Gediminas Vagnorius. Landsbergis announced the end of the suspension of the declaration of independence. Soviet troops fired on civilians gathered around the Vilnius television tower; 13 people were killed and 500 were injured. (In August 1999 six former officers of the CPL were convicted of complicity in attempts to overthrow the Government, and sentenced to between three and 12 years' imprisonment.).

9 February 1991: A referendum on independence took place in Lithuania: some 84% of the population participated, of which 90.5% voted in favour of independence. Lithuania refused to participate officially in the all-Union referendum on the future of the USSR in the following month.

August 1991: Military vehicles entered Vilnius during an attempted coup in the Soviet capital, Moscow. The Supreme Council joined in the condemnation of the coup and, upon its collapse, the Lithuanian Government ordered the withdrawal of Soviet forces from the republic.

6 September 1991: The State Council of the USSR formally acknowledged Lithuania's independence.

10 September 1991: Lithuania became a member of the Conference on Security and Co-operation in Europe (CSCE, renamed the Organization for Security and Co-operation in

Europe—OSCE in December 1994); one week later the country was admitted to the UN.

January 1992: Lithuania and Poland signed a Declaration on Friendly Relations and Neighbourly Co-operation (a formal treaty of friendship and co-operation was finally signed in April 1994); it guaranteed the rights of the respective ethnic minorities in each country and also recognized the existing border between the countries.

25 May 1992: A proposal to introduce an executive presidency was rejected in a referendum.

July 1992: A vote of 'no confidence' in Vagnorius won a majority in the Seimas (formerly the Supreme Council); Aleksandras Abišala replaced him as Prime Minister.

1 October 1992: Lithuania ceased to belong to the 'rouble zone'. A provisional monetary unit, the talonas, was introduced. It was replaced, on 25 June 1993, by the litas.

25 October 1992: The first round of voting in a general election took place. A new Constitution, which established a presidency, was overwhelmingly approved in a referendum; it was formally adopted on 6 November.

15 November 1992: The second round of voting in the parliamentary elections gave the former CPL, renamed the Lithuanian Democratic Labour Party (LDLP), a final total of 76 of the 141 seats in the Seimas; Sąjūdis won 49 seats.

December 1992: Bronislovas Lubys, a member of the Abišala Government, was appointed Prime Minister; a coalition Government was formed, including six ministers from the previous administration and only three LDLP members.

14 February 1993: Algirdas Brazauskas was elected President, securing some 60% of the votes cast (from December 1992 he had been acting head of state in his capacity as Chairman of the new Seimas).

March 1993: Adolfas Šleževičius, a member of the LDLP, was appointed Prime Minister.

May 1993: Lithuania became a full member of the Council of Europe.

31 August 1993: The last of the former Soviet (Russian) troops remaining on Lithuanian territory were withdrawn.

November 1993: Lithuania signed a number of bilateral agreements with Russia, including a 'most-favoured nation' treaty and social guarantees for ex-servicemen. Later disagreements over military transits delayed the implementation of the trade agreements.

January 1994: Lithuania joined the North Atlantic Treaty Organization's (NATO) 'Partnership for Peace' programme of military co-operation. Lithuania had already expressed its intent to become a full member of NATO and had denounced Russian claims to be entitled to station troops on former Soviet territory.

February 1996: The Seimas, by 94 votes to 26, approved a presidential decree dismissing Šleževičius from office (he also later resigned as leader of the LDLP and, in October, was charged with abuse of power while in office). Laurynas Mindaugas Stankevičius, previously Minister of Government Reforms and Local Governments, was appointed Prime Minister and chose a new cabinet.

20 October and 10 November 1996: After two rounds of voting in the general election, the Conservative Party (CP) secured 70 seats in the Seimas and the Christian Democratic Party of Lithuania (CDPL) 16; the LDLP won only 12 seats, the nationalist Centre Union won 13 and the Lithuanian Social Democratic Party (LSDP) obtained 12. The CP and the CDPL formed a coalition, supported by the Centre Union, and later in the month Landsbergis became parliamentary speaker and Vagnorius returned as premier (both were Conservatives).

October 1997: President Brazauskas made the first official visit to Russia by a Baltic head of state since the collapse of the USSR; he signed a state border delimitation treaty and agreed on bilateral co-operation.

21 December 1997: The two leading candidates in the first round of the presidential election were Arturas Paulauskas, a former prosecutor, who received 45% of the votes cast, and Valdas Adamkus, a retired environmental-protection executive who had mainly lived in the USA, with 28%.

4 January 1998: In the second round of the presidential election Adamkus received 50.4% of the votes cast, Paulauskas 49.6% (Adamkus was sworn in as President on 26 February).

December 1998: In accordance with the European Convention on Human Rights and Fundamental Freedoms, the Seimas voted to abolish the death penalty.

May 1999: Vagnorius, increasingly criticized, resigned as premier, with Irena Degutienė appointed to replace him for the interim. Later that month the Mayor of Vilnius, Rolandas Paksas, was appointed Prime Minister; his Government mainly comprised members of the CP and the CDPL.

October 1999: Paksas resigned as Prime Minister, following a dispute over the sale of the state-owned Mažeikiai NAFTA petroleum refinery to a US oil company, Williams International. Degutienė, who was once again appointed acting premier, declined the invitation to form a government. The First Deputy Chairman of the Seimas, Andrius Kubilius, became Prime Minister and a new, largely unaltered, Government was appointed on 3 November.

11 December 1999: At a summit of European Union (EU) heads of government in Helsinki, Finland, Lithuania, which had applied for EU membership in 1995, was invited to begin accession negotiations from 28 March 2000.

May 2000: In anticipation of the general election, the two largest left-wing parties, the LDLP and the LSDP, formed an electoral alliance which, with the addition of two smaller parties, became known as the A. Brazauskas Social Democratic Coalition (SDC).

13 June 2000: The Seimas passed legislation claiming compensation from Russia for damage caused to the country during Soviet occupation; despite President Adamkus' opposition to the legislation, the Chairman of the Seimas, Landsbergis, signed the law.

8 October 2000: In the legislative elections the SDC obtained 51 of the 141 seats in the Seimas; the Lithuanian Liberal Union, led by Paksas, secured 34 seats and the left-wing New Union, led by Arturas Paulauskas, 29. The CP, owing to a split in the party earlier in the year, won only nine seats.

12 October 2000: The Lithuanian Liberal Union, the New Union, the Centre Union and the Modern Christian Democratic Union signed a coalition agreement, becoming known as the New Policy bloc; agreements with several smaller parties ensured the bloc would have the support of a majority of deputies in the Seimas. Paulauskas was then elected Chairman of the new Seimas, and Paskas became Prime Minister, his Lithuanian Liberal Union-New Union Government being approved by the Seimas on 9 November.

18 June 2001: The New Union members of the coalition cabinet resigned, following the refusal of Prime Minister Paksas to stand down. On 20 June, after unsuccessful efforts to form a minority government, Paksas finally acceded. The Deputy Chairman of the Lithuanian Liberal Union, Eugenijus Gentvilas, was appointed acting Prime Minister.

3 July 2001: Former President Brazauskas became Prime Minister and a new cabinet was approved two days later.

21 December 2001: Paksas and 10 other deputies, including the former Minister of the Economy, Eugenijus Maldeikis (who had resigned in February), left the parliamentary faction of the Lithuanian Liberal Union, owing, in part, to the party's failure to nominate Paksas as First Deputy Chairman of the Seimas; the deputies were formally expelled from the party in January 2002.

9 March 2002: Paksas and other former members of the Lithuanian Liberal Union founded the Party of Lithuanian Liberal Democratic Party (LLDP), with Paksas as its Chairman.

11 June 2002: The Government formally agreed to EU demands to decommission the Ignalina nuclear power plant, in return for a substantial contribution from the EU towards the anticipated €2,400m. cost of the endeavour. The first reactor was to close by 2005, and the second by 2009.

21 November 2002: At a NATO summit meeting, held in Prague, Czech Republic, Lithuania was one of seven countries formally invited to join the Alliance in 2004.

13 December 2002: Lithuania was among 10 countries formally invited to join the EU from 1 May 2004.

22 December 2002: Valdas Adamkus failed to secure an overall majority in the first round of the presidential election, obtaining 35.5% of the votes cast; Rolandas Paksas received 19.7%. In local elections held on the same day the ruling LSDP won the overwhelming majority of municipal mayoralties.

5 January 2003: In a second round of voting in the presidential election, Paksas obtained 54.7% of the votes cast, compared with the 45.3% of the votes received by Adamkus.

26 February 2003: Paksas was inaugurated as President; he subsequently resigned from the chairmanship of the LLDP.

4 March 2003: Algirdas Brazauskas was reappointed as Prime Minister, replacing only one member of the Council of Ministers.

10–11 May 2003: In a national referendum 89.95% of participants voted in favour of EU membership.

27 May 2003: The Russian State Duma finally ratified the state border delimitation treaty signed in 1997 (and ratified by the Seimas in October 1999), in order to facilitate travel arrangements for Russian citizens travelling to and from the exclave of Kaliningrad.

History

Dr KĘSTUTIS GIRNIUS

EARLY HISTORY

The Lithuanian state emerged in the early 13th century, when the regional chieftain, Mindaugas (Mindouh), imposed his rule on the majority of Lithuanian tribes. The last pagan outpost in Europe, Lithuania was under constant attack by crusaders until the 15th century. However, the Lithuanian Grand Dukes, by a skilful blend of conquest, marriage alliances and compromise with the local nobility, expanded Lithuania's southern and eastern borders to the Black Sea and beyond Smolensk (Russia). In 1386 the Lithuanian Grand Duke, Jogaila (Jagiełło, baptized Władysław in 1386), married the Polish Queen Jadwiga (Hedwig), instituting an alliance that lasted until the late 18th century. When the Polish-Lithuanian Commonwealth was partitioned, ethnographic Lithuania was absorbed into the Russian Empire.

The alliance with Poland was a mixed blessing for Lithuania. Although its links with Poland ensured the country's integration into Western Christendom, the nobility and burghers were 'polonized', dividing the country into two distinct blocs—a literate élite that could not speak Lithuanian and the illiterate peasantry that did. During the early years of Russian rule (1795–1915) the authorities generally ignored the peasantry. However, following the insurrection of 1863, they opted for a policy of sustained russification, banning the publication of Lithuanian language books in the Latin script, and imposing restrictions on the activity of the Roman Catholic Church. This assault on language and religion had the reverse effect, for it galvanized the Church and a small body of intellectuals into efforts to preserve the national identity. Newspapers were published in Prussia and the USA and smuggled into Lithuania. Furthermore, political consciousness matured, and there were demands for autonomy, if not independence.

INDEPENDENT LITHUANIA

The collapse of the Russian and German Empires in the aftermath of the First World War permitted the rebirth of the Lithuanian state. Germany, which occupied Lithuania in 1915, allowed the formation of the Council of Lithuania, expecting it to supply a veneer of popular support for Lithuania's annexation. However, on 16 February 1918 the Council declared Lithuania's independence. Defeat on the western front ended German efforts to modify the declaration, and by the end of the year Lithuanians began to assume control of the country's administration.

Securing independence required two years of intermittent warfare and the loss of a significant amount of territory, in particular the Vilnius (Wilno) region, which was occupied by Polish troops in October 1920. The loss of this region was offset in part by Lithuania's seizure in 1923 of the former German territory of Klaipėda (Memel), then under the jurisdiction of the League of Nations. Most Western countries extended diplomatic recognition to Lithuania by the end of 1922.

The Constituent Assembly, elected in April 1920, ratified a Constitution that established a democratic republic, in which the parliament had extensive powers, including the right to elect the President. From 1920 to 1926 the Christian Democratic Party (CDP) and its allies dominated parliament, passing legislation that set the framework for communal life. When a coalition of leftists and minorities assumed power following the elections in May 1926, disgruntled army officers, Christian Democrats and members of the Nationalist Party organized a *putsch* on 16 December. Antanas Smetona, the leader of the Nationalist Party and former Chairman of the Council of Lithuania, was chosen to be President by the rightist 'rump' parliament. Smetona maintained power until the Soviet occupation in 1940. Although opposition political parties were banned and the media was censored, the population generally tolerated the mildly authoritarian regime.

During the period between the First and Second World Wars the economy was rebuilt. The radical agrarian reform of 1922 ensured a measure of social justice. The standard of living rose steadily, even during the economic Depression. Although the country remained underdeveloped industrially, it created a comprehensive educational system, fostered the arts and developed an adequate health system. The most important achievement, however, was the revival of a flagging national consciousness and the growth of civic and national pride.

THE YEARS OF OCCUPATION

The Molotov-Ribbentrop, or Nazi-Soviet Pact, signed on 23 August 1939, prepared the way for Lithuania's occupation by dividing Eastern Europe into spheres of influence. The Soviet authorities wasted little time in asserting their claims under the 'Secret Protocols' of the Pact. On 10 October Lithuania was coerced into signing a Treaty of Mutual Assistance that allowed the Soviet Red Army to establish bases on Lithuanian territory. On 15 June 1940 large units of the Red Army marched into Lithuania. Within two months, on 3 August, Lithuania became a Union Republic of the USSR.

The communist Government imposed quickly the Soviet model of society on Lithuania. Industry was nationalized, censorship introduced, all non-communist organizations were banned. Massive repression accompanied the sovietization of Lithuanian society. The deportation of about 20,000 people, including women and children, just one week before the German attack on the USSR convinced many Lithuanians that the communists had embarked on a policy of genocide.

At the beginning of the German–Soviet conflict on 22 June 1941, thousands of Lithuanians rose up against the withdrawing Soviets. A Provisional Government announced the re-establishment of Lithuanian independence. However, the Germans replaced the Government with their own administration, the chief task of which was to ensure that Lithuania contributed to the Nazi military machine. Nonetheless, for many Lithuanians the German occupation was less harsh than the Soviet one. Jews were the major exception; about 90% of Lithuania's 200,000 Jews were murdered under the Nazi regime.

The return of the Red Army in 1944 was greeted with trepidation. More than 60,000 individuals, including a disproportionate number of intellectuals, fled to the West, and thousands of young men withdrew into the forest, joining partisan bands that engaged in conflict with Soviet security forces. Organized guerrilla resistance spread throughout the country and lasted until 1952. As many as 30,000 partisans died in the struggle. The communists responded with mass arrests and deportations and the collectivization of agriculture. Deportations occurred almost annually until 1951. Estimates of the number of victims of communist repression vary, but 200,000, or about 10% of the total population, is a frequent figure.

Terror eased after the death of Stalin (Iosif V. Dzhugashvili) in 1953, as did hopes of Western intervention. Owing to a higher birth-rate in the villages, a smaller influx of Russians and previous industrial underdevelopment, ethnic Lithuanians still constituted 80% of the population and, by 1970, 67% of the members of the Communist Party of Lithuania (CPL), as well as a majority among leading government and party cadres.

Undeniable progress in some spheres occurred during Soviet rule. Illiteracy was eliminated, higher education was improved and made accessible to a broader cross-section of the population. Medical care became universally available. After two decades of decline, agricultural output improved dramatically and surpassed that of most Soviet republics. Industrialization gathered momentum in the 1970s, with the construction of several gigantic complexes. The standard of living rose steadily until 1985. Relative economic welfare conferred substantial legitimacy on the regime.

Undercurrents of dissatisfaction remained strong, however. Although the Government's campaign against the Roman Catholic Church was relentless, the Church succeeded in retaining both genuine independence and the sympathy of many Lithuanians, who came to consider it the chief defender of patriotic values. In the face of renewed repression in the early 1970s, militant priests began to publish the underground *Chronicle of the Catholic Church in Lithuania*, which the authorities never managed to suppress. Lay Roman Catholics and anti-communist intellectuals followed the lead of the Chronicle and founded a number of independent, *samizdat* publications, most of which were rapidly suppressed and their editors imprisoned.

THE ROAD TO INDEPENDENCE

Lithuania regained its independence in an astonishingly brief period. At the end of 1987 conservative, if not reactionary, elements were firmly in control of the CPL and were planning a new campaign against clericalism and nationalism. Barely two years later, on 11 March 1990, Lithuania declared the re-establishment of its independence. The founding meeting of the Lithuanian Movement for Reconstruction (Sąjūdis) on 3 June 1988 is generally considered to be the starting-point of Lithuania's national rebirth. The Movement's initial goals were modest: co-operation with the Government in fostering reform; the creation of separate republican citizenship; greater economic, cultural, and political autonomy. Several propitious decisions ensured the future of Sąjūdis, in particular its rejection of the tutelage of the CPL and its decision to mobilize the population in support of its programme.

On 20 October 1988 the CPL elected the popular Algirdas Brazauskas as its First Secretary. A conciliatory attitude adopted by Brazauskas and the leaders of Sąjūdis soon fell victim to the dictates of political reality and to rising expectations. The CPL supported moderate reforms but aimed to retain its hegemony, while Sąjūdis refused to be a junior partner. For several months Sąjūdis, under the leadership of Vytautas Landsbergis, and the CPL vied for public support. Sąjūdis was the clear winner. In the March 1989 elections to the all-Union Congress of People's Deputies, Sąjūdis candidates won 37 of the 42 seats in Lithuania. Endowed with electoral legitimacy, Sąjūdis began to demand the dismantling of fundamental features of the Soviet state. The defeat in the elections was a sobering experience for the CPL, for it realized that without a radical change in policy it would face a similar debacle in the elections to the Lithuanian Supreme Soviet in 1990. Younger CPL activists, aware that urging anything less than severance of formal links with the USSR would be tantamount to political suicide, pressed for the establishment of an independent Communist Party of Lithuania. On 20 December 1989 the Party Congress voted in favour of doing so. Despite disapproval by the central authorities and a visit by Soviet leader Mikhail Gorbachev to Lithuania in January 1990, Lithuania's communists did not rescind their decision.

Although the secession from the Communist Party of the Soviet Union (CPSU) led to an increase in the popularity of the CPL, Sąjūdis easily won a majority of seats in the elections to the Lithuanian Supreme Soviet on 24 February 1990. On 11 March, in its first session, the newly elected parliament approved a declaration proclaiming the restoration of Lithuanian sovereignty. On the same day Landsbergis was elected Chairman of the Supreme Council (as the parliament had been renamed), easily defeating Brazauskas. Kazimiera Prunskienė was appointed Prime Minister and asked to form a government.

CONSOLIDATION OF INDEPENDENCE

The Soviet central authorities reacted harshly to Lithuania's actions. A campaign of intimidation commenced almost immediately and was supplemented by an economic blockade on 18 April 1990. Many Western governments urged Lithuania to seek a compromise, but the Sąjūdis majority in the Supreme

Council refused to accept any accord that could be interpreted as mandating a suspension of the acts of independence.

The initial euphoria that accompanied the surge to independence soon dissolved. Parliament and the Government quarrelled over the division of powers and duties. Landsbergis and Prunskienė disagreed sharply on policy towards the USSR. Prunskienė was more willing to make concessions, while Landsbergis feared that compromises on matters of principle would only encourage the all-Union authorities to increase their demands. Tension mounted until Prunskienė and the Government were forced to resign on 10 January 1991. The new Prime Minister, Gediminas Vagnorius, was a firm supporter of Landsbergis. In January the USSR resorted to force in its attempts to restore its authority in Lithuania. Airborne troops and the special KGB (Committee of State Security) Alpha unit were sent to Vilnius, where they occupied various buildings. On 13–14 January a column of tanks fired on a crowd of civilians gathered around the Vilnius television tower, killing 15 and wounding hundreds. The violence was counterproductive, as ordinary citizens rallied to support the Government.

Although Soviet forces did not launch any further large-scale operations, the killings created a sense of uncertainty. The failure of the conservative coup attempt in the Russian and Soviet capital, Moscow, in August 1991 and the resulting ascendancy of the Russian President, Boris Yeltsin, resolved the impasse. Western countries quickly began to recognize Lithuania's independence, as did the new Soviet State Council on 6 September.

Independence did not, however, herald an era of political consensus. Although Landsbergis and Sąjūdis now seemed invincible and their policies vindicated, political fortunes changed dramatically. Problems, which had not been voiced publicly, owing to fears that they might undermine the quest for independence, emerged. The standard of living of most Lithuanians decreased sharply, economic reforms were ineffective and the dismantling of the collective farms led to chaos and anger in the countryside. Parliamentary debate became querulous and bitter, engendering popular disgust with politics. Internal disputes hindered the effectiveness of the Vagnorius Government, while Landsbergis continued his efforts to establish a powerful presidency, despite strong parliamentary opposition. On 25 May 1992 a referendum on strengthening the role of the presidency failed to win the necessary majority. On 9 July the Supreme Council decided to hold new elections and, five days later, Vagnorius was deposed by a vote of 'no confidence'.

The results of the elections of 25 October and 15 November 1992 were unexpected. The former CPL, reconstituted as the Lithuanian Democratic Labour Party (LDLP) in December 1990, won 76 of the 141 seats in the Seimas (as the Supreme Council had been renamed), pro-Landsbergis Sąjūdis candidates won 49, with the remainder of the seats divided among several minor groupings. Three factors played a central role in the LDLP's victory: Brazauskas' popularity; anger at Sąjūdis's confrontational style of politics; and dissatisfaction with the worsening economic situation. Proving that the parliamentary election results were not fortuitous, Brazauskas was elected President of the Republic, when he easily defeated Lithuania's ambassador to the USA, Stasys Lozoraitis, an *émigré*, in the direct presidential elections of 14 February 1993.

Initial fears that the LDLP would pursue populist programmes and halt economic reforms proved to be unfounded. Adolfas Šleževičius, who served as Prime Minister from 10 March 1993 to 8 February 1996, continued and, in some respects, accelerated Lithuania's integration into the market economy. None the less, success alternated with failure. Despite sharp declines in industrial production and the

standard of living, the Government fulfilled the austere conditions of the economic memorandum signed with the IMF. The expected improvement of the economy did not materialize, however.

The public's dissatisfaction with the Government's inability to solve economic problems paled in comparison to the anger caused by its indifference to corruption. The authorities ignored blatant cases of public officials living beyond their means, the asset stripping that characterized privatization, and complaints by foreign businessmen that nothing could be done without bribes. In late December 1995 the press revealed that Prime Minister Šleževičius had used unofficial information to withdraw his savings from troubled banks that were to be closed two days later. Initially the LDLP rallied to the support of Šleževičius, but when public anger failed to subside, President Brazauskas called for his removal. On 8 February 1996 the Seimas dismissed him from his duties. Nevertheless, the public's anger was not assuaged; it was clear that the LDLP had defended Šleževičius longer than decency and loyalty required. The new Prime Minister, Laurynas Mindaugas Stankevičius, took charge of what was clearly an interim administration.

In the parliamentary elections, held on 20 October and 10 November 1996, the Conservative Party (CP), led by Vytautas Landsbergis and consisting primarily of members of Sąjūdis, won a decisive victory, obtaining 70 of 141 seats, while its allies, the Christian Democratic Party of Lithuania (CDPL), garnered a further 16. The LDLP suffered a defeat, the magnitude and scope of which was as unexpected as the party's triumph four years earlier. It obtained only 12 seats, and one-sixth of the votes that it had won in 1992. Landsbergis was elected Chairman of the Seimas, while Gediminas Vagnorius once again became Prime Minister.

The CP formed a coalition government with the CDPL. Possessing an overwhelming majority in the Seimas, they undertook a series of reforms and easily overrode objections by the President. Frustrated by growing political isolation, in October 1997 Brazauskas announced that he would not seek a second presidential term in the election, to be held in December. In the second round of elections, held in early January 1998, Valdas Adamkus, an *émigré* who had fled Lithuania in 1944, narrowly defeated (by less than 1% of the votes) the left-wing former Prosecutor-General, Artūras Paulauskas. The new President quickly assumed an active role in political life, seeking to increase the power of the presidency. The Government concentrated its efforts on economic reform and expansion, more aggressive tax collection, and improving the standard of living. Such policies were quite successful until the effects of the Russian financial crisis in August 1998 led to a recession in 1999. However, earlier disagreements between the party's two leaders—Landsbergis and Vagnorius—had already begun to undermine the CP's unity.

In early 1999 Prime Minister Vagnorius became embroiled in a bitter quarrel with President Adamkus, following the latter's public criticism of what he believed to be the Government's failure to eradicate corruption in the public sector and his demands for Vagnorius' resignation. Although the Seimas expressed its support for Vagnorius in April, the Prime Minister resigned on 3 May. Two weeks later Rolandas Paksas, the Mayor of Vilnius, was appointed Prime Minister. However, the new Government proved incapable of formulating a clear policy for dealing with the financial and economic crisis and lacked the resolve to address other major issues. Paksas resigned as premier on 27 October, protesting against the decision of the majority of the cabinet to approve the sale of the Mažeikiai NAFTA petroleum refinery to the US company, Williams International. Andrius Kubilius, hitherto First Deputy Chairman of the Seimas, was sworn in as Prime Minister on 3 November. The new Prime Minister succeeded in reducing the budgetary deficit, limiting government spending, and renegotiating an agreement with the IMF. However, the measures were not enough to resuscitate his party's flagging political fortunes.

The parliamentary elections, held on 8 October 2000, introduced another change of direction in Lithuanian politics. The CP won only nine seats, while the A. Brazauskas Social Democratic Coalition, an alliance led by the Lithuanian Social Democratic Party (LSDP) and the Lithuanian Democratic Labour Party (LDLP), with the former President as Honorary Chairman, obtained the greatest amount of votes and seats (51). However, the newly founded Lithuanian Liberal Union, chaired by Paksas, and the New Union (Social Liberals), led by Paulauskas, received enough seats (34 and 29, respectively) and the support of several minor parties to form the new ruling coalition. Paulauskas was elected Chairman of the Seimas, and Paksas became Prime Minister. The new coalition was fragile from the outset, as the Liberal Union was pro-business and right of centre, while the New Union had a populist and leftist orientation. Internal squabbling, growing voter dissatisfaction, and the upsurge in the popularity of the LSDP (the Coalition had united into a single party in January 2001) strengthened the position of the radicals in the New Union, who had initially hoped to form a coalition with the Social Democrats. The crisis came in mid-June, when the New Union withdrew its ministers from the cabinet. Paksas' efforts to form a new coalition failed, and he resigned on 20 June. Algirdas Brazauskas, the leader of the LSDP, became the Prime Minister of the new Government that was appointed on 5 July. Dealing from a position of strength, the LSDP did not even offer a coalition agreement to the New Union, which had to be satisfied with an informal accord and six of the 13 portfolios.

The new Government continued the progress made by its predecessors in reducing the budgetary deficit, supporting market reforms and working on the legislation required to ensure entry into the European Union (EU). Several years of solid economic growth had helped to consolidate the Government's popularity, despite discontent from within two of its core constituencies—unskilled urban workers and farmers—who had expected more generous funding of social programmes. The LSDP performed strongly in the regional and municipal elections held in December 2002, winning substantially more seats than any other party. The Government remained firmly in control and no major political challenges were expected, as the centre-right continued to be plagued by internal disputes.

In an unexpected political development, Rolandas Paksas defeated the popular incumbent Valdas Adamkus in the second round of the presidential elections, held on 5 January 2003 (following an initial inconclusive round on 22 December 2002), to become Lithuania's third President since 1992. Paksas, who founded the Lithuanian Liberal Democratic Party (LLDP) in March 2002, after he failed to be re-elected as Chairman of the Lithuanian Liberal Union, won 55% of the votes cast in the second round, compared with Adamkus's 45%. Paksas had little support within the Seimas, and was not expected to inaugurate major changes in either domestic or foreign policy.

The defeat of Adamkus in the presidential elections appeared to be a further case of the electorate simply choosing to vote against the incumbent. Similarly, every parliamentary election held had led to the defeat of the ruling coalition. All the major parties, with the singular exception of the LSDP, had experienced internal conflicts, resulting in formal splits and the founding of new parties. However, the frequent changes in government had not led to significant alterations in economic or foreign policy. The commitment of all the principal parties to membership of the North Atlantic Treaty Organization (NATO) and the EU, and to fulfilling agreements with the IMF and other international lending institutions, established tight parameters that limited the range of policies that were seriously to be considered. Lithuania's basic tax structure, welfare and labour policies, and the level of government regulation of the economy had not been subject to major reforms in almost a decade, and there were no major political forces that might challenge the status quo.

FOREIGN RELATIONS

Following the re-establishment of independence, Lithuania placed the highest priority on the integration of the country into Western economic and security structures, while maintaining reasonably good links with Russia. There were fluctuations and changes in emphasis concerning the best means of implementing such policy, but a broad consensus supported by all major political forces emerged from 1994. This consistency of purpose was fruitful, and in early 2003 Lithuania signed accession treaties with both the EU and NATO.

The Sąjūdis Government bluntly insisted on its sovereign right to determine its foreign policy and brushed aside Russian objections to its efforts to join NATO as unjustified attempts to interfere in its internal affairs. It took some time to convince the left, in particular the LDLP, to assent to a clear Western orientation. Initially, the LDLP sought to conduct what it called a 'balanced' foreign policy, but which in effect constituted an inclination towards neutrality. However, Russia disregarded the LDLP's conciliatory approach, refused to implement a treaty granting Lithuania 'most favoured nation' status in trade and imposed prohibitive tariffs on Lithuanian goods. In January 1994 the LDLP reversed its policy: President Brazauskas visited Brussels, Belgium, and Lithuania joined NATO's 'Partnership for Peace' programme.

Integration into Western organizations proceeded at a steady pace. On 14 May 1993 Lithuania became a full member of the Council of Europe. A free-trade agreement with the EU entered into effect on 1 January 1995, and on 12 June Lithuania signed an association agreement with the EU (the so-called Europe agreement), which came into force in February 1998. In December 1999 the EU invited Lithuania to commence accession negotiations. Lithuania's progress in the negotiations was rapid, and by the end of 2001 it was considered one of the leading candidates for admission. At the EU's Copenhagen summit in Denmark in December 2002 Lithuania completed its negotiations with the EU. Lithuania was to receive more assistance per head than any of the other nine countries that were scheduled to accede in 2004, with special funding for the closure of the Ignalina nuclear power plant and the implementation of the new transit procedures for travellers crossing Lithuanian territory to reach the Russian exclave of Kaliningrad. In a referendum, held on 10–11 May 2003, 90% of Lithuanians voted in favour of EU membership. Lithuania was formally to join the Union on 1 May 2004.

Lithuania was equally determined and successful in its pursuit of NATO membership. After the LDLP's initial reluctance to develop closer links with NATO had been overcome, Lithuania became a very active participant in the Partnership for Peace programme and its soldiers participated in NATO peace-keeping operations in the Balkans and elsewhere. The modernization of Lithuania's armed forces was evaluated favourably by NATO officials. By mid-2002 even Russia accepted the inevitability of Lithuanian membership, although it continued to express its doubts about the wisdom of NATO expansion. At a NATO summit meeting, held in Prague, the Czech Republic, in late November 2002, Lithuania received the long-awaited formal invitation to join the Alliance. During a visit to Vilnius in the same month, the US President, George W. Bush, made explicit the USA's commitment to Lithuania's security.

Despite Russian opposition to NATO membership for the Baltic states, relations with Russia improved steadily in the 1990s. Initial disagreements concerning the withdrawal of Russian troops from Lithuanian territory and the regulation of Russian military transit to the Kaliningrad exclave were resolved. The granting of Lithuanian citizenship to all members of the Russian minority who sought it eliminated a potential source of conflict. In 1997 Lithuania became the first country outside the Commonwealth of Independent States (CIS—comprising the countries of the former USSR, with the exception of the Baltic states) to sign a treaty with Russia, delimiting their common border. On 27 May 2003 the Russian State Duma finally ratified the treaty, which included an agreement on the land border, as well as an agreement on the exclusive economic zone and the continental shelf in the Baltic Sea. At a summit meeting in Moscow in March 2001 the Presidents of both countries issued a joint declaration, reiterating their commitment to maintaining their good relationship. However, disagreements arose the following year concerning transit arrangements to Kaliningrad. Russia insisted that it continue to be visa-free, while Lithuania demanded strict controls in conformity with the EU's Schengen Agreement on common borders. An accord was eventually reached, stipulating that after 1 July 2003 Russian citizens travelling to Kaliningrad would require 'facilitated' travel documents, which, in effect, were more easily obtainable visas.

Lithuania retained cordial links with Belarus and even adopted the role of mediator between the Belarusian Government and the EU, after the latter accused Belarus of human rights violations. At the beginning of the 2000s, however, Lithuanian-Belarusian relations were strained, owing to Lithuania's decision to allow political opponents of the Government of Belarus to reside in Vilnius. Lithuania continued to urge the West to engage in critical dialogue with Belarus. In March 2002 Lithuania and Poland launched a joint initiative to request a mandate from the Council of Europe to commence discussions with Belarus, aimed at reducing the international isolation of that country.

Lithuania's traditionally close ties with Estonia and Latvia have been reinforced by the development of an impressive institutional structure to ensure Baltic co-operation. Regular meetings at the presidential, governmental and parliamentary levels helped to overcome some misunderstandings that arose in the mid 1990s, owing to minor trade disputes and competition over foreign investment and membership of the EU and NATO. Military co-operation has always been excellent. In the late 1990s the three countries established a joint international peace-keeping battalion (BALTBAT), as well as a defence college, a naval unit and an air observation system. Lithuania placed special importance on further improving its relations with Poland, a country with which it had strong historical, if not always friendly, links. In 1997 joint councils at presidential, governmental and parliamentary levels were established to resolve emerging problems and broaden the range of co-operative ventures. Poland vigorously supported Lithuania's efforts to join NATO. Lithuania also has close relations with the Nordic countries, especially Denmark, which actively supported the Lithuanian cause in European forums. Lithuania participated in wider regional initiatives; it was a founding member of the Council of Baltic Sea States in 1992, and assumed its presidency in 1999.

Despite occasional complaints regarding the growth of foreign influence, both cultural and commercial, and restraints on the country's sovereignty, Lithuania's political élite and the majority of its population believe that NATO membership will guarantee the country's national security, while entry into the EU should ensure the country's domestic prosperity. The benefits of close ties with neighbouring states are also widely recognized. Thus, the main tenets of Lithuanian foreign policy are likely to remain constant for many years.

The Economy

Dr KĘSTUTIS GIRNIUS

In the latter half of the 20th century the Lithuanian economy underwent two fundamental transformations that gravely disrupted the established patterns of economic activity. Following the Soviet occupation of 1940, Lithuania's industrially underdeveloped, primarily agricultural, but capitalist economy was subjected to the dictates of the central planning authorities in Moscow, the Russian and Soviet capital. Its agriculture was collectivized, its industry and commerce nationalized. Economic development was sporadic under the Soviet regime, but by 1980 Lithuanian industry compared favourably in quality, technical level and labour productivity to the USSR as a whole, and the standard of living was one of the highest among the republics.

The disadvantages of a centrally planned economy became evident after the collapse of the USSR in 1991, when Lithuania began its transition to a market economy. Owing to the availability of inexpensive natural resources, the industrial sector had become excessively energy intensive, inefficient in its utilization of resources, and incapable of manufacturing internationally competitive products. More than 90% of Lithuania's trade was with the rest of the USSR, which supplied Lithuanian industry with raw materials and a market for its outputs. The need to sever these trading links and to downsize the inefficient industrial sector led to serious economic difficulties.

By 2003 the Lithuanian economy had undergone a successful and fundamental transformation. In March 2001 the European Commission stated that Lithuania could 'be regarded as a functioning market economy and should be able to cope with competitive pressure and market forces within the Union in the medium term'. This evaluation was supported by the USA in February 2003. On the positive side, Lithuanian trade had been redirected towards the West, the current-account deficit on the balance of payments had been reduced radically, the majority of firms had been privatized, the national currency, the litas, was stable, and from 2 February 2002 its fixed rate of exchange was linked to the common European currency, the euro, instead of the US dollar. The economy also made an impressive recovery from a major downturn in the late 1990s, showing its ability to adjust to changed circumstances. However, major shortcomings in the economy still existed. Lithuanian industry remained vulnerable to outside pressures, productivity was low, rural areas remained blighted, and the unemployment rate had remained stubbornly above 10%.

Relative success accompanied the first steps in the transition process. By 1991 Lithuania had passed legislation for the privatization of state property, distributed investment vouchers to citizens to facilitate the privatization process, and dismantled most collective farms. By liberalizing prices well ahead of Russia, and by utilizing the favourable terms of trade, Lithuania managed to mitigate the effects of sharp decreases in production until early 1992. However, the cumulative effects of the industrial downturn, the lack of investment, disruption of trade, and lax monetary policy resulted in a sharp decline in the gross domestic product (GDP), an increase in the rate of inflation and a consequent decrease in the standard of living.

In 1991 an economic downturn commenced and accelerated sharply in the following two years. In 1991 GDP declined by 5.7%. It declined by 21.3% in 1992 and by 16.2% in 1993. The situation improved slightly in 1994, when the decline in GDP slowed to 9.8%, and in 1995 the Lithuanian economy registered growth, of 3.3%, as reforms began to have some effect. The decline in GDP and industrial production was accompanied by a dangerous surge in inflation that also reached its apex in 1992. The adoption of a currency board helped stabilize the currency, and more substantial growth was registered in the following years. Privatization of most small and medium-sized enterprises continued at a steady pace. By December 1995 a reported 83% of state-owned assets designated for privatization had been transferred to private ownership, and most Lithuanians owned their residences. By early 1996 macroeconomic stability had been achieved. In 1996 GDP increased by 4.7%, and it grew by 7.3% in 1997 and by 5.1% in 1998.

In 1999, owing to the consequences of the Russian financial crisis (beginning with a dramatic devaluation of the Russian currency, the rouble, in August of the previous year) and the Government's inadequate response to the emerging problems, Lithuania fell into recession and GDP declined by 4.2% in real terms. Industrial production declined by almost 14%. In 2000 the Lithuanian economy began a modest recovery, as GDP grew by 4.9%, caused primarily by a 7.6% rise in the added value of industry. The economic upturn accelerated in 2001 and 2002 with GDP increasing by 6.3% and by 6.2%, respectively. The transport, trade and construction sectors made the major contributions to this increase. According to provisional figures for 2002 GDP was calculated at US $13,900m., or $3,988 per head. Continued growth was forecast for 2003.

DOMESTIC SECTORS

The structure of the Lithuanian economy underwent major changes in the last decade of the 20th century. The role of industry and agriculture declined steadily in the 1990s, while the services sector assumed an ever more important role. The contribution of industry (including mining, manufacturing and power) to overall GDP decreased from some 65% in 1991 to about 24% in 2002. In turn, the services sector registered steady growth in the same period, accounting for some 61% of GDP in 2001.

The structure of industry also altered greatly throughout the decade. The sectors that had the closest links with Russian industry were the most adversely affected. The manufacture of machinery, which comprised 27% of industrial output in 1990, had fallen to a mere 2.5% by 1997; production of electronic equipment registered a similar decline.

The giant industrial plants that were the pride of Soviet Lithuanian industry fared badly. The first unit of the Ignalina power plant, which had the world's largest Russian Graphite Moderated Channel Tube (RBMK or 'Chornobyl'-type) reactors and supplied about 85% of Lithuania's energy, is to be closed by 2005, at the insistence of the European Union (EU); the second reactor is to be closed by 2009. In June 2002 the EU agreed to make a substantial contribution towards the cost of decommissioning the plant, expected to reach €2,400m. Since exports of electricity to all its immediate neighbours, as well as Estonia, have risen sharply in recent years, Lithuania is canvassing the EU and its Baltic neighbours for financial support for the construction of a new nuclear power plant.

One-third of the shares of the Mažeikiai NAFTA petroleum refinery, which accounted for about 10% of GDP, were sold to the US company, Williams International, in 1999. However, Williams experienced great difficulties in reaching an agreement with Russian companies for the long-term supply of petroleum, partly owing to their desire to acquire the refinery. In September 2002 the Russian petroleum company Yukos signed several agreements that left it with a 53.7% share of the company, while the state retained 40.7%, with the remaining 5.7% distributed among various minor shareholders. The company remained unprofitable in 2002, but losses were 41.3% less than in 2001. Overall, industrial production increased by 7.5% in 2002, as quarrying of stone and clay, the manufacture of motor vehicle parts, furniture, paper and wood products recorded strong growth.

In the early 1990s capital was scarce in Lithuania, and foreign firms invested primarily in the food, clothing and textiles industries, which could be privatized quickly and refurbished to produce competitive goods for export. Phillip Morris of the USA and its subsidiary, Kraft Jacobs Suchard, were the first foreign companies to make major investments in Lithuania. Mid-sized German firms followed their lead. By the end of 1997 the new contours of the industrial landscape were evident. The food and beverages industry received the largest share, followed by petroleum processing, chemicals and related products, textiles, clothing and fur processing. By the early 2000s the largest proportion of new investment was directed towards manufacturing (see below). The construction industry, which languished in the early 1990s, had made a strong recovery, and accounted for some 6% of GDP in 2001; in 2002 production increased by 13%. More than 50% of all construction work is done in Vilnius, and another 25% in Kaunas and Klaipėda.

The role of agriculture in the economy also declined from the 1990s. The sectoral share of GDP declined from some 30% in 1991 to 7.2% in 2001, as the huge collective and state farms, which produced meat and dairy products for the USSR, were dismantled. Most agricultural land was returned to its previous owners or their heirs. These individual farms accounted for almost three-quarters of total agricultural production, even though their average size was less than 20 ha, and their future viability remained in doubt.

Animal husbandry, which accounted for two-thirds of aggregate value of agricultural production in Soviet years, declined dramatically in the 1990s. The number of cattle, hogs, and poultry more than halved. Limited changes occurred in the use of agricultural land, most of which was sown with grain and forage crops, the remainder with potatoes, flax and sugar beet. Only the larger farmers experimented with the production of industrial crops.

The loss of its traditional markets, competition from the West, and higher energy and fertilizer prices combined to weigh heavily on the agricultural sector. The upturn that commenced in 1994 ended with the collapse of the traditional Russian market in 1998. However, the modest recovery that began in 2000 had been further consolidated. In 2002 crop output increased by 8.5% compared with the previous year, but productivity remained far below Western European levels, and various support programmes consumed some 10% of state spending; in 2002 17.8% of the population continued to be employed in agriculture. Efforts to reduce subsidies faltered because government purchases of milk and other products were the only source of income for many of the inhabitants of the countryside.

Wholesale and retail trade, transportation and communications, and real estate dominated the services sector. Retail trade did not emerge from the downturn of 1999 until 2001, when it increased by 7.4%. It grew by a healthy 12.4% in 2002, as consumer confidence was re-established. The transport sector, which had declined slightly in 2001, rebounded as a result of increased turnover at the port of Klaipėda. However, the port's future remained in doubt, as Russia continued to pressure its own firms to favour domestic ports. At the beginning of 2003 the Lithuanian fixed-line telecommunications market was formally deregulated, and the five-year monopoly of Lietuvos Telekomas came to an end. Major changes in service and pricing were not expected. The mobile telephone market had grown steadily for more than five years, and its penetration rate at the beginning of 2003 was 45%.

FOREIGN TRADE AND PAYMENTS

The composition and origin of Lithuania's international trade altered significantly in the years following independence. Dependence on Russia diminished in the 1990s, while commercial links with the countries of the EU increased to a lesser degree than did those of the other Baltic states. The volume of both imports and exports continued to grow, although there was a sharp decline in 1998 and 1999, owing to the effects of the collapse of the Russian market.

In 1991 more than 93% of Lithuania's total trade was with the other Soviet nations, while only 7% was with Western nations. Trade was rapidly reorientated towards the EU, as Scandinavian and German countries took the lead in forging ties with the newly independent country. In 2002 the EU was Lithuania's main trading partner by a strong margin, accounting for some 48% of Lithuanian exports and 45% of its imports, representing a slight increase compared with the previous year. The United Kingdom had emerged as Lithuania's leading export partner, accounting for 13.4% of total exports in 2002, followed by Russia, Germany and Latvia. Lithuania's exports to the EU states were primarily raw materials, such as wood, and low-cost goods, such as textiles and clothing. There was also an increase in the export of assembled goods, such as machinery and transport equipment and electronics, as well as food products, which were produced to meet EU health standards. Chemicals and plastics formed the main exports to Russia. The Commonwealth of Independent States (CIS—the countries of the former USSR, excluding the three Baltic states) remained an important trading partner. In 2002 CIS countries received 19.2% of Lithuania's exports and provided 26.2% of its imports. Lithuania remained dependent on Russia for petroleum and other raw materials, and as a market for some of its less competitive products, such as food products, wood pulp and plastics.

Lithuania had a substantial trade deficit from 1994. The sale of raw materials, semi-finished products, textiles and agricultural goods did not offset the cost of imports of natural gas and petroleum from Russia, and automobiles, heavy machinery and high-technology products from the West. The imbalance between imports and exports was exacerbated further by the fact that the local currency, the litas, 'pegged' (or fixed) as it was to the US dollar, appreciated against the EU and CIS currencies, making exports less competitive. Exports increased steadily from 1999, and increased by more than 20% in both 2000 and 2001. Exports rose by another 10.6% in 2002, to a value of some €5,900m. However, imports increased by 11.0%, and the balance of trade remained negative, at €2,289m.

Lithuania gradually reduced trade barriers in the 1990s, and in April 2001 the Seimas (Parliament) completed the ratification process that made official Lithuania's entry into the World Trade Organization (WTO). In the late 1990s the growing trade deficit contributed to an uncomfortably high current-account deficit on the balance of payments. It was equivalent to 10.3% of GDP in 1997, to 12.1% in 1998 and to 11.2% in 1999. A dramatic improvement occurred in 2000, when the deficit declined by 43.5% compared with the previous year, and represented only 6.0% of GDP. Central bank

officials attributed the decline to improvements not only in the balance of trade, but also in the services surplus, particularly in the transport, communications and construction services. In 2001 the current-account deficit declined to below 5.0% of GDP, a striking improvement, in less than four years. In 2002 the deficit was €696m., or 4.8% of GDP.

Foreign direct investment (FDI) in Lithuania has increased in recent years, even though privatization is nearing completion. The Government was consistently eager to sell small and medium-sized businesses. However, it was initially reluctant to privatize the largest firms, particularly in the energy sector, primarily because of fears that their sale to foreign, especially Russian firms, would render Lithuania subject to manipulation by foreign countries. By 1998 most industrial firms had been privatized, while the last state-run bank was sold to the Norddeutsche Landesbank Girozentrale (Germany) in March 2002. Although fears of foreign control have not been allayed completely, the Government was in the process of selling off the energy and transport sectors. The sale of a second 34% share in Lietuvos Dujos (Lithuanian Gas) to Russia's Gazprom was postponed in 2003, owing to disagreements over the price, and a condition imposed by Lithuania stating that at least 70% of the company's gas exports to Lithuania should be channelled through Lithuanian Gas. However, the privatization of the major elements of the electricity sector was expected to be completed in 2003. The Government intended to sell 12%–15% of shares in Mažeikiai NAFTA to the European Bank for Reconstruction and Development (EBRD) by the end of 2003. Efforts to sell 34% of the shares in Lithuanian Airlines, the national carrier, seemed to have failed, however, and there were some difficulties in selling the remaining shipping firms. None the less, FDI in Lithuania increased by 23.7% in 2002, to total €3,820m. at 1 January 2003. The total remained less per head than in Estonia and Latvia, in part because perceptions of favouritism, corruption and lack of transparency had a restraining effect on investment until the late 1990s. The Nordic countries, in particular Denmark and Sweden, were major investors, and they were joined by Estonia, Germany and the USA in 2002. The structure of foreign investment had also altered somewhat: in 2001–02 manufacturing received the largest proportion of new investments (29.3%), followed by financial intermediation (20.1%), the retail and wholesale trade (17.3%), and communications services (13.9). Portfolio investment had never been significant.

MONETARY AND FISCAL POLICY

A strict monetary policy allowed Lithuania to moderate inflation and establish a stable national currency. Lithuania withdrew from the 'rouble zone' on 1 October 1992, when the country was on the verge of 'hyperinflation'. The rate of inflation for 1992 was 1,020%. The introduction of the litas in 1993 did not dampen inflation—410% in 1993—as the exchange rate remained subject to sharp fluctuations. The decisive measure, taken on 1 April 1994, was the adoption of the currency-board system. According to the system, all litai in circulation were supported by foreign currency and gold reserves and were exchangeable on demand. The rate of four litai to one US dollar that was established at this time remained in force, despite occasional attacks on the litas and the soaring current-account deficits of the late 1990s. By 1996 price inflation had declined to an annual average of 24.6% and the rate decreased steadily thereafter, reaching 5.1% in 1998. The annual rate of increase in consumer prices was just 0.8% in 1999 and 0.9% in 2000, and it was 1.3% in 2001. The stability of the litas and the efficiency of the currency board were no longer questioned. On 1 February 2002 the litas was 'repegged' to the euro at the rate of 3.45 litai to one euro. The switch reflected Lithuania's changing trade patterns, reduced exchange-rate fluctuations with Lithuania's main trading partners and provided a stable environment for continued growth. The rate of consumer-price inflation was 0.3% in 2002.

For most of the 1990s government deficits were modest, averaging about 2% of GDP. This was the result of prudent fiscal policies, and of improved tax collection, which aimed to restrict the 'shadow' economy. During the recession of 1999, however, the situation worsened, and the budgetary deficit increased to about 5.7% of GDP as the Government continued its expansionary fiscal policies during the Russian financial crisis. With encouragement from the IMF, the Government introduced an austerity budget in 2000 that reduced the deficit to 2.0% of GDP. Strong economic growth helped pare down the budget deficit to 1.2% of GDP in 2002. From its founding, the social-security system, Valstybinio socialinio draudimo sistema (SoDRA), operated with a budgetary deficit, which reached US $126m. in 2000. With a rapidly ageing population and a potentially unsustainable long-term debt, the Government reduced benefits for working pensioners and raised the qualifying pensionable age. In 2001 a modest budgetary surplus of $250,000 was achieved, marking important progress in improving revenue flows and reducing administrative costs. In March 2002, in another indication of growing confidence in the stability of the banking system, the Bank of Lithuania reduced the minimum required reserve ratio for commercial banks from 8% to 6%. In early 2003 the Bank announced its intention to reduce the reserve ratio to the EU norm of 2% within two years.

Total public-sector debt was increasing steadily, but remained manageable. At the end of 2002 it amounted to €3,815m., or 26.2% of GDP. Of the total, 75% was foreign debt, the majority of which comprised loans from commercial banks and financial institutions.

STANDARD OF LIVING AND EMPLOYMENT

The economic turmoil unleashed by the demise of the USSR had severe consequences for most of Lithuania's inhabitants. Inflation in 1991–96 destroyed the savings of most of the population, real wages and pensions decreased sharply (by almost 50%, according to some estimates), leading to the impoverishment of a significant portion of the population. Social inequality also increased markedly. With the decline in earning power, a disproportionate share of income was spent on necessities. In 1994 the average family spent 60% of their budget on food, a portion that would have been greater if not for changes in eating habits. Since then living standards have improved markedly, and expenditure on food account for 32% of the budget in the early 2000s. None the less, a substantial number of Lithuanians were still immured in poverty, with no prospect of betterment. In 2000 around 1% of the population lived in extreme poverty, defined as an income of less than US $32 per month, and a further 16% had incomes below the official poverty line of $65 per month; 24% of the population subsisted on pensions and other government benefits, and 37% of households, primarily in rural areas, had no adequate sanitation.

Real wages increased from 1995, except in 1999–2000. In 2002 wages increased by some 5%. In January 2002 the average pre-tax monthly wage was approximately €342, which was in line with the average for the region. Wage levels in the private sector continued to be lower than in the public sector; agricultural wages remained the lowest, and those in the financial and energy sectors the highest. The wage differential between men and women was substantial. The tax burden remained high, particularly the proportional tax of 33% on personal income.

The restructuring of industry and agriculture, as well as the reduction in the size of the public sector, swelled the ranks of the unemployed. The official rate of unemployment increased two-fold, rising from 6.2% in mid-1998 to 13.8% in 2002. Real unemployment was believed to be significantly higher: 17.5%, according to the International Labour Organization (ILO) methodology. Furthermore, about 7.5% of the labour force had been unemployed for over three years. The slow pace of job creation, limited job retraining opportunities, the concentration of employment opportunities in the three major cities, coupled with lack of affordable accommodation there, precluded any significant improvements in the labour market in the near future. The Ministry of Social Security and Labour estimated that slightly more than 200,000 citizens, mostly the young and better-educated, were working abroad; their number was expected to rise significantly in the coming years. Although their absence reduced pressure on the internal job market, fears were growing that Lithuania was losing the skilled workers it required to be competitive in the EU.

PROSPECTS

The performance of the economy after the recession of 1999 is a mark of its successful transition to a market economy. Despite two periods of reverse, 1991–93 and 1998–2000, the economy has shown steady, if unspectacular growth. GDP and real wages have grown, inflation had been brought under control, the currency was stabilized and the volatile banking sector was strengthened. Lithuania's budgetary deficit and foreign debt were modest. Lithuania consistently fulfilled its commitments to the IMF, and international ratings agencies revised upwards Lithuania's long-term ratings. Trade was redirected towards the West and the tax system was modernized. Prices and trade had been liberalized and the general investment climate improved. Lithuanian laws and regulations were adjusted to conform to EU norms. Lithuania also managed to cash in on its numerous positive intangibles: political stability, lack of ethnic strife, good geographical location, cordial ties with all its neighbours, including Russia, and membership of the EU by 2004.

Nevertheless, shortcomings remained. The Government showed great reluctance to relinquish control over so-called strategic assets, particularly in the energy and transportation sectors. State controls were intrusive, and investors still had to contend with a lethargic and corrupt bureaucracy. Laws regulating business were complicated and subject to frequent changes. The securities market was underdeveloped, hindering investment and plans to reform the pension system. Mortgages, venture capital, and loans to small business were almost unavailable. Although productivity had been increasing at an annual rate of around 4% since 1995, the productivity of many sectors was still but a fraction of that of leading industrial nations, thus undermining the advantages of inexpensive labour.

Cash-flow problems and the lack of working capital forced many companies to resort to barter arrangements to settle debts. An inflexible labour market limited the options available to both employers and employees. Despite increased investment, many branches of industry, especially the energy sector, were in need of modernization. Agricultural subsidies were a major drain on government resources. Industrial and agricultural products encountered difficulties in finding new markets. Living standards and life expectancy in the countryside were much lower than in urban areas, while mortality and morbidity rates were significantly higher. Revitalizing the rural areas remained one of the country's major economic challenges. The rigidity of the labour market had created a substantial class of the permanently unemployed, while the great upward mobility of the last decades had limited severely the chances of recent college graduates to assume positions of responsibility.

The two economic downturns helped rouse the Government from its relative complacency. Among the long-overdue measures initiated after 1999 were a reduction in state subsidies and the number of government employees, a consolidation of the budget, increased financial control over public activities and a reduction, if not an elimination, of the many regulations that impeded development of the business sector. Structural reforms were implemented in municipal finances, banking, and other financial sectors. Changes were made in the tax system. Progress was also made in modernizing the social-security system by supplementing the state-run pension with voluntary private schemes. The results are clearly visible. In 2003 Lithuania was ranked 36th in the global competitiveness report of the World Economic Forum. Inflation in 2001 and 2002 was less than 1.5%, while the country's commercial banks reported an aggregate unaudited profit of €42,500m., the highest level since the recovery of independence. That the economic downturn was soon brought under control, and that solid growth was registered in 2001–02, when the world economy teetered on the brink of a recession, was a tribute to the resilience that the Lithuanian economy had gained through the process of reform. Despite these achievements many Lithuanians have been relegated to the margins of economic life, and the country as a whole still has far to go; according to some estimates, the real GDP level in 2002 was only 77% of that in 1989, an implacable reminder that much remains to be done.

Statistical Survey

Source (unless otherwise indicated): Department of Statistics to the Government of Lithuania (Statistics Lithuania), Gedimino pr. 29, Vilnius 2600; tel. (523) 64822; fax (523) 64845; e-mail statistika@mail.std.lt; internet www.std.lt.

Area and Population

AREA, POPULATION AND DENSITY

Area (sq km).	65,301*
Population (census results)	
12 January 1989†	3,674,802
6 April 2001	
Males	1,629,148
Females.	1,854,824
Total	3,483,972
Population (official estimates at 1 January)	
2001	3,486,998
2002	3,475,586
2003‡	3,462,600
Density (per sq km) at 1 January 2003	53.0

* 25,213 sq miles.
† Figure refers to the *de jure* population. The *de facto* total was 3,689,779.
‡ Provisional figure, rounded.

POPULATION BY ETHNIC GROUP
(permanent inhabitants at 2001 census)*

	'000	%
Lithuanian	2,907.3	83.5
Polish	235.0	6.7
Russian	219.8	6.3
Belarusian	42.9	1.2
Total (incl. others)	3,484.0	100.0

* Figures are provisional.

ADMINISTRATIVE DIVISIONS
(2001 census)

County	Area (sq km)	Population	Density (per sq km)
Alytus	5,425	187,769	34.6
Kaunas	8,170	701,529	85.9
Klaipėda	5,746	385,768	67.1
Marijampolė	4,463	188,634	42.3
Panevėžys.	7,881	299,990	38.1
Šiauliai	8,751	370,096	42.3
Tauragė	3,874	134,275	34.7
Telšiai	4,139	179,885	43.5
Utena	7,201	185,962	25.8
Vilnius.	9,650	850,064	88.1
Total	65,301	3,483,972	53.4

PRINCIPAL TOWNS
(population at 2001 census)

Vilnius (capital) . .	542,287		Šiauliai	133,883
Kaunas	378,943		Panevėžys. . . .	119,749
Klaipėda	192,954		Alytus	71,491

2002 (official estimate at 1 January): Vilnius 553,373.

BIRTHS, MARRIAGES AND DEATHS

	Registered live births		Registered marriages		Registered deaths	
	Number	Rate (per 1,000)	Number	Rate (per 1,000)	Number	Rate (per 1,000)
1995 . .	41,195	11.4	22,150	6.1	45,306	12.5
1996 . .	39,066	10.8	20,433	5.7	42,896	11.9
1997 . .	37,812	10.6	18,796	5.3	41,143	11.5
1998 . .	37,019	10.4	18,486	5.2	40,757	11.5
1999 . .	36,415	10.3	17,868	5.1	40,003	11.3
2000 . .	34,149	9.8	16,906	4.8	38,919	11.1
2001 . .	31,546	9.1	15,764	4.5	40,399	11.6
2002* . .	30,153	8.7	16,162	4.7	41,162	11.9

* Provisional figures.

Expectation of life (WHO estimates, years at birth): 72.9 (males 72.6; females 72.9) in 2001 (Source: WHO, *World Health Report*).

IMMIGRATION AND EMIGRATION
('000 persons)

	1999	2000	2001
Immigrants	2.7	1.5	4.7
Emigrants.	1.4	2.6	7.3

EMPLOYMENT
(annual averages, '000 persons)*

	2001	2002
Agriculture, hunting, forestry and fishing . .	233.9	250.6
Mining and quarrying	2.8	4.3
Manufacturing	243.2	260.6
Electricity, gas and water	35.1	28.4
Construction	84.8	93.2
Wholesale and retail trade; repair of motor vehicles, motorcycles and personal and household goods	205.7	211.2
Hotels and restaurants	25.8	28.0
Transport, storage and communications . . .	86.0	87.4
Financial intermediation	10.9	14.0
Real estate, renting and business activities . .	41.1	54.9
Public administration and defence; compulsory social security	71.9	81.3
Education	155.0	138.9
Health and social work	99.6	94.6
Other community, social and personal service activities	51.9	53.8
Other activities not adequately defined . . .	4.2	4.9
Total	1,351.8	1,405.9
Unemployed	284.0	224.4
Total labour force	1,635.8	1,630.3
Males	830.1	828.9
Females	805.7	801.4

* Official estimates based on results of 2001 census.

Health and Welfare

KEY INDICATORS

Total fertility rate (children per woman, 2001)	1.3
Under-5 mortality rate (per 1,000 live births, 2001) . . .	9
HIV/AIDS (% of persons aged 15–49, 2001)	0.07
Physicians (per 1,000 head, 1998)	3.95
Hospital beds (per 1,000 head, 2000)	10.1
Health expenditure (2000): US $ per head (PPP)	420
Health expenditure (2000): % of GDP	6.0
Health expenditure (2000): public (% of total)	72.4
Human Development Index (2000): ranking	49
Human Development Index (2000): value	0.808

For sources and definitions, see explanatory note on p. vi.

Agriculture

PRINCIPAL CROPS
('000 metric tons)

	1999	2000	2001
Wheat	870.9	1,237.6	1,076.3
Barley	741.6	859.6	776.2
Rye	260.9	311.4	231.1
Oats	67.1	82.9	84.3
Buckwheat	8.6	14.8	12.7
Triticale (wheat-rye hybrid)	85.1	130.9	36.7
Other cereals	14.4	20.6	19.8
Potatoes	1,708.0	1,791.6	1,054.4
Sugar beet	870.9	881.6	900.0
Dry peas	46.5	49.7	30.0
Other pulses*	16.4	23.5	22.2
Rapeseed	115.0	81.0	64.8
Cabbages	119.6	125.7	121.3
Tomatoes	6.8	5.1	4.4
Cucumbers and gherkins . . .	12.0*	12.0	8.0
Dry onions	23.1	20.3	22.7
Carrots	47.4	65.3	61.6
Green peas*	5.0	6.0	5.0
Other vegetables*	111.2	98.3	99.0
Apples	100.0	98.6	151.1
Pears	9.2	3.0	4.0
Grapes†	22.0	20.0	n.a.

* Unofficial figure(s).
† FAO estimates.

Source: FAO.

LIVESTOCK
('000 head at 1 January)

	1999	2000	2001
Horses	74	75	68
Cattle	923	898	748
Pigs	1,159	936	856
Sheep	16	14	12
Goats	24	25	23
Chickens	6,749	6,372	5,576
Turkeys	377*	400†	400†
Rabbits	102	85	82

* Unofficial figure.
† FAO estimate.

Source: FAO.

LIVESTOCK PRODUCTS
('000 metric tons, unless otherwise indicated)

	1999	2000	2001
Beef and veal	77.3	75.4	63.9
Pig meat	91.0	84.5	91.6
Poultry meat	23.0	17.2*	18.5*
Cows' milk	1,714.2	1,724.7	1,794.0
Cheese	37.2	43.6	47.0
Butter	26.2	19.3	21.0
Eggs	40.1	36.4	37.4
Honey	0.8	0.8	0.8
Cattle hides (fresh)†	9.2	10.7	8.1

* Unofficial figure.
† FAO estimates.

Source: FAO.

Forestry

ROUNDWOOD REMOVALS
('000 cubic metres, excl. bark)

	1999	2000	2001
Sawlogs, veneer logs and logs for sleepers	2,535	2,900	2,850
Pulpwood	1,240	1,100	1,150
Other industrial wood	25	50	50
Fuel wood	1,124	1,450	1,650
Total	4,924	5,500	5,700

Source: FAO.

SAWNWOOD PRODUCTION
('000 cubic metres, incl. railway sleepers)

	1999	2000	2001
Coniferous (softwood)	850	1,000	950
Broadleaved (hardwood) . . .	300	300*	300*
Total	1,150	1,300	1,250

* FAO estimate.

Source: FAO.

Fishing

(metric tons, live weight)

	1998	1999	2000
Capture	66,578	33,594	78,987
Atlantic cod.	3,296	4,371	4,721
Atlantic redfishes . . .	1,769	3,884	6,687
Jack and horse mackerels . .	11,902	2,641	25,464
Atlantic herring . . .	2,368	1,313	1,198
Sardinellas	10,575	2,814	6,324
European sprat . . .	4,460	3,117	1,682
European anchovy	3,612	1,067	16,137
Chub mackerel	5,420	549	3,871
Atlantic mackerel . . .	2,823	4,936	2,085
Largehead hairtail . . .	9,708	2	32
Northern prawn	3,340	4,167	6,376
Aquaculture	1,516	1,650	1,996
Common carp	1,516	1,650	1,921
Total catch	68,094	35,244	80,983

Source: FAO, *Yearbook of Fishery Statistics*.

Mining

('000 metric tons, unless otherwise indicated)

	2000	2001	2002
Crude petroleum	232	316	471
Dolomite ('000 cubic metres) . .	735	524	384
Limestone	1,060	850	894
Clay ('000 cubic metres) . . .	247	177	171
Peat	380	259	259

Industry

SELECTED PRODUCTS
('000 metric tons, unless otherwise indicated)

	1999	2000	2001
Sausages and smoked meat products	54.1	55.2	54.2
Flour	215.3	204.9	211.5
Mayonnaise	7.9	8.6	10.2
Refined sugar	121.2	126.6	108.7
Beer ('000 hectolitres) . .	184.8	210.5	219.3
Wine ('000 hectolitres) . . .	646	403	429
Cigarettes (million)	8,200	7,200	n.a.
Cotton fabrics (million sq m) .	57.0	55.1	44.3
Linen fabrics (million sq m) .	20.0	17.8	13.8
Fabrics of man-made fibres . .	39.2	17.7	8.0
Footwear—excl. rubber and plastic ('000 pairs)	1,800	700	900
Rubber and plastic footwear ('000 pairs)	500	400	400
Plywood ('000 cubic metres) . .	14.3	21.2	27.6
Particle board ('000 cubic metres)	101.9	172.2	197.4
Paper	9.6	12.3	13.9
Paperboard	27.6	41.0	54.3
Motor spirit (petrol)	4,507	4,659	6,544
Sulphuric acid	800	809	465
Mineral and chemical fertilizers	885	924	832
Nitrogenous fertilizers . . .	557	595	611
Cement	666	570	500*
Cast iron	23.4	23.2	24.6
Television receivers ('000) . .	186.5	207.2	143.2
Refrigerators and freezers ('000)	229.2	216.3	320.4
Bicycles ('000)	188	254	323
Electric energy (million kWh) . .	13,535	11,400*	14,700*

* Figure is rounded.

Finance

CURRENCY AND EXCHANGE RATES

Monetary Units
  100 centas = 1 litas (plural: litai).

Sterling, Dollar and Euro Equivalents (30 May 2003)
  £1 sterling = 4.812 litai;
  US $1 = 2.921 litai;
  €1 = 3.453 litai;
  100 litai = £20.78 = $34.24 = €28.96.

Note: In June 1993 Lithuania reintroduced its national currency, the litas, replacing a temporary coupon currency, the talonas, at a conversion rate of 1 litas = 100 talonai. The talonas had been introduced in May 1992, initially circulating alongside (and at par with) the Russian (formerly Soviet) rouble. An official mid-point exchange rate of US $1 = 4.00 litai was in operation from 1 April 1994 until 1 February 2002. From 2 February 2002 the litas was linked to the euro, with the exchange rate set at €1 = 3.4528 litai.

BUDGET
(million litai)*

Revenue†	1999	2000	2001
Tax revenue	10,452.0	10,316.8	10,697.4
Taxes on income, profits and capital gains	1,398.8	1,334.7	1,273.0
Corporate	360.8	311.7	259.2
Individual	1,038.0	1,023.0	1,013.8
Social security contributions	3,405.5	3,597.7	3,678.0
Domestic taxes on goods and services	5,433.5	5,239.5	5,596.9
Excises	1,643.4	1,459.8	1,643.0
General sales, turnover or value-added taxes . . .	3,741.9	3,698.2	3,831.4
Taxes on international trade	192.6	142.9	133.8
Other current revenue . . .	585.6	775.8	1,032.6
Administrative fees and charges, non-industrial and incidental sales	207.9	188.2	537.7
Capital revenue	13.4	42.7	29.2
Total	11,051.0	11,135.3	11,759.2

Expenditure‡	1999	2000	2001
General public services	530.9	519.2	599.6
Defence	440.4	589.3	755.4
Public order and safety	871.6	829.7	833.0
Education	749.3	724.0	925.5
Health	1,945.0	1,956.6	2,028.9
Social security and welfare . . .	4,519.8	4,574.6	4,480.1
Recreational, cultural and religious affairs and services	272.4	232.7	233.4
Economic affairs and services . .	1,540.3	1,577.6	1,527.2
Agriculture, forestry, fishing and hunting	561.1	731.6	587.7
Transport and communications .	833.5	720.6	680.6
Other purposes	2,386.1	1,443.5	1,233.7
Interest payments	626.7	771.0	741.7
Total	13,260.8	12,447.3	12,616.8
Current	11,120.9	11,533.6	11,499.5
Capital	2,139.9	913.7	1,117.3

* Figures refer to the consolidated accounts of the central Government, comprising the operations of the central budget, the Guarantee Fund and Fund for Financial Support to Bankrupted Enterprises, Privatization Funds, the Road Fund, Social Security Funds and others.
† Excluding grants received (million litai): 239.9 in 2001.
‡ Excluding lending minus repayments (million litai): 796.8 in 1999; −727.3 in 2000; −445.9 in 2001.

Source: IMF, *Government Finance Statistics Yearbook*.

INTERNATIONAL RESERVES
(US $ million at 31 December)

	2000	2001	2002
Gold*	47.10	51.47	63.82
IMF special drawing rights . . .	1.32	18.43	53.44
Reserve position in IMF	0.02	0.02	0.02
Foreign exchange	1,310.21	1,599.27	2,302.78
Total	1,358.65	1,669.19	2,420.06

* National valuation.

Source: IMF, *International Financial Statistics*.

MONEY SUPPLY
(million litai at 31 December)

	2000	2001	2002
Currency outside banks	2,658.3	2,919.9	3,756.4
Demand deposits at banking institutions	3,002.6	3,808.0	4,553.0
Total money (incl. others) . .	5,672.6	6,744.5	8,329.2

Source: IMF, *International Financial Statistics*.

COST OF LIVING
(Consumer Price Index; base: 1993 = 100)

	1999	2000	2001
Food (incl. beverages)	17,997.5	17,562.6	18,193.3
Fuel and light	783.6	914.8	933.0
Clothing	343.7	341.0	326.7
Rent	682.1	698.0	714.8
All items (incl. others)	19,750.8	19,937.4	20,195.9

Source: ILO.

2002 (base: 2001 = 100): All items 100.3.

NATIONAL ACCOUNTS
(million litai at current prices)

Expenditure on the Gross Domestic Product

	1999	2000	2001
Final consumption expenditure .	37,146.7	38,566.7	40,124.1
Households	27,441.8	28,580.7	30,407.3
Non-profit institutions serving households	71.2	132.3	119.2
General government . . .	9,633.8	9,853.7	9,597.6
Gross capital formation	9,858.2	9,025.9	9,979.8
Gross fixed capital formation .	9,614.2	8,565.3	9,784.6
Changes in inventories . . .	229.1	448.9	186.0
Acquisitions, *less* disposals, of valuables	14.9	11.7	9.2
Total domestic expenditure . .	47,004.9	47,592.6	50,103.9
Exports of goods and services . .	16,952.9	20,436.5	24,182.3
Less Imports of goods and services	21,349.5	23,331.2	26,788.6
GDP in market prices . . .	42,608.3	44,697.9	47,497.6
GDP at constant 2000 prices	42,608.3	44,697.9	47,497.6

Gross Domestic Product by Economic Activity

	1999	2000	2001
Agriculture, hunting and forestry	3,191.8	3,174.3	3,039.8
Fishing	22.9	26.7	28.8
Mining and quarrying	178.8	279.0	317.6
Manufacturing	6,985.1	7,981.6	8,767.7
Electricity, gas and water supply	1,660.1	1,540.9	1,786.1
Construction	2,949.4	2,429.9	2,597.0
Wholesale and retail trade . . .	6,065.9	6,685.0	7,478.3
Hotels and restaurants	652.1	619.0	676.7
Transport, storage and communications	4,003.7	5,013.1	5,384.6
Financial intermediation . . .	868.2	881.0	987.5
Real estate, renting and business activities	3,186.4	3,403.7	3,554.6
Public administration and defence	2,678.2	2,786.9	2,474.6
Education	2,655.2	2,595.9	2,722.6
Health and social work . . .	1,542.6	1,466.3	1,464.7
Other community, social and personal service activities . .	1,237.7	1,302.8	1,404.1
Private households with employed persons	31.0	37.6	43.6
Sub-total	37,909.3	40,223.8	42,728.3
Less Financial intermediation services indirectly measured . .	612.7	590.5	593.4
Gross value added in basic prices	37,296.6	39,633.3	42,134.9
Taxes *less* subsidies on products	5,311.7	5,064.5	5,362.8
GDP in purchasers' values . .	42,608.3	44,697.8	47,497.7

BALANCE OF PAYMENTS
(US $ million)

	1999	2000	2001
Exports of goods f.o.b.	3,146.7	4,050.4	4,889.0
Imports of goods f.o.b.	−4,551.3	−5,154.1	−5,997.0
Trade balance	−1,404.6	−1,103.8	−1,108.0
Exports of services	1,091.5	1,058.8	1,157.0
Imports of services	−786.1	−678.7	−700.3
Balance on goods and services	−1,099.1	−723.7	−651.4
Other income received . . .	114.8	185.5	205.7
Other income paid	−372.6	−379.3	−385.5
Balance on goods, services and income	−1,356.8	−917.5	−831.1
Current transfers received . . .	167.4	246.8	262.0
Current transfers paid	−4.6	−4.3	−4.5
Current balance	−1,194.1	−674.9	−573.6
Capital account (net)	−3.3	2.2	1.4
Direct investment abroad . . .	−8.6	−3.7	−7.1
Direct investment from abroad . .	486.5	378.9	445.8
Portfolio investment assets . . .	−2.0	−141.4	26.2
Portfolio investment liabilities . .	512.7	405.9	238.0
Financial derivatives assets . .	—	—	18.3
Financial derivatives liabilities .	—	—	−19.6
Other investment assets . . .	−182.5	39.9	−225.0
Other investment liabilities . .	259.8	22.8	300.9
Net errors and omissions . . .	−42.2	128.3	153.6
Overall balance	−178.7	158.0	359.0

External Trade

PRINCIPAL COMMODITIES
(million litai)

Imports c.i.f.	2000	2001	2002
Vegetable products	698.4	692.7	712.1
Prepared foodstuffs; beverages, spirits and vinegar; tobacco and manufactured substitutes . .	874.0	990.7	1,003.1
Mineral products	5,082.2	5,385.8	5,030.9
Products of the chemical or allied industries	1,986.2	2,338.7	2,447.4
Plastics, rubber and articles thereof	1,201.9	1,340.9	1,479.3
Textiles and textile articles . . .	2,038.4	2,226.7	2,244.8
Base metals and articles thereof .	1,156.7	1,328.5	1,922.0
Machinery and mechanical appliances; electrical equipment; sound and television apparatus .	3,418.1	4,250.6	4,939.6
Vehicles, aircraft, vessels and associated transport equipment .	1,900.3	2,923.2	4,624.3
Total (incl. others)	21,826.0	25,413.2	28,562.2

Exports f.o.b.	2000	2001	2002
Live animals and animal products	809.9	853.6	788.3
Vegetable products	309.1	497.1	412.9
Prepared foodstuffs; beverages, spirits and vinegar; tobacco and manufactured substitutes . .	650.5	886.3	914.2
Mineral products	3,234.3	4,287.9	3,830.8
Products of the chemical or allied industries	1,201.3	1,179.9	1,306.7
Plastics, rubber and articles thereof	475.8	536.5	571.3
Wood cork and articles thereof; wood charcoal; manufactures of straw, esparto, etc.	901.1	964.6	1,094.3
Textiles and textile articles . . .	2,836.3	2,994.1	3,058.1
Base metals and articles thereof .	634.3	680.9	958.1
Machinery and mechanical appliances; electrical equipment; sound and television apparatus .	1,619.7	1,960.2	2,030.8
Vehicles, aircraft, vessels and associated transport equipment .	1,034.9	1,694.0	3,247.5
Miscellaneous manufactured articles	643.0	769.8	1,001.4
Total (incl. others)	15,237.5	18,332.0	20,290.7

PRINCIPAL TRADING PARTNERS
(million litai)

Imports c.i.f.	2000	2001	2002
Belarus	394.4	483.4	424.2
Belgium	430.8	497.9	529.8
China, People's Republic . . .	336.2	500.2	673.6
Czech Republic	299.3	344.1	367.1
Denmark	675.7	742.0	832.8
Estonia	254.1	274.9	n.a.
Finland	557.1	582.3	648.1
France	922.1	956.7	1,099.8
Germany	3,285.1	4,377.7	4,851.2
Italy	788.7	1,073.0	1,386.1
Japan	406.1	482.4	609.9
Kazakhstan	90.3	37.0	400.5
Latvia	360.1	392.4	454.7
Netherlands	496.2	598.2	642.1
Norway	168.9	245.0	416.2
Poland	1,076.2	1,233.0	1,366.3
Russia	5,973.1	6,428.0	6,070.7
Spain	242.3	323.5	n.a.
Sweden	743.2	771.4	932.3
Ukraine	330.8	414.3	466.2
United Kingdom	985.3	851.8	939.0
USA	517.4	771.9	811.8
Total (incl. others)	21,826.0	25,413.2	28,562.2

Exports f.o.b.	2000	2001	2002
Belarus	442.8	714.5	650.8
Belgium	241.3	299.5	388.7
Denmark	743.9	822.2	1,037.9
Estonia	343.0	595.2	773.9
Finland	194.1	255.1	239.1
France	667.6	601.3	834.3
Germany	2,183.5	2,303.1	2,103.9
Italy	356.4	369.3	565.8
Latvia	2,287.8	2,316.3	1,955.0
Netherlands	730.4	538.6	639.2
Norway	170.6	239.1	485.0
Poland	832.3	1,148.3	721.7
Russia	1,083.7	2,019.7	2,469.9
Spain	182.0	247.4	n.a.
Sweden	667.5	671.3	853.3
Switzerland	193.5	107.7	337.2
Turkey	266.8	260.2	352.8
Ukraine	670.8	618.9	527.5
United Kingdom . . .	1,185.9	2,532.6	2,727.2
USA	739.2	696.8	714.7
Total (incl. others)	15,237.5	18,332.0	20,290.7

Transport

RAILWAYS
(traffic)

	2000	2001	2002
Passenger journeys ('000) . . .	8,852	7,718	7,217
Passenger-km (million)	611	533	498
Freight transported ('000 metric tons)	30,712	29,174	36,650
Freight ton-km (million) . . .	8,919	7,741	9,767

ROAD TRAFFIC
(public transport and freight)

	2000	2001	2002
Passenger journeys ('000) . . .	372,684	346,401	347,783
Passenger-km (million)	2,154	2,119	2,046
Freight transported ('000 metric tons)	45,013	45,075	45,047
Freight ton-km (million) . . .	7,769	8,274	10,709

ROAD TRAFFIC
(motor vehicles in use at 31 December)

	1999	2000	2001
Passenger cars	1,089,334	1,172,394	1,133,477
Buses and coaches	15,590	15,069	15,171
Lorries and vans	86,824	88,346	89,373
Motorcycles and mopeds . . .	19,515	19,842	20,244

INLAND WATERWAYS

	2000	2001	2002
Passenger journeys ('000) . . .	1,299.9	1,323.6	2,890.2
Passenger-km (million)	2	1	3
Freight transported ('000 metric tons)	852.4	543.3	515.0
Freight ton-km (million) . . .	1	1	1

SHIPPING

Merchant Fleet
(registered at 31 December)

	2000	2001	2002
Number of vessels	185	175	184
Total displacement ('000 grt) . .	434.2	393.3	435.3

Source: Lloyd's Register-Fairplay, *World Fleet Statistics*.

International Sea-borne Freight Traffic
('000 metric tons)

	1999	2000	2001
Goods loaded	12,864	18,552	18,144
Goods unloaded	2,796	4,296	4,224

Source: UN, *Monthly Bulletin of Statistics.*

CIVIL AVIATION
(traffic on scheduled services)

	2000	2001	2002
Passengers carried ('000) . . .	343	363	376
Passenger-km (million)	461	484	524
Freight transported (million metric tons)	3.3	3.3	3.4

Source: UN, *Statistical Yearbook.*

Kilometres flown: 10 million in 1998.

Tourism

FOREIGN VISITORS BY COUNTRY OF ORIGIN
(arrivals at accommodation establishments)

	1999	2000	2001
Belarus	12,971	14,034	19,195
Estonia	12,499	11,425	14,011
Finland	20,960	22,775	21,282
Germany	48,390	52,089	54,479
Latvia	27,354	24,750	27,252
Poland	33,288	37,477	45,820
Russia	24,890	28,282	44,859
Sweden	14,099	15,174	14,013
United Kingdom	13,332	13,383	11,138
USA	12,479	13,120	13,310
Total (incl. others)	293,247	299,938	349,662

Source: Lithuanian State Department of Tourism, Vilnius.

Receipts from tourism (US $ million): 550.4 in 1999; 391.3 in 2000; 383.0 in 2001 (Source: Bank of Lithuania).

Communications Media

	1999	2000	2001
Television receivers ('000) . . .	1,555	1,560	n.a.
Telephones ('000 main lines in use)	1,152.6	1,187.7	1,151.7
Mobile cellular telephones ('000 subscribers).	332.0	524.0	932.0
Personal computers ('000 in use) .	220	240	260
Internet users ('000).	103	225	250

1997: Radio receivers ('000 in use) 1,900; Facsimile machines (number in use) 6,200.

1999: Book titles (incl. brochures) 4,097; Newspapers 377 (number), 2,188 (average circulation, '000 copies); Other periodicals 418.

2002: Telephones ('000 main lines in use) 935.9; Mobile cellular telephones ('000 subscribers) 1,631.6.

Sources: International Telecommunication Union; UNESCO, *Statistical Yearbook* ; UN, *Statistical Yearbook* and Ministry of Education and Science, Vilnius.

Education

(2002/03)

	Institutions	Teachers*	Students*
Comprehensive schools	2,172	50,200	594,300
Vocational schools	82	4,700	44,400
Schools of further education . .	51	5,300	48,600
Universities	19	8,900	119,600

* Figures are rounded.

Source: Ministry of Education and Science, Vilnius.

Teachers (1999): Pre-primary schools 12,526; Primary and general secondary schools 52,000; Vocational schools 5,032.

Adult literacy rate (UNESCO estimates): 99.6% (males 99.5%; females 99.7%) in 2000 (Source: UN Development Programme, *Human Development Report*).

Directory

The Constitution

The Constitution was approved in a national referendum on 25 October 1992 and adopted by the Seimas on 6 November. The following is a summary of its main provisions:

THE STATE

The Republic of Lithuania is an independent and democratic republic; its sovereignty is vested in the people, who exercise their supreme power either directly or through their democratically elected representatives. The powers of the State are exercised by the Seimas (Parliament), the President of the Republic, the Government and the Judiciary. The most significant issues concerning the State and the people are decided by referendum.

The territory of the republic is integral. Citizenship is acquired by birth or on other grounds determined by law. With certain exceptions established by law, no person may be a citizen of Lithuania and of another state at the same time. Lithuanian is the state language.

THE INDIVIDUAL AND THE STATE

The rights and freedoms of individuals are inviolable. Property is inviolable, and the rights of ownership are protected by law. Freedom of thought, conscience and religion are guaranteed. All persons are equal before the law. No one may be discriminated against on the basis of sex, race, nationality, language, origin, social status, religion or opinion. Citizens may choose their place of residence in Lithuania freely, and may leave the country at their own will. Citizens are guaranteed the right to form societies, political parties and associations. Citizens who belong to ethnic communities have the right to foster their language, culture and customs.

SOCIETY AND THE STATE

The family is the basis of society and the State. Education is compulsory until the age of 16. Education at state and local government institutions is free of charge at all levels. State and local government establishments of education are secular, although, at the request of parents, they may offer classes in religious instruction. The State recognizes traditional Lithuanian and other churches and religious organizations, but there is no state religion. Censorship of mass media is prohibited. Ethnic communities may independently administer the affairs of their ethnic culture, education, organizations, etc. The State supports ethnic communities.

NATIONAL ECONOMY AND LABOUR

Lithuania's economy is based on the right to private ownership and freedom of individual economic activity. Every person may freely choose an occupation, and has the right to adequate, safe and healthy working conditions, adequate compensation for work, and social security in the event of unemployment. Trade unions may be freely established and may function independently. Employees have the right to strike in order to protect their economic and social interests. The state guarantees the right of citizens to old-age and disability pensions, as well as to social assistance in the event of unemployment, sickness, widowhood, etc.

THE SEIMAS

Legislative power rests with the Seimas. It comprises 141 members, elected for a four-year term on the basis of universal, equal and direct suffrage by secret ballot. Any citizen who has attained 25 years of age may be a candidate for the Seimas. Members of the Seimas may not be found criminally responsible, may not be arrested, and may not be subjected to any other restrictions of personal freedom, without the consent of the Seimas. The Seimas convenes for two regular four-month sessions every year.

The Seimas considers and enacts amendments to the Constitution; enacts laws; adopts resolutions for the organization of referendums; announces presidential elections; approves or rejects the candidature of the Prime Minister, as proposed by the President of the Republic; establishes or abolishes government ministries, upon the recommendation of the Government; supervises the activities of the Government, with the power to express a vote of 'no confidence' in the Prime Minister or individual ministers; appoints judges to the Constitutional Court and the Supreme Court; approves the state budget and supervises the implementation thereof; establishes state taxes and other obligatory payments; ratifies or denounces international treaties whereto the republic is a party, and considers other issues of foreign policy; establishes administrative divisions of the republic; issues acts of amnesty; imposes direct administration and martial law, declares states of emergency, announces mobilization, and adopts decisions to use the armed forces.

THE PRESIDENT OF THE REPUBLIC

The President of the Republic is the Head of State. Any Lithuanian citizen by birth, who has lived in Lithuania for at least the three preceding years, who has reached 40 years of age and who is eligible for election to the Seimas, may be elected President of the Republic. The President is elected by the citizens of the republic, on the basis of universal, equal and direct suffrage by secret ballot, for a term of five years. No person may be elected to the office for more than two consecutive terms.

The President resolves basic issues of foreign policy and, in conjunction with the Government, implements foreign policy; signs international treaties and submits them to the Seimas for ratification; appoints or recalls, upon the recommendation of the Government, diplomatic representatives of Lithuania in foreign states and international organizations; appoints, upon the approval of the Seimas, the Prime Minister, and charges him/her with forming the Government, and approves its composition; removes, upon the approval of the Seimas, the Prime Minister from office; appoints or dismisses individual ministers, upon the recommendation of the Prime Minister; appoints or dismisses, upon the approval of the Seimas, the Commander-in-Chief of the armed forces and the head of the Security Service.

THE GOVERNMENT

Executive power is held by the Government of the republic (Council of Ministers), which consists of the Prime Minister and other ministers. The Prime Minister is appointed and dismissed by the President of the Republic, with the approval of the Seimas. Ministers are appointed by the President, on the nomination of the Prime Minister.

The Government administers the affairs of the country, protects the inviolability of the territory of Lithuania, and ensures state security and public order; implements laws and resolutions of the Seimas as well as presidential decrees; co-ordinates the activities of the ministries and other governmental institutions; prepares the draft state budget and submits it to the Seimas; executes the state budget and reports to the Seimas on its fulfilment; drafts legislative proposals and submits them to the Seimas for consideration; establishes and maintains diplomatic representation with foreign countries and international organizations.

JUDICIAL SYSTEM

The judicial system is independent of the authority of the legislative and executive branches of government. It consists of a Constitutional Court, a Supreme Court, a Court of Appeal, and district and local courts (for details, see section on Judicial System below).

The Government

HEAD OF STATE

President: ROLANDAS PAKSAS (elected 5 January 2003; inaugurated 26 February 2003).

COUNCIL OF MINISTERS
(July 2003)

Prime Minister: ALGIRDAS MYKOLAS BRAZAUSKAS.

Minister of the Economy: PETRAS ČĖSNA.

Minister of Finance: DALIA GRYBAUSKAITĖ.

Minister of National Defence: LINAS ANTANAS LINKEVIČIUS.

Minister of Culture: ROMA ŽAKAITIENĖ.

Minister of Social Security and Labour: VILIJA BLINKEVIČIŪTĖ.

Minister of Justice: VYTAUTAS MARKEVIČIUS.

Minister of Transport and Communications: ZIGMANTAS BALČYTIS.

Minister of Health Care: JUOZAS OLEKAS.

Minister of Foreign Affairs: ANTANAS VALIONIS.

Minister of the Interior: VIRGILIJUS BULOVAS.

Minister of Agriculture and Forestry: JERONIMAS KRAUJELIS.

Minister of Education and Science: ALGIRDAS MONKEVIČIUS.

Minister of the Environment: ARŪNAS KUNDROTAS.

MINISTRIES

Office of the President: S. Daukanto 3/8, Vilnius 2008; tel. (526) 28986; fax (521) 26210; e-mail info@president.lt; internet www .president.lt.

Office of the Prime Minister: Gedimino pr. 11, Vilnius 2039; tel. (526) 63874; fax (521) 63877; e-mail kasp@lrvk.lt; internet www.lrvk .lt.

Ministry of Agriculture and Forestry: Gedimino pr. 19, Vilnius 2025; tel. (523) 91001; fax (521) 24440; e-mail zum@zum.lt; internet www.zum.lt.

Ministry of Culture: J. Basanavičiaus 5, Vilnius 2600; tel. (526) 19486; fax (526) 23120; e-mail culture@muza.lt; internet www.muza .lt.

Ministry of the Economy: Gedimino pr. 38/2, Vilnius 2600; tel. (526) 22416; fax (526) 23974; e-mail pr@po.ekm.lt; internet www .ekm.lt.

Ministry of Education and Science: A. Volano 2/7, Vilnius 2691; tel. (527) 43126; fax (526) 12077; e-mail smmin@smm.lt; internet www.smm.lt.

Ministry of the Environment: Jakšto 4/9, Vilnius 2694; tel. (526) 16148; fax (521) 20847; e-mail kanceliarja@aplinkuma.lt; internet www.gamta.lt.

Ministry of Finance: J. Tumo-Vaižganto 8A/2, Vilnius 2600; tel. (523) 90005; fax (521) 26387; e-mail finmin@finmin.lt; internet www .finmin.lt.

Ministry of Foreign Affairs: J. Tumo-Vaižganto 2, Vilnius 2600; tel. (523) 62444; fax (523) 13090; e-mail urm@urm.lt; internet www .urm.lt.

Ministry of Health Care: Vilniaus 33, Vilnius 2001; tel. (526) 21625; fax (521) 24601; e-mail webmaster@sam.lt; internet www .sam.lt.

Ministry of the Interior: Šventaragio 2, Vilnius 2600; tel. (527) 18451; fax (527) 18551; e-mail atstovasspaudai@vrm.lt; internet www.vrm.lt.

Ministry of Justice: Gedimino pr. 30/1, Vilnius 2600; tel. (526) 24670; fax (526) 25940; e-mail tm1@utic.tm.lt.

Ministry of National Defence: Totorių 25/3, Vilnius 2001; tel. (526) 24821; fax (521) 26082; e-mail vis@kam.lt; internet www.kam .lt.

Ministry of Social Security and Labour: A. Vivulskio 11, Vilnius 2693; tel. (526) 03790; fax (526) 03813; e-mail post@socmin.lt; internet www.socmin.lt.

Ministry of Transport and Communications: Gedimino pr. 17, Vilnius 2679; tel. (523) 93911; fax (521) 24335; e-mail transp@transp .lt; internet www.transp.lt.

President and Legislature

PRESIDENT

Presidential Election, First Ballot, 22 December 2002

Candidates	Valid votes cast	% of valid votes cast
Valdas Adamkus	514,154	35.53
Rolandas Paksas	284,559	19.66
Artūras Paulauskas	120,238	8.31
Vytautas Šerenas	112,215	7.75
Vytenis Povilas Andriukaitis	105,584	7.30
Kazimieras Prunskienė	72,925	5.04
Juozas Edvardas Petraitis	54,139	3.74
Eugenijus Gentvilas	44,562	3.08
Julius Veselka	32,293	2.23
Algimantas Matulevičius	32,137	2.22
Others	74,311	5.14
Total	1,447,117	100.00

Second Ballot, 5 January 2003

Candidates	Valid votes cast	% of valid votes cast
Rolandas Paksas	777,769	54.71
Valdas Adamkus	643,870	45.29
Total	1,421,639	100.00

SEIMAS
(Parliament)

Gedimino pr. 53, Vilnius 2002; tel. (523) 96880; fax (523) 99607; e-mail bendrasis@lrs.lt; internet www.lrs.lt.

Chairman: ARTŪRAS PAULAUSKAS.

First Deputy Chairman: ČESLOVAS JURŠĖNAS.

Deputy Chairmen: VYTENIS ANDRIUKAITIS, ARTŪRAS SKARDŽIUS, GINTARAS STEPONAVIČIUS.

General Election, 8 October 2000

Parties	% of votes	Seats
A. Brazauskas Social Democratic Coalition*	31.1	51
Lithuanian Liberal Union	17.3	34
New Union (Social Liberals)	19.6	29
Conservative Party of Lithuania	8.6	9
Lithuanian Farmers' Party	4.1	4
Christian Democratic Party of Lithuania	3.1	2
Lithuanian Centre Union	2.9	2
Lithuanian Poles' Electoral Action	1.9	2
Christian-Democratic Union	4.2	1
Moderate Conservative Union	2.0	1
Lithuanian Freedom Union	1.3	1
Young Lithuania National Party	1.2	1
Modern Christian-Democratic Union	—	1
Independents	—	3
Others	2.6	0
Total	100.0	141

*Comprising the Lithuanian Democratic Labour Party and the Lithuanian Social Democratic Party (the two parties formally merged under the latter name in 2001), the New Democracy Party (which merged with the Lithuanian Peasants' Party to form the Peasants' and New Democracy Union in 2002) and the Lithuanian Russians' Union.

Local Government

The system of local government in Lithuania comprises two levels. The lower level consists of 61 districts, of which 12 are cities and 49 are rural regions. The higher level consists of 10 counties, each with a governor, directly appointed by the Prime Minister. Municipal elections were held on 22 December 2002.

Association of Local Authorities in Lithuania: Gedimino pr. 24, Vilnius 260; tel. (526) 16063; fax (526) 15366; e-mail lsa3@vilnius.lt; internet www.lsa.lt; Foreign Relations Adviser JUSTAS SAKENAS.

County Councils

Vilnius County Council: Gedimino pr. 14, Vilnius 2001; tel. (521) 23082; fax (521) 26118; e-mail apskriti@vilnius.aps.lt; internet www.vilnius.aps.lt; Governor ALIS VIDŪNAS.

Alytus County Council: Tvirtovės 1/2, Alytus 4580; tel. (315) 71233; fax (315) 71473; e-mail aps@alytus.aps.lt; internet www.alytus.aps.lt; Governor RAIMUNDAS MARKAUSKAS.

Kaunas County Council: L. Sapiegos 10, Kaunas 3000; tel. (372) 22752; fax (372) 09191; e-mail kava@kaunas.aps.lt; internet www.kaunas.aps.lt; Governor VALENTINAS KALINAUSKAS.

Klaipėda County Council: Danės 17, Klaipėda 5800; tel. (463) 12483; fax (463) 14907; e-mail urs@klaipeda.aps.lt; internet www.klaipeda.aps.lt; Governor VIRGINIJA LUKOŠIENĖ.

Marijampolė County Council: Vytauto 28, Marijampolė 4520; tel. (343) 50250; fax (343) 91240; e-mail mara@aps.lt; internet www.marijampole.aps.lt; Governor ALBINAS MITRULEVIČIUS.

Panevėžys County Council: Respublikos 38, Panevėžys 5319; tel. (455) 05700; fax (454) 65517; e-mail apskritis@pava.lt; internet www.pava.lt; Governor RIMANTAS SANKAUSKAS.

Šiauliai County Council: Vilniaus 263, Šiauliai 5414; tel. (415) 24531; fax (415) 24536; e-mail apskritis@siauliai.aps.lt; internet www.siauliai.aps.lt; Governor ALVYDAS ŠEDŽIUS.

Tauragė County Council: 16 Vasario 6, Tauragė 5900; tel. (446) 52727; fax (446) 52881; e-mail apskritis@taurage.aps.lt; Governor ARŪNAS BEIŠYS.

Telšiai County Council: Žemaitės 14, Telšiai 5610; tel. (444) 52262; fax (444) 51442; e-mail apskritis@telsiai.aps.lt; internet www.is.lt/telsiai.aps; Governor KAZYS LEČKAUSKAS.

Utena County Council: Aušros 22, Utena 4910; tel. (389) 57500; fax (389) 59536; e-mail apskritis@utena.aps.lt; Governor RIMANTAS DIJOKAS.

District Councils

Akmenė Regional Council: Respublikos 2, Naujoji Akmenė 5464; tel. (425) 57144; fax (425) 5659; e-mail info@akmene.lt; internet www.akmene.lt; Mayor ANICETAS LUPEIKA.

Alytus City Council: Rotušės 4, Alytus 4580; tel. (315) 55118; fax (315) 55191; e-mail alytus@ams.lt; internet www.ams.lt; Mayor VYTAUTAS KIRKLIAUSKAS.

Alytus Regional Council: Pulko 21, Alytus 4580; tel. (315) 55530; fax (315) 74716; Mayor ALGIRDAS VRUBLIAUSKAS.

Anykščiai Regional Council: J. Biliūno 23, Anykščiai 4930; tel. (381) 51442; fax (381) 53630; e-mail anyr@is.lt; internet www.anyksciai.lt; Mayor SAULIUS NEFAS.

Birštonas City Council: Jaunimo 2, Birštonas 4440; tel. (319) 56233; fax (319) 56565; e-mail savivaldybe@birstonas.lt; internet sav.birstonas.lt; Mayor ANTANAS ZENKEVIČIUS.

Biržai Regional Council: Vytauto 38, Biržai 5280; tel. (450) 31233; fax (450) 32485; e-mail birzai@sav.lt; internet www.birzai.lt; Mayor REGIMANTAS RAMONAS.

Druskininkai City Council: Vilniaus 18, Druskininkai 4690; tel. (313) 55355; fax (313) 55376; e-mail info@druskininkai.lt; internet www.druskininkai.lt; Mayor ALGIMANTAS MAKNYS.

Elektrenai Regional Council: Elektrinės 8, Elektrėnai 4061; tel. (528) 58000; fax (528) 58005; e-mail elektrenu.savivsldybe@is.lt; internet www.elektrenai.lt; Mayor KĘSTUTIS VAITUKAITIS.

Ignalina Regional Council: Laisvės 70, Iganalina 4740; tel. (386) 52442; fax (386) 53148; e-mail info@ignalina.lt; internet www.ignalina.lt; Mayor BRONIS ROPĖ.

Jonava Regional Council: Žeimių g. 13, Jonava 5000; tel. (349) 61040; fax (349) 51309; e-mail savivaldybe@jonava.lt; internet www.jonava.lt; Mayor EGIDIJUS SINKEVIČIUS.

Joniškis Regional Council: Livonijos 4, Joniškis 5150; tel. (426) 69142; fax (426) 69143; e-mail savivaldybe@joniskis.lt; internet www.siauliai.aps.lt/joniskis/; Mayor EDMUNDAS GRIGALIŪNAS.

Jurbarkas Regional Council: S. Dariaus ir S. Girėno 96, Jurbarkas 4430; tel. (447) 70153; fax (447) 70166; e-mail jurbarkas@lsa.lt; internet www.jurbarkas.lt; Mayor ALOYZAS ZAIRYS.

Kaišiadorys Regional Council: Bažnyčios 4, Kaišiadorys 4230; tel. (346) 51233; fax (346) 51244; e-mail kaissav@is.lt; internet www.kaisiadorys.lt; Mayor PRANAS ZAVECKAS.

Kalvarijos Regional Council: Laisvės 1, Kalvarijos 1; tel. and fax (343) 23894; e-mail info@kalvarija.lt; internet www.kalvarija.lt; Mayor JONAS K. DZIRMEIKA.

Kaunas City Council: Laisvės 96, Kaunas 3000; tel. (372) 26058; fax (372) 23078; e-mail meras@kaunas.sav.lt; internet www.kaunas.lt; Mayor ARVYDAS GARBARAVIČIUS.

Kaunas Regional Council: Savanorių 371, Kaunas 3042; tel. (373) 05500; fax (373) 05501; e-mail meras@krs.lt; internet www.krs.lt; Mayor PETRAS MIKELIONIS.

Kazlu Ruda Regional Council: M. Valaneičaus 12, Kazlu Ruda 4500; tel. (343) 95052; fax (343) 95276; e-mail krs@is.lt; Mayor VALDAS KAZLAS.

Kėdainiai Regional Council: J. Basanavičiaus 36, Kėdainiai 5030; tel. (347) 55758; fax (347) 61125; e-mail kedainiai@lsa.lt; internet www.kedainiai.lt; Mayor VIKTORAS MUNTIANAS.

Kelmė Regional Council: Vytauto Dižiojo 58, Kelmė 5470; tel. (427) 51233; fax (427) 53490; e-mail kelme@lsa.lt; internet www.kelme.lt; Mayor K. ARVASEVIČIUS.

Klaipėda City Council: Liepų 11, Klaipėda 5800; tel. (463) 96000; fax (463) 96015; e-mail meras@klaipeda.lt; internet www.klaipeda.lt; Mayor RIMANTAS TARAŠKEVIČIUS.

Klaipėda Regional Council: Klaipėdos 2, Gargždai 5840; tel. (464) 52233; fax (464) 72005; e-mail audrkamp@takas.lt; internet www.klaipedos-r.lt; Mayor ČESLAVAS BANEVIČIUS.

Kretinga Regional Council: J. K. Chodkaevičiaus 10, Kretinga 5700; tel. (445) 51442; fax (445) 52448; e-mail kretinga@lsa.lt; internet www.kretinga.lt; Mayor V. KUBILIUS.

Kupiškis Regional Council: Vytauto 2, Kupiškis 4880; tel. (459) 35500; fax (459) 35510; e-mail info@kupiskis.lt; internet www.kupiskis.lt; Mayor LEONAS APŠEGA.

Lazdijai Regional Council: Vilniaus 1, Lazdijai 4560; tel. (318) 51233; fax (318) 51351; e-mail lazdijai@sav.lt; internet www.lazdijai.lt; Mayor JONAS MATULEVIČIUS.

Marijampolė City Council: J. Basanavičiaus 1, Marijampolė 4520; tel. (343) 90003; fax (343) 90014; e-mail mms@marijampole.lt; internet www.marijampole.lt; Mayor VIDMANTAS BRAZYS.

Marijampolė Regional Council: Vytauto 17, Marijampolė 4520; tel. (343) 51233; fax (343) 54265; e-mail valdyba@mari.omnitel.net; Mayor JUOZAS VAIČIULIS.

Mažeikiai Regional Council: Laisvės 8/1, Mažeikiai 5500; tel. (443) 98202; fax (443) 26165; e-mail maz.saviv@pikuolis.omnitel.net; internet www.mazeikiai.lt; Mayor BRONIUS KRYŽIUS.

Molėtai Regional Council: Vilniaus 44, Molėtai 4150; tel. (383) 51233; fax (383) 51442; e-mail info@moletai.lt; internet www.moletai.lt; Mayor VALENTINAS STUNDYS.

Neringa City Council: Taikos 2, Neringa 5870; tel. (469) 52234; fax (469) 52572; e-mail meras@neringa.lt; internet www.neringainfo.lt; Mayor STASYS MIKELIS.

Pagegiai Regional Council: Vilniaus 9, Pagegiai 5760; tel. (441) 57294; fax (441) 57874; Mayor VACLOVAS MISEIKIS.

Pakruojis Regional Council: Kęstučio 4, Pakruojis 5220; tel. (421) 69070; fax (421) 69090; e-mail pakruojis@lsa.lt; internet www.siauliai.aps.lt/pakruojis/; Mayor JUOZAS JUOZAPAITIS.

Palanga City Council: Vytauto 73, Palanga 5720; tel. (460) 48705; fax (460) 40216; e-mail valdyba@palanga.lt; internet www.palanga.lt; Mayor PRANAS ŽEIMYS.

Panevėžys City Council: Laisvės 20, Panevėžys 5319; tel. (455) 01350; fax (455) 01353; e-mail savspauda@panevezys.sav.lt; internet www.panevezys.sav.lt; Mayor VITAS MATUZAS.

Panevėžys Regional Council: Vasario 16–27, Panevėžys 5319; tel. (455) 82947; fax (455) 82975; e-mail meras@panrs.lt; internet www.panrs.lt; Mayor ALFREDAS PEKELIŪNAS.

Pasvalys Regional Council: Vytauto Didžiojo 1, Pasvalys 5250; tel. (451) 52546; fax (451) 52889; e-mail pasvalys@lsa.lt; internet www.pasvalys.lt; Mayor GINTAUTAS GEGUŽINSKAS.

Plungė Regional Council: Vytauto 12, Plungė 5640; tel. (448) 72232; fax (448) 71608; e-mail plunge@lsa.lt; internet www.plunge.lt; Mayor ALEKSANDRAS LUKAS.

Prienai Regional Council: Laisvės 12, Prienai 4340; tel. (319) 61102; fax (319) 61199; e-mail prienai@lsa.lt; internet www.prienai.lt; Mayor ANTANAS GUSTAITIS.

Radviliškis Regional Council: Aušros 10, Radviliškis 5120; tel. (422) 69001; fax (422) 69000; e-mail nadu.meras@siauliei.aps.lt; internet www.siauliei.aps.lt/radviliskis; Mayor VYTAUTAS SIMELIS.

Raseiniai Regional Council: V. Kudirkos 5, Raseiniai 4400; tel. (428) 51347; fax (428) 51604; e-mail raseiniai@lsa.lt; Mayor RIMAS STANKŪNAS.

Rietavas Regional Council: Plungės 13, Rietavas 5663; tel. (448) 68556; fax (448) 68446; e-mail savivaldybe@rietavas.lt; internet www.rietavas.lt; Mayor ANTANAS ČERNECKIS.

Rokiškis Regional Council: Respublikos 94, Rokiškis 4820; tel. (458) 71233; fax (458) 54420; e-mail rokiskis@lsa.lt; internet www.rokiskis.lt; Mayor EGIDIJUS VILIMAS.

Šakiai Regional Council: Bažnyčios 4, Šakiai 4460; tel. (345) 51233; fax (345) 52472; e-mail sakiai.sav@is.lt; internet www.sakiai.lt; Mayor JUOZAS PUODŽIUKAITIS.

Šalčininkai Regional Council: Vilniaus 49, Šalčininkai 4090; tel. (380) 51332; fax (380) 51244; e-mail meras@salcininkai.lt; internet www.salcininkai.lt; Mayor JOSIFAS RYBAKAS.

Šiauliai City Council: Vasario 16–62, Šiauliai 5400; tel. (415) 24100; fax (415) 24116; e-mail meras@siauliai.sav.lt; internet www.siauliai.sav.lt; Mayor VYTAUTAS JUŠKUS.

Šiauliai Regional Council: Vilniaus 263, Šiauliai 5419; tel. (415) 23888; fax (415) 24115; e-mail meras@siauliai-r.sav.lt; internet www.siauliai-r.sav.lt; Mayor RAIMUNDAS JAKUTIS.

Šilalė Regional Council: J. Basanavičiaus 2/1, Šilalė 5920; tel. (449) 74233; fax (449) 74154; e-mail silalesav@is.lt; Mayor ZITA LAZDAUSKIENĖ.

Šilutė Regional Council: S. Dariaus ir S. Girėno 1, Šilutė 5730; tel. (441) 79227; fax (441) 51517; e-mail meras@pamarys.lt; internet www.silute.lt; Mayor ARVYDAS JAKAS.

Širvintos Regional Council: Vilniaus 61, Širvintos 4100; tel. (382) 51233; fax (382) 53770; e-mail sirvintos@lsa.lt; Mayor VYTAS ŠIMONĖLIS.

Skuodas Regional Council: Vilniaus 13, Skuodas 5670; tel. (440) 73933; fax (440) 73984; e-mail skuodas@lsa.lt; Mayor LIUDVIKAS ŽUKAUSKAS.

Švenčionys Regional Council: Vilniaus 19, Švenčionys 4730; tel. (387) 66372; fax (387) 66365; e-mail savivaldybe@svencionys.lt; internet www.svencionys.lt; Mayor VYTAUTAS VIGELIS.

Tauragė Regional Council: Respublikos 2, Tauragė 5900; tel. (446) 51233; fax (446) 53446; e-mail taurage@lsa.lt; internet www.taurage.lt; Mayor PETRAS JAKUBAUSKAS.

Telšiai Regional Council: Žemaitės 14, Telšiai 5610; tel. (444) 52233; fax (444) 51244; e-mail telsiai@lsa.lt; Mayor JUOZAS BUTKEVIČIUS.

Trakai Regional Council: Vytauto 33, Trakai 4050; tel. (528) 55549; fax (528) 55524; e-mail trakai@lsa.lt; internet www.trakai.lt; Mayor VYTAUTAS MIKALAUSKAS.

Ukmergė Regional Council: Kęstučio 3, Ukmergė 4120; tel. (340) 63432; fax (340) 63370; e-mail ukmerge@sav.lt; internet www.ukmerge.lt; Mayor JANINA AKSTINAVIČIENĖ.

Utena Regional Council: Utenio 4, Utena 4910; tel. (389) 61611; fax (389) 61615; e-mail infosav@utena.sav.lt; internet www.utena.lt; Mayor ALVYDAS KATINAS.

Varėna Regional Council: Vytauto 12, Varėna 4640; tel. (310) 31500; fax (310) 51200; e-mail meras@varena.lt; internet www.varena.lt; Mayor VIDAS MIKALAUSKAS.

Vilkaviškis Regional Council: S. Nėries 1, Vilkaviškis 4270; tel. (342) 60060; fax (342) 60066; e-mail vilkaviskis@lsa.lt; internet www.vilkaviskis.lt; Mayor ALGIRDAS BAGUŠINSKAS.

Vilnius City Council: Gedimino pr. 9, Vilnius 2600; tel. (526) 20160; fax (521) 26057; e-mail meras@vilnius.lt; internet www.vilnius.lt/new/en/vadovybe.php; Mayor ARTŪRAS ZUOKAS.

Vilnius Regional Council: Rinktinės 50, Vilnius 2600; tel. (527) 50987; fax (527) 30068; e-mail vrsa1@aiva.lt; Mayor LEOKADIJA JANUŠAUSKIENĖ.

Visaginas City Council: Parko 14, Visaginas 4761; tel. (386) 31233; fax (386) 31286; internet www.visaginas.lt; Mayor ANTANAS IVANAUSKAS.

Zarasai Regional Council: Sėlių 22, Zarasai 4780; tel. (385) 30901; fax (385) 51240; e-mail z.rejest@is.lt; Mayor KOSTAS ZALECKAS.

Political Organizations

In mid-2003 37 political parties were registered with the Ministry of Justice.

Conservative Party of Lithuania (CP) (Homeland Union—Lithuanian Conservatives, Christian Democrats and Freedom Fighters): Gedimino pr. 15, Vilnius 2001; tel. and fax (523) 96450; e-mail info@tslk.lt; internet www.tslk.lt; f. 1993; from elements of Sąjūdis; Chair. ANDRIUS KUBILIUS; Exec. Sec. JURGIS RAZMA; 15,000 mems.

Lithuanian Christian Democrats: Pylimo 36/2, Vilnius 2001; tel. (526) 26126; fax (521) 27387; e-mail lkdp@takas.lt; internet www.lkdp.lt; f. 1904; re-est. 1989; formed in 2001 by merger of the Christian Democratic Party of Lithuania and the Christian Democratic Union; Chair. KAZYS BOBELIS; 12,000 mems.

Lithuanian Citizens' Alliance: Vilnius; tel. (527) 33394; f. 1996; Chair. MEČISLAV VAŠKOVIČ.

Lithuanian Economic Party: Vilnius; tel. (526) 31564; fax (526) 51380; f. 1995; Chair. KLEMENSAS ŠEPUTIS; 1,500 mems.

Lithuanian Freedom Union: Donelaičio 6, Kaunas; tel. (372) 02594; f. 1994; Chair. VYTAUTAS ŠUSTAUSKAS.

Lithuanian Green Party: Antakalnio 46–40, Vilnius 2055; tel. (374) 25566; fax (374) 25207; e-mail zigmasvaisvila@lrs.lt; internet www.zalieji.lt; f. 1989; Chair. RŪTA GAJAUSKAITE; 400 mems.

Lithuanian Humanistic Party: Vilnius; tel. (527) 35831; f. 1990; Chair. LEOPOLDAS TARAKEVIČIUS.

Lithuanian Justice Party: Nemuno 19, Kaunas; tel. (372) 09382; f. 1995; Chair. BRONIUS SIMANAVIČIUS.

Lithuanian Liberal Democratic Party (LLDP): Pylimo 27/14, Vilnius 2000; tel. (526) 23493; e-mail sekretoriatas@ldp.lt; internet www.ldp.lt; f. 2002; right-wing; Chair. VALENTINAS MAZURONIS; 1,500 mems.

Lithuanian Liberal and Centre Union: A. Jakšto 9, Vilnius 2001; tel. (523) 13264; fax (527) 91910; e-mail lls@lls.lt; internet www.lls.lt; f. 2003; by a merger of the Lithuanian Centre Union, the Lithuanian Liberal Union and the Modern Christian-Democratic Union; Chair. ARTŪRAS ZUOKAS; over 5,000 mems.

Lithuanian Life Logics Party: Vilnius; f. 1996; Chair. VYTAUTAS BERNATONIS.

Lithuanian National Union: Gedimino pr. 22, Vilnius 2600; tel. (526) 24935; fax (526) 17310; e-mail lietauta@takas.lt; internet www.lts.lt; f. 1924; refounded 1989; Chair. GEDIMINAS SAKALNIKAS; 3,000 mems.

Lithuanian People's Party: Pelesos 1/2, Vilnius; tel. (526) 30429; f. 1996; Chair. VYTAUTAS LAZINKA.

Lithuanian Poles' Electoral Action (AWPL): Didžioji 40, Vilnius 2601; tel. (521) 23388; f. 1994; Chair. WALDEMAR TOMASZEWSKI; 1,000 mems.

Lithuanian Polish People's Party (Polska Partia Ludowa): Vilnius; Chair. ANTONINA POLTAWIEC.

Lithuanian Political Prisoners' Party: Kipro Petrausko pr. 38, Kaunas 3005; tel. and fax (377) 95494; f. 1995; Chair. ZIGMAS MEDINECKAS.

Lithuanian Reform Party: Gedimino pr. 2, Vilnius; tel. (521) 25800; f. 1996; Chair. ALGIRDAS PILVELIS.

Lithuanian Republican Party: Pramonės pr. 3–62, Kaunas 3031; tel. (373) 51214; e-mail respublikos_varpai@takas.lt; internet respublikosvarpai.5u.com; active 1922–29; re-est. 1991; Chair. KAZIMIERAS PETRAITIS; 2,450 mems.

Lithuanian Rightist Union: A. Jakšto 9, Vilnius 2001; f. 2001 by the merger of the Lithuanian Independence Party, the Lithuanian Democratic Party, the Lithuanian Freedom League and the Homeland People's Union; planned merger with the Conservative Party of Lithuania in 2003; Chair. ARŪNAS ZEBRIUNAS; 2,000 mems.

Lithuanian Russians' Union: Savanorių pr. 11–70, Vilnius 2015; tel. (523) 96636; fax (526) 24248; e-mail sergejus.dmitrijevas@lrs.lt; internet www.sojuzrus.visiems.lt; f. 1995; contested the 2000 legislative election as part of the A. Brazauskas Social Democratic Coalition; Chair. SERGEJ DMITRIJEV; 1,200 mems.

Lithuanian Social Democratic Party (LSDP): Barboros Radvilaites 1, Vilnius 2600; tel. (526) 13907; fax (526) 15420; e-mail info@lsdp.lt; internet www.lsdp.lt; absorbed the Lithuanian Democratic Labour Party in 2001; Chair. ALGIRDAS BRAZAUSKAS; 11,000 mems.

Lithuanian Social Justice Union: Žirmūnų 30A–42, Vilnius; tel. (527) 32055; f. 1996; Chair. KAZIMIERAS JONAS JOCIUS.

Lithuanian Socialist Party: Šeškinės 65/58, Vilnius 2010; tel. (524) 19765; f. 1994; Chair. ALBINAS VISOCKAS; 800 mems.

Lithuanian Union of Political Prisoners and Deportees: Laisvės 39, Kaunas 3000; tel. (373) 23214; fax (377) 74100; e-mail tremtinys@takas.lt; internet www.lpkts.lt; f. 1988; planned merger with the Conservative Paty of Lithuania in 2003; Pres. POVILAS JAKUČIONIS; 60,000 mems.

Moderate Conservative Union: Odminių g. 5, Vilnius 2002; tel. (521) 26876; fax (521) 26880; e-mail info@nks.lt; internet www.nks.lt; f. 2000; centre-right; Chair. GEDIMINAS VAGNORIUS.

National Centre Party (NCP): Vilnius; f. 2003 by former members of the Lithuanian Centre Union unwilling to merge into the Lithuanian Liberal and Centre Union (q.v.); Chair. ROMUALDAS OZOLAS; 1,000 mems.

National Progress Party: Vilnius ; tel. (523) 96656; fax (523) 96779; e-mail egidijus.klumbys@lrs.lt; internet www.tpp.lt; active 1916–24, re-est. 1994; Chair. EGIDIJUS KLUMBYS; 1,100 mems.

New Union (Social Liberals): Gedimino pr. 10/1, Vilnius 2001; tel. (521) 07600; fax (521) 07602; e-mail centras@nsajunga.lt; internet www.nsajunga.lt; f. 1998; centre-left; Chair. ARTŪRAS PAULAUSKAS.

Peasants' and New Democracy Union: A. Jakšto 9–22, Vilnius 2001; tel. and fax (526) 15613; e-mail ndpartija@takas.lt; internet www.5ci.lt/ndmp; f. 2001 by the merger of the New Democracy Party and the Lithuanian Peasants' Party (Lithuanian Farmers' Party); Chair. KAZIMIERAS PRUNSKIENĖ; 1,500 mems.

Young Lithuania National Party ('Jaunoji Lietuva'): Čiurlionio 9/2, Vilnius 2009; tel. (372) 26254; fax (527) 03217; e-mail jaunalietuviai@is.lt; internet www.is.lt/jaunalietuviai; f. 1994; Chair. STANISLOVAS BUŠKEVIČIUS; 1,000 mems.

Diplomatic Representation

EMBASSIES IN LITHUANIA

Austria: Gaono g. 6, Vilnius; tel. (526) 60580; fax (527) 91363; e-mail a80645@post.omnitel.net; Ambassador MICHAEL SCHWARZINGER.

Belarus: Mindango 13, Vilnius 2600; tel. (526) 62200; fax (526) 62212; internet www.belarus.lt; Ambassador VLADIMIR GARKUN.

China, People's Republic: Algirdo 36, Vilnius 2006; tel. (521) 62861; fax (521) 62682; e-mail chinaemb_lithuania@mfa.gov.ch; internet www.chinaembassy.lt; Ambassador CHEN YUMING.

Czech Republic: Tilto g. 1–2, Vilnius 2000; tel. (526) 61040; fax (526) 61066; e-mail cz.embassy.vilnius@post.omnitel.net; Ambassador PETR VOZNICA.

Denmark: T. Kosciuškos 36, Vilnius 2001; tel. (521) 53434; fax (523) 12300; e-mail vnoamb@um.dk; internet www.denmark.lt; Ambassador EVA JANSON.

Estonia: Mickevičiaus 4A, Vilnius 2004; tel. (527) 80200; fax (527) 80201; e-mail sekretar@estemb.lt; Ambassador REIN OIDEKIVI.

Finland: Klaipėdos 6, Vilnius 2600; tel. (521) 21621; fax (521) 22463; e-mail sanomat.vil@formin.fi; internet www.finland.lt; Ambassador TAINA KIEKKO.

France: Švarco g. 1, Vilnius 2600; tel. (521) 22979; fax (521) 24211; e-mail ambafrance.vilnius@diplomatie.gouv.fr; internet www.ambafrance-lt.org; Ambassador JEAN-BERNARD HARTH.

Germany: Z. Sierakausko 24/8, Vilnius 2600; tel. (521) 31815; (521) 31812; e-mail germ.emb@takas.lt; internet www.deutschebotschaft-wilna.lt; Ambassador Dr ALEXANDER VON ROM.

Holy See: Kosciuškos g. 28, Vilnius 2001; tel. (521) 23696; fax (521) 24228; e-mail nuntiusbalt@aiva.lt; Apostolic Nuncio Most Rev. PETER STEPHAN ZURBRIGGEN (Titular Archbishop of Glastonia, Glastonbury).

Italy: Tauro 12, Vilnius 2001; tel. (521) 20620; fax (521) 20405; e-mail ambasciata@ambitvilnius.lt; Ambassador BERNARDO UGUCCIONI.

Kazakhstan: Birutes 20A/35 , Vilnius 2004; tel. (521) 22123; fax (521) 33701; e-mail kazakhstan@embassy.lt; internet kazakhstan.embassy.lt; Ambassador RASHID IBRAYEV.

Latvia: M. K. Čiurlionio 76, Vilnius 2600; tel. (521) 31260; fax (521) 31130; e-mail lietuva@latvia.balt.net; internet latvia.balt.net; Ambassador MAIRA MORA.

Norway: D. Poškos 59, Vilnius 2004; tel. (527) 26926; fax (527) 26964; e-mail emb.vilnius@mfa.no; internet www.norvegija.lt; Ambassador KÅRE HAUGE.

Poland: Smėlio 20A, Vilnius 2055; tel. (527) 09001; fax (527) 09007; internet www.polandembassy.lt; Ambassador JERZY BAHR.

Romania: Vivulskio 19, Vilnius; tel. (523) 10527; fax (523) 10652; e-mail ambromania@post.omnitel.net; internet www.romania.lt; Ambassador LUCIAN FATU.

Russia: Latvių 53/54, Vilnius 2600; tel. (527) 21763; fax (527) 23877; e-mail rusemb@rusemb.lt; Ambassador YURII A. ZUBAKOV.

Sweden: Didzioji 16, Vilnius 2600; tel. (526) 85010; fax (526) 85030; e-mail ambassaden.vilnius@foreign.ministry.se; internet www.swedishembassy.lt; Ambassador JAN PALMSTIERNA.

Turkey: Didžioji 37, Vilnius 2001; tel. (526) 49570; fax (523) 23277; e-mail turemvil@eunet.lt; Ambassador ALI NAZIM BELGER.

Ukraine: Teatro 4, Vilnius 2600; tel. (521) 21536; fax (521) 20475; e-mail ukrembassy@post.5ci.lt; internet www.5ci.lt/ukrembassy; Ambassador MYKOLA DERKACH.

United Kingdom: Antakalnio 2, Vilnius 2055; tel. (524) 62900; fax (524) 62901; e-mail be-vilnius@britain.lt; internet www.britain.lt; Ambassador JEREMY HILL.

USA: Akmenų 6, Vilnius 2600; tel. (521) 23031; fax (523) 12819; e-mail mail@usembassy.lt; internet www.usembassy.lt; Ambassador STEPHEN D. MULL.

Judicial System

The organs of justice are the Supreme Court, the Court of Appeal, district courts, local courts of administrative areas and a special court—the Commercial Court. The Seimas (Parliament) appoints and dismisses from office the judges of the Supreme Court in response to representations made by the President of the Republic (based upon the recommendation of the chairman of the Supreme Court). Judges of the Court of Appeal are appointed by the President with the approval of the Seimas (on the recommendation of the Minister of Justice), while judges of district and local courts are appointed and dismissed by the President. The Council of Judges submits recommendations to the President of the Republic concerning the appointment of judges, as well as their promotion, transfer or dismissal from office.

The Constitutional Court decides on the constitutionality of acts of the Seimas, as well as of the President and the Government. It consists of nine judges, who are appointed by the Seimas for a single term of nine years; one-third of the Court's members are replaced every three years.

The Office of the Prosecutor-General is an autonomous institution of the judiciary, comprising the Prosecutor-General and local and district prosecutors' offices which are subordinate to him. The Prosecutor-General and his deputies are appointed for terms of seven years by the President, subject to approval by the Seimas, while the prosecutors are appointed by the Prosecutor-General. The Office of the Prosecutor-General incorporates the Department for Crime Investigation. The State Arbitration decides cases of business litigation. A six-volume Civil Code, in accordance with European Union and international law, came into effect in 2001, replacing the Soviet civil legal system, which had, hitherto, remained in operation.

Constitutional Court: Gedimino pr. 36, Vilnius 2600; tel. (521) 26398; fax (521) 27975; e-mail mailbox@lrkt.lt; internet www.lrkt.lt; f. 1993; Chair. EDIGIJUS KURIS.

Court of Appeal: Gedimino pr. 40/1, Vilnius 2600; tel. (526) 26876; fax (526) 18039; Chair. VYTAUTAS MILIUS.

Supreme Court: Gynėjų 6, Vilnius 2725; tel. (526) 10560; fax (526) 27950; e-mail lat@tic.lt; internet www.lat.litlex.lt; Chair. VYTAUTAS GREIČIUS.

Office of the Prosecutor-General: A. Smetonos 4, Vilnius 2709; tel. (526) 62305; fax (526) 62317; e-mail cekelil@lrgp.lt; Prosecutor-General ANTANAS KLIMAVIČIUS.

Religion

Lithuania adopted Christianity at the end of the 14th century. However, the country's geographical position and history have long predetermined a diversity of religious communities. The restoration of independence, in 1991, stimulated the revival of religious practice, which was widely suppressed or banned during the Soviet period. Traditional religious communities were re-established and new ones came into existence. In 2001 there were 923 traditional and 176 non-traditional religious organizations registered in the country.

CHRISTIANITY

The Roman Catholic Church

Roman Catholicism has been the principal religious affiliation in Lithuania for more than 600 years (it was adopted by the Lithuanian State in 1387). The Roman Catholic Church in Lithuania comprises two archdioceses and five dioceses. There are seminaries at Vilnius, Kaunas and Telšiai. At 31 December 2001 the Roman Catholic Church estimated there to be 1.9m. adherents in Lithuania.

Lithuanian Bishops' Conference
(Conferentia Episcopalis Lituaniae)

Skapo 4, Vilnius 2001; tel. (521) 25455; fax (521) 20972; e-mail lvk@post.omnitel.net.

f. 1996; Pres. Cardinal AUDRYS JUOZAS BAČKIS (Archbishop of Vilnius).

Archbishop of Kaunas: Most Rev. SIGITAS TAMKEVIČIUS, Rotušės 14A, Kaunas 3000; tel. (374) 09026; fax (373) 20090; e-mail kurija@kn.lcn.lt; internet www.kaunas.lcn.lt.

Archbishop of Vilnius: Cardinal AUDRYS JUOZAS BAČKIS, Šventaragio 4, Vilnius 2001; tel. (526) 27098; fax (521) 22807; e-mail vilncnsis@takas.lt.

The Byzantine Rite Catholic (Uniate) Church

Established in 1596 by the Lithuanian Brasta (Brest) Church Union, the Uniate Church is headed by the Metropolitan Archbishop of Lviv (Ukraine) and is under the judicial protection of the Roman Catholic Church of Lithuania. At 1 January 1996 there were five commun-

ities, with three priests, one monastic order and one church returned to the adherents in Vilnius.

Representation of the Order of St Basil the Great in Lithuania: Aušros Vartų 7B, Vilnius 2001; tel. (521) 22578; Centre of the Byzantine Rite Catholics (Uniates) in Lithuania; Superior PAVLO JACHIMEC.

Orthodox Churches

Russian Orthodox Church

The first communities appeared during the 12th century and the first monastery was established in Vilnius in 1597. While Lithuania formed part of the Russian Empire (1795–1915), Orthodoxy was considered the state religion. The Vilnius and Lithuanian Eparchy of the Russian Orthodox Church is under the jurisdiction of the Moscow Patriarchate. At 1 January 1996 there were 41 communities (with 30 clergymen and 41 churches). There were an estimated 180,000 adherents in 2001.

Vilnius and Lithuanian Eparchy of the Russian Orthodox Church: Aušros Vartų 10, Vilnius 2001; tel. (521) 27765; Metropolit CHRYZOSTOM (Georgii Martishkin).

Lithuanian Old Believers Pomor Church

The first communities settled in Lithuania in 1679 and the Church was established in 1709. At 1 January 1996 there were approximately 34,000 adherents (mainly ethnic Russians) in 58 communities, with 23 clergymen and 50 churches.

Supreme Council of the Old Believers (Pomor) Church in Lithuania: Naujininkų 20, Vilnius 2030; tel. (526) 95271; f. 1925; Chair. MARK SEMIONOV (acting).

Protestant Churches

Lithuanian Evangelical Lutheran Church

The first parishes were established in 1539–69. In 1563 the Evangelical Church divided into Lutheran and Reformed Churches. Church attendance revived after 1990. The Lithuanian Evangelical Lutheran Church comprises one diocese. At 1 January 1998 there were approximately 30,000 adherents in 54 parishes (with 18 priests and 41 churches).

Consistory of the Lithuanian Evangelical Lutheran Church: Tumo-Vaizganto 50, Tauragė 5900; tel. and fax (446) 61145; e-mail konsistorija@takas.lt; Bishop JONAS KALVANAS.

Lithuanian Evangelical Reformed Church

The first parishes were established after 1563. At 1 January 1996 there were approximately 12,000 adherents in 11 parishes (with two pastors and nine churches).

Lithuanian Evangelical Reformed Church: POB 661, Vilnius 2049; tel. and fax (524) 50656; Pres. of Synodie Collegium POVILAS A. JAŠINSKAS.

Lithuanian Baptist Union and Other Churches

Parliament awarded the Baptist Union 'recognized' status in July 2001, the first religious community to be awarded this status. There has been a Baptist presence in Lithuania since the 18th century. The United Methodist Church, the New Apostolic Church, the Pentecostal Union and the Adventist Church ETH are all similarly seeking such status, beyond their current one of simply being registered.

ISLAM

Sunni Islam is the religion of the ethnic Tatars of Lithuania. The first Tatar communities settled there in the 14th century. The first mosque in Vilnius was erected in 1558. At 1 January 1996 there were five Tatar religious communities (with 10 clergymen, four mosques and one prayer house). In 2001 there were an estimated 5,000 adherents in Lithuania.

Lithuanian Muslims' Religious Community: A. Vivulskio 3, Vilnius 2009; tel. (526) 52051; Imam MIKAS CHALECKAS.

JUDAISM

The first Jewish communities appeared in Lithuania in the 15th century. In the 15th–17th centuries Lithuania was an important centre of Jewish culture and religion. Before the Second World War approximately 250,000 Jews lived in Lithuania; an estimated 90% were murdered during the German occupation (1941–44). At 1 January 1996 there were five Judaic religious communities, with two synagogues (in Vilnius and Kaunas). There were an estimated 5,000 adherents in Lithuania in 2001.

Jewish Community of Lithuania: Pylimo 4, Vilnius 2001; tel. (526) 13003; fax (521) 27915; e-mail jewishcom@post.5ci.lt; internet www.litjews.org; f. 1992 to replace and expand the role of the Jewish Cultural Society; Chair. SIMONAS ALPERAVIČIUS; Chief Rabbi SAMUEL KAHN (London, United Kingdom).

The Press

In 1999 there were 377 newspapers and 418 periodicals published in Lithuania.

The publications listed below are in Lithuanian, except where otherwise indicated.

PRINCIPAL NEWSPAPERS

Kauno diena (Kaunas Daily): Vytauto pr. 27, Kaunas 3687; tel. (373) 41971; fax (374) 23404; e-mail redakcija@kaunodiena.lt; internet www.kaunodiena.lt; f. 1945; 6 a week; Editor-in-Chief AUŠRA LEKA; circ. 50,000.

Klaipėda: Šauliu 21, Klaipėda 5800; tel. (463) 97701; e-mail office@klaipeda.daily.lt; internet www.klaipeda.daily.lt; Editor ANTANAS STANEVIČIUS.

Kurier Wileński (Vilnius Express): Laisvės pr. 60, Vilnius 2056; tel. (524) 27901; fax (524) 27265; f. 1953; 5 a week; in Polish; Editor-in-Chief CZESŁAW MALEWSKI; circ. 8,000.

Lietuvos aidas (Echo of Lithuania): Maironio 1, Vilnius 2710; tel. (526) 15208; fax (521) 24876; e-mail centr@aidas.lt; internet www.aidas.lt; f. 1917; re-est. 1990; 5 a week; Editor-in-Chief ROMA GRINIŪTĖ-GRINBERGIENĖ; circ. 20,000.

Lietuvos rytas (Lithuania's Morning): Gedimino pr. 12A, Vilnius 2001; tel. (527) 43600; fax (527) 43700; e-mail daily@lrytas.lt; internet www.lrytas.lt; f. 1990; 6 a week in Lithuanian, with 3 supplements per week; Editor-in-Chief GEDVYDAS VAINAUSKAS; circ. 65,000 (Mon.–Fri.), 200,000 (Sat.).

Lietuvos zinios Kęstučiog. 4, Vilnius; tel. (527) 54904; fax (527) 53131; e-mail lzinios@lzinios.lt; internet www.lzinios.lt; 6 a week; Editor-in-Chief RYTAS STASELIS.

Respublika (Republic): A. Smetonos 2, Vilnius 2600; tel. (521) 23112; fax (521) 23538; f. 1989; 6 a week in Lithuanian, with 5 Russian editions per week; Editor-in-Chief VITAS TOMKUS; circ. 55,000.

Vakarinės naujienos (Evening News): Laisvės pr. 60, Vilnius 2056; tel. (524) 28052; fax (524) 28563; e-mail info@vnaujienos.lt; internet www.vnaujienos.lt; f. 1958; 5 a week; in Lithuanian and Russian; Editor RIČARDAS JARMALAVIČIUS; circ. 15,000.

Vakarų ekspresas (Western Express): H. Manto 2, Klaipėda 5800; tel. (462) 18074; fax (463) 10102; e-mail sek.ve@balt.net; internet www.vakaru-ekspresas.lt; f. 1990; 6 a week; Editor-in-Chief GINTARAS TOMKUS; circ. 15,000.

PRINCIPAL PERIODICALS

Apžvalga (Review): Pylimo 362, Vilnius 2001; tel. (526) 11151; fax (526) 10503; f. 1990; fortnightly; publ. by Christian Democratic Party of Lithuania; Editor-in-Chief DARIUS VILIMIAS; circ. 2,000.

Artuma: M. Daukšos 21, Kaunas 3000; tel. and fax (372) 09683; f. 1989; monthly; Editor-in-Chief VANDA IBIANSKA; circ. 3,000.

Dienovidis (Midday): Pilies 23A, Vilnius 2001; tel. (521) 21911; fax (521) 23101; e-mail dienovidis@takas.lt; f. 1990; weekly; Editor-in-Chief ALDONA ŽEMAITYTĖ; circ. 4,500.

Ekho Litvy (Echo of Lithuania): Laisvės pr. 60, Vilnius 2056; tel. (524) 28463; fax (524) 28463; e-mail echo.litvy@aunet.lt; f. 1940; daily; in Russian; Editor-in-Chief ALGIMANTAS ZHUKAS; circ. 5,000.

Genys (Woodpecker): Geležinio Vilko 12, Vilnius 2001; tel. (523) 13621; fax (523) 13622; f. 1940; monthly; illustrated; for 8–12-year-olds; Editor-in-Chief VYTAUTAS RAČICKAS; circ. 5,000.

Kultūros barai (Domains of Culture): Latako 3, Vilnius 2001; tel. (526) 16696; fax (526) 10538; e-mail kulturosbarai@takas.lt; f. 1965; monthly; Editor-in-Chief BRONYS SAVUKYNAS; circ. 3,000.

Liaudies kultūra (Ethnic Culture): Barboros Radvilaitės 8, Vilnius 2600; tel. (526) 13412; fax (521) 24033; e-mail lfcc@lfcc.lt; internet neris.mii.lt/heritage/lfcc/lfcc.html; f. 1988; 6 a year; Editor-in-Chief DALIA ANTANINA RASTENIENĖ; circ. 1,100.

Lietuvos sportas (Lithuanian Sports): Odminių 3, Vilnius 2600; tel. and fax (526) 16757; f. 1922; re-est. 1992; 3 a week; Editor-in-Chief BRONIUS ČEKANAUSKAS; circ. 18,000.

Lietuvos ūkis (Lithuanian Economy): Algirdo 31, Vilnius 2600; tel. (521) 36718; fax (522) 36445; f. 1921; monthly; Editor-in-Chief ALGIRDAS JASIONIS; circ. 3,000.

Literatūra ir menas (Literature and Art): Z. Sierakausko 15, Vilnius 2009; tel. (523) 33189; fax (523) 33181; e-mail lmenas@takas.lt; internet www.culture.lt/lmenas; f. 1946; weekly; publ. by the Lithuanian Writers' Union; Editor-in-Chief KORNELIJUS PLATELIS; circ. 3,000.

Lithuania in the World: T. Vrublevskio 6, Vilnius 2600; tel. (526) 14432; fax (526) 13521; e-mail lw.magazine@post.omnitel.net; internet www.kryptis.lt/lithuania; f. 1993; 6 a year; in English; Editor-in-Chief STASYS KAŠAUSKAS; circ. 15,000.

Magazyn Wileński (Vilnius Journal): Laisvės pr. 60, Vilnius 2056; tel. (524) 27718; fax (524) 29065; e-mail magazyn@magwil.lt; internet www.magwil.lt; f. 1990; monthly; political, cultural; in Polish; Editor-in-Chief MICHAŁ MACKIEWICZ; circ. 5,000.

Metai (Year): K. Sirvydo 6, Vilnius 2600; tel. (526) 17344; f. 1991; monthly; journal of the Lithuanian Writers' Union; Editor-in-Chief DANIELIUS MUŠINSKAS; circ. 2,000.

Mokslas ir gyvenimas (Science and Life): Antakalnio 36, Vilnius 2055; tel. and fax (523) 41572; internet ausis.gf.vu.lt/mg/; f. 1957; monthly; popular science; Editor-in-Chief JUOZAS BALDAUSKAS; circ. 3,500.

Moksleivis (Schoolmate): A. Jakšto 8–10, Vilnius 2600; tel. (526) 27604; f. 1959; monthly; Editor-in-Chief ALGIMANTAS ZURBA; circ. 14,000.

Moteris (Woman): Vykinto 7, Vilnius 2004; tel. and fax (521) 24741; e-mail redakcija@moteris.lt; internet www.moteris.lt; f. 1952; monthly; popular, for women; Editor-in-Chief EGLE STRIAUKIENE; circ. 40,000.

Mūsų gamta (Our Nature): Rudens 33B, Vilnius 2600; tel. (526) 96964; f. 1964; 6 a year; Editor-in-Chief VYTAUTAS KLOVAS; circ. 2,500.

Naujasis Židinys (New Hearth): Tilto g. 8/3, Vilnius 2001; tel. (522) 20311; fax (521) 22363; f. 1991; monthly; religion and culture; Editor-in-Chief SAULIUS DRAZDAUSKAS; circ. 1,200.

Nemunas: Gedimino 45, Kaunas 3000; tel. (373) 22244; f. 1967; monthly; journal of the Lithuanian Writers' Union; Editor-in-Chief ALGIMANTAS MIKUTA; circ. 1,500.

Panele (Young Miss): Vykinto 7, Vilnius 2004; tel. (527) 15900; fax (527) 15901; e-mail magazine@panele.lt; internet www.panele.lt; f. 1994; monthly; popular, for ages 12–25; Editor-in-Chief JURGA SIMKIENE; circ. 66,000.

7 meno dienos (7 Days of Art): Bernardinų 10, Vilnius 2001; tel. (526) 13039; fax (526) 11926; e-mail 7md@culture.lt; internet www.culture.lt/7menodienos; f. 1992; weekly; Editor-in-Chief LINAS VILDŽIŪNAS; circ. 2,000.

Sandora (Covenant): Dominikonų 6, Vilnius 2001; tel. (521) 22141; fax (521) 20598; e-mail sandora@hotmail.com; f. 1989; monthly; Editor-in-Chief ELVYRA KUČINSKAITĖ; circ. 9,000.

Švyturys (Beacon): Maironio 1, Vilnius 2600; tel. (526) 10791; fax (526) 14690; f. 1949; monthly; politics, economics, history, culture, fiction; Editor-in-Chief JUOZAS BAUSYS; circ. 10,000.

Tremtinys (Deportee): Laisvės 39, Kaunas 3000; tel. (372) 09530; f. 1988; weekly; publ. by the Lithuanian Union of Political Prisoners and Deportees; Editor-in-Chief ROMUALDAS JURGELIONIS; circ. 4,000.

Valstiečių laikraštis (Farmer's Newspaper): Laisvės pr. 60, Vilnius 2056; tel. and fax (524) 21281; e-mail redakcija@valstietis.lt; internet www.valstietis.lt; f. 1940; 2 a week; Editor-in-Chief JONAS ŠVOBA; circ. 78,000.

Vasario 16 (16 February): J. Gruodžio 9–404, Kaunas 3000; tel. (372) 25219; f. 1988; fortnightly; journal of the Lithuanian Democratic Party; Sec. PRIMAS NOREIKA; circ. 1,600.

NEWS AGENCIES

Baltic News Service (BNS): Jogailos g. 9/1, Vilnius 2001; tel. (523) 12410; fax (526) 81515; e-mail bns@bns.lt; f. 1991; Dir RIMANTAS ŠIMKUS.

ELTA (Lithuanian News Agency): Gedimino pr. 21/2, Vilnius 2600; tel. (526) 28864; fax (526) 19507; e-mail zinias@elta.lt; internet www.elta.lt; f. 1920; Dir KĘSTUTIS JANKAUSKAS.

Publishers

Alma littera: A. Juozapavičiaus 6/2, Vilnius 2600; tel. (527) 28246; fax (5) 28026; e-mail post@almali.lt; internet www.almali.lt; f. 1990; fiction, children's books, textbooks; Dir-Gen. ARVYDAS ANDRIJAUSKAS.

Baltos lankos (White Meadows): Mėsinių 4, Vilnius 2001; tel. (521) 20126; fax (521) 20152; e-mail baltos.lankos@post.omnitel.net; internet www.baltoslankos.lt; f. 1992; literature, humanities, social sciences, fiction and textbooks; Editor SAULIUS ŽUKAS.

Eugrimas: Šilutės 42A, Vilnius 2042; tel. (523) 00075; e-mail eugrimas@eugrimas.com; internet www.eugrimas.com; f. 1995; eco-

nomics, education, law, politics and philosophy; Dir EUGENIJA PETRU-
LIENĖ.

Katalikų pasaulis (Catholic World): Dominikonų 6, Vilnius 2001;
tel. (521) 22422; fax (526) 26462; f. 1990; Dir KĘSTUTIS LATOŽA.

Lietuvos rašytojų sąjungos leidykla (Lithuanian Writers' Union
Publishers): K. Sirvydo 6, Vilnius 2600; tel. (526) 28643; fax (526)
28945; e-mail rsleidykla@is.lt; internet www.rsleidykla.lt; f. 1990;
fiction, essays, literary heritage, children's books; Dir GIEDRE SOR-
IENE.

Mintis (Idea): Z. Sierakausko 15, Vilnius 2600; tel. (523) 32943; fax
(521) 63157; f. 1949; philosophy, history, law, economics, tourist
information; Dir ALEKSANDRAS KRASNOVAS.

Mokslo ir enciklopedijų leidybos institutas (Science and Encyclopaedia Publishing Institute): L. Asanavičiūtės 23, Vilnius 2050;
tel. (524) 58526; fax (524) 58537; e-mail meli@meli.lt; internet www
.meli.lt; f. 1992; science and reference books, dictionaries, encyclopaedias, higher education textbooks, books for the general reader;
Dir RIMANTAS KARECKAS.

Presvika: Pamėnkalnio 25/11, Vilnius 2001; tel. (526) 23182; fax
(526) 23110; e-mail presvika@post.5ci.lt; f. 1996; educational literature and textbooks; Dir VIOLETA BILAIŠYTĖ.

Šviesa (Light): Vytauto 25, Kaunas 3000; tel. (373) 41834; fax (373)
42032; e-mail sviesa@balt.net; internet www.sviesa.lt; f. 1945; textbooks and pedagogical literature; Dir JONAS BARCYS.

Tyto alba: J. Jasinskio 10, Vilnius 2001; tel. and fax (524) 98602;
e-mail tytoalba@taide.lt; internet www.tytoalba.lt; f. 1993; literature in translation; Dir LOLITA VARANAVIČIENĖ.

Vaga (Furrow): Gedimino pr. 50, Vilnius 2600; tel. (526) 26443; fax
(526) 16902; e-mail vaga@post.omnitel.net; internet www.lietus.lt/
vaga; f. 1945; fiction, non-fiction, art, children's books; Dir ARTURAS
MICKEVIČUS.

Vyturys (Lark): J. Tumo-Vaižganto 2, Vilnius 2600; tel. and fax
(526) 29407; f. 1985; fiction and non-fiction for children and youth;
Dir ALEKSAS BOČIAROVAS.

PUBLISHERS' ASSOCIATION

Lithuanian Publishers' Association: K. Sirvydo 6, Vilnius 2000;
tel. and fax (526) 17740; e-mail lla@centras.lt; f. 1989; Pres. SAULIUS
ZUKAS.

Broadcasting and Communications

TELECOMMUNICATIONS

Regulatory Authority

Communications Regulatory Authority (Ryšių Reguliavimo
Tarnyba): Algirdo 27, Vilnius 2006; tel. (521) 05633; fax (521) 61564;
e-mail rrt@rrt.lt; internet www.rrt.lt; f. 2001; Dir TOMAS BARA-
KAUSKAS.

Major Service Provider

Lietuvos Telekomas AB: Savanorių pr. 28, Vilnius 2001; tel. (521)
27755; fax (521) 26655; e-mail info@telecom.lt; internet www
.telecom.lt; f. 1992; privatized 1998; operates public telecommunications network, repairs telecommunications equipment; Pres. and
Gen. Man. TAPIO PAARMA; 5,200 employees.

BROADCASTING

Lietuvos Radijo ir televizijos komisija (Radio and Television
Commission of Lithuania): Vytenio 6, Vilnius 2009; tel. (523) 30660;
fax (526) 47125; e-mail lrtk@rtk.lt; internet www.rtk.lt.

Radio

Lietuvos radijas ir televizija (Lithuanian Radio and Television):
S. Konarskio 49, Vilnius 2600; tel. (523) 63000; fax (523) 63208;
e-mail forel@lrtv.lt; internet www.lrtv.lt; f. 1926; govt-owned; Chair.
MARCELIJUS MARTINAITIS; Gen. Dir KĘSTUTIS PETRAUSKIS.

Lietuvos radijas (Lithuanian Radio): S. Konarskio 49, Vilnius
2600; tel. (523) 63010; fax (521) 35333; internet www.lrtv.lt/lt_lr
.htm; f. 1926; broadcasts in Lithuanian, Russian, Polish, Yiddish,
Belarusian and Ukrainian; Dir JŪRATĖ LAUČIŪTĖ.

A2: Vilnius; tel. (526) 41229; e-mail a2@post.inet.lt; internet www
.a2.lt; private, commercial.

Aukštaitijos radijas: Laisvės 1, Panevėžys 5300; tel. and fax (455)
96969; e-mail armac@laineta.lt; private, commercial; Dir ALGIRDAS
ŠATAS.

Bumsas: Smiltelės 13–64, Klaipėda 5802; tel. (463) 20909; fax (463)
22020; e-mail bumsas@bumsas.lt; internet www.bumsas.lt; private,
commercial; Dir DALIUS NOREIKA.

FM 99: Rotuses 2, POB 119, Alytus 4580; tel. (315) 77711; fax (315)
74646; e-mail fm99@fm99.lt; internet www.fm99.lt; private, commercial; Dir LIUDAS RAMANAUSKAS.

Kapsai: P. Armino 71, Marijampolė 4520; tel. and fax (343) 54512;
e-mail kapsai@mari.omnitel.net; internet www1.omnitel.net/
kapsai; private, commercial; Dir RAIMUNDAS MARUSKEVIČIUS.

Kauno fonas 105.4: Radastu 2, Kaunas 3000; tel. (373) 30390; fax
(373) 30368; e-mail reklama@kaunoradijas.lt; internet www
.kaunoradijas.lt; private, commercial; Dir ORESTAS MINDERIS.

Labas FM: Naugarduko 91, Vilnius 2006; tel. (521) 63591; internet
www.labasfm.lt; Dir DARIUS UZKURAITIS.

Laisvoji banga: Naugarduko 91, Vilnius 2006; tel. (521) 63836; fax
(521) 63591; e-mail radio@lbanga.lt; internet www.lbanga.lt; private, commercial; Dir VYTAUTAS BARTKUS.

Laluna: M. Mazvydo 11, Klaipėda 5800; tel. and fax (463) 43232;
e-mail laluna@laluna.lt; internet www.laluna.lt; private, commercial; Dir RUSLANAS ALEKSANDRAVIČIUS.

M-1: Laisvės pr. 60, Vilnius 2056; tel. (523) 60360; fax (523) 60366;
e-mail m-1@m-1.lt; internet www.m-1.lt; private, commercial; Dir-
Gen. HUBERTAS GRUSNYS.

Mazeikiu aidas: Sodu 13–93, Mazeikiai 5500; tel. (443) 65095; fax
(443) 65600; private, commercial; Dir ALINA JONIKAITĖ.

Nevėžio radijas: Kniaudiskiu 87/84 P.d. 107, Panevėžys 5304; tel.
(454) 23922; fax (455) 96888; e-mail rolka@nradijas.lt; private, commercial; Dir ALVYDAS ADUKONIS.

Pukas: Šaldytuvu 25, Kaunas 3002; tel. (373) 42424; fax (373)
42434; e-mail boss@pukas.lt; f. 1991; private, commercial; Dir KĘS-
TUTIS PŪKAS.

Radiocentras: Laisvės pr. 60, Vilnius 2056; tel. (521) 28706; fax
(524) 29073; e-mail biuras@radiocentras.lt; internet www
.radiocentras.lt; private, commercial; Dir-Gen. M. GARBERIS.

Ratekona: P.d. 3300, Vilnius 2013; tel. (685) 76840; fax (521) 52171;
e-mail consult@zilionis.cjb.net; f. 1994; private, commercial; Dir
SIGITAS ZILIONIS.

Saules radijas: Dvaro 88, Šiauliai 5400; tel. (414) 22431; fax (414)
32816; e-mail src@siauliai.aiva.lt; private, commercial; Editor-in-
Chief VALENTINAS DIDZGALVIS.

Tau: Draugystės 19, Kaunas 3031; tel. (373) 52790; fax (373) 52128;
e-mail info@tau.balt.net; internet www.tau.lt; private, commercial;
Dir ALGIRDAS KEPEŽINSKAS.

Titanika: Sporto 6, Kaunas 3000; tel. (372) 03404; fax (372) 08222;
e-mail titanika@kaunas.sav.lt; internet www.kaunas.sav.lt/
titanika/; private, commercial.

Ventus: Montuotoju 2, Mazeikiai 5500; tel. (443) 96225; fax (443)
96226; e-mail admin@ventus.lt; internet www.ventus.lt; private,
commercial; Dir-Gen. GIEDRIUS STELMOKAS.

V. Mečkausko firma 'Versmės' radijas ir televizija: Pergalės
57–9, Elektrėnai 4061; tel. (528) 39543; fax (528) 39616; e-mail
mesta@one.lt.

Všį Kauno radijas ir televizija: S. Daukanto 28A, Kaunas 3000;
tel. (373) 21010; fax (373) 22570; e-mail kaunas@lrtv.lt; Dir P.
GARNYS.

Žemaitijos radijas: Mažeikių 18, Telšiai 5610; tel. (444) 74433; fax
(444) 75445; e-mail zemaitijos@radijas.lt; internet www.radijas.lt;
private, commercial; Dir ALGIMANTAS GINČIAUSKIS.

UAB Znad Wilii radijo stotis: Laisvės pr. 60, Vilnius 2056; tel.
(524) 90870; fax (527) 84446; e-mail radio@znadwilii.lt; internet
www.znadwilii.lt; f. 1992; private, commercial; Dir-Gen. MIROSLAVAS
JUCHNEVIČIUS.

Television

Lietuvos radijas ir televizija: see Radio.

Lietuvos televizija: S. Konarskio 49, Vilnius 2600; tel. (523)
63100; fax (521) 63282; e-mail romas@litv.lt; programmes in Lithuanian, Russian, Polish, Ukrainian and Belarusian; Dir ROMAS
JANKAUSKAS.

Aidas: Birutes 42, Trakai 4050; tel. (528) 52480; mainly relays
German programmes; private, commercial; Dir ČESLOVAS RULEVIČIUS.

Baltijos televizija: Laisvės pr. 60, Vilnius 2056; tel. (524) 28917;
fax (524) 26623; e-mail webmaster@btv.lt; internet www.btv.lt;
broadcasts own programmes and relays German, Polish and US
broadcasts; private, commercial; Dir-Gen. GINTARAS SONGAILA.

Kaunas plius: P.d. 2040, Kaunas 3000; tel. (372) 20650; fax (372)
20640; private, commercial; Pres. HENRIKAS ZUKAUSKAS.

LNK TV (Laisvas Nepriklausomas Kanalas): Šeškinės 20, Vilnius 20010; tel. (521) 24061; fax (521) 23924; e-mail lnk@lnk.lt; internet www.lnk.lt; private, commercial; Dir PAULIUS KOVAS.

PAN-TV: Laisvės 26–211, Panevėžys 5300; tel. (454) 64267; fax (454) 35889; private, commercial; Dir SAULIUS BUKELIS.

Raseiniu TV: Vytauto Didziojo 10, Raseiniai 4400; tel. (428) 53955; fax (428) 53735; e-mail mirkliai@raseiniai.omnitel.net; Dir KĘSTUTIS SKAMARAKAS.

Šiaulių TV: Aušros al. 48, Šiauliai 5400; tel. and fax (415) 23809; private; Dir STASYS SUŠINSKAS.

TV3: Nemencines 4, Vilnius 2016; tel. (523) 16131; fax (527) 64253; e-mail postmaster@tv3.lt; internet www.tv3.lt; broadcasts own programmes (20% of schedule) in Lithuanian and English, and relays international satellite channels; private, commercial; Dir VILMA MARČIULEVIČIUTE.

Vilniaus TV: Vivulskio 23, Vilnius 2600; tel. (521) 35560; fax (523) 37904; e-mail vk@mail.iti.lt; internet www.vtv.lt; f. 1994; private, commercial; Dir LEONAS REMEIKA.

Finance

(cap. = capital; res = reserves; dep. = deposits; m. = million; brs = branches; amounts in litai, unless otherwise stated)

BANKING

In the early 1990s, following independence, comprehensive reforms were made in Lithuania's banking system, beginning with the establishment of a central bank, the Bank of Lithuania. During 1995 several of the smaller commercial banks became bankrupt, culminating in the collapse in December of the two largest, the Lithuanian Joint-Stock Innovation Bank (LJIB) and Litimpex Bank. The crisis resulted in the eventual closure of 16 of the 28 banks in operation at that time. As a result, the Government devised a programme, in consultation with the IMF and the World Bank, to secure and restructure the banking system. At the end of 2001 nine banks were operating under a licence from the Bank of Lithuania; there were also four branches of foreign banks, and five representative offices of foreign banks in Lithuania.

Central Bank

Bank of Lithuania (Lietuvos bankas): Gedimino pr. 6, Vilnius 2001; tel. (526) 80029; fax (526) 28124; e-mail bank_of_lithuania@lbank.lt; internet www.lbank.lt; f. 1922; re-est. 1990; central bank, responsible for bank supervision; cap. 100m., res 1,813.4m. (Feb. 2002); Chair. of Bd REINOLDIJUS ŠARKINAS.

Commercial Banks

Agricultural Bank of Lithuania (AB Lietuvos Žemės Ūkio Bankas): J. Basanavičiaus 26, Vilnius 2600; tel. (523) 93553; fax (521) 39058; e-mail lzub-info@lzub.lt; internet www.lzub.lt; f. 1924 as Žemės Bankas; re-founded in 1992 as successor to Agropramoninis Bankas; 93.08% owned by Norddeutsche Landesbank Girozentrale (Germany); cap. 102.8m., res 25.6m., dep. 1,273.1m. (Dec. 2001); Chair. of Bd THOMAS STEPHAN BUERKLE; 46 brs.

Bank of Vilnius (Vilniaus bankas AB): Gedimino pr. 12, Vilnius 2600; tel. (526) 82514; fax (526) 26557; e-mail info@vb.lt; internet www.vb.lt; f. 1990 as Spaudos Bankas; absorbed AB Bankas Hermis in 2000; 98% owned by Skandinaviska Enskilda Banken (Sweden); cap. 154.4m., res 430.8m., dep. 5,165.3m. (Dec. 2001); Chair. and Chief Exec. JULIUS NIEDVARAS; 18 brs.

AB Bankas Hansa-LTB: Savanoriu pr. 19, Vilnius 2009; tel. (526) 84444; fax (522) 32433; e-mail info@ltb.lt; internet www.hansa.lt; f. 2001 by merger of Lieutuvos Taupomasis Bankas and Hansabankas; owned by Hansapank (Estonia); cap. 370.3m., res 32.3m., dep. 3,429.4m. (Dec. 2001); Chair. of Bd ARŪNAS ŠIKŠTA.

Medical Bank (Medicinos Bankas): Pamėnkalnio 40, Vilnius 2600; tel. (521) 23321; fax (526) 24481; e-mail info@medbank.lt; internet www.medbank.lt; f. 1992; cap. 34.4m., res 2.1m., dep. 92.2m. (Dec. 2001); Chair. of Bd KĘSTUTIS OLSAUSKAS; 7 brs.

AB Parex Bankas: K. Kalinausko 13, Vilnius 2009; tel. (526) 64600; fax (526) 64601; e-mail info@parex.lt; internet www.parex.lt; f. 1996; cap. 31.0m. , res 0.9m., dep. 128.1m. (Dec. 2002); Chair. and Chief Exec. JANIS TUKANS; 6 brs.

UAB Sampo Bankas: Gelezinio Vilko 18A, Vilnius 2004; tel. (521) 09400; fax (521) 09409; f. 1994; fmrly Lithuanian Development Bank; present name adopted 2001; 99.99% owned by Sampo plc (Finland); cap. 37.1m., res 3.3m., dep. 129.9m. (Dec. 2001); Chair. of Bd GINTAUTAS GALVANAUSKAS.

Šiaulių Bank: Tilžės 149, Šiauliai 5400; tel. (415) 22117; fax (414) 30774; e-mail info@sb.lt; internet www.sb.lt; f. 1992; cap. 34.0m., res 1.8m., dep. 263.1m. (Dec. 2001); Chair. ALGIRDAS BUTKUS; 8 brs.

Snoras Bank: A. Vivulskio 7, Vilnius 2600; tel. (526) 62700; fax (523) 10155; e-mail info@snoras.com; internet www.snoras.com; f. 1992; cap. 163.5m. (Dec. 2001), dep. 655.1m., total assets 884.0m. (Dec. 2001); Chair. of Management Bd RAIMONDAS BARANAUSKAS; 10 brs.

Tauro Bank: K. Kalinausko 13, Vilnius 2600; tel. (521) 25030; fax (521) 25066; f. 1991; cap. 36.0m., dep. 152.6m. (Dec. 1996); Chair. GINTARAS TERLECKAS; 9 brs.

AB Ūkio Bankas: J. Gruodžio 9, Kaunas 3000; tel. (373) 01301; fax (373) 23188; e-mail ub@ub.lt; internet www.ub.lt; f. 1989; cap. 90.7m. (Dec. 2002), dep. 633.4m. (Dec. 2001); Chair. of Bd and Chief Exec. EDITA NAVICKAITE; 12 brs.

Lithuanian Savings Bank (AB Lietuvos Taupomasis Bankas): Savanorių pr. 19, Vilnius 2009; tel. (521) 32370; fax (521) 32431; f. 1919; 90.7% owned by Hansapank (Estonia); cap. 167.3m., res 86.4m., dep. 2,980.5m. (Dec. 2000); scheduled for privatization; Chair. of Bd ARŪNAS ŠIKŠTA.

Property Banks

Nuosavybes Bank (Property Bank): Vilnius; loan-recovery agency.

Turto Bank: Kestucio 46, Vilnius 2600; tel. (527) 80900; fax (527) 51155; e-mail info@turtas.lt; internet www.turtas.lt; f. 1996; cap. 8.9m., total assets 1,001.9m. (Dec. 2000); recovery of non-performing loans, administration of Ministry of Finance loans; Chair. of Bd STEPONAS VYTAUTAS JURNA; 6 brs.

Banking Association

Association of Lithuanian Banks: Ankštoji g. 5, Vilnius 2600; tel. (524) 96669; fax (524) 96139; e-mail info@lba.lt; f. 1991; Pres. EDUARDAS VILKELIS; 10 mems.

COMMODITY EXCHANGES

National Commodity Exchange: Laisvės 35, Kaunas 3000; tel. (372) 24498; fax (376) 20726; f. 1992; Pres. VYTAUTAS VINKLERIS; 16 mems.

Baltic Exchange: Pylimo 2/6, Vilnius 2001; tel. (521) 61195; fax (521) 26842; f. 1991; Pres. VYTAUTAS JAKELIS; 16 mems.

STOCK EXCHANGE

National Stock Exchange: Ukmergės 41, Vilnius 2600; tel. (527) 23871; fax (527) 24894; e-mail office@nse.lt; internet www.nse.lt; f. 1993; Pres. RIMANTAS BUSILA.

Trade and Industry

GOVERNMENT AGENCIES

Fund for State Property and Restoration of People's Savings: Vilnius; f. 1997; supervises distribution and uses of revenues derived from privatization.

Lithuanian State Enterprise State Property Fund: Vilnius 16, Vilnius 2600; tel. (526) 84902; fax (526) 84997; e-mail info@vtf.lt; internet www.vtf.lt; f. 1995; privatization and management of state-owned and municipal property; Dir POVILAS MILAŠAUSKAS.

CHAMBERS OF COMMERCE

Association of Lithuanian Chambers of Commerce, Industry and Crafts: J-Tumo-Vaižganto 9/1–63A, Vilnius 2001; tel. (526) 12102; fax (526) 12112; e-mail lppra@post.omnitel.net; internet www.lithuaniachambers.lt; f. 1992; mem. of International Chamber of Commerce and of Asscn of European Chambers of Commerce and Industry; Dir-Gen. RIMAS VARKULEVIČIUS.

Kaunas Chamber of Commerce, Industry and Crafts: K. Donelaičio 8, Kaunas 3000; POB 2111, Kaunas; tel. (372) 01491; fax (372) 08330; e-mail chamber@chamber.lt; internet www.chamber.lt; f. 1925; re-est. 1991; Pres. M. RONDOMANSKAS.

Klaipėda Chamber of Commerce, Industry and Crafts: POB 148, Klaipėda 5800; tel. (464) 10628; fax (464) 10626; e-mail krppr@klaipeda.omnitel.net; Pres. SIGITAS PAULAUSKAS; Dir VIKTORAS KROLIS.

Marijampolė Chamber of Commerce and Industry: Kęstučio 9/20, Marijampolė 4520; tel. (343) 55568; fax (343) 56346; Pres. VYGANDAS MATULIS.

Panevėžys Chamber of Commerce, Industry and Crafts: Respublikos 34, Panevėžys 5319; tel. (454) 63687; fax (454) 62227; e-mail panevezys@chambers.lt; internet www.ccic.lt; f. 1991; Pres. VYTAUTAS ŠIDLAUSKAS; Gen. Dir VYTAUTAS KAZAKEVIČIUS.

Šiauliai Chamber of Commerce, Industry and Crafts: Vilniaus 88, Šiauliai 5400; tel. (414) 27709; fax (414) 39973; e-mail siauliai-cci@siauliai.omnitel.net; Dir-Gen. DAILIS BARAKAUSKAS.

Vilnius Chamber of Commerce, Industry and Crafts: Algirdo 31, Vilnius 2600; tel. (521) 35550; fax (521) 35542; e-mail vilnius@cci.lt; internet www.cci.lt; f. 1991; Pres. VYTAS NAVICKAS; 427 mems.

INDUSTRIAL ASSOCIATION

Lithuanian Industrialists' Confederation: A. Vienuolio 8, Vilnius 2001; tel. (521) 25217; fax (527) 23320; f. 1989; Pres. BRONISLOVAS LUBYS.

EMPLOYERS' ORGANIZATION

Lithuanian Business Employers' Confederation: A. Rotundo 5, Vilnius 2600; tel. (526) 29729; fax (521) 20448; e-mail lvdk@post.omnitel.net; internet 195.182.80.20/lvdk; f. 1999; Pres. VIKTOR USPASKICH.

UTILITIES

Energy System of Lithuania: Zveju 14, Vilnius 2600; tel. (527) 34638; fax (521) 26736; Gen. Dir ANZELMAS BACIALISKAS.

Electricity

Lietuvos energija AB (Lithuanian Power): Zveju 14, Vilnius 2600; tel. (527) 82406; fax (521) 26736; e-mail lietuvos.energija@lpc.lt; internet www.lpc.lt; f. 1995; restructured in 2000; Man. Dir RYMANTAS JUOZAITIS; 11,500 employees.

Alytus Electric Utility: Pramonės 7, Alytus 4580; tel. (315) 25745; fax (315) 34827; e-mail aet@lpc.lt; f. 1962; transmission and distribution; 127,000 customers (Dec. 1996); Dir VITAS BLAZAUSKAS.

Klaipėda Electric Utility: Liepu 64A, Klaipėda 5799; tel. (463) 15054; fax (463) 15056; f. 1957; transmission and distribution; 218,000 customers (Dec. 1996); Dir VYTAUTAS GIRDVAINIS.

Rytų Skirstomieji Tinklai AB: Senamiesčio 102B, Panevėžys 5319; tel. (455) 04459; fax (454) 81394; e-mail pet@pet.lt; internet rytis.rst.lt; f. 1957; distribution of electricity; 156,000 customers (Dec. 2002); Dir LEONAS MIKALAJŪNAS.

Šiauliai Electric Utility: Tilžės 68, Šiauliai 5409; tel. (415) 94459; fax (415) 53041; e-mail info@set.lpc.lt; f. 1957; transmission and distribution; 190,000 customers (Jan. 2002); Dir VINCAS PONELIS.

Utena Electric Utility: Uzpaliu 87, Utena 4910; tel. (389) 62150; fax (389) 62196; e-mail utenoset@uet.lpc.lt; f. 1964; transmission and distribution; 113,900 customers (Jan. 2001); Dir JURGIS DUMBRAVA.

JSC Vakaru skirstomieji tinklai: Kestučio 36, Kaunas 3000; tel. (373) 09259; fax (373) 09269; e-mail vest@vest.lt; internet www.vest.lt; f. 2001; distribution in central and western Lithuania; 263,000 customers (Dec. 1996); Chief Exec. ARŪNAS KESERAUSKAS; 3,000 employees.

Vilnius Electric Utility: Motoru 2, Vilnius 2038; tel. (521) 67465; fax (521) 67467; f. 1957; transmission and distribution; 268,000 customers (Dec. 1996); Dir RIMANTAS MILISAUSKAS.

Gas

Lietuvos Dujos (Lithuanian Gas): Aguonų 24, Vilnius 2600; tel. (523) 60210; fax (523) 60200; e-mail lt@lietuvosdujos.lt; internet www.dujos.lt; f. 1995; natural gas transmission and distribution; 34% of shares divested to Ruhrgas AS and E.ON Energie AG (Germany) in June 2002; scheduled for further privatization; Gen. Man. VIKORAS VALENTUKEVIČIUS; 4,300 employees.

MAJOR COMPANIES

By 1991 the privatization of state property had been approved and vouchers for investment distributed to citizens. In December 1995 it was reported that 83% of state-owned assets designated for privatization had been transferred to private ownership. In November 1997 the Seimas approved legislation which fully substituted a cash system for the voucher system of privatization.

Achema AB: Jonalaukio k., Ruklos sen., Jonava 5004; tel. (349) 56237; fax (349) 56004; e-mail rvs@achema.com; internet www.achema.com; f. 1965 as Jonava Nitrogen Fertilizers Enterprise; privatized in 1999; produces chemical fertilizers, resins and water treatment chemicals; Gen. Dir JONAS SIRVYDIS; 1,200 employees.

Akmenės Cementas AB: J. Dalinkevičiaus 2, Naujoji Akmenė 5464; tel. (425) 58323; fax (425) 56198; e-mail sekretoriatas@cementas.lt; f. 1952; sales 112.6m. litai (1999); produces cement, sorted limestone; Man. Dir PRANAS KRIŠTOPAITIS; 822 employees.

Alga AB: Gamyklu 4, Marijampolė 4520; tel. (343) 98700; fax (343) 98701; e-mail alga@alga.lt; internet www.alga.lt; f. 1990; manufactures metal constructions for industry, aluminium and PVC windows and doors, and other constructions; Pres. ANDRIUS LINKUS; 194 employees.

Alita JSC: Miškininkų 17, Alytus 4580; tel. (315) 79243; fax (315) 57264; e-mail market@alita.lt; internet www.alita.lt; f. 1963; joint-stock co; produces sparkling wines, wines, spirits, concentrated juices; Dir-Gen. VYTAUTAS JUNEVIČIUS; 500 employees.

Alytaus Tekstilė AB: Pramonės pr. 1, Alytus 4580; tel. (315) 57357; fax (315) 57366; e-mail alytaus-tekstile@post.omnitel.net; internet www.tekstile.lt; f. 1969; cotton yarn and fabrics; Dir MATTI HAARAJOKI; 3,000 employees.

Atrama AB: Raudondvario 162, Kaunas 3021; tel. (373) 62052; fax (373) 62542; e-mail info@atrama.lt; internet www.atrama.lt; f. 1940; joint-stock co; boilers, water meters and gas cylinders; Dir ALVYDAS SVEDAS; 140 employees.

Audėjas AB: Zarasų 24/1, Vilnius 2600; tel. (526) 60100; fax (526) 14676; e-mail audejas@audejas.lt; internet www.audejas.lt; f. 1947; sales 35m. litai (2000); manufactures jacquard, velvet and linen fabrics for upholstery and interiors; Dir JONAS KARČIAUSKAS; 260 employees.

Aurida: Pramonės pr. 8, Panevėžys 5319; tel. (454) 64193; fax (454) 22951; f. 1959; manufactures compressors for motor vehicles and domestic use, aluminium and iron castings, bicycle pumps; Gen. Dir JUOZAS BRONUSAS; 1,500 employees.

Baltija Shipbuilding Yard JSC: Pilies 8, Klaipėda 5799; tel. (463) 98100; fax (463) 98245; e-mail baltija@baltijas.lt; internet www.baltijas.lt; f. 1952; joint-stock co; ship-building; Dir-Gen. VIKTORAS STULPINAS; 1,500 employees.

Baltijos Automobiliu Technika UAB (Baltic Automobile Technology): Vilniaus 10, Klaipėda 5800; tel. (464) 96500; fax (464) 96501; f. 1993; joint-stock co; cables for vehicles; Dir MAXIMILIAN FUCHSSCHWANZ; 1,700 employees.

Baltik Vairas: Tilžės 74, Šiauliai 5410; tel. (414) 52134; fax (414) 23906; e-mail baltic.vairas@siauliai.omnitel.net; joint Lithuanian-German venture; bicycle manufacturer; Dir DIRK ZWICK; 630 employees.

Dirbtinis Pluostas AB: Pramones pr. 4, Kaunas 3711; tel. (377) 60023; fax (377) 64075; e-mail dp.general@kaunas.omnitel.net; joint-stock co; yarns and fabrics; sales 190m. litai (1998); Chair. GIEDRIUS PUKAS; 1,652 employees.

Dovana: Vilnius 2050; tel. (524) 58860; fax (524) 58829; f. 1967; designs and produces clothing and soft furnishings; Chair. and Gen. Dir BRONIUS VINTYS; 2,100 employees.

Drobė: Jonavos 60, Kaunas 3000; tel. (373) 63282; fax (373) 63474; e-mail market@drobe.lt; f. 1920; wool-mixture fabrics; Dir V. GUBAVIČIUS; 1,300 employees.

Ekinsta AB: Visoriu 27, Vilnius 2057; tel. (527) 61574; fax (527) 00253; e-mail ekinsta@yahoo.com; f. 1968; sales 22.3m. litai (2000); construction, wood processing, produces wooden windows and doors; joint-stock co; Dir VYTAUTAS KIAUŠAS; 300 employees.

Ekranas AB: Elektronikos 1, Panevėžys 5139; tel. (454) 63450; fax (454) 23415; e-mail info@ekranas.lt; internet www.ekranas.lt; f. 1962; sales 179m. litai (1999); electronic components; Dir EIMUTIS ŽVYBAS; 3,500 employees.

Elfa State Electrotechnical Enterprise: Vytenis 50, Vilnius 2654; tel. (526) 31531; fax (526) 60709; f. 1940; production of electric motors; Gen. Dir ALGIMANTAS ZAJANKAUSKAS; 2,000 employees.

Elnias AB: Vilniaus 72, Šiauliai 5419; tel. and fax (414) 33855; f. 1877; leather footwear; Chief Exec. VYTAUTAS PERDIČIUS; 815 employees.

Fasa AB: Sporto 9, Marijampolė 4520; tel. (343) 70562; fax (343) 70469; e-mail fasa@mari.omnitel.lt; internet www.fasa.lt; f. 1960; sales 7.3m. litai (2000); manufactures automatic packaging machines for meat and dairy products; Dir ARUNAS ADOMAVIČIUS; 390 employees.

Gražtai AB: Birželio 23-iosios/10, Vilnius 2600; tel. (521) 30515; fax (521) 61065; e-mail office@graztai.lt; internet www.graztai.lt; f. 1957; produces drills for quick-cutting steel, solid alloy, wood-working tools; Dir P. RAMANAUKASKAS; 190 employees.

Grigiškes AB: Vilniaus 10, Grigiskes 4058; tel. (46) 333904; fax (46) 651486; e-mail grigiskes@auste.elnet.lt; internet www.grigiskes.com; f. 1923; sales 25m. litai (1998); manufactures paper and paper products; Gen. Dir ROMALDAS JADENKUS; 1,260 employees.

Inkaras AB: Raudondvario 127, Kaunas 3021; tel. (372) 60520; fax (372) 60231; e-mail batas@kaunas.omnitel.net; f. 1933; production of rubber and rubber goods; Pres. ANDRIUS PAULIUKAITIS; 850 employees.

Jiesia AB: Chemijos pr. 29, Kaunas 3031; tel. (374) 52963; fax (374) 53541; internet www.jiesia.lt; f. 1938; sales 4.8m. litai (1999); manufactures porcelain, stoneware and ceramic products; Dir RUSTENIS MIDVIKIS; 320 employees.

Juodupes Nemunas AB: Pergales 4, Juodupe 4822; tel. (278) 52067; fax (278) 53481; e-mail j.nemunas@post.omnitel.net; f. 1907; joint-stock co; textiles; Chair. DARIUS AUSMANAS; 682 employees.

Katra Ltd: Taikos pr. 113, Kaunas 3036; tel. (373) 13020; fax (373) 13421; e-mail info@katra.lt; internet www.katra.lt; f. 1991; sales US $11.5m. (1999); manufacture of water meters, heating meters, district heating substations, parking meters and payphones; Pres. ALBINAS BACILIUNAS; 324 employees.

Kauno Audiniai AB: Griunvaldo 3/5, Kaunas 3697; tel. (372) 26484; fax (372) 28323; e-mail kaudiniai@kaunas.omnitel.net; f. 1930; joint-stock co; sales 36.4m. litai (1998); silk, fabrics; Pres. RAMUNAS GARBARAVIČIUS; 447 employees.

Kauno baldai AB: Drobės 66, Kaunas 3002; tel. (377) 40687; fax (377) 40425; f. 1880; joint-stock co; furniture products; Dir ZYDRUNAS MATUŠEVIČIUS; 650 employees.

Kauno Elektra AB: Piliakalnio 3, Kaunas 3019; tel. (372) 28103; fax (372) 98938; f. 1958; electric motors, grinders; Dir S. STANKEVIČIUS; 625 employees.

Kauno Ketaus Liejykla AB: R. Kalantos 49, Kaunas 3014; tel. (373) 51090; fax (373) 51260; e-mail ketus@takas.lt; internet ketus.biznis.lt; joint-stock co; produces cast-iron mouldings; Dir RYMANTAS KULBOKAS.

Kausta AB: Naglio 4A, Kaunas 3014; tel. (377) 51490; fax (377) 64212; e-mail kausta@kainas.aiva.net; f. 1961; industrial construction and renovation; Gen. Dir ANTANAS BURKAS; 1,750 employees.

Klaipėdos Kartonas AB: Nemuno 2, Klaipėda 5800; tel. (463) 95601; fax (463) 95600; e-mail kl.kartonas@klaipeda.omnitel.net; internet www.omnitel.net/kl-kartonas; f. 1898; sales 32.6m. litai (1999); produces paper and paperboard; Gen. Man. A. PASVENSKAS; 556 employees.

Klaipėdos Maistas AB: Šilutes 79, Klaipėda 5799; tel. (463) 41200; fax (463) 90279; e-mail info@maistas.com; internet www.maistas.com; f. 1928; sales 164.2m. litai (1998); joint-stock co; produces tinned meat and sausages; Chair. VALANČIUS GINTARAS; 1,372 employees.

Kuro Aparatūra AB: Kalvarijų 143, Vilnius 2650; tel. (527) 66463; fax (527) 22408; f. 1959; sales 59m. litai (1998); produces fuel pumps for diesel engines and fuel jets; Dir PETRAS ZAIKAUSKAS; 3,300 employees.

Lietkabelis AB: Janonio 4, Panevėžys 5319; tel. (455) 02685; fax (454) 24501; e-mail laidas@post.omnitel.net; internet www.lietkabelis.lt; f. 1959; sales 24m. litai (1999); joint-stock co; manufacture and sale of enamelled copper wire; Chair. ALGIS BUCAS; 450 employees.

Lifosa AB: Juodkiškio 50, Kėdainiai 5030; tel. (347) 66483; fax (347) 66166; e-mail info@lifosa.com; internet www.lifosa.com; f. 1963; sales 400m. litai (1998); joint-stock co; chemical production; Chair. DANAS TVARIJONAVIČIUS; 1,500 employees.

Linas AB: S. Kerbedžio 23, Panevėžys 5319; tel. (455) 06100; fax (454) 22607; e-mail linas@mail.linas.lt; internet www.linas.lt; f. 1957; sales 74.8m. litai (2000); joint-stock co; linen fabrics; Pres. RAMUNAS LENČIAUSKAS; 1,651 employees.

Linu Audiniai AB: Birutes 43, Plungė 5640; tel. (448) 52632; fax (448) 51321; e-mail audiniai@klaipeda.aiva.lt; f. 1913; fabrics and linens; Dir ALVYDAS VITKEVIČIUS; 1,066 employees.

Litoda AB: Pramonės pr. 4, Plungė 5640; tel. (448) 53237; fax (448) 57812; e-mail oda@pvilnius.omnitel.net; f. 1971; production and sale of vinyl leather for the clothing, footwear and furniture industries, and vinyl leather products; Pres. and Chair. A. GIRLEVIČIUS; 500 employees.

Marijampolės Pieno Konservai AB: Kauno 114, Marijampolė 4520; tel. (343) 71498; fax (343) 79731; e-mail mpk.pienas@pikuolis.omnitel.net; f. 1977; sales 81.3m. litai (1999); 49% owned by State Property Fund; production and export of tinned dairy products, bottling and packing of juices and soft drinks; Dir ZENONAS SKIBINIAUSKAS; 1,349 employees.

Mastis AB: Pramonės 11, Telšiai 5610; tel. and fax (444) 53341; fax (444) 54154; f. 1932; joint-stock co; knitted fabrics and clothing; Gen. Dir GINTAUTAS JUCIUS; 820 employees.

Mažeikiai NAFTA (Petroleum Refinery): Juodeikiai District, Mažeikiai 5526; tel. (443) 70639; fax (443) 92525; e-mail leonas@nafta.lt; internet www.nafta.lt; f. 1980; 53.7% of shares sold to Yukos (Russia) in Sept. 2002, 40.7% state-owned; sales 2,800m. litai (1998); petroleum derivatives, liquefied gas, sulphur; Dir-Gen. JIM SCHEEL; 3,650 employees.

Medienos Plaušas: Savanorių pr. 183, Vilnius 2600; tel. (527) 06280; fax (522) 30686; e-mail medienos_plausas@post.omnitel.net; f. 1956; sales 41.8m. litai (1998); manufacture of corrugated cardboard and packaging, soft fibreboard and egg boxes; Man. Dir HEIKKI PIETILÄINEN; 470 employees.

Naujoji Ruta AB: Bielskio 15, Šiauliai 5402; tel. (414) 42281; fax (414) 41556; e-mail prekyba@nruta.lt; sales 27.8m. litai (1999); production and sale of caramel, chocolate, liqueur chocolates, marshmallows and other confectionery; Dir EMILIJA BUTIENE; 273 employees.

Nemunas AB: R. Kalantos 83, Kaunas 3014; tel. (377) 65030; fax (377) 66881; e-mail nemunas@kaunas.omnitel.net; f. 1951; produces wire, wire netting, nails and agricultural tools; Dir VITALIJUS GRAUNAS; 420 employees.

Neris: Pramonės 97, Vilnius 2048; tel. (526) 70023; fax (526) 71815; e-mail neris@nkm.lt; f. 1958; produces trucks for the timber industry, metal constructions, repairs and modernizes railway carriages; Dir-Gen. RIMAS KELPŠA; 300 employees.

Oruva AB: Ventos 8, Mažeikiai 5500; tel. (443) 66465; fax (443) 66956; f. 1965; sales 30.6m. litai (1998); compressors for household refrigerators, air-cooled diesel engines and household appliances; Pres. RIMVYDAS KROLIS; 1,591 employees.

Panevėžio Aurida UAB: Pramonės 8, Panevėžys 5319; tel. (454) 61101; fax (454) 64193; e-mail pan-aurida@post.omnitel.net; f. 1959; manufacture of compressors for motor vehicles and domestic use, production of alumunium castings and steel forgings, machining of components; Dir REDAS KLUPŠAS; 300 employees.

Panevėžio Pienas AB: Tinklu 9, Panevėžys 5319; tel. (455) 02077; fax (455) 02073; e-mail info@pienine.lt; f. 1942; joint-stock co; sales 32m. litai (Jan.–June 2000); dairy; Dir ALBERTAS BALČIUNAS; 800 employees.

Panevėžio Stiklas (Glass-Works): Pramonės 10, Panevėžys 5319; tel. (454) 63747; fax (454) 65703; e-mail abstiklas@glassw.lt; internet www.glassw.lt; f. 1965; joint-stock co; sales 95.7m. litai (1998); manufacturing and processing of glass products; Dir A. BAKONIS; 996 employees.

Pas Juozapa AB: Laivšes pr. 125, Vilnius 2022; tel. (524) 81696; fax (524) 81641; e-mail pasjuozapa@auste.elnet.lt; f. 1993; wholesale and retail trade in foodstuffs and general merchandise, operation of supermarkets; Pres. Dr JUOZAPAS BUDRIKIS; 700 employees.

Pergales Koncernas UAB: Kaunakiernio 5, Kanuas 3000; tel. (374) 25473; fax (374) 29310; e-mail perkon@kaunas.omnitel.net; internet www.lda.lt/go/pergalesk; f. 1867; joint-stock co; manufacture of marine machinery, heating equipment, wheels and containers; Dir LEONARDAS KRUPENKOVAS; 350 employees.

Plasta AB: Savanorių pr. 180, Vilnius 2644; tel. (526) 39876; fax (521) 63429; e-mail plastampt@plasta.aiva.lt; internet www.statyba.lt; f. 1961; sales 45.3m. litai (1998); polythene pipe, bags and film; Dir ALGIRDAS GUSKEVIČIUS; 1,200 employees.

Satrija AB: Vilniaus 5, Rašeiniai 4400; tel. (428) 53263; fax (428) 52161; e-mail satrija@raseiniai.omnitel.net; f. 1955; joint-stock co; sales 33.8m. litai (1998); clothing; Man. Dir JONAS STRAVINSKAS; 1,300 employees.

Šenukai Group JSC: Pramonės pr. 6, Kaunas 3031; tel. (373) 04801; fax (373) 04803; e-mail marketing@senukai.lt; internet www.senukai.lt; f. 1995; joint-stock co; sales US $75m. (2000); wholesale and retail construction materials, electrical repair and lighting equipment, chemicals, hardware, sports and leisure goods, domestic appliances, gardening products, metal processing, glass cutting, manufacture of furniture and other wooden products, aluminium windows, doors, façades, shower cubicles and other metal constructions, freight transport; Pres. AUGUSTIN RAKAUSKAS; 1,400 employees.

Šiaulių Pienas AB: Bielsko 18, Šiauliai 5402; tel. (414) 41020; fax (414) 21688; e-mail pienas@siauliai.alva.lt; f. 1957; joint-stock co; sales 66.5m. litai (1998); dairy; Dir STANISLOVAS AMBRASAS; 991 employees.

Šiaulių Tauro Televizorial: Pramonės 15, Šiauliai 5402; tel. (414) 52445; fax (415) 40570; f. 1994; televisions and television equipment; Dir R. ZUKAUSKAS; 352 employees.

Sirijus: Artojų 7, Klaipėda 5799; tel. (462) 12757; fax (462) 16833; f. 1931; galvanic elements and batteries; Dir L. MAKŪNAS; 530 employees.

Skaiteks JSC: Aukštaičių 7, Vilnius 2600; tel. (526) 43415; fax (526) 43405; e-mail export@skaiteks.lt; internet www.skaiteks.lt; f. 1949; produces electricity meters; Gen. Dir ROMUALDAS URBANAVIČIUS; 650 employees.

Snaigė AB: Pramonės 6, Alytus 4580; tel. (315) 77580; fax (315) 77612; e-mail snaige@snaige.lt; internet www.snaige.lt; f. 1963; joint-stock co; sales 174m. litai (1998); produces household refrigerators, freezers, display coolers, and thermo-insulation panels; Pres. ANTANAS ANDRIULIONIS; 1,996 employees.

Stumbras AB: K. Bugos 7, Kaunas 3000; tel. (372) 26185; fax (372) 22939; e-mail stumbras@kaunas.alva.lt; f. 1906; joint-stock co; sales 85m. litai (1998); produces vodka and liqueurs, ethyl alcohol, carbonic acid, beer, hops extract, potato starch and mineral water; Dir JONAS ZUKAUŠKAS; 820 employees.

Švyturys AB: Kuliu vartu 7, Klaipėda 5799; tel. (464) 48000; fax (464) 84009; e-mail svyturys@svyturys.com; internet www.svyturys.lt; joint-stock co; 95% owned by Carlsberg A/S (Denmark); sales 75.3m. litai (1999); production and sale of beer; Dir TOOMAS KUČINSKAS; 360 employees.

Telebaltika (Lithuanian Consortium of Radioelectronics): Žamaiciu 31, Kaunas 3031; tel. (372) 07750; fax (377) 33769; production of radioelectronic equipment; Pres. SIGITAS GODELIS; 24,000 employees.

Trikotažas AB: Savanorių 255, Kaunas 3009; tel. (377) 30202; fax (377) 34013; e-mail trico@taide.lt; f. 1935; joint-stock co; knitted fabrics; Gen. Dir JONAS ZAKAITIS; 1,479 employees.

Utenos Gerimai AB: Pramonės 12, Utena 4910; tel. (389) 52787; fax (389) 69047; e-mail gvenslovas@ug.omnitel.net; f. 1977; joint-stock co; produces beer, non-alcoholic beverages and malt; Dir STASYS KRASAUŠKAS; 860 employees.

Utenos Trikotažas: J. Basanavičiaus 122, Utena 4910; tel. (389) 51445; fax (389) 69358; e-mail trikotut.lt@post.omnitel.net; f. 1967; sales 101m. litai (1998); knitwear and yarn; Dir NIJOLE DUMBLIAUSKIENĖ; 1,810 employees.

Vakaru Laivu Remontas AB: Minijos 180, Klaipėda 5816; tel. (463) 55031; fax (463) 55114; joint-stock co; construction and repair of ships; Gen. Dir ALGIRDAS RENKAUSKAS; 1,500 employees.

Vienybe AB: Kauno 120, Ukmergė 4120; tel. (340) 63516; fax (340) 63544; e-mail vienybe@vienybe.lt; internet www.vienybe.com; f. 1919; sales 28m. litai (2000); manufacture of machine components; Man. Dir ARTURAS GRIBACAUSKAS; 685 employees.

Vilkas AB: Raudondvario 101, Kaunas 3026; tel. (373) 63155; fax (373) 61988; e-mail abvilkas@kaunas.omnitel.net; internet www.dokeda.lt/vilkas; f. 1932; joint-stock co; processing of fur and hides, production of leather and fur clothing and household products; Man. Dir PETRAS TEREŠKEVIČ; 400 employees.

Vilniaus Mesos Kombinatas AB: Savanorių pr. 219, Vilnius 2665; tel. (526) 53354; fax (526) 53317; e-mail vmkdir@takas.lt; f. 1994; sales 57m. litai (2000); produces meat and meat products; Dir ARNOLDAS VYSNIAUSKAS; 480 employees.

Vilniaus Prekybos Mazmena UAB: Naugarduko 99, Vilnius 2609; tel. (526) 86787; fax (526) 86700; f. 1995; sales 745.9m. litai (1998); wholesalers and retailers in food and general goods; Dir RENATAS VAITKEVIČIUS; 2,800 employees.

Vilniaus Vingis AB: Savanorių pr. 176, Vilnius 2600; tel. (523) 92500; fax (523) 92555; e-mail vingis@vingis.lt; internet www.vingis.lt; f. 1959; sales 120.4m. litai (2000); electrical components and equipment; Dir-Gen. VACLOVAS ŠLEINOTA; 2,244 employees.

Vingriai JSC: Smolensko 10, Vilnius 2006; tel. (523) 99030; fax (521) 31171; e-mail commerce@vingriai.lt; internet www.aiva.lt/vingriai; f. 1959 as Vilnius State Plant of Grinding-Machines; present name adopted 2002; produces milling and grinding machines, vacuum chambers and metal parts; Dir ČESLOVAS KRINICKAS.

Žalgiris: Pramonės 141, Vilnius 2048; tel. (526) 71476; fax (526) 74774; f. 1947; metal-cutting machines, milling machines; Dir JURIJUS SIVICKIS.

Žemaitijos Pienas UAB: Sedos 35, Telšiai 5610; tel. (444) 22201; fax (444) 74897; e-mail z-pienas@telsiai.omnital.net; f. 1993; sales 156m. litai (2000); dairy; Dir ALGIRDAS PAŽEMECKAS; 1,188 employees.

Žuvu Konservai AB: Nemuno 20, Klaipėda 5084; tel. (463) 40986; fax (462) 72821; e-mail fish@klaipeda.omnitel.net; joint-stock co; 80% owned by Govt, 20% owned by employees; production and sale of canned, salted and smoked fish; Dir RUTA LASTOČKINA; 600 employees.

TRADE UNIONS

Christian Farmers' Union of Lithuania: V. Mykolaičio-Putino 5, Vilnius 2009; tel. and fax (523) 12029; f. 1919; re-est. 1995; 10 regional brs; 6,000 mems; Chair. JUOZAS ALEKNAVIČIUS.

Lithuanian Labour Federation: V. Mykolaičio-Putino 5/140, Vilnius 2600; tel. and fax (523) 12029; e-mail ldforg@ldf.lt; internet www.ldf.lt; f. 1919; re-est. 1991; 20,000 mems; Chair. KAZIMIERAS KUZMINSKAS; Sec.-Gen. REGINA REKEŠIENĖ.

Lithuanian Trade Unions Centre: Basanavičiaus 29A, Vilnius 2600; tel. (526) 14888; fax (526) 60217; f. 1993; 13 affiliated unions with 140,000 mems; Chair. ALGIRDAS KVEDARAVIČIUS.

Lithuanian Union of Free Trade Unions: J. Jasinskio 9, Vilnius 2600; tel. (526) 10921; fax (526) 19078; f. 1992; 8 affiliated unions with 50,000 mems; Chair. ALGIRDAS SYSAS.

Lithuanian Workers' Union: V. Mykolaičio-Putino 5, Vilnius 2009; tel. (526) 21743; fax (521) 33295; e-mail ltds@takas.lt; internet www.darbininkas.lt; f. 1989; 28 regional brs; 7 federations; 52,000 mems; Pres. ALDONA BALSIENĖ.

Transport

RAILWAYS

In 2001 there were 1,696 km of railway track in use in Lithuania; in the same year some 122 km of track were electrified. Main lines link Vilnius with Rīga (Latvia), Minsk (Belarus), Kaliningrad (Russia) and Warsaw (Poland), via the Belarusian town of Grodno.

Lithuanian Railways (Lietuvos geležinkeliai AB): Mindaugo 12–14, Vilnius 2600; tel. (526) 93300; fax (526) 18323; e-mail 24@litrail.lt; internet www.litrail.lt; f. 1991; Gen. Dir K. DIRGELA; 15,500 employees.

ROADS

In 2001 the total length of the road network was 76,573 km. The motorway network totalled 417 km and some 91% of roads were paved.

Lithuanian Road Administration (Lietuvos automobilių kelių direkcija): J. Basanavicius 36/2, Vilnius 2009; tel. (521) 31361; fax (521) 31362; e-mail info@lra.lt; internet www.lra.lt; Gen. Dir VIRGAUDAS PUODZIUKAS.

SHIPPING

The main port is at Klaipėda. During the Soviet period the port was used as an important transit facility, with some 90% of its total traffic being transit trade to and from the republics of the USSR. This role diminished with the establishment of Lithuanian independence in 1991 and the disruption of traditional trading patterns following the dissolution of the USSR. The Lithuanian Shipping Company was formerly part of the Soviet merchant shipping system. In the early 1990s it was restructured as an independent enterprise, although it was adversely affected by declining trade and a largely obsolete fleet. In 2000 the World Bank funded an investment project for the reconstruction of the port gate and protection measures for the environment.

Port Authority

Klaipėda State Seaport Authority: J. Janonio 24, Klaipėda 5800; tel. (464) 99799; fax (464) 99777; e-mail info@port.lt; internet www.port.lt.

Shipowning Company

Public Company Lithuanian Shipping Company (AB Lietuvos Jūrų Laivininkystė): Malunininku 3, Klaipėda 5813; tel. (463) 93105; fax (463) 93119; e-mail gp@ljl.lt; internet www.ljl.lt; f. 1969; partially privatized in June 2001; 73.24% state-owned; transportation of cargo; Gen. Dir VYTAUTAS VISMANTAS.

CIVIL AVIATION

Lithuania has air links with Western European destinations and with cities in the former USSR. The state airline, Lietuvos avialinijos, is based at the international airports at Vilnius and Kaunas. An airport at Šiauliai opened for international flights at the end of 1993.

Directorate of Civil Aviation (Oro Navigacija): Rodūnės kelias 2, Vilnius 2023; tel. (527) 39102; fax (527) 39161; e-mail info@ans.lt; internet www.ans.lt; Gen. Dir ALGIMANTAS RAŠČIUS.

Lithuanian Airlines (Lietuvos avialinijos): A. Gustaičio 4, Vilnius 2038; tel. (523) 06017; fax (521) 66828; e-mail info@lal.lt; internet www.lal.lt; f. 1991; state-owned; scheduled for privatization in 2002; operates passenger and cargo flights to regional and European destinations; Dir-Gen. STASYS JARMALAVIČIUS.

Aviakompanija Lietuva (Air Lithuania): Veiverių 132, Karmelava Airport, Kaunas 3018; tel. (373) 91420; fax (372) 26030; e-mail hdoffice@airlithuania.lt; internet www.airlithuania.lt; f. 1991; state-owned; operates passenger and cargo services to Europe; became subsidiary of Lithuanian Airlines in August 1997; Chair. and Dir-Gen. TOMAS LAURINAITIS.

Tourism

Tourist attractions in Lithuania include the historic cities of Vilnius, Kaunas, Kėdainiai, Trakai and Klaipėda, coastal resorts, such as Palanga and Kuršių Nerija, and picturesque countryside. There were some 350 private travel agencies in operation in 1999 and some 349,662 tourists visited the country in 2001; tourist receipts in that year totalled US $383.0m.

Lithuanian State Department of Tourism: Vilniaus 4/35, Vilnius 2600; tel. (526) 22610; fax (521) 26819; e-mail tb@tourism.lt; internet www.tourism.lt; Dir ALVITIS LUKOSEVICIUS.

Culture

NATIONAL ORGANIZATION

Ministry of Culture: see section on The Government (Ministries).

Department of Cultural Heritage Protection (Kultūros Paveldo Centras): Ašmenos 10, Vilnius 2600; tel. (526) 22926; fax (521) 22191; e-mail kpcb@kpc.lt; internet www.kpc.lt; f. 1995; Dir VITAS KARČIAUSKAS.

CULTURAL HERITAGE

Art Museum of Lithuania: Didžioji 4, Vilnius 2001; tel. (526) 28030; fax (521) 26006; e-mail idm@aiva.lt; internet www.ldm.lt; f. 1933; over 202,045 items; library of 30,000 vols; Dir ROMUALDAS BUDRYS.

Contemporary Art Centre: Vokiečių 2, Vilnius 2001; tel. (526) 29851; fax (526) 23954; e-mail cac.info@cac.lt; internet www.cac.lt; f. 1968; Lithuanian and international art exhibitions, performances, video and film screenings; Dir KĘSTUTIS KUIZINAS.

Cultural Foundation of Lithuania: Jakšto 9, Vilnius 2600; tel. (526) 17634; fax (526) 20508; f. 1989; promotes the arts and culture of Lithuania; Chair. JURGIS DVARIONAS.

Institute of Lithuanian Language: P. Vileisio 5, Vilnius 2055; tel. (523) 46472; fax (523) 47200; e-mail lki@ktl.mii.lt; internet www .lki.lt; f. 1939; Dir GIEDRIUS SUBAČIUS.

Institute of Lithuanian Literature and Folklore: Antakalnio 6, Vilnius; tel. (526) 21943; e-mail llti@ktl.mii.lt; f. 1939; attached to the Lithuanian Academy of Sciences; Dir ALGIS KALĖDA.

Lithuanian Ethnographic Museum: Rumšiškės, Kaišiadorys 4237; tel. and fax (346) 51589; Dir STASYS GUTAUTAS.

Lithuanian Folk Culture Centre (LFCC): B. Radvilaitės 8, Vilnius 2600; tel. (526) 14763; fax (526) 12607; e-mail lfcc@lfcc.lt; internet www.lfcc.lt; Dir JUOZAS MIKUTAVIČIUS.

Lithuanian Institute of Culture and Arts: Tilto g. 4, Vilnius 2001; tel. (526) 13646; fax (526) 10989; e-mail mastac@aiva.lt; internet www.aiva.lt/kultura_ir_menas/; f. 1990; research institute; Dir ARVYDAS MATULIONIS.

Lithuanian Music Information and Publishing Centre: A. Mickevičiaus 29, Vilnius 2600; tel. (527) 26986; fax (521) 20939; e-mail info@mic.lt; internet www.mic.lt; f. 1997; promotes Lithuanian music, maintains collection of manuscripts and recordings, publishes biannual newsletter, *Lithuanian Music*; Dir DAIVA PARULSKIENE.

Lithuanian Sea Museum: Smiltynė 3, Klaipėda 5800; tel. (463) 91119; fax (463) 91101; e-mail director@juru.muziejus.lt; f. 1979; exhibits and breeds sea animals; Dir ALOYZAS KAŽDALIS.

Lithuanian Training Centre for Cultural Administrators: Saltoniškių 58, Vilnius 2600; tel. (527) 52777; fax (527) 90304; e-mail lkdtc@takas.lt; mem. of European Network of Cultural Administrators Training Centres; Dir LINA BANIENĖ.

M. K. Čiurlionis National Art Museum: Vlado Putvinskio 55, Kaunas 3000; tel. (372) 29738; fax (372) 04612; f. 1921; Lithuanian and European art, folk art, oriental and Ancient Egyptian art, numismatics; library of 24,000 vols; Dir OSVALDAS DAUGELIS.

Martynas Mažvydas National Library of Lithuania: Gedimino pr. 51, Vilnius 2635; tel. (526) 29023; fax (526) 27129; e-mail info@ lnb.lt; internet www.lnb.lt; f. 1919; 5.2m. vols; Dir Dr VLADAS BULAVAS.

National Museum of Lithuania: Arsenalo 1, Vilnius 20; tel. (526) 27774; fax (526) 11023; e-mail muziejus@lnm.lt; internet www.lnm .lt; f. 1855; over 854,000 exhibits; special archaeological, numismatic, historical, ethnographical and iconographical collections; library of over 56,000 vols; Dir BIRUTĖ KULNYTĖ.

Trakai Historical Museum: Kęstučio 4, Trakai; tel. (528) 51274; f. 1948; local history; Dir VIRGILIJUS POVILIŪNAS.

Vilnius Gaono Jewish State Museum: Pamėnkalnio 12, Vilnius 2001; tel. (526) 24590; fax (526) 27083; e-mail jmuseum@puni.osf.lt; f. 1989; researches the history of the Jews of Lithuania; organizes conferences and exhibitions; Dir EMANUEL ZINGERIS.

War Museum of Vytautas the Great: K. Donelaičio 64, Kaunas 3000; tel. (372) 29606; fax (372) 22756; f. 1921; approx. 200,000 exhibits; library of approx. 13,000 vols; Dir J. JUREVIČIUS.

SPORTING ORGANIZATIONS

Lithuanian State Department of Physical Training and Sports: J. Žemaitės 6, Vilnius 2600; tel. (523) 35353; fax (521) 33221; e-mail kksd@kksd.lt; internet www.kksd.lt; govt agency; Dir-Gen. VYTAS NĖNIUS.

National Olympic Committee of Lithuania: Olimpiečių 15, Vilnius 2051; tel. (527) 80642; fax (527) 80660; e-mail komitetas@ltok .lt; internet www.ltok.lt; f. 1924; Pres. ARTŪRAS POVILIŪNAS; Sec-Gen. VYTAUTAS ZUBERNIS.

PERFORMING ARTS

Juozo Miltinio Drama Theatre: Laisvės 5, Panevėžys 5319; tel. (455) 84596; fax (455) 84597; e-mail jmteatras@takas.lt; Dir RIMANTAS TERESAS.

Kaunas State Academic Drama Theatre: Laisvės 71, Kaunas 3000; tel. (372) 24198; fax (372) 07693; e-mail info@dramosteatras .lt; internet www.dramosteatras.lt; f. 1920; Dir V. BARTULIS.

Klaipėda Drama Theatre: Teatro 2, Klaipėda 5800; tel. (462) 19801; fax (462) 19484; Dir R. KORKŪZIENĖ.

Lithuanian Academic Drama Theatre: Gedimino pr. 4, Vilnius 2600; tel. (526) 22045; fax (526) 20051; Artistic Dir RIMAS TUMINAS.

Lithuanian National Opera and Ballet Theatre: Vienuolio 1, Vilnius 2600; tel. (526) 20093; fax (523) 14065; e-mail administracija@opera.lt; internet www.opera.lt; f. 1920; Dir-Gen. K. MINDERIS.

Lithuanian National Philharmonic: Aušros Vartų 5, Vilnius 2001; tel. (526) 65210; fax (526) 65266; e-mail info@filharmonija.lt; internet www.fiharmonija.lt; f. 1940; comprises symphony and chamber orchestras, choir, string quartets and soloists; Dir-Gen. EGIDIJUS MIKŠYS.

Lithuanian Puppet Theatre: Arklių 5, Vilnius 2600; tel. (526) 14047; fax (526) 28159; Dir P. ŠVOMBARIS.

Lithuanian State Symphony Orchestra (Lietuvos Valstybinis Symfoninis Orkestras): Zygimantu 6, Vilnius 2600; tel. (526) 28127; fax (521) 20966; e-mail lvso@lvso.lt; internet www.lvso.lt; f. 1989; Dir JURGIS BANEVIČIUS.

Lithuanian Youth Theatre (Valstybinis Jaunimo Teatras): Arklių 5, Vilnius 2600; tel. (526) 25556; fax (526) 25558; e-mail info@ jaunimoteatras.lt; internet www.jaunimoteatras.lt; Dir A. LATĖNAS.

Russian Drama Theatre: J. Basanivičiaus 13, Vilnius; tel. (521) 21801; fax (526) 52167; e-mail lrdt@takas.lt; f. 1947; Dirs VLADIMIR TARASOV, IGOR MARKOV.

Šiauliai Drama Theatre: Tilžės 144, Šiauliai 5400; tel. (414) 33577; fax (414) 32614; Dir R. ATKOČIŪNAS.

ASSOCIATIONS

Architects Association of Lithuania: Kalvarijų 1, Vilnius 2600; tel. (527) 56483; fax (527) 24825; e-mail architektu.sajunga@takas .lt; f. 1925 as the Engineers and Architects Association of Lithuania; organizes exhibitions, seminars and training; Chair. VYTAUTAS JURGIS DIČIUS.

Cultural Foundation of Lithuania: Jakšto 9, Vilnius 2600; tel. (526) 17634; fax (526) 20508; f. 1989; restoration of Lithuanian cultural heritage; Chair. JURGIS DVARIONAS.

Lithuanian Artists' Association: Vokiečių 4/2, Vilnius 2600; tel. (526) 22557; fax (526) 21986; e-mail info@artistasassociation.lt; internet www.artistasassociation.lt; f. 1935; Chair. VACLOVAS KRUTINIS; 1,227 mems.

Lithuanian Association of Artists: K. Sirvydo 6, Vilnius 2600; tel. (521) 23919; fax (526) 16996; e-mail eleres@takas.lt; internet eleres.prantel.lt; Pres. V. MARTINKUS.

Lithuanian Choirs' Union: Radvilaitės 8, Vilnius 2600; tel. (526) 12530; fax (521) 24033; Pres. VYTAUTAS MIŠKINIS.

Lithuanian Composers' Union: A. Mickevičiaus 29, Vilnius 2600; tel. (521) 23611; fax (521) 20939; e-mail gaida@lks.lt; internet www .mic.lt; f. 1941; organizes festivals, such as the Gaida Baltic Music Festival, the Lithuanian Music Spring; Chair. GINTARAS SODEIKA.

Lithuanian Designers' Union: Juozapavičiaus 11, Vilnius 2600; tel. (527) 21734; fax (527) 21893; e-mail disajunga@centras.lt; f. 1987; Chair. JONAS MALINAUSKAS.

Lithuanian Film-makers' Union: Birutės18; Vilnius 2004; tel. and fax (521) 20759; e-mail lks1@auste.elnet.lt; f. 1931; Chair. GYTIS LUKŠAS.

Lithuanian Folk-Art Society: Stiklių 16, Vilnius 2001; tel. and fax (521) 20564; f. 1966; Chair. J. RUDZINSKAS.

Lithuanian Journalists' Union: Vilniaus 33, Vilnius 2600; tel. (526) 11790; fax (521) 21571; f. 1957; Chair. RIMGAUDAS EILUNAVIČIUS.

Lithuanian Musician's Society: Gedimino pr. 32/2, Vilnius 2001; tel. (526) 23043; fax (521) 20302; e-mail muzsajunga@takas.lt; Pres. Prof. RIMVYDAS ŽIGAITIS.

Lithuanian Photographers' Union: Universiteto 4, Vilnius 2001; tel. and fax (526) 11665; Chair. A. SUTKUS.

Lithuanian Society for Study of Local Lore: Traku 2, Vilnius 2001; tel. (526) 24929; fax (521) 21126; f. 1926; Chair. IRENA SELIU-KAITE.

Lithuanian Theatre Union: Gedimino pr. 1, Vilnius 2001; tel. (526) 23586; fax (526) 10814; f. 1987; Chair. HEGIS MATULIOUIS.

Lithuanian Writers' Union: K. Sirvydo 6, Vilnius 2600; tel. (521) 23919; fax (526) 19696; e-mail eleres@takas.lt; internet www.eleres .prantel.lt; f. 1940; Chair. VALENTINAS SVENTICKAS.

Motherland (Teviske): Tilto g. 8/2, Vilnius 2600; tel. (526) 13580; fax (526) 24092; f. 1964; Chair. VACLOVAS SAKALAUSKAS.

PEN Centre of Lithuania: K. Sirvydo 6, Vilnius 2600; tel. (526) 19486; fax (526) 16902; e-mail almantsam@yahoo.com; internet www.pen.lt; f. 1989; Pres. ALMANTAS SAMALAVIČIUS; Sec. LAIMANTAS JONUŠYS; 36 mems.

Polish Union of Lithuania: Didzioji 40, Vilnius 2601; tel. (521) 23388; e-mail nasz-ozas@mail.tl; internet nasz-ozas.tripod.com; f. 1988; organizes cultural and educational activities; Chair. RYSZARD MACIEJKIANIEC.

Education

Under the terms of the 1992 Constitution, education in Lithuania is free of charge and is compulsory between the ages of seven and 18. There are three principal levels of education: comprehensive (from seven to 18 years of age), vocational and schools of further education (16–18 years), and higher. From January 2003 a uniform tuition fee was to be introduced for students of higher education, although there were to be exemptions for the highest achievers. There are three main types of comprehensive school: primary, basic and secondary. In the 2000/01 academic year primary enrolment was equivalent to 94.7% of the relevant age-group. The corresponding figure for secondary enrolment was 88.4%. In 2002/03 there were 2,172 comprehensive schools, with a total enrolment of 594,300 students. There were 82 vocational schools, 51 schools of further education, and 19 universities in that year. Lithuanian is the main language of instruction, although in 1999/2000 7.7% of students at comprehensive schools were taught in Russian and 3.8% were taught in Polish. In 2001 the state budget allocated 925.5m. litai (7.3% of expenditure) to education.

UNIVERSITIES

International School of Management: Kaunas; f. 1999; from the Business Training Centre; affiliated to the Norwegian School of Management BI; 70 students.

Kaunas University of Technology: K. Donelaičio 73, Kaunas 3006; tel. (373) 00011; fax (373) 24144; e-mail rastine@cr.ktu.lt; internet www.ktu.lt; f. 1922; languages of instruction: Lithuanian, English, French, German and Russian; 14 faculties; 1,133 teachers; 13,942 undergraduate students, 3,904 post-graduate students; Rector Prof. RAMUTIS BANSEVIČIUS.

Klaipėda University: H. Manto 84, Klaipėda 5808; tel. (463) 98900; fax (463) 98999; e-mail rektorius@rekt.ku.lt; internet www .ku.lt; f. 1991; 689 teachers, 4,259 students; Rector Prof. STATYS VAITEKUNAS.

Vilnius Gediminas Technical University: Saulėtekio 11, Vilnius 2040; tel. (527) 00478; fax (527) 00112; e-mail urd@adm.vtu.lt; internet www.vtu.lt; f. 1956; languages of instruction: Lithuanian, English, French; 8 faculties, 1 institute; 739 teachers; 9,500 students; Rector EDMUNDAS KAZIMIERAS ZAVADSKAS.

Vilnius University: Universiteto 3, Vilnius 2734; tel. (526) 87010; fax (526) 87096; e-mail infor@cr.vu.lt; internet www.vu.lt; f. 1579; language of instruction: Lithuanian; 1,169 teachers; 19,120 students; Rector Prof. BENEDIKTUS JUODKA (acting).

Vytautas Magnus University: Donelaicio 28, Kaunas 3000; tel. (372) 22739; fax (372) 03858; e-mail rektorius@abm.vdu.lt; internet

www.vdu.lt; f. 1922; closed 1950, reopened 1989; language of instruction: Lithuanian; 7 faculties, 24 institutes, 25 departments; 444 teachers; 6,282 students; Rector VYTAUTAS KAMINSKAS.

Social Welfare

A comprehensive state-funded health system was introduced in Lithuania under Soviet rule. Some reforms were introduced in 1990, including the legalization of private practices. In October 1991, shortly after the re-establishment of Lithuanian independence, a National Health Concept was adopted, which strongly criticized the Soviet system and emphasized the need for substantial reforms. Implementation of reform, however, was slow. In 2000 there were 10.1 hospital beds and 3.8 physicians per 1,000 inhabitants. The rate of infant mortality in 2001 was 9 per 1,000 live births. Total government expenditure on health in 2001 was 2,028.9m. litai (representing 16.1% of total spending).

Under the terms of the 1992 Constitution citizens were entitled to old-age and disability pensions, as well as social assistance in the event of unemployment, sickness, widowhood, etc. The social security system (SODRA—Valstybinio socialinio draudimo sistema Lietuvoje) comprises a social insurance scheme (financed by the independent Social Insurance Fund) and a social assistance scheme, administered by local authorities. A private social insurance system, funded from insurance funds and including the establishment of pension funds, was envisaged in 1998; former Lithuanian political prisoners and deportees were to receive higher old-age pensions. Women retire at the age of 60.0 years, whereas men retire at 62.5 years. In 2001 there were 947,600 pensioners and expenditure on pensions in that year was 3,557.5m. litai (equivalent to 7.4% of GDP). In that year the average old-age pension was 317.6 litai per month. The monthly minimum wage was to be increased from 430 litai to 450 litai per month from 1 September 2003. Total government expenditure on social security and welfare in 2001 was 4,480.1m. litai (35.5% of total spending).

NATIONAL AGENCIES

Department of Labour Safety: Jaksto 1/25, Vilnius 2600; tel. (526) 61854; Dir-Gen. JONAS SIMKUNAS.

Ministry of Health Care: see section on The Government (Ministries).

Ministry of Social Security and Labour: see section on The Government (Ministries).

Social Policy Unit (Socialinės Politikos Grupé): Vivulskio 10–26, Vilnius 2009; tel. (26) 50506; fax (26) 50026; e-mail spg@tdd.lt; internet www.spg.lt; analyses the main aspects of human development, the social situation and the social security system and publishes the Lithuanian Human Development Report; Dir JOLANTA RIMKUTĖ.

State Social Insurance Fund Board of Lithuania (SoDra) (Valstybinio Socialinio Draudimo Fondo Valdyba): Konstitucijos 12, Vilnius 2600; tel. (527) 24864; fax (527) 24254; e-mail sodrainfo@ sodra.lt; internet www.sodra.lt; Dir ČESLAVA ZABULĖNIENĖ.

HEALTH AND WELFARE ORGANIZATIONS

Association for the Physically Disabled of Lithuania: Vilnius 2723; tel. (526) 29807; fax (526) 27415; Chair. JONAS MAČIUKEVIČIUS.

Children's Fund of Lithuania: Zygimantu 12, Vilnius 2600; tel. (526) 28836; fax (526) 27180; f. 1988; Chair. JUOZAS NEKROŠIUS; Dir ROMANAS BURBA.

Lithuanian Association of the Blind and Visually Handicapped: Labdariŭ 7/11, Vilnius 2600; tel. (526) 24866; fax (521) 21464; e-mail ausra@lass.vno.osf.lt; f. 1944; Pres. OSVALDAS PETRAUSKAS.

Lithuanian Red Cross Society: Gedimino pr. 3A, Vilnius 2600; tel. (526) 28947; fax (526) 19923; e-mail redcross@tdd.lt; internet www .redcross.lt/; f. 1919; social work, training and international relations; Sec.-Gen. REGIMANTAS BUDSYS.

Lithuanian Society of the Deaf: Kazimiero 3, Vilnius 2600; tel. (526) 28115; Chair. ALGIRDAS JAKAITIS.

The Environment

In November 2002 the Seimas ratified the 1997 Kyoto Protocol to the UN Convention on Climate Change, which requires signatories to reduce emissions of 'greenhouse' gases. The area of the Curonian spit, bordered by both Russia (Kaliningrad) and Lithuania on the Baltic Sea, was included on the UN Educational, Scientific and Cultural Organization's (UNESCO) World Heritage List in 2001. In

2003 UNESCO intervened to request the Russian company Lukoil (Kaliningradmorneft) to postpone its planned drilling of the D-6 (Kravcovskoye) oilfield in the region and to receive an international assessment team, owing to environmental concerns and the fact that Lithuania had not yet had access to, or participation in, an environmental appraisal of the project.

GOVERNMENT ORGANIZATIONS

Ministry of the Environment: see section on The Government (Ministries).

State Environmental Inspectorate: Juozapaviciaus 9, Vilnius 2005; tel. and fax (527) 22766; e-mail vaai@nt.gamta.lt; f. 1997; Chief RIMANTAS SALKAUSKAS.

Lithuanian Environmental Investment Fund (LEIF): Lukiòki 5–201, Vilnius 2600; tel. (26) 11978; fax (22) 24535; e-mail laaif@iti .lt; internet www.laaif.lt; f. 1996; funded by receipts from environmental pollution tax and grants from the EU's PHARE programme.

Lithuanian Geological Survey (Lietuvos Geologijos Tarnyba): S. Konarskio 35, Vilnius 2600; tel. (523) 32889; fax (523) 36156; e-mail lgt@lgt.lt; internet www.lgt.lt; Dir JUOZAS MOCKEVIČIUS.

ACADEMIC INSTITUTES

Centre for Environmental Studies, Vilnius University: M. K. Čiurlionio 21–27, Vilnius 2009; tel. (526) 50866; fax (526) 50855; Dir Dr STASYS SINKEVIČIUS.

Lithuanian Academy of Sciences: Gedimino pr. 3, Vilnius 2600; tel. (526) 13651; fax (526) 18464; e-mail prezidum@ktl.mii.lt; f. 1941; several attached institutes involved in scientific research; organizes workshops and conferences; Pres. BENEDIKTAS JUODKA.

Institute of Botany: Želiųjų 49, Vilnius 2021; tel. (527) 11618; fax (527) 29950; e-mail botanika@botanika.lt; internet www .botanika.lt/bi; f. 1959 to conduct research into botany, mycology, bacteriology and virology; publishes quarterly periodical, *Botanica Lithuanica*; Dir Dr VALERIUS RAŠOMAVIČIUS; Chair. of Council Dr HABIL JŪRATE DARGINAVIČIENE.

Institute of Ecology, Vilnius University: Akademijos 2, Vilnius 2600; tel. (527) 29275; fax (527) 29257; e-mail ekoi@ekoi.lt; internet www.ekoi.lt; f. 1945; ecological research; Dir Prof. Dr JUOZAS VIRBICKAS.

Lithuanian Energy Institute: Breslaujos 3, Kaunas 3035; tel. (373) 51403; fax (373) 51271; e-mail birute@isag.lei.lt; internet www .lei.lt; f. 1956; Dir JURGIS VILEMAS.

NON-GOVERNMENTAL ORGANIZATIONS

Aplinkosaugos Valdymo ir Technologiju Centras (Environmental Centre for Administration and Technology—ECAT): Lydos 4, Kaunas 3000; tel. (374) 23053; fax (374) 22797; e-mail ecat@ecat .lt; internet www.ecat.lt; f. 1997; supports and promotes ecological activities in municipalities, provides training, information and consultation services; Dir AUDRONE ALISOSIUTE.

Lietuvos Ekologu Draugija (Lithuanian Ecologists Society): Akademijos 2, Vilnius 2600; tel. (527) 29275; fax (527) 29257; e-mail ekoi@ekoi.lt; Contact JANINA BARSIENE.

Lietuvos Gamtos Draugija (Lithuanian Nature Society): Algirdo 31–120, Vilnius 2006; tel. (523) 10039; e-mail algirdas.gaigalas@gf .vu.lt; nature education and conservation; Contact ALGIRDAS GAIGALAS.

Lietuvos Gamtos Fondas (LGF) (Lithuanian Fund for Nature): Klaipėdos 5–16, Vilnius 2001; tel. and fax (526) 25152; e-mail info@ glis.lt; internet www.glis.lt; f. 1991; nature research and conservation programmes; Sec.-Gen. P. MIERAUSKAS.

Lithuanian Green Movement/Friends of the Earth Lithuania: POB 156, Kaunas 3000; tel. (372) 07250; fax (372) 09274; e-mail atgaja@kaunas.omnitel.net; f. 1988; directed by a Co-ordination Council; Chair. of Council RIMANTAS BRAZIULIS.

Lithuanian Green Party: Pylimo 38–1, POB 8000, Vilnius 2055; tel. (523) 49653; fax (527) 25676; e-mail zigmas@parexliz.lt; f. 1989; environmental political party; Chair. RŪTA GAJAUSKAITĖ; 300 mems.

Ne Pelno Organizacija 'Ekologinio Svietimo Centras' (Ecological Education Centre): S. Stankevičiaus 47–41, Vilnius 2029, POB 2311; tel. (524) 76351; Contact AUGUSTAS UKVERTIS.

Defence

Before regaining independence in 1991, Lithuania had no armed forces separate from those of the USSR. In October of that year the Department of State Defence (established in April 1990) was reformed as the Ministry of Defence (now the Ministry of National Defence). Military service is compulsory and lasts for 12 months. In August 2002 Lithuania's total active armed forces numbered an estimated 13,510 (including a 1,960-strong Voluntary National Defence Force and 1,800 centrally controlled personnel), consisting of an army of 8,100 (including 3,027 conscripts), a navy of 650 (including 300 conscripts) and an air force of 1,000. There was also a paramilitary force of 13,850, including a border guard of 5,000. The 2001 budget allocated 755.4m. litai (6.0% of expenditure) to defence. It was also planned to restructure the defence forces, in order to conform to North Atlantic Treaty Organization (NATO) standards. Lithuania was to become a full member of NATO in 2004. In 1998 the Baltic states agreed to establish a joint airspace observation system (BALTNET), a defence college and a peace-keeping battalion (BALTBAT). A Baltic naval unit (BALTRON) was created and a joint Polish-Lithuanian battalion was planned.

Commander-in-Chief of the Armed Forces: Brig.-Gen. JONAS KRONKAITIS.

Commander of the Defence Staff: VITALIJUS VAIKSNORAS.

Bibliography

Alonso-Gamo, Patricia *et al. Lithuania: History and Future of the Currency Board Arrangement*. Washington, DC, IMF, 2002.

Ashbourne, A. *Lithuania: The Rebirth of a Nation, 1991–1994*. Oxford, Lexington Books, 1999.

Darst, R. G. *Smokestack Diplomacy*. Cambridge, MA, MIT Press, 2001.

Eidintas, A. *Lithuania in European Politics: The Year of the First Republic, 1918–1940*. Auckland, St Martin's Press, 1999.

Gerner, K., and Hedlund, S. *The Baltic States and the End of the Soviet Empire*. London, Routledge, 1993.

Gordon, H. *The Shadow of Death: The Holocaust in Lithuania*. Lexington, KY, University Press of Kentucky, 2000.

Krickus, R. J. *Showdown: The Lithuanian Rebellion and the Breakup of the Soviet Empire*. London, Brasseys, 1997.

Lukowski, J. *Liberty's Folly: The Polish-Lithuanian Commonwealth in the 18th Century, 1697–1795*. London, Routledge, 1991.

Musteikis, A. *The Reformation in Lithuania: Religious Fluctuations in the 16th Century*. Boulder, CO, East European Monographs, 1988.

Navickas, K. *The Struggle of the Lithuanian People for Statehood*. Vilnius, Gintaras, 1971.

Oleszczuk, J. *Political Justice in the USSR: Dissent and Repression in Lithuania*. Boulder, CO, East European Monographs, 1988.

Popovski, V. *National Minorities and Citizenship Rights in Lithuania, 1988–93 (Studies in Russia and East Europe)*. Auckland, St Martin's Press, 2000.

Remeikis, T. *Opposition to Soviet Rule in Lithuania, 1945–1980*. Chicago, IL, Institute of Lithuanian Studies Press, 1980.

Senn, A. *Lithuania Awakening*. Los Angeles, CA, University of California Press, 1990.

Vardys, V. *Lithuania: The Rebel Nation*. Oxford, Westview Press, 1996.

The Catholic Church, Dissent and Nationality in Soviet Lithuania. Boulder, CO, and New York, NY, East European Quarterly—Columbia University Press, 1978.

'Lithuanian National Politics', in *Problems of Communism*, Vol. 38 (1989).

See also the Select Bibliography in Part Four.

THE FORMER YUGOSLAV REPUBLIC OF MACEDONIA

Geography

PHYSICAL FEATURES

The former Yugoslav republic of Macedonia (FYRM, or, according to its Constitution, the Republic of Macedonia) lies in South-Eastern Europe, on the Balkan Peninsula. Roughly rectangular in shape, Macedonia is a land-locked state, having a northern border with Serbia and Montenegro (the Serbian province of Kosovo and Metohija to the north-west and Serbia proper to the north-east). To the west lies Albania, to the south, Greece, and to the east, Bulgaria.

The historical region of Macedonia is divided between the country that uses its name, and Greece and Bulgaria. The Republic of Macedonia, which is sometimes known as Vardar Macedonia (Pirin Macedonia is that part of the territory in Bulgaria and Aegean Macedonia in Greece), has a total area of 25,713 sq km (9,928 sq miles). The country is mountainous. It is bisected by the Vardar (Axiós) river, which flows from north-west to south-east, across the centre of the country and in to Greece, where it enters the Aegean Sea.

CLIMATE AND POPULATION

Macedonia has a mild, Mediterranean climate, although winters, especially in the mountainous areas, are cold and snow cover can last for several months. It has a mean summer-time temperature of 27°C (80°F). According to official estimates, the total population of Macedonia was some 2,049,000. at the end of 2002, with a population density of 79.7 per sq km. According to the census of June 1994, the total population of the Republic of Macedonia was 1,945,932 (of whom 974,255 were males and 971,677 females). The capital is Skopje (Skoplje or, in Turkish, Usküb), anciently a capital of the Serbs, which is located on the Vardar, in the central north of the country, and had a population of 444,299 in June 1994. Other principal towns included Bitola, in south-west Macedonia (77,464), Prilep, in the centre (68,148), Kumanovo, in the north (71,853) and Tetovo, west of Skopje, the centre of Albanian settlement (50,344).

According to the census of 1994, ethnic Macedonians accounted for 66.6% of the national population and ethnic Albanians for some 22.7%. The Macedonians are a Southern Slav people, closely related to Bulgarians. However, the separate existence of a Macedonian ethnic group was acknowledged neither by Bulgaria nor Greece (which described its own 'Macedonian' minority as Slav-speaking Greeks) or many Serbs. Most Albanians were concentrated in the west of the country, particularly the north-west, where they tended to

live in distinct communities, mostly in the countryside. Most of the population was nominally Christian and of the Eastern Orthodox faith. The Macedonians were adherents of the Macedonian Orthodox Church, which was autocephalous or independent, but was not recognized by the other Orthodox. Most of the Albanians were Muslim, although there were some Roman Catholics in Skopje (immigrants from the Prizren area of Kosovo) and some Orthodox near Ohrid. Most of the remaining minority groups were also Muslim. In 1994 some 4.0% of the population were ethnic Turks, 2.3% Roma (Gypsies) and 2.1% Serbs, mostly in Skopje and Kumanovo. There were also a number of Slav Muslims (known as Torbeshes, Poturs or Pomaks—comprising 0.8% of the population in 1994) and some 8,601 Vlahs or Vlachs (Koutsovlahs, Aromani, Cincari), Macedonia being the main former Yugoslav territory of this traditionally nomadic, Romanian-speaking people. The official language of the country, under the 1991 Constitution, was originally stipulated as Macedonian. Constitutional amendments, which were adopted in November 2001, accorded minority languages, such as Albanian, the status of official languages in communities where speakers constituted 20% of the population.

Chronology

6th century BC: The ancient kingdom of Macedon, with capitals at Pella and Aigai (Edessa), was established on the borders of the Hellenic territories.

336–323 BC: Reign of Alexander III ('the Great') of Macedon, the most famous of the ancient kings; he secured Macedon's hegemony over the Greeks and conquered the Persian Empire. His empire disintegrated after his death into a number of Hellenistic kingdoms, of which Macedon became the territory of the Antigonid dynasty.

168 BC: Macedon was finally defeated by the Roman Empire and the kingdom was divided into four semi-autonomous territories.

148 BC: After an uprising the Roman province of Macedonia (an area that included large parts of modern-day northern Greece and western Bulgaria) was created.

AD 395: Following a division of the administration of the Roman Empire, Macedonia and Illyria to the north-west formally came under the authority of the Eastern Roman ('Byzantine') Emperor in Constantinople (now İstanbul, Turkey).

6th century: Southern Slav peoples began to move from Pannonia into the Balkans.

7th century: The ancestors of the Bulgars moved south of the Danube and merged with the Slavs and the autochthonous inhabitants of Macedonia.

865: Boris, the Khan of the Bulgars, converted to Eastern Orthodox Christianity following the missionary activity of the Byzantine brothers, SS Cyril and Methodius; a Slavonic liturgy (based on a dialect of the western Bulgar territory of Macedonia) was introduced with a written language, in the Cyrillic script, which remains common to all the Eastern and Balkan Slavic peoples.

1014: Final defeat of the western Bulgarian, or Macedonian, realm under Samuel (Samuil) by the Byzantine Emperor, Basil II.

1187: The Emperor in Constantinople acknowledged Serb independence and the establishment of the second Bulgarian Empire (which was to include much of Macedonia and the surrounding territories).

1330: The Serbs defeated the Bulgarians and the Greek Byzantines at the Battle of Velbuzhde (Küstendil).

1346: Establishment of a Serbian patriarchate and the coronation of Stefan Dušan 'the Great' of Raška, who reigned (1331–55) as Tsar of the Serbs and Greeks, at Skopje; however, he failed in his ambition to conquer Constantinople (Carigrad).

1389: The Turkish Ottoman Empire secured its conquest of Macedonia and the region by its victory against the Serbian nobility at a battle on the plain of Kosovo Polje; the Ottoman Empire was administered by the confessional *millet* system, which placed the Orthodox of Macedonia (after 1453) under the jurisdiction of the Greek Ecumenical Patriarch in Constantinople.

1870: The Bulgarians declared an Exarchate for their Church—that is they proclaimed their autonomy from the Ecumenical Patriarchate and introduced the Slavonic liturgy; they contested with the Greek Church for adherents in the Macedonian region.

March 1878: The Treaty of San Stefano concluded the war between Russia, in support of the Orthodox Slavs, and the Ottomans; however, the Great Powers rejected the settlement, which created a 'Greater Bulgaria'.

July 1878: At the Congress of Berlin, Bulgaria was denied the annexation of Macedonia, while Serbia and Montenegro secured their independence; many Macedonians fled to Bulgaria after this treaty.

1893: Foundation of the Internal Macedonian Revolutionary Organization (IMRO), which opposed the partition of Macedonia, but supported the idea of a Southern Slav ('Yugoslav') federation.

1895: The foundation of the External Organization of Supremacists (based in Sofia, Bulgaria) divided Macedonian nationalism, as it favoured the incorporation of Macedonia into Bulgaria.

2 August 1903: The Ilinden Uprising against the Ottomans, in what is now Bulgarian (Pirin) Macedonia, was organized by IMRO and led by Gotse Delchev; the revolt was suppressed, but remains commemorated by both Macedonian and Bulgarian nationalists.

May 1913: The Peace of London concluded the First Balkan War, in which a league of Bulgaria, Greece, Montenegro and Serbia succeeded in removing the Turks from the bulk of their European possessions.

June 1913: Hoping to secure its claim to Macedonia, Bulgaria attacked Serbia, which had occupied Skopje (Usküb) after defeating the Ottomans at nearby Kumanovo (November 1912); Serbia was supported by Greece, Montenegro, Romania and the Turks.

August 1913: The Peace of Bucharest concluded the Second Balkan War; Bulgaria lost most of Macedonia, which was divided between Serbia (Vardar Macedonia or 'South Serbia') and Greece (Aegean Macedonia); Albanian independence was recognized.

28 July 1914: Habsburg Austria-Hungary declared war on Serbia; this started the First World War between the Central Powers, of Austria-Hungary and Germany, and the Entente Powers, of France, Russia, Serbia and the United Kingdom.

1915: Serbian Macedonia was occupied by Bulgaria, which joined the Central Powers in the conquest of Serbia.

4 December 1918: Proclamation of the Kingdom of Serbs, Croats and Slovenes, which united Serbia (including Vardar Macedonia) and Montenegro with the former Habsburg lands, under the Serbian monarchy.

3 October 1929: Following the imposition of a royal dictatorship, the country was formally named Yugoslavia.

March 1941: A *coup d'état* reversed previous policies and aligned Yugoslavia with the Allied Powers of the Second World War.

April 1941: German and Italian forces invaded Yugoslavia, which was partitioned; Macedonia was again occupied by Bulgaria, which lost much local support to the communists.

29 November 1945: Following elections for a Provisional Assembly, the Federative People's Republic of Yugoslavia was proclaimed, with Tito (Josip Broz, leader of the communist resistance forces) as Prime Minister. By this time a Macedonian alphabet and orthography had been prepared and accepted by the communist authorities, which wished to foster a distinct Macedonian identity.

January 1946: A Soviet-style Constitution established a federation of six republics and two autonomous regions in Yugoslavia; one of the republics was Macedonia. This was not only an acknowledgement of Macedonian nationalism, but an attempt to resolve the competing claims of Serbia and Bulgaria (until 1948 Tito had ambitions of a greater federation including the latter).

1958: The archdiocese of Ohrid, an ancient see, was established, despite the protests of the Serbian Orthodox hierarchy, which resented the move towards separation.

April 1963: A new Constitution changed the country's name to the Socialist Federal Republic of Yugoslavia (SFRY).

18 July 1967: The autocephaly of the Macedonian Orthodox Church was declared, but the Serbian Church refused to acknowledge it and was backed by the Ecumenical Patriarch and the other established Orthodox Churches.

November 1968: Demonstrations in Tetovo by ethnic Albanians, present in large numbers in western Macedonia, demanded the creation of a seventh federal republic, for the Albanians of Yugoslavia.

4 May 1980: Tito died; his responsibilities were transferred to the collective State Presidency and to the Presidium of the ruling League of Communists of Yugoslavia (LCY).

1981: Protests by Albanians in the neighbouring Serbian Autonomous Province of Kosovo (officially renamed Kosovo and Metohija from September 1990) provoked measures by the Macedonian authorities against Albanian nationalism.

1988: There were further demonstrations in the republic, not only about economic conditions and in favour of reform, but also by Albanian students.

1989: The communist regime amended the republican Constitution to allow a multi-party system; however, ethnic tension increased when further amendments declared that Macedonia was a 'nation-state' of the ethnic Macedonians, omitting mention of the Albanian minority.

February 1990: The Movement for All-Macedonian Action (MAMA) was founded; although a nationalist party, it disclaimed any territorial ambitions for the republic.

June 1990: The Internal Macedonian Revolutionary Organization—Democratic Party for Macedonian National Unity (IMRO—DPMNU), a more extreme nationalist party, was founded and elected Ljubčo Georgievski as leader.

July 1990: Ante Marković, the federal Prime Minister, formed the Alliance of Reform Forces (ARF), an all-Yugoslav party, which supported his Government and advocated Western-style reforms.

November 1990: Two rounds of elections to a new, unicameral 120-seat Assembly (Sobranie) were held in Macedonia.

9 December 1990: The final round of voting in Macedonia produced an inconclusive result, with the nationalist opposition, IMRO—DPMNU, winning the largest number of seats (37); the League of Communists of Macedonia—Party of Democratic Reform (LCM—PDR, the former ruling communists) won 31 seats, the republican ARF 19 (subsequently the Liberal Party) and the two predominantly Albanian parties, the Party of Democratic Prosperity (PDP) and the People's Democratic Party, together, 25.

7 January 1991: The IMRO—DPMNU, the LCM—PDR and the Macedonian ARF agreed on a coalition administration (subsequently Stojan Andov of the ARF was elected President of the Sobranie and, eventually, Kiro Gligorov of the LCM—PDR President of the Republic, with Ljubčo Georgievski of the IMRO—DPMNU as Vice-President); however, an administration under Milo Djukanović did not satisfy the competing demands of the parties.

25 January 1991: The Sobranie unanimously adopted a declaration of Macedonia's sovereignty, including a statement of its right to secede from the SFRY.

March 1991: Nikola Kljušev became premier of a new administration, composed of non-political 'experts'.

7 June 1991: The Sobranie changed the state's name to the Republic of Macedonia; among other constitutional amendments and against a background of increasing tension in Croatia and Slovenia, which were attempting to secede from the federation, the Sobranie declared Macedonian neutrality and also provided that it alone could authorize a state of emergency (this was done on 4 August).

8 September 1991: Some 95% of the two-thirds of eligible voters who participated in the referendum were in favour of an independent and sovereign Macedonia; the large ethnic Albanian minority boycotted the poll.

October 1991: Croatia and Slovenia declared their final independence. The IMRO—DPMNU announced that it was to leave the Government, following the resignation of Ljubčo Georgievski as Vice-President. Later, the Macedonian Government announced that more than 60% of federal bases in the republic had been evacuated; the total withdrawal of federal troops was completed in March of the following year.

17 November 1991: The new Constitution was enacted, despite opposition from the majority of the ethnic Albanian deputies and three of the IMRO—DPMNU deputies; with the promulgation of the new Constitution Macedonia was declared to be an independent country.

January 1992: An unofficial referendum conducted among the ethnic Albanian population resulted in a 99.9% vote in favour of territorial and political autonomy for the Albanian population. The Commission of the European Community (EC—known as the European Union, EU, from November 1993) acknowledged that Macedonia fulfilled the requirements for official recognition; however, Greek objections to the use of the name 'Macedonia' and the use of the Star of Vergina (an emblem associated with Alexander the Great) on the Macedonian national flag ensured that EC recognition for Macedonia was not forthcoming. Nevertheless, on 16 January Bulgaria became the first country officially to recognize Macedonia; Turkey followed suit early in the following month.

April 1992: The new Constitution of the Federal Republic of Yugoslavia (FRY) referred only to Serbia and Montenegro, effectively acknowledging the secession of Macedonia. Diplomatic relations were established with Croatia.

June 1992: Negotiations between the Macedonian Minister of Foreign Relations and the Greek Prime Minister, Konstantinos Mitsotakis, ended in failure.

July 1992: Following a vote of 'no confidence' passed in the Sobranie, and after demonstrations by more than 100,000 people in the capital protesting at its failure to gain recognition for an independent Macedonia, the Government resigned.

September 1992: Branko Crvenkovski, leader of the Social Democratic Alliance of Macedonia (SDAM, known as the LCM—PDR until 1991), was appointed Chairman (Prime Minister) of a new coalition Government.

October 1992: A new citizenship law stipulating a 15-year residency requirement prior to granting citizenship came into effect, angering many ethnic Albanians.

December 1992: The UN Security Council authorized the dispatch of troops, civilian police and military observers to Macedonia in order to monitor the inter-ethnic tensions, following an increase in sometimes violent unrest.

April 1993: Macedonia was admitted to the UN, despite Greek objections, but under the name of the 'former Yugoslav republic of Macedonia' (FYRM).

May 1993: A new currency, the new Macedonian denar, was introduced.

September 1993: Negotiations between the FYRM and Greece, held in New York, the USA, under UN auspices, failed to resolve the dispute over the former Yugoslav republic's name.

December 1993: The United Kingdom established full diplomatic relations with the FYRM, followed, in a co-ordinated move, by France, Germany and the Netherlands before the end of the year.

16 February 1994: Greece suspended diplomatic relations with the FYRM and prohibited the country from using the Greek port of Thessaloníki, except for humanitarian aid.

17 February 1994: The PDP split, with the more radical faction later forming the Party of Democratic Prosperity of the Albanians in Macedonia (PDPAM).

16 October 1994: Kiro Gligorov, a candidate of the Alliance for Macedonia (consisting of the SDAM, the Liberal Party and the Socialist Party of Macedonia—SPM) was re-elected to the presidency by an overwhelming majority (78.37% of the valid votes cast). His only opponent in the election was Ljubiša Georgievski, representing the IMRO—DPMNU. The first round of voting in the general election was also held; a second round of voting, held on 30 October, was boycotted by the IMRO—DPMNU which, having won no seats in the first round, made allegations of widespread fraud.

13 November 1994: A third round of legislative elections was held in some constituencies, owing to irregularities in earlier rounds. Final results confirmed that the Alliance for Macedonia had won the majority of seats (of which 58 went to the SDAM, 29 to the Liberals and eight to the SPM); the PDP won 10 seats. The Sobranie subsequently approved an SDAM-led administration, again headed by Crvenkovski and including the PDP.

17 February 1995: Violent disturbances occurred in Tetovo, following the opening of an 'illegal' Albanian-language university, resulting in the death of an Albanian. A few days later the rector of the institution, Fadil Sulejmani, was arrested and was subsequently sentenced to two-and-a-half years' imprisonment.

31 March 1995: The Macedonian contingent of UN peace-keeping forces in the former Yugoslavia was named the UN Preventive Deployment Force (UNPREDEP); it became an independent command in February 1996 and its mandate was eventually extended until February 1999.

13 September 1995: The FYRM and Greece signed an agreement establishing diplomatic relations and economic ties between the two countries: Greece was to lift its embargo in return for Macedonia relinquishing its claim to the Star of Vergina for its national flag.

3 October 1995: President Gligorov was seriously injured in a car-bomb attack.

12 October 1995: The FYRM was accepted into the Organization for Security and Co-operation in Europe (OSCE), with the ending of Greek objections; the country had become a member of the Council of Europe earlier in the month.

23 February 1996: A new Government, in which the Liberal Party was unrepresented, was approved by the Sobranie, following the collapse of the Alliance for Macedonia.

8 April 1996: The FYRM and the FRY established full diplomatic relations in an accord on normalizing relations and promoting co-operation; both countries recognized the other's sovereignty, independence and territorial integrity.

July 1996: Parliamentary and popular protests were made by ethnic Albanian deputies over the status of the Albanian-language university at Tetovo, culminating in a demonstration outside Tetovo prison where the rector, Sulejmani (whose sentence had been reduced to one year), was incarcerated (he was released on 1 February 1997); sporadic protests continued.

17 November 1996: In the first round of voting in local elections, the SDAM received the greatest number of votes, followed by the IMRO—DPMNU-led alliance and then the PDP; the PDPAM and the People's Democratic Party (which were to merge in 1997) obtained an increased proportion of the ethnic Albanian vote.

February 1997: Further municipal elections in Tetovo (where voting had to be repeated) resulted in victory for the PDPAM, prompting renewed displays of nationalist sentiment by ethnic Albanians.

9 April 1997: An increase in civil unrest in neighbouring Albania led to additional troops being deployed on the FYRM–Albanian border.

22 May 1997: The Constitutional Court forbade the use of the Albanian flag in the FYRM, causing protests by ethnic Albanians.

29 May 1997: The Sobranie approved Crvenkovski's new Government, which remained led by the SDAM, but including the PDP and the SPM.

8 July 1997: The Sobranie adopted legislation stipulating that the use of the Albanian flag, and flags of other nationalities, would only be permitted on national holidays, with the Macedonian flag being displayed at the same time; government officials forcibly removed Albanian flags displayed at municipal buildings in Gostivar and Tetovo, leading to violent clashes between protesting ethnic Albanians and security forces, which resulted in three deaths and the arrests of 500 protesters.

5–6 March 1998: Some 50,000 ethnic Albanians attended a rally in Skopje in support of the ethnic Albanians in the neighbouring Serbian province of Kosovo and Metohija and to demand international intervention in the region; at the demonstration an Albanian flag was hoisted and the Albanian national anthem was played—ethnic Albanian leaders were later charged with inciting ethnic unrest.

13 April 1998: The Democratic Party of Albanians (DPA—formed in 1997 by the merger of the PDPAM and the People's Democratic Party) announced that it was to withdraw its members from all government institutions in protest at the continuing imprisonment of Rufi Osmani, the former mayor of Gostivar, who had been sentenced to a term of imprisonment in September 1997 for inciting ethnic tension and rebellion in the July flag troubles.

31 August 1998: The PDP and the DPA announced the establishment of a political co-operation agreement, including an electoral alliance, to promote the cause of ethnic Albanians in the FYRM.

26 September 1998: The FYRM signed an agreement with Albania, Bulgaria, Greece, Italy, Romania and Turkey on the establishment of multinational forces in South-Eastern Europe, to operate under UN auspices.

18 October 1998: In the first round of voting in elections to the Sobranie, the IMRO—DPMNU won 26.9% of the valid votes cast, followed by the SDAM with 23.8%; the alliance of ethnic Albanian parties won 19.6% of the votes cast, while the newly-formed Democratic Alternative (DA) won 10.8%, the Liberal-Democratic Party (LDP—the Liberal Party had merged with the Democratic Party of Macedonia in 1996) 6.9% and the Movement for Cultural Tolerance and Civic Co-operation, a coalition of the SPM and five parties representing various ethnic minorities, 4.1%.

1 November 1998: After a second round of voting the 'For Changes' alliance (which comprised the IMRO—DPMNU and the DA) gained 58 seats in the Sobranie, followed by the SDAM with 29 and the PDP-DPA grouping with a total of 24. A further round of voting in two electoral districts was held on

15 November, in which For Changes and the PDP-DPA each won a further seat.

23 November 1998: Georgievski was invited to form a coalition Government; his Cabinet, appointed in early December, comprised 14 representatives from the IMRO—DPMNU, eight from the DA and five members from the DPA; following its inclusion in the administration the DPA reversed its decision to withdraw its representatives from government institutions.

7 December 1998: A 2,300-strong North Atlantic Treaty Organization (NATO) 'extraction force' was deployed in the FYRM to assist in the evacuation of OSCE monitors in Kosovo in the event of a large-scale conflict there.

29 December 1998: The Sobranie approved legislation providing for the early release of some 8,000 prisoners, including Osmani. Overriding a presidential veto, the legislature approved the law for a second time on 4 February 1999; Osmani was released two days later.

26 February 1999: The People's Republic of China vetoed a UN Security Council resolution to extend the UNPREDEP mandate for a further six months, following a decision by the FYRM Government to recognize China (Taiwan), which had prompted the People's Republic of China to suspend diplomatic relations with Macedonia. UNPREDEP formally ended its six-year mission on 1 March.

7 March 1999: Local elections were held in Gostivar and Tetovo. No candidate was elected in Gostivar, owing to low voter participation. Murtezan Ismaili of the DPA was elected Mayor of Tetovo.

April 1999: Following an escalation in the conflict in neighbouring Kosovo, about 14,000 further NATO troops were deployed near the Macedonian–Serbian border; the number of forces was further increased, to 16,000, in June, when the border was repeatedly closed to prevent further influxes of refugees.

20 June 1999: Following the FRY Government's acceptance of a peace plan to end NATO's air campaign, the return of refugees from Macedonia to Kosovo began.

31 October and 14 November 1999: In the first round of the presidential election, Tito Petkovski, the candidate of the SDAM, obtained 32.7% of the votes cast, while the IMRO—DPMNU nominee, Boris Trajkovski, won 20.8% and the DA leader, Vasil Tupurkovski, 16%. As nobody secured a majority, a second ballot took place on 14 November between the two leading candidates, which Trajkovski won, with 52.8% of the votes cast. The SDAM disputed the results, claiming widespread malpractice, particularly in the western regions where the population of ethnic Albanians was high. The accusations were supported by the OSCE.

27 November 1999: The Supreme Court upheld a legal appeal by the SDAM against the election results and ruled that a further ballot should take place in some regions in the west of the country.

5 December 1999: A partial round of elections took place for 10% of the electorate. The overall results were virtually unchanged; Trajkovski won with 52.9% of votes cast. The SDAM continued to claim irregularities; nevertheless, on 15 December, Trajkovski was inaugurated as President.

14 April 2000: The Sobranie approved legislation making compulsory the return of property expropriated under the communist regime.

25 July 2000: New legislation on education was adopted, which permitted the use of Albanian and other languages in private tertiary institutions. A new, private university, with instruction in Albanian and Macedonian, opened in Tetovo in November 2001, after its construction was funded by the international community.

10 September 2000: Municipal elections were held throughout the FYRM. International observers criticized the conduct of the elections and 27 of the 123 municipalities required a repeated first ballot.

24 September 2000: The second ballots and, where required, repeated first ballots of the municipal elections were held. Electoral irregularities were also reported in this round and repeated ballots were scheduled to continue in individual municipalities for several months. Final results indicated that the governing coalition secured approximately 75 of the country's 123 municipalities, principally in rural areas.

6 November 2000: Tensions between two of the partners in the governing coalition were resolved when the IMRO—DPMNU and the DA agreed on a programme of alterations to electoral legislation and increased DA participation in negotiations with international institutions.

30 November 2000: The DA formally withdrew from the coalition with the IMRO—DPMNU, although three individual members of the party chose to remain in the reconstituted governing coalition, with the IMRO—DPMNU, the DPA and numerous members of smaller parties and independents. The new coalition had the support of 63 of the 120 members of the Sobranie. The President of the Sobranie, Savo Klimovski, a member of the DA, resigned, and Stojan Andov was elected to succeed him.

13 December 2000: The principal border crossing between the FYRM and Greece was reopened. Representatives of both countries' Governments held negotiations aimed at improving bilateral relations.

29 December 2000: President Trajkovski visited the capital of the FRY, Belgrade, for a meeting with the federal President, Vojislav Koštunica. A number of bilateral agreements were signed and both countries emphasized the need to improve their bilateral relations.

26 February 2001: Violent clashes between Macedonian security forces and ethnic Albanian rebels, identified as members of the self-styled National Liberation Army (NLA), erupted near the Macedonian border village of Tanusevci. The Government appealed to NATO for assistance in combating the rebels.

21 March 2001: The UN Security Council adopted Resolution 1345, condemning extremist violence in the FYRM, which constituted a threat to the stability of the region.

13 May 2001: Following inter-party discussions, a new Government of national unity, which included the SDAM, the DPA and the PDP, was formed, and approved by the Sobranie.

18 June 2001: The Ministers of Foreign Affairs of the FYRM and the People's Republic of China agreed to re-establish diplomatic relations, prompting China (Taiwan) immediately to announce its intention to close its embassy in Skopje.

29 June 2001: NATO formally approved a plan to dispatch a 3,000-member force to the FYRM to assist in the disarmament of ethnic Albanian rebels, which was, however, conditional on a lasting peace agreement in the country.

5 July 2001: The Government announced that a NATO-mediated cease-fire agreement had been reached with the rebels.

22 July 2001: The cease-fire collapsed, with ethnic Albanian rebels attacking government forces near the major town of Tetovo.

26 July 2001: It was announced that the cease-fire between government forces and ethnic Albanian rebels, who had agreed to withdraw from newly captured territory, had been restored.

13 August 2001: Government and ethnic Albanian leaders signed a framework peace accord at Ohrid, providing for the amendment of the Constitution to grant greater rights to the ethnic Albanian community. It was agreed that NLA members would cede armaments to NATO troops.

22 August 2001: NATO released the activation order for the establishment of a mission, Operation Essential Harvest, which was to comprise up to 4,500 troops with a mandate to disarm former NLA combatants and destroy their weapons within 30 days of its deployment.

26 September 2001: NATO's 30-day disarmament programme was declared to have been successful, and the establishment of a further, reduced NATO mission, Operation Amber Fox, was authorized. On the following day it was announced that the NLA had been formally dissolved.

16 November 2001: The Sobranie adopted 15 main constitutional amendments, which incorporated reforms agreed in August. The principal amendments were: the revision of the Constitution to include a reference to members of non-ethnic Macedonian communities as citizens of the country; the introduction in the Sobranie of a 'double majority' system, whereby certain legislation would also require the approval of a majority of deputies from an ethnic group; the recognition of a minority language as official in communities where speakers comprised more than 20% of the population; and the right to proportional representation for ethnic Albanians in the Constitutional Court, all areas of government administration, and the security forces.

21 November 2001: The SDAM and the allied LDP withdrew from the coalition Government, which was subsequently re-organized.

19 June 2002: The Sobranie approved legislation making Albanian an official language, in accordance with the August 2001 Ohrid peace agreement.

18 July 2002: In accordance with the peace agreement, the Sobranie was officially dissolved, prior to legislative elections, which were scheduled for 15 September and were to be monitored by some 750 EU observers.

15 September 2002: A 10-party alliance (led by the SDAM and the LDP), known as Together for Macedonia, secured 60 of the 120 seats in the Sobranie. IMRO—DPMNU won 33 seats and the newly established Democratic Union for Integration (DUI) 16 seats.

1 November 2002: A new, 18-member administration, comprising members of the SDAM, the LDP and the DUI, and headed by Branko Crvenkovski, was officially approved by the Sobranie.

14 December 2002: Operation Amber Fox was replaced by a 450-member mission, Allied Harmony.

31 March 2003: Allied Harmony was replaced by a 350-member, EU-led mission, known as Operation Concordia, which was to maintain security in order to facilitate the implementation of the Ohrid peace agreement.

4 April 2003: The FYRM became a member of the World Trade Organization.

24 April 2003: Georgievski announced his resignation from the leadership of IMRO—DPMNU.

History

Dr KEITH BROWN

THE MACEDONIAN REGION

The name 'Macedonia' was used in the fifth century BC by Greek historians to refer to a region to the north of Greece. Until the fourth century BC, Macedonia or Macedon remained a marginal kingdom, situated between the city-states of the Greek mainland and the tribal peoples of the Balkans. Among the latter were the Paeonians and the Illyrians. Whereas city-states like Athens were by this time proud democracies, Macedonia was a monarchy, and as such viewed as somewhat underdeveloped by many southern neighbouring states. In 359 BC Philip II acceded to the throne, and early in his reign gained control of silver mines around Mt Pangaion, near Kavalla at the mouth of the River Struma. Putting these economic resources to efficient use, Philip subdued the city-states of Greece. His son, Alexander III (known as Alexander the Great) then led a campaign of conquest against the Persian Empire, reaching India before his army, after a decade, rebelled against his command. When Alexander died in Babylon in 323 BC his vast empire was divided into a number of Hellenistic kingdoms. The great campaign of expansion to the east, initiated by Philip and Alexander, left Macedonia weakened. The kingdom was conquered by the Roman Empire in 168 BC, and Macedon was divided into four semi-autonomous territories (becoming a province of the Empire 20 years later).

At its height, Roman rule extended over much of the Balkans, bringing with it the Latin language, new cities, and new roads. A major route, the Via Egnatia, extended from the Adriatic coast in modern Albania, to Thessaloníki, which had been established by Cassander, one of Alexander's successors, providing a crucial connection between the western and eastern parts of the Roman Empire. In 326 AD Emperor Constantine moved his capital to Byzantium (now İstanbul, Turkey). Constantine had previously converted to Christianity, and Constantinople, as it was then renamed, became the capital of a Christian empire. It endured for more than 1,000 years, and exerted a strong political and cultural influence over the southern Balkans.

Under Byzantine rule, the demography of the Balkans changed significantly. Two major groups of peoples made their way there from the north and the east. The great Slav migrations of the sixth and seventh centuries brought people south from the territory of modern Russia to settle in lands that were previously thinly populated. In the second half of the seventh century the Bulgars, a people related to the Tatars, swept into the region from Central Asia. Roman settlers and indigenous peoples, who had in some cases adopted Roman customs and in others preserved their own languages and ways of livelihood, were either assimilated or driven south and west into the mountains. It was after this period that Slavic languages came to dominate much of the Balkans. Latin survived in modern Romanian and in Vlah or Vlach, spoken across the region. Modern Albanian is a distinct language, providing part of the basis for the nationalist argument that Albanians are direct descendants of the Illyrians. Romany, the language spoken by the substantial Rom, or Gypsy, population of the Balkans, has Indic origins, and probably also reached the region during Byzantine rule.

In the ninth century SS Cyril and Methodius, who originated from Thessaloníki, led Christian missions northward and eastward, and became instrumental in the introduction of Old Church Slavonic, the basis of all subsequent Slavic literary languages. The Serbs adopted Orthodox Christianity through this medium, as did the Bulgars. In both cases, rulers aspired to secular and religious authority. Bulgar power reached its height in the ninth and 10th centuries, under King Simeon, before being curtailed by a strong Byzantine military response. One of the last bastions of Bulgar autonomy that survived was the kingdom of Samuil, with its capital in Ohrid. In the 13th century Stefan Nemanja established a Serbian kingdom, and his brother, St Sava, became head of an autonomous Serbian church. The kingdom reached the height of its powers in the mid-14th century, under Stefan Dušan of Raška, and again stretched into the territory of modern Macedonia. Like the Bulgarian rulers before him, he aspired to conquer Constantinople, but died on his way to attack the city.

Although the Byzantine Empire defeated such challenges in the region, it came under increasing pressure from other enemies. In 1204 the crusading armies of the Christian feudal states of Western Europe seized the city on their way to the Holy Land, and the Empire became divided. Subsequently, the expanding power of the Ottoman Empire reduced the former Byzantine Empire to the size of one city, and advanced into the Balkans. From the defeat of a Serbian army at the plain of Kosovo Polje in 1389 until the early 20th century, the Ottoman Empire maintained control of the territory of modern Albania and Macedonia, as well as parts of modern Greece and modern Bulgaria, and much of Kosovo.

THE OSMANLı (OTTOMAN) TURKISH PERIOD, AND THE RISE OF NATIONALISM

The Ottoman Empire was Islamic in character, with its own methods of managing religious and cultural diversity among its subjects. The Empire permitted the practice of religions other than Islam, and relied on the co-operation of religious leaders to maintain order. Individuals were, none the less, encouraged or coerced to convert, and did so in especially large numbers where the two Christian faiths, Eastern Orthodoxy and Western Catholicism, competed for adherents, in Albania and in Bosnia. When they did convert, however, they were not permitted to worship through the medium of their own language: in the late 19th and early 20th centuries the Empire was especially hostile to Albanian attempts to learn or worship in Albanian.

The relationship between the Orthodox Church and the Ottoman regime was of particular importance in the Balkans. When the Ottomans took over the Balkan Peninsula, there were patriarchates at Constantinople, Pec and Ohrid. The former used Greek liturgy, the latter two Old Church Slavonic. Each was a legacy of a prior empire (Byzantine, Serb and Bulgar, respectively). Following Serb rebellion, and because both Slavonic language churches also had links to Russia, another important enemy, the Sultan reduced the status of both the Pec and Ohrid patriarchates in 1767, thus increasing the authority of the so-called 'Greek' patriarchate of Constantinople.

As was the case with the Byzantine Empire, Ottoman authority was overthrown by forces external to the Balkans. Ideals of self-determination were the basis for the Serb rebellion of 1804, and played a role in the Greek War of Independence (1821–30), which resulted in the creation of Greece after British, French and Russian assistance. In 1878 an uprising in Bulgaria was followed by Russian intervention and another negotiated settlement, known as the Treaty of San Stefano, which briefly created a 'greater Bulgaria', encompassing much of modern Macedonia and extending as far as Lake Ohrid on its western border. The other European powers intervened to reverse this resolution, which created an overpowerful satellite state to Russia. Nevertheless, Bulgaria soon joined Serbia and Greece as an autonomous state with ambitions for further expansion.

In what was left of the Ottoman Empire in the Balkans, internal activism also emerged. In 1878 the League of Prizren, an Albanian cultural association, was established, and in 1909 and 1910 the Albanian population revolted against Ottoman rule. In 1893 a secret Macedonian revolutionary organization had been formed by a group of teachers and other activists from the region's Orthodox Christian population. The organization, known as the Internal Macedonian Revolutionary Organization (IMRO), suffered from internal divisions, as some of its members favoured close links with Bulgaria, while others pursued greater autonomy. In August 1903 the organization staged the Ilinden Uprising against Ottoman rule, but its hopes of external intervention from the European powers, as had occurred elsewhere, were disappointed. The Ottoman army and Muslim population launched savage reprisals, and the organization split into leftist (later communist) and rightist (generally pro-Bulgarian) factions, which continued hostilities with Ottoman forces, Greek and Serbian militia groups, and each other.

By 1912 Greece, Serbia and Bulgaria had negotiated a strategy whereby they would combine their military resources. In the first Balkan War, together with Montenegro, they defeated Ottoman forces on every front. The Bulgarians made the smallest advances, and after the war requested that Serbia transfer territory to them, as the alliance had agreed. Serbia, however, refused, keeping the area around Ohrid, Bitola and Skopje as recompense for the territory in Albania they had expected, but which the Great Powers had turned into a new nation-state. Bulgaria then launched the second Balkan War against its former allies, and was quickly defeated. The modern Republic of Macedonia comprises the area taken by Serbia and claimed by Bulgaria.

THE WORLD WARS, AND THE CREATION OF YUGOSLAVIA

Following the end of the First World War, the Ottoman Empire was finally dissolved. At the Versailles (France) Peace Conference of 1919, US President Woodrow Wilson's doctrine of self-determination provided the mechanism for redelineating boundaries in Eastern and South-Eastern Europe. At the same time the victorious powers rewarded their allies. A new South Slavic state, known as the Kingdom of Serbs, Croats and Slovenes, and headed by the Serbian monarchy, was created. The country comprised Serbia, Montenegro, the areas that both had won during the Balkan Wars, and parts of the former Austro-Hungarian Empire, and was formally renamed Yugoslavia in 1929. Delegations to Versailles from Macedonia, arguing either for autonomy or for union with Bulgaria on ethnic grounds, were ignored.

The issue of 'lost territory' remained of concern in Bulgaria, where a large number of Slavic-speaking Orthodox refugees had fled from the territory of the new 'greater Serbia'. They were joined there in exile by others from northern Greece, who were part of a voluntary population exchange agreed between Greece and Bulgaria. During the Second World War Bulgaria allied itself with Germany, in return for the promise of expansion into Macedonia. In 1941–44 Bulgaria occupied more than 50% of the territory of the modern Republic of Macedonia, as well as areas of northern Greece. Bulgaria pursued an aggressive policy of assimilative nationalization that alienated significant sections of the population. Since 1921 the Communist Party had enjoyed some success in the region, and pledges by Tito (Josip Broz, the leader of the communist resistance forces) of greater autonomy for the Macedonian people also won support. The Federative People's Republic of Yugoslavia, with Tito as Prime Minister, was proclaimed in November 1945. Macedonia emerged as a republic in the new federal state and its Slav-speaking majority was recognized as a nation for the first time. Opposition continued in two forms:

those who remained pro-Bulgarian, and those who aspired to create a sovereign non-Yugoslav 'greater' Macedonia. Although Tito (who became President of Yugoslavia in January 1953) also had ambitions to incorporate western Bulgaria and northern Greece into an enlarged Macedonian republic, he remained committed to the federal concept. When relations with Bulgaria were suspended, following Tito's split with Soviet communism, and the Greek communists were defeated in the civil war in Greece, the Yugoslav Government took measures to suppress both forms of opposition. Symbolic nationalism was, none the less, encouraged: the language was quickly codified, and the autocephaly of the Macedonian Orthodox Church restored in 1967 (on the 200th anniversary of the closure of the Ohrid Bishopric under Ottoman rule). Tito also continued to use the Macedonian issue to further his foreign policy when necessary, contrasting the 'free' expression of Macedonian identity in Yugoslavia with its denial in Bulgaria and Greece.

Within the Socialist Federal Republic of Yugoslavia, Macedonia progressed well, although, in economic and cultural terms, it was dependent on Yugoslavia, and especially its large neighbouring republic, Serbia. However, tension between the Slavic majority and the rising ethnic Albanian minority in western Macedonia increasingly dominated politics in the country. Between 1951 and 1981 Albanian cultural rights in Macedonia steadily improved; however, demonstrations in Priština, in the neighbouring Serbian Autonomous Province of Kosovo, in 1981, concerned the Macedonian authorities, which followed the Serbian example in taking repressive measures against Albanian nationalism.

THE END OF YUGOSLAVIA

Throughout the 1980s, as Yugoslavia's economic situation deteriorated, many Macedonians, nevertheless, remained loyal to the ideal of federalism. As elsewhere, however, nationalist parties gained support by claiming incompetence or inefficiency at federal level. The results of democratic elections to a new, unicameral legislature in late 1990 demonstrated the divisions in Macedonian politics. A new nationalist coalition, headed by the Internal Macedonian Revolutionary Organization—Democratic Party for Macedonian National Unity (IMRO—DPMNU, which revived the name of the 1893 IMRO), won 37 seats. The League of Communists of Macedonia—Party of Democratic Reform (LCM—PDR, the former ruling Communists) secured 31 seats, while the Alliance of Reform Forces (ARF) of the federal Prime Minister, Ante Marković, won 19 seats. Macedonia's Albanian community, in an early indication that it viewed its political future in different terms, voted for ethnically-defined parties, the largest of which was the Party for Democratic Prosperity (PDP), with 24 seats. The newly elected, 120-member Assembly (Sobranie) elected Kiro Gligorov, a prominent member of the LCM—PDR as President, while Ljubčo Georgievski of the IMRO—DPMNU became Vice-President. As Yugoslavia approached its collapse in 1991, Gligorov co-operated with the President of Bosnia and Herzegovina, with the aim of achieving a resolution in the form of a looser federation. Macedonia's representative to the collective presidency, Vasil Tupurkovski, also pursued the same agenda, in an effort to reach a compromise arrangement.

After a referendum in November 1991 (which was, however, boycotted by the Albanian community) a new Constitution declaring the sovereignty of the Republic of Macedonia was adopted. The Macedonian authorities applied for recognition from the Commission of the European Community (EC, now European Union, EU), a panel of experts created to determine EC policy on the recognition of Yugoslavia's republics as sovereign states. The Commission acknowledged that Macedonia fulfilled the requirements for official recognition; however, the EC did not follow the recommendation, owing to objections by the Greek Government, which perceived in the creation of an independent republic under the name 'Macedonia' the possibility of future claims on territory in northern Greece. President Gligorov, nevertheless, successfully negotiated the withdrawal of Yugoslav federal troops from Macedonia in March 1992, which, together with the adoption of a new Constitution in the Federal Republic of Yugoslavia (FRY), marked Yugoslav acceptance of Macedonian secession. In December the UN Security Council approved the deployment of the UN Protection Force (UNPROFOR) along the Macedonian border with the FRY and Albania, in an effort to prevent inter-ethnic unrest. (In March 1995 the operation was renamed the UN Preventative Deployment Force—UNPREDEP.) Economically, however, Macedonia suffered considerably as a result of the severe disruption of its trade links with Serbia, following the imposition of UN sanctions against the FRY.

GREECE AND THE NEW MACEDONIA

The adoption of a new flag in Macedonia in August 1992 attracted particular opposition from Greece, which objected to the depiction outside Greece of the 'Vergina Star' (regarded as an ancient Greek symbol of Philip of Macedon and Alexander the Great). In February 1993 Greece agreed to international arbitration over the issue of Macedonia's name, undertaking to abide by its final outcome. On 8 April the republic was admitted to the UN under the temporary name of 'the former Yugoslav republic of Macedonia' (FYRM), pending settlement of the issue of a permanent name by international mediators. In October, however, the Greek Government announced that Greece was to withdraw from UN-sponsored negotiations on the issue of a permanent name. From February 1994 Greece blocked all non-humanitarian shipments to Macedonia from the port of Thessaloníki, and also prevented road and rail transport into or from the republic; it subsequently closed its consulate in Skopje. In March 1995 it was announced that Greece had accepted a resumption of negotiations with the FYRM, under the auspices of the UN, commencing in April; in May the Organization for Security and Co-operation in Europe announced that it was to join the mediation efforts. In September an interim accord was signed at the UN headquarters in New York, the USA, by the Macedonian Minister of Foreign Affairs and his Greek counterpart. The agreement provided for the mutual recognition of existing frontiers and respect for the sovereignty and political independence of each state, and for the free movement of goods and people between the two countries. Greece was to withdraw its trade embargo and end its veto on the FYRM's entry into international organizations, while the Macedonian authorities undertook to abandon the use of the Vergina emblem in any form, and to amend parts of the Constitution that had been regarded by Greece as 'irredentist'. (The issue of a permanent name for the FYRM was to be the subject of further negotiations.) In early October the Sobranie approved a new state flag, depicting an eight-rayed sun in place of the Vergina emblem. The interim accord was ratified by the Sobranie on 9 October, and was formally signed in Skopje by representatives of the FYRM and Greece on 13 October. The border between the two countries was subsequently reopened.

DOMESTIC POLITICS, 1992–98

The IMRO—DPMNU left the governing coalition in October 1991. Following the collapse of the first administration of technocrats in July 1992, the LCM—PDR, which had been renamed the Social Democratic Alliance of Macedonia (SDAM), led by Branko Crvenkovski, formed a Government in September. The new Cabinet included representatives from several parties, including the Albanian PDP. Nevertheless, pressure from sections of the country's Albanian population that sought improved rights continued. At the same time the ruling coalition also came under continuous attack from Macedonian nationalists operating through the IMRO—DPMNU, who resisted any concession to Albanian demands, sought greater distance from Serbia, and took stances apparently designed to make dialogue with Greece impossible.

Despite continuous domestic and international pressure, the Government survived its first electoral challenge in 1994, when legislative and presidential elections took place concurrently. The IMRO—DPMNU, again led by Georgievski, enrolled a famous theatre director, Ljubiša Georgievski (no relation), as presidential candidate. However, Gligorov's personal standing resulted in him securing a second term, and the first round of voting in parliamentary elections indicated that the alliance led by the SDAM had defeated the opposition challenge. Claiming that electoral fraud had taken place, the IMRO—DPMNU boycotted the second round, with the result that the SDAM alliance secured 97 of the 120 seats in the Sobranie.

Prior to the elections, the principal Albanian party, the PDP, had divided, with a more radical faction, under the leadership of Arben Xhaferi, forming a new organization, the Party of Democratic Prosperity of the Albanians in Macedonia (PDPAM), later in 1994. Meanwhile, following the boycott of the referendum and census in 1991, radical factions, which campaigned for greater cultural rights and constitutional reform, emerged. Violent clashes occurred between Albanians and security forces on several occasions, the most notable being in the north-western town of Tetovo, after an 'illegal' Albanian-language university was opened in late 1994. During confrontations between ethnic Albanians and security forces, who were attempting to close the university, one ethnic Albanian was killed. In 1997, in Gostivar, a dispute occurred over the display of Turkish and Albanian flags at a local government office, which was again declared illegal and prevented by police action. There were also sporadic border incidents and bomb attacks, indicating that armed and militant factions existed among the ethnic Albanian population. During the period after 1994 illicit economic activities increased further in the FYRM. War profiteers, who had already been engaged in smuggling in the early years of international sanctions against the FRY, diversified their operations. Gligorov himself, 78 years of age, narrowly survived a car bomb in September 1995. Public discontent grew, as reports of insider 'buy-outs' of state assets became widely known, and other scandals emerged, including the collapse of a pyramid savings bank in Bitola in 1997.

DOMESTIC AND INTERNATIONAL ISSUES: IMRO—DPMNU IN POWER, 1998–2001

In 1998–2001 the IMRO—DPMNU remained without parliamentary representation, undertaking party reorganization, consolidating its support at local level, and conducting public protests. Conscious of the necessity of gaining international credibility, the party publicly transformed itself from nationalist to centre-right. Prior to the legislative elections in late 1998, the IMRO—DPMNU also created an alliance with a new party, the Democratic Alternative (DA), established by the popular Yugoslav-era politician, Vasil Tupurkovski. Tupurkovski (who had mainly resided in the USA since 1990) pledged economic recovery through foreign investment. The IMRO—DPMNU, meanwhile, mobilized the strong popular support it had gained throughout the country. The results of the 1998 elections were unexpected: the alliance between the IMRO—DPMNU and the DA took 58 of the 120 seats, while the SDAM, which had split from its former coalition partners, won only 29. Even more unexpected was the subsequent

announcement of a governing coalition between the IMRO—DPMNU and the DA, and Xhaferi's Democratic Party of Albania (DPA—which had been reconstituted from the PDPAM). The DPA had contested the elections in alliance with the PDP (despite the differences between the two parties), and the grouping had obtained a total of 24 seats.

The co-operation between parties formerly considered as radical nationalists was perceived by international observers as a welcome sign of progress in the republic, and some viewed it as an indication of Tupurkovski's unique skills of reconciliation. Shortly after the victory, he announced that, in exchange for support he had secured from the Taiwanese Government to fulfil his pre-election commitment, the FYRM would extend diplomatic recognition to Taiwan. This decision had immediate political consequences, prompting the People's Republic of China, in protest, to suspend diplomatic relations with the FYRM and to veto the extension of the UNPREDEP mission in the republic at the UN Security Council. (With the escalation of tension in the province of Kosovo, NATO forces deployed under the UN mandate remained deployed at the border with Kosovo.) The agreement with Taiwan collapsed, and Tupurkovski was widely discredited, although it was still largely assumed that he would be submitted as a coalition candidate in the presidential election in 1999, at the expiry of Gligorov's term of office. In the event, all three government coalition parties contested the election, as did a further three candidates. Tupurkovski was eliminated in the first round; in the second round, which took place on 14 November, Boris Trajkovski, the IMRO—DPMNU candidate, was elected to the presidency with 52.8% of the votes cast, defeating Tito Petkovski of the SDAM.

The campaign of the 1999 presidential election was characterized by fierce anti-Albanian rhetoric from the SDAM candidate, and afterwards by opposition accusations of widespread electoral malpractice, especially in western areas with a high Albanian population, where Trajkovski received overwhelming support. At the government level, co-operation between Albanian and Macedonian parties continued, including agreement on a mainly Albanian-language university in Tetovo (funded by international donors), and progress toward greater decentralization. Relations with Bulgaria, Albania and Greece improved (although the issue with Greece over the use of the name 'Macedonia' remained unresolved), and the international community clearly welcomed the new administration's pragmatism. The Government survived the conflict in Kosovo in March–June 1999, when over 250,000 Kosovar Albanians found refuge in the country, and NATO's presence in the FYRM expanded considerably to support the international Kosovo Force (KFOR) deployed in the province. Nevertheless, mutual distrust between the Macedonian and Albanian communities continued to rise: the NATO bombardment of the FRY and subsequent deployment in Kosovo were widely believed to demonstrate that NATO, and especially the USA, strongly favoured the Albanian population. Many Macedonians became disenchanted with the new Government, believing that it was privatizing national industry for short-term personal profit, and permitting Albanian criminal networks to operate unchecked in western Macedonia. Party membership was also perceived as being more significant than before in securing state employment. Meanwhile, even within the Government, ethnic Albanians continued to demand constitutional change and greater regional autonomy in the FYRM. Following numerous scandals and inter-party disputes, the DA withdrew from the Government in November 2000 (and disaffected members of the IMRO—DPMNU established a breakaway faction earlier that year), but the coalition of the IMRO—DPMNU and the DPA survived, with the DPA assuming an increasing prominence. Local elections in September 2000, which the opposition attempted to exploit as a vote on the Government's performance, were characterized by low participation and widespread irregularities.

2001–02: CIVIL CONFLICT AND ITS CONSEQUENCES

The demarcation of the FYRM's northern border with the FRY was finally confirmed, after nine years of indeterminacy, in early 2001. Immediately afterwards a Macedonian border village, Tanuševci, was occupied by armed Albanians belonging to the National Liberation Army (NLA), a newly emerged paramilitary movement, led by Ali Ahmeti (a Macedonian Albanian with strong associations with the large Albanian diaspora in Switzerland, Scandinavia and the USA). With some assistance from KFOR troops across the border, Macedonian security forces finally succeeded in recapturing the village. The NLA regrouped and expanded its activities to villages around Tetovo and Kumanovo, in north and north-western Macedonia, subsequently advancing to Aračinovo, on the outskirts of Skopje. Within the FYRM, demands for a new partition or exchange of populations were expressed, as was open anti-Albanian sentiment in the Macedonian-language media, especially after prominent Albanian politicians from the FYRM signed a common agenda with Kosovo Liberation Army (KLA) leaders. The EU and the USA led mediation efforts between Albanian and Macedonian parliamentary parties, while sporadic fighting continued, displacing thousands of civilians, and resulting in at least 100 deaths. Atrocities against civilians on both sides were reliably reported. Following heavy pressure from the international community, a peace accord was signed in Ohrid in mid-August by representatives of the four largest parties represented in the Sobranie: the IMRO—DPMNU, the SDAM, the PDP and the DPA. NATO troops supervised a 30-day process of disarmament, which was completed in late September. On 16 November the Sobranie adopted a number of the constitutional amendments agreed under the peace settlement, providing for pledges of considerable assistance for the war-damaged economy by international donors in early 2002.

The constitutional changes of the Ohrid Agreement were introduced to provide greater rights for the FYRM's minorities (referred to in the agreement as 'Communities') in national and local politics, education, and the state employment sector. It emphasized in particular a system known as the double majority method, whereby legislation affecting minorities required not only a majority of parliamentary votes, but also a majority of votes cast by those deputies who were not members of the ethnic majority. The agreement also stipulated as a target that ethnic groups' representation in institutions, including the judiciary, police and civil service, should be equal to their respective percentage of the country's population. A new census was therefore an integral part of the political process, and initial results were released in January 2003. This followed a general election in September 2002, in which the Government led by IMRO—DPMNU was removed. After four years in power, IMRO—DPMNU and the DPA had won reputations for cronyism and corruption, especially with regard to the sale of national assets and a policy of rewarding the party faithful with state-sector jobs. The reputations of both parties and their leaders also suffered in the war and its outcome. As a result, even in coalition with the Liberal-Democratic party, IMRO—DPMNU received only 33 seats in the Sobranie, and the DPA seven. The SDAM's new coalition 'Together for Macedonia' won 60 seats, and the new party formed by Ali Ahmeti, the Democratic Union for Integration,

won 16 seats. After protracted negotiations, these two groupings formed a new coalition Government, which was again headed by Crvenkovski. The new Government has continued with the implementation of the Ohrid Agreement and, like the other former Yugoslav republics, aims eventually to accede to the EU. The country, none the less, continues to face significant challenges, many of which are related to continuing inter-ethnic tensions. In April 2003, following his resignation as leader of IMRO—DPMNU, the former Prime Minister, Ljubčo Georgievski, publicly demanded that the republic be partitioned along ethnic lines. Such rhetoric also serves the interests of those parts of the FYRM's Albanian population that, even after the political reforms of Ohrid, still pursue the goal of a 'greater Albania'. Some ideologues, notably Hashim Thaçi (a former KLA leader, whose political party is represented in the Kosovo Assembly) have pledged commitment to the creation of mono-ethnic states as the basis for long-term regional stability. Continuing sporadic violence in the western part of the country clearly serves the interests of those who do not wish for a stable and peaceful multi-ethnic Macedonian state.

FUTURE PROSPECTS

In the rhetoric and practice of the NLA in 2001, it was possible to trace three different trends in Albanian activism in the FYRM. Some announcements suggested that the insurgency was concerned with reform, and as such represented an extension of other forms of political action aimed only at achieving constitutional change and greater collective rights. At other times, the NLA's actions seemed to be co-ordinated with the former KLA in Kosovo, and with Albanian insurgents in southern Serbia, suggesting a more far-reaching agenda of eventual secession and possible unification with other 'historically Albanian' territory. Clearly, Ohrid did not satisfy this objective, and, in this context, could be viewed merely as a stage towards attaining full autonomy and union with Kosovo. Finally, for some people in the region, especially those who have been systematically excluded from legal means to achieving prosperity, conflict and instability is advantageous and they aim to perpetuate such conditions, which continuously provide opportunities for personal financial profit. In the illicit trading of cigarettes, petrol, drugs and munitions, the former Yugoslav Albanian mafia has taken a leading role, and is also an increasing force in organized crime in Europe, particularly in northern Italy. The networks created for the illicit transit of commodities are also used both by male labour migrants, travelling from the Middle East and Asia to the Balkans and thence to Europe, and for trafficking in women, who are then forced into prostitution. There is some evidence that the KLA, and subsequently the NLA, were supported by such activities, and that their former members remain dependent on the continuation of these networks.

These three types of political activism (reformist, nationalist and criminal) remain relevant in the FYRM, where the economy is weak, unemployment is high, and many of the country's more talented citizens regard their futures as being abroad. The republic now faces the additional challenge of waning international interest and support. A full decade after the disintegration of the former Yugoslavia, Macedonia continues to address the issues of economic dependency and nationalist unrest that precipitated crisis then, and its tools for doing so remain limited. Unless able to demonstrate tangible and positive results, the reformists may yet lose the advantages they have struggled to maintain in recent years.

The Economy

Dr DAVID A. DYKER

INTRODUCTION

A Turkish colony until 1913, unrecognized as anything more than 'South Serbia' in the period between the First and Second World War, emerging as a Yugoslav republic in 1945, but remaining until the collapse of Yugoslavia one of its poorest regions, Macedonia was unique among the countries of the Balkans. It was a developing country, but also a post-communist country, and it had difficult relations with some neighbouring countries. Greece took issue with the very notion of an independent Macedonian state, fearing, it seemed, a destabilizing effect on Greek Macedonia and on its Slav-speaking minority. In 1994–95 Greece imposed an economic blockade on Macedonia over this issue. The successive regional conflicts have had a particularly adverse affect on the economy. The former Yugoslav republic of Macedonia (FYRM) had a population of over 2m. and a gross domestic product (GDP) of only US $3,700m. (at prevailing exchange rates) in 2002. Although mountainous, it had fertile agricultural land, much of it suitable for growing subtropical crops like tobacco. However, the country was not rich in industrial raw materials, with the exception of some ferrous metals. The FYRM was critically dependent on foreign trade, both for markets for its specialist agricultural crops and for supplies for its industry, with exports representing 30% and imports 49% of GDP in 2002. In this context, the FYRM's less than cordial relations with some neighbouring states were a distinct disadvantage. The Macedonian leadership had skilfully avoided any direct involvement in the conflicts arising from the collapse of the former Yugoslavia. However, they were unable to avoid domestic conflict between the Slav Macedonian population and the substantial Albanian minority, which erupted into hostilities in 2001. The August 2001 agreement between the Government and the Albanian insurgents restored peace in the FYRM, but tension between the ethnic groups remained high, further complicating the task of economic policy-making.

THE STRUCTURE OF THE MACEDONIAN ECONOMY

The production profile of the Macedonian economy was the product of an evolution familiar across the transition region. Agriculture, industry (excluding construction) and mining, which together accounted for over one-half of national income in 1994, contributed less than 42% of GDP in 2002. Conversely, the services sector accounted for a total of almost 60% of GDP by 2002.

Manufacturing still accounted for three-quarters of total exports in 2002, but industry and mining as a whole were dominated by low-value-added activities. Low levels of productivity and widespread managerial inefficiency reflected the still heavy burden of the communist legacy. Under pressure from the IMF and the World Bank, the Government has pursued a policy of privatization, but progress has been slow, and there has been little investment in terms of new capital and expertise.

A DIFFICULT ECONOMIC TRANSITION

The FYRM's transition to a market economy progressed slowly. Although a privatization programme was drafted as early as 1992, it remained largely unimplemented through the early years of independence. By March 1996 only 604 companies had been privatized, largely through management 'buy-outs' (the managers were usually from the communist period), with an additional 25 very large industrial state enterprises undergoing a special pre-privatization restructuring process sponsored by the World Bank, which resulted in the loss of around 20,000 jobs. Only in 1998 did strategic foreign investors begin to feature seriously in Macedonian privatization. The private sector's share of GDP was still, however, only 60% in that year. Progress with the programme of privatization in the late 1990s remained very slow. The country's only petroleum refinery, the OKTA Oil Refinery, was partially privatized in mid-1999, when Hellenic Petroleum of Greece acquired a majority share. However, attempts by the Government in late 1999 and early 2000 to negotiate the sale of other companies largely failed. The exceptions were the Bitola Brewery and the Karpos Decorative Fabrics Factory, for which buyers were found. Under pressure from the international financial organizations, progress in privatization accelerated in late 2000. In December of that year the Frotirka textiles firm and the Jegunovce ferro-alloy installation, two of the 12 enterprises targeted for privatization by the IMF and the World Bank, were sold. In January 2001 a 51% share in the highly profitable state telecommunications company, Makedonski Telekomunikacii (MT), was acquired by the Hungarian enterprise, Matáv. Later in the same year the Porcelanka ceramics firm at Veles was sold to an Austrian company, Exclusiva. The Hemteks polyester-fibres enterprise, the Frinko refrigerator and freezer factory, and the FAS Oktombri bus-manufacturing company have been closed down. Tenders for the Sasa mine at Makedonska Kamenica and the Zletovo battery-manufacturing firm were announced in 2002, but by 2003 no progress had been made with the sale of these companies. The privatization of the state electricity company, Elektrostopanstvo na Makedonija, was also envisaged, but at mid-2003 had proceeded no further. At the beginning of 2003 1,688 enterprises, employing 83% of the total work-force, had been privatized, with a further 84 companies, employing a total of 3.7% of the work-force, in the process of privatization. The Government continued to hold shares in 512 companies, of which it had a controlling interest in 282.

It was remarkable, however, that any economic transition at all occurred in the FYRM. In terms of macroeconomic indicators, the achievements were considerable. During 1994–95, when the country suffered the effects both of the UN sanctions on Serbia, which isolated Macedonia from its traditional markets, and the Greek embargo, which denied it access to its traditional port, Thessaloníki, the country managed to maintain budgetary balance and to preserve stability of prices far better than most transitional economies. In the following years the Macedonian Government continued to report above-average macroeconomic performance. The budgetary deficit was restrained to less than 2% of GDP throughout 1996–98, and small surpluses were recorded in 1999 and 2000. A deficit equivalent to 6% of GDP appeared in 2001, under the pressure of the domestic political crisis, but the deficit was reduced to 4.8% in 2002, partly owing to generous foreign aid. In accordance with Macedonia's agreement with the IMF, the budget deficit for 2003 was projected at just 1.6% of GDP. However, independent projections indicated that the deficit would be nearer 3% of GDP. The annual inflation rate averaged only 2.5% in 1997. Consumer prices actually fell by 0.1% in 1998 and 0.7% in 1999, before increasing again, by 5.8%, in 2000, as a result of the impact of higher international petroleum prices and the introduction of value-added tax (VAT) in April. The inflation rate declined slightly to 5.5% in 2001, and to an estimated 2.4% in 2002 (when the government target was 2%). The exchange rate against the US dollar remained largely unchanged in 1997–99. It declined by some 16% in 2000, in accordance with inflation, and by 3.2%, rather less than the rate of inflation, in 2001. In 2002 the denar recovered by some 5.7% against the dollar, while remaining stable against the euro. The price of relative stability, in terms of production and employment levels, was certainly high. GDP declined by an annual average of 25% in 1991–95, and while positive economic growth resumed in 1996, the average growth rate in 1996–2000 was just 2.5%. Under the impact of the domestic political crisis, GDP actually contracted by 4.6% in 2001. The trend was reversed in 2002, but with a growth rate of just 0.3%. The rate of unemployment, as defined by the International Labour Organization, was 31.9% in 2002, having reached some 40% in late 1999, following the mass influx of refugees from the neighbouring Serbian province of Kosovo and Metohija. In 2002 GDP per head was about US $1,800, but average monthly personal income in the same year was some $210, reflecting the fact that the 'parallel' economy accounted for 30%–40% of the aggregate real economy. While economic growth of more than 5% per year would be perfectly feasible for the FYRM, it might be many years before the legal part of the economy would be able to provide employment for the great majority of the labour force.

THE 'PARALLEL' ECONOMY

The predominance of the 'parallel' economy was, paradoxically, the greatest strength and the greatest weakness of the Macedonian economy. It was the country's illegal economic activity, particularly prohibited imports and exports, that allowed it to survive the years of embargo. The Kosovo conflict created further opportunities for illicit trading, especially across Macedonia's border with Serbia. Offers of assistance from the international community to combat crime were evidently aimed at suppressing the drugs-transit trade, in which narcotics were transported from the Middle East, via Macedonia, to Western Europe. Once an increase in legitimate trade appeared, it was the interests of the powerful drugs-traffickers, and the corrupt politicians that co-operated with them, that were likely to operate as obstacles to sustained recovery. Consequently, the Macedonian Government decided that it was essential to take measures to ensure that the corrupt officials were not allowed to dominate the economy.

Legislation that was adopted in 1998, with the aim of discouraging unofficial privatization and strengthening creditors' rights in case of bankruptcy, represented a clear incentive to foreign capital investors to become involved in the FYRM. By mid-2000 foreign investment, by Greece and Slovenia in particular, had begun to benefit the economy. It was unrealistic, however, to expect foreign capital to meet all of the FYRM's investment requirements; by the end of 2002 cumulative foreign direct investment in Macedonia totalled just US $843m., representing about $420 per head (about the same as Bulgaria). The largest privatization took place in January 2001, when Matáv bought the 51% share in MT for $321m., but foreign direct investment largely ceased thereafter, again partly owing to the domestic political crisis. Over the first three quarters of 2002, gross inflow of foreign direct investment into the Macedonian economy totalled just $67.7m. Most of this modest inflow was directed to the manufacturing sector, maintaining the prospect that this key sector of the economy might, in time, be transformed into an efficient, export-orientated production system. Investment in the FYRM does, however, remain crucially dependent on the domestic banking system.

THE REORGANIZATION OF THE BANKING SECTOR

Macedonian government policy on banking reform was based on three main elements: pluralization and privatization of the banking system; rehabilitation, rather than bankruptcy, as the principal instrument of restructuring; and recapitalization of the whole system. The main practical implication of the first element was that a proportion of the assets of Stopanska Banka, which previously accounted for around 65% of the total banking assets in the FYRM, was to be used to create six smaller, regionally-based and privately-owned banks. The first of these, the Ohrid Bank, was formed in 1995 on the basis of about 10% of the assets of Stopanska Banka. The aim was to reduce Stopanska Banka's share of total banking business in Macedonia to no more than 1.8% higher than that of the Komercijalna Banka of Skopje, the next largest bank. Stopanska Banka itself was privatized in April 2000 through the sale of a majority share to the National Bank of Greece. In 2002 another major bank, Kreditna Banka, was sold to the Alpha Banka group, also of Greece, and renamed Alpha Banka.

Recapitalization of the whole banking system represented the most difficult, and the most important, element of creating a banking system that could genuinely support the new private economy. The privatization of the banks, as such, was carried out primarily through management takeovers. This was a reasonably convenient means of transition from a market-socialist structure to a capitalist structure, but it did not provide any new revenue. In the case of Stopanska Banka that was achieved by means of an issue of new shares.

The Macedonian banking reform was a sensible, if not very radical, programme. In practice, however, the policy of developing a new commercial banking system was fraught with difficulties. Attempts to foster institutions specializing in lending to small businesses sometimes failed, and the scandal surrounding the collapse of several 'pyramid' financial schemes in 1997 continued adversely to affect Macedonian politics until 2000, when a settlement was finally reached. Attempts to ensure transparent accounting and prevent banks from exercising favouritism in lending policy were only partially successful; over the first nine months of 2000 some 37.3% of all bank loans were classified as 'high risk', a rather higher proportion than had prevailed in 1998. Overall bank liquidity, however, improved by 42.1% in 2000, compared with 1999. It continued to improve in 2001, but declined sharply again in 2002. The level of bank lending was virtually static between December 2000 and December 2001. Over the succeeding 12 months it grew by just 6.2%. New banking legislation, which was introduced in July 2000, was designed to be the first measure towards harmonization with European Union (EU) directives on banking, and moved the Macedonian system closer to the Core Basle Principles for Effective Banking Supervision imposed by the Basle Committee on Banking Supervision (all in accordance with Macedonia's long-standing aim to join the EU). The new legislation was followed in November by the adoption of changes to the regulations in foreign-exchange operations by commercial banks, which effectively allowed the banks more freedom in this area. The level of foreign-currency lending by the banks was stable throughout 2001, but increased by some 17% between December 2001 and December 2002. In December 2002 the commercial banks took over control of the clearing function from the Payments Operations Agency. There are currently 20 commercial banks and 23 specialist savings institutions in the FYRM.

THE STOCK EXCHANGE

The creation of a Macedonian stock exchange reinforced and supplemented banking reform by providing a venue for trading in shares in the banks themselves, and supplying an alternative channel for the mobilization of savings. Established in September 1995, the Skopje Stock Exchange, sponsored by the United Kingdom, commenced trading in March 1996. Its initial capital of DM 1m. was provided by 11 commercial banks, two insurance companies and four specialist savings institutions. The Macedonian stock market performed poorly in 1999, with turnover declining by more than 60%, compared with the previous year. However, it recovered in 2000, with a five-fold increase in year-on-year turnover, generated by the sale of a number of large enterprises to foreign investors, the issuance and trade in treasury bills in settlement of claims relating to the old hard-currency savings deposits, and further improvements in the regulatory framework of the market. In 2001 turnover increased by a further 400%, as a result of the privatization of MT in January, and brisk trade in the treasury bills concerning hard-currency savings deposits. In 2002, however, turnover declined to 5,700m. new denars, 26% less than the level recorded in 2000. The Macedonian stock market remained a very small operation, restricted by the predominance of insiders in the ownership structure of the economy and highly vulnerable to political disturbances. It was, nevertheless, an important symbol of the FYRM's future as a market economy.

MULTILATERAL FINANCIAL SUPPORT

The IMF, the World Bank, the International Finance Corporation (IFC—part of the World Bank), the International Development Association (IDA), the European Bank for Reconstruction and Development (EBRD, based in the United Kingdom) and the EU's PHARE programme (originally Poland/Hungary Aid for Restructuring of Economies) all extended support to the FYRM. The enhanced structural-adjustment facility (ESAF) extended by the IMF to Macedonia in 1997 was suspended in mid-1999, as the conflict in Kosovo worsened. However, the IMF approved an Extended Fund Facility (EFF) of US $31m. in November 2000 and a Poverty Reduction and Growth Facility (PRGF) of $13m. in the following month. In November 2001, however, these were suspended because of Macedonia's failure to reach the objectives of the Facilities. In January 2003 a new, 15-month loan of $27m. was agreed between the Fund and the Macedonian Government. In December 2000 the World Bank approved a second Financial and Enterprise Sector Adjustment Programme (FESAL), valued at $50.3m., to continue until the end of 2003. The FESAL was conditional on the Macedonian Government completing the process of sale or liquidation of large, loss-making enterprises. The Government continued to request more time over the matter, while the Bank insisted on rapid and decisive action. At the beginning of 2003 there were still 24 state-owned, loss-making enterprises awaiting privatization. These difficulties, combined with the onset of the political crisis in 2001, have largely resulted in the suspension of new World Bank project financing to Macedonia. In December 2001, however, an Emergency Economic Recovery Credit, targeted mainly at public sector reform, was approved. The Stability Pact for South Eastern Europe, signed by most of the Balkan countries after the end of the Kosovo conflict in June 1999, was expected to provide a channel for new sources of funding for Balkan reconstruction. In March 2000 €1,700m. was pledged to fund various programmes in the region. The only major project for the FYRM, however, was the development and modernization of the border post at Blace, between Macedonia and Kosovo. A new donors' conference was convened in March 2002, which produced pledges of aid totalling $578m. During the 1990s overall the EU delivered some

€452m. in aid to the FYRM. A Stabilization and Association Agreement (SAA), which was signed with the EU in April 2001, provided significant indicators of the FYRM's economic future. Unlike the association agreements that many Central and South-Eastern European countries had reached with the EU, the SAA did not commit the EU to eventual Macedonian accession to the Union. It was expected, nevertheless, greatly to benefit the FYRM's economy.

In late 2001 the EU approved an emergency aid package for the FYRM of some €12m., following the €12.8m. pledged in August, immediately after the fighting had ended. The funds were to be allocated to the restoration of electricity and water supplies in areas affected by the fighting, and the reconstruction of damaged houses. Subsequently, in December the European Commission adopted a five-year 'community assistance for reconstruction, development and stabilization' strategy for the FYRM, involving transfers to Macedonia until the end of 2004. At the donors' conference in March 2002 the European Commission announced that total aid to the FYRM during 2001–02 would total €188m. In June 2000, following one year of negotiations, a free trade agreement was signed between Macedonia and the European Free Trade Association (EFTA). In April 2003 Macedonia joined the World Trade Organization (WTO).

TRANSPORT AND COMMUNICATIONS INFRASTRUCTURE

Owing to the FYRM's geographical position in the Balkans, the development of its transport links was of crucial importance. International financial support played an essential role in the modernization of the Macedonian infrastructure. In December 1995 the EBRD was the first to administer a loan of 9.7m. ECU (the ECU was replaced by the euro on 1 January 1999), to finance the modernization of Skopje airport. Subsequently, emphasis was placed on the development of road, rail and telecommunications networks. In April 2000 the EU donated €182m. towards five 'swift start' projects, which were designed to improve infrastructure, the electric power system and the road network. In June of the same year Bulgaria and the FYRM signed a protocol to improve bilateral trade and economic relations, particularly in the sectors of transport, communications and energy. The European Investment Bank loan for motorway construction was part of a series of loans for infrastructural development, a number of which were to be used to modernize the railways. The World Bank and a Japanese enterprise, Marubeni, were also involved in the modernization of the Macedonian railways. The privatization of MT, originally scheduled for 1998, was finally implemented in January 2001 (see above). The expectation was that the agreement would provide MT not only with finance, but also with the technology required to upgrade the whole telecommunications network. MT continued to develop its mobile communications system, and the Government sold a second mobile operator's licence to the Hellenic Telecommunications Organization (Greece) in November 2001 for US $25m. The aggregate number of mobile subscribers increased from 115,700 in 2000 to 384,000 in 2002. The use of internet services was also increasing rapidly.

The domestic conflict of 2001 caused a severe reverse to the FYRM's efforts to modernize its transport and communications infrastructure. Direct damage was minor, except to the electricity transmission network. However, as a result of the outbreak of fighting, there was effectively no investment during that year in transport networks, which already desperately required upgrading. Traffic in goods has continued to decline on both road and rail, as has passenger traffic on the railways. Further aid flows in 2002 and 2003 were expected to assist the Macedonian authorities in recovering from these adverse effects, but the transport network, in particular, was likely to remain a significant impediment to economic progress for the foreseeable future.

DEVELOPING THE POLICY AGENDA

At early 2001 the FYRM Government could view the economic policy agenda with some equanimity. Relations with Serbia and Greece were improving steadily, and the basis for a long-term partnership with the EU had been established. Improvements in significant macroeconomic indicators, such as GDP growth, balance of trade and inflation, were expected. Budgetary deficits were to be restrained to low levels.

By mid-2003, as the FYRM Government endeavoured to maintain the fragile peace established in August 2001, the outlook had changed fundamentally. The authorities continued efforts to control the budgetary deficit, and GDP was expected to recover only slowly from the negative impact of 2001. Current-account deficits were at a level of about 10% of GDP, and would certainly not fall below 5% of GDP in the short to medium term; foreign aid was unlikely to be sufficient to cover all of these deficits. Prospects for completion of the privatization programme, and for the maintenance of steady relations with the IMF were reasonably favourable, while the general improvement in the FYRM's relations with neighbouring states and the EU continued. However, the nature of the political compromise that had ended the civil conflict in 2001 was such as to cast serious doubt on the future of economic policy-making in the FYRM. The broad-based Government that had emerged from the elections of 1998, led by the Macedonian nationalist party, included representatives with dubious commitment to the August 2001 peace settlement, and the tenuous coalition appeared particularly ill-suited to the task of implementing austerity policies in difficult conditions. In the legislative elections of September 2002, however, the incumbent Government was removed from power. The new governing coalition was headed by the Social Democratic Alliance of Macedonia (former communists), and also included a newly established Albanian party, the Democratic Union for Integration. The election result caused some stabilization of the FYRM's ethnic politics, and promised to create a more favourable environment for economic policy. Ethnic tensions remained high, however, and the underlying problem of how to forge a proactive policy consensus remained unresolved. At mid-2003 the prospects of the FYRM emerging from long-term poverty to take its place among the European nations remained deeply uncertain.

Statistical Survey

Source (unless otherwise indicated): State Statistical Office of the Republic of Macedonia, 91000 Skopje, Dame Gruev 4, POB 506; tel. (2) 114904; fax (2) 111336; e-mail info@stat.gov.mk; internet www.stat.gov.mk.

Area and Population

AREA, POPULATION AND DENSITY

Area (sq km)	25,713*
Population (census results)	
31 March 1991†	2,033,964
20 June 1994‡	
Males	974,255
Females	971,677
Total	1,945,932
Population (official estimates at 31 December)	
2001	2,031,112
2002	2,049,000
Density (per sq km) at 31 December 2002	79.7

* 9,928 sq miles.

† The total refers to the *de jure* population, i.e. persons with a permanent residence in the country, including residents temporarily abroad (regardless of the duration of their absence). Other persons present in Macedonia were excluded.

‡ Figures from the 1994 census refer to persons with an official place of residence in the country (including those temporarily abroad for less than a year) and persons from other countries who have been granted a residence permit in Macedonia and have been present there for at least a year.

PRINCIPAL ETHNIC GROUPS
(census results)

	1991	1994
Macedonian	1,328,187	1,295,964
Albanian	441,987	441,104
Turkish	77,080	78,019
Roma (Gypsy)	52,103	43,707
Serbian	42,775	40,228
Muslim	31,356	15,418
Vlach	7,764	8,601
Total (incl. others)	2,033,964	1,945,932

PRINCIPAL TOWNS
(population at 1994 census)

Skopje (capital) . .	444,299	Veles	46,798
Bitola	77,464	Štip	41,730
Kumanovo . . .	71,853	Ohrid	41,146
Prilep	68,148	Strumica	34,067
Tetovo	50,344		

BIRTHS, MARRIAGES AND DEATHS*

	Registered live births		Registered marriages		Registered deaths	
	Number	Rate (per 1,000)	Number	Rate (per 1,000)	Number	Rate (per 1,000)
1994 . .	33,487	17.2	15,736	8.1	15,771	8.1
1995 . .	32,154	16.3	15,823	8.0	16,338	8.3
1996 . .	31,403	15.8	14,089	7.1	16,063	8.1
1997 . .	29,478	14.8	14,072	7.0	16,596	8.3
1998 . .	29,244	14.6	13,993	7.0	16,870	8.4
1999 . .	27,309	13.5	14,172	7.0	16,789	8.3
2000 . .	29,308	14.5	14,255	7.0	17,253	8.5
2001 . .	27,010	13.3	13,267	6.5	16,919	8.3

* Prior to 1994, rates per 1,000 are not comparable with figures for later years.

Expectation of life (WHO estimates, years at birth): 71.8 (males 68.9; females 74.9) in 2001 (Source: WHO, *World Health Report*).

ECONOMICALLY ACTIVE POPULATION
(sample surveys, '000 persons aged 15 years and over, at April)

	2001*	2002
Agriculture, hunting and forestry.	149.2	133.6
Fishing	0.3	0.7
Mining and quarrying	9.3	6.9
Manufacturing	149.2	132.4
Electricity, gas and water	16.5	14.8
Construction	35.6	32.8
Wholesale and retail trade, repair of motor vehicles, motorcycles and articles for personal use and for households	66.7	64.3
Hotels and restaurants.	12.4	11.2
Transport, storage and communications.	33.2	32.6
Financial intermediation	8.8	8.4
Real estate, renting and business activities.	10.4	11.1
Public administration and defence, compulsory social security.	33.9	33.0
Education.	27.0	33.7
Health and social work.	26.9	26.2
Total employed†	**599.3**	**561.3**

* October.
† Including others.

Source: IMF, *Former Yugoslav Republic of Macedonia: Selected Issues and Statistical Appendix* (May 2003).

Health and Welfare

KEY INDICATORS

Total fertility rate (children per woman, 2001).	1.6
Under-5 mortality rate (per 1,000 live births, 2001)	26
HIV/AIDS (% of persons aged 15–49, 2001).	<0.10
Physicians (per 1,000 head, 2001)	4.4
Hospital beds (per 1,000 head, 2001)	10.0
Health expenditure (2000): US $ per head (PPP)	300
Health expenditure (2000): % of GDP	6.0
Health expenditure (2000): public (% of total)	84.5
Human Development Index (2000): ranking	65
Human Development Index (2000): value	0.772

For sources and definitions, see explanatory note on p. vi.

Agriculture

PRINCIPAL CROPS
('000 metric tons)

	1999	2000	2001
Wheat	377.8	299.0	246.0
Rice (paddy)*	21.3	19.0	19.0
Barley	126.0	110.0	91.5
Maize	200.2	127.0	118.3
Rye	11.0	7.0†	7.0*
Potatoes	165.0	164.0	176.0
Sugar beet.	67.0	56.0	38.0
Dry beans*	13.7	13.6	13.5
Sunflower seed	14.0	10.0*	12.0†
Cabbages	69.5	70.4	75.3
Tomatoes	128.4	134.7	126.3
Cucumbers and gherkins*	22	22	22
Chillies and green peppers*	109.0	110.0	110.0
Dry onions	38.3	36.3	30.6
Green beans*	17.8	17.7	17.5
Other vegetables.	23.0	22.5	23.1
Apples	73.0	84.3	38.4
Pears	9.8	8.9	6.5
Peaches and nectarines	9.0	9.5	4.6
Plums	28.1	23.4	13.3
Cherries (incl. sour)	9.5	9.8*	11.1*
Grapes.	230.1	264.3	229.8
Watermelons and melons	121.3	122.0*	122.0*
Other fruits	10.9	10.6	7.4
Tobacco (leaves)	32.0	28.0†	28.0*

* FAO estimate(s).
† Unofficial figure.

Source: FAO.

LIVESTOCK
('000 head, year ending September)

	1999	2000	2001
Horses	60	57	57*
Cattle	267	270	265†
Pigs	197	226	204
Sheep	1,315	1,289	1,251
Poultry.	3,339	3,350*	3,350*

* FAO estimate.
† Unofficial figure.

Source: FAO.

LIVESTOCK PRODUCTS
('000 metric tons)

	1999	2000	2001
Beef and veal.	7.7	7.0*	9.0*
Mutton and lamb.	4.4	4.5†	5.9†
Pig meat	9.2	9.0†	8.8†
Poultry meat†.	12	12	12
Cows' milk	208.7	200.0†	200.0†
Sheep's milk	39.1	40.0†	40.0†
Butter†	9.3	9.5	9.5
Cheese.	1.4	1.4†	1.4†
Poultry eggs	20.7†	20.5	20.6†
Honey	1.6	1.5†	1.6†
Wool: greasy	2.0	2.0†	2.0†
Cattle hides†	1.4	1.3	1.3
Sheepskins†	0.9	0.9	0.9

* Unofficial figure.
† FAO estimate(s).

Source: FAO.

Forestry

ROUNDWOOD REMOVALS
('000 cubic metres, excl. bark)

	1999	2000	2001
Sawlogs, veneer logs and logs for sleepers.	113	164	125
Pulpwood*.	5	5	5
Other industrial wood	5	8	10
Fuel wood	699	875	605
Total	**822**	**1,052**	**745**

* FAO estimates.

Source: FAO.

SAWNWOOD PRODUCTION
('000 cubic metres, incl. railway sleepers)

	1998	1999	2000
Coniferous (softwood)	6	10	8
Broadleaved (hardwood).	21	27	28
Total	**27**	**37**	**36**

Source: FAO.

Fishing

(metric tons, live weight)

	1998	1999	2000
Capture	131	135	208
Freshwater fishes	113	113	77
Trouts	18	22	131
Aquaculture	1,257	1,669	1,626
Common carp	135	215	238
Bleak	236	130	110
Other freshwater fishes . . .	258	210	330
European eel	72	60	50
Trouts	324	788	705
Huchen	214	244	173
White fishes	18	22	20
Total catch	1,388	1,804	1,834

Source: FAO, *Yearbook of Fishery Statistics*.

Mining

('000 metric tons)

	1997	1998	1999
Lignite	7,442.9	8,144.7	7,277.6
Copper concentrates* . . .	46.8	39.1	37.8
Lead concentrates*	19.5	16.8	12.3
Zinc concentrates*	15.5	14.3	10.2
Chromium concentrates* . . .	1.5	—	—
Gypsum (crude)	51.4	55.0	76.2

* Figures refer to the metal content of concentrates.

2000 ('000 metric tons): Zinc concentrates (metal content) 12.2 (Source: US Geological Survey).

Industry

SELECTED PRODUCTS

('000 metric tons, unless otherwise indicated)

	1997	1998	1999
Vegetable oils: refined	21.0	18.8	11.3
Flour	164.4	154.2	140.4
Refined sugar	35.2	40.4	43.0
Wine ('000 hectolitres)	957.6	1,227.1	911.9
Beer ('000 hectolitres)	600.1	578.2	651.9
Soft drinks ('000 hectolitres) . .	941.9	816.5	685.2
Cigarettes (million)	9,678	7,009	17,758
Wool yarn: pure and mixed . . .	4.4	3.3	0.5
Cotton yarn: pure and mixed . .	4.0	4.1	2.3
Woven cotton fabric (million sq metres)	9.8	13.7	6.1
Woven woollen fabrics (million sq metres)	5.4	5.2	0.8
Leather footwear ('000)	1,138	1,382	1,837
Sulphuric acid	105.0	100.8	87.8
Caustic soda (Sodium hydroxide) .	3.4	24.1	0.6
Motor spirit (petrol)	97.3	152.8	266.8
Gas-diesel (distillate fuel) oil . .	122.7	272.1	203.6
Residual fuel oils (Mazout) . . .	128.9	289.6	248.2
Cement	610.8	461.2	563.3
Ferro-alloys	85.9	106.7	77.5
Lead: unwrought	56.6	57.7	46.8
Zinc: unwrought	3.1	8.6	4.0
Refrigerators ('000)	11.7	4.0	—
Electric energy (million kWh) . .	6,718.8	7,036.5	6,821.7

Finance

CURRENCY AND EXCHANGE RATES

Monetary Units
100 deni = 1 new Macedonian denar.

Sterling, Dollar and Euro Equivalents (30 May 2003)
£1 sterling = 85.55 new denars;
US $1 = 51.92 new denars;
€1 = 61.38 new denars;
1,000 new denars = £11.69 = $19.26 = €16.29.

Average Exchange Rate (new denars per US $)
2000   65.904
2001   68.037
2002   64.354

Note: The Macedonian denar was introduced in April 1992, replacing (initially at par) the Yugoslav dinar. In May 1993 a new Macedonian denar, equivalent to 100 of the former units, was established as the sole legal tender.

BUDGET

(million new denars)*

Revenue†	2000	2001	2002
Tax revenue	51,115	47,564	54,387
Personal income tax	10,793	7,247	7,514
Profit tax	2,793	3,006	2,625
Sales tax	17,452	17,133	20,521
Excises	12,281	10,681	10,715
Import duties	7,733	6,111	6,335
Non-tax revenue	3,028	3,370	2,395
Capital revenue	424	462	576
Total	54,142	50,934	56,782

Expenditure	2000	2001	2002
Current expenditure	45,027	56,683	59,310
Wage, salaries and allowances .	16,285	16,407	18,339
Other purchases of goods and services	6,137	19,825	13,803
Refugees and poverty-related expenditure	1,482	582	389
Transfers	17,174	15,669	23,452
Interest payments	3,949	4,200	3,328
Capital expenditure	5,751	7,380	8,221
Enterprise sector reform . . .	344	239	1,389
Public administration reform . .	60	944	443
Statistical discrepancy	184	−49	827
Total‡	51,520	65,363	70,378

* Figures refer to transactions of the central Government, excluding the operations of extrabudgetary funds.
† Excluding foreign grants received (million new denars): 3,239 in 2000; 415 in 2001; 0 in 2002.
‡ Including transfers to reserves (million new denars): 154 in 2000; 166 in 2001; 187 in 2002.

Source: IMF, *Former Yugoslav Republic of Macedonia: Selected Issues and Statistical Appendix* (May 2003).

INTERNATIONAL RESERVES

(US $ million at 31 December)

	2000	2001	2002
Gold*	30.7	53.7	67.8
IMF special drawing rights . .	0.7	2.2	6.1
Foreign exchange	428.7	742.9	715.9
Total	460.1	798.8	789.8

* National valuation.

Source: IMF, *International Financial Statistics*.

MONEY SUPPLY
(million new denars at 31 December)

	2000	2001	2002
Currency outside banks	9,522	14,134	14,136
Demand deposits at deposit money banks	11,896	11,168	12,255
Total (incl. others)	22,392	n.a.	27,722

Source: IMF, *International Financial Statistics.*

COST OF LIVING
(Consumer price index; base: 1990=100)

	1999	2000	2001
Food (incl. beverages) . . .	38,216	38,061	40,685
Fuel and light	33,051	42,107	43,753
Clothing (incl. footwear). . .	38,492	37,607	38,094
Rent and water	99,307	108,046	120,253
All items (incl. others)	43,154	45,665	48,176

Source: ILO.

NATIONAL ACCOUNTS
(million new denars at current prices)

National Income and Product

	1994	1995	1996
Compensation of employees. . .	95,546	104,503	109,183
Operating surplus	9,218	17,337	18,587
Domestic factor incomes. .	104,764	121,840	127,770
Consumption of fixed capital . .	20,558	23,290	23,628
Gross domestic product (GDP) at factor cost	125,322	145,130	151,398
Indirect taxes.	25,315	27,781	28,235
Less Subsidies	4,228	3,390	3,190
GDP in purchasers' values . .	146,409	169,521	176,444
Factor income from abroad . . .	432	1,206	1,778
Less Factor income paid abroad .	2,462	2,283	2,966
Gross national product (GNP) .	144,379	168,445	175,256
Less Consumption of fixed capital .	20,558	23,290	23,628
National income in market prices	123,821	145,155	151,628
Other current transfers from abroad	17,711	16,320	18,997
Less Other current transfers paid abroad	7,819	7,494	10,518
National disposable income. .	133,713	153,981	160,106

Expenditure on the Gross Domestic Product

	1998	1999	2000
Government final consumption expenditure.	39,504	43,009	43,021
Private final consumption expenditure.	141,078	145,693	175,965
Increase in stocks	9,426	6,461	12,351
Gross fixed capital formation . .	33,982	34,710	38,332
Total domestic expenditure. .	223,990	229,873	269,669
Exports of goods and services . .	80,343	88,143	114,209
Less Imports of goods and services	109,355	109,007	147,489
GDP in purchasers' values . .	194,979	209,010	236,389
GDP at constant 1995 prices .	179,879	187,684	196,223

Gross Domestic Product by Economic Activity

	2000	2001	2002*
Agriculture, hunting and forestry	23,756	22,933	24,398
Fishing	14	24	25
Industry†	53,163	50,940	48,423
Construction	13,361	11,801	11,462
Wholesale and retail trade . .	25,402	26,076	29,077
Hotels and restaurants . . .	3,463	3,410	3,788
Transport and communications.	21,261	21,694	24,213
Financial services	7,342	7,420	8,445
Real estate and business services‡	17,931	18,935	18,804
Public administration and defence	14,333	14,445	15,249
Education	8,266	8,048	8,353
Health care and social work . .	8,987	8,690	9,119
Other community, social and personal services	5,217	5,552	5,699
Sub-total	202,496	199,968	207,055
Less Imputed bank service charge	5,153	4,738	5,393
GDP at basic prices. . . .	197,344	195,230	201,660
Taxes on products . . . . . } *Less* Subsidies on products . . }	39,045	38,611	37,230
GDP in purchasers' values .	236,389	233,841	238,890

* Estimates.
† Including mining, manufacturing and electricity. Figures exclude crafts and trades, listed separately.
‡ Including imputed rents of owner-occupied dwellings.

BALANCE OF PAYMENTS
(US $ million)

	1999	2000	2001
Exports of goods f.o.b.	1,192.1	1,317.1	1,153.5
Imports of goods f.o.b.	−1,602.2	−1,875.2	−1,574.9
Trade balance	−410.1	−558.0	−421.4
Exports of services	248.4	303.1	233.8
Imports of services	−323.8	−357.8	−336.7
Balance on goods and services.	−485.5	−612.7	−524.3
Other income received . . .	22.5	42.2	48.1
Other income paid	−66.3	−87.3	−88.6
Balance on goods, services and income.	−529.4	−657.8	−564.8
Current transfers received . . .	750.3	923.1	872.5
Current transfers paid	−330.2	−372.4	−632.0
Current balance	−109.3	−107.2	−324.3
Capital account (net)	4.4	0.3	1.3
Direct investment abroad . . .	—	0.6	−0.9
Direct investment from abroad. .	30.1	175.6	443.2
Portfolio investment assets . .	−0.4	—	3.2
Portfolio investment liabilities . .	0.5	−0.1	—
Other investment assets . . .	−81.0	−81.1	8.8
Other investment liabilities . .	240.4	290.2	−66.1
Net errors and omissions . . .	34.5	−46.0	25.9
Overall balance	119.2	232.3	91.1

Source: IMF, *International Financial Statistics.*

External Trade

PRINCIPAL COMMODITIES
(distribution by SITC, US $ million)

Imports c.i.f.	1999	2000	2001
Food and live animals	212.1	211.6	194.1
Meat and meat preparations	69.2	63.3	61.8
Cereals and cereal preparations	31.7	40.1	31.3
Crude materials (inedible) except fuels	56.5	54.5	47.1
Mineral fuels, lubricants, etc.	162.4	289.8	233.9
Petroleum, petroleum products etc.	135.1	255.7	192.4
Chemicals and related products	184.4	188.5	171.4
Basic manufactures	272.7	270.2	206.3
Iron and steel	46.9	57.2	34.8
Machinery and transport equipment	355.4	409.8	283.0
Machinery specialized for particular industries	62.6	63.6	51.4
General industrial machinery equipment and parts	53.4	51.7	44.0
Electrical machinery, apparatus etc. (excl. telecommunications and sound equipment)	48.5	61.7	47.6
Road vehicles and parts*	113.3	137.8	62.2
Miscellaneous manufactured articles	97.5	103.3	105.0
Total (incl. others)	1,776.2	2,093.9	1,687.6

* Data on parts exclude tyres, engines and electrical parts.

Exports f.o.b.	1999	2000	2001
Food and live animals	67.0	65.8	65.3
Vegetables and fruit	37.4	30.5	30.1
Beverages and tobacco	159.9	129.4	121.5
Beverages	46.9	44.3	46.5
Tobacco and tobacco manufactures	113.0	85.1	75.0
Crude materials (inedible) except fuels	50.8	49.0	37.4
Chemicals and related products	55.1	59.8	60.4
Basic manufactures	354.2	487.3	372.2
Textile yarn, fabrics, etc.	40.4	36.9	37.2
Iron and steel	182.4	289.4	195.4
Non-ferrous metals	73.5	90.4	73.4
Machinery and transport equipment	83.1	83.2	76.0
Electrical machinery, apparatus etc. (excl. telecommunications and sound equipment)	45.4	46.5	46.4
Miscellaneous manufactured articles	372.3	378.2	374.2
Clothing and accessories (excl. footwear)	320.3	317.9	319.4
Footwear	34.1	38.4	36.9
Total (incl. others)	1,191.3	1,322.6	1,155.1

PRINCIPAL TRADING PARTNERS
(US $ million)

Imports c.i.f.	1999	2000	2001
Argentina	3.3	8.0	7.5
Austria	44.5	41.7	43.9
Bulgaria	91.6	97.6	103.4
Croatia	62.2	57.9	46.4
France	40.4	38.6	30.3
Germany	245.8	253.3	213.4
Greece	164.5	201.6	184.4
Hungary	20.0	31.4	17.5
Italy	92.7	111.1	107.7
Japan	17.9	22.0	16.7
Netherlands	39.5	45.3	45.8
Poland	22.6	20.9	15.2
Russia	91.2	191.9	139.3
Slovenia	156.7	144.2	118.9
Sweden	25.1	31.7	18.8
Switzerland-Liechtenstein	22.7	28.2	24.0
Turkey	53.7	52.4	46.4
Ukraine	114.8	205.8	86.0
United Kingdom	33.6	32.0	26.2
USA	54.7	83.1	51.5
Yugoslavia	183.9	190.4	157.2
Total (incl. others)	1,776.2	2,093.9	1,687.6

Exports f.o.b.	1999	2000	2001
Albania	15.0	12.8	10.1
Belgium	17.2	23.9	7.4
Bosnia and Herzegovina	19.4	23.2	16.2
Bulgaria	26.1	26.9	20.7
Croatia	49.0	47.7	58.4
Cyprus	15.4	20.9	1.6
France	12.7	14.9	16.0
Germany	254.3	257.5	237.5
Greece	85.9	84.1	101.4
Italy	77.6	90.8	88.7
Netherlands	40.5	36.0	45.3
Russia	15.1	10.4	13.9
Slovenia	34.0	26.4	20.9
Spain	8.8	13.2	21.4
Switzerland-Liechtenstein	23.0	35.7	40.5
United Kingdom	27.5	27.2	26.6
USA	136.1	165.7	99.7
Yugoslavia	254.5	335.1	266.8
Total (incl. others)	1,191.3	1,322.6	1,687.6

Transport

RAILWAYS
(traffic)

	1999	2000	2001
Passenger journeys ('000)	1,662	1,862	1,344
Passenger-km (million)	150	176	133
Freight carried ('000 metric tons)	2,166	3,231	2,799
Freight net ton-km (million)	380	527	462

ROAD TRAFFIC
(motor vehicles in use at 31 December)

	1999	2000	2001
Motorcycles	3,506	3,729	4,483
Passenger cars	289,860	299,588	309,562
Buses	2,479	2,498	2,620
Commercial vehicles	20,011	20,763	21,727
Special vehicles	7,610	8,552	9,554
Tractors and working vehicles	1,777	1,417	1,560

INLAND WATERS
(lake transport)

	1998	1999	2000
Passengers carried ('000) . . .	15.0	9.5	10.3
Passenger-km ('000)	375	265	321

CIVIL AVIATION
(traffic on scheduled services)

	1997	1998	1999
Kilometres flown (million) . . .	5	5	7
Passengers carried ('000) . . .	250	295	488
Passenger-kilometres (million) . .	285	328	599
Total ton-kilometres (million) . .	27	31	57

Source: UN, *Statistical Yearbook*.

Tourism

TOURISTS BY COUNTRY OF ORIGIN*

	1999	2000	2001
Albania	21,248	24,747	6,419
Bulgaria	18,770	27,623	8,484
Croatia.	3,260	4,651	2,609
France	4,735	4,768	2,313
Germany	12,370	10,349	4,860
Greece	10,152	21,304	10,637
Italy	6,259	4,410	2,511
Netherlands	5,953	6,809	1,564
Russia	3,366	3,078	1,647
Slovenia	4,606	5,288	2,658
Turkey	5,038	6,700	3,101
Ukraine	622	6,347	3,405
United Kingdom	9,126	6,693	4,357
USA	13,900	15,312	7,099
Yugoslavia	29,346	35,522	16,429
Total (incl. others)	180,788	224,016	98,946

* Figures refer to arrivals from abroad at accommodation establishments.

Tourism receipts (US $ million): 15 in 1998; 40 in 1999; 37 (preliminary) in 2000 (Source: World Tourism Organization).

Communications Media

	1998	1999	2000
Television receivers ('000 in use) .	500	550	570
Telephones ('000 main lines in use)	439.2	471.0	516.0
Mobile cellular telephones ('000 subscribers).	30.1	47.7	115.7
Internet users ('000)	20.0	30.0	n.a.
Book production: titles*	738	733	727
Book production: copies ('000)* . .	2,101	1,858	968
Daily newspapers: titles . . .	4	5	6
Daily newspapers: average circulation ('000 copies) . . .	32,060	32,988	32,640
Non-daily newspapers: titles . .	26	29	33
Non-daily newspapers: average circulation ('000 copies) . . .	2,818	3,139	2,619

* Including pamphlets.

2001: Telephones ('000 main lines in use) 538.5; Mobile cellular telephones ('000 subscribers) 223.3; Internet users ('000) 70.0.

Radio receivers ('000 in use): 410 in 1997.

Facsimile machines (number in use): 3,000 in 1997.

Sources: mainly International Telecommunication Union; UNESCO, *Statistical Yearbook*; and UN, *Statistical Yearbook*.

Education

(2000/01, unless otherwise indicated)

	Institutions	Teachers	Students
Primary	1,010	13,329	246,490
Secondary	95	5,467	90,990
University level*	29	1,501	43,587
Other higher*	1	60	1,123

* 2001/02 figures.

Adult literacy rate (latest available): Males 97%; Females 91% (Source: UNICEF, *The State of the World's Children*).

Directory

The Constitution

The Constitution of the former Yugoslav republic of Macedonia was promulgated on 17 November 1991. The September 1995 interim agreement with Greece required guarantees that the Macedonian Constitution enshrined or implied no claim to territory beyond the country's existing borders. Some amendment of the 1991 document was thus necessitated. Following the framework agreement between the principal Macedonian and ethnic Albanian parties, reached in August 2001 (see Recent History), the Constitution was revised on 16 November to include 15 principal amendments. The following is a summary of the main provisions of the Constitution, which describes the country as the Republic of Macedonia:

GENERAL PROVISIONS

The Republic of Macedonia is a sovereign, independent, democratic state, where sovereignty derives from democratically elected citizens, referendums and other forms of expression. The citizens of the Republic of Macedonia are defined as the Macedonian people, as well as citizens living within its borders who are, *inter alia*, ethnic Albanians, ethnic Turks, ethnic Serbs and Vlach. The fundamental values defined by the Constitution are: basic human rights, free expression of nationality, the rule of law, a policy of pluralism and the free market, local self-government, entrepreneurship, social justice and solidarity, and respect for international law. State power is divided into legislative, executive and judicial power.

BASIC RIGHTS

The following rights and freedoms are guaranteed and protected in the Republic: the right to life, the inviolability of each person's physical and moral integrity, the right to freedom of speech, public appearance, public information, belief, conscience and religion, and the freedom to organize and belong to a trade union or a political party. All forms of communication and personal data are secret, and the home is inviolable.

The Macedonian language is the official language in use throughout the Republic of Macedonia. Any other language spoken by at least 20% of the population (such as Albanian) is also an official language. The official personal documentation of citizens speaking an official language other than Macedonian will also be issued in that language.

Military and semi-military associations, which do not belong to the Armed Forces of the Republic, are prohibited.

Any citizen who has reached the age of 18 years has the right to vote and to be elected to organs of government. The right to vote is equal, general and direct, and is realized in free elections by secret ballot. The proportional representation of each community must be assured in the public services and in all areas of public life. Citizens enjoy equal freedoms and rights without distinction as to sex, race, colour, national and social origin, political and religious conviction, material and social position. All religious creeds are separate from the State and are equal under the law. They are identified, *inter alia*, as the Macedonian Orthodox Church, the Islamic Community of Macedonia, the Roman Catholic Church, the Evangelic Methodist

Church and the Jewish Community. The members of all such communities are free to establish schools and other charitable institutions in the fields of culture, art and education.

GOVERNMENT

Legislature

Legislative power resides with the Sobranie (assembly), which consists of between 120 and 140 deputies elected for four years. The Sobranie adopts and amends the Constitution, enacts laws and gives interpretations thereof, adopts the budget of the Republic, decides on war and peace, chooses the Government, elects judges and releases them from duty. The Sobranie may decide, by a majority vote, to call a referendum on issues within its competence. A decision is adopted at a referendum if the majority of voters taking part in the ballot votes in favour of it and if more than one-half of the electorate participates in the vote. The Sobranie forms a Council for Inter-Ethnic Relations, comprising seven representatives from each of the ethnic Macedonian and Albanian communities, and five representatives of other nationalities living in the state. Parliamentary legislation on issues of culture and identity, particularly in the areas of language and education, can only be adopted if a majority of the deputies representing these communities votes in favour, in addition to the overall majority. Three of the nine judges of the Constitutional Court and three of the seven members of the Republican Judicial Council must also be elected by a double majority vote.

President

The President of the Republic represents the country and is responsible for ensuring respect for the Constitution and laws. He is Commander of the Armed Forces and appoints the Prime Minister. He appoints three members of the Security Council of the Republic (of which he is President) and ensures that the Council reflects the composition of the country's population.

Ministers

Executive power in the Republic resides with the Prime Minister and Ministers, who are not permitted concurrently to be deputies in the Sobranie. The Ministers are elected by the majority vote of all the deputies in the Sobranie. The Ministers implement laws and the state budget, and are responsible for foreign and diplomatic relations.

Judiciary

Judicial power is vested in the courts, and is autonomous and independent. The Supreme Court is the highest court. The election and dismissal of judges is proposed by the Republican Judicial Council.

Local Government

Legislation at local and municipal level is adopted by a two-thirds' majority vote of the total number of representatives. Legislation regulating such areas as local finance, elections and municipal boundaries must be adopted by a majority of the representatives representing the minority communities, as well as by an overall majority. In units of local self-government, citizens participate in decision-making on issues of local relevance directly, and through representatives.

OTHER PROVISIONS

The Sobranie elects an Ombudsman to ensure that constitutional rights are upheld, particularly the principles of non-discrimination and fair representation of the respective communities in public life. Revision of the Constitution must be approved by a two-thirds' majority in the Sobranie. Certain articles, such as the Preamble and those relating to local councils and minority rights, also require a majority of the vote by deputies from the minority communities.

The Government

President of the Republic: BORIS TRAJKOVSKI (inaugurated 15 December 1999).

GOVERNMENT
(July 2003)

A coalition of the Social Democratic Alliance of Macedonia (SDAM), the Liberal-Democratic Party (LDP) and the Democratic Union for Integration (DUI).

Prime Minister: BRANKO CRVENKOVSKI (SDAM).

Deputy Prime Ministers and Minister of Finance: PETAR GOSEV (LDP).

Deputy Prime Minister, with responsibility for Political Systems: MUSA XHAFERI (DUI).

Deputy Prime Minister, with responsibility for European Integration: RADMILA SEKERINSKA (SDAM).

Minister of Defence: VLADO BUCHKOVSKI (SDAM).

Minister of Internal Affairs: HARI KOSTOVI (SDAM).

Minister of Justice: ISMAIL DARDHISHTA (DUI).

Minister of Foreign Affairs: ILINKA MITREVA (SDAM).

Minister of the Economy: ILIJA FILIPOVSKI (SDAM).

Minister of Transport and Communications: MILAIM AJDINI (DUI).

Minister of Agriculture, Forestry and Water Resources: SLAVKO PETROV (LDP).

Minister of Labour and Social Welfare: JOVAN MANASIEVSKI (LDP).

Minister of Education and Science: AZIZ POLLOZHANI (DUI).

Minister of Culture: BLAGOJA STEFANOVSKI (SDAM).

Minister of Health: REXHEP SELMANI (DUI).

Minister of Local Self-Government: ALEKSANDAR GESTAKOVSKI (SDAM).

Minister of the Environment and Urban Planning: LJUBOMIR JANEVI (SDAM).

Minister without Portfolio: VLADO POPOVSKI (LDP).

MINISTRIES

Office of the President: 1000 Skopje, 11 Oktomvri bb; tel. (2) 3113318; fax (2) 3112147; internet www.president.gov.mk.

Office of the Prime Minister: 1000 Skopje, Ilindenska bb; tel. (2) 3115455; fax (2) 3112561; e-mail office@primeminister.gov.mk; internet www.primeminister.gov.mk.

Ministry of Agriculture, Forestry and Water Resources: 1000 Skopje, Leninova 2; tel. (2) 3134477; fax (2) 3239429; internet www.mzsv.gov.mk.

Ministry of Culture: 1000 Skopje, Ilindenska bb; tel. (2) 3118022; fax (2) 3127112; internet www.gov.mk/kultura.

Ministry of Defence: 1000 Skopje, Orce Nikolov bb; tel. and fax (2) 3119577; fax (2) 3227835; e-mail info@morm.gov.mk; internet www.morm.gov.mk.

Ministry of the Economy: 1000 Skopje, Bote Bocevski 9; tel. (2) 384470; fax (2) 384472; e-mail ms@mt.net.mk; internet www.ms.gov.mk.

Ministry of Education and Science: 1000 Skopje, Dimitrija Čupovski 9; tel. (2) 3117896; fax (2) 3118414; e-mail mofk@mofk.gov.mk; internet www.mofk.gov.mk.

Ministry of the Environment and Urban Planning: 1000 Skopje, ul. Drezdenska 52; tel. (2) 3366930; fax (2) 3366931; e-mail info@moe.gov.mk; internet www.moe.gov.mk.

Ministry of Finance: 1000 Skopje, Dame Gruev 14; tel. (2) 3117288; fax (2) 3117280; internet www.finance.gov.mk.

Ministry of Foreign Affairs: 1000 Skopje, Dame Gruev 6; tel. (2) 3115266; fax (2) 3115790; e-mail mailmnr@mnr.gov.mk; internet www.mnr.gov.mk.

Ministry of Health: 1000 Skopje, Vodnjanska bb; tel. (2) 3147147; fax (2) 3113014; internet www.zdravstvo.com.mk.

Ministry of Internal Affairs: 1000 Skopje, Dimitar Mirchev bb; tel. (2) 3117222; fax (2) 3112468.

Ministry of Justice: 1000 Skopje, Dimitrija Čupovski 9; tel. (2) 3117277; fax (2) 3226975; internet www.covekovi-prava.gov.mk.

Ministry of Labour and Social Welfare: 1000 Skopje, Dame Gruev 14; tel. (2) 3117787; fax (2) 3118242; e-mail mtsp@mt.net.mk; internet www.mtsp.gov.mk.

Ministry of Local Self-Government: 1000 Skopje, Dimitrija Čupovski 9; tel. (2) 3106302; fax (2) 3106303; internet www.mls.gov.mk.

Ministry of Sports and Youth: 1000 Skopje, Jurij Gagarin 15; tel. (2) 3393408; fax (2) 3384472.

Ministry of Transport and Communications: 1000 Skopje, plostad Crvena skopska opstina 4; tel. (2) 3126228; fax (2) 3123292.

President and Legislature

PRESIDENT

Presidential Election, First Ballot, 31 October 1999

Candidate	% of votes
Tito Petkovski (SDAM)	33.2
Boris Trajkovski (IMRO—DPMNU)*	20.6
Vasil Tupurkovski (DA)*	16.0
Muharem Nexipi (DPA)*	14.8
Stojan Andov (LDP)	11.2
Muhamet Halili (PDP)	4.2
Total	**100.0†**

*The IMRO—DPMNU, the DPA and the DA constituted the 'For Changes' alliance.
† Including invalid and spoilt votes.

Second Ballot, 14 November 1999*

Candidate	% of votes†
Boris Trajkovski (IMRO—DPMNU)	52.9
Tito Petkovski (SDAM)	45.9
Total	**100.0**

*A further partial round was conducted on 5 December 1999.
† Including invalid and spoilt votes.

SOBRANIE
(Assembly)

President: NIKOLA POPOVSKI, 1000 Skopje, 11 Oktomvri bb; tel. (2) 3112255; fax (2) 3237947; e-mail sgjorgiøsembly.gov.mk; internet www.sobranie.mk.

General Election, 15 September 2002*

Party	Votes	% of votes	Seats
Together for Macedonia†	494,744	40.46	60
IMRO—DPMNU‡	298,404	24.41	33
DUI	114,913	11.85	16
DPA	63,695	5.21	7
PDP	28,397	2.32	2
NDP	26,237	2.15	1
SPM	25,976	2.12	1
Others	140,345	11.48	—
Total	**1,222,711**	**100.00**	**120**

*Of the 120 members of the Assembly, 85 were elected in single-member constituencies. The remaining 35 were elected by a national system of proportional representation, in which voters chose from lists of candidates submitted by individual parties or by groups of parties.
† Electoral coalition of 10 parties, led by the SDAM.
‡ The IMRO—DPMNU contested the elections in alliance with the LPM.

Local Government

After some debate the Sobranje finalized new arrangements for local government on 12 September 1996. Macedonia was to comprise 123 administrative-territorial units or municipalities, of which seven constituted the city of Skopje. The new system made few concessions to the demands among ethnic Albanians for a degree of autonomy in those areas where they formed a majority, largely in the north-west of the country. Local elections in the new municipalities were held on 17 November. Of the 123 elected mayors, the majority (55) represented the Social Democratic Alliance of Macedonia (SDAM), although its candidates were not elected in Skopje, Prilep or Ohrid. Further local government elections took place in two rounds on 10 and 24 September 2000, amid reports of numerous violent incidents. A further round of voting subsequently took place, as a result of the electoral irregularities. It was announced at the end of the month that the parties belonging to the government coalition had secured 75 of the 123 municipalities.

Political Organizations

Democratic Alliance: Skopje; f. 2000; Chair. ASLLAN SELMANI.

Democratic Alliance of Serbs in Macedonia (Demokratski Savez Srba u Makedoniji—DSSM): Skopje; f. 1994; Chair. BORIVOJE RISTIĆ.

Democratic Alternative (DA) (Demokratska Alternativa): c/o Sobranje, 1000 Skopje, 11 Oktomvri bb; tel. (2) 3062713; fax (2) 3063089; internet www.da.org.mk; f. 1998; formed an electoral alliance with the IMRO—DPMNU; Chair. VASIL TUPURKOVSKI.

Democratic League—Liberal Party: Skopje, Gale Hristov k. 3-6; tel. (2) 3263523; Leader XHEMIL IDRIZI.

Democratic Muslim Party: Skopje; f. 2001; Leader TEFIK KADRI.

Democratic Party of Albanians (DPA): Tetovo, Maršal Tito 2; tel. (44) 31534; f. July 1997 by a merger of the Party of Democratic Prosperity of Albanians in Macedonia (f. 1994) and the National Democratic Party (f. 1990); officially registered in July 2002; absorbed the National Democratic Party (f. 2001) and the Republican Party of Albanians (f. 2002) in June 2003; Chair. ARBEN XHAFERI.

Democratic Party of Serbs in Macedonia (DPSM): Skopje, 27 Mart 11; tel. (2) 3254274; f. 1996; Pres. DRAGISA MILETIĆ.

Democratic Party of Turks in Macedonia (DPTM) (Demokratska Partija na Turcite va Makedonija): Skopje, bul. Krste Misirkova 67; tel. (2) 3114696; Leader ERDOGAN SARACH.

Democratic Party of Yugoslavs of Macedonia (DPYM) (Demokratska Partija Jugoslovena Makedonije—DPJM): Skopje; f. 1993; Chair. ZIVKO LEKOSKI; Gen. Sec. BOGDAN MICKOSKI.

Democratic Union for Integration (DUI) (Demokratska Unija za Integracija): Tetovo; f. 2002; ethnic Albanian, dominated by former mems of rebel National Liberation Army; Chair. ALI AHMETI.

Front for Albanian National Unification (FANU): emerged in 2003 as political wing of rebel Albanian National Army; supports creation of 'greater Albania'; Sec.-Gen. ALBAN VJOSA.

Internal Macedonian Revolutionary Organization ('Real') ('Real' IMRO) (Vnatrešno-Makedonska Revolucionerna Organizacija—VMRO): Skopje; f. 2000 by fmr mems of the IMRO—DPMNU; centre-right; Chair. BORIS ZMEJKOVSKI.

Internal Macedonian Revolutionary Organization—Democratic Party for Macedonian National Unity (IMRO—DPMNU) (Vnatrešno-Makedonska Revolucionerna Organizacija—Demokratska Partija za Makedonsko Nacionalno Edinstvo—VMRO—DPMNE): 1000 Skopje, Petar Drapshin br. 36; tel. (2) 3111441; fax (2) 3211586; e-mail info@vmro-dpmne.org.mk; internet www.vmro-dpmne.org.mk; nationalist; formed an electoral alliance with the Democratic Alternative; Pres. NIKOLA GRUEVSKI; Sec. DEN DONCEV.

Liberal-Democratic Party (LDP) (Liberalno-Demokratska Partija): Skopje, Ilindenska bb; tel. and fax (2) 3116106; internet www.ldp.org.mk; f. 1996 by a merger of the Liberal Party and the Democratic Party; Leader RISTO GUSTEROV.

Liberal Party of Macedonia (LPM) (Liberalna Partija na Makedonije): Skopje; Leader STOJAN ANDOV.

Macedonian Democratic Party: Tetovo, Bazaar 3; tel. (44) 20826; fax (44) 24860; Leader TOMISLAV STOJANOVSKI.

Movement for all-Macedonian Action (MAAK)—Conservative Party: Skopje, Maksim Gorki 18/111; tel. (2) 116540; f. 1996; right-wing nationalist; Leader STRASO ANGELOVSKI.

Party of Democratic Action—Islamic Way (Stranka Demokratske Akcije—Islamski Put): Tetovo, Ilindenska 191; tel. (44) 32113; Leader MAZLAM KENAN.

Party for Democratic Prosperity (PDP) (Partija za Demokratski Prosperitet): Tetovo, Karaorman 62; tel. (44) 25709; f. 1990; split 1994; predominantly ethnic Albanian and Muslim party; Chair. ABDURAHMAN ALITI; Sec.-Gen. NASER ZYBERI.

Party for the Full Emancipation of Romanies in Macedonia (Demokratska Progresivna Partija na Romite od Makedonija): Skopje, Shuto Orizari bb; tel. (2) 3612726; Leader FAIK ABDIĆ.

Social Democratic Alliance of Macedonia (SDAM) (Socijaldemokratski Sojuz na Makedonije—SDSM): 1000 Skopje, Bihačka 8; tel. (2) 3135380; fax (2) 3120462; e-mail contact@sdsm.org.mk; internet www.sdsm.org.mk; f. 1943; name changed from League of Communists—Party of Democratic Reform in 1991; led alliance, Together for Macedonia, which was elected to govt in Sept. 2002; Chair. BRANKO CRVENKOVSKI; Gen. Sec. GEORGI SPASOV.

Social Democratic Party of Macedonia (Socijaldemokratska Partija na Makedonije): Skopje, bul. Kliment Ohridski 54; tel. and fax (2) 3223681; Leader BRANKO JANEVSKI.

Socialist Party of Macedonia (SPM) (Socijalistiska Partija na Makedonije): 1000 Skopje, 11 Oktomvri 17; tel. (2) 3228015; fax (2) 3220075; f. 1990; left-wing; Chair. LJUBISAV IVANOV; Vice-Chair. BLAGOJE FILIPOVSKI.

Union of Ethnic Croats: Skopje; f. 1996; Pres. Marija Damja-novska.

Union of Roma in Macedonia (Sojuz na Romite od Makedonija): Skopje.

Diplomatic Representation

EMBASSIES IN THE FORMER YUGOSLAV REPUBLIC OF MACEDONIA

Albania: 1000 Skopje, Hristijan Todorovski-Karposh 94; tel. (2) 2614636; fax (2) 2614200; e-mail ambshquip@lotus.mpt.com.mk; Ambassador Vladimir Prelja.

Austria: 1000 Skopje, Vasil Stefanovski 7; tel. (2) 3109550; fax (2) 3130237; e-mail austramb@unet.com.mk; Ambassador Harald W. Kotschy.

Bulgaria: 1000 Skopje, Zlatko Shnaider 3; tel. (2) 3229444; fax (2) 3116139; e-mail bgemb@unet.com.mk; Ambassador Aleksandar Yordanov.

Canada: 1000 Skopje, Mitropolit Teodosie Gologanov 104, POB 68; tel. (2) 3125228; fax (2) 3122681; e-mail dfaitmk@unet.com.mk; Ambassador Raphael Girard.

China, People's Republic: 1000 Skopje; tel. (2) 3134392; fax (2) 3133405; Ambassador Zhang Wanxue.

Croatia: 1000 Skopje, Mitropolit Teodosij Gologanov 59; tel. (2) 3127350; fax (2) 3127417; e-mail velhrskp@mpt.com.mk; Ambassador Vitomir Miro Lasić.

France: 1000 Skopje, Salvador Aljende 73; tel. (2) 3118749; fax (2) 3117760; e-mail franamba@nic.mpt.com.mk; Ambassador Jean-François Terral.

Germany: 1000 Skopje, Dimitrija Čupovski 26; tel. (2) 3110507; fax (2) 3117713; e-mail dtboskop@unet.com.mk; internet www.deutschebotschaft-skopje.com.mk; Ambassador Dr Irene Hinrichsen.

Hungary: 1000 Skopje, Mirka Ginova 27; tel. (2) 3063423; fax (2) 3063070; Ambassador József Szász.

Iran: 1000 Skopje, Gjorgji Peskov 6; tel. (2) 3118020; fax (2) 3118502; e-mail iri-emb@unet.cpm.mk; Chargé d'affaires a.i. Moslem Saberi.

Italy: 1000 Skopje, 8 Udarna brig. 22; tel. (2) 3117430; fax (2) 3117087; internet www.ambasciata.org.mk; Ambassador Dr Antonio Tarelli.

Netherlands: 1000 Skopje, Leninova 69–71; tel. (2) 3129319; fax (2) 3129309; Ambassador Johannes Hendricus Maria Wolfs.

Norway: 1000 Skopje, Mitropolit Teodosie Gologanov 59/2a; tel. (2) 3129165; fax (2) 3111138; Chargé d'affaires a.i. Vibeke Lilloe.

Poland: 1000 Skopje, Djuro Djakovic 50; tel. and fax (2) 3119744; e-mail ambpol@unet.com.mk; Chargé d'affaires a.i. Andrzej Dobrzyński.

Romania: 1000 Skopje, Londonska 11a; tel. (2) 3070144; fax (2) 3061130; e-mail romanamb@rsc.com.mk; Chargé d'affaires Nicolae Mares.

Russia: 1000 Skopje, Pirinska 44; tel. (2) 3117160; fax (2) 3117808; e-mail rusembas@mol.com.mk; f. 1994; Ambassador Asatur Agaron.

Serbia and Montenegro: 1000 Skopje, Pitu Guli 8; tel. (2) 3129298; fax (2) 3129427; Ambassador Biserka Matić Spasojević.

Slovenia: 1000 Skopje, Vodnjanska 42; tel. (2) 3178730; fax (2) 3176631; Ambassador Mitja Štrukelj.

Switzerland: Skopje 1000, Naroden Front 19; tel. (2) 3128300; fax (2) 3116205; Ambassador Stefan Mellen.

Turkey: 1000 Skopje, Slavej Planina bb; tel. (2) 3113270; fax (2) 3117024; e-mail turkish@mol.com.mk; Ambassador Mehmet Taser.

United Kingdom: 1000 Skopje, Dimitrija Čupovski 26, 4th Floor; tel. (2) 3299299; fax (2) 3299236; e-mail beskopje@mt.net.com; internet www.britishembassy.org.mk; Ambassador George Edgar.

USA: 1000 Skopje, Ilindenska bb; tel. (2) 3116180; fax (2) 3118105; e-mail usis@usemb-skopje.mpt.com.mk; internet usembassy.mpt.com.mk; Ambassador Lawrence Butler.

Judicial System

The FYRM has 27 Courts of First Instance and three Courts of Appeal. The Republican Judicial Council, which comprises seven members elected by the Sobranie for a term of six years, proposes the election or dismissal of judges to the Sobranie. The Constitutional Court, comprising nine judges elected by the Sobranie with a mandate of nine years, is responsible for the protection of constitutional and legal rights, and ensures that there is no conflict in the exercise of legislative, executive and judicial powers. The Supreme Court is the highest court in the country, and guarantees the equal administration of legislation by all courts

Constitutional Court of the Republic of Macedonia: 1000 Skopje, 12 Udarna brig. 2; tel. (2) 3165153; fax (2) 3119355; e-mail usud@usud.gov.mk; Pres. Dr Todor Džunov.

Supreme Court: 1000 Skopje, Krste Misirkova bb; tel. (2) 3234064; fax (2) 3237538; Pres. Simeon Gelevski.

Republican Judicial Council: 1000 Skopje, Lazar Lichenoski 13; tel. (2) 3213084; fax (2) 3116458; Pres. Tihomir Velkovski.

Office of the Public Prosecutor: 1000 Skopje, Krste Misirkova bb; tel. (2) 3229314; Public Prosecutor Aleksandr Prcevski.

Religion

Most ethnic Macedonians are adherents of the Eastern Orthodox Church, and since 1967 there has been an autocephalous Macedonian Orthodox Church. However, the Serbian Orthodox Church refuses to recognize it, and has persuaded the Ecumenical Patriarch and other Orthodox Churches not to do so either. There are some adherents of other Orthodox rites in the country. Those Macedonian (and Bulgarian) Slavs who converted to Islam during the Ottoman era are known as Pomaks and are included as an ethnic group of Muslims. The substantial Albanian population is mostly Muslim (mainly Sunni, but some adherents of a Dervish sect); there are a few Roman Catholic Christians and a small Jewish community.

CHRISTIANITY

Macedonian Orthodox Church: Skopje, Betovenova bb, POB 69; tel. (2) 3230697; fax (2) 3230685; Metropolitan See of Ohrid revived in 1958; autocephaly declared 1967; 1.5m. mems; comprises seven bishoprics in Macedonia and three abroad; Head of Church and Archbishop of Ohrid and Macedonia Metropolitan Archbishop Mihail Ríć (of Skopje).

The Roman Catholic Church

The diocese of Skopje, suffragan to the archdiocese of Vrhbosna (Bosnia and Herzegovina), covers most of the FYRM. The Bishop is also Apostolic Exarch for Catholics of the Byzantine Rite in the FYRM. At 31 December 2001 there were an estimated 4,000 adherents of the Latin Rite in the diocese, and the country had 11,000 adherents of the Byzantine Rite.

Bishop of Skopje: Rt Rev. Joakim Herbut, Biskupski Ordinarijat, 1000 Skopje, Risto Šiškov 31; tel. and fax (2) 3164123; e-mail katbiskupija@mt.net.mk.

ISLAM

Islamic Community of Macedonia: Skopje, Chairska 52; tel. (2) 3117530; fax (2) 3117883; e-mail bim@bim.org.mk; internet www.bim.org.mk; formerly headquarters of the Skopje Region, one of the four administrative divisions of the Yugoslav Muslims; Leader Hadži Arif Emini.

JUDAISM

Jewish Community: 1000 Skopje, Borka Taleski 24.

The Press

In 2000 a total of 39 newspapers and 116 magazines were published in the FYRM.

PRINCIPAL DAILY NEWSPAPERS

Bechuk: 1000 Skopje, MOST Ltd, Dame Gruev 5; tel. (2) 3117377; fax (2) 3118638; e-mail vesnik@utrinski.com.mk; internet www.int.utrinskivesnik.com.mk; Dir Erol Rizaov; Editor-in-Chief Branko Trickovski.

Denes: 1000 Skopje, M.ºH. Jasmin 50; tel. (2) 3110239; fax (2) 3110150; e-mail denes@unet.com.mk; internet www.denes.com.mk; Dir Georgi Ajanovski; Editor Nik Denes.

Dnevnik: 1000 Skopje, Teodosij Gologanov 28; tel. (2) 3297555; fax (2) 3297554; e-mail dnevnik@dnevnik.com.mk; internet www.dnevnik.com.mk; independent; Editor-in-Chief Branko Geroski.

Flaka e vëllazërimit (Flame of Brotherhood): 1000 Skopje, Mito Hadživasilev bb; tel. (2) 3112025; fax (2) 3224829; f. 1945; re-launched 1994; Albanian-language newspaper; Editor-in-Chief ABDULHADI ZULFIQARI; circ. 4,000.

Nova Makedonija: 1000 Skopje, Mito Hadživasilev bb; tel. (2) 3237455; fax (2) 3118238; internet www.novamakedonija.com.mk; f. 1944; morning; in Macedonian; Editor-in-Chief GEORGI AJANOVSKI; circ. 25,000.

Večer: 1000 Skopje, Mito Hadživasilev bb; tel. (2) 3111537; fax (2) 3238327; internet www.vecer.com.mk; f. 1963; evening; in Macedonian; Editor-in-Chief STOJAN NASEV; circ. 29,200.

PERIODICALS

Delo: Skopje, Petar Drapshin 26; tel. (2) 3231949; fax (2) 3115748; f. 1993; weekly; nationalist; Editor-in-Chief BRATISLAV TASKOVSKI.

Fokus: Skopje, Železniča 53; tel. (2) 3111327; fax (2) 3111685; weekly; independent; Editor-in-Chief NIKOLA MLADENOV.

Macedonian Times: 1000 Skopje, Vasil Gorgov 39; tel. and fax (2) 3121182; e-mail mian@mian.com.mk; internet www.unet.com.mk/mian; f. 1994; monthly; politics and current affairs; English; Editor-in-Chief JOVAN PAVLOSKI.

Puls: 1000 Skopje, Mito Hadživasilev bb; tel. (2) 3117124; fax (2) 3118024; weekly; Editor-in-Chief VASIL MICKOVSKI.

Roma Times: Skopje; e-mail mail@dostae.net.mk; internet www.dostae.net.mk/mk/press_mk_roma.htm; f. 2001; 3 a week; circ. 3,000.

Sport Magazine: 1000 Skopje, Mito Hadživasilev Jasmin bb; tel. and fax (2) 3116254; e-mail lav@unet.com.mk; f. 1991; weekly; circ. 6,000.

Trudbenik: Skopje, Udarna brigada 12; weekly; organ of Macedonian Trade Unions; Editor SIMO IVANOVSKI.

NEWS AGENCIES

Macedonian Information Agency: 1000 Skopje, Bojmija K/2; tel. (2) 2461600; fax (2) 2464048; e-mail mia@mia.com.mk; internet www.mia.com.mk; f. 1992; 24-hr news service in Macedonian, Albanian and English; Exec. Dir ZIVKO GEORGIEVSKI.

Makfax: 1000 Skopje, 11 Oktomvri 36/3, POB 738; tel. (2) 3110125; fax (2) 3110184; e-mail makfax@unet.com.mk; internet www.makfax.com.mk; f. 1993; independent; provides daily regional news service; Macedonian, Albanian and English.

PRESS ASSOCIATION

Journalists' Association of Macedonia: 1000 Skopje, Gradskizid 13, POB 498; tel. and fax (2) 3116447; Pres. STOJAN NASEV.

Publishers

Detska radost/Nova Makedonija: 1000 Skopje, Mito Hadživasilev Jasmin bb; tel. (2) 3213059; fax (2) 3225830; f. 1944; children's books; Dir KIRIL DONEV.

Kultura: 1000 Skopje, Sv. Kliment Ohridski 68A; tel. (2) 3111332; fax (2) 3228608; e-mail ipkultura@simt.com.mk; f. 1945; history, philosophy, art, poetry, children's literature and fiction; in Macedonian; Dir DIMITAR BAŠEVSKI.

Kulturen Život: 1000 Skopje, Ruzveltova 6; tel. (2) 3239134; f. 1971; Editor LJUBICA ARSOVSKA.

Makedonska kniga: 1000 Skopje, 11 Oktomvri; tel. (2) 3224055; fax (2) 3236951; f. 1947; arts, non-fiction, novels, children's books; Dir SANDE STOJČEVSKI.

Matica Makedonska: 1000 Skopje, ul. Maršal Tito br. 43/1-6; tel. (2) 3230358; fax (2) 3229244; f. 1991; Dir RADE SILJAN.

Metaforum: 1000 Skopje, Goce Delčev 6; tel. (2) 3114890; fax (2) 3115634; f. 1993; Dir RUŽICA BILKO.

Misla: 1000 Skopje, Partizanski odredi 1; tel. (2) 3221844; fax (2) 3118439; f. 1966; modern and classic Macedonian and translated literature; Pres. ZLATA BUNTESLEA.

Naša kniga: 1000 Skopje, Maksim Gorki 21, POB 132; tel. (2) 3228066; fax (2) 3116872; f. 1948; Dir STOJAN LEKOVSKI.

Nova Makedonija: 1000 Skopje, Mito Hadživasilev Jasmin bb; tel. (2) 3116366; fax (2) 3118238; newspapers, general publishing; Chief Exec. SLOBODAN CASULE; Editor-in-Chief NOVE CVETANOVSKI.

Prosvetno delo: 1000 Skopje, Dimitrija Čupovski 15; tel. (2) 3117255; fax (2) 3225434; f. 1945; works of domestic writers and textbooks in Macedonian for elementary, professional and high schools; fiction and scientific works; Dir Dr KRSTE ANGELOVSKI.

Tabernakul: 1000 Skopje, POB 251, Mihail Cokov; tel. and fax (2) 3115329; e-mail tabervt@mol.com.mk; internet www.tabernakul.com; f. 1989; Dir CVETAN VRAŽIVIRSKI.

Broadcasting and Communications

TELECOMMUNICATIONS

Makedonski Telekomunikacii (MT): 1000 Skopje, Direkcija, Orce Nikolov bb; tel. (2) 3141141; fax (2) 3126244; e-mail info@mpt.com.mk; internet www.mt.com.mk; 51% of shares divested to the Matáv Hungarian Telecommunications Co in Jan. 2001; Chief Exec. DAN DONCEV.

BROADCASTING

Radio

Makedonska Radio-Televizija (MRT): 1000 Skopje, Goce Delčev bb; tel. (2) 3236839; fax (2) 3111821; e-mail mkrtvcor@mt.com.mk; internet www.mkrtv.com.mk; f. 1944; fmrly Radiotelevizija Skopje, name changed 1991; 3 radio channels; broadcasts in Macedonian, Albanian, Turkish, Serb, Roma and Vlach; Dir-Gen. GORDANA STOSIĆ; Dir of Radio GRIGORI POPOVSKI.

Antenna 5 Radio: 1000 Skopje, Tetovska 35; tel. (2) 3111911; fax (2) 3113281; e-mail mail@antenna5.com.mk; internet www.antenna5.com.mk; 12 transmitters broadcast to 80% of the country.

Television

Makedonska Radio-Televizija (MRT): 1000 Skopje, Goce Delčev bb; tel. (2) 3112200; fax (2) 3111821; e-mail gstosic@unet.com.mk; internet www.mkrtv.com.mk; f. 1964; fmrly Radiotelevizija Skopje, name changed 1991; state broadcasting co; 3 television services; broadcasts in Macedonian, Albanian, Turkish, Serb, Roma and Vlach; Dir-Gen. GORDANA SIOSIE; Dir of Television LJUBČO TOZIJA.

A1 Television: 1000 Skopje, Pero Nakov bb; tel. (2) 2550350; fax (2) 2551970; e-mail altv@a1.com.mk; internet www.a1.com.mk; Gen. Man. DARKO PERUSEVSKI.

SITEL Television: Skopje; tel. (2) 3116566; fax (2) 3114898; e-mail sitel@unet.com.mk; internet www.sitel.com.mk; Gen. Man. GOVAN IVANOVSKI.

Finance

(cap. = capital; res = reserves; dep. = deposits; m. = million; amounts in new Macedonian denars, unless otherwise indicated; brs = branches)

BANKS

At the end of September 2001 there were 20 commercial banks in the FYRM; of these, the two largest banks (Stopanska Banka and Komercijalna Banka) accounted for more than one-half of the banking system assets and about two-thirds of the deposits. At that time a total of six banks had majority foreign shareholders. The privatization of the banking sector was completed in early 2000.

National Bank

Narodna Banka na Makedonija (National Bank of the Republic of Macedonia): 1000 Skopje, POB 401, Kompleks banki bb; tel. (2) 3112177; fax (2) 3113481; e-mail nbmdevre@nlc.mpt.com.mk; internet www.nbrm.gov.mk; central bank and bank of issue; total assets 112.1m. (Dec. 1999); Gov. LJUBE TRPEVSKI.

Selected Banks

Alpha Banka a.d.—Skopje: 1000 Skopje, Dame Gruev 1, POB 564; tel. (2) 3116433; fax (2) 3116830; e-mail kreditnabank@mt.net.mk; f. 1993 as Kreditna Banka a.d.; name changed as above in 2002; cap. 185.8m., res 601.5m., dep. 1,151.6m. (Dec. 2002); Chair. SPYROS FILARETOS; 3 brs.

Balkanska Banka: 1000 Skopje, Maksim Gorki 6; tel. (2) 3286100; fax (2) 3130448; e-mail balkbank@mt.net.mk; internet www.bbs.com.mk; f. 1993; cap. 292.3m., res 309.9m., dep. 1,418.4m. (Dec. 2001); Gen. Man. KIRIL PENDEV.

Eksport-Import Banka a.d.—Skopje: 91000 Skopje, DTC Paloma Bjanka, Dame Gruev 16; tel. (2) 3133411; fax (2) 3112744; e-mail info@eximb.com.mk; internet www.eximb.com.mk; f. 1994; cap. 601.4m., res 162.6m., dep. 1,645.3m. (Dec. 2001); Pres. METODIJA SMILENSKI.

Izvozna I. Kreditna Banka a.d.: 1000 Skopje, Partizanski odredi 3, POB 421; tel. (2) 3129147; fax (2) 3122393; e-mail ikbanka@

ikbanka.com.mk; internet www.ikbanka.com.mk; f. 1993; cap. 408.3m., res 276.2m., dep. 883.0m. (Dec. 2002); Pres. PANCE MANCEVSKI.

Komercijalna Banka a.d.—Skopje: 1000 Skopje, Kej Dimitar Vlahov 4; tel. (2) 3107107; fax (2) 3111780; e-mail contact@kb.com .mk; internet www.kb.com.mk; f. 1955 as Komunalna Banka; name changed as above in 1991; cap. 2,137.9m., res 950.1m., dep. 22,406.1m. (Dec. 2001); Pres. LJUBOMIR MIHAJLOVIĆ; 33 brs.

Makedonska Banka a.d.—Skopje: 91000 Skopje, Blok 12/2, bul. VMRO br. 3, POB 505; tel. (2) 3117111; fax (2) 3117191; e-mail info@ makbanka.com.mk; internet www.makbanka.com; f. 1972; name changed in 1994; cap. 239.6m., res 515.2m., dep. 1,813.2m. (Dec. 2000); Pres. ALEKSANDAR NIKOLOVSKI.

Ohridska Banka a.d.—Ohrid: 6000 Ohrid, Makedonski Prosvetiteli 19; tel. (46) 206600; fax (46) 254130; internet www.ob.com.mk; cap. 636.8m., res 136.7m., dep. 2,929.4m. (Dec. 2002); Pres. NAUM HADZILEGA; Chair. VANGEL NIKOLOSKI.

Stopanska Banka a.d.—Bitola: 97000 Bitola, Dobrivoe Radosavljević 21; tel. (47) 37048; fax (47) 223876; e-mail stbbt@mt.net .mk; f. 1948 as Komunalna Banka Bitola; name changed as above in 1995; cap. 844.6m., res 193.0m., dep. 2,094.5m. (Dec. 2001); Pres. VANGEL TORKOV.

Stopanska Banka a.d.—Skopje: 1000 Skopje, 11 Oktomvri 7; tel. (2) 3295295; fax (2) 3114503; e-mail sbank@stb.com.mk; internet www.stb.com.mk; f. 1944; cap. 3,602.2m., res 1.1m., dep. 18,116.7m. (Dec. 2002); privatized in April 2000; Chair. THEODOROS KARATZAS; 23 brs.

Teteks—Kreditna Bank a.d.: 1000 Skopje, POB 198; tel. (2) 3119206; fax (2) 3222370; e-mail tebank@mol.com.mk; f. 1993 as Teteks Banka; name changed as above, following merger with Kreditna Banka a.d. Bitola; cap. 272.9m., res 2.2m., dep. 784.4m. (Dec. 1995); Pres. GLIGORIE GOGOVSKI.

Tutunska Banka: 1000 Skopje, 12-ta Udarna brigada bb, POB 702; tel. (2) 3105600; fax (2) 3231114; e-mail tutban@mpt.com.mk; internet www.tb.com.mk; f. 1985; cap. 506.3m., res 1,026.3m., dep. 4,560.0m. (Dec. 2001); Pres. BORIS ZAKRAJSEK.

STOCK EXCHANGE

Skopje Stock Exchange: 1000 Skopje, Mito Hadživasilev Jasmin 20; tel. (2) 3122055; fax (2) 3122069; e-mail mse@unet.com.mk; internet www.mse.org.mk; f. 1996; Chair. EVGENI ZOGRAFSKI.

INSURANCE

Stock Co for Insurance and Reinsurance 'Makedonija'— Skopje: 1000 Skopje, 11 Oktomvri 25; tel. (2) 3115188; fax (2) 3115374; internet www.qbe.com; f. 1945; stock company for insurance and reinsurance.

Trade and Industry

GOVERNMENT AGENCY

Agency of Information: 1000 Skopje, Guro Gakovik 64; tel. (2) 3214723; fax (2) 3115659; e-mail sinf@sinf.gov.mk; internet www .sinf.gov.mk; Dir VEBI BEXHETI.

Privatization Agency of the Republic of Macedonia: 1000 Skopje, Nikola Vapcarov 7, POB 410; tel. (2) 3117564; fax (2) 3126022; e-mail agency@mpa.org.mk; internet www.mpa.org.mk; Dir MARINA NAKEVA-KAVRAKOVA.

Securities and Exchange Commission: 1000 Skopje, Kuzman Josifovski Pitu 1, POB 859; tel. and fax (2) 3114199; e-mail khv@sec .gov.mk; internet www.sec.gov.mk; Pres. NIKOLA GRUEVSKI.

CHAMBERS OF COMMERCE

Economic Chamber of Macedonia: 1000 Skopje, Dimitrija Čupovski 13; tel. (2) 3118088; fax (2) 3116210; e-mail ic@ic .mchamber.org.mk; internet www.mchamber.org.mk; f. 1962; Pres. DUŠAN PETRESKI.

Regional Chamber of Commerce of Skopje: 1000 Skopje, Partizanski odredi 2, POB 509; tel. (2) 3112511; fax (2) 3116419; e-mail regkomsk@regkom.org.mk; Pres. BORIS DIMOVSKI.

UTILITIES

Electricity

Electric Power Industry of Macedonia (Elektrostopanstvo na Makedonija): 1000 Skopje, Bate Bacevski br. 9; tel. (2) 3111077; fax (2) 3227827; production, transfer and distribution of electric power.

MAJOR COMPANIES

By the beginning of 2003 1,688 enterprises, employing over 80% of the labour force, had been privatized; a further 84 companies were in the process of privatization. The Government continued to hold shares in 512 companies, and retained a controlling interest in 282.

Alkaloid a.d.: 1000 Skopje, bul. Aleksandar Makedonski 12; tel. (2) 3265020; fax (2) 3612531; e-mail trajcem@unet.com.mk; internet www.alkaloid.mk; f. 1936; producers of medicines and chemicals; Gen. Man. TRAJCE MUKAJETOV; 1,750 employees.

Alumina: 1000 Skopje, Ivo R. Lola 164; tel. (2) 3064166; fax (2) 3064272; e-mail alummk@lotus.mpt.com.mk; internet www.mpt .com.mk/~alummk; aluminium products; Gen. Dir VASIL KOSTOJČI-NOSKI; 1,595 employees.

Brako: 91400 Veles, Novi Veles 12; tel. (93) 26655; fax (93) 23210; main areas of activity incl. caravans, boat trailers, beekeepers' trailers, etc.; Dir DORDI MANČEVSKI; 650 employees.

Fabrika za Kvasec i Alkohol: 7000 Bitola, ul. Industriska; tel. (47) 220494; fax (47) 32433; e-mail kvasara@mt.net.mk; yeast and alcohol production.

Frotirka: 2320 Delcevo, ul. Industriska 8; tel. (33) 411455; fax (33) 411119; e-mail frotirka@mt.net.mk; f. 1961; privatized in 2000; production of towels and terry cloth; Gen. Man. JOVAN POPOV.

Granit Construction Co: 1000 Skopje, POB 569, ul. Dmitrija Cupaskog; tel. (2) 3227752; fax (2) 3112318; e-mail granit@unet.com .mk; internet www.granit.com.mk; f. 1952; Gen. Dir STRASO MILKOVSKI; 5,600 employees.

Industrija a.d. Ruen Kočani: 92300 Kočani, 29 Noemvri 32; tel. (33) 21600; fax (33) 21223; f. 1952; production of clutches and metal goods for all types of vehicles; Dir JORDAN SREBENOV; 1,500 employees.

Karpos Decorative Fabrics Factory: 91330 Kriva Palanka, Maršal Tito 7; tel. (31) 75201; fax (31) 74335; decorative upholstery products and taffeta fabrics; privatized in 2000; Gen. Dir RUSE DIMOVSKI.

Makpetrol Co: 1000 Skopje, POB 537, Mito Hadži Vasilev Jasmin bb 4; tel. (2) 3112144; fax (2) 3111525; f. 1947; import and export of petroleum products; Dir ANDREJA JOSIFOVSKI; 500 employees.

MZT Hepos a.d.: 1000 Skopje, Pero Nakov bb; tel. (2) 2549800; fax (2) 2549848; e-mail mzthepos@mt.net.mk; internet www.hepos.com .mk; f. 1953; development and manufacture of brake equipment for different types of trains; Man. Dir VLADO ATANOSOVSKI; 425 employees.

OKTA Oil Refinery: 1000 Skopje, s. Miladinovci; tel. (2) 3231702; fax (2) 3761001; fmr state-owned petroleum refinery; 54% stake sold to Hellenic Petroleum SA of Greece in 1999.

Organsko Hemijska Industrija (OHIS): 1000 Skopje, Provmajska bb; tel. (2) 3112199; fax (2) 3110250; internet www.ohis.com .mk; manufactures polyacrylonitrillic fibre, PVC powder, etc.; Man. Dir JORGO ČUKA; 5,774 employees.

Otex a.d. Holding Co: 6000 Ohrid, ul. 7-mi Noemvri 181; tel. (46) 205355; fax (46) 260181; e-mail otex@mt.net.mk; internet www.otex .org.mk; Pres. VLATKO SIMJANOSKI; 1,700 employees.

Porcelanka: Veles, ul. Industriska bb; tel. (43) 34255; fax (43) 34210; f. 1954; under Austrian ownership from 2001; production of china and ceramics.

Rafinerija na Nafte—Skopje: 1000 Skopje, POB 66; tel. (2) 3239511; fax (2) 3236920; production of gasoline and other fuels; Gen. Dir VANGEL ARANUTOV; 1,432 employees.

Rudnici i Zelezarnica Skopje (Skopje Mines and Iron Works): 1000 Skopje, POB 54; tel. (2) 3221076; fax (2) 3221257; engaged in all stages, from iron ore mining to production of steel sheets and related products; privatized in 1998; 11,000 employees.

Sasa: Makedonska Kamenica, ul. Marsal Tito bb; tel. (33) 431222; fax (33) 431402; production of zinc and lead ores; Gen. Man. LJUBČO DIMITROVSKII.

Sileks a.d.: 91320 Kratovo, Goce Delčev; tel. (31) 116238; fax (31) 114898; f. 1936; mining, industry, tourism and trade; Dir LJUBČO IVANOV; 2,600 employees.

Skopje Technical Gases (Tehnicki Gasovi Skopje a.d.): 1000 Skopje, ul. Proleterska 4; tel. (2) 3041447; fax (2) 3032354; e-mail tgs@unet.com.mk; production of technical gases; Gen. Man. TRAJCE NIKOLOVSKI.

Technometal-Vardar a.d.: 1000 Skopje, Veljko Vlahović 11; tel. (2) 3229411; fax (2) 3113435; e-mail tehvar01@unet.com.mk; internet www.tehnometal-vardar.com.mk; exports and imports metals, metal products and chemical products, machinery, vehicles and other consumer goods; Gen. Man. SLAVKO GEORGIEVSKI; 1,000 employees.

Teteks a.d.: 91220 Tetovo, B. Miladovini; tel. (44) 20006; fax (44) 22126; e-mail teteks@mpt.com.mk; internet www.teteks.com; production of fabrics and clothing; Gen. Dir GLIGORIE GOGOVSKI; 3,700 employees.

Treska: 1000 Skopje, Ive Lole Ribara 130; tel. (2) 3223222; timber industry and wood-working; 10,000 employees.

Zletovo Baterii a.d.: Probistip; tel. (42) 483816; fax (42) 483656; internet www.unet.com.mk/mbc/zletovo.htm; scheduled for privatization; production of batteries; Gen. Man. G. VASILEVSKA.

TRADE UNIONS

Federation of Trade Unions of Macedonia: 1000 Skopje; tel. (2) 3231374; fax (2) 3115787; Pres. VANCO MURATOVSKI; 320,000 mems.

Transport

RAILWAYS

In 2001 the rail network totalled 699 km, of which 233 km were electrified. From 2000 the European Investment Bank made a series of loans to finance the modernization of the railways.

Makedonski Železnici (MZ) (Macedonian Railways): 1000 Skopje, železnička 50; tel. (2) 3227903; fax (2) 3462330; e-mail mzdir@mt.net .mk; f. 1992; Dir-Gen. RATKO STEFANOVSKI.

ROADS

The FYRM's road network totalled 12,927 km in 2001, of which about 6,710 km were paved. The principal road links Tabanovtse, at the border with Serbia and Montenegro, and Bogoroditsa, at the border with Greece. In July 2003 the European Bank for Reconstruction and Development (EBRD) granted the FYRM a US $45m. loan in support of two major road-construction projects.

Fund for National and Regional Roads: 1000 Skopje, Dame Gruev 14; tel. (2) 3118044; fax (2) 3220535; e-mail tanjam@mpt.net .mk.

CIVIL AVIATION

The FYRM has two international airports, at Petrovets, 25 km from Skopje, and at Ohrid.

Adria Airways: 1000 Skopje, Gradski zid, blok 11; tel. (2) 3117009; fax (2) 3235531.

Avioimpex: 1000 Skopje, Oktomvri K14 11; tel. (2) 3239933; fax (2) 3119348; e-mail axx@lotus.mpt.com.mk; internet www.avioimpex .com; f. 1992; flights within Europe; Pres. ILIJA SMILEV.

Macedonian Airlines (MAT): 1000 Skopje, Vasil Glavinov 3; tel. (2) 3292333; fax (2) 3229576; e-mail mathq@mat.com.mk; internet www.mat.com.mk; f. 1994; domestic services and flights within Europe; Man. Dir DUSKO GRUEVSKI.

Palair Macedonian Airlines: 1000 Skopje, Kuzman Jusifovski Pitu bb; tel. (2) 3115868; fax (2) 3238238; f. 1991; domestic services and flights within Europe and to the USA, Canada and Australia; Chair. BITOLJANA VANJA.

Tourism

Following independence in 1991, the FYRM's tourist industry (formerly a major source of foreign exchange) experienced a decline, largely owing to the country's proximity to the conflict in other republics of the former Yugoslavia, domestic instability and the sanctions imposed by Greece. Receipts from tourism were estimated at US $37m. in 2000. However, continuing regional instability, including fighting in the north of the country in 2001, has adversely affected tourism. Tourist arrivals declined dramatically, from 224,016 in 2000 to 98,946 in 2001.

Tourist Association of Macedonia: 1000 Skopje, Dame Gruev 28/5; tel. (2) 3290862; e-mail tarm@mt.net.mk; internet www.tarm .org.mk.

Tourist Association of Skopje: 1000 Skopje, POB 399, Dame Gruev, blok 3; tel. (2) 3118498; fax (2) 3230803.

Culture

NATIONAL ORGANIZATIONS

Ministry of Culture: see section on The Government (Ministries).

Ministry of Education and Science: see section on the Government (Ministries).

Committee for Education, Culture and Physical Culture: 1000 Skopje, Veljko Vlahović 9; tel. (2) 3117896; fax (2) 3118414; Dir DIMITRIE CUPOVSKI.

Cultural and Information Centre (Kulturno-Informativni Centar): 1000 Skopje, Moše Pijade bb; tel. (2) 3230206; fax (2) 3238158; f. 1957; Dir LJUBČO MALENKOV.

Republican Institute for the Protection of Cultural Monuments of Macedonia (Republički Zavod za Zaštita na Spomenicite na Kulturata): 1000 Skopje, POB 225, Evlija Celebija bb; tel. (2) 3232436; fax (2) 3227240; f. 1949; Dir JOVAN RISTOV.

CULTURAL HERITAGE

Archives of Macedonia (Arhiv na Makedonija): 1000 Skopje, Grigor Prličev 3; tel. and fax (2) 3115783; e-mail arhiv@unet.com .mk; internet www.soros.org.mk/archive/index.htm; f. 1951; Dir ZORAN TODOROVSKI.

Art Gallery (Umetnička Galerija): 1000 Skopje, Kruševska 1A; tel. (2) 3133102; f. 1948; Dir DRAGAN BOŠNAKOVSKI.

Bitola Art Gallery (Umetnička Galerija—Bitola): 97000 Bitola, Maršal Tito bb; f. 1958; Dir LJILJANA HRISTOVA.

Borka Talevski Municipal Library (Gradska Biblioteka Borka Talevski): 97000 Prilep, Maršal Tito bb; tel. (47) 24344; f. 1951; Dir SLAVE RISTESKI.

Braka Miladinovci Municipal Library (Gradska Biblioteka Braka Miladinovci): 1000 Skopje, Partizanski odredi bb; tel. (2) 3232544; f. 1935; Dir VASE MANČEV.

Clement of Ohrid Municipal and University Library (Matična i Universitetska Biblioteka Kliment Ohridski): 97000 Bitola, Laninova 39; tel. (47) 33208; f. 1945; Dir DOBRI PETREVSKI.

Clement of Ohrid National and University Library (Narodna i Univerzitetska Biblioteka Kliment Ohridski): 1000 Skopje, Goce Delčev bb 6; tel. (2) 3115177; fax (2) 3226848; e-mail kliment@nubsk .edu.mk; internet www.nubsk.edu.mk; f. 1944; Dir POSKOL GILEVSKI.

Grigor Prličev Municipal Library (Gradska Biblioteka Grigor Prličev): 96000 Ohrid, Kosta Abraševik 22; tel. (46) 22064; f. 1944; Dir SLAVE BANAROVSKI.

Institute for the Protection of Cultural Monuments and Natural Rarities in Bitola (Zavod za Zaštita na Spomenicite na Kulturata i Prirodnite Retkosti): 97000 Bitola, Kliment Ohridski bb; tel. (47) 35387; f. 1975; contains museum and gallery; Dir NIKOLA IVANOVSKI.

Institute for the Protection of Cultural Monuments in Ohrid (Zavod za Zaštita na Spomenicite na Kulturata—Ohrid): 96000 Ohrid, Boro Šain 10; tel. (46) 22498; f. 1951; Dir NADA NOVAKOVSKA.

Institute for the Protection of Cultural Monuments in Skopje (Zavod za Zaštita na Spomenicite na Kulturata—Skopje): 1000 Skopje, Makarie Frčkovski br. 8, POB 328; tel. (2) 3233812; f. 1963; Dir ŽIVKO GELEVSKI.

International Colony of Art in Prilep (Medjunaroda kolonja na sovermena umetnost vo Prilep): 98000 Prilep, Kičevsko džada bb; tel. (48) 25788; Dir BORISLAV KONESKI.

Kočo Racin Municipal Library (Matična Biblioteka 'Kočo Racin'): 91220 Tetovo, Todor Cipovski Merdžan 64; tel. (44) 32194; e-mail nbkrte@soros.org.mk; f. 1945; Dir VLADIMIR KOČOSKI.

Marko Cepenkov Institute of Folklore (Institut za Folklor 'Marko Cepenkov'): 1000 Skopje, Ruzveltova 3, POB 319; tel. (2) 3380176; fax (2) 3380177; f. 1950; Principal Officer Dr TRPKO BICEVSKI.

Museum of Contemporary Art (Muzej na Sovremena Umetnost): 1000 Skopje, Samoilova bb, POB 482; tel. (2) 3117735; f. 1964; Dir ZORAN PETROVSKI.

Museum of Macedonia (Muzej na Makedonija): 1000 Skopje, Ćurčiska bb; tel. (2) 3116044; fax (2) 3116439; e-mail musmk@mt .net.mk; internet www.museummk.com; f. 1924; research, collection, documentation and exhibition of archeology, history, ethnology and medieval art; library of 5,700 vols; Dir Dr DRAGI MITREVSKI.

Museum of Skopje (Muzej na Grad Skopje): 1000 Skopje, Mito Hadživasilev bb; tel. (2) 3115367; f. 1949; Dir KLIME KOROBAR.

Pane Georgievski National Library (Narodna Biblioteka Pane Georgievski): 91300 Kumanovo, Narodna revolucija 1; tel. (31) 21415; f. 1945; Dir NADA TVANOVSKA.

Youth Cultural Centre—Skopje (Mladinski Kulturen Centar—Skopje): 1000 Skopje, Kej Dimitar Vlahov bb; tel. (2) 3115225; fax (2) 3115906; f. 1972; Dir GOCE DIMOVSKI.

SPORTING ORGANIZATION

Macedonian Olympic Committee: 1000 Skopje, Kuzman Josifovski Pitu 17, Blok 1, Kompleks Skopjanka; tel. (2) 3162506; fax (2)

3116068; e-mail mok@mol.com.mk; internet www.mok.org.mk; f. 1992; Pres. Dr Vasil Tupurkovski; Gen. Sec. Zoran Gapić.

PERFORMING ARTS

Theatre

Bitola National Theatre (Naroden Teatar—Bitola): 97000 Bitola, Maršal Tito 66; tel. (47) 232370; fax (47) 227970; f. 1944; Dir Blagoja Stefanovski.

Drama Theatre (Dramski Teatar): 1000 Skopje, Šekspirova 15; tel. (2) 3250005; fax (2) 3256598; f. 1946; Dir Blagoja Čorevski.

Kumanovo Folk Theatre (Naroden Teatar—Kumanovo): 91300 Kumanovo, Kiril i Metodij bb; tel. (31) 23950; f. 1948; Dir Tomislav Spasovski.

Macedonian National Theatre (Drama) (Makedonski Naroden Teater): 1000 Skopje, Dimitar Vlahov bb; tel. (2) 3114511; fax (2) 3114060; f. 1945; Gen. Dir Ljubčo Petruševski.

Macedonian National Theatre (Opera and Ballet) (Makedonski Naroden Teater): 1000 Skopje, Bitpazarska bb; tel. (2) 3114691; Dir Ljubčo Petruševski.

Theatre for Children and Youth (Teatar za Deca i Mladinci): 1000 Skopje, POB 169, JNA bb; tel. (2) 3222619; fax (2) 3223118; f. 1989; Dir Ljubomir Čdikovski.

Theatre of Minorities (Teatar na Narodnostite): 1000 Skopje, Nikola Martinovski 41; tel. (2) 3111017; fax (2) 3222570; f. 1950; Dir Saladin Bilal (Turkish Drama); Dir Sefedin Nuredini (Albanian Drama).

Vojdan Černodrinski Folk Theatre—Prilep (Naroden Teatar Vojdan Černodrinski—Prilep): 98000 Prilep, Borka Taleski 111; tel. (48) 28644; f. 1950; Dir Stojan Damčevski.

Youth Open Theatre (Mlad Otoveren Teatar): c/o Youth Cultural Centre, 1000 Skopje, Kej Dimitar Vlahov bb; tel. (2) 3111508; fax (2) 3115906; f. 1975.

Music

Macedonian Philharmonic Orchestra (Makedonska Filharmonija): 1000 Skopje, Makedonija bb; tel. (2) 3118450; fax (2) 3235753; e-mail makfilnic@mpt.com.mk; f. 1944; concerts, promotion of Macedonian music culture and exchange of musicians; Chief Conductor Angel Šurev; Dir Ganka Svetanova.

Macedonian Radio and Television Choir (Hor na Makedonskata Radio-Televizija—MRT): 1000 Skopje, Goce Delčev bb; tel. (2) 3113231; fax (2) 3225212; Chief Conductor Dragan Suplevski.

May Opera Evenings (Majski Operski Večeri): 1000 Skopje, POB 153, MRT Kej Dimitar Vlahov bb; tel. (2) 3114908; fax (2) 3114060; f. 1973.

Skopje International Jazz Festival (Internacionalen Skopje Džez Festival): c/o Youth Cultural Centre, 1000 Skopje, Kej Dimitar Vlahov bb; tel. (2) 3111508; fax (2) 3115906; f. 1980.

Skopje MRT Big Band (Plesni Orkestar MRT Skopje): 1000 Skopje, Nov dom na MRT; tel. (2) 3227205; Chief Conductor Aleksandar Dzambazov.

Skopje MRT Chamber Orchestra (Kamerni Orkestar MRT Skopje): 1000 Skopje, Nov dom na MRT; tel. (2) 3227205.

Film

Film Library of Macedonia (Kinoteka): 1000 Skopje, Goce Delčev bb; tel. (2) 3228064; fax (2) 3220062; organizes an annual international film festival; f. 1976.

Horizont Film: 1000 Skopje, ul. Franklin Ruzvelt 2–8; tel. and fax (2) 3231447; e-mail mitri@lotus.mpt.com.mk; f. 1991; private production company; short documentary and feature films; Dir Antonio Mitrikeski.

Makedonija Film: 1000 Skopje, POB 534, Nikola Vapcarov 7; tel. (2) 3118614; fax (2) 3118065; f. 1947; Dir Dobri Boškovski.

Pegas: 1000 Skopje, 8-mi Mart 4; tel. (2) 3117038; production company; f. 1991; Dir Panta Mižimakov.

Vardar Film: 1000 Skopje, ul. 8 Mart 4; tel. (2) 3117527; fax (2) 3117038; f. 1947; production company; Dir Stevan Acovski.

ASSOCIATIONS

Academic Cinema Club (Akademski Kino Klub): 1000 Skopje, Pirinska bb; tel. (2) 3259537; f. 1959; 80 members; Pres. Vićentie Dorčevski; Sec. Branko Ristovski.

Association of Macedonian Composers (Društvo na Kompozitorite na Makedonija): 1000 Skopje, Maksim Gorki 18; tel. (2) 3220567; fax (2) 3235854; f. 1947; Pres. Vlastimir Nikolovski; Sec. Marko Kolovski; 49 mems.

Association of Sciences and Arts (Društvo za nauka i umetnost): 97000 Bitola, POB 145; tel. (47) 22683; f. 1960; Pres. Sotir Panovski; Sec.-Gen. Trajko Ogenovski.

Egyptian Association of Citizens: Ohrid; f. 1990; group who reject Roma ethnicity and claim to be Egipcani or Egyptians; allowed separate registration in Macedonian census of 1991; Leader Nazim Arifi.

Macedonian–Turkish Friendship and Co-operation Society: Skopje; f. 1994; promotes friendly relations between Macedonia and Turkey through culture, trade, science, art, tourism and sport.

Musical Youth of Macedonia (Muzička mladina na Makedonija): 1000 Skopje, Ilindenska bb; tel. (2) 3117882; fax (2) 3116545; f. 1963.

Phralipe (Brotherhood—Roma Union of Macedonia): 1000 Skopje, Suto Orizari; f. 1948; cultural asscn of the Roma (Gypsies).

Society of Caricaturists of Macedonia (Združenie na karikaturistite na Makedonija): 1000 Skopje, Mito Hadživasilev bb, POB 530; tel. (2) 3116366; f. 1980; Pres. Ane Vasilevski; 40 mems.

Society of Film Workers of Macedonia (Društvo na filmski rabotnici na Makedonija): 1000 Skopje, 8-mi Mart 4; tel. (2) 3211811; f. 1950; Pres. Delčo Mihajlov; 82 mems.

Society of Literary Translators of Macedonia (Društvo na leteraturnite preveduvači na Makedonija): 1000 Skopje, POB 3; f. 1955; Pres. Ilija Korubin; Sec. Taško Širilov; 250 mems.

Society of Musical Artists of Macedonia (Združenie na muzička umetnici na Makedonija): 1000 Skopje, Maksim Gorki 18; tel. (2) 3220567; fax (2) 3235854; f. 1947; Pres. Milan Firfov; 62 mems.

Society of Plastic Arts of Macedonia (Društvo na Likovnite Umetnike na Makedonija): 1000 Skopje, 13 Noemvri bb, POB 438; f. 1946; Pres. Gligor Čemerski; Sec. Branislav Mirčevski; 333 mems.

Society of Writers of Macedonia (Društvo na Pisatelite na Makedonija): 1000 Skopje, Maksim Gorki 18; tel. (2) 3117668; fax (2) 3228345; f. 1947; protection of authors' rights and promotion of Macedonian literature; Pres. Jovan Pavlovski; Sec. Paskal Gilovski; Sec. Svetlana Hristova-Jocić; 194 mems.

Union of Associations for Macedonian Language and Literature (Sojuz na Društvata za Makedonski Jakiz i Literatura): Filoški fakultet, 1000 Skopje, Krste Misirkov bb; f. 1954; Pres. Elena Bendevska; Sec. Ljubčo Mitrevski; 700 mems.

Education

Elementary education is free and compulsory for all children between the ages of seven and 15. Various types of secondary school, beginning at 15 and lasting for four years, are available to those who qualify. In 1999/2000 primary enrolment included 93.6% of children in the relevant age-group (males 94.0%; females 93.1%), while the comparable ratio for secondary education was equivalent to 83.6% (males 85.0%; females 82.2%). According to the terms of the Constitution, nationals are granted the right to elementary and secondary education in their mother tongue. In 2000/01 Albanian was the language of education in 273 primary schools and 23 secondary schools, Turkish in 56 primary schools and five secondary schools, and Serbian in 14 primary schools. There are universities at Skopje and Bitola; a third, Albanian-language university, which was founded in Tetovo by the Albanian minority in December 1994, was declared illegal by the Government. New legislation on education was adopted in July 2000, permitting the use of Albanian and other languages in private tertiary institutions. A new, private university (the South-East Europe University), with instruction in Albanian and Macedonian, opened in Tetovo in November 2001, with the help of funding from the international community. In July 2003 it was announced that, under amendments to legislation on higher education, Tetovo University had gained the opportunity to be granted legal status later that year (thereby becoming the third state-funded institution of higher education). In 2001/02 some 44,710 students were enrolled in higher education. Expenditure on education by the central Government in 2002 was budgeted at 7,591m. denars (11.4% of total expenditure).

UNIVERSITIES

South-East Europe University (SEEU): Tetovo; f. 2001; Dir Aljadin Abazi.

SS Cyril and Methodius University of Skopje (Univerzitet 'Sv. Kiril I Metódij'): 1000 Skopje, POB 576, Krste Misirkov bb; tel. (2) 3116323; fax (2) 3116370; e-mail postmaster@ukim.edu.mk; f. 1949; state-controlled; 24 faculties; 10 research institutes; 1,300 teachers; 25,967 students; Rector Prof. Dr Radmila Kiprijanova.

University of Bitola (Univerzitet Bitolj): 97000 Bitola, 1 Maj bb; tel. (47) 23788; f. 1979; Rector Prof. Dr Dame Nestorovski.

Social Welfare

While Macedonia formed part of the former Yugoslav federation, the region enjoyed the same welfare provisions as the rest of the country. There was an obligatory social insurance scheme for anyone in employment and their families, which provided for health insurance, money payments and grants, in case of sickness, accident, disability and old age. All workers were entitled to annual leave. In the 1980s the republics assumed increasing responsibility for social welfare, for which Macedonia, following its independence in 1991, assumed total responsibility. Thereafter, resources were more severely restricted. Unemployment benefit was restricted, particularly because the numbers without work were extremely high. The country received international financial support and a significant degree of humanitarian aid. In 1998 the Government announced plans to reform the social-security system, including an increase in pensions, the abolition of university fees and an increase in the number of student grants. At the same time, however, fees for medical services were to be introduced and parents were to pay 10%–20% of the cost of their child's medical treatment. In 2001 the FYRM had 16 general hospitals, 21 clinics and institutes, 17 specialized hospitals and nine other in-patient facilities, with a total of 10,045 beds. There were 4,459 physicians (including 2,894 specialists), 1,125 dentists and 309 pharmacists working in the country. Of total estimated expenditure by the central Government in 2002, 332m. denars (0.5% of anticipated expenditure) were allocated to health services and 14,951m. denars (22.5% of expenditure) to social security and welfare.

Ministry of Health: see section on The Government (Ministries).

Ministry of Labour and Social Welfare: see section on The Government (Ministries).

The Environment

The problem of industrial pollution in the FYRM, originating largely from industrial sites in urban areas such as Skopje, Tetovo and Veles, was first addressed by a range of policies devised by the Environmental Action Programme for Central and Eastern Europe, adopted in 1993. Subsequently, Macedonia's environmental policy was structured according to a framework environmental law and a National Environmental Action Plan (NEAP), both implemented in 1996. The NEAP identified the areas that required immediate action, such as problems in air quality, water quality, solid-waste management, biodiversity conservation and forest preservation. In addition, Macedonia aimed to reach EU environmental standards as part of its effort to achieve the long-term goal of EU integration. In June 1999 Macedonia and Albania reached agreement on the implementation of environmental protection projects around Lakes Ohrid and Prespa. In June 2000 Macedonia signed a bilateral treaty on co-operation in environmental protection.

GOVERNMENT ORGANIZATIONS

Ministry of Agriculture, Forestry and Water Resources: see section on The Government (Ministries).

Ministry of the Environment and Urban Planning: see section on The Government (Ministries).

Hydro-Meteorological Institute: 1000 Skopje, ul. Skupe bb; tel. (2) 3097004; e-mail lile@meteo.gov.mk; Dir LJILJANA TODOROVSKA-TALEVSKA.

Regional Environment Centre: 1000 Skopje, ul. Ivo Lola Ribar 39/II-2; tel. (2) 3131904; fax (2) 3109240; e-mail recmk@mol.com.mk; local rep. KATARINA STOJKOVSKA.

Republic Institute for Health Protection: 1000 Skopje, 50-ta Divizija 6; tel. (2) 3125044; fax (2) 3223354; e-mail rzzz@unet.com .mk; management of air quality, surface and drinking water and food; Dir Dr DANAIL SIMOVSKI.

ACADEMIC INSTITUTES

Macedonian Academy of Sciences and Arts (Makedonska Akademija na Naukite i Umetnostite): 1000 Skopje, bul. Krste Misirkov 2, POB 428; tel. (2) 3114200; fax (2) 3115903; e-mail makakad@ manu.edu.mk; f. 1967; Pres. Acad. GEORGI EFREMOV.

Institute of Chemistry: 1000 Skopje, Arhimedova 5; tel. (2) 3117055; e-mail trajcest@iunona.pmf.ukim.edu.com; Pres. TRAJCE STAFILOV.

Institute of Engineering and Scientific Societies and Unions of Macedonia: 1000 Skopje, Dame Gruev 14A, IT House, POB 139; tel. (2) 3229040; conferences and seminars in the fields of engineering, technical sciences, architecture, agriculture, environmental matters and ecology; Pres. Prof. G. M. DIMIROVSKI.

Institute of Occupational Medicine: 1000 Skopje, II Makedonska Brigada Br. 43, POB 910; tel. and fax (2) 2621428; e-mail occhemed@informa.mk; f. 1970; monitoring of the working and living environment and assessment of the effects of the environment on human health; Principal Officer Ass. STEFAN TODOROV.

Water Development Institute of Macedonia (Zavod za Vodostopanstvo Na Republika Makedonija): 1000 Skopje, Zeleznička 62, POB 310; tel. (2) 3228028; fax (2) 3239401; f. 1952; publication of *Water Development Problems* (Vodostopanski problemi); research in water development, ecology, applied hydraulics and erosion; Dir Ing. METODI BOEV.

NON-GOVERNMENTAL ORGANIZATIONS

Ecological Movement of Macedonia (Dviženje na Ekologistite na Makedonija—DEM): 1000 Skopje, ul. Vasil Giorgov bb, POB 6; tel. and fax (2) 3220518; e-mail bimadem@mpt.com.mk; f. 1990; co-operation with Macedonian environmental non-governmental organizations; Contact MARJAN DODVSKI.

Enhalon Ecological Association (Opštinsko Ekološko Društvo 'Enhalon'): 96330 Struga, Vojdan Černodrinski 24; tel. (46) 71308; f. 1990; Principal Officer MATE GOGOSKI.

Flora Ecological Association: 91330 Kriva Palanka, Goce Delchev 26; tel. (31) 375594; fax (31) 375138; f. 1990; environmental conservation; Principal Officer Dr GORGI KEROVSKI.

Golak Ecological Association (Ekološko Društvo Golak): 92320 Delcevo, M. M. Brico bb; tel. and fax (33) 84864; f. 1994; Contact KIRO GORGIEV.

Grašnica Ecological Association: 96000 Ohrid, Sarplaninska 30; tel. (46) 53502; f. 1991; environmental protection, especially of Lake Ohrid; Principal Officer ŽIVKO MARTINOVSKI.

Lake Ohrid Conservation Project: 96000 Ohrid, Dimitar Vlahov; tel. (46) 263743; e-mail Anita_Kodozman@yahoo.com; Dir ANITA KODOZMAN.

Macedonian Ecological Society: 1000 Skopje, POB 162; tel. (2) 3117055; fax (2) 3228141; e-mail melovski@iunona.pmf.ukim.edu .mk; f. 1972; scientific and ecological projects, nature conservation, publication of scientific journals, scientific symposia, congresses and workshops; Principal Officer LJUBČO GRUPČE; Principal Officer LJUBČO MELOVSKI.

Mariovo Ecological Association: 97000 Prilep, Krume Volnaroski 29; tel. (48) 29293; fax (48) 22571; f. 1991; preservation of the Mariovo region; Contact RISTO NIKOLOSKI.

Molika Environmental Movement (Dviženje za Oklinata Molika): 97000 Bitola, M. Tito 47/1; tel. and fax (47) 48469; e-mail molika@mpt.com.mk; Contact MICHAILO MOJSOV.

Odek Ecological Association: 91430 Kavadarci, JNA 16; tel. (93) 77439; co-ordination of ecological activities in Kavadarci; Principal Officer Prof. TOME LISIČANEC; Principal Officer DUŠKO PETROV.

Ozone Ecological Association: 92400 Strumica, Leninova 134; tel. and fax (32) 31450; environmental monitoring; Principal Officer RISTO VUCKOV.

Prilep Ecological Association: 97500 Prilep, Marksova 54A; tel. (48) 22280; f. 1991; environmental conservation in the Prilep region; Principal Officer Dr ILIJA BAŠEKI.

Priroda Ecological Association: Tikvesh, Ilo Vilarov 36; f. 1990; Contact IVANOV ATANOS.

Resen Youth Council (Mladinski sovet—Resen): 96310 Resen, Korculanska 32; tel. (46) 42352; f. 1990; ecological education in schools; Co-ordinator ARON PRTSULOVSKI.

Vila Zora Ecological Association (Ekološko Društvo 'Vila Zora'): 91400 Veles, Dimitar Vlahov bb; tel. and fax (43) 33023; environmental protection of the Beles region; Principal Officer PANDORA NIKUŠEVA.

Zdravec Environmental Association (Ekološko Društvo Zdravec): 92304 M Kamenica, Dom na rudari 'Sasa' 110; tel. (33) 86865; e-mail zdravec@informa.mk; Contact LILJANA DIMITROVSKA.

Defence

In August 2002 the army totalled 12,300 (including 7,600 conscripts); the air force numbered about 800. Conscription, which was introduced in April 1992, lasted for nine months until January 2003, when the term of service was reduced to six months. Paramilitary forces comprised a police force of some 7,600. On 31 March 2003 the existing NATO contingent in the country was replaced by a mission led by the European Union (EU), known as Operation Concordia, comprising 350 military personnel; 13 EU member states and 14 non-EU nations contributed to the operation. In 2002 defence expenditure by the central Government was budgeted at 7,620m. denars (equivalent to 3.0% of GDP).

Commander in Chief of the Macedonian Armed Forces: President of the Republic.

Chief of Staff of the Macedonian Army: Gen. METODIJA STAMBOLISKI.

Bibliography

Aarbakke, V. *Ethnic Rivalry and the Quest for Macedonia, 1870–1913*. New York, NY, East European Monographs, 2003.

Brown, K. *Past in Question: Modern Macedonia and the Uncertainties of Nation*. Princeton, NJ, Princeton University Press, 2003.

Cowan, J. K. (Ed.). *Macedonia: the Politics of Identity and Difference (Anthropology, Culture and Society Series)*. London, Pluto Press, 2000.

Donnelly Carney, E. *Women and Monarchy in Macedonia*. Norman, OK, University of Oklahoma Press, 2000.

Errington, R. *A History of Macedonia*. Berkeley, CA, University of California Press, 1990.

Institute for Balkan Studies. *Macedonia, Past and Present: Reprints from 'Balkan Studies'*. Thessaloníki, 1992.

Pettifer, J. (Ed.). *The New Macedonian Question*. New York, NY, Palgrave, 1999.

Porter, D. *Your Woman in Skopje: Letters from Macedonia, 1995–99*. Philadelphia, PA, Xlibris Corpn, 2001.

Poulton, H. *Who are the Macedonians?* London, C. Hurst, 2000.

Roudometof, V. (Ed.). The Macedonian Question New York, NY, Columbia University Press, 2000.

Siotas, J. C. *Siatista-Macedonia: The Spirit of Hellenism*. Raleigh, NC, Pentland Press, 2000.

Sokalski, H. *Ounce of Prevention: Macedonia and the UN Experience in Preventative Diplomacy*. Washington, DC, US Institute of Peace, 2003.

Sowards, S. *Austria's Policy of Macedonian Reform*. Boulder, CO, East European Monographs, 1989.

Szajkowski, B. *Macedonia (Postcommunist States and Nations)*. London, Routledge, 2003.

Tarkas, A. *Athens–Skopje: Behind Closed Doors* (in Greek). Lavrinthos, 1995.

Vukmanović-Tempo, S. *Struggle for the Balkans*. London, Merlin Press, 1990.

Williams, A. *Preventing War*. Lanham, MD, Rowman and Littlefield, 2000.

Wyzan, M. *First Steps to Economic Independence in Macedonia*. Stockholm, Stockholm Institute of Soviet and Eastern European Economics (Östekonomiska Institutet), 1992.

See also the Select Bibliography in Part Four.

POLAND

Geography

PHYSICAL FEATURES

The Republic of Poland is located to the north of central Europe, with a 520-km (323-mile) coastline along the Baltic Sea. To the west lies Germany, to the south-west the Czech Republic and to the south Slovakia. The eastern frontiers are with former Soviet states; to the north is the Russian enclave around Kaliningrad (formerly Königsberg) on the Baltic coast; there is a short border with Lithuania to the north-east; while Belarus lies beyond the northern part of the eastern border, and Ukraine the southern. After the Second World War Poland lost a considerable amount of territory to the USSR, while gaining the former German provinces of Pomerania and Silesia in the west, and part of East Prussia in the east. Poland's borders are now marked by the Oder (Odra) and Neisse (Nysa) rivers in the west, the River Bug in the east, the Sudetic Mountains in the south-west and the Carpathian range of mountains in the south-east. The country has an area of 312,685 sq km (120,728 sq miles), some 20% less than in 1939.

Poland is a predominantly low-lying country, the average altitude being only 173 m (474 ft). The highest point in the country is 2,499 m, at Rysy on the border with Slovakia. The most developed and most highly populated region is the central plain, which covers more than one-third of the country. The plain is crossed by Poland's two major rivers, the Oder and the Vistula (Wisła), which rise in the Sudetic and Carpathian mountains, respectively, along the southern borders, and flow into the Baltic Sea. South of the plain there is a plateau (average height 700 m) which is drained by the Bug, San and Vistula rivers. On the southern border of Poland, between the Sudetic range in the west and the western reaches of the Carpathians in the east, lies the broad depression of the Moravian Gate, which is the traditional route into Central Europe. North of the central plains there are belts of shallow lakes, surrounded by undulating and wooded countryside. North of this lake district are the coastal lowlands, which are most extensive near the estuaries of the Oder and Vistula. Most of the coastline is covered by sand dunes. There are many beaches and lagoons and few natural harbours.

CLIMATE

Poland's climate is largely continental, with hot summers and cold winters, although it is more temperate in the west than in the east. The average July temperature in Warsaw (Warszawa) is 18°C (65°F), while the average for January is –4°C (25°F). Warsaw has an average annual rainfall of 560 mm, whereas Kraków (Cracow), in the south, has an annual average of 745 mm.

POPULATION

Ethnic Poles now constitute some 97% of the total population, making Poland one of the most ethnically homogenous countries in the world. Most of the substantial pre-1939 Ukrainian and Jewish populations either fled the country or were killed during the Nazi occupation. There are still minor communities of Belarusians, Ukrainians and Jews, and small numbers of Greeks, Macedonians, Russians, Lithuanians, Slovaks, Czechs and Roma (Gypsies). Some ethnic Germans remain in the former German territories of Silesia and Pomerania, although most of the Germans living in Poland or in the lands granted to Poland in 1945 were deported after the War. The official language is Polish, a member of the Western Slavonic group. Most of the inhabitants profess Christianity, 95.6% of the population being nominal adherents of the Roman Catholic Church in 1997.

The total population at the end of December 2002 was estimated at 38,610,000, giving a population density of 123.5 persons per sq km. According to provisional data from the census conducted in May 1995, the population at that time numbered 38,620,000. In December 1998 it was estimated that 1,618,468 people lived in the capital, Warsaw. Other important towns included Łódź (population 806,728), a major industrial centre, and Kraków (population 740,666), an important centre of culture and learning. Since the Second World War there has been a significant movement of the population from rural to urban areas: in 2000 only 38.2% of the population lived in the countryside, compared with 68% in 1946.

Chronology

966: The first historical ruler of Poland, Prince Mieszko I, converted to Latin Christianity.

1320: Lidisław I was crowned King of a reunited Poland.

1386: The Grand Duke of Lithuania became King, as Władysław II, by marriage to Jadwiga of Poland; they founded the Jagiellonian dynasty (1386–1572) and established a personal union of Poland with Lithuania.

1493: A two-chamber Sejm (parliament) was established.

1569: Under Sigismund II a permanent union with Lithuania was established, by the Union of Lublin, which was to last until the final dismemberment of the Polish-Lithuanian Commonwealth in 1795.

1764: Election of Stanisław II, who ruled until 1795.

1772: The First Partition of Poland, between Russia, Prussia and Austria, took place.

1791: Stanisław II created Europe's first modern constitution.

1793: The Second Partition of Poland.

1795: The Third Partition extinguished the Polish state.

1807: The Grand Duchy of Warsaw was established by Napoleon I of France.

1815: The 'Congress Kingdom of Poland' was formed under Russian patronage.

1905–07: Revolution in Russian Poland.

1915: The Russian occupation was ended by German victory on the eastern front in the First World War.

1916: Restoration of an 'independent' Kingdom of Poland by Germany.

3 June 1918: The Entente Governments recognized the principle of Polish independence.

11 November 1918: Józef Piłsudski assumed power in Warsaw; Poland was declared an independent republic.

28 June 1919: The Treaty of Versailles recognized Polish independence.

13–19 August 1920: Soviet forces were defeated at the Battle of Warsaw.

18 March 1921: The Treaty of Rīga was signed by Poland, Ukraine and Soviet Russia, formally concluding the Soviet–Polish war and defining the frontiers in the region.

1922: Stanisław Wojciechowski was elected Head of State.

12 May 1926: Piłsudski seized power in a *coup d'état*.

25 January 1932: A non-aggression pact was signed with the USSR.

26 January 1934: A non-aggression pact was signed with Germany.

23 March 1935: A new Constitution was enacted.

12 May 1935: Death of Piłsudski.

31 March 1939: France and the United Kingdom announced guarantees of Poland's independence, in response to German territorial demands.

23 August 1939: The Nazi-Soviet Pact was signed, including a secret agreement between the USSR and Germany to partition Poland.

1 September 1939: Germany invaded Poland, which caused the beginning of the Second World War.

17 September 1939: The USSR invaded Poland.

30 September 1939: A Government-in-Exile was formed in Paris, France, under Gen. Władysław Sikorski, moving to London, the United Kingdom, in 1940.

22 June 1941: Germany invaded the USSR; all of Poland was occupied by Nazi forces.

5 January 1942: The Polish Workers' Party (PWP) was founded.

April 1943: The Warsaw Ghetto uprising was suppressed by German troops.

25 April 1943: German investigators discovered, at Katyn in the USSR, the bodies of 4,000 Polish officers, who had been murdered by Soviet secret police in 1940 (the USSR only admitted its responsibility in April 1990).

4 July 1943: Gen. Sikorski, Prime Minister of the Government-in-Exile, died in an air crash.

23 July 1944: The Polish Committee of National Liberation (Lublin Committee—PKWN) was established under Soviet auspices.

1 August–2 October 1944: The Warsaw Rising was eventually suppressed by German troops.

February 1945: German forces withdrew from Warsaw. The British, Soviet and US leaders, Winston Churchill, Stalin (Iosif V. Dzhugashvili) and Franklin D. Roosevelt, met in the Crimean town of Yalta (now in Ukraine): the 'Curzon line' was agreed as Poland's eastern border; Stalin promised 'free and unfettered elections' in Poland after the War.

21 April 1945: A Soviet-Polish Treaty of Friendship was signed.

6 July 1945: The USA and the United Kingdom formally recognized the 'Provisional Government of National Unity', which was dominated by members of the Soviet-backed PKWN, but included Stanisław Mikołajczyk and a few others from the Government-in-Exile.

17 July–2 August 1945: The Potsdam Conference: the Allies agreed to give former German territories east of the Oder–Neisse line to Poland.

19 January 1947: Elections to the Sejm were won by the Democratic Bloc, a grouping dominated by the PWP and led by Władysław Gomułka; the United Kingdom and the USA complained that the elections did not meet the requirements agreed at Yalta.

6 February 1947: The People's Republic of Poland was declared; Bolesław Bierut took office as President.

October 1947: Mikołajczyk fled to London after threats to his life.

September 1948: Gomułka was forced to admit 'political errors' and was dismissed as party leader; in 1949 he was arrested, accused of 'rightist and nationalist deviations'.

December 1948: The founding congress of the Polish United Workers' Party (PZPR) took place after the PWP merged with the Polish Socialist Party; Bierut was appointed party First Secretary.

22 July 1952: A new Soviet-style Constitution was adopted.

1954: Bierut was succeeded by Józef Cyrankiewicz as Chairman of the Council of Ministers, but remained party First Secretary.

14 May 1955: The Treaty of Warsaw founded the Soviet bloc military organization known as the Warsaw Pact.

28–29 June 1956: Seventy-four people died in riots in Poznań protesting against food price rises.

October 1956: Władysław Gomułka was appointed First Secretary and began to introduce some political liberalization.

March 1968: Nation-wide anti-Government student protests took place, followed by a party-inspired campaign against Jews and intellectuals.

April 1968: Marshal Marian Spychalski was appointed Head of State.

November 1968: The Soviet leader, Leonid Brezhnev, announced the 'Brezhnev Doctrine' (declaring the right of the USSR to intervene in the affairs of its Warsaw Pact allies) in Warsaw.

December 1970: Gomułka and Spychalski resigned after workers were killed when police suppressed strikes and protests in the Baltic ports; Piotr Jaroszewicz replaced Józef Cyrankiewicz (who became Head of State) as Chairman of the Council of Ministers; Edward Gierek was appointed First Secretary.

7 December 1970: A treaty was signed by Poland and the Federal Republic of Germany (West Germany), confirming the post-1945 Polish western border.

1972: Gierek launched a 'modernization programme' of large-scale investment funded chiefly by Western banks.

September 1976: The Workers' Defence Committee (KOR) was formed after striking miners were arrested at Radom.

16 October 1978: Cardinal Karol Wojtyła, Archbishop of Kraków, was elected head of the world-wide Roman Catholic Church as Pope John Paul II.

February 1980: Piotr Jaroszewicz was replaced as Chairman of the Council of Ministers by Edward Babiuch at the party Congress.

July 1980: Food-price rises led to strikes and workers' protests; unofficial strike committees were formed to press for pay increases and, subsequently, for political demands to be met.

14 August 1980: Some 17,000 workers at the Lenin Shipyards in Gdańsk (formerly Danzig) went on strike; the strike spread to Szczecin (formerly Stettin) one week later and involved over 150,000 workers.

24 August 1980: Babiuch resigned and was replaced by Józef Pińkowski as Chairman of the Council of Ministers.

31 August 1980: Following negotiations with Lech Wałęsa and other union delegates, the Gdańsk and Szczecin agreements were signed: the Government agreed to the unions' demands, including the right to form free trade unions and the right to strike.

5 September 1980: Gierek was replaced as First Secretary by Stanisław Kania.

17 September 1980: Representatives from some 35 independent trade-union committees met to form the independent trade union, Solidarity (Solidarność), which was officially recognized on 10 November.

10–11 February 1981: Pińkowski was replaced as Chairman of the Council of Ministers by Gen. Wojciech Jaruzelski. Jaruzelski replaced Kania as party First Secretary in October.

13 December 1981: Jaruzelski declared martial law. A Military Council of National Salvation was established; Wałęsa and other Solidarity activists were arrested and imprisoned.

13 December 1982: Martial law was suspended (Wałęsa had been released from gaol the previous month).

22 July 1983: Martial law was formally lifted; the Military Council of National Salvation was dissolved.

5 October 1983: Lech Wałęsa was awarded the Nobel Peace Prize.

October 1984: Jerzy Popiełuszko, a pro-Solidarity priest, was murdered by security forces.

October 1985: Some multi-candidate ballots were allowed in legislative elections; Solidarity urged a boycott and, later, challenged the results.

6 November 1985: Jaruzelski resigned as the Chairman of the Council of Ministers, becoming President of the Council of State (Head of State); he was succeeded by Prof. Zbigniew Messner.

June 1988: Only 55% of the electorate participated in local elections after Solidarity urged a boycott, following months of continuing civil and industrial unrest.

19 September 1988: Zbigniew Messner's Government resigned; Dr Mieczysław Rakowski became Chairman of a more reformist Council of Ministers.

31 October 1988: Large-scale protests took place after the Government announced the closure of the Lenin Shipyards in Gdańsk.

6 February 1989: 'Round table' negotiations between the Government and opposition leaders, headed by Lech Wałęsa, opened in Warsaw. Following two months of talks, a negotiated agreement was reached: Solidarity was to be re-legalized; partly free elections were to be held; and economic reforms were promised. Two days later appropriate constitutional amendments were adopted, including the creation of a new, bicameral National Assembly; 65% of seats in the lower chamber (Sejm) were to be reserved for communists.

17 May 1989: Full legal status was granted to the Roman Catholic Church (diplomatic relations with the Holy See were restored in July) and freedom of conscience guaranteed.

June 1989: Elections to the National Assembly took place (in two rounds): Solidarity won 99% of the freely elected seats.

28–29 July 1989: Jaruzelski, having been narrowly elected President on 19 July, resigned all party posts; he was replaced as First Secretary by Mieczysław Rakowski.

August 1989: Solidarity having refused a coalition with the communists the previous month, Lt-Gen. Czesław Kiszczak was chosen as premier, but he failed to form a government. President Jaruzelski then accepted Solidarity's earlier proposal of a coalition with the United Peasants' Party and the Democratic Party; Tadeusz Mazowiecki was asked to lead a new, multi-party administration.

29–30 December 1989: The National Assembly approved amendments to the Constitution, including an end to the PZPR's monopoly of power, and the restoration of the official name and flag of pre-war Poland. Finance minister Leszek Balcerowicz's economic reform plan (already approved by the IMF) was approved by the Sejm.

November 1990: Poland's western border was confirmed by the signature of a treaty with the reunified Germany.

25 November 1990: The presidential election took place: Wałęsa received some 43% of the votes cast, but premier Mazowiecki was forced into third place by a maverick candidate, Stanisław Tymiński; Mazowiecki's Government resigned the next day.

9 December 1990: Wałęsa won the second round of the presidential election with 74% of the votes cast.

January 1991: Jan Bielecki was approved as Chairman of the Council of Ministers by the Sejm, and his proposed Government was also accepted. The Citizens' Parliamentary Club (the group of Solidarity deputies in the National Assembly) was split by the formation of the Democratic Union (UD).

4 April 1991: The first of the 50,000 Soviet troops remaining in Poland were withdrawn.

27 October 1991: Only 43.2% of the electorate participated in Poland's first fully free elections to the Senat (the upper house of the National Assembly) and the Sejm; a total of 29 parties won representation in the Sejm: the largest, with 62 of the 460 seats (12.3% of the votes cast), being the UD; the Democratic Left Alliance (SLD), led by the Social Democracy of the Republic of Poland (SRP, as the PZPR was known from 1990), won 60 seats (11.9%).

December 1991: Following weeks of negotiations, Jan Olszewski of the Centre Alliance was appointed Chairman of the Council of Ministers (Prime Minister).

June 1992: Following its lack of progress with economic reform, and disputes with President Wałęsa, a motion of 'no confidence' in the Government was passed by the Sejm. The leader of the Polish People's Party (PSL), Waldemar Pawlak, was appointed premier, but failed to form a government.

July 1992: Hanna Suchocka of the UD became Prime Minister and formed a seven-party coalition to govern.

8 December 1992: An interim Constitution, the 'Small Constitution', entered into force while a comprehensive revision of the 1952 Constitution was in progress.

28 May 1993: As a result of continuing dissatisfaction over government economic and social policies, a vote of 'no confidence' in the Suchocka Government was passed in the Sejm; however, President Wałęsa refused to accept the Prime Minister's resignation and dissolved parliament.

19 September 1993: A general election took place, under a new electoral law designed to minimize the fragmentation of parliamentary representation; the SLD and the PSL, also dominated by former communists, obtained the most votes (20.4% and 15.4%, respectively) and between them took 303 of the 406 seats.

October 1993: The PSL leader, Pawlak, was appointed Prime Minister and formed a Government of SLD and PSL members, plus one Union of Labour member and an independent.

April 1994: Poland formally applied for membership of the European Union (EU).

February 1995: Relations between President Wałęsa and the Government deteriorated as the former demanded Pawlak's resignation. This achieved, Józef Oleksy of the SLD, the speaker of the Sejm and a former communist minister, was appointed premier and formed a new Government in early March.

5 and 19 November 1995: The first round of the presidential election was contested by 13 candidates; Aleksander Kwaśniewski, Chairman of the SRP, obtained 35.1% of the votes cast, and Wałęsa 33.1%. In the second round of voting Kwaśniewski won 51.7% of the votes cast and Wałęsa 48.3%.

23 December 1995: After the Supreme Court dismissed claims of electoral malpractice against him by supporters of Wałęsa, Aleksander Kwaśniewski took office as President.

January 1996: Oleksy resigned as Prime Minister, to be elected leader of the SRP, in succession to Kwaśniewski. The President appointed Włodzimierz Cimoszewicz, a former Minister of Justice, as premier.

November 1996: Poland became a full member of the Organisation for Economic Co-operation and Development.

6 March 1997: The announcement that 3,000 Gdańsk shipyard workers were to lose their jobs followed months of industrial unrest and provoked demonstrations and pickets of government offices throughout the country.

2 April 1997: The National Assembly approved a new Constitution, which slightly reduced presidential powers and committed the country to a social market economy; it was endorsed in the following month by 52.7% of the votes cast in a national referendum and took effect on 17 October.

21 September 1997: In the general election the Solidarity Election Action, a coalition comprising 36 parties, emerged as the strongest grouping, securing 201 seats in the Sejm and 51 in the Senat; the SLD retained 164 seats in the Sejm and 28

in the Senat, while the PSL retained only 27 and three, respectively; the third party, therefore, was the Freedom Union (UW), with 60 deputies and eight senators.

15 October 1997: Jerzy Buzek, a member of Solidarity since its formation, was nominated as Prime Minister and eventually agreed a coalition with the UW later in the month.

8 January 1998: The National Assembly ratified the Concordat, an agreement governing relations between the State and the Roman Catholic Church, which had been reached in 1993, but approval of which had been repeatedly delayed by the previous SLD-led coalition Government.

July 1998: Six AWS deputies withdrew their support for the Government, in protest at the decision to sell the bankrupt Gdańsk shipyard, birthplace of the Solidarity movement. This followed the ruling coalition's loss of nine other deputies in preceding weeks.

1 September 1998: The death penalty was abolished.

11 October 1998: Local government elections indicated continuing support for the ruling AWS-led coalition, although the SLD secured the largest number of seats in nine of the 16 voivodships.

18 December 1998: The Institute of National Remembrance Act, which allowed citizens access to secret-service files compiled on them in the communist era, was enacted, after the Sejm voted to discount a presidential veto; the act came into effect in January 1999.

12 March 1999: Poland was formally admitted to NATO, along with the Czech Republic and Hungary.

December 1999: Solidarity announced that it was to withdraw from politics and become an 'organization of employees'; the movement's voting rights within the AWS were transferred to the Social Movement of Solidarity Election Action (RS AWS), founded in December 1997, and led by Buzek.

12 April 2000: All foreign-exchange controls on the złoty were lifted and the 'crawling-peg' mechanism (which progressively reduced the value of the złoty against a 'basket' of Western currencies, including the US dollar) was abandoned.

19 May 2000: Prime Minister Buzek suspended the Government of Warsaw's central commune (a coalition of the UW and the SLD), replacing it with a centrally appointed commissioner; leaders of the UW demanded Buzek's resignation.

8 June 2000: Negotiations aimed at maintaining the governing coalition ended in failure, and the withdrawal of the UW from the Government was formalized; Buzek subsequently formed a minority Government comprising AWS members.

11 July 2000: President Kwaśniewski became the first Polish head of state since the collapse of communist rule in 1989 to make an official visit to Russia; both countries pledged to improve bilateral relations.

August 2000: A court investigating allegations of collaboration by public figures with the communist-era security forces acquitted both President Kwaśniewski and Wałęsa of any such involvement.

8 October 2000: Kwaśniewski was re-elected to the presidency, receiving 53.9% of the votes cast. Andrzej Olechowski (an independent and former minister in Solidarity and AWS Governments) obtained 17.3% of the ballot, Marian Krzaklewski (the official AWS candidate) 15.6% and Jarosław Kalinowski of the PSL 6.0%.

8 December 2000: Leszek Balcerowicz, who had resigned the leadership of the UW, was nominated to succeed Hanna Gronkiewicz-Waltz as President of the National Bank of Poland, and later approved by the Sejm. The UW elected Bronisław Geremek as its new leader. In the same month five of the largest parties in the AWS coalition agreed to merge formally into a single party, to be led by Buzek (thus displacing Krzaklewski).

7 March 2001: The National Assembly voted in favour of reinstating or providing compensation for property seized from Polish citizens by the state between 1944 and 1989. President Kwaśniewski, however, expressed the reservations that this would exclude Jewish claimants who fled Poland during or after the Second World War, and would also place the nation under considerable financial strain.

23 September 2001: Legislative elections took place to both the Sejm and the Senat. The incumbent Solidarity Electoral Action of the Right (AWSP, as the AWS had been restyled in May) failed to win any seats in the Sejm; instead, a leftist coalition of the SLD and the Union of Labour (UP) secured the greatest number of seats, winning 75 of the 100 seats in the Senat and 216 of the 460 seats in the Sejm.

9 October 2001: A coalition agreement was signed by the SLD, the UP and the PSL (which had obtained 44 seats in the Sejm), to secure an overall majority in the lower house. A new Government was sworn in on 19 October, led by Leszek Miller.

29 November 2001: Andrzej Lepper's refusal to resign as Vice-Marshal of the Sejm, following an attack on the Minister of Foreign Affairs over concessions made to the EU on the issue of land sales, resulted in his dismissal. On 25 January 2002 the Sejm voted to remove Lepper's parliamentary immunity from prosecution. In February he was charged with seven counts of slander, and in March he was sentenced to one year's imprisonment (conditionally suspended for four years) for his role in organizing illegal blockades in 1999.

2 July 2002: Marek Belka resigned as Minister of Finance. Three days later Grzegorz Kołodko, who had been Minister of Finance in 1994–97, was appointed as Belka's replacement.

27 October 2002: Direct local elections took place, in which the ruling SLD-UP coalition won 33.7% of the votes cast. A second round of voting took place on 10 November.

13 December 2002: At an historic EU summit meeting in Copenhagen, Denmark, Poland was among 10 countries formally invited to join the Union from 1 May 2004.

6 January 2003: Prime Minister Miller carried out a cabinet reshuffle. The ministries of economy and of labour were consolidated into a new Ministry of Economy, Labour and Social Policy, under Jerzy Hausner.

10 January 2003: A law regulating media ownership was suspended, pending the results of an inquiry, following allegations by the newspaper *Gazeta Wyborcza* that the film producer Lew Rywin had attempted, on behalf of the Prime Minister, to solicit a bribe from the newspaper, in return for the approval of amendents to the legislation, which would have enabled the newspaper's parent company to purchase a TV station.

1 March 2003: Miller expelled the PSL from the Government, after it supported opposition deputies in voting against new tax legislation.

14 March 2003: The governing coalition formed a parliamentary alliance with the Peasant Democratic Party (PLD).

7–8 June 2003: In a national referendum on EU membership, 77% of the votes cast were in favour of the country's accession.

11 June 2003: Following the resignation of Kołodko as Minister of Finance, Hausner was nominated to be Deputy Prime Minister, while retaining the economy, labour and social policy portfolio. Two days later the Council of Ministers won a vote of confidence in the Sejm.

29 June 2003: Miller was re-elected to the leadership of the SLD.

History

JAN REPA

EARLY HISTORY

Poland emerged as a state in the 10th century, when several Slav-speaking tribes united under the leadership of the Polanians ('dwellers of the cultivated fields'). The conversion of Mieszko I (Mieczysław) to Catholic Christianity in 966 determined Poland's subsequent Western orientation. Following a period of political fragmentation in the 12th and 13th centuries, when the province of Silesia defected to the German empire, the Polish kingdom was restored in the early 1300s, and brought to a new level of power by Casimir 'the Great' (1333–70), who codified laws, promoted trade, encouraged immigration by Jews and other communities, and began Poland's territorial expansion eastwards. In 1386 Queen Hedwig (Jadwiga) married Jagiełło, the Grand Duke of Lithuania. The consequent Lithuanian union brought significant territorial gains, including modern Belarus and central Ukraine. Renaissance humanism exerted a strong influence on Poland's élites, engendering a cult of the Latin language and the civic values of the Roman Republic, as demonstrated by the statute of 1503, prohibiting the introduction of new laws without the consent of parliament.

Upon the death of Sigismund Augustus, the last of the Jagiellonian dynasty, in 1572, Poland became a 'Commonwealth', with a constitutional monarch elected by the Szlachta (nobility), which comprised 8%–10% of the population. Absorbing the native nobilities of the eastern territories, the Szlachta developed a popular but highly exclusive culture, based on social origin, equality, free elections, the right of rebellion in a just cause and, increasingly, defence of the Roman Catholic faith. Politically marginalized, the towns and cities began a gradual decline. Attempts to strengthen central government and create a large standing army of peasant conscripts were rejected as a threat to liberty and Poland's élite cavalry regiments dominated the battlefields of East Europe. Military campaigns were waged against Cossacks, Russians, Swedes, Tatars and Turks; the Russian city of Moscow was captured in 1611 and the Ottoman Turks were defeated at Vienna, Austria, in 1683. However, this was taking place against a background of steadily dwindling resources. By the early 1700s Poland had become virtually ungovernable—a condition encouraged by the leaders of neighbouring states, who in 1733 pledged themselves by secret treaty to 'uphold Polish liberties' (maintain the state of near-anarchy).

Increasing internal pressure for reform provoked a ruthless response from the surrounding countries. In 1772 Austria, Prussia and Russia annexed one-third of Poland's territory by an Act of Partition. The reformers, cautiously supported by Poland's last king, Stanisław II Poniatowski, maintained their programme, creating the world's first ministry of education in 1773. In 1791 the Sejm (parliament) enacted a new Constitution, which abolished the elective monarchy, strengthened the executive and enfranchised the bourgeoisie. Prussia and Russia invaded once more and imposed a further partition. An unsuccessful uprising led by Tadeusz Kósciuszko was followed in 1795 by the Third Partition, after which Poland disappeared from the map.

Polish hopes of a national revival initially rested with Revolutionary France. The French leader, Napoleon I Bonaparte, created a Grand Duchy of Warsaw (1807–15) from parts of the Austrian and Prussian zones, encompassing a small part of former Polish territory. Poles fought in Napoleon I's armies, contributing up to 100,000 troops for the Russian campaign of 1812. After his fall from power, Poland was again partitioned, most of the Grand Duchy of Warsaw becoming a dominion of the Russian Tsar. Unpopular Russian policies contributed to major insurrections in 1830–31 and 1863–64, followed by intensified repression, including the closure of the universities in Warsaw and Wilno (Vilnius, now in Lithuania), and the emigration of a large part of Poland's political and cultural élite. The Prussian Government pursued a long campaign of germanization in its Polish territories, with little success, although, in other respects, Prussian Poland was prosperous and well-managed. Austrian Poland (Galicia) was granted self-government in 1867—providing a new focus for national politics—although the cultural brilliance of cities like Kraków (Cracow) and the regional capital, Lwów (Lemberg—now Lviv, Ukraine) contrasted with much rural poverty. In the late 19th century, the Polish-speaking peasantry acquired a strong national consciousness. But Polish aspirations were increasingly challenged by the emerging nationalism of former subject peoples (Jews, Lithuanians and Ukrainians), each promoting their own political agenda.

REBIRTH OF THE POLISH STATE

During the First World War, the Polish territories endured heavy fighting between Russia and the Central Powers of Austria-Hungary and Germany, on what was known as the Eastern Front. With the War about to end and the three partitioning empires in a state of collapse, the Poles proclaimed independence in October 1918—a political *fait accompli* officially recognized in the following year by the Treaty of Versailles. Poland's borders were not fixed, however, until the resolution of a number of plebiscites, armed conflicts with Germans, Czechs, Lithuanians and Ukrainians, and a major war with Bolshevik Russia (1919–21). The new Poland was just over one-half the size of the old Commonwealth. Despite this, national minorities (Belarusians, Germans, Jews and Ukrainians) accounted for 30% of the population. In addition, there were significant Polish-speaking communities in neighbouring countries. The new state was established as a parliamentary republic, although the dominant political figure was Marshal Józef Piłsudski, a former socialist activist and military leader in the period of national rebirth. Much effort was expended on reintegrating three distinct regions, characterized by different legal systems, living standards, political traditions and mentality. Poland encountered severe economic difficulties, partly inherited from the Partition era and exacerbated by the world economic depression of the 1930s. Politically, the country was polarized between the National Democrats and their allies, who wanted a centralized state and the assimilation of minorities; and the supporters of Piłsudski, who saw the Poles as potential leaders of an extensive Eastern European federation. Impatient with political instability characterized by a succession of short-lived coalition governments, Piłsudski led a *coup d'état* in 1926, establishing a personal regime, which his followers continued after his death in 1935.

THE SECOND WORLD WAR

German and Soviet opinion remained largely unreconciled with the territorial losses occasioned by Poland's re-emergence. Polish foreign policy was intended to balance the country between Germany and the USSR and follow a principle of equidistance. However, in 1939 the German Chancellor, Adolf Hitler, presented a series of demands, including a repositioning of the frontier and Poland's accession to the Anti-Comintern Pact signed by Germany, Italy and Japan. Poland refused, and on 1 September 1939 German troops invaded the country, followed by Soviet forces on the 17 September. Warsaw capitulated to the Germans later that month and Poland was again partitioned. France and the United Kingdom declared war on Germany in response, effectively beginning the Second World War. In 1941 Germany invaded the USSR, bringing all Polish territory under its control. During the War over 6m. Polish citizens died, including almost the entire Jewish population. Both Germany and the USSR, in their positions as occupying powers, were responsible for the persecution and eradication of local communities and the deliberate killing of people with education and social standing. Poland also became the site of a number of special camps for the systematic extermination of Europe's Jews and other groups. Resistance activity continued throughout the war, formally led by a broadly based Government-in-Exile in London, the United Kingdom, under General Władysław Sikorski, which established diplomatic relations with the USSR in 1941. Following his death in 1943, Sikorski was succeeded as premier by the Peasant Party leader, Stanisław Mikołajczyk.

In 1943, with the war against Germany turning in its favour, the USSR severed relations with the Polish Government and began forming a future Polish administration under its own supervision. At the summit meeting held in Tehran, Iran, in December 1943, the United Kingdom and the USA agreed that the USSR would recover most of the Polish territory annexed in 1939. Poland would be compensated at Germany's expense and would form part of a new Soviet 'sphere of influence'. In July 1944 a Committee of National Liberation (PKWN) was established, under Soviet auspices, gradually assuming the administration of Polish territories from which the Soviet army had expelled German forces and civilians.

THE PERIOD OF COMMUNIST RULE

In January 1945 the PKWN transformed itself into a 'Provisional Government of National Unity'. At the Allied summit in Yalta (Ukraine, then part of the USSR) the following month, Stalin (Iosif V. Dzhugashvili) agreed, as a concession to Western leaders, to reconstitute the Provisional Government with the participation of a number of members of the Government-in-Exile, including Mikołajczyk. This amended Government was recognized by the United Kingdom and the USA on 6 July 1945. The communists also undertook to hold 'free and unfettered elections' as soon as practicable. In reality, only political groups acceptable to the USSR were allowed to participate. During the electoral campaign 16 wartime resistance leaders were arrested and tried in Moscow, the Soviet capital. In conditions of widespread intimidation and electoral malpractice, the general election was held in January 1947. The Democratic Bloc, led by the communist Polish Workers' Party, gained an expected victory. Mikołajczyk fled the country with US assistance. The following year the communists renamed themselves the Polish United Workers' Party (PZPR), after a merger with the rump of the pre-war Socialist Party.

The new Poland differed greatly from the pre-war Republic. Its population had declined from 35m. to 24m. Geographically, its territory had been relocated several hundred kilometres to the west. Major centres of Polish culture, such as Lwów and Wilno were incorporated into the USSR (in the Ukrainian and Lithuanian republics, respectively) and their Polish inhabitants expelled. An estimated 8m. Germans fled or were expelled from Poland's new 'western territories'. For the first time since the early Middle Ages, Poland was an ethnically homogenous country, Polish-speakers accounting for some 98% of the population.

Poland's first communist leader, Władysław Gomułka, attempted to pursue a distinctively Polish Socialist policy, but he was forced to resign in September 1948. Bolesław Bierut, a long-standing Comintern agent, assumed power. His period in office coincided with Poland's darkest period of repressive Stalinism, characterized by subservience to Soviet policy, a significant expansion of the internal security forces (UB), the imprisonment of political opponents and members of the Resistance, the forced development of heavy industry and the direct exploitation of Polish resources by the USSR.

In 1953 Stalin died. Three years later the denunciation of Stalin by the new Soviet leader, Nikita Khrushchev, the death of Bierut, and the violent suppression of a demonstration against communist rule in the city of Poznań combined to create a major crisis for the Polish regime. The immediate result was the rehabilitation of Gomułka and his reinstatement as leader of the PZPR; he reiterated his belief in a 'Polish road' to socialism. Khrushchev threatened military intervention, although such intervention never occurred. Several thousand Soviet 'advisers' were ordered to return to the USSR. The collectivization of agriculture was halted, cultural policy was relaxed and cautious economic reforms initiated. By the end of the mid-1960s, however, it was clear that Gomułka's 'stabilization' had been unable to maintain its early successes. The economy remained heavily centralized. Communist control was re-established in cultural and professional life, albeit without the open intimidation of the Stalin era. In the absence of genuine political pluralism, the Roman Catholic Church successfully asserted its role as 'guardian' of Poland's national traditions. In 1966 (the 1,000th anniversary of Poland's conversion to Christianity) the Church initiated a major public campaign, presenting itself as the authentic 'leading force' in the nation.

By 1968 Gomułka's control over the PZPR was slipping. He was challenged by Edward Gierek, the leader of the PZPR in the industrial region of Silesia, and by the 'Partisan' faction, which proclaimed a mixture of Stalinism and nationalism. The banning of a theatre production of a classic 19th century play, containing criticism of tsarist Russia, led to student unrest, demanding an end to censorship. Gomułka blamed the protests on 'Zionist elements', strengthening the Partisans' position. The subsequent anti-Jewish purges in the PZPR and professions adversely affected Poland's image in the West for many years. In December 1970 a decision to increase food prices caused violent unrest in the Baltic Sea ports. The shooting of protesting workers precipitated Gomułka's removal from office and his replacement by Edward Gierek.

Gierek, a trade union activist in Belgium and France in the 1930s, was presented to the Polish public as a pragmatist with 'first-hand experience' of the West. Gierek attempted to revitalize the faltering economy by borrowing large sums from Western banks. This was intended to propagate a Polish 'economic miracle' based on the implementation of new technology and cheap local labour. The central economic planning system was largely unreformed, however. By the mid-1970s a debt crisis had developed as planned exports failed to materialize. Allegations of corruption among PZPR officials became increasingly frequent. Renewed labour unrest in 1976 was suppressed by force, although on this occasion critics of the regime established a Workers' Defence Committee (KOR). The organization's ideology centred on the human-rights provisions of the Helsinki Final Act of the Conference on Security and Co-operation in Europe, signed in 1975; its members sought to increase co-operation between intellectuals and workers and gradually developed an extensive network of legal assistance and clandestine publications. The intention was to challenge the Polish regime's actual behaviour, rather than its ideology or its relationship with the USSR.

By the end of the 1970s the PZPR leadership was demoralized, with no coherent strategy for dealing with the political and economic problems that it had, at least in part, generated. In October 1978 the election of Cardinal Archbishop Karol Wojtyła of Kraków as Pope John Paul II—the first Pole to lead the Roman Catholic Church—represented a turning point in Polish history. His triumphant return to his homeland brought hundreds of thousands of Poles on to the streets, expressing a new confidence in their own strength and shared values in contrast to the enfeebled communist apparatus. In early 1980 Poland experienced further widespread industrial unrest, which soon affected the entire state economy. Amid growing political and industrial unrest, Gierek resigned on the grounds of 'ill health'.

THE RISE OF SOLIDARITY

The discontent of mid-1980 led to confrontation between Gdańsk shipyard workers and government officials, who eventually agreed to the establishment of Solidarity (Solidarność), the first independent trade union in the Eastern bloc. The shipyard negotiators were assisted by a group of intellectuals associated with KOR; although the world media concentrated on the charismatic leader of Solidarity, Lech Wałęsa, a shipyard electrician. Solidarity soon claimed 10m. members. Government censorship of the press effectively collapsed and the communists promised reforms, although they were subsequently accused of delaying their implementation. Solidarity's advisers advocated a 'self-limiting revolution', maintaining the appearance of communist rule in order to forestall armed intervention. However, the reluctance of the regime to expedite political change, combined with a worsening economic situation, radicalized attitudes. The appointment of the defence minister, Gen. Wojciech Jaruzelski, to the positions of Prime Minister and PZPR leader in February 1981 suggested change was imminent.

On 13 December 1981 Jaruzelski declared martial law as leader of a Military Council of National Salvation. Solidarity was proscribed and its leaders, including Wałęsa, imprisoned. Through what was, ostensibly a military *coup d'état*, Jaruzelski attempted to restore the hegemony of the PZPR. Although the response of the French and German Governments was muted, the US President, Ronald Reagan, used the event to reinvigorate ideological rivalry with Russia, demanding that it 'let Poland be Poland', and increasing the US military budget. Jaruzelski struggled to establish domestic stability and to gain international acceptance. Amid continued political unrest, Wałęsa was released in November 1982. In July 1983 martial law was formally ended; the Military Council of National Salvation was dissolved; and an amnesty for all political prisoners was declared. In October Wałęsa was awarded the Nobel Peace Prize.

The relaxation of the regime's policies continued, and its efforts to secure international acceptance began to yield some success. These efforts were undermined in October 1984, however, when a young pro-Solidarity priest, Fr Jerzy Popiełuszko, was abducted and killed. Four officials from the Ministry of Internal Affairs were subsequently convicted of his murder. Popiełuszko's funeral became a mass protest against the regime. Legislative elections were held in October 1985, voters having a choice of two officially vetted candidates for 410 of the 460 seats in the Sejm. Solidarity urged voters to boycott the poll, and subsequently disputed the Government's claim that 79% of the electorate had participated. In November Jaruzelski resigned as premier, being replaced by Prof. Zbigniew Messner, and became Head of State.

In the late 1980s there was a marked relaxation of policies, prompted by Poland's deteriorating economic situation and a growing recognition of popular discontent with the regime, manifested by repeated violent unrest. A further factor was the accession of Mikhail Gorbachev to power in the USSR in 1985. Gradually, his more liberal policies permeated the political structures of the Warsaw Pact states. In 1988 Gorbachev announced that force would no longer be used to keep the Eastern European regimes in power.

In 1989 'round table' talks between the communists and opposition representatives, led by Wałęsa, resulted in the restoration of Solidarity's legality and, in June 1989, in Poland's first legislative election under rules of 'controlled democracy'. Solidarity secured all but one of the seats in the new upper chamber (Senat) and all 35% of the seats that it was allowed to contest in the lower chamber (Sejm). The remainder were reserved for the communists and their client-parties (including the Democratic Party and the United Peasants' Party). Jaruzelski was elected by deputies to the newly created office of President by a majority of one. When the communists' former allies withdrew their support, the way was cleared for Tadeusz Mazowiecki, a prominent Roman Catholic journalist and Solidarity adviser, to become, on 24 August 1989, the first non-communist premier in the Eastern bloc.

The two principal responsibilities of the new Government were political reform and the reversal of decades of economic mismanagement. A radical monetary reform was introduced in January 1990 with IMF approval. Named the 'Balcerowicz Plan', after the new finance minister, Leszek Balcerowicz, it aimed at creating the preconditions for a successful move from a centrally planned economy to one run according to market forces. Politically, Mazowiecki moved more cautiously, declaring he would 'draw a line' over the past.

DISINTEGRATION OF THE SOLIDARITY CONSENSUS

The mood of optimism that greeted the formation of the Solidarity-led Government in 1989 abated in the following year as real wages and productivity decreased and unemployment rose rapidly. Divisions within Solidarity became increasingly evident as Wałęsa considered he was being marginalized by supporters of Mazowiecki. Wałęsa argued for faster political and economic change, including Solidarity's own transformation into competing parties and an accelerated programme of privatization. Jaruzelski resigned in September 1990 to permit a direct presidential election to be held; both Wałęsa and Mazowiecki were candidates. A confrontational campaign ensued, following which Mazowiecki was eliminated in the first ballot. Wałęsa went on to win, and was inaugurated in December. However, the volatility of the electorate was indicated by the unexpected level of support for the Polish-Canadian businessman, Stanisław Tymiński, who emerged as Wałęsa's main contender. Mazowiecki resigned as premier in November and was succeeded by Jan Krzysztof Bielecki, hitherto an economist and journalist.

The Bielecki Government remained in office until August 1991 when, exasperated by the obstructiveness of a politically unsympathetic Sejm, it offered its resignation. Poland's first completely free legislative elections were arranged for 27 October. Owing to the extreme form of proportional representation adopted, 29 parties won representation in the Sejm. The most successful were the Democratic Union (Unia Democratyczne—UD), representing the old Mazowiecki faction, with 12.3% of the votes cast (62 seats), and the Democratic Left Alliance (Sojusz Lewicy Demokratycznej—SLD), an electoral coalition led by former communists espousing the Western European model of social democracy.

Following several weeks of negotiations, in December 1991 a centre-right coalition Government was formed by Jan Olszewski, a human rights lawyer and former Solidarity activist. However, after only seven months in office it was obliged to resign, rendered powerless by constant infighting and a series of disputes with President Wałęsa. After representatives of other parties had failed to form an administration, Hanna Suchocka of the UD became Poland's first female Prime Minister in July 1992, leading a seven-party coalition Government. Despite her personal popularity, her administration was swiftly beset by familiar problems—coalition infighting and labour unrest. On 28 May 1993 a vote of 'no confidence' proposed by Suchocka's nominal allies, the parliamentary Solidarity group, was passed by a margin of one vote and the Government resigned.

The period from 1989 to 1993 was marked by factionalism, personality clashes and policy confusion among the post-Solidarity parties. A broad consensus existed in support of democracy and a broadly Western orientation; however, there were also fears of a potential loss of new-found sovereignty and of Western dominance. Some on the left wing of Solidarity even advocated seeking a common platform with the former communists. Political figures on the right argued for the exclusion of former communists from the political process and a renewed emphasis on Poland's ethnic identity and Roman Catholic faith. A further problem was the uncertain delineation of presidential powers. Wałęsa favoured a more active style of presidency; while his opponents wanted the President to remain largely a symbolic head of state. An attempt to find a compromise was made in the 'Small Constitution' of August 1992, which included a major concession by the Sejm: the granting to the President of the right, upon changes of government, to nominate candidates for three key ministries: defence, interior and foreign affairs.

THE RETURN OF THE LEFT

Following the resignation of the Suchocka Government, President Wałęsa dissolved the Sejm, scheduling a legislative election for 19 September 1993. New electoral rules were enacted, excluding from parliamentary representation any party receiving fewer than 5% of the votes cast (apart from the German minority, for which four seats were reserved). The election resulted in a decisive victory for the left. The SLD and the Polish People's Party (Polskie Stronnictwo Ludowe—PSL) together obtained 35.8% of the votes cast and, under the new rules, won over 65% of the seats in the lower house. In the Senat, the two parties won a combined 73 of the 100 seats. The UD was the most successful of the centre-right parties, obtaining 10.6% of the ballot and winning 74 seats in the Sejm.

On 18 October 1993 Waldemar Pawlak, the leader of the PSL, was nominated as premier by President Wałęsa and, following protracted negotiations, formed a coalition Government with the SLD. Among the opposition, the UD merged with the Liberal Democratic Congress in 1994 to form the Freedom Union (Unia Wolności—UW). Nevertheless, there were few signs of right-wing consensus. President Wałęsa's relations with the Government and the Sejm (dominated by former communists) quickly deteriorated. His frequent use of the presidential veto and his readiness to involve himself directly in government affairs compounded the impression of disunity. Furthermore, the governing coalition was beset by internal differences. Disagreement over the privatization of Bank Śląski in December 1993 led to the dismissal of the Deputy Minister of Finance, Stefan Kawalec of the SLD, and the subsequent resignation of the Minister of Finance, Marek Borowski (also of the SLD).

Pawlak resigned as premier in February 1995, after a sustained political campaign by President Wałęsa. He was replaced by Józef Oleksy of the SLD, the first former communist to become Prime Minister in post-1989 Poland. Oleksy had previously been Marshal (speaker) of the Sejm. The choice of Oleksy confounded some observers, who had expected Wałęsa to invite Aleksander Kwaśniewski, his potential rival for the presidency, to form a government.

Despite political instability, the Polish economy had quietly revived. In 1993 the country's gross domestic product (GDP) registered 3.8% growth; this expansion continued, reaching 7.0% in 1995. A significant factor in this expansion was the strong performance of small and medium-scale private enterprise, particularly in the services sector. In addition, the rate of inflation declined throughout the decade. Foreign visitors also noted a new sense of social dynamism, exemplified by successful young entrepreneurs with little obvious interest in party politics. Some even drew parallels between Poland and post-war Italy.

THE 'RED TRIANGLE'

The first round of the 1995 presidential election, held on 5 November, resulted in Kwaśniewski and Wałęsa leading the poll, with 35.1% and 33.1%, respectively, of the votes cast. The SLD leader ran an effective campaign, emphasizing youthful sophistication and an openness to new ideas. The second round of voting, a direct contest between left and right, brought Kwaśniewski a narrow victory, by 51.7% to 48.3%. Both houses of the National Assembly and the presidency were now controlled by the former communist left—Polish politics was dominated by the so-called 'red triangle'.

Despite the polarization of politics, which had improved his chances of re-election, Wałęsa's record in office—his capricious, interventionist and confrontational behaviour—proved unpopular with the electorate. Opinion polls suggested many, especially younger, voters considered his time to have passed. Against a background of accusations that Kwaśniewski had misled the public about his academic qualifications, Wałęsa refused to participate in the new President's inauguration ceremony in December 1995.

The result of the presidential election was also a disappointment for the Roman Catholic Church, itself divided between conservatives, who saw the fall of communism as an opportunity to promote Poland as a 'model' Roman Catholic society; and 'modernizers', who argued that the Church needed to adapt to life in a pluralistic democracy. Under the Solidarity-based Governments, the Church had succeeded in having much of its agenda inscribed in law: the reintroduction of religious education in state schools, highly restrictive abortion legislation, and a legal obligation on the state broadcast media to reflect 'Christian values'. Despite internal advice in favour of neutrality, the Church openly supported Wałęsa in the election campaign.

In early 1996 the (pro-Wałęsa) Minister of Internal Affairs, Andrzej Milczanowski, announced the discovery of documents suggesting that Oleksy had been a Soviet (and subsequently Russian) agent since the 1980s. Oleksy strongly denied the charge, but was forced to resign so that the evidence could be examined by the official prosecutor. It was eventually decided that insufficient evidence existed to conduct a prosecution, and Oleksy was exonerated in an official report published in October 1996.

As successor to Oleksy, President Kwaśniewski turned to Włodzimierz Cimoszewicz, an academic lawyer and former communist. The formation of the new Government in January 1996 was marked by none of the intrigues and procrastination that accompanied changes of administration under the previous President. Nevertheless, from mid-1996 there was renewed infighting among the coalition partners. In addition,

there was a series of industrial disputes, with state-sector workers demanding a greater share of the relative prosperity that economic growth and foreign investment were bringing and resisting the redundancies implicit in industrial restructuring. In June 1996 a major dispute developed over the fate of the loss-making Gdańsk shipyard, the birthplace of Solidarity. The Government's decision to file for the shipyard's bankruptcy provoked protests organized by that movement; nevertheless, by August the shipyard had been officially declared bankrupt. Protests continued into the following year, and 3,000 employees were eventually made redundant in March 1997. Other disputes at this time involved doctors and coal miners.

As the 1997 legislative elections approached, relations with the Roman Catholic Church again came to prominence. This was partly the result of a revival in the political fortunes of the centre-right opposition. Mindful of the failures caused by past disunity, 36 parties and pressure groups, including the Centre Alliance (Porozumienie Centrum—PC) and the National Christian Union (Zjednoczenie Chrześcijańsko-Narodowe—ZChN), coalesced around the Solidarity 'rump', to form an electoral bloc called Solidarity Electoral Action (Akcja Wyborcza Solidarność—AWS). A major role in this process was played by Solidarity's new leader, Marian Krzaklewski.

On 2 April 1997, after four years of parliamentary negotiations, the National Assembly adopted a new Constitution, subsequently approved in a national referendum on 25 May. The Constitution slightly reduced the powers of the presidency and committed Poland to a social market economy based on the freedom of economic activity and private ownership. The Roman Catholic Church failed to secure a paragraph in the Constitution's preamble recognizing its 'special status' in Polish life. Its efforts to secure a Concordat—an agreement with the State, defining the Church's legal rights and prerogatives—were also defeated, owing to opposition from the SLD.

THE 1997 ELECTION AND ITS AFTERMATH

The general election was held on 21 September 1997. The AWS became the strongest group in both chambers of the National Assembly, securing 201 seats in the Sejm (with 33.8% of the votes cast) and 51 in the Senat. The SLD won 27.1% of the votes cast (equating to 164 seats in the Sejm) and 28 upper-house seats. The UW obtained 60 seats in the Sejm and eight in the Senat, while the PSL saw its representation reduced to 27 seats in the lower house and three in the Senat. Marian Krzaklewski declined to assume the premiership (widely regarded as confirming his intention to contest the presidential election in October 2000). In mid-October Jerzy Buzek, a Protestant academic and longstanding, if not prominent, Solidarity activist, was appointed Prime Minister. Later in that month the AWS signed a coalition agreement with the UW and a new Council of Ministers was formed. Among the UW representatives in the new cabinet were the party's leader, Leszek Balcerowicz (the author of the monetary reform undertaken in 1990), who was appointed Deputy Prime Minister; Minister of Finance and Chairman of the Economic Committee. The programme of the new Government, which prioritized European Union (EU) and North Atlantic Treaty Organization (NATO) membership, was approved by the Sejm in early November.

The Government was committed to accelerating the process of administrative and economic reform, which it claimed had been neglected under the previous administration. In January 1998 a projected reorganization of local government was announced, involving a reduction in the number of voivodships (provinces) from 49 to 12 and the restoration of an intermediate tier of local government, in the form of some 300 powiats (counties). Following considerable opposition from

President Kwaśniewski and from politicians and voters in the threatened provincial centres, a compromise establishing 16 provinces was signed into law in July.

The Buzek Government encountered continued industrial unrest, despite its enthusiasm for further economic restructuring. An additional incentive was the commencement of membership negotiations with the EU in March 1998. In April the Government presented its plan for the coal industry, envisaging a 50% reduction of the work-force and the closure of 24 of the country's 65 mines. Further restructuring projects were announced, involving the railways and the steel industry. Despite these plans, in May 1998 the European Commission announced a suspension of its programme of development aid, owing to the insufficient number of viable projects presented by the Government. The suspension resulted in the dismissals of Poland's chief EU negotiator, Ryszard Czarnecki, of the ZChN, and his deputy, Piotr Nowina-Konopka, of the UW.

The Government was also embarrassed by the activity of an extreme-right group, led by a disaffected former Solidarity activist, Kazimierz Switon, which began erecting hundreds of wooden crosses outside the Second World War concentration camp at Auschwitz, after Jewish pressure to have a large cross, erected there after a papal visit, removed. The Roman Catholic hierarchy was also embarrassed; the Polish Primate, Cardinal Józef Glemp, had initially supported the action. After protracted legal manoeuvres, during which Switon claimed to be the victim of a Judaeo-Masonic conspiracy, the crosses were removed. In January 2000 Switon was convicted of incitement to racial hatred and given a six-month suspended prison sentence.

In January 1999 the Government began four ambitious reforms simultaneously, involving education, health, local government and pensions. These reforms were ostensibly aimed at reducing the role of the state and introducing an element of competition in the relevant sectors. The resulting bureaucratic confusion, although predictable, increased public dissatisfaction with the Government, and there was increasing industrial unrest throughout the year, culminating, in late September, in a demonstration in Warsaw attended by some 35,000 people. In addition, the rate of economic growth had slowed, owing to the effects of the Russian financial crisis of August 1998 and a significant rise in unemployment as industrial restructuring began to take effect. In December Balcerowicz threatened to resign, when the AWS rejected his proposals for a 'flat-rate' income tax as excessively radical and socially divisive.

Tensions within the governing coalition were expressed in May by Buzek's suspension of the Government of Warsaw's central district, hitherto administered by a coalition led by members of the UW which, in response, demanded Buzek's resignation. In the same month certain AWS deputies voted against the UW's proposed taxation reforms; the UW subsequently reiterated its demand for Buzek to resign and announced the withdrawal of its five ministers. The UW's withdrawal was formalized in June. The AWS formed a minority Government with Buzek remaining as Prime Minister. The Polish right was fragmented and unpopular, and had difficulty in agreeing on a candidate to contest the presidential election, scheduled for October. Meanwhile, the popularity of the incumbent President, Kwaśniewski, was increasing.

THE PENDULUM SWINGS BACK

The presidential election proved a disaster for the ex-Solidarity camp. Aleksander Kwaśniewski was re-elected in the first ballot, with 54% of the votes cast, whereas Krzaklewski came third, with only 16%, and voters humiliated Lech Wałęsa, who received just 1%. Krzaklewski eventually

resigned from the leadership of the AWS, which in May 2001 transformed itself into a single party, Solidarity Electoral Action of the Right (AWSP), under Buzek.

In October 2000 Leszek Balcerowicz became the Governor of Poland's central bank and resigned as leader of the UW. In an indecisive election, Bronisław Geremek, the former foreign minister, became head of the UW, prompting the withdrawal from the party of the Liberal faction led by Donald Tusk. In January 2001 a new political movement, the Civic Platform, was announced by Andrzej Olechowski (Poland's former negotiator with the EU, who had come second in the recent presidential elections, with 17% of the votes cast), Donald Tusk and the parliamentary speaker, Maciej Plazyński, a defector from the AWS. The organization advocated a state administration free from party-political patronage and a conservative-liberal political orientation. It enjoyed strong early popularity.

In 2001 the economy experienced significantly lower rates of growth. The central bank was criticized for maintaining excessively high interest rates, which was attributed to the Government's failure to control public spending. Critics accused both the Government and the central bank of neglecting the needs of small businesses. By the end of the first quarter unemployment had reached 16% of the labour force and the closure of coal mines and heavy industry plants continued.

The resolution of historical issues took on great significance in 2001, with the resumption of the trial of 78-year old Gen. Jaruzelski for ordering troops to repress Solidarity protesters in 1970, which had resulted in 44 deaths. President Kwaśniewski was also prompted to apologize formally for the massacre of the Jewish inhabitants of the town of Jedwabne in 1941, by their Polish neighbours, following the discovery that this was not committed by Nazi occupiers. The revelation caused widespread controversy throughout the country, with the Roman Catholic Church expressing regret, but refusing to add its name to an apology.

With the next parliamentary elections scheduled to be held in September 2001, opinion polls indicated victory for the SLD opposition. Meanwhile, the incumbent Government had been beset by the dismissal and resignation of three ministers in July, most notably the Minister of Post and Telecommunications, who was alleged to have been implicated in corrupt activities. In early September the elderly Minister of Foreign Affairs (and war hero), Wladysław Bartoszewski, resigned, claiming that he had been marginalized with regard to decisions relating to the diplomatic service. The Government maintained an unyielding policy in membership negotiations with the EU, insisting that subsidies should be available to Poles from the outset of membership and pressing for membership by 2003. However, the Government was swift to welcome the election of George W. Bush, who took office as President of the USA in January 2001, and President Bush visited Warsaw in June, describing Poland as the USA's 'trusted friend' and alluding to further NATO enlargement in 2002.

SOLIDARITY'S DEMISE

The legislative elections, held on 23 September 2001 as scheduled, represented a significant turning point in Polish politics. The former Solidarity parties of the AWSP and the UW failed to win any seats and a coalition of the SLD and the Union of Labour (UP) won a total of 291 seats (in the upper and lower houses, combined). The Civic Platform was the second-placed party, with 65 seats in the Sejm, and the new Law and Justice Party, formed by former justice minister Lech Kaczynski, won 44 seats. Equally important was the support given to three openly anti-EU parties: the PSL, the populist Self Defence Party, and the right wing, 'Catholic-nationalist' League of

Polish Families, with a combined total of 133 seats in the Sejm. An SLD-UP-PSL coalition Government took office in October under Prime Minister Leszek Miller, a former member of the communist Politburo. Following its defeat, the AWSP retreated from politics, while Geremek resigned as leader of the UW, to be replaced by Władysław Frasyniuk, although the party's future remained in doubt.

ON THE WAY TO EU MEMBERSHIP

The Miller Government quickly set about improving Poland's foreign relations (see below). Although Miller's coalition partner, the PSL, protested at the conduct of EU negotiations, in March 2002 Poland's Roman Catholic bishops involved the Church in politics once again, endorsing future Polish membership of the EU, albeit with some reservations. Thus, the main challenge to the Government remained the economy. By 2002 the rate of unemployment had risen to 18%. The central bank, under Balcerowicz, continued to concentrate on the rate of inflation, which eventually declined to just above 1%. Poland received conflicting advice on how to manage its economic situation. In April the European Commission criticized the lack of co-ordination between the Ministry of Finance and the central bank; meanwhile, the European Central Bank suggested that Poland should aim to increase growth, even at the risk of a moderate increase in inflation.

In July 2002 the Minister of Finance, Marek Belka, unexpectedly resigned. The appointment of a leftward-leaning academic, Grzegorz Kołodko (who had held the post in 1994–97), was regarded as marking a change in emphasis, from orthodox monetary discipline, to an attempt to balance the need for sound finances with economic expansion. The second half of 2002 was dominated by the negotiations for EU membership, which culminated in their successful conclusion at an EU summit held in Copenhagen, Denmark, in December, after agreement was reached with the Polish delegation on improved terms for farmers.

By early 2003 there were signs that Poland's economy was improving, with annual growth for 2003 projected at 3%, but the Government's position had weakened. In December 2002 a daily newspaper, *Gazeta Wyborcza*, published allegations that financial interests linked to the governing SLD had solicited bribes from a major Polish-US consortium, in return for promises to amend proposed media ownership legislation in its favour. The resulting televised parliamentary inquiry, while failing to establish guilt, created the impression of a political class characterized by endemic corruption and cronyism, and consequently the Government's opinion poll ratings declined dramatically. In January 2003 Prime Minister Miller merged the ministries of economy and labour, creating a new Ministry of the Economy, Labour and Social Policy, under the increasingly prominent Jerzy Hausner. In March Miller terminated the coalition agreement with the PSL, remaining in charge of a minority Government.

On 7–8 June 2003 Poland's electorate approved EU membership in a referendum. Of the votes cast, 77% were in favour of accession, and the rate of participation was 59%; the Pope had previously expressed support for Poland's membership of the Union. Miller immediately attempted to use the referendum result to reinforce his position. Within days, Kołodko had resigned, after refusing to accept Miller's proposals for a uniform rate of personal and corporate tax, and overall control of economic strategy was transferred to Hausner's new 'superministry'. Miller subsequently won a parliamentary vote of confidence and was re-elected to the leadership of the SLD unopposed later in June. However, President Kwaśniewski, whose second and final term was to end in 2005, had expressed support for the creation of a broad political coalition to oversee EU entry in May 2004, and there were widespread

suggestions that he was manoeuvring against the Prime Minister.

INTERNATIONAL RELATIONS

The alternation of former Solidarity and former communist governments appeared to have had little effect on Poland's international relations. From 1993 all governments insisted their aim was membership of the EU and of NATO, and the latter was achieved in March 1999. Poland gave strong support to NATO's intervention in the Federal Republic of Yugoslavia in the same month, less than two weeks after joining the Alliance—a stance which, if opinion polls are to be believed, enjoyed considerable public support. Poland's relations with the EU subsequently strengthened rapidly, with the successful conclusion of membership negotiations in December 2002, and accession to the EU scheduled for 1 May 2004. The form that the new, expanded EU would take was less than clear, however. At an EU summit meeting in Nice, France, in December 2000, Poland was promised 27 votes in the EU Council of Ministers—the same number as Spain, and only three fewer than France, Germany, Italy and the United Kingdom—and was fighting to retain this relatively privileged position. During the latter stages of EU negotiations, Prime Minister Miller, Minister of Foreign Affairs Włodzimierz Cimoszewicz, and the minister responsible for European affairs, Danuta Hübner, made several concessions, including agreement on lower initial agricultural subsidies and on an option whereby Austria and Germany would be permitted to exclude Polish workers from their labour markets for a period of seven years.

Despite divided public opinion, Poland gave strong support to the US-led military action in Iraq in March 2003, sending 200 combat troops. The USA subsequently offered Poland the opportunity to run one of three planned reconstruction zones in Iraq, under overall US command. This close involvement with US policy led to serious strains in Poland's relations with France, and to a lesser extent with Germany. Poles remained suspicious of French proposals for a European security role independent of the USA; five Polish leaders have said that they want Poland to be the USA's 'closest ally' in Central and South-Eastern Europe. Polish officials countered French allegations that Poland had departed from a 'European' policy on Iraq, by declaring that no such agreed policy existed.

From the early 1990s Poland placed particular emphasis on relations with its immediate Western neighbour, Germany. The electoral defeat of the German Christian Democrats in October 1998 and the replacement of Helmut Kohl as Chancellor by the Social Democrat Gerhard Schröder was regarded by Poland as a reverse for bilateral relations. This, in conjunction with an awareness of French ambivalence about EU enlargement, led Poland to re-emphasize its links with other countries, such as the United Kingdom, although British hesitation over the adoption of the single European currency, the euro, and further European integration limited its influence.

Relations with Russia remained tense in the early 2000s. In March 2000 President Kwaśniewski attempted to improve relations with Russia by inviting that country's newly elected President, Vladimir Putin, to Poland, and in July Kwaśniewski paid an official visit to Russia. In January 2002 Putin visited Poland in the first such visit by a Russian head of state since 1993; he laid a wreath at the Warsaw monument to the Polish Wartime Resistance and Miller declared the visit to represent a breakthrough in relations. None the less, opinion polls suggested that Poles regarded the *rapprochement* with caution. However, Russia appeared reluctantly to have accepted Polish membership of NATO and there were signs that President Putin wanted to emphasize pragmatic issues over questions of national prestige. Poland strongly favoured the further expansion of NATO, which was to include the Baltic states from 2004, and it continued to attempt to draw Ukraine westwards. However, Poland's Ukrainian policy remained limited by political uncertainty and the lack of reform in Ukraine, and by lingering 'grass-roots' animosity in the areas either side of the Polish–Ukrainian border.

The Economy
Prof. GEORGE BLAZYCA

INTRODUCTION

The post-Second World War settlement between the victorious powers not only dismembered Germany, but also resulted in significant movement of frontiers and people in Central Europe. The Poland that emerged from the War looked, in a geographic sense, substantially different from the independent Poland of the inter-war years. Its frontiers shifted westwards by around 180 km (112 miles), with lost territory in the east absorbed by the USSR and compensation in the form of formerly German lands in the west. Mass movements of population accompanied the changes to the political map of Europe. All this meant that early post-war Poland could not easily be compared in an economic sense to the pre-war Republic. Politically, post-war Poland was firmly in the Soviet bloc, where it remained until 1989, when the Berlin Wall was breached and a new Europe began to be constructed. In terms of its economic system Poland inherited Soviet-style central planning, with all its characteristic features and defects. As in other communist economies the severe, and eventually terminal, shortcomings of command planning were masked for a time by impressive output growth rates and radical shifts in economic structure. The relatively poor and weakly developed economies of most of Central Europe were about to embark on a great wave of forced industrialization, promising badly needed economic reconstruction and modernization. Throughout the 1950s, 1960s and even, in the case of Poland, to the mid-1970s, this modernization had a great impact. Urbanization also proceeded at a fast pace and welfare states brought health care, education and generally better living conditions to the bulk of the population. However, by the late 1970s it was becoming plain that what had been achieved was not sustainable: central planning was showing greater wear and tear and the attempts to mend it had only limited and short-term impact. In particular, the technological gap with the market economies in the West grew wider and with it the East–West divergence in living standards became more pronounced and, for populations in Central Europe, less acceptable. After Mikhail Gorbachev emerged as Soviet leader in 1985 political developments accelerated, culminating in 1989 in the final self-destruction of the European planned economies and of the communist system generally. In August–September 1989, much to its surprise, the Solidarity (Solidarność) protest movement was suddenly thrust into power and faced the task of transforming itself from Gdańsk-based opposition to Warsaw-based government. Meanwhile an academic economist, little known outside Poland, Leszek Balcerowicz, was invited to become Minister of Finance and to devise a means of moving from a planned to a market economy, from state- to privately-owned economy, from communism to capitalism. The task was immense and made all the more difficult in 1989–90 because of a sharp deterioration in macroeconomic conditions, when output declined dramatically and price inflation accelerated.

POST-COMMUNIST ECONOMIC POLICY AND PERFORMANCE

When the 'Balcerowicz Plan' was launched in January 1990 its major aim was to stabilize the 'hyperinflating' economy. With inflation running, in late 1989, at a monthly rate in excess of 30% there was no doubt that unless price growth was brought under control, the market mechanism could not function. Nevertheless, in addition to 'shock therapy' to stabilize the economy, Balcerowicz was also intent on liberalization (removing barriers to price movement, to entrepreneurship and to foreign trade) and privatization. Later, a deeper economic restructuring would, it was hoped, transform the over-industrialized, largely obsolete and environmentally unfriendly Polish economy into one that much more resembled a modern economy of the Western European type. Although much was accomplished in the decade following communism, by the early 2000s that task had not yet been completed.

Stabilization was achieved fairly quickly, but at a high cost, with a much deeper than expected post-transition recession, which was partly the result of the shock-therapy approach and partly owing to the collapse of the socialist bloc's trading arrangements (organized through the Council for Mutual Economic Assistance—CMEA or Comecon). Polish gross domestic product (GDP), as officially recorded, fell by almost 18% between 1989 and 1991. The decline in industrial production was on a par with the Great Depression of the early 1930s—industrial production declined by 37% in 1929–32 and by almost 34% in 1989–91. However, from 1992 the economy began once again to grow. After expanding by 2.6% that year, real GDP growth accelerated steadily, reaching an average of 5.4% per year in 1993–95. The growth rate peaked at 7.0% in 1995, but remained impressive in 1996 and 1997 (6.0% and 6.8%, respectively), and Poland was the first post-communist economy to recover from the shock of transition when, in 1996, it regained its 1989 level of GDP output. From 1998 until 2000 economic growth slowed, in part owing to the effect of the Czech financial crisis of 1997 and, more importantly, the collapse of the Russian rouble in 1998. Then, in 2001, reflecting the serious downturn in international economic conditions, the GDP growth rate decelerated rapidly to reach only 1.1% where, more or less, it remained in 2002 (at 1.3%).

In the early to mid-1990s, recovery was given considerable impetus by domestic consumption, with exports playing a subsidiary role. However, domestic (and, later, foreign) investment became more significant in 1995–97. By the second half of the 1990s foreign direct investment (FDI) inflows began also, after a slow start, to increase. Foreign investors came to appreciate Poland's dual appeal as a low-cost export base with a relatively strong physical and skills infrastructure and a thirsty domestic market. Inward investment flows accelerated sharply in the mid-1990s, but were to decline later, at the beginning of the 2000s, alongside the global economic downturn. The inward investment agency, Panstwówa Agencja Inwestycji Zagranicznych (PAIZ), reported FDI inflows increasing from US $2,500m. in 1995 to $10,600m. in 2000, before declining to only $6,100m. in 2002.

Exports played a useful if somewhat sporadic role in supporting recovery in the 1990s, but one that became more pronounced in 2001–02, suggesting that economic restructuring was achieving results. The large volume of informal cross-border purchases by Germans and Russians was another useful addition to net exports, peaking at US $7,100m. in 1995, but severely affected thereafter by the Russian crisis, and declining to $3,600m. in 1999, with a slight recovery, to $4,400m. in 2001, before dropping slightly, to $4,100m. in 2002. Meanwhile, total export earnings remained surprisingly strong at the beginning of the 2000s, given the decline in the world economy, expanding from $28,256m. in 2000 to $30,275m. in 2001 and to $32,983m. in 2002, according to central bank figures. This robust increase in exports was somewhat unexpected and taken by many observers as evidence of successful restructuring in the economy during the late 1990s. Polish businesses, many believed, had become more tightly connected to the international production systems of the multinational firms responsible for the flow of investment into the country. In the earlier period impressive mid-1990s GDP growth was largely the result of strong domestic demand, something that worried the central bank. Its main concern was that consumer spending was increasing too quickly, fuelled by a rapid growth of credit and real wages. The strong złoty also fuelled a dramatic increase in the consumption of imports, especially of cars and household durables. As domestic economic pressures increased, the current account of the balance of payments came under pressure. In 1996 it slipped into deficit and the first signs of the economic 'over-heating' that was to be the principal concern of policy-makers in the mid-1990s became evident. If the current-account deficit was small in 1996 and manageable over 1997–98, by 1999 it had escalated to 7.6% of GDP and official concern was rising. The forced devaluation in May 1997 of the previously reliable Czech koruna, as short-term capital took flight, alongside the rouble crisis of 1998, heightened international investors' sensitivity towards large current-account deficits in emerging markets. In this context the Polish authorities became understandably preoccupied with reducing the current-account deficit.

During the 1990s and into the following decade the monetary authorities kept real interest rates at high levels, much to the dismay of the Ministry of Finance, causing a serious ongoing rift between policy-makers. The Ministry of Finance maintained that high interest rates were part of the problem of the Polish economy rather than a solution, in that they attracted speculative capital and contributed to an excessively strong exchange rate. The tension between central bank and Ministry of Finance remained a feature of the Polish policy-making scene and one that had a wider political aspect. The central bank, the National Bank of Poland, is fiercely independent and has always been strongly (its critics say too strongly) committed to a 'tight' monetary policy and the struggle against inflation. The bank's monetary policy committee (MPC) sets its own inflation targets and its goal for the medium term, first announced in 1998 and steadfastly adhered to thereafter, was to reduce inflation to 4% by the end of 2003. The MPC freely, and sometimes dramatically, used the only real weapon at its disposal (interest rates) to bear down on inflationary pressures. From 1999 and into 2000, fearful that inflationary pressures were accelerating, the MPC aggressively pushed rates up, but in early 2001, amid nervousness as to the state of the world economy and evident domestic weaknesses, it sent rates into reverse. That process continued into 2003, and by the end of May the reference interest rate stood at 5.5%, but a steady decline in monthly inflation, down to 0.3% in April, meant that interest rates remained high, in real terms.

Throughout the 1990s, despite political tremors, and the comings and goings of numerous prime ministers and finance ministers, economic policy in the broader sense enjoyed substantial continuity. The commitment to building a market economy remained intact, banking and tax reforms were introduced, privatization proceeded, and trade remained firmly fixed in its new Western orbit. The reorientation from a Russian/Soviet-centred to German/EU-centred trade was a remarkable structural adjustment of the early 1990s. Germany quickly asserted itself in the place previously held by the USSR, as Poland's main trading partner. Even in 2002, when the German economy was in some trouble, Germany accounted for 32% of Polish exports and 24% of imports. By the mid-1990s Poland was fully interacting with Western institutions. Foreign debt had been successfully rescheduled, the IMF had endorsed macroeconomic policy, an EU Association Agreement was in place and Poland was a member of the Organisation for Economic Co-operation and Development (OECD). Poland was committed to, and on course for, EU membership. At the EU summit held in Copenhagen, Denmark, in December 2002 the long process of accession negotiation was brought to a successful conclusion, when 10 aspirant members, including Poland, were invited to join the Union in May 2004.

RESTRUCTURING THE ECONOMY

From the 1990s economic restructuring was largely propelled by the evolving private sector, the contribution of which to GDP rose from around 18% in 1989 to 63% in 2001. The privately employed labour force (employed persons, *pracujacy*), including agriculture, amounted to almost 75% of the total in 2001, compared with 33% in 1989–90 (when it was already ahead of Hungary's 25% and Czechoslovakia's 6%). Structural transformation was also evident in significant changes in GDP composition during the 1990s. Industry's share of GDP declined from 41.7% in 1988 to 20.8% in 2002, while the share of GDP accounted for by the services sector continued to expand (reaching 44% by 2002). In this respect, Poland, like other formerly centrally planned economies, was adapting rapidly to the market economy pattern, where typically 60%–70% of GDP is generated by services.

While economic activity and employment shifted rapidly from the state to the private sector, from manufacturing to services, agriculture remained more resistant to change, giving Poland a distinctive employment pattern in which the farming community retains immense social, political and cultural importance. Indeed, at the end of 2001 28.8% of the work-force was engaged in agriculture (including forestry and fishing), compared with 25.3% in industry (including construction, mining, manufacturing and utilities). By this measure, 4.3m. people were employed in agriculture, compared with 3.8m. in industry, a structure strongly diverging from the typical Western pattern, where agriculture employs very few. However it should be noted that the precise extent of agricultural employment is somewhat ambiguous. Alternative methods of calculation generated much lower figures; for example, agriculture provides a 'significant' income for an estimated 18% of the work-force, while the OECD believes that on the basis of 'significant' time commitment (at least 2,120 hours per year) agriculture's employment share declines to just 9%. Whatever its real weight in employment terms, the agricultural contribution to GDP was unambiguously small and had declined sharply (from some 13% in 1988 to 3.3% in 2001).

EU support for restructuring and investment in the rural infrastructure should begin to flow to Poland on a substantial scale after EU entry, even though the Polish authorities failed to wrest from the EU identical treatment for Polish and EU farmers post-entry. This means that for Poland, as for other new EU members, the level of support will begin in the range 25%–40% of existing Common Agricultural Policy (CAP) levels and will slowly increase to 100% over 10 years. A dramatic decline in farm employment seems inevitable and investment in the rural, non-agricultural infrastructure will be crucial to minimizing social and political problems. Some short-term problems include doubts regarding the absorption capacity on the Polish side for these aid and investment flows. Much needs to be done: the rural infrastructure is poorly developed, with improvements to communications (especially telephones) and environmental (including water) management taking place slowly. The presidential election held in October 2000 showed support for candidates campaigning on rural issues, demonstrating once again that, in Polish economic conditions, agriculture is a policy area that cannot be ignored. This was reinforced in the September 2001 general election, when the radical farmers' party, the Self Defence Party of the Republic of Poland (Partia Samoobrona Rzeczypospolitej Polskiej), emerged unexpectedly as the third force in Polish politics, obtaining 10.2% of the votes and 53 seats in the 460-seat lower house of parliament.

AGRICULTURE

In mid-2001 just under 1.9m. 'farms' were said to exist in Poland. However, relatively few of these units were farms in the sense understood in the West. The number fell slightly in the 1990s (down from 2.1m. in 1990), with little change to the average farm size (up slightly to 8 ha). These small, fragmented units were worked largely with old-fashioned methods. Around one-half of farms produced only for subsistence. In 2001 23% of farms were smaller than 2 ha in size, and a further 34% were between 2 ha and 5 ha. Only a few large farms existed (i.e. with an area greater than 15 ha), their number increasing from 6.1% of the total in 1990 to 9.4% in 2001. In land area Poland is the ninth-largest European country, and its agriculture accounts for a high proportion of European output; Poland's agricultural specialities include cereals, meat and dairy products. Poland occupies third place in Europe (excluding Russia) in terms of rye production, and is Europe's most significant producer of potatoes, accounting for 14.3% of the European total in 2001 (a bad year, with output down from 24.2m. metric tons in 2000 to 19.4m. metric tons). Poland is also a major producer of sugar beet, accounting for 6.9% of the European total in 2001, and is a significant producer of wheat and barley, as well as animal products, especially pork, beef, milk and eggs. This addition to EU food-production capacity caused complications for accession and helped focus attention on the need for CAP reform. Despite the considerable capacity of Polish agriculture, the country is a net importer of foodstuffs, particularly of vegetable products, fats and oils. The CAP made it relatively difficult to export to the EU, and Russia had traditionally been Poland's most important food export market, with sales worth US $611m. in 1998, although Germany was second with $537m., followed by Ukraine ($194m.) and Italy ($155m.). After the 1998 rouble collapse food exports to Russia declined sharply (they reached only $215m. in 2000, while Polish farmers complained that they were pushed out of the market by highly subsidized EU exports). Grievances over such matters, and declining agricultural prices, easily ignite noisy farmers' protests, with the Self Defence Party frequently co-ordinating such events.

BASIC INDUSTRIES—COAL, COPPER, SULPHUR AND STEEL

Traditional extractive and heavy industry have been immensely important to Polish economic development. The country has abundant reserves of coal, sulphur and copper, which created a natural base for the development of heavy industry and semi-processing. Although Polish hard coal extraction was declining, in 1998 the country remained the seventh-largest producer in the world, accounting for 3.1% of world output. Coal and steel are regionally concentrated in

Upper Silesia, in the conurbation around the city of Katowice. However, the heavy industry bias in production was changing, albeit slowly, by the turn of the 20th century. Mining and quarrying accounted for 5.4% of industrial production sold in 2002, down from some 8% in 1995. The number of people employed in the sector was 209,000 in late 2002, 8.3% of the total for industry as a whole. The coal sector (black and brown), with its work-force of 168,000 in late 2002, was still important, although it accounted for only 3.8% of total industry sales and 6.9% of all industrial employment. Poland's deep coal-mining industry was under pressure throughout the post-1989 period as demand declined: Poland's power stations used much less coal than one decade previously (52.1m. metric tons in 2001, compared with some 82m. tons in 1990) and costs had risen sharply. In 1998 a restructuring plan was agreed that won miners' support (thanks to generous redundancy arrangements). Production of hard coal declined rapidly from a pre-transformation peak of 193m. tons in 1988 to 103m.–104m. tons per year in 2000–02. Exports continue to account for a significant proportion of the coal produced (23m. tons in 2001), but Poland has moved a long way from the heavy reliance on coal as an export earner that was characteristic of the communist period.

Copper production has long been a Polish speciality, reflecting good resource endowments and supporting a well-established electric-cables sector. One giant semi-privatized enterprise, KGHM Polska Miedź, provides all Poland's output of refined copper (509,000 metric tons in 2002). KGHM is Europe's largest and the world's fifth-largest copper producer, its fortunes inextricably bound to the world market price for copper.

The steel industry suffers from serious over-capacity. In 1992 consultants recommended the closure of one-half of the country's 25 steelworks by 2002. This proved too radical for either the Solidarity-backed governments or their successors to implement, but output did decline, from some 20m. metric tons in the late 1980s to 10.5m. tons in 2000, and then sharply in the subsequent downturn, to 8.4m. tons in 2002. Some restructuring has taken place and a few smaller plants were closed on environmental grounds in the early transformation period. One major steelworks, Huta Warszawa, was privatized and sold to an Italian concern, Lucchini. Most steel production (around 60% of the total) was accounted for by the two largest plants (Huta Katowice and Huta Sedzimira, the latter near Kraków), and most employment in the steel industry (around 72% of the total) was concentrated in the Katowice area. A number of privatization attempts focused on Huta Katowice and Huta Sedzimira had come to nothing by 2002, when the Government embarked on another steel consolidation exercise, bringing together the leading plants in a holding company, Polish Steel Mills (Polskie Huty Stali—PHS), prior to another attempt at privatization. In 2003 two Western groups were in the running for Polish steel privatization: the British-owned LNM Group, and US Steel.

MANUFACTURING

In late 2002 industry employed 2.5m. people, with 2.1m. in manufacturing. Manufacturing also accounted for 82% of industry sales. Food and drink was the largest branch, accounting for 20% of all industry sales. Chemicals and chemical products accounted for 6.2% of such sales, metals 3.9%, metal products 4.5%, and machinery and equipment 4.2%. Transport vehicles was a very promising growth sector of the later 1990s: sales amounted to 3.6% of the industry total in 1995, and to 7.0% in 2000, but declined to 5.7% by 2002, as the sector became a victim of general growth deceleration. Western producers were drawn into assembly operations in the 1990s, and it seemed for a time that motor manufacture was a pinnacle of transformation restructuring success. However, in late 2000, encountering a sudden reduction in demand, even firms long established in the Polish market began to retrench. Food-processing, already important in domestic terms, has the potential to become a key export industry in an enlarged EU. The wood and paper sector (especially furniture) was a particular export success in the 1990s. Throughout the transformation period of the 1990s the question uppermost in the minds of many observers was where Polish manufacturing specializations would lie as the country reintegrated into the world economy. Furniture and textiles were successful, but were often based on the so-called outward processing trade (OPT). As foreign investment increased, Poland should have become more deeply integrated in the international economy via the activity of multinational companies, and it seemed from the surprisingly strong export performance of 2001–02, noted earlier, that this may indeed have been the case.

THE FINANCIAL SECTOR

Bank reform and privatization began in Poland in 1989, when the National Bank of Poland (NBP) was transformed into a Western-style central bank. Its network of nine regional branches was to be the framework for a new private banking sector. In 1993 the first of its former regional branches, the Poznań-based Wielkopolski Bank Kredytowy, was privatized. The Katowice-based Bank Śląski followed in early 1994, in the early days of the post-communist coalition Government that ruled from 1993 to 1997. The sale was, however, plunged into political controversy when the bank's share price escalated 13-fold on the first day of trading, convincing the opposition that it had been undersold and prompting accusations of profiteering and ministerial negligence. This fuelled a mid–1990s view that for many sectors (not least banking and insurance) privatization should be preceded by commercialization (a halfway step to disposal) and in some cases by sectoral consolidation, a policy that the SLD-UP-PSL coalition returned to in 2002. Some straightforward bank privatization did continue, however, in the 1990s. The Kraków-based Bank Przemysłowo-Handlowy was floated at the beginning of 1995 and Bank Gdański later that year. Then, to accelerate privatization, bank consolidation proposals were revived, with some of the remaining NBP regional banks brought together with another leading Polish bank, Pekao. The Pekao group was privatized in 1999. Bank Handlowy, perhaps the best known of all the Polish banks, because of its role in foreign trade, was originally to form the nucleus of a second consolidated banking group, but successfully pleaded its case to stay independent, and was privatized in mid-1997. In 2000 it merged with the Citibank Group of the USA. Genuinely new private banks also emerged, of which perhaps the best known was the Bank Inicjatyw Gospodarczych (BIG), established in 1989. In 1997 it took a controlling share in Bank Gdański and from then traded as BIG Bank Gdański; but, with the exception of BIG BG, most domestic private banks were small. By 2003 two large banks were still to be privatized: Powszechna Kasa Oszczędności Bank Państwowy—PKO Bank Polski (PKO BP) and Bank Gospodarki Żywnościowej (the grouping of rural co-operative banks). These two, in a concession to political pressure, were to be sold with preference to domestic capital and, for the same reasons, the new Government was in no hurry to accelerate their disposal. Nevertheless, with privatization revenues declining to significantly below target in 2002, and probably also in 2003, the Government was likely at least partially to privatize the PKO BP in 2004.

At the beginning of the privatization process, in the early 1990s the commercial banks had serious bad-debt problems from years of politically directed lending to state enterprises, but in 1993 a highly effective debt-restructuring scheme was introduced. The NBP also operated a shrewd policy of issuing licences to foreign banks only where they agreed also to take over smaller and weaker Polish banks. Partly because of these licensing restrictions, Western banks were initially slow to enter the market. Privatization, however, accelerated in the later 1990s. In 1999, in addition to its 60% stake in Wielkopolski Bank Kredytowy, Allied Irish Banks (Ireland) took an 80% stake in Bank Zachodni, creating a strong presence in western Poland. In the same year UniCredito Italiano (Italy) and Allianz (Germany) bought a 52% stake in Pekao. The sale, however, rekindled controversy, as some argued that Pekao was sold too cheaply to relatively weak purchasers, and three former finance ministers wrote to the incumbent Minister of Finance, Balcerowicz, to question the choice of UniCredito. Concerns over foreign control of Polish banking and finance became more strident. The insurance sector (property and life business) was, in 2000, still dominated by the largely state-owned Powszechny Zakład Ubezpieczeń (PZU), with around 60% of the market. Meanwhile, the market's growth potential had attracted a number of foreign insurers into joint ventures, especially in life insurance. The privatization of PZU had been mired in controversy for several years, as successive governments had challenged allegedly unfavourable deals made by their predecessors. This process was challenged by the Netherlands-based Eureko group, which turned to the international courts for support in its attempt to obtain a larger stake in the lucrative PZU.

The Warsaw Stock Exchange (WSE) had only five listed companies when it reopened in April 1991, but by 2002 some 220 stocks were listed. Despite this growth the WSE was not a major source of investment finance. Stock-market capitalization remained fairly low, equivalent to around 17% of GDP in early 2001, compared with 21% in the Czech Republic and Hungary and 19% in Russia. However, the Polish exchange is widely reckoned to be one of the most transparent and best regulated in all the post-communist economies (a factor, according to some, that has inhibited its growth). In Poland the market has, like others, faced significant fluctuation, but trading scandals have been relatively few and market collapse (unlike in Russia or the Czech Republic) has been avoided.

THE EU MEMBERSHIP PROCESS

Poland has been placed firmly in an EU trade orbit since the early 1990s, when the EU accounted for about two-thirds of all Polish trade, but full EU membership was always the major long-term goal. This was to take place in May 2004. Full EU membership should bring significant advantages, including the removal of almost all remaining trade barriers (especially important in agriculture and foodstuffs), greater FDI, access to EU structural funds for the improvement of physical and social infrastructure, and some measure (initially at least 25% of EU levels) of CAP support. The direct input in EU policy-making was also a great attraction, as was the notion (to Polish governments) that the country could play a key role in shaping the EU's Eastern policy.

Of course serious problems remain. The gap in income per head between Poland and the EU is wide and Poland can expect substantial regional and structural fund inflows. Poland's immediate problem is in improving absorption capacity. Polish agriculture, as noted above, always posed the most serious difficulties in negotiating EU entry terms, but the matter had been resolved, at least until the EU returned to the issue of fundamental CAP reform. That reform seemed to be on a slow adjustment path from price subsidy to direct income support, as well as a new focus on rural restructuring and development. The latter could be of immense benefit to Poland.

SOME PROBLEMS AND HOPES FOR THE FUTURE

Although considerable achievements were made in the first decade of transformation, in 2002–03 Poland continued to encounter pressing economic and social challenges, the most serious of which was an unemployment rate that was approaching 20%. A substantially market-based economic system existed, where the private sector was dominant, but restructuring was not yet complete. In 2003 heavy industry remained state-owned (largely because finding private buyers in the context of weak international conditions had proved impossible) and regional as well as rural imbalances persisted and were, in some cases, becoming more severe. Economic growth slowed substantially in 2001 and 2002, although inflationary pressures, reflecting international trends, were subdued. The current-account deficit was much reduced from its early 1999 peak of 7.6% of GDP (down to 3.6% in early 2003), but it was uncertain whether this improvement would persist, especially if import growth were to follow any more general economic recovery. Apart from unemployment, the main economic problem in Poland was the severe decline in investment, which decreased by 8.8% in 2001 and by 7.2% in 2002. For the domestic economy in the longer term, rural restructuring remains a critical challenge. Inequalities were also increasing, both in terms of income distribution and spatial considerations. In early 2002 the new Government presented a set of medium-term policies (enterprise, growth and jobs) designed to return the country to a solidly respectable growth path, of an over-optimistic 3.5% in 2003 and 5% in 2004. In addition to this domestic initiative the hope was that EU membership, and with it the flow of substantial new resources to Poland, would help overcome underlying problems. However, this, as noted earlier, raised questions as to the domestic economy's capacity to absorb such inflows. The Government's controversial decision to buy US (Lockheed Martin) F16 aircraft for its airforce, while a blow to its European partners, meant that Poland had won potentially huge US investment as part of the off-set deal to the purchase. The Polish Government also sought a substantial dividend to its support for the US military action in Iraq, in terms of reconstruction work. For the medium term, large aid and investment inflows seem likely to strengthen the currency, putting greater pressure on Polish exporters and threatening to undermine their competitiveness. It is interesting in this context to note wider discussion among Polish policy-makers on the advisability of rapid entry into the single currency (euro) zone. Discussing the adoption of the euro was relatively straightforward, however; finding the right exchange rate to do so, then achieving it without inducing excessive depreciation would be considerably more challenging. This will be one of the key problems for policy-makers in Poland from 2004, but in 2003 the most pressing problem to be addressed was, without any doubt, unemployment, especially among the young.

Statistical Survey

Source (unless otherwise indicated): Główny Urząd Statystyczny (Central Statistical Office), 00-925 Warsaw, Al. Niepodległości 208; tel. (22) 6252215; fax (22) 6251525; internet www.stat.gov.pl.

Area and Population

AREA, POPULATION AND DENSITY

Area (sq km)	
Land	304,465
Inland water	8,220
Total	312,685*
Population (census results)†	
7 December 1988.	37,878,641
17 May 1995 (provisional)	
Males	18,771,000
Females.	19,849,000
Total	38,620,000
Population (official rounded estimates at 31 December)†	
2000	38,644,200
2001	38,632,500
2002	38,610,000‡
Density (per sq km) at 31 December 2002	123.5

* 120,728 sq miles.

† Figures exclude civilian aliens within the country and include civilian nationals temporarily outside the country.

‡ Rounded figure.

VOIVODSHIPS

(estimated population at 31 December 2001)

	Area (sq km)	Total ('000)	Density (per sq km)
Dolnośląskie	19,948	2,970.1	148.9
Kujawsko-Pomorskie	17,970	2,101.7	117.0
Lubelskie	25,114	2,227.6	88.7
Lubuskie	13,984	1,024.5	73.3
Łódzkie	18,219	2,632.9	144.5
Malopolskie	15,144	3,240.9	214.0
Mazowieckie	35,597	5,079.0	142.7
Opolskie.	9,412	1,080.5	114.8
Podkarpackie	17,926	2,131.4	118.9
Podlaskie	20,180	1,219.9	60.5
Pomorskie	18,293	2,204.4	120.5
Śląskie	12,294	4,830.4	392.9
Świętokrzyskie	11,672	1,319.6	113.1
Warmińsko-Mazurskie . . .	24,203	1,469.3	60.7
Wielkopolskie	29,826	3,366.0	112.9
Zachodniopomorskie	22,902	1,734.3	75.7
Total	312,685	38,632.5	123.6

PRINCIPAL TOWNS
(estimated population at 31 December 1998)

Warszawa (Warsaw, the capital)	1,618,468	Olsztyn	170,904
Łódź	806,728	Rzeszów	162,049
Kraków (Cracow) .	740,666	Ruda Śląska . . .	159,665
Wrocław	637,877	Rybnik	144,582
Poznań	578,235	Wałbrzych . . .	136,923
Gdańsk	458,988	Tychy	133,178
Szczecin	416,988	Dąbrowa Górnicza .	131,037
Bydgoszcz	386,855	Płock	131,011
Lublin	356,251	Elbląg	129,782
Katowice	345,934	Opole	129,553
Białystok	283,937	Gorzów Wielkopolski	126,019
Częstochowa . . .	257,812	Włocławek . . .	123,373
Gdynia	253,521	Chorzów	121,708
Sosnowiec	244,102	Tarnów	121,494
Radom	232,262	Zielona Góra . . .	118,182
Kielce	212,383	Koszalin	112,375
Gliwice	212,164	Legnica	109,335
Toruń	206,158	Kalisz	106,641
Bytom	205,560	Grudziądz	102,434
Zabrze	200,177	Słupsk	102,370
Bielsko-Biała . . .	180,307	Jastrzębie-Zdrój . .	102,294

2001 (estimate): Warsaw 1,609,800.

BIRTHS, MARRIAGES AND DEATHS

	Registered live births		Registered marriages		Registered deaths	
	Number	Rate (per 1,000)	Number	Rate (per 1,000)	Number	Rate (per 1,000)
1994 . .	481,285	12.5	207,689	5.4	386,398	10.0
1995 . .	433,109	11.2	207,081	5.4	386,084	10.0
1996 . .	428,203	11.1	203,641	5.3	385,496	10.0
1997 . .	412,635	10.7	204,850	5.3	380,201	9.8
1998 . .	395,619	10.2	209,430	5.4	375,354	9.7
1999 . .	382,002	9.9	219,398	5.7	381,415	9.9
2000 . .	378,348	9.8	211,150	5.5	368,000*	9.5
2001 . .	368,205	9.5	195,122	5.0	363,200*	9.4

* Number rounded to the nearest 100.

Expectation of life (WHO estimates, years at birth): 74.0 (males 69.9; females 78.1) in 2001 (Source: WHO, *World Health Report*).

IMMIGRATION AND EMIGRATION*

	1999	2000	2001
Immigrants	7,525	7,331	6,625
Emigrants	21,536	26,999	23,368

* Figures refer to immigrants arriving for permanent residence in Poland and emigrants leaving for permanent residence abroad.

ECONOMICALLY ACTIVE POPULATION*
('000 persons aged 15 years and over)

	1999†	2000‡	2001‡
Agriculture, hunting and forestry	4,322.4	4,304.6	4,296.0
Fishing	11.6	10.3	7.9
Mining and quarrying . . .	256.7	223.2	216.6
Manufacturing	2,923.0	2,674.7	2,545.4
Electricity, gas and water supply	246.9	236.5	246.1
Construction	915.0	814.6	772.0
Wholesale and retail trade; repair of motor vehicles, motorcycles and personal and household goods	2,093.9	2,074.6	2,096.2
Hotels and restaurants . . .	216.3	225.7	231.5
Transport, storage and communications	838.2	779.3	733.9
Financial intermediation . . .	388.7	298.6	285.9
Real estate, renting and business activities	775.8	822.6	841.3
Public administration and defence; compulsory social security	439.5	492.6	526.6
Education	908.3	902.8	915.6
Health and social work . . .	967.0	908.2	865.0
Other community, social and personal service activities . .	388.4	390.9	383.1
Total employed	15,691.7	15,159.2	14,963.1
Unemployed	2,177.8	2,702.6	3,115.1
Total labour force	17,869.5	17,861.8	18,078.2
Males	9,165.1	n.a.	n.a.
Females	8,704.4	n.a.	n.a.

* Excluding persons employed in budgetary entities conducting activity within the scope of national defence and public safety.
† At 30 September.
‡ At 31 December.

Health and Welfare

KEY INDICATORS

Total fertility rate (children per woman, 2001)	1.3
Under-5 mortality rate (per 1,000 live births, 2000) . . .	10
HIV/AIDS (% of persons aged 15–49, 1999)	0.10
Physicians (per 1,000 head, 1997)	2.36
Hospital beds (per 1,000 head, 1998)	5.3
Health expenditure (2000): US $ per head (PPP)	578
Health expenditure (2000): % of GDP	6.0
Health expenditure (2000): public (% of total)	69.7
Human Development Index (2000): ranking	37
Human Development Index (2000): value	0.833

For sources and definitions, see explanatory note on p. vi.

Agriculture

PRINCIPAL CROPS
('000 metric tons)

	1999	2000	2001
Wheat	9,051.3	8,502.9	9,283.0
Barley	3,401.1	2,783.4	3,330.5
Maize	599.4	923.3	1,361.9
Rye	5,180.7	4,003.0	4,863.6
Oats	1,446.3	1,070.2	1,305.2
Buckwheat and millet . .	60.3	73.4	58.7
Triticale (wheat-rye hybrid) . .	2,096.9	1,901.0	2,697.9
Mixed grain	3,914.3	3,083.4	4,059.5
Potatoes	19,926.7	24,232.4	19,378.9
Sugar beet	12,563.6	13,134.4	11,363.9
Dry beans	44.3	47.2	40.9
Dry peas	55.1	45.6	39.8
Other pulses	217.5*	221.3†	233.9
Rapeseed	1,131.9	958.1	1,063.6
Cabbages	1,709.2	1,899.0	1,709.6
Tomatoes	333.1	311.5	273.7
Cauliflowers	225.4	248.2	250.4
Cucumbers and gherkins . . .	385.0	356.0	350.0†
Dry onions	688.3	720.3	625.9
Carrots	906.5	946.7	921.9
Mushrooms†	100	100	100
Other vegetables*	1,277.5	1,309.6	1,206.5
Apples	1,604.2	1,450.4	2,433.9
Pears	66.5	81.6	77.4
Cherries (incl. sour)	179.6	178.1	224.4
Plums	90.7	106.9	131.9
Strawberries	178.2	171.3	242.1
Raspberries	43.2	39.7	44.8
Currants	153.4	146.8	175.3
Other fruit*	69.0	69.1	70.2
Tobacco (leaves)	43.7	29.5	23.9

* Unofficial figure(s).
† FAO estimate(s).
Source: FAO.

LIVESTOCK
('000 head year ending September)

	1999	2000	2001
Horses	551	550	550*
Cattle	6,455	6,093	5,734
Pigs	18,538	17,122	17,106
Sheep	392	362	343
Chickens	50,017	49,526	48,274
Geese	608	764	614
Turkeys	672	713	802
Ducks	2,953	3,551	3,571

* FAO estimate.
Source: FAO.

LIVESTOCK PRODUCTS
('000 metric tons)

	1999	2000	2001
Beef and veal	384.6	348.5	316.3
Pig meat	2,043.0	1,923.0	1,849.1
Horse meat	9.1	9.1*	9.1*
Game meat*	12.1	11.0	11.0
Chicken meat	573.1	585.2	691.5
Duck meat*	11.0	13.0	15.0
Turkey meat*	18.0	19.0	20.0
Goose meat*	7.4	9.2	7.5
Cows' milk	12,284.4	11,889.3	11,884.0
Cheese	481.1	475.3	460.1
Butter	166.0	161.6	178.9
Hen eggs	414.9	423.7	449.3
Honey	8.9	8.6	9.5
Cattle hides (fresh)* . . .	43	39	34

* FAO estimate(s).
Source: FAO.

Forestry

ROUNDWOOD REMOVALS
('000 cubic metres, excl. bark)

	1999	2000	2001
Sawlogs, veneer logs and logs for sleepers	10,946	11,609	10,641
Pulpwood	9,901	10,988	11,171
Other industrial wood . . .	1,995	1,892	1,765
Fuel wood	1,426	1,536	1,691
Total	24,268	26,025	25,268

Source: FAO.

SAWNWOOD PRODUCTION
('000 cubic metres, incl. railway sleepers)

	1999	2000	2001
Coniferous (softwood)	3,349	3,532	2,850
Broadleaved (hardwood) . . .	788	730	700
Total	4,137	4,262	3,550

Source: FAO.

Fishing

('000 metric tons, live weight)

	1998	1999	2000
Capture	247.0	235.1	218.4
Atlantic cod	27.7	28.1	23.3
Alaska pollock	81.9	65.5	33.2
Atlantic herring	21.9	19.2	24.5
European sprat	59.1	71.7	84.3
Antarctic krill	15.6	18.6	20.7
Aquaculture	29.8	33.7	35.8
Common carp	19.4	21.4	22.6
Rainbow trout	9.0	11.1	11.4
Total catch	276.8	268.8	254.1

Source: FAO, *Yearbook of Fishery Statistics*.

Mining

('000 metric tons, unless otherwise indicated)

	1998	1999	2000
Hard coal	115,726	111,894	103,331
Brown coal (incl. lignite) . . .	62,820	60,839	59,484
Crude petroleum	360	425	653
Salt (unrefined)	3,284	3,411	4,307
Native sulphur (per 100%) . .	1,348	1,175	1,369
Copper ore (metric tons)* . . .	436,200	523,120	525,000†
Lead ore (metric tons)* . . .	73,814	81,849	65,000†
Magnesite ore—crude . . .	38,300	54,800	50,000†
Silver (metric tons)*	1,108	1,100	1,144
Zinc ore (metric tons)* . . .	157,874	160,082	155,000†
Natural gas (million cu metres) .	4,852	4,757	4,956

* Figures refer to the metal content of ores.
† Estimate.

Source: US Geological Survey.

Industry

SELECTED PRODUCTS
(metric tons, unless otherwise indicated)

	1998	1999	2000
Sausages and smoked meat. . .	888,000	873,000	n.a.
Refined sugar ('000 metric tons) .	2,102	1,821	2,014
Margarine.	363,000	367,000	n.a.
Wine and mead ('000 hectolitres) .	4,500	4,490	n.a.
Beer ('000 hectolitres)	21,000	23,400	24,900
Cigarettes (million)	96,700	95,100	83,500
Cotton yarn[1]	82,200	67,300	n.a.
Woven cotton fabrics ('000 metres)[2]	207,000	179,000	n.a.
Wool yarn[1]	27,100	18,200	n.a.
Woven woollen fabrics ('000 metres)[2] . .	29,500	22,400	n.a.
Cellulosic staple and tow . . .	3,700	2,400	n.a.
Leather footwear ('000 pairs) . .	24,400	22,600	16,800
Mechanical wood pulp	113,000	126,000	130,000
Chemical wood pulp	722,000	698,000	746,000
Newsprint ('000 metric tons) . .	92.2	149.0	211.0
Other paper ('000 metric tons) . .	1,434	1,484	n.a.
Paperboard	192,000	206,000	n.a.
Synthetic rubber	95,000	97,500	n.a.
Rubber tyres ('000)[3]	14,410	14,660	23,329
Sulphuric acid—100% ('000 metric tons).	1,707	1,482	n.a.
Nitric acid—100% ('000 metric tons).	1,671	1,635	n.a.
Caustic soda—96% ('000 metric tons).	807	737	394
Soda ash—98% ('000 metric tons)	983	910	1,018
Nitrogenous fertilizers (a) ('000 metric tons)[4]	1,406	1,272	1,610
Phosphate fertilizers (b) ('000 metric tons)[4]	593	535	530
Plastics and synthetic resins ('000 metric tons).	940	1,114	1,340
Motor spirit—Petrol ('000 metric tons)[5]	n.a.	n.a.	4,435
Distillate fuel oils ('000 metric tons)	6,031	6,041	n.a.
Residual fuel oils ('000 metric tons)	4,129	4,758	n.a.
Coke-oven coke ('000 metric tons)	9,944	8,575	9,000*
Cement ('000 metric tons) . . .	14,970	15,600	14,800
Pig-iron ('000 metric tons)[6] . .	6,129	5,233	6,492
Crude steel ('000 metric tons) . .	9,915	8,853	10,504
Rolled steel products ('000 metric tons).	7,987	6,991	7,530
Aluminium—unwrought[7] . .	54,168	50,974	46,941
Refined copper—unwrought . .	446,837	470,494	486,002
Refined lead—unwrought . . .	64,300	63,895	45,412
Zinc—unwrought[7]	178,016	177,804	161,000
Radio receivers ('000) . . .	154	138	109
Television receivers ('000) . .	4,436	5,121	6,287
Merchant ships launched (gross reg. tons)	598,000	n.a.	n.a.
Passenger motor cars (number) .	592,355	647,232	532,427
Lorries and tractors (number) . .	56,100	62,714	58,112
Domestic washing machines (number)	416,000	448,000	457,000
Domestic refrigerators (number) .	714,000	726,000	693,000
Construction: dwellings completed (number)	80,594	81,979	n.a.
Electric energy (million kWh) . .	142,789	142,128	145,148
Manufactured gas from cokeries (million cu metres)	4,145	3,876	n.a.

* Estimate.

[1] Pure and mixed yarns. Cotton includes tyre cord yarn.

[2] Pure and mixed fabrics, after undergoing finishing processes. Cotton and wool include substitutes.

[3] Tyres for passenger motor cars and commercial vehicles, including inner tubes and tyres for animal-drawn road vehicles, and tyres for non-agricultural machines and equipment.

[4] Fertilizer production is measured in terms of (a) nitrogen or (b) phosphoric acid. Phosphate fertilizers include ground rock phosphate.

[5] Including synthetic products.

[6] Including blast-furnace ferro-alloys.

[7] Figures refer to both primary and secondary metal. Zinc production includes zinc dust and remelted zinc.

Sources: partly UN, *Industrial Commodity Statistics Yearbook* and *Monthly Bulletin of Statistics*; IRF, *World Road Statistics*.

Finance

CURRENCY AND EXCHANGE RATES

Monetary Units
100 groszy (singular: grosz) = 1 new złoty.

Sterling, Dollar and Euro Equivalents (30 May 2003)
£1 sterling = 6.114 new złotys;
US $1 = 3.711 new złotys;
€1 = 4.387 new złotys;
100 new złotys = £16.36 = $26.95 = €22.80.

Average Exchange Rate (new złotys per US dollar)
2000   4.3461
2001   4.0939
2002   4.0800

Note: On 1 January 1995 Poland introduced a new złoty, equivalent to 10,000 of the former units.

STATE BUDGET
(million new złotys)

Revenue	1999	2000	2001
Domestic revenue	125,856.8	135,530.1	139,354.0
Taxation	112,776.9	119,643.9	119,101.3
Value-added tax. . . .	48,803.6	51,749.8	52,893.1
Excises	25,208.1	27,312.0	28,860.5
Taxes on earnings . . .	38,175.6	39,956.3	36,663.9
Other current revenue . . .	13,079.9	15,886.2	20,252.7
Customs duties	5,566.0	5,080.3	4,060.5
External revenue.	65.4	133.8	1,172.9
Total	**125,922.2**	**135,663.9**	**140,526.9**

Expenditure	1999	2000	2001*
Education	2,920.2	1,959.9	1,780.4
Higher education.	5,070.5	5,326.7	6,370.7
Health care	6,312.6	4,300.0	4,600.8
Social welfare.	10,142.8	11,978.1	14,634.5
State administration. . . .	5,972.5	6,655.9	6,150.0
Public safety	6,473.2	7,040.1	7,757.7
Finance	20,975.2	20,578.3	21,005.0
Social security	29,436.4	36,698.6	46,065.6
National defence	9,448.4	9,943.7	8,875.1
Subsidies	2,573.0	n.a.	n.a.
Total (incl. others)	**138,401.2**	**151,054.9**	**172,885.2**
Current	131,012.5	143,627.2	n.a.
Capital.	7,388.7	7,427.7	n.a.

* Data not strictly comparable with previous years.

INTERNATIONAL RESERVES
(US $ million at 31 December)

	2000	2001	2002
Gold*	901.5	914.7	1,134.0
IMF special drawing rights . .	17.7	25.8	39.5
Reserve positition in IMF . .	224.4	461.0	651.0
Foreign exchange.	26,319.9	25,161.6	27,959.2
Total	**27,463.5**	**26,563.1**	**29,783.7**

* National valuation (US $400 per troy ounce).

Source: IMF, *International Financial Statistics*.

MONEY SUPPLY
(million new złotys at 31 December)

	2000	2001	2002
Currency outside banks . . .	34,112.7	38,212.6	42,192.7
Demand deposits at commercial banks	48,419.6	51,940.9	70,683.1
Total money (incl. others) . .	**82,574.2**	**94,157.8**	**112,889.0**

Source: IMF, *International Financial Statistics*.

COST OF LIVING
(Consumer Price Index; base: 1998 = 100)

	1999	2000	2001
Food (incl. beverages)	102.0	111.6	116.8
Fuel and light	106.1	115.4	n.a.
Clothing (incl. footwear). . . .	107.7	113.6	n.a.
Rent	120.2	114.4	n.a.
All items (incl. others)	107.3	118.1	124.6

Source: ILO, *Yearbook of Labour Statistics*; UN, *Monthly Bulletin of Statistics*.

NATIONAL ACCOUNTS
(million new złotys at current prices)
Composition of the Gross National Product

	1998	1999	2000
Compensation of employees . .	250,314.0	276,363.0	297,820.6
Operating surplus . . . . } Consumption of fixed capital . }	227,649.6	250,783.0	293,518.2
Gross domestic product (GDP) at factor cost . . .	477,963.6	527,146.0	591,338.8
Indirect taxes	82,681.1	94,680.5	100,153.3
Less Subsidies	6,763.1	6,711.2	6,566.0
GDP in purchasers' values .	553,881.6	615,115.3	684,926.1
Factor income received from abroad. . . . . . . } *Less* Factor income paid abroad }	−4,115.6	−4,007.2	−6,350.1
Gross national product . .	549,766.0	611,108.1	678,576.0

Expenditure on the Gross Domestic Product

	1998	1999	2000
Government final consumption expenditure.	85,497.3	95,586	106,314
Private final consumption expenditure.	352,062.7	396,361	447,397
Increase in stocks	5,800.6	5,595	8,132
Gross fixed capital formation . .	139,204.5	156,690	170,430
Total domestic expenditure. .	582,565.1	654,232	732,272
Exports of goods and services .	155,873.8	160,787	201,001
Less Imports of goods and services	184,878.8	199,904	248,347
GDP in purchasers' values . .	553,560.1	615,115	684,926

Gross Domestic Product by Economic Activity

	1999	2000	2001
Agriculture, hunting and forestry .	21,083.5	22,083.3	24,533.2
Fishing	229.0	201.4	198.7
Mining and quarrying	14,117.8	16,067.9	15,283.4
Manufacturing	112,938.6	124,416.7	118,590.1
Electricity, gas and water . . .	18,155.0	19,607.1	24,213.6
Construction	47,142.7	51,292.1	48,194.5
Trade and repairs	110,605.5	126,799.7	134,351.1
Hotels and restaurants . . .	6,724.9	7,990.4	8,293.9
Transport, storage and communications	36,259.1	42,981.8	48,191.9
Financial intermediation . .	11,580.0	14,302.9	13,830.5
Real estate, renting and business activities* . .	63,282.8	77,509.7	86,856.7
Public administration and defence	26,892.3	39,663.0	45,155.9
Education	23,770.7	28,724.0	33,679.8
Health care and social work . .	21,210.8	25,591.0	26,575.3
Other community, social and personal services	21,831.8	25,604.2	28,140.6
Private households with employed persons	4.5	5.1	5.5
GDP at basic prices . . .	535,829.0	622,840.3	656,094.7
Taxes, *less* subsidies, on products .	87,969.3	100,506.1	105,261.5
GDP in purchasers' values . .	623,798.3	723,346.4	761,356.2

* Including imputed rents of owner-occupied dwellings.

BALANCE OF PAYMENTS
(US $ million)

	1999	2000	2001
Exports of goods f.o.b.	30,060	35,902	41,664
Imports of goods f.o.b.	−45,132	−48,210	−49,324
Trade balance	−15,072	−12,308	−7,660
Exports of services	8,363	10,387	9,755
Imports of services	−6,982	−8,994	−8,951
Balance on goods and services.	−13,691	−10,915	−6,856
Other income received . . .	1,837	2,250	2,625
Other income paid	−2,847	−3,713	−4,015
Balance on goods, services and income	−14,701	−12,378	−8,246
Current transfers received . .	2,898	3,008	3,737
Current transfers paid	−684	−628	−848
Current balance	−12,487	−9,998	−5,357
Capital account (net) . . .	55	32	75
Direct investment abroad . .	−31	−17	89
Direct investment from abroad. .	7,270	9,341	5,713
Portfolio investment assets . .	−548	−89	46
Portfolio investment liabilities . .	691	3,422	1,067
Financial derivatives assets . .	579	269	n.a.
Financial derivatives liabilities .	−10	—	−336
Other investment assets . .	−3,339	−3,870	−4,071
Other investment liabilities . .	5,850	1,148	664
Net errors and omissions . .	2,126	387	1,682
Overall balance	156	625	−428

Source: IMF, *International Financial Statistics*.

External Trade

PRINCIPAL COMMODITIES
(US $ million)

Imports c.i.f.	1999	2000	2001
Food and live animals	2,537	2,558	2,724
Crude materials (inedible) except fuels	1,419	1,643	1,578
Mineral fuels, lubricants, etc. . .	3,281	5,297	5,081
Chemicals and related products .	6,584	6,881	7,337
Basic manufactures	9,526	9,789	10,333
Machinery and transport equipment	17,544	18,114	18,324
Miscellaneous manufactured articles	4,380	4,218	4,416
Total (incl. others)	45,911	48,940	50,275

Exports f.o.b.	1999	2000	2001
Food and live animals	2,328	2,366	2,669
Crude materials (inedible) except fuels	839	894	915
Mineral fuels, lubricants, etc. . .	1,377	1,610	2,043
Chemicals and related products .	1,695	2,151	2,278
Basic manufactures	6,986	7,856	8,614
Machinery and transport equipment	8,278	10,820	13,055
Miscellaneous manufactured articles	5,750	5,804	6,355
Total (incl. others)	27,407	31,651	36,092

Source: IMF, *Republic of Poland: Selected Issues and Statistical Appendix* (June 2002).

PRINCIPAL TRADING PARTNERS
(million new złotys)*

Imports c.i.f.	1998	1999	2000
Austria.	3,154.5	3,512.0	4,141.8
Belgium	4,625.6	5,149.4	5,543.4
China, People's Republic	4,092.7	4,850.1	6,015.8
Czech Republic	5,110.5	5,854.9	6,810.6
Denmark	3,207.9	3,274.6	3,414.4
Finland	2,766.0	3,334.1	3,854.9
France.	10,599.0	12,444.0	13,701.9
Germany	42,036.7	45,968.5	50,938.6
Hungary	2,072.8	2,486.5	3,353.5
Italy	15,371.1	17,061.4	17,726.9
Japan	3,161.1	3,682.0	4,587.1
Korea, Republic	4,488.3	4,705.4	3,225.9
Netherlands	6,257.2	6,825.3	7,570.6
Russia.	8,278.7	10,680.1	20,116.2
Slovakia	2,060.4	2,253.2	3,144.5
Spain	4,191.1	4,508.3	5,191.6
Sweden	4,748.3	5,757.2	6,121.4
Switzerland	2,255.8	2,698.2	2,830.7
Taiwan.	1,719.8	1,918.3	2,001.6
United Kingdom	8,057.2	8,362.7	9,476.1
USA	6,167.0	6,523.6	9,423.4
Total (incl. others)	162,963.0	182,400.0	213,071.8

Exports f.o.b.	1998	1999	2000
Austria.	1,929.4	2,200.0	2,783.9
Belgium	2,422.1	3,016.6	4,067.4
Czech Republic	3,574.5	4,130.2	5,228.1
Denmark	2,712.6	3,332.5	3,724.5
France.	4,637.9	5,269.9	7,156.4
Germany	35,767.8	39,240.9	48,078.1
Hungary	1,641.8	2,141.1	2,837.9
Italy	5,790.7	7,110.5	8,702.4
Netherlands	4,732.7	5,725.1	6,960.5
Norway	810.4	1,354.6	1,472.3
Russia.	5,566.3	2,829.6	3,770.5
Slovakia	1,179.0	1,418.1	1,913.4
Spain	1,365.1	1,649.8	2,201.8
Sweden	2,359.9	2,690.9	3,753.6
Ukraine	3,790.0	2,800.1	3,488.0
United Kingdom	3,845.0	4,366.5	6,178.8
USA	2,643.1	2,996.3	4,342.2
Total (incl. others)	98,647.9	108,757.9	137,908.7

* Imports by country of purchase; exports by country of sale.

Transport

POLISH STATE RAILWAYS
(traffic)

	1999	2000	2001
Paying passengers ('000 journeys)	395,850	360,687	332,218
Freight ('000 metric tons)	186,846	187,247	166,856
Passenger-kilometres (million).	26,198	24,092	22,469
Freight ton-kilometres (million)	55,471	54,448	47,913

ROAD TRAFFIC
(motor vehicles registered at 31 December)

	1998	1999	2000
Passenger cars	8,890,763	9,282,816	9,991,260
Lorries and vans	1,578,818	1,682,887	1,783,008
Buses and coaches	80,827	78,717	82,356
Motorcycles and scooters	1,563,513	1,441,691	802,618
Road tractors	79,212	85,013	97,348

Source: IRF, *World Road Statistics*.

INLAND WATERWAYS
(traffic)

	1999	2000	2001
Passengers carried ('000)	1,121	1,265	1,637
Freight ('000 metric tons)	8,382	10,433	10,255
Passenger-kilometres (million).	18	26	42
Freight ton-kilometres (million)	1,028	1,173	1,264

SHIPPING
Merchant Fleet
(registered at 31 December)

	2000	2001	2002
Number of vessels	429	393	383
Displacement ('000 gross registered tons).	1,119.2	618.3	585.6

Source: Lloyd's Register-Fairplay, *World Fleet Statistics*.

Sea Transport
(Polish merchant ships only)

	1998	1999	2000
Passengers carried ('000)	609	622	625
Freight ('000 metric tons)	25,362	22,747	22,774
Passenger-kilometres (million).	172	131	129
Freight ton-kilometres (million)	166,095	164,236	133,654

International Sea-borne Shipping at Polish Ports

	1998	1999	2000
Vessels entered ('000 net reg. tons)	41,164	40,565	n.a.
Passengers ('000): arrivals	1,175	1,572	2,260
Passengers ('000): departures	1,134	1,545	2,205
Cargo ('000 metric tons): loaded*	32,314	33,361	31,524
Cargo ('000 metric tons): unloaded*	18,294	15,866	15,810

* Including ships' bunkers and transhipments.

Source: Ministry of Transport and Maritime Economy.

CIVIL AVIATION
Polish Airlines—'LOT'
(scheduled and non-scheduled flights)

	1999	2000	2001
Passengers carried ('000)	2,621	2,880	3,436
Passenger-kilometres (million).	5,629	6,034	6,412
Cargo (metric tons)	29,000	28,000	27,000
Cargo ton-kilometres ('000).	94,000	88,000	79,000

Source: partly Ministry of Transport and Maritime Economy.

Tourism

FOREIGN TOURIST ARRIVALS
('000, including visitors in transit)

Country of residence	2000	2001	2002
Belarus	5,920	5,197	4,242
Czech Republic	11,985	9,276	8,313
Germany	48,903	31,010	23,655
Lithuania	1,414	1,393	1,398
Russia.	2,275	1,969	1,844
Slovakia	3,914	2,642	2,126
Ukraine	6,184	6,418	5,853
Total (incl. others)	84,515	61,431	50,735

Receipts from tourism (US $ million): 4,500 in 2002.

Source: Institute of Tourism.

Communications Media

	1998	1999	2000
Radio licences ('000)*	9,577	9,461	n.a.
Television receivers ('000 in use)‡	14,500	15,000	15,500
Telephones ('000 main lines in use)*	8,808	10,076	10,740
Mobile cellular telephones ('000 subscribers)	1,944	3,956	6,748
Personal computers ('000 in use)‡	1,900	2,400	2,670
Internet users ('000)‡	1,581	2,100	2,800
Book production: titles†	16,462	19,192	21,647
Book production: copies ('000)† .	84,999	78,078	102,800
Daily newspapers: number . .	52	46	42
Daily newspapers: average circulation ('000 copies) . .	4,167	3,870	3,928
Non-daily newspapers: number .	29	28	n.a.§
Non-daily newspapers: average circulation ('000 copies) . . .	871	722	n.a.§
Other periodicals: number . . .	5,297	5,518	5,314
Other periodicals: average circulation ('000 copies) . . .	72,336	65,997	68,368

* At 31 December.

† Including pamphlets (1,753 titles and 7,461,000 copies in 1998; 1,644 titles and 5,554,000 copies in 1999).

‡ Source: International Telecommunication Union.

§ In 2000 there were 71 daily and non-daily newspapers, with a combined average circulation of 4,566,000 copies.

Facsimile machines (estimate, 1995): 55,000 in use (Source: UN, *Statistical Yearbook*).

2001: Telephones ('000 main lines in use) 11,394; Mobile cellular telephones ('000 subscribers) 10,050; Personal computers ('000 in use) 3,300; Internet users ('000) 3,800 (Source: International Telecommunication Union).

2002: Mobile cellular telephones ('000 subscribers) 14,000 (Source: International Telecommunication Union).

Education

(2001/02)

	Institutions	Teachers ('000)	Students ('000)
Pre-primary*	20,429	74.8	956.8
Primary	15,836	242.4	3,105.1
Lower secondary	6,423	123.9	1,743.1
Secondary	10,514	158.2	1,852.9
General	2,296	52.6	716.8
Technical and vocational	8,218	105.6	1,136.1
Post-secondary	2,625	n.a.	211.0
Tertiary	344	82.1	1,718.7

* 1998/99 figures.

Adult literacy rate (UNESCO estimates): 99.7% (males 99.7%; females 99.7%) in 2000 (Source: UN Development Programme, *Human Development Report*).

Directory

The Constitution

The Constitution of the Republic of Poland was adopted by the National Assembly on 2 April 1997 and endorsed by popular referendum on 25 May of that year. The following is a summary of the main provisions of the Constitution, which came into force on 17 October 1997:

THE REPUBLIC

The Republic of Poland shall be a unitary, democratic state, ruled by law, and implementing the principles of social justice. The Republic of Poland shall safeguard the independence and integrity of its territory, ensure the freedom and rights of persons and citizens, and safeguard the national heritage. The Constitution shall be the supreme law of the Republic of Poland, which shall respect international law binding upon it. Legislative power shall be vested in the Sejm and the Senat, executive power shall be vested in the President and the Council of Ministers, and judicial power shall be vested in courts and tribunals.

The Republic of Poland shall ensure freedom for the creation and functioning of political parties, trade unions and other voluntary associations. The financing of political parties shall be open to public inspection. Political parties and other organizations whose programmes are based upon totalitarian methods and the modes of activity of nazism, fascism and communism, as well as those whose programmes or activities sanction racial or national hatred, or the application of violence for the purpose of obtaining power or to influence the State's policy, or provide for the secrecy of their own structure or membership, shall be forbidden. The Republic of Poland shall ensure freedom of the press and other means of social communication.

A social market economy, based on the freedom of economic activity, private ownership, and solidarity, dialogue and co-operation between social partners, shall be the basis of the economic system of Poland.

Churches and other religious organizations shall have equal rights. Public authorities shall be impartial in matters of personal conviction, whether religious or philosophical, or in relation to outlooks on life, and shall ensure their freedom of expression within public life. The Armed Forces shall observe neutrality regarding political matters and shall be subject to civil and democratic control.

Polish shall be the official language in the Republic of Poland. The image of a crowned eagle upon a red field shall be the coat-of-arms, and white and red shall be the colours of the Republic of Poland. The national anthem shall be the *Mazurka Dąbrowskiego*. The capital of the Republic of Poland shall be Warsaw.

THE FREEDOMS, RIGHTS AND OBLIGATIONS OF PERSONS AND CITIZENS

All persons shall be equal before the law. Men and women shall have equal rights. The Republic of Poland shall ensure Polish citizens belonging to national or ethnic minorities the freedom to maintain and develop their own language, to maintain customs and traditions, and to develop their own culture.

The Republic of Poland shall ensure the legal protection of the life of every human being; the inviolability of the person and of the home; freedom of movement; freedom of faith and religion; and the freedom to express opinions. The freedom of peaceful assembly and association shall be guaranteed. At the age of 18 every citizen shall have the right to participate in a referendum, and to vote in presidential, legislative and local elections. Everyone shall have the right to own property; the freedom to choose and pursue his occupation; the right to health protection; and the right to education. Everyone shall have the right to compensation for any harm done to him by any action of an organ of public authority contrary to law.

SOURCES OF LAW

The sources of universally binding law of the Republic of Poland shall be the Constitution, statutes, ratified international agreements, and regulations.

THE SEJM AND THE SENAT

The Sejm shall be composed of 460 Deputies. Elections to the Sejm shall be universal, equal, direct and proportional and conducted by secret ballot. The Senat shall be composed of 100 Senators. Elections to the Senat shall be universal, direct and conducted by secret ballot.

The Sejm and the Senat shall be elected for a four-year term of office. At the ages of 21 and 30, respectively, every citizen having the right to vote shall be eligible for election to the Sejm and the Senat.

The Sejm shall elect from amongst its members a Marshal and Vice-Marshalls. The Sejm adopts laws; may adopt a resolution on a state of war; may order a nationwide referendum; and may appoint investigative committees to examine particular matters.

The Senat reviews laws adopted by the Sejm; it may adopt amendments or resolve upon complete rejection. The Senat can be overriden by the Sejm by an absolute majority vote in the presence of at least one-half of the statutory number of Deputies.

In instances specified in the Constitution, the Sejm and the Senat, sitting in joint session, shall act as the National Assembly (Zgromadzenie Norodowe). The right to introduce legislation shall belong to Deputies, to the Senat, to the President of the Republic, to the Council of Ministers, and to a group of at least 100,000 citizens having the right to vote in elections to the Sejm.

THE PRESIDENT OF THE REPUBLIC OF POLAND

The President of the Republic of Poland shall be the supreme representative of the Polish State and the guarantor of the continuity of state authority. The President shall ensure observance of the Constitution, safeguard the sovereignty and security of the State, as well as the inviolability and integrity of its territory. The President shall be elected in universal, equal and direct elections by secret ballot. The President shall be elected for a five-year term, and may be re-elected only once. Only a Polish citizen aged over 35 years, with full electoral rights in elections to the Sejm, may be elected President. Any such candidature shall be supported by the signatures of at least 100,000 citizens having the right to vote in elections to the Sejm. If the President of the Republic is unable to discharge the duties of his office, the Marshal of the Sejm shall temporarily assume presidential duties.

The President's duties include the calling of elections to the Sejm and the Senat; heading the Armed Forces; nominating and appointing the Prime Minister; appointing senior public officials; and representing the State in foreign affairs.

Bringing an indictment against the President shall be done by resolution of the National Assembly, passed by a majority of at least two-thirds of the statutory number of members, on the motion of at least 140 members.

THE COUNCIL OF MINISTERS AND GOVERNMENT ADMINISTRATION

The Council of Ministers shall conduct the internal affairs and foreign policy of the Republic of Poland, and shall manage the government administration. The President shall nominate a Prime Minister who shall propose the composition of a Council of Ministers. The Prime Minister shall, within 14 days following his appointment, submit a programme of activity of the Council of Ministers to the Sejm, together with a motion requiring a vote of confidence.

The members of the Council of Ministers shall be responsible to the Sejm, both collectively and individually. The Sejm shall pass a vote of no confidence in the Council of Ministers by a majority of votes of the statutory number of Deputies, on a motion of at least 46 Deputies, specifying the name of a candidate for Prime Minister.

LOCAL SELF-GOVERNMENT

The commune (*gmina*) shall be the basic unit of local self-government. Other units of regional and/or local self-government shall be specified by statute. Public duties aimed at satisfying the needs of a self-governing community shall be the direct responsibility of such units. Units of local self-government shall perform their duties through constitutive and executive organs. Units of local self-government shall be assured public funds for the performance of the duties assigned to them.

COURTS AND TRIBUNALS

The courts and tribunals shall constitute a separate and independent power. The administration of justice in the Republic of Poland shall be implemented by the Supreme Court, the common courts, administrative courts and military courts. Judges, within the exercise of their office, shall be independent and subject only to the Constitution and statutes. A judge shall not belong to a political party or trade union, or perform public activities incompatible with the principles of independence of the courts and judges. The Supreme Court shall exercise supervision over common and military courts.

The Constitutional Tribunal

The Constitutional Tribunal shall adjudicate on the conformity of statutes and other normative acts issued by central state organs to the Constitution. Its judgments shall be universally binding and final. Judges of the Tribunal shall be independent and subject only to the Constitution.

The Tribunal of State

Persons holding high state positions (as specified in the Constitution) shall be accountable to the Tribunal of State for violations of the Constitution or statutes. The First President of the Supreme Court shall be chairperson of the Tribunal. Its members shall be independent and subject only to the Constitution and statutes.

ORGANS OF STATE CONTROL AND FOR THE DEFENCE OF RIGHTS

The Supreme Chamber of Control shall be the chief organ of state order, and shall be subordinate to the Sejm. It shall audit the activity of the organs of government administration, the National Bank of Poland, state legal persons and other state organizational units. The Commissioner for Citizens' Rights shall safeguard the freedoms and rights of persons and citizens as specified in the Constitution and other normative acts. The National Council of Radio and Television Broadcasting shall safeguard freedom of speech and the right to information, as well as the public interest regarding radio and television broadcasting.

PUBLIC FINANCES

The National Bank of Poland, as the central bank of the State, shall have an exclusive right to issue money as well as to formulate and implement monetary policy. It shall be responsible for the value of the Polish currency.

The Council for Monetary Policy, presided over by the President of the National Bank, shall annually formulate the aims of monetary policy and present them to the Sejm at the same time as the submission of the Council of Ministers' draft Budget.

EXTRAORDINARY MEASURES

In situations of particular danger, if ordinary constitutional measures are inadequate, any of the following appropriate extraordinary measures may be introduced in a part or upon the whole territory of the State: martial law, a state of emergency or a state of natural disaster.

The Government

HEAD OF STATE

President: ALEKSANDER KWAŚNIEWSKI (elected 19 November 1995; re-elected 8 October 2000).

COUNCIL OF MINISTERS
(July 2003)

A coalition of the Democratic Left Alliance (SLD) and the Freedom Union (UW).

Prime Minister and Chairman of the European Integration Committee: LESZEK MILLER (SLD).

Deputy Prime Minister and Minister of the Economy, Labour and Social Policy: JERZY HAUSNER (SLD).

Deputy Prime Minister and Minister of Infrastructure: MAREK POL (UP).

Minister of Foreign Affairs: WŁODZIMIERZ CIMOSZEWICZ (SLD).

Minister of National Defence: JERZY SZMAJDZIŃSKI (SLD).

Minister of Finance: ANDRZEJ RACZKO (SLD).

Minister of the Treasury: PIOTR CZYŻEWSKI (SLD).

Minister of Justice: GRZEGORZ KURCZUK (SLD).

Minister of Internal Affairs and Administration: KRZYSZTOF JANIK (SLD).

Minister of Education: KRYSTYNA ŁYBACKA (SLD).

Minister of Culture: WALDEMAR DĄBROWSKI (Ind.).

Minister of Health: LESZEK SIKORSKI (SLD).

Minister of the Environment: CZESŁAW ŚLEZIAK (SLD).

Minister of Science: MICHAŁ KLEIBER (SLD).

Minister of Agriculture and Rural Development: ANDRZEJ OLEJNICZAK (SLD).

Minister without Portfolio: LECH NIKOLSKI (SLD).

Minister without Portfolio: DANUTA HÜBNER (Ind.).

MINISTRIES

Chancellery of the Prime Minister: 00-583 Warsaw, Al. Ujazdowskie 1/3; tel. (22) 6946000; fax (22) 6252637; e-mail cirinfo@kprm .gov.pl; internet www.kprm.gov.pl.

Ministry of Agriculture and Rural Development: 00-930 Warsaw, ul. Wspólna 30; tel. (22) 6231000; fax (22) 6232750; e-mail kanceleria@minrol.gov.pl; internet www.minrol.gov.pl.

Ministry of Culture: 00-71 Warsaw, ul. Krakowskie Przedmieście 15/17; tel. (22) 8267331; fax (22) 8261922; e-mail rzecznik@mk.gov .pl; internet www.mk.gov.pl.

Ministry of the Economy, Labour and Social Policy: 00-513 Warsaw, ul. Nowogrodzka 1/3/5; tel. (22) 6610100; e-mail bpi@mpips .gov.pl; internet www.mpips.gov.pl.

Ministry of Education and Sport: 00-918 Warsaw, Al. Szucha 25; tel. (22) 6280461; fax (22) 6288561; e-mail minister@menis.waw.pl; internet www.men.waw.pl.

Ministry of the Environment: 02-922 Warsaw, ul. Wawelska 52/54; tel. (22) 5792377; fax (22) 5792511; e-mail info@mos.gov.pl; internet www.mos.gov.pl.

Ministry of Finance: 00-916 Warsaw, ul. Świętokrzyska 12; tel. (22) 6945555; fax (22) 8260180; internet www.mf.gov.pl.

Ministry of Foreign Affairs: 00-580 Warsaw, Al. Szucha 23; tel. (22) 5239000; fax (22) 6290287; e-mail dsi@msz.gov.pl; internet www .msz.gov.pl.

Ministry of Health: 00-952 Warsaw, ul. Miodowa 15; tel. (22) 6349600; fax (22) 6358783; e-mail kancelaria@mz.gov.pl; internet www.mz.gov.pl.

Ministry of Infrastructure: 00-928 Warsaw, ul. Chałubińskiego 4/6; tel. (22) 6301000; fax (22) 6301116; e-mail info@mtigm.gov.pl; internet www.mi.gov.pl.

Ministry of Internal Affairs and Administration: 02-514 Warsaw, ul. Batorego 5; tel. (22) 6014427; fax (22) 8497494; e-mail wp@mswia.gov.pl; internet www.mswia.gov.pl.

Ministry of Justice: 00-950 Warsaw, Al. Ujazdowskie 11; tel. (22) 5212888; fax (22) 6215540; e-mail nagorska@ms.gov.pl; internet www.ms.gov.pl.

Ministry of National Defence: 00-909 Warsaw, ul. Klonowa 1; tel. (22) 6280031; fax (22) 8455378; e-mail bpimon@wp.mil.pl; internet www.wp.mil.pl.

Ministry of Science: 00529 Warsaw, ul. Wspólna 1/3; tel. (22) 5292718; internet www.mnii.gov.pl.

Ministry of the Treasury: 00-522 Warsaw, ul. Krucza 36; tel. (22) 6958000; fax (22) 6280872; e-mail minister@mst.gov.pl; internet www.msp.gov.pl.

Other Government Departments

European Integration Committee: 00-918 Warsaw, Al. Ujazdowskie 9; tel. (22) 4555500; fax (22) 6294888; e-mail info@mail.ukie .gov.pl; internet www.ukie.gov.pl.

Government Centre for Strategic Studies: 00-926 Warsaw, ul. Wspólna 4; tel. (22) 6618600; e-mail info@mail.rcss.gov.pl; internet www.rcss.gov.pl.

President and Legislature

PRESIDENT

Presidential election, 8 October 2000

	Votes	%
Aleksander Kwaśniewski	9,485,224	53.90
Andrzej Olechowski	3,044,141	17.30
Marian Krzaklewski	2,739,621	15.57
Jarosław Kalinowski	1,047,949	5.95
Andrzej Lepper	537,570	3.05
Janusz Korwin-Mikke	252,499	1.43
Lech Wałęsa	178,590	1.01
Jan Lopuszanski	139,682	0.79
Dariusz Grabowski	89,002	0.51
Piotr Ikonowicz	38,672	0.22
Tadeusz Wilecki	28,805	0.16
Bogdan Pawlowski	17,164	0.10
Total*	17,789,231	100.00

* Including 190,312 invalid votes.

ZGROMADZENIE NARODOWE
(National Assembly)

Senat

Senat: 00-072 Warsaw, ul. Wiejska 4/6; tel. (22) 6942500; fax (22) 2290968; internet www.senat.gov.pl.

Marshal: LONGIN HIERONIM PASTUSIAK (SLD-UP).

Vice-Marshals: JOLANTA DANIELAK (SLD-UP), RYSZARD JARZEMBOWSKI (SLD-UP), KAZIMIERZ KUTZ (Blok Senat 2001).

Election, 23 September 2001

Parties and alliances	Seats
Democratic Left Alliance (SLD)/Union of Labour (UP)	75
Blok Senat 2001*	15
Polish People's Party (PSL)	4
Self Defence Party of the Republic of Poland	2
League of Polish Families (LPR)	2
Independents	2
Total	100

* An electoral alliance comprising Solidarity Electoral Action of the Right, the Citizens' Platform, the Law and Justice Party, the Freedom Union and the Movement for the Reconstruction of Poland.

Sejm

Sejm: 00-902 Warsaw, ul. Wiejska 4/6; tel. (22) 285927; internet www.sejm.gov.pl.

Marshal: MAREK BOROWSKI (SLD-UP).

Vice-Marshals: TOMASZ NAŁĘCZ (SLD-UP), DONALD TUSK (PO), JANUSZ WOJCIECHOWSKI (PSL).

Election, 23 September 2001

Parties and alliances	% of votes	Seats
Democratic Left Alliance (SLD)/Union of Labour (UP)	41.0	216
Civic Platform (PO)	12.7	65
Self Defence Party of the Republic of Poland	10.2	53
Law and Justice Party (PiS)	9.5	44
Polish People's Party (PSL)	9.0	42
League of Polish Families (LPR)	7.9	38
Solidarity Electoral Action of the Right (AWSP)	5.6	—
Freedom Union (UW)	3.1	—
German Minority (MN)	0.4	2
Others	0.6	—
Total	100.0	460

Local Government

In 1998 a major reform of the structure of local government was undertaken. Legislation was enacted to reduce the number of voivodships from 49 to 16, with these new regional jurisdictions controlled partly by governors appointed by the central Government and partly by elected councils (sejmiks). A new tier of local government was introduced with the creation of 308 counties (powiats), which are governed by elected councils. The basic unit of local government remains the commune (gmina), of which there are 2,489. Elections to the newly created voivodship and powiat councils were held on 11 October 1998 and the new structure became effective on 1 January 1999. Direct local elections took place on 27 October and 10 November 2002.

VOIVODSHIPS

Dolnośląskie: 50-951 Wrocław, pl. Powstańców Warszawy 1; tel. (71) 3406100; fax (71) 3432028; e-mail www@uwoj.wroc.pl; internet www.uwoj.wroc.pl; Gov. RYSZARD NAWRAT.

Kujawsko-Pomorskie: 85-950 Bydgoszcz, ul. Jagiellońska 3; tel. (52) 3497913; fax (52) 3497294; e-mail rpras@uwoj.bydgoszcz.pl; internet www.uwoj.bydgoszcz.pl; Gov. ROMUALD KOSIENIAK.

Lubelskie: 20-914 Lublin, ul. Spokojna 4; tel. (81) 5324543; fax (81) 5324826; e-mail wojewoda@uw.lublin.pl; internet www.uw.lublin.pl; Gov. HENRYK MAKAREVICZ.

Lubuskie: 66-400 Gorzów, ul. Jagiellończyka 8; tel. and fax (95) 7202355; e-mail wojewoda@uwoj.gorzow.pl; internet www .wojewodalubuski.pl; Gov. ANDRZEJ J. KORSKI.

Łódzkie: 90-926 Łódź, ul. Piotrkowska 104; tel. (42) 6363301; fax (42) 6365276; e-mail wojewoda@lodz.uw.gov.pl; internet www.uw .lodz.pl; Gov. KRYSZTOF MAKOWSKI.

Małopolskie: 31-156 Kraków, ul. Basztowa 22; tel. (12) 6160200; fax (12) 4227208; e-mail redakcja@uwoj.krakow.pl; internet www .uwoj.krakow.pl; Gov. JERZY ADAMIK.

Mazowieckie: 00-950 Warsaw, pl. Bankowy 3–5; tel. (22) 6956251; fax (22) 6203704; e-mail wojmaz@mazowsze.uw.gov.pl; internet www.mazowsze.uw.gov.pl; Gov. LESZEK MIZIELIŃSKI.

Opolskie: 45-082 Opole, ul. Piastowska 14; tel. (77) 4524252; fax (77) 4544575; e-mail wojewoda@opole.uw.gov.pl; internet www .opole.uw.gov.pl; Gov. LESZEK POGAN.

Podkarpackie: 35-959 Rzeszów, ul. Grunwaldzka 15; tel. (17) 8627511; fax (17) 8627181; e-mail sekrwoj@uw.rzeszow.pl; internet www.uw.rzeszow.pl; Gov. ZDISŁAW SIEWIERSKI.

Podlaskie: 15-213 Białystok, ul. Mickiewicza 3; tel. (85) 7415978; fax (85) 7322486; internet www.bialystok.uw.gov.pl; Gov. MAREK STRZALINSKI.

Pomorskie: 80-810 Gdańsk, ul. Okopowa 21–27; tel. (58) 3077695; fax (58) 3011417; e-mail rzecznik@uwgda.gov.pl; internet www.uw .gda.pl; Gov. JAN RYSZARD KURYLCZYK.

Śląskie: 40-032 Katowice, ul Jagiellońska 25; tel. (32) 2551225; fax (32) 2564245; e-mail wojwoda@katowice.uw.gov.pl; internet www .katowice.uw.gov.pl; Gov. LECHOSŁAW JARZĘBSKI.

Świętokrzyskie: 25-955 Kielce, al. IX Wieków Kielc 3; tel. (41) 3442956; fax (41) 3444832; e-mail head12@kielce.uw.gov.pl; internet www.kielce.uw.gov.pl; Gov. WŁODZIMIERZ WÓJCIK.

Warmińsko-Mazurskie: 10-959 Olsztyn, al. J. Piłsudskiego 7–9; tel. (89) 5233200; fax (89) 5237754; e-mail mawww@uw.olsztyn.pl; internet www.uw.olsztyn.pl; Gov. STANISŁAW LESKEK SZATKOWSKI.

Wielkopolskie: 61-713 Poznań, al. Niepodległości 16–18; tel. (61) 8541071; fax (61) 8541150; e-mail nowakowski@poznan.uw.gov.pl; internet www.poznan.uw.gov.pl; Gov. ANDRZEJ NOWAKOWSKI.

Zachodniopomorskie: 70-502 Szczecin, Wały Chrobrego 4; tel. (91) 4303300; fax (91) 4338522; e-mail zuw@szczecin.pl; internet www.szczecin.uw.gov.pl; Gov. STANISŁAW WZIĄTEK.

Political Organizations

Under the 1990 law, political parties are not obliged to file for registration. By January 1998 the number of registered parties operating in Poland had declined from some 360 to 60, as a result of new regulations, which obliged existing parties to apply for re-registration by the end of 1997, presenting a list of a minimum of 1,000 supporting signatures, instead of the previous 15.

Alliance of Polish Christian Democrats (Porozumienie Polskich Chrzescijanskich Demokratów—PPChD): e-mail biuro@chadecja .org.pl; internet www.ppchd.org.pl; f. 1999 by the merger of the Centre Alliance, the Movement for the Republic of Poland and the Party of Christian Democrats; Chair. ANTONI TOKARCZUK; Head of Political Council PAWEŁ LACZKOWSKI.

All-Polish Alliance of the Unemployed (OSB): f. 2001; leader BEATA CHORAZY-RYSZKO.

Christian Democratic Party of the Third Republic (ChDTRP): Warsaw, Al. Jerozolimskie 11/19; tel. (22) 6291329; fax (22) 6291081; e-mail chdrp@chdrp.org.pl; internet www.chdrp.org .pl; f. 1997; Chair. MAREK GUMOWSKI.

Christian National Union (Zjednoczenie Chrześcijańsko Narodowe—ZChN): Warsaw, ul. Mokotowska 555/50; tel. (22) 6227120; e-mail biuro@zchn.waw.pl; internet www.zchn.waw.pl; f. 1989; about 10,000 mems; Chair. STANISŁAW ZAJAC.

Civic Platform (PO): 00-548 Warsaw, al. Ujazdowskie 18; tel. (22) 6227548; fax (22) 6225386; internet www.platforma.org.pl; f. 2001 by a popular independent presidential candidate and factions of the UW and the AWS; also known as the Citizens' Platform; contested the elections to the Senat in 2001 as part of the Blok Senat; formed co-operation agreement with the Law and Justice Party for the 2002 local elections; Leader DONALD TUSK.

Confederation for an Independent Poland (Konfederacja Polski Niepodległej—KPN): 00-920 Warsaw, ul. Nowy Świat 18/20; tel. (22) 8261043; fax (22) 8261400; e-mail kpnwa@poczta.onet.pl; internet www.lion.transprojekt.krakow.pl/sk/; f. 1979; centre-right; about 35,000 mems; Chair. LESZEK MOCZULSKI.

Confederation for an Independent Poland (Patriotic Camp—KPN OP): e-mail skus@kpn.org.pl; Leader ADAM SLOMKA.

Conservative Peasant Party-New Poland Movement (SKL-RNP): Warsaw; e-mail webmaster@skl.org.pl; f. 2002 by the merger of the Conservative Peasant Party and the Alliance of Polish Christian Democrats right-wing; Chair. ARTUR BALAZS.

Democratic Left Alliance (Sojusz Lewicy Demokratycznej—SLD): Warsaw; internet www.sld.org.pl; f. 1991 as an electoral coalition of Social Democracy of the Republic of Poland (Socjaldemokracja Rzeczypospolitej Polskiej—SdRP) and the All Poland Trade Unions Alliance; reorganized as a party in 1999, when the SdRP was disbanded;

formed electoral and government alliance with the Union of Labour in 2001; led by LESZEK MILLER.

All Poland Trade Unions Alliance (Ogólnopolskie Porozumienie Związków Zawodowych—OPZZ): see section on Trade and Industry (Trade Unions).

Democratic Party (Stronnictwo Demokratyczne—SD): 00-021 Warsaw, ul. Chmielna 9; tel. (22) 269571; fax (22) 274051; f. 1937; 12,000 mems (1999); Chair. ANDRZEJ ARENDARSKI.

Freedom Union (Unia Wolności—UW): 00-683 Warsaw, ul. Marszałkowska 77/79; tel. (22) 8275047; fax (22) 8277851; e-mail uw@uw.org.pl; internet www.uw.org.pl; f. 1994 by merger of Democratic Union (Unia Demokratyczna—UD) and the Liberal Democratic Congress (Kongres Liberalno-Demokratyczny—KLD); contested the election to the Senat in 2001 as part of the Blok Senat; 12,500 mems; Leader WLADYSŁAW FRASYNIUK; Dep. Leader TADEUSZ SYRYJCZYK.

German Minority (Mniejszość Niemiecka—MN): Leader HENRYK KRÓL.

Labour Party (Stronnictwo Pracy—SP): Warsaw; tel. (22) 291611; fax (22) 6252095; f. 1937; reactivated 1989; merged with Christian Democracy group in 1994; merged with Peasant-Independence Coalition in 2000; formerly known as the Christian Democratic Labour Party; 2,750 mems; Chair. TOMASZ JACKOWSKI; Gen. Sec. ZBIGNIEW JECZMYK.

Law and Justice Party (Prawo i Sprawieliwość—PiS): 00-564 Warsaw, ul. Koszykowa 10; tel. (22) 6216767; fax (22) 6215035; e-mail biuro@pis.org.pl; internet www.pis.org.pl; f. 2001; conservative; contested the election to the Senat in 2001 as part of the Blok Senat; formed co-operation agreement with the Civic Platform for the 2002 local elections; Leader LECH KACZYNSKI.

League of Polish Families (Liga Polskich Rodzin—LPR): f. 2001 as alliance comprising the National Party, All-Poland Youth, the Polish Accord Party, the Catholic National movement and the Peasant National Bloc; Christian, nationalist, anti-EU; Leader ROMAN GIERTYCH; Chief of Staff ZYGMUNT WRZODAK.

Movement for the Reconstruction of Poland (Ruch Odbudowy Polski—ROP): Warsaw; f. 1995; conservative; contested the election to the Senat in 2001 as part of the Blok Senat; 12,000 mems; Leader JAN OLSZEWSKI.

National Pensioners' Party (Krajowa Partia Emerytówi Rencistów—KPEiR): Chair. ZENON ZUMIŃSKI.

Non-Party Bloc in Support of Reforms (Bezpartyjny Blok Wspierania Reform—BBWR): Warsaw; f. 1993 by Lech Wałęsa; Leader LESZEK ZIELIŃSKI; Chair. Prof. ZBIGNIEW RELIGA.

Party of Real Politics (Stronnictwo Polityki Realnej): Warsaw; f. 1996 following a split in the Polish Union of Real Politics; right-wing; Chair. MARIUSZ DZIERZAWSKY.

Party X: Warsaw; tel. (22) 427160; f. 1991; advocates free-market economy, expansion of industry and agriculture, gradual elimination of unemployment and universal access to education, culture and health; 9,000 mems; Leader JÓZEF KOSSECKI.

Peasant Democratic Party (Partia Ludowo Demokratyczna—PLD): f. 1998; Leader ROMAN JAGIELIŃSKI.

Polish People's Party (Polskie Stronnictwo Ludowe—PSL): 00-131 Warsaw, ul. Grzybowska 4; tel. (22) 6206020; fax (22) 6545383; e-mail biuronkw@nkw.psl.org.pl; internet www.psl.org.pl; f. 1990 to replace United Peasant Party (Zjednoczone Stronnictwo Ludowe; f. 1949) and Polish Peasant Party—Rebirth (Polskie Stronnictwo Ludowe—Odrodzenie; f. 1989); centrist, stresses development of agriculture and social-market economy; 200,000 mems; Chair. JAROSŁAW KALINOWSKI.

Polish Socialist Party (Polska Partia Socjalistyczna—PPS): 00-325 Warsaw, ul. Krakowskie Przedmieście 6; tel. (22) 8262054; fax (22) 8266908; e-mail info@polskapartiasocjalisticzyna.org; internet www.pps.org.pl; f. 1892; re-established 1987; 5,000 mems; Leader PIOTR IKONOWICZ.

Self Defence Party of the Republic of Poland (Partia Samoobrona Rzeczypospolitej Polskiej): 00-024 Warsaw, Al. Jerozolimskie 30; tel. (22) 6250472; fax (22) 6250477; e-mail samoobrona@ samoobrona.org.pl; internet www.samoobrona.org.pl; f. 2000 by trade union leaders opposed to the Government's social and economic policies to contest the parliamentary elections in 2001; agrarian, conservative, anti-EU; Leader ANDRZEJ LEPPER.

Social Movement (Ruch Społeczny—RS): 00-683 Warsaw, ul. Marszałkowska 77/79; tel. (22) 6223146; fax (22) 6218224; e-mail biuro@rsaws.pl; internet www.rsaws.pl; f. 1997 as the political wing of the Solidarity trade union; name shortened from Social Movement of Solidarity Electoral Action—RS AWS in 2002; Chair. KRZYSZTOF PIESIEWICZ.

Socio-Cultural Association of Germans of Upper Silesia (Towarzystwo Społeczno-Kulturalne Niemców Województwa Katowickiego): Katowice.

Solidarity Electoral Action of the Right (AWSP): Warsaw; f. 1996 as Solidarity Electoral Action, an electoral alliance of over 30 centre-right parties; formed a renewed alliance of four principal parties, Social Movement of Solidarity Electoral Action, the Christian National Union, the Alliance of Polish Christian Democrats and the Conservative Peasant Party, in Dec. 2000; name changed as above in 2001, upon the withdrawal of the latter party; formed an alliance with the Movement for the Reconstruction of Poland in 2001, and contested the election to the Senat as part of the Blok Senat; Leader JERZY BUZEK; Gen. Sec. MAREK KOTLARSKI.

Union of Labour (Unia Pracy—UP): 00-513 Warsaw, ul. Nowogrodzka 4; tel. and fax (22) 6256776; e-mail biuro@uniapracy.org.pl; internet www.uniapracy.org.pl; f. 1993; formed electoral and government coalition with the Democratic Left Alliance in 2001; Leader MAREK POL.

Union of Real Politics (Unia Polityki Realnej—UPR): 00-042 Warsaw, ul. Nowy Świat 41; tel. and fax (22) 8267477; internet www.upr.org.pl; f. 1996; Leader STANISŁAW MICHALKIEWICZ.

Diplomatic Representation

EMBASSIES IN POLAND

Afghanistan: 03-930 Warsaw, ul. Nobla 3; tel. (22) 6173173; fax (22) 6163777; Chargé d'affaires a.i. ABDUL H. HAIDER.

Albania: 00-789 Warsaw, ul. Słoneczna 15; tel. (22) 8498427; fax (22) 8484004; e-mail albos@warman.com.pl; Ambassador SOKOL GJOKA.

Algeria: 03-932 Warsaw, ul. Dąbrowiecka 21; tel. (22) 6175855; fax (22) 6160081; e-mail ambalgva@zigzag.pl; Ambassador TEDJINI SALAOUANDJI.

Angola: 02-635 Warsaw, ul. Balonowa 20; tel. (22) 6463529; e-mail embaixada@emb-angola.pl; Ambassador LISETH NAWANGA SATUMBO PENA.

Argentina: 03-973 Warsaw, ul. Brukselska 9; tel. (22) 6176028; fax (22) 6177162; e-mail secons@ikp.atm.com.pl; Ambassador CARLOS ALBERTO PASSALACQUA.

Armenia: 02-908 Warsaw, ul. Waszkowskiego 11; tel. (22) 8408130; fax (22) 6420643; e-mail main@embarmenia.it.pl; Ambassador ASHOT HOVAKIMIAN.

Australia: 00-513 Warsaw, ul. Nowogradzka 11, Nautilus Bldg, 3rd Floor; tel. (22) 5213444; fax (22) 6273500; e-mail ambasada@australia.pl; internet www.australia.pl; Ambassador PATRICK LAWLESS.

Austria: 00-748 Warsaw, ul. Gagarina 34; tel. (22) 8410081; fax (22) 8410085; e-mail austria@it.com.pl; Ambassador GEORG WEISS.

Bangladesh: Warsaw; tel. (22) 8483200; fax (22) 8484974; e-mail bangla@it.com.pl; Ambassador ASHFAQUR RAHMAN.

Belarus: 03-978 Warsaw, ul. Ateńska 67; tel. (22) 6172391; fax (22) 6178441; Ambassador PAVEL LATUSHKA.

Belgium: 00-095 Warsaw, ul. Senatorska 34; tel. (22) 8270233; fax (22) 8285711; e-mail ambabel.warsaw@pol.pl; e-mail warsaw@diplobel.org; Ambassador BRUNO NÈVE DE MÉVERGNIES.

Brazil: 03-931 Warsaw, ul. Poselska 11, Saska Kepa; tel. (22) 6174800; fax (22) 6178689; e-mail polbrem@polbrem.it.pl; Ambassador CARLOS ALBERTO DE AZEVEDO PIMENTEL.

Bulgaria: 00-540 Warsaw, Al. Ujazdowskie 33/35; tel. (22) 6294071; fax (22) 6282271; e-mail office@bgemb.com.pl; Ambassador LATCHEZAR Y. PETKOV.

Canada: 00-481 Warsaw, ul. Matejki 1/5; tel. (22) 5843100; fax (22) 5843190; e-mail wsaw@dfait-maeci.gc.ca; Ambassador RALPH J. LYSYSHYN.

Chile: 02-925 Warsaw, ul. Okrężna 62; tel. (22) 8582330; fax (22) 8582329; e-mail embajada@embachile.pl; Ambassador LEOPOLDO DURÁN VALDÉS.

China, People's Republic: 00-203 Warsaw, ul. Bonifraterska 1; tel. (22) 8313836; fax (22) 6354211; e-mail ambchina@pol.pl; Ambassador ZHOU XIAOPEI.

Colombia: 03-936 Warsaw, ul. Zwycięzców 29; tel. (22) 6177157; fax (22) 6176684; e-mail embcol@medianet.com.pl; Ambassador DORY SÁNCHEZ DE WETZEL.

Costa Rica: 02-954 Warsaw, ul. Kubickiego 9, m. 5; tel. (22) 8589112; fax (22) 6427832; e-mail embajada.cr@supermedia.pl; Chargé d'affaires JOHNNY SÁUREZ SANDÍ.

Croatia: 02-628 Warsaw, ul. Ignacego Krasickiego 10; tel. (22) 8441225; fax (22) 8440567; e-mail croemb@pol.pl.

Cuba: 02-516 Warsaw, ul. Rejtana 15, m. 8; tel. (22) 8481715; fax (22) 8482231; e-mail embacuba@medianet.pl; Ambassador JORGE FERNANDO LEFEBRE NICOLÁS.

Czech Republic: 00-555 Warsaw, ul. Koszykowa 18; tel. (22) 6287221; fax (22) 6298045; e-mail warsaw@embassy.mzv.cz; internet www.mfa.cz/warsaw; Ambassador BEDŘICH KOPECKÝ.

Denmark: 02-517 Warsaw, ul. Rakowiecka 19; tel. (22) 8482600; fax (22) 8487580; e-mail wawamb@wawamb.um.dk; internet www.danskeambassade.pl; Ambassador LAURIDS MIKAELSEN.

Ecuador: 02-516 Warsaw, ul. Rejtana 15, m. 15; tel. (22) 8487230; fax (22) 8488196; e-mail mecuapol@it.com.pl; Ambassador GALO FERNANDO LARREA DONOSO.

Egypt: 03-972 Warsaw, ul. Alzacka 18; tel. (22) 6176973; fax (22) 6179058; e-mail embassyofegypt@zigzag.pl; Ambassador HAMDI SANAD LOZA.

Estonia: 02-639 Warsaw, ul. Karwińska 1; tel. (22) 6464480; fax (22) 6464481; e-mail saatkond@varssavi.vm.ee; internet www.estemb.pl; Ambassador AIVO ORAV.

Finland: 00-559 Warsaw, ul. Chopina 4/8; tel. (22) 6294091; fax (22) 6213442; e-mail sanomat.var@formin.fi; Ambassador HANNU HÄMÄLÄINEN.

France: 02-515 Warsaw, ul. Pulawska 17; tel. (22) 5293000; fax (22) 5293001; e-mail presse@ambafrance.org.pl; internet www.france.org.pl; Ambassador PATRICK GAUTRAT.

Germany: 03-932 Warsaw, ul. Dąbrowiecka 30; tel. (22) 6173011; fax (22) 6173582; internet www.ambasadaniemiec.pl; e-mail info@ambasadaniemiec.pl; Ambassador REINHARD SCHWEPPE.

Greece: 00-432 Warsaw, ul. Górnośląska 35; tel. (22) 6229460; fax (22) 6229464; e-mail embassy@greece.pl; internet www.greece.pl; Ambassador NIKOLAOS VAMVOUNAKIS.

Holy See: 00-582 Warsaw, Al. J. Ch. Szucha 12, POB 163 (Apostolic Nunciature); tel. (22) 6288488; fax (22) 6284556; e-mail nuncjatura@episkopat.pl; Apostolic Nuncio Most Rev. JÓZEF KOWALCZYK (Titular Archbishop of Eraclea).

Hungary: 00-559 Warsaw, ul. Chopina 2; tel. (22) 6284451; fax (22) 6218561; e-mail magyar@optimus.waw.pl; Ambassador MIHÁLY GYÖR.

India: 02-516 Warsaw, ul. Rejtana 15, m. 2–7; tel. (22) 8495800; fax (22) 8496705; e-mail ss-com@it.com.pl; Ambassador RAJAMANI LAKSHMI NARAYAN.

Indonesia: 03-903 Warsaw, ul. Estońska 3–5, POB 33; tel. (22) 6175179; fax (22) 6121885; e-mail comwar@polbox.pl; internet www.indonezja.plocman.pl; Ambassador IBNU SANYOTO.

Iran: 03-928 Warsaw, ul. Królowej Aldony 22; tel. (22) 6174293; fax (22) 6178452; e-mail iranemb@warman.com.pl; internet www.iranemb.warsaw.pl; Ambassador SEYED MOUSA KAZEMI.

Ireland: 00-789 Warsaw, ul. Humańska 10; tel. (22) 8496633; fax (22) 8498431; e-mail ambasada@irlandia.pl; internet www.irlandia.pl; Ambassador THELMA DORAN.

Israel: 02-078 Warsaw, ul. Krzywickiego 24; tel. (22) 8250923; fax (22) 8251607; e-mail itonut@israel.pl; internet www.israel.pl; Ambassador Prof. SHEWACH WEISS.

Italy: 00-055 Warsaw, Pl. Dąbrowskiego 6; tel. (22) 8263471; fax (22) 8278507; e-mail ambvars@polbox.com.pl; Ambassador GIANCARLO LEO.

Japan: 00-464 Warsaw, ul. Szwoleżerów 8; tel. (22) 6965000; fax (22) 6965001; e-mail info-cul@emb-japan.pl; internet www.emb-japan.pl; Ambassador MASAKI ONO.

Kazakhstan: 02-954 Warsaw, ul. Królowej Marysieńki 14; tel. (22) 6425388; fax (22) 6423427; e-mail kazdipmis@hot.pl; Ambassador KONSTANTIN ZHIGALOV.

Korea, Democratic People's Republic: 00-728 Warsaw, ul. Bobrowiecka 1A; tel. (22) 8405813; fax (22) 8405710; Ambassador KIM PYONG IL.

Korea, Republic: 00-867 Warsaw, ul. Chlodna 51, Warsaw Trade Tower, 24th Floor; tel. (22) 8483337; fax (22) 52825000; e-mail jnchung89@mofat.go.kr; Ambassador SONG MIN-SOON.

Laos: 02-516 Warsaw, ul. Rejtana 15, m. 26; tel. (22) 8484786; Chargé d'affaires a.i. SENGPHET HOUNGBOUNGNUANG.

Latvia: 02-516 Warsaw, ul. Rejtana 15, m. 28; tel. (22) 8481947; fax (22) 8480201; e-mail amlotewl@warman.com.pl; Ambassador ULDIS VITOLIŅŠ.

Lebanon: 02-516 Warsaw, ul. Starościńska 1B, m. 10–11; tel. (22) 8445065; fax (22) 6460030; e-mail embleban@pol.pl; Ambassador AHMED IBRAHIM.

Libya: 03-934 Warsaw, ul. Kryniczna 2; tel. (22) 6174822; fax (22) 6175091; e-mail alfath2@ikp.atm.com.pl; Ambassador GIUMA IBRAHIM FERJANI.

Lithuania: 00-580 Warsaw, Al. J. Ch. Szucha 5; tel. (22) 6253368; fax (22) 6253440; e-mail litwa_amb@waw.pdi.net; Ambassador DARIUS DEGUTIS.

Macedonia, former Yugoslav republic: 02-954 Warsaw, ul. Królowej Marysieńki 40; tel. (22) 6517291; fax (22) 6517292; e-mail ambrmwar@zigzag.pl; Ambassador KOSTE STOIMENOVSKI.

Malaysia: 03-902 Warsaw, ul. Gruzińska 3; tel. (22) 6174413; fax (22) 6177920; e-mail emwwarsaw@it.com.pl; Ambassador Dato NG BAK HAI.

Mexico: 02-516 Warsaw, ul. Starościńska 1B, m. 4/5; tel. (22) 6468800; fax (22) 6464222; e-mail embamex@ikp.pl; Ambassador FRANCISCO JOSÉ CRUZ GONZÁLEZ.

Moldova: 02-634 Warsaw, ul. Miłobędzka 12; tel. (22) 8447278; fax (22) 6462099; e-mail ammd_pol@yahoo.com; Ambassador EUGEN CARPOV.

Mongolia: 02-516 Warsaw, ul. Rejtana 15, m. 16; tel. (22) 8482063; fax (22) 8499391; e-mail mongamb@ikp.atm.com.pl; internet www .ambmong.net7.pl; Ambassador TUGALKHUU BAASANSUREN.

Morocco: 02-516 Warsaw, ul. Starościńska 1, m. 11/12; tel. (22) 8496341; fax (22) 8481840; e-mail sifamava@pol.pl; Ambassador HASSAN ABADI.

Netherlands: 00-791 Warsaw, ul. Chocimska 6; tel. (22) 8492351; fax (22) 8488345; e-mail nlgovwar@ikp.pl; Ambassador JAN EDWARD CRAANEN.

Nigeria: 00-791 Warsaw, ul. Chocimska 18; tel. (22) 8486944; fax (22) 8485379; e-mail nigemb@ant.pl; Ambassador ZUBAIRU DADA.

Norway: 00-559 Warsaw, ul. Chopina 2A; tel. (22) 6964030; fax (22) 6280938; e-mail emb.warsaw@mfa.no; Ambassador STEN LUNDBO.

Pakistan: 02-516 Warsaw, ul. Starościńska 1, m. 1/2; tel. (22) 8494808; fax (22) 8491160; e-mail parepwarsaw@mailer.cst.tpsa.pl; Ambassador FAUZIA NAZREEN.

Peru: 02-516 Warsaw, ul. Starościńska 1, m. 3–4; tel. (22) 6468806; fax (22) 6468617; e-mail embperpl@atomnet.pl; internet www .perupol.pl; Ambassador MARTÍN YRIGOYEN YRIGOYEN.

Portugal: 03-941 Warsaw, ul. Zwycięzców 12; tel. (22) 6176021; fax (22) 6174498; Ambassador MARIA MARGARIDA DE ARAÚJO DE FIGUEIREDO.

Romania: 00-559 Warsaw, ul. Chopina 10; tel. (22) 6283156; fax (22) 6285264; e-mail embassy@roembassy.com.pl; Ambassador IRENI COMAROSCHI.

Russia: 00-761 Warsaw, ul. Belwederska 49; tel. (22) 6213453; fax (22) 6253016; e-mail ambrus@poczta.fm; Ambassador NIKOLAI AFANASIEVSKII.

Saudi Arabia: 00-739 Warsaw, ul. Stępińska 55; tel. (22) 8400000; fax (22) 8406003; Ambassador OSAMAH A. AL-SANOSI.

Serbia and Montenegro: 00-540 Warsaw, Al. Ujazdowskie 23/25; tel. (22) 6285161; fax (22) 6297173; e-mail yuabapl@zigzag.pl; Ambassador ZORAN NOVAKOVIĆ.

Slovakia: 00-581 Warsaw, ul. Litewska 6; tel. (22) 5258110; fax (22) 5258122; e-mail slovakia@waw.pdi.net; internet www .ambasada-slovacji.pdi.pl; Ambassador MAGDALÉNA VÁŠÁRYOVÁ.

Slovenia: 02-516 Warsaw, ul. Starościńska 1, m. 23–24; tel. (22) 8498282; fax (22) 8484090; e-mail sloemb@it.com.pl; Ambassador ZVONE DRAGAN.

South Africa: 00-675 Warsaw, 6th floor, IPC Business Centre, ul. Koszykowa 54; tel. (22) 6256228; fax (22) 6256270; e-mail saembassy@supermedia.pl; Ambassador SIKOSI MIJI.

Spain: 00-459 Warsaw, ul. Myśliwiecka 4; tel. (22) 6224250; fax (22) 6225408; e-mail embesp@medianet.pl; Ambassador MIGUEL ÁNGEL NAVARRO PORTERA.

Sri Lanka: 02-520 Warsaw, ul. Wiśniowa 40, m.12–13; tel. (22) 6464394; fax (22) 6464435; e-mail lankaemb@medianet.pl; Ambassador RATNAYAKE MUDIYANSELANGE RANJITH CHULA BANDARA.

Sweden: 00-585 Warsaw, ul. Bagatela 3; tel. (22) 6408900; fax (22) 6408983; e-mail ambassaden.warszawa@foreign.ministry.se; internet www.swedishembassy.pl; Ambassador MATS STAFFANSSON.

Switzerland: 00-540 Warsaw, Al. Ujazdowskie 27; tel. (22) 6280481; fax (22) 6210548; e-mail swiemvar@mailer.cst.tpsa.pl; Ambassador ANDRÉ VON GRAFFENREID.

Syria: 02-536 Warsaw, ul. Narbutta 19A; tel. (22) 8491456; fax (22) 8491847; Chargé d'affaires a.i. FARES CHAHINE.

Thailand: 00-790 Warsaw, ul. Willowa 7; tel. (22) 8492655; fax (22) 8492630; e-mail thaiemb@ids.pl; Ambassador VONGTIVA SURAPOLBHICHET.

Tunisia: 00-459 Warsaw, ul. Myśliwiecka 14; tel. (22) 6286330; fax (22) 6216298; e-mail at.varsovie@it.com.pl; Ambassador ALI BOUSNINA.

Turkey: 02-622 Warsaw, ul. Malczewskiego 32; tel. (22) 6464323; fax (22) 6463757; e-mail turkemb@it.com.pl; Ambassador CANDAN AZER.

Ukraine: 00-580 Warsaw, Al. J. Ch. Szucha 7; tel. (22) 6250127; fax (22) 6298103; e-mail emb_pl@mfa.gov.ua; Ambassador OLEKSANDR NYKONENKO.

United Kingdom: 00-556 Warsaw, Al. Róż 1; tel. (22) 6281001; fax (22) 6217161; e-mail info@britishembassy.pl; internet www .britishembassy.pl; Ambassador The Hon. MICHAEL PAKENHAM.

USA: 00-540 Warsaw, Al. Ujazdowskie 29/31; tel. (22) 6283041; fax (22) 6288298; internet www.usaemb.pl; Ambassador CHRISTOPHER HILL.

Uruguay: 02-516 Warsaw, ul. Rejtana 15, m. 12; tel. (22) 8495040; fax (22) 6466887; e-mail uropol@ikp.atm.com.pl; Ambassador CARLOS AMORIN.

Venezuela: 02-516 Warsaw, ul. Rejtana 15, m. 10/11; tel. (22) 6461846; fax (22) 6468761; e-mail embavenez.pl@qdnet.pl; Ambassador DANIELA SZOKOLOCZI.

Viet Nam: 02-589 Warsaw, ul. Kazimierzowska 14; tel. (22) 8446021; fax (22) 8446723; e-mail vso@warman.com.pl; Ambassador DINH XUAN LUU.

Yemen: 03-941 Warsaw, ul. Zwycięzców 18; tel. (22) 6176025; fax (22) 6176022; Ambassador ABDULAZIZ AHMED ALI BAEISA.

Judicial System

SUPREME COURT

Supreme Court

00-951 Warsaw, pl. Krasińskich 2/4/6; tel. (22) 5308213; fax (22) 5309065; e-mail press@sn.pl; internet www.sn.pl.

The highest judicial organ; exercises supervision over the decision-making of all other courts; its functions include: the examination of cassations of final decisions made by courts of appeal; the adoption of resolutions aimed at providing interpretation of legal provisions that give rise to doubts. Justices of the Supreme Court are appointed by the President of the Republic on motions of the National Council of Judiciary and serve until the age of retirement. The First President of the Supreme Court is appointed (and dismissed) from among the Supreme Court Justices by the Sejm on the motion of the President of the Republic, and serves a six-year term. The other presidents of the Supreme Court are appointed by the President of the Republic from among the Supreme Court Justices.

First President: Prof. Dr hab. LECH GARDOCKI.

OTHER COURTS

The Supreme Administrative Court examines, in one procedure, complaints concerning the legality of administrative decisions; it is vested exclusively with the powers of court of cassation.

President: Prof. Dr hab. WALERIAN SANETRA.

Religion

CHRISTIANITY

The Roman Catholic Church

The Roman Catholic Church was granted full legal status in May 1989, when three laws regulating aspects of relations between the Church and the State were approved by the Sejm. The legislation guaranteed freedom of worship, and permitted the Church to administer its own affairs. The Church was also granted access to the media, and allowed to operate its own schools, hospitals and other charitable organizations. A Concordat, agreed by the Polish Government and the Holy See in 1993, was ratified in January 1998.

For ecclesiastical purposes, Poland comprises 14 archdioceses (including one for the Catholics of the Byzantine-Ukrainian rite) and 26 dioceses (including one for the Catholics of the Byzantine-Ukrainian Rite and one Military Ordinariate). At 31 December 2001 there were 20.1m. adherents in Poland.

Bishops' Conference: Konferencja Episkopatu Polski, 01-015 Warsaw, Skwer Kardynała Stefana Wyszyńskiego 6; tel. (22) 8389251; fax (22) 8380967; f. 1969; statutes approved 1995; Pres. Cardinal JÓZEF GLEMP (Archbishop of Warsaw).

Latin Rite

Archbishop of Warsaw and Primate of Poland: Cardinal JÓZEF GLEMP, Sekretariat Prymasa Polski, 00-246 Warsaw, ul. Miodowa 17/19; tel. (22) 5317200; fax (22) 6354324; e-mail prymas@perytnet .pl.

Archbishop of Białystok: Most Rev. WOJCIECH ZIEMBA, 15-087 Białystok, Pl. Jana Pawła II 1, Kuria Metropolitalna; tel. and fax (85) 7416473; e-mail kuria@bialystok.opoka.org.pl.

Archbishop of Częstochowa: Most Rev. STANISŁAW NOWAK, 42-200 Częstochowa, Al. Najśw. Maryi Panny 54, Kuria Metropolitalna; tel. (34) 3241044; fax (34) 3651182; e-mail kuria@czestochowaopoka.org .pl.

Archbishop of Gdańsk: Most Rev. TADEUSZ GOCŁOWSKI, 80-330 Gdańsk (Oliwa), ul. Cystersów 15, Kuria Metropolitalna; tel. (58) 5520051; fax (58) 5522775; e-mail kuria@gsd.gda.pl.

Archbishop of Gniezno: Most Rev. HENRYK MUSZYŃSKI, 62-200 Gniezno, ul. Kanclerza Jana Łaskiego 7; tel. (61) 4262102; fax (61) 4262105; e-mail kuriagni@gniezno.opoka.org.pl.

Archbishop of Katowice: Most Rev. DAMIAN ZIMOŃ, 40-043 Katowice, ul. Jordana 39, Kuria Metropolitalna; tel. (32) 2512160; fax (32) 2514830; e-mail kuria@katowice.opoka.org.pl.

Archbishop of Kraków: Cardinal FRANCISZEK MACHARSKI, 31-004 Kraków, ul. Franciszkańska 3, Kuria Metropolitalna; tel. (12) 6288100; fax (12) 4294617; e-mail kuria@diecezja.krakow.pl.

Archbishop of Łódź: Most Rev. WŁADYSŁAW ZIÓŁEK, 90-458 Łódź, ul. Ks Ignacego Skorupki 1, Kuria Arcybiskupia; tel. (42) 6375844; fax (42) 6361696; e-mail kuria@archidiecezja.lodz.pl.

Archbishop of Lublin: Most Rev. JÓZEF MIROSŁAW ŻYCIŃSKI, 20-105 Lublin, ul. Ks Prymasa Stefana Wyszyńskiego 2, Skr. p. 198, Kuria Metropolitalna; tel. (81) 5321058; fax (81) 5346141; e-mail j .zycinski@kuria.lublin.pl.

Archbishop of Olsztyn(Warmia): Most Rev. EDMUND PISZCZ, 10-006 Olsztyn, ul. Pieniężnego 22; tel. and fax (89) 5272280.

Archbishop of Poznań: Most Rev. STANISŁAW GADECKI, 61-109 Poznań ul. Ostrów Tumski 2, Kuria Arcybiskupia; tel. (61) 8524282; fax (61) 8519748; e-mail kuria@archpoznan.org.pl.

Archbishop of Przemyśl: Most Rev. JÓZEF MICHALIK, 37-700 Przemyśl, Pl. Katedralny 4A,Kuria Metropolitalna; tel. (16) 6786694; fax (16) 6782674; e-mail kuria@przemysl.opoka.org.pl.

Archbishop of Szczecin-Kamień: Most Rev. ZYGMUNT KAMIŃSKI, 71-459 Szczecin, ul. Papieża Pawła VI 4, Kuria Metropolitalna; tel. (91) 4542292; fax (91) 4536908; e-mail kuria@szczecin.opoka.org.pl.

Archbishop of Wrocław: Cardinal HENRYK ROMAN GULBINOWICZ, 50-328 Wrocław, ul. Katedralna 13, Kuria Metropolitalna; tel. (71) 3271111; fax (71) 3228269; e-mail kuri@archidiecezja.wroc.pl.

Byzantine-Ukrainian Rite

Archbishop of Przemyśl-Warsaw: Most Rev. IVAN MARTYNIAK, 37-700 Przemyśl, ul. Basztowa 13; tel. and fax (16) 6787868.

Old Catholic Churches

Mariavite Catholic Church in Poland (Kościół Katolicki Mariawitów w RP): Felicjanów, 09-470 Bodzanów, k. Płocka; tel. (24) 2607010; f. 1893; 2,470 mems (2002); Archbishop JÓZEF M. RAFAEL WOJCIECHOWSKI.

Old Catholic Mariavite Church (Kościół Starokatolicki Mariawitów): 09-400 Płock, ul. Wielkiego 27; tel. and fax (24) 2623086; f. 1906; 25,250 mems (1992); Chief Bishop ZDZISŁAW WŁODZIMIERZ JAWORSKI.

Polish Catholic Church in Poland (Kościół Polskokatolicki w RP): 02-635 Warsaw, ul. Balonowa 7; tel. (22) 8484617; f. 1920; 52,400 mems (1995); Prime Bishop Most Rev. WIKTOR WYSOCZAŃSKI.

The Orthodox Church

Polish Autocephalous Orthodox Church (Polski Autokefaliczny Kościół Prawosławny): 03-402 Warsaw, Al. Solidarności 52; tel. (22) 6190886; internet www.orthodox.pl; 870,600 mems (1989); Archbishop of Warsaw and Metropolitan of All Poland SAWA (MICHAŁ HRYCUNIAK); Archbishop of Łódź and Poznań SZYMON (SZYMON ROMAŃCZUK); Archbishop of Przemyśl and Nowy Sącz ADAM (ALEKSANDER DUBEC); Archbishop of Wrocław and Szczecin JEREMIASZ (JAN ANCHIMIUK); Archbishop of Lublin and Chełm ABEL (ANDRZEJ POPŁAWSKI); Bishop of Białystok and Gdańsk JAKUB (JAKUB KOSTIUCZUK); Bishop of Hajnówka MIRON (MIROSŁAW CHODAKOWSKI); Bishop of Bielsk Podlaski GRZEGORZ (JERZY CHARKIEWICZ).

Protestant Churches

In 1999 there were an estimated 148,738 Protestants in Poland.

Baptist Union of Poland (Kościół Chrześcijan Baptystów w RP):

00-865 Warsaw, ul. Walic ów 25; tel. and fax (22) 6242783; e-mail baptist@hsn.com.pl; f. 1844; 4,000 baptized mems; Pres. Rev. Dr GRZEGORZ BEDNARCZYK; Gen. Sec. RYSZARD GUTKOWSKI.

Evangelical Augsburg (Lutheran) Church in Poland (Kościół Ewangelicko-Augsburski w RP): 00-246 Warsaw, ul. Miodowa 21; tel. (22) 8870200; fax (22) 8870218; e-mail biskup@luteranie.pl; internet www.luteranie.pl; 87,000 mems, 132 parishes (2002); Bishop and Pres. of Consistory JANUSZ JAGUCKI.

Evangelical-Reformed Church (Kościół Ewangelicko-Reformowany): 00-145 Warsaw, Al. Solidarności 76A ; tel. (22) 8314522; fax (22) 8310827; e-mail reformanda@wp.pl; f. 16th century; 4,500 mems (1996); Bishop MAREK IZDEBSKI; Pres. of the Consistory WITOLD BRODZINSKI.

Pentecostal Church (Kościół Zielonoświątkowy): 00-825 Warsaw, ul. Sienna 68/70; tel. (22) 6248575; fax (22) 6204073; e-mail nrk@kz .pl; f. 1910; 20,000 mems (2000); Pres. Bishop MIECZYSŁAW CZAJKO.

Seventh-day Adventist Church in Poland (Kościół Adwentystów Dnia Siódmego): 00-366 Warsaw, ul. Foksal 8; tel. (22) 8277611; fax (22) 8278619; f. 1921; 10,024 mems, 81 preachers (1997); Pres. WŁADYSŁAW POLOK; Sec. ANDRZEJ SICINSKI.

United Methodist Church (Kościół Ewangelicko-Metodystyczny w RP): 00-561 Warsaw, ul. Mokotowska 12; tel. and fax (22) 6285328; e-mail tep@elc.com.pl; internet www.kem.com.pl; f. 1921; 5,000 mems; Gen. Supt/Bishop Rev. Dr EDWARD PUŚLECKI.

There are also several other small Protestant churches, including the Church of Christ, the Church of Evangelical Christians, the Evangelical Christian Church and the Jehovah's Witnesses.

ISLAM

In 1999 there were about 5,125 Muslims of Tartar origin in Białystok Province (eastern Poland), and smaller communities in Warsaw, Gdańsk and elsewhere.

Religious Union of Muslims in Poland (Muzułmański Związek Religijny): 15-426 Białystok, Rynek Kosciuszki 26, m. 2; tel. (85) 414970; Chair. STEFAN MUCHARSKI.

JUDAISM

Union of Jewish Communities in Poland (Związek Gmin Wyznaniowych Żydowskich w Rzeczypospolitej Polskiej): 00-950 Warsaw, ul. Twarda 6; tel. (22) 6204324; fax (22) 6201037; 14 synagogues and about 2,500 registered mems; Pres. PAWEŁ WILDSTEIN.

The Press

Legislation to permit the formal abolition of censorship and to guarantee freedom of expression was approved in April 1990. In 1999 there were 46 daily newspapers in Poland, with a total circulation of 3,870,000. A total of 71 daily and non-daily newspapers were published in 2000, with a total circulation of 4,566,000. In that year there were 5,314 periodicals, with a combined circulation of 68.4m. copies.

PRINCIPAL DAILIES

Białystok

Gazeta Współczesna (Contemporary Daily): 15-950 Białystok, POB 193, ul. Suraska 1; tel. (85) 420935; f. 1951; Editor JERZY KOSTRZEWSKI; circ. 35,000.

Bydgoszcz

Gazeta Pomorska: Bydgoszcz; tel. (52) 221928; fax (52) 221542; f. 1948; local independent newspaper for the provinces of Bydgoszcz, Toruń and Włocławek; Editor MACIEJ KAMIŃSKI; circ. 100,000 (weekdays), 300,000 (weekends).

Gdańsk

Dziennik Bałtycki (Baltic Newspaper): 80-886 Gdańsk, Targ Drzewny 3/7; tel. (58) 3012651; fax (58) 3013560; f. 1945; non-party; Editor KRZYSZTOF KRUPA; circ. 180,000.

Głos Wybrzeża: Gdańsk; tel. (58) 3011572; f. 1991; Editor-in-Chief MAREK FORMOLA; circ. 50,000.

Katowice

Dziennik Zachodni: 40-950 Katowice, ul. Młyńska 1; tel. (32) 1539084; fax (32) 1538196; e-mail dziennik@dz.com.pl; internet www.dz.com.pl; f. 1945; non-party; Chief Editor MAREK CHYLIŃSKI; circ. 510,000.

Trybuna Śląska (Silesian Tribune): 40-098 Katowice, ul. Młyńska 1; tel. (32) 2537822; fax (32) 2537997; e-mail tsl@trybuna-slaska.com.pl; internet www.trybuna-slaska.com.pl; f. 1945; fmrly Trybuna Robotnicza; independent; Editor ROMUALD ORZET; circ. 180,000 (weekdays), 800,000 (weekends).

Kielce

Słowo Ludu (Word of the People): 25-363 Kielce, ul. Wesoła 47/49; tel. (41) 3442480; fax (41) 3446979; e-mail redakcja@slowoludu.com.pl; internet www.slowoludu.com.pl; f. 1949; independent; Editor GRZEGORZ ŚCIWIARSKI; circ. 50,000 (weekdays), 130,000 (weekends).

Koszalin

Głos Pomorza (Voice of Pomerania): 75-604 Koszalin, ul. Zwycięstwa 137/139; tel. (94) 422693; fax (94) 423309; f. 1952; Editor-in-Chief WIESŁAW WIŚNIEWSKI; circ. 60,000 (weekdays), 130,000 (weekends).

Kraków

Czas Krakowski (Cracow Time): Kraków; tel. (12) 4225355; fax (12) 4217502; f. 1848; reactivated 1990; independent; Editor JAN POLKOWSKI; circ. 150,000 (weekdays), 260,000 (weekends).

Dziennik Polski: 31-072 Kraków, ul. Wielopole 1; tel. (12) 6199200; fax (12) 6199276; e-mail redakcja@dziennik.krakow.pl; internet www.dziennik.krakow.pl; Editor PIOTR ALEKSANDROWICZ.

Echo Krakowa: Kraków; tel. (12) 4224678; f. 1946; independent; evening; Editor WITOLD GRZYBOWSKI; circ. 60,000 (weekdays), 90,000 (weekends).

Gazeta Krakowska: Kraków; tel. (12) 4220985; fax (12) 4221563; f. 1949; Editor-in-Chief JERZY SADECKI; circ. 60,000 (weekdays), 150,000 (weekends).

Łódź

Dziennik Łódzki: 90-532 Łódź, ul. ks. Skorupki 17/19; tel. (42) 6303565; fax (42) 6377364; e-mail dziennik@dziennik.lodz.pl; internet www.dziennik.lodz.pl; f. 1945; non-party; Editor JULIAN BECK; circ. 50,000 (weekdays), 110,000 (weekends).

Lublin

Dziennik Lubelski: 20-601 Lublin, ul. Zana 38c ; tel. (81) 558000; f. 1990; fmrly Sztandar Ludu; Editor ALOJZY LESZEK GZELLA; circ. 45,000 (weekdays), 210,000 (weekends).

Dziennik Wschodni: 20-081 Lublin, ul. Staszica 20; tel. (81) 5340600; fax (81) 5340601; e-mail redakcja@dw.lublin.pl; internet www.dw.lublin.pl; Editor STANISŁAW SOWA.

Kurier Lubelski: 20-950 Lublin, POB 176; tel. (81) 5326634; fax (81) 5326835; e-mail redakcja@kurierlubelski.pl; internet www.kurier.lublin.pl; f. 1830; independent; evening; Editor PAWEŁ CHROMCEWICZ; circ. 40,000 (weekdays), 100,000 (weekends).

Olsztyn

Gazeta Olsztyńska (Olsztyn Gazette): 10-417 Olsztyn, ul. Towarowa 2; tel. (889) 330277; fax (889) 332691; f. 1886; renamed 1970; independent; Editor-in-Chief TOMASZ ŚRUTKOWSKI; circ. 45,000 (weekdays), 90,000 (weekends).

Opole

Nowa Trybuna Opolska: 45-086 Opole, ul. Powstańców Śląskich 9; tel. (77) 4567041; fax (77) 4543737; e-mail nto@nto.com.pl; internet www.nto.com.pl; f. 1952; independent; Editor WOJCIECH POTOCKI; circ. 80,000.

Poznań

Gazeta Poznańska: 60-782 Poznań, ul. Grunwaldzka 19; tel. (61) 8665568; e-mail gp@gp.pl; internet www.gp.pl; f. 1991; part of the Polskapresse group; Editor JAROSŁAW GOJTOWSKI; circ. 80,000 (weekdays), 320,000 (weekends).

Głos Wielkopolski (Voice of Wielkopolska): 60-959 Poznań, ul. Grunwaldzka 19; tel. (61) 8694100; fax (61) 8659672; e-mail glosmar@sylaba.poznan.pl; internet www.glos.com; f. 1945; independent; Editor-in-Chief MAREK PRZYBYLSKI; circ. 110,000 (weekdays), 160,000 (weekends).

Rzeszów

Gazeta Codzienna 'Nowiny': 35-959 Rzeszów, ul. Unii Lubelskiej 3; tel. (17) 628471; fax (17) 628836; f. 1949; evening; Editor JAN MUSIAŁ; circ. 100,000.

Szczecin

Głos Szczeciński (Voice of Szczecin): 70-550 Szczecin, Pl. Hołdu Pruskiego 8; tel. (91) 4341306; fax (91) 4345472; e-mail glos@dragon.com.pl; internet www.glosszczecinski.com.pl; f. 1947; Editor-in-Chief ROBERT CIEŚLAK; circ. 30,000 (weekdays), 100,000 (weekends).

Kurier Szczeciński: 70-550 Szczecin, Pl. Hołdu Pruskiego 8; tel. and fax (91) 4345741; e-mail redakcja@kurier.szczecin.pl; internet www.kurier.szczecin.pl; Editor ANDRZEJ ŁAPCIEWICZ.

Warsaw

Express Wieczorny (Evening Express): 02-017 Warsaw, Al. Jerozolimskie 125/127; tel. (22) 6285231; fax (22) 6284929; f. 1946; non-party; Editor ANDRZEJ URBAŃSKI; circ. 140,000 (weekdays), 400,000 (weekends).

Gazeta Wyborcza: 00-732 Warsaw, ul. Czerska 8/10; tel. (22) 415513; fax (22) 416920; e-mail listy@gazeta.pl; internet wyborcza.gazeta.pl; f. 1989; non-party; national edn and 20 local edns; weekend edn: Gazeta Świateczna; special supplements; Editor-in-Chief ADAM MICHNIK; circ. 516,000 (daily), 686,000 (weekends).

Kurier Polski: 00-018 Warsaw, ul. Zgoda 11; tel. (22) 8278081; fax (22) 8270552; e-mail kpkurier@kurier.pl; f. 1729; Editor BOŻENA SKUPIŃSKA; circ. 150,000 (weekdays), 190,000 (weekends).

Nasz Dziennik (Our Newspaper): 04-476 Warsaw, ul. Żeligowskiego 16/20; tel. (22) 6734819; fax (22) 6734817; e-mail redakcja@naszdziennik.pl; internet www.naszdziennik.pl; national; Editor EWA SOŁOWIEJ; circ. 250,000.

Nowa Europa: Warsaw; tel. (22) 6200966; fax (22) 6209145; Editorial Dir ANDRZEJ WROBLEWSKI.

Polska Zbrojna: 00-950 Warsaw, ul. Grzybowska 77; tel. (22) 6204293; fax (22) 6242273; f. 1943; fmrly Żolnierz Wolności, name changed 1990; Editor JERZY ŚLĄSKI; circ. 50,000.

Przegląd Sportowy (Sports Review): 02-017 Warsaw, Al. Jerozolimskie 125/127, POB 181; tel. (22) 6289116; fax (22) 218697; f. 1921; Editor MACIEJ POLKOWSKI; circ. 110,000.

Rzeczpospolita (The Republic): 02-015 Warsaw, Pl. Starynkiewicza 7; tel. (22) 6283401; fax (22) 6280588; e-mail p.aleksandrowicz@rzeczpospolita.pl; internet www.rzeczpospolita.pl; f. 1982; 51% owned by Orkla (Norway); Editor-in-Chief MACIEJ LUKASIEWICZ; circ. 275,000.

Super Express: 00-939 Warsaw, ul. Jubilerska 10; tel. (22) 5159000; fax (22) 5159010; e-mail listy@superexpress.com.pl; internet www.se.com.pl; f. 1991; Pres. and Chief Exec. IZABELLA JABLONSKA; Editor-in-Chief EWA JAROSŁAWSKA; circ. 371,106.

Trybuna: 00-835 Warsaw, ul. Miedziana 11; tel. (22) 6253015; fax (22) 6204100; e-mail redakcja@trybuna.com.pl; f. 1990; fmrly Trybuna Ludu; organ of Social Democracy of the Republic of Poland; Editor-in-Chief ANDRZEJ URBAŃCZYK; circ. 110,000 (weekdays), 150,000 (weekends).

Wprost: 02-017 Warsaw, Al. Jerozolimskie 123, Reform Plaza; tel. (22) 5291100; fax (22) 8529016; e-mail redakcja@wprost.pl; internet www.wprost.pl; Editor MAREK KRÓL.

Życie Warszawy (Warsaw Life): Warsaw; tel. (22) 6256990; fax (22) 6226031; e-mail zycie@zw.com.pl; internet www.zw.com.pl; f. 1944; independent; Editor-in-Chief ANDRZEJ BOBER; circ. 250,000 (weekdays), 460,000 (weekends).

Wrocław

Gazeta Robotnicza: 50-010 Wrocław, ul. Podwale 62; tel. (71) 335756; fax (71) 335756; f. 1948; Editor ANDRZEJ BUŁAT; circ. 30,000 (weekdays), 315,000 (weekends).

Gazeta Wrocławska: Wrocław; e-mail redakcja@gazeta.wroc.pl; internet www.gazeta.wroc.pl; part of the Polskapresse group; circ. 48,600.

Zielona Góra

Gazeta Lubuska: 65-042 Zielona Góra, POB 120, Al. Niepodległości 25; tel. (68) 3254661; fax (68) 3253555; e-mail redakcja@gazetalubuska.pl; internet www.gazetalubuska.pl; f. 1952; independent; Editor MIROSŁAW RATAJ; circ. 60,000 (weekdays), 150,000 (weekends).

PERIODICALS

Computerworld Poland: 04-228 Warsaw, ul. Tytoniowa 10; tel. (22) 121390; fax (22) 154495; internet www.comnet.com.pl/cw; weekly; information technology; circ. 14,400.

Le Courrier de Varsovie: Warsaw; internet www.courrierdevarsovie.pl; daily, monthly; in French; Dir JAN KRAUZE.

Dom i Wnętrze (House and Interior): Warsaw; tel. (22) 6211038; fax (22) 6211030; e-mail ipaco@domiwnetrze.com.pl; f. 1991; illustrated monthly; Editor WIESŁAW KEDZIERSKI.

Dziecko (Child): 02-651 Warsaw, ul. Garażowa 7; tel. (22) 6077700; fax (22) 6077704; e-mail dziecko@proszynski.com.pl; f. 1995;

monthly; women's magazine concerning children's affairs; Editor JUSTYNA DĄBROWSKI; circ. 95,000.

Dziewczyna (Girl): Warsaw; tel. (22) 6363681; fax (22) 6365281; e-mail mpc@saxon.pip.com.pl; f. 1990; monthly; lifestyle magazine for young women; Editor AGNIESZKA LESIAK; circ. 420,000.

Elle: 02-119 Warsaw, ul. Pruszkowska 17; tel. (22) 6689083; fax (22) 6689183; e-mail elle@elle.com.pl; f. 1994; monthly; women's fashion; Editor-in-Chief MARZENA WILKANOWICZ DEVOUD; circ. 190,000 (1998).

Filipinka: Warsaw; tel. (22) 312221; f. 1957; fortnightly; illustrated for teenage girls; Editor HANNA JAWOROWSKA-BŁOŃSKA; circ. 125,600.

Film: Warsaw; tel. (22) 455325; fax (22) 454651; f. 1946; monthly; illustrated magazine; Editor-in-Chief LECH KURPIEWSKI; circ. 105,000.

Forum: 00-656 Warsaw, ul. Śniadeckich 10; tel. (22) 6289503; fax (22) 6256150; f. 1965; weekly; political, social, cultural and economic; Editor-in-Chief BOGDAN HERBICH; circ. 33,000.

Gazeta Bankowa: Warsaw; tel. (22) 6287272; fax (22) 6212653; e-mail bankowa@ikp.atm.com.pl; internet www.bankowa.com.pl; f. 1988; weekly; business and finance; Editor-in-Chief ADA KOSTRZ-KOSTECKA; circ. 35,000.

Gazeta Targowa: 61-707 Poznań, ul. Libelta; tel. (61) 8528582; fax (61) 8526108; e-mail gazetarg@soho.online.com; finance; Editor-in-Chief SAWOMIR ERKIERT.

Głos Nauczycielski (Teachers' Voice): 00-389 Warsaw, ul. Smulikowskiego 6/8; tel. (22) 276630; fax (22) 276630; f. 1917; weekly; organ of the Polish Teachers' Union; Editor WOJCIECH SIERAKOWSKI; circ. 40,000.

Gromada-Rolnik Polski: Warsaw; tel. (22) 278815; fax (22) 278815; f. 1951; 3 a week; agricultural; Editor ZBIGNIEW LUBAK; circ. 281,800.

Kobieta i Życie (Woman and Life): Warsaw; tel. and fax (22) 6283030; f. 1946; weekly; women's; Editor ZOFIA KAMIŃSKA; circ. 400,000.

Lubie Gotować (I Love Cooking): 02-651 Warsaw, ul. Garażowa 7; tel. (22) 6077620; fax (22) 6461270; e-mail kuchnia@proszynski.com.pl; internet www.proszynski.com.pl; f. 1988; monthly; cookery; Editor HANNA GRYKALOWSKA; circ. 202,727.

Nie (No): 00-789 Warsaw, ul. Słoneczna 25; tel. (22) 8484420; fax (22) 8497258; e-mail nie@redakija.nie.com.pl; internet www.nie.com.pl; f. 1990; satirical weekly; Editor JERZY URBAN; circ. 500,000.

Nie z tej Ziemi (Out of this World): Warsaw; tel. (22) 241485; fax (22) 241481; f. 1990; monthly; para-science, ghost stories, etc.; Editor TADEUSZ LACHOWICZ; circ. 150,000.

Nowa Fantastyka: 00-640 Warsaw, ul. Mokotowska 5/6; tel. (22) 8253475; fax (22) 8252089; f. 1982; monthly; science fiction and fantasy; Editor MACIEJ PAROWSKI; circ. 57,000.

Nowa Wieś: Warsaw; tel. and fax (22) 6284583; f. 1948; weekly; illustrated peasant magazine; Editor KAZIMIERZ DŁUGOSZ; circ. 60,000.

Panorama: 40-082 Katowice, ul. Sobieskiego 11; tel. (3) 1538595; fax (3) 1538374; f. 1960; weekly; socio-cultural magazine; Editor ADAM JAZWIECKI; circ. 150,000.

Państwo i Prawo (State and Law): 00-330 Warsaw, ul. Nowy Świat 72; tel. (22) 6288296; f. 1946; monthly organ of the Polish Academy of Sciences; Editor Dr LESZEK KUBICKI; circ. 3,000.

Polityka (Politics): 00-835 Warsaw, ul. Miedziana 11, POB 86; tel. (22) 6353491; fax (22) 6351797; e-mail polityka@polityka.com.pl; internet polityka.onet.pl; f. 1957; weekly; political, economic, cultural; Editor JERZY BACZYŃSKI; circ. 340,000.

Poradnik Gospodarski (Farmers' Guide): 60-837 Poznań, ul. A. Mickiewicza 33; tel. and fax (61) 8476001; f. 1889; monthly; agriculture; Editor-in-Chief WAWRZYNIEC TRAWIŃSKI; circ. 10,000.

Prawo i Gospodarka: Warsaw; tel. (22) 6727961; fax (22) 6727976; e-mail z.maciag@pg.com.pl; internet www.seonet.pl; Editor ZBIGNIEW MACIĄG.

Przegląd Tygodniowy (Weekly Review): Warsaw; tel. (22) 6207290; fax (22) 6544711; e-mail przegtyg@medianet.pl; internet www.przeglad-tygodniowy.pl; f. 1981; weekly; political, economic, social, historical, cultural, scientific and artistic; Editor-in-Chief JERZY DOMAŃSKI; circ. 150,000.

Przekrój (Review): 00-490 Warsaw, ul. Wiejska 16; tel. (22) 6272306; fax (22) 6272305; e-mail nowy.przekroj@edipresse.pl; f. 1945; weekly; illustrated; cultural; Editor-in-Chief JACEK RAKOWIECKI; circ. 77,500.

Przyjaciółka (Friend): 00-490 Warsaw, ul. Wiejska 16; tel. (22) 6280583; fax (22) 6285866; f. 1948; weekly; women's magazine; Editor EWA NIEZBECKA; circ. 720,000.

Res Publica Nowa: 00-950 Warsaw 1, POB 856, ul. Smolna 12; tel. (22) 263047; fax (22) 262329; f. 1987; monthly; political and cultural; Editor MARCIN KRÓL; circ. 5,000.

Sport: 40-082 Katowice, ul. Sobieskiego 11, POB 339; tel. (3) 1539995; fax (3) 1537138; f. 1945; 5 a week; Editor ADAM BARTECZKO; circ. 135,000.

Spotkania (Meetings): Warsaw; tel. (22) 399022; fax (22) 241423; f. 1990; weekly; illustrated; political, social, economic, cultural and scientific magazine; Editor MACIEJ IŁOWIECKI; circ. 80,000.

Sprawy Międzynarodowe (International Affairs): 00-950 Warsaw, ul. Warecka 1A; tel. (22) 5239086; fax (22) 5239027; e-mail warecka@qdnet.pl; internet www.qdnet.pl/warecka; f. 1948; quarterly; published by the Polish Foundation of International Affairs; also English edition, *The Polish Quarterly of International Affairs* (f. 1992); Editor HENRYK SZLAJFER; circ. 900.

Swiat Nauki (World of Science and Technology): 02-651 Warsaw, ul. Garażowa 7; tel. (22) 6077640; fax (22) 6077645; e-mail swiatnauki@proszynski.com.pl; internet www.proszynski.com.pl/swiatnauki; f. 1991; monthly; Editor-in-Chief JOANNA ŻIMAKOWSKA.

Szpilki: Warsaw; tel. (22) 6280429; f. 1935; weekly; illustrated satirical; Editor JACEK JANCZARSKI; circ. 100,000.

Teatr: 03-902 Warsaw, ul. Jakubowska 14; tel. (22) 6175594; fax (22) 6174298; f. 1945; monthly; illustrated; theatrical life; Editor JANUSZ MAJCHEREK; circ. 4,000.

Tygodnik Gospodarczy (Economic Weekly): 00-511 Warsaw, ul. Nowogrodzka 31; tel. (22) 6280593; fax (22) 6299614; e-mail redakcja@tygodnikgospodarczy.pl; internet www.waw.pdi.net/sigma; f. 1991; weekly; international business and economics; Publr TADEUSZ JACEWICZ; circ. 52,000.

Tygodnik Solidarność: Warsaw; tel. (22) 6352037; fax (22) 317858; f. 1981; reactivated 1989; weekly; Editor ANDRZEJ GELBREG; circ. 60,000.

The Warsaw Voice: 00-950 Warsaw, POB 28; tel. (22) 8375138; fax (22) 8371995; e-mail voice@warsawvoice.com.pl; internet www.warsawvoice.com.pl; f. 1988; weekly; economic, political, social, cultural and economic; in English; Editor ANDRZEJ JONAS; Gen. Dir JULIUSZ KŁOSOWSKI; circ. 15,000.

Wiedza i Życie (Knowledge and Life): 02-651 Warsaw, ul. Garażowa 7; tel. (22) 6077630; fax (22) 6077645; e-mail wiedza@proszynski.com.pl; internet www.proszynski.com.pl/wiedzaizycie; f. 1926; monthly; popular science; Editor ANDRZEJ GORZYM; circ. 112,000.

Żołnierz Polski (Polish Soldier): 00-800 Warsaw, ul. Grzybowska 77; tel. (22) 204286; fax (22) 202127; f. 1945; monthly; illustrated magazine primarily about the armed forces; Editor IRENEUSZ CZYŻEWSKI; circ. 40,000.

Życie Gospodarcze (Economic Life): Warsaw; tel. (22) 6289493; fax (22) 6210034; f. 1945; weekly; economic; Editor STANISŁAW CHETSTOWSKI; circ. 35,700.

NEWS AGENCIES

Polska Agencja Informacyjna (PAI) (Polish Information Agency): 04-028 Warsaw, Al. Stanów Zjednoczonych 53; tel. (22) 134605; fax (22) 134924; f. 1967; bulletins and news services on Polish culture, foreign policy and economics; Editor-in-Chief JAN FOROWICZ.

Polska Agencja Prasowa (PAP) (Polish Press Agency): 00-950 Warsaw, Al. Jerozolimskie 7; tel. (22) 6280001; fax (22) 6286407; e-mail webmaster@pap.com.pl; internet www.pap.com.pl; f. 1944; brs in 28 Polish towns and 22 foreign capitals; 274 journalist and photojournalist mems; information is transmitted abroad in English only; Pres. ROBERT BOGDAŃSKI; Vice-Pres. PIOTR CIOMPA.

Foreign Bureaux

Agence France-Presse (AFP): 00-582 Warsaw, Al. Szucha 16, m. 34; tel. (22) 6272409; fax (22) 6223499; e-mail afpwaw@pol.pl; Correspondent PIERRE-ANTOINE DONNET.

Agencia EFE (Spain): 00-656 Warsaw, ul. Śniadeckich 18, Lokal 16; tel. (22) 6282567; fax (22) 6215989; Bureau Chief JORGE RUIZ LARDIZÁBAL.

Agenzia Nazionale Stampa Associata (ANSA) (Italy): 00-672 Warsaw, ul. Piękna 68, p. 301; tel. (22) 298413; fax (22) 299843; Bureau Chief MAURIZIO SALVI.

Associated Press (AP) (USA): 00-433 Warsaw, ul. Profesorska 4; tel. (22) 6287231; fax (22) 6295240; internet www.ap.org; Correspondent ANDRZEJ STYLIŃSKI.

Bulgarska Telegrafna Agentsia (BTA) (Bulgaria): Warsaw; tel. (22) 278059; Correspondent WESELIN JANKOW.

Česká tisková kancelář (ČTK) (Czech News Agency): 03-946 Warsaw, ul. Brazyliоska 14A/9; tel. and fax (22) 6728780; e-mail ctk@ctk.if.pl; Correspondent JAN MELICHAR.

Deutsche-Presse Agentur (dpa) (Germany): 03-968 Warsaw, ul. Saska 7A ; tel. (22) 6171058; fax (22) 6178481; Correspondent DANIEL BRÖSSLER.

Informatsionnoye Telegrafnoye Agentstvo Rossii—Telegrafnoye Agentstvo Suverennykh Stran (ITAR—TASS) (Russia): Warsaw; tel. (22) 292192; fax (22) 296131; Correspondent ALEKSANDR L. POTEMKIN.

Kyodo News Service (Japan): 05-220 Warsaw, Zielonka Prosta 14; tel. and fax (22) 7810246; Chief JUN IWAWAKI.

Magyar Távirati Iroda Rt. (MTI) (Hungary): 02-954 Warsaw, ul. Jakuba Kubickiego 19, m. 11; tel. (22) 6517675; e-mail pkovacs@ipgate.pl; Correspondent PÉTER KOVÁCS.

Reuters (United Kingdom): 00-854 Warsaw, Al. Jana Pawła II 23; tel. (22) 6539700; fax (22) 6539780; internet www.reuters.com.pl; Correspondent ANTHONY BARKER.

Rossiiskoye Informatsionnoye Agentstvo—Novosti (RIA—Novosti) (Russia): Warsaw; tel. (22) 6283092; 6 correspondents.

Tlačová agentúra Slovenskej republiky (TASR) (Slovakia): Warsaw; tel. and fax (22) 6780399; Correspondent IGOR RABATIN.

Xinhua (New China) News Agency (People's Republic of China): 00-203 Warsaw, ul. Bonifraterska 1; tel. (22) 313876; Correspondents TANG DEQIAO, DONG FUSHENG, SCHAO JIN.

PRESS ASSOCIATION

Stowarzyszenie Dziennikarzy Polskich (SDP) (Polish Journalists' Association): 00-366 Warsaw, ul. Foksal 3/5; tel. and fax (22) 8278720; f. 1951; dissolved 1982, legal status restored 1989; 2,320 mems; Pres. KRYSTYNA MOKROSIŃSKA; Vice-Pres. ANDRZEJ KRAJEWSKI; Gen. Sec. J. MARCIN MAKOWIECKI.

Publishers

Bertelsmann Media Sp. z o.o.: 02-786 Warsaw, ul. Rosoła 10; tel. (22) 6458200; fax (22) 6484732; e-mail poczta@swiatksiazki.com.pl; internet www.swiatksiazki.com.pl; f. 1994 as Bertelsmann Publishing Świat Książki Sp. z o.o.; belles-lettres, science-fiction, popular science, albums, books for children and teenagers; Pres. ANDRZEJ KOSTARCZYK; Editor-in-Chief BOGUSŁAW DĄBROWSKI.

Dom Wydawniczy ABC Sp. z o.o.: 01-231 Warsaw, ul. Płocka 5A; tel. (22) 5358000; fax (22) 5358001; e-mail info@abc.com.pl; internet www.abc.com.pl; f. 1989; legal, business and financial books; part of Polskie Wydawnictwa Profesjonalne Sp. z o.o.; owned by Wolters Kluwer (Netherlands); Owners WŁODZIMIERZ ALBIN, KRZYSZTOF BRZESKI.

Dom Wydawniczy Bellona: 00-844 Warsaw, ul. Grzybowska 77; tel. (22) 6204291; fax (22) 6522695; e-mail bellona@bellona.pl; f. 1947; fiction, history and military; Dir ZBIGNIEW CZERWIŃSKI; Pres. Col JÓZEF SKRZYPIEC.

Dom Wydawniczy Rebis Sp. z o.o.: 60-171 Poznań, ul. Żmigrodzka 41/49; tel. (61) 8678140; fax (61) 8673774; e-mail rebis@rebis.com.pl; internet www.rebis.com.pl; f. 1990; psychology, self-help books and parental guides; Pres. and Man. Dir TOMASZ SZPONDER.

Drukarnia i Księgarnia św. Wojciecha (St Adalbert Printing and Publishing Co): 60-967 Poznań, Pl. Wolności 1; tel. (61) 8529186; fax (61) 8523746; e-mail wydawnictwo.ksw@archpoznan.org.pl; f. 1895; textbooks and Catholic publications; Dir Rev. BOGDAN REFORMAT; Editor-in-Chief BOŻYSŁAW WALCZAK.

Egmont Sp. z o.o.: 00-810 Warsaw, ul. Srebrna 16; tel. (22) 6255005; fax (22) 6252949; f. 1990; books and comics for children and teenagers; Dir JACEK BEŁDOWSKI; Editor-in-Chief HANNA BALTYN.

Instytut Wydawniczy Pax (Pax Publishing Institute): 00-390 Warsaw, Wybrzeże Kościuszkowskie 21A ; tel. (22) 6253398; fax (22) 6251378; e-mail iwpax@it.com.pl; internet www.iwpax.com.pl; f. 1949; theology, philosophy, religion, history, literature; Man. Dir JACEK KRZEKOTOWSKI; Editor-in-Chief KAROL KLAUZA.

Ludowa Spółdzielnia Wydawnicza (People's Publishing Co-operative): 00-131 Warsaw, ul. Grzybowska 4/8; tel. (22) 6205718; fax (22) 6207277; f. 1949; fiction, poetry and popular science; Chair. and Editor-in-Chief JAN RODZIM.

Muza SA: 00-590 Warsaw, ul. Marszałkowska 8; tel. (22) 6211776; fax (22) 6292349; e-mail muza@muza.com.pl; f. 1991; albums, encyclopedias, lexicons, handbooks, dictionaries, belles-lettres, books for children and youth; Man. Dir MARCIN GARLINSKI.

Niezależna Oficyna Wydawnicza NOWA (Independent Publishing House NOWA): 00-251 Warsaw, ul. Miodowa 10; tel. and fax (22) 6359994; f. 1972; belles-lettres, memoirs, essays, recent history, politics; Pres. GRZEGORZ BOGUTA; Editor-in-Chief MIROSŁAW KOWALSKI.

Oficyna Literacka: Kraków; tel. (12) 4117365; f. 1982; clandestinely, 1990 officially; belles-lettres, poetry, including débuts, essays; Editor-in-Chief HENRYK KARKOSZA.

Oficyna Wydawnicza Volumen: Warsaw; tel. and fax (22) 6357557; f. 1984 (working clandestinely as WERS), 1989 officially; science, popular history, anthropology and socio-political sciences; Dir ADAM BOROWSKI.

Pallottinum—Wydawnictwo Stowarzyszenia Apostolstwa Katolickiego: 60-959 Poznań, Al. Przybyszewskiego 30, POB 23; tel. (61) 8675233; fax (61) 8675238; e-mail pallottinum@pallottinum.pl; internet www.pallottinum.pl; f. 1947; religious and philosophical books; Dir Mgr STEFAN DUSZA.

Państwowe Wydawnictwo Rolnicze i Leśne (State Agricultural and Forestry Publishers): 00-950 Warsaw, Al. Jerozolimskie 28; tel. and fax (22) 8276338; f. 1947; professional publications on agriculture, forestry, health and veterinary science; Dir and Editor-in-Chief JOLANTA KUCZYŃSKA.

Państwowy Instytut Wydawniczy (State Publishing Institute): 00-372 Warsaw, ul. Foksal 17; tel. (22) 8260201; fax (22) 8261536; e-mail piw@piw.pl; internet www.piw.pl; f. 1946; Polish and foreign classical and contemporary literature, fiction, literary criticism, biographies, performing arts, culture, history, popular science and fine arts; Dir and Editor-in-Chief TADEUSZ NOWAKOWSKI.

Polskie Przedsiębiorstwo Wydawnictw Kartograficznych im. E. Romera SA (Romer Polish Cartographical Publishing House Co): 00-410 Warsaw, ul. Solec 18; tel. (22) 5851800; fax (22) 5851801; e-mail ppwk@ppwk.com.pl; internet www.ppwk.com.pl; f. 1951; maps, atlases, travel guides, books on geodesy and cartography; Man. Dir JACEK BŁASCZYŃSKI.

Polskie Wydawnictwa Profesjonalne: 01-231 Warsaw, ul. Płocka 5A ; tel. (22)_ 5358000; fax (22) 5358001; e-mail info@abc.com.pl; internet www.abc.com.pl; country's largest legal publisher, produces CD-rom databases and periodicals; online; Pres. ALBIN WŁODZIMIERZ.

Polskie Wydawnictwo Ekonomiczne SA (Polish Publishing House for Economic Literature): 00-099 Warsaw, ul. Canaletta 4; tel. (22) 8264182; fax (22) 8275567; e-mail pwe@pwe.com.pl; internet www.pwe.com.pl; f. 1949; economics books and magazines; Man. Dir ALICJA RUTKOWSKA; Editor MARIOLA ROMUS.

Polskie Wydawnictwo Muzyczne (Polish Publishing House for Music): 31-111 Kraków, Al. Krasińskiego 11A ; tel. (12) 4227044; fax (12) 4220174; e-mail pwm@pwm.com.pl; internet www.pwm.com.pl; f. 1945; music and books on music; Man. Dir and Editor LESZEK POLONY.

Prószyński i S-ka: 02-651 Warsaw, ul. Garazowa 7; tel. (22) 6077700; fax (22) 8497317; e-mail ksiazki@proszynski.pl; internet www.proszynski.pl; f. 1990; poetry, fiction, non-fiction, educational text and reference books, popular science etc.; 400 employees.

Spółdzielnia Wydawnicza Czytelnik (Reader Co-operative Publishing House): 00-490 Warsaw, ul. Wiejska 12A ; tel. (22) 6289508; fax (22) 6283178; e-mail sekretariat@czytelnik.pl; internet www.czytelnik.pl; f. 1944; general, especially fiction and contemporary Polish literature; Pres. MAREK ŻAKOWSKI; Editor-in-Chief HENRYK CHŁYSTOWSKI.

Spółdzielnia Wydawniczo-Handlowa 'Książka i Wiedza' (Trade Co-operative Publishing House): 00-375 Warsaw, ul. Smolna 13; tel. (22) 8275401; fax (22) 8279423; e-mail publisher@kiw.com.pl; internet www.kiw.com.pl; f. 1948; philosophy, religion, linguistics, literature and history; Dir STANISŁAW SOŁTYS; Editor MARIA ZWOLAK.

Wydawnictwa Artystyczne i Filmowe (Art and Film Publications): 02-595 Warsaw, ul. Puławska 61; tel. (22) 8455301; fax (22) 8455584; f. 1959; theatre, cinema, photography and art publications and reprints; Pres. and Dir JANUSZ FOGLER.

Wydawnictwa Komunikacji i Łączności (Transport and Communications Publishing House): 02-546 Warsaw, ul. Kazimierzowska 52; tel. (22) 8492314; fax (22) 8492322; e-mail wkl@wkl.com.pl; internet www.wkl.com.pl; f. 1949; technical books on motorization, electronics, radio engineering, television and telecommunications, road, rail and air transport; Dir JERZY KOZŁOWSKI; Editor-in-Chief BOGUMIŁ ZIELIŃSKI.

Wydawnictwa Naukowo-Techniczne (Scientific-Technical Publishers): 00-048 Warsaw, ul. Mazowiecka 2/4, POB 359; tel. (22) 8267271; fax (22) 8268293; e-mail wnt@pol.pl; internet www.wnt.com.pl; f. 1949; scientific and technical books on mathematics, physics, chemistry, foodstuffs industry, electrical and electronic engineering, computer science, automation, mechanical engineering, light industry; technological encyclopedias and dictionaries; Man. Dir and Editor Dr ANIELA TOPULOS.

Wydawnictwa Normalizacyjne ALFA-WERO (Standardization Publishing House): 01-067 Warsaw, ul. Piaskowa 6/8/10; tel. and fax (22) 6366925; f. 1956; standards, catalogues and reference books on standardization, periodicals, political and historical literature, science fiction, general; Man. Dir ANDRZEJ ŚWIĘCICKI; Editor MAREK NOWOWIEJSKI.

Wydawnictwa Polskiej Agencji Ekologicznej SA (Polish Ecological Publishing House): Warsaw; tel. (22) 8494927; fax (22) 8495081; e-mail ekologia@pae.com.pl; f. 1953; geology; Dir JERZY CHODKOWSKI.

Wydawnictwa Szkolne i Pedagogiczne (WSiP) (Polish Educational Publishers): 00-950 Warsaw, POB 480, Pl. Dąbrowskiego 8; tel. (22) 8265451; fax (22) 8279280; e-mail wsip@wsip.com.pl; internet www.wsip.com.pl; f. 1945; privatized in 1998; joint-stock co; school textbooks and popular science books, scientific literature for teachers, visual teaching aids, periodicals for teachers and youth; Chair. RAFAŁ GRUPIŃSKI.

Wydawnictwo Amber Sp. z o.o.: 00-108 Warsaw, ul. Zielna 39; tel. (22) 6204013; fax (22) 6201393; e-mail right@amber.supermedia.pl; reference books, fiction, biography and autobiography; Dir ZBIGNIEW FONIOK; Editor MAŁGORZATA CEBO-FONIOK.

Wydawnictwo Arkady: 00-959 Warsaw, ul. Dobra 28, POB 137; tel. (22) 8269316; fax (22) 8274194; e-mail arkady@arkady.com.pl; internet www.arkady.com.pl; f. 1957; publications on building, town planning, architecture and art; Dir and Pres. JANINA KRYSIAK.

Wydawnictwo Buffi: 43-300 Bielsko-Biała, ul. Poniatowskiego 6; tel. (33) 8146927; fax (33) 8149535; f. 1992; albums, calendars, postcards; Dir MAREK BUFFI.

Wydawnictwo C. H. Beck.: 01-518 Warsaw, ul. Gen. Zajączka 9; tel. (22) 3377600; fax (22) 3377601; e-mail redakcja@beck.pl; internet www.beck.pl; f. 1993; law and economics; Man. Dir PAWEŁ ESSE.

Wydawnictwo Czasopism i Książek Technicznych SIGMA NOT, Sp. z o.o. (Sigma Publishers of Technical Periodicals and Books, Ltd): 00-950 Warsaw, ul. Ratuszowa 11, POB 1004; tel. (22) 8180918; fax (22) 6192187; e-mail infor.sigma@pol.pl; internet www.pol.pl/sigma_not; f. 1949; popular and specialized periodicals and books on general technical subjects; Dir and Editor-in-Chief Dr ANDRZEJ KUSYK.

Wydawnictwo Dolnośląskie Sp. z o.o.: 50-206 Wrocław, ul. Strażnicza 1/3; tel. (71) 3288914; fax (71) 3288954; e-mail sekretariat@wd.wroc.pl; internet www.wd.wroc.pl; f. 1986; belles-lettres, essays, memoirs, translations, general non-fiction; Pres. of Bd ANDRZEJ ADAMUS.

Wydawnictwo Europa: 50-011 Wrocław, ul. Kościuszki 35; tel. (71) 3463010; fax (71) 3463015; e-mail europa@wydawnictwo-europa.pl; internet www.wydawnictwo-europa.pl; f. 1990; belles-lettres, non-fiction, educational publications, dictionaries, encyclopedias and atlases; Man. Dir and Editor WOJCIECH GŁUCH.

Wydawnictwo Gebethner: Warsaw; tel. (22) 8310113; fax (22) 8311417; f. 1990; publishes and distributes foreign language teaching material, imports scientific books; Pres. ZYGMUNT GEBETHNER.

Wydawnictwo Infor Sp. z o.o.: 01-938 Warsaw, ul. Wóycickiego 1/3; tel. (22) 7514400; fax (22) 7514411; f. 1987; law, economics, marketing, management; Pres. DARIUSZ PIEKARSKI.

Wydawnictwo Interpress Polskiej Agencji Informacyjnej SA (Polish Information Agency's Interpress Publishers): 00-585 Warsaw, ul. Bagatela 12; tel. (22) 6282818; fax (22) 6289331; f. 1968; Poland past and present, handbooks, monographs, guide-books; publishing co-operation; Editor-in-Chief ANDRZEJ TUŁOWIECKI.

Wydawnictwo 'Iskry' Sp. z o.o. (Iskry Publishing House Ltd): 00-375 Warsaw, ul. Smolna 11; tel. and fax (22) 8279415; e-mail iskry@polbox.pl; f. 1952; travel, Polish and foreign fiction, science fiction, essays, popular science, history, memoirs; Dir Dr WIESŁAW UCHAŃSKI; Editor KRZYSZTOF OBŁUCKI.

Wydawnictwo Kurpisz: 01-341 Poznań, ul. Przemysława 46; tel. (61) 8331517; f. 1991; belles-lettres, reprints, dictionaries, encyclopedias, periodicals; Dir KAZIMIERZ GRZESIAK.

Wydawnictwo Lekarskie PZWL Sp. z o.o. (Medical Publishers Ltd): 00-238 Warsaw, ul. Długa 38/40; tel. (22) 8312161; fax (22) 8310054; e-mail promocja@pzwl.pl; internet www.pzwl.pl; f. 1945; medical literature and manuals, lexicons, encyclopedias; Pres. ZOFIA ŻAKOWSKA.

Wydawnictwo Literackie (Literary Publishing House): 31-147 Kraków, ul. Długa 1; tel. (12) 4232254; fax (12) 4225423; e-mail redakcja@wl.net.pl; internet www.wl.net.pl; f. 1953; works of literature and belles-lettres; Dir BARBARA DRWOTA; Editor-in-Chief MAŁGORZTA NYCZ.

Wydawnictwo Nasza Księgarnia Sp. z o.o. (Nasza Księgarnia Publishing House Ltd): 02-868 Warsaw, ul. Sarabandy 24c; tel. (22) 6439389; fax (22) 6437028; e-mail naszaksiegarnia@nk.com.pl; f. 1921; books and periodicals for children and young readers; educa-

tional publications; Pres. AGNIESZKA TOKARCZYK; Editor JOLANTA SZTUCZYŃSKA.

Wydawnictwo Naukowe PWN SA (Polish Scientific Publishers PWN): 00-251 Warsaw, ul. Miodowa 10; tel. (22) 6954001; fax (22) 6954288; e-mail international@pwn.com.pl; internet www.pwn.com.pl; f. 1951; publications and journals on sciences and humanities, university textbooks, encyclopedias, dictionaries, multimedia; Pres. PETER WHISKERD-WĘGORZEWSKI; Man. Dir MICHAŁ SZEWIELOW; Editor-in-Chief RYSZARD BUREK.

Wydawnictwo Ossolineum (Ossolineum Publishing House): 50-062 Wrocław, Pl. Solny 14A ; tel. (71) 3436961; fax (71) 3448103; e-mail osso-bn@pwr.wroc.pl; internet www.ossolineum.wroc.pl; f. 1817; privatized; publishing house of the Polish Academy of Sciences; academic publications in humanities and sciences; Man. Dir Dr WOJCIECH KARWACKI.

Wydawnictwo Podsiedlik-Raniowski Sp. z o.o.: 60-171 Poznań, ul. Żmigrodzka 41/49; tel. (61) 8679546; fax (61) 8676850; e-mail office@priska.com.pl; f. 1990; popular and children's literature, poetry, prose, classical works, educational books; Pres. KRZYSZTOF RANIOWSKI; Dir MICHAŁ STECKI.

Wydawnictwo Prawnicze Sp. z o.o. (Legal Publishing House Ltd): 02-520 Warsaw, ul. Wiśniowa 50; tel. (22) 494151; fax (22) 499410; e-mail wp@wp.com.pl; f. 1952; Dir and Editor-in-Chief Dr JERZY KOWALSKI.

Wydawnictwo Prószyński Ska SA: 02-651 Warsaw, ul. Garażowa 7; tel. (22) 6077000; fax (22) 8497317; e-mail wydawnictwo@proszynski.com.pl; internet www.proszynski.com.pl; f. 1990; handbooks, belles-lettres, educational books; Pres. MIECZYSŁAW PRÓSZYŃSKI; Editor DOROTA MALINOWSKA.

Wydawnictwo RTW: 01-780 Warsaw, ul. Broniewskiego 9A ; tel. (22) 6337010; fax (22) 6637474; e-mail rtw@wydawrtw.media.pl; internet www.wydawrtw.media.pl; f. 1992; education, geography, geology, history, science, atlases, dictionaries, encyclopedias and audio books.

Wydawnictwo Śląsk Sp. z o.o. (Silesia Publishing House Ltd): 40-161 Katowice, Al. W. Korfantego 51; tel. (32) 580756; fax (32) 583229; e-mail biuro@slaskwn.com.pl; f. 1952; social, popular science, technical and regional literature; Pres. TADEUSZ SIERNY.

Wydawnictwo Wam: 31-501 Kraków, ul. Kopernika 26; tel. (12) 4291888; fax (12) 4295003; e-mail wam@wydawnictwowam.pl; internet www.wydawnictwowam.pl; f. 1872; textbooks, encyclopedias, non-fiction, fiction and children's books; Dir HENRYK PIETRAS.

Wydawnictwo Wiedza Powszechna (General Knowledge): 00-054 Warsaw, ul. Jasna 26; tel. and fax (22) 8269592; e-mail wiedza@medianet.pl; internet www.wiedza.pl; f. 1952; popular science books, Polish and foreign language dictionaries, foreign language textbooks, encyclopedias and lexicons; Dir TERESA KORSAK.

Wydawnictwo Wilga Sp. z o.o.: 00-389 Warsaw, ul. Smulikowskiego 1/3; tel. (22) 8260882; fax (22) 8260643; e-mail wilga@ternet.pl; f. 1993; education and fiction; Pres. JAN WOJNITKO; Editor-in-Chief OLGA WOJNITKO.

Wydawnictwo Zysk SA: 64-774 Poznań, ul. Wielka 10; tel. (61) 8532767; fax (61) 8532751; f. 1994; belles-lettres, popular, scientific and religious literature; Pres. TADEUSZ ZYSK.

Zakład Wydawnictw Statystycznych (Statistical Publishing Establishment): 00-925 Warsaw, Al. Niepodległości 208; tel. (22) 6083210; fax (22) 6083867; f. 1971; statistics and theory of statistics, economics, social sciences, periodicals; Dir ANDRZEJ STASIUN.

Znak Społeczny Instytut Wydawniczy (Znak Social Publishing Institute): 30-105 Kraków, ul. Kościuszki 37; tel. (12) 4219776; fax (12) 4219814; e-mail redakcja@znak.com.pl; internet www.znak.com.pl; f. 1959; religion, philosophy, belles-lettres, essays, history; Chief Exec. HENRYK WOŹNIAKOWSKI; Editor-in-Chief JERZY ILLG.

PUBLISHERS' ASSOCIATION

Polskie Towarzystwo Wydawców Książek (Polish Society of Book Editors): 00-048 Warsaw, ul. Mazowiecka 2/4; tel. and fax (22) 8260735; f. 1921; Pres. JANUSZ FOGLER; 500 mems.

Broadcasting and Communications

TELECOMMUNICATIONS

Telecommunications Regulatory Office (URT): 00-582 Warsaw, ul. Kasprzaka 18/20; tel. (22) 6088270; e-mail prasowy@urt.gov.pl; internet www.urt.gov.pl; f. 2001; Chair. MAREK ZDROJEWSKI.

Polkomtel SA: 02-001 Warsaw, Al. Jerozolimskie 81; tel. (22) 6071905; fax (22) 6071902; f. 1996; operates the Plus GSM mobile cellular telephone network; Chair. JAROSŁAW PACHOWSKI; Pres. WŁADYSŁAW BARTOSZEWICZ.

Polska Telefonia Cyfrowa (PTC) Sp zoo: Warsaw; tel. (22) 6996000; fax (22) 6996109; f. 1996; operates the Era GSM mobile cellular telephone network; largest mobile phone operator; Chair. and Gen. Dir BOGUSŁAW KUŁAKOWSKI; 1,000 employees.

Telekomunikacja Polska (TPSA): 00-945 Warsaw, ul. Swiętokrzyska 3; tel. (22) 8268742; fax (22) 8268528; internet www.tpsa.pl; f. 1992; partial privatization in 1998, a further 35% sold in 2000; Chief Exec. PAWEŁ RZEPKA; 72,000 employees.

BROADCASTING

Regulatory Authority

Polish National Radio and Television Broadcasting Council (KRRiTV): 00-015 Warsaw, Skwer Kardinala Wyszyńskiego, Prymasa Polski 9; tel. (22) 6359925; fax (22) 8383501; internet www.krrit.gov.pl; f. 1993; f. 1992; Chair. DANUTA WANIEK.

Radio

There are 180 radio broadcasting institutions, of which 17 are public, and seven national channels, of which four are public.

Polskie Radio SA (Polish Radio): 00-977 Warsaw, Al. Niepodległości 77/85; tel. (22) 6459259; fax (22) 6455924; e-mail polskie.radio@radio.com.pl; internet www.radio.com.pl; Pres. KRZYSZTOF MICHALSKI; Dir of International Relations HANNA DĄBROWSKA.

Home Service: there are four national channels broadcasting 90 hours per day; one long-wave transmitter (600 kW) broadcasting on 225 kHz; 11 medium-wave transmitters and 18 relay stations; 137 VHF transmitters covering all four programmes and 17 local programmes.

Foreign Service: Five transmitters broadcast on 10 frequencies on short-wave, one transmitter broadcasting on medium-wave. Programmes in Polish, English, Esperanto, German, Russian, Belarusian, Ukrainian, Lithuanian, Slovak and Czech.

Radio Maryja: 87-100 Torun, ul. Zwirki i Wigury 80; tel. (56) 552361; fax (56) 552362; internet www.radiomaryja.pl; Catholic station; Dir TADEUSZ RYDZYK.

Radio Musyka Fakty (RMF FM): 30-204 Kraków, Al. Waszyngtona 1, Kopiec Kosciuszki; tel. (12) 4219696; fax (12) 4217895; e-mail redakcja@rmf.pl; internet www.rmf.pl; Pres. STANISŁAW TYCZYNSKI; Dir JOLANTA WIŚNIEWSKA.

Radio Zet: 00-503 Warsaw, ul. Żurawia 8; tel. (22) 5833382; fax (22) 5833356; e-mail radiozet@radiozet.com.pl; internet www.radiozet.com.pl; f. 1990; independent; 24 hours; has broadcast nationally since 1994; wholly owned by the Eurozet media group; Pres. and Editor-in-Chief ROBERT KOZYRA.

Television

There are 26 television broadcasting institutions, of which 12 are public. Of the national public channels, one broadcasts for 22 hours, the other for 16 hours per day via 84 transmitters and 134 relay stations. A third national public channel was launched in early 2002. In addition, there is one national private channel, broadcasting for 18 hours per day, and one satellite channel of Polish Television, TV Polonia, broadcasting for 16 hours per day. As well as the various local programmes for Gdańsk, Katowice, Szczecin, Wrocław (seven hours per day) and Lublin (four hours per day), there are regional programmes for Bydgoszcz, Kraków, Łódź, Poznań, Rzeszów and Warsaw (three hours per day). Poland's first private (commercial) TV station began operating in Wrocław in early 1990. Broadcasting is regulated by the Broadcasting Bill, enacted in 1993. Poland's first digital television service was launched in April 1998.

Telewizja Polska SA (Polish Television): 00-999 Warsaw, ul. J. P. Woronicza 17, POB 211; tel. (22) 5476550; fax (22) 5477719; e-mail pr@tvp.pl; internet www.tvp.pl; f. 1952; Chair. ROBERT KWIATKOWSKI; Vice-Chair. ANNA POPOWICZ; 6,730 employees.

PolSat: 04-028 Warsaw, Al. Stanów Zjednoczonyck 53; tel. (22) 104001; fax (22) 134295; internet www.polsat.com.pl; f. 1992; Polish satellite company, awarded Poland's first national, private television licence in 1994; Propr. ZYGMUNT SOLORZ.

TVN Sp. z o.o.: 02-981 Warsaw, ul. Augustówka 3; tel. (22) 8566060; fax (22) 8566666; e-mail widzowie@tvn.pl; internet www.tvn.pl; f. 1997; broadcasts in northern Poland, Łódź and Warsaw; Pres. PIOTR WALTER.

Finance

(cap. = capital; res = reserves; dep. = deposits; m. = million; amounts in new złotys unless otherwise indicated; brs = branches)

BANKING

In accordance with Poland's association agreement with the EU, foreign banks were permitted to operate freely in the country from 1997. In September 1996 Poland's first banking group was created, the Grupa Pekao SA. In 2000 there were 75 commercial banks and 757 co-operative banks operating in Poland.

On 1 January 1995 a new złoty, equivalent to 10,000 old złotys, was introduced. All figures given below are in terms of new złotys.

National Bank

Narodowy Bank Polski—NBP (National Bank of Poland): 00-919 Warsaw, ul. Świętokrzyska 11/21, POB 1011; tel. (22) 6531000; fax (22) 6208518; e-mail nbp@nbp.pl; internet www.nbp.pl; f. 1945; state central bank; cap. 400.0m., res 22,283.3m., dep. 61,688.2m. (Dec. 2001); Pres. LESZEK BALCEROWICZ; First Deputy Pres. JERZY STOPYRA; 16 brs.

Other Banks

ABN Amro Bank (Polska) SA: 02-134 Warsaw, ul. l-go Sierpnia 8A, Wisniowy Business Park, POB 417; tel. (22) 5730500; fax (22) 5730501; internet www.abnamro.com; f. 1994 through takeover of Interbank SA; 100% owned by ABN AMRO Bank, NV (Netherlands); cap. 146.2m., res 48.3m., dep. 3,003.4m (Dec. 2001); Man. H. KESSELER.

Bank Amerykański w Polsce SA—AmerBank (American Bank in Poland Inc.): 00-102 Warsaw, ul. Marszałkowska 115; tel. (22) 6248505; fax (22) 6249981; e-mail amerbank@amerbank.pl; internet www.amerbank.pl; f. 1991; 95.2% owned by DZ Bank AG Deutsche Zentral-Genossenschaftsbank (Germany); commercial bank; cap. 23.1m., res 91.9m., dep. 1,450.3m. (Dec. 2001); Chair of Bd. PETER DIECKMAN; Pres. SŁAWOMIR SIKORA.

Bank Gospodarki Żywnościowej SA—BGZ (Bank of Food Economy): 01-211 Warsaw, ul. Kasprzaka 10/16; tel. (22) 8604000; fax (22) 8605000; e-mail info@bgz.pl; internet www.bgz.pl; f. 1919; present name adopted 1994; universal commercial bank; finances agriculture, forestry and food processing; cap. 23.1m., res 874.6m., dep. 15,596.6m. (Dec. 2001); Exec. Pres. MICHAŁ MACHLEID; Man. Dir JERZY BUSZ; 353 brs and sub-brs.

Bank Gospodarstwa Krajowego—BGK (National Economy Bank): 00-955 Warsaw, Al. Jerozolimskie 7, POB 41; tel. (22) 5229127; fax (22) 6270378; e-mail bgk@bgk.com.pl; internet www.bgk.com.pl; f. 1924; state-owned; cap. 178.9 m., res 1,942.0m., dep. 1,669.7m. (Dec. 2001); Pres. of Bd RYSZARD PAZURA; 7 brs.

Bank Handlowy w Warszawie SA (Trade Bank of Warsaw): 00-923 Warsaw, ul. Senatorska 16; tel. (22) 6903000; fax (22) 8300113; e-mail listybh@citicorp.com; internet www.citihandlowy.pl; f. 1870; merged with Citibank (Poland) SA in 2001; trade and finance bank; specializes in corporate and investment banking; 92.1% owned by Citibank Overseas Investment Corpn (USA); cap. 430.3m., res 5,311.7m., dep. 22,317.9m. (Dec. 2001); Pres. CEZARY STYPULKOWSKI; Chair. STANISŁAW SOLTYSINSKI; 61 brs.

Bank Millennium: 00-924 Warsaw, ul. Kopernika 36/40; tel. (22) 6575720; fax (22) 8267180; e-mail wojciech.kaczorowski@bankmillennium.pl; internet www.bankmillennium.pl; f. 1989 as Bank Inicjatyw Gospodarczych BIG SA; renamed BIG Bank Gdański SA in 1997, present name adopted 2001; 50.0% owned by Banco Comercial Portugues (Portugal); cap. 849.2m., res 520.3m., dep. 15,867.2m. (Dec. 2001), total assets 18,612.5m. (Dec. 2002); Chair. BOGUSŁAW KOTT; 172 brs.

Bank Ochrony Środowiska SA—BOS (Environmental Protection Bank): 00-950 Warsaw 1, Al. Jana Pawła II 12, POB 150; tel. (22) 8508735; fax (22) 8508891; e-mail bos@bosbank.pl; internet www.bosbank.pl; f. 1991; 47.0% owned by Skandinaviska Enskilda Banken AB (Sweden), 44.36% by Polish National Fund for the Protection of the Environment and Water; cap. 132.0m., res 435.8m., dep. 4,394.2m. (Dec. 2001); Pres. of Exec. Bd JOSEF KOZIOL; 48 brs.

Bank Polska Kasa Opieki—Bank Pekao SA: 00-950 Warsaw, ul. Grzybowska 53/57; tel. (22) 6560000; fax (22) 6560004; e-mail info@pekao.com.pl; internet www.pekao.com.pl; f. 1929; universal bank; absorbed Bank Depozytowo-Kredytowy, Pomorski Bank Kredytowy and Powszechny Bank Gospodarczy in 1999; 53.2% owned by Uno-Credito Italiano SpA (Italy); cap. 165.8m., res 5,431.8m., dep. 60,628.1m. (Dec. 2001); Chair. ALESSANDRO PROFUMO; 720 brs and sub-brs.

Bank Przemysłowo-Handlowy PBK SA—Bank BPH-BPK (Industrial and Commercial Bank): 31-548 Kraków, Al. Pokoju 1; tel. (12) 6186888; fax (12) 6186863; e-mail bank@bphpbk.pl; internet www.bphpbk.pl; f. 1988; merged with Hypovereinsbank Polska (1999), Powszechny Bank Kredytowy (2000) and Bank Przemysłowo-Handlowy (2001); present name adopted 2002; cap. 143.6m., res 5,159.4m., dep. 38,252.1m. (Dec. 2001); Chair. of Sup. Bd ALICJA KORNASIEWICZ; Pres. JÓZEF WANCER; 75 brs and 172 sub-brs.

Bank Wspólpracy Europejskiej—BWE SA (European Co-operative Bank): 00-082 Warsaw, ul. Senatorska 14, POB 85; tel. (22) 8299800; fax (22) 8260261; e-mail promocja@bwe.pl; internet www .bwe.pl; f. 1990; commercial bank for tourism industry; present name adopted 1997; cap. 117.3m., res 40.1m., dep. 946.8m. (Dec. 2001); Exec. Pres. PIOTR PUCZYNSKI (acting); 9 brs.

Bank Zachodni WBK SA (Western Bank): 50-950 Wrocław, Rynek 9/11; tel. (71) 3701000; fax (71) 3702771; e-mail dorota.bernatowicz@ bzwbk.pl; internet www.bzwbk.pl; f. 1989; present name adopted 2001; absorbed Wielkopolski Bank Kredytowy SA in 2001; 70.5% owned by AIB European Investments Ltd (Ireland); cap. 729.6m., res 1,276.3m., dep. 20,884.1m. (Dec. 2001); Pres. JACEK KSEŃ; 433 brs.

BNP Paribas Bank Polska SA: 00-108 Warsaw, ul. Zielna 41/43; tel. (22) 6972308; fax (22) 6972309; e-mail warsaw.office@ bnpparibas.com; internet www.bnpparibas.com; f. 1994; 100% owned by BNP Paribas (France); present name adopted 2001; cap. 193.4m., res 104.1m., dep. 1,207.5m. (Dec. 2001); Man. Dir YVES DRIEUX.

BRE Bank SA: 00-950 Warsaw, ul. Senatorska 18, POB 728; tel. (22) 8290000; fax (22) 8290033; e-mail info@brebank.com.pl; internet www.brebank.com.pl; f. 1987 as Bank Rozwoju Eksportu; 50% owned by Commerzbank AG (Germany); present name adopted 1999; specializes in corporate banking; cap. 91.9m., res 2,004.6m., dep. 16,637.8m. (Dec. 2001); Chair. of Bd KRZYSZTOF SWARC; Pres., Chief Exec. and Gen. Man. WOJCIECH KOSTRZEWA; 12 brs.

Crédit Lyonnais Bank Polska SA: 00-697 Warsaw, al. Jerozolimskie 65/97, LIM Centre, POB 50; tel. (22) 6306888; fax (22) 6354500; f. 1991 as Międzynarodowy Bank w Polsce SA; present name adopted 1997; 100% owned by Crédit Lyonnais Global Banking (France); cap. 22.8m., res 145.6m., dep. 1,088.5m. (Dec. 2001); Chair. of Bd BERNARD MIGNUCCI; Pres. BERNARD SZLACHETKA.

Deutsche Bank 24 SA: 31-047 Kraków, ul. Józefa Sarego 2/4, POB 234; tel. (12) 6182116; fax (12) 4295686; e-mail info@db-24.pl; internet www.db-24.pl; f. 1991; present name adopted 2001; 92.6% owned by Deutsche Bank 24 Aktiengesellschaft (Germany); cap. 336.3m., res −166.5m., dep. 1,704.8m. (Dec. 2001); Chair. of Sup. Bd and Chief Exec. Dr HERBERT WALTER; Pres. MAREK KULCZYCKI.

Deutsche Bank Polska SA: 00-609 Warsaw, al. Armii Ludowej 26; tel. (22) 5799000; fax (22) 5799001; e-mail public.relations@db.com; internet www.deutsche-bank.pl; f. 1995; 100% owned by Deutsche Bank AG (Germany); cap. 230.0m., res 273.4m., dep. 2,802.2m. (Dec. 2001); Chief Exec. STAN SZCZUREK; Dir-Gen. WOLFGANG NIEDENHOFF.

Fortis Bank Polska SA: 02-676 Warsaw, ul. Postępu 15; tel. (22) 5669000; fax (22) 5669010; e-mail info@fortisbank.com.pl; internet www.fortisbank.com.pl; f. 1990; fmrly Pierwszy Polsko-Amerykański Bank Kraków SA; present name adopted 2000; 99.1% owned by Fortis Bank (Belgium); cap. 30.2m., res 448.8m., dep. 3,417.3m. (Dec. 2001); Pres. JEAN-MARIE DE BAERDEMAEKER; Chair. LUC DELVAUX.

Górnośląski Bank Gospodarczy—GBG Bank SA: 40-006 Katowice, ul. Warszawska 6, POB 1138; tel. (32) 2008500; fax (32) 2008685; e-mail gbg@gbg.com.pl; internet www.gbg.com.pl; f. 1990; 68.8% owned by Bank Przemysłowy-Handlowy PBK SA; cap. 62.2m., res 77.5m., dep. 2,760.9m. (Dec. 2001); Pres. TADEUSZ WNUK (acting); Chair. ANDRZEJ PODSIADLO; 44 brs.

ING Bank Śląski SA: 40-086 Katowice, ul. Sokolska 34; tel. (32) 3577000; fax (32) 588308; e-mail info@ing.pl; internet www.ing.pl; f. 1989; present name adopted 2001; acquired Wielkopolski Bank Rolniczy SA in 2001; 87.8% owned by ING Bank NV (Netherlands); cap. 130.1m., res 2,380.5m., dep. 22,112.6m. (Dec. 2001); Chair. ANDRZEJ WROBLEWSKI; Pres. MARIAN CZAKANSKI; 332 brs and sub-brs.

Kredyt Bank SA: 01-211 Warsaw, ul. Kasprzaka 2/8, POB 93; tel. (22) 6345400; fax (22) 6345335; e-mail bew@kredytbank.com.pl; internet www.kredytbank.com.pl; f. 1997 by merger; present name adopted 1999; 58.2% owned by KBC Bank NV (Belgium), 18.4% by Deutsche Bank Trust Co Americas (USA); cap. 739.5m., res 1,598.0m., dep. 18,204.6m. (Dec. 2001); Chair. ANDRZEJ WITKOWSKI; Pres. STANISŁAW PACUK; 75 brs.

LG Petro Bank SA: 93-172 Lódź, ul. Rzgowska 34/36; tel. (42) 819060; fax (42) 6846192; internet www.lgpetro.com.pl; f. 1990; present name adopted 1996; cap. 111.3m., res 131.5m., dep. 1,372.9m. (Dec. 1999); Pres. DONG CHANG PARK.

Powszechna Kasa Oszczędności Bank Państwowy—PKO Bank Polski SA (PKO BP SA) (State Savings Bank): 00-975 Warsaw, ul. Pulawska 15, POB 183; tel. (22) 5218067; fax (22) 5218068; internet www.pkobp.pl; f. 1919; state-owned joint-stock co;

cap. 1,340.3m., res 1,457.4 m., dep. 71,039.1m. (Dec. 2001); Pres. of Man. Bd. ANDRZEJ PODSIADLO; Chair. of Sup. Bd. KRZYSZTOF PIETRASZKIEWICZ; 1,153 brs and sub-brs.

Powszechny Bank Kredytowy SA w Warszawie (Warsaw Credit Bank): 00-958 Warsaw, ul. Towarowa 25A, POB 3; tel. (22) 5318000; fax (22) 5318786; e-mail info@pkb.pl; internet www.pbk.pl; f. 1989; privatized, and absorbed Bank Morski in 1997; in 1999 acquired Pierwszy Komercyjny Bank SA; in 2000 merged with Bank Austria Creditanstalt Poland SA; cap. 146.7m., res 1,939.0m., dep. 19,130.4m. (Dec. 2000); Chair. CHRISTINE BOGDANOWICZ-BINDERT; Pres. of Bd ANDRZEJ PODSIADLO; 338 brs.

Raiffeisen Bank Polska SA: 00-549 Warsaw, ul. Piekna 20, POB 53; tel. (22) 5852000; fax (22) 5852585; internet www.raiffeisen.pl; f. 1991; present name adopted 2000; 100% owned by Raiffeisen Zentralbank Österreich AG (Austria); cap. 332.0m., res 126.8m. dep. 5,011.0m. (Dec. 2001); Chair. HERBERT STEPIC; 21 brs.

STOCK EXCHANGE

The Warsaw Stock Exchange was re-established in April 1991. In March 1999 it had 37 member companies and listed shares in 205 firms, in addition to 43 issues of Treasury bonds. In January 1998 a derivatives market was launched, listing index and USD futures.

Polish Securities and Exchange Commission (Komisja Papierów Wartościowych i Gield): Warsaw, Pl. Powstańców Warszawy 1; tel. (22) 5560800; fax (22) 8268100; e-mail kpwig@kpwig.gov .pl; internet www.kpwig.gov.pl; Pres. JACEK SOCHA; Dir JERZY WALCZAK.

Warsaw Stock Exchange: 00-498 Warsaw, ul. Książęca 4; tel. (22) 6283232; fax (22) 6281754; e-mail gielda@wse.com.pl; internet www .wse.com.pl; opened for trading in 1991; Pres. and Chief Exec. Dr WIESŁAW ROZUCKI.

INSURANCE

In early 2000 there were 56 insurance companies operating in Poland. The largest companies were Polish National Insurance (Państwowy Zakład Ubezpieczeń—PZU), which dominated the property insurance market, and Warta Insurance and Reinsurance, which specialized in vehicle insurance, and foreign business. PZU's subsidiary, PZU Life, was the largest life insurance company.

Grupa Powszechny Zakład Ubezpieczeń (PZU) (Polish National Insurance Group): 00-133 Warsaw, Al. Jana Pawła II 24; tel. (22)5823400; fax (22) 5823401; e-mail poczta@pzu.pl; internet ww.pzu.pl; f. 1803; insurance group comprising two principal companies dealing in various areas of insurance, and six support companies; 55% state-owned; Pres. ZDISŁAW MONTKIEWICZ; 400 brs; 14,000 employees.

> **PZU SA:** internet www.pzu.pl/pzusa; property insurance products; claimed 55.5% of the market in 1999; owner of the PZU Capital Group.

> **PZU Życie SA:** e-mail kontact@pzuzycie.pl; internet www .pzuzycie.com.pl; life insurance products; claimed 56.4% of the market in 1999; 99.9% of shares held by PZU SA; founder of Powschne Towarzystwo Emerytalne PZU SA—PZU SA Pension Society; President BOGUSŁAW KASPRZYK.

Towarzystwo Ubezpieczeń i Reasekuracji Warta SA (Warta Insurance and Reinsurance Co Ltd): 00-805 Warsaw, ul. Chmielna 85/87; tel. (22) 5810100; fax (22) 5811374; e-mail info@warta.pl; internet www.warta.pl; f. 1920; marine, air, motor, fire, luggage and credit; deals with all foreign business; Pres. AGENOR JAN GAWRZYAL; 25 brs; representatives in London (United Kingdom) and New York (USA).

Trade and Industry

GOVERNMENT AGENCIES

Mass Privatization Programme: c/o Department of National Investment Funds, Ministry of the Treasury, 00-522 Warsaw, ul. Krucza 36; tel. (22) 6958453; fax (22) 6958701; responsible for the divestment of various state-owned enterprises.

Polish Agency for Foreign Investment (PAIZ): 00-599 Warsaw, Al. Róż 2; tel. (22) 6210706; fax (22) 6226169; e-mail post@paiz.gov .pl; internet www.paiz.gov.pl; Pres. ADAM PAWŁOWICZ.

DEVELOPMENT ORGANIZATION

State Office for Housing and Urban Development: 00-926 Warsaw, ul. Wspólna 2; tel. (22) 6618111; fax (22) 6284030; e-mail umieszk@umirm.gov.pl; internet www.umirm.gov.pl; f. 1997; development of government housing policy; Pres. SŁAWOMIR NAJNIGIER.

CHAMBERS OF COMMERCE

Krajowa Izba Gospodarcza (Polish Chamber of Commerce): Head Office, 00-074 Warsaw, ul. Trębacka 4, POB 361; tel. (22) 6309600; fax (22) 8274673; internet www.kig.pl; f. 1990; Pres. ANDRZEJ ARENDARSKI; Chair. KAZIMIERZ PAZGAN; 150 mems.

Izba Przemysłowo-Handlowa Inwestorów Zagranicznych (Chamber of Industry and Trade for Foreign Investors): 00-071 Warsaw, ul. Krakowskie Przedmieście 47/51; tel. (22) 8261822; fax (22) 8268593.

UTILITIES

Energy Regulatory Authority (Urząd Regulacji Energetyki): 00–872 Warsaw, ul. Chłodna 64; tel. (22) 6616107; fax (22) 6616152; e-mail ure@ure.gov.pl; internet www.ure.gov.pl; Pres. Dr LESZEK JUCHNIEWICZ.

Electricity

Polish Power Grid Company (Polskie Sieci Elektroenergetyczne SA—PSE): 00-496 Warsaw, ul. Mysia 2; tel. (22) 6931580; fax (22) 6285964; f. 1990; Pres. Prof. Dr hab. STANISŁAW DOBRZAŃSKI.

State Atomic Energy Agency (Państwowa Agencja Atomistyki): 00-921 Warsaw, ul. Krucza 36; tel. (22) 6282722; fax (22) 6290164; e-mail niewodniczanski@paa.gov.pl; internet www.paa.gov.pl; f. 1982; responsible for the development and safe application of nuclear technologies, as well as for nuclear research and radiation protection; Pres. Prof. JERZY NIEWODNICZAŃSKI.

STOEN Stołeczny Zakład Energetyczny SA (STOEN Capital Power Distribution Company Ltd): 00-347 Warsaw, Wybrzeże Kopciuszkowskie 41; tel. (22) 8213387; fax (22) 8213122; f. 1993; distributes electric energy; Pres. KRZYSZTOF ZIĘBA; Chair. KAZIMIERZ PAWE BISEK.

Gas

EuRoPol GAZ SA: 04-028 Warsaw, Al. Stanów Zjednoczonych 61; tel. (22) 5174000; fax (22) 5174040; e-mail konto@europolgaz.com.pl; f. 1993; joint venture between PGNiG and the Russian gas company, Gazprom; Pres. KAZIMIERZ ADAMCZYK.

Polish Oil and Gas Company (PGNiG): 00-537 Warsaw, 6 ul. Krucza 14; tel. (22) 6235601; fax (22) 6235856; e-mail nowak@pgnig.com.pl; internet www.pgnig.com.pl; f. 1982; state-owned natural-gas producer and supplier; Pres. ALEKSANDER FINDZIŃSKI; 47,300 employees.

MAJOR COMPANIES

Agora SA: 00-732 Warsaw, ul. Czerska 8/10; tel. (22) 5554202; fax (22) 8400067; e-mail contact@agora.pl; internet www.agora.pl; f. 1989; publishes newspapers, operates radio stations and internet portal; Pres. WANDA RAPACZYŃSKI; 3,260 employees.

Agromet-Motoimport Co. Ltd: 02-923 Warsaw, ul. Kolobrzeska 36; tel. (22) 6428545; fax (22) 6420242; e-mail agro@agromet-motoimport.com.pl; internet www.agromet-motoimport.com.pl; f. 1950; import and export of agricultural machinery and equipment; Gen. Dir ZBIGNIEW KONOPIŃSKI.

Agros Holding SA: 00-613 Warsaw, ul. Chałubińskiego 8; tel. (22) 8300614; fax (22) 8300615; e-mail ajozwik@agrostrade.com.pl; internet www.agros.com.pl; f. 1989; financing of and investment in production, trade and services in the food and agricultural industries; Chair. ZOFIA GABER; 7,000 employees.

Agros Trading Spółka z o.o.: 00-613 Warsaw, ul. Chałubińskiego 8; tel. (22) 8302736; fax (22) 8300791; e-mail info@agrostrade.com.pl; internet www.agrostrade.com.pl; f. 1966; wholesale trade in farm supplies, groceries and related products; Man. Dir ZOFIA GABER-SOBIERALSKA; 216 employees.

Animex SA: 02-256 Warsaw, Al. Krakowska 110–114; tel. (22) 3345900; fax (22) 3345901; e-mail animex@animex.com.pl; internet www.animex.com.pl; f. 1951; formerly Animex Export-Import; 92.5% owned by Smithfield Foods (USA); imports and exports slaughtering and breeding animals, meat and meat products, poultry, game; Pres. and Gen. Dir ROBERT ŻULEWSKI; 230 employees.

Ars Polona: 00-068 Warsaw, ul. Krakowskie Przedmieście 7, POB 1001; tel. (22) 8261201; fax (22) 8266240; e-mail arspolona@arspolona.com.pl; internet www.arspolona.com.pl; f. 1953; import and export of books, newspapers, stamps, coins, musical instruments, records, contemporary works of art and silver jewellery; Gen. Dir MONIKA BIAŁECKA; 100 employees.

AUTOSAN SA: 38-500 Sanok, ul. Lipińskiego 109; tel. (13) 4650111; fax (13) 4650430; e-mail marketing@autosan.com.pl; internet www.autosan.com.pl; f. 1945; manufacture and export of motor buses, and agricultural and goods trailers; Chair. ANDRZEJ KRZANOWSKI; Marketing Dir ROMAN MAJEWSKI; 1,530 employees.

Azoty Puławy—Zakłady Azotowe Puławy w Puławach: 24-110 Puławy, Al. 1000-lecia, Państwa Polskiego 13; tel. (81) 875555; fax (81) 875444; f. 1961; chemicals, incl. fertilizers, melamine, nitrates and polyethelene; Gen. Dir MIROSŁAW MALINOWSKI.

Baltona SA: 81-537 Gdynia, ul. Łuzycka 3; tel. (58) 6224504; fax (58) 6222055; e-mail marketing@baltona.pl; internet www.baltona.com.pl; f. 1946; import and export of food and industrial goods; supplier to retail shops, ships, airlines, duty-free shops, diplomatic offices; Pres. and Gen. Dir STANISŁAW DEBICKI; 200 employees.

Befama SA: 43-300 Bielsko Biała, ul. Piekarska 130, POB 67; tel. (33) 8123061; fax (33) 8221293; e-mail sales@befama.com.pl; internet www.befama.com.pl; f. 1851; design, production and sale of textile machinery; Man. Dir JERZY PYTLARZ; 400 employees.

Bełchatów, Kopalnia Węgla Brunatnego SA: 97-400 Bełchatów, Rogowiec, POB 100; tel. (44) 7373000; fax (44) 7373456; e-mail info@kwb-belchatow.pl; internet www.kwb-belchatow.pl; f. 1974; coal and lignite mining; state-owned; Pres. CZESŁAW WOJCIECHOWSKI; 10,200 employees.

Budimex SA: 00-517 Warsaw, ul. Marszałkowska 82; tel. (22) 6236164; fax (22) 6294831; e-mail info@budimex.com.pl; internet www.budimex.com.pl; f. 1968; holding company, industrial building, civil engineering, housing, assembly works, land reclamation; Pres. MAREK MICHAŁOWSKI; 210 employees.

Bumar, Przedsiębiorstwo Handlu Zagranicznego, Spółka zo.o. (Foreign trade Enterprise Bumar, Ltd): 00-828 Warsaw, Al. Jana Pawła II 11; tel. (22) 6249168; fax (22) 6243807; internet www.phzbumar.com.pl; f. 1971; trade in construction and industrial equipment; Pres. and Gen. Man. ROMAN BACZYŃSKI.

Bumar Łabędy SA: 44-109 Gliwice, ul. Mechaników 9; tel. (32) 7342164; fax (32) 7345002; internet www.bumar.gliwice.pl; f. 1951; steel machinery and parts for agriculture and construction; Pres. and Gen. Dir HENRYK PFEIFER; 4,180 employees.

H. Cegielski-Poznań SA: 61-485 Poznań, ul. 28 Czerwca 1956 r. 223/229; tel. (61) 8311102; fax (61) 8311372; internet www.hcp.com.pl; f. 1846; manufacture and export of power equipment, marine engines, railway locomotives and carriages, etc.; Man. Dir WACŁAW PIOTROWSKI; 2,360 employees.

Centrala Produktow Naftowych (CPN) SA: 00-950 Warsaw, ul. Bankiewicza 4; tel. (22) 6953550; fax (22) 6287728; f. 1944; petroleum distribution and sales; operation of filling stations, terminals and depots; Pres. and Gen. Dir JERZY MAŁYSKA; 7,000 employees.

Centromor SA: 80-819 Gdańsk, ul. Okopowa 7; tel. (58) 3081000; fax (58) 3019428; e-mail info@centromor.com.pl; internet www.centromor.com.pl; f. 1950; import and export of ships and marine equipment; Man. Dir RYSZARD FERWORN; 200 employees.

Centrozap SA: 40-085 Katowice, ul. Mickiewicza 29; tel. (32) 2513401; fax (32) 2598658; e-mail cent@centrozap.com.pl; internet www.centrozap.com.pl; f. 1951; imports and exports complete plants, machines and equipment for the metallurgical, foundry and mining industries, air conditioning, etc.; Dir-Gen. IRENEUSZ KRÓL.

Chemobudowa-Kraków SA: 30-103 Kraków, ul. Stachowicza 18; tel. (12) 4272230; fax (12) 4272220; e-mail biuro@chemobudowa.pl; internet www.chemobudowa.pl; f. 1949; civil engineering; Pres. TADEUSZ ZAJĄC; 1,700 employees.

Ciech SA: 00-950 Warsaw, ul. Powazkowska 46–50, POB 271; tel. (22) 6391000; fax (22) 6391451; e-mail ciech@ciech.waw.pl; internet www.ciech.waw.pl; f. 1945; 51.9% state-owned; largest chemicals conglomerate in Poland; imports and exports organic and inorganic chemicals, dyestuffs, fertilizers, paints, varnishes, enamels, cosmetics, petroleum products, plastics, sulphur and pharmaceutical products; Pres. LUDWIK KLINKOSZ; 490 employees.

Daewoo FSO Motor Spółka zo.o.: 00-992 Warszawa, ul. Jagiellońska 88; tel. (22) 6763000; fax (22) 8115239; internet www.daewoo.com.pl/fso; f. 1950; vehicle manufacturer; Pres. and Gen. Man. JIN CHOOL SUK.

Dal SA: 00-683 Warsaw, Al. Jerozolimskie 65/79; tel. (22) 300460; fax (22) 300461; international trading company, barter and compensation transactions, mediation through its affiliated companies all over the world; Dir MAREK PIETKIEWICZ.

Diora SA: 58-200 Dzierżoniów, ul. Świdnicka 38; tel. (74) 8322200; fax (74) 8318561; e-mail diora@diora.com.pl; internet www.diora.com.pl; f. 1945; joint-stock co; production of audio and visual electronic equipment; Chair. and Gen. Dir JANUSZ MĄKOSA; 680 employees.

Dromex SA: 02-261 Warsaw, ul. Trojańska 7; tel. (22) 8462045; fax (22) 8462555; internet www.dromex.com; f. 1967; export of road, bridge, railway and airfield construction work; Pres. and Gen. Dir DARIUSZ SŁOTWIŃSKI; 600 employees.

Elana SA: 87-100 Torún, ul. M. Skłodowskiej-Curie 73; tel. (56) 6562200; fax (56) 6561565; e-mail elana@elana.pl; internet www.elana.pl; f. 1960; synthetic fibres; Chair. STANISŁAW MAŃKA.

Elektrim SA: 00-950 Warsaw, ul. Pańska 77/79; tel. (22) 6528705; fax (22) 6528700; internet www.elektrim.pl; f. 1945; imports and exports power engineering technology, transmission, electrical and telecommunication equipment telecommunications and internet services; 49% owned by Vivendi; Chair. of Sup. Bd DAVOOD SYED; 12,000 employees.

Elwro SA: 53-238 Wrocław, ul. Ostrowskiego 30; tel. (71) 3631347; fax (71) 3447359; f. 1993; manufacture and export of computer systems, microcomputers, other computer equipment (hardware and software), calculators, etc.; Man. Dir WŁADYSŁAW KIERZKOWSKI; 194 employees.

Energomontaz-Północ SA: 00-450 Warsaw, ul. Przemyslowa 30; tel. (22) 6211041; fax (22) 6296324; e-mail info@energomontaz.com.pl; internet www.energomontaz.com.pl; f. 1952; holding company; manufacture and service of power and industrial engineering installations; Chair. JÓZEF JEDRUCH; 3,600 employees.

Energopol Trade SA: 00-950 Warsaw, ul. Nowogrodzka 21, POB 367; tel. (22) 6298081; fax (22) 6290412; e-mail bhexport@energopol.com.pl; internet www.energopol.com.pl; f. 1991; contractors and designers, civil engineering projects, pipelines; Pres. WŁODIMIERZ ZAŁAPIC; 750 employees.

Exbud SA: 25-323 Kielce, ul. Manifestu Lipcowego 34; tel. (41) 3326307; fax (41) 3322122; e-mail info@exbud.com.pl; internet www.exbud.com.pl; f. 1977; privatized 1990; 94% owned by Skanska Europe AB; construction, manufacture of construction materials and components; Pres. LESZEK WALCZYK; 15,400 employees.

Film Polski Film Agency: 00-048 Warsaw, ul. Mazowiecka 6/8; tel. (22) 8268455; fax (22) 8275784; e-mail info@filmpolski.com.pl; f. 1964; promotion of Polish film, imports and exports films for television and the cinema, production services, distribution; Dir ANDRZEJ GOLENIEWSKI.

Furnel SA: 03-911 Warsaw, ul. Marokańska 16; tel. (22) 6715203; fax (22) 6715211; e-mail furnel@furnel.com.pl; internet www.furnel.com.pl; f. 1988; 8 regional offices; production and export of furniture, wooden goods, electronic and telecommunication equipment; Pres. and Gen. Man. STEFAN MAJCHRZAK; 2,400 employees.

Gdanska Stocznia Remontowa: Gdańsk 80-958, ul. Ostrowiu 1; tel. (58) 3071600; fax (58) 3012532; e-mail remontowa@remontowa.com.pl; internet www.remontowa.com.pl; ship repairs and conversions; Gen. Dir PIOTR SOYKA.

Geokart Spółka z o.o.: 35-113 Rzeszów, ul. Wita Stwosza 44; tel. (22) 8565304; fax (22) 8564947; e-mail geokart@geokart.com.pl; internet www.geokart.com.pl; f. 1989; geodesic and cartographic work and service; Exec. Man. ŁUCJAN PIETLUCH; 70 employees.

Gliwicka Spółka Węglowa SA: 44-100 Gliwice, ul. Jasna 31; tel. and fax (32) 2394507; e-mail gsw@gsw.pl; internet www.gsw.pl; f. 1993; coal mining; state-owned; Pres. and Gen. Man. BOGUSŁAW BOBROWSKI; 35,935 employees.

C. Hartwig Warszawa: 00-950 Warsaw, ul. Poznańska 15; tel. (22) 6296031; fax (22) 6211581; e-mail promocja@c.hartwig.com.pl; internet www.c.hartwig.pl; f. 1858; also Gdańsk, Katowice, Poznań, Wrocław; sole forwarding agent for rail, air, sea, river and road transport; Pres. GRZEGORZ OCIESA.

Hortex Holding SA: 00-034 Warsaw, ul. Warecka 11A ; tel. (22) 5510000; fax (22) 5510101; e-mail hortex@hortex.com.pl; internet www.hortex.com.pl; f. 1958; fresh, frozen and processed fruits and vegetables for industrial and consumer use; Pres. WOJCIECH MADALSKI; employees 4,539.

Huta Katowice SA: 41-308 Dąbrowa Górnicza, Al. Piłsudskiego 92; tel. (32) 7945333; fax (32) 7955200; e-mail zbhz@hutakatowice.com.pl; internet www.hutakatowice.com.pl; partial privatization scheduled; steel mill; Pres. MIROSŁAW WRÓBEL; 6,500 employees.

Huta Stalowa Wola SA: 37-450 Stalowa Wola, ul. Kwiatkowskiego 1; tel. (16) 8434212; fax (16) 8721210; f. 1937; heavy construction equipment, steel foundry products; Chair. and Gen. Dir RYSZARD KARDASZ; 14,500 employees.

Huta im. Tadeusza Sendzimira SA: 30-969 Kraków, ul. Ujastek 1; tel. (12) 6448866; fax (12) 6447496; internet www.hts.com.pl; f. 1954; rolled steel, galvanized steel and steel products; Gen. Dir PIOTR JANECZEK; 11,400 employees.

Impexmetal SA: 00-842 Warsaw, ul. Łucka 7/9, POB 62; tel. (22) 6586000; fax (22) 6200544; e-mail info@impexmetal.com.pl; internet www.impexmetal.com.pl; f. 1951; exports non-ferrous metals and their alloys; Chair and Gen. Dir JERZY KAMINSKI; Financial Dir KRZYSTOF ADAMSKI; 147 employees.

Inco Veritas SA: 00-519 Warsaw, ul. Wspólna 25; tel. (22) 6216471; fax (22) 6280775; e-mail inco-bzs@it.com.pl; internet www.inco-veritas.com.pl; f. 1947; stationery, books, artifacts, glass objects, tools, chemicals, toiletries and cleaning products; Pres. and Gen. Dir BOGUSŁAW DĘBSKI; 3,400 employees.

Intraco: 00-950 Warsaw, POB 912, ul. Stawki 2; tel. (22) 6356002; fax (22) 6355418; exports building services, interior architecture; imports equipment and spare parts; Dir JERZY PIETRULA.

KGHM Polska Miedź SA: 59-301 Lublin, ul. M. Skłodowskiej-Curie 48; tel. (76) 8478200; fax (70) 8478500; e-mail pr@bz.kghm.com.pl; internet www.kghm.com.pl; f. 1961; Europe's largest producer of copper; mining of non-ferrous metal ore and processing of refined metals; Pres. MARIAN KRZEMINSKI; 18,560 employees.

Kolmex: 00-844 Warsaw, ul. Grzybowska 80/82, POB 236; tel. (22) 6615000; fax (22) 6209381; f. 1964; imports and exports railway rolling-stock and containers; Pres. ANDZREJ NAŁĘCZ; 85 employees.

Kopex SA: 40-172 Katowice, ul. Grabowa 1, POB 245; tel. (32) 2586031; fax (32) 2035180; e-mail kopex@kopex.com.pl; internet www.kopex.com; f. 1962; exports and imports fuels, machinery, equipment and appliances for mining, drilling and other engineering industries; consultancy services; Chair. and Man. Dir KRZYSTOF PYTEL; 170 employees.

Labimex Spółka z o.o.: 00-950 Warsaw, Krakowskie Przedmieście 79, POB 261; tel. (22) 266431; fax (22) 260810; f. 1973; exports and imports medical, scientific and research apparatus, teaching aids, laboratory equipment, optical and geodetic instruments; Dir-Gen. JERZY RYCHTER.

Lasy Państwowe: 00-922 Warsaw, ul. Wawelska 52; tel. (22) 8256028; fax (22) 8258556; f. 1924; forestry, land and wildlife conservation and management; Man. Dir KONRAD TOMASZEWSKI; 36,727 employees.

Maspex Wadowice: 34–100 Wadowice, ul. Legionow 37; tel. (33) 8731075; fax (33) 8739778; internet www.maspex.com.pl; f. 1990; soft beverages manufacturer; 3,000 employees.

Metalexport Spółka z o.o.: 00-950 Warsaw, ul. Mokotowska 49, POB 442/642; tel. (22) 6600222; fax (22) 6286561; e-mail infomex@metalexport.pl; internet www.metalexport.pl; f. 1949; exports and imports technological and military equipment, complete engineering plants, tools and machine tools; Pres. Dr PIOTR BÜCHNER; 100 employees.

Metronex SA: 02-325 Warsaw, ul. Białobrzeska 53, POB 198; tel. and fax (22) 8239806; f. 1965; exports and imports measurement instruments, process control devices, medical equipment, computers, software, office equipment, etc.; Dir ANDRZEJ ZIAJA; 100 employees.

Minex SA.: 00-613 Warsaw, ul. Chałubínskiego 8, POB 1002; tel. (22) 302326; fax (22) 8300926; e-mail chairman@minex.com.pl; internet www.minex.com.pl; f. 1949; exports and imports minerals, cement, glass and ceramics; Dir MIROSŁAW PIETA; 120 employees.

Nadwiślańska Spółka Węglowa SA (Nadwiślańska Coal Mine Co): 43-100 Tychy, ul. Bałuckiego 4; tel. (32) 3245000; fax (32) 3245309; e-mail infor.nsw@nsw.com.pl; internet www.nsw.com.pl; f. 1993; coal-mining services; Pres. and Man. Dir LECH WIZNER; 42,000 employees.

Navimor Import-Export Co. Ltd: 80-890 Gdańsk, ul. Heweliusza 11, POB 423; tel. (58) 318624; fax (58) 314497; ship repairs, import and export of shipyard installations, floating docks and pontoons, yachts, river vessels and coasters, fishing vessels, marine equipment, motors for small craft; Pres. KRZYSZTOF BANASZAK.

Orbis SA: 00-028 Warsaw, ul. Bracka 16; tel. (22) 8260271; fax (22) 8273301; internet www.orbis.pl; f. 1920; hotels; Pres. MACIEJ GRELOWSKI; 9,934 employees.

Pagart: 00-078 Warsaw, Pl. Marszałka Józefa Piłsudskiego 9; tel. (22) 8260145; fax (22) 8276405; e-mail pagart@pagart.com.pl; internet www.pagart.com.pl; f. 1957; represents Polish artists abroad and organizes guest performances of foreign artists in Poland; Pres. ANDRZEJ SOWINSKI.

Paged SA: 00-950 Warsaw, Pl. Trzech Krzyzy 18, POB 991; tel. (22) 6238100; fax (22) 6281396; e-mail paged@paged.com.pl; internet www.paged.com.pl; f. 1932; imports machinery and equipment for wood and paper industries, exports furniture, pulp and paper, boards and wooden products; Dir-Gen. MIRON TRZECIAK; 210 employees.

Petrobaltic Spółka z o.o.: 80-958 Gdańsk, Stary Dwór 9; tel. (58) 3013061; fax (58) 3014311; e-mail petrobaltic@osnet.pl; f. 1990; petroleum and natural gas exploration, drilling and field services; Pres. and Man. Dir JAN KUREK; 400 employees.

Pezetel SA: 04-028 Warsaw 50, Al. Stanów Zjednoczonych 61, POB 88; tel. (22) 8108001; fax (22) 8132356; e-mail board@pezetel.com.pl; internet www.pezetel.com.pl; f. 1971; import and export of aircraft, helicopters, sailplanes, turbo-shaft, jet, and radial-piston aircraft engines, diesel engines, generators, air equipment, electric carts, pneumatics, hydraulics, aviation and agricultural services; Pres. ANDRZEJ JESIONEK; 55 employees.

Polcargo Inspection: 81-963 Gdynia, ul. Zeromskiego 32, POB 223; tel. (58) 6205371; fax (58) 6216819; e-mail polcargo@gd.onet.pl; f. 1949; international superintendence and testing services; Man. Dir SŁAWOMIR WŁADYKO.

Polcoop SA: 00-950 Warsaw, ul. Kopernika 30; tel. (22) 8264060; fax (22) 8271053; f. 1957; exports foodstuffs, agricultural products, incl. fruit, vegetables and meat; imports fertilizers, fresh and processed fruit and vegetables, machinery, equipment, spare parts, etc.; Pres. STANISŁAW NIECKARZ; 580 employees.

Polimex-Cekop SA: 00-950 Warsaw, ul. Czackiego 7/9, POB 815; tel. (22) 8297100; fax (22) 8260493; e-mail info@polimex-cekop.pl; internet www.polimex-cekop.pl; f. 1945; exports and imports machines and complete plants; Man. Dir MACIEJ MĘCLEWSKI; 9,250 employees.

POL-MOT Holding SA: 00-220 Warsaw, ul. Rajców 10; tel. (22) 8310790; fax (22) 8310890; e-mail plomot@warman.com.pl; internet www.polmot.pl; f. 1968; holding co dealing in farm machinery, automobiles and construction; also Pol Mot Praszka SA; Gen. Dir ANDRZEJ ZARAJCZYK.

Polservice: 00-613 Warsaw, ul. Chałubinskiego 8; tel. (22) 8139526; fax (22) 8139526; f. 1961; export and import of consulting and technical services, transfer of technology; Dir-Gen. JERZY FIJAŁKOWSKI; 400 employees.

Polski Koncern Naftowy, PKN–ORLEN SA: 09-411 Płock, ul. Chemików 7; tel. (24) 3655381; fax (24) 3655448; e-mail media@orlen.pl; internet www.orlen.pl; f. 1999 by the merger of Petrochemia Płock and Centrala Produktow Naftowych; crude petroleum processing and manufacture of petrochemical products; largest domestic enterprise in 2001; 28.4% state-owned; Pres. and Man. Dir ZBIGNIEW WROBEL; 10,700 employees.

Polskie Huty Stali (PHS) (Polish Steelworks Co): f. 2002 by the State Treasury as a holding co to consolidate the Katowice, Sedzimir (Kraków), Florian (Swietochlowice) and Cedler (Sosnowiec) Steelworks in preparation for privatization; Chair. JERZY PODSIADLO.

Polskie Wydawnictwo Muzyczne: 31-111 Kraków, Al. Krasińskiego 11A ; tel. (12) 4227044; fax (12) 4220174; e-mail pwm@pwm.com.pl; internet www.pwm.com.pl; f. 1945; import and export of musical material; Man. Dir LESZEK POLONY; see also under Publishers; 100 employees.

Poczta Polska: 00-940 Warsaw, ul. Małachowskiego 2; tel. (22) 6565000; fax (32) 8273256; e-mail webmaster@poczta-polska.pl; internet www.poczta-polska.pl; f. 1992; postal services; Gen. Man. RAJMUND JAROSZEK, GRZEGORZ SZERMANOWICZ; 95,000 employees.

Polskie Zakłady Lotnicze-Mielec SA (Polish Aviation Factory): 39-300 Mielec, ul. Wojska Polskiego 3; tel. (17) 7887000; fax (17) 7886587; e-mail pzl@ptc.pl; internet www.pzl-mielec.pl; f. 1938; manufactures aircraft and vehicles; Pres. and Man. Dir A. SZORTYKA; 1,500 employees.

Prokom Software: f. 1985; hardware and software; designs and installs technical infrastructure; Pres. RYSZARD KRAUZE; 2,000 employees.

Rafineria Gdańska SA: 80-718 Gdańsk, ul. Elbląska 135; tel. (58) 3087111; fax (58) 3018888; e-mail lotos@rafineria.gda.pl; internet www.rafineria.gda.pl; f. 1975; petroleum refinery; Chair. and Man. Dir WOJCIECH ZURAWIK; 1,630 employees.

Rolimpex SA: 02-305 Warsaw, Al. Jerozolimskie 146D ; tel. (22) 5702110; fax (22) 5702112; e-mail execdep@rolimpex.waw.pl; internet www.rolimpex.waw.pl; f. 1951; exports and imports agricultural products of vegetable origin; Gen. Dir ROMAN MŁYNIEC; 210 employees.

Ruch SA: internet www.ruch.com.pl; f. 1900; trade in books, newspapers and periodicals; Chair. MIROSŁAWA NYKIEL; 11,450 employees.

Rybnicka Spółka Węglowa SA: 44-200 Rybnik, ul. Jastrzębska 10; tel. (36) 7394510; fax (36) 7220201; f. 1993; coal mining services; Pres. KRYSTIAN ZAJĄC; 28,900 employees.

SGS-PTK Supervise SP Zoo: 81-369 Gdynia, ul. Derdowskiego 7, POB 167; tel. (58) 6216685; fax (58) 6615152; f. 1947; quality and quantity control, supervisions, appraisals and evaluations for privatizations and joint ventures, risk management, environmental services; Gen. Dir MAREK SZWAJ; 162 employees.

Shipcontrol: 81-334 Gdynia, ul. Polska 21; tel. (58) 207096; fax (58) 210212; f. 1963; tallying, weighing and gauging of cargo, stowage plans and supervision, inspection of containers, etc.; Dir BOGDAN OBSZARSKI.

Siarkopol: 39-405 Tarnobrzeg, ul. Zakładowa 50; tel. (15) 8221561; fax (15) 8225193; e-mail piekarz@siarkopol.com.pl; f. 1953; sulphur mine and manufacturer of battery acid; Man. Dir TADEUSZ PUKA; 2,700 employees.

Stalexport SA: 40-085 Katowice, ul. Mickiewicza 29, POB 401; tel. (32) 2512211; fax (32) 251264; e-mail stalex@stalexport.com.pl; internet www.stalexport.com.pl; f. 1962; exports and imports rolled steel products, high quality steel, tubes, ores, pig iron, ferro alloys, power-generating units, ceramic tiles; Chair. JÓZEF OKOLSKI; Pres. EMIL WASACZ; 340 employees.

Statoil Polska Spólka z o.o.: 00-465 Warsaw, ul. 10 Listopada 29; tel. (22) 6221950; fax (22) 6221931; f. 1992; operates petroleum stations; Gen. Man. PAUL O'GORMAN; 800 employees.

Stocznia Gdynia SA (Gdynia Shipyard): 81-969 Gdynia 2, ul. Czechosłowacka 3; tel. (58) 6271500; fax (58) 6210879; e-mail mm@stocznia.gdynia.pl; f. 1922; ship-building; Pres. JANUSZ SZLANTA; 9,000 employees.

Stocznia Szczecińska Porta Holding SA: 71-642 Szczecin, ul. Hutnicza 1; tel. (91) 4232434; fax (91) 4231872; f. 1948; renationalized in 2002, owing to bankruptcy; ship-building and repairing; 6,500 employees.

Stomil Olsztyn SA: 10-454 Olsztyn, ul. Leonharda 9; tel. (89) 5330741; fax (89) 5336597; f. 1967; manufactures tyres and inner tubes; Pres. RENE FONTES; 4,400 employees.

Textilimpex Co Ltd: 90-950 Łódź, ul. Traugutta 25, POB 320; tel. (42) 6325180; fax (42) 6367760; e-mail tx.tarqil@textilimpex.com.pl; internet www.textilimpex.com.pl; f. 1949; import and export of textile goods and raw materials for the textile industry, exhibition services; Gen. Dir STANISŁAW DYBILES; 197 employees.

Turów, Kopalnia Węgla Brunatnego: 59-916 Bogatynia, ul. Bogatynina 3; tel. (75) 7735300; fax (75) 7755400; f. 1947; state-owned; coal mining exploration; Gen. Man. ANDRZEJ SZWARNOWSKI; 6,430 employees.

UNITRA Trading and Industrial Corporation: 00-950 Warsaw, ul. Nowogrodzka 50, POB 66; tel. (22) 213382; fax (22) 214761; hi-tech equipment, industrial systems, electronic and other goods; consultancy and promotional services; Dir JAN BRUKSZO.

Universal SA: 00-950 Warsaw, Al. Jerozolimskie 44, POB 370; tel. (22) 6936091; fax (22) 6936367; f. 1959; company dealing in electrical household appliances, metal, plastic and glass household goods, sports and recreational equipment, heating and air-conditioning equipment; Gen. Dir DARIUSZ PRZYWIECZERSKI; 200 employees.

Ursus SA: 02-945 Warsaw, ul. Traktorzystów 10; tel. (22) 6672323; fax (22) 6679054; f. 1945; owned by Ursus Trading Sp Zoo; tractor manufacturers; Pres. STANISŁAW BORTKIEWICZ; Gen. Dir JANUSZ SCISKALSKI; 12,200 employees.

Varimex: 00-950 Warsaw, ul. Wilcza 50/52, POB 263; tel. (22) 6235000; fax (22) 6218619; e-mail headoffice@varimex.com.pl; f. 1945; import and export of medical and photographic equipment, valves and fittings, fire-fighting equipment, building hardware, catering and typographic equipment; import of textile machines; Gen. Dir ANDRZEJ SOBCZYK; 160 employees.

Węglokoks SA: 40-085 Katowice, ul. A. Mickiewicza 29; tel. (32) 7573226; fax (32) 515463; f. 1952; imports and exports coal, coke, gas; Chair. and Gen. Dir SEBASTIAN CZYPIONKA, MICHAŁ KWIATKOWSKI; 320 employees.

Zakłady Chemiczne Police: 72-010 Police, ul. Kuznicka 1; tel. (91) 173888; fax (91) 173446; e-mail kontakt@zchpolice.pl; internet www.zchpolice.pl; f. 1964; fertilizers, acids and titanium dioxide; 4,400 employees.

Zakłady Wlokien Chemicznych Stilon SA: 66-407 Gorzów Wielkopolski, ul. Walczaka 25; tel. (95) 732011; fax (95) 7325040; f. 1951; textiles products and audio tapes; Pres. and Gen. Man. JANUSZ GRAMZA; 3,500 employees.

ZELMER (Zakłady Zmechanizowanego Sprzetu Domwego): 35-016 Rzeszów, ul. Hoffmanowej 19; tel. (17) 8522666; fax (17) 8523622; e-mail marketing@zelmer.pl; internet www.zelmer.pl; f. 1951; domestic and kitchen appliances; Gen. Dir Dr BOGUSŁAW MADERA; 3,700 employees.

Zespół Elektrociepłowni w Łodzi SA: 90-972 Łódź, ul. Andrzejewski 5; tel. (42) 6755000; fax (42) 6755190; f. 1960; energy conservation research and consultation; Pres. MARIAN STRUMIŁO; 3,400 employees.

TRADE UNIONS

All Poland Trade Unions Alliance (Ogólnopolskie Porozumienie Związków Zawodowych—OPZZ): 00-924 Warsaw, ul. Kopernika 36/40; tel. (22) 8267106; fax (22) 8265102; e-mail opzz@opzz.org.pl; internet www.opzz.org.pl; f. 1984; 2.3m. mems (2000); Chair. MACIEJ MANICKI.

Independent Self-governing Trade Union—Solidarity (NSZZ Solidarność): 80-855 Gdańsk, Wały Piastowskie 24; tel. (58) 3016737; fax (58) 3010143; e-mail zagr@solidarnosc.org.pl; internet www.solidarnosc.org.pl; f. 1980; outlawed 1981–89; 1.2m. mems; Chair. JANUSZ SNIADEK.

Rural (Private Farmers') Solidarity: Leader ROMAN WIERZBICKI.

Transport

RAILWAYS

At the end of 2000 there were 22,560 km of railway lines making up the state network, of which 11,826 km were electrified and 985 km were narrow gauge. Substantial modernization, with assistance from the World Bank and other sources, was planned.

General Railway Inspectorate (Główny Inspektorat Kolejnictwa): 00-928 Warsaw, ul. Chałubinskiego 4/6; e-mail gik@gik.gov.pl; internet www.gik.gov.pl; Gen. Inspector BOLESŁAW MUSIAŁ; Dir-Gen. LIDIA OSTROWSKA.

Polish State Railways Plc (Polskie Koleje Państwowe Spótka Akcyjna—PKP SA): 00-973 Warsaw, ul. Szczęśliwicka 62; tel. (22) 5249000; fax (22) 5249020; e-mail infopkp@pkp.com.pl; internet www.pkp.com.pl; f. 1926; freight and passenger transport; scheduled for privatization after 2001; Pres. KRZYSZTOF CELIŃSKI; 152,586 employees.

ROADS

In December 2000 there were 364,656 km of roads, of which 358 km were motorways. Poland launched a road construction scheme in mid-2002, partly funded by the European Union, which aimed to enhance the country's position as a major transit route between Western Europe and the countries of the former USSR. The project, which was to concentrate on road construction, also aimed to modernize some 1,500 km of existing roads.

General Directorate of Public Roads and Motorways (Generalna Dyrekcja Dróg Krajowych i Autostrad): 00-921 Warsaw, ul. Wspólna 1/3; tel. (22) 6217072; fax (22) 6219557; internet www.gddp.gov.pl; Dir TADEUSZ SUVARA.

Państwowa Komunikacja Samochodowa (PKS) (Polish Motor Communications): Warsaw; tel. (22) 363594; fax (22) 366733; f. 1945; state enterprise organizing inland road transport for passengers and goods. Bus routes cover a total of 121,000 km; passengers carried 1,039,409 (1995).

Pekaes SA: 01-204 Warsaw, ul. Siedmiogrodzka 1/3; tel. (22) 6322251; fax (22) 6321092; e-mail info@pekaes.com.pl; f. 1958; road transport of goods to all European and Middle Eastern countries; Pres. ALBERT BOROWSKI.

INLAND WATERWAYS

Poland has 6,850 km of waterways, of which 3,813 km were navigable in 2000. The main rivers are the Wisła (Vistula, 1,047 km), Odra (Oder, 742 km in Poland), Bug (587 km in Poland), Warta (808 km), San, Narew, Noteć, Pilica, Wieprz and Dunajec. There are some 5,000 lakes, the largest being the Śniardwy, Mamry, Łebsko, Dąbie and Miedwie. In addition, there is a network of canals (approximately 348 km).

About 1,637,000 passengers and 10.3m. metric tons of freight were carried on inland water transport in 2001.

SHIPPING

Poland has three large harbours on the Baltic Sea: Gdynia, Gdańsk and Szczecin. At 31 December 2002 the Polish merchant fleet had 57 cargo-carrying ships, with a total displacement of 457,773 grt.

Authority of Szczecin and Świnoujście Authority SA: 70-603 Szczecin, ul. Bytomska 7; tel. (91) 4308240; fax (91) 4624842; e-mail info@port.szczecin.pl; internet www.port.szczecin.pl; f. 1950; Pres. and Man. Dir ANDRZEJ MONTWIŁŁ.

Port of Gdańsk Authority SA: 80-955 Gdańsk, ul. Zamknieta 18; tel. (58) 3439300; fax (58) 3439485; e-mail info@portgdansk.pl; internet www.portgdansk.pl; Pres. and Gen. Dir MARIAN SWITEK.

Port of Gdynia Authority SA: 81-337 Gdynia, ul. Rotterdamska Str. 9; tel. (58) 6274002; fax (58) 6203191; e-mail marketing@port.gdynia.pl; internet www.port.gdynia.pl; f. 1922; Pres. JANUSZ JAROSINSKI.

Principal shipping companies:

Polskie Linie Oceaniczne (PLO) (Polish Ocean Lines): 81-364 Gdynia, ul. 10 Lutego 24, POB 265; tel. (58) 6278222; fax (58) 6278480; e-mail pol@pol.com.pl; internet www.pol.com.pl; f. 1951; holding co for six shipping cos operating within PLO group; Dir-Gen. KRZYSZTOF KREMKY.

Polska Żegluga Bałtycka SA— Polferries (Polish Baltic Shipping Co—POLFERRIES): 78-100 Kołobrzeg, ul. Portowa 41; tel. (94) 3552102 (from June 2003); fax (94) 3526612; e-mail info@polferries.pl; internet www.polferries.pl.

Polska Żegluga Morska (PZM) (Polish Steamship Co): 70-419 Szczecin, Pl. Rodła 8; tel. (91) 3595595; fax (91) 4340574; e-mail pzmmanagement@polsteam.com.pl; internet www.polsteam.com.pl; f. 1951; world-wide tramping; fleet of 103 vessels for bulk cargoes totalling nearly 3m. dwt; Gen. Dir PAWE BRZEZICKI.

CIVIL AVIATION

Okęcie international airport is situated near Warsaw. There are also international airports at Kraków, Gdańsk and Katowice. Domestic flights serve Gdańsk, Gołeniow, Katowice, Kraków, Poznań, Rzeszów, Szczecin, Warsaw and Wrocław.

General Inspectorate of Civil Aviation (Główny Inspektorat Lotnictwa Cywilnego): 00-928 Warsaw, ul. Chałubinskiego 4/6; tel. and fax (22) 6298689; e-mail gilc@polbox.pl; internet www.gilc.gov.pl; Gen. Inspector ZBIGNIEW MĄCKA.

Air Silesia: Katowice; f. 2002; low-cost regional passenger and cargo carrier; Chair. EUGENIUSZ PIECHOCZEK.

Polskie Linie Lotnicze (LOT SA) (Polish Airlines—LOT): 00-906 Warsaw, ul. 17 Stycznia 39; tel. (22) 6066111; fax (22) 8460909; e-mail lot@lot.com; internet www.lot.com; f. 1929; 90 air routes, domestic services and international services to the Middle East, Africa, Asia, Canada, USA, and throughout Europe; due to be privatized in 2003; Pres. JAN LITWIŃSKI; Vice-Pres. ZBIGNIEW KISZCZAK.

Tourism

The Polish Tourist and Country-Lovers' Association is responsible for tourism and maintains about 420 branches across the country. The Association runs about 250 hotels, hostels and campsites. Poland is rich in historic cities, such as Gdańsk, Wrocław, Kraków, Poznań and Warsaw. There are 30 health and climatic resorts, while the mountains, forests and rivers provide splendid scenery and excellent facilities for touring and sporting holidays. In 2002 Poland was visited by some 50.7m. foreign tourists, 46.6% of whom were from Germany.

National Administration of Tourism and Physical Culture (Urząd Kultury Fizycznej i Turystyki): 00-916 Warsaw, ul. Świętokrzyska 12; tel. (22) 6945555; fax (22) 8262172.

Polish Tourist and Country-Lovers' Society (Polskie Towarzystwo Turystyczno-Krajoznawcze): 00-075 Warsaw, ul. Senatorska 11; tel. (22) 265735; fax (22) 262505; f. 1950; Chair. ADAM CHYŻEWSKI; the Society has about 250 tourist accommodation establishments; 89,919 mems (1998).

Culture

NATIONAL ORGANIZATIONS

Ministry of Culture: see section on The Government (Ministries); includes:

Institute of Culture (Instytut Kultury): 01-532 Warsaw, ul. Skazańców 25; tel. (22) 8391234; fax (22) 8399570; e-mail instkult@warman.com.pl; internet www.institute-of-culture.pl; f. 1974; research centre for Polish culture; Dir Dr JAN STANISŁAW WOJCIECHOWSKI.

Polish Cultural Foundation (Fundacja Kultury Polskiej): 00-252 Warsaw, ul. Podwale 1/3; tel. (22) 6357628; fax (22) 6355264; f. 1988; promotes Polish culture of all kinds both in Poland and world-wide; Chair. Prof. TADEUSZ POLAK; Pres. BEATA TYSZKIEWICZ.

State Committee of Polish Cinematography: 00-071 Warsaw, Krakowskie Przedmieście 21–23; tel. (22) 8267489; fax (22) 8276233; Chair. TADEUSZ ŚCIBOR-RYLSKI.

CULTURAL HERITAGE

Auschwitz-Birkenau State Museum (Państwowe Muzeum Auschwitz-Birkenau w Oświęcimiu): 32-620 Oświęcim, ul. Więźniów Oświęcimia 20; tel. (33) 8432022; fax (33) 8431934; e-mail muzeum@auschwitz.org.pl; internet www.auschwitz.org.pl; f. 1947; UNESCO World Heritage Site.

History Museum of the City of Kraków (Muzeum Historyczne m. Krakowa): 31-011 Kraków, Krzysztofory, Rynek Główny 35; tel. (12) 223264; f. 1899; Dir ANDRZEJ SZCZYGIEŁ.

History Museum of the City of Warsaw (Muzeum Historyczne m. st. Warszawy): 00-272 Warsaw, Rynek Starego Miasta 28; tel. (22) 6351625; fax (22) 8319491; f. 1947; collections covering the history of Warsaw from the 10th century onwards; Dir Prof. Dr JANUSZ DURKO.

Jagiellonian Library (Biblioteka Jagiellońska): 30-059 Kraków, al. Mickiewicza 22; tel. (12) 6336377; fax (12) 6330903; e-mail ujbj@ if.uj.edu.pl; internet www.bj.uj.edu.pl; f. 1364; national library for books up to 1800; Dir Dr Krzysztof Zamorski.

National Library (Biblioteka Narodowa): 02-086 Warsaw 22, POB 36, Al. Niepodległości 213; tel. (22) 6082999; fax (22) 8255251; e-mail biblnar@bn.org.pl; internet www.bn.org.pl; f. 1928; *c.* 7m. vols; Dir Michał Jagiełło.

National Museum in Warsaw (Muzeum Narodowe): 00-495 Warsaw, Al. Jerozolimskie 3; tel. (22) 6211031; fax (22) 6228559; e-mail muzeum@mnw.art.pl; internet www.mnw.art.pl; f. 1862; historical and art collections; Dir Ferdynand Ruszczyc.

National Museum in Kraków (Muzeum Narodowe w Krakowie): 30-062 Kraków, Al. 3 Maja 1; tel. (12) 2955600; fax (12) 2955555; e-mail dyrekcja@muz-nar.krakow.pl; internet www.museum .krakow.pl; f. 1879; historical and art collections; Dir Zofia Gołubiev.

Polish State Archives (Archiwa Państwowe): 00–950 Warsaw, POB 1005, ul. Długa 6; tel. (22) 8313206; e-mail ndap@archiwa.gov .pl; internet www.archiwa.gov.pl; Dir Daria Nałęcz.

State Archaeological Museum (Państwowe Muzeum Archeologiczne): 00-950 Warsaw, ul. Długa 52, POB 69; tel. (22) 8313221; fax (22) 8315195; e-mail pma@ternet.pl; f. 1923; Dir Dr Jan Jaskanis.

State Ethnographic Museum in Warsaw (Państwowe Muzeum Etnograficzne w Warszawie): 00-056 Warsaw, ul. Kredytowa 1; tel. (22) 277641; f. 1888; Polish and non-European collections; Dir Dr Jan Witold Suliga.

SPORTING ORGANIZATION

Olympic Committee of the Republic of Poland: 00-483 Warsaw, ul. Frascati 4; tel. (22) 6285038; fax (22) 6298862; f. 1918; Pres. Stanisław Paszczyk; Gen. Sec. Janusz Tatera.

Polish Sport Confederation (Polska Konfederacja Sportu): 00–916 Warsaw, ul. Świętokrzyska 12; tel. (22) 8265864; fax (22) 8262172; e-mail pksport@pksport.pl; internet www.pksport.pl; Pres. Andrzej Kraśnicki.

PERFORMING ARTS

Theatre

Drama Theatre (Teatr Dramatyczny): 00-901 Warsaw, Pałac Kultury i Nauki; tel. (22) 8263872; internet www.teatrdramatyczny.pol .pl; Dir Anna Sapiego, Piotr Cieślak.

National Folk Theatre of Kraków (Państwowy Teatr Ludowy w Krakowie): 31-943 Kraków, ul. ós Teatralne 34; tel. (12) 443626.

National Theatre (Teatr Narodowy): 00-077 Warsaw, Pl. Teatralny 3; tel. (22) 6920770; fax (22) 6920741; internet www.narodowy .pol.pl; Dir Krzysztof Torończyk.

National Theatre of Poland in Warsaw (Państwowy Teatr Polski w Warszawie): 00-327 Warsaw, ul. Karasia 2; tel. (22) 8264880; fax (22) 8269278; e-mail sekretariat@teatrpolski.waw.pl; internet www .teatr-polski.art.pl; f. 1913; Dir Jerzy Zaleski; Artistic Dir Jarosław Kilian.

National Modern Theatre in Warsaw (Państwowy Teatr Nowy w Warszawie): 02-503 Warsaw, ul. Puławska 37/39.

Warsaw Contemporary Theatre (Teatr Współczesny w Warszawie): 00-640 Warsaw, ul. Mokotowska 13.

Opera Houses

Kraków Opera and Operetta (Opera i Operetka w Krakowie): 31-005 Kraków, ul. Bracka 2; fax (12) 4220879.

National Baltic Opera (Państwowe Opera Bałtycka): 80-219 Gdańsk, Al. Zwycięstwa 15; tel. and fax (58) 7634912; e-mail opera@ operabaltycka.pl; internet www.operabaltycka.pl; Dir Włodzimierz Nawotka.

Polish National Opera—Grand Theatre (Opera Narodowa—Teatr Wielki): 00-950 Warsaw, Pl. Teatralny 1, Teatr Wielki; tel. (22) 6920200; fax (22) 8260423; e-mail office@teatrwielki.pl; internet www.teatrwielki.pl; f. 1778; includes museum; Dir Jacek Kaspszyk.

Warsaw Chamber Opera (Warszawska Opera Kameralna): 00-695 Warsaw, ul. Nowogrodzka 49; tel. (22) 6283096; fax (22) 6293223; e-mail publicrelations@wok.pol.pl; internet www.woc.pol .p; f. 1961; Dir Stefan Sutkowski.

Warsaw National Operetta (Państwowa Operetka w Warszawie): Warsaw, ul. Nowogrodzka 49; tel. (22) 6287071; fax (22) 6217233; Dir Bogusław Kaczyński.

Orchestras

Kraków Philharmonic (Karol Szymanowski) Orchestra (Filharmonia im. Karola Szymanowskiego w Krakowie): 31-103 Kraków, ul. Zwierzyniecka 1; tel. and fax (12) 4224312; e-mail pfk@ filharmonia.dnd.com.pl; internet www.filharmonia.dnd.com.pl.

Warsaw National Philharmonic Orchestra (Filharmonia Narodowa w Warszawie): 00-950 Warsaw, ul. Jasna 5; tel. (22) 5517111; fax (22) 5517200; e-mail filharmonia@filharmonia.pl; internet www .filharmonia.pl; f. 1901; Dir Kazimierz Kord.

ASSOCIATIONS

Art Historians Association (Stowarzyszenie Historyków Sztuki): 00-272 Warsaw, Rynek Starego Miasta 27; tel. (22) 8313773; fax (22) 6359074; f. 1934; Pres. Prof. Dr hab. Maria Poprzęcka; Sec.-Gen. Dr Katarzyna Nowakowska-Sito; 1,473 mems.

Association of Polish Architects (Stowarzyszenie Architektów Polskich): 00-950 Warsaw, ul. Foksal 2; tel. (22) 8278712; fax (22) 8278713; e-mail sarp@sarp.org.pl; internet www.sarp.org.pl; f. 1934; Pres. Krzysztof Chwalibóg; Sec.-Gen. Jerzy Grochulski; 6,000 mems.

Association of Polish Film-makers (Stowarzyszenie Filmowców Polskich): 00-071 Warsaw, ul. Krakowskie Przedmieście 41; tel. (22) 8276785; fax (22) 8286423; f. 1966; Pres. Jacek Bromski.

Association of Polish Musicians (Stowarzyszenie Polskich Artystów Muzyków): 00-660 Warsaw, ul. Lwowska 15/12; tel. (22) 8212802; fax (22) 6282835; Pres. Antoni Wicherek.

Central Association of Authors (ZaiKS): 00-950 Warsaw, ul. Hipoteczna 2; tel. (22) 8281705; fax 8289204; e-mail sekretariat@ zaiks.org.pl; internet www.zaiks.org.pl; f. 1918.

Plastic Arts Association of Poland (Związek Polskich Artystów Plastyków): 00-496 Warsaw, ul. Nowy Świat 7/6; tel. (22) 6210137; fax (22) 6211365; internet www.zpap.org.pl; Pres. Rafał Strent.

Polish PEN Club (Polski PEN Club): 00-079 Warsaw, ul. Krakowskie Przedmieście 87/89; tel. (22) 8282823; fax (22) 8265784; e-mail penclub@ikp.atm.com.pl; f. 1925; Pres. Jacek Bocheński.

Polish Republic's Photoclub Association of Authors (Fotoklub Rzeczypospolitej Polskiej Stowarzyszenie Twórców): 02-094 Warsaw, ul. Grójecka 75; tel. (22) 8223917; fax (22) 8252940; Pres. Mieczysław Cybulski.

Polish Society of Graphic Arts and Design (Stowarzyszenie Polskich Artystów Grafików, Projektantów): 00-496 Warsaw, ul. Nowy Świat 7, m. 6; tel. (22) 217819; Pres. Stanisław Wieczorek.

Education

Children up to the age of seven years may attend crèches (złobki) and kindergartens (przedszkola). In 1998/99 49.6% of children between the ages of three and six years attended kindergarten, with 95.4% of all six-year olds attending a pre-school establishment in 2000/01. A reform of primary and secondary education began to take effect in 1999 and will be fully implemented by the 2004/05 academic year. Education is free and compulsory for all children between the ages of seven and 16 years. Basic schooling begins at the age of seven years with primary school (szkoła podstawowa), for which there is a common curriculum throughout the country. The reformed programme of primary education lasts for six years (reduced from eight), divided into two equal cycles. In 2000/01 enrolment in primary schools and lower secondary schools was equivalent to 100% of the relevant age group. The reforms also introduced a new cycle of education, conducted at lower secondary schools (Gimnazjum). Attendance at these schools is compulsory for three years.

The reforms of secondary education ensured that students would enter the secondary cycle at 16 years rather than at 13. Three years of education leading to college or university entrance is available at general secondary schools (liceum ogólnokształcące) to pupils who are successful in the entrance examination. In 2000/01 enrolment at secondary schools was equivalent to 90.1% of the children in the relevant age-group. Other secondary school pupils attend vocational and technical schools (technika zawodowe) or basic vocational schools (zasadnicze szkoły). Vocational and technical schools provide four- and five-year courses combining vocational and general secondary education, and can lead to qualifications for entry into higher education. Basic vocational schools provide three-year courses consisting of three days' theoretical and three days' practical training per week; in addition, some general secondary education is provided. New post-secondary schools (szkoła policealna) were introduced in the 1999 reforms to prepare students from technical and vocational schools for skilled jobs. Secondary education is provided free of charge to candidates who are successful in the entrance examination.

There is a small number of private schools, administered under state supervision, and, in 1989, the Roman Catholic Church was granted the right to operate its own schools. In 2001/02 there were 344 higher education establishments in Poland and there were 15 universities in 1999/2000. In 2001 government expenditure on education amounted to 8,151.1m. złotys, which represented 4.7% of total budgetary expenditure.

UNIVERSITIES

Adam Mickiewicz University in Poznań (Uniwersytet im. Adama Mickiewicza w Poznaniu): 61-712 Poznań, ul. Henryka Wieniawskiego 1; tel. (61) 8526425; fax (61) 8294444; e-mail rectorof@amu.edu.pl; internet www.amu.edu.pl; f. 1919; 13 faculties; 2,536 teachers; 43,726 students; Rector Prof. Dr hab. STANISŁAW LORENC.

Catholic University of Lublin (Katolicki Uniwersytet Lubelski): 20-950 Lublin, al. Racławickie 14; tel. (81) 4454105; fax (81) 4454191; e-mail dwz@kul.lublin.pl; internet www.kul.lublin.pl; f. 1918; 7 faculties; 884 teachers; 18,970 students; Rector Rev. Prof. ANDRZEJ SZOSTEK.

Jagiellonian University (Uniwersytet Jagielloński): 31-007 Kraków, ul. Gołębia 24; tel. (12) 4221033; fax (12) 4226306; e-mail rektor@adm.uj.edu.pl; internet www.uju.edu.pl; f. 1364; 11 faculties; 3,200 teachers; 29,000 students; Rector Prof. Dr hab. FRANCISZEK ZIEJKA.

Marie Curie-Skłodowska University (Uniwersytet Marii Curie-Skłodowskiej): 20-031 Lublin, Plac Marii Curie-Skłodowskiej 5; tel. (81) 5375107; fax (81) 5375102; f. 1944; 10 faculties; 1,760 teachers; 23,592 students, incl. 10,255 extra-mural students; Rector Prof. Dr hab. KAZIMIERZ GOBEL.

Nicholas Copernicus University of Toruń (Uniwersytet Mikołaja Kopernika w Toruniu): 87-100 Toruń, ul. Gagarina 11; tel. (56) 6542951; fax (56) 6542944; f. 1945; 10 faculties; 2,706 teachers; 29,644 students; Rector Prof. Dr JAN KOPCEWICZ.

Szczecin University (Uniwersytet Szczeciński): 70-453 Szczecin, al. Jedności Narodowej 22A ; tel. (91) 4342536; fax (91) 44342992; e-mail rektorat@univ.szczecin.pl; internet www.univ.szczecin.pl; f. 1985; 6 faculties, 1 institute; 1,008 teachers; 26,793 students; Rector Prof. Dr hab. ZDZISŁAW CHMIELEWSKI.

University of Gdańsk (Uniwersytet Gdański): 80-952 Gdańsk, ul. Bazyńskiego 1A ; tel. (58) 5529043; fax (58) 5520311; e-mail rekug@univ.gda.pl; internet www.univ.gda.pl; f. 1970; 9 faculties; 1,571 teachers; 28,060 students; Rector Prof. Dr hab. ANDRZEJ CEYNOWA.

University of Łódź (Uniwersytet Łódzki): 90-131 Łódź, ul. Narutowicza 65; tel. (42) 6354002; fax (42) 6783924; e-mail rektorat@krysia.uni.lodz.pl; internet www.uni.lodz.pl; f. 1945; 11 faculties; 2,069 teachers; 41,496 students; Rector Prof. Dr hab. STANISŁAW LISZEWSKI.

University of Silesia (Uniwersytet Śląski): 40-007 Katowice, ul. Bankowa 12; tel. (32) 599601; fax (32) 599605; e-mail dwz@usl.adm.us.edu.pl; f. 1968; 10 faculties; 1,777 teachers; 37,935 students; Rector Prof. Dr TADEUSZ SŁAWEK.

University of Warmia and Mazury in Olsztyn (Uniwersytet Warmińsko-Mazurski w Olsztynie): 10-952 Olsztyn, ul. Oczapowskiego 2; tel. (89) 5273310; fax (89) 5240408; f. 1999; 25,000 students; Rector Prof. Dr hab. RYSZARD J. GÓRECKI.

University of Warsaw (Uniwersytet Warszawski): 00-927 Warsaw, Krakowskie Przedmieście 26/28; tel. (22) 6200381; tel. (22) 8263263; e-mail bip@mercury.ci.uw.edu.pl; internet www.uw.edu.pl; f. 1816; 18 faculties, 24 other units; 2,678 teachers; 52,733 students; Rector Prof. PIOTR WĘGLEŃSKI.

University of Wrocław (Uniwersytet Wrocławski): 50-137 Wrocław, Plac Uniwersytecki 1; tel. (71) 402212; fax (71) 402800; e-mail rek@bu.uni.wroc.pl; internet www.uni.wroc.pl; f. 1702; 8 faculties; 1,815 teachers; 33,222 students; Rector Prof. Dr hab. ROMUALD GELLES.

Technical and Agricultural Universities

August Cieszkowski Agricultural University (Akademia Rolnicza im. Augusta Cieszkowskiego): 60-637 Poznań, ul. Wojska Polskiego 28; tel. (61) 8470334; fax (61) 8487146; e-mail rektorat@owl.au.poznan.pl; f. 1951; 7 faculties; 782 teachers; 9,016 students; Rector Prof. Dr JERZY PUDEŁKO.

Białystok Technical University (Politechnika Białostocka): 15-351 Białystok, ul. Wiejska 45A ; tel. (85) 7443073; fax (85) 7422393; e-mail rektorat@cksr.ac.bialystok.pl; internet www.bialystok.pl/pd-info; f. 1949; 6 faculties, 1 institute; 677 teachers; 11,068 students; Rector Prof. Dr hab. Inż. MICHAŁ BOŁTRYK.

Częstochowa Technical University (Politechnika Częstochowska): 42-201 Częstochowa, ul. Dąbrowskiego 69; tel. (34) 3612580; fax (34) 3612385; e-mail rektorat@adm.pcz.czest.pl; internet www.matinf.pcz.czest.pl; f. 1949; 6 faculties; 698 teachers; 15,495 students; Rector Prof. Dr hab. Inz. JANUSZ SZOPA.

Kielce University of Technology (Politechnika Świętokrzyska): 25-314 Kielce, al. Tysiąclecia Państwa Polskiego 7; tel. (41) 24100;

fax (41) 42997; f. 1965; 3 faculties; 370 teachers; 4,300 students; Rector Prof Dr hab. HENRYK FRĄCKIEWICZ.

Kraków University of Technology (Politechnika Krakowska im. Tadeusza Kościuszki): 31-155 Kraków, ul. Warszawska 24; tel. (12) 6282201; fax (12) 6335773; e-mail r-0@admin.pk.edu.pl; f. 1945; 7 faculties; 1,080 teachers; 13,500 students; Rector Prof. Dr hab. KAZIMIERZ FLAGA.

Łódź Technical University (Politechnika Łódzka): 90-924 Łódź, Ks. I. Skorupki 6/8; tel. (42) 6312001; fax (42) 6368522; e-mail rector@sir.p.lodz.pl; internet www.p.lodz.pl; f. 1945; 11 faculties, 1 institute; 1,750 teachers; 20,000 students; Rector Prof. Dr hab. JÓZEF MAYER.

Poznań Technical University (Politechnika Poznańska): 60-965 Poznań, pl. Skłodowskiej-Curie 5; tel. (61) 8313237; fax (61) 8330217; e-mail rector@put.poznan.pl; f. 1919; 7 faculties; 2,000 teachers; 12,400 students; Rector Prof. Dr hab. JERZY DEMBCZYNSKI.

Rzeszów Technical University (Politechnika Rzeszowska): 35-959 Rzeszów, POB 85, ul. W. Pola 2; tel. (17) 8651100; fax (17) 8541260; e-mail rektor@prz.rzeszow.pl; internet www.prz.rzeszow.pl; f. 1974 as a university; 5 faculties; 612 teachers; 16,000 students; Rector Prof. TADEUSZ MARKOWSKI.

Silesian Technical University (Politechnika Śląska): 44-100 Gliwice, ul. Akademicka 2A ; tel. (32) 2312349; fax (32) 2371655; e-mail rek.sekr@polsl.gliwice.pl; internet www.polsl.gliwice.pl; f. 1945; 11 faculties; 2,000 teachers; 26,000 students; Rector Assoc. Prof. BOLESŁAW POCHOPIEŃ.

Stanisław Staszic University of Mining and Metallurgy (Akademia Górniczo-Hutnicza im. Stanisława Staszica w Krakowie): 30-059 Kraków, Al. Mickiewicza 30; tel. (12) 6334998; fax (12) 6334672; e-mail rektorat@uci.agh.edu.pl; internet www.agh.edu.pl; f. 1919; 15 faculties; 1,950 teachers; 28,553 students; Rector Prof. Dr hab. Inż. RYSZARD TADEUSIEWICZ.

Technical University of Gdańsk (Politechnika Gdańska): 80-952 Gdańsk, ul. G. Narutowicza 11/12; tel. (58) 3415791; fax (58) 3415821; e-mail rektor@pg.gda.pl; internet www.pg.gda.pl; f. 1904; 10 faculties; 1,160 teachers; 16,500 students; Rector Prof. ALEKSANDER KOŁODZIEJCZYK.

Technical University of Lublin (Politechnika Lubelska): 20-950 Lublin, ul. Bernardyńska 13; tel. (81) 5322201; fax (81) 5327364; e-mail tul@rekt.pol.lublin.pl; f. 1953; 4 faculties; 555 teachers; 9,00 students; Rector Prof. Dr hab. Inz. KAZIMIERZ SZABELSKI.

Technical University of Szczecin (Politechnika Szczecińska): 70-310 Szczecin, Al. Piastów 17; tel. (91) 4346751; fax (91) 4494014; e-mail rektor@ps.pl; internet www.ps.pl; f. 1946; 6 faculties; 829 teachers; 11,024 students; Rector Prof. Dr hab. Inz. MIECZYSŁAW WYSIECKI.

University of Agriculture in Lublin (Akademia Rolnicza w Lublinie): 20-934 Lublin, ul. Akademicka 13; tel. and fax (81) 33549; f. 1955; 5 faculties; 599 staff; 5,100 students; Rector Prof. Dr hab. MARIAN WESOŁOWSKI.

Warsaw Agricultural University (Szkoła Główna Gospodarstwa Wiejskiego Warszawie): 02-787 Warsaw, ul. Nowoursynowska 166; tel. and fax (22) 8438588; e-mail rector@sggw.waw.pl; f. 1816; 11 faculties; 1,100 teachers; 11,000 students; Rector Prof. Dr W. KLUCIŃSKI.

Warsaw University of Technology (Politechnika Warszawska): 00-661 Warsaw, Pl. Politechniki 1; tel. (22) 6607419; fax (22) 6216892; e-mail soltyski@rekt.pw.edu.pl; internet www.pw.edu.pl; f. 1826; 17 faculties; 2,390 teachers; 31,900 students; Rector Prof. Dr hab. Inz. STANISŁAW MAŃKOWSKI.

Wrocław University of Technology (Politechnika Wrocławska): 50-370 Wrocław, Wybrzeże Wyspiańskiego 27; tel. (71) 3202217; fax (71) 3286565; e-mail sekrpwr@ac.pwr.wroc.pl; internet www.pwr.wroc.pl; f. 1945; 12 faculties; 2,035 teachers; 27,024 students; Rector Prof. TADEUSZ LUTY.

Social Welfare

The Polish social-welfare system is controlled by the Ministries of Health and of the Economy, Labour and Social Policy. Locally, the system is administered by the Health and Social Welfare Departments of the Presidiums of the National Councils. In April 2002 a strategy was adopted to replace the 17 regional patients' boards with a single National Health Protection Fund (supervised by the premier and the Minister of Health) in 2003. Medical care is provided free for all workers and the rural population. Radical reforms to the health-care scheme were introduced in January 1999, creating a market within the field of health care. The 2001 central government budget allocated a total of 7,757.7m. złotys, which was 4.5% of total budget expenditure, to public safety, and a further 14,634.5m. złotys (8.5%) to social welfare and 46,065.6m. złotys (26.6%) to social security.

At the end of 2000 there were 85,031 physicians and 11,758 dental surgeons in practice (22.0 and 3.0 per 10,000 of the population, respectively). There were 190,952 general hospital beds, and a total of 716 general hospitals were in operation. The Polish Red Cross organizes and undertakes the care of the sick at home and general home assistance to those who are incapacitated through ill health, etc. Alimony is assured by law to single mothers. Welfare benefits are available to the unemployed. A major reform of the pensions system was undertaken in 1998, with legislation passed to introduce a three-tier structure, becoming operational on 1 January 1999. The first tier is a modified state scheme, to which all employees will contribute; the second consists of mandatory private funds; and the third tier groups optional private funds. Those under 30 make mandatory payments into a selected private fund; those between 30 and 50 have the option of starting a private pension; and those over 50 remain within the state scheme.

NATIONAL AGENCIES

Ministry of Health: see section on The Government (Ministries).

National Health Fund (Narodowy Fundusz Zdrowia): 02–390 Warsaw, ul. Grójecka 186; tel. (22) 5726000; fax (22) 5726333; internet www.nfz.gov.pl; Pres. MACIEJA TOKARCZYKA.

Ministry of the Economy, Labour and Social Policy: see section on The Government (Ministries).

Social Security Institute (Zakład Ubezpieczeń Społecznych): 00–701 Warsaw, ul. Czerniakowska 16; tel. (22) 6233000; fax (22) 8402610; internet www.zus.pl.

State Fund for the Rehabilitation of Disabled People (Państwowy Fundusz Rehabilitacji Osób Niepełnosprawnych): 00–828 Warsaw, Al. Jana Pawła II 13; tel. (22) 6200351; internet www.pfron .org.pl; Dir ROMAN SROCZYŃSKI.

HEALTH AND WELFARE ORGANIZATIONS

Foundation for the Handicapped (Fundacja osób Niepełnosprawnych): 00-160 Warsaw, ul. Zamenhofa 8; tel. (22) 8314004; fax (22) 8314992; internet www.fon.org.pl.

Institute of Labour and Social Affairs (Instytut Pracy i Spraw Socjalnych): 00-389 Warsaw, ul. Bellotiego 3B ; tel. (22) 6367200; e-mail instprac@ipiss.com.pl; internet www.ipiss.com.pl; f. 1963; research on labour, wages, income distribution, living standards, social security and social insurance, and labour laws etc; Dir Dr BOŻENNA BALCERZAK-PARADOWSKA.

Marie Skłodowska-Curie Memorial Cancer Centre and Institute of Oncology (Centrum Onkologii, Instytut im. Marii Skłodowskiej-Curie): 02-781 Warsaw, ul. W. K. Roentgena 5; tel. (22) 6440200; fax (22) 6440208; e-mail kchjg@coi.waw.pl; f. 1932; Dir Prof. MAREK P. NOWACKI.

National Institute of Cardiology (Instytut Kardiologii): 04-628 Warsaw, ul. Alpejska 42; tel. (22) 153011; fax (22) 152524; Dir Prof. ZYGMUNT SADOWSKI.

Polish Association of the Blind (Polski ZwiązekNiewidomych): 00-216 Warsaw, ul. Konwiktorska 9; tel. (22) 8312271; e-mail pzn@ pzn.org.pl; internet www.pzn.org.pl.

Polish Association of the Deaf (Polskich Związek Głuchych): 00-261 Warsaw, ul. Podwale 23; tel. (22) 8314071; fax (22) 6357536; internet www.pzg.org.pl; f. 1946; Pres. KAZIMIERZ DIEHL.

Polish Red Cross (Polski Czerwony Krzyż): 000950 Warsaw, ul. Mokotowska 14, POB 47; tel. (22) 6285201; fax (22) 6284168; e-mail head.office@pck.org.pl; internet www.pck.org.pl; Pres. ALEKSANDER MALACHOWSKI.

Tuberculosis and Pulmonary Diseases Institute (Instytut Gruźlicy i Chorób Płuc): 01-138 Warsaw, ul. Płocka 26; tel. (22) 6912128; f. 1948; Dir Prof. Dr hab. med. KAZIMIERZ ROSZKOWSKI-SIŻ.

Union of Belarusian Refugees in Poland (ZBUP): Bialystok; f. 2001; provides legal, financial and advisory support; Chair. JAN ABADOUSKI.

The Environment

The environmental movement in Poland became of significance in the early 1980s, with several groups emerging from within the Solidarity trade-union movement. There are more than 40 major ecological groups and several Green parties. The Polish Government maintains membership of the World Conservation Union—IUCN (based in Gland, Switzerland) and the Environmental Partnership for Central Europe. The country is also a member of the Council of Baltic Sea States (founded in 1992), which in 1995 agreed the Baltic

Sea Comprehensive Environmental Action Programme. This identified Poland as the main source of waste entering the marine environment of the Baltic. Other major concerns included air and water pollution caused by antiquated industrial plant and the burning of low-quality fuel, including lignite (brown coal). In 1999 it was estimated that the state would be required to spend US $30,000–$35,000m. in order to conform with environmental standards specified by the European Union. In the same year, the European Commission urged Poland to accelerate its programme of environmental legislation, while praising the country's efforts to reduce pollution. According to official sources 6,570.3m. złotys was spent on environmental protection in 1999, which amounted to 0.1% of GDP. In April 2001 the Government passed the Environmental Protection Act.

GOVERNMENT ORGANIZATIONS

Ministry of the Environment: see section on The Government (Ministries); incl.:

National Fund for Environmental Protection and Water Management (Narodowy Fundusz Ochrony Środowiska i Gospodarki Wodnej): 02–673 Warsaw, ul. Konstruktorska 3A; tel. (22) 8490079; fax (22) 8497272; e-mail fundusz@nfosigw.gov.pl; internet www.nfosigw.gov.pl; Pres. JERZY SWATOŃ.

Senate Committee on the Environment: 00-902 Warsaw, ul. Wiejska 6–8; tel. and fax (22) 6941639; formulation of legislation concerned with environmental protection; Chair. RYSZARD OCHWAT.

State Council for Nature Conservation in Poland (Państwowa Rada Ochrony Przyrody): 00-922 Warsaw, ul. Wawelska 52–54; tel. (22) 5792605; fax (22) 5792555; e-mail bozena.haczek@ mos.gov.pl; f. 1921; advises the Govt on environmental matters; Chair. Prof. Dr ANDRZEJ GRZYNACZ.

State Inspectorate for Environmental Protection: 00-922 Warsaw, ul. Wawelska 52/54; tel. (22) 8250001; fax (22) 8256376; internet www.pios.gov.pl; Gen. Dir MAREK MROCZKOWSKI.

The Ministry of Agriculture and Rural Development is also concerned with environmental matters (see section on The Government—Ministries)

ACADEMIC INSTITUTES

Polish Academy of Sciences (PAN) (Polska Akademia Nauk—PAN): 00-901 Warsaw, POB 24, Palac Kultury i Nauki; tel. (22) 6566000; fax (22) 6207651; f. 1952; Pres. Prof. LESZEK KUZNICKI; attached research insts incl.:

Institute of Ecology (Instytut Ekologii PAN): 05-092 Łomianki, Dziekanów Lesny, ul. M. Konopnickiej 1; tel. (22) 7513157; fax (22) 7513100; f. 1952; operates research stations in Gdańsk, Lublin, Mikołajki and Świdwie; Dir Prof. Dr LESZEK GRÜM.

Institute of Environmental Engineering (Instytut Podstaw Inzynierii Środowiska PAN): 41-819 Zabrze, ul. M. Skłodowskiej-Curie 34; tel. (32) 2716481; fax (32) 2717470; e-mail ipis@ipis .zabrze.pl; internet www.ipis.zabrze.pl; f. 1961; research and consultancy in environmental management systems; Dir Assoc. Prof. JAN KAPAŁA.

Institute of Environmental Protection (Instytut Ochrony Środowiska—IOS): 00-548 Warsaw, ul. Krucza 5/11; tel. (22) 6251005; fax (22) 6295263; internet www.ios.edu.pl; research centre into major environmental issues; Dir Prof. BARBARA GWOREK.

Institute of Nature Conservation (Instytut Ochrony Przyrody PAN): 31-512 Kraków, ul. Lubicz 46; tel. and fax (12) 4210348; e-mail noudenisi@cyf-kr.edu.pl; internet botan.ib-pan.krakow.pl/ przyroda/index.htm; f. 1952; research into natural biological processes, preservation of biodiversity and rare and threatened plant and animal species; research into the degradation of natural resources, changing ecosystems, water resources and landscape; Dir Prof. Dr ZYGMUNT DENISIUK.

Institute of Physical Planning and Municipal Economy (Instytut Gospodarki Przestrzennej i Komunalnej): 02-078 Warsaw, ul. Krzywickiego 9; tel. and fax (22) 8250937; f. 1949; research on physical planning, municipal economy and architecture; Dir Dr JACEK MALASEK.

Polish Academy of Sciences, Legal Studies Institute (Instytut Nauk Prawnych Polskiej Akademii Nauk): 00-330 Warsaw, Nowy Świat 72 (Palac Staszica); tel. and fax (22) 8267853; e-mail inp@inp.pan.pl; internet www.inp.pan.pl; f. 1956; activities include research into environmental law; Dir Prof. Dr MARIA KRUK-JAROSZ.

Forestry Research Institute (Instytut Badawczy Leśnictwa): 00-973 Warsaw, ul. Bitwy Warszawskiej 1920, r. 3; tel. (22) 8223201; fax (22) 8224935; e-mail ibl@ibles.waw.pl; internet www.ibles.waw .pl; f. 1930; part-funded by the Ministry of Environmental Protection; comprises 12 scientific sections; Dir Prof. Dr A. KLOCEK.

Institute of Meteorology and Water Management (Instytut Meteorologii i Gospodarki Wodnej): 01–673 Warsaw, ul. Podleśna 61; tel. (22) 8341851; fax (22) 8341801.

Institute for Sustainable Development (ISD) (Instytut na rzecz Ekorozwoju—INE): 00-743 Warsaw, Nabielaka 15 lok. 1; tel. (22) 8510402; fax (22) 8510400; e-mail ine@ine-isd.org.pl; internet www .ine-isd.org.pl; f. 1990; Principal officer Dr ANDRZEJ KASSENBERG.

Polish Geological Institute (Państwowy Instytut Geologiczny): 00–975 Warsaw, ul. Rakowiecka 4; tel. (22) 8495351; fax (22) 8495342; internet www.pgi.waw.pl; f. 1919; 740 staff; 6 regional branches; Dir Prof. LESZEK MARKS.

Research Centre for Agricultural and Forest Environmental Studies PAN (Zakład Badan Środowiska Rolniczego i Leśnego PAN): 60-809 Poznań, ul. Bukowska 19; tel. (61) 8475603; fax (61) 8473668; e-mail ryszagro@man.poznan.pl; f. 1979; Dir Prof. Dr hab. LECH RYSZKOWSKI.

NON-GOVERNMENTAL ORGANIZATIONS

Biuro Obsługi Ruchu Ekologicznego (BORE) (Service Office for the Environmental Movement—SOEM): 03-727 Warsaw, Al. Zieleniecka 6/8; Principal Officer JOLANTA PAWLAK.

Club of Environmental Journalists: 00-922 Warsaw, ul. Wawelska 52/54; tel. (22) 259056; fax (22) 258556; Contact SLAWOMIR TRZASKOWSKI.

Ecological Library Foundation: 61-715 Poznań, ul. Kościuszki 79; tel. (61) 8524139; fax (61) 8528276; e-mail rceebepz@free.ngo.pl; ecological library, protects endangered species in Poland; Pres. JACEK PURAT; Dir JAREK FISZER.

Ecology and Health Foundation: 02-904 Warsaw, ul. Bernardyńska 5/73A; tel. (22) 6427337; fax (22) 318443; e-mail ecoheal@ikp .atm.com.pl; provides information on environmental threats to health; Principal Officer Dr MAREK SIEMIŃSKI, Dr STEFAN BOGUSŁAWSKI, Dr JANUSZ OLTON.

Forest Management and Geodesy Bureau (Biuro Urzą dzania Lasu i Geodezji Leśnej): 00-922 Warsaw, ul. Wawelska 52/54; fax (22) 258399; e-mail buligl@buligl.pl; Dir ADAM SZEMPLIŃSKI.

Foundation for the Support of Ecological Initiatives: 31-121 Kraków, ul. Czysta 17/4 12/24; tel. (12) 6315730; fax (12) 6315731; e-mail zarzad@fwie.eco.pl; internet www.fwie.eco.pl; Contact PIOTR WIMAROWICZ.

> **Green Brigades Publishing House:** 31-014 Kraków, ul. Sławkowska 12; tel. and fax (12) 4222147; e-mail zb@eco.pl; internet www.zb.eco.pl; f. 1989; publishes books and magazines on environmental subjects; Principal Officer ANDRZEJ ŻWAWA.

League of Nature Conservation (Liga Ochrony Przyrody—LOP): 00-355 Warsaw, apt. 2, ul. Tamka 37; tel. (22) 8288171; fax (22) 8286580; e-mail ecekol@ecekol.edu.pl; internet www.ecekol.edu.pl; f. 1928; official nature conservation asscn; Pres. WŁADYSŁAW SKALNY; 268,000 mems.

National Foundation for Environmental Protection (NEEP): 01-445 Warsaw, ul. E. Ciotka 13; tel. (22) 8772359; fax (22) 8772360; e-mail nfos@nfos.org.pl; internet www.nfos.org.pl; f. 1989; Sec. ANNA KORYCKA.

Polish Ecological Club (Polski Klub Ekologiczny—PKE): 44–100 Gliwice, ul. Kaszubska 2; tel. (32) 2318591; e-mail biuro@pkegliwice .pl; internet www.pkegliwice.pl; f. 1988 as part of Solidarity; major independent asscn, affiliated to Friends of the Earth Int.; promotes sustainable development, human ecology, environmental education, waste recycling, conservation strategies; federation of regional groups; Mem. Bd Prof. STANISŁAW JUCHNOWICZ.

Polish Green Network (Polska Zielona Sieć—PZS): 31–008 Kraków, ul. Św. Anny 9; tel. (12) 4225906; e-mail info@zielonasiec .pl; internet www.zielonasiec.pl.

Regional Ecological Centre (REC): 00-515 Warsaw, ul. Żurawia 32/34, lok. 18; tel. (22) 6293665; fax (22) 6299352; e-mail recpl@data .pl; internet www.rec.org.pl; headquarters in Hungary.

Social Institute for Ecology: 03-127 Warsaw, ul. Zieleniecka 6/8; tel. (22) 6183781; fax (22) 6182884; e-mail bore@plearn.edu.pl; Pres. JUSTYNA KRYNACKA.

UNESCO Environmental Club—Workshop for Biodiversity: 21-050 Piaski, ul. Partyzantów 19; tel. (81) 5821001; e-mail bel@dtm .dtm.lublin.pl; Contact JANUSZ KUSMIERCZYK.

REGIONAL ORGANIZATIONS

Environmental Partnership for Central Europe (Fundacja Partnerstwo dla Środowiska): 31-005 Kraków, ul. Bracka 6/6; tel. (12) 4225088; fax (12) 4294725; e-mail biuro@epce.org.pl; internet www.epce.org.pl; f. 1992 as a Programme Office of the German Marshall Fund of the USA; changed name and registered as not-for-profit foundation in 1997; provides support for non-governmental organizations, small business and local communities in establishing and managing environmental partnerships for sustainable development; Dir RAFAL SERAFIN; Finance Dir RADOSŁAW TENDERA.

European Association of Environment and Resource Economists, Polish Division: 30-067 Kraków, ul. Gramatyka 10; tel. and fax (12) 6373529; e-mail preisner@wzn4.zarz.agh.edu.pl; f. 1990; Pres. Dr LESZEK PREISNER.

LOP European Environmental Centre: 02-384 Warsaw, ul. Włodarzewska 13–15; tel. (22) 6580135; fax (22) 6580164; e-mail ecekol@ecekol.edu.pl; internet www.ecekol.edu.pl; f. 1994; Dir TOMASZ CIEŚLIK.

Defence

In August 2002 Poland's armed forces were estimated to number 163,000, of which 81,000 were conscripts. Of the total, 104,050 were in the army, 14,300 in the navy and 36,450 in the air force. In addition, the border troops numbered 14,100 and the prevention units of the police 7,300. There were also 8,200 centrally controlled staff. Military service lasts for 12 months in all services, although graduates serve only six months. A six-year programme of modernization and restructuring began in March 2001, including significant pay rises to compensate for the aim of reducing the number of troops to 150,000 by 2003. Since 1988 conscientious objectors have been permitted to perform an alternative community service. Service in the reserve lasts until the age of 60 and in August 1999 membership totalled 406,000. In 2001 expenditure on defence was totalled 8,875.1m. new złotys (5.1% of total spending).

Poland was a member of the Warsaw Pact until its final dissolution in July 1991. Withdrawals of all former Soviet troops from Poland were completed by November 1992, although some Russian troops remained in order to supervise the transit arrangements for former Soviet troops withdrawing from Germany. In January 1994 the restructuring of the armed forces was announced in order to allow for the implementation of NATO's programmes. Poland joined NATO's 'Partnership for Peace' programme in the same year. It became a full member of the Alliance in March 1999.

Commander-in-Chief of the Armed Forces: President of the Republic.

Chief of Staff of the Defence Forces: Gen. CZESŁAW PIATAS.

Bibliography

Ascherson, N. *The Polish August: The Self-Limiting Revolution.* Harmondsworth, Penguin, 1981.

> *The Struggles for Poland.* London, Michael Joseph, 1987.

Boyes, R. *Nagi prezydent: çzycie polityczne Lecha Wałensy, The Naked President.* London, Martin Secker and Warburg, 1994.

Brock, P. de Beauvoir. *Nationalism and Populism in Partitioned Poland.* London, Orbis, 1973.

Bromke, A. *Poland's Politics: Idealism vs. Realism* (Russian Research Center Studies). Cambridge, MA, Harvard University Press, 1967.

Davies, N. *God's Playground: A History of Poland*, 2 vols. Oxford, Oxford University Press, 1982.

> *Heart of Europe: A Short History of Poland.* Oxford, Oxford University Press, 1986.

Dziewanowski, M. K. *The Communist Party of Poland: An Outline History* (Russian Research Center Studies). Cambridge, MA, Harvard University Press, 1967.

Garlinski, J. *Poland in the Second World War.* Basingstoke, Macmillan, 1985.

Garton Ash, T. *The Polish Revolution: Solidarity 1980–82* (revised edn). London, Granta (in asscn with Penguin), 1991.

Gomułka, S., and Polansky, A. (Eds). *Polish Paradoxes.* London, Routledge, 1990.

Kolankiewicz, G., and Lewis, P. *Poland. Politics, Economics, Society* (Marxist Regimes Series). London, Pinter, 1988.

Kołodko, G. W. *From Shock to Therapy: The Political Economy of Post-socialist Transformation.* Oxford, Oxford University Press, 2000.

Kubik, J. *The Power of Symbols Against the Symbols of Power: The Rise of Solidarity and the Fall of State Socialism in Poland.* University Park, PA, Pennsylvania University Press, 1994.

Landau, Z., and Tomaszewski, J. *The Polish Economy in the Twentieth Century.* London, Croom Helm, 1985.

Lane, D., and Kolankiewicz, G. (Eds). *Social Groups in Polish Society.* London, Macmillan, 1973.

Lukowski, J., and Zawadzki, H. *A Concise History of Poland.* Cambridge, Cambridge University Press, 2001.

Majkowski, W. *People's Poland: Patterns of Social Inequality and Conflict.* Westport, CO, Greenwood, 1985.

Millard, F. *The Anatomy of the New Poland.* Aldershot, Edward Elgar, 1994.

Miłosz, C. *The Captive Mind* (translated by Jane Zielomko), new edn. Harmondsworth, Penguin, 1980.

Polonsky, A. *Politics in Independent Poland: The Crisis of Constitutional Government, 1921–39.* Oxford, Clarendon Press, 1972.

  The Great Powers and the Polish Question, 1941–45: A Documentary Study in Cold War Origins. London, London School of Economics, 1976.

Roos, H. *A History of Modern Poland: From the Foundation of the State in the First World War to the Present Day* (translated by J. R. Foster). London, Eyre and Spottiswoode, 1966.

Rostowski, J. *Macroeconomic Instability in post-Communist Countries.* Oxford, Oxford University Press, 1998.

Sachs, J. *Poland's Jump to the Market Economy.* Cambridge, MA, MIT Press, 1993.

Sanford, G. *Military Rule in Poland: The Rebuilding of Communist Power, 1981–83.* London, Croom Helm, 1986.

Sanford, G., and Gozdecka-Sanford, A. *Historical Dictionary of Poland.* London, Scarecrow Press, 1994.

Staar, R. F. (Ed.). *Transition to Democracy in Poland.* New York, NY, St Martin's Press, 1998.

Staniszkis, J. *Poland's Self-Limiting Revolution* (edited by Jan. T. Gross). Princeton, NJ, Princeton University Press, 1984.

Swidlicki, A. *Political Trials in Poland, 1981–86.* London, Croom Helm, 1987.

Szajkowski, B. *Next to God . . . Poland: Politics and Religion in Contemporary Poland.* London, Frances Pinter, 1983.

Tworzecki, H. *Parties and Politics in post-1989 Poland.* Boulder, CO, Westview Press, 1996.

Wandycz, P. *The Lands of Partitioned Poland, 1795–1918* (A History of East Central Europe, Vol. 7). Seattle, WA, University of Washington Press, 1975.

Watt, R. M. *Bitter Glory: Poland and its Fate 1918–1939.* New York, NY, Hippocrene Books, 1998.

Weydenthal, J. B. de. *The Communists of Poland: An Historical Outline.* Stanford, CA, Hoover Institution Press, 1986.

Woodall, Jean (Ed.). *Policy and Politics in Contemporary Poland.* London, Frances Pinter, 1982.

Zamoyski, A. *The Polish Way: A Thousand-Year History of the Poles and Their Culture.* New York, NY, Hippocrene Books, 1998.

ROMANIA

Geography

PHYSICAL FEATURES

Romania (formerly the Socialist Republic of Romania) is a republic in South-Eastern Europe; much of the country forms part of the Balkan peninsula. In the south-east of the country there is a coastline of about 250 km (150 miles) along the Black Sea. The southern border is with Bulgaria and the south-western border is with Serbia (Serbia and Montenegro). Hungary lies to the north-west, Ukraine to the north and Moldova to the north-east. Romania has a total area of 238,391 sq km (92,043 sq miles).

The Carpathian Mountains form a horseshoe through central Romania, running south-east from the northern border and then, as the Transylvanian Alps or Southern Carpathians, traversing central Romania from east to west. The Transylvanian Alps rise to over 2,000 m in places, the mountain of Negoiul being the highest point in Romania, at 2,548 m (8,360 ft). South and east of the mountains lies the fertile Romanian Plain, the lowlands of Wallachia (along the Danube) and Moldavia (along the Siret and Prut Rivers, tributaries of the Danube). Most of the southern confines of Romania are marked by the River Danube (Dunărea). However, in the west of the country, the Banat region has a land border with Vojvodina, a part of Serbia. The Iron Gates hydroelectric power and navigation system is on the border with Serbia. In the east, before it reaches the Black Sea, the Danube turns north and flows parallel to the coast before entering the sea at the Delta Dunării (Mouths of the Danube), which forms a border with Ukraine. This area between the Danube and the Black Sea, which features Romania's only land border with Bulgaria, is the Dobrogea (Dobrudzha). The River Prut defines the north-eastern border and divides Romanian Moldavia from the former Soviet state of Moldova, or Moldavia. The plateau-land of north-west Romania, across the Carpathians from the plains, is known as Transylvania and was formerly a province of Hungary.

CLIMATE

The climate is continental, with cold, snowy winters and hot summers. Summers are milder and wetter in the mountains, and the Black Sea moderates the winters on the coast. The north and east suffer from drought if the summer is dry. The average summer temperature is 23°C (73°F) and the winter average is –3°C (27°F). The average annual rainfall for the whole of Romania is 637 mm (25 in), ranging from 1,000 mm in the mountains to 400 mm in the Danube delta.

POPULATION

Romanian is a Romance language, which evolved from the Latin spoken in Central Europe at the time of the Roman Empire, but with many archaic forms and influences from the

Slavonic languages, Hungarian, French and Turkish. It is the official language, although Hungarian (Magyar), German and other minority languages are also spoken. According to the census of March 2002, 89.5% of the total population were ethnic Romanians, 6.6% were ethnic Hungarians and 2.5% were Roma (Gypsies). There are also communities of Germans, Ukrainians (Ruthenians), Carpatho-Rusyns and Turks. Most of the population profess Christianity and are adherents of the Eastern Orthodox Church; about 87% of the population are members of the Romanian Orthodox Church. About 6% of the population are members of the Roman Catholic Church, using not only the Latin rite, but also Romanian (Uniate) and Armenian rites. Protestant churches are particularly strong among the Hungarian and German populations. There are also communities of the Old-Rite Christian Church (an Orthodox sect) and the Armenian-Gregorian Church. The Turks and Tatars are predominantly Muslim and, despite the decline in numbers caused by emigration, there is still a significant Jewish community.

The principal and capital city is Bucharest (Bucureşti), which is located in the south of the country, in the east of the historic territory of Wallachia. At March 2002 it had an estimated population of 1,921,751. Other major cities are: Iaşi (321,580), in the north-east, near the border with Moldova; Cluj-Napoca (318,027) in central Transylvania; Timişoara (317,651) in the west, in what was known as the Banat; Constanţa (310,526), a port on the Black Sea; Craiova (302,622), in the Jiu valley in the south; Galaţi (298,584), on the Danube near the borders with Moldova and Ukraine; and Braşov (283,901), in the centre of the country. The total population of the country at the 2002 census was 21,698,181, according to provisional results, and the population density was 91.0 per sq km. The Bucharest Municipality was the most densely populated region (8,074.6 per sq km in March 2002).

Chronology

106: Emperor Trajan made Dacia a province of the Roman Empire.

270: Rome abandoned Dacia to Visigothic invaders, the first of many incursions by peoples from the north and east.

1365: Emergence of independent principalities in Moldavia (now north-east Romania and parts of Moldova and Ukraine) and Wallachia (now south-west Romania), having formerly been Hungarian banates or border lordships.

1394: Wallachia became a dependency of the Ottoman Empire.

1457–1504: Reign of Ştefan III ('the Great') of Moldavia.

1512: Moldavia recognized Ottoman overlordship.

1593–1601: Reign of Mihail ('the Brave') of Wallachia, who briefly united Moldavia and Transylvania with his realm.

April 1856: Under the terms of the Treaty of Paris the principalities of Wallachia and Moldavia were unified, but remained under Turkish suzerainty; the Moldavian Bojar, Cuza, became the ruler.

1866: A prince of the House of Hohenzollern-Sigmaringen replaced the ousted Cuza as Carol I of Romania.

13 July 1878: By the Treaty of Berlin, Romania was recognized as an independent state and was ceded part of the Dobrogea.

27 March 1881: Romania was recognized as a kingdom.

1916: Romania entered the First World War after generous promises of territory by the Entente Powers; however, much of the country was occupied by the Axis Powers.

1919–20: Following the post-First World War peace treaties, Romania received Bessarabia, Bucovina, Transylvania, the Banat and Crisana-Maramureş.

1938: King Carol II established a royal dictatorship, suspending the Constitution and banning political parties.

27 June 1940: Romania ceded Bessarabia and Northern Bucovina to the USSR.

August 1940: Romania ceded southern Dobrogea to Bulgaria and northern Transylvania to Hungary.

September 1940: Carol II abdicated in favour of his son, Michael (Mihail), after having appointed Gen. Ion Antonescu as Prime Minister.

22 June 1941: Romania joined the German invasion of the USSR.

23 August 1944: Antonescu was arrested and Romania became a supporter of the Allied cause.

31 August 1944: Soviet troops entered Bucharest.

6 March 1945: The Soviets installed a 'puppet' government under Petru Groza.

November 1946: Elections were held and won by the communist-led National Democratic Front.

30 December 1947: The Romanian People's Republic was proclaimed following the abdication of King Michael under pressure from the ruling Romanian Workers' Party (RWP).

24 September 1952: A new Constitution, based on the Soviet model, was approved by the Grand National Assembly.

30 November 1952: Elections were held for the Grand National Assembly. Gheorghe Gheorghiu-Dej, First Secretary of the RWP, became absolute leader.

March 1965: Following Gheorghiu-Dej's death, Nicolae Ceauşescu was elected First Secretary of the RWP.

June 1965: The RWP changed its name to the Romanian Communist Party (RCP).

August 1965: A new Constitution was adopted; the country's name was changed to the Socialist Republic of Romania.

December 1967: Ceauşescu became President of the State Council.

1968: Romania refused to join in the Warsaw Pact's suppression of the 'Prague Spring' revolt in Czechoslovakia.

1971: Romania was admitted to the General Agreement on Tariffs and Trade (GATT—known as the World Trade Organization, WTO, from January 1995).

1972: Romania was admitted to the IMF and the World Bank.

March 1974: Ceauşescu became President of the Republic.

15 November 1987: Thousands of workers in Braşov demonstrated against the Government's economic policy; the local RCP headquarters was sacked.

December 1987: Protests took place in Timişoara and other cities. Following a three-day conference of the RCP, Ceauşescu announced improvements in food supplies and wage increases.

June 1988: Following a demonstration by 50,000 Hungarians outside the Romanian embassy in Budapest, the Romanian Government ordered the closure of the Hungarian consulate in Cluj-Napoca.

March 1989: In an open letter to the President, six retired RCP officials questioned Ceauşescu's uncompromising policies, accusing him of disregard for the Constitution.

15–17 December 1989: Mounting protests in Timişoara over attempts to arrest László Tőkes, an ethnic Hungarian pastor, culminated in the army opening fire on demonstrators.

21 December 1989: Ceauşescu was interrupted by hostile chanting during a speech in the centre of Bucharest. During a subsequent demonstration the police and army shot dead many of the protesters.

22–25 December 1989: Ceauşescu and his wife fled Bucharest, but were later captured near Târgovişte, summarily tried by a military tribunal and executed. Meanwhile, anti-Ceauşescu forces seized control of the radio and television stations, and a Council of the National Salvation Front (NSF) was formed.

26 December 1989: Ion Iliescu was declared President and Petre Roman was made Prime Minister.

27 December 1989: A final Securitate (secret police) assault on the television station was driven back by the army.

28 December 1989: The name of the country was changed by decree to Romania.

1 January 1990: The NSF Council abolished the Securitate.

24–29 January 1990: Following an announcement that the NSF would contest the elections that were to be held in May, anti-NSF demonstrations were held; these were dispersed by NSF loyalists, who later attacked the offices of parties opposed to the NSF.

February 1990: The NSF and opposition parties agreed on the formation of a 253-seat Provisional National Unity Council (PNUC), which elected a 21-member Executive Bureau with Iliescu as its President. A demonstration against Iliescu and the NSF was followed by one in support of the NSF by miners from the Jiu valley.

March 1990: Opposition groups led by George Serban drew up the Timişoara Declaration, which urged the banning of former communists from office and democratic reforms. There were disturbances between ethnic Hungarians and nationalist Romanians.

22 April 1990: Opposition supporters began an occupation of University Square in Bucharest.

20 May 1990: The NSF won decisively in the first free elections since 1937. Ion Iliescu was elected President with over 85% of the votes cast.

13–15 June 1990: Police forcibly removed the opposition supporters who had been occupying University Square, prompting unrest in which the police headquarters was set on fire and there was an attempt to take over the television station. Miners from the Jiu valley were transported to the capital by the Government, and later attacked anyone in Bucharest suspected of being an anti-Government sympathizer; at least six people were killed.

20 June 1990: Ion Iliescu (who later resigned the leadership of the NSF) was sworn in as President and appointed Petre Roman to head a new Government.

August 1990: Anti-Government demonstrations resumed in University Square, but the Mayor of Bucharest subsequently declared an indefinite ban on meetings and demonstrations in Bucharest's squares.

November 1990: The Prime Minister, Roman, was granted special powers by the National Assembly to rule by decree and hasten the reforms for the free-market economy, following the introduction of emergency economic measures in the previous month. There were various demonstrations, in Bucharest and elsewhere, against the Government's economic policies, against the re-emergence of the RCP as the Socialist Labour Party and demanding reunification with Soviet Moldova.

December 1990: President Iliescu met union leaders in an attempt to avoid a general strike being called over worsening living conditions; the Government agreed to demands that the second stage of its price liberalization programme be postponed.

26 December 1990: The former sovereign, King Michael, was expelled from the country during a 24-hour visit.

February 1991: Trading in foreign currencies commenced at six authorized Romanian banks. Land-reform legislation came into effect, returning arable land to agricultural workers.

14 August 1991: The Privatization Law was approved, providing for the distribution of 30% of the capital of state commercial companies by voucher to the general public, and for the sale of the remaining 70%.

27 August 1991: The Government announced its recognition of Moldova immediately after its parliament had declared its independence from the USSR; however, the following day President Iliescu referred to the inevitability of Moldova and Romania being reunited.

23–26 September 1991: Coal-miners in the Jiu valley went on strike over pay and conditions; when they demonstrated in Bucharest (as they had done in June, but relatively peacefully) violence broke out. The Roman Government resigned to enable the creation of a government of 'national opening'.

October 1991: Theodor Stolojan (former finance minister and President of the National Privatization Agency), at the invitation of President Iliescu, formed a new Government, which included members of the NSF, the National Liberal Party (NLP), the Agrarian Democratic Party and the Romanian Ecological Movement.

8 December 1991: A referendum approved the new Constitution, passed by the legislature in November.

March 1992: Local elections in February–April confirmed the decline in the popularity of the NSF and provoked a split in

the ruling party: a pro-Iliescu wing formed the Democratic National Salvation Front—DNSF, while a 'rump' NSF retained Roman as leader.

27 September 1992: Legislative and presidential elections were held. The DNSF won the greatest number of seats, with 117 of the 328 elective seats in the Assembly of Deputies, the lower chamber of Parliament, and 49 of the 143 seats in the Senate; the Democratic Convention of Romania (DCR), an opposition alliance, won 82 seats in the Assembly of Deputies and 34 seats in the Senate. Iliescu narrowly failed to win the required majority for immediate election as President.

11 October 1992: In a second round of voting, Iliescu, with 61% of the votes cast, defeated Emil Constantinescu, of the DCR, to be elected President.

November 1992: After extended negotiations, Nicolae Văcăroiu, a nominally independent bureaucrat, formed a Government consisting of equal numbers of DNSF members and independents.

May 1993: Price subsidies for many basic commodities and services were abolished, precipitating renewed industrial unrest.

9–10 July 1993: At its second national conference, the DNSF changed its name to the Party of Social Democracy of Romania (PSDR) and merged with several left-wing parties.

7 October 1993: After its application for membership had been rejected earlier in the year owing to its poor civil-liberties record, Romania was finally admitted to the Council of Europe.

26 January 1994: Romania became the first former communist country to sign a 'Partnership for Peace' agreement with the North Atlantic Treaty Organization (NATO).

18 August 1994: Two members of the ultra-nationalist Romanian National Unity Party (RNUP) were appointed to the Council of Ministers. In January 1995 the extreme nationalist parties in Parliament, the RNUP, the Greater Romania Party and the Socialist Labour Party (SLP), formally agreed to co-operate with the ruling PSDR.

May 1995: Romania ratified the Council of Europe's Framework Convention, which was that organization's first-ever legally binding instrument devoted to the general protection of national minorities.

June 1995: Following an increase in widespread dissatisfaction with the Government's economic record, workers in the energy sector, supported by the coal-miners and railway employees, held a three-day strike. Meanwhile, Romania formally applied for membership of the European Union (EU), with the backing of all political parties.

1 August 1995: The mass privatization scheme was instigated, with each Romanian over 18 years of age receiving vouchers worth 975,000 lei, which could be exchanged for shares in 4,000 state-owned enterprises.

June 1996: The ruling PSDR won the largest number of mayoral and council posts in local elections; however, there were allegations of electoral malpractice.

16 September 1996: Romania and Hungary signed a treaty of historic reconciliation, the Treaty of Understanding, Co-operation and Good Neighbourliness, in Timişoara, under which Hungary renounced claims to parts of Transylvania while Romania guaranteed a range of rights to its ethnic Hungarian population.

3 November 1996: In the general elections, the DCR won 122 of the 328 elective seats in the lower house and 53 of the Senate's 143 seats, while the PSDR took 91 and 41 seats, respectively, and the recently formed Social Democratic Union (SDU—a merger of the Democratic Party–DP, as the NSF was now known, and the Romanian Social Democratic

Party) obtained seats for 53 deputies and 23 senators. In the first round of the simultaneous presidential election Iliescu won 32.3% of the ballot, while his closest rival, Constantinescu, who was again the DCR's candidate, took 28.2%.

17 November 1996: In a second round of voting in the presidential election Iliescu was defeated by Constantinescu, who obtained 54.4% of the valid votes cast.

19 November 1996: The former trade unionist and Mayor of Bucharest, Victor Ciorbea, was nominated as Prime Minister. He later announced a radical economic reform programme.

12 December 1996: A coalition Government dominated by the DCR, but also including representatives of the SDU and the Democratic Alliance of Hungarians in Romania (DAHR), was sworn in.

8 August 1997: Some 20,000 workers took part in nationwide demonstrations against the announcement of the closure of 17 loss-making state enterprises.

11 August 1997: Several leading members of the PSDR, who had resigned from the party in the previous month, formed a new, centre-left party, the Alliance for Romania (AFR), led by a former foreign minister, Teodor Melescanu; the AFR held 13 seats in the lower house and two in the Senate.

19 November 1997: A rally in Bucharest organized by trade unions as part of an ongoing protest at increasing poverty was attended by some 40,000 people.

7 February 1998: Ciorbea announced the formation of a new Council of Ministers, which included members of the DCR as well as the DAHR and five independents; however, the DP refused to support the administration until Ciorbea was removed from office.

30 March 1998: Following increasing pressure from within the coalition, as well as continued social unrest, Ciorbea resigned as premier; President Constantinescu appointed the interior minister, Gavril Dejeu, as an interim Prime Minister.

15 April 1998: Radu Vasile, Secretary-General of the Christian Democratic National Peasants' Party (CDNPP—part of the DCR alliance), was confirmed as the new premier; his proposed coalition cabinet and his programme for accelerated market reform were also approved by the legislature.

25 June 1998: The Senate voted to forbid former secret police agents from holding public office; consequently, the Minister of Health, Francisc Baranyi, was dismissed from the Council of Ministers after admitting that he had collaborated with the Securitate.

4 January 1999: Miners in the Jiu valley went on strike, demanding a 35% pay increase and the reversal of a decision to close two coal mines. Following the Vasile Government's refusal to negotiate over the issue, 10,000–20,000 miners marched on Bucharest; however, violent clashes broke out between marchers and the security forces.

21 January 1999: Amid severe criticism of the security forces' management of the protest, the Minister of the Interior, Gabril Dejeu, was forced to resign. The following day an agreement was reached between the premier and the miners' leader, Miron Cozma, ending the strike.

15 February 1999: Cozma was sentenced *in absentia* to 18 years' imprisonment for his role in the miners' protests of 1991. In response, Cozma led a protest march of up to 4,000 miners; violence ensued between protesters and security forces, during which one miner died and more than 100 people were injured. Several hundred protesters, including Cozma, were arrested.

17 April 1999: Ciorbea and other members of the CDNPP resigned from the party in order to form the Christian Democratic National Alliance (CDNA).

19 June 1999: The Chamber of Deputies voted in favour of allowing the public access to the files of the Securitate; the legislation was promulgated by the President in December.

31 May 1999: The Chamber of Deputies approved amendments to the electoral law, increasing the threshold for parliamentary legislation from 3% to 5%, with alliances required to obtain a further 3% for each member party.

16 July 1999: The Supreme Court of Justice sentenced Gen. Victor Athanasie Stănculescu and Gen. Mihai Chiţac to 15 years' imprisonment for ordering the security forces to open fire on protesters during the Timişoara uprising in 1989; an appeal against the sentences was rejected in February 2000.

10 December 1999: Romania was one of six countries invited to begin negotiations on entry into the EU. Formal accession talks commenced on 15 February 2000.

13 December 1999: Amid continuing social unrest, President Constantinescu dismissed Vasile, after all seven CDNPP ministers and three NLP ministers had resigned from the cabinet, withdrawing their support for the premier; the Minister of Labour and Social Protection, Alexandru Athanasiu, was appointed interim Prime Minister.

17 December 1999: Constantinescu nominated the Governor of the National Bank of Romania, Mugur Isărescu, as Prime Minister. The legislature subsequently approved his appointment and that of a new Council of Ministers, which was largely unchanged.

30 January 2000: A cyanide spill at the Baia Mare gold mine released approximately 22m. gallons of the chemical into the Lapus river, poisoning the ecological system of the Tisza river and 2,000 km of the Danube.

3 February 2000: Following his expulsion from the CDNPP, Vasile established the far-right Romanian People's Party.

March 2000: A US $21m. plan to clear the wreckage of three bridges across the river Danube (Dunărea), destroyed during NATO air-strikes against Yugoslavia in April 1999, was announced; the blockage had resulted in financial losses of around $800m. in 1999. In the same month an agreement was reached between Romania and Bulgaria on the position of the new bridge on the Danube, to be funded by the EU-led Stability Pact for South Eastern Europe.

18 June 2000: The PSDR won the largest number of mayoral and council posts in local elections, obtaining 36.7% of the votes cast, followed by the DP, with 12.7% and the DCR, with 11.1%.

27 June 2000: Following his election as Mayor of Bucharest, Trăian Băşescu, hitherto Minister of Transport, was replaced by Anca Boangiu.

16 July 2000: Decebal Trăian Remes tendered his resignation as Minister of Finance, but Isărescu declined to accept the resignation. Remes resigned from the National Liberal Party in August, citing a perceived leftward shift in the party's policies.

26 November 2000: Legislative and presidential elections were held in Romania. Ion Iliescu of the PSDR received 36.4% of the votes cast in the first ballot of the presidential election, compared with 28.3% received by the second-placed candidate, Corneliu Vadim Tudor of the right-wing Greater Romania Party (GRP). In the legislative election, the PSDR won 155 seats in the Chamber of Deputies and 65 in the Senate, the GRP won 84 in the Chamber of Deputies and 37 in the Senate, with the DP and the NLP each obtaining 30 deputies and 13 Senate mandates.

10 December 2000: In the second ballot of the presidential election, Iliescu received 66.8% of the valid votes cast, compared with 33.2% obtained by Tudor. Iliescu assumed the presidency on 20 December and subsequently invited Adrian Năstase of the PSDR to form a minority government.

28 December 2000: Năstase's proposed Government was endorsed by the legislature, agreements having been signed with a number of opposition parties (although not the GRP).

19 January 2001: Năstase became the new leader of the PSDR, in place of Iliescu.

7 February 2001: A new law on the restitution of property nationalized in the communist era was promulgated by Iliescu.

6 March 2001: The CDNA re-merged with the CDNPP, from which it had broken away in 1999. Andrei Marga became the Chairman of the new party until July, when he was replaced by the former premier, Victor Ciorbea.

18 May 2001: Petre Roman was replaced as leader of the DP by Trăian Băsescu.

16 June 2001: The PSDR and the RSDP merged, to form the Social Democratic Party (SDP) under the leadership of Prime Minister Năstase.

29 September 2001: The Socialist Party of National Revival, a breakaway faction of the GRP, held its inaugural meeting and elected Ioan Radu, the Deputy Mayor of Bucharest, as its leader.

29 November–5 December 2001: Large-scale protests against declining living standards and government austerity were held in Bucharest and Brașov.

17 January 2002: The NLP and the AFR formally merged under the name of the former.

6 March 2002: The Government signed a 'social pact' with three of the five largest trade unions.

29 March 2002: The Government established a new National Anti-corruption Prosecution office, which was to commence operations in September.

23 August 2003: The Government ended a moratorium on the international adoption of Romanian children (following pressure from the USA); the ban had been imposed on EU advice.

24 August 2002: Former Prime Minister Theodor Stolojan was elected Chairman of the NLP.

12 September 2002: The Senate approved a law requiring all political parties to re-register by 31 December and to comprise a minimum of 10,000 members from at least 21 of the country's 41 administrative regions.

October 2002: Hungarian President Ferenc Mádl paid the first official visit to Romania by a Hungarian head of state.

10 November 2002: Local elections took place in 21 regions, with the SDP receiving the most votes.

21 November 2002: At a summit meeting held in Prague, Czech Republic, Romania was one of seven countries formally invited to join NATO in 2004; US President George W. Bush subsequently visited the country.

17 June 2003: The Presidents of Romania and Ukraine signed an accord confirming their mutual land border, as it was delineated in 1961, with the exception of the disputed border along the contintental shelf of the Black Sea.

19 June 2003: In a cabinet reorganization, the number of ministries was reduced from 23 to 14, and three new ministers were introduced: Minister of Health Mircea Buran, Minister of Education, Research and Youth Alexandru Athanasiu, and Minister of Labour, Social Solidarity and Family Affairs Elena Dumitriu.

4 July 2003: President Iliescu and President Vladimir Putin of Russia signed a Treaty on Friendly Relations and Co-operation, on which negotiations had begun in 1992 (leaving the contentious issue of the repatriation of Romanian gold and cultural items confiscated by the USSR for resolution by a separate joint commission).

History

Prof. TOM GALLAGHER

INTRODUCTION

Communist rule under Nicolae Ceaușescu ended violently and abruptly in Romania in 1989, but in the 1990s a protracted and incomplete transition from that social system occurred. A legacy of foreign occupation stretching over centuries, combined with sharp internal divisions—economic, cultural and, above all, ethnic—retarded the progress of democratization.

Romania peacefully acquired its independence in stages between 1856 and 1881, when it was recognized as a kingdom under a branch of the German Hohenzollern dynasty. The self-image of Romania as a Latin country, which has always believed itself to be an extension of the West towards the East, meant that it often differentiated itself from its neighbours. It might share the Orthodox religion with its Slav neighbours, but it stayed aloof from most of them, particularly Russia, which was seen as a long-term foe of Romanian independence. It is significant that independence was acquired through the skill of Romanian politicians in dealing with the Western powers, ensuring that Ottoman overlordship was not substituted by Russian control.

Along with Hungary, Romania was the only non-Slavic nation-state in the Danubian basin; however, co-operation was thwarted by the debilitating quarrel over Transylvania, part of Romania since 1918, but often under Hungarian rule for centuries before that. It was only at the beginning of the 21st century that reconciliation between the two peoples appeared to be making cautious progress. It was hardly surprising that recently acquired independence and dire threats to territorial integrity allowed nationalism to occupy a salient role in political culture. Nor was it any more surprising that, often against a background of misrule, rulers consistently sought legitimacy from citizens by invoking nationalism and portraying themselves as executors of 'the national mission'.

From 1881 to 1938 Romania enjoyed stable constitutional rule, which distinguished it from all other states in South-Eastern Europe; nevertheless, during this time institutions and civic culture were not democratic. The inability of a poorly institutionalized state to integrate new territories with large minority populations acquired after 1918 contributed to the collapse of democracy 20 years later; in 1945 Soviet forces effectively occupied the country. For the next 60 years indigenous forms of development were pursued in turn by right-wing populists and national communists, following an interlude of communist rule shaped by internationalist (in reality pro-Soviet) norms.

Between 1947 and 1989 the determination of the communist regime to retain absolute control over politics and society and oppose any liberal initiatives in economics, prevented the possibility of a democratic transition largely resourced and driven from within. The West indirectly contributed to the chain of events that led to the violent collapse of the dictatorship of Nicolae Ceauşescu in 1989. Although Western countries preferred to overlook systematic human rights abuse until the last years of Ceauşescu's rule, substantial loans were made available to the dictator. These were used to finance ill-conceived industrialization schemes that resulted in massive policy failures. At considerable cost to his people, Ceauşescu strove to repay these loans by 1990, but in December 1989 popular protests and a rebellion by second-ranking communists brought about his downfall.

THE FIRST PRESIDENCY OF ION ILIESCU

The state and party bureaucracy supported the former *apparatchik*, Ion Iliescu, once he appeared capable of defending its privileges in uncertain times. The promise of social protection secured Iliescu's election as President in May 1990 (he had been declared President in late 1989) and his re-election in 1992. Voters feared that the opposition's commitment to radical free market ideas would result in their further impoverishment, and its qualifications to govern were certainly far from impressive. The personality-based opposition parties with their fierce anti-communism had been a disincentive to change. President Iliescu gained popularity by relaxing the savage austerity of the Ceauşescu era. Collectivized villagers, elderly citizens and workers in heavy industry, all with reason to feel insecure about the future, found noisy electoral competition unsettling and were more comfortable with socialist paternalism.

In the early 1990s the ruling National Salvation Front (NSF—known as the Party of Social Democracy of Romania—PSDR, from 1993, and the Social Democratic Party—SDP, from 2001) was able to draw up a new Constitution and restructure on its own terms, or leave relatively unaltered, institutions such as the judiciary, the intelligence services and the armed forces. Pacts between government and opposition to shape the new political institutions, such as occurred in Poland and Hungary, were absent in Romania. The 1991 Romanian Constitution, largely forced through by the NSF, was opposed by most of the opposition. It contained no provision for the separation of powers between the executive, the legislature and the judiciary, and it allowed for centralized republican government, with the head of state enjoying important discretionary powers.

President Iliescu ruled on behalf of those who had benefited from the communist-era changes, which had seen property owners disinvested and a huge bureaucracy created to oversee a socialist state hostile to private initiative. In the 1990s large state subsidies were poured into loss-making industries, the managers of which often diverted public resources for their own private benefit. A poorly conceived attempt to create the semblance of a market economy occurred as Romania witnessed the emergence of a new oligarchy, largely composed of 'nomenklatura capitalists', mainly to be found in the privatized retail and service sectors. As early as 1992, what the media dubbed 'cardboard millionaires' were able to use their political connections to divert more than US $2,000m. from the largest state bank, BANCOREX, which they obtained in credits owing to their closeness to the NSF. BANCOREX continued to operate in this way for most of the 1990s, the Government ultimately paying for the losses out of the budget. A further source of illicit wealth were the 'hard' currency accounts Ceauşescu had amassed in foreign banks: former intelligence officers gained control of these and some became highly influential in the economic realm.

By exploiting nationalism, a poorly institutionalized and incompetent regime facing problems beyond its capacity nevertheless managed to remain in power into the second half of the 1990s. However, Iliescu, unlike Ceauşescu, could never enjoy a monopoly over nationalism. Separate nationalist parties emerged, which regarded foreign models of politics and economic change with suspicion and refused to abide by international norms in handling national minorities. These chauvinist parties were often drawn from the large body of functionaries who had benefited from the dictatorship's strategy of promoting ethnic Romanian interests at the expense of minority ones. They appealed to groups in the population most strongly conditioned by totalitarian rule or memories of foreign oppression. President Iliescu needed Western financial support to revive the economy and he desired a normalization of relations with the West to improve the legitimacy of his regime. For some years he adroitly manoeuvred between his chauvinist domestic allies and international bodies monitoring Romanian efforts to break with the communist past. However, Romania's gradual entry into a liberal international community limited his ability to manoeuvre. The external monitoring of human rights and government practices that Iliescu allowed meant that the façade democracy that, perhaps, he would have been most comfortable with, slowly gave way to a competitive system with enough genuine elements to secure his peaceful removal from office in 1996.

Iliescu hoped that Romania could benefit from Western economic and diplomatic support while being able to shape its own semi-authoritarian course. The restoration of 'most favoured nation' trading status by the US Congress in October 1992 was followed by the signing, on 17 November, of an association agreement with the European Community (known as the European Union—EU from November 1993), the first two major diplomatic successes enjoyed by Romania since 1990.

Evidence that Iliescu was still far from certain about whether to align with the West even in an opportunistic way was provided when Romania broke UN sanctions against Yugoslavia and became the only former communist country to sign a comprehensive treaty with the USSR. This treaty of friendship, signed in April 1991, gave the USSR an effective right of veto over any Romanian alliance with a Western country; however, it was abrogated by the collapse of the USSR six months later.

The need to delegitimize conflictual nationalism in South-Eastern Europe as a whole became a priority for the Western democracies from the mid-1990s onwards. Pressure was brought to bear on President Iliescu to sever links with the ultra-nationalist parties that had been part of the PSDR-led coalition since 1994. US persuasion also contributed to a breakthrough in Romanian-Hungarian state relations in 1996, with the signature of a bilateral treaty between the two states on 16 September.

REFORMIST INTERLUDE 1996–2000

The presidential and parliamentary elections of November 1996 coincided with widespread hopes that Romania stood a real chance of drawing closer to mainstream Europe. Many of the industrial workers who had kept President Iliescu in power since 1990 rejected him because his poorly institutionalized regime, with a daunting record of incompetence, was perceived to be jeopardizing their interests. By 1996 42% of the Romanian population lived below the subsistence level and a 35% decrease in living standards had occurred since 1989. The average monthly salary in early 1996 was equivalent to US $110, the second-lowest in the region. The majority of the population spent 60% of their income on food, the price of many basic commodities, above all foodstuffs, equalling or exceeding prices in Western Europe. Owing to malnutrition and inadequate heating, the incidence of tuberculosis in Romania increased in 1996 to 10 times the European average. The 1990s were in many ways a continuation of the tragic era encompassing much of the 20th century in which Romania experienced the disintegration of democracy, foreign occupations in both World Wars and the brutal replacement of a Western-leaning social system with a totalitarian state.

The election of Emil Constantinescu to the presidency in late 1996 constituted the first peaceful transfer of power in Romania since the 1930s. Hopes were growing that political parties would, for the first time, actually represent citizens' interests. The unexpected transfer of power to the opposition alliance known as the Democratic Convention of Romania (DCR) was a repudiation of the previous regime, rather than a positive endorsement for the opposition. No plan for economic reform had been formulated in advance by the Christian Democratic National Peasants' Party of Romania (CDNPP), the dominant force in the victorious alliance and the only major party of pre-Second World War age in the entire region to be restored to government in the 1990s. To form a viable administration, the DCR entered a coalition with the Democratic Party (DP), which had broken away from the pro-Iliescu wing of the NSF in 1992. The coalition was an ill-matched combination of inveterate anti-communists and reformist junior former communists.

It was the Prime Minister, Victor Ciorbea, who bore the brunt of the challenge of reform. He soon discovered how great was the shortage of loyal and competent officials willing to carry out overdue reforms. The Ciorbea Government emphasized a policy of *rapprochement* with neighbours and reconciliation with minorities. Where the new administration broke most decisively with the longstanding tradition of Romanian state nationalism was in its relations with Hungary and the 1.6m.-strong Hungarian minority resident in Romania. The domestic image of Romanians and ethnic Hungarians as 'insiders' and 'outsiders', respectively, locked in a majority-minority power relationship, was gradually abandoned and replaced by one that emphasized mutual co-operation. The party that represented the interests of the Hungarian minority, the Democratic Alliance of Hungarians in Romania (DAHR), was part of the governing coalition.

Despite having been elected to force through bold economic changes, the Ciorbea Government decided to concentrate most of its efforts on achieving membership of NATO. Doubts that Romania would be a consumer rather than a provider of security proved too strong, and in July 1997 Romania discovered that its membership bid had been unsuccessful. Soon the two main partners in the coalition Government, the CDNPP and the DP, were embroiled in disputes over patronage. Except for attempts to liberalize prices, economic reforms, hastily worked out at the end of 1996, were never really implemented. The IMF and other Western creditors lost patience with the Ciorbea Government, particularly over its failure to restructure state energy utilities. Under President Iliescu, the energy sector was well-funded because managers and workers provided a vital support base for a regime opposed to genuine privatization. The electricity, gas and petroleum utilities continued to operate, largely independent of the Government, while generating huge losses, which were covered by the state budget. The failure of the Ciorbea Government to match rhetoric with deeds had a dispiriting effect domestically and eroded foreign confidence in the ability of Romania to cast off a totalitarian legacy. On 30 March 1998 Ciorbea resigned. The CDNPP was demoralized and faction-ridden; it had shown itself unprepared for government and unable to define its priorities.

In mid-April 1998 a new premier, Radu Vasile, was appointed. He was contested by elements within his own party, the CDNPP, and distrusted by the President, who resented his greater popularity. His negotiating skills proved vital in the first months of 1999 when rebellious coal-miners, encouraged by the ultra-nationalist Greater Romania Party (GRP), marched on Bucharest to protest a series of mine closures that were intended to regain IMF confidence. Vasile persuaded the miners to desist from their march after they had routed police in several pitched battles. Order was restored in February after the arrest of the union leader, Miron Cozma, and the concessions, which Vasile had agreed under duress, were rescinded.

Under Vasile's influence relations slowly improved with the IMF, and in August 1999 a new loan was extended to Romania. In 1999 Romania avoided defaulting on a loan by paying just over US $2,500m. to service a debt of $9,000m., mainly acquired during the Iliescu period.

Powerful bureaucratic obstacles impeded the consolidation of democracy in the 1990s. A particularly damaging legacy of the Iliescu presidency was the existence of state bodies with near-identical functions, which often sought to neutralize each other's effectiveness. The existence of at least nine intelligence services attached to different military and civilian branches of state was the best known example. It was widely believed that the influence of the intelligence community stemmed from the fact that before 1989 many people active in public life across the political spectrum acted as informers, either voluntarily or through coercion. (In 1999 a new law still gave the main intelligence force significant control over millions of Securitate files, some of which had been selectively leaked since 1998 to discredit reformist politicians.)

The bicameral nature of Parliament proved troublesome for post-1996 administrations. The division of responsibilities between the lower and upper houses was unclear and the complexity of procedures delayed important reforms. The intricate nature of the Romanian justice system also impeded reform. The Supreme Court, the Constitutional Court and the Supreme Council of Magistrates had overlapping authority that rendered the system ineffectual. Few of the financiers arrested in 1997 on serious fraud charges had been successfully tried by the late 1990s.

The judiciary and prosecution services were among the branches of the state most damaged by communism. After 1989 low salaries and continuous political interference made the law-enforcement agencies prone to corruption. Moreover, there was a veritable army of bureaucrats who had no vested interest in seeing integration with Euro-Atlantic institutions succeed, because it would endanger the status quo. At the end of the 1990s, therefore, inexperienced reformers, grappling with the challenges of European integration, depended on an administrative élite steeped in authoritarian and collectivist values.

EXTERNAL SUCCESSES AND REPUDIATION AT HOME

In 1998 the European Commission decided that pre-accession states least prepared for entry would receive a disproportionately large share of funds from the EU in order to catch up with 'fast-track' candidates. Of potentially great significance was the proposal, made in October 1999 by Günther Verheugen, the EU Commissioner for Enlargement, for a partnership between the EU, other multilateral bodies and the Romanian Government, to advance a medium-term reform programme and rebuild administrative institutions. The Vasile Government accepted Verheugen's request that the EU would play an active role in supervising the formulation and implementation of a development strategy in 2000–04.

The event that undoubtedly strengthened Romania's European standing was the Government's support of NATO's intervention in the Yugoslav (Serb) province of Kosovo in 1999 following systematic human rights violations against its Albanian population. Faced with a choice between religious and historical ties with Serbia and persisting, in dangerous circumstances, with a pro-Western foreign policy, the Romanian Government quickly concluded that it had no alternative but to align with NATO. The pro-NATO stance of a previously fractured Government was bold, especially in light of the fact that public opinion, under the influence of a nationalist media, was turning against the Western Alliance.

Three days after Romania was formally invited to begin EU accession negotiations, on 13 December 1999, Radu Vasile was dismissed as Prime Minister, following the resignation of most of his ministers. Serious doubts regarding the constitutional validity of Vasile's dismissal by the President were outweighed by the fact that he was in conflict with Constantinescu, as well as most of his party and the privatization chief. A similar, multi-party coalition was quickly reassembled, under the leadership of Mugur Isărescu, Governor of the National Bank of Romania since 1991 (the longest an important state position had been held by any one person). As Governor of the National Bank, he had provided financial stability at a time when the economy otherwise lacked a strong reformist momentum.

Divided reformers accepted the active assistance of multilateral organizations in order to draw up a strategy for economic recovery. However, drawing closer to the West was unable to save them from electoral rejection at home. By 2000 most of the population, around 40% of which was facing absolute poverty, was no longer prepared to accept further economic misery in return for progress on foreign-policy goals. A nervous President Constantinescu abandoned a second-term bid for power in July, rather than face the wrath of voters on the campaign trail.

With presidential and parliamentary elections due in November 2000, the PSDR entered the campaign with a decisive lead. Iliescu had a strong following among one-third of the electorate, represented in the rural, elderly, and poorly-educated sections of the population, whose loyalty had proved unshakeable, regardless of the accusations about his record in government.

The PSDR obtained a near majority of seats in the legislative election of 26 November 2000 (155 of the 346 seats in the Chamber of Deputies, and 65 of the 140 Senate seats), but it was the beneficiary of a frustrated vote rather than the repository of hopes that it would perform better in government than the outgoing coalition. Far more unsettling was the remarkable success of the anti-Western GRP, which reconciled the political extremes of left and right. It secured many of the votes of the collapsed centre, as well as those of younger voters, acquiring about 25% of the seats in parliament (84 in the Chamber of Deputies, and 37 in the Senate), compared with a combined total of just 27 in 1996. Its fiercely anti-minority leader Corneliu Vadim Tudor, formerly Ceauşescu's propagandist, became the prime beneficiary of the rift between the main parties and society at large, where the chief political players were often viewed as remote and ready to promote their group interests at the expense of most ordinary Romanians.

In the presidential election, also held on 26 November 2000, Iliescu obtained only 8% more of the votes cast than Tudor, failing to achieve the required majority, which resulted in a second round of voting on 10 December. The GRP's electoral campaign concentrated on the elimination of corruption, as had the campaign that helped to secure Emil Constantinescu's unexpected victory in the presidential election of 1996. The fact that sections of the GRP, as well as its leader, had had close ties with ex-members of the Ceauşescu-era intelligence services, who had flourished through operating in the 'black' economy, scarcely diluted the party's appeal. The GRP was regarded as having an unblemished record, because it was the only sizeable party not to have been in government after 1989; the fact that Vadim lacked a record of administrative failure enabled many voters to project on to him their wishes for the future.

REFORMIST HOPES INVESTED IN THE SDP

Iliescu won the second round of the presidential election, held on 10 December 2000, with 67% of the votes cast. International agencies and major governments, which had been working to integrate Romania with mainstream European institutions, welcomed the result. In previous months, the PSDR had striven hard to shed an anti-Western image. Despite being a late convert to economic reform, it was hoped that the incoming Prime Minister, Adrian Năstase, would emerge as a vigorous proponent of Euro-Atlantic integration.

The PSDR had already agreed to support the development plan for 2000–04, worked out between the Isărescu Government and the EU and intended to prepare Romania for EU membership. However, Năstase adopted a more independent stance towards the IMF than his recent predecessors. The IMF was unhappy with Năstase's plan to maintain a budgetary deficit of 4.0%–4.5%, in order to provide a social 'safety net' for lower-income voters in areas of economic decline. In talks with the Fund in March 2001, however, he argued that the Romanian population could not endure further economic privation and that structural reforms involving the closure of loss-making factories were only feasible politically if economic provisions to mitigate the effects of mass redundancies were quickly put in place. The IMF regarded banking reform and the privatization of the energy utilities as vital, in order to create a viable foundation for the functioning of a successful market economy. It agreed with the view, expressed in March by the EU's Permanent Representative to Romania, that Romania could not yet be regarded as a functioning market economy. By 2002 only one-third of the economy had been privatized, but it was this sector that provided almost all the tax revenue. A stand-by loan was agreed with the IMF in October 2001, but the Fund continued to be unhappy about the Government's slowness in restructuring the energy sector and its failure to reduce the level of arrears owed to the budget by state companies. However, a major breakthrough had been the privatization of the Sidex steel mill at Galaţi, the largest in Central and South-Eastern Europe, which was sold to LNM/ISPAT, an Anglo-Indian consortium, in July. The ailing plant accounted for 5% of gross domestic product (GDP) and had been a huge drain on state finances. In 2002 economic indicators were healthier than they had been since the mid-1990s, and in 2001 the economy grew at a rate of 5.3%, ending four years of contraction or minimal growth. This, and other improvements, led credit ratings agencies to upgrade Romania's country risk score.

In 2001 Năstase replaced Iliescu as Chairman of the ruling party (by this time renamed the SDP) and attempted to establish his long-term political dominance, as the SDP extended its influence into every corner of political life. Năstase was not afraid to promote nationalism in an attempt to detach voters from the extremist GRP, and he insisted that the central state retain its primacy after encountering demands for regional autonomy from both Romanians and the large ethnic Hungarian minority in Transylvania. However, he was willing to abandon a confrontational stance towards the Hungarian minority party, the DAHR. By not regularly demanding concessions from its partners as a price for staying in government, the DAHR had been a rare stabilizing factor in the previous Government. It gave the SDP parliamentary support in return for a range of concessions meant to preserve the cultural identity of the Hungarian minority. However, there was concern among normally moderate DAHR representatives that the party had conceded too much, and a split in the party took place in March 2003.

In 2002 Năstase proposed altering the Constitution to permit the President to be elected by Parliament rather than by the electorate, an idea that was quashed by Iliescu. Parliament was one of the most unpopular institutions in the country, and if the right to elect a President was transferred to it, the credibility of a still-fragile democracy would have been undermined. In general, however, the chronic weakness of the opposition enabled legislation to work its way through Parliament more speedily. This made Năstase's Government the most stable that Romania had known since 1989. However, the lack of effective parliamentary scrutiny was a disadvantage, and the Prime Minister would need to retain a strong grip on his party in order to prevent authoritarian instincts and a desire to treat state property as its own from harming both the SDP's image and that of Romania. In January 2002 Năstase reacted strongly to a report, which had been distributed electronically to foreign embassies and news agencies, focusing on the personal wealth of the Prime Minister and his family. Most of the claims had already been published by the press or aired in parliamentary debates; nevertheless, on 17 January the Prosecutor-General's Office ordered the detention of those allegedly involved in the report's distribution. Four days later Năstase admitted that the authorities had overreacted and that the Government and public institutions were still learning how to cope with criticism. The affair focused attention on the fact that although Năstase headed a left-wing party, he was one of Romania's wealthiest politicians. Trained in international law, he was one of the few relatively young officials who had been permitted to travel freely by the 'hardline' communist regime.

In 2002, despite Romania having made halting progress on the domestic reform front, the USA was willing to draw up a less onerous set of conditions than before to enable Romania to enter NATO. The catalyst for this change of approach was the suicide attacks on the USA of 11 September 2001, carried out by Islamist extremists. Henceforth, the strategic importance of countries bordering, or adjacent to, the Black Sea, and by extension the Middle East, increased significantly, particularly as the prospect of US-led military action to remove from power the regime of the Iraqi President, Saddam Hussein, steadily mounted. The USA increasingly regarded foreign-policy dangers and threats in terms of terrorism, judging its allies and partners on their readiness to show purposeful engagement in countering that threat. Both Romania and Bulgaria made clear their willingness to assist the USA. Accordingly, their chances of being invited to join NATO had increased dramatically by March 2002, when a summit meeting of the candidate countries for NATO membership was held in Bucharest. The USA for the first time gave a clear official indication that it desired the widest possible NATO enlargement, declaring that no country would be left out of NATO on geographical or historical criteria, or owing to pressure from any outside power. On 1 August Romania became one of the first countries in the world to sign a contentious bilateral agreement with the USA, granting US soldiers and diplomats immunity from prosecution by the International Criminal Court (ICC), a global war crimes court under UN jurisdiction—a request disputed by many US allies. The USA was thus the driving force behind the second phase of NATO expansion, decided at the Alliance's summit held in Prague, the Czech Republic, on 21–22 November 2002. Romania subsequently gave conspicuous endorsement to the USA's military campaign in Iraq, against strong disapproval from such European powers as France and Germany.

Peace-keeping was the main thrust of the EU's emerging Common Foreign and Security Policy, and in August 2002 the European Commission condemned Romania for pursuing its own unilateral course. In its 2002 report on Romania's progress towards accession, the Commission declared that Romania was the only candidate country that continued to lack a market economy; this was despite the fact that Romania was the second-largest recipient of EU funding

designed to prepare it to withstand the rigours of full membership. The EU required a far deeper transformation of the Romanian state than did NATO. The NATO entry requirements were largely technical, involving the need to reduce in size and modernize the armed forces. In the past, NATO had also insisted on political pluralism and economic reform, but the emphasis on issues of governance and human rights became gradually more muted as other concerns took priority. On 21 November 2002 Romania obtained its greatest foreign-policy success for many years, when it was invited to open negotiations to join NATO in 2004, and on 26 March 2003 it signed the Accession Protocol, which made full membership almost certain.

In late 2002 several thousand US military personnel arrived in Romania to refit and occupy installations near the port of Constanța. However, with the major Western democracies divided over the merits of forcibly imposing regime change in Iraq, many in the EU felt by early 2003 that Romania was unlikely to be a reliable advocate of a common foreign policy. There was deep unease in Romania when, at a special EU summit on the Iraq crisis, French President Jacques Chirac criticized candidate countries for expressing support for military action, while their position remained uncertain with regard to EU accession. Of the former communist countries of the 'new Europe', which had allied themselves with the USA over Iraq, Romania was particularly vulnerable to EU retaliation, owing to the scale of its economic problems and the lengths to which it had gone to co-operate with the USA. The President of the European Commission, Romano Prodi, declared in February that EU candidate countries could not expect to 'share their economy with the EU and their security with the USA'.

The EU also made clear its concerns over corruption, specifically with regard to the €1,000m. that Romania was due to receive from the EU by 2006 in pre-accession support, and stipulated that it would monitor Romania's ability to absorb such sums before EU accession was approved. By this time, it was becoming impossible for the EU to ignore the emergence of an oligarchy based around the ruling SDP. It had taken shape during the Government's first extended period in office until 1996, when a wealthy new class had emerged, as state property was informally transferred to private hands, lucrative contracts were granted to government supporters, and virtually interest-free bank loans were awarded to SDP and state officials. The political protectors of this oligarchy returned to office in 2000, just as large amounts of EU funds began to pour into the country. The EU had failed to devise a customized strategy for Romania that took into account the problems arising from the nature of its totalitarian legacy, with a political class largely composed of individuals who, despite the communist backgrounds of many, were essentially concerned with acquiring personal fortunes courtesy of the state, and subsequently the EU. The Union lacked the capacity to check that all pre-accession funds were spent in the manner intended. In some quarters, directing huge amounts of funding to a country where the public service continued to display a chronic lack of professionalism, and where most government parliamentarians ran their own businesses, was considered to be a major stimulus for corruption.

Most SDP notables do not welcome a strong foreign presence in the economy if it results in the implementation of business practices and a stringent regulatory framework at variance with their informal approaches to money-making. Many prefer the Government to subsidize failing state industries or indebted utilities because of the favourable links that they have built up with the state sector over the years. Under pressure from both the EU and the IMF, Romania declared its determination in early 2003 to sell 70 large and mostly insolvent state companies by the end of the year. The privatization agency hoped to attract investors who would maintain the same company activities and minimize staff reductions. However, such an objective was unlikely to be realized, owing to the weak international economy and lack of investor confidence in Romania. The survival of these economic giants prevented Romania from becoming a functioning market economy, and may prevent it from completing its negotiations for EU entry by 2007, the official target date. With much reform still only at the planning stage, Romania would have to close negotiations by the end of 2004, if 2007 was to be a realistic date for accession. Some observers argued that Romania was unlikely to be ready for EU accession until 2010, at the earliest. A communique issued at an EU summit, held in Athens, Greece, in April, confirming the scheduled accession of 10 countries (many of them from Central and South-Eastern Europe) to the EU in 2004, made no mention of Romania as a future member, nor of 2007 as a target date for further expansion.

Resolute action must be taken to combat corruption. In 2001 Transparency International, an organization that measures perceived corruption world-wide, classified Romania as among the worst-offending countries in Eastern Europe, just above Russia. To satisfy EU concerns, a package of anti-corruption measures was passed by Parliament at the end of March 2003. It was the latest in a series of laws creating specialist structures within different ministries to target the issue. However, the Government delayed submitting the legislation to international scrutiny by civil society representatives, and was subsequently criticized for key failings. The legislation did not require the detailed listing of assets, and officials were only required to reveal ownership of a bank account, not the amount in it. This made it difficult to establish whether an official had accumulated significant assets while in office. Moreover, many valuable assets, such as land not used for farming, certain kinds of property, jewellery, and art collections, did not need to be declared. The law also stipulated that only assets and services with a value exceeding €300 each needed be declared by officials who received them during their period of duty—a high maximum level for a country where the monthly wage is half that sum.

An affair relating to the collapse of the National Investment Fund represented a test of the Romanian authorities' determination to tackle corruption. The Fund had collapsed in 2000, causing some 300,000 people to lose their savings. Branches of the Fund were largely run by former intelligence agents and the domestic intelligence agency appeared to have shown little interest in elucidating the causes for its collapse. The affair resurfaced in March 2003, when Ioana Maria Vlas,

the Fund's former manager, returned to Romania from Israel to co-operate with the authorities; she was alleged to have been involved in advising leading notables to withdraw their investments before the collapse of the Fund.

The much weakened centre-right parties in opposition had failed to capitalize on the Government's failings. Instead, polls showed the extremist GRP in second place to the ruling party. It suited the SDP surreptitiously to boost the prospects of the GRP, since Năstase could then present it to the West as the only alternative to his own party. Fears that the SDP was attempting to acquire a monopoly of power were intensified by various laws passed from 2001. In 2003 new legislation ensured that officials appointed to administrative posts on political criteria could occupy them indefinitely, even in the event of a change of government. Meanwhile, according to a law adopted in 2002, new political parties required 25,000 founding members in order to register, and each party was required to have members from at least one-half of the country's administrative divisions, thus obstructing the creation of local or regional parties. In addition, the media was threatened with the imposition a draft law, allowing those perceived to have shown contempt for the Romanian nation through the written or spoken word to be imprisoned for between two and five years. In parts of Romania where powerful SDP figures dominated the local administration, the opposition media had been subjected to systematic harassment. Ironically, the only direct check on the SDP came from the party's founder, Iliescu, who was nearing the end of the second full presidential term permitted him by the Constitution. He had invested his political might in the eradication of corruption from the SDP, and in February 2003 he criticized Năstase during a televised broadcast, accusing him of arrogance and authoritarianism. However, Iliescu had his own senior allies in the party, who had acquired their wealth, in the past, by exploiting the party's monopoly of power. The main motive for his offensive against Năstase's regime appeared to be a desire to remain the dominant figure in the SDP when he stepped down as Head of State at the end of 2004. As mentioned above, there was growing concern in the EU that numerous power-holders in Romania were primarily interested in diverting EU funds for private gain, rather than using the funds to reform the country. It was difficult to see how Romania could be allowed to join the EU in the foreseeable future with vital reforms still very much at the planning stage. Were EU accession to occur, however, some EU states feared the large-scale migration of the population westwards, as ordinary Romanians seek to take advantage of the opportunity to begin new lives in better-governed nations.

The Economy

ALAN SMITH

INDUSTRIALIZATION AND EXTERNAL ECONOMIC RELATIONS IN THE COMMUNIST PERIOD

The economic policies pursued during the communist period and during the era of Nicolae Ceauşescu (1965–89) in particular, complicated the process of transition to a market economy in Romania. Economic policy in the communist period entailed an extreme variant of the Stalinist policy of rapid industrialization. This involved the construction of a heavy industrial base in a predominantly agrarian economy, the collectivization of agriculture and the transfer of labour from agriculture to industry, together with the introduction of a highly centralized system of economic management and restrictions on the private sector.

Industrial growth was achieved by allocating a large (and growing) proportion of national income to investment, concentrated in heavy industry. A low priority was given to investment in infrastructure and social and cultural facilities. The strategy of industrialization was accelerated when Ceauşescu came to power in 1965, with greater emphasis on investment in the machine-tool and petrochemical industries. Ceauşescu's over-ambitious targets for industrial development created major imbalances between the demand for energy and raw materials and domestic sources of supply.

In 1967 the Ceauşescu Government embarked on the strategy of 'import-led' growth. The strategy was intended to facilitate imports of Western machinery and equipment and to encourage the development of 'joint ventures' and 'co-operation agreements' with Western multinational corporations in order to modernize Romanian industry. However, the strategy suffered from basic flaws. It attempted to build up a technological base in advanced engineering industries (including aviation), in which Romania had little experience and expertise, rather than developing and enhancing Romania's traditional strengths in the production of food and beverages, clothing, furniture, footwear, light industrial products and household goods. Multinationals were reluctant to invest in advanced engineering industries and Romania was forced to borrow 'hard' currency to make direct purchases of machinery and equipment to a far greater degree than was intended. The new industries failed to generate sufficient exports to the West to service debt and to finance a continued flow of imports of machinery and equipment, and energy, raw materials and components and spare parts to keep imported equipment in operation. By the mid-1970s Romania was experiencing major balance-of-payments difficulties and encountered growing problems in servicing its external debt. These were exacerbated by a decline in output of crude petroleum following an earthquake in 1977, with its epicentre in the major crude petroleum-producing regions, which turned Romania into a net petroleum importer. The increase in world petroleum prices in 1979 and Romania's dependence on crude petroleum imported from the Organization of the Petroleum Exporting Countries (OPEC) resulted in unsustainable balance-of-payment deficits and external debt, which forced Romania to suspend interest payments and to reschedule debt in 1982.

The need to reschedule debt resulted in an abrupt change in Romanian economic policy in the 1980s as Ceauşescu gave priority to the repayment of hard-currency debt. The low level of competitiveness of Romanian exports in Western markets meant that surpluses in the balances of trade and payments could only be achieved by a drastic reduction in imports, followed by the export of items with a low level of processing, such as food, energy and other basic consumer goods that were also in high domestic demand. By 1989 imports from the industrial West had been reduced to one-third of their 1980 levels and in April 1989 Ceauşescu announced that Romanian external debt had been eliminated.

The repayment of debt created enormous hardship for the majority of the population, and caused major damage to industry and infrastructure. Romania became a net exporter of food, while severe food shortages and food queues appeared in major cities. The Government also imposed draconian restrictions on household energy consumption, while prioritizing energy supplies to industry. Imports of machinery and equipment were drastically restricted, resulting in the failure to modernize industry and infrastructure, including transport and telecommunications. At the same time, valuable resources allocated to investment were squandered on grandiose 'prestige' investment projects, such as the Presidential Palace in Bucharest and the Danube–Black Sea Canal.

PROBLEMS OF THE TRANSITION TO A MARKET ECONOMY

The transition to a market economy, the restructuring of industry and agriculture and macroeconomic stabilization were implemented far more slowly in Romania following the collapse of communism than in the transition economies of Central Europe. This reflected a combination of adverse starting conditions, lack of political support for radical reforms and bureaucratic obstruction. The high degree of concentration of power and centralization of the economic system, added to the greater degree of isolation of citizens from foreign ideas and contacts during the Ceauşescu era, meant that the population at large had very limited experience of market-type reforms under communism. A population

that had already endured nearly a decade of extreme austerity during the debt-repayment programme was reluctant to withstand the impact of the radical economic changes associated with a rapid transition to a market economy. This strengthened the position of those members of the former elite who opposed structural change. However, the delay in creating the mechanisms of a functioning market economy and in restructuring and modernizing obsolete industries created further problems, including a major growth in inequality and poverty. Successive governments experienced difficulties in balancing budgets when confronted with a low tax base and pressures for expenditure on welfare, which resulted in high rates of monetary growth and inflation. The slow pace of modernization of industry and agriculture also contributed to the survival of an uncompetitive economy, producing relatively obsolete products, with high levels of overstaffing. This resulted in unsustainably high deficits in the balances of trade and payments, while low levels of foreign investment forced Romania to rely on 'stand-by' credits from the IMF to finance current-account deficits. This, in turn, required governments to submit to IMF conditions to pursue more restrictive financial and monetary policies and to accelerate reforms, which met with only modest success.

The internal problems experienced by Romania were aggravated by geographical and international factors. The greater distance from the richer members of the European Union (EU) added to the costs and difficulty of exporting to Western Europe, and made Romania a less attractive destination for foreign direct investment. The civil conflict in the former Yugoslavia compounded problems of developing trade links with Western Europe.

ECONOMIC POLICY IN THE TRANSITION

The transition to a market economy from 1989 until 2003 can be divided into three distinct political phases. The first covered the Governments of 1990–96 of the National Salvation Front (NSF—known as the Party of Social Democracy of Romania—PSDR, from 1993–2001, and subsequently renamed the Social Democratic Party—SDP). These Governments pursued a gradual (or partial) transition to a market economy, which involved a slow pace of privatization, the continuation of large subsidies to loss-making, state-owned industries (including coal-mining, power-generation, metallurgy and engineering, railways and air transport), limited reforms to the agrarian sector and highly limited reforms to the financial sector. The slow pace of macroeconomic stabilization resulted in high budgetary deficits and continued high rates of inflation, while ongoing subsidies to loss-making industries diverted government expenditure away from investment in infrastructure, housing, education and the development of an effective system of public welfare. The diversion of resources to loss-making industries also impeded industrial modernization and the development of industrial and services sectors that were responsive to consumers' demands.

The second phase began in November 1996, when the PSDR administration was replaced by a coalition Government led by the centre-right Democratic Convention of Romania (DCR). The change in administration marked a major shift of emphasis in economic policy, towards market-orientated reforms constructed with the assistance of the IMF and modelled on the experience of the more successful transition economies of Central and South-Eastern Europe. However, the implementation of market-orientated policies was impeded by continual policy disputes within the Government itself and by resistance to reforms by the Parliament, state bureaucrats and managers of state-owned enterprises. The DCR Government presided over a period of economic decline, growing unemployment, resurgent open inflation, and a decline in real wages and real incomes, which contributed to growing popular discontent with the Government. The Government was heavily defeated in the parliamentary and presidential elections, held in November–December 2000. This resulted in the return of a minority Government formed by the PSDR and the beginning of the third political phase of economic policy since the collapse of communism. The new parliamentary leadership of the PSDR was dominated by the reformist wing of the party, which made membership of the EU a major objective. This required the Government to attempt to accelerate economic reform and to implement a macroeconomic stabilization programme with the support of the IMF and subject to IMF conditionality. Although by mid-2003 it had met with only moderate success, the new Government had demonstrated far greater competence in implementing a reform strategy than its predecessor.

Gradualist Economic Policies and Restructuring, 1990–96

The immediate priority of the Government of the NSF, which took power following the December 1989 revolution, was to win popular support by improving consumption, suppressed during the policy of debt-repayment. Constraints on household consumption were eased as exports of food and energy were restricted and imports of the most urgently needed items were increased. Retail prices in state stores remained at their communist levels until November 1990, a control that required growing subsidies from the state budget, while total money incomes from all sources grew by 25%. These policies could not be sustained in the long term. In late 1990 the Prime Minister, Petre Roman, introduced a programme of structural reforms, intended to bring about the transition to a market economy within a two-year period. The programme included the gradual liberalization of prices and the removal of subsidies to basic consumer goods, including food products. A stabilization programme, involving strict fiscal and monetary policies, was drawn up with the approval of the IMF. Wages and salaries were only partially indexed to price rises, to prevent an inflationary wage-price spiral, resulting in a decline in real wages. These measures provoked public hostility, reflected in the violent demonstrations by miners in Bucharest in September 1991, which led directly to the collapse of the Roman Government.

The overthrow of the Roman administration heralded a return to a slower pace of privatization of industry and banking, more gradual structural change and more relaxed macroeconomic policies. Roman's immediate replacement as Prime Minister, Theodor Stolojan, was unable to implement the austerity policies required to bring down inflation, which reached 223% in 1991 and 199% in 1992, or to bring about structural reforms that could have resulted in large-scale unemployment.

Following elections in September 1992 a minority Government was formed, headed by the pro-Iliescu wing of the NSF, which ruled with the support of socialist and nationalist parties that were broadly opposed to a rapid transition to a market economy, with Nicolae Văcăroiu as Prime Minister. The Government's half-hearted commitment to structural reform and inflationary macroeconomic policies brought it into conflict with the IMF. The Government continued to grant subsidies to loss-making state-owned enterprises and tolerated major overstaffing and high wage levels in public utilities. This resulted in high costs of production, which contributed to inflation and adversely affected the competitiveness of domestic industry. By the end of 1995 only 8% of state-owned industrial capital had been privatized. The development of a small-scale private sector *de novo* was slower than that of the Czech Republic, Hungary and Poland, as the financial sector remained predominantly under state control and failed to provide the nascent private sector with capital for development, while the services sector expanded far less rapidly than in other transition economies.

A brief attempt was made to bring about macroeconomic stabilization in 1993–94. The National Bank of Romania (NBR), under the governance of Mugur Isărescu, introduced a strategy that included more restrictive monetary and fiscal policies and the maintenance of a stable nominal exchange rate after a sharp devaluation. The strategy had some initial success. Annual consumer-price inflation was reduced from 256% in 1993 to 28% in 1995. Economic growth, which had started at a modest 1.5% in 1993 (after a decline in gross domestic product—GDP—of 25% in 1990–92), accelerated to 3.9% in 1994 and to 7.1% in 1995. Nevertheless, the improvement in economic performance proved to be short-lived, as the Government attempted to expand domestic demand from the beginning of 1995, with parliamentary and presidential elections approaching in November 1996. Inflation increased, to 57% in 1996, and the current-account deficit surged to US $2,671m. The full impact of the inflationary pressures that had been released by expansionary policies was suppressed by the maintenance of price controls over large-scale state-owned industry. The Government also introduced controls over the foreign-exchange market, which effectively involved the rationing of foreign exchange to favoured customers. This prevented the exchange rate from falling to a level of equilibrium, thereby preventing an increase in the price of imported goods and also denied potential importers access to foreign exchange, preventing a further deterioration in the balance of payments. This policy brought the Government into direct conflict with the IMF, which suspended its stand-by agreement in April 1996.

Economic Policy and Reforms in 1996–2000

The elections of November 1996 resulted in the return of a centre-right, DCR-dominated, coalition Government, under the leadership of Victor Ciorbea. The Government announced plans to implement a policy, drawn up in consultation with the IMF, which was broadly similar to the 'shock-therapy' programme implemented in Poland in the early 1990s. The policy involved tighter fiscal and monetary policies, including a major reduction in the budgetary deficit and the elimination of 'soft' credits by the central bank to agriculture and industry. This necessitated reductions in government expenditure and increases in value-added tax (VAT) and in duties on alcohol and tobacco. The Government also announced that it would accelerate measures to restructure the economy and would pursue a more market-orientated microeconomic policy. This included: the removal of price controls; the elimination of subsidies on consumer goods, including fuel and foodstuffs; the removal of subsidies to loss-making enterprises and public utilities; and the liberalization of the foreign-exchange market and the abolition of import controls. The Government's economic programme included proposals to accelerate the privatization of industry and the banking sector; to restructure public utilities, particularly in the energy sector; to close loss-making coal-mines and a number of enterprises in the metallurgical, engineering and petrochemical industries; and to undertake agricultural reforms.

The Government's macroeconomic policy resulted in a substantial reduction in real incomes. The liberalization of the foreign-exchange market resulted in the halving of the nominal value of the leu between November 1996 and February 1997. Price liberalization released repressed inflationary pressures, resulting in an annual inflation rate of 154.8% in 1997. Real wages fell by one-third in the first three months after the elections, with income inequality widening and a large number of low-wage earners falling into poverty, as salaries failed to keep pace with price increases for energy and foodstuffs. In 1997 real GDP declined by 6.9% and industrial output by 5.9%. This partly resulted from the restructuring and closure of loss-making industries, and partly from reductions in real wages, which affected demand for consumer goods and services, compounding the problems of the *de novo* private sector.

Programmes to accelerate privatization and industrial restructuring fell badly behind schedule in 1997. The closure of loss-making enterprises was accompanied by generous redundancy payments, which threatened the macroeconomic stabilization programme, as budgetary deficits continued at high levels and monetary policy was relaxed in the second half of 1997. This brought the Government into further dispute with the IMF, which withheld financial support. Major disagreements within the coalition Government from the end of 1997 led to Victor Ciorbea's replacement as Prime Minister by Radu Vasile, in April 1998. Vasile drafted a new set of reform proposals, which were again intended to accelerate the privatization of state-owned enterprises and banks, to restructure public utilities and to close major loss-making enterprises. However, economic performance continued to deteriorate throughout 1998. GDP declined by 7.3%, annual inflation, although lower than the previous year, still stood at 59.1%, and the trade deficit widened to US $2,625m. Disagreements within the governing coalition hindered the implementation of reforms and in December 1998 President Constantinescu announced yet another crisis programme to accelerate development.

The economic situation continued to deteriorate in 1999; the decline in GDP slowed to 3.2%, but inflation remained high, at 45.8%. However, the closure of enterprises and coal-mines resulted in a resurgence of violent public demonstrations throughout the year, involving clashes with the police, outbreaks of strikes and widespread labour unrest, which was uncommonly severe in the public-utilities sector. An agreement for further credits from the IMF, concluded in April, was suspended in the last quarter of 1999. However, after delays owing to financial difficulties, the stand-by loan was finally released in mid-2000. In December 1999 President Constantinescu dismissed Vasile and appointed as Prime Minister Mugur Isărescu, Governor of the National Bank of Romania since 1990. Isărescu announced a new set of proposals to accelerate privatization and to stabilize the economy, together with fiscal reforms intended to reduce the tax burden on private companies. The economy staged a minor recovery in 2000. GDP grew by 1.8%, largely as a result of a growth of exports and investment which contributed to a decrease in unemployment. However, the return to economic growth for the first year since 1996 could not disguise the major problems facing the economy. Real wages and consumption continued to decline. Inflation remained at over 40% as fiscal policy was relaxed in an attempt to stimulate growth, by easing the tax burden on companies and individuals. The resulting growth in the budget deficit brought the Government into renewed disagreement with the IMF. Little progress was made in accelerating privatization in 2000 and progress in structural reforms remained slow. In November both the IMF and the EU published reports that were highly critical of Romanian economic policy and the lack of progress made in structural reforms. The EU concluded that Romania did not have a functioning market economy and would not be capable of withstanding competitive pressures inside the Union. The IMF criticized the Government for its failure to reduce government expenditure, slow progress in privatization and the continued subsidization of large loss-making state-owned enterprises. Attempts to increase welfare payments, minimum wages and wages for state-sector personnel prior to the legislative election put further strain on the budget, aggravated relations with the IMF and failed to impress the electorate.

Economic Policy and Performance following the General Election of November 2000

The PSDR became the single largest party in the new Parliament after the elections of November 2000, and formed a minority Government under Adrian Năstase. Mugur Isărescu, the outgoing Prime Minister, returned to his post as Governor of the National Bank, in which role he played a key part in implementing the Government's macroeconomic strategy. The successor Government made membership of western institutions, including the North Atlantic Treaty Organization (NATO) and the EU, its major foreign policy objective. This required it to tighten macroeconomic policies and to accelerate economic reforms. Policies agreed by the Government with the EU, the IMF and the World Bank include the reduction of costs and the elimination of losses in state-owned enterprises; the privatization, and if necessary, the closure of large loss-making state-owned enterprises; the restructuring of the financial sector and the privatization of banks; a radical overhaul of the inefficient and loss-making energy sector, including the privatization of gas and electricity production and distribution, and the profitable state-owned petroleum company, Petrom; and the implementation of a macroeconomic stabilization policy under the surveillance of the IMF. The new Government proved to be more successful than its predecessors in enacting the legislation required to facilitate economic reform (although it relied over-heavily on government decrees to enforce policies before gaining parliamentary approval), in restructuring the institutions associated with such reform, and in conducting negotiations with domestic unions, the EU, the IMF and the World Bank. The Government secured a new, 18-month stand-by agreement with the IMF in October 2001, which required it progressively to reduce budgetary deficits, the growth of money supply and inflation; to implement strict controls on wages in state-owned enterprises; to eliminate losses in the state sector; to increase energy prices to world market levels and to reduce losses in the energy sector; and to eliminate enterprise arrears to the budget and to energy suppliers. The agreement also required the Government to accelerate privatization and the restructuring of state-owned industries prior to privatization, and to improve bank supervision and regulation. The Government had some success in meeting the macroeconomic targets contained in the agreement with the IMF in 2001–02. The budgetary deficit was reduced to 3.5% of GDP in 2001 and to 2.8% in 2002. The end-of-year inflation rate was reduced from 45.7% in 2000, to 30.3% in 2001, and to 17.8% in 2002. However, this figure remained high by the standards of transition economies in Central Europe. The Government planned to reduce inflation to single digits in 2004, but this target might prove to be over-optimistic. Economic growth accelerated in 2001, assisted by a good harvest, with GDP growing by 5.7% and, despite a poor harvest in 2002, GDP grew by 4.9% in that year. However, the resumption of economic growth led to a surge in imports of machinery, components and raw and semi-processed materials. The trade deficit reached US $2,969m. in 2001, resulting in a current-account deficit of $2,317m. Notwithstanding the unfavourable international economic situation in 2002, exports increased by 21.8% and the trade deficit was reduced to $2,613m., resulting in a current-account deficit of $1,573m. Remittances from Romanian workers abroad were a major source of income (with some sources estimating them to be as high as $3,000m. in 2002, including cash brought home by workers, which is then sold on the domestic foreign-exchange market) to offset the trade deficit. The need to finance continued current-account deficits caused foreign debt to increase, reaching $15,500m. by the end of 2002.

Nevertheless, the Government encountered problems in meeting the structural targets contained in the IMF stand-by agreement. The IMF has repeatedly warned about the large-scale losses of state-owned enterprises, as well as the high level of wages (which are rising faster than in the private sector) and overstaffing, and the level of both inter-enterprise arrears and those owed to energy suppliers, as well as arrears in payments to the state budget. There has been specific criticism of high production-costs and losses among energy companies and of the failure to privatize the sector. These problems resulted in further delays in releasing the second tranche of lending under the IMF stand-by agreement in early 2002, raising the possibility that Romania would fail to complete an agreement for an unprecedented sixth time. Despite the Government's failure to limit wages or reduce staff levels, its success in meeting macroeconomic targets persuaded the IMF to extend the agreement until August 2003 (although there was a major disagreement about increases to the minimum wage in January 2003), and to release the second and third tranches of credits in 2003. However, attempts to limit government expenditure in order to meet budget-deficit targets resulted in problems in meeting plans for expenditure on policies to alleviate poverty, for investment in infrastructure and state-owned enterprises, and for projects associated with entry to the EU and NATO. By mid-2003 the health service was experiencing a major financial crisis, which threatened the breakdown of the system.

The IMF's principal reservations concerned the slow pace of privatization, and the privatization of the energy sector, in particular. Although most small and medium-sized companies had been privatized by the end of 2002, the pace of privatization of large, frequently loss-making, state-owned enterprises remained slow, in comparison with other countries in the region. In 2001 the Government abolished the State Ownership Fund, which was widely regarded as a major impediment to the privatization of large-scale industry, and replaced it with the State Privatization Agency (APAPS), under government control. The APAPS introduced a strategy of accelerated privatization in 2002, which involved selling companies relatively cheaply, with a commitment from the new owners to invest in the modernization of the business and to maintain employment levels for a specified period—a restriction that deterred some potential investors. The strategy had some success, and some high-profile privatizations were achieved in the industrial sector in 2001–02, including the sale of the region's largest steel producer, Sidex at Galaţi; the aluminium companies Alro Slatina and Alprom Slatina; the Vulcan engineering plant; and the Constanţa shipyard. In the financial sector, the APAPS successfully divested the country's third largest bank, Banca Agricola, Banc Post, and the Astra insurance company. The liberalization of the telecommunications sector was also achieved, allowing new, predominantly foreign, companies to enter the market following the sale of a majority stake in the fixed-line telecommunications company, Romtelecom. At the end of 2002 private ownership had been extended to 54.8% of the country's capital stock, to become the dominant form of ownership. The APAPS retained shares in 350 companies, including 80 large state-owned enterprises, but proposed to dispose of the majority of its holdings by the end of 2003, while 20 of the more difficult state-owned enterprises were to be privatized with the assistance of the World Bank in 2004. To this end, the organization announced proposals to implement substantial job reductions in 23 state-owned enterprises in 2003, which resulted in further conflict with the unions. The greatest problems occurred in the commercialization of the energy sector where, despite the sale of the RAFO petroleum refinery, progress has been painfully slow. Four major gas and electricity distribution companies were scheduled to be opened to public investment in 2003–04. Another reverse,

however, was the failure to privatize the largest remaining state-owned bank, Banca Commercială Română, which was a condition of the Government's stand-by agreement with the IMF; two bids were rejected at the end of 2002, but it was hoped that the sale would be resolved by 2004.

The EU's annual report on progress towards accession, published in October 2002, noted that the country had made considerable progress over the preceding year, but concluded that Romania, alone among the candidate, did not yet have a functioning market economy and consequently did not satisfy the economic criteria for entry into the EU. However, the EU offered Romania the possibility of entry in 2007, and issued a detailed programme specifying stringent conditions that would have to be satisfied in order to meet the economic standards for entry. The EU also offered increased financial assistance to Romania in the pre-accession period. The plan for accession specified conditions that were similar to those agreed with the IMF, but with the need for some additional structural reforms, such as reductions in public-sector wages and employment, reforms to the tax system, improvements in the financial sector (which it regarded as failing to provide proper intermediation between savers and lenders), the completion of the privatization of the banking sector, and further reforms to the public sector. The EU also repeated its long-standing concerns at pervasive corruption and instructed the Government to take stronger action in this area.

PROSPECTS

Despite the difficulties outlined above, at mid-2003 prospects for the Romanian economy had improved over the preceding year and seemed substantially better than at any time in the previous decade. The Government remained committed to reform, and there appeared to be a far wider acceptance of the measures that would be required to bring about sustained economic recovery among the population as a whole. The economy had started to grow and inflation was being reduced progressively. The National Bank had pursued a prudent policy under Mugur Isărescu and Romania's credit ratings had improved, allowing the Bank to return to international capital markets as the country successfully built up gold and foreign-exchange reserves to safe levels, thereby averting the likelihood of a financial crisis. Nevertheless, poverty remained high and increases in energy prices affected the poorest households. Romania expected to join the EU in 2007, but had to meet stringent economic conditions, which could prove too challenging.

Exports and investment will continue to be the main drivers of economic growth. Romanian exports, concentrated on the EU market, mainly comprise labour-intensive and low value-added products, such as clothing, footwear and furniture and resource-intensive products, including iron and steel products and non-ferrous metals, which have relatively low levels of value-added, while these exports also encounter major competition from low-wage economies. The Government hoped that a sustained recovery could be based on growth in foreign direct investment, urgently required to modernize and create industrial sectors with the potential to export higher value-added goods to EU markets, but will continue to experience difficulties in attracting investment before it completes structural reforms. Romania will continue to incur balance-of-payments deficits over the following few years and will be required to maintain sound relations with the IMF, both as a source of finance to enable it to continue to service its debt in the mid-2000s, and as an indicator of its reliability to potential private investors. This will impose major constraints on domestic economic policy in the medium term and will leave the Government with little room to increase expenditure on welfare programmes or investment in infrastructure.

Statistical Survey

Source (unless otherwise indicated): Institutul National de Statistică (National Institute of Statistics), Bucharest, Bd. Libertatii 16; tel. (21) 3124875; fax (21) 3124873; e-mail romstat@insse.ro; internet www.insse.ro/index.html.

Area and Population

AREA, POPULATION AND DENSITY

Area (sq km)	238,391*
Population (census results)	
7 January 1992	22,810,035
18–27 March 2002 (preliminary)	
Males	10,581,350
Females.	11,116,831
Total	21,698,181
Population (official estimates at 1 January)	
1999	22,489,000
2000	22,456,000
2001	22,430,000
Density (per sq km) at 2002 census†	91.0

* 92,043 sq miles.
† Based on preliminary results.

POPULATION BY ETHNIC GROUP
(2002 census)

	Number	% of total
Romanian.	19,409,400	89.5
Hungarian	1,434,377	6.6
Gypsy	535,520	2.5
Ukrainian	61,091	0.3
German	60,088	0.3
Carpathio-Rusyns	36,397	0.2
Turks	32,596	0.2
Others and unknown	128,712	0.6
Total	**21,698,181**	**100.0**

ADMINISTRATIVE DIVISIONS
(at census of March 2002)

	Area (sq km)	Estimated population	Density (per sq km)	Administrative capital (with population)
Alba	6,242	382,999	61.4	Alba Iulia (66,369)
Arad	7,754	461,730	59.5	Arad (172,824)
Argeş	6,826	653,903	95.8	Piteşti (168,756)
Bacău	6,621	708,751	107.0	Bacău (175,921)
Bihor	7,544	600,223	79.6	Oradea (206,527)
Bistriţa-Năsăud .	5,355	312,325	58.3	Bistriţa (81,467)
Botoşani . . .	4,986	454,023	91.1	Botoşani (115,344)
Brăila	4,766	373,897	78.5	Brăila (216,929)
Braşov	5,363	588,366	109.7	Braşov (283,901)
Buzău	6,103	494,982	81.1	Buzău (133,116)
Călăraşi . . .	5,088	324,629	63.8	Călăraşi (70,046)
Caraş-Severin. .	8,520	333,396	39.1	Reşiţa (83,985)
Cluj.	6,674	703,269	105.4	Cluj-Napoca (318,027)
Constanţa. . .	7,071	715,172	101.1	Constanţa (310,526)
Covasna . . .	3,710	222,274	59.9	Sfântu Gheorghe (61,512)
Dâmboviţa. . .	4,054	541,326	133.5	Târgovişte (89,429)
Dolj.	7,414	734,823	99.1	Craiova (302,622)
Galaţi	4,466	619,522	138.7	Galaţi (298,584)
Giurgiu . . .	3,526	298,022	84.5	Giurgiu (69,587)
Gorj.	5,602	387,407	69.2	Târgu Jiu (96,562)
Harghita . . .	6,639	326,020	49.1	Miercurea-Ciuc (41,852)
Hunedoara . .	7,063	487,115	69.0	Deva (69,390)
Ialomiţa . . .	4,453	296,486	66.6	Slobozia (52,677)
Iaşi	5,476	819,044	149.6	Iaşi (321,580)
Ilfov*	1,593	300,109	189.6	Bucharest (1,921,751)
Maramureş . .	6,304	510,688	81.0	Baia Mare (137,976)
Mehedinţi . . .	4,933	306,118	62.1	Drobeta-Turnu-Severin (104,035)
Mureş	6,714	579,862	86.4	Târgu Mureş (149,577)
Neamţ	5,896	557,084	94.5	Piatra-Neamţ (105,499)
Olt	5,498	490,276	89.2	Slatina (79,171)
Prahova . . .	4,716	829,224	175.8	Ploieşti (232,452)
Sălaj	3,864	248,407	64.3	Zalău (63,305)
Satu Mare. . .	4,418	369,096	83.5	Satu Mare (115,630)
Sibiu	5,432	422,224	77.7	Sibiu (155,045)
Suceava . . .	8,553	690,941	80.8	Suceava (106,138)
Teleorman. . .	5,790	436,926	75.5	Alexandria (50,591)
Timiş	8,697	677,744	77.9	Timişoara (317,651)
Tulcea	8,499	258,639	30.4	Tulcea (92,762)
Vâlcea	5,765	413,570	71.7	Râmnicu Vâlcea (107,656)
Vaslui	5,318	455,550	85.7	Vaslui (70,267)
Vrancea . . .	4,857	390,268	80.4	Focşani (103,219)
Bucharest Municipality* .	228	1,921,751	8,074.6	Bucharest (1,921,751)
Total	**238,391**	**21,698,181**	**91.0**	

* The Bucharest Municipality is a separate administrative division, but the city is also the capital of the adjacent Ilfov region. The area and population of Bucharest are included only in figures for the municipality.

PRINCIPAL TOWNS
(at census of March 2002)

Bucureşti (Bucharest, the capital)	1,921,751	Piteşti	168,756
Iaşi	321,580	Arad	172,824
Cluj-Napoca	318,027	Sibiu	155,045
Timişoara	317,651	Târgu Mureş	149,577
Constanţa	310,526	Baia Mare	137,976
Craiova	302,622	Buzău	133,116
Galaţi	298,584	Satu Mare	115,630
Braşov	283,901	Botoşani	115,344
Ploieşti	232,452	Râmnicu-Vâlcea	107,656
Brăila	216,929	Suceava	106,138
Oradea	206,527	Piatra-Neamţ	105,499
Bacău	175,921	Drobeta-Turnu-Severin	104,035

BIRTHS, MARRIAGES AND DEATHS

	Registered live births		Registered marriages		Registered deaths	
	Number	Rate (per 1,000)	Number	Rate (per 1,000)	Number	Rate (per 1,000)
1994	246,736	10.9	154,221	6.8	266,101	11.7
1995	236,640	10.4	153,943	6.8	271,672	12.0
1996	231,348	10.2	150,388	6.7	286,158	12.7
1997	236,891	10.5	147,105	6.5	279,316	12.4
1998	237,297	10.5	145,000	6.5	269,166	12.0
1999	235,000	10.5	140,000	6.2	265,000	11.8
2000	233,000	10.4	136,000	6.1	255,100	11.4
2001	220,368	9.8	n.a.	n.a.	259,603	11.6

Sources: partly UN, *Demographic Yearbook* and *Population and Vital Statistics Report*.

Expectation of life (WHO estimates, years at birth): 71.1 (males 67.8; females 74.5) in 2001 (Source: WHO, *World Health Report*).

ECONOMICALLY ACTIVE POPULATION
(labour force surveys, '000 persons aged 15 years and over)

	1999	2000	2001
Agriculture, hunting and forestry	4,491.6	4,598.7	4,523.1
Fishing	7.6	7.9	3.7
Mining and quarrying	186.3	163.2	150.0
Manufacturing	2,164.8	2,053.8	2,024.8
Electricity, gas and water	223.5	195.8	198.9
Construction	397.0	403.4	430.0
Wholesale and retail trade; repair of motor vehicles, motorcycles and personal and household goods	926.3	928.4	951.9
Hotels and restaurants	123.9	122.8	130.9
Transport, storage and communications	499.8	511.3	519.4
Financial intermediation	87.0	92.6	75.9
Real estate, renting and business services	141.1	132.3	124.1
Public administration	532.7	563.1	581.4
Education	423.2	415.0	409.3
Health and social assistance	340.5	345.8	350.6
Other services	230.3	229.6	222.9
Total employed	10,775.7	10,763.8	10,696.9
Unemployed	789.9	821.2	750.0
Total labour force	11,565.6	11,585.0	11,446.9
Males	6,261.6	6,253.8	6,155.4
Females	5,304.0	5,331.2	5,291.5

Registered unemployed ('000 persons): 1,130.3 in 1999; 1,007.1 in 2000; 826.9 in 2001.

Source: ILO.

Health and Welfare

KEY INDICATORS

Total fertility rate (children per woman, 2001)	1.3
Under-5 mortality rate (per 1,000 live births, 2001)	21
HIV/AIDS (% of persons aged 15–49, 2001)	<0.10
Physicians (per 1,000 head, 1994)	1.84
Hospital beds (per 1,000 head, 1998)	7.56
Health expenditure (1998): US $ per head (PPP)	190
Health expenditure (1998): % of GDP	2.9
Health expenditure (1998): public (% of total)	63.8
Access to water (% of persons, 1999)	58
Access to sanitation (% of persons, 1999)	53
Human Development Index (2000): ranking	63
Human Development Index (2000): value	0.775

For sources and definitions, see explanatory note on p. vi.

Agriculture

PRINCIPAL CROPS
('000 metric tons)

	1999	2000	2001
Wheat	4,661.4	4,434.4	7,735.1
Barley	1,018.6	867.0	1,580.0
Maize	10,934.8	4,898.0	9,119.2
Rye	21.1	21.8	28.6
Oats	389.6	244.0	382.4
Potatoes	3,957.1	3,469.8	3,997.1
Sugar beet	1,414.9	666.9	875.5
Dry beans	47.7	21.8	36.5
Dry peas	27.0	14.2	21.7
Walnuts	33.1	31.5	33.9
Soybeans (Soya beans)	183.4	69.5	72.7
Sunflower seed	1,300.9	721.0	823.5
Rapeseed	108.2	76.1	101.8
Cabbages	885.4	731.9	819.2
Lettuce	24.0	20.0†	26.2†
Tomatoes	708.6	628.7	651.7
Pumpkins, squash and gourds	154.0†	120.0†	152.0*
Cucumbers and gherkins	145.0†	110.0†	138.0*
Chillies and green peppers	212.3	174.8	184.8
Dry onions	401.1	296.3	396.5
Garlic	84.5	68.3	82.9
Green beans	52.4	40.1	50.8
Green peas	22.2	17.7	22.6
Other vegetables†	333.2	296.8	335.3
Apples	315.0	490.3	507.4
Pears	63.5	70.6	71.6
Cherries	71.6	73.7	91.2
Apricots	31.5	28.4	28.3
Peaches	16.1	18.3	16.7
Plums	361.3	549.6	557.2
Strawberries	14.6	11.7	18.4
Grapes	1,117.4	1,295.3	1,121.7
Cantaloupes and other melons	853.2	900.0*	945.0*
Other fruits†	102.5	97.0	41.4
Pimento*	28	30	30
Tobacco (leaves)	14.8	10.9	10.1

* FAO estimate(s).
† Unofficial figure(s).

Source: FAO.

LIVESTOCK
('000 head, year ending September)

	1999	2000	2001
Horses	839	858	860*
Cattle	3,143	3,051	2,870
Pigs	7,194	5,848	4,797
Sheep	8,409	8,121	7,657
Goats	585	558	538
Chickens	69,480	69,143	70,076

* FAO estimate.

Source: FAO.

LIVESTOCK PRODUCTS
('000 metric tons)

	1999	2000	2001
Beef and veal	153	162	145
Mutton and lamb.	54	49	49
Goat meat	4.3	4.0	3.8
Pig meat	595.1	502.3	460.1
Horse meat†	8.6	9.0	9.0
Poultry meat	268.5	259.4	283.9
Other meat†	7.8	7.8	8.0
Cows' milk	4,360.3	4,301.3	4,457.4
Sheep's milk	342.4	321.5	323.7
Cheese.	42.4	40.6	38.7
Butter	9.2	6.0	6.5
Hen eggs	266.2	262.8	276.2
Other poultry eggs . . .	28.3	22.7	23.8
Honey	11.2	11.7	12.6
Wool: greasy	19.0	18.0	16.9
Wool: scoured	11.4	10.8	12.0*
Cattle hides (fresh)* . . .	32.5	30.7	31.2
Sheepskins (fresh)* . . .	14.1	13.4	11.8

* Unofficial figure(s).
† FAO estimates.
Source: FAO.

Forestry

ROUNDWOOD REMOVALS
('000 cubic metres, excluding bark)

	1999	2000	2001
Sawlogs, veneer logs and logs for sleepers	5,287	6,146	5,638
Pulpwood	1,425	1,652	2,150
Other industrial wood . . .	2,772	2,318	2,018
Fuel wood	3,220	3,032	2,618
Total	12,703	13,148	12,424

Source: FAO.

SAWNWOOD PRODUCTION
('000 cubic metres, including railway sleepers)

	1999	2000	2001
Coniferous (softwood) . . .	1,845	2,077	1,805
Broadleaved (hardwood). . .	973	1,319	1,254
Total	2,818	3,396	3,059

Source: FAO.

Fishing

('000 metric tons, live weight)

	1998	1999	2000
Capture	9.0	7.8	7.4
Goldfish	1.1	1.2	1.2
Silver carp	0.4	1.3	0.6
Whiting	0.6	0.3	0.3
European sprat . . .	3.3	1.9	1.8
Aquaculture	9.6	9.0	9.7
Common carp	1.9	1.9	2.3
Goldfish	1.8	1.5	1.3
Bighead carp	1.4	1.0	2.1
Silver carp	3.6	3.1	3.2
Total catch	18.6	16.8	17.1

Source: FAO, *Yearbook of Fishery Statistics.*

Mining
('000 metric tons, unless otherwise indicated)

	1998	1999	2000
Brown coal (incl. lignite) . . .	26,037	22,881	29,279
Crude petroleum	6,309	6,154	6,038
Iron ore*	459	365	290
Bauxite	161.9	136	135
Copper concentrates† . . .	19.1	16.5	16.1
Lead concentrates† . . .	15.1	17.5	18.7
Zinc concentrates† . . .	25.7	26.5	27.5
Salt (unrefined)	2,220	2,133	2,215
Natural gas (million cu metres) .	14,441	14,577	14,577

* Figures refer to gross weight.
† Figures refer to the metal content of concentrates.

Source: US Geological Survey.

Industry

SELECTED PRODUCTS
('000 metric tons, unless otherwise indicated)

	1997	1998	1999
Refined sugar	243	321	246
Margarine	25.8	36.1	36.1
Wine ('000 hectolitres) . . .	7,314	5,071	5,661
Beer ('000 hectolitres) . . .	7,651	9,989	11,133
Tobacco products	26	29	31
Cotton yarn—pure and mixed .	43	36	28
Cotton fabrics—pure and mixed (million sq metres) . . .	173	170	143
Woollen yarn—pure and mixed .	28	20	17
Woollen fabrics—pure and mixed (million sq metres) . .	34	22	18
Silk fabrics—pure and mixed (million sq metres)* . .	52	40	32
Flax and hemp yarn—pure and mixed . . .	5	5	4
Linen, hemp and jute fabrics—pure and mixed (million sq metres) .	17	8	7
Chemical filaments and fibres . .	75	48	28
Footwear (million pairs). . .	36	31	31
Chemical wood pulp	197	162	178
Paper and paperboard . . .	330	306	302
Synthetic rubber	29	23	16
Rubber tyres ('000)	3,110	3,002	2,834
Sulphuric acid	329	229	234
Caustic soda (sodium hydroxide) .	323	310	297
Soda ash (sodium carbonate) . .	547	462	415
Nitrogenous fertilizers (a)† . .	669	318	612
Phosphatic fertilizers (b)† . . .	136	99	101
Pesticides	8	5	4
Plastics and resins	338.6	319.9	298.4
Motor spirit (petrol)	3,642	3,627	3,017
Kerosene and white spirit . .	168	181	205
Distillate fuel oils	3,952	4,035	3,137
Residual fuel oils	2,083	1,941	1,825
Petroleum bitumen (asphalt) . .	305	241	204
Liquefied petroleum gas. . .	242	304	261
Coke	3,317	3,312	1,716
Cement	6,553	7,300	6,252
Pig-iron	4,556	4,541	2,969
Crude steel	6,675	6,336	4,392
Aluminium—unwrought . . .	164	175	174
Refined copper—unwrought . .	23	21	21
Radio receivers ('000) . . .	28	10	n.a.
Television receivers ('000) . . .	89	134	56
Merchant ships launched ('000 deadweight tons)	43	58	231
Passenger motor cars ('000). . .	109	104	89
Motor tractors, lorries and dump trucks (number)	1,956	1,263	900
Tractors ('000)	10.5	9.6	4.5
Sewing machines ('000) . . .	3	1	1
Domestic refrigerators ('000) . .	429	366	323
Domestic washing machines ('000)	82	36	28
Domestic cookers ('000) . . .	339	310	285
Electric energy (million kWh) . .	57,148	53,496	50,713

* Including fabrics of artificial silk.
† Production in terms of (a) nitrogen or (b) phosphoric acid.

Finance

CURRENCY AND EXCHANGE RATES

Monetary Units
100 bani (singular: ban) = 1 Romanian leu (plural: lei).

Sterling, Dollar and Euro Equivalents (30 May 2003)
£1 sterling = 52,980.2 lei;
US $1 = 32,156.0 lei;
€1 = 38,013.9 lei;
100,000 Romanian lei = £1.888 = $3.110 = €2.631.

Average Exchange Rate (lei per US $)
2000   21,708.7
2001   29,060.8
2002   33,055.4

STATE BUDGET
('000 million lei)

Revenue*	1998	1999	2000
Current revenue	62,681.0	88,649.7	119,763.5
Tax revenue	60,677.9	85,019.0	114,394.5
Direct taxes	22,714.2	26,560.8	31,472.5
On profits	10,845.6	16,646.0	19,927.3
Indirect taxes	37,963.6	58,458.2	82,922.0
Value-added tax . .	22,493.2	32,471.2	50,438.7
Customs duties . . .	5,741.4	7,846.7	8,702.4
Excises	8,431.3	16,167.9	20,636.3
Other indirect taxes . . .	1,297.8	1,972.3	3,144.7
Non-tax revenue	2,003.1	3,630.7	5,369.0
Capital revenue	3,228.1	4,201.2	121.0
Total	65,909.1	92,850.9	119,884.5

Expenditure†	1998	1999	2000
General public services	2,866.9	4,108.5	7,683.1
Defence	6,707.6	8,347.2	14,060.0
Public order and safety	5,205.1	7,535.6	13,947.7
Education	10,801.6	13,996.2	20,173.4
Health	3,183.9	3,517.5	3,710.4
Social security and welfare . .	6,815.7	9,069.9	11,242.1
Housing and community amenities	946.8	1,827.8	2,762.0
Recreational, cultural and religious affairs	1,466.4	1,746.6	3,077.3
Economic affairs	10,682.6	15,817.7	24,388.3
Agriculture	4,539.8	4,974.6	9,091.8
Transport and communications	3,357.5	7,211.3	9,769.7
Other	10,196.1	6,994.4	4,879.4
Total	58,872.7	72,931.4	105,923.1

* Excluding grants received ('000 million lei): 1,306.5 in 1998; 388.9 in 1999; 211.3 in 2000.
† Excluding lending minus repayments ('000 million lei): 18,743.9 in 1998; 33,955.3 in 1999; 43,244.1 in 2000.

2001 ('000 million lei): Revenue 148,203.1; Expenditure 184,021.2.

INTERNATIONAL RESERVES
(US $ million at 31 December)

	2000	2001	2002
IMF special drawing rights . . .	1	7	2
Foreign exchange	3,921	5,435	7,209
Total (excl. gold)	3,922	5,442	7,211

Source: IMF, *International Financial Statistics*.

MONEY SUPPLY
('000 million lei at 31 December)

	2000	2001	2002
Currency outside banks	25,742	35,635	45,577
Demand deposits at deposit money banks	18,579	25,968	38,329
Total money	44,320	61,603	83,907

Source: IMF, *International Financial Statistics*.

COST OF LIVING
(Consumer Price Index; base: Oct. 1990 = 100)

	1998	1999	2000
Food and beverages	53,830.6	68,822.0	98,906.8
Other goods	50,346.8	76,686.9	110,426.6
Services	64,032.5	117,842.6	181,315.3
All items	53,437.7	77,914.2	113,494.9

NATIONAL ACCOUNTS
('000 million lei at current prices)

Expenditure on the Gross Domestic Product

	1998	1999	2000
Government final consumption expenditure	51,649.8	81,179.5	99,634.6
Private final consumption expenditure	255,886.2	388,984.5	588,303.6
Increase in stocks	−1,350.9	−4,546.0	7,680.6
Gross fixed capital formation . .	61,209.8	97,169.8	147,209.6
Total domestic expenditure .	367,394.9	539,356.9	842,828.4
Exports of goods and services			
Less Imports of goods and services	−28,724.9	−23,430.9	−46,294.7
GDP in purchaser' values . .	338,670.0	539,356.9	796,533.7

Gross Domestic Product by Economic Activity

	1998	1999	2000
Agriculture, hunting, fishing and forestry	54,077.1	72,096.0	90,929.3
Mining and quarrying			
Manufacturing	107,305.6	146,054.2	219,861.1
Electricity, gas and water . . .			
Construction	17,496.6	26,260.2	38,127.3
Services	128,050.1	243,648.6	370,916.4
Sub-total	306,929.4	488,059.0	719,834.1
Less Imputed bank service charge	1,567.4	7,970.8	9,600.8
GDP at basic prices	305,362.0	480,088.2	710,233.3
Taxes (less subsidies) on products	33,308.0	59,268.7	86,300.4
GDP in purchasers values .	338,670.0	539,356.9	796,533.7

BALANCE OF PAYMENTS
(US $ million)

	1999	2000	2001
Exports of goods f.o.b.	8,503	10,366	11,385
Imports of goods f.o.b.	−9,595	−12,050	−14,354
Trade balance	−1,092	−1,684	−2,969
Exports of services	1,365	1,767	1,994
Imports of services	−1,785	−2,021	−2,203
Balance on goods and services	−1,512	−1,938	−3,178
Other income received	152	325	455
Other income paid	−563	−606	−737
Balance on goods, services and income	−1,923	−2,219	−3,460
Current transfers received . . .	804	1,079	1,417
Current transfers paid	−178	−219	−274
Current balance	−1,297	−1,359	−2,317
Capital account (net)	45	36	95
Direct investment abroad . . .	−16	11	17
Direct investment from abroad . .	1,041	1,025	1,157
Portfolio investment assets . . .	9	28	−8
Portfolio investment liabilities . .	−724	74	583
Other investment assets . . .	246	−407	−44
Other investment liabilities . . .	141	1,212	1,233
Net errors and omissions . . .	794	286	819
Overall balance	239	906	1,535

Source: IMF, *International Financial Statistics*.

External Trade

PRINCIPAL COMMODITIES
(US $ million)

Imports c.i.f.	1997	1998	1999
Prepared foodstuffs beverages and tobacco	426	524	416
Mineral products	2,408	1,687	1,252
Mineral fuels and oils; bituminous substances; mineral waxes	2,131	1,431	1,051
Chemical products . . .	940	1,028	974
Plastics, rubber and articles thereof	444	512	477
Plastics and articles thereof . .	325	392	385
Textiles and textile articles	1,565	1,825	1,937
Synthetic or man-made filaments	236	295	316
Synthetic or man-made staple fibres	320	369	392
Base metals and articles of base metal	670	790	687
Machinery and mechanical appliances; electrical equipment; sound and image recorders and players . .	2,593	2,723	2,435
Boilers, turbines, engines mechanical apparatus and devices, parts thereof . . .	1,685	1,516	1,344
Electric machinery, appliances and equipment; TV sound and image recorders and players	908	1,207	1,091
Vehicles and associated transport equipment . . .	384	485	314
Vehicles, tractors and other ground vehicles	292	423	236
Total (incl. others)	11,280	11,838	10,395

Exports f.o.b.	1997	1998	1999
Mineral products	638	507	502
Mineral fuels and oils; bituminous substances; mineral waxes	518	393	414
Chemical products	560	336	327
Wood and articles of wood, excl. furniture	338	385	495
Wood, wood charcoal and articles of wood	330	378	489
Textiles and textile articles	1,942	2,162	2,197
Knitted or crocheted clothing and accessories	310	409	454
Non-knitted clothing and accessories	1,415	1,544	1,571
Footwear, headgear, umbrellas and similar articles	545	609	683
Footwear and parts thereof	540	603	678
Base metals and articles of base metal	1,557	1,583	1,310
Pig-iron, iron and steel . .	917	865	665
Products of pig-iron, iron and steel	315	374	288
Aluminium and articles thereof	253	247	255
Machinery and electrical appliances; electrical equipment; sound and image recorders and players . .	737	790	968
Boilers, turbines, engines mechanical apparatus and devices, parts thereof . . .	485	432	555
Electrical machinery appliances and equipment; TV sound and image recorders and players .	252	358	413
Vehicles and associated transport equipment . .	448	427	466

Exports f.o.b.— *continued*	1997	1998	1999
Miscellaneous manufactured articles	526	519	502
Furniture; lighting fittings and other similar articles; prefabricated buildings. . .	475	473	457
Total (incl. others)	8,431	8,302	8,503

PRINCIPAL TRADING PARTNERS
(US $ million)*

Imports c.i.f.	1998	1999†	2000†
Austria	347.4	311	332
Belgium-Luxembourg . . .	226.6	194	203
Brazil	143.4	128	181
China, People's Republic . .	177.5	145	174
Czech Republic	194.9	173	196
France (incl. Monaco) . .	815.4	704	799
Germany	2,064.5	1,841	1,923
Greece	204.6	198	372
Hungary	546.9	414	513
Israel	110.8	98	84
Italy	2,060.7	2,062	2,443
Japan	84.8	118	170
Korea, Republic	254.6	277	212
Netherlands	277.8	243	284
Poland	145.5	160	193
Russia	1,062.3	704	1,120
Spain	121.3	109	130
Sweden	147.7	145	177
Switzerland-Liechtenstein . .	138.1	128	154
Turkey	271.5	237	271
Ukraine	167.5	109	196
United Kingdom	396.8	444	536
USA	499.0	370	391
Total (incl. others)	11,835.4	10,557	13,055

Exports f.o.b.	1998	1999	2000†
Austria	249.2	242.5	251
Belgium-Luxembourg . . .	155.1	151.0	178
Bulgaria	77.9	136.7	290
Egypt	184.0	153.2	171
France (incl. Monaco) . .	491.5	530.4	722
Germany	1,628.6	1,510.0	1,627
Greece	201.4	216.7	324
Hungary	219.2	270.8	355
Israel	95.0	65.7	77
Italy	1,839.9	1,990.4	2,319
Moldova	128.6	101.0	142
Netherlands	313.1	327.0	329
Poland	82.2	120.0	102
Spain	84.2	106.9	114
Turkey	323.0	469.4	627
United Kingdom	303.2	412.9	546
USA	320.0	316.9	380
Yugoslavia	118.6	85.9	138
Total (incl. others)	8,300.9	8,487.0	10,367

* Imports by country of production; exports by country of last consignment.
† Figures are rounded.

Source: partly UN, *International Trade Statistics Yearbook*.

Transport

RAILWAYS
(traffic)

	1998	1999	2000
Passenger journeys (million) . .	146.8	129.3	117.5
Passenger-km (million)	13,422	12,304	11,632
Freight transported (million metric tons) . .	76.5	62.9	71.5
Freight ton-km (million) . . .	19,708	15,927	17,982

ROAD TRAFFIC
(motor vehicles in use at 31 December)

	1998	1999	2000
Passenger cars	2,822,254	2,980,014	3,128,782
Buses and coaches	45,546	47,305	48,142
Lorries and vans	380,312	410,159	413,493
Motorcycles and mopeds . . .	325,675	325,150	315,685

Source: IRF, *World Road Statistics.*

INLAND WATERWAYS
(traffic)

	1998	1999	2000
Passenger journeys ('000) . . .	1,923	1,654	133
Passenger-km (million)	13.1	11.0	15.0
Freight transported ('000 metric tons).	14,856	13,976	13,102
Freight ton-km (million) . . .	4,203	2,802	2,634

SHIPPING

Merchant Fleet
(registered at 31 December)

	2000	2001	2001
Number of vessels	264	240	237
Total displacement ('000 grt) . .	766.9	637.7	622.0

Sources: Lloyd's Register-Fairplay, *World Fleet Statistics.*

International Sea-borne Freight Traffic
('000 metric tons)

	1998	1999	2000
Goods loaded	10,860	14,376	12,648
Goods unloaded	17,344	11,100	12,828

Sources: Ministry of Transport, Bucharest, and UN, *Monthly Bulletin of Statistics.*

CIVIL AVIATION
(traffic)

	1998	1999	2000
Passenger journeys ('000) . . .	1,008	1,048	1,282
Passenger-km (million)	1,827	1,887	2,212
Freight transported ('000 metric tons).	10.0	8.0	8.0
Freight ton-km (million) . . .	22.0	20.0	19.0

Tourism

FOREIGN VISITOR ARRIVALS
('000)*

Country of origin	1999	2000	2001
Bulgaria	489	363	392
Germany	249	255	328
Hungary	1,031	1,203	1,131
Italy	158	189	219
Moldova	1,455	1,436	1,033
Poland	103	102	106
Russia	78	83	86
Slovakia	92	80	84
Turkey.	281	253	61
Ukraine	319	330	324
Yugoslavia	152	143	127
Total (incl. others)	5,224	5,264	4,938

* Figures refer to arrivals at frontiers of visitors from abroad. Excluding same-day visitors (excursionists), the total number of tourist arrivals (in '000) was: 3,209 in 1999; 3,274 in 2000; n.a. in 2001.
Source: World Tourism Organization, *Yearbook of Tourism Statistics).*

Receipts from Tourism (US $ million): 260 in 1998; 254 in 1999; 364 in 2000 (Source: World Bank, *World Bank Atlas*).

Communications Media

	1999	2000	2001
Television receivers ('000 in use)	7,000	8,500	n.a.
Telephones ('000 main lines in use)	3,740.0	3,899.2	4,116.0
Mobile cellular telephones ('000 subscribers).	1,355.5	2,499.0	3,845.1
Personal computers ('000 in use) .	600	713	800
Internet users ('000)	600	800	1,000

1996: Book production (incl. pamphlets) 7,199 titles (38,374,000 copies); Daily newspapers 106; Other periodicals 1,207.

1997: Radio receivers ('000 in use) 7,200.

2002: Internet users ('000) 1,800.

Sources: mostly UNESCO, *Statistical Yearbook*; UN, *Statistical Yearbook*; International Telecommunication Union.

Education

(2000/01)

	Institutions	Pupils	Teachers
Kindergartens	10,080	611,036	34,023
Primary and gymnasium schools	12,709	2,411,505	162,606
Secondary schools	1,367	687,919	64,018
Vocational schools	93	239,550	4,894
Specialized technical schools	108	91,105	1,493
Higher education	126	533,152	27,959

Adult literacy rate (UNESCO estimates): 98.1% (males 99.0%; females 97.3%) in 2000 (Source: UN Development Programme, *Human Development Report*).

Directory

The Constitution

Following its assumption of power in December 1989, the National Salvation Front decreed radical changes to the Constitution of 1965. The name of the country was changed from the Socialist Republic of Romania to Romania. The leading role of a single political party was abolished, a democratic and pluralist system of government being established.

The combined chambers of the legislature elected in May 1990, working as a constituent assembly, drafted a new Constitution (based on the Constitution of France's Fifth Republic), which was approved in a national referendum on 8 December 1991.

Under the 1991 Constitution, political power in Romania belongs to the people and is exercised according to the principles of democracy, freedom and human dignity, of inviolability and inalienability of basic human rights. Romania is governed on the basis of a multi-party democratic system and of the separation of the legal, executive and judicial powers. Romania's 486-seat legislature, consisting of the Chamber of Deputies (the lower house) and the Senate (the upper house), and Romania's President are elected by universal, free, direct and secret vote, the President serving a maximum of two terms. The term of office of the legislature and of the President is four years. Citizens have the right to vote at the age of 18, and may be elected at the age of 21 to the Chamber of Deputies and at the age of 30 to the Senate, with no upper age limit. Those ineligible for election include former members of the Securitate (the secret police of President Ceauşescu) and other former officials guilty of repression and abuses. Independent candidates are eligible for election to the Chamber of Deputies and to the Senate if supported by at least 251 electors and to the Presidency if supported by 100,000 electors. Once elected, the President may not remain a member of any political party. The President appoints the Prime Minister, who in turn appoints the Council of Ministers.

The Government

HEAD OF STATE

President: ION ILIESCU (elected 10 December 2000).

COUNCIL OF MINISTERS
(July 2003)

Prime Minister: ADRIAN NĂSTASE.

Minister of Foreign Affairs: MIRCEA DAN GEOANĂ.

Minister of European Integration: HILDEGARD CAROLA PUWAK.

Minister of Public Finance: MIHAI NICOLAE TĂNĂSESCU.

Minister of Justice: MIHAELA RODICA STĂNOIU.

Minister of National Defence: IOAN MIRCEA PAŞCU.

Minister of the Interior and Public Administration: IOAN RUS.

Minister of Labour, Social Solidarity and Family Affairs: ELENA DUMITRIU.

Minister of Economy and Commerce: IOAN-DAN POPESCU.

Minister of Agriculture, Forestry, Water and Environmental Protection: ILIE SÂRBU.

Minister of Transport, Construction and Tourism: MIRON TUDOR MITREA.

Minister of Education, Research and Youth: ALEXANDRU ATHANASIU.

Minister of Culture and Religious Affairs: RĂZVAN THEODORESCU.

Minister of Health: MIRCEA BEURAN.

Minister of Communications and Information Technology: DAN NICA.

Minister Co-ordinating the General Secretariat of Government: PETRU ŞERBAN MIHĂILESCU.

Minister-delegate for Relations with Parliament: ACSINTE GASPAR.

Minister-delegate for Public Administration: GABRIEL OPREA.

Minister-delegate, Chief Negotiator for European Integration: VASILE PUŞCAŞ.

Minister-delegate for Co-ordinating the Control Authorities: IONEL BLĂNCULESCU.

Minister-delegate for Relations with Social Partners: MARIAN SÂRBU.

Minister-delegate for Commerce: EUGEN DIJMĂRESCU.

MINISTRIES

Office of the Prime Minister: 71201 Bucharest, Piaţa Victoriei 1; tel. (21) 3131450; fax (21) 3122436; e-mail prim.ministru@guv.ro; internet www.guv.ro.

Ministry of Agriculture, Forestry, Water and Environmental Protection: 70312 Bucharest, Bd. Carol I 24; tel. (21) 6144020; fax (21) 3124410; internet www.maap.ro.

Ministry of Communications and Information Technology: Bucharest, Bd. Libertatii 14; internet www.mcti.ro.

Ministry of Culture and Religious Affairs: 71341 Bucharest, Piaţa Presei Libere 1; tel. (21) 2228479; fax (21) 2245440; e-mail tudor.maruntelu@cultura.ro; internet www.ministerulculturii.ro.

Ministry of Education, Research and Youth: 70738 Bucharest, Str. Gen. Berthelot 28–30, Sector 1; tel. (21) 6133315; fax (21) 3124719; internet www.edu.ro.

Ministry of European Integration: Bucharest, Str. Apolodor 17, Sector 5; tel. (21) 3011502; fax (21) 3368509; internet www.mie.ro.

Ministry of Foreign Affairs: 71274 Bucharest, Al. Alexandru 33; tel. (21) 2302071; fax (21) 2314090; e-mail maero@mae.kappa.ro; internet www.mae.ro.

Ministry of Health: 70109 Bucharest, Str. Ministerului 1–3; tel. (21) 2223850; fax (21) 3124916; internet www.ms.ro.

Ministry of the Interior and Public Administration: 70622 Bucharest, Sector 6, Str. Mihai Vodă 6; tel. (21) 3158616; fax (21) 3149718; e-mail drp@mi.ro; internet www.mi.ro.

Ministry of Justice: 70663 Bucharest, Str. Apolodor 17; tel. (21) 3112266; fax (21) 3155389; internet www.just.ro.

Ministry of Labour, Social Solidarity and Family: 70119 Bucharest, Str. Demetru Dobrescu 2B, Sector 1; tel. (21) 3156563; fax (21) 3122768; internet www.mmss.ro.

Ministry of National Defence: 77303 Bucharest, Str. Izvor 13–15, Sector 5; tel. (21) 4106876; fax (21) 3120863; e-mail drp@mapn.ro; internet www.mapn.ro.

Ministry of Public Administration: 71201 Bucharest, Piaţa Victoriei 1; tel. (21) 3123687; fax (21) 3113641; internet www.mapgov.ro.

Ministry of Public Finance: 70663 Bucharest, Str. Apolodor 17; tel. (21) 4103400; fax (21) 3122077; e-mail presa@mail.mfinante.ro; internet www.mfinante.ro.

Ministry of Transport, Construction and Tourism: Bucharest, Bd. Dinicu Golescu 38; tel. (21) 4101933; fax (21) 4111138; internet www.mt.ro.

Ministry for Relations with Parliament: 71201 Bucharest, Piaţa Victoriei 1; tel. (21) 2223677; fax (21) 2223652; e-mail mrp-ministru@gov.ro.

President

Presidential Election, 26 November and 10 December 2000

Candidates	First ballot votes cast %	Second ballot votes cast	Number %
Ion Iliescu (PSDR)	36.35	6,696,623	66.8
Corneliu Vadim Tudor (GRP) .	28.34	3,324,247	33.2
Teodor Dumitru Stolojan (NLP)	11.78	—	—
Constantin Mugurel Isărescu (Ind.)	9.54	—	—
Gheorghe Frunda (DAHR) . .	6.22	—	—
Petre Roman (DP)	2.99	—	—
Teodor Melescanu (Ind.) . . .	1.91	—	—
Others	2.87		
Total	100.00	10,020,870	100.0

In addition, a total of 160,264 invalid votes were cast in the second ballot.

Legislature

PARLIAMENT

Chairman of the Chamber of Deputies: VALERIU DORNEANU.

Chairman of the Senate: NICOLAE VĂCĂROIU.

General Election, 26 November 2000

	Seats	
Parties	Chamber of Deputies	Senate
Party of Social Democracy of Romania (PSDR)	155	65
Greater Romania Party (GRP)	84	37
Democratic Party (DP).	31	13
National Liberal Party (NLP)	30	13
Democratic Alliance of Hungarians in Romania (DAHR).	27	12
Minority parties*	19	0
Total	346	140

* These included the 'Bratstvo' Community of Bulgarians in Romania; the Community of Lipovenian Russians in Romania; the Croatian Union of Romania; the Cultural Union of Albanians in Romania; the Cultural Union of Ruthenians in Romania; the Democratic Union of Czechs and Slovaks in Romania; the Democratic Union of Serbs and Carasovenians in Romania; the Democratic Union of the Turco-Muslim Tatars in Romania; the Federation of Jewish Communities in Romania; the German Democratic Forum of Romania; the General Union of Ethnic Associations of Romania; the Hellenic Union of Romania; the Italian Community of Romania; the Roma Party; the Slav Macedonian Association of Romania; the Turkish Democratic Union of Romania; the Union of Armenians in Romania; the Union of Poles in Romania; the Union of Ukrainians in Romania.

Local Government

The system of local government in Romania was reformed under the terms of the Constitution of 1991. The basic principle of local government is local autonomy and the decentralization of public services. The lowest tier of local government is the local council of a city or commune; mayors and council members are elected by constituents in each relevant area, to serve for a period of four years. The activities of local councils are co-ordinated by county councils, which are also elected by their constituents. The county councils, in turn, elect a president and vice-president. A prefect for each county is appointed by the central Government as its representative at the local level, and has the power to challenge acts of all tiers of local government. Romania consists of 40 administrative divisions (counties) and the municipality of Bucharest, the capital city, which is itself divided into administrative sectors. Local elections were held on 10 November 2002.

Bucharest Municipal Council: 70602 Bucharest, Bd. Elisabeta 47; tel. (21) 3158429; fax (21) 3120030; e-mail pmb@pmb.ro; internet www.pmb.ro; Mayor TRĂIAN BĂŞESCU; Prefect PETRU ENESCU BOTEZATU.

Alba County Council: 2500 Alba Iulia, Str. I. C. Brătianu 1; tel. (258) 811254; fax (258) 813325; Pres. AUGUSTIN PRESECAN.

Arad County Council: 2900 Arad, Bd. Revoluţiei 75; tel. (257) 211474; fax (257) 250170; e-mail euro@cjarad.ro; internet www.cjarad.ro; Pres. CAIUS MIHAI PARPALĂ.

Argeş County Council: 0300 Piteşti, Piaţa Vasile Milea 1; tel. (248) 219299; fax (248) 219200; e-mail cabinet@cjarges.ro; internet www.cjarges.ro; Pres. ION MIHAILESCU.

Bacău County Council: 5500 Bacău, Str. Mărăşeşti 2; tel. (234) 134481; fax (234) 135012; e-mail consjdbc@mic.ro; internet www.csjbacau.ro; Pres. NECULAI LUPU.

Bihor County Council: 3700 Oradea, Parcul Traian 10; tel. (259) 437484; fax (259) 437484; e-mail cjbh@rdsor.ro; internet www.cjbihor.ro; Pres. STEFAN SEREMI.

Bistriţa-Năsăud County Council: 4400 Bistriţa, Piaţa Petru Rareş 1; tel. (263) 231474; fax (263) 214750; e-mail pres.cjbn@karma.ro; internet www.consjudbn.8m.com; Pres. GHEORGHE MARINESCU.

Botoşani County Council: 6800 Botoşani, Piaţa Revoluţiei 1–3; tel. (231) 514712; fax (231) 515020; e-mail egner@petar.ro; internet www.cjbotosani.ro; Pres. FLORIN SIMION EGNER.

Brăila County Council: 6100 Brăila, Piaţa Independenţei 1; tel. (239) 619945; fax (239) 611765; e-mail consiliu@cibnet.flex.ro; internet www.cjbraila.ro; Pres. AUREL GABRIEL SIMIONESCU.

Braşov County Council: 2200 Braşov, Bd. Eroilor 5; tel. (268) 410777; fax (268) 476905; e-mail cjbv@deuroconsult.ro; internet www.brasovcounty.ro; Pres. ARISTOTEL CANCESCU.

Buzău County Council: 5100 Buzău, Bd. Nicolae Bălcescu 48; tel. (238) 445542; fax (238) 423862; e-mail cjbuzau@buzau.astral.ro; internet www.cjbuzau.ro; Pres. VIOREL CONSTANTINESCU.

Călăraşi County Council: 8500 Călăraşi, Str. 1 December 1918 1; tel. (242) 311301; fax (242) 33160; e-mail cjcalarasi@nex.ro; Pres. MIHAI ARBAGIC.

Caraş-Severin County Council: 1700 Reşiţa, Piaţa 1 Decembrie 1918/1; tel. (255) 211420; fax (255) 211127; e-mail cjcs@cs.ro; internet www.cs.ro/conciliul_judetean/index.html; Pres. ILIE MUSTACILA.

Cluj County Council: 3400 Cluj-Napoca, Bd. 21 Decembrie 1989/58; tel. (264) 193677; fax (264) 196726; e-mail serban@cjcluj.ro; internet www.cjcluj.ro; Mayor GHEORGHE FUNAR; Pres. SERBAN GRATIAN.

Constanţa County Council: 8700 Constanţa, Bd. Tomis 51; tel. (241) 708001; fax (241) 708453; e-mail consjud@cjc.ro; internet www.cjc.ro; Pres. STELIAN DUTU.

Covasna County Council: 4000 Sfântu Gheorghe, Str. Libertăţii 4; tel. (267) 311544; fax (267) 351228; e-mail office@consjud.covasna.ro; internet www.covasna.info.ro; Pres. JÁNOS DEMETER.

Dâmboviţa County Council: 0200 Târgovişte, Bd. Independenţei 1; tel. (245) 611466; fax (245) 634520; e-mail consjdb@cjd.ro; internet www.cjd.ro; Pres. AUREL CUCU.

Dolj County Council: 1100 Craiova, Str. Unirii 19; tel. (251) 418042; fax (251) 411210; internet www.dass.ro; Pres. ION VOICULESCU.

Galaţi County Council: 6200 Galaţi, Str. Domnească 56; tel. (236) 411099; fax (236) 460703; e-mail consiliu@xnet.ro; internet www.cjgalati.ro; Pres. DAN-LILION GOGONCEA.

Giurghiu County Council: 8375 Giurghiu, Str. C. Dobrogeanu-Gherea 3–5; tel. (246) 215685; fax (246) 216511; e-mail cjg@pcnet.ro; internet www.cjgiurgiu.ro; Pres. VICTOR BOIANGIU.

Gorj County Council: 1400 Târgu Jiu, Piaţa Victoriei 2–4; tel. (253) 214006; fax (253) 212023; e-mail consjud@cjgorj.ro; internet www.cjgorj.ro; Pres. NICOLAE MISCHIE.

Harghita County Council: 4100 Miercurea-Ciuc, Str. Libertăţii 5; tel. (266) 111568; fax (266) 154013; internet www.cchr.ro; Pres. VILMOS ZSONBORI.

Hunedoara County Council: 2700 Deva, Str. 1 Decembrie 35; tel. (254) 211624; fax (254) 214130; e-mail conjudhd@e-mailrecep.ro; internet www.cjhunedoara.ro; Pres. MIHAIL NICOLAE RUDEANU.

Ialomiţa County Council: 8400 Slobozia, Str. Matei Basarab 29; tel. (243) 232000; fax (243) 230250; e-mail savu@cicnet.ro; internet www.cicnet.ro; Pres. GHEORGHE SAVU.

Iaşi County Council: 6600 Iaşi, Bd. Ştefan cel Mare şi Sfânt 69; tel. (232) 210330; fax (232) 210336; e-mail info@icc.ro; internet www.icc.ro; Pres. LUCIAN FLAISER.

Ilfov County Council: Bucharest, Str. Gheorghe Manu 18; tel. (21) 2125698; fax (21) 2125699; Pres. BEBE IVANOVICI.

Maramureş County Council: 4800 Baia Mare, Str. Gh. Şincai 46; tel. (262) 412110; fax (262) 413945; e-mail office@cjmm.multinet.ro; internet www.cjmm.multinet.ro; Pres. ALEXANDRU COSMA.

Mehedinţi County Council: 1500 Turnu-Severin, Str. Traian 89; tel. (252) 312717; fax (252) 312417; e-mail cjmehedinti@cjmehedinti.ro; internet www.cjmehedinti.ro; Pres. CONSTANTIN SÂRBULESCU.

Mureş County Council: 4300 Târgu Mureş, Str. Primăriei 2; tel. (265) 163211; fax (265) 160380; e-mail cjmures@orizont.net; internet www.cjmures.ro; Pres. GYORGI LAJOS VIRAG.

Neamţ County Council: 5600 Piatra-Neamţ, Str. Alexandru cel Bun 27; tel. (233) 213670; fax (233) 211569; e-mail cj.neamt@decebal.ro; Pres. RAUL CONSTANTIN BOBEANU.

Olt County Council: 0500 Slatina, Bd. Alexandru I. Cuza 14; tel. (249) 432807; fax (249) 431122; e-mail cjolt@slatina.ro; internet www.slatina.ro/cjolt/; Pres. MARIN IONICA.

Prahova County Council: 2200 Ploieşti, Bd. Republicii 2; tel. (244) 114820; fax (244) 115816; e-mail cons_jud@interplus.ro; Pres. MIRCEA COSMA.

Sălaj County Council: 4700 Zalău, Piaţa 1 Decembrie 1918/12; tel. (260) 662035; fax (260) 661097; e-mail office@cjsj.ro; internet www.cjsj.ro; Pres. LEONTIN BORDAS.

Satu Mare County Council: 3900 Satu Mare, Piaţa 25 Octombrie 1; tel. (261) 716994; fax (261) 712651; e-mail cpr@cjsm.ro; internet www.cjsm.ro; Pres. STEFAN SZABO.

Sibiu County Council: 2400 Sibiu, Str. Gen. Magheru 14; tel. (269) 416368; fax (269) 218159; e-mail judet@cjsibiu.ro; internet www .cjsibiu.ro; Pres. CONSTANTIN MORAR.

Suceava County Council: 5800 Suceava, Str. Ştefan cel Mare 36; tel. (230) 522915; fax (230) 522784; internet www.consiliu.suceava .ro; Pres. GAVRIL MIRZA.

Teleorman County Council: 0700 Alexandria, Str. Dunării 178; tel. (247) 311301; fax (247) 312494; e-mail cjt@cictelnet.ro; internet www.cictelnet.ro; Pres. NICOLAE LIVIU DRAGNEA.

Timiş County Council: Timişoara, Bd. Revoluţiei 17; tel. (256) 190592; fax (256) 190591; internet www.cjtimis.ro; Pres. DAN IOAN SIPOS.

Tulcea County Council: 8800 Tulcea, Str. Păcii 20; tel. (240) 511930; fax (240) 513071; e-mail office@cjtulcea.ro; internet www .cjtulcea.ro; Pres. TRIFON BELACURENCU.

Vâlcea County Council: 1000 Râmnicu Vâlcea, Str. General Praporgescu 5; tel. (250) 731027; fax (250) 735617; e-mail consjvl@unet .ro; internet www.cjvalcea.ro; Pres. IULIAN COMANESCU.

Vaslui County Council: 6500 Vaslui, Str. Ştefan cel Mare 79; tel. (235) 311962; fax (235) 312391; e-mail consiliu@cjvs.quantum.ro; internet www.vaslui.ro; Pres. ION MANOLE.

Vrancea County Council: 5300 Focşani, Bd. Dimitre Cantemir 1; tel. (237) 613211; fax (237) 612228; e-mail consiliu.judetean@ vrancea.ro; internet www.vrancea.ro; Pres. MARIAN OPRISAN.

Political Organizations

Following the downfall of President Ceauşescu in December 1989, numerous political parties were formed or re-established in preparation for the holding of free elections. By 1996 there were some 90 registered political parties. A law approved in September 2002 required all political parties to re-register by 31 December.

Christian Democratic National Peasants' Party of Romania (CDNPP) (Partidul Naţional Ţărănesc Creştin-Democrat din România—PNŢCD): 73231 Bucharest, Bd. Carol I 34; tel. (21) 6154533; fax (21) 6143277; internet www.pntcd.ro; f. 1989 by merger of centreright Christian Democratic Party and traditional National Peasant Party; f. 1869; banned 1947, revived Dec. 1989 original party re-established in Aug. 1990 by separate group; supports pluralist democracy and the restoration of peasant property; 615,000 mems; Chair. VICTOR CIORBEA; Sec.-Gen. CONSTANTIN DUDU IONESCU.

Civic Alliance (Alianţa Civică): Bucharest, Piaţa Amzei 13, etaj 2, Sector 1; tel. and fax (21) 6595903; f. 1990 as alliance of opposition groupings outside legislature; Chair. ANA BLANDIANA.

Democratic Alliance of Hungarians in Romania (DAHR) (Uniunea Democrată Maghiară din România—UDMR): Bucharest, Str. Avram Iancu 8; tel. (21) 3146849; fax (21) 3144583; e-mail elhivbuk@ dial.kappa.ro; internet www.rmdsz.ro; f. 1990; supports the rights of Hungarians in Romania; Pres. BÉLA MARKÓ; Exec. Pres. CSABA TAKÁCS.

Democratic Alliance Party: Sibiu; f. 1995; supports the rights of Gypsies in Romania; Leader FLORIN CIOABĂ.

Democratic Convention of Romania 2000 (DCR): 70401 Bucharest, Splaiul Independenţei 7, Bl. 101, Sector 5; tel. and fax (21) 3124014; alliance of 5 centre-right parties and other organizations formed to contest the legislative election of November 2000; Pres. ION DIACONESCU.

Democratic Party (DP) (Partidul Democrat—PD): 71274 Bucharest, Al. Modrogan 1; tel. and fax (21) 2301332; e-mail office@ pd.ro; internet www.pd.ro; f. 1993; fmrly Democratic Party—National Salvation Front; was to absorb the National Alliance in mid-2001; centre-left; advocates a modern and social-democratic Romania, with a free-market economy, and respect for the rights and freedoms of national minorities; Pres. TRĂIAN BĂSESCU; Sec.-Gen. VASILE BLAGA.

Greater Romania Party (GRP) (Partidul România Mare—PRM): 70101 Bucharest, Str. G. Clemenceau 8–10; tel. (21) 6130967; fax (21) 3126182; internet www.romare.ro; f. 1991; nationalist; Chair. CORNELIU VADIM TUDOR; Sec.-Gen. GHEORGHE FUNAR.

Humanist Party of Romania (Partidul Umanist din România): Bucharest, Calea Victoriei 118, etaj 5, Sector 1; tel. (21) 2125302; fax (21) 2125301; e-mail pur@itcnet.ro; internet www.pur.ro; f. 1991; Pres. DAN VOICULESCU.

Liberal Monarchist Party of Romania (Partidul Liberal Monarhist din România): Bucharest, Bd. George Coşbuc 1; tel. (21) 6134940; f. 1990; advocates the restoration of the monarchy; Pres. DAN CERNOVODEANU.

National Liberal Alliance: Bucharest; f. 1996; alliance of the Party of the Civic Alliance and the Liberal Party 1993; Leader NICOLAE MANOLESCU.

National Liberal Party (NLP) (Partidul Naţional Liberal—PNL): 70112 Bucharest, Bd. Aviatorilor 86; tel. (21) 2310795; fax (21) 2317511; e-mail dre@pnl.ro; internet www.pnl.ro; f. 1869; banned 1947; merged with Liberal Party in 1993, and with Party of the Civic Alliance and Liberal Party of Romania in 1998, absorbed Alliance for Romania AFR in 2002 and the Union of Right-Wing Forces in 2003; supports EU and NATO integration, advocates freedom of expression and religion, observance of the equal rights of all minorities, the privatization of enterprises, decentralization of state powers and a free and competitive market; Chair. THEODOR STOLOJAN.

National Union of the Centre: f. 1996; alliance of the Agrarian Democratic Party of Romania and the Romanian Humanistic Party; supports agrarian, ecological and humanitarian policies.

Patriotic Party of Reconciliation (PPR): Bucharest; f. 1998; centre-right; Leader Prince PAUL of Romania.

Popular Action (Actiunea Populara): f. 2003 by members of the Christian Democratic National Peasant's Party of Romania; scheduled to merge with the Popular Christian Party; Leader EMIL CONSTANTINESCU.

Popular Christian Party (PPC): Bucharest; f. 2001 by former members of the CDNPP; scheduled to merge with Popular Action in 2003; Leaders ANDREI MARGA, VASILE LUPU, CALIN CATALIN CHIRITA.

Romanian Communist Party: fmrly Romanian Workers' Party renamed as above in 1997; Leader CRISTIAN ION NICULAE.

Romanian Ecological Federation (REF) (Federaţia Ecologistă din România): 73226 Bucharest, Str. Matei Voievod 102; tel. (21) 6352743; alliance incl. the Romanian Ecological Movement; Leader GUGUI EDWARD.

Romanian Ecological Movement (Mişcarea Ecologistă din România): 70259 Bucharest, Str. Alexandru Phillippide 11; tel. (21) 2116943; fax (21) 2116858; f. 1990; advocates protection of the environment and the pursuit of democratic, pacifist and humanist values; Chair. TOMA GHEORGHE MAIORESCU.

Romanian Ecological Party (Partidul Ecologist Român): 70476 Bucharest, Str. Stelea Spătarul 10A; tel. (21) 6158285; merged with the Green Alternative Party of Ecologists and the Ecologist Convention in 2003; Chair. CORNELIU PROTOPOPESCU.

Romanian People's Party: f. 2000; far-right; Pres. RADU VASILE; Exec. Pres. SORIN LEPSA.

Social Democratic Party (SDP) (Partidul Social Democrat—PSD): 71271 Bucharest 2, Str. Kiseleff 10; tel. (21) 2222958; fax (21) 2223272; internet www.psd.ro; f. 2001 by the merger of the Romanian Social Democratic Party and the Party of Social Democracy of Romania; absorbed the Party of Moldovans in 2002; a merger with the Socialist Labour Party and the Socialist Party of National Revival was due to be completed in Sept. 2003; Chair. ADRIAN NĂSTASE; Pres. of National Council ALEXANDRU ATHANASIU; Sec.-Gen. DAN MATEI AGATHON.

Traditional National Liberal Party (PNL-T): Bucharest; f. 2000; previously known as PNL-Bratianus; part of Romanian Democratic Convention 2000; Leader DECEBAL TRĂIAN REMES.

Traditional Social Democratic Party of Romania (Partidul Social Democrat Tradiţional din România): 70208 Bucharest 2, Str. Aaron Florian 1; tel. (21) 2110479; fax (21) 2101707; f. 1991 by merger of Traditional Social Democratic Party and National Democratic Party; supports the Party of Social Democracy of Romania; centre-left; Pres. LUCIAN CERNESCU.

Diplomatic Representation

EMBASSIES IN ROMANIA

Albania: 71274 Bucharest, Str. Duiliu Zamfirescu 7, Sector 1; tel. (21) 2119829; fax (21) 2108039; e-mail albemb@dataline.ro; Ambassador LEONIDHA MERTIRI.

Algeria: 71111 Bucharest, Bd. Lascar Catargiu 29; tel. (21) 2115150; fax (21) 2115695; Ambassador MOHAMED LAICHOUBI.

Argentina: 70258 Bucharest, Str. Drobeta 11; tel. (21) 2117290; fax (21) 2101412; Ambassador DIANA BERRUHET.

Armenia: Bucharest 3, Str. Calotesti 1, ap. 2; tel. (21) 3215930; fax (21) 3215679; e-mail armembro@starnets.ro; Ambassador YEGISHE SARKISSIAN.

Austria: 70254 Bucharest, Str. Dumbrava Roşie 7; tel. (21) 2104354; fax (21) 2100885; e-mail bukarest-ka@bmaa.gv.at; Ambassador Dr CHRISTIAN ZEILEISSEN.

Azerbaijan: Bucharest, Str. Ion Caragea Voda 23; tel. (21) 2113044; fax (21) 2110513.

Belarus: Bucharest, Şos. Pavel Kiseleff 55, Vila 6; tel. (21) 2233510; fax (21) 2231763; e-mail ambasada.belarus@vipnet.ro; Ambassador ANATOLY I. BUTEVICH.

Belgium: 70256 Bucharest, Bd. Dacia 58; tel. (21) 2102969; fax (21) 2102803; e-mail ambabuc@ines.ro; Ambassador XAVIER VAN MIGEM.

Bolivia: Bucharest, Str. Mihai Eminescu 44–48, ap. 14; tel. (21) 2102600; fax (21) 2101338; e-mail embolivia@mail.roknet.ro; Ambassador HERNANDO GARCÍA SUÁREZ.

Brazil: 71248 Bucharest, Str. Praga 11; tel. (21) 2301130; fax (21) 2301599; e-mail braembuc@starnets.ro; Ambassador JERONIMO MOSCARDO DE SOUZA.

Bulgaria: 71272 Bucharest, Str. Rabat 5; tel. (21) 2122150; fax (21) 2307654; Ambassador NIKOLAI MILKOV.

Canada: 71118 Bucharest, Str. Nicolae Iorga 36; tel. (21) 3075000; fax (21) 3075015; e-mail bucst@dfait-maeci.gc.ca; internet www.dfait-maeci.gc.ca/Bucharest; Ambassador RAPHAEL A. GIRARD.

Chile: 71113 Bucharest, Str. Sevastopol 13–17; tel. (21) 3127239; fax (21) 3127246; e-mail embachile@consuladochile.ro; Ambassador MANUEL ENRIQUE HINOJOSA MUÑOZ.

China, People's Republic: 71512 Bucharest, Şos. Nordului 2; tel. (21) 2328858; fax (21) 2330684; Ambassador CHEN DELAI.

Colombia: 70188 Bucharest, Str. Poloná 35, ap. 3; tel. (21) 2115106; fax (21) 2100155; e-mail embcolro@bx.logicnet.ro; Ambassador ENRIQUE ARIAS JIMÉNEZ.

Congo, Democratic Republic: Bucharest, Str. Mihai Eminescu 50–54, ap. 15, Sector 2; tel. (21) 2108265; Ambassador GOMEZ DUMBA KIMBAYA.

Congo, Republic: Bucharest, Bd. Pachge Protopopescu 14; tel. and fax (21) 3153371; Chargé d'affaires GEORGES AMBARA.

Croatia: Bucharest, Str. Dr Burghelea 1, Sector 2; tel. (21) 3130457; fax (21) 3130384; e-mail crobuc@canad.ro; Ambassador ŽELJKO KUPRESAK.

Cuba: 71148 Bucharest, Str. Mihai Eminescu 44–48; tel. and fax (21) 2118916; Ambassador LÁZARO MÉNDEZ CABRERA.

Czech Republic: 70418 Bucharest, Str. Ion Ghica 11; tel. (21) 3159142; fax (21) 3122539; e-mail bukurest@ines.ro; Ambassador RADEK PECH.

Denmark: 73102 Bucharest, Str. Dr Burghelea 3; tel. (21) 3120352; fax (21) 3120358; e-mail buhamb@um.dk; Ambassador ERIK BOM.

Ecuador: Bucharest; tel. (21) 2103791; fax (21) 2103790; Chargé d'affaires a.i LEÓN PABLO AVILES SALGADO.

Egypt: 70185 Bucharest, Bd. Dacia 21; tel. (21) 2110938; fax (21) 2100337; e-mail egyptemb@canad.ro; Ambassador WAFAA ASHRAF MOUHARAM BASSIMN.

Finland: 71217 Bucharest, Str. Atena 2 bis; tel. (21) 2307504; fax (21) 2307505; e-mail finland@dnt.ro; internet www.finlandia.ro; Ambassador PEKKA HARTTILA.

France: 70172 Bucharest, Str. Biserica Amzei 13–15; tel. (21) 3120217; fax (21) 3120200; internet www.ambafrance-ro.org; Ambassador PHILIPPE ETIENNE.

Germany: 71272 Bucharest, Str. Aviator Gh. Demetriade 68; tel. (21) 2029830; fax (21) 2305846; e-mail botshaft@deutschebotshaft-bukarest.ro; Ambassador WILFRED GRUBER.

Greece: 71108 Bucharest, Str. Orlando 6; tel. (21) 2125688; fax (21) 2125690; e-mail hellas@com.pcnet.ro; internet www.grembassy.ro; Ambassador THEODORA GROSSOMANIDOU.

Holy See: 70749 Bucharest, Str. Pictor C. Stahi 5–7 (Apostolic Nunciature); tel. (21) 3139490; fax (21) 3120316; e-mail nuntius@fx.ro; Apostolic Nuncio Most Rev. JEAN-CLAUDE PÉRISSET (Titular Archbishop of Iustiniana prima).

Hungary: 70203 Bucharest, Str. Jean-Louis Calderon 63; tel. (21) 6146621; fax (21) 3120467; e-mail hunembro@ines.ro; internet hungaryemb.ines.ro; Ambassador ISTVÁN IJGYÁRTÓ.

India: 712663 Bucharest, Str. Uruguay 11; tel. (21) 2225451; fax (21) 2232681; e-mail indem@dnt.ro; Ambassador JAWAHAR LAL.

Indonesia: 71108 Bucharest, Str. Orlando 10; tel. (21) 3120742; fax (21) 3120214; e-mail indo.bucharest@itcner.ro; Ambassador TOTO SOEGIHARTO.

Iran: 71112 Bucharest 1, Bd. Lascar Catargiu 39; tel. (21) 3120493; fax (21) 3120496; Ambassador Dr AHMAD FARD HOSSEINI.

Israel: 751211 Bucharest, Bd. Dimitrie Cantemir 1; tel. (21) 3304149; fax (21) 3300750; e-mail israel.embassy@algoritma.ro; Ambassador SANDU MAZOR.

Italy: 711192 Bucharest, Str. Henri Coandă 7–9; tel. (21) 3113465; fax (21) 3124269; e-mail primosegretario@ambitalia.ro; internet www.ambitalia.ro; Ambassador ANNA BLEFARI MELAZZI.

Japan: 70189 Bucharest 1, Str. Polonă 4; tel. (21) 2100790; fax (21) 2100272; e-mail embjpn@mb.roknet.ro; Ambassador HIDEKATA MITSUHASHI.

Jordan: 702542 Bucharest, Str. Dumbrava Roşie 1; tel. (21) 2104705; fax (21) 2100320; e-mail jordan.embassy@pcnet.ro; Ambassador AZMI A. MIRZA.

Korea, Democratic People's Republic: 715145 Bucharest, Şos. Nordului 6; tel. and fax (21) 2329665; Ambassador KIM CHUN GIL.

Korea, Republic: 71293 Bucharest, Bd. Mircea Eliade 14; tel. (21) 2307198; fax (21) 2307629; e-mail koreaemb@kappa.ro; internet www.uriel.net/~romemb; Ambassador KIM EUN-KI.

Lebanon: 71271 Bucharest, Str. Atena 28, ap.1; tel. (21) 2309205; fax (21) 2307534; e-mail embassy.Lebanon@allnet.ro; Ambassador ABDEL MAJID EL KASSIR.

Liberia: 72111 Bucharest, Str. Mihai Eminescu 82–88, etaj 1, ap. 19–20; tel. (21) 6193029; Chargé d'affaires G. MARCUS KELLEY.

Libya: 71111 Bucharest, Bd. Lascar Catargiu 15; tel. (21) 6507105; fax (21) 3120232; Chargé d'affaires SALEH KHALIFA GWEIDA.

Macedonia, former Yugoslav Republic: Bucharest, Str. Gral Eremia Grigorescu 16; tel. (21) 2100880; fax (21) 2117295; e-mail ammakbuk@mb.roknet.ro; Ambassador BLAGOJ ZASOV.

Malaysia: Bucharest, Str. Mihai Eminescu 124A, etaj 3, ap. 8; tel. (21) 2113801; fax (21) 2100270; e-mail mwbucrst@itcnet.ro; Chargé d'affaires AZIZAN ISMAIL.

Mexico: 702281 Bucharest, Str. Armeneasca 35, Sector 2; tel. (21) 2104417; fax (21) 2104713; Ambassador ENRIQUE FERNÁNDEZ ZAPATA.

Moldova: 71273 Bucharest 1, Al. Alexandru 40; tel. (21) 2300474; fax (21) 2307790; e-mail moldova@customers.digiro.net; Ambassador EMIL CIOBU.

Morocco: 70256 Bucharest, Bd. Dacia 75; tel. (21) 2102945; fax (21) 2102767; e-mail ambmarbuc@xnet.ro; Ambassador TAHAR NEJJAR.

Netherlands: 72271 Bucharest, Str. Atena 18; tel. (21) 2086030; fax (21) 2307620; e-mail bkr@minbuza.nl; internet www.olanda.ro; Ambassador P. J. WOLTHERS.

Nigeria: 71108 Bucharest, Str. Orlando 9; tel. (21) 3128685; fax (21) 3120622; e-mail nigeremb@canad.ro; Ambassador M. G. S. SAMAKI.

Norway: 70254 Bucharest, Str. Dumbrava Roşie 4; tel. (21) 2100274; fax (21) 2100275; e-mail emb.bucharest@mfa.ro; Ambassador ARNT MAGNE RINDAL.

Pakistan: 71304 Bucharest 1, Str. Barbu Delavrancea 22; tel. (21) 2225736; fax (21) 2225737; e-mail parepbuc@k.ro; Ambassador NAZAR ABBAS.

Peru: Bucharest, Şos. Kiseleff 18; tel. (21) 2231253; fax (21) 2231088; e-mail embaperu@bx.logicnet.ro; Ambassador JOSÉ AUGUSTO TENORIO BENAVIDES.

Philippines: 71039 Bucharest, Str. Carol Davila 107; tel. (21) 2248058; fax (21) 2233500; e-mail daciafil@dnt.ro; Ambassador MARIA ROSARIO JANOLO.

Poland: 71273 Bucharest, Al. Alexandru 23; tel. (21) 2302330; fax (21) 2307832; e-mail ampolemb@mail.flamingo.ro; internet ampolbuk.kappa.ro/ambassada.html; Ambassador MICHAL KLINGER.

Portugal: 71249 Bucharest 1, Str. Paris 55; tel. (21) 2304136; fax (21) 2304117; e-mail embporrom@fx.ro; Ambassador ZOZIMO JUSTO DA SILVA.

Qatar: Bucharest, Str. Venezuela 10A; tel. (21) 2304741; fax (21) 2305446; Ambassador ALI SULTAN AL-ZAMAN.

Russia: 71269 Bucharest, Şos. Kiseleff 6; tel. (21) 2223170; fax (21) 2229450; e-mail rab@mb.roknet.ro; internet www.romania.mid.ro; Ambassador ALEKSANDR TOLKACH.

Serbia and Montenegro: 71132 Bucharest, Calea Dorobanţilor 34; tel. (21) 2119871; fax (21) 2100175; Ambassador DUŠAN FRANCUSKI.

Slovakia: 70206 Bucharest 2, Str. Otetari 3; tel. (21) 3126822; fax (21) 3122435; e-mail zusrbuh@fx.ro; Ambassador JAN SOTH.

Spain: 71274 Bucharest, Str. Tirana 1; tel. (21) 2121730; fax (21) 2307626; Ambassador JESÚS ATIENZA SERNA.

Sudan: 70256 Bucharest, Bd. Dacia 71; tel. (21) 2114967; fax (21) 2111217; e-mail sudanbuc@mb.roknet.ro; internet www.sudanbuc.net; Ambassador BASHIR MOHAMED EL-HASSAN.

Sweden: 71276 Bucharest, Str. Sofia 5; tel. (21) 2302184; fax (21) 2306256; e-mail ambassaden.bukarest@foreign.ministry.se; Ambassador SVANTE KILANDER.

Switzerland: 70152 Bucharest 1, Str. Pitar Moş 12; tel. (21) 2100299; fax (21) 2100324; e-mail vertretung@buc.rep.admin.ch; Ambassador FRANÇOIS CHAPPUIS.

Syria: 71114 Bucharest, Bd. Lascar Catargiu 50; tel. (21) 2124186; fax (21) 3129554; e-mail embsyrom@yahoo.com; Ambassador Dr BECHARA KHAROUF.

Thailand: Bucharest, Str. Vasile Conta 12; tel. (21) 3110031; fax (21) 3110044; Ambassador SURIYA ROSHANABUDDI.

Turkey: 71142 Bucharest, Calea Dorobanţilor 72; tel. (21) 2100279; fax (21) 2100407; e-mail bozkir@easynet.ro; Ambassador OMER ZEYTINOĞLU.

Ukraine: 71132 Bucharest, Calea Dorobanţilor 16; tel. (21) 2116986; fax (21) 2116949; e-mail emb_ro@mfa.gov.ua; Ambassador ANTON BUTEIKO.

United Kingdom: 70154 Bucharest, Str. Jules Michelet 24; tel. (21) 2017200; fax (21) 2017299; e-mail press.bucharest@fco.gov.uk; internet www.britain.ro; Ambassador QUINTON QUAYLE.

USA: Bucharest, Str. Tudor Arghezi 7–9; tel. (21) 2104042; fax (21) 2100395; internet www.usembassy.ro; Ambassador MICHAEL GUEST.

Uruguay: 70188 Bucharest, Str. Polonă 35, Scara A, ap. 5; tel. (21) 2118212; fax (21) 2100348; e-mail urubucar@bx.logicnet.ro; Ambassador JUAN DELMIRO PODESTÁ PIÑON.

Venezuela: 71312 Bucharest 1, Str. Pictor G.D. Mirea 18; tel. (21) 2225874; fax (21) 2226183; e-mail embavero@kappa.ro; Ambassador (vacant).

Viet Nam: 73112 Bucharest, Str. C. A. Rosetti 35; tel. (21) 3111604; fax (21) 3121626; e-mail ambviet@ebony.ro; Ambassador LE VAN TOAN.

Yemen: 71279 Bucharest, Bd. Aviatorilor 50; tel. (21) 2313272; fax (21) 2307679; Chargé d'affaires ABDELELAH M. AL-ERYANY.

Judicial System

SUPREME COURT

The Supreme Court of Justice, which was reorganized under Law 56 of 9 July 1993, exercises control over the judicial activity of all courts. It ensures the correct and uniform application of the law. The members of the Supreme Court are appointed by the President of Romania at the proposal of the Superior Council of Magistrates.

President: Prof. Dr GHEORGHE UGLEAN, 70503 Bucharest, Calea Rahovei 2–4; tel. (21) 3353750; fax (21) 3125890; internet www.sjc.ro.

CONSTITUTIONAL COURT

According to the Constitution approved by referendum on 8 December 1991, a Constitutional Court was to be established within six months. The first Constitutional Court of Romania was duly established in June 1992, under Law 47 of 18 May.

President: NICOLAE POPA, Bucharest, Parliament Palace, Calea 13 Septembrie 2, Sector 5; tel. (21) 3132531; fax (21) 3125480; e-mail ccr@ccr.ro; internet www.ccr.ro.

COUNTY COURTS AND LOCAL COURTS

The judicial organization of courts at the county and local levels was established by Law 92 of 4 August 1992. In each of the 40 counties of Romania there is a county court and between three and six local courts. The county courts also form 15 circuits of appeal courts, where appeals against sentences passed by local courts are heard, which are generally considered courts of first instance. There is also a right of appeal from the appeal courts to the Supreme Court. In both county courts and local courts the judges are professional magistrates.

MILITARY COURTS

Military courts were reorganized through Law 54 of 9 July 1993. Generally they judge contraventions of the law by service personnel at one of the two military courts in the country. These are the Territorial Military Court, with a right of appeal to the Appeal Military Court. There is also a military department within the Supreme Court which judges appeals in some special cases. The judges are professional lawyers and career officers.

GENERAL PROSECUTING MAGISTRACY

The General Prosecuting Magistracy functions under Law 92 of 4 August 1992. There are prosecuting magistracies operating through each court, under the authority of the Minister of Justice.

Prosecutor-General: TANASE JOITE, 76105 Bucharest 5, Bd. Libertăţi i 14; tel. (21) 4102727; fax (21) 3113939; e-mail pg@kappa.ro; internet www.mp.pcnet.ro.

Religion

In Romania there are 15 religious denominations and more than 400 religious associations recognized by the state. According to census figures, about 87% of the population belonged to the Romanian Orthodox Church in January 1992.

State Secretariat for Religious Affairs: 70136 Bucharest, Str. Nicolae Filipescu 40; tel. (21) 2118116; fax (21) 2109471; e-mail ssc@mediasat.ro; f. 1990; Minister Sec. of State LAURENŢIU TĂNASE.

CHRISTIANITY

The Romanian Orthodox Church

The Romanian Orthodox Church is the major religious organization in Romania (with more than 19m. believers) and is organized as an autocephalous patriarchate, being led by the Holy Synod, headed by a patriarch. The Patriarchate consists of five metropolitanates, nine archbishoprics and 12 bishoprics.

Holy Synod: 70666 Bucharest, Str. Antim 29; tel. (21) 3570803; fax (21) 3370822; Sec. Bishop TEOFAN SINAITUL.

Romanian Patriarchate
(Patriarhia Română)

70526 Bucharest, Al. Dealul Mitropoliei 25; tel. (21) 3374035; fax (21) 3370097; e-mail patriarhia@dnt.ro; internet www.patriarhia.ro.

Patriarch, Metropolitan of Muntênia and Dobrogea and Archbishop of Bucharest: TEOCTIST ARĂPAŞU, 70526 Bucharest, Str. Patriarhiei 21; tel. (21) 3372776.

Metropolitan of Banat and Archbishop of Timişoara and Caransebeş: Dr NICOLAE CORNEANU, 1900 Timişoara, Bd. Constantin Diaconovici Loga 7; tel. (256) 190960.

Metropolitan of Moldova and Bucovina and Archbishop of Iaşi: Dr DANIEL CIOBOTEA, 6600 Iaşi, Bd. Ştefan cel Mare şi Sfânt 16; tel. (232) 214771; fax (232) 212656; e-mail iecum@mail.dntis.ro.

Metropolitan of Oltenia and Archbishop of Craiova: TEOFAN, 1100 Craiova, Str. Mitropolit Firmilian 3; tel. (251) 415054; fax (251) 418369; e-mail mitrop_teofan@m-ol.ro; internet www.m-ol.ro.

Metropolitan of Transylvania, Crişana and Maramureş and Archbishop of Sibiu: Dr ANTONIE PLĂMĂDEALĂ, 2400 Sibiu, Str. Mitropoliei 24; tel. (269) 412867.

Archbishop of Suceava and Rădăuti: PIMEN ZAINEA, 5800 Suceava, Str. Ioan Vodă Viteazul 2; tel. (230) 215796.

Archbishop of Târgovişte: Dr NIFON MIHAITA, 0200 Târgovişte, Str. Mihai Bravu 5-8; tel. (245) 211588; e-mail ips-nifon@k.ro.

Archbishop of Tomis: LUCIAN FLOREA, 8700 Constanţa, Str. Muzeelov 23; tel. (241) 614257.

Archbishop of Vad, Feleac and Cluj: BARTOLOMEU ANANIA, 3400 Cluj-Napoca, Piaţa Avram Iancu 18; tel. (264) 559010; e-mail rev-renasterea@personal.ro.

The Roman Catholic Church

Catholics in Romania include adherents of the Armenian, Latin and Romanian (Byzantine) Rites.

Latin Rite

There are two archdioceses and four dioceses. At 31 December 2001 there were 1,256,512 adherents of the Latin Rite (about 5.8% of the total population).

Archbishop of Alba Iulia: Most Rev. GYÖRGY-MIKLÓS JAKUBÍNYI, 2500 Alba Iulia, Str. Mihai Viteazul 21; tel. (258) 811689; fax (258) 811454; e-mail albapress@apulum.ro.

Archbishop of Bucharest: Most Rev. IOAN ROBU, 70749 Bucharest, Str. Gen. Berthelot 19; tel. (21) 3154955; fax (21) 3121208.

Romanian Rite

There is one metropolitan and four dioceses. At 31 December 2001 there were 747,500 adherents of the Romanian Rite.

Metropolitan of the Romanian Uniate Church and Archbishop of Făgăraş and Alba Iulia: Most Rev. LUCIAN MUREŞAN, 3175 Blaj, Str. Petru Pavel Aron 2; tel. (258) 712057; fax (258) 710608; e-mail mitropoliablaj@albacomp.ro.

Protestant Churches

Baptist Union of Romania: 78152 Bucharest 1, Str. Dîmbovitei 9–11, Sector 6; tel. (21) 2205053; fax (21) 4302942; 1,450 churches; Pres. Pastor VASILE ALEXANDRU TALOŞ.

Evangelical Church of the Augsburg Confession in Romania: 2400 Sibiu, Str. General Magheru 4; tel. and fax (269) 217864; e-mail ev.landeskon@logon.ro; founded in the 16th century; comprises some 15,813 mems; mainly of German nationality; Bishop of Sibiu Dr CHRISTOPH KLEIN (tel. (69) 230202; fax (69) 217864); Gen. Sec. FRIEDRICH GUNESCH.

Reformed (Calvinist) Church

700,000 mems; two bishoprics.

Bishop of the Transylvanian Reformed Church District: Rev. GÉZA PAP, 3400 Cluj-Napoca, Str. I. C. Brătianu 51; tel. (264) 197472; fax (264) 195104; e-mail office@reformatus.ro.

Bishop of Oradea: LÁSZLÓ TŐKÉS, 3700 Oradea, Str. J. Calvin 1; tel. (259) 432837; e-mail partium@rdsor.ro; internet www .kiralyhagomellek.ro.

Romanian Evangelical Church: 76207 Bucharest, Str. Carol Davila 48; tel. (21) 6381004.

Evangelical-Lutheran Church of the Augsburg Confession in Romania: 3400 Cluj-Napoca, Bul. 22 Decembrie 1; tel. (264) 196614; fax (264) 193897; e-mail luthphkolozsvar@zortec.ro; comprises about 26,500 Hungarians, 4,000 Slovaks and 200 Romanians; Superintendent ÁRPÁD MÓZES.

Unitarian Church: 3400 Cluj-Napoca, Str. 21 Decembrie 9; tel. (264) 193236; fax (264) 195927; e-mail unitarian@mail.dntcj.ro; f. 1568; comprises about 75,000 mems of Hungarian nationality; 125 churches and 30 fellowships; Bishop ÁRPÁD SZABÓ.

Other Christian Churches

Armenian-Gregorian Church: 70228 Bucharest, Str. Armenească 9; tel. (21) 6139070; fax (21) 3121083; 5,000 mems; Archbishop TIRAIR MARTICHIAN.

Bulgarian Church: 70014 Bucharest, Str. Doamnei 18, Sector 4; tel. (21) 6135881.

Jehovah's Witnesses: 73217 Bucharest, Str. Teleajen 84, Sector 2; tel. (21) 3027500; fax (21) 3027501; e-mail ormi@zappmobile.ro.

Old-Rite Christian Church: 6100 Brăila, Str. Zidari 5; tel. (239) 647023; 50,000 mems of Russian nationality; Metropolitan TIMON GAVRILA.

Open Brethren Church: Head MELITON LAZAROVICI.

Pentecostal Church: 76252 Bucharest, Str. Carol Davila 81; tel. (21) 2126419; fax (21) 2204303; e-mail cuvadev@fx.ro; f. 1922; 2,455 churches, 525 pastors (Dec. 2001); 450,000 mems; Pres. Rev. RIVIS TIPEI PAVEL; Gen. Sec. Rev. IOAN GURĂU.

Serbian Orthodox Church: 1900 Timişoara, Piaţa Unirii 4; tel. and fax (256) 130426; Administrator Bishop LUKIJAN.

Seventh-day Adventist Church: 72900 Voluntari, Ilfov, Str. Erou Iancu Nicolae 38; tel. (21) 4908590; fax (21) 4908570; e-mail communicatii@adventist.ro; internet www.adventist.ro; f. 1920; 67,000 mems; Pres. of the Union Rev. ADRIAN BOCANEANU; Sec.-Gen. TEODOR HUTANU.

Ukrainian Orthodox Church: 4925 Sighetu Marmaţiei, Str. Bogdan Vodă 12; tel. (262) 511879.

Union of Brethren Assemblies: 72461 Bucharest, Andronache 60A; tel. and fax (21) 2407865; f. 1925; Pres. MIRCEA CIOATĂ.

BAHA'I FAITH

Baha'i Community: 70122 Bucharest, Bd. Nicolae Bălcescu 38, etaj 7, ap. 28; tel. (21) 6506120.

ISLAM

The Muslim Community comprises some 55,000 members of Turkish-Tatar origin.

Grand Mufti: OSMAN NEGEAT, 8700 Constanţa, Bd. Tomis 41; tel. (241) 611390.

JUDAISM

In 1999 there were about 14,000 Jews, organized in some 70 communities, in Romania.

Federation of Jewish Communities: 70478 Bucharest, Str. Sf. Vineri 9–11; tel. (21) 3132538; fax (21) 3120869; e-mail asivan@ pcnet.ro; Great Rabbi MENACHEM HACOHEN; Pres. Prof. Dr NICOLAE CAJAL.

The Press

The Romanian press is highly regionalized, with newspapers and periodicals appearing in all of the administrative districts. In 1996 there were a total of 1,313 newspapers and periodicals in circulation in Romania, including 106 daily newspapers. Some 106 newspapers and periodicals are published in the languages of co-inhabiting nationalities in Romania, including Hungarian, German, Serbian, Ukrainian, Armenian and Yiddish. The Ministry of Culture relinquished control of the press in June 1990.

The publications listed below are in Romanian, unless otherwise indicated.

PRINCIPAL DAILY NEWSPAPERS

Adevărul (Truth): 71341 Bucharest, Piaţa Presei Libere 1; tel. (21) 2240067; fax (21) 2243612; e-mail redactia@adevarul.kappa.ro; internet adevarul.kappa.ro; f. 1888; daily except Sun.; independent; Dir CHRISTIAN TUDOR POPESCU; circ. 200,000.

Azi (Today): 70101 Bucharest, Calea Victoriei 39A; tel. (21) 3144215; fax (21) 3120128; e-mail office@cicero.kappa.ro; f. 1990; independent; Editor-in-Chief OCTAVIAN ŞTIREANU.

Cotidianul (The Daily): 77107 Bucharest, Calea Plevnei 114; tel. (21) 3102052; fax (21) 3123764; e-mail rhpress@cotidianul.ro; internet www.cotidianul.ro; f. 1991; daily except Sun.; Dir of Marketing IOANA SAMAREANU; circ. 120,000.

Cronica Română: 75121 Bucharest, Calea Şerban Vodă 22–24; tel. (21) 3126363; fax (21) 3126813; f. 1992; daily; Dir HORIA ALEXANDRESCU; circ. 29,000.

Curierul Naţional (National Messenger): 70109 Bucharest, Str. Ministerului 2–4; tel. (21) 3159512; fax (21) 3121300; e-mail curiernr@bx.logicnet.ro; f. 1991; Dir-Gen. VALENTIN PAUNESCU; Editor-in-Chief MARIUS PETREAN; circ. 55,000.

Dimineata (Morning): Bucharest, Str. Roma 48; tel. (21) 2120337; fax (21) 2120496; f. 1990; Dir SORIN STEFAN STANCIU.

Evenimentul Zilei (Event of the Day): 71341 Bucharest, Piaţa Presei Libere 1; tel. (21) 2226381; fax (21) 2226382; f. 1991; tabloid; Editor-in-Chief GHEORGHE VOICU; circ. 200,000.

Gazeta Sporturilor (Sports Gazette): 70139 Bucharest, Str. Vasile Conta 16; tel. (21) 2111135; fax (21) 2100153; f. 1924; daily except Sun.; independent; Editor-in-Chief AURELIAN BREBEANU; circ. 50,000.

Jurnalul National (National Journal): Bucharest, Şos. Ficusului 44A; tel. (21) 2322467; fax (21) 2307944; f. 1993; Editor-in-Chief MARIUS TUCĂ; circ. 70,000.

Libertatea (Freedom): 70711 Bucharest, Şos. Fabrica de Glucoza Nr. 5, Sector 2; tel. (21) 2035646; fax (21) 2030830; internet www .libertatea.ro; f. 1989; daily except Sun.; morning paper; Editor-in-Chief ADRIAN HALPERT; circ. 140,000.

România Liber (Free Romania): 71341 Bucharest, Piaţa Presei Libere 1; tel. (21) 2224770; fax (21) 2232071; f. 1877; daily except Sun.; independent; Exec. Dir PETRE MIHAI BACANU; circ. 100,000.

Tineretul Liber (Free Youth): 71341 Bucharest, Piaţa Presei Libere 1; tel. (21) 2225040; fax (21) 2223313; f. 1989; daily except Sun. and Mon.; Editor-in-Chief ARISTOTEL BUNESCU.

Vocea Romaniei (Romanian Voice): Bucharest; tel. (21) 2227205; fax (21) 2226347; f. 1993; govt newspaper; Dir D. D. RUJAN.

Zina (The Day): Bucharest, Str. Ion Cimpineanu 4; tel. and fax (21) 3113155; f. 1930; Dir SORIN ROSCA STANESCU.

DISTRICT NEWSPAPERS

Alba

Ardealul: Alba Iulia; tel. (258) 13026; f. 1990; daily; Editor-in-Chief IOAN MAIER.

Unirea (The Union): 2500 Alba Iulia, Str. Decebal 27; tel. (258) 811420; f. 1990; independent; daily except Sun.; Gen. Man. GHEORGHE CIUL; Editor-in-Chief GHEORGHE YURCA; circ. 32,000.

Arad

Adevărul (The Truth): 2900 Arad, Bd. Revoluţiei 81; tel. (257) 213302; fax (257) 280655; f. 1989; independent; daily; Dir DOREL ZAVOIANU; circ. 53,000.

Argeş

Argeşul Liber (Free Argeş): Piteşti; tel. (276) 30490; f. 1990; independent; daily; Editor-in-Chief MARIN MANOLACHE.

Bacău

Deşteptărea (The Awakening): 5500 Bacău, Str. Vasile Alecsandri 63; tel. (234) 111272; fax (234) 124794; f. 1989; Man. CORNEL GALBEN; Editor-in-Chief IOAN ENACHE; circ. 50,000.

Bihor

Erdélyi Napló: 3700 Oradea, Sirul Canonicilor 25; tel. (259) 417158; fax (259) 417126; e-mail erdelyinaplo@rdslink.ro; internet www.hhrf.org/erdelyinaplo; f. 19901; in Hungarian; weekly; Editor-in-Chief LÁSZLÓ DÉNES.

Bistriţa-Năsăud

Răsunetul (Sound): 4400 Bistriţa, Str. Bistricioarei 6; tel. (290) 11684; f. 1990; journal of the National Salvation Front, Bistriţa-Năsăud County; Editor-in-Chief VASILE TABĂRĂ.

Botoşani

Gazeta de Botoşani: 6800 Botoşani, Bd. Mihai Eminescu 91; tel. (240) 851106; f. 1990; fmrly Clopotul; daily; Editor-in-Chief GHEORGHE ZANEA.

Brăila

Libertatea (Freedom): 6100 Brăila, Piaţa Independenţei 1; tel. (294) 635946; f. 1989; independent; daily; Editor-in-Chief RODICA CANĂ.

Braşov

Bună Zina Braşov (Good Afternoon Braşov): Braşov; tel. (268) 411073; fax (268) 411072; f. 1995; Dir DORU ŞUPEALĂ; circ. 30,000.

Gazeta de Transilvania (Transylvanian Gazette): 2200 Braşov, Str. M. Sadoveanu 3; tel. (268) 8142029; fax (268) 8152927; f. 1838; ceased publication 1946, re-established 1989; daily except Mon.; independent; Editor-in-Chief EDUARD HUIDAN.

Buzău

Opinia (Opinion): Buzău; tel. (238) 412764; fax (238) 711063; f. 1990; independent; daily; Editor-in-Chief CALIN BOSTAN.

Călăraşi

Pământul (Free Earth): 8500 Călăraşi, Str. Bucureşti 187; tel. (2911) 15840; fax (2911) 313630; f. 1990; socio-political; weekly; Editor-in-Chief GHEORGHE FRANGULEA.

Caraş-Severin

Timpul (The Times): 1700 Reşiţa, Piaţa Republicii 7; tel. (240) 412739; fax (240) 416709; f. 1990; independent daily; Editor-in-Chief GHEORGHE JURMA.

Cluj

Adevărul de Cluj (Truth of Cluj): 3400 Cluj-Napoca, Str. Napoca 16; tel. (264) 111032; fax (264) 192828; f. 1989; daily; independent; Editor-in-Chief ILIE CĂLIAN; circ. 200,000.

Szabadság (Freedom): 3400 Cluj-Napoca, Str. Napoca 16, POB 340; tel. (264) 198985; fax (264) 197206; e-mail szabadsag@mail.dntcj.ro; internet www.hhrf.org/szabadsag/szamok.htm; f. 1989; daily except Sun.; in Hungarian; Editor-in-Chief ÁRON BALLÓ; circ. 12,000.

Constanţa

Cuget Liber (Free Thinking): 8700 Constanţa, Bd. I. C. Brătianu 5; tel. (241) 665110; fax (241) 665606; f. 1989; independent; daily; Dir ARCADI STRAHILEVICI.

Covasna

Cuvântul nou (New Word): 4000 Sfântu Gheorghe, Str. Pieţei 8; tel. (240) 2311388; f. 1968; new series 1990; daily except Mon.; Editor-in-Chief DUMITRU MÂNOLĂCHESCU.

Háromszék (Three Chairs): 4000 Sfântu Gheorghe, Str. Presei 8A; tel. (240) 67351504; fax (240) 67351253; e-mail hpress@3szek.ro; internet www.3szek.ro; f. 1989; socio-political; daily; in Hungarian; Editor-in-Chief FARKAS ÁRPÁD.

Dâmboviţa

Dâmboviţa: 0200 Târgovişte, Str. Unirii 32; f. 1990; independent; daily; Editor-in-Chief ALEXANDRU ILIE.

Dolj

Cuvântul Libertăţii (Word of Liberty): 1100 Craiova, Str. Lyon 8; tel. (251) 2457; fax (251) 4141; f. 1989; daily except Sun.; Editor-in-Chief DAN LUPESCU; circ. 40,000.

Galaţi

Viaţa Libera (Free Life): 6200 Galaţi, Str. Domnească 68; tel. (23) 6456800; fax (23) 6457528; f. 1990; independent; daily; Dir RADU MACOVEI.

Giurgiu

Cuvântul Liber (Free Word): 8375 Giurgiu, Str. 1 Decembrie 1918 60A; tel. (2912) 21227; f. 1990; weekly; Editor-in-Chief ION GAGHII; circ. 10,000.

Gorj

Gorjanul: 1400 Târgu Jiu, Str. Constantin Brâncuşi 15; tel. (2929) 17464; f. 1990; socio-political; daily; Editor-in-Chief NICOLAE BRÎNZAN.

Harghita

Adevărul Harghitei (Truth of Harghita): 4100 Miercurea-Ciuc, Str. Leticeni 45; tel. (258) 13019; f. 1990; independent; daily; Editor-in-Chief MIHAI GROZA.

Új Sport (New Sport): 4100 Miercurea-Ciuc; tel. (258) 15940; fax (258) 152514; independent sports; daily; in Hungarian; Editor-in-Chief PÉTER LÁSZLÓ.

Hunedoara

Cuvântul Liber (Free Word): 2700 Deva, Str. 1 Decembrie 35; tel. (256) 11275; fax (256) 18061; f. 1949; daily except Mon.; Editor-in-Chief NICOLAE TÎRCOB; circ. 25,000.

Ialomiţa

Tribuna Ialomiţei (Ialomiţa Tribune): 8400 Slobozia, Str. Dobro-geanu-Gherea 2; f. 1969; weekly; Editor-in-Chief TITUS NIŢU.

Iaşi

Evenimentul: 6600 Iaşi, Str. Ştefan cel Mare 4; tel. (232) 112023; fax (232) 112025; e-mail evenimentul@mail.dntis.ro; f. 1991; daily; Editor-in-Chief CONSTANTIN PALADUTA.

Monitorul: 6600 Iaşi, Str. Smârdan 5; tel. (232) 271271; fax (232) 270415; daily; Editor-in-Chief DAN RADU; circ. 40,000.

Opinia (Opinion): 6600 Iaşi, Str. Vasile Alecsandri 8; tel. (232) 452105; f. 1990; social, political and cultural; daily; Editor-in-Chief VASILE FILIP.

Maramureş

Graiul Maramureşului (Voice of Maramureş): 4800 Baia Mare, Bd. Bucureşti 25; tel. (262) 221017; fax (262) 224871; e-mail graiul@sintec.ro; f. 1989; independent; daily; Editor-in-Chief AUGUSTIN COZMUŢA.

Bányavidéki Új Szó (Miner's New Word): 4800 Baia Mare, Bd. Bucureşti 25; tel. (262) 274465; fax (262) 432585; e-mail genius@sintec.ro; f. 1989; weekly; in Hungarian; Editor-in-Chief MARIA SZILVESZTER.

Mehedinţi

Datina (Tradition): 1500 Drobeta-Turnu-Severin, Str. Traâan 89; tel. (2978) 119950; f. 1990; independent; daily; Editor-in-Chief GHEORGHE BUREŢEA.

Mureş

Cuvântul Liber (Free Word): 4300 Târgu Mureş, Str. Gh. Doja 9; tel. (265) 36636; f. 1990; independent; daily; Editor-in-Chief LAZĂR LADARIU.

Népújság (People's Journal): 4300 Târgu Mureş, Str. Gh. Doja 9; tel. (265) 166780; fax (265) 166270; e-mail impress@netsoft.ro; f. 1990; daily; in Hungarian; Editor-in-Chief JÁNOS MAKKAI.

Neamţ

Ceahlăul: 5600 Piatra-Neamţ, Al. Tiparului 14; tel. and fax (233) 625282; f. 1989; daily; Editor-in-Chief VIOREL TUDOSE; circ. 20,000.

Olt

Glasul Adevărului (Voice of the Truth): 0500 Slatina, Str. Filimon Sârbu 5; tel. (244) 22131; f. 1990.

Prahova

Prahova: 2000 Ploieşti, Bd. Republicii 2; tel. (244) 141245; fax (244) 111206; f. 1870; Editor-in-Chief DUMITRU CÂRSTEA; circ. 17,000.

Sălaj

Graiul Sălajului (Voice of Sălaj): 4700 Zalău, Piaţa Unirii 7; tel. (299) 614120; f. 1990; daily; Editor-in-Chief IOAN LUPA.

Szilágyság (Word from Sălaj): 4700 Zalău, Piaţa Libertăţii 9, POB 68; tel. (299) 633736; f. 1990; organ of Hungarian Democratic Union of Romania; weekly; Editor-in-Chief János Kui.

Satu Mare

Ardealul: 3900 Satu Mare; tel. (261) 730661; f. 1990; organ of Christian Democratic National Peasants' Party; weekly; Dir Nae Antonescu.

Szatmári Friss Újság: 3900 Satu Mare, Str. M. Viteazu 32; tel. (261) 712024; fax (261) 714654; e-mail szfu@multiarea.ro; internet www.hhrf.org/frissujsag; f. 1990; daily except Sun.; in Hungarian; Editor-in-Chief Veres István.

Sibiu

Tribuna: Sibiu, Str. Dr Ratiu 7; tel. (292) 413833; fax (292) 412026; f. 1884; daily; independent; Editor-in-Chief Octavian Rusu; circ. 40,000.

Suceava

Crai nou: 5800 Suceava, Str. Mihai Viteazul 32; tel. (230) 214723; fax (230) 530285; e-mail redactie@crainou.ro; f. 1990; daily; Editor-in-Chief Teodorescu Dumitru.

Teleorman

Teleormanul Liber (Free Teleorman): 0700 Alexandria, Str. Ion Creangă 63, jud. Teleorman; tel. (247) 311950; fax (247) 323871; e-mail etl@starnets.ro; f. 1990; daily; Editor-in-Chief Gheorghe Filip.

Timiş

Renasterea Banateana: Timişoara, Bd. Revolutiei 8; tel. (256) 197176; fax (256) 190370; f. 1990; Editor-in-Chief Adrian Pop; circ. 50,000.

Timişoara: 1900 Timişoara, Str. Brediceanu 37A; tel. (256) 123401; fax (256) 146170; f. 1990; daily; Dirs George Serban, Lucian Vasile Szabo.

Tulcea

Delta (The Delta): 8800 Tulcea, Str. Spitalului 4; tel. (2405) 12406; fax (2405) 16616; f. 1885; new series 1990; daily except Mon.; Editor-in-Chief Neculai Amihulesei.

Vaslui

Adevărul (Truth): 6500 Vaslui, Str. Ştefan cel Mare 79; tel. (2983) 12203; socio-cultural publication; twice weekly; f. 1990; Editor-in-Chief Teodor Praxiu.

Vâlcea

Curierul de Vâlcea (Courier of Vâlcea): 1000 Râmnicu Vâlcea, Calea lui Traian 127; tel. (250) 718394; fax (250) 732423; f. 1990; independent; daily except Mon.; commerce; Dir Ioan Barbu.

Vrancea

Milcovul Liber (Free Milcov): 5300 Focşani, Bd. Unirii 18; tel. (237) 614579; fax (237) 613588; f. 1989; weekly; Dir Ovidiu Butuc.

PRINCIPAL PERIODICALS

Bucharest

22: 70179 Bucharest, Calea Victoriei 120; tel. (21) 3141776; fax (21) 3112208; e-mail r22@r22.sfos.ro; f. 1990; weekly; published by the Group for Social Dialogue; Editor-in-Chief Gabriela Adameşteanu; circ. 13,000.

Academia Catavencu (Dubious Academy): Bucharest; tel. (21) 4209459; fax (21) 6362760; f. 1991; weekly; satirical; Dir Mircea Dinescu; circ. 85,000.

Astrologia (Astrology): Bucharest, Piaţa Presei Libere 1; f. 1996; monthly; Editor-in-Chief Aurora Indan.

Auto Pro: Bucharest; tel. (21) 4113225; fax (21) 4111043; f. 1994; monthly; motor-vehicles; Editor-in-Chief Dan Vardie; circ. 50,000.

Bursa: Bucharest, Str. Balcesti 7, Sector 3; tel. (21) 3228691; fax (21) 3124556; e-mail marketing@bursa.ro; f. 1990; finance; Editor-in-Chief Florian Goldstein; circ. 35,000.

Capital: Bucharest, Şos. Fabrica de Glucoza 5, Sector 2; tel. (21) 2030802; fax (21) 2425359; e-mail office@capital.ro; internet www .capital.ro; f. 1990; weekly; Editor-in-Chief Ionut Popescu; circ. 60,000.

Doina: 71341 Bucharest, Piaţa Presei Libere 1; tel. (21) 2223346; fax (21) 2244801; f. 1991; monthly; Dir Vasile Tincu.

Economistul (The Economist): Bucharest, Calea Grivitei 21; tel. (21) 6507820; fax (21) 3129717; f. 1990; daily; Editor-in-Chief Ioan Erhan.

Contemporanul—Ideea Europeană: 71341 Bucharest, Piaţa Presei Libere 1; tel. (21) 177316; f. 1881; weekly; cultural, political and scientific review, published by the Ministry of Culture; Dir Nicolae Breban.

Expres Magazin: 71341 Bucharest 1, Piaţa Presei Libere 1; tel. (21) 2225119; fax (21) 3128381; independent; weekly; Dir Cornel Nistor-escu; circ. 98,000.

Familia Moderna (Modern Family): 71341 Bucharest, Piaţa Presei Libere 1; tel. (21) 2223209; fax (21) 2227810; f. 1995; Dir Vasile Tincu.

Femeia Moderna (Modern Woman): 71341 Bucharest, Piaţa Presei Libere 1; tel. (21) 2223346; fax (21) 2224801; f. 1868; monthly; Dir Vasile Tincu.

Flacăra (The Flame): 71341 Bucharest 1, Piaţa Presei Libere 1; tel. (21) 2243688; fax (21) 2273713; e-mail redactia@flacara21.ro; internet www.flacara21.ro; f. 1911; monthly; Editor-in-Chief Alex-andru Arion; circ. 30,000.

Fotbal (Football): 79778 Bucharest, Vasile Conta 16; tel. (21) 2111288; fax (21) 2100153; f. 1966; weekly; independent; Editor-in-Chief Laurentiu Dumitrescu; circ. 55,000.

Jurnalul Afacerilor (Business Journal): Bucharest, Piaţa Presei Libere 1; tel. (21) 2223760; fax (21) 2230691; f. 1990; Dir Marcel Barbu; circ. 25,000.

Luceafărul (The Morning Star): 71102 Bucharest, Calea Victoriei 133; tel. (21) 596760; f. 1958; weekly; published by the Writers' Union; Dir Laurentiu Ulici.

Magazin (The Magazine): Bucharest, Piaţa Presei Libere 1; tel. (21) 2225111; fax (21) 2230866; f. 1958; Dir Filip Dumitru.

Magazin istoric (Historical Magazine): 70711 Bucharest, Piaţa Valter Mărăcinea; tel. (21) 3126877; fax (21) 3150991; e-mail mistoric@itcnet.ro; internet www.itcnet.ro/history/magazin.htm; f. 1967; monthly; review of historical culture; Chief Editor Dorin Matei; circ. 35,000.

Meridian: Bucharest; tel. (21) 6155332; fax (21) 3121706; f. 1993; Editor-in-Chief Constantin Zlibut.

Panoramic Radio-TV: 79757 Bucharest, Str. Molière 2–4; tel. (21) 2307501; fax (21) 156992; e-mail micara.dumutrescu@tvr.ro; f. 1990; weekly; Dir Stefan Dimitriu; Editor-in-Chief Adrian Ionescu; circ. 50,000.

PC World Romania: 71316 Bucharest, Bd. Mareşal Averescu 8–10, Sector 1; tel. and fax (21) 2241132; e-mail pcworld@idg.ro; internet www.pcworld.ro; f. 1993; monthly; computing and internet magazine; Editor-in-Chief Bogdan Learschi; circ. 15,000.

Revista Română de Statistică (Romanian Review of Statistics): 70542 Bucharest, Bd. Libertăţii 16; tel. (21) 4106744; fax (21) 3124873; e-mail munteanu@cns.kappa.ro; f. 1952; monthly; organ of the National Statistics Commission; Editor-in-Chief Nicolae Gâr-ceag.

România Literară (Literary Romania): 71102 Bucharest, Calea Victoriei 133; tel. (21) 6506286; fax (21) 6503369; e-mail romlit@ romlit.ro; internet www.romlit.ro; f. 1968 as successor to Gazeta Literară; weekly; literary, artistic and political magazine; published by the Fundation România Literară (Writers' Union); Dir Nicolae Manolescu; Editor-in-Chief Alex Ştefănescu.

România Mare (Greater Romania): 70101 Bucharest, Calea Victoriei 39A; tel. (21) 6156093; fax (21) 3125396; f. 1990; weekly; independent nationalist; Editor-in-Chief Corneliu Vadim Tudor; circ. 90,000.

Romanian Panorama: 71341 Bucharest, Piaţa Presei Libere 1, Corp B, POB 33–38; tel. (21) 2242162; fax (21) 2243608; e-mail rps@ dial.kappa.ro; internet www.wsp.ro; f. 1955; monthly; in English, French, German, Russian and Spanish; economy, politics, social questions, science, history, culture, sport, etc.; published by the Foreign Languages Press Group; Dir Nicolae Şarambei; circ. 166,000.

Super Magazin: Bucharest, Piaţa Presei Libere 1; tel. (21) 2223323; fax (21) 2226382; f. 1993; Editor-in-Chief Gheorghe Voicu; circ. 200,000.

Tehnium: 79784 Bucharest, Piaţa Presei Libere 1; tel. (21) 2223711; f. 1970; monthly; hobbies; Editor-in-Chief Ing. Ilie Mihăescu; circ. 100,000.

Telecom Romania: Bucharest; tel. (21) 2120340; f. 1994; bi-monthly; networking and telecommunications; Editor-in-Chief Andrei Savu.

Tribuna economică (Economic Tribune): 70159 Bucharest, Bd. Magheru 28–30; tel. (21) 6592270; fax (21) 6595158; e-mail tribunae@dnt.ro; f. 1886; weekly; Editor-in-Chief BOGDAN PADURE; circ. 25,000.

Vânătorul şi Pescarul Român (The Romanian Hunter and Angler): 70344 Bucharest, Calea Moşilor 128; tel. (21) 3133363; fax (21) 3136804; f. 1948; monthly review; published by the General Association of Hunters and Anglers; Editor-in-Chief GABRIEL CHEROIU.

Cluj-Napoca

Korunk (Our Time): 3400 Cluj-Napoca, Str. Iasilor 14; tel. and fax (264) 432154; e-mail korunk@mail.dntcj.ro; internet www.hhrf.org/korunk; f. 1926; monthly; social review; in Hungarian; Editor-in-Chief LAJOS KÁNTOR; circ. 1,500.

Napsugár (Sun Ray): 3400 Cluj-Napoca, Str. L. Rebreanu 58/28, POB 137; tel. and fax (264) 141323; e-mail napsugar@mail.dntcj.ro; internet www.dntcj.ro/ngos/napsugar; f. 1956; monthly illustrated literary magazine for children aged 7–10 years; in Hungarian; Editor-in-Chief EMESE ZSIGMOND; circ. 18,000.

Szivárvány (Rainbow): 3400 Cluj-Napoca, Str. L. Rebreanu 58/28, POB 137; tel. and fax (264) 141323; e-mail napsugar@mail.dntcj.ro; f. 1980; monthly illustrated literary magazine for children aged 3–6 years; in Hungarian; Editor-in-Chief EMESE ZSIGMOND; circ. 21,500.

Tribuna: 3400 Cluj-Napoca, Str. Universităţii 1; tel. (264) 117548; f. 1884; weekly; cultural review; Editor-in-Chief AUGUSTIN BUZURA.

Iaşi

Cronica: 6600 Iaşi, Str. Vasile Alecsandri 6; tel. (232) 146433; fax (232) 211086; e-mail valerist@mail.dntis.ro; f. 1966; monthly; cultural review; Editor-in-Chief VALERIU STANCU; circ. 5,000.

Timişoara

Orizont (Horizon): 1900 Timişoara, Piaţa Sf. Gheorghe 3; tel. and fax (256) 133376; f. 1949; weekly; review of the Writers' Union (Timişoara branch); Editor-in-Chief MIRCEA MIHAIES.

Târgu Mureş

Erdélyi Figyelö (Transylvanian Observer): 4300 Târgu-Mureş, Str. Primăriei 1; tel. (265) 166910; fax (265) 168688; f. 1958; fmrly Uj Élet; trimestrial; illustrated magazine; in Hungarian; Editor-in-Chief JÁNOS LÁZOK.

Lató (Visionary): 4300 Târgu Mureş, Str. Tuşnad 5; tel. and fax (265) 167087; f. 1953; fmrly Igaz Szó; monthly; in Hungarian; literature; Editor-in-Chief BÉLA MARKÓ; circ. 1,000.

NEWS AGENCIES

ROMPRES (Romanian National News Agency): 71341 Bucharest, Piaţa Presei Libere 1; tel. (21) 2228340; fax (21) 2220089; e-mail webmaster@rompres.ro; internet www.rompres.ro; f. 1949; fmrly Agerpres; provides news and photo services to more than 110 subscribers in Romanian media and 40 overseas news agencies; daily news released in English and French; publs news and feature bulletins in English and French; Chamber of Deputies reassumed control in Feb. 2002; Gen. Man. CONSTANTIN BADEA.

Nord-Est Press: 6600 Iaşi, Str. Smirdan 5; tel. and fax (232) 144776; independent regional news agency for north-east Romania; Editor MONA DIRTU.

Foreign Bureaux

Agence France-Presse (AFP): 70151 Bucharest, Str. Pitar Moş 25, ap. 26; tel. (21) 2100261; Correspondent FRANÇOISE MICHEL.

Agenzia Nazionale Stampa Associata (ANSA) (Italy): 70401 Bucharest, Bd. Unirii 8, Bl. 7A; tel. and fax (21) 6335325; f. 1970; Chief Correspondent GIAN MARCO VENIER.

Allgemeiner Deutscher Nachrichtendienst (ADN) (Germany): Bucharest; tel. (21) 111214; Correspondent MICHAEL HUBE.

Associated Press (AP) (USA): 70122 Bucharest, Bd. Nicolae Bălcescu 30, ap. 14; tel. (21) 3120288.

Bulgarska Telegrafna Agentsia (BTA) (Bulgaria): Bucharest, Str. Mihai Eminescu 124, Inter B, etaj 5, ap. 12; tel. (21) 191880; Correspondent PETYO PETKOV.

Deutsche Presse-Agentur (dpa) (Germany): Bucharest; tel. (21) 121481; fax (21) 123079; Correspondent JOACHIM SONNENBERG.

Informatsionnoye Telegrafnoye Agentstvo Rossii– Telegrafnoye Agentstvo Suverennykh Stran (ITAR—TASS) (Russia): Bucharest, Str. Armeneasca 41; tel. (21) 2106050; fax (21) 2107490; e-mail itartass@mb.roknet.ro; Correspondent NIKOLAI N. MOROZOV.

Magyar Távirati Iroda (MTI) (Hungary): 72238 Bucharest, Al. Alexandru 10, ap. 1; tel. and fax (21) 2307741; e-mail mtibuc@pcnet.ro; internet www.mti.hu; Correspondent ISTVÁN GOZON.

Polska Agencja Prasowa (PAP) (Poland): Bucharest; tel. (21) 206870; Correspondent STANISŁAW WOJNAROWICZ.

Reuters (UK): Bucharest; tel. (21) 3158772; fax (21) 6158448.

Rossiiskoye Informatsionnoye Agentstvo—Novosti (RIA—Novosti) (Russia): 76100 Bucharest, Pandur Hw. 15, Block P18, ap. 6, Sector 5; tel. (21) 4108855; fax (21) 4115812; Correspondent VYACHESLAV SAMOSHIN.

Xinhua (New China) News Agency (People's Republic of China): 71512 Bucharest, Şos. Nordului 2; tel. (21) 2329675; fax (21) 2320258; e-mail xinhua@dial.kappa.ro; Correspondent CHEN JIN.

PRESS ASSOCIATIONS

Society of Romanian Journalists—Federation of All Press Unions (Societatea Ziariştilor din România—Federaţia Sindicatelor din Întreaga Presă): Bucharest, Piaţa Presei Libere 1; tel. (21) 2228351; fax (21) 2224266; f. 1990; affiliated to International Organization of Journalists and to International Federation of Journalists; Pres. RADU SORESCU; 5,000 mems.

The Union of Professional Journalists (Pres. ŞTEFAN MITROI) was established in 1990, as was the Democratic Journalists' Union (Pres. P. M. BACANU). There is also an Association of Hungarian Journalists of Romania (Pres. LAJOS KANTOR).

Publishers

Editura Academiei Române (Publishing House of the Romanian Academy): 76117 Bucharest, Calea 13 Septembrie 13; tel. (21) 4119008; fax (21) 4103983; e-mail edacad@ns.ear.ro; internet www.ear.ro; f. 1948; important books and periodicals on original scientific work, 96 periodicals in Romanian and foreign languages; Dir GHEORGHE MIHĂILĂ.

Editura Albatros: 71341 Bucharest, Piaţa Presei Libere 1, Of. 33; tel. (21) 2228493; f. 1971; Editor-in-Chief GEORGETA DIMISIANO.

Editura Artemis (Artemis Publishing House): 71341 Bucharest, Piaţa Presei Libere 1; tel. (21) 2226661; f. 1991; fine arts, fiction, children's literature, history; Dir MIRELLA ACSENTE.

Editura Cartea Românească (Publishing House of the Romanian Book): Bucharest; tel. (21) 3123733; fax (21) 3110025; f. 1969; Romanian contemporary literature; Dir DAN CRISTEA.

Editura Ceres: 71341 Bucharest, Piaţa Presei Libere 1; tel. (21) 2224836; f. 1953; books on agriculture and forestry; Dir MARIA DAMIAN.

Editura Dacia SA (Dacia Publishing House): 3400 Cluj-Napoca, Str. Paul Chinezul 2; tel. and fax (264) 194912; f. 1969; classical and contemporary literature, science fiction, academic, technical, philosophical and scientific books in Romanian and Hungarian; Gen. Man. IOAN VĂDAN.

Editura Didactică şi Pedagogică (Educational Publishing House): 70738 Bucharest, Str. Spiru Haret 12; tel. and fax (21) 3122885; e-mail edp@totalnet.ro; internet www.edituradp.ro; f. 1951; school, university, technical and vocational textbooks; pedagogic literature and methodology; teaching materials; Gen. Man. Prof. MIHAELA ZĂRNESCU-ENCEANU.

Editura Eminescu (Eminescu Publishing House): 701141 Bucharest, bd. Nicolae Bălcescu 33, Bloc UMIC, sc. B, Ap. 7; tel. and fax (21) 3137410; e-mail edituraeminescu@yahoo.com; internet www.edituraeminescu.com; f. 1969; contemporary original literary works and translations of world literature; Dir SILVIA CINCA.

Editura Enciclopedică (Encyclopaedic Publishing House): 71341 Bucharest, Piaţa Presei Libere 1; tel. and fax (21) 2243667; f. 1968; merged with Scientific Publishing House, as Editura Ştiinţifică şi Enciclopedică, 1974–90; encyclopaedias, dictionaries, bibliographies, chronologies, monographs, reference books and children's books; popular and informational literature; provides photographs and encyclopaedic and statistical data about Romania for publishing houses abroad; Dir MARCEL POPA.

Editura Humanitas (Humanitas Publishing House): 79734 Bucharest, Piaţa Presei Libere 1; tel. (21) 2228546; fax (21) 2243632; e-mail editors@agora.humanitas.ro; internet www.humanitas.ro; f. 1990; philosophy, religion, political and social sciences, economics, history, fiction, textbooks, art, literature, practical books; Dir GABRIEL LIICEANU.

Editura Ion Creangă SA (Ion Creangă Publishing House): 71341 Bucharest, Piaţa Presei Libere 1; tel. (21) 2223254; fax (21) 2231112; f. 1969; children's books; Dir DANIELA CRĂSNARU.

Editura Junimea (Junimea Publishing House): 6600 Iaşi, Str. Cuza Vodă 29, POB 28; tel. (232) 117290; f. 1969; Romanian literature, art books, translations, scientific and technical books; Dir CONSTANTIN DRAM.

Editura Kriterion (Kriterion Publishing House): 70002 Bucharest, str. Franceza 6/1; tel. and fax and fax (21) 3146246; e-mail krit@dnt .ro; internet www.kriterion.ro; f. 1969; classical and contemporary literature, reference books in science and art in Hungarian, German, Romanian, Russian, Serbian, Slovak, Tatar, Turkish, Ukrainian and Yiddish; translations in Romanian, Hungarian and German; Dir GYULA H. SZABÓ.

Editura Litera (The Letter Publishing House): Bucharest; tel. and fax (21) 2224829; f. 1969; original literature; Dir VIORICA OANCEA.

Editura Medicală SA (Medical Publishing House): 70406 Bucharest, Str. Smârdan 5; tel. (21) 6143252; fax (21) 3124879; f. 1954; medical literature; Dir Prof. AL. C. OPROIU.

Editura Meridiane (Meridiane Publishing House): 71341 Bucharest, Piaţa Presei Libere 1; tel. (21) 2243623; fax (21) 2223037; f. 1952; arts, history, biographies, religion, social sciences, cultural studies, media, anthropology, essays, medicine, travel, archaeology, linguistics; Dir ELENA-VICTORIA JIQUIDI; Senior Editors LIVIA SZASZ CÂMPEANU, ANDREI NICULESCU.

Editura Militară (Military Publishing House): 70764 Bucharest, Str. Gen. Constantin Cristescu 3–5; tel. and fax (21) 3112191; f. 1950; military history, theory, science, technics, medicine and fiction; Dir LUCIAN JUMĂTATE.

Editura Minerva (Minerva Publishing House): 71341 Bucharest, Piaţa Presei Libere 1; tel. and fax (21) 2224823; f. 1969; Romanian classical literature, world literature, original literary works, literary criticism and history; Dir ONDINE DASCĂLIŢA.

Editura Muzicală (Musical Publishing House): 71102 Bucharest, Calea Victoriei 141; tel. and fax (21) 3129867; e-mail editura_muzicala@hotmail.com; f. 1957; books on music, musicology and musical scores; Dir MARIUS VASILEANU.

Editura pentru Turism (Tourism Publishing House): 70161 Bucharest 1, Bd. Gh. Magheru 7; tel. (21) 6145160; f. 1990; tourism; Dir VICTOR CRĂCIUN.

Editura Porto-Franco (Porto-France Publishing House): 6200 Galati, Bd. George Coşbuc 223A; tel. (236) 464602; fax (236) 461204; f. 1990; literary and scientific books, translations; Dir ADRIANA ALDEA.

Editura Presa Libera (Free Press Publishing House): 71341 Bucharest, Piaţa Presei Libere 1; f. 1954; newspapers, magazines.

Editura Scrisul Românesc (Romanian Writing Publishing House): 1100 Craiova, Str. Mihai Viteazul 4; tel. (241) 413763; fax (251) 419506; e-mail scrisulromanesc@topedge.ro; f. 1922; socio-political, technical, scientific and literary works; Dir MARIUS GHICA.

Editura Sport-Turism (Sport-Tourism Publishing House): 79736 Bucharest, Str. Vasile Conta 16; tel. (21) 107480; f. 1968; sport, tourism, monographs, translations, postcards, children's books; Dir MIHAI CAZIMIR.

Editura Ştiinţifică (Scientific Publishing House): 71341 Bucharest, Piaţa Presei Libere 1; tel. and fax (21) 2223330; f. 1990; fmrly Editura Ştiinţifică şi Enciclopedică; language dictionaries, bibliographies, monographs, chronologies, reference books, popular and informational literature; Dir DINU GRAMA.

Editura Tehnică (Technical Publishing House): 71341 Bucharest, Piaţa Presei Libere 1; tel. (21) 2228348; fax (21) 2242164; e-mail tehnica@mail.tehnica.ro; internet www.tehnica.ro; f. 1950; technical and scientific books, technical dictionaries; Dir ROMAN CHIRILĂ.

Editura Univers: 79379 Bucharest, Piaţa Presei Libere 1; tel. (21) 2226629; fax (21) 2243765; e-mail univers@rnc.ro; f. 1961; translations from world literature, criticism, essays, literary history, philosophy of culture, educational; Dir Prof. Dr MIRCEA MARTIN.

Editura de Vest (West Publishing House): 1900 Timişoara, Piaţa Sfântul Gheorghe 2; tel. (256) 18218; fax (256) 14212; f. 1972 as Editura Facla; socio-political, technical, scientific and literary works in Romanian, Hungarian, German and Serbian; Dir VASILE POPOVICI.

Rao International Publishing: 78217 Bucharest, Bd. 1 Mai 125; tel. (21) 2104588; fax (21) 2228059; educational books.

Tribuna Press and Publishing House: 2400 Sibiu, Str. George Coşbuc 38; tel. (224) 12810; fax (224) 12026; f. 1991; Dir EMIL DAVID.

PUBLISHERS' ASSOCIATIONS

Cultura Naţională: 79715 Bucharest, Piaţa Presei Libere 1; tel. (21) 6181255; state organization attached to Ministry of Culture; administration, production and distribution of literary magazines and books of national interest; organization of imports and exports.

Romanian Association of Publishers (Asociaţia Editorilor din România): 701641 Bucharest, Bd. Magheru 35, Et. 4, Ap. 42; tel. (21) 2125162; fax (21) 2125178; e-mail info@aer.ro; internet www.aer.ro; f. 1993; 50 mems; Pres. GABRIEL LIICEANU.

WRITERS' UNION

Romanian Writers' Union (Uniunea Scriitorilor din România): 71102 Bucharest, Calea Victoriei 115; tel. (21) 6507245; fax (21) 3129634; f. 1949; Pres. LAURENTIU ULICI.

Broadcasting and Communications

TELECOMMUNICATIONS

Connex (MobiFon SA): 74228 Bucharest, Str. Nerva Traian 3; tel. (21) 3021111; fax (21) 3021413; e-mail contact@connex.ro; internet www.connex.ro; f. 1996; operates mobile cellular telephone network in 10 cities; Pres. AL TOLSTOY.

Mobil Rom: internet www.mobil-rom.com; f. 1996; operates mobile cellular telephone network; owned by Orange Plc (United Kingdom); Exec. Dir PIERRE MATTEI.

Romtelecom SA: 70060 Bucharest 5, Bd. Libertăţii 14—16; tel. (21) 4001212; fax (21) 4105581; e-mail contact@romtelecom.ro; internet www.romtelecom.ro; f. 1933; joint-stock co; former state monopoly; 54% owned by Hellenic Telecommunications Organization (Greece); Dir-Gen. FLORIN ANGHEL.

Telemobil SA: Bucharest, 2 B Bis, Balotesti, Jud. Ilfov; tel. (21) 4024444; fax (21) 4024456; internet www.telemobil.ro; f. 1999; operates mobile cellular telephone network; Man. Dir and Chief Exec. DIWAKER SINGH.

BROADCASTING

Radio

Radiodifuziunea Română: 70747 Bucharest, Str. Gral Berthelot 60–64, POB 63-1200; tel. (21) 3031432; fax (21) 3121057; e-mail adimitriu@radio.ror.ro; f. 1928; 39 transmitters on medium-wave, 69 transmitters on VHF; 114 relays; News, Cultural, Youth and Music Programmes, plus two local and six regional programmes; foreign broadcasts on one medium-wave and eight short-wave transmitters in Arabic, Bulgarian, Chinese, English, German, Greek, Hungarian, Italian, Portuguese, Romanian, Russian, Serbian, Spanish, Turkish and Ukrainian; Chair. DRAGOS SEULEANU.

Radioteleviziunea Română (Romanian Radio and Television): 71281 Bucharest 1, Calea Dorobanţilor 191, POB 63–1200; tel. (21) 2307032; fax (21) 2300381; e-mail tcr@tvr.ro; internet www.tvr.ro; f. 1955; Pres. CRISTIAN HADJI-CULEA; Exec. Dir ALEXANDRU LAZESCU.

Radio 'Nord-Est': 6600 Iaşi, Str. Gării 22; tel. (232) 211570; fax (232) 146363; e-mail rneiasi@mail.dntis.ro; f. 1992; independent; Station Man. ANCA CIOBANU.

Societatea Natională de Radiocommunicaţii, SA (National Radiocommunications Co.): 70060 Bucharest, Bd. Libertaţii 14; tel. (21) 4001101; fax (21) 4001228; e-mail rarmanag@com.pcnet.ro; state-owned.

Television

Romania's first regional television station (at Timişoara) was registered in 1989. The first satellite television channel, Tele 7 ABC, was launched in 1994.

Televiziunea Română—Telecentrul Bucureşti (Romanian Television—Bucharest TV Centre): 71281 Bucharest, Calea Dorobanţilor 191, POB 63-1200; tel. (21) 6334710; fax (21) 2121427; state-owned; 39 transmitters; daily transmissions; Pres. and Dir-Gen. CRISTIAN-VALERIU HADJI-CULEA.

Antena Independenta: 71561 Bucharest, Şos. Bucureşti-Ploieşti 25–27; tel. (21) 2121844; first independent television station.

Channel 2 TV Română: Bucharest; f. 1992 as a jt venture; 80% owned by Atlantic Television Ltd (UK-Canada), 20% by Radioteleviziunea Română; independent commercial channel; to broadcast six hours of programmes daily; Man. Dir ROBIN EDWARDS.

Pro TV: Bucharest, Bd. Carol I 109, etaj 2; tel. (21) 3124218; fax (21) 3124228.

Radioteleviziunea Română (Romanian Radio and Television): see Radio.

Finance

(cap. = capital; res = reserves; dep. = deposits; m. = million; amounts in lei (unless otherwise indicated); brs = brs)

BANKING

In April 1997 legislation providing for the privatization of state-owned banks was approved; Banca Română Pentru Dezvoltare SA was the first to be sold, in December 1998.

Central Bank

National Bank of Romania (Banca Națională a României): 70421 Bucharest 3, Str. Lipscani 25; tel. (21) 3130410; fax (21) 3123831; internet www.bnro.ro; f. 1880; central bank and bank of issue; manages monetary policy; supervises commercial banks and credit business; cap. and res 25,578,300m., dep. 152,782,700m. (Dec. 2001); Gov. MUGUR CONSTANTIN ISĂRESCU; 22 brs.

Other Banks

Alpha Bank Romania SA: 712811 Bucharest 1, Calea Doroban-tilor 237B; tel. (21) 2092100; fax (21) 2316570; e-mail bbr@alphabank.ro; internet www.alphabank.ro; f. 1994 as Banca București, present name since 2000; cap. US $22,995.0m.(Dec. 2002), res 641,281m., dep. 7,955,599m. (Dec. 2000); Pres. ELEFTHERIOS IOANNOU.

Banc Post SA: 761062 Bucharest 5, Bd. Libertății, Bl. 104; tel. (21) 3361124; fax (21) 3360772; e-mail bpt@bancpost.ro; internet www.bancpost.ro; f. 1991; 19.3% owned by EFG Eurobank Ergasias SA (Greece), 17.0% by Banco Portugues de Investimento SA (Portugal); cap. 2,086,946m., res 844,282m., dep. 11,038,684m. (Dec. 2001); Pres., Chair. and Chief Exec. ELENA PETCULESCU.

Banca Comercială Carpatica SA: 2400 Sibiu, Bd. Mihai Viteazu 42; tel. (269) 233815; fax (269) 233371; e-mail extern@carpatica.ro; internet www.carpatica.ro; f. 1999; cap. 278,978m., dep. 365,824m., total assets 654,771m. (Dec. 2001); Pres. and Chair. NICOLAE HOANTA.

Banca Comercială 'Ion Tiriac'—Banca Tiriac: 74228 Bucharest, Str. Nerva Traian 3, Complex M101; tel. (21) 3032600; fax (21) 3025700; e-mail bancatriac@cbit.ro; internet www.bancatiriac.ro; f. 1991; cap. 5,621,450m., res 61,815m., dep. 9,705,328m. (Dec. 2001); Chair. and Chief Exec. ANTHONY VAN DER HEIJDEN; 44 brs and sub-brs.

Banca Comercială Robank—Robank SA: 741382 Bucharest 3, Bd. Unirii 59; tel. (21) 3225700; fax (21) 3226885; e-mail office@robank.ro; internet www.robank.ro; f. 1995; cap. 165,468m., res 232,589m., dep. 2,335,259m. (Dec. 2001); Pres. and Chair. MUSTAFA AYAN; 5 brs.

Banca Comercială Română SA—BCR (Romanian Commercial Bank): 70348 Bucharest 3, Bd. Regina Elisabeta 5; tel. (21) 3126185; fax (21) 3122096; e-mail marketing@bcr.ro; internet www.bcr.ro; f. 1990; absorbed operations of Banca Română de Comert Exterior (BANCOREX) in Oct. 1999; commercial banking services for domestic and foreign customers; 70% state-owned, pending privatization; cap. 7,924,688mm., res 14,464,916m., dep 92,235,741m. (Dec. 2001); Pres. and Chair. NICOLAE DĂNILĂ; 285 brs and agencies.

Banca Comercială West Bank: 2900 Arad, Bd. Revolutiei 88; tel. (257) 284888; fax (257) 285998; e-mail westbank@rdslink.ro; f. 1996; 72.4% by Sanpaolo IMI SpA (Italy); cap. 270,428m., res 180,963m., dep. 1,150,106m. (Dec. 2001); Pres. CORNEL PIRTEA.

Banca Daewoo (Romania) SA: Bucharest, 1/F, International Business Centre, Bd. Carol I 34–36; tel. (21) 2505711; fax (21) 2505831; e-mail daewoo@fx.ro; f. 1996; 99.99% owned by Daewoo Securities Co Ltd (Rep. of Korea); cap. US $22.7m., dep. US $39.9m., total assets US $67.6m. (Dec. 2000); Pres. BUM-SHIK BAE.

Banca de Credit și Dezvoltare (ROMEXTERRA) SA (Bank of Credit and Development): 4300 Târgu Mureș, Mureș, bd. 1 Decembrie 1918 93; tel. (265) 166640; fax (265) 166047; e-mail info@romexterra.ro; internet www.romexterra.ro; f. 1993; cap. 444,000m., res 1,458,5330m., dep. 2,228,120m. (Dec. 2002); Pres. VASILE IFRIM; 22 brs.

Banca de Export-Import a României—Eximbank SA: 761042 Bucharest 5, Str. Splaiul Independentei 15; tel. (21) 3361134; fax (21) 3366176; e-mail relatii@eximbank.ro; f. 1992; 87.4% owned by State Privatization Agency; cap. 316,986m., res 6,367,845m., dep. 1,304,820m. (Dec. 2001); Chair. and Chief Exec. Dr MARIANA DIACONESCU.

Banca Pentru Mică- Industrie și Liberă-Inițiativă SA—MINDBANK) (Bank for Small Industry and Free Enterprise—MINDBANK): 78104 Bucharest 1, Calea Grivitei 24; tel. (21) 3030700; fax (21) 3030732; e-mail mindbank@bx.logicnet.ro; f. 1990; cap. 200,000m., res 240,733m., dep. 720,106m. (Dec. 2001); privately-owned; Chair. IOAN PRUNDUS; Dep. Chair. EMIL RADU, SERGIU IOAN MANEA; 12 brs.

Banca Română Pentru Dezvoltare SA-Groupe Société Générale (Romanian Bank for Development): 70016 Bucharest 3, Str. Doamnei 4; tel. (21) 3130571; fax (21) 3159600; e-mail communication@brd.ro; internet www.brd.ro; f. 1990 to replace Investment Bank (f. 1923); financial and banking services and operations to individual and private and small cos, etc.; 51.9% owned by Société Générale (France); cap. 1,742,253m., res 13,938,420m., dep. 44,662,823m. (Dec. 2001); Chair. BOGDAN BALTAZAR; Chief Exec. PATRICK GELIN; 191 brs.

Banca Română Pentru Relansare Economica—Libra Bank SA (Romanian Bank for Economic Revival–Libra Bank): 712791 Bucharest 1, Bd. Aviatorilor 46; tel. (21) 2303333; fax (21) 2306565; e-mail informatii@librabank.ro; internet www.librabank.ro; f. 1996; cap. 182,248m. (Dec. 2001), dep. 187,258m., total assets 405,774m. (Dec. 2000); Pres. DAN CONSTANTINESCU.

Banca Românească SA (Romanian Bank): 70401 Bucharest, Bd. Unirii 35, Bloc A3; tel. (21) 3211601; fax (21) 3213624; e-mail office@brom.ro; internet www.brom.ro; f. 1993; 71.9% owned by Romanian-American Enterprise Fund (USA); cap. 692,064m., res 71,432m., dep. 1,696,253m. (Dec. 2001); Chief Exec. and Chair. of Bd PETRU RARES.

Banca Transilvania SA (Transylvanian Bank): 3400 Cluj-Napoca, Bd. Eroilor 36; tel. (264) 198833; fax (264) 198832; e-mail bancatransilvania@bancatransilvania.ro; internet www.bancatransilvania.ro; f. 1994; cap. 396,160m., res 666,102m., dep. 3,953,515m. (Dec. 2001); Pres. IOSIF POP; 32 brs.

Casa de Economii și Consemnațiuni—CEC SA (Savings and Consignation Bank): 79104 Bucharest 3, Calea Victoriei 13; tel. (21) 3122895; fax (21) 3143970; e-mail office@rsb.ro; internet www.rsb.ro; f. 1864; state-owned; handles private savings, loans for the interbanking market and mortgages; cap. 642,000m., res 1,409,830m., dep. 19,522,479m. (Dec. 2000); Chair. CONSTANTIN TECULESCU; 42 brs.

Citibank Romania SA: 712042 Bucharest 1, Bd. Lancu de Hunedoara 8, POB 63-5; tel. (21) 2101850; fax (21) 2101854; internet www.citibank.ro; f. 1996; 99.6% owned by Citigroup Overseas Investment Corpn (USA); cap. US $22.0m., dep. US $317.9m., total assets US $370.4m (Dec. 2001); Pres. and Chair. ZDENEK TUREK.

Commercial Bank of Greece (Romania) SA: 70759 Bucharest 1, Str. Berzei 19, Sector 1; tel. (21) 3159783; fax (21) 3103964; e-mail bank@cbg.ro; internet www.cbg.ro; f. 1996; cap. 338,915.7m., dep. 640,163.4m., total assets 999,889,4m. (Dec. 2001); Pres. SPYRIDON KOSKINAS.

Egnatia Bank (Romania) SA: 70744 Bucharest, Str. Gral. C. Budisteanu 28C, BP 22-155; tel. (21) 3032100; fax (21) 3032181; f. 1998 as BNP-Dresdner Bank (Romania) SA; present name adopted 2001; 99.9% owned by Egnatia Bank (Greece); Pres. MARINIS STRATOPOULOS.

Eurom Bank SA: 71000 Bucharest, Bd Aviatorilor 45; tel. (21) 2067077; fax (21) 2067050; e-mail office@eurombank.ro; internet dacia-felix.ro; f. 1991 as Banca Dacia Felix SA; present name adopted 2001; 94.0% owned by Kolal BV (Netherlands); cap. 58,609m., res 1,540,064m., dep. 1,319,203m. (Dec. 1999); Chair. BENESH AVITAL.

Finansbank (Romania) SA: 751012 Bucharest 4, Str. Splaiul Unirii 12, Bl. B6; tel. (21) 3017100; fax (21) 3310970; e-mail hoffice@finansbank.ro; internet www.finansbank.ro; f. 1993; adopted present name 2000; 63.6% owned by Finansbank AS (Turkey); cap. 671,661m., dep. 1,956,994m., total assets 2,370,614m. (Dec. 2001); Pres. BEKIR DILDAR.

HVB Bank Romania SA: 71278 Bucharest 1, Str. Dr Grigore Mora 37; tel. (21) 2032222; fax (21) 2308485; e-mail contact@ro.hwb-cee.com; internet www.hvb.ro; f. 1997 as Creditanstalt SA; present name adopted 2001; 99.7% owned by Bank Austria Creditanstalt AG; cap. 100,001m., res 104,337m., dep. 4,067,163m. (Dec. 2000); Pres. and Chair. DAN PASCARIU.

Nova Bank SA: 71411 Bucharest 2, Bd. D. Cantemir 2, Bl. P3, T II; tel. (21) 3360856; fax (21) 3362414; e-mail office@nova-bank.ro; internet www.nova-bank.ro; f. 1997 as Banca Comerciala Unirea; Gen. Man. ZOE GHINESCU.

Piraeus Bank Romania SA: Bucharest 2, Bd. Carol I 34–36, International Business Centre; tel. (21) 2506798; fax (21) 2501799; internet www.piraeusbank.ro; f. 1995; present name adopted 2000; 99.99% owned by Piraeus Bank (Greece); cap. 521,090.6m., dep. 610,067.0m., total assets 1,078,355.8m. (Dec. 2000); Pres., Chief Exec. and Chair. EMANUEL ODOBESCU; Dir-Gen. SOFRONIS STRINOPOULOS; 3 brs.

Raiffeisen Bank SA: 742141 Bucharest 3, Bd. Mircea Voda 44; tel. (21) 3230031; fax (21) 3236027; e-mail centrala@raiffesien.ro; f. 2002 by merger of Banca Agricola-Raiffeisen SA and Raiffeisenbank (Romania) SA; 94.2% owned by Raiffeisen Zentralbank Osterreich AG (Austria); Pres. STEVEN VAN GRONINGEN.

Romanian International Bank: 70401 Bucharest 3, Bd. Unirii 68, Bloc K2; tel. (21) 3227005; fax (21) 3237272; e-mail office@roib.ro; f. 1998; privately owned; Chair. of Bd Ion Ghica.

Unicredit Romania SA: 70401 Bucharest 4, Bd. Splaiul Unirii 16; tel. (21) 3302900; fax (21) 3303992; e-mail office@unicredit.ro; internet www.unicredit.ro; f. 1997 as DEMiRBANK Romania SA; ; name changed as above in 2001; 99.84% owned by Unicredito Italiano (UCI); cap. 404,066m., res 110,010m., dep. 1,134,548m. (Dec. 2001); Pres. of Man. Bd Fausto Petteni; Chief Exec. Selçuk Saldirak; 15 brs.

BANKING ASSOCIATION

Romanian Banking Association (Asociaţia Română a Băncilor): 76100 Bucharest, Str. Mihai Eminescu 88; tel. (21) 2112007; fax (21) 2112100; e-mail arb@arexim.ro; Chair. Radu Gilţea; Sec.-Gen. Radu Negrea.

STOCK EXCHANGE

Bucharest Stock Exchange (Bursa de Valori Bucureşti): 70421 Bucharest, Str. Doamnei 8; tel. (21) 3158209; fax (21) 3158149; e-mail bvbrel@ccir.ro; internet bse.ccir.ro; f. 1882; reopened 1995 (ceased operations 1948); 128 listed cos; Pres. Sergiu Oprescu; Gen. Man. Stere Farmache.

INSURANCE

Allianz-Tiriac Asigurări: 71139 Bucharest, Cáderea Bastiliei 80–84; tel. (21) 2082222; fax (21) 2082211; e-mail office@allianztiriac.ro; internet www.allianztiriac.ro.

Arad: 71421 Bucharest, Şos. Ştefan cel Mare 7–9; tel. (21) 6113162; fax (21) 6113279.

Asigurareo Românescô SA (ASIROM) (Romanian Insurance): 70332 Bucharest 2, Bd. Carol I 31–33; tel. (21) 2504271; fax (21) 2504145; f. 1991; all types of insurance, including life insurance; Gen. Man. Angela Toncescu; 41 brs.

Astra SA: 71291 Bucharest, Str. Puşkin 10; tel. (21) 2305288; fax (21) 2305248.

Carom SA: 70406 Bucharest, Str. Smârdan 5; tel. (21) 6150519; fax (21) 3124710.

Cascom SA: 77102 Bucharest, Calea Plevnei 46–48; tel. (21) 6151810.

Metropol SA: 75121 Bucharest, Bd. Dimitrie Cantemir 1; tel. (21) 3304706; fax (21) 3304725; f. 1991; all types of insurance and reinsurance; Chair. and Man. Dir Dr Joseph Noupadja.

Romanian-Canadian Insurance Co (AROCA) SA: 70414 Bucharest, Str. Doamnei 17–19; tel. and fax (21) 3135605; e-mail aroca@fx.ro.

Insurance Association

Uniunea Naţională a Societăţilor de Asigurare şi Reasigurare din România: 70406 Bucharest, Str. Smârdan 5; tel. (21) 6130358.

Trade and Industry

GOVERNMENT AGENCIES

Agency for Foreign Investments: Bucharest; f. 2002 to promote investment in Romania.

Romanian Development Agency (Agenţia Română de Dezvoltare): 70161 Bucharest, Bd. Magheru 7; tel. (21) 3122886; fax (21) 3120371; f. 1991; promotes foreign investment in Romanian industry; Pres. Sorin Fodoreanu.

State Privatization Agency (APAPS): 70205 Bucharest, Str. C.A. Rosetti 21; tel. (21) 2118018; fax (21) 2104459; successor org. to the State Ownership Fund; Gen. Dir Gabriel Mihut.

CHAMBER OF COMMERCE

Chamber of Commerce and Industry of Romania and the Municipality of Bucharest: Bucharest 3, Bd. Octavian Goga 2; tel. (21) 3229536; fax (21) 3229542; e-mail ccir@ccir.ro; internet www.ccir.ro; f. 1868; non-governmental organization; Pres. Gheorge Cojocaru.

EMPLOYERS' ASSOCIATIONS

National Confederation of Romanian Employers (Confederaţia Naţională a Patronatului Român): 70169 Bucharest, Str. Mendeleev 36–38; tel. (21) 3124715; fax (21) 3124745.

Romanian Private Farmers' Federation (Federaţia agricultorilor privatizaţi din România): 70111 Bucharest 1, Bd. Nicolae Bălcescu 17–19; tel. (21) 6131869; fax (21) 6133043; f. 1991; represents 4,000 farming co-operatives and 41 district unions; Pres. Gheorghe Predila.

UTILITIES

Electricity

Hidroelectrica SA: 70219 Bucharest, Str. Constantin Nacu 3, Sector 2; tel. (21) 3112231; fax (21) 3111174; e-mail generala@hidroelectrica.ro; internet www.hidroelectrica.ro; state-owned; administers 120 hydropower plants and 4 pumping stations through 10 regional subsidiaries; Gen. Man. Eugen Pena.

Nuclearelectrica SA: Bucharest; f. 2000; Gen. Dir Ioan Rotaru.

Termoelectrica SA: internet www.termoelectrica.ro; f. 2000.

SC Electrica SA: Bucharest, Str. Grigore Alexandrescu 9, Sector 1; tel. (21) 2085999; fax (21) 2085998; internet www.electrica.ro; f. 2002 following the reorganization of the National Electricity Company CONEL; electricity distributor and supplier; 8 regional branches; Chair. Cristian Istodorescu.

Transelectrica SA: internet portal.transelectrica.ro; f. 2000; formerly part of the National Electricity Company CONEL; state-owned; transmission system operator of the Romanian power system; includes 8 subsidiaries and OPCOM SA power market operator; Chair. Dorin Mucea; Gen. Dir Gheorghe Olteanu.

Gas

SNTGN Transgaz SA: 3125 Mediaş, Str. Unirii 4; tel. (269) 842262; fax (269) 839031; e-mail cabinet@romgaz.ro; internet www.transgaz.ro; state-owned; exploration, transmission and distribution of natural gas; Pres. and Gen. Dir Gabriel Coconea.

SNGN Romgaz SA: 3125 Medias, Str. Unirii 4; tel. (269) 801014; fax (269) 841769; e-mail contact@exprogaz.ro; internet www.exprogaz.ro; gas exploration, storage and production; also operates under the name Exprogaz.

MAJOR COMPANIES

In 2002 54.8% of companies were privately owned.

Arcom International SA: 77106 Bucharest, Str. Virgiliu 81; tel. (21) 6382137; fax (21) 3120129; e-mail arcom@hades.ro; internet www.arcom.ro; f. 1969; civil and industrial constructions, mechanical and electrical installations, engineering and technical assistance services; Gen. Man. Ionel Mocanu; 3,250 employees.

Arpechim SA: 3000 Piteşti, Judet Argeş, Str. Petrochimistilor 127; tel. (248) 632049; fax (248) 213600; e-mail marketing@arpechim.ro; internet www.arpechim.ro; f. 1966; Gen. Man. Gheorghe Matei; 6,200 employees.

Auto-Dacia SA: 0401 Colibaşi, Judet Argeş, Str. Uzinei 1–3; tel. (248) 634800; fax (248) 630788; f. 1968; manufacture, export and import of road vehicles, vehicle parts and special purpose vehicles; privatized in 1999; Pres. Constantin Stroe; 14,300 employees.

Clujana SA: 3400 Cluj-Napoca, 1 May Sq. 4–5; tel. (264) 437157; fax (264) 437044; e-mail creatie@mail.dntcj.ro; internet www.clujana.twf.ro; f. 1911; manufactures footwear; Gen. Man. Mihail Maties; 700 employees.

Combinatul de Oteluri Speciale (COST) SA: 0200 Târgovişte, Judet Dâmbovita, Şos. Găesti 9–11; tel. (245) 632553; fax (245) 614582; e-mail cost@starnets.ro; internet www.starnets.ro/cost; f. 1973; production of stainless steel, carbon and alloys; Dir Ioan Ferariu; 5,700 employees.

Covtex SA: 2437 Sibiu, Str. Transilvaniei 43, Cisnădie; tel. (269) 562201; fax (269) 213330; f. 1874; manufacturers of carpets, rugs and other woollen products; Dir Petre Boldsor; 3,500 employees.

Daewoo Automobile Romania SA: 1100 Craiova, Judet Dolj, Str. Caracal KM3; tel. (251) 147800; fax (251) 144875; e-mail publrel@rodae.ro; internet www.rodae.ro; f. 1994; manufactures motor vehicles; owned by Daewoo (Republic of Korea); Pres. Cho Sung-Yang; 4,100 employees.

Daewoo Mangalia Heavy Industries SA: 8727 Mangalia, Str. Portului 1; tel. (241) 753340; fax (241) 756060; e-mail drahi@drahi.ct.ro; internet www.dmhi.ct.ro; f. 1997; shipbuilding, ship repair and conversion; Pres. Hong Soon-Gab; 3,400 employees.

Elektronica SA: Bucharest 2, Bd Dimitrie Pompei 5–7; tel. (21) 3122258; fax (21) 3122260; f. 1960; manufactures audio, broadcasting and electronic equipment; Chair. Efrahim Rottman; 5,600 employees.

Electroputere SA: 1100 Craiova, Str. Bucureşti 144; tel. and fax (251) 437700; e-mail electroputere@electroputere.ro; internet www

.electroputere.com; f. 1949; manufactures electrical machinery and vehicles; Gen. Dir PETRU SABAILA; 6,000 employees.

Energomontaj SA: 71223 Bucharest 1, Str. Dorobanţilor 103–105; tel. (21) 2321020; fax (21) 2307765; e-mail saemprog@saem.logicnet .ro; internet www.logicnet.ro/saem; f. 1949; industrial and utilities construction; Chair. FLORIN KESLER; 6,300 employees.

Hidroconstructia SA: 71223 Bucharest 1, Str. Dorobanţilor 103–105; tel. (21) 2300259; fax (21) 2307764; e-mail hidrocom@mail .totalnet.ro; civil and hydraulic engineering; Gen. Dir IURIE DRUTA; 14,000 employees.

Iame SA: 4000 Sfântu Gheorghe, Str. Constructorilor 2; tel. (267) 352950; fax (267) 351914; e-mail markiame@iame.ro; internet www .iame.ro; f. 1973; production of electric motors and electric components for vehicles; Man. Dir VLADIMIR FURDUI; 1,070 employees.

Industrialexport SA: 79185 Bucharest 1, Bd. Dacia 13; tel. (21) 2118905; fax (21) 2116211; e-mail ie@starnets.ro; f. 1953; exports oilfield, mining and food equipment; contractor for complete industrial projects, mainly for refineries, chemical and petrochemical industries; imports and exports pumps and industrial valves and fittings; barter operations and general trading; Pres. and Gen. Man. Eng. GEORGES CONSTANTIN; 216 employees.

Maşinexportimport Industries SA: 70033 Bucharest 3, Bd. Carol I 12, POB 37-152; tel. (21) 3124314; fax (21) 3120150; e-mail cruceru@mexim.com.ro; f. 1962; producer, exporter and importer of machine tools for metal-working and manufactured and consumer goods; also exports woodworking and textiles machinery; Gen. Dir TRAIAN CRUCERU; 117 employees.

Mecanoexportimport SA: 79522 Bucharest 1, Bd. Dacia 30, POB 22–107; tel. (21) 2119855; fax (21) 2107894; e-mail mecano@kappa .ro; internet www.mecanoexport.ro; f. 1969; imports and exports road construction equipment, metal railway sleepers, diesel and electric railway engines, rolling stock, air compressors, lifting and conveying equipment; Gen. Dir CORNEL ANGHEL; 60 employees.

Metalexportimport SA: Bucharest 1, Str. Mendeleev 21–25; tel. (21) 3120447; fax (21) 3111841; e-mail metall@rnc.ro; f. 1948; exports and imports rolled steel products, welded and seamless tubes, ferro-alloys, non-ferrous metals; Pres. and Gen. Man. FOCA CREŢU; 140 employees.

Navlomar SA: Bucharest, Str. C. A. Rosetti; tel. (21) 2113445; fax (21) 2114123; e-mail navlomar@fx.ro; f. 1969; shipbrokers, Danube River chartering agents, cargo transit and transhipment, ship agents, ship-chandlers, consultancy and legal assistance, export and import; Dir NICK EFTIMIE; 55 employees.

Oltchim SA: 1000 Râmnicu Vâlcea, Str. Uzinei 1; tel. (250) 736101; fax (250) 736188; e-mail oltchim@oltchim; internet www.oltchim .onix.ro; f. 1966; produces and exports chemicals and food products; Pres. Dr CONSTANTIN ROIBU; 7,350 employees.

Petrolexportimport: 741291 Bucharest 3, Bd. Unirii 72, Bloc J3C; tel. (21) 3208452; fax (21) 3208460; e-mail office@petex.ro; internet www.petex.ro; f. 1948; export of petroleum products; import of raw materials for petrochemical industry; Chair. VALERIU IANCU; 75 employees.

SNP PETROM SA (Romanian National Oil Corporation): 70176 Bucharest, Calea Victoriei 109; tel. (21) 2125001; fax (21) 3102213; internet www.petrom.ro; f. 1997; exploration, production, refining, and sale of petroleum and natural gas; Pres. ION POPA; 90,000 employees.

Petrostar SA: 2000 Ploieşti, Bd. Bucureşti 37; tel. (244) 175963; fax (244) 175412; e-mail petrostar@interplus.ro; internet www .petrostar.net; f. 1949; petroleum production, storage, and distribution, and research, design, engineering, and consulting for the petroleum and gas industries; Pres. and Gen. Man. CONSTANTIN ILIESCU; 500 employees.

Regia Autonoma a Tutunului din Romania: Bucharest 6, Bd Regiei 2; tel. (21) 6374443; fax (21) 3121076; f. 1881; production of tobacco products; Gen. Dir ADRIAN POPESCU; 8,500 employees.

Roman SA Truck Co (Autocamione Braşov): 2200 Braşov, Str. Poienilor 5; tel. (268) 311992; fax (268) 311333; e-mail roman@ roman.ro; internet www.roman.ro; f. 1921; manufacture and export of trucks and vehicles; Gen. Dir CAROL RUGACS; 8,652 employees.

Românoexport SA: 704 Bucharest 3, Str. Doamnei 17–19, POB 594; tel. (21) 6133699; fax (21) 3121103; f. 1948; exports: fabrics, knitwear, carpets, and blankets; imports: wool, cotton, jute, dyestuffs, felts, etc.; Man. Dir PETRU CRIŞAN; 300 employees.

Romenergo SA: 71101 Bucharest, Calea Floreasca 242–246, POB 1–736; tel. (21) 2330771; fax (21) 2330855; e-mail parvescu@ romenergo.ro; internet www.romenergo.ro; f. 1979; engineering and power generation equipment for hydro, thermal and nuclear power projects, boilers, turbines, generators; studies, training, service, etc.; Pres. and Man. Dir ALEXANDRU PARVESCU; 1,700 employees.

Romferchim SA: 77206 Bucharest, Splaiul Independenţei 202A, POB 12–226; tel. (21) 6385305; fax (21) 3121141; e-mail office@ romferchim.ro; internet www.romferchim.ro; f. 1991; exports fertilizers, pharmaceuticals, cosmetics, cellulose, fibres, chemical products, etc.; imports phosphorites, apatite, acids, complete plants and equipment for chemical and petro-chemical industry; Man. Dir MIHAI IONESCU; 125 employees.

Romproject SA: 78101 Bucharest 1, Calea Griviţei 6; tel. (21) 3120529; fax (21) 3120131; e-mail rompro@starnets.ro; f. 1981; exports design and drafting services, technical assistance for building and irrigation works, mass housing programmes, construction management; Dir PETRE IONIŢA; 210 employees.

ROMSILVA SA: 70164 Bucharest, Bd. Gen. Gh. Magheru 31; tel. (21) 6592020; fax (21) 2228428; e-mail rnp@rosilva.ro; internet www .rosilva.ro; f. 1991; produces timber, forest fruit, honey, seeds and game and wickerwork items, manages state forests; Dir DORIN CIUCA; 40,000 employees.

Romtrans SA: 75268 Bucharest 5, POB 1–893, Calea Rahovei 196; tel. (21) 3358930; fax (21) 3372840; e-mail office@romtrans.pcnet.ro; internet www.romtrans.ro; f. 1952; international transport and freight forwarding agency; Dir EUGEN BÂR; 2,250 employees.

Sidex SA: 6200 Galaţi, Str. Smârdan 1; tel. (236) 411990; fax (236) 432017; e-mail office@sidex.ro; internet www.sidex.ro; f. 1961; largest iron and steel works in Central and South-Eastern Europe; privatized in 2001; Gen. Man. ION FLORENTIN SANDU; 27,700 employees.

Tehnoforestexport SA: Bucharest 2, Piaţa Rosetti 4; tel. (21) 6136717; fax (21) 6154020; f. 1948; exports furniture and other finished wooden products; imports raw materials for wood-working industry; timber processing; marketing; Man. Dir CONSTANTIN POPA; 381 employees.

Uzinexportimport SA: 70033 Bucharest 1, Bd. Iancu de Hunedoara 8, Bldg H-3; tel. (21) 2307676; fax (21) 2306623; e-mail rasvan@mb.roknet.ro; internet www.uzin.roknet.ro; f. 1966; export and import of complex installations and basic equipment for the machine-building industry and ships and shipbuilding industry and cement industries, metallurgical and iron and steel plants; Chair. and CEO MATACHE NICOLAIDE; 210 employees.

SC Vulcan SA: 76305 Bucharest 5, Str. Sebastian 88; tel. (21) 4105396; fax (21) 4100185; e-mail vulcan@ns.vulcan.ro; internet www.vulcan.ro; f. 1904; production of boilers, pressure boiler parts, oil pumping units, and power plant components; Gen. Man. DANIEL SURDEANU; 2,006 employees.

TRADE UNIONS

The regulations governing trade unions were liberalized in early 1990. The Uniunea Generală a Sindicatelor din România (UGSR) was dissolved. Several new trade union organizations have since been established.

Alpha Cartel (Cartelul Alfa): f. 1990; 1.1m. mems; Leader BOGDAN HOSSU.

Confederation of Democratic Trade Unions of Romania: Bucharest; f. 1994; 34 branch federations; 640,000 mems; Leader IACOB BACIU.

Confederation of Romanian Miners' Trade Unions: Pres. ILIE DORSAN.

COSIN Confederation (Confederaţia COSIN): f. 1990; 10,000 mems.

Fides Confederation (Confederaţia Fides): 180,000 mems; Leader CĂTĂLIN CROITORU.

Hercules Confederation (Confederaţia Hercules): Bucharest; f. 1990; transport workers.

Inter-union Confederative Alliance of 15 November (Alianţa Confederativă Intersindicală 15 Noiembrie): 2200 Braşov, Str. Michael Weiss 13; tel. and fax (268) 151936; f. 1991; 120,000 mems; Pres. ADRIAN LAHARIA.

National Trade Union Bloc (Blocul Naţional Sindical): 77208 Bucharest, Splaiul Independenţei 202A; tel. (21) 4115184; fax (21) 4115185; e-mail bns@bns.ro; internet www.bns.ro; f. 1991; merged with National Free Trade Union Confederation of Romania—Brotherhood; c. 3.4m. mems; Pres. DUMITRU COSTIN; Gen. Sec. MATEI BRĂTIANU.

Other organizations include Infratirea, the Justice and Brotherhood Union and the Convention of Non-Aligned Union Confederations (Pres. ION MACHEDON).

Transport

RAILWAYS

In 2002 there were 11,002 km of track in operation (of which 3,929 km were electrified lines in 1998). In January 1996 the World Bank approved a loan of US $120m. to help finance the restructuring of Romania's railways. In September 1998 the Societatea Nationale a Căilor Ferate Române (SNCFR—National Romanian Railway Company) was divided into five companies.

Company for Railways Assets Management (SAAF): 77113 Bucharest, Bd. Dinicu Golescu 38; tel. (21) 6373252; fax (21) 2227877; Gen. Man. MIRCEA DINU.

National Railways Company for Freight Traffic (CFR Marfa SA): 77113 Bucharest, Bd. Dinicu Golescu 38; tel. (21) 2249336; fax (21) 3124700; e-mail vtulbure@marfa.cfr.ro; f. 1988; after the reorganization of the SNCFR; main railway freight transport operator in Romania; Gen. Man. VASIK TULBURE.

National Passenger Railway Transport Co (CFR Calatori): 77113 Bucharest, Bd. Dinicu Golescu 38; tel. (21) 2222518; fax (21) 4112054; e-mail irina.vlad@cfr.ro; internet www.cfr.ro; divided into eight regional administrations since 1999; reorganized in Feb. 2001 and merged with eight regional companies; operates all local, regional, long-distance and international rail services; Gen. Man. VALENTIN BOTA.

National Railways Company (CFR SA): 77113 Bucharest, Bd. Dinicu Golescu 38; tel. (21) 2223637; fax (21) 3123200; e-mail virgil .daschievici@cfr.ro; internet www.cfr.ro; management railway infrastructure; Gen. Dir MIHAI MECOLAICIUC; 41,486 employees.

Rail Management Services Company (SMF): 77113 Bucharest, Bd. Dinicu Golescu 38; tel. (21) 2233560; fax (21) 6384530; e-mail spopeanga@central.cfr.ro; provides financial, judicial and accounting services; Gen. Man. SILVIA POPEANGA.

Societatea de Constructii Cai de Comunicatii SA: Bucharest 1, Bd. Dinicu Golescu 38; tel. (21) 2223615; fax (21) 3125903; f. 1876; production of materials for railway construction and vehicles; Pres. NICOLAE CONSTANTINESCU; 13,300 employees.

Metropolitan Transport

The Bucharest underground railway network totals 63.5 km in length. There are currently plans to modernize the underground system.

Societatea Comerciala de Transport cu Metroul Bucureşti–METROREX SA : 79917 Bucharest 1, Bd. Dinicu Golescu 38; tel. (21) 2248975; fax (21) 3125149; e-mail contact@metrorex.ro; internet www.metrorex.ro; f. 1977; Gen. Man. MARIUS IONEL LAPADAT.

ROADS

At the end of 2000 there were 198,603 km of roads, of which 113 km were motorways, 14,711 km national roads and 63,791 km secondary roads. Under the 1991–2005 road development programme, more than 3,000 km of motorways were to be built and 4,000 km of existing roads were to be modernized.

CCCF Bucharest SA: 77113 Bucharest 1, Bd. Dinicu Golescu 38; tel. (21) 6387375; fax (21) 6385335; f. 1879; construction of roads, railways, bridges and tunnels; Gen. Man. NICOLAE CONSTANTINESCU; 8,000 employees.

National Administration of Roads (Regia Autonomă Administraţia Naţională a Drumurilor—AND): Ministerul Transporturilor, 77113 Bucharest 1, Bd. Dinicu Golescu 38, Rm 55; tel. (21) 2233606; fax (21) 3120984; Dir-Gen. Dr Ing. DANILA BUCSA.

Road and Bridge Corporation (Regia Autonomă de Drumuri şi Poduri): Bucharest, Şos. Bucureşti-Ploieşti, km 18; tel. (21) 6130123.

INLAND AND OCEAN SHIPPING

Navigation on the River Danube is open to shipping of all nations. The Danube–Black Sea Canal was officially opened to traffic in 1984, and has an annual handling capacity of 80m. metric tons. Work on the 85-km Danube–Bucharest Canal was abandoned in early 1990. The first joint Romanian-Yugoslav Iron Gates (Porţile de Fier) power and navigation system on the Danube was completed in 1972, and Iron Gates-2 opened to navigation in 1984. Romania's principal seaports are Constanţa (on the Black Sea), Tulcea, Galaţi, Brăila and Giurgiu (on the Danube). In August 1995 Romania launched its first ferry service to Turkey, operating between Constanţa and Samsun. In 2001 Romania's merchant fleet had 240 vessels, with a total displacement of 637,700 grt. Of the River Danube, 1,075 km flowed through Romanian territory, with 524 km of secondary branches and 64km of canals; the total length of canals in the country was some 132 km.

Galaţi Corporation for the Administration of the Lower Danube (Regia Autonomă Administraţia Fluvială a Dunării de Jos

Galaţi): 6200 Galaţi, Str. Portului 28–30; tel. (236) 460812; fax (236) 460847; Gen. Man. MIHAI OCHIALBESCU.

National Company for the Administration of the Maritime Port of Constanţa SA: 8700 Constanţa, Portului Incinta, Gara Maritima; tel. (241) 611540; fax (241) 619512; e-mail apmc@ constantza-port.ro; internet www.constantza-port.ro; f. 1991; also administrates Midia, Mangalia and Tomis ports; Gen. Man. GHEORGHE MOLDOVEANU.

National Company for the Administration of Maritime Ports on the Danube: 6200 Galaţi, Str. Portului 34; tel. (236) 460660; fax (236) 460140; Gen. Man. ALEXANDROS GALIATATOS.

National Company for the Administration of Navigable Canals SH: 8700 Constanţa, Str. Ecluzei Agigea 1, POB 93; tel. (241) 738505; fax (241) 639402; e-mail compania@acn.ro; internet www.acn.ro; fmrly Constanţa Corpn for Navigable Channels; Gen. Man. SEVASTIAN STEFAN.

National Company for the Administration of River Ports on the Danube: 8375 Giurgiu, Şos. Portului 1; tel. (246) 213003; fax (246) 3110521; e-mail apdf@infogrup.pcnet.ro; internet www .intelsev.ro/apdf; f. 1998; Gen. Man. CRISTIAN NEMTESCU.

NAVROM—Romanian Shipping Co: 8700 Constanţa, Portului Incinta; tel. (241) 615166; fax (241) 618413; organizes sea transport; operates routes to most parts of the world; Gen. Man. MANEA GHIOCEL.

Petromin Shipping Co: Constanţa, Portului Incinta, Poarta 2; tel. (241) 617802; fax (241) 619690; e-mail office@petromin.cunet.ro; merchant fleet of 30 ships and tankers totalling 1.778m. gross registered tons; Chair. ANDREI CARAIANI.

Romline: 8700 Constanţa, Poarta 2 Hostel; tel. (241) 617285; fax (241) 615647; f. 1990; merchant shipping company.

CIVIL AVIATION

There are international airports at Bucharest-Baneasa, Bucharest-Otopeni, M. Kogălniceanu-Constanţa, Timişoara, Arad, Sibiu, Oradea and Târgu Mureş.

Romanian Civil Aeronautic Authority (Regia Autonomă Autoritatea Aeronautică Civilă Română): 71557 Bucharest, Şos. Bucureşti–Ploieşti, km 16.5; tel. (21) 3121938; fax (21) 2302942; Gen. Man. GAVRIL GHEORGHE.

Angel Airlines: 712961 Bucharest, Str. 18 Amiral Constantin Basescu; tel. (21) 2315944; fax (21) 2315947; internet www .angelairlines.ro; f. 2001; scheduled domestic flights; Chair. and Chief Exec. KHOSRO AZAD.

Carpatair: Bucharest, 1 Dr Iacob Felix 55; tel. (21) 3130308; fax (21) 3130500; internet www.carpatair.com; f. 1998 as Veg Air, assumed present name in 1999; scheduled domestic and regional flights to Hungary, Italy and Moldova; Pres. NICOLAE PETROV.

Compania Nationala de Transporturi Aeriene Române SA—TAROM (Romanian Air Transport): 79154 Bucharest, Şos. Bucureşti–Ploieşti, km 16.5, Otopeni Airport; tel. (21) 2322494; fax (21) 3125686; e-mail secrgen@tarom.logicnet.ro; internet www.tarom .digiro.net; f. 1954; joint-stock company; scheduled to be privatized in 2002; services to 43 cities throughout Europe, the Middle East, Asia and the USA and extensive internal flights; Pres. GHEORGHE RACARU.

Jaro International: Bucharest; tel. (21) 2322273; fax (21) 2307781; f. 1990; private charter airline; Pres. and Dir-Gen. MIRICA DIMITRESCU.

Liniile Aeriene Romane (LAR) (Romanian Airlines): 70733 Bucharest, Şos. Ştirbei Vodă 2–4; tel. (21) 3153206; fax (21) 3120148; e-mail dorin@baneasa.biz; f. 1975 by TAROM to operate passenger charter services; re-established as independent airline in 1990; Man. Dir DORIN IVAŞCU.

Romavia Romanian Aviation Co: 75121 Bucharest, Bd. Dimitrie Cantemir 1; tel. (21) 3301160; fax (21) 3301049; f. 1991; owned by Ministry of National Defence; state VIP and chartered and scheduled passenger and cargo flights; Man. Dir IULIU-ADRIAN GOLEANU.

Tourism

The Carpathian Mountains, the Danube delta and the Black Sea resorts (Mamaia, Eforie, Mangalia and others) are the principal attractions. In 2000 there were 4.9m. tourist arrivals (including same-day visitors).

Tourism Promotion Office: 70663 Bucharest, Str. Apolodor 17; tel. (21) 4100491; fax (21) 4100579; e-mail turism@kappa.ro; govt org.; Gen. Dir CRISTIAN CUTAS.

National Association of Travel Agencies (Asociaţia Naţională a Agenţiilor de Turism——ANAT): 74288 Bucharest 3, Str. Foişorului 8, Bloc 3c, Sc. 2, ap. 41; tel. (21) 3230855; fax (21) 3211908; e-mail anatr@starnets.ro; Pres. Cornel Gaina.

Culture

NATIONAL ORGANIZATIONS

Ministry of Culture and Religious Affairs: see section on The Government (Ministries).

Institute for Cultural Memory (Institutul de Memorie Culturala): internet www.cimec.ro; f. 1978; national centre for cultural heritage record, primarily financed by the Ministry of Culture; Dir Dan Matei.

Romanian Cultural Foundation (Fundaţia Culturală Română): 71273 Bucharest, Al. Alexandru 38; tel. (21) 2301373; fax (21) 2307559; e-mail fcr@algoritma.ro; internet www.fcr.ro; f. 1990; aims to promote Romanian culture world-wide; Pres. Augustin Buzura.

Romanian National Commission for UNESCO (Comisia Naţională a României pentru UNESCO): 71291 Bucharest, Str. Anton Cehov 8; tel. (21) 2223048; fax (21) 2307636; e-mail cnr@wsp.ro; f. 1956; Pres. Prof. Andrei Marga; Sec.-Gen. Prof. Victor Iancu.

CULTURAL HERITAGE

Bucharest Museum of History and Art (Muzeul de Istorie şi Artă al Municipiului Bucureşti): 70058 Bucharest 3, Bd. I. C. Brătianu 2; tel. (21) 3156858; fax (21) 6138515; e-mail historie@sunu.rnc.ro; f. 1921; 50,000-vol. library; 11 affiliated museums; Dir Ionel Ioniţă.

Library of the Romanian Academy (Biblioteca Academiei Române): 711021 Bucharest, Calea Victoriei 125; tel. (21) 2121284; fax (21) 2125856; e-mail biblacad@bar.acad.ro; internet www.bar.acad.ro; f. 1867; 9.7m. items; Dir Prof. Dr G. Strempel.

Museum of Romanian Literature (Muzeul Literaturii Române): 71116 Bucharest, Bd. Dacia 12; tel. (21) 2125845; fax (21) 2125846; e-mail info@mlr.ro; internet www.mlr.ro; f. 1957; 5 affiliated museums; Dir Alexandru Dan Condeescu.

National Archives of Romania (Arhivele Naţionale ale României): Bucharest, Bd. Elisabeta 49; tel. (21) 3137637; fax (21) 3125841; e-mail arhnet@mi.ro; f. 1831; Dir-Gen. Prof. Dr Corneliu Mihail Lungu.

National History Museum of Romania (Muzeul Naţional de Istorie a României): 70012 Bucharest, Calea Victoriei 12; tel. (21) 3158207; fax (21) 3113356; e-mail direct@mnir.ro; internet www.mnir.ro; f. 1972; historical artefacts from all periods; archaeological and numismatic research; 45,000-vol. library; Dir Dr Crişan Muşeteanu.

National Library of Romania (Biblioteca Naţională a României): 79708 Bucharest 3, Bd. Ion Ghica 4; tel. (21) 3157063; fax (21) 3123381; e-mail go@bibnat.ro; internet www.bibnat.ro; f. 1955; 8.6m. items; 2 brs in Alba Iulia and Craiova; Dir Ion Dan Erceanu.

National Museum of Art of Romania (Muzeul Naţional de Artă al României): 701012 Bucharest, Calea Victoriei 49–53; tel. (21) 3155193; fax (21) 3124327; e-mail national@art.museum.ro; internet art.museum.ro; f. 1948; 4 affiliated museums; Dir Roxana Theodorescu.

National Museum of the History of Transylvania (Muzeul Naţional de Istorie a Transilvaniei): 3400 Cluj-Napoca, Str. Constantin Daicoviciu 2; tel. and fax (264) 191718; e-mail secretariat@mnit.museum.utcluj.ro; internet www.museum.utcluj.ro; Dir Constantin Daicoviciu.

Village Museum (Muzeul Satului): 713211 Bucharest, Şos. Kiseleff 28–30; tel. (21) 2229110; fax (21) 2229068; e-mail muzeulsatului@xnet.ro; internet www.cimec.ro; f. 1936; ethnographic open-air museum, folk art, rural architecture, agricultural machinery, etc.; Dir-Gen. Dr Georgeta Stoica.

SPORTING ORGANIZATION

Romanian Olympic Committee: 70206 Bucharest, Str. Otetari 2; tel. (21) 2111600; fax (21) 3150490; e-mail noc_romania@cor.ro; internet www.cor.ro; f. 1914; Pres. Ion Tiriac; Gen. Sec. Dan Popper.

PERFORMING ARTS

Theatres

Bucharest Jewish Theatre: Bucharest, Str. Dr Juliu Barasch 15; tel. (21) 3234530; fax (21) 3232746; e-mail tes@tes.ro; internet www.tes.ro; f. 1948; Dir Harry Eliad.

I. L. Caragiale National Theatre (Teatrul Naţional 'I. L. Caragiale'): 701211 Bucharest, Bd. Nicolae Bălcescu 2; tel. (21) 3139437; fax (21) 3123169; e-mail tncaragiale@yahoo.com; internet tnb.kappa.ro; f. 1834; Gen. Dir Dinu Saranu.

Comedy Theatre (Teatrul de Comedie): 70000 Bucharest, Str. Sf. Dimitru 2; tel. (21) 3159137; fax (21) 3120926; e-mail tcomedie@rins.ro; Dir Dan Vasiliu.

Ion Creangă Theatre (Teatrul 'Ion Creangă'): 701531 Bucharest, Str. Pictor Verona 15; tel. (21) 2111169; fax (21) 2110061; Dir Ioan Gârnacea.

State German Theatre (Teatrul German de Stat Timişoara): 1900 Timişoara, Str. Mărăsesti 2; tel. (256) 201291; e-mail teatgerm@mail.dnttm.ro; internet www.infotim.ro/tgst; f. 1956; Dir Alexandra Gandi Ossau.

Romanian Athenaeum (Ateneul Român): Bucharest, Str. Franklin 1; tel. (21) 3152567; fax (21) 312983; e-mail nlicaret@hotmail.com; f. 1888; hosts the George Enescu Bucharest Philharmonic Orchestra; Dir-Gen. Cristian Mandeal; Artistic Dir Nicolae Licaret.

Ţăndărică Puppet Theatre (Teatrul Ţăndărică): Bucharest, Str. Eremia Grigorescu 24; tel. (21) 2113288; fax (21) 2106294; f. 1949; Artistic Man. Calin Mocanu.

Opera Houses

National Opera House (Opera Naţionale): 706091 Bucharest, Bd. Mihail Kogălniceanu 70–72; tel. (21) 3157939; fax (21) 3157849; e-mail onb@kappa.ro; internet www.operanb.ro; Dir Ludovic Spiess.

Hungarian State Opera House: 3400 Cluj-Napoca, Str. Emil Isac 26–28; tel. (264) 193463; f. 1948; Dir Simon Gabor.

Ion Dacian Operetta Theatre (Teatrul de Operetă 'Ion Dacian'): 701211 Bucharest, Bd. Nicolae Bălcescu 2; tel. and fax (21) 3126583; Dir Amza Salceanu.

ASSOCIATIONS

Architects' Union of Romania (Uniunea Arhitecţilor din România): 701091 Bucharest, Str. Academiei 18–20; tel. (21) 3123053; fax (21) 3120956; e-mail rna@com.pcnet.ro; internet www.ong.ro/ong/uar; f. 1952; Pres. Arch. Alexandru Beldiman.

Artists' Association of Bucharest (Asociaţia Artiştilor Plastici—Bucureşti): 70036 Bucharest, Piaţa Rosetti 2; tel. (21) 3133860; f. 1973; Pres. Dan Segărceanu.

Association of Photographic Artists (Asociaţia Artiştilor Fotografi): 70700 Bucharest, POB 1223; tel. (21) 6149558; f. 1956; f. 1956.

Bessarabia and Bucovina Cultural Association (Asociaţia Culturală 'Pro Basarabia şi Bucovina'): 703481 Bucharest, Bd. Regina Elisabeta 19; tel. (21) 6140359; f. 1983; Exec. Pres. Nicolae Radu Halippa.

Composers' and Musicologists' Union of Romania (Uniunea Compozitorilor şi Muzicologilor din România): 71102 Bucharest, Calea Victoriei 141; tel. (21) 2107211; fax (21) 6502825; e-mail smei@itcnet.ro; f. 1920; reorganized 1949; Pres. Adrian Iorgulescu.

Ethnology Society of Romania (Societatea de Etnologie din România): 707142 Bucharest, Str. Zalomit 12; tel. (21) 6535846; f. 1990; Pres. Dr Romulus Vulcănescu; Sec. George Anca.

European Cultural Centre (Centrul European de Cultură): 712973 Bucharest, Bd. Primăverii 50; tel. (21) 2232619; fax (21) 2302292; e-mail cti@com.pcnet.ro; internet www.rotravel.com/cti; f. 1990; Pres. Dan Berindei.

Film-makers' Union of Romania (Uniunea Cineaştilor din România): 70169 Bucharest, Str. Mendeleev 28–30; tel. (21) 2127963; fax (21) 3111246; e-mail czucin@rnc.ro; f. 1963; reorganized 1990; provides professional, social and financial support for film-makers; Pres. Mihnea Gheorghiu; Dir Constantin Pivniceru.

PEN Club România: 711021 Bucharest, Calea Victoriei 115; tel. (21) 6507245; Pres. Ana Blandiana.

Romanian Union of Fine Arts (Uniunea Artiştilor Plastici din România): 711171 Bucharest, Str. Nicolae Iorga 21; tel. (21) 6504920; fax (21) 3113572; e-mail uap@dnt.ro; internet www.uap.ro; f. 1950 to promote the work of its members; awards scholarship; Pres. Prof. Zamfir Dumitrescu.

Romanian Union of War Veterans (Uniunea Veteranilor de Război): 71102 Bucharest, Calea Victoriei 135; tel. (21) 6507969; f. 1989; preservation of war monuments; publishes historical information; Pres. Ştefan Cucu.

Romanian Writers' Union: see section on Publishers (Writers' Union).

Theatre Union of Romania (Uniunea Teatrală din România): 701411 Bucharest, Str. Georghe Enescu 2–4; tel. (21) 3153636; fax (21) 3120913; e-mail uniter@buc.soros.ro; f. 1990; Pres. ION CARAMITRU.

Education

Education is free and compulsory between the ages of six and 16 years. Before reaching the age of six years, children may attend crèches (creşe) and kindergartens (grădiniţe de copii); in 1999/2000 65.2% of pre-school age children were attending kindergarten. Between the ages of six and 16 years children attend the general education school (şcoală de cultură generală de zece ani). In 1998 primary enrolment was 95.7% of children in the relevant age-group, while the ratio for secondary education in 1996 was 73% (males 72%; females 74%).

There are five types of secondary school. The general secondary school (liceul), for which there is an entrance examination, provides a specialized education suitable for preparation of students for admission to university or college. Vocational secondary schools (şcoli profesionale de ucenici), where training is given for careers in, for example, industry or agriculture, along with some general education. (Courses in these schools are also available to adults requiring retraining.) Secondary art schools (şcoală medie de artă) provide a general secondary education, but with an emphasis on music, art and the theatre. Secondary physical education schools (şcoala medie de educaţie fizică) also provide a general secondary education, but with an emphasis on physical fitness and training. In 2000/01 the total enrolment in secondary education was 687,919. Finally, teacher-training secondary schools (şcoala pedagogică de Onvăţători and şcoală pedagogică de educatoare) provide courses to prepare students for work as kindergarten and general education teachers.

Tuition in minority languages, particularly Hungarian and German, is available. In June 1999 legislation providing for the establishment of a minority-language university was approved. There are 49 public higher educational institutes in Romania, 38 of which are universities; enrolment in tertiary education was equivalent to 28.0% in 1999/2000. There is an increasing number of private institutes. In 2000 spending of 20,173,400m. lei, equivalent to 19.0% of total expenditure in that year, was allocated to education.

UNIVERSITIES

Alexandru Ioan Cuza University of Iaşi (Universitatea 'Alexandru Ioan Cuza' Iaşi): 6600 Iaşi, Bd. Carol I11; tel. (232) 201022; fax (232) 201201; e-mail livran@uaic.ro; internet www.uaic.ro; f. 1860; 14 faculties; 927 teachers; 16,382 students; Rector Prof. Dr GHEORGHE POPA.

Cluj-Napoca Babeş-Bolyai University (Universitatea 'Babeş-Bolyai' Cluj-Napoca): 3400 Cluj-Napoca, Str. Mihail Kogălniceanu 1; tel. (264) 194315; fax (264) 191906; e-mail staff@staff.ubbcluj.ro; internet www.ubbcluj.ro; f. 1919; 18 faculties; 1,664 teachers; 23,122 students; Rector Prof. Dr ANDREI MARGA.

Dunarea de Jos University of Galaţi (Universitatea 'Dunarea de Jos' din Galaţi): 6200 Galaţi, Str. Domnească 47; tel. (236) 413602; fax (236) 461352; f. 1948; f. 1974 as university; 9 faculties; 583 teachers; 8,869 students; Rector Prof. EMIL CONSTANTIN.

Petroleum and Gas University of Ploieşti (Universitatea Petrol-Gaze din Ploieşti): 2000 Ploieşti, Bd. Bucureşti 39; tel. (244) 173171; fax (244) 175847; internet www.upg-ploiesti.ro; f. 1948 as Institute of Petroleum and Gas, 1992 as a university; 4 faculties; 690 teachers; 7,500 students; Chancellor Prof. N. N. ANTONESCU.

Transylvanian University of Braşov (Universitatea 'Transilvania' din Braşov): 2200 Braşov, Bd. Eroilor 29; tel. (268) 142576; fax (268) 410525; e-mail rectorat@unitbv.ro; internet www.unitbv.ro; f. 1948; 10 faculties; 2,022 teachers; 11,504 students; Rector Prof. Dr Eng. SERGIU T. CHIRIACESCU.

University of Bucharest (Universitatea din Bucureşti): 70609 Bucharest, Bd. Mihail Kogălniceanu 34–46; tel. (21) 3077301; fax (21) 3131760; e-mail secretariat@unibuc.ro; internet www.unibuc.ro; f. 1864; assumed present status 1990; 20 faculties; 14 colleges; 1,490 teachers; 24,650 students; Rector Prof. Dr IOAN MIHĂILESCU.

University of Craiova (Universitatea din Craiova): 1100 Craiova, Str. Al. I. Cuza 13; tel. (251) 414398; fax (251) 411688; e-mail relint@entral.ucv.ro; internet www.central.ucv.ro; f. 1947; 14 faculties; 1,100 teachers; 15,000 students; Rector Prof. Dr MIRCEA IVANESCU.

University of the West in Timişoara (Universitatea de Vest din Timişoara): 1900 Timişoara, Bd. V. Pârvan 4; tel. (256) 194068; fax (256) 190009; e-mail rector@rectorat.uvt.ro; internet www.uvt.ro; f. 1944; 10 faculties; 672 teachers; 10,000 students; Rector Prof. Dr DUMITRU GAŞPAR.

Technological Universities

Cluj-Napoca Technical University (Universitatea Tehnică din Cluj-Napoca): 3400 Cluj-Napoca, Str. Constantin Daicoviciu 15; tel. (264) 195699; fax (264) 192055; e-mail int.rel.office@staff.utcluj.ro; f. 1922; 8 faculties; 660 teachers; 10,615 students; Rector Dr Eng. GHEORGHE LAZEA.

Gheorghe Asachi Technical University (Universitatea Technică 'Gheorghe Asachi'): Iaşi, Bd. D. Mangeron 67; tel. (232) 212322; fax (232) 211667; e-mail rectorat@stoff.tuiasi.ro; internet www.tuiasi.ro; f. 1912; 10 faculties; 1,813 teachers; 13,703 students; Rector Prof. Dr Ing. MIHAI CRETU.

Gr. T. Popa University of Medicine and Pharmacy of Iaşi (Universitatea de Medicină şi Farmacie 'Gr. T. Popa' Iaşi): 6600 Iaşi, Str. Universităţii 16; tel. (232) 211818; fax (232) 211820; e-mail rectorat@umfiasi.ro; internet www.umfiasi.ro; f. 1879; 4 faculties and 4 colleges; 970 teachers; 5,022 students; Pres. Prof. Dr CAROL STANCIU.

Iuliu Hatieganu University of Medicine and Pharmacy of Cluj-Napoca (Universitatea de Medicină şi Farmacie 'Iuliu Hatieganu' Cluj-Napoca): 3400 Cluj-Napoca, Str. Emil Isac 13; tel. (264) 195516; fax (264) 197257; e-mail dri@umfcluj.ro; f. 1919; 3 faculties; 616 teachers; 3,901 students; Rector Prof. Dr MARIUS TRAIAN BOJITA.

Technical University of Timişoara (Universitatea 'Politehnica' din Timişoara): Timişoara, Piaţa Victoriei 2; tel. (256) 220373; fax (256) 190321; e-mail relint@rectorat.utt.ro; internet www.utt.ro; f. 1920; 9 faculties; 902 teachers; 11,774 students; Rector Prof Dr Ing. IOAN GHEORGHE CARTIŞ.

University of Agricultural Science of the Banat in Timişoara (Universitatea de Ştiinţe Agricole a Banatului Timişoara): 1900 Timişoara, Calea Aradului 119; tel. (256) 141424; fax (256) 200296; e-mail usabtm@mail.dnttm.ro; f. 1945; 6 faculties; 287 teachers; 3,387 students; Rector Prof. Dr IOAN PĂUN OTIMAN.

University of Medicine and Pharmacy (Universitatea de Medicină şi Farmacie): 4300 Târgu-Mureş, Str. Gheorghe Marinescu 38; tel. (265) 213127; fax (265) 210407; f. 1948; 3 faculties; 333 teachers; 2,084 students; Rector Prof. Dr ION PASCU.

University Polytechnic of Bucharest (Universitatea 'Politehnica' din Bucureşti): 77206 Bucharest, Splaiul Independenţei 313; tel. (21) 4100391; fax (21) 4115365; f. 1819; 12 faculties; 1,696 teachers; 22,921 students; Rector Prof. Dr IOAN DUMITRACHE.

Social Welfare

Following the revolution of December 1989, international attention was focused on the orphanages in Romania housing large numbers of unwanted and neglected children (contraception and abortion having been illegal during the Ceauşescu years), many of whom were found to be suffering from Acquired Immunodeficiency Syndrome (AIDS), hepatitis and other serious illnesses, owing to poor medical treatment. In May 1998 there were 98,872 children under the age of 18 years housed in 650 orphanages in Romania. The incidence of tuberculosis increased during the early 1990s (from 64 sufferers per 100,000 in 1990 to 92.7 per 100,000 in the first quarter of 1993), and up to 10% of the population were reported to be carrying the hepatitis B virus. In 2001 Romania's infant mortality rate was high, at 21 per 1,000 live births.

Romania has a comprehensive state insurance scheme, premiums being paid by enterprises and institutions on behalf of their employees. A new law on unemployment allowance was adopted in January 1991. In addition, funds are allotted to sickness benefits, children's allowances, pensions and the provision of health resorts. Medical care is provided free of charge. In 1998 there were 184.0 doctors and 23.9 dentists per 100,000 of the population; in that year there were 7.56 per 1,000 people. State spending of 3,710,400m. lei was allocated to health in 2000, representing 3.5% of total expenditure, while 11,242,100m. lei (10.6% of total expenditure) was allocated to social welfare. In July 2002 the Government approved a new social programme for 2002–03, to support the poorest members of the population.

NATIONAL AGENCIES

Ministry of Health: see section on The Government (Ministries).

National Health Insurance Body (Casa Naţională de Asigurări de Sănătate—CNAS): Bucharest, Calea Calarasilor 248, Bl. S19, Sector 3; tel. (21) 3026200; internet www.casan.ro; Pres. EUGENIU TURLEA.

Ministry of Labour, Social Solidarity and Family: see section on The Government (Ministries).

National Authority for Child Protection and Adoption: Bucharest, Bd. Magheru 7, Sector 1; tel. (21) 3100790; fax (21)

3127474; e-mail office@anpca.ro; internet www.copii.ro; f. 1997; contains Romanian Adoption Cttee; Sec. of State CRISTIAN LIVIU TĂBĂCARU.

State Department for the Disabled: Bucharest, Calea Victoriei 194; tel. (21) 6593000; fax (21) 6593970; Sec. of State GABRIELA POPESCU.

HEALTH AND WELFARE ORGANIZATIONS

Association of Deaf Persons: Bucharest, Str. Armand Călinescu 3; tel. (21) 3102338; fax (21) 3113061; Pres. BARBU FLOREA.

Association of Former Political Prisoners of Romania: 70387 Bucharest, Str. Mântuleasa 10; tel. (21) 6139359; fax (21) 2106089; Pres. CONSTANTIN TICU DUMUSTRESCU.

Association for Human Rights Protection in Romania—Helsinki Committee: 704012 Bucharest, Nicolae Tonitza 8; tel. and fax (21) 3124528; e-mail apador@dnt.ro; internet www.apador .org; Pres. MONICA MACOVEI.

Human Rights Protection League: 70119 Bucharest, Str. Dem. I. Dobrescu 11; tel. (21) 6137190; fax (21) 3121728; f. 1990; deals with complaints regarding infringement of human rights; develops education programmes; Pres. NICOLAE ŞTEFĂNESCU DRĂGĂNEŞTI.

Institute of Hygiene and Public Health (Institutul de Igienă şi Sănătate Publică Bucureşti): 76256 Bucharest, Str. Dr Leonte 1–3; tel. (21) 6383970; fax (21) 3123426; f. 1927; Dir Prof. MANOLE CUCU.

Institute of Research for the Quality of Life (Institutul de Cercetare a Calităţii Vieţii): Bucharest 6, Splaiul Independenţei 202A; tel. (21) 6383375; f. 1990; formulates economic and social policy for improvement of standards of living in Romania; Dir Dr CĂTĂLIN ZAMFIR.

National Committee for UNICEF: 70732 Bucharest, Str. Ştirbel Vodă 37; tel. (21) 6157627.

National Society for Physically Handicapped Persons (Societatea Naţională a Handicapaţilor Fizic): 78171 Bucharest, Bd. Banu Manta 9; tel. (21) 2225220; fax (21) 2223137; Pres. SIMON FRANCISC.

Research Institute for Labour Safety (Institutul de Cercetări pentru Protecţia Muncii): 70744 Bucharest 1, Str. Gral. Budişteanu 15; tel. (21) 6150531; f. 1951; Dir Dr Ing. ALEXANDRU DARABONT.

Romanian Association of Blind People (Asociaţia Nevăzătorilor din România): 73305 Bucharest, Str. Vatra Luminoasă 108 bis; tel. (21) 2506615; fax (21) 2500519; e-mail cc@anor.ro; Pres. TEODOR LEPĂDATU.

Romanian Medical Association (Asociaţia Medicală Română): 70754 Bucharest, Str. Ionel Perlea 10; tel. (21) 3141071; fax (21) 3121357; f. 1873; Pres. Prof. Dr VALERIU POPESCU; Sec.-Gen. Prof. Dr EMANOIL POPESCU.

Romanian Red Cross Society: 70172 Bucharest, Str. Biserica Amzei 29; tel. (21) 6593385; fax (21) 3128452; internet www.ifrc.org; Pres. Prof. NICOLAE NICOARĂ.

Save The Children Organization (Organizatia Salvati Copii): 77116 Bucharest, Intrarea Ştefan Furtună 3; tel. (21) 6375716; fax (21) 3124486; Pres. GABRIELA ALEXANDRESCU.

The Environment

The first Romanian law on environmental protection was passed in 1930. Environmental problems caused some concern under the communist regime, and a Law on Environmental Protection was passed in 1973. The extent of heavy pollution and environmental damage in Romania became fully apparent after the revolution of December 1989. The Romanian Government is a member of the Danube Commission (based in Hungary), the Joint Danube Fishery Commission (Slovakia) and the IUCN (Gland, Switzerland). There are about 600 protected areas in Romania, covering some 12,500 sq km. The Danube Delta because of its bird population, the Retezat National Park (in the Southern Carpathians) and the Rodua National Park (in the Eastern Carpathians) are recognized by the United Nations Educational, Scientific and Cultural Organization (UNESCO) as being of special ecological importance.

On 30 January 2000 an accidental spillage of some 22m. gallons of cyanide at the Baia Mare gold mine, resulted in the poisoning of the ecosystem of the Lapus and Tisza Rivers in Hungary and a 2,000 km stretch of the Danube river. However, the rivers subsequently recovered better than had been expected. A report published in May 2000 by the Ministry of Waters, Forestry and Environmental Protection drew attention to extensive water, air and soil contamination in Romania. In July the Ministry ordered the partial closure of the Turnu Magurele chemical plant, owing to the leaks of ammonia polluting the air in the vicinity of the site. Romania's poor environmental record was one of the main obstacles to the country joining

the European Union (EU); however, it did become a member of the EU's European Environment Agency.

GOVERNMENT ORGANIZATIONS

Ministry of Agriculture, Forestry, Water and Environmental Protection: see section on The Government (Ministries).

Administration of Biosphere Reservation of the Danube Delta: 8800 Tulcea, Str. Taberei 32; tel. (2405) 50950.

Agency of Environmental Protection and Surveillance: Bucharest, Bd. Mihail Kogălniceanu 27; tel. (21) 6135535.

Romsilva (National Forestry Organization): 70164 Bucharest 1, Bd. Gen. Gh. Magheru 31; tel. (21) 6592020; fax (21) 2228428; e-mail rnp@rosilva.ro; internet www.rosilva.ro; manages state forests, conservation, processing and maintenance work.

ACADEMIC INSTITUTES

Academy of Agricultural and Forest Sciences 'Gheorghe Ionescu-Şişeşti' (Academia de Ştiinţe Agricole şi Silvice 'Gheorghe Ionescu-Şişeşti'): Bucharest, Bd. Mărăşti 61; tel. (21) 2227834; fax (21) 2229139; f. 1969; Pres. Prof. CORNELIU RĂUŢĂ; particularly involved in environmental matters through the activities of.

    Central Research Station for Soil Erosion Control (Staţiunea Centrală de Cercetări pentru Combaterea Eroziunii Solului): Perieni jud. Vaslui; tel. (235) 413770; fax (235) 412837; e-mail perieni@axel.ro; internet www.spectral.ro/perieni; f. 1954; Dir Ing. D. NISTOR.

    Danube Delta National Institute for Research and Development (Institutul de Cercetăre şi Projectare Delta Dunării): 8800 Tulcea, Str. Babadag 165; tel. (240) 531520; fax (240) 533547; e-mail office@indd.tim.ro; internet www.indd.timm.ro; f. 1970; conservation of the diverse ecology of the Danube delta, monitoring of the wetlands, fish ecology, tourism research; Exec. Dir Ing. ROMULUS STIUCA.

    Environmental Engineering and Research Institute (Institutul de Cercetări pentru Inginerea Mediului): 71552 Bucharest, Splaiul Independenţei 294; tel. (21) 6373035; fax (21) 2229139; Dir Dr V. ROJANSKI.

    Forest Research and Management Plans Institute (Institutul de Cercetări şi Amenajări Silvice——ICAS): Bucharest 2, Şos. Stefăneşti 128; tel. and fax (21) 6556845; f. 1933; silviculture, genetics, ecology, game management, trout farming, protection against soil erosion; Gen. Man. Dr M. IANCULESCU.

    National Institute of Meteorology and Hydrology: 71552 Bucharest, Şos. Bucureşti-Ploieşti 97; tel. (21) 2303166; fax (21) 2303143; e-mail relatii@meteo.inmh.ro; internet www.inmh.ro; f. 1884; Dir IOANA MARINEL.

    Romanian Marine Research Institute (Institutul Român de Cercetări Marine): 70259 Bucharest, Alexandru Philippide 11; tel. (21) 6412943; fax (21) 6104858; e-mail rmri@alpha.rmri.ro; internet www.rmri.ro; f. 1970; studies Black Sea hydrology, ecosystems and pollution; biochemistry, extraction and utilization of aquatic living resources; aquaculture; fishery resources; marine technology; Dir Dr Eng. TOMA GEORGE MAIORESCU.

Energy Information and Documentation Centre (Centrul de Informare Documentară pentru Energetică): 74568 Bucharest 3, Bd. Energeticienilor 8; tel. and fax (21) 3239552; e-mail cide@mail.gsci .vsat.ro; f. 1966; information relating to power plants, heat distribution and utilization, environmental protection, electricity generation and power system technology; Dir CONSTANTIN TUICĂ.

National Institute of Metrology (Institutul Naţional de Metrologie): 75669 Bucharest, Şos. Vitan-Bârzeşti 11; tel. (21) 6343520; fax (21) 3121533; f. 1951; Dir A. MILLEA.

National Research-Development Institute for Environmental Protection (Institutul National de Cercetare-Dezvoltare pentru Protectia Mediului): 77703 Bucharest 78, Spl. Independentei 294, Sector 6; tel. (21) 2210990; fax (21) 2219204; internet www.icim .ro; f. 1952.

Romanian Academy (Academia Română): 71102 Bucharest, Calea Victoriei 125; tel. (21) 6507680; fax (21) 3120209; e-mail esimion@ acad.ro; internet www.acad.ro; f. 1866 as Societatea Literară Română, present name 1948; concerned with protection of both natural and human environments; research into numerous scientific and cultural subjects; includes a publishing house and a library; Pres. EUGEN SIMION.

NON-GOVERNMENTAL ORGANIZATIONS

The **Romanian Ecological Movement** (Mişcarea Ecologistă din România) and the **Romanian Ecological Party** (Partidul Ecologist Român) (see section on Political Organizations) form part of the

Romanian Ecological Federation—REF of political parties. There are several other small 'Green' parties

ECO Black Sea: 8700 Constanţa, Bd. Mamaia 294; tel. (241) 664392; e-mail cier@impromex.ro; internet www.sitex.ro/cier; committed to environmental issues concerning the Black Sea; also associated with the Information, Education and Resource Centre for the Black Sea; Man. IONICĂ BUCUR.

Eco-Council Association (Asociatia Eco Conseil): 2200 Braşov, Bd. Barbu Lautaru 11/27/C/5; tel. (268) 189587; fax (268) 315436; e-mail ecoenvironment@hotmail.com; Contact RUSU CONSTANTIN MARIUS.

Eco-Development Foundation: 74538 Bucharest, Papiu Ilarian 4; Contact CARMELA FLOROIU.

ECODELTA: Tulcea, Piaţa Republicii 2; tel. (2405) 514660.

Ecology Society: Sighetu Marmatiei, Str. T. Vladimirescu 55; tel. (262) 512660.

European Foundation for Ecological Education and Culture: Bucharest, Şos Kiseleff 31; tel. (21) 2225916; ContactTOMA GEORGE MAIORESCU.

Infoterra Romania: Bucharest, POB 42–82, Bd. Libertatii 12, Sector 5; tel. (21) 3113308; e-mail infoterra@mappm.ro; internet www.mappm.ro/infoterra/; office of environmental information and references, part of the United Nations Environment Programme; maintains the Environment Library of Romania; Dir SANDA ODIATIU.

National Centre for Ecological and Tourist Information: 6600 Iaşi, Al. Rozelor 38. Bl. 10, Sc A, Apt 9; tel. (232) 139838; fax (232) 213545; Contact ADRIAN PODOLEANU.

Nature and Environmental Protection Association (Asociatia pentru Protectia Mediului si a Naturii): 76256 Bucharest, Dr Leonte 1/3; tel. (21) 6384010; fax (21) 6374202; Contact Prof. MANOLE CUCU.

Romanian Ecological Action (Actiunea Ecologica Romana): 1100 Craiova, Nicolae Titulescu 38; tel. (251) 196686; Contact CODRESI TECLU.

Romanian Ecological Foundation: 72442 Bucharest, Şos Colentina 56, Bl. 100, Apt 69; tel. and fax (21) 6553355; Contact ILIE IZVORANU PUIU.

Romanian Ecological Management for Sustainable Development Association: Bucharest, Calea Victoriei 125, Et. 1, Cam 31; tel. (21) 6504889; fax (21) 3125342.

Romanian Wildlife Society: 73232 Bucharest, Intr Plut Luicu Vasile 2; tel. and fax (21) 6351761; Contact HORIA ALMASAN.

Training, Information and Mediation Centre for Eco-Development: 2000 Ploieşti, Bd. Bucureşti 39; tel. (244) 118457; fax (244) 116549; e-mail timced@csd.univ.ploesti.ro; Contact ADRIAN GEORGESCU.

UNESCO Pro Natura: Bucharest, Calea Plevnei 61; tel. (21) 3112644; fax (21) 3121920; e-mail pronatura@ccs.ro; internet www.pronatura.ro/en; member of the World Conservation Union; Pres. MAXIM IURIE.

World Environmental Centre (Centrul Mondial de Protectie a Mediului): 73546 Bucharest, Şos. Pantelimon 309/8, Apt. 158; tel. (21) 6272004; fax (21) 3128063; Contact LIVIU IONESCU.

Defence

Prior to its dissolution in 1991, Romania was a member of the Warsaw Pact, although it allowed no Pact troops on to its soil and did not participate in military exercises. In July 2003 the South-Eastern European Brigade (SEEBRIG) for Military Co-operation, active since 1999, moved its headquarters to the Black Sea port of Constanţa. Military service is compulsory and lasts for eight months. In August 2002 regular forces totalled an estimated 99,200 (including 35,000 conscripts and 10,000 in centrally controlled units); of these, 66,000 were in the army (including 21,000 conscripts), 17,000 in the air force and 6,200 in the navy. In addition, there were 22,900 border guards and a gendarmerie of 57,000 (under the control of the Ministry of the Interior). Spending of 28,400,000m. lei was allocated to defence in the 2001 state budget. Romania was scheduled to become a full member of the North Atlantic Treaty Organization (NATO) in 2004.

Commander-in-Chief of the Armed Forces: The President of Romania.

Chief of Staff of the Army: Gen. MIHAI POPESCU.

Bibliography

Almond, M. *The Rise and Fall of Nicolae and Elena Ceauşescu.* London, Chapman, 1992.

Boia, L. *History and Myth in Romanian Consciousness.* New York, NY, Central European University Press, 2001.

Romania: Borderland of Europe. London, Reaktion Books, 2002.

Cartwright, A. L. *The Return of the Peasant: Land Reform in Post-Communist Romania.* Aldershot, Ashgate, 2001.

Deletant, D. *Ceauşescu and the Securitate: Coercion and Dissent in Romania, 1965–89.* London, Hurst and Co, 1995.

Communist Terror in Romania. London, Hurst and Co, 1999.

Fischer, M. *Nicolae Ceauşescu. A Study in Political Leadership.* Boulder, CO, and London, Lynn Rienner Publishers, 1989.

Twentieth Century Romania. New York, NY, and London, Columbia University Press, 1991.

Gallagher, T. *Romania After Ceauşescu: The Politics of Intolerance.* Edinburgh, Edinburgh University Press, 1995.

Romania after Communism: Distrusting Democracy. London, Hurst and Co, 2003.

Georgescu, V. *The Romanians: A History.* London, I. B. Tauris, 1991.

Gilberg, T. *Nationalism and Communism in Romania.* Boulder, CO, and Oxford, Westview Press, 1990.

Govrin, Y. *Israeli-Romanian Relations at the End of the Ceauşescu Era.* London, Frank Cass, 2002.

Heidhues, F., and Schrieder, G. (Eds). *Romania—Rural Finance in Transition Economies,* (Development Economics and Policy, Vol. 14). Vienna, Peter Lang, 2000.

Hitchins, K. *The Romanians 1774–1866.* Oxford, Oxford University Press, 1996.

Rumania, 1866–1947. Oxford, Oxford University Press, 1994.

International Business Publications. *Romania Business Intelligence Report.* International Business Publications, USA, 2001.

Ioanid, R. *The Holocaust in Romania: the Destruction of Jews and Gypsies under the Antonescu Regime, 1940–1944.* Chicago, IL, Ivan R. Dee, 2000.

Jackson, M. *Romania's Debt Crisis: Its Causes and Consequences,* (East European Economies: Slow Growth in the 1980s, Vol. 3). Washington, DC, USGPO (Joint Economic Committee of the US Congress), 1986.

Lazar, I., and Simon, A. I. (Eds). *Transylvania: A Short History.* La Vergne, TN, and Milton Keynes, Simon Publications, 2001.

Light, D., and Phinnemore, D. (Eds). *Post-Communist Romania: Coming to terms with Transition.* Houndsmill, Palgrave, 2001.

Livezeanu, I. *Cultural Politics In Greater Romania: Regionalism, Nation-Building, and Ethnic Struggle, 1918–30.* Ithaca, NY, and London, Cornell University Press, 1995.

Mitu, S. *National Identity of Romanians in Transylvania.* New York, NY, Central European University Press, 2001.

Nelson, D. N. (Ed.). *Romania After Tyranny.* Boulder, CO, and London, Westview Press, 1992.

Patterson, W. *Rebuilding Romania: Energy, Efficiency and the Economic Transition.* London, Earthscan Publications Ltd, 1995.

Pop, I. A. *Romanians and Romania.* New York, NY, and London, Columbia University Press, 2000.

Pridham, G., and Gallagher, T. (Eds). *Experimenting with Democracy: Regime Change in the Balkans.* London, Routledge, 2000.

Rady, M. *Romania in Turmoil.* London and New York, NY, I. B. Tauris, 1992.

Ronnas, P. *Urbanization in Romania.* Stockholm, Economic Research Institute, Stockholm School of Economics, 1984.

'The Economic Legacy of Ceauşescu', in *Economic Change in the Balkan States,* O. Sjoberg and M. L. Wyzan (Eds). London, Frances Pinter, 1991.

Roper, S. D. *Romania: The Unfinished Revolution.* Amsterdam, Harwood Academic, 2000.

Shafir, M. *Romania: Politics, Economics and Society.* London, Frances Pinter, 1985.

Siani-Davis, P, and M. *Romania* (World Bibliographic Series), Oxford, Clio Press, 1998.

Smith, A. H. 'Is There a Romanian Crisis? The Problems of Energy and Indebtedness', in *Crisis in the East European Economy*, J. Drewnowski (Ed.). Beckenham, Croom Helm, 1982.

The Planned Economies of Eastern Europe. Beckenham, Croom Helm, 1983.

'Romania: International Economic Developments and Foreign Economic Relations', in *The Economies of Eastern Europe and their Foreign Economic Relations*, P. Joseph (Ed.). Brussels, NATO, 1987.

'The Romanian Economy: Policy and Prospects for the 1990s', in *The Central and East European Economies in the 1990s: Prospects and Constraints*, R. Weichardt (Ed.). Brussels, NATO, 1991.

Verdery, K. *National Ideology Under Socialism: Identity and Cultural Politics in Ceauşescu's Romania*. Berkeley, CA, University of California Press, 1995.

SERBIA AND MONTENEGRO

Geography

PHYSICAL FEATURES

The State Union of Serbia and Montenegro, reconstituted from the Federal Republic of Yugoslavia (FRY) in February 2003, and formerly part of the Socialist Federal Republic of Yugoslavia (SFRY), is situated in the central Balkan Peninsula, in South-Eastern Europe. It has a western coastline along the Adriatic Sea (part of the Mediterranean). The land-locked territories of Serbia (with an area of 88,361 sq km), occupy the larger part of the country, and Montenegro (with an area of 13,182 sq km), lies in the south-west, on the Adriatic coast; the country has a total area of 102,173 sq km (39,449 sq miles). Serbian territory includes two formerly autonomous provinces: Kosovo and Metohija (formerly known as Kosovo and renamed in 1990) and Vojvodina. Kosovo and Metohija (with an area of 10,887 sq km) occupies the plateau-lands in the south-west of Serbia, and Vojvodina (21,506 sq km) is in the north of the republic. Serbia and Montenegro is bordered by Hungary to the north, Romania and Bulgaria to the east, the former Yugoslav republic of Macedonia to the south-east and Albania to the south. In the extreme south-western corner there is a short border with Croatia on the Adriatic coast, but the main border with that country is in the north-west, and the central western border is with Bosnia and Herzegovina.

The River Danube (Dunav) forms part of Serbia and Montenegro's western border with Croatia and runs across the northern half of the country to form part of the eastern frontier with Romania. The fertile plains of Vojvodina and northern Serbia are also watered by the Tisa (Tisza), Drava and Sava rivers, the last of which flows eastwards from Bosnia and Herzegovina to join the Danube at Belgrade (Beograd). Another river to flow into the Danube on these plains is the Morava, which passes through a deep valley from the mountainous south. Serbia and Montenegro has a rugged mountainous terrain, except in the north where the Pannonian plains begin. The highlands of the south-west are known as the Black Mountains (Crna Gora), from which Montenegro takes its name. Montenegro is also traversed by some fertile river valleys which cut southwards towards the lowlands around Lake Scutari (Skadarsko Jezero). There are some coastal lowlands around the harbour of Kotor (formerly Cattaro—on the Boka Kotorska bay) and to the south of the Adriatic city of Bar and Lake Scutari.

CLIMATE

The climate is continental in the hilly interior and Mediterranean on the coast, with steady rainfall throughout the year. The average summer temperature in Belgrade is 22°C (71°F) and in winter the average temperature is 0°C (32°F). The average annual rainfall is 635 mm (25 in) in Belgrade.

POPULATION

Serbia and Montenegro is dominated by Southern Slavic peoples, predominantly the Serbs. The Serbs made up 63% of the population of the FRY, according to the census of 1991. The principal language in the country is Serbo-Croat in its Serbian form, *ekavian*, and is written in the Cyrillic script. The Montenegrins (5% of the total population of the FRY at the 1991 census, but 62% of the population of Montenegro) also speak a Serbo-Croat dialect (*ijekavian*), use the Cyrillic script and are a Serb people. The non-Slavic ethnic Albanians

were actually the second largest group in the country (17% of the total population in 1991). They were predominantly present in the province of Kosovo. The other main non-Slavic group in the country was that of the Hungarians (Magyars—3%). The province of Vojvodina, in the north of the country, was formerly part of the Banat, a border territory of the Habsburg realm. Although it is an area of very mixed ethnic composition, originally it had a large Hungarian population. However, by the latter part of the 20th century it was dominated by Serbs. Those, usually of mixed parentage, who chose to define themselves as ethnic 'Yugoslavs' also made up some 3% of the country's total population in 1991. The Slav Muslims (3%) lived mainly in the Sandžak region, on the Serbian–Montenegrin border and to the north of Kosovo (the chief city of the region is Novi Pazar—anciently Raška). Other minority communities in the FRY included Roma (Gypsies), Vlahs (Vlachs), Bulgarians, Czechs, Slovaks and Ruthenians (Ukrainians).

A reflection of the Serb and Montenegrin majority is the predominance of Orthodox Christianity. Some 41% of the population adhere to the Eastern Orthodox Church (which introduced the Cyrillic alphabet), as represented by the Serbian Orthodox Church. There are followers of other Orthodox rites, some Roman Catholics (in Vojvodina and among the Albanian minority) and a few Protestants. Islam is the religion of a significant minority, but it is concentrated in the south of the country, among Slav Muslims and most of the Albanian population. There is also a small Jewish community.

According to official estimates, in mid-2002 the FRY had a total population of 10,664,300. The population density was, therefore, 104.4 per sq km. At mid-2001 the estimated population of Serbia was 9,993,000, and the population of Montenegro was 658,000. The capital and largest city is Belgrade (in Serbia—also the capital of that republic), which had a population of 1,687,000 at mid-2001, according to UN estimates. The Montenegrin capital is Podgorica (formerly Titograd), which had a population of 117,875 at the census of March 1991. The Serbian province of Kosovo had a population of 1,956,196 at March 1991 (an increase of some 23% compared with 1981, the highest rate of population growth of any region in the SFRY). However, following the conflict there in 1999 the population dramatically decreased. The provincial capital is Priština (155,499). Serbia's other province, Vojvodina, had a population of 2,031,889; its capital is Novi Sad, which had 179,626 inhabitants in 1991. Other important towns in Serbia and Montenegro include Niš (175,391 in 1991), Kragujevać (147,305), Subotica (100,386) and Zrenjanin (81,316).

Chronology

168 BC: Illyria (which included modern-day Serbia and Montenegro) was annexed by the Roman Empire and Macedon was finally defeated.

AD 395: Following a division of the administration of the Roman Empire, Illyria was ruled by the Eastern Roman ('Byzantine') Emperor in Constantinople (now İstanbul, Turkey).

5th century: Southern Slav peoples began to move from Pannonia into Illyria and the Balkans.

812: By the Treaty of Aix-la-Chapelle (Aachen), the Byzantine Emperor, Michael I, acknowledged the Frankish (German) ruler, Charles ('the Great'—Charlemagne), as Emperor in the West; German influence over the Slovene-inhabited areas of Carinthia and Carniola was established.

863: The missionary activity of the Byzantine brothers, SS Constantine (Cyril) and Methodius, led to the conversion of the Serbs (including the ancestors of the Bosnians and Montenegrins) and the Bulgars (and Macedonians) to Eastern Orthodox Christianity; a Slavonic liturgy (based on a Macedonian dialect) was introduced with a written language, in the Cyrillic script, which remained common to all the Eastern and Balkan Slavic peoples.

1014: Final defeat of the western Bulgarian, or Macedonian, realm under Samuel by the Byzantine Emperor, Basil II. Later in the century Byzantine influence began to decline.

1102: Croatia's personal union with Hungary effectively, if not finally, linked it to the Hungarian Crown.

1169: Accession of Stefan I Nemanja as Grand Župan (ruler) of Raška; he united the Serb tribes and established a Serbian state.

1187: The Emperor in Constantinople acknowledged Serbian independence, Hungarian conquests in Croatia and Bosnia and the establishment of the second Bulgarian Empire.

1219: St Sava, brother of the Serbian king, Stefan II, was consecrated the first autocephalous archbishop of the Serbian Orthodox Church, at Žiča.

1330: The Serbs defeated the Bulgarians and the Greek Byzantines at the Battle of Velbuzhde (Küstendil).

1346: Establishment of a Serbian patriarchate and the coronation of Stefan Dušan ('the Great') of Raška (1331–55) as Uroš IV, Tsar of the Serbs and Greeks, at Skopje; however, he failed in his ambition to conquer Constantinople (Carigrad).

1377: Stefan (Stjepan) Trvtko I (1353–91) proclaimed himself Tsar of the Bosnians and Serbs, ruling a Bosnia that was now dominated by the heretical 'Church of Bosnia' (*ecclesia Sclavoniae*).

28 June 1389: The Turkish Ottoman Empire, which had already conquered Macedonia, destroyed the Serbian nobility at a battle on the plain of Kosovo Polje (sometimes referred to as 'the Field of Blackbirds').

1459–83: The Ottomans finally incorporated the rest of Serbia into the Empire, following the fall of the Serbian stronghold of Smederovo, and completed the subjugation of Bosnia and Herzegovina; the Montenegrins (Serbs of the principality of Zeta) maintained a semi-independence.

1490: Death of the Hungarian King, Matthias I Corvinus, who had secured modern Croatia and Vojvodina (Slavonia and the Banat) for Hungary and, temporarily, conquered the Habsburg lands.

1526: Louis II and the Hungarian forces were destroyed by the Ottomans at the Battle of Mohács; the Hungarian Crown was claimed as a hereditary possession of the House of Habsburg, but the kingdom itself was subsequently partitioned between the Habsburgs (Croatia) and the Ottomans (Slavonia).

1690: Serbs ('the 30,000 Families', led by Patriarch Arsenije III Crnojević), retreating with Habsburg armies, first settled in Vojvodina.

1697: The Petrović-Njegoš family established the rule of a joint prince and bishop in Montenegro (under the title of Vladika), reigning over the principality until 1918.

1718: The Peace of Passarowitz confirmed the Habsburg liberation of Hungary, including Croatia and Slavonia; the Ottomans ceded the Banat and northern Serbia (but the latter was held only until 1739).

1796: Montenegro, never completely subdued by the Ottomans, was acknowledged as an independent principality.

1804–13: A revolt of the Serbian peasantry against the local Turkish garrison became a popular revolt for autonomy (the First Serbian Uprising), led by Kara Djordje ('Black George') Petrović.

1815: The Congress of Vienna confirmed Austrian rule over Istria and Dalmatia, which were formerly Venetian.

1817: Serbia became an autonomous principality, after the Second Serbian Uprising under Miloš Obrenović, whose house was, from then on, in constant rivalry with the Karadjordjević dynasty.

1848: At a time of revolution in Habsburg and other territories, the Croatian assembly, in Agram (Zagreb), was forced to end consideration of a Southern Slav state.

1851: Danilo II became Vladika of Montenegro, but renounced the title, and the episcopacy, early the next year—he married and reigned as Prince until his assassination in 1860 (a Metropolitan Primate for the Montenegrin Church was appointed in 1855).

1868: Croatia, united with Slavonia, was granted autonomy by Hungary, which, since the *Ausgleich* or Compromise of the previous year, was a partner in the Habsburg 'Dual Monarchy'.

March 1878: The Treaty of San Stefano concluded the war between Russia, in support of the Orthodox Slavs, and the Ottomans, but the Great Powers rejected the settlement.

July 1878: At the Congress of Berlin, Bulgaria was denied the annexation of Macedonia, Montenegro's independence was confirmed and Serbia's tributary status was ended (it was awarded territory around Niš); Austria-Hungary secured administration rights in Bosnia and Herzegovina and ensured that the Ottomans remained in the Sandžak of Novi Pazar and in Kosovo, as a restraint on Serbian expansion.

1881: Final abolition of the 'Military Frontier' or Krajina (now in Croatia), in which, since the 17th century, the Habsburgs had allowed some autonomy to Serb settlers defending the borders against the Ottomans.

1882: Serbia was proclaimed a kingdom under Milan Obrenović, whose regime was conservative and pro-Habsburg.

1903: Assassination of King Aleksandar I of Serbia; accession of Petar I Karadjordjević, leader of the Radical Party, who was anti-Habsburg and saw the rise of the Southern Slav movement ('Yugoslavism').

1908: The 'Young Turk' uprising in the Ottoman Empire led to disturbances in the Balkans; Austria-Hungary annexed Bosnia and Herzegovina, despite international objections, but its ally, Germany, prevented war against Serbia.

1910: Nikola I, nephew and heir of Danilo II, proclaimed himself King of Montenegro. The secret, Greater Serb society, Union or Death (the 'Black Hand'), was founded by Col Dimitrijević-Apis.

May 1913: The Peace of London concluded the First Balkan War, in which a league of Bulgaria, Greece, Montenegro and Serbia succeeded in removing the Turks from the bulk of their European possessions.

June 1913: Bulgaria attacked Serbia, which was supported by Greece, Montenegro, Romania and the Turks.

August 1913: The Peace of Bucharest concluded the Second Balkan War; Bulgaria lost Macedonia, which was divided between Serbia and Greece; the Sandžak was divided between Serbia and Montenegro; but Austria-Hungary and Italy succeeded in preventing Serbia from gaining access to the Adriatic, notably by the recognition of Albanian independence.

28 June 1914: The heir to the Habsburg throne, Archduke Francis Ferdinand, and his wife were assassinated in Sarajevo, the Bosnian capital, by a student, Gavrilo Princip, who was acting for the Serb Black Hand group.

28 July 1914: Austria-Hungary declared war on Serbia, which started the First World War between the Central Powers of Austria-Hungary and Germany, and the Entente Powers, of France, Russia, Serbia and the United Kingdom.

1915: Serbia, including Macedonia, was conquered by the Central Powers and Bulgaria.

1916: Habsburg troops invaded Montenegro.

July 1917: Serbia and the other Southern Slavs (excluding the Bulgarians) declared their intention to form a unitary state, under the Serbian monarchy.

YUGOSLAVIA 1918–91

29 October 1918: Following the defeat and dissolution of the Danubian Monarchy, the Southern Slav (Yugoslav) peoples separated from the Austro-Hungarian system of states (a Southern Slav republic was established on 15 October); Dalmatia, Croatia-Slavonia, Bosnia and Herzegovina, parts of Carinthia, Carniola and the Banat were, subsequently, ceded formally to the new state.

4 December 1918: Proclamation of the Kingdom of Serbs, Croats and Slovenes, which united Serbia and Montenegro with the former Habsburg lands.

August 1921: Prince Aleksandar, Regent of Serbia since 1914 and of the new Kingdom since its formation, became King, upon the ratification of the so-called Vidovdan (St Vitus Day) Constitution. Nikola II, who still maintained a government-in-exile, died in the same year, the last of the Petrović-Njegoš family to have reigned in Montenegro.

3 October 1929: Following the imposition of a royal dictatorship, the country was formally named Yugoslavia.

1931: The dictatorship was suspended by the introduction of a new Constitution, although this did not prevent Croat unrest and the rise of the Fascist Ustaša (Rebel) movement.

October 1934: King Aleksandar I of Yugoslavia was assassinated in France by Croatian extremists; his brother, Prince Pavle, became Regent, on behalf of the young King Petar II.

1937: Josip Broz (Tito) became General-Secretary of the Communist Party of Yugoslavia (CPY), which was to become the main partner in the Partisan (National Liberation Army) resistance to the German invasion.

March 1941: A *coup d'état* by air-force officers ousted the Regent and installed King Petar II, who reversed previous policies and aligned himself with the Allied Powers of the Second World War.

10 April 1941: An Independent State of Croatia was established (including much of Bosnia and Herzegovina), with an Ustaše Government under Ante Pavelić.

17 April 1941: German and Italian forces invaded Yugoslavia: Germany annexed Lower Styria and parts of Carinthia; Italy annexed Ljubljana and Dalmatia, and the nominally independent Montenegro became its client; Albania (in personal union with the Italian Crown) annexed Kosovo; part of Vojvodina (eastern Slavonia) was annexed by Hungary; Macedonia was occupied by Bulgaria; the remainder of Serbia was placed under German military administration.

29 November 1943: In the Bosnian town of Jajce, following fierce resistance and civil conflict with the royalist Četniks (Yugoslav Army of the Fatherland) of western Serbia and with the Ustaše regime, Gen. (later Marshal) Tito's Partisans proclaimed their own government for liberated areas (mainly in Bosnia, Croatia and Montenegro); Tito's leadership was subsequently acknowledged by the Allies and the royal Government-in-Exile, although the following year King Petar II was declared deposed.

20 October 1944: Aided by the Soviet Red Army, Belgrade was liberated from German occupying forces.

29 November 1945: Following elections for a Provisional Assembly, the Federative People's Republic of Yugoslavia was proclaimed, with Tito as Prime Minister.

January 1946: A Soviet-style Constitution, establishing a federation of six republics and two autonomous regions, was adopted.

28 June 1948: Yugoslavia was expelled from the Soviet-dominated Cominform; the break with the USSR ended Yugoslav ambitions for a Balkan federation with Albania and Bulgaria.

November 1952: The Communist Party was renamed the League of Communists of Yugoslavia (LCY) and several liberal reforms were adopted.

January 1953: A new Constitution was adopted, with Tito becoming President of the Republic.

1954: Istria was partitioned between Italy, which gained the city of Trieste, and Yugoslavia. The so-called Novi Sad Agreement proclaimed Serbo-Croat to be one language with two scripts and a number of variants.

1955: Relations with the USSR were normalized.

April 1963: A new Constitution changed the country's name to the Socialist Federal Republic of Yugoslavia (SFRY).

1966: Monetary reform and economic liberalization were introduced; later in the year the reformists secured the fall of Vice-President Aleksandar Ranković, the head of the secret police and an advocate of strong central government.

July 1971: Following the granting of the rights of autonomy to the federal units, Tito introduced a system of collective leadership and the regular rotation of posts; a collective State Presidency for Yugoslavia was established, with Tito as its head.

November 1971: Tito criticized the reformist Croatian leadership, causing it to resign; the suppression of the Croatian 'mass movement', or *Maspok,* and a purge of liberals throughout Yugoslavia followed.

February 1974: A new Constitution was adopted.

May 1979: The principle of rotating leadership was extended to the secretaryship of the LCY.

4 May 1980: Tito died; his responsibilities were transferred to the collective State Presidency and to the Presidium of the LCY.

March 1981: Protests by students in Priština led to demonstrations by Albanian nationalists throughout Kosovo; the unrest was to continue sporadically throughout the 1980s.

1986: Slobodan Milošević, leader of the Belgrade Communists, became leader of the League of Communists of Serbia.

24–25 April 1987: Thousands of Serbs and Montenegrins, who had gathered at Kosovo Polje to protest at harassment by the Albanian population, clashed with police.

November 1988: Some 100,000 ethnic Albanians demonstrated in Priština, demanding the reinstatement of two Kosovo Party leaders who had been pressured into resigning. An estimated 1m. people demonstrated in Belgrade, against alleged discrimination by the Albanian population of Kosovo. Public demonstrations were banned in Kosovo.

December 1988: Against a background of increasing popular dissatisfaction with economic conditions, Branko Mikulić, the President of the Federal Executive Council (Yugoslav), and his Government were forced to resign following the Federal Assembly's rejection of the proposed state budget for 1989; three months later a new Government was appointed under Ante Marković.

January 1989: In Montenegro the State Presidency and the Presidium of the local League of Communists resigned as a result of public pressure (a similar situation had occurred in Vojvodina three months previously).

February 1989: Azem Vlasi, a prominent Albanian from Kosovo, was dismissed from the LCY Central Committee, provoking protests in Kosovo, during which federal troops intervened.

May 1989: Slobodan Milošević was elected President of the Serbian State Presidency (and re-elected, in direct elections, in November).

September 1989: The Slovenian Assembly reaffirmed the sovereignty of their Republic and declared its right to secede from the SFRY; thousands demonstrated in Serbia and Montenegro against the perceived threat to the unity of the SFRY.

November 1989: The first direct, secret ballot in Serbia since before the Second World War was held for local, parliamentary and presidential elections, although the communists continued to dominate the electoral and candidate lists.

December 1989: Serbian enterprises were instructed to sever all links with Slovenia, which retaliated by closing its border with Serbia and implementing reciprocal economic sanctions.

20–23 January 1990: The LCY voted to abolish its leading role in society, but rejected Slovenian proposals to restructure the federal Party; the League of Communists of Slovenia suspended its links with the LCY.

February 1990: The Yugoslav People's Army (YPA—Jugoslovenska Narodna Armija) was deployed in Kosovo for the first time and the federal State Presidency subsequently approved any action by the YPA needed to maintain the *status quo* in Kosovo. The Slovenian Communists changed the name of their party and renounced its links with the LCY.

22 April 1990: In Slovenia Milan Kučan, the leader of the former communists, was elected as President of the republican Presidency; the opposition DEMOS coalition, which had already won the direct elections to the main Socio-Political Chamber, emerged as the winner in the Chamber of Municipalities.

6–7 May 1990: The Croatian Democratic Union (CDU), the nationalist opposition party, obtained 205 of the eventual 351 seats.

15 May 1990: Dr Borisav Jović (Serbia) took over as President of the federal State Presidency.

26 June 1990: The Kosovo Assembly was suspended and its responsibilities assumed by the Serbian Assembly.

2 July 1990: The Slovenian Assembly proclaimed the full sovereignty of the Republic. In a referendum, a majority of Serbians approved the proposed new republican Constitution, which, among other matters, effectively removed the distinct status of the Autonomous Provinces of Kosovo and Vojvodina; 114 deputies of the 180-member Kosovo Assembly declared that Kosovo was, thenceforth, independent of Serbia and a constituent republic of the SFRY; in response, the Serbian Assembly declared the provincial legislation dissolved.

17 July 1990: The League of Communists of Serbia merged with the republican Socialist Alliance of the Working People (a communist mass organization), to form the Socialist Party of Serbia (SPS); Slobodan Milošević was elected leader.

25 July 1990: The Croatian Assembly approved constitutional changes that reasserted Croatian sovereignty. The leaders of the Serb minority in Croatia, who had formed a 'Serb National Council', proclaimed the right to sovereignty and autonomy for all Croatian Serbs.

13 September 1990: The 111 members of the Kosovo Assembly, who, at a secret session in Kačanik on 7 September, had declared the Assembly to have been re-formed, proclaimed a 'Constitution of the Republic of Kosovo'.

28 September 1990: Serbia's new Constitution formally took effect: the word 'Socialist' was removed from the Republic's title; a multi-party system was established (in accordance with federal provisions of the previous month); the independence of the institutions of the Autonomous Provinces was effectively removed; and Kosovo was renamed Kosovo and Metohija.

19 October 1990: Stipe Mesić was endorsed, by the Federal Assembly, as the new Croatian member of the State Presidency and Vice-President of the collective body.

9 December 1990: Three nationalist parties won most of the seats after the final round of elections to the Assembly of Bosnia and Herzegovina. In similar elections in Macedonia the nationalist opposition, the Internal Macedonian Revolutionary Organization—Democratic Party for Macedonian National Unity (IMRO—DPMNU), won the largest number of seats in the Assembly. In Serbia a presidential election was won by Milošević, with 65% of the votes cast; the first round of the elections to the Assembly was held, despite an opposition boycott. The first round elections to the presidency and to a new, unicameral Assembly were also held in Montenegro.

16 December 1990: The final round of voting in the Montenegrin Assembly elections took place; the ruling League of Communists of Montenegro won 83 of the 125 seats.

21 December 1990: The Croatian Assembly promulgated a new Constitution, which proclaimed the Republic's full sovereignty and its right to secede from Yugoslavia.

23 December 1990: A referendum, in which an overwhelming majority voted in favour of secession, was held in Slovenia, despite federal warnings of unconstitutionality and economic sanctions. No candidate having won an overall majority in the Montenegrin presidential election, a second round was held and was won by Momir Bulatović, of the League of Communists. The second round of elections to the Serbian Assembly was held; the final results gave 194 of the 250 seats to the ruling SPS.

15 January 1991: The Serbian Assembly elected Dragutin Zelenović, until then the Vojvodina member of the federal State Presidency, as the republican premier.

25 January 1991: The Macedonian Assembly unanimously adopted a declaration of the Republic's sovereignty, including a statement of its right to secede from the federation.

20–21 February 1991: Slovenia initiated its process of 'dissociation' from Yugoslavia, and Croatia asserted the primacy of its Constitution and laws over those of the federation; both Republics, which had declared a mutual defence pact in the previous month, declared their willingness to negotiate a future for Yugoslavia.

9 March 1991: Massive demonstrations, demanding less confrontational policies by the SPS and resignations from the Serbian Government, began in Belgrade; many opposition leaders were among those arrested, notably Vuk Drašković of the nationalist Serbian Renewal Movement; President Milošević demanded the deployment of federal troops to suppress the disturbances.

15–21 March 1991: Jović, the President of the federal State Presidency, resigned and, supported by the members for Kosovo and Metohija, Montenegro and Vojvodina, demonstrated the power of the 'Serbian bloc' to render the State Presidency inquorate; however, the YPA rejected political involvement (which was what the Serbian Government was demanding) and the crisis passed when Jović withdrew his resignation.

6 May 1991: The USA suspended all economic aid to Yugoslavia, because of alleged human rights abuses in Kosovo and Metohija and the 'destabilization' of the State Presidency.

THE DEMISE OF THE SFRY

6 June 1991: A summit of the republican presidents considered a proposal to make Yugoslavia an alliance of states; by this time an overwhelming majority had voted for independence in Croatia (although the Serb region of Krajina rejected such moves) and Slovenia had enacted legislation enabling its eventual assumption of independent power.

25 June 1991: The Croatian and Slovenian Assemblies declared the independence and sovereignty of their republics, beginning the process of dissociation from the federation.

27 June 1991: The YPA began military operations, mainly in Slovenia, mobilizing to secure the international borders of the SFRY.

30 June 1991: Under pressure from the European Community (EC—known as the European Union from November 1993), Stipe Mesić, a Croat, was confirmed as President of the federal State Presidency (he was due to assume office on 15 May, but was not endorsed by the Serbian bloc, leaving the body in abeyance).

1–5 July 1991: The emergency committee of senior officials of the Conference on Security and Co-operation in Europe (CSCE) and the CSCE Conflict Prevention Centre met for the first time, to discuss the situation in Yugoslavia; the CSCE meetings supported the EC's peace efforts, which continued with agreement on an arms embargo (endorsed by the USA on 8 July), a decision to send in cease-fire observers and the suspension of financial aid to Yugoslavia.

7–8 July 1991: The EC mediating team and representatives of the State Presidency, Croatia and Slovenia agreed that all fighting should cease immediately and that Slovenia and Croatia should have a three-month moratorium on further implementation of their declarations of dissociation. However, fighting continued to escalate in Croatia.

21 August 1991: The federal State Presidency and the republican authorities reached an agreement that provided for the basic economic and political operation of the federation for three months.

26 August 1991: The presidential cease-fire commission collapsed with the resignation of its secretary, who stated that the July agreement had been breached some 200 times and that more than 70 people had been killed. The next day condemnation of Serbia, as the aggressor in the Yugoslav conflict, was general at an EC meeting (a view echoed by the USA on 29 August); the EC proposed new peace measures, but Milošević refused to endorse them.

7 September 1991: An EC-sponsored peace conference on the future of Yugoslavia opened in The Hague, the Netherlands, chaired by the former British foreign minister and NATO Secretary-General, Lord Carrington; the federal State Presidency met with all eight members for the last time.

25 September 1991: The UN Security Council unanimously ordered an arms embargo on Yugoslavia.

3 October 1991: The Serbian bloc on the federal State Presidency announced that, because of the imminent threat of war, Serbia was to assume certain powers of the Federal Assembly; the other four Presidency members were not present and repudiated the decision of this 'rump' Presidency and refused to participate in further activities of the body.

8 October 1991: The Croatian Assembly declared all federal laws null and void. Slovenia's independence declaration took effect and recalled all its citizens in federal institutions.

15 October 1991: The Assembly of Bosnia and Herzegovina declared the Republic's sovereignty, emphasizing the inviolability of its borders and its willingness to consider a form of Yugoslav association. As in Croatia, however, the Serb areas rejected such declarations.

19 October 1991: Following a referendum in the province, the Kosovo Assembly-in-Exile declared Kosovo to be an independent and sovereign Republic; the Assembly appointed a provisional coalition government.

26 October 1991: In the Sandžak region (mainly in Serbia, but partly in Montenegro) the Slav Muslims voted for autonomy in a referendum banned by the Serbian authorities.

9–10 November 1991: A referendum of Serbs in Bosnia and Herzegovina indicated overwhelming support for remaining in a common Serb state.

17 November 1991: A new Constitution was enacted in Macedonia, which declared it to be an independent country.

5 December 1991: Stipe Mesić resigned from his post as President of the federal State Presidency, declaring that Yugoslavia had ceased to exist.

20 December 1991: Ante Marković, the federal Prime Minister, resigned following a vote of 'no confidence'; further resignations followed.

10 January 1992: Sanctions, imposed on Montenegro and Serbia by the EC in the previous year, were lifted from Montenegro.

15 January 1992: The EC recognized the independence of Croatia and Slovenia; numerous countries followed. The Montenegrin Constitution, adopted in November 1991, was amended in order to comply with EC criteria for recognition.

9 March 1992: The first UN peace-keeping forces arrived in the former Yugoslavia, following the endorsement of their deployment by the 'rump' federal State Presidency the previous December. The first in several days of mass protests by opponents of the Serbian Government occurred in Belgrade.

27 April 1992: By adopting a new federal Constitution, Montenegro and Serbia effectively acknowledged the secession of the other four republics, although they claimed to be a continuation of the SFRY, rather than one of a number of successor states, and claimed all international functions of the Federation. Under the new Constitution a Federal Republic of Yugoslavia (FRY) was created, with a bicameral legislature and a single head of state replacing the collective State Presidency; the 1990 Serbian abolition of the autonomous status of Kosovo and Vojvodina was confirmed.

THE FEDERAL REPUBLIC OF YUGOSLAVIA

11 May 1992: Alleging Serbian involvement in the continued fighting in Croatia and in Bosnia and Herzegovina, the Governments of the EC countries announced their decision to withdraw their ambassadors from the FRY.

24 May 1992: Elections, declared illegal by the Serbian authorities, were held in Kosovo; the Democratic Alliance of Kosovo (DAK) won a majority of seats in this Assembly and its leader, Ibrahim Rugova, was elected President of the self-proclaimed 'Republic of Kosovo'. The 'Kosovo Assembly' was prevented from holding its inaugural session by several hundred Serbian police.

30 May 1992: Economic sanctions were imposed on Serbia and Montenegro by the UN, because of their involvement in the wars in Croatia and Bosnia and Herzegovina.

31 May 1992: The opposition boycotted elections to the new Federal Assembly and the SPS won an overwhelming number of seats in the parliament. The Serbian Democratic Movement (SDM) was formed by a broad alliance of opposition parties; Vuk Drašković was elected leader.

15 June 1992: Dobrica Ćosić was elected President of the FRY.

14 July 1992: Milan Panić, a US businessman of Serbian origin, was elected Prime Minister of the FRY.

26–27 August 1992: At the conference on the former Yugoslavia, held in London, the United Kingdom, Panić declared that there was no federal involvement in the conflict in Bosnia and Herzegovina. The state of emergency in Kosovo and Metohija (in force from 1989) was revoked, following a visit to the area by Panić.

12 October 1992: A new Montenegrin Constitution was adopted, defining the republic as part of the FRY.

12–13 October 1992: There was rioting in Kosovo and Metohija following the arrest of two ethnic Albanian deputies from the 'Kosovo Assembly' and the banning of an Albanian-language newspaper; Panić attended UN-EC sponsored negotiations in Priština to discuss the reopening of Albanian schools in Kosovo. There were terrorist attacks on Muslims in Pljevlja, in the Sandžak. Supporters of Milošević surrounded the Federal Ministry of Internal Affairs with 48,000 Serbian police and blockaded the building for several weeks.

20 December 1992: Ćosić was re-elected President of Yugoslavia, in a direct election, with some 85% of the votes cast. At a general election the SPS won 47 of the 138 seats in the Federal Assembly. The SPS was also successful in the republican elections, winning 101 of the 250 seats in the Serbian Assembly. The SPS leader, Milošević, was re-elected President of Serbia, with 56% of the votes cast, compared with

Panić, who obtained 34%. The opposition accused the SPS of electoral malpractice.

29 December 1992: Panić was replaced as Federal Prime Minister by a Montenegrin, Rade Kontić.

10 January 1993: Momir Bulatović, of the ruling Democratic Party of Montenegrin Socialists (DPMS), was re-elected President of Montenegro in a second round of voting.

3 February 1993: A new Federal Government, comprising the SPS and the DPMS, was formed. The SDM, which had won 49 seats at the December elections, began a boycott of the Serbian Assembly.

10 February 1993: A new Serbian Government, comprised of SPS members and led by Nikola Sainović, officially took office.

5 March 1993: Milo Djukanović formed a new coalition Government in Montenegro.

1 June 1993: Ćosić was removed from office by the Federal Assembly, following accusations that he had conspired with army generals to oust Milošević; there were mass demonstrations in Belgrade in protest at his dismissal. Miloš Radulović was appointed acting President by the Federal Assembly. On 25 June Zoran Lilić was elected President of the FRY.

19 December 1993: In further Serbian parliamentary elections the SPS received some 37% of votes cast and 123 seats in the Assembly; the opposition SDM obtained 18% of the ballot and 45 seats; the nationalist Serbian Radical Party (SRP) came third with 15.6% of the votes cast and 39 seats. The Democratic Party of Serbia (DPS) won seven seats.

17 March 1994: The Serbian Assembly approved the election of a new republican Government, with Mirko Marjanović as premier.

August 1994: Against a background of increasing tension between President Milošević and the Bosnian Serb leadership, the Serbian Assembly endorsed a peace plan, sponsored by the 'Contact Group' (consisting of France, Germany, Russia, the United Kingdom and the USA), which had earlier been rejected by the Serb Assembly in Bosnia and Herzegovina.

September 1994: A smaller, 14-member Federal Government was appointed, with Kontić retaining the post of Prime Minister. The UN suspended some sanctions against the FRY (mainly relating to travel, sport and culture) after the Serbian leadership imposed a blockade on the Bosnian Serbs.

August 1995: Following a major military offensive by Croatian government troops in the Serb-controlled enclave of the Krajina (in Croatia), over 100,000 Croatian Serbs sought refuge in the FRY, particularly Vojvodina, prompting protests from Hungarians in that region. The Bosnian Serb leadership agreed to allow the FRY to act as its representative during peace negotiations on Bosnia and Herzegovina.

1–21 November 1995: At an air base near Dayton, Ohio, the USA, a number of agreements on peace in the former Yugoslavia was reached by the leaderships of Bosnia and Herzegovina, Croatia and the FRY. Later in the month, Milošević dismissed several leading members of the SRP who were opposed to the terms of the Dayton accords. All international sanctions against the FRY were suspended.

14 December 1995: The Dayton accords were signed into treaty in Paris, France.

February 1996: The Yugoslav Government suspended its blockade of Bosnian Serb territories.

23 August 1996: The FRY and Croatian Governments finally normalized relations with a treaty of mutual recognition.

3 November 1996: There were federal, Montenegrin and local elections. The SPS-led United List obtained 64 of the 138 seats in the federal Chamber of Citizens, followed by the opposition electoral alliance, Zajedno, with 22 seats; ethnic Albanians in Kosovo boycotted the elections. The DPMS won the majority of seats in elections to the Republican Assembly in Montenegro, and also secured control of the majority of municipal assemblies in the republic. The results of the municipal elections in Serbia were unclear.

17 November 1996: Following a second round of voting in local elections in Serbia, provisional results showed that Zajedno had secured control of 14 cities, including Belgrade; however, Zajedno's victory was annulled by the courts, leading to mass demonstrations; a third round of voting was held on 27 November, but was largely boycotted. Further protests against the rulings led to two deaths.

2 January 1997: After an Organization for Security and Co-operation in Europe (OSCE) delegation had declared the Serbian local election results to be valid, the Serbian Orthodox Church, which had hitherto supported Milošević's SPS, issued a statement in support of the opposition's electoral victory.

11 February 1997: After further anti-Government demonstrations, the Serbian National Assembly reinstated the municipal election results; opposition leaders announced an end to the protests, although students continued to agitate in support of political reform. The National Assembly also approved a reorganization of the Serbian cabinet.

23 June 1997: The DPMS voted to support the candidacy of Milošević for the federal presidency, but rejected proposals that there should be direct presidential elections in the future, fearing the reduction of Montenegrin influence in Yugoslavian affairs.

15 July 1997: Milošević was elected to be President of the FRY by the Federal Assembly, following the expiry of Lilić's mandate; the conflicts within the DPMS caused the ballot to be held earlier than scheduled. Opposition deputies boycotted the vote and declared its result invalid.

6 August 1997: Bulatović was re-elected leader of the DPMS and nominated as the party's candidate for the Montenegrin presidency. Although the Montenegrin courts invalidated his candidature (as Djukanović was also endorsed as the DPMS nominee), the federal Constitutional Court overturned this decision on 28 August.

21 September 1997: In Serbian legislative elections the United List failed to secure an outright majority, while the nationalist SRP increased its representation to 82 seats and Drašković's Serbian Renewal Movement (SRM) obtained 45 seats. In the Serbian presidential contest Lilić, the candidate of the United List, attracted the most votes, but not enough to avoid a second round.

5 October 1997: Vojislav Šešelj narrowly defeated Lilić in the second round of the Serbian presidential election, but the election was declared constitutionally invalid as less than 50% of the electorate had participated. In the Montenegrin presidential election Bulatović obtained 48% of the valid votes cast and Djukanović 47% and, as the two leading candidates, had to contest a second round of voting.

19 October 1997: After a second round of voting, Djukanović was elected President of Montenegro, with 50.8% of the votes cast; the OSCE deemed the election generally fair, despite objections from the rival candidate, Bulatović, the incumbent President.

7 December 1997: In a new election to the Serbian presidency none of the candidates obtained more than 50% of the votes cast. (The United List candidate was now Milan Milutinović, hitherto Federal Minister of Foreign Affairs, following Lilić's appointment to the Federal Government in November).

21 December 1997: In the second round of the Serbian presidential election, Milutinović secured 59.2% of the votes cast, compared with Šešelj, who obtained 37.5%.

15 January 1998: Djukanović was inaugurated as President of Montenegro, despite violent disturbances following protests by the supporters of Bulatović; the federal premier, Kontić, brokered an agreement between the DPMS factions providing for early legislative elections and a transitional Government (approved in early February).

23 February 1998: The UN further relaxed international sanctions against the FRY, in recognition of its support for the continuing peace process in Bosnia and Herzegovina.

3 March 1998: An international arms embargo was imposed on the FRY, in response to a major offensive by Serbian forces against the separatist insurgents of the Kosovo Liberation Army (KLA)—up to 80 Kosovars died, some of them, allegedly, civilians.

24 March 1998: The Serbian Prime Minister, Marjanović, announced the establishment of a coalition Government comprising 13 SPS members, four from the Yugoslav United Left and 15 representatives of the SRP, including Šešelj, who became a deputy premier.

7 April 1998: The leadership of the 'Republic of Kosovo', Rugova and the DAK, refused to negotiate with the Serbian President, Milutinović, reiterating that it would only deal with the federal authorities, and with foreign mediation.

15 May 1998: Under considerable pressure from the international community (led by the Contact Group prominent in the Bosnian conflict) the federal President, Milošević, met Rugova in Belgrade; the US-brokered meeting was followed by the opening of negotiations between delegations from the two sides in Priština.

19 May 1998: President Milošević appointed Bulatović the new federal premier, having dismissed Kontić the previous day (the Federal Government had lost a confidence vote); Djukanović, the President of Montenegro, immediately declared the new administration to be illegal.

31 May 1998: In elections to an enlarged, 78-seat Republican Assembly in Montenegro, For a Better Life, an alliance led by Djukanović's DPMS, secured an outright majority (42 seats); Bulatović's Socialist People's Party of Montenegro won 29 seats.

13 June 1998: The Contact Group threatened the use of force to bring about an end to the fighting in Kosovo and the withdrawal of Serbian troops, which were allegedly attacking civilians.

17 June 1998: The new Republican Assembly withdrew all 20 Montenegrin members of the upper Chamber of Republics in the Federal Assembly and replaced them with delegates loyal to Djukanović, to ensure that President Milošević could not command the two-thirds majority necessary for constitutional amendments.

16 July 1998: A new Montenegrin Government, headed by Filip Vujanović and comprising representatives of the DPMS, the People's Party of Montenegro and the Social-Democratic Party of Montenegro, was appointed.

23 September 1998: With Resolution 1199 the UN Security Council demanded an immediate cease-fire in Kosovo, the withdrawal of Serbian troops, unrestricted access for humanitarian aid and meaningful negotiations; it threatened further action, assumed by most to include the use of force, if its demands were not met.

28 September 1998: The Serbian Government announced the end of military activity in Kosovo and promised an amnesty to any remaining KLA members; the Serbian legislature agreed to establish a multi-ethnic Interim Executive Council in the province. There were, however, reports of a new

Serbian offensive, in which ethnic Albanian civilians, including women and children, had been massacred.

8 October 1998: Following reports of a new Serbian offensive, the international community issued an ultimatum that military force would be employed against the FRY unless UN demands were met by 27 October.

13 October 1998: President Milošević agreed to the presence of a 2,000-strong, OSCE 'verification force' (the Kosovo Diplomatic Observer Mission), to monitor the implementation of the Security Council's demands, and to NATO surveillance flights in FRY airspace; in return, Serbia would retain sovereignty over Kosovo and Metohija, pending negotiations on autonomy for the province. The first members of the Observer Mission arrived in Priština five days later.

7 December 1998: A proposed peace plan for Kosovo was rejected by the Kosovan Government.

14 December 1998: Serbian security forces attacked KLA troops attempting to transport supplies of armaments from Albania, killing 31; tensions in the region further increased following the discovery, four days later, of the body of the Serbian mayor of Kosovo Polje, Zvonko Bojanić. Heavy fighting subsequently broke out. A 2,300-member NATO 'extraction force' was deployed near the Kosovo border in Macedonia, to effect the evacuation of the OSCE monitors in the event of an attack.

2 January 1999: The cease-fire declared the previous October 1998 was broken; episodes of violence occurred throughout January.

13 January 1999: Serb military and ethnic Albanian prisoners were released following an agreement between the KLA and the Serbian Government.

15 January 1999: The discovery of the bodies of 45 ethnic Albanians in the village of Račak, 30 km south-west of Priština prompted international condemnation of Serbia.

6 February 1999: A peace conference, organized by the Contact Group and attended by all groups, convened in Rambouillet, near Paris, France.

23 February 1999: The Serbian and ethnic Albanian delegations, including KLA representatives, agreed, in principle, to accept the peace plan.

18 March 1999: Following a second round of the peace negotiations, the ethnic Albanian delegation formally signed the peace agreement. The Serbian delegation, however, continued to object to certain clauses.

20 March 1999: OSCE monitors left Kosovo; a further 30,000 Serbian forces were subsequently deployed in and around the region.

24 March 1999: Following the collapse of negotiations between the US envoy, Richard Holbrooke, and President Milošević, the 19 members of NATO approved a NATO-led aerial bombardment of air defences and military installations in the FRY, notably in Belgrade, Novi Sad, Priština and Podgorica. In response, the Federal Government declared a state of war (which the Montenegrin Government refused to recognize).

30 March 1999: NATO rejected an offer by President Milošević gradually to reduce Serbian security forces in Kosovo if an immediate cease-fire was declared.

April 1999: Serbian security forces in Kosovo intensified the campaign of mass expulsions and large-scale massacres of the Kosovan Albanian civilian population, resulting in an exodus of refugees from the province; by early April over 470,000 ethnic Albanians had fled Kosovo.

6 April 1999: The FRY Government announced that Serbian security forces had unilaterally ceased all operations against the KLA and that negotiations with Rugova had commenced.

NATO dismissed the cease-fire announcement as inadequate and continued its operation.

14 April 1999: NATO aircraft mistakenly attacked a convoy of ethnic Albanian refugees in Kosovo, killing about 64.

20 April 1999: The President of Montenegro, Milo Djukanović, refused to comply with an order from President Milošević to place Montenegrin security forces under federal military command.

22 April 1999: The Federal Government and Russia, which had opposed NATO's action, agreed on a proposal for an international presence in Kosovo, under UN auspices and including Russian personnel. NATO, however, reiterated its stance that it should lead any international protection force in the region.

27 May 1999: The UN International Criminal Tribunal for the former Yugoslavia (ICTY) in The Hague announced the indictment of President Milošević, the Serbian President Milutinović, the Federal Deputy Prime Minister, Nikola Sainović, the Chief of Staff of the federal army, Gen. Dragoljub Ojdanić, and the Serbian Minister of the Interior, Vlajko Stojiljković, on charges of crimes against humanity.

3 June 1999: Following mediation by the President of Finland, Martti Ahtisaari, the Serbian National Assembly formally approved a peace plan presented to the FRY Government by EU and Russian envoys. The agreement, based on proposals agreed in May, by the Group of Eight (comprising the seven industrial nations and Russia), provided for the withdrawal of Serbian forces from Kosovo, and the deployment of a joint NATO-Russian peace-keeping force (to be known as KFOR), numbering about 50,000 personnel. Refugees were to be allowed to return to Kosovo, and the province was to achieve some autonomy under an interim administration.

9 June 1999: A Military Technical Agreement, providing for the complete withdrawal of Serbian forces within 11 days, was signed by the FRY and NATO representatives.

10 June 1999: The UN Security Council adopted Resolution 1244 (with the People's Republic of China abstaining) approving the peace plan for Kosovo. NATO formally approved the establishment of the Kosovo Peace Implementation Force (KFOR) and divided Kosovo into five sectors, to be under the control of a member country. The UN Interim Administration Mission in Kosovo (UNMIK) was to assume authority in the region.

14 June 1999: SRP ministers and legislative deputies temporarily suspended participation in the Serbian Government, in protest at President Milošević's acceptance of the Kosovo peace plan.

18 June 1999: Following discussions between the US Defence Secretary, William Cohen, and his Russian counterpart, an agreement was reached whereby 3,600 Russian troops would serve as part of KFOR under NATO command.

20 June 1999: NATO announced the official end to the air campaign, following the withdrawal of Serbian forces from Kosovo; NATO signed an agreement with the KLA whereby the latter was to disarm within 90 days. The Serbian National Assembly formally ended the state of war in the FRY.

16 July 1999: The first meeting was held of the Kosovo Transitional Council (KTC), created as a consultative body to UNMIK; it comprised representatives of the main political parties and ethnic groups in Kosovo.

August 1999: Despite the efforts of KFOR troops to enforce order, increasing violence in Kosovo, particularly in Priština, caused most of the remaining Serbian residents to leave the capital. According to the UN High Commissioner for Refugees, the Serbian population of Priština had decreased from 40,000 to less than 2,000 within a few months.

5 August 1999: The Montenegrin Government drafted a proposal to abolish the federation and replace it with an Association of the States of Serbia and Montenegro and announced that a referendum on independence for the republic would be held if Milošević failed to agree to the demands.

20 September 1999: NATO agreed to the reconstitution of the KLA as a 5,000-member civil emergency security force, to be known as the Kosovo Protection Corps; two days later, Serbian representatives to the KTC withdrew participation in protest.

28 September 1999: An escalation in violence between Serbs and Kosovar Albanians culminated in a grenade attack on the market of Kosovo Polje, south of Priština, in which two Serbs were killed and 40 wounded.

15 October 1999: KFOR troops intervened to suppress violent rioting by ethnic Albanians in the northern town of Titova Mitrovice, which was divided into separate Kosovar Albanian and Serbian regions following the conflict.

2 November 1999: Montenegro adopted the Deutsche Mark as its official currency; the decision was subsequently ruled illegal by the federal Constitutional Court.

15 January 2000: The Serbian paramilitary leader and war-crimes suspect, Zeljko Raznatović (known as Arkan), was shot and killed in Belgrade.

7 February 2000: The Federal Minister of Defence, Pavle Bulatović, was killed in Belgrade. President Milošević subsequently appointed Gen. Dragoljub Ojdanić, who had been indicted by the ICTY, to replace Bulatović.

3 April 2000: Serbian representatives announced that they were to resume participation in the KTC and another multi-ethnic body established by UNMIK, in an effort to encourage Western governments to prevent ethnic violence against the Serb community.

3 May 2000: In what was seen as an attempt by President Milošević to consolidate his position in the event of an opposition victory in federal legislative elections, due to be held later in the year, the Serbian parliament elected a 20-member delegation from the ruling coalition parties to the federal Chamber of Republics. The SRM boycotted the legislative session.

13 May 2000: Bosko Perošević, President of the Provincial Government of Vojvodina, was killed in Novi Sad. The Federal Government accused opposition groups of involvement in the killing.

17 May 2000: Following the Serbian Government's decision to close several independent newspapers and television stations, some 30,000 people attended a protest rally in Belgrade; two days earlier an estimated 20,000 had attended a demonstration organized by opposition parties in support of early elections in the republic.

22 May 2000: A Serbian court in Niš sentenced 143 Kosovar Albanians, alleged to be members of the KLA, to between seven and 13 years' imprisonment on charges of terrorism.

11 June 2000: Local elections were held in Podgorica and Herceg Novi; the ruling coalition, For a Better Life, won a majority of seats in the Montenegrin capital's municipal assembly. In Herceg Novi the pro-Milošević Coalition for Yugoslavia, led by Bulatović's Socialist People's Party of Montenegro, won 19 out of a possible 35 local council seats, followed by For a Better Life with 14.

12 June 2000: The mandates for the 20 newly-elected deputies from the Serbian Assembly to the Chamber of Republics were verified, causing anger amongst Montenegrin deputies, whose 20-member delegation was ignored by the Federal Assembly in early May.

24 July 2000: The federal Chamber of Republics approved amendments to the Constitution, allowing for the direct election of the federal President and of deputies to the Chamber; a proposal giving the federal legislature the power to appoint and dismiss members of the Federal Government, including the Prime Minister, was also approved. The amendments allowed President Milošević, whose term of office had been due to end in 2001, to stand for re-election for two more terms. Opposition parties in both republics condemned the changes.

27 July 2000: President Milošević announced that federal legislative and presidential elections were to be held on 24 September; Djukanović immediately declared that Montenegro would not participate in the elections.

7 August 2000: An alliance of Serbian opposition parties, the Democratic Opposition of Serbia (DOS), nominated Vojislav Koštunica, the leader of the Democratic Party of Serbia (DPS), as its joint presidential candidate.

24 September 2000: The federal elections took place, amid allegations of electoral malpractice made against Milošević.

26 September 2000: The Federal Election Commission announced that Koštunica had received 48% of the votes cast in the presidential election, compared with 40% for Milošević, thus necessitating a second round of voting. However, external electoral monitoring organizations estimated that Koštunica had secured over 50% of the ballot, and consequently Koštunica refused to participate in a second round. In legislative elections to the federal Chamber of Citizens, the DOS won 43.9% of the valid votes cast, and 58 of the 108 Serbian seats, the SPS received 33.0% (44 seats), the SRP 8.7% (five seats) and the Socialist People's Party of Montenegro 2.2% of the votes cast (28 of the 30 Montenegrin seats). In elections to the 20 Serbian seats in the federal Chamber of Republics, the DOS received 46.2% of the valid votes cast (10 seats) and the SPS won 32.7% (seven seats); and in elections to the 20 Montenegrin seats the Socialist People's Party of Montenegro received 83.3% of votes (19 seats).

28 September 2000: Amid increasing pressure from the international community for Milošević to accept defeat, the Serb Orthodox Church announced that it considered Koštunica to have been elected President. The Chief of General Staff of the Yugoslav Army, Gen. Nebojsa Pavković, declared that his forces would not interfere in the political process.

29 September 2000: Vojislav Šešelj, the leader of the SRP, one of the partners in the ruling coalition, officially withdrew his party's support and transferred his allegiance to Koštunica.

1 October 2000: Demonstrations began throughout Yugoslavia in support of Koštunica, urging Milošević to accept that he had lost the presidential election.

5 October 2000: Amid continued popular demonstrations against Milošević in Belgrade, opposition supporters took control of the parliament buildings and the headquarters of the state broadcasting service. Koštunica declared himself the elected President of the FRY, with the support of the state-controlled news agency. Milošević conceded defeat the following day.

7 October 2000: Koštunica was sworn in as President during a joint session of the new federal legislature. The Government of Serbia resigned on the following day, announcing that legislative elections would be brought forward to December.

9 October 2000: Canada, the USA and the EU agreed to remove sanctions imposed on the FRY during the Kosovo conflict. Numerous countries, which had suspended diplomatic relations with the FRY, subsequently agreed to their restoration. Momir Bulatović, the federal premier, resigned.

17 October 2000: The SPS and the DOS reached an agreement on the joint governance of Serbia, pending legislative elections on 23 December. The Prime Minister was to be a member of the SPS, making decisions in conjunction with deputy prime ministers from the DOS and the Serbian Renewal Movement.

18 October 2000: The Montenegrin Government announced that it remained committed to independence from the FRY. Koštunica had previously stated that he opposed Montenegrin independence, but was prepared for a referendum to be held on the issue. In the following month the Montenegrin Government announced that a referendum on independence would be held in 2001.

21 October 2000: During a visit to the capital of Bosnia and Herzegovina, Koštunica declared that diplomatic relations between that country and the FRY would be re-established and that the FRY would henceforth co-operate with the ICTY.

24 October 2000: Koštunica admitted that Serbian forces had been responsible for killings in Kosovo; a film detailing atrocities committed by Serbian forces in the province was shown on Yugoslav television in November. The Serbian legislature approved the new transitional Government.

26 October 2000: The FRY was accorded full membership of the EU-initiated Stability Pact for South Eastern Europe.

28 October 2000: In municipal elections held in the province of Kosovo and Metohija the Democratic League of Kosovo (DLK), led by Rugova, secured 58.1% of the votes cast and won control of 21 of the 30 municipalities, including the five major cities. The ethnic Serb population boycotted the elections and the head of the UN administration in Kosovo, Bernard Kouchner, announced he would appoint councillors in Serb-dominated municipalities, pending the arrangement of further elections.

1 November 2000: The FRY, which had previously declined to apply for membership of the UN since the dissolution of the SFRY, was admitted to the organization after an application made by the new regime was accepted.

4 November 2000: The new, multi-party Federal Government, led by Zoran Žižić of the Socialist People's Party of Montenegro, was endorsed by the federal parliament.

26 November 2000: The FRY was admitted to membership of the OSCE.

15 December 2000: The FRY was admitted to the European Bank for Reconstruction and Development.

23 December 2000: In the legislative election in Serbia, the DOS secured 64.1% of the votes cast, equating to 176 of the 250 seats in the National Assembly; the SPS received 13.8% of the ballot (37 seats), the SRP 8.6% (23 seats) and the Serbian Unity Party 5.3% (14 seats).

27 December 2000: Zoran Djindjić, the principal figure in the DOS campaign, was named as Serbian Prime Minister designate; he was to propose a government by early January 2001.

25 January 2001: The Serbian National Assembly approved by a large majority the DOS-dominated Government proposed by Djindjić.

24 February 2001: The former head of the secret service, Radovan Marković, was arrested in connection with an assassination attempt against the opposition leader, Vuk Drašković, in October 1999.

1 April 2001: Following increasing international pressure on the new Federal Government, Milošević was taken into custody for questioning on charges of corruption during his term in public office.

5 April 2001: The ICTY submitted the original indictment against Milošević to the FRY authorities.

22 April 2001: Elections to the 77-member Montenegrin Republican Assembly took place. The pro-independence alliance, led by Djukanović, known as Victory Belongs to Mon-

tenegro, secured 36 seats in the legislature, narrowly defeating Bulatović's alliance opposing independence, Together for Yugoslavia, with 33 seats.

22 May 2001: Following the increase in ethnic Albanian rebel activity, the FRY armed forces returned to the demilitarized zone in Kosovo (which had been under the control of KFOR under the military agreement signed in June 1999).

23 June 2001: The Federal Government approved a decree, providing for the extradition of Milošević to the ICTY.

26 June 2001: Some 10,000 supporters of Milošević demonstrated in Belgrade in protest at his proposed extradition.

28 June 2001: Following the temporary suspension of the government decree by the federal Constitutional Court, Milošević was taken from the central prison in Belgrade and extradited to The Hague.

29 June 2001: The Federal Prime Minister, Zoran Žižić, resigned in protest at Milošević's extradition to the ICTY.

2 July 2001: The Montenegrin legislature approved a new coalition Government for the republic, which was again headed by Vujanović.

3 July 2001: Milošević was formally charged at the ICTY with crimes against humanity. He refused to acknowledge the authority of the Tribunal.

24 July 2001: A reorganized Federal Government, proposed by the new Prime Minister, Dragiša Pesić (a member of the Socialist People's Party of Montenegro), was approved in the legislature.

17 August 2001: Following increasing division with Djindjić, Koštunica withdrew the ministers belonging to his DPS from the Serbian Government.

10 September 2001: The UN Security Council adopted a resolution ending the embargo on armaments that had been imposed against the FRY in March 1998.

17 November 2001: Elections to 100 seats of a 120-member Kosovo Assembly took place, as part of a plan to establish partial self-government in the province. Rugova's DLK secured 47 seats, while the Democratic Party of Kosovo (DPK) of Hashim Thaçi won 26 seats.

23 November 2001: Milošević, who had already been indicted on charges relating to Croatia and Kosovo, was for the first time charged with genocide, in connection with crimes committed in Bosnia in 1992–95.

10 December 2001: The opening session of the new Kosovo Assembly in Priština was boycotted by DPK deputies. The refusal of the DPK to participate in votes prevented the election of Rugova as President of Kosovo.

5 January 2002: The Federal Minister of Finance, who opposed a decision by the National Bank of Yugoslavia, tendered his resignation.

21 January 2002: A German diplomat, Michael Steiner, was appointed head of UNMIK.

23 January 2002: The Serbian legislature voted in favour of restoring partial autonomy to the northern province of Vojvodina.

12 February 2002: Milošević's trial at the ICTY officially commenced. He continued to refuse to recognize the authority of the ICTY, and to deny all charges.

4 March 2002: After a compromise agreement was reached between the DLK and the DPK, the Kosovo Assembly finally elected Rugova President of the province. A member of the DPK, Bajram Rexhepi, became Prime Minister, heading a 10-member Cabinet.

14 March 2002: Following negotiations on the issue of Montenegro's independence, the government leaders of the FRY and the two entities signed a framework agreement, providing for the reconstitution of Yugoslavia as a joint state, to be known as 'Serbia and Montenegro'.

19 March 2002: One of the Serbian Deputy Prime Ministers, Gen. Momčilo Perišić, resigned from his post, having been arrested on charges of espionage.

11 April 2002: Following increasing pressure from the US Government, which suspended economic aid to the FRY at the end of March, the Federal Assembly finally approved legislation providing for the extradition of indicted war criminals, and the issue of arrest warrants for those who refused to surrender to the ICTY. Of 10 former Yugoslav state officials indicted, six subsequently agreed to surrender to the Tribunal.

19 April 2002: Vujanović resigned from the office of Montenegrin Prime Minister, after four pro-independence ministers withdrew from his Government in protest at the Republican Assembly's approval of the union agreement.

2 May 2002: A former Yugoslav Deputy Prime Minister, Nikola Sainović, who had been indicted in May 1999, was voluntarily transferred to the ICTY.

31 May 2002: The Federal Assembly officially approved the agreement on the creation of a joint state (which had been ratified by the legislatures of both entities in April). It was envisaged that a new constitution would be adopted later that year, followed by national elections to the new joint legislature.

17 June 2002: A reorganization of the Serbian Government was approved in the National Assembly .

24 June 2002: President Koštunica replaced the Chief of General Staff of the Yugoslav Army, Col-Gen. Nebojsa Pavković, who initially refused to accept his dismissal.

11 July 2002: The former Yugoslav President, Zoran Lilić, was arrested and extradited to the ICTY, having been subpoenaed as a prosecution witness in the trial of Milošević. He refused to testify unless he was himself guaranteed immunity from prosecution.

18 July 2002: It was announced that presidential elections in Serbia would be brought forward to 29 September, to allow the extradition of Milutinović (who had been indicted in 1999) to the ICTY.

19 July 2002: Following the failure of Vujanović to secure majority support for a new government, the Republican Assembly was dissolved and further legislative elections in Montenegro were scheduled for October.

26 July 2002: The ruling Serbian DOS coalition formally expelled the DPS. (DPS deputies had withdrawn from the National Assembly in June.)

29 September 2002: At the first round of elections for the Serbian presidency, Koštunica received 30.9% of the votes cast, while Miroljub Labus, the Federal Deputy Prime Minister, who was supported by Djindjić, won 27.4%, and Šešelj 23.2%. A second round between Koštunica and Labus was scheduled for 13 October.

13 October 2002: The second ballot to the Serbian presidency, at which Koštunica secured some 68.4% of votes cast, was declared invalid, owing to the participation rate of only 44.0% of the electorate (lower than the required minimum level of 50%).

20 October 2002: At elections to the Montenegrin Republican Assembly, Djukanović's pro-independence coalition, now known as the Democratic List for a European Montenegro, secured 39 of the 75 seats, with the Together For Change alliance, led by Socialist People's Party of Montenegro, which had opposed the proposed creation of a looser union with Serbia, obtaining 30 seats.

8 December 2002: A third presidential poll in Serbia was again declared invalid, owing to a rate of participation of only about 45.0% of the registered electorate; Koštunica had won 57.7% of votes cast.

22 December 2002: The presidential election in Montenegro was also invalidated by a participation level of 45.9%, following a boycott organized by the opposition; Vujanović (representing the Democratic List for a European Montenegro) had consequently secured 83.7% of votes cast in the ballot, which was contested by 11 candidates. A further election to the Montenegrin presidency was scheduled for 9 February 2003.

30 December 2002: Milutinović was replaced, on an interim basis, by the Speaker of the Serbian National Assembly, Nataša Mićić.

8 January 2003: A new Montenegrin Cabinet, headed by Djukanović, was finally approved by the Republican Assembly.

20 January 2003: Milutinović was voluntarily extradited to the ICTY, where he subsequently pleaded not guilty to charges relating to crimes perpetrated during the 1999 conflict in Kosovo.

SERBIA AND MONTENEGRO

4 February 2003: Both chambers of the Federal Assembly approved the Constitutional Charter (which had been endorsed by the legislatures of both entities at the end of January), thereby officially replacing the FRY with the State Union of Serbia and Montenegro.

9 February 2003: The presidential ballot in Montenegro (at which Vujanović secured 82.0% of votes cast) was again declared invalid, with a rate of participation of 46.6% of the registered electorate. The Montenegrin authorities announced that electoral regulations would be amended to abolish the legal minimum requirement of 50% voter participation, and a third round was scheduled for 11 May.

25 February 2003: In accordance with the Constitutional Charter, the existing federal and entity legislatures elected a 126-member Assembly of Serbia and Montenegro, comprising 91 Serbian and 35 Montenegrin deputies.

7 March 2003: A former Speaker of the Republican Assembly, Svetozar Marović, was elected unopposed as President of Serbia and Montenegro by the new legislature.

12 March 2003: Djindjić was shot dead by an unknown assailant in Belgrade. Mićić immediately imposed a state of emergency in Serbia, and some 1,200 suspects were arrested in connection with the assassination.

18 March 2003: A former Federal Minister of Internal Affairs, Zoran Živković, nominated by the DP to replace Djindjić as party leader, was approved by the Assembly as the new Serbian Prime Minister. A five-member national Cabinet, headed by Marović (who was also Prime Minister), was approved by the Assembly of Serbia and Montenegro.

3 April 2003: Serbia and Montenegro became a member of the Council of Europe.

24 April 2003: Milošević and eight others were officially charged with involvement in the killing of the former Serbian President, Ivan Stambolić, whose remains had been discovered in March.

29 April 2003: Some 45 suspects, including Šešelj, were formally charged in connection with the assassination of Djindjić.

11 May 2003: At the third poll in Montenegro, Vujanović was elected to the presidency, with 63.3% of the votes cast. (Although only about 48% of the electorate had participated in the ballot, regulations had been amended to end the 50% minimum requirement.)

13 June 2003: Vujanović was officially inaugurated as President of Montenegro.

19 June 2003: Serbia and Montenegro formally applied to join NATO's 'Partnership for Peace' programme.

1 July 2003: The Assembly of Serbia and Montengro approved the establishment of a special prosecutor's office to investigate crimes perpetrated in Serbia and to improve co-operation with the ICTY.

25 July 2003: The UN Secretary-General appointed a former Finnish Prime Minister, Harri Holkeri, as the new head of UNMIK in Kosovo, replacing Steiner.

History

Dr DAVID NORRIS

EARLY HISTORY TO THE 20TH CENTURY

The Federal Republic of Yugoslavia (FRY), declared on 27 April 1992, consisted of the republics of Serbia and Montenegro from the former Socialist Federal Republic of Yugoslavia (SFRY). The SFRY had, in addition, included the republics of Bosnia and Herzegovina, Croatia, Macedonia and Slovenia. The Serbs of Serbia, Bosnia and Herzegovina and Croatia, and many Montenegrins, regarded themselves as part of the Serb nation. They dated the beginning of their statehood from 1169, when Stefan Nemanja declared himself the Grand Župan of Raška. The kingdom gradually grew in wealth and political prestige under the influence of Byzantine culture. It reached its greatest territorial extent during the reign of Stefan Dušan the Great (1331–55) from the Danube in the north to the Peloponnese in the south. However, the state could not resist the Ottoman Empire's attempts to subjugate the Balkans and was defeated at the Battle of Kosovo Polje on 28 June 1389. The last Serbian fortress at Smederevo fell in 1459. Serbia was to remain under Ottoman power until the 19th century, although Montenegro was spared conquest because of its mountainous terrain.

The First Serbian Uprising (1804–13) against Ottoman rule ultimately failed and the leaders, under Kara Djordje ('Black George') Petrović, fled the country. The Second Serbian Uprising (1815–17) had more success and the Sultan granted a degree of local autonomy to a small area of Serbia comprising Belgrade and Šumadija to the south. He recognized Miloš Obrenović, leader of the Second Uprising, as the first Knez (Prince) of the region. The houses of Obrenović and Karadjordjević became rivals for power in 19th-century Serbia. Prince Mihailo Obrenović secured the removal of the Ottoman Pasha (Governor) from Serbia in 1867. His successor, Milan, was recognized as king of a sovereign state in 1882.

The successor to Milan, King Aleksandar I Obrenović of Serbia, a conservative and pro-Habsburg monarch, was deposed by a coup in 1903 and his dynastic rival, Petar Karadjordjević, acceded to the throne. During the Balkan Wars of 1912–13 Serbia expanded into Macedonia at the expense of the Ottoman Empire, which lost most of its European possessions. Habsburg annexation of Bosnia and Herzegovina in 1908 was designed to intimidate Serbia. With the acquisition of this region, Austro-Hungarian land now obstructed Serbia's easy outlet to the sea. Bosnian resentment at Habsburg imperialist policy motivated Gavrilo Princip to assassinate the heir to the Habsburg throne, Archduke Francis Ferdinand, on 28 June 1914. On 28 July Austria-Hungary declared war on Serbia, which precipitated the First World War between the Central Powers of Austria-Hungary, Germany and their allies, and the Entente Powers of France, Russia, Serbia and the United Kingdom.

THE KINGDOM OF SERBS, CROATS AND SLOVENES

Serbia, after some initial military success against the Habsburg Empire, was conquered in 1915. The Serbian Government-in-Exile met Croat and Slovene representatives on Corfu (then a British territory, now Greek) in 1917. They agreed to form a unitary Southern Slav state under the Karadjordjević dynasty after the War. Such a state had been the aim of the Southern Slav or 'Yugoslavist' movement which had developed during the 19th century. The Kingdom of Serbs, Croats and Slovenes was proclaimed on 1 December 1918, uniting Serbia and Montenegro with the former Habsburg lands. The Serbs were the largest single national group and maintained a monopoly of political power. Croatian opposition led a Serb nationalist deputy to assassinate the leader of the Croatian Peasant Party in June 1928. Confronted with the collapse of the parliamentary system of government, King Aleksandar I Karadjordjević installed himself as dictator. The country was formally named Yugoslavia on 3 October 1929. King Aleksandar was assassinated by Ustaše Croat extremists in 1934, in France. His cousin, Prince Pavle, became Regent on behalf of Aleksandar's son, Petar II, but he too failed to solve the problem of Serb–Croat relations, although he granted limited local autonomy to Croatia in 1939.

Prince Pavle signed a treaty with the Axis Powers of Germany and Italy in March 1941, in the hope of preventing an Axis invasion of his divided country. A *coup d'état* followed, on 26–27 March, in which Petar was installed as ruler and the treaty revoked. German and Italian forces invaded Yugoslavia in early April, and, on 17 April, the Yugoslav high command surrendered. Yugoslavia was dismembered: Germany annexed Lower Styria and parts of Carinthia; Italy annexed Ljubljana and Dalmatia, and the nominally independent Montenegro became its client; Albania (in personal union with the Italian Crown) annexed Kosovo; part of Vojvodina was annexed by Hungary; Macedonia was occupied by Bulgaria; the remainder of Serbia was placed under German military administration (nominally under the leadership of Gen. Milan Nedić). On 10 April an Independent State of Croatia (including much of Bosnia and Herzegovina) had been formed, with an Italian, Duke Aimone of Spoleto, as King and a fascist Ustaše Government headed by Ante Pavelić. Atrocities committed by the Ustaše against the Serbs forced many to resist this new order.

There were two resistance groups against the Ustaše regime and occupying forces: one was organized by the royalist Četniks (Yugoslav Army of the Fatherland); and the other by the Partisans (National Liberation Army), led by Josip Broz (Tito) and the Communist Party of Yugoslavia (CPY). A civil war was fought between the various internal forces. The United Kingdom transferred its support from the Četniks to the Partisans in mid-1943 and began supplying them with arms. Belgrade was liberated from German occupying forces, on 20 October 1944, with the help of the Soviet Red Army. The CPY won an overwhelming majority in the Constituent Assembly, on 11 November 1945, which voted to abolish the monarchy and establish the Federative People's Republic of Yugoslavia (FPRY), with Tito as Prime Minister, on 29 November. In January 1946 a new, Soviet-style Constitution was adopted, establishing a federation of six republics and two autonomous regions.

THE TITO YEARS

The six republics of the FPRY were based on the country's five principal nationalities (Croat, Macedonian, Montenegrin, Serb and Slovene) and Bosnia and Herzegovina. Serbia was sub-divided into three parts: 'Narrow' or 'Inner' Serbia (comprising Belgrade, Šumadija and southern Serbia), and the Autonomous Provinces of Kosovo and Vojvodina. Kosovo contained a large Albanian minority and Vojvodina a substantial Hungarian population. The Federal Assembly had two chambers: the Federal Council; and the Council of Nationalities, in which republics and provinces had equal representation. Routine business was dealt with by a small group in the Presidium of the Federal Assembly, although real power was held by the CPY's Central Committee. The centralization of functions was symbolized by Tito simultaneously holding the posts of state President, leader of the CPY and Commander-in-Chief of the Yugoslav People's Army (YPA—Jugoslovenska narodna armija).

Although under Tito the rapid nationalization of Yugoslavia's main assets was achieved, between 1945 and 1948, and private property was redistributed to the peasantry, the Yugoslav leader also pursued policies not in keeping with those of his Communist neighbours. His independent style of leadership resulted, on 28 June 1948, in the federation's expulsion from the Soviet-dominated Cominform. Once isolated from its former partners in the Communist bloc of Eastern Europe, the FPRY was guided by two aims: firstly, to obtain trade treaties and credits from Western countries without having to establish Western parliamentary pluralism; secondly, to distance itself from the highly centralized Soviet system. To these ends, Yugoslav self-management developed, combining the principles of workers' co-operatives with a mass participatory political system of interlocking delegations. Rudimentary and limited economic decentralization was adopted in the 1950 Basic Law on the Management of State Economic Enterprises by Working Collectives. Workers' councils operated factories alongside managers appointed by the CPY. The Party was renamed the League of Communists of Yugoslavia (LCY) at its Sixth Congress in November 1952, when it was decided that Party members should play a more educative role in their campaign to further socialism. However, this apparent liberalism did not extend to internal discipline.

The Yugoslav political system contained obvious contradictions. The process of decentralization continued and standards of living rose rapidly. In July 1965 a series of economic measures was approved which further relaxed state controls on foreign investment and the banking system. However, commercial decisions were still taken for political reasons. In the mid-1960s the Federal Government began to transfer resources from the wealthy north of the country (Slovenia, parts of Croatia and Serbia) to the poorer southern areas (Kosovo, Bosnia and Herzegovina, Macedonia, Montenegro). The tension between decentralization and the LCY's monopoly of political power led to demands for political change. In November 1968 there were demonstrations in Kosovo in support of the province becoming a republic. In 1971 there were demonstrations in Croatia for increased autonomy. Tito purged the LCY in Croatia and imprisoned some opposition figures. He then began a purge of reformers and liberals in other republics, such as the head of the Serbian League of

Communists, Marko Nikezić, who was removed from his post in October 1972.

These repressive measures were soon followed by concessions. The 1974 Constitution strengthened the status of the republics and granted similar internal powers to Serbia's Autonomous Provinces. The collective federal State Presidency, introduced in 1971, was reformed to include one representative from each of the eight constituent parts of the Socialist Federal Republic of Yugoslavia (SFRY—the country had been renamed in April 1963), with Tito as President for life. However, a significant effect of these changes was to transfer the power base of delegated authority from the federal level to the republics.

The many contradictions of Tito's regime deepened in the last years before his death in May 1980. In reality, the federation's unity was achieved by exploiting the fear of hostile neighbours outside the country and of animosity between different national groups inside. The nationality issue was partially resolved through compromise; positions of power and influence were rotated among representatives of different national groups in sensitive areas. In addition, federal cohesion was promoted by Tito's personal influence and by the combined power of the LCY and the YPA as pan-Yugoslav institutions.

AFTER TITO: 1980–87

Following Tito's death on 4 May 1980, his responsibilities were transferred to the collective State Presidency and to the Presidium of the LCY. The President of the State Presidency acted as titular head of state, a post which rotated annually among the delegates. Major problems arose owing to nationalist tensions and the worsening economic situation. Self-management, as it had developed after the 1974 Constitution, had serious structural deficiencies. The delegate system was cumbersome and expensive and there had been a shift of real power from the federal to the republican governments.

The first crisis to befall the post-Tito regime occurred in March 1981, when protests by students over living conditions, in Priština, led to demonstrations by Albanian nationalists throughout Kosovo. The Government declared a state of emergency in the Autonomous Province, but demonstrations recurred intermittently in the mid-1980s. From 1986 the Presidency of Serbia, and the Serbian delegate to the federal State Presidency, Ivan Stambolić, demanded constitutional reform which would give the Serbian parliament more control over its provinces. The demands were refused, however, as other delegates sensed an attempt to increase Serbian influence in the federation. The 1974 Constitution had transferred the balance of power in Kosovo to the ethnic Albanian community; 100,000 Serbs emigrated from the region during the 1970s, and a further 30,000 in 1981–87. On 24–25 April 1987 thousands of Serbs and Montenegrins attended a rally, addressed by the leader of the Serbian Communists, Slobodan Milošević, at Kosovo Polje, to protest at harassment by the Albanian population.

THE DISSOLUTION OF THE SFRY: 1987–92

The late 1980s and early 1990s in Serbian and Montenegrin politics were dominated by Slobodan Milošević's rise to power and the dissolution of the SFRY. Milošević was supported by Stambolić in his early Party career. He became leader of the Belgrade League of Communists in 1984, and of the Serbian League of Communists in 1986. He succeeded in bringing about the fall of Stambolić by the end of 1987. He was elected President of the State Presidency of Serbia in May 1989, and continued to lead the Serbian Communists, from 17 July 1990 under a new name, the Socialist Party of Serbia (SPS).

Having purged the Serbian League of Communists of opponents in the late 1980s, Milošević sought to broaden his popular appeal in Serbia and Montenegro. A main source of discontent at this time was the special status of Serbia's two Autonomous Provinces, which effectively limited the power of the republic of Serbia. He initiated a movement known as the 'Anti-Bureaucratic Revolution', notably with demonstrations in Novi Sad that caused the resignation of the Vojvodina Party leadership in October 1988. He also increased his support by organizing mass demonstrations throughout Serbia in support of the Serbs in Kosovo. Mass demonstrations also took place in Montenegro in support of the Serbs in Kosovo and in protest at the Montenegrin Government, which resigned in the following January. In November 1988, in Belgrade, a rally protesting against discrimination by the Albanian authorities in Kosovo attracted almost 1m. demonstrators. On 1 February 1990 federal troops arrived in Kosovo, following an escalation of the violence in the region, mainly prompted by the dismissal and detention of a prominent ethnic Albanian Communist official, Azem Vlasi. In a referendum, held on 2 July, a majority of voters in Serbia approved the proposed new republican Constitution, which effectively removed the autonomous status of the provinces of Kosovo and Vojvodina. The Kosovo provincial Assembly and Government were dissolved by the Serbian authorities three days later.

The fragility of the federation was further evidenced by the increasing differences between the Serbian and the Slovenian leadership after 1989. Both sides wished to maintain the unity of the SFRY, but by incompatible means. The Slovenians argued in favour of a confederation with looser links between central government and the republics, while Milošević insisted on the collective responsibility imposed by democratic centralism. An Emergency Congress of the LCY was held on 20–22 January 1990, when Slovenian proposals to restructure the federal Party were rejected. The Slovenian delegation withdrew from the Congress and the republican League of Communists suspended its links with the LCY, signifying the end of the LCY as a federal organization.

In February 1990 the Slovenian Party confirmed its formal secession from the federal LCY and changed its name to the Party of Democratic Reform. The Communists of Croatia and Macedonia subsequently made similar changes. Slovenia and Croatia elected nationalist governments in April and May 1990. In December multi-party elections were held in several republics. In Montenegro the Communists succeeded in retaining the Presidency and in securing a majority of seats in the Assembly. In Serbia Milošević was elected President under the new Serbian Constitution. However, opposition to his Government grew in 1991, culminating in a large rally in Belgrade and demands for his resignation on 9 March.

The six republican Presidents met in late March 1991, in a renewed attempt to resolve their country's crisis. Both Croatia and Slovenia declared their intention to secede from the SFRY if a solution was not found. Tension between Serbs and Croats increased when, on 15 May, the normally automatic transfer of the Presidency of the federal State Presidency, this year scheduled for the Croatian delegate, Stjepan ('Stipe') Mesić, was not endorsed by the Serbian, Kosovan and Vojvodinian members (the Montenegrin member abstained). Croatia and Slovenia declared their independence from the SFRY on 25 June 1991. The federal premier, Ante Marković, ordered the YPA to reassume control of the Slovenian borders as the legitimate territory of the SFRY. The army advanced into Slovenia, but retreated by the end of June. At the same time a cease-fire agreement, brokered by the European Community (EC, known as the European Union—EU, from November 1993), resulted in Serbian acceptance of Mesić as President of the federal State Presidency. In Croatia, meanwhile, hostilities broke out in Eastern Slavonia and in the newly established 'Serb Autonomous Region of Krajina', where the YPA worked with local Serb paramilitary units. The withdrawal of federal troops from Slovenia began in July and, in the same month, discussions on the future of Yugoslavia between the State Presidency members and the six republican Presidents began.

In the latter half of 1991 fighting intensified and spread to other parts of Croatia, despite a number of cease-fire agreements. On 8 October the Croatian and Slovenian declarations of independence took effect, while later in the month Bosnia and Herzegovina proclaimed its sovereignty. Marković and the federal Secretary for Foreign Affairs resigned from their posts after a vote of 'no confidence' in the Federal Assembly in November and, in the following month, Mesić resigned, claiming that Yugoslavia had ceased to exist. On 15 January 1992 the EC, at Germany's insistence, initiated general recognition of Slovenian and Croatian independence. A UN peacekeeping force (UN Protection Force in Yugoslavia—UNPROFOR) was deployed in Croatia in March. International recognition of Bosnia and Herzegovina as an independent state, on 6 April 1992, led to the beginning of the worst civil war to occur on the territory of the former SFRY.

THE FEDERAL REPUBLIC OF YUGOSLAVIA

As the other republics had formally seceded from the SFRY, in April 1992 Serbia and Montenegro claimed all the federation's international functions. On 27 April the 83 deputies of Serbia and Montenegro to the Federal Assembly of the SFRY voted to adopt a Constitution, which created the FRY, comprising Serbia and Montenegro. Both republics kept their own governments and a bicameral Federal Assembly was established. The lower federal chamber was elected by constituencies, while the upper house had equal numbers of Serbian and Montenegrin deputies.

Elections were held on 31 May 1992 for representatives to the new Federal Assembly. These resulted in widespread success for the SPS, owing to a boycott by opposition parties. However, Milošević faced strong opposition in mid-1992, with the formation, in late May, of a broad opposition alliance, the Serbian Democratic Movement (SDM). Dobrica Ćosić was appointed federal President and, on 14 July, a US businessman of Serbian origin, Milan Panić, became federal Prime Minister. In the remainder of 1992 a political battle developed between Milošević and Panić. Presidential and parliamentary federal and republican elections were scheduled for 20 December 1992. Panić, during his campaign for the Serbian presidency, publicly attacked the Serb leaders in Croatia and Bosnia and Herzegovina, Goran Hadžić and Radovan Karadžić, respectively. Recognizing the territorial integrity of the former Yugoslav republics, he also offered appeasement to ethnic Albanians in Kosovo and Metohija. In the elections, boycotted by the ethnic Albanians of Kosovo and Metohija and the Sandžak Muslims, the federal President, Ćosić, retained his post, winning some 85% of the votes cast. Milošević was re-elected President of Serbia and the SPS won 47 of the 138 seats in the Federal Assembly. Panić was removed from office on 29 December 1992, following a vote of 'no confidence' passed by the new Federal Assembly. He was replaced as federal Prime Minister by a Montenegrin, Rade Kontić. On 3 February 1993 a new FRY Government, comprising the SPS and the Democratic Party of Montenegrin Socialists (DPMS), was formed.

The FRY's first years were largely shaped by the civil wars in the territories of the former Yugoslavia, and by international sanctions imposed against Serbia and Montenegro. The international community exerted pressure on Milošević to persuade the Bosnian Serbs to halt their offensive in Bosnia and Herzegovina. Governments of EC countries withdrew their ambassadors from Yugoslavia and, on 30 May 1992, UN sanctions were imposed against Serbia and Montenegro.

The FRY was severely affected by the UN-imposed economic sanctions. By late 1992 there were shortages of many basic items, there was hyperinflation, productivity was decreasing rapidly and the rate of unemployment was rising, as all international trade and banking relations were suspended. Greater sanctions were imposed in April 1993, in an attempt to persuade the Bosnian Serbs to accept the plan for the 'cantonization' of Bosnia and Herzegovina, proposed by Cyrus Vance and Lord Owen, the Co-Chairmen of the UN-EC negotiating initiative on the former Yugoslavia. Milošević and Ćosić persuaded Radovan Karadžić, the leader of the Serbs in Bosnia and Herzegovina, to accept the plan on 2 May, although it was later rejected by the Bosnian Serb Assembly. Milošević, President Franjo Tudjman of Croatia and President Alija Izetbegović of Bosnia and Herzegovina, as well as the Bosnian Serb leader, Karadžić, and the Bosnian Croat leader, Mate Boban, attended a summit meeting, in Geneva (Switzerland), on 16 June, where the Serb and Croat representatives agreed a peace initiative under which Bosnia and Herzegovina would be divided into three ethnically based states. The Bosnian Muslim leader, Izetbegović, however, refused to ratify any plans which would lead to a serious decentralization of power.

Milošević's support for the Vance-Owen Plan indicated a change in government policy. Sanctions were adversely affecting the FRY and it was essential to persuade the international community to lift them. However, his support prompted internal opposition. His main adversary was his former ally, Vojislav Šešelj, leader of the Serbian Radical Party (SRP). In September 1993 Šešelj and the SRP members of the Serbian parliament proposed a vote of 'no confidence' in Milošević's Government. In response, the Government dissolved parliament and announced new elections, to be held on 19 December. The SPS increased its majority, at the expense of the SRP, winning 123 seats. Milošević consolidated his position as Serbian President throughout 1993. Following allegations that he had plotted with military commanders to depose Milošević, federal President Ćosić was dismissed on 1 June, and replaced by the less influential Zoran Lilić. On 26 August some 43 members of the General Staff were retired and replaced by personnel thought to be more loyal to the Serbian President, including a new Chief of Staff for the Yugoslav Army (as the YPA had been renamed), Col-Gen. Momčilo Perišić.

The international community continued to demand support for its plans to resolve the civil war in Bosnia and Herzegovina. A 'Contact Group', consisting of representatives from France, Germany, Russia, the United Kingdom and the USA, was established to consider and put forward various options. This Group proposed the division of Bosnia and Herzegovina into two 'entities', one consisting of a Croat-Muslim Federation (formed by an accord signed in the US capital, Washington, DC, in March 1994), covering 51% of Bosnian territory, and the other to consist of a Serb Republic, to co-exist in a unified state, in the remaining 49% of the country. The rejection of the Contact Group Plan by Bosnian Serbs in a referendum was endorsed by their parliament on 1 September. Milošević supported the Contact Group's proposals and reacted to this rejection by closing the FRY's border with Bosnia and Herzegovina. He allowed international monitors to inspect the border crossings. In response to his support the international community ended sanctions on international air traffic and cultural and sporting links in September 1994.

There was little change in Bosnia and Herzegovina until August 1995 when, in response to Bosnian Serb attacks on Muslim enclaves declared to be 'safe areas' by the UN Security Council, the North Atlantic Treaty Organization (NATO) began a series of air strikes against Serb communication and supply lines. In co-ordination with these strikes, Croatian government forces, armed and trained by the USA, attacked the Serb region of Krajina (Croatia) creating some 250,000 civilian refugees who fled across northern Bosnia and Herzegovina to Serbia. Having defeated the Krajina Serbs, in September the Croatian army pursued a joint campaign with the forces of the Muslim-led Bosnian Government against the Serbs in western and central Bosnia. Their assault was successful, and Karadžić was forced to accept the Contact Group's proposal.

A peace conference (the so-called Peace Proximity Talks) was held at the Wright-Patterson Air Force Base near Dayton, Ohio (USA), during November 1995. Following intense US pressure, it had been agreed in August that Milošević would represent the Bosnian Serbs, as Karadžić, among others, had been named as a suspected war criminal by the International Criminal Tribunal for the former Yugoslavia (ICTY), based in The Hague (Netherlands). The aim of the negotiations, attended by the President of Croatia, Tudjman, and the President of Bosnia and Herzegovina, Izetbegović, as well as the Serbian leader, was to agree internal borders between the two entities, as outlined in the Contact Group Plan. After the signing of the Dayton accords all other sanctions on the economy and trade were suspended and the FRY's re-integration into the international community became a priority.

Western Governments restored diplomatic links with the FRY, at ambassadorial level. Nevertheless, the so-called 'outer wall' of sanctions was maintained, which barred the FRY from membership of international organizations such as the Organization for Security and Co-operation in Europe (OSCE), prohibited the International Bank for Reconstruction and Development (World Bank) and the International Monetary Fund (IMF) from launching investment programmes in the country and barred foreign governments from offering trade credits. Thus, sanctions continued to have a debilitating effect on the FRY's economy and domestic discontent with Milošević's Government increased. By the end of 1996 the FRY's trade deficit stood at US $2,200m., while official reserves in the National Bank were $300m.

Local elections were held in Serbia and Montenegro on 17 November 1996. In Serbia, an opposition coalition known as Zajedno (Together), composed of the Serbian Renewal Movement (SRM), led by Vuk Drašković, the Democratic Party (DP), led by Zoran Djindjić and Vesna Pešić's Civic Alliance of Serbia, defeated Milošević's SPS in 14 major cities, including Belgrade, Novi Sad, Niš and Kragujevac. Milošević refused to recognize the opposition's electoral gains, a stance which immediately provoked public protests. The protest movement was peaceful and persistent. In view of daily demonstrations the Serbian President finally acknowledged Zajedno's gains on 4 February 1997. Zajedno took control of the 14 cities and Djindjić became mayor of Belgrade. (He was voted from office in September 1997.)

On 23 July 1997 Milošević resigned as President of Serbia and was formally inaugurated as federal President, having been elected by the Federal Assembly one week earlier. In elections to the Serbian legislature the government coalition (comprising the SPS, New Democracy and Yugoslav United Left, the last led by Milošević's wife, Mirjana Marković) lost its overall majority, while the SRP made electoral gains, proving itself to be a credible political force in Serbia. President Milošević attempted to draw Drašković away from the Zajedno coalition by opening negotiations with him. Drašković agreed to participate in the Serbian presidential elections, held concurrently, while the rest of the opposition, urged by Djindjić, boycotted them. Lilić, representing the government coalition, gained 35.9% of the first round votes, followed by Vojislav Šešelj of the SRP, with 28.6%, and

Drašković, representing the SRM, with 22%. A final round of elections to the republican presidency was held on 7 December, by which time Lilić had been replaced as candidate for the government coalition by Milan Milutinović. He was elected President of Serbia in a second round of voting, defeating Šešelj with 59.2% of the votes to his opponent's 37.5%.

In January 1998 the Serbian government coalition opened negotiations with Drašković's SRM, in order to gain the support of that party's deputies. The talks were prolonged and inconclusive. However, on 24 March, in a surprise move, negotiations were swiftly concluded with Šešelj and it was announced that a new coalition Government, comprising the SPS, the SRP and the Yugoslav United Left, was to be formed. Šešelj was appointed Deputy Prime Minister and his party given a share of ministerial portfolios. Drašković and the SRM became marginalized political forces, both in relation to the Government and to the opposition.

In general, President Milošević was able to depend on the support of the Montenegrin President, Momir Bulatović. However, disputes emerged between the Governments of Serbia and Montenegro and within the Federal Assembly over the issue of republican autonomy. The Montenegrin Government wanted firm, local autonomy and was beginning increasingly to resent Serbian attempts to dominate the Federal Government. Milošević's administration favoured strong, central government and Serbia continued to exercise authority in the federation. A power struggle emerged in the ruling DPMS between the President, Bulatović, supported by Milošević, and the Prime Minister, Milo Djukanović. Djukanović had supported Bulatović in the latter's presidential campaign in 1990 and had been appointed Montenegrin premier in 1991. He lost support in the mid-1990s, when he encouraged the protest movement in Serbia.

A presidential election was held in Montenegro on 5 October 1997, contested by Bulatović and Djukanović. The latter campaigned for reform of the economy and electoral reform, which would ensure parliamentary representation for the Albanian and Muslim minorities in the Montenegrin parliament. Djukanović also maintained contacts with Djindjić's DP in Serbia as part of an anti-Milošević position. He was supported in his presidential candidacy by the EU and the USA, and despite his associations with the previous, Milošević-sponsored regime in Montenegro, he was regarded abroad as a liberal and a modernizer. The incumbent, Bulatović, narrowly won the first round of the presidential elections. However, Djukanović won the second round of elections held two weeks later, taking just over 50% of the vote. Although the ballot was declared free and fair by the OSCE, the outgoing President refused to recognize his defeat and tried to organize a series of popular demonstrations to protest at alleged electoral fraud. The demonstrations did not attract the support that Bulatović expected. The Federal Prime Minister, Kontić, succeeded in brokering an agreement between the two sides, whereby legislative elections would be held in May, in Montenegro. Djukanović and his allies (who contested the elections as the For A Better Life alliance) won 42 of the 78 seats in the Montenegrin parliament on 31 May. His Government adopted a policy of reform within the framework of the FRY, but did not deny the possibility of Montenegro's secession from the federation.

Relations between Montenegro and Serbia deteriorated in 1999. In January the Montenegrin Government agreed to open a border crossing with Croatia without consulting the Federal Government. During the NATO military campaign against the FRY in March–June (see below), Djukanović tried to distance his republic from Serbia by refusing to declare a state of emergency and by not allowing Montenegrin police forces to come under the military command of the Yugoslav Army. However, Podgorica and other Montenegrin cities came under NATO attack. When hostilities ceased Djukanović received international support for his attempts to increase independence from the Federal Government in Belgrade. In June he met the US President, Bill Clinton, in Slovenia, and in October the ban on international civilian air traffic with the FRY was lifted with respect to Montenegro.

At the beginning of November 1999 the Montenegrin Government adopted the Deutsche Mark as an official parallel currency with the Yugoslav dinar in order to forestall inflationary pressures resulting from the Federal Government's economic policy (the federal Constitutional Court ruled the move illegal in January 2000). Meanwhile, the federal authorities continued to oppose efforts by the Montenegrin Government to pursue independence. By March trade between the two republics had virtually ceased. In an attempt by the federal President to challenge Djukanović, in March Serbia imposed a full economic blockade on Montenegro (this was relaxed in May). In May Montenegro's participation in the Federal Assembly was undermined with the rejection of its 20-member delegation to the Chamber of Republics. In early July constitutional changes were passed, allowing the direct election of the federal President and of deputies in the Chamber of Republics. The changes were approved by the Federal Assembly in late July and, a few days later, Milošević announced that federal legislative and presidential elections were to be held on 24 September. Djukanović, who had reacted to the changes to the Constitution by encouraging secession from the FRY and asserting Montenegro's economic strength, immediately declared that Montenegro would not participate in the elections. Local elections in Podgorica and Herceg Novi in June 2000, however, demonstrated that support for the pro-Milošević Coalition for Yugoslavia remained, and would not be easily defeated.

CONFLICT IN KOSOVO

Dissent in the southern Serbian province of Kosovo and Metohija (as the region was named in the 1990 Constitution), where ethnic Albanians made up almost 90% of the population, brought the FRY to a crisis point in 1999. Following the 1990 referendum in favour of the new Serbian Constitution, which removed Kosovo's autonomous status, the ethnic Albanian population followed a policy of non-violent civil disobedience, under the leadership of Ibrahim Rugova and his Democratic Alliance of Kosovo (DAK). A parallel state was created, in which ethnic Albanians distanced themselves from all state institutions and established their own schools, health centres, media outlets and governmental structures, while boycotting all republican and federal elections.

Armed resistance against Serbian authority increased in Kosovo from the mid-1990s. A paramilitary movement, the Kosovo Liberation Army (KLA), which proposed that the only acceptable solution was independence for the region, announced that it intended to achieve its aim through armed resistance. The Contact Group demanded negotiations between President Milošević and Rugova, while condemning the activities of both the KLA and the Serbian Government, which, in January 1998, dispatched troops and special police units to the region to quell KLA activity. Western Governments, concerned that the conflict should not escalate into a large-scale regional conflict, maintained that Kosovo was an integral part of the FRY, but that foreign mediation was required in order to achieve enhanced status for the province. The Contact Group, however, was not unanimous in its position regarding the province, with Russia maintaining that the conflict in Kosovo was an internal matter for the FRY.

Limited action had been agreed by EU foreign ministers at the beginning of September 1998, when flights to member countries by Yugoslav Airlines (Jugoslovenski Aerotransport—JAT) were banned. On 23 September the UN Security Council voted to demand an immediate cease-fire, the withdrawal of Serbian security forces, unrestricted access for humanitarian agencies and negotiations with international involvement to end the conflict in Kosovo. However, the UN Security Council did not vote to endorse NATO military intervention against the FRY. Nevertheless, NATO began to increase its military capability in the region, in preparation for an air offensive against the FRY. On 8 October the US special envoy, Richard Holbrooke, delivered an ultimatum to President Milošević, on behalf of NATO, that without full compliance with all the Security Council's demands, air strikes would be launched. In late October there were reports of renewed fighting in Kosovo between Serbian government forces and the KLA and, in early 1999, there was an alleged massacre of 45 Kosovo Albanians by Serbian forces in the village of Račak. Increasingly frustrated by the lack of progress, the Contact Group invited representatives from the Serbian Government, the DAK 'government' and the KLA to Rambouillet (France) for negotiations, which began on 6 February.

At the peace conference Serbian and Albanian representatives failed to agree proposals on interim autonomy for the region, the conditions for a cease-fire, the numbers of future Serbian police and security forces to be stationed in Kosovo, and the presence of NATO troops. The US Secretary of State, Madeleine Albright, despite Russian protests, warned the FRY that NATO would attack the country if agreement was not reached. The Kosovo Albanian delegations demanded an agreement that would promise eventual independence for the region. The first round of negotiations ended on 23 February 1999, with a commitment to reconvene on 15 March, when negotiations based on the proposed Rambouillet Accord (Interim Agreement for Peace and Self-Government in Kosovo) recommenced. On 18 March the ethnic Albanian representatives signed the Accord, although it made no specific guarantee of future independence for Kosovo. The Serbian delegation objected strongly to the lack of a role for the UN in the Accord and rejected the clause that gave NATO military personnel the right to unrestricted access to all parts of the FRY, given in the military appendix to the Accord. Nevertheless, the NATO Governments in the Contact Group announced that the Accord was not a matter for negotiation and that military targets inside the FRY would be attacked if the Serbian delegation refused to sign. The following day the meeting ended. Western Governments withdrew their diplomatic staff from the FRY and the OSCE withdrew its monitors from Kosovo. On 24 March NATO launched its first attack on the FRY, using aircraft and cruise missiles.

The People's Republic of China and Russia immediately criticized the NATO action and called for an end to the military campaign against the FRY. Headquarters of the Yugoslav Army reported renewed attacks by the KLA against police and army units in Kosovo. The refugee crisis worsened as Serbian security forces intensified their offensive in response. Many ethnic Albanians either fled or were forcibly moved out of Kosovo. Many people also fled because of the dangers posed by NATO attacks on the major towns and suspected military sites in the countryside. President Milošević, whose Government was seriously threatened at the beginning of 1997 by a series of popular demonstrations, enjoyed an increase in support as the population united against the NATO military campaign.

At the beginning of the air offensive NATO's only targets were military. It had difficulty, however, in locating smaller, mobile units and inflicted little damage on the FRY's military capability. However, in April 1999 it intensified its campaign, extending its targets to include transport infrastructure and industrial facilities, including factories and oil refineries. The large number of attacks by aircraft and cruise missiles resulted in the destruction of numerous non-military targets and consequent civilian deaths, to international protest. The destruction of the embassy of the People's Republic of China in Belgrade on 8 May caused anti-NATO demonstrations in the Chinese capital, Beijing, and other Chinese cities. On 27 May President Milošević and four other leading functionaries in the FRY were indicted for war crimes in Kosovo by the ICTY.

On 13 April 1999 Albright met the Russian foreign minister, Igor Ivanov, for talks in Oslo (Norway), resulting in the appointment of the former Prime Minister, Viktor Chernomyrdin, as Russia's special envoy to the Balkans. The US Deputy Secretary of State, Strobe Talbot, was appointed his US counterpart. On 14 May President Martti Ahtisaari of Finland, a former UN diplomat, was brought into the peace process by the UN Secretary-General, Kofi Annan. On 2 June, following intense diplomatic negotiations between Governments of the EU, the USA and Russia, Ahtisaari and Chernomyrdin visited Belgrade for talks with President Milošević. The following day agreement was reached on a peace plan, the terms of which included: a verifiable withdrawal of all Serbian security forces from Kosovo; the stationing in Kosovo of an international civilian and military presence under a UN mandate; the return of all refugees under surveillance of the UN High Commissioner for Refugees (UNHCR); demilitarization of the KLA; and autonomy for the region within the framework of the FRY. On 9 June representatives of the Yugoslav Army and of NATO forces signed the Military Technical Agreement in Kumanovo, in the former Yugoslav republic of Macedonia (FYRM). This document went some way towards fulfilling the conditions laid down by the FRY at the Rambouillet negotiations. NATO troops were given access to Kosovo only through the FYRM and Albania with no right of access to the remainder of the FRY and there was explicit UN involvement in the interim civilian administration of the region. On 10 June the UN Security Council adopted Resolution 1244, with the People's Republic of China abstaining, approving the peace agreement. The last of the Serbian security forces left Kosovo on 20 June.

On 2 July 1999 Bernard Kouchner was appointed head of the UN's Interim Mission Administration in Kosovo (UNMIK). Attempts were made to establish an interim government for the region but serious disagreements emerged between Rugova's DAK, which had been elected as a regional 'government' before the conflict, and Hashim Thaçi's KLA, which claimed recognition for its role in ending direct rule from the Federal Government. In early August the KLA appointed its own Provisional Government, despite the UN Security Council Resolution confirming that UNMIK was the only legitimate government. Facing retribution from returning ethnic Albanians, many Serbs left Kosovo and on 24 August the UNHCR estimated that there remained a Serbian population of 30,000 in the region, out of more than 200,000 before the conflict began. In early 2000 the failure of the NATO-Russian Kosovo Peace Implementation Force (KFOR) and UNMIK to protect the Serb minority in Kosovo was widely criticized. In April, following weeks of disagreement between the EU and USA regarding the approach to security in the region, Eurocorps, the European defence force, took over the command of the international peace-keeping force in Kosovo. Negotiations continued at the Kosovo Transitional Council (KTC), created as a consultative body to UNMIK.

Following the NATO campaign, Milošević made use of the increased economic hardship in the country to improve his own position by appealing to anti-NATO sentiment. Opposition parties were left in disarray, with no co-operation between Djindjić's DP and Drašković's SRM. NATO's policy of international isolation reinforced the vulnerability of the opposition in Serbia. On 14 February 2000, at a meeting of EU ministers in Brussels, Belgium, it was decided to suspend the ban on civilian air traffic with the FRY for a period of six months. However, all significant trading and political contacts with the FRY were prohibited.

THE END OF THE MILOŠEVIĆ ERA

In late February 2000 President Milošević was re-elected President of the SPS. Having led his country into conflict with NATO, he attempted to claim the final result to be a victory for his Government. The FRY's economic and political isolation only served to maintain him in power by isolating the opposition from sources of external support. Constitutional changes, adopted in July, introduced a system of direct election to the presidency, allowing him to seek a further term. Federal presidential and legislative elections took place on 24 September; however, a boycott of the voting in Montenegro, urged by Djukanović in protest at the constitutional changes, was widely observed, to Milošević's advantage. In Serbia 18 opposition parties formed a coalition, known as the Democratic Opposition of Serbia (DOS), which supported Vojislav Koštunica, the leader of the small Democratic Party of Serbia (DPS), as candidate for federal President. It was eventually declared that, according to provisional results released by the Federal Election Commission, Koštunica had won about 48% of the votes cast and Milošević 40%, and that, since neither candidate had an overall majority, a second round of elections would take place on 8 October. The DOS disputed the results, claiming that Milošević had caused the figures to be falsified, and that its own estimates indicated that Koštunica had won the election. The opposition alliance decided not to contest second round, on the grounds that its participation would validate the credibility of the official result, and instead urged a general strike and mass demonstrations, to take place on 5 October outside the Federal Assembly in Belgrade. Security forces erected roadblocks on the main roads leading to Belgrade, but these failed to prevent the arrival of protesters from all parts of Serbia. Frequent clashes occurred between members of the security forces and demonstrators in the capital, and tear gas was used to disperse the crowds. Demonstrators subsequently took control of the Federal Assembly building and the main media institutions. The security forces withdrew without taking further action against the protesters, and the Chief of General Staff of the Yugoslav Army, Col-Gen. Nebojsa Pavković, insisted that the armed forces would also refrain from intervention. On the following day, 6 October, Milošević, having lost the support of the state security forces and the official media, acknowledged Koštunica's electoral victory. The election of the new President and democratic change in the FRY was immediately welcomed by the international community.

The population of the FRY expected rapid improvements in political life and social conditions, following the installation of Koštunica's administration in October 2000. However, the new Government was beset by numerous difficulties. Concern was expressed at the level of the country's co-operation with the ICTY, the issue of Kosovo, the need for economic reform, and the relationship between Serbia and Montenegro. An immediate problem was caused by the many factions within the political establishment, some of which were supporters of the defeated Milošević. Koštunica was only able to form a Federal Government with the support of Montenegrin deputies from Bulatović's Socialist People's Party of Montenegro, who were opposed to Djukanović's pro-independence policy. The Serbian National Assembly was dominated by deputies from the SPS, who refused to co-operate with the new federal administration. The impasse prompted concern that the legitimate authority of government would collapse. A compromise was reached that resulted in the establishment of an interim republic government for Serbia, with principal posts shared

between the DOS and SPS (thereby allocating joint control of, for example, the police and the judiciary). Elections to the Serbian National Assembly were scheduled for 23 December 2000. Fearful of possible recriminations some prominent members of the previous regime fled from the country, including Milošević's son, Marko. On 25 November Milošević's presidency of the SPS was confirmed at a party congress. However, under his leadership the SPS managed to secure only 13.8% of the votes in the December elections to the Serbian National Assembly. The DOS won an overall majority and the leader of the DP, Zoran Djindjić, became Prime Minister. Milan Milutinović, the SPS President of Serbia, remained in office, but with no party support in the legislature he became marginalized, while power was effectively commanded by the Prime Minister.

As soon as Koštunica came to office in October 2000 several foreign Governments urged that Milošević be extradited to the ICTY for trial on numerous charges of war crimes. The USA, in particular, increased pressure on the Yugoslav President, finally making economic aid conditional upon the arrest and extradition of Milošević. Koštunica, a constitutional lawyer, refused the demands, insisting that Milošević should first be tried in the FRY for corruption and other crimes committed during his 13 years in public office. On 1 April 2001 Milošević was arrested and, following increasing international pressure, the Serbian Government finally approved a decree providing for his extradition, and he was dispatched to The Hague via Bosnia and Herzegovina on 28 June. Koštunica and the Federal Government had not consented to this measure and a series of recriminations over the legality and necessity of Milošević's extradition ensued. The Federal Prime Minister, a Montenegrin deputy from Bulatović's SPP, resigned in protest prompting an immediate constitutional difficulty. Koštunica required a further Montenegrin to be appointed in order to maintain the delicate balance of power within the federal administration. The issue was finally resolved by the appointment of Dragiša Pešić (also a member of the SPP) as the new Prime Minister.

On 3 July 2001 Milošević was formally charged at the ICTY, with crimes against humanity relating to the conflicts in Croatia, Bosnia and Herzegovina, and Kosovo. In November the charges against him in connection with the war crimes perpetrated in Bosnia and Herzegovina were increased to include genocide. In Serbia Djindjić accused Koštunica of refusing to co-operate fully with the ICTY, and US insistence resulted in the withholding of further economic aid at the end of March 2002. However, in April the Federal Assembly finally ceded to pressure and adopted new legislation to allow the extradition of suspected war criminals. Attention was focused on the former Serbian Minister of the Interior, Vlajko Stojiljković, the former Deputy Federal Prime Minister, Nikola Šainović, and the former Yugoslav Army Chief of Staff, Dragoljub Ojdanović. Stojiljković committed suicide rather than be extradited for trial, while Ojdanović surrendered to the Tribunal.

The issue of Kosovo and its status remained and was broadened to include the question of the ethnic Albanian population in the neighbouring FYRM. Koštunica, supported by President Vladimir Putin of Russia, insisted that Kosovo be an integral part of the FRY, as defined in the UN Security Council's Resolution 1244 (which stipulated that the province be awarded substantial autonomy but not independence). On 28 October 2000 local government elections were conducted in Kosovo. Rugova's Democratic League of Kosovo (DLK, which had been formed as a successor organization to the DAK) won control of 21 of the 30 municipal councils, including the provincial capital Priština, in many cases ousting the Democratic Party of Kosovo (DPK), led by the former Commander of the KLA, Hashim Thaçi. Both the DLK and the DPK supported future independent status for Kosovo.

With Western support for the FRY's new administration causing a perceived loss of support for independence for Kosovo, an extremist breakaway group of the former KLA, known as the Liberation Army of Preševo, Medvedja and Bujanovac (LAPMB), emerged. Members of this organization commenced incursions from Kosovo into the demilitarized security zone separating the province from the FRY and into southern Serbia. Their aim was to extend Kosovo's borders to include the Preševo valley, situated in Serbia, with its substantial ethnic Albanian population and to provoke a Yugoslav military response. The KFOR troops stationed on Kosovo's borders were unable to prevent these cross-border raids. NATO commended the Yugoslav Army for acting with restraint and began negotiations to allow a phased introduction of Yugoslav troops in the security zone, who had hitherto been denied access into the security zone by the conditions of the Technical Military Agreement, which had been reached to end the NATO bombardment in June 1999. On 16 February 2001 a civilian bus carrying Serbian women and children was blown up by ethnic Albanian extremists in the north of the province. On 15 May it was announced that the introduction of Yugoslav patrols into the security zone would be completed later that month in the most sensitive regions on the border with the Preševo valley.

International fears for regional security and stability increased on 25 January 2001, when ethnic Albanian extremists from Kosovo claimed responsibility for a rocket attack on a police station over the border in the FYRM. By the end of February another KLA breakaway group, the self-styled National Liberation Army (NLA), was regularly in conflict with government security forces in the FYRM. KFOR troops were unable to prevent the transit of rebels and armaments across the border from Kosovo into the neighbouring country. The NLA aimed to establish an independent country for the ethnic Albanian population of Kosovo and the FYRM. Peace was only restored to the FYRM when an internationally-mediated cease-fire was reached on 13 August 2001.

In November 2001 Rugova's DLK maintained its support in elections to the new Kosovo Assembly, securing 47 of the 100 elective seats, while Thaçi's DPK won 26 seats. Rugova was eventually appointed President at the beginning of March 2002. By then the main issues concerning the international community had changed and the future status of Kosovo was of secondary importance. The focus of international concern was on regional security and greater emphasis was placed on the necessity for successful economic reform in Serbia, and increasing pressure for Montenegrin independence which threatened the stability of the FRY.

The economic situation in the country following the political changes of October 2000 remained critical: inflation and unemployment rates increased further, energy restrictions were imposed during winter, and productivity continued to decline. The cost of repairing the damage to the industrial sector and infrastructure caused by NATO's 1999 bombing campaign against the FRY was estimated at some £20,000m. The sanctions imposed against the previous regime had officially ended, but restrictions preventing the FRY's access to international financial institutions remained in force. A programme of economic reforms was proposed aimed at facilitating the planned privatization programme. Support from abroad was pledged, although aid and investment were not disbursed as rapidly as initially expected and were often conditional upon other demands relating to co-operation with the ICTY and further reform measures. The prices of manufactured goods, foodstuffs and public utilities rose, taxes were increased, and the four largest banks were put into liquidation. Such measures were seen by the IMF and World Bank

as part of the necessary transformation of the economy and were a common feature of other countries in transition in Eastern Europe. As in those other countries, in the FRY dissatisfaction was expressed in many areas of society and the popularity of the new administration was placed under pressure.

Relations between the Federal Government and Djukanović's administration in Montenegro remained uneasy. In December 2000 Djukanović announced that elections to the Montenegrin Republican Assembly (which would effectively act to determine public opinion on the issue of independence from the FRY) would be conducted in April 2001. Voting to the Republican Assembly took place on 22 April. The elections developed largely into a contest between two coalitions; the pro-independence Victory Belongs to Montenegro, led by Djukanović, won by a narrow margin, taking about 42% of the votes cast, while the federalist Together for Yugoslavia, led by Bulatović, secured some 41% of the votes. Consequently, neither side had an overall majority but both claimed a moral victory. Djukanović was only able to form a government that received approval in the Montenegrin legislature with the support of the Liberal Alliance of Montenegro, which strongly supported independence for the entity and insisted that a referendum on the issue be conducted. However, the international community, concerned lest the position of President Koštunica be undermined, urged Djukanović to be cautious and to seek constitutional changes within the framework of the FRY.

Djukanović, who was under considerable pressure from his alliance partners within the Republican Assembly, refused to acknowledge the announcement by Koštunica in July 2001 that Pešić had been appointed to replace Zizić as Federal Prime Minister. He insisted that he would discuss relations between Serbia and Montenegro within the FRY only with Djindjić, bypassing all federal institutions. With international concern over possible consequences increasing, the EU dispatched its High Representative responsible for foreign and security policy, Javier Solana Madariaga, to Belgrade in order to mediate in negotiations between the Federal, Serbian and Montenegrin delegations. On 14 March 2002 the discussions resulted in the signing of a framework Agreement on Restructuring of Relations between Serbia and Montenegro, which was to be ratified by the Republican and Federal Assemblies. Under the accord, the reconstituted state was to be named the State Union of Serbia and Montenegro, thereby ending the term Yugoslavia. The two entities would have their own administrations, while a joint, unicameral legislature would elect the President, who would propose the composition of a Council of Ministers with five departments: foreign affairs, defence, international economic relations, internal economic relations, protection of human and minority rights. The agreement included guarantees of Montenegrin proportionate representation in diplomatic offices abroad, and provided for quotas for Montenegrin representatives in the legislature, and parity in representation in international organizations through a system of rotation. The EU promised assistance in the implementation of the articles of the agreement. After a period of three years, either Serbia or Montenegro was entitled to initiate proceedings to withdraw from the State Union, under the terms of a Provision on Reconsideration. Under this article, in the event that Montenegro withdrew from the union, international rulings related to the FRY, in particular UN Security Council Resolution 1244 on Kosovo, would fully apply to Serbia as the successor state.

From the establishment of the new administration in October 2000, Djindjić, as leader of the largest party in the governing coalition, frequently tried to assert his office over that of Koštunica in an effort to reduce his political authority. Under the new arrangements for Serbia and Montenegro, the

President was to be a much weaker figure. Facing a substantial loss of influence in the politics of the new state, Koštunica decided to contest the Serbian presidency in the elections on 29 September 2002 to replace Milan Milutinović. His main opponent, Miroljub Labus, was an economist who negotiated loans with the IMF and World Bank for the new administration, and the Federal Deputy Prime Minister. Vojislav Šešelj also contested the election, criticizing his opponents, Djindjić, in particular, for alleged connections with the Serbian criminal underworld. No candidate won a majority of votes and a second ballot was held on 13 October between Koštunica and Labus. Koštunica won a substantial majority in the second ballot, but only 45.5% of the electorate voted, thereby invalidating the result. A third ballot was held on 8 December, but again fewer than the required 50% of the electorate voted. Following these expressions of disillusionment by the electorate at the internal disagreements in the DOS, Koštunica was marginalized and Djindjić became the most powerful figure in Serbian politics. Under the terms of the Constitution, without an elected President, the Speaker of the Serbian National Assembly, Nataša Mićić, became acting President of Serbia. In January 2003 Milan Milutinović, who had been indicted for war crimes at the same time as Milošević, no longer being President, lost his immunity from extradition and surrendered to the ICTY. Šešelj was also indicted by the ICTY for crimes against humanity against the non-Serb population in Croatia and Bosnia in 1991–95. On 24 February he surrendered to the Tribunal, where he was charged on several counts.

At the end of February 2003 Djindjić survived an assassination attempt, allegedly by Dejan Milenković, a known Belgrade criminal. Milenković was held in custody, but then released by the order of a local court. On 12 March Djindjić was assassinated by a sniper as he left the main government building. Acting President Mićić declared a state of emergency and Zoran Živković, nominated as the new leader of the DP, became Prime Minister of Serbia. Immediate action was taken to arrest those responsible and an investigation into the circumstances surrounding Djindjić's death was ordered. It was soon revealed that the conspiracy involved former and current members of the state security services, Belgrade's criminal community and senior government functionaries. Some 4,000 people were taken into custody for questioning as part of the investigation. Numerous people were dismissed from their posts including the President of the Serbian Supreme Court, the Chief Prosecutor and many judges, for taking bribes and for their involvement with organized criminal gangs. Inquiries by the security services also led to the arrest of many criminals who were alleged to be involved with Djindjić's assassination. The state of emergency declared by the Government was broadly welcomed in Serbia for its robust action against corrupt officials and criminals. Immediate investigations revealed the involvement of the state security apparatus in the planning and execution of the assassination. In particular, the authorities were anxious to question the former commander of the elite special unit known as the 'Red Berets' and leader of one of Belgrade's most powerful criminal gangs, the Zemun clan, Milorad Luković. He had been responsible for Milošević's bodyguard protection, and then placed his support behind Djindjić and the DOS during the October 2000 coup. It has been alleged that Djindjić, in return for this support, protected Luković from extradition to The Hague and did not interfere in his criminal activities. However, Djindjić came under increasing pressure to discontinue such favours and to initiate a public campaign against crime and corruption in the weeks before his assassination. Further investigations revealed a longer involvement of the state security apparatus in illegal affairs. The remains of Ivan Stambolić, a former opponent of Milošević, who disappeared on 25 August 2000, were discovered buried in northern Serbia. His death was viewed as a political assassination carried out by the state security services on Milošević's orders. On 24 April 2003 Milošević was charged with ordering Stambolić's kidnap and murder. Also in April Serbian police made it known that they wished to question Šešelj, being held in The Hague, over matters concerning Djindjić's assassination. By May Luković had not been detained and his whereabouts remained unknown. The assassination of Djindjić, and in particular the revelations that followed, under close public scrutiny, caused a state of general shock in Serbia. The close relationship between government officials, the state security apparatus and organized crime showed the extent of corruption fostered during the years of Milošević's administration, taking advantage of the chaos perpetrated by war in Bosnia and Herzegovina and isolation under international sanctions. The Serbian Government faced serious challenges in issues of regional stability, uncertainty over Kosovo, the need for economic reform and the demand for democratic accountability of the Government.

The Economy

Dr DAVID A. DYKER

INTRODUCTION

The economy of the Federal Republic of Yugoslavia (FRY) was dominated by political obstacles and war from the collapse of the former Yugoslavia in 1991 until the removal from power of Slobodan Milošević in October 2000. Successive wars in Croatia, Bosnia and Herzegovina and Kosovo and Metohija drained the economy of resources, distorted its structure, and brought upon the country a catalogue of international economic sanctions. The regime of Milošević, the federal President from July 1997, showed superficial interest in the cause of economic transition, but in reality delayed any action on principal issues, such as privatization and price reform. Isolated from the world economy and effectively controlled by President Milošević and a small group of his closest associates, in 2000 the federal economy still displayed many of the features of a communist system.

ECONOMIC PERFORMANCE

The performance of the economy of the FRY was poor throughout the Milošević period, and did not improved dramatically after the fall of Milošević. National income in 2002 was some 48% of the 1989 level, and gross domestic product (GDP) per head, calculated on the basis of the free-market exchange rate, only just exceeded US $1,000. There was a precipitous decline in real wages in 1999, with the average real wage in November 1999 representing slightly over 50% of the corresponding figure for November 1998. The trend was reversed in 2000, but only to the extent of a modest year-on-year increase in real wages of 6.1%. In 2001, however, the year-on-year rate of growth in real earnings increased to 13.3%, and in 2002 it increased again, to 21%. During 2002, according to the Federal Statistical Office, monthly net salaries averaged 9,113 dinars. It was expected that the rate of growth in real wages would fall sharply in 2003. GDP was expected to increase by 4%–5% in that year, a level of growth that would allow further improvement in the real living standards of the population, but would not permit continuation of the pattern of increases of the previous two years.

In 1993 the FRY surpassed all records for 'hyperinflation' (116,540,000m.%). The monetarist policy introduced at the beginning of 1994 sharply reduced inflation, which averaged just 3.3% in that year. Thereafter, the rate of growth of consumer prices increased: owing to the conflict in Kosovo, the related deterioration in the current account of the balance of payments, and economic sanctions; end of year inflation increased to 113.5% in 2000. However, the end of year inflation rate declined dramatically, to 39.0% in 2001, and further, to an estimated 14.2% in 2002 (less than the target level of 20%), after the new Government implemented a stabilization programme. (The rate of inflation in Montenegro at the end of 2002 was estimated at 9.4%). Foreign trade largely declined throughout the Milošević decade, exports in the late 1990s, accounting for only some 10%–20% of national income. Exports increased by nearly 20% in 2002, compared with the previous year, but imports grew by over 30%, with the result that imports were covered by exports to the extent of only 36%. Consequently, the trade deficit in 2002 was estimated at US $3,908m., compared with $2,834m. in 2001 and $1,788m. in 2000. In 2002 the current-account deficit was estimated at $2,012m. (equivalent to 12.8% of GDP), compared with $1,119m. in 2001 and $610m. in 2000.

THE STRUCTURE OF THE ECONOMY

The most striking structural features of the economy of the FRY under Milošević were derived directly from the country's military involvement in the area of the former Yugoslavia: the size of the military establishment, which claimed 70% of the federal budget, the extent of the second economy, which might have accounted for as much as 30%–40% of the total real economy, and the prevalence of organized crime. The conservatism of government economic policy, however, meant that even within the officially reported civilian economy there was much less structural change during 1991–2000 than in the corresponding period in other transition economies. In particular, the FRY did not experience the upsurge of the services sector that took place in nearly all the other transition economies, even in those where patterns in aggregate GDP were slow-moving. Thus, in 1998 services accounted for slightly more than 30% of social product, compared with nearly 60% of GDP for neighbouring former Yugoslav republic of Macedonia. The difference was rather less dramatic in real terms because social product does not include government services. According to any estimate of the 'true' GDP of the FRY, however, the gap was still very large. Thus, one of the central paradoxes of the FRY economy under Milošević was that, while industry and agriculture were in a critical state, the economy remained crucially dependent on those sectors in a way that was unlike any other transition economy. The damage caused by the North Atlantic Treaty Organization's (NATO) aerial bombardment in March–June 1999 to the industrial infrastructure, especially the energy infrastructure, was partially repaired in the second half of 1999 and the first half of 2000, and industrial production increased in 2000 by 10.9%, compared with 1999. However, the industrial recovery had already slowed down at the time of the political crisis, and the downward trend in growth rates of industrial production continued in the post-Milošević period. In 2001 the average level of industrial production remained constant compared with the previous year. In the following year positive growth resumed, but only to the extent of about 2%. In 2000 the agricultural sector suffered considerably; the physical volume of agricultural production fell by 17% year-on-year,

with the impact of the severe water shortages of the summer exacerbated by disorganization and mismanagement. In 2001, however, favourable weather conditions produced an exceptionally good harvest, with aggregate agricultural output increasing by 25%. The 5.5% growth in GDP in that year was, indeed, almost entirely a result of the performance of the agricultural sector. However, 2002 was a relatively poor year for agriculture, with aggregate output falling by 2%. While the services sector was expected to emerge as the main focus of economic growth, the weak performance of industry was a cause of some concern to the Government. Agriculture also remained an overpopulated and undercapitalized sector, with low levels of technical efficiency and a high incidence of poverty. Government policy on agriculture was, however, generally liberal in orientation, and price support was abandoned in 2002, as part of the reform programme.

ECONOMIC POLICY

Fiscal and monetary policy

The pattern of public spending in the FRY under Milošević in many ways reflected the peculiar situation in which the country found itself. Federal expenditure was dominated by military outgoings, and the Serbian consolidated budget, which accounted for a large percentage of total budgetary spending in the federation, was dominated by social security payments. After the conflict in Kosovo, substantial portions were also reserved for post-war reconstruction. Explicit funding for support for industry and agriculture in this period amounted to a small percentage of the total budget, although it is possible that elements of such support were concealed under other headings. Officially, the budget was always balanced; however, in practice, deficits were covered through the issue of Treasury Bills. Latterly, these were all under the control of the National Bank of Yugoslavia. This mode of financing was, of course, inherently inflationary, and targets for the expansion of the money supply consistently failed to be met. It was such financing of the budget that caused the hyperinflation of the mid-1990s. The authorities subsequently maintained better control over expenditure. However, the relatively good performance of consumer prices (by FRY standards) in 1999 owed more to the reimposition of price controls than to monetary policy. The new Government removed price controls, while tightening monetary policy and the money supply (M1) actually fell by 1.4% between the end of December 2000 and the end of February 2001 (although this figure partially reflected the decision by the National Bank to stop including the part of the money supply previously allocated to Montenegro, where the dinar had been replaced by the German Deutsche Mark—DM—as the legal tender). Between the end of February and the end of December 2001, however, M1 more than doubled, and it increased by a further 78.6% between the end of December 2001 and the end of December 2002. There has, nevertheless, been a real improvement in monetary discipline, and the National Bank forecast an increase in money supply of just 14%–15% over 2003. How well the Government would be able to implement such targets would depend on the success of its efforts to reduce the budgetary deficit. The federal budget produced a surplus for 2001, while a small deficit in the Serbian budget, equivalent to 1.2% of GDP, was recorded for that year. In 2002 the Serbian budget deficit widened to 5% of GDP, though foreign aid, notably the support of the IMF under the March 2002 agreement, ensured that this slippage would not destabilize the domestic economy. The Serbian budgetary deficit for 2003 was projected at 4.3% of GDP. Most of this deficit was expected to be covered by foreign aid and loans, with National Bank lending to the Government, worth 0.5% of GDP in 2002, being reduced to zero. The heavy dependence on inflows of foreign assistance introduced an element of risk into the 2003 budget projections, but the continued support of the IMF meant that the risk was not an onerous one. Overall, it was probable that monetary policy would not be disrupted by problems of fiscal balance in 2003.

Privatization

The process of privatization began in the early 1990s. However, legislation passed by the Serbian National Assembly in July 1994 effectively halted the process and by the late 1990s little had changed, with the private sector still accounting for only some 15%–20% of the total business sector. The laws on the enterprise and on 'basic changes in the ownership of social capital' approved in 1997 were never properly implemented, and in April 2000 only 37% of enterprises had conformed to its requirements. In this context, the 1998 Law on Privatization remained essentially ineffectual, and indeed in 2000 it was not yet legally possible to trade in shares of enterprises privatized under the 1998 legislation. The stock market still did not operate effectively, partly owing to legal constraints as discussed above, and partly because enterprises were, for the most part, still under the control of corrupt employees, who often manipulated the prices of stock-market offers in order to exclude external buyers. With the installation of the new Government, privatization again became a primary issue. The basic principle of current privatization policy has been to favour cash sales, as a means of raising revenue, and in order to ensure that state-owned companies were taken over by 'strategic investors' (outsiders with technological expertise and business dynamism, as well as funds), rather than insiders with few assets, except good political connections. Privatization has, however, remained a weak point of government policy, proceeding at a hesitant pace, and often impeded by disagreements between different levels of government. In July 2002, however, new legislation was introduced to facilitate privatization, especially privatization by auction. At March 2003 about 250 companies had already been privatized by the procedure of 'accelerated auction', with a further 1,000 firms slated by the Government for privatization by this procedure before the end of the year. With 1,228 companies preparing for accelerated auction privatization and 799 privatization programmes already submitted to the privatization agency, it was expected that the target could be exceeded. By mid-2003 the Government expected to be holding auctions on a daily basis. A further 700 companies were expected to be privatized in the second round of privatization by accelerated auction. Insider manipulation, however, remained a major problem.

MONTENEGRO

The republican Government of Montenegro, the diminutive, junior partner in the FRY, always insisted on pursuing its own economic policy. It sought to approach privatization more radically than its republican partner in the FRY throughout the late 1990s, albeit not always to great effect. The development of political tension between Montenegro and Serbia over the Kosovo conflict, however, brought the issue of Montenegrin economic self-determination to a new and higher level. By the end of 1999 Montenegro's main new priority was the establishment of an independent monetary system. The foundation for this was laid in November 1999 when the DM was officially declared legal tender in Montenegro, with the dinar retaining its legal tender status, but at a much depreciated exchange rate (the federal Constitutional Court subsequently declared the move illegal). In March 2000 Serbia retaliated against Montenegro's currency reform by imposing an economic and financial boycott on the republic. However, the boycott was relaxed in May and abandoned after the change of government in October of that year. With Montenegro and Serbia operating separate customs and banking systems, however, economic discourse between the two parts of the Federation had still not been normalized, and the differential widened in January 2002, when Montenegro adopted the euro as its legal tender. Finally, under heavy pressure from the European Union (EU) a framework agreement was signed between Serbia and Montenegro on 14 March. Under the agreement, the two entities of the FRY were to continue to have separate currencies, tax and budgetary systems, customs services, banking systems and systems of financial supervision. There were to be joint ministries for internal and external economic relations, in addition to a shared diplomatic service and army, and freedom of movement of people and capital. The constituent republics of the new 'State Union of Serbia and Montenegro' were to work towards the harmonization of trade and customs policy, with the EU arbitrating on any disagreements in this context, within the framework of a future Stabilization and Association Agreement between the EU and the joint state. There was considerable general scepticism regarding the feasibility of the new union, and many observers expected it to serve merely as a transitional arrangement, prior to complete separation of the republics. In the event, sustained pressure from the multilateral organizations and the EU kept the new state union project on course, with customs and tax matters proving the most difficult to resolve. Negotiations on these issues were continuing in 2003.

By early 2003 Montenegro's mass privatization campaign had been completed, and 50% of Montenegrin companies had been privatized. However, the course of privatization in the republic has not always proceeded smoothly, with a 120-day strike in 2002 at the Nikčic Brewery, now owned by the Belgian Interbrew company. The Montenegrin Government has, furthermore, struggled to divest principal state-owned enterprises. In 2002 the Jugopetrol oil company was sold to Hellenic Petroleum, which raised the level of foreign direct investment per head in Montenegro to US $459, the highest level in the region. However, attempts to find foreign buyers for Telekom Crne Gore, the Kombinat Aluminijuma plant, the Željezara steel works at Nikčic, and the Podgorica cigarette plant had not been successful. There were also plans to privatize the national rail and electricity companies. A number of service providers, including road construction and maintenance and hotel management organizations, were also slated for privatization. The Montenegrin Government was also seeking to develop social programmes for the employees of companies to be privatized, to make them more attractive to investors.

KOSOVO AND METOHIJA

The occupation of Kosovo by NATO and the UN following the conflict in 1999 raised a whole series of difficult problems of economic administration. Although the principle of Yugoslav sovereignty over the region was clear in general political terms, it was difficult to observe rigidly in practical economic terms. In the context of the monetary vacuum, the UN had to introduce a form of currency into Kosovo for its own administrative purposes. The choice, once again, was the DM. This was followed, in November 1999, by the establishment of a Banking and Payments Authority of Kosovo (BPK). The BPK was to fulfil all the traditional roles of a central bank except for the issue of currency. In addition to performing the functions of a banker for the UN in Kosovo, the BPK was charged with the task of developing a commercial banking system in the province. In January 2002 the DM was replaced by the euro as the legal tender in Kosovo. Macroeconomic stabilization policy in the province has been relatively successful, with inflation in 2002 at only 5%–6%.

Economic recovery in Kosovo proceeded very slowly. It was difficult for the UN administration to establish conditions for business activity, and the uncertainty over the province's political future made strategic policy-making difficult. The UN administration has, however, proceeded with privatization. The Kosovo Loan Agency, operating under the aegis of the EAR (European Agency for Reconstruction) was expected to privatize 400 Kosovan companies. The Trepča mining complex, the biggest company in the province, was to be privatized under a special, separate programme. It was reported that some privatization functions were to be transferred from UNMIK to the provisional administration of Kosovo in the course of 2003. In late 2002 the Serbian Ministry of Economic Affairs and Privatization won the agreement of UNMIK to proceed with no privatizations until all interested creditors from Serbia have been registered. Discussions between UNMIK and the Serbian administration over privatization in Kosovo ensued. In mid-2003, following the adoption of legislation regulating foreign direct investment, the Kosovo Trust Agency, under the jurisdiction of UNMIK, announced the launch of a privatization programme for the 500 'socially-owned enterprises' (SOEs) under its management. These SOEs operated throughout Kosovo in all sectors of the economy and represented both small- and large-scale enterprises, active in agro-industrial, textiles, wineries, retail and trade, hotels, building materials, mining and metal processing.

Owing to the large-scale expenditure that it incurred, not all of which could be financed from transfers from outside the province, the UN administration was forced to establish a system of revenue collection. This was frequently a point of disagreement between UNMIK and the Serbian Government throughout 2001 and 2002. In early 2003, however, as the UN sought to reduce its commitment in Kosovo, and UNMIK made plans to reduce its staff by up to 60%, preparations began for the transfer of responsibility for the tax system to the provisional administration. Kosovo's GDP was just US $2,000m. in 2002, some $900 per head. The province has a huge balance-of-trade deficit, with exports in 2002 estimated at $100m., compared to imports of $900m. The rate of unemployment was estimated at 57% at mid-2003. With EU aid to the province falling from $134m. in 2002 to a projected $50m. in 2003, this could become an acute problem. With donations projected to cover planned budgetary expenditures to the extent of just 7% in 2003, the possibility of the emergence of a 'double deficit' crisis is very real. The solution is foreign direct investment, but there appeared to be no prospect of any dramatic increase in that variable.

THE BANKING SYSTEM

One of the most burdensome legacies bequeathed by Milošević to the new Government was a banking system that effectively failed to function either as a clearing network or as a mobilizer of investible funds. The commercial banking system had not taken over responsibility for the clearing of accounts from the state-owned Payments Agency, and the implementation of legislation specifying that each bank should have a minimum basic capital of US $5m. continued to encounter resistance. It was estimated in 2001 that the cost of restructuring the Yugoslav commercial banking system would total DM 21,100m. ($9,700m.), equivalent to 93% of estimated GDP for 2001. In the event, the Government decided on a drastic approach to the problem, and in early 2002 four of Yugoslavia's biggest banks were liquidated. The 'shock therapy' seemed to work, and in the course of 2002 the banking sector increased its staffing levels substantially. Mortgages were a key growth point, with foreign banks taking the lead. Subsequently, at the beginning of 2003 the clearing function was finally transferred from the Payments Agency to the commer-

cial banks. The changeover did not take place entirely smoothly, and in February the Government announced that it was taking back some clearing functions. Overall, however, the switch has been pronounced a success. In business terms, the Serbian banking sector continues to struggle. Over the first nine months of 2002, it made an aggregate loss of 2,400m. dinars. This was partly on account of repayments of hard-currency savings deposits frozen by Milošević in the early 1990s. (It was estimated that, but for the hard-currency repayments, the banking sector would have make aggregate profits of 4,000m. dinars.) However, the sector remains structurally weak, and fewer than one-half of Serbia's companies view banks as a realistic source of investment finance. The resolution of all the problems of the Serbian banking sector is, at best, a medium-term prospect.

FOREIGN ECONOMIC RELATIONS

Despite nearly a decade of intermittent conflict with its neighbours and the West, and despite all efforts to increase the level of self-sufficiency, shortly before the change of administration in 2000 the FRY remained significantly dependent on foreign trade with Western nations. Under the new Government the trend strengthened, and Yugoslavia's export orientation to the EU intensified in 2000 and 2001. The country struggled throughout the Milošević period to export enough to pay for vital imports, with balance-of-trade deficits reaching an average of nearly US $2,000m. per year in 1995–2000. The problem remained unresolved in the post-Milošević period. In 2002 the trade deficit was estimated at $3,908m., with the current-account deficit at about $2,012m. Gross external debt at the end of January 2003 totalled $12,079m. The November 2001 agreement between Yugoslavia and the Paris Club of official creditors was specially designed to ensure that Yugoslavia would be able to service the rescheduled debt on a regular basis, based on projections of GDP growth and international economic conditions. By 2003 bilateral agreements had been signed with all Paris Club members except Denmark, Sweden, Russia, Italy, Japan and Finland. Agreement with the London Club of commercial creditors, however, remained elusive. At the official meeting between the two sides, in April 2002 the Club offered to cancel between 30% and 40%; however, the Yugoslav Government held out for a 66% 'write-off'. There were serious doubts as to whether the Club was likely to improve its offer, except possibly in terms of a partial cancellation of penalty interest on the defaulted debt, but the National Bank remained optimistic. The price of Yugoslav debt on the secondary market rose from 10 cents to the dollar of nominal debt in the late Miloševic era, to 48 cents to the dollar at the end of 2002. The official position of the Government was that the country could not afford to pay back more than one-third of the London Club debt. A complicating factor was that around 15% of the debt is held by the country's nationals, many of them close associates of Milošević. There were further, unofficial, meetings between the Government and the London Club of commercial debtors at the end of November 2002, but these did not appear to have made significant further progress. The Belgrade Institute of Economic Sciences estimated that Serbia and Montenegro's debt-service ratio will rise to 19.2% (of visible and invisible exports) in 2005, 23% in 2006, and some 27% in 2007. That could portend a crisis of debt service in the medium term.

Following the conflict in Kosovo, and in view of 10 years of negligible net investment, large-scale foreign capital inflow was a desperate necessity, for the real economy, and to maintain external financial equilibrium. The Serbian Government estimated that Serbia would need a total of US $4,500m. in aid and loans over the period 2003–04, if reforms were to continue and critical gaps in infrastructure were to be filled. With the change in government in 2000, the political obstacles to such inflow had been largely, but not wholly, removed. In 2003 Serbia hoped to receive $800m.–$900m. in aid. Of that, $140m. was due to come from the USA. If Serbia failed to satisfy the US Government that it was fully co-operating with the ICTY, however, the money would not be disbursed. Fears that the EU might take a similarly conditional stance over its Community Assistance for Reconstruction, Development and Stabilization (CARDS) aid programme to Serbia appeared to be unfounded. The IMF stand-by arrangement, agreed in March 2002, was designed to ensure that the Yugoslav and Serbian Governments would meet their fiscal commitments in 2002. At the beginning of 2003 there was some doubt as to whether the Fund would continue to support the Union of Serbia and Montenegro, although on technical economic and financial, rather than political grounds. In the event, the Fund agreed disbursement of a further tranche of the stand-by loan in April 2003. By the beginning of 2003, however, it was becoming evident that full-scale reconstruction of the Serbian and Montenegrin economy would require substantial increases in the inflow of private foreign investment, even on the most optimistic assumptions about official aid. Foreign direct investment into the State Union totalled $500m. in 2002. It was projected by the Serbian Government at $1,000m. for 2003. In the aftermath of the assassination of the Serbian Prime Minister, Zoran Djindjić, however, that figure could well prove to be overly optimistic.

CONCLUSION

As the largest republic in the former Yugoslavia, Serbia played an important role in the remarkable success of the Yugoslav system of market socialism in the 1950s and 1960s. It suffered, along with the other Yugoslav republics, from the economic stagnation of the 1980s, and was particularly adversely affected by the collapse of the Iraqi market, after the war in the Persian (Arabian) Gulf in 1991, and of the Council for Mutual Economic Assistance with the end of Communism within the Soviet bloc. From that time, misconceived domestic policies and international sanctions pushed Serbia and Montenegro into long-term poverty. With gross fixed investment at less than 14% of social product (it would be an even smaller percentage of GDP), at the beginning of the 21st century the existing capital stock of the FRY was not even being maintained, and the damage caused by the Kosovo conflict in 1999 only exacerbated this underlying problem. Lack of investment, and the absence of any effective policies to restructure the industrial profile inherited from communism, meant that the huge balance-of-trade deficit became a deep-seated structural feature of the economy. These problems represented the legacy of Milošević to the new Government. The resolution of these difficulties required the Government to proceed decisively with the modernization of the country's damaged and obsolete infrastructural capital stock, while at the same time preserving fiscal balance as a primary condition for the maintenance of price stability. It was further to require a radical banking reform of a type and on a scale that has proved difficult and painful to implement. Finally, the Government needed to discover a means of financing the current-account deficit, which was likely to total about US $1,000m.–$2,000m. per year for the foreseeable future. In view of the extent of unused resources in the economy, it seemed possible that GDP growth might average more than 10% annually for the next 10 years. With that level of growth, domestic problems of financial balance would eventually be resolved, and the prospect of indefinite sustained growth would increase. At 2003, however, the immediate prospects for Serbia and Montenegro were less favourable. Despite striking achievements in the area of macroeconomic stabilization, the Government had not been able to revive industrial growth. The assassination of Djindjić in March was a major shock to business confidence, and indicated that there are still serious elements of political instability in the country. In that context, annual growth of around 3%–4% seemed a more realistic prospect, a prospect that would leave Serbia and Montenegro struggling to make any significant impression in the enormous gap, in terms of GDP per head, that has opened up between itself and the EU.

Statistical Survey

Sources: Savezni zavod za statistiku (Federal Statistical Office), 11000 Belgrade, Kneza Miloša 20; tel. (11) 681999; fax (11) 642368; internet www.szs.sv .gov.yu ; National Bank of Yugoslavia, 11000 Belgrade, bul. Revolucije 15; tel. (11) 3248841; internet www.nbj.yu.

Note: Unless otherwise indicated, figures in this Survey refer to the territory of the Federal Republic of Yugoslavia (FRY), comprising the two republics of Serbia and Montenegro (now the nion of Serbia and Montenegro). Where data for the FRY are not available, the Survey has retained tables relating to the former Socialist Federal Republic of Yugoslavia (SFRY), which comprised six republics. Such tables are indicated by the phrase 'former SFRY' after the heading.

Area and Population

AREA, POPULATION AND DENSITY

Area (sq km)	102,173*
Population (census results)	
31 March 1981	9,897,986
31 March 1991	
Males	5,157,120
Females	5,236,906
Total	10,394,026
Population (official estimates at mid-year)	
2000	10,633,500
2001	10,651,600
Serbia†	9,993,000
Montenegro†	658,000
2002	10,664,300
Density (per sq km) at mid-2002	104.4

* 39,449 sq miles.
† Figures are rounded.

REPUBLICS
(census of 31 March 1991)

Republic	Area (sq km)	Population	Density (per sq km)	Capital (with population)
Serbia	88,361	9,778,991	111	Belgrade (1,168,454)
Vojvodina* . .	21,506	2,013,889	94	Novi Sad (179,626)
Kosovo and Metohija* .	10,887	1,956,196	180	Priština (155,499)
Montenegro . .	13,812	615,035	45	Podgorica† (117,875)
Total	102,173	10,394,026	102	—

* Provinces within Serbia.
† Formerly Titograd.

PRINCIPAL TOWNS
(population at 1991 census)

Beograd (Belgrade, the capital)	1,168,454	Podgorica*	117,875
Novi Sad	179,626	Subotica	100,386
Niš	175,391	Zrenjanin	81,316
Kragujevac	147,305	Pančevo	72,793
Priština	155,409	Čačak	71,550

* Formerly Titograd.

Mid-2001 (UN estimate, incl. suburbs): Belgrade 1,687,000 (Source: UN, *World Urbanization Prospects: The 2001 Revision*).

POPULATION BY ETHNIC GROUP
(1991 census)

Ethnic group	Population ('000)	%
Serbs	6,504	62.6
Albanians	1,715	16.5
Montenegrins	520	5.0
Yugoslavs	350	3.4
Hungarians	344	3.3
Muslims	336	3.2
Total (incl. others)	10,394	100.0

BIRTHS, MARRIAGES AND DEATHS

	Registered live births		Registered marriages		Registered deaths	
	Number	Rate (per 1,000)	Number	Rate (per 1,000)	Number	Rate (per 1,000)
1995	140,504	13.3	60,325	5.7	107,535	10.2
1996	137,312	13.0	56,719	5.4	111,146	10.5
1997*	131,400	12.4	56,200	5.3	111,800	10.5
1998*	128,500	12.1	54,800	5.3	113,300	10.5
1999*	124,000	11.7	53,000	5.0	115,500	10.9
2000*	125,900	11.8	58,300	5.5	118,100	11.1
2001*	130,200	12.2	57,200	5.4	113,100	10.6
2002*	132,200	12.4	57,800	5.4	119,100	11.2

* Rounded figures. Data for Kosovo and Metohija are estimates (Source: Federal Statistical Office, Belgrade).

Source: UN, *Demographic Yearbook*.

Expectation of life (WHO estimates, years at birth): 72.2 (males 69.7; females 74.8) in 2001 (Source: WHO, *World Health Report*).

ECONOMICALLY ACTIVE POPULATION
('000 employees, average at 30 September)

	2000	2001	2002*
Agriculture, forestry, fishing and water works	95	90	87
Mining and quarrying	43	41	40
Manufacturing	668	643	591
Public utilities	54	55	53
Construction	111	104	97
Wholesale and retail trade	235	226	226
Hotels and restaurants	44	44	41
Transport, storage and communications	143	140	138
Financial intermediation	49	45	35
Real estate and property	50	56	52
Public administration and social security	70	73	72
Education	129	134	139
Health and social care	170	173	174
Other community, social and personal services	55	55	55
Private shop workers and owners	322	361	401
Total employed	2,237	2,241	2,201
Unemployed	806	850	924
Total labour force	3,043	3,091	3,125

* Estimates.

Health and Welfare

KEY INDICATORS

Total fertility rate (children per woman, 2001)	1.6
Under-5 mortality rate (per 1,000 live births, 2001)	19
HIV/AIDS (% of persons aged 15–49, 2001)	0.19
Physicians (per 1,000 head, 1998)	2.04
Hospital beds (per 1,000 head, 1995)	5.31
Health expenditure (2000): US $ per head (PPP)	237
Health expenditure (2000): % of GDP	5.6
Health expenditure (2000): public (% of total)	51

For sources and definitions, see explanatory note on p. vi.

Agriculture

PRINCIPAL CROPS
('000 metric tons)

	1999	2000	2001
Wheat	2,035.0	2,056.0	2,529.9
Barley	300.0	252.2	423.5
Maize	6,140.0	2,968.0	5,930.9
Oats	122.0	96.2	126.2
Sugar beet	2,427.6	1,070.0	1,806.4
Potatoes	865.0	690.4	1,015.0
Dry beans	73.0	33.9	31.6
Other pulses†	65.0	71.0	71.5
Walnuts	21.5	23.8	23.6†
Soybeans	294.0	170.6	207.1
Sunflower seed	273.0*	223.0*	317.9
Cabbages	282.0	285.3	283.9
Tomatoes	176.6	180.0†	175.2
Cucumbers and gherkins†	34.8	34.8	34.8
Chillies and green peppers	131.0	131.0†	132.5
Dry onions	120.0	120.0†	137.0
Garlic	36.5*	36.5†	28.2
Carrots	58.0†	60.0†	63.6
Apples	98.0	105.0†	197.5
Pears	70.0	60.0†	43.4
Cherries (incl. sour)	99.0	81.5	73.0
Peaches and nectarines	44.0	41.6	41.7
Plums	380.0	370.0	333.1
Strawberries	23.5†	25.1	34.7
Raspberries	60.0*	56.1	77.8
Grapes	213.0	362.6	380.8
Watermelons and melons	285.0*	244.4	253.9
Tobacco (leaves)	14.5	11.3	16.6

* Unofficial figure.
† FAO estimate(s).

Source: FAO.

LIVESTOCK
('000 head, year ending 30 September)

	1999	2000	2001
Horses	76	49	49*
Cattle	1,831	1,452	1,831*
Buffaloes	21	29	29*
Pigs	4,372	4,087	3,578
Sheep	2,195	1,917	1,448
Goats	326	241	164
Chickens	26,492†	21,118†	21,100*

* FAO estimate.
† Unofficial figure.

Source: FAO.

LIVESTOCK PRODUCTS
('000 metric tons)

	1999	2000	2001
Beef and veal	104.0	98.2	92.5
Mutton and lamb	22.0	22.0*	17.2
Pig meat	640.0†	655.4*	590.0*
Poultry meat	93.6	88.6*	82.8
Cows' milk	1,825.0	1,830.0*	1,625.3
Sheep's milk	34.0	26.0*	18.0
Cheese	12.7	12.0*	13.8
Butter	2.2	2.2*	2.3
Hen eggs	76.3	72.0	67.7
Honey	2.5	2.5*	2.3
Wool: greasy	3.0	3.0*	2.2
Wool: scoured	1.8	1.8*	1.8*
Cattle hides*	20.1	20.0	20.0
Sheep skins*	4.3	4.3	4.3

* FAO estimate(s).
† Unofficial figure.

Source: FAO.

Forestry

ROUNDWOOD REMOVALS
('000 cubic metres, excl. bark)

	1999	2000	2001
Sawlogs, veneer logs and logs for sleepers	972	1,266	1,006
Pulpwood	103	189	140
Fuel wood	1,282	1,772	1,277
Total	2,357	3,227	2,423

Source: FAO, *Yearbook of Forest Products*.

SAWNWOOD PRODUCTION
('000 cubic metres, incl. railway sleepers)

	1999	2000	2001
Coniferous (softwood)	94	106	95
Non-coniferous (hardwood)	270	398	297
Total	364	504	391

Source: FAO.

Fishing

('000 metric tons, live weight)

	1998	1999	2000
Capture	2.6*	1.3	1.1
Freshwater fishes	2.2*	0.8	0.7
Aquaculture	6.6	3.4	2.8
Rainbow trout	6.6	3.4	2.8
Total catch	9.2	4.7	3.9

* FAO estimate.

Source: FAO, *Yearbook of Fishery Statistics*.

Mining

('000 metric tons, unless otherwise indicated)

	1998	1999	2000
Coal	44,072	31,429	34,124
Crude petroleum	913	705	805
Lead and zinc ore*	1,249	349	602
Bauxite	226	500	630
Natural gas (million cubic metres)	731	679	729

* Figures refer to gross weight of ores extracted. In the former Socialist Federal Republic of Yugoslavia lead and zinc ore contained 2.7% lead and 2.3% zinc in 1989 and 1990.

Source: US Geological Survey.

Industry

SELECTED PRODUCTS
('000 metric tons, unless otherwise indicated)

	1999	2000	2001
Wine*	136.6	197.3	198.0
Oil of sunflower seed*	77	70	85
Beer ('000 hectolitres)	6,786	6,734	6,063
Cotton yarn ('000 metric tons)	8.5	9.8	n.a.
Wool yarn	4.8	5.0	n.a.
Leather footwear ('000 pairs)	3,586	3,983	4,278
Cement	1,575	2,117	2,418
Sulphuric acid	30	98	68
Motor spirit (petrol)	237	n.a.	n.a.
Residual fuel oil	450	n.a.	n.a.
Pig-iron	128	560	n.a.
Crude steel	226	682	598
Aluminium—unwrought	73	88	100
Refined copper—unwrought	50	46	32
Refined lead—unwrought	n.a.	1.2	n.a.
Zinc—unwrought	0.8	8.9	n.a.
Television receivers ('000 units)	13	6	5
Tractors (number)	1,867	2,310	1,757
Lorries (number)	407	711	590
Motor cars ('000)	8	12	7
Bicycles ('000)	18	16	n.a.
Electric energy (million kWh)†	33,892	34,360	34,583

* FAO figures, referring to production during crop year ending 30 September.
† Estimates.

Source: partly UN, *Industrial Commodity Statistics Yearbook*.

Finance

CURRENCY AND EXCHANGE RATES

Monetary Units
100 para = 1 Yugoslav dinar.

Sterling, Dollar and Euro Equivalents (28 February 2003)
£1 sterling = 91.53 dinars;
US $1 = 57.83 dinars;
€1 = 53.64 dinars;
1,000 Yugoslav dinars = £10.925 = $17.292 = €18.644.

Average Exchange Rate (new dinars per US $)
1989	2.876
1990	11.318
1991	19.638

Note: On 1 January 1990 the new dinar, equivalent to 10,000 old dinars, was introduced in the Socialist Federal Republic of Yugoslavia (SFRY). After the disintegration of the SFRY, the Federal Republic of Yugoslavia (FRY) continued to use the Yugoslav dinar as its currency. Meanwhile, the other republics of the former SFRY introduced their own currencies to replace (initially at par) the Yugoslav dinar. As a result of rapid inflation in the FRY, the value of the Yugoslav dinar depreciated sharply. By the end of May 1993 the exchange rate was about 89,000 dinars per US dollar. After further devaluations, the currency was redenominated from 1 October, with the introduction of another new dinar, worth 1,000,000 of the former units. However, the depreciation of the currency continued, and on 30 December the new dinar was replaced by a further dinar, worth 1,000 million of its predecessors. In January 1994 there was another currency reform, with the establishment of a dinar officially valued at 1 Deutsche Mark (DM, equivalent to 13 million former dinars). In November 1999 Montenegro, one of the two constituent republics of the FRY, announced the introduction of the DM as its official currency. In September of that year the UN had decided to adopt the DM as the currency for official transactions in the Serbian province of Kosovo and Metohija. Euro notes and coins were introduced on 1 January 2002, replacing the DM, at an exchange rate of €1 = 1.95583 DM.

CONSOLIDATED BUDGET*
('000 million dinars)

Revenue†	2000	2001‡	2002§
Current revenue	140.2	300.5	419.8
Tax revenue	126.4	273.8	385.3
Personal income tax . .	12.7	36.2	52.8
Social security contributions .	44.8	85.5	112.9
Retail sales tax	32.9	75.8	110.5
Excises	10.7	28.4	50.3
Taxes on international trade and operations	10.3	16.0	23.9
Other current revenue . . .	13.8	26.6	34.6
Capital revenue	—	—	1.2
Total	140.2	300.5	421.0

Expenditure‖	2000	2001‡	2002§
Current expenditure. . . .	131.2	292.6	435.9
Expenditure on goods and services	66.4	134.5	178.9
Wages and salaries . .	36.0	73.0	98.6
Subsidies and other current transfers	62.5	152.4	239.0
Transfers to households . .	54.5	126.5	197.0
Capital expenditure	11.8	10.0	30.5
Total	143.0	310.2	477.0

* Comprising a consolidation of the Federal Budget, and the budgets of the Republic of Serbia and the Republic of Montenegro.
† Excluding grants received ('000 million dinars): 2.8 in 2000; 6.4 in 2001.
‡ Preliminary figures.
§ Projected figures.
‖ Excluding lending minus repayments ('000 million dinars): 0.3 in 2000; 9.6 in 2001.

Source: IMF, *Federal Republic of Yugoslavia: Selected Issues and Statistical Appendix* (May 2002).

INTERNATIONAL RESERVES
(former SFRY, US $ million at 31 December)

	1989	1990	1991
Gold*	80	81	81
IMF special drawing rights . .	—	13	—
Foreign exchange.	4,136	5,461	2,682
Total	4,216	5,555	2,763

* Valued at US $42.22 per troy ounce.

Source: IMF, *International Financial Statistics*.

Foreign exchange (FRY, US $ million at 31 December): 663.0 in 1999; 890.0 in 2000; 1,808.6 in 2001.

MONEY SUPPLY
(million dinars at 31 December)

	1999	2000	2001
Currency in circulation . . .	6,688	10,932	25,273
Demand deposits	7,864	14,848	31,259
Total money (incl. others) . .	14,552	25,780	56,532

Source: IMF, *Federal Republic of Yugoslavia: Selected Issues and Statistical Appendix* (May 2002).

COST OF LIVING
(Consumer Price Index; base: previous year = 100)

	2000	2001	2002
Food	205	188	107
Clothing and footwear . . .	171	184	117
Housing	145	227	146
Fuel and light	147	220	152
All items (incl. others)	186	189	117

NATIONAL ACCOUNTS
Gross Domestic Product by Economic Activity
(million dinars at current prices)*

	1997	1998	1999
Agriculture, hunting, forestry and fishing	19,875	25,274	37,331
Mining and quarrying . . .	5,671	6,845	7,144
Manufacturing	23,555	32,934	42,958
Electricity, gas and water . . .	4,900	6,030	7,879
Construction	5,460	7,170	8,220
Wholesale and retail trade . . .	7,249	11,637	15,588
Restaurants and hotels . . .	1,459	1,962	2,081
Transport, storage and communications	8,832	13,709	16,439
Financial intermediation . .	5,281	7,477	10,815
Real estate, renting and business activities	3,599	4,228	6,097
Public administration and defence; compulsory social security . .	5,016	6,033	10,274
Education	3,595	4,371	4,753
Health and social work	5,129	6,230	6,780
Other	3,539	4,949	5,600
GDP at factor cost	103,160	138,849	181,959
Indirect taxes, *less* subsidies . .	9,196	13,402	14,557
GDP in purchasers' values . .	112,355	152,251	196,516

2000: GDP in purchasers' values 358,056m. dinars*.

* Foreign trade transactions at official exchange rates, and Federal Statistics Office estimates of change in stocks; excluding Kosovo and Metohija.

Source: IMF, *Federal Republic of Yugoslavia: Selected Issues and Statistical Appendix* (May 2002).

BALANCE OF PAYMENTS
(US $ million)

	1998	1999	2000
Exports of goods f.o.b.	2,858	1,498	1,723
Imports of goods c.i.f.	−4,849	−3,296	−3,711
Trade balance	−1,991	−1,798	−1,988
Exports of services	914	471	624
Imports of services	−421	−243	−293
Balance on goods and services	−1,498	−1,570	−1,657
Other income received	57	43	53
Other income paid	−49	−35	−42
Balance on goods, services and income	−1,490	−1,562	−1,646
Private transfers received . . .	688	501	632
Private transfers paid	−378	−280	−284
Current balance	−1,180	−1,341	−1,298
Foreign direct investment (net) .	113	112	25
Medium- and short-term loans: disbursements	50	29	377
Medium- and short-term loans: amortization	−25	−17	−143
Short-term loans and deposits (net)	−35	−37	−33
Other capital inflows	78	30	92
Net errors and omissions . . .	884	1,113	1,207
Overall balance	−115	−111	227

External Trade

PRINCIPAL COMMODITY GROUPS
(distribution by SITC, US $ million)

Imports c.i.f.	2000	2001	2002
Food and live animals	279	441	527
Crude materials (inedible) except fuels	221	188	208
Mineral fuels, lubricants, etc.	745	1,001	1,070
Chemicals and related products	556	698	856
Basic manufactures	772	948	1,270
Machinery and transport equipment	820	1,029	1,629
Miscellaneous manufactured articles	237	356	553
Total (incl. others)	3,711	4,837	6,320

Exports f.o.b.	2000	2001	2002
Food and live animals	255	275	482
Crude materials (inedible) except fuels	123	102	118
Chemicals and related products	145	132	169
Basic manufactures	632	653	713
Machinery and transport equipment	215	243	254
Miscellaneous manufactured articles	270	363	369
Total (incl. others)	1,723	1,903	2,275

PRINCIPAL TRADING PARTNERS
(US $ million)*

Imports c.i.f.	1999	2000	2001
Austria	114	114	147
Bosnia and Herzegovina	187	174	135
Bulgaria	149	324	153
Germany	404	479	589
Greece	147	132	218
Hungary	101	123	194
Italy	333	390	500
Romania	108	145	175
Russia	274	319	685
Slovenia	24	35	145
Total (incl. others)	3,296	3,711	4,837

Exports f.o.b.	1999	2000	2001
Bosnia and Herzegovina	303	254	249
France	41	43	43
Germany	175	177	231
Greece	74	75	63
Hungary	32	62	63
Italy	167	223	312
Macedonia, former Yugoslav republic	157	210	176
Russia	77	86	80
Switzerland	106	107	160
United Kingdom	42	34	56
Total (incl. others)	1,497	1,723	1,903

* Imports by country of origins; exports by country of destination.

Source: IMF, *Federal Republic of Yugoslavia: Selected Issues and Statistical Appendix* (May 2002).

Transport

RAILWAYS
(traffic)

	1999	2000	2001
Passengers carried ('000)	9,904	12,221	10,985
Passenger-kilometres (million)	860	1,436	1,262
Freight carried ('000 metric tons)	6,657	9,287	9,376
Freight ton-kilometres (million)	1,308	1,970	2,040

ROAD TRAFFIC
(motor vehicles in use at 30 June)

	1997	1998	1999
Passenger cars	1,500,888	1,598,262	1,593,183
Buses and coaches	11,640	11,857	11,181
Goods vehicles	125,144	131,893	130,026
Motorcycles and mopeds	39,585	40,048	35,547

Source: IRF, *World Road Statistics*.

INLAND WATERWAYS

Fleet
(number of vessels)

	1994
Tugs	143
Motor barges	67
Barges	421
Tankers	100
Passenger vessels	8

Traffic
('000 metric tons)

	2000	2001
Goods carried	3,729	3,609
Ton-km (million)	980	983

SHIPPING

Merchant Fleet
(registered at 31 December)

	2000	2001	2002
Number of vessels	8	7	3
Displacement ('000 gross registered tons)	4.4	3.5	28.2

Source: Lloyd's Register-Fairplay, *World Fleet Statistics*.

International Sea-borne Freight Traffic
('000 metric tons, unless otherwise indicated)

	1998	1999	2000
Goods loaded	40	30	16
Goods unloaded	61	81	94

CIVIL AVIATION
(traffic)

	1999	2000	2001
Passengers carried ('000)	489	1,122	1,215
Passenger-kilometres (million)	332	978	1,003
Cargo carried ('000 tons)	1,091	3,187	3,859
Ton-kilometres (million)	1.6	7.6	4.3

Tourism

FOREIGN TOURIST ARRIVALS
(at accommodation establishments)

Country of origin	1999	2000	2001
Austria.	2,933	5,189	10,059
Bosnia and Herzegovina . . .	58,447	75,902	73,533
Bulgaria	5,946	8,605	10,562
Croatia.	3,585	7,920	13,775
Czech Republic and Slovakia . .	3,057	8,668	21,186
Germany	3,907	8,327	18,850
Hungary	2,477	4,808	9,743
Italy	8,133	12,605	16,813
Macedonia, former Yugoslav republic.	11,787	19,484	25,846
Romania	4,309	7,611	10,931
Russia	6,946	14,025	18,393
Slovenia	3,131	7,336	20,851
United Kingdom	2,171	3,225	7,586
USA	2,148	2,740	8,908
Total (incl. others)	151,650	238,957	351,333

Tourism Receipts (US $ million): 17 in 1999.

Source: mainly World Tourism Organization, *Yearbook of Tourism Statistics*.

Communications Media

	2000	2001	2002
Television receivers ('000 in use)	3,000	n.a.	n.a.
Telephones ('000 main lines in use)	2,406.2	2,443.9	2,493.0
Mobile cellular telephones ('000 subscribers).	1,303.6	1,977.8	2,750.4
Personal computers ('000 in use)	250	250	290
Internet users ('000)	400	600	640

Facsimile machines ('000 in use): 19,860 in 1999.

Radio receivers ('000 in use): 3,150 in 1997.

Books (titles published): 5,367 in 1996.

Daily newspapers: 18 in 1996 (average circulation 1,128,000).

Non-daily newspapers: 602 in 1996 (average ciculation 3,935,000).

Periodicals: 411 in 1994 (average annual circulation 3,191,000).

Source: partly International Telecommunication Union.

Education

(2001/02, unless otherwise indicated)

	Institu-tions	Teachers	Students Males	Students Females	Students Total
Pre-primary* . . .	1,748	17,198	94,139	87,986	182,125
Primary	4,079	48,993	n.a.	n.a.	771,250
Secondary	519	27,037	n.a.	n.a.	346,565
General*	n.a.	n.a.	270,006	278,947	548,953
Teacher training* .	n.a.	n.a.	88	239	327
Vocational* . . .	n.a.	n.a.	140,322	125,427	265,749
Higher	142	12,113	n.a.	n.a.	190,819
High schools . . .	52	1,577	n.a.	n.a.	49,350
Faculties and art academies . . .	90	10,356	n.a.	n.a.	141,469

* 1996/97 figure.

Source: partly UNESCO, *Statistical Yearbook*.

Adult literacy rate: 93.3% (males 97.6%; females 89.2%) in 1991 (Source: UNESCO, *Statistical Yearbook*).

Directory

The Constitution*

The Constitution of the Federal Republic of Yugoslavia, comprising Serbia and Montenegro, was adopted on 27 April 1992. Its main provisions are summarized below:

The Federal Republic of Yugoslavia (FRY) is a sovereign federal state, based on the principle of equality of its citizens and its member republics. The FRY comprises the Republic of Serbia and the Republic of Montenegro, and there are constitutional provisions for it to be joined by other republics. The FRY covers a unified territory consisting of the territories of the member republics. The FRY borders are inviolable.

Each member republic will have sovereignty over issues which, under the Federal Constitution, do not come within the competence of the FRY. In the FRY, power is in the hands of citizens, who exercise it either directly or through their freely-elected representatives. The FRY is based on the rule of law. The FRY recognizes and guarantees human liberties and citizens' rights as recognized by international law. The FRY recognizes and guarantees the rights of national minorities to preserve, develop and express their ethnic, cultural, linguistic and other characteristics, and their right to use their own national symbols in accordance with international law.

Authority in the FRY is shared between legislative, executive and judicial organs of state. Under the Constitution, the FRY is a single economic space with a single market. Political pluralism is a condition for, and a guarantee of, a democratic political system in the FRY.

In the FRY all citizens are equal before the law, regardless of their national affiliation, race, sex, language, religion, political or other convictions, education, social origin, property status and any other personal characteristic. Each citizen has a duty to respect the freedoms and rights of others and will be accountable for it.

The freedom of work and enterprise is guaranteed in the FRY. The right to private ownership is guaranteed. Nobody can be deprived of property, nor can it be limited (except when general interests require, as envisaged by the law and provided that compensation not lower than the market value of the property is paid to the owner). A foreigner assumes the right to private ownership and the right to enterprise under the conditions of reciprocity.

The FRY establishes policies, adopts and implements federal laws, other regulations and general documents, and secures constitutional and judicial protection in the following areas: human liberties, citizens' rights and duties as laid down in the Federal Constitution, the single market, the development of the FRY, communications and technical and technological systems, safety in all types of transport, the health service, international relations, and the defence and security of the FRY.

Bodies of the FRY are: the Federal Assembly, the President of the Republic, the Federal Government, the Federal Court, the Federal Public Prosecutor and the National Bank of Yugoslavia. Provision is made for the power and composition of the Federal Constitutional Court.

The FRY has an army which protects its sovereignty, territory, independence and constitutional system. The Yugoslav Army has both active and reserve staff. The active staff comprises professional soldiers and conscripts engaged in national service. The President of the Republic commands the Army both in time of peace and in time of war, in accordance with decisions of the Supreme Defence Council. The Supreme Defence Council consists of the President of the Republic and presidents of member republics. The FRY President is the President of the Supreme Defence Council. National service in the FRY is compulsory. A citizen who does not wish to perform regular military service on account of religious or other conscientious objections can participate in national service in the Yugoslav Army without weapons or in civilian service.

* On 4 February 2003 the legislature of the Federal Republic of Yugoslavia (FRY—comprising the two republics of Serbia and Montenegro) approved a Constitutional Charter, thereby officially reconstituting the FRY as the State Union of Serbia and Montenegro. Under the Constitutional Charter, a 126-member Assembly of Serbia and Montenegro, comprising 91 Serbian and 35 Montenegrin deputies, is directly elected for a four-year term. The Assembly elects a joint President of Serbia and Montenegro, who is also the Prime Minister of the Union, for a four-year term. A five-member joint Cabinet is approved by the Assembly. At republican level legislative power continues to be vested, respectively, in the National Assembly of Serbia and the Republican Assembly of Montenegro, both of which are directly elected. Each republic has its own President and Government. The member states of Serbia and Montenegro are to amend their respective Constitutions, in accordance with the Constitutional Charter. After three years each state may decide by referendum to gain independence.

The Government

HEAD OF STATE

President of Serbia and Montenegro: SVETOZAR MAROVIĆ (elected 7 March 2003).

COUNCIL OF MINISTERS
(July 2003)

Prime Minister: SVETOZAR MAROVIĆ.

Minister of Foreign Economic Relations: BRANKO LUKOVAC.

Minister of Foreign Affairs: GORAN SVILANOVIĆ.

Minister of Defence: BORIS TADIĆ.

Minister of Internal Economic Relations: AMIR NURKOVIĆ.

Minister of Human and Minority Rights: RASIM LJAJIĆ.

MINISTRIES

Office of the Prime Minister: Belgrade; tel. (11) 334281.

Ministry of Defence: 11000 Belgrade, Kneza Miloša 37; tel. (11) 656122.

Ministry of Foreign Affairs: 11000 Belgrade, Kneza Miloša 24; tel. (11) 682555; fax (11) 682668; e-mail smip@smip.sv.gov.yu; internet www.mfa.gov.yu.

Ministry of Foreign Economic Relations: Belgrade.

Ministry of Internal Economic Relations: 11070 Belgrade, Bulevar Lenjina 2; tel. (11) 2223550; fax (11) 195244.

Ministry of Human and Minority Rights: Belgrade.

President and Legislature

PRESIDENT

The President of Serbia and Montenegro is elected for a four-year term by the Assembly.

SKUPŠTINA SRBIJE I CRNE GORE
(Assembly of Serbia and Montenegro)

The Assembly of Serbia and Montenegro comprises 126 deputies, who are directly elected for a four-year term (91 from Serbia and 35 from Montenegro). The first Assembly was elected on 25 February by the existing federal and republican legislatures.

Speaker: DRAGOLJUB MIĆUNOVIĆ.

Election, 25 February 2003

Party	Seats
Democratic Opposition of Serbia*	37
Democratic List for European Montenegro†	19
Democratic Party	17
Together for Changes‡	14
Socialist Party of Serbia	12
Serbian Radical Party	8
Social Democratic Party of Montenegro	5
Party of Serbian Unity	5
Christian Democratic Party of Serbia	2
Democratic Alternative	2
Others	5
Total	**126**

* Alliance of 18 political parties.
† Coalition, principally comprising the Democratic Party of Montenegrin Socialists, the Social-Democratic Party of Montenegro and the Citizens' Party of Montenegro.
‡ Coalition, comprising the Socialist People's Party of Montenegro, the Serbian People's Party of Montenegro and the People's Party of Montenegro.

Local Government

Local government in the FRY was based on the municipality or commune. For administrative purposes, Montenegro was divided into municipalities (for details, see section on the Republics—Montenegro), of which there were 21. Serbia is divided into administrative regions (for details, see section on the Republics–Serbia), of which there were 29, including the territories of the formerly autonomous provinces of Kosovo and Metohija and Vojvodina. Following the enactment of the 1990 Serbian Constitution, and subsequently of the FRY Constitution of 27 April 1992, Vojvodina retained its provincial Assembly. However, the provincial Assembly of Kosovo and Metohija was dissolved, although it declared a 'Republic of Kosovo' (denounced as illegitimate by the Serbian authorities). Following the conflict in Kosovo in 1999, the UN Interim Administration in Kosovo (UNMIK) assumed responsibility for all civilian administration in Kosovo. The UN established the Kosovo Transitional Council (KTC), a consultative body. An Interim Administrative Council (IAC) was established in December to manage the province. The 'Republic of Kosovo' was dissolved in February 2000. In May 2001 UNMIK agreed to establish partial provincial self-government in Kosovo. In January 2002 the Serbian National Assembly voted to restore partial autonomy to Vojvodina. For details on the provinces, see section on the Republics—Serbia. In October 1991 the Slav Muslims of the Sandžak area voted for autonomy in a banned referendum.

Political Organizations

Alliance of Peasants of Serbia Party: Belgrade; tel. (11) 789235; f. 1990 as Peasants' Party of Serbia; Pres. MILOMIR BABIĆ.

Citizens' Party of Montenegro (Gradanska Partija Crne Gore): Podgorica; mem. of Democratic List for European Montenegro electoral coalition.

Democratic Alliance of Albanians in Montenegro (Demokratski Savez U Crnoj Gori—DSCG): Podgorica; mem. of Albanians Together electoral coalition; Chair. MEHMED BARDHI.

Democratic Community of Vojvodina Hungarians (Demokratska zajednica vojvodjanskih Madjara—DZVM): tel. (24) 852248; f. 1990; supports interests of ethnic Hungarian minority in Vojvodina; c. 20,000 mems; Chair. SANDOR PAL.

Democratic League of Kosovo: Priština; f. 2000 as successor to the Democratic Alliance of Kosovo; ethnic Albanian grouping; party with largest representation in Kosovo Assembly after Nov. 2001 elections; Chair. Dr IBRAHIM RUGOVA.

Democratic League of Montenegro: Podgorica; Leader MEHNED BARDHI.

Democratic League of Vojvodina (Liga Socijaldemokrata Vojvodine—LSV): Novi Sad, Trg Mladenaca 10; tel. and fax (21) 29139; internet www.lsv.org.yu; Pres. NENAD ČANAK.

Democratic Party of Kosovo: Priština; fmrly Party for the Democratic Party of Kosovo; represented in Kosovo Assembly after Nov. 2001 elections; Chair. HASHIM THAÇI.

Democratic Opposition of Serbia (DOS) (Demokratska Opozicija Srbije): 11000 Belgrade, Brace Jugovica 2a; tel. and fax (11) 3340620; e-mail info@dos.org.yu; internet www.dos.org.yu; alliance of 18 political parties, which secured a majority in legislative elections in December 2000; Leader ZORAN ŽIVKOVIĆ.

Alliance of Vojvodina's Hungarians: 24000 Subotica, Age Mamuzica 13; tel. (24) 553801; e-mail office@vmsz.org.yu; internet www.vmsz.org.yu; f. 1993; supports autonomous status for Vojvodina; Chair. JOŽEF KASA.

Christian Democratic Party of Serbia: 11000 Belgrade, Hadži Nikole Živkovića 2-II; tel. and fax (11) 3284695; e-mail dhss@net .yu; internet www.dhss.org.yu; Pres. Dr VLADAN BATIĆ.

Civic Alliance of Serbia: 11000 Belgrade, Terazije 3; tel. and fax (11) 3341696; e-mail gss@gradjanskisavez.org.yu; internet www .gradjanskisavez.org.yu; Pres. GORAN SVILANOVIĆ.

Coalition Sumadija: 34000 Kragujevac, ul. Branka Radicevića; tel. and fax (34) 67973; e-mail sumadija@infosky.net; internet www.sumadija.org.yu; Pres. BRANISLAV KOVACEVIĆ.

Coalition Vojvodina: Panačevo, Trg Slobode 3; tel. and fax (13) 353629; e-mail info@koalicijavojvodina.org.yu; internet www .koalicijavojvodina.org.yu; Pres. DRAGAN VESELINOV.

Democratic Alternative: Belgrade, Makedonska 5; tel. and fax (11) 3343471; e-mail da@da.org.yu; internet www.da.org.yu; Pres. NEBOJSA ČOVIĆ.

Democratic Centre: Belgrade, Terazije 3; tel. (11) 3229925; e-mail centar@idc.org.yu; internet www.dc.org.yu; Pres. DRAGOLJUB MICUNOVIĆ.

Democratic Party (DP) (Demokratska Stranka): 11000 Belgrade, Krunska 69; tel. and fax (11) 3443003; e-mail info@ds.org .yu; internet www.ds.org.yu; f. 1990; Pres. ZORAN ŽIVKOVIĆ.

League of Social-Democrats of Vojvodina: 21000 Novi Sad, trg Mladenaca 10/II; tel. (21) 29139; e-mail office@lsv.org.yu; internet www.lsv.org.yu; Pres. NENAD CANAK.

Movement for Democratic Serbia: Belgrade, Francuska 12; tel. (11) 3229821; fax (11) 3234730; e-mail pokret@pokret.org.yu; internet www.pokret.org.yu; Pres. MOMČILO PERISIĆ.

New Democracy: Belgrade, Proleterskih brigada 76; tel. (11) 4440677; fax (11) 3444230; e-mail izv.odbor@novademokratija.org .yu; internet www.novademokratija.org.yu; f. 1990 as New Democracy–Movement for Serbia; Chair. DUŠAN MIHAILOVIĆ; Sec.-Gen. TAHIR HASANOVIĆ.

New Serbia: 11000 Belgrade, Dragoslava Jovanovića 7; tel. and fax (11) 3238225; e-mail info@nova-srbija.org.yu; internet www .nova-srbija.org.yu; Pres. VELIMIR ILIĆ, MIHAJLO MARKOVIĆ.

Party of Democratic Action: 36300 Novi Pazar, Poštanskifah 101; tel. (20) 311454; Pres. RASIM LJAJIĆ.

Reform Democratic Party of Vojvodina: 21000 Novi Sad, Ilje Ognjanovića 10/II; tel. (21) 29561; e-mail rdsv@eunet.yu; internet www.rdsv.org.yu; f. 1992; Pres. MIODRAG ISAKOV.

Serb Resistance Movement–Democratic Movement: Priština; Pres. MOMČILO TRAJKOVIĆ.

Social-Democracy: 11000 Belgrade, Kralja Milana 23/I; tel. (11) 3342753; fax (11) 3343792; e-mail info@socijaldemokratija.org.yu; internet www.socijaldemokratija.org.yu; Pres. VUK OBRADOVIĆ.

Social-Democratic Union: 11000 Belgrade, Beogradska 8/II; tel. and fax (11) 434107; e-mail info@sdu.org.yu; internet www .sdu.org.yu; Pres. ZARKO KORAC.

Democratic Party of Montenegrin Socialists (DPMS) (Demokratska Partija Socijalista): 81000 Podgorica, Jovana Tomaśevića 33; tel. (81) 225830; fax (81) 242101; e-mail dps4@mn.yu; internet www.dps.cg.yu; name changed from League of Communists of Montenegro in 1991; supports the independence of Montenegro; division within the party emerged in mid-1997; Chair. MILO DJUKANOVIĆ.

Democratic Party of Serbia (DPS) (Demokratska stranka Srbije): Belgrade, Braće Jugovića 2A; tel. and fax (11) 3282886; e-mail info@dss.org.yu; internet www.dss.org.yu; f. 1992 following split from Democratic Party; withdrew from Govt in Aug. 2001, although officially remained in Democratic Opposition of Serbia; Leader Dr VOJISLAV KOŠTUNICA.

Democratic Reform Party of Muslims (Demokratska reformska stranka Muslimana): 38400 Prizren, Koritnik 3; tel. (29) 22322; party of ethnic Muslims; left-wing; Pres. AZAR ZULJI.

Democratic Union of Albanians (DUA) (Demokratska partija Albanaca): Preševo, Selami Halaci bb; f. 1990; Pres. FUAD NIMANI.

League of Communists—Movement for Yugoslavia of Montenegro: Podgorica; Chair. RADE LAKUSIĆ.

Liberal Alliance of Montenegro (LAM): Podgorica; e-mail webmaster@lscg.cmagora.com; internet www.lscg.cmagora.com; pro-independence; Leader MIODRAG ZIVKOVIĆ.

Liberal Party (Liberalna Stranka): Valjevo, Dr Pantića 70; tel. (14) 222659; f. 1989; favours a free-market economy; Leader PREDRAG M. VULETIĆ.

Party of Democratic Action of Kosovo and Metohija (PDA-KM): Vitomirića; party of ethnic Muslims; affiliated to the PDA of Bosnia and Herzegovina; Chair. NUMAN BALIĆ.

Party of Democratic Action—Montenegro: Rozaj; Slav Muslim party, affiliated to PDA of Bosnia and Herzegovina; Leader HARUN HADŽIĆ.

Party of Democratic Action of Sandžak (PDA-S): 36300 Novi Pazar, trg Maršala Tita 2; tel. (20) 25667; f. 1990; party of ethnic Muslims of Sandžak; affiliated to the PDA of Bosnia and Herzegovina; advocates autonomy for the Sandžak region; Chair. Dr SULEJMAN UGLJANIN.

Party of Natural Law: Belgrade; Leader MILAN MILO RADULOVIĆ.

Party of Serbian Unity: coalition, comprising Party of Serbian Progress, Party of Serbian Unity, Peasants' Party of Serbia and United Pensioners' Party; Leader ŽELJKO RAZNJATOVIĆ.

People's Assembly Party (Narodna saborna stranka): 11040 Belgrade, Masarikova 5/VIII; tel. (11) 685490; fax (11) 656818; f. 1992 as Democratic Movement of Serbia (Depos), a coalition of four parties and a party faction; reconstituted as a political party and renamed in 1995; Pres. SLOBODAN RAKITIĆ.

People's Party of Montenegro (Narodna Stranka Crne Gore): 11000 Belgrade, Srpskih Vladara 14; e-mail narodna@cg.yu; internet www.narodnastranka.cg.yu; Chair. DRAGAN SOC.

People's Socialist Party of Montenegro: Podgorica; Leader DUSKO JOVANOVIĆ.

Povratak (Return): Priština; Serbian coalition with representation in Kosovo Assembly after Nov. 2001 elections.

Radical Party of the Left 'Nikola Pasić': Belgrade.

Regeneration of Serbia (Preporod Srbije): Belgrade; f. 2000; Leader MILOVAN DRECUN.

Serbian People's Party of Montenegro (Srpska Narodna Stranka Crne Gore): 81000 Podgorica, Bratstva i jedinstva 53; tel. (81) 620324; e-mail sns@cg.yu; internet www.sns.cg.yu.

Serbian Popular Party: Belgrade; Leader ŽELIDRAG NIKČEVIĆ.

Serbian Radical Party (SRP) (Srpska Radikalna Stranka—SRS): 11000 Belgrade, Ohridska 1; tel. (11) 457745; f. 1991; extreme nationalist; advocates a 'Greater Serbian' state; Leader Dr VOJISLAV ŠEŠELJ; Gen. Sec. ALEKSANDAR VUCIĆ.

Serbian Renewal Movement (SRM) (Srpski pokret obnove—SPO): Belgrade, Krez Mihajlovna 48; tel. (11) 635281; fax (11) 628170; internet www.spo.org.yu; f. 1990; right-wing; nationalist; Pres. VUK DRAŠKOVIĆ.

Serb National Council: Priština; Leader RADA TRAJKOVIĆ.

Social-Democratic Party of Montenegro (SDP): 81000 Podgorica, Jovana Tomasévića bb; tel. (81) 248648; fax (81) 612133; e-mail sdp@cg.yu; internet www.sdp.cg.yu; Pres. RANKO KRIVOKAPIĆ.

Socialist People's Party of Montenegro (Socijalistička Narodna Partija Crne Gore—SNP): Podgorica; e-mail admin@snp.cg.yu; internet www.snp.cg.yu; Leader MOMIR BULATOVIĆ.

Socialist Party of Serbia (SPS) (Socijalistička partija Srbije): 11000 Belgrade, bul. Lenjina 6; tel. (11) 634921; fax (11) 628642; internet www.sps.org.yu; f. 1990 by merger of League of Communists of Serbia and Socialist Alliance of Working People (SAWP) of Serbia; Pres. BOGOLJUB BJELICA; Gen. Sec. ZORAN ANDJELKOVIĆ.

United Democratic Movement: Priština; f. 1998 by fmr mems of the Democratic Alliance of Kosovo; ethnic Albanian party; Chair. REXHEP QOSJA.

United Radical Party of Serbia: Belgrade; Leader SLOBODAN JOVIĆ.

Vojvodina Democratic Opposition: Novi Sad; f. 2000.

Yugoslav Green Party: Belgrade, Mutapova 12; tel. (11) 4447030; f. 1990; open to all citizens regardless of national, religious or racial affiliation; Pres. DRAGAN JOVANOVIĆ.

Yugoslav United Left: Belgrade; internet www.jul.org.yu; f. 1994; alliance of 23 left-wing organizations; Pres. MIRJANA MARKOVIĆ.

Diplomatic Representation

EMBASSIES IN SERBIA AND MONTENEGRO

Albania: 11000 Belgrade, Bulevar Mira 25A; tel. (11) 3065350; fax (11) 665439; Chargé d'affaires a.i. EDMOND HAXHINASTO.

Algeria: 11000 Belgrade, Maglajska 26B; tel. (11) 668211; Ambassador MOULOUD HAMAI.

Angola: 11000 Belgrade, Vase Pelagića 32 51; tel. (11) 3690241; fax (11) 3690191; Ambassador FILIPE FELISBERTO MONIMAMBU.

Argentina: 11000 Belgrade, Knez Mihajlova 24/I; tel. (11) 623569; fax (11) 622630; Ambassador CARLOS ABEL MARTESE.

Australia: 11000 Belgrade, Čika Ljubina 13; tel. (11) 624655; fax (11) 624029; e-mail austemba@eunet.yu; internet www.australia .org.eu; Ambassador JOHN OLIVER.

Austria: 11000 Belgrade, Kneza Sime Markovića 2; tel. (11) 635955; fax (11) 635500; Ambassador HANNES PORIAS.

Belarus: 11000 Belgrade, Deligradska 13; tel. (11) 3616836; fax (11) 3616938; e-mail bvalerij@eunet.yu; Ambassador VLADIMIR MATSKEVICH.

Belgium: 11000 Belgrade, Krunska 18; tel. (11) 3230016; fax (11) 3244394; e-mail embassy@belgium.org.yu; Ambassador WILFRIED NARTUS.

Bosnia and Herzegovina: Milana Tankosića 8; tel. (11) 3291277; fax (11) 766507; Chargé d'affaires a.i. RADOMIR BOGDANOVIĆ.

Brazil: 11000 Belgrade, Krunska 14; tel. (11) 3239781; fax (11) 3230653; e-mail brasbeig@eunet.yu; Ambassador RUBEM AMARAL JUNIOR.

Bulgaria: 11000 Belgrade, Birčaninova 26; tel. (11) 3613980; fax 3611136; Ambassador YANI MILCHAKOV.

Canada: 11000 Belgrade, Kneza Miloša 75; tel. (11) 3063000; fax (11) 3063042; e-mail bgrad@dfait-maeci.gc.ca; internet www.canada .org.yu; Ambassador DONALD P. McLENNAN.

Chile: 11000 Belgrade, Cakorska 3; tel. (11) 3670403; fax (11) 3670405; Ambassador AGUSTÍN PÍO GARCÍA.

China, People's Republic: 11000 Belgrade, Lackovićeva 6; tel. (11) 662737; fax (11) 653538; Ambassador WEN XIGUI.

Congo, Democratic Republic: 11000 Belgrade, Diplomatska kolonija 3; tel. (11) 664131; Chargé d'affaires a.i. PAUL EMILE TSHINGA AHUKA.

Croatia: 11000 Belgrade, Kneza Miloša 62; tel. (11) 3610535; fax (11) 3610032; e-mail croambg@eunet.yu; Ambassador DAVOR BOŽINOVIĆ.

Cuba: 11000 Belgrade, Vasilija Gaćeše 9b; tel. (11) 3692441; fax (11) 647858; Ambassador JUAN SANCHEZ MONROE.

Cyprus: 11040 Belgrade, Diplomatska Kolonija 9; tel. (11) 3672725; fax (11) 3671348; e-mail cyprus@eunet.yu; Ambassador STAVROS AMVROSIOU.

Czech Republic: 11000 Belgrade, bul. Kralja Aleksandra 22; tel. (11) 3230133; fax (11) 3230134; e-mail belgrade@embassy.mzv.cz; Ambassador JUDITA ŠTOURAČOVÁ.

Denmark: 11040 Belgrade, Neznanog Junaka 9A; tel. (11) 3670443; fax (11) 660759; e-mail ambadane@eunet.yu; Chargé d'affaires a.i. JÖRGEN V. ANDERSEN.

Egypt: 11000 Belgrade, Andre Nikolića 12; tel. (11) 651225; fax (11) 652036; Ambassador AMR KHODEIR YEHYA MOSTAFA KHODEIR.

Finland: 11000 Belgrade, Birčaninova 29; tel. (11) 3065400; fax (11) 3065375; e-mail finembas@eunet.yu; Ambassador HANNU MÄNTYVAARA.

France: 11000 Belgrade, Pariska 11; tel. (11) 636200; fax (11) 636274; e-mail amba_fr@eunet.yu; Ambassador GABRIEL KELLER.

Germany: 11000 Belgrade, Kneza Miloša 74–76; tel. (11) 3064300; fax (11) 3064303; e-mail germemba@eunet.yu; Ambassador KURT LEONBERGER.

Ghana: 11000 Belgrade, Ognjena Price 50; tel. (11) 3440856; fax (11) 3440071; e-mail ghana@eunet.yu; Chargé d'affaires a.i. KARK ASMAH.

Greece: 11000 Belgrade, Francuska 33; tel. (11) 3226523; fax 3344746; e-mail office@greekemb.co.yu; Ambassador MICHELL SPINELLIS.

Guinea: 11000 Belgrade, Ohridska 4; tel. (11) 431830; fax (11) 451391; Ambassador Dr FARA MILLIMONO.

Holy See: 11000 Belgrade, Svetog Save 24; tel. (11) 3085356; fax (11) 3085216; Apostolic Nuncio Most Rev. EUGENIO SBARBARO (Titular Archbishop of Tiddi).

Hungary: 11000 Belgrade, Proleterskih brigada 72; tel. (11) 4440472; fax (11) 4445708; e-mail hunemblg@eunet.yu; Ambassador JÓZSEF PANDUR.

India: 11000 Belgrade, Generala Hanrisa 37; tel. (11) 466192; fax (11) 465043; Ambassador ARUN KUMAR.

Indonesia: 11000 Belgrade, bul. Mira 18; tel. (11) 3674062; fax (11) 3672984; Chargé d'affaires a.i. ALOYSIUS BOENTARMAN.

Iran: 11000 Belgrade, Proleterskih brigada 9; tel. (11) 338782; fax (11) 3223676; Ambassador ALI ABOLHASSANI SHAHREZA.

Iraq: 11000 Belgrade, Teodora Drajzera 38; tel. (11) 3671580; fax (11) 3671590; Ambassador Dr SAMI SAOUN KHATI AL-KINANI (pending new appointment).

Israel: 11000 Belgrade, bul. Mira 47; tel. (11) 3672400; fax (11) 3670304; Ambassador YORAM SHANI.

Italy: 11000 Belgrade, Birčaninova 11; tel. (11) 3066100; fax (11) 3249413; e-mail italbelg@eunet.yu; internet www.italy.org.yu; Ambassador GIOVANNI CARACCIOLO DI VIETRI.

Japan: 11070 Novi Belgrade, Vladimira Popovica 6; tel. (11) 3012800; fax (11) 3118258; Ambassador RYUICHI TANABE.

Korea, Republic: 11070 Belgrade, Hyatt Regency, Milentija Popovića 5; tel. (11) 3011194; fax (11) 3011195; Ambassador RYU JIN-KYU.

Lebanon: 11000 Belgrade, Vase Pelagića 38; tel. (11) 3691178; fax (11) 3693108; e-mail ambaleb@eunet.yu; Chargé d'affaires a.i. NIDAL YEHYA.

Libya: 11000 Belgrade, Mirka Tomića 6; tel. (11) 663445; fax (11) 3670805; e-mail libyaamb@eunet.yu; Chargé d'affaires a.i. AISHA MOKHTAR TRHUNI.

Macedonia, former Yugoslav republic: 11000 Belgrade, Gospodar Jevremova 34; tel. (11) 633348; fax (11) 182287; Ambassador VIKTOR DIMOVSKI.

Mexico: 11000 Belgrade, Cara Dušana 58/V; tel. (11) 638111; fax (11) 629566; e-mail embamex@net.yu; Ambassador CARLOS ALEJANDRO RODRIGUEZ Y QUEZADA.

Morocco: 11000 Belgrade, Sanje Živanović 4; tel. (11) 651775; Chargé d'affaires a.i. KAMAL FAQIR BENAISSA.

Myanmar: 11000 Belgrade, Kneza Miloša 72; tel. (11) 645420; fax (11) 3614968; e-mail mebel@eunet.yu; Ambassador U KYAR NYO CHIT PE.

Netherlands: 11000 Belgrade, Simina 29; tel. (11) 3282332; fax (11) 628986; e-mail nlgovbel@eunet.yu; Ambassador KEES J. R. KLOMPENHOUWER.

Nigeria: 1100 Belgrade, Geršićeva 14A; tel. (11) 413411; fax (11) 401305; e-mail nigeria@bits.net; Ambassador MOHAMMED BUBA AHMED.

Norway: 11000 Belgrade, Kablarska 30; tel. (11) 3690154; fax (11) 3690158; Ambassador HANS OLA URSTAD.

Pakistan: 11000 Belgrade, bul. Mira 62; tel. (11) 661676; fax (11) 661667; Chargé d'affaires a.i. ARSHED SAUD KHOSA.

Peru: 11000 Belgrade, Terazije 1/II; tel. (11) 3221197; fax (11) 3228694; Chargé d'affaires a.i. HÉCTOR FRANCSICO MATALLANA MARTINEZ.

Poland: 11000 Belgrade, Kneza Miloša 38; tel. (11) 3615287; fax (11) 3616939; e-mail ambrpfrj@eunet.yu; Chargé d'affaires a.i. TADEUSZ DIEM.

Portugal: 11000 Belgrade, Vladimira Gaćinovića 4; tel. (11) 662895; fax (11) 662892; e-mail embporbg@yubc.net; Ambassador AGUSTO RUSSO DIAS.

Romania: 11000 Belgrade, Kneza Miloša 70; tel. (11) 3618327; fax (11) 3618339; Ambassador STEFAN GLAVAN.

Russia: 11000 Belgrade, Deligradska 32; tel. (11) 657533; fax (11) 657845; Ambassador VLADIMIR IVANOVSKI.

Slovakia: 11070 Belgrade, bul. Umetvosti 18; tel. (11) 3010000; fax (11) 3010020; Ambassador MIROSLAV LAJČÁK.

Slovenia: Belgrade, Zmaj Jovina 33a; tel. (11) 3284458; fax (11) 625884; Ambassador BORUT ŠUKLJE.

Spain: 11000 Belgrade, Prote Mateje 45; tel. (11) 3440231; fax (11) 3444203; e-mail embajada@sezampro.yu; Ambassador MARIANO GARCÍA MUNOZ.

Sweden: 11000 Belgrade, Pariska 7; tel. (11) 3031600; fax (11) 3031601; e-mail swedeemb@eunet.yu; Ambassador MICHAEL SAHLIN.

Switzerland: 11000 Belgrade, Birčaninova 27; tel. (11) 3065820; fax (11) 657253; Ambassador GAUDENZ B. RUF.

Syria: 11000 Belgrade, Mlade Bosne 31; tel. (11) 3443671; fax (11) 3440121; Chargé d'affaires a.i. MOHAMMAD ALI OBEID.

Tunisia: 11000 Belgrade, Vase Pelagića 19; tel. (11) 3691961; fax (11) 3690642; e-mail at.belgr@eunet.yu; Ambassador RIDHA TNANI.

Turkey: 11000 Belgrade, Krunska 1; tel. (11) 3235431; fax (11) 3235433; e-mail turem@eunet.yu; Ambassador HASAN SERVET ÖKTEM.

Ukraine: 11000 Belgrade, Josipa Slavenskog 27; tel. (11) 3671516; fax (11) 36781; Ambassador ANATOLY SHOSTAK.

United Kingdom: 11000 Belgrade, Generala Ždanova 46; tel. (11) 645055; fax (11) 659651; e-mail britemb@eunet.yu; Ambassador CHARLES CRAWFORD.

USA: 11000 Belgrade, Kneza Miloša 50; tel. (11) 3619344; fax (11) 3615489; e-mail billmont@aol.com; Ambassador WILLIAM D. MONTGOMERY.

Zimbabwe: 11000 Belgrade, Tolstojeva 51; tel. (11) 3672996; fax (11) 3671218; e-mail zimbegd@eunet.yu; Ambassador LLOYD GUNDU.

Judicial System

Judicial functions are to be discharged within a uniform system, and the jurisdiction of the courts shall be established and altered only by law. In general, court proceedings are conducted in public (exceptionally the public may be excluded to preserve professional secrets, public order or morals) in the national language of the region in which the court is situated. Citizens who do not know the language in which the proceedings are being conducted may use their own language.

The judicial system comprises courts of general jurisdiction, i.e. communal courts, county courts, republican supreme courts and the Federal Court. The courts of general jurisdiction are organized in accordance with individual republican legislation. In general, the courts are entitled to proceed in criminal, civil and administrative matters. Military courts, headed by the Supreme Military Court, proceed in criminal and administrative matters connected with military service or national defence. Economic or trade matters are under the jurisdiction of economic courts. They proceed also in penal-economic matters. Judges are elected or replaced by the republican assemblies or the Assembly of Serbia and Montenegro (see below).

The Federal Court and federal Constitutional Court were to continue functioning under the Constitutional Charter, adopted on 4 February 2003, until otherwise specified by this law. The Assembly of Serbia and Montenegro, which was established on 25 February, approved legislation providing for the creation of the Court of Serbia and Montenegro. Unfinished cases before the existing federal Constitutional Court and Federal Court within the remit of the Court of Serbia and Montenegro on the basis of the Constitutional Charter were to be transferred to that Court. The Court of Serbia and Montenegro was to have constitutional court and administrative court functions, and was to decide on the harmonization of court practice between the member states. The administrative court function was to be exercised in relation with administrative acts of the joint Council of Ministers. The Court of Serbia and Montenegro has an equal number of judges from the member states, who are elected by the Assembly of Serbia and Montenegro.

THE JUDICIARY OF SERBIA AND MONTENEGRO

Constitutional Court

This court decides on the conformity of the Constitutions of the member republics with the state Constitution. The court has seven judges, who elect the President of the Court from among themselves.

President of the Constitutional Court: MILOVAN BUZADZIĆ.

Federal Court

This is the highest organ of justice. The Federal Court comprises 11 judges who are elected and replaced by the Assembly of Serbia and Montenegro. The judges of the Federal Court elect the President of the Court from among themselves.

President of the Federal Court: Dr RAFAEL CIJAN, 11000 Belgrade, Svetozara Markovića 21; tel. (11) 3242547.

THE REPUBLICAN JUDICIARIES

Montenegro

The courts in Montenegro are supervised by the republican Ministry of Justice. The highest courts in the republican judicial system are the Supreme Court and the Constitutional Court.

Constitutional Court of the Republic of Montenegro: 81000 Podgorica, Lenjina 3; tel. (81) 41846; Pres. NIKOLA VUJANOVIĆ.

Supreme Court: 81000 Podgorica, Njegoševa 6; tel. (81) 43070; Pres. STEVAN DAMJANOVIĆ.

Office of the Public Prosecutor: 81000 Podgorica, Njegoševa 6; tel. (81) 43053; Public Prosecutor ZORAN RADONJIĆ.

Serbia

All courts in Serbia are within the jurisdiction of the republican Ministry of Justice. The Supreme Court and the Constitutional Court are the highest courts in the republican judicial system.

Constitutional Court of the Republic of Serbia: 11000 Belgrade, Nemanjina 22–26; tel. (11) 658755; Pres. Dr BALŠA SPADIJER.

Supreme Court of Serbia: 11000 Belgrade, Nemanjina 22–26; tel. (11) 658755; Pres. LEPOSAVA KARAMARKOVIĆ.

Office of the Public Prosecutor of the Republic of Serbia: 11000 Belgrade, Nemanjina 22–26; tel. (11) 658755; Public Prosecutor MILOMIR JAKOVLJEVIĆ.

Provincial Secretariat of Justice for the Province of Kosovo and Metohija: Zejnel Salihu br. 4; fax (38) 31929.

Provincial Secretariat for National Minorities, Administration and Regulations for the Province of Vojvodina: 21000 Novi Sad, bul. Mihaila Pupina 16; tel. (21) 56170; fax (21) 56137.

Religion

Most of the inhabitants of Serbia and Montenegro are, at least nominally, Christian, but there is a significant Muslim minority. The main Christian denomination is Eastern Orthodox, but there is a strong Roman Catholic presence. There are also small minorities of Old Catholics, Protestants and Jews.

CHRISTIANITY

The Eastern Orthodox Church

Serbian Orthodox Church: Headquarters: 11001 Belgrade, Kralja Petra 5, POB 182; tel. (11) 638161; fax (11) 182780; e-mail pravoslavlje@spc.yu; internet www.spc.yu; 11m. adherents; Patriarch of Serbia His Holiness PAVLE (Archbishop of Peć and Metropolitan of Belgrade-Karlovci); Sec. Archdeacon MOMIR LEČIĆ.

Head of the Orthodox Church in Montenegro: Cetinje; acknowledges the jurisdiction of the Patriarch of Serbia and commands the allegiance of most of the Orthodox in Montenegro; AMFILOHIJE RADOVIĆ (Metropolitan of Crna Gora and Primorje).

Montenegrin Orthodox Church: Cetinje; autocephalous until 1920, when it was dissolved against the Constitution and canon law and annexed to the Serbian Orthodox Church; restored 1993 by the Committee of the Restoration of the Autocephaly of the Montenegrin Orthodox Church; Patriarch of Montenegro His Excellency MIHAILO DEDEIĆ (Metropolitan of Montenegro).

The Roman Catholic Church

Serbia and Montenegro, and the former Yugoslav republic of Macedonia together comprise two archdioceses (including one, Bar, directly responsible to the Holy See) and four dioceses. At 31 December 2001 the estimated number of adherents was equivalent to 4.6% of the total population.

Archbishop of Bar: Most Rev. JOSIP ZEF GASHI, Nadbiskupski Ordinarijat, 85000 Bar, Popovići 98; tel. (85) 313863; fax (85) 313817.

Archbishop of Belgrade: Most Rev. STANISLAV HOČEVAR, Nadbiskupski Ordinarijat, 11000 Belgrade, Svetozara Markovića 20; tel. (11) 3234846; fax (11) 3344613; e-mail nadbisbg@eunet.yu.

Old Catholic Church

Old Catholic Church in Serbia and Vojvodina: 11000 Belgrade; Dir of Bishop's Diocese JOVAN AJHINGER.

Protestant Churches

Christian Assemblies—Church of Christ's Brethren: 21470 Bački Petrovac, Janka Kralja 4; tel. (21) 780153; Pres. of Elders SAMUEL RYBAR.

Christian Church Jehovah's Witnesses: 11000 Belgrade, Milorada Mitrovića 4; tel. (11) 450383.

Christian Nazarene Community: Hrišćanska nazarenska zajednica, 21000 Novi Sad, Vodnikova br. 12; tel. (21) 401049; Pres. KAROL HRUBIK VLADIMIR.

Christian Reformed Church: 24323 Feketic, Bratsva 26; tel. and fax (24) 738070; f. 1919; 22,000 mems; Bishop ISTVAN CSETE-SZEMISI.

Evangelical Christian Church of the Augsburg Confession in Serbia-Vojvodina: 24000 Subotica, Brace Radiča 17; tel. and fax (24) 721048; e-mail dolinski@suonline.net; Superintendent DOLINSKY ÁRPÁD.

Evangelical Church of Republic of Croatia, Republic of Bosnia and Herzegovina and Vojvodina: 10000 Zagreb, Gundulićeva 28; tel. (48) 55622; fax (48) 54289; e-mail evang.lut.c.o.zg@email.hinet.hr; 7,500 mems; Pres. Dr VLADO L. DEUTSCH.

Seventh-Day Adventist Church: Hrišćanska adventistička crkva, 11000 Belgrade, Božidara Adzije 4; tel. (11) 453842; fax (11) 3442631; e-mail rantic@eunet.yu; Pres. RADIŠA ANTIĆ; Sec. JOVAN MIHALJČIĆ.

Slovak Evangelical Church of the Augsburg Confession: 21000 Novi Sad, Karadžićeva 2; tel. (21) 611882; Lutheran; 51,500 mems (1990); Bishop Dr ANDREJ BEREDI.

Union of Baptist Churches in Serbia: 11000 Belgrade, Slobodanke D. Savic 33; tel. and fax (11) 410964; f. 1992; Gen. Sec. Rev. AVRAM DEGA.

United Methodist Church: 21000 Novi Sad, L. Mušičkoga 7; tel. and fax (21) 613122; e-mail emc@eunet.yu; f. 1898; 3,000 mems; Superintendent MARTIN HOVAN.

ISLAM

Almost 20% of the Montenegrin population profess Islam as their faith, many being ethnic Muslims of the Sandžak region (which was partitioned between Montenegro and Serbia in 1913). Most Muslims in Serbia are ethnic Albanians, mainly resident in the Province of Kosovo and Metohija, but there are also ethnic Slav Muslims in the part of Sandžak located in south-west Serbia. Serbian Islam is predominantly Sunni, although a Dervish sect, introduced in 1974, is popular among the Albanians (some 50,000 adherents, mainly in Kosovo and Metohija).

Islamic Community in the Republic of Serbia: 38000 Priština; Pres. of the Mesihat Dr REDZEP BOJE.

JUDAISM

Federation of Jewish Communities in Yugoslavia: Belgrade, Kralja Petra 71A /III, POB 512; tel. (11) 621837; fax (11) 626674; e-mail savezjev@infosky.net; f. 1919, revived 1944; Pres. ACA SINGER.

The Press

In 2000 some 629 newspapers and 564 periodicals were published in the then FRY (of which 583 newspapers and 539 periodicals were published in Serbia).

PRINCIPAL DAILIES
(In Serbo-Croat, except where otherwise stated)

Belgrade

Blic: 11000 Belgrade, Masarikova 5; tel. (11) 3619148; fax (11) 3619271; e-mail sveseline@yahoo.com; internet www.blic.com; f. 1996; Editor-in-Chief VESLIN SIMONOVIĆ; circ. 230,000.

Borba: 11000 Belgrade, trg Marksa i Engelsa 7; tel. (11) 334531; fax (11) 344913; f. 1922; morning; taken under govt control in 1994; Editor-in-Chief ZARKO OBRADOVIĆ; circ. 46,000.

Danas: 11000 Belgrade, Alekse Nenadovica 19–23 V; tel. and fax (11) 3441186; e-mail danas@eunet.yu; internet www.danas.co.yu; banned Oct. 1998; independent; Dir DUSAN MITROVIĆ; Editor GRUJICA SPAŠOVIĆ.

Dnevni Telegraf: 11000 Belgrade, trg Nikole Pašić 7; tel. (11) 334531; fax (11) 344913; morning; banned Oct. 1998; independent; Editor-in-Chief (vacant).

Nacional: Belgrade; f. 2000; Editor-in-Chief PREDRAG POPOVIĆ.

Naša Borba: Belgrade, 29 Novembar 68B; tel. (11) 3020000; fax (11) 753734; e-mail nasa_borba@yurope.com; f. 1995 by journalists from *Borba* who rejected imposition of govt control, banned Oct. 1998; independent; Editor-in-Chief MIHAL RAMAĆ; circ. 35,000.

Newsday: 11001 Belgrade, Obiličev Venac 2, POB 439; f. 1983; Mon.–Fri; published in English by Tanjug and *Privredni Pregled*.

Politika: 11000 Belgrade, Makedonska 29; tel. (11) 3221836; fax (11) 3248768; f. 1904; Dir-Gen. and Editor-in-Chief HADŽI DRAGAN ANTIĆ; circ. 300,000.

Politika Ekspres: 11000 Belgrade, Makedonska 29; tel. (11) 325630; evening; Editor-in-Chief MILE KORDIĆ; circ. 76,000.

Privredni Pregled: 11000 Belgrade, Marsala. Birjuzova 3; tel. (11) 182888; fax (11) 627591; f. 1950; business and economics; Dir and Chief Editor DUŠAN DJORDJEVIĆ; circ. 14,000.

Sport: 11000 Belgrade, trg Marksa i Engelsa 7/III; tel. (11) 33451; fax (11) 344913; e-mail jslsport@bits.net.yu; internet www.jsl-sport.co.yu; f. 1945; Editor ZORAN MILOVIĆ; circ. 50,000.

Večernje novosti: 11000 Belgrade, trg Nikole Pašića 7; tel. (11) 334531; fax (11) 344913; e-mail vnovosti@eunet.yu; f. 1953; evening; Chief and Executive Editor RADISAV BRAJOVIĆ; circ. 270,000.

Niš

Narodne Novine: 18000 Niš, Vojvode Gojka 14; morning; Chief Editor LJUBIŠA SOKOLOVIĆ (acting); circ. 7,210.

Novi Sad

Dnevnik: 21000 Novi Sad, 23; internet www.dnevnik.co.yu; f. 1942 as *Slobodna Vojvodina*; morning; Editor-in-Chief DRAGAN RADEVIĆ; circ. 61,000.

Magyar Szó: 21000 Novi Sad, V. Mišića 1; f. 1944; morning; in Hungarian; Editor-in-Chief (vacant); circ. 25,590.

Podgorica

Pobjeda: Podgorica, Bulevar Revolucije 11; tel. (81) 246701; fax (81) 244475; e-mail pobjeda@cg.yu; internet www.pobjeda.co.yu; morning; Editor-in-Chief VIDOJE KONTAR (acting); circ. 17,959.

Publika: Podgorica, Crnogorskih serdara 8; tel. (81) 601430; fax (81) 625123; e-mail info.publika@cg.yu; internet www.publika.co.yu.

Priština

Bujku: Priština; in Albanian; banned by Serbian authorities October 1992; Editor-in-Chief BINAK KELMENDI.

Jedinstvo: 38000 Priština, Srpskih Vladara 41; morning; Editor-in-Chief DRAGAN MALOVIĆ; circ. 2,465.

Koha Ditore: Priština; published in Albanian; Editor VETON SURROI.

PERIODICALS

Belgrade

4. Jul.: Belgrade, trg Bratstva i Jedinstva 9/III–IV; weekly; organ of Federation of Veterans of the People's Liberation War of Yugoslavia; Dir and Editor-in-Chief RAJKO PAVIČEVIĆ; circ. 10,000.

Duga (Rainbow): Belgrade; 2 a month; news magazine; Editor-in-Chief ILIJA REPAIĆ.

Ekonomist: Belgrade; f. 1948; quarterly; journal of the Yugoslav Association of Economists; Editor Dr HASAN HADŽIOMEROVIĆ.

Ekonomska Politika: 11000 Belgrade, trg Nikole Pašića 7; tel. (11) 3398298; f. 1952; weekly; Man. PRETPLATE RADOJKA KOLAROVIĆ.

Evropljanin: Belgrade; current affairs; weekly; Publr IVAN TADIĆ.

Finansije: Belgrade, Jovana Ristića 1; f. 1945; 6 a year; Editor BOGOLJUB LAZAREVIĆ.

Front: Belgrade, Proleterskih brigada 13; f. 1945; fortnightly; illustrated review; Editor-in-Chief STEVAN KORDA; circ. 263,000.

Ilustrovana Politika: 11000 Belgrade, Macetenska 39; tel. (11) 326938; fax (11) 32255602; f. 1958; weekly illustrated review; Editor-in-Chief JEVERN DAMNJANOVIĆ; circ. 90,000.

Jisa Info: 11000 Belgrade, Zmaj Jovina 4; tel. (11) 3282447; fax (11) 626576; e-mail jisa@yubc.net; internet www.jisa.org.yu; Editor DUBRAVKA DJURIĆ.

Književne Novine: Belgrade, Francuska 7; f. 1948; fortnightly; review of literature, arts and social studies; Editor-in-Chief (vacant); circ. 7,500.

Književnost: Belgrade, Čika Ljubina 1; tel. (11) 620130; fax (11) 627465; f. 1946; monthly; literary review; Editor VUK KRNJEVIĆ; circ. 1,800.

Medjunarodna Politika (Review of International Affairs): Belgrade, Nemanjina 34, POB 413; e-mail intenaff@eunet.yu; f. 1950 by the Federation of Yugoslav Journalists; published in English and Serbian; Editor-in-Chief Dr RANKO PETKOVIĆ; Gen. Man. MILIVOJE OBRADOVIĆ.

Medjunarodni Problemi: Belgrade, Makedonska 25; tel. (11) 3221433; fax (11) 3224013; e-mail branam@eunet.yu; f. 1949; quarterly; review of the Institute of International Politics and Economics; Editor B. MARKOVIĆ; circ. 1,000.

Mikro/PC World: 11030 Belgrade, Pozeska 81a; tel. (11) 5447971; fax (11) 542397; e-mail pisma@mikro.co.yu; internet www.mikro.co.yu; f. 1997; 11 a year; computing; Editor MILENKO VASIĆ; circ. 23,000.

NIN (Nedeljne informativne novine): Belgrade, Cetinjska 1, POB 208; tel. (11) 3224410; fax (11) 3221272; e-mail nin@eunet.yu; f. 1935; weekly; Editor-in-Chief MILIVOJE GLIŠIĆ; Gen. Man. TOMISLAV DZADZIĆ; circ. 35,000.

Novi Glasnik: Belgrade; f. 1993; 6 a year; military magazine; Editor-in-Chief Col MILE SUSNJAR.

Official Gazette of the Federal Republic of Yugoslavia: 11000 Belgrade, Jovana Ristića 1; f. 1945; editions in Serbo-Croat, Slovene, Albanian, Hungarian and Macedonian; Dir VELJKO TADIĆ; circ. 73,000.

Ošišiani Jež: 11000 Belgrade, Generala Ždanova 28/IV; tel. (11) 3232211; fax (11) 3232423; f. 1935; fortnightly; humour and satire; Editor RADIVOJE BOJIČIĆ; circ. 50,000.

Politikin Zabavnik: Belgrade, Makedonska 29; f. 1939; weekly; comic; Editor RADOMIR ŠOŠKIĆ; circ. 41,000.

Pravoslavlje: 11000 Belgrade, Kralja Petra 5; tel. (11) 3282596; fax (11) 630865; e-mail pravoslavlje@spc.yu; f. 1967; fortnightly; religious; published by the Serbian Orthodox Church; Editor RADOMIR RAKIĆ; circ. 7,600.

Rad: Belgrade, trg Nikole Pašića 5; tel. (11) 330927; weekly; organ of the Confederation of Trade Unions; Dir RADOSLAV ROSO; Editor-in-Chief STANISLAV MARINKOVIĆ; circ. 70,000.

Svet Kompjutera: 11000 Belgrade, Makedonska 29; tel. and fax (11) 3373181; e-mail editors@sk.co.yu; internet sk.beograd.com; f. 1984; monthly; computing; Editor ZORÁN MOSORINSKI; 26,000.

Tehničke novine: 11000 Belgrade, Hajduk Veljkov venac 12; tel. (11) 657415; e-mail ivladan@net.yu; internet solair.eunet.yu/_ivladan; monthly; technical; Chief Editor SAŠA IMPERL; circ. 75,000.

Viva: 11000 Belgrade, Cetinjska 1V; tel. (11) 3220132; fax (11) 3220552; e-mail viva@politika.co.uk; internet www.politika.co.yu; monthly; health; Editor DRAGUTIN GREGORIĆ; circ. 25,000.

Vojska: Belgrade, Proleterskih brig. 13; f. 1945; weekly; Yugoslav Army organ; Dir MILAN KAVGIĆ; Editor-in-Chief Col MILORAD PANTELIĆ.

Yugoslav Journal of Operations Research: 11000 Belgrade, Faculty of Organizational Sciences, University of Belgrade, Jove Ilica 154; tel. (11) 3972383; fax (11) 461221; e-mail yujor@fon.fonbg.ac.yu; internet jujor.fon.bg.ac.yu; 2 a year; systems science and management science; Editor RADIVOJ PETROVIĆ; circ. 700.

Yugoslav Law (1975–): Belgrade, Terazije 41; tel. and fax (11) 3233213; 3 a year; in English and French; publ. by the Institute of Comparative Law and the Union of Jurists' Asscn; Editor Dr OLIVER ANTIĆ.

Yugoslav Survey: Belgrade, Moše Pijade 8/1, POB 677; tel. (11) 3233610; fax (11) 3240291; f. 1960; quarterly; general reference publication of basic documentary information about Yugoslavia in English; Dir ILE KOVAČEVIĆ; Editor-in-Chief TOMO KOSOVIĆ (acting); circ. 3,000.

Niš

Bratstvo: Niš; Bulgarian-language magazine; Dir VENKO DIMITROV.

Novi Sad

Letopis Matice Srpske: Novi Sad, Matice srpske 1; f. 1824; monthly; literary review; Editor Dr SLAVKO GORDÍC.

Podgorica

Koha (Time): Podgorica; f. 1978; Albanian-language magazine; circ. 2,000 (estimated).

Stvaranje: Podgorica, Revolucije 78; f. 1946; monthly; literary review; publ. by the Literary Asscn of Montenegro; Man. RANKO JOVOVIĆ.

Priština

Koha (Time): Priština; f. 1994; Albanian-language magazine; Editor-in-Chief VETON SUROI.

Zeri: Priština; political weekly; in Albanian; Editor-in-Chief BLERIM SHALA.

NEWS AGENCY

Novinska Agencija Tanjug: 11001 Belgrade, Obilićev Venac 2, POB 439; tel. (11) 332230; f. 1943; 90 correspondents in Serbia and Montenegro and 30 offices abroad; press and information agency governed by self-management; news service for domestic press, radio and television; news and features service for abroad in English, French and Spanish; photo and telephoto service; economic and financial services for home and abroad; publishes EITI, service for trade, industry and banking in Serbo-Croat, English and French; computerized commodity service for domestic businesses and banks; Dir and Editor-in-Chief DUŠAN DJORDJEVIĆ.

Foreign Bureaux

Agence France-Presse (AFP) (France): 11000 Belgrade, trg Nikole Pasica 2; tel. (11) 3232622; fax (11) 620638; e-mail afpbgd@eunet.yu; Bureau Chief JEAN-EUDES BARBIER.

Agenzia Nazionale Stampa Associata (ANSA) (Italy): 11000 Belgrade, Braće Jugovića 5; tel. (11) 620221; fax (11) 628225; Bureau Chief LUCIANO CAUSA.

Allgemeiner Deutscher Nachrichtendienst (ADN) (Germany): 11000 Belgrade, Šiva Stena 1A; tel. (11) 461752; Correspondent Dr WILLFRIED MUCH.

Associated Press (AP) (USA): 11000 Belgrade, Dositejeva 12; tel. (11) 631553; Correspondent IVAN STEFANOVIĆ.

Bulgarska Telegrafna Agentsia (BTA) (Bulgaria): Belgrade; tel. (11) 636361; fax (11) 636361; Correspondent NIKOLA KITSEVSKI.

Česká tisková kancelář (ČTK) (Czech Republic): 11070 Belgrade, 190/Stan. 6/III, Blok 37; tel. (11) 134892; Correspondent MIROSLAV JILEK.

Informatsionnoye Telegrafnoye Agentstvo Rossii—Telegrafnoye Agentstvo Suverennykh Stran (ITAR—TASS) (Russia): Belgrade, Ognjena Price 17; tel. (11) 4446928; Correspondent MIKHAIL ABELEV.

Korean Central News Agency (KCNA) (Democratic People's Republic of Korea): Belgrade, Dr Milutina Ivkovića 9; tel. (11) 668426; Bureau Chief KIM JONG SE.

Magyar Távirati Iroda (MTI) (Hungary): 11030 Belgrade, Vladimira Rolovica 176; tel. (11) 506508; Correspondent GYÖRGY WALKO.

Rossiiskoye Informatsionnoye Agentstvo—Novosti (RIA—Novosti) (Russia): Belgrade, Strahinjića Bana 50; tel. (11) 629419; Bureau Chief SERGEI GRIZUNOV.

United Press International (UPI) (USA): 11000 Belgrade, Generala Zdanova 19; tel. (11) 342490; Correspondent NESHO DJURIĆ.

Xinhua (New China) News Agency (People's Republic of China): Belgrade; tel. (11) 493789; Correspondent YANG DAZHOU.

PRESS ASSOCIATIONS

Federation of Yugoslav Journalists (Savez Novinara Jugoslavije): Belgrade, trg Republike 5/III; tel. (11) 624993; f. 1945; 11,500 mems; Pres. MILISAV MILIĆ.

Independent Association of Journalists of Serbia: Belgrade; f. 1994; Pres. DRAGAN NIKITOVIĆ.

Yugoslav Newspaper Publishers' Association: Belgrade; Dir RASTKO GUZINA.

There is also an **Association of Professional Journalists of Montenegro**

Publishers

Alfa-Narodna knjiga: 11000 Belgrade, Šafarikova 11; tel. (11) 3227426; fax (11) 3227946; e-mail tea@eunet.yu; internet www.narodnaknjiga.co.yu; f. 1950; fiction, non-fiction, children's books and dictionaries; Gen. Man. MILIČKO MIJOVIĆ.

BIGZ (Beogradski izdavačko-grafički zavod): 11000 Belgrade, bul. vojvode Mišića 17/VI; tel. (11) 650627; fax (11) 648626; f. 1831; literature and criticism, children's books, pocket books, popular science, philosophy, politics; Dir SNEŽANA KNEŽEVIĆ.

Dečje novine: 32300 Gornji Milanovac, T. Matijevića 4; tel. (32) 711195; fax (32) 711248; general literature, children's books, science, science fiction, textbooks; Gen. Dir MIROSLAV PETROVIĆ.

Forum: Novinsko-izdavačka i štamparska radna organizacija, 21000 Novi Sad, Vojvode Mišića 1, POB 200; tel. (21) 611300; f. 1957; newspapers, periodicals and books in Hungarian; Dir GYULA GOBBY.

Gradjevinska Knjiga: 11000 Belgrade, trg Nikole Pašića 8/II; tel. (11) 3233565; fax (11) 3233563; f. 1948; technical, scientific and educational textbooks; Dir LJUBINKO ANDELIĆ.

IP Matice srpske: 21000 Novi Sad, trg Toze Markovića 2; tel. (21) 420199; fax (21) 27281; e-mail m.grujic@sezampro.yu; f. 1826; Yugoslav and foreign fiction and humanities; Man. Dir MILORAD GRUJIĆ.

Jedinstvo: 38000 Priština, Dom štampe bb, POB 81; tel. (38) 27549; fax (38) 29809; poetry, novels, general literature, science, children's books; Dir JORDAN RISTIĆ.

Jugoslovenska knjiga: 11000 Belgrade, trg Republike 5/VIII, POB 36; tel. (11) 621992; fax (11) 625970; art, economics and culture; Dir ZORAN NIKODIJEVIĆ.

Medicinska knjiga: 11001 Belgrade, Mata Vidakovića 24–26; tel. (11) 458165; f. 1947; medicine, pharmacology, stomatology, veterinary; Dir MILE MEDIĆ.

Minerva: Izdavačko-štamparsko preduzeće, 24000 Subotica, trg 29 novembra 3; tel. (24) 25712; fax (24) 23208; novels and general; Dir LADISLAV ŠEBEK.

Naučna knjiga: 11000 Belgrade, Uzun Mirkova 5; tel. (11) 637220; f. 1947; school, college and university textbooks, publications of scientific bodies; Dir Dr BLAŽO PEROVIĆ.

Nolit: 11000 Belgrade, Terazije 27/II; tel. (11) 3245017; fax (11) 627285; f. 1928; Yugoslav and other belles-lettres, philosophy and fine art; scientific and popular literature; Dir-Gen. RADIVOJE NEŠIĆ; Editor-in-Chief RADIVOJE MIKIĆ.

Obod: 81250 Cetinje, Njegoševa 3; tel. (86) 21331; fax (86) 21953; general literature; Dir VASKO JANKOVIĆ.

Panorama: Priština; f. 1994; publishes newspapers and journals in Serbian, Albanian and Turkish; Dir JORDAN RISTIĆ.

Pobjeda: 81000 Podgorica, Južni bul. bb; tel. (81) 44433; f. 1974; poetry, fiction, lexicography and scientific works.

Proex Commerce: 11000 Belgrade, Terazije 16; tel. (11) 686978; fax (11) 641052; e-mail gbproex@eunet.yu; internet www.proex.co .yu; editorial and typographic co-productions; export and import of books and periodicals.

Prosveta: 11000 Belgrade, Čika Ljubina 1/I; tel. (11) 629843; fax (11) 182581; f. 1944; general literature, art books, dictionaries, encyclopaedias, science, music; Dir BUDIMIR RUDOVIĆ.

Rad: 11000 Belgrade, Dečanska 12; tel. (11) 3239998; fax (11) 3230923; e-mail rad@radbooks.co.yu; internet www.radbooks.co.yu; f. 1949; politics, economics, sociology, psychology, literature, biographies; Man. Dir SIMON SIMONOVIĆ; Editor-in-Chief NOVICA TADIĆ.

Rilindja: 38000 Priština, Dom štampe bb; tel. (38) 23868; popular science, literature, children's fiction and travel books, textbooks in Albanian; Dir NAZMI RRAHMANI.

Savremena administracija: 11000 Belgrade, Crnotravska 7–9; tel. (11) 667633; fax (11) 667277; f. 1954; economy, law, science university textbooks; Dir TOMISLAV JOVIĆ.

Sportska knjiga: 11000 Belgrade, Makedonska 19; tel. (11) 320226; f. 1949; sport, chess, hobbies; Dir BORISLAV PETROVIĆ.

Srpska književna zadruga: 11000 Belgrade, Srpskih Vladara 19/I; tel. (11) 330305; fax (11) 626224; f. 1892; works of classical and modern Yugoslav writers, and translations of works of foreign writers; Pres. RADOVAN SAMARDŽIĆ; Editor RADOMIR RADOVANAĆ.

Svetovi: 21000 Novi Sad, Arse Teodorovića 11; tel. (21) 28032; fax (21) 28036; general; Dir JOVAN ZIVLAK.

Tehnička Knjiga: 11000 Belgrade, Vojvode Stepe 89; tel. (11) 468596; fax (11) 473442; f. 1948; technical works, popular science, reference books, 'how to' books, hobbies; Dir RADIVOJE GRBOVIĆ.

Vuk Karadžič: 11000 Belgrade, Kraljevića Marka 9, POB 762; tel. (11) 628066; fax (11) 623150; scientific literature, popular science, children's books, general; Gen. Man. VOJIN ANČIĆ.

Zavod za udžbenike i nastavna sredstva: 11000 Belgrade, Obilićev Venac 5; tel. (11) 637426; e-mail zavodudz@eunet.yu; internet www.zavod.co.yu; fax (11) 630014; f. 1957; textbooks and teaching aids; Dir RADOSLAV PETKOVIĆ.

PUBLISHERS' ASSOCIATION

Association of Yugoslav Publishers and Booksellers (Udruženje izdavača i knjižara Jugoslavije): 11000 Belgrade, Kneza Miloša 25, POB 570; tel. (11) 642533; fax (11) 646339; e-mail ognjenl@eunet.yu; f. 1954; organizes Belgrade International Book Fair; Dir OGNJEN LAKIĆEVIĆ; 116 mem. organizations.

Broadcasting and Communications

TELECOMMUNICATIONS

Telecom Serbia: 11000 Belgrade, Takovska 2; tel. (11) 3234414; fax (11) 3232141; e-mail drasko.Petrovic@telekom.yu; 49% transferred to Hellenic Telecommunications Organization and Telecom Italia SpA in 1997; Dir-Gen. DRAŠKO PETROVIĆ.

BROADCASTING

Jugoslovenska Radiotelevizija (JRT) (Association of Yugoslav Radio and Television Organizations): 11000 Belgrade, Generala Ždanova 28; tel. (11) 3230194; fax (11) 434023; f. 1952; Exec. Dir NIKOLIĆ VJERA.

Radio

Radio D: Podgorica; f. 2000; independent radio station.

Radio Jugoslavija: 11000 Belgrade, Hilandarska 2/IV, POB 200; tel. (11) 346884; fax (11) 332014; e-mail radioyu@bitsyu.net; internet www.radioyu.org; f. 1951; foreign service; broadcasts in Serbo-Croat,

Arabic, English, French, German, Russian and Spanish; Dir Dr DRAGAN MARKOVIĆ.

Radiotelevizija Crne Gore: 81000 Podgorica, Cetinjski put bb; tel. (81) 41800; fax (81) 43640; f. 1944; 2 radio programmes; broadcasts in Serbo-Croat; Dir-Gen. ZORAN JOCOVIĆ.

Radiotelevizija Srbije (RTS): 11000 Belgrade, Takovska 10; tel. (11) 3229780; fax (11) 3229788; f. 1929; 5 radio programmes; Dir-Gen. DRAGOLJUB MILANOVIĆ; Asst Dir-Gen. MILIVOJE PAPLOVIĆ; comprises:

Radiotelevizija Beograd: 11000 Belgrade, Hilandarska 2; tel. (11) 346801; fax (11) 326768; f. 1929; 5 radio programmes; Dir-Gen. DOBROSAV BJELETIĆ; Dir of Radio DRAGOSLAV NIKITOVIĆ (acting).

Radiotelevizija Novi Sad: 21000 Novi Sad, Ignata Pavlasa 3Ž; tel. (21) 611588; fax (21) 26624; f. 1949; 7 radio programmes; broadcasts in Serbo-Croat, Slovak, Romanian, Hungarian and Ruthenian; Gen. Man. PETAR JOVANOVIĆ.

Radiotelevizija Priština: 38000 Priština, Marsala Tita bb; tel. (38) 26255; fax (38) 25355; f. 1944; 3 radio programmes; broadcasts in Serbo-Croat, Romany and Turkish; Dir-Gen. RICHARD LUCAS; Dir of Radio MILORAD VUJOVIĆ.

B92: Belgrade, Makedonska 22; tel. (11) 3248577; fax (11) 3248075; f. 1989; independent radio station; Editor-in-Chief VERAN MATIĆ.

Mir: Tuza; tel. (81) 875305; e-mail dino@co.yu; f. 1998; independent Albanian-language station; Chair. DINO RAMOVIĆ.

Radio TV Bajina Basta: 31250 Bajina Basta, Svetosavska 34; tel. (31) 851688; fax (31) 853162; e-mail office@bajinabasta.org; internet www.bajinabasta.org; f. 1986; independent radio and television station; Dir BOBAN TOMIĆ.

Television

Radiotelevizija Crne Gore: 81000 Podgorica; f. 1971; 2 television programmes; Dir of Television MILUTIN RADULOVIĆ (acting).

Radiotelevizija Srbije: see Radio.

Radiotelevizija Beograd: 11000 Belgrade, Takovska 10; tel. (11) 342001; fax (11) 543178; f. 1958; 3 television programmes; in Serbo-Croat; Dir of Television SLOBODAN IGNJATOVIĆ.

Radiotelevizija Novi Sad: 21000 Novi Sad, Sutjeska 1; tel. (21) 615144; fax (21) 613959; f. 1975; 2 television programmes; broadcast in 8 languages; Gen. Man. PETAR JOVANOVIĆ.

Radiotelevizija Priština: 38000 Priština, Zejnel Ajdini 12; tel. (38) 31211; fax (38) 32073; f. 1975; 1 television programme; Dir of Television NIKOLA SARIĆ.

RTV BK Television: 1070 Belgrade, Nikole Tesle 42a; tel. (11) 3013555; fax (11) 3013526; e-mail info@bkt.com; internet www.bktv .com; f. 1994; independent television station; Dir-Gen. Dr TIMOHIR SIMIĆ; Editor-in-Chief MILOMIR MARIĆ.

Kosava Television: Belgrade; f. 1998; Dir MARIJA MILOŠEVIĆ.

Studio B: Belgrade; Editor-in-chief LJUBISLAV ALEKSIĆ.

TV Srbijasume 92: Belgrade; f. 2000; state-sponsored youth television station.

Uzice Television S: Uzice; f. 2000.

Finance

(cap. = capital; res = reserves; dep. = deposits; m. = million; amounts in convertible Yugoslav dinars unless otherwise stated; br. = branch)

BANKING

Central Banking System

Under the Constitution of 2003, the National Bank of Yugoslavia became Serbia's central bank, and was renamed the National Bank of Serbia. Its functions include the issue of money, provision of credit to banks and government authorities, control of credits and bank activities, recommendation of legislation relating to the activities, recommendation of legislation relating to the foreign exchange system and its implementation, management of gold and foreign exchange reserves, control of foreign exchange operations and other special activities. The National Bank of Montenegro, which was established in 2000, is also recognized by the Constitution.

National Bank of Serbia (Narodna banka Srbije): 11000 Belgrade, Kralja Petra 12, POB 1010; tel. (11) 3027100; fax (11) 3027113; e-mail kabinet@nbj.sv.gov.yu; internet www.nbj.yu; f. 1884, restructured 1963; National Bank of Yugoslavia until 2003; cap. and res 2,391.9m., dep. 16,120.0m. (Dec. 1999); total assets 147,883m. (Dec. 2001); Gov. KORI UDOVICKI; 4 brs.

National Bank of Montenegro: 81000 Podgorica, Blaža Jovanovića 7; tel. (81) 43381; Gov. Krunislav Vukčević.

Bank for International Economic Co-operation

**Jugoslovenska Banka Za Medjunarodnu Ekonomsku Sar-
adnju** (Yugoslav Bank for International Economic Co-operation):
11000 Belgrade, Bulevar Avnoja 121, POB 219; tel. (11) 3115270; fax
(11) 3110217; e-mail jubmes@jubmes.co.yu; internet www.jubmes.co
.yu; f. 1979; focuses on the financing of export-orientated and development projects; cap. 581.1m., res 174.3m., dep. 504.1m. (2001);
Pres. Darko Čukić; Vice-Pres. Branko Mijanović.

Other Banks

Alco Banka: 11000 Belgrade, Požeška 65b; tel. (11) 3050300; fax
(11) 3540930; e-mail banka@alcoyu.co.yu; f. 1996; cap. 277.1m., res
2.9m., dep. 369.2m. (2000); Chair. Miroljub Aleksić.

Delta Banka a.d. Beograd: 11070 Belgrade, Narodnih heroja 43;
tel. (11) 3113850; fax (11) 693808; e-mail dbanka@deltabanka.co.yu;
internet www.deltabanka.co.yu; f. 1991; cap. 2,011.7m., res 561.6m.,
dep. 11,390.5m. (Dec. 2001); Pres. Miroslav Mišković; 34 brs.

Jubanka a.d. Beograd: 11000 Belgrade, Kralja Milana 11; tel. (11)
3234931; fax (11) 3246840; e-mail jubanka@jubanka.com; internet
www.jubanka.com; f. 1956; cap. 2,191.7m., res 1,779.8m., dep.
31,395.7m. (2001); Dir-Gen. Borislav Djokić; 14 brs.

Komercijalna Banka a.d. Beograd: 11000 Belgrade, Svetog Save
14; tel. (11) 3080100; fax (11) 3442372; e-mail posta@kombank.com;
internet www.kombank.com; cap. 1,445.8m., res 271.6m., dep.
12,803.1m. (2001); Pres. Ljubomir Mihajlović.

Micro Finance Banka a.d. Beograd: 11000 Belgrade, Gospodar
Jevremova 9; tel. and fax (11) 3025605; e-mail infobel@mfbbanka
.com; internet www.mfbbanka.com; f. 2001; cap. 406.0m., dep.
2,152.3m. (2001); Gen. Man. Klaus Müller.

Yu Garant Banka a.d.: 11000 Beograd, 25 Slobodana Penezica; tel.
(11) 656999; fax (11) 644854; internet www.yugb.co.yu; cap.
1,115.1m., res 203.2m., dep. 4,165.2m. (Dec. 2000); Gen. Man. Dr
Vuk Obradović.

Zepter Banka a.d. Beograd: 11070 Belgrade, Bulevar Lenjina
117; tel. (11) 3113233; fax (11) 138603; e-mail zepterb@bitsyu.net;
internet www.banka.zepter.co.yu; cap. 404.0m., res 147.2m., dep.
635.4m. (2000); Pres. Philip Zepter.

Vojvodina

Metals Banka a.d. Novi Sad: 21000 Novi Sad, Bulevar Cara
Lazara 7A; tel. (21) 450695; fax (21) 350611; f. 1990; cap. 554.0m., res
165.4m., dep. 908.3m. (2001); Gen. Man. Ananije Pavićević.

Panonska Banka a.d.: 21001 Novi Sad, 76 Bulevar Oslobodjenja,
POB 351; tel. (21) 612444; fax (21) 613939; e-mail office@panban.co
.uk; internet www.panban.co.yu; f. 1974 as branch of Vojvodjanska
Banka-Centrala; cap. and res 972m., dep. 2,217m. (Nov. 2001); Gen.
Man. Raško Božović; 8 brs.

Vojvodjanska Banka, a.d.: 21001 Novi Sad, POB 391, Trg Slobode
7; tel. (21) 421077; fax (21) 624859; e-mail marketing@voban.co.yu;
internet www.voban.co.yu; f. 1962; cap. 4,574.4m., res 676.5m., dep.
19,888.7m. (Dec. 2001); Pres. Života Mihajlović; 275 brs.

Banking Association

Association of Banks of Serbia and Montenegro (Udruženje
banaka Srbije i Crne Gore): 11001 Belgrade, Bulevar kralja Aleksandra 86; tel. (11) 3020760; fax (11) 3370179; e-mail ubj@fimmet.co
.yu; f. 1955; association of business banks; works on improving interbank co-operation, organizes agreements of mutual interest for
banks, gives expert assistance, establishes co-operation with foreign
banks, other financial institutions and their associations, represents
banks in relations with the Government and the National Bank of
Serbia and Montenegro; Pres. Prof. Vojin Bjelica; Sec.-Gen. Mileta
Babović.

STOCK EXCHANGE

Belgrade Stock Exchange: 11070 Belgrade, Omladinskih brigada
1, POB 214; tel. (11) 3117297; fax (11) 138242; e-mail marketing@
belex.co.yu; internet www.belex.co.yu; f. 1894.

INSURANCE

Kompanija 'Dunav Osiguranje' (Dunav Insurance Company):
11001 Belgrade, Makedonska 4, POB 624; tel. (11) 3224001; fax (11)
624652; f. 1974; all types of insurance.

Trade and Industry

GOVERNMENT AGENCIES

Foreign Trade Institute (Institut za Spoljnu Trgovinu): 11000
Belgrade, Moše Pijade 8; tel. (11) 339041; Dir Dr Slobodan Mrkša.

Kosovo Trust Agency: Green Bldg, Rruga Vellusha II, Priština;
tel. (38) 400255; fax (38) 248076; e-mail soetenders@eumik.org;
internet www.kta-kosovo.org; Kosovo's privatization agency, supervised by UN mission in the province.

Serbian Investment and Export Promotion Agency (SIEPA):
11000 Belgrade, Terazije 23; tel. (11) 3248040; fax (11) 3248227;
e-mail marketing@siepa.sr.gov.yu; internet www.siepa.sr.gov.yu.

CHAMBERS OF COMMERCE

**Chamber of Commerce and Industry of Serbia and Mon-
tenegro** (Privredna Komora Srbije i Crne Gore): 11000 Belgrade,
Terazije 23, POB 1003; tel. (11) 3248123; fax (11) 3248754; e-mail
info@pkj.co.yu; internet www.pkj.co.yu; f. 1990; independent organization affiliating all domestic economic organizations; promotes
economic and commercial relations with foreign countries; Pres. Dr
Slobodan Korać.

Chamber of Commerce of Montenegro (Privredna Komora Crne
Gore): 81000 Podgorica, Novaka Miloševa 29/II; tel. (81) 31071; fax
(81) 34926; Pres. Vojin Djukanović.

Chamber of Commerce of Serbia (Privredna Komora Srbije):
11000 Belgrade, Gen. Zdanova 13–15; tel. (11) 3240611; fax (11)
3230949; e-mail pksrbije@pks.co.yu; internet www.pks.co.yu; Pres.
Radoslav Veselinović.

UTILITIES

Electricity

Elektroprivreda Crne Gore (Elektroprivreda Montenegro):
81400 Nicšić, Vuka Karadžića 2; tel. (83) 212177; production, transmission and distribution of electric power; 3,480 employees.

Elektroprivreda Srbije (Elektroprivreda Serbia): 11000 Belgrade,
Balkanska 7; tel. (11) 620921; fax (11) 629489; state-owned; Pres.
Dragan Kostić; 528 employees.

Gas

Naftna Industrija Srbije (NIS) (Serbian Oil Industry): 21000
Novi Sad, Sutjeska 1; tel. (21) 615144; fax (21) 25037; f. 1990 as
Naftagas-Hip-Jugopetrol by merger of 42 social enterprises, previously affiliated to 3 composite orgs of associated labour; petroleum
and natural gas exploration and production in Yugoslavia and
abroad; refines crude petroleum and natural gas, producing a
variety of petroleum derivatives and associated products, incl. mineral fertilizers and synthetic rubber; also operates petro-chemical
and chemical plants; Pres. Arvo Suppi; 18,694 employers.

MAJOR ENTERPRISES AND COMPANIES

Adriatic Shipyard—'Bijela': 85343 Bijela; tel. (88) 72068; fax (88)
71108; e-mail bijela@cg.yu; ship repair services and reconstruction;
f. 1927; Gen. Man. Stanko Zloković; 805 employees.

Agrovojvodina Elnos: 21000 Novi Sad, Sentandrejski put 165; tel.
(21) 412751; fax (21) 412096; e-mail elnos@eunet.yu; internet www
.elnos.eunet.yu; f. 1991; wholesale and retail trade of agricultural
machinery, construction equipment, chemicals, tools, etc.; Dir
Bjelica Zoran; 215 employees.

Bambi: 12000 Požarevac, Djure Djakovića bb; tel. (12) 223071; fax
(12) 213183; e-mail bambi@beotel.yu; internet www.bambi.co.yu; f.
1967; state-owned; production of confectionery; Dir Miroslav
Miletić; 1,768 employees.

Centrotextil: 11000 Belgrade, Knez Mihailova 1–3; tel. (11)
637749; fax (11) 635794; design, manufacture and sale of textiles,
clothing, leather goods and footwear; Man. Dir Goran Aleksić; 1,800
employees.

DMB (Dvadesetprvi Maj): 11090 Rakovica, Oslobodenja 1; tel. (11)
592111; fax (11) 593967; production of engines, transmissions and
equipment; Dir-Gen. Aleksandar Laković; 5,500 employees.

Duga d.d.: 11000 Belgrade, Viline Vode 6; tel. and fax (11) 754883;
e-mail duga@duga.ibl.com; internet www.duga.ibl.com; production
and sale of paints, polymers and chemicals; Gen. Man. Zlatan
Batalović; 707 employees.

Energoprojekt Holding Corporation: 11070 Novi Beograd; tel.
(11) 2221826; fax (11) 3114200; e-mail ep@energoprojekt.co.yu;
internet www.energoprojekt.co.yu; f. 1951; Pres. Milan Branković;
1,620 employees.

Galenika-Oour—Galenika Farmaceutsko-Hemijska Industrija: 11080 Zemun, Batajnicki Drum bb; tel. (11) 190810; fax (11) 199424; pharmaceutical and chemical production; Gen. Dir MARIA KURSTAIĆ; 6,000 employees.

Genex—Generalexport: 11070 Belgrade, Narodnih Heroja br. 43; tel. (11) 696992; fax (11) 609228; general trading internationally and in the execution of export-import business on a large scale; Gen. Dir MILORAD SAVICEVIĆ; 5,228 employees.

Goša Holding Corporation: 11420 Smederevska Palanka, Industrijska 70; tel. (26) 321253; fax (26) 321472; f. 1923; state-owned company; design, production and assembly of vehicles, engineering, power-generating and agricultural equipment; Pres. BRANISLAV MILANOVIĆ; 7,000 employees.

Hemijska Industrija, Pancevo (Pancevo Chemical Industry): 26000 Pancevo, Spoljnostarcevacka 80; tel. (13) 45953; fax (13) 45926; engaged in the production of petrochemicals, fertilizers; inorganic chemicals, fine and special chemicals, etc.; Gen. Dir VASILJE RADUNOVIĆ; 1,910 employees.

Holding Korporacija 'Krušik' d.d. ('Krušik' Holding Corporation): 14000 Valjevo, ul. Valjevskog nop Odreda 59; tel. (14) 223121; fax (14) 220516; e-mail hkkrusik@ptt.yu; manufactures military products, textile machinery, water and sanitary fittings, etc.; Gen. Man. MILADIN PIRIN; 16,000 employees.

IHP Prahovo: 19330 Prahovo; tel. (19) 512551; fax (19) 511765; production of mineral fertilizers; Gen. Dir RADOMIR SLADOJEVIĆ; 1,500 employees.

Industrija Kablova Holding (Cables Manufacturing Industry of Svetozarevo): 35000 Jagodina, Gine Pajević; tel. (35) 221102; fax (35) 231141; e-mail institut@fk.co.yu; internet www.fks.co.yu; Yugoslavia's largest cables manufacturer; Pres. ZIVADIN ANTONIJEVIĆ; 9,038 employees.

Industrija Masina i Traktora—IMT a.d.: 11000 Belgrade, Novi Beograd, Tošin Bunar 268; tel. (11) 150747; fax (11) 153576; manufacture of agricultural machinery; 3,950 employees.

Inex Interexport a.d.: 11000 Belgrade, Marta 69 27; tel. (11) 3376060; fax (11) 3376103; import and export, manufacturing and transportation; Gen. Dir VLADIMIR BRUSIĆ; 2,170 employees.

Istra—Fabrika Armatura Istra Deonicarsko Drustvo: 25230 Kula, Ise Sekičkog 30; tel. (25) 722122; fax (25) 722173; manufactures sanitary fittings; Gen. Dir ROMODA DJORDJE; 1,500 employees.

Ites 'Lola Ribar' a.d.: 25250 Odžaci, POB 5, Lola Ribara 40; tel. (25) 742113; fax (25) 742419; e-mail ites@ites.co.yu; manufactures tufted carpets, hemp yarn, twines, cordage and polypropylene products; Gen. Man. VOJISLAV MILENKOVIĆ; 1,200 employees.

Ivo Lola Ribar: 11000 Belgrade, bul. Revolucije 84; tel. (11) 4447744; fax (11) 433085; designs and manufactures drilling and milling machinery, industrial cranes and computers, etc; Man. Dir DRAGAN JOVANČEVIĆ; 8,500 employees.

Jugopetrol d.d.: 11070 Novi Beograd, Milentija Popovića 4; tel. (11) 2223311; fax (11) 2224816; internet www.jugopetrol.co.yu; exploration, sale and distribution of petroleum derivatives; Dir DRAGAN TOMIĆ; 4,500 employees.

Kombinat Aluminijuma, Podgorica: 81000 Podgorica, POB 22, Dajbabe bb; tel. (81) 620616; fax (81) 620955; e-mail kap.board@cg.yu; f. 1969; metal processing; Dir VOJIN DJUKANOVIĆ; 4,103 employees.

Leskoteks: 16000 Leskovac, AVNOJ-a 95; tel. (16) 43042; fax (16) 53364; manufacture of woollen fabrics and garments; Gen. Dir JELICA KOCIĆ; 9,550 employees.

Metallurgical and Metalworking Corporation (MMK): Nikšić, tel. (83) 41422; fax (83) 44750; manufacture of crude steel, steel castings, etc.; Pres. ZARKO MIJUSKOVIĆ; 6,500 employees.

Metalservis: 11000 Belgrade, POB 337, Karadjordjeva 65; tel. (11) 3281345; fax (11) 626325; e-mail msholding.co.yu; supplies tools, machines and equipment, building materials, electrical meterials, chemical products; Gen. Dir SLAVKA DJURIĆ; 314 employees.

Milan Blagojević: 32240 Lucani, Radnicka bb; tel. (32) 817100; fax (32) 818916; f. 1948 as manufacturer of defence products, has developed a chemical industry with a wide product assortment; Gen. Dir MILIJA JANKOVIĆ; 3,700 employees.

Miloje Zakić: 37000 Krusevac, Srpskih Vladara bb; tel. (37) 22328; fax (37) 23517; rubber processing, manufacture of industrial explosives and production of environmental protection equipment; 7,000 employees.

Minel Holding Corporation: 11000 Belgrade, Cara Lazara br. 3; tel. (11) 628935; fax (11) 625493; e-mail minelhol@eunet.yu; a group of enterprises designing, manufacturing equipment and constructing industrial projects; produces thermal power equipment, electrical power equipment and food-processing facilities; Pres. MILOSAV FILIPOVIĆ; 4,500 employees.

Nevena Chemical Industry d.d.: 16000 Leskovac, Djordja Stamenkovica; tel. (16) 242320; fax (16) 248311; e-mail nevena@cent.co.yu; f. 1872; production of cosmetics and toiletries; Gen. Man. PREDRAG DIMITRIJEVIĆ; 836 employees.

Obod d.d.: 81250 Cetinje, Njegošova 143; tel. (86) 31730; fax (86) 31731; e-mail obods@cg.yu; trade in electrical appliances; Dir ALEKSANDER MIJATOVIĆ; 2,869 employees.

Pik-Bicej: 21220 Becej, Mose Pijade 2; tel. (21) 811180; fax (21) 812049; agricultural production, being one of Yugoslavia's largest producers of milk and meat; 4,500 employees.

Proleter: 23000 Zrenjanin, Temisvarski drum bb; tel. (23) 44210; fax (23) 49138; produces machine-woven carpets, machine-tufted carpets and yarn; Gen. Dir JOKO IVANCEVIĆ; 1,500 employees.

Prvi Maj: 18300 Pirot; tel. (10) 32255; fax (10) 35116; produces clothing and knitwear; Gen. Man. HRISTIVOJE KOSTIĆ; 6,000 employees.

Ratko Mitrović: 11000 Belgrade, Koste Glavinića 8; tel. (11) 650522; fax (11) 650356; design, construction, civil engineering and manufacture of building materials; 7,000 employees.

Reik Kolubara: 14220 Lazarevac, Slobonana Kozareva bb; tel. (11) 810226; mining of lignite coal; estimated production of 33m. metric tons in 1992; 15,500 employees.

Rudarsko Topionicarski Basen, Bor: 19210 Bor, Srpskih Vladara 29; tel. (30) 230252; fax (30) 34462; extraction and processing of copper, precious metals and minerals; manufacture of chemicals and provision of engineering services; 24,000 employees.

Rudnici Boksita Nikšić Oour Prerada (Nikšić Bauxite Mines): 81000 Nikšić, var 13 Jula 30; tel. (83) 24122; non-ferrous metallurgy; 1,600 employees.

Simpo: 11000 Belgrade, Svetonikolski trg 6; tel. (11) 625792; fax (11) 637700; manufacturer and exporter of furniture, mattresses and decorative upholstery fabrics; Pres. DRAGOMIR TOMIĆ; 4,475 employees.

Sintelon: 21400 Backa Palanka, Industrija Zona d.d.; tel. (21) 742012; fax (21) 742677; manufacture of PVC floor coverings and machine-woven carpets; Pres. NIKOLA PAVIČIĆ; 1,689 employees.

Sirmium: 22000 Sremska Mitrovića, trg Brace Radica 4; tel. (22) 221122; primary agriculture, food processing, trade, catering and tourism services; 21,000 employees.

Sportstar d.d.: 11060 Belgrade, Visnijicka 84; tel. (11) 771333; fax (11) 782882; f. 1946; produces and sells sporting goods; Gen. Man. ZORAN PERUČIĆ; 1,200 employees.

Valjaonića Bakra i Aluminijuma 'Slobodan Penezić' (Krcun—Copper and Aluminium Rolling Mill): 31205 Sevojno; tel. (31) 21015; processing metal into products; 7,870 employees.

Velefarm d.d.: 11000 Belgrade, Vojvode Stepe 414A; tel. (11) 3090100; fax (11) 3971300; e-mail velefarm@velefarm.co.yu; internet www.velefarm.co.yu; trade in medical equipment and pharmaceuticals; Dir DRAGAN VUČIĆEVIĆ; 500 employees.

Viskoza Loznića: 15300 Loznića, Gradiliste bb; tel. (15) 82411; fax (15) 82047; production and processing of viscose fibres and foils; Pres. PAVLE DJOKIĆ; 10,386 employees.

Vojvodina: 22000 Sremska Mitrovića, Parobrodska 2/I; tel. (22) 222284; forestry, processing of timber; manufacture of furniture, cellulose, paper; foreign trade; 14,000 employees.

Zastava Group: 34000 Kragujevac, trg Topolivaca br. 4; tel. (34) 323187; fax (34) 323301; e-mail t.savic@zastavadd.co.yu; manufacture, sales and maintenance of passenger vehicles, lorries and firearms for police units, hunting and sports use; Chair. MILAN BEKO; Vice-Pres. (Marketing) TOMA SAVIĆ; 37,300 employees.

Zavarivac: 11000 Belgrade, Brankova 23; tel. (11) 633125; fax (11) 620560; manufactures load-bearing steel structures, steel locks and specialist processing equipment for the petrochemical, chemical and food industries; Gen. Dir NOVIĆA JANKOVIĆ; 2,400 employees.

Zmaj Co: 11080 Zemun-Belgrade, Autoput 18; tel. (11) 600452; fax (11) 601490; e-mail ipm@zmaj.co.yu; internet www.zmaj.co.yu; production and development of agricultural machinery and equipment; Gen. Man. BRANISLAV SAVIĆ; 1,300 employees.

TRADE UNIONS

Association of Free and Independent Trade Unions: 11000 Belgrade, Karadjordjeva 50; tel. and fax (11) 623671; e-mail asns@asns.org.yu; internet www.asns.org.yu; mem. of the Democratic Opposition of Serbia alliance which won Sept. 2000 elections; Pres. DRAGAN MILOVANOVIĆ.

Confederation of Autonomous Trade Unions of Serbia and Montenegro (Savez Samostalnih Sindikata Srbije i Crne Gore): 11000 Belgrade, trg Nikola Pašić 5; tel. (11) 3230922; fax (11) 3241911; 1.9m. mems.

Trade unions comprising the Confederation of Autonomous Trade Unions of Serbia and Montenegro:

Agricultural, Food and Tobacco Industry Workers' Union (Sindikat radnika poljprivrede, prehrambene i duvanske industrije): Pres. Federal Cttee ERNE KIČI.

Building Workers' Union (Sindikat radnika gradjevinarstva): Pres. Federal Cttee MILOŠ ŽORIĆ.

Catering and Tourism Workers' Union (Sindikat radnika u ugostiteljstvu i turizmu): Pres. Federal Cttee MILAN FRKOVIĆ.

Chemistry and Non-Metallic Industry Workers' Union (Sindikat radnika hemije i nemetala): Pres. Federal Cttee STOJMIR DOMAZETOVSKI.

Commerce Workers' Union (Sindikat radnika u trgovini): Pres. Federal Cttee LJUBICA BRAČKO.

Education, Science and Culture Workers' Union (Sindikat radnika delatnosti vaspitanja, obrazovanja, nauke i kulture): Pres. Federal Cttee BORIS LIPUŽIĆ.

Energy Workers' Union (Sindikat radnika energetike): Pres. Federal Cttee VASKRSIJE SAVIČIĆ.

Forestry and Wood Industry Workers' Union (Sindikat radnika šumarstva i prerade drveta): Pres. Federal Cttee DRAGOLJUB OBRADOVIĆ.

Health and Social Care Workers' Union (Sindikat radnika delatnosti zdravstva i socijalne zaštite): Pres. Federal Cttee LJILJANA MILOŠEVIĆ.

Metal Production and Manufacturing Workers' Union (Sindikat radnika proizvodnje i prerade metala): Pres. Federal Cttee SLAVKO URŠIĆ.

Public Utilities and Handicrafts Workers' Union (Sindikat radnika u komunalnoj privredi i zanatstvu): Pres. Federal Cttee JOSIP KOLAR.

Printing, Newspaper, Publishing and Information Workers' Union (Sindikat radnika grafičke, novinsko-izdavačke i informativne delatnosti): Pres. Federal Cttee BORIS BIŚĆAN.

State Administration and Finance Workers' Union (Sindikat radnika državne uprave i finansijskih organa): Pres. Federal Cttee RAM BUĆAJ.

Textile, Leather, and Footwear Workers' Union (Sindikat radnika industrije tekstila, kože i obuće): Pres. Federal Cttee JOZEFINA MUSA.

Transport and Communications Workers' Union (Sindikat radnika saobraćaja i veza): Belgrade; tel. (11) 646321; Pres. Federal Cttee HASAN HRNJIĆ.

Transport

Much international transport activity to or from the FRY was halted in 1992–94 as a result of UN sanctions. In 2000 it was announced that the FRY was to receive aid from the Stability Pact for South Eastern Europe for transport projects. The construction of the road and railway bridge across the River Danube in Novi Sad was completed in May. Work on the construction of the Belgrade–Novi Sad highway began in June.

RAILWAYS

In 2000 there were 4,058 km of railway track in use, of which 1,364 km were electrified. In March 2002 the Government signed an agreement with the European Union on an €80m. loan for the reconstruction of the major rail route.

Zajednica Jugoslovenskih Železnica (Yugoslav Railways): 11000 Belgrade, Nemanjina 6, POB 553; tel. (11) 3616722; fax (11) 3616797; Gen. Man. SVETOLIK KOSTADINOVIĆ.

ROADS

In 2000 there were an estimated 44,777 km of roads, of which 28,061 km were paved.

INLAND WATERWAYS

About 3.7m. metric tons of freight were carried on inland water transport in 2000.

SHIPPING

With the dissolution of the SFRY, Yugoslavia lost much of its access to the sea; the principal coastal outlet is the Montenegrin port of Bar, which is linked to Bari (Italy) by a regular ferry service. In 1992–95 many Yugoslav vessels were impounded abroad, as a result of UN sanctions. In 1996 the maritime fleet resumed operations.

Jugoslovenska Oceanska Plovidba (Yugoslav Ocean Lines): 85330 Kotor; tel. (82) 25011; Pres. ANTON MOŠKOV.

Jugoslovenska Pomorska Agencija (Yugoslav Shipping Agency): 11070 Belgrade, bul. Mihaila Pupina 165A, POB 210; tel. (11) 3115994; fax (11) 3112070; e-mail jugentyu@eunet.yu; f. 1947; charter services, liner and container transport, port agency, passenger service, air cargo service; Gen. Man. MIROSLAV PAVLIČIĆ.

CIVIL AVIATION

There are international airports at Belgrade and Podgorica, as well as several domestic airports.

Jugoslovenski Aerotransport (JAT) (Yugoslav Airlines): 11070 Belgrade, Bulevar umetnosti 16; tel. (11) 3114222; fax (11) 3112853; e-mail pr@jat.com; internet www.jat.com; f. 1947; 51% owned by Govt of Serbia; re-establishing former network of commercial flights following the lifting of the ban by the EU in February 2000; renewed regular flights to Lebanon, Saudi Arabia and Syria in July; operates two domestic routes; Dir-Gen. PREDRAG VUJOVIC.

Smaller operators included:

Air Jugoslavia: 11000 Belgrade, Bul Utmetnosti 16; tel. (11) 2221454; fax (11) 327832; f. 1969; wholly-owned subsidiary of JAT; Gen. Man. NEOLO LOZIĆ.

Air Montenegro: 81000 Podgorica, Airport Podgorica, POB 073; tel. (81)230641; fax (81) 623762; e-mail contact@mgr.cg.yu; internet www.montenegro-airlines.com; f. 1991; operations commenced 1997; regular domestic and international charter services; Pres. ZORAN DURLJIĆ.

Aviogenex: 11070 Belgrade, Vladimira Popovića 8; tel. (11) 3119385; fax (11) 3111017; e-mail agxdir@icg.co.yu; f. 1968; passenger flights within Europe; Man. Dir BRATISLAV PEJKOVIĆ.

Tourism

Prior to the disintegration of the SFRY, tourism was a major source of foreign exchange (receipts were estimated at US $2,700m. in 1990); most foreign tourists were, however, attracted to Croatia and Slovenia. The great lake of Scutari, in Montenegro, is a notable tourist attraction, as is Montenegro's Adriatic coastline. The Yugoslav tourist industry was adversely affected by the imposition of UN sanctions, in May 1992. Although some recovery in the tourism industry was subsequently achieved, the NATO air offensive against the FRY, which commenced in March–June 1999, resulted in the suspension of tourist activity. In that year the number of tourist arrivals declined to 151,650, compared with 282,639 in 1998. Tourist arrivals recovered to 238,957 in 2000 and to 351,333 in 2001.

National Tourism Organization of Montenegro: 81000 Podgorica, Omladinskih brigada 7; tel. (81) 230959; fax (81) 230979; e-mail tourism@cg.yu; internet www.visit-montenegro.com; Man. Dir PREDRAG JELUSIĆ.

National Tourism Organization of Serbia (Turistička Organizacija Srbije): 11000 Belgrade, POB 433, Dobrinska 11; tel. (11) 3612754; fax (11) 686804; e-mail ntos@eunet.yu; internet www.serbia-info.com/ntos; f. 1953; produces information and conducts market research and promotion in the field of tourism; Dir JOVAN POPESKU.

Yugotours: 11000 Belgrade, Zmaj Jovina 4; tel. (11) 626163; fax (11) 625380; f. 1957; organizes travel and accommodation arrangements for foreign and domestic tourists; 3 branch offices, 2 European; Man. Dir SLOBODAN ŚĆEPANOVIĆ.

Culture

Although, following periods of conflict in the 1990s, the FRY did not maintain cultural links with most countries, in 2000 there were signs of progress. In May Yugoslav and Iraqi foreign ministers signed a programme of co-operation in science, education and culture. The programme envisaged co-operation between universities and exchanges of scholarships and delegations. It was hoped that co-operation in the fields of literature and sport would also commence. In the same month, the Federal Government signed a three-year programme of cultural and educational co-operation with the People's Republic of China. The republican Government of Montenegro signed a memorandum of cultural co-operation with the Albanian Government in April.

GOVERNMENT ORGANIZATIONS

Ministry of Culture of the Republic of Montenegro: see section below on The Republics—Government of Montenegro (Ministries).

Ministry of Culture of the Republic of Serbia: see section below on The Republics—Government of Serbia (Ministries).

Ministry of Sport and Education of the Republic of Serbia: see section below on The Republics—Government of Serbia (Ministries).

Cultural Centre of Novi Sad (Kulturni Centar grada Novog Sada): 21000 Novi Sad, Katolička porta 5; tel. and fax (21) 616358; e-mail kcns@eunet.yu; f. 1945; organizes literary and philosophical-sociological presentations, concerts, exhibitions, film-viewing, theatre productions and festivals, including the International Festival of Alternative and New Theatre (INFANT); publishes books and literary magazines; Dir DRAGAN SREĆKOV.

Historical Institute of Montenegro (Istoriski Institut Crne Gore): 81000 Podgorica, Naselje Kruševac; f. 1948.

Montenegrin Academy of Sciences and Arts (Crnogorska Akademija Nauka i Umjetnosti): 81000 Podgorica, Rista Stijovića 5; tel. (81) 631095; Pres. DRAGUTIN VUKOTIĆ; Gen. Sec. MILINKO ŠARANOVIĆ.

Montenegrin Centre for Cultural and Artistic Activities (Republički Centar za Kulturno-umjetničke Delatnosti): 81000 Podgorica, Vasa Raičkovića 27; tel. (81) 44270; Dir MILAN POPOVIĆ; Programme Organizer VESELIN RADUNOVIĆ.

Montenegrin Institute for the Protection of Cultural Monuments (Republički Zavod za Zaštitu Spomenika Kulture): 81250 Cetinje, Bajova 150; tel. (86) 31039; fax (86) 31753; e-mail rzzsk@cg.yu; f. 1948; research, registration and protection of cultural property in Montenegro; Dir Dr ČEDOMIR MARKOVIĆ.

Serbian Academy of Arts and Sciences: 11001 Belgrade, Kneza Mihaila 35, POB 366; tel. (11) 3342400; fax (11) 182825; e-mail sasapres@bib.sanu.ac.yu; internet www.sanu.ac.yu; f. 1886; Pres. DEJAN MEDAKOVIĆ.

CULTURAL HERITAGE

Archiv Jugoslavije: 11000 Belgrade, Vase Pelagića 33, POB 65; tel. (11) 3690252; fax (11) 652740; e-mail arhiv@gov.yu; internet www.arhiv.sv.gov.yu; f. 1950; Dir MOMČILO MIĆOVIĆ.

Ethnographical Museum (Etnografski muzej): 11000 Belgrade, trg Studentski 13, p.p 357; tel. (11) 3281888; fax (11) 621284; e-mail sekretar@etnomuzej.co.yu; internet www.etnomuzej.co.yu; f. 1901; Dir MITAR MIHIĆ.

Gallery of the Matica srpska ('Matica srpska' Galerija): 21000 Novi Sad, trg Galerija 1; tel. and fax (21) 421455; f. 1847; collection of Serbian art in Vojvodina from the end of the 17th century to the present; Dir LEPOSAVA ŠELMIĆ.

Library Matica srpska: 21000 Novi Sad, Matice srpske 1; tel. (21) 420199; fax (21) 420199; e-mail bms@bms.ns.ac.yu; Dir MIRO VUKSANOVIĆ.

Maritime Museum of Montenegro (Pomorski muzej Crne Gore): 81330 Kotor; f. 1900; Dir JOVAN MARTINOVIĆ.

Museum of Applied Art (Muzej primenjene umetnosti): 11001 Belgrade, Vuka Karadžića 18; tel. (11) 626841; fax (11) 629121; f. 1951; Dir SVETLANA ISAKOVIĆ.

Museum of Contemporary Art: 11070 Belgrade, Novi Beograd, Ušće Save bb; tel. (11) 3115771; fax (11) 3112955; e-mail msub@eunet.yu; internet www.msub.org.yu; f. 1958, opened 1965; Dir BRANISLAVA DIMITRIJEVIĆ.

Museum of Vojvodina (Muzej Vojvodine): 21000 Novi Sad, Dunavska 35–37; tel. (21) 26766; fax (21) 25059; f. 1947; sections on archaeology, ethnology, history and applied art; Dir LUBIVOJE CEROVIĆ.

National Library of Serbia: Belgrade, Skerlićeva 1; tel. (11) 451750; fax (11) 451289; e-mail injac@nbs.bg.ac.yu; internet www.nbs.bg.ac.yu; Dir STRETEN UGRICIĆ.

National Museum (Narodni muzej): 11000 Belgrade, trg Republike 1A; tel. (11) 624322; fax (11) 627721; e-mail yugo@yubusiness.co.yu; internet www.yubusiness.co.yu/nmuzej.htm; f. 1844; archeological collections and art gallery; Dir BOJANA BORIĆ-BREŠKOVIĆ.

State Museum of Montenegro (Državni muzej Crne Gore): 81250 Cetinje, Novice Cerovića; e-mail mncgb@cg.yu; departments of history, ethnography, archaeology and arts; Dir PETAR ĆUKOVIĆ.

University Library 'Svetozar Marković': Belgrade, Bulevar revolucije 71; tel. (11) 3370509; fax (11) 3370354; e-mail info@unilib.bg.ac.yu; internet www.unilib.bg.ac.yu; f. 1921; Dir NIKOLA MARKOVIĆ (acting).

SPORTING ORGANIZATIONS

Yugoslav Olympic Committee: 11040 Belgrade, Generala Vasica 5; tel. (11) 3671574; fax (11) 3671887; e-mail jok@eunet.yu; internet www.jok.org.yu; f. 1919, recognized in 1920; Pres. DRAGAN KICANOVIĆ; Gen. Sec. PREDRAG MANOJLOVIĆ.

PERFORMING ARTS

Belgrade Drama Theatre: 11000 Belgrade, Save Kovačevića 64A; tel. (11) 423183; internet www.narodnopozoriste.co.yu; f. 1948; theatre productions, contemporary and classical drama; Gen. Man. GORAN SULTANOVIĆ.

Bitef Theatre: 11000 Belgrade, Terazije 29/I; tel. (11) 3243109; fax (11) 3236324; e-mail bitef@bitef.co.yu; f. 1989; theatre production, touring, international cultural co-operation, BITEF festival organization; Gen. Man. NENAD PROKIĆ.

National Theatre of Montenegro (Crnogorsko Narodno Pozorište): 81000 Podgorica, Stanka Dragojevića 12; tel. (81) 43293; drama, ballet, opera; Dir BLAGOTA ERAKOVIĆ.

National Theatre of Belgrade (Narodno Pozorište): 11000 Belgrade, Francuska 3; tel. (11) 3281333; fax (11) 622560; internet www.infosky.net/~clsavic; Dir of Opera DEJAN SAVIĆ; Dir of Ballet LIDJA PILPENKO.

Theatre Atelier 212: 11000 Belgrade, Lole Ribara 21; tel. (11) 3246146; fax (11) 3236215; e-mail scvetko@bits.net; f. 1956; Man. SVETOZAR CVETKOVIĆ.

Ujvideki Szinhaz Theatre of Novi Sad: 21000 Novi Sad, Jovana Subotica 3–5; tel. (21) 622306.

Yugoslav Drama Theatre: 11000 Belgrade, Srpskih Vladara 50; tel. (11) 657766.

Music

Belgrade Opera Orchestra (Orkestar Beogradske opere): 11000 Belgrade, Francuska 3; tel. (11) 624565; fax (11) 622560; e-mail operanp@eunet.yu; internet www.narodnopozoriste.co.yu; Gen. Man. DEJAN SAVIĆ.

Belgrade Strings ('Dušan Skovran' String Orchestra) (Beogradski gudački orkestar 'Dušan Skovran'): Sava centar, 11070 Belgrade, Milentija Popovića 9; tel. (11) 143456; fax (11) 147134; e-mail bstrings@yuonline.net; internet www.belgradestrings.org.yu; f. 1965; Music Dir and Principal Conductor ALEKSANDAR PAVLOVIĆ; Man. ZORICA PREMATE.

Belgrade Philharmonic Orchestra (Beogradska Filharmonija): 11000 Belgrade, Studentski trg 11; tel. (11) 635518; fax (11) 187533; f. 1923; Dir BRANKA CVEJIĆ-MEZEI; Chief Conductor EMIL TABAKOV.

'Collegium Musicum' Women's Choir ('Collegium Musicum' hor): c/o Fakultet muzičke umetnosti, 11000 Belgrade, Srpskih vladara 50; tel. (11) 642414; fax (11) 3613451; e-mail colegium@eunet.yu; f. 1971; Chief Conductor DARINKA MATIĆ MAROVIĆ.

Niš Symphony Orchestra (Niški Sinfonijski Orkestar): 18000 Niš, Stanka Paunovića 16; tel. and fax (18) 522634; Gen. Man. NENAD KATANIĆ; Chief Conductor DEJAN SAVIĆ.

Pro Musica Chamber Orchestra (Kamerni Orkestar 'Pro Musica'): c/o Djura Jakšić, 11000 Belgrade, Požeška 92; tel. (11) 552580; Conductor DJURA JAKŠIĆ.

Radio-television Belgrade (RTV Belgrade) Jazz Band (Jazz orkestar RTV Beograd): 11000 Belgrade, Hilandarska 2; tel. (11) 346801; Conductors VOJISLAV SIMIĆ, ŽVONIMIR SKERL.

RTV Belgrade Mixed Choir (Mešoviti hor RTV Beograd): 11000 Belgrade, Hilandarska 2; tel. (11) 346801; Chief Conductor VLADIMIR KRANJČEVIĆ.

RTV Belgrade Symphony Orchestra (Simfonijski orkestar RTV Beograd): 11000 Belgrade, Hilandarska 2; tel. (11) 346801; Conductor VANCO CAVDARSKI.

RTV Novi Sad Big Band (Plesni orkestar RTV Novi Sad): 21000 Novi Sad, Žarka Zrenjanina 3; tel. (21) 611588; Chief Conductor RUDOLF TOMŠIĆ.

Symphony Orchestra of Montenegro RTV (Simfonijski orkestar Crnogorske RTV): 81000 Podgorica, Cetinjski put bb; Chief Conductor RADOVAN PAPOVIĆ.

Yugoslav Army Symphony Orchestra (Sinfonijski orkestar umetničkog ansambla JNA): Dom JNA, 11000 Belgrade, Braće Jugovića 19; tel. (11) 339551; Chief Conductor MAJOR ILIJA ILIJEVSKI.

ASSOCIATIONS

Historical Society (Istorijski Institut): 11000 Belgrade, Kneza Mihaila 35; tel. (11) 638418; fax (11) 185504; e-mail istorinst@bib.sanu.ac.yu; f. 1947; Pres. TIBOR ŽIVKOVIĆ.

Library Association of Serbia (Bibliotekarsko društvo Srbije): 11000 Belgrade, Skerlićeva 1; tel. (11) 451242; tel. 12208; fax (11) 452952; f. 1947; Pres. DOBRIVOJE MLADENOVIĆ; Sec. VERA CRLJIĆ.

Montenegrin PEN Centre: 81250 Cetinje, Njegoševa 7, POB 117; tel. (86) 21303; f. 1990; Pres. PAVLE MIJOVIC; Sec. MLADEN LOMPAR.

Roma Union of Serbia (Društva Rom Srpska): 11000 Belgrade; f. 1930; federation of some 60 local asscns; Pres. SAIT BALIĆ.

Serbian Literary Association (Srpska književna zadruga): 11000 Belgrade, Srpskih vladara 19/I; tel. (11) 330305; f. 1892; special collection of 19th-century periodicals; Pres. (vacant); Sec.-Gen. RAD-IVOJE KONSTANTINOVIĆ; c. 2,500 mems.

Serbian PEN Centre: 11000 Belgrade, Francuska 7; f. 1926, re-formed 1962; Pres. MIODRAG PERIŠIĆ; Sec. KOSTA ČAVOŠKI.

Serbian Society (Matica srpska): 21000 Novi Sad, Matice srpske 1; e-mail maticadm@eunet.yu; f. 1826; literary, scientific, cultural and publishing society; Pres. Prof. Dr BOŽIDAR KOVAĆEK.

Society of Serbian Language and Literature (Društvo za srpski jezik i književnost): University of Belgrade, 11000 Belgrade, Studentski trg 1; f. 1910; Pres. P. STEVANOVIĆ; Sec. D. PAVLOVIĆ.

Education

The educational system of Serbia and Montenegro is organized at republican level. Elementary education is free and compulsory for all children between the ages of seven and 15, when children attend the 'eight-year school'. Various types of secondary education are available to all who qualify, but the vocational and technical schools are the most popular. Alternatively, children may attend a general secondary school (gymnasium) where they follow a four-year course which will take them up to university entrance.

At the secondary level there are also a number of art schools, apprentice schools and teacher-training schools. In 1996 primary enrolment was equivalent to 71% of children in the appropriate age-group (boys 71%; girls 72%), while the comparable ratio for secondary education was 64% (boys 62%; girls 66%). Those who have attended the technical schools may pursue their education further at one of the two-year post-secondary schools, created in response to the needs of industry and the social services. In the 2001/02 academic year the country had 4,079 primary schools, attended by 771,250 students, and 519 secondary schools, attended by 346,565 students. In 2000/01 there were 51 post-secondary schools, and 87 institutes of higher education (including six universities) in the country.

UNIVERSITIES

Kragujevac University (Univerzitet u Kragujevcu): 34000 Kragujevac, Jovana Cvijica bb; tel. (34) 370270; fax (34) 370168; e-mail unikg@knez.uis.kg.ac.yu; internet www.uis.kg.ac.yu; f. 1976; 11 faculties; 700 teachers; 12,500 students; Rector Prof. MIRKO ROSIĆ.

University of Arts in Belgrade (Univerzitet Umetnosti u Beogradu): 11000 Belgrade, Kosančićev venac 29; tel. (11) 625166; fax (11) 629785; e-mail rektorat.arts@bg.ac.yu; f. 1957 as Academy of Arts, became University in 1973; 4 faculties; 430 teachers; 2,183 students; Rector Prof. RADMILA BAKOČEVIĆ.

University of Belgrade (Univerzitet u Beogradu): 11001 Belgrade 6, trg Studentski 1; tel. (11) 635153; e-mail ubqinfo@rect.bg.ac.yu; internet www.bq.ac.yu; f. 1863, reorganized 1905 and 1954; 28 faculties; 3,201 teachers; 49,890 students; Rector Prof. Dr DRAGUTIN VELIČKOVIĆ.

University of Montenegro, Podgorica (Univerzitet Crne Gore, Podgorica): 81000 Podgorica, Cetinjski put bb; tel. (81) 214484; fax (81) 42301; f. 1974; 14 faculties, one Academy of Music; five institutes; 833 teachers; 8,828 students; Rector Prof. Dr RATKO DUKA-NOVIĆ.

University of Niš (Univerzitet u Nišu): 18000 Niš, Universitetski trg 2; tel. (18) 547970; fax (18) 547950; e-mail uniuni@ni.ac.yu; internet www.ni.ac.yu; f. 1965; 12 faculties; 1,300 teachers; 24,000 students; Rector Prof. Dr BRANIMIR DJORDJEVIĆ.

University of Novi Sad (Univerzitet u Novom Sadu): 21000 Novi Sad, trg Dositeja Obradovića 5; tel. (21) 350622; fax (21) 450418; e-mail rektorat@uns.ns.ac.yu; internet www.ns.ac.yu; f. 1960; 13 faculties; 2,700 academic staff; 30,000 students; Rector Prof. FUADA STANKOVIĆ.

Social Welfare

All employed persons and their families are covered by obligatory social insurance schemes, providing for health insurance, money and grants in kind in case of sickness, accidents, disablement, old age and death. Insured persons are entitled to medical care, including compensation for an unlimited period during sick leave, rehabilitation and preventive care. The retirement pension is usually equivalent to 85%–87% of average monthly income during the last five years of employment. Women and young children enjoy special protection under the health-insurance scheme. Employed women are entitled to at least 270 days' paid leave before and after childbirth. Confinements in hospital and maternity care are free of charge. Women are entitled to shorter working hours when their child is ill. All workers are entitled to annual leave, which varies from 18 to 36 days. The NATO aerial bombardment of the FRY in March–June 1999 resulted in widespread damage to infrastructure and power supplies, severe food shortages and the contamination of water sources. Following the agreement to a peace plan in June, the UN Office of the High Commissioner for Refugees was allocated responsibility for the resettlement of refugees, the Organization for Security and Co-operation in Europe (OSCE) for the establishment of democratic institutions, and the EU for economic reconstruction.

GOVERNMENT AGENCIES

Ministry of Health of the Republic of Montenegro: see section below on The Republics—Government of Montenegro (Ministries).

Ministry of Health and Environmental Protection of the Republic of Serbia: see section below on The Republics—Government of Serbia (Ministries).

Ministry of Labour and Social Welfare: see section below on The Republics—Government of Montenegro (Ministries).

Ministry of Labour and Employment of the Republic of Serbia: see section below on The Republics—Government of Serbia (Ministries).

HEALTH AND WELFARE ORGANIZATIONS

Council for the Defence of Human Rights and Freedoms: Priština; affiliated to International Federation of Human Rights; Pres. ADEM DEMAQI.

Helsinki Committee of Human Rights of Sanđak: Novi Pazar; Pres. SEFKO ALOMEROVIĆ.

Red Cross of Yugoslavia: 11000 Belgrade, Ruzveltov 61; tel. (11) 761063; national federation of republican societies.

Serbian Society for the Fight against Cancer: 11000 Belgrade, Pasterova 14; tel. and fax (11) 656386; e-mail serbca@ncrc.ac.yu; f. 1927; publishes 'The Best Cure is Prevention' (Bolje sprečiti nego lečiti); Pres. Dr PREDRAG BRZAKOVIĆ; 42,000 mems.

Soros Yugoslavia Foundation: 11000 Belgrade, Tolstojeva 5; tel. (11) 660937; fax (11) 669683; e-mail newsflash@soros.zer.de; f. 1991; part of Soros foundations network; provides medical supplies to hospitals and assists organization of clinical seminars on medical topics; distributes food, clothes and educational material to refugee centres; Man. Dir SLOBODAN NAKARADA.

Yugoslav Commission for Humanitarian Issues and Missing Persons: Belgrade; Head PAVLE TODOROVIĆ.

The Environment

The level of pollution in the FRY increased as a result of the conflict in Kosovo in 1999. A report by the Regional Environmental Centre for Central and Eastern Europe claimed that radioactive air pollution had been detected in some areas of the FRY as a result of NATO's use of uranium-tipped shells during the NATO air offensive in March–June. In March 2002 it was reported that the UN Environment Programme had discovered areas in the Preševo valley (Serbia) and Cape Arza (Montenegro) that were still contaminated with depleted uranium. The FRY was also adversely affected by the mineral waste leak from a Romanian mine, which contaminated the Tisza River. In April 2000 the clearing of the Novi Sad bridge over the River Danube, destroyed during NATO aerial bombardment, commenced. The EU pledged to cover 85% of the costs incurred.

GOVERNMENT ORGANIZATIONS

Ministry of the Environment and Town Planning of the Republic of Montenegro: see section below on The Federal Republics—Government of Montenegro (Ministries).

Ministry of Health and Environmental Protection of the Republic of Serbia: see section below on The Federal Republics—Government of Serbia (Ministries).

Co-ordinating Committee for the Environment: 11070 Belgrade, SIV, Lenjina 2; tel. (11) 330349.

Hydrometeorological Service of the Republic of Serbia: 11000 Belgrade, POB 100, Kneza Višeslava 66; tel. (11) 545240; fax (11)

545378; network of stations involved in meteorological and hydrological forecasting, agricultural meteorology, environmental control and radar monitoring; Dir Nikola Dutina; Deputy Dir Vladimir Dimitrijević.

ACADEMIC INSTITUTES

Centre for Socio-Ecological Research and Documentation (Centar za Socio-Ekoloska Istraživanja i Dokumentaciju—EKO CENTAR): 11000 Belgrade, Rige od Fere 4; tel. (11) 183178; fax (11) 638941; e-mail irenam@eunet.yu; Contact Vukasin Pavlović.

Institute for Plant Protection and the Environment: 11000 Belgrade, POB 936, T. Drajzera 9; tel. (11) 660049; f. 1945; Dir Dr Dmitrije Matijević.

NON-GOVERNMENTAL ORGANIZATIONS

Belgrade Ecological Camp (Beogradski Ekoloski Kamp): 11000 Belgrade, Kneza Viseslava 27; tel. (11) 3248035; fax (11) 543873.

Blue Dragon Centre (Nezavisni Istraživacki Centar 'Plavi Zmaj'): 21205 Stremski Karlovci, M. Stratimirovića 3, P. fah. 7; tel. and fax (21) 881662.

Ecological Movement of Belgrade (Ekoloski Pokret Beograda—EKOB): 11000 Belgrade, Agostina Neta 28–42; tel. and fax (11) 161824; Contact Mladen Gvero.

Ecological Movement of Novi Sad (Ekoloski Pokret grada Novog Sada): 21000 Novi Sad, Vojvodanskih brigada 17; tel. and fax (21) 29096; e-mail zelenis@eunet.yu; internet www.go.to/ekopokret; f. 1990; environmental protection, affiliated with over 150 organizations, mostly schools and institutes; Gen. Man. Nikola Aleksić.

Green Circle Ecological Society (Ekolosko Drustvo 'Zeleni Krug'): 11000 Belgrade, Brače Nedića 29.

Josif Pancić Biological Research Society (Biolosko Istrazivacko Drustvo 'Josif Pancić'): 11000 Belgrade, Bioloski fakultet, Studentski trg 16; tel. (11) 3226221; e-mail bid@classroom.opennet.org; Contact Branko Karapandza.

Yugoslav Green Party: Belgrade, Mutapova 12; tel. (11) 4447030; f. 1990; environmental party open to all citizens regardless of national, religious or racial affiliation; Pres. Dragan Jovanović.

Žubor Independent Ecological Movement: 11400 Mladenovac, Postanski fah 76; tel. (11) 8213060; fax (11) 8220145; e-mail ekozubar@www.yu; f. 1990; Pres. Malisa Milosević.

Defence

In August 2002 the estimated total strength of the armed forces of the Federal Republic of Yugoslavia (now Serbia and Montenegro) was some 74,500 (including 60,000 conscripts), comprising an army of some 60,000, a navy of an estimated 3,500 and an air force of 11,000. There were also some 400,000 reserves. The length of military service, which is compulsory for men, was reduced to nine months at the end of 2001. Voluntary military service for women was introduced in 1983.

In June 1999 the North Atlantic Treaty Organization's (NATO) air offensive against the FRY was suspended, following the Federal Government's signing of a peace agreement. Under the subsequent UN Security Council Resolution 1244, the NATO-led international Kosovo Force (KFOR) was deployed in the province of Kosovo and Metohija. The UN Security Council established the UN Interim Administration Mission in Kosovo (UNMIK) as the supreme legal and executive authority in the province. In September 1999, following the disarmament of the paramilitary organization, the Kosovo Liberation Army, NATO agreed that the movement be reconstituted as a 5,000-member civil emergency security force, known as the Kosovo Protection Corps. At the end of May 2003 UNMIK comprised 4,097 civilian police officers, 38 military personnel, and a further 4,189 local and international civilian personnel. At July KFOR (which had originally numbered its maximum authorized strength of 50,000) totalled some 23,000 troops; a further reduction in the size of the contingent by the end of 2003 was planned. In June Serbia and Montenegro formally applied to join NATO's Partnership for Peace programme. As part of extensive reforms of the armed forces stipulated by NATO, the military's central command was placed under the control of the Ministry of Defence; it was announced that the period of national service was to be reduced.

Commander-in-Chief of the Army of Serbia and Montenegro: President of Serbia and Montenegro.

Chief of Staff of the Army of Serbia and Montenegro: Col-Gen. Branko Krga.

THE REPUBLICS

Under the Constitution adopted on 27 April 1992, the Federal Republic of Yugoslavia (FRY) comprised the Republics of Montenegro and Serbia. The abolition of the autonomy of the Serbian provinces of Kosovo (Kosovo and Metohija) and Vojvodina was confirmed. The adoption of the Constitutional Charter on 4 February 2003 officially replaced the FRY with the State Union of Serbia and Montenegro. (A new flag, national symbols and anthem were expected to be adopted by the end of 2003.)

MONTENEGRO

(CRNA GORA)

Introduction

The Republic of Montenegro lies in the south-west of Serbia and Montenegro, on the Adriatic Sea. Montenegro had an area of 13,812 sq km and, according to the March 1991 census, a population of 615,035, making a population density of 45 per sq km. In mid-2001 Montenegro had an estimated population of 658,000. The old royal capital, in the highlands above the Adriatic, is Cetinje. The modern capital of Montenegro is Podgorica (formerly Titograd), with a population of 117,875 at the 1991 census.

Montenegro is a Serb territory, first settled by the Slavs in the sixth century AD. The Serbs converted to Eastern Orthodox Christianity in the ninth century. Mihajlo (Michael) of Zeta first united the Serbs in one kingdom in the 11th century. The principality of Zeta was the original Montenegrin state, consisting of the Southern Slav tribes in the inaccessible mountains of the modern Montenegro ('Black Mountains'). Zeta shared the fate of the Serbs generally for the rest of the Middle Ages, eventually falling under Serbian (Raška) rule. Despite the Ottoman advance into Europe, the Montenegrins maintained a precarious independence, emerging as an identifiable political entity by the 15th century. The Montenegrins resisted complete domination by the Venetians or, from the 16th century, by the Ottoman Turks. They remained faithful to the Serbian Orthodox Church, but did not establish a unitary state, being ruled by a succession of different dynasties. Owing to the isolation of Montenegro, the Church, like the state, was effectively independent, ruled by the Vladika (Prince-Bishop) from 1697, a man who was both primate and prince, selected from and by the predominant dynasty of Petrović-Njegoš. The modern principality emerged during the 19th century, its independence having been acknowledged in 1796 and confirmed in 1878. Danilo II (1851–60) renounced the title of Vladika two months after his accession, in January 1852, and assumed the style of Prince. He appointed a cousin as head of the Montenegrin Church in 1855, but himself married. Upon his assassination he was succeeded by his nephew, Nikola.

With the revival of a Serbian principality, Montenegrin policy was guided by its ethnic-Serb roots and an alignment with its co-religionists. In 1910 Montenegro was proclaimed a kingdom, under Nikola I. Montenegro supported Serbia in the Balkan Wars of 1912–13 and gained part of the Sandžak, on its north-eastern borders. Montenegro also supported Serbia in the First World War, but was occupied by Habsburg troops in 1916. During the War the Montenegrins joined in negotiations to form a common Southern Slav state. The Montenegrin royal family did not acquiesce in the loss of its power (maintaining a government-in-exile until the death of Nikola I in 1921), but, nevertheless, the Serbian dynasty occupied the new throne of the Kingdom of Serbs, Croats and Slovenes (from 1929, Yugoslavia). In the Second World War Montenegro regained a nominal independence, as a client of Fascist Italy, but support for Tito's (Josip Broz) Partisan resistance was strong and after the War Montenegro, with the additional territory of the city-state of Cattaro (now Kotor), became a constituent republic of federal Yugoslavia.

The Montenegrins were well represented in the ruling Communist party and in the Yugoslav People's Army (YPA). During the 1980s, following the death of Tito, Montenegro's traditional alliance with Serbia once more became evident. In 1988 this was ensured by allegedly Serbian-organized demonstrations, which brought about the replacement of the Montenegrin communist leadership with conservatives in sympathy with the Serbian leader, Slobodan Milošević. Similarity to the Serbian situation was further demonstrated by the elections of 1990. The ruling communists amended the republican Constitution, to provide for a unicameral Assembly, with 125 seats, and a directly elected State President, replacing the previous collective Presidency. In the elections of 9 December the ruling League of Communists of Montenegro (subsequently named the Democratic Party of Montenegrin Socialists—DPMS) won a majority of seats (83), while the republican branch of the Alliance of Reform Forces (ARF) won 17. The communist presidential candidate, Momir Bulatović, defeated the ARF candidate in a second round of voting, on 23 December.

During the early 1990s Montenegro loyally supported Serbia in the political crises of Yugoslavia. Bulatović, the President of Montenegro, did cause some surprise when he accepted European Community (EC) peace proposals, in October 1991. Serbia, alone of the Yugoslav republics, had rejected the plan. There was some tension in relations between Montenegro and Serbia following this action and the declaration of sovereignty adopted by the Montenegrin Assembly, on 18 October. The assertion of republican over federal law was prompted by uneasiness with the civil war and, it was believed, as a pragmatic response to the disintegration of Yugoslavia. It was a formality, intended to ensure proper representation at any future negotiations on the federation, more than a symptom of a distinct Montenegrin nationalism. On 10 January 1992 EC sanctions, imposed on Montenegro in the previous year, were lifted, and, five days later, the Montenegrin Constitution, adopted in November 1991, was amended in order to comply with EC criteria for recognition.

In April 1992, one month after its inhabitants had voted overwhelmingly in a referendum to remain within a federal Yugoslavia, Montenegro joined with Serbia in claiming all the international functions of the Socialist Federal Republic of Yugoslavia (SFRY), following the secession from it of the other four republics. The Federal Republic of Yugoslavia (FRY), comprising Serbia and Montenegro, was created on 27 April. From 30 May UN sanctions were imposed on the new country. On 12 October Montenegro adopted a new Constitution, in which the republic was defined as part of the FRY. On 10 January 1993 Bulatović was re-elected President of the republic, after defeating his nationalist rival, Branko Kostić, by a substantial margin. On 5 March Milo Djukanović, the republican premier, formed a coalition Government.

Montenegro's relations with Serbia deteriorated in the mid-1990s. Following the imposition, in mid-1993, of an import-export licensing system by Serbia, Montenegro retaliated by introducing similar trade controls. Furthermore, Serbia's endeavours to disestablish both republics' defence and foreign ministries were seen as further attempts to erode Montenegrin sovereignty and to undermine Bulatović's power. Increasingly, in 1993, Montenegro pursued foreign relations independently of Serbia, concluding trade agreements with Italy and Albania. The Montenegrin foreign minister tried to station UN monitors on the republic's borders with Bosnia and Herzegovina to ensure no sanctions were being broken. Although the various elements of the Montenegrin coalition Government held differing views on the future form that their state should take, all agreed on the preservation of the republic's sovereignty when confronted with Serbia's attempts to erode it.

President Bulatović had spoken in favour of Montenegro's autonomy, if not outright independence. By mid-1995, however, he seemed to be fully supportive of the policies of Slobodan Milošević, the Serbian President, even over such controversial issues as the resettlement of Serb refugees from the Krajina (Croatia) in August 1995, and the fate of the Bosnian Serb military commander, Ratko Mladić, whom he endorsed. Later, Bulatović also backed Milošević in his demands for the resignation of Radovan Karadžić, President of the Serb Republic of Bosnia and Herzegovina.

Despite this apparent reversal, members of the republican Government again sought to determine Montenegro's own foreign policy. The Prime Minister, Djukanović, publicly announced his desire for the rapid integration of the republic into the international community, including such institutions as the World Bank and the International Monetary Fund. The Serbian and Federal Governments, on the other hand, refused to seek admission to such organizations, arguing that the 'rump' Yugoslavia was the legitimate continuation of the SFRY, and, as such, its membership should be automatic. Further disagreements between the two republics in the mid-1990s included the progress of privatization, which was much further advanced in Montenegro, and Serbian attempts to assert ownership over two airports and other state property in Montenegro.

The Prime Minister, Djukanović, stated in May 1996 that the majority of Montenegrins would be in favour of remaining within the FRY; however, relations between the republican governments continued to deteriorate in the late 1990s. The Serbian Government's annulment of local election results in late 1996 was opposed by Djukanović's new administration (elections to the Republican Assembly in November had given the DPMS an increased parliamentary majority). In early 1997 Djukanović publicly declared Milošević unfit to hold public office, an opinion which led not only to inter-republican division, but also contributed to a rift between the premier and his former mentor, Bulatović, the Montenegrin President. In March the premier's refusal to remove any anti-Milošević ministers from his Cabinet, on the orders of Bulatović, contributed to his dismissal as deputy leader of the DPMS. The factionalism within the ruling DPMS deepened during 1997. In June Djukanović's supporters opposed the party's backing of Milošević's candidature in the federal presidential election and, in the following month, dismissed Bulatović from the DPMS leadership, claiming he was too closely allied with the Serbian Government. Elections to the republican presidency, held on 5 and 19 October, were dominated by acrimony between the incumbent President and the premier, who were both DPMS candidates, albeit for opposing factions. Djukanović was eventually elected President, although Bulatović declared the result invalid.

On the eve of Djukanović's inauguration, in January 1998, supporters of the outgoing President stormed government buildings in Podgorica, killing two policemen. Following continuing violent protests, an agreement was reached which provided for early legislative elections, on 31 May. The Republican Assembly approved the establishment of a transitional Government in early February, of which Djukanović's DPMS faction formed the majority. Bulatović's bloc refused to participate in the new administration and formed the Socialist People's Party of Montenegro. The results of elections to the Republican Assembly in May confirmed the popularity of Djukanović's anti-Milošević stance, his party winning an outright majority. A new coalition Government was appointed in July, dominated by the 'rump' DPMS and led by Filip Vujanović.

Montenegrin suspicions of Serbia's insidious domination of the FRY was further fuelled in May 1998, when Bulatović was appointed Prime Minister of a new Federal Government, which the Republican Assembly refused to recognize. Bulatović annulled the regulation whereby both republics had to be consulted on federal appointments and began to remove Montenegrin officials from the FRY's institutions. This was in response to the replacement, in June, of Montenegrin members of the federal Chamber of Republics by DPMS representatives, in an attempt to curtail any attempts by Milošević to increase his presidential powers. In early August the Montenegrin administration announced that it would suspend links with the Federal Government until Bulatović resigned from his office in favour of a pro-Djukanović candidate. However, this stance was not heeded and Bulatović remained in power.

The situation worsened in early 1999, with the Montenegrin administration refusing to acknowledge decisions taken by the increasingly Serbian-dominated Federal Government. The escalating ethnic conflict in Kosovo and Metohija involved the Serbian security forces and ethnic Albanians; however, the ensuing NATO-led aerial bombardment of the FRY in March–June affected Montenegro as well as Serbia. Despite assurances from NATO that it would attempt to fulfil the request made in late April, to save the Republic from bombing, Montenegro suffered even greater damage. The Federal Government responded to the commencement of the air offensive by declaring a state of war, which the Montenegrin Government refused to recognize and instead demanded a halt to Milošević's policy. Montenegrin citizens were divided in their opinion and it was feared that the NATO aerial attack would provoke a civil war between supporters of Milošević and the Republic's anti-Milošević, relatively pro-Western, Government. In March the Republican Assembly adopted a resolution that requested all parties to work to preserve domestic peace and tolerance and the foreign ministry issued a statement excluding itself from the federal decision to sever diplomatic links with several NATO members. On 20 April Djukanović refused to comply with an order from President Milošević to place Montenegrin security forces under federal military command.

In mid-May 1999 Djukanović met Western European leaders, creating further tension between the two Republics. After a peace agreement was enforced in June the Republican Government drafted a proposal to abolish the federation and replace it with an association of the states of Serbia and Montenegro. It announced that a referendum on independence for the Republic would be held if Milošević failed to agree to the demands. Although by August 2000 a referendum had not taken place, relations between Montenegro and Serbia continued to deteriorate. The adoption of a citizenship law by the republican legislature, in October 1999, was seen as a step towards eventual secession. Furthermore, in November, following the failure of inter-republic negotiations, the Montenegrin Government adopted the German Deutsche Mark as its official currency alongside the depreciated dinar, hitherto the most significant attempt to achieve greater independence. The Federal Government responded by imposing a partial economic blockade on the Republic and, in January 2000, its Constitutional Court ruled Montenegro's adoption of the German currency to be illegal. In December 1999 the federal army's temporary seizure of Montenegro's main airport at Podgorica raised concern amongst Montenegrins of the FRY's willingness to use force to undermine republican authority. In January 2000 Serbian police blocked the export of food to Montenegro, thus raising the price of basic foods and increasing the high unemployment rate. At the beginning of March Serbia imposed a full economic embargo on Montenegro. In May the republican premier, Filip Vujanović, declared that the Yugoslav federation no longer existed, having been reduced to a loose confederation of Montenegro and Serbia.

As a result of growing discontentment with the Serbian domination of the Federal Assembly and foreign policy, Montenegro aimed to be accepted and treated as an independent and equal player in international relations. The Republic concentrated on improving relations with Albania and on securing funding from Western Governments. In June 2000 Vujanović met the Chief Prosecutor for the International Criminal Tribunal for the former Yugoslavia to discuss co-operation and, in the same month, ministers attended a session of the UN Security Council to give their views regarding the situation in the FRY. In July Djukanović refused to condemn NATO aggression against the FRY. Such actions infuriated federal President Milošević, who repeatedly demonstrated his power, politically and militarily, over the smaller republic. In May the Federal Assembly ignored the Montenegrin Assembly's nomination of a 20-member delegation to the Chamber of Republics. In the following month, the approval of anti-terrorism federal legislation was perceived to be an infringement of Montenegrins' constitutional rights. Constitutional changes, introduced in July, allowed the federal President and Chamber of Republics to be directly elected. This development reinforced Serbian domination of the FRY and thus further alienated Montenegrin leaders. Djukanović claimed inter-republican relations were at an all-time low, and sent a warning to the international community that, unless Serbian authority was curbed, the region faced further crisis. He also announced that Montenegro would not participate in federal elections, to be held in September.

Several changes in the Montenegrin Government took place in 1999–2000. In December 1999 the Minister of Foreign Affairs, Branko Perović, resigned after being charged by an Italian court for involvement in the illegal import and export of goods to the Italian 'mafia'. He was replaced by Branko Lukovac. In July 2000 Savo Djurdjevac was elected Deputy Prime Minister and

Miodrag Gomilanović appointed the Minister of the Environment.

Despite many discussions over Montenegro's possible secession, most ministers preferred an equal union with a reformed, democratic and Europe-orientated Serbia. The partial municipal elections held on 11 June 2000 were considered a reliable indicator of the results of a referendum on Montenegro's future status in the FRY, with the results showing that public opinion was divided. The ruling 'For a Better Life' coalition won 28 out 54 possible seats in the Podgorica municipal assembly. The pro-Milošević Coalition for Yugoslavia, led by Bulatović, won 22 seats. Milošević supporters made even greater gains in Herceg Novi, where the Coalition for Yugoslavia won 19 of 35 seats. The ruling coalition gained only 14 seats. The pro-independence Liberal Alliance of Montenegro (LAM), which precipitated the elections by leaving the governing coalition, fared worse, winning only four seats in Podgorica and two in Herceg Novi. The results were a disappointment to Djukanović's Government. The assassination of Goran Zugić, an adviser to Djukanović, 10 days before the elections, raised the fear that the federal authorities were trying to encourage instability in Montenegro. However, despite Milošević's evident control over republican matters, by mid-2000 Montenegro had succeeded in increasing its role in international affairs and had gained the support of neighbouring countries and major Western powers.

In July 2000 the Montenegrin Republican Assembly voted to reject constitutional amendments, approved by the federal legislature, which provided for direct election to the federal presidency and Chamber of Republics and effectively reduced Montenegro's status within the FRY. The Montenegrin Government subsequently announced that the republic would not participate in the federal and legislative elections on 24 September, in protest at the amendments. Since only about 30% of the Montenegrin electorate participated in the elections, as a result of Djukanović's boycott, the new Federal President, Dr Vojislav Koštunica, was obliged to form a government with the Socialist People's Party (the only Montenegrin party to be represented in the legislature). Later that month Djukanović announced proposals that the Yugoslav federation become a loose union of two internationally-recognized, separate states. At the end of December the People's Party of Montenegro, which supported the continuation of the federation, withdrew from the governing coalition in the entity. Djukanović subsequently announced that elections to the Montenegrin Republican Assembly would take place in April 2001.

At the elections to the 77-member Montenegrin Republican Assembly, which were conducted on 22 April 2001, the pro-independence alliance, 'Victory Belongs to Montenegro', led by the DPMS, won 36 seats, while the coalition opposing independence, 'Together for Yugoslavia', led by the Socialist People's Party of Montenegro, won 33 seats, and the Liberal Alliance of Montenegro six seats. Despite having failed to secure a majority in the legislature, Djukanović announced that he would continue to pursue his aim of organizing a referendum on independence. (However, it was unlikely that Djukanović would be able to command the two-thirds' majority required to amend the Constitution.) In May a co-operation agreement was signed between the DPMS, the Social-Democratic Party of Montenegro (SDP) and the LAM, whereby a LAM representative was to become speaker of the Republican Assembly. In late June Vujanović (who had been reappointed Prime Minister) formed a new coalition Government, comprising representatives of the DPMS, the SDP and a junior member of the DPMS alliance, the Democratic Union of Albanians.

Following protracted negotiations on the issue of Montenegro's independence (which were mediated by the EU from November 2001), the government leaders of the FRY and the two entities signed a framework agreement on 14 March 2002, providing for the establishment of a 'Union of States' (to be known as 'Serbia and Montenegro'). Under the accord, the two republics were to maintain separate economies, but share foreign and defence policies, and elect a joint presidency and legislature (in which Montenegro would be guaranteed equal representation to Serbia). (However, Montenegro was entitled to refer the issue of independence to a referendum after a period of three years.) Later in March the LAM withdrew from Djukanović's coalition (thereby ending its narrow majority in the Republican Assembly), in protest at the agreement, which prompted widespread criticism from pro-independence supporters. Nevertheless, on 9 April the Montenegrin Republican Assembly approved the accord by 58 of the 77 deputies (with the LAM

representatives opposing). Four principal pro-independence ministers subsequently resigned from the Montenegrin Government, forcing Vujanović to tender his resignation on 19 April. He was subsequently reappointed to the office of Prime Minister by Djukanović, but, despite further discussions, proved unable to secure majority support in the legislature for a new government. On 19 July, in accordance with the Constitution, the Republican Assembly was officially dissolved and further legislative elections in Montenegro, following the failure of Vujanović to secure majority support for a new government, were scheduled for October.

Elections to the Montenegrin Republican Assembly took place on 20 October 2002: Djukanović's pro-independence coalition, now known as Democratic List for a European Montenegro, secured 39 of the 75 seats, with the Together for Changes coalition (led by Bulatović's Socialist People's Party of Montenegro), which had opposed the planned creation of a looser union with Serbia, receiving 30 seats. In November Djukanović resigned from the office of President (prior to becoming the new Prime Minister), and a presidential election in Montenegro was scheduled for December. The presidential election in Montenegro on 22 December was invalidated by a participation level of 45.9%, following a boycott organized by the Socialist People's Party of Montenegro and the LAM; Vujanović (representing the Democratic List for a European Montenegro) had consequently secured 83.7% of votes cast in the ballot, which was contested by 11 candidates. It was subsequently announced that a further election to the Montenegrin presidency would take place on 9 February 2003. Following protracted disagreement in the Republican Assembly between the DPMS and the allied SDP over the allocation of ministerial portfolios, a new Cabinet, headed by Djukanović, was finally approved by the legislature on 8 January 2003. Meanwhile, in November 2002 a major scandal emerged, after a Moldovan woman claimed that she had been forced to work in a Montenegrin brothel visited by senior Montenegrin officials. The deputy state prosecutor was subsequently arrested on charges of involvement in human trafficking. (In June 2003, however, the charges against him were abandoned, prompting domestic and international protests.)

On 4 February 2003 both chambers of the Federal Assembly approved the Constitutional Charter (which was adopted by the Montenegrin Republican Assembly on 29 January), thereby officially replacing the FRY with the State Union of Serbia and Montenegro. The presidential ballot in Montenegro on 9 February (at which Vujanović secured 82.0% of votes cast) was again declared invalid, with a rate of participation of 46.6% of the registered electorate. The Together for Changes alliance was deeply divided regarding the establishment of the new Union, and again failed to present a candidate. The Montenegrin authorities announced that electoral regulations would be amended to abolish the legal minimum requirement of 50% voter participation, and a third round was scheduled for 11 May. On 25 February, in accordance with the Constitutional Charter, the existing federal and entity legislatures elected a 126-member Assembly of Serbia and Montenegro, comprising 91 Serbian and 35 Montenegrin deputies. On 7 March a former Speaker of the Republican Assembly, Svetozar Marović, was elected unopposed as President of Serbia and Montenegro by the new Assembly. Marović also became Prime Minister, heading a five-member Cabinet, which was approved by the Assembly on 18 March.

At the third poll in Montenegro on 11 May 2003, Vujanović was elected to the presidency, with 63.3% of the votes cast. (Although only about 48% of the electorate had participated in the ballot, regulations had been amended to end the 50% minimum requirement.) Vujanović (who had agreed to the compromise arrangement of a looser union with Serbia following pressure from the EU) subsequently announced that a referendum on the issue of independence would be conducted in Montenegro within three years.

Directory

THE GOVERNMENT

STATE PRESIDENT

President of the Republic: Filip Vujanović (elected 11 May 2003; took office 13 June 2003).

MINISTERS
(July 2003)

A coalition of the Democratic Party of Montenegrin Socialists (DPMS), the Social-Democratic Party of Montenegro (SDP) and the Democratic Union of Albanians (DUA).

Prime Minister: MILO DJUKANOVIĆ (DPMS).

Deputy Prime Minister, with responsibility for the Political System and Internal Affairs: DRAGAN DJUROVIĆ (DPMS).

Deputy Prime Minister, with responsibility for the Financial System and Public Spending: JUSUF KALOMPEROVIĆ (SDP).

Deputy Prime Minister, with responsibility for Economic Policy and Economic Development: BRANIMIR GVOZDENOVIC (DPMS).

Minister of Justice: ZELJKO STURANOVIĆ (DPMS).

Minister of Internal Affairs: MILAN FILIPOVIĆ (Ind.).

Minister of Finance: MIROSLAV IVANISEVIĆ (DPMS).

Minister of Foreign Affairs: DRAGIŠA BURZAN (SDP).

Minister of Education and Science: SLOBODAN BACKOVIĆ (DPMS).

Minister of Culture: VESNA KILIBARDA (Independent).

Minister of Economic Affairs: DARKO USKOKOVIĆ (DPMS).

Minister of Maritime Industry and Transport: ANDRIJA LOMPAR (SDP).

Minister of Agriculture, Forestry and Water Management: MILUTIN SIMOVIĆ (DPMS).

Minister of Tourism: PREDRAG NENEZIĆ (DPMS).

Minister of Trade: SLAVICA MILACIĆ (DPMS).

Minister of the Environment and Town Planning: RANKO RADOVIĆ (Independent).

Minister of Health: MIODRAG PAVLICIĆ (SDP).

Minister of Labour and Social Welfare: SLAVOLJUB STILJEPOVIĆ (DPMS).

Minister for the Protection of Human Rights of Ethnic Groups and National Minorities: JEZIM HAJDINAGA (DUA).

Minister without Portfolio: SUAD NUMANOVIĆ (DPMS).

MINISTRIES

All ministries are based in Podgorica.

Office of the President: Podgorica; fax (81) 42329.

Office of the Prime Minister: Podgorica, Jovana Tomaševića bb; tel. (81) 52833; fax (81) 52246.

Ministry of Agriculture, Forestry and Water Management: 81000 Podgorica, Stanka Dragojevića 2; tel. (81) 242106; fax (81) 246553.

Ministry of Culture: 81000 Podgorica, Njegoševa 2; tel. (81) 225408; fax (81) 224878.

Ministry of Education and Science: 81000 Podgorica, Vuka Karadžića 3; tel. (81) 612999; fax (81) 612996.

Ministry of Finance: 81000 Podgorica, Stanka Dragojevića 2; tel. (81) 242835; fax (81) 224450.

Ministry of Foreign Affairs: 81000 Podgorica, Stanka Dragojevića 2; tel. (81) 246357; fax (81) 224609; e-mail mip@cg.yu.

Ministry of Health: 81000 Podgorica, Trg 'Vektra' bb; tel. (81) 242276; fax (81) 242762.

Ministry of Internal Affairs: Podgorica, Lenjina 6; tel. (81) 5223; fax (81) 52919.

Ministry of Justice: Podgorica, Vuka Karadžića 3; tel. (81) 51355; fax (81) 612780.

Ministry of Labour and Social Welfare: 81000 Podgorica, Vuka Karadžić 3; tel. and fax (81) 612986.

Ministry of Maritime Industry and Transport: 81000 Podgorica, Stanka Dragojevića 2; tel. (81) 245720; fax (81) 243081.

Ministry of Tourism: 81000 Podgorica, Cetinjski Put bb, Poslovna Zgrada 'Vektra'; tel. (81) 234116; fax (81) 234168; e-mail e-mail ministarstvo.turizma@mn.yu; internet www.mturizma.cg.yu.

PRESIDENT AND LEGISLATURE

President

Presidential Election, First Ballot, 22 December 2002

Candidate	Votes	% of votes
Filip Vujanović (Democratic List for European Montenegro) *	175,328	83.7
Dragan Hajduković (Independent)	12,319	5.9
Aleksandar Vasiljević (Serbian Radical Party)	6,448	3.1
Milan Milo Radulović (Party of Natural Law)	3,115	1.5
Others	7,294	3.4
Total †	204,504	100.0

* Coalition, principally comprising the Democratic Party of Montenegrin Socialists, the Social-Democratic Party of Montenegro and the Citizens' Party of Montenegro.
† Excluding 5,094 invalid votes. Percentage of votes is based on total votes cast.

Second Ballot, 9 February 2003

Candidate	Votes	% of votes
Filip Vujanović (Democratic List for European Montenegro) *	174,536	82.0
Dragan Hajduković (Independent)	14,556	6.8
Aleksandar Vasiljević (Serbian Radical Party)	8,734	4.1
Milan Milo Radulović (Party of Natural Law)	3,218	1.5
Others	4,727	5.6
Total †	205,771	100.0

* Coalition, principally comprising the Democratic Party of Montenegrin Socialists, the Social-Democratic Party of Montenegro and the Citizens' Party of Montenegro.
† Excluding 7,001 invalid votes. Percentage of votes is based on total votes cast.

Third Ballot, 11 May 2003

Candidate	Votes	% of votes
Filip Vujanović (Democratic List for European Montenegro)†	141,000	63.3
Dragan Hajduković (Independent)	69,000	30.8
Miodrag Zivković (Liberal Alliance of Montenegro)	8,000	3.9
Total‡	218,000	100.0

* Estimated number of votes cast.
† Coalition, principally comprising the Democratic Party of Montenegrin Socialists, the Social-Democratic Party of Montenegro and the Citizens' Party of Montenegro.
‡ Total excludes an estimated 4,500 invalid votes. Percentage of votes is based on total votes cast.

Republican Assembly

Speaker: RANKO KRIVOKAPIĆ.

Election, 20 October 2002

Party	Votes	% of votes	Seats
Democratic List for European Montenegro	167,166	47.97	39
Together for Changes	133,900	38.43	30
Liberal Alliance of Montenegro	20,365	5.83	4
Albanians Together	8,498	2.44	2
Total (incl. others)	330,199	100.00	75

* Coalition, principally comprising the Democratic Party of Montenegrin Socialists, the Social-Democratic Party of Montenegro and the Citizens' Party of Montenegro.
† Coalition, comprisingthe Socialist People's Party of Montenegro, the Serbian People's Party of Montenegro and the People's Party of Montenegro.
‡ Coalition, principally comprising the Democratic Union of Albanians and the Democratic Alliance of Albanians in Montenegro.
§ Excluding 9,851 invalid votes.

LOCAL GOVERNMENT

For administrative purposes, Montenegro is divided into 21 municipalities. Elections were held on 3 November 1996, in which the DPMS gained control of the majority of municipal councils; further local elections were held in Podgorica and Herceg Novi on 11 June 2000. Elections were again held in 19 municipalities on 15 May 2002, in which a coalition of the DPMS and Social-Democratic Party of Montenegro won control of 10 municipal councils.

Andrijevica (1): Andrijevica; tel. (871) 43338; fax (871) 43171; Pres. of the Assembly VESELIN BAKIĆ.

Bar (2): Bar; tel. (81) 12065; fax (81) 12833; Pres. of the Assembly BORISLAV LALEVIĆ.

Bijelo Polje (3): Bijelo Polje; tel. and fax (84) 32630; Pres. of the Assembly DJORDJIJE LUKIĆ.

Berane (4): Berane; tel. (871) 31954; fax (871) 33357; Pres. of the Assembly SVETO MITROVIĆ.

Budva (5): Budva; tel. (86) 51211; fax (86) 51257; Pres. of the Assembly DJORDJIJE PRIBILOVIĆ.

Danilovgrad (6): Danilovgrad; tel. (81) 812022; fax (81) 811920; Pres. of the Assembly MILORAD KADIĆ.

Žabljak (7): Žabljak; tel. (872) 61717; fax (872) 61222; Pres. of the Assembly DOBRICA ŠLJIVANČANIN.

Kolašin (8): Kolašin; tel. (81) 865907; fax (81) 965143; Pres. of the Assembly MILETA BULATOVIĆ.

Kotor (9): Kotor; tel. (82) 13150; fax (82) 13404; Pres. of the Assembly NIKOLA KONJEVIĆ.

Mojkovac (10): Mojkovac; tel. (84) 72117; fax (84) 72715; Pres. of the Assembly MILISAV ĆORIĆ.

Nikšić (11): Nikšić; tel. (83) 213116; fax (83) 213096; Pres. of the Assembly Dr MILORAD DRLJEVIĆ.

Plav (12): Plav; tel. (871) 51475; fax (871) 51420; Pres. of the Assembly ORHAN REDŽEPAGIĆ.

Plužine (13): Plužine; tel. (83) 71103; fax (83) 71139; Pres. of the Assembly MIJUŠKO BAJAGIĆ.

Pljevlja (14): Pljevlja; tel. (872) 81013; fax (872) 81002; Pres. of the Assembly RADOMAN GOGIĆ.

Rožaje (15): Rožaje; tel. (871) 72975; fax (871) 71383; Pres. of the Assembly NUSRET KALAČ.

Tivat (16): Tivat; tel. (82) 61225; fax (82) 61301; Pres. of the Assembly ZORAN JANKOVIĆ.

Podgorica (17): Podgorica; tel. (81) 224275; fax (81) 224035; Mayor MIOMIR MUGOSA.

Ulcinj (18): Ulcinj; tel. (85) 81413; fax (85) 51909; Pres. of the Assembly SKENDER HODŽA.

Herceg Novi (19): Herceg Novi; tel. (82) 51564; fax (82) 53976; Mayor DJURO CVETKOVIĆ.

Cetinje (20): Cetinje; tel. (86) 31755; fax (86) 31316; Pres. of the Assembly SAVO PARAČA.

Šavnik (21): Šavnik; tel. and fax (83) 66127; Pres. of the Assembly MIOMIR VUJAČIĆ.

SERBIA

(SRBIJA)

Introduction

The Republic of Serbia is a land-locked territory forming the most part of Serbia and Montenegro. The Republic also includes the province of Kosovo and Metohija (formerly known as Kosovo) and the province of Vojvodina, both of which were formerly federal units of the old Yugoslav federation (as Autonomous Provinces within Serbia). Kosovo and Metohija occupies the south-west corner of the republic and Vojvodina comprises the northern part. The capital of Serbia is the federal capital, Belgrade (Beograd—with a population of 1,168,454 in 1991), which lies in the very north of 'Inner' Serbia. At the census of March 1991, the total population of the republic was 9,778,991. Its total area was 88,361 sq km and its population density, therefore, was 111 per sq km. In mid-2001 the population of Serbia was estimated to be 9,993,000.

Serbs settled in the Roman province of Illyria in the sixth century AD. Their conversion to Eastern Orthodox Christianity strengthened the claims of the Eastern Roman ('Byzantine') Empire to suzerainty, although, in the ninth and 10th centuries, the main Southern Slav power was the Bulgarian Empire. Despite Bulgarian, Byzantine and Hungarian pressures, a Serbian kingdom was established in the 12th century. It did not include the northern parts of modern Serbia; the territories of the Serbs were in southern and central Serbia, based on the principality of Raška (Rascia), but including the principalities of Zeta (Montenegro) and Rama or Bosnia. Stefan I of the Nemanjid dynasty was able to end Byzantine rule and, in 1187, Serbian independence was acknowledged by the Emperor. In 1219 St Sava, the son of Stefan I, was consecrated the autocephalous archbishop of the Serbs. The Serbian Orthodox Church was to become the repository of national culture and identity, particularly following the destruction of the medieval empires.

The Serbian state of the Nemanjids declined, but a period of Balkan pre-eminence was secured by the destruction of the Bulgarian and Byzantine armies at Velbuzhde (Küstendil) in 1330. The following year Stefan Dušan ('the Great') succeeded to the principality of Raška and he led the Serbs in campaigns against the other Orthodox powers for dominance in the Balkans. In 1346, as Uroš IV, he was crowned Tsar of the Serbs and Greeks and established a Serbian patriarchate. His capital was at Skopje (Macedonia), although he hoped to conquer Constantinople (Carigrad—now İstanbul, Turkey) and inherit the legitimate claims of the Roman Empire. Dušan the Great (Uroš IV) was succeeded by Uroš V (1355–67), under whom the kingdom disintegrated into feudal despotates. One of the more powerful of the ruling noblemen, Lazar of Raška, attempted to unite the despotates against the advance of the Ottoman Turks, but the power of the Serbs was crushed on the plains of Kosovo Polje (of disputed etymology, but usually translated as 'the Field of Blackbirds'), in 1389. In 1459 Serbia was finally absorbed by the Ottoman Empire. During the following centuries the Serbs preserved their Orthodox Christian culture and proved to be valuable recruits against the Turks, even for the Roman Catholic Habsburgs (Vojvodina became a Habsburg territory, as was, in the early 18th century, northern Serbia).

The modern Serbian state was established during the 19th century. For the details of this, see the Chronology and History. Serbian expansion was opposed by Austria-Hungary, and this consequent involvement of Great-Power politics in the Balkans led to the First World War. Thus, from 1915 Serbia was occupied by forces of the Central Powers, and the exiled Serbian Government agreed to the formation of a Southern Slav (Yugoslav) state to include Montenegro and various Habsburg territories. With the defeat of the Central Powers and the dissolution of the Habsburg Monarchy, this decision was effected. On 4 December 1918 a Kingdom of Serbs, Croats and Slovenes was proclaimed, uniting Serbia, including Macedonia and Kosovo, with Montenegro and the Habsburg lands (modern Croatia, Slovenia and Vojvodina). In August 1921, upon the agreement and ratification of the Constitution, the Serbian Regent from 1914, Prince Aleksandar Karadjordjević, became King Aleksandar I of a Serb-dominated state.

The other nationalities resented Serbian domination of the Kingdom (known as Yugoslavia from 1929) and this added to the violence of the civil war, which erupted after the German invasion of 1941, during the Second World War. The royal family and the Government fled into exile and Serbia was partitioned between the Fascist Croatian state, Hungary and Bulgaria; the 'rump' Serbia was placed under German military administration, the nominal leader being the quisling general, Milan Nedić. The occupation was fiercely resisted, however, and the Allied Powers gave their support to the communist-dominated Partisans of Josip Broz (Tito). They declared King Petar II deposed in 1944 and, after the War, Serbia became part of a federal Yugoslav state. Serbia was one of the constituent republics of communist Yugoslavia, but it included two autonomous regions, Kosovo and Vojvodina, which were also distinct units of the federation (see below).

Serbia remained dissatisfied with the federal arrangement, as the two Autonomous Provinces were *de facto* republics, particularly after the adoption of a new Constitution in 1974. Tito had supported the gradual decentralization of Yugoslavia, but Serb aspirations were placated by their domination of the Yugoslav People's Army (YPA) and of the Communist Party. After Tito's death in 1980 the Serbian authorities began to seek a rearrangement of the balance of power within the republic and in the federation.

In May 1989 Slobodan Milošević became President of the republican State Presidency. A conservative communist, he appealed to Serbian nationalism and granted some constitutional reforms. Thus, in November he secured his position by being re-elected President of the Presidency, in the first direct, secret ballot in Serbia since before the Second World War. On 9 December 1990 he was elected, with over 65% of the votes cast, as the sole President of Serbia, under the new Serbian Constitution. This Constitution made Serbia a republic, rather than a socialist republic, and effectively removed the autonomy of Kosovo (which was renamed Kosovo and Metohija) and Vojvodina. It was approved by referendum in July 1990. The Constitution (which effectively gave Serbia control of three votes, instead of one, in the federal institutions) was not entirely in accordance with the federal Constitution, but Milošević was not challenged. Serbia continued to veto proposals for federal reform and, instead, advocated more centralization.

Opposition to Milošević's Government increased in 1991. The main opposition to Milošević's Socialist Party of Serbia (SPS—as the Serbian League of Communists was renamed in July 1990) was the nationalist Serbian Renewal Movement (SRM). In early 1991 the SRM leader, Vuk Drašković, emerged as the main figure in an anti-communist alliance of opposition parties, which found increasing support in the republic. In March there were mass anti-communist demonstrations in Belgrade against Milošević's policies.

With the onset of civil war, in June 1991, however, the immediate pressure of the opposition abated and the SPS was again able to exploit the nationalism engendered by the conflict, although opposition criticism did not cease completely. With the support of the State Presidency members for Kosovo, Vojvodina and Montenegro, Serbia took effective control of the 'rump' federal Presidency. Internationally, Serbia was widely held to be primarily responsible for the civil war and, in May 1992, UN sanctions were imposed on Serbia.

Following the secession of the other republics from the SFRY, in April 1992 Serbia, along with Montenegro, claimed to be the legitimate successor of the old federation, renaming the country the Federal Republic of Yugoslavia (FRY). In late May a broad opposition alliance, the Serbian Democratic Movement (SDM or DEPOS), was formed, partly as a response to the electoral success that the SPS had enjoyed in the recent federal elections. Republican elections were scheduled for 20 December and Milan Panić, the federal Prime Minister, stood against Milošević for the post of Serbian President.

Although Panić's electoral campaign was initially popular it began to lose momentum in late 1992. The opposition to Milošević was fragmented and the UN did not respond to Panić's request to suspend sanctions during the election period. Milošević, however, had inherited the property and organization of the communists, controlled most of the mass media and exploited his opponent's failure to secure UN concessions. Consequently, he succeeded in being re-elected President, winning 56.3% of the votes cast. His party, the SPS, won the largest share of the seats (101) in the 250-seat Serbian Assembly. The ultra-nationalist Serbian Radical Party (SRP), led by Vojislav Šešelj, took 73 seats and the SDM 49. However, the leader of the SDM and of the SRM, Drašković, claimed that the election was fraudulent and, from 3 February 1993, the SDM deputies began a boycott of the Serbian Assembly. On 2 June, during anti-Government demonstrations in Belgrade, Drašković and his wife were detained by police and badly beaten.

Throughout 1993 tension within the government coalition of the SPS and Šešelj's SRP increased. In October a motion of 'no confidence' in the Government was debated, and supported by the opposition SRM. Threatened by the imminent fall of his Government, President Milošević, on 20 October, dissolved the Serbian parliament and scheduled elections for 19 December.

The political issues of the election campaign were overshadowed by personal rivalry between Milošević and Šešelj. On 5–6 November 1993 numerous SRP members were arrested for various capital crimes. The parts of the media under the Serbian Government's control made much of the events, linking Šešelj to various war crimes in Bosnia and Herzegovina. Šešelj retaliated with counter-accusations of atrocities. An estimated 62% of those able to vote participated in the elections. The SPS won 123 seats in the Assembly, compared to the SDM's 45 and the SRP's 39 seats. The Democratic Party (DP), led by Zoran Djindjić, made the largest gains in the elections, winning 29 seats (compared to the seven it had previously held). The nationalist Democratic Party of Serbia (DPS) won seven seats and the remaining seven seats went to ethnically-based political groups.

Thus, Milošević succeeded in reaffirming his control of the Serbian Government, and in increasing the parliamentary representation of the SPS. Continuing to distance himself from his former nationalist allies, in February 1994 he negotiated the establishment of a coalition with the New Democracy (ND) party, which had been a member of the SDM coalition during the parliamentary elections. A campaign against the independent media followed.

In the mid-1990s, however, there were signs that opposition to Milošević's regime was increasing. The Serbian leadership's blockade of the Bosnian Serbs in September 1994 and the participation of Milošević in the negotiations for a Bosnian peace settlement in November 1995 were unpopular with several nationalist parties and with influential members of the Serbian Orthodox Church. Although in March 1996 Milošević was re-elected leader of the SPS virtually unopposed, he was seen to rely increasingly on figures outside his party for loyalty and support. The Yugoslav United Left movement (YUL)—a coalition of over 20 left-wing organizations, which was dominated by Milošević's wife, Mirjana Marković—consequently gained in influence.

Following the signing of the General Framework Agreement for Peace in Bosnia and Herzegovina in December 1995 the SRM, the DP and the Civic Alliance of Serbia (CAS) agreed to create an informal coalition opposition to the Serbian Government. The coalition, which by now included the DPS, contested the municipal elections, held in November 1996. Zajedno, as the coalition was known, gained control of 14 principal towns, including Belgrade. However, the results were annulled by the SPS-controlled municipal courts, a decision which was upheld by the Serbian Supreme Court. Throughout December mass demonstrations in protest at the invalidation of the results were held, which developed into general protests against the Milošević regime. The Government responded aggressively, closing radio stations, which had reported the protests and imposing a ban on demonstrations, which security forces violently enforced.

The municipal election results (which had been verified by the Organization for Security and Co-operation in Europe—OSCE) were eventually reinstated by the National Assembly in February 1997, following foreign criticism and the threat of international sanctions. Demands for political reform continued throughout the year, however. Nevertheless, in 1997 divisions emerged among the opposition, particularly over the choice of a joint candidate for the forthcoming presidential election. Drašković was nominated as Zajedno's candidate. In May he accused Djindjić of secretly negotiating with the SPS and, in the following month the SRM withdrew from the coalition. In fact, it co-operated with the SPS to remove Djindjić from the mayoralty of Belgrade.

Elections to the republican legislature and presidency were held on 21 September 1997. The United List coalition, led by the SPS, failed to secure an outright majority in the National Assembly, winning 110 of the 250 seats, while the SRP increased its representation to 82 and the SRM gained 45 seats. In the first round of the presidential election none of the candidates secured the requisite majority of the votes. A second round was held on 5 October, in which Zoran Lilić, the United List candidate, was narrowly defeated by the SRP's Šešelj. However, the result was declared invalid as the rate of voter participation had been less than 50%. This was owing, in part, to a legislative boycott staged by Djindjić's supporters. A further election was scheduled for 7 and 21 December, after which Milan Milutinović, who had replaced Lilić as the United List nominee, was declared the republican President. There were doubts as to the validity of the ballot, which, nevertheless, was endorsed by the Serbian election commission. A coalition Government, again headed by Mirko Marjanović and comprising SRP, SPS and YUL members, was eventually formed in March 1998. Šešelj was appointed Deputy Prime Minister.

The new administration's main concern in 1998 and 1999 was the conflict in Kosovo and Metohija (see below) and the effects of the international sanctions imposed on the region. In October 1998 the Government attempted to quell growing domestic unrest by imposing a ban on foreign media broadcasts and suspending publication of independent newspapers. The peace plan for Kosovo accepted by the federal authorities in the following month was severely criticized by the Serbian Government. The discovery, in January 1999, of the bodies of 45 ethnic Albanians in the Kosovo village of Račak provoked international condemnation of Serbian authorities, which were increasingly considered the aggressors in the escalating violence. In May the Serbian Minister of the Interior, Vlajko Stojiljković, was indicted by the International Criminal Tribunal for the former Yugoslavia (ICTY), in The Hague, Netherlands, on charges of war crimes.

On 14 June 1999 ministers and legislative deputies from the SRP temporarily withdrew from the Serbian Government and parliament in protest at the federal authorities' acceptance of the peace plan proposed by the international community. Nevertheless, on 24 June the Serbian National Assembly voted to end the state of war in the FRY, declared in March following the commencement of the NATO aerial bombardment. In October Drašković claimed that an automobile collision, in which he was injured and four SRM officials killed, had been a deliberate attempt to kill him. Indeed, the hitherto unknown Serbian Liberation Army subsequently claimed responsibility for the attack. In early 2000 opposition leaders demanded that local government, legislative and presidential elections be conducted in Serbia by the end of April. In January the Serbian paramilitary leader and war-crimes suspect, Zeljko Raznatović (Arkan), was killed in Belgrade. In the following month Milošević was re-elected President of the SPS.

Several changes occurred in the composition of the republican National Assembly and Government in 2000. In May the SRM boycotted the parliamentary sessions, in protest at the Serbian Government's refusal to make public the names of those suspected of killing the four SRM officials in October 1999. As a result of the opposition boycott, all the candidates chosen to represent Serbia in the federal upper house were from the pro-Milošević ruling coalition. This was in spite of legislation, passed in April 2000, providing for deputies to be elected to the Chamber of Republics according to a proportional system, in order to reflect the multi-party composition of the Serbian Assembly. Of the 20 deputies elected, nine represented the Milošević-led SPS, nine were from the SRP, and two were delegates of the YUL. In mid-June Drasković was shot and slightly injured. The Serbian authorities were widely believed to have been involved in the attack; however, the Government maintained that Montenegro was responsible for the assassination attempt and accused the USA of inciting unrest in Serbia.

Anti-Government rallies in May 2000, led by the student resistance movement, Otpor, were frequent and often led to violent clashes. In mid-May the Serbian Government took control of the independent television station, Studio B, as well as two other independent radio stations, resulting in further protests. Serbian relations with Montenegro worsened as the Montenegrin Government continued its attempts to seek independence, and in March Serbia imposed an economic blockade on Montenegro.

At federal presidential and legislative elections on 24 September 2000 Milošević was defeated by Dr Vojislav Koštunica, the leader of an alliance of 18 opposition parties, known as the Democratic Opposition of Serbia (DOS). Following considerable domestic and international pressure, Milošević finally relinquished the presidency on 6 October, and Koštunica was inaugurated on the following day. All remaining international sanctions in force against Serbia were subsequently ended. Despite continued hostility from supporters of Milošević, the DOS negotiated an agreement with the SPS in mid-October; the Serbian legislature was to be dissolved, and a transitional cabinet installed in the entity, pending elections to the Serbian National Assembly. The new transitional Serbian Government, in which

the SPS retained the premiership, was installed later that month. In the elections to the 250-member Serbian National Assembly on 23 December 2000 the DOS secured a substantial majority, with 176 seats, while the SPS won 37 seats and the SRP 23 seats. In January 2001 Djindjić (whose DP was a prominent party in the DOS) was elected to the Serbian premiership, and a new Government, comprising representatives of the alliance, was installed later that month.

In late June 2001, following continued international pressure for the authorities to co-operate with the ICTY, the Serbian Government approved a decree, providing for the extradition of Milošević and other indicted war criminals to the ICTY. Supporters of Milošević subsequently staged a large demonstration in Belgrade, in protest at his proposed extradition. The Serbian Government refused to comply with a ruling by the federal Constitutional Court that the decree was invalid, and on 28 June (shortly before an important international donor conference was to take place) Milošević was extradited to the ICTY. On the following day Zoran Žižić resigned from the office of Federal Prime Minister, in protest at Milošević's extradition (which had been strongly opposed by the Socialist People's Party of Montenegro—SPP). In July Koštunica appointed Dragiša Pešić, also a member of the SPP and hitherto Federal Minister of Finance, to the post. Later that month a reorganized Federal Government, proposed by Pešić, was approved in the legislature.

In August 2001 the division between Koštunica and Djindjić, resulting from the Serbian Government's decision to extradite Milošević, was further exacerbated by the killing in Belgrade of a security agent, who had reportedly been investigating alleged connections of prominent state officials to organized crime. Koštunica accused Djindjić's administration of failing to address widespread crime, and withdrew the DPS ministers from the Government (although the party officially remained within the DOS coalition). At the end of August a district court in The Hague dismissed a legal challenge by Milošević against his detention and arraignment at the ICTY, on the grounds that the Dutch judiciary had no jurisdiction over the Tribunal. In early September Djindjić declared that Milutinović (who had also been indicted in May 1999) had official immunity from prosecution during the tenure of his presidency.

In October 2001 the initial indictment against Milošević relating to Kosovo was amended, henceforth alleging that he had organized security-force operations against Kosovar Albanians, which had resulted in the expulsion of 80,000 civilians from the province. (In September investigators announced that five mass graves, containing remains of civilians killed during the conflict in Kosovo, had been discovered.) Also in October Milošević was further indicted in connection with war crimes perpetrated in Croatia in 1991–92; he was accused of ordering the forcible removal of the majority of the non-Serb population from one-third of the territory of Croatia, with the aim of incorporating the region into a Serb-dominated state. The former Commander of the Yugoslav Navy, Pavle Strugar, surrendered to the ICTY later in October 2001, and a further senior officer travelled voluntarily to The Hague in early November. Later in November Milošević (hitherto indicted for crimes against humanity, breaches of the 1949 Geneva Convention, and violations of the laws or customs of war) was charged, for the first time, with genocide, in connection with the atrocities perpetrated by Serbian forces during the planned removal of Muslims and Croats from large areas of Bosnia and Herzegovina in 1992–95. He continued to refuse to recognize the authority of the ICTY, and 'not guilty' pleas were submitted on his behalf for all three indictments. In December the European Court of Human Rights announced that Milošević had initiated a further challenge to the legality of his detention and trial in the Netherlands. Milošević's trial officially commenced on 12 February 2002 (with testimony on the charges relating to Kosovo), and was expected to continue for at least two years. Milošević, who had decided to conduct his own defence, continued to deny all charges, and strongly condemned the NATO bombardment of Serbia in 1999.

In December 2001 the Speaker of the Serbian National Assembly, who was the deputy leader of the DPS and a close associate of Koštunica, was obliged to resign from the post, after accusing parties belonging to the DOS coalition of electoral malpractice. In January 2002 the Federal Minister of Finance, who had opposed a decision by the National Bank of Yugoslavia to declare four Serbian banks insolvent (in accordance with structural reforms), also tendered his resignation. In March one of the Serbian Deputy Prime Ministers, Momčilo Perišić, was arrested, and subsequently resigned, after military intelligence sources claimed to have evidence that he had given classified information to a US diplomat. Djindjić rejected demands by Koštunica that he also submit his resignation over the issue, and requested the dismissal of the head of the military security service responsible for Perišić's arrest. Perišić claimed that the charges had been fabricated, in an attempt to cause the dissolution of Djindjić's Government. In June the DPS withdrew from the Serbian National Assembly, in protest at the expulsion of 21 DPS deputies. The Serbian Government was reorganized in the same month. In July it was announced that presidential elections in Serbia would be brought forward to 29 September, to allow the extradition of Milutinović to the ICTY. At the end of July the DOS coalition formally expelled the DPS.

In June 2002 a reorganization of the Serbian Government was approved in the National Assembly. It was announced that presidential elections in Serbia would be brought forward to 29 September, to allow the extradition of Milutinović (who had been indicted in 1999) to the ICTY. In July the ruling Serbian DOS coalition formally expelled the DPS. (DPS deputies had withdrawn from the National Assembly in June.)

In August 2002 Koštunica announced that he intended to seek election to the Serbian presidency in September (since the office of Federal President was no longer to exist under the agreement for the creation of a joint state). The other most prominent presidential candidate was Miroljub Labus, the incumbent Federal Deputy Prime Minister and Minister of Foreign Trade, who was supported by Djindjić. In the same month Milošević, from The Hague, appointed Bogoljub Bjelica as leader of the SPS (rejecting the candidate nominated by the party). At the Serbian presidential election, which was conducted on 29 September, Koštunica won some 30.9% of the votes cast, while Labus received 27.4% and Šešelj 23.2% of the votes; the rate of participation was 55.5% of the registered electorate. Since no candidate had secured an outright majority of votes, a second round between Koštunica and Labus was scheduled for 13 October. However, this second ballot, at which Koštunica secured some 68.4% of the votes cast, was declared invalid, owing to participation of only 44.0% of the electorate (lower than the required minimum level of 50%). (Šešelj had urged his supporters not to participate in the poll, while it was reported that Djindjić had also unofficially supported a boycott.)

A third presidential poll in Serbia on 8 December was again annulled, owing to a voter turnout of only about 45.0% of the registered electorate; Koštunica had won 57.7% of votes cast. On 30 December, under the terms of the Constitution, Milutinović was replaced, on an interim basis, by the Speaker of the Serbian National Assembly, Nataša Mićić.

On 20 January 2003 Milutinović was voluntarily transferred to the ICTY, where he subsequently pleaded not guilty to charges relating to crimes perpetrated during the 1999 conflict in Kosovo. On 4 February 2003 both chambers of the Federal Assembly approved the Constitutional Charter (which was adopted by the Serbian National Assembly on 27 January), thereby officially replacing the FRY with the State Union of Serbia and Montenegro (see the chapter on Montenegro). Ethnic Albanians in Kosovo voiced their opposition to the province's inclusion in the new Union as part of Serbia, and continued to demand independence. Later in February Šešelj surrendered to the ICTY, where he was charged on several counts in connection with the forcible removal of the non-Serb population from parts of the former Yugoslavia in 1991–95.

On 12 March 2003 Djindjić, having survived an apparent assassination attempt in February, was shot dead by an unknown assailant outside government buildings in Belgrade. Mićić immediately imposed a state of emergency in Serbia. A government statement attributed Djindjić's killing to leaders of an organized criminal group, known as the Zemun Clan. Some 1,200 suspects, including a former Serbian Minister of Security, were subsequently arrested for questioning, some for their alleged connections with the Zemun Clan. The former Federal Minister of Internal Affairs, Zoran Živković, was nominated by the DP to replace Djindjić, and was approved by the Assembly as the new Serbian Prime Minister on 18 March. He immediately took measures to address organized crime and corruption, gaining the approval of the internaitonal community. At the end of March copies of security forces discovered the remains of Ivan Stambolić, who had been abducted in August 2000. The Serbian authorities issued an international arrest warrant for Mirjana Marković and her son (who were in hiding in Russia), in connection with the killing of Stambolić; Milošević (who had become

an enemy of Stambolić in the 1980s) was subsequently also charged. Later that month the state of emergency in Serbia was ended and some 45, including Šešelj, were charged with alleged involvement in the assassination of Djindjić. These suspects were accused of arranging his killing with leaders of the Zemun Clan, as part of a conspiracy to overthrow the Government and reinstate an administration of former associates of Milošević, which would reverse the policy of co-operation with the ICTY. Some 10 of those charged, including a principal suspect, Milorad Luković, the former head of a special security unit, remained at large. In early May a former Serbian Minister of Security, Jovica Stanišić and his deputy, Franko Simatović, already in detention in Belgrade in connection with Djindjić's assassination, were also indicted by the ICTY for war crimes perpetrated against Croats and Muslims. Simatović was transferred to the ICTY at the end of May, and Stanišić in early June. Later in June the Serbian authorities finally arrested Col Veselin Sljivancanin, who had been indicted by the ICTY for the murder of more than 200 Croats captured during the Serb occupation of the Croatian town of Vukovar in 1991. He pleaded guilty at the Tribunal in early July. On 30 July the Serbian Government appointed a special prosecutor for war crimes, in the hope that the ICTY would assign some of its cases to Serbian courts.

Kosovo

The former autonomous province of Kosovo, officially known as Kosovo and Metohija from 1990, lies in south-west Serbia. Its capital is Priština. Kosovo (Kosova to the Albanians) is populated by a large ethnic Albanian majority. The region was important historically to the Serbs as well as to the Albanians (the Albanian national revival began here in 1878, with the foundation of the League of Prizren). The Serbs remained suspicious of ambitions for a 'Greater Albania' and seldom tolerated nationalist aspirations. Under President Milošević, the Serbian Government implemented policies designed to encourage resettlement of Kosovo by ethnic Serbs, a total of 50,000 Serbs and Montenegrins having left the province from 1981.

The Albanians did achieve some national rights under the federal state, notably the achievement of the status of an Autonomous Province and participation in communist Yugoslavia as a federal unit. Serbs and Montenegrins dominated the provincial administration and the communist apparatus until the fall of the Serb head of the security services, Aleksandar Ranković, in 1966. There were then demands for a Kosovo republic, and some concessions were granted to both the Autonomous Provinces (the other being Vojvodina—see below) by the federal authorities in 1968. These rights were confirmed in the new Yugoslav Constitution of 1974. However, the federal and Serbian authorities remained repressive of nationalist groups, accusing them of separatist sympathies. Certainly the Albanians of Kosovo were not culturally threatened and the leadership of the local League of Communists and provincial administration was predominantly ethnic Albanian. The main demand of the nationalists was for republican status.

In March and April 1981 there were nationalist riots in Kosovo, mainly in Priština, which were vigorously repressed after a state of emergency had been declared. The communist authorities instituted a policy of 'differentiation', which involved the purging of any Party member or official who did not actively denounce the campaign for a seventh republic. Between 1981 and 1990, according to the United Kingdom-based human-rights group, Amnesty International, over 7,000 Albanians were arrested and imprisoned in Kosovo, for nationalist activities.

The rise of Serb nationalism, from the mid-1980s, exacerbated tensions in the province. From 1985 the issue of Serb and Montenegrin emigration became of note in the Serbian media, with allegations of harassment by the ethnic Albanians. By 1987 Serbian nationalists were regularly citing incidents of what was increasingly described as 'genocide'. The rise of Slobodan Milošević to the Presidency of Serbia was indicative of the increasingly nationalist mood of the Serbs. The 1974 Constitution was perceived to be against Serbian interests and the new leadership sought to reduce the autonomy of the two provinces.

In November 1988, under pressure from Serbia, the prominent Albanian politician, Azem Vlasi, resigned from the Kosovo politburo, causing widespread protests in the province. In February 1989 he was dismissed from the Central Committee of the League of Communists of Yugoslavia, causing further protests in Kosovo. In March he was arrested, together with other Albanian leaders, and charged with 'counter-revolutionary' activities; their trial became a source of continuing tension, until their release in April 1990. The situation deteriorated in this year and, in March, Serbia assumed direct control of the Kosovo police force, causing the resignation of Yusuf Zehjnulahu, the Chairman (premier) of the Executive Council (Government) of Kosovo, and, by May, of every ethnic Albanian member of the provincial Government.

The new Serbian Constitution of 1990 removed the remaining vestiges of autonomy from the two provinces. A republic-wide referendum on the new Serbian Constitution, largely boycotted by the Albanians, was conducted on 2 July (it was formally promulgated on 28 September, from when Kosovo was known as Kosovo and Metohija) resulted in a majority of Serbs approving the new Constitution. In response to the holding of the constitutional referendum, 114 of 180 deputies in the Kosovo Assembly met and declared Kosovo independent of Serbia and itself a constituent republic of the SFRY. On 5 July the Serbian authorities dissolved the provincial Assembly and Government. The Kosovo Presidency resigned in protest and Serbia introduced a special administration. By September some 15,000 ethnic Albanian officials had been dismissed and measures limiting the number of Albanians in the education system had been implemented.

The dependence of the provincial administration on central Serbian authority, however, was demonstrated in the federal constitutional crisis of March 1991. The Albanian member for Kosovo on the federal State Presidency was dismissed by the Serbian Assembly on 16 March, and on 18 March the functions of the Kosovo Presidency were temporarily suspended. This action by Serbia, and alleged rights abuses in Kosovo, however, was what the USA used to justify its termination of economic aid to Yugoslavia. Meanwhile, on 7 September 1990, at a meeting in Kačanik, 111 members of the old representative body declared the Kosovo Assembly to have been reconvened and, six days later, proclaimed a basic law of the 'Republic of Kosovo'. As the Kosovo Assembly-in-Exile, based in Zagreb (Croatia), it organized a referendum on independence from Serbia on 26–30 September 1991 (although it was banned by Serbia), which overwhelmingly was in favour of Kosovo becoming a sovereign republic. Elections, also declared illegal by Serbian authorities, were held in the province on 24 May 1992. The Democratic Alliance of Kosovo (DAK) secured the most seats in the 130-seat Assembly, and the DAK leader, Ibrahim Rugova, was elected President of the self-proclaimed 'Republic of Kosovo'.

The new Yugoslav Constitution of April 1992 confirmed Kosovo's loss of status as according to the 1990 Serbian Constitution: the Federal Republic of Yugoslavia (FRY) comprised only the republics of Montenegro and Serbia, with reference made to Kosovo and Metohija and to Vojvodina as 'former autonomous provinces'. The ethnic Albanians in Kosovo did not participate in the 1992 Serbian presidential and parliamentary elections and there were allegations of malpractice by the Serbian authorities. In March 1993, following reports of increased harassment of Kosovar Albanians, the USA threatened to send troops to the area. In July Serbia expelled international monitors working in the region. Controversy continued in 1993–94 over issues such as the closure of Albanian-language schools, the dissolution of the Kosovo Academy of Sciences and renewed Serbian attempts to settle Slavs in the province. In December 1993 republican elections were boycotted in Kosovo, and, in early 1994, the situation remained tense, with reports of a growing armed resistance by Kosovar Albanians, and a large Serbian police and military presence.

Throughout the mid-1990s there were reports of harassment of Kosovar Albanians by Serbian police. The attempted resettlement of Serb refugees in the province, following the August 1995 offensive in the Krajina by the Croatian army, was strongly opposed by the Kosovar Albanians, although the refugees were usually unwilling to locate there. The situation deteriorated further in 1996 with the emergence, in February, of an ethnic Albanian terrorist organization, the Kosovo Liberation Army (KLA—Ushtria Clirimtave e Kosoves). Members of this group, which was based in Switzerland, claimed responsibility for the murder of several Serbs, some of them policemen, in separate incidents in 1996 and 1997. In January 1998, following increased unrest in the region, the KLA announced its intention to achieve independence for Kosovo through armed resistance against the Serbian authorities. Special Serbian security forces were dispatched to the region, leading to the outbreak of open armed conflict. For the details of this, see the Chronology and History.

The response of the international community to the unrest in Kosovo was a further source of discontent to its Albanian population. Limited commitment to resolving the situation had been made: in June 1996 a US Information Agency office was opened in Priština, with a view to initiating Serbian-Kosovan negotiations and in early 1998 the EU's offer to open a monitoring office was rejected by the Serbian authorities. Following the signing of the so-called Dayton accords on peace in the former Yugoslavia in November–December 1995, the maintenance of an 'outer wall' of sanctions against the FRY was mooted by the UN Security Council, if the federation failed to comply fully with the accords or to address the situation of its ethnic minorities. The 'outer wall' included a veto on admission to international organizations, such as the UN and the IMF.

Following the outbreak of armed conflict in the region in 1998, as with Bosnia and Herzegovina, the West seemed primarily concerned with preserving international boundaries. In March the UN Preventive Deployment Force in Macedonia (UNPREDEP) had increased its presence on the border with the FRY. The international community condemned Serbian military action in the province, reimposing sanctions and continually threatening to employ military force against the FRY. However, Western Governments did not formally recognize the 'Republic of Kosovo' and maintained that the province was an integral part of the FRY. Although the 'Contact Group' of Western nations insisted that foreign intervention, in the form of mediation, was essential to ensure the restoration of Kosovo's autonomy, no offer of international support was made to the Kosovar 'government', despite pleas from the DAK.

Negotiations regarding the implementation of a cease-fire in Kosovo and the withdrawal of Serbian security forces continued throughout 1998 and on 13 October Milošević agreed to a proposed peace plan. The DAK, however, opposed the plan, maintaining that independence was Kosovo's main aim. From late October intermittent violations of the cease-fire occurred and on 6 November the deployment of OSCE observers in Kosovo commenced. In December clashes between Serbian security forces and the KLA escalated. In January 1999 the bodies of 45 ethnic Albanians were discovered in the village of Račak. It appeared that those killed were unarmed civilians, although the Serbian Government claimed that they were KLA members. In February–March Serbian and ethnic Albanian delegations, including KLA representatives, attended a peace conference in Rambouillet, Paris (France). Following the resignation from the delegation of the hardliner Adem Demaçi, the Kosovar Albanian delegation signed the peace agreement on 18 March. Negotiations with federal representatives, however, failed, and on 24 March a NATO-led aerial bombardment of the FRY commenced. Serbian security forces in Kosovo subsequently intensified the mass expulsions and large-scale massacres of the ethnic Albanian civilian population, resulting in the continued exodus of refugees from the province. In April NATO aircraft bombed a convoy of ethnic Albanian refugees in Kosovo, killing around 64, apparently owing to confusion over Serbian military targets. By mid-May it was estimated that about 600,000 ethnic Albanian refugees had fled Kosovo to neighbouring countries.

On 3 June 1999 a peace agreement providing for the withdrawal of Serbian forces from Kosovo and the deployment of a joint NATO-Russian Kosovo Peace Implementation Force (KFOR), was approved by the Serbian National Assembly. Under the peace plan's terms, refugees were to be allowed to return and the province was to achieve some autonomy under an Interim Administrative Council, which was formally established in December. Once the Serbian security forces had commenced their withdrawal from Kosovo, NATO suspended its air strikes and the province was divided into five sectors, under the respective control of the United Kingdom, Germany, France, the USA and Italy. The UN Interim Administration Mission in Kosovo (UNMIK) assumed supreme legal and executive authority in the region. In July the first meeting of the newly-formed Kosovo Transitional Council (KTC), a consultative body to UNMIK comprising representatives of the principal political parties and ethnic groups in Kosovo, including the KLA, was held. Rugova, who at first boycotted the KTC, agreed to join the Council in August.

By mid-July 1999 an estimated 700,000 Kosovar Albanians had returned to the province. However, at the same time, some 70,000 Serbian civilians had fled Kosovo, particularly Priština, fearing retaliatory attacks. Indeed, from September violence escalated to include KFOR troops, as well as Serbs and ethnic

Albanians. In the same month NATO acceded to KLA demands that it be reconstituted as a 5,000-member civil emergency security force. The Serbian representatives withdrew from the KTC in protest at the decision (they rejoined in April 2000, when they also agreed to participate, as observers, in the Interim Administration Council). In October 1999 violent rioting by ethnic Albanians in the northern town of Kosovska Mitrovica, which had been divided into separate ethnic Albanian and Serbian regions, broke out. Shortly after this, and following the killing in Priština of a UN official, it was announced that the strength of the UNMIK police force was to be increased. In February 2000, following further ethnic clashes, NATO approved a reinforcement of KFOR, which numbered 30,000 at this time. Nevertheless, intermittent violence continued, and UNMIK and KFOR attracted increasing criticism for failing to protect the region's Serbian minority.

In February 2000 Rugova announced the dissolution of the 'Republic of Kosovo' and of the DAK, signifying a move towards the creation of a single administration, representing Kosovar Albanians and Serbs. In April Eurocorps, the European defence force created in 1993, took over command of KFOR from NATO. The issue of the return of refugees continued to cause problems. At the end of April clashes occurred in Kosovska Mitrovica between Serbs and French KFOR troops over the return of the majority of ethnic Albanians, whom the Serbs claimed had never lived there. In May it was estimated that the return to the region of the vast majority of Serb refugees had not begun. According to the President of the Provisional Executive Council of Kosovo, only 270 ethnic Serbs remained in Priština by the end of May. However, by this time about 822,000 of the estimated 900,000 ethnic Albanian refugees had returned. Campaigns for the release of prisoners were also prevalent. In May a Kosovo Albanian Council urged international organizations to obtain the release of 3,500 ethnic Albanians believed to be held in Serbia. The KTC also demanded the release of prisoners and in April–May ethnic Albanian prisoners in Kosovska Mitrovica threatened to starve themselves until prisoners were liberated from Serbia. Demonstrations also took place. In May, in Niš, 143 Kosovar Albanians, alleged to be members of the KLA, were sentenced to a total of 1,632 years' imprisonment, after being convicted of charges of terrorism. The sentences provoked international condemnation, as well as ethnic Albanian protests.

Following the completion of a voter registration process, local government elections took place in Kosovo on 28 October 2000. Rugova's Democratic League of Kosovo (DLK—which had been formed as a successor organization to the DAK) secured 58% of votes cast to 30 municipal councils, while the Democratic Party of Kosovo (DPK), led by a former KLA Commander, Hashim Thaçi, won 27% of the votes. In late November members of a separatist movement, the Liberation Army of Preševo, Medvedja and Bujanovac (believed to be related to the dissolved KLA) launched an offensive in the Preševo region in southern Serbia, near the border with Kosovo. Attacks against a number of local government officials in Priština were also reported. Serbian authorities threatened to dispatch troops to the region (which formed part of the demilitarized zone under the June 1999 agreement), if KFOR troops failed to suppress the rebel activity. In January 2001 the Danish Minister of Defence, Hans Hækkerup, was nominated by the UN to replace Bernard Kouchner as head of UNMIK. In the same month the UN announced that it had discovered evidence of radioactivity in Kosovo, as a result of the depleted uranium ammunition used by NATO during its air bombardments. Violence continued in the province between the KFOR and ethnic Albanian separatists, who staged numerous attacks against Serbian civilians. In early March the ethnic Albanian rebels signed a cease-fire agreement, after NATO agreed for the first time to allow Serbian forces to enter the demilitarized zone; the troops were to provide support to KFOR in suppressing separatist activity in the province and to deter infiltration into Macedonia by ethnic Albanian militants (see the chapter on the former Yugoslav republic of Macedonia).

In May 2001 UNMIK announced that elections to a legislative assembly would take place in Kosovo on 17 November, under a programme for establishing partial provisional self-government in the province. The assembly would have powers in the sectors of health, education and authority, although supreme executive authority would be retained by the head of UNMIK (who was to retain ultimate executive authority, and control over the province's finances and judiciary). By the stipulated date for the certification of political parties in late July some 28 organizations had registered to contest the elections. Elections to 100 seats of the 120-member Kosovo Assembly were conducted peacefully on 17 November, as scheduled. (The remaining 20 seats were allocated proportionally to Serbs and other ethnic groups.) Rugova's DLK secured 47 seats, while the DPK won 26 seats and a coalition of Serbian parties, known as Povratak (Return), 22 seats. A seven-member presidency for the legislature was established in December. However, repeated attempts to elect Rugova as President of Kosovo proved unsuccessful, owing to a boycott of the vote by the other parties represented in the legislature. In January 2002 a German diplomat, Michael Steiner, replaced Hækkerup as head of UNMIK. On 4 March, following protracted inter-party discussions, Rugova was finally elected President of Kosovo, after it was agreed that a member of the DPK, Bajram Rexhepi, would become Prime Minister. A 10-member Government (in which the DLK held four portfolios and the DPK a further two) was subsequently established. In April the Povratak coalition finally agreed to join the provincial Government.

In early May 2002 Rugova testified against Milošević at the ICTY, providing evidence that the former Yugoslav President had been aware of the war crimes perpetrated by Serb forces in Kosovo. Rugova denied claims by Milošević (who was conducting his own defence) that the KLA had been a terrorist and criminal organization. Steiner announced at the end of July that some 68 parties had registered to contest elections to the four-year term municipal councils, scheduled for October. He also stated that discussions on the future status of Kosovo were dependent on the implementation of the provisional institutions. Voter turnout in the local government elections, which were conducted on 26 October, was estimated at 54%. The DLK won control of 11 of 30 municipalities, including Priština, although this represented a deline in support compared with the previous elections (in which they secured 20 municipalities). The DPK won a majority in four municipalities, while a newly-emerged organization, Alliance for the Future of Kosovo, led by Ramush Haradinaj, won the third-highest number of votes, although not gaining control of a municipality. Serbian parties won a majority in five municipalities. On 25 November UNMIK finally took control of the Serb side of the hitherto divided Kosovska Mitrovica, following an agreement reached with the Serbian Government.

In February 2003 KFOR arrested three prominent members of the KLA, who were subsequently extradited to the ICTY and pleaded not guilty crimes committed at a detention camp during the Kosovo conflict. A fourth suspect evaded arrest in Kosovo, but was detained in Slovenia and transferred to The Hague later in February. The inclusion of Kosovo in the new State Union of Serbia and Montenegro prompted protests among the ethnic Albanian population in Kosovo, who continued to demand independence for the province. Steiner, however, declared that the issue of Kosovo's future status could not be resolved at that time. Following an EU summit meeting in June, which was attended by both Albanian and Serbian representatives from Kosovo, it was agreed that the Kosovan authorities would enter into discussions with the Government of Serbia and Montenegro in July. Direct negotiations were to be conducted on a number of important issues, including energy and transport links, and the return of some 230,000 Kosovar refugees from Serbia and Montenegro. (At that time only about 7,000 refugees had returned to the province since 2000.) On 25 July 2003 the UN Secretary-General appointed a former Finnish Prime Minister, Harri Holkeri, to replace Steiner as head of UNMIK. In early August a deterioration in relations between Kosovan officials and UNMIK was reported. On 3 August an UNMIK police-officer was killed in an ambush near Kosovska Mitrovica (the first fatality suffered by the UN Mission since 1999).

Vojvodina

The other former autonomous province, Vojvodina, was also affected by the changes in Serbia, although the ethnic Serb majority there made them less controversial. Vojvodina had originally been a Hungarian marcher territory or banate, in which the Habsburgs had settled other ethnic groups to defend Christendom against the Ottomans. A large Serb population had first settled there in 1690, when the so-called '30,000 Families', led by Patriarch Arsenije III Crnojević, migrated from the Ottoman-dominated south. In the 19th century the Habsburgs had created a province of Serbian Vojvodina, hoping to satisfy the aspirations of the Serb nationalists. At the end of the Second World War more Serbs had settled there and they became the dominant ethnic group.

Until the late 1980s Vojvodina retained some provincial independence. In October 1988 demonstrations allegedly organized by the Milošević faction secured a communist leadership sympathetic to the new Serbian rulers. The Hungarian Government expressed concern for the rights of the ethnic Hungarian (Magyar) minority, during 1990 and 1991, particularly following the effective removal of Vojvodina's autonomous status in the 1990 Serbian Constitution. This was confirmed by the April 1992 new federal Constitution, which recognized these changes introduced in Serbia's organic law. However, Vojvodina did retain a provincial Assembly to represent the region as a whole. There were a great number of ethnic minorities in Vojvodina, all of which had political or social organizations to represent them. The largest was the Democratic Community of Vojvodina Hungarians (DCVH), which, unlike the Albanian parties of Kosovo and Metohija, did not boycott the Serbian elections of December 1993 and secured representation in the new parliament. With a Serb majority in the province, the republican authorities were more tolerant of manifestations of cultural autonomy for minorities in Vojvodina than in Kosovo.

In the mid- and late 1990s there were signs that opposition was increasing among the inhabitants of Vojvodina to the province's domination by Serbia. On 13 May 1996 a total of 17 political parties, associations and organizations signed a Manifesto for Vojvodina Autonomy. This move was the beginning of a campaign to amend the Serbian Constitution of 1990 and the federal Constitution of 1992 to restore the province's autonomous status, with full legislative, judicial and executive powers. It was feared that the conflict in Kosovo in the late 1990s would spread to Vojvodina or at least encourage calls for independence or further autonomy. Potential conflict emerged in May 2000, following the assassination of SPS member and President of the Provincial Government, Boško Perosević. Opposition parties were blamed for his murder. He was replaced by Damnjan Radenković. Furthermore, in the same month, the Serbian Government's decision to take control of the Studio B television station in Novi Sad, the capital of Vojvodina, led to demonstrations and violent clashes that lasted for several weeks. At the beginning of June opposition parties established a united Vojvodina Democratic Opposition, which demanded political change. The governing coalition in Vojvodina opposed the constitutional changes instigated by President Milošević in July and threatened to declare independence in protest. Elections to the Vojvodina Assembly took place on 24 September, with a second round on 8 October. The Democratic Opposition of Serbia for Vojvodina secured 71.7% of votes cast, and 86 of the 120 seats in the provincial legislature. On 21 January 2002 the Serbian legislature voted in favour of restoring partial autonomy to Vojvodina. In March the Government of the province was reorganized to exclude members of the Democratic Party of Serbia (which had opposed the new legislation in the Serbian National Assembly).

Directory

THE GOVERNMENT

State President

President of the Republic: NATAŠA MIĆIĆ (acting).

MINISTERS
(July 2003)

Prime Minister: ZORAN ZIVKOVIĆ.

Deputy Prime Minister and Minister of Internal Affairs: DUŠAN MIHAJLOVIĆ.

Deputy Prime Ministers: NEBOJSA COVIĆ, ZARKO KORAĆ, JOŽEF KASA, CEDOMIR JOVANOVIĆ.

Minister of Finance and Economy: BOZIDAR DJELIĆ.

Minister of Energy and Mining: (vacant).

Minister of Religious Affairs: VOJISLAV MILOVANOVIĆ.

Minister of Foreign Trade Relations: GORAN PITIĆ.

Minister of Economic Affairs and Privatization: ALEKSANDAR VLAHOVIĆ.

Minister of Transport and Telecommunications: MARIJA RASETA VUKOSAVLJEVIĆ.

Minister of Sport and Education: GAŠO KNEŽEVIĆ.

Minister of Social Welfare: GORDANA MATKOVIĆ.

Minister of Science, Technology and Development: DRAGAN DOMAZET.

Minister of Construction and Town Planning: DRAGOSLAV ŠUMARAĆ.

Minister of Health and Environmental Protection: TOMICA MILOSAVLJEVIĆ.

Minister of Culture: BRANISLAV LEČIĆ.

Minister of Justice and Local Authority: VLADAN BATIĆ.

Minister of Labour and Employment: DRAGAN MILOVANOVIĆ.

Minister of Agriculture: STOJAN JEVTIĆ.

Minister of Trade, Tourism and Services: SLOBODAN MILOSAVLJEVIĆ.

MINISTRIES

Office of the President: 11000 Belgrade, Andrićev venac 1; tel. (11) 184162; fax (11) 3617865; e-mail kprs@ptt.yu.

Office of the Prime Minister: 11000 Belgrade, Nemanjina 11; tel. (11) 685872; fax (11) 659682.

Ministry of Agriculture: 11000 Belgrade, Nemanjina 26; tel. (11) 642276; fax (11) 659146.

Ministry of Construction and Town Planning: 11000 Belgrade, Nemanjina 22–26; tel. (11) 3614652; fax (11) 3614653; e-mail murgs@eunet.yu.

Ministry of Culture: 11000 Belgrade, 11 Nikola Pasic Sq; tel. (11) 3346330; fax (11) 3346100; e-mail kabinet@min-cul.sr.gov.yu; internet www.min-cul.sr.gov.yu.

Ministry of Economic Affairs and Privatization: Belgrade, Srpskih vladara 16; tel. tel. (11) 3617599; fax (11) 3617640; e-mail officemprov@mpriv.sr.gov.yu; internet www.mpriv.sr.gov.yu.

Ministry of Energy and Mining: 11000 Belgrade, 36 Kralja Milana (Srpskih vladara) St; tel. (11) 3346755; fax 3616603; e-mail ljubica.todorovic@mem.sr.gov.yu; internet www.mem.sr.gov.yu.

Ministry of Finance and Economy: 11000 Belgrade, Nemanjina 22–26; tel. (11) 3616361; fax (11) 3616535; e-mail bdjelsc@mfin.sr.gov.yu; internet www.mfin.sr.gov.yu.

Ministry of Foreign Trade Relations: 11000 Belgrade, Gračanička 8; tel. (11) 3617628; fax (11) 3633142; e-mail office@mier.sr.gov.yu.

Ministry of Health and Environmental Protection: 11000 Belgrade, Nemanjina 22–26; tel. (11) 3616298; fax (11) 3616596; e-mail rminzd@eunet.yu.

Ministry of Internal Affairs: 11000 Belgrade, Kneza Miloša 103; tel. (11) 3612589; fax (11) 3617814; e-mail muprs@mup.sr.gov.yu; internet www.mup.sr.gov.yu.

Ministry of Justice and Local Authority: 11000 Belgrade, Nemanjina 26; tel. (11) 3616548; fax (11) 3616419; e-mail ksenija@mpravde.sr.gov.yu.

Ministry of Labour and Employment: 11000 Belgrade, Nemanjina 22; tel. (11) 3616253; fax (11) 3617498; e-mail mrz@mrz.sr.gov.yu; internet www.mrz.sr.gov.yu.

Ministry of Religious Affairs: 11000 Belgrade, Nemanjina 11; tel. and fax (11) 3346649; fax (11) 3617595; e-mail min_vera@uzzpro.sr.gov.yu.

Ministry of Science, Technology and Development: 11000 Belgrade, Nemanjina 22–26; tel. (11) 3616516; fax (11) 3616584; e-mail administrator@mnt.bg.ac.yu; internet www.nauka.ac.yu.

Ministry of Social Welfare: 11000 Belgrade, Nemanjina 22–26; tel. (11) 3616294; fax (11) 3616259; e-mail goga@msoc.sr.gov.yu; internet www.msoc.sr.gov.yu.

Ministry of Sport and Education: 11000 Belgrade, Nemanjina 22–26; tel. (11) 3616489; fax (11) 3616491; e-mail min.edu.sr@yubc.net.

Ministry of Trade, Tourism and Services: 11000 Belgrade, Nemanjina 22–26; tel. (11) 3631136; fax (11) 3610258.

Ministry of Transport and Telecommunications: 11000 Belgrade, Nemanjina 22–26; tel. (11) 3616426; fax (11) 3617486; e-mail info@minsaotel.sr.gov.yu; internet www.msaotel.sr.gov.yu.

PRESIDENT AND LEGISLATURE

President

Presidential Election, First Ballot, 29 September 2002

Candidate	Votes	% of votes
Vojislav Koštunica (Democratic Party of Serbia)	1,123,420	30.89
Mirolujub Labus (Independent)	995,200	27.36
Dr Vojislav Šešelj (Serbian Radical Party)	845,308	23.24
Vuk Drašković (Serbian Renewal Movement)	159,959	4.40
Borislav Pelević (Party of Serbian Unity)	139,047	3.82
Velimir Zivojinović (Socialist Party of Serbia)	119,052	3.27
Nebojsa Pavković (Independent)	75,662	2.08
Others	179,394	4.93
Total	**3,637,042**	**100.00**

* Excluding invalid vote.

Second Ballot, 13 October 2002

Candidate	Votes	% of votes
Vojislav Koštunica (Democratic Party of Serbia)	1,974,450	68.40
Mirolujub Labus (Indpendent)	911,567	31.60
Total	**2,886,017**	**100.00**

* Excluding invalid votes.

Third Ballot, 8 December 2002

Candidate	Votes	% of votes
Vojislav Koštunica (Democratic Party of Serbia)	1,699,098	57.66
Vojislav Šešelj (Serbian Radical Party)	1,063,296	36.08
Borislav Pelević (Party of Serbian Unity)	103,926	3.53
Total*	**2,866,320**	**100.00**

* Excluding 80,396 invalid votes. Percentage of votes is based on total votes cast.

National Assembly

Chairman: Nataša Mićić.

Election, 23 December 2000

Party	Votes	% of votes	Seats
Democratic Opposition of Serbia*	2,402,387	64.1	176
Socialist Party of Serbia	515,845	13.8	37
Serbian Radical Party	322,333	8.6	23
Party of Serbian Unity†	199,847	5.3	14
Others	n.a.	8.2	—
Total	n.a.	100.00	250

* Alliance of 18 political parties.

† Coalition of Party of Serbian Progress, Party of Serbian Union, Peasants' Party of Serbia and United Pensioners' Party.

LOCAL GOVERNMENT

For administrative purposes, Serbia is divided into regions, of which there are 29, including territories of the formerly autonomous provinces of Kosovo and Metohija and Vojvodina. Municipal elections were held on 3, 17 and 27 November 1996. Following some controversy over the results (see above), the opposition coalition, Zajedno, gained control of 14 municipal assemblies, including Belgrade. Following the enactment of the 1990 Serbian Constitution and, subsequently, of the federal Constitution of 1992, Vojvodina retained its provincial Assembly. However, the provincial Assembly of Kosovo was dissolved, although a 'Kosovo Assembly-in-Exile' was formed, based in Zagreb, Croatia, which proclaimed a 'Republic of Kosovo'. In March 1998 a presidential election was won by Ibrahim Rugova, leader of the Democratic Alliance of Kosovo (DAK) and of the 'Republic of Kosovo'. The DAK also organized elections to a provincial assembly, which were held in the same month. Following international military intervention in Kosovo in 1999, in June the UN Interim Administration in Kosovo (UNMIK) assumed authority in the province. A consultative body to UNMIK, known as the Kosovo Transitional Council (KTC), was established in the following month, comprising representatives of all ethnic groupings. In February 2000 the DAK disbanded. Local government elections took place in Kosovo on 28 October 2000, and on 26 October 2002 (see above). On 21 January 2002 the Serbian legislature voted in favour of restoring partial autonomy to Vojvodina, restoring local authority over some 20 regions. (The legislation was regarded as a temporary measure, pending the adoption of a new constitution in Serbia.)

Under a programme to establish partial provisional self-government in the province, elections to a 120-member Kosovo Assembly took place, monitored by the Organization for Security and Co-operation in Europe (OSCE), on 17 November 2001. In March 2002 a President was elected for the province, and a Government was established. Under the structure of the Provisional Institutions of Self-Government, the head of UNMIK retains supreme executive authority, and governs in conjunction with the Kosovo Assembly. The Kosovo Assembly comprises 100 elective seats and 20 seats that are allocated proportionally to Serbs and other minority groups. The President of Kosovo is elected by the Assembly, having been nominated by the party with the largest number of seats, or at least 25 deputies. The President nominates the Prime Minister, who proposes a Government for the approval of the Assembly. The Government is empowered to propose draft legislation. The judicial system comprises a Supreme Court, district courts, municipal courts, and minor offence courts. The head of UNMIK appoints judges and prosecutors from a list of candidates approved by the Assembly.

Municipal elections took place in 18 Serbian regions on 4 November 2001. On 28 July 2002, under an agreement reached by the Serbian authorities and ethnic Albanian separatists in May 2001, elections to new multi-ethnic local governments in the municipalities of Preševo, Medvedja and Bujanovac were conducted. The OSCE reported that voting had taken place peacefully.

North Bačka (1): 24000 Subotica, Lazara Nesica 1; tel. (24) 25361; fax (24) 53272; CEO Dragan Bozinivić.

Central Banat (2): Zrenjanin, trg Slobode 10; tel. (23) 66007; CEO Jovan Subotić.

North Banat (3): 23300 Kikinda, Srpskih dobrovoljaca 12; tel. (23) 21008; fax (23) 22921; CEO Zdravko Galić.

South Banat (4): 26000 Pancevo, Kralja Petra 12/4; tel. (13) 45580; fax (13) 46940; CEO Vladimir Sarić.

Western Bačka (5): Sombor, trg Cara Urisa 1; tel. (25) 56311; CEO Mile Capić.

Southern Bačka (6): Novi Sad, Maršala Tita 16; tel. (21) 56311; CEO Jovo Ubiparip.

Srem (7): 22000 Sremska Mitrovica, 13 Sv. Dimitrije; tel. (22) 221053; CEO Zikica Dronjak.

Macva (8): Sabac, Maršala Tita 6/III; tel. (15) 25500; fax (15) 24203; CEO Radenko Stepić.

Kolubara (9): Valjevo, Vuka Karadzica 16/II; tel. (14) 21655; fax (14) 26112; CEO Aleksa Jokić.

Podunavlje (10): Smederevo, trg Republike 5; tel. (26) 223636; fax (26) 223646; CEO Stevan Zezelj.

Branicevo (11): Pozarevać, Drinska 2; tel. (12) 223999; fax (26) 223646; CEO Miroslav Sretenović.

Sumadija (12): Kragujeva, Save Kovacevica 7; tel. (34) 69206; CEO Vladeta Miletić.

Pomoravlje (13): Svetozarevo (Jagodina), Maršala Tita 82; tel. (35) 221516; fax (35) 224515; CEO Vladimir Jovanović.

Bor (14): 19219 Bor, Moše Pijade 5; tel. (30) 22956; fax (30) 21687; CEO Nedeljko Magdalenović.

Zaječar (15): 19000 Zaječar, Generala Gambete 44; tel. (19) 21587; fax (19) 21626; CEO Sreten Trojanecević.

Zlatibor (16): 31000 Uzice, Dimitrija Tucovica 52; tel. (31) 22262; CEO Slobodan Vermezović.

Morava (17): 32000 Cacak, Zupana Stracimira 2; tel. (32) 23310; CEO Milos Nešović.

Raška (18): Kraljevo, trg Bratstva i Jedinstva 3; tel. (36) 332133; fax (36) 22235; CEO Milos Nešović.

Rasina (19): Kruševać, Pana Djukića 1; tel. (37) 29795; fax (37) 39962; CEO Vladimir Tasić.

Nišava (20): Niš, Vozdova 11; tel. (18) 40626; fax (18) 23742; CEO Jovan Zlatić.

Toplica (21): Prokuplje, Tatkova 2; tel. (27) 21070; fax (27) 24316; CEO Ratko Zecević.

Pirot (22): Pirot, Maršala Tita 125; tel. (18) 22471; CEO Nesko Madić.

Jablanica (23): 16000 Leskovać, Pane Djukica 9–11; tel. (16) 50131; CEO Zivojin Stefanović.

Pčinja (24): 17500 Vranje, Peti Kongress 1; tel. and fax (17) 31330; CEO Svetislav Ljubić.

Kosovo (25): 38000 Priština, Maršala Tita 2; tel. (38) 27790; fax (38) 27791; CE O Milos Simović, Veljko Odalović.

Peć (26): 38300 Peć, Maršala Tita bb; tel. (39) 31043; fax (39) 22442; CEO Miladin Ivanović.

Prizren (27): 38400 Prizren, Marsala Tita bb; tel. and fax (29) 44342; CEO Blazo Damjanović.

Kosovska Mitrovica (28): 38220 Kosovska Mitrovica, Edvarda Kardelja; tel. and fax (28) 31880; CEO Dragan Pelević.

Kosovsko Pomoravlje (29): 38250 Gnjilane, Kralja Petra bb; tel. and fax (28) 22042; CEO Predrag Kovacević.

Kosovo and Metohija

Head of the UN Interim Administration Mission in Kosovo (UNMIK): Harri Holkeri.
President of Kosovo: Ibrahim Rugova.
President of the Kosovo Assembly: Nexhat Daçi.
Prime Minister: Dr Bajram Rexhepi.

Vojvodina

President of the Provincial Assembly: Nenad Canak.
Provincial President: Damnjan Radenković.
Premier: Djordje Djukić.

Bibliography

Akhavan, P., and Howse, R. (Eds). *Yugoslavia, the Former and the Future*. Washington, DC, Brookings Institution, 1995.

Allcock, J. B. *Explaining Yugoslavia*. New York, NY, Columbia University Press, 2000.

Anzulović, B. *Heavenly Serbia: From Myth to Genocide*. New York, NY, New York University Press, 1999.

Auty, P. *Tito: A Biography*. Harmondsworth, Penguin, 1974.

Bacevich, A. J., and Cohen, E. A. (Eds). *War Over Kosovo*. New York, NY, Columbia University Press, 2002.

Banać, I. *The National Question in Yugoslavia: Origins, History, Politics*. Ithaca, NY, Cornell University Press, 1984.

Bennett, C. *Yugoslavia's Bloody Collapse*. London, Hurst, 1995.

Benson, L. *Yugoslavia: a Concise History*. New York, NY, Palgrave Macmillan, 2002.

Berg, S. *Conflict and Cohesion in Socialist Yugoslavia: Political Decision Making Since 1966*. Princeton, NJ, Princeton University Press, 1983.

Bojičić, V., and Dyker, D. 'Sanctions on Serbia: Sledgehammer or Scalpel?' in *Working Papers in Contemporary European Studies*, No. 1. Sussex European Institute, University of Sussex, 1993.

Buckley, W. J. (Ed.). *Kosovo: Contending Voices on Balkan Interventions*. Cambridge, MI, 2000.

Bujošević, D. and Radovanović, I. *The Fall of Milošević; the October 5 24–Hour Coup*. New York, NY, Palgrave, 2003.

Carpenter, T. G. (Ed.). *NATO's Empty Victory*. Washington, DC, Cato Institute, 2000.

Cohen, L. J. *The Socialist Pyramid: Elites and Power in Yugoslavia*. London, Tri-Service Press, 1989.

Broken Bonds: The Disintegration of Yugoslavia, 2nd Edn. Boulder, CO, Westview Press, 1995.

Colović, I. *Politics of Identity in Serbia*. New York, NY, New York University Press, 2002.

Daalder, I. H., and O'Hanlon, M. E. *Winning Ugly: NATO's War to Save Kosovo*. Washington, DC, Brookings Institution, 2000.

Danchev, A., and Halverson, H. (Eds). *International Perspectives on the Yugoslav Conflict*. London, Macmillan, 1996.

Djilas, M. *Tito: The Story from Inside*. London, Weidenfeld and Nicolson, 1981.

Djokić, D. (Ed.) *Yugoslavism: Histories of a Failed Idea, 1918–1992*. Madison, WI, University of Wisconsin Press.

Dragnich. A. N. *Serbs and Croats: The Struggle in Yugoslavia*. London, Harcourt Brace Jovanovich, 1992.

Dragović-Soso, J. *'Saviours of the Nation': Serbia's Intellectual Opposition and the Revival of Nationalism*. Montreal, McGill-Queen's University Press, 2002.

Dyker, D. *Yugoslavia: Socialism, Development and Debt*. London, Routledge, 1990.

Dyker, D., and Vejvoda, I. *Yugoslavia and After—A Study in Fragmentation, Despair and Rebirth*. New York, NY, Longman, 1999.

Glenny, M. *The Fall of Yugoslavia: The Third Balkan War*. London, Penguin, 1992.

Gruenwald, O. *The Yugoslav Search for Man: Marxist Humanism in Contemporary Yugoslavia*. South Hadley, MA, J. F. Bergin, 1983.

Hammond, H., and Herman, E. (Eds). *Degraded Capability: the Media and the Kosovo Crisis*. London, Pluto Press, 2000.

Hudson, K. *The Breaking of the South Slav Dream: the Rise and Fall of Yugoslavia*. London, Pluto Press, 2003.

Job, C. *Yugoslavia's Ruin: the Bloody Lessons of Nationalism: a Patriot's Warning*. Lanham, MD, Rowman and Littlefield, 2002.

Johnstone, D. *Fools' Crusade: Yugoslavia, Nato, and Western Delusions*. New York, NY, Monthly Review Press, 2003.

Judah, T. *Kosovo: War and Revenge*. Yale, Yale University Press, 2000.

The Serbs: History, Myth and the Destruction of Yugoslavia. New Haven, CT, Yale University Press, 2000.

Kardelj, E. *Reminiscences: the Struggle for Recognition and Independence: The New Yugoslavia 1944–57*. London, Blond and Briggs, 1984.

Lawrence, S. *Montenegro*. New York, NY, Berkley Publishing Group, 1998.

Lydall, H. *Yugoslav Socialism: Theory and Practice*. Oxford, Clarendon Press, 1984.

Yugoslavia in Crisis. Oxford, Clarendon Press, 1989.

Macdonald, D. B. *Balkan Holocausts? Serbian and Croatian Victim Centered Propaganda and the War in Yugoslavia*. Manchester, Manchester University Press, 2003.

Magaš, B. *The Destruction of Yugoslavia: Tracking the Break-Up 1980–92*. London and New York, NY, Verso, 1993.

Mahmutcehajić, R. *Sarajevo Essays: Politics, Ideology and Tradition*. New York, NY, 2003.

Malcolm, N. *Kosovo: A Short History*. New York, NY, New York University Press, 1998.

McAllester, M. *Beyond the Mountains of the Damned*. New York, NY, New York University Press, 2002.

Naimark. N. M., and Case, H. *Yugoslavia and its Historians: Understanding the Balkan Wars of the 1990s*. Stanford, CA, Stanford University Press, 2003.

Parenti, M. *To Kill a Nation: the Attack on Yugoslavia*. London, Verso Books, 2001.

Pavlowitch, S. K. *Yugoslavia*. London, Ernest Benn, 1971.

The Improbable Survivor: Yugoslavia and its Problems 1918–1988. London, C. Hurst, 1988.

Tito—Yugoslavia's Great Dictator: A Reassessment. London, C. Hurst, 1993.

Serbia: the History Behind the Name. London, Hurst, 2002.

Serbia: the History of an Idea. New York, NY, New York University Press, 2002.

Perica, V. *Balkan Idols: Religion and Nationalism in Yugoslav States*. New York, NY, Oxford University Press, 2002.

Ramet, S. *Nationalism and Federalism in Yugoslavia, 1963–1990*. Bloomington, IN, Indiana University Press, 1992.

Balkan Babel: the Disintegration of Yugoslavia from the Death of Tito to the Fall of Milošević. Boulder, CO, Westview Press, 2002.

Ramet, S., and Adamovich, L. *Beyond Yugoslavia*. Boulder, CO, Westview Press, 1995.

Ridley, J. *Tito*. London, Constable, 1995.

Sell, L. *Slobodan Milošević and the Destruction of Yugoslavia*. Durham, NC, Duke University Press, 2002.

Silber, L. *Yugoslavia: Death of a Nation*. New York, NY, Penguin, 1997.

Singleton, F. *A Short History of the Yugoslav Peoples*. Cambridge, Cambridge University Press, 1985.

West, R. *Tito: The Rise and Fall of Yugoslavia*. London, Sinclair-Stevenson, 1994.

Whealey, R. H. *American Intervention in Yugoslavia: a Diplomatic History Since 1991*. New York, NY, Prometheus Books, 2003.

See also the Select Bibliography in Part Four.

SLOVAKIA

Geography

PHYSICAL FEATURES

The Slovak Republic, or Slovakia, which, together with the Czech Republic, formed Czechoslovakia between 1918 and 1992, is bordered to the west by the Czech Republic, to the north by Poland, to the east by Ukraine, to the south by Hungary and to the south-west by Austria. The country covers an area of 49,033 sq km (18,932 sq miles).

The terrain is largely mountainous, rising, in the north, to Slovakia's highest point, Gerlach (Gerlachovsky) Peak (2,655 m—8,711 ft), in the High Tatras. The High Tatras (Vysoké Tatry), on the northern border with Poland, and the Low Tatras (Nízké Tatry), in the centre and east, are the principal mountain ranges. They form the westernmost branch of the Carpathian mountain chain. The mountains are drained by numerous rivers, flowing south to the lowland areas, including the Váh, the Nitra, the Hron and the Hornád. Part of the southern border is marked by the River Danube (Dunaj). There are lowland areas in the south-west and south-east of the country, which are extensions of the Pannonian Plain and are the main areas for settlement and agriculture. More than two-fifths of Slovakia is forested, and only one-third is cultivated land.

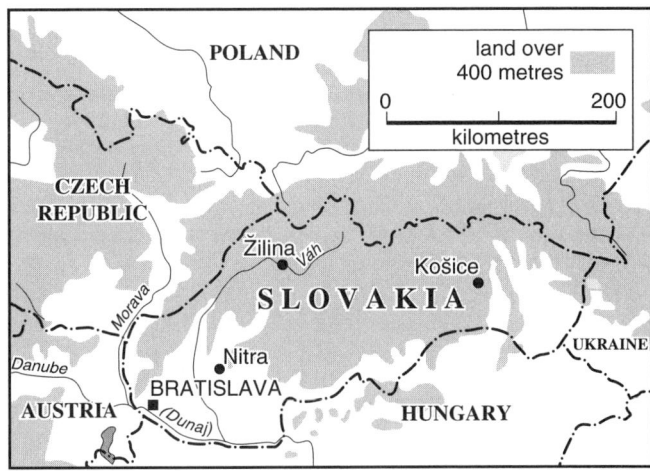

CLIMATE

The climate is of a typical continental type, with average temperatures in Bratislava varying from –0.7°C (30.7°F) in January to 21.1°C (70.0°F) in July. However, average temperatures in the mountainous centre of the country are as much as 10°C lower. Temperature inversions during the winter frequently cause pollution problems in the more populous and industrialized areas. Average annual rainfall in Bratislava is 649 mm.

POPULATION

According to official estimates, at mid-2002 the total population of Slovakia was 5,378,595. The country's population density at this time was, therefore, 109.7 per sq km. According to the 2001 census, 4,614,854 (85.8%) of the country's inhabitants were ethnic Slovaks, 520,528 (9.7%) Hungarians (Magyars), who are concentrated along the southern border with Hungary, 89,920 Roma (Gypsies) and 46,968 Czechs (including Moravians and Silesians). There were also small communities of Ruthenians and Ukrainians (35,015), Germans (5,405) and Poles (2,602). (It was believed that there was considerable underenumeration of the Roma community, many of whom claimed other nationalities, particularly Hungarian; in the mid-1990s they were estimated to number 400,000.) Slovak, a member of the Western Slavonic group of languages (and closely related to Czech), is the official language. The Hungarian community use their own language; there are Hungarian-language newspapers and periodicals and Hungarian-language broadcasting. The language law of 1990, which established Slovak as the official language in the Slovak Republic over two years before formal separation, restricted official use of minority languages to areas where at least 20% of the population were members of an ethnic minority; legislation enacted in 1996 prohibited official use of all languages other than Slovak, although a further law, enacted in July 1999, restored conditions similar to those in force under the 1990 legislation. Christianity is the major religion, the Roman Catholic Church being the largest denomination.

The capital of Slovakia is Bratislava (formerly known as Pressburg), situated in the extreme south-west of the country, on the River Danube, and only 50 km (31 miles) from Vienna (the capital of Austria). At 31 December 2001 the city had a population of 428,094. Other important towns include Košice (236,036) and Prešov (92,720), in the east, Nitra (87,308), in the south, Žilina (85,384), on the River Váh in the north, and Banská Bystrica (82,961), in the centre.

Chronology

5th–7th centuries: Slavic tribes migrated to central Europe from the eastern plains.

830: The Great Moravian Empire was established, eventually including Slovakia and Bohemia.

907: The Hungarians destroyed the Moravian forces at the Battle of Bratislava (Pressburg).

11th century: Slovakia was incorporated into the Kingdom of Hungary, although parts were subsequently claimed by the Kingdom of Bohemia.

1491: The Peace of Pressburg acknowledged Habsburg claims to the throne of Hungary.

1526: The Austrian Habsburgs inherited their claim to Hungary upon the death of Louis II, at the battle of Mohács. The Kingdom was partitioned between the victorious Ottomans, the principality of Transylvania and the Habsburgs, who retained control of the Slovak territories; Pressburg became the capital of Hungary, and Hungarian monarchs were crowned there for the next three centuries.

1781–85: Serfdom was abolished in both the Czech and Slovak lands.

1844: The first grammar of the Slovak language, written by Ľudovít Stur, was published.

1848: There was an unsuccessful Slovak rebellion against Hungarian rule.

1861: A National Congress of Slovaks issued the Memorandum of the Slovak Nation, which demanded autonomy for Slovakia.

1867: The *Ausgleich* (Compromise) creating the Habsburg Dual Monarchy of Austria-Hungary restored full Hungarian control over Slovakia; a policy of 'magyarization' soon commenced, contributing to a high rate of emigration.

30 May 1918: The Pittsburgh Agreement, which provided for the creation of a common Czech-Slovak state, was signed between Slovak and Czech exiles in the USA.

28 October 1918: The Republic of Czechoslovakia was proclaimed (for details on Czechoslovakia, see the chapter on the Czech Republic).

29 September 1938: The Munich Agreement between the United Kingdom, France, Italy and Germany permitted the cession of the Czechoslovak territories known as Sudetenland to Germany. This also caused the collapse of the Czechoslovak First Republic.

October 1938: Slovakia and Carpatho-Ruthenia (after 1945 part of the USSR—Ukraine) gained autonomy; the Hlinka Slovak National People's Party (HSNPP), under the pro-Fascist leadership of Mgr Jozef Tiso, was declared the only authorized party in Slovakia.

2 November 1938: Hungary annexed parts of southern Slovakia.

14 March 1939: The day before Nazi Germany began the occupation of the Czech Lands Adolf Hitler, the German leader, agreed to a separate Slovak state.

1941: The Tiso regime adopted a Jewish Code that enabled it to begin a policy of extermination of Jews.

29 August 1944: An uprising against HSNPP rule began in Slovakia. By the end of October it had been suppressed by German troops.

April 1945: The Government-in-Exile returned to Czechoslovakia; it agreed to some limited Slovak autonomy.

16 May 1946: In national elections the Czechoslovak Communist Party (CPCz) won 38% of the votes cast; in Slovakia, however, it won only some 30%, with the Democratic Party winning 62%.

1947: Gustáv Husák organized a communist 'coup' in Slovakia, by accusing many members of the Democratic Party of being sympathetic to the HSNPP.

February–June 1948: The communists effectively seized power in the whole country and introduced a new Constitution.

1954: Husák and other prominent Slovak Communists, accused of 'Slovak nationalism', were the latest victims of the purges in the CPCz.

1960: A new Constitution formally limited Slovak autonomy, dissolving the local executive and removing legislative authority from the Slovakian National Council.

January 1968: Alexander Dubček, leader of the Communist Party of Slovakia (CPS), became First Secretary of the CPCz and initiated the so-called 'Prague Spring' reforms.

August 1968: After a meeting in Bratislava the countries of the Warsaw Pact (except Romania) sent troops to invade Czechoslovakia; Dubček and other government and Party leaders were abducted.

1 January 1969: A federal system of government was introduced, despite the ending of other reforms, with the country comprising the Slovak and Czech Socialist Republics.

April 1969: Husák, rehabilitated in the early 1960s, replaced Dubček as First Secretary of the CPCz.

1975: Ludvík Svoboda resigned as President and was replaced by Husák.

1 January 1977: A group of Czechoslovak dissidents published the 'Charter 77' manifesto, which demanded an end to the abuse of civil and political rights.

1987: Miloš Jakeš replaced Husák as leader of the CPCz.

1988: Towards the end of the year large anti-Government demonstrations began to occur and this escalated in 1989.

November 1989: Opposition activists formed an anti-Government coalition known as Public Against Violence (PAV—the Czech equivalent was Civic Forum). The leadership of Civic Forum and PAV began discussions with the communist leadership, as protests continued to increase throughout the country. At the end of the month the Federal Assembly abolished the CPCz constitutional monopoly on power.

December 1989: Demonstrations in Prague, Bratislava and other cities continued. A new federal Government was announced, with a majority of non-communist members. Dubček was elected Chairman of the Federal Assembly. Husák resigned as President and was replaced by the dissident Czech playwright, Václav Havel.

April 1990: As part of a continuing process of reform and liberalization the name of the country was changed to the Czech and Slovak Federative Republic.

June 1990: Elections to the Federal Assembly took place; PAV (in Slovakia) and Civic Forum (in Bohemia and Moravia) won an overall majority. In elections to the Slovakian National Council, the republican legislature, PAV emerged as the largest party, with some 35% of the votes cast and 48 of the 150 seats; Vladimír Mečiar of PAV was elected premier of Slovakia.

December 1990: Constitutional changes delimited the powers of the federal, Czech and Slovakian Governments.

March 1991: Mečiar, the premier of the Slovak Republic, left PAV over the issue of Czech-Slovakian relations and his advocacy of more autonomy. There were also large demonstrations in favour of independence; President Havel was attacked by crowds when he visited Bratislava.

April 1991: Mečiar and seven members of his cabinet were dismissed by the Presidium of the Slovakian National Council, because of their defection from the disintegrating PAV; Jan Čarnogurský, leader of the Christian Democratic Movement (CDM), was appointed as premier instead.

June 1991: Mečiar was elected Chairman of the newly formed Movement for a Democratic Slovakia (MDS).

September 1991: A group of Slovakian politicians, mostly members of the MDS and the Slovak National Party (SNP), formed the Initiative for a Sovereign Slovakia (mainly as an attempt to forestall a referendum authorized by the Federal Assembly in June).

5–6 June 1992: Elections to the federal and republican legislatures took place; the MDS emerged as the dominant Slovakian party, winning some 37% of the votes cast and 74 seats in the Slovakian National Council. The former communists, the Party of the Democratic Left (PDL), won 29 seats, the CDM 18 and the SNP 15. The remaining 14 seats were won by a coalition of Hungarian parties; Mečiar was elected to lead an MDS-dominated Slovakian Government.

17 July 1992: The Slovakian National Council overwhelmingly approved a declaration of sovereignty and the dissolution of the federation came to appear inevitable.

1 September 1992: The Slovakian National Council adopted a new Constitution for the Republic, which was to come into effect upon the dissolution of Czechoslovakia.

October 1992: Slovakia, without the agreement of Hungary, started to divert the River Danube into a newly constructed canal, part of the Gabčíkovo dam scheme.

November 1992: At the third attempt, and by only three votes, the Federal Assembly approved the legislation which would end the federation, despite opposition even from Slovakian deputies.

1 January 1993: With the dissolution of all federal structures, the Slovak Republic became a sovereign nation, as did the Czech Republic.

February 1993: Separate Slovakian and Czech currencies (both called koruna) were introduced. The parliament, the National Council of the Slovak Republic, finally elected a President for the country, Michal Kováč, deputy leader of the MDS and a former Chairman of the Czechoslovak Federal Assembly.

June 1993: Slovakia became a member of the Council of Europe and finalized its association agreement with the European Community (EC, known as the European Union—EU—from November).

October 1993: The MDS and the SNP (which had left the previous coalition in March) agreed to form a new coalition Government.

March 1994: Following a number of splits in the ruling parties a motion of 'no confidence' in Mečiar's Government was passed in the National Council. A new Government was formed, with Jozef Moravčík (leader of the newly formed Democratic Union of Slovakia—DUS) as Prime Minister, which included representatives of six former opposition parties and groupings.

30 September–1 October 1994: In the general election the MDS was the most successful party, winning, in alliance with the Farmers' Party of Slovakia, some 35% of the votes cast and a total of 61 seats. Of the remaining seats the Common Choice bloc (an alliance of left-wing parties, led by the PDL) secured 18, a coalition of Hungarian parties 17, the CDM 17, the DUS 15, the newly formed Association of Workers of Slovakia (AWS) 13 and the SNP nine.

December 1994: After protracted negotiations Mečiar and the MDS formed a new government coalition, with the nationalist SNP and the left-wing AWS.

August 1995: The President's son, also called Michal Kováč, was abducted and taken to Austria, before being detained in that country on an international arrest warrant issued by a court in Munich, Germany, investigating charges of embezzlement. President Kováč claimed that there was evidence to suggest Slovak Intelligence Service (SIS) involvement in his son's abduction; the Austrian courts eventually decided against his extradition to Germany and he was permitted to return to Slovakia in February 1996.

15 November 1995: A law was passed restricting the official use of any language other than Slovak, provoking domestic and international criticism, notably from Hungarians.

March 1996: Parliamentary approval of a friendship treaty with Hungary, signed in March 1995, required significant amendments to the document and, as a condition of co-operation by the more radical members of the government coalition, a Law on the Protection of the Republic (controversial anti-subversion legislation eventually rejected by parliament in February 1996).

May 1996: After several months of mutual accusations by the President and Prime Minister, Kováč filed libel charges against Mečiar; this followed the latter's public claim that the President had been personally involved in an alleged fraud which had led to the German demands for his son's extradition.

January 1997: A civic movement, Charter 97, was formed to monitor observance of the Constitution and of civil rights.

10 July 1997: The Slovak Democratic Coalition (SDC), a new grouping of five opposition parties including the CDM and the DUS, demanded Mečiar's resignation after announcements that, for failing to fulfil political criteria, Slovakia would not be among the first former communist countries to join the North Atlantic Treaty Organization (NATO) or the EU.

10 December 1997: The Constitutional Court ruled that the President's five-year term of office would end on the anniversary of his inauguration rather than of his election, as advocated by Mečiar.

29 January 1998: The National Council failed to obtain the three-fifths' majority required to elect a new President; the MDS had not nominated a candidate to succeed Kováč, leading to opposition allegations that Mečiar deliberately sought to leave the presidency vacant; further attempts to elect a president in the following month also failed.

2 March 1998: President Kováč's term expired without a replacement having been elected; Mečiar, as Prime Minister, constitutionally assumed most of the functions of head of state.

22 April 1998: Three parties of the Hungarian minority merged to form the Party of the Hungarian Coalition (PHC), following government proposals to legislate for representation in parliament to be limited only to those parties obtaining more than 5% of the votes cast. The National Council approved the amended electoral legislation on 20 May.

8 June 1998: The Mochovce nuclear power plant in western Slovakia was activated, despite an adverse safety report and international concern (particularly from neighbouring Austria).

25–26 September 1998: The MDS emerged from the general election as the largest party, with 27.0% of the votes cast (43 seats); the SNP won 9.1% of the votes cast (14 seats) and the AWS failed to reach the 5% threshold. Four opposition groups secured representation: the SDC (26.3%—42 seats), the PDL (14.7%—23 seats), the PHC (9.1%—15 seats) and the Party of Civic Understanding (PCU—8.0%—13 seats).

30 October 1998: The new Government, a coalition of the SDC (nine ministerial seats), the PDL (six), the PHC (three) and the PCU (two), was appointed, with the SDC's Mikuláš Dzurinda as Prime Minister.

January 1999: The National Council approved a constitutional amendment introduced by the new Government, providing for direct election of the President.

15 May 1999: In the first direct presidential election the governing coalition's candidate, Rudolf Schuster (the mayor of Košice and chairman of the PCU), obtained 47.4% of the votes cast, Mečiar 37.2%; in the second round of voting two weeks later, Schuster received 57.2% of the votes cast and was duly elected President.

10 December 1999: Slovakia was formally invited to begin negotiations with the EU about accession, in recognition of its progress with reform and transition.

January 2000: Dzurinda announced the formation of a new political party, the Slovak and Democratic Christian Union (SDCU), to contest the legislative elections scheduled for 2002 and in an attempt to concentrate the SDC into a single party; several other members of the Government subsequently announced their intention to join the SDCU.

April 2000: Mečiar was arrested and charged with fraud and abuse of power, relating to payments made to members of his Government while he was premier; he was also fined for refusing to give evidence in the investigation into the abduction of Michal Kováč, junior. The Government was criticized for the excessive use of force used during his arrest.

10 May 2000: The MDS, having failed to carry motions of 'no confidence' earlier in the year, began a boycott of the parliamentary session, in protest at the supposed politicization of the judicial process, including the investigations into Lexa and Mečiar; the boycott ended on 6 June.

22 May 2000: Dzurinda and his Czech counterpart, Miloš Zeman, signed an agreement formally resolving disputes over the division of Czechoslovak property between the two successor states upon the dissolution of Czechoslovakia at the end of 1992.

3 July 2000: Dzurinda and the Chairman of the National Council, Jozef Migaš, signed an agreement providing for an emergency division of presidential powers during President Schuster's incapacity (he had been taken ill in the previous month), there being no procedure identified in the Constitution for the temporary replacement of an indisposed President—Dzurinda was to represent Slovakia abroad and control the armed forces, while Migaš controlled the presidency's legislative assent.

31 July 2000: President Schuster made his first public appearance following his illness and officially resumed the exercise of his presidential powers.

18 November 2000: The SDC effectively collapsed, as the SDCU attempted to become the single party to replace it, but was challenged by those wishing to keep the constituent parties of the Coalition distinct. Dzurinda was elected leader of the SDCU.

27 November 2000: The National Council having removed his immunity in August, the head of the SIS during Mečiar's premiership, Ivan Lexa, was charged *in absentia* with the abduction of former President Kováč's son, alleged to have been committed by the SIS under his leadership.

December 2000: Slovakia formally joined the Organisation for Economic Co-operation and Development (OECD).

February 2001: New legislation provided for institutions designed to strengthen the independence of the judiciary and amended the Constitution to provide for regional government; these reinforced earlier reforms such as the restoration of minority-language rights in 1999 and the freedom of information rights which took effect at the beginning of the year.

23 April 2001: The creation of another pro-reform, centre-right party, the New Civic Alliance (NCA), was announced by Pavol Ruško, the owner of a major Slovakian broadcasting company.

1 and 15 December 2001: The MDS was the most successful party at local government elections, securing six of the country's eight gubernatorial posts and 146 of the 401 seats contested in regional councils; the elections were notable for the low level of voter participation.

18 July 2002: Ivan Lexa was extradited from South Africa to Slovakia. He was detained in December, but denied all the charges against him.

20–21 September 2002: At legislative elections, Mečiar's MDS, despite obtaining the highest proportion of votes cast (19.5%) and 36 seats in the National Council, failed to secure an overall majority. The SDCU won 28 seats, a centre-right party, known as Direction (Směr), 25 seats, the PHC 20 seats, the CDM 15 seats, and the NCA 15 seats.

8 October 2002: Following Mečiar's failure to negotiate alliances with other parties, Schuster invited Dzurinda to form an administration and four reformist parties (the SDCU, the PHC, the CDM and the NCA) formed a coalition agreement.

16 October 2002: Schuster officially appointed a new coalition Government (which also included the Chairman of the Democratic Party).

21 November 2002: At a summit meeting held in Prague, Czech Republic, Slovakia was formally invited to become a member of NATO in 2004.

6–7 December 2002: Elections to municipality self-government bodies took place; the government coalition parties secured most of the 2,926 mayoral offices, while the MDS reportedly won only 384.

13 December 2002: At an historic EU summit meeting, in Copenhagen, Denmark, Slovakia was invited to become a full member of the Union on 1 May 2004.

16–17 May 2003: At a national referendum, 92.5% of the votes cast (with some 52% of the electorate participating) were in favour of Slovakia becoming a member of the EU.

History

Dr ANDREW RYDER

INTRODUCTION

The territory now known as Slovakia was initially settled by Illyrian, Celtic and then Germanic tribes. Slavic tribes arrived from the east in the sixth or seventh centuries. In the ninth century the land was part of the Great Moravian Empire, which also included Bohemia and neighbouring territories. Following the dissolution of the Great Moravian Empire, however, in the 10th century, the Czechs and Slovaks were divided, as the latter came under Hungarian rule, a state which persisted, in different forms, for some 1,000 years. Even when it was part of the Habsburg Empire, the transport infrastructure and economy of Slovakia remained orientated towards Budapest, the leading city of the Hungarian-dominated area, while the Czech Lands (Bohemia and Moravia) were orientated towards Vienna, the imperial capital of Austria. There was little evidence of significant cultural development in Slovakia until the late 18th century, when a movement of national renaissance began. Slovak was not recognized as an independent language until the mid-19th century, and the first grammar was not written until 1844. However, it continued often to be treated as a dialect of Czech rather than as a language in its own right (indeed, the first Czechoslovak Constitution referred to a single Czechoslovak language). In the 19th century Slovak nationalists were supported by the Austrian Habsburgs, who were attempting to limit the growing influence of the Hungarians. A Slovak legion came to the assistance of Emperor Francis Joseph I in suppressing the Hungarian revolt of 1848–49; in return the Slovaks were granted a limited amount of autonomy. In 1861 a National Congress, organized by leading Slovak intellectuals, issued a Memorandum, demanding autonomy for Slovakia. However, after the Austro-Hungarian *Ausgleich* (Compromise) of 1867, the Hungarians regained full control over Slovakia and instituted a policy of 'magyarization', which resulted in considerable emigration, in particular to the USA. While Slovakia was a mainly agricultural country with few large cities and little industry, the Czech Lands were relatively urbanized and became the leading industrial region of the Austro-Hungarian Empire, supplying a market which stretched across Central Europe. During the First World War Slovaks joined with Czechs in campaigning for an independent state, composed of the Czech Lands and Slovakia. In 1918, in the USA, the leading campaigners signed the Czech-Slovak Pittsburgh Agreement, in which the Czech and Slovak exile groups agreed to coexist in a common, democratic state.

CZECHOSLOVAKIA 1918–38

The Pittsburgh Agreement envisaged some autonomy for Slovakia, but, when Czechoslovakia's first Constitution was promulgated in 1920, there was no provision for a proper federal system. During the existence of the First Republic (1918–38) the authorities in Prague rejected proposals to grant Slovakia genuine self-government, although, from 1928, the country was divided into four territorial administrative areas: Bohemia, Moravia-Silesia, Slovakia and Carpatho-Ruthenia. The early years of the Czechoslovak state found both the Czech Lands and Slovakia disadvantaged, and although the Czech Lands experienced considerable economic development between the First and Second World Wars, Slovakia remained largely undeveloped. The new Czechoslovak republic, therefore, was characterized by great disparities in living standards, infrastructure and economic development between different regions, and by poor transport links between the Czech and Slovakian parts of the country and within Slovakia itself. Slovaks constituted 23% of the population of the new state, but produced only 12% of the national income and 8% of the total national industrial product. Moreover, the productivity of Slovakian agriculture was only 60% of that in the Czech Lands, and Slovakia produced only 22% of the country's agricultural output. Per-head incomes in Slovakia were only 42% of the Czech average. These differences persisted throughout the first two decades of Czechoslovakia's existence.

The centrist policies of the Czechoslovak Government, dominated by Czech rather than Slovak interests, paid most attention to maintaining the nation's industrial base, and tended to ignore problems that were specific to Slovakia. This led, therefore, to a more radical approach on the part of the Slovaks. The main Slovak national party, the Hlinka Slovak National People's Party (HSNPP), combined elements of Fascism with a fusion of Roman Catholicism and nationalism. In October 1938, following the Munich Agreement (which permitted the cession of the Czechoslovak Sudetenland territories to Germany) and the end of the First Republic, the HSNPP declared autonomy for Slovakia and became the only authorized party there, after banning all other political groups.

WARTIME SLOVAKIA

In November 1938 Hungary annexed some southern parts of Slovakia where the population was predominantly Hungarian. On 14 March 1939, the day before the German occupation of the Czech Lands, the German leader, Adolf Hitler, agreed to the establishment of a separate Slovak state, under the leadership of Jozef Tiso, a Slovak nationalist and Roman Catholic priest, and Slovakia became independent for the first time in its history. The wartime Slovak state (March 1939–April 1945) was based on a combination of German and Italian Fascist principles. Any opposition to the Tiso regime was ruthlessly suppressed and the treatment of Jews, especially after the adoption of the Jewish Code in 1941, was particularly severe. Between March and October 1942 an estimated 58,000 Jews were deported to Nazi German extermination camps. In August 1944, however, an armed uprising against

the HSNPP regime began. It lasted two months before being suppressed by German troops, which were invited into Slovakia by Tiso. Despite its failure, the Slovak National Rising did provide legitimacy for Slovak exiles who were opposed to Tiso. The Czechoslovak Government-in-Exile, however, was unwilling to grant genuine autonomy to the Slovaks in a post-Second World War state, and Slovakia and the Czech Lands were reunited; the Slovak territory seized by Hungary was returned to Czechoslovak control.

CZECHOSLOVAKIA 1945–89

Although economic and other disparities between Slovakia and the Czech Lands persisted, the relative differences between the two parts of the country had changed for several reasons. The expulsion of ethnic Germans and the loss of Carpatho-Ruthenia from the restored Czechoslovak state increased the Slovak proportion of the population. Moreover, Czech industry, controlled by Germany for six years, had not only been reoriented towards military needs, but had suffered from over-intensive use and insufficient new investment. Consequently, by 1948 Slovakia had almost 28% of the country's population, and produced over 19% of the national income, over 13% of the national industrial output and almost 31% of agricultural output. There were certain political concessions, including the devolution of some powers to the Slovakian National Council and the establishment of a weak governmental structure in Slovakia, the Board of Commissioners. Even this small degree of federalization was largely negated by the seizure of power by the Communists, in Slovakia in late 1947, and in the whole of the country in 1948. The communist coup d'état in Slovakia was led by Gustáv Husák, later to be General Secretary of the Communist Party of Czechoslovakia (CPCz), on the pretext of preventing the re-emergence of supporters of the Tiso regime (Tiso himself was hanged in 1947).

In the aftermath of the communist take-over the new leadership attempted to reduce any sense of Slovak nationhood. Husák did not remain in power in Slovakia for long. In 1954 he was sentenced to life imprisonment, along with four other Slovak communists, on charges of Slovak separatism. Under the communist regime expressions of Slovak nationalism were severely suppressed, and any formal power that Slovakian national institutions maintained was nullified by the highly centralized structure of the CPCz.

It was not until the 1960s, with the appointment of Alexander Dubček (an ethnic Slovak) as leader of the Communist Party of Slovakia (CPS) and the beginning of the reform movement, that the issue of Slovakian autonomy re-emerged in public debate. In 1968 the Government approved plans for the creation of a federal system of two equal republics. Despite the Soviet invasion, in August, the new federal system was introduced on 1 January 1969. Slovakia became the Slovak Socialist Republic, with a Slovakian Government and a National Council with wide constitutional powers. However, the reimposition of centralized communist rule, under the leadership of the rehabilitated Husák, left these new institutions largely powerless.

The communist Government pursued a policy of industrializing the entire country, and paid special attention to Slovakia. Slovakia's eastern border was, at that time, with the USSR; furthermore, the fraternal socialist (communist) states of Poland and Hungary virtually surrounded the territory, which was a comfortable distance away from the border with the Federal Republic of Germany, the main focus of interest for the North Atlantic Treaty Organization (NATO). Consequently, and as had been the case in the 1930s, investment and production in the defence industry increased sharply, as did investment in those industries that relied on imports from the USSR, such as the steel industry, which used iron ore from

Ukraine. Moreover, the state made a concerted effort to distribute employment and production in such a way as to reflect the relative proportions of population between the Czech and Slovakian parts of Czechoslovakia, and also concentrated on eliminating differences in wages and living standards. Although disparities persisted, they were relatively slight: by 1989 the Slovak Republic contained 34% of the federation's population, produced 30% of its national income, 33% of its gross agricultural output and almost 30% of gross industrial output. Labour productivity increased from 62% of the Czech average to 96%, and the average wage increased to 99% of the Czech average.

POST-COMMUNIST CZECHOSLOVAKIA

With the 'velvet revolution' of 1989, Slovaks began to demand real changes in their status within the federation. It was at this time that political and economic differences between the two Republics again became evident. Policies at the federal level were adopted on economic and moral grounds, regardless of their regional impacts, and before a consensus had been reached on how to mitigate their effects. These effects were felt more strongly, and more rapidly, in Slovakia than in the Czech Republic. In November 1989 a coalition of independent groups, called Public Against Violence (PAV), had been formed in opposition to the communist regime. (PAV was the Slovakian counterpart to, and ally of, the Czech Civic Forum.) It retained a wide degree of support at the first free elections to be held since 1946, both to the Federal Assembly and to the Czech and Slovakian National Councils, which took place on 8 and 9 June 1990. PAV won 34.5% of the votes and took 48 of the 150 seats in the Slovakian National Council. Vladimír Mečiar, the leader of PAV, was elected Prime Minister of the Slovak Republic. At the federal level PAV, in alliance with its Czech partner, Civic Forum, was also the dominant party.

However, as its name implies, PAV was less a political party than a loose coalition of reformers, and by 1991 it had divided. Mečiar was forced to resign, and founded his own party, the Movement for a Democratic Slovakia (MDS—Hnutie za demokratické Slovensko). Meanwhile, Ján Čarnogurský of the Christian Democratic Movement (CDM—Kresťansko-demokratické hnutie), the second largest party in the Slovakian National Council, became Prime Minister. Mečiar and the MDS became a rallying point for those in Slovakia who favoured outright independence. Further general elections at federal and republican levels were held in June 1992. Not only did the MDS establish itself as the dominant party in the Slovakian National Council, where it won 74 of the 150 seats (but only 37% of votes cast), but it also won 57 seats in the 300-member Federal Assembly, second only to the Civic Democratic Party, the principal party to emerge from the Czech Civic Forum. In the Slovakian National Council the principal advocate of a continued federation, the CDM, obtained only 18 seats. Mečiar once again became Prime Minister in Slovakia, and relentlessly moved the Republic towards independence. On 17 July the Slovakian National Council approved a declaration of Slovakian sovereignty by an overwhelming majority. Although the Civic Democratic Party and the MDS did agree to form a new federal Government in late July, its objective was merely to supervise the dissolution of Czechoslovakia by the end of the year, after Czech politicians realized that Slovakian opposition would curtail or even block their economic reform programme. Mečiar favoured a continuation of government intervention in the economy, and Slovaks stood to suffer economically far more than their Czech neighbours, with unemployment already three times higher, at 12%, in Slovakia than in the Czech Republic.

INDEPENDENT SLOVAKIA

Post-independence Slovakia evolved through two distinct phases; the MDS-dominated administration (under Mečiar) which governed from independence until September 1998, and the pro-West successor coalition with its reform-orientated agenda.

To a considerable extent, Mečiar and his party, the MDS, were the main force behind the move towards independence. The new Slovakian Constitution was adopted, with overwhelming support in the Slovakian National Council, on 1 September 1992. However, there was resistance in the Federal Assembly to adoption of legislation allowing the dissolution of Czechoslovakia. It was only in late November, at the third attempt and by just three votes, that the Federal Assembly finally approved the necessary legislation. Among other matters then decided was that some federal property would continue to be shared by the two Republics, and also that the Czechoslovak currency, the koruna (crown), would remain, at least for the first six months of independence. However, in practice there was some urgency in the setting up of separate national institutions, and in February 1993 separate currencies (both also called the koruna) were established, prompted by an outflow of convertible ('hard') currency from Slovakia.

The existing MDS-dominated Government remained in place upon separation at 1 January 1993, and the Slovakian National Council became the unicameral legislature, with the new, official title of the National Council of the Slovak Republic. The President was to be elected by the National Council to serve a five-year term of office. It had been anticipated that the veteran politician and 1960s communist reformer, Alexander Dubček, would be elected as Slovakia's first President. However, he died in November 1992 as the result of injuries received in an automobile accident. In two rounds of voting in January 1993 none of the four presidential candidates, one from each of the leading parties, obtained the necessary 60% of votes cast. In mid-February Michal Kováč, Deputy Chairman of the MDS, was presented to the National Council as the sole candidate and was duly appointed President. Although Kováč and Mečiar had been political allies, relations between them soon deteriorated and politics in Slovakia became characterized by feuding between the President and the Government.

After independence Mečiar attempted to broaden his support in parliament and within the country at large by bringing the leader of the Slovak National Party (SNP—Slovenská národná strana), Ľudovít Černák, into his Government. However, the early months of independence were marked by political infighting, not only between parties (Černák resigned as Minister of the Economy over the appointment of a former communist as minister responsible for defence), but also within the MDS. In March 1993 the leading advocate of westernization within the MDS, Milan Kňažko, was obliged to resign his position as Deputy Prime Minister and Minister for Foreign Affairs, after unsuccessfully standing for the leadership of the party against Mečiar. Subsequently, Kňažko and seven other members of the National Council left the MDS and announced their intention to form a rival party, the Alliance of Democrats of the Slovak Republic (ADSR).

By early 1994 Mečiar's Government had lost majority support in the National Council, with only part of the SNP remaining loyal to him. In February six SNP deputies left the party to form what became the National Democratic Party—New Alternative (NDP—NA), with Černák as leader; Ján Slota became leader of the SNP. In the same month Jozef Moravčík, Minister of Foreign Affairs, and Roman Kováč, First Deputy Prime Minister, resigned from the Government, subsequently forming another new opposition party, the Democratic Union of Slovakia (DUS—Demokratická uniá Slovenska). These new factions, along with the ADSR, entered into negotiations to form a moderate party capable of replacing the MDS-SNP coalition, which they accused of becoming increasingly authoritarian and ultra-nationalist.

The Government was defeated in a vote of 'no confidence' on 12 March 1994, and was dismissed two days later. President Kováč invited Jozef Moravčík to form a new government, and a five-party coalition was hastily agreed, comprising the CDM and the PDL, as well as the three new parties, the NDP—NA, the DUS and the ADSR (the last was subsequently absorbed into the DUS). With only an interim mandate, the Government's first act was to approve the holding of early elections on 30 September and 1 October.

Nevertheless, the MDS won 61 seats in the 1994 general election, with 35% of the votes cast, becoming the largest party in the National Council, its success being generally attributed to Mečiar's populist campaign. In late October, following the failure of inter-party negotiations to agree a new coalition, President Kováč invited Mečiar to form a new government. By mid-December Mečiar had created an alliance with the far-right SNP and the left-wing Association of Workers of Slovakia (AWS), which gave him control of 83 seats in the National Council.

A central feature of the new Government was the continuing personal enmity between Mečiar and President Kováč. After taking office, Mečiar worked hard to reduce the influence of the President, and purged opposition supporters from government agencies. Another feature of Mečiar's administration was the alleged political role played by the Slovakian police force and the Slovakian Intelligence Service (SIS). A notable example occurred in August 1995. The son of President Kováč, also called Michal Kováč, was taken by unknown assailants across the border into Austria, where he was detained on the basis of an international arrest warrant which had been issued in Munich, Germany, in connection with allegations of embezzlement. A court in Vienna, Austria, denied the German extradition request, freed Kováč on 20 February 1996, on the grounds that he had been taken to Austria against his will, and implicated the SIS in his abduction.

The episode was widely regarded as an attempt by Mečiar to discredit the President. The Mečiar administration was increasingly subject to criticism from other governments and from international organizations for its intolerance of opposition and its erosion of civil and minority rights. Commentators noted the increasing tendency towards pro-government bias in the broadcasting of the state television and radio stations, which prompted the Organization for Security and Co-operation in Europe (OSCE) to express concern about the lack of freedom in Slovakia's media. Political infighting and the erosion of civil rights undermined Slovakia's chances of joining the first group of transition states invited to participate in NATO and European Union (EU) accession negotiations.

President Kováč's term of office expired on 2 March 1998 but, although efforts to replace him had begun in January, parliament was unable to elect a successor. Mečiar's Government controlled only 82 votes in the National Council, eight votes less than the three-fifths' majority required to elect a President. The Constitution contained provision for the transfer of many presidential powers to the Government in the event of a vacant presidency, and there were suspicions that Mečiar was actively pursuing such an eventuality. With Kováč's departure from office, Mečiar halted all criminal proceedings relating to the abduction of Kováč's son in 1995, and gave amnesties to those implicated. Mečiar also purged the diplomatic corps, replacing 28 of Slovakia's ambassadors (more than one-half of the total). In addition, the MDS appointed two members of parliament to replace deputies who

had defected to the opposition, despite this being declared illegal. Mečiar's actions were strongly criticized by the EU and the USA, and the 15 EU states issued a joint statement warning that this could further damage Slovakia's prospects for EU membership.

At the end of May 1998, despite vigorous resistance from the opposition, the National Council approved government-sponsored amendments to electoral legislation, which would exclude from parliamentary representation those parties that received fewer than 5% of the votes cast in the general election (scheduled for 25–26 September), even those within coalitions. This legislation marked a turning point in domestic politics by galvanizing the opposition into the formation of more concerted alliances. In anticipation of such a move by Mečiar, the Slovak Democratic Coalition (SDC—a grouping of five opposition parties, established in July 1997, which included the CDM, the DUS, the Social Democratic Party of Slovakia—SDP, the Democratic Party and the Green Party) had registered as a single party. In April 1998 three Hungarian minority parties (the Coexistence Party, the Civic Party, and the Hungarian Christian Democratic Party of Slovakia) joined to create the Party of the Hungarian Coalition (PHC—Strana madarskej koalicie). In August Mečiar's MDS tried once again to undermine the opposition, challenging the SDC's right to participate in the general election on the basis that the party registration was illegal since the SDC was not a single party but remained a coalition; the Supreme Court overruled the challenge.

THE SEPTEMBER 1998 ELECTIONS AND THE GOVERNMENT OF MIKULÁŠ DZURINDA

The general election of September 1998 transformed Slovak domestic and foreign policy, as well as bringing about a series of upheavals in the political landscape. The MDS emerged from the general election as the strongest single party, with 27.0% of the votes cast (43 seats), but with little or no chance of forming a government. The only parties prepared to co-operate with Mečiar were the SNP, which won 9.1% of the votes cast (14 seats), and the AWS, which failed to reach the 5% threshold. Four opposition parties secured representation: the SDC (26.3% and 42 seats), the Party of the Democratic Left (PDL, 14.7% and 23 seats), the PHC (9.1% and 15 seats) and the Party of Civic Understanding (PCU, which won 8.0% of the votes cast and 13 seats). These parties expressed their readiness to form a coalition and, with a combined 93 seats in the 150-strong chamber, they would also have the three-fifths' majority necessary to enact constitutional amendments and to elect a candidate to the still-vacant presidency. The formation of the new Government required more than one month of negotiations. Reluctance to admit the PHC into the coalition was overcome when the party agreed that it would not promote the creation of autonomous Hungarian regions or work for the repudiation of the Beneš Decrees (which led to the expulsion of ethnic Germans and Hungarians after the Second World War). The new Government, led by Mikuláš Dzurinda, was appointed on 30 October 1998 and was the first post-independence Government to have ethnic Hungarian representatives. The SDC was allocated nine ministerial posts, the PDL six, the Hungarian coalition three, and the PCU two.

After becoming Prime Minister, Dzurinda attempted to transform the SDC into a real political party, with the aim of creating a power base and eliminating the prospect of further electoral instability. The process started in January 2000, when he announced the creation of a new party, the Slovak Democratic and Christian Union (SDCU), which attracted support from within the five-party coalition. However, the holding of the new party's first conference in November, when Dzurinda was elected Chairman, precipitated the final collapse of the SDC. (This had been likely to occur anyway, since dual party membership was to become illegal at the end of March 2001.)

Although there was frequent speculation that the coalition Government would collapse, not only did it last its four-year term, but the legislative elections of September 2002 confirmed Prime Minister Dzurinda's hold on power. Rising unemployment and the decline in real wages steadily eroded popular support for the parties represented in the Government. However, this was not matched by an increase in support for the MDS. Public antipathy towards Mečiar remained high, and the party suffered. Instead, voters showed support for a new party, Smĕr (Direction), established in October 1999 by Robert Fico. Fico was a member of the communist nomenklatura before 1989, and later served as Slovakia's representative at the European Court of Human Rights. Initially a centre-right party, Smĕr consistently adopted a more nationalist stance throughout 2000, and gained not only at the expense of the MDS, but also of parties in the government coalition. Smĕr and the MDS were often viewed as potential partners in a future government, but Fico stated that he would never co-operate with the MDS as long as Mečiar remained the party leader. In April 2001 the establishment of another new pro-reform party, New Civic Alliance (NCA), was announced by Dr Pavol Ruško, the owner of Slovakia's main television station, Markiza TV. However, regional government elections held in December showed strong support for the MDS, although often in coalition. The MDS took control of two regional legislatures outright, and another three as part of local coalitions. In addition, the MDS won six of eight governships. The SDCU (along with its future coalition partners) won control of the Bratislava regional assembly, and the PHC won control of the Nitra legislature.

The September 2002 elections gave the MDS the largest share of the vote, with 19.5%, but this was well below its 1998 level, followed by the SDCU, with 15.1%. The PHC secured 11.2% of the vote, the CDM 8.3%, and Ruško's NCA another 8.0%. On 8 October these parties agreed to form a new coalition government, again headed by Dzurinda, with 78 seats (a majority of three) in the National Council. The coalition's chances of success were enhanced, when the leader of the Democratic Party told its supporters to vote for the SDCU. To some extent, other right wing and populist parties have gained from the support lost by the MDS, in particular Smĕr, which obtained 13.5% of the vote. Parties on the left wing of the political spectrum also suffered. The SDP, a member of the coalition after 1998, attracted only 2% of the vote, owing partly to a split in April 2002, when a pro-reform group formed a breakaway party. However, the unreformed Communist Party of Slovakia won 6.3% of the vote, obtaining representation in the National Council for the first time.

In local elections on 6–7 December 2002, the MDS also did relatively badly, taking just 16.6% of about 25,000 council seats, and 384 of 2,926 mayoralties. Support for the MDS was strongest in small settlements in mainly rural areas. Voters in cities tended to favour reformist parties. However, the pattern of election results at the local level differs dramatically from the national results. The former coalition party, the PDL, won 128 mayoralties, while independent candidates won 951.

By June 2003 the MDS had fallen to second place in opinion polls, with the support of just 17.7% of the electorate. Fico's Smĕr was the leading party, with 25%. However, support for the coalition members remained strong: the SDCU had 12.7%, the PHC 10.3%, NCA 9.4%, and the CDM 9.1% of the votes.

To some extent the success of the coalition since 1998 has been the result of the political acumen of Dzurinda, but it has also been helped by the creation of a coalition council which convenes regularly to resolve disputes among different coalition members over policy and proposed legislation. However,

the wide range of political parties within the first coalition made it difficult to tackle some political sensitive issues, particularly the reform of the public sector. The new coalition has a more uniform centre-right orientation, which should simplify the ongoing reform process. However, disputes within the coalition over legislation, particularly between the CDM and NCA, have threatened its stability.

Dzurinda and the coalition Government have also been helped by the turbulent nature of Slovak politics, which is characterized less by a division between left-wing and right-wing than between populist and reformist political parties, most of which are organized around a single leader (although NCA, both established and led by Ruško is somewhat populist and reformist). The MDS and Smĕr, the most popular party in opinion polls in mid-2003, have charismatic leaders and are populist in orientation. However, although populist parties and politicians attract considerable support in opinion polls, they often lack internal democracy, despite formal congresses and meetings, and are prone to fragment. This happened to the MDS prior to the 2002 elections, and again in early 2003. In the first case, Ivan Gašparović, a former parliamentary deputy, left the party when he was refused an electoral candidacy, and established his own party, the Movement for Democracy, in July 2002. In the second case, 11 deputies, under the leadership of Vojtech Tkac, broke away to form a new party, the People's Union (L'udová uniá) in late March 2003. Tkac and his associates cited the internal authoritarian methods of the MDS as their reason for leaving, and pledged to remain in opposition. However, that party failed to reach the 5% threshold. At its congress in mid-June, the MDS renamed itself the People's Party—Movement for a Democratic Slovakia. Similarly, the SNP split in October 2001, when Jan Slota left to establish his own party, the Real Slovak National Party. In the September 2002 elections neither party reached the 5% threshold, and consequently at the end of May 2003 the SNP and Real SNP decided to reunite, with Slota as the new Chairman, and Anna Malikova, former Chairman after Slota left, as first Vice-Chairman. The reunification occurred after an acrimonious SNP conference in April failed to elect a new party leader. In addition, the MDS and SNP politicians were repeatedly charged with violations of the law, and even Mečiar in mid-2003 remained the subject of an investigation into the source of some 40m. Slovak koruny used to pay for the reconstruction of a residence while he was Prime Minister. The many enterprises privatized under Mečiar's Government were also controversial, and in early July a former Minister of the Economy under Mečiar, Karol Cesnek, was one of eight people accused of fraud and abuse of power in embezzling money from a holding company, which took over a major armaments manufacturer in the town of Martin in 1994.

In its first four years the Dzurinda Government created the financial and institutional foundation for development, and from September 2002 it concentrated on building the infrastructure. In its first term, the Government completed the privatization of large firms, reorganized public administration, undertook reform of the courts, made the legislative, judicial and administrative systems more transparent, and initiated the depoliticization of the economy and state administration. To a considerable extent, the agenda was determined by EU issues prior to membership. During the next four years the Government is likely to concentrate on the further reform of institutions, including the courts and civil service, the reduction of corruption, the structural reform of enterprises and enterprise taxation, and the clearing up of politically contentious areas of the economy, including pensions, state benefits, and the railways.

Slovakia was originally expected to join NATO and the Organisation for Economic Co-operation and Development

(OECD) at the same time as the Czech Republic, but was excluded from those two organizations owing to a failure to undertake economic and political reforms and to respect human rights. For the same reasons, it was excluded from the EU accession process. During the first few years in power, the Dzurinda Government was forced to make up for lost time, renationalizing and then reprivatizing several enterprises, and instituting reforms which had been abandoned or delayed under Mečiar. These included the restoration of democracy, readjusting and rebuilding international relations, restoring confidence in and bringing transparency to the economy, restructuring politically-motivated privatizations, reorganizing and revitalizing the banking sector, rescuing mismanaged enterprises, and enforcing fiscal rectitude on enterprises. As a consequence, Slovakia was rapidly back on course to meet the conditions of the EU, OECD and NATO.

One of the first acts of the Government formed in 1998 was to enact a law requiring that the President of the Republic be directly elected for a five-year term. The first such election was held on 15 May 1999, with a second round of voting taking place two weeks later. The governing coalition's candidate, Rudolf Schuster, the leader of the PCU, obtained 57% of the votes cast in the second round, defeating Mečiar, who won 43% of the votes.

The Government also announced that it would investigate the actions of the previous administration and the SIS, with particular regard to the abduction of the then President's son in August 1995. The head of the SIS at the time, Ivan Lexa, although he had fled abroad in 2000, was eventually charged *in absentia* later that year. In 2002, after it was discovered that he was living in South Africa, he was extradited to Slovakia in July and arrested. These investigations were part of a broader review of appointments and actions taken by the previous Government. In April 2000 Mečiar was arrested and charged with fraud and abuse of power. He was released later on the same day, having been fined for refusing to answer questions relating to the abduction of Michal Kováč and charges previously made against Lexa. The means used to apprehend Mečiar (large numbers of armed police used explosives to gain entry to his home) were criticized by opposition groups. However, opinion polls showed that almost two-thirds of the electorate supported the arrest.

As part of its attempts to reinvigorate democracy, the Government restored language rights for minority groups within the country in 1999. At the end of February 2001 the National Council enacted constitutional amendments that introduced the right of regional self-government and a new law that strengthened the independence of the judiciary by creating a council of judges. The Government also enhanced the status of the Constitutional Court and of the state audit office, and adopted freedom of information legislation, which came into effect at the beginning of 2001.

Five years after the departure of Mečiar's Government, the SIS retained a reputation for malpractice. In December 2002 the SIS was accused in an article of being involved in a variety of illicit activities. Subsequently, a scandal erupted over the illegal recording of the telephone conversations of Ruško, the leader of the NCA. The SIS and the Interior Ministry were believed to be responsible, although the NCA was a coalition partner. The Minister of the Interior, Vladimír Palko, claimed that the SIS and not the Ministry had effective control of the system. In February 2003 a second scandal developed, when a newspaper and a television station received transcripts of 25 mobile telephone conversations, in which Gabriel Palacka, a former transport minister and member of the SDCU, appeared to be implicated in embezzlement.

Finally, on 11 March 2003, the head of the SIS, Vladimír Mitro, resigned, after strong criticism of his appointment of Peter Tóth as head of counter-intelligence in late February.

Tóth allegedly accused Palko of manipulating the database of recorded telephone conversations for political advantage, and Palko responded by filing suit against Tóth for libel and defamation. Mečiar incited more controversy by publicly declaring that not only was it possible to order the 'tapping' of an opponent's telephone by the SIS, but that he had witnessed such activities himself. Mitro was replaced by Ladislav Pittner, an SDCU member and a former Minister of the Interior, on 2 April. The series of scandals also fostered dissension within the coalition, particularly between the CDM and the NCA, the latter arguing that it should be given a role in managing the SIS and Ministry of the Interior institutions, which were under the control of members of the SDCU and CDM, respectively. The SIS annual report, released in June, made no mention of these scandals, but did claim that spies from former Soviet bloc countries had been discovered operating inside Slovakia.

To the frustration of many critics of the SIS, Lexa was released from detention in June 2003. However, he was to stand trial on charges of involvement in the murder of a former police-officer, believed to have been involved in providing evidence in the kidnapping of Michal Kováč, junior. Lexa was also accused of sabotage, fraud, trafficking in illegal weapons and abuse of office. In early 2003 it was announced that he would face an additional three charges of misuse of power, including espionage relating to Michal Kováč, planting an explosive device at a CDM pre-election meeting, and the alleged theft of a 'tapping' system from the SIS. Meanwhile, from May 2003 the public was allowed to examine files held on them, compiled by a former Czechoslovak security agency, with the creation of a National Memory Institute, operating at the Ministry of Justice. It was estimated that, of some 70,000 original files formerly under the control of the SIS, about two-thirds remained.

In many ways the Lexa case clearly demonstrated the problems facing the legal system, including a backlog of court cases and long delays in bringing cases to trial. In 2001 civil cases continued for an average of 14 months, and criminal cases for four months. Reform of the legal system and courts has been under way since May 2001, with the adoption of a series of new legislation and amendments increasing the independence of the judiciary and legal system. In April 2002 the Act on the Judicial Council was adopted, creating an elected Council of 18 members, all of whom must be lawyers, and nine of whom must be judges. However, in the first half of 2003, the Council failed to elect a new Chairman of the Supreme Court. The term of the incumbent, Štefan Harabin, ended in February, and he failed to win re-election after two attempts. Previous candidates were prohibited from further attempts at election, and by June three new candidates were proposed to be elected for a five-year term.

The Code of Criminal procedure was amended in June 2002 with the aim of simplifying pre-trial procedures, removing overlaps in duties between police and prosecutors, and increasing transparency in investigation procedure. It also introduced conciliation as a means of resolving disputes. Under proposals for the reorganization of the court system in 2003, two regional courts would be closed, and the remaining six courts would be renamed higher courts, and serve mainly to hear appeals; 55 district courts would be replaced by 25 local courts and 17 'detached branches'. However, foreign observers suggested that the boundaries between the courts and the executive and legislative branches of government remain uncertain, noting among other things the lack of an independent budget and appropriations process. In the case of the court reorganization, for example, judges were not consulted beforehand, and countered by suggesting that reducing administration would help to improve productivity.

Civil service reform has been another goal of the Dzurinda Government. The Civil Service Act of July 2001 established a Civil Service Office to ensure compliance with the act, and to carry out tasks in connection with management and development of the civil service. In 2002, after consultation with European partners, it developed a strategic plan for the development of the Civil Service, examining ways of improving the selection process, and grading and job evaluation. Additional work has looked at the question of civil service pay. Following the 2002 elections, the coalition continued to pursue the reform of democratic institutions. Within the National Council, there were demands for the elimination of spending limits on political campaigns, and their replacement with tougher controls on sources of party incomes. At 2003, pre-election spending was limited to 12m. Slovak koruny. There were also demands to amend the Constitution to reduce the immunity of deputies.

As part of a series of extensive economic reforms, the Government reassessed the privatization process. The VSŽ steel works, which had been sold cheaply to a Mečiar associate, was taken back into public ownership when the company collapsed. After some restructuring, VSŽ was sold to US Steel in 2000, with guarantees of investment, minimal job losses and some government responsibility for inherited debts. Likewise, what was effectively renationalization took place in the banking sector, followed by reorganization and a second privatization. A dramatic increase in direct foreign investment accompanied these actions, enhanced by the end of the policy of retaining firms in so-called strategic sectors in state ownership. Such reforms also ended the 'soft' loans and government intervention that had kept many firms functioning. In mid-2000 it was estimated that over one-half of all enterprises in the country were making a loss. However, earlier that year the Government introduced a new bankruptcy law, designed to emulate US legislation, which encouraged the process towards keeping firms as ongoing concerns.

Encouraging macroeconomic figures from Slovakia were greeted favourably by foreign observers, and the EU became much more positive about Slovakia's progress towards membership of the Union (see below), and in Slovakia support for EU membership increased steadily throughout 2000 and 2001. According to an opinion poll taken in December 2000, 79.6% of the population fully or partly supported membership, one of the highest levels of support among the former communist countries. At the referendum on accession on 16–17 May 2003 the rate of voter participation was just over 52%, despite concern that the referendum would fail to attract the required minimum of 50% of the electorate to be valid. Some 92.5% of those who voted were in favour of joining the EU. On 1 July the National Council approved the accession treaty, which only the Communist Party of Slovakia opposed.

MINORITY RIGHTS IN SLOVAKIA

Slovakia has not eliminated ethnic frictions, but since the late 1990s efforts have been made to reduce discrimination and increase opportunity, particularly for the Roma (Gypsy) minority. Hungarians account for nearly 10% of the population, according to the census of 2001, while the population of Roma increased to 89,920 (about 1.7% of the total). However, it is widely believed that the census under-enumerated the Roma population, and estimates range from 350,000 to 500,000.

Hungarian-speaking Slovakians are represented by the PHC, which regularly takes about 10% of the votes in elections, and as such constitutes a stable political bloc. After 1998 it formed part of the Government, which gave the Hungarian minority some part in policy-making, although as the debate over the restoration of language rights demonstrated, the influence of the party was limited. Both the MDS

and Smĕr expressed anti-Hungarian bias, leaving the party no choice but to support the coalition Government. Despite its participation in the governing coalition, the party's support in opinion polls did not wane in the same way as support for the other constituent parties. Although Slovakia and Hungary signed a Treaty of Friendship and Co-operation in early 1995, which guaranteed the rights of ethnic minorities in each republic and confirmed the existing border, under the Mečiar Government relations between Slovakia and Hungary remained cool. Among Slovaks, there were fears, heightened by some statements from Hungarian politicians, that Hungary, which had controlled parts of Slovakia in 1938–44, had not given up revisionist hopes of expanding its boundaries. Then, in March 1996 the National Council approved the reorganization of local government, which came into effect in July of that year, creating a situation in which Hungarians remained a minority in every administrative region. This, in turn, could lead to a decline in the representation of Hungarians in the National Council. There had been a number of earlier disputes, involving the prohibition from January 1996 of the official use of any language other than Slovak, the removal of bilingual road signs and the compulsory Slovak styling of female Hungarian names, despite an adverse ruling by the Slovakian Constitutional Court.

As well as the conciliatory approach taken by the Dzurinda Government, the prospect of membership in the EU has also helped to foster a greater degree of minority rights for Hungarians and Roma. The PHC became a member of the coalition, and by mid-1999 the Dzurinda Government had adopted new minority-language legislation allowing Hungarians and other minorities to use their own language when dealing with local government. However, the law, which was drafted after extensive consultation with the EU and the OSCE, only covered minority groups in areas where they comprised 20% or more of the population. Thus, 158 communities, with a total population of about 100,000, were excluded. The PHC protested this restriction, and proposed various amendments, but the law was passed unchanged. A European Charter on minority languages entered into force on 1 January 2002, obligating Slovakia to provide better access to higher education for minorities. On 12 March 2003 the Slovak cabinet agreed to open a Hungarian language university in the town of Komárno by September 2004.

In 1999–2000 the Dzurinda Government adopted a strategy for Roma, which aimed at eliminating discrimination and disadvantages that contributed to the marginalization of Roma. However, the strategy was criticized for consisting mainly of short-term projects and focusing on social issues, such as training, unemployment, and housing, rather than confronting broader issues such as discrimination. To some extent, Government recognized the problem. In early 2003 it announced plans to spend 50m. Slovak koruny (€1.2m.) on Roma projects in that year. In addition, EU funds were expected become available after 2004.

However, Roma problems remain severe. The cabinet identified 620 Roma settlements in the country, mainly in the east, where about 139,560 Roma live. Many of these settlements lack running water and electricity. It is reported that in some settlements, 90% and even 100% of residents are unemployed, and many have not worked since 1989. Initiatives to encourage municipal authorities to build additional housing have not been well received, and some have argued that such housing would simply reinforce patterns of Roma segregation. It has also been noted that many settlements are 'squatter' settlements, where the legal ownership of land is unclear, leaving residents vulnerable to eviction. The health of Roma is also generally poor. The average lifespan of the Roma is only 54.5 years for males and 68.5 years for females, compared with a Slovak average of 73.1 years.

The Roma population is also characterized by low levels of education, compared with the rest of the population. According to the 1991 census, only 0.8% had completed secondary education. As part of the commitment to guarantee protection for minority languages, in early 2003 the Government announced plans to open three Roma high schools with teaching in Romany language and history. The first, with a focus on foreign languages and technology, was to open in Košice, in September 2003.

Unlike the Hungarians, the Roma are not politically organized; they have no political parties, and lack representation in government. In July 1995 a particularly brutal attack by extreme right-wing youths, in Banská Bystrica, led to the death of a Roma. This was followed by a suggestion from Ján Slota, the leader of the SNP, that Roma be housed in separate villages because it had not proved possible to integrate them into society. In February 2003 Slota, by this time the leader of the Real Slovak National Party, proposed that the legislature should pass a law offering to pay Roma men to be sterilized. The proposal came only a few weeks after allegations that Roma women from eastern Slovakia had been forced into sterilization, raising serious questions about the situation of Roma in Slovakia. The rise in racially motivated crimes, directed mainly at Roma and those of African and Asian origin, rose almost three-fold in 2002.

The problems of ongoing discrimination and violence were emphasized from October 1997, when, following the broadcast on Slovakian television of a documentary about Slovakian refugees in the United Kingdom, large numbers of Slovakian Roma sought refuge in the West. In October 1998 the United Kingdom imposed a visa requirement on Slovakian nationals visiting the country after an inflow of several thousand Roma refugees. Similarly, in July 1999 there was an exodus of over 1,000 Roma to Finland, prompting the Finnish Prime Minister to warn that treatment of the Roma could harm Slovakia's chances of joining the EU. A number of other European countries also imposed visa requirements in the late 1990s. Despite continued efforts at integration and de-marginalization, in March 2003 the Czech Government announced that in the first 12 weeks of the year as many as 20,000 Roma from Eastern Slovakia had migrated to the Czech Republic.

FOREIGN POLICY

Since 1993 foreign policy has centred around several main issues. These include relations with the Czech Republic and Hungary, and the EU, NATO and other European institutions. Early post-independence relations with the Czech Republic were dictated by the division of the previous Czechoslovak state's assets. As the Czechs retained control of certain pivotal assets, such as the state airline and travel agency, the Slovaks claimed that they were entitled to some form of compensation. Furthermore, Slovakians were initially prevented from taking up the shares that they had bought in Czech companies privatized during 1992. In July 1993 controls were introduced on the Czech–Slovakian border, in a development provoked by the increased movement of immigrants around Central and South-Eastern Europe, particularly of those hoping to reach and settle in Germany. However, an agreement ensured that restrictions on movement between the two countries would not apply to nationals of the Czech Republic and Slovakia.

Slovak-Czech relations remained volatile. On 10 April 1997 the Czech President, Václav Havel (the last President of Czechoslovakia), who had opposed the dissolution of the Czechoslovak state, publicly criticized Mečiar for his attitude to the involvement of NATO in Eastern Europe. The Slovakian Government, in turn, accused Havel of insulting Mečiar and of interfering in Slovakia's internal affairs. The Slovakian ambassador was recalled from Prague, and a planned summit meeting between the two countries' premiers was cancelled. When the meeting finally took place in October 1997, only minor disputes between the two countries were resolved.

Although Mečiar's Government repeatedly affirmed its commitment to the pursuit of EU and NATO membership, its actions indicated quite the reverse, demonstrating a suspicion of Western institutions and a desire to orientate Slovakia towards the east. Russia offered loans and assistance to help complete the Russian-designed Mochovce nuclear power station, in the west of the country, which became operational in June 1998. Its inauguration adversely affected relations with Austria, which was concerned about the plant's safety. Also, it was alleged that Russia was supplying petroleum, gas and other raw materials to Slovakia at below-market prices.

As a successor to the Czechoslovak state, Slovakia was a member of the Visegrad Group and of the Central European Free Trade Association (CEFTA). Following independence, in October 1993 Slovakia signed an association agreement with the European Community (known as the EU from November of that year). Upon independence, the country had associate status with the OECD, through its Partners in Transition programme. After being invited to become a full member in July 2000, Slovakia joined in December of that year. During the mid-1990s the Mečiar Government drew increasingly forthright criticism from international organizations for its lack of commitment to democratic reform and to civil rights. European institutions issued a number of statements warning the Slovakian Government that its actions were in conflict with the general aims of the EU. Finally, in July 1997 Slovakia learnt that it had been excluded from the first group of former communist states to be invited to join NATO and the list of countries to participate in early EU accession negotiations. The Government's intolerance of opposition and the fragility of democracy were cited as the principal reasons.

The victory of the opposition in the September 1998 general election occasioned a reversal in Slovakian foreign policy. The Dzurinda Government, which took office in October, was outspoken in its enthusiasm for Western European institutions, declaring its intent to seek early membership of both the EU and NATO. After being congratulated by the EU on its progress towards meeting the criteria for admission, Slovakia was invited, on 10 December 1999, to begin accession negotiations. This was facilitated once the President of the European Commission, Romano Prodi, decided on a policy of flexible negotiations, characterized by a multi-speed accession process. On 15 February 2000 official discussions commenced, with substantive negotiations beginning on 28 March. One year later Slovakia had provisionally closed 16 chapters of the EU's *acquis communautaire*, and had caught up with the original 'first-wave' applicants. On 13 December 2002 the Government concluded accession talks, and was invited to join the EU on 1 May 2004. The National Council approved the Treaty of Accession on 10 April 2003, and it was signed on 16 April in Athens, Greece.

The Dzurinda Government improved relations with the Czech Republic, ending those disputes which had persisted since the dissolution of the Czech and Slovak Federation in 1993. The Slovakian central bank sold a 24% share in Československa Obchodní Banka at the end of December 1999, for US $400m. This was the same as the price of the Czech Government's 66% share, which had been sold to a foreign investor in May. In November of that year the two countries had settled their last remaining financial disputes over 5% of the former federation's assets. They agreed to cancel mutual financial claims, to the benefit of Slovakia, which owed the Czech central bank about $740m. The Czech central bank also gave Slovakia 4.1m. metric tons of gold that it had retained. In addition, the two countries exchanged state-held shares in two banks: Slovakia's 13.6% share in the

Czech Komerční banka was exchanged for the Czech Republic's 16.9% share in the Slovak Všeobecná úverová banka, enabling both banks to be privatized. According to opinion polls conducted in early 2003, 10 years after independence, only 43% of Czechs believed that the split had been beneficial. Within Slovakia, concerns have been expressed that Czech children are losing the ability to understand Slovak, while Slovaks continue to understand Czech. (Czech television is available in Slovakia, but Slovak television is not available in Czech Republic.) However, after Václav Klaus (whose wife is Slovak) was elected President of the Czech Republic on 28 February, he expressed concern at the decline in trade between the two countries and urged the development of closer links with Slovakia.

Improved relations with Hungary were also a priority for the Government. As well as the enactment of new minority-language legislation, a sign of the improved relations between the two countries was the decision, agreed in September 1999, to build a new bridge across the Danube. This would replace the one destroyed by German forces at the end of the Second World War, the only such bridge not to have been replaced. The bridge and the consequent reductions in distances for travellers would not only enable ethnic Hungarians on both sides of the border to visit and trade, but was expected to help revitalize the local economies of peripheral regions in both Hungary and Slovakia—a major concern, with unemployment in the immediate region of Slovakia nearing 30%. The Dzurinda Government also defused another source of contention between the two countries, the Gabčíkovo-Nagymaros hydroelectric project. This scheme was initiated by the Governments of Czechoslovakia and Hungary in 1978, involving the construction of two dams and the diversion of the River Danube, was another ongoing source of conflict between Hungary and Slovakia. In 1989 Hungary abandoned the project on the grounds that it was environmentally harmful, but the Czechoslovak and later Slovak Governments proceeded unilaterally. Towards the end of 1992 the Slovak Government diverted the Danube and initial operations of the Gabčíkovo dam system began in 1994. In March 1993 Slovakia and Hungary agreed to forward the dispute to the International Court of Justice (ICJ—based in The Hague, Netherlands). In September 1997 the ICJ ruled that both countries had breached international law and that they were required to negotiate to fulfil the original agreement. After the Dzurinda Government assumed office in 1998, additional discussion led to the decision to submit the issue to a panel of experts.

Perhaps the most obvious sign of Hungarian-Slovakian détente was the Slovakian Government's approval, in late September 2000, of the sale of a 36.2% share of Slovnaft, a petroleum refiner and operator of fuel stations, to the Hungarian Oil and Gas Company Ltd (Magyar Olaj és Gázipari Rt—MOL). This allowed MOL an option to purchase a controlling interest in Slovnaft within two years. In March 2003 MOL exercised the option, taking an additional 32% share in the Slovnaft refinery, in addition to a 2% stake acquired from shareholders. This was described by the Chairman of MOL as the 'most important transaction in the history of Slovakia and Hungary'. However, although relations between Hungary and Slovakia were much improved, there were still some areas of friction.

In June 2001 the Hungarian legislature approved the so-called 'Status' or 'Benefit' Law, which came into effect at the beginning of 2002. The law aimed to promote an Hungarian identity among ethnic Hungarians living abroad, to encourage Hungarians in other countries to study in Hungarian, and to create a sense of a greater Hungarian community. The law was criticized by the Council of Europe and, after consultation with Hungarians living abroad, was amended by the Hungarian legislature in June 2003, to state that after Hungary joined the EU it would be implemented in accordance with EU regulations. Although the amended law met with EU approval, the Slovak Government continued to argue that it compromised Slovak sovereignty. However, in July the Ministers of Foreign Affairs of Hungary and Slovakia reached a potential solution for the implementation of the law.

Interestingly, the Hungarian Status Law inspired a similar Slovak government initiative, first raised in March 2003, to create a law supporting Slovak foreign communities, including the creation of an Office for Slovaks Abroad. The office would place all responsibility for dealing with the overseas Slovak community in one office, and help to promote and maintain a Slovak identity among members of the Slovak diaspora. It was noted that in the 1990 US census, 1.9m. people identified themselves as being of Slovak origin, but in the 2000 census, the figure had fallen to 900,000. In the Czech Republic the number of Slovaks had fallen from 320,000 to 220,000 in 1991–2001. The World Association for Slovaks Living Abroad suggested that the way in which the Hungarian Government supported ethnic Hungarians abroad could serve as an example, and pointed out that in 2003 Hungary spent almost €33m. on such support, compared with about €71,000 spent by Slovakia.

Slovakia also improved relations with Austria. A new nuclear power plant with two reactors was opened at Mochovce in 1998, despite the objections of the Austrian Government. Further expansion of the plant was postponed, and in response to representations from Austria, another nuclear plant at Bohunice was to be closed between 2006 and 2008. This second plant relied on Soviet era reactors, and was the site of two accidents, one in 1972, and the second in 1977. The EU has been providing money to prepare for the closure through the PHARE (originally Poland/Hungary Assistance for the Restructuring of Economies) programme.

In early 2003, prior to a visit by the Pope later in the year, the CDM proposed a treaty with the Vatican that would allow public servants to express 'conscientious objection', and refuse to undertake any act that contradicted their religion or ethics. This was strongly opposed by some parties, particularly Smer, which argued that the CDM was attempting to impose a Roman Catholic lifestyle on all levels of society. However, according to census figures, since 1991 the number of Slovaks acknowledging a religious affiliation had increased sharply, to 84.1% in 2001, from 72.8% in 1991. The share of Roman Catholics of the total population increased from 60.4% to 68.9%.

In November 2002 Slovakia finally received a formal invitation to become a member of NATO in 2004. Consequently, in February 2003 the Government decided to send an anti-chemical unit of 75 soldiers to Iraq as part of a broader initiative to develop a NATO-EU unit. The troops returned to Slovakia in June. Meanwhile, in late May plans were announced for the creation of a special military unit, specializing in peace-keeping, mine-clearing and reconstruction, to be deployed with NATO or EU peace-keeping forces. However, a survey taken in early June suggested that an increasing amount of criticism was directed towards the USA in the aftermath of the US-led military action in Iraq.

In April 2003 members of the National Council criticized Cuba for violating human rights, after arresting people accused of conspiring with the USA, and Robert Fico, the head of Smer, was publicly criticized by members of the government coalition for a June visit to Belarus, on the grounds that it gave legitimacy to the undemocratic regime of President Alyaksandr Lukashenka. Thus, by mid-2003 Slovak foreign policy had completed a total reversal from the position of 1989.

RELATIONS WITH THE EU

Preparation for EU accession had dominated, and continued to dominate, the legislative agenda and political scene. There was widespread concern that the country would not be prepared to obtain the full amount of accession and post-accession funds to which it was entitled, owing to a lack of administrative capacity at all levels of government, unfamiliarity with EU rules, and insufficient budgetary resources to enable governments to pay their share of funding. To some extent, fears about funding were based on Slovakia's experience with pre-accession funds, particularly the Special Pre-accession Programme for Agriculture and Rural Development (SAPARD), one of three sources of pre-accession funding. SAPARD was created to support projects related to agriculture and regional development. The other two sources of funding are the Instrument for Structural Policies for Pre-Accession (ISPA), aimed at supporting transport and infrastructure projects, and PHARE, created at the very beginning of the transition process in 1989 to support a variety of accession measures, but reorientated in 1997 to support EU accession. After 2004, these programmes were to be replaced by structural and cohesion funds. ISPA funding was obtained relatively quickly, because Slovakia had a range of road and rail projects and water and sewer treatment projects in development, but SAPARD funding was slower in coming. The initial agreement to commit funds was signed in 1999, but it was not until April 2002 that Slovakia's SAPARD agency was accredited and the European Commission decided to confer the management of SAPARD aid to the Slovak authorities. From January 2004 Slovakia would be able to submit proposals for structural funds. In March 2003 the National Council adopt a national development plan, prepared by the Ministry for Construction and Public Works, which was submitted to the EU; however, at the end of May the EU returned strategic documents concerned with accessing structural funds to the Slovak Government, stating that they were characterized by a lack of clarity and had little input from regional governments. After 2004 EU funds were to be directed to areas where GDP per head was less than 75% of the EU average, which included the whole country, with the exception of the Bratislava region.

At mid-2003 it appeared that Slovakia was the least-prepared candidate country. However, although some Slovaks suggested that corruption was a major problem, EU officials stated that lack of training was the main issue. At the end of April just over 300 officials were involved in EU matters, but that number was to increase to 600 by the end of August. Recruitment was hampered by high turnover and lack of skills, and the Government announced that in order to attract and retain qualified staff, wages were to be relatively high, up to 45,000 koruny per month in the Ministry of Construction and Public Works, compared with an average monthly wage of just 14,000 koruny. The Ministry of Construction and Public Works offered a special course on structural funds, in conjunction with eight universities from Austria and Slovakia, which was attended by 380 people from state and regional government administrations, non-governmental organizations, and professional associations in 2001. In early 2003, in response to the need for trained staff, the Government announced the creation of an instruction programme based in the European Affairs section of the Government, the Continuous Professional Training (CPT) Slovakia Project. The Government aimed to use the Project to train 400 employees of the central and regional Governments and as many as 25 members of the National Council.

Concern was also expressed that the national and regional administrations were ill-prepared to support EU bids. Although funds required co-financing, there were no provisions in the national budget, nor in the budgets of the eight regional Governments, for matching funds, and in March 2003 the head of an EU delegation to Slovakia expressed concern as to whether regional Governments understood the nature of, and were ready to deal with, structural funds. Moreover, in early May it was noted that few projects were being developed to take advantage of funding, although project applications were to be accepted from January 2004.

Meanwhile, it is widely expected that wages would rise after accession, partly owing to the need to prevent skilled workers from emigrating once freedom of movement in the EU was established. Initially, freedom of movement will be restricted: countries have two years in which to open their labour markets to citizens of the accession states, but this can be extended by an additional three years if necessary, and by a further two years if it is thought likely to destabilize national labour markets. However, Denmark, Greece, Ireland, the Netherlands, Sweden and the United Kingdom announced that their labour markets would be opened up to accession nationals from 2004. Increases in property prices are also predicted when, after a transitional period, Slovakia is forced to open its property market to all EU nationals.

The Economy

Dr ANDREW RYDER

INTRODUCTION

From independence in 1993, the Slovakian economy consistently exceeded expectations. However, much of this period was characterized by political instability during the Governments of Vladimír Mečiar, the Prime Minister in 1993–98. By mid-2003, despite extremely high levels of unemployment, the economy appeared to be one of the more successful of the former communist bloc states, characterized by a low rate of inflation and rising gross domestic product (GDP). By this time it was estimated that GDP had recovered to 111% of its 1989 level, a rate of recovery from the severe recession of 1989–91 exceeded in the region only by Hungary, Poland and Slovenia. After 1989 the economy was characterized by a shift from reliance on industry to services and a move from state to private ownership. Between 1990 and 2003 the proportion of GDP accounted for by industry declined from 52.7% to an estimated 26.7%, and agriculture's share fell slightly from 5.7% to 3.9%, while that of services increased from 34.2% to almost 64%.

In 1990 prices and the rate of inflation in the Czech and Slovak Republics were similar, but in 1991 the Slovakian rate of inflation accelerated. Higher inflation was initially expected to persist throughout the mid-1990s; however, the rate of inflation rose more slowly in Slovakia than in the Czech Republic in that period.

At the time of separation Slovakia agreed to assume responsibility for US $2,600m. worth of Czechoslovakia's $9,500m. debt, and to adhere to a free-trade zone, the Central European Free Trade Area (CEFTA), originally comprising its partners in the Visegrad Group, the Czech Republic, Hungary and Poland (so named after the Hungarian town in which the leaders of the latter two countries and Czechoslovakia met in 1991), which came into effect at the beginning of March 1993 (Slovakia withdrew from CEFTA in March 2003). However, the separation of the Czech and Slovak Republics failed to clarify long-term bilateral economic relations. Moreover, it imposed new administrative costs on Slovakia, such as those involved in setting up diplomatic representation abroad and new ministries and state bureaux.

The separation of the Czech and Slovak Republics was considered a 'velvet divorce', and public statements suggested that close economic and political relations would be maintained. However, relations between the two countries were often difficult. Plans for the two countries to use a common currency for at least six months proved short lived. Fears that high inflation and the outflow of convertible ('hard') currency from Slovakia would destabilize the crown (koruna) led to the Czech Government withdrawing from the currency agreement within six weeks of the separation. Each country established a new koruna. Pressure to devalue the new Slovak currency swiftly emerged, although the central bank insisted on maintaining parity with the Czech version until July 1993. Inflation accelerated, owing in part to the imposition of value-added tax (VAT), but also owing to the need to eliminate subsidies and price controls.

Although the economies of the two states were highly interdependent, the system of payments between enterprises in the different republics was confused by the creation of separate currencies. This affected the 'voucher' privatization programme, which had started before the dissolution of the federation. At the beginning of 1993 Slovak commercial banks owed 24,700m. koruny to the successor to the Central Bank of Czechoslovakia, an amount equal to the former subsidy paid by the Czechs to the Slovaks. By early March Slovak firms owed 16,800m. koruny to the Czech Republic. Moreover, there was still debate over the proper division of federal assets. During the first round of privatization carried out by the Federal Government in 1992, Slovak investment in Czech companies had considerably exceeded Czech investment in Slovak firms, and the Czech Government refused to distribute further vouchers to Slovak citizens.

Customs posts appeared at 18 crossings along the new border, despite a proposed customs union. Telephone calls between the Czech and Slovak Republics, formerly charged at a domestic rate, were now charged at an international one, and quintupled in price. Trade and banking relations were also complicated—even before the dissolution of Czechoslovakia, trade between the two republics had declined sharply, and the contraction was exacerbated by the separation. However, the two countries shared a common external tariff, averaging 8%, even though goods from third countries did not circulate freely between them. A clearing system using the European Currency Unit (ECU) as the accounting unit operated in 1993–95, providing for controlled fluctuations of the two currencies, before being abandoned as part of the move towards implementing full currency convertibility, and a customs union was eventually established.

The shift to world market prices for fuel and raw materials, and the collapse of traditional markets in the old communist bloc of Central and South-Eastern Europe and the former USSR, affected the balance of trade, and impeded the manufacturing sector and exporters in general. In 1999 trade with the Czech Republic still accounted for almost 20% of the country's total trade, although the share continued to decline thereafter, falling to just 14.5% of imports and 14.5% of exports in the first five months of 2003.

Real GDP within the Slovak Republic declined in 1990–93. GDP grew annually from 1994, reaching a rate of 6.6% in 1996. Recession in the Czech Republic and in Russia in the late 1990s slowed GDP growth, with the economy expanding

by 4.4% in 1998, but by only an estimated 1.9% in 1999. This contraction was exacerbated by the austerity programme imposed by the new Government of Mikuláš Dzurinda. The slower growth in GDP was accompanied by a decline in industrial output in 1999, with the textiles and manufacturing sectors particularly affected. However, by the last quarter of that year, output had resumed its previous upward trend. Industrial output had contracted sharply in 1989–93, but increased for almost all the remainder of the decade (contracting again only in 1999). Subsequently, GDP growth was positive, reaching an annual rate of 4.4% in 2002, and remaining at 4.1% in the first quarter of 2003.

AGRICULTURE

Agriculture in Slovakia is shaped by relief. The country's farming regions can be divided into four zones, which follow the relief from north to south. These are the warm southern plains, suitable for the cultivation of maize and vines; a cooler zone, which extends across the entire country and in which wheat, barley and sugar beet are grown; a slightly larger belt suitable for growing rye, oats and potatoes; and a mountain region used mainly for grazing, which dominates the central part of the country, covering about one-quarter of the total area. In total, 51% of the area of the country is used for farming, and just over 40% of the territory is covered by forests.

Until 1989 Slovakia was self-sufficient in basic foodstuffs, and is still essentially self-sufficient in basic products. Leading cereal crops included wheat, barley and maize; other major crops included oil seeds, sugar beets, fruits and vegetables and poppy seeds. From the start of the transition process, agriculture declined in importance, its share of GDP falling from 8.2% in 1990 to 3.5% in 2002. The area sown generally remained stable, but, according to World Bank figures, agricultural value added declined by an annual average of 0.2% in 1990–97. By the end of the 1990s the sector had stabilized, as indicated by revised World Bank figures including the final two years of the decade, showing a bare overall growth of 0.7% per year. Cereal production declined from 4.4m. metric tons in 1988 to 3.2m. tons in 1993, but recovered to 3.9m. tons by 1996, and remained at about that level in 2001. Sugar-beet production fell from 1.8m. metric tons in 1988 to 1.1m. tons in 1993, although it recovered to 1.7m. tons in 1996, before declining again, to 1.3m. tons, by 1998. Sugar-beet output declined to less than 1m. in 2000, but rose to 1.3m. in 2001. Potato production fluctuated, amid a general trend of decline, from 669,000 metric tons in 1991 to 412,000 tons in 1998; output declined slightly to 387,300 in 2001. Livestock figures decreased sharply: between 1989 and 2001 the number of cattle fell from 1,623,000 to 645,000 head; sheep declined from 621,000 to 358,000, and pigs from 2.7m. to 1.5m. Milk production decreased from 1,995m. litres in 1989 to about 1,160m. litres in 2001. Hothouses also declined in area, falling to about one-third of 1989 levels by 1995. Employment in agriculture also steadily contracted; in 1990 the sector (including forestry and fishing) employed 14.7% of those employed; by the end of 2002 the average for the year was just 6.2% of the labour force, and in the first quarter of 2003 employment in the sector had fallen year-on-year by 10,000. By late 2000 the contribution of the food sector (including livestock, food products and tobacco) to total exports had fallen to just 2.9%, although the share of agricultural trade in total trade in that year was 5.0%. This was the result of imports: in 2000 Slovakia had a negative balance in agricultural trade of US $382m. Subsequently, although exports were further damaged by the appearance of 'mad cow disease' (BSE) in the country in September 2001, agriculture accounted for 3.7% of exports in 2001. However, 10 additional cases of BSE were reported in the following 12 months, and in

July 2003 one more case was discovered in the course of a routine sample. Moreover, during the second quarter of 2003 a prolonged drought threatened incomes and output. Declining unemployment in 2003 and an improving economic climate increased demand for farm products, but farmers remain worried about the impact of European Union (EU) accession on farm prices and incomes.

Investment in agriculture declined by 7.6% between 1989 and 1993, the entire sector being beset by shortages of investment and of essential equipment. In addition, agricultural subsidies were reduced by over 40%. When inflation is taken into account, subsidies decreased sharply and agricultural incomes declined sharply, in real terms. In 1993 producer support equalled about 30% of farm revenue; by 2000 it had fallen to just 3%, among the lowest in the transition countries. To some extent this represented much-needed reform in the sector. Communist Governments had traditionally encouraged autarky, necessitating certain crops to be grown on unsuitable land. Not only were subsidies required to make this possible, but investment was also frequently diverted from other activities which might have been more productive.

At independence, agriculture in Slovakia was almost entirely collectivized or organized in co-operatives. The privatization process was initially slow, owing to poor land-ownership records and conflicting claims; nevertheless, by 1995 about 98% of all farms were in private hands. Some 85% were owned by self-employed farmers, the remainder being owned by joint-stock companies and co-operatives. The latter group averaged 1,600 ha in area and accounted for about 70% of all farmland, and in 2000 the share of rural land in individual use was just 9%. Although the average farm area was about 250 ha, more than one-half of all farms were under five ha, and almost three-quarters were under 20 ha. Despite this, the European Bank for Reconstruction and Development (EBRD) viewed the reform process in agriculture as being relatively advanced, placing Slovakia among the leading six transition countries. However, reform has come at a considerable cost. Education levels in rural areas remains relatively low, only 42% of the population having more than primary education, which means that most farmers are ill-equipped to participate in the new post-socialist economy. Rural unemployment in 2002 was more than 20%, slightly higher than the national average, and 6.7% of rural income was derived from home consumption, and another 23.9% from state benefits.

INDUSTRY AND CONSTRUCTION

At the time of independence Slovakia contained two of Central and South-Eastern Europe's most modern metallurgy plants: the Slovalco aluminium smelter in Žiar nad Hronom; and the Eastern Slovakian Steelworks (VSŽ) in Košice. Together the two consumed over 15% of the whole country's total electricity output. With heavy industry consuming 60% of Slovakia's electricity (and 60% of that accounted for by only 20 large enterprises), industry in Slovakia was obviously energy-intensive. Between 1989 and 1994 energy consumption decreased by 16%, but later rose slightly when GDP resumed growth. After independence Slovakia attempted to reduce its dependence on energy imports, preferring to rely on nuclear power and electricity produced by the Gabčíkovo-Nagymoros hydroelectric system. High energy consumption and heavy industry left a legacy of environmental damage. In 1995 it was estimated that annual investment needed to reach EU emission standards and improve the regulation of pollution was equivalent to 2.8% of 1990 GDP, amounting to over ECU 1,128 per person. In 1988, the year before the end of communist rule, industry was estimated to have accounted for 50.7% of GDP; by 2001 its share had declined to 25.0%, with construction accounting for a further 4.7% in that year.

Pre-independence Slovakia had a narrower industrial base than the Czech Republic, and much of its industrial capacity was concentrated in large enterprises with many thousands of employees. Companies employing 500 or more people accounted for 62% of the industrial labour force. Moreover, within Czechoslovakia and the Council for Mutual Economic Assistance, the republic had specialized in armaments, electrical goods and quality steel. Within the former federation, Slovakia was the only producer of refrigerators, freezers, colour televisions and small motorcycles; these industries often required subsidies for energy, raw materials and transport, and relied on obsolete technology.

After 1989 industrial production in Slovakia declined sharply. Certain sectors were particularly badly affected—between 1989 and 1993 footwear production fell by 60%, for example. Employment in industry also fell sharply after 1989, declining by over 28% between 1990 and 1995, but later remaining stable. In 2002 the sector (excluding construction) employed 30.1% of the employed labour force. In addition to problems facing consumer-goods industries, the important armaments industry was particularly badly affected by the dissolution of the Warsaw Pact. Production was further damaged by a federal government decision to end armaments production in Czechoslovakia. By 1992 armaments production in the Slovak Republic had declined to just 7.2% of 1988 levels. Furthermore, employment in armaments production was concentrated in just a few areas, where it was, by far, the most important sector of the economy. Attempts were made to convert weapons plants to civilian production, but the long-term future of many factories remained uncertain.

Construction also slowed after independence, to less than one-half of 1991 totals by 1994, although there was a substantial recovery, between 1994 and 1996, with output increasing by almost one-half, and by 2002 8.3% of the labour force was employed in the sector. Policy-makers argued that transport was an important activity in Slovakia, owing to its central position in Europe, and that investment in the country's hitherto poor infrastructure would increase the country's attractiveness to investors. In the mid-1990s the Government announced a scheme to expand the motorway system, which envisaged new north–south and east–west motorway links, bringing the total length of the Slovakian motorway network to 659.3 km by 2005, despite estimates suggesting that demand might not warrant such construction. This programme was intended to reduce unemployment in construction and machinery production. Support for the motorway programme contributed to the country's worsening budgetary position—it moved from a surplus equivalent to 0.2% of GDP in 1995 to an estimated deficit equivalent to 2.6% of GDP in 1998, destabilizing the currency and leading to higher interest rates. By late 2000 90 km of new motorway had been completed, but the programme was truncated by the Dzurinda Government.

There were positive aspects to the post-independence Slovakian economy. Despite the country's financial difficulties, a growing number of companies opened up representative offices in Bratislava, rather than serving Slovakia from the Czech capital, Prague, as had been the case in the past. Early companies to make major investments included the Swiss food group, Nestlé, the German electronics company, Siemens, and the American firm, Whirlpool, as well as Volkswagen. In addition to the privatization of large firms through the voucher scheme (which took place before the Slovak Republic withdrew from the Czech and Slovak Federation), most small-scale enterprises were privatized during the scheme, or were sold to the employees who worked in them. By the end of 1997 98.5% of all small companies had been privatized.

Between 1993 and 1998 progress in the sale of larger Slovakian firms was erratic, largely as a result of political instability. Progress was also complicated by the lack of foreign investment and disputes over the best method of privatization, and the voucher privatization scheme was halted.

Political and legal instability discouraged foreign investment, and the privatization process lacked transparency. In June 1997, for example, the National Property Fund (NPF—the agency responsible for privatizing state-owned assets) sold a 15% stake in Slovnaft, a partially privatized petrochemical company, to its management for 20% of the publicly traded price. Suspicions were also raised regarding the sales of VSŽ and of Nafta (a gas exploration company sold to a prominent Mečiar supporter in 1996 for less than one-sixth of its market valuation). This, together with the erosion of democratic rights and political crisis over the institution of the presidency, led to Slovakia being excluded from the first group of states to be admitted to the North Atlantic Treaty Organization (NATO), and failing to join the Organisation for Economic Co-operation and Development (OECD) with the Czech Republic. Moreover, the country was excluded from the first group of potential entrants to the EU, and was only invited to begin accession negotiations in December 1999. As a consequence, foreign direct investment (FDI) remained relatively low, totalling just US $1,762m. between 1989 and 1998, or about $326 per head. With the election of the Dzurinda Government, however, FDI soared to an estimated $1,500m. in 2000, owing to the privatization programme pursued by the administration, and by the end of 2002 Slovakia was fourth in terms of FDI among the EU accession countries, when measured both in terms of the total amount received since 1989, and per head.

Despite the erratic pace of privatization, by the end of 2000 the private sector generated an estimated 85% of both GDP and industrial employment, and by the end of 2002 accounted for about 88% of GDP. Measured in terms of output, 98.9% of agriculture was based in the private sector, 46.2% of forestry, 79.3% of industry, 99.5% of construction, 62.9% of transportation, and 99.8% of trade. The growth of small and medium-sized enterprises (SMEs) played an important role in the growth of the private sector, and by 2000 they accounted for almost 17% of the labour force, and individual entrepreneurs accounted for almost 23%. According to the Statistical Office of the Slovak Republic they numbered 356,306 at end of 2002 (almost 315,000 of which comprised individual entrepreneurs), although this represented a decline of about 10,000 from the previous year. About three new SMEs were being created each day, and 104 individuals were registering for business licences. Industrial output increased by 4.7% in 1994 and by 8.3% in 1995. Subsequently, it increased more slowly, showing growth of 2.7% in 1996, 1.2% in 1997 and 4.0% in 1998, but declining by 3.4% in 1999, before resuming growth, of 9.1% in 2000, 4.6% in 2001 and 6.6% in 2002. More importantly, labour productivity improved, and employment in industry, after contracting sharply between 1989 and 1994, increased slightly in 1996–98, and continued to improve thereafter. By the end of the decade a distinction could be drawn between small, often privately owned firms, which increased their profitability and were relatively well adapted to market forces, and large, increasingly unprofitable, enterprises, dependent on 'soft' loans from a technically insolvent banking sector, and failing to pay taxes and debts. Inter-enterprise arrears amounted to 370,000m. koruny, equivalent to about 50% of GDP, compared with 18% of GDP in 1997 and 27% in 1993. Moreover, of those firms employing 25 or more persons, 45% showed no profit by the end of 1996. In June 2000 the Dzurinda Government introduced a new bankruptcy law, which embraced a shift in policy towards keeping firms as ongoing concerns throughout the bankruptcy and restructuring process. Creditors' rights were improved, adminis-

trators were given more autonomy and the process was limited to 18 months. However, in mid-2000 over one-half of all Slovakian enterprises were loss-making. Of these, around 20% would be profitable but for debt-service costs. The remainder, about 12,000, or one-third of the national total, were candidates for complete liquidation. They employed a substantial proportion of the labour force; companies already ready for liquidation and awaiting adjudication accounted for 140,000 jobs.

One of the most important elements of the post-independence economy was the VSŽ steelworks in Košice, privatized in 1992. The company became a successful producer and exporter, accounting for up to 30% of Slovakia's foreign-exchange earnings in the mid-1990s, although this figure declined to under 20% later in the decade. Steel exports from Slovakia to the EU were initially limited by EU regulations, although these were removed from 1 January 1996, and Slovakia was allowed to export steel freely to the EU. Foreign investment also helped to increase industrial production. Hydro Aluminium (Norway) purchased a share in the Slovalco works at Žiar nad Hronom, and improved energy and environmental efficiency and increased output. Hydro Aluminium first bought a share in the plant in 1994, and in March 2001 announced that it was co-operating with the EBRD to buy additional stakes in the firm from the state-owned ZNSP, which would give the Norwegian company a controlling interest. ZNSP was left with a 20% holding. Hydro Aluminium was given the option to buy the EBRD shares by the end of 2006, which would give it 80% of the voting shares. Hydro Aluminium subsequently created a new production line, which would allow annual production of almost 150,000 metric tons, making the plant one of Europe's leading producers.

The German automobile company, Volkswagen, first invested in Slovakia in May 1991, establishing a joint operation with Bratislavske Automobilove Závod to produce gear-boxes and assemble vehicles. In 1994 Volkswagen assumed complete control of the company, becoming the largest single investor in Slovakia. A new factory, located in existing buildings, was ranked 12th in terms of productivity among Volkswagen's 60 factories. Production growth exceeded expectations and, by the end of the 1990s, had reached 125,000 vehicles, increasing further to 225,000 in 2002. In 1999 Volkswagen invested in a components plant in Martin, in north-central Slovakia. This area was the centre of the Slovakian armaments industry before 1989, and, owing to the collapse of that sector, suffered from persistent unemployment. The successful expansion of Volkswagen production in Slovakia led to the attraction of foreign suppliers to the Martin region and generated a growth effect in related manufacturing branches. By 2002 exports from the automotive sector amounted to 27% of all Slovak exports, and sales in the sector equalled 20% of all industrial sales. Volkswagen's successful track record attracted other car and components manufacturers, most notably Peugeot Citroen. In January 2003 it announced that it had selected Slovakia over Poland, Hungary and the Czech Republic and would invest €700m. to build a plant in Trnava, about 45 km north-east of Bratislava, which would open in 2006 and be able to produce 300,000 small cars annually. Initially, the plant was to employ 3,500 people, but it was eventually expected to create up to 6,000 additional jobs. The investment was one of the largest in the history of Slovakia, and was made possible by state aid consisting of tax and other incentives totalling 4,200 koruny (about €101m.) and infrastructure investment worth 6,500m. koruny (about €157m.). Slovakia's gains came at the expense of Western Europe. In late 2002 Volkswagen announced that it was transferring production from Spain and Navarre in France to Bratislava, and in June 2003 the Spanish manufacturer of car upholstery,

Jobels, announced plans to open a plant near Košice—making a 150m. koruny investment in the first phase, and a further 90m. koruny in the second phase (a total of about €5.8m.). In early 2003 the South Korean car manufacturer, Hyundai, was considering locating a new car plant in eastern Slovakia, and several Peugeot suppliers were reported to be interested in building plants near Trnava. However, heavy dependence on the car industry made the economy vulnerable to downturns. In June 2003 Siemens automotive, supplying Ford, made 500 of a labour force of 1,800 redundant from its plant in Košice.

Whirlpool Slovakia, initially a joint venture between the US domestic-appliance manufacturer, Whirlpool, and the Slovakian manufacturer, Tatramat, located in the eastern town of Poprad, was another successful enterprise. In 1996 Whirlpool took full control of the firm, and subsequently concentrated European production there. In 2002 it transferred production of top-loading washing machines from Amiens, France, to Slovakia, and in early 2003 announced that it would be moving production from Germany to the plant in October, making it Europe's largest producer of washing machines. In 1992 annual production was just 92,000; in 2002 it was close to 1m., and by 2005 production is targeted to reach 2m. units. After receiving promises of government support and assistance, Whirlpool announced investments of over 50,000m. koruny, and over the short term was to create 700 new jobs, almost doubling the work-force.

In addition, 'greenfield' investments included a Samsung plant to manufacture computer monitors and television sets, which opened in the western town of Galanta. By mid-2003 over €13m. had been invested in the plant, and the Government planned for it to become Samsung's main European production centre. It employed about 730 people, but employment was expected to double by the end of 2004.

ENERGY

Slovakia had about one-half of the petroleum-refining capacity of the former Czechoslovakia, and is crossed by petroleum and gas pipelines which were supplied by the former USSR. A transit agreement was made to supply the Czech Republic with 8,000m. cu m of natural gas, and the network was linked to Western European networks. Slovnaft, the national refinery enterprise, expanded into the Czech Republic, Hungary, and Poland in the mid-1990s, and had two stations in Ukraine. However, by the late 1990s Slovnaft was itself the subject of interest from foreign firms. A natural-gas field was discovered in the eastern part of the country, which was expected to produce between 200m. and 250m. cu m of gas annually, thus doubling the country's previous output, which stood at 257m. cu m in 1998. In late September 2000 the Slovakian competition office approved the sale of a 36.2% stake of Slovnaft to be sold to the Hungarian Oil and Gas Company Ltd for US $262m. The Hungarian Oil and Gas Company Ltd was given the option to buy up to a 50%-plus-one share interest within two years, and in March 2003 exercised part of the option, taking an additional 32% stake in the Slovnaft refinery, in addition to a 2% stake acquired from shareholders.

Aside from natural gas, Slovakia had few domestic sources of energy. Brown coal (lignite) deposits were of poor quality, expensive to mine and insufficient to meet local demand. Despite this, and despite requiring government subsidies, the policy of the Movement for a Democratic Slovakia (MDS) Governments, led by Mečiar, was for them to remain open until at least 2005. However, within the country, energy consumption declined sharply between 1989 and 1994, largely as a result of the declines in industrial production and incomes. The Government aimed to achieve self-sufficiency in energy, having imported about 15% of its electricity in the early 1990s. This objective was assisted by the development of the hydroelectric plant at Gabčíkovo and the controversial opening of the nuclear power station at Mochovce in 1998, despite the objections of Austria, although a condition for EU consent to this opening was an agreement to close the Soviet-era reactors at Bohunice in 2006–08. The Bohunice plant relied on Soviet era VER 440 and V230 reactors, and was the site of two accidents, in 1972 and in 1977. The EU provided money to prepare for the closure through the PHARE (originally Poland/Hungary Assistance for the Restructuring of Economies) programme.

In 1993 the Surgut treaty ensured the supply of Russian gas to Slovakia at below market prices. Although this guaranteed low fuel and electricity prices, it also discouraged improvements in energy efficiency and by the late 1990s energy efficiency remained well below European averages. In 1997 the state-owned gas company signed an exclusive supply contract, lasting until 2008, with the Russian natural gas firm, Gazprom. The new coalition Government signed a further agreement with Russia, ensuring Slovakia's dependence on Russian natural gas supplies until 2014. This dependency was the cause of the trade deficit with Russia, which reached 33,900m. koruny in September 1999. Under the Mečiar Government, the energy sector was one of several strategic sectors reserved for state ownership, but this policy was abandoned by the succeeding coalition. From 2000, the Government undertook the sale of 49% of the shares in the energy sector, part of a general policy of privatizing natural monopolies. Initially, the electricity system was divided into three regional distributors and a generating enterprise, Slovenské Elektrárne (SE). In November 2000 the Government started the energy privatization process with Transpetrol, a crude petroleum pipeline operator, aiming to sell a 49% stake, and much of the energy sector was partly privatized during 2002. In January a 49% share in Transpetrol was sold to the Russian oil company, Yukos, which took over management of the firm. That was followed by a sale of 49% of the gas pipeline operator Slovenský Plynárenský Priemysel (SPP) to a consortium of Ruhrgaz and Gaz de France for US $2,700m. in July, and the three regional electricity distribution companies: Zapadoslovenske Energetika (ZSE) in September to the German firm, Eon, and Stredoslovenske Energetika (SSE) to Électricité de France in October. In January 2003 a 49% share in Vychodoslovenske Energetika (VSE), the smallest of the distribution firms, was sold to German firm RWE. In total, the sale of the energy enterprises raised $3,403.4m. Plans envisaged the privatization of SE in 2003–04, although the final organization of the firm had not been decided by mid-2003. Eight potential bidders existed, but none wanted to buy it as a single unit. In 2002, prior to privatization, SE made 1,434 of a labour force of about 11,200 redundant, and was considering a further 630 in 2003. In addition, in October 2001 Gazprom signed a letter of intent with four Western European firms to build a new gas pipeline that would bypass Ukraine, and link up with the existing Slovakian pipeline via Poland.

EXTERNAL TRADE AND FOREIGN RELATIONS

Since 1993 Slovakia's share of imports into the EU has grown as fast as Hungary's, and faster than that of the Czech Republic and Poland. Wages remain below those in the Czech Republic, Poland, and Hungary, and this rapid growth reflects the end of managed trade, closer economic relations with EU, new inward investment, and the continued competitiveness of the Slovak economy. A substantial amount of foreign investment has been related to 'greenfield' investment, which accounted for over 10% in 2001, and more in 2002. Nevertheless, the country remains vulnerable to economic downturns through its reliance on a few major exporters. For example, Volkswagen alone accounted for a 15% share of all exports in 2000. The dissolution of Czechoslovakia at the end of 1992 converted much of Slovakia's domestic trade into international trade. Within the Czechoslovak federation, the Slovak economy was considered to have the greater dependence on exports to the other republic, and the Slovak economy was also more reliant on exports to other countries within the socialist bloc. Before the dissolution of the federation, sales to the Czech lands accounted for almost 27% of all Slovak goods sold. Overall, Slovakia's economy was more dependent on imports than was the Czech economy, and a substantially higher proportion of its imports came from the communist bloc than did those to the Czech Republic, most notably imports of fuel. The collapse of the socialist system thus left Slovakia disadvantaged, as the sharp increase in fuel prices had repercussions on the cost of transport and manufacturing. The existence of some of the Slovak Republic's main employers (and main consumers of energy) was directly threatened by federal free-market policies.

In 1992 the Czech Republic accounted for 48.5% of Slovak exports. Fears that trade between the two Republics would decline following independence were well-founded. By 1999 the Czech Republic accounted for just 18.1% of exports and 18.4% of imports (c.i.f.), and in 2002 the Czech Republic took 15.2% of exports, and accounted for 15.1% of imports. In the first five months of 2003 trade between the two countries declined still further, the Czech Republic accounting for 13.9% of exports and 14.5% of imports. Germany (22.6% of imports and 26.0% of exports in 2002) had become the Slovakia's pre-eminent trading partner.

Trade with Slovakia's former communist partner states also declined after 1989. However, trade within CEFTA increased after 1994. By 1995 the overall trade balance was in deficit, as was the current account on the balance of payments from 1996. The devaluation of the koruna in October 1998 improved export prospects while increasing the cost of imports. In the late 1990s Slovakian trade with the countries of the Commonwealth of Independent States (CIS) was greater than that by other non-CIS transition countries, and its overall share of trade with Western Europe was about two-thirds of the corresponding level of other transition states. From 1998 the situation changed, as trade with the West increased at the expense of that with Russia and the CIS, although Russia remained the second-largest source of imports: 12.5% in 2002, mainly owing to imports of fuel. The deficit with Russia amounted to more than 90.4% of the total trade deficit. In 2002 trade with the EU accounted for 50.3% of imports and 60.5% of exports, and the country had a positive trade balance with the EU. Trade within CEFTA, including with the Czech Republic, accounted for 23% of imports and 28.3% of exports, and again Slovakia had a positive trade balance, although its balance with the Czech Republic was negative. In 1998 Slovakia's trade deficit stood at US $2,351m., while the deficit on the current account was $2,126m. The trade deficit declined by over one-half between 1998 and 1999, and in 2000 declined again, to just $895m., before rising to about $2,115m. in 2002. This increase was mainly owing to the growth of FDI, but also to increased imports of consumer goods. The budget deficit declined by almost 60%, falling from the equivalent of 10.8% of GDP in 1998 to just 3.2% at the end of 2001, but reached an estimated 5.5% in 2002. In 2003 the Government planned to reduce the deficit to no more than 4.9% of GDP. Currency restrictions imposed after independence to improve the state's hard-currency reserves forced Slovakian companies to operate on credit, restricting trade, and it was only after the koruna became fully convertible that trade with Western countries grew.

Until 1993 Slovakia was a leading candidate among the transition countries for early membership of NATO and the EU. The country joined the European Free Trade Association in July 1992, while still part of the Czechoslovak Federation, and signed an association agreement with the EU in June 1993. However, after independence, MDS administrations favoured trade with Russia. Other sources of income included pipeline fees for the trans-shipment of Russian petroleum and gas. Trade with Russia grew as the country fell increasingly behind in its original quest to join the EU and NATO. Unfortunately, this dependence left Slovakia highly vulnerable to any downturn in the Russian economy and the Republic was seriously affected by the Russian financial crisis of August 1998. Unemployment, which had declined to an average 11.1% for 1996, rose again, reaching 15.6% by the end of 1998, and rose still further thereafter, reaching 20.5% in January 2000. Another contributory factor was the new Government's abandonment of MDS employment-support policies. Unemployment remained high throughout 2000 and early 2001, in some months dropping below 17%, but generally averaging between 18% and 20% of the labour force. At the end of 2002 the rate of unemployment was estimated at 18%.

In common with many countries in the region, Slovakia was adversely affected by the conflict in the Federal Republic of Yugoslavia (FRY) from March 1999. Thus, the bombing of bridges across the Danube at Novi Sad in Serbia closed the river to traffic. As a result, Bratislava Sturovo, and Komarno, Slovakia's main ports, were stranded from access to the Black Sea and world markets, and industries that depended on water transport suffered as a result. Europe's largest inland shipmaker, Slovenské Lodenice, was unable to deliver ships to customers, and in 2000 was forced into bankruptcy. The successor firm, Slovenské Lodenice Komarno Bratislava, was wholly owned by the National Property Fund, but in 2003 plans to sell a minority stake were announced. The fall of the old regime in the FRY in late 2000 and the consequent re-establishment of relations with the West led to the resumption of Danube trade.

The Government of Mikuláš Dzurinda attempted to improve relations with Slovakia's neighbours from October 1998. In November 1999 a solution was reached regarding the final division of state assets of the former Czechoslovakia. The 24% share in the Československá Obchodní Banka held by the Slovakian central bank was sold in December 1999 for US $400m., the same price paid for the Czech Government's 66% share sold in May. In early October the two Governments agreed to exchange Slovakia's 13.6% stake in the Czech Kommerční banka for the 16.9% share in Všeobecná úverová banka held by the Czech Government, allowing the restructuring and reprivatization of both banks to proceed. On 24 November the last financial disputes between the two countries were settled. The Republics cancelled mutual financial claims, to the benefit of Slovakia, which owed the Czech central bank $740m., resulting from the division of the assets and liabilities of the former Czechoslovak National Bank. Slovakia, which disputed this debt, also received 4.1m. metric tons of gold, which had been withheld in response by the Czech central bank. Relations with Hungary also improved, and in September 1999 the two countries agreed to build a new bridge across the Danube, replacing one destroyed during the Second World War. The aim was to promote cross-border trade, and revitalize the local economy on both sides of the border. The EU agreed partially to fund the project, and in 2003 the Hungarian Oil and Gas Company Ltd took a controlling share in Slovnaft (see above).

From the end of 2002 preparation for EU accession dominated the legislative agenda and political scene. In 2004 Slovakia was expected to pay 10,000m. koruny to the EU (about €240m.), but was to receive up to 23,000m. koruny in various structural and cohesion funds (€556m.). Between 2004 and 2006 Slovakia would be entitled to more than

€1,000m. in structural funds, and the application process for structural funds would begin at the beginning of January 2004. However, the Slovak Government would have to provide at least an additional €370m., and the private sector was expected to contribute a further €300m. By May 2003 concern was being expressed that the country would be unable to obtain the full amount of funds to which it was entitled, owing to a lack of administrative capacity at all levels of government, unfamiliarity with EU rules, and insufficient budgetary resources to enable the authorities to pay their share of funding. However, the Government remained optimistic that it would be able to meet the necessary requirements.

ECONOMIC AND LABOUR POLICY

After independence, the Slovakian central bank pursued a strict monetary policy, and the Government succeeded in maintaining budget deficits within the limit of 5% of GDP imposed by the IMF. On 1 January 1993 a new tax system, including VAT at 23% for most goods and 5% for certain goods and services, was introduced. Rates were increased to 25% and 6%, respectively, in July 1993. Personal and corporate income taxes and a social-security tax also existed at this time. In 1999 the lower rate of VAT was raised to 10%, and prices of utilities, rents, and transport were raised, although further price increases were later postponed. These and other moves helped to reduce the budget deficit to 4% of GDP by the end of 1999, and the current-account deficit by one-half, enabling the bank to reduce interest rates from December 1999 and throughout 2000.

The head of the central bank until July 1999, Vladimír Masár, maintained the bank's independence and implemented a strict monetary policy, in opposition to government policy of stimulating employment by expanding government spending. As a result, the budget deficit and interest rates increased, impeding industrial expansion by making the cost of borrowing more expensive. Masár was responsible for the decision to remove exchange controls on the koruna in 1998. He was replaced by his deputy, Marián Jusko, who announced in December 1999, that the central bank would thenceforth control monetary policy by manipulating interest rates, abandoning the policy of trading bonds on the open market. Subsequently, in December 2000, an amendment was passed to the central bank law, altering the focus of policy from maintaining exchange-rate stability to maintaining price stability.

In 1994 Slovakia's official foreign-exchange reserves were equivalent to the revenue from just one month of merchandise exports. Consequently, a temporary 10% surcharge was imposed on all imported consumer goods, comprising 12% of total imports. By 1997 the surcharge had been eliminated, after a considerable increase in foreign-exchange reserves, from US $120m. in 1990 to $3,302m. at the end of 1997. However, the increasing current-account deficit prompted the Government to implement austerity measures in June 1999, which included a reintroduction of a surcharge of 7%, affecting 80% of all imports, although the surcharge was to be eliminated by the end of 2000. At the end of September 2000 reserves, excluding gold, stood at $4,166m. On 1 October 1995 the koruna became fully convertible. Although this action was prompted by the Czech Republic's abandonment of the clearing mechanism and move to convertibility, it also reflected growing confidence on the part of the Government and the central bank. Initially linked to a 'basket' of five currencies, the koruna was subsequently 'pegged' to the US dollar (40% weighting) and the German Deutsche Mark (60%). In early 1999 the koruna was linked to the common European currency, the euro, as its base currency. At the time that convertibility was implemented, the central bank widened the fluctuation band for the koruna from 1.5% to 3.0%, and in 1996 the band was further widened, to 7.0%. Sub-

sequently, the bank abandoned the fixed peg in October 1998, and allowed the currency to become freely convertible.

Meanwhile, unemployment increased in the mid-1990s. In some areas, particularly in southern regions where there was a large ethnic Hungarian population, levels of unemployment exceeded 20%. By 1996 the rate of unemployment, particularly in disadvantaged areas, was over 25%. Under the MDS the distribution of resources for regional development was highly political. Bratislava, an opposition stronghold, lost its status as a separate region in 1996, and saw its allocations from the state budget sharply reduced after 1994. Initially, the numbers of unemployed were increased not only by redundancies, but also by new entrants to the labour force.

Much of the creation of new jobs took place in the services sector. In 2002 the services sector employed 55.4% of the active labour force, compared with 39.9% in 1989. In 2001 the sector accounted for 57.2% of GDP, of which non-market and housing services contributed 11.8% and wholesale and retail trade 15.0%. From 1993, when it contributed 58.2% of GDP, the contribution of services to the economy gradually increased, while that of industry diminished. By 1995 95% of all prices were uncontrolled, the principal exceptions being energy and public services. Many uncontrolled prices could be maintained at low levels by these controlled energy prices. In September of that year a new price law was enacted, extending the power to regulate prices to local authorities, especially when such regulation was said to be in the public interest. This was seen by many as a retrograde step in the reform process; however, by the end of 1995 the rate of inflation had declined to 7.3%, among the lowest levels in the region, remaining below 7% in 1996–98. After the coalition Government led by Dzurinda came in power in October 1998, a combination of austerity measures, including increases in VAT, price liberalization in 1999, and a short lived import surcharge of 7%, contributed to a sharp increase in the annual rate of inflation, which increased to 10.6% in 1999. Price liberalization continued thereafter, with prices annually being increased for rents, transport, gas, electricity, rail transport and bus transport, and water and sewerage services. This contributed to bursts of steeply rising inflation within a general downward trend in the average rate of increase in prices. Thus, by 2002 inflation had declined to about 3.3%. However, in 2003 regulated prices were to be increased sharply for electricity, water, gas, sewage and rents, which were to be almost doubled. In addition, rail and bus fares were to increase by almost 20%, adding up to 4.5 percentage points to inflation. Consequently, inflation for the year was expected to be close to 9%. As part of the austerity measures, the corporate tax was reduced from 40% to 29%, in an attempt to stimulate the creation and growth of private SMEs, although cumulative tax arrears amounted to 48,200m. koruny (US $1,165m.) by mid-1999. VAT arrears, much owed by large, uneconomic companies, constituted the major proportion of tax arrears. By the late 1990s tax evasion was widespread and by 1998 the Slovakian Central Bank estimated that the informal economy was equivalent to 12% of GDP. Also, in October the Central Bank abandoned the fixed peg on the koruna, which resulted in a sharp decline against the dollar and other currencies. However, by early 2000 the currency had recovered substantially, particularly against the euro, before declining sharply between March and May. After this short period it came under strong upward pressure as the amount of inward investment grew.

In November 2000 the Government created a new financial regulator, the Financial Markets Authority, for capital markets, aimed at reforming and injecting new investment into the stock market. Initially, it licensed and supervised capital markets and the insurance industry, but in 2002 banking and pensions were to be added to its remit. Members of its board were appointed by the Government, and it was only able to propose legislation to the Ministry of Finance. The Government was also encountered the problem of finding revenue to redeem bonds issued by the National Property Fund after Mečiar cancelled the second round of voucher privatization in 1995. About 40% of the bonds were redeemed between August 1996 and November 2000. However, the Fund was technically insolvent when the Dzurinda Government came to power, but the bonds were due to expire from 1 January 2000, and the Fund was obligated to repay them within one year. Funds from the sale of Slovenská sporiteľna were to be used to finance the Fund, although this would only cover about 60% of the outstanding liabilities.

From 1998 the Government pursued fiscally conservative policies, restraining spending and services. There have been ongoing efforts to reform the social support system, the tax system, and, particularly since the 2002 elections, the pension system. As part of the reform process, the coalition agreed in late May 2003 to introduce a uniform rate of 19% for income tax and VAT, effective from January 2004. Some criticized this measure as regressive, but others argued that it would enhance the country's attractiveness to foreign investors. As part of the reform, excise taxes increased at the beginning of July 2003, increasing prices for fuel, beer, wine, spirits and tobacco. The increase in VAT would lead to higher prices for some items, such as drugs, on which VAT had already been raised from 10% to 14% in 2002. The aim in the longer term was to pass a new tax law with a vastly simplified tax structure, including the imposition of an annual vehicle tax, and basing property tax rates on value rather than area. However, in July 2003 the President refused to sign the legislation, sending it back to the National Council for a second vote.

The Government also attempted to reform the labour market. In March 2003, after prolonged negotiations with trade union leaders, the cabinet approved proposals for a new labour code, which loosened restrictions on engaging and dismissing labour, permitted the employment of spouses, increased types of part-time jobs, and classified employees according to job description rather than educational level. In particular, the right of trade unions to intervene in production was curtailed. In compensation, there would be increased over-time and compulsory employer insurance contributions for part-time workers. The Government also proposed substantial alterations to unemployment benefits, which lasted for up to nine months and equalled 40% of the average net wage. Plans are also under way to reform child benefit, and deliver a large proportion of the monthly benefit through tax relief. The aim was to shift the delivery of benefits to tax relief in order to encourage more people to work.

The introduction and raising of fees for various services was related to the process of tax reform. Fees for health care services, including hospital stays and prescriptions, were introduced on 1 June 2003. Initially, there was some confusion, since fees were based on age, condition and financial situation, but in late June it was reported that the number of prescriptions had declined by 30%. The Government had also increased fees for a variety of routine services, including passports and land registration.

In March 2003 the Government announced plans to introduce fees for university students, despite protests from the Slovak Rector's Congress (representing university administrations) and students. At the same time, it announced plans to increase the amount students could borrow in any one year. Initial proposals were for annual fees of 7,000–12,000 koruny per year (about €170 to €290), and student loans were to be doubled from 20,000 koruny to 40,000 koruny.

In accordance with recommendations from the IMF and the support of the World Bank, since the mid-1990s Slovakia has been reforming the pension system, which is not fully funded. Before 1994 health benefits, disability benefits and pensions were paid by the same agency, but in that year the Social Insurance Act established the Social Insurance Agency (SIA) as the provider of pension and disability insurance. Until the late 1990s, the pension system was in surplus, but from 1999 onwards the pensions deficit equalled about 0.5% of GDP. This was the result of a decline in contributions: expenditure as a proportion of GDP remained at the same level, at about 7.5%. However, revenue had declined from 8% to 7% of GDP, and was expected to decline further as a consequence of high unemployment and slow wage growth. Thus far, the deficit has been paid from the state budget, including privatization revenues, but over the long term this will not be sustainable. Under the existing scheme, pensions are based on a mandatory 'pay-as-you-go' system. Of wages, 28.0% are allocated to social insurance, 21.6% of which is provided by employers, and 6.4% by employees. The link between total wages and benefits is weak, and periods of unemployment or extended leave are not reflected in final pensions.

In April 2002 the legislature adopted a new Labour Code, and it had steadily tightened the link between benefits and contributions. At 50.8%, payroll taxes were among the highest in the OECD countries, and were marginally higher than those in the Czech Republic, Hungary and Poland. Of the wage bill, 28% was allocated to the pensions system, 4.8% to disability insurance, 14% to health insurance, and 4% to unemployment insurance, of which employers paid 38% and employees 12.8% (this compared with an EU average rate of 37%, of which 23% was for pensions). In late June 2003 the Government announced that it planned to begin reducing payroll taxes, initially from 50.8% to 47.5% of total salary, the reductions in tax coming from the employers' share of the payments.

A debate about pensions reform began in June 2003. Plans called for the creation of a 'three-pillar' pension system, to comprise the existing pay-as-you-go system as the first pillar; a new, mandatory, so-called capitalization pillar, which was to be fully funded by employee contributions; and a voluntary third pillar, also fully funded by employee contributions, and managed entirely in the private sector. The second pillar was to consist of individual accounts managed by management companies of the employee's choice, under the supervision of the social insurance agency. The third, voluntary pillar would take the form of individual retirement accounts, and had already been in existence since 1996; since 1999 it has been open to both employees and the self-employed.

In late June 2003 the Ministry of Labour, Social Affairs and the Family proposed that the minimum monthly wage be increased to 5,950 koruny per month (€143) from 1 January 2004, compared with the existing 5,570 koruny. Nation-wide, it was estimated that only 1,300 workers received the minimum wage, whereas 3,500 were expected to fall within the new wage threshold. The unions demanded a higher minimum, but the Government argued that a higher increase would result in dismissals and increased unemployment. Pensions were raised by 6% in July 2003, after a vote in the National Council overruled a presidential veto.

PRIVATIZATION

By June 2003 the privatization process was essentially complete, except for government holdings in so-called strategic firms, where the Government was allowed to sell only 49% of the shares. These include Slovenské Elektrárne (SE), three regional electricity distributors, the SPP gas utility and the Transpetrol pipeline. In 2003 the Government announced plans to abandon the requirement that it hold a strategic stake, although even if the sale of strategic shares is approved, it does not mean that privatization will follow.

Earlier privatizations have brought in dividend income on those shares the Government retained. By the beginning of 2003 the share of GDP accounted for by the private sector had reached about 88%. As early as the end of 1994 the country had 35,000 registered SMEs, with a total of 425,000 registered employees. By 1996 two-thirds of all enterprises employed fewer than 25 people. However, privatization had taken place at a considerable cost. The privatization of many formerly state-owned firms was flawed, and from 1998 the new Government moved to renationalize some firms, cancel the privatization of others, and arrange for the reorganization and reprivatization of several enterprises and banks.

The first round of voucher privatization was completed before Slovakia's independence. A second round was scheduled to take place soon after independence, but was suspended and then cancelled in mid-1995, even though 3.5m. citizens had bought vouchers. A new scheme, offering five-year government bonds rather than vouchers, became law in September. Privatization continued in the form of direct sales of assets to management and employees by the NPF. Assets were sold for an initial payment of as little as 10%–20% of the book value, and loans granted to cover the remainder of the cost. Subsequent loan instalments could be offset against the value of investments made by new owners. The government bonds issued to replace vouchers could be spent on retirement or health insurance, the purchase of property, or the purchase of shares in the NPF and selected privatized companies. In November 1996 the Constitutional Court ruled that the Government, and not the NPF, was responsible for the direct sale of state property. In February 1996 the National Council had amended the privatization law to reduce the level of worker participation in the privatization process, eliminating the requirement that a portion of shares in privatized companies be sold to employees and limiting the maximum share sold in this way to 10%, as opposed to the former limit of 34%. However, the new laws eliminated transparency in the privatization process, and frequently the new ownership structure of companies was not made public. Protection for minority shareholders was removed, undermining both domestic and foreign confidence in the privatization process.

The privatization law reserved 29 major companies in 'strategic' sectors, including utilities, arms production and telecommunications, for state ownership. The state also attempted to retain a degree of control in 50 other firms, including Slovnaft and VSŽ. At the same time, private investment funds were prevented from taking part in decision-making in firms in which they held a stake, although the Constitutional Court subsequently declared this ban to be invalid. By mid-1997 firms with a book value of some US $1,000m. were still awaiting privatization. Proceeds from the sales were to be used to repay the privatization bonds, which became due in 2000, although the average sale price of shares remained less than 40% of book value and, with purchasers allowed to offset payment for shares against capital investments in the firm, the NPF was unlikely to gather much income from the sales.

After coming to power, the Dzurinda Government reviewed privatizations that had occurred under the previous administration. It also reviewed the entire privatization strategy, abolishing the requirement that 'strategic' companies remain under state ownership. Under the new strategy, state ownership was to vary according to three categories of firm: natural monopolies, such as the railways and the postal service, which would remain publicly owned; certain energy production and distribution companies in which the state would retain a controlling interest; and the remainder of companies in which no minimum level of state ownership was defined. The National Council was given the right to debate privatizations, although, constitutionally, privatization was an executive rather than a legislative, responsibility. In addition, the Government invited Transparency International, an international agency monitoring corruption, to oversee the privatization process.

The new Government effectively renationalized most of the banking sector, with the aim of improving the reputation of the sector by reorganization and then by reprivatization. The state acquired controlling interests in two of the largest banks, Slovenská sporiteľňa and Všeobecná úverová banka, in 1999, the other, Investičná a rozvojová banka, having already been acquired. The Government intended to return the banks swiftly to the private sector, but first had to augment its holdings, increase capital and assume 'bad' loans, which were transferred to a new specialized agency. Bids were invited for Slovenská sporiteľňa, the Savings Bank, in July and December 2000, Austria's Erste Bank won control of an 87% share for €425m. (18,400m. koruny), about twice the book value. However, the Government had to take over 32,400m. koruny of problem loans, inject 4,300m. koruny in capital, and guarantee the adjusted book value of 11,900m. koruny. Bids were formally invited for the Všeobecná úverová banka in mid-June 2001, with a decision on a purchaser planned by the end of the year. The state also assumed the 'social loans' granted by the previous administration, amounting to 8,500m. koruny, as well as 5,400m. koruny in non-performing loans made to the national power generator to fund the construction of the nuclear power station at Mochovce. In addition, the Government was committed to loan guarantees worth about 100,000m. koruny. It was hoped that some of these could be repaid through the exchange of shares in newly privatized firms, but other liabilities included debts of public-sector organizations, such as the NPF, and loans made to rail, water and electricity monopolies. Once the reforms of the Dzurinda Government began to take effect, the dramatic increase in FDI made it possible to use revenues from the privatization process to pay outstanding obligations.

The Government was also compelled to renationalize or restructure large, formerly state-owned firms, which had been sold below their market value. These companies had relied on generous loans from banks, and been supported by loan guarantees from the Government. Their accounts were not transparent, minority shareholders had no representation in management, and the Mečiar Government's employment policy encouraged the companies to retain labour. The firms included Nafta, in which the state had sold a 45.9% holding to a Mečiar supporter in 1996 for less than one-sixth of its stock-market value. However, the plan to renationalize Nafta encountered difficulties and eventually led to the dismissal of the head of the NPF.

However, the most important reprivatization was that of the steel-maker, VSŽ, one of the most modern steel companies in the region. VSŽ, the country's largest firm and, until the late 1990s, its leading exporter, defaulted on a US $35m. loan in December 1998, causing other banks to call in their loans. The company was forced into administration and the creditor banks assumed voting rights in the firm's shares. VSŽ had 13,000m. koruny ($369m.) of debt, of which 11,000m. koruny was in foreign currency. In addition, it had accumulated substantial tax arrears. The administrators' first aim was to restructure the firm, reducing the number of subsidiaries from some 120 to 20–30, and shedding 2,000 jobs from a labour force of 26,000. Extreme acquisitions, such as Sparta Prague, a leading football club in the Czech Republic, were sold. VSŽ's problems included illegal outflows, mismanagement and exclusive contracts with suppliers and distributors. In March 2000 US Steel agreed to acquire the steel business of VSŽ, and the sale was approved by 99% of shareholders on 12 October. As an inducement, the Slovakian Government offered 10 years of tax reductions, but, in turn, US steel was obligated to reduce the work-force only by natural wastage during that period.

Privatizations completed under the Mečiar Government were likely to cause problems for some time. For example, PPS Detva, once a major armaments manufacturer, was privatized in 1995, and management unsuccessfully attempted to transform into a manufacturer of automobile components. In 1997, facing bankruptcy, they transferred the company's assets to a new firm, PPS Detva Holding, but soon ran up debts to insurance companies, banks, utilities and suppliers. In March 2002 the Supreme Court challenged the legality of the transfer, and the management resigned, forcing the firm into bankruptcy. At mid-2003 it employed 560 out of an original 1,800 people, and in July the courts approved its sale to a holding firm which hoped to develop links with the Swedish firm, Volvo.

Privatization of smaller state-owned enterprises was likely to continue, not only to raise more revenue to finance ambitious reform packages, but also further to remove corruption and inefficiency in management. For example, there were plans to convert the State Forestry Company, Lesy SR, which controls about one-half of the forests in the Slovak Republic, from a state enterprise to a state-owned joint-stock company, in order to make accounting more transparent.

INVESTMENT

Since the first Dzurinda Government took office, Slovakia has seen a remarkable increase in FDI; once among the lowest four non-CIS transition countries in terms of FDI, it has become the fourth-highest, both cumulatively and in 2002. This is owing in large measure to the delayed privatization (and reprivatization) process, but is also a result of new inward investment; in 2002 17% of the FDI coming into the country was a result of new investment. FDI reached US $182,000m. in 2002, almost twice the previous record in 2000. Of this, $152,000m. was privatization revenue, but non-privatization investment also increased by 13% compared with 2001. The uniform tax rate was cited as a factor in attracting inward investment, as well as the country's low wages.

Between 1990 and 1992 Slovakia received only 12.8% of the total of US $1,801m. foreign investment in Czechoslovakia. As the country moved towards independence, foreign investment declined sharply, and the banking and foreign-exchange problems encountered by the new country initially had an inhibiting effect on investment. After independence, investment was discouraged by the policies of the Mečiar Government. Political and legal instability discouraged foreign investment, and the privatization process lacked transparency. By the end of 1998 Slovakia had attracted an estimated cumulative total of $1,762m. in FDI. This amounted to $326 per head, among the lowest levels of all the non-CIS transition countries. Only Romania, Albania, Macedonia, and Bulgaria had attracted less. The country also had a commitment of $583m. to various development institutions, including the World Bank and the EBRD, accumulated between 1990 and 1994.

More than one-half of all foreign investment was concentrated in the Bratislava area, which a German research organization rated the most attractive region within Central Europe, based on criteria that included access to markets, infrastructure, labour-force skills and costs. Moreover, despite a relatively low rating by investment agencies, in the late 1990s the country was generally considered among the best transition countries with regard to reform and the overall climate for investment. By mid-1999 the EBRD viewed the privatization process as essentially completed, and gave a high ranking to the trade and foreign-exchange system. Although it viewed the reform of enterprise governance and restructuring as incomplete, as well as price liberalization

and competition policy, Slovakia compared favourably with its neighbours in terms of its rankings, trailing only in the areas of banking reform and related non-bank institutions.

However, investment rose sharply after the coalition Government took office in October 1998. The privatization of hitherto protected state firms, the impact of reform, improved investment ratings, and the renewed prospect of early EU membership all encouraged inward investment. In 2000 total investment (about US $1,200m.) amounted to about one-third of the total investment during the previous 10 years, and over two-thirds of the investment total of $1,700m. between 1993 and 1999.

In June 2000 the Government formed a new agency, the Slovak Investment and Trade Development Agency (SARIO), to act as a 'one-stop shop' to promote inward investment. The new agency replaced the Slovak National Agency for Foreign Investment and Development, which was heavily criticized for poor service and lack of co-ordination. It brought together six ministries and the National Property Fund to promote investment opportunities and conduct regional studies. Initially, the new agency was funded by both the Government and a €5.5m. grant from the EU's PHARE scheme. However, conflicts of interests among senior staff led to their resignation; the EU delayed funding and SARIO almost became bankrupt in May 2001, when the Government failed to transfer its budget on time. In August the agency was transformed into a joint-stock company. It announced that it had helped to attract 30 investment projects worth €335m. and some 6,500 jobs between October 2001 and September 2002, and in 2003 it played a key role in attracting Peugeot Citroen to the country (see above). In 2002 alone, the agency claimed to have created 5,356 new jobs, with a planned increase to 7,896, from 25 investment projects worth €310m.

Slovakia continues to suffer from pronounced regional inequalities. Although unemployment had fallen to 14.8% by the end of May 2003, there was widespread regional variation, ranging from 3.6% in Bratislava to 22.0% in Košice. According to employment offices, an east–west divide does exist in labour markets. Growth is concentrated in the western part of the country, where demand for skilled staff is high. However, in the eastern part of the country, demand is mainly seasonal, and most jobs are for the relatively unskilled; there are said to be few jobs for university graduates. At the same time, national surveys compiled in early 2003 suggested that migrants were leaving rural areas in search of jobs.

Interestingly, in 2002 average wages rose faster outside Bratislava; wages rose 7% on average, employees in non-Slovak firms receiving the highest average increase, of 11%. However, the lowest paid workers remained those in agriculture, who received just 54.7 koruny per hour, despite a rise of 28% in 2002. Average wages at the end of 2002 were 93.3 koruny per hour. Not surprisingly, unemployment is correlated with 'black market' activity. In late April 2003 it was claimed that Slovakia had the smallest black market economy of the transition countries, accounting for just 18.3% of GDP in 2001–02. However, in Bratislava it accounted for just 3.7% of output. The Government argued that reform of the unemployment benefit system, linking benefits to previous income, would reduce the shadow economy.

Since the fall of communism, the railways have lost money, and by the beginning of 2003 the total debt had reached 50,000m. koruny (€1,200m.). As well as plans to expand the motorway system, the mid- and late 1990s saw a planned improvement of Slovakia's railway infrastructure, most notably the creation of new, electrified links with Austria, Hungary and Poland. Passenger travel declined by more than one-half from 1989, and the railways' profitability was also undermined by the collapse of freight traffic, which declined in volume from 128m. metric tons in 1989 to just 60m. tons in

1997, and 53.6m. tons in 2001. Under the Mečiar Government, rail fares were subsidized, and the labour force unchanged; the railways were the largest single employer in Slovakia. In July 1999 the European Investment Bank made a loan of $240m., to be repaid over two years, to the state rail company, to help it integrate with pan-European routes. However, a condition of the loan was that the company would reduce its 52,000-strong labour force and increase fares towards market levels. The Dzurinda Government raised rail fares and reduced subsidies and expenditure, in an attempt to control the budget deficit. On 1 January 2002 the rail system was divided into two sections: Slovak State Railways manages the rail infrastructure, and Železnicna Spolocnost manages passenger and freight services. In this way, the finances of rail operations can be made more transparent, and the high operating subsidies for freight and passenger services can be separated from capital costs. From the late 1990s, the Government attempted to stem the railways deficit, but the unions resisted strongly. In 2001 employment had fallen only slightly to 44,500, compared with the 1995 level of 53,000, despite a collapse in passenger and freight traffic. Productivity remained low (at 62.4% of 1989 levels, according to the EBRD), and hovered at this level throughout most of the 1990s. At the beginning of 2003 the Government ended services on 25 regional rail lines and eliminated 200 train services. Claiming that the closure of lines and cancellation of trains would undermine the integrity of the network and that the closures would have a disproportionate impact on areas of high unemployment, the unions took strike action at the end of January, which was suspended after three days by a court order. Freight transport makes up about 75% of total rail revenues, and the strike had wide-ranging impact on manufacturing and transit traffic, as well as proving costly to the rail system. Service on 11 lines was restored at the end of May at a cost of 50m. koruny, but the unions, fearing that line closures would lead to job losses, continued to press for an 8% increase in wages. Existing plans demanded that the budgets of the two railway companies be balanced by 2010, and a rescue package was announced in late March 2003, estimated at 30,000m. Slovak koruny (about €720m.) over the next four years. Meanwhile, in July the Government announced that it would transfer liabilities of the two companies worth 21,000m. Slovak koruny to the overall state debt, and subsidize investments by 2,500m. koruny in 2004.

In response to the financial problems, some regional Governments have taken over the control of lines; the Bratislava region created the Bratislava Regional Rail Company in May 2003, to run passenger and freight traffic. The Košice regional authorities also expressed interest in taking over local lines and services.

Rail operating costs absorb resources from capital investments in both the road and rail network. In 2003 it was announced that over one-third of class two and three roads in country were in a poor or dangerous condition. Regional Governments pay part of the cost of repairs, but lack the resources to maintain the road system. The annual shortfall is estimated at about 500m. koruny. Some 600m. koruny was spent on road maintenance and repairs to roads, and 8,400m. koruny on motorway construction. In 2004 the total budget for road maintenance and repair was to be raised to 2,360m. koruny. However, new motorways were needed to attract investment. The current priority is a motorway running through the northern part of the country from Bratislava to Košice, which will cost a total of 80,000m. koruny. Several segments have already been completed, and completion was scheduled for 2010, but spending was only about one-quarter of the amount needed, which could delay completion by up to 10 years. In early 2003 a government coalition party demanded that cheaper routes be constructed through the

southern part of the country, linking Bratislava to Košice, and passing through seven of the eight regional capitals and through regions with some of the highest unemployment rates in the country. They claimed that this could be built in five years for 50,000m.–55,000m. koruny. However, although the northern route runs through more difficult terrain, it also links up existing industrial areas, connecting to international corridors, and can create potential tourist areas in the Tatras. In June the Government announced a compromise: 60% of the state budget for new roads would be spent on building the northern route, which is scheduled for completion in seven years, and 25% would be allocated to upgrading roads in the south, creating dual carriageways along the proposed southern route.

The prospect of EU membership is also increasingly reflected in local and regional development plans. For example, since the beginning of the 1990s it has been suggested that the under-used Bratislava airport could serve the Vienna region of Austria and provide some relief for crowding at Vienna's Schwechat Airport. Poor road and rail connections, and later border controls imposed by the Schengen Agreement after Austria joined the EU in 1995, prevented the realization of this project, by deterring cross-border travel to the under-used Bratislava airport. However, in late April 2003 officials representing the Bratislava regional Government, Vienna city and regional officials, and Vienna airport announced an EU-financed project to link the two airports in a single system, in advance of the implementation of the Schengen accord in 2006. After 2006, the aim is to increase direct connections from Bratislava airport, and increase the speed of road and rail connections between two capitals, effectively making Bratislava a second Vienna airport. A new airline, SkyEurope, based in Bratislava airport, was founded in 2001, based on the idea of offering cheap flights to major cities from Bratislava. It started with just one 30-seater plane flying between Bratislava and Košice, but one year later had expanded to some 15 destinations in Slovakia and abroad.

PROSPECTS

Upon independence, prospects for Slovakia's economy, with its traditional concentration on defence and heavy industry, were unpromising. The transition to a modern market and service economy was expected to be a lengthy and painful procedure. However, by the beginning of 1996 Slovakia had the lowest inflation rate in the region. By 2003 GDP had grown consistently since 1994, as had gross industrial output. Much of the growth in industry and construction was concentrated in the private sector. The average monthly wage in the country increased from US $161 in 1992 to $368 (€325) in 2002, although it remained below those of Poland, Hungary and the Czech Republic. Moreover, the devaluation of the koruna in October 1998, coupled with relatively low rates of inflation, made the country's wage levels still more competitive. Despite the koruna's subsequent appreciation in value, wages remained competitive. Mečiar's defeat in the legislative elections of September 1998 substantially altered both the direction of Slovakia's economic policy and the country's prospects for closer integration with Western economic institutions. The new Government was strongly committed to reform, and willing to undertake the political and economic changes necessary to prepare Slovakia for EU and NATO membership. Originally, Slovakia had been expected to join the EU, the OECD and NATO at the same time, or close to the same time, as its partners in CEFTA. Only in late July 2000 was the country invited to become a full member of the OECD, and towards the end of 2002 it was invited to join NATO and the EU. The Slovak economy continued to perform well in 2002, exceeding expectations. In that year GDP increased by 4.4% overall, including an upsurge in the last quarter, when year-on-year growth reached 5.4%. In April 2003 the OECD praised the Government's economic policies, and predicted that growth was likely to continue. It noted that, although inflation was likely to increase as a result of increasing energy prices, the Government's ambitious structural programmes would ensure continued growth. Although businessmen claim that influence still plays a role in economic success, the EBRD rates the legal system, including financial regulations and commercial law, relatively highly, although it notes that enterprise regulation remains complex and non-transparent. Inflation is relatively controlled, although increases in regulate prices are expected to raise it from 3.3% in 2002 to almost 9% in 2003, and the current-account deficit is considered high, at an estimated 8.2% of GDP in 2002. However, this was a decline from the 8.8% recorded in 2001, and the Government aimed to limit the deficit to 6.2% of GDP in 2003. The aim was to reduce it to 3% by 2007 or 2008, to allow Slovakia to join the single European currency. The budget deficit was also high, at about 5.5% in 2002 (owing perhaps to extra spending in the campaign for the September elections), but the aim was to restrain it to no more than 4.9% in 2003. Although the trade balance remained negative, in May, for the first time in several years, the balance was positive, stimulated by exports in the car sector.

Reform has taken place at some cost. Unemployment surged upwards to new highs after the Dzurinda Government took office, and began to abate only in 2003, when it had fallen to under 15% by the end of June. However, it was estimated that some 600,000 people lived in poverty, and in some sectors, pay remains low. Teachers have been described as being among the country's worst paid professionals, and went on strike in May and June, closing 90% of all schools, including nursery, primary and secondary, and 22 universities. Only private schools were unaffected. Farmers had also threatened strike action, motivated by a lack of price support and price declines for pork and milk, leading to a possible loss of up to 1,000m. koruny. Crime also rose in 2002, and health surveys taken in 2002–03 showed that as many as 55% of all deaths in country were due to cardio-vascular problems, as opposed to about one-third in Western Europe. Despite this, Slovakia has undergone a second revolution since 1998, which has led to a date for entry to the EU and NATO and laid the foundations for future economic growth and development.

Statistical Survey

Source: Statistical Office of the Slovak Republic, Miletičova 3, 824 67 Bratislava; tel. (2) 5023-6340; fax (2) 5556-1361; e-mail agnesa.kralikova@statistics.sk; internet www.statistics.sk.

Area and Population

AREA, POPULATION AND DENSITY

Area (sq km)	49,033*
Population (census results)	
3 March 1991.	5,274,335
26 May 2001	
Males	2,612,515
Females.	2,766,940
Total	5,379,455
Population (official estimates at mid-year)	
2000	5,400,679
2001	5,379,780†
2002	5,378,595‡
Density (per sq km) at mid-2001	109.7

* 18,932 sq miles.
† Adjusted to take account of 2001 census.
‡ Preliminary figure.

POPULATION BY NATIONALITY
(at 2001 census)

	Number	%
Slovak.	4,614,854	85.79
Hungarian	520,528	9.68
Gypsy	89,920	1.67
Czech, Moravian, Silesian	46,968	0.87
Ruthenian and Ukrainian	35,015	0.65
German	5,405	0.10
Polish	2,602	0.05
Russian	1,590	0.03
Others (incl. undeclared)	62,573	1.16
Total	5,379,455	100.00

REGIONS
(at 2001 census)

	Area (sq km)	Population	Density (per sq km)
Bratislava	2,053	599,015	292
Trnava	4,148	551,003	133
Trenčín	4,501	605,582	135
Nitra	6,343	713,422	112
Žilina	6,788	692,332	102
Banská Bystrica	9,455	662,121	70
Prešov	8,993	789,968	88
Košice	6,753	766,012	113
Total	49,034	5,379,455	110

PRINCIPAL TOWNS
(estimated population at 31 December 2001)

Bratislava (capital) .	428,094	Trnava	70,189
Košice	236,036	Martin. . . .	60,055
Prešov	92,720	Trenčín	57,813
Nitra	87,308	Poprad. . . .	56,241
Žilina	85,384	Prievidza . . .	52,947
Banská Bystrica .	82,961	Zvolen	43,796

BIRTHS, MARRIAGES AND DEATHS

	Registered live births		Registered marriages		Registered deaths	
	Number	Rate (per 1,000)	Number	Rate (per 1,000)	Number	Rate (per 1,000)
1995 . .	61,427	11.4	27,489	5.1	52,686	9.8
1996 . .	60,123	11.2	27,484	5.1	51,236	9.5
1997 . .	59,111	11.0	27,955	5.2	52,124	9.7
1998 . .	57,582	10.7	27,494	5.1	53,156	9.9
1999 . .	56,223	10.4	27,340	5.1	54,402	9.8
2000 . .	55,151	10.2	25,903	4.8	52,724	9.8
2001 . .	51,136	9.5	23,795	4.4	51,980	9.7
2002 . .	50,841	9.5	25,062	4.7	51,532	9.6

Expectation of life (WHO estimates, years at birth): 73.1 (males 69.3; females 77.4) in 2001 (Source: WHO, *World Health Report*).

EMPLOYMENT
(labour force surveys, '000 persons)

	2000	2001	2002
Agriculture, hunting, forestry and fishing	139.8	130.6	131.4
Mining and quarrying . . .	24.8		
Manufacturing	540.4	628.8	640.9
Electricity, gas and water . .	50.1		
Construction	167.7	169.5	176.0
Wholesale and retail trade; repair of motor vehicles, motorcycles and personal and household goods	324.9	327.3	340.0
Hotels and restaurants . . .			
Transport, storage and communications	167.1	162.1	154.4
Financial intermediation . .	37.1	38.3	39.8
Real estate, renting and business services	90.8	104.3	103.3
Public administration and defence; compulsory social security	158.3	157.8	149.7
Education	161.6	168.9	162.8
Health and social work . . .	147.9	143.6	141.5
Other community, social and personal service activities .	86.6	87.0	79.1
Private households with employed persons	3.9	4.7	7.9
Activities not adequately defined	0.8	1.0	0.6
Total	2,101.7	2,123.7	2,127.0
Males	1,137.3	n.a.	n.a.
Females	964.4	n.a.	n.a.

Registered unemployed (annual averages, '000 persons): 482.2 in 2000; 508.0 in 2001.

Health and Welfare

KEY INDICATORS

Total fertility rate (children per woman, 2001)	1.3
Under-5 mortality rate (per 1,000 live births, 2001) . . .	9
HIV/AIDS (% of persons aged 15–49, 2001)	<0.10
Physicians (per 1,000 head, 1998)	3.53
Hospital beds (per 1,000 head, 1996)	7.48
Health expenditure (2000): US $ per head (PPP)	690
Health expenditure (2000): % of GDP	5.9
Health expenditure (2000): public (% of total)	89.6
Access to water (% of persons, 2000)	100
Access to sanitation (% of persons, 2000)	100
Human Development Index (2000): ranking	36
Human Development Index (2000): value	0.835

For sources and definitions, see explanatory note on p. vi.

Agriculture

PRINCIPAL CROPS
('000 metric tons)

	1999	2000	2001
Wheat	1,187.3	1,254.3	1,894.1
Barley	723.7	396.7	685.2
Maize	779.3	440.4	616.0
Rye	69.6	64.2	118.6
Oats	48.4	25.0	35.6
Triticale	—	19.3	33.4
Potatoes	384.4	418.8	387.3
Sugar beet	1,404.9	961.5	1,286.2
Dry peas	48.0	18.2	23.0
Sunflower seed	125.1	117.3	118.4
Rapeseed	237.1	113.8	240.3
Cabbages (white)	198.5	98.6	30.9
Tomatoes	70.4	73.0	35.0
Chillies and green peppers . . .	40.4	35.4	36.0*
Cucumbers and gherkins . . .	40.7	44.7	44.0*
Onions	50.1	26.3	15.8
Carrots	74.6	51.2	14.1
Apples	68.3	81.5	50.2
Grapes	61.2	61.1	71.6
Watermelons	41.2	29.2	28.0*
Other fruit*	146.6	142.3	120.9
Tobacco (leaves)	1.3	1.9	2.0

* FAO estimate(s).

Source: FAO.

LIVESTOCK
('000 head, year ending 30 September)

	1999	2000	2001
Cattle	705	664	645
Pigs	1,593	1,562	1,488
Sheep	326	348	358
Goats	51	51	51
Horses	10	9	9*
Chickens†	12,644	14,036	14,621

* FAO estimate.
† Unofficial figures.

Source: FAO.

LIVESTOCK PRODUCTS
('000 metric tons, unless otherwise indicated)

	1999	2000	2001
Beef and veal	50.2	48.0	38.2
Pig meat	175.5	163.6	153.0
Poultry meat	82.7	89.9	91.7
Cows' milk	1,162.6	1,067.0	1,147.2
Goats' milk	13.2	13.2	13.3
Butter	16.1	16.1	17.0
Cheese	55.0	54.5	58.1
Hen eggs	64.8	60.8	64.3
Other poultry eggs*	10	10	10
Cattle hides (fresh)*	5.4	4.8	0.0

* FAO estimates.

Source: FAO.

Forestry

ROUNDWOOD REMOVALS
('000 cubic metres, excl. bark)

	1998	1999	2000
Sawlogs, veneer logs and logs for sleepers	2,176	2,303	2,396
Pulpwood	2,890	2,717	2,613
Other industrial wood	60	55	37
Fuel wood	404	193	167
Total	5,530	5,268	5,213

Source: FAO.

2001: Figures assumed to be unchanged from 2000, except for fuel wood (194,000 cubic metres).

SAWNWOOD PRODUCTION
('000 cubic metres, incl. railway sleepers)

	1997	1998	1999
Coniferous (softwood)	501	845	541
Broadleaved (hardwood)	266	420	203
Total	767	1,265	744

2000: Production as in 1999 (FAO estimates).

Source: FAO.

Fishing

(metric tons, live weight)

	1998	1999	2000
Capture	1,414	1,391	2,255
Common carp	778	822	928
Rainbow trout	17	16	771
Northern pike	68	69	77
Breams	99	98	94
Aquaculture	648	872	887
Common carp	63	157	74
Rainbow trout	487	630	752
Total catch (incl. others)	2,062	2,263	3,142

Source: FAO, *Yearbook of Fishery Statistics*.

Mining

('000 metric tons, unless otherwise indicated)

	1998	1999	2000
Brown coal	2,764.9	2,513.0	2,485.5
Lignite	1,200.0	1,211.3	1,101.3
Iron ore	41.7	40.0	32.1
Crude petroleum	54.0	32.4	29.9
Natural gas (million cu metres)	257.0	409.6	358.8
Limestone	3,291.5	3,158.9	3,841.4
Natural sands	608.8	507.5	421.9
Gravel	4,750.4	2,633.6	2,572.5

Industry

SELECTED PRODUCTS
('000 metric tons, unless otherwise indicated)

	1998	1999	2000
Wheat flour	349.6	319.4	327.0
Bread	124.7	125.5	124.3
Sugar	211.8	197.0	122.9
Pasta	19.0	17.9	20.8
Beer ('000 hectolitres)	4,477.8	4,473.2	4,491.4
Wine ('000 hectolitres)	514.4	544.9	476.4
Spirits and distillates (million litres)	39	34	35
Cotton yarn	5.2	3.7	3.3
Footwear ('000 pairs)	11,630	9,426	10,069
Paper and paperboard	625.6	646.5	703.7
Paints and enamels	30.2	31.0	32.6
Chemical fibres	63.3	73.2	65.5
Black-coal coke	1,515	1,615	1,705
Engine and petrochemical petrol	1,520	1,120	1,473
Gas-diesel (distillate fuel) oil	1,900	1,445	880
Cement*	4,705.0	4,717.9	4,509.9
Pig-iron	2,797	2,987	3,166
Crude steel	3,179	3,419	3,520
Aluminium	229.0	239.8	251.2
Household refrigerators and freezers (number)	257,178	240,122	198,948
Passenger motor cars (number)	125,467	126,561	180,804
Lorries and vans (number)	312	76	40
Motorcycles	7,011	4,106	2,196
Colour television receivers	304,127	311,294	431,177
Electric energy (million kWh)	26,308.8	27,746.2	30,607.4

* Including cement clinker.

Finance

CURRENCY AND EXCHANGE RATES

Monetary Units

100 halierov (singular: halier) = 1 Slovenská koruna (Slovak crown or Sk; plural: koruny).

Sterling, Dollar and Euro Equivalents (30 May 2003)
£1 sterling = 58.02 koruny;
US $1 = 35.21 koruny;
€1 = 41.63 koruny;
1,000 koruny = £17.24 = $28.40 = €24.02.

Average Exchange Rate (koruny per US $)
2000   46.035
2001   48.355
2002   45.327

Note: In February 1993 Slovakia introduced its own currency, the Slovak koruna, to replace (at par) the Czechoslovak koruna.

STATE BUDGET
('000 million koruny)

Revenue	1999	2000	2001*
Tax revenue	274.6	303.9	298.8
Personal income tax	46.1	41.3	44.2
Corporate income tax	23.0	26.4	21.7
Value-added tax	58.9	70.6	73.6
Excise taxes	25.2	28.5	28.4
Custom duties and import surcharge	12.5	13.2	3.9
Other taxes	7.6	8.3	9.2
Social security contributions	101.3	115.7	117.9
Total	339.5	347.6	351.8

Expenditure	1999	2000	2001*
Current expenditure	311.1	338.8	347.9
Wages	55.8	59.7	63.3
Education†	2.5	2.0	1.8
Health	43.6	48.8	51.3
Other consumption . . .	42.2	46.0	50.9
Subsidies to enterprises . . .	26.3	35.3	25.9
Interest payments	23.5	23.7	23.7
Social expenditure	117.2	123.3	131.0
Investment expenditure . . .	30.8	34.5	37.2
Net lending	25.6	5.8	6.2
Total	367.5	379.1	391.4

* Estimates.
† Excluding wages.
Source: IMF, *Slovak Republic: Selected Issues and Statistical Appendix* (September 2002).

INTERNATIONAL RESERVES
(US $ million at 31 December)

	2000	2001	2002
Gold*	53	45.3	54.8
IMF special drawing rights . .	0.49	0.66	1.15
Foreign exchange	4,022	4,140	8,808
Total	4,075	4,186	8,863

* National valuation.
Source: IMF, *International Financial Statistics*.

MONEY SUPPLY
(million koruny at 31 December)

	2000	2001	2002
Currency outside banks . . .	67,048	80,963	84,211
Demand deposits at commercial banks	118,916	144,603	160,560
Total money	185,964	225,566	244,771

Source: IMF, *International Financial Statistics*.

COST OF LIVING
(Consumer Price Index; base December 1995 = 100))

	1999	2000	2001
Foodstuffs and non-alcoholic beverages	116.5	122.7	129.5
Alcoholic beverages and tobacco .	123.9	135.8	140.2
Clothing and footwear	129.0	133.0	136.2
Housing, water, electricity, gas and other fuels	151.7	201.0	235.5
All items (incl. others)	128.6	144.0	154.6

Source: IMF, *Slovak Republic: Selected Issues and Statistical Appendix* (September 2002).

NATIONAL ACCOUNTS

Expenditure on the Gross Domestic Product
(million koruny at current prices, provisional figures)

	2000	2001	2002
Government final consumption expenditure	180,330	197,580	214,050
Private final consumption expenditure	510,680	560,240	603,880
Increase in stocks	−22,080	7,180	14,980
Gross fixed capital formation . .	267,930	309,610	319,750
Total domestic expenditure . .	936,860	1,074,610	1,152,660
Exports of goods and services . .	652,430	732,350	781,410
Less Imports of goods and services	674,490	816,040	857,930
GDP in purchasers' values . .	908,800	989,300	1,073,610

Source: IMF, *International Financial Statistics*.

Gross Domestic Product by Economic Activity
('000 million koruny, current prices)

	1999	2000	2001
Agriculture and forestry . . .	33.2	36.0	40.6
Industry*	215.6	233.1	241.3
Construction	42.4	42.3	45.6
Market services	343.3	388.2	437.5
Communications	23.6	23.6	27.6
Transport	57.8	66.5	83.3
Wholesale and retail trade . .	114.1	134.2	144.9
Other market services . . .	147.7	163.9	181.6
Non-market services	101.7	106.1	113.8
Total	815.3	887.2	964.6

* Principally mining, manufacturing, electricity, water and gas.
Source: IMF, *Slovak Republic: Selected Issues and Statistical Appendix* (September 2002).

BALANCE OF PAYMENTS
(US $ million)

	1998	1999	2000
Exports of goods f.o.b.	10,720	10,201	11,896
Imports of goods f.o.b.	−13,071	−11,310	−12,791
Trade balance	−2,351	−1,109	−895
Exports of services	2,292	1,899	2,241
Imports of services	−2,276	−1,844	−1,805
Balance on goods and services	−2,334	−1,054	−459
Other income received . . .	437	268	268
Other income paid	−595	−568	−623
Balance on goods, services and income	−2,492	−1,353	−814
Current transfers received . . .	645	466	344
Current transfers paid	−279	−268	−224
Current balance	−2,126	−1,155	−694
Capital account (net)	70	158	91
Direct investment abroad . . .	−145	376	−22
Direct investment from abroad . .	562	354	2,052
Portfolio investment assets . . .	−57	247	−195
Portfolio investment liabilities . .	841	405	1,016
Other investment assets . . .	190	1,713	−973
Other investment liabilities . .	520	−1,307	−407
Net errors and omissions . . .	−333	−14	51
Overall balance	−478	777	920

Source: IMF, *International Financial Statistics*.

External Trade

COMMODITY GROUPS
(distribution by SITC, million koruny)

Imports f.o.b.	1998	1999	2000
Food and live animals	24,249	24,121	26,468
Crude materials (inedible) except fuels	17,669	17,894	22,907
Mineral fuels, lubricants, etc. . .	50,291	60,665	103,321
Chemicals and related products .	48,843	52,869	64,669
Basic manufactures	82,984	85,765	104,187
Machinery and transport equipment	185,625	176,935	210,535
Miscellaneous manufactured articles	45,758	44,480	51,807
Total (incl. others)	460,736	468,892	590,275

Exports f.o.b.	1998	1999	2000
Food and live animals	12,144	12,849	13,874
Crude materials (inedible) except fuels	13,565	16,276	17,814
Mineral fuels, lubricants, etc. . .	13,235	20,126	38,376
Chemicals and related products .	33,579	33,417	43,519
Basic manufactures	113,284	116,385	146,618
Machinery and transport equipment	141,144	166,899	216,836
Miscellaneous manufactured articles	47,967	54,543	68,193
Total (incl. others)	377,807	423,648	548,527

2001 (million koruny): *Imports f.o.b.:* Prepared foodstuffs, beverages and tobacco, 22,779; Mineral products 117,890; Products of the chemical or allied industries 61,769; Rubber and plastics, and articles thereof 37,035; Wood pulp, cellulose and paper, and articles thereof 20,882; Textiles and textile articles 40,625; Base metals and articles of base metal 59,533; Machinery and electrical equipment 180,458; Vehicles, aircraft, vessels and transport equipment 89,858; Optical, photographic, measuring and medical apparatus; clocks and watches; musical instruments 16,715; Total (incl. others) 713,898. *Exports f.o.b.:* Mineral products 47,519; Products of the chemical or allied industries 30,126; Rubber and plastics, and articles thereof 32,499; Wood and articles of wood 14,848; Wood pulp, cellulose and paper, and articles thereof 31,376; Textiles and textile articles 41,578; Articles of stone, plaster, cement, asbestos, mica; ceramic products; glass 14,365; Base metals and articles of base metal 92,402; Machinery and electrical equipment 114,424; Vehicles, aircraft, vessels and transport equipment 126,077; Total (incl. others) 611,325.

2002 (million koruny): *Imports f.o.b.:* Prepared foodstuffs, beverages and tobacco, 24,959; Mineral products 109,175; Products of the chemical or allied industries 65,650; Rubber and plastics, and articles thereof 45,560; Wood pulp, cellulose and paper, and articles thereof 22,472; Textiles and textile articles 41,993; Base metals and articles of base metal 66,886; Machinery and electrical equipment 191,471; Vehicles, aircraft, vessels and transport equipment 95,423; Optical, photographic, measuring and medical apparatus; clocks and watches; musical instruments 17,807; Total (incl. others) 714,071. *Exports f.o.b.:* Mineral products 46,618; Products of the chemical or allied industries 31,023; Rubber and plastics, and articles thereof 37,854; Wood and articles of wood 15,249; Wood pulp, cellulose and paper, and articles thereof 31,692; Textiles and textile articles 43,297; Articles of stone, plaster, cement, asbestos, mica; ceramic products; glass 15,534; Base metals and articles of base metal 93,481; Machinery and electrical equipment 122,763; Vehicles, aircraft, vessels and transport equipment 137,560; Total (incl. others) 651,256.

PRINCIPAL TRADING PARTNERS
(million koruny)

Imports f.o.b.	2000	2001	2002
Austria.	23,248	29,608	31,480
Belgium	9,399	11,927	13,501
Czech Republic	86,852	107,622	113,290
France	19,759	27,577	32,960
Germany	147,867	176,187	169,188
Hungary	12,401	18,227	20,423
Italy	36,449	45,579	51,529
Japan	9,955	11,466	13,873
Netherlands	9,107	10,512	13,143
Poland	18,046	23,175	24,088
Russia	100,577	105,433	93,848
Switzerland	7,374	9,178	10,169
Ukraine	8,737	9,387	8,473
United Kingdom	14,293	18,158	18,957
USA	12,223	13,797	15,961
Total (incl. others)	590,275	714,071	747,883

Exports f.o.b.	2000	2001	2002
Austria.	45,885	49,651	50,053
Belgium	11,467	14,699	13,531
Czech Republic	95,414	101,576	99,023
France	25,427	24,102	27,202
Germany	146,856	165,525	169,200
Hungary	26,700	32,855	35,528
Italy	50,334	54,015	69,916
Netherlands	14,560	17,209	19,806
Poland	32,095	35,598	34,761
Russia	4,917	6,306	6,494
Switzerland	9,411	9,371	8,155
Ukraine	6,796	7,037	7,064
United Kingdom	10,366	15,030	15,457
USA	7,776	7,837	9,387
Total (incl. others)	548,527	611,325	651,256

Transport

	1999	2000	2001
Railway transport:			
freight ('000 tons)	49,115	54,177	53,588
passengers (million)	69	67	63
Public road transport:			
freight ('000 tons)*	33,920	39,680	34,773
passengers (million)	622	604	566
Waterway transport: freight ('000 tons)	1,507	1,607	1,551

* Road transport for transport organizations including non-incorporated tradesmen.

ROAD TRAFFIC
(motor vehicles in use at 31 December)

	1998	1999	2000
Passenger cars	1,196,109	1,236,396	1,274,244
Buses and coaches	11,293	11,101	10,920
Goods vehicles	111,081	115,981	110,714
Motorcycles*	100,891	44,215	45,647

* Excluding scooters.

CIVIL AVIATION
(traffic on scheduled services)

	1998	1999	2000
Passengers carried ('000) . .	232.6	168.4	158.9
Freight carried (metric tons) . .	637	776	697
Passenger-km (million)	316.0	260.5	250.9
Freight ton-km ('000)	338	262	220

Tourism

FOREIGN TOURIST ARRIVALS
(visitors at accommodation facilities)

Country of origin	1999	2000	2001
Austria.	32,643	36,779	44,046
Czech Republic	275,031	277,401	327,607
France	14,833	16,015	19,523
Germany	137,964	155,129	172,446
Hungary	53,057	59,322	73,937
Italy	27,076	28,097	32,737
Netherlands	16,540	18,772	22,068
Poland	173,135	201,082	264,631
Russia	22,361	30,861	19,876
Ukraine	31,732	24,212	18,863
USA	23,310	28,851	28,183
Total (incl. others)	975,105	1,045,614	1,219,099

Receipts from tourism (US $ million): 489 in 1999; 461 in 2000 (Source: World Bank).

Communications Media

	1998	1999	2000
Radio receivers (licensed) . . .	1,255,624	1,368,863	1,347,477
Television receivers (licensed) . .	1,392,883	1,241,663	1,211,773
Telephones in use	1,539,283	1,655,380	1,697,982
Telefax stations (registered) . .	54,037	n.a.	n.a.
Mobile cellular telephones			
(subscribers)	493,868	662,511	1,109,888
Personal computers ('000 in use)* .	470	590	n.a.
Internet users ('000)*	500	600	650
Newspapers and periodicals: titles	1,269	1,290	1,465

2001:* Main telephone lines in use 1,556,300; Personal computers in use 800,000; Mobile cellular subscribers 2,147,300.

2002:* Main telephone lines in use 1,402,700; Personal computers in use 970,000; Internet users 862,800; Mobile cellular subscribers 2,923,400.

* Source: International Telecommunication Union.

Book production (1996): 3,800 titles (Source: UNESCO, *Statistical Yearbook*).

Education

(2000/01)

	Institutions	Teachers	Students
Kindergarten	3,263	15,229	154,232
Primary (basic).	2,447	39,745	650,966
Secondary: grammar	212	6,259	82,147
Secondary: specialized. . . .	372	9,882	104,301
Secondary: vocational	368	11,255	111,128
Higher*	20	9,047	125,896

* Full-time study only.

Directory

The Constitution*

On 1 September 1992 the Slovak National Council adopted the Constitution of the Slovak Republic (which entered into force on 1 January 1993), the main provisions of which, as amended in January 1999, are summarized below:

FUNDAMENTAL PROVISIONS

The Slovak Republic is a democratic and sovereign state, ruled by law. It is bound neither to an ideology, nor to a religion. State power belongs to the people, who exercise it either through their representatives or directly. The state authorities shall act only on the basis of the Constitution and to the extent and in the manner stipulated by law.

The territory of the Slovak Republic is integral and indivisible. The conditions for naturalization or deprival of state citizenship of the Slovak Republic are regulated by law. No person may be deprived of citizenship against his/her will. The Slovak language is the state language in the republic. The use of languages other than the state language in administrative relations is regulated by law. The capital of the republic is Bratislava.

BASIC RIGHTS AND FREEDOMS

The people are free and equal, and the rights and freedoms of every citizen are guaranteed, irrespective of sex, race, colour, language, faith, political or other conviction, national or social origin, nationality or ethnic origin. No person may be tortured, nor be subjected to cruel, inhuman or humiliating treatment or punishment. Capital punishment is not practised.

Every person has the right to own property. The place of abode is inviolable. The freedom of migration and the freedom of domicile are guaranteed.

The freedom of expression and the right to information are guaranteed. Censorship is prohibited. The right to assemble peacefully is guaranteed. Every person has the right to be a member of a union, community, society or any other association. Citizens have the right to found political parties and movements. Such parties and movements, as well as other associations, are separate from the state.

The citizens have the right to participate in the administration of public affairs, either directly or through the free election of their representatives. The right to vote is universal, direct and equal and is exercised by secret ballot.

The universal advancement of citizens who are members of national minorities and ethnic groups is guaranteed, above all the right to develop their own culture, to broadcast and receive information in their mother tongue, to join national associations and to found and maintain educational and cultural institutions. The languages of national minorities may also be used in administrative relations.

Every person has the right to the free choice of profession and vocational training as well as to do business and to perform other commercial activities. Employees are entitled to fair and satisfactory working conditions. Citizens may form free associations to protect their economic and social interests. Trade unions are independent of the state. The right to strike is guaranteed.

Every citizen is entitled to adequate old-age and disability benefits; widow's allowances; free health care; family support; and education.

NATIONAL COUNCIL OF THE SLOVAK REPUBLIC

Supreme legislative power is vested in the National Council of the Slovak Republic, which has 150 deputies, elected for a four-year term. The deputies represent the citizens and are elected by them in general, equal and direct elections, by secret ballot.

The National Council has the power to: adopt the Constitution, constitutional and other laws and supervise their execution; elect and recall the President of the Slovak Republic by secret ballot; decide on proposals to call a referendum; prior to their ratification, give consent to international political, economic or other agreements; establish ministries and other bodies of state administration; supervise the activities of the Government and pass a vote of confidence or censure on the Government or its members; approve the state budget and supervise its execution; elect judges, including the Chairman and Vice-Chairmen of the Supreme Court and of the Constitutional Court; adopt a resolution to declare war if the Slovak Republic is attacked, or if such a declaration ensues from the obligations of international treaties.

THE PRESIDENT OF THE REPUBLIC

The President is the Head of State of the Slovak Republic. He/she is directly elected by universal adult suffrage for a five-year term. The President is responsible to the National Council. He/she may not be elected for more than two consecutive terms.

The President represents the Slovak Republic internationally; negotiates and ratifies international agreements; receives and gives credentials to envoys; convenes constituent sessions of the National Council; may dissolve the National Council; signs laws; appoints and recalls the Prime Minister and other members of the Government and receives their resignation; grants amnesty, pardons and commutes sentences imposed by courts; may declare a state of emergency on the basis of constitutional law; may declare a referendum.

THE GOVERNMENT

The Government of the Slovak Republic is the highest organ of executive power. It is composed of the Prime Minister and Ministers. The Prime Minister is appointed by the President of the Republic. On the Prime Minister's recommendation, the President appoints and recalls the members of the Government and puts them in charge of their ministries. For the execution of office, the Government is responsible to the National Council.

The Government has the power to prepare bills; issue decrees; adopt fundamental provisions for economic and social policy; authorize drafts for the state budget and closing account of the year; decide international agreements; decide principal questions of internal and international policy; submit bills to the National Council; request the legislature for a vote of confidence.

*Further revisions to the Constitution were approved in February 2001 and officially entered into effect on 1 July. The amendments redefined the relationship between national and international law, incorporated Slovakia's aim of joining foreign alliances, strengthened the powers of the Constitutional Court, granted greater independence to the judiciary (by the establishment of a new judicial council), and provided for public administration reform, with the creation of a higher level of regional self-government.

The Government

HEAD OF STATE

President of the Republic: RUDOLF SCHUSTER (inaugurated 15 June 1999).

GOVERNMENT
(July 2003)

The Government comprises members of the Slovak Democratic and Christian Union (SDCU), the Christian Democratic Movement (CDM), the Party of the Hungarian Coalition (PHC), the New Civic Alliance (NCA) and the Democratic Party (DP).

Prime Minister: MIKULÁŠ DZURINDA (SDCU).

Deputy Prime Minister for European Integration, Human Rights and Minorities: PÁL CSÁKY (PHC).

Deputy Prime Minister and Minister of Finance: IVAN MIKLOŠ (SDCU).

Deputy Prime Minister and Minister of Justice: DANIEL LIPŠIĆ (CDM).

Deputy Prime Minister, and Minister of the Economy, and Administration and Privatization of National Property: ROBERT NEMCSICS (NCA).

Minister of Foreign Affairs: EDUARD KUKAN (SDCU).

Minister of Defence: IVAN ŠIMKO (SDCU).

Minister of the Environment: LÁSZLÓ MIKLÓS (PHC).

Minister of the Interior: VLADIMIR PALKO (CDM).

Minister of Labour, Social Affairs and the Family: L'UDOVÍT KANÍK (DP).

Minister of Culture: RUDOLF CHMEL (NCA).

Minister of Education: MARTIN FRONC (CDM).

Minister of Health: RUDOLF ZAJAC (ANC).

Minister of Agriculture: SIMON ZSOLT (PHC).

Minister of Transport, Posts and Telecommunications: PAVOL PROKOPOVIĆ (SDCU).

Minister of Construction and Public Works: ISTVÁN HARNA (PHC).

MINISTRIES

Office of the Government of the Slovak Republic: nám. Slobody 1, 813 70 Bratislava; tel. (2) 5729-5111; fax (2) 5249-7603; e-mail tio@government.gov.sk; internet www.government.gov.sk.

Ministry of Agriculture: Dobrovičova 12, 812 66 Bratislava; tel. (2) 5296-6111; fax (2) 5296-1834; e-mail majkut@mpsr.sanet.sk; internet www.mpsr.sk.

Ministry of Construction and Public Works: Špitálska 8, 816 44 Bratislava; tel. (2) 5975-1111; fax (2) 5293-1203; e-mail informacie@build.gov.sk; internet www.build.gov.sk.

Ministry of Culture: nám. SNP, 81101 Bratislava; tel. (2) 5939-1111; fax (2) 5926-6457; e-mail webmaster@culture.gov.sk; internet www.culture.gov.sk.

Ministry of Defence: Kutuzovova 7, 832 28 Bratislava; tel. (2) 4425-0320; fax (2) 4425-3242; e-mail linka.dovery@mod.gov.sk; internet www.mod.gov.sk.

Ministry of the Economy, and Administration and Privatization of National Property: Mierová 19, 827 15 Bratislava; tel. (2) 4854-1111; fax (2) 4333-7827; e-mail icom@economy.gov.sk; internet www.economy.gov.sk.

Ministry of Education: Stromová 1, 813 30 Bratislava; tel. (2) 5937-4315; fax (2) 5477-3766; e-mail kancmin@education.gov.sk; internet www.education.gov.sk.

Ministry of the Environment: nám. L'. Štúra 1, 812 35 Bratislava; tel. (2) 5956-1111; fax (2) 5956-2031; e-mail info@lifeenv.gov.sk; internet www.lifeenv.gov.sk.

Ministry of Finance: Štefanovičova 5, 817 82 Bratislava; tel. (2) 5958-1111; fax (2) 5249-8042; e-mail inform@mfsr.sk; internet www.finance.gov.sk.

Ministry of Foreign Affairs: Hlboká cesta 2, 833 36 Bratislava; tel. (2) 5978-1111; fax (2) 5978-2213; internet www.foreign.gov.sk.

Ministry of Health: Limbová 2, 831 05 Bratislava; tel. (2) 5937-3111; fax (2) 5477-7983; e-mail office@health.gov.sk; internet www.health.gov.sk.

Ministry of the Interior: Pribinova 2, 812 72 Bratislava; tel. (2) 5091-1111; fax (2) 5094-4017; e-mail www@minv.sk; internet www.minv.sk.

Ministry of Justice: Župné nám. 13, 813 11 Bratislava; tel. (2) 5935-3111; fax (2) 5441-5952; e-mail tlacove@justice.gov.sk; internet www.justice.gov.sk.

Ministry of Labour, Social Affairs and the Family: Špitálska 4–6, 816 43 Bratislava; tel. (2) 5975-1111; fax (2) 5292-1258; internet www.employment.gov.sk.

Ministry of Transport, Posts and Telecommunications: nám. Slobody 6, 810 05 Bratislava; tel. (2) 5949-4111; fax (2) 5249-4794; e-mail info@telecom.gov.sk; internet www.telecom.gov.sk.

President

Presidential Election, 15 and 29 May 1999

Candidates	First ballot votes cast %	Second ballot votes cast Number	%
Rudolf Schuster	47.38	1,727,398	57.18
Vladimír Mečiar . . .	37.24	1,293,642	42.82
Magda Vášáryová . . .	6.60	—	—
Ivan Mjartan	3.59	—	—
Ján Slota	2.50	—	—
Others	2.69	—	—
Total	100.00	3,021,040	100.00

Legislature

NATIONAL COUNCIL OF THE SLOVAK REPUBLIC

Chairman: PAVOL HRUŠOVSKÝ.

Deputy Chairmen: ZUZANA MARTINÁKOVÁ, BÉLA BUGÁR, Dr PAVOL RUSKO, VILIAM VETEŠKA.

General Election, 20–21 September 2002

Party	Votes	% of votes	Seats
Movement for a Democratic Slovakia	560,691	19.50	36
Slovak Democratic and Christian Union	433,953	15.09	28
Direction (Smer)	387,100	13.46	25
Party of the Hungarian Coalition .	321,069	11.16	20
Christian Democratic Movement .	237,202	8.25	15
New Civic Alliance	230,309	8.01	15
Communist Party of Slovakia . .	181,872	6.32	11
Others	522,885	18.19	—
Total*	2,875,081	100.00	150

* Excluding 34,917 invalid votes.

Local Government

Slovakia is divided into eight 'higher territorial units', (each with a regional council), the principal units of local administration, which are subdivided into 79 electoral districts. The ethnic Hungarian parties have a declared aim of an autonomous ethnic Hungarian region within Slovakia. Local elections took place in December 2001. Elections to municipality self-government bodies took place in December 2002.

Association of Towns and Communities of Slovakia: Bezrucova 9, 811 09 Bratislava; tel. (2) 5296-4243; fax (2) 5296-4256; e-mail centr@zmos.sk; internet www.zmos.sk; Dir-Gen. GEJZA BALOGH.

REGIONS

Banská Bystrica: L. Štúra nám. 1, 975 41 Banská Bystrica; tel. (48) 430-6111; fax (48) 413-6558; Gov. MILAN MARCOK.

Bratislava: Staromestská 6, 814 71 Bratislava; tel. (2) 5931-2111; fax (2) 5443-1282; Gov. L'UBO ROMAN.

Košice: Komenského 52, 041 26 Košice; tel. (55) 600-1102; fax (55) 633-6718; Gov. RUDOLF BAUER.

Nitra: Štefánikova 69, 949 80 Nitra; tel. (37) 549-111; fax (37) 515-329; Gov. MILAN BELICA.

Prešov: Mieru nám. 3, 080 01 Prešov; tel. (51) 708-1111; fax (51) 772-1423; Gov. PETER CHUDIK; Chair. Ing. JOZEF POLAČKO.

Trenčín: Hviezdoslavova 3, 911 49 Trenčín; tel. (32) 411-111; fax (32) 434-686; Gov. ŠTEFAN STEFANEĆ.

Trnava: Trnava; tel. (33) 5564-111; fax (33) 5512-320; Gov. PETER TOMEČEK.

Žilina: ul. Janka Krála 4, 010 40 Žilina; tel. (41) 677-7111; fax (41) 651-428; Gov. JOZEF TARCAK.

DISTRICTS

Bratislava I: Medená 2, 814 99 Bratislava; tel. (2) 384-6111; fax (2) 366-554; Chair. Ing. IVAN ŠULKO.

Bratislava II: Tomášikova 20, 826 09 Bratislava; tel. (2) 4342-4431; fax (2) 4333-7462; Chair. PETR KOLESÁR.

Bratislava III: Junácka 1, 832 29 Bratislava; tel. (2) 4425-8768; fax (2) 4425-8438; Chair. Ing. IVAN DUTKA.

Bratislava IV: Karloveská 2, 842 10 Bratislava; tel. (2) 6549-2111; fax (2) 6542-8961; Chair. L'UBICA NAVRÁTILOVÁ.

Bratislava V: Kutlíkova 17, 852 12 Bratislava; tel. (2) 6382-2601; fax (2) 6383-2203; e-mail simka.vladislav@ba5.vs.sk; Chair. Ing. VLADISLAV ŠIMKA.

Malacky: Záhorácka 116, 901 01 Malacky; tel. (34) 772-5737; fax (34) 772-3854; e-mail ouma@ha.vs.sk; internet www.ouma.sk; Chair. MILAN VAŠKOR.

Pezinok: Štefánikova 10, 902 01 Pezinok; tel. (33) 411-172; fax (33) 411-113; Chair. Dr RENÉ BÍLIK.

Senec: Lichnerova 61, 903 01 Senec; tel. (2) 4592-3338; fax (2) 4592-5466; Chair. ŠTEFAN HAJDUCH.

Dunajská Streda: Slobody nám. 1194, 929 01 Dunajská Streda; tel. (31) 552-2112; fax (31) 552-6286; Chair. PAVEL KESZEGH.

Galanta: Mierové nám. 1, 924 26 Galanta; tel. (31) 780-2201; fax (31) 780-3980; Chair. Ing. LADISLAV POMOTHY.

Hlohovec: Jarmočná 5, 920 01 Hlohovec; tel. (33) 742-4835; fax (33) 742-1311; Chair. Ing. MICHAL JAVOR.

Piešt'any: Krajinská cesta 5053/13, 921 01 Piešt'any; tel. (33) 776-1111; fax (33) 776-1213; Chair. MÁRIA GAŠPARÍKOVA.

Senica: Vajanského 17, 905 01 Senica; tel. (34) 512-851; fax (34) 513-120; Chair. Ing. ŠTEFAN MIKULA.

Skalica: Slobody nám. 15, 909 01 Skalica; tel. (34) 644-214; fax (34) 645-194; Chair. JAROSLAV RIHA.

Trnava: Vajanského 22, 917 01 Trnava; tel. (33) 555-0111; fax (33) 242-01; Chair. Ing. IVAN MIČKA.

Bánovce nad Bebravou: Sládkovičova 60, 957 63 Bánovce nad Bebravou; tel. (38) 603-775; fax (38) 602-744; Chair. Ing. LADISLAV RAUČINA.

Ilava: Mierové nám. 81/18, 019 01 Ilava; tel. (42) 451-224; fax (42) 451-226; Chair. Ing. RUDOLF LACKO.

Myjava: M. R. Štefánika 561, 907 01 Myjava; tel. (34) 213-941; fax (34) 212-557; Chair. Ing. DUŠN HOLOTA.

Nové Meste nad Váhom: Odborárska 1, 915 41 Nové Meste nad Váhom; tel. (32) 712-875; fax (32) 712-819; Chair. Ing. MILOSLAV MALÍK.

Partizánske: SNP nám. 212/4, 958 01 Partizánske; tel. (37) 924-72; fax (37) 931-00; Chair. PAVOL HORŇAN.

Považská Bystrica: Centrum 1/1, 017 11 Považská Bystrica; tel. (42) 300-111; fax (42) 325-970; Chair. Ing. PAVEL PETRÍK.

Prievidza: Šumperská 1, 971 73 Prievidza; tel. (46) 542-3021; fax (46) 542-2169; e-mail prednosta@pd.vs.sk; Chair. Ing. MIROSLAV ŠTORCEL.

Púchov: ul. 1 Mája 896, 020 58 Púchov; tel. (42) 460-2302; fax (42) 460-2303; e-mail prednosta@pu.vs.sk; Chair. Ing. ONDREJ DIVÍNSKY.

Trenčin: M. R. Štefánika 20, 911 49 Trenčín; tel. (32) 743-1551; fax (32) 743-1758; e-mail prednosta@tn.vs.sk; Chair. MÁRIOU DEDÍKOVOU.

Komárno: M. R. Štefánika 10, 945 36 Komárno; tel. (35) 769-111; fax (35) 701-692; Chair. MERGIT KESZEGHOVÁ.

Levice: L'udovíta Štúra 53, 934 26 Levice; tel. (36) 502-231; fax (36) 622-5212; Chair. Ing. PAVEL ZACHAR.

Nitra: Štefánikova 69, 949 80 Nitra; tel. (37) 522-875; fax (37) 526-870; Chair. Ing. JURAJ HOTVÁTH.

Nové Zámky: F. Kapisztóryho 1, 940 36 Nové Zámky; tel. (35) 225-11; fax (35) 423-161; Chair. Ing. LADISLAVE MARENČÁK.

Šal'a: Sv. Trojice nám. 7, 927 15 Šal'a; tel. (31) 770-2351; fax (31) 770-6021; e-mail primator@sala.sk; internet www.sala.sk; Chair. Ing. ŠTEFAN SZELES.

Topol'čany: L'. Štúra 1738, 955 01 Topol'čany; tel. (38) 353-111; fax (38) 321-192; Chair. Ing. L'UBOMIR BOŠANSKÝ.

Zlaté Moravce: Sládkovičova 3, 953 33 Zlaté Moravce; tel. (37) 401-111; fax (37) 218-08; Chair. Ing. RUDOLF RAGAS.

Bytča: Zámok 104, 014 01 Bytča; tel. (41) 552-2782; fax (41) 553-3783; e-mail okresny.urad@by.vs.sk; internet www.vs.sk; Chair. Ing. ELENA ŠUTEKOVÁ.

Čadca: Palárikova 1158, 022 23 Čadca; tel. (41) 217-40; fax (41) 215-35; Chair. Ing. PETR ŠPITA.

Dolný Kubín: Slobody nám. 1, 026 01 Dolný Kubín; tel. (43) 863-371; fax (43) 862-395; Chair. Ing. L'UBOMÍR ONDIRKO.

Kysucké Nové Mesto: Litovelská 670, 024 01 Kysucké Nové Mesto; tel. (41) 420-3226; fax (41) 420-3345; e-mail oo_oiss@km.vs.sk; Chair. Ing. JANA SVRČKOVA.

Liptovský Mikuláš: Osloboditel'ov nám. 1, 031 41 Liptovský Mikuláš; tel. (44) 529-999; fax (44) 523-513; Chair. JAROSLAV LEHOTSKÝ.

Martin: Vajanského nám. 1, 036 58 Martin; tel. (43) 804-361; fax (43) 329-27; Chair. JOZEF ORSZÁGH.

Námestovo: A. Bernoláka nám. 381/4, 029 01 Námestovo; tel. (43) 502-111; fax (43) 523-164; Chair. ELENA KRAUSOVÁ.

Ružomberok: Slobody nám. 9, 034 50 Ružomberok; tel. (44) 312-111; fax (44) 322-871; Chair. Ing. IVETA HATALOVÁ.

Turčianske Teplice: Partizánska 12, 039 01 Turčianske Teplice; tel. (43) 492-4003; fax (43) 492-2320; Chair. MILAN LITVA.

Tvrdošín: Medvedzie 131, 027 45 Tvrdošín; tel. (43) 302-111; fax (43) 322-029; Chair. Ing. JURAJ BERNAT'ÁK.

Žilina: A. Kmet'a 17, 010 01 Žilina; tel. (41) 677-2111; fax (41) 620-323; Chair. Ing. TIBOR MINTÁL.

Banská Bystrica: Čsl. armády nám. 26, 974 01 Banská Bystrica; tel. (48) 433-0101; fax (48) 411-3575; e-mail masa@misbb.sk; Chair. Ing. JÁN KRÁLIK.

Banská Štiavnica: Križovatka 4, 969 54 Banská Štiavnica; tel. (45) 691-3344; fax (45) 691-3342; e-mail prednosta@bs.vs.sk; Chair. Ing. PETER ZORVAN.

Brezno: Rázusova 40, 977 01 Brezno; tel. (48) 611-5681; fax (48) 611-5684; Chair. Ing. JAROSLAV DEMIAN.

Detva: Záhradná 12, 962 12 Detva; tel. (45) 545-6412; fax (45) 545-6153; Chair. Ing. JÁN ŠUFLIARSKY.

Krupina: Priemyselná 1, 963 01 Krupina; tel. (45) 551-1222; fax (45) 551-1016; Chair. Ing. ANTON POLIAK.

Lučenci: Republiky nám. 8, 984 36 Lučenec; tel. (47) 432-1246; fax (47) 432-2038; Chair. JÁN JACKULIAK.

Poltár: Sklárska 51, 987 01 Poltár; tel. (47) 422-3100; fax (47) 421-0330; Chair. Ing. VÍT'AZOLAV ZÁKOPČAN.

Revúca: ul. Gen. Viesta 1103/4, 050 01 Revúca; tel. (58) 218-05; fax (58) 442-2371; Chair. Ing. JOZEF FOL'TN.

Rimavská Sobota: Mihálya Tompu nám. 2, 979 11 Rimavská Sobota; tel. (47) 562-1575; fax (47) 532-2415; Chair. Ing. ZOLTÁN BOROS.

Vel'ký Krtíš: I. Madácha 2, 990 11 Vel'ký Krtíš; tel. (47) 483-0191; fax (47) 483-0895; Chair. BOHUSLAV BEŇO.

Zvolen: SNP nám. 35, 961 08 Zvolen; tel. (45) 533-0622; fax (45) 533-1258; Chair. PETER RANDUŠKA.

Žarnovica: Dolná 14, 966 81 Žarnovica; tel. (45) 413-285; fax (45) 413-059; Chair. KAMIL DANKO.

Žiar nad Hronom: Matice slovenskej nám. 3, 965 01 Žiar nad Hronom; tel. (45) 722-323; fax (45) 722-277; Chair. Ing. PETER KLIMENT.

Bardejov: Dlhý rad 16, 085 77 Bardejov; tel. (54) 471-0329; fax (54) 474653; e-mail oo_oiss@bj.vs.sk; Chair. JÁN PATAKY.

Humenné: Kukorelliho 1, 066 01 Humenné; tel. (57) 775-2001; fax (57) 632-47; Chair. Ing. MIROSLAV SEMAN.

Kežmarok: Dr Alexandra 61, 060 01 Kežmarok; tel. (52) 524-380; fax (52) 524-382; e-mail oo_oiss@kk.vs.sk; Chair. Ing. JÁN SOLIAR.

Levoča: Majstra Pavla nám. 4, 054 01 Levoča; tel. (53) 451-1333; fax (53) 514-333; Chair. Ing. PETER TUREK.

Medzilaborce: Cintorínska 2, 068 33 Medzilaborce; tel. (57) 212-60; fax (57) 210-21; Chair. Dr MICHAL PAČUTA.

Poprad: Popradské nábrežie 16, 058 44 Poprad; tel. (52) 716-0111; fax (52) 626-48; Chair. Ing. MILAN BARAN.

Prešov: Mieru nám. 2, 080 73 Prešov; tel. (51) 732-958; fax (51) 723-566; Chair. Ing. MILAN BENČ.

Sabinov: Slobody nám. 85, 083 01 Sabinov; tel. (51) 521-624; fax (51) 521-712; Chair. Ing. PAVEL SLANINKA.

Snina: ul. Partizánska 1057, 069 01 Snina; tel. (57) 768-5621; fax (57) 762-2380; Chair. SVÄTOSLAV HUSŤÁK.

Stará Ľubovňa: M. R. Štefánika 1, 064 16 Stará Ľubovňa; tel. (52) 432-3931; fax (52) 223-96; Chair. Dr ANDREJ MOKRIŠ.

Stropkov: Športová 2, 091 01 Stropkov; tel. (54) 742-3871; fax (54) 742-3790; Chair. Ing. JOZEF ŠIMKO.

Svidník: Sov. hrdinov 102, 089 17 Svidník; tel. (54) 212-55; fax (54) 229-04; Chair. Ing. VLADIMÍR POPÍK.

Vranov nad Topľou: Slobody nám. 5, 093 01 Vranov nad Topľou; tel. (57) 212-41; fax (57) 228-92; Chair. IGOR PRIBULA.

Gelnica: Hlavná 1, 056 01 Gelnica; tel. and fax (53) 482-1628; e-mail prednosta@gl.vs.sk; internet www.vs.sk/ougl; Chair. Dr MICHAL KUCHTA.

Košice I: Hviezdoslavova 7, 040 01 Košice; tel. (55) 622-2001; fax (55) 622-5329; Chair. Ing. MARTA LASKOVSKÁ.

Košice II: Popradská 74, 040 11 Košice; tel. (55) 643-4100; fax (55) 643-8484; e-mail prednosta@ke2.vs.sl; Chair. Ing. LADISLAV HERMAN.

Košice III: Adlerova 2, 040 22 Košice; tel. (55) 717-831; fax (55) 718-261; Chair. Dr VLADIMÍR KUŽILLA.

Košice IV: Textilná 6, 040 12 Košice; tel. (55) 623-1111; fax (55) 623-1413; Chair. Ing. BORIS FARKAŠOVSKÝ.

Košice-okolie: Hroncova 13, 040 11 Košice; tel. (55) 600-4111; fax (55) 632-2792; Chair. Ing. ĽUBOŠ PASTOR.

Michalovce: Slobody nám. 1, 071 01 Michalovce; tel. (56) 644-1398; fax (56) 240-36; Chair. Ing. VLADIMÍR JAKUB.

Rožňava: Mája nám. 1, 048 00 Rožňava; tel. (58) 732-1740; fax (58) 732-3946; Chair. Ing. JÁN LIPTÁK.

Sobrance: Michalovská 55, 073 01 Sobrance; tel. (56) 652-4044; fax (56) 652-3398; Chair. Ing. PETER STANKO.

Spišská Nová Ves: Štefánikovo nám. 1, 052 80 Spišská Nová Ves; tel. (53) 442-2251; fax (53) 442-1305; Chair. Dr JURAJ BEŇA.

Trebišov: M. R. Štefánika 1161/184, 075 01 Trebišov; tel. (56) 672-2611; fax (56) 672-5740; Chair. Ing. JÁNOS JUHÁSZ.

Political Organizations

Association of Workers of Slovakia (AWS) (Združenie robotníkov Slovenska): Horná 83, 974 01 Banská Bystrica; tel. (88) 742-703; f. 1994; Chair. JÁN ĽUPTÁK.

Christian Democratic Movement (CDM) (Kresťansko-demokratické hnutie): Žabotova 2, 811 04 Bratislava; tel. (2) 396-308; fax (2) 396-313; e-mail kdh@kdh.sk; internet www.kdh.sk; f. 1990; Chair. PAVOL HRUŠOVSKY.

Civic Conservative Party: Bratislava; f. Dec. 2001 by breakaway mems of the Democratic Party; Chair. PETER TATAR.

Communist Party of Slovakia (Komunistická strana Slovenska—KSS): 83103 Bratislava, Hattalova 12A; tel. and fax (2) 4437-2540; e-mail sekr@kss.sk; internet www.kss.sk; Pres. JOZEFA ŠEVCA.

Democratic Party (Demokratická strana): Šancová 70, 813 47 Bratislava; tel. (2) 5249-6927; fax (2) 5249-5893; e-mail secret@demstrana.sl; internet www.demstrana.sl; f. 1944; in 1994 absorbed the Civic Democratic Union, Civic Democratic Party of Slovakia, Democrats '92, Czech-Slovak Understanding and the Green League; conservative; breakaway faction (Leader FRANTIŠEK SEBEJ), f. Feb. 2001; Chair. LUDOVIT KANIK; 3,000 mems.

Democratic Union of Slovakia (DUS) (Demokratická únia Slovenska): Medená 10, 811 04 Bratislava; tel. and fax (2) 361-637; internet www.demunia.sk; f. 1994 by former members of the Movement for a Democratic Slovakia; in 1995 absorbed the National Democratic Party—New Alternative; splinter group, Liberal Democratic Union, f. in 2000; Chair. ĽUBOMÍR HARACH; First Dep. Chair. MILAN KŇAŽKO.

Direction (Smēr): Sumračna 27, 821 02 Brastislava; tel. and fax (2) 4342-6297; e-mail kancelaria@asistent.sk; internet www .strana-smer.sk; f. 1999; absorbed the Party of Civic Understanding in 2003; centre-right, pro-EU, pro-NATO; Chair. ROBERT FICO.

Green Party in Slovakia (Strana zelených na Slovensku): Palisády 56, 811 06 Bratislava; tel. (2) 323-231; fax (2) 364-848; f. 1989; Chair. LADISLAV AMBROS.

Movement for a Democratic Slovakia (MDS) (Hnutie za demokratické Slovensko): Tomášikova 32A, 830 00 Bratislava; tel. (2) 4329-3800; fax (2) 4341-0225; e-mail webmaster@hzds.sk; internet www.hzds.sk; f. 1991; renamed People's Party—Movement for a Democratic Slovakia June 2003; Chair. VLADIMÍR MEČIAR.

Movement for Democracy: Bratislava; f. 2002 by former members of the MDS (q.v.); Chair. IVAN GASPAROVIČ.

New Agrarian Party: Bratislava; f. 1997; coalition of the Farmers' Movement of Slovakia and the Farmers' Party of Slovakia; Chair. PAVEL DELINGA.

Farmers' Movement of Slovakia (Hnutie poľnohospodárov Slovenska): Sama Chalúpku 18, 071 01 Bratislava; tel. (2) 215-291; Chair. JOZEF KLEIN.

Farmers' Party of Slovakia (Roľnícka strana Slovenska): Trenčianska 55, 821 09 Bratislava; tel. (2) 215-800; Chair. PAVEL DELINGA.

New Civic Alliance (Aliancia Nového Občana—ANO): 84101 Bratislava, Drobného 27; tel. (2) 6920-2919; fax (2) 6920-2920; e-mail ano@ano-aliancia.sk; internet www.ano-aliancia.sk; f. April 2001; centre-right, pro-reform; Dir PAVOL RUŠKO.

Party of the Democratic Centre (Strana demokratického stredu): Kopčianska 94A, 851 01 Bratislava; tel. (2) 6828-7291; fax (2) 6383-0572; e-mail strana@sds.sk; internet www.sds.sk; f. 1999; Chair. IVAN MJARTAN.

Party of the Democratic Left (PDL) (Strana demokratickej ľavice): Gunduličova 12, 811 05 Bratislava; tel. (2) 5443-3617; fax (2) 5443-5574; e-mail hovorca@sdl.sk; internet www.sdl.sk; f. 1991 by mems of the fmr Communist Party of Slovakia; Chair. PAVEL KONCOŠ.

Party of the Hungarian Coalition (PHC) (Strana madarskej koalicie): Žabotova 2, 811 04 Bratislava; tel. (2) 5249-7684; fax (2) 5249-5791; e-mail webmaster@smk.sk; internet www.mkp.sk; f. 1998 by Coexistence, the Hungarian Christian Democratic Movement and the Hungarian Civic Party to contest the 1998 parliamentary elections as a single party; Chair. BÉLA BUGÁR.

Coexistence (Spolužitie/Együttélés): Pražská 7, POB 44, 814 09 Bratislava; tel. and fax (2) 497-877; represents ethnic Hungarian interests; Leader MIKLÓS DURAY.

Hungarian Christian Democratic Movement: Žabotova 2, Bratislava; tel. (2) 395-164; fax (2) 395-264; e-mail bugar@nciz.tsa .de; Pres. BÉLA BUGÁR; Vice-Pres. PÁL CSÁKY.

Hungarian Civic Party: Žabotova 2, 811 04 Bratislava; tel. (2) 397-684; fax (2) 395-791; Chair. LÁSZLÓ A. NAGY.

Party of Labour and Development (Strana prace a rozvoja): Bratislava; f. 2000; left-wing; Chair. JAN KALEJA.

People's Union (Ľudová uniá): Bratislava; f. March 2003 by breakaway mems of the Movement for a Democratic Slovakia.

Romany Civic Initiative: represents interests of Romany population; Chair. GEJZA ADAM.

Slovak Democratic and Christian Union (SDCU) (Slovenská Demokratická a Krestanská Unia): Ružinovska 28, 821 03 Bratislava; tel. (2) 4341-4102; fax (2) 4341-4106; e-mail sdku@sdkuonline.sk; internet www.sdkuonline.sk; f. 2000 to contest legislative elections in 2002; Leader MIKULÁŠ DZURINDA; Gen. Sec. IVAN HARMAN.

Slovak National Party (SNP) (Slovenská národná strana): Šafárikovo nám. 3, 814 99 Bratislava; tel. (2) 5292-4260; fax (2) 5296-6188; e-mail sns@isnet.sk; internet www.sns.sk; Chair. JAN SLOTA; Vice-Chair. ANNA MALIKOVA.

Slovak Social Democratic Union: f. 1997 by former members of the Social Democratic Party of Slovakia; left-wing; Chair. JOZEF SKULTETY.

Social Democratic Alternative (Sociálnodemokratická alternatíva—SDA): 81107 Bratislava, Karadžičova 41; tel. and fax (2) 5564-8627; e-mail sda@sdalternativa.sk; f. Feb. 2002 by breakaway mems of Party of the Democratic Left; Chair. MILAN FTÁČNIK.

Social Democratic Party of Slovakia (Sociálno-demokratická strana Slovenska): Žabotova 2, 811 04 Bratislava; tel. and fax (2) 5249-4621; e-mail sdss@ba.psg.sk; internet www.sdss.sk; re-established 1990; Chair. JAROSLAV VOLF.

Diplomatic Representation

EMBASSIES IN SLOVAKIA

Angola: Jančova 8, BII/4, 811 02 Bratislava; tel. (2) 6280-3373; fax (2) 6280-3364; e-mail embangol@netax.sk; Ambassador MANUEL QUARTA 'PUNZA'.

Austria: Venturska 10, 811 01 Bratislava; tel. (2) 5443-2985; fax (2) 5443-2486; e-mail ambasada@austria.isternet.sk; Ambassador GABRIELE MATZNER-HOLZER.

Belgium: Fraňa král'a 5, 811 05 Bratislava; tel. (2) 5249-1338; fax (2) 5249-4296; e-mail ambabelbratis@gtinet.sk; Ambassador FRANÇOIS DEL MARMOL.

Bulgaria: Kuzmányho 1, 811 06 Bratislava; tel. (2) 5441-5308; fax (2) 5441-2404; e-mail bulembassy@stonline.sk; internet www.stonline.sk/bg_embassy/; Ambassador JANI MILČAKOV.

China, People's Republic: Údolná 7, 811 06 Bratislava; tel. (2) 5441-5304; fax (2) 5441-6551; Ambassador TAO MIAOFA.

Croatia: Mišikova 21, 811 06 Bratislava; tel. (2) 5443-3647; fax (2) 5443-5365; Ambassador GJURO DEŽELIĆ.

Cuba: Somolického 1, 811, 05 Bratislava; tel. (2) 5249-2777; fax (2) 5249-4200; e-mail embacuba@zutom.sk; Chargé d'affaires a.i. LAUREANO CARDOSO TOLEDO.

Czech Republic: 29 Augusta 5, 810 00 Bratislava; tel. (2) 5293-1204; fax (2) 5293-1209; e-mail bratislava@embassy.mzv.cz; Ambassador RUDOLF SLANSKY.

France: Hlavné nám. 7, 811 01 Bratislava; tel. (2) 5934-7111; fax (2) 5934-7199; e-mail diplo@france.sk; internet www.france.sk; Ambassador JACQUES FAURE.

Germany: Hviezdoslavovo nám. 10, 813 03 Bratislava; tel. (2) 5290–4400; fax (2) 5443–1480; e-mail info@germanembassy.sk; internet www.germanembassy.sk; Ambassador Dr UTA MAYER-SCHALBURG.

Greece: Hlavné nám. 4, 811 01 Bratislava; tel. (2) 5443-9841; fax (2) 5443-9854; e-mail embassy@greece.sk; internet www.greece.sk; Ambassador VASSILIOS IKOSSIPENTARCHOS.

Holy See: Nekrasovova 17, 811 04 Bratislava (Apostolic Nunciature); tel. (2) 5479-3528; fax (2) 5479-3529; Apostolic Nuncio Most Rev. HENRYK JÓZEF NOWACKI (Titular Archbishop of Blera).

Hungary: Sedlárska 3, 814 25 Bratislava; tel. (2) 5443-0541; fax (2) 5443-5484; Ambassador MIKLÓS BOROS.

India: Radlinkkého 2, 811 02 Bratislava; tel. (2) 5293-1700; fax (2) 5293-1690; e-mail india@indembassy.sk; internet www.eindia.sk; Ambassador UPENDRA CHANDRA.

Indonesia: Mudroňova 51, 811 02 Bratislava; tel. (2) 5441-9886; fax (2) 5441-9890; e-mail indonesia@indonesia.sk; internet www.indonesia.sk; Ambassador MALIKUS SUAMIN.

Italy: Červeňova 19, 811 03 Bratislava; tel. (2) 5441-2585; fax (2) 5441-3202; e-mail amb@ambitaba.sk; internet www.caambitaba.sk; Ambassador EGONE RATZENBERGER.

Netherlands: Fraňa Kral'a 5, 811 05 Bratislava; tel. (2) 5262–5081; fax (2) 5249-1075; e-mail hollandembassy@internet.sk; internet www.netherlandsembassy.sk; Ambassador L. L. STOKVIS.

Poland: ul. Zelena 6, 814 26 Bratislava; tel. (2) 5443-2744; fax (2) 5443-2007; e-mail polskyobchradca@brh.sk; internet www.polskyobchracdca.sk; Ambassador JAN KOMORNICKI.

Romania: Fraňa Král'a 11, 811 05 Bratislava; tel. (2) 5249-1665; fax (2) 5244-4056; e-mail ro-embassy@ba.sknet.sk; Chargé d'affaires a.i. GHEORGHE LUPES.

Russia: Godrova 4, 811 06 Bratislava; tel. (2) 5441-5823; fax (2) 5443-4910; e-mail embrus@gtinet.sk; Ambassador ALEKSEI BORODAVKIN.

Serbia and Montenegro: Búdková 38, 811 04 Bratislava; tel. (2) 5443-1927; fax (2) 5443-1933; e-mail embas_yu@isternet.sk; Ambassador VELJKO ĆURČIĆ.

Slovenia: Moyzesova 4, 813 15 Bratislava; tel. (2) 5245-0005; fax (2) 5245-0009; Ambassador ROBERT KOKALJ.

Spain: Prepoštská, 811 01 Bratislava; tel. (2) 5441-5724; fax (2) 5441-7565; e-mail embespsk@mail.mae.es; Ambassador ESTANISLAO DE GRANDES PASCUAL.

Turkey: Holubyho 11, 811 03 Bratislava; tel. (2) 5441-5504; fax (2) 5441-3145; e-mail testta@nextra.sk; Ambassador INCI TÜMAY.

Ukraine: Radvaňská 35, 811 01 Bratislava; tel. (2) 5443-1672; fax (2) 5441-2651; Ambassador JURIJ RYLACH.

United Kingdom: Panská 16, 811 01 Bratislava; tel. (2) 5441-9632; fax (2) 5441-0002; e-mail bebra@internet.sk; internet www.britemb.sk; Ambassador RICK TODD.

USA: Hviezdoslavovo nám. 4, 811 02 Bratislava; tel. (2) 5443-3338; fax (2) 5443-0096; e-mail hengeldc@state.gov; internet www.usis.sk; Ambassador RONALD WEISER.

Judicial System

The judicial system of Slovakia has three levels: District Courts (55), Regional Courts (eight) and the Supreme Court. Regional Courts serve as courts of appeal to the District Courts, as well as serving as Courts of First Instance in some cases: the Supreme Court is the highest judicial authority in the country, operating as a Court of Cassation and appeal for Regional Courts. There is also a Constitutional Court to ensure compliance with the Constitution. In April 2002 an 18-member Judicial Council was elected, all of whom were lawyers, and nine of whom were judges. Three members are nominated by the President, three by the legislature, three by the Government, and eight elected by the judges themselves. The final member is the Chairman of the Supreme Court. The Council proposes candidates for judgeships, decides on the assignment of judges, comments on the budget, and elects the Chief Justice of the Supreme Court.

Chairman of the Supreme Court: (vacant).

Prosecutor-General: MICHAL HANZEL.

Chairman of the Constitutional Court: JÁN MAZÁK.

Religion

The principal religion in Slovakia is Christianity, of which the largest denomination (representing some 69% of the total population according to the census of May 2001) is the Roman Catholic Church. About 10% of the population profess no religious belief.

CHRISTIANITY

The Roman Catholic Church

Slovakia consists of two archdioceses and five dioceses, including one (directly responsible to the Holy See) for Catholics of the Slovak (Byzantine) rite, also known as 'Greek' Catholics or Uniates. At 31 December 2001 the estimated number of adherents represented about 69.6% of the total population.

Bishops' Conference: Konferencia biskupov Slovenska, Kapitulská 11, 81499 Bratislava; tel. (2) 5443-5234; fax (2) 5443-5913; e-mail kbs@kbs.sk; internet www.rcc.sk; f. 1993; Pres. Rt Rev. FRANTIŠEK TONDRA (Bishop of Spiš).

Latin Rite

Archbishop of Bratislava-Trnava: Most Rev. JÁN SOKOL, Arcibiskupský úrad, Hollého 10, 917 66 Trnava; tel. (33) 591-2111; fax (33) 551-1224; e-mail abu@abu.sk.

Archbishop of Košice: Most Rev. ALOJZ TKÁČ, Arcibiskupský úrad, Hlavná 28, 041 83 Košice; tel. (55) 682-8111; fax (55) 622-1034; e-mail abukosica@kbs.sk.

Slovak Rite

Bishop of Prešov: Rt Rev. JÁN HIRKA, Gréckokatolícky biskupský úrad, Hlavná ul. 1, 081 35 Prešov; tel. (51) 772-2814; fax (51) 772-2723; e-mail grkbupo@nextra.sk; internet www.home.nextra.sk/greckoka; 175,000 adherents, 199 parishes (Dec. 1999).

The Orthodox Church

Orthodox Church of the Czech Lands and Slovakia

Theological Faculty of Prešov University, Masaryková 15, Prešov, 080 80 Slovakia; POB 655, 111 21 Prague 1, Czech Republic; tel. (2) 431-5015.

Divided into four eparchies in the former Czechoslovakia: Prague and Olomouc (Czech Republic), Prešov and Michalovce (Slovakia); Archbishop of Prague and Metropolitan of the Czech Lands and Slovakia DOROTHEOS; 53,613 mems (March 1991); 127 parishes; Theological Faculty in Charles University, Prague, Czech Republic.

Archbishop of Prešov: Rev. NIKOLAJ, Budovatelská 1, 080 01 Prešov; e-mail mrpc@orthodox.sk.

Bishop of Michalovce: Rev. JOHN, Štefánikova, 071 44 Michalovce.

Protestant Churches

Baptist Union of Slovakia: Súl'ovská 2, 821 05 Bratislava; tel. and fax (2) 4342-1145; e-mail jozef-kulacik@computel.sk; f. 1994; 2,038 mems (April 2000); Pres. Rev. TOMÁŠ KRIŠKA; Gen. Sec. Rev. Dr JOZEF KULAČÍK.

Evangelical Church of the Augsburg Confession in Slovakia (Lutheran Church): Palisády 46, POB 289, 811 00 Bratislava; tel. (2) 5443-2842; fax (2) 5443-2940; e-mail tlac@ecav.sk; internet www .ecav.sk; presided over by the Bishop-General and Inspector-General; 327 parishes in 14 seniorates and two districts; 374,000 mems (Nov. 2001); Bishop-Gen. JÚLIUS FILO; Inspector-Gen. JÁN HOLČÍK.

Reformed Christian Church of Slovakia: Jókaiho 34, 945 01 Komárno; tel. (35) 770-1826; fax (35) 770-1827; e-mail rkc@freemail .hu; 109,735 mems and 325 parishes (2001); Bishop Dr GÉZA ERDÉLYI; Dir Mgr MIHÁLY TÓTH.

United Methodist Church in Slovakia: Panenská 10, 811 03 Bratislava; tel. and fax (2) 5441-4468; e-mail ecmrso@ba.psg.sk; internet www.slovaknet.sk/cirkev-metodisticka; 400 mems and 7 parishes; Superintendent PAVEL PROCHÁZKA.

Other Christian Churches

Apostolic Church: Sreznevského 2, 831 03 Bratislava; tel. and fax (2) 4425-0913; e-mail acs@gtinet.sk; internet www.acs-net.sk; f. 1956; 4,000 mems; Pres. JÁN LACHO.

JUDAISM

Union of the Jewish Religious Communities in the Slovak Republic (Ústredný zväz židovských náboženských obcí v Slovenskej republike): Kozia ul. 21/II, 814 47 Bratislava; tel. (2) 5441-2167; fax (2) 5441-1106; e-mail uzzno@netax.sk; 3,300 mems; Hon. Pres. Prof. PAVEL TRAUBNER; Exec. Chair. FERO ALEXANDER; Rabbi BARUCH MYERS.

The Press

In 2000 there were 1,465 newspapers and periodicals published in Slovakia, of which 16 were daily newspapers. In 1998 there were 39 titles published in Hungarian, seven in German, four in Ukrainian and two in Ruthenian.

The publications listed below are in Slovak, unless otherwise indicated.

PRINCIPAL DAILIES

Banská Bystrica

Smer dnes (Direct Today): Čs. armády 26, 974 01 Banská Bystrica; tel. (48) 433-43; fax (48) 433-41; f. 1948; independent; Editor-in-Chief JURAJ KUČERA; circ. 20,000.

Večerník (Evening Paper): nám. SNP 3, 974 00 Banská Bystrica; tel. (48) 539-01; fax (48) 526-03; Editor-in-Chief EVA BENČÍKOVÁ; circ. 5,000.

Bratislava

Hospodárske noviny (Economic News): Pribinova 25, 810 11 Bratislava; tel. (2) 5063-3627; fax (2) 5063-4724; e-mail hn@hnx.sk; morning; Editor-in-Chief SLAVOMÍR MALIČKAY; circ. 40,000.

Národná obroda (National Renewal): Mickiewiczova 1, 810 05 Bratislava; tel. (2) 323-973; fax (2) 323-983; e-mail extro@savba.sk; f. 1990; independent; economic; Editor-in-Chief ŠTEFAN MESÁROŠ; circ. 28,000 (March 1998).

Nový čas (New Time): Gorkého 5, 812 78 Bratislava; tel. (2) 363-070; fax (2) 363-104; f. 1991; morning; Editor-in-Chief ZUZANA RAČKOVÁ; circ. 230,000.

Práca (Labour): Odborárske nám. 3, 814 99 Bratislava; tel. (2) 5023-9316; fax (2) 5542-2985; e-mail marketing@praca.sk; internet www .praca.sk; f. 1946; publ. by the Confederation of Trade Unions of the Slovak Republic; Editor-in-Chief (vacant); circ. 80,000.

Pravda (Truth): Pribinova 25, 810 11 Bratislava; tel. (2) 367-503; fax (2) 210-4759; f. 1920; independent; left-wing; Editor-in-Chief PAVOL MINARIK; circ. 165,000.

Roľnícke noviny (Agricultural News): Dobrovičova 12, 813 78 Bratislava; tel. (2) 368-449; fax (2) 321-282; f. 1946; Editor-in-Chief JURAJ ŠESTÁK; circ. 20,000.

Slovenská republika (Slovak Republic): Ružová dolina 6, 824 70 Bratislava; tel. (2) 5022-1505; fax (2) 5022-1500; e-mail redakcia@ republika.sk; Editor-in-Chief EDUARD FAŠUNG; circ 78,000.

Sme (We Are): Mytná 33, 810 05 Bratislava; tel. (2) 498-726; fax (2) 498-306; f. 1993; Editor-in-Chief MARTIN SIMECKA; circ. 50,000.

Šport (Sport): Svätoplukova 2, 819 23 Bratislava; tel. (2) 600-53; fax (2) 211-380; Editor-in-Chief ZDENO SIMONIDES; circ. 85,000.

Új szó (New Word): Prievozská 14A, 820 06 Bratislava; tel. (2) 523-8320; fax (2) 523-8321; f. 1948; midday; Hungarian-language paper; Editor-in-Chief ATTILA LOVÁSZ; circ. 42,000.

Večerník (Evening Paper): Pribinova 25, 819 16 Bratislava; tel. (2) 325-085; fax (2) 210-4521; f. 1956; evening; Editor-in-Chief MARTIN PODSTUPKA; circ. 30,000.

Košice

Košický večer (Košice Evening): tr. SNP 24, 042 97 Košice; tel. (55) 429-820; fax (55) 421-214; f. 1990; Editor-in-Chief MIKULÁŠ JESENSKÝ; circ. 25,000.

Lúč (Ray): B. Němcovej 32, 042 62 Košice; tel. (55) 633-2117; fax (55) 359-090; f. 1992; Editor-in-Chief EDITA PAČAJOVÁ-KARDOŠOVÁ; circ. 15,000.

Slovenský východ (Slovak East): Letná 45, 042 66 Košice; tel. (55) 539-79; fax (55) 539-50; Editor-in-Chief DUŠAN KLINGER; circ. 30,000.

Prešov

Prešovský večerník (Prešov Evening Paper): Jarkova 4, 080 01 Prešov; tel. (51) 724-563; fax (51) 723-398; f. 1990; Editor-in-Chief PETER LIČÁK; circ. 13,000.

PRINCIPAL PERIODICALS

A Het (The Week): Bratislava; weekly; Hungarian-language magazine; Editor-in-Chief ATTILA LOVÁSZ.

Deák–Avízo: Pribišova 19A, 841 05 Bratislava; tel. (2) 722-485; fax (2) 714-655; 3 a week; advertising and information; Dir ERNEST DEAK; circ. 70,000.

Dievča (Girl): Mudroňova 12, 815 05 Bratislava; tel. (2) 311-920; monthly; publ. by the Slovak Union of Women; Editor-in-Chief DANA VIESTOVÁ; circ. 18,000.

Domino Efekt: Hlavná 68, 040 01 Košice; tel. and fax (55) 622-7692; f. 1992; weekly; Editor-in-Chief ANDREJ HRICO; circ. 20,000.

Elektrón + Zenit: Pražská 11, 812 84 Bratislava; tel. (2) 417-225; fax (2) 493-385; monthly; science and technology for young people; Editor-in-Chief LADISLAV GYORFFY; circ. 22,000.

Eurotelevízia (Eurotelevision): Pribinova 25, 819 14 Bratislava; tel. (2) 5063-4194; fax (2) 5063-4152; e-mail etv@euroskopringier.sk; weekly; Editor-in-Chief TAŇA LUCKÁ; circ. 290,000.

Eva: Pribinova 25, 819 39 Bratislava; tel. (2) 5063-3340; fax (2) 5063-4128; e-mail eva@euroskop.sk; internet www.euroskop.riniger .sk; monthly; magazine for women; Editor-in-Chief KATARINA PATVAROŠOVÁ; circ. 120,000.

International: Štúrova 4, 815 80 Bratislava; tel. (2) 367-808; fax (2) 326-685; weekly; current affairs; Editor-in-Chief TATIANA JAGLOVÁ; circ. 60,000.

Kamarát (Friend): POB 73, 820 14 Bratislava; tel. and fax (2) 240-8777; f. 1950; fortnightly; magazine for teenagers; Editor-in-Chief VLADIMÍR TOPERCER; circ. 30,000.

Katolícke noviny (Catholic News): Kapitulská 20, 815 21 Bratislava; tel. (2) 533-1790; fax (2) 533-3178; f. 1849; weekly; Editor-in-Chief MÁRIA KOTESOVÁ; circ. 116,000.

Krásy Slovenska (Beauty of Slovakia): Vajnorská 100A, 832 58 Bratislava; tel. (2) 279-0641; fax (2) 279-0587; illustrated bimonthly; Editor-in-Chief MILAN KUBIŚ; circ. 10,000.

Línia: Pribišova 19A, 841 05 Bratislava; tel. (2) 6025-1123; fax (2) 6025-1130; monthly; life-style; Editor-in-Chief JÁN HANUŠKA; circ. 25,000.

Móda (Fashion): Štefánikova 4, 812 64 Bratislava; tel. (2) 765-704; fax (2) 491-191; quarterly; Editor-in-Chief DANA LAPŠANSKÁ; circ. 20,000.

Ohník (Little Flame): Pražská 11, 812 84 Bratislava; tel. (2) 417-233; monthly; youth; Editor-in-Chief STANISLAV BEBJAK; circ. 35,000.

Plus 7 dní: Ružová dolina 27, 825 06 Bratislava; tel. (2) 656-83; fax (2) 201-6309; weekly; social magazine; Editor-in-Chief MILOŠ LUKNÁR; circ. 60,000.

Poradca podnikateľa (Entrepreneurs' Adviser): Národná 13, POB 29, 010 01 Žilina; tel. (89) 734-1112; fax (89) 734-1180; e-mail mesticka@pp_holding.sk; internet www.pp_holding.sk; f. 1993; monthly; Gen. Dir ZOJA ŽIDEKOVÁ; Editor-in-Chief MÁRIA MESTICKÁ; circ. 70,000.

Rodina (Family): Pribinova 25, POB 122, 810 11 Bratislava; tel. (2) 210-4027; monthly; family magazine; Editor-in-Chief M. VÁROŠ; circ. 145,000.

Romano ľil nevo: Jarková 4, 080 01 Prešov; tel. (41) 772-5238; fax (41) 773-3439; e-mail romskylist@vadium.sk; internet www.rnj .vadium.sk; f. 1991; in Romany and Slovak; publ. by the Association Jekhetane-Spolu-Together; Editor-in-Chief DANIELA HIVEŠOVÁ-ŠILANOVÁ; circ. 8,500.

Slovenka (Slovak Woman): Jaskový rad 5, 833 80 Bratislava; tel. (2) 5478-9652; fax (2) 5477-6118; e-mail slovenka@slovenka.sk; f. 1948;

weekly; illustrated magazine; Editor-in-Chief Zuzana Krútka; circ. 220,000.

Slovenské národné noviny (Slovak National News): Matica slovenská, Mudroňová 1, 036 52 Martin; tel. and fax (43) 345-35; f. 1845; weekly; organ of Matica slovenská cultural organization; Editor-in-Chief Peter Mišák; circ. 7,000.

Slovenský profit: Pribinova 25, 810 11 Bratislava; tel. (2) 563-3817; fax (2) 563-4581; economic weekly; Editor-in-Chief Iveta Seifertová; circ. 25,000.

Stop: Exnárova 57, 820 12 Bratislava; tel. (2) 522-5052; fax (2) 522-0554; fortnightly; motoring; Editor-in-Chief L'uboš Kríž; circ. 47,000.

Szabad újság (Free Journal): Michalská 9, 814 99 Bratislava; tel. (2) 333-012; fax (2) 330-519; f. 1991; Hungarian-language economic weekly; Editor-in-Chief Géza Szabó; circ. 40,000.

Trend: Rezedova 5, POB 31, 820 07 Bratislava; tel. (2) 4341-1652; fax (2) 4333-1336; e-mail redakcia@trend.sk; internet www.trend.sk; f. 1991; weekly; for entrepreneurs; publ. by Trendy Ltd; Editor-in-Chief Jaroslav Matyas; circ. 25,000.

Vasárnap (Sunday): Pribinova 25, 819 15 Bratislava; tel. (2) 323-220; fax (2) 364-529; f. 1948; weekly; independent Hungarian-language magazine; Editor-in-Chief József Szilvássy; circ. 97,000.

Výber (Digest): Kominárska 2, 832 03 Bratislava; tel. (2) 203-4486; fax (2) 203-4521; f. 1968; weekly; digest of home and foreign press; Editor-in-Chief Miroslava Avramovová; circ. 15,000.

Život (Life): Pribinova 25, 819 37 Bratislava; tel. (2) 210-4135; fax (2) 210-4145; f. 1951; illustrated family weekly; Editor-in-Chief Milan Vároš; circ. 255,000.

Zmena (Change): Sabinovská 14, 821 02 Bratislava; tel. (2) 237-758; fax (2) 522-6420; f. 1989; weekly; independent; Editor-in-Chief Vladimír Mohorita; circ. 20,000.

NEWS AGENCIES

SITA: internet www.sita.sk; f. 1997; independent; Dir-Gen. Pavol Mudry.

Tlačová agentúra Slovenskej republiky (TASR) (News Agency of the Slovak Republic): Pribinova 23, 819 28 Bratislava; tel. (2) 5921-0152; fax (2) 5296-2468; e-mail market@tasr.sk; internet www.tasr.sk; f. 1992; has overseas bureaux in Russia, Germany, Czech Republic and Belgium; Dir Peter Nedavska.

Foreign Bureaux

Česká tisková kancelář (ČTK) (Czech Republic): Pribinova 25, 819 02 Bratislava; tel. (2) 210-4633; fax (2) 210-4605.

Informatsionnoye Telegrafnoye Agentstvo Rossii– Telegrafnoye Agentstvo Suverennykh Stran (ITAR—TASS) (Russia): Jancova 8A, 811 01 Bratislava; tel. (2) 315-797; Correspondent Valerii I. Rzhevskii.

The following news agencies are also represented in Slovakia: Reuters (UK), Deutsche Presse-Agentur (Germany), Austria Presse-Agentur (Austria), Agence France-Presse (France), Magyar Távirati Iroda (Hungary), RIA—Novosti (Russia), Polska Agencja Prasowa (Poland), Agenzia Nazionale Stampa Associata (Italy), Novinska Agencija Tanjug (Serbia and Montenegro) and Viet Nam News Agency (Viet Nam).

PRESS ASSOCIATIONS

Slovenský syndikát novinárov (Slovak Syndicate of Journalists): Župné nám. 7, 815 68 Bratislava; tel. (2) 5443-5071; fax (2) 5443-4534; e-mail ssn@internet.sk; internet www.ssn.sk; f. 1968; reorganized 1990; 2,600 mems; Chair. Stanislava Benicka.

Združenie slovenských novinárov (Association of Slovak Journalists): Šafárikovo nám. 4, 811 02 Bratislava; tel. and fax (2) 363-184; f. 1992; 700 mems; Chair. Ján Smolec.

Publishers

Alfa-press: Križkova 9, 811 04 Bratislava; tel. and fax (2) 399-837; technical and economic literature, dictionaries; Dir Jozef Bednárik.

Matica slovenská: J. C. Hronského, 036 52 Martin; tel. (43) 413-2454; fax (43) 413-3188; e-mail sprava@matica.sk; internet www.matica.sk; f. 1863; literary science, bibliography, biography and librarianship; literary archives and museums; Man. Ing. Jozef Markuš, Dr Miroslav Bielik.

Mladé letá (Young Years): Sasinkova 5; tel. (2) 5556-4293; fax (2) 5542-5714; e-mail mleda@medlab.sk; f. 1950; literature for children and young people; Dir Ing. Jaroslav Janković.

Obzor (Horizon): Špitálska 35, 815 85 Bratislava; tel. (2) 361-015; fax (2) 361-237; f. 1953; educational encyclopaedias, popular scientific, fiction, textbooks, law; Editor-in-Chief Margita Svitková.

Osveta (Education): Osloboditeľov 21, 036 54 Martin; tel. (43) 341-21; fax (43) 350-60; f. 1953; medical, health, photographic, fiction; Gen. Dir Ing. Martin Farkaš.

Práca (Labour): Štefánikova 19, 812 71 Bratislava; tel. (2) 333-779; fax (2) 330-046; f. 1946; law, guides, cookery, fiction, etc.; Dir Miroslav Bernáth.

Príroda a.s. (Nature): Križkova 9, 811 04 Bratislava; tel. (2) 396-335; fax (2) 397-564; e-mail priroda@priroda.bts.sk; f. 1949; school textbooks, encyclopaedias, reference books, etc. for children and youth; Chair. Ing. Emilia Jankovitsová.

Slovenské pedagogické nakladeteľstvo: Sasinkova 5, 815 19 Bratislava; tel. (2) 5557–2454; fax (2) 5557-1894; e-mail spn@slovanet.sk; internet www.spn.sk; f. 1920; pedagogical literature, educational, school texts, dictionaries; Dir Mária Sedláková.

Slovenský spisovateľ a.s. (Slovak Writer): A. Pla'vku 12, 813 67 Bratislava; tel. (2) 399-734; fax (2) 399-736; fiction, poetry; Dir Martin Chovanec.

Smena (Change): Pražská 11, 812 84 Bratislava; tel. (2) 498-018; fax (2) 493-305; f. 1949; fiction, literature for young people, newspapers and magazines; Dir Ing. Jaroslav Šišolák.

Šport: Vajnorská 100/A, 832 58 Bratislava; tel. (2) 691-95; sport, physical culture, guide books, periodicals; Dir Dr Bohumil Golian.

Tatran: Michalská 9, 815 82 Bratislava; tel. (2) 5443-5849; fax (2) 5443-5777; f. 1949; fiction, art books, children's books, literary theory; Dir Dr Eva Mládeková.

Veda (Science): Bradáčova 7, 852 86 Bratislava; tel. (2) 832-254; fax (2) 832-254; f. 1953; publishing house of the Slovak Academy of Sciences; scientific and popular scientific books and periodicals; Man. Eva Majeská.

PUBLISHERS' ASSOCIATION

Združenie vydavateľov a kníhkupcov Slovenskej republiky (Publishers' and Booksellers' Asscn of Slovakia): Gregorovej 8, 821 03 Bratislava; tel. and fax (2) 4333-6700; e-mail austo@post.sk; Pres. Dr Alex Aust.

WRITERS' UNION

Asociácia organizácií spisovateľov Slovenska (Asscn of Writers' Organizations in Slovakia): Laurinská 2, 815 08 Bratislava; tel. (2) 5443-5368; fax (2) 5443-4117; e-mail aoss@nextra.sk; f. 1949; reorganized 1990; 330 mems; Pres. Vasil Dacej.

Broadcasting and Communications

TELECOMMUNICATIONS

Regulatory Authority

Telecommunications Office of the Slovak Republic: Jarošova 1, POB 76, 830 08 Bratislava 38; tel. (2) 4425-4328; fax (2) 4425-9577; e-mail roman.vavro@teleoff.gov.sk; internet www.teleoff.gov.sk; Chair. Milan Luknár.

Major Service Providers

Eurotel: f. 1997; 60% owned by Slovak Telecom; operates mobile cellular telephone network; Chair. and CEO Artur Bobovnicky.

Globtel: Prievozská 6, 821 09 Bratislava; f. 1997; operates mobile cellular telephone network; Gen. Man. Bruno Duthoit.

Slovak Telecom (Slovenské Telekomunikácie): nám. Slobody 6, 817 62 Bratislava; tel. (2) 5249-2324; fax (2) 5249-2492; e-mail sekr.gr@st.sk; internet www.telecom.sk; scheduled for privatization in 2000; Dir-Gen. Emil Hubinák.

BROADCASTING

Slovak Radio (Slovenský rozhlas): Mýtna 1, POB 55, 817 55 Bratislava; tel. (2) 5727-3560; fax (2) 5249-8923; e-mail interrel@slovakradio.sk; internet www.slovakradio.sk; f. 1926; Dir-Gen. Jaroslav Reznik.

Television

Slovenská televízia (STV) (Slovak Television): Mlynská dolina 28, 845 45 Bratislava; tel. (2) 6542-3001; fax (2) 6542-2341; internet www.stv.sk; f. 1956; public broadcasting co; Chair. of Council Jaroslav Franek; Dir Richard Rybníček.

Slovenska Televizna Spolocnost: Palisady 39, 811 06 Bratislava; tel. (2) 531-6610; fax (2) 531-4061; f. 1996; broadcasts as Markiza TV; first privately owned television channel; owned by Central European Media Enterprises; Dir-Gen. PAVOL RUSKO.

TA3: Gagarinova 12, POB 31, 820 15 Bratislava; e-mail web@ta3 .com; internet www.ta3.com; f. 2001; privately owned; Dir-Gen. MARTIN LENGYEL; Editor-in-Chief ZDENEK SAMAL.

TV Joj: Grešákova 10, 040 01 Kosiče; tel. (55) 622-2664; fax (55) 6221-027; e-mail joj@joj.sk; internet www.joj.sk; f. 2002; privately owned subsidiary of Nova TV (Czech Republic); Dir-Gen. VLADIMÍR ŽELEZNÝ; Dir MILAN KNAŽKO.

Finance

(cap. = capital; res = reserves; dep. = deposits; m. = million; brs = branches; amounts in Slovak koruny)

BANKING

Central Bank

National Bank of Slovakia (Národná banka Slovenska): Štúrova 2, 813 25 Bratislava; tel. (2) 5953-1111; fax (2) 5413-1167; e-mail info@nbs.sk; internet www.nbs.sk; f. 1993; total assets 279,652.0m. (Dec. 2001); determines monetary policy, issues banknotes and coins, controls circulation of money, co-ordinates payments and settlements between banks, supervises the performance of banking activities; Gov. MARIÁN JUSKO.

Commercial Banks

Banka Slovakia, a.s.: Janka Krála, POB 76, 974 01 Banská Bystrica; tel. (48) 431-7111; fax (48) 413-2222; e-mail sekretar@basl .sk; internet www.basl.sk; f. 1996; cap. 756.9m., res 35.7m., dep. 3,261.5m. (Dec. 2000); Pres. ALENA LONGAUEROVÁ.

Citibank (Slovakia), a.s.: Viedenská cesta 5, 851 01 Bratislava; tel. (2) 6827-8111; fax (2) 6827-8200; e-mail citibank.slovakia@ citibank.com; internet www.citibank.sk; f. 1995; cap. 1,650m., res 827.3m., dep. 22,026.9m. (Dec. 2001); Gen. Dir TIRAD MAHMOUD.

Crédit Lyonnais Bank Slovakia, a.s.: Klemensova 2A, POB 70, 811 09 Bratislava; tel. (2) 5926-2111; fax (2) 5926-2248; internet www.creditlyonnais.sk; f. 1994; cap. 500.0m., res 69.5m., dep. 21,500.0m. (Dec. 2001); Dir-Gen. JEAN-MICHEL GIOVANNETTI.

Devín banka, a.s.: Františkánske nám. 8, 813 10 Bratislava; tel. (2) 5936-6102; fax (2) 5443-2311; e-mail devinbanka@devinbanka.sk; f. 1992; total assets 13,177m.; cap. 993.5m., dep. 10,891m. (Dec. 1999); Gen. Dir PAVEL RUSNAK; 26 brs.

HVB Bank Slovakia, a.s.: Mostovà 6, 814 16 Bratislava; tel. (2) 5969-1111; fax (2) 5969-9406; e-mail infobacask@sk.bacai.com; internet www.hvb-bank.sk; f. Sept. 2001 by merger of Bank Austria Creditanstalt Slovakia and Hypo-Vereinsbank Slovakia; cap. 60.2m., res 57.0m., dep. 640.5m. (Dec. 2001); Chair. CHRISTIAN SUP-PANZ.

Istrobanka, a.s.: Laurinská 1, POB 109, 811 00 Bratislava; tel. (2) 5939-7111; fax (2) 5443-1744; e-mail info@istrobanka.et.sk; internet www.istrobanka.sk; f. 1992; cap. 1,300m., res 250.6m., dep. 21,960.7m. (Dec. 2001); Chair. and Dir-Gen. MIROSLAV PAULEN; 11 brs.

Komerční Banka Bratislava, a.s.: Medená 6, 810 00 Bratislava; tel. (2) 5293-2153; fax (2) 5296-4801; e-mail koba@koba.sk; internet www.koba.sk; f. 1995; cap. 500.0m., res 20.7m., dep. 5,427.8m. (Dec. 2001); Chair. IVAN DUDA.

Ľudová banka, a.s. (People's Bank, Inc.): Vysoká 9, POB 81, 810 00 Bratislava; tel. (2) 5965-1111; fax (2) 5441-2453; e-mail market@ luba.sk; internet www.luba.sk; f. 1992; cap. 670.0m., res 1,134.5m., dep. 24,107.8m. (Dec. 2001); Chair. JOZEF KOLLÁR; 12 brs.

OTP Banka Slovensko, a.s. (Investment and Development Bank, Inc.): Štúrova 5, 813 54 Bratislava; tel. (2) 5979-1111; fax (2) 5296-3484; e-mail info@otpbank.sk; internet www.otpbank.sk; f. 1992 as Investična a rozvojová banka; 95.7% of shares divested to NSB Ltd (Hungary) in April 2002; Aug. 2002 name changed as above; cap. 1,044m., res 798.9m., dep. 19,183.1m. (Dec. 2001); Pres. KAROLY HODOSSY; 53 brs.

Poštová banka, a.s. (Postal Bank, Inc.): Gorkého 3, POB 149, 814 99 Bratislava; tel. (2) 5960-3333; fax (2) 5960-3344; e-mail silvia_valekova@pabk.sk; internet www.pabk.sk; f. 1993; scheduled for privatization; cap. 2,269.6m., res 55.2m., dep. 18,302.0m. (Dec. 2001); Pres. and Chair. LIBOR CHRÁST; 24 brs.

Prvá komunálna banka, a.s. (First Municipal Bank, Inc.): Hodžova 11, 010 11 Žilina; tel. (41) 511-1101; fax (41) 562-4129; e-mail

webinfo@pkb.sk; internet www.pkb.sk; f. 1993; cap. 1,002.0m., res 73.4m., dep. 20,344.7m. (Dec. 2001); Pres. JOZEF MIHALIK; 45 brs.

Tatra banka, a.s.: Vajanského nábr. 5, POB 50, 810 11 Bratislava; tel. (2) 6865-1111; fax (2) 5292-4760; e-mail info@tatrabanka.sk; internet www.tatrabanka.sk; f. 1990; cap. 1,044.3m., res 5,144.0m., dep. 95,390.8m. (Dec. 2001); Chair. and Gen. Man. RAINER FRANZ; 30 brs.

UniBanka, a.s.: Vajnorská 21, 832 65 Bratislava; tel. (2) 4437-3964; fax (2) 4437-3975; internet www.unibanka.sk; f. 1990; April 2002 name changed as above from Poľnobanka; cap. 2,717.6m., res 1.9m., dep. 27,463.8m. (Dec. 2001); Chair. of Bd JIŘI KUNERT; 10 brs.

Všeobecná úverová banka, a.s. (General Credit Bank, Inc.): Mlynské Nivy 1, POB 90, 829 90 Bratislava 25; tel. (2) 5055-1111; fax (2) 5556-6650; e-mail webmaster@vub.sk; internet www.vub.sk; f. 1990; sold to Banka Intesa (Italy) in 2001; cap. 12,978.0m., res 1,294.0m., dep. 154,479.0m. (Dec. 2001); Pres. LADISLAV VAŠKOVIČ; 42 brs.

Savings Banks

Prvá stavebná sporiteľňa, a.s.: Bajkalská 30, POB 48, 829 48 Bratislava; tel. (2) 5823-1111; fax (2) 5341-1131; f. 1992; cap. 1,000m.; Chair. of Bd JÁN ROLAND BURGER.

Slovenská sporiteľňa, a.s. (Slovak Savings Bank): Suché mýto 4, 816 07 Bratislava; tel. (2) 5957-4500; fax (2) 5957-4503; e-mail postmaster@slsp.sk; internet www.slsp.sk; f. 1969; fmrly state-owned; absorbed operations of Priemyselná banka (Industrial Bank) in 1999; privatized in 2000, majority stake bought by Erste Bank (Austria); total assets 202,058.0m. (Dec. 2001); Chair. REGINA OVENSKY-STRAKA; 638 brs and agencies.

COMMODITY AND STOCK EXCHANGES

Bratislava Commodity Exchange (Komoditná burza Bratislava): Ul. 29 Augusta 2, 811 07 Bratislava; tel. (2) 5293-1010; fax (2) 5293-1007; e-mail burza@kbb.sk; internet www.kbb.sk; Gen. Sec. IGOR KREJČÍ.

Bratislava Stock Exchange (Burza cenných papierov v Bratislave a.s.): Vysoká 17, POB 151, 814 99 Bratislava; tel. (2) 4923-6111; fax (2) 4923-6102; e-mail info@bsse.sk; internet www.bsse.sk; Dir-Gen. MÁRIA HURAJOVÁ.

INSURANCE

Slovak Insurance Co (Slovenská poisťovňa, a.s.): Strakova 1, 815 74 Bratislava; tel. (2) 533-2949; fax (2) 533-1272; majority stake divested to Allianz (Germany) in Dec. 2001; Chair. and Pres. RUDOLF JANAC.

Trade and Industry

GOVERNMENT AGENCIES

National Property Fund: Drieňová 27, 821 01 Bratislava; tel. (2) 4827-1448; fax (2) 4827-1289; e-mail fnm@natfund.gov.sk; internet www.natfund.gov.sk/index.htm; f. 1993; supervises the privatization process; Pres. JOZEF KOJDA; Vice-Pres. PAVOL HULÍK.

Slovak Investment and Trade Development Agency: Martinèekova 17, 821 01 Bratislava; tel. (2) 5810-0310; fax (2) 5819–0319; e-mail sario@sario.sk; internet www.sario.sk; f. 1991; Gen. Dir LADISLAV BALKO.

CHAMBERS OF COMMERCE

Slovak Chamber of Commerce and Industry (Slovenská obchodná a priemyselná komora): Gorkého 9, 816 03 Bratislava; tel. (2) 5443-3291; fax (2) 5413-1159; e-mail sopkurad@scci.sk; internet www.scci.sk; Pres. Prof. PETER MIHÓK.

Banská Bystrica Chamber of Commerce and Industry: Svermeva 43, 974 01 Banská Bystrica; tel. (48) 345-057; fax (48) 363-88; e-mail sopkrbb@sopk.sk; internet www.bb.scci.sk.

Košice Chamber of Commerce and Industry: Južná Trieda 2A, 040 01 Košice; tel. (45) 641-9477; fax (45) 641-9470; e-mail sopkrkke@scci.sk; internet www.sopk.sk/ko/; Dir STEFAN KARAŠ.

Trenčín Chamber of Commerce and Industry: Jilemnickeho St 2, 911 01 Trenčín; tel. (32) 652-3834; fax (32) 652-1023; e-mail sopkrktn@scci.sk; internet www.commerce-and-industry.com.

Žilina Chamber of Commerce and Industry: Vysokoskolakov 4, 010 08 Žilina; tel. (41) 459-59; fax (41) 451-82; e-mail sopkrkza@scci .sk; internet www.sopk.sk/za/an/; Dir JAN MISURA.

UTILITIES

Electricity

Slovenské electrárne (SE): Hraničná 12, 827 36 Bratislava; tel. (2) 5069-1111; fax (2) 5341-7533; e-mail valovic_jozef@hq.seas.sk; internet www.seas.sk; largest state-owned utility; External Relations Dir JOZEF VALOVIC.

Gas

Nafta a.s.: Naftárska 965, 908 45 Gbely; tel. (34) 921-500; fax (34) 921-103; f. 1918; privatized 1996, renationalized 1999; gas exploration and production; Chair. JURAJ GREBÁČ; 2,588 employees.

Slovenský Plynárenský Priemysel (SPP) (Slovak Gas Company): Mlynské nivy 44A, 825 11 Bratislava; tel. (2) 5869-2111; fax (2) 5341-5590; e-mail spp@spp.sk; internet www.spp.sk; partially privatized in July 2002; Gen. Dir JÁN DUCKÝ.

MAJOR COMPANIES

Bučina, a.s.: Lučenecká 1335/21, 960 96 Zvolen; tel. (45) 530-1421; fax (45) 530-1138; e-mail bucina@bucina.sk; internet www.bucina .sk; f. 1946; primary and secondary wood production; some foreign trade activities; Pres. Ing. PETER LISPUCH; 1,450 employees.

Bukóza Progres, a.s.: Hencovská 2073, 093 02 Hencovce; tel. (57) 461-152; fax (57) 431-562; f. 1948; manufactures timber products; kraft pulp, viscose pulp, furfural, D-xylose, beech timber, railway sleepers, veneers, furniture, etc.; Gen. Man. PAVOL KENDRA; 1,978 employees.

Chemko, a.s. Strážske: Priemyselná 720, 072 22 Strážske; tel. (56) 649-1614; fax (56) 649-1416; e-mail market@chemko.sk; internet www.chemko.sk; f. 1952; production and sale of organic and inorganic chemical products; Chair. DUŠAN HORDOŠ; 2,358 employees.

Chemlon, a.s.: Chemlonská 1, 066 76 Humenné; tel. (57) 672-49; fax (57) 772-0640; e-mail michal.halko@chemlon.sk; internet www .chemlon.sk; f. 1959; manufactures PA-6 fibres and chips, polyester fibres; Gen. Dir MICHAL HALKO; 3,150 employees.

Chemosvit, a.s.: Štúrova 101, 059 21 Svit; tel. (52) 715-1111; fax (52) 715-2740; e-mail saleswe@chemosvit.sk; internet www .chemosvit.sk; f. 1934; production of OPP films, LDPE films, cellophane films, barrier cast films, machinery and PP fibres; Chair. MICHAL L'ACH; 1,500 employees.

Doprastav, a.s.: Drieňová 27, 826 56 Bratislava 2; tel. (2) 4333-4319; fax (2) 4333-7063; e-mail doprastav@doas.sk; f. 1953; civil engineering; construction; manufacture of building materials; Chair. and Man. Dir IVAN ŠESTÁK; 2,621 employees.

Duslo, a.s.: Kopanica 1778, 927 03 Šal'a; tel. (31) 775-1111; fax (31) 775-3040; e-mail duslo@duslo.sk; internet www.duslo.sk; f. 1958; production and sale of ammonia, nitrogen fertilizers, anti-oxidants and other chemicals; Chair. and Gen. Dir JOZEF KOLLÁR; 3,200 employees.

Elektrosvit Holding a.s.: Komárňanská 3, 940 37 Nové Zámky; tel. (35) 642-6074; fax (35) 642-6067; e-mail elsvit@nz.psg.sk; internet www.elektrosvit.sk; f. 1950; fmly Elektrosvit a.s.; manufacture of electric lighting fixtures, electric motors, freezers, air-conditioning services, etc.; provides foreign business and economic services; Pres. JOZEF ŠUTKA; 1,000 employees.

Grafobal Group, a.s.: Mazúrova 2, 909 87 Skalica; tel. (34) 664-5230; fax (34) 664-5105; e-mail grafobal@grafobal.sk; internet www .grafobal.sk; f. 1905; manufactures paper and paper-based packaging; printing; Chair. and Man. Dir PAVOL HORVÁTH; 1,366 employees.

Hornonitrianske bane Prievidza, a.s.: Matice Slovenskej 10, 971 71 Prievidza; tel. (46) 542-3121; fax (46) 543-2106; e-mail cicmanec@ hbp.sk; internet www.hbp.sk; f. 1996; coal production; Chair. PETER ČIČMANEC; 8,100 employees.

Hutne stavby, a.s., Košice: Letná 45, 041 91 Košice; tel. (55) 633-2531; fax (55) 632-0441; f. 1951; construction; manufacture of building materials; Pres. JURAJ KAMARAS; 1,400 employees.

Hydrostav, a.s.: Miletičova 21, POB 45, 824 87 Bratislava; tel. (2) 5057-1111; fax (2) 5557-7180; e-mail info@hds.sk; f. 1951; construction; manufacture of building materials; transport and other services; Dir STANISLAV KLIKÁČ; 7,450 employees.

IDC Holding, a.s.: Drieňová 3, 821 09 Bratislava; tel. (2) 4333-0440; fax (2) 4333-0220; f. 1906; manufacture and sale of confectionary; Chair. PAVOL JAKUBEC; 1,600 employees.

Inžinierske stavby, a.s.: Priemyselná 7, 042 45 Košice; tel. (55) 633-9455; fax (55) 633-7831; e-mail marketing@inzierske-stavby .sk; internet www.inzierske-stavby.sk; f. 1951; civil engineering and grounds works; Chair. BRAŇO PRIELOŽNÝ; 1,700 employees.

Istrochem, a.s.: Nobelova 34, 836 05 Bratislava; tel. (2) 4425-5888; fax (2) 4951-2310; e-mail istroch@istrochem.sk; internet www .istrochem.sk; f. 1873; manufacture of synthetic fibres, chemicals, industrial explosives and plastic mouldings; Chair. MICHAL GREGA; 2,602 employees.

Jas, a.s.: Slovenská 14, 085 14 Bardejov; tel. (54) 722-301; fax (54) 722-498; f. 1957; production and sale of shoes and shoe materials; Exec. Dir JOZEF VARALI; 4,000 employees.

Juhoslov: Továrenská 1, 943 03 Sturovo; tel. (36) 561-111; fax (36) 204-0; f. 1963; production of paper, boxes, packaging, etc.; Exec. Dir JURAJ KUCERA; 2,600 employees.

Kerametal, a.s.: Jašíkova 2, 826 05 Bratislava; tel. (2) 4829-1580; fax (2) 4829-1581; e-mail kerametal@kerametal.sk; f. 1970; conducts import and export activities; special commercial transactions and services; Man. Dir IGOR JUNAS; 95 employees.

KLF-ZVL, a.s.: Kukučinová, 024 11 Kysucke Nové Mesto; tel. (41) 421-2611; fax (41) 421-2519; e-mail klfzvl@netlab.sk; internet www .omnia-odbyt.sk; f. 1950; manufacture of specialist engineering tools and equipment; Dir JÁN SMATANA; 3,050 employees.

Makyta: 1. Mája 882/46, 020 25 Púchov; tel. (42) 631-410; fax (42) 631-105; e-mail makyta@px.psg.sk; internet www.makyta.sk; f. 1939; production and sale of clothing; Chair. and Gen. Dir MARIÁN VIDOMAN; 4,200 employees.

Matador, a.s. Púchov: Terézie vansovej 1054/45, 020 32 Púchov; tel. (42) 461-1111; fax (42) 464-2403; e-mail reklama@matador.sk; internet www.matador.sk; f. 1950; manufacture, wholesale and retail of rubber products, incl. tyres and conveyor belts; Chair. and Gen. Dir JOZEF VOZÁR; 3,775 employees.

Merina, a.s.: M. R. Štefánika 379/19, 911 60 Trenčín; tel. (32) 741-4600; fax (32) 741-4605; internet www.merina.sk; f. 1907; manufacture of natural yarns and woven fabrics; Chair. LIBOR MIŠÁK; 1,495 employees.

Mier: Pílska 7–9, 955 13 Topol'čany; tel. (815) 323-303; fax (815) 321-087; f. 1988; manufacture of furniture, upholstery, etc.; Gen. Man. MILAN VANÍK; 1,050 employees.

Nováčke chemické závody, a.s.: M. R. Štefánika 1, 972 71 Nováky; tel. (46) 568-1111; fax (46) 546-1138; e-mail marketing@ nchz.sk; internet www.nchz.sk; f. 1940; production of chemical products and plastic materials; Chair. and Man. Dir ALEXANDER PÁLFFY; 2,190 employees.

Nový Calex, a.s.: Továrenská 49, 953 36 Zlaté Moravce; tel. (37) 210-08; fax (37) 424-365; e-mail ndh@ndh.sk; internet www.ndh.sk; manufactures compressors, other machinery (including pneumatic tools), refrigerators and freezers; Exec. Dir KOLOMAN ISTRIK.

Oravské ferozliatinárske závody (OFZ) (Orava Ferro-alloys Works): 027 53 Istebné nad Oravou; tel. (43) 580-4111; fax (43) 589-2370; e-mail office@ofz.sk; internet www.ofz.sk; f. 1952; production of ferro-alloys; Gen. Dir Ing. VLADIMÍR KLOCOK; 1,619 employees.

Ozeta odevné závody, a.s.: Vel'komoravská 9, 911 05 Trenčín; tel. (32) 656-2111; fax (32) 652-3240; e-mail oztrencin@ozeta.sk; internet www.ozeta.sk; f. 1938; clothing manufacturer; Chair. and Gen. Dir ŠTEFAN BRATKO; 4,815 employees.

Petrimex, a.s.: Dr Vladimíra Clementisa 10, 826 02 Bratislava; tel. (2) 4828-2111; fax (2) 4333-8148; imports and exports chemicals, raw materials and pharmaceutical products; Man. Dir MARIÁN MOJŽIŠ; 184 employees.

Severoslovenské celulózky a papierne, a.s. (North Slovak Cellulose and Paper Works): Bystrická 13, 034 17 Ružomberok; tel. (44) 432-2223; fax (44) 432-7701; e-mail scp@scprbk.sk; internet www .scprbk.sk; f. 1988; production of cellulose, pulp, paper, cardboard, softwood timber, etc.; Gen. Dir Ing. JÁN LÍŠKA; 2,650 employees.

Slovakofarma, a.s.: Nitrianska 100, 920 27 Hlohovec; tel. (33) 736-1111; fax (33) 730-0890; e-mail info@slofa.sk; internet www .slovakofarma.sk; f. 1941; food products; chemical, botanical and pharmaceutical products; Chair. and Chief Exec. ONDŘEJ GATTNAR; 1,680 employees.

Slovalco, a.s.: Priemyselná 12, 965 63 Žiar nad Hronom; tel. (45) 608-9999; fax (45) 608-7905; e-mail mail@slovalco.sk; internet www .slovalco.sk; production and sale of aluminium; Chair. JOZEF PITTNER; 701 employees.

Slovenská armatúrka myjava, a.s.: Kpt. M. Uhra 57/3, 907 16 Myjava; tel. (34) 212-641; fax (34) 213-310; f. 1937; production and distribution of plumbing and hosing fittings, tyre valves, plastic products, aluminium and brass castings, etc.; Gen. Dir LADISLAV PAVLÍČEK; 2,700 employees.

Slovenský Hodváb, s.p.: Továrenská 532, 905 01 Senica; tel. (34) 695-1111; fax (34) 695-1296; e-mail futrikanic@slovhodvab.sk; internet www.slovhodvab.sk; f. 1920; production of man-made fibres and the PET synthetic polymer; Gen. Dir JOZEF FUTRIKANIČ; 1,525 employees.

Slovnaft, a.s.: Vlčie Hrdlo, 824 12 Bratislava 23; tel. (2) 5859-1111; fax (2) 4524-3750; e-mail info@slovnaft.sk; internet www.slovnaft.sk; f. 1895 as Apollo, current name adopted 1949; petroleum refining; production of fuels, lubricants, solvents, plastics and other petrochemical products; Chief Exec. VRATKO KAŠŠOVIC; 4,221 employees.

Tatramat a.s.: Hlavná 1, 058 92 Poprad; tel. (52) 712-7398; fax (52) 712-7500; e-mail tatramat@tatramat.sk; internet www.tatramat.sk; f. 1945; manufacture of domestic appliances; Chair. JÁN MIŠKO; 500 employees.

Tatrasvit Svit—Socks, a.s.: Mierova 1, 059 21 Svit; tel. (52) 712-6111; fax (52) 712-6163; e-mail info@tatrasvit.sk; internet www.tatrasvit.sk; fmrly Tatrasvit, a.s.; f. 1952; production of textiles and knitwear; Gen. Dir PETER STUPKA; 950 employees.

Tatravagónka, a.s.: Štefánikova 887/53, 058 01 Poprad; tel. (52) 772-3275; fax (52) 772-1732; e-mail julius.vachmansky@tatravagonka.sk; internet www.tatravagonka.sk; f. 1994; production of rail transport units; Exec. Dir JÚLIUS VACHMANSKÝ; 2,167 employees.

Technopol International, a.s.: Kutlíkova 17, 852 50 Bratislava; tel. (2) 6828-6130; fax (2) 6381-2180; e-mail techinter@technopol.sk; internet www.techopol.sk; f. 1997; exports and imports machinery and equipment for the food, chemical, defence, telecommunications and timber industries; Gen. Dir ALEXANDER ČEREVKA; 57 employees.

Tesla Piešťany, a.s.: Vrbovská 2617/102, 921 72 Piešťany; tel. (33) 521-1111; fax (33) 762-3747; f. 1961; manufacture of semi-conductors and other electronic instruments; wholesale of electrical and radio components; retail of radio and television sets, electrical products; research and development services; Pres. and Gen. Dir MILAN GABIK; 170 employees.

Transpetrol, a.s.: Šumavská 38, 821 08 Bratislava; tel. (2) 526-1010; fax (2) 526-7105; e-mail transpetrol@transpetrol.sk; internet www.transpetrol.sk; 49% of shares divested to Yukos (Russia) in Dec. 2001; crude-petroleum pipeline operator; Chair. JOZEF KAISER; 492 employees.

Trnavské automobilové závody (Trnava Automobile Works): Čoburgova, POB 62, 917 48 Trnava; tel. (33) 203-51; fax (33) 265-17; f. 1986; vehicles, special machines, spare parts, sheet metal products, etc.; Man. Ing. JOZEF PUSCHENREITER; 2,309 employees.

Vab Sipox, a.s.: 957 01 Banovce nad Bebravou; tel. (38) 602-591; fax (38) 604-012; e-mail vab@vab.sk; internet www.vab.sk; f. 1951; manufacture of agricultural and construction machinery, machine tools, precision machinery, timber-processing equipment, etc.; Pres. Ing. JOZEF MAJSKY; 3,000 employees.

Volkswagen Slovakia, a.s.: Devínska Nová Ves, 843 02 Bratislava 49; tel. (2) 6964-1111; fax (2) 6964-2300; e-mail jozef.uhrik@volkswagen.sk; f. 1991; fmrly Volkswagen Bratislava s.p.o.l. s.r.o.; manufacture of motor vehicles; Dir JOZEF UHRÍK; 4,500 employees.

VSŽ, a.s.: Vstupný areál VSŽ, 044 54 Košice; tel. (55) 673-4107; fax (55) 622-6041; internet www.vsz.sk; f. 1959; controlling interest acquired by US Steel Group in 2000; manufacture of fabricated metal products, iron and steel; Chair. and Pres. Dr GABRIEL EICHLER; 24,600 employees.

Whirlpool Slovakia: Jašíkova 2, POB 23, 820 09 Bratislava; tel. (2) 4341–2170; e-mail whirlpool.sk@whirlpool.com; internet www.whirlpool.sk; Europe's largest washing-machine producer.

Závod Slovenského národného povstania a.s. (ZSNP): Priemyselná 12, 965 63 Žiar nad Hronom; tel. (45) 601-2501; fax (45) 672-5152; e-mail zsnp_zom@zsnp.sk; internet www.zsnp.sk; f. 1953; manufacture of secondary building materials; aluminium extraction; production of aluminium sheets, foils and other products; Gen. Dir JOZEF PITTNER; Marketing Dir TEODOR KVAPIL; 2,955 employees.

Zlaty Bazant: Hurbanovo; brewery and malting plant; 66% stake owned by Heineken (Netherlands); 600 employees.

ZPA Krizik, a.s.: Solivarská 1/A, 080 01 Prešov; tel. (51) 723-265; fax (51) 723-100; e-mail krizik@vadium.sk; automation engineering, control engineering, manufacture of ecological devices; Chair. STANISLAV COREJ; 1,864 employees.

ZTS Dubnica nad Váhom, a.s.: Areal ZTS 924, 018 41 Dubnica nad Váhom; tel. (42) 442-0247; fax (42) 442-2052; e-mail or@ztsdubnica.sk; internet www.ztsdubnica.sk; f. 1937; development and manufacture of weapons, hydroelectric power plants and waterworks, railway vehicles, torsion bars, hydraulic breaking hammers, machines and equipment for rubber and glass industry, etc.; Dir-Gen. ALEXANDER WOLF; 2,500 employees.

ZTS TEES, a.s.: Csl armády 3/1697, 036 57 Martin; tel. (43) 413-2307; fax (43) 413-1036; e-mail jbalogh@zts-tees.sk; internet www.zts-tees.sk; f. 1949; manufacture of agricultural machinery; Chair. JAROSLAV BALOGH; 1,632 employees.

TRADE UNIONS

Confederation of Trade Unions of the Slovak Republic (Konfederácia odborových zväzov Slovenskej republiky): Odborárské nám. 3, 815 70 Bratislava; tel. (2) 622-65; fax (2) 213-303; e-mail press@kozsr.sk; internet www.internet.sk/kozsr/; Pres. IVAN SAKTOR; 1.1m. members; affiliated unions include.

Metalworkers' Federation: Miletičova 24, 815 70 Bratislava; tel. (2) 5556-5383; fax (2) 5556-5387; e-mail oskovo@kovo.sk; Pres. EMIL MACHYNA.

Trade Union of Workers in Agriculture: Vajnorská 1, 815 70 Bratislava; tel. (2) 542-4186; fax (2) 542-1673; Pres. SVETOZÁR KORBEL'.

Trade Union of Workers in the Chemical Industry: Osadná 6, 831 03 Bratislava; tel. (2) 273-527; fax (2) 273-538; Pres. JURAJ BLAHÁK.

Trade Union of Workers in Construction and Construction Materials: Vajnorská 1, 815 70 Bratislava; tel. (2) 5542-4180; fax (2) 5542-2764; e-mail stavba@nextra.sk; Pres. DUŠAN BARČÍK.

Trade Union of Workers in Cultural and Social Organizations: Vajnorská 1, 815 70 Bratislava 1; tel. and fax (2) 5542-3760; e-mail sozkaso@nextra.sk; Pres. MÁRIA KRIŠTOFIČOVÁ.

Trade Union of Workers in Energy: Vajnorská 1, 815 70 Bratislava; tel. and fax (2) 542-1622; f. 1992; Pres. VLADIMIR MOJŠ.

Trade Union of Workers in the Food-processing Industry: Vajnorská 1, 815 70 Bratislava; tel. (2) 5542-1575; fax (2) 566-2506; e-mail ozp@isnet.sk; Pres. MAGDALENA MELLENOVA.

Trade Union of Workers in the Glass Industry: ul. Matice Slovenskej 19, 911 05 Trenčín; tel. (32) 743-7200; Pres. MIROSLAV BUČEK.

Trade Union of Workers in the Health and Social Services: Vajnorská 1, 815 70 Bratislava 3; tel. (2) 5542-3965; fax (2) 5542-5330; Pres. ANDREJ KUČINSKÝ.

Trade Union of Workers in Radio, Television and Newspapers: Vajnorská 1, 815 70 Bratislava; tel. (2) 211-844; Pres. PETER JÁCHIN.

Trade Union of Workers in the Textile, Clothing and Leather Industry: Vajnorská 1, 815 70 Bratislava; tel. (2) 213-389; fax (2) 526-2570; Pres. Ing. KONŠTANTÍN BALÁŽ.

Trade Union of Workers in the Wood-working, Furniture and Paper Industries: Vajnorská 1, 815 70 Bratislava; tel. (2) 213-660; fax (2) 213-163; Pres. BORISLAV MAJTÁN.

Transport

RAILWAYS

In early 2001 the total length of railways in Slovakia was estimated at 3,600 km, of which 1,400 km were electrified.

Železnica Spolocnost: Bratislava; f. 2001; state-owned co established to operate passenger and freight services and maintain rolling stock.

Železnice Slovenskej republiky (Slovak State Railways): Klemensova 8, 813 61 Bratislava; tel. (2) 5058-7007; fax (2) 5296-2296; e-mail gr@zsr.sk; internet www.zsr.sk; f. 1993; became a joint-stock co with responsibility for management of rail infrastructure in 2001, when responsibility for operations was transferred to the newly established state-owned concern, Železnica Spolocnost; Dir-Gen. ANDREJ EGYED.

Dopravný podnik Bratislava, a.s. (Bratislava Transport): Olejkárska 1, 814 52 Bratislava; tel. (2) 5950-1111; fax (2) 5950-1400; e-mail zad@dpb.sk; internet www.dpb.sk; tramway being upgraded to light-rail system; 11 routes with 154 stops; Dir-Gen. J. ZACHAR.

ROADS

In early 2001 the total road system (including motorways) was estimated at 17,880 km.

Slovenská správa ciest (Slovak Road Administration): Mileticová 19, 826 19 Bratislava; tel. (2) 5556-8008; fax (2) 5556-8011; internet www.ssc.sk; Dir DUŠAN FAKTOR.

INLAND WATERWAYS

The total length of navigable waterways in Slovakia (on the River Danube) is 172 km. The Danube provides a link with Germany, Austria, Hungary, Serbia and Montenegro, Bulgaria, Romania and the Black Sea, although it was closed to traffic in the then Federal Republic of Yugoslavia after damage caused during the conflict in that country in 1999. The main river ports are Bratislava and Komárno.

Štátna plavebná správa (State Shipping Authority): ul. Prístavná 10, 810 11 Bratislava; tel. (2) 5556-6336; fax (2) 5556-6335; internet www.sps.sk; Dir Ing. JÁN JURIA.

Slovenská plavba a prístavy (Slovak Shipping and Ports): Pribinova 24, 815 24 Bratislava; tel. (2) 5292-5798; fax (2) 5296-3002; e-mail spap@spap.sk; internet www.spap.sk; Gen. Man. OLDŘICH STRUMINSKÝ.

CIVIL AVIATION

There are five international airports in Slovakia: Bratislava (M. R. Štefánik Airport), Košice, Piešťany, Poprad and Sliač. Until Slovak Airlines, the national carrier, began operations in March 1998, ČSA (Czech Airlines) provided air transport services for both Slovakia and the Czech Republic.

Air Slovakia: M. R. Štefánik Airport, 823 11 Bratislava; tel. (2) 4342-2742; fax (2) 4342-2742; internet www.airslovakia.sk; f. 1993; scheduled passenger flights to Israel, Kuwait, Bulgaria, Cyprus, Greece and Spain; charter and cargo services; Gen. Dir AUGUSTIN BERNAT.

SkyEurope Airlines: Ivanská 26, 821 04 Bratislava; tel. (2) 4850-1111; fax (2) 4850-1000; internet www.skyeurope.com; f. 2001; first budget airline in Central Europe; joint venture with Spanish and Belgian interests; scheduled and charter passenger and cargo services; domestic and international services; Chief Execs CHRISTIAN MANDL, ALAIN SKOWRONEK.

Slovak Airlines: Trnavská cesta 56, 821 02 Bratislava; tel. (2) 4445-0096; fax (2) 4445-0097; e-mail sll@sll.sk; internet www.sll.sk; f. 1995; 34% state-owned; scheduled and charter passenger and cargo services; domestic services to Košice; international charter services to Russia, Spain, Italy, Bulgaria, Cyprus, Turkey, Greece and Tunisia; Chair. and Gen. Dir PAVOL MLADY.

Slovenská správa letísk (Slovak Airports Authority): M. R. Štefánik Airport, 823 11 Bratislava; tel. (2) 4342-4633; fax (2) 4342-2146; e-mail saa@ssl.sk; Dir-Gen. JAN KASSAK.

Tatra Air, a.s.: M. R. Štefánik Airport, 823 14 Bratislava; tel. (2) 292-318; fax (2) 294-259; f. 1990; joint-stock airline co; Exec. Dir BOHUŠ HURAJ.

Tourism

Slovakia's tourist attractions include ski resorts in the High and Low Tatras and other mountain ranges, more than 20 spa resorts (with thermal and mineral springs), numerous castles and mansions, and historic towns, including Bratislava, Košice, Nitra, Bardejov, Kežmarok and Levoča. In 2001 1,219,099 foreign tourists visited Slovakia; revenue from tourism was US $461m. in 2000.

Slovak Tourist Board: Namestie L. Stura 1, POB 35, 974 05 Banska Bystrica; tel. (48) 413-6146; fax (48) 413-6149; e-mail sacr@sacr.sk; internet www.slovakiatourism.sk.

SATUR: Bratislava; f. 1993 from the former Czechoslovak state travel agency, Čedok; has 52 brs throughout Slovakia.

Slovakoturist: Volgogradská 1, Bratislava; tel. (2) 552-47.

Tatratour: Bajkalská 25, 827 27 Bratislava; tel. (2) 521-4826; fax (2) 521-2722.

Culture

NATIONAL ORGANIZATION

Ministry of Culture: see section on The Government (Ministries).

CULTURAL HERITAGE

Gallery of Eastern Slovakia (Východoslovenská galéria): Leninova 72, 040 01 Košice; tel. (55) 211-87; art gallery; Dir Dr LADISLAV ZOZUĽÁK.

Matica Slovenská: L. Novomeského 32, Martin; tel. (43) 324-54; f. 1863; Slovak cultural org.; Chair. Ing. IMRICH SEDLÁCH.

Municipal Gallery of Bratislava (Galéria mesta Bratislavy): Mirbachov palác, Františkánske nám. 11, 815 35 Bratislava; tel. (2) 5443-5102; fax (2) 5443-2611; e-mail gmb@nextra.sk; Dir Dr IVAN JANČAR.

Municipal Museum of Bratislava (Mestské múzeum v Bratislava): Stara Radnica, Primaciálne nám. 3, 815 18 Bratislava; tel. (2) 5543-4742; fax (2) 5443-4631; e-mail mmba@bratislava.sk; f. 1868; displays on history, social history, art; library of 21,400 vols; Dir Dr PETER HYROSS.

Slovak National Gallery (Slovenská národná galéria): Riečna 1, 815 13 Bratislava; tel. (2) 5443-0437; fax (2) 5443-3971; e-mail info@sng.sk; internet www.sng.sk; f. 1948; paintings, sculpture, prints, drawings, applied art and facsimiles; library of 65,000 vols, 80,000 documents; Dir KATARINA BAJCUROVA.

Slovak National Museum (Slovenské národné múzeum): Vajanského nábr. 2, 814 36 Bratislava; tel. (2) 5296-6867; fax (2) 5292-4344; e-mail riad@snm.sk; internet www.snm.sk; f. 1893; archaeology, ethnography, musicology, numismatics, history of Slovakia, natural history; Dir Prof. Dr MATUŠ KUČERA.

State Gallery Banská Bystrica (Statna galéria v Banskej Bystrici): Dolna 8, 975 90 Banská Bystrica; tel. and fax (48) 412-4167; e-mail sgbb@isternet.sk; museum of fine arts; Dir Dr ALENA VRBANOVA.

SPORTING ORGANIZATION

Slovak Olympic Committee: Junácka 6, 832 80 Bratislava; tel. (2) 4924-9271; fax (2) 4924-9575; e-mail office@olympic.sk; internet www.olympic.sk; f. 1992; Pres. FRANTISEK CHMELAR; Sec.-Gen. MARTIN BENKO.

PERFORMING ARTS

Bratislava Music Festival (Bratislavské hudobné slávnosti): Michalská 10, 815 36 Bratislava; tel. (2) 334-528; fax (2) 332-652; Dir Dr LADISLAV MOKRÝ.

Divadlo korzo '90: Suché mýto 17, Dunajská 1, Bratislava; tel. (2) 330-739; theatre; Dir ĽUBOMÍR GREGOR.

Eastslowak Theatre of Košice: Hlavná 58, 040 01 Košice; tel. (55) 622-1231; fax (55) 622-8235; state theatre, opera and ballet house; Theatre Dir ŠTEFAN FEJKO; Opera Dir FRANTIŠEK BALÚN.

Košice State Philharmonic Orchestra (Štátna filharmónia Košice): Dom umenia, Moyzesova 66, 041 23 Košice; tel. and fax (55) 622-4509; e-mail sfk@sfk.sk; internet www.sfk.sk; Dir Dr IRENA MEDŇANSKÁ; Principal Conductor Dr JOHANNES WILDNER.

Nitra International Theatre Festival (Divadelná Nitra): Svätoplukovo nám. 4, 950 53 Nitra; tel. and fax (37) 652-4870; e-mail nitrafest@nr.nitrafest.sk; internet www.nitrafest.sk; festival dates 20–25 Sept.; Artistic and Man. Dir DARINA KÁROVÁ.

Nová scéna: Živnostenská 1, 812 92 Bratislava; tel. (2) 532-30; theatre; Dir ĽUBO ROMAN.

Slovak National Theatre (Slovenské národné divadlo): Gorkého 4, 815 86 Bratislava; tel. (2) 323-861; e-mail snd@snd.sk; internet www.snd.sk; f. 1920; comprises separate opera, ballet and drama ensembles.

Slovak Philharmonic Orchestra (Slovenská filharmónia): Medená 3, 816 01 Bratislava; tel. (2) 5443-3351; fax (2) 5443-5956; e-mail filharm@filharm.sk; internet www.filharm.sk; Dir Ing. JOZEF TKÁCIK; Principal Conductor and Music Dir ONDREJ LENÁRD.

Slovak Radio Symphony Orchestra (Symfonický orchester slovenského rozhlasu): Mýtna 1, POB 55, 810 05 Bratislava; tel. (2) 5727-3475; fax (2) 5727-3386; e-mail jurkovic@slovakradio.sk; internet www.slovakradio.sk/sosr; Chief Conductor CHARLES OLIVIERI-MUNROE; Man. Dir Prof. MILOŠ JURKOVIČ.

ASSOCIATIONS

Association of Hungarian Writers: Bratislava; f. 1989.

Association of Slovak Theatre Professionals (Združenie divadelníkov na Slovensku): Dunajská 36, 812 92 Bratislava; tel. (2) 332-107; fax (2) 326-677; f. 1990; theatrical association.

Association of Writers' Organizations in Slovakia (Asociácia organizácií spisovateľov Slovenska): Laurinská 2, 815 08 Bratislava; tel. and fax (2) 533-4117; f. 1949; reorganized in 1990; 330 mems; Pres. MILAN SÚTOVEC.

Centre of Folk Art Production (Ústredie ľudovel umeleckej výroby): Obchodná 64, 816 11 Bratislava; tel. (2) 533-5296; fax (2) 531-7667; e-mail uluv@gtinek.sk; internet www.gratex.sk; f. 1945; aims to preserve and develop traditional arts and crafts; training courses; exhibitions; Dir Dr EMÍLIA FULKOVÁ.

Csemadok: cultural union of Hungarians in Slovakia; Gen. Dir PETER KOLAR.

Fine Art Foundation (Fond výtvarných umeni): Trnavská 112, 826 33 Bratislava; tel. (2) 235-340; fax (2) 236-282.

Music Centre Slovakia (Hudobné centrum): Michalská 10, 815 36 Bratislava; tel. (2) 5443-4003; fax (2) 5443-0379; e-mail hc@hc.sk; internet www.hc.sk; Dir Dr OĽGA SMETANOVÁ.

Slovak Architects' Society (Spolok architektov Slovenska): Panská 15, 811 01 Bratislava; tel. (2) 533-1431; fax (2) 533-5744; f. 1990; Pres. MARTIN KUSÝ; Dir FRANTIŠEK KYSELICA; 1,900 mems.

Slovak Design Centre (Slovenské Design centrum): Baštová 4, 811 01 Bratislava; tel. (2) 331-371.

Slovak Film Union (Slovenský filmový zväz): Mostová 6, 811 02 Bratislava; tel. (2) 331-071; Chair. ILJA RUPPELDT; Sec. PETER ŇUKOVIČ.

Slovak Music Association (Slovenská hudobná asociácia): Jakubovo nám. 12, 811 06 Bratislava; tel. (2) 333-794.

Slovak Music Foundation (Slovenský hudobný fond): Medená 29, 811 02 Bratislava; tel. (2) 533-3412; fax (2) 533-1110; Dir Ing. MILOŠ KOCIÁN.

Slovak Music Union (Slovenská hudobná únia): Michalská 10, 815 36 Bratislava; tel. (2) 5443-5291; fax (2) 5443-0188; e-mail hudobnaunia@stonline.sk; Chair. EGON KRÁK.

Slovak Union of Visual Arts (Slovenská výtvarná únia): Partizánská 21, 813 51 Bratislava; tel. (2) 5313-623; fax (2) 5333-154; f. 1990; organization of exhibitions, creative symposia; Pres. VIKTOR HULÍK; 1,800 mems.

Union of Slovak Composers and Concert Performers (Zväz slovenských skladateľov a koncertných umelcov): Sládkovičova 11, Bratislava; tel. (2) 330-188; f. 1955; 290 mems; Pres. Prof. Dr OTO FERENCZY; Sec. ALOJZ LUKNÁR.

Union of Slovak Dramatists (Zväz slovenských dramatických umelcov): Gorkého 4, 812 92 Bratislava; Pres. OSVALD ZAHRADNIK.

Education

Education is provided free of charge at all levels by state-controlled and church-affiliated schools. Most children between the ages of three and six attend kindergarten (mateřska škola). Compulsory education begins at six years, when children attend basic school (základná škola). Courses at basic school last for nine years, although the last of these is optional. Most children continue their studies after basic school, either at a secondary grammar school (gymnázium), of which there were 212 in the 2000/01 academic year, a secondary specialized school (stredná odborná škola), of which there were 372, or a secondary vocational school (stredné odborné učilište), of which there were 368. In each type of institution students follow four-year courses. The establishment of private and religious schools was legalized in 1990. In the 2000/01 school year 297,576 children attended secondary school. There were 125,896 students enrolled at Slovakia's 20 institutions of higher education in 2000/01. Primary enrolment in 2000/01 included 89.4% of the relevant age-group (males 88.8%; females 90.0%), while the comparable ratio for secondary enrolment was estimated at 74.9% (males 74.6%; females 75.2%). Of total current government expenditure (excluding wages) in 2001, an estimated 1,800m. koruny (0.5%) was allocated to education.

UNIVERSITIES

Comenius University of Bratislava (Univerzita Komenského Bratislava): Šafárikovo nám. 6, 818 06 Bratislava; tel. (2) 5292-1594; fax (2) 5296-3836; e-mail kr@rec.uniba.sk; internet www.uniba.sk; f. 1467 as Academia Istropolitana, reopened under present name 1919; 12 faculties; 1,956 teachers; 25,290 students; Rector Prof. Ing. FERDINAND DEVÍNSKY.

Šafárik University (Univerzita Pavla Jozefa Šafárika): Šrobárova 2, 041 80 Košice; tel. (55) 622-2608; fax (55) 766-959; e-mail zahrodd@kosice.upjs.sk; internet www.upjs.sk; f. 1959; 4 faculties; 2 institutes; 400 teachers; 4,100 students; Rector Prof. Ing. DUŠAN PODHRADSKÝ.

Slovak Agricultural University in Nitra (Slovenská poľnohospodárska univerzita v Nitre): A. Hlinku 2, 949 76 Nitra; tel. (37) 650-8111; fax (37) 741-2626; e-mail admin-www@uniag.sk; internet www.uniag.sk; f. 1946; languages of instruction: Slovak and English; 4 faculties; 494 teachers; 9,700 students; Rector Prof. IMRICH OKENKA.

Slovak University of Technology in Bratislava (Slovenská technická univerzita v Bratislave): Vazovova 5, 812 43 Bratislava; tel. (2) 5729-4323; fax (2) 5729-4326; e-mail zahran@vm.stuba.sk; internet www.stuba.sk; f. 1938; 6 faculties; 1,500 teachers; 15,700 students; Chancellor Dr IVETA FABIÁNOVÁ.

Technical University of Košice (Technická univerzita v Košiciach): Letná 9, 042 00 Košice; tel. (55) 602-1111; fax (55) 633-2748; e-mail maria.mrazova@tuke.sk; internet www.tuke.sk; f. 1952; 8 faculties; 850 teachers; 11,900 students; Rector Prof. JURAJ SINAY.

University of Economics in Bratislava (Ekonomická Univerzita v Bratislave): Odbojárov 10, 832 20 Bratislava; tel. (2) 526-7139; fax (2) 526-7117; e-mail stern@euba.sk; internet www.euba.sk; f. 1940; 5 faculties, 1 attached institute; 425 teachers; 11,733 students; Rector Prof. Dr JURAJ STERN.

University of Veterinary Medicine (Univerzita veterinárskeho Lekárstva): Komenského 73, 041 81 Košice; tel. (55) 633-0127; fax (55) 633-5641; e-mail rektor@uvm.sk; internet www.uvm.sk; f. 1949; languages of instruction: Slovak and English; 153 teachers; 785 students; Rector Prof. RUDOLF CABADAJ.

University of Žilina (Žilinská univerzita): Moyzesova 20, 010 26 žilina; tel. (41) 5621-781; fax (41) 724-7702; f. 1953; 7 faculties; 618 teachers; 9,070 students; Rector Prof. JÁN BUYŇÁK.

Zvolen Technical University (Technická Univerzita vo Zvolene): T. G. Masaryka 24, 960 53 Zvolen; tel. (45) 335-111; fax (45) 330-027; e-mail rektor@vsld.tuzvo.sk; internet www.tuzvo.sk; f. 1807; reorganized as College of Forestry and Wood Technology 1952, acquired university status 1991; 4 faculties; 243 teachers; 2,200 students; Rector Prof. MIKULAŠ SUPIN.

Social Welfare

Following the dissolution of Czechoslovakia in 1993, the two successor states announced plans to introduce changes to the existing social-welfare system. The health service was to remain largely under state control in Slovakia, although there were plans to privatize certain elements, particularly spas and pharmacies. In March 2003 parliament approved legislation aimed at reforming the health care system, introducing provisions whereby patients (with the exception of pregnant women and children under the age of six years) would be required to pay a proportion of the cost of visiting their doctor or receiving hospital treatment. On 1 January 1995 two independent institutions were established: the Social Insurance Agency (for sickness insurance and pensions security) and the General Health Insurance Agency (financing health care). Payments into the agencies were to be made by employees, employers, the self-employed and the state. In 2000 there were 19,303 physicians working in Slovakia (including 8,520 in the private sector), and a total of 56,261 beds in health care establishments. Of total general government expenditure in 2001, an estimated 131,000m. koruny (33.5% of spending) was allocated to social expenditure, and a further 51.3m. koruny (13.1%) was allocated to health.

In 1994 the Government established an Employment Fund, responsible for distributing benefits to the unemployed, and for making social insurance contributions on their behalf. Unemployment benefits may be paid for a period of up to nine months, at a rate of 40% of the average net wage.

GOVERNMENT AGENCIES

Ministry of Labour, Social Affairs and the Family: see section on The Government (Ministries).

General Health Insurance Agency: Bratislava; f. 1995; provides sickness insurance and pensions security.

Social Insurance Agency (Sociálna Poisťovňa): ul. 29 augusta 8–10, 813 63 Bratislava; tel. (2) 323-592; fax (2) 323-168; f. 1995; administers health, sickness and pension insurance schemes; Dir Dr IGOR LIPTÁK.

NON-GOVERNMENTAL AGENCY

Slovak Red Cross: Grösslingova 24, 814 46 Bratislava; tel. (2) 5292-2305; fax (2) 52923279; Pres. Dr MILAN KRUCAY; Sec.-Gen. Ing. BOHDAN TELGÁRSKY.

The Environment

As in most of the countries of Eastern Europe, pollution and environmental damage was widespread, resulting from communist mismanagement, particularly of the energy industry. During the communist period the region was highly dependent on locally produced lignite coal (brown coal), which has a low energy value and a high sulphur and ash content. In the mid-1990s there was also growing concern over Slovakia's Soviet-designed nuclear power plants, both over the safety of old reactors and plans to complete construction of a new plant at Mochovce. The Mochovce plant began operations in 1998, amid fears expressed by Slovakia's neighbours (most notably Austria) that it did not meet international safety standards. Slovakia subsequently agreed to close the reactors at an older power station in 2006–08. The Gabčíkovo hydroelectric plant on the country's border with Hungary, which had involved the diversion of the Danube river, was also opposed by environmentalists, and caused an international dispute between the two countries, after Slovakia proceeded to build and operate the dam without Hungarian consent. Not only did the river's diversion result in the fall of its water level, but there were fears that it might destroy the surrounding wetlands, harm local farming and affect the local aquifer. In 1996–2000 progress was made in the development of environmental legislation, under the terms of the National Environmental Action Plan, which received parliamentary approval in 1996. Total disbursements by the national environmental protection fund amounted to 1,243.9m. koruny in 2000, of which the largest share (some 42%) was allocated to waste water treatment plants and sewerage. Adherence of new legislation to European Union (EU) regulations was a priority, as Slovakia was due to become a full member in May 2004.

GOVERNMENT ORGANIZATIONS

Ministry of the Environment: see section on The Government (Ministries).

Slovak Environmental Agency (Slovenská agentúra životného prostredia): Tajovského 28, 975 90 Banská Bystrica; tel. (48) 413-5131; fax (48) 423-0409; e-mail toncik@sazp.sk; internet www.sazp.sk; Dir Ing. MIROSLAV TONČÍK.

Slovak National Parks Administration (Správa národných parkov SR): Hodžova 11, 031 01 Liptovský Mikuláš; tel. (44) 244-98; fax (44) 514-125; e-mail snpsr@za.sk; Dir Ing. IVAN GAŠINEC.

Slovak Caves Administration (Správa slovenských jaskýň): Hodžova 11, 031 01 Liptovský Mikuláš; tel. (44) 536-101; fax (44) 536-311; e-mail caves@ssj.sk; internet www.ssj.sk; Dir Ing. JOZEF HLAVÁČ.

ACADEMIC INSTITUTES

Slovak Academy of Sciences (Slovenská Académia Vied): Štefánikova 49, 814 38 Bratislava; tel. (2) 5249-6131; fax (2) 5249-5689; e-mail kovac@up.upsav.sk; internet www.savba.sk; f. 1953; Pres. ŠTEFAN LUBY.

Institute of Botany (Botanický ústav): Dúbravská cesta 14, 842 23 Bratislava; tel. (2) 373-507; fax (2) 371-948; e-mail botunist@savba.sk; internet nic.savba.sk/inst/botu; f. 1964; research into the flora and vegetation of Slovakia, plant physiology, embryology and pathology; Dir IVAN JAROLIMEK.

Institute of Dendrobiology (Arboretum Mlyňany—Ústav dendrobiológie): 951 52 Slepčany; tel. (37) 948-33; fax (37) 948-36; f. 1892; re-established 1954; research into horticulture and landscape architecture; Dir Assoc. Prof. IVAN TOMAŠKO.

Institute of Evolutionary and Applied Landscape Ecology: Andreja Kmeťa 13, 969 00 Banská Štiavnica; tel. (45) 218-06; fax (45) 238-16; Principal Officers Dr PETER MÚDRY, Dr YOZEF ŠTEFFEK.

Institute of Forest Ecology (Ústav ekológie lesa): Štúrova 2, 960 53 Zvolen; tel. (45) 223-12; fax (45) 274-85; e-mail bublinec@uvt.tuzvo.sk; f. 1981; study of ecology, the environment, soil science, forest eco-systems, tree species; Dirs EDUARD BUBLINEC, JOZEF VÁLKA.

Institute of Geography (Geografický ústav): Štefánikova 49, 814 73 Bratislava; tel. (2) 5249-5587; fax (2) 5249-1340; e-mail geogsekr@savba.sk; f. 1943; research in geography, regional matters and the environment; Dir Assoc. Prof. ANTON BEZÁK.

Institute of Hydrology (Ústav hydrológie a hydrauliky): Račianská 75, 830 08 Bratislava; tel. (2) 253-021; fax (2) 259-404; Dir JÚLIUS SUTOR.

Institute of Landscape Ecology (Ústav krajinnej ekológie SAV): Štefánikova 3, POB 254, 814 99 Bratislava; tel. (2) 5249-3882; fax (2) 5249-4508; e-mail director@uke.savba.sk; research centres in Nitra and Východná; Dir JÚLIUS OSZLÁNYI.

Centre for Environmental Impact Assessment: Faculty of Natural Sciences, Comenius University of Bratislava, Mlynská dolina B-2, 842 15 Bratislava; tel. (2) 6029-6579; fax (2) 6542-8938; e-mail pavlickova@fns.uniba.sk; f. 1993; training, documentation, education and information centre; Dirs Dr KATARÍNA PAVLIČKOVÁ, Assoc. Prof. MARÍA KOZOVÁ.

ENVIRO—Information Branch: c/o Ministry for the Environment, Hlbolá 2, 812 35 Bratislava; tel. (2) 725-968; fax (2) 728-441.

Forest Research Institute (Lesnícky výskumný ústav): T. G. Masaryka 22, 960 92 Zvolen; tel. (45) 533-5716; fax (45) 532-1883; e-mail ilavsky@fris.sk; f. 1898; forestry management and ecological research; Dir Dr JÁN ILAVSKÝ.

Trnava Nuclear Power Plant Research Institute, Inc. (Výskumný ústav jadrových elektrárni Trnava, a.s.): Okružná 5, 918 64 Trnava; tel. (33) 599-1356; fax (33) 599-1193; e-mail korec@vuje.sk; internet www.vuje.sk; f. 1977; environmental impact and operational risk assessment; development of radioactive-waste disposal technologies; management of emergency situations; Dir JÁN KOREC.

Water Research Institute (Výskumný ústav vodného hospodárstva): nábr. L. Svobodu 5, 812 49 Bratislava; tel. (2) 343-111; fax (2) 315-743; f. 1951; Dir VLADIMÍR HOLČÍK.

NON-GOVERNMENTAL ORGANIZATIONS

Environmental Partnership for Central Europe—Slovak Office: Skvteckého 30, 974 00 Banská Bystrica; tel. and fax (48) 401-259; e-mail medved@seps.bb.sanet.sk; Country Dir JURAJ MESÍK.

Green Party in Slovakia: see section on Political Organizations.

Green Perspective Foundation (Nadácia Zelená nádej): 082 13 Tulčik 27; tel. and fax (51) 778-9138; e-mail main@gpf.sk; internet www.gpf.sk; campaigns for environmental conservation and responsible use of biosystems; campaigns to save the Čergov forest in north-east Slovakia; Dirs JURAJ LUKÁČ, PETER MEDVED, RADOSLAV POTOČNÝ.

Greenpeace Slovakia: POB 58, 815 99 Bratislava; tel. (2) 5293-1340; fax (2) 5293-1641; e-mail slovakia@greenpeace.sk; internet www.greenpeace.sk.

IUCN Slovakia: Vysoká 18, 811 06 Bratislava; tel. (2) 536-1175; national office of the World Conservation Union (IUCN); Dir PETER SABO.

Society for Sustainable Living in Slovakia (Spoločnosť pre Trvalo Udržateľný život v SR): Staroturský chodník 1, 811 01 Bratislava; tel. (2) 363-462; fax (2) 313-968; e-mail huba@savba.sk; internet www.fns.uniba.sk/zp; f. 1993; Chair. Dr MIKULÁŠ HUBA.

Slovak Ecological Society (Slovenská ekologická spoločnosť): Akademická 2, POB 23/B, 949 01 Nitra; tel. (37) 356-01; fax (37) 356-08; e-mail nrukhala@savba.savba.sk; f. 1992; Pres. Dr PAVOL ELIÁŠ.

Slovak Union of Nature and Landscape Conservationists (Slovensky zväz ochrancov prírody a krajiny—SZOPK): Godrova 3, 811 06 Bratislava; tel. (2) 531-3968; fax (2) 531-3291; environmental education; protection of natural resources and biodiversity; protection of historical monuments and the landscape; Dirs Dr MIROSLAV FULÍN, Dr JOZEF GREGOR; 353 local groups; 14,000 mems.

Tree of Life (Strom života): Pražská 11, 813 36 Bratislava; tel. (2) 398-473; fax (2) 398-703; organizes environmental and cultural education and training projects for young people, teachers and the general public; Dir OTO MAKÝŠ.

Defence

In August 2002 the total strength of Slovakia's armed forces numbered 26,200; the army numbered 13,000 (including 10,400 conscripts), the air force 10,200 and there were some 3,000 centrally-controlled staff and logistical and support staff. In addition there were an estimated 1,700 border police, 250 guard troops, 1,400 railway defence troops and 1,350 civil defence troops. Military service in Slovakia is compulsory and lasts for 12 months. The budget allocation for defence spending in 2001 was estimated at 18,200m. koruny. Slovakia became a member of the North Atlantic Treaty Organization's NATO 'Partnership for Peace' programme in February 1994, and was to accede to full membership in 2004.

Commander-in-Chief: President of the Republic.

Chief of the General Staff: Lt-Gen. MILAN CEROVSKÝ.

Bibliography

For publications on Czechoslovakia see the Bibliography of the Czech Republic chapter.

Brock, P. *The Slovak National Awakening: An Essay in the Intellectual History of East-Central Europe*. Toronto, University of Toronto Press, 1976.

European Bank for Reconstruction and Development. *Transition Report*. London, EBRD, annually.

Goldman, M. F. *Slovakia since Independence: a Struggle for Democracy*. Westport, CT, Praeger, 1998.

Harris, E. *Nationalism and Democratisation: Politics of Slovakia and Slovenia*. Burlington, VT, Ashgate Publishing Company, 2002.

Henderson, K. *Slovakia (Postcommunist States and Nations)*. London, Routledge, 2002.

Jablonický, J., and Pivovarči, J. *The Slovak National Uprising*. Bratislava, Obzor, 1969.

Kirschbaum, S. J. *A History of Slovakia: The Struggle for Survival*. New York, NY, St Martin's Press, 1994.

    Historical Dictionary of Slovakia. Lanham, MD, Scarecrow Press, 1998.

Kirschbaum, S. J., and Roman, C. R. (Eds). *Reflections on Slovak History*. Toronto, Slovak World Congress, 1987.

Kuijs, L. *Monetary Policy Transmission Mechanisms and Inflation in Slovakia*. Washington, DC, IMF, 2002.

Lettrich, J. *History of Modern Slovakia*. Toronto, Slovak Research and Studies Centre, 1987.

Mallakh, D. H. *The Slovak Autonomy Movement, 1935–1939: A Study in Unrelenting Nationalism*. New York, NY, Columbia University Press, 1979.

Matovcik, A. (Ed.) *Slovak Biographical Dictionary*. Illinois, IL, Bolchazy Carducci, 2002.

McQuibban, P., Save-Soderbergy, B., and Sanchez-Moron, A. *Advancing Democracy in Slovakia Through Local Self-Governance*. Stockholm, International IDEA, 2002.

Smith, A. 'Uneven Development and the Restructuring of the Arms Industry in Slovakia' in *Transactions of the Institute of British Geographers*, Vol. 19, No. 4, 1994.

    Reconstructing the Regional Economy: Industrial Transformation and Regional Development in Slovakia. Cheltenham, Edward Elgar, 1998.

Steiner, E. *The Slovak Dilemma*. Cambridge, Cambridge University Press, 1973.

See also the Select Bibliography in Part Four.

SLOVENIA

Geography

PHYSICAL FEATURES

The Republic of Slovenia, formerly a constituent partner in the Socialist Federal Republic of Yugoslavia (SFRY), lies in south-central Europe. Slovenia has frontiers with Italy in the west, Austria to the north, Hungary along a short border in the east, and its southern border is with Croatia. In the southwest of the country there is a short coastal strip (40 km—25 miles) on the Adriatic Sea, around the Istrian port of Koper (Capodistria).

Slovenia is an Alpine area, being dominated by the Julian and Karawanken Alps (Julijske Alpe and Karavanke). Slovenia's highest peak, Triglav (2,863 m—9,394 ft), is in the Julian Alps, close to the northern part of the border with Italy. Most of the territory is mountainous, the main areas of lower terrain being in the south-west near the coast, in the central southern areas, along the Sava river, and in the north-east around the Mura river, where Slovenia becomes a narrowing strip of territory abutting on to the Pannonian plains. The country's river valleys and its Karst region (a limestone plateau in the Dinaric Alps) contribute to the agricultural territory and much of its area is forested.

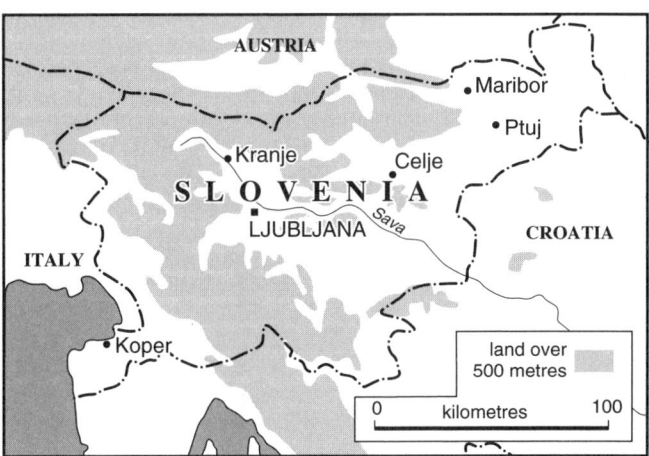

CLIMATE

The climate in Slovenia is Mediterranean near the coast, and continental inland. Mountainous areas have a colder climate with heavy snowfall in winter. Average daily temperatures range from between 0°C (32°F) and 22°C (71.6°F) inland, and between 2°C (35.6°F) and 24°C (75.2°F) on the coast. Average annual rainfall ranges from 800 mm in the east to 3,000 mm in the north-west.

POPULATION

According to census results, the total population of Slovenia was 1,964,036 at 31 March 2002, which gave it a population density of 96.9 per sq km. At that time 83.1% of the population were ethnic Slovenes. There were also Slovene communities in other former republics of the SFRY, and in Austria and Italy. The largest minority ethnic groups in Slovenia were Serbs (2.0% of the total population in 2002) and Croats (1.8%). There were also small numbers of Bosnian Muslims (Bosniaks), Hungarians, Albanians, Macedonians, Montenegrins and Italians. The official language is Slovene, a Southern Slavonic tongue, related to but distinct from Serbo-Croat. The traditional religion of the Slovenes is Christianity, as practised by the Roman Catholic Church, to which most of the population adhere. There are small communities of other Christian denominations, including Eastern Orthodox Christians, of Muslims (mainly guest workers) and Jews. The capital of Slovenia is Ljubljana, the largest city in the country, with an estimated population of 265,881 at 31 March 2002. It is located in the centre-west of Slovenia. Other important towns include Maribor (population 110,668 in 2002), Kranj (51,225), Celje (48,081) and Koper (47,539).

Chronology

168 BC: Illyria (in the north of which lay the territory which is now Slovenia) was annexed by the Roman Empire.

AD 395: Following a division of the administration of the Roman Empire, Illyria was ruled by the Eastern Roman ('Byzantine') Emperor in Constantinople (now İstanbul, Turkey).

5th century: Southern Slav peoples began to move from Pannonia into Illyria and the Balkans.

7th century: Western Slavic tribes associated themselves with the Slavic Duchy of Carinthia (based in modern Austria), while Western Christian missionaries from Salzburg were active among these ancestors of the Slovenes, introducing the Latin script and a Western cultural orientation.

745: Carinthia fell under the influence of the Frankish (German) empire, becoming a mark or marcher lordship in 788; the Slav conversion to Christianity was, therefore, secured.

812: By the Treaty of Aix-la-Chapelle (Aachen), the Byzantine Emperor, Michael I, acknowledged the Frankish ruler, Charles ('the Great'—Charlemagne), as Emperor in the West; German influence over the Slovene-inhabited areas of Carinthia and Carniola was thus established, although Byzantine (and Venetian) influence remained on the Istrian coast.

869–74: Kocelj briefly established a Slovene principality in Lower Pannonia (southern Hungary).

1335: Carniola and Carinthia became hereditary possessions of the Austrian House of Habsburg, within the Holy Roman Empire.

1490: Death of the Hungarian King, Matthias I Corvinus, who had, temporarily, conquered the Habsburg lands.

1551: A minister of the Protestant (Calvinist) Church of Carniola, Primož Trubar, published a catechism, which was the first book in the Slovene language.

1584: Jurij Dalmatin translated the Bible into Slovene and Adam Bohorič wrote a Slovene grammar.

1599: The Counter-Reformation secured the Slovenes for Roman Catholicism by the final extinction of the Church of

Carniola, the writings of which, however, had already provided the basis of Slovene literature.

1815: The Congress of Vienna confirmed Austrian rule over Istria and Dalmatia, which were formerly Venetian.

1848: A group of Slovene intellectuals formulated the first political manifesto advocating a united Slovenia.

1867: The *Ausgleich,* or Compromise, created, in the Habsburg territories, the 'Dual Monarchy' of Austria-Hungary; the Slovenes were found in four of the 15 Austrian crownlands: Carniola (where they formed a majority); Carinthia; Styria; and the Coastal Lands around Trieste (ancient Aquileia).

28 June 1914: The heir to the Habsburg throne, Archduke Francis Ferdinand, and his wife were assassinated in Sarajevo (Bosnia and Herzegovina), which led to the start of the First World War.

July 1917: Prominent Slovenes, together with other Southern Slavs (excluding the Bulgarians), declared their intention to form a unitary state, under the Serbian monarchy.

29 October 1918: Following the defeat and dissolution of the Danubian Dual Monarchy, the Southern Slav (Yugoslav) peoples separated from the Austro-Hungarian system of states (a Southern Slav republic was established on 15 October); Carniola and parts of the Coastal Lands, Styria and Carinthia, among other territories, were subsequently ceded formally to the new state.

4 December 1918: Proclamation of the Kingdom of Serbs, Croats and Slovenes, which united the former Habsburg lands with Serbia and Montenegro.

3 October 1929: Following the imposition of a royal dictatorship, the country was formally named Yugoslavia.

1937: Josip Broz (Tito) became General Secretary of the Communist Party of Yugoslavia (CPY), which was to become the main partner in the Partisan (National Liberation Army) resistance to the German invasion.

April 1941: German and Italian forces invaded Yugoslavia, which was dismembered, with Germany annexing Lower Styria and parts of Carinthia, and Italy annexing Ljubljana and Istria; the Liberation Front, which was to become the Slovene wing of the Partisan movement, was founded.

29 November 1945: A Provisional Assembly proclaimed the Federative People's Republic of Yugoslavia, elections having taken place after fighting ended in Carinthia and Styria in May.

January 1946: A Soviet-style Constitution, establishing a federation of six republics (including a Socialist Republic of Slovenia) and two autonomous regions, was adopted.

November 1952: The Communist Party was renamed the League of Communists of Yugoslavia (LCY) and several liberal reforms were adopted.

1954: Istria was partitioned between Italy (which gained the city of Trieste) and Yugoslavia (most of the territory was awarded to Slovenia, which thereby gained a coastline, but the southern Istrian peninsula became part of Croatia).

April 1963: A new Constitution changed the country's name to the Socialist Federal Republic of Yugoslavia (SFRY).

1971: Following the granting of the rights of autonomy to the federal units, Tito introduced a system of collective leadership and the regular rotation of posts; a collective State Presidency for Yugoslavia was established, with Tito as its head. However, later in the year, there was a purge of 'nationalist' liberals throughout Yugoslavia.

1975: The Treaty of Osimo formally established the Yugoslav–Italian borders.

4 May 1980: Tito died; his responsibilities were transferred to the collective State Presidency and to the Presidium of the LCY.

1988: Against a background of increasing dissatisfaction with the state of the economy, the military trial of journalists on *Mladina* magazine and of an army officer provoked the first demands for Slovenian independence.

27 September 1989: With rising dissatisfaction throughout Yugoslavia, the Slovenian Assembly reaffirmed the sovereignty of their Republic and declared its right to secede from the SFRY.

December 1989: Serbian enterprises were instructed to sever all links with Slovenia, which retaliated by closing its borders to Serbian goods and implementing reciprocal economic sanctions. Six of the main opposition parties united in the Democratic Opposition of Slovenia (DEMOS), which advocated economic independence.

20–23 January 1990: At its 14th (Extraordinary) Congress, the LCY voted to abolish its leading role in society, but rejected Slovenian proposals to restructure the federal party; the Slovenian delegation withdrew from the Congress and the League of Communists of Slovenia suspended its links with the LCY.

4 February 1990: A conference of the League of Communists of Slovenia renounced its links with the LCY and decided to change its name to the Party of Democratic Reform.

8 March 1990: The Slovenian Assembly renamed the territory the Republic of Slovenia.

April 1990: The opposition DEMOS coalition won the direct elections to the Assembly's main Socio-Political Chamber (obtaining 47 of the 80 seats); and emerged as the winner in the Chamber of Municipalities (the Chamber of Associated Labour was elected on a non-party basis). At the second round of voting Milan Kučan, the leader of the former communists, was elected President of the republican Presidency. The following month Lojze Peterle, leader of the Slovenian Christian Democratic Party (a member of DEMOS), was elected President of the Executive Council (premier).

2 July 1990: The Assembly proclaimed the full sovereignty of Slovenia.

28 September 1990: The Assembly asserted its jurisdiction over the Slovenian Territorial Defence Force; the move was denounced by the federal authorities, which, in January 1991, ordered that all 'unauthorized' armed units should surrender their weapons.

23 December 1990: A referendum, in which an overwhelming majority voted in favour of secession, was held in Slovenia, despite federal warnings of unconstitutionality and economic sanctions.

20 February 1991: The Slovenian Assembly adopted a resolution initiating its process of 'dissociation' from Yugoslavia, although it declared its willingness to negotiate on the federation's future as well as the details of secession.

8 May 1991: With the failure of various attempts to negotiate a new federation, Slovenia announced that it would secede from Yugoslavia by 26 June, resulting in tension between the Territorial Defence Force and the federal Yugoslav People's Army (YPA). Slovenia subsequently formed a new Slovenian Territorial Army.

25 June 1991: The Slovenian and Croatian Assemblies declared the independence and sovereignty of their Republics, formally beginning dissociation from the federation.

27 June 1991: The YPA began military operations in Slovenia, mobilizing to secure the international borders of the SFRY and bombing Ljubljana airport. Fighting continued intermittently over the next few weeks, despite European Community (EC) efforts to negotiate a cease-fire.

7–8 July 1991: The EC mediated a cease-fire in the former Yugoslavia and a three-month moratorium on further implementation of the Slovenian and Croatian declarations of dissociation.

2 October 1991: The Slovenian Assembly resolved to end all involvement in Yugoslavia after 7 October, the last day of the EC-negotiated moratorium. The last YPA troops left Slovenia, by sea, on 26 October.

23 December 1991: The Slovenian Constitution was enacted, providing for a bicameral legislature, with elections scheduled for 1992. In the same month the DEMOS coalition was dissolved.

15 January 1992: Slovenia was officially recognized by the EC (known as the European Union—EU after November 1993), having been recognized by Germany the previous month. The USA recognized the country in April and, on 22 May, it was admitted to the UN.

May 1992: As a result of a vote of 'no confidence' by the National Assembly (Državni zbor), Lojze Peterle resigned as Prime Minister. His successor was Dr Janez Drnovšek, leader of the Liberal Democratic Party (LDP) and a former President of the SFRY State Presidency.

6 December 1992: The first presidential and parliamentary elections since Slovenian independence were held; Kučan, the incumbent Head of State, was elected President of the Republic and Drnovšek was confirmed as Prime Minister, leading a coalition Government, composed mainly of members of the LDP (which later merged with three other parties to form the Liberal Democracy of Slovenia—LDS), the Slovenian Christian Democrats (SCD) and the United List alliance (subsequently known as the United List of Social Democrats—ULSD).

23 July 1993: Arms illegally destined for Bosnia and Herzegovina were discovered at Maribor airport; several leading Slovenian politicians were implicated in the scandal, including the Minister of Defence, Janez Janša.

April 1994: The Social Democratic Party of Slovenia (SDPS) left the coalition in protest at the dismissal from the cabinet of its President, Janša, the previous month.

June 1995: A meeting between the premiers of Croatia and Slovenia resolved most of the border dispute between them, although other issues remained subject to further negotiations.

November 1995: Slovenia recognized the Federal Republic of Yugoslavia (FRY—Serbia and Montenegro) following agreements on peace in the former SFRY.

26 January 1996: The ULSD became the second party to withdraw from the coalition, considerably limiting the Government's power to enact legislation.

10 June 1996: Having reached an accord with Italy, which had previously objected to Slovenia's application, the country finally signed an Association Agreement (Europe Agreement) with the EU. Later that month it was admitted, as an associate partner, to the Western European Union defence organization.

10 November 1996: Legislative elections were held; the Liberal Democracy of Slovenia (LDS) obtained 25 seats in the 90-seat Državni zbor, and subsequently increased its parliamentary bloc to 45, after securing the support of the ULSD, the Democratic Party of Pensioners of Slovenia (DeSUS), the Slovenian National Party (SNP) and the two deputies of the Hungarian and Italian minorities; however, an electoral alliance, known as the Slovenian Spring, comprising the Slovenian People's Party (SPP), the SDPS and the SCD, also obtained 45 seats.

9 January 1997: Following protracted negotiations over the nomination of a Prime Minister, which ended only when an SCD deputy defected from the Slovenian Spring to become an independent and agreed to support Drnovšek's candidacy, the new Državni zbor re-elected Drnovšek to the premiership; a coalition Government was approved in late February.

14 July 1997: In order to meet the requirements for ratification of the Europe Agreement, signed in June 1996, the Državni zbor voted in favour of amending an article of the Constitution, to allow foreigners to purchase land in Slovenia.

23 November 1997: In a presidential election Kučan won a second (and final) term of office, obtaining 55.6% of the votes cast.

26 November 1997: A new, 40-member National Council (Državni svet—parliament's upper house) was indirectly elected by an electoral college for a five-year term.

25 August 1998: Slovenia and Croatia agreed to begin negotiations on the future status of the jointly-owned Krško nuclear power station, which Slovenia had privatized in the previous month. In November it was announced that the dispute would be resolved on the basis of co-ownership.

10 November 1998: Accession negotiations on Slovenia's full EU membership began. The first meeting of the EU-Slovenia Association Council was held on 22 February 2000.

21 January 2000: The Minister of Foreign Affairs, Boris Frlec, resigned; he was replaced by a former Minister of Foreign Affairs and hitherto ambassador to the USA, Dimitrij Rupel, on 2 February.

3 April 2000: Following the announcement, in mid-March, that nine ministers belonging to the SPP were to resign their posts in mid-April (after which the SPP was to merge with the SCD), Drnovšek attempted to form a new Government, nominating eight independents to replace the SPP ministers; however, his proposals were defeated in the Državni zbor five days later and, no longer enjoying a parliamentary majority, he was obliged to resign.

3 May 2000: Andrej Bajuk, the nominee of Coalition Slovenia, an alliance formed by the new SPP–SCD party and the SDPS, narrowly won endorsement as premier in the Državni zbor in a third round of voting. Bajuk's administration was approved by parliament on 7 June; the new Government was to govern until legislative elections were held later in the year.

4 August 2000: Bajuk was elected chairman of a new political party, having resigned from the SPP. The new party would contest the legislative election as New Slovenia—Christian People's Party (NSi).

15 October 2000: In the general election the LDS obtained 36.3% of the votes cast, receiving 34 seats in the 90-member Državni zbor; the SDPS received 15.8% of the ballot (14 seats), the ULSD 12.1% (11 seats) and the SPP–SCD 9.6% (nine seats); NSi won eight seats.

1 December 2000: The Državni zbor endorsed the appointment of a new coalition Government led by Drnovšek and supported by the LDS, the ULSD, the SPP and DeSUS.

9 December 2000: Diplomatic relations were established between Slovenia and the FRY.

19 July 2001: Slovenia and Croatia signed agreements intended to resolve their outstanding border issues and confirming their joint management of the Krško nuclear plant.

24 January 2002: Janez Potocnik, in charge of negotiations on Slovenia's accession to the EU, was also appointed as a Minister without Portfolio, responsible for European Affairs.

15 April 2002: Former Prime Minister and Chairman of the Slovenian Parliamentary Commission for European Affairs, Lojze Peterle, was elected to represent the accession countries in the presidency of the Convention on the Future of the EU.

21 November 2002: At a summit meeting of the North Atlantic Treaty Organization (NATO), held in Prague, Czech Republic, Slovenia and six other countries were invited to accede to the Alliance in 2004.

1 December 2002: Drnovšek was elected President of the Republic, at a second round of voting (the first took place on 10 November), receiving 56.5% of the votes cast and defeating Barbara Brezigar, a state prosecutor supported by the SDPS and the NSi.

13 December 2002: At an historic EU summit meeting, held in Copenhagen, Denmark, Slovenia was one of 10 countries formally invited to become full members of the Union from 1 May 2004.

19 December 2002: The Državni zbor approved the composition of a new Government, headed by Anton Rop, a member of the LDS and hitherto Minister of Finance.

23 March 2003: At two national plebiscites, 89.6% of votes cast were in favour of Slovenia's accession to the EU, and 66.1% were in favour of NATO membership. The overall rate of participation in the referendums was 60.4%.

History

Dr CATHIE CARMICHAEL

EARLY HISTORY

The ancestors of the modern Slovenes probably settled in the Eastern Alps in the fifth or sixth centuries and formed part of a wave of migration from the East by Slavonic tribes. The oldest piece of writing in the Slovene language, the Freising Fragments from the ninth century, is also claimed variously by modern Czechs and Slovaks as an early example of their language. The extent of Slavonic settlement in the Alps was initially much wider, but this territory shrank over the centuries and by the 21st century Slovene was only spoken by small minorities in Austria and Italy, whose traditional culture had come under various assimilatory pressures. As a political state Slovenia was a relative latecomer, really only coming into existence as a Yugoslav republic at the end of 1945. Nevertheless, Slovenia's national history covered several centuries, as a discernible national consciousness clearly existed by the 16th century and probably predated this period. In the seventh century the Slovenes had an elaborate investiture ceremony (stoličevanje), which determined who would be Duke of Karantanija (roughly equivalent to modern Carinthia). Although the ducal stone used for this ceremony is in modern-day Austria, the modern Slovene state resisted Kosovo-style irredentism (by not using this as a national symbol) and pursued a policy of good relations with its neighbour. After 745 AD, the Slovenes lived under the domination of the Franks and were incorporated into the Holy Roman Empire and the Western Catholic Church.

THE SLOVENES UNDER HABSBURG DOMINATION

The Habsburg dynasty acquired Styria in 1278, followed by Carniola and Carinthia in 1335 and Trieste in 1385. Excluding only a small area of Italy, the vast majority of Slovenes lived under the rule of the Habsburgs until 1918. On the whole Slovene was the language of the peasants ruled over by a German-speaking nobility, although this dichotomy is rather simplistic; sections of the nobility such as the Dukes of Celje in the 15th century had a good deal of autonomy and it is evident from inventories of books in the 16th century that many also read Slovene. The 16th century was a great turning point in Slovene history. In 1573 a vast peasant rebellion uniting Slovenes and Kajkavian Croats and led by Matija Gubec was put down with brute force. The Habsburg authorities also suppressed the Slovene Reformation, which had led to the production of a vernacular Bible in 1584. Like Croatia, Slovenia also became the frontier of Christendom in the 16th century and experienced frequent Turkish incursions. There was a reduction in Slovene-language publication in the 17th and 18th centuries, but it experienced a rapid revival in the 19th century.

In 1791 the first recognizably modern history of the Slovenes was produced by Anton Linhart and in 1797 Valentin Vodnik produced the first Slovene newspaper. During the Napoleonic Wars (1803–15), the Slovene lands were incorporated into the Illyrian Provinces (1809–13) and vernacular publication was encouraged. Reincorporation into the Habsburg lands in 1815 meant that the Slovenes were gradually influenced by Central European cultural nationalism. Jernej Kopitar produced a standardized Slovene grammar in 1808 and the poet France Prešeren (1800–49) produced some of the greatest work in the language, including the national anthem 'Zdravljica'. In economic life, Dr Janez Bleiweis founded an agricultural society in 1843, which was to evolve into the Slovene People's Party in 1905. By 1848, with the outbreak of revolutions across the Habsburg monarchy, some Slovenes were to call for a *zedinjena Slovenija* (United Slovenia). Cultural nationalist activities then continued with the foundation of the Society of St Hermagoras in 1851 and also the establishment of *Slovenska matica* (Slovene Society) in 1864. After the reorganization of the state as a 'dual monarchy' in 1867 to accommodate Hungarian demands, Slovenes became increasingly involved in a 'trialist' solution to the monarchy's problems, which would recognize the Slavs as the third great element. South Slav political solutions also became increasingly attractive to the Slovenes in the years immediately preceding the First World War, although many, including the writer Ivan Cankar, had misgivings as to whether ethnic groups as different as the Serbs and Slovenes would be able to live comfortably in a single state, given their vastly different historical experiences. In the early 20th century notions of 'race' dominated political life and, from 1915–18, Slovene commitment to Yugoslavism increased, particularly with the formation of 'home rule' national councils in mid-1918. The defection of the Slovenes, particularly the influential cleric Anton Korošec, helped to bring down the old Habsburg dynasty in October. The Slovenes then rapidly moved into a new state ruled by the Karadjordjević dynasty, the Kingdom of Serbs, Croats and Slovenes, formed in December 1918

THE SLOVENES AND THE TWO YUGOSLAVIAS

The formation of the Yugoslav kingdom (formally renamed Yugoslavia in 1929) divided the Slovenes as a nation for virtually the first time in history. Slovenes living in the Klagenfurt basin decided to stay within Austria after a plebiscite in October 1920, although this was difficult to achieve in some areas, notably near the border. The Italians had been promised Slovene ethnic territory in the Treaty of London of 1915 (the punitive terms of which had helped to cement the Yugoslav orientation of Slovene politics) and, under the terms of the Treaty of Rapallo in November 1920, Italy gained the Adriatic littoral, Gorizia and a section of the Julian Alps. Italy and Austria then embarked on programmes designed to eradicate Slovene language and culture. Under the Italian Fascist leader, Benito Mussolini, Slavs were obliged to italianize their names and many intellectuals were moved to other parts of Italy to accelerate assimilation. The town of Ljubljana succeeded Klagenfurt (Celovec) and Trieste (Trst) as the central point of Slovene culture, a position it retained into the 21st century.

The Karadjordjević kingdom, which was considered by many of its subjects to be Serb-dominated, was beset with national problems from its inception, although it is fair to say that many Slovenes participated willingly in the new state, particularly the Slovene leader, Korošec, who became Prime Minister. The liberal Vidovdan Constitution of 1921 was suspended in 1929 when King Aleksandar (Alexander) began to rule as dictator until his assassination in 1934 by aggrieved Croatian and Macedonian nationalists. Aleksandar was replaced by a weak regency, and by 1939 Yugoslavia was disintegrating, with some Slovenes pressing for the same autonomies for their province of 'Dravska' that Croatia had gained in the so-called *Sporazum* (Mutual Understanding) of the same year.

Yugoslavia collapsed in April 1941, when German and Italian forces invaded and its Government fled to London, the United Kingdom. Slovene Styria and a part of Carniola were annexed to the German Third Reich, while control of the south, including Ljubljana, went to the Italians. A Liberation Front, composed of liberals, Christian socialists (including one of Slovenia's greatest writers, Edvard Kocbek) and communists (including Boris Kidrić; and Edvard Kardelj, a Stalinist theorist of the national question who, after the war ended, would become the most influential mind in the Yugoslav leader Tito's inner circle) was formed on 27 April to oppose the occupation. Nationalists formed the so-called *Domobranci* (Home Defence) and frequently collaborated with the occupying forces against the combined left. Nevertheless, the divisions in Slovene politics were never quite as extreme as elsewhere in continental Europe either in the 1940s or the 1990s. The Liberation Front joined forces with the Yugoslav partisans, led by Josip Broz (Tito), and by 1945 drove out the remaining Germans, who had taken over from the Italians after the latter's collapse in 1943. In addition, these combined forces also liberated Trieste in May 1945.

The victorious communists chose to remake Yugoslavia as a federal state of national republics, modelled closely on the USSR. They duly proclaimed a Socialist Republic of Slovenia in January 1946 and added a small Adriatic littoral, consisting of the towns of Koper, Izola and Piran to the territory (although this area had only a small historically Slovene population). Italians and Germans fled the new communist state and their homes were taken by the local Slavs, a process that made Slovenia remarkably ethnically homogeneous by Central European standards. Although the Yugoslavs had wished to retain Trieste, they were overruled by the Soviet leader, Stalin (Iosif V. Dzhugashvili), and the Western Allies, which insisted that the status of the city be resolved by the UN's Free Territory of Trieste, in 1946. The city was then partitioned into zones A and B. Only the latter zone, which contained the suburbs but no economically important features, was retained by Yugoslavia. The loss of Trieste (which was confirmed in 1954) with its Slovene-speaking proletariat was an incalculable economic and cultural blow for the fledgling republic. However, the existence of Slovene communities outside the communist republic ensured that there was a free-flow of ideas from the West as well as a flourishing black market (the parallel, illegal economy).

From 1948 Kardelj set about reshaping the ideological bases of Yugoslav socialism, including economic decentralization (which, his critics stated, favoured Slovenia) and an international policy of non-alignment. Nevertheless, the second Yugoslavia, like the first, was beset by nationalist problems, which began to emerge in the 1960s. Inter-republican tensions erupted in mid-1969 when the Slovenes protested to the central Government over the redirection of funds lent by the World Bank to rebuild the Karawanken tunnel (linking Slovenia to Austria). In 1974 a new Constitution was introduced, intended to devolve power even further by giving more authority to the republics, which had the theoretical right to secede from the Federation.

THE DISINTEGRATION OF YUGOSLAVIA 1980–91

The deaths of Edvard Kardelj in 1979 and of Tito in May 1980 marked the end of an era in Slovenian politics. Tito was not replaced by a strong leader to unite all Yugoslavs, and Slovene nationalism began to emerge as a response to this power vacuum. In 1981 the journal *Nova revija* was founded and its editors were clearly inspired by the Polish *Solidarność* (Solidarity) movement. In 1987 it published an edition on the 'Slovenian National Programme' that looked at the perceived negative position of the Slovenes within the Socialist Federal Republic of Yugoslavia (SFRY—as the country had been renamed in 1963). Slovenia also experienced a cultural revolution in the 1980s, led by the youth journals *Mladina* and *Katedra* and the independent Radio Študent. Intellectuals and artists flirted with previously forbidden ideas and concepts, including the idea of an independent Slovenia. The Slovenes also began to create closer ties with their non-communist neighbours through organizations such as *Alpe-Adria*. Within the SFRY, Slovenia defended the civil liberties of the Kosovar Albanians who lived under martial law after riots in 1986. In 1987 the election of a Serbian leader willing to use extreme Serb nationalism to legitimize his own position unleashed a dangerous factor into Yugoslav politics. For Slobodan Milošević and his supporters, Slovenian freedom of expression was anathema; from the mid-1980s the small Alpine republic was provoked with economic boycotts and with threats of rallies.

On 27 September 1989 a majority in the Slovenian Assembly adopted a constitutional amendment asserting republican sovereignty. On 13 December the newly formed opposition coalition, Democratic Opposition of Slovenia (DEMOS), announced its alternative political programme, which included economic sovereignty for Slovenia, the suspension of federal legislation, the introduction of a temporary Slovenian monetary unit and a commitment to a plebiscite on independence. In January 1990 the entire Slovenian delegation withdrew from an emergency congress of the Yugoslavian League of Communists. The League of Communists of Slovenia (LCS) officially left the League of Communists of Yugoslavia in the following month, having renamed itself the Party of Democratic Reform (PDR) and arranged for democratic elections to be held. Although DEMOS won an overall majority in the elections of April 1990, with 126 of the 240 contested seats, the PDR candidate, Milan Kučan, defeated the DEMOS candidate, Jože Pučnik, to be President. The Christian Democrat, Lojze Peterle, became Prime Minister. On 2 July, by an overwhelming majority, the Državni zbor (Slovenian National Assembly) declared Slovenia to be an independent state, without explicitly confronting the issue of secession. From that time, Slovenian laws were to take precedence over federal laws. In September Slovenia refused to accept the authority of the Federal Constitution on the grounds that the Kosovar Albanians had effectively been excluded from the Federal Assembly.

The question of Slovenian involvement in the Yugoslavian People's Army (YPA), which had played a notable role in the republic's politics in the late 1980s, when several journalists, including the future Minister of Defence, Janez Janša, had been arrested and charged with leaking military secrets, emerged again in 1990. In February Slovenia withdrew its units from Kosovo and announced its intention to control its own frontier posts and the YPA units within the country. In July the YPA seized territorial defence weapons, including most of Slovenia's heavy artillery, and ignored an ultimatum issued for their return by 10 August. When the YPA refused to allow Slovenian conscripts to carry out their military service solely in Slovenia, the republican Government suspended military payments in retaliation. Following the crisis in 1988, when the communist authorities had effectively protected citizens against the wrath of the YPA, the Government, including Janša, reorganized their territorials into a republican army. In October 1990 the YPA forcibly took control of the republican army's headquarters in Ljubljana, which led Slovenia to accelerate its plans. In the same month Croatia and Slovenia proposed a restructuring of Yugoslavia into an alliance of sovereign states, which would control their own foreign policies, with only a consultative parliament remaining in Belgrade. The Slovenian Government then organized a plebiscite on independence. Of the 93.5% of the electorate who voted on 26 December, 88.5% supported full independence. Over the next six months the Slovenian Government made the necessary arrangements to finalize the transfer of power from federal to republican bodies. In January 1991 Croatia and Slovenia signed mutual defence agreements, and in March conscription to the YPA was suspended.

THE REPUBLIC OF SLOVENIA FROM 1991

On 25 June 1991 Slovenia and Croatia declared full independence from the SFRY and ordered their own territorial forces to take control of borders. The YPA initially restricted its troop movements to the seizure of international borders on 27 and 28 June, but an impasse was reached when the Slovenes refused to countenance a cease-fire until the YPA had returned to barracks. Over the following week there was aerial bombardment of Brnik (Ljubljana) airport, a number of ambushes, blockades of military bases and mass desertions from the YPA. Official figures stated that 79 were killed, some of whom were Turkish lorry drivers caught up in an ambush. The Slovenian Government also waged a 'diplomatic war', which effectively secured Slovenian independence and a non-military defeat of Yugoslav forces.

On 28 June 1991 a 'troika' of European Community (EC, known as the European Union—EU from November 1993) foreign ministers from Italy, Luxembourg and the Netherlands initiated negotiations for a cease-fire between the federal authorities, the YPA and the Slovenian Government. This included a three-month suspension of Slovenian independence and a return to barracks by YPA troops. By 5 July Slovenia had demobilized 10,000 men and the EC had imposed an arms embargo on Yugoslavia. Further plans, agreed on 7 July, allowed an unarmed European mission to monitor the cease-fire and gave control of the international borders to the Slovenian police. YPA troops were to be withdrawn from Slovenia by 25 October. On 7 October Slovenia issued its own currency, the tolar. In December a new Constitution was adopted, based upon the principle of the division of power between the judiciary, executive and legislature. The 90-member Državni zbor was to be elected for a four-year term and the directly elected President was to serve for five years. On 15 January 1992 the countries of the EC officially recognized Slovenian independence, followed by the USA in April. Slovenia was admitted to the UN in May 1992, and served a two-year mandate between January 1998 and 2000 as a member of the UN Security Council.

On 6 December 1992 Slovenia held its first post-independence parliamentary and presidential elections. Milan Kučan was confirmed in the largely ceremonial post of President, winning 63.9% of the votes cast. On 10 November 1997 Kučan was re-elected for a second, final term with 55.6% of the votes

cast. Despite the fact that his powers were limited, Kučan was considered to have a stabilizing influence on politics. It was noteworthy that Slovenia managed to avoid excessive recriminations about its communist past and individuals associated with the old regime were not isolated from the mainstream as they were, for example, in the Czech Republic. The 1992 elections failed to secure a majority for any party. Janez Drnovšek, an economist and a former member of the Yugoslavian presidium, who had taken over from Peterle in May 1992, formed a coalition Government in January 1993, comprising his own party, the Liberal Democratic Party of Slovenia (LDS), the Slovenian Christian Democrats (SCD), the United List (an alliance including some former communists, later renamed the United List of Social Democrats—(ULSD), and the Social Democratic Party of Slovenia (SDPS). Although often pilloried in the Slovenian satirical press, Kučan's personal popularity grew from the time of his election, and he remained President until late 2002, serving two full terms of office (see below).

The importance of personalities in Slovenian politics has often been noted by commentators; in part this is probably owing to the small size of the political elite. Individuals also change roles with reasonable frequency. Dimitrij Rupel, a former academic and a nationalist ideologue, was Slovenia's first Minister of Foreign Affairs at the time of independence. He subsequently became Mayor of Ljubljana, in 1992–97, prior to serving as ambassador to the USA. In February 2000, following the resignation of Boris Frlec, he was re-appointed Minister of Foreign Affairs, a position that he retained in Drnovšek's new Government, appointed in December.

The first coalition Government was particularly characterized by ill-tempered infighting, partly because of the volatile personality and influence of Janez Janša. In July 1993, as Minister of Defence and leader of the SDPS, he was implicated in an arms-trading scandal. Following his dismissal from the Government, in March 1994, Janša withdrew his party from the coalition. In April 1998 the SDPS alleged that Drnovšek had violated the Constitution by signing a secret security agreement with Israel in 1995. Janša's proposal that Drnovšek be impeached the following month was rejected by the Državni zbor in June and indirectly led to Janša's own resignation as head of Slovenia's delegation to the North Atlantic Treaty Organization (NATO) in the same month. In September 1994 Peterle resigned as Minister of Foreign Affairs in protest at what he believed was disproportionate LDS representation in the Government. (In the same year the LDS had merged with the Greens of Slovenia—Eco-Social Party and a number of other smaller left-wing groups.) Peterle was replaced by Zoran Thaler, another LDS member.

In 1994 the Italian Government stated that until Slovenia agreed to compensate Italian nationals who had fled from Istria after the Second World War and had thereby lost their property, it would obstruct Slovenian efforts to join the EU. This action delayed scheduled Slovenian-EU accession negotiations by several years and it was not until May 1996 that the two countries reached a compromise agreement. Slovenia was to amend its Constitution to allow EU nationals to purchase property within four years of the Association Agreement (Europe Agreement) being ratified; EU citizens who had previously been resident in Slovenia for three years would be allowed to purchase property immediately. Although this excluded the Italian nationals, it was seen by some politicians as a betrayal of Slovenia's national interest and the SCD proposed a motion of 'no confidence' in Thaler. On the same day Drnovšek, angered by the attempt to destabilize his Government, dissolved the coalition, although he reversed this decision the next day and retained Thaler as acting Minister of Foreign Affairs. Thaler resigned from this post in July 1997, following opposition claims that Slovenia's accession to the EU would be on less favourable terms than other states (his negotiated agreement on EU accession had been ratified by the Državni zbor in the same month).

In legislative elections, held on 10 November 1996, the LDS increased its number of deputies to 25 and forged a strong coalition with the ULSD, the Democratic Party of Pensioners of Slovenia (DeSUS), the Slovenian National Party (SNP), and the Italian and Hungarian minorities parties, bringing its overall parliamentary representation to 45. However, an electoral alliance known as the Slovenian Spring, comprising the Slovenian People's Party (SPP), the SCD and the SDPS, also obtained 45 seats. President Kučan proposed that Drnovšek continue as premier; however, it was not until January 1997 that he was re-elected by the Državni zbor, after an SDPS deputy had become an independent. Finally, in February the SPP agreed to join a government coalition with the LDS and DeSUS.

In March 2000, in an attempt to broaden the appeal of the centre-right parties, the SPP and the SCD announced that they were to merge in the following month, at which time the nine SPP ministers would withdraw from the governing coalition. In early April Drnovšek, who no longer commanded a parliamentary majority, nominated eight independents to replace the departing ministers. However, his proposed new Government failed to receive endorsement in the Državni zbor, and the premier was forced to resign. Following their merger, the SPP and the SCD formed an electoral alliance known as Coalition Slovenia, which then nominated Andrej Bajuk as a candidate for the leadership; he was confirmed as Prime Minister in May. His interim coalition administration, which included Peterle as Minister of Foreign Affairs and Janša as Minister of Defence, governed until the legislative elections were held on 15 October.

The elections were a decisive rejection of Bajuk's style of government and right-wing orientation, in particular his 'special relationship' with the Roman Catholic Church and largesse in appointing close associates to principal posts. Drnovšek's LDS increased its share of the votes cast by 9%, obtaining 36.3% and 34 seats. The ULSD obtained 12.1% of the votes cast, while Janša's SDPS took 15.8% of the votes cast (down slightly on its 1996 total), but the real loser of the election was the newly merged New Slovenia—Christian People's Party (NSi), formed following a split in the SPP (which had merged with the SCD in April 2000), with 8.6% of the votes. The remnants of the SPP secured 9.6%, compared with a combined total of 29.0% for the SPP and the SCP in 1996. Drnovšek formed a new coalition Government, which included the LDS, the ULSD, the SPP and DeSUS, in December 2000.

Kučan was succeeded as President in late 2002 by Janez Drnovšek. The latter received 44.4% of votes cast in the first round of voting, on 10 November, but encountered a serious challenge from Barbara Breziger (who received 30.8%, contesting the election as an independent, but with the support of the SPDS and NSi). In the second round polls, on 1 December, Drnovšek received 56.5% of the popular vote, clearly indicating that Slovenians prefer continuity to change in political life. Following the appointment of Anton Rop of the LDS as premier in mid-December, most of the key posts in the Government remained unchanged.

FOREIGN RELATIONS

Independent Slovenia sought closer integration into the international community, particularly the EU and NATO. In May 1993 Slovenia joined the Council of Europe and participated in NATO's 'Partnership for Peace' programme. Slovenian troops formed part of the NATO-led stabilization force (SFOR) in Bosnia and Herzegovina in 1996–98 and were deployed in Albania in 1997. They also formed part of the NATO-Russian peace-keeping force, KFOR, in Kosovo after 1999. Never-

theless, Slovenia's application to be included in the first round of NATO enlargement was rejected in 1997. During his time as Prime Minister, Drnovšek continued to regard membership as a key policy objective and argued that Slovenia's long-term interests lay with that Organization. US President Bill Clinton visited Slovenia in mid-1999, as did his successor, George W. Bush, in June 2001 (when he visited Slovenia to participate in a summit with Russian President Vladimir Putin), cementing already good Slovenian-US relations, and the Slovenian Government tried to promote itself as a 'bridge' between East and West. Drnovšek saw the eventual success of this policy when in November 2002, at a NATO summit held in Prague, Czech Republic, Slovenia was formally invited to join in the next round of NATO expansion in 2004. It is perhaps because of this success rather than his personal charisma that Drnovšek was able to succeed the popular Kučan as President.

At the time of independence, Slovenia's politicians expressed the hope that Slovenia would enjoy closer relations with Western European institutions and countries. In 1998 Slovenia began its 'Strategy for Accession to the European Union'. By early 2002 it had harmonized most of its laws with the *acquis communautaire* of the EU (that is, the body of EU legislation, treaties and case law) and closed its 'duty free' shops in July 2001. In April 2002 there was a public outcry over the planned sale of stakes in the state-owned banks, Nova Ljubljanska Banka and Nova Kreditna Banka Maribor, to foreign owners (in line with EU recommendations on privatization), indicating that some popular resentment about the implementation of strict EU norms remained. Also in April former Prime Minister Peterle was elected to represent candidate countries at the presidency of the Convention on the Future of the EU in Brussels, Belgium, seemingly in acknowledgement of his crucial role in negotiations with the EC in 1991–92. In December 2002 Slovenia was invited to become a full member of the EU, moving away from its associate member status with the signature of the Treaty of Accession in Athens, Greece, in April 2003, in the expectation that it would join the Union on 1 May 2004, at the same time as nine other countries. The Slovenian public voted in favour of both NATO and EU membership in a referendum held on 23 March 2003. Of the votes cast, 89.6% supported accession to the EU and 66.1% favoured membership of NATO.

Relations with neighbouring Austria were somewhat strained in the mid-1990s, echoing the problems that Slovenia faced with Italy. The Slovenian press were critical of the nationalist Austrian Freedom Party (FPÖ), particularly its leader (and Governor of Kärnten—Carinthia) Jörg Haider, for many years, as they witnessed concerted attacks on the civil rights of the Slovene minority in the neighbouring republic. Slovenia was also unwilling to endorse the claim in some Austrian quarters that it had a minority of Slovenes of German origin or that it might owe compensation to ethnic Germans who lost their properties in 1945 as a result of the so-called AVNOJ resolutions, which sought to expel ethnic Germans from communist-controlled Yugoslavia.

Relations with Croatia were also problematic at times. The nuclear plant at Krško was divided between the two republics in 1995, but in July 1998 Slovenia disconnected power lines to Croatia after the latter refused to pay for its energy supply (supply was subsequently restored). In November both sides agreed to resolve the Krško dispute on the basis of co-ownership. Although the Governments of both republics were united in their opposition to Istrian autonomy and keen to retain the terms of the 1975 Treaty of Osimo, which had delineated the Yugoslavian–Italian border, the two countries could not always agree where their mutual borders should lie. By 1993 there were eight disputed border territories, of which the Piran region in Istria proved to be the most awkward, although 98% of the disputed border territories had been attributed by June 1995. After January 2000, with the installation of a new Croatian Government, bilateral relations improved markedly and previously difficult issues had been largely resolved by July 2001.

On the whole, Slovenia supported NATO's aerial bombardment of the Federal Republic of Yugoslavia (FRY—now Serbia and Montenegro) in 1999 and participated in the UN Interim Administration Mission in Kosovo (UNMIK). After the fall of Milošević, following the Yugoslav presidential election of September 2000, Slovenia established diplomatic and economic relations with the FRY and cultivated the new President, Vojislav Koštunica, as a potential ally. Relations with Montenegro, which entered into a three-year bilateral agreement with Serbia in 2002, also improved considerably. In foreign

affairs, independent Slovenia avoided the extremes of some of the other former Yugoslav countries and its Western neighbours, particularly Austria and Italy. Although Slovenia has its own far-right party, the SNP, which obtained 4.4% of the votes cast in the October 2000 election, while its leader, Zmago Jelinčič, managed to secure over 8% of the votes cast in the presidential elections in 2002, on the whole Slovenian politics has coalesced around the political centre. Many Yugoslavs living in Slovenia in 1991 chose to remain and take Slovenian citizenship, even though the 1991 Constitution did not give them the same rights as the tiny Hungarian and Italian populations. Although cultural 'Yugo-nostalgia' was not uncommon in the Alpine republic, at the beginning of the 21st century Slovenia could no longer be meaningfully regarded as part of the Balkans.

The Economy

Dr DAVID A. DYKER

INTRODUCTION

Slovenia was the most developed of the republics of the former Yugoslavia. By the 1960s it was reporting levels of national income per head of nearly twice the Yugoslav average and it consistently accounted for the bulk of Yugoslavia's hard-currency exports. These strengths carried over into the transition period. By the beginning of the 21st century Slovenia was by far the richest of the Central and South-Eastern European countries, with a gross domestic product (GDP) per head in 2002 of US $10,495, compared with $6,780 in the Czech Republic, $6,370 in Hungary and $4,924 in Poland. Slovenia was the only one of these countries that did not suffer from recurrent weakness in the balance of payments throughout the 1990s and into the early 2000s. It was an ethnically and geographically compact country, with no serious problems relating to ethnic minorities or critical regional economic imbalances. Nevertheless, there were problem areas in Slovenia's relations with some of its neighbours. Although Slovenia's involvement in the wars in the former Yugoslavia in the late 1990s was marginal, the increase in popularity of the far right in Austrian politics (from a base in the Slovenian-minority area of Austria) caused difficulties in relations with Slovenia's northern neighbour. Furthermore, Slovenia had not completely resolved its disagreement with Croatia over territorial waters and other issues. However, by late 2002 serious negotiations were under way on the possible sale of the Croatian share in the disputed Krško nuclear power station to Slovenia, while a provisional regime for fishing rights in the disputed Bay of Piran was in effective operation. None of these problems was on a scale that would seriously affect Slovenia's economic relations with its neighbours, or its steady progress towards membership of the European Union (EU). Indeed the prospect of the latter, for Croatia as well as for Slovenia, was one the main driving forces for better relations between the two countries. Slovenia's sustained efforts to accommodate the requirements of the EU *acquis communautaire* (the list of important regulations and common policies taken to define it as a single market) were rewarded in December 2002, when the EU's Copenhagen summit (Denmark) approved the accession of Slovenia to the EU, along with seven other transition countries (as well as Cyprus and Malta), to take effect in May 2004, following approval of membership by a referendum held in March 2003.

ECONOMIC PERFORMANCE

Slovenia's economic performance over the years of transition was steady rather than spectacular. Following an initial de-

cline in 1991–92, from 1993 GDP increased at an average annual rate of around 4%. Real GDP increased by 5.2% in 1999, by 4.6% in 2000 and by 2.9% in 2001. The growth rate held steady at 3.2% in 2002, and growth of 2.7% was anticipated in 2003. The rate of unemployment was 5.9% (according to ILO definitions) in 2001, considerably lower than in most Central and South-Eastern European countries. Provisional data suggested that the unemployment rate remained at about the same level in 2002. The annual inflation rate declined from 7.9% in 1998 to 6.1% in 1999, but increased slightly in 2000, to 8.8%. Thereafter it registered a steady decline, measuring 8.4% in 2001 and 7.5% in 2002. Slovenia's record on budgetary balance was one of the best in the transition region, with a fiscal deficit in 2001 of just 1.6% of GDP. Provisional data for 2002 suggested a deficit in that year of just under 1% of GDP, and the Government was aiming to maintain that pattern in 2003–04. Economic activity had been successfully reorientated towards the countries of the EU; in 1990 the Yugoslav market accounted for 62% of total Slovenian deliveries outside its borders, while in 2002 nearly as high a percentage of Slovenian exports went to the EU market. In 2001 somewhat less than one-fifth of Slovenian exports were to the successor states of the former Socialist Federal Republic of Yugoslavia. All of this took place in the context of a significant, but not dramatic, structural reorientation away from industry, towards services. Thus, the contribution of industry to GDP as a whole fell from over 40% in 1991 to 36.8% in 2001. In that year the sector engaged 38.1% of the employed labour force. In contrast, the contribution of the services sector to the economy increased at an average annual rate of 2.0% per year in the 1990s. In 2001 it contributed 60.1% of GDP and employed 52.1% of the employed labour force. Against that background the export of manufactured products remained Slovenia's principal source of foreign currency, with manufacturing accounting for 93.6% of total exports in 2001, and for 93.5% in 2002. The manufacturing sector as a whole contributed 26.8% of GDP in 2001, and subsidies by the state to manufacturing represented just 3% of GDP generated in that sector in 2000, compared with 9.5% in 1998. Some other important sectors of the economy, however, remained heavily dependent on state support. Thus state aid accounted for 32.9% of agricultural GDP and 6.5% of mining GDP in 2000. Overall, state aid to the economy accounted for 2.1% of GDP in 2000, compared with 3.5% in 1998. It has been agreed that a number of Slovenian state aid programmes, notably in the areas of mining, agriculture and the environment, will continue after EU accession, with a final closing date of December 2009. Central government consumption was equivalent to 21.3% of GDP in 2001. A substantial proportion of gross fixed investment expenditure, which in total accounted for 24.9% of GDP in 2001, was also in the government sector.

There was, then, no 'shock therapy' in Slovenia. Given the country's 40-year experience of a quasi-market economy under the Yugoslav system of 'self-managed socialism', and a relatively high level of economic development at the outset of transition, this was, perhaps, not surprising. Yet for all Slovenia's success, there were indications that the structural evolution of the economy was rather slow-moving. Unit values of exports dropped steadily throughout the 1990s and at the end of the decade a significant deficit in the balance of payments emerged. Until 1997 the country's current account of the balance of payments was in surplus (US $50.4m. in 1997). However, in 1998 this turned into a deficit of $118.0m. and in 1999 the deficit increased, to $698.3m., before steadying at $547.7m. in 2000. A modest surplus, of $30.9m. was achieved in 2001, with a much more substantial surplus of $374.8m. (equivalent to 1.8% of GDP) recorded in 2002. The trade deficit was over $1,400m. in both 1999 and 2000, but was reduced to just under $1,000m. in 2001, owing to an increase in exports of machinery and equipment. During the transition years the Slovenian corporate sector as a whole never recorded a net profit. In consequence, levels of new investment in manufacturing remained at a relatively low level. Gross fixed investment grew slowly in absolute terms through the early 2000s, but fell as a proportion of GDP, from 27.4% in 1999 to 24.9% in 2001.

PRIVATIZATION

The pace of privatization in Slovenia was slow, and in 1999 the private sector accounted for just 55% of GDP, compared with 80% in Hungary. At the turn of the century many large companies in the steel, aluminium and petroleum industries remained a part of the state-owned Development Corporation of Slovenia. Where privatization was implemented, it was usually on the basis of a management-employee buy-out. This tended to reinforce 'insider' interest, which, to a considerable extent, controlled enterprises under the old self-management system and made it difficult for external strategic investors to impose restructuring programmes. The pace of privatization began to accelerate in early 2001, with the focus on the banking sector. In January of that year the Slovenian Government began to make preparations for the privatization of Nova Ljubljanksa Banka d.d. (NLB), the largest bank in the country, and Nova Kreditna Banka Maribor d.d. (NKBM), another of the leading banks. In 2002 a 34% stake in NLB was sold to KBC Bank NV of Belgium, with the state retaining a 33% share. By late 2002, however, it appeared that the Government wished to maintain a controlling interest in NKBM, with NKBM merging with one of the smaller banks to give it a stronger base for competing with NLB. A similar story seemed to be unfolding in the insurance sector, with the largest company, Triglav Insurance Co d.d., about to be privatized, and plans to use the second largest company, Maribor Insurance Co d.d., as the focal point of a consolidation drive. The deadline for privatizing Telekom Slovenije has been put back from 2003 until 2005, but in the mean time the state had reduced its stake to 65%. Overall, the maintenance of a degree of insider control, and of effective domestically-owned competition, continued to be among the major features of the process of privatization in Slovenia.

FOREIGN INVESTMENT

The stock of foreign direct investment (FDI) per head in Slovenia was quite high, in relation to the transition region as a whole. In 1999 Slovenia had a cumulative FDI per head of just over US $2,000, compared with $2,500 in Hungary, the front-runner on FDI among the transition countries. However, while FDI had been a sustained trend in Hungary for a period of 10 years, the Slovenian figure largely reflected the privatization of NLB in 2002, when the stock of FDI in Slovenia nearly doubled. Until 2001 trends in FDI in Slovenia were, in fact, rather weak. The $320.8m. of investment reported in 1997 was a record, but the impetus was not maintained and in 1998 only $165.0m. was invested in the country. The figure declined further in 1999, to $143.5m., and to under $100m. in 2000. In 2001, however, the figure rose to $503m., before soaring to $1,865m. in 2002.

The pattern of privatization as it developed in the 1990s, which favoured those already employed in the enterprise being divested, rather than outside investment, effectively served to inhibit foreign take-overs of existing companies. However, the need to assimilate the requirements of the *acquis communautaire* as a condition of EU accession compelled the Slovenian Government and legislature to remove significant barriers to FDI, such as restrictions on the rights of foreigners to buy land in Slovenia, and restrictions relating to the capital account of the balance of payments. Therefore, there was little genuinely new foreign investment in Slovenia in the late 1990s, and indeed by 2000 the great bulk of annual FDI in Slovenia was represented by the re-invested profits of existing foreign investors. The recovery in FDI during 2001 reflected a spate of new developments—in the banking sector the takeover of SKB Banka by Société Générale of France in May 2001, the acquisition of the mobile telecommunications operator, SI.MOBIL d.d., by Mobilkom Austria in February, and the take-over of the Pivovarna Union brewery by Belgium's Interbrew in October, prior to the sale, in 2002, of the 34% stake in NLB. It is perhaps a little early to proclaim Slovenia a high-FDI country on a parallel with Hungary, with so much of the total being the consequence of a single deal. None the less, by 2003 Slovenia was beginning to show the kind of FDI profile that would be expected on the basis of its endowment in human capital and infrastructure.

THE BANKING AND FINANCIAL SYSTEM

In 2000 as much as 41.3% of the assets of the Slovenian banking system remained in the possession of state-owned banks (compared with just over 10% in Hungary). In January 1999 new banking legislation was passed, which, for the first time, allowed foreign banks to establish branches in Slovenia. Restrictions remained, however: such branches would have to obtain a licence from the Bank of Slovenia, would be subject to minimum capital requirements and would have to submit to central bank supervision. The first branch of a foreign bank in Slovenia (Kärntner Sparkasse of Austria) was duly established in June 1999. However, no immediate influx on the part of other foreign banks to obtain a share in the Slovenian retail banking market subsequently occurred. Foreign banks did increase their aggregate share of total lending in Slovenia during 2000 and early 2001, but the trend was reversed in the second half of 2001. Developments in 2001 and 2002 changed the situation substantially. By early 2003 some 30%–35% of Slovenian banking assets were foreign-owned, and the effective degree of foreign control of the industry was substantially higher, with the great bulk of bank credit now originating from banks with a dominant foreign interest. Until Slovenia acceded to the EU, however, foreign banks would continue to be barred from retail bank activity except through a branch or subsidiary. The Ljubljana Stock Exchange remained underdeveloped, with market capitalization standing at just 10.4% of GDP at 31 December 2002. Market capitalization did, however, grow by as much as 57.6% in 2002, reflecting in part a series of liberalizing measures implemented by the Bank of

Slovenia. The comparative buoyancy of the stock market in 2002 was also related to the increase in the value of shares in the Lek Pharmaceutical and Chemical Company d.d., prior to its takeover by the Swiss Novartis company.

THE TECHNOLOGY FACTOR

The Slovenian economy in transition was generally characterized by a relatively weak impetus to structural change, with company management dominated by conservative insider interests closely associated with the state, while foreign investment, banks and the stock market remained insufficiently developed to provide genuine strategic alternatives. However, while in Slovenia FDI did not play the critical role in upgrading technology that it had in, for example, Hungary, there was a clear correlation between foreign investment and the closeness of networking between Slovenian companies and foreign ones. This meant that foreign investment helped Slovenian firms to develop the kind of relationship with foreign firms that maximized the scope for technology transfer into Slovenia. Nor was it solely the foreign-owned Slovenian companies that developed relationships with foreign companies. A number of domestically owned companies also enjoyed the status of first-tier supplier *vis-à-vis* major multinationals. That meant that they supplied complex parts (engines or gear-boxes to an automobile manufacturer, for example) and were actively involved in the design and development of these parts. The status of first-tier supplier maximized the scope for technology transfer through industrial networking. However, to be a first-tier supplier, the company needed to be already at a very high technological level. It was striking that Slovenia was the only transition country where there were a significant number of domestically owned first-tier suppliers. While this basically reflected the technological legacy left to Slovenia by the former Yugoslavia, the legacy was reinforced by government measures. The industrial clustering programme, introduced in 1999, was aimed explicitly at the strengthening of industrial networking and specialization. Other government programmes targeted best practice benchmarking and support measures for international marketing, while support was also given to technology-based small and medium-sized enterprises (SMEs). Therefore, while state aid played an ambivalent role in the process of restructuring the Slovenian economy, often being disbursed on an *ad hoc* basis and poorly targeted towards new investment, other policy elements were clearly orientated to structural and technological dynamism.

Despite outstanding performance by individual firms and sensible government policies, however, the overall technological level of the Slovenian economy remained low at the beginning of the 21st century. In a 2003 survey of levels of national competitiveness of the world's most advanced economies, conducted by the International Institute for Management Development (IMD—based in Lausanne, Switzerland), Slovenia was ranked only 56th of 50 countries and nine regions in the science, technology and human resources category. The general trend in Slovenia's international competitiveness, nevertheless, registered a clear, if modest, improvement during 2000–03, in terms of absolute IMD survey scores, if not in terms of rankings. Slovenia showed up particularly well in IMD surveys of general productivity growth, ranking seventh in the 2002 survey. Indeed the growth of labour productivity in manufacturing accelerated throughout 1999, and averaged 6.9% in 2000 year-on-year, before easing back to 2.1% in 2001. As a result, real unit labour costs fell by 2.9% in 2000, and again by 0.4% in 2001, despite substantial increases in wages. Significant real appreciation of the tolar during 2001 and 2002, however, resulted in a decline in international competitiveness in the early 2000s.

EU ACCESSION

In negotiating full membership of the EU with the European Commission, Slovenia faced a range of problems common to all the accession countries. In essence the EU did not negotiate over accession; rather it presented aspiring members with the *acquis communautaire* and requested that potential members bring their own existing regulations and policies into alignment as a prior condition of accession. Slovenia's accession task list could be divided into two principal categories: achieving alignment with the *acquis communautaire* and preparing the economy for the competition it would face upon entry.

By the end of 2001 Slovenia had provisionally closed negotiations with the European Commission on 26 of the 29 chapters of the *acquis*, leaving just agriculture, regional policy and budgetary provisions outstanding. Progress had been particularly impressive in relation to sensitive areas, such as the environment and law enforcement. Slovenia was especially commended by the European Commission for the relative efficiency and probity of its legal and administrative institutions, which were to play a key role after accession in terms of supervising the implementation of the treaties of the EU. However, a number of major problem areas remained. In the report on Slovenia's progress towards EU accession published in mid-2002, the European Commission identified insufficient progress in the areas of price liberalization, labour-law reform, judicial reform and support measures for SMEs. Among substantive issues, agriculture and state aids were among the most difficult to resolve. In particular, Slovenia disapproved of the Commission's proposal, announced in January 2002, that the farmers of candidate countries would be paid only partial income support for several years after accession. In September some 10,000 farmers demonstrated outside the Slovenian parliament, demanding greater public-sector funding and enhanced protection after EU accession. However, in October, at a European Council meeting in Brussels, Belgium, a compromise was reached, whereby farmers in all the new member states would initially receive 25% of the income support payable to farmers in existing member states. The figure would rise by 5% per year until 2007, and subsequently by 10% per year, bringing farmers from new member states up to the full income support level in 2013, assuming accession in 2004 and subject to the imposition of a maximum level of total EU expenditure on agriculture. The system of state aid to the economy presented similar problems; in particular, any such aid would be required to originate from the EU's Structural Funds and Cohesion Fund, and through EU and national research and development funds. Again, in the event, a compromise was reached, with the European Commission agreeing to a number of transition periods for Slovenian state aid; notably, state assistance for the closure and restoration of former mines was to be permitted until 2004, that related to agricultural restructuring until 2006, assistance to environmental projects until 2008, and state aid to organizations in special economic zones was to be permitted until 2009. The Slovenian Government proposed that Slovenia be divided into three regions—Ljubljana, the West and the East—for the purposes of the Regional Fund, thereby ensuring that the country be a net recipient of EU funds after accession. However, the European Commission was unhappy with this proposal, and resolution of the issue appeared unlikely before 2005.

Slovenian accession to the EU would not deter the Government from its pursuit of economic restructuring policies. It would, however, greatly reduce the scope for it to disburse *ad hoc* grants, and force it to concentrate on increasing technical assistance and support for research and development. With this in mind, legislation on support for research and development was drafted by the Slovenian Government for the period

2000–03. The legislation envisaged a system of incentives for research and development activity at the level of individual companies, regions and specific sectors. The regional and sectoral programmes would focus primarily on the establishment of technology centres and science and technology parks and the consolidation of consultancy networks.

At the economic level, Slovenia's position *vis-à-vis* accession was relatively strong. By 2003 Slovenia had a greater number of economically viable companies per head than did most of the accession countries, and it appeared likely that many of these companies were well placed to enjoy continued growth. However, the processes necessitated by greater integration with the EU were by no means automatic, and their success would depend critically on the quality of leadership shown by both Slovenian and foreign entrepreneurs active in the economy, and also by the further evolution of public policy in the post-accession period, particularly in relation to the key issue of restructuring.

Statistical Survey

Source (unless otherwise indicated): Statistični letopis (Statistical Yearbook), published by Statistical Office of the Republic of Slovenia, 1000 Ljubljana, Vožarski pot 12; tel. (61) 1255322; fax (61) 216932; e-mail indok@gov.si; internet www.sigov.si/zrs.

Area and Population

AREA, POPULATION AND DENSITY

Area (sq km)	20,273*
Population (census results)	
31 March 1991	1,913,355
31 March 2002	
Males	958,576
Females	1,005,460
Total	1,964,036
Population (official estimates at 31 December)	
2000	1,990,094
2001	1,994,026
2002	1,995,033
Density (per sq km) at 31 December 2002	98.4

* 7,827 sq miles.

POPULATION BY ETHNIC GROUP
(2002 census)

Ethnic group	Number	%
Slovenes	1,631,363	83.1
Serbs	38,964	2.0
Croats	35,642	1.8
Bosniaks	21,542	1.1
Muslims*	10,467	0.5
Hungarians	6,243	0.3
Albanians	6,186	0.3
Macedonians	3,972	0.2
Montenegrins	2,667	0.1
Italians	2,258	0.1
Total (incl. others)	1,964,036	100.0

* Including persons claiming Muslim ethnicity rather than religious adherence.

PRINCIPAL TOWNS
(population at 2002 census)

Ljubljana (capital) .	265,881	Koper (Capodistria) .	47,539
Maribor	110,668	Novo mesto . . .	40,925
Kranj	51,225	Nova Gorica . . .	35,640
Celje	48,081		

BIRTHS, MARRIAGES AND DEATHS

	Registered live births		Registered marriages		Registered deaths	
	Number	Rate (per 1,000)	Number	Rate (per 1,000)	Number	Rate (per 1,000)
1994 . .	19,463	9.8	8,314	4.2	19,359	9.7
1995 . .	18,980	9.5	8,245	4.2	18,968	9.5
1996 . .	18,788	9.5	7,555	3.8	18,620	9.4
1997 . .	18,165	9.1	7,500	3.8	18,928	9.5
1998 . .	17,856	9.0	7,528	3.8	19,039	9.6
1999 . .	17,533	8.8	7,716	3.9	18,885	9.5
2000 . .	18,180	9.1	7,201	3.6	18,588	9.3
2001 . .	17,477	8.8	6,935	3.5	18,508	9.3

Expectation of life (years at birth): 75.9 (males 72.1; females 79.5) in 2001 (Source: WHO, *World Health Report*).

IMMIGRATION AND EMIGRATION

	1999	2000	2001
Long-term immigrants	4,941	6,185	7,803
Long-term emigrants	2,606	3,570	4,811

ECONOMICALLY ACTIVE POPULATION
('000 persons aged 15 years and over, at May each year)

	1999	2000	2001
Agriculture, hunting, forestry and fishing	96	85	90
Mining and quarrying	6	7	5
Manufacturing	278	269	277
Electricity, gas and water supply .	8	10	11
Construction	45	48	55
Wholesale and retail trade; repair of motor vehicles, motorcycles and personal and household goods	109	119	113
Hotels and restaurants	34	34	34
Transport, storage and communications	54	60	57
Financial intermediation	21	22	24
Real estate, renting and business activities	49	43	45
Public administration and defence; compulsory social security . .	49	53	48
Education	60	57	62
Health and social work	45	46	47
Other social and personal services	36	34	33
Private households with employed persons	—	—	1
Activities not adequately defined	3	6	12
Total employed	892	894	914
Unemployed	71	69	57
Total labour force	963	963	972
Males	519	517	527
Females	444	446	445

Health and Welfare

KEY INDICATORS

Total fertility rate (children per woman, 2001)	1.2
Under-5 mortality rate (per 1,000 live births, 2001) . . .	5
HIV/AIDS (% of persons aged 15–49, 2001)	<0.10
Physicians (per 1,000 head, 1998)	2.28
Health expenditure (2000): US $ per head (PPP)	1,462
Health expenditure (2000): % of GDP	8.6
Health expenditure (2000): public (% of total)	78.9
Access to water (% of persons, 2000)	100
Human Development Index (2000): ranking	29
Human Development Index (2000): value	0.879

For sources and definitions, see explanatory note on p. vi.

Agriculture

PRINCIPAL CROPS
('000 metric tons)

	1999	2000	2001
Wheat	117.3	162.6	180.4
Barley	33.1	38.2	43.2
Maize	308.0	282.4	257.5
Rye	2.6	1.8	2.3
Oats	5.6	5.4	4.7
Mixed grain	1.4	3.2	3.6*
Potatoes	194.2	186.2	148.3
Sugar beet	467.1	349.1	185.7
Dry beans	3.0*	5.8	0.5
Walnuts	1.6	2.9	2.3
Cabbages	45.2*	27.0	17.2
Tomatoes	9.4*	3.4	3.1
Dry onions	1.1*	6.3	5.4
Garlic	1.4*	0.1	0.1
Carrots	5.6*	2.8	2.3
Apples	81.2	129.7	76.9
Pears	9.0	15.4	8.8
Cherries	2.4	3.3	2.2
Peaches and nectarines	9.7	12.2	5.3
Plums	3.8	6.3	6.0
Grapes	98.3	126.7	126.8*
Hops	2.7	2.0	2.0*

* FAO estimate.
Source: FAO.

LIVESTOCK
('000 head)

	1999	2000	2001
Cattle	453.1	471.4	493.7
Pigs	592.4	558.5	603.6
Sheep	72.5	72.5	96.2
Goats	16.8	14.6	22.0
Horses	12.1	14.3	14.6*
Chickens*	7.2	7.2	7.2

* FAO estimate(s).
Source: FAO.

LIVESTOCK PRODUCTS
('000 metric tons)

	1999	2000	2001*
Beef and veal	43.1	42.2	42.2
Pig meat	67.3	58.5	60.0
Chicken meat	54.5	54.5*	54.5
Cows' milk	634.4	649.3	649.3
Cheese	21.0	21.7	22.0
Butter	4.3	3.5	3.5
Hen eggs	23.4	22.7	22.9

* FAO estimate(s).
Source: FAO.

Forestry

ROUNDWOOD REMOVALS
('000 cubic metres, excl. bark)

	1999	2000	2001
Sawlogs, veneer logs and logs for sleepers	992	1,120	1,144
Pulpwood	434	396	410
Other industrial wood	137	205	408
Fuel wood	505	532	295
Total	2,068	2,253	2,257

SAWNWOOD PRODUCTION
('000 cubic metres, incl. railway sleepers)

	1999	2000	2001
Coniferous (softwood)	338	300	302
Broadleaved (hardwood) . . .	117*	139	157
Total	455	439	459

* FAO estimate.
Source: FAO.

Fishing

(metric tons, live weight)

	1999	2000	2001
Freshwater fishes	1,330	1,313	1,314
Marine fishes	1,885	1,746	1,774
Crustaceans and molluscs . . .	65	77	226
Total catch	3,215	3,039	3,088

Mining

('000 metric tons, unless otherwise indicated)

	1998	1999	2000
Brown coal	1,277	1,163	1,175
Lignite	4,122	3,726	3,718
Natural gas (million cubic metres) .	16.1	18.4	n.a.
Crude petroleum	900	100	100
Aluminium	73.8	77.2	100.0
Kaolin	10	10	10
Gypsum	10	10	10*
Pumice*	40	40	40
Salt	5	5*	2*

* Estimate(s).
Source: partly US Geological Survey.

Industry

SELECTED PRODUCTS
('000 metric tons, unless otherwise indicated)

	1998	1999	2000
Wine ('000 hectolitres)	466	365	413
Beer ('000 hectolitres)	2,000	2,022	2,571
Cigarettes (million)	7,555	8,032	7,855
Wool yarn	1.1	1.0	1.0
Cotton yarn	n.a.	7.2	0.8
Woven woollen fabrics (million sq metres)	n.a.	1.2	1.6
Footwear (excl. rubber) ('000 pairs)	5,641	4,779	3,404
Veneer sheets ('000 cubic metres)	22	21	21
Plywood ('000 cubic metres) . .	32	53	35
Mechanical wood pulp	30	33	32
Chemical wood pulp	112	120	121
Newsprint	68	67	61
Other printing and writing paper	240	200	200
Household and sanitary paper . .	52	57	61
Wrapping and packaging paper and paperboard	120	78	78
Hydrochloric acid	22.1	6.6	8.3
Sulphuric acid	128	126	133
Rubber tyres ('000)*	6,320	4,924	5,629
Roofing tiles (million)	17	12	24
Cement	1,149	1,222	1,252
Crude steel	95	76	n.a.
Aluminium	10.2	9.0	8.8
Refined lead	7.3	8.2	8.5
Refrigerators for household use ('000)	756	780	841
Washing machines (household) ('000)	474	447	488
Television receivers ('000) . . .	231	244	349
Passenger motor cars ('000) . .	n.a.	119	123
Bicycles ('000)	61	99	142
Electric energy (million kWh) . .	13,718	13,262	13,624

* Tyres for road motor vehicles only.

Source: mainly UN, *Industrial Commodity Statistics Yearbook*.

Finance

CURRENCY AND EXCHANGE RATES

Monetary Units
100 stotins = 1 tolar (SIT).

Sterling, Dollar and Euro Equivalents (30 May 2003)
£1 sterling = 324.8 tolars;
US $1 = 197.1 tolars;
€1 = 233.0 tolars;
1,000 tolars = £3.079 = $5.073 = €4.291.

Average Exchange Rate (tolars per US $)
2000 222.66
2001 242.75
2002 240.25

Note: The tolar was introduced in October 1991, replacing (initially at par) the Yugoslav dinar.

BUDGET
('000 million tolars)*

Revenue	1999	2000	2001
Tax revenue	1,499	1,600	1,798
Taxes on income and profits . .	274	311	358
Taxes on payroll, property etc.	82	95	116
Social security contributions . .	496	553	621
Domestic taxes on goods and services	601	603	673
Value-added tax	207	399	439
Excises	70	134	166
Taxes on international trade and transactions	46	38	30
Other current revenue	80	95	139
Capital revenue and grants . . .	11	17	21
Total	**1,590**	**1,727**	**1,968**

Expenditure†	1999	2000	2001
Current expenditure (excl. transfers)	708	797	924
Wages and salaries	351	388	456
Expenditure on goods and services	296	336	386
Interest payments	51	61	73
Current transfers	738	813	908
Subsidies	63	59	63
Transfers to households . . .	648	731	817
Capital expenditure (excl. transfers)	109	111	128
Capital transfers	58	60	71
Total	**1,613**	**1,781**	**2,031**

* Figures represent a consolidation of the accounts of the central Government (State Budget, Pension Fund and Health Insurance Fund) and local administrative authorities.
† Excluding net lending.

INTERNATIONAL RESERVES
(US $ million at 31 December)

	2000	2001	2002
Gold*	0.09	67.22	83.25
IMF special drawing rights . .	3.69	5.03	6.98
Reserve position in IMF . . .	82.33	80.63	120.69
Foreign exchange	3,110.00	4,244.33	6,852.57
Total	**3,196.01**	**4,397.21**	**7,063.48**

* Valued at market-related prices.

Source: IMF, *International Financial Statistics*.

MONEY SUPPLY
(million tolars at 31 December)

	2000	2001	2002
Currency outside banks . . .	119,818	142,110	143,054
Demand deposits at commercial banks	263,472	317,305	376,570*
Total money (incl. others) . .	**385,881**	**462,532**	**523,760***

* Rounded figure.

Source: IMF, *International Financial Statistics*.

COST OF LIVING
(Consumer Price Index for urban areas; base: 1990 = 100)

	1999	2000	2001
Food (incl. beverages) . . .	1,554.5	1,639.6	1,787.7
Fuel and light	1,879.7	2,340.5	2,585.1
Clothing (incl. footwear) . . .	1,539.6	1,644.8	1,679.2
Rent	3,366.9	3,555.4	4,043.9
All items (incl. others)	**1,647.0**	**1,793.4**	**1,944.4**

Source: ILO.

NATIONAL ACCOUNTS

National Income and Product
(million tolars at current prices)

	1998	1999	2000
Compensation of employees. . .	1,700,323	1,889,714	2,122,115
Operating surplus	472,084	535,628	586,717
Domestic factor incomes. .	2,172,407	2,425,342	2,708,832
Consumption of fixed capital . .	580,989	634,144	706,093
Gross domestic product (GDP) at factor cost	2,753,396	3,059,486	3,414,925
Indirect taxes	572,126	668,115	697,701
Less Subsidies	71,771	79,200	77,108
GDP in purchasers' values .	3,253,751	3,648,401	4,035,518
Factor income from abroad . .	69,279	74,352	87,689
Less Factor income paid abroad	64,230	80,602	102,630
Gross national product . . .	3,258,799	3,642,151	4,020,577
Less Consumption of fixed capital	580,989	634,144	706,093
National income in market prices	2,677,810	3,008,007	3,314,484
Other current transfers from abroad	54,842	63,756	79,018
Less Other current transfers paid abroad	34,141	40,866	51,209
National disposable income	2,698,511	3,030,897	3,342,294

Expenditure on the Gross Domestic Product
('000 million tolars at current prices)

	2000	2001	2002
Final consumption expenditure .	3,234.8	3,627.4	3,982.4
Households . . . . . } Non-profit institutions serving } households . . . . . }	2,391.9	2,653.1	2,896.4
General government . . .	842.9	974.3	1,086.0
Gross capital formation . .	1,138.3	1,141.6	1,227.2
Gross fixed capital formation .	1,085.9	1,132.0	1,209.1
Changes in inventories . . . } Acquisitions, less disposals, of } valuables . . . . . }	52.4	9.6	18.1
Total domestic expenditure .	4,373.1	4,769.0	5,209.6
Exports of goods and services .	2,387.3	2,746.6	3,055.2
Less Imports of goods and services	2,538.1	2,774.6	2,980.3
GDP in purchasers' values .	4,222.4	4,741.0	5,284.5
GDP at constant 1995 prices .	2,747.0	2,825.5	2,915.3

Source: IMF, *International Financial Statistics*.

Gross Domestic Product by Economic Activity
(million tolars at current prices)

	1999	2000	2001
Agriculture, hunting and forestry	114,552	115,101	124,161
Fishing	520	534	460
Mining and quarrying . . .	36,825	36,763	36,393
Manufacturing	859,603	970,014	1,082,244
Electricity, gas and water supply	98,108	112,768	134,556
Construction	195,879	214,935	236,420
Wholesale and retail trade; repair of motor vehicles, motorcycles and personal and household goods	365,101	403,227	460,079
Hotels and restaurants . .	94,979	111,721	131,266
Transport, storage and communications	259,090	282,646	313,330
Financial intermediation . .	134,177	156,326	176,644
Real estate, renting and business activities	380,744	421,884	489,887
Public administration and defence; compulsory social security	178,540	203,034	236,766
Education	177,098	205,041	240,022
Health and social work . . .	169,420	195,243	227,855
Other community, social and personal services	115,126	133,145	153,066
Sub-total	3,179,760	3,562,382	4,043,150
Less Imputed bank service charge	69,351	77,324	79,058
GDP at basic prices	3,110,409	3,485,059	3,964,092
Taxes on products	591,242	602,030 }	602,099
Less Subsidies on products . .	53,250	51,570 }	
GDP in purchasers' values .	3,648,401	4,035,518	4,566,191

BALANCE OF PAYMENTS
(US $ million)

	2000	2001	2002
Exports of goods f.o.b.	8,807.9	9,342.8	10,472.6
Imports of goods f.o.b.	−9,946.9	−9,962.3	−10,715.7
Trade balance	−1,138.9	−619.5	−243.0
Exports of services	1,887.6	1,959.6	2,291.5
Imports of services	−1,437.9	−1,457.5	−1,736.1
Balance on goods and services.	−689.2	−117.4	312.4
Other income received . . .	434.0	462.6	487.8
Other income paid	−407.8	−443.4	−559.1
Balance on goods, services and income	−663.0	−98.2	241.1
Current transfers received . .	340.8	390.0	451.4
Current transfers paid . . .	−225.4	−260.8	−317.7
Current balance	−547.7	30.9	374.8
Capital account (net)	3.5	−3.6	1.6
Direct investment abroad . . .	−65.3	−132.8	−117.0
Direct investment from abroad. .	135.9	503.3	1,865.3
Portfolio investment assets . . .	−58.4	−107.5	−94.1
Portfolio investment liabilities . .	246.0	188.9	27.0
Other investment assets . . .	−519.2	206.6	−887.2
Other investment liabilities . .	941.3	545.7	662.8
Net errors and omissions . . .	42.1	53.0	33.6
Overall balance	178.3	1,284.6	1,866.9

Source: IMF, *International Financial Statistics*.

External Trade

PRINCIPAL COMMODITIES
(distribution by SITC, million euros)

Imports c.i.f.	1999	2000	2001
Food and live animals	507.4	558.1	603.7
Crude materials (inedible) except fuels	444.9	593.9	568.0
Mineral fuels, lubricants, etc.	605.8	997.4	916.3
Petroleum, petroleum products, etc.	445.5	776.5	663.0
Chemicals and related products	1,112.9	1,361.0	1,442.0
Basic manufactures	2,042.2	2,405.5	2,597.7
Textile yarn, fabrics, etc.	330.8	375.1	407.9
Iron and steel	393.6	477.7	491.3
Non-ferrous metals	276.3	384.8	424.0
Other metal manufactures	365.8	406.2	414.6
Machinery and transport equipment	3,501.8	3,748.2	3,815.5
Power-generating machinery and equipment	263.7	267.3	290.6
Machinery specialized for particular industries	327.3	319.9	334.0
General industrial machinery equipment and parts	453.9	531.2	502.2
Electrical machinery, apparatus etc.	548.5	689.5	728.2
Road vehicles (incl. air-cushion vehicles) and parts (excl. tyres engines and electrical parts)	1,284.0	1,190.7	1,212.1
Miscellaneous manufactured articles	1,158.3	1,210.2	1,292.6
Clothing and accessories (excl. footwear)	373.6	385.7	391.8
Total (incl. others)	9,477.6	10,984.2	11,344.4

Exports f.o.b.	1999	2000	2001
Chemicals and related products	880.3	1,062.9	1,968.0
Medicinal and pharmaceutical products	358.2	432.9	524.9
Basic manufactures	2,102.4	2,590.4	2,768.7
Paper, paperboard and articles thereof	319.5	431.2	431.5
Textile yarn, fabrics, etc.	268.3	310.9	367.9
Iron and steel	233.6	296.4	298.4
Non-ferrous metals	277.0	361.5	399.5
Other metal manufactures	347.2	430.7	462.2
Machinery and transport equipment	2,849.9	3,411.3	3,738.4
General industrial machinery equipment and parts	357.3	409.1	467.2
Electrical machinery, apparatus etc.	867.1	1,065.3	1,149.3
Road vehicles (incl. air-cushion vehicles) and parts (excl. tyres engines and electrical parts)	1,037.3	1,157.6	1,196.6
Miscellaneous manufactured articles	1,686.9	1,830.6	1,978.8
Furniture and parts; bedding mattresses, etc.	576.6	636.7	713.3
Clothing and accessories (excl. footwear)	431.9	421.2	421.2
Total (incl. others)	8,030.8	9,491.6	10,346.8

PRINCIPAL TRADING PARTNERS
(million euros)*

Imports c.i.f.	1999	2000	2001
Austria	757.3	905.7	943.8
Belgium	140.2	159.0	176.4
China, People's Republic	127.2	148.6	176.8
Croatia	417.9	486.6	451.2
Czech Republic	264.2	273.5	278.0
France	1,032.5	1,127.4	1,204.6
Germany	1,945.4	2,082.4	2,178.3
Hungary	251.9	320.0	352.4
Italy	1,586.2	1,916.8	2,004.0
Japan	179.5	180.5	162.6
Korea, Republic	97.2	78.1	70.3
Netherlands	195.4	230.1	219.5
Poland	104.0	149.8	160.7
Russia	149.6	250.8	314.8
Slovakia	85.7	143.7	159.6
Spain	219.3	286.2	295.3
Sweden	174.7	179.7	114.8
Switzerland	203.4	175.3	170.4
United Kingdom	289.7	336.9	292.2
USA	274.7	325.1	332.8
Total (incl. others)	9,477.6	10,984.2	11,344.5

Exports f.o.b.	1999	2000	2001
Austria	584.0	713.8	773.3
Belgium	125.3	106.3	111.9
Bosnia and Herzegovina	341.8	408.3	444.8
Croatia	631.3	749.5	894.4
Czech Republic	149.3	164.5	187.9
France	459.6	671.7	702.2
Germany	2,465.9	2,574.5	2,714.6
Hungary	136.0	183.3	174.9
Italy	1,101.8	1,288.7	1,289.7
Macedonia, former Yugoslav republic	166.8	171.4	147.1
Netherlands	134.9	163.6	172.4
Poland	178.7	245.2	271.1
Russia	121.8	209.9	315.4
Switzerland	84.0	110.8	108.3
United Kingdom	160.1	202.6	289.6
USA	243.1	293.5	272.7
Yugoslavia	80.5	156.7	263.6
Total (incl. others)	8,030.8	9,491.6	10,346.8

* Imports by country of origin; exports by country of destination.

Transport

RAILWAYS
(traffic)

	1999	2000	2001
Passenger journeys ('000)	13,756	15,010	14,484
Passenger-kilometres (million)	623	705	715
Freight carried ('000 metric tons)	14,226	15,064	14,919
Freight ton-kilometres (million)	2,784	2,857	2,837

ROAD TRAFFIC
(registered motor vehicles at 31 December)

	1999	2000	2001
Motorcycles and mopeds	9,978	11,308	11,723
Passenger cars	829,674	847,941	862,648
Buses and coaches	2,319	2,257	2,212
Lorries	42,088	44,251	45,811
Agricultural tractors	61,312	64,028	66,088

SHIPPING

Merchant Fleet
(at 31 December)

	2000	2001	2002
Number of vessels	10	10	11
Displacement (gross registered tons)	1,767	1,891	2,251

Source: Lloyd's Register-Fairplay, *World Fleet Statistics*.

International Sea-borne Freight Traffic
('000 metric tons)

	1999	2000	2001
Goods loaded	189	184	180
Goods unloaded	2,760	2,679	2,791

CIVIL AVIATION
(traffic)

	1999	2000	2001
Kilometres flown ('000)	12,841	13,661	12,836
Passengers carried ('000) . . .	780	866	801
Passenger-kilometres (million) . .	832	866	790
Freight carried (metric tons) . .	4,147	4,556	4,173
Freight ton-kilometres ('000) . .	4,160	4,495	4,108

Tourism

FOREIGN TOURIST ARRIVALS
('000)*

Country of origin	1999	2000	2001
Austria	126.4	150.3	174.4
Bosnia and Herzegovina . . .	26.3	28.9	27.9
Croatia	82.0	91.3	95.5
Czech Republic	22.6	26.7	29.0
France	17.9	22.2	23.5
Germany	157.5	204.0	234.2
Hungary	25.1	30.4	32.6
Italy	207.2	256.2	269.3
Netherlands	21.0	31.5	34.8
Russia	10.4	12.1	15.5
United Kingdom	23.7	31.2	40.4
USA	18.9	25.4	28.3
Total (incl. others)	884.0	1,089.5	1,218.7

* Figures refer to arrivals at accommodation establishments.

Tourism receipts (US $ million): 1,088 in 1998; 954 in 1999; 961 in 2000.

Communications Media

	1999	2000	2001
Telephone subscribers ('000) . .	786.2	808.8	945.3
Facsimile machines (subscribers)	18,290	19,739	11,072
Mobile cellular telephones (subscribers)	325,048	468,351	662,619
Radio licences ('000)	533.1	n.a.	n.a
Television licences ('000) . . .	471.3	n.a.	n.a
Personal computers ('000 in use)	500	548	550
Internet users ('000)	250	300	600
Book production (titles published)*	3,976	3,917	3,598
Daily newspapers	5	5	6
Non-daily newspapers	221	200	227
Other periodicals	1,332	1,296	1,515

* Including pamphlets.
Sources: partly UNESCO, *Statistical Yearbook*; UN, *Statistical Yearbook*; and International Telecommunication Union.

Education

(1999/2000, unless otherwise indicated)

	Institutions	Teachers	Students Males	Students Females	Students Total
Pre-primary . . .	806	7,329	33,512	30,639	64,151
Elementary*† . . .	476	15,489	98,294	93,407	191,701
Upper secondary† . .	275	13,043	60,829	61,589	122,418
Higher education . .	37‡	4,666	36,300§	51,800§	88,100§

* 1998/99.
† Including education of adults.
‡ 1995/96.
§ Excluding post-graduate students, 2001/02 figures.

Pre-primary: Students 63,328 in 2000/01.

Adult literacy rate (UNESCO estimates): 99.6% (males 99.7%; females 99.6%) in 2000 (Source: UN Development Programme, *Human Development Report*).

Directory

The Constitution

The Constitution of the Republic of Slovenia was enacted on 23 December 1991. Its provisions for the independence and sovereignty of Slovenia had been endorsed by a plebiscite held on 23 December 1990. The following is a summary of the Constitution's main articles:

INTRODUCTION

Slovenia is a democratic republic, governed by the rule of law. Slovenia is a territorially indivisible state. Human rights and fundamental freedom—including the rights of the autochthonous Italian and Hungarian ethnic communities—are protected. Slovenia attends to the welfare of the autochthonous Slovenian minorities in neighbouring countries and of Slovenian emigrants and migrant workers abroad.

The separation of church and state is guaranteed. Religious groups enjoy equal rights under the law and are guaranteed freedom of activity.

The autonomy of local government in Slovenia is guaranteed. The capital of the republic is Ljubljana. The official language of Slovenia is Slovene. In those areas where Italian or Hungarian ethnic communities reside, the official language is also Italian or Hungarian.

HUMAN RIGHTS AND FUNDAMENTAL FREEDOMS

All persons are guaranteed equal human rights and fundamental freedoms, irrespective of national origin, race, sex, language, religion, political or other beliefs, financial status, birth, education or social status, and all persons are equal before the law. Human life is inviolable, and there is no capital punishment. No person may be subjected to torture, inhuman or humiliating punishment or treatment. The right of each individual to personal liberty is guaranteed.

Respect for the humanity and dignity of the individual is guaranteed in all criminal or other proceedings. The use of violence of any sort on any person whose liberty has been restricted in any way is forbidden. Except for certain situations (as determined by statute), all court proceedings are conducted in public and all judgments are delivered in open court. Each person is guaranteed the right of appeal. Any person charged with a criminal offence is presumed innocent until proven guilty by due process of the law.

Each person has the right to freedom of movement, to choose his place of residence, to leave the country and to return at any time he wishes. The right to own and to inherit property is guaranteed. The dwellings of all persons are inviolable, and the protection of personal data relating to the individual is guaranteed. Freedom of expression of thought, freedom of speech and freedom to associate in public, together with freedom of the press and of other forms of public communication and expression, are guaranteed. The right to vote is universal and equal. Each citizen who has attained the age of 18 years is eligible both to vote and to stand for election.

The freedom of work is guaranteed. Each person may freely choose his employment. Forced labour is forbidden. All citizens who fulfil such conditions as are laid down by statute, have the right to social security. The State regulates compulsory health, pension, disability and other social insurance, and ensures the proper administration thereof. Education is free, and the State provides the opportunity for all citizens to obtain a proper education.

Each person is entitled freely to identify with his national grouping or ethnic community, to foster and give expression to his culture and to use his own language and script. All incitement to ethnic, racial, religious or other discrimination, as well as the inflaming of ethnic, racial, religious or other hatred or intolerance, is unconstitutional, as is incitement to violence or to war. The autochthonous Italian and Hungarian ethnic communities are guaranteed the right freely to use their national symbols and to establish organizations, to foster economic, cultural, scientific and research activities, as well as activities associated with the mass media and publishing. These two communities have the right to education and schooling in their own languages. They are also entitled to establish autonomous organizations in order to exercise their rights. The Italian and Hungarian communities are directly represented both at the local level and in the National Assembly (Državni zbor). The status and special rights of Gypsy (Roma) communities living in Slovenia are determined by statute.

ECONOMIC AND SOCIAL RELATIONS

The State is responsible for the creation of opportunities for employment. Each person has the right to a healthy environment, and the State is responsible for such an environment. The protection of animals from cruelty is regulated by statute. State and local government bodies are responsible for the preservation of the natural and cultural heritage.

Free enterprise is guaranteed. The establishment of trade unions, and the operation and membership thereof, is free. Workers enjoy the right to strike. The State creates the conditions necessary to enable each citizen to obtain proper housing.

ADMINISTRATION OF THE STATE

The National Assembly (Državni zbor)

The Državni zbor consists of 90 deputies, who serve a four-year term; 40 deputies are directly elected, while 50 are elected on a proportional basis by the parties represented in the chamber (which are required to hold a minimum of 3% of the votes). The Italian and Hungarian ethnic communities are entitled to elect one deputy each to the Državni zbor. The President of the Državni zbor (Speaker) is elected by a majority vote of all elected deputies.

The Državni zbor enacts laws; makes other decisions; authorizes adherence to international agreements; may call a referendum; may proclaim a state of war or a state of emergency, at the initiative of the Government; may establish parliamentary inquiries with respect to matters of public importance.

The National Council (Državni svet)

The Državni svet represents social, economic, trade and professional and local interests. It is composed of 40 councillors: four representing employers; four representing employees; four representing farmers, small business persons and independent professional persons; six representing non-profit-making organizations; and 22 representing local interests. Councillors are elected for a five-year term.

The Državni svet may: propose the enactment of statutes by the Državni zbor; demand that the Državni zbor reconsider statutes prior to their proclamation; demand the holding of a referendum; and demand the establishment of a parliamentary inquiry. The Državni zbor may require the Državni svet to provide its opinions on specific matters. A councillor of the Državni svet may not be simultaneously a deputy of the Državni zbor.

The President of the Republic

The President of the Republic of Slovenia is Head of State and Commander-in-Chief of the Defence Forces. The President is elected on the basis of universal, equal and direct suffrage by secret ballot. The President's term of office is five years (with a maximum of two consecutive terms). Only a citizen of Slovenia may be elected President of the Republic. Presidential elections are called by the President of the Državni zbor. The office of President of the Republic is incompatible with other public offices or other employment. In the event that the President of the Republic is permanently incapacitated, dies, resigns or is otherwise permanently unable to perform his functions, the President of the Državni zbor temporarily occupies the office of the President of the Republic until such time as a replacement is elected.

The President of the Republic is empowered to: call elections to the Državni zbor; proclaim statutes; appoint state officers and functionaries; accredit, and revoke the accreditation of, Slovenian ambassadors to foreign states, and to accept the credentials of foreign diplomatic representatives; grant amnesties; and confer state honours, decorations and honorary titles.

If, in the course of carrying out his office, the President of the Republic acts in a manner contrary to the Constitution or commits a serious breach of the law, he may be brought before the Constitutional Court upon the request of the Državni zbor. The President may be dismissed from office upon the vote of no less than two-thirds of all of the judges of the Constitutional Court.

The Government

The Government is composed of the Prime Minister and ministers. The Government is independent, and individual ministers are independent within their own particular portfolios. Ministers are accountable to the Državni zbor. After consultations with the leaders of the various political groups within the Državni zbor, the President of the Republic proposes to the Državni zbor a candidate for the office of Prime Minister. The Prime Minister is elected by the Državni zbor by a majority vote. Ministers in the Government are appointed or dismissed by the Državni zbor, upon the proposal of the Prime Minister. The Prime Minister is responsible for the political unity, direction and administrative programme of the Government and for the co-ordination of the work of the various ministers. The Državni zbor may, upon the motion of no fewer than 10 deputies and by a majority vote, elect a new Prime Minister (such a vote is deemed a vote of 'no confidence' in the Government). Furthermore, the Državni zbor may bring the Prime Minister or any minister before the Constitutional Court to answer charges relating to breaches of the Constitution.

The Judiciary

Judges independently exercise their duties and functions in accordance with the Constitution and with the law. The Supreme Court is the highest court for civil and criminal cases in the republic. The Državni zbor elects judges upon the recommendation of the Judicial Council, which is composed of 11 members. The office of a judge is incompatible with office in any other state body, local government body or organ of any political party.

The Office of the Public Prosecutor

The Public Prosecutor is responsible for the preferment of criminal charges, for prosecuting criminal matters in court and for the performance of such other duties as are prescribed by statute.

LOCAL SELF-GOVERNMENT

Slovenians exercise local government powers and functions through self-governing municipalities and other local government organizations. A municipality may comprise a single community or a number of communities, whose inhabitants are bound together by common needs and interests. The State supervises the proper and efficient performance of municipalities and wider self-governing local administrative bodies. Municipalities raise their own revenue. Municipalities are at liberty to join other municipalities in establishing wider self-governing local administrative bodies or regional local government bodies to exercise administrative powers and to deal with matters of wider common interest. Citizens may join together and form self-governing local bodies to further their common interests.

PUBLIC FINANCE

The State and local government bodies fund the performance of their respective duties and functions from taxes and other mandatory charges levied by them and from such other income as they may derive from their assets. All revenues raised, and all monies expended, for public purposes by the State and by local government bodies must be accounted for in their respective budgets.

The Auditor General's office is the body with ultimate responsibility for auditing state finances, the state budget and monies expended for public purposes. The Auditor General's office is independent in the performance of its functions. Officers of the Auditor General's office are appointed by the Državni zbor.

The Bank of Slovenia is the central bank. It is independent in its operations and accountable to the Državni zbor. The Governor of the Bank of Slovenia is appointed by the Državni zbor.

THE CONSTITUTIONAL COURT

The Constitutional Court is composed of nine judges, elected by the Državni zbor, upon the nomination of the President of the Republic, for a term (non-extendable) of nine years. The President of the

Constitutional Court is elected by the judges from amongst their own number to hold office for a period of three years.

The Constitutional Court is empowered to decide upon matters relating to: the conformity of statutes with the Constitution and with international agreements; complaints of breaches of the Constitution involving individual acts infringing human rights and fundamental freedoms; juridical disputes between the state and local government bodies or among such local government bodies; juridical disputes between the Državni zbor, the President of the Republic and the Government; and unconstitutional acts or activities of political parties.

The Government

HEAD OF STATE

President: Dr JANEZ DRNOVŠEK (elected 1 December 2002; inaugurated 22 December 2002).

GOVERNMENT
(July 2003)

A coalition of the Liberal Democracy of Slovenia, the United List of Social Democrats and the Slovenian People's Party.

Prime Minister: Dr ANTON ROP.

Minister of Finance: Dr DUŠAN MRAMOR.

Minister of Internal Affairs: Dr RADO BOHINC.

Minister of Foreign Affairs: Dr DIMITRIJ RUPEL.

Minister of Justice: IVAN BIZJAK.

Minister of Defence: Dr ANTON GRIZOLD.

Minister of Labour, Family and Social Affairs: Dr VLADO DIMOVSKI.

Minister of the Economy: Dr TEA PETRIN.

Minister of Agriculture, Forestry and Food: FRANC BUT.

Minister of Culture: ANDREJA RIHTER.

Minister of the Environment, Physical Planning and Energy: JANEZ KOPAČ.

Minister of Transport: JAKOB PRESEČNIK.

Minister of Education, Science and Sport: Dr SLAVKO GABER.

Minister of Health: Dr DUŠAN KEBER.

Minister of the Information Society: Dr PAVEL GANTAR.

Minister without Portfolio, responsible for European Affairs: JANEZ POTOČNIK.

Minister without Portfolio, responsible for Regional Development: ZDENKA KOVAČ.

MINISTRIES

Office of the President: 1000 Ljubljana, Erjavčeva 17; tel. (1) 4781205; fax (1) 4781357; internet www.sigov.si/up-rs.

Office of the Prime Minister: 1000 Ljubljana, Gregorčičeva 20; tel. (1) 4781000; fax (1) 4781607; e-mail gp.upv@gov.si; internet www.sigov.si/pv.

Ministry of Agriculture, Forestry and Food: 1000 Ljubljana, Dunajska 56–58; tel. (1) 1789103; fax (1) 4789013; e-mail franc.but@gov.si; internet www.sigov.si/mkgp.

Ministry of Culture: 1000 Ljubljana, Cankarjeva 5; tel. (1) 4785900; fax (1) 4785901; e-mail mkinfo@gov.si; internet www.sigov.si/mk.

Ministry of Defence: 1000 Ljubljana, Kardeljeva ploščad 25; tel. (1) 1331111; fax (1) 1318164; e-mail soi@oub.mo-rs.si; internet www.mo-rs.si.

Ministry of the Economy: 1000 Ljubljana, Kotnikova 5; tel. (1) 4783600; fax (1) 4331031; e-mail kabinet@gov.si; internet www2.gov.si/mg/mgslo.nsf.

Ministry of Education, Science and Sport: 1000 Ljubljana, Župančičeva 6; tel. (1) 4784600; fax (1) 4784719; e-mail vprasajte.mszs@gov.si; internet www.mszs.si.

Ministry of the Environment, Physical Planning and Energy: 1000 Ljubljana, Dunajska c. 48; tel. (1) 4787400; fax (1) 4787422; e-mail info.mop@gov.si; internet www.sigov.si/mop.

Ministry of Finance: 1502 Ljubljana, Župančičeva 3; tel. (1) 4785211; fax (1) 4785655; internet www.gov.si/mf.

Ministry of Foreign Affairs: 1000 Ljubljana, Prešernova 25; tel. (1) 4782294; fax (1) 4782340; e-mail info.mzz@gov.si; internet www.sigov.si/mzz.

Ministry of Health: 1000 Ljubljana, Štefanova 5; tel. (1) 4786001; fax (1) 4786058; e-mail ministrstvo.zdravje@gov.si; internet www.gov.si/mz.

Ministry of the Information Society: 1508 Ljubljana, Langusova 4; tel. (1) 4788000; fax (1) 4788375; e-mail mid@gov.si; internet www.gov.si/mid.

Ministry of Internal Affairs: 1501 Ljubljana, Štefanova 2; tel. (1) 4325125; fax (1) 1214330; e-mail ssj@mnz.si; internet www.mnz.si.

Ministry of Justice: 1000 Ljubljana, Župančičeva 3; tel. (1) 3695200; fax (1) 3695519; internet www.sigov.si/mp.

Ministry of Labour, Family and Social Affairs: 1000 Ljubljana, Kotnikova 5; tel. (1) 4783450; fax (1) 4783456; e-mail vlado.dimovski@gov.si; internet www.sigov.si/mddsz.

Ministry of Transport: 1535 Ljubljana, Langusova ul. 4; tel. (1) 4788000; fax (1) 4788139; e-mail mpz.info@gov.si; internet www.sigov.si/mpz.

President and Legislature

PRESIDENT

Presidential Election, First Ballot, 10 November 2002

Candidate	Votes	% of votes
Janez Drnovšek (Liberal Democracy of Slovenia)	506,800	44.40
Barbara Brezigar (Independent)	351,049	30.76
Zmago Jelinèiè Plemeniti (Slovenian National Party)	97,103	8.51
France Arhar (Independent)	86,678	7.60
Franc Bucar (Independent)	36,989	3.24
Lev Kreft (United List of Social Democrats)	25,655	2.25
Anton Bebler (Independent)	21,096	1.85
Gorazd Drevensek (New Party)	9,772	0.86
Jure Cekuta (Independent)	6,188	0.54
Total*	1,141,330	100.00

* Excluding 15,019 invalid votes.

Second Ballot, 1 December 2002

Candidate	Votes	% of votes
Janez Drnovšek (Liberal Democracy of Slovenia)	583,570	56.54
Barbara Brezigar (Independent)	448,482	43.46
Total*	1,032,052	100.00

* Excluding 13,803 invalid votes.

DRŽAVNI ZBOR
(National Assembly)

President: BORUT PAHOR, 1000 Ljubljana, Šubičeva 4; tel. (1) 4789400; fax (1) 4789845; e-mail borut.pahor@dz-rs.si; internet www.dz-rs.si.

General Election, 15 October 2000

	Votes	% of votes	Seats
Liberal Democracy of Slovenia	389,485	36.26	34
Social Democratic Party of Slovenia	169,957	15.82	14
United List of Social Democrats	129,749	12.10	11
Slovenian People's Party	102,550	9.55	9
New Slovenia—Christian People's Party	92,823	8.64	8
Democratic Party of Pensioners of Slovenia	55,468	5.16	4
Slovenian National Party	47,095	4.38	4
Youth Party of Slovenia	46,594	4.34	4
Others*	40,311	3.75	2
Total†	1,074,032	100.00	90

*Two of the 90 seats in the National Assembly are reserved for representatives of the Italian and Hungarian minorities.
† Excluding 36,813 invalid votes.

DRŽAVNI SVET
(National Council)

President: TONE HROVAT, 1000 Ljubljana, Šubičeva 4; tel. (1) 4789802; fax (1) 4789851; e-mail tone.hrovat@ds-rs.si; internet www .ds-rs.si.

There are 40 councillors in the Državni svet, who are indirectly elected for a five-year term by an electoral college.

Local Government

The system of local government in Slovenia was restructured in 1994. By 2003 193 municipalities had been established, each of which had an elected mayor and council; of these, some 11 were designated as city muncipalities.

Association of Municipalities and Towns (Skupnost občin Slovenije): 2000 Maribor, Partizanska 1; tel. (2) 2502690; fax (2) 2515725; e-mail info@skupnostobcin.si; internet www .skupnostobcin.si; f. 1994; 108 mems; Sec.-Gen. JASMINA VIDMAR.

MUNICIPALITIES

Ajdovščina Municipality: 5270 Ajdovščina, cesta 5 Maja 6A; tel. (5) 3659100; fax (5) 3659130; e-mail obcina.ajdovscina@siol.net; Mayor MARJAN POLJSAK.

Beltinci Municipality: 9231 Beltinci, Mladinska ul. 2; tel. (2) 5413535; fax (2) 5413570; e-mail obcina@beltinci.si; internet www .beltinci.si; Mayor MILAN KERMAN.

Benedikt Municipality: 2234 Benedikt, Benedikt 16A; tel. (2) 7031423; fax (2) 7036081; e-mail obcina.benedikt@siol.net; internet www.benedikt.si; Mayor MILAN GUMZAR.

Bistrica ob Sotli Municipality: 3256 Bistrica ob Sotli, Bistrica ob Sotli 9; tel. (3) 8001500; fax (3) 5804327; e-mail obcina .bistricaobsotli@siol.net; Mayor JOŽEF PREGRAD.

Bled Municipality: 4269 Bled, cesta Svobode 13; tel. (4) 5750100; fax (4) 5751243; e-mail obcina.bled@bled.si; internet www.bled.si; Mayor JOŽE ANTONIČ.

Bloke Municipality: 1385 Nova vas, Nova vas 4A; tel. (1) 7098916; fax (1) 7098917; e-mail zupan@bloke.si; Mayor JOŽE DOLES.

Bohinj Municipality: 4264 Bohinjska Bistrica, Triglavska 35; tel. (41) 757091; e-mail obcina@bohinj.si; internet www.bohinj.si; Mayor EVGENIJA KEGL KOROŠEC.

Borovnica Municipality: 1353 Borovnica, Paplerjeva 22; tel. (1) 7548330; fax (1) 7546126; internet www.borovnica.net; Mayor ALOJZ MOČNIK.

Bovec Municipality: 5230 Bovec, Trg golobarskih žrtev 8; tel. (5) 3841900; fax (5) 3841915; e-mail obcina.zupan@bovec.si; internet www.bovec.si; Mayor DANIJEL KRIVEC.

Braslovče Municipality: 3314 Braslovče, Braslovče 29; tel. (3) 7038400; fax (3) 7038410; e-mail obcina@braslovce.com; internet www.braslovce.com; Mayor MARKO BALANT.

Brda Municipality: 5212 Dobrovo, Trg 25 Maja 2; tel. (5) 3351030; fax (5) 3351039; e-mail obcina.brda@guest.arnes.si; internet www2 .arnes.si/~ngobcib1; Mayor FRANC MUŽIČ.

Brežice Municipality: 8250 Brežice, cesta prvih borcev 18; tel. (7) 4991500; fax (7) 4990052; e-mail ferdo.pinteric@brezice.si; internet www.turizem-brezice.info; Mayor ANDREJ VIZJAK.

Brezovica Municipality: 1351 Brezovica, Tržaška cesta 390; tel. (1) 3601770; fax (1) 3601771; e-mail info@brezovica.si; internet www .brezovica.si; Mayor DRAGO STANOVNIK.

Cankova Municipality: 9261 Cankova, Cankova 25; tel. (2) 5409030; fax (2) 5409031; Mayor DRAGO VOGRINČIČ.

Celje City Municipality: 3000 Celje, trg Celjskih Knezov 9; tel. (3) 4265300; fax (3) 4265682; e-mail ue.celje@gov.si; internet www.celje .si; Mayor BOJAN ŠROT.

Cerklje na Gorenjskem Municipality: 4207 Cerklje na Gorenjskem, ul. Franca Barleta 23; tel. (4) 2780100; fax (4) 2521027; e-mail info@cerklje.si; internet www.cerklje.si; Mayor FRANC ČEBULJ.

Cerknica Municipality: 1380 Cerknica, cesta 4 Maja 53; tel. (1) 7093313; fax (1) 7091110; e-mail helena.slajnar@cerknica.si; internet www.cerknica.si; Mayor MIROSLAV LEVAR.

Cerkno Municipality: 5282 Cerkno, Bevkova 9; tel. (5) 3734640; fax (5) 3899211; e-mail obcina@cerkno.si; internet www.cerkno.si; Mayor JURIJ KAVČIČ.

Cerkvenjak Municipality: 2236 Cerkvenjak, Cerkvenjak 25; tel. (2) 7034115; fax (2) 7034042; internet cerkvenjak.obcina.com; Mayor JOŽEF KRANER.

Črenšovci Municipality: 9232 Črenšovci, ul. prekmurske čete 20; tel. (2) 5735756; fax (2) 5735758; e-mail obcina.crensovci@siol.net; internet www.obcina-crensovci.si; Mayor ANTON TÖRNAR.

Črna na Koroškem Municipality: 2393 Črna na Koroškem, Centre 101; tel. (2) 8704810; fax (2) 8704821; e-mail obcina.crna@ nicsi.net; internet www.crna.si; Mayor JANEZ ŠVAB.

Črnomelj Municipality: 8340 Črnomelj, trg Svobode 3; tel. (7) 3061100; fax (7) 3061130; e-mail urad.zupana@crnomelj.si; internet www.crnomelj.si; Mayor ANDREJ FABJAN.

Destrnik Municipality: 2253 Destrnik, Vintarovci 50; tel. (2) 7520900; fax (2) 7520902; e-mail obcina.destrnik@siol.net; Mayor FRANC PUKŠIČ.

Divača Municipality: 6215 Divača, Kraška 32; tel. (5) 7310930; fax (5) 7310940; e-mail obcina@divaca.si; Mayor RAJKO VOJTKOVSZKY.

Dobje Municipality: 3224 Dobje pri Planini, Dobje 26; tel. (3) 5796000; fax (3) 5796001; e-mail obcinadobje@siol.net; Mayor FRANC SALOBIR.

Dobrepolje Municipality: 1312 Dobropolje, Videm—Dobropolje 35; tel. (1) 7867010; fax (1) 7807923; e-mail obcina.dobrepolje@siol .net; Mayor ANTON JAKOPIČ.

Dobrna Municipality: 3204 Dobrna, Dobrna 19; tel. (3) 7801050; fax (3) 7801060; e-mail obcina@dobrna.si; Mayor MARTIN BRECL.

Dobrova-Polhov Gradec Municipality: 1356 Dobrova, ul. Vladimirja Dolničarja 2; tel. (1) 3641458; fax (1) 3642211; e-mail info@ dobrova-polhovgradec.si; internet www.dobrova-polhovgradec.si; Mayor MRAK LOVRO.

Dobrovnik Municipality: 9223 Dobrovnik, Dobrovnik 297; tel. (2) 5776880; fax (2) 5776887; e-mail obcina.dobrovnik@siol.net; internet www.dobrovnik.si; Mayor MARJAN KARDINAR.

Dol pri Ljubljani Municipality: 1262 Dol pri Ljubljani, Dol pri Ljubljani 1; tel. (1) 5303240; fax (1) 5303249; e-mail obcina@dol.si; internet www.dol.si; Mayor PRIMOŽ ZUPANČIČ.

Dolenjske Toplice Municipality: 8350 Dolenjske Toplice, Zdraviliški trg 8; tel. (7) 3845180; fax (7) 3845182; e-mail obcina.dtoplice@ siol.net; internet www.dolenjske-toplice.si; Mayor FRANC VOVK.

Domžale Municipality: 1230 Domžale, Ljubljanska 69; tel. (1) 7220100; fax (1) 7214231; e-mail urada.zupane@domzale.si; internet www.domzale.si; Mayor CVETA ZALOKAR-ORAŽEM.

Dornava Municipality: 2252 Dornava, Dornava 125; tel. (2) 7540110; fax (2) 7550791; e-mail obcina-dornava@siol.net; Mayor FRANC ŠEGULA.

Dravograd Municipality: 2370 Dravograd, trg 4 Julija 7; tel. (2) 8783011; fax (2) 8783284; e-mail obcina@dravograd.si; internet www .dravograd.si; Mayor MARIJANA CIGALA.

Duplek Municipality: 2241 Spodnji Duplek, cesta 4 Julija 106; tel. (2) 6814101; fax (2) 6819471; e-mail obcina@duplek.si; internet www.duplek.si; Mayor JANEZ RIBIČ.

Gorenja vas-Poljane Municipality: 4224 Gorenja vas, Poljanska cesta 87; tel. (4) 5183100; fax (4) 5183101; e-mail info@obcina-gvp.si; internet www.obcina-gvp.si; Mayor JOŽE BOGATAJ.

Gorišnica Municipality: 2272 Gorišnica, Gorišnica 54; tel. (2) 7431111; fax (2) 7431120; e-mail obcina.gorisnica@siol.net; internet www.gorisnica.si; Mayor JOŽEF KOKOT.

Gornja Radgona Municipality: 9250 Gornja Radgona, Partizanska 13; tel. (2) 5611671; fax (2) 5621438; e-mail tajnistvo .zupana@gor-radgona.si; internet www.gor-radgona.si; Mayor ANTON KAMPUŠ.

Gornji Grad Municipality: 3342 Gornji Grad, Attemsov trg 3; tel. (3) 5843300; fax (3) 5843068; e-mail obcina.gornji-grad@siol.net; Mayor ANTON RIFELJ.

Gornji Petrovci Municipality: 9203 Gornji Petrovci, Gornji Petrovci 3D; tel. (2) 5569000; fax (2) 5569001; e-mail obcina.gpetrovci@ siol.net; Mayor FRANC ŠLIHTHUBER.

Grad Municipality: 9264 Grad, Grad 172; tel. (2) 5509120; fax (2) 5531525; e-mail obcina.grad@siol.net; Mayor DANIEL KALAMAR.

Grosuplje Municipality: 1290 Grosuplje, Kolodvorska ul. 2; tel. (1) 7888750; fax (1) 7888764; e-mail obcina.grosuplje@ob.grosuplje.si; internet www.grosuplje.si; Mayor JANEZ LESJAK.

Hajdina Municipality: 2288 Hajdina, Zgornja Hajdina 45; tel. (2) 7883030; fax (2) 7883031; e-mail uprava@hajdina.si; internet www .hajdina.si; Mayor RADOSLAV SIMONIČ.

Hoče Slivnica Municipality: 2311 Hoče, Pohorska cesta 15; tel. (2) 6165321; fax (2) 6165330; e-mail anton.obreht@hoce-slivnica.si; internet www.hoce-slivnica.si; Mayor ANTON OBREHT.

Hodoš—Hodos Község Municipality: 9205 Hodoš, Hodoš 52; tel. (2) 5598021; fax (2) 5598020; e-mail obcina-hodos-kozseg@siol.net; Mayor LUDVIK ORBAN.

Horjul Municipality: 1354 Horjul, Horjul 57; tel. (1) 7500210; fax (1) 7549146; Mayor DANIJEL FORTUNA.

Hrastnik Municipality: 1430 Hrastnik, pot Vitka Pavliča 5; tel. (3) 5654350; fax (3) 5644041; e-mail janez.karner@hrastnik.si; Mayor MIRAN JERIČ.

Hrpelje-Kozina Municipality: 6240 Kozina, Reška cesta 14; tel. (5) 6800150; fax (5) 6800180; e-mail obcinahrpeljekozina@hrpelje.si; Mayor ALBERT PECAR.

Idrija Municipality: 5280 Idrija, Mestni trg 1; tel. (5) 3726100; fax (5) 3771340; e-mail obcina.idrija@idrija.si; Mayor DAMJAN KRAPŠ.

Ig Municipality: 1292 Ig, Ig 72; tel. (1) 2862806; fax (1) 2862229; e-mail obcina-ig@siol.net; Mayor JANEZ CIMPERMAN.

Ilirska Bistrica Municipality: 6250 Ilirska Bistrica, Bazoviška 14; tel. (5) 7141361; fax (5) 7141284; Mayor ANTON ŠENKINC.

Ivančna Gorica Municipality: 1295 Ivančna Gorica, Sokolska 8; tel. (1) 7878385; fax (1) 7877697; e-mail obc.ivancna.gorica@siol.net; internet www.ivancna-gorica.si; Mayor JERNEJ LAMPRET.

Izola Municipality: 6310 Izola, Sončno nabrežje 8; tel. (5) 6600100; fax (5) 6600110; e-mail breda.pecan@izola.si; Mayor BREDA PEČAN.

Jesenice Municipality: 4270 Jesenice, cesta Titova 78; tel. (4) 5869200; fax (4) 5869270; e-mail obcina.jesenice@jesenice.si; internet www.jesenice.si; Mayor BORIS JANEZ BREGANT.

Jezersko Municipality: 4206 Zgornje Jezersko, Zgornje Jezersko 57; tel. (4) 2545110; fax (4) 2545111; e-mail obcina.jezersko@siol.net; Mayor MILAN KOCJAN.

Juršinci Municipality: 2256 Juršinci, Juršinci 3B; tel. (2) 7582141; fax (2) 7582461; e-mail obcina.jursinci@s5.net; Mayor ALOJZIJ KAUČIČ.

Kamnik Municipality: 1240 Kamnik, Glavni trg 24; tel. (1) 8318102; fax (1) 8318119; e-mail sprejemna.pisarna@kamnik.si; internet www.kamnik.si; Mayor TONE SMOLNIKAR.

Kanal ob Soči Municipality: 5213 Kanal, trg Svobode 23; tel. (5) 3981200; fax (5) 3981223; e-mail obcina.kanal@siol.net; Mayor IPAVEC MIRAN.

Kidričevo Municipality: 2325 Kidričevo, ul. Borisa Kraigherja 25; tel. (2) 7990610; fax (2) 7990619; e-mail obcina.kidricevo@siol.net; internet www.kidricevo.si; Mayor ZVONIMIR HOLC.

Kobarid Municipality: 5222 Kobarid, trg Svobode 2; tel. (5) 3899200; fax (5) 3899211; e-mail obcina.kobarid@siol.net; internet www.kobarid.si; Mayor PAVEL GREGORČIČ.

Kobilje Municipality: 9227 Kobilje, Kobilje 35; tel. (2) 5799221; fax (2) 5799220; e-mail obcina.kobilje@siol.net; Mayor PAVEL NAMET.

Kočevje Municipality: 1330 Kočevje, Ljubljanska cesta 26; tel. (1) 8938220; fax (1) 8938230; e-mail oobcina.kocevje@siol.net; internet www.kocevje.si; Mayor JANKO VEBER.

Komen Municipality: 6223 Komen, Komen 86; tel. (5) 7310450; fax (5) 7310460; e-mail obcina@komen.si; internet www.komen.si; Mayor UROŠ SLAMIČ.

Komenda Municipality: 1218 Komenda, Zajčeva ul. 23; tel. (1) 8343210; fax (1) 8341323; e-mail obcina.komenda@siol.net; internet www.komenda.si; Mayor TOMAŽ DROLEC.

Koper (Capodistria) City Municipality: 6000 Koper, Verdijeva ul. 10; tel. (5) 6646100; fax (5) 6271602; e-mail obcina@koper.si; internet www.koper.si; Mayor BORIS POPOVIČ.

Kostel Municipality: 1336 Vas, Vas 1; tel. (1) 8948006; fax (1) 8948007; e-mail obcina.kostel@siol.net; Mayor VALENTIN JUŽNIČ.

Kozje Municipality: 3260 Kozje, Kozje 37; tel. (3) 8001400; fax (3) 5801075; e-mail obcina.kozje@siol.net; Mayor ANDREJ KOCMAN DUŠAN.

Kranj City Municipality: 4000 Kranj, Slovenski trg 1; tel. (4) 2373000; fax (4) 2373100; e-mail obcina.kranj@kranj.si; internet www.kranj.si; Mayor MOHOR BOGATAJ.

Kranjska Gora Municipality: 4280 Kranjska Gora, Kolodvorska 1A; tel. (4) 5809800; fax (4) 5809824; e-mail obcina@kranjska-gora.si; internet www.breg.si/kg; Mayor JURE ŽERJAV.

Križevci Municipality: 9242 Križevci pri Ljutomeru, Križevci 11; tel. (2) 888140; fax (2) 5871031; e-mail obcina.krizevci@siol.net; Mayor FELIKS MAVRIČ.

Krško Municipality: 8270 Krško, cesta krških žrtev 14; tel. (7) 4981100; fax (7) 4922221; e-mail obcina.krsko@krsko.si; internet www.krsko.si; Mayor FRANC BOGOVIČ.

Kungota Municipality: 2201 Zg. Kungota, Plintovec 1; tel. (2) 6550505; fax (2) 6550506; e-mail obcina@kungota.si; internet www.kungota.si; Mayor JOŽEF KARNER.

Kuzma Municipality: 9263 Kuzma, Kuzma 24; tel. (2) 5558016; fax (2) 5558018; e-mail obcina.kuzma@moj.net; Mayor JOŽEF ŠKALIČ.

Laško Municipality: 3270 Laško, Mestna ul. 2; tel. (3) 7338700; fax (3) 7338740; e-mail obcina@lasko.si; internet www.lasko.si; Mayor JOŽE RAJH.

Lenart Municipality: 2230 Lenart, trg Osvoboditve 7; tel. (2) 7291311; fax (2) 7207352; e-mail obcina@lenart.si; internet www.lenart.si; Mayor IVAN VOGRIN.

Lendava Municipality: 9220 Lendava, trg Ljudske pravice 5; tel. (2) 5789400; fax (2) 5751252; e-mail obcina@lendava.si; internet www.lendava.net; Mayor ANTON BALAŽEK.

Litija Municipality: 1270 Litija, Jerebova ul. 14; tel. (1) 8983211; fax (1) 8983835; e-mail info@litija.net; internet www.litija.net; Mayor MIROSLAV KAPLJA.

Ljubljana City Municipality: 1000 Ljubljana, Mestni trg 1; tel. (1) 3061000; fax (1) 3061021; e-mail int.relations@ljubljana.si; internet www.ljubljana.si; Mayor DANICA SIMŠIČ.

Ljubno Municipality: 3333 Ljubno ob Savinji, Cesta v Rastke 12; tel. (3) 8391770; fax (33) 5841415; e-mail obcina.ljubno@siol.net; Mayor ANKA RAKUN.

Ljutomer Municipality: 9240 Ljutomer, Vrazova 1; tel. (2) 5849044; fax (2) 5811610; e-mail osgz@siol.net; Mayor JOŽEF ŠPINDLER.

Logatec Municipality: 1370 Logatec, Tržaška cesta 15; tel. (1) 7590600; fax (1) 7590620; e-mail obcina.logatec@logatec.si; internet www.obcina-logatec.com/obcina.htm; Mayor JANEZ NAGODE.

Loška dolina Municipality: 1386 Stari trg pri Ložu, cesta Notranjskego odreda 2; tel. (1) 7057808; fax (1) 7057805; Mayor JANEZ STERLE.

Loški potok Municipality: 1318 Loški potok, Hrib 17; tel. (1) 8350100; fax (1) 8350102; Mayor JANEZ NOVAK.

Lovrenc na Pohorju Municipality: 2344 Lovrenc na Pohorju, Spodnji trg 8; tel. (2) 6751701; fax (2) 6751601; e-mail obcina@lovrenc.si; internet www.lovrenc.si; Mayor FRANC LADINEK.

Luče Municipality: 3334 Luče, Luče 106; tel. (3) 8393550; fax (3) 8393551; e-mail obcina.luce@siol.net; Mayor CIRIL ROSC.

Lukovica Municipality: 1225 Lukovica, Lukovica 46; tel. and fax (1) 7235119; e-mail obcina.lukovica@lukovica.si; internet www.lukovica.si; Mayor MATEJ KOTNIK.

Majšperk Municipality: 2322 Majšperk, Majšperk 32A; tel. (2) 7950830; fax (2) 7944221; e-mail natasa.obc.majsperk@siol.net; Mayor DARINKA FAKIN.

Maribor City Municipality: 2000 Maribor, ul. Heroja Staneta 1; tel. (2) 2201000; fax (2) 2201230; e-mail mestna.obcina@maribor.si; internet www.maribor.si; Mayor BORIS SOVIČ.

Markovci Municipality: 2281 Markovci, Markovci 43; tel. (2) 7888880; fax (2) 7888881; e-mail info@markovci.si; internet www.markovci.si; Mayor FRANC KEKEC.

Medvode Municipality: 1215 Medvode, cesta komandanta Staneta 12; tel. (1) 3619510; fax (1) 3611686; e-mail obcina@medvode.si; internet www.medvode.si; Mayor STANISLAV ŽAGAR.

Mengeš Municipality: 1234 Mengeš, Slovenska cesta 30; tel. (1) 7237081; fax (1) 7238981; e-mail obcina@menges.si; internet www.menges.si; Mayor TOMAŽ ŠTEBE.

Metlika Municipality: 8330 Metlika, Mestni trg 24; tel. (7) 3063100; fax (7) 3637402; e-mail obcina.metlika@siol.net; internet www.metlika.si; Mayor SLAVKO DRAGOVAN.

Mežica Municipality: 2392 Mežica, Trg svobode 1; tel. (2) 8279350; fax (2) 8279359; e-mail info@mezica.si; internet www.mezica.si; Mayor JANEZ PRADER.

Miklavž na Dravskem polju Municipality: 2204 Miklav, na Dravskem polju, Nad izviri 6; tel. (2) 6296820; fax (2) 6296828; e-mail obcina.miklavz@miklavz.si; internet www.miklavz.si; Mayor LEOPOLD KREMŽAR.

Miren-Kostanjevica Municipality: 5291 Miren, Miren 129; tel. (5) 3304670; fax (5) 3304682; e-mail tajnistvo@miren-kostanjevica.si; internet www.miren-kostanjevica.si; Mayor ZLATKO MARTIN MARUŠIČ.

Mirna Peč Municipality: 8216 Mirna Pě, Trg 2; tel. (7) 3078706; fax (7) 3078707; e-mail obcina.mirnapec@siol.net; Mayor ZVONKO LAH.

Mislinja Municipality: 2382 Mislinja, Šolska cesta 34; tel. (2) 8856081; fax (2) 8856065; e-mail info@mislinja.si; Mayor VIKTOR ROBNIK.

Moravče Municipality: 1251 Moravče, Trg svobode 4; tel. (1) 7232702; fax (1) 7231035; e-mail obcina.moravce@siol.net; Mayor LJUDMILA NOVAK.

Moravske Toplice Municipality: 9226 Moravske Toplice, Kranjčeva 3; tel. (2) 5481765; fax (2) 5381502; e-mail obcina

.moravsketoplice@moj.net; internet www.moravske-toplice.si; Mayor FRANC CIPOT.

Mozirje Municipality: 3330 Mozirje, Savinjska cesta 7; tel. (3) 8393300; fax (3) 8393305; e-mail obcina.mozirje@siol.net; Mayor IVAN SUHOVERŠNIK.

Murska Sobota City Municipality: 9000 Murska Sobota, Kardoševa ul. 2; tel. (2) 5311000; fax (2) 5303324; Mayor ANTON SLAVIĆ.

Muta Municipality: 2366 Muta, Glavni trg 17; tel. (2) 8761823; fax (2) 8761114; e-mail obcina.muta@muta.si; internet www.muta.si; Mayor BORIS KRALJ.

Naklo Municipality: 4202 Naklo, Glavna cesta 24; tel. (4) 2771100; fax (4) 2771111; e-mail obcina.naklo1@siol.net; Mayor IVAN JANEZ ŠTULAR.

Nazarje Municipality: 3331 Nazarje, Savinjska cesta 4; tel. (3) 8391600; fax (3) 8391615; e-mail obcina.nazarje@siol.net; Mayor IVAN PURNAT.

Nova Gorica City Municipality: 5000 Nova Gorica, Trg Edvarda Kardelja 1; tel. (5) 3350111; fax (5) 3021233; e-mail mestna.obcina@nova-gorica.si; internet www.nova-gorica.si; Mayor MIRKO BRULC.

Novo mesto City Municipality: 8000 Novo mesto, Seidlova cesta 1; tel. (7) 3939202; fax (7) 3939208; e-mail mestna.obcina@novomesto.si; internet www.novomesto.si/si; Mayor BOŠTJAN KOVAČIČ.

Odranci Municipality: 9233 Odranci, Panonska 33; tel. and fax (2) 5737176; e-mail obcina.odranci@siol.net; Mayor IVAN MARKOJA.

Oplotnica Municipality: 2317 Oplotnica, Grajska cesta 1; tel. (2) 8450900; fax (2) 8450909; e-mail obcina.oplotnica@siol.net; internet www.oplotnica.si; Mayor VLADIMIR GLOBOVNIK.

Ormož Municipality: 2270 Ormož, Ptujska cesta 6; tel. (2) 7415300; fax (2) 7415327; e-mail obcina.urad@ormoz.si; internet www.ormoz.si; Mayor VILI TROFENIK.

Osilnica Municipality: 1337 Osilnica, Osilnica 11; tel. and fax (1) 8941505; e-mail obcina@osilnica.si; internet www.osilnica.si/obcina/index.html; Mayor ANTON KOVAČ.

Pesnica Municipality: 2211 Pesnica pri Mariboru, Pesnica pri Mariboru 39A; tel. (2) 6542309; fax (2) 6530791; e-mail obcina.pesnica@medinet.si; Mayor VENČESLAV SENEKOVIČ.

Piran (Pirano) Municipality: 6330 Piran, Tartinijev trg 2; tel. (5) 6710315; fax (5) 6710308; e-mail obcina.piran@piran.si; internet www.piran.si; Mayor VOJKA ŠTULAR.

Pivka Municipality: 6257 Pivka, Kolodvorska 5; tel. (5) 7210100; fax (5) 7210102; e-mail obcina@pivka.si; internet www.pivka.si; Mayor ROBERT SMRDELJ.

Podčetrtek Municipality: 3254 Podčetrtek, Trška cesta 5; tel. (3) 8182780; fax (3) 5829198; e-mail tajnistvo@podcetrtek.si; internet www.podcetrtek.si; Mayor MARJAN DROFENIK.

Podlehnik Municipality: 2286 Podlehnik, Podlehnik 9; tel. and fax (2) 7884060; e-mail obcina.podlehnik@amis.net; internet www2.arnes.si/~osmbmkpo1s/obcina/obcina/obcina.htm; Mayor VEKOSLAV FRIC.

Podvelka Municipality: 2363 Podvelka, Podvelka 20; tel. (2) 8769510; fax (2) 8766216; e-mail obcina@podvelka.si; Mayor ANTON KOVŠE.

Polzela Municipality: 3313 Polzela, Polzela 8; tel. (3) 7033200; fax (3) 7033223; e-mail obcina@polzela.si; Mayor LJUBO ŽNIDAR.

Postojna Municipality: 6230 Postojna, Ljubljanska 4; tel. (5) 7280700; fax (5) 7280780; e-mail obcina@postojna.si; internet www.postojna.si; Mayor JERNEJ VERBIČ.

Prebold Municipality: 3312 Prebold, Hmeljarska cesta 3; tel. (3) 7036400; fax (3) 7036405; e-mail obcina.prebold@siol.net; Mayor VINKO DEBELAK.

Preddvor Municipality: 4205 Preddvor, Dvorski trg 10; tel. (4) 2751000; fax (4) 2751020; e-mail obcina.zupan@preddvor.si; internet www.preddvor.si; Mayor FRANC EKAR.

Prevalje Municipality: 2391 Prevalje, trg 2A; tel. (2) 8246100; fax (2) 3461024; e-mail obcina@prevalje.si; internet www.prevalje.si; Mayor Dr MATIC TASIČ.

Ptuj City Municipality: 2250 Ptuj, Mestni trg 1; tel. (2) 7482999; fax (2) 7482998; e-mail info@ptuj.si; internet www.ptuj.si; Mayor Dr ŠTEFAN ČELAN.

Puconci Municipality: 9201 Puconci, Puconci 80; tel. (2) 5459100; fax (2) 5459101; Mayor LUDVIK NOVAK.

Rače-Fram Municipality: 2327 Rače, Grajski trg 14; tel. (2) 6096017; fax (2) 6096018; e-mail obcina.race.fram@siol.net; Mayor BRANKO LEDINEK.

Radeče Municipality: 1433 Radeče, ul. Milana Majcna 1; tel. (1) 5685155; fax (1) 5685285; Mayor FRANC LIPOGLAVŠEK.

Radenci Municipality: 9252 Radenci, Radgonska cesta 9; tel. (2) 5669610; fax (2) 5669620; Mayor JOŽEF TOPLAK.

Radlje ob Dravi Municipality: 2360 Radlje ob Dravi, Mariborska cesta 7; tel. (2) 8871401; fax (2) 8871285; Mayor ALAN BUKOVNIK.

Radovljica Municipality: 4240 Radovljica, Gorenjska cesta 19; tel. (4) 5372300; fax (4) 5314684; e-mail obcina.radovljica@radovljica.si; internet www.radovljica.si; Mayor JANKO S. STUŠEK.

Ravne na Koroškem Municipality: 2390 Ravne na Koroškem, Gačnikova pot 5; tel. (2) 8705510; fax (2) 8705541; e-mail obcina@ravne.si; internet www.ravne.si; Mayor MAKSIMILIJAN VEČKO.

Razkrižje Municipality: 9240 Ljutomer, Šafarsko 42; tel. (2) 5849900; fax (2) 8549901; e-mail obcinarazkrizje@siol.net; internet www.razkrizje.si; Mayor STANKO IVANUŠIČ.

Ribnica Municipality: 1310 Ribnica, Gorenjska cesta 3; tel. (1) 8372000; fax (1) 8361091; e-mail obcina.ribnica@siol.net; internet www.ribnica.si; Mayor ALOJZ MARN.

Ribnica na Pohorju Municipality: 2364 Ribnica na Pohorju, Ribnica na Pohorju 1; tel. (2) 8880556; fax (2) 8880558; e-mail obcina@ribnicanapohorju.si; internet www.ribnicanapohorju.si; Mayor MARIJA SGERM.

Rogaška Slatina Municipality: 3250 Rogaška Slatina, ul.Izletniška 2; tel. (3) 8181700; fax (3) 8181724; e-mail obcina@rogaska-slatina.si; internet www.rogaska-slatina.si; Mayor BRANKO KIDRIČ.

Rogašovci Municipality: 9262 Rogašovci, Svetij Jurij 15A; tel. (2) 5588404; fax (2) 5571607; e-mail obcina.rogasovci@siol.net; Mayor JANKO HALB.

Rogatec Municipality: 3252 Rogatec, Ceste 11; tel. (3) 8121000; fax (3) 8121012; e-mail obcina.rogatec@siol.net; Mayor MARTIN MIKOLIČ.

Ruše Municipality: 2342 Ruše, Trg Vstaje 11; tel. (2) 6690640; fax (2) 6690647; e-mail info@ruse.si; internet www.ruse.si; Mayor VILI REZMAN.

Šalovci Municipality: 9204 Šalovci, Šalovci 162; tel. (7) 5598050; fax (7) 5598054; e-mail obcina.salovci@siol.net; Mayor ALEKSANDER ABRAHAM.

Selnica ob Dravi Municipality: 2352 Selnica ob Dravi, Slovenski trg 4; tel. (2) 6730202; fax (2) 6730214; e-mail obcina.selnica@kksonline.com; Mayor VLADIMIR SABOLEK.

Semič Municipality: 8333 Semič, Štefanov trg 9; tel. (7) 3565360; fax (7) 3565365; e-mail obcina.semic@siol.net; internet www.semic.si; Mayor IVAN BUKOVEC.

Šempeter-Vrtojba Municipality: 5290 Šempeter pri Gorici, Cesta Goriške fronte 11; tel. (5) 3351000; fax (5) 3351007; e-mail obcina.sempeter-vrtojba@siol.net; internet www.sempeter-vrtojba.si; Mayor DRAGAN VALENČIČ.

Šenčur Municipality: 4208 Šenčur, Kranjska cesta 11; tel. (4) 2519100; fax (4) 2519111; e-mail obcina@sencur.si; internet www.sencur.si; Mayor MIRO KOZELJ.

Šentilj Municipality: 2212 Šentilj, Šentilj 69; tel. (2) 6511331; fax (2) 6511351; e-mail obcina@sentilj.si; Mayor EDVARD ČAGRAN.

Šentjernej Municipality: 8310 Šentjernej, Trubarjeva cesta 5; tel. (7) 3933560; fax (7) 3933577; e-mail sentjernej@siol.net; internet www.sentjernej.si; Mayor FRANC HUDOKLIN.

Šentjur pri Celju Municipality: 3230 Šentjur, Mestni trg 10; tel. (3) 7471280; fax (3) 7471285; e-mail stefan.tisel@obc-sentjur.si; internet obcina.sentjur.com; Mayor ŠTEFAN TISELJ.

Sevnica Municipality: 8290 Sevnica, Glavni trg 19A; tel. (7) 8161200; fax (7) 8161210; e-mail obcina.sevnica@siol.net; internet www.obcina-sevnica.si; Mayor KRISTIJAN JANC.

Sežana Municipality: 6210 Sežana, Partizanska cesta 4; tel. (5) 7310101; fax (5) 7310123; e-mail urad.zupana@sezana.si; internet www.sezana.si; Mayor MIROSLAV KLUN.

Škocjan Municipality: 8275 Škocjan, Škocjan 67; tel. and fax (7) 3076310; e-mail skocjan.obcina@siol.net; Mayor ANTON ZUPET.

Škofja Loka Municipality: 4220 Škofja Loka, Poljanska 2; tel. (4) 5112300; fax (4) 5112318; e-mail obcina@skofjaloka.si; internet www.skofjaloka.si; Mayor IGOR DRAKSLER.

Škofljica Municipality: 1291 Škofljica, Šmarska cesta 3; tel. (1) 3666311; fax (1) 3667872; e-mail info@skofljica.si; internet www.skofljica.si; Mayor Dr JOŽE JURKOVIČ.

Slovenj Gradec City Municipality: 2380 Slovenj Gradec, Šolska ul. 5; tel. (2) 8812110; fax (2) 8812118; e-mail matjaz.zanoskar@slovenj-gradec.si; internet www.slovenj-gradec.si; Mayor MATJAŽ ZANOŠKAR.

Slovenska Bistrica Municipality: 2310 Slovenska Bistrica, Kolodvorska ul. 10; tel. (2) 8181241; fax (2) 8181141; e-mail obcina.sl .bistrica@amis.net; Mayor Dr IVAN ŽAGAR.

Slovenske Konjice Municipality: 3210 Slovenske Konjice, Stari trg 29; tel. (3) 7573350; fax (3) 7574328; e-mail info@ slovenskekonjice.si; internet www.slovenskekonjice.si; Mayor JANEZ JAZBEC.

Šmarje pri Jelšah Municipality: 3240 Šmarje pri Jelšah, Aškerčev trg 12; tel. (3) 8171600; fax (3) 8171626; e-mail obcina@ smarje-pri-jelsah.si; internet www.smarje-pri-jelsah.si; Mayor JOŽEF ČAKŠ.

Šmartno ob Paki Municipality: 3327 Šmartno ob Paki, Šmartno ob Paki 72; tel. (3) 8984950; fax (3) 8984960; e-mail obcina.smartno@ net.rr-vel.si; internet www.rr-vel.si/smartno; Mayor ALOJZ PODG-ORŠEK.

Šmartno pri Litiji Municipality: 1275 Šmartno pri Litiji, Toma-zinova 2; tel. and fax (1) 8987867; e-mail obcina@smartno-litija.si; internet www.smartno-litija.si; Mayor MILAN IZLAKAR.

Sodražica Municipality: 1317 Sodražica, Trg 25 Maja 3; tel. (1) 8366075; fax (1) 8371004; e-mail obcina.sodrazica@siol.net; Mayor ANDREJ POGORELEC.

Solčava Municipality: 3335 Solčava, Solčava 16; tel. (3) 8392750; fax (3) 8392755; e-mail obcina.solcava@siol.net; Mayor VOJTEH KLE-MENŠEK.

Šoštanj Municipality: 3325 Šoštanj, Trg Svobode 12; tel. (3) 8984300; fax (3) 8984333; e-mail obcina@sostanj.si; internet www .sostanj.si; Mayor MILAN KOPUŠAR.

Starše Municipality: 2205 Starše, Starše 93; tel. (2) 6864800; fax (2) 6864810; e-mail obcina@starse.si; Mayor VILI DUCMAN.

Štore Municipality: 3220 Štore, cesta XIV Divizije 15; tel. (3) 7803840; fax (3) 7803850; e-mail obcina.store@siol.net; Mayor FRANC JAZBEC.

Sveta Ana Municipality: 2233 Sveta Ana, Sveta Ana 17; tel. (2) 7295800; fax (2) 7295885; e-mail obcina.sv.ana@siol.net; internet www.sv-ana.si; Mayor BOGOMIR RUHITEL.

Sveti Andraž v Slovenskih goricah Municipality: 2255 Vito-marci, Vitomarci 71; tel. (2) 7579530; fax (2) 7574921; e-mail obcina .sv.andraz@siol.net; Mayor FRANC KREPŠA.

Sveti Jurij Municipality: 9244 Svetij Jurij ob Ščavnici, Biserjane 1a; tel. and fax (2) 5681004; e-mail obcina.sv.jurij@siol.net; Mayor ANTON SLANA.

Tabor Municipality: 3304 Tabor, Tabor 25; tel. (3) 7057080; fax (3) 7047081; e-mail obcina.tabor@siol.net; Mayor VILKO JAZBINŠEK.

Tišina Municipality: 9261 Tišina, Tišina 4; tel. (2) 5391710; fax (2) 5391711; e-mail obcina.tisina@siol.net; Mayor JOŽEF POREDOŠ.

Tolmin Municipality: 5220 Tolmin, Padlih borcev 2; tel. (5) 3819500; fax (5) 3819533; e-mail obcina.tolmin@siol.net; Mayor JOŽEF ERNEST KEMPERLE.

Trbovlje Municipality: 1420 Trbovlje, Leninov trg 4; tel. (3) 5634800; fax (3) 5627986; e-mail zupan.trb@siol.net; internet www .trbovlje.si; Mayor BOGDAN BAROVIČ.

Trebnje Municipality: 8210 Trebnje, Goliev trg 5; tel. (7) 3481100; fax (7) 3481131; internet www.trebnje.si; Mayor MARICA ŠKODA.

Trnovska vas Municipality: 2254 Trnovska vas, Trnovska vas 42; tel. (2) 7579510; fax (2) 7571661; e-mail spletni.urednik@ trnovska-vas.si; internet www.trnovska-vas.si; Mayor KARL VURCER.

Tržič Municipality: 4290 Tržič, Trg Svobode 18; tel. (4) 5971510; fax (4) 5971513; e-mail obcina.trzic@trzic.si; internet www.trzic.si; Mayor PAVEL RUPAR.

Trzin Municipality: 1236 Trzin, Mengeška cesta 9; tel. (1) 7226100; fax (1) 7211060; e-mail info@obcina-trzin.si; internet www .obcina-trzin.si; Mayor ANTON PERŠAK.

Turnišče Municipality: 9224 Turnišče, ul. Štefana Kovača 73; tel. (2) 5721370; fax (2) 5735041; e-mail obcina.turnisce@siol.net; Mayor JOŽE KOCET.

Velenje City Municipality: 3320 Velenje, Titov trg 1; tel. (3) 8961600; fax (3) 8961654; e-mail info@velenje.si; internet www .velenje.si; Mayor SREČKO MEH.

Velika Polana Municipality: 9225 Velika Polana, Velika Polana 111; tel. (2) 5737030; fax (2) 5737032; e-mail obcina@velika-polana .si; Mayor ANDREJ LEBAR.

Velike Lašče Municipality: 1315 Velike Lašče, Levstikov trg 1; tel. and fax (1) 7889238; e-mail zupan@velike-lasce.si; internet www .velike-lasce.si; Mayor ANTON ZAKRAJŠEK.

Veržej Municipality: 9241 Veržej, ul. bratstva in enotnosti 8; tel. (2) 5888180; fax (2) 5888181; e-mail obcina.verzej@siol.net; Mayor DRAGO LEGEN.

Videm Municipality: 2284 Videm pri Ptuju, Videm pri Ptuju 54; tel. (2) 7619400; fax (2) 7649401; e-mail info@videm.si; Mayor FRI-DERIK BRAČIČ.

Vipava Municipality: 5271 Vipava, Glavni trg 15; tel. (5) 3643410; fax (5) 3643412; e-mail obcina.vipava@siol.net; Mayor IVAN PRINCES.

Vitanje Municipality: 3205 Vitanje, Grajski trg 1; tel. (3) 7574350; fax (3) 7574351; e-mail info@vitanje.si; internet www.vitanje.si; Mayor VETRIH SLAVKO.

Vodice Municipality: 1217 Vodice, Kopitarjev trg 1; tel. (1) 8332610; fax (1) 8332630; e-mail vodice@siol.net; internet www .vodice.si; Mayor BRANE PODBORŠEK.

Vojnik Municipality: 3212 Vojnik, Keršova ul. 1; tel. (3) 7800620; fax (3) 7800637; e-mail obcina@vojnik.si; internet www.vojnik.si; Mayor BENEDIKT PODERGAJS.

Vransko Municipality: 3305 Vransko, Vransko 59; tel. (3) 7032800; fax (3) 7032816; e-mail obcina.vransko@vransko.si; internet www.vransko.si; Mayor FRANC SUŠNIK.

Vrhnika Municipality: 1360 Vrhnika, Tržaška cesta 1; tel. (1) 7555412; fax (1) 7505158; e-mail zupan.obcina@vrhnika.si; internet www.vrhnika.si; Mayor Dr MARJAN RIHAR.

Vuzenica Municipality: 2367 Vuzenica, Mladinska ul. 1; tel. (2) 8791220; fax (2) 8791221; e-mail obcina.vuzenica@siol.net; internet www.vuzenica.si; Mayor MIRAN KUS.

Zagorje ob Savi Municipality: 1410 Zagorje ob Savi, cesta 9 avgusta 5; tel. (1) 5655700; fax (1) 5664011; e-mail obcina.zagorje@ zagorje.si; internet www.zagorje.si; Mayor MATJAŽ ŠVAGAN.

Žalec Municipality: 3310 Žalec, ul. Savinjske čete 5; tel. (3) 7136400; fax (3) 7136464; e-mail obcina.zalec@eunet.si; internet www.zalec.si; Mayor ALOJZ POSEDEL.

Zavrč Municipality: 2283 Zavrč, Zavrč 11; tel. (2) 7610482; fax (2) 7610483; e-mail obcina.zavrc@siol.net; Mayor MIRAN VUK.

Železniki Municipality: 4228 Železniki, Češnjica 48; tel. (4) 5000000; fax (4) 5000020; e-mail uprava@obcina.zelezniki.si; internet www.zelezniki.si; Mayor MIHAEL PREVC.

Žetale Municipality: 2287 Žetale, Žetale 1; tel. (2) 7610644; fax (2) 7695721; e-mail obcina.zetale@siol.net; internet zetale.cjb.net; Mayor ANTON BUTOLEN.

Žiri Municipality: 4226 Žiri, Trg Svobode 2; tel. (4) 5050700; fax (4) 5105444; Mayor BOJAN STARMAN.

Žirovnica Municipality: 4274 Žirovnica, Breznica 3; tel. (4) 5809100; fax (4) 5809109; e-mail obcina@zirovnica.si; internet www .zirovnica.si; Mayor FRANC PFAJFAR.

Zreče Municipality: 3214 Zreče, Cesta na Roglo 13B; tel. (3) 7571700; fax (3) 5762498; e-mail info@zrece.si; internet www.zrece .si; Mayor JOŽEF KOŠIR.

Žužemberk Municipality: 8360 Žužemberk, Grajski trg 33; tel. (7) 3885180; fax (7) 3885181; e-mail obcina.zuzemberk@siol.net; Mayor FRANC ŠKUFCA.

Political Organizations

Christian Social Union (KSU) (Krščansko-Socialna unija): 1000 Ljubljana, Mariborska 26; f. 1995; Pres. FRANC MIKLAVIČ; Sec.-Gen. IVAN KEPIČ.

Democratic Party of Pensioners of Slovenia (DeSUS) (Demok-ratična stranka upokojencev Slovenije): 1000 Ljubljana, Kersnikova 6; tel. (1) 324171; fax (1) 1314113; internet www.desus.si; Pres. JANKO KUSAR.

Democratic Party of Slovenia (Demokratska stranka Slovenije): 1000 Ljubljana, Linhartova 13; tel. (1) 1261073; fax (1) 1255077; f. 1994 by mems of Democratic Party who opted not to join the LDS (see below); Pres. ANTON PERŠAK; 2,200 mems.

Greens of Slovenia (Zeleni Slovenije): 1000 Ljubljana; f. 1989; in 1993 the party split into two factions, one retaining the original name, the other, more radical wing adopting the title, Greens of Slovenia—Eco-Social Party; Leader VANE GOŠNIK.

Liberal Democracy of Slovenia (LDS) (Liberalna demokracija Slovenije): 1000 Ljubljana, Republike trg 3; tel. (1) 2000310; fax (1) 1256150; e-mail lds@lds.si; internet www.lds.si; f. 1994 by a merger of the Liberal Democratic Party, the Greens of Slovenia—Eco-Social Party, the Democratic Party and the Socialist Party of Slovenia; Pres. Dr JANEZ DRNOVŠEK; Gen. Sec. GREGOR GOLOBIČ; 18,000 mems.

National Democratic Party (NDP) (Narodna demokratska stranka): 1000 Ljubljana; withdrew from SCD 1994; Pres. MARJAN VIDMAR.

New Party (Nova Stranka): 1000 Ljubljana, Linhartova cesta 13; tel. (1) 3063995; fax (1) 2310567; e-mail info@nova-stranka.si; internet www.nova-stranka.si; Pres. Dr GORAZD DREVENŠEK.

New Slovenia—Christian People's Party (NSi) (Nova Slovenija—Krščanska ljudska stranka): 1000 Ljubljana, Cankarjeva 11; tel. (1) 5004180; fax (1) 5004190; e-mail tajnistvo@nsi.si; internet www.nsi.si; f. Aug. 2000 by disaffected mems of the Slovenian People's Party; Pres. Dr ANDREJ BAJUK.

Party of Albanian Democratic Union: Ljubljana; f. 2000; Chair. BESNIK TALLAJ.

Slovenian National Party (SNP) (Slovenska nacionalna stranka—SNS): 1000 Ljubljana, Tivolska 13; tel. and fax (1) 4325207; internet www.sns.si; f. 1991; right-wing nationalist party; Pres. ZMAGO JELINČIČ; Vice-Pres. SAŠO PEČE; Sec.-Gen. MIŠA GLAŽAR; 5,500 mems.

Slovenian National Right (SNR) (Slovenska nacionalna desnica): f. 1993 by a 'breakaway' faction of the SNP; Pres. SAŠO LAP.

Slovenian People's Party (SPP) (Slovenska ljudska stranka—SLS): 1000 Ljubljana, Zarnikova 3; tel. (1) 301891; fax (1) 301871; internet www.sls.si; f. 1989 as the Slovenian Farmers' Association; conservative; merged with the Slovenian Christian Democrats in April 2000; Pres. FRANC ZAGOZEN; Chair. JOŽE ZUPANCIC.

Social Democratic Party of Slovenia (SDPS) (Socialdemokratska stranka Slovenije—SDS): 1000 Ljubljana, Komenskega 11; tel. (1) 4345450; fax (1) 4345452; e-mail tajnistvo@sds.si; internet www.sds.si; f. 1989; centre-right; mem. of European People's Party; Pres. JANEZ JANŠA; Sec.-Gen. DUŠAN STRNAD; Parl. Group Leader ANDREJ VIZJAK; 20,000 mems.

United List of Social Democrats (ULSD) (Združena lista socialnih demokratov—ZLSD): 1000 Ljubljana, Levstikova 15; tel. (1) 2515897; fax (1) 4261170; e-mail info@zlsd.si; internet www.zlsd.si; f. 1992 as the United List, an electoral alliance of the Democratic Party of Pensioners, the Party of Democratic Reform of Slovenia, the Social Democratic Union and the Workers' Party of Slovenia; in 1993 it became a single party and adopted its current name; Pres. BORUT PAHOR; Gen. Sec. DUSAN KUMER; 23,000 mems.

Youth Party of Slovenia (Stranka mladih Slovenije—SMS): 1000 Ljubljana, Rimska cesta 8; tel. (1) 4211400; e-mail info@sms.si; internet www.sms.si; Pres. DOMINIK S. ČERNJAK.

Diplomatic Representation

EMBASSIES IN SLOVENIA

Albania: 1000 Ljubljana, Ob Ljubljanici 12; tel. (1) 4322324; fax (1) 4322053; e-mail albania@siol.net; Ambassador DAUT GUMENI.

Austria: 1000 Ljubljana, Prešernova cesta 23; tel. (1) 4790700; fax (1) 2521717; e-mail laibach-ob@bmaa.gv.at; Ambassador Dr FERDINAND MAYRHOFER-GRUNBUHEL.

Belgium: 1000 Ljubljana, Republike trg 3/IX; tel. (1) 2006010; fax (1) 4266395; e-mail ljubljana@si-diplobel.org; Ambassador GEORGES GODART.

Bosnia and Herzegovina: 1000 Ljubljana, Korlajeva 26; tel. (1) 4324042; fax (1) 4322230; Ambassador MLADEN BOSIĆ.

Bulgaria: 1000 Ljubljana, Stari trg 1; tel. (1) 4265744; fax (1) 4258845; Chargé d'affaires a.i. Dr TODOR DRAZHEV.

China, People's Republic: 1111 Ljubljana, Legatova ul. 2; tel. (1) 2005810; fax (1) 2005832; Ambassador YANG HEXIONG.

Croatia: 1000 Ljubljana, Gruberjevo nabrežje 6; tel. (1) 4256220; fax (1) 4258106; e-mail croemb.slovenia@siol.net; Ambassador CELESTIN SARDELIĆ.

Czech Republic: 1000 Ljubljana, Riharjeva 1; tel. (1) 4202450; fax (1) 2839259; e-mail ljubljana@embassy.mzv.cz; Ambassador TOMÁŠ SZUNYOG.

Denmark: 1000 Ljubljana, Tivolska 48; tel. (1) 4380800; fax (1) 4317417; e-mail ljuamb@danish-embassy.si; Ambassador LARS MØLLER.

France: 1000 Ljubljana, Barjanska cesta 1; tel. (1) 4790400; fax (1) 4790410; e-mail info@ambafrance.si; internet www.ambafrance.si; Ambassador OLIVIER DE LA BAUME.

Germany: 1000 Ljubljana, Prešernova cesta 27; tel. (1) 2516166; fax (1) 4250899; e-mail germanembassy-slovenia@siol.net; Ambassador HEIKE ZENKER.

Greece: 1000 Ljubljana, Mestni trg 8; tel. (1) 4201400; fax (1) 2811114; e-mail emb.gr.slo@siol.net; Ambassador GEORGE NICOLAIDIS.

Holy See: 1000 Ljubljana, Krekov trg 1; tel. (1) 4339204; fax (1) 4315130; e-mail nun-slo@siol.net; Apostolic Nuncio Most Rev. MARIAN OLEŚ (Titular Archbishop of Ratiaria).

Hungary: 1210 Ljubljana, Konrada Babnika 5; tel. (1) 5121882; fax (1) 5121878; e-mail huemblju@siol.net; Ambassador GÁBOR BAGI.

Italy: 1000 Ljubljana, Snežniška 8; tel. (1) 4262194; fax (1) 4253302; e-mail amblubiana@siol.net; Ambassador NORBERTO CAPPELLO.

Macedonia, former Yugoslav republic: 1000 Ljubljana, Dunajska 104; tel. (1) 5684454; fax (1) 5685181; Ambassador ILJAZ SABRIU.

Netherlands: 1000 Ljubljana, Palača Kapitelj, Polijanski nasip 6; tel. (1) 4201462; fax (1) 4201417; Ambassador JAN C. HENNEMAN.

Poland: 1000 Ljubljana, Rožna dolina XV, št. 18; tel. (1) 4232882; fax (1) 4232881; e-mail ambpol.si@siol.net; internet www.poland-embassy.si; Ambassador JANUSZ JESIONEK.

Romania: 1000 Ljubljana, Podlimbarskega 43; tel. (1) 5058294; fax (1) 5055432; e-mail embassy.of.romania@siol.net; Ambassador VICTOR CHIUJDEA.

Russia: 1000 Ljubljana, Tomšičeva 9; tel. (1) 4256875; fax (1) 4256878; e-mail ambrus.slo@siol.net; Ambassador VYACHESLAV I. DOLGOV.

Serbia and Montenegro: 1000 Ljubljana, Vogelna ul. 8; tel. and fax (1) 4380110; Ambassador Dr IVO VISKOVIĆ.

Slovakia: 1000 Ljubljana, Tivolska cesta 4; tel. and fax (1) 4255425; e-mail velepos.slovakia@siol.net; Ambassador Dr ROMAN PALDAN.

Spain: 1000 Ljubljana, Trnovski pristan 24; tel. (1) 4202330; fax (1) 4202333; Ambassador LUIS FELIPE FERNÁNDEZ DE LA PEÑA.

Sweden: 1000 Ljubljana, Ajdovščina 4/8; tel. (1) 3000270; fax (1) 3000271; Ambassador JOHN-CHRISTER AHLANDER.

Switzerland: 1000 Ljubljana, Republike trg 3/VI; tel. (1) 2008640; fax (1) 2008669; Ambassador PAUL KOLLER.

Turkey: 1000 Ljubljana, Livarska 4; tel. (1) 4368149; fax (1) 4368148; e-mail vrtucije@siol.net; Ambassador HALIL AKINCI.

United Kingdom: 1000 Ljubljana, Republike trg 3/IV; tel. (1) 2003910; fax (1) 4250174; e-mail info@british-embassy.si; internet www.british-embassy.si; Ambassador HUGH ROGER MORTIMER.

USA: 1000 Ljubljana, Prešernova cesta 31; tel. (1) 2005500; fax (1) 2005555; e-mail email@usembassy.si; internet www.usembassy.si; Ambassador JOHNNY YOUNG.

Judicial System

The Slovenian Constitution guarantees the independence of the judiciary.

The 44 district courts decide minor cases (criminal acts incurring a maximum sentence of three years' imprisonment, property disputes where the value of the disputed property is not more than SlT 2m., and certain other civil cases). The 11 regional courts act as courts of the first instance in all cases other than those for which the district courts have jurisdiction. Four regional courts act as courts of the second instance. There are, in addition, labour courts, which have jurisdiction in labour disputes, and social courts, which adjudicate in disputes over pensions, welfare allocations and other social benefits. A higher labour and social court has jurisdiction in the second instance. The Supreme Court is the highest authority for civil and criminal law. There is also a Constitutional Court, composed of nine judges, each elected for a single term of nine years, which determines, *inter alia*, the conformity of national legislation and all other regulations with the Constitution.

Constitutional Court of the Republic of Slovenia: 1000 Ljubljana, Beethovnova 10; tel. (1) 4776400; fax (1) 2510451; e-mail info@us-rs.si; internet www.us-rs.si; Pres. DRAGICA WEDAM-LUKIČ.

Supreme Court: 1000 Ljubljana, Tavčarjeva 9; tel. (1) 3005310; fax (1) 3005318; e-mail mitja.deisinger@sodisce.si; internet www.sodisce.si; Pres. MITJA DEISINGER.

Office of the Public Prosecutor: 1511 Ljubljana, Dunajska 22; tel. (1) 2320396; fax (1) 4310381; e-mail sebastijan.rakovec@dt-rs.si; Public Prosecutor ZDENKA CERAR.

Office of the Public Attorney: 1000 Ljubljana, Cankarjeva 5; Public Attorney JOŽE GREGORIČ.

Religion

Most of the population are Christian, predominantly adherents of the Roman Catholic Church. The Archbishop of Ljubljana is the most senior Roman Catholic prelate in Slovenia. There is also a

Slovene Old Catholic Church. There are few Protestant Christians, despite the importance of a Calvinist sect (the Church of Carniola) to the development of Slovene literature in the 16th century. There are some members of the Eastern Orthodox Church, some Muslims and a small Jewish community.

CHRISTIANITY

The Roman Catholic Church

The Roman Catholic Church in Slovenia comprises one archdiocese and two dioceses. At 31 December 2001 there were an estimated 1,642,000 adherents (equivalent to about 81.9% of the total population).

Bishops' Conference

Slovenska Škofovska Konferenca, 1000 Ljubljana, p.p. 121/III, Ciril Metodov trg 4; tel. (1) 2342600; fax (1) 2342612.

f. 1993; Pres. Most Rev. FRANC RODÉ (Archbishop of Ljubljana).

Archbishop of Ljubljana: Most Rev. FRANC RODÉ, 1001 Ljubljana, p.p. 1990, Ciril Metodov trg 4; tel. (1) 2342600; fax (1) 2314169; e-mail nadskofija.ljubljana@rkc.si.

Old Catholic Church

Slovene Old Catholic Church: 1000 Ljubljana; Maribor, Vita Kraigherja 2; f. 1948; Bishop Rev. JOSIP KVOČIĆ.

Protestant Church

Evangelical Lutheran Church of Slovenia: 9226 Moravske Toplice, 11 Levstikova; tel. (2) 5381323; fax (2) 5381324; e-mail evang.cerkev.si@siol.nt; f. 1561; 20,000 mems; Chair. GEZA ERNIŠA.

JUDAISM

Jewish Community of Slovenia: 1000 Ljubljana, Trzaska 2, POB 37; tel. and fax (1) 2521836; e-mail jss@siol.net; Pres. ANDREJ KOŽAR BECK.

The Press

The publications listed below are in Slovene, unless otherwise indicated.

PRINCIPAL DAILIES

Delo (Event): 1509 Ljubljana, Dunajska 5; tel. (1) 4727402; fax (1) 4737406; e-mail webmaster@delo.si; internet www.delo.si; f. 1959; morning; Editor-in-Chief MITJA MERŠOL; circ. 93,781.

Dnevnik (Daily): 1510 Ljubljana, Kopitarjeva 2; tel. (1) 3082100; fax (1) 3082189; e-mail info@dnevnik.si; internet www.dnevnik.si; f. 1951; evening; independent; Man. Dir BRANKO BERGANT; Editor-in-Chief ZLATKO ŠETINC; circ. 63,000.

Slovenske novice (Slovene News): 1509 Ljubljana, Dunajska 5; tel. (1) 1737700; fax (1) 1737352; f. 1991; Editor-in-Chief MARJAN BAUER; Man. Editor TIT DOBERSEK; circ. 80,000.

Večer (Evening): 2000 Maribor, Svetozarevska 14; tel. (2) 2353500; fax (2) 2353368; e-mail desk@vecer.com; internet www.vecer.si; f. 1945; Dir BORIS CEKOV; Editor-in-Chief MILAN PREDAN; circ. 70,000.

PERIODICALS

Antena: 1000 Ljubljana, Slovenska 15; tel. (1) 1253418; fax (1) 1253367; f. 1965; weekly; youth magazine concerned with popular culture; Editor-in-Chief JASMIN PETAN MALACHOVSKY; circ. 20,000.

Ars Vivendi: 1000 Ljubljana, Poljanska 6; tel. and fax (1) 317058; f. 1987; quarterly; visual arts and design; publ. in Slovene and English; Editor-in-Chief SONJA TOMAŽIČ; circ. 10,000.

Avto magazin: 1000 Ljubljana, Dunajska 5; tel. (1) 1738251; fax (1) 1738220; f. 1967; fortnightly; cars, motorcycles and sports; Editor BOŠTJAN JEVŠEK; circ. 16,000.

Delavska enotnost: 1000 Ljubljana, Dalmatinova 4; tel. (1) 1310033; fax (1) 1313942; f. 1942; weekly; trade union issues; Dir and Editor-in-Chief MARJAN HORVAT; circ. 16,000.

Dolenjski list: 8000 Novo Mesto, Glavni trg 24; tel. (7) 3323606; fax (7) 3322898; f. 1950; weekly; general and local information; Editor-in-Chief MARJAN LEGAN; circ. 24,000.

Družina: 1000 Ljubljana, Krekov trg 1; tel. (1) 1316202; fax (1) 1316152; e-mail druzina@siol.net; f. 1952; Christian; Editor-in-Chief JANEZ GRIL; circ. 70,000.

Finance: 1509 Ljubljana, Dunajska 5; tel. (1) 1330137; fax (1) 1312223; internet www.finance-on.net; f. 1992; 2 a week; Editor-in-Chief JOŽE PETROVČIČ; circ. 8,500.

Flaneur: 1000 Ljubljana, Šaranovičeva 12; f. 1992; bi-monthly; English; politics, economy, culture and leisure; Editor-in-Chief TADEJ ČATER; circ. 2,500.

Gea: 1536 Ljubljana, Slovenska 29; tel. (1) 2413230; fax (1) 1252836; e-mail gea@mkz-lj.si; internet www.mkz-lj.si; f. 1990; monthly; popular science; Editor-in-Chief JANA LESKOVEC; circ. 23,000.

Gorenjski glas: 4000 Kranj, Zoisova ul. 1; tel. (4) 2014200; fax (4) 2014213; f. 1947; 2 a week; general and regional information; Editor-in-Chief MARIJA VOLEJAK; circ. 23,300.

Gospodarski vestnik: 1509 Ljubljana, Dunajska 5; tel. (1) 3091700; fax (1) 3091705; e-mail gvrevija@gvestnik.si; internet www.gvestnik.si; f. 1952; weekly; business; Editor-in-Chief JOŽE PETROVČIČ; circ. 9,500.

Jana: 1509 Ljubljana, Dunajska 5; tel. (1) 319260; fax (1) 1334320; f. 1972; weekly; women's interest; Editor-in-Chief BERNARDA JEKLIN; circ. 62,000.

Kaj: 62000 Maribor, Svetozarevska 14; tel. (2) 26951; fax (2) 227736; f. 1984; weekly; popular; Editor-in-Chief MILAN PREDAN; circ. 16,500.

Kmečki glas: 1000 Ljubljana, p.p. 47, Železna 14; tel. (1) 1735350; fax (1) 1735376; weekly; general and agricultural news; Dir BORIS DOLNIČAR; circ. 38,000.

Lipov list: 1000 Ljubljana, Miklosičeva 38/6; tel. (1) 312087; fax (1) 1332338; e-mail tzs@siol.net; monthly; Editor-in-Chief MARJETICA NOVAK.

Mag: 1000 Ljubljana, Njegoševa 14; tel. (1) 319480; fax (1) 1329158; f. 1995; weekly; news and politics; Editor-in-Chief DANILO SLIVNIK.

Manager: 1000 Ljubljana, Dunajska 5; tel. (1) 3091990; fax (1) 3091705; internet www.gvrevija.com/manager; f. 1990; monthly; business management; Editor-in-Chief JOŽE PETROVČIČ; circ. 3,000.

Mladina: 1000 Ljubljana, Resljeva 16; tel. (1) 1328175; fax (1) 1331239; f. 1942; weekly; news magazine; Editor-in-Chief JANI SEVER; circ. 30,000.

Moj mikro: 1509 Ljubljana, Dunajska 5; tel. (1) 4738261; fax (1) 4738109; e-mail marjan.kodelja@delo-revije.si; internet www.delo-revije.si; monthly; personal computers; Editor-in-Chief MARJAN KODELJA.

Muska: 1000 Ljubljana, Kersnikova 4; tel. (1) 1317039; fax (1) 322570; e-mail kaja.sivic@kiss.uni_lj.si; monthly; music; Editor-in-Chief KAJA SIVIČ.

Naš Čas (Our Time): 63320 Velenje, Foltova 10; tel. (3) 855450; fax (3) 851990; f. 1956; weekly; general and regional information; Editor-in-Chief STANE VOVK; circ. 6,250.

Nedeljski dnevnik (Weekly Record): 1000 Ljubljana, Kopitarieva 2; tel. (1) 1325261; fax (1) 1321020; f. 1961; weekly; popular; Editor-in-Chief ZLATKO ŠETINC; circ. 171,000.

Novi tednik (New Weekly): 3000 Celje, Prešernova 19; tel. (3) 442500; fax (3) 441032; f. 1945; weekly; general and local information; Editor-in-Chief BRANE STAMEJČIČ; circ. 16,980.

Obrtnik: 1000 Ljubljana, Celovška 71; tel. (1) 5830507; fax (1) 5193496; e-mail revija.obrtnik@ozs.si; internet www.ozs.si; f. 1971; monthly; small businesses; Editor-in-Chief MIRAN JAREC; circ. 60,000.

Pavliha: 1000 Ljubljana, Slovenska 15; tel. (1) 221661; monthly; satire; Editor-in-Chief JOZE PETELIN.

PIL: 1000 Ljubljana, Nazorjeva 1; tel. (1) 2413220; fax (1) 4252836; e-mail pil@mkz-lj.si; internet www.mkz-lj.si; teenagers' interest; Editor-in-Chief YANA ZIZKELBACH; circ. 30,000.

Podjetnik: 1000 Ljubljana, Dunajska 51; tel. (1) 1330102; fax (1) 1330450; f. 1992; monthly; business and management; Editor-in-Chief JOŽE VILFAN; circ. 8,500.

Primorske novice (News from the Coast): 6000 Koper, OF ul. 12; tel. (5) 6648100; fax (5) 6272350; e-mail editors@prim-nov.si; internet www.prim-nov.si; f. 1947; 3 a week; general and regional information; Editor-in-Chief BOJAN GLUHAK; circ. 28,000.

Profit: 1000 Ljubljana, Dunajska 7; tel. (1) 4304310; fax (1) 2318940; e-mail profit.uredmistvo@sid.net; 2 a month; business; Editor-in-Chief JOŽE SIMČIČ.

Rodna gruda (Native Bosom): 1000 Ljubljana, Cankarjeva 1/II, Združenje Slovenska izseljenska matica; tel. (1) 2410286; fax (1) 4251673; e-mail rodna.gruda@zdruzenje-sim.si; internet sim.kivi-com.si/default2.asp?type=2&MenuID=1535; f. 1951; monthly; ethnic issues and news; Editor-in-Chief JOŽE PREŠEREN; circ. 4,000.

7D: 2000 Maribor, Svetozarevska 14; tel. (2) 224221; fax (2) 211264; f. 1972; weekly; general, travel; Man. Dir BOŽO ZORKA; Editor-in-Chief MILAN PREDAN; circ. 20,000.

Slovenia Weekly: 1000 Ljubljana, Hradeckega 38; tel. (1) 4261412; fax (1) 5402027; e-mail marketing@vitrum.si; internet weekly.vitrum.si; f. 1994; weekly; politics and business; Editor-in-Chief TOMAŽ GERDINA; circ. 3,000.

Slovenian Business Report: 1000 Ljubljana, Dunajska 5; tel. (1) 3091924; fax (1) 3091705; f. 1991; monthly; in English; economic affairs; Editor-in-Chief Jože Petrovčić; circ. 4,000.

Slovenija: 1000 Ljubljana, Cankarjeva 1/II; tel. (1) 2410284; fax (1) 4251673; e-mail sim@siol.net; internet sim.kivi-com.si/default3 .asp?type=3&MenuID=1512; f. 1987; quarterly; in English; ethnic issues and news; Man. Editor Jože Prešeren; circ. 3,500.

Slovenske brazde (Slovenian Tracks): 1000 Ljubljana, Zarnikova 3; tel. (1) 4301891; fax (1) 4301871; f. 1990; weekly; Man. Editor Nace Potocnik.

Stop: 1000 Ljubljana, Dunajska 5; tel. (1) 319190; fax (1) 1330403; f. 1967; weekly; leisure, film, theatre, pop music, radio and television programmes; Editor Igor Savič; circ. 44,600.

Tednik: 2250 Ptuj, Raičeva 6; tel. (2) 7493410; fax (2) 7493435; e-mail tednik@radio-tednik.si; internet www.radio-tednik.si; f. 1948; weekly; politics, local information; Editor-in-Chief Jože Šmigoc; circ. 12,000.

Tretji dan (Third Day): 1000 Ljubljana, Jurčičev trg 2; tel. (1) 1263071; fax (1) 223864; weekly; Editor-in-Chief Dr Tone Jamnik.

Tribuna: 1000 Ljubljana, Kersnikova 4; tel. (1) 319496; fax (1) 319448; 3 a week; student newspaper; Editor-in-Chief Bojan Korenini.

Vestnik Murska Sobota (Murska Sobota Herald): 9000 Murska Sobota, ul. Arhitekta Novaka 13; tel. (2) 5311960; fax (2) 5321175; e-mail vestnik@eunet.si; internet www.p-inf.si; f. 1949; weekly; popular; Editor-in-Chief Janez Votek; circ. 20,000.

Zdravje (Health): 1000 Ljubljana, Cigaletova 5; tel. (1) 2319360; e-mail gasamil@k2.net; monthly; Editor-in-Chief Gasa Milivojevič.

PRESS AGENCIES

Morel: 1000 Ljubljana, Reboljeva 13, statti Parmova 41-45; tel. (1) 4361222; fax (1) 4361223; e-mail morel@si21.com; internet www .morel.si; f. 1993; Dir and Chief Editor Emil Lukančič-Mori.

Slovenska Tiskovna Agencija (STA): 1000 Ljubljana, Cankarjeva 5, p.p. 145; tel. (1) 2410100; fax (1) 4266050; e-mail desk@sta.si; internet www.sta.si; f. 1991; Dir-Gen. Igor Vezovnik; Editor-in-Chief Tadeja Šergan.

Publishers

Cankarjeva Založba: 1000 Ljubljana, Kopitarjeva 2; tel. (1) 3603720; fax (1) 3603787; e-mail import.books@cankarjeva-z.si; internet www.cankarjeva-z.si; f. 1945; philosophy, science and popular science; dictionaries and reference books; Slovenian and translated literature; import and export; international co-productions; Dir-Gen. Jože Korinšek.

DZS d.d.: 1538 Ljubljana, Mestni trg 6; tel. (1) 4251269; fax (1) 4251183; e-mail info@dzs.si; internet www.dzs.si; f. 1945; textbooks, manuals, world classics, natural sciences, art books, encyclopedias, dictionaries, educational CD-ROMS; import and export; Mans Irena Junkar, Mima Šuštaršič Hvastija.

Mladinska Knjiga Založba d.d.: 1000 Ljubljana, Slovenska 29; tel. (1) 2413288; fax (1) 4252294; e-mail intsales@mkz-lj.si; f. 1945; books for youth and children, including general, fiction, science, travel and school books, language courses, magazines and videos; international co-operation; Dir Milan Matos.

Slovenské Matica: 1000 Ljubljana, Kongresni trg 8; tel. and fax (1) 2514200; e-mail drago.jancar@siol.net; f. 1864; poetry, science, philosophy; Pres. Prof. Dr Joža Mahnič.

Založba Lipa Koper: 66000 Koper, Muzejski trg 7; tel. (5) 6274883; fiction; Dir Prof. Jože A. Hočevar.

Založba Obzorja d.d. Maribor: 2000 Maribor, Partizanska 3–5; tel. (2) 2348100; fax (2) 2348135; e-mail info@zalozba-obzorja.si; internet www.zalozba-obzorja.si; f. 1950; popular science, general literature, periodicals, etc.; Man. Dir Gorazd Zemljarič.

Broadcasting and Communications

TELECOMMUNICATIONS

Telecommunications Agency (Agencija za telekomunikacije, radiodifuzijo in pošto Republike Slovenije—ATRP): 1000 Ljubljana, Kotnikova 19A; tel. (1) 4734900; fax (1) 4328036; e-mail urst.box@gov .si; internet www.atrp.si; Dir Jože Klešnik (acting).

MOBITEL: 1537 Ljubljana, Vilharjeva 23; tel. (1) 4722200; fax (1) 4722950; e-mail ma@mobitel.si; internet www.mobitel.si; f. 1991; Dir Anton Majzelj; 700 employees.

SI.MOBIL d.d.: 1000 Ljubljana, Šmartinska cesta 134B; tel. (1) 5440000; fax (1) 5440099; e-mail info@simobil.si; internet www .simobil.com; f. 1999; shares acquired by Mobilkom Austria in Feb. 2001; Chair. of Bd Bojan Dremelj.

Telekom Slovenije: 1000 Ljubljana, Cigaletova 15; tel. (1) 4334111; fax (1) 4322013; internet www.telekom.si; f. 1949; scheduled for privatization; Chief Exec. (acting) and Chair. of Bd Peter Grašek; 3,350 employees.

BROADCASTING

Regulatory Authority

Slovenian Broadcasting Council: 1000 Ljubljana, Parmova 53; tel. (1) 1363596; fax (1) 1363595; e-mail info.srdf@srd.gov.si; internet www.sigov.si/srd; f. 1994; nine mems; protects independence of radio and television programmes; supervises the activities of broadcasting and cable operators.

Radio

In 1996 49 regional and local radio stations were operating in Slovenia.

Radiotelevizija Slovenija (RTV Slo): 1550 Ljubljana, Kolodvorska 2; tel. (1) 4752154; fax (1) 4752150; e-mail webmaster@rtvslo .si; internet www.rtvslo.si/html/radio-slo; f. 1928; 3 radio programmes nationally; broadcasts in Slovene, Hungarian and Italian; Gen. Man. Aleks Štakul.

Radio Koper Capodistria: 6000 Koper, OF ul. 15; tel. (5) 6485483; fax (5) 6485488; e-mail radio.koper@rtvslo.si; internet www.rtvslo .si; Dir Dragomir Mikelić .

Radio Maribor: 2000 Maribor, Ilichova 33; tel. (2) 4299132; fax (2) 4299215; e-mail srecko.trglec@rtvslo.si; internet www.rtvslo.si; Editor Srečko Trglec.

Radio Murski val: 9000 Murska Sobota, Arhitekta Novaka ul. 13; tel. (2) 5311960; fax (2) 5321175; e-mail radio-murski.val@siol.net; internet www.p-inf.si; f. 1958; Editor-in-Chief Marjan Dora.

Radio Ptuj: 2250 Ptuj, Raiceva 6; tel. (2) 7493410; fax (2) 7493435; e-mail nabiralnik@radio-tednik.si; internet www.radio-teknik.si.

Television

In 1996 42 regional television stations were operating as part of Televizija Slovenia. Three private television stations and more than 20 local cable television stations were also broadcasting in Slovenia.

Radiotelevizija Slovenija (RTV Slo): 1550 Ljubljana, Kolodvorska 2; tel. (1) 4752154; fax (1) 4752150; e-mail webmaster@rtvslo .si; internet www.rtvslo.si/html/radio-slo; f. 1928; 2 television programmes (TV1 and TV2) nationally; broadcasts in Slovene, Hungarian and Italian; Gen. Man. Aleks Štakul.

Kanal A: 1000 Ljubljana, Tivolska 50; tel. (1) 1334133; fax (1) 1334222; Pres. Douglas Fulton.

Pop TV: 1000 Ljubljana, Kranjčeva 26; tel. (1) 1893200; fax (1) 1612022; Editor Tomaž Perovič.

TV 3: 1210 Ljubljana, Štula 23; tel. (1) 1831200; fax (1) 1521512; Editor-in-Chief Mladen Sichrovsky.

Finance

BANKS

(cap. = capital; res = reserves; dep. = deposits; m. = million; amounts in Slovene tolars unless otherwise stated; brs = branches)

The Slovenian banking sector is currently undergoing a rationalization process, involving a conversion to commercial banking (new regulations took effect in January 1995) and the merging of smaller banks.

National Bank

Banka Slovenije (Bank of Slovenia): 1505 Ljubljana, Slovenska 35; tel. (1) 4719000; fax (1) 2515516; e-mail bsl@bsi.si; internet www.bsi .si; formerly National Bank of Slovenia, as part of the Yugoslav banking system; assumed central bank functions in 1991; bank of issue since Oct. 1991; res 199,911.7m., dep. 1,202,090.6m., total assets 1,594,811.6m. (Dec. 2002); Gov. Mitja Gaspari.

Selected Banks

Abanka d.d. Ljubljana (Abanka Joint-Stock Company): 1517 Ljubljana, Slovenska 58, POB 368; tel. (1) 1718100; fax (1) 4325165; e-mail info@abanka.si; internet www.abanka.si; f. 1955 as Ljubljana Branch of Yugoslav Bank for Foreign Trade, adopted current name 1989; cap. 5,156.7m., res 7,977.7m., dep. 133,646.0m. (Dec. 2000); Pres. and Chief Exec. Aljoša Tomaž; 32 brs.

Bank Austria Creditanstalt d.d. Ljubljana: 1000 Ljubljana, Smartinska 140; tel. (1) 5876600; fax (1) 5411860; e-mail info@si .bacai.com; internet www.ba-ca.si; f. 1991; cap. 3,101.4m., res 6,669.2m., dep. 79,057.6m. (Dec. 2000); Chair. JOACHIM REITMEIER.

Banka Celje d.d.: 3000 Celje, Vodnikova 2, POB 431; tel. (3) 5431000; fax (3) 5483511; e-mail info@banka-celje.si; internet www .banka-celje.si; cap. 6,131.9m., res 14,602.1m., dep. 134,946.8m. (Dec. 2000); Pres. NIKO KAČ; 16 brs.

Banka Koper d.d.: 6502 Koper, Pristaniška 14; tel. (5) 6651100; fax (5) 6397472; e-mail info@banka-koper.si; internet www.banka-koper .si; f. 1955; cap. 5,313.6m., res 13,999.6m., dep. 158,127.6m. (Dec. 2000); Man. Dir VOJKO ČOK; 9 brs.

Banka Vipa d.d.: POB 52, 5000 Nova Gorica, Erjavceva ul. 2; tel. (5) 3385000; fax (5) 3028506; e-mail int@banka-vipa.si; f. 1992; cap. 1,895.8m., res 3,289.4m., dep. 45,863.0m. (Dec. 2000); Chair. EGIDIJ BIRSA.

Factor Banka: 1000 Ljubljana, Železna cesta 16; tel. (1) 4311136; fax (1) 4328066; e-mail info@factorb.si; internet www.factorb.si; f. 1993; cap. 1,452.5m., res 384.6m., dep. 17,182.4m. (Dec. 2000); Chair. BORIS PESJAK.

Gorenjska Banka d.d. Kranj: 4000 Kranj, Bleiweisova cesta 1, POB 147; tel. (4) 2084000; fax (4) 2021718; e-mail info@gbkr.si; internet www.gbkr.si; f. 1955; cap. 3,779.2m., res 21,347.8m., dep. 99,560.6m. (Dec. 2000); Man. Dir ZLATKO KAVČIČ; 5 brs.

Nova Kreditna Banka Maribor d.d. (NKBM): 2505 Maribor, Vita Kraigherja 4; tel. (2) 2292290; fax (2) 2524333; e-mail info@nkbm.si; internet www.nkbm.si; f. 1955; adopted present name 1994; scheduled for partial privatization; cap. 5,600m., res 29,699m., dep. 285,443m. (Dec. 2000); Pres. and Chief Exec. Dr JOŽE GLOGOVŠEK; 81 brs and sub-brs.

Nova Ljubljanska Banka d.d. (NLB): 1520 Ljubljana, Republike trg 2; tel. (1) 4250155; fax (1) 4250331; e-mail info@nlb.si; internet www.nlb.si; f. 1994; commercial, investment and savings bank; 34% of shares divested to KBC Bank NV (Belgium) in May 2002; cap. 13,800m., res 25,790m., dep. 794,574m. (Dec. 2000); Pres. and Chief Exec. MARKO VOLJC; 16 brs.

Raiffeisen Krekova Banka d.d.: 2000 Maribor, Slomškov trg 18; tel. (2) 2293100; fax (2) 2223502; e-mail info@r-kb.si; internet www .r-kb.si; f. 1992; cap. 2,058.0m., res 4,233.4m., dep. 55,602.8m. (Dec. 2000); Chair. ALEŠ ŽAJDELA; 14 brs.

SKB Banka d.d.: 1000 Ljubljana, Ajdovščina 4; tel. (1) 4715918; fax (1) 4715757; e-mail info@skb.si; internet www.skb.si; f. 1978; shares acquired by Société Générale in May 2001; cap. 16,499.3m., res 6,509.1m., dep. 213,298.7m. (Dec. 2000); Pres. and Chief Exec. JEAN-LOUIS MATTEI.

Slovenska Zadružna Kmetijska Banka d.d. Ljubljana: 1000 Ljubljana, Kolodvorska 9; tel. (1) 4727100; fax (1) 4727411; e-mail info@szkbanka.si; internet www.szkbanka.si; f. 1990; cap. 1,759.2m., res 4,379.0m., dep. 39,321.9m. (Dec. 2000); Man. Dir MILAN KNEŽEVIČ; 5 brs.

STOCK EXCHANGE

Ljubljana Stock Exchange d.d.: 1000 Ljubljana, Slovenska 56; tel. (1) 4710211; fax (1) 4710213; e-mail info@ljse.si; internet www .ljse.si; f. 1989; operative 1990; Pres. and Chief Exec. Dr DRAŠKO VESELINOVIČ.

INSURANCE

Adriatic Insurance Co d.d.: 6503 Koper, Ljubljanska cesta 3A; tel. (5) 6643100; fax (5) 6643303; e-mail info@adriatic.si; internet www .adriatic.si; f. 1990.

Grawe Insurance Co d.d.: 2000 Maribor, Gregorčičeva 39; tel. (2) 2285500; fax (2) 2285526; e-mail prima@prima.si.

Maribor Insurance Co d.d.: 2507 Maribor, Cankarjeva 3; tel. (2) 224111.

Merkur Insurance Co d.d.: 1000 Ljubljana, Dunajska 58; tel. (1) 3005450; fax (1) 4361092; e-mail info@merkur-zav.si; internet www .merkur-zav.si; f. 1992; Gen. Man. DENIS STROLIGO; Marketing Man. ANDREJ OSTERC; Financial Man. MOJCA ANDROJNA.

Triglav Insurance Co d.d. (Zavarovalnica Triglav d.d.): 1000 Ljubljana, Miklošičeva 19; tel. (1) 1747200; e-mail info-triglav@ zav-triglav.si; internet www2.zav-triglav.si; privatization proposed in 2003; Chair. MILAN TOMAŽEVIČ; Dir-Gen. FRANC ŠKUFCA.

Trade and Industry

GOVERNMENT AGENCY

Agency of the Republic of Slovenia for Restructuring and Privatization: 1000 Ljubljana, Kotnikova 28; tel. (1) 1316030; fax (1) 1316011; e-mail webmaster@arspip.si; internet www.arspip.si; Dir MIRA PUC.

DEVELOPMENT ORGANIZATION

Development Corporation of Slovenia: 1000 Ljubljana, Dunajska 160; tel. (1) 1894800; fax (1) 1894819; e-mail jana .bogdanovski@srd.si; Pres. BOGDAN TOPIČ; Chair. MARJAN REKAR.

CHAMBERS OF COMMERCE

Chamber of Commerce and Industry of Slovenia: 1504 Ljubljana, Dimičeva 13; tel. (1) 5898313; fax (1) 5898317; e-mail irma .butina@gzs.si; internet www.gzs.si; Pres. MARTA TURK; Sec.-Gen. IRMA BUTINA; 55,000 mems.

> **Slovene Businessmen's Association:** 1504 Ljubljana, Dimičeva 13; tel. (1) 1898312; fax (1) 1898317; e-mail romana.tomc@gzs .si; internet www.gzs.si; f. 1994 as autonomous part of Chamber of Economy of Slovenia; Pres. MARTA TURK; Sec.-Gen. ROMANA TOMC LAMPIČ; 48,000 mems.

Chamber of Small Businesses of Slovenia: 1000 Ljubljana, Celovška 71; tel. (1) 4593241; fax (1) 4559270; Pres. MIHA GRAH; Sec. ANTON FILIPIČ; 50,000 mems.

UTILITIES

Electricity

Elektro-Slovenija d.o.o. (ELES): 1000 Ljubljana, Hajdrihova 2; tel. (1) 1301440; fax (1) 1250333; e-mail info@eles.si; internet www .eles.si; national electricity distributor; Chief Exec. VEKOSLAV KOROŠEC; 530 employees.

Nuklearna Elektrarna p.o. (NEK): 8270 Krško, Vrbina 12; tel. (7) 4802000; fax (7) 4921528; internet www.nek.si; f. 1974; jtly owned by Slovenia and Croatia, pending privatization; production and distribution of electricity; Man. Dir STANE ROŽMAN; 610 employees.

Gas

GEO PLIN d.o.o.: 1000 Ljubljana, Ljubljanska brigade 11; tel. (1) 5820600; fax (1) 5820601; e-mail info@geoplin.si; internet www .geoplin.si; f. 1975; nat. gas co; Gen. Man. JANEZ MOŽINA; 145 employees.

MAJOR COMPANIES

Alpina d.d. žiri: 4226 Žiri, Strojarska ul. 2; tel. (4) 5191461; fax (4) 5192163; e-mail alpina@alpina.si; internet www.alpina.si; f. 1947; manufacture of ski boots, sports footwear and fashion shoes; Pres. FRANCI MLINAR; 1,100 employees.

Belinka Chemical Industries d.d.: 1001 Ljubljana, cesta Zasavska 95, POB 4973; tel. (1) 5886299; fax (1) 5886303; e-mail info-pk@belinka.si; internet www.belinka.si; f. 1948; chemical production; Pres. MARJAN CERAR; 120 employees.

Cinkarna Celje d.d.: 3000 Celje, Kidričeva 26; tel. (3) 5419610; fax (3) 5419598; e-mail info@cinkarna.si; internet www.cinkarna.si; manufacture of dyes and pigments; aluminium production; forging, pressing, stamping and roll-forming of metal; powder metallurgy; Gen. Man. MARJAN PRELEČ; 1,265 employees (2002).

Droga Portorož d.d.: 6310 Izola, Industrijksa cesta 21; tel. (5) 6747214; fax (5) 6746215; e-mail info@droga.si; internet www.droga .si; f. 1964; processing and packaging of comestibles; Gen. Man. MATJAŽ CAČOVIČ; 6,135 employees (2002).

ETI Elektroelement d.d.: 1411 Izlake, Obrazija 5; tel. (3) 5673512; fax (3) 5674077; e-mail eti@eti.si; internet www.eti.si; makers of electrotechnical products and technical ceramic products; Gen. Man. JOŽEF SMRKOLJ; 950 employees (2002).

Gorenje d.d.: 3320 Velenje, Partizanska 12, POB 107; tel. (3) 8991000; fax (3) 8992800; e-mail marketing@gorenje.si; internet www.gorenje.si; f. 1950; fmrly Gorenje gospodinjski aparati d.d.; manufacturers of heating equipment and domestic appliances; Pres. and Chief Exec. JOŽE STANIČ; 6,615 employees (2002).

Helios d.d. Domžale: 1230 Domzale, Količevo 2; tel. (1) 7213007; fax (1) 7241234; e-mail info@helios.si; internet www.helios.si; f. 1924; makers of resins and paints for the automotive industry, protective coatings for metal, wood and mineral surfaces, industrial adhesives; Pres. UROŠ SLAVINEC; 715 employees (2002).

Impol d.d.: 2310 Slovenska Bistrica, Partizanska 38; tel. (2) 8187421; fax (2) 8181219; e-mail info@impol.si; internet www.impol.si; f. 1825; casting of light metals; Man. Dir JERNEJ ČOKL; 891 employees (2002).

Industrija Usnja Vrhnika d.d.: 1360 Vrhnika, Tržaška 31, POB 43; tel. (1) 7558700; fax (1) 7558800; e-mail exp@iuv.si; internet www.iuv.si; f. 1946; leather garments and footwear manufacturer; Pres. IZIDOR DERGANC; 1,900 employees.

Intereuropa Koper d.d.: 6000 Koper, Vojkovo Nabrezje 32; tel. (5) 6641000; fax (5) 6642674; e-mail info@intereuropa.si; internet www.intereuropa.si; international freight carriers; Pres. JOŽE KRANJC; 2,472 employees (2002).

Iskra Avtoelektrika d.d.: 5290 Šempeter pri Gorici, Polje 15; tel. (5) 3393000; fax (5) 3393801; e-mail info@iskra-ae.com; internet www.iskra-ae.com; f. 1960; manufacturer of automotive electrical parts, tools and specialist machinery; Pres. ALEŠ NEMEČ; 2,036 employees (2002); comprises 28 cos, including:

Iskra Avtoelektrika Nova Gorica: 5291 Šempeter pri Gorici, Polje 15; tel. (5) 6531211; fax (5) 6532371; f. 1960; manufacturers of electrical automotive parts; Dir ALES NEMEC; 1,425 employees.

Iskra Kondenzatorji d.d.: 8333 Semič, Vajdova ul. 71; tel. (7) 3849200; fax (7) 3067110; e-mail iskra.semic@iskra-semic.si; internet www.iskra-semic.si; f. 1951; manufacturers of electrical equipment; Chair. and Dir-Gen. KAREL GEROLT; 1,100 employees (2002).

Iskraemeco d.d.: 4000 Kranj, Savska loka 4; tel. (4) 2064000; fax (4) 2064376; e-mail info@iskraemeco.si; internet www.iskraemeco.si; f. 1945; production of electricity meters and energy management systems; Man. Dir NIKOLAJ BEVK; 2,100 employees (2002).

Jeklotehna Trgovina d.o.o.: 2000 Maribor, Svetozarevska 10; tel. and fax (2) 2510391; internet www.jeklotehna-trgovina.si; trades in metals, textiles, plastic, tools and machines; Dir FRANC GRADISNIK.

Jutranjka d.d.: 8290 Sevnica, Radna 3; tel. (7) 8141223; fax (7) 8141649; e-mail uprava@jutranjka.si; internet www.jutranjka.si; f. 1962; manufacturers of children's clothing; Man. Dir DRAGO PERC (acting); 1,074 employees.

Kemofarmacija d.d: 1000 Ljubljana, cesta na Brdo 100; tel. (1) 4709800; fax (1) 4709970; e-mail info@kemfarm.si; internet www.kemfarm.si; f. 1947; pharmaceutical products; Pres. and Man. Dir VOJMIR URLEP; 178 employees.

Konus Konex d.o.o.: 3210 Slovenske Konjice, Mestni trg 18; tel. (3) 7573100; fax (3) 5754368; e-mail info@konuskonex.com; internet www.konuskonex.com; f. 1894; manufacture of leather goods, man-made fibres; Dir SAVO GRILJ; 175 employees.

Kovinoplastika Lož d.d.: 1386 Stari trg Lož, cesta 19 Oktobra 57, POB 50; tel. (1) 7095100; fax (1) 7058466; e-mail info@kovinoplastika.si; internet www.kovinoplastika.si; f. 1954; domestic fittings and industrial tools; Pres. and Chief Exec. ALOJZ MAZIJ; 1,185 employees.

Krka d.d.: 8501 Novo mesto, Šmarješka cesta 6; tel. (7) 3312111; fax (7) 3321537; e-mail info@krka.si; internet www.krka.si; pharmaceutical products; f. 1954; Pres. and Chief Exec. MILOŠ KOVAČIČ; 2,740 employees.

Labod d.d.: 8000 Novo mesto, Seidova cesta 35, POB 213; tel. (7) 3917400; fax (7) 3917409; e-mail labod@labod.si; internet www.labod.si; f. 1924; clothing manufacturer; Man. Dir ANDREJ KIRM; 480 employees (2002).

Lek Pharmaceutical and Chemical Company d.d.: 1526 Ljubljana, Verovškova 57, POB 81; tel. (1) 5882111; fax (1) 5683517; e-mail info@lek.si; internet www.lek.si; f. 1946; 99.07% stake acquired by Novartis (Switzerland) in 2002; pharmaceuticals, chemicals, cosmetics and medical products; Pres. and Chief Exec. METOD DRAGONJA; 3,429 employees.

Lip Bled d.d.: 4260 Bled, Ljubljanska 32; tel. (4) 5795000; fax (4) 5741202; e-mail lipbl@lip-bled.si; internet www.lip-bled.si; f. 1948; sawmill operators, makers of wooden furniture; Man. Dir JAKOB REPE; 920 employees.

Ljubljanske mlekarne d.d.: 1000 Ljubljana, Tolstojeva 63; tel. (1) 5881500; fax (1) 5685436; e-mail info@lj-mlek.si; internet www.lj-mlek.si; f. 1956; manufacture of dairy products; Pres. ANTON VRHOVNIK; 800 employees.

Mehano d.o.o: 6310 Izola, Polje 9, POB 83; tel. (5) 6608100; fax (5) 6608101; e-mail mehano@mehano.si; internet www.mehano.si; f. 1952; manufacturer of battery-operated toys; Gen. Man. MOJCA ČERNE; 433 employees.

Merkur d.d.: 4202 Naklo, Cesta ne Okroglo 7; tel. (4) 2588000; fax (4) 2588805; e-mail info@merkur.si; internet www.merkur.si; f. 1896; wholesale and retail of technical consumer products, construction materials, installation and electrical fittings, industrial

technical goods and ferrous metallurgy products; Pres. and Chief Exec. BINE KORDEŽ; 1,568 employees.

Metalna Ecce d.o.o.: 2105 Maribor, Zagrebška 20; tel. (2) 4612511; fax (2) 4613027; e-mail metalna@medinet.si; internet www.metalna-ecce.si; f. 1920; machine building; Pres. SILVO ŠMARČAN; 600 employees.

Mura European Fashion Design d.d.: 9000 Murska Sobota, Plese 2; tel. (2) 5132100; fax (2) 5321513; e-mail pr@mura.si; internet www.mura.si; f. 1925; production of ready-made garments and fashion design; Gen. Man. BORUT MEH; 5,525 employees (2002).

Nafta Lendava d.o.o.: 9220 Lendava, Rudarska 1, POB 36; tel. (2) 5772100; fax (2) 5772345; e-mail info@nafta-lendava.si; internet www.nafta-lendava.si; f. 1945; petroleum refinery; manufacture of organic base chemicals; Pres. CVETO ŽALIK; 595 employees.

Peko Tržič d.d.: 4290 Tržič, Ste Marie aux Mines 5; tel. (4) 5379100; fax (4) 5379119; e-mail info@peko.si; internet www.peko.si; manufacture and sale of footwear; Chair. of Bd MARTA GORJUP BREJC,; 955 employees.

Perutnina Ptuj d.d.: 2250 Ptuj, Potrceva 10; tel. (2) 7490100; fax (2) 7490134; e-mail info@perutnina.si; internet www.perutnina.si; f. 1905; poultry slaughterers; Dir ROMAN GLASER; 1,280 employees (2002).

Petrol d.d.: 1527 Ljubljana, Dunajska 50; tel. (1) 4714234; fax (1) 4714809; e-mail petrol@petrol.si; internet www.petrol.si; f. 1945; petroleum and petrochemical products; also operate petrol stations and hotels; Dir JANEZ LOTRIČ; 2,000 employees (2002).

Pivovarna Union: 1000 Ljubljana, Pivovarniška 2; tel. (1) 4717217; fax (1) 4717316; e-mail info@pivo-union.si; internet www.pivo-union.sil; owned by Interbrew (Belgium); producer of Union beer, Sola soft drinks and Zala mineral water; Gen. Man. DIMITRIJ LAVRIČ; 485 employees (2002).

Planika Kranj d.d.: 4000 Kranj, Savska loka 21, POB 157; tel. (4) 2014500; fax (4) 2014506; e-mail planika@planika.si; internet www.planika.si; 57% state-owned; manufacture of footwear; Man. Dir MILAN BAJŽELJ; 1,130 employees (2002).

Poslovni sistem Mercator d.d.: 1000 Ljubljana, Dunajska cesta 107; tel. (1) 5601000; fax (1) 5601063; e-mail info@mercator.si; internet www.mercator.si; sale of food products; privatized in 1995; Chief Exec. ZORAN JANKOVIČ; 14,129 employees.

Rudnik Trbovlje-Hrastnik d.o.o. (Trbovlje-Hrastnik Colliery): 1420 Trbovkje, trg Revolucije 12, POB 80; tel. (3) 5626144; fax (3) 5626642; e-mail rth@rth.si; f. 1996; coal mining; Man. Dir ALJOŠA KINK; 1,300 employees.

Salonit Anhovo Holding d.d.: 5210 Anhovo, Vojkova 1, POB 15; tel. (5) 3921000; fax (5) 3921700; e-mail salonit@salonit.si; internet www.salonit.si; building materials; Man. Dir JOŽE FUNDA; 535 employees (2002).

Sava Rubber and Chemical Industries d.d.: 4502 Kranj, Skofjeloška 6, POB 2650; tel. (4) 2021711; fax (4) 2021114; e-mail info@sava.si; internet www.sava.si; f. 1920; privatized as joint-stock co in 1996; major tyre manufacturer; Gen. Man. JANEZ BOHORIČ; 900 employees (2002).

SCT d.d.: 1000 Ljubljana, Slovenska cesta 56, POB 469; tel. (1) 4345204; fax (1) 4345280; e-mail sct@sct.si; internet www.sct.si; f. 1947; civil engineering; Pres. and Gen. Man. IVAN ZIDAR; 2,604 employees (2002).

Steklarna Rogaška d.d.—Rogaška Crystal: 3250 Rogaška Slatina, ul. Talcev 1; tel. (3) 8180170; fax (3) 8180326; e-mail info@stek-rogaska.si; internet www.stek-rogaska.si; f. 1927; crystal glass makers; Man. Dir DAVORIN ŠKRINJARIČ; 1,065 employees (2002).

Stol d.d.: 1241 Kamnik, Ljubljanska 45; tel. (1) 8301000; fax (1) 8313356; e-mail andrej.trpin@stol.si; internet www.stol.si; manufacturers of wooden furniture; Dir BOGOMIR BOGATAJ; 1,100 employees.

SŽ ZJ (Slovenske železarne) Acroni d.o.o.: 4270 Jesenice, Kidričeva 44; tel. (4) 5841000; fax (4) 5841111; e-mail uprava@acroni.si; internet www.acroni.si; f. 1993; manufacture of basic iron and steel and of ferroalloys; Gen. Man. Dr VASILIJ PREŠERN; 1,475 employees (2002).

Talum d.d.: 2325 Kidričevo, Tovarniška 10, POB 2325; tel. (2) 7995100; fax (2) 7995139; e-mail quest@talum.si; internet www.talum.si; f. 1947; aluminium production; manufacture of chemical products; Gen. Man. DANILO TOPLEK; 970 employees.

Tekstil d.d.: 1122 Ljubljana, Letališka 34; tel. (1) 5866100; fax (1) 5866162; e-mail info@tekstil.si; internet www.tekstil.si; f. 1947; shoe and textiles manufacturers; Dir-Gen. STANISLAV ZIDAR; 175 employees.

Tobačna Grosist d.o.o.: 1000 Ljubljana, Tobačna ul. 5, POB 487; tel. (1) 4777100; fax (1) 4259415; e-mail tobacna@tobacna.si;

internet www.tobacna.si; f. 1871; privatized in 1991; member of Imperial Tobacco Group (United Kingdom); production and sale of cigarettes; Gen. Man. BOJAN SIMONIČ; 500 employees.

Unior Kovaška industrija d.d.: 3214 Zreče, Kovaška cesta 10; tel. (3) 7578100; fax (3) 5762103; e-mail unior@unior.si; internet www .unior.si; f. 1919; producer of hand and machine tools, etc.; Pres. MATELA REŽUN; 2,500 employees.

Zlatorog d.d.: 2000 Maribor, ul. Sokoloska 46; tel. (2) 4216715; fax (2) 4216729; e-mail monika.paluc@zlatorog.si; internet www .zlatorog.si; manufacturers of soap and detergents; Dir DITA KAS-TELIC.

TRADE UNIONS

The Association of Independent Trade Unions of Slovenia: 1000 Ljubljana, Dalmatinova 4; tel. (1) 4317983; fax (1) 4318294; Pres. DUŠAN SEMOLIČ.

Independence—Confederation of New Trade Unions of Slovenia: 1000 Ljubljana, Linhartova 13; tel. (1) 4329141; fax (1) 4302868; Pres. FRANCE TOMŠIČ.

Transport

RAILWAYS

The rail link between western Europe and Greece, Turkey and the Near and Middle East runs through Slovenia. In 1999 there were 1,201 km of railway lines in Slovenia, of which 499 km were electrified.

Slovenske Železnice (SŽ) (Slovenian Railways): 1506 Ljubljana, Kolodvorska 11; tel. (1) 2912100; fax (1) 2914813; e-mail info@ slo-zeleznice.si; internet www.slo-zeleznice.si; Chief Exec. BLAŽ MIKLAVČIČ.

ROADS

In 2000 the country had 20,177 km of roads, of which 427 km were motorways, 1,112 km were highways, main or national roads and 4,733 km were secondary or regional roads. An 84-km motorway links Ljubljana, Postojna and Sežana with the coastal region in the south-west, and a 25-km motorway connects the capital with Kranj and the Gorenjska region in the north-east. A motorway construction programme was approved by the Government in January 1998. The plan envisaged the completion of 519 km of motorway sections by 2004.

Directorate of the Republic of Slovenia for Roads: Ministry of Transport, 1535 Ljubljana, Langusova ul. 4; tel. (1) 1788000; fax (1) 1788139; e-mail drsc-info@gov.si.

SHIPPING

Slovenia's principal international trading port, at Koper, handles some 6m. tons of freight annually, and has terminals for general, bulk and liquid cargo, containers and 'roll on, roll off' traffic, as well as warehousing facilities. The port is a duty-free zone. There are also major ports at Portorož and Izola.

Luka Koper d.d.: 6501 Koper, Vojkovo nabrežje 38; tel. (5) 6656100; fax (5) 6395020; e-mail portkoper@luka-kp.si; internet www.luka-kp.si; f. 1957; Chief Exec. BRUNO KORELIČ.

Principal Shipping Company

Splošna Plovba Ltd: 6320 Portorož, Obala 55, POB 60; tel. (5) 6766000; fax (5) 6766130; e-mail plovba@5-plovba.si; transport of all types of cargo; regular liner service; Man. Dir ALDO KREJAČIČ.

CIVIL AVIATION

There are three international airports in Slovenia, at Brnik (Ljubljana), Maribor and Portorož.

Adria Airways: 1000 Ljubljana, Kuzmičeva 7; tel. (1) 3691000; fax (1) 4369233; e-mail info@adria.si; internet www.adria.si; f. 1961; operates international scheduled services to destinations in Europe and the Near and Middle East; Pres. BRANKO LUCOVNIK.

Tourism

Slovenia offers a variety of tourist attractions, including Mediterranean beaches to the west, the Alps to the north and the 'karst' limestone regions, with more than 6,000 caves. The number of foreign tourist arrivals has increased steadily from the mid-1990s, reaching 1,218,700 in 2001. Tourism receipts totalled US $961m. in 2000.

Slovenian Tourist Board: 1000 Ljubljana, Dunajska 156; tel. (1) 5891840; fax (1) 5891841; e-mail info@slovenia-tourism.si; internet www.slovenia-tourism.si; Exec. Man. BOJAN MEDEN.

Culture

NATIONAL ORGANIZATIONS

Ministry of Culture: see section on The Government (Ministries).

Cultural and Congress Centre (Cankarjev dom): 1000 Ljubljana, Prešernova 10; tel. (1) 2417100; fax (1) 2417322; e-mail cankarjev .dom@cd-cc.si; internet www.cd-cc.si; f. 1980; organizes theatre, opera and dance productions; distributes art films; presents fine arts exhibitions; organizes and accommodates international congresses, symposia, seminars and conferences; Gen. Dir MITJA ROTOVNIK.

Cultural Heritage Office of Slovenia (Uprava Republike Slovenije za kulturno dediščino): 1001 Ljubljana, POB 176, Plečnikov trg 2; tel. (1) 2513267; fax (1) 4266547; e-mail urskd@gov.si; internet www.sigov.si/ukd/; f. 1913; central administration for preservation and care of cultural heritage and monuments; central register of cultural monuments; 7 regional orgs; Dir STANISLAV MRVIČ.

Festival Ljubljana: 1000 Ljubljana, Trg francoske revolucije 1–2; tel. (1) 2416000; fax (1) 2416037; e-mail info@festival-lj.si; internet www.festival-lj.si; f. 1952; annual cultural event; Pres. of Council STANE BREZOVAR.

CULTURAL HERITAGE

Academy for Fine Arts (Akademija Za Likovno Umetnost): 1000 Ljubljana, Erjavčeva 23; tel. (1) 2512726; fax (1) 2519071; e-mail alu-dekanat@uni-lj.si; internet www.alu.uni-lj.si; Dir BOGOSLAV KALAŠ.

Archives of the Republic of Slovenia (Arhiv Republike Slovenije): 1127 Ljubljana, Zvezdarska 1, p.p. 21; tel. (1) 2414200; fax (1) 2414269; e-mail ars@gov.si; internet www.gov.si/ars/index.html; f. 1887; collection of material from the 12th century onwards dealing with territory populated by Slovenes; archive of Slovene film production since 1905; Chief VLADIMIR ŽUMER.

International Centre of Graphic Arts (Mednarodni Grafični Likovni Center): 1000 Ljubljana, Grad Tivoli, Pod turnom 3; tel. (1) 4265240; fax (1) 1219752; e-mail info@mglc-lj.si; internet www .mglc-lj.si; f. 1986; collection of contemporary international graphics and artists' books; Dir LILIJANA STEPANČIČ.

Museum of Modern Art (Moderna galerija): 1000 Ljubljana, Tomšičeva 14; tel. (1) 2416800; fax (1) 2514120; e-mail info@mg-lj.si; internet www.mg-lj.si; f. 1947; 20th-century Slovenian and international art collection; temporary exhibitions of national and international contemporary art; maintains an information centre, a photographic archive, a library of 39,000 vols and a restoration studio; Dir ZDENKA BADOVINAC.

National Gallery (Narodna galerija): 1000 Ljubljana, Puharjeva 9; tel. (1) 2415434 ; fax (1) 2415403; e-mail info@ng-slo.si; internet www.ng-slo.si; f. 1918; library of 30,000 vols; Dir Dr ANDREJ SMREKAR.

National Museum of Slovenia (Narodni muzej Slovenije): 1000 Ljubljana, Muzejska 1; tel. (1) 2414400; fax (1) 2414422; e-mail info@ narmuz-lj.si; internet www.narmuz-lj.si; f. 1821; library of 150,000 vols; Dir Dr PETER KOS.

National and University Library (Narodna in Univerzitetna Knjižnica—NUK): 1000 Ljubljana, Turjaška 1; tel. (1) 2001110; fax (1) 4257293; e-mail uprava@nuk.uni-lj.si; internet www.nuk.uni-lj .si; f. 1774; 2.3m. vols; Man. Dir LENART ŠETINC.

Regional Archives of Maribor (Pokrajinski Arhiv Maribor): 2000 Maribor, Glavni trg 7; tel. (2) 2285000; fax (2) 2522564; e-mail slavica.tovsak@pamb.pokarh-mb.si; internet www.pokarh-mb.si; f. 1933; Dir SLAVICA TOVSAK.

Restoration Centre of the Republic of Slovenia (Restavratorski Center Republike Slovenije): 1000 Ljubljana, Poljanska 40; tel. (1) 2343100; fax (1) 2343176; Dir JOSIP KOROŠEC.

SPORTING ORGANIZATION

Olympic Committee of Slovenia: 1000 Ljubljana, Celovska 25; tel. (1) 1323240; fax (1) 1323303; e-mail info@olympic.si; internet www.oks-zsz.si; f. 1991; Pres. JANEZ KOCIJANČIC; Sec.-Gen. TONE JAGODIC.

PERFORMING ARTS

Academy for Theatre, Radio, Film and Television (Akademija za gledališče, radio, film in televizijo—AGRFT): 1000 Ljubljana, Nazorjeva 3; tel. (1) 2510412; fax (1) 2510450; e-mail agrft-gledalisce@uni-lj.si; internet www.agrft.uni-lj.si; f. 1945 as

Academy for Dramatic Arts;; present name adopted 1963; faculty of Ljubljana University (q.v.) since 1975; Dean MIRAN ZUPANIČ.

City Theatre of Ljubljana: 1000 Ljubljana, Čopova 14; tel. (1) 4258222; fax (1) 2517044; e-mail info@mgl.si; internet www.mgl.si; f. 1949; Gen. Man. and Artistic Dir BORIS KOBAL.

Slovenian National Theatre—Drama, Ljubljana (Slovensko narodno gledališče Drama Ljubljana): 1000 Ljubljana, Erjavčeva 1; tel. (1) 2521462; fax (1) 2523885; e-mail info@sngdrama-lj.si; internet www.sngdrama-lj.si; Dir JANEZ PIPAN.

Slovenian National Theatre—Drama and Opera, Maribor (Slovensko narodno gledališče—SNG—Drama in Opera Maribor): 2000 Maribor, Slovenska ul. 27; tel. (2) 2506100; fax (2) 2521207; e-mail sng.maribor@sng-mb.si; internet www.sng-mb.si; Dir TEO PAJNIK.

Slovenian National Theatre—Opera and Ballet, Ljubljana (Slovensko narodno gledališče—SNG—Opera in Balet Ljubljana): 1000 Ljubljana, Zupančičeva 1; tel. (1) 2411700; fax (1) 4262249; e-mail tatjana.regent@guest.arnes.si; internet www.operainbalet-lj .si; Dir BORUT SMREKAR.

Mladinsko Theatre (Slovensko mladinsko gledališče—SMG): 1000 Ljubljana, Vilharjeva 11; tel. (1) 2310610; fax (1) 4335025; e-mail info@mladinsko-gl.si; internet www.mladinsko-gl.si; f. 1955; Man. Dir PETAR JOVIČ; Artistic Dir TOMAŽ TOPOROŠIČ.

Music

Music Academy (Akademija za glasbo): 1000 Ljubljana, Stari trg 34; tel. (1) 2427300; fax (1) 1254857; e-mail ag-dekanat@uni-lj.si; internet www.ag.uni-lj.si; faculty of the University of Ljubljana (q.v.); Dean PAVEL MIHELČIČ.

Slovenian Philharmonic Orchestra (Slovenska filharmonija): 1000 Ljubljana, Kongresni trg 10; tel. (1) 2410800; fax (1) 2410900; e-mail smateja.kralj@filharmonija.si; internet www.filharmonija.si; f. 1701; Chief Conductor MARKO LETONJA.

Slovenian RTV Big Band (Plesni orkester/Big Band RTV Slovenija): 1550 Ljubljana, Kolodvorska 2; tel. (1) 1752469; fax (1) 1752471; f. 1945; Chief Conductor LOJZE KRAJNČAN.

Slovenian RTV Chamber Orchestra (Camerata Labacensis RTV Slovenija): 1000 Ljubljana, Dunajska 21; tel. (1) 1752469; fax (1) 1752471; f. 1974; Artistic Dir ANTON NANUT.

Slovenian RTV Symphony Orchestra (Simfonijski orkester RTV Slovenija): 1550 Ljubljana, Kolodvorska 2; tel. (1) 1752469; fax (1) 1752471; internet www.rtvslo.si/simfoniki/slo/01_splosno.htm; f. 1955; Chief Conductor DAVID DE VILLIERS.

ASSOCIATIONS

Film Fund of the Republic of Slovenia (Filmski sklad Republike Slovenije): 1000 Ljubljana, Miklošičeva 38; tel. (1) 4313175; fax (1) 4337250; e-mail info@film-sklad.si; internet www.film-sklad.si; Dir SAŠA JOVANOVIČ.

Historical Association of Slovenia (Zveza zgodovinskih društev Slovenije): 1000 Ljubljana, Aškerčeva 2; tel. (1) 2411200; fax (1) 4259337; f. 1839; library of 5,215 vols; Pres. Dr JURE PEROVŠEK.

Slovene Society (Slovenska matica): 1000 Ljubljana, Kongresni trg 8; tel. and fax (1) 2514200; e-mail drago.jancar@siol.net; f. 1864; Pres. Prof. Dr JOŽA MAHNIČ; Sec. DRAGO JANČAR.

Slovene Writers' Association (Društvo Pisateljev Slovenije): 1000 Ljubljana, Tomšičeva 12; tel. (1) 2514144; fax (1) 4216430; e-mail barbara.subert@guest.arnes.si; internet www.drustvo-dsp.si; Chair. TONE PERŠAK.

Society for Slavic Studies of Slovenia (Slavistično društvo Slovenije): 1000 Ljubljana, Aškerčeva 2/II; tel. (1) 1250001; f. 1935; Chair. Dr FRANCE NOVAK.

Society for Slovene Composers (Društvo slovenskih skladateljev): 1000 Ljubljana, Trg francoske revolucije 6/I; tel. (1) 2415600; fax (1) 2415666; e-mail info@drustvo-dss.si; internet www .drustvo-dss.si; f. 1945; Sec. MAKS STRMČNIK.

Education

Education in Slovenia is free of charge and is compulsory between the ages of six and 15 years. In 1999/2000 some 7,329 teaching staff were employed in 806 pre-primary educational institutions, which were attended by a total of 63,328 pupils in 2000/01. In ethnically mixed regions, two methods of schooling have been developed: bilingual or with instruction in the minority languages. The system of primary and secondary education, established in the 1990s, lasts nine years, with an optional 10th year. In 1998/99 enrolment in compulsory education was equivalent to almost 100% of the relevant age group (males 100%; females 99%). In the same year a total of

191,701 students attended 476 elementary schools, which employed 15,489 teachers.

Various types of secondary education, beginning at 15 and lasting between two and a half and four years, were also available. In 1999/2000 there were 275 upper secondary schools attended by 191,701 students. In 1996 secondary enrolment was equivalent to 92% of the relevant age group (males 90%; females 93%). In 2000/01 4,760 students attended 17 tertiary vocational colleges, which employed 133 staff. Slovenia's two universities are situated in Ljubljana and Maribor, with 54,312 and 28,082 students, respectively, in 2001/02. Enrolment in tertiary education in 2000/01 was 82,812 full- and part-time students in undergraduate studies and more than 3,000 post-graduate students.

Ministry of Education, Science and Sport: see section on The Government (Ministries).

UNIVERSITIES

University of Ljubljana (Univerza v Ljubljani): 1000 Ljubljana, Kongresni trg 12; tel. (1)2418500; fax (1) 1254053; e-mail ul-rektorat@uni-lj.si; internet www.uni-lj.si; f. 1595; reconstituted 1810, reopened 1919; 22 faculties, three academies, two higher schools; 1,800 teachers; 40,000 students; Rector Prof. Dr JOŽE MENCINGER.

University of Maribor (Univerza v Mariboru): 2000 Maribor, Slomškov trg 15; tel. (2) 2523611; fax (2) 2513541; e-mail university@uni-mb.si; internet www.uni-mb.si; f. 1975; nine faculties; 653 teachers; 20,572 students; 1 attached school and 2 attached colleges; Rector Prof. Dr LUDVIC TOPLAK.

Social Welfare

The social-welfare system in Slovenia is extensive and consists of three separate schemes: pensions and disability allowances; health protection and health insurance; and unemployment benefit. The financing for each scheme comes from contributions from employers and employees. These are paid to the funds of the Institute of Pension and Disability Insurance, to the Institute of Health Insurance (both independent public bodies) or, in the case of unemployment benefits, to the state budget. Child-care benefits and income-related benefits for maternity leave are financed by general taxation. Social-assistance schemes are funded partly by central government and partly by local government. Expenditure on child allowances and social-security allowances in 2000 amounted to 112,060m. tolars (equivalent to 6.3% of total expenditure).

Pensions in Slovenia are income related, and are calculated on the basis of the average monthly wage of the insured person for the 10 most favourable consecutive years of insurance. The official retirement age was 63 years for men and 61 years for women. The minimum gross monthly wage in Slovenia in December 1995 was 31,666 tolars. In that year the average weekly hours worked (per person in manufacturing) were 40.7. A reform of the pension system began in 1999; the retirement age and pension qualifying period were increased, while the pension took into account factors such as time spent caring for children, work done before the age of 18 and the continuation of work after retirement. Expenditure on pensions in 2000 was 490,682m. tolars (equivalent to 27.5% of total government expenditure).

In March 1992 a new health-care system came into effect in Slovenia, whereby the rights of individuals to health care were determined by the level of their contributions. The Institute for Health Insurance was established to implement compulsory health insurance. A system of voluntary health insurance was introduced in 1993. In 1997 the Government contributed SIT 196,636m. to the Health Insurance Fund, equivalent to 14.8% of total expenditure. Private medical practice in most fields was also introduced in 1992. In 1998 there were 228 physicians, 681 nurses, 60.8 dentists and 36.3 pharmacists per 100,000 inhabitants.

Unemployment benefit in Slovenia is paid by the National Employment Office. The level of benefit is calculated using the average monthly wage for the 12 months previous to unemployment. The minimum level of benefit is 100% of the guaranteed minimum wage, while the maximum level is three times the minimum.

NATIONAL AGENCIES

Ministry of Health: see section on The Government (Ministries).

Ministry of Labour, Family and Social Affairs: see section on The Government (Ministries).

Health Insurance Institute of Slovenia (Zavod za zdravstveno zavarovanje Slovenije): 1507 Ljubljana, Miklošičeva 24; tel. (1) 3077200; fax (1) 2312182; e-mail webmaster@zzzs.si; internet www .zzzs.si; f. 1992; Gen. Dir FRANC KOŠIR.

Housing Fund of the Republic of Slovenia (Stanovanjski sklad Republike Slovenije): 1001 Ljubljana, Poljanska cesta 31, p.p. 2044; tel. (1) 4710500; fax (1) 4710503; e-mail ssrsinfo@ stanovanjskisklad-rs.si; internet www.stanovanjskisklad-rs.si; f. 1991; Chair. JANEZ KOPAČ.

National Employment Office (Zavod Republike Slovenije za zaposlovanje): 1000 Ljubljana, Glinška ul. 12, p.p. 2962; tel. (1) 2002350; fax (1) 4259823; e-mail info@ess.gov.si; internet www.ess .gov.si; Gen. Dir JOŽE GLAZER.

Office for Equal Opportunities (Urad za enake možnosti): 1000 Ljubljana, Tržaška 19A; tel. (1) 47884609; fax (1) 4788471; e-mail uem@gov.si; internet www.uem-rs.si; Dir TANJA SALECL.

Old-Age and Disibility Pension Insurance Institute of Slovenia (Zavod za pokojninsko in invalidsko zavarovanje Slovenije—ZPIZ): 1000 Ljubljana, Kolodvorska ul. 15; tel. (1) 3061878; fax (1) 3061880; e-mail informacije@zpiz.si; internet www.zpiz.si; f. 1992; Gen. Dir JANEZ PRIJATELJ.

HEALTH AND WELFARE ORGANIZATIONS

SOŽITJE National Association for the Mentally Handicapped (Zveza drustev za pomoč duševno prizadetim Slovenija): 1000 Ljubljana, Samova 9/2; tel. (1) 4369750; fax (1) 4362406; e-mail info@zveza-sozitje.si; internet www.zveza-sozitje.si; Chair. Dr ALENKA ŠELIH.

National Committee of the Red Cross (Rdeči križ Slovenije): 1000 Ljubljana, Mirje 19; tel. (1) 2414300; fax (1) 2414344; e-mail rdeci.kriz@rks.si; internet www2.arnes.si/~ljrksl/; f. 1991; Pres. Dr JANKO PREDAN.

National Committee for UNICEF: 1000 Ljubljana, Pavšičeva 1; tel. (1) 5838080; fax (1) 5838081; e-mail info@unicef-slo.si; internet www.unicef-slo.si; Pres. ANDREJA ČRNAK-MEGLIČ.

ŠENT Association for Mental Health (Slovensko združenje za duševno zdravje): 1000 Ljubljana, Vilharjeva 22; tel. (1) 4319408; fax (1) 4313156; e-mail sent@hotmail.com; internet www.drogart.s5.net/ sent/; seven regional branches.

Slovenska Karitas: 1000 Ljubljana, Kristanova ul. 1; tel. (1) 3005960; fax (1) 2323186; e-mail info@karitas.si; internet www .karitas.si; f. 1990; Roman Catholic charitable organization; brs in Ljubljana, Maribor and Koper.

Youth Aid Centre Asscn (Društvo Center za pomoč mladim): 1000 Ljubljana, Kersnikova 4; tel. (1) 4382210; fax (1) 4382214; e-mail ursa.rozman@guest.arnes.si; internet www.cpm-drustvo.si; information, training and counselling for 15–25 year olds; brs in Ljubljana and Maribor.

The Environment

Environmental concerns are not as prevalent in Slovenia as in other Central or South-Eastern European countries, although in 1989 the Citizens' Green Party of Slovenia (later the Greens of Slovenia) was the first formal party of opposition to the League of Communists in the old Yugoslav federation. In July 1991, shortly before Slovenia's secession, the federal authorities signed a declaration on the eco-logical protection of the Adriatic, implementing the Adriatic Initiative agreed with Albania, Greece and Italy in 1989. Slovenia accepted its obligations under this accord. Slovenia has a National Environment Action Programme and a Nature Protection Act was passed in 1999.

GOVERNMENT ORGANIZATIONS

Council for Environmental Protection of the Republic of Slovenia (Svetza za varstvo okolja Republike Slovenije—CEPRS): 1000 Ljubljana, Slovenska cesta 56; tel. (1) 4306070; fax (1) 4306075; e-mail svo@svo-rs.si; internet www.sigov.si/svo/; f. 1994; Pres. FRANC LOBNIC; Sec.-Gen. SLAVICA ANDOLJŠEK.

Ministry of Agriculture, Forestry and Food: see section on The Government (Ministries).

Ministry of the Environment, Physical Planning and Energy: see section on The Government (Ministries).

ACADEMIC INSTITUTE

University of Ljubljana—Biotechnical Faculty: 1000 Ljubljana, Jamnikarjeva 101; tel. (1) 4231161; fax (1) 2565782; e-mail dekan@bf.uni-lj.si; internet www.bf.uni-lj.si; departments include agronomy, biology, food science and technology, forestry, landscape architecture, microbiology, wood science and technology, zoology; Dean Dr JOŽE RESNIK.

NON-GOVERNMENTAL ORGANIZATIONS

Greens of Slovenia (Zelena Slovenije—ZS): see section on Political Organizations.

Society for Natural Sciences of Slovenia: 1000 Ljubljana, Novi trg 4/IV; f. 1934; 3,000 mems; Pres. R. KAVČIČ; Sec. T. WRABER.

Slovenian Fund for Nature: 1000 Ljubljana, Novi trg 2; tel. and fax (1) 221914.

Umanotera—Slovenian Foundation for Sustainable Development: 1000 Ljubljana, Metelkova 6, p.p. 4440; tel. (1) 4397100; fax (1) 4397105; e-mail info@umanotera.org; internet www.umanotera .org; Chair. JOŽE VILFAN.

Defence

Military service in Slovenia is compulsory and lasts for a period of seven months; however, compulsory military service is expected to be abolished by 2004, with the armed forces set to become fully professional in 2010. In August 2002 Slovenia had active armed forces of 9,000, with 20,000 reserves. Slovenian paramilitary forces comprised 4,500 armed police and 5,000 reserves. The estimated defence budget for 2001 was SIT 66,700m. Slovenia was scheduled to become a full member of the North Atlantic Treaty Organization (NATO) in 2004.

Commander-in-Chief of the Armed Forces: President of the Republic.

Chief of Staff of the Slovenian Army Supreme Headquarters: Col-Gen. IZTOK PODBREGAR, 1000 Ljubljana, Prežihova 4; tel. (1) 219748; fax (1) 219764.

Bibliography

Ballinger, P. *History in Exile: Memory and Identity at the Borders of the Balkans.* Princeton, NJ, Princeton University Press, 2002.

Benderly, J., and Kraft, E. *Independent Slovenia: Origins, Movements, Prospects.* New York, NY, St Martin's Press, 1994.

Bister, F. J. *Majestät, es ist zu spät...: Anton Korosec und die slovenische Politik im Wiener Reichsrat bis 1918* Bóhlau, Vienna, 1995.

Bukowski, C., and Sabic, Z. *Small States in the Post-Cold War World: Slovenia and NATO Enlargement.* Westport, CT, Praeger, 2002.

Carmichael, C. *Slovenia.* Oxford, World Bibliographical Series, ABC-Clio, 1986.

Chetkovich, S., and Chetkovich, S. *Monetary reform: the case of Slovenia.* Stockholm Institute of Soviet and East European Economics, 1992.

Englefield, G. *Yugoslavia, Croatia, Slovenia: Re-emerging Boundaries.* Durham, International Boundaries Research Unit (IBRU) Press, 1992.

Ferfila, B., and Phillips, P. A. *Slovenia.* Lanham, MD, University Press of America, 2000.

Fink Hafner, D., and Robbins, J. R. *Making a New Nation: The Formation of Slovenia.* Aldershot, Dartmouth Publishing Co, 1997.

Gow, J. and Carmichael, C. *Slovenia and the Slovenes. A Small State and the New Europe.* Bloomington, IN, Indiana University Press, 2000.

Harris, E. *Nationalism and Democratisation: Politics of Slovakia and Slovenia.* Burlington, VT, Ashgate Publishing Company, 2002.

Jazbec, M. *The Diplomacies of New Small States: The case of Slovenia with some comparison from the Baltics.* Aldershot, Ashgate Publishing, 2001.

Požun, B. J. *Shedding the Balkan Skin: Slovenia's Quiet Emergence in the New Europe.* Central Europe Review Ltd (internet publisher), 2000.

PART THREE
Political Profiles of the Region

POLITICAL PROFILES

ABDIĆ, Fikret: Bosnian former politician; b. 1940; ethnic Bosnian Muslim (Bosniak). *Career:* in 1967 he became manager of Agrokomerc, a state agroindustrial company, which he built into a large, successful enterprise, thereby bringing prosperity to the surrounding region of Cazinska Krajina (north-west Bosnia) and earning popularity among its inhabitants (who named him 'Babo', an affectionate term for father). He was a member of the Presidium of the Central Committee of the League of Communists of Bosnia and Herzegovina and was a representative in the Federal Chamber of the Yugoslav Federal Assembly in the 1980s. In August 1987 he was accused of corruption and imprisoned for almost two years during his investigation and trial. He was eventually acquitted, owing to insufficient evidence. In mid-1990 he joined the predominantly Bosniak Party for Democratic Action (PDA), declaring that he was acting according to the will of the people of Cazinska Krajina, and was elected to the Bosnian state Presidency in November. He increasingly opposed the President of the state Presidency, Alija Izetbegović (q.v.), after the outbreak of civil war in Bosnia and Herzegovina, arguing for the partition of the republic and an end to the 'suicidal war'. On 27 September 1993 his followers proclaimed an 'Autonomous Republic of Western Bosnia' and elected him President. He was subsequently expelled from the PDA and dismissed from the state Presidency, and his control of territory in the Bihać region was contested by the Fifth Corps of the Bosnian army. Government troops failed to oust Abdić until August 1994, when he fled to the Serb-held Krajina region of Croatia. In July 1995, assisted by the Krajina Serbs, Abdić and his supporters attempted to recapture the Bihać region, but were once again driven across the Croatian border by Bosnian and Croatian government forces. Despite the Bosniak-Croat alliance, Croatia subsequently refused to hand over Abdić to the Bosnian authorities, notwithstanding a promise of amnesty. In April 1996 Abdić founded the Democratic People's Union, which contested the September election; his party failed to obtain representation in the state Parliamentary Assembly, but returned three deputies in the Federation's House of Representatives. Abdić was also a Bosniak candidate in the concurrently held election to the state Presidency. In August he was indicted by the public prosecutor's office in Bihać on various charges, including that of war crimes. However, he contested the election for the Bosniak member of the state Presidency in September 1998, in which he was placed second, behind Izetbegović. Abdić was arrested in Rijeka in June 2001 on the war crimes charge, which included the murder of three prisoners-of-war and the deaths of some 121 civilians in a bombardment of the Bihać region in November 1994. He pleaded not guilty at his trial, which commenced in Karlovac, Croatia, in July 2001. Proceedings were subsequently adjourned until late June 2002. At the end of July Abdić was found guilty of war crimes and sentenced to 20 years' imprisonment.

ADAMKUS, Valdas: former President of Lithuania; b. 3 Nov. 1926, in Kaunas; m. Alma Adamkiene in 1951. *Education:* University of Munich, Germany, and University of Illinois, the USA. *Career:* during the Nazi (German) occupation of Lithuania from 1941, he ran a clandestine newspaper, before joining a nationalist unit supported by the Nazis, which fought against the Soviet forces. In 1944, as the USSR occupied the country, he fled to the West. After working in a sports car factory in Chicago, the USA, he was employed for 27 years at the US Environmental Protection Agency (EPA), being appointed regional director for the US Midwest before his retirement. He began regular visits to Lithuania as an EPA official in 1972, then, after independence was restored in 1991, participated in local politics. He was granted Lithuanian citizenship in 1992. In October 1997 a local court ruled that he fulfilled the three-year residence requirement, and

might contest the presidential election. He conducted an energetic electoral campaign; however, it was felt that his age and poor command of the Lithuanian language might count against him. He secured 27.9% of the votes cast in the first round in December 1997, in second place to Artūras Paulauskas (q.v.). In the second round, held in January 1998, he obtained 50.4% of the votes, narrowly defeating Paulauskas. He was inaugurated as President on 26 February. His election, which surprised many, could partly be attributed to a widespread desire for a fresh start in the country, with Adamkus' well-preserved good looks and promotion of a spirit of openness and initiative representative of coveted Western attributes. He proved an accomplished mediator and advocate of parliamentary co-operation. In 1999 Adamkus asserted his power by bringing about the resignation of the Prime Minister, Gediminas Vagnorius, openly criticizing the latter's 'authoritarian' style of government. He was subsequently instrumental in appointing the former President, Algirdas Brazauskas (q.v.), to the premiership in mid-2001; after the appointment, he made clear his intention to intervene if the Government took action that he considered likely to jeopardize reform. Adamkus sought re-election to the presidency in December 2002, but, faced with 16 rivals, was unable to secure a majority of the votes cast. He was defeated by the former Prime Minister, Rolandas Paksas, in a second round of voting in January 2003; some observers attributed the defeat to complacency, an unimpressive campaign and a low participation rate. He remained popular, however, and successfully campaigned for a vote in favour of accession to the European Union at the referendum held in May 2003.

AHMETI, Ali: Macedonian politician and former rebel leader; b. 1959, in Zajas; m. with two c. *Education:* University of Priština. *Career:* he was involved in radical politics as a student, and was imprisoned for a few months. After participating in an uprising of Albanian students in Priština in 1981, he fled to Switzerland, where he reportedly continued to play a role in Albanian nationalist and Marxist-Leninist exile politics. He later joined the LPK (Popular Movement for Kosovo), the main precursor of the Kosovo Liberation Army (KLA), and may have fought in the KLA uprising in Kosovo in 1998–99. He was leader of the National Liberation Army (NLA, which emerged as the successor movement to the KLA) by the time hostilities started in the former Yugoslav republic of Macedonia (FYRM) in February 2001. Quelling talk of territorial gains, Ahmeti insisted that the NLA's aim was simply to accelerate the process of obtaining equal status and rights for ethnic Albanians in the FYRM, including through the recognition of Albanians as a constituent nationality of the country and the acceptance of Albanian as an official language. Keen not to alienate the West, he reiterated that he wished Macedonia to remain a unitary, multi-ethnic state. In mid-August Macedonian and ethnic Albanian leaders signed a framework peace agreement, providing for constitutional changes in exchange for the disarmament of the NLA. On 27 September Ahmeti announced that the NLA had been formally dissolved, following the completion of the disarmament process—cease-fire violations were strongly condemned by Ahmeti, who urged the continuation of the peace process. After much prevarication on the part of the Sobranie (Assembly), the constitutional amendments were adopted in November. Towards the end of 2001 Ahmeti began to restyle himself as a 'social democrat', claiming that he wanted to release Macedonians from the 'ethnic mindset' and move towards a political system based on programmes and policy. In February 2002 the former NLA leadership, together with the three principal ethnic Albanian political parties, established a Co-ordinating Council of Albanians, intended to ensure the implementation of the framework peace agreement and to unite politically all ethnic Albanians in the country. Ahmeti subsequently founded a new party, the Democratic Union for Integration (DUI). The party gained support among ethnic Albanians, and won 16 of the 120 seats in the Sobranie at the legislative elections held in September 2002. Ahmeti subsequently agreed to participate in a new governing coalition, with the Together for Macedonia alliance led by Branko Crvenkovski (q.v., who became Prime Minister). However, resentment of Ahmeti's past raised security fears if he were to attend sessions of the Sobranie with regularity. His new position as a constitutional politician led to increased international acceptance of his role in Macedonian affairs, and he made a number of international visits in 2003, reaffirming that he did not seek the partition of the country. While enjoying great respect among ethnic Albanians, he remained hindered by the fact that he spoke little Macedonian and lacked Macedonian citizenship papers. *Address:* Democratic Union for Integration, Tetovo, FYRM.

ASHDOWN, Sir Jeremy John Durham (Paddy): High Representative of the International Community in Bosnia and Herzegovina and former British politician; b. 27 Feb. 1941, in Delhi, India; m. Jane Courtenay, with two c. *Education:* Bedford School, United Kingdom. *Career:* he served in the British Royal Marines in 1959–71, and subsequently joined the diplomatic service, working at the UN in Geneva, Switzerland, in 1971–76. He later became active in British politics and served as Liberal Democrat leader in 1988–99. On 27 May 2002 he succeeded Wolfgang Petritsch as High Representative of the International Community in Bosnia and Herzegovina. Ashdown, who was to oversee the implementation of the remaining civil aspects of the Dayton accords, identified combating corruption and organized crime as his initial priority, stating that although the nationalist hold on power had weakened, criminal activity was increasingly widespread. He also aimed to increase employment, through reform. Ashdown acted decisively, dismissing the ministers responsible for finance in both entities in mid-June, after criticizing malpractice in the customs agencies. In April 2003 Ashdown removed all references to statehood from the Serb entity's Constitution, and abolished the Serb Republic Supreme Military Council, and in July he suspended the financial accounts of 14 Bosnian Serbs who were suspected of being connected with war crime suspects. His determination to act against corruption and malpractice in the country's administration led to some international criticism of his style, and of the role's lack of accountability. However, he consistently expressed his dissatisfaction with some of his considerable powers (described by some as 'discretionary' and 'draconian'), claiming that they led to a perception of him as the governor of an international protectorate, while he saw his role as that of a 'servant of the people'. *Address:* 71000 Sarajevo, Emerika Bluma 1, Bosnia and Herzegovina; tel. (1) 283500; fax (1) 283501; internet www.ohr.int.

BALCEROWICZ, Dr Leszek: President of the central bank of Poland; b. 19 Jan. 1947, in Lipno; m., with two s. and one d. *Education:* graduated from the Warsaw School of Planning and Statistics (1970); studied business administration at St John's University, New York (USA) until 1974. *Career:* he was a staff member at the Institute of International Economy Relations in 1970–80 and then worked at the Economic Development Institute. He was a member of the Polish Union of Workers' Party in 1969–81. A member of Solidarity, in 1989–91 he served as Minister of Finance, introducing reforms (the so-called Balcerowicz Plan) that provided for a 'shock therapy' move to a free-market economy. Although Balcerowicz had always been considered a highly intelligent and able economist, during this period he was seen by many as a bureaucrat and disciplinarian, remote from the hardships of the population. Nevertheless, credited as the architect of Poland's post-communist economic transformation, in April 1995 he was elected Chairman of the Freedom Union (UW), a party formed by the merging of two centre-right groups in the previous year. In this role he finally became a politician, travelling widely within Poland to communicate the party's secular message of prosperity through reform, and reaching out to the country's nascent middle-class, the party's natural constituency. Following the general election of September

1997, the UW became the junior partner in a coalition Government formed by Solidarity Election Action (AWS) and led by Jerzy Buzek. Balcerowicz was given the posts of Deputy Prime Minister, Minister of Finance and Chairman of the Economic Committee, and pledged to accelerate the processes of privatization and industrial restructuring. His enthusiasm for continued radical reform was not shared by certain members of the AWS, however, and the UW left the coalition Government in June 2000, after numerous policy conflicts. Balcerowicz resigned as leader of the UW in November. His reputation as an economist remained formidable, however. In January 2001 he was appointed President of the National Bank of Poland (NBP) for a six-year term. Strongly in favour of the adoption of the euro, he faced a challenging economic environment. He fiercely defended the independence of the central bank—his refusal, in June 2003, to assent to a plan devised by the Minister of Finance, Grzegorz Kołodko (q.v.), to use foreign-exchange reserves to lower the country's budget deficit, led to Kołodko's resignation. Balcerowicz was publicly perceived as remote, inflexible and committed to excessively aggressive reforms, although he remained an internationally respected administrator. *Address:* Narodowy Bank Polski (National Bank of Poland), 00-919 Warsaw, ul. Świętokrzyska 11/21, POB 1011, Poland; tel. (22) 6531000; fax (22) 6208518; e-mail nbp@nbp.pl.

BĂSESCU, Trăian: Romanian politician; b. 4 Nov. 1951; m. with two d. *Education:* studied at the Faculty of Navigation, Institute of Civil Marine; carried out further studies in maritime transport at the Norwegian Academy; he speaks English and French. *Career:* he began his professional career as a marine officer, becoming a Captain in the Merchant Navy in 1981. In 1987–89 he was Head of the Navrom Agency in the Netherlands. After the fall of communism in 1989, he joined the National Salvation Front, which ran the country first on a broad front and then as a vehicle of President Ion Iliescu (q.v.). Băsescu served as Minister of Transport in 1991–92, a period when much of the Romanian merchant fleet was sold in disputed circumstances. He aligned with Petre Roman, Iliescu's chief rival in the early 1990s, and helped him to establish the Democratic Party (DP) as a credible moderate leftist force. He was again Minister of Transport in the coalition of mainstream parties aligned against Iliescu and his party, which was in office from 1996 to 2000. Băsescu was regarded as a capable minister by the commission that channelled investment into the transport sector to help prepare the country for European Union entry. He also enjoyed a higher popularity rating than his party leader, Roman, because of his straight-talking and approachable image. He proved adept at dealing with the infighting that increasingly undermined the coalition and, in the local elections of June 2000, was narrowly elected Mayor of Bucharest. This was an isolated success for the coalition forces, which were crushed in the national elections at the end of the year by the resurgent Party of Social Democracy of Romania (PSDR), later Social Democratic Party (SDP), of Iliescu. Băsescu launched an energetic campaign to reduce the vast number of stray dogs in Bucharest, but his bolder plans to modernize the run-down Romanian capital were frustrated by the PSDR, which resented his popularity. In May 2001 he ousted Roman as DP leader, with the support of 62% of delegates at the party's national convention. Many second-ranking officials of the DP defected to the ruling SDP, lured by the offer of lucrative positions in a party that lacked real political ability. Fierce personal rivalry developed between Băsescu and the Prime Minister, Adrian Năstase, who feared Băsescu might threaten his chances of becoming President in 2004. Băsescu's popularity remained high, but his party languished in the polls. Although he tried to reach out to nationalists and present himself as the chief foe of corruption, he struggled to preserve the cohesion of the DP, as leading notables defected to the SDP at a time when political analysts insisted that only a merger with the rival National Liberal Party would enable it to remain a major contender in national politics. *Address:* Democratic Party (DP), 71274 Bucharest, Al. Modrogan 1, Romania; tel. and fax (21) 2301332; e-mail office@pd.ro.

BELKA, Prof. Marek: international administrator and former Minister of Finance and Deputy Prime Minister of Poland; b. 1952; m. with two c. *Education:* studied Economics at the University of Łódź, Columbia University and the University of Chicago (USA) and the London School of Economics (United Kingdom). *Career:* in parallel with an academic career (specializing in macroeconomics, monetary policy and the history of economic theory), he worked as an adviser and consultant in the Central Planning Office and the Ministries of Finance and Privatization in 1990–96. He was Vice-President of the Council of Socio-Economic Strategy in the Council of Ministers in 1994–96 and then served as Economic Adviser to the President, Aleksander Kwaśniewski (q.v.). He was appointed Deputy Prime Minister and Minister of Finance under Włodzimierz Cimoszewicz in February 1997, but returned to advise the President in November of that year, remaining in this position until October 2001. A member of the Democratic Left Alliance (SLD), which led the coalition Government formed after the legislative election of September 2001, Belka was once again appointed Deputy Prime Minister and Minister of Finance. Faced with a challenging economic environment, he proposed an austere package of reforms designed to improve the country's finances. However, he resigned from the Government in July 2002, citing fatigue and other personal reasons—the złoty declined in value on international markets after the announcement. Rumours of a disagreement between Belka and the Prime Minister, Leszek Miller, over the independence of the Ministry of Finance were seemingly confirmed by Belka later in the year. In May 2003 he was unexpectedly appointed to the leadership of the International Consultative Committee for Foreign Affairs in the US-led interim administration in Iraq—Poland's support for the USA in the conflict had caused some controversy in its relations with other European countries, and Belka's appointment was seen by many as a 'reward' from the USA for Polish assistance. Belka himself described the International Consultative Committee as an attempt to 'internationalize the coalition's presence' in Iraq. Belka's principal task in his early months in the job appeared to be the co-ordination of international donations for the reconstruction of the country's infrastructure.

BERISHA, Dr Sali: Albanian politician and former President; b. 1 Aug. 1944, in Tropoje. *Education:* he studied at Tirana University. *Career:* a cardiologist, he co-founded the main anti-communist opposition group, the Democratic Party of Albania (DPA), with Gramoz Pashko, in December 1990. He soon demonstrated his political acumen, withdrawing DPA support from the Bufi Government in December 1991 and thus bolstering his own authority as head of the radical, more militant wing of the party. His combative, populist campaigning style proved highly successful, and he was elected President after the electoral defeat of the communists (renamed the Socialist Party of Albania—SPA) in March 1992. Berisha's presidency was marked by an increasingly authoritarian approach to government, particularly after the publication, in November 1994, of a draft basic law that extended the powers of the executive, and of the 'Genocide Law' of September 1995. The latter effectively banned the leading members of the opposition from holding government office and led to an electoral boycott that allowed the DPA an uncontested victory in the general election of mid-1996. In 1997 the widely held belief that members of Berisha's Government had profited personally from the collapsed 'pyramid' investment schemes fuelled the nation-wide insurgency. By the time of Berisha's resignation on 24 July, following the DPA's defeat in the general election, his presidency had been largely discredited. However, in opposition Berisha continued to demonstrate the aggressive style that had taken him to power. Exploiting the historic Gheg (north)–Tosk (south) rivalry, he encouraged rioters in the northern town of Shkodër (a traditional DPA stronghold) in February 1998 and, in September, led his armed supporters in anti-Government protests that led to the resignation of the Prime Minister, Fatos Nano (q.v.). The DPA failed to unseat the ruling SPA in the June–July 2001 legislative elections, but performed strongly in the north of the country, accentuating the political

divide between the two regions. The DPA boycotted parliament after the election, declaring there to have been electoral violations. In December Berisha was re-elected to the party's leadership, with a substantial majority of the votes cast. Berisha strongly opposed Nano's intention to stand as a presidential candidate in the election of mid-2002, and the two party leaders eventually approved Alfred Moisiu (q.v.) as a compromise candidate. In his capacity as leader of the opposition, he remained a determined opponent of Nano, repeatedly accusing him and his party of links with organized crime and of exercising undue control over the country's media. *Address:* Democratic Party of Albania (Partia Demokratike e Shqipërisë—PDSH), Rruga Punetoret e Rilindjes, Tirana, Albania; tel. (4) 228091; fax (4) 223525; e-mail profsberisha@albaniaonline.net.

BĒRZIŅŠ, Andris: former Prime Minister of Latvia; b. 4 Aug. 1951, in Rīga; m., with two c. *Education:* a graduate in history and philosophy from the University of Latvia. *Career:* before entering politics he worked as a teacher and in state personnel training. In 1993, as a member of the newly formed Latvian Way, which performed well in the June general election, he became the State Minister of Labour, in a coalition Government led by Valdis Birkavs. Following the formation of a new coalition Government in September 1994, this time led by Māris Gailis, he was appointed Deputy Prime Minister and Minister of Welfare, retaining this post until late 1995. In 1997 he was elected Mayor of Rīga, a position he held until he was invited by President Vaira Viķe-Freiberga (q.v.) in May 2000 to form a government, following the resignation of Andris Šķēle. Bērziņš formed a centre-right coalition Government, comprising Latvian Way, the People's Party, the Conservative Union 'For Fatherland and Freedom'/LNNK and the New Party. Despite being the largest party in the coalition comprising Latvia's longest-serving Government since independence, Latvian Way had little chance of success in the legislative election held in October 2002. Indeed, it failed to secure the 5% of the votes cast required to win seats in parliament. Bērziņš retreated from politics, resigned as chairman of Latvian Way and, in June 2003, established a consulting company.

BOROWSKI, Marek: Polish politician; b. 4 January 1946, in Warsaw; m., with one s. *Education:* he studied international economic relations at the Warsaw School of Planning and Statistics. *Career:* A leader of student demonstrations against communist rule, he was not permitted to complete his university education, and began working in a department store, rising to the post of financial director before leaving in 1982 to enter government service. He became Director of the Ministry of the Domestic Market and in the late 1980s played a central role in the first economic reforms made in Poland. He became Deputy Minister in the same department in October 1989. He left government in 1991, having overseen numerous privatizations and reforms, but became a member of the Sejm (the lower chamber of parliament) in the same year, representing the Social Democraic Party. He served on the principal economic committee of the chamber until his appointment as Deputy Prime Minister and Minister of Finance in October 1993. He resigned four months later, in protest at the dismissal of his deputy. He served in the cabinet office until February 1996, when he became Vice-Marshal (deputy speaker) of the Sejm. Following the elections held in October 2001 he was elected Marshal. *Address:* 00–902 Warsaw, ul. Wiejska 4/6, Poland; internet www.sejm.gov.pl.

BRAZAUSKAS, Algirdas: Prime Minister and former President of Lithuania; b. 22 Sept. 1932, in Rokškis; m. Julija Styraite-Brazauskiene, with two d. *Education:* Kaunas Polytechnic Institute. *Career:* he began his career as an engineer, gradually being promoted in the energy sector, until he became Minister for the Construction Materials Industry of the Lithuanian SSR in 1967–77. He meanwhile rose through the ranks of the Central Committee of the Lithuanian Communist Party, becoming First Secretary in 1988. In 1990 he was elected Chairman of the Democratic Labour Party and of the Presidium of the Lithuanian SSR, Deputy Chairman of the USSR Supreme Soviet, and deputy premier of Lithuania. In 1992 he became acting President of Lithuania, and in the following year formally took office as President, a post that he retained until 1997. In January 2001 he was elected Chairman of the Lithuanian Social Democratic Party (LSDP—which had merged with the Lithuanian Democratic Labour Party—LDLP), having been Honorary Chairman of the A. Brazauskas Social Democratic Coalition, which obtained 31% of the votes in the legislative election of October 2000. In July 2001, following the collapse of the coalition Government, Brazauskas was appointed Prime Minister. He pledged to maintain Lithuania's commitment to economic reforms and to membership of the North Atlantic Treaty Organization (NATO) and the European Union (EU), in addition to seeking a greater emphasis on social reforms. His popularity—although still widespread—declined somewhat during 2001 and 2002, partly owing to hostility from the media, and this decline prevented him from participating in the presidential election held in December 2002. He remained as Prime Minister, where his objectives remained eventual membership of the EU and NATO and the improvement of relations with Russia, particularly regarding the Kaliningrad enclave. *Address:* Office of the Prime Minister, Gedimino pr. 11, Vilnius 2039, Lithuania; tel. (526) 63874; fax (521) 63877; e-mail kasp@lrvk.lt.

BUCHKOVSKI, Vlado: Minister of Defence of the former Yugoslav republic of Macedonia (FYRM); b. 2 Dec. 1962, in Skopje. *Education:* he studied law at the University of Skopje. *Career:* he studied for a doctorate in law, which he was awarded in 1998. In the same year he was appointed to the country's electoral commission. A member of the Social Democratic Alliance of Macedonia, he became Vice-President of the party in 1999. He was elected Chairman of Skopje city council in 2000, but left the position the following year when he was appointed Minister of Defence in the Government of national unity led by Ljubčo Georgievski (q.v.). The deteriorating security situation in the country, as attacks by ethnic Albanian rebel groups grew in frequency and severity, made this a crucial position. A North Atlantic Treaty Organization (NATO) force was sent to the country in August 2001, after a cease-fire was agreed by the rebels. Buchkovski resigned in November, claiming that full-scale civil war had been averted, and that he no longer wished to remain in government. He returned to the position in October 2002, however, after the victory of the centre-left alliance led by Branko Crvenkovski (q.v.). Although he expressed concern that the security situation in the country was once again deteriorating, a number of reforms that he oversaw, combined with the presence of the NATO (and subsequently European Union) force and the products of negotiations with rebel groups, led to an improvement by mid-2003. *Address:* Ministry of Defence, 1000 Skopje, Orce Nikolov bb, FYRM; tel. (2) 3230928; internet www.morm .gov.mk.

BUDIŠA, Dražen: Croatian politician; b. 25 July 1948, in Drniš; m. Nada Budiša, with three s. *Education:* University of Zagreb. *Career:* he came to prominence through his participation as an independent student leader in the 'Croatian Spring' movement of 1970 and his subsequent four-year prison term. He became leader of the Croatian Social-Liberal Party (CSLP) in 1990 and, one year later, became a minister in the Government of the newly independent Croatia. He was elected to the Sabor in 1992, retaining his seat in subsequent elections. In the late 1990s he concentrated on creating a strong opposition to the ruling Croatian Democratic Union (CDU). For the legislative election of January 2000 his CSLP formed a coalition with the Social Democratic Party (SDP) and defeated the CDU, securing 47% of the votes cast. Following the coalition's victory, Budiša stood as the SDP/CSLP candidate in the presidential election, also held in January. In the first round he polled 27.7% of the votes cast; however, in a second ballot against former Yugoslav President Stipe Mesić (q.v.) in February, he was defeated, winning 43.8% of the votes, compared with Mesić's 56.2%. In July 2001 four ministers belonging to the CSLP resigned from the Government, in protest at a decision by the authorities to extradite two war crimes suspects for trial at the International Criminal Tribunal for the former Yugoslavia (ICTY, based in The Hague, the Netherlands). As a result of the ensuing rift within the CSLP over the issue, Budiša announced his resignation from the leadership of the party. Just months later, however, he decided to return to politics, and in early February 2002 was re-elected to the presidency of the CSLP. At the end of February he removed the First Deputy Prime Minister, Goran Granić, and two other CSLP ministers from the Government, reportedly questioning their loyalty to the party, owing to their failure to support his stance of opposition to co-operation with the ICTY. The remaining three CSLP members in the Government then resigned, to demonstrate their disagreement with the party leadership. Budiša was appointed First Deputy Prime Minister by Ivica Račan (q.v.) on 21 March, apparently in a bid to avoid the collapse of the Government (CLSP representatives were also nominated to assume the other vacant posts). However, in early July Budiša finally withdrew the CSLP from the governing coalition, after an agreement on joint ownership of the Krško nuclear power installation in Slovenia was ratified in the Sabor, despite the opposition of 17 of the 23 CSLP deputies. Budiša led the CSLP to a centrist, anti-Government position, and was fiercely critical of Račan and Mesić over their policies towards the ICTY. In mid-2003 he participated in a series of meetings with leaders of other centrist parties, with a view to the formation of a coalition to contest the next legislative election (despite previous assertions that the CSLP would 'fight alone'). *Address:* Croatian Social-Liberal Party (Hrvatska Socijalno-Liberalna Stranka—HSLS), 10000 Zagreb, trg N. Š. Zrinskog 17, Croatia; tel. (1) 4810401; fax (1) 4810404; e-mail hsls@hsls .hr.

ČAVIĆ, Dragan: President of the Serb Republic of Bosnia and Herzegovina; b. 10 March 1958, in Zenica; ethnic Serb; m., with one s. and one d. *Education:* he graduated in economics from the University of Banja Luka. *Career:* he worked as an economist, before becoming finance director of a number of industrial companies. He was elected to the National Assembly of the Serb Republic (Republika Srpska) of Bosnia and Herzegovina in 1998, representing the Serbian Democratic Party (SDP). His mandate was revoked by the High Representative of the International Community, Carlos Westendorp, in October of that year, after comments regarding the situation in the Serbian province of Kosovo and Metohija were deemed to have jeopardized the administration of the Dayton accords. Westendorp's successor, Wolfgang Petritsch, restored Čavić's mandate in July 1999. He was elected to the Vice-Presidency of the Serb Republic in November 2000, as the running-mate of Mirko Sarović, remaining in office until the elections held in October 2002, at which he was elected President, securing 35.9% of the votes cast. His presidency suffered a scandal almost immediately, when it was revealed that a Bosnian firm had been selling arms illegally to Iraq. A presidential investigation, concluded in January 2003, reported that the illegal sales had begun under the presidency of Biljana Plavsić (q.v.), and that she and the contemporary administrations bore primary responsibility. The report was widely criticized by opposition parties and the international community. A subsequent report by Western intelligence agencies suggested that Sarović had known about the exports (he was forced to resign from the state Presidency)—Čavić claimed the report was biased and inaccurate. In April 2003 he ordered the disbandment of a military intelligence unit, which had been caught undertaking an espionage mission against forces of the North Atlantic Treaty Organization stationed in the country. A strident nationalist, he repeatedly stated that he considered the defence of the Serb nation to be a 'mission from God'. *Address:* Office of the President, 78000 Banja Luka, Republika Srpska of Bosnia and Herzegovina; internet www.predsjednikrs.net.

CHRISOCHOIDHIS, Michalis: Greek politician; b. 31 October 1955, in Imathia. *Education:* he studied law at the Aristotle University of Thessaloníki. *Career:* a member of the Panhellenic Socialist Movement (PASOK) since its establishment in 1974, he was a leading figure in the party's regional structure, and held numerous elected posts at local level. He entered the national parliament in 1989 and was elected to the party's central committee the following year. He became Deputy Minister of Commerce in July 1994, and deputy

Minister of Development in January 1996. In February 1999 he was appointed to the cabinet, as Minister for Public Order. This post gave him responsibility for many of Greece's most pressing issues, notably the security situation, in the light of increased terrorist activity by the November 17 organization and the preparations for the Olympic Games to be held in Athens in 2004. The detention, in July 2002, of a man believed to be the leading figure in November 17 was seen by many as a crucial event in the attempt to neutralize terrorism in Greece, and was widely considered a personal triumph for Chrisochoidhis. In July 2003 he was elected Secretary-General of PASOK and left the cabinet. *Address:* Odos Charilaou Trikoupi 50, Athens, Greece; tel. (21) 03232049; e-mail pasok@pasok.gr; internet www.pasok.gr.

CHRISTODOULAKIS, Nikolaos (Nikos): Minister of the Economy and Finance of Greece; b. 1952, in Armeni, Chania; m., with one d. *Education:* studied at Athens Polytechnic and the University of Cambridge, the United Kingdom. *Career:* linked to the 1973 student uprising at the Athens Polytechnic, Christodoulakis began his career as an academic, securing research and professorial positions at a number of universities in Greece and abroad. From 1991 he served on various policy committees of the Panhellenic Socialist Movement (PASOK). In 1993 he was appointed General Secretary of the Ministry of Research and Technology in the PASOK-led Government, and in 1996 became Economics Counsellor to the Prime Minister, Konstantinos (Costas) Simitis (q.v.). He served as deputy economy minister in 1996–2000, setting up a modern debt-management system, and as Minister of Development in 2000–01, when he oversaw the partial liberalization of the energy market, winning praise from the European Union (EU). In the October 2001 cabinet reshuffle he was granted the dual portfolios of Minister of National Economy (a new post) and Minister of Finance. The reshuffle, which removed most traditionalists from the cabinet, gave seniority to the Ministry of Finance, and Christodoulakis became, in effect, Simitis's deputy, heading the reformist camp. A self-described market-friendly socialist, his stated priorities include reducing unemployment through boosting economic growth, fully integrating into the euro zone, strengthening business activity and encouraging faster deregulation, to attract investment. He oversaw the introduction of the euro to the country in 2002, and responded to public discontent at perceived price rises after its adoption by restricting price increases on certain goods. It was reported in March 2003 that his predecessor, who had become the Minister of National Defence, Ioannis Papantoniou (q.v.), had urged his resignation, although this was swiftly denied by all parties. He wrote extensively on economic subjects and—belying his generally dry, academic image—was also an art enthusiast, arranging a loan in 2000 to keep a leading collection of modern art within the country. *Address:* Ministry of the Economy and Finance, Odos Nikos 5–7, 101 80 Athens, Greece; tel. (21) 03332000.

CHRISTODOULOS, Archbishop: Orthodox Primate of Greece; b. 1939, in Xanthi. *Education:* studied law and theology (in which he received a doctorate) and languages (speaking French, English, Italian and German). *Career:* he was ordained a deacon in the Greek Orthodox Church in 1961 and a priest in 1965. He served as a preacher and senior spiritual father for nine years and as Secretary of the Holy Synod of the Orthodox Church for seven years. He was elected Metropolitan of Demetrias in 1974 and Archbishop of Athens and all Greece in April 1998, becoming the youngest archbishop to lead the church in Greece. He was enthroned in May, in a ceremony boycotted both by the President, Konstantinos (Costas) Stefanopoulos (q.v.), and the Prime Minister, Konstantinos (Costas) Simitis (q.v.), while human rights groups criticized his nationalist stance towards Catholics, Jews, Muslims and other minorities. Outspoken and prone to making fiery speeches, Christodoulos promised to make the improvement of relations with other Orthodox Churches a priority and emphasized the need to modernize the Greek Church (later, in an unexpected move, he announced that boys in the church would be permitted to wear earrings). In May 2001 he grudgingly agreed, after considerable political pressure, to welcome

Pope John Paul II (regarded as a heretic by the Orthodox Church) on his one-day visit to Athens. The Pope used his visit to ask forgiveness for past Roman Catholic transgressions, notably the sacking of Constantinople by Catholic crusaders in 1204. The statement was applauded by Christodoulos, who embraced the pontiff, although few held hopes for a speedy reconciliation between the two Churches. After orchestrating large-scale demonstrations in Athens in mid-2001, in August Christodoulos demanded that a referendum be held on proposals to remove all reference to religious affiliation from government-issued identity cards—a measure he said had been proposed by the Jewish community. In 2003 Christodoulos organized a campaign for a reference to Europe's 'historic past' (a phrase used to indicate Christian hegemony) to be made in any future European constitution. *Address:* Orthodox Church of Greece, Odos Ioannou Gennadiou 14, 115 21 Athens, Greece; tel. (21) 07218381.

CONSTANTINESCU, Emil: former President of Romania; b. 19 Nov. 1939, in Tighina (Moldova); m. Nadia Ileana, with one s. and one d. *Education:* he graduated from Bucharest University with a degree in law and a doctorate in geology. *Career:* a jurist, geologist and former professor and rector of the University of Bucharest, he benefited from the political sponsorship of the elderly Corneliu Coposu, who enjoyed national stature because of his long-standing resistance to communism. In 1996 Constantinescu was elected President of Romania, at the second attempt, at the head of an opposition alliance, the Democratic Convention of Romania (DCR), founded by Coposu. He was obliged to share power with the moderate-left Democratic Party in order to obtain a governing majority. Over the following four yeas, he proved unable to contain in-fighting between coalition members, largely over the spoils of office. He concentrated on foreign-policy goals and the most significant foreign-policy decision of his presidency, arguably, was his decision in 1999 to support unconditionally the North Atlantic Treaty Organization (NATO) in its military action in the Federal Republic of Yugoslavia. Romania was invited to open negotiations for entry to the European Union at the end of that year. However, Constantinescu's initially high popularity ratings decline dramatically owing to his support for the NATO action, and his failure to combat corruption and promote effective governance. He withdrew unexpectedly from the race for a second presidential term in July 2000. As a result the coalition forces had little time to find a substitute, and this deepened their internal conflict, enabling ultra-nationalists to fill the vacuum, on a platform that combined authoritarian solutions with anti-corruption measures. After the publication of excerpts from his diaries in 2002, Constantinescu attempted to re-enter politics. The ephemeral Popular Action movement was regarded as his vehicle, but he was distrusted by former allies owing to his largely unimpressive record in office. *Address:* Popular Action, Bucharest, Romania.

ČOVIĆ, Dragan: Chairman of the state Presidency of Bosnia and Herzegovina; b. 20 Aug. 1956, in Mostar; ethnic Croat; m., with two d. *Education:* he studied at the Universities of Mostar and Sarajevo. *Career:* he joined an engineering company in Mostar, remaining in employment there for 21 years. Following the conflict in the country he studied for a doctorate, and became active in the nationalist Croat Democratic Union of Bosnia and Herzegovina (CDU—BH). Despite being in dispute with the local branch of the party in Mostar, he was appointed Deputy Prime Minister and Minister of Finance of the Federation in November 1998. In 2001 he was among a group of ministers dismissed by the High Representative of the International Community, Wolfgang Petritsch, following allegations that they had diverted state funds to churches in exchange for the insertion of pro-CDU—BH statements in sermons. The dismissed ministers were subsequently prominent in a plan to establish a third, Croat, entity within Bosnia and Herzegovina, and a number of meetings in support of the plan descended into violent unrest. The plan received little support from other parties, and almost none from the international community, and Petritsch authorized UN forces to restore order. Criminal proceedings based on the allegations of embezzlement were begun in April. In July 2002 he was chosen as the candidate of the CDU—BH for the election to the ethnic Croat position on the state Presidency, stating that he would not pursue the creation of a third entity if elected. He won 61.5% of the votes cast in the election in October, and assumed his position on the Presidency soon after. He assumed the Chairmanship of the Presidency in June 2003, stating that his aims were to ensure the continuity of judicial and political stability within the country. Allegations of corruption relating to his time as Deputy Prime Minister of the Federation continued to be made against him, and his participation in the attempt to establish a third entity contributed to his unpopularity among ethnic Bosniaks and Serbs. His nationalism and charismatic speaking style ensured that he retained widespread support among those of his own ethnicity, however. *Address:* Office of the Presidency, 71000 Sarajevo, Musala 5, Bosnia and Herzegovina; tel. (33) 664941; fax (33) 472491; internet www.predsjednistvobih.ba.

CRVENKOVSKI, Branko: Prime Minister of the former Yugoslav republic of Macedonia (FYRM); b. 12 Oct 1962, in Sarajevo (Bosnia and Herzegovina). *Education:* University of Skopje. *Career:* a member of the Macedonian League of Communists (which, after several name changes, became the Social Democratic Alliance of Macedonia—SDAM), he worked as a computer engineer before succeeding Kiro Gligorov as leader when the latter became President of the Republic. As leader of one of the main parties he was appointed Chairman (Prime Minister) of a new coalition Government on 4 September 1992. Despite the economic crisis caused by the blockade by Greece, imposed in February 1994, the SDAM, part of the Alliance of Macedonia, won the largest number of seats of any party in the Sobranie (Assembly) elected in October, and Crvenkovski was asked to form a new coalition Government. He remained premier after the collapse of the Alliance of Macedonia in February 1996, with the withdrawal from government of the Liberal Party. He then provided a greater role for the ethnic Albanian party, the Party for Democratic Prosperity, in the subsequent ruling coalition. He thereby reinforced a policy of maintaining the constitutional involvement of the Albanian minority within the state structures of the former Yugoslav republic of Macedonia, which had preserved a relative degree of stability since independence. He remained Prime Minister until the general election of October–November 1998, having resisted demands for the Government's resignation following the financial scandal of March 1997, in which many public officials were implicated. Thereafter, he stayed on as Chairman of the SDAM, which formed the largest opposition party in the Sobranie. Together for Macedonia, an electoral coalition of 10 parties, led by the SDAM, secured 40.5% of the votes cast and 60 of the 120 seats in the Sobranie in the parliamentary election of 15 September 2002. Crvenkovski subsequently formed a new coalition Government with the Democratic Union for Integration of Ali Ahmeti (q.v.), which was approved on 1 November. *Address:* Office of the Prime Minister, 1000 Skopje, Ilindenska bb, FYRM; tel. (2) 115389; fax (2) 112561; e-mail office@ primeminister.gov.mk.

DÁVID, Dr Ibolya: Hungarian politician. *Career:* a lawyer by training, Dávid was appointed Minister of Justice in the Government led by Victor Orbán (q.v.) in 1998. Her party, the Hungarian Democratic Forum (HDF), had formed an alliance with Orbán's Federation of Young Democrats—Hungarian Civic Party (FYD—HCP) to contest the May election. The only female minister in the cabinet, she supported traditional conservative and Christian values, and made a number of controversial and hitherto unprecedented decisions, including reversing a pardon issued by the then President, Árpád Göncz, and introducing strict drugs and crime laws. As leader of the HDF, she renewed the electoral alliance with the FYD—HCP for the 2002 general election, but the grouping failed to secure sufficient seats to give it a majority in the National Assembly; it duly ceded power to an alliance of the Hungarian Socialist Party and the Alliance of Free Democrats. Dávid remained as leader of the HDF, and continue to play a prominent role on the political scene (opinion polls in 2003 suggesting that she was the country's most popular politician), with suggestions that she hoped, ultimately, to become Hungary's first female Prime Minister. *Address:* Hungarian Democratic Forum (HDF) (Magyar Demokrata Fórum—MDF), 1026 Budapest, Szilágyi Erszébet fasor 73, Hungary; tel. (1) 212-2828; fax (1) 225-2290.

DJELIĆ, Božidar: Serbian and Montenegrin (Serbian) politician; Minister of Finance and Economy of Serbia; b. 1 April 1965; m., with two c. *Education:* Institut d'Études Politiques (France) and Harvard (USA); speaks English, French, Russian, German and Polish. *Career:* he lived and worked outside Yugoslavia for 15 years, serving as an economic adviser to a number of foreign governments and businesses. He specialized in the difficulties of transforming economies based on socialist principles and, among other things, initiated the voucher privatization schemes in Poland and Russia. Following the collapse of the regime of President Slobodan Milošević (q.v.) in 2000, he was recalled to Yugoslavia and, following a meeting with the Serbian Prime Minister, Zoran Djindjć, was appointed Serbian Minister of Finance and Economy in early 2001. He faced an enormous task in rebuilding the republic's economy, devastated by almost a decade of sanctions and the North Atlantic Treaty Organization's aerial bombardment of 1999. He swiftly entered into an ambitious reform programme, supported by the World Bank, as part of which, among other reforms, four of Yugoslavia's leading banks were closed. He adopted a higher profile in the Government in the aftermath of the assassination of Djindjić in March 2003. In July he accused the Governor of the central bank, Mladjan Dinkić, of blackmail, after the latter threatened to publicize allegations of government corruption if early elections were not arranged. The relationship between the two deteriorated, and Djelić asserted that he would resign if any allegations of corruption against him were proven. A new Governor of the National Bank was appointed later in the month. *Address:* Ministry of Finance and Economy, 11000 Belgrade, Nemanjina 22–26, Serbia and Montenegro; tel. (11) 3616361; fax (11) 3616535; e-mail bdjelsc@mfin.sr.gov.yu.

DJUKANOVIĆ, Milo: Serbian and Montenegrin (Montenegrin) politician; Prime Minister of Montenegro; b. 15 Feb. 1962, in Nikšić, Montenegro; m. Lidija Kuč, with one s. *Education:* he graduated in economics from Titograd (later Podgorica) University in 1986. *Career:* a former successful basketball player, he joined the League of Communists of Yugoslavia in 1979. In early 1989 the Montenegrin communist leadership was forced to resign and was replaced by a relatively young group of communists, including Djukanović. This group favoured a Montenegrin renaissance, although its members remained loyal allies of Serbia. The new leadership was among the first in Yugoslavia to agree to the holding of multi-party elections, which took place in December 1990 and were won by the League of Communists of Yugoslavia (subsequently renamed the Democratic Party of Montenegrin Socialists—DPMS). On his 29th birthday, in 1991, Djukanović was asked to lead a DPMS Government. Following elections in December 1992, he formed a coalition Government. His relations with the federal and Serbian Governments became increasingly strained during the mid-1990s, particularly as a result of his pursuit of an independent Montenegrin foreign policy, and partly owing to his support for the protest movement in Serbia, in late 1996. He was opposed to the increasing control exercised by the Serbian and, later federal, President, Slobodan Milošević (q.v.), on Montenegrin politics and in February 1997 incurred the latter's wrath by publicly declaring him to be unfit to hold public office. Relations with his former mentor and DPMS ally, the Montenegrin President, Momir Bulatović, also became increasingly strained, owing to the latter's alliance with Milošević. In the bitterly fought presidential election of 1997 Djukanović and Bulatović opposed each other, representing different factions of the DPMS. Djukanović obtained 50.8% of the votes cast and succeeded to office in January 1998. Despite his communist past, Djukanović proved a liberal reformer, whose regime received the approval of Western Governments. During the escalating ethnic conflict in the Serbian province of Kosovo and Metohija in 1999, he disagreed with Milošević's domestic and foreign policy and excluded his administration from any federal decisions. He refused to condemn the aerial bombardment of the Federal Republic of Yugoslavia (FRY) by the North Atlantic Treaty Organization in March–June 1999. In July Djukanović announced that Montenegro would not participate in the elections for the federal presidency or to the Federal Assembly scheduled for September, in protest at the amendments to the Constitution allowing Milošević to seek direct election to the presidency. In December he announced proposals for greater independence for Montenegro, prompting the People's Party of Montenegro to withdraw from the republican governing coalition. Consequently, legislative elections took place in Montenegro on 22 April 2001: Djukanović's pro-independence alliance, Victory Belongs to Montenegro, secured 36 of the 77 seats in the republican Assembly, narrowly defeating Bulatović's Together for Yugoslavia alliance, which won 33 seats. Djukanović formed a minority Government supported by the more radical nationalist Liberal Alliance of Montenegro (LAM). After lengthy negotiations on the issue of Montenegrin independence, mediated by the EU from November 2001, the Government leaders of the FRY and of Serbia and Montenegro signed a framework agreement on 14 March 2002, providing for the establishment of a 'Union of States', to be known as 'Serbia and Montenegro'. Under the agreement, the two republics were to maintain separate economies, but were to share foreign and defence policies, and elect a joint presidency and legislature, in which Montenegro would have equal powers to Serbia. In protest at the agreement, the LAM withdrew from the coalition, thereby ending Djukanović's narrow majority in the republican Assembly. Despite widespread criticism from pro-independence supporters, who were not mollified by the provision in the agreement for Montenegro to refer the issue of independence to a referendum after a period of three years, the Montenegrin legislature approved the accord in April. However, amid worsening political chaos, the Government collapsed, prompting concern that the implementation of the agreement would be delayed. Internationally, Djunkanović's personal importance had lessened following the removal of Milošević. At the same time, the problems inherent in Montenegro, ignored while Milošević was in power, received greater attention. In mid-2002 Italy's anti-Mafia directorate launched an investigation against Djukanović for alleged cigarette-smuggling. The President strenuously denied the allegations, which threatened further to sully Montenegro's image abroad. Following a dispute over the new constitutional arrangements, which led to the collapse of the Government, Djukanović was compelled to dissolve the Republican Assembly and arrange new elections for October. In September it was announced that he would stand as his party's candidate for Prime Minister, and that, to this end, he was to resign as President if the party was successful in the legislative elections to be held the following month. His coalition won 39 of the 75 seats in the Assembly, and Djukanović resigned from the presidency in late November—he was appointed Prime Minister-designate shortly afterwards, and his cabinet was endorsed in early January 2003. The disputes over the new constitutional arrangements continued, with Djukanović attracting criticism (for different reasons) in both republics. However, he was able to obtain parliamentary support for the new constitutional charter of 'Serbia and Montenegro' in late January, which entered into force in early February. Djukanović saw his immediate priority thereafter as the creation of a plan of economic reform. Allegations of corruption continued to surface with regularity, but Djukanović appeared as central to the Montenegrin political scene as ever. *Address:* Office of the Prime Minister of Montenegro, Podgorica, Jovana Tomaševića bb, Serbia and Montenegro; tel. (81) 52833; fax (81) 52246.

DOGAN, Ahmed: Bulgarian politician; b. 29 March 1954; ethnic Turk. *Education:* doctorate in philosophy. *Career:* it was revealed in 1997 that he had worked for Bulgaria's communist intelligence services from 1974 to 1988. However, under the communist regime, he was also prosecuted for his championing of ethnic Turkish rights and, in June 1989, was arrested and sentenced to 10 years in prison for being a founder and leader of an 'anti-state organization', the Movement for Rights and Freedoms (MRF). He was amnestied in

December of the same year. He was elected as a deputy in June 1990 and, after the October 1991 election, his party was the third largest in the National Assembly and agreed to support a Government of the Union of Democratic Forces (UDF). In December 1992 the MRF nominated Lyuben Berov as Prime Minister, and subsequently, with the majority of members of the Bulgarian Socialist Party and a schismatic section of the UDF, provided him with a strong base of support in the National Assembly. Although the MRF's representation in parliament was reduced following the election in November 1994, and the party experienced internal disputes, in the late 1990s Dogan remained a strong representative of the Muslim minority in Bulgaria. In April 1997 the Alliance for National Salvation, a coalition dominated by the MRF, won 19 seats in the election to the National Assembly, reflecting continuing popular support for the party's policies. The MRF signed a coalition agreement on 20 July 2001 with the National Movement Simeon II, following the legislative election of 17 June, in which it secured 21 seats. Thus, the MRF gained power for the first time in its history, although Dogan did not form part of the cabinet approved in late July. Dogan said of the new Government that 'dialogue, tolerance and a new political style' would create opportunities for Bulgaria to progress; however, he repeatedly predicted difficulties for the administration, arising from public discontent at crime and lack of investment. Dogan was viewed as a figure with substantial power, if not a seat, in the administration, his apparent aims being increased investment and spending of European Union funds in areas primarily populated by his support base. While publicly supportive of the Prime Minister, Simeon Saxe-Coburg-Gotha (q.v.), Dogan was critical of many other ministers, and by June 2003 his desire for a reshuffle was evident. *Address:* Movement for Rights and Freedoms (Dvizhenie za Prava i Svobodi), Sofia, Bulgaria; tel. (2) 988-18-23.

DRAŠKOVIĆ, Vuk: Serbian and Montenegrin (Serbian) politician; b. 29 Nov. 1946, in Media, in the Banat region of Vojvodina; m. Dania Drašković. *Education:* he studied law at Belgrade University. *Career:* an ardent nationalist, he was vociferous in demands for resistance to the Croats and the Albanians of Kosovo (Kosovo and Metohija). His right-wing tendencies were said to have contributed to his poor showing in the presidential election of 1990, when he obtained only 20% of the votes cast. In March 1991, however, he emerged as the leading opposition figure during the anti-Government demonstrations in Belgrade. His party, the Serbian Renewal Movement (SRM), was the largest opposition group in the Serbian parliament until 1992, when it entered into an electoral coalition, named the Democratic Movement of Serbia (DMS or DEPOS), which obtained 49 seats in the December 1992 election. After the election, claiming fraud, Drašković and other DMS deputies began a boycott of parliament. During anti-Government demonstrations in June, Drašković was detained by police for five weeks and badly beaten. Charges of attempting to overthrow the constitutional order were eventually dropped. In the December 1993 election the DMS obtained 45 seats. Drašković consistently spoke out against the alleged atrocities carried out by Bosnian Serbs during the civil conflict in Bosnia and Herzegovina, and as a result became increasingly isolated among nationalists in Serbia. He was also critical of the administration led by Slobodan Milošević, and in early 1996 was the victim of a virulent campaign by the Government-led media, after writing a letter to Western Governments denouncing the alleged abuse of civil rights and press freedoms in Serbia. His position was strengthened in 1996 by a *rapprochement* between the SRM, the Democratic Party and the Civic Alliance of Serbia, which led to the formation of an opposition coalition, Zajedno (Together), which contested the 1996 local elections. Zajedno gained control of 14 major Serbian cities, but its electoral successes were annulled by the authorities, leading to violent disturbances by its supporters. In February 1997 the election results were eventually declared valid and Drašković found himself in a position to help reinforce Zajedno's gains. However, the alliance was weakened by infighting and was dissolved later in the year. The SRM obtained 45 seats in the elections to the National Assembly in September

1997 and Drašković stood as a Serbian presidential candidate in December, securing the third-largest number of votes. He was appointed Deputy Prime Minister of the Federal Republic of Yugoslavia (FRY), but was dismissed in April 1999, during the NATO bombardment of the country, for expressing views in contradiction to the position of the federal Government. In October he was injured in an automobile collision that was later accepted as having been a deliberate attempt to kill him. (In February 2001 a former head of Milošević's secret service, Radovan Marković, was detained in connection with the incident.) Despite Drašković's popularity among the opponents of Milošević, his personal rivalries with other leaders prevented the opposition from establishing a serious challenge to the incumbent regime. In June 2000 he was shot and injured in his home. The SRM did not join the broad alliance of parties, the Democratic Opposition of Serbia (DOS), formed to oppose Milošević in 2000, and failed to secure any seats in the federal legislature following elections in September. In elections to the Serbian National Assembly in December, the party did not secure the 5% of votes needed for parliamentary representation, and Drašković's personal influence was greatly reduced. In early 2002 he demanded that new elections to be held by the end of the year, and announced that he planned to hold a series of rallies across Serbia. He sought election to the presidency in the first round of voting held in September, but received less than 5% of the votes cast. In April 2003 Milošević and others were charged with the attack on Drašković in June 2000. *Address:* Serbian Renewal Movement (SRM) (Srpski pokret obnove—SPO), Belgrade, Krez Mihajlovna 48, Serbia and Montenegro; tel. (11) 635281; fax (11) 628170.

DRNOVŠEK, Dr Janez: President of Slovenia and former Yugoslav head of state; b. 17 May 1950, in Izlake. *Education:* Maribor University, where he received a doctorate in economics; he speaks English, French, German, Spanish and Serbo-Croat. *Career:* he worked variously as an industrialist, banker and diplomat. In May 1989 he was elected, in a direct popular ballot, as Slovenia's representative on the Yugoslavian federal State Presidency. Despite anxieties about his political inexperience, he was elected by the Presidency for Slovenia's turn as President of the federal state. He served in this capacity until May 1990. He then remained a member of the State Presidency until 8 October 1991, when Slovenia formally recalled all its citizens from participation in federal institutions. He became President of the Liberal Democratic Party (which later merged with three other organizations to form Liberal Democracy of Slovenia—LDS) and, following the resignation of Lojze Peterle in May 1992, he was appointed Prime Minister of Slovenia. He retained this post after the general election at the end of the year. During his time as premier he survived a series of disputes and scandals within the ruling coalition. In January 1996 the withdrawal from the Government of one of the LDS's coalition partners left the administration without a parliamentary majority. After the general election of November 1996 the LDS and its potential allies controlled exactly the same number of seats as the newly formed opposition alliance, Slovenian Spring. The impasse was broken in January 1997 when Drnovšek was re-elected Prime Minister. Following the merger of the LDS's coalition partner, the Slovenian People's Party (SPP), with an opposition party, the Slovenian Christian Democrats, in April 2000, Drnovšek was again left without a parliamentary majority. The National Assembly rejected his reconstituted Government and he was obliged to resign. He retained the presidency of the LDS, however, and led the party in its campaign for the legislative election, held on 15 October, in which his party obtained 36% of the votes cast and 34 seats in the National Assembly. Consequently, Drnovšek was re-elected to the premiership in early November. A coalition Government was formed, with the United List of Social Democrats, the SPP and the Democratic Party of Pensioners of Slovenia. In mid-2002 Drnovšek announced his intention to stand as a candidate in the presidential election scheduled for November. He won 44.4% of the votes cast in the first ballot, and was elected following the second round, in which he won 56.6% of the votes. He resigned as Prime Minister and as chairman of the LDS immediately thereafter, and was inaug-

urated as President in late December. He nominated the Minister of Finance, Anton Rop (q.v.) to succeed him as premier. He expressed satisfaction at the support for membership of the European Union and the North Atlantic Treaty Organization expressed by the Slovenian people at a referendum in March 2003. *Address:* Office of the President, 1000 Ljubljana, Erjavčeva 17, Slovenia; tel. (1) 4781205; fax (1) 4781357.

DZURINDA, Mikuláš: Prime Minister of Slovakia; b. 4 Feb. 1955, in Spiššky Štvrok; m., with two c. *Education:* University of Transport and Communications in Žilina. *Career:* a telecommunications expert, he became leader of the Slovak Democratic Coalition (SDC) upon its formation in July 1997. The SDC emerged from the general election of September 1998 as the second-largest party, behind the Movement for a Democratic Slovakia (MDS) of the incumbent Prime Minister, Vladimír Mečiar (q.v.). Mečiar could not muster the support needed to establish another governing coalition and Dzurinda was therefore given the task of forming a new government. The new Government was eventually appointed in October, with Dzurinda as Prime Minister. He immediately began to work to end the period of dogmatic, authoritarian government—and Slovakia's increasing isolation from Western military, political and economic institutions—that had prevailed under Mečiar. In January 2000 Dzurinda announced the formation of a new party, the Slovak Democratic Christian Union (SDCU), following the failure of negotiations aimed at concentrating the constituent parties of the governing coalition into a single party. Several ministers from across the coalition left their parties to join the SDCU. Dzurinda denied accusations that he was attempting to discredit his coalition partners in preparation for advanced legislative elections. He was elected Chairman of the SDCU at the party's opening congress in November, when the SDC ceased to exist. In July Dzurinda assumed some of the powers of the President, Rudolf Schuster (q.v.), while the latter was incapacitated through ill health. Relations between the coalition partners remained difficult, and in January 2002 Dzurinda was obliged to dismiss the Minister of Finance, Brigita Schmögnerová, following objections to her actions in the Government from her own party, the Party of the Democratic Left (PDL). With opinion polls showing him to be the least popular politician in Slovakia, the SDCU and its allied parties were not expected to be re-elected to Government in the September legislative election. However, the return to political prominence of Mečiar assisted Dzurinda, and he began to rebuild his popularity. Further assisted by the establishment of numerous new parties, most notably Direction, led by Robert Fico (q.v.), Dzurinda was able to guide the SDCU to secure 15.1% of the votes cast, and 28 seats, compared with the 19.5% of the ballot and 36 seats won by Mečiar's MDS. Dzurinda formed a coalition with four other parties, and he was confirmed as Prime Minister at the end of the month. His re-election was seen as a boost for Slovakian hopes of membership of the European Union and the North Atlantic Treaty Organization (a date for the latter being confirmed at a summit meeting of the Alliance in November), such was Dzurinda's popularity abroad. A keen runner, Dzurinda travelled to New York, the USA, in October 2001 to run the city marathon, as a sign of solidarity with the USA following the suicide attacks of the previous month. Such a gesture was expected to help his country's relations with the USA. *Address:* Office of the Government of the Slovak Republic, nám. Slobody 1, 813 70 Bratislava, Slovakia; tel. (2) 5729-5111; fax (2) 5249-7603; e-mail tio@government.gov.sk.

FICO, Robert: Slovakian politician; b. 1965. *Career:* Part of a new generation of younger politicians in Slovakia, he was formerly a member of the Party of the Democratic Left (PDL). He founded the Direction (Smêr) party in December 1999, as an alternative to the existing parties, and quickly became one of the most popular politicians in the country, in part owing to the unpopularity of the ruling coalition. Holding strong anti-minority views, he initially sought to distance his party from the Movement for a Democratic Slovakia (MDS) of former premier Vladimír Mečiar (q.v.), regarding it as a close rival, but later made a distinction between his party and Mečiar's, saying that he would not rule out co-operation under a new leader. By mid-2001 Direction had an estimated 4,000 members and was playing a part in local and regional government. Fico had a particularly strong support base among the young, with his success based largely on his personal charisma (he employed an image consultant), rather than clearly defined policies. At the legislative election held in September 2002 Direction won 13.5% of the votes cast, and won 25 seats in parliament. Fico entered opposition, stating that he intended to make life difficult for the governing coalition. Although Fico was popular and widely trusted, opinion polls revealed that voters did not consider him to be a serious candidate for the presidency (the election was scheduled to be held in May 2004). *Address:* Direction (Směr), Sumračna 27, 821 02 Bratislava, Slovakia; tel. and fax (2) 4342-6297; e-mail kancelaria@asistent.sk.

FUNAR, Gheorghe: Romanian politician; b. 29 Sept. 1949; m., with one s. *Education:* he studied at the Faculty of Economic Science, Cluj in 1969–73, and obtained a doctorate from that institution in 1999. *Career:* he was an agronomist, specializing in the collective arm system, which dominated agriculture in the communist era. In 1990 he joined the Party of Romanian National Unity (PRNU) founded by professional people who had benefited from the Ceauşescu dictatorship's bid to assimilate the large Hungarian minority located in the province of Transylvania, and who feared losing their privileges after the collapse of communism. Funar profited from the survival of ethnic tensions in Cluj, the capital of Transylvania, and was elected the city's Mayor in 1992. Twice re-elected, he soon acquired the reputation of being one of Romania's most controversial politicians. He praised Ceauşescu as a patriot and erected a statue in honour of the wartime dictator Ion Antonescu, despite his persecution of the Jews. He also tried to eradicate Hungarian influence in his city, the large historic centre of which was largely constructed by Hungarians before Romania acquired Transylvania in 1918. He was head of the PRNU in 1992–97 and in 1992 he received 10% of the votes cast when he stood for president on an ultra-nationalist platform. His party held the balance of power from 1992 until 1996, a period when Funar flouted conventions that required city mayors to co-operate with central government. In 1993–94 his city was at the centre of the Caritas scandal, when a 'pyramid' bank of that name acquired the savings of several million Romanians before defaulting. Despite identifying with Caritas, Funar survived by reaffirming the alleged Hungarian danger, and he ordered his ministers to leave the government when Romania and Hungary signed a treaty of friendship in 1996. Funar's unpredictable and autocratic style alienated many ultra-nationalists and the PRNU split in the late 1990s. He found a new home as deputy leader of the Greater Romania Party, which in 2000 became the country's largest opposition force. Under Funar, Cluj had become an isolated city, losing is potential to act as a 'bridge' with Western Europe. Major foreign investment had been discouraged, for fear that it would open up the city to new ideas and thus dispel the nationalist suspicions skillfully exploited by Funar. *Address:* 3400 Cluj-Napoca, Bd. 21 Decembrie 1989, Romania.

GAVRIYSKI, Svetoslav: Governor of the Bulgarian National Bank; b. 18 Dec. 1948, in Svishtov. *Education:* graduated in foreign trade relations from the Karl Marx Higher Institute of Economics, Sofia. *Career:* from 1972 he worked as an economic expert in, successively, the Foreign Trade Office, the Ministries of Economy and Finance and the Foreign Finances Office. He was prominent in negotiating an IMF loan in March 1996. Having served as deputy finance minister, without party affiliation, since 1992, he was appointed Minister of Finance in the interim, non-partisan Government of Stefan Sofianski in February 1997, formed to stabilize the political situation. On 11 June, as one of several efforts by the newly appointed Government of Ivan Kostov to impose fiscal discipline on the economic sector, he was appointed Governor of the central bank, in succession to Lyubomir Filipov. Placed in charge of an entirely new senior staff, he was responsible for the implementation of the currency-board monetary system, approved by the IMF, in July.

Under this, the central bank surrendered the function of monetary supervision. Despite widespread doubts about the system, it proved successful in restoring economic stability to the country. His mandate expired in June 2003 and, although he had announced his intention to seek a second six-year term of office, he was not believed to have the support of the governing parties. He remained as acting Governor while the country's principal political parties attempted to resolve differences preventing the organization of the required election. *Address:* Bulgarian National Bank (Bulgarska Narodna Banka), 1000 Sofia, Blvd Aleksandur Battenberg 1, Bulgaria; tel. (2) 914-51-203; fax (2) 980-24-25; e-mail press_office@bnbank.org.

GENTVILAS, Eugenijus: Lithuanian politician; b. 14 March 1960. *Education:* he obtained a doctorate in geography from the University of Vilnius. *Career:* from 1983 he worked at the Department of Ecological Problems and as a junior research fellow at the Academy of Sciences. He was active in the 'green' movement at the end of the 1980s. In 1990 Gentvilas was elected to the Supreme Council of Lithuania in Klaipėda, serving as speaker in 1991–92. Following an electoral defeat in 1992, he returned to academia, at the University of Klaipėda. He was elected to the Klaipėda City Council in 1995, where he enthusiastically promoted free trade in the region. In 1995–97 he was also director of a Lithuanian-US joint venture. He was elected Mayor of Klaipėda in 1997. Gentvilas had been appointed Chairman of the Lithuanian Liberal Union in early 1996, but handed over the position to Rolandas Paksas (q.v.) when the latter joined the party at the end of 1999, owing to Paksas' perceived greater popularity. Gentvilas became First Deputy Chairman of the party. After the legislative election of October 2000, the Liberal Union, with 34 seats in the Seimas (Parliament), formed a coalition Government with the New Union, with Paksas as Prime Minister. Gentvilas was appointed Minister of the Economy in March 2001, following the resignation of Eugenijus Maldeikis, resigning the mayorship in order to assume the portfolio; his stated priorities as minister were energy and business issues. However, the coalition Government collapsed in mid-June, with the resignation of six New Union cabinet members, followed by that of Paksas. Gentvilas was appointed interim Prime Minister, but was unable to resurrect the coalition, and Algirdas Brazauskas (q.v.) took over as premier in early July. Following demands from within the party, Paksas resigned from the Liberal Union in September; Gentvilas was appointed acting Chairman and was confirmed in the position the following month. He was a candidate in the presidential election held in December 2002, but received only 3.1% of the votes cast. Following the election, plans were announced for a merger between the Lithuanian Liberal Union, the Lithuanian Centre Union (the presidential candidate of which had also performed poorly) and the Christian-Democratic Union. The Liberal and Centre Union was formally constituted in late May 2003. Gentvilas did not seek election to the party chairmanship, and it remained to be seen what role he would take as the new movement developed. *Address:* Lithuanian Liberal and Centre Union, A. Jakšto 9, Vilnius 2001, Lithuania; tel. (523) 13264; fax (527) 91910; e-mail lls@lls.lt.

GEOANA, Mircea Dan: Minister of Foreign Affairs of Romania; b. 14 July 1958; m. Mihaela, with one s. and one d. *Education:* he studied at the Polytechnic Institute and the Law School at the University of Bucharest, and graduated from the École Nationale d'Administration in Paris (France) in 1992. He was studying for a doctorate in world economy at the Academy for Economic Sciences in Bucharest in 2000. He is fluent in English, French and Spanish. *Career:* he joined the Foreign Service in 1990, immediately after the Romanian revolution, and was quickly promoted to Director of the European Affairs Department. In February 1996 he was appointed ambassador to the USA, shortly after President Ion Iliescu had decided to align Romania firmly with the West. His diplomatic skills enabled him to be retained in the USA when a change of government took place at the end of 1996. In December 2000 he was appointed Minister of Foreign Affairs in the cabinet of Adrian Năstase after the Party of Social

Democracy of Romania, later the Social Democratic Party (SDP), was returned to office. In 2001 he served as Organization for Security and Co-operation in Europe Chairman-in-Office, and Romania won praise for showing that it could effectively co-ordinate a range of high-profile international initiatives in unstable parts of the Caucasus and the Balkans. His familiarity with US policy-making enabled him to seize the initiative and successfully promote Romania's claim for membership of the North Atlantic Treaty Organization (NATO) when US attention returned to the Balkans after the suicide attacks of 11 September 2001 on the USA. He is associated with the wing of the SDP that appeared to desire a final break with communist-era mentalities, and he is widely expected to progress to further political advancement. *Address:* Ministry of Foreign Affairs, 71274 Bucharest, Al. Alexandru 33, Romania; tel. (21) 2302071; fax (21) 2314090; e-mail maero@mae.kappa.ro.

GEORGIEVSKI, Ljubčo: former Prime Minister of the former Yugoslav republic of Macedonia (FYRM); b. 17 Jan. 1966, in Štip. *Education:* University of Skopje. *Career:* a published poet, he was elected leader of a new nationalist party, the International Macedonian Revolutionary Organization—Democratic Party for Macedonian National Unity (IMRO—DPMNU) in June 1990, one year after the republican Communist Party amended the Constitution to allow a multi-party system. At the parliamentary election of November–December 1990 Georgievski's party won the largest number of seats in the Sobranie (Assembly) and formed part of a coalition Government from January 1991. He was elected Vice-President of the republic, under Kiro Gligorov, later that month. In October, however, Georgievski resigned his position and the IMRO—DPMNU joined the opposition, claiming that it had not been sufficiently consulted with regard to policy-making. Although the IMRO—DPMNU was unrepresented in the Sobranie after the general election in October 1994, it continued to play a significant role in opposition. In the general election of October–November 1998 an electoral alliance of the IMRO—DPMNU and the Democratic Alternative won the largest number of seats (58) in the Sobranie, although it failed to secure an outright majority. Nevertheless, Georgievski was invited to form a coalition government. Hostilities between Macedonian government forces and ethnic Albanian rebels in the north of the country from late February 2001 prompted fears of large-scale civil conflict. Following inter-party discussions, ethnic Albanian opposition parties agreed to join a new Government of National Unity, again headed by Georgievski. During subsequent negotiations between the coalition Government and the ethnic Albanian rebels, mediated by Western envoys, Georgievski was reported to have angrily opposed ethnic Albanian demands. He also strongly criticized the Western mediators, whom he perceived as sympathetic towards the ethnic Albanian minority. Dissent between the governing parties increased, and the coalition splintered in November, with the Social Democratic Alliance and the Liberal Democrats leaving the Government, as hostilities waned. With the IMRO—DPMNU behind in the opinion polls, Georgievski postponed the legislative election expected in January 2002 until later in the year. It was eventually held in September, but the IMRO—DPMNU was unable to improve its fortunes, obtaining only 33 of the 120 seats in the Sobranie, compared with the 60 won by the Together for Macedonia alliance. Georgievski reacted angrily to the signature of a coalition agreement between Branko Crvenkovski (q.v.) of Together for Macedonia and Ali Ahmeti (q.v.), the former leader of the Albanian rebels, and leader of the Democratic Union for Integration, which held 16 parliamentary seats. Georgievski withdrew from the leadership of the IMRO—DPMNU in May 2003, becoming the party's Honorary Chairman. *Address:* International Macedonian Revolutionary Organization—Democratic Party for Macedonian National Unity, 1000 Skopje, Petar Drapshin br. 36, FYRM; tel. (2) 3111441.

GLEMP, Cardinal Archbishop Józef: Roman Catholic Primate of Poland; b. 18 Dec. 1929, in Inowrocław. *Education:* studied Polish literature at Warsaw and Toruńc and gained a double doctor's degree in canon law and civil law at the Lateran and Gregorianum Universities in Rome (Italy). *Career:* he was ordained in 1956 and studied in Rome in 1958–64. After joining the secretariat of the Polish Primate in 1967, he was appointed Archbishop-Metropolitan of Gniezno and Warsaw and Primate of Poland in 1981. He became a Cardinal in 1983. In the early 1980s he was prominent in the political changes in the country, working on various government committees. From March 1992 he was Archbishop of Warsaw (remaining Primate). The Church was widely perceived to have earned little credit during the period of non-communist Government, particularly over the issues of abortion and the restitution of ecclesiastical property. It also actively opposed the successful presidential candidate, Aleksander Kwaśniewski (q.v.), in 1995, although he sought an early meeting with Glemp in 1996. The Solidarity union and the Roman Catholic Church in Poland enjoyed a mutually supportive relationship during the 1980s, and the accession of a Solidarity-led coalition Government, following the general election of September 1997, made closer relations possible once again. The immediate result of this was the ratification of the Concordat, an agreement governing relations between the state and the Roman Catholic Church, approval of which had been repeatedly delayed by the previous coalition Government of former communists. Nevertheless, the influence of the Church was restrained by the presence of the secular Freedom Union (UW) within the governing coalition and of Kwaśniewski in the President's office. In May 2000 Glemp admitted the wrongs committed by many clergy in the period of communist rule, including manifestations of anti-Semitism. The Church attracted criticism, owing to its initial reluctance to assign the blame for the wartime massacre of the Jewish population in the village of Jedwabne to the Poles rather than the Nazis. This was compounded when the Primate stated that Jews had been known to betray Roman Catholic citizens under the Bolsheviks, during the Second World War. An unprecedented requiem service of penitence was conducted by the Primate and other bishops in May 2001, to express regret at the atrocities committed during the War, but this did not entirely defuse tensions. In late 2001 Glemp came out strongly in favour of Poland joining the European Union (EU) and in 2002 insisted that a religious reference be included in the EU Constitution; its exclusion when the draft document was published in mid-2003 was criticized. By this point, however, the church was facing a decline in both political and social influence, its image further tarnished by sexual allegations against the Archbishop of Poznań. *Address:* Konferencja Episkopatu Polski, 01-015 Warsaw, Skwer Kardynała Stefana Wyszyńskiego 6, Poland; tel. (22) 8389251; fax (22) 8380967.

GRANIĆ, Dr Mate: Croatian politician; b. 19 Sept. 1947, in Baska Voda; m. Jadranka Granić, with one s. and two d. *Education:* University of Zagreb. *Career:* a trained physician specializing in the treatment of diabetes, having initially pursued an academic career, he joined the ruling party, the Croatian Democratic Union (CDU), and was part of the coalition Government of Democratic Unity appointed by President Franjo Tudjman and confirmed by the Croatian Assembly in August 1991. He succeeded Zdenko Škrabako as foreign minister in 1993, serving in this position until late 1999, and became a key figure in the negotiations to end the civil conflict in Croatia and in neighbouring Bosnia and Herzegovina. He also figured in the subsequent implementation of the Bosnian peace settlement, particularly the reunification of Mostar in mid-1996. He negotiated Croatia's normalization of relations with the Federal Republic of Yugoslavia (FRY) in August 1996, but was opposed to Croatia joining any regional organizations, preferring a closer identification with Western Europe, rather than with the country's Balkan neighbours. By the late 1990s, however, this ambition was frustrated by the distaste of Western institutions for the authoritarian style of government in Croatia. Following the death of Tudjman, in December 1999, Granić participated unsuccessfully in the presidential election of January 2000, as a candidate of the CDU. Soon after this defeat, in March, he left the CDU and established a new, moderate party with Vesna Skare-Ozbolt, called Croatian Democratic Centre. By mid-2000 the new party, the stated aims of which were to build a wealthy, stable, just and European-orientated Croatia, commanded as much popular support as the CDU. However, as the 2000s progressed the new party's support declined steadily, as that of the CDU was rejuvenated. Granić himself retained substantial personal popularity, however, and was re-elected to the party's presidency in April 2003. *Address:* Croatian Democratic Centre (Demokratski Centar), Trg Bana Josipa Jelacica 1/11, 1000 Zagreb, Croatia.

GUSA, Cosmin: Romanian politician; b. 2 July 1970 , in Câmpia Turzii. *Education:* he obtained a doctorate in management from the University of Babeş-Bolyai in Cluj in 2000. *Career:* he worked as a marketing director and administrator in the Romanian media in 1994–2000, acquiring a senior position in the media empire headed by Dan Niculescu, controller of the country's most popular private television station, Antena 1. In 2001 Guza was appointed head of the ruling Social Democratic Party (SDP) by Prime Minster Adrian Năstase (q.v.). He was seeking a capable lieutenant, ready to enforce his will in a party that remained dominated by figures loyal to President Ion Iliescu (q.v.). The beneficiary of several periods of study in the fields of public relations and management in the USA, Gusa strengthened the efficiency of the SDP. He expelled from this nominally left-wing party a series of deputies who had expressed open concern about the SDP's close ties with large-scale business and its image problem regarding corruption. He was also a faithful ally of the Prime Minister, as he and Iliescu disputed the leadership of the SDP. However, when they settled their differences Gusa lost his position in June 2003, and left the party one month later. None the less, Gusa was the most visible representative of a new type of Romanian politician, with no background in communism, and able to interact effectively with Western officials, whose managerial language and mannerisms he effectively displayed. Without a firm ideological outlook, he appeared destined to enjoy an uninterrupted political rise regardless of future political shifts.

HAUSNER, Jerzy: Deputy Prime Minister and Minister of the Economy, Labour and Social Policy of Poland; b. 6 October 1949. *Education:* he studied at the Economic Academy of Kraków. *Career:* he pursued a career in academia, and taught at his alma mater from 1972 onwards, becoming one of the country's most respected economists. In 1994 he was appointed Director-General of the Prime Minister's office by Waldemar Pawłak. In this post he had responsibility for many aspects of the country's programme of economic reform, as an adviser to the Deputy Prime Minister and Minister of Finance, Grzegorz Kołodko (q.v.). Following the accession to the premiership of Włodzimierz Cimoszewicz he became the Government's commissioner for social-security reform. The reforms he proposed were widely seen as harsh, leading many critics to describe him as a remote academic, with little knowledge of the needs of ordinary Poles. This criticism intensified in some quarters when he was appointed Minister of Labour and Social Policy in the new Government led by Leszek Miller (q.v.) in October 2001. In early 2002 he proposed a series of measures aimed at the liberalization of the labour market, and was criticized by trade unions for making it easier for companies to dismiss staff. In January 2003 Miller dismissed the Minister of the Economy, following failings in the privatizations of the country's coal and steel industries. The economy portfolio was merged into that held by Hausner. His responsibilities were further expanded in June, when Miller transferred the overall responsibility for the country's economic policy from the Minister of Finance, Kołodko, to Hausner, and nominated him to be a Deputy Prime Minister. Kołodko resigned shortly afterwards. Although his remit made a lack of public popularity almost inevitable, Hausner's background as an economist rather than a politician helped as well as hindered him, and signs of growing public respect for him were beginning to emerge. *Address:* Ministry of the Economy, Labour and Social Policy, ul. Nowogrodzka 1/3/5, 00–513 Warsaw, Poland; tel. (22) 6610100; e-mail bpi@mpips .gov.pl; internet www.mpips.gov.pl.

HAVEL, Václav: former President of the Czech Republic; b. 5 Oct. 1936, in Prague; m. 1st Olga Šplíchalová in 1964; m.

2nd Dagmar Veškrnová in 1997. *Education:* studied drama at the Academy of Arts, Prague. He was excluded from further education in the 1950s because of his wealthy background, and instead attended evening classes. *Career:* a playwright by profession, he worked at the Theatre on the Balustrade from 1959, and published his first play, *The Garden Party*, to great critical acclaim, in 1963. His theatrical career was blocked after 1968, as he became increasingly active in dissident circles. He was a co-founder and leader of Charter 77, helped establish the Committee for the Defence of the Rights of the Unjustly Persecuted (VONS) in 1978 and was imprisoned three times between 1977 and 1989 for his political activities. During this period he developed the theories that would later guide his 'legitimate' political career, coming to believe that a confident, moral civil society was an essential foundation for success, that partisanship was antithetical to progress and that dissident groups could serve as a model for post-totalitarian society. In November 1989 Havel helped establish Civic Forum, an informal alliance of pro-democracy groups, and became the figurehead of the 'velvet revolution'. He was elected President of Czechoslovakia on 29 December 1989, and was re-elected on 5 July 1990. He was active in the constitutional negotiations between the federal and republican authorities but, when it became clear that the federation was to be dissolved, he resigned. He was elected President of the independent Czech Republic in January 1993. Subsequently, the rewritten Czech Constitution confined Havel's role within narrow parameters, giving him little or no influence over domestic policy-making. When the conservative Civic Democratic Party (CDP) of Václav Klaus (q.v.), which had emerged from Civic Forum as the strongest single party, began to exhibit precisely the brand of prescriptivist arrogance that Havel had feared, he set out to restore some balance, with weekly broadcasts to the nation, using his moral authority to inculcate a sense of responsibility and civic pride. Havel was permitted more freedom in foreign affairs and wielded all his influence to ensure that the Czech Republic made rapid progress towards integration into Western economic and military structures. In November 1997 Havel used the collapse, owing to financial irregularities, of Klaus' CDP Government as an opportunity to berate the country's politicians for neglecting the rule of law and reneging on their moral duties. In the late 1990s the respect and affection of the Czech people for Havel faltered somewhat, for reasons ranging from domestic political problems to public antipathy towards his second wife (whom he married shortly after the death of his first). Although he was re-elected for a second, and final, term as President in January 1998, he received only a narrow majority, in an election marred by infighting. His political influence waned during his second presidential term, as was evident from the decision of the CDP to agree to support a minority Czech Social Democratic Party (CSDP) Government, ignoring Havel's attempts to mediate the formation of a centre-right coalition. In 2000 Havel criticized the renewal of the two largest parties' co-operation agreement and the amendments to the country's electoral law that the two proposed—and was, in turn, criticized for politicizing the presidency. In June Havel underwent major surgery for the third time during his terms of office; a former heavy smoker, his health remained poor, and he was repeatedly hospitalized in 2001–02. Nevertheless, he continued to play an active role in the political life of the country, and in June 2002 he expressed frustration at the animosity and conspiratorial ethos that he felt had come to dominate Czech politics. His second term in the presidency expired in February 2003, amid much domestic and international media attention. In his final address, he thanked the Czech people, stating that, when he had first taken office, he had only expected to remain in the post for a matter of weeks. He declared himself to be 'not greatly perturbed' by the failure of parliament to elect a successor before his departure (Klaus was eventually elected nearly four weeks later), and announced his intentions to withdraw 'as far as possible, but perhaps not totally', from public view, to read as much as possible, and to resume writing.

ILIESCU, Ion: President of Romania; b. 3 March 1930, in Oltenița, Ilfov District; m. Elena Iliescu in 1951. *Education:* studied at the Bucharest Polytechnic Institute, before going to Moscow (Russia/USSR) to study water engineering at the Power Engineering Institute; he speaks French, English and Russian. *Career:* he was the son of a pre-war communist and was active in the party's youth movement after Soviet forces installed it in power in 1946. In 1968 he was elected to the central committee, but his communist party career stalled in 1971 when he disassociated himself from the desire of the country's ruler Nicolae Ceaușescu to model Romania's future on that of North Korea. Until 1989 he served as a party boss in the provinces, and then as head of the water company, before being relegated to the directorship of a technical publishing company. In 1989, however, he returned to prominence when the Ceaușescu dictatorship collapsed, following popular protests and a *putsch* mounted by second-ranking party and top military figures. On 26 December 1989, the day after Ceaușescu's execution, Iliescu was appointed head of the council of the National Salvation Front (NSF), the body that had taken charge of the country and became, in effect, interim President. Iliescu won the support of party and state officials who wished to maintain, or recover, their privileges and were content with pursuing a cautious realignment with the West while they retained their dominance. Initially, he was seen abroad as a reformer in the mould of the Soviet leader, Mikhail Gorbachev. However, his image suffered when the NSF used forcible methods to cement its hold on power. This initially broad front fell under the control of communist-era notables, and early elections were announced for 20 May 1990 before a non-leftist opposition could properly organize itself. Iliescu was elected President for two years while a new Constitution was drawn up. It took him years to recover from a decision, in June 1990, to mobilize coal-miners to break up an encampment of protesters in central Bucharest, opposed to the NSF's continuation in office. The miners attacked opposition party and civil society offices and, in September 1991, were used to drive Iliescu's rival, Petre Roman, from the premiership. Iliescu was widely viewed then as an old-style communist finding it difficult to abide by democratic rules and ready to exploit nationalism in order to retain an advantage over his opponents. On 11 October 1992 he won a second-round election for the presidency, but the ruling party lost its overall majority and had to rely on ultra-nationalist parties. Although personally austere, Iliescu presided over a 'get rich quick' strategy, which benefited several close associates and his party's economic allies. In the November 1996 presidential election, he lost in the second round to Emil Constantinescu (q.v.). He resumed the leadership of his party and opposed the poorly implemented reforms of the centre-right coalition. Its unpopularity enabled him to be re-elected in the second round of presidential voting in December 2000. In the last term the Constitution allows him to serve, he substantially transformed his image. He affected a reconciliation with leading opposition figures, who came to view him as a welcome check on the power of Prime Minister Adrian Năstase (q.v.). He welcomed former King Michael back to the country in 2001, and returned part of his estates to him after blocking his return to Romania in the early 1990s. He insisted that foreign-policy successes, such as Romania's admission to NATO (scheduled for 2004), belonged to all the mainstream political forces. Approaching the end of his presidency, he displayed no inclination to retire from politics. He sided with the opposition in ensuring that revisions to the Constitution did not concentrate undue power in the executive, and publicly insisted that the ruling Social Democratic Party (SDP) take energetic steps to bury its image as a corrupt party, asking its leading figures to avoid conflicts of interest by withdrawing from the boards of companies. His energetic approach to his presidential duties caused growing friction with premier Năstase, who preferred Iliescu to act as an elder statesman. Iliescu identified with the left-wing of the SDP and his interference was resented by the businessmen who had flourished under Năstase. A split in the party was predicted unless they could find a better way to work together. Iliescu had rebranded his image from that of a communist apparatchik to a multilingual reformer with broad appeal who was at ease in the company of Western leaders. *Address:* Office of the President, 76238 Bucharest, Cotroceni Palace, Bd. Geniuliu 1-3, Sector 5, Romania; tel. (21) 4100581.

ISĂRESCU, Mugur Constantin: Romanian banker and politician; b. 1 Aug. 1949, in Drăgășani. *Education:* in 1971 he graduated in international economic relations from the Academy of Economic Studies in Bucharest, and he obtained a doctorate from the same institution in 1989. *Career:* he lectured and researched in international economics and financial subjects until 1990, when he joined the foreign ministry, which needed competent experts in a bid to normalize economic relations with Western countries. In 1990 he was appointed head of the National Bank of Romania (central bank) by Prime Minister Petre Roman and, with a break of one year, has held that important state post ever since. He proved a shrewd guardian of the national finances at a time when chronic mismanagement was a feature of many other branches of economic decision-making. On 13 December 1999, in a surprise move, he was nominated as Prime Minister of the centrist coalition, which had one year of its mandate to run. He established good relations with the European Commission, the President of which, Romano Prodi, praised him for his serious approach to economic reform. He established his authority over the squabbling coalition parties, which needed to restore their credibility before the voters. In 2000 he was persuaded to stand for president by the incumbent, Emil Constantinescu (q.v.), when he conceded that his own chances of obtaining a renewed mandate on a centre-right platform were slim. Isărescu fought a understated campaign, emphasizing his ability to revive parts of the economy and his strong ties with the European Union (EU). He was harmed by allegations that he had failed to act decisively to halt the collapse of the National Investment Fund, as a result of which 300,000 savers lost money. He obtained only 9.5% of the votes cast in the presidential election, but the incoming Social Democratic Government reinstated him as central bank chief after strong representations were made on his behalf by the EU. In 2002 he was named the best central bank governor in the world by a British financial publication. *Address:* National Bank of Romania, 70421 Bucharest 3, Str. Lipscani 25, Romania; tel. (21) 3130410; fax (21) 3123831.

IZETBEGOVIĆ, Dr Alija: former President of the Presidency of Bosnia and Herzegovina; b. 8 Aug. 1925, in Bosanski Šamac; ethnic Bosnian Muslim (Bosniak); m., with one s. and two d. *Education:* he studied law at the University of Sarajevo. *Career:* a legal adviser, he was a prominent dissident and political prisoner under the communist regime. He was imprisoned for three years in 1946, for 'pan-Islamist activity', and again in 1983, for 14 years, although he was released in an amnesty of 1988. In 1970 he wrote the *Islamic Declaration*, on the all-inclusive nature of Islam. His book *Islam between East and West* (published in 1982), which attempts to define the unique position of Bosnian (Bosniak) Muslims, was the reason for his imprisonment in 1983. He was a strict Muslim, but claimed not to be a fundamentalist; the party he founded, in May 1990, the Party of Democratic Action (PDA), although the first Bosnian party founded on nationalist grounds, was centrist politically. On 20 December, as the leader of the largest party, he was elected President of the seven-member state Presidency of Bosnia and Herzegovina (*de facto* republican head of state). Izetbegović warned of the outbreak of civil conflict in Bosnia and Herzegovina after the recognition by the European Community of independent Croatia and Slovenia in January 1992. Throughout the Bosnian war (1992–95), he remained faithful to the idea of a 'Citizens' Bosnia', a unitary state controlled by a rotating Presidency based in Sarajevo. His endorsement, therefore, of the US-brokered General Framework Agreement for Peace in Bosnia and Herzegovina in November 1995, which allowed for the co-existence of two separate 'entities' within Bosnia and Herzegovina, came only after considerable prevarication and pressure from his US allies. Izetbegović was reported to have led an increasingly reclusive lifestyle during the war and was regarded, even by loyal associates, as more suited to a life of religious contemplation than a career in politics. Nevertheless, he maintained a high level of support within the Bosniak community, both with intellectuals and the military. He suffered heart problems in February 1996, but in September secured election as the Bosniak member of the new Presidency of Bosnia and Herzegovina. As the member who had gained the highest number of votes, he was the first President of that body. In 1996–98 he met with opposition from within the Presidency, in the form of the nationalist Croat member, Krešimir Zubak. In the election of September 1998 he was once again successful as the Bosniak member of the state Presidency (obtaining almost 87% of the valid votes cast) and took over the state Presidency in turn in February 2000. In October he retired from the Presidency, owing to ill health. However, he remained Chairman of the PDA until October 2001, and retained influence within the party thereafter. In early December 2001 he travelled to Dubai, the United Arab Emirates, to receive an 'Islamic Personality of the Year' award from that country's Government. Later that month he was flown to Saudi Arabia for treatment of a heart condition, remaining there until January 2002; he underwent heart surgery in Slovenia later in the year. The authorities of the Serb Republic (Republika Srpska) had submitted an indictment against Izetbegović to the International Criminal Tribunal for the former Yugoslavia (ICTY), in The Hague, the Netherlands, claiming him to be guilty of war crimes during the conflict of 1992–95. At mid-2003 the ICTY had yet to initiate any action against him, although it was expected that further pressure for such action would be made during a visit of the ICTY's chief prosecutor to the Serb Republic, scheduled for mid-July.

JÁRAI, Zsigmond: Governor of the National Bank of Hungary; b. 1951, in Biharkeresztes; m., with two c. *Education:* studied at the Karl Marx University of Economics, Budapest. *Career:* he was employed by the State Development Bank in the 1970s and 1980s, where he dealt with the introduction of capital movement to Hungary. He was subsequently appointed head of the securities division at Budapest Bank. As President of the Stock Exchange Council in 1988-89, he co-founded the Budapest exchange, before leaving Hungary to pursue a career in the United Kingdom. He returned to Hungary in 1993 as head of the Budapest branch of a British merchant bank. In 1995 Járai was appointed head of Magyar Hitel Bank, and oversaw its privatization in 1996. The new owners, ABN Amro (of the Netherlands), appointed him President and Chief Executive Officer. In the same year he became Chairman of the Budapest Stock Exchange. In June 1996 he became an adviser to the National Bank of Hungary, and soon afterwards was appointed Minister of Finance in the Government of Viktor Orbán (q.v.), following the general election in May 1998. The Government embarked on an economic programme that aimed to stimulate economic growth, reduce inflation and lower tax rates, with the goal of attaining the necessary economic conditions for accession to the European Union (EU). Járai became Governor of the central bank in March 2001, and retained a central involvement in the EU accession process. He aimed to keep strict controls on the forint and the Hungarian economy, in order to facilitate EU accession. In 2003 he stated that economic conditions dictated that Hungary would not be ready to adopt the euro until at least 2008. *Address:* National Bank of Hungary (Magyar Nemzeti Bank), 1850 Budapest, Szabadság tér 8–9, Hungary; tel. (1) 269-4760; fax (1) 332-3913.

JARUZELSKI, Gen. Wojciech: former President of Poland; b. 6 July 1923, in Kurów; m. Barbara, with one d. *Education:* Infantry Officers' School, Karol Swierczewski General Staff Academy, Warsaw. *Career:* he served with the Polish Armed Forces and was promoted to various senior posts, before becoming Minister of National Defence in 1968–83, in which position he was responsible for the invasion of Czechoslovakia. He was appointed Chairman of the Council of Ministers (Prime Minister) and First Secretary of the Central Committee (PZPR) in 1981. In December of that year, heading a Military Council of National Salvation, Jaruzelski declared martial law, in a move he later claimed was intended to prevent a Soviet invasion. The Solidarity movement was proscribed and its leaders, including Lech Wałęsa (q.v.), were imprisoned, as Jaruzelski attempted to restore the hegemony

of the PZPR. Wałęsa was released the following year and martial law formally ended in June 1983, when the Military Council was dissolved. In November 1985 Jaruzelski resigned as Chairman of the Council of Ministers, in order to become President of the Council of State (Head of State). In December 1986, in an effort to boost support for the regime, he established a 56-member Consultative Council, attached to the Council of State, which included former members of the Solidarity movement. However, public discontent intensified. The new Solidarity-led legislature narrowly elected Jaruzelski—the sole candidate—to the post of executive President (with a six-year mandate) in 1989, mainly in the hope of ensuring a peaceful transition of power. Jaruzelski agreed to resign in September of the following year, to permit a direct presidential election to take place. The vote was won by Wałęsa. In 1998 a trial opened against Jaruzelski, relating to an incident that occurred in 1970, when 44 shipyard workers were shot and killed during a protest in Gdańsk, allegedly on his orders as Minister of National Defence. The trial was later abandoned owing to his ill health, but resumed, after numerous delays, in late 2001, with Jaruzelski pleading not guilty to murder. However, the trial was abandoned until February 2002 after the judge became ill. Further procedural delays meant that the trial was still in its early stages at mid-2003. In July, to widespread bemusement, a presidential dinner was held in honour of Jaruzelski's 80th birthday, focusing on his role in the end of communist rule in 1989.

KALLAS, Siim: former Prime Minister of Estonia; b. 2 Oct. 1948, in Tallinn; m. to Kristi Kallas, with one s. and one d. *Education:* graduate of Tartu University. *Career:* a banker by profession, he was Chief Specialist at the Estonian SSR Ministry of Finance in 1975–79, before becoming General Manager of the Estonian Savings Bank until 1986. In 1991 he was appointed President of the Bank of Estonia (Eesti Pank), a post he held until 1995. As central bank governor, he was credited with much of the success of the policies of economic transformation of the early 1990s, and earned national and international popularity. In 1994 he founded, and subsequently led, the pro-business Estonian Reform Party (ERP), which obtained 19 seats in the Riigikogu in the 1995 legislative election. In October 1995 his party was invited to form a coalition Government with Tiit Vähi's Estonian Coalition Party (ECP) and the Rural Union. Kallas was appointed Minister of Foreign Affairs, a post he held until 1996, when he and five other ERP ministers resigned in protest at the signing of a coalition agreement between the ECP and the Estonian Centre Party. In early March 1999 he was cleared by the Tallinn municipal court of charges in connection with the disappearance of US $10m. from the North Estonia Bank. His acquittal opened the way for his re-entry into government in the same month, this time as Minister of Finance, following the formation of a centre-right coalition Government by the ERP, the Pro Patria (Fatherland) Union and the People's Party Moderates. In December 2001, in an apparent attempt to distance itself from the increasingly unpopular national Government in which it continued to participate, the ERP left the governing coalition of Tallinn City Council, protesting at financial mismanagement. Developments following the withdrawal prompted the resignation of the national Government led by Mart Laar (q.v.) in early January 2002. The ERP and Estonian Centre Party signed an agreement on the formation of an interim, coalition Government, to include ministers from both parties (despite their ideological differences), with the support of the Estonian People's Union. On 22 January Kallas was approved as Prime Minister in the Riigikogu, by 62 votes to 31. He took office on 28 January, pledging to work to combat social injustice and to move towards membership of the European Union (EU) and the North Atlantic Treaty Organization (NATO). Despite a strong performance from the ERP in the legislative election held in March 2003, the new Res Publica movement, led by Juhan Parts (q.v.) obtained more seats, and was in the strongest position in the coalition negotiations. Kallas and Parts eventually agreed on the composition of a coalition Government (again with the support of the Estonian People's Union), under the latter's premiership (Kallas declined a cabinet post). He was re-elected to the leadership of the ERP in May, and remained one of the country's most prominent political figures, despite his absence from the Government. *Address:* Estonian Reform Party (ERP), Tõnismagi 3A–15, Tallinn 0001, Estonia; tel. 611-2909; fax 611-2908; e-mail erl@erl.ee.

KARADŽIĆ, Dr Radovan: Bosnian politician and former President of the Serb Republic of Bosnia and Herzegovina; b. 19 June 1945, in Montenegro, Yugoslavia; ethnic Serb; m. Ljiljana Zelen-Karadzić, with one s. and one d. *Career:* as a trained psychiatrist, specializing in neuroses and depression, he worked with the Sarajevo football team before entering politics. He was imprisoned in Yugoslavia during the period of communist rule, allegedly on charges of fraud. As the leader of the nationalist Serbian Democratic Party of Bosnia and Herzegovina (SDP), which he co-founded in 1990, he did not accept any government posts, but did agree to a coalition with the main Bosniak and Croat parties after the 1990 election. However, as the Yugoslav crisis of 1991 escalated, he became less able to accept consensus decisions. He articulated the Serb desire to remain in the Yugoslav federation, although he was accused of threatening the other ethnic groups of the heterogeneous republic. Following the onset of civil war in Bosnia and Herzegovina, he pursued a policy of 'cantonization', envisaging the division of the republic on ethnic grounds, and the eventual union of Serb-controlled territory with Serbia. He was regarded by many as the architect of the practice of 'ethnic cleansing' (the expulsion by one ethnic group of others in an attempt to create a homogenous population), adopted by Bosnian Serbs in their efforts to implement this policy. Karadžić was named President of the 'Serb Republic of Bosnia and Herzegovina' at its proclamation on 27 March 1992. A champion of the interests of extreme nationalists, he became increasingly isolated during the civil war, owing to his failure to compromise on the terms of a peace settlement, which also, ultimately, ended his alliance with the Serbian President, Slobodan Milošević (q.v.). He also lost some of his support among extremist Serbs following a public rift with the Bosnian Serb commander, Ratko Mladić (q.v.), in 1995. In the same year he was indicted as a war crimes suspect by the International Criminal Tribunal for the former Yugoslavia (ICTY—based in The Hague, the Netherlands). He was later formally charged with genocide and crimes against humanity. As a suspected war criminal, the implementation of the Bosnian peace settlement, the General Framework Agreement for Peace in Bosnia and Herzegovina, was conditional on his removal from power. The international community became increasingly impatient at the failure of the North Atlantic Treaty Organization (NATO)-led Implementation Force and the Yugoslav authorities to apprehend him. In July 1996, after an international warrant was issued for his arrest, he eventually resigned as Bosnian Serb President, in favour of his deputy, Biljana Plavšić (q.v.), against whom he engaged in a bitterly fought power struggle in 1997. Her defeat in the 1998 presidential election by his close ally, Nikola Poplasen, was indicative of the immense power he continued to wield in the Serb Republic. As an international fugitive, he assumed the role of the *éminence grise* of a Serb leadership still, it seemed, implacably opposed to the idea of reintegration. In July 2001 the Bosnian Serb Republic Government drafted legislation pledging closer co-operation with the ICTY, thereby providing for the extradition of Karadžić, once apprehended, to the Tribunal. In December the SDP voted to expel all war crimes suspects, including Karadžić, from the party, following considerable international pressure; Karadžić was duly replaced by Dragan Kalinić in March 2002. Karadžić, who was apparently writing his autobiography (he also wrote poetry, and was reported to have published a satirical play and a children's book in 2002), was widely believed to be moving between locations in the Bosnian Serb Republic and the republic of Montenegro, the Federal Republic of Yugoslavia, in early 2002, and the USA increased the reward offered for information leading to his arrest to US $5m. However, raids near the southern Bosnian Serb town of Foca in February–March, in the largest such operation mounted by NATO forces, failed to locate him, and Karadžić continued to command widespread popular support in the

Serb Republic. In April Karadžić wrote a letter expressing his 'regret' at being unable to appear before the ICTY, which he declared had been established illegally. In July, following a search of Karadžić's former home in Pale, NATO forces claimed to have seized evidence of his involvement in organized criminal activities. NATO forces made another high-profile attempt to locate Karadžić in the Foca area in mid-August, but this was also unsuccessful. The UN High Representative, Paddy Ashdown (q.v.), announced a change of strategy in March 2003, stating that efforts to apprehend Karadžić would henceforth concentrate on attacking the networks supporting his clandestine existence. However, despite claims of numerous successes in this regard, Karadžić remained at large in mid-2003.

KAVAN, Jan: Czech politician; Chairman of the UN General Assembly; b. 17 Oct. 1946, in London, the United Kingdom; m., with four c. *Education:* he was expelled from university in Czechoslovakia and emigrated to the United Kingdom, where he studied international relations at the London School of Economics and history and politics at the Universities of Oxford and Reading. *Career:* he worked as a journalist in the United Kingdom, establishing the Palach Press Agency and two foundations, with the aim of gaining publicity and support in the Western media for Czech opposition parties and political prisoners. He also founded and edited the *East European Reporter*. In 1979 he was stripped of his Czechoslovakian citizenship. He remained in the United Kingdom until the collapse of communist rule, whereupon he returned to Czechoslovakia and was elected to the Federal Assembly, representing the Civic Forum, in 1990. Following the dissolution of Czechoslovakia he lectured in the USA, before returning and joining the Czech Social Democratic Party (CSDP). He was elected to the Senate in 1996 and became Minister of Foreign Affairs in 1998. Following resignations from the Government in December 1999, he was elevated to the position of Deputy Prime Minister. Kavan became involved in controversy in April 2000 following the publication of a book—shortly after he had been appointed Minister in charge of the Czech Security Services—alleging that he had maintained contacts with the Czechoslovak security forces while in the United Kingdom. Following the legislative elections of June 2002, and the subsequent appointment of a new coalition Government, Kavan was elected President of the 57th Session of the UN General Assembly in July.

KLAUS, Dr Václav: President of the Czech Republic; b. 19 June 1941, in Prague; m. Livia Klausová in 1968, with two s. *Education:* attended Prague School of Economics and Cornell University (New York, USA). *Career:* an economist, banker and academic, Klaus was a leading member of Civic Forum and became Minister of Finance in the federal Government in December 1989. He was reappointed in June 1990, after the election. He became Chairman of the conservative Civic Democratic Party (CDP) when Civic Forum split in 1991 and quickly remodelled the party in his own image—disciplined, resourceful and pragmatic—turning it into the most powerful political force to emerge from Civic Forum's tangle of opposition groups. Having been a Deputy Prime Minister in the federal Government, following the dissolution of Czechoslovakia he accepted the position of Prime Minister of the Czech Republic, leading a new coalition Government. He remained Prime Minister when the Czech Republic gained independence on 1 January 1993. His Government's combination of pragmatism and reformist zeal led initially to the most successful economic reform programme of all the former Soviet satellites. Much of its achievement, however, was perceived, rather than real. Moreover, the administration's *laissez-faire* approach to the activities of lending banks and of the stock exchange provoked widespread criticism when it was discovered that many of the Czech Republic's new entrepreneurs were enriching themselves at the expense of the country at large. When evidence emerged, in November 1997, that the CDP had received a substantial donation from a businessman who had later bid successfully in the privatization of a steelworks, the coalition Government collapsed, and the CDP's reputation for careless accounting was apparently confirmed. However, Klaus remained a popular figure and the CDP performed reasonably well in the general election of June 1998, winning only five seats fewer than in 1996, despite having split following the scandal of 1997. Nevertheless, the Czech Social Democratic Party (CSDP) of Miloš Zeman (q.v.) had become the strongest party in parliament, owing to a consolidation of support on the left. Although Zeman and Klaus were personal rivals, the latter agreed to pledge the CDP's support for a minority CSDP Government, in exchange for the influential position of parliamentary speaker. This so-called 'opposition' agreement was renewed in January 2000, but relations between Klaus and Zeman remained difficult; moreover, the CSDP leader, Vladimír Špidla (q.v.), made it clear that he did not intend to co-operate with Klaus following the legislative election of June 2002. In the election, the CDP registered its worst performance since the party's establishment (although it obtained 24.5% of the votes cast), and Klaus announced that he would not seek election to the presidency while the incumbent Government remained in office. By October, however, he had changed his mind, and announced both that he would accept candidacy if proposed and that he would not seek re-election as chairman of the CDP at the party's congress in December. Shortly afterwards he was nominated as his party's official presidential candidate. His campaign centred on the differences between him and Havel, of whom he had been a fierce critic. Following several inconclusive rounds of voting, Klaus was eventually elected to the presidency on 28 February 2003, by a margin of one vote, defeating the new candidate of the governing coalition, Jan Sokol (q.v.). He was inaugurated on 7 March, amid lingering public discontent at the failure of the country's politicians to elect a President at an earlier stage. Despite his previous lack of enthusiasm for the European Union, he publicly stated his commitment to the process leading to Czech accession, although his silence in the prelude to the referendum held in June was taken by many as a signal of his continued opposition to Czech membership. He was criticized early in his presidency by Špidla, who claimed that Klaus was interfering with the Government's programme after the President vetoed amendments to tax legislation. *Address:* Office of the President of the Republic, 119 08 Prague-Hradčany, Czech Republic.

KOŁODKO, Grzegorz Witold: former Deputy Prime Minister and Minister of Finance of Poland; b. 28 Jan. 1949, in Tczew; m. with two d. *Education:* attended Warsaw School of Economics. *Career:* A Professor of Economics from 1972, and a member of the Polish United Workers' Party (PZPR) from 1968, he was Director of the Institute of Finance in 1989–94, and published extensively on economic theory and policy. He was Deputy Prime Minister and Minister of Finance in 1994–97, under Prime Minster Waldemar Pawlak, but resigned following a reprimand from President Włodzimierz Cimoszewicz over an unsanctioned foreign trip. He achieved a significant reduction in the rates of inflation and unemployment, as well as increased production, but was criticized for over-spending, over-stimulating the economy and failing to restructure industry. His tenure was also marked by conflict with the central bank. From 2000 he was Director of Transformation, Integration and Globalization Economic Research (TIGER), but in July 2002 he was again appointed Deputy Prime Minister and Minister of Finance by Prime Minister Leszek Miller (q.v.), amid widespread public approval; however, his appointment was regarded with caution by the international financial community. A keen advocate of European Union membership, he promised a continuity of policy, and the reduction of unemployment as a principal objective, as well as conciliation with the central bank, with which the Government was again in conflict. It was hoped that his popularity might help to restore the Government's image in the face of economic stagnation. Far from providing conciliation, his relationship with the head of the central bank, Leszek Balcerowicz (q.v.) was often fractious, as the two men's views on many issues of economic policy contrasted as starkly as their popularity levels. It was a disagreement with Balcerowicz that led to Kołodko's resignation in June 2003, as the head of the central bank refused to assent to Kołodko's plan to use the proceeds of a surplus in the country's foreign-

exchange reserves to be transferred to the budget. *Address:* ul. Malcuzynskiego 7 m. 12, 02-973 Warsaw, Poland; tel. (22) 5192108; fax (22) 8140870; e-mail kolodko@tiger.edu.pl; internet www.tiger.edu.pl.

KOŠTUNICA, Dr Vojislav: former President of the Federal Republic of Yugoslavia (FRY—now Serbia and Montenegro); b. 24 April 1944, in Belgrade; m. Radmila Arandjelović. *Education:* studied law at Belgrade University. *Career:* a former constitutional lawyer, he came to prominence just prior to the presidential and legislative elections of September 2000. An alliance of 18 parties, the Democratic Opposition of Serbia (DOS), nominated him, as the leader of one of the alliance's two principal parties, the Democratic Party of Serbia (DPS), as a compromise candidate to contest the presidential election. His campaign was understated and mild-mannered, and championed the democratic rights of the Serbian people. He demanded political reform and the removal from office of President Slobodan Milošević (q.v.), but was cautious not to undermine the broad nationalist sentiment still popular in Serbia, which had previously been a highly effective instrument in Milošević's hold on power. International, and especially Western, support for Koštunica was also a vital ingredient in his rise to power. He was inaugurated on 7 October 2000, after domestic and international pressure forced Milošević to relinquish the presidency. Koštunica subsequently opposed Milošević's extradition to the International Criminal Tribunal for the former Yugoslavia (ICTY, in The Hague, Netherlands), saying that this contravened the state's constitutional order, and favoured his trial in the FRY on charges of corruption. In early 2002 he strongly criticized the conduct of the trial at the ICTY, describing it as legally inconsistent and claiming that the Court had an anti-Serb bias. Some observers felt that these comments were designed to prevent him from losing credibility domestically, given the defiant stance adopted by Milošević. There were increasing divisions between Koštunica and the Prime Minister of Serbia, Zoran Djindjić, after the latter facilitated the extradition of Milošević to The Hague; Koštunica withdrew the DPS from the DOS coalition in August 2001, and subsequently demanded both early elections and the resignations of various officials, including Djindjić. Having overseen the process of creating the new constitutional charter that transformed Yugolslavia into 'Serbia and Montenegro', Koštunica decided to stand in the election to the Serbian presidency held in October 2002. He obtained the most votes in the election, but the poll was invalidated, owing to the fact that less than 50% of the electorate took part (Koštunica unsuccessfully challenged the decision). A second atempt to elect a President in early December was also unsuccessful. Frustrated at the electoral process, Koštunica withdrew from the contest, and he subsequently resigned the federal presidency, as part of the process of transformation of the country into Serbia and Montenegro in February 2003. *Address:* Democratic Party of Serbia (DPS), Belgrade, Braće Jugovića 2A, Serbia and Montenegro.

KOVÁCS, László: Hungarian Minister of Foreign Affairs. *Career:* a member of the Hungarian Socialist Party (HSP), he was appointed foreign minister in a coalition Government led by Gyula Horn in June 1994, following the HSP's victory in the legislative election of the previous month. One of the priorities of his foreign policy was support for ethnic Hungarians abroad, notably in Romania. Such a policy initially led to a deterioration in relations between the two countries, particularly after Kovács referred to the possibility of 'peaceful border changes'. He was, however, keen to placate foreign opinion and agreed treaties with both Romania and Slovakia in 1995 and 1996, earning the criticism of nationalists. Kovács was also active in beginning the process of Hungary's accession to the European Union (EU) and the North Atlantic Treaty Organization (NATO). Following the HSP's defeat in the general election of May 1998, Horn resigned as party leader and, in September, Kovács was elected to the post. Considered by many to be lacking in leadership skills, he failed to unite the party. After a particularly divisive power struggle in 2001, he stated that he would not stand as the party's candidate for the post of Prime Minister in the 2002 election; a compromise candidate, Péter Medgyessy (q.v.), was agreed upon instead. The HSP secured a small advantage in the first round of the election in early April. After a second round of voting, the party had obtained 46.1% of the votes cast and, forming an alliance with the Alliance of Free Democrats, entered power. Medgyessy, who became Prime Minister, appointed Kovács as Foreign Minister. He resumed his previous policies of improving relations with Hungary's neighbours and preparing for EU membership. In January 2003 Kovács publicly accused the previous Prime Minister, Viktor Orbán (q.v.), of providing unofficial support to groups campaigning against Hungarian EU accession, while publicly stating it to be the country's goal. *Address:* Ministry of Foreign Affairs, 1027 Budapest, Bem rkp. 47; tel. (1) 458-1000; fax (1) 212-5981.

KRAFT, Vahur: President of the Bank of Estonia; b. 11 March 1961, in Tartu; m. with one c. *Education:* a 1984 graduate of the Department of Finance and Credit at Tartu University, he speaks English and Russian. *Career:* Kraft worked in a series of banks, including Eesti Hoiupank and Eesti Sotsiaalpank, from 1984. In 1992 he was appointed Vice-Governor in Estonia of the IMF, before being elevated, three years later, to Governor. In the same year he was appointed President of Eesti Pank (the Bank of Estonia). As central bank governor, he played a major role in the country's economic reform programme in the 1990s. Kraft was briefly succeeded, when his term came to an end in April 2000, by Vello Vensel, who resigned shortly after his appointment on the grounds of ill-health; Kraft was re-elected as President of the Bank in June. The development of economic stability and of a financial 'safety net' were among his stated priorities, and his period of office coincided with strong economic growth in the country. *Address:* Bank of Estonia (Eesti Pank), Estonia pst. 13, Tallinn 15095, Estonia; tel. 668-0719; fax 668-0836; e-mail info@epbe.ee.

KRAJIŠNIK, Momčilo: former Bosnian politician and former Co-President of Bosnia and Herzegovina; b. 20 Jan. 1945, in Zabrjle, Bosnia and Herzegovina; ethnic Serb. *Career:* a member of the nationalist Serbian Democratic Party of Bosnia and Herzegovina (SDP), he was elected as a deputy to the Republican Assembly in December 1990. Following the coalition agreement between the three main parties, the SDP was allowed to nominate the candidate for parliamentary speaker, and Krajišnik was duly elected. On 14 October 1991 he attempted to prevent the Bosniak (Bosnian Muslim) and Croat deputies from declaring the Republic's sovereignty, by ending the parliamentary session. He was subsequently elected speaker of the unilaterally proclaimed 'Assembly of the Serb Nation' (comprising Serb deputies of the Bosnian Assembly and constituted on 24 October), which declared its adherence to the Yugoslav federation. This parliament established a 'Serb Republic' and became known as the People's Assembly. Despite being a fervent nationalist, Krajišnik maintained cordial relations with representatives of the international community, and played a particularly significant role as mediator and spokesman in mid-1996, during the time of the dismissal of the moderate Bosnian Serb premier, Rajko Kasagić, and the long-awaited resignation of the Serb Republic's President, Radovan Karadžić (q.v.), a close ally of Krajišnik. Although under international investigation for war crimes, Krajišnik was not charged, and in September 1996 was elected to the three-member state Presidency of Bosnia and Herzegovina, with the second largest number of votes. His term as Co-President was characterized by infighting; he refused to attend the constituent assembly of the new Bosnian parliament, claiming his life would be put at risk, although many suspected that to be a pretext for refusing to swear loyalty to a unified Bosnian state, to which he was opposed. Indeed, he frequently refused to attend meetings of the Presidency and attempted to prevent the implementation of the Dayton accords. During 1997 he became increasingly opposed to the policies of the new Bosnian Serb President, Biljana Plavšić (q.v.), particularly following her supporters' seizure of transmitters of the national television station, of which he was a board member. In September 1998 his failure to win re-election to the state Presidency was one of the few results in

the various elections to be greeted with satisfaction by the international community. Nevertheless, for a short while he remained a powerful force in Bosnian Serb politics, particularly while his ally, Nikola Poplasen, was Bosnian Serb President. In April 2000 he was arrested by the Stabilization Force (SFOR) on charges of war crimes. He was extradited to the International Criminal Tribunal for the former Yugoslavia (ICTY—based in The Hague, Netherlands), to await trial, having pleaded not guilty to all charges. In October 2001 the ICTY refused to release him on bail, a freedom it had granted Plavšić, on the grounds that he could not be trusted to return. Krajišnik began a legal challenge to his continued detention, causing his trial, initially scheduled to commence in 2002, to be delayed. Following the unsuccessful conclusion of this challenge, the trial was assigned to begin in May 2003 (by which time Plavšić had been convicted and sentenced to 11 years' imprisonment), but was subsequently subject to further postponement.

KUČAN, Milan: former President of Slovenia; b. 14 Jan. 1941, in Križevci; m. Stefka Kučan, with two d. *Education:* he graduated in law from Ljubljana University in 1963. *Career:* he was president of the official communist youth organization, the Slovenian Socialist Youth League, in 1968–69 and a member of its secretariat from 1969–73. He worked as secretary of the Socialist Alliance for Slovenia between 1973 and 1978 and was President of the Slovenian National Assembly in 1978–82. In 1986 he was appointed leader of the League of Communists of Slovenia. As with other communists who espoused nationalist causes, he retained some popularity and, in the republican presidential election of April 1990, he was elected President of the five-member State Presidency in a direct, popular ballot, despite the opposition parties winning the parliamentary contest. With the failure of attempts to reform the Yugoslav federation, he became head of state of an independent Slovenia in 1991. On 6 December 1992 he was directly elected as President of the Republic. Under the terms of the 1991 Constitution this had become a largely ceremonial post, but he was considered to be an influential and stabilizing force in the fractious political scene. During 1993 he was accused by several leading politicians of protecting corrupt officials of the former communist regime. Apart from this incident, however, he remained widely respected for his role in the careful handling of Slovenia's transition to independence and to a market economy. In November 1997 he was re-elected for a second (and final) term as President. In May 2000 Kučan advocated early legislative elections, following the collapse of the Government led by Janez Drnovšek (q.v.). Relations with Drnovšek's successor, Andrej Bajuk, were strained, but the situation improved when Drnovšek was re-elected in October 2000. Kučan's main objective, prior to the end of his term in December 2002, was to enable the accession of Slovenia to both the North Atlantic Treaty Organization (NATO) and the European Union (EU), and by the end of 2002 Slovenia had received formal invitations to accede to both organizations in 2004. In May 2003 Kučan testified against the former Yugoslav leader, Slobodan Milošević (q.v.), in the proceedings against him at the International Criminal Tribunal for the former Yugoslavia (ICTY) in The Hague, the Netherlands; Milošević conducted an aggressive cross-examination of Kučan, and the two former Presidents accused each other of fomenting the dissolution of Yugoslavia.

KUKAN, Eduard: Minister of Foreign Affairs of Slovakia; b. 26 Dec. 1939, in Trnovec nad Váhom; m., with one s. and one d. *Education:* he studied at the Moscow Institute of International Relations, Russia, and Charles University, in Prague, the Czech Republic. *Career:* he joined the Czechoslovak Foreign Service in 1964 and served in a number of diplomatic posts, including the Czechoslovak embassy in the USA (1977–81). He was appointed Permanent Representative of Czechoslovakia to the UN in New York, the USA, in 1990–93, and of Slovakia until 1994. In that year he was elected to the Slovak parliament, and served as Minister of Foreign Affairs from March until December. He was a member of the Executive Committee of the Democratic Union of Slovakia (DUS), and subsequently Chairman (1997–98) and then Vice-Chairman of the Slovak Democratic Coalition (SDC). In 1998 he was re-appointed Minister of Foreign Affairs and, in 1999, during the crisis in the Serbian province of Kosovo, in the Federal Republic of Yugoslavia, acted as the UN's Special Envoy to the Balkans. In 2000 he became Vice-Chairman of the Slovak Democratic and Christian Union (SDCU), formed by Mikuláš Dzurinda (q.v.) in that year, in an attempt to unite the parties of the governing coalition. As Minister of Foreign Affairs, Kukan supported his country's efforts to join the North Atlantic Treaty Organization (NATO) and the European Union (EU), and in late 2002 Slovakia received invitations to accede to both organizations in 2004. Kukan was a highly popular figure among the electorate, and opinion polls in 2003 revealed him to be the most popular choice for the country's next President (a presidential election was scheduled to take place in May 2004). *Address:* Ministry of Foreign Affairs, Hlboká cesta 2, 833 36 Bratislava, Slovakia; tel. (2) 5978-1111; fax (2) 5978-2213.

KUNCZE, Gábor: Hungarian politician; b. 1950. *Career:* a former economist and engineer, Kuncze became Minister of the Interior in 1994, after his party, the Alliance of Free Democrats (AFD), signed a coalition agreement with the Hungarian Socialist Party (HSP). Kuncze was elected leader of the AFD in 1997. After the disastrous performance by the party in the 1998 general election (when it attained just 7% of the votes, slightly above the threshold of 5% required for parliamentary representation), he resigned the leadership, which was assumed by Gabor Demszky. Kuncze resumed the role in 2001 in preparation for the 2002 general election. In the poll, the AFD obtained 5.2% of the votes—widely considered to be an unexpectedly strong performance—and agreed to co-operate with the HSP once again, thereby enabling a Socialist-led Government to take power in May. Kuncze portrayed the party as a political bridge between the left and right of the country. He promised his supporters that he would oblige the Government, led by Péter Medgyessy (q.v.), to implement key AFD policies, including tax reductions, reforms to health care and a reduction in corruption. He was true to his word during the Government's first year, as he regularly made critical public pronouncements, particularly on the issue of taxation—in July 2003 he intimated that the coalition might be in peril if tax rates were not reduced within one year. *Address:* Alliance of Free Democrats (AFD) (Szabad Demokraták Szövetsége—SzDSz), 1143 Budapest, Gizella u. 36, Hungary; tel. (1) 223-2050; fax (1) 221-0579; e-mail zsolt .udvarvolgyi@szdsz.hu.

KWAŚNIEWSKI, Aleksander: President of Poland; b. 15 Nov. 1954, in Białogard, Koszalin; m. Jolanta Konty in 1979, with one d. *Education:* graduated from the Department of Transportation Economics of the University of Gdańsk in 1978. *Career:* an activist in the Socialist Union of Polish Students, he became editor-in-chief of *Itd* in 1981–84 and held the same post on *Sztandar Mlodych* in 1984–85. In 1985 he was appointed Minister without Portfolio (responsible for youth), remaining in this post until 1987. In the following year he was appointed Chairman of the Polish Olympic Committee, a post that he retained until 1991. He was elected leader of Social Democracy of the Republic of Poland (SRP, the former Communists) at its first congress in January 1990 and remained leader until his election as President. Kwaśniewski was also leader of the SRP's electoral coalition with the All Poland Trade Unions Alliance, the Democratic Left Alliance (SLD). He gained a seat in the Sejm in 1991 and retained this in the 1993 election. He presided over the National Assembly's Constitutional Commission from 1993–95. Kwaśniewski won the greatest number of votes in both rounds of the presidential election in November 1995, securing 51.7% of the valid ballot in the second round, against Lech Wałęsa (q.v.). He was inaugurated as President on 23 December. As President, he oversaw the parliamentary adoption of a new Constitution in April 1997 and the ratification of the Concordat, governing relations between the state and the Roman Catholic Church, in January 1998. He demonstrated his political acumen after the accession of the centre-right coalition Government in October 1997, using disagreements within the administration to strengthen his position. Amid allegations that he was influenced by his own communist past, he vetoed legislation

permitting citizens access to security-service files compiled on them during the communist era; however, the veto was discounted by the Sejm and the legislation was enacted. His exoneration from charges of collaboration with communist-era security services allowed him to stand again in the presidential election in October 2000, when he was re-elected in a first round of voting, with 54% of the votes cast. In March 2001 he vetoed a law aimed at compensating those who had lost property nationalized under the communist regime. In July of that year he issued a formal apology—controversial in some quarters—for the alleged involvement of Polish citizens in the wartime massacre of Jews in the village of Jedwabne. Kwaśniewski also worked to improve relations with Russia, and in mid-2002 advocated further advances in social welfare, in order to protect democracy in the country. Despite widespread disaproval of his support for the US-led military intervention in Iraq in early 2003, he remained popular with the public, presenting a smooth, liberal image. *Address:* Chancellery of the President, 00902 Warsaw, ul. Wiejskaio, Poland.

LABUS, Miroljab: Serbian and Montenegrin (Serbian) politician; b. 28 February 1947, in Mala Krsna; m., with two d. *Education:* he studied law and economics at the University of Belgrade. *Career:* he briefly practised law before returning to academia. He entered politics in the 1980s, and was a deputy to the Yugoslav federal parliament in 1992–96, becoming Vice-President of the Democratic Party in 1993. In 1997 he was the co-founder of the 'G-17' group, a non-party-based campaign group established to oppose the economic policies of the Yugoslav President, Slobodan Milošević (q.v.). In 2000 he was appointed Deputy Prime Minister in the Government of Serbia led by his party colleague, Zoran Djindjić. He was an advocate of an international outlook for Serbia, claiming that the nationalistic and eastward-looking policies of previous governments had proved a massive hindrance to the country, when compared with its neighbours. He stood for election to the Serbian presidency in September 2002. In common with many academics-turned-politicians in the region he was criticized for being out of touch with ordinary people, criticisms exploited by his principal opponent, federal President Vojislav Koštunica (q.v.). Labus received the second-highest number of votes and advanced to a second round against Koštunica in October, but the second poll was annulled after it was revealed that less than 50% of the electorate had voted (Koštunica had been the clear choice of those who had). Labus withdrew from the presidential contest before a new election was organized, and concentrated on the transformation of G-17 into a political party—he was elected its Chairman in December. *Address:* c/o G-17 Institute, Knez Mihajlova 10, Belgrade, Serbia and Montenegro.

LÁSZLÓ, Csaba: Minister of Finance of Hungary; b. 1962. *Career:* respected in the financial world, László was appointed as an independent Minister of Finance in the new coalition Government led by Péter Medgyessy (q.v.) of the Hungarian Socialist Party in May 2002, following the general election of the previous month. The financial markets, which had feared a severe swing to the politics of the right or left, or the establishment of a minority Government, responded well to László's appointment. László would have to seek to keep the Hungarian economy stable, in preparation for accession to the European Union (EU), which was anticipated in 2004. In addition, he outlined the following short-term priorities: adjusting the state budget to EU standards; addressing taxation issues; and opening up government finances to public scrutiny (in contrast to the opaque practices of the previous Government). He was a strong advocate of Hungarian membership of the euro at the earliest possible opportunity, although by 2003 he accepted the view of the Governor of the central bank, Zsigmond Járai (q.v.), that the Hungarian economy would not be ready for membership until 2008. *Address:* Ministry of Finance, 1051 Budapest, József Nádor tér 2–4, Hungary; tel. (1) 318-2066; fax (1) 318-2570.

LEPPER, Andrzej: Polish politician. *Career:* A former boxer and labourer, he led the Self-Defence Trade Union (Samoobrona) in protests against the restructuring programme of the Solidarity-led coalition Government in the late 1990s. Samoobrona organized road blockades and took other forthright measures, including the depositing of manure outside government buildings. In late 1999, with the protests generating increasing violence, Lepper announced that he would form a new anti-Government coalition with other farmers' organizations and trade unions: the Self Defence Party of the Republic of Poland was formally established in January 2000. To broaden its support base, it also aimed to support industrial workers and to address issues relating to natural resources. Lepper contested the presidential election of October 2000, obtaining 3.1% of the votes cast. In May 2001 he was sentenced to 16 months in gaol, for slandering politicians, including the President, Aleksander Kwaśniewski (q.v.), and two former ministers; he launched an appeal against the sentence. Considered to be a coarse populist by many urban Poles, he gained support from the disaffected rural poor, and in the legislative election of September 2001 the Self Defence Party took 53 seats in the Sejm (with 10.2% of the votes cast). Announcing his readiness to blockade parliament to obtain concessions, it was clear that neither Lepper's manner nor his tactics had changed. In particular, he remained adamantly opposed to admission to the European Union (EU), considering this body to have impoverished Polish farmers. This stance proved popular among his rural constituency, raising concerns among other parties that it could tip the balance of support away from admission, in the forthcoming referendum. Lepper was also strongly opposed to co-operation with the IMF and the World Bank. In November Lepper was dismissed as Vice-Marshal of the Sejm (a position to which he had been appointed the previous month), after verbally attacking the Minister of Foreign Affairs over concessions made to the EU on the issue of land sales. His parliamentary immunity from prosecution was removed in January 2002 and he was subsequently fined for having insulted the President, and charged with seven counts of slander. In March he received a suspended one-year prison sentence for his role in the organization of illegal blockades of 1999. He led an occupation by his supporters of the agriculture ministry in May 2002, and was widely criticized for attempting to subvert the democratic process. He was re-elected to the leadership of the Self Defence Party in May 2003, and remained a controversial figure, being vehemently opposed to many viewpoints (not least EU membership) which were held almost unanimously among the remainder of the country's political class. In July Lepper expelled four deputies from the Self Defence Party, after they questioned his financial and administrative management of the party. *Address:* Self Defence Party of the Republic of Poland (Partia Samoobrona Rzeczypospolitej Polskiej), 00-024 Warsaw, Al. Jerozolimskie 30, Poland; tel. (22) 6250472; fax (22) 6250477; e-mail sambroona@sambroona.org.pl.

LOZANCIĆ, Niko: President of the Federation of Bosnia and Herzegovina; b. 1957, in Kakanj; ethnic Croat. *Education:* he trained as a lawyer. *Career:* he practised law before becoming an active member of the Croat Democratic Union of Bosnia and Herzegovina (CDU—BH), first as a municipal councillor, then as a member of the House of Peoples of the Federation parliament. He became Chairman of the House of Peoples in 2000, and caused controversy in February 2001 by refusing to convene a session of the house, despite being instructed to do so by the High Representative of the International Community, Wolfgang Petritsch (he claimed that the electoral regulations were disadvantageous to the ethnic Croat community and that the resulting chamber did not adequately represent the electorate). The session eventually began without Lozancić, and the remainder of the CDU—BH delegation, who boycotted the chamber in protest. Previously, in December 2000, he had accepted the post of Secretary-General of the unofficial Croat assembly, and in August 2001 he and the other members of the body accompanied the former Chairman of the state Presidency, Ante Jelavić, to court to answer charges of jeopardizing the country's territorial integrity. Lozancić became deputy Chairman of the CDU—BH in early 2002, but refused to replace Jelavić as chairman after the latter was disqualified from political office. Following the elections held in the country in October 2002, in December he was proposed for the presidency of the Federation, and was

confirmed in office the following month. He maintained that the constitutional arrangements of the Federation favoured the Bosniaks, and early in his presidency stated that he did not trust the country's security services, implying that police officers had delayed his car and left him open to a possible assassination attempt. *Address:* Office of the President of the Federation, 71000 Sarajevo, Bosnia and Herzegovina; tel. (33) 472618.

MÁDL, Dr Ferenc: President of Hungary; b. 29 Jan. 1931, in Bánd, Veszprem; m. in 1955, with one s. *Education:* studied at the University of Pécs and Eötvös Loránd University in Budapest; awarded doctorates in law and political sciences. *Career:* he worked at the Institute of State and Legal Sciences at the Hungarian Academy of Sciences until 1973. He was then a lecturer at the Eötvös Loránd University and became Director of its Institute of Civil Sciences in 1978. In 1985 he was appointed head of the University's Faculty of International Private Law. In 1990–93 he served as Minister without Portfolio, without party affiliation, in the Government of József Antall, later becoming Minister of Culture and Public Education. In June 1995 he stood as the joint candidate of the opposition bloc in the presidential election, but was overwhelmingly defeated by Árpád Göncz. He was appointed Chairman of the Hungarian Association of Civic Co-operation in 1996. In 1999 he became a member of the Government's scientific advisory body and received the Schenyi award for his internationally recognized research in law. In early May 2000 he was nominated by the Independent Smallholders' and Civic Party as a candidate in the election to succeed President Göncz. His nomination was subsequently endorsed by all political parties, with the exception of the right-wing Hungarian Justice and Life Party, led by István Csurka. Although he was the sole presidential nominee, Mádl failed to obtain the requisite two-thirds' majority in two National Assembly ballots. Eventually, in a third round of voting on 6 June, in which only a simple majority was required, he secured the presidency. Mádl declared that, as President, his priorities would be Hungary's entry into the European Union (EU) and the maintenance of stability in Central and South-Eastern Europe, particularly in the Balkans. He took office on 4 August. In August 2002 it was reported that he was being investigated by a commission on political figures' links with communist-era security services. Mádl announced that he considered the commission unconstitutional, but subsequently stated that he was willing to co-operate with it. *Address:* Office of the President, 1055 Budapest, Kossuth Lajos tér 3–5, Hungary; tel. (1) 441-4103.

MAJKO, Pandeli: Albanian Minister of Defence; b. 15 Nov. 1967; m. with one c. *Education:* degrees in engineering and law. *Career:* a former student leader, he was active in the street protests in 1990 that helped to depose the country's isolationist, Stalinist regime. In 1991 he was one of the founders of the Euro-Socialist Youth Forum, which he headed until 1995. As a member of the Socialist Party of Albania (SPA), and a parliamentary deputy from 1992, Majko established a reputation for pragmatism and honesty. In 1996 he assumed responsibility for public affairs in the SPA and in 1997 replaced Rexhep Mejdani (q.v.) as General-Secretary of the party, when Mejdani was elected the country's President. In that year Majko proved an effective mediator in feuds between the SPA Government of Fatos Nano (q.v.) and the opposition Democratic Party of Albania (DPA) of Sali Berisha (q.v.). As a compromise candidate, Majko won his party's nomination to succeed Nano as Prime Minister, following the latter's resignation in September 1998, and subsequently became Albania's youngest leader, at 30 years of age, heading a broad-based coalition. Unlike other SPA leaders, Majko was never a member of the former communist party, and was therefore considered to have the best chance of establishing a new paradigm in Albanian politics, based on consensus government and public accountability. It was also hoped that he would be able to restore law and order, which had disintegrated under the Nano administration. Majko won respect abroad for his handling of the Kosovo crisis, which he made a priority, but was criticized at home for failing to combat corruption and smuggling (he claimed political squabbling had hindered his efforts). After being ousted by Nano as leader of the SPA at a party congress in October 1999, he resigned from the premiership, and was succeeded by the vice-premier, Ilir Meta (q.v.). Majko continued to serve as Minister of Defence under Meta. When Meta resigned his position in January 2002, he proposed Majko to succeed him. Majko was duly re-appointed Prime Minister by Mejdani on 7 February. At the expiry of Mejdani's mandate, however, the SPA and the DPA reached consensus on the election of Alfred Moisiu (q.v.) to the presidency. On 25 July Majko was obliged to resign from the office of Prime Minister in favour of Nano, after the SPA General Steering Committee decided that the party Chairman should be Head of Government. Majko (who was reported to have negotiated with Nano prior to tendering his resignation) was subsequently returned to the post of Minister of Defence in Nano's new Government. He became a passionate advocate of Albanian involvement in international organizations and military actions, overseeing the preparations for the country's possible North Atlantic Treaty Organization entry, and committing an Albanian force to the US-led operations in Iraq in 2003. *Address:* Ministry of Defence, Bulevardi Dëshmorët e Kombit, Tirana; tel. (4) 222103; fax (4) 228325; e-mail info@mod.gov.al.

MAKSIM, His Holiness Patriarch: Head of the Bulgarian Orthodox Church, Chairman of the Bulgarian Patriarchy; b. 29 April 1914, in Oreshak village, Lovech region. *Education:* a graduate of Sofia Academy of Theology. *Career:* originally Marin Naydenov Minkov, he graduated in 1935 and served the Church in Ruse and Lovech. He became a monk in 1941, when he took the name of Maksim; in 1947 he was appointed Archimandrite and Coadjutor in the Ruse diocese. In 1950–55 he represented the Bulgarian Church in Moscow, Russia, and in 1955 became Secretary-General of the Holy Synod. He was ordained bishop in 1956. In 1960 he was appointed Bishop of Lovech and in 1971 he was elected Bishop of Sofia and Patriarch of Bulgaria. In 1992 his authority was challenged when a schism emerged in the Bulgarian Church: several bishops rejected the authority of the Patriarchy, even after a visit by the Ecumenical Patriarch of Constantinople in 1993. Patriarch Maksim complained that elements within the Bulgarian establishment had provoked the schism, eventually resolved in October 1998 by an International Orthodox Synod, which recognized Patriarch Maksim as sole head of the Church in Bulgaria. Although the Synod recommended that he retire to a monastery, Patriarch Maksim continued to play a role in public life, attending the inauguration ceremony of Simeon Saxe-Coburg Gotha (q.v.) in July 2001 (the new Prime Minister pledged his oath on a bible, indicating support for the country's Orthodox Christian traditions) and that of Georgi Parvanov (q.v.), the country's new President, in January 2002, as well as leading public prayers. He was a strong supporter of legislation enacted on religious affairs in December. The new law guaranteed freedom of religion for all Bulgarians, prohibiting governmental interference in religious affairs, while describing Orthodox Christianity as the country's 'traditional religion' (this last stipulation was opposed by representatives of other faiths). Maksim suggested that such legislation, had it been in force in 1992, might have prevented the schism. *Address:* 1090 Sofia, Oborishte St 4, Synod Palace, Bulgaria; tel. (2) 87-56-11; fax (2) 89-76-00.

MARKÓ, Béla: Romanian politician; b. 8 Sept. 1951, in Târgul Secuiesc; ethnic Hungarian; m., with two c. *Education:* he graduated from the faculty of philology in the University of Babeş-Bolyai in Cluj in 1974. *Career:* one of the Hungarian minority's best-known poets, he taught until the end of the communist regime in 1989. In 1990 he emerged as a leading figure in the Democratic Alliance of Hungarians in Romania (DAHR), which represented the interests of the ethnic Hungarian (Magyar) minority in Romania. In 1992 he became the DAHR's leader, advocating autonomy, but not outright separation for those parts of the province of Transylvania where Hungarians were in a majority. The DAHR had ministries in the government from 1996 until 2000, following the electoral defeat of President Ion Iliescu (q.v.) and his Party of Social Democracy of Romania (PSDR), later Social Democratic Party (SDP), then flatly opposed to making concessions to the Hun-

garian minority. Markó remained outside government and concentrated on managing the affairs of the DAHR, which viewed itself as a platform for Hungarian interests, rather than as a conventional party. Initially, under Western pressure, Iliescu's party signed a co-operation agreement with the DAHR upon winning the 2000 election. The DAHR supported the Government with its parliamentary votes, in return for concessions in the fields of education, local government, and property restitution. Younger critics inside the DAHR argued that Markó had bestowed legitimacy upon a former fierce opponent of the Hungarians in Romania, in return for paltry concessions, and insisted that the prime beneficiaries of the pact with the SDP were some of Markó's deputies, who they claimed had benefited financially from their access to government. Markó was re-elected head of the DAHR in February 2003, but his most vocal internal critic, Tibor Tőrő, broke away, claiming that the DAHR was in danger of abandoning its democratic mechanisms and becoming a hierarchical party on the Romanian model. Markó thus faced the challenge of limiting the split, to ensure that in future the DAHR could obtain the 5% threshold of votes without which it was disqualified from sitting in parliament. *Address:* Democratic Alliance of Hungarians in Romania (DAHR) (Uniunea Democrata Maghiara din România—UDMR), Bucharest, Str. Avram Iancu 8, Romania; tel. (21) 3146849; fax (21) 3144583; e-mail elhivbuk@dial.kappa.ro.

MARKOVIĆ, Mirjana (Mira): Serbian and Montenegrin (Serbian) politician; b. 1943; m. Slobodan Milošević (q.v.), with one d. and one s. *Education:* graduated from the State University of Niš; gained a doctorate in sociology in 1978. *Career:* a lecturer in sociology at Belgrade University, in 1990 she was one of the founder members of the League of Communists—Movement for Yugoslavia, the successor to the all-Yugoslav Communist Party. A committed Marxist, she believed that the future of Serbia lay in its development along the lines of Chinese communism. In 1994 she established the Yugoslav United Left (YUL), an alliance of socialist organizations. Aided by her position as the wife of Milošević, the Serbian President, the movement formed a coalition with the ruling party, his Socialist Party of Serbia (SPS), and rapidly gained influence within the Government. From 1996 the YUL became increasingly influential, with greater representation in both the republican and federal Governments. Following her husband's election as federal President in mid-1997, the SPS and the YUL enjoyed an even closer alliance. The YUL formed part of the new Serbian Government of Mirko Marjanović announced in March 1998. After a reorganization of the federal Government in August 1999, the YUL's influence within that body increased. After the defeat of the SPS and YUL alliance by the Democratic Opposition of Serbia (DOS) in the federal presidential and legislative elections in September 2000, Milošević was forced from power (Marković, however, gained a seat in the lower house of parliament, after standing for election in a move that many considered a final attempt to shore up support for her husband's regime). The alliance also lost control of the Serbian Government, following legislative elections in the republic in December. Milošević was eventually arrested early on 1 April 2001, after the couple and their daughter, Marija, were surrounded at their residence in the town of Pozarevać by security forces. Marković was subsequently obliged to leave Pozarevać, as a result of local hostility. She continued to visit her husband during his detention in the central prison in Belgrade, and his subsequent extradition to the International Criminal Tribunal for the former Yugoslavia (ICTY, in The Hague, Netherlands), vociferously asserting his innocence. Devoted to Milošević—an emotion that was clearly reciprocated—she was considered by many to have been the real power behind the former President; she continued to deny steadily-mounting accusations of involvement in killings and other criminal activities while her husband was in power. She was apparently reluctant to return from The Hague to the FRY (now Serbia and Montenegro), where many believed it likely that she would herself eventually come under investigation. Her fears were realized when, in April 2003, a warrant was issued for her arrest in connection with the assassination of the former Serbian President, Ivan Stambolić, in August 2000 (her husband was also charged with involvement in the murder). She severed her links with the YUL in May 2003, by which time it was believed she had sought refuge in Russia. *Address:* 11000 Belgrade, bul. Lenjina 6, Serbia and Montenegro; e-mail jul@jul.org.yu.

MAROVIĆ, Svetozar: President of Serbia and Montenegro (Montenegrin); b. 31 March 1955, in Kotor; m., with two c. *Education:* he studied law at the University of Podgorica. *Career:* he worked in public administration before entering politics as a co-founder of the pro-independence Montenegrin party, the Democratic Party of Socialists (DPS). He was elected to the Republican Assembly in Montenegro in 1990, and represented the DPS in the republican legislature throughout the 1990s and early 2000s, being speaker in 1998–2002. He also served in the federal parliament. In December 2002 it was announced that he would stand for the post of President of the new state of Serbia and Montenegro, scheduled for the coming February. In the event, he was the sole candidate and he took office in early March 2003, declaring his aims to be economic development, closer relations with other countries in Europe, and co-operation with the International Criminal Tribunal for the former Yugoslavia (ICTY), based in The Hague, Netherlands. He assented to the imposition of a state of emergency in Serbia following the assassination of the Serbian Prime Minister, Zoran Djindjić, in the same month. *Address:* Office of the President, 11000 Belgrade, Serbia and Montenegro.

MEČIAR, Vladimír: Slovak politician and former Prime Minister; b. 26 July 1942, in Zvolen; m. Margita Mečiarová, with two s. and two d. *Education:* graduated in law from Comenius University, Bratislava in 1973. *Career:* a former pugilist, from 1959 he spent several years working in the Communist youth movement. In 1969 he was accused of supporting the reformists. He was expelled from the Communist Party of Czechoslovakia in 1970. While studying law he worked as a welder in Dubnica. He then worked as an enterprise lawyer until November 1989, when he became Minister of the Interior and the Environment in the new Government of Slovakia. He became premier after the election of June 1990, but split from the ruling Public Against Violence movement (Slovakia's counterpart to the Czech Civic Forum) to found the Movement for a Democratic Slovakia (MDS) in March 1991, which he also led. On 23 April 1991 he was dismissed as premier by the Slovak National Council. However, following the election in June 1992, in which the MDS emerged as the dominant Slovakian party, the National Council re-elected Mečiar as premier, leading a Government composed primarily of MDS members. After Slovakia gained independence, the Government became increasingly divided, as Mečiar indulged in nationalistic politics, while failing to promote economic reform. However, Mečiar remained in office when a new coalition was formed in November 1993. On 12 March 1994 this Government received a vote of 'no confidence' in the National Council and, with the support of the President, Mečiar was dismissed two days later. In December, after lengthy negotiations in the wake of the legislative election, Mečiar was reappointed Prime Minister of a coalition Government. On resuming the premiership, he immediately installed people loyal to him in important state positions. He attempted to gain control of the police force, which he accused of being corrupt. Another priority was a reduction in the powers of President Michal Kováč, an aim that served to exacerbate the feud between the two men. This bitter dispute was a distraction to the real business of government and the latter years of Mečiar's premiership were marked by an increasingly erratic and autocratic style, as he traded insults with the President, rejected his coalition allies—only to embrace them once again when he could find no others—manipulated the democratic process in an attempt to ensure his own survival and, all the while, ignored the protests of foreign governments and international organizations. During the 1998 general election campaign the principal independent television broadcaster was taken over by a company with MDS links, with alleged security services involvement, and state broadcasters were reduced to government propagandists. Nevertheless, Mečiar's MDS-led coalition was outnumbered in the parlia-

ment elected in September, and he was forced to resign the premiership. He subsequently announced his retirement from public life, but returned in May 1999 to contest the country's first direct presidential election as the MDS candidate. He was defeated by the candidate supported by the governing coalition, Rudolf Schuster (q.v.). In April 2000 Mečiar was arrested on charges of abuse of power and fraud (later abandoned). He was fined for refusing to answer questions relating to the abduction of Kováč's son in 1995, in which his security forces were believed to have been involved, but was then released. Returning to the leadership of the MDS, he remained an influential figure in the country, and retained his popularity, especially with older people and in rural constituencies. In mid-2001 he began a serious process of reinvention. He declared the MDS to be firmly committed to European Union and North Atlantic Treaty Organization membership (even organizing a meeting on accession to the latter in late 2001), although in parliament the party continued to oppose the reforms needed for entry. For their part, Western countries remained unconvinced, and made it clear that support for Mečiar in the September 2002 election would threaten relations. In preparation for the election, Mečiar removed many of the 'old guard' of the MDS—apparently to rejuvenate the party—thereby strengthening his hold on power. He expressed his readiness to co-operate with incumbent ruling parties after the election (although those parties appeared less favourable towards the idea), while continuing to antagonize the leader of the Direction (Smer) party, a clear rival of the MDS, Robert Fico (q.v.). In local elections in December 2001, in which the rate of voter participation was low, MDS representatives secured 146 of the 401 seats in the regional councils and six of the eight gubernatorial posts. The party, and Mečiar, continued to perform well in opinion polls as the election approached, although he did have the effect of concentrating support for the Prime Minister, Mikuláš Dzurinda (q.v.), hitherto highly unpopular. The MDS's electoral prospects were also damaged by reports that Mečiar had assaulted a journalist in the weeks prior to the election, and by his poor performance when faced with familiar allegations of corruption in televised debates. In the event, the MDS became the largest party in parliament following the election in September 2002, winning 19.5% of the votes cast and 36 seats. However, distaste at Mečiar's personal style ensured that none of the other significant parties were willing to form a coalition with the MDS—Dzurinda was able to form a new coalition, and Mečiar was again excluded from government. It was reported in 2003 that senior MDS figures considered Mečiar to be a liability, and were preparing a leadership challenge. However, he was re-elected as Chairman in June. He remained the one figure who was able to polarize public opinion in Slovakia—those who supported him did so fervently, those who did not tended to dislike him with equal vigour. *Address:* Movement for a Democratic Slovakia (Hnutie za demokratické Slovensko), Tomášikova 32A, 830 00 Bratislava, Slovakia; tel. (2) 4329-3800; fax (2) 4341-0225; e-mail webmaster@hzds.sk.

MEDGYESSY, Dr Péter: Prime Minister of Hungary; b. 1942, in Budapest. *Education:* obtained a doctorate from the University of Economics, Budapest; speaks French and Romanian. *Career:* regarded as a reformist communist, he worked at the Ministry of Finance from the 1960s, rising to become Minister of Finance in 1987, in which role he established a banking and taxation system designed to meet the requirements of a market economy. He served as Deputy Prime Minister with responsibility for economic affairs in 1988–89, under Miklós Németh. In 1990–94 he worked in banking in Hungary, latterly as Chairman and Chief Executive Officer of the Hungarian Bank for Investment and Development. He became Minister of Finance once again in March 1996–July 1998, replacing Dr Lajos Bokros, and won praise for his proposals on pension reform. He returned to banking in October 1998. In mid-2001 the Hungarian Socialist Party (HSP), which was suffering from increasing internal divisions, nominated Medgyessy, then affiliated to no political party, as its candidate for Prime Minister in the 2002 election. Just before the election Medgyessy was investigated by the

Hungarian police over allegations of illegal property dealings. He described the investigation as politically motivated and was later successful in a libel action on the issue. The HSP obtained a small advantage in the first round of the election in early April. In contrast to the public demonstrations of support staged by the ruling party prior to the second round, Medgyessy promoted the HSP's 'quiet strength', and in the second round the HSP secured 46.1% of the votes cast and, forming an alliance with the Alliance of Free Democrats (AFD), entered government in May, after a number of recounts and legal appeals; Medgyessy was sworn in as Prime Minister on 27 May. He immediately promised to work to heal the serious divisions engendered by the close-run contest. Expressing his desire to promote a 'new left' in politics, he proposed the creation of a 'social contract' with the poor, and promised a 50% pay rise for those in the health, education and public administration sectors. He pledged to work to improve relations with the country's Central European neighbours—damaged by the nationalist rhetoric of the previous Prime Minister, Victor Orbán (q.v.)—and was expected to lead Hungary into the European Union (he signed the country's accession treaty in April 2003). A more reserved character than Orbán, his supporters depicted him as a man of greater integrity. In June, however, following media allegations in an opposition newspaper, Medgyessy admitted that he had served as a counter-intelligence officer at the Ministry of Finance in 1977–82, but denied that he had worked as an 'informant'. At the beginning of August he defended his past in front of a specially-convened parliamentary committee, asserting that he had worked merely to ensure Hungary's financial independence from the USSR. The committee's report stated that, while it considered Medgyessy's co-operation with it to have been incomplete, there was nothing in his past to disqualify him from the premiership. Despite the controversy, and numerous demands from opposition parties for his resignation (the public appeared relatively content for him to remain), he survived in office and the crisis appeared to abate. Medgyessy attracted domestic criticism when he signed a letter stressing the importance of European-US unity in the prelude to the US-led intervention in Iraq. He effected a minor reorganization of his Government in May 2003, claiming that the new structure was more responsive to the country's political situation. *Address:* Office of the Prime Minister, 1055 Budapest, Kossuth Lajos tér 1–3, Hungary; tel. (1) 441-4000; fax (1) 268-3050.

MEJDANI, Dr Rexhep: former President of Albania; b. 17 Aug. 1944, in Tirana; m., with two c. *Education:* he studied physics at the University of Tirana. *Career:* from 1977 he was a lecturer of physics at the University of Tirana. In the early 1990s he spent time as a visiting scientist and professor at various universities. He was also the Dean of the Faculty of Natural Sciences at the University of Tirana from 1989 and became Head of Theoretical Physics in 1992. In July 1996 he joined the Socialist Party of Albania (SPA) and, one month later, was voted General-Secretary. Mejdani was elected President by the People's Assembly following the mid-1997 general election defeat of the Democratic Party of Albania (DPA) and the subsequent resignation from the presidency of Sali Berisha (q.v.). His election marked a significant change in the division of power between different branches of the Albanian administration. It was soon clear that under the SPA Government of Fatos Nano (q.v.), President Mejdani was to have primarily an honorary role, with the Prime Minister's office adopting more executive functions. In 1999 he played an instrumental part in the conflict in neighbouring Kosovo and Metohija, bringing together Kosovar Albanian factions and ensuring their presence at peace negotiations. Overall, he aimed to promote stabilization in the Balkans and prevent the polarization of Albanian politics. In 1999 he was awarded the Romanian national Order, the 'Golden Star of Romania' and in 2000 received the 'Order of Gratitude', on the 30th anniversary of the founding of Priština University (Federal Republic of Yugoslavia), for his contribution to the University. Mejdani's term of office expired in late July 2002. Although, according to the terms of the Constitution, he had been eligible to stand for a second five-year term, his close links

with the SPA had meant that he was unlikely to secure conservative support in the People's Assembly, and he was succeeded by retired general Alfred Moisiu (q.v.). *Address:* c/o Socialist Party of Albania (Partia Socialiste e Shqipërisë—PSS), Tirana, Albania; tel. (4) 227409; fax (4) 227417.

MESIĆ, Stjepan ('Stipe'): President of Croatia and former President of the Yugoslav federal State Presidency (head of state); b. 24 Dec. 1934, in Orahovića; m. with two d. *Education:* University of Zagreb. *Career:* a member of the Croatian Democratic Union (CDU), which won the republican election in Croatia, he was made premier (Prime Minister) of the republic in May 1990. In August he was elected as the Croatian member of the federal State Presidency and, consequently, its Vice-President. An anti-Communist and Croat nationalist, he was also one of the Presidency members who refused to vote for the Serbian request for a state of emergency in March 1991. The Serbian-dominated establishment, therefore, refused to countenance what should have been the automatic election of the Croatian member as President of the federal Presidency, in May. Following the declarations of 'dissociation' by Croatia and Slovenia, and an EC-negotiated cease-fire at the start of the civil war, he was elected Yugoslav President, at the end of June 1991 (the first non-Communist President). However, the Presidency was increasingly revealed as too divided to function effectively, and the armed forces proved reluctant to obey the orders of a Croat who supported his republic's attempted secession. In October the 'Serbian bloc' of Presidency members began to meet without Mesić or the members for Bosnia and Herzegovina, Macedonia or Slovenia. Mesić's position was rendered more ambiguous by Croatia's recall of its citizens from federal institutions. On 5 December he formally resigned his federal post, but pursued a political career in Croatia, where he was one of the most popular politicians. Following the parliamentary election held on 2 August 1992 he was elected President of the Croatian Assembly (Sabor), a post which he held until May 1994. In the previous month, having become increasingly opposed to the anti-Muslim and undemocratic views of the Croatian President, Franjo Tudjman, he had left the ruling party, the CDU, to co-found the Croatian Independent Democrats (CID) with another prominent liberal, Josip Manolić. This party formed part of an opposition electoral alliance that won 16 seats (the second largest bloc) in the 80-seat Chamber of Representatives in the general election of October 1995. In January 2000 he stood as the candidate of a coalition of the four main opposition parties in the presidential election, winning 41% of the votes cast in the first round. In a second ballot, on 7 February, he defeated Dražen Budiša, winning 56% of the votes cast. He was inaugurated as President on 18 February, having resigned from the CID three days earlier. His election to the presidency was heralded by many as the beginning of a new era in Croatian politics. He pledged to introduce democratic reforms, in conjunction with the new Prime Minister, Ivica Račan (q.v.), and to integrate Croatia into Western European structures, particularly the European Union (EU) and the North Atlantic Treaty Organization (NATO). Negotiations towards EU membership proceeded successfully in 2001, but other reforms were obstructed by infighting within the administration. In July 2001 Mesić backed the move to hand over two war crimes suspects to the International Criminal Tribunal for the former Yugoslavia (ICTY, based in The Hague, the Netherlands), describing this as an 'unavoidable' international obligation. In January 2002, on the 10th anniversary of the EU's recognition of Croatia, he declared that it was time to 'speak the truth'. In a speech to parliament, he declared that the Croatian leadership had goaded the minority Serb population in the 1990s, and also denounced the territorial aspirations of the Tudjman Government in Bosnia and Herzegovina. In addition, he deplored the continuing violations of democracy in Croatia. In February 2002 it was reported that he was prepared to testify against Slobodan Milošević (q.v.) at the ICTY, and in October he became the first head of state to give evidence to the tribunal, making numerous serious allegations against Milošević in his testimony. Milošević, conducting his own defence, cross-examined Mesić fiercely, claiming that he had ordered atrocities against

Serbs during the conflict, something Mesić vehemently denied. Despite criticism of his conduct regarding Croatian war crimes suspects and their trials in Croatia and at the ICTY (both from the suspects' supporters and those determined that they be prosecuted), opinion polls in mid-2003 revealed that Mesić remained the country's most popular political figure. *Address:* Office of the President, 10000 Zagreb, Banksi Dvori, Croatia; e-mail office@president.hr.

META, Ilir: Albanian politician and former Prime Minister; b. 1969. *Education:* he studied economics at the University of Tirana. *Career:* In the early 1990s he was among the leaders of the student movement that helped to precipitate the collapse of the Communist regime in Albania. In 1992, as a candidate of the Socialist Party of Albania (SPA), he was elected to the People's Assembly. In 1993 he was elected Deputy Chairman of the Presidency, in charge of foreign affairs, and three years later became Deputy Chairman of the Parliamentary Commission on Foreign Affairs. In October 1998 he was appointed Secretary of State for European Integration at the Ministry of Foreign Affairs, before being promoted, later in the year, to the post of Deputy Prime Minister and Minister of Government Co-ordination in the cabinet of Pandeli Majko (q.v.). On 27 October 1999, after Majko's resignation, President Rexhep Mejdani (q.v.) nominated Meta to lead a new Government. His appointment as Prime Minister was seen as a compromise between the two factions of the SPA. The SPA retained the support of the electorate in the legislative election of June–July 2001, but after the poll the leader of the party, Fatos Nano (q.v.), demanded the resignation of certain ministers, whom he accused of corruption. Nano's supporters proceeded to block the replacements proposed by Meta. In January 2002, having failed to reach agreement with Nano on a reshuffle, Meta resigned, amid much acrimony. Although Majko was subsequently appointed to the office of Prime Minister as a compromise candidate, he was replaced by Nano on 25 July. Meta became Deputy Prime Minister and Minister of Foreign Affairs in Nano's new Government. However, his relationship with Nano remained strained, and public enmity returned in July 2003, when he resigned, claiming that the Prime Minister was attempting to assume control of the Ministry of Foreign Affairs.

MIĆIĆ, Nataša: acting President of Serbia and President of the National Assembly of Serbia; b. 11 August 1965, in Uzice; m., with one c. *Education:* she studied law at the University of Belgrade. *Career:* she practised law before entering politics. A member of the Civic Alliance, she became deputy speaker of the Serbian parliament in 2000, and was elected speaker one year later. Despite her youth, she proved herself to be a capable and determined holder of the office. Following the failure of two attempts to elect a new Serbian President in late 2002, Mićić was appointed acting President in late December. The country was thrown into crisis in March 2003 when the Prime Minister, Zoran Djindjić, was assassinated, and Mićić declared a state of emergency. With little willingness to attempt to elect a new President in the wake of the assassination and of the constitutional transformation of Yugoslavia into Serbia and Montenegro, she remained acting President into the second half of 2003. *Address:* Office of the President of Serbia, Andrićev venac 1, 11000 Belgrade, Serbia and Montenegro; tel. (11) 3030866; fax (11) 3030868; e-mail kprsa@ptt.yu.

MIKLOŠ, Ivan: Minister of Finance of Slovakia; b. 2 June 1960, in Svidník; m., with two c. *Education:* he studied economics at the University of Bratislava. *Career:* he pursued higher studies in economics, before entering Czechoslovak politics as Minister for Privatization in 1991. He left government upon the separation of the two countries the following year, and returned to his job as an economist. He was a co-founder of Slovakia's Conservative Party in 1993 and was elected President of the Democratic Party in 1994, after the two groups had merged. In September 1998 he was elected to parliament, representing the Slovak Democratic Coalition, one of the parties of the governing alliance, and was named Deputy Prime Minister for the Economy shortly thereafter. He was returned to parliament in September 2002, and was named Deputy Prime Minister and Minister of Finance. His

programme of reforms proved unpopular with many, although he was widely credited with improving Slovakia's economic position to such an extent that membership of the European Union (EU), unthinkable in the mid-1990s, was by 2004. *Address:* Ministry of Finance, Štefanovičova 5, 817 82 Bratislava, Slovakia; tel. (2) 5958-1111; fax (2) 5249-8042; e-mail inform@mfsr.sk; internet www.finance.gov.sk.

MILLER, Leszek: Prime Minister of Poland; b. 3 July 1946, in Zyradów; m. Aleksandra Borowiec, with one s. *Education:* Higher School of Social Sciences. *Career:* he was a staff member of the Central Committee of the Polish United Workers' Party (PUWP) in 1977–86, and Secretary to the Central Committee in 1989–90, as well as a member of the Politburo Central Committee. He was elected as a deputy to parliament in 1991, becoming Minister of Labour and Social Policy in 1993–96, and thereafter, minister with responsibility for the office of the Council of Ministers in 1996 and Minister of Internal Affairs and Administration in 1997. In 1999 he became Chairman of the Democratic Left Alliance (SLD), having been Chairman of one of its two constituent parties, the Social Democracy of the Republic of Poland, from 1997. The SLD gained in popularity in 2000–01 and, as support for the incumbent administration declined, Miller began to prepare for his party's anticipated electoral win, studying English and economics and meeting a number of foreign leaders. In the September 2001 legislative election the SLD, in coalition with the Union of Labour (UP), won 216 seats in the Sejm (with 41% of the votes), but failed to secure an overall majority. After signing a coalition agreement with the Polish People's Party (PSL), Miller was sworn in as Prime Minister on 19 October. Faced with an extremely difficult economic environment, he immediately pledged to carry out measures designed to rescue the public finances and to reduce unemployment. While some economists doubted his abilities in this area, his sense of discipline and single-mindedness could not be called into question. Miller was also Chairman of Poland's European Integration Committee; accession to the European Union (EU) was regarded as a priority for the country, although a significant degree of opposition to entry persisted. Miller announced that a referendum on admission would be held in mid-2003, and that his Government would resign if the plebiscite failed to gain support for entry. However, in March 2003 the PSL (which held two senior government posts) left the governing coalition, and Miller was forced to reconstitute the Government as an SLD-UP minority administration. The referendum, held in June 2003, produced a comfortable majority in favour of Polish membership. The relative weakness of Lepper's administration (by this point 11 ministers, including two Ministers of Finance, had left the Government since Miller became Prime Minister) caused Miller to seek a vote of confidence in the Sejm immediately after the result of the referendum was announced. The Government won the vote, but doubts remained over its commitment to the strict financial policy required for EU accession. *Address:* Chancellery of the Prime Minister, 00-583 Warsaw, Al. Ujazdowskie 1/3, Poland; tel. (22) 6946000; fax (22) 6252637; e-mail cirinfo@kprm.gov.pl.

MILOŠEVIĆ, Slobodan: former President of the Federal Republic of Yugoslavia; b. 20 Aug. 1941, in Pozarevać, Serbia; m. Mirjana Marković (q.v.), with one d. and one s. *Education:* he graduated in law from Belgrade University in 1964. *Career:* a conservative communist, he worked in local Government, industry and banking as a modest bureaucrat, displaying little interest in active politics until the 1980s. He was leader of the Belgrade Communists from 1984 until 1986, when he was made leader of the League of Communists of Serbia. He was initially sponsored by the Serbian President, Ivan Stambolić, who was the first major victim of Milošević's habit of ruthlessly discarding former political allies. Milošević initiated an 'anti-bureaucratic revolution' and espoused nationalist rhetoric, thereby maintaining the popularity of the ruling party (subsequently renamed the Socialist Party of Serbia—SPS). In May 1989 he was made President of the republican State presidency. In December 1990 he was elected, by direct ballot, to the new post of sole, executive President, and was re-elected in December 1992 and in

December 1993. His centralizing and pan-Serb policies played a significant part in provoking the dissolution of the old federation, while helping to secure parliamentary majorities at both the federal and republican levels, assisted by his control of the mass media and divisions in the opposition. Milošević's administration was condemned for its involvement in the civil wars in Croatia and in Bosnia and Herzegovina, and sanctions were imposed on Serbia and Montenegro (constituting the Federal Republic of Yugoslavia—FRY—from April 1992). Involved in such controversial policies, and with international isolation exacerbating economic hardship, Milošević was careful to ensure the loyalty of the Serbian and federal establishments in the 1990s. He also began to present himself as a peacemaker, being eager to end the FRY's isolation. An excellent negotiator, in August 1995 he pressured the Bosnian Serbs into allowing the FRY to act as their representative. The ensuing negotiations culminated in the signing of the General Framework Agreement for Peace in Bosnia and Herzegovina the following month in Paris (France) and the suspension of most of the sanctions against the FRY by the end of that year. Following the expiry of his mandate as Serbian President, he consolidated his power-base through his election to the federal presidency in July 1997. His desire to ensure loyalty at republican level led to a deterioration in relations with Montenegro from the mid-1990s, but his attempt to prevent an opponent, Milo Djukanović (q.v.), from taking presidential office in Montenegro in early 1998 ended in failure. Regarded by many as a war crimes suspect, he nevertheless managed to preserve his credibility within the international community until 1998, when his brutal suppression of an uprising by ethnic Albanian separatists in Kosovo and Metohija met with international condemnation and the reimposition of sanctions. His defiance of international demands and threats, including that of an air offensive by Western forces against Serbia itself, appeared to be motivated by a desire to unite the Serbs behind him, although economic hardship was meanwhile undermining his support. Despite growing evidence of domestic opposition, he remained firmly in control of the state apparatus. He was believed to rely on a close coterie of friends and drinking companions, and maintained a privacy that included mysterious disappearances from public view for sometimes significant periods. Following the failure of multilateral peace negotiations in March 1999, and the continuing repression of ethnic Albanians by the Serbian security forces, the North Atlantic Treaty Organization (NATO) began an air offensive. Support for Milošević increased sharply in Serbia during the bombardment, with one missile reportedly hitting the presidential residence. In May Milošević was indicted by the International Criminal Tribunal for the former Yugoslavia (ICTY, in The Hague, Netherlands), on charges of war crimes. He accepted peace proposals in June and, although Kosovo was removed from his authority, remained strong within the rest of Serbia. However, in 2000 his popularity within Serbia began to decline, with widespread anti-Government demonstrations and increased co-operation among opposition movements. Nevertheless, in February he was re-elected president of the SPS. In July the Federal Assembly adopted an amendment to the Constitution providing for the direct election of the federal President, thus allowing Milošević to contest the next presidential election. Milošević lost the first round of the election to the candidate of the Democratic Opposition of Serbia (DOS) alliance, Vojislav Koštunica (q.v.), but refused to acknowledge that his challenger had won the first round outright. In early October, shortly before a second round was due to be held, a popular uprising forced him to concede defeat. He remained leader of the SPS, but his hopes of continuing as a political force were diminished after the Serbian legislative election in December significantly reduced the strength of his party. He was arrested by security forces early on 1 April 2001, after a violent stand-off, and was expected to stand trial in the FRY on charges of corruption while in public office. During his detention in the central prison in Belgrade, he was taken to hospital, reportedly for heart problems. Following heavy pressure on the federal Government from the international community, an extradition decree was approved, which he attempted to contest.

However, on 28 June he was extradited to the ICTY, becoming the first former head of state to appear before such a court. He was formally charged with crimes against humanity at the ICTY in early July, but continued to refuse to recognize the authority of the Tribunal. Legal challenges by Milošević and his supporters against his detention in 2001 and 2002 were dismissed, as were appeals for him to be released from detention to prepare his defence. Further indictments were brought against him in October and November 2001, including, for the first time, the charge of genocide, in connection with atrocities perpetrated by Serbian forces in Bosnia and Herzegovina in 1992–95. His trial officially commenced on 12 February 2002, and was expected to last for at least two years. Milošević, who was conducting his own defence, denied all charges, and instead attempted to focus attention on the NATO bombardment of Serbia in 1999. He held lengthy cross-examinations of the early witnesses (particularly, in October 2002, the Croatian President, Stipe Mesić—q.v.), making strident assertions and accusations, and announced his intention to call prominent Western politicians as later witnesses. Many observers accused his supporters of involvement in the assassination of the Serbian Prime Minister, Zoran Djindjić, in March 2003. The following month he was charged with involvement in the attempted assassination of Vuk Drašković (q.v.) in June 2000 and in the murder of the former Serbian President, Ivan Stambolić, in August 2000. He retained some degree of support in Serbia, particularly among the rural population, but many of his erstwhile supporters were beginning to look at the results of his regime more dispassionately.

MILUTINOVIĆ, Milan: Serbian and Montenegrin (Serbian) politician; former President of Serbia; b. 12 Dec. 1942, in Belgrade; m. Olga Milutinovića, with one c. *Education:* he studied law at Belgrade University. *Career:* a former member of the Communist Youth League of Yugoslavia's Presidium, he was appointed deputy head of the socio-political council of the Federal Assembly in 1969. In 1983–87 he was director of the Serbian National Library and a published writer, before becoming involved in full-time politics as a member of the Socialist Party of Serbia (SPS), the successor to the Serbian Communist Party. Following the dissolution of the Socialist Federative Republic of Yugoslavia, he was ambassador to Greece from 1989–95, and held the post of Serbian Minister of Science and Education. In 1995 he was appointed Federal Minister of Foreign Affairs, a post he held until late 1997 when, as the SPS candidate (replacing Zoran Lilić), he unexpectedly won a repeat election to the Serbian presidency. His election was marred by allegations of vote-rigging. He was regarded as a loyal, but lacklustre, ally of the federal President, Slobodan Milošević (q.v.), and was expected to carry out the latter's policies. Prior to the North Atlantic Treaty Organization's (NATO) aerial bombardment of the Federal Republic of Yugoslavia (FRY) in 1999, however, he supported signing the proposed peace agreement, leading Milošević and his supporters to claim that he was organizing a campaign against the federal President. In May he was indicted by the International Criminal Tribunal for the former Yugoslavia (ICTY, in The Hague, Netherlands) on charges of war crimes, including the deportation of 740,000 ethnic Albanians and the murder of over 300 people. In August he was placed under close scrutiny by the security forces, following apparent accusations of disloyalty to the federal President. In April 2000 he underwent heart surgery. Milutinović remained President of Serbia following the popular uprising against Milošević in October 2000, but lost all political influence after Milosević was forced from office. In early September 2001 the Serbian Prime Minister, Zoran Djindjić, declared Milutinović to have official immunity from prosecution; however, after immense international pressure, in April 2002 the Federal Assembly approved legislation providing for the extradition of all indicted war crimes suspects and the issue of arrest warrants for those who failed to surrender. By mid-2002 Milutinović was the only indicted suspect still to be holding high office. His presidential term expired in December 2002, and he surrendered to the ICTY in late January 2003, pleading not guilty to the charges against him at his first appearance shortly thereafter.

MLADIĆ, Gen. Ratko: Bosnian; military leader; b. 12 March 1943, in Kalinovik; ethnic Serb; m., with one s. *Career:* a radical Serb nationalist, his father was killed by Croatian Fascist collaborators during the Second World War. He became a tank officer in the Yugoslav People's Army (YPA) in Bosnia and Herzegovina and, during the civil war in Croatia in 1991, gained popularity among the Serbs for his support of their claim to the enclave of Krajina. In 1992 he was appointed commanding officer of the YPA and subsequently commanded the siege of Sarajevo and the 'ethnic cleansing' (forcible expulsions from 'Serb' areas) of numerous Bosnian Muslim (Bosniak) communities. Paranoid about the danger of German expansionism and Muslim aggression, which he considered to be sponsored by Middle Eastern countries, Mladić aimed to bring about the 'total military defeat of the Muslims' and the formation of a 'Greater Serbia'. He had a huge popular following among Bosnian Serbs, as he strongly opposed any peace settlement to the Bosnian civil war, including the November 1995 General Framework Agreement for Peace in Bosnia and Herzegovina. Despite his intransigence, and unlike his one-time ally, the former President of the Serb Republic, Radovan Karadžić (q.v.), Mladić remained on good terms with the Serbian President, Slobodan Milošević (q.v.), who angered the international community by failing to order his arrest in Yugoslavia, following his indictment as a war criminal in April 1995. Mladić subsequently resided in Belgrade, under the protection of Milošević, but, following the latter's arrest by the Yugoslav authorities in April 2001 and subsequent extradition to the International Criminal Tribunal for the former Yugoslavia (ICTY—based in the Hague, the Netherlands), he became more vulnerable, and went into hiding. In July the Bosnian Serb Republic Government drafted legislation pledging closer co-operation with the ICTY, thereby providing for the arrest and extradition of Mladić and Karadžić to the Tribunal. In February 2002 a high-ranking Serbian government minister reportedly stated that Mladić was in Serbia, but that he could not be persuaded to surrender to the ICTY. According to the minister, who was not identified, Mladić had been warned that he was no longer afforded the protection of the Yugoslav Army (although it was reported later in that year that certain factions within the miltary continued to protect him). The USA had increased the reward offered for information leading to his arrest to US $5m. A report issued by the Netherlands Institute for War Documentation in April 2002 held Mladić to be principally responsible for the massacre of up to 8,000 people in Srebreniča in 1995. Following the assassination of the Serbian Prime Minister, Zoran Djindjić, in March 2003 the Serbian authorities detained a number of supporters of Milošević, some of whom were believed to have provided support and protection to Mladić, and hopes that he would be unable to remain in hiding were raised. However, despite this, and the efforts by NATO forces to find and arrest him, Mladić continued to evade capture into 2003.

MOISIU, Gen. (retd) Alfred: Albanian President; b. 1 Dec. 1929, in Shkodër; m., with three d. and one s. *Education:* military Academy of Engineering in Moscow, graduating in 1958 with Gold Medal. *Career:* served in the engineering division of the Ministry of Defence. Minister of Defence following the country's first multi-party elections in 1991, he subsequently served as adviser to the Minister of Defence in 1992–97. Prior to standing in the presidential election of June 2002, he headed the Albanian Atlantic Council, which promoted ties between Albania and the North Atlantic Treaty Organization (NATO). The initial candidate for the presidential election that was held in the People's Assembly on 24 June, Albania's ambassador to the European Union (EU), Artur Kuko, had refused to stand. The election of Moisiu, the sole candidate, was, therefore, regarded as a compromise, particularly since an attempt had been made to select a candidate on the basis of consensus between Fatos Nano (q.v.), the leader of the Socialist Party of Albania (SPA), and Sali Berisha, the leader of the Democratic Party of Albania (DPA), following EU recommendations that the country reduce polarization. Moisiu received 97 votes out of a potential 140 cast in the People's Assembly, and took office on 24 July

2002. He announced at his inauguration that his aim was to see the end of corruption in the country and increasing partnership with Western nations. *Address:* c/o Office of the Council of Ministers, Këshilli i Ministrave, Tirana, Albania.

NANO, Fatos: Albanian Prime Minister; b. 1952. *Career:* an economist and a reformist communist, Nano became leader of the newly renamed Socialist Party of Albania (SPA—the former Communists) in June 1992. He occupied the post of Prime Minister of Albania in February–June 1991 and from July 1997 to September 1998. In June 1991 his resignation from the premiership was provoked by widespread unrest at the deteriorating economic situation, and in September 1998 he was forced out by armed supporters of the former President, Sali Berisha (q.v.), who brought two days of violence to the capital, Tirana. In July 1993 Nano was arrested, along with other former Communist leaders, on charges of financial impropriety, which the SPA claimed were politically motivated. He went on trial for these charges in March 1994 and, the following month, was found guilty and sentenced to 12 years' imprisonment. International human rights organizations denounced the charges against Nano as spurious, but failed to secure his release. He remained in prison until March 1997, when he was freed during that month's insurgency, and was subsequently granted an official pardon by Berisha. In January 1999 he resigned from the party chairmanship of the SPA, declaring his intention to withdraw from politics; however, he stood as a candidate in the SPA leadership contest in September, and was subsequently re-elected to the post. Following the victory of the SPA in the 2001 legislative elections, Nano demanded the resignation of particular government ministers, whom he accused of corruption. A number of ministers stepped down, and Nano's supporters proceeded to block the replacements proposed by the Prime Minister, Ilir Meta (q.v.). The resulting feud between Nano and Meta paralyzed the Government and resulted, in January 2002, in Meta's resignation, the latter claiming that he had been subject to 'irresponsible accusation and defamation' by Nano. Although Nano had been widely expected stand as the party's candidate for the presidency in 2002, the requirement that the two main political parties reached consensus on who was to stand, in fulfilment of European Union (EU) demands that Albania reduce polarization, precluded his candidacy. At the expiry of the mandate of the incumbent President, the SPA and the opposition Democratic Party of Albania reached consensus on the election of Alfred Moisiu (q.v.) to the presidency. On 25 July Moisiu appointed Nano as Prime Minister (replacing the Prime Minister designate, Pandeli Majko—q.v.), after the SPA General Steering Committee decided that the party Chairman should be Head of Government. Nano's new coalition Government surprisingly including Meta as Minister of Foreign Affairs, was approved at the end of July. He announced that the priorities of his Government were to combat trafficking and organized crime in Albania, to improve foreign relations, and, in particular, to expedite the country's accession to the EU. He was swiftly attacked by opposition figures, most notably by Berisha, who accused him of links with organized crime and of exercising undue influence on the media. Meta resigned in July 2003, claiming that Nano was exceedingly autocratic and was attempting to take control of the country's foreign affairs portfolio. The Minister for Integration, Sokol Nako, a close ally of Meta, also resigned. Nano swiftly appointed replacements, and denied that the Government was in crisis. *Address:* Office of the Council of Ministers, Këshilli i Ministrave, Tirana, Albania; tel. (4) 228210; fax (4) 227888.

NĂSTASE, Adrian: Prime Minister of Romania; b. 22 June 1950, in Bucharest; m. Daniela Miculescu in 1986, with two s. *Education:* studied at the University of Bucharest, achieving a law degree (1978), a Master's degree in sociology (1978) and a doctorate in international law (1987); he speaks English and French. *Career:* Trained in international law, he was one of the shrinking number of officials allowed to study abroad by the increasingly rigorous communist regime in the 1980s. His father-in-law, Angelo Miculescu, was a long-standing minister and ambassador under Nicolae Ceaușescu, which enabled Năstase to avoid the worst of communist-era privations. He became Minister of Foreign Affairs in June 1990 and tried to strengthen the country's image after regime-inspired violence against its opponents had brought much unwelcome publicity. From 1992 to 1996 he deputized for Ion Iliescu (q.v.) as head of the ruling party, while he served as Romania's President. He was also President of the Chamber of Deputies and it was his job to preserve the Government's slim parliamentary majority. From 1996 to 2000 he led the offensive of the Party of Social Democracy of Romania (PSDR) against the centre-right coalition in office. He spoke out strongly against Romania's support for military action by the North Atlantic Treaty Organization (NATO) in the Federal Republic of Yugoslavia (FRY) in 1999, and he was a stern critic of concessions made to the Hungarian minority. In the 2000 elections, he supervised the successful campaign of the PSDR and was invited by Iliescu, newly re-elected as President, to form a government. He formed a parliamentary alliance with the representatives of the Hungarian minority, which gave the PSDR a working majority and signified an end to the poor relations between the two formations. In January 2001 Năstase became the leader of the PSDR, and in June the party was renamed the Social Democratic Party (SDP). His government has benefited from improving economic indicators and increasingly close links with the EU and NATO. But his close links with the economic oligarchy that has flourished under the SDP, including members of the pre-1989 intelligence services, made him a contested figure. In March 2003 he attracted publicity by arriving in Belgrade for the funeral of the murdered Serbian premier, Zoran Djindjić, in bullet-proof clothing. Only under international pressure was the Government willing to pass laws designed to stem corruption and prevent a concentration of power in few hands. Năstase's wealth and penchant for collecting art made him an incongruous figure in a party mainly supported by the poorest sections of Romanian society. His relations with Iliescu suffered as he moved, perhaps over-hastily, to elevate the SDP's founder to a largely ceremonial position within the party. Iliescu sided with elements in the party and wider politics who wished to curb Năstase's ambitions. He was respected as a capable administrator, who got on well with European Union (EU) leaders, but it was by no means a foregone conclusion that he would succeed Iliescu as President in 2004, despite his party's strong lead in the polls. *Address:* Office of the Prime Minister, 71201 Bucharest, Piaţa Victoriei 1, Romania; tel. (21) 3131450; fax (21) 3122436; e-mail prim.ministru@guv.ro.

OLECHOWSKI, Andrzej: Polish politician; b. 9 Sept. 1947, in Kraków; m., with two s. *Education:* he studied at the Warsaw School of Planning and Statistics. *Career:* he worked as an economist for a number of international organizations, and became an adviser to the Governor of the central bank of Poland in 1987. He was appointed Deputy Governor of the central bank in 1989. He joined the Government in February 1992, when he was appointed Minister of Finance. However, he resigned three months later, stating that planned social-security reforms threatened the country's economic future. He was appointed an economic adviser to the President shortly afterwards. He returned to the Government, as Minister of Foreign Affairs, in 1993, serving until the collapse of the Government in March 1995. He re-entered politics in 2000, helping to form (but not actually joining) a new party, the Civic Platform, with the intention of contesting the impending presidential election. He drew his support chiefly from the middle classes, but proved more popular with the voters than other centre-right candidates. In the event, he received 17.3% of the votes cast, and finished in second place to the incumbent, Aleksander Kwaśniewski (q.v.). Olechowski formally joined the Civic Platform in 2003, and was reputedly considering a new challenge for the presidency in 2005. *Address:* 00113 Warsaw, ul. Emilii Plater 53, Poland.

ORBÁN, Viktor: former Prime Minister of Hungary; b. 31 May 1963, in Székesfehérvár; m., with four c. *Education:* Eötvös Loránd University, Budapest. *Career:* while employed as a sociologist at the Ministry of Agriculture and the Food Industry in 1988, he co-founded the Federation of Young Democrats (FYD) as a dissident youth group. Under his leadership, the group was transformed into a centrist political party. He was elected to parliament in the general election of 1990, and led the parliamentary FYD. After a poor result in the 1994 general election, Orbán presided over a rightward shift of the FYD's policies. Later that year he was appointed Chair of the Parliamentary Committee on European Integration Affairs. In 1995 the party changed its name to the Federation of Young Democrats—Hungarian Civic Party (FYD—HCP). Following a substantial increase in support in the general election held in May 1998, the FYD—HCP, which won 147 of the 386 seats, was able to form a coalition with the Independent Smallholders' and Peasants' Party (ISPP), which obtained 48 seats, and the Hungarian Democratic Forum (HDF), which secured 18 seats. In June Orbán was appointed Prime Minister. The financial markets reacted adversely to the new Government, believing that the inexperience of the FYD—HCP and the nationalism of the ISPP would impede foreign investment and detract from the progress made under the previous administration. By 2000, however, foreign investment had increased and economic growth was healthy. In addition, Hungary acceded to the North Atlantic Treaty Organization (NATO) in March 1999, with Orbán's administration gaining credit internationally for its role in NATO's operation in the Federal Republic of Yugoslavia in the same year. Orbán also managed to guide Hungary through the effects of the 1998 economic crisis in Russia, forestalling the collapse of several banks. In February 2000 he resigned as Chairman of the FYD—HCP to concentrate on his role as Prime Minister. In late 2001 the FYD—HCP formed an electoral alliance with the HDF, deputies from the Independent Smallholders' and Civic Party (ISCP, as the ISPP had been renamed), and the ethnic Roma Lungo Drom Alliance, in preparation for the 2002 general election. As the election approached, Orbán's rhetoric—and actions—became increasingly nationalistic. In June 2001 the National Assembly passed a 'Status' or 'Benefit' Law granting ethnic Hungarians living in adjacent countries education, employment and medical rights in Hungary. The law appeared designed to draw votes away from the extreme-right Hungarian Justice and Life Party (HJLP), led by István Csurka. Orbán's demand for the repeal of the Beneš Decrees—under which Hungarians, and many Germans, were expelled from Czechoslovakia and had their property confiscated after the Second World War—was, likewise, widely regarded as a deliberately controversial, populist measure. The Prime Minister's skill as an orator, and his telegenic, charismatic qualities, continued to ensure a high degree of popularity among the electorate. However, in the first round of the election of April 2002 the FYD—HCP obtained 40.3% of the votes cast, compared with the 41.2% of the votes secured by the Hungarian Socialist Party (HSP). Government supporters held a huge rally prior to the second round, in which the FYD—HCP obtained 48.7% of the votes cast, compared with the HSP's 46.1%. Lacking coalition partners to secure a majority in the National Assembly, the FYD—HCP was eventually obliged to cede power to an alliance of the HSP and the Alliance of Free Democrats. Following Orbán's defeat, an estimated 500,000 people gathered in Budapest to demonstrate their support for him. Relations with the new Government remained uncomfortable, and Orbán was not permitted to have an office in parliament. He subsequently formed a new coalition of opposition forces, 'Alliance for the Nation', also popularly known as 'Go Hungary!'. He was among the most prominent of those who urged the Prime Minister, Péter Medgyessy (q.v.), to resign, following revelations of his employment by the secret service in the communist era. Although somewhat isolated by the main parties, Orbán remained an important public figure. *Address:* c/o National Assembly, 1055 Budapest, Kossuth Lajos tér 1–3, Hungary; tel. (1) 441-4000; fax (1) 441-5000.

PAKSAS, Rolandas: President of Lithuania; b. 10 June 1956, in Telsiai; m., with two c. *Education:* Vilnius Institute of Higher Engineering and Leningrad Institute of Civil Aviation. *Career:* he was a flight instructor for much of his early career, as well as serving in the Voluntary National Defence Service. In 1992–97 he was President of the construction company Restako, and in 1997 was elected as Mayor of Vilnius. In May 1999 he became Prime Minister and also adviser for special tasks to the President. However, he resigned in late October of that year, after the Council of Ministers approved the divestment of the Mažeikiai NAFTA petroleum refinery to a US company, on unfavourable terms. Amid political disagreements, he also resigned from the Conservative Party of Lithuania in mid-November 1999, and in early December was elected Chairman of the Lithuanian Liberal Union. Following the legislative election in October 2000, Paksas was again nominated as Prime Minister, leading a coalition Government of the Lithuanian Liberal Union and the New Union (Social Liberals). However, the Government was beset by problems, with a fundamental policy conflict between the coalition parties. The divisions consistently frustrated Paksas in his efforts to implement reform and accelerate privatization. In June the New Union demanded Paksas' resignation and, following his refusal, six New Union cabinet members resigned. Paksas finally tendered his resignation, in an unsuccessful attempt to preserve the coalition. Algirdas Brazauskas (q.v.) was appointed his successor and Paksas became leader of the parliamentary opposition. Paksas resigned as Chairman of the Lithuanian Liberal Union in September 2001, after losing the support of the party. With 10 other party deputies, he left the parliamentary faction of the Liberal Union in late December, after indications that it was not prepared to support him in a bid for the presidency in 2002. Paksas and the other deputies were formally expelled in January 2002, and in March they formed a new party, the Party of Lithuanian Liberal Democrats (PLLD). Paksas was elected to the presidency in January 2003, defeating Valdus Adamkus (q.v.) in a second round of voting. *Address:* Office of the President, S. Daukanto 3/8, Vilnius, Lithuania; tel. (526) 28986; fax (521) 26210.

PAPANDREOU, Georgios: Minister of Foreign Affairs of Greece; b. 16 June 1952, in St Paul, MN, USA; m. Ada, with one s. and one d. *Education:* studied at Amherst College, Maryland, the USA, the University of Stockholm, Sweden, and the London School of Economics, the United Kingdom. *Career:* he entered Parliament as a deputy for the Panhellenic Socialist Movement (PASOK) in 1981; following the general election, his father, Andreas, formed Greece's first socialist Government. Papandreou became a member of the Central Committee of PASOK in 1984 and was appointed Minister of Education and Religious Affairs in 1988. Upon PASOK's return to power in 1993, still led by his father, he was appointed Deputy Minister of Foreign Affairs. Having been born in the USA, he was seen as potentially able to attract US support for Greek policies. He remained in this post after his father's deteriorating health caused him to resign the premiership in 1996. The new Prime Minister, Konstantinos Simitis (q.v.), valued his good relations with the USA and in February 1999, after the resignation of the Minister of Foreign Affairs, Theodoros Pangalos, Papandreou was appointed to the vacant position. He was forthright in his criticism of the North Atlantic Treaty Organization's military intervention in the conflict in the Federal Republic of Yugoslavia in March–June 1999. His policy of *rapprochement* with Greece's historic rival, Turkey, extended to support for Turkey's candidacy to membership of the European Union (EU); in January 2000 he became the first Greek Minister of Foreign Affairs to visit Turkey since 1962. With occasional reverses, often relating to the issue of the potential accession of Cyprus to the EU, relations between the two countries were strengthened thereafter, and co-operation agreements signed relating to a range of subjects. The possibility of the reunification of Cyprus encouraged this process. Papandreou retained the foreign affairs portfolio, despite a number of government reshuffles, and it was clear that Simitis valued his expertise in this area. *Address:* Ministry of Foreign Affairs, Odos Akadimias 1, 106 71 Athens, Greece; tel. (21) 03681000; fax (21) 03624195; e-mail mfa@mfa.gr.

PAPANTONIOU, Ioannis: Minister of National Defence of Greece; b. 1949; two s. and one d. *Education:* Universities of Athens, Wisconsin, the USA, Paris, France, and Cambridge, the United Kingdom. *Career:* he lectured at the Department of Economics at the University of Athens and worked as a researcher at the Centre of Planning and Economic Research

in 1977–78. In 1978–81 he worked at the Organisation for Economic Co-operation and Development (OECD) in Paris, and subsequently served as a Panhellenic Socialist Movement (PASOK) member of the European Parliament in 1981–84. After working as a special adviser to the Prime Minister on European Community Affairs, he served as Deputy Minister for the National Economy in 1985–89, briefly as Minister of Trade in 1989, and from 1989 as a member of Parliament. He assumed the national economy and finance portfolios in 1994, where he was credited with curbing spending and reducing the bloated state sector. He retained the positions after the general election of April 2000, but in a cabinet reshuffle in October 2001 was moved to the Ministry of National Defence, replacing Akis Tsohatzopoulos (q.v.), regarded as the main party rival of the Prime Minister, Konstantinos Simitis (q.v.). Papantoniou was expected to prioritize streamlining the Government's significant expenditure on defence and was also responsible for security issues relating to the Olympic Games, which were due to be held in Athens in 2004. In March 2003 reports of a rift in the cabinet between Papantoniou and his successor as Minister of Finance, Nikolaos Christodoulakis (q.v.) were strongly denied. *Address:* Ministry of National Defence, Mesogion Pentagono, Athens, Greece; tel. (21) 06555911; fax (21) 06443832; e-mail epyetha@mod.gr.

PARAVAĆ, Borislav: member of the state Presidency of Bosnia and Herzegovina; b. 18 February 1943; ethnic Serb; m., with two c. *Education:* he studied economics at the University of Zagreb. *Career:* he worked as an accountant, auditor and company manager, becoming a local councillor in the 1980s and Mayor of Doboj in 1990. Representing the Serbian Democratic Party (SDP), he was elected to the National Assembly of the Bosnian Serb Republic (Republika Srpska) in 1996. Upon his election to the Bosnia and Herzegovina House of Representatives in October 2002 he became a deputy chairman of that chamber. He was nominated by the SDP to the Serb position in the three-member Presidency in April 2003, following the resignation of Mirko Sarović. As the ethnic Serb member of the presidency held the chairmanship at the time of his election, Paravać assumed that post until June, when it passed to the Croat member, Dragan Čović (q.v.). Paravać was considered a determined Bosnian Serb nationalist, and opponents immediately began speculation as to his role during the conflict in the country. His perceived hostility towards the media caused controversy in his first days in the Presidency. His stated aim was for the country to concentrate on the future—to this end, he urged the settlement of a minor border dispute with Croatia, and an end to a number of international law suits between the countries of the former Yugoslavia. *Address:* 71000 Sarajevo, Musala 5, Bosnia and Herzegovina; tel. (33) 664941; fax (33) 472491.

PARTS, Juhan: Prime Minister of Estonia; b. 27 Aug. 1966, in Tallinn; divorced, with one s. and one d. *Education:* he graduated in law from the University of Tartu. *Career:* he worked in the Ministry of Justice, and was active in the development of the newly independent Estonia's legal and judicial systems. In 1998 he was appointed Auditor General, and attracted public attention by urging the dismissal of numerous ministers when financial irregularities were discovered. The European Union (EU) audit committee praised the transparency and thoroughness of the regime he established. He resigned in May 2002 and became a member of Res Publica, which had been founded as a political club as long ago as 1989, but had only recently re-emerged as a centre-right, pro-business political party. He immediately announced his intention to stand for the party leadership, and was elected to the post in August (in October he was formally censured by parliament for leaving his previous position before the expiry of his term of office, and for taking up a role in politics before he had officially left the position). Res Publica swiftly attracted support throughout the country, and at the general election held in March 2003 won 28 seats in the 101-seat Riigikogu (parliament), the same number as the Estonian Centre Party (ECP), although the latter party won a slightly greater percentage of the votes cast. The leader of the ECP, Edgar Savisaar (q.v.), was consequently asked to form a new government, but coalition negotiations between Res Publica and a number of other parties were already well advanced, and Savisaar realized he had little alternative but to cede the opportunity to Parts. Following protracted negotiations, a three-party coalition, controlling 60 seats, was agreed, and Parts' Government was confirmed in office in early April. He saw his primary task as leading Estonia into the EU (a referendum on membership was scheduled for September). *Address:* Office of the Prime Minister, Tallinn 15161, Rahukohtu 3, Estonia; tel. 631-6701; fax 631-6704; e-mail peaminister@rk.ee; internet www.riik.ee/primeminister.

PARVANOV, Georgi (Sedefchov): President of Bulgaria; b. 28 June 1957, in Sirishtnik; m. Zorka Parvanova. *Education:* studied history. *Career:* he replaced Zhan Videnov as Chairman of the Bulgarian Socialist Party (BSP—previously the Bulgarian Communist Party—BCP) after Videnov unexpectedly resigned as party leader and Prime Minister in December 1996. In 1997, amid intensifying street protests against the BSP Government, Parvanov went against a party ruling and refused an offer to form a new administration. He gained widespread respect for this action, which defused the political situation but moved the party into opposition. Parvanov gradually steered the BSP in the direction of social democracy, managing to avoid alienating older members of the party. In May 1998 he was re-elected Chairman of the party, with 58% of the votes cast. In November 2001, after a colourful campaign with a focus on social issues, he gained 36.4% of the votes cast in the first round of the presidential election, while the incumbent, Petar Stoyanov, secured 34.9%. In the second round Parvanov confirmed his lead, obtaining 51.4% of the votes cast. The result was somewhat unexpected, given the electorate's rejection of the BSP in the legislative election held in June that year, and appeared to reflect both public disillusionment (the rate of participation was extremely low) and a desire for change. Parvanov, who was inaugurated as President on 19 January 2002, pledged his commitment to gaining admission to both the North Atlantic Treaty Organization (NATO) and the European Union (EU). Although Parvanov was considered well able to compromise, some observers expressed concern as to whether the former communist would be able to work successfully with the Prime Minister and former Tsar, Simeon Saxe-Coburg Gotha (q.v.), and his National Movement Simeon II-led Government. These fears appeared to be justified in early 2003 when Parvanov first vetoed legislation that would have excluded certain privatizations from judicial investigation, then publicly disagreed with the Government's decision to support the US-led intervention in Iraq. *Address:* Office of the President, Blvd Dondukov 2, 1123 Sofia, Bulgaria; tel. (2) 923-93-33; e-mail press@president.bg.

PAULAUSKAS, Artūras: Lithuanian politician; b. 1954; m. Jolanta Paulauskiene, with two s. and one d. *Education:* Vilnius State University. *Career:* having trained as a lawyer, he served as Prosecutor-General in the communist era and continued in that office thereafter, gaining much recognition for his efforts to combat organized crime. Following the decision by Algirdas Brazauskas (q.v.) not to stand for a second term in the presidency, he was the main opponent of Valdas Adamkus (q.v.) in the election of 1997–98. Opinion polls consistently presented him as the favoured candidate, and he appeared comfortably in the lead in the first round of voting, obtaining 45.28% of the votes cast. Vytautas Landsbergis, defeated in the first round, announced his support for him. However, he was narrowly beaten in the second round in January 1998, securing 49.63% of the votes cast, to Adamkus' 50.37%. In late April 1998 Paulauskas founded a new, left-wing political party, the New Union. The party aimed to promote a spirit of co-operation and active public participation in politics, especially by young people. It enjoyed an increase in popularity in 2000 as voters became disenchanted with older parties, and secured enough votes to form a coalition Government with the Lithuanian Liberal Union in the legislative election held in October. Paulauskas was subsequently elected Chairman of the Seimas. However, in June 2001, as divisions between the coalition parties worsened, the New Union withdrew from the Government, which collapsed. The Union subsequently entered into co-operation with the new

Social Democratic Government led by Brazauskas. Paulauskas contested the presidency in December 2002, but obtained only 8.3% of the votes cast in the first round of voting; some observers believed his popularity to have been weakened by his party's performance in government, and there was also a sense that he had changed loyalties too frequently to engender trust. *Address:* New Union (Social Liberals), Gedimino pr. 10/1, Vilnius 2001, Lithuania; tel. (521) 07600; fax (521) 07602; e-mail centras@nsajunga.lt.

PETKOV, Prof. Dr Krustyu: Bulgarian trade union leader; b. 18 Nov. 1943, in Dimovo, Vidin region; m., with two c. *Education:* educated as an economist, he has a doctorate. *Career:* a professor of labour sociology, he was involved in the official trade union movement of communist Bulgaria. He led the communist-dominated Bulgarian Professional Union in its renunciation of any political affiliation and, in February 1990, its transformation into the Confederation of Independent Trade Unions in Bulgaria, of which he became Chairman. It remained the largest trade union body in the country. Petkov headed the United Labour Bloc (ULB), a political party established in 1997. The ULB was one of 15 left and left-of-centre parties to contest the legislative election of June 2001 as part of the Bulgarian Socialist Party-led Coalition for Bulgaria. *Address:* Confederation of Independent Trade Unions in Bulgaria, 1040 Sofia, Blvd Makedonia 1, Bulgaria; tel. (2) 917-04-79; fax (2) 988-59-69.

PICULA, Tonino: Minister of Foreign Affairs of Croatia; b. 31 Aug. 1961, in Mali Lošinj. *Education:* he studied sociology at the University of Zagreb. *Career:* a participant in the civil war of the early 1990s, following Croatia's secession from Yugoslavia, he has been professionally involved in politics since 1989 (he had previously worked in publishing). He became the International Secretary of the Social Democratic Party (SDP), the successor party to the League of Communists, in 1993 and in 1997 was elected SDP councillor in the Zagreb County Assembly. In January 2000 he was elected to the lower house of parliament and was appointed Minister of Foreign Affairs in the new coalition Government of Ivica Račan (q.v.). On taking office, he affirmed the country's commitment to the Dayton accords and said that improving relations with Bosnia and Herzegovina was a priority. He declared Croatia ready to co-operate with the International Criminal Tribunal for the former Yugoslavia (ICTY, based in The Hague, the Netherlands), and said that Croatian courts should make renewed efforts to deal with war crimes suspects. These issues, and the negotiations regarding Croatia's possible accession to the European Union, were the principal matters of concern during his first three years in government. *Address:* Ministry of Foreign Affairs, 10000 Zagreb, trg Nikole Šubića Zrinskog 7–8; Croatia; tel. (1) 4569964; fax (1) 4569977; e-mail mvp@mvp.hr.

PLAVŠIĆ, Prof. Biljana: Bosnian politician and former President of the Serb Republic of Bosnia and Herzegovina; b. 1930, in Tuzla; ethnic Serb. *Education:* studied biochemistry in the USA. *Career:* she held the post of faculty dean at the University of Sarajevo before embarking on a political career. She was elected to the collective rotating state Presidency in November 1991, but left the all-Bosnian Government at the beginning of the civil war to help form the 'Serb Republic of Bosnia and Herzegovina'. During the Bosnian war (1992–95) she served as co-Vice President of the Serb Republic and was strongly in favour of expelling all Bosniaks from eastern Bosnia. Known as the 'Iron Lady of the Bosnian Serbs', she was reported to hold even more extreme nationalist views than her leader, Radovan Karadžić (q.v.), and regarded herself as the epitome of the qualities of the *Velka Srpkinja* (Greater Serbian Women) group. She was effectively banned from Serbia (Yugoslavia) after 1993, when she campaigned against a peace settlement for Bosnia and Herzegovina that the Serbian President, Slobodan Milošević (q.v.), had personally endorsed. She was seen as Karadžić's heir and was granted some of his powers, including responsibility for negotiations with the international community, in May 1996, and named as acting President in July. In September she was elected President of the Serb Republic. She was expected to rule in accordance with Karadžić's wishes, but instead

Plavšić, a shrewd opportunist and pragmatist, adopted increasingly moderate policies, in order to gain Western approval for her regime (and, thus, the legitimacy that would precede aid). Alleging corruption, she began to dismiss allies of Karadžić. During 1997 a bitter power struggle developed between the two leaders. In this she was opposed by the entity's National Assembly, which was dominated by those loyal to Karadžić, but she enjoyed the support of the international community, which regarded her as the lesser of two evils. Following her expulsion from Karadžić's Serb Democratic Party (SDP) in July, she formed the Serb National Alliance (SNA), which was represented in the coalition Government formed following elections in November. Her appointment of the moderate reformer, Milorad Dodik, as premier confirmed her pro-Western stance. However, she was defeated by the nationalist candidate in the presidential election of September 1998. In May 2000 she tendered her resignation as SNA Chairman, following disagreements with the main committee, although she remained party leader. In January 2001 Plavšić unexpectedly surrendered to the International Criminal Tribunal for the former Yugoslavia (ICTY—in The Hague, the Netherlands), after having learned of the existence of an indictment issued against her in April 2000. The first woman to be indicted by the Tribunal, she subsequently pleaded not guilty to a number of charges, which included genocide and crimes against humanity. The ICTY granted her provisional release in August, pending her trial, she lived in Belgrade under the surveillance and protection of the Yugoslav police. Upon the resumption of her trial she pleaded guilty to one charge of crimes against humanity, while the remaining seven charges were dropped. Plavšić's legal representatives denied speculation that she had agreed to testify in any other cases before the ICTY. In February 2003 she was sentenced to 11 years' imprisonment, the Tribunal accepting that there were strong mitigating factors, including her age, guilty plea, and testimony as to her involvement in the negotiation of the Dayton Peace Accords made by the former US Secretary of State, Madeleine Albright. She began her sentence in a Swedish prison in June, following that country's agreement to be responsible for her detention. Although she was the highest-profile figure to have been convicted at the ICTY, and had been closely linked to other indictees, the implications for other cases remained unclear.

POL, Marek: Deputy Prime Minister of Poland; b. 8 Dec. 1953, in Słupsk; m., with one s. and one d. *Education:* studied mechanical engineering at the Poznań Polytechnic and Economics at the Poznań Academy of Economics. *Career:* he began work at the Agricultural Vehicle Factory in Antoninek, rising to the position of Deputy Director for Financial and Commercial Affairs and carrying out the privatization of the factory. He remained professionally associated with the motor industry. One of the founding members of the Union of Labour (UP) in 1993, Pol was elected Chairman in 1998. In October 1993 he entered the cabinet as Minister of Industry and Trade in the administration led by Waldemar Pawlak. He remained in this position until 1995, when he assumed responsibility for reform of the central economic administrations in the cabinets of two successive Prime Ministers, Józef Oleksy and Włodzimierz Cimoszewicz. In the legislative election of September 2001 the UP, in coalition with the Democratic Left Alliance (SLD), obtained 216 seats in the Sejm, with 41% of the votes. To secure a majority in parliament, the two parties signed a coalition agreement with the Polish People's Party (PSL). Pol was appointed Deputy Prime Minister and Minister of Infrastructure, under Leszek Miller (q.v.); as Minister of Infrastructure, he also controlled issues of communications and regional policy in the country. His plans to introduce road pricing led to a vote of 'no confidence' in him in September 2002, which was defeated. After the withdrawal of the PSL from the coalition in March 2003 another motion of 'no confidence' in Pol was put before the Sejm—this too was defeated. His enthusiasm for road pricing continued to be a point of contention between him and Miller, but he remained a keen member of the Government. *Address:* Union of Labour (Unia Pracy—UP), 00-513 Warsaw, Nowogrodzka 4, Poland; tel. and fax (22) 6256776; e-mail biuro@uniapracy.org.pl.

RAČAN, Ivica: Prime Minister of Croatia; b. 24 Feb. 1944, in Ebersbach, Germany. *Education:* University of Zagreb. *Career:* he became a member of the presidency of the Central Committee of the League of Communists of Croatia (LCC) in 1972, and of its federal equivalent in 1986. From 1982 to 1986 he was director of the Josip Broz Tito political school and editor of *Kumoreèki Zapisi*. In 1989, as President of the Central Committee of the LCC and a firm advocate of political pluralism, he announced the holding of the first democratic multi-party elections in Croatia. At the same time, following a confrontation with Serbian leader Slobodan Milošević (q.v.), he withdrew the LCC from a federal congress. In 1990 he was elected to the Croatian House of Representatives, where he reformed the LCC and renamed it, firstly as the Party of Democratic Change, and then, finally, as the Social Democratic Party (SDP) in 1991. In 1992 and 1995 he was re-elected to the legislature. In the late 1990s he developed the SDP into a strong opposition to the ruling Croatian Democratic Union (CDU). In 1998 he signed a coalition agreement with the President of the Croatian Social Liberal Party (CSLP), Dražen Budiša (q.v.), for the 2000 legislative election. In January 2000 this coalition, comprising the SDP, CSLP and four smaller parties, gained a majority of seats in the House of Representatives and, on 27 January, Račan was appointed Prime Minister. Račan's Government proved slow to institute economic reforms, principally owing to a lack of experience and to administrative inefficiency. In May 2001, however, he announced that Croatia was to sign a Stabilization and Association Agreement with the European Union (EU), as the first move towards full membership of the organization (the agreement was ratified by parliament in December). In July his Government won a motion of confidence, after four CSLP ministers resigned in protest at a decision to extradite two war crimes suspects to the International Criminal Tribunal for the former Yugoslavia (ICTY, based in The Hague, the Netherlands). At the same time, a statement reaffirming his policy of co-operation with the ICTY was approved. The four CSLP ministers rejoined Parliament, while Budiša, who continued strenuously to oppose extradition, resigned from the leadership of the CSLP. The question continued to cause difficulties in the country; a demonstration organized by war veterans in October demanded Račan's resignation. In February 2002 Budiša, by this time re-elected to the party leadership, removed the First Deputy Prime Minister, Goran Granić, and two other CSLP ministers from the Government, apparently for failing to support his stance of continued opposition to co-operation with the ICTY. In a bid to avert the collapse of his Government, Račan appointed Budiša First Deputy Prime Minister on 21 March. In early July, however, Budiša finally withdrew the CSLP from the government coalition, after an agreement on joint ownership of a nuclear power installation in Slovenia was ratified in the legislature, despite the opposition of the CSLP. Račan subsequently resigned, following the collapse of his administration. He was returned to the office of Prime Minister later that month, after his reappointment was supported in the legislature and, following agreement with the leaders of the other political parties belonging to the ruling coalition, a new Council of Ministers was established at the end of July. Following the installation of his new Government, Račan declared the necessity of introducing unpopular economic reforms. He strongly favoured Croatia's eventual accession to the European Union, overseeing the country's formal application for membership in February 2003, and continued to urge full co-operation with the ICTY. *Address:* Office of the Prime Minister, 10000 Zagreb, trg sv. Marka 2, Croatia; tel. (1) 4569201; fax (1) 432041.

REPŠE, Einārs: Prime Minister of Latvia; b. 9 Dec. 1961, in Jelgava; m. Diana Vagale 1988 (divorced), with two s. and one d. *Education:* graduated in physics from the University of Latvia. *Career:* he helped to form the Latvian independence movement in the late 1980s and was elected to the Supreme Council in 1990. Having taught himself economics, he became a member of the parliamentary Economics Commission. In September 1991 he was appointed Governor of the Bank of Latvia. He was credited with the smooth transition of the

Latvian economy from a Soviet centrally planned structure to a successful product of monetary reform. By the mid-1990s the country was enjoying relative economic stability. In August 1995 Repše survived a vote of 'no confidence' in the Saeima (legislature), following a crisis in the banking sector. Continuing with a restrictive monetary policy, he succeeded in maintaining economic stability and in strengthening the currency. In 1997 he was reappointed Governor for a second six-year term. Perceived as an astute economist capable of surviving political turmoil, he continued to command great respect internationally and significant domestic popular approval. In November 2001, one year before his term of office was due to expire, he resigned the governorship to found a new political party, New Era. The centre-right party attracted immediate popular support, despite a delay in declaring its policy objectives. Repše was elected Chairman at the party's founding congress in early February 2002. He stressed that he wanted New Era to appeal to those who had not previously been politically active. The party was to be based on the principles of honesty, professionalism and openness, and would promote social welfare and freedom, while aiming to reduce bureaucracy and corruption. The Prime Minister, Andris Bērziņš (q.v.), welcomed Repše's return to politics, and said he hoped the move would support the development of the centre-right in Latvia. However, New Era swiftly gained widespread support, largely at the expense of his own Latvian Way, and at the legislative election of October 2002 New Era became the largest group in the Saemia, with 26 seats. Repše was invited to form a government, and took office as Prime Minister in November, having agreed a coalition with three other parties. He pledged to build on the good works of his predecessors and produce better results through his own policies where the other administrations had failed. However, by mid-2003 his Government was attracting criticism over its perceived lack of acheivement and ambition. In June a motion of 'no confidence' in the Government brought by the People's Party was easily defeated. *Address:* Office of the Prime Minister, Brīvības bulv. 36, Rīga 1050, Latvia.

RIMŠĒVIČS, Ilmārs: Governor of the Bank of Latvia; b. 30 April 1965, in Rīga. *Education:* studied economics and international trade relations at Rīga Technical University; carried out further studies at St Lawrence University (USA) and received an MBA from Clarkson University (USA). *Career:* he served as Deputy Chairman of the Economics Committee of the Popular Front of Latvia (PFL) in 1989–90, during which time he worked on the economic crisis and monetary reform programmes that would transform Latvia into a market economy. In 1990–92 he was Manager of the Foreign Operations Department and Head of the Securities Department at Latvijas Zemen Banka (a commercial bank). In mid-1992 he was appointed Deputy Governor of the Bank of Latvia and Chairman of the Executive Board. His term as Deputy Governor was renewed in 1998. After the resignation of the Governor, Einārs Repše (q.v.), in November 2001 to form a new political party, Rimšēvičs—Repše's nominated successor—was appointed Governor on 20 December, for a six-year term. Like his predecessor, he was committed to the maintenance of a tight monetary policy and macroeconomic stability, the continuation of structural reforms and improvements to the country's investment environment. He retained this view after Repše's election to the premiership, expressing concern as to the Government's budgetary policy on several occasions in 2003. *Address:* Bank of Latvia, K. Valdemāra iela 2a, Rīga 1050; tel. 702-2300; fax 702-2420; e-mail info@bank .lv.

ROP, Anton: Prime Minister of Slovenia; b. 27 December 1960, in Ljubljana. *Education:* he studied economics at the University of Ljubljana. *Career:* he worked as an economist, becoming an adviser on privatization to the Government of Slovenia in 1992. The following year he was appointed State Secretary at the Ministry of Economic Relations and Development, charged with overseeing the privatization process. In 1996 he became Minister of Labour, Family and Social Affairs, and held that portfolio until the general election held in late 2000. Following the return to office of the Prime Minister, Janez Drnovšek (q.v.), Rop was appointed Minister of

Finance. Drnovšek was successful in his campaign to be elected President in late 2002, and made it known that Rop was his preferred successor. He was confirmed in the premiership by parliament in December 2002. As Prime Minister, he maintained his focus on economic affairs, aiming to ensure that Slovenia's economy was prepared for entry into the European Union, scheduled for 2004. Indeed, he attracted criticism from some quarters for concentrating too fully on this issue, leaving all others aside. *Address:* Office of the Prime Minister, 1000 Ljubljana, Gregorčičeva 20, Slovenia; tel. (1) 4781000; fax (1) 4781607; e-mail gp.upv@gov.si; internet www.sigov.si/pv.

RUGOVA, Dr Ibrahim: Serbian and Montenegrin (Serbian/Kosovan) politician; b. in 1944, in Kosovo (now Kosovo and Metohija), Serbia; ethnic Albanian. *Education:* studied linguistics at the Sorbonne University, Paris (France). *Career:* a prominent dissident writer, and Professor of Albanian literature, he consistently championed the rights of the ethnic Albanian (Kosovar) population. In 1990 he founded and became leader of the Democratic Alliance of Kosovo (DAK), which became the mass party of the ethnic Albanians after its effective takeover of the provincial Socialist Alliance of Working People. Rugova led the boycott of the 1990 constitutional referendum and election. He supported the creation of Kosovo as the ethnic Albanian 'home' republic, in the Yugoslav federation, although union with Albania had considerable support in the province. On 24 May 1992 he was elected President of the self-proclaimed 'Republic of Kosovo' and his party gained the most seats in an Assembly declared illegitimate by the Serbian authorities. In spite of a lack of recognition of the 'shadow state' by the international community throughout the mid-1990s, he remained committed to the idea of Kosovan autonomy through peaceful means. The Kosovar Albanians refused to participate in federal and republican elections from 1996. Following the rise in popularity of the Kosovo Liberation Army (KLA), which advocated separatism for Kosovo through armed resistance, and the subsequent outbreak of armed conflict in the region in 1998, Rugova's authority in Kosovo declined slightly. Nevertheless, in March 1998 he was re-elected President of the 'Republic of Kosovo', obtaining more than 90% of the votes cast. The Serbian authorities declared the election illegal, and his attempt, later in the year, to convene a parliament, was broken up by the police. However, in April the Serbian administration agreed to hold discussions with his 'Government'. Rugova at first refused, but later met the federal President, Slobodan Milošević (q.v.), to open negotiations between the two sides. The US-brokered peace plan for the region, accepted by the Yugoslav authorities in October, after much international mediation, was condemned by Rugova. In 1999 the ethnic conflict escalated further, with ethnic Albanians generally favouring the radical KLA above Rugova's DAK. In March Rugova agreed to the peace proposals, which were, however, rejected by Milošević. During the subsequent aerial bombardment of the Federal Republic of Yugoslavia (FRY), Rugova met Milošević, in a televised encounter that provoked intense criticism in Kosovo. Rugova subsequently removed to Rome (Italy), where he remained until the bombardment ended. He returned once a peace agreement had been enforced and participated in the creation of an Interim Administrative Council (IAC), which gave a degree of autonomy to the province, in December 1999. In February 2000 the 'Republic of Kosovo' was dissolved and Rugova established the Democratic League of Kosovo (DLK) as a successor organization to the DAK. In May 2001 the UN Interim Administration Mission in Kosovo (UNMIK), established in June 1999, presented a plan granting provisional self-government for Kosovo, and announced that elections to a legislative assembly would take place in the province on 17 November 2001. Rugova's DLK secured 47 of the 100 seats under contest in the Kosovo Assembly in these polls. Repeated attempts to elect Rugova as President proved unsuccessful, as other parties boycotted the votes, but in early March 2002, after lengthy discussions, he finally achieved the presidency, after agreeing that a member of the rival Democratic Party of Kosovo (DPK), Bajram Rexhepi, would become Prime Minister. A 10-member Cabinet was subsequently established. Rugova said that his Government would work towards the creation of a 'free, democratic, peaceful, prosperous and independent Kosovo'. The integration of all ethnic groups into political and economic life was recognized as a principal objective. However, ultimate executive authority was retained by the head of UNMIK, who also continued to exert control over the province's finances and judiciary. Rugova appeared as an early witness at the trial of Milošević at the International Criminal Tribunal for the former Yugoslavia (ICTY, in The Hague, the Netherlands) in May 2002, where the two exchanged accusations relating to the Kosovo conflict. The following month he was re-elected to his party's leadership. He was involved in a car accident in December 2002, but was unhurt. In early 2003 he restated his opposition to direct bilateral negotiations with the authorities. In mid-2003 he urged displaced ethnic Serbs to return to their homes in Kosovo, although many doubted the sincerity (and the potential effectiveness) of the request. *Address:* Democratic League of Kosovo, Priština, Serbia and Montenegro.

RUPEL, Dr Dimitrij: Minister of Foreign Affairs of Slovenia; b. 7 April 1946, in Ljubljana; m. *Education:* he studied world literature and sociology at Ljubljana University (with one year at the University of Essex, United Kingdom) and obtained a doctorate in sociology at Brandeis University (Massachusetts, USA); he speaks English, German, Italian and French. *Career:* he worked as a journalist, translator and editor—and as an academic in Canada and the USA, as well as Slovenia—and was considered a dissident for his criticism of the communist regime. In 1987 he founded and edited the political journal *Nova Revija*. He established the opposition Slovenian Democratic Party in 1989, and became Minister of Foreign Affairs in the first elected Government in 1990, remaining in this position until 1993. At the end of 1994 he was elected Mayor of Ljubljana, where he served until being appointed ambassador to the USA in 1997. He returned to Slovenia in early 2000, to assume the post of Minister of Foreign Affairs under Janez Drnovšek (q.v.), resuming the post in the new Government led by Drnovšek in December 2000. He made clear his desire to forge links with the most advanced countries and organizations, in order to bolster Slovenia's international and regional position. Rupel played an important role in negotiations regarding Slovenian accession to the European Union and the North Atlantic Treaty Organization, and was popular both within Slovenia and among the international community. *Address:* Ministry of Foreign Affairs, 1000 Ljubljana, Prešernova 25, Slovenia; tel. (1) 4782294; fax (1) 4782340; e-mail info.mzz@gov.si.

RÜÜTEL, Arnold: President of Estonia; b. 10 May 1928, in Saaremaa; m. Ingrid Rüütel in 1958, with two d. *Education:* trained as an agronomist at the Estonian Agricultural Academy, of which he later was Rector. *Career:* before entering politics he was a senior agronomist in Estonia. In 1964 he joined the Communist Party, becoming First Deputy Chairman of the Estonian SSR Council of Ministers in 1979, Chairman of the Estonian Supreme Soviet in 1983 and Deputy Chairman of the all-Union Supreme Soviet in 1984. Following Estonia's denunciation of Soviet authority in 1990, Rüütel became Chairman of the Supreme Council of Estonia, as the Supreme Soviet had been renamed. In September 1992 he stood as a presidential candidate, polling 42.2% of the valid votes cast, but was passed over in favour of Lennart Meri (q.v.) by the Riigikogu (as the Supreme Council had been renamed), when no candidate secured an overall majority of the ballot. In 1994 he formed the Estonian Country People's Party, which established an alliance, the Rural Union, with other agrarian parties to contest the parliamentary election of March 1995. The Rural Union, allied with the Estonian Coalition Party (ECP), won the largest number of seats in the legislature and subsequently formed a Government. It was also involved in the three coalition Governments formed in 1995–98. Rüütel was elected Deputy Speaker of the Riigikogu following the election of March 1995, before resigning the position to contest the presidential election held in 1996. In the election Rüütel was again President Meri's strongest contender, preventing the incumbent from winning the necessary two-thirds' majority, even after three rounds of voting in August. How-

ever, in the second round of voting in a larger electoral college in September, Meri was successful; Rüütel won 126 votes. In 2000 the Rural Union merged with the Estonian Pensioners' and Families' Party to form the Estonian People's Union, of which Rüütel was elected Chairman. Rüütel entered the presidential election of 2001 in September, following inconclusive rounds of voting in the previous month. An electoral body was convened on 21 September, and Rüütel emerged the victor after a second round of voting, defeating Toomas Savi of the governing Estonian Reform Party (ERP). Rüütel, who secured 186 votes, received strong support from delegates representing rural areas suffering from high unemployment. He was sworn in as President on 8 October, and pledged to work to combat unemployment, create equal opportunities for education and restore population growth. Some Estonians were concerned at the effect the election of a former Communist president would have on the country's relations with the West. However, Rüütel's signing, in December 2001, of a bill abolishing the requirement that candidates for public office must be proficient in Estonian, was seen as deepening the process of democracy in the country, and as further progress towards membership of the European Union (EU) and the North Atlantic Treaty Organization (NATO). Although constantly reminded of his past as a senior figure in Soviet Estonia by his nickname, 'Red Arnold', he was generally popular with Estonians. He refused to comment on the possibility of his seeking a second term in the presidency (it was likely that the Constitution would be amended to provide for a direct election by the time his first term expired), although his wife publicly discounted a second term shortly before his 75th birthday in May 2003. *Address:* Office of the President, Weizenbergi 39, Tallinn 15050, Estonia.

SAVISAAR, Edgar: Mayor of Tallinn City Government and former Prime Minister of Estonia; b. 31 May 1950, in Harjumaa. *Education:* a graduate of economics from Tartu State University. *Career:* he was a communist until January 1990, but also became a leader of the Estonian Popular Front, which was founded in April 1988. From July 1989 he was a deputy premier in the Estonian Government and, upon the 1990 electoral victory of the Front, was appointed to lead the Council of Ministers. In January 1992, despite the hitherto relatively strong performance of the Estonian economy, he was obliged to ask for emergency powers because of the increasing shortage of supplies. Shortly afterwards he resigned as premier, but was elected to the post of Deputy Speaker of the Riigikogu following the parliamentary election of 20 September. In the legislative election held in March 1995, the Estonian Centre Party, of which Savisaar was by that time leader, won the third largest number of seats. Savisaar was appointed Deputy Prime Minister and Minister of the Interior in the coalition Government of Tiit Vähi of the Estonian Coalition Party (ECP). However, in October it was revealed that Savisaar had made secret tape and video recordings of conversations he had held with other politicians, following the election, concerning the formation of a new coalition. In the ensuing scandal he was dismissed from his ministerial posts. The Estonian Centre Party refused to accept his dismissal and, as a result of the effective collapse of the coalition, the remainder of the Council of Ministers was forced to resign. Savisaar resigned as Chairman of the Estonian Centre Party and announced his departure from politics. In March 1996, however, following a split in the party, he was reappointed leader. In November of that year the ECP, again part of the ruling coalition, signed a co-operation agreement with the Estonian Centre Party, without informing the Estonian Reform Party (ERP), the other member of the coalition. The subsequent anger of the ERP precipitated the collapse of the Government. In the late 1990s the Estonian Centre Party remained popular with the electorate, winning the largest number of seats (28) in the legislative election of March 1999. However, Savisaar's party was unable to form a majority coalition. Following his defeat in the Tallinn mayoral election in June 2001, Savisaar remained vigorously active in leading the centrist opposition. In December the ERP announced that it was to withdraw from the Government of Tallinn City Council because of financial mismanagement, and signed a coalition agreement with the Estonian Centre Party. The Mayor of Tallinn, Tõnis Palts, was subsequently forced to resign, when a censure motion, brought by the Estonian Centre Party, was passed by a significant majority. Savisaar was duly elected Mayor of Tallinn in mid-December. The ERP's withdrawal from the City Council, and subsequent developments, prompted the resignation of the Government of Mart Laar in January 2002. The ERP and Estonian Centre Party hastily signed an agreement to form an interim, coalition Government, to include ministers from both parties, despite their contrasting political viewpoints. The administration, led by Siim Kallas (q.v.) and relying on the support of the Estonian People's Union, took office later in January. Savisaar remained as Mayor of Tallinn, with a strong influence on the Government. His lack of enthusiasm for Estonian membership of the European Union was rare among Estonian politicians, even within his own party. Prior to the legislative election held in March 2003 it appeared that Saavisar's party would be the largest in the Riigikogu following the election. However, the Estonian Centre Party (which obtained the largest share of votes cast) and the new Res Publica movement, led by Juhan Parts (q.v.), each won 28 of the 110 seats. As the leader of the most successful party, Savisaar was asked to form a government, although it soon became obvious that Parts had already agreed a coalition with the ERP, an agreement which would make any other coalition unviable. Savisaar entered opposition (and restated his commitment to his post as Mayor of Tallinn) while Parts became Prime Minister. *Address:* Estonian Centre Party (Eesti Keskerkond), Toom-Rüütli 3/5, POB 3737, Tallinn 0090, Estonia; tel. 627-3460; fax 627-3461; e-mail keskerakond@keskerakond.ee.

SAXE-COBURG GOTHA, Simeon Borisov (Saxe-Coburgotski): Prime Minister of Bulgaria; b. 16 June 1937, in Sofia; m. Margarita Gomez-Acebo y Cejeula, with four s. and one d. *Education:* he studied in Egypt, Spain and the USA. *Career:* Deposed as Tsar (King) Simeon II on 15 September 1946, after a referendum in Bulgaria demanding the establishment of a republic, he was educated in Egypt, then lived in exile in Spain. He worked as a financial consultant and businessman in both Spain and the USA, while continuing to build up contacts in Bulgaria and elsewhere. Following a ruling by the Constitutional Court that the communist confiscation of property was illegal, Saxe-Coburg Gotha began to pay visits to Bulgaria in the late 1990s. In April 2001 he returned to Bulgaria, and was elected leader of the newly formed National Movement. In late April the Supreme Court of Appeal upheld a ruling of the City Court of Sofia denying the Movement permission to register for participation in the forthcoming legislative election, stating that its leader did not fulfil all of the necessary eligibility criteria. The National Movement subsequently formed an alliance with two smaller, registered parties, forming the National Movement Simeon II, led by Vesela Draganova, in order to take part. The alliance obtained a decisive victory in the election of 17 June, securing 42.73% of the votes cast, to obtain 120 seats in parliament. Saxe-Coburg Gotha subsequently agreed, with apparent reluctance, to accept the role of premier, and formed an alliance with the minority Movement for Rights and Freedoms (MRF—representing the country's Muslim minority). With a patriotic, young cabinet, Saxe-Coburg Gotha intended to implement a programme to bring about a dramatic improvement to the economy within 800 days, building on the market reforms instigated by his predecessor, Ivan Kostov. He also wished to lead the country into the North Atlantic Treaty Organization (NATO) and the European Union (EU). Criticism of his Government initially centred on the perceived failure to bring about the promised economic advances, although other issues, most notably the agreement to close two reactors at the Kozloduy nuclear power plant as part of pre-accession negotiations with the EU, came to prominence as the administration developed. By July 2003 three motions of 'no confidence' in Saxe-Coburg Gotha's Government, and one specifically directed at the Prime Minister himself, had been defeated. Although by now a seasoned and committed democratic politician, he acknowledged that he still thought of himself as King. *Address:* c/o Council of Ministers, 1000 Sofia,

Blvd Dondukov 1, Bulgaria; tel. (2) 940-27-70; fax (2) 980-20-56; e-mail iprd@government.bg.

SCHUSTER, Rudolf: President of Slovakia; b. 4 Jan. 1934, in Košice; m. Irene Trojáková, with one s. and one d. *Education:* he studied at the Slovak Technical University in Bratislava and at Košice Technical University. *Career:* he worked at the Slovak Academy of Sciences, before joining the VSŽ steelworks in Košice. He joined the Communist Party in 1964 and remained a member until 1990. He was elected to Košice city council in 1974 and was Mayor 1983–86. He became Chairman of the Eastern Slovak Regional National Council in 1986 and 1989-90 was Chairman of the Slovak National Council. Schuster was appointed ambassador to Canada of the Czech and Slovak Federation in 1990, before becoming the first Minister of Foreign Affairs of independent Slovakia in 1993–94. In 1994–99 he was again Mayor of Košice, and was a member of the National Council 1998–99, having joined the Party of Civic Understanding (PCU), a member of the coalition that formed a Government after the legislative election of September 1998. In early 1999 he was proposed as the coalition's candidate for the vacant presidency in the country's first direct presidential election. He defeated Vladimír Mečiar (q.v.) in the second round of voting on 29 May and was inaugurated in June. He subsequently resigned his positions as Mayor of Košice and Chairman of the PCU. During his first year in office he was often critical of the antagonistic nature of politics in Slovakia, urging the governing coalition and the opposition Movement for a Democratic Slovakia (MDS) to co-operate. In June 2000 he was hospitalized with a serious abdominal complaint and—allegedly after failings in his treatment—was transferred to Austria for emergency surgery, when serious complications developed. He was maintained in a controlled coma for two weeks before recovering, returning to Slovakia to resume his duties in mid-August. In May 2001, in a 'state of the nation' address highly critical of the Government, Schuster warned that political fighting was obstructing economic reform. He proved himself willing to use the presidential veto on draft legislation, most notably in July 2003 on amendments to the law on abortion. *Address:* Office of the President of the Republic, 810 00 Bratislava, POB 128, Slovakia.

ŠEŠELJ, Vojislav: Serbian and Montenegrin (Serbian) politician; b. 1 October 1954, in Sarajevo (Bosnia and Herzegovina); m., with two s. *Education:* he studied at the University of Sarajevo, becoming the youngest holder of a doctorate in Yugoslavia. *Career:* he was imprisoned in his twenties for writing an article advocating the replacement of Yugoslavia with a so-called 'Greater Serbia'. Following his release, in 1989 he became the leader of the Chetnik movement (a royalist, nationalist group echoing the Serbian militia that fought in the Second World War). In 1990 he established the Serbian Radical Party, with an extreme nationalist platform, and he was elected to the Serbian parliament in the same year. A number of paramilitary groups which fought in the wars against the secessionist republics (and were accused of atrocities) were formally linked to the party. Previously an ally of Slobodan Milošević (q.v.), they became opponents when the latter attempted to negotiate an end to the Bosnian conflict in 1993—Šešelj claimed that Milošević was betraying the Serb people, and made allegations of war crimes against him. Šešelj was himself wanted for questioning in connection with similar offences. In 1997 he was appointed Deputy Prime Minister of Serbia, and he stood in the presidential election held in the same year, being defeated in the second ballot by Milan Milutinović (q.v.). The unrest among ethnic Albanians in the Serbian province of Kosovo and Metohija prompted a reconciliation with Milošević—Šešelj advocated the expulsion of all ethnic Albanians form Serbia. The fervour of his nationalist rhetoric increased after the beginning of the bombardment of Yugoslavia by North Atlantic Treaty Organization (NATO) forces in March 1999. He resigned from the Government in June of that year, following Milošević's acceptance of a peace plan to end the conflict in Kosovo and the NATO bombing—the plan involved the deployment of a NATO force in Kosovo, which Šešelj vehemently opposed. However, he and his party resumed participation in government shortly afterwards. Allegations of his involvement in war crimes resurfaced thereafter, and following the indictment of Milošević by the International Criminal Tribunal for the former Yugoslavia (ICTY, based in the Hague, Netherlands), it was considered likely that charges against Šešelj would follow. He again sought election to the Serbian presidency in late 2002—Milošević, by now on trial and in custody in the Netherlands, expressed his support for him. Both elections were annulled owing to insufficient participation, Šešelj having been the third most popular choice in the first election, and the voters' second choice in the second poll. In February 2003 he was indicted by the ICTY; he voluntarily surrendered to the custody of the Tribunal later in the month. He retained a significant element of popular support, and a rally held in Belgrade before his departure was reported to have attracted some 10,000 people. In April he was charged, in absentia, with involvement in the assassination of the Serbian Prime Minister, Zoran Djindjić, the previous month. Following a number of disputes with the ICTY over the procedure of his trial, he was reported to have begun a hunger strike in May. *Address:* c/o Serbian Radical Party, Ohridska 1, 11000 Belgrade, Serbia and Montenegro; tel. (11) 457745.

SIMITIS, Konstantinos (Costas): Prime Minister of Greece; b. 23 June 1936, in Athens; m. Daphne Arkadiou, with two c. *Education:* he studied law at the University of Marburg, Germany, and economics at the London School of Economics, the United Kingdom. *Career:* a member of a renowned left-wing family, he practised law from 1961. In 1963 he founded a socialist movement and subsequently became a member of the Panhellenic Liberation Movement (PAK) during the 'regime of the colonels' (1967–74). He left Greece in 1971 and took up teaching posts at universities in Germany, where he remained until 1975. While in exile he was convicted *in absentia* of arson and use of explosives. Upon the restoration of democracy in Greece in 1974, he was a founder member of the Panhellenic Socialist Movement (PASOK) and was co-author of the party's charter. In 1977 he was appointed Professor of Commercial Law at the University of Athens. His disagreements with PASOK's leader and the country's Prime Minister, Andreas Papandreou, were frequent—he resigned from the party's executive committee in 1979 and was omitted from the list of candidates for the general election held in 1991 for this reason. Nevertheless, he was Minister of Agriculture in 1981–85 and Minister of National Economy in 1985–87. He resigned from his positions as Minister of Industry, Energy and Technology and of Commerce in September 1995, citing interference from PASOK officials. Having become known as a modernizer within PASOK, he urged Papandreou to resign the premiership, owing to his poor health and the slow pace of reform within the party. Upon Papandreou's resignation in January 1996, Simitis was elected Prime Minister by PASOK deputies. His stated priority was to prepare Greece for membership of the European Union's programme of economic and monetary union (EMU). The measures of fiscal austerity that his Government introduced to achieve this aim were frequently criticized, even by members of his own party, but PASOK retained an absolute majority of parliamentary seats in the general election held on 9 April 2000, and Simitis was able to form a new Government. The following month Greece's application to join EMU was accepted by the European Commission. The popularity of Simitis and his Government declined in April 2001, as a result of government plans to overhaul the pensions system, which led to widespread protests and general strikes. Following international criticism of the country's sluggish progress in its preparations for the 2004 Olympic Games (to be held in Athens), Simitis reshuffled the Cabinet in October 2001, replacing traditionalists with Western-minded reformers. The new Government aimed to prioritize development policy, social convergence and the strengthening of the country's international position. Re-elected to the party leadership with over 70% of the votes in October, Simitis announced his intention of leading PASOK into the 2004 general election. Simitis carried out a further minor reshuffle in July 2003, with ostensibly the same motive, claiming that he had needed to revitalize his Government prior to the legislative elections. However, commentators had

expected a more wide-ranging reorganization, and claimed that Simitis had lost momentum. *Address:* Office of the Prime Minister, Maximos Mansion, Herodou Atticou 19, 106 74 Athens, Greece; tel. (21) 03385242; fax (21) 07241776; e-mail mail@primeminister.gr.

SOKOL, Jan: Czech university professor and former presidential candidate; b. 18 April 1936, in Prague; m., with three c. *Education:* he studied mathematics at Charles University, Prague. *Career:* he worked as a clockmaker before beginning his studies, and as computer programmer and software developer during his course and after its completion. He was a dissident against communist rule and a signatory of the original Charter 77 document. Following the collapse of communism he was elected to the Czechoslovak Federal Assembly in 1990, where he gained a reputation as a mediator, chairing a committee on the relationship between Czech and Slovak interest. He left parliament in 1992, and returned to university, completing first a master's degree and then a doctorate in philosophy before taking up a teaching post. Though not a member of any political party, he returned to public life in 1997, serving as education minister in the interim Government that took office following the resignation of Václav Klaus (q.v.). Returning to academia he was appointed Dean of the Faculty of Humanities at Charles University in 2000. He unexpectedly returned to prominence in early 2003 when, following the failure of two attempts by parliament to elect a successor to President Václav Havel, he was approached by the Prime Minister, Vladimír Špidla (q.v.), to be the candidate of the governing coalition in a third election, in which he would oppose Klaus. It was hoped that his apolitical status would attract a broad base of support. In the event, Klaus won the election by one vote in a third ballot, after gaining the support of communist deputies and a number from parties of the governing coalition. Sokol returned to his university post, and considered it unlikely that he would again enter the political sphere. A Roman Catholic, the bible was one of the numerous books he had translated into Czech. *Address:* Faculty of Humanities, Charles University, Krize 4–10, 150 00 Prague 5, Czech Republic.; tel. 224491111; e-mail uk@cuni.cz; internet www.cuni.cz.

ŠPIDLA, Vladimír: Czech politician; b. 22 April 1951, in Prague; m. twice, with four c. *Education:* in 1970–76 he studied at the Faculty of Philosophy at Charles University in Prague. *Career:* after working in various manual jobs in the period of 'normalization', he served in local administration in Jindřichův Hradec in 1990–96. A founding member of the Czech Social Democratic Party (CSDP) and a member of its Presidium from 1992, he was elected to parliament in 1996. He served as President of the party's Social Policy and Health Service Committee and as Chairman of its regional organization in South Bohemia in 1996–98. Mild-mannered and tenacious, Špidla was appointed Deputy Prime Minister and Minister of Labour and Social Affairs in 1998. In April 2001 he succeeded Miloš Zeman (q.v.) as leader of the CSDP. Following a modest victory by the CSDP in parliamentary elections conducted in June 2002, on 15 July he was appointed Prime Minister in a new coalition Government, which was expected to be more pluralistic than previous cabinets. The Government was particularly affected by the public consternation at the protracted presidential election process, and the eventual success of Václav Klaus (q.v.), a determined opponent of Špidla, was thought likely to jeopardize the Government's programme. Indeed, Špidla reacted to the defeat of the governing coalition's presidential candidate by proposing a motion of confidence in the Government shortly after Klaus's election—the Government's one-seat notional majority was maintained. Špidla dismissed a minister who had supported Klaus in the presidential election shortly thereafter. He considered his policy towards the European Union vindicated when a referendum showed more than three-quarters of voters to be in favour of accession. However, the opposing views on many matters of President and Prime Minister seemed likely to dominate Czech politics in the near term. *Address:* Czech Social Democratic Party (Česká strana sociálně demokratická), Lidovy dům, Hybernská 7, 110 00

Prague 1, Czech Republic; tel. and fax 224219911; e-mail info@socdem.cz.

STANISHEV, Sergey: Bulgarian politician; b. 5 May 1966, in Ukraine. *Education:* he graduated from the Faculty of History at the Moscow State University, Russia, in 1989 and obtained a doctorate in history in 1994; he conducted further studies in political science in 1998. *Career:* in 1994–95 he worked as a journalist. In 1995 he began work as an expert in the Foreign Policy and International Relations Department of the Supreme Council of the Bulgarian Socialist Party (BSP), becoming Chief of the Department in 1996, a position that he retained until 2001. He was a visiting fellow in international relations at the London School of Economics and Political Science, the United Kingdom, in 1999–2000. In May 2000 he was elected a member of the BSP Supreme Council and became the party's International Secretary. He entered the National Assembly in the legislative election of June 2001 (although the BSP, as a whole, performed poorly in the poll, which it contested as part of the Coalition for Bulgaria, formed in January with 14 smaller left and left-of-centre parties). Following the election of Georgi Parvanov (q.v.) to the presidency in November 2001, Stanishev—Parvanov's nominated successor—was elected Chairman of the party (and thus of the Coalition for Bulgaria) on 15 December, obtaining 67% of the votes cast. He affirmed his party's commitment to securing Bulgaria's membership of the European Union (EU) and the North Atlantic Treaty Organization (NATO). He was re-elected as leader of the BSP in June 2002, following which the party's criticism of the Government intensified, Stanishev being a particularly harsh critic of the decisions to close reactors at the Kozloduy nuclear plant and to support the US-led military intervention in Iraq in early 2003. *Address:* Bulgarian Socialist Party (Bulgarska Sotsialisticheska Partiya), Positano St 20, POB 382, Sofia, Bulgaria; tel. (2) 980-12-91; fax (2) 980-52-91; e-mail bsp@mail.bol.bg.

STEFANOPOULOS, Konstantinos (Costas): President of Greece; b. 1926, in Patras; m. Eugenia El. Stounopoulou in 1959, with two s. and one d. *Education:* he studied law at the University of Athens. *Career:* he practised law before entering Parliament in 1964 as a member of the National Radical Union. He joined the New Democracy (ND) party upon its foundation in 1974, and was appointed Minister of the Interior in the first democratic Government after the end of the military regime; he subsequently served in ND governments as Minister of Social Services and Minister in the Prime Minister's Office. Stefanopoulos twice stood unsuccessfully for the leadership of ND. Following the second of these defeats in 1984 he became disenchanted with the party, and the following year he and nine other deputies left ND and founded the Democratic Renewal Party (DIANA). The party won one seat in Parliament in the general election held in April 1990, which Stefanopoulos himself took; his support enabled ND, led by Konstantinos Mitsotakis, to form Greece's first single-party Government since 1981. He formally joined the ND parliamentary grouping two months later. After DIANA failed to win any seats at the election to the European Parliament in 1994 Stefanopoulos disbanded the party and retired from politics. He returned to public life in March 1995, when he was elected to the presidency, having been nominated by the Political Spring party. Stefanopoulos secured the support of 181 of the 300 members of Parliament, but was opposed by ND members. In February 2000 he was re-elected by Parliament, this time with the support of both major parties. By 2003 his position was something of an inconvenience to some senior figures in the ND, who urged him to resign, and thus precipitate an advanced legislative election. Stefanopoulos showed no inclination to do so, however, and any such comments were rejected by the ND leadership. *Address:* Office of the President, Odos Vas. Georgiou 7, 106 74 Athens, Greece; tel. (21) 07283111; fax (21) 07248938.

STOLOJAN, Theodor: Romanian politician and economist; b. 24 Oct. 1943, in Târgovişte; m., with two c. *Education:* he studied at the Academy of Economic Studies in Bucharest from 1961 to 1966 and obtained a doctorate from the same institute in 1980. *Career:* he was an economist in the Ministry of Finance from 1972 to 1990. He was Minister of Finance

from April 1990 to April 1991 and head of the privatization agency until his appointment as Prime Minister on 1 October 1991. He helped stabilize a volatile situation after his predecessor had been forcibly ousted by a mob of coal-miners. He acquired a reputation as a conciliator towards the Hungarian minority at a time when inter-ethnic relations were marked by tension. However, he was criticized for nationalizing hard currency bank deposits, preventing their withdrawal until their value had depreciated as a result of inflation. He left politics, although he supported Iliescu in his unsuccessful re-election bid in 1996. From 1993 to 1998 he was a senior economist at the World Bank, where he was involved with economic recovery programmes in former Soviet Central Asia. In 1998 he joined the Tofan group of Romanian companies, which enjoyed a reputation for sound business practices often lacking elsewhere. The crisis of the centre-right parties, following the political failures of the 1996–2000 coalition Government, led him to accept an invitation from the National Liberal Party (NLP) to be its presidential candidate in 2000; he was third-placed, with 11.8% of the votes. On 24 August 2002 he was elected leader of the NLP, which was the main centrist challenger to the ruling Social Democratic Party. *Address:* National Liberal Party, 70112 Bucharest, Bd. Aviatorilor 86, Romania.; tel. (21) 2310795; fax (21) 2317511.

SVILANOVIĆ, Goran: Minister of Foreign Affairs of Serbia and Montenegro; b. 1963, in Gnjilane; m., with one d. and one s. *Education:* Belgrade Law School. *Career:* he took a strong interest in civil and human rights, and served as an assistant professor at Belgrade Law School from 1989 to 1998, when he was among a group of academics removed from their posts for opposing new legislation on universities. He was briefly spokesman (1997) and then Vice-President of the opposition Civic Alliance of Serbia (1998), and in 1999 was elected President of that group. After the fall of President Slobodan Milošević (q.v.) in October 2000, Svilanović was appointed Minister of Foreign Affairs in the new reformist Government. In this capacity he favoured improved relations with the West, especially with regard to the economic sphere. However, he initially supported the view of the federal President, Vojislav Koštunica (q.v.), that war crimes suspects should be tried in the FRY, rather than extradited to the International Criminal Tribunal for the former Yugoslavia (ICTY, in The Hague, the Netherlands). After significant international pressure, legislation providing for the extraditions was finally approved. He retained his position following the country's transition to the new constitutional arrangements (as Serbia and Montenegro) in February 2003. He created controversy when, in June, he celebrated his country's defeat of Croatia at the European Water Polo Championships by jumping into the pool to congratulate the players. Violence erupted in the stadium, and in Belgrade, where the Croatian mission was stormed by Serb nationalists. Svilanović apologized for his exuberant celebrations shortly afterwards. In July 2003 he was criticized by the Montenegrin Minister of Foreign Affairs for taking an excessively pro-Serbian position in his post, a criticism he rejected. *Address:* Ministry of Foreign Affairs, 11000 Belgrade, Kneza Milosa 24, Serbia and Montenegro; tel. (11) 682555; fax (11) 682668; e-mail smip@smip.sv.gov.yu.

TEOCTIST, His Holiness Patriarch: Head of the Romanian Orthodox Church, Patriarch of the Metropolitan of Muntênia and Dobrogea and Archbishop of Bucharest; b. 1915, in Tocileni. *Education:* studied at the Faculty of Orthodox Theology at Bucharest University. *Career:* born Teoctist Arăpaşu, he enrolled as a monk in the Orthodox Church at a period when many church officials rallied around the ultra-right-wing Iron Guard movement, which enjoyed a huge popular following in the 1930s. The release of his secret police file in 2001 showed that he had been an active 'legionary' in the movement and had participated in the Legionary uprising of January 1941, in which the Jewish minority was a primary target. Teoctist joined the hierarchy of the Church in 1949, one year after the new communist authorities had removed church elements hostile to their rule. He was made Bishop of the Romanian Missionary Diocese in the USA in 1963, but failed to obtain a residency permit. In March 1973 he became Archbishop of Craiova, Metropolitan of Oltenia-Craiova and, later, Metropolitan of Moldavia and Suceava. In October 1977 he was appointed Archbishop of Iași. In 1986 he was elected Patriarch of the Romanian Orthodox Church at a time when the communist dictator, Nicolae Ceaușescu, was demolishing historic churches in Bucharest. A telegram in Teoctist's name, released in the final days of the regime, praised Ceaușescu for his 'brilliant activity', 'wise guidance', and 'daring thinking', and hailed his re-election at the 14th party congress in November 1989. It also claimed that the Romanians were living 'in a Golden Age, properly and righteously bearing (Ceaușescu's) name'. He offered his resignation in January 1990, but was reinstated in April owing to the absence of an obvious successor. Teoctist tried to re-establish Orthodoxy at the forefront of national life. He lobbied for its elevation as the state religion and he was a fierce opponent of proselytizing Western religions, as well as of the legalization of homosexuality. Under him the Church largely stayed outside active politics and pursued some striking ecumenical initiatives, which placed it ahead of other Orthodox Churches in the region. In May 1999 he received Pope John Paul II, whose visit to Romania was the first official one he made to an Orthodox country. In October 2002 an historic landmark occurred in Orthodox-Christian relations when the Pope and Teoctist celebrated a common religious service in the Vatican. *Address:* Office of the Patriarch, Metropolitan of Muntênia and Dobrogea, 70526 Bucharest, Str. Patriarhiei 21, Romania; tel. (21) 3372776.

TERZIĆ, Adnan: Prime Minister of Bosnia and Herzegovina; b. 1960; ethnic Bosnian Muslim (Bosniak). *Education:* he graduated in geodetic engineering. *Career:* while working as a geodetic engineer he became increasingly sympathetic to the cause of Bosnian Muslim (Bosniak) nationalism. The conflict in the country in the early 1990s encouraged him to enter politics, and he joined the Party of Democratic Action (PDA), founded by Dr Alija Izetbegović (q.v.). He became Mayor of Travnik following the Dayton peace agreement, and in 1996 issued a denial in response to allegations that ethnic Croat families had been expelled from the area. He was elected Governor of the Central Bosnia canton for 1997–98, and oversaw the return of numerous refugees to the canton. He served in the same position in 2000–01 and continued his previous policies. As the PDA became more liberal, Terzić was elected Vice-President of the party in October 2001, and he was a central figure in the party's campaign for the legislative elections held in 2002 (at which the PDA and the other nationalist parties performed strongly). In December 2002, in accordance with the amended Constitution, he was elected to a four-year term as Prime Minister (the post had previously been allocated to members of the three ethnic communities in turn, changing every eight months). *Address:* Office of the Prime Minister, 71000 Sarajevo, Vojvode Putnike 3, Bosnia and Herzegovina; tel. (33) 664941; fax (33) 443446.

THAÇI, Hashim: Yugoslav (Serbian/Kosovan) politician; former Chief of the Kosovo Liberation Army (KLA) in Kosovo and Metohija (Federal Republic of Yugoslavia—FRY); b. 1970. *Career:* as Chief of the KLA he fought against Serbian security forces for Kosovo's independence. Also known as 'Commander Snake', he was leader of the ethnic Albanian delegation at the peace conference in Rambouillet (France) in February–March 1999. In March a Serbian judge issued an order for his arrest, claiming that he had been tried and sentenced to 10 years' imprisonment *in absentia*. Nevertheless, he continued his efforts as the leader of the Party of Democratic Progress in Kosovo (renamed the Democratic Party of Kosovo—DPK). By September the KLA had been demilitarized and reconstituted as a civil emergency security force. In December Thaçi became one of the ethnic Albanian members of the Interim Administrative Council (IAC) established in Kosovo, and worked to establish a suitable governing body in the province. In local government elections, conducted in Kosovo on 28 October 2000, the DPK secured 27% of the votes cast, compared with the 58% of the votes won by the rival Democratic League of Kosovo (DLK) led by Dr Ibrahim Rugova (q.v.), and gained control of six of the 30 municipalities. Thaçi remained as one of the four Kosovo representatives in the IAC. In May 2001 the UN Interim Administration Mission in Kosovo (UNMIK) pre-

sented a plan granting provisional self-government for Kosovo, and announced that elections to a legislative assembly would take place in November. The DPK won 26 of the 100 contested seats, compared with 47 for the DLK. On the first day of the new assembly's operation, in December, Thaçi walked out, after he was prevented from making a political statement. Tensions between the parties represented in the parliament persisted, particularly over the issues of representation in Government and the appointment of the new President. In March 2002, after lengthy inter-party negotiations, Rugova was elected President, having agreed that a member of the DPK, Bajram Rexhepi, would become Prime Minister. Thaçi was re-elected DPK leader in June 2002. In June 2003 it was reported that he had been briefly detained by the Hungarian authorities while in transit through Budapest, on the basis of a Yugoslav arrest warrant for 'terrorism', issued during the presidency of Slobodan Milošević. The Hungarian Government subsequently denied these reports, although many observers believed them to be true—his arrest was criticized by the Kosovo Government, while Serbian officials were critical of his release. *Address:* Democratic Party of Kosovo, Priština, Kosovo and Metohija, Serbia and Montenegro.

TIHIĆ, Sulejman: member of the state Presidency of Bosnia and Herzegovina; b. 26 Nov. 1951, in Bosanski Samac; ethnic Bosnian Muslim (Bosniak); m., with two s. and one d. *Education:* he graduated in law from the University of Sarajevo. *Career:* he worked as a public prosecutor and, subsequently, a judge, before entering private practice in 1983. He was imprisoned by Bosnian Serb forces during the conflict in the country. Following his release, he entered the diplomatic service, working as head of the consular department at the country's embassy in Berlin (Germany). In 1996 he returned to Bosnia and Herzegovina, becoming an adviser to the Minister of Foreign Affairs; in the same year he was elected to the parliament of the Bosnian Serb Republic (Republika Srpska), representing the Party for Democratic Action (PDA). He was elected a deputy chairman of the PDA shortly afterwards, and frequently acted as parliamentary spokesman for the coalition of Bosniak parties in the Serb Republic. He was elected deputy speaker of the chamber in 2000. Upon the retirement from the party leadership of Alija Izetbegović (q.v.) in October 2001, Tihić was elected to succeed him, and in May 2002 he was nominated as the PDA's candidate for the Bosniak seat on the state Presidency, to be contested in October. He received 37% of the votes cast in the presidential election, defeating two other candidates, and was inaugurated on 28 October. Although the PDA was nominally a 'single-ethnicity' party, Tihić repeatedly stressed his wish that ethnic Croats and Serbs would support and join the movement. In general, he was a fervent advocate of 'multi-ethnicity', supporting the return of refugees from all the nation's communities to their original homes, campaigning for the Serb Republic to adopt a less ethnically specific name, and stating his enthusiasm for the eventual restoration of a unitary state in Bosnia and Herzegovina. *Address:* Office of the Presidency, 71000 Sarajevo, Musala 5, Bosnia and Herzegovina; tel. (33) 664941; fax (33) 472491.

TRAJKOVSKI, Boris: President of the former Yugoslav republic of Macedonia; b. 25 June 1956, in Strumića; m. Vilma Trajkovska, with one s. and one d. *Education:* graduated in law from SS Cyril and Methodius University, Skopje. *Career:* until 1997 he was head of the legal department of the Sloboda construction company in Skopje. A member of the International Macedonian Revolutionary Organization—Democratic Party for Macedonian National Unity (IMRO—DPMNU), in 1997–98 he served as Chief of Office for the Mayor of Kisela Voda municipality in Skopje. In January 1999 he was appointed Deputy Minister of Foreign Affairs in the cabinet of Ljubčo Georgievski (q.v.). As the IMRO—DPMNU candidate in the presidential election of October 1999, he obtained 52.8% of the votes cast in the second round, thereby securing the presidency. Supporters of the defeated candidate from the Social Democratic Alliance, Tito Petkovski, claimed widespread malpractice and a third ballot was held in some regions of the country. The overall results were virtually unchanged, however, and Trajkovski was inaugurated as President on 15 December. He pledged to instil greater democracy in the country and to work towards improving the economy. Following the onset of hostilities between Macedonian government forces and ethnic Albanian rebels in February 2001, Trajkovski played a significant role in peace negotiations. He urged the Sobranie (Assembly) to adopt amendments to the Constitution providing for greater rights for the ethnic Albanian minority, while admitting the imperfections of the framework peace agreement reached in August. With the adoption of the amendments in November, he called on the international community to increase its assistance to, and recognition of, Macedonia. At the end of 2001, to ensure the continuation of the peace process, Trajkovski pardoned a number of prisoners accused of being former members of the ethnic Albanian National Liberation Army (NLA). His priority continued to be the establishment of peace, prosperity and stability in the country. To this end, he sponsored the Ohrid accord, which went some way towards normalizing the relationship betwenn the ethnic Albanian minority and the state, and made Albanian an official second language of the country. *Address:* Office of the President of the Republic, 1000 Skopje, 11 Oktomvri bb, former Yugoslav republic of Macedonia; tel. (2) 3113318; fax (2) 3112147.

TSOHATZOPOULOS, Apostolos-Athanassios (Akis): Minister of Development of Greece; b. 1939; m. Gudrun Moldenhauer, with one s. and one d. *Education:* he studied at the Technical University of Munich, Germany. *Career:* he was active in the Panhellenic Liberation movement in the 1960s and, like many others, was deprived of Greek citizenship by the military regime. He was a leading figure in the foundation and early administration of the Panhellenic Socialist Movement (PASOK). In 1981 he was elected to Parliament and was appointed Minister for Public Works by Andreas Papandreou. His proximity to Papandreou was demonstrated when, upon the return of PASOK to government in 1986, he was appointed Minister to the Prime Minister. He subsequently served as Minister of the Interior on three separate occasions and was General Secretary of PASOK in 1990–95. When Papandreou was incapacitated by ill health in November 1995, Tsohatzopoulos assumed his duties. In the election within the PASOK parliamentary grouping to nominate a new premier in January 1996, he was defeated by Konstantinos Simitis (q.v.). Simitis replaced many of Papandreou's closest associates in his new Government, but kept Tsohatzopoulos as Minister for National Defence. Tsohatzopoulos retained this position until October 2001, when Simitis reshuffled and enlarged the cabinet, following international criticism of the country's slow progress in preparations for the 2004 Olympic Games, which were to be held in Athens. The only 'traditionalist' remaining in the cabinet, Tsohatzopoulos was moved to the Ministry of Development—the Prime Minister had earlier stated that national development was a priority for Greece. Although the move was seen by many as a means of marginalizing him, he adopted his new portfolio with enthusiasm, particularly in the field of energy development, and he remained in the post following the cabinet reshuffle effected in July 2003. However, Tsohatzopoulos remained a vocal critic of the painful economic and social reforms advocated by the reformers in the Government. *Address:* Ministry of Development, Odos Mihalakopoulou 80, 101 92 Athens, Greece; tel. (21) 07482770; fax (21) 07788279.

TUDOR, Corneliu Vadim: Romanian politician; b. 28 Nov. 1949; m., with two d. *Education:* studied at the Faculty of Philosophy at the University of Bucharest; speaks Italian, French and English. *Career:* a former communist propagandist, he was the court poet for the Ceauşescu family, before heading the ultranationalist Greater Romania Party (GRP), and managing its associated newspaper, *Romania Mare (Greater Romania)* A deputy since 1992, Tudor gained prominence in the run-up to the November 2000 presidential election, in which he took 33.2% of the votes in the second round, as increased levels of hardship and unemployment in the country led to a surge in support for populist forces that had never been in government. Vadim's mastery of the televised media contributed to his success, as did his decision to

suspend his customary nationalism and campaign on an anti-corruption platform. He was the prime beneficiary of the rift between the major parties and society at large, much of which regarded the conventional political class as ready to promote its group interests at the expense of ordinary Romanians. The GRP became the second largest party in the legislature, Vadim bringing in his wake figures associated with repression in the communist era, or others keen to obtain parliamentary immunity to avoid prosecution for criminal offences. However, he was isolated in Parliament as the other parties struck agreements. A flamboyant character, Tudor's xenophobic rhetoric against Roma (Gypsies), ethnic Hungarians and Jews caused unease both in the region and among the European Union (EU) leadership. In mid-2001 a group of Romanian journalists published a book entitled 'The Anthology of Shame', including poems and stories written by Tudor, with the aim of revealing details of Tudor's past to the electorate. Defections had dented its credibility, but the GRP continued to enjoy high poll ratings. *Address:* Greater Romanian Party—GRP (Partidul România Mare—PRM), 70101 Bucharest, Str. G. Clemenceau 8-10, Romania; tel. (21) 6130967; fax (21) 3126182.

TŮMA, Zdeněk: Governor of the Czech National Bank; b. 19 Oct. 1960, in České Budějovice. *Education:* he studied at the University of Economics in Prague. *Career:* joined the Institute for Forecasting of the Czechoslovak Academy of Sciences as a postgraduate researcher, and subsequently served as an adviser to the Ministry of Industry and Trade, in 1993–95. From 1995 he served as Chief Economist at Patria Finance, until June 1998, when he became Executive Director of the European Bank for Reconstruction and Development (EBRD), representing the Czech Republic, Slovakia, Hungary and Croatia on the Board of Directors. He joined the Czech National Bank in early 1999 as a Vice-Governor and board member, being appointed Governor in December 2000 to replace Josef Tošovský. Between 1990 and 1998 he also lectured on macroeconomics at Charles University, Prague. He regularly published articles on macroeconomics and monetary policy in professional journals and the press. During the presidential election 'crisis' of early 2003 Tůma commented that he hoped the new president, whoever it may be, would not 'politicize' the central bank. He was a supporter of the campaign for a vote in favour of accession to the European Union in the referendum held in June 2003. *Address:* Czech National Bank, Na Příkopě 28, 115 03 Prague 1, Czech Republic; tel. (2) 24411111; fax (2) 24413708; e-mail pavel.zubek@cnb.cz.

VASSILEV, Nikolai Vassilev: Deputy Prime Minister and Minister of Transport and Communications of Bulgaria; b. 28 Nov. 1969. *Education:* he graduated from the Budapest University of Economic Science and Public Administration, Hungary, and subsequently studied business administration, international economics and finance in the USA and Japan. *Career:* he worked as a financial consultant and analyst for various large international firms, eventually becoming Senior Vice-President and Head of Central and East European Research at Lazard Capital Markets in the City of London, the United Kingdom. While abroad, he was a member of the Bulgarian City Club, which brought together expatriate Bulgarians to discuss political issues. Vassilev was appointed to the new cabinet of the former monarch, Simeon Saxe-Coburg Gotha (q.v.), following the victory of the National Movement Simeon II in the June 2001 legislative election. He announced his intention to pursue privatization, combat corruption, reinforce capital markets and introduce tax reform to encourage re-investment. His handling of the economy drew criticism from many observers, however, and he became increasingly unpopular among the electorate as promised improvements in living standards failed to materialize. He was moved from the position in the cabinet reshuffle of July 2003, assuming the expanded transport portfolio, while remaining Deputy Prime Minister. *Address:* Ministry of Transport and Communications, 1000 Sofia, Bulgaria; tel. (2) 988-55-32; fax (2) 980-26-90; e-mail s.bozukova@mi.government.bg.

VELCHEV, Milen Emilov: Minister of Finance of Bulgaria; b. 24 March 1966, in Sofia. *Education:* studied business administration in financial engineering at the Massachusetts

Institute of Technology, Cambridge, MA, USA, and conducted further studies in business management and international relations in New York, USA, and Sofia. *Career:* he was an attaché at the International Organizations Division of the Bulgarian Ministry of Foreign Affairs in 1990–92. In 1995–2001 he worked for an investment bank, in the City of London, the United Kingdom. He was also a member of the Bulgarian City Club, founded by expatriate Bulgarians for the purpose of political discussion. Simeon Saxe-Coburg Gotha (q.v.) appointed him to his cabinet, following the victory of the National Movement Simeon II in the legislative election of June 2001. Despite widespread criticism of the Government's handling of the economy, little was directed at Velchev, considered by many commentators to be highly competent, not least in his dealings with the International Monetary Fund. He remained in his position following the cabinet regorganization effected by Saxe-Coburg Gotha in July 2003. *Address:* Ministry of Finance, 1000 Sofia, Rakovski St 102, Bulgaria; tel. (2) 985-920-20; fax (2) 87-05-81; e-mail feedback@minfin.government.bg.

VIĶE-FREIBERGA, Vaira: President of Latvia; b. 1 Dec. 1937, in Rīga; m. Imants Freiberg in 1960, with one s. and one d. *Education:* studied at the University of Toronto and McGill University (Canada), gaining a postgraduate degree in psychology and a doctorate in experimental psychology; she speaks English, French, Latvian, Spanish and German. *Career:* Viķe-Freiberga's parents emigrated to Canada at the end of the Second World War. She worked as a clinical psychologist in Toronto Psychiatric Hospital in the early 1960s. In 1965 she was appointed Assistant Professor of Clinical Psychology at the University of Montreal, becoming Professor in 1977. In 1984 she was appointed Vice-Chairman of the Science Council of Canada. She moved back to Latvia in 1998, becoming Director of the Latvian Institute, in Rīga. After seven rounds of voting in the Saeima (legislature), she was elected President of Latvia on 17 June 1999, the first woman to assume the presidency of a Central European country. She was inaugurated on 8 July. As President, Viķe-Freiberga enjoyed only limited powers; however, she put her Western credentials to use diplomatically, working hard to convince the European Union (EU) and the North Atlantic Treaty Organization (NATO) of the case for Latvia's accession. In February 2001 she met the President of Russia, Vladimir Putin, and agreed to open a 'new chapter' in relations between the two countries. it was considered likely that this new relationship was a factor in her decision to veto some elements of new lagislation on language in Latvia, which, according to some, would have severely restricted the rights of Russian speakers. Viķe-Freiberga was highly popular in Latvia, as many thought her pro-Western style had helped the country increase its international standing, reflected in its possible membership of the European Union. She was re-elected to the presidency in June 2003, the absence of candidates opposing her indicating the esteem in which she was held. She enjoyed an international reputation as a scientist and had been awarded a number of honours and fellowships. *Address:* Chancery of the President, Pils lauk. 3, Rīga 1900, Latvia; tel. 737-7548; fax 709-2106; e-mail chancery@president.lv.

VUJANOVIĆ, Filip: President of Montenegro; b. 1 Sept. 1954, in Belgrade; m., with two d. and one s. *Education:* he studied law at the University of Belgrade. *Career:* a Democratic Party of Montenegrin Socialists (DPMS) member and an ally of the then republican premier, Milo Djukanović (q.v.), he held the post of Montenegrin Minister of Internal Affairs in 1996–97, at a time when Montenegro was keen to distance itself from the Serbian and federal authorities. Following Djukanović's election to the republican presidency, he was appointed head of a transitional Government in February 1998 and, in May, reappointed Prime Minister. He pledged to secure equal status for Montenegro within the Federal Republic and to continue the reformist policies of his predecessor. His new Government, which comprised representatives of the DPMS, the People's Party of Montenegro and the Social-Democratic Party of Montenegro, became even further estranged from the federal Government by refusing to recog-

nize the federal administration of Momir Bulatović (q.v.). In late 1998 Vujanović consolidated his position, with promotion to the deputy leadership of the DPMS. During the conflict in the Serbian province of Kosovo and Metohija in early 1999 he sought to distance Montenegro from the actions of the federal Government and emphasized his Government's opposition to many of the policies of the federal President, Slobodan Milošević (q.v.). His relations with the federal Government deteriorated still further in 1999, following his open condemnation of Milošević's domestic and foreign policy. He strongly opposed the amendment to the federal Constitution passed in July 2000 providing for the direct election of the federal President, claiming that this further consolidated Milošević's power and reduced Montenegro's influence in federal matters. After the DPMS-led alliance supporting Djukanović's plans for independence for Montenegro secured a narrow victory in elections to the Republican Assembly in April 2001, Vujanović was reappointed Prime Minister in June, and subsequently formed a new coalition Government. Negotiations on the issue of independence for Montenegro, mediated by the EU from November 2001, resulted in the Government leaders of the FRY and the two republics signing a framework agreement on 14 March 2002, providing for the establishment of a 'Union of States' (to be known as 'Serbia and Montenegro'). The agreement allowed the two republics to maintain separate economies, but provided for them to share foreign and defence policies and to elect a joint presidency and legislature (in which Montenegro would have equal powers to Serbia). The agreement also permitted Montenegro to refer the issue of independence to a referendum after three years. Nevertheless, the accord, which was approved by the Montenegrin legislature in April (and by the Serbian legislature at the same time, and the Federal Assembly in June), provoked discontent among pro-independence supporters. Four prominent pro-independence ministers, belonging to the radical nationalist Liberal Alliance of Montenegro (LAM) and the Social-Democratic Party of Montenegro (SDP), resigned from the Montenegrin Government, leaving it without a majority. On 19 April Vujanović submitted his resignation, and the Government was dissolved. He was returned to the office of Prime Minister, but failed to secure majority support for a new government; consequently, in accordance with the Constitution, further legislative elections in Montenegro were scheduled for 6 October. His party won 39 of the 75 seats in the Assembly and, with Djukanović poised to become Prime Minister, Vujanović was elected President of the Assembly. Following Djukanović's resignation from the presidency in November, Vujanović became acting President by virtue of his office. He then announced that he would be the governing coalition's candidate in the presidential election. He obtained the most votes in the election, held on 22 December, but it was annulled after it was calculated that less than one-half of eligible voters had participated. In a second election in February 2003 (by which time the federation had been transformed into 'Serbia and Montenegro'), Vujanović again received more than 80% of the votes cast, but again the participation rate was less than 50%, and the election was annulled. Parliament subsequently changed the electoral law, deleting the requirement for 50% participation in any round of voting other than the first. A third election was held on 11 May, and Vujanović obtained some 63% of the votes cast, and was duly elected. He immediately announced that, in accordance with the new Constitution of Serbia and Montenegro, he would organize a referendum on Montenegro's secession in three years, as soon as permitted. *Address:* Office of the President, Podgorica, Serbia and Montenegro.

WAŁĘSA, Leszek ('Lech'): former President of Poland; b. 29 Sept. 1943, in Popowo, in the Włocławek district; m. Danuta Wałęsa in 1969, with four s. and four d. *Career:* he worked as an electrician for a collective farm, fulfilling his two years' military service in 1963–65. In 1967 he began work at the Lenin Shipyard in Gdańsk. By December 1970 he was the head of a strike committee; six years later he was dismissed for his protests about working conditions, voiced at a union meeting. Having found work repairing machinery, in 1979 he again lost his job, for commemorating the 1970 strike. In

August 1980 he joined strikers at the Lenin Shipyard and became head of their 'inter-factory' committee. His success in negotiations with the Government led to the signing of the so-called Gdańsk accords, which permitted free trade unions and the right to strike. By 1981 Wałęsa was Chairman of the Solidarity union and movement, which was banned under the martial law introduced in December. He was arrested and interned in 1981–82. In 1983 he was awarded the Nobel Peace Prize, but refused to leave Poland to collect it, as a sign of support for imprisoned trade union members. In 1998 Wałęsa participated in negotiations with the Government, resulting in the lifting of the ban on Solidarity and the prospect of democratic reform. He then headed the coalition that defeated Communist rule in the legislative election of 1989, and was elected President in December 1990, resigning as leader of Solidarity. As President he acquired a reputation for attempting to dominate government policy. While this was not always unpopular under the Communist-dominated parliament, disputes with successive Governments over his presidential role occurred throughout the early 1990s. The situation was exacerbated by his creation of presidential councils involved in policy-making decisions. Wałęsa formed the Non-Party Bloc for Political Reform, which participated in the 1993 legislative election. However, the election was won by former communist and other left-wing parties, and in 1994 and 1995 Wałęsa was again involved in disagreements with parliament and the Government over the extent of his powers. Many believed that he thereby hoped to recover his reputation as the champion of opposition to communism but, appearing increasingly contentious and authoritarian, he even alienated many of his erstwhile allies from the Solidarity movement. He was narrowly defeated by Aleksander Kwaśniewski (q.v.) in the second round of voting in the presidential election of November 1995; he subsequently failed to attend Kwaśniewski's inauguration. Before leaving office Wałęsa ensured that the premier, Józef Oleksy, was obliged to resign in January 1996. He continued to embarrass the Government and, many claimed, the public, by reapplying for his old job as an electrician at the Gdańsk shipyard, as part of a claim for a suitable pension (this was eventually arranged). Wałęsa re-emerged onto the political scene following the victory of Solidarity Election Action (AWS) in the general election of September 1997, with the announcement that he had formed a new party, the Christian Democratic Party of the Third Republic (ChDTRP). The party, he said, was positioned to inherit the reformist mantle of the AWS, although many observers believed that it was simply intended as a foundation for a presidential bid in 2000. The party formed an electoral alliance known as Lech Wałęsa's Camp with other, smaller parties in 1999. Wałęsa remained a totemic figure in Polish politics and a symbol of the victory of democracy, but in the presidential election of October 2000 he was decisively rejected by the electorate, securing just 1% of the votes cast. Having announced his retirement from politics, he stood down as Chairman of the ChDTRP in June 2001. However, one month later he became Honorary Chairman of the new Christian Democracy Civic Forum. He was much in demand as a lecturer and public speaker abroad, and in 2002 he announced his return to politics. In the same year he accepted a management position with a US-based business software company. In 2003 he presented a television programme on fishing, and while he had little involvement in politics he continued to attract international attention. *Address:* Gdańsk-Oliwa, ul. Polanki 54, Poland.

XHAFERI, Arben: Macedonian politician; b. 1948; ethnic Albanian. *Education:* studied philosophy in Belgrade (Yugoslavia). *Career:* involved in radical student politics, he helped to organize demonstrations in Tetovo, the main ethnic Albanian town in Macedonia. After his studies he moved to Kosovo, where he was appointed senior editor at the staterun television station in Priština. He was dismissed when the 'hardline' Serb administration led by Slobodan Milošević (q.v.) removed all ethnic Albanians from the station. Xhaferi returned to Macedonia and resumed his political activity, joining the predominantly Albanian Party for Democratic Prosperity (PDP). The PDP split into two factions in February

1994; that led by Xhaferi made the more radical demands for improved rights for ethnic Albanians in Macedonia. Xhaferi was elected to parliament as an independent in the October 1994 general election. In July 1997, his faction, which had been renamed the Party of Democratic Prosperity of Albanians in Macedonia (PDPAM), merged with the National Democratic Party (NDP) to create the Democratic Party of Albanians (DPA), headed by Xhaferi. Having formed an electoral alliance with the other faction of the PDP for the October 1998 general election, and obtained 24 seats, the DPA joined the coalition Government led by Ljubčo Georgievski (q.v.) of the International Macedonian Revolutionary Organization—Democratic Party for Macedonian National Unity (IMRO—DPMNU). The DPA also participated in the coalition Government formed in December 1999. In government, the DPA maintained its pressure for the rights of ethnic Albanians to be given greater prominence. When hostilities by the ethnic Albanian National Liberation Army (NLA) began in the north of the country in late February 2001, the party, while stressing the importance of resolving problems through the political sphere, put pressure on the Government to enter into negotiations with the rebels. At one point Xhaferi threatened to remove the DPA from government unless his demands were met. Nevertheless, the DPA formed part of the new Government of National Unity, also led by Georgievski, established in May 2001 to try to contain the situation. Popular and charismatic, Xhaferi enjoyed a great deal of influence throughout the crisis, despite ill health. It remained unclear how much contact or co-operation existed between the NLA and the DPA leadership; each side was critical of the other's tactics, but supported the same overall aims. When consitutional amendments improving the rights of ethnic Albanians were finally adopted in November 2001, Xhaferi said that the country's next move must be to 'repair the mentality' that had caused ethnic conflicts. Strengthening the cohesion and force of the ethnic Albanian side, however, in February 2002 the DPA, PDP and NDP formed a Co-ordinating Council of Albanians with the former NLA leadership. The Council was intended to unify ethnic Albanian politics in Macedonia and to ensure the implementation of the framework peace agreement. The DPA, PDP and the new Democratic Union for Integration (DUI), led by the former NLA leader Ali Ahmeti (q.v.) were unable to agree a common platform for the general election due to take place in September. At the election the DUI proved popular with Albanian voters, and won 16 seats, compared with the DPA's seven seats. Excluded from a governing coalition in which the DUI participated, Xhaferi decided not to take up his parliamentary mandate. However, he remained the leader of the DPA, and was re-elected as such in July 2003, stating that the party continued to advocate self-determination for the country's Albanian minority. In April 2002 Xhaferi was present at a café in Tetovo when it came under attack; the motive, and the attackers themselves, remained unknown. *Address:* Democratic Party of Albanians (DPA), Maršal Tito 2, Tetovo, former Yugoslav republic of Macedonia; tel. (44) 331534.

ZAORÁLEK, Lubomír: Czech politician; b. 6 September 1956. *Education:* he studied at the University of Ostrava. *Career:* He entered national politics in 1990, as a deputy to the Federal Assembly from North Moravia, but lost his seat following the free legislative elections held later in that year. He re-entered parliament in 1996, and quickly gained influence, becoming Chairman of the foreign affairs committee. Following the legislative elections held in June 2002, he was elected Chairman of the Chamber of Deputies, defeating the former Prime Minister, Václav Klaus (q.v.) in a second round of voting. During the period between the departure from the presidency of Václav Havel (q.v.) and the inauguration of his successor, Klaus, Zaorálek exercised some of the duties of the presidency. He was seen as a capable statesman, a fervent supporter of Czech membership of the European Union, and a passionate advocate of his region, one of the poorest in the country. *Address:* Office of the Chairman of the Chamber of Deputies, Prague, Czech Republic.

ZEMAN, Miloš: former Prime Minister of the Czech Republic; b. 29 Jan. 1944, in Kolín; m. Ivana Bednarčíková, with one s. and one d. *Education:* graduated from the Prague School of Economics. *Career:* a teacher and economic forecaster, Zeman joined the Communist Party in 1968 but, two years later, was expelled, along with other reformers, for his opposition to the invasion by Warsaw Pact troops. In February 1993, following the dissolution of Czechoslovakia, he became Chairman of the Czech Social Democratic Party (CSDP), although his mandate as a parliamentary deputy had expired with the federal institutions. Despite fears that his affinity with the radical wing of the party and his controversial political style might result in internal divisions, under his leadership the CSDP's popularity increased. He was in favour of free-market reform, although in a less radical form than that advocated by the governing coalition. His party became the main opposition party in the election to the Chamber of Deputies in May–June 1996, winning the second largest number of seats, of which one was his. In late June, in order to obtain the support of the CSDP, the minority governing coalition was obliged to agree to Zeman's election as parliamentary speaker. Zeman used his position to apply pressure to the Government, which was led by the Civic Democratic Party (CDP) and his long-standing political rival, Václav Klaus (q.v.). He continued to pursue aggressively the CSDP's agenda when that Government was replaced by Josef Tošovský's interim coalition, accusing the Government of enacting right-wing policies without a mandate to do so. In the general election of June 1998 the CSDP emerged as the strongest single party and, after other parties proved unable to form a centre-right coalition, Zeman became Prime Minister, leading a minority CSDP Government, with tacit CDP support. Despite marked policy differences, the 'opposition' agreement with the CDP was renewed in January 2000, although Zeman was obliged to reorganize the Council of Ministers and support amendments to electoral legislation. Zeman led the Czech Republic into the North Atlantic Treaty Organization (NATO), and was active in pursuit of membership of the European Union (EU). He stepped down as leader of the CSDP in April 2001, and was replaced by Vladimír Špidla (q.v.), but remained Prime Minister pending the 2002 parliamentary election. Relations with Klaus—and with sections of the media—continued to be strained. In late 2000 and early 2001 Zeman condemned the actions of demonstrators protesting against the appointment of Jiří Hodac as Director-General of the state television service (the protestors—supported by the President, Václav Havel—feared that Hodac's affiliation with the CDP would lead to political bias in news coverage). Following the legislative election of June 2002, in which the CSDP secured a narrow majority, Zeman was replaced as premier by Špidla, who formed a new, coalition Government. *Address:* Czech Social Democratic Party (Česká strana sociálně demokratická), Lidovy dům, Hybernská 7, 110 00 Prague 1, Czech Republic; tel. and fax (2) 24219911; e-mail info@socdem.cz.

ŽIVKOVIĆ, Zoran: Prime Minister of Serbia; b. 22 December 1960, in Niš; m., with one s. and one d. *Education:* he studied economics at the University of Belgrade. *Career:* an independent businessman, he was a founder member of the Democratic Party of Serbia (DPS). He was elected to the Serbian National Assembly in 1993, and became Vice-President of the DPS in the following year. He became Mayor of Niš in 1996, leaving the Serbian parliament shortly afterwards. He was attacked by nationalists in 1999 when, following the bombardment of the country by North Atlantic Treaty Organization (NATO) forces, he authorized the acceptance by the city of Niš of aid packages from NATO member countries. Within the DPS he was a loyal supporter of Zoran Djindjić, and when the latter became Prime Minister in 2001 he appointed Živković Minister of the Interior. Following the assassination of Djindjić in March 2003, Živković was elected to the premiership by parliament, and he formed a new Government shortly afterwards, claiming that he was retaining the same policies and the same people. He maintained the policy of co-operation with the International Criminal Tribunal for the former Yugoslavia (ICTY, based in The Hague, Netherlands), and stated that he would search for any fugitive indictees, and either arrest them or prove that they were not in Serbia. *Address:* Office of the Prime Minister, 11000 Belgrade, Nemanjina 11, Serbia and Montenegro; tel. (11) 3030866; fax (11) 3617609.

PART FOUR
Regional Information

THE UNITED NATIONS

Address: United Nations, New York, NY 10017, USA.

Telephone: (212) 963-1234; **fax:** (212) 963-4879; **internet:** www.un .org.

The United Nations (UN) was founded on 24 October 1945. The organization, which has 191 member states, aims to maintain international peace and security and to develop international co-operation in addressing economic, social, cultural and humanitarian problems. The principal organs of the UN are the General Assembly, the Security Council, the Economic and Social Council (ECOSOC), the International Court of Justice and the Secretariat. The General Assembly, which meets for three months each year, comprises representatives of all UN member states. The Security Council investigates disputes between member countries, and may recommend ways and means of peaceful settlement: it comprises five permanent members (the People's Republic of China, France, Russia, the United Kingdom and the USA) and 10 other members elected by the General Assembly for a two-year period. The Economic and Social Council comprises representatives of 54 member states, elected by the General Assembly for a three-year period: it promotes co-operation on economic, social, cultural and humanitarian matters, acting as a central policy-making body and co-ordinating the activities of the UN's specialized agencies. The International Court of Justice comprises 15 judges of different nationalities, elected for nine-year terms by the General Assembly and the Security Council: it adjudicates in legal disputes between UN member states.

Secretary-General: KOFI ANNAN (Ghana) (1997–2006).

MEMBER STATES IN CENTRAL AND SOUTH-EASTERN EUROPE
(with assessments for percentage contributions to the UN budget for 2003, and year of admission)

Albania	0.00300	1955
Bosnia and Herzegovina	0.00400	1992
Bulgaria	0.01300	1955
Croatia	0.03900	1992
Czech Republic*	0.20300	1993
Estonia	0.01000	1991
Greece	0.53900	1945
Hungary	0.12000	1955
Latvia	0.01000	1991
Lithuania	0.01700	1991
Macedonia, former Yugoslav republic	0.00600	1993
Poland	0.37800	1945
Romania	0.05800	1955
Serbia and Montenegro†	0.02000	2000
Slovakia*	0.04300	1993
Slovenia	0.08100	1992

* Czechoslovakia, which had been a member of the UN since 1945, ceased to exist as a single state on 31 December 1992. In January 1993, as Czechoslovakia's legal successors, the Czech Republic and Slovakia were granted UN membership, and seats on subsidiary bodies that had previously been held by Czechoslovakia were divided between the two successor states.

† Admitted as the Federal Republic of Yugoslavia. Present name was adopted in February 2003.

PERMANENT MISSIONS TO THE UNITED NATIONS
(with Permanent Representatives—July 2003)

Albania: 320 East 79th St, New York, NY 10021; tel. (212) 249-2059; fax (212) 535-2917; e-mail albania@un.int; ZEF MAZI.

Bosnia and Herzegovina: 866 United Nations Plaza, Suite 580, New York, NY 10017; tel. (212) 751-9015; fax (212) 751-9019; e-mail bosnia@un.int; internet www.un.int/bosnia; MIRZA KUSLJUGIC.

Bulgaria: 11 East 84th St, New York, NY 10028; tel. (212) 737-4790; fax (212) 472-9865; e-mail bulgaria@un.int; internet www.un .int/bulgaria; STEFAN TAFROV.

Croatia: 820 Second Ave, 19th Floor, New York, NY 10017; tel. (212) 986-1585; fax (212) 986-2011; e-mail croatia@un.int; internet www.un.int/croatia; Dr IVAN ŠIMONOVIĆ.

Czech Republic: 1109-1111 Madison Ave, New York, NY 10028; tel. (212) 535-8814; fax (212) 772-0586; e-mail un.newyork@embassy .mzv.cz; internet www.czechembassy.org; HYNEK KMONICEK.

Estonia: 600 Third Ave, 26th Floor, New York, NY 10016; tel. (212) 883-0640; fax (212) 883-0648; e-mail mission.newyork@mfa.ee; MERLE PAJULA.

Greece: 866 Second Ave, 13th Floor, New York, NY 10017; tel. (212) 888-6900; fax (212) 888-4440; e-mail mission@greeceun.org; internet www.greeceun.org; ADAMANTIOS VASSILAKIS.

Hungary: 227 East 52nd St, New York, NY 10022; tel. (212) 752-0209; fax (212) 755-5395; e-mail hungary@un.int; internet www.un .int/hungary; LÁSZLÓ MOLNÁR.

Latvia: 333 East 50th St, New York, NY 10022; tel. (212) 838-8877; fax (212) 838-8920; e-mail irppanony@aol.com; GINTS JEGERMANIS.

Lithuania: 420 Fifth Ave, 3rd Floor, New York, NY 10018; tel. (212) 354-7820; fax (212) 354-7833; e-mail lithuania@un.int; internet www.un.int/lithuania; GEDIMINAS SERKSNYS.

Macedonia, former Yugoslav republic: 866 United Nations Plaza, Suite 517, New York, NY 10017; tel. (212) 308-8504; fax (212) 308-8724; e-mail macedonia@un.int; internet www.un.int/ macedonia; Dr SRGJAN KERIM.

Poland: 9 East 66th St, New York, NY 10021; tel. (212) 744-2506; fax (212) 517-6771; e-mail poland@un.int; internet www.un.int/ poland; JANUSZ STANCZYK.

Romania: 573–577 Third Ave, New York, NY 10016; tel. (212) 682-3273; fax (212) 682-9746; e-mail romania@un.int; internet www.un .int/romania; MIHNEA IOAN MOTOC.

Serbia and Montenegro: 854 Fifth Ave, New York, NY 10021; tel. (212) 879-8700; fax (212) 879-8705; e-mail yugoslavia@un.int; internet www.un.int/serbia-montenegro; DEJAN ŠAHOVIĆ.

Slovakia: 866 United Nations Plaza, Suite 494, New York, NY 10017; tel. (212) 980-1558; fax (212) 980-3295; e-mail slovakia@un .int; PETER TOMKA.

Slovenia: 600 Third Ave, 24th Floor, New York, NY 10016; tel. (212) 370-3007; fax (212) 370-1824; e-mail mny@mzz-dkp.gov.si; internet www.un.int/slovenia; ROMAN KIRN.

OBSERVERS

European Community: European Commission Delegation in New York, 305 East 47th St, New York, NY 10017; tel. (212) 371-3804; fax (212) 758-2718; e-mail euinfo@delusny.cec.eu.int; internet www .europa-eu-un.org; Liaison Office of the General Secretariat of the Council of Ministers of the European Union, 345 East 46th St, 6th Floor, New York, NY 10017; tel. (212) 292-8600; fax (212) 681-6266; the Observer is the Permanent Representative to the UN of the country currently exercising the Presidency of the Council of Ministers of the European Union.

International Committee of the Red Cross: 801 Second Ave, 18th Floor, New York, NY 10017; tel. (212) 599-6021; fax (212) 599-6009; e-mail mail@icrc.delnyc.org; SYLVIE JUNOD.

International Organization for Migration: 122 East 42nd St, Suite 1610, New York, NY 10168; tel. (212) 681-7000; fax (212) 867-5887; e-mail unobserver@iom.int; ROBERT G. PAIVA.

International Seabed Authority: 1 United Nations Plaza, Room 1140, New York, NY 10017; tel. (212) 963-6470; fax (212) 963-0908.

International Tribunal for the Law of the Sea: 1 United Nations Plaza, Room 1142, New York, NY 10017; tel. (212) 963-6480; fax (212) 963-0908.

Organization of the Islamic Conference: 130 East 40th St, 5th Floor, New York, NY 10016; tel. (212) 883-0140; fax (212) 883-0143; e-mail oic@un.int; internet www.un.int/oic; MOKHTAR LAMANI.

World Conservation Union—IUCN: 406 West 66th St, New York, NY 10021; tel. and fax (212) 734-7608.

The Council of Europe, the Economic Co-operation Organization, the Organization of the Black Sea Economic Co-operation and the Organization for Security and Co-operation in Europe are among a number of intergovernmental organizations that have a standing invitation to participate as Observers, but do not maintain permanent offices at the United Nations.

United Nations Information Centres/Services

Czech Republic: nam. Kinských 6, 150 00 Prague 5; tel. (2) 57199831; fax (2) 47316761; e-mail unicprg@terminal.cz; internet www.unicprague.cz.

Greece: 36 Amalia Ave, 105 58; Athens; tel. (1) 5230640; fax (1) 5233639; e-mail unicgre@unic.gr; internet www.unic.gr; also covers Cyprus and Israel.

Poland: 00-608 Warsaw, Al. Niepodległości 186; 02-514 Warsaw, POB 1; tel. (22) 8259245; fax (22) 8255785; e-mail unic.pl@undp.org; internet www.unic.un.org.pl.

Romania: POB 1-701, 16 Aurel Vlaicu St, Bucharest; tel. (1) 2113242; fax (1) 2113506; e-mail unic@undp.ro.

ECONOMIC COMMISSION FOR EUROPE—ECE

Address: Palais des Nations, 1211 Geneva 10, Switzerland.

Telephone: (22)-917-44-44; **fax:** (22)-917-05-05; **e-mail:** info.ece@unece.org; **internet:** www.unece.org.

The UN Economic Commission for Europe was established in 1947. It provides a regional forum for governments from European countries, the USA, Canada, Israel and central Asian republics to study the economic, environmental and technological problems of the region and to recommend courses of action. ECE is also active in the formulation of international legal instruments and the setting of international norms and standards.

MEMBERS

Albania	Liechtenstein
Andorra	Lithuania
Armenia	Luxembourg
Austria	Macedonia, former Yugoslav
Azerbaijan	republic
Belarus	Malta
Belgium	Moldova
Bosnia and Herzegovina	Monaco
Bulgaria	Netherlands
Canada	Norway
Croatia	Poland
Cyprus	Portugal
Czech Republic	Romania
Denmark	Russia
Estonia	San Marino
Finland	Serbia and Montenegro
France	Slovakia
Georgia	Slovenia
Germany	Spain
Greece	Sweden
Hungary	Switzerland
Iceland	Tajikistan
Ireland	Turkey
Israel	Turkmenistan
Italy	Ukraine
Kazakhstan	United Kingdom
Kyrgyzstan	United Kingdom
Latvia	Uzbekistan

Organization

(July 2003)

COMMISSION

ECE, with ECAFE (now ESCAP), was the earliest of the five regional economic commissions set up by the UN Economic and Social Council. The Commission holds an annual plenary session and several informal sessions, and meetings of subsidiary bodies are convened throughout the year.

Chairman: CLYDE KULL (Estonia).

SECRETARIAT

The secretariat services the meetings of the Commission and its subsidiary bodies and publishes periodic surveys and reviews, including a number of specialized statistical bulletins on timber, housing, building, and transport (see list of publications below). It maintains close and regular liaison with the United Nations Secretariat in New York, with the secretariats of the other UN regional commissions and of other UN organizations, including the UN Specialized Agencies, and with other intergovernmental organizations. The Executive Secretary also carries out secretarial functions for the Executive Body of the 1979 Convention on Longrange Transboundary Air Pollution and its protocols. The ECE and UN Secretariats also service the ECOSOC Committee of Experts on the Transport of Dangerous Goods.

Executive Secretary: BRIGITA SCHMÖGNEROVÁ (Slovakia).

Activities

The guiding principle of ECE activities is the promotion of sustainable development. Within this framework, ECE's main objectives are to provide assistance to countries of central and eastern Europe in their transition from centrally-planned to market economies and to achieve the integration of all members into the European and global economies. Environmental protection, transport, statistics, trade facilitation and economic analysis are all principal topics in the ECE work programme, which also includes activities in the fields of timber, energy, trade, industry, and human settlements.

The 52nd plenary session of the ECE, held in April 1997, introduced a programme of reform, reducing the number of principal subsidiary bodies from 14 to seven, in order to concentrate resources on the core areas of work listed below, assisted by sub-committees and groups of experts. The Commission also determined to strengthen economic co-operation within Europe and to enhance co-operation and dialogue with other sub-regional organizations.

Committee on Environmental Policy: Provides policy direction for the ECE region and promotes co-operation among member governments in developing and implementing policies for environmental protection, rational use of natural resources, and sustainable development; supports the integration of environmental policy into sectoral policies; seeks solutions to environmental problems, particularly those of a transboundary nature; assists in strengthening environmental management capabilities, particularly in countries in transition; prepares ministerial conferences (normally held every four years—2003: Kiev, Ukraine); develops and promotes the implementation of international agreements on the environment; and assesses national policies and legislation. In April 2003 a committee was established to ensure compliance by governments with the Aarhus Convention on environmental decision-making and information dissemination.

Committee on Human Settlements: Reviews trends and policies in the field of human settlements; undertakes studies and organizes seminars; promotes international co-operation in the field of housing and urban and regional research; assists the countries of central and eastern Europe, which are currently in the process of economic transition, in reformulating their policies relating to housing, land management, sustainable human settlements, and planning and development.

Committee on Sustainable Energy: Exchanges information on general energy problems; work programme comprises activities including labelling classification systems and related legal and policy frameworks; liberalization of energy markets, pricing policies and supply security; harmonization of energy policies and practices; development of regional sustainable energy strategies for the 21st century; rational use of energy, efficiency and conservation; energy infrastructure including interconnection of electric power and gas networks; coal and thermal power generation in the context of sustainable energy development; Energy Efficiency 21 Project; promotion and development of a market-based Gas Industry in Economies in Transition—Gas Centre programme; and technical assistance and operational activities in energy for the benefit of countries with economies in transition.

Committee for Trade, Industry and Enterprise Development: A forum for studying means of expanding and diversifying trade among European countries, as well as with countries in other regions, and for drawing up recommendations on how to achieve these ends. Analyses trends, problems and prospects in intra-European trade; explores means of encouraging the flow of international direct investment into the newly opening economies of central and eastern Europe; promotes new or improved methods of trading by means of marketing, industrial co-operation, contractual guides, and the facilitation of international trade procedures (notably through the Electronic Data Interchange for Administration, Commerce and Transport—UN/EDIFACT, a flexible single international standard).

Conference of European Statisticians: Promotes improvement of national statistics and their international comparability in economic, social, demographic and environmental fields; promotes co-ordination of statistical activities of international organizations active in Europe and North America; and responds to the increasing need for international statistical co-operation both within the ECE region and between the region and other regions. Works very closely with FAO, OECD and the EU.

Inland Transport Committee: Promotes a coherent, efficient, safe and sustainable transport system through the development of international agreements, conventions and other instruments covering a wide range of questions relating to road, rail, inland water and combined transport, including infrastructure, border-crossing facilitation, road traffic safety, limitation of air pollution and noise, requirements for the construction of road vehicles and other transport regulations, particularly in the fields of transport of dangerous goods and perishable foodstuffs. Also considers transport trends and economics and compiles transport statistics. Assists central and eastern European countries, as well as ECE member states from central Asia, in developing their transport systems and infrastructures.

Timber Committee: Regularly reviews markets for forest products; analyses long-term trends and prospects for forestry and timber; keeps under review developments in the forest industries, including environmental and energy-related aspects. Subsidiary bodies run jointly with FAO deal with forest technology, management and training and with forest economics and statistics.

SUB-REGIONAL PROGRAMMES

Southeast European Co-operative Initiative—SECI: initiated in December 1996, in order to encourage co-operation among countries of the sub-region and to facilitate their access to the process of European integration. Nine *ad hoc* Project Groups have been established to undertake preparations for the following selected projects: trade facilitation; transport infrastructure, in particular road and rail networks; financial policies to promote small and medium-sized enterprises; co-operation to combat crime and corruption; energy efficiency demonstration zone networks; interconnection of natural gas networks; co-operation among securities markets; and the recovery programme for rivers, lakes and adjacent seas (with particular emphasis on the Danube River Basin). Activities are overseen by a SECI Agenda Committee and a SECI Business Advisory Council. Participating countries: Albania, Bosnia and Herzegovina, Bulgaria, Croatia, Greece, Hungary, the former Yugoslav republic of Macedonia, Moldova, Romania, Slovenia and Turkey.

Special Programme for the Economies of Central Asia—SPECA: initiated in March 1998 as a joint programme of the ECE and ESCAP. Aims to strengthen sub-regional co-operation, in particular in the following areas: the development of transport infrastructure and facilitation of cross-border activities; the rational use of energy and water; regional development and attraction of foreign investment; and development of multiple routes for pipeline transportation of hydrocarbons to global markets. In February 2002 SPECA's Regional Advisory Committee endorsed the terms of reference for the establishment of a Business Advisory Council of SPECA, which aimed to bring together business representatives from participating countries and from their major trading and economic partners. The inaugural session of the Council was held in June, in Almaty, Kazakhstan. Participating countries: Kazakhstan, Kyrgyzstan, Tajikistan, Turkmenistan and Uzbekistan.

Finance

ECE's budget for the two years 2002–03 was US $40.0m.

Publications

ECE Annual Report.

Annual Bulletin of Housing and Building Statistics for Europe and North America.

Annual Bulletin of Transport Statistics for Europe and North America.

ECE Highlights (3 a year).

The ECE in the Age of Change.

Economic Survey of Europe (2 a year).

Statistical Journal of the UNECE (quarterly).

Statistical Standards and Studies.

Statistics of Road Traffic Accidents in Europe and North America.

Timber Bulletin (6 a year).

Timber Committee Yearbook (annually).

Trends in Europe and North America: Statistical Yearbook of the ECE (annually).

UN Manual of Tests and Criteria of Dangerous Goods.

UN Recommendations on the Transport of Dangerous Goods.

UNECE International Legal Instruments, Norms and Standards.

The UNECE Works for Quality and Safety: Norms and Standards.

Women and Men in Europe and North America.

World Robotics (annually).

Studies on air pollution, forestry and timber, water, gas, energy; environmental performance reviews; country profiles on the housing sector; transport agreements; customs conventions; maps; trade and investment briefings and guides; reports on fertility and family, gender, migration and population ageing; statistical bulletins; sectoral studies; discussion papers.

Reports, proceedings of meetings, technical documents, codes of conduct, codes of practice, guide-lines to governments, etc.

UNITED NATIONS CHILDREN'S FUND—UNICEF

Address: 3 United Nations Plaza, New York, NY 10017, USA.

Telephone: (212) 326-7000; **fax:** (212) 887-7465; **e-mail:** info@unicef.org; **internet:** www.unicef.org.

UNICEF was established in 1946 by the UN General Assembly as the UN International Children's Emergency Fund, to meet the emergency needs of children in post-war Europe and China. In 1950 its mandate was changed to respond to the needs of children in developing countries. In 1953 the General Assembly decided that UNICEF should continue its work, as a permanent arm of the UN system, with an emphasis on programmes giving long-term benefits to children everywhere, particularly those in developing countries. In 1965 UNICEF was awarded the Nobel Peace Prize.

Organization

(July 2003)

EXECUTIVE BOARD

The Executive Board, as the governing body of UNICEF, comprises 36 member governments from all regions, elected in rotation for a three-year term by ECOSOC. The Board establishes policy, reviews programmes and approves expenditure. It reports to the General Assembly through ECOSOC.

SECRETARIAT

The Executive Director of UNICEF is appointed by the UN Secretary-General in consultation with the Executive Board. The administration of UNICEF and the appointment and direction of staff are the responsibility of the Executive Director, under policy directives laid down by the Executive Board, and under a broad authority delegated to the Executive Director by the Secretary-General. In December 2001 there were some 5,600 UNICEF staff positions, of which about 85% were in the field.

Executive Director: CAROL BELLAMY (USA).

REGIONAL OFFICE

UNICEF has a network of eight regional and 126 field offices serving 162 countries and territories. Its offices in Tokyo, Japan, and Brussels, Belgium, support fund-raising activities; UNICEF's supply division is administered from the office in Copenhagen, Demark. A research centre concerned with child development is based in Florence, Italy.

Central and Eastern Europe, Commonwealth of Independent States and Baltic States: Palais des Nations, 1211 Geneva, Switzerland; tel. (22) 9095600; fax (22) 9095909; e-mail ceecisro@unicef.ch.

NATIONAL COMMITTEES

UNICEF is supported by 37 National Committees, mostly in industrialized countries, whose volunteer members, numbering more than 100,000, raise money through various activities, including the sale of greetings cards. The Committees also undertake advocacy and awareness campaigns on a number of issues and provide an important link with the general public.

Activities

UNICEF is dedicated to the well-being of children, adolescents and women and works for the realization and protection of their rights within the frameworks of the Convention on the Rights of the Child, which was adopted by the UN General Assembly in 1989 and by 2003 was almost universally ratified, and of the Convention on the Elimination of All Forms of Discrimination Against Women, adopted by the UN General Assembly in 1979. Promoting the full implementation of the Conventions, UNICEF aims to ensure that children world-wide are given the best possible start in life and attain a good level of basic education, and that adolescents are given every opportunity to develop their capabilities and participate successfully in society. The Fund also continues to provide relief and rehabilitation assistance in emergencies. Through its extensive field network in some 162 developing countries and territories, UNICEF undertakes, in co-ordination with governments, local communities and other aid organizations, programmes in health, nutrition, education, water and sanitation, the environment, gender issues and development, and other fields of importance to children. Emphasis is placed on low-cost, community-based programmes. UNICEF programmes are increasingly focused on supporting children and women during critical periods of their life, when intervention can make a lasting difference, i.e. early childhood, the primary school years, adolescence and the reproductive years. Priorities include early years development, immunization strategies, girls' education, combating the spread and impact of HIV/AIDS, and strengthening the protection of children against violence, exploitation and abuse.

UNICEF was instrumental in organizing the World Summit for Children, held in September 1990 and attended by representatives from more than 150 countries, including 71 heads of state or government. The Summit produced a Plan of Action which recognized the rights of the young to 'first call' on their countries' resources and formulated objectives for the year 2000, including: (i) a reduction of the 1990 mortality rates for infants and children under five years by one-third, or to 50–70 per 1,000 live births, whichever is lower; (ii) a reduction of the 1990 maternal mortality rate by one-half; (iii) a reduction by one-half of the 1990 rate for severe malnutrition among children under the age of five; (iv) universal access to safe drinking water and to sanitary means of excreta disposal; and (v) universal access to basic education and completion of primary education by at least 80% of children. UNICEF supported the efforts of governments to achieve progress towards these objectives. The Fund played a leading role in helping governments and other partners prepare for the UN General Assembly special session on Children, which was held in May 2002 to assess the outcome of the 1990 summit and to determine a set of actions and objectives for the next 10 years. At the session the General Assembly adopted a document entitled 'A World Fit for Children', reaffirming its commitment to the agenda of the 1990 summit, and outlining a plan of action for the attainment of new goals and targets in the areas of education, health and the protection of children. A database of economic and social indicators is available at www.unicef.org/information/databases.

The UNICEF Regional Monitoring Project (MONEE) was initiated in 1992 to monitor the effects of economic and social transition on children in Central and South-Eastern Europe and the former USSR. UNICEF publishes on an annual basis a report entitled *Young People in Changing Societies,* assessing the situation of young adults (aged from 15–24 years) residing in Eastern European and Central Asian states with economies in transition. In May 2001 UNICEF supported a conference of high-level representatives of European and Central Asian countries, convened under the auspices of the Governments of Bosnia and Herzogovina and Germany, in Berlin, Germany, to formulate a communal agenda concerning the welfare of children in the region over the coming decade.

In 2000 UNICEF launched a new initiative, the Global Movement for Children—comprising governments, private- and public-sector bodies, and individuals—which aimed to rally world-wide support to improve the lives of all children and adolescents. In April 2001 a 'Say Yes for Children' campaign was adopted by the Global Movement, identifying 10 critical actions required to further its objectives. These were: eliminating all forms of discrimination and exclusion; putting children first; ensuring a caring environment for every child; fighting HIV/AIDS; eradicating violence against and abuse and exploitation of children; listening to children's views; universal eduation; protecting children from war; safeguarding the earth for children; and combating poverty. UNICEF was to co-ordinate the campaign.

UNICEF, in co-operation with other UN agencies, promotes universal access to and completion of basic and good quality education. The Fund, with UNESCO, UNDP, UNFPA and the World Bank, co-sponsored the World Conference on Education for All, held in Thailand in March 1990, and undertook efforts to achieve the objectives formulated by the conference, which included the elimination of disparities in education between boys and girls. UNICEF participated in and fully supports the objectives and framework for action adopted by the follow-up World Education Forum in Dakar, Senegal, in April 2000. The Fund supports education projects in sub-Saharan Africa, South Asia and countries in the Middle East and North Africa, and implements a Girls' Education Programme in more than 60 developing countries, which aims to increase the enrolment of girls in primary schools. More than 120m. children world-wide, of whom nearly 53% are girls, remain deprived of basic education. In December 2002 UNICEF initiated the '25 by 2005' initiative, which aimed to eliminate gender disparities in education in 25, mainly African and Asian, countries by 2005.

Through UNICEF's efforts the needs and interests of children were incorporated into Agenda 21, which was adopted as a plan of action for sustainable development at the UN Conference on Environment and Development, held in June 1992. In mid-1997, at the UN General Assembly's Special Session on Sustainable Development, UNICEF highlighted the need to improve safe water supply, sanitation and hygiene, and thereby reduce the risk of diarrhoea and other water-borne diseases, as fundamental to fulfilment of child rights. The Fund has supported initiatives to provide the benefits of safe water, sanitation and hygiene education to communities in developing countries. UNICEF also works with UNEP to promote environment issues of common concern and with the World Wide Fund for Nature to support the conservation of local ecosystems.

UNICEF aims to break the cycle of poverty by advocating for the provision of increased development aid to developing countries, and aims to help poor countries obtain debt relief and to ensure access to basic social services. To this end it supports NetAid, an internet-based strategy to promote sustainable development and combat extreme poverty. UNICEF is the leading agency in promoting the 20/20 initiative, which was endorsed at the World Summit for Social Development, held in Copenhagen, Denmark, in March 1995. The initiative encourages the governments of developing and donor countries to allocate at least 20% of their domestic budgets and official development aid respectively, to health care, primary education and low-cost safe water and sanitation.

UNICEF estimates that the births of some 50m. children annually are not officially registered, and urges universal registration in order to prevent the abuse of children without proof of age and nationality, for example through trafficking, forced labour, early marriage and military recruitment. The Fund, which vigorously opposes the exploitation of children as a violation of their basic human rights, works with ILO and other partners to promote an end to exploitative and hazardous child labour, and supports special projects to provide education, counselling and care for the estimated 250m. children between the ages of five and 14 years working in developing countries. UNICEF played a major role at the World Congress against Commercial Sexual Exploitation of Children, held in Stockholm, Sweden, in 1996, which adopted a Declaration and Agenda for Action to end the sexual exploitation of children. UNICEF also actively participated in the International Conference on Child Labour held in Oslo, Norway, in November 1997. The Conference adopted an Agenda for Action to eliminate the worst forms of child labour, including slavery-like practices, forced labour, commercial sexual exploitation and the use of children in drugs-trafficking and other hazardous forms of work. UNICEF supports the 1999 ILO Worst Forms of Child Labour Convention, which aims at the prohibition and elimination of the worst forms of child labour. In 1999 UNICEF launched a global initiative, Education as a Preventive Strategy Against Child Labour, with the aim of providing education to children forced to miss school because of work. The Fund helped to draft and promotes full ratification and implementation of an Optional Protocol to the Convention of the Rights of the Child concerning the sale of children, child prostitution and pornography, which was adopted in May 2000 and entered into force in January 2002. UNICEF co-sponsored and actively participated in the Second Congress Against Commercial Sexual Exploitation of Children held in Yokohama, Japan, in December 2001.

Child health is UNICEF's largest programme sector, accounting for some 40% of programme expenditure in 2000. UNICEF estimates that around 10m. children under five years of age die each year, mainly in developing countries, and the majority from largely preventable causes. UNICEF has worked with WHO and other partners to increase global immunization coverage against the following six diseases: measles, poliomyelitis, tuberculosis, diphtheria, whooping cough and tetanus. In 2000 UNICEF, in partnership with WHO, governments and other partners, helped to immunize 550m. children under five years of age in 53 countries against polio. In 1999

UNICEF, WHO, the World Bank and a number of public- and private-sector partners launched the Global Alliance for Vaccines and Immunization (GAVI), which aimed to protect children of all nationalities and socio-economic groups against vaccine-preventable diseases. GAVI's strategy included improving access to sustainable immunization services, expanding the use of existing vaccines, accelerating the development and introduction of new vaccines and technologies and promoting immunization coverage as a focus of international development efforts. UNICEF and WHO also work in conjunction on the Integrated Management of Childhood Illness programme to control diarrhoeal dehydration, a major cause of death among children under five years of age in the developing world. UNICEF-assisted programmes for the control of diarrhoeal diseases promote the low-cost manufacture and distribution of pre-packaged salts or home-made solutions. The use of 'oral rehydration therapy' has risen significantly in recent years, and is believed to prevent more than 1m. child deaths annually. During 1990–2000 diarrhoea-related deaths were reduced by one-half. UNICEF also promotes the need to improve sanitation and access to safe water supplies in developing nations in order to reduce the risk of diarrhoea and other water-borne diseases (see 20/20 initiative, above). To control acute respiratory infections, another leading cause of death in children under five in developing countries, UNICEF works with WHO in training health workers to diagnose and treat the associated diseases. As a result, the level of child deaths from pneumonia and other respiratory infections has been reduced by one-half since 1990. Around 1m. children die from malaria every year, mainly in sub-Saharan Africa. In October 1998 UNICEF, together with WHO, UNDP and the World Bank, inaugurated a new global campaign, Roll Back Malaria, to fight the disease. UNICEF supports control programmes in more than 30 countries.

According to UNICEF estimates, around 27% of children under five years of age are underweight, while each year malnutrition contributes to about one-half of the child deaths in that age group and leaves millions of others with physical and mental disabilities. More than 2,000m. people world-wide (mainly women and children in developing countries) are estimated to be deficient in one or more essential vitamins and minerals, such as vitamin A, iodine and iron. UNICEF supports national efforts to reduce malnutrition, for example, fortifying staple foods with micronutrients, widening women's access to education, improving household food security and basic health services, and promoting sound child-care and feeding practices. Since 1991 more than 15,000 hospitals in at least 136 countries have been designated 'baby-friendly', having implemented a set of UNICEF and WHO recommendations entitled '10 steps to successful breast-feeding'. In 1996 UNICEF expressed its concern at the impact of international economic embargoes on child health, citing as an example the extensive levels of child malnutrition recorded in Iraq. UNICEF remains actively concerned at the levels of child malnutrition and accompanying diseases in Iraq and in the Democratic People's Republic of Korea, which has also suffered severe food shortages centres.

UNICEF estimates that almost 515,000 women die every year during pregnancy or childbirth, largely because of inadequate maternal health care. For every maternal death, approximately 30 further women suffer permanent injuries or chronic disabilities as a result of complications during pregnancy or childbirth. With its partners in the Safe Motherhood Initiative—UNFPA, WHO, the World Bank, the International Planned Parenthood Federation, the Population Council, and Family Care International—UNICEF promotes measures to reduce maternal mortality and morbidity, including improving access to quality reproductive health services, educating communities about safe motherhood and the rights of women, training midwives, and expanding access to family planning services.

UNICEF is concerned at the danger posed by HIV/AIDS to the realization of children's rights. It is estimated that one-half of all new HIV infections occur in young people. At the end of 2002 3.2m. children under 15 were living with HIV/AIDS. Some 800,000 children under 15 were newly infected during that year, while 610,000 died as a result of AIDS. It was estimated that about one-half of all new HIV infections during 2002 occurred in young people, aged 15–24. It is estimated that more than 13m. children worldwide have lost one or both parents to AIDS since the start of the epidemic. UNICEF's priorities in this area include prevention of infection among young people, reduction in mother-to-child transmission, care and protection of orphans and other vulnerable children, and care and support for children, young people and parents living with HIV/AIDS. UNICEF works closely in this field with governments and co-operates with other UN agencies in the Joint UN Programme on HIV/AIDS (UNAIDS), which became operational on 1 January 1996. In July 2002 UNICEF, UNAIDS and WHO jointly produced a study entitled *Young People and HIV/AIDS: Opportunity in Crisis*, examining young people's sexual behaviour patterns and knowledge of HIV/AIDS.

At December 2001 it was estimated that 85,000 females aged from 15–24 and 340,000 males in that age group were living with HIV/AIDS in Central Europe, South-Eastern Europe and the CIS.

UNICEF provides emergency relief assistance, supports education, health, mine-awareness and psychosocial activities and helps to demobilize and rehabilitate child soldiers in countries and territories affected by violence and social disintegration. It assists children orphaned or separated from their parents and made homeless through armed conflict. In recent years several such emergency operations have been undertaken, including in Afghanistan, Angola, Burundi, Kosovo, Liberia, Sierra Leone and Sudan. In 1999 UNICEF adopted a Peace and Security Agenda to help guide international efforts in this field. Emergency education assistance includes the provision of 'Edukits' in refugee camps and the reconstruction of school buildings. In the area of health the Fund co-operates with WHO to arrange 'days of tranquility' in order to facilitate the immunization of children in conflict zones. Psychosocial assistance activities include special programmes to assist traumatized children and help unaccompanied children to be reunited with parents or extended families.

An estimated 300,000 children are involved in armed conflicts as soldiers, porters and forced labourers. UNICEF encourages ratification of the Optional Protocol to the Convention on the Rights of the Child on the involvement of children in armed conflict, which was adopted by the General Assembly in May 2000 and entered into force in February 2002, and bans the compulsory recruitment of combatants below 18 years. The Fund also urges states to make unequivocal statements endorsing 18 as the minimum age of voluntary recruitment to the armed forces. UNICEF was an active participant in the so-called 'Ottawa' process (supported by the Canadian Government) to negotiate an international ban on anti-personnel land-mines which, it was estimated, killed and maimed between 8,000 and 10,000 children every year. The Convention on the Prohibition of the Use, Stockpiling, Production and Transfer of Anti-Personnel Mines and on their Destruction was adopted in December 1997 and entered into force in March 1999. By January 2003 the Convention had been ratified by 131 countries. UNICEF is committed to campaigning for its universal ratification and full implementation, and also supports mine-awareness campaigns.

Finance

UNICEF is funded by voluntary contributions from governments and non-governmental and private-sector sources. Total income in 2000 amounted to US $1,139m., of which 64% was from governments and intergovernmental organizations. Total expenditure in 2000 amounted to $1,111m.

UNICEF's income is divided into contributions for 'regular resources' (used for country programmes of co-operation approved by the Executive Board, programme support, and management and administration costs) and contributions for 'other resources' (for special purposes, including expanding the outreach of country programmes of co-operation and ensuring capacity to deliver critical assistance to women and children for example during humanitarian crises). In 2000 contributions for 'regular resources' totalled US $563m. and those for 'other resources' amounted to $576m.

Publications

Facts and Figures (in English, French and Spanish).

The State of the World's Children (annually, in Arabic, English, French, Russian and Spanish and about 30 other national languages).

UNICEF Annual Report (in English, French and Spanish).

UNICEF at a Glance (annually, in English, French and Spanish).

Reports; series on children and women; nutrition; education; children's rights; children in wars and disasters; working children; water; sanitation and the environment; analyses of the situation of children and women in individual developing countries.

UNITED NATIONS DEVELOPMENT PROGRAMME— UNDP

Address: One United Nations Plaza, New York, NY 10017, USA.
Telephone: (212) 906-5295; **fax:** (212) 906-5364; **e-mail:** hq@undp
.org; **internet:** www.undp.org.

The Programme was established in 1965 by the UN General Assembly. Its central mission is to help countries to eradicate poverty and achieve a sustainable level of human development, an approach to economic growth that encompasses individual well-being and choice, equitable distribution of the benefits of development, and conservation of the environment. UNDP advocates for a more inclusive global economy.

Organization

(July 2003)

UNDP is responsible to the UN General Assembly, to which it reports through ECOSOC.

EXECUTIVE BOARD

The Executive Board is responsible for providing intergovernmental support to, and supervision of, the activities of UNDP and the UN Population Fund (UNFPA). It comprises 36 members: eight from Africa, seven from Asia, four from eastern Europe, five from Latin America and the Caribbean and 12 from western Europe and other countries.

SECRETARIAT

In recent years UNDP has implemented a process aimed at restructuring and improving the efficiency of its administration. Offices and divisions at the Secretariat include: an Operations Support Group; Offices of the United Nations Development Group, the Human Development Report, Audit and Performance Review, and Communications; and Bureaux for Crisis Prevention and Recovery, Resources and Strategic Partnerships, Development Policy, and Management. Five regional bureaux, all headed by an assistant administrator, cover: Africa; Asia and the Pacific; the Arab states; Latin America and the Caribbean; and Europe and the Commonwealth of Independent States. There is also a Division for Global and Interregional Programmes.

Administrator: MARK MALLOCH BROWN (United Kingdom).

Associate Administrator: Dr ZÉPHIRIN DIABRÉ (Burkina Faso).

Assistant Administrator and Director, Regional Bureau for Europe and the CIS: KALMAN MIZSEI (Hungary).

COUNTRY OFFICES

In almost every country receiving UNDP assistance there is an office, headed by the UNDP Resident Representative, who usually also serves as UN Resident Co-ordinator, responsible for the co-ordination of all UN technical assistance and operational development activities, advising the Government on formulating the country programme, ensuring that field activities are undertaken, and acting as the leader of the UN team of experts working in the country. The offices function as the primary presence of the UN in most developing countries.

OFFICES OF UNDP RESIDENT REPRESENTATIVES IN CENTRAL AND SOUTH-EASTERN EUROPE

Albania: Desh Moret E4, Rruga Shkurtit 35, Tirana; tel. (42) 33122; fax (42) 32075; e-mail fo.alb@undp.org; internet www.al.undp.org; Rep. ANNA-KRISTINA STJARNERKLINT.

Bosnia and Herzegovina: 71000 Sarajevo, Marsala Tita 48; tel. (71) 276800; fax (71) 665681; e-mail fo.bih@undp.org; internet www .undp.ba; Rep. HENRIK KOLSTRUP.

Bulgaria: 1784 Sofia, Tzarigradsko St, 7th Floor; tel. (2) 969-61-00; fax (2) 974-30-89; e-mail registry.bg@undp.org; internet www.undp .bg; Rep. MARTA RUEDAS.

Croatia: 10000 Zagreb, Ilica 207; tel. (1) 371-2631; fax (1) 371-2634; e-mail registry.hr@undp.org; Rep. CORNELIS KLEIN.

Kosovo: Pristina, St 14; tel. (38) 549-066; fax (38) 549-065; e-mail registry.ks@undp.org; internet www.ks.undp.org; Rep. ROBERT PIPER.

Latvia: Pils iela 21, Rīga 1167; tel. 750-3600; fax 750-3601; e-mail fo .lva@undp.org; internet www.undp.riga.lv; Rep. JAN SAND SORENSEN.

Lithuania: J. Tumo-Vaizganto 2, Vilnius 2000; tel. (2) 210-7400; fax (2) 210-7401; e-mail registry@undp.lt; internet www.undp.lt; Rep. CIHAN SULTANOGLU.

Macedonia, former Yugoslav republic: 1000 Skopje, ul. Dimitrie Cupovski 8; tel. (2) 116335; fax (2) 118261; e-mail registry.mk@undp .org; internet www.undp.org.mk; Rep. BERNARD FERY.

Poland: 00-608 Warsaw, ul. Niepodleglosci 186; tel. (22) 825-9245; fax (22) 825-4958; e-mail registry.pl@undp.org; internet www.undp .org.pl; Rep. COLIN GLENNIE.

Romania: 79362 Bucharest, Str. Aurel Vlaicu 16; tel. (1) 211-88-55; fax (1) 211-34-94; e-mail registry.ro@undp.org; internet www.undp .ro; Rep. SOKNAN HAN.

Regional Support Centre and Sub-regional Resource Facility (also covers Czech Republic, Hungary, Slovakia and Slovenia): Grösslingova 35, 811 09 Bratislava, Slovakia; tel. (7) 5933-7111; fax (7) 5933-7450; e-mail registry.sk@undp.org; internet www.undp.sk; Senior Regional Co-ordinator BEN SLAY.

Serbia and Montenegro: 11001 Belgrade, Internacionale Brigada 69; tel. (11) 3444-400; fax (11) 3444-300; e-mail undp@undp.org.yu; Rep. FRANCIS O'DONNELL.

Activities

As the world's largest source of grant-funded technical assistance for developing countries, UNDP provides advisory and support services to governments and UN teams. Assistance is mostly non-monetary, comprising the provision of experts' services, consultancies, equipment and training for local workers, including fellowships for advanced study abroad. UNDP supports programme countries in attracting aid and utilizing it efficiently. The Programme is committed to allocating some 88% of its regular resources to low-income developing countries. Developing countries themselves contribute significantly to the total project costs in terms of personnel, facilities, equipment and supplies.

Since the mid-1990s UNDP has strengthened its focus on results, streamlining its management practices and promoting clearly defined objectives for the advancement of sustainable human development. Under 'UNDP 2001', an extensive internal process of reform initiated during the late 1990s, UNDP placed increased emphasis on its activities in the field and on performance and accountability, focusing on the following priority areas: democratic governance; poverty reduction; crisis prevention and recovery; energy and environment; promotion of information and communications technology; and combating HIV/AIDS. In 2001 UNDP established six Thematic Trust Funds, covering each of these areas, to enable increased support of thematic programme activities. Gender equality and the provision of country-level and co-ordination services are also important focus areas. In accordance with the more results-oriented approach developed under the 'UNDP 2001' process the Programme introduced a new Multi-Year Funding Framework (MYFF), the first phase of which covered the period 2000–03. The MYFF outlines the country-driven goals around which funding is to be mobilized, integrating programme objectives, resources, budget and outcomes. It provides the basis for the Administrator's Business Plans for the same duration and enables policy coherence in the implementation of programmes at country, regional and global levels. A Results-Oriented Annual Report (ROAR) was produced for the first time in 2000 from data compiled by country offices and regional programmes. It was hoped that UNDP's greater focus on performance would generate increased voluntary contributions from donors, thereby strengthening the Programme's core resource base. In September 2000 the first ever Ministerial Meeting of ministers of development co-operation and foreign affairs and other senior officials from donor and programme countries, convened in New York, USA, endorsed UNDP's shift to a results-based orientation.

From the mid-1990s UNDP also determined to assume a more active and integrative role within the UN system-wide development framework. UNDP Resident Representatives—usually also serving as UN Resident Co-ordinators, with responsibility for managing inter-agency co-operation on sustainable human development initatives at country level—were to play a focal role in implementing this approach. In order to promote its co-ordinating function UNDP allocated increased resources to training and skill-sharing programmes. In late 1997 the UNDP Administrator was appointed to chair the UN Development Group (UNDG), which was established as part of a series of structural reform measures initiated by the UN Secretary-General, with the aim of strengthening collaboration between all UN funds, programmes and bodies concerned with development. The UNDG promotes coherent policy at country level through the system of UN Resident Co-ordinators (see above), the Common Country Assessment mechanism (CCA, a country-based process for evaluating national development situations), and the UN Development Assistance Framework (UNDAF, the foundation for planning and co-ordinating development operations at country level, based on the CCA. Within the framework of the Administrator's Business Plans for 2000–03 a new Bureau for Resources and Strategic Partnerships was established to build and strengthen working partnerships with other UN bodies, donor and programme countries, international financial institutions and development banks, civil society organizations and the private sector. The Bureau was also to serve UNDP's regional bureaux and country offices through the exchange of information and promotion of partnership strategies.

UNDP has a catalyst and co-ordinating function as the focus of UN system-wide efforts to achieve the so-called Millennium Development Goals (MDGs), pledged by governments attending a summit meeting of the UN General Assembly in September 2000. The objectives included a reduction by 50% in the number of people with income of less than US $1 a day and those suffering from hunger and lack of safe drinking water by 2015. Other commitments made concerned equal access to education for girls and boys, the provision of universal primary education, the reduction of maternal mortality by 75%, and the reversal of the spread of HIV/AIDS and other diseases. UNDP plays a leading role in efforts to integrate the MDGs into all aspects of the UN activities at country level. The Programme supports the formulation of MDG Reports for all developing countries.

UNDP aims to help governments to reassess their development priorities and to design initiatives for sustainable human development. UNDP country offices support the formulation of national human development reports (NHDRs), which aim to facilitate activities such as policy-making, the allocation of resources and monitoring progress towards poverty eradication and sustainable development. In addition, the preparation of Advisory Notes and Country Co-operation Frameworks by UNDP officials helps to high-light country-specific aspects of poverty eradiction and national strategic priorities. In January 1998 the Executive Board adopted eight guiding principles relating to sustainable human development that were to be implemented by all country offices, in order to ensure a focus to UNDP activities. A network of nine Sub-regional Resource Facilities (SURFs) has been established to strengthen and co-ordinate UNDP's technical assistance services. Since 1990 UNDP has published an annual *Human Development Report*, incorporating a Human Development Index, which ranks countries in terms of human development, using three key indicators: life expectancy, adult literacy and basic income required for a decent standard of living. In 1997 a Human Poverty Index and a Gender-related Development Index, which assesses gender equality on the basis of life expectancy, education and income, were introduced into the Report for the first time.

UNDP's activities to facilitate poverty eradication include support for capacity-building programmes and initiatives to generate sustainable livelihoods, for example by improving access to credit, land and technologies, and the promotion of strategies to improve education and health provision for the poorest elements of populations (with a focus on women and girls). In 1996 UNDP launched the Poverty Strategies Initiative (PSI) to strengthen national capacities to assess and monitor the extent of poverty and to combat the problem. All PSI projects were to involve representatives of governments, the private sector, social organizations and research institutions in policy debate and formulation. In early 1997 a UNDP scheme to support private-sector and community-based initiatives to generate employment opportunities, MicroStart, became operational. UNDP supports the Caribbean Project Development Facility and the Africa Project Development Facility, which are administered by the International Finance Corporation and which aim to develop the private sector in these regions in order to generate jobs and sustainable livelihoods. With the World Bank, UNDP helps governments of developing countries applying for international debt relief to draft Poverty Reduction Stategy Papers.

Approximately one-quarter of all UNDP programme resources support national efforts to ensure efficient and accountable governance and to build effective relations between the state, the private sector and civil society, which are essential to achieving sustainable development. UNDP undertakes assessment missions to help ensure free and fair elections and works to promote human rights, a transparent and competent public sector, a competent judicial system and decentralized government and decision-making. Within the context of the UN System-wide Special Initiative on Africa, UNDP supports the Africa Governance Forum which convenes annually to consider aspects of governance and development. In July 1997 UNDP organized an International Conference on Governance for Sustainable Growth and Equity, which was held in New York,

USA. At the World Conference on Governance held in Manila, the Philippines, in May/June 1999, UNDP sponsored a series of meetings held on the subject of Building Capacities for Governance. In April of that year UNDP and the Office of the High Commissioner for Human Rights launched a joint programme to strengthen capacity-building in order to promote the integration of human rights issues into activities concerned with sustainable human development.

In 1997 the Regional Bureau for Europe and the CIS (RBEC) initiated a programme to provide technical support to countries making the transition towards democratic institutions and free-market economies. The programme aimed to focus on public sector reform; decentralization, including strengthening local governments; support for parliaments; establishment of ombudsman institutions; participation and strengthening of civil society; and supreme audit and evaluation capacity, in order to promote transparency, accountability and effective management.

UNDP plays a role in developing the agenda for international cooperation on environmental and energy issues, focusing on the relationship between energy policies, environmental protection, poverty and development. UNDP supports the development of national programmes that emphasize the sustainable management of natural resources, for example through its Sustainable Energy Initiative, which promotes more efficient use of energy resources and the introduction of renewable alternatives to conventional fuels. UNDP is also concerned with forest management, the aquatic environment and sustainable agriculture and food security. Within UNDP's framework of urban development activities the Local Initiative Facility for Urban Environment (LIFE) undertakes small-scale environmental projects in low-income communities, in collaboration with local authorities and community-based groups. Other initiatives include the Urban Management Programme and the Public–Private Partnerships Programme for the Urban Environment, which aimed to generate funds, promote research and support new technologies to enhance sustainable environments in urban areas. In 1996 UNDP initiated a process of collaboration between city authorities world-wide to promote implementation of the commitments made at the 1995 Copenhagen summit for social development (see below) and to help to combat aspects of poverty and other urban problems, such as poor housing, transport, the management of waste disposal, water supply and sanitation. The first Forum of the so-called World Alliance of Cities Against Poverty was convened in October 1998, in Lyon, France. The second Forum took place in April 2000 in Geneva, Switzerland, and the third Forum was held in April 2002 in Huy, Belgium.

UNDP collaborates with other UN agencies in countries in crisis and with special circumstances to promote relief and development efforts, in order to secure the foundations for sustainable human development and thereby increase national capabilities to prevent or pre-empt future crises. In particular, UNDP is concerned to achieve reconciliation, reintegration and reconstruction in affected countries, as well as to support emergency interventions and management and delivery of programme aid. In 1995 the Executive Board decided that 5% of total UNDP regular resources be allocated to countries in 'special development situations', i.e. urgently requiring major, integrated external support. Special development initiatives include the demobilization of former combatants, rehabilitation of communities for the sustainable reintegration of returning populations, the restoration and strengthening of democratic institutions, and clearance of anti-personnel land-mines. UNDP has established a mine action unit within its Bureau for Crisis Prevention and Recovery (formerly the Emergency Response Division), in order to strengthen national de-mining capabilities. In December 1996 UNDP launched the Civilian Reconstruction Teams programme, creating some 5,000 jobs for former combatants in Liberia to work on the rehabilitation of that country's infrastructure. In January 2002 UNDP, the World Bank and the Asian Development Bank announced the results of a jointly-prepared preliminary 'needs assessment' report for reconstruction efforts in Afghanistan: it was estimated that US $15,000m. in donor financing would be required over 10 years, of which $5,000m. would need to be provided in the first 2.5 years. UNDP is the focal point within the UN system for strengthening national capacities for natural disaster reduction (prevention, preparedness and mitigation relating to natural, environmental and technological hazards). UNDP's Disaster Management Programme oversees the system-wide Disaster Management Training Programme.

From October 1998–January 2000 UNDP and the UN Department for Disarmament Affairs undertook a joint project in Albania, the Gramsh Pilot Project of Weapons in Exchange for Development, holding arms collections and implementing 12 small-scale community-based development projects. A similar scheme, known as the Weapons for Development Project, was undertaken in the Elbasan and Diber districts during the period June 2000–February 2002, including a weapons destruction component. A new two-year Small Arms and Light Weapons Control project was initiated in April 2002.

UNDP is a co-sponsor, jointly with WHO, the World Bank, UNICEF, UNESCO, UNDCP, ILO and UNFPA, of the Joint UN

Programme on HIV and AIDS (UNAIDS), which became operational on 1 January 1996. UNAIDS co-ordinates UNDP's HIV and Development Programme. UNDP regards the HIV/AIDS pandemic as a major challenge to development, and advocates for making HIV/AIDS a focus of national planning; supports decentralized action against HIV/AIDS at community level; helps to strengthen national capacities at all levels to combat the disease; and aims to link support for prevention activities, education and treatment with broader development planning and responses. UNDP places a particular focus on combating the spread of HIV/AIDS through the promotion of women's rights. Within the UN system UNDP also has responsibility for co-ordinating activities following global UN conferences. In March 1995 government representatives attending the World Summit for Social Development, which was held in Copenhagen, Denmark, approved initiatives to promote the eradication of poverty, to increase and reallocate official development assistance to basic social programmes and to promote equal access to education. The Programme of Action adopted at the meeting advocated that UNDP support the implementation of social development programmes, co-ordinate these efforts through its field offices and organize efforts on the part of the UN system to stimulate capacity-building at local, national and regional levels. The PSI (see above) was introduced following the summit. A special session of the General Assembly to review the implementation of the summit's objectives was convened in June 2000. Following the UN Fourth World Conference on Women, held in Beijing, People's Republic of China, in September 1995, UNDP led inter-agency efforts to ensure the full participation of women in all economic, political and professional activities, and assisted with further situation analysis and training activities. (UNDP also created a Gender in Development Office to ensure that women participate more fully in UNDP-sponsored activities.) In June 2000 a special session of the General Assembly (Beijing + 5) was convened to review the conference. UNDP played an important role, at both national and international levels, in preparing for the second UN Conference on Human Settlements (Habitat II), which was held in İstanbul, Turkey, in June 1996 the (see UN Human Settlements Programme). At the conference UNDP announced the establishment of a new facility, which was designed to promote private-sector investment in urban infrastructure. A special session of the UN General Assembly, entitled Istanbul + 5, was held in June 2001 to report on the implementation of the recommendations of the Habitat II conference.

UNDP aims to ensure that, rather than creating an ever-widening 'digital divide', ongoing rapid advancements in information technology are harnessed by poorer countries to accelerate progress in achieving sustainable human development. UNDP advises governments on technology policy, promotes digital entrepreneurship in programme countries and works with private-sector partners to provide reliable and affordable communications networks. The Bureau for Development Policy operates the Information and Communication Technologies for Development Programme, which aims to promote sustainable human development through increased utilization of information and communications technologies globally. The Programme aims to establish technology access centres in developing countries. A Sustainable Development Networking Programme focuses on expanding internet connectivity in poorer countries through building national capacities and supporting local internet sites. UNDP has used mobile internet units to train people even in isolated rural areas. In 1999 UNDP, in collaboration with an international communications company, Cisco Systems, and other partners, launched NetAid, an internet-based forum (accessible at www.netaid.org) for mobilizing and co-ordinating fundraising and other activities aimed at alleviating poverty and promoting sustainable human development in the developing world. With Cisco Systems and other partners, UNDP has worked to establish academies of information technology to support training and capacity-building in developing countries. By February 2002 70 academies had been established in 34 countries. UNDP and the World Bank jointly host the secretariat of the Digital Opportunity Task Force, a partnership between industrialized and developing countries, business and non-governmental organizations that was established in 2000. UNDP is a partner in the Global Digital Technology Initiative, launched in 2002 to strengthen the role of information and communications technologies in achieving the development goals of developing countries.

In 1996 UNDP implemented its first corporate communications and advocacy strategy, which aimed to generate public awareness of the activities of the UN system, to promote debate on development issues and to mobilize resources by increasing public and donor appreciation of UNDP. UNDP sponsors the International Day for the Eradication of Poverty, held annually on 17 October.

Finance

UNDP and its various funds and programmes are financed by the voluntary contributions of members of the United Nations and the Programme's participating agencies, as well as through cost-sharing by recipient governments and third-party donors. In 2001 total voluntary contributions amounted to an estimated US $2,580m, of which $652m. was for regular (core) resources. Donor co-finance, including trust funds and cost-sharing by third parties, amounted to $672m. in 2001, while cost-sharing by programme country governments amounted to more than $1,100m. In 2001 field programme expenditure under UNDP's regular programme totalled $1,526.2m.

Publications

Annual Report of the Administrator.

Choices (quarterly).

Global Public Goods: International Co-operation in the 21st Century.

Human Development Report (annually, also available on CD-ROM).

Poverty Report (annually).

Results-Oriented Annual Report.

Associated Funds and Programmes

UNDP is the central funding, planning and co-ordinating body for technical co-operation within the UN system. A number of associated funds and programmes, financed separately by means of voluntary contributions, provide specific services through the UNDP network. UNDP manages a trust fund to promote economic and technical co-operation among developing countries.

GLOBAL ENVIRONMENT FACILITY—GEF

The GEF, which is managed jointly by UNDP, the World Bank and UNEP, began operations in 1991 and was restructured in 1994. Its aim is to support projects concerning climate change, the conservation of biological diversity, the protection of international waters, reducing the depletion of the ozone layer in the atmosphere, and (since October 2002) arresting land degradation and addressing the issue of persistent organic pollutants. The GEF acts as the financial mechanism for the Convention on Biological Diversity and the UN Framework Convention on Climate Change. UNDP is responsible for capacity-building, targeted research, pre-investment activities and technical assistance. UNDP also administers the Small Grants Programme of the GEF, which supports community-based activities by local non-governmental organizations, and the Country Dialogue Workshop Programme, which promotes dialogue on national priorities with regard to the GEF. In August 2002 32 donor countries pledged $2,920m. for the third periodic replenishment of GEF funds (GEF-3), covering the period 2002–06. During 1991–2002 the GEF allocated $4,000m. in grants and raised $12,000m. in co-financing from other sources in support of more than 1,000 projects in more than 140 developing nations.

Chair. and CEO: MOHAMMED T. EL-ASHRY.

MONTREAL PROTOCOL

UNDP assists countries to eliminate the use of ozone-depleting substances (ODS), in accordance with the Montreal Protocol to the Vienna Convention for the Protection of the Ozone Layer, through the design, monitoring and evaluation of ODS phase-out projects and programmes. In particular, UNDP provides technical assistance and training, national capacity-building and demonstration projects and technology transfer investment projects. By mid-2001, through the Executive Committee of the Montreal Protocol, UNDP had completed 822 projects and activities concerned with eliminating ozone-depleting substances.

UNITED NATIONS DEVELOPMENT FUND FOR WOMEN— UNIFEM

UNIFEM is the UN's lead agency in addressing the issues relating to women in development and promoting the rights of women worldwide. The Fund provides direct financial and technical support to enable low-income women in developing countries to increase earnings, gain access to labour-saving technologies and otherwise improve the quality of their lives. It also funds activities that include women in decision-making related to mainstream development projects. In 2001 UNIFEM approved 67 new projects and continued to support some 204 ongoing programmes world-wide. In that year UNIFEM's Trust Fund in Support of Actions to Eliminate Violence Against Women (established in 1996) provided grants to 21 national and regional programmes. During 1996–2001 the Trust Fund awarded grants totalling US $5.3m. in support of 127 initiatives in more than 70 countries. UNIFEM has supported the preparation of national reports in 30 countries and used the priorities identified in these reports and in other regional initiatives to formulate a Women's Development Agenda for the 21st century. Through these efforts, UNIFEM played an active role in the preparation for the UN Fourth World Conference on Women, which was held in Beijing, People's Republic of China, in September 1995. UNIFEM participated at a special session of the General Assembly convened in June 2000 to review the conference, entitled Women 2000: Gender Equality, Development and Peace for the 21st Century (Beijing + 5). In March 2001 UNIFEM, in collaboration with International Alert, launched a Millennium Peace Prize for Women. In January 2002 UNIFEM appealed for US \$12m. to support women's leadership in the ongoing peace-building and reconstruction process in Afghanistan. UNIFEM maintains that the empowerment of women is a key to combating the HIV/AIDS pandemic, in view of the fact that women and adolescent girls are often culturally, biologically and economically more vulnerable to infection and more likely to bear responsibility for caring for the sick. In March 2002 UNIFEM launched a three-year programme aimed at making the gender and human rights dimensions of the pandemic central to policy-making in ten countries. A new online resource (www.genderandaids.org) on the gender dimensions of HIV/AIDS, was launched in February 2003. UNIFEM was a co-founder of WomenWatch (accessible online at www.un.org/womenwatch), a UN system-wide resource for the advancement of gender equality. Programme expenditure in 2001 totalled \$25.4m.

Headquarters

304 East 45th St, 15th Floor, New York, NY 10017, USA; tel. (212) 906-6400; fax (212) 906-6705; e-mail unifem@undp.org; internet www.unifem.undp.org.

Director: NOELEEN HEYZER (Singapore).

UNITED NATIONS VOLUNTEERS—UNV

The United Nations Volunteers is an important source of middle-level skills for the UN development system supplied at modest cost, particularly in the least-developed countries. Volunteers expand the scope of UNDP project activities by supplementing the work of international and host-country experts and by extending the influence of projects to local community levels. UNV also supports technical co-operation within and among the developing countries by encouraging volunteers from the countries themselves and by forming regional exchange teams comprising such volunteers. UNV is involved in areas such as peace-building, elections, human rights, humanitarian relief and community-based environmental programmes, in addition to development activities.

The UN International Short-term Advisory (UNISTAR) Programme, which is the private-sector development arm of UNV, has increasingly focused its attention on countries in the processof economic transition. Since 1994 UNV has administered UNDP's Transfer of Knowledge Through Expatriate Nationals (TOKTEN) programme, which was initiated in 1977 to enable specialists and professionals from developing countries to contribute to development efforts in their countries of origin through short-term technical assignments.

At 31 January 2003 3,201 UNVs were serving in 130 countries. At that time the total number of people who had served under the initiative amounted to more than 30,000 in some 140 countries.

From mid-2000 600 UNVs participated in efforts to implement the electoral registration process in Kosovo and Metohija, as well as to support other reconstruction projects.

Headquarters

POB 260111, 53153 Bonn, Germany; tel. (228) 8152000; fax (228) 8152001; e-mail information@unvolunteers.org; internet www .unvolunteers.org.

Executive Co-ordinator: SHARON CAPELING-ALAKIJA.

UNITED NATIONS ENVIRONMENT PROGRAMME— UNEP

Address: POB 30552, Nairobi, Kenya.

Telephone: (20) 621234; **fax:** (20) 624489; **e-mail:** cpiinfo@unep .org; **internet:** www.unep.org.

The United Nations Environment Programme was established in 1972 by the UN General Assembly, following recommendations of the 1972 UN Conference on the Human Environment, in Stockholm, Sweden, to encourage international co-operation in matters relating to the human environment.

Organization

(July 2003)

GOVERNING COUNCIL

The main functions of the Governing Council, which meets every two years, are to promote international co-operation in the field of the environment and to provide general policy guidance for the direction and co-ordination of environmental programmes within the UN system. It comprises representatives of 58 states, elected by the UN General Assembly, for four-year terms, on a regional basis. The Council is assisted in its work by a Committee of Permanent Representatives.

HIGH-LEVEL COMMITTEE OF MINISTERS AND OFFICIALS IN CHARGE OF THE ENVIRONMENT

The Committee was established by the Governing Council in 1997, with a mandate to consider the international environmental agenda and to make recommendations to the Council on reform and policy issues. In addition, the Committee, comprising 36 elected members, was to provide guidance and advice to the Executive Director, to enhance UNEP's collaboration and co-operation with other multilateral bodies and to help to mobilize financial resources for UNEP.

SECRETARIAT

Offices and divisions at UNEP headquarters include the the Office of the Executive Director; the Secretariat for Governing Bodies: Offices for Evaluation and Oversight, Programme Co-ordination and Man-

agement, and Resource Mobilization; and divisions of communications and public information, early warning and assessment, policy development and law, policy implementation, technology and industry and economics, regional co-operation and representation, environmental conventions, and GEF co-ordination.

Executive Director: Dr KLAUS TÖPFER (Germany).

REGIONAL OFFICE

Europe: 11–13 chemin des Anémones, 1219 Châtelaine, Geneva, Switzerland; tel. (22) 9178279; fax (22) 9178024; e-mail roe@unep .ch; internet www.unep.ch/roe.

OTHER OFFICES

Agreement on the Conservation of Small Cetaceans of the Baltic and North Seas—ASCOBANS: c/o Sea Mammal Research Unit, High Cross, Madingley Rd, Cambridge CB3 0ET, United Kingdom; tel. and fax (1223) 301282; e-mail ascobans@smru.ac.uk; internet www.wcmc.org.uk/cms; Exec. Sec. JETTE JENSEN; f. 1994; encourages co-operation on habitat conservation and management; research to assess population status and dynamics, seasonal movements and important feeding and breeding areas; pollutant analyses; legislation advice; information and education.

Convention on International Trade in Endangered Species of Wild Fauna and Flora— CITES: 15 chemin des Anémones, 1219 Châtelaine, Geneva, Switzerland; tel. (22) 9178139; fax (22) 7973417; e-mail cites@unep.ch; internet www.cites.org; Sec.-Gen. WILLEM WOUTER WIJNSTEKERS (Netherlands).

Global Programme of Action for the Protection of the Marine Environment from Land-based Activities: POB 16227, 2500 The Hague, Netherlands; tel. (70) 3114460; fax (70) 3456648; e-mail gpa@unep.nl; internet www.gpa.unep.org; Co-ordinator Dr VEERLE VANDEWEERD.

Secretariat of the Basel Convention: CP 356, 13–15 chemin des Anémones, 1219 Châtelaine, Geneva, Switzerland; tel. (22) 9178218; fax (22) 7973454; e-mail sbc@unep.ch; internet www.basel.int; Exec. Sec. SACHIKO KUWABARA-YAMAMOTO.

Secretariat of the Convention on Biological Diversity: World Trade Centre, 393 St Jacques St West, Suite 300, Montréal, QC, Canada H2Y 1N9; tel. (514) 288-2220; fax (514) 288-6588; e-mail secretariat@biodiv.org; internet www.biodiv.org; Exec. Sec. HAMDALLAH ZEDAN.

Secretariat of the Multilateral Fund for the Implementation of the Montreal Protocol: 1800 McGill College Ave, 27th Floor, Montréal, QC, Canada H3A 3J6; tel. (514) 282-1122; fax (514) 282-0068; e-mail secretariat@unmfs.org; internet www.unmfs.org; Chief Dr OMAR EL-ARINI.

Secretariat of the UN Framework Convention on Climate Change: Haus Carstanjen, Martin-Luther-King-Str. 8,53175 Bonn, Germany; tel. (228) 815-1000; fax (228) 815-1999; e-mail secretariat@unfccc.de; internet www.unfccc.de; Exec. Sec. JOKE WALLER-HUNTER.

UNEP/CMS (Convention on the Conservation of Migratory Species of Wild Animals) Secretariat: Martin-Luther-King-Str. 8, 53175 Bonn, Germany; tel. (228) 8152401; fax (228) 8152449; e-mail cms@unep.de; internet www.wcmc.org.uk/cms; Exec. Sec. ARNULF MÜLLER-HELMBRECHT.

UNEP Chemicals: International Environment House, 11–13 chemin des Anémones, 1219 Châtelaine, Geneva, Switzerland; tel. (22) 9171234; fax (22) 7973460; e-mail chemicals@unep.ch; internet www.chem.unep.ch; Dir JAMES B. WILLIS.

UNEP Co-ordinating Unit for the Mediterranean Action Plan—MEDU: Leoforos Vassileos Konstantinou 48, POB 18019, 11610 Athens, Greece; tel. (210) 7273100; fax (210) 7253196; e-mail unepmedu@unepmap.gr; internet www.unepmap.org; Co-ordinator LUCIEN CHABASON.

UNEP Division of Technology, Industry and Economics: Tour Mirabeau, 39–43, Quai André Citroën, 75739 Paris Cédex 15, France; tel. 1-44-37-14-41; fax 1-44-37-14-74; e-mail unep.tie@unep.fr; internet www.uneptie.org/; Dir JACQUELINE ALOISI DE LARDEREL.

UNEP International Environmental Technology Centre—IETC: 2–110 Ryokuchi koen, Tsurumi-ku, Osaka 538-0036, Japan; tel. (6) 6915-4581; fax (6) 6915-0304; e-mail ietc@unep.or.jp; internet www.unep.or.jp; Dir STEVE HALLS.

UNEP Ozone Secretariat: POB 30552, Nairobi, Kenya; tel. (20) 623850; fax (20) 623913; e-mail ozoneinfo@unep.org; internet www.unep.org/ozone/; Officer-in-Charge MICHAEL GRABER.

UNEP Secretariat for the UN Scientific Committee on the Effects of Atomic Radiation: Vienna International Centre, Wagramerstrasse 5, POB 500, 1400 Vienna, Austria; tel. (1) 26060-4330; fax (1) 26060-5902; e-mail norman.gentner@unvienna.org; internet www.unscear.org; Sec. Dr NORMAN GENTNER.

Activities

UNEP serves as a focal point for environmental action within the UN system. It aims to maintain a constant watch on the changing state of the environment; to analyse the trends; to assess the problems using a wide range of data and techniques; and to promote projects leading to environmentally sound development. It plays a catalytic and co-ordinating role within and beyond the UN system. Many UNEP projects are implemented in co-operation with other UN agencies, particularly UNDP, the World Bank group, FAO, UNESCO and WHO. About 45 intergovernmental organizations outside the UN system and 160 international non-governmental organizations have official observer status on UNEP's Governing Council, and, through the Environment Liaison Centre in Nairobi, UNEP is linked to more than 6,000 non-governmental bodies concerned with the environment. UNEP also sponsors international conferences, programmes, plans and agreements regarding all aspects of the environment.

In February 1997 the Governing Council, at its 19th session, adopted a ministerial declaration (the Nairobi Declaration) on UNEP's future role and mandate, which recognized the organization as the principal UN body working in the field of the environment and as the leading global environmental authority, setting and overseeing the international environmental agenda. In June a special session of the UN General Assembly, referred to as the 'Rio + 5', was convened to review the state of the environment and progress achieved in implementing the objectives of the UN Conference on Environment and Development (UNCED), held in Rio de Janeiro, Brazil, in June 1992. The meeting adopted a Programme for Further Implementation of Agenda 21 (a programme of activities to promote sustainable development, adopted by UNCED) in order to intensify efforts in areas such as energy, freshwater resources and technology transfer. The meeting confirmed UNEP's essential role in advancing the Programme and as a global authority promoting a coherent legal and political approach to the environmental challenges of sustainable development. An extensive process of restructuring and realign-

ment of functions was subsequently initiated by UNEP, and a new organizational structure reflecting the decisions of the Nairobi Declaration was implemented during 1999. UNEP played a leading role in preparing for the World Summit on Sustainable Development (WSSD), held in August/September 2002 in Johannesburg, South Africa, to assess strategies for strengthening the implementation of Agenda 21. Governments participating in the conference adopted the Johannesburg Declaration and WSSD Plan of Implementation, in which they strongly reaffirmed commitment to the principles underlying Agenda 21 and also pledged support to all internationally-agreed development goals, including the UN Millennium Development Goals adopted by governments attending a summit meeting of the UN General Assembly in September 2000. Participating governments made concrete commitments to attaining several specific objectives in the areas of water, energy, health, agriculture and fisheries, and biodiversity. These included a reduction by one-half in the proportion of people world-wide lacking access to clean water or good sanitation by 2015, the restocking of depleted fisheries by 2015, a reduction in the ongoing loss in biodiversity by 2010, and the production and utilization of chemicals without causing harm to human beings and the environment by 2020. Participants determined to increase usage of renewable energy sources and to develop by 2005 integrated water resources management and water efficiency plans. A large number of partnerships between governments, private sector interests and civil society groups were announced at the conference.

In May 2000 UNEP sponsored the first annual Global Ministerial Environment Forum (GMEF), held in Malmö, Sweden, and attended by environment ministers and other government delegates from more than 130 countries. Participants reviewed policy issues in the field of the environment and addressed issues such as the impact on the environment of population growth, the depletion of earth's natural resources, climate change and the need for fresh water supplies. The Forum issued the Malmö Declaration, which identified the effective implementation of international agreements on environmental matters at national level as the most pressing challenge for policy-makers. The Declaration emphasized the importance of mobilizing domestic and international resources and urged increased co-operation from civil society and the private sector in achieving sustainable development. The second GMEF, held in Nairobi in February 2001, addressed means of strengthening international environmental governance, establishing an Open-Ended Intergovernmental Group of Ministers or Their Representatives (IGM) to prepare a report on possible reforms. GMEF-3, held in Cartagena, Colombia, in February 2002, considered UNEP's participation in the forthcoming WSSD, with a focus on environmental guidance issues.

ENVIRONMENTAL ASSESSMENT AND EARLY WARNING

The Nairobi Declaration resolved that the strengthening of UNEP's information, monitoring and assessment capabilities was a crucial element of the organization's restructuring, in order to help establish priorities for international, national and regional action, and to ensure the efficient and accurate dissemination of emerging environmental trends and emergencies.

In 1995 UNEP launched the Global Environment Outlook (GEO) process of environmental assessment. UNEP is assisted in its analysis of the state of the global environment by an extensive network of collaborating centres. Reports on the process are issued every two–three years. (The first *Global Environment Outlook, GEO-1*, was published in January 1997, and the second, *GEO 2000*, in September 1999, and *GEO-3* in May 2002.) UNEP is leading a major Global International Waters Assessment (GIWA) to consider all aspects of the world's water-related issues, in particular problems of shared transboundary waters, and of future sustainable management of water resources. UNEP is also a sponsoring agency of the Joint Group of Experts on the Scientific Aspects of Marine Environmental Pollution and contributes to the preparation of reports on the state of the marine environment and on the impact of land-based activities on that environment. In November 1995 UNEP published a Global Biodiversity Assessment, which was the first comprehensive study of biological resources throughout the world. The UNEP–World Conservation Monitoring Centre (UNEP–WCMC), established in June 2000, provides biodiversity-related assessment. UNEP is a partner in the International Coral Reef Action Network—ICRAN, which was established in 2000 to manage and protect coral reefs world-wide. In June 2001 UNEP launched the Millennium Ecosystems Assessment, which is expected to be completed in 2004. Other major assessments under way in 2002 included GIWA (see above); the Assessment of Impact and Adaptation to Climate Change; the Solar and Wind Energy Resource Assessment; the Regionally-Based Assessment of Persistent Toxic Substances; the Land Degradation Assessment in Drylands; and the Global Methodology for Mapping Human Impacts on the Biosphere (GLOBIO) project.

UNEP's environmental information network includes the Global Resource Information Database (GRID), which converts collected data into information usable by decision-makers. The INFOTERRA programme facilitates the exchange of environmental information through an extensive network of national 'focal points'. By early 2003 177 countries were participating in the network. Through INFOTERRA UNEP promotes public access to environmental information, as well as participation in environmental concerns. UNEP aims to establish in every developing region an Environment and Natural Resource Information Network (ENRIN) in order to make available technical advice and manage environmental information and data for improved decision-making and action-planning in countries most in need of assistance. UNEP aims to integrate its information resources in order to improve access to information and to promote its international exchange. This has been pursued through UNEPnet, an internet-based interactive environmental information- and data-sharing facility, and Mercure, a telecommunications service using satellite technology to link a network of 16 earth stations throughout the world.

UNEP's information, monitoring and assessment structures also serve to enhance early-warning capabilities and to provide accurate information during an environmental emergency.

POLICY DEVELOPMENT AND LAW

UNEP aims to promote the development of policy tools and guidelines in order to achieve the sustainable management of the world environment. At a national level it assists governments to develop and implement appropriate environmental instruments and aims to co-ordinate policy initiatives. Training workshops in various aspects of environmental law and its applications are conducted. UNEP supports the development of new legal, economic and other policy instruments to improve the effectiveness of existing environmental agreements.

UNEP was instrumental in the drafting of a Convention on Biological Diversity (CBD) to preserve the immense variety of plant and animal species, in particular those threatened with extinction. The Convention entered into force at the end of 1993; by December 2002 187 countries and the European Community were parties to the CBD. The CBD's Cartagena Protocol on Biosafety (so-called as it had been addressed at an extraordinary session of parties to the CBD convened in Cartagena, Colombia, in February 1999) was adopted at a meeting of parties to the CBD held in Montreal, Canada, in January 2000. The Protocol regulates the transboundary movement and use of living modified organisms resulting from biotechnology (such as genetically modified—GM—seeds and crops), in order to reduce any potential adverse effects on biodiversity and human health. It establishes an Advanced Informed Agreement procedure to govern the import of such organisms. By December 2002 the Protocol had been ratified by 45 states. In January of that year UNEP launched a major project aimed at supporting developing countries with assessing the potential health and environmental risks and benefits of GM crops, in preparation for the Protocol's entry into force. In February the parties to the CBD and other partners convened a conference, in Montreal, to address ways in which the traditional knowledge and practices of local communities could be preserved and used to conserve highly-threatened species and ecosystems. The sixth conference of parties to the CBD, held in April 2002, adopted detailed voluntary guide-lines concerning access to genetic resources and sharing the benefits attained from such resources with the countries and local communities where they originate; a global work programme on forests; and a set of guiding principles for combating alien invasive species. UNEP supports co-operation for biodiversity assessment and management in selected developing regions and for the development of strategies for the conservation and sustainable exploitation of individual threatened species (e.g. the Global Tiger Action Plan). It also provides assistance for the preparation of individual country studies and strategies to strengthen national biodiversity management and research. UNEP administers the Convention on International Trade in Endangered Species of Wild Flora and Fauna (CITES), which entered into force in 1975.

UNEP is the lead UN agency for promoting environmentally sustainable water management. It regards the unsustainable use of water as the most urgent environmental and sustainable development issue, and estimates that two-thirds of the world's population will suffer chronic water shortages by 2025, owing to rising demand for drinking water as a result of growing populations, decreasing quality of water because of pollution, and increasing requirements of industries and agriculture. In 2000 UNEP adopted a new water policy and strategy, comprising assessment, management and co-ordination components. The Global International Waters Assessment (see above) is the primary framework for the assessment component. The management component includes the Global Programme of Action (GPA) for the Protection of the Marine Environment from Land-based Activities (adopted in November 1995), and UNEP's freshwater programme and regional seas programme. The

GPA for the Protection of the Marine Environment for Land-based Activities focuses on the effects of activities such as pollution on freshwater resources, marine biodiversity and the coastal ecosystems of small-island developing states. UNEP aims to develop a similar global instrument to ensure the integrated management of freshwater resources. It promotes international co-operation in the management of river basins and coastal areas and for the development of tools and guide-lines to achieve the sustainable management of freshwater and coastal resources. UNEP provides scientific, technical and administrative support to facilitate the implementation and co-ordination of 14 regional seas conventions and 13 regional plans of action, and is developing a strategy to strengthen collaboration in their implementation. The new water policy and strategy emphasizes the need for improved co-ordination of existing activities. UNEP aims to play an enhanced role within relevant co-ordination mechanisms, such as the UN openended informal consultation process on oceans and the law of the sea.

In 1996 UNEP, in collaboration with FAO, began to work towards promoting and formulating a legally-binding international convention on prior informed consent (PIC) for hazardous chemicals and pesticides in international trade, extending a voluntary PIC procedure of information exchange undertaken by more than 100 governments since 1991. The Convention was adopted at a conference held in Rotterdam, Netherlands, in September 1998, and was to enter into force on being ratified by 50 signatory states. It aimed to reduce risks to human health and the environment by restricting the production, export and use of hazardous substances and enhancing information exchange procedures. By March 2003 the Convention had been ratified by 41 signatory states.

In conjunction with UN-Habitat, UNDP, the World Bank and other organizations and institutions, UNEP promotes environmental concerns in urban planning and management through the Sustainable Cities Programme, as well as regional workshops concerned with urban pollution and the impact of transportation systems. In 1994 UNEP inaugurated an International Environmental Technology Centre (IETC), with offices in Osaka and Shiga, Japan, in order to strengthen the capabilities of developing countries and countries with economies in transition to promote environmentally-sound management of cities and freshwater reservoirs through technology co-operation and partnerships.

UNEP has played a key role in global efforts to combat risks to the ozone layer, resultant climatic changes and atmospheric pollution. UNEP worked in collaboration with the World Meteorological Organization to formulate the UN Framework Convention on Climate Change (UNFCCC), with the aim of reducing the emission of gases that have a warming effect on the atmosphere, and has remained an active participant in the ongoing process to review and enforce the implementation of the Convention and of its Kyoto Protocol. UNEP was the lead agency in formulating the 1987 Montreal Protocol to the Vienna Convention for the Protection of the Ozone Layer (1985), which provided for a 50% reduction in the production of chlorofluorocarbons (CFCs) by 2000. An amendment to the Protocol was adopted in 1990, which required complete cessation of the production of CFCs by 2000 in industrialized countries and by 2010 in developing countries; these deadlines were advanced to 1996 and 2006, respectively, in November 1992. In 1997 the ninth Conference of the Parties (COP) to the Vienna Convention adopted a further amendment which aimed to introduce a licensing system for all controlled substances. The eleventh COP, meeting in Beijing, People's Republic of China, in November/December 1999, adopted the Beijing Amendment, which imposed tighter controls on the import and export of hydrochlorofluorocarbons, and on the production and consumption of bromochloromethane (Halon-1011, an industrial solvent and fire extinguisher). The Beijing Amendment entered into force in December 2001. A Multilateral Fund for the Implementation of the Montreal Protocol was established in June 1990 to promote the use of suitable technologies and the transfer of technologies to developing countries. UNEP, UNDP, the World Bank and UNIDO are the sponsors of the Fund, which by July 2001 had approved financing for some 3,850 projects in 124 developing countries at a cost of US $1,200m. Commitments of $440m. were made to the fourth replenishment of the Fund, covering the three-year period 2000–02.

POLICY IMPLEMENTATION

UNEP's Division of Environmental Policy Implementation incorporates two main functions: technical co-operation and response to environmental emergencies.

With the UN Office for the Co-ordination of Humanitarian Assistance (OCHA), UNEP has established a joint Environment Unit to mobilize and co-ordinate international assistance and expertise for countries facing environmental emergencies and natural disasters. In mid-1999 UNEP and UN-Habitat jointly established a Balkan Task Force (subsequently renamed UNEP Balkans Unit) to assess the environmental impact of NATO's aerial offensive against the Federal Republic of Yugoslavia (now Serbia and Montenegro). In

November 2000 the Unit led a field assessment to evaluate reports of environmental contamination by debris from NATO ammunition containing depleted uranium. A final report, issued by UNEP in March 2001, concluded that there was no evidence of widespread contamination of the ground surface by depleted uranium and that the radiological and toxicological risk to the local population was negligible. It stated, however, that considerable scientific uncertainties remained, for example as to the safety of groundwater and the longer-term behaviour of depleted uranium in the environment, and recommended precautionary action. In December 2001 UNEP established a new Post-conflict Assessment Unit, which replaced, and extended the scope of, the Balkans Unit. In 2002 the Post-conflict Assessment Unit was undertaking activities in Afghanistan as well as the Balkans.

UNEP, together with UNDP and the World Bank, is an implementing agency of the Global Environment Facility (GEF), which was established in 1991 as a mechanism for international co-operation in projects concerned with biological diversity, climate change, international waters and depletion of the ozone layer. UNEP services the Scientific and Technical Advisory Panel, which provides expert advice on GEF programmes and operational strategies.

TECHNOLOGY, INDUSTRY AND ECONOMICS

The use of inappropriate industrial technologies and the widespread adoption of unsustainable production and consumption patterns have been identified as being inefficient in the use of renewable resources and wasteful, in particular in the use of energy and water. UNEP aims to encourage governments and the private sector to develop and adopt policies and practices that are cleaner and safer, make efficient use of natural resources, incorporate environmental costs, ensure the environmentally sound management of chemicals, and reduce pollution and risks to human health and the environment. In collaboration with other organizations and agencies UNEP works to define and formulate international guide-lines and agreements to address these issues. UNEP also promotes the transfer of appropriate technologies and organizes conferences and training workshops to provide sustainable production practices. Relevant information is disseminated through the International Cleaner Production Information Clearing House. UNEP, together with UNIDO, has established eight National Cleaner Production Centres to promote a preventive approach to industrial pollution control. In October 1998 UNEP adopted an International Declaration on Cleaner Production, with a commitment to implement cleaner and more sustainable production methods and to monitor results; the Declaration had 267 signatories at December 2001, including representatives of 45 governments. In 1997 UNEP and the Coalition for Environmentally Responsible Economies initiated the Global Reporting Initiative, which, with participation by corporations, business associations and other organizations and stakeholders, develops guide-lines for voluntary reporting by companies on their economic, environmental and social performance. In April 2002 UNEP launched the 'Life-Cycle Initiative', which aims to assist governments, businesses and other consumers with adopting environmentally-sound policies and practice, in view the upward trend in global consumption patterns.

UNEP provides institutional servicing to the Basel Convention on the Control of Transboundary Movements of Hazardous Wastes and their Disposal, which was adopted in 1989 with the aim of preventing the disposal of wastes from industrialized countries in countries that have no processing facilities. In March 1994 the second meeting of parties to the Convention determined to ban the exportation of hazardous wastes between industrialized and developing countries. The third meeting of parties to the Convention, held in 1995, proposed that the ban should be incorporated into the Convention as an amendment. The resulting so-called Ban Amendment (prohibiting exports of hazardous wastes for final disposal and recycling from states parties belonging to the OECD and, or, European Union, and from Liechtenstein, to any other state party to the Convention) required ratification by three-quarters of the 62 signatory states present at the time of adoption before it could enter into effect; by February 2003 the Ban Amendment had been ratified by 36 parties. In 1998 the technical working group of the Convention agreed a new procedure for clarifying the classification and characterization of specific hazardous wastes. The fifth full meeting of parties to the Convention, held in December 1999, adopted the Basel Declaration outlining an agenda for the period 2000–10, with a particular focus on minimizing the production of hazardous wastes. At February 2003 the number of parties to the Convention totalled 155. In December 1999 132 states adopted a Protocol to the Convention to address issues relating to liability and compensation for damages from waste exports. The governments also agreed to establish a multilateral fund to finance immediate clean-up operations following any environmental accident.

The UNEP Chemicals office was established to promote the sound management of hazardous substances, central to which was the International Register of Potentially Toxic Chemicals (IRPTC).

UNEP aims to facilitate access to data on chemicals and hazardous wastes, in order to assess and control health and environmental risks, by using the IRPTC as a clearing house facility of relevant information and by publishing information and technical reports on the impact of the use of chemicals.

UNEP's OzonAction Programme works to promote information exchange, training and technological awareness. Its objective is to strengthen the capacity of governments and industry in developing countries to undertake measures towards the cost-effective phasing-out of ozone-depleting substances. UNEP also encourages the development of alternative and renewable sources of energy. To achieve this, UNEP is supporting the establishment of a network of centres to research and exchange information of environmentally-sound energy technology resources.

REGIONAL CO-OPERATION AND REPRESENTATION

UNEP maintains six regional offices. These work to initiate and promote UNEP objectives and to ensure that all programme formulation and delivery meets the specific needs of countries and regions. They also provide a focal point for building national, subregional and regional partnership and enhancing local participation in UNEP initiatives. Following UNEP's reorganization a co-ordination office was established at headquarters to promote regional policy integration, to co-ordinate programme planning, and to provide necessary services to the regional offices.

UNEP provides administrative support to several regional conventions, for example the Lusaka Agreement on Co-operative Enforcement Operations Directed at Illegal Trade in Wild Flora and Fauna, which entered into force in December 1996 having been concluded under UNEP auspices in order to strengthen the implementation of the CBD and CITES in Eastern and Central Africa. UNEP also organizes conferences, workshops and seminars at national and regional levels, and may extend advisory services or technical assistance to individual governments.

CONVENTIONS

UNEP aims to develop and promote international environmental legislation in order to pursue an integrated response to global environmental issues, to enhance collaboration among existing convention secretariats, and to co-ordinate support to implement the work programmes of international instruments.

UNEP has been an active participant in the formulation of several major conventions (see above). The Division of Environmental Conventions is mandated to assist the Division of Policy Development and Law in the formulation of new agreements or protocols to existing conventions. Following the successful adoption of the Rotterdam Convention in September 1998, UNEP played a leading role in formulating a multilateral agreement to reduce and ultimately eliminate the manufacture and use of Persistent Organic Pollutants (POPs), which are considered to be a major global environmental hazard. The agreement on POPs, concluded in December 2000 at a conference sponsored by UNEP in Johannesburg, South Africa, was adopted by 127 countries in May 2001.

UNEP has been designated to provide secretariat functions to a number of global and regional environmental conventions (see above for list of offices).

COMMUNICATIONS AND PUBLIC INFORMATION

UNEP's public education campaigns and outreach programmes promote community involvement in environmental issues. Further communication of environmental concerns is undertaken through the media, an information centre service and special promotional events, including World Environment Day, photograph competitions, and the awarding of the Sasakawa Prize (to recognize distinguished service to the environment by individuals and groups) and of the Global 500 Award for Environmental Achievement. In 1996 UNEP initiated a Global Environment Citizenship Programme to promote acknowledgment of the environmental responsibilities of all sectors of society.

Finance

UNEP derives its finances from the regular budget of the United Nations and from voluntary contributions to the Environment Fund. A budget of US $119.9m. was authorized for the two-year period 2002–03, of which $100m. was for programme activities (see below), $14.9m. for management and administration, and $5m. for fund programme reserves.

Publications

Annual Report.

APELL Newsletter (2 a year).

Cleaner Production Newsletter (2 a year).
Climate Change Bulletin (quarterly).
Connect (UNESCO-UNEP newsletter on environmental degradation, quarterly).
Earth Views (quarterly).
Environment Forum (quarterly).
Environmental Law Bulletin (2 a year).
Financial Services Initiative (2 a year).
GEF News (quarterly).
Global Environment Outlook (every 2–3 years).
Global Water Review.
GPA Newsletter.
IETC Insight (3 a year).

Industry and Environment Review (quarterly).
Leave it to Us (children's magazine, 2 a year).
Managing Hazardous Waste (2 a year).
Our Planet (quarterly).
OzonAction Newsletter (quarterly).
Tierramerica (weekly).
Tourism Focus (2 a year).
UNEP Chemicals Newsletter (2 a year).
UNEP Update (monthly).
World Atlas of Coral Reefs.
World Atlas of Biodiversity.
World Atlas of Desertification.
Studies, reports, legal texts, technical guide-lines, etc.

UNITED NATIONS HIGH COMMISSIONER FOR REFUGEES—UNHCR

Address: CP 2500, 1211 Geneva 2 dépôt, Switzerland.
Telephone: (22) 7398111; **fax:** (22) 7397312; **e-mail:** unhcr@unhcr.ch; **internet:** www.unhcr.ch.
The Office of the High Commissioner was established in 1951 to provide international protection for refugees and to seek durable solutions to their problems.

Organization

(July 2003)

HIGH COMMISSIONER

The High Commissioner is elected by the United Nations General Assembly on the nomination of the Secretary-General, and is responsible to the General Assembly and to the UN Economic and Social Council (ECOSOC).
High Commissioner: RUUD LUBBERS (Netherlands).
Deputy High Commissioner: MARY ANN WYRSCH (USA).

EXECUTIVE COMMITTEE

The Executive Committee of the High Commissioner's Programme (ExCom), established by ECOSOC, gives the High Commissioner policy directives in respect of material assistance programmes and advice in the field of international protection. In addition, it oversees UNHCR's general policies and use of funds. ExCom, which comprises representatives of 57 states, both members and non-members of the UN, meets once a year.

ADMINISTRATION

Headquarters include the Executive Office, comprising the offices of the High Commissioner, the Deputy High Commissioner and the Assistant High Commissioner. There are separate offices for the Inspector General, the Special Envoy in the former Yugoslavia, and the Director of the UNHCR liaison office in New York. The other principal administrative units are the Division of Communication and Information, the Department of International Protection, the Division of Resource Management, and the Department of Operations, which is responsible for the five regional bureaux covering Africa; Asia and the Pacific; Europe; the Americas and the Caribbean; and Central Asia, South-West Asia, North Africa and the Middle East. At July 2002 there were 268 UNHCR field offices in 114 countries. At that time UNHCR employed 5,523 people, including short-term staff, of whom 4,654 (or 84%) were working in the field.

Activities

The competence of the High Commissioner extends to any person who, owing to well-founded fear of being persecuted for reasons of race, religion, nationality or political opinion, is outside the country of his or her nationality and is unable or, owing to such fear or for reasons other than personal convenience, remains unwilling to accept the protection of that country; or who, not having a nationality and being outside the country of his or her former habitual residence, is unable or, owing to such fear or for reasons other than personal convenience, is unwilling to return to it. This competence may be extended, by resolutions of the UN General Assembly and decisions of ExCom, to cover certain other 'persons of concern', in addition to refugees meeting these criteria. Refugees who are assisted by other UN agencies, or who have the same rights or obligations as nationals of their country of residence, are outside the mandate of UNHCR.

In recent years there has been a significant shift in UNHCR's focus of activities. Increasingly UNHCR has been called upon to support people who have been displaced within their own country (i.e. with similar needs to those of refugees but who have not crossed an international border) or those threatened with displacement as a result of armed conflict. In addition, greater support has been given to refugees who have returned to their country of origin, to assist their reintegration, and UNHCR is working to enable local communities to support the returnees, frequently through the implementation of Quick Impact Projects (QIPs).

At December 2001 the refugee population world-wide provisionally totalled 12.1m. and UNHCR was concerned with an estimated further 940,791 asylum-seekers, 462,723 recently returned refugees and 6.3m. others (of whom an estimated 5.0m. were internally displaced persons—IDPs).

World Refugee Day, sponsored by UNHCR, is held annually on 20 June.

INTERNATIONAL PROTECTION

As laid down in the Statute of the Office, UNHCR's primary function is to extend international protection to refugees and its second function is to seek durable solutions to their problems. In the exercise of its mandate UNHCR seeks to ensure that refugees and asylum-seekers are protected against *refoulement* (forcible return), that they receive asylum, and that they are treated according to internationally recognized standards. UNHCR pursues these objectives by a variety of means that include promoting the conclusion and ratification by states of international conventions for the protection of refugees. UNHCR promotes the adoption of liberal practices of asylum by states, so that refugees and asylum-seekers are granted admission, at least on a temporary basis.

The most comprehensive instrument concerning refugees that has been elaborated at the international level is the 1951 United Nations Convention relating to the Status of Refugees. This Convention, the scope of which was extended by a Protocol adopted in 1967, defines the rights and duties of refugees and contains provisions dealing with a variety of matters which affect the day-to-day lives of refugees. The application of the Convention and its Protocol is supervised by UNHCR. Important provisions for the treatment of refugees are also contained in a number of instruments adopted at the regional level. These include the 1969 Convention Governing the Specific Aspects of Refugee Problems adopted by OAU (now AU) member states in 1969, the European Agreement on the Abolition of Visas for Refugees, and the 1969 American Convention on Human Rights.

UNHCR has actively encouraged states to accede to the 1951 United Nations Refugee Convention and the 1967 Protocol: 144 states had acceded to either or both of these basic refugee instruments by September 2002. An increasing number of states have also adopted domestic legislation and/or administrative measures to implement the international instruments, particularly in the field of procedures for the determination of refugee status. UNHCR has sought to address the specific needs of refugee women and children, and has also attempted to deal with the problem of military attacks on refugee camps, by adopting and encouraging the acceptance of a set of principles to ensure the safety of refugees. In recent years it has formulated a strategy designed to address the fundamental causes of refugee flows. In 2001, in response to widespread concern about perceived high numbers of asylum-seekers and large-scale international economic migration and human trafficking, UNHCR initiated a series of Global Consultations on International Protection with the signatories to the 1951 Convention and 1967 Protocol, and other interested parties, with a view to strengthening both the application and scope of international refugee legislation. A consultation of 156 Governments, convened in Geneva, in December, reaffirmed commitment to the central role played by the Convention and Protocol. The final consultation, held in May 2002, focused on durable solutions and the protection of refugee women and children. Subsequently, based on the findings of the Global Consultations process, UNHCR developed an Agenda on Protection with six main objectives: strengthening the implementation of the 1951 Convention and 1967 Protocol; the protection of refugees within broader migration movements; more equitable sharing of burdens and responsibilities and building of capacities to receive and protect refugees; addressing more effectively security-related concerns; increasing efforts to find durable solutions; and meeting the protection needs of refugee women and children. The Agenda was endorsed by the Executive Council in October.

ASSISTANCE ACTIVITIES

The first phase of an assistance operation uses UNHCR's capacity of emergency preparedness and response. This enables UNHCR to address the immediate needs of refugees at short notice, for example, by employing specially-trained emergency teams and maintaining stockpiles of basic equipment, medical aid and materials. A significant proportion of UNHCR expenditure is allocated to the next phase of an operation, providing 'care and maintenance' in stable refugee circumstances. This assistance can take various forms, including the provision of food, shelter, medical care and essential supplies. Also covered in many instances are basic services, including education and counselling.

As far as possible, assistance is geared towards the identification and implementation of durable solutions to refugee problems—this being the second statutory responsibility of UNHCR. Such solutions generally take one of three forms: voluntary repatriation, local integration or resettlement in another country. Voluntary repatriation is increasingly the preferred solution, given the easing of political tension in many regions from which refugees have fled. Where voluntary repatriation is feasible, the Office assists refugees to overcome obstacles preventing their return to their country of origin. This may be done through negotiations with governments involved, or by providing funds either for the physical movement of refugees or for the rehabilitation of returnees once back in their own country.

When voluntary repatriation is not an option, efforts are made to assist refugees to integrate locally and to become self-supporting in their countries of asylum. This may be done either by granting loans to refugees, or by assisting them, through vocational training or in other ways, to learn a skill and to establish themselves in gainful occupations. One major form of assistance to help refugees reestablish themselves outside camps is the provision of housing. In cases where resettlement through emigration is the only viable solution to a refugee problem, UNHCR negotiates with governments in an endeavour to obtain suitable resettlement opportunities, to encourage liberalization of admission criteria and to draw up special immigration schemes. During 2000 an estimated 39,500 refugees were resettled under UNHCR auspices.

In the early 1990s UNHCR aimed to consolidate efforts to integrate certain priorities into its programme planning and implementation, as a standard discipline in all phases of assistance. The considerations include awareness of specific problems confronting refugee women, the needs of refugee children, the environmental impact of refugee programmes and long-term development objectives. In an effort to improve the effectiveness of its programmes, UNHCR has initiated a process of delegating authority, as well as responsibility for operational budgets, to its regional and field representatives, increasing flexibility and accountability. An Evaluation and Policy Analysis Unit reviews systematically UNHCR's operational effectiveness.

CENTRAL AND SOUTH-EASTERN EUROPE

The political changes in Central and Eastern Europe during the early 1990s resulted in a dramatic increase in the number of asylum-seekers and displaced people in the region. UNHCR was the agency designated by the UN Secretary-General to lead the UN relief operation to assist those affected by the conflict in the former

Yugoslavia. It was responsible for the supply of food and other humanitarian aid to the besieged capital of Bosnia and Herzegovina, Sarajevo, and to Muslim and Croatian enclaves in the country, under the armed escort of the UN Protection Force. Assistance was provided not only to Bosnian refugees in Croatia and displaced people within Bosnia and Herzegovina's borders, but also, in order to forestall further movements of people, to civilians whose survival was threatened. The operation was often seriously hampered by armed attacks (resulting, in some cases, in fatalities), distribution difficulties and underfunding from international donors. The Dayton peace agreement, which was signed in December 1995 bringing an end to the conflict, secured the right for all refugees and displaced persons freely to choose their place of residence within the new territorial arrangements of Bosnia and Herzegovina. Thus, the immediate effect of the peace accord was further population displacement, including a mass exodus of almost the entire Serb population of Sarajevo. Under the peace accord, UNHCR was responsible for planning and implementing the repatriation of all Bosnian refugees and displaced persons, then estimated at 2m.; however, there were still immense obstacles to freedom of movement, in particular for minorities wishing to return to an area dominated by a different politico-ethnic faction. By the end of 2001 there was still an estimated total Bosnian refugee population of some 425,979, of whom some 166,134 were receiving assistance from UNHCR. The majority of the Bosnian refugee population were in the Federal Republic of Yugoslavia (FRY, now Serbia and Montenegro). In addition, there were 18,665 recently returned refugees and 80,172 returned IDPs of concern to UNHCR in Bosnia and Herzegovina and 438,253 IDPs who had yet to return home. Returns by refugees and IDPs (including significant numbers of refugees returning to areas where they represented minority ethnic communities) accelerated during 2000 and 2001, owing to an improvement in security conditions. In 2001 so-called 'minority returns' totalled 92,061, bringing the total number of minority returns since 1998 to 287,000. In July 2002 the heads of state of Bosnia and Herzogovina, Croatia and the FRY met in Sarajevo with a view to resolving a number of outstanding issues including the return of remaining refugees.

From March 1998 attacks by Serbian forces against members of a separatist movement in the southern Serbian province of Kosovo and Metohija resulted in large-scale population displacement. Of particular concern were some 50,000 people who had fled to the surrounding mountains, close to the Albanian border, without shelter or adequate provisions. In October the withdrawal of Serbian troops and the involvement of the international community in the provision of aid and monitoring of the situation in Kosovo was thought to have prompted substantial numbers to have returned home. However, in December there were reports of renewed attacks by Serbian forces on the local Albanian population, which persisted into 1999. The failure of peace negotiations prompted further displacement, and in late March an estimated 95,000 people fled their homes following the withdrawal of international observers of the OSCE and the commencement of a NATO operation, which aimed to halt the Serbian attacks and compel the FRY to agree to a peace settlement. By mid-April UNHCR estimated that up to 1.3m. Kosovar Albanians had been displaced since the fighting began in 1998, with reports that thousands had been forcibly expelled by Serbian troops in recent weeks. UNHCR attempted to provide emergency relief to the thousands of refugees who fled to neighbouring countries, and expressed concern for those remaining in the province, of whom up to 400,000 were thought to be living without shelter. In early April 1999 UNHCR condemned the decision of the authorities in the former Yugoslav republic of Macedonia (FYRM) forcibly to evacuate some 30,000 refugees from camps in Blace, near the FRY border, and subsequently to close the border to further refugees. At that time UNHCR helped to co-ordinate an international effort to evacuate substantial numbers of the refugees to third countries, and issued essential identity and travel documents. In Albania UNHCR funded transport to relocate an estimated 250,000 people from the border town of Kukës, where resources and the local infrastructure were strained by the massive population influx, to other sites throughout the country. At the start of June the Kosovar refugee population totalled some 443,300 people in Albania, 247,800 in the FYRM, 69,300 in Montenegro, and 21,700 in Bosnia and Herzegovina, while under a joint Humanitarian Evacuation Programme with the International Organization for Migration, more than 90,000 refugees had been evacuated to 29 countries. UNHCR organized host families to receive a large proportion of the refugees, while additional shelter was provided in the form of tented camps and collective centres. In mid-June, following a cease-fire accord and an agreement by the FRY to withdraw all forces and paramilitary units, UNHCR initiated a large-scale registration operation of Kosovar refugees and began to deliver emergency provisions to assist the displaced population within Kosovo. Despite warnings of anti-personnel devices and lack of shelter, UNHCR estimated that some 477,000 refugees had returned in a spontaneous repatriation movement by the end of June. Meanwhile, it was reported that a total of 170,000 Serbs left Kosovo, fearing reprisal attacks by returning ethnic Albanians; in addition, some 50,000 members of the Roma minority moved out of the province. In September UNHCR estimated that one-third of all homes in Kosovo had been destroyed or seriously damaged during the conflict, prompting concerns regarding the welfare of returning refugees and IDPs in the coming winter months. UNHCR distributed 'shelter kits' to assist the process of reconstruction of homes, and proceeded to accelerate the distribution of blankets and winter clothing, as well as of fuel, food, water, and the provision of medical care throughout Serbia and Montenegro. By the end of 1999 the majority of refugees had returned to Kosovo. In mid-2000 UNHCR scaled down its emergency humanitarian activities in Kosovo and provided a UN Humanitarian Co-ordinator to oversee the transition to long-term reconstruction and development, in co-operation with the UN Interim Administration Mission in Kosovo (UNMIK). UNHCR and OSCE have periodically jointly assessed the situation of minority communities in Kosovo; in May 2002 the two organizations reported that discrimination against and intimidation of minorities in the province was prevalent, hindering minority returns and integration. From mid-2001 more than 5,000 ethnic Albanians returned to Serbia from Kosovo, where they had sought refuge.

In response to the mounting insecurity in the FYRM from early 2001, as conflict escalated between ethnic Albanian rebels and government troops, 81,000 Macedonian refugees fled to Kosovo (of whom several thousand repatriated promptly) and 12,000 to southern Serbia during February–August, while over that period more than 50,000 people became displaced within the FYRM. In June UNHCR appealed for funds to finance the provision of emergency humanitarian assistance to the Macedonian refugees, and opened a registration centre in Kosovo. Repatriations accelerated following the conclusion in August of a framework peace agreement between the opposing parties; by April 2002 some 4,000 Macedonian refugees remained in Kosovo, while 16,800 persons remained displaced withing the FYRM; in many cases the latter feared returning to communities in which they would belong to an ethnic minority.

In recent years Albania has become a major point of transit for economic migrants and asylum-seekers travelling to Western Europe; significant illegal human-trafficking activities have been reported in that country. UNHCR participates in a care programme to assist migrants stranded in Albania.

CO-OPERATION WITH OTHER ORGANIZATIONS

UNHCR works closely with other UN agencies, intergovernmental organizations and non-governmental organizations (NGOs) to increase the scope and effectiveness of its operations. Within the UN system UNHCR co-operates, principally, with the World Food Programme in the distribution of food aid, UNICEF and the World Health Organization in the provision of family welfare and child immunization programmes, OCHA in the delivery of emergency humanitarian relief, UNDP in development-related activities and the preparation of guide-lines for the continuum of emergency assistance to development programmes, and the Office of the UN High Commissioner for Human Rights. UNHCR also has close working relationships with the International Committee of the Red Cross and the International Organization for Migration. In 2002 UNHCR worked with 510 NGOs as 'implementing partners', enabling UNHCR to broaden the use of its resources while maintaining a co-ordinating role in the provision of assistance.

TRAINING

UNHCR organizes training programmes and workshops to enhance the capabilities of field workers and non-UNHCR staff, in the following areas: the identification and registration of refugees; people-orientated planning; resettlement procedures and policies; emergency response and management; security awareness; stress management; and the dissemination of information through the electronic media.

Finance

The United Nations' regular budget finances a proportion of UNHCR's administrative expenditure. The majority of UNHCR's programme expenditure (about 98%) is funded by voluntary contributions, mainly from governments. The Private Sector and Public Affairs Service, established in 2001, aims to increase funding from non-governmental donor sources, for example by developing partnerships with foundations and corporations. Following approval of the Unified Annual Programme Budget any subsequently-identified requirements are managed in the form of Supplementary Programmes, financed by separate appeals. The total budget for 2002 amounted to US $925.4m.

Publications

Refugees (quarterly, in English, French, German, Italian, Japanese and Spanish).
Refugee Resettlement: An International Handbook to Guide Reception and Integration.
Refugee Survey Quarterly.
The State of the World's Refugees (every 2 years).
UNHCR Handbook for Emergencies.
Press releases, reports.

Statistics

POPULATIONS OF CONCERN TO UNHCR IN CENTRAL AND SOUTH-EASTERN EUROPE
('000 persons, at 31 December 2001, provisional figures)

	Refugees	Asylum-seekers	Returned refugees*	Others of concern†
Bosnia and Herzegovina	32.7	0.4	18.7	518.4
Bulgaria	3.0	1.5	—	—
Croatia	21.9	0.1	11.9	34.1
Czech Republic	1.2	11.6	—	—
Greece	6.9	6.2	—	—
Hungary	4.7	2.4	—	—
Macedonia	4.4	0.1	90.0	74.5
Poland	1.3	—	—	—
Slovenia	2.4	0.3	—	4.5
Yugoslavia	400.3	0.1	25.6	351.1

* Refugees who returned to their place of origin during 2001.
† Mainly internally displaced persons (IDPs) of concern to UNHCR, and former IDPs who returned to their place of origin during 2001; also includes 85,000 'local residents at risk' in the Federal Republic of Yugoslavia (now Serbia and Montenegro).

UNITED NATIONS PEACE-KEEPING

Address: Department of Peace-keeping Operations, Room S-3727-B, United Nations, New York, NY 10017, USA.

Telephone: (212) 963-8077; **fax:** (212) 963-9222; **internet:** www.un.org/Depts/dpko/.

United Nations peace-keeping operations have been conceived as instruments of conflict control. The UN has used these operations in various conflicts, with the consent of the parties involved, to maintain international peace and security, without prejudice to the positions or claims of parties, in order to facilitate the search for political settlements through peaceful means such as mediation and the good offices of the Secretary-General. Each operation is established with a specific mandate, which requires periodic review by the Security Council. United Nations peace-keeping operations fall into two categories: peace-keeping forces and observer missions.

Peace-keeping forces are composed of contingents of military and civilian personnel, made available by member states. These forces assist in preventing the recurrence of fighting, restoring and maintaining peace, and promoting a return to normal conditions. To this end, peace-keeping forces are authorized as necessary to undertake negotiations, persuasion, observation and fact-finding. They conduct patrols and interpose physically between the opposing parties. Peace-keeping forces are permitted to use their weapons only in self-defence.

Military observer missions are composed of officers (usually unarmed), who are made available, on the Secretary-General's request, by member states. A mission's function is to observe and report to the Secretary-General (who, in turn, informs the UN Security Council) on the maintenance of a cease-fire, to investigate violations and to do what it can to improve the situation.

The UN's peace-keeping forces and observer missions are financed in most cases by assessed contributions from member states of the organization. In recent years a significant expansion in the UN's peace-keeping activities has been accompanied by a perpetual financial crisis within the organization, as a result of the increased financial burden and some member states' delaying payment. At 31 December 2002 outstanding assessed contributions to the peace-keeping budget amounted to some US $1,340m.

UNITED NATIONS INTERIM ADMINISTRATION MISSION IN KOSOVO— UNMIK

Address: Headquarters: Priština, Kosovo.

Special Representative of the UN Secretary-General and Head of Mission: HARRI HOLKERI (Finland).

Principal Deputy Special Representative of the UN Secretary-General: CHARLES H. BRAYSHAW (USA).

Deputy Special Representative for Police and Justice: JEAN-CHRISTIAN CADY (France).

Deputy Special Representative for Civil Administration: FRANCESCO BASTAGLI (Italy).

Deputy Special Representative for (OSCE) Institution Building in Kosovo: PASCAL FIESCHI (France).

Deputy Special Representative for (EU) Reconstruction in Kosovo: ANDY BEARPARK (United Kingdom).

In June 1999 NATO suspended a 10-week aerial offensive against the then Federal Republic of Yugoslavia (now Serbia and Montenegro), following an agreement by the Serbian authorities to withdraw all security and paramilitary forces from the southern province of Kosovo and Metohija, where Serbian repression of a separatist movement had prompted a humanitarian crisis and co-ordinated international action to resolve the conflict. On 10 June the UN Security Council adopted Resolution 1244, which outlined the terms of a political settlement for Kosovo and provided for the deployment of international civilian and security personnel. The security presence, termed the Kosovo Peace Implementation Force (KFOR), was to be led by NATO, while the UN was to oversee all civilian operations. UNMIK was established under the terms of Resolution 1244 as the supreme legal and executive authority in Kosovo, with responsibility for all civil administration and for facilitating the reconstruction and rehabilitation of the province as an autonomous region. For the first time in a UN operation other organizations were mandated to co-ordinate aspects of the mission in Kosovo, under the UN's overall jurisdiction. The four key elements, or Pillars, of UNMIK were (i) humanitarian affairs (led by UNHCR); (ii) civil administration; (iii) democratization and institution-building (OSCE); and (iv) economic reconstruction (EU). At the end of the first year of UNMIK's presence the element of humanitarian assistance was phased out. A new Pillar, concerned with police and justice, was established in May 2001, under the direct leadership of the UN. On arriving in the province at the end of June 1999 UNMIK and KFOR established a Joint Implementation Commission to co-ordinate and supervise the demilitarization of the Kosovo Liberation Army. UNMIK initiated a mass information campaign (and later administered new radio stations in Kosovo) to urge co-operation with the international personnel in the province and tolerance for all ethnic communities. A Mine Co-ordinating Centre supervised efforts to deactivate anti-personnel devices and to ensure the safety of the returning ethnic Albanian population. In mid-July the UN Secretary-General's permanent Special Representative took office, and chaired the first meeting of the Kosovo Transitional Council (KTC), which had been established by the UN as a multi-ethnic consultative organ, the highest political body under UNMIK, to help to restore law and order in the province and to reintegrate the local administrative infrastructure. In August a Joint Advisory Council on Legislative Matters was constituted, with representatives of UNMIK and the local judiciary, in order to consider measures to eliminate discrimination from the province's legal framework. At the end of July UNMIK personnel began to supervise customs controls at Kosovo's international borders. Other developments in the first few months of UNMIK's deployment included the establishment of joint commissions on energy and public utilities, education, and health, a Technical Advisory Commission on establishing a judiciary and prosecution service, and, in October, the establishment of a Fuel Supervisory Board to administer the import, sale and distribution of petroleum. Central financial institutions for the province were inaugurated in November. In

the same month UNMIK established a Housing and Property Directorate and Claims Commission in order to resolve residential property disputes. In September the KTC agreed to establish a Joint Security Committee, in response to concerns at the escalation of violence in the province, in particular attacks on remaining Serbian civilians. In mid-December the leaders of the three main political groupings in Kosovo agreed on provisional power-sharing arrangements with UNMIK for the administration of Kosovo until the holding of elections, scheduled for 2000. The agreement on the so-called Kosovo-UNMIK Joint Interim Administrative Structure established an eight-member executive Interim Administrative Council and a framework of administrative departments. The KTC was to maintain its consultative role. In January 2000 UNMIK oversaw the inauguration of the Kosovo Protection Corps, a civilian agency comprising mainly former members of the newly-demilitarized Kosovo Liberation Army, which was to provide an emergency response service and a humanitarian assistance capacity, to assist in de-mining operations and contribute to rebuilding local infrastructure. In August UNMIK, in view of its mandate to assist with the regeneration of the local economy, concluded an agreement with a multinational consortium to rehabilitate the important Trepca non-ferrous mining complex. During mid-2000 UNMIK organized the voter registration process for the forthcoming territory-wide municipal elections. These were held in late October with a strong voter turnout, although participation by minority communities was low. In mid-December the Supreme Court of Kosovo was inaugurated, comprising 16 judges appointed by the Special Representative. During 2000 UNMIK police and KFOR co-operated in conducting joint security operations; the establishment of a special security task force to combat ethnically-motivated political violence, comprising senior UNMIK police and KFOR members, was agreed in June. From January 2001 UNMIK international travel documents were distributed to Kosovars without Yugoslav passports. From early June, in response to ongoing concern at violence between ethnic Albanians and security forces in the former Yugoslav republic of Macedonia (FYRM), UNMIK designated 19 authorized crossing points at Kosovo's international borders with Albania and the FYRM, and its boundaries with Montenegro and Serbia. In mid-May the Special Representative of the Secretary-General signed the Constitutional Framework on Interim Self-Government, providing for the establishment of a Constitutional Assembly; elections to the proposed Assembly were scheduled to take place in mid-November. UNMIK undertook efforts to register voters, in particular those from minority ethnic groups, and to continue to facilitate the return of displaced persons to their home communities. The last session of the KTC was held in October, and a general election was conducted, as scheduled, on 17 November. In December the Special Representative of the Secretary-General inaugurated the new 120-member Assembly. However, disagreements ensued among the three main political parties represented in the Assembly concerning the appointment of the positions of President and Prime Minister. In February 2002 Michael Steiner, then the Special Representative of the Secretary-General, negotiated an agreement with the leaders of the main political parties that resolved the deadlock in establishing the Interim Government. Accordingly, in March the new President, Prime Minister and Interim Government were inaugurated, enabling the commencement of the process of developing self-governing institutions. In November the mission established the UNMIK Administration—Mitrovica, superseding parallel institutions that had operated hitherto in Serb-dominated northern Mitrovica, and thereby extending UNMIK's authority over all Kosovo. During that month a second series of municipal elections took place.

Reporting to the UN Security Council in February 2003 Steiner detailed his priorities for that year as: intensifying efforts to facilitate a reduction in politically and ethnically motivated violence, organized crime and corruption; institution-building and developing the legal system to provide a solid basis for attracting investment to Kosovo, with a view to creating jobs and reducing unemployment; consolidating a multi-ethnic society; and transferring competencies from UNMIK to the provisional institutions of self-government. In March a Transfer Council was established with responsibility for the latter process. In June, in conjunction with UNDP, UNMIK launched a Rapid Response Returns Facility (RRRF) to assist returnees from inside and outside Kosovo through the provision of housing and socio-economic support; by July more than 7,000 returns had been reported. In July the outgoing Special Representative promulgated a new Criminal Code and Criminal Procedure Code, to enter into force in April 2004.

At July 2003 UNMIK comprised 4,097 civilian police, 1,005 international civilian personnel, 3,184 local civilian personnel, and 38 military personnel. The General Assembly apportioned US $329.7m. to finance the operation during the period 1 July 2003–30 June 2004.

WORLD FOOD PROGRAMME—WFP

Address: Via Cesare Giulio Viola 68, Parco dei Medici, 00148 Rome, Italy.

Telephone: (06) 6513-1; **fax:** (06) 6513-2840; **e-mail:** wfpinfo@wfp .org; **internet:** www.wfp.org.

WFP, the principal food aid organization of the United Nations, became operational in 1963. It aims to alleviate acute hunger by providing emergency relief following natural or man-made humanitarian disasters, and supplies food aid to people in developing countries to eradicate chronic undernourishment, to support social development and to promote self-reliant communities.

Organization

(July 2003)

EXECUTIVE BOARD

The governing body of WFP is the Executive Board, comprising 36 members, 18 of whom are elected by the UN Economic and Social Council (ECOSOC) and 18 by the Council of the Food and Agriculture Organization (FAO). The Board meets four times each year at WFP headquarters.

SECRETARIAT

WFP's Executive Director is appointed jointly by the UN Secretary-General and the Director-General of FAO and is responsible for the management and administration of the Programme. In 2001 there were 2,567 permanent staff members, of whom about 70% were working in the field. WFP administers some 87 country offices, in order to provide operational, financial and management support at a more local level, and has established seven regional bureaux, located in Bangkok, Thailand (for Asia), Cairo, Egypt (for the Middle East, Central Asia and the Mediterranean), Rome, Italy (for Eastern Europe), Managua, Nicaragua (for Latin America and the Caribbean), Yaoundé, Cameroon (for Central Africa), Kampala, Uganda (for Eastern and Southern Africa), and Dakar, Senegal (for West Africa).

Executive Director: James T. Morris (USA).

Activities

WFP is the only multilateral organization with a mandate to use food aid as a resource. It is the second largest source of assistance in the UN, after the World Bank group, in terms of actual transfers of resources, and the largest source of grant aid in the UN system. WFP handles more than one-third of the world's food aid. WFP is also the largest contributor to South–South trade within the UN system, through the purchase of food and services from developing countries. WFP's mission is to provide food aid to save lives in refugee and other emergency situations, to improve the nutrition and quality of life of vulnerable groups and to help to develop assets and promote the self-reliance of poor families and communities. WFP aims to focus its efforts on the world's poorest countries and to provide at least 90% of its total assistance to those designated as 'low-income food-deficit'. At the World Food Summit, held in November 1996, WFP endorsed the commitment to reduce by 50% the number of undernourished people, no later than 2015. During 2001 WFP food assistance benefited some 77m. people world-wide, of whom 20m. received aid through development projects, 43m. through emergency operations, and 14m. through rehabilitation programmes. Total food deliveries amounted to 4.2m. metric tons in 82 countries.

WFP aims to address the causes of chronic malnourishment, which it identifies as poverty and lack of opportunity. It emphasizes the role played by women in combating hunger, and endeavours to address the specific nutritional needs of women, to increase their access to food and development resources, and to promote girls' education. It also focuses resources on supporting the food security of households and communities affected by HIV/AIDS and on promoting food security as a means of mitigating extreme poverty and vulnerability and thereby combating the spread of HIV/AIDS. In February 2003 WFP and the Joint UN Programme on HIV/AIDS (UNAIDS) concluded an agreement to jointly address the relationship between HIV/AIDS, regional food shortages and chronic hunger, with a particular focus on Africa, South-East Asia and the Caribbean.

In the early 1990s there was a substantial shift in the balance between emergency relief and development assistance provided by WFP, owing to the growing needs of victims of drought and other natural disasters, refugees and displaced persons. By 1994 two-thirds of all food aid was for relief assistance and one-third for development, representing a direct reversal of the allocations five years previously. In addition, there was a noticeable increase in aid given to those in need as a result of civil war, compared with commitments for victims of natural disasters. Accordingly, WFP has developed a range of mechanisms to enhance its preparedness for emergency situations and to improve its capacity for responding effectively to situations as they arise. A new programme of emergency response training was inaugurated in 2000, while security concerns for personnel was incorporated as a new element into all general planning and training activities. Through its Vulnerability Analysis and Mapping (VAM) project, WFP aims to identify potentially vulnerable groups by providing information on food security and the capacity of different groups for coping with shortages, and to enhance emergency contingency-planning and long-term assistance objectives. In early 2003 VAM field units were operational in more than 50 countries. WFP also co-operates with other UN agencies including FAO (undertaking joint activities in 24 countries in 2001), IFAD (conducting joint activities in 14 countries in that year) and UNHCR. The key elements of WFP's emergency response capacity are its strategic stores of food and logistics equipment, stand-by arrangements to enable the rapid deployment of personnel, communications and other essential equipment, and the Augmented Logistics Intervention Team for Emergencies (ALITE), which undertakes capacity assessments and contingency-planning. During 2000 WFP led efforts, undertaken with other UN humanitarian agencies, for the design and application of local UN Joint Logistics Centre facilities, which aimed to co-ordinate resources in an emergency situation. In 2001 a new UN Humanitarian Response Depot was opened in Brindisi, Italy, under the direction of WFP experts, for the storage of essential rapid response equipment. In that year the Programme published a set of guide-lines on contingency planning.

In 2001 WFP delivered emergency food assistance valued at US $90m. to the Federal Republic of Yugoslavia (now Serbia and Montenegro), the former Yugoslav republic of Macedonia—FYRM, and Albania. WFP has conducted several assessment missions in Serbia and Montenegro and the FYRM to evaluate the food requirements of vulnerable local populations, low-income householders, IDPs and refugees. WFP terminated its activities in Kosovo in June 2002.

Through its development activities, WFP aims to alleviate poverty in developing countries by promoting self-reliant families and communities. Food is supplied, for example, as an incentive in development self-help schemes and as part-wages in labour-intensive projects of many kinds. In all its projects WFP aims to assist the most vulnerable groups and to ensure that beneficiaries have an adequate and balanced diet. Activities supported by the Programme include the settlement and resettlement of groups and communities; land reclamation and improvement; irrigation; the development of forestry and dairy farming; road construction; training of hospital staff; community development; and human resources development such as feeding expectant or nursing mothers and schoolchildren, and support for education, training and health programmes. In 2001 WFP supported development projects in 55 countries, which benefited some 20m. people. School feeding projects benefited 15m. children during that year. During 2001 WFP initiated a new Global School Feeding Campaign to strengthen international co-operation to expand educational opportunities for poor children and to improve the quality of the teaching environment.

Following a comprehensive evaluation of its activities, WFP is increasingly focused on linking its relief and development activities to provide a continuum between short-term relief and longer-term rehabilitation and development. In order to achieve this objective, WFP aims to integrate elements that strengthen disaster mitigation into development projects, including soil conservation, reafforestation, irrigation infrastructure, and transport construction and rehabilitation; and to promote capacity-building elements within relief operations, e.g. training, income-generating activities and environmental protection measures. In 1999 WFP adopted a new Food Aid and Development policy, which aims to use food assistance both to cover immediate requirements and to create conditions conducive to enhancing the long-term food security of vulnerable populations. During that year WFP began implementing Protracted Relief and Recovery Operations (PRROs), where the emphasis is on fostering stability, rehabilitation and long-term development for victims of natural disasters, displaced persons and refugees. PRROs were to be introduced no later than 18 months after the initial emergency operation, and to last no more than three years. When undertaken in collaboration with UNHCR and other international agencies, WFP was to be responsible for mobilizing basic food commodities and for related transport, handling and storage costs. In 2001 PRROs, involving the provision of 818,700 metric tons of food, were being undertaken in 41 countries.

Finance

The Programme is funded by voluntary contributions from donor countries and intergovernmental bodies such as the European Union. Contributions are made in the form of commodities, finance and services (particularly shipping). Commitments to the International Emergency Food Reserve (IEFR), from which WFP provides the majority of its food supplies, and to the Immediate Response

Account of the IEFR (IRA), are also made on a voluntary basis by donors. In 2001 contributions by donors provided 83% of WFP's food requirements. WFP's operational expenditure in that year amounted to some US $1,744m., while administrative costs totalled $244.7m. for the two-year period 2000–01.

Publications

Annual Report.
Food and Nutrition Handbook.
School Feeding Handbook.

FOOD AND AGRICULTURE ORGANIZATION OF THE UNITED NATIONS—FAO

Address: Viale delle Terme di Caracalla, 00100 Rome, Italy.
Telephone: (06) 5705-1; **fax:** (06) 5705-3152; **e-mail:** fao.hq@fao .org; **internet:** www.fao.org.
FAO, the first specialized agency of the UN to be founded after the Second World War, aims to alleviate malnutrition and hunger, and serves as a co-ordinating agency for development programmes in the whole range of food and agriculture, including forestry and fisheries. It helps developing countries to promote educational and training facilities and the creation of appropriate institutions.

European Union: blvd Simon Bolivar, 1000 Brussels, Belgium; tel. (2) 203-8587; fax (2) 203-8589; e-mail fao-lobr@fao.org; Dir MANFRED LINDAU.

United Nations: Suite DC1-1125, 1 United Nations Plaza, New York, NY 10017, USA; tel. (212) 963-6036; fax (212) 963-5425; e-mail fao-lony@field.fao.org; Dir HOWARD W. HJORT.

Organization

(July 2003)

CONFERENCE

The governing body is the FAO Conference of member nations. It meets every two years, formulates policy, determines the Organization's programme and budget on a biennial basis, and elects new members. It also elects the Director-General of the Secretariat and the Independent Chairman of the Council. Every other year, FAO also holds conferences in each of its five regions (see below).

COUNCIL

The FAO Council is composed of representatives of 49 member nations, elected by the Conference for staggered three-year terms. It is the interim governing body of FAO between sessions of the Conference. The most important standing Committees of the Council are: the Finance and Programme Committees, the Committee on Commodity Problems, the Committee on Fisheries, the Committee on Agriculture and the Committee on Forestry.

SECRETARIAT

The total number of FAO staff in May 2002 was 3,700, of whom 1,500 were professional staff and 2,200 general service staff. About one-half of the Organization's staff were based at headquarters. Work is supervised by the following Departments: Administration and Finance; General Affairs and Information; Economic and Social Policy; Agriculture; Forestry; Fisheries; Sustainable Development; and Technical Co-operation.
Director-General: JACQUES DIOUF (Senegal).

REGIONAL AND SUB-REGIONAL OFFICES

Europe: Viale delle Terme di Caracalla, Room A-304, 00100 Rome, Italy; tel. (06) 57051; fax (06) 5705 3152; internet www.fao.org/ regional/europe; Regional Rep. CLAUDE FORTHOMME.

Sub-regional Office for Central and Eastern Europe: 1068 Budapest, Benczur u. 34, Hungary; tel. (1) 461-2000; fax (1) 351-7029; e-mail fao-seur@fao.org; Sub-regional Rep. PETER ROSENEGGER.

JOINT DIVISION AND LIAISON OFFICES

Joint FAO/IAEA Division of Nuclear Techniques in Food and Agriculture: Wagramerstrasse 5, 1400 Vienna, Austria; tel. (1) 20600; fax (1) 20607.

Activities

FAO aims to raise levels of nutrition and standards of living by improving the production and distribution of food and other commodities derived from farms, fisheries and forests. FAO's ultimate objective is the achievement of world food security, 'Food for All'. The organization provides technical information, advice and assistance by disseminating information; acting as a neutral forum for discussion of food and agricultural issues; advising governments on policy and planning; and developing capacity directly in the field.

In November 1996 FAO hosted the World Food Summit, which was held in Rome and was attended by heads of state and senior government representatives of 186 countries. Participants approved the Rome Declaration on World Food Security and the World Food Summit Plan of Action, with the aim of halving the number of people afflicted by undernutrition, at that time estimated to total 828m. world-wide, by no later than 2015. A review conference to assess progress in achieving the goals of the summit, entitled World Food Summit: Five Years Later, held in June 2002, reaffirmed commitment to this objective. During that month FAO announced the formulation of a global 'Anti-Hunger Programme', which aimed to promote investment in the agricultural sector and rural development, with a particular focus on small farmers, and to enhance food access for those most in need, for example through the provision of school meals, schemes to feed pregnant and nursing mothers and food-for-work programmes. In late 2002 FAO reported that an estimated 840m. people were undernourished during the period 1998–2000; of these 799m. resided in developing countries, 30m. in states with economies in transition and 11m. in industrialized countries.

In November 1999 the FAO Conference approved a long-term Strategic Framework for the period 2000–15, which emphasized national and international co-operation in pursuing the goals of the 1996 World Food Summit. The Framework promoted interdisciplinarity and partnership, and defined three main global objectives: constant access by all people to sufficient nutritionally adequate and safe food to ensure that levels of undernourishment were reduced by 50% by 2015 (see above); the continued contribution of sustainable agriculture and rural development to economic and social progress and well-being; and the conservation, improvement and sustainable use of natural resources. It identified five corporate strategies (each supported by several strategic objectives), covering the following areas: reducing food insecurity and rural poverty; ensuring enabling policy and regulatory frameworks for food, agriculture, fisheries and forestry; creating sustainable increases in the supply and availability of agricultural, fisheries and forestry products; conserving and enhancing sustainable use of the natural resource base; and generating knowledge. The November 2001 FAO Conference adopted a medium-term plan covering 2002–07 and a work programme for 2000–03, both on the basis of the Strategic Framework.

FAO organizes an annual series of fund-raising events, 'TeleFood', some of which are broadcast on television and the internet, in order to raise public awareness of the problems of hunger and malnutrition. Since its inception in 1997 public donations to Tele-Food have exceeded US $10m., financing more than 1,000 'grass-roots' projects in more than 100 countries. The projects have provided tools, seeds and other essential supplies directly to small-scale farmers, and have been especially aimed at helping women.

In 1999 FAO signed a memorandum of understanding with UNAIDS on strengthening co-operation. In December 2001 FAO, IFAD and WFP determined to strengthen inter-agency collaboration in developing strategies to combat the threat posed by the HIV/AIDS epidemic to food security, nutrition and rural livelihoods. During that month experts from those organizations and UNAIDS held a technical consultation on means of mitigating the impact of HIV/AIDS on agriculture and rural communities in affected areas.

The Technical Cooperation Department has responsibility for FAO's operational activities, including policy development assistance to member countries; investment support; and the management of activities associated with the development and implementation of country, sub-regional and regional programmes. The Department manages the technical co-operation programme (TCP, which funds 13% of FAO's field programme expenditures), and mobilizes resources.

AGRICULTURE

FAO's most important area of activity is crop production, accounting annually for about one-quarter of total field programme expenditure. FAO assists developing countries in increasing agricultural production, by means of a number of methods, including improved seeds and fertilizer use, soil conservation and reforestation, better water resource management techniques, upgrading storage facilities, and improvements in processing and marketing. FAO places special emphasis on the cultivation of under-exploited traditional food crops, such as cassava, sweet potato and plantains.

In 1985 the FAO Conference approved an International Code of Conduct on the Distribution and Use of Pesticides, and in 1989 the Conference adopted an additional clause concerning 'Prior Informed Consent' (PIC), whereby international shipments of newly banned or restricted pesticides should not proceed without the agreement of importing countries. Under the clause, FAO aims to inform governments about the hazards of toxic chemicals and to urge them to take proper measures to curb trade in highly toxic agrochemicals while keeping the pesticides industry informed of control actions. In 1996 FAO, in collaboration with UNEP, publicized a new initiative which aimed to increase awareness of, and to promote international action on, obsolete and hazardous stocks of pesticides remaining throughout the world (estimated in 2001 to total some 500,000 metric tons). In September 1998 a new legally-binding treaty on trade in hazardous chemicals and pesticides was adopted at an international conference held in Rotterdam, Netherlands. The so-called Rotterdam Convention required that hazardous chemicals and pesticides banned or severely restricted in at least two countries should not be exported unless explicitly agreed by the importing country. It also identified certain pesticide formulations as too dangerous to be used by farmers in developing countries, and incorporated an obligation that countries halt national production of those hazardous compounds. The treaty was to enter into force on being ratified by 50 signatory states. FAO was co-operating with UNEP to provide an interim secretariat for the Convention. In July 1999 a conference on the Rotterdam Convention, held in Rome, established an Interim Chemical Review Committee with responsibility for recommending the inclusion of chemicals or pesticide formulations in the PIC procedure. As part of its continued efforts to reduce the environmental risks posed by over-reliance on pesticides, FAO has extended to other regions its Integrated Pest Management (IPM) programme in Asia and the Pacific on the use of safer and more effective methods of pest control, such as biological control methods and natural predators (including spiders and wasps), to avert pests. In February 2001 FAO warned that some 30% of pesticides sold in developing countries did not meet internationally accepted quality standards. A revised International Code of Conduct on the Distribution and Use of Pesticides, adopted in November 2002, aimed to reduce the inappropriate distribution and use of pesticides and other toxic compounds, particularly in developing countries.

FAO's Joint Division with the International Atomic Energy Agency (IAEA) tests controlled-release formulas of pesticides and herbicides that gradually free their substances and can limit the amount of agrochemicals needed to protect crops. The Joint FAO/IAEA Division is engaged in exploring biotechnologies and in developing non-toxic fertilizers (especially those that are locally available) and improved strains of food crops (especially from indigenous varieties). In the area of animal production and health, the Joint Division has developed progesterone-measuring and disease diagnostic kits, of which thousands have been delivered to developing countries. FAO's plant nutrition activities aim to promote nutrient management, such as the Integrated Plant Nutritions

Systems (IPNS), which are based on the recycling of nutrients through crop production and the efficient use of mineral fertilizers.

The conservation and sustainable use of plant and animal genetic resources are promoted by FAO's Global System for Plant Genetic Resources, which includes five databases, and the Global Strategy on the Management of Farm Animal Genetic Resources. An FAO programme supports the establishment of gene banks, designed to maintain the world's biological diversity by preserving animal and plant species threatened with extinction. FAO, jointly with UNEP, has published a document listing the current state of global livestock genetic diversity. In June 1996 representatives of more than 150 governments convened in Leipzig, Germany, at a meeting organized by FAO (and hosted by the German Government) to consider the use and conservation of plant genetic resources as an essential means of enhancing food security. The meeting adopted a Global Plan of Action, which included measures to strengthen the development of plant varieties and to promote the use and availability of local varieties and locally-adapted crops to farmers, in particular following a natural disaster, war or civil conflict. In November 2001 the FAO Conference adopted the International Treaty on Plant Genetic Resources for Food and Agriculture, which was to provide a framework to ensure access to plant genetic resources and to related knowledge, technologies and funding. The Treaty was to enter into force once it had been ratified by 40 signatory states; at February 2003 it had been ratified by 15 states.

An Emergency Prevention System for Transboundary Animal and Plant Pests and Diseases (EMPRES) was established in 1994 to strengthen FAO's activities in the prevention, early warning of, control and, where possible, eradication of pests and highly contagious livestock diseases (which the system categorizes as epidemic diseases of strategic importance, such as rinderpest or foot-and-mouth; diseases requiring tactical attention at international or regional level, e.g. Rift Valley fever; and emerging diseases, e.g. bovine spongiform encephalopathy—BSE). EMPRES has a desert locust component, and has published guide-lines on all aspects of desert locust monitoring. FAO has assumed responsibility for technical leadership and co-ordination of the Global Rinderpest Eradication Programme (GREP), which has the objective of eliminating the disease by 2010. Following technical consulations in late 1998, an Intensified GREP was launched. In November 1997 FAO initiated a Programme Against African Trypanosomiasis, which aimed to counter the disease affecting cattle in almost one-third of Africa. EMPRES promotes Good Emergency Management Practices (GEMP) in animal health. The system is guided by the annual meeting of the EMPRES Expert Consultation.

FAO's organic agriculture programme provides technical assistance and policy advice on the production, certification and trade of organic produce. In July 2001 the FAO/WHO Codex Alimentarius Commission adopted guide-lines on organic livestock production, covering organic breeding methods, the elimination of growth hormones and certain chemicals in veterinary medicines, and the use of good quality organic feed with no meat or bone meal content.

ENVIRONMENT

At the UN Conference on Environment and Development (UNCED), held in Rio de Janeiro, Brazil, in June 1992, FAO participated in several working parties and supported the adoption of Agenda 21, a programme of activities to promote sustainable development. FAO is responsible for the chapters of Agenda 21 concerning water resources, forests, fragile mountain ecosystems and sustainable agriculture and rural development. FAO was designated by the UN General Assembly as the lead agency for co-ordinating the International Year of Mountains (2002), which aimed to raise awareness of mountain ecosystems and to promote the conservation and sustainable development of mountainous regions.

FISHERIES

FAO's Fisheries Department consists of a multi-disciplinary body of experts who are involved in every aspect of fisheries development from coastal surveys, conservation management and use of aquatic genetic resources, improvement of production, processing and storage, to the compilation and analysis of statistics, development of computer databases, improvement of fishing gear, institution-building and training. In November 1993 the FAO Conference adopted an agreement to improve the monitoring and control of fishing vessels operating on the high seas that are registered under 'flags of convenience', in order to ensure their compliance with internationally accepted marine conservation and management measures. In March 1995 a ministerial meeting of fisheries adopted the Rome Consensus on World Fisheries, which identified a need for immediate action to eliminate overfishing and to rebuild and enhance depleting fish stocks. In November the FAO Conference adopted a Code of Conduct for Responsible Fishing, which incorporated many global fisheries and aquaculture issues (including fisheries resource conservation and development, fish catches, seafood and fish processing, commercialization, trade and research) to promote the sustainable development of the sector. In February 1999 the FAO Committee on Fisheries adopted new international measures, within the framework of the Code of Conduct, in order to reduce over-exploitation of the world's fish resources, as well as plans of action for the conservation and management of sharks and the reduction in the incidental catch of seabirds in longline fisheries. The voluntary measures were endorsed at a ministerial meeting, held in March and attended by representatives of some 126 countries, which issued a declaration to promote the implementation of the Code of Conduct and to achieve sustainable management of fisheries and aquaculture. In March 2001 FAO adopted an international plan of action to address the continuing problem of so-called illegal, unreported and unregulated fishing (IUU). In that year FAO estimated that about one-half of major marine fish stocks were fully exploited, one-quarter under-exploited, at least 15% over-exploited, and 10% depleted or recovering from depletion. IUU was estimated to account for up to 30% of total catches in certain fisheries. In October FAO and the Icelandic Government jointly organized the Reykjavik Conference on Responsible Fisheries in the Marine Ecosystem, which adopted a declaration on pursuing responsible and sustainable fishing activities in the context of ecosystem-based fisheries management (EBFM). EBFM involves determining the boundaries of individual marine ecosystems, and maintaining or rebuilding the habitats and biodiversity of each of these so that all species will be supported at levels of maximum production. FAO promotes aquaculture (which contributes almost one-third of annual global fish landings) as a valuable source of animal protein and income-generating activity for rural communities. In February 2000 FAO and the Network of Aquaculture Centres in Asia and the Pacific (NACA) jointly convened a Conference on Aquaculture in the Third Millennium, which was held in Bangkok, Thailand, and attended by participants representing more than 200 governmental and non-governmental organizations. The Conference debated global trends in aquaculture and future policy measures to ensure the sustainable development of the sector. It adopted the Bangkok Declaration and Strategy for Aquaculture Beyond 2000. In December 2001 FAO issued a report based on the technical proceedings of the conference.

FORESTRY

FAO focuses on the contribution of forestry to food security, on effective and responsible forest management and on maintaining a balance between the economic, ecological and social benefits of forest resources. The Organization has helped to develop national forestry programmes and to promote the sustainable development of all types of forest. FAO administers the global Forests, Trees and People Programme, which promotes the sustainable management of tree and forest resources, based on local knowledge and management practices, in order to improve the livelihoods of rural people in developing countries. FAO's Strategic Plan for Forestry was approved in March 1999; its main objectives were to maintain the environmental diversity of forests, to realise the economic potential of forests and trees within a sustainable framework, and to expand access to information on forestry.

NUTRITION

The International Conference on Nutrition, sponsored by FAO and WHO, took place in Rome in December 1992. It approved a World Declaration on Nutrition and a Plan of Action, aimed at promoting efforts to combat malnutrition as a development priority. Since the conference, more than 100 countries have formulated national plans of action for nutrition, many of which were based on existing development plans such as comprehensive food security initiatives, national poverty alleviation programmes and action plans to attain the targets set by the World Summit for Children in September 1990. In October 1996 FAO, WHO and other partners jointly organized the first World Congress on Calcium and Vitamin D in Human Life, held in Rome. In January 2001 a joint team of FAO and WHO experts issued a report concerning the allergenicity of foods derived from biotechnology (i.e. genetically modified—GM foods). In July the Codex Alimentarius Commission agreed the first global principles for assessing the safety of GM foods, and approved a series of maximum levels of environmental contaminants in food. FAO and WHO jointly convened a Global Forum of Food Safety Regulators in Marrakech, Morocco, in January 2002. In April the two organizations announce a joint review of their food standards operations, including the activities of the Codex Alimentarius Commission.

PROCESSING AND MARKETING

An estimated 20% of all food harvested is lost before it can be consumed, and in some developing countries the proportion is much higher. FAO helps reduce immediate post-harvest losses, with the introduction of improved processing methods and storage systems. It also advises on the distribution and marketing of agricultural produce and on the selection and preparation of foods for optimum nutrition. Many of these activities form part of wider rural development projects. Many developing countries rely on agricultural prod-

ucts as their main source of foreign earnings, but the terms under which they are traded are usually more favourable to the industrialized countries. FAO continues to favour the elimination of export subsidies and related discriminatory practices, such as protectionist measures that hamper international trade in agricultural commodities. FAO has organized regional workshops and national projects in order to help member states to implement World Trade Organization regulations, in particular with regard to agricultural policy, intellectual property rights, sanitary and phytosanitary measures, technical barriers to trade and the international standards of the Codex Alimentarius. FAO evaluates new market trends and helps to develop improved plant and animal quarantine procedures. In November 1997 the FAO Conference adopted new guide-lines on surveillance and on export certification systems in order to harmonize plant quarantine standards. FAO participates in PhAction, a forum of 12 agencies that was established in 1999 to promote post-harvest research and the development of effective post-harvest services and infrastructure.

FOOD SECURITY

FAO's policy on food security aims to encourage the production of adequate food supplies, to maximize stability in the flow of supplies, and to ensure access on the part of those who need them. In 1994 FAO initiated the Special Programme for Food Security (SPFS), designed to assist low-income countries with a food deficit to increase food production and productivity as rapidly as possible, primarily through the widespread adoption by farmers of improved production technologies, with emphasis on areas of high potential. FAO was actively involved in the formulation of the Plan of Action on food security that was adopted at the World Food Summit in November 1996, and was to be responsible for monitoring and promoting its implementation. In March 1999 FAO signed agreements with IFAD and WFP that aimed to increase co-operation within the framework of the SPFS. A budget of US $10.5m. was allocated to the SPFS for the two-year period 2002–03. In early 2003 the SPFS was operational in 74 countries categorized as 'low-income food-deficit', of which 42 were in Africa. The Programme promotes South–South co-operation to improve food security and the exchange of knowledge and experience. By March 2002 26 bilateral co-operation agreements were in force, for example, between Pakistan and Swaziland and Viet Nam and Benin.

In 2002 three countries in Europe were categorized as 'low-income food-deficit': Albania, Bosnia and Herzegovina, and the former Yugoslav republic of Macedonia—FYRM. The SPFS was operational in Albania and Bosnia and Herzegovina. An SPFS operation for the FYRM was under preparation.

FAO's Global Information and Early Warning System (GIEWS), which become operational in 1975, maintains a database on and monitors the crop and food outlook at global, regional, national and sub-national levels in order to detect emerging food supply difficulties and disasters and to ensure rapid intervention in countries experiencing food supply shortages. It publishes regular reports on the weather conditions and crop prospects in sub-Saharan Africa and in the Sahel region, issues special alerts which describe the situation in countries or sub-regions experiencing food difficulties, and recommends an appropriate international response. FAO's annual publication *State of Food Insecurity in the World* is based on data compiled by the Organization's Food Insecurity and Vulnerability Information and Mapping Systems programme.

FAO INVESTMENT CENTRE

The Investment Centre was established in 1964 to help countries to prepare viable investment projects that will attract external financing. The Centre focuses its evaluation of projects on two fundamental concerns: the promotion of sustainable activities for land management, forestry development and environmental protection, and the alleviation of rural poverty. In 2000–01 90 projects were approved, representing a total investment of some US $4,670m.

EMERGENCY RELIEF

FAO works to rehabilitate agricultural production following natural and man-made disasters by providing emergency seed, tools, and technical and other assistance. Jointly with the United Nations, FAO is responsible for WFP, which provides emergency food supplies and food aid in support of development projects. FAO's Division for Emergency Operations and Rehabilitation was responsible for preparing the emergency agricultural relief component of the 2002 UN inter-agency appeals for 17 countries and regions.

INFORMATION

FAO collects, analyses, interprets and disseminates information through various media, including an extensive internet site. It issues regular statistical reports, commodity studies, and technical manuals in local languages (see list of publications below). Other materials produced by the FAO include information booklets, reference papers, reports of meetings, training manuals and audio-visuals.

FAO's internet-based interactive World Agricultural Information Centre (WAICENT) offers access to agricultural publications, technical documentation, codes of conduct, data, statistics and multimedia resources. FAO compiles and co-ordinates an extensive range of international databases on agriculture, fisheries, forestry, food and statistics, the most important of these being AGRIS (the International Information System for the Agricultural Sciences and Technology) and CARIS (the Current Agricultural Research Information System). Statistical databases include the GLOBEFISH databank and electronic library, FISHDAB (the Fisheries Statistical Database), FORIS (Forest Resources Information System), and GIS (the Geographic Information System). In addition, FAOSTAT provides access to updated figures in 10 agriculture-related topics.

In June 2000 FAO organized a high-level Consultation on Agricultural Information Management (COAIM), which aimed to increase access to and use of agricultural information by policy-makers and others. The second COAIM was held in September 2002.

World Food Day, commemorating the foundation of FAO, is held annually on 16 October.

FAO Councils and Commissions

(Based at the Rome headquarters unless otherwise indicated)

European Commission on Agriculture: f. 1949 to encourage and facilitate action and co-operation in technological agricultural problems among member states and between international organizations concerned with agricultural technology in Europe.

European Commission for the Control of Foot-and-Mouth Disease: internet www.fao.org/ag/AGA/AGAH/EUFMD/default .htm; f. 1953 to promote national and international action for the control of the disease in Europe and its final eradication.

European Forestry Commission: f. 1947 to advise on the formulation of forest policy and to review and co-ordinate its implementation on a regional level to exchange information and to make recommendations; 27 member states.

European Inland Fisheries Advisory Commission: internet www.fao.org/fi/body/eifac/eifac.asp; f. 1957 to promote improvements in inland fisheries and to advise member governments and FAO on inland fishery matters; 34 mems.

FAO/WHO Codex Alimentarius Commission: internet www .codexalimentarius.net; f. 1962 to make proposals for the co-ordination of all international food standards work and to publish a code of international food standards; established Intergovernmental Task Force on Foods Derived from Biotechnology in 1999; 165 member states.

General Fisheries Council for the Mediterranean—GFCM: internet www.fao.org/fi/body/rfb/index.htm; f. 1952 to develop aquatic resources, to encourage and co-ordinate research in the fishing and allied industries, to assemble and publish information, and to recommend the standardization of equipment, techniques and nomenclature.

International Poplar Commission: f. 1947 to study scientific, technical, social and economic aspects of poplar and willow cultivation to promote the exchange of ideas and material between research workers, producers and users; to arrange joint research programmes, congresses, study tours; to make recommendations to the FAO Conference and to National Poplar Commissions.

International Rice Commission: internet www.fao.org/ag/AGP/ AGPC/doc/field/commrice/welcome.htm; f. 1949 to promote national and international action on production, conservation, distribution and consumption of rice, except matters relating to international trade; 60 member states.

Finance

FAO's Regular Programme, which is financed by contributions from member governments, covers the cost of FAO's Secretariat, its Technical Co-operation Programme (TCP) and part of the cost of several special action programmes. The proposed budget for the two years 2002–03 totalled US $651.8m. Much of FAO's technical assistance programme is funded from extra-budgetary sources, predominantly by trust funds that come mainly from donor countries and international financing institutions. The single largest contributor is the United Nations Development Programme (UNDP). In 2001 total field programme expenditure amounted to $367m.

Publications

Animal Health Yearbook.

Commodity Review and Outlook (annually).

Environment and Energy Bulletin.

Ethical Issues in Food and Agriculture.

Fertilizer Yearbook.

Food Crops and Shortages (6 a year).

Food Outlook (5 a year).

Food Safety and Quality Update (monthly; electronic bulletin).

Forest Resources Assessment.

Plant Protection Bulletin (quarterly).

Production Yearbook.

Quarterly Bulletin of Statistics.

The State of Food and Agriculture (annually).

The State of Food Insecurity in the World (annually).

The State of World Fisheries and Aquaculture (every two years).

The State of the World's Forests (every 2 years).

Trade Yearbook.

Unasylva (quarterly).

Yearbook of Fishery Statistics.

Yearbook of Forest Products.

World Animal Review (quarterly).

World Watch List for Domestic Animal Diversity.

Commodity reviews; studies; manuals.

INTERNATIONAL BANK FOR RECONSTRUCTION AND DEVELOPMENT—IBRD (WORLD BANK)

Address: 1818 H St, NW, Washington, DC 20433, USA.

Telephone: (202) 477-1234; **fax:** (202) 477-6391; **e-mail:** pic@worldbank.org; **internet:** www.worldbank.org.

The IBRD was established in December 1945. Initially it was concerned with post-war reconstruction in Europe; since then its aim has been to assist the economic development of member nations by making loans where private capital is not available on reasonable terms to finance productive investments. Loans are made either directly to governments, or to private enterprises with the guarantee of their governments. The World Bank, as it is commonly known, comprises the IBRD and the International Development Association (IDA). The affiliated group of institutions, comprising the IBRD, the IDA, the International Finance Corporation (IFC), the Multilateral Investment Guarantee Agency (MIGA) and the International Centre for Settlement of Investment Disputes (ICSID, see below), is now referred to as the World Bank Group.

Organization

(July 2003)

Officers and staff of the IBRD serve concurrently as officers and staff in the IDA. The World Bank has offices in New York, Brussels, Paris (for Europe), Frankfurt, London, Geneva and Tokyo, as well as in more than 100 countries of operation. Country Directors are located in some 28 country offices.

BOARD OF GOVERNORS

The Board of Governors consists of one Governor appointed by each member nation. Typically, a Governor is the country's finance minister, central bank governor, or a minister or an official of comparable rank. The Board normally meets once a year.

EXECUTIVE DIRECTORS

The general operations of the Bank are conducted by a Board of 24 Executive Directors. Five Directors are appointed by the five members having the largest number of shares of capital stock, and the rest are elected by the Governors representing the other members. The President of the Bank is Chairman of the Board.

PRINCIPAL OFFICERS

The principal officers of the Bank are the President of the Bank, four Managing Directors, two Senior Vice-Presidents and 23 Vice-Presidents.

President and Chairman of Executive Directors: JAMES D. WOLFENSOHN (USA).

Vice-President, Europe and Central Asia: JOHANNES F. LINN.

Activities

FINANCIAL OPERATIONS

IBRD capital is derived from members' subscriptions to capital shares, the calculation of which is based on their quotas in the International Monetary Fund. At 30 June 2002 the total subscribed capital of the IBRD was US $189,505m., of which the paid-in portion was $11,476m. (6.1%); the remainder is subject to call if required. Most of the IBRD's lendable funds come from its borrowing, on commercial terms, in world capital markets, and also from its retained earnings and the flow of repayments on its loans. IBRD loans carry a variable interest rate, rather than a rate fixed at the time of borrowing.

IBRD loans usually have a 'grace period' of five years and are repayable over 15 years or fewer. Loans are made to governments, or must be guaranteed by the government concerned, and are normally made for projects likely to offer a commercially viable rate of return. In 1980 the World Bank introduced structural adjustment lending, which (instead of financing specific projects) supports programmes and changes necessary to modify the structure of an economy so that it can restore or maintain its growth and viability in its balance of payments over the medium term.

The IBRD and IDA together made 229 new lending and investment commitments totalling US $19,519.4m. during the year ending 30 June 2002, compared with 225 (amounting to $17,250.6m.) in the previous year. During 2001/02 the IBRD alone approved commit-

ments totalling $11,451.8m. (compared with $10,487.1m. in the previous year), of which $4,894.7m. (43%) was allocated to Europe and Central Asia. Disbursements by the IBRD in the year ending 30 June 2002 amounted to $11,256m.

IBRD operations are supported by medium- and long-term borrowings in international capital markets. During the year ending 30 June 2002 the IBRD's net income amounted to US $2,778m.

The World Bank's primary objectives are the achievement of sustainable economic growth and the reduction of poverty in developing countries. In the context of stimulating economic growth the Bank promotes both private-sector development and human resource development and has attempted to respond to the growing demands by developing countries for assistance in these areas. In March 1997 the Board of Executive Directors endorsed a 'Strategic Compact', providing for a programme of reforms, to be implemented over a period of 30 months, to increase the effectiveness of the Bank in achieving its central objective of poverty reduction. The reforms included greater decentralization of decision-making, and investment in front-line operations, enhancing the administration of loans, and improving access to information and co-ordination of Bank activities through a knowledge management system comprising four thematic networks: the Human Development Network; the Environmentally and Socially Sustainable Development Network; the Finance, Private Sector and Infrastructure Development Network; and the Poverty Reduction and Economic Management Network. In 2000/01 the Bank adopted a new two-year Strategic Framework which emphasized two essential approaches for Bank support: strengthening the investment climate and prospects for sustainable development in a country, and supporting investment in the poor. In September 2001 the Bank announced that it was to join the UN as a full partner in implementing the so-called Millennium Development Goals, and was to make them central to its development agenda. The objectives, which were approved by governments attending a special session of the UN General Assembly in September 2000, included a reduction by 50% in the number of people with an income of less than US $1 a day and those suffering from hunger and lack of safe drinking water by 2015. The Bank was closely involved in preparations for the International Conference on Financing for Development, which was held in Monterrey, Mexico, in March 2002. The meeting adopted the Monterrey Consensus, which outlined measures to support national development efforts and to achieve the Millennium Development Goals.

The Bank's efforts to reduce poverty include the compilation of country-specific assessments and the formulation of country assistance strategies (CASs) to review and guide the Bank's country programmes. Since August 1998 the Bank has published CASs, with the approval of the government concerned. In 1998/99 the Bank's Executive Directors endorsed a Comprehensive Development Framework (CDF) to effect a new approach to development assistance based on partnerships and country responsibility, with an emphasis on the interdependence of the social, structural, human, governmental, economic and environmental elements of development. The Framework, which aimed to enhance the overall effectiveness of development assistance, was formulated after a series of consultative meetings organized by the Bank and attended by representatives of governments, donor agencies, financial institutions, non-governmental organizations, the private sector and academics.

In December 1999 the Bank introduced a new approach to implement the principles of the CDF, as part of its strategy to enhance the debt relief scheme for heavily indebted poor countries (see below). Applicant countries were requested to formulate a national strategy to reduce poverty, to be presented in the form of a Poverty Reduction Strategy Papers (PRSP). In cases where there might be some delay in issuing a full PRSP, it was permissible for a country to submit a less detailed 'interim' PRSP (I-PRSP) in order to secure the preliminary qualification for debt relief. During 2001/02 seven countries completed PRSPs and nine countries issued interim papers. In 2000/01 the Bank introduced a new Poverty Reduction Support Credit to help low-income countries to implement the policy and institutional reforms outlined in their PRSP. The first credits were approved for Uganda and Viet Nam in May and June respectively. In January 2002 a PRSP public review conference, attended by more than 200 representatives of donor agencies, civil society groups, and developing country organizations was held as part of an ongoing review of the scheme by the Bank and the IMF.

In September 1996 the World Bank/IMF Development Committee endorsed a joint initiative to assist heavily indebted poor countries (HIPCs) to reduce their debt burden to a sustainable level, in order to make more resources available for poverty reduction and economic growth. A new Trust Fund was established by the World Bank in November to finance the initiative. The Fund, consisting of an initial allocation of US \$500m. from the IBRD surplus and other contributions from multilateral creditors, was to be administered by IDA. In early 1999 the World Bank and IMF initiated a comprehensive review of the HIPC initiative. In June the G-7 and Russia, meeting in Cologne, Germany, agreed to increase contributions to the HIPC Trust Fund and to cancel substantial amounts of outstanding debt, and proposed more flexible terms for eligibility. In September the Bank and IMF reached an agreement on an enhanced HIPC scheme, with further revenue to be generated through the revaluation of a percentage of IMF gold reserves. It was agreed that, in order to qualify for debt relief and additional concessional lending, countries were to formulate a PRSP, and should demonstrate prudent financial management in the implementation of the strategy for at least one year. Those countries still deemed to have an unsustainable level of debt at the pivotal 'decision point' of the process were to qualify for assistance. In the majority of cases a sustainable level of debt was targeted at 150% of the net present value (NPV) of the debt in relation to total annual exports (compared with 200%–250% under the original HIPC scheme). Other countries with a lower debt-to-export ratio were to be eligible for assistance under the initiative, providing that their export earnings were at least 30% of GDP (lowered from 40%) and government revenue at least 15% of GDP (reduced from 20%).

In addition to providing financial services, the Bank also undertakes analytical and advisory services, and supports learning and capacity-building, in particular through the World Bank Institute (see below), the Staff Exchange Programme and knowledge-sharing initiatives. The Bank has supported efforts, such as the Global Development Gateway, to disseminate information on development issues and programmes

TECHNICAL ASSISTANCE

The provision of technical assistance to member countries has become a major component of World Bank activities. The economic and sector work (ESW) undertaken by the Bank is the vehicle for considerable technical assistance. In addition, project loans and credits may include funds earmarked specifically for feasibility studies, resource surveys, management or planning advice, and training. The Economic Development Institute has become one of the most important of the Bank's activities in technical assistance. It provides training in national economic management and project analysis for government officials at the middle and upper levels of responsibility. It also runs overseas courses aiming to build up local training capability, and administers a graduate scholarship programme.

The Bank serves as an executing agency for projects financed by the UN Development Programme. It also administers projects financed by various trust funds.

Technical assistance (usually reimbursable) is also extended to countries that do not need Bank financial support, e.g. for training and transfer of technology. The Bank encourages the use of local consultants to assist with projects and stimulate institutional capability.

The Project Preparation Facility (PPF) was established in 1975 to provide cash advances to prepare projects that may be financed by the Bank. In December 1994 the PPF's commitment authority was increased from US \$220m. to \$250m. In 1992 the Bank established an Institutional Development Fund (IDF), which became operational on 1 July; the purpose of the Fund was to provide rapid, small-scale financial assistance, to a maximum value of \$500,000, for capacity-building proposals.

ECONOMIC RESEARCH AND STUDIES

In the 1990s the World Bank's research, conducted by its own research staff, was increasingly concerned with providing information to reinforce the Bank's expanding advisory role to developing countries and to improve policy in the Bank's borrowing countries. The principal areas of current research focus on issues such as maintaining sustainable growth while protecting the environment and the poorest sectors of society, encouraging the development of the private sector, and reducing and decentralizing government activities.

The Bank chairs the Consultative Group on International Agricultural Research (CGIAR), which was founded in 1971 to raise financial support for international agricultural research work for improving crops and animal production in the developing countries; it supports 16 research centres.

CO-OPERATION WITH OTHER ORGANIZATIONS

The World Bank co-operates closely with other UN bodies, at the project level, particularly in the design of social funds and social action programmes. It collaborates with the IMF in implementing economic adjustment programmes in developing countries. The Bank holds regular consultations with the European Union and

OECD on development issues, and the Bank-NGO Committee provides an annual forum for discussion with non-governmental organizations (NGOs). In September 1995 the Bank initiated the Information for Development Programme (InfoDev) with the aim of fostering partnerships between governments, multilateral institutions and private-sector experts in order to promote reform and investment in developing countries through improved access to information technology. Strengthening co-operation with external partners was a fundamental element of the Comprehensive Development Framework, which was adopted in 1998/99 (see above). In 2001/02 a Partnership Approval and Tracking System was implemented to provide information on the Bank's regional and global partnerships.

In June 1995 the World Bank joined other international donors (including regional development banks, other UN bodies, Canada, France, the Netherlands and the USA) in establishing a Consultative Group to Assist the Poorest (CGAP), which was to channel funds to the most needy through grass-roots agencies. An initial credit of approximately US \$200m. was committed by the donors. The Bank manages the CGAP Secretariat, which is responsible for the administration of external funding and for the evaluation and approval of project financing. The CGAP provides technical assistance, training and strategic advice to microfinance institutions and other relevant bodies. As an implementing agency of the Global Environment Facility (GEF, see p. 698) the Bank assists countries to prepare and supervise GEF projects relating to biological diversity, climate change and other environmental protection measures.

In 1997 a Partnerships Group was established to strengthen the Bank's work with development institutions, representatives of civil society and the private sector. The Group established a new Development Grant Facility, which became operational in October, to support partnership initiatives and to co-ordinate all of the Bank's grant-making activities. Also in 1997 the Bank, in partnership with the IMF, UNCTAD, UNDP, the World Trade Organization (WTO) and International Trade Commission, established an Integrated Framework for Trade-related Assistance to Least Developed Countries, at the request of the WTO, to assist those countries to integrate into the global trading system and improve basic trading capabilities.

The Bank is a lead organization in providing reconstruction assistance following natural disasters or conflicts, usually in collaboration with other UN agencies or international organizations, and through special trust funds. In April 1999 the World Bank and the IMF convened an international meeting of governments and agencies to review the immediate response of the international community to meet the humanitarian, economic and financial needs of the six Balkan countries most affected by the conflict in Kosovo and Metohija, and to consider areas for future co-operation and measures to promote economic recovery and growth in those countries. Following the end of the conflict, the Bank was mandated, within the framework of a Stability Pact (signed at a special meeting of ministers of foreign affairs, representatives of international organizations and regional institutions held in June), to co-ordinate a comprehensive approach to economic assistance and regional development in South East Europe, in collaboration with the European Commission. A funding conference was convened in March 2000, at which donor countries pledged US \$2,400m. towards assistance projects. In late June 2001 the Bank and European Commission organized a conference, attended by representatives of 42 countries and 25 international organizations, to generate support for a new Economic Recovery and Transition Programme for the Federal Republic of Yugoslavia that had been prepared in co-operation with the authorities in that country (now Serbia and Montenegro). Some \$1,280m. was pledged in order to implement the programme and pursue the process of reform.

The Bank conducts co-financing and aid co-ordination projects with official aid agencies, export credit institutions, and commercial banks. During the year ending 30 June 2002 a total of 109 IBRD and IDA projects involved co-financers' contributions amounting to US \$4,700m., or 26% of total bank lending.

EVALUATION

The Operations Evaluation Department is an independent unit within the World Bank, which studies and publishes the results of projects after a loan has been fully disbursed, so as to identify problems and possible improvements in future activities. In 1996 a Quality Assurance Group was established to monitor the effectiveness of the Bank's operations and performance.

In September 1993 the Bank's Board of Executive Directors agreed to establish an independent Inspection Panel, consistent with the Bank's objective of improving project implementation and accountability. The panel, which became operational in September 1994, was to conduct independent investigations and report on complaints concerning the design, appraisal and implementation of development projects supported by the Bank. By mid-2002 the panel had received 26 formal requests for inspection.

IBRD INSTITUTIONS

World Bank Institute (WBI): founded in March 1999 by merger of the Bank's Learning and Leadership Centre, previously responsible for internal staff training, and the Economic Development Institute (EDI), which had been established in 1955 to train government officials concerned with development programmes and policies. The new Institute aimed to emphasize the Bank's priority areas through the provision of training courses and seminars relating to poverty, crisis response, good governance and anti-corruption strategies. The Institute co-ordinated a process of consultation and dialogue with researchers and other representatives of civil society to examine poverty for the 2000/01 *World Development Report.* During 1999/2000 the WBI expanded its programmes through distance learning, global knowledge networks, and use of new technologies. Under the EDI a World Links for Development programme was initiated to connect schools in developing countries with partner establishments in industrialized nations via the internet. A new initiative, Global Development Learning Network (GDLN), aimed to expand access to information and learning opportunities through the internet, videoconferences and organized exchanges. At mid-2002 37 GDLN distance learning centers were operational and 42 sites were under development; Vice-Pres. FRANNIE LÉAUTIER (Tanzania/France).

International Centre for Settlement of Investment Disputes (ICSID): founded in 1966 under the Convention of the Settlement of Investment Disputes between States and Nationals of Other States. The Convention was designed to encourage the growth of private foreign investment for economic development, by creating the possibility, always subject to the consent of both parties, for a Contracting State and a foreign investor who is a national of another Contracting State to settle any legal dispute that might arise out of such an investment by conciliation and/or arbitration before an impartial, international forum. The governing body of the Centre is its Administrative Council, composed of one representative of each Contracting State, all of whom have equal voting power. The President of the World Bank is (*ex officio*) the non-voting Chairman of the Administrative Council.; At December 2002 136 countries had signed and ratified the Convention to become ICSID Contracting States. At that time the Centre had considered 68 cases, while 46 were pending.; Sec.-Gen. KO-YUNG TUNG (Japan).

Publications

Abstracts of Current Studies: The World Bank Research Program (annually).

Annual Report on Operations Evaluation.

Annual Report on Portfolio Performance.

Annual Review of Development Effectiveness.

EDI Annual Report.

Global Commodity Markets (quarterly).

Global Development Finance (annually, also on CD-Rom and online).

Global Economic Prospects (annually).

ICSID Annual Report.

ICSID Review—Foreign Investment Law Journal (2 a year).

Joint BIS-IMF-OECD-World Bank Statistics on External Debt (quarterly, also available on the internet at www.worldbank.org/data/jointdebt.html).

New Products and Outreach (EDI, annually).

News from ICSID (2 a year).

Poverty Reduction Strategies Newsletter (quarterly).

Research News (quarterly).

Staff Working Papers.

Transition (every 2 months).

World Bank Annual Report.

World Bank Atlas (annually).

World Bank Economic Review (3 a year).

The World Bank and the Environment (annually).

World Bank Research Observer.

World Development Indicators (annually, also on CD-Rom and online).

World Development Report (annually, also on CD-Rom).

Statistics

IBRD Loans Approved, 1 July 2001–30 June 2002
(US $ million)

Country	Purpose	Amount
Croatia . . .	.Structural adjustment loan	202.0
Latvia	Housing project learning and innovation investment	2.0
Lithuania	Education improvement	25.4
	Vilnius district heating project	17.1
Poland. . . .	.Second hard coal sector adjustment loan	100.0
Romania . . .	.Rural development adaptable programme	40.0
	Second social development fund adaptable programme	20.0
Slovakia . . .	.Social benefits reform	23.5
	Enterprise and financial sector adjustment	177.3

INTERNATIONAL DEVELOPMENT ASSOCIATION—IDA

Address: 1818 H Street, NW, Washington, DC 20433, USA.
Telephone: (202) 477-1234; **fax:** (202) 477-6391; **internet:** www
.worldbank.org/ida.

The International Development Association began operations in
November 1960. Affiliated to the IBRD, IDA advances capital to the
poorer developing member countries on more flexible terms than
those offered by the IBRD.

Organization

(July 2003)

Officers and staff of the IBRD serve concurrently as officers and staff
of IDA.

President and Chairman of Executive Directors: JAMES D.
WOLFENSOHN (ex officio).

Activities

IDA assistance is aimed at the poorer developing countries (i.e. those
with an annual GNP per capita of less than US $885 in 2001 dollars
qualified for assistance in 2002/03). Under IDA lending conditions,
credits can be extended to countries whose balance of payments
could not sustain the burden of repayment required for IBRD loans.
Terms are more favourable than those provided by the IBRD; credits
are for a period of 35 or 40 years, with a 'grace period' of 10 years, and
carry no interest charges. At mid-2002 81 countries were eligible for
IDA assistance, including several small-island economies with a
GNP per head greater than $885, but which would otherwise have
little or no access to Bank funds, and 14 so-called 'blend borrowers'
(such as India), which are entitled to borrow from both the IDA and
IBRD. IDA administers a Trust Fund, which was established in
November 1996 as part of a World Bank/IMF initiative to assist
heavily indebted poor countries (HIPCs, see IBRD).

IDA's total development resources, consisting of members' subscriptions and supplementary resources (additional subscriptions
and contributions), are replenished periodically by contributions
from the more affluent member countries. In November 1998 representatives of 39 donor countries agreed to provide US $11,600m. for
the 12th replenishment of IDA funds, enabling total lending to
amount to an estimated $20,500m. in the period July 1999–June
2002. The new IDA-12 resources were to be directed towards the
following objectives: investing in people; promoting good governance; promoting broad-based growth; and protecting the environment. Discussions on the 13th replenishment of IDA funds commenced in February 2001, and for the first time involved representatives of borrowing countries, civil society and other public groups. A
final commitment, providing for some US $23,000m. in resources in
the period 1 July 2002–30 June 2005, was concluded in early July
2002.

During the year ending 30 June 2001 IDA credits totalling US
$8,067.6m. were approved. Some 70% of new lending was for invest-

ment projects, in particular for the provision of basic social services
and public administration, some 25% was in the form of adjustment
credits.

Publication

Annual Report.

IDA OPERATIONS AND RESOURCES, 1998–2002
(US $ million, years ending 30 June)

	1997/98	1998/99	1999/2000	2000/01	2001/02
Commitments* .	7,508	6,812	4,358	6,764	8,068
Disbursements .	5,630	6,023	5,177	5,492	6,612

* Excluding HIPC development grants.

Source: *World Bank Annual Report 2002.*

Statistics

IDA Credits Approved, 1 July 2001–30 June 2002
(US $ million)

Country	Purpose	Amount
Albania . . .	.Road maintenance credit	17
	Financial sector adjustment credit	15.0
	Poverty reduction support credit	20.0
	Power sector rehabilitation and restructuring investment credit	29.9
	Pilot fishery investment credit	5.6
Bosnia and Herzegovina .	.Solid waste management project	18.0
	Business environment adjustment credit	44.0
	Road management and safety project	30.0
	Private sector credit financial intermediary loan	10.0
Macedonia, former Yugoslav republic	Community development	5.0
	Public sector management adjustment	15.0
	Emergency economic recovery investment credit	15.0
Yugoslavia	Trade and Transport Facilitation in Southeast Europe project	6.8
	Private and financial sector adjustment credit	85.0
	Education improvement invesetment credit	10.0
	Structural adjustment credit	70.0

Source: *World Bank Annual Report 2002.*

INTERNATIONAL FINANCE CORPORATION—IFC

Address: 2121 Pennsylvania Ave, NW, Washington, DC 20433, USA.

Telephone: (202) 473-9331; **fax:** (202) 974-4384; **e-mail:** information@ifc.org; **internet:** www.ifc.org.

IFC was founded in 1956 as a member of the World Bank Group to stimulate economic growth in developing countries by financing private-sector investments, mobilizing capital in international financial markets, and providing technical assistance and advice to governments and businesses.

Organization

(July 2003)

IFC is a separate legal entity in the World Bank Group. Executive Directors of the World Bank also serve as Directors of IFC. The President of the World Bank is *ex officio* Chairman of the IFC Board of Directors, which has appointed him President of IFC. Subject to his overall supervision, the day-to-day operations of IFC are conducted by its staff under the direction of the Executive Vice-President.

PRINCIPAL OFFICERS

President: JAMES D. WOLFENSOHN (USA).

Executive Vice-President: PETER L. WOICKE (Germany).

OFFICES IN THE REGION

Albania: Rruga Deshmoret e4 Shkurtit 34, Tirana; tel. (42) 30017; fax (42) 40590; Programme Co-ordinator ELIRA SAKIQI.

Bosnia and Herzegovina: 71000 Sarajevo, H. Kresevljakovica 19; tel. (33) 440293; fax (33) 440108; Officer HARIS KUSHKUNOVIC.

Bulgaria: 1057 Sofia, Dragan Tzankov Blvd 36, World Trade Centre; tel. (2) 9181-42-25; fax (2) 971-20-45; Programme Co-ordinator GEORGE ALEXANDROV.

Croatia: 10000 Zagreb, Kennedyev trg 6B; tel. (1) 2387236; fax (1) 2387233; Programme Co-ordinator VEDRAN ANTOLJAK.

Czech Republic: Husova 5, 110 00 Prague 1; tel. (2) 24401402; fax (2) 24401410; Head of Special Operations CHARLES VAN DER MANDELE.

Macedonia, former Yugoslav republic: 91000 Skopje, Leninova 34; tel. (91) 117159; fax (91) 117627; Programme Officer SLOBODANKA MATAKOVA.

Poland: 00-113 Warsaw, Emilii Plater 53, Warsaw Financial Centre, 9th Floor; tel. (22) 5206100; fax (22) 5206101; Regional Rep. LAURENCE CARTER.

Romania: Bucharest 2, Blvd Dacia 83; tel. (1) 2112866; fax (1) 2113141; Chief of Mission ANA MARIA MIHAESCU.

Activities

IFC aims to promote economic development in developing member countries by assisting the growth of private enterprise and effective capital markets. It finances private sector projects, through loans, the purchase of equity, quasi-equity products, and risk management services, and assists governments to create conditions that stimulate the flow of domestic and foreign private savings and investment. IFC may provide finance for a project that is partly state-owned, provided that there is participation by the private sector and that the project is operated on a commercial basis. IFC also mobilizes additional resources from other financial institutions, in particular through syndicated loans, thus providing access to international capital markets. IFC provides a range of advisory services to help to improve the investment climate in developing countries and offers technical assistance to private enterprises and governments.

To be eligible for financing, projects must be profitable for investors, as well as financially and economically viable, must benefit the economy of the country concerned, and must comply with IFC's environmental and social guide-lines. IFC aims to promote best corporate governance and management methods and sustainable business practices, and encourages partnerships between governments, non-governmental organizations and community groups. In mid-2002 IFC published its first Sustainability Review, reflecting its emphasis on sustainability as a key strategic and corporate priority.

IFC's authorized capital is US $2,450m. At 30 June 2002 paid-in capital was $2,360m. The World Bank was originally the principal source of borrowed funds, but IFC also borrows from private capital markets. IFC's net income amounted to $215m. in 2001/02, compared with $345m. in the previous year.

In the year ending 30 June 2002 project financing approved by IFC amounted to US $5,835m. for 223 projects in 63 countries and regions (compared with $5,357m. for 240 projects in 77 countries in the previous year). Of the total approved, $4,006m. was for IFC's own account, while $1,829m. was in the form of loan syndications and underwriting of securities issues and investment funds by more than 100 participant banks and institutional investors. Generally, the IFC limits its financing to less than 25% of the total cost of a project, but may take up to a 35% stake in a venture (although never as a majority shareholder). Disbursements for IFC's account amounted to $1,498m. in 2001/02 (compared with $1,535m. in the previous year).

During 2001/02 total financing commitments for 204 new projects amounted to US $3,610m. The largest proportion of commitments was allocated to Latin America and the Caribbean (41%); East Asia and the Pacific and Europe and Central Asia both received 21%, South Asia and sub-Saharan Africa 7%, and the Middle East and North Africa received 4%. The Corporation invests in a wide variety of business and financial institutions in a broad range of sectors. In 2001/02 more than one-third of total financing committed (34%) was for financial services. Other financing included transportation, warehousing and utilities (17%), information technologies (9%), construction and real estate (8%), and non-metallic mineral product manufacturing (6%).

IFC offers risk-management services, assisting institutions to avoid financial risks that arise from changes in interest rates, in exchange rates or in commodity prices. In 2001/02 IFC approved 11 risk-management projects for companies and banks, bringing the total number of projects approved since the introduction of the service in 1990 to 104 in 39 countries.

In 1999/2000 the IFC and World Bank advisory services were integrated into the Private Sector Advisory Services (PSAS). PSAS advises governments and private enterprises on policy, transaction implementation and foreign direct investment. The Foreign Investment Advisory Service (FIAS), established in 1986, provides advice on promoting foreign investment and strengthening the country's investment framework at the request of governments. During 2001/02 FIAS completed 50 advisory projects. Under the Technical Assistance Trust Funds Program (TATF), established in 1988, IFC manages resources contributed by various governments and agencies to provide finance for feasibility studies, project identification studies and other types of technical assistance relating to project preparation.

IFC's SME Department also works with external donors to establish development facilities. In September 2000 the Southeast Europe Enterprise Development (SEED) initiative was formally launched at its headquarters in Sarajevo, Bosnia and Herzegovina, as a five-year scheme to support the development of the private-sector in Albania, Bosnia and Herzegovina, Kosovo, the former Yugoslav republic of Macedonia, and the Federal Republic of Yugoslavia (now Serbia and Montenegro). In June of that year the IFC approved the establishment of a China Project Development Facility to support the development of SMEs within the People's Republic of China. The Facility's headquarters in Chengdu, Sichuan Province, became operational in 2001/02. Both these initiatives highlighted the following three strategic targets: to provide support services at enterprise level; to assist the development of local private sector support institutions; and to advocate ways to improve the business-enabling environment. Also in 2000 a Private Enterprise Partnership, jointly funded by IFC and donor governments, was initiated to implement programmes to develop financial markets in the former Soviet Union, as well as to improve corporate governance practices and business support services in order to enhance the investment and business environment. An SME Capacity Building Facility provides financial support for local projects and development facilities which aim to stimulate small business growth.

Publications

Annual Report.

Emerging Stock Markets Factbook (annually).

Impact (quarterly).

Lessons of Experience (series).

Results on the Ground (series).

Review of Small Businesses (annually).

Discussion papers and technical documents.

MULTILATERAL INVESTMENT GUARANTEE AGENCY— MIGA

Address: 1818 H Street, NW, Washington, DC 20433, USA.
Telephone: (202) 473-6163; **fax:** (202) 522-2630; **internet:** www .miga.org.

MIGA was founded in 1988 as an affiliate of the World Bank. Its mandate is to encourage the flow of foreign direct investment to, and among, developing member countries, through the provision of political risk insurance and investment marketing services to foreign investors and host governments, respectively.

Organization
(July 2003)

MIGA is legally and financially separate from the World Bank. It is supervised by a Council of Governors (comprising one Governor and one Alternate of each member country) and an elected Board of Directors (of no less than 12 members).

President: JAMES D. WOLFENSOH (USA).

Executive Vice-President: MOTOMICHI IKAWA (Japan).

Activities

The convention establishing MIGA took effect in April 1988. Authorized capital was US $1,082m. In April 1998 the Board of Directors approved an increase in MIGA's capital base. A grant of $150m. was transferred from the IBRD as part of the package, while the capital increase (totalling $700m. callable capital and $150m. paid-in capital) was approved by MIGA's Council of Governors in April 1999. A three-year subscription period then commenced, covering the period April 1999–March 2002. At 30 June 2002 total subscriptions to the capital stock amounted to $1,713m., of which $328m. was paid-in.

MIGA guarantees eligible investments against losses resulting from non-commercial risks, under four main categories:

(i) transfer risk resulting from host government restrictions on currency conversion and transfer;

(ii) risk of loss resulting from legislative or administrative actions of the host government;

(iii) repudiation by the host government of contracts with investors in cases in which the investor has no access to a competent forum;

(iv) the risk of armed conflict and civil unrest.

Before guaranteeing any investment, MIGA must ensure that it is commercially viable, contributes to the development process and is not harmful to the environment. During the fiscal year 1998/99 MIGA and IFC appointed the first Compliance Advisor and Ombudsman to consider the concerns of local communities directly affected by MIGA or IFC sponsored projects. In February 1999 the Board of Directors approved an increase in the amount of political risk insurance available for each project, from US $75m. to $200m.

During the year ending 30 June 2002 MIGA issued 58 investment insurance contracts for 33 projects in 24 countries with a value of US $1,357m., compared with 66 contracts valued at $2,000m. in the previous financial year. The amount of direct investment associated with the contracts in 2001/02 totalled approximately $4,700m. (compared with $5.200m. in 2000/01), bringing the total estimate investment facilitated since 1988 to $45,800m. through 597 contracts.

MIGA administers two investment guarantee trust funds, for Bosnia and Herzegovina and for the West Bank and Gaza Strip, to underwrite investment in post-conflict reconstruction activities.

MIGA also provides policy and advisory services to promote foreign investment in developing countries and in transitional economies, and disseminates information on investment opportunities. In October 1995 MIGA established a new network on investment opportunities, which connected investment promotion agencies (IPAs) throughout the world on an electronic information network. The so-called IPA*net* aimed to encourage further investments among developing countries, to provide access to comprehensive information on investment laws and conditions and to strengthen links between governmental, business and financial associations and investors. A new version of IPA*net* was launched in 1997 (and can be accessed at www.ipanet.net). In June 1998 MIGA initiated a new internet-based facility, 'PrivatizationLink', to provide information on investment opportunities resulting from the privatization of industries in developing economies. In October 2000 a specialized facility within the service was established to facilitate investment in Russia (russia.privatizationlink.com). During 2000/01 an office was established in Paris, France, to promote and co-ordinate European investment in developing countries, in particular in Africa and Eastern Europe. In September 2002 a new regional office was inaugurated in Singapore, in order to facilitate foreign investment in Asia. In April MIGA launched a new service, 'FDIXchange', to provide potential investors, advisors and financial institutions with up-to-date market analysis and information on foreign direct investment opportunities in emerging economies (accessible at www.fdixchange.com).

Publications

Annual Report.
Investment Promotion Quarterly (electronic news update).
MIGA News (quarterly).

INTERNATIONAL MONETARY FUND—IMF

Address: 700 19th St, NW, Washington, DC 20431, USA.
Telephone: (202) 623-7300; **fax:** (202) 623-6220; **e-mail:** publicaffairs@imf.org; **internet:** www.imf.org.

The IMF was established at the same time as the World Bank in December 1945, to promote international monetary co-operation, to facilitate the expansion and balanced growth of international trade and to promote stability in foreign exchange.

Organization
(July 2003)

Managing Director: HORST KÖHLER (Germany).

First Deputy Managing Director: ANNE KRUEGER (USA).

Deputy Managing Directors: SHIGEMITSU SUGISAKI (Japan), EDUARDO ANINAT (Chile).

Directors, European Department: MICHAEL C. DEPPLER, JOHN ODLING-SMEE.

BOARD OF GOVERNORS

The highest authority of the Fund is exercised by the Board of Governors, on which each member country is represented by a Governor and an Alternate Governor. The Board normally meets annually. The voting power of each country is related to its quota in the Fund. An International Monetary and Financial Committee (formerly the Interim Committee) advises and reports to the Board on matters relating to the management and adaptation of the international monetary and financial system, sudden disturbances that might threaten the system and proposals to amend the Articles of Agreement.

BOARD OF EXECUTIVE DIRECTORS

The 24-member Board of Executive Directors is responsible for the day-to-day operations of the Fund. The USA, the United Kingdom, Germany, France and Japan each appoint one Executive Director. There is also one Executive Director from the People's Republic of China, Russia and Saudi Arabia, while the remainder are elected by groups of the remaining countries.

REGIONAL OFFICE

Regional Office for Europe: 64–66 ave d'Iena, 75116 Paris, France; tel. 1-40-69-30-70; fax 1-47-23-40-89; Dir FLEMMING LARSEN.

Activities

The purposes of the IMF, as defined in the Articles of Agreement, are:

(i) To promote international monetary co-operation through a permanent institution which provides the machinery for consultation and collaboration on monetary problems;

(ii) To facilitate the expansion and balanced growth of international trade, and to contribute thereby to the promotion and maintenance of high levels of employment and real income and to the development of members' productive resources;

(iii) To promote exchange stability, to maintain orderly exchange arrangements among members, and to avoid competitive exchange depreciation;

(iv) To assist in the establishment of a multilateral system of payments in respect of current transactions between members and in the elimination of foreign exchange restrictions which hamper the growth of trade;

(v) To give confidence to members by making the general resources of the Fund temporarily available to them, under adequate safeguards, thus providing them with the opportunity to correct maladjustments in their balance of payments, without resorting to measures destructive of national or international prosperity;

(vi) In accordance with the above, to shorten the duration of and lessen the degree of disequilibrium in the international balances of payments of members.

In joining the Fund, each country agrees to co-operate with the above objectives. In accordance with its objective of facilitating the expansion of international trade, the IMF encourages its members to accept the obligations of Article VIII, Sections two, three and four, of the Articles of Agreement. Members that accept Article VIII undertake to refrain from imposing restrictions on the making of payments and transfers for current international transactions and from engaging in discriminatory currency arrangements or multiple currency practices without IMF approval. By mid-2002 152 members had accepted Article VIII status.

The financial crises of the late 1990s, notably in several Asian countries, Brazil and Russia, contributed to widespread discussions concerning the strengthening of the international monetary system. In April 1998 the Executive Board identified the following fundamental aspects of the debate: reinforcing international and domestic financial systems; strengthening IMF surveillance; promoting greater availability and transparency of information regarding member countries' economic data and policies; emphasizing the central role of the IMF in crisis management; and establishing effective procedures to involve the private sector in forestalling or resolving financial crises. During 1999/2000 the Fund implemented several measures in connection with its ongoing efforts to appraise and reinforce the global financial architecture, including, in March 2000, the adoption by the Executive Board of a strengthened framework to safeguard the use of IMF resources. During 2000 the Fund established the IMF Center, in Washington, DC, which aimed to promote awareness and understanding of its activities. In September the Fund's new Managing Director announced his intention to focus and streamline the principals of conditionality (which links Fund financing with the implementation of specific economic policies by the recipient countries) as part of the wider reform of the international financial system. A comprehensive review was undertaken, during which the issue was considered by public forums and representatives of civil society. New guide-lines on conditionality, which *inter alia* aimed to promote national ownership of policy reforms and to introduce specific criteria for the implementation of conditions given different states' circumstances, were approved by the Executive Board in September 2002. In 2000/01 the Fund established an International Capital Markets Department to improve its understanding of financial markets and a separate Consultative Group on capital markets to serve as a forum for regular dialogue between the Fund and representatives of the private sector.

In early 2002 a position of Director for Special Operations was created to enhance the Fund's ability to respond to critical situations affecting member countries. In February the newly-appointed Director immediately assumed leadership of the staff team working with the authorities in Argentina to help that country to overcome its extreme economic and social difficulties. In September the IMFC approved further detailed consideration of a sovereign debt restructuring mechanism (SDRM), which aimed to establish a procedure to enable countries with an unsustainable level of debt to renegotiate loans more effectively. In January 2003 the IMF hosted a conference for representatives from the financial sector and civil society and other public officials and academics to discuss aspects of the SDRM.

SURVEILLANCE

Under its Articles of Agreement, the Fund is mandated to oversee the effective functioning of the international monetary system. Accordingly, the Fund aims to exercise firm surveillance over the exchange rate policies of member states and to assess whether a country's economic situation and policies are consistent with the objectives of sustainable development and domestic and external stability. The Fund's main tools of surveillance are regular, bilateral consultations with member countries conducted in accordance with Article IV of the Articles of Agreement, which cover fiscal and monetary policies, balance of payments and external debt developments, as well as policies that affect the economic performance of a country, such as the labour market, social and environmental issues and good governance, and aspects of the country's capital accounts, and finance and banking sectors. In April 1997, in an effort to improve the value of surveillance by means of increased transparency, the Executive Board agreed to the voluntary issue of Press Information Notices (PINs) (on the internet and in *IMF Economic Reviews)*, following each member's Article IV consultation with the Board, to those member countries wishing to make public the Fund's views. Other background papers providing information on and analysis of economic developments in individual countries continued to be made available. In addition, World Economic Outlook discussions are held, normally twice a year, by the Executive Board to assess policy implications from a multilateral perspective and to monitor global developments.

The rapid decline in the value of the Mexican peso in late 1994 and the financial crisis in Asia, which became apparent in mid-1997, focused attention on the importance of IMF surveillance of the economies and financial policies of member states and prompted the Fund to enhance the effectiveness of its surveillance and to encourage the full and timely provision of data by member countries in order to maintain fiscal transparency. In April 1996 the IMF established the Special Data Dissemination Standard (SDDS), which was intended to improve access to reliable economic statistical information for member countries that have, or are seeking, access to international capital markets. In March 1999 the IMF undertook to strengthen the Standard by the introduction of a new reserves data template. By late 2002 52 countries had subscribed to the Standard. In December 1997 the Executive Board approved a new General Data Dissemination System (GDDS), to encourage all member countries to improve the production and dissemination of core economic data. The operational phase of the GDDS commenced in May 2000. The Fund maintains a Dissemination Standards Bulletin Board (accessible at dsbb.imf.org), which aims to ensure that information on SDDS subscribing countries is widely available.

In April 1998 the then Interim Committee adopted a voluntary Code of Good Practices on Fiscal Transparency: Declaration of Principles, which aimed to increase the quality and promptness of official reports on economic indicators, and in September 1999 it adopted a Code of Good Practices on Transparency in Monetary and Financial Policies: Declaration of Principles. The IMF and World Bank jointly established a Financial Sector Assessment Programme (FSAP) in May 1999, initially as a pilot project, which aimed to promote greater global financial security through the preparation of confidential detailed evaluations of the financial sectors of individual countries. Assessments were undertaken of 12 industrialized countries, emerging market economies and developing countries. During 2000 the FSAP was extended to cover a further 24 countries. It remained under regular review by the Boards of Governors of the Fund and World Bank. As part of the FSAP, Fund staff may conclude a Financial System Stability Assessment (FSSA), addressing issues relating to macroeconomic stability and the strength of a country's financial system. A separate component of the FSAP are Reports on the Observance of Standards and Codes (ROSCs), which are compiled after an assessment of a country's implementation and observance of internationally recognized financial standards. In March 2000 the IMF Executive Board adopted a strengthened framework to safeguard the use of IMF resources. All member countries making use of Fund resources were to be required to publish annual central bank statements audited in accordance with internationally accepted standards. It was also agreed that any instance of intentional misreporting of information by a member country should be publicized. In the following month the Executive Board approved the establishment of an Independent Evaluation Office to conduct objective evaluations of IMF policy and operations. In August the Executive Board adopted a Code of Conduct to guide its activities.

In April 2001 the Executive Board agreed on measures to enhance international efforts to counter money-laundering, in particular through the Fund's ongoing financial supervision activities and its programme of assessment of offshore financial centres. In November the IMFC, in response to the terrorist attacks against targets in the USA, which had occurred in September, resolved, *inter alia,* to strengthen the Fund's focus on surveillance, and, in particular, to extend measures to counter money-laundering to include the funds of terrorist organizations. It determined to accelerate efforts to assess offshore centres and to provide technical support to enable poorer countries to meet international financial standards.

SPECIAL DRAWING RIGHTS

The special drawing right (SDR) was introduced in 1970 as a substitute for gold in international payments, and was intended eventually to become the principal reserve asset in the international monetary system. SDRs are allocated to members in proportion to their quotas. In October 1996 the Executive Board agreed to a new allocation of SDRs in order to achieve their equitable distribution among member states (i.e. all members would have an equal number of SDRs relative to the size of their quotas). In particular, this was deemed necessary since 38 countries that had joined the Fund since the last allocation of SDRs in 1981 had not yet received any of the units of account. In September 1997 at the annual meeting of the Executive Board, a resolution approving a special allocation of SDR 21,400m. was passed, in order to ensure an SDR to quota ratio of 29.32%, for all member countries. The resolution was to come into effect following its acceptance by 60% of member countries, having 85% of the total voting power. (At 30 April 2002 118 members, holding 73% of the voting power, had agreed to the proposal.)

From 1974 to 1980 the SDR was valued on the basis of the market exchange rate for a basket of 16 currencies, belonging to the members with the largest exports of goods and services; since 1981 it has been based on the currencies of the five largest exporters (France, Germany, Japan, the United Kingdom and the USA), although the list of currencies and the weight of each in the SDR valuation basket is revised every five years. In January 1999 the IMF incorporated the new currency of the European Economic and Monetary Union, the euro, into the valuation basket; it replaced the French and German currencies, on the basis of their conversion rates with the euro as agreed by the EU. From 1 January 2001 the relative weights assigned to the currencies in the valuation basket were redistributed. The value of the SDR averaged US $1.29484 during 2002, and at 31 December 2002 stood at $1.35952.

The Second Amendment to the Articles of Agreement (1978) altered and expanded the possible uses of the SDR in transactions with other participants. These 'prescribed holders' of the SDRs have the same degree of freedom as Fund members to buy and sell SDRs and to receive or use them in loans, pledges, swaps, donations or settlement of financial obligations. In 2001/02 there were 16 'prescribed holders': the African Development Bank and the African Development Fund, the Arab Monetary Fund, the Asian Development Bank, the Bank of Central African States, the Bank for International Settlements, the Central Bank of West African States, the East African Development Bank, the Eastern Caribbean Central Bank, the European Central Bank, the International Bank for Reconstruction and Development, the International Development Association, the International Fund for Agricultural Development, the Islamic Development Bank, the Latin American Reserve Fund and the Nordic Investment Bank.

QUOTAS

MEMBERSHIP AND QUOTAS IN EUROPE *
(million SDR)

Country	July 2003
Albania	48.7
Bosnia and Herzegovina	169.1
Bulgaria	640.2
Croatia	365.1
Czech Republic	819.3
Estonia	65.2
Greece	823.0
Hungary	1,038.4
Latvia	126.8
Lithuania	144.2
Macedonia, former Yugoslav republic	68.9
Poland	1,369.0
Romania	1,030.2
Serbia and Montenegro	467.7
Slovakia	357.5
Slovenia	231.7

* The Special Drawing Right (SDR) was introduced in 1970 as a substitute for gold in international payments and was intended eventually to become the principal reserve asset in the international monetary system. Its value (which was US $1.39927 at 30 July 2003 and averaged $1.29484 in 2002) is based on the currencies of the five largest exporting countries (France, Germany,

Japan, the United Kingdom and the USA from 1981). In January 1999 the IMF incorporated the new common European currency, the euro, into the SDR valuation 'basket'; it replaced the French and German currencies, on the basis of their conversion rate with the euro, as agreed by the European Union. Each member is assigned a quota related to its national income, monetary reserves, trade balance and other economic indicators. A member's subscription is equal to its quota and is payable partly in SDRs and partly in its own currency. The quota determines a member's voting power and determines its access to the financial resources of the IMF, and its allocation of SDRs. Quotas are reviewed at intervals of not more than five years, to take into account the state of the world economy and members' different rates of development. In January 1998 the Board of Governors adopted a resolution in support of an increase in quotas of 45%, subject to approval by member states constituting 85% of total quotas (as at December 1997). Sufficient consent had been granted by January 1999 to enable the 11th General Review of quotas to enter into effect. The Twelfth General Review was concluded at the end of January 2003 without an increase in quotas. At July 2003 total quotas in the Fund amounted to SDR 212,772.8m.

RESOURCES

Members' subscriptions form the basic resource of the IMF. They are supplemented by borrowing. Under the General Arrangements to Borrow (GAB), established in 1962, the 'Group of Ten' industrialized nations (G-10—Belgium, Canada, France, Germany, Italy, Japan, the Netherlands, Sweden, the United Kingdom and the USA) and Switzerland (which became a member of the IMF in May 1992 but which had been a full participant in the GAB from April 1984) undertake to lend the Fund as much as SDR 17,000m. in their own currencies, to assist in fulfilling the balance-of-payments requirements of any member of the group, or in response to requests to the Fund from countries with balance-of-payments problems that could threaten the stability of the international monetary system. In 1983 the Fund entered into an agreement with Saudi Arabia, in association with the GAB, making available SDR 1,500m., and other borrowing arrangements were completed in 1984 with the Bank for International Settlements, the Saudi Arabian Monetary Agency, Belgium and Japan, making available a further SDR 6,000m. In 1986 another borrowing arrangement with Japan made available SDR 3,000m. In May 1996 GAB participants concluded an agreement in principle to expand the resources available for borrowing to SDR 34,000m., by securing the support of 25 countries with the financial capacity to support the international monetary system. The so-called New Arrangements to Borrow (NAB) was approved by the Executive Board in January 1997. It was to enter into force, for an initial five-year period, as soon as the five largest potential creditors participating in NAB had approved the initiative and the total credit arrangement of participants endorsing the scheme had reached at least SDR 28,900m. While the GAB credit arrangement was to remain in effect, the NAB was expected to be the first facility to be activated in the event of the Fund's requiring supplementary resources. In July 1998 the GAB was activated for the first time in more than 20 years in order to provide funds of up to US $6,300m. in support of an IMF emergency assistance package for Russia (the first time the GAB had been used for a non-participant). The NAB became effective in November, and was used for the first time as part of an extensive programme of support for Brazil, which was adopted by the IMF in early December.

DRAWING ARRANGEMENTS

Exchange transactions within the Fund take the form of members' purchases (i.e. drawings) from the Fund of the currencies of other members for the equivalent amounts of their own currencies. Fund resources are available to eligible members on an essentially short-term and revolving basis to provide members with temporary assistance to contribute to the solution of their payments problems. Before making a purchase, a member must show that its balance of payments or reserve position makes the purchase necessary. Apart from this requirement, reserve tranche purchases (i.e. purchases that do not bring the Fund's holdings of the member's currency to a level above its quota) are permitted unconditionally.

With further purchases, however, the Fund's policy of 'conditionality' means that a member requesting assistance must agree to adjust its economic policies, as stipulated by the IMF. All requests other than for use of the reserve tranche are examined by the Executive Board to determine whether the proposed use would be consistent with the Fund's policies, and a member must discuss its proposed adjustment programme (including fiscal, monetary, exchange and trade policies) with IMF staff. Purchases outside the reserve tranche are made in four credit tranches, each equivalent to 25% of the member's quota; a member must reverse the transaction by repurchasing its own currency (with SDRs or currencies specified by the Fund) within a specified time. A credit tranche purchase is usually made under a 'Stand-by Arrangement' with the Fund, or under the Extended Fund Facility. A Stand-by Arrangement is normally of one or two years' duration, and the amount is made available in instalments, subject to the member's observance of 'performance criteria'; repurchases must be made within three-and-a-quarter to five years. An Extended Arrangement is normally of three years' duration, and the member must submit detailed economic programmes and progress reports for each year; repurchases must be made within four-and-a-half to 10 years. A member whose payments imbalance is large in relation to its quota may make use of temporary facilities established by the Fund using borrowed resources, namely the 'enlarged access policy' established in 1981, which helps to finance Stand-by and Extended Arrangements for such a member, up to a limit of between 90% and 110% of the member's quota annually. Repurchases are made within three-and-a-half to seven years. In October 1994 the Executive Board approved a temporary increase in members' access to IMF resources, on the basis of a recommendation by the then Interim Committee. The annual access limit under IMF regular tranche drawings, Stand-by Arrangements and Extended Fund Facility credits was increased from 68% to 100% of a member's quota, with the cumulative access limit remaining at 300% of quota. The arrangements were extended, on a temporary basis, in November 1997.

In addition, special-purpose arrangements have been introduced, all of which are subject to the member's co-operation with the Fund to find an appropriate solution to its difficulties. During late 1999 the Fund undertook a review of its non-concessional lending facilities. The Buffer Stock Financing Facility (BSFF), established in 1969 in order to enable members to pay their contributions to the buffer stocks which were intended to stabilize markets for primary commodities, was abolished in January 2000, having last been used in 1984. In January 2000 the Executive Board also resolved to eliminate the contingency component of the former Compensatory and Contingency Financing Facility, established in 1988, reforming it as the Compensatory Financing Facility (CCF). The CCF provides compensation to members whose export earnings are reduced as a result of circumstances beyond their control, or which are affected by excess costs of cereal imports. In December 1997 the Executive Board established a new Supplemental Reserve Facility (SRF) to provide short-term assistance to members experiencing exceptional balance-of-payments difficulties resulting from a sudden loss of market confidence. Repayments were to be made within one to one-and-a-half years of the purchase, unless otherwise extended by the Board. The SRF was activated immediately to provide SDR 9,950m. to the Republic of Korea, as part of a Stand-by Arrangement amounting to SDR 15,550m., the largest amount ever committed by the Fund. (With additional financing from governments and international institutions, the total assistance 'package' for the Republic of Korea reached an estimated US $57,000m.) In July 1998 SDR 4,000m. was made available to Russia under the SRF and, in December, some SDR 9,100m. was extended to Brazil under the SRF as part of a new Stand-by Arrangement. In January 2001 some SDR 2,100m. in SRF resources were approved for Argentina as part of an SDR 5,187m. Stand-by Arrangement augmentation. (In January 2002 the Executive Board approved an extension of one year for Argentina's SRF repayments.) In April 1999 an additional facility, the Contingent Credit Lines (CCL), was established to provide short-term financing on similar terms to the SRF in order to prevent more stable economies being affected by adverse international financial developments and to maintain investor confidence. Under the CCL member countries were to have short-term access to up to 500% of their quota, subject to meeting various economic criteria stipulated by the Fund. No funds under the CCL were committed in 2001/02.

In October 1995 the Interim Committee of the Board of Governors endorsed recent decisions of the Executive Board to strengthen IMF financial support to members requiring exceptional assistance. An Emergency Financing Mechanism was established to enable the IMF to respond swiftly to potential or actual financial crises, while additional funds were made available for short-term currency stabilization. (The Mechanism was activated for the first time in July 1997, in response to a request by the Philippines Government to reinforce the country's international reserves, and was subsequently used during that year to assist Thailand, Indonesia and the Republic of Korea, and, in July 1998, Russia.) Emergency assistance was also to be available to countries in a post-conflict situation, in addition to existing arrangements for countries having been affected by natural disasters, to facilitate the rehabilitation of their economies and to improve their eligibility for further IMF concessional arrangements.

In November 1999 the Fund's existing facility to provide balance-of-payments assistance on concessional terms to low-income member countries, the Enhanced Structural Adjustment Facility, was reformulated as the Poverty Reduction and Growth Facility (PRGF), with greater emphasis on poverty reduction and sustainable development as key elements of growth-orientated economic strategies. Assistance under the PRGF (for which 77 countries were deemed eligible) was to be carefully matched to specific national requirements. Prior to drawing on the facility each recipient country was, in collaboration with representatives of civil society, non-governmental organizations and bilateral and multilateral institutions, to develop a national poverty reduction strategy, which was to be presented in a Poverty Reduction Strategy Paper (PRSP). PRGF loans carry an interest rate of 0.5% per year and are repayable over 10 years, with a five-and-a-half-year grace period; each eligible country is normally permitted to borrow up to 140% of its quota (in exceptional circumstances the maximum access can be raised to 185%). A PGRF Trust replaced the former ESAF Trust.

The PRGF supports, through long-maturity loans and grants, IMF participation in a joint initiative, with the World Bank, to provide exceptional assistance to heavily indebted poor countries (HIPCs), in order to help them to achieve a sustainable level of debt management. The initiative was formally approved at the September 1996 meeting of the Interim Committee, having received the support of the 'Paris Club' of official creditors, which agreed to increase the relief on official debt from 67% to 80%. Resources for the HIPC initiative are channelled through the PRGF Trust. In early 1999 the IMF and World Bank initiated a comprehensive review of the HIPC scheme, in order to consider modifications of the initiative and to strengthen the link between debt relief and poverty reduction. A consensus emerged among the financial institutions and leading industrialized nations to enhance the scheme, in order to make it available to more countries, and to accelerate the process of providing debt relief. In September the IMF Board of Governors expressed its commitment to undertaking an off-market transaction of a percentage of the Fund's gold reserves (i.e. a sale, at market prices, to central banks of member countries with repayment obligations to the Fund, which were then to be made in gold), as part of the funding arrangements of the enhanced HIPC scheme; this was undertaken during the period December 1999–April 2000. Under the enhanced initiative it was agreed that countries seeking debt relief should first formulate, and successfully implement for at least one year, a national poverty reduction strategy (see above). By November 2002 a total of $25,102m. in NPV terms had been committed, of which the Fund's share was $2,043m.

During 2001/02 the IMF approved funding commitments for new arrangements amounting to SDR 41,219m., compared with SDR 14,333m. in the previous year. Of the total amount, SDR 39,438m. was committed under nine new Stand-by Arrangements and the augmentation of two already in place (for Argentina and Turkey). Nine new PRGF arrangements were approved in 2001/02, amounting to SDR 1,781m., while augmentations of four existing commitments were also approved. During 2001/02 members' purchases from the general resources account amounted to SDR 29,194m., compared with SDR 9,599m. in the previous year, with the main users of IMF resources being Turkey (SDR 16,200m.), Argentina (SDR 5,922m.) and Brazil (SDR 5,277m.). Outstanding IMF credit at 30 April 2002 totalled SDR 58,698m., compared with SDR 48,662m. as at the previous year. In August the Fund approved its largest ever Stand-by credit amounting to SDR 22,800m. in support of the Brazilian Government's efforts to secure economic and financial stability.

During the financial year 2001/02 Stand-by Arrangements were agreed for Bulgaria (SDR 240.0m.), Lithuania (SDR 86.5m.), Romania (SDR 300m.) and the Federal Republic of Yugoslavia (now Serbia and Montenegro) (SDR 200.0m.).

TECHNICAL ASSISTANCE

Technical assistance is provided by special missions or resident representatives who advise members on every aspect of economic management, while more specialized assistance is provided by the IMF's various departments. In 2000/01 the IMFC determined that technical assistance should be central to IMF's work in crisis prevention and management, in capacity-building for low-income countries, and in restoring macroeconomic stability in countries following a financial crisis. Technical assistance activities subsequently underwent a process of review and reorganization to align them more closely with IMF policy priorities and other initiatives, for example the Financial Stability Assessment Programme. The majority of technical assistance is provided by the Departments of Monetary and Exchange Affairs, of Fiscal Affairs and of Statistics, and by the IMF Institute. The Institute, founded in 1964, trains officials from member countries in financial analysis and policy, balance-of-payments methodology and public finance; it also gives assistance to national and regional training centres.

Publications

Annual Report.

Balance of Payments Statistics Yearbook.

Direction of Trade Statistics (quarterly and annually).

Finance and Development (quarterly, published jointly with the World Bank).

Global Financial Stability Report (quarterly).

Government Finance Statistics Yearbook.

IMF Economic Reviews (3 a year).

IMF Research Bulletin (quarterly).

IMF Survey (2 a month).

International Financial Statistics (monthly and annually, also on CD-ROM).

Joint BIS-IMF-OECD-World Bank Statistics on External Debt (quarterly).

Staff Papers (quarterly).

World Economic Outlook (2 a year).

Occasional papers, economic and financial surveys, pamphlets, booklets.

UNITED NATIONS EDUCATIONAL, SCIENTIFIC AND CULTURAL ORGANIZATION—UNESCO

Address: 7 place de Fontenoy, 75352 Paris 07 SP, France.

Telephone: 1-45-68-10-00; **fax:** 1-45-67-16-90; **e-mail:** scg@unesco.org; **internet:** www.unesco.org.

UNESCO was established in 1946 'for the purpose of advancing, through the educational, scientific and cultural relations of the peoples of the world, the objectives of international peace and the common welfare of mankind'.

Organization

(July 2003)

GENERAL CONFERENCE

The supreme governing body of the Organization, the Conference meets in ordinary session once in two years and is composed of representatives of the member states.

EXECUTIVE BOARD

The Board, comprising 58 members, prepares the programme to be submitted to the Conference and supervises its execution; it meets twice or sometimes three times a year.

SECRETARIAT

Director-General: KOICHIRO MATSUURA (Japan).

CO-OPERATING BODIES

In accordance with UNESCO's constitution, national Commissions have been set up in most member states. These help to integrate work within the member states and the work of UNESCO.

PRINCIPAL REGIONAL OFFICES

European Centre for Higher Education—CEPES: Str. Stirbei Vodà 39, 70732 Bucharest, Romania; tel. (1) 3159956; fax (1) 3123567; e-mail cepes@cepes.ro; internet www.cepes.ro; Dir JAN SADLAK.

Regional Office for Science and Technology for Europe: Palazzo Loredan degli Ambasciatori, 1262/A Dorsoduro, 30123 Venice, Italy; tel. (041) 522-5535; fax (041) 528-9995; e-mail roste@unesco.org; internet www.unesco.org/venice; Dir Prof. PIERRE LASSERRE.

Activities

In November 2001 the General Conference approved a medium-term strategy to guide UNESCO during the period 2002–07. The Conference adopted a new unifying theme for the organization: 'UNESCO contributing to peace and human development in an era of globalization through education, the sciences, culture and communication'. UNESCO's central mission as defined under the strategy was to contribute to peace and human development in the globalized world through its four programme domains (Education, Natural and Social and Human Sciences, Culture, and Communication and Information), incorporating the following three principal dimensions: developing universal principles and norms to meet emerging challenges and protect the 'common public good'; promoting pluralism and diversity; and promoting empowerment and participation in the emerging knowledge society through equitable access, capacity-building and knowledge-sharing. Programme activities were to be focused particularly on supporting disadvantaged and excluded groups or geographic regions. The organization aimed to decentralize its operations in order to ensure more country-driven pro-

gramming. UNESCO's overall work programme for 2002–03 comprised the following major programmes: education; natural sciences; social and human sciences; culture; and communication and information. Basic education; fresh water resources and ecosystems; the ethics of science and technology; diversity, intercultural pluralism and dialogue; and universal access to information, especially in the public domain, were designated as the priority themes. The work programme incorporated two transdisciplinary projects—eradication of poverty, especially extreme poverty; and the contribution of information and communication technologies to the development of education, science and culture and the construction of a knowledge society. UNESCO aims to promote a culture of peace. The UN General Assembly designated UNESCO as the lead agency for co-ordinating the International Decade for a Culture of Peace and Non-Violence for the Children of the World (2001–10), with a focus on education, and the UN Literacy Decade (2003–12). In the implementation of all its activities UNESCO aims to contribute to achieving the UN Millennium Goal of halving levels of extreme poverty by 2015.

EDUCATION

Since its establishment UNESCO has devoted itself to promoting education in accordance with principles based on democracy and respect for human rights.

In March 1990 UNESCO, with other UN agencies, sponsored the World Conference on Education for All. 'Education for All' was subsequently adopted as a guiding principle of UNESCO's contribution to development. UNESCO advocates 'Literacy for All' as a key component of 'Education for All', regarding literacy as essential to basic education and to social and human development. In April 2000 several UN agencies, including UNESCO and UNICEF, and other partners sponsored the World Education Forum, held in Dakar, Senegal, to assess international progress in achieving the goal of 'Education for All' and to adopt a strategy for further action (the 'Dakar Framework'), with the aim of ensuring universal basic education by 2015. The Forum launched the Global Initiative for Education for All. The Dakar Framework emphasized the role of improved access to education in the reduction of poverty and in diminishing inequalities within and between societies. UNESCO was appointed as the lead agency in the implementation of the Framework. UNESCO's role in pursuing the goals of the Dakar Forum was to focus on co-ordination, advocacy, mobilization of resources, and information-sharing at international, regional and national levels. It was to oversee national policy reforms, with a particular focus on the integration of 'Education for All' objectives into national education plans, which were to be produced by all member countries by 2002. UNESCO's work programme on Education for 2002–03 aimed to promote an effective follow-up to the Forum and comprised the following two main components: Basic Education for All: Meeting the Commitments of the Dakar World Education Forum; and Building Knowledge Societies through Quality Education and a Renewal of Education Systems. 'Basic Education for All', signifying the promotion of access to learning opportunities throughout the lives of all individuals, including the most disadvantaged, was designated as the principal theme of the programme and was deemed to require urgent action. The second part of the strategy was to improve the quality of educational provision and renew and diversify education systems, with a view to ensuring that educational needs at all levels were met. This component included updating curricular programmes in secondary education, strengthening science and technology activities and ensuring equal access to education for girls and women. (UNESCO supports the UN Girls' Education Initiative, established following the Dakar Forum.) The work programme focused on the importance of knowledge, information and communication in the increasingly globalized world, and the significance of education as a means of empowerment for the poor and of enhancing basic quality of life.

Within the UN system, UNESCO is responsible for providing technical assistance and educational services in the context of emergency situations. This includes providing education to refugees and displaced persons, as well as assistance for the rehabilitation of national education systems.

UNESCO is concerned with improving the quality, relevance and efficiency of higher education. It assists member states in reforming their national systems, organizes high-level conferences for Ministers of Education and other decision-makers, and disseminates research papers. A World Conference on Higher Education was convened in October 1998 in Paris, France. The Conference adopted a World Declaration on Higher Education for the 21st Century, incorporating proposals to reform higher education, with emphasis on access to education, and educating for individual development and active participation in society. The Conference also approved a framework for Priority Action for Change and Development of Higher Education, which comprised guide-lines for governments and institutions to meet the objectives of greater accessibility, as well as improved standards and relevancy of higher education.

The International Institute for Educational Planning and the International Bureau of Education undertake training, research and the exchange of information on aspects of education. A UNESCO Institute for Education, based in Hamburg, Germany, researches literacy activities and the evolution of adult learning systems. UNESCO aims to promote the use of new information and communication technologies in the expansion of learning opportunities. A joint UNESCO/ILO committee of experts has been established to consider strategies for enhancing the status of the teaching profession.

The April 2000 World Education Forum recognized the global HIV/AIDS pandemic to be a significant challenge to the attainment of 'Education for All'. UNESCO, as a co-sponsor of UNAIDS, takes an active role in promoting formal and non-formal preventive health education.

NATURAL SCIENCES

In November 1999 the General Conference endorsed a Declaration on Science and the Use of Scientific Knowledge and an agenda for action, which had been adopted at the World Conference on Science, held in June/July 1999, in Budapest, Hungary. UNESCO was to coordinate the follow-up to the conference and, in conjunction with the International Council for Science, to promote initiatives in international scientific partnership. The following were identified as priority areas of UNESCO's work programme on Natural Sciences for 2002–03: Science and Technology: Capacity-building and Management; and Sciences, Environment and Sustainable Development. Water Security in the 21st Century was designated as the principal theme, involving addressing threats to water resources and their associated ecosystems. UNESCO was the lead UN agency involved in the preparation of the first *World Water Development Report*, issued in March 2003. UNESCO was a joint co-ordinator of the International Year of Freshwater (2003), which aimed to raise global awareness of the importance of improving the protection and management of fresh water resources. The Science and Technology component of the programme focused on the follow-up of the World Conference on Science, involving the elaboration of national policies on science and technology; strengthening science education; improving university teaching and enhancing national research capacities; and reinforcing international co-operation in mathematics, physics, chemistry, biology, biotechnology and the engineering sciences. UNESCO aims to contribute to bridging the divide between community-held traditional knowledge and scientific knowledge.

UNESCO aims to improve the level of university teaching of the basic sciences through training courses, establishing national and regional networks and centres of excellence, and fostering co-operative research. In carrying out its mission, UNESCO relies on partnerships with non-governmental organizations and the world scientific communities. With the International Council of Scientific Unions and the Third World Academy of Sciences, UNESCO operates a short-term fellowship programme in the basic sciences and an exchange programme of visiting lecturers. In September 1996 UNESCO initiated a 10-year World Solar Programme, which aimed to promote the application of solar energy and to increase research, development and public awareness of all forms of ecologically-sustainable energy use.

UNESCO has over the years established various forms of intergovernmental co-operation concerned with the environmental sciences and research on natural resources, in order to support the recommendations of the June 1992 UN Conference on Environment and Development and, in particular, the implementation of 'Agenda 21' to promote sustainable development. The International Geological Correlation Programme, undertaken jointly with the International Union of Geological Sciences, aims to improve and facilitate

global research of geological processes. In the context of the International Decade for Natural Disaster Reduction (declared in 1990), UNESCO conducted scientific studies of natural hazards and means of mitigating their effects and organized several disaster-related workshops. The International Hydrological Programme considers scientific aspects of water resources assessment and management; and the Intergovernmental Oceanographic Commission(focuses on issues relating to oceans, shorelines and marine resources, in particular the role of the ocean in climate and global systems. The IOC has been actively involved in the establishment of a Global Coral Reef Monitoring Network and is developing a Global Ocean Observing System. An initiative on Environment and Development in Coastal Regions and in Small Islands is concerned with ensuring environmentally-sound and sustainable development by strengthening management of the following key areas: freshwater resources; the mitigation of coastline instability; biological diversity; and coastal ecosystem productivity. UNESCO hosts the secretariat of the World Water Assessment Programme on freshwater resources.

UNESCO's Man and the Biosphere Programme supports a world-wide network of biosphere reserves (comprising 425 sites in 95 countries in February 2003), which aim to promote environmental conservation and research, education and training in biodiversity and problems of land use (including the fertility of tropical soils and the cultivation of sacred sites). In October 2002 UNESCO announced that the 138 biospheres in mountainous areas would play a leading role in a new Global Change Monitoring Programme aimed at assessing the impact of global climate changes. Following the signing of the Convention to Combat Desertification in October 1994, UNESCO initiated an International Programme for Arid Land Crops, based on a network of existing institutions, to assist implementation of the Convention.

SOCIAL AND HUMAN SCIENCES

UNESCO is mandated to contribute to the world-wide development of the social and human sciences and philosophy, which it regards as of great importance in policy-making and maintaining ethical vigilance. The structure of UNESCO's Social and Human Sciences programme takes into account both an ethical and standard-setting dimension, and research, policy-making, action in the field and future-oriented activities. UNESCO's work programme for 2002–03 on Social and Human Sciences comprised three main components: The Ethics of Science and Technology; Promotion of Human Rights, Peace and Democratic Principles; and Improvement of Policies Relating to Social Transformations and Promotion of Anticipation and Prospective Studies. The priority Ethics of Science and Technology element aimed to reinforce UNESCO's role as an intellectual forum for ethical reflection on challenges related to the advance of science and technology; oversee the follow-up of the Universal Declaration on the Human Genome and Human Rights (see below); promote education in science and technology; ensure UNESCO's role in promoting good practices through encouraging the inclusion of ethical guiding principles in policy formulation and reinforcing international networks; and to promote international co-operation in human sciences and philosophy. The Social and Human Sciences programme had the main intellectual and conceptual responsibility for the transdisciplinary theme 'eradication of poverty, especially extreme poverty'.

UNESCO aims to promote and protect human rights and acts as an interdisciplinary, multicultural and pluralistic forum for reflection on issues relating to the ethical dimension of scientific advances, for example in biogenetics, new technology, and medicine. In May 1997 the International Bioethics Committee, a group of 36 specialists who meet under UNESCO auspices, approved a draft version of a Universal Declaration on the Human Genome and Human Rights, in an attempt to provide ethical guide-lines for developments in human genetics. The Declaration, which identified some 100,000 hereditary genes as 'common heritage', was adopted by the UNESCO General Conference in November and committed states to promoting the dissemination of relevant scientific knowledge and co-operating in genome research. The November Conference also resolved to establish an 18-member World Commission on the Ethics of Scientific Knowledge and Technology (COMEST) to serve as a forum for the exchange of information and ideas and to promote dialogue between scientific communities, decision-makers and the public. UNESCO hosts the secretariat of COMEST. COMEST met for the first time in April 1999 in Oslo, Norway. Its second meeting, which took place in December 2001 in Berlin, Germany, focused on the ethics of energy, fresh water and outer space.

In 1994 UNESCO initiated an international social science research programme, the Management of Social Transformations (MOST), to promote capacity-building in social planning at all levels of decision-making. UNESCO sponsors several research fellowships in the social sciences. In other activities UNESCO promotes the rehabilitation of underprivileged urban areas, the research of socio-cultural factors affecting demographic change, and the study of family issues.

UNESCO aims to assist the building and consolidation of peaceful and democratic societies. An international network of institutions and centres involved in research on conflict resolution is being established to support the promotion of peace. Other training, workshop and research activities have been undertaken in countries that have suffered conflict. The Associated Schools Project (ASPnet—comprising 6,483 institutions in 166 countries in early 2003) has, for 50 years, promoted the principles of peace, human rights, democracy and international co-operation through education. An International Youth Clearing House and Information Service (INFOYOUTH) aims to increase and consolidate the information available on the situation of young people in society, and to heighten awareness of their needs, aspirations and potential among public and private decision-makers. UNESCO also focuses on the educational and cultural dimensions of physical education and sport and their capacity to preserve and improve health. Fundamental to UNESCO's mission is the rejection of all forms of discrimination. It disseminates scientific information aimed at combating racial prejudice, works to improve the status of women and their access to education, and promotes equality between men and women.

CULTURE

In undertaking efforts to preserve the world's cultural and natural heritage UNESCO has attempted to emphasize the link between culture and development. In November 2001 the General Conference adopted the UNESCO Universal Declaration on Cultural Diversity, which affirmed the importance of intercultural dialogue in establishing a climate of peace. The work programme on Culture for 2002–03 included the following interrelated components: Reinforcing Normative Action in the Field of Culture; Protecting Cultural Diversity and Promoting Cultural Pluralism and Intercultural Dialogue; and Strengthening Links between Culture and Development. The focus was to be on all aspects of cultural heritage, and on the encouragement of cultural diversity and dialogue between cultures and civilizations. Under the 2002–03 programme UNESCO aimed to launch the Global Alliance on Cultural Diversity, a six-year initiative to promote partnerships between governments, non-governmental bodies and the private sector, with a view to supporting cultural diversity through the strengthening of cultural industries and the prevention of cultural piracy. UNESCO was designated as the lead agency for co-ordinating the UN Year for Cultural Heritage, celebrated in 2002.

UNESCO's World Heritage Programme, inaugurated in 1978, aims to protect historic sites and natural landmarks of outstanding universal significance, in accordance with the 1972 UNESCO Convention Concerning the Protection of the World Cultural and Natural Heritage, by providing financial aid for restoration, technical assistance, training and management planning. By July 2003 the 'World Heritage List' comprised 754 sites in 128 countries, of which 582 had cultural significance, 149 were natural landmarks, and 23 were of 'mixed' importance. Examples include: the ancient city of Nessebar (Bulgaria), Plitvice Lakes National Park (Croatia), the historic centre of Prague (Czech Republic), the old town of Tallinn (Estonia), the Acropolis (Greece), the Hollokö settlement (Hungary), the historic centre of Rīga (Latvia), the historic centre of Vilnius (Lithuania), the Ohrid region (Macedonia), Auschwitz concentration camp (Poland), the Danube Delta (Romania), the Vlkolinec settlement (Slovakia), the Skocjan Caves (Slovenia), and Durmitor National Park (Yugoslavia). UNESCO also maintains a list of World Heritage in Danger, comprising 35 sites at July 2003; these included the archaeological site of Butrint in Albania.

The formulation of a Declaration against the Intentional Destruction of Cultural Heritage was authorized by the General Conference in November 2001. In addition, the November General Conference adopted the Convention on the Protection of the Underwater Cultural Heritage, covering the protection from commercial exploitation of shipwrecks, submerged historical sites, etc., situated in the territorial waters of signatory states. UNESCO also administers the 1954 Hague Convention on the Protection of Cultural Property in the Event of Armed Conflict and the 1970 Convention on the Means of Prohibiting and Preventing the Illicit Import, Export and Transfer of Ownership of Cultural Property. In 1992 a World Heritage Centre was established to enable rapid mobilization of international technical assistance for the preservation of cultural sites. Through the World Heritage Information Network (WHIN), a world-wide network of more than 800 information providers, UNESCO promotes global awareness and information exchange.

UNESCO supports efforts for the collection and safeguarding of humanity's non-material 'intangible' heritage, including oral traditions, music, dance and medicine. In May 2001 UNESCO awarded the title of 'Masterpieces of the Oral and Intangible Heritage of Humanity' to 19 cultural spaces (i.e. physical or temporal spaces hosting recurrent cultural events) and popular forms of expression deemed to be of outstanding value. UNESCO produces an *Atlas of the World's Languages in Danger of Disappearing*. The most recent edition, issued in February 2002, reported that, of some 6,000 languages spoken world-wide, about one-half were endangered.

UNESCO encourages the translation and publication of literary works, publishes albums of art, and produces records, audiovisual programmes and travelling art exhibitions. It supports the development of book publishing and distribution, including the free flow of books and educational material across borders, and the training of editors and managers in publishing. UNESCO is active in preparing and encouraging the enforcement of international legislation on copyright.

In December 1992 UNESCO established the World Commission on Culture and Development, to strengthen links between culture and development and to prepare a report on the issue. The first World Conference on Culture and Development was held in June 1999, in Havana, Cuba. Within the context of the UN's World Decade for Cultural Development (1988–97) UNESCO launched the Silk Roads Project, as a multi-disciplinary study of the interactions among cultures and civilizations along the routes linking Asia and Europe, and established an International Fund for the Promotion of Culture, awarding two annual prizes for music and the promotion of arts. In April 1999 UNESCO celebrated the completion of a major international project, the *General History of Africa*.

COMMUNICATION AND INFORMATION

In 2001 UNESCO introduced a major programme, 'Information for All', as the principal policy-guiding framework for the Communication and Information sector. The organization works towards establishing an open, non-exclusive knowledge society based on information-sharing and incorporating the socio-cultural and ethical dimensions of sustainable development. It promotes the free flow of, and universal access to information, knowledge, data and best practices, through the development of communications infrastructures, the elimination of impediments to freedom of expression, and the promotion of the right to information; through encouraging international co-operation in maintaining libraries and archives; and through efforts to harness informatics for development purposes and strengthen member states' capacities in this field. Activities include assistance with the development of legislation and training programmes in countries where independent and pluralistic media are emerging; assistance in the monitoring of media independence, pluralism and diversity; promotion of exchange programmes and study tours; and improving access and opportunities for women in the media. UNESCO recognizes that the so-called global 'digital divide', in addition to other developmental differences between countries, generates exclusion and marginalization, and that increased participation in the democratic process can be attained through strengthening national communication and information capacities. UNESCO promotes the upholding of human rights in the use of cyberspace. The organization was to participate in the World Summit on the Information Society, scheduled to take place in Geneva, Switzerland, in December 2003. The work programme on Communication and Information for 2002–03 comprised the following components: Promoting Equitable Access to Information and Knowledge Especially in the Public Domain, and Promoting Freedom of Expression and Strengthening Communication Capacities. During 2002–03 UNESCO was to evaluate its interactive internet-based WebWorld Portal, which aims to provide global communication and information services at all levels of society. UNESCO's Memory of the World project aims to preserve in digital form, and thereby to promote wide access to, the world's documentary heritage.

In regions affected by conflict UNESCO supports efforts to establish and maintain an independent media service. This strategy is largely implemented through an International Programme for the Development of Communication (IPDC, see below). In Cambodia, Haiti and Mozambique UNESCO participated in the restructuring of the media in the context of national reconciliation and in Bosnia and Herzegovina it assisted in the development of independent media. In December 1998 the Israeli–Palestinian Media Forum was established, to foster professional co-operation between Israeli and Palestinian journalists. IPDC provides support to communication and media development projects in the developing world, including the establishment of news agencies and newspapers and training editorial and technical staff. Since its establishment in 1982 IPDC has financed some 1,000 projects in more than 130 countries.

In March 1997 the first International Congress on Ethical, Legal and Societal Aspects of Digital Information ('InfoEthics') was held in Monte Carlo, Monaco. At the second 'InfoEthics' Congress, held in October 1998, experts discussed issues concerning privacy, confidentiality and security in the electronic transfer of information. UNESCO maintains an Observatory on the Information Society, which provides up-to-date information on the development of new information and communications technologies, analyses major trends, and aims to raise awareness of related ethical, legal and societal issues. A UNESCO Institute for Information Technologies in Education was established in Moscow, Russia in 1998. In 2001 the UNESCO Institute for Statistics was established in Montréal, Canada.

Finance

UNESCO's activities are funded through a regular budget provided by contributions from member states and extrabudgetary funds from other sources, particularly UNDP, the World Bank, regional banks and other bilateral Funds-in-Trust arrangements. UNESCO co-operates with many other UN agencies and international non-governmental organizations.

UNESCO's Regular Programme budget for the two years 2002–03 was US $544.4m., the same as for the previous biennium. Extra-budgetary funds for 2002–03 were estimated at $320m.

Publications

(mostly in English, French and Spanish editions; Arabic, Chinese and Russian versions are also available in many cases)

Atlas of the World's Languages in Danger of Disappearing.

Copyright Bulletin (quarterly).

Encyclopedia of Life Support Systems (internet-based).

International Review of Education (quarterly).

International Social Science Journal (quarterly).

Museum International (quarterly).

Nature and Resources (quarterly).

Prospects (quarterly review on education).

UNESCO Courier (monthly, in 27 languages).

UNESCO Sources (monthly).

UNESCO Statistical Yearbook.

World Communication Report.

World Educational Report (every 2 years).

World Heritage Review (quarterly).

World Information Report.

World Science Report (every 2 years).

Books, databases, video and radio documentaries, statistics, scientific maps and atlases.

WORLD HEALTH ORGANIZATION—WHO

Address: Ave Appia 20, 1211 Geneva 27, Switzerland.
Telephone: (22) 7912111; **fax:** (22) 7913111; **e-mail:** info@who.int; **internet:** www.who.int.

WHO, established in 1948, is the lead agency within the UN system concerned with the protection and improvement of public health.

Organization

(July 2003)

WORLD HEALTH ASSEMBLY

The Assembly meets in Geneva, once a year; it is responsible for policy making and the biennial programme and budget; appoints the Director-General, admits new members and reviews budget contributions.

EXECUTIVE BOARD

The Board is composed of 32 health experts designated by, but not representing, their governments; they serve for three years, and the World Health Assembly elects 10–12 member states each year to the Board. It meets at least twice a year to review the Director-General's programme, which it forwards to the Assembly with any recommendations that seem necessary. It advises on questions referred to it by the Assembly and is responsible for putting into effect the decisions and policies of the Assembly. It is also empowered to take emergency measures in case of epidemics or disasters.

Chairman: KYAW MYINT (Myanmar).

SECRETARIAT

Director-General: Dr JONG-WOOK LEE (Republic of Korea).

Executive Directors: Dr ANARFI ASAMOA-BAAH (Ghana) (Health Technology and Pharmaceuticals), MARYAN BAQUEROT (General Management), Dr DAVID L. HEYMANN (USA) (Communicable Diseases), Dr CHRISTOPHER MURRAY (Evidence and Information for Policy), Dr DAVID NABARRO (United Kingdom) (Sustainable Development and Healthy Environments), Dr TOMRIS TÜRMEN (Turkey) (Family and Community Health), Dr DEREK YACH (South Africa) (Non-communicable Diseases and Mental Health), NADIA YOUNES (Egypt) (External Relations and Governing Bodies).

Chef de Cabinet (Office of the Director-General): DENIS AITKIN (United Kingdom).

REGIONAL OFFICE

Europe: 8 Scherfigsvej, 2100 Copenhagen Ø, Denmark; tel. (1) 39-17-17-17; fax (1) 39-17-18-18; e-mail webmaster@who.dk; internet www.who.dk; Dir Dr MARC DANZON (France).

Activities

WHO's objective is stated in the constitution as 'the attainment by all peoples of the highest possible level of health'. 'Health' is defined as 'a state of complete physical, mental and social well-being and not merely the absence of disease and infirmity'. In November 2001 WHO issued the International Classification of Functioning, Disability and Health (ICF) to act as an international standard and guide-lines for determining health and disability.

WHO acts as the central authority directing international health work, and establishes relations with professional groups and government health authorities on that basis.

It provides, on request from member states, technical and policy assistance in support of programmes to promote health, prevent and control health problems, control or eradicate disease, train health workers best suited to local needs and strengthen national health systems. Aid is provided in emergencies and natural disasters.

A global programme of collaborative research and exchange of scientific information is carried out in co-operation with about 1,200 national institutions. Particular stress is laid on the widespread communicable diseases of the tropics, and the countries directly concerned are assisted in developing their research capabilities.

It keeps diseases and other health problems under constant surveillance, promotes the exchange of prompt and accurate information and of notification of outbreaks of diseases, and administers the International Health Regulations. It sets standards for the quality control of drugs, vaccines and other substances affecting health. It formulates health regulations for international travel.

It collects and disseminates health data and carries out statistical analyses and comparative studies in such diseases as cancer, heart disease and mental illness.

It receives reports on drugs observed to have shown adverse reactions in any country, and transmits the information to other member states.

It promotes improved environmental conditions, including housing, sanitation and working conditions. All available information on effects on human health of the pollutants in the environment is critically reviewed and published.

Co-operation among scientists and professional groups is encouraged. The organization negotiates and sustains national and global partnerships. It may propose international conventions and agreements, and develops and promotes international norms and standards. The organization promotes the development and testing of new technologies, tools and guide-lines. It assists in developing an informed public opinion on matters of health.

HEALTH FOR ALL

WHO's first global strategy for pursing 'Health for all' was adopted in May 1981 by the 34th World Health Assembly. The objective of 'Health for all' was identified as the attainment by all citizens of the world of a level of health that would permit them to lead a socially and economically productive life, requiring fair distribution of available resources, universal access to essential health care, and the promotion of preventive health care. In May 1998 the 51st World Health Assembly renewed the initiative, adopting a global strategy in support of 'Health for all in the 21st century', to be effected through regional and national health policies. The new approach was to build on the primary health care approach of the initial strategy, but was to strengthen the emphasis on quality of life, equity in health and access to health services. The following have been identified as minimum requirements of 'Health for All':

Safe water in the home or within 15 minutes' walking distance, and adequate sanitary facilities in the home or immediate vicinity;

Immunization against diphtheria, pertussis (whooping cough), tetanus, poliomyelitis, measles and tuberculosis;

Local health care, including availability of essential drugs, within one hour's travel;

Trained personnel to attend childbirth, and to care for pregnant mothers and children up to at least one year old.

WHO's technical programmes are divided into nine groups, or 'clusters', each headed by an Executive Director, as follows: Communicable Diseases; Non-communicable Diseases and Mental Health; Family and Community Health; Sustainable Development and Healthy Environments; Health Technology and Pharmaceuticals; Evidence and Information for Policy; External affairs and Governing Bodies; General Management; and Office of the Director-General (including audit, oversight and legal activities). In 2000 WHO adopted a new corporate strategy, entailing a stronger focus on performance and programme delivery through standardized plans of action, and increased consistency and efficiency throughout the organization.

The Tenth General Programme of Work, for the period 2002–05, defined a policy framework for pursuing the principal objectives of building healthy populations and combating ill health. The Programme took into account: increasing understanding of the social, economic, political and cultural factors involved in achieving better health and the role played by better health in poverty reduction; the increasing complexity of health systems; the importance of safeguarding health as a component of humanitarian action; and the need for greater co-ordination among development organizations. It incorporated four interrelated strategic directions: lessening excess mortality, morbidity and disability, especially in poor and marginalized populations; promoting healthy lifestyles and reducing risk factors to human health arising from environmental, economic, social and behavioural causes; developing equitable and financially fair health systems; and establishing an enabling policy and an institutional environment for the health sector and promoting an effective health dimension to social, economic, environmental and development policy.

COMMUNICABLE DISEASES

WHO identifies infectious and parasitic communicable diseases as a major obstacle to social and economic progress, particularly in developing countries, where, in addition to disabilities and loss of productivity and household earnings, they cause nearly one-half of all deaths. Emerging and re-emerging diseases, those likely to cause epidemics, increasing incidence of zoonoses (diseases passed from animals to humans either directly or by insects) attributable to environmental changes, outbreaks of unknown etiology, and the undermining of some drug therapies by the spread of antimicrobial resistance are main areas of concern. In recent years WHO has noted the global spread of communicable diseases through international travel, voluntary human migration and involuntary population displacement.

WHO's Communicable Diseases group works to reduce the impact of infectious diseases world-wide through surveillance and response; prevention, control and eradication strategies; and research and product development. Combating malaria and tuberculosis (TB) are organization-wide priorities and, as such, are supported not only by their own areas of work but also by activities undertaken in other areas. The group seeks to identify new technologies and tools, and to foster national development through strengthening health services and the better use of existing tools. It aims to strengthen global monitoring of important communicable disease problems. The group advocates a functional approach to disease control. It aims to create consensus and consolidate partnerships around targeted diseases and collaborates with other groups at all stages to provide an integrated response. In April 2000 WHO and several partner institutions in epidemic surveillance established a Global Outbreak Alert and Response Network. Through the Network WHO aims to maintain constant vigilance regarding outbreaks of disease and to link world-wide expertise to provide an immediate response capability. From March 2003 WHO, through the Network, was co-ordinating the international investigation into the global spread of Severe Acute Respiratory Syndrome (SARS), a previously unknown atypical pneumonia. A Global Fund to Fight AIDS, TB and Malaria was established, with WHO participation, in 2001 (see below).

In July 1998 WHO declared the control of malaria a priority concern, and in October the organization formally launched the 'Roll Back Malaria' programme, in conjunction with UNICEF, the World Bank and UNDP, which aimed to halve the prevalence of malaria by 2010. The disease kills an estimated 1m. people each year, and affects a further 300m.–500m. people, some 90% of whom live in sub-Saharan Africa.

In 1995 WHO established a Global Tuberculosis Programme to address the challenges of the TB epidemic, which had been declared a global emergency by the Organization in 1993. According to WHO estimates, one-third of the world's population carries the TB bacillus, and 2m.–3m. people die from the disease each year. WHO provides technical support to all member countries, with special attention given to those with high TB prevalence, to establish effective national tuberculosis control programmes. WHO's strategy for TB control includes the use of DOTS (direct observation treatment, short-course), standardized treatment guide-lines, and result accountability through routine evaluation of treatment outcomes. Simultaneously, WHO is encouraging research with the aim of further disseminating DOTS, adapting DOTS for wider use, developing new tools for prevention, diagnosis and treatment, and containing new threats such as the HIV/TB co-epidemic. In March 1999 WHO announced the launch of a new initiative, 'Stop TB', in partnership with the World Bank, the US Government and a coalition of non-governmental organizations, which aimed to promote DOTS to ensure its use in 85% of detected cases by 2005 (compared with around one-quarter in 1999). The global target for case detection by 2005 was 70%. However, inadequate control of DOTS in some areas, leading to partial and inconsistent treatments, has resulted in the development of drug-resistant and, often, incurable strains of the disease. The incidence of so-called multidrug-resistant TB (MDR-TB) strains, that are unresponsive to the two main anti-TB drugs, has risen in recent years. During 2001 WHO was developing and testing DOTS-Plus, a strategy for controlling the spread of MDR-TB in areas of high prevalence. In 2001 WHO estimated that more than 8m. new cases of TB were occurring world-wide each year, of which the largest concentration was in south-east Asia. It envisaged a substantial increase in new cases by 2005, mainly owing to the severity of the HIV/TB co-epidemic. TB is the principal cause of death for people infected with the HIV virus. In March 2001 the Global TB Drug Facility was launched under the 'Stop TB' initiative; this aimed to increase access to high-quality anti-TB drugs for sufferers in developing countries. In October the 'Stop TB' partnership announced a Global Plan to Stop TB, which envisaged the expansion of access to DOTS; the advancement of MDR-TB prevention measures; the development of anti-TB drugs entailing a shorter treatment period; and the implementation of new strategies for treating people with HIV and TB.

In 2000 the WHO regional office for Europe reported that the level of MDR-TB infection in Estonia, Latvia and Lithuania ranked amongst the highest in the world.

One of WHO's major achievements was the eradication of smallpox. Following a massive international campaign of vaccination and surveillance (begun in 1958 and intensified in 1967), the last case was detected in 1977 and the eradication of the disease was declared in 1980. In May 1996 the World Health Assembly resolved that, pending a final endorsement, all remaining stocks of the smallpox virus were to be destroyed on 30 June 1999, although 500,000 doses of smallpox vaccine were to remain, along with a supply of the smallpox vaccine seed virus, in order to ensure that a further supply of the vaccine could be made available if required. In May 1999, however, the Assembly authorized a temporary retention of stocks of the virus until 2002. In late 2001, in response to fears that illegally-held virus stocks could be used in acts of biological terrorism (see below), WHO reassembled a team of technical experts on smallpox. In January 2002 the Executive Board determined that stocks of the virus should continue to be retained, to enable research into more effective treatments and vaccines.

In 1988 the World Health Assembly declared its commitment to the eradication of poliomyelitis by the end of 2000 and launched the Global Polio Eradication Initiative. WHO's regional office for Europe declared the continent to be 'polio-free' in June 2002.

WHO is committed to the elimination of leprosy (the reduction of the prevalence of leprosy to less than one case per 10,000 population). The use of a highly effective combination of three drugs (known as multi-drug therapy—MDT) resulted in a reduction in the number of leprosy cases world-wide from 10m.-12m. in 1988 to 597,000 in 2000. The Global Alliance for the Elimination of Leprosy, launched in November 1999 by WHO, in collaboration with governments of affected countries and several private partners, including a major pharmaceutical company, aims to bring about the eradication of the disease by the end of 2005, through the continued use of MDT treatment. Most cases occur in Africa, South America and the Far East.

The objective of providing immunization for all children by 1990 was adopted by the World Health Assembly in 1977. Six diseases (measles, whooping cough, tetanus, poliomyelitis, tuberculosis and diphtheria) became the target of the Expanded Programme on Immunization (EPI), in which WHO, UNICEF and many other organizations collaborated. As a result of massive international and national efforts, the global immunization coverage increased from 20% in the early 1980s to the targeted rate of 80% by the end of 1990. This coverage signified that more than 100m. children in the developing world under the age of one had been successfully vaccinated against the targeted diseases, the lives of about 3m. children had been saved every year, and 500,000 annual cases of paralysis as a result of polio had been prevented. In 1992 the Assembly resolved to reach a new target of 90% immunization coverage with the six EPI vaccines; to introduce hepatitis B as a seventh vaccine (with the aim of an 80% reduction in the incidence of the disease in children by 2001); and to introduce the yellow fever vaccine in areas where it occurs endemically.

In June 2000 WHO released a report entitled 'Overcoming Antimicrobial Resistance', in which it warned that the misuse of antibiotics could render some common infectious illnesses unresponsive to treatment. At that time WHO issued guide-lines which aimed to mitigate the risks associated with the use of antimicrobials in livestock reared for human consumption.

NON-COMMUNICABLE DISEASES AND MENTAL HEALTH

The Non-communicable Diseases and Mental Health group comprises departments for the surveillance, prevention and management of uninfectious diseases, such as those arising from an unhealthy diet, and departments for health promotion, disability, injury prevention and rehabilitation, mental health and substance abuse. Surveillance, prevention and management of non-communicable diseases, tobacco, and mental health are organization-wide priorities.

Tobacco use, unhealthy diet and physical inactivity are regarded as common, preventable risk factors for the four most prominent non-communicable diseases: cardiovascular diseases, cancer, chronic respiratory disease and diabetes. WHO aims to monitor the global epidemiological situation of non-communicable diseases, to co-ordinate multinational research activities concerned with prevention and care, and to analyse determining factors such as gender and poverty. In mid-1998 the organization adopted a resolution on measures to be taken to combat non-communicable diseases; their prevalence was anticipated to increase, particularly in developing countries, owing to rising life expectancy and changes in lifestyles. For example, between 1995 and 2025 the number of adults affected by diabetes was projected to increase from 135m. to 300m. In 2001 chronic diseases reportedly accounted for about 59% of the estimated 56.5m. total deaths globally and for 46% of the global burden of disease. In February 1999 WHO initiated a new programme, 'Vision 2020: the Right to Sight', which aimed to eliminate avoidable blindness (estimated to be as much as 80% of all cases) by 2020. Blindness was otherwise predicted to increase by as much as twofold, owing to the increased longevity of the global population. In co-operation with the International Association for the Study of Obesity WHO has studied obesity-related issues. The International Task Force on Obesity, affiliated to the IASO, aims to encourage the development of new policies for managing obesity. WHO and FAO jointly commissioned an expert report on the relationship of diet, nutrition and physical activity to chronic diseases, which was published in March 2003.

WHO's programmes for diabetes mellitus, chronic rheumatic diseases and asthma assist with the development of national initiatives, based upon goals and targets for the improvement of early detection, care and reduction of long-term complications. WHO's cardiovascular diseases programme aims to prevent and control the major cardiovascular diseases, which are responsible for more than 14m. deaths each year. It is estimated that one-third of these deaths could have been prevented with existing scientific knowledge The programme on cancer control is concerned with the prevention of cancer, improving its detection and cure and ensuring care of all cancer patients in need. In 1998 a five-year programme to improve cancer care in developing countries was established, sponsored by private enterprises.

The WHO Human Genetics Programme manages genetic approaches for the prevention and control of common hereditary diseases and of those with a genetic predisposition representing a major health importance. The Programme also concentrates on the further development of genetic approaches suitable for incorporation into health care systems, as well as developing a network of international collaborating programmes.

WHO works to assess the impact of injuries, violence and sensory impairments on health, and formulates guide-lines and protocols for the prevention and management of mental problems. The health promotion division promotes decentralized and community-based health programmes and is concerned with developing new approaches to population ageing and encouraging healthy life-styles and self-care. It also seeks to relieve the negative impact of social changes such as urbanization, migration and changes in family structure upon health. WHO advocates a multi-sectoral approach—involving public health, legal and educational systems—to the prevention of injuries, which represent 16% of the global burden of disease. It aims to support governments in developing suitable strategies to prevent and mitigate the consequences of violence, unintentional injury and disability. Several health promotion projects have been undertaken, in collaboration between WHO regional and country offices and other relevant organizations, including: the Global School Health Initiative, to bridge the sectors of health and education and to promote the health of school-age children; the Global Strategy for Occupational Health, to promote the health of the working population and the control of occupational health risks; Community-based Rehabilitation, aimed at providing a more enabling environment for people with disabilities; and a communication strategy to provide training and support for health communications personnel and initiatives. In 2000 WHO, UNESCO, the World Bank and UNICEF adopted the joint Focusing Resources for Effective School Health (FRESH Start) approach to promoting life skills among adolescents.

In July 1997 the fourth International Conference on Health Promotion (ICHP) was held in Jakarta, Indonesia, where a declaration on 'Health Promotion into the 21st Century' was agreed. The fifth ICHP was convened in June 2000, in Mexico City, Mexico.

Mental health problems, which include unipolar and bipolar affective disorders, psychosis, epilepsy, dementia, Parkinson's disease, multiple sclerosis, drug and alcohol dependency, and neuropsychiatric disorders such as post-traumatic stress disorder, obsessive compulsive disorder and panic disorder, have been identified by WHO as significant global health problems. Although, overall, physical health has improved, mental, behavioural and social health problems are increasing, owing to extended life expectancy and improved child mortality rates, and factors such as war and poverty. WHO aims to address mental problems by increasing awareness of mental health issues and promoting improved mental health services and primary care.

The Substance Abuse department is concerned with problems of alcohol, drugs and other substance abuse. Within its Programme on Substance Abuse (PSA), which was established in 1990 in response to the global increase in substance abuse, WHO provides technical support to assist countries in formulating policies with regard to the prevention and reduction of the health and social effects of psychoactive substance abuse. PSA's sphere of activity includes epidemiological surveillance and risk assessment, advocacy and the dissemination of information, strengthening national and regional prevention and health promotion techniques and strategies, the development of cost-effective treatment and rehabilitation approaches, and also encompasses regulatory activities as required under the international drugs-control treaties in force.

The Tobacco or Health Programme aims to reduce the use of tobacco, by educating tobacco-users and preventing young people from adopting the habit. In 1996 WHO published its first report on the tobacco situation world-wide. According to WHO, about one-third of the world's population aged over 15 years smoke tobacco, which causes approximately 3.5m. deaths each year (through lung cancer, heart disease, chronic bronchitis and other effects). In 1998 the 'Tobacco Free Initiative', a major global anti-smoking campaign, was established. In May 1999 the World Health Assembly endorsed the formulation of a Framework Convention on Tobacco Control (FCTC) to help to combat the increase in tobacco use (although a number of tobacco growers expressed concerns about the effect of the convention on their livelihoods). The draft Framework Convention was finalized in March 2003 and was adopted by the World Health Assembly in May. The greatest increase in tobacco use is forecast to occur in developing countries.

FAMILY AND COMMUNITY HEALTH

WHO's Family and Community Health group addresses the following areas of work: child and adolescent health, research and programme development in reproductive health, making pregnancy safer, women's health, and HIV/AIDS. Making pregnancy safer and HIV/AIDS are organization-wide priorities. The group's aim is to improve access to sustainable health care for all by strengthening health systems and fostering individual, family and community development. Activities include newborn care; child health, including promoting and protecting the health and development of the child through such approaches as promotion of breast-feeding and use of the mother-baby package, as well as care of the sick child, including diarrhoeal and acute respiratory disease control, and support to women and children in difficult circumstances; the promotion of safe motherhood and maternal health; adolescent health, including the promotion and development of young people and the prevention of specific health problems; women, health and development, including addressing issues of gender, sexual violence, and harmful traditional practices; and human reproduction, including research related to contraceptive technologies and effective methods. In addition, WHO aims to provide technical leadership and co-ordination on reproductive health and to support countries in their efforts to ensure that people: experience healthy sexual development and maturation; have the capacity for healthy, equitable and responsible relationships; can achieve their reproductive intentions safely and healthily; avoid illnesses, diseases and injury related to sexuality and reproduction; and receive appropriate counselling, care and rehabilitation for diseases and conditions related to sexuality and reproduction.

In September 1997 WHO, in collaboration with UNICEF, formally launched a programme advocating the Integrated Management of Childhood Illness (IMCI), following successful regional trials in more than 20 developing countries during 1996–97. IMCI recognizes that pneumonia, diarrhoea, measles, malaria and malnutrition cause some 70% of the approximately 11m. childhood deaths each year, and recommends screening sick children for all five conditions, to obtain a more accurate diagnosis than may be achieved from the results of a single assessment. WHO's Division of Diarrhoeal and Acute Respiratory Disease Control encourages national programmes aimed at reducing childhood deaths as a result of diarrhoea, particularly through the use of oral rehydration therapy and preventive measures. The Division is also seeking to reduce deaths from pneumonia in infants through the use of a simple case-management strategy involving the recognition of danger signs and treatment with an appropriate antibiotic.

The HIV/AIDS epidemic represents a major threat to human well-being and socio-economic progress. Some 95% of those known to be infected with HIV/AIDS live in developing countries, and AIDS-related illnesses are the leading cause of death in sub-Saharan Africa. At December 2002 an estimated 42m. adults and children world-wide were living with HIV/AIDS, of whom 5m. were newly infected during that year. WHO's Global Programme on AIDS, initiated in 1987, was concluded in December 1995. A Joint UN Programme on HIV/AIDS (UNAIDS) became operational on 1 January 1996, sponsored by WHO, the World Bank, UNICEF, UNDP, UNESCO and UNFPA. (The UN International Drug Control Programme became the seventh sponsoring agency of UNAIDS in 1999, and in 2001 ILO became the eighth sponsor.) The UNAIDS secretariat is based at WHO headquarters. WHO established an Office of HIV/AIDS and Sexually-Transmitted Diseases in order to ensure the continuity of its global response to the problem, which included support for national control and education plans, improving the safety of blood supplies and improving the care and support of AIDS patients. In addition, the Office was to liaise with UNAIDS and to make available WHO's research and technical expertise. Sufferers of HIV/AIDS in developing countries have often failed to receive advanced antiretroviral (ARV) treatments that are widely available in industrialized countries, owing to their high cost. In May 2000 the World Health Assembly adopted a resolution urging WHO member states to improve access to the prevention and treatment of HIV-related illnesses and to increase the availability and affordability of drugs. WHO, with UNAIDS, UNICEF, UNFPA, the World Bank, and major pharmaceutical companies, participates in the 'Accelerating Access' initiative, which aims to expand access to care, support and ARVs for people with HIV/AIDS. In March 2002, under its 'Access to Quality HIV/AIDS Drugs and Diagnostics' programme, WHO published a comprehensive list of HIV-related medicines deemed to meet standards recommended by the Organization. In April WHO issued the first treatment guide-lines for HIV/AIDS cases in poor communities, and endorsed the inclusion of HIV/AIDS drugs in its *Model List of Essential Drugs* (see below) in order to encourage their wider availability. The secretariat of the International HIV Treatment Access Coalition, founded in December 2002 by governments, non-governmental organizations, donors and others to facilitate access to ARVs for people in low and middle income countries, is based at WHO headquarters. In June 2001 governments participating in a special session of the UN General Assembly on HIV/AIDS adopted a Declaration of Commitment on HIV/AIDS. A WHO-UNAIDS HIV Vaccine Initiative was launched in 2000. In July a meeting of the Group of Seven industrialized nations and Russia (G-8), convened in Genoa, Italy, announced the formation of a new Global Fund to Fight AIDS, TB and Malaria (as previously proposed by the UN Secretary-General and recommended by the World Health Assembly). The Fund, a partnership between governments, UN bodies (including WHO) and other agencies, and private-sector interests, aimed to disburse US $700m.–$800m. in grants during 2002, thereby increasing annual global expenditure on combating those diseases by about 50%. WHO supports governments in developing effective health-sector responses to the HIV/AIDS epidemic through enhancing the planning and managerial capabilities, implementation capacity, and resources of health systems. In February 2003 WHO and FAO jointly published a manual on nutritional care for people living with HIV/AIDS.

In 1990 the WHO Regional Committee for Europe established the EUROHEALTH programme in Central and Eastern Europe. The programme was to establish reforms in health care and environment, to control communicable and non-communicable diseases, and to improve the health of women and children.

Joint UN Programme on HIV/AIDS (UNAIDS): 20 ave Appia, 1211 Geneva 27, Switzerland; tel. (22) 7913666; fax (22) 7914187; e-mail unaids@unaids.org; internet www.unaids.org; Established in 1996 to lead, strengthen and support an expanded response to the global HIV/AIDS pandemic; activities focus on prevention, care and support, reducing vulnerability to infection, and alleviating the socioeconomic and human effects of HIV/AIDS; co-sponsors: WHO, UNICEF, UNDP, UNFPA, UNDCP, ILO, UNESCO, the World Bank; Exec. Dir PETER PIOT (Belgium).

SUSTAINABLE DEVELOPMENT AND HEALTHY ENVIRONMENTS

The Sustainable Development and Healthy Environments group focuses on the following areas of work: health in sustainable development; nutrition; health and environment; food safety; and emergency preparedness and response. Food safety is an organization-wide priority.

WHO promotes recognition of good health status as one of the most important assets of the poor. The Sustainable Development and Healthy Environment group seeks to monitor the advantages and disadvantages for health, nutrition, environment and development arising from the process of globalization (i.e. increased global flows of capital, goods and services, people, and knowledge); to integrate the issue of health into poverty reduction programmes; and to promote human rights and equality. Adequate and safe food and nutrition is a priority programme area. WHO collaborates with FAO, the World Food Programme, UNICEF and other UN agencies in pursuing its objectives relating to nutrition and food safety. An estimated 780m. people world-wide cannot meet basic needs for energy and protein, more than 2,000m. people lack essential vitamins and minerals, and 170m. children are estimated to be malnourished. In December 1992 WHO and FAO hosted an international conference on nutrition, at which a World Declaration and Plan of Action on Nutrition was adopted to make the fight against malnutrition a development priority. Following the conference, WHO promoted the elaboration and implementation of national plans of action on nutrition. WHO aims to support the enhancement of member states' capabilities in dealing with their nutrition situations, and addressing scientific issues related to preventing, managing and monitoring protein-energy malnutrition; micronutrient malnutrition, including iodine deficiency disorders, vitamin A deficiency, and nutritional anaemia; and diet-related conditions and non-communicable diseases such as obesity (increasingly affecting children, adolescents and adults, mainly in industrialized countries), cancer and heart disease. In 1990 the World Health Assembly resolved to eliminate iodine deficiency (causing mental retardation); a strategy of universal salt iodization was launched in 1993. In collaboration with other international agencies, WHO is implementing a comprehensive strategy for promoting appropriate infant, young child and maternal nutrition, and for dealing effectively with nutritional emergencies in large populations. Areas of emphasis include promoting health-care practices that enhance successful breast-feeding; appropriate complementary feeding; refining the use and interpretation of body measurements for assessing nutritional status; relevant information, education and training; and action to give effect to the International Code of Marketing of Breast-milk Substitutes. The food safety programme aims to protect human health against risks associated with biological and chemical contaminants and additives in food. With FAO, WHO establishes food standards (through the work of the Codex Alimentarius Commission and its subsidiary committees) and evaluates food additives, pesticide residues and other contaminants and their implications for health. The programme provides expert advice on such issues as food-borne pathogens (e.g. listeria), production methods (e.g. aquaculture) and food biotechnology (e.g. genetic modification). In July 2001 the Codex Alimentarius Commission adopted the first global principles for assessing the safety of GM foods. In March 2002 an intergovernmental task force established by the Commission finalized 'principles for the risk analysis of foods derived from biotechnology', which were to provide a framework for assessing the safety of genetically-modified—GM foods and plants. In the following month WHO and FAO announced a joint review of their food standards operations. In February 2003 the The FAO/WHO Project and Fund for Enhanced Participation in Codex was launched to support the participation of poorer countries in the Commission's activities.

WHO's programme area on environment and health undertakes a wide range of initiatives to tackle the increasing threats to health and well-being from a changing environment, especially in relation to air pollution, water quality, sanitation, protection against radiation, management of hazardous waste, chemical safety and housing hygiene. Some 1,100m. people world-wide have no access to clean drinking water, while a further 2,400m. people are denied suitable sanitation systems. WHO helped launch the Water Supply and Sanitation Council in 1990 and regularly updates its *Guidelines for Drinking Water Quality*. In rural areas, the emphasis continues to be on the provision and maintenance of safe and sufficient water supplies and adequate sanitation, the health aspects of rural housing, vector control in water resource management, and the safe use of agrochemicals. In urban areas, assistance is provided to identify local environmental health priorities and to improve municipal governments' ability to deal with environmental conditions and health problems in an integrated manner; promotion of the 'Healthy City' approach is a major component of the Programme. Other Programme activities include environmental health information development and management, human resources development, environmental health planning methods, research and work on problems relating to global environment change, such as UV-radiation. A report considering the implications of climate change on human health, prepared jointly by WHO, WMO and UNEP, was published in July 1996. The WHO Global Strategy for Health and Environment, developed in response to the WHO Commission on Health and Environment which reported to the UN Conference on Environment and Development in June 1992, provides the framework for programme activities. In December 2001 WHO published a report on the relationship between macroeconomics and health.

WHO's work in the promotion of chemical safety is undertaken in collaboration with ILO and UNEP through the International Programme on Chemical Safety (IPCS), the Central Unit for which is located in WHO. The Programme provides internationally-evaluated scientific information on chemicals, promotes the use of such information in national programmes, assists member states in establishment of their own chemical safety measures and programmes, and helps them strengthen their capabilities in chemical emergency preparedness and response and in chemical risk reduction. In 1995 an Inter-organization Programme for the Social Management of Chemicals was established by UNEP, ILO, FAO, WHO, UNIDO and OECD, in order to strengthen international co-operation in the field of chemical safety. In 1998 WHO led an international assessment of the health risk from bendocine disruptors (chemicals which disrupt hormonal activities). In January 2001 WHO sent a team of experts to Kosovo and Metohija (Federal Republic of Yugoslavia—FRY, now Serbia and Montenegro) to assess the potential impact on the health of the local population of exposure to depleted uranium, which had been used by NATO in ammunition during its aerial offensive against the FRY in 1999.

Following the major terrorist attacks perpetrated against targets in the USA in September 2001, WHO focused renewed attention on the potential deliberate use of infectious diseases, such as anthrax and smallpox, or of chemical agents, in acts of biological or chemical terrorism. In September 2001 WHO issued draft guide-lines entitled 'Health Aspects of Biological and Chemical Weapons'.

Within the UN system, WHO's Department of Emergency and Humanitarian Action co-ordinates the international response to emergencies and natural disasters in the health field, in close co-operation with other agencies and within the framework set out by the UN's Office for the Co-ordination of Humanitarian Affairs. In this context, WHO provides expert advice on epidemiological surveillance, control of communicable diseases, public health information and health emergency training. Its emergency preparedness activities include co-ordination, policy-making and planning, awareness-building, technical advice, training, publication of standards and guide-lines, and research. Its emergency relief activities include organizational support, the provision of emergency drugs and supplies and conducting technical emergency assessment missions. The Division's objective is to strengthen the national capacity of member states to reduce the adverse health consequences of disasters. In responding to emergency situations, WHO always tries to develop projects and activities that will assist the national authorities concerned in rebuilding or strengthening their own capacity to handle the impact of such situations In May 2001 WHO participated with governments and other international agencies in a joint exercise to evaluate national and international procedures for responding to a nuclear emergency.

WHO provided emergency medical supplies to refugees fleeing the conflict that erupted in Kosovo in March 1999, as well as support for the health authorities in neighbouring host countries. WHO also conducted post-conflict surveillance of the public health situation in Kosovo; co-ordinated agencies providing health care; prepared a plan of action for the rehabilitation and improvement of health services in the region; and conducted a study to determine the threat caused by anti-personnel land mines. In 2001 the WHO humanitarian office in Kosovo co-ordinated medical assistance for refugees sheltering from unrest in the former Yugoslav republic of Macedonia.

HEALTH TECHNOLOGY AND PHARMACEUTICALS

WHO's Health Technology and Pharmaceuticals group, made up of the departments of essential drugs and other medicines, vaccines and other biologicals, and blood safety and clinical technology, covers the following areas of work: essential medicines—access, quality and rational use; immunization and vaccine development;

and world-wide co-operation on blood safety and clinical technology. Blood safety and clinical technology are an organization-wide priority.

In January 1999 the Executive Board adopted a resolution on WHO's Revised Drug Strategy which placed emphasis on the inequalities of access to pharmaceuticals, and also covered specific aspects of drugs policy, quality assurance, drug promotion, drug donation, independent drug information and rational drug use. Plans of action involving co-operation with member states and other international organizations were to be developed to monitor and analyse the pharmaceutical and public health implications of international agreements, including trade agreements. In April 2001 experts from WHO and the World Trade Organization participated in a workshop to address ways of lowering the cost of medicines in less developed countries. In the following month the World Health Assembly adopted a resolution urging member states to promote equitable access to essential drugs, noting that this was denied to about one-third of the world's population. WHO participates with other partners in the 'Accelerating Access' initiative, which aims to expand access to antiretroviral drugs for people with HIV/AIDS (see above).

WHO reports that 2m. children die each year of diseases for which common vaccines exist. In September 1991 the Children's Vaccine Initiative (CVI) was launched, jointly sponsored by the Rockefeller Foundation, UNDP, UNICEF, the World Bank and WHO, to facilitate the development and provision of children's vaccines. The CVI has as its ultimate goal the development of a single oral immunization shortly after birth that will protect against all major childhood diseases. An International Vaccine Institute was established in Seoul, Republic of Korea, as part of the CVI, to provide scientific and technical services for the production of vaccines for developing countries. In September 1996 WHO, jointly with UNICEF, published a comprehensive survey, entitled *State of the World's Vaccines and Immunization*. In 1999 WHO, UNICEF, the World Bank and a number of public- and private-sector partners formed the Global Alliance for Vaccines and Immunization (GAVI), which aimed to expand the provision of existing vaccines and to accelerate the development and introduction of new vaccines and technologies, with the ultimate goal of protecting children of all nations and from all socio-economic backgrounds against vaccine-preventable diseases.

WHO supports states in ensuring access to safe blood, blood products, transfusions, injections, and health-care technologies.

EVIDENCE AND INFORMATION FOR HEALTH POLICY

The Evidence and Information for Health Policy group addresses the following areas of work: evidence for health policy; health information management and dissemination; and research policy and promotion and organization of health systems. Through the generation and dissemination of evidence the Evidence and Information for Health Policy group aims to assist policy-makers assess health needs, choose intervention strategies, design policy and monitor performance, and thereby improve the performance of national health systems. The group also supports international and national dialogue on health policy.

WHO co-ordinates the Health InterNetwork Access to Research Initiative (HINARI), which was launched in July 2001 to enable relevant authorities in developing countries to access more than 2,000 biomedical journals through the internet at no or greatly reduced cost, in order to improve the world-wide circulation of scientific information; some 28 medical publishers participate in the initiative.

Finance

WHO's regular budget is provided by assessment of member states and associate members. An additional fund for specific projects is provided by voluntary contributions from members and other sources, including UNDP and UNFPA.

A regular budget of US $842.7m. was proposed for the two years 2002–03, of which some 6.3%, or $52.8m., was provisionally allocated to Europe.

Publications

Action against Infection (newsletter).
Bulletin of WHO (monthly).
Environmental Health Criteria.
International Digest of Health Legislation (quarterly).
International Classification of Functioning, Disability and Health—ICF.

International Statistical Classification of Diseases and Related Health Problems (Tenth Revision, 1992–1994 (versions in 37 languages)).

Model List of Essential Drugs (biennially).

Weekly Epidemiological Record.

WHO Drug Information (quarterly).

WHO Model Formulary.

World Health Report (annually).

World Health Statistics Annual.

Technical report series; catalogues of specific scientific, technical and medical fields available.

OTHER UN ORGANIZATIONS ACTIVE IN THE REGION

INTERNATIONAL CRIMINAL TRIBUNAL FOR THE FORMER YUGOSLAVIA—ICTY

Address: Public Information Unit, POB 13888, 2501 The Hague, Netherlands.

Telephone: (70) 512-5233; **fax:** (70) 512-5355; **internet:** www.un .org/icty.

In May 1993 the Security Council, acting under Article VII of the UN Charter, adopted Resolution 827, which established an *ad hoc* 'war crimes' tribunal. The so-called International Tribunal for the Prosecution of Persons Responsible for Serious Violations of International Humanitarian Law Committed in the Territory of the Former Yugoslavia (also referred to as the International Criminal Tribunal for the former Yugoslavia—ICTY) was inaugurated in The Hague, Netherlands, in November. The ICTY consists of a Chief Prosecutor's office, and 16 permanent judges, of whom 11 sit in three trial chambers and five sit in a seven-member appeals chamber (with the remaining two appeals chamber members representing the ICTR, see below). In addition, a maximum at any one time of 9 *ad litem* judges, drawn from a pool of 27, serve as required. Public hearings were initiated in November 1994. The first trial proceedings commenced in May 1996, and the first sentence was imposed by the Tribunal in November. In July and November 1995 the Tribunal formally charged the Bosnian Serb political and military leaders Radovan Karadžić and Gen. Ratko Mladić, on two separate indictments, with genocide, crimes against humanity, violation of the laws and customs of war and serious breaches of the Geneva Conventions. In July 1996 the Tribunal issued international warrants for their arrest. Amended indictments, confirmed in May 2000, and announced in October and November, respectively, included the withdrawal of the fourth charge against Mladić. Karadžić and Mladić remained at large in early 2003. In April 2000 Momčilo Krajišnik, a senior associate of Karadžić, was detained by the ICTY, charged with genocide, war crimes and crimes against humanity. Biljana Plavšić, a further former Bosnian Serb political leader, surrendered to the Tribunal in January 2001, also indicted on charges of genocide, war crimes and crimes against humanity. In the following month three Bosnian Serb former soldiers were convicted by the ICTY of utilizing mass rape and the sexual enslavement of women as instruments of terror in wartime. In February 2003 Plavšić was sentenced to eleven years' imprisonment, having pleaded guilty in October 2002 to one of the charges against her (persecutions: a crime against humanity). (Under a plea agreement reached with the Tribunal the remaining charges had been withdrawn.) In mid-1998 the ICTY began investigating reported acts of violence against civilians committed by both sides in the conflict in the southern Serbian province of Kosovo and Metohija. In early 1999 there were reports of large-scale organized killings, rape and expulsion of the local Albanian population by Serbian forces. In April ICTY personnel visited refugee camps in neighbouring countries in order to compile evidence of the atrocities, and obtained intelligence information from NATO members regarding those responsible for the incidents. In May the then President of the then Federal Republic of Yugoslavia (FRY, renamed Serbia and Montenegro in February 2003), Slobodan Milošević, was indicted, along with three senior government ministers and the chief-of-staff of the army, charged with crimes against humanity and violations of the customs of war committed in Kosovo since 1 January 1999; international warrants were issued for their arrests. In June, following the establishment of an international force to secure peace in Kosovo, the ICTY established teams of experts to investigate alleged atrocities at 529 identified grave sites. The new FRY administration, which had assumed power following legislative and presidential elections in late 2000, contested the impartiality of the ICTY, proposing that Milošević and other members of the former regime should be tried before a national court. In April 2001 Milošević was arrested by the local authorities in Belgrade. Under increasing international pressure, the Federal Government approved his extradition in June, and he was immediately transferred to the ICTY, where he was formally charged with crimes against humanity committed in Kosovo in 1999.

A further indictment of crimes against humanity committed in Croatia during 1991–92 was confirmed in October 2001, and a third indictment, which included charges of genocide committed in Bosnia and Herzegovina in 1991–95, was confirmed in November 2001. In early February 2002 the Appeals Chamber ordered that the three indictments be considered in a single trial. The trial commenced later in that month. Milošević, however, continued to protest at the alleged illegality of his arrest and refused to recognize the jurisdiction of the Court. The case was expected to continue until the end of 2004. In August 2001 the ICTY passed its first sentence of genocide, convicting a former Bosnian Serb military commander, Gen. Radislav Kristić, for his role in the deaths of up to 8,000 Bosnian Muslim men and boys in Srebreniča in July 1995. In January 2003 Fatmir Limaj, an ethnic Albanian deputy in the Kosovo parliament and former commander of the Kosovo Liberation Army (KLA), was indicted by the ICTY on several counts of crimes against humanity and war crimes that were allegedly committed in mid-1998 against Serb and Albanian detainees at the KLA's Lapusnik prison camp. Limaj was arrested in Slovenia in February 2003 and transferred to ICTY custody in early March. At that time 23 arrest warrants remained outstanding. Of those who had appeared in proceedings before the Tribunal, 13 were awaiting appeal, nine were serving sentence and nine had been acquitted. Five people had completed their sentences. It was envisaged that the Tribunal's trial activities would be terminated by 2008.

President of the ICTY: THEODOR MERON (USA).

OFFICE FOR THE CO-ORDINATION OF HUMANITARIAN AFFAIRS—OCHA

Address: United Nations Plaza, New York, NY 10017, USA.

Telephone: (212) 963-1234; **fax:** (212) 963-1312; **e-mail:** ochany@ un.org; **internet:** www.reliefweb.int/ocha_ol/.

The Office was established in January 1998 as part of the UN Secretariat, with a mandate to co-ordinate international humanitarian assistance and to provide policy and other advice on humanitarian issues. It administers the Humanitarian Early Warning System, as well as Integrated Regional Information Networks to monitor the situation in different countries and a Disaster Response System.

Under Secretary-General for Humanitarian Affaris and Emergency Relief Co-ordinator: JAN EGELAND (Norway).

OFFICE FOR DRUG CONTROL AND CRIME PREVENTION —ODCCP

Address: Vienna International Centre, POB 500, 1400 Vienna, Austria.

Telephone: (1) 26060-0; **fax:** (1) 26060-5866; **e-mail:** odccp@odccp .org; **internet:** www.odccp.org.

The Office was established in November 1997 to strengthen the UN's integrated approach to issues relating to drug control, crime prevention and international terrorism. It comprises two principal components: the United Nations International Drug Control Programme (UNDCP) and the Centre for International Crime Prevention, both headed by the ODCCP Executive Director.

Executive Director: ANTONIO MARIA COSTA (Italy).

OFFICE OF THE UNITED NATIONS HIGH COMMISSIONER FOR HUMAN RIGHTS

Address: Palais Wilson, 52 rue de Paquis, 1201 Geneva, Switzerland.

Telephone: (22) 9179290; **fax:** (22) 9179022; **e-mail:** scrt.hchr@ unog.ch; **internet:** www.unhchr.ch.

The Office is a body of the UN Secretariat and is the focal point for UN human-rights activities. Since September 1997 it has incorporated the Centre for Human Rights. The High Commissioner is the

UN official with principal responsibility for UN human-rights activities.

High Commissioner: SERGIO VIEIRA DE MELLO (Brazil).

UNITED NATIONS HUMAN SETTLEMENTS PROGRAMME—UN-Habitat

Address: POB 30030, Nairobi, Kenya.

Telephone: (20) 621234; **fax:** (20) 624266; **e-mail:** infohabitat@unhabitat.org; **internet:** www.unhabitat.org.

UN-Habitat was established, as the United Nations Centre for Human Settlements, in October 1978 to service the intergovernmental Commission on Human Settlements. It became a full UN programme on 1 January 2002, serving as the focus for human settlements activities in the UN system.

Executive Director: ANNA KAJUMULO TIBAIJUKA (Tanzania).

UNITED NATIONS CHILDREN'S FUND—UNICEF

Address: 3 United Nations Plaza, New York, NY 10017, USA.

Telephone: (212) 326-7000; **fax:** (212) 888-7465; **e-mail:** netmaster@unicef.org; **internet:** www.unicef.org.

UNICEF was established in 1946 by the UN General Assembly as the UN International Children's Emergency Fund, to meet the emergency needs of children in post-war Europe and China. In 1950 its mandate was changed to emphasize programmes giving long-term benefits to children everywhere, particularly those in developing countries who are in the greatest need.

Executive Director: CAROL BELLAMY (USA).

Regional Office for the Middle East and North Africa: POB 1551, UNICEF House, Tl'a al-Ali al Dahak Bin Soufian St, 11821 Amman, Jordan; tel. (6) 5539977; fax (6) 5538880; e-mail menaro@unicef.org.jo.

UNITED NATIONS CONFERENCE ON TRADE AND DEVELOPMENT—UNCTAD

Address: Palais des Nations, 1211 Geneva 10, Switzerland.

Telephone: (22) 9071234; **fax:** (22) 9070057; **e-mail:** ers@unctad.org; **internet:** www.unctad.org.

UNCTAD was established in 1964. It is the principal organ of the UN General Assembly concerned with trade and development, and is the focal point within the UN system for integrated activities relating to trade, finance, technology, investment and sustainable development. It aims to maximize the trade and development opportunities of developing countries, in particular least-developed countries, and to assist them to adapt to the increasing globalization and liberalization of the world economy. UNCTAD undertakes consensus-building activities, research and policy analysis and technical co-operation.

Secretary-General: RUBENS RICÚPERO (Brazil).

UNITED NATIONS POPULATION FUND—UNFPA

Address: 220 East 42nd St, New York, NY 10017, USA.

Telephone: (212) 297-5020; **fax:** (212) 297-4911; **internet:** www.unfpa.org.

Created in 1967 as the Trust Fund for Population Activities, the UN Fund for Population Activities (UNFPA) was established as a Fund of the UN General Assembly in 1972 and was made a subsidiary organ of the UN General Assembly in 1979, with the UNDP Governing Council (now the Executive Board) designated as its governing body. In 1987 UNFPA's name was changed to the United Nations Population Fund (retaining the same acronym).

Executive Director: THORAYA A. OBAID (Saudi Arabia).

UN SPECIALIZED AGENCIES

INTERNATIONAL ATOMIC ENERGY AGENCY—IAEA

Address: POB 100, Wagramerstrasse 5, 1400 Vienna, Austria.

Telephone: (1) 26000; **fax:** (1) 26007; **e-mail:** official.mail@iaea.org; **internet:** www.iaea.org/worldatom.

The Agency was founded in 1957 as an autonomous intergovernmental organization, although it is administratively part of the UN system and reports annually to the UN General Assembly. Its main objectives are to enlarge the contribution of atomic energy to peace, health and prosperity throughout the world, and to ensure that materials and services provided by the Agency are not used to further any military purpose.

Director-General: Dr MOHAMMAD EL-BARADEI (Egypt).

INTERNATIONAL CIVIL AVIATION ORGANIZATION—ICAO

Address: 999 University St, Montréal, QC H3C 5H7, Canada.

Telephone: (514) 854-8219; **fax:** (514) 954-6077; **e-mail:** icaohq@icao.org; **internet:** www.icao.int.

ICAO was founded in 1947, on the basis of the Convention on International Civil Aviation, signed in Chicago, in 1944, to develop the techniques of international air navigation and to help in the planning and improvement of international air transport.

Secretary-General: TAIEB CHERIF (Algeria).

Regional Office for Europe: 3 bis, Villa Emile-Bergerat, 92522 Neuilly-sur-Seine Cédex, France; tel. 1-46-41-85-85; fax 1-46-41-85-00; e-mail icaoeurnat@paris.icao.int; internet www.icao.int/eurnat.

INTERNATIONAL FUND FOR AGRICULTURAL DEVELOPMENT—IFAD

Address: Via del Serafico 107, 00142 Rome, Italy.

Telephone: (06) 54591; **fax:** (06) 5043463; **e-mail:** ifad@ifad.org; **internet:** www.ifad.org.

IFAD was established in 1977, following a decision by the 1974 UN World Food Conference, with a mandate to combat hunger and eradicate poverty on a sustainable basis in the low-income, food-deficit regions of the world. Funding operations began in January 1978.

President and Chairman of Executive Board: LENNART BÅGE (Sweden).

INTERNATIONAL LABOUR ORGANIZATION—ILO

Address: 4 route des Morillons, 1211 Geneva 22, Switzerland.

Telephone: (22) 7996111; **fax:** (22) 7988685; **e-mail:** ilo@ilo.org; **internet:** www.ilo.org.

ILO was founded in 1919 to work for social justice as a basis for lasting peace. It carries out this mandate by promoting decent living standards, satisfactory conditions of work and pay and adequate employment opportunities. Methods of action include the creation of international labour standards; the provision of technical co-operation services; and training, education, research and publishing activities to advance ILO objectives.

Director-General: JUAN O. SOMAVÍA (Chile).

Regional Office for Europe and Central Asia: 4 route des Morillons, 1211 Geneva 22, Switzerland; tel. (22) 7996650; fax (22) 7996061; e-mail europe@ilo.org.

INTERNATIONAL MARITIME ORGANIZATION—IMO

Address: 4 Albert Embankment, London, SE1 7SR, United Kingdom.

Telephone: (20) 7735-7611; **fax:** (20) 7587-3210; **e-mail:** info@imo.org; **internet:** www.imo.org.

The Inter-Governmental Maritime Consultative Organization (IMCO) began operations in 1959, as a specialized agency of the UN to facilitate co-operation among governments on technical matters affecting international shipping. Its main aims are to improve the safety of international shipping, and to prevent pollution caused by ships. IMCO became IMO in 1982.

Secretary-General: WILLIAM A. O'NEIL (Canada).

INTERNATIONAL TELECOMMUNICATION UNION—ITU

Address: Place des Nations, 1211 Geneva 20, Switzerland.

Telephone: (22) 7305111; **fax:** (22) 7337256; **e-mail:** itumail@itu.int; **internet:** www.itu.int.

Founded in 1865, ITU became a specialized agency of the UN in 1947. It acts to encourage world co-operation for the improvement and use of telecommunications, to promote technical development, to harmonize national policies in the field, and to promote the extension of telecommunications throughout the world.

Secretary-General: YOSHIO UTSUMI (Japan).

UNITED NATIONS INDUSTRIAL DEVELOPMENT ORGANIZATION—UNIDO

Address: Vienna International Centre, POB 300, 1400 Vienna, Austria.

Telephone: (1) 260260; **fax:** (1) 2692669; **e-mail:** unido@unido.org; **internet:** www.unido.org.

UNIDO began operations in 1967 and became a specialized agency in 1985. Its objectives are to promote sustainable and socially equitable industrial development in developing countries and in countries with economies in transition. It aims to assist such countries to integrate fully into global economic system by mobilizing knowledge, skills, information and technology to promote productive employment, competitive economies and sound environment.

Director-General: CARLOS ALFREDO MAGARIÑOS (Argentina).

UNIVERSAL POSTAL UNION—UPU

Address: Weltpoststr., 3000 Berne 15, Switzerland.

Telephone: (31) 3503111; **fax:** (31) 3503110; **e-mail:** info@upu.int; **internet:** www.upu.int.

The General Postal Union was founded by the Treaty of Berne (1874), beginning operations in July 1875. Three years later its name was changed to the Universal Postal Union. In 1948 UPU became a specialized agency of the UN. It aims to develop and unify the international postal service, to study problems and to provide training.

Director-General: THOMAS E. LEAVEY (USA).

WORLD INTELLECTUAL PROPERTY ORGANIZATION— WIPO

Address: 34 chemin des Colombettes, 1211 Geneva 20, Switzerland.

Telephone: (22) 3389111; **fax:** (22) 7335428; **e-mail:** wipo.mail@wipo.int; **internet:** www.wipo.int.

WIPO was established in 1970. It became a specialized agency of the UN in 1974 concerned with the protection of intellectual property (e.g. industrial and technical patents and literary copyrights) throughout the world. WIPO formulates and administers treaties embodying international norms and standards of intellectual property, establishes model laws, and facilitates applications for the protection of inventions, trademarks etc. WIPO provides legal and technical assistance to developing countries and countries with economies in transition and advises countries on obligations under the World Trade Organization's agreement on Trade-Related Aspects of Intellectual Property Rights (TRIPS).

Director-General: Dr KAMIL IDRIS (Sudan).

WORLD METEOROLOGICAL ORGANIZATION—WMO

Address: 7 bis, ave de la Paix, 1211 Geneva 2, Switzerland.

Telephone: (22) 7308111; **fax:** (22) 7308181; **e-mail:** ipa@wmo.ch; **internet:** www.wmo.ch.

WMO was established in 1950 and was recognized as a Specialized Agency of the UN in 1951, aiming to improve the exchange of information in the fields of meteorology, climatology, operational hydrology and related fields, as well as their applications. WMO jointly implements the UN Framework Convention on Climate Change with UNEP.

Secretary-General: Prof. G.O.P. OBASI (Nigeria).

COUNCIL OF BALTIC SEA STATES—CBSS

Address: Strömsborg, POB 2010, 103 11 Stockhölm, Sweden.
Telephone: (8) 440-19-20; **fax:** (8) 440-19-44; **e-mail:** cbss@cbss.st;
internet: www.cbss.st.
The Council of Baltic Sea States (CBSS) was established in 1992 to
develop co-operation between member states.

MEMBERS

Denmark	Iceland	Poland
Estonia	Latvia	Russia
Finland	Lithuania	Sweden
Germany	Norway	

The European Commission also has full membership status.

Organization

(July 2003)

PRESIDENCY

The presidency is occupied by member states for one year, on a
rotating basis. Summit meetings of heads of government are convened every two years. The last summit meeting was held in St
Petersburg, Russia, in June 2002.

COUNCIL

The Council comprises the ministers of foreign affairs of each
member state and a representative of the European Commission.
The Council meets annually and aims to serve as a forum for
guidance, direction of work and overall co-ordination among participating states. The minister of foreign affairs of the presiding
country acts as Chairman of the Council and is responsible for co-
ordinating the Council's activities between ministerial sessions,
with assistance from the Committee of Senior Officials. (Other
ministers also convene periodically, on an *ad hoc* basis by their own
decision.)

COMMITTEE OF SENIOR OFFICIALS—CSO

The Committee consists of senior officials of the ministries of foreign
affairs of the member states and of the European Commission. It
serves as a discussion forum for matters relating to the work of the
Council and undertakes inter-sessional activities. The Chairman of
the Committee, from the same country serving as President of the
CBSS, meets regularly with the previous and future Chairmen. The
so-called Troika aims to maintain information co-operation, promote
better exchange of information, and ensure more effective decision-
making.

SECRETARIAT

In October 1998 the presidency inaugurated a permanent secretariat in Stockholm. The tasks of the secretariat include the preparation of summit meetings, annual sessions of ministers of foreign
affairs, and other meetings of high-level officials and experts, the
provision of technical support to the presidency regarding the implementation of plans, maintaining contacts with other sub-regional
organizations, and strengthening awareness of the Council and its
activities. The Secretariat includes an Energy Unit (established in
April 2000), Baltic 21 Unit (January 2001) and a Children's Unit
(June 2002).

Director: HANNU HALINEN (Finland).

COMMISSIONER ON DEMOCRATIC DEVELOPMENT

Amagertorv 14, POB 1165, 1010 Copenhagen K, Denmark; tel. 33-
91-22-88; fax 33-91-22-96; e-mail mail@cbsscommissioner.org;
internet www.cbss-commissioner.org.

The ministerial session held in May 1994 agreed to appoint an
independent Commissioner on democratic institutions and human
rights to serve a three-year term of office, from October of that year.
In July 1997, at the sixth ministerial session held in Riga, Latvia,
the Commissioner's term of office was extended by a further three
years. The ninth ministerial session, held in Bergen, Norway, in
June 2000, revised and renewed the Commissioner's mandate, until
September 2003.

Commissioner on Democratic Development: HELLE DEGN (Denmark).

Activities

The CBSS was established in March 1992 as a forum to enhance and
strengthen co-operation between countries in the Baltic Sea region.
At a meeting of the Council in Kalmar, Sweden, in July 1996,
ministers adopted an Action Programme as a guide-line for CBSS
activities. The main programme areas covered stable and participatory political development; economic integration and prosperity;
and protection of the environment. The third summit meeting of
CBSS heads of government, held at Kolding, Denmark, in April
2000, recommended a restructuring of the organization to consolidate regional intergovernmental, multilateral co-operation in all
sectors. In June the ninth meeting of the CBSS Council approved the
summit's recommendations. The 10th ministerial session, held in
Hamburg, Germany, in June 2001, adopted a set of guide-lines
regarding the strengthening of the CBSS.

At the first Baltic Sea States summit, held in Visby, Sweden, in
May 1996, heads of government agreed to establish a Task Force on
Organized Crime (TF-OC) to counter drugs-trafficking, strengthen
judicial co-operation, increase the dissemination of information,
impose regional crime-prevention measures, improve border controls and provide training. In January 1998 the second summit
meeting, convened in Riga, Latvia, agreed to extend the mandate of
the Task Force until the end of 2000 and to enhance co-operation in
the areas of civic security and border control. In April 2000 the third
Baltic Sea States summit prolonged the Task Force's mandate
further, until the end of 2004. The 2000 summit also authorized the
establishment of a Task Force on Communicable Disease Control
(TF-CDC), which was mandated to formulate a joint plan aimed at
improving disease control throughout the region, and also to
strengthen regional co-operation in combating the threat to public
health posed by a significant increase in communicable diseases.

The Council has founded a number of working groups, comprising
experts in specific fields, which aim to report on and recommend
action on issues of concern to the Council. In mid-2003 there were
five groups working under the auspices of the CSO: the Working
Group on Assistance to Democratic Institutions (WGDI), based in
Berlin, Germany; the Working Group on Economic Co-operation
(WGEC), based in Tallinn, Estonia; the Working Group on Nuclear
Radiation Safety (WGNRS), based in Stockholm, Sweden; the
Working Group on Youth Affairs, based in Helsinki, Finland; and
the Working Group for Co-operation on Children at Risk (WGCC),
based in Riga, Latvia. There was also an *ad hoc* Working Group on
Transport, based in Warsaw, Poland.

A Baltic Business Advisory Council (BAC) was established in 1996
with the aim of facilitating the privatization process in the member
states in transition and promoting small and medium-sized enterprises.

In January 2001 the CBSS Council agreed to establish a unit in
the CBSS secretariat to implement Baltic 21, the regional variant
(adopted by the CBSS in 1998) of 'Agenda 21', the programme of
action agreed by the UN Conference on Environment and Development, held in Rio de Janeiro, Brazil, in June 1992. Baltic 21
comprised a programme of 30 projects throughout the region, which
aim to promote sustainable development in the agriculture, forestry
and fisheries, energy, industry, tourism, transport, and spatial
planning sectors. The Baltic Sea Region Energy Co-operation
(BASREC) has its own secretariat function and council of senior
energy officials, administered by the CBSS secretariat. BASREC
also has *ad hoc* groups on electricity markets, gas markets, energy
efficiency and climate change.

The CBSS contributed to the implementation of the European
Union's Northern Dimension Action Plan (NDAP) for 2000–03
through the formulation, in collaboration with other regional groupings, of a 'List of Priorities and Projects'. In March 2003 the Committee of Senior Officials met to consider the organization's contribution to the NDAP for 2004–06.

Finance

Contributions of the governments of the Council's 11 member states
finance the Secretariat and the Commissioner on Democratic Development. Ongoing activities and co-operation projects are funded
through voluntary contributions from member states on the basis of
special contribution schemes.

Publication

Newsletter (monthly).

THE COUNCIL OF EUROPE

Address: 67075 Strasbourg Cédex, France.
Telephone: 3-88-41-20-00; **fax:** 3-88-41-27-81; **e-mail:** pointi@coe
.int; **internet:** www.coe.int.

The Council was founded in May 1949 to achieve a greater unity
between its members, to facilitate their social progress and to uphold
the principles of parliamentary democracy, respect for human rights
and the rule of law. Membership has risen from the original 10 to 44.

MEMBERS*

Albania	Liechtenstein
Andorra	Lithuania
Armenia	Luxembourg
Austria	Macedonia, former Yugoslav
Azerbaijan	republic
Belgium	Malta
Bulgaria	Moldova
Bosnia and Herzegovina	Netherlands
Croatia	Norway
Cyprus	Poland
Czech Republic	Portugal
Denmark	Romania
Estonia	Russia
Finland	San Marino
France	Slovakia
Georgia	Slovenia
Germany	Spain
Greece	Sweden
Hungary	Switzerland
Iceland	Turkey
Ireland	Ukraine
Italy	United Kingdom
Latvia	

* The Holy See, Canada, Japan, Mexico and the USA have observer
status with the organization. The Serbia and Montenegro parliament has special 'guest status' at the Parliamentary Assembly,
while the parliaments of Canada, Israel and Mexico have observer
status with the Assembly.

Organization

(July 2003)

COMMITTEE OF MINISTERS

The Committee consists of the ministers of foreign affairs of all
member states (or their deputies); it decides with binding effect all
matters of internal organization, makes recommendations to governments and draws up conventions and agreements; it also discusses matters of political concern, such as European co-operation,
compliance with member states' commitments, in particular concerning the protection of human rights, and considers possible co-
ordination with other institutions, such as the European Union (EU)
and the Organization for Security and Co-operation in Europe
(OSCE). The Committee meets weekly at deputies level and twice a
year (usually in May and November) at ministerial level.

CONFERENCES OF SPECIALIZED MINISTERS

There are 19 Conferences of specialized ministers, meeting regularly
for intergovernmental co-operation in various fields.

PARLIAMENTARY ASSEMBLY

President: Peter Schieder (Austria).

Chairman of the Socialist Group: Terry Davis (United Kingdom).

Chairman of the Group of the European People's Party: René
van der Linden (Netherlands).

**Chairman of the European Democratic (Conservative)
Group:** David Atkinson (United Kingdom).

Chairman of the Liberal Democratic and Reformers' Group:
Mátyás Eörsi (Hungary).

Chairman of the Unified European Left Group: Jaakko Laakso
(Finland).

Members are elected or appointed by their national parliaments
from among the members thereof; political parties in each delegation
follow the proportion of their strength in the national parliament.
Members do not represent their governments, speaking on their own
behalf. At January 2003 the Assembly had 306 members (and 301

substitutes): 18 each for France, Germany, Italy, Russia and the
United Kingdom; 12 each for Poland, Spain, Turkey and Ukraine; 10
for Romania; seven each for Belgium, the Czech Republic, Greece,
Hungary, the Netherlands and Portugal; six each for Austria, Azer-
baijan, Bulgaria, Sweden and Switzerland; five each for Bosnia and
Herzegovina, Croatia, Denmark, Finland, Georgia, Moldova,
Norway and Slovakia; four each for Albania, Armenia, Ireland and
Lithuania; three each for Cyprus, Estonia, Iceland, Latvia, Lux-
embourg, the former Yugoslav republic of Macedonia, Malta and
Slovenia; and two each for Andorra, Liechtenstein and San Marino.
The parliaments of Israel, Canada and Mexico have permanent
observer status, while that of Serbia and Montenegro has special
'guest status'. (Belarus's special status was suspended in January
1997.)

The Assembly meets in ordinary session once a year. The session
is divided into four parts, generally held in the last full week of
January, April, June and September. The Assembly submits Recommendations to the Committee of Ministers, passes Resolutions, and
discusses reports on any matters of common European interest. It is
also a consultative body to the Committee of Ministers, and elects
the Secretary-General, the Deputy Secretary-General, the Secretary-General of the Assembly, the Council's Commissioner for
Human Rights, and the members of the European Court of Human
Rights.

Standing Committee: represents the Assembly when it is not in
session, and may adopt Recommendations to the Committee of
Ministers and Resolutions on behalf of the Assembly. Consists of the
President, Vice-Presidents, Chairmen of the Political Groups,
Chairmen of the Ordinary Committees and Chairmen of national
delegations. Meets usually three times a year.

Ordinary Committees: political; legal and human rights; economic
and development; social, health and family affairs; culture, science
and education; environment, agriculture, and local and regional
authorities; migration, refugees and demography; rules of procedure
and immunities; equal opportunities; honouring of obligations and
commitments by member states of the Council of Europe.

CONGRESS OF LOCAL AND REGIONAL AUTHORITIES OF
EUROPE—CLRAE

The Congress was established in 1994, incorporating the former
Standing Conference of Local and Regional Authorities, in order to
protect and promote the political, administrative and financial
autonomy of local and regional European authorities by encouraging
central governments to develop effective local democracy. The Congress comprises two chambers—a Chamber of Local Authorities and
a Chamber of Regions—with a total membership of 306 elected
representatives (and 306 elected substitutes). Annual sessions are
mainly concerned with local government matters, regional planning,
protection of the environment, town and country planning, and
social and cultural affairs. A Standing Committee, drawn from all
national delegations, meets between plenary sessions of the Congress. Four Statutory Committees (Institutional; Sustainable Development; Social Cohesion; Culture and Education) meet twice a year
in order to prepare texts for adoption by the Congress.

The Congress advises the Council's Committee of Ministers and
the Parliamentary Assembly on all aspects of local and regional
policy and co-operates with other national and international organizations representing local government. The Congress monitors
implementation of the European Charter of Local Self-Government,
which was opened for signature in 1985 and provides common
standards for effective local democracy. Other legislative guide-lines
for the activities of local authorities and the promotion of democracy
at local level include the 1980 European Outline Convention on
Transfrontier Co-operation, and its Additional Protocol which was
opened for signature in 1995, a Convention on the Participation of
Foreigners in Public Life at Local Level (1992), and the European
Charter for Regional or Minority Languages (1992). In addition, the
European Urban Charter defines citizens' rights in European towns
and cities, for example in the areas of transport, urban architecture,
pollution and security.

President: Herwig Van Staa (Austria).

SECRETARIAT

Secretary-General: Dr Walter Schwimmer (Austria).

Deputy Secretary-General: Maud de Boer-Buquicchio (Netherlands).

Secretary-General of the Parliamentary Assembly: Bruno
Haller (France).

Activities

In an effort to harmonize national laws, to put the citizens of member countries on an equal footing and to pool certain resources and facilities, the Council of Europe has concluded a number of conventions and agreements covering particular aspects of European co-operation. Since 1989 the Council has undertaken to increase co-operation with all countries of the former Eastern bloc and to facilitate their accession to the organization. In October 1997 heads of state or government of member countries convened for only the second time (the first meeting took place in Vienna, in October 1993—see below) with the aim of formulating a new social model to consolidate democracy throughout Europe. The meeting endorsed a Final Declaration and an Action Plan, which established priority areas for future Council activities, including fostering social cohesion; protecting civilian security; promoting human rights; enhancing joint measures to counter cross-border illegal trafficking; and strengthening democracy through education and other cultural activities. In addition, the meeting generated renewed political commitment to the Programme of Action against Corruption, which has become a key element of Council activities.

A Multidisciplinary Group on International Action against Terrorism, established in 2001, has updated the 1977 European Convention on the Suppression of Terrorism. In 2001 the Council's Committee of Ministers adopted a set of 'Guide-lines on Human Rights and the Fight against Terrorism'.

HUMAN RIGHTS

The promotion and development of human rights is one of the major tasks of the Council of Europe. The European Convention for the Protection of Human Rights and Fundamental Freedoms (European Convention on Human Rights) was opened for signature in 1950. The Steering Committee for Human Rights is responsible for intergovernmental co-operation in the field of human rights and fundamental freedoms; it works to strengthen the effectiveness of systems for protecting human rights, to identify potential threats and challenges to human rights, and to encourage education and provide information on the subject. The Committee has been responsible for the elaboration of several conventions and other legal instruments including Protocol No. 12 of the European Convention on Human Rights, adopted in June 2000, which enforces a general prohibition of discrimination; and Protocol No. 13, adopted in May 2002, which guarantees the abolition of the death penalty in all circumstances (including in time of war).

The Committee was responsible for the preparation of the European Ministerial Conference on Human Rights, held in Rome in November 2000, which commemorated the 50th anniversary of the adoption of the European Convention on Human Rights. The Conference highlighted, in particular, 'the need to reinforce the effective protection of human rights in domestic legal systems as well as at the European level'.

The 1993 Vienna summit meeting also agreed to restructure the control mechanism for the protection of human rights, mainly the procedure for the consideration of cases, in order to reduce the length of time before a case is concluded. As a result, Protocol (No. 11) to the European Convention on Human Rights was opened for signature by member states in May 1994. The then existing institutions (i.e. the European Commission of Human Rights and the European Court of Human Rights) were consequently replaced in November 1998 (when Protocol No. 11 entered into force) by a single Court, working on a full-time basis.

The second summit meeting of the Council's heads of state and government, held in Strasbourg, France, in October 1997, welcomed a proposal to institute a Council of Europe Commissioner for Human Rights to promote respect for human rights in member states; this office was established by a resolution of the Council's Committee of Ministers in May 1999.

The November 2000 European Ministerial Conference on Human Rights commemorated the 50th anniversary of the European Convention on Human Rights and agreed an agenda for the Council's future human rights activities. This included work on a future reform of the control system of the Convention, in order to preserve its effectiveness despite the rising number of individual applications. In November 2002, in this regard, the Committee of Ministers adopted a Declaration on The Court of Human Rights for Europe.

Commissioner for Human Rights: ALVARO GIL-ROBLES (Spain).

European Court of Human Rights

The Court has compulsory jurisdiction and is competent to consider complaints lodged by states party to the European Convention and by individuals, groups of individuals or non-governmental organizations claiming to be victims of breaches of the Convention's guarantees. The Court comprises one judge for each contracting state. The Court sits in three-member Committees, empowered to declare applications inadmissible in the event of unanimity and where no further examination is necessary, seven-member Cham-

bers, and a 17-member Grand Chamber. Chamber judgments become final three months after delivery, during which period parties may request a rehearing before the Grand Chamber, subject to acceptance by a panel of five judges. Grand Chamber judgments are final. The Court's final judgments are binding on respondent states and their execution is supervised at regular intervals by the Committee of Ministers. Execution of judgments includes payment of pecuniary just satisfaction awarded by the Court, adoption of specific individual measures to erase the consequences of the violations found (such as striking out of impugned convictions from criminal records, reopening of judicial proceedings, etc.), and general measures to prevent new similar violations (e.g. constitutional and legislative reforms, changes of domestic case-law and administrative practice, etc.) At January 2002 18,383 applications were pending before the Court.

President: LUZIUS WILDHABER (Switzerland).

Registrar: PAUL MAHONEY (United Kingdom).

European Committee for the Prevention of Torture and Inhuman or Degrading Treatment or Punishment—CPT

The Committee was established under the 1987 Convention for the Prevention of Torture as an integral part of the Council of Europe's system for the protection of human rights. The Committee, comprising independent experts, aims to examine the treatment of persons deprived of their liberty with a view to strengthening, if necessary, the protection of such persons from torture and from inhuman or degrading treatment or punishment. It conducts periodic visits to police stations, prisons, detention centres, and all other sites where persons are deprived of their liberty by a public authority, in all states parties to the Convention, and may also undertake *ad hoc* visits when the Committee considers them necessary. By January 2003 the Committee had undertaken 98 periodic visits and 48 *ad hoc* visits. After each visit the Committee drafts a report of its findings and any further advice or recommendations, based on dialogue and co-operation.

President: SILVIA CASALE (United Kingdom).

European Social Charter

The European Social Charter, in force since 1965, is the counterpart of the European Convention on Human Rights, in the field of protection of economic and social rights. A revised Charter, which amended existing guarantees and incorporated new rights, was opened for signature in May 1996, and entered into force on 1 July 1999. By January 2003 43 of the 44 member states had signed the Charter, some 32 of which had ratified it. Rights guaranteed by the Charter concern all individuals in their daily lives in matters of housing, health, education, employment, social protection, movement of persons and non-discrimination. The European Committee of Social Rights considers reports submitted to it annually by member states. It also considers collective complaints submitted in the framework of an Additional Protocol (1995), providing for a system which entered into force in July 1998, permitting trade unions, employers' organizations and NGOs to lodge complaints on alleged violations of the Charter. The Committee, composed of 13 members (to be expanded to 15 from January 2005), decides on the conformity of national situations with the Charter. When a country does not bring a situation into conformity, the Committee of Ministers may, on the basis of decisions prepared by a Governmental Committee (composed of representatives of each Contracting Party), issue recommendations to the state concerned, inviting it to change its legislation or practice in accordance with the Charter's requirements.

President of the European Committee of Social Rights: JEAN-MICHEL BELORGEY (France).

FRAMEWORK CONVENTION FOR THE PROTECTION OF NATIONAL MINORITIES

In 1993 the first summit meeting of Council of Europe heads of state and government, held in Vienna, mandated the Committee of Ministers to draft 'a framework convention specifying the principle that States commit themselves to respect in order to assure the protection of national minorities'. A special committee was established to draft the so-called Framework Convention for the Protection of National Minorities, which was then adopted by the Committee in November 1994. The Convention was opened for signature in February 1995, entering into force in February 1998. Contracting parties (35 States at January 2003) are required to submit reports on the implementation of the treaty at regular intervals to an Advisory Committee composed of 18 independent experts. The Advisory Committee adopts an opinion on the implementation of the Framework Convention by the contracting party, on the basis of which the Committee of Ministers adopts a resolution. At January 2003 23 opinions and 14 resolutions had been adopted.

President of the Advisory Committee: RAINER HOFMANN.

RACISM AND INTOLERANCE

In October 1993 heads of state and of government, meeting in Vienna, resolved to reinforce a policy to combat all forms of intolerance, in response to the increasing incidence of racial hostility and intolerance towards minorities in European societies. A European Commission against Racism and Intolerance (ECRI) was established by the summit meeting to analyse and assess the effectiveness of legal, policy and other measures taken by member states to combat these problems. It became operational in March 1996. Members of ECRI are designated by governments on the basis of their recognized expertise in the field, although participate in the Commission in an independent capacity. ECRI undertakes activities in three programme areas: country-by-country approach; work on general themes; and ECRI and civil society. In the first area of activity, ECRI analyses the situation regarding racism and intolerance in each of the member states, in order to advise governments on measures to combat these problems. In December 1998 ECRI completed a first round of reports for all Council members. A follow-up series of reports were prepared during the four-year period 1999–2002. ECRI's work on general themes includes the preparation of policy recommendations and guide-lines on issues of importance to combating racism and intolerance. ECRI also collects and disseminates examples of good practices relating to these issues. Under the third programme area ECRI aims to disseminate information and raise awareness of the problems of racism and intolerance among the general public.

A Committee on the Rehabilitation and Integration of People with Disabilities supports co-operation between member states in this field and undertakes studies in order to promote legislative and administrative action.

MEDIA AND COMMUNICATIONS

Article 10 of the European Convention on Human Rights (freedom of expression and information) forms the basis for the Council of Europe's mass media activities. Implementation of the Council of Europe's work programme concerning the media is undertaken by the Steering Committee on the Mass Media (CDMM), which comprises senior government officials and representatives of professional organizations, meeting in plenary session twice a year. The CDMM is mandated to devise concerted European policy measures and appropriate legal instruments. Its underlying aims are to further freedom of expression and information in a pluralistic democracy, and to promote the free flow of information and ideas. The CDMM is assisted by various specialist groups and committees. Policy and legal instruments have been developed on subjects including: exclusivity rights; media concentrations and transparency of media ownership; protection of journalists in situations of conflict and tension; independence of public-service broadcasting, protection of rights holders; legal protection of encrypted television services; media and elections; protection of journalists' sources of information; and the independence and functions of broadcasting regulatory authorities. These policy and legal instruments (mainly in the form on non-binding recommendations addressed to member governments) are complemented by the publication of studies, analyses and seminar proceedings on topics of media law and policy. The CDMM has also prepared a number of international binding legal instruments, including the European Convention on Transfrontier Television (adopted in 1989 and ratified by 25 countries by 31 December 2002), the European Convention on the legal protection of services based on or consisting of conditional access (signed by eight countries and ratified by two at the end of 2002), and the European Convention relating to questions on copyright law and other rights in the context of transfrontier broadcasting by satellite (ratified by two countries and signed by seven other member states and the European Community at the end of 2002). CDMM areas of activity in 2002 included: self-regulation of internet services; credibility of information disseminated online; media and privacy; the regulation of digital broadcasting services; and media and terrorism.

SOCIAL COHESION

In June 1998, the Committee of Ministers established the European Committee for Social Cohesion (CDCS). The CDCS has the following responsibilities: to co-ordinate, guide and stimulate co-operation between member States with a view to promoting social cohesion in Europe, to develop and promote integrated, multidisciplinary responses to social issues, and to promote the social standards embodied in the European Social Charter and other Council of Europe instruments, including the European Code of Social Security. The CDCS is also responsible for executing the terms of reference of the European Code of Social Security, the European Convention on Social Security and the European Agreement on 'au pair' Placement. The CDCS has agreed on policy guide-lines on access to employment, housing and social protection. In November 2002 it adopted a report on *Access to Social Rights in Europe*, and in early 2003 it was drafting a Recommendation on the subject. It also supervises a programme of work on families and children.

The European Code of Social Security and its Protocol entered into force in 1968; by March 2003 the Code and Protocol had been ratified by Belgium, Germany, Luxembourg, the Netherlands, Norway, Portugal and Sweden, while the Code alone had, additionally, been ratified by Cyprus, the Czech Republic, Denmark, France, Greece, Ireland, Italy, Spain, Switzerland, Turkey and the United Kingdom. These instruments set minimum standards for medical care and the following benefits: sickness, old-age, unemployment, employment injury, family, maternity, invalidity and survivor's benefit. A revision of these instruments, aiming to provide higher standards and greater flexibility, was completed for signature in 1990 and had been signed by 14 states at March 2003.

The European Convention on Social Security, in force since 1977, now applies in Austria, Belgium, Italy, Luxembourg, the Netherlands, Portugal, Spain and Turkey; most of the provisions apply automatically, while others are subject to the conclusion of additional multilateral or bilateral agreements. The Convention is concerned with establishing the following four fundamental principles of international law on social security: equality of treatment, unity of applicable legislation, conservation of rights accrued or in course of acquisition, and payment of benefits abroad. In 1994 a Protocol to the Convention, providing for the enlargement of the personal scope of the Convention, was opened for signature. By March 2003 it had been signed by Austria, the Czech Republic, Greece and Luxembourg, and had been ratified by Portugal.

HEALTH

Through a series of expert committees, the Council aims to ensure constant co-operation in Europe in a variety of health-related fields, with particular emphasis on patients' rights, for example: equity in access to health care, quality assurance, health services for institutionalized populations (prisoners, elderly in homes), discrimination resulting from health status and education for health. These efforts are supplemented by the training of health personnel.

Improvement of blood transfusion safety and availability of blood and blood derivatives has been ensured through European Agreements and guide-lines. Advances in this field and in organ transplantation are continuously assessed by expert committees.

Eighteen states co-operate in a Partial Agreement to protect the consumer from potential health risks connected with commonplace or domestic activities. The committees of experts of the Public Health Committee provide the scientific base for national and international regulations regarding products which have a direct or indirect impact on the human food chain, pesticides, pharmaceuticals and cosmetics.

The 1992 Recommendation on A Coherent Policy for People with Disabilities contains the policy principles for the rehabilitation and integration of people with disabilities. This model programme recommends that governments of all member states develop comprehensive and co-ordinated national disability policies taking account of prevention, diagnosis, treatment education, vocational guidance and training, employment, social integration, social protection, information and research. It has set benchmarks, both nationally and internationally. The 1995 Charter on the Vocational Assessment of People with Disabilities states that a person's vocational abilities and not disabilities should be assessed and related to specific job requirements. The 2001 Resolution on Universal Design aims to improve the accessibility, recommending the inclusion of Universal Design principles in the training for vocations working on the built environment. The 2001 Resolution on New Technologies recommends formulating national strategies to ensure that people with disabilities benefit from new technologies. Current activities include: air travel, community living, disability prevention, and women with disabilities. Tailor-made programmes for Central and Eastern European countries take account of their specific requirements. The Council of Europe designated 2003 as the European Year of People with Disabilities.

In the co-operation group to combat drug abuse and illicit drugs trafficking (Pompidou Group), 34 states work together, through meetings of ministers, officials and experts, to counteract drug abuse. The Group follows a multidisciplinary approach embracing in particular legislation, law enforcement, prevention, treatment, rehabilitation and data collection.

The Convention on the Elaboration of a European Pharmacopoeia (establishing legally binding standards for medicinal substances, auxiliary substances, pharmaceutical preparations, vaccines for human and veterinary use and other articles) entered into force in eight signatory states in May 1974: in January 2003 30 states and the European Union were parties to the Convention. WHO and 16 European and non-European states participate as observers in the sessions of the European Pharmacopoeia Commission. In 1994 a procedure on certification of suitability to the European Pharmacopoeia monographs for manufacturers of substances for pharmaceutical use was established. In 2002 almost 1,100 certificates were granted. A network of official control laboratories for human and veterinary medicines was established in 1995, open to all signatory countries to the Convention and observers at the Pharmacopoeia Commission. The fourth edition of the European Pharmacopoeia, in force since 1 January 2002, is updated three times a year in its electronic version, and includes some 1,800 harmonized European standards, or 'monographs', 300 general methods of analysis and 2,002 reagents.

In April 1997 the first international convention on biomedicine was opened for signature at a meeting of health ministers of member states, in Oviedo, Spain. The so-called Convention for the Protection of Human Rights and the Dignity of Human Beings with Respect to the Applications of Biology and Medicine incorporated provisions on scientific research, the principle of informed patient consent, organ and tissue transplants and the prohibition of financial gain and disposal of a part of the human body. It entered into force on 1 November 1999 (see below).

POPULATION AND MIGRATION

The European Convention on the Legal Status of Migrant Workers, in force since 1983, has been ratified by France, Italy, the Netherlands, Norway, Portugal, Spain, Sweden and Turkey, and was signed by Moldova in July 2002. The Convention is based on the principle of equality of treatment for migrant workers and the nationals of the host country as to housing, working conditions, and social security. The Convention also upholds the principle of the right to family reunion. An international consultative committee, representing the parties to the Convention, monitors the application of the Convention.

In 1996 the European Committee on Migration concluded work on a project entitled 'The Integration of Immigrants: Towards Equal Opportunities' was concluded and the results were presented at the sixth conference of European ministers responsible for migration affairs, held in Warsaw, Poland. At the conference a new project, entitled 'Tensions and Tolerance: Building better integrated communities across Europe' was initiated; it was concluded in 1999. The Committee was responsible for activities concerning Roma/Gypsies in Europe, in co-ordination with other relevant Council of Europe bodies. The Committee is also jointly responsible, with the *ad hoc* Committee of Experts on the legal aspects of territorial asylum, refugees and stateless persons, for the examination of migration issues arising at the pan-European level.

The European Population Committee, an intergovernmental committee of scientists and government officials responsible for population matters, monitors and analyses population trends throughout Europe and informs governments, research centres and the public of demographic developments and their impact on policy decisions. It compiles an annual statistical review of demographic developments (covering 46 European states) and publishes the results of studies on population issues, such as *Fertility and new types of households and family formation in Europe* (2001), and *Trends in mortality and differential mortality in Europe* (2001). Future publications were to include studies on the demographic characteristics of immigrant populations, the demographic consequences of economic transition in the countries of central and eastern Europe, and social exclusion.

COUNCIL OF EUROPE DEVELOPMENT BANK

The Council of Europe Development Bank was established in April 1956 by the Committee of Ministers, initially as the Resettlement Fund, and later as the Council of Europe Social Development Fund, and then renamed again in November 1999. It is a multilateral development bank with a social mandate, promoting social development by granting loans for projects with a social purpose. Projects aimed at solving social problems related to the presence of refugees, displaced persons or forced migrants are a priority. In addition, the Bank finances projects in other fields that contribute directly to strengthening social cohesion in Europe: job creation and preservation in small and medium-sized enterprises; social housing; improving urban living conditions; health and education infrastructure, protection of the environment, and rural modernisation; protection and rehabilitation of the historic heritage. At November 2002 the Bank had a subscribed capital of €3,160m. It is currently funding 167 projects in 28 countries. Its lending activities have been increasingly targeted at central and eastern European countries. Since 1995 the Bank has approved 66 projects in 14 transition countries, supported by a cumulative total of €1,800m. worth of loans.

EQUALITY BETWEEN WOMEN AND MEN

The Steering Committee for Equality between Women and Men (CDEG—an intergovernmental committee of experts) is responsible for encouraging action at both national and Council of Europe level to promote equality of rights and opportunities between the two sexes. Assisted by various specialist groups and committees, the CDEG is mandated to establish policies, studies and evaluations, to examine national policies and experiences, to work out concerted policy strategies and measures for implementing equality and, as necessary, to prepare appropriate legal and other instruments. It is also responsible for preparing the European Ministerial Conferences on Equality between Women and Men. The main areas of CDEG activities are the comprehensive inclusion of the rights of women (for example, combating violence against women and trafficking in human beings) within the context of human rights; the issue of equality and democracy, including the promotion of the participation of women in political and public life; projects aimed at studying the specific equality problems related to cultural diversity, migration and minorities; positive action in the field of equality between men and women and the mainstreaming of equality into all policies and programmes at all levels of society. In October 1998 the Committee of Ministers adopted a Recommendation to member states on gender mainstreaming; in May 2000 it approved a Recommendation on action against trafficking in human beings for the purpose of sexual exploitation; and in April 2002 it adopted a Recommendation on the protection of women against violence.

LEGAL MATTERS

The European Committee on Legal Co-operation develops co-operation between member states in the field of law, with the objective of harmonizing and modernizing public and private law, including administrative law and the law relating to the judiciary. The Committee is responsible for expert groups which consider issues relating to administrative law, efficiency of justice, family law, nationality, information technology and data protection.

Numerous conventions and Recommendations have been adopted, and followed up by appropriate committees or groups of experts, on matters which include: efficiency of justice, nationality, legal aid, rights of children, data protection, information technology, children born out of wedlock, animal protection, adoption, information on foreign law, and the legal status of non-governmental organizations. In addition, a new draft Convention on contact concerning children was adopted in May 2002.

In December 1999 the Convention for the Protection of Human Rights and the Dignity of Human Beings with Respect to the Applications of Biology and Medicine: Convention on Human Rights and Biomedicine entered into force, as the first internationally-binding legal text to protect people against the misuse of biological and medical advances. It aims to preserve human dignity and identify, rights and freedoms, through a series of principles and rules. Additional protocols develop the Convention's general provisions by means of specialized texts. A Protocol prohibiting the medical cloning of human beings was approved by Council heads of state and government in October 1997 and entered into force on 1 March 2001. A Protocol on the transplantation of human organs and tissue was opened for signature in January 2002. Work on draft protocols relating to biomedical research, protection of the human embryo and foetus, and genetics is ongoing. A draft Recommendation on xenotransplantation is currently being considered by the Committee of Ministers.

In 2001 an Additional Protocol to the Convention for the protection of individuals with regard to automatic processing of personal data was adopted. The Protocol, which opened for signature in November, concerned supervisory authorities and transborder data flows. By April 2003 it had been signed by 21 states, and ratified by three (Germany, Slovakia and Sweden).

In 2001 the the European Committee for Social Cohesion (CDCS) approved three new conventions on contact concerning children, legal aid, and 'Information Society Services'. In 2002 the CDCS approved a Recommendation on mediation on civil matters and a resolution establishing the European Commission for the Efficiency of Justice (CEPEJ). The aims of the CEPEJ are: to improve the efficiency and functioning of the justice system of memeber states, with a view to ensuring that everyone within their jurisdiction can enforce their legal rights effectively, increasing citizen confidence in the system; and enabling better implementation of the international legal instruments of the Council of Europe concerning efficiency and fairness of justice.

The Consultative Council of European Judges has prepared a framework global action plan for judges in Europe. In addition, it has contributed to the implementation of this programme by the adoption of opinions on standards concerning the independence of the judiciary and the irremovability of judges, and on the funding and management of courts.

A Committee of Legal Advisors on Public and International Law (CAHDI), comprising the legal advisors of ministers of foreign affairs of member states and of several observer states, is authorized by the Committee of Ministers to examine questions of public international law, and to exchange and, if appropriate, to co-ordinate the views of member states. The CAHDI functions as a European observatory of reservations to international treaties. Recent activities of the CAHDI include the preparation of a Recommendation on reactions to inadmissible reservations to international treaties, the publication of a report on state practice with regard to state succession and recognition, and another on expression of consent of states to be bound by a treaty. In 2002 the CAHDI was conducting research into the practice of states with regard to immunities of states and their property.

An *ad hoc* Committee of Experts on the Legal Aspects of Territorial Asylum, Refugees and Stateless Persons (CAHAR) proposes solutions to practical and legal problems relating to its area of expertise and works towards harmonizing rules and practices to be followed in Europe in matters of asylum and refugees. It reviews national and international developments and formulates appropriate legal instruments (mainly Recommendations) for discussion and adoption by the Committee of Ministers. Over the years the Committee has drafted a number of pan-European standards, and in 2002 it prepared a draft recommendation relating to the detention of asylum seekers. The CAHAR has also adopted a series of opinions for the Committee of Ministers on issues relating to refugees and displaced persons in member states. It works closely with other international bodies, in particular UNHCR and the Council's Parliamentary Assembly.

With regard to crime, expert committees and groups operating under the authority of the European Committee on Crime Problems have prepared conventions on such matters as extradition, mutual assistance, recognition and enforcement of foreign judgments, transfer of proceedings, suppression of terrorism, transfer of prisoners, compensation payable to victims of violent crime, money-laundering, confiscation of proceeds from crime, cybercrime and corruption. In 2002 member states concluded an additional Protocol to the 2001 Convention on cybercrime relating to the criminalization of acts of a racist and xenophobic nature committed through computer systems.

The Group of States Against Corruption (GRECO) became operational in 1999 and became a permanent body of the Council in 2002. By the end of that year it had 34 members (33 member states of the Council of Europe and the USA). A monitoring mechanism, based on mutual evaluation and peer pressure, GRECO assesses members' compliance with Council instruments for combating corruption. Its First Round Evaluations were completed by the end of 2002. A Second Round Evaluation commenced in 2003, reviewing Proceeds of Corruption, Public Administration and Corruption, and Legal Persons and Corruption. It was then to cover member states' compliance with, *inter alia*, requirements of the Criminal Law Convention on Corruption, which entered into force in July 2002. The evaluation procedure of GRECO is confidential but it has become practice to make reports public after their adoption.

The select committee of Experts on the Evaluation of Anti-Money laundering Measures (MONEYVAL) became operational in 1998. It is responsible for mutual evaluation of the anti-money laundering measures in place in 25 Council of Europe states that are not members of the Financial Action Task Force (FATF). The MONEYVAL mechanism is based on FATF practices and procedures. States are evaluated against the relevant international standards in the legal, financial and law enforcement sectors. In the legal sector this includes evaluation of states' obligations under the Council of Europe Convention on Laundering, Search Seizure and Confiscation of the Proceeds from Crime. After the terrorist attacks against targets in the USA on 11 September 2001, the Comittee of Ministers adopted revised terms of reference, which specifically include the evaluation of measures to combat the financing of terrorism. MONEYVAL completed its first round of onsite visits in 2000 and subsequently adopted all first round reports. Its second round, focusing even more closely on the effectiveness of national systems, began in 2001 and was expected to be completed during 2003. The evaluations of MONEYVAL are confidential, but summaries of adopted reports are made public.

A Criminological Scientific Council, composed of specialists in law, psychology, sociology and related sciences, advises the Committee and organizes criminological research conferences and colloquia. A Council for Penological Co-operation organizes regular high-level conferences of directors of prison administration and is responsible for collating statistical information on detention and community sanctions in Europe. The Council prepared the European Prison Rules in 1987 and the European Rules on Community Sanctions (alternatives to imprisonment) in 1992. A council for police matters was established in 2002.

In May 1990 the Committee of Ministers adopted a Partial Agreement to establish the European Commission for Democracy through Law, to be based in Venice, Italy. The so-called Venice Commission was enlarged in February 2002 and at early 2003 comprised all Council of Europe member states. The Commission is composed of independent legal and political experts, mainly senior academics, supreme or consitutional court judges, members of national parliaments, and senior public officers. Its main activity is constitutional assistance and may supply opinions upon request, made through the Committee of Ministers, by the Parliamentary Assembly, the Secretary-General or any member states of the Commission . Other states and international organizations may request opinions with the consent of the Committee of Ministers. The Commission is active throughout the constitutional domain, and has worked on issues including legislation on constitutional courts and national minor-ities, electoral law and other legislation with implications for national democratic institutions. The creation of the Council for Democratic elections institutionalized co-operation in the areaof elections between the Venice Commission, the Parliamentary Assembly of the Council of Europe, and the Congress of Regional and Local Authorities of Europe.The Commission disseminates its work through the UniDem (University for Democracy) programme of seminars, the CODICES database, and the *Bulletin of Constitutional Case-Law.*

The promotion of local and regional democracy and of transfrontier co-operation constitutes a major aim of the Council's intergovernmental programme of activities. The Steering Committee on Local and Regional Democracy (CDLR) serves as a forum for representatives of member states to exchange information and pursue co-operation in order to promote the decentralization of powers, in accordance with the European Charter on Local Self-Government. The CDLR's principal objective is to improve the legal, institutional and financial framework of local democracy and to encourage citizen participation in local and regional communities. In December 2001 the Committee of Ministers adopted a Recommendation on citizens' participation in public life at local level, drafted on the basis of the work conducted by the CDLR. The CDLR publishes comparative studies and national reports, and aims to identify guide-lines for the effective implementation of the principles of subsidiarity and solidarity. Its work also constitutes a basis for the provision of aid to central and eastern European countries in the field of local democracy. The CDLR is responsible for the preparation and follow-up of Conferences of Ministers responsible for local and regional government.

Intergovernmental co-operation with the CDLR is supplemented by specific activities aimed at providing legislative advice, supporting reform and enhancing management capabilities and democratic participation in European member and non-member countries. These activities are specifically focused on the democratic stability of central and eastern European countries. The programmes for democratic stability in the field of local democracy draw inspiration from the European Charter of Local Self-Government, operating at three levels of government: at intergovernmental level, providing assistance in implementing reforms to reinforce local or regional government, in compliance with the Charter; at local or regional level, co-operating with local and regional authorities to build local government capacity; and at community level, co-operating directly with individual authorities to promote pilot initiatives. Working methods include: awareness-raising conferences; legislative opinion involving written opinions, expert round-tables and working groups; and seminars, workshops and training at home and abroad.

The policy of the Council of Europe on transfrontier co-operation between territorial communities or authorities is implemented through two committees. The Committee of Experts on Transfrontier Co-operation (LR-CT), working under the supervision of the CDLR, aims to monitor the implementation of the European Outline Convention on Transfrontier Co-operation between Territorial Communities or Authorities; to make proposals for the elimination of obstacles, in particular of a legal nature, to transfrontier and interterritorial co-operation; and to compile 'best practice' examples of transfrontier co-operation in various fields of activity. In 2002 the Committee of Ministers adopted a draft recommendation on the mutual aid and assistance between central and local authorities in the event of disasters affecting frontier areas. A Committee of Advisers for the development of transfrontier co-operation in central and eastern Europe is composed of six members appointed or elected by the Secretary-General, the Committee of Ministers and the Congress of Local and Regional Authorities of Europe. Its task is to guide the promotion of transfrontier co-operation in central and eastern European countries, with a view to fostering good neighbourly relations between the frontier populations, especially in particularly sensitive regions. Its programme comprises: conferences and colloquies designed to raise awareness on the Outline Convention; meetings in border regions between representatives of local communities with a view to strengthening mutual trust; and legal assistance to, and restricted meetings with, national and local representatives responsible for preparing the legal texts for ratification and/or implementation of the Outline Convention. The priority areas which had been outlined by the Committee of Advisers include South-East Europe, northern Europe around the Baltic Sea, the external frontiers of an enlarged European Union, and the Caucasus.

EDUCATION, CULTURE AND HERITAGE

The European Cultural Convention covers education, culture, heritage, sport and youth. Programmes on education, higher education, culture and cultural heritage are managed by four steering committees.

The education programme consists of projects on education for democratic citizenship and human rights, history teaching, the

European dimension of education and interreligious dialogue, instruments and policies for plurilingualism, equitable education policies responding to new social, economic and technological realities, and bilateral co-operation for education renewal. Other activities include the partial agreement for the European Centre for Modern Languages located in Graz, Austria, the In Service Educational Staff Training Programme, the Network for School Links and Exchanges, and the European Schools Day competition, organized in co-operation with the European Union. The Council of Europe's main focus in the field of higher education is on the Bologna Proccess aiming to establish a European Higher Education Area by 2010.

In December 2000 the Committee of Ministers adopted a Declaration on Cultural Diversity, formulated in consultation with other organizations (including the European Union and UNESCO), which created a framework for developing a European approach to valuing cultural diversity. A European Charter for Regional or Minority languages entered into force in 1998, with the aim of protecting regional or minority languages, which are considered to be a threatened aspect of Europe's cultural heritage. It was intended to promote the use in private and public life of languages traditionally used within a state's territory. The Charter provides for a monitoring system enabling states, the Council of Europe and individuals to observe and follow up its implementation.

The Council of Europe's activities related to cultural policy focus on the following prioriy areas: standard-setting; cultural policy reviews; conflict prevention; comparative studies on cultural diversity, and partnership programmes; archives; the MOSAIC and STAGE projects (co-operation with South-East Europe and the South Caucasus, respectively); and the Action Plan for Russia.

The European Convention for the Protection of Audiovisual Heritage and its Protocol were opened for signature in November 2001. The Eurimages support fund helps to finance co-production of films. The Convention for the Protection of the Architectural Heritage and the Protection of the Archaeological Heritage provide a legal framework for European co-operation in these areas. The European Heritage Network is a being developed to facilitate the work of professionals and state institutions and the dissemination of good practices in more than 30 countries of the states party to the European Cultural Convention.

YOUTH

In 1972 the Council of Europe established the European Youth Centre (EYC) in Strasbourg. A second residential centre was created in Budapest in 1995. The centres, run with and by international non-governmental youth organizations representing a wide range of interests, provide about 50 residential courses a year (study sessions, training courses, symposia). A notable feature of the EYC is its decision-making structure, by which decisions on its programme and general policy matters are taken by a Programming Committee composed of an equal number of youth organizations and government representatives.

The European Youth Foundation (EYF) aims to provide financial assistance to European activities of non-governmental youth organizations and began operations in 1973. Since that time more than 380 organizations have received financial aid for carrying out international activities, while more than 210,000 young people have participated in meetings supported by the Foundation. The European Steering Committee for Intergovernmental Co-operation in the Youth Field conducts research in youth-related matters and prepares for ministerial conferences.

SPORT

The Committee for the Development of Sport, founded in November 1977, oversees sports co-operation and development on a pan-European basis, bringing together all the 48 states party to the European Cultural Convention. Its activities focus on the implementation of the European Sport Charter and Code of Sports Ethics (adopted in 1992 and revised in 2002), the role of sport in society, the provision of assistance in sports reform to new member states in central and eastern Europe, and the practice of both recreational and high level sport. A Charter on Sport for Disabled Persons was adopted in 1986. The Committee also prepares the Conferences of European Ministers responsible for Sport and has been responsible for drafting two important conventions to combat negative influences on sport. The European Convention on Spectator Violence and Misbehaviour at Sport Events (1985) provides governments with practical measures to ensure crowd security and safety, particularly at football matches. The Anti-Doping Convention (1989) has been ratified by nearly 40 European countries, and is also open to non-European states.

ENVIRONMENT AND SUSTAINABLE DEVELOPMENT

In 1995 a pan-European biological and landscape diversity strategy, formulated by the Committee of Ministers, was endorsed at a ministerial conference of the UN Economic Commission for Europe, which was held in Sofia, Bulgaria. The strategy was to be implemented jointly by the Council of Europe and UNEP, in close co-operation with the European Community. In particular, it provided for implementation of the Convention on Biological Diversity.

At March 2002 45 states and the European Community had ratified a Convention on the Conservation of European Wildlife and Natural Habitats, which entered into force in June 1982 and gives total protection to 693 species of plants, 89 mammals, 294 birds, 43 reptiles, 21 amphibians, 115 freshwater fishes, 113 invertebrates and their habitats. The Convention established a network of protected areas known as the 'Emerald Network'. The Council's NATUROPA Centre provides information and documentation on the environment, through periodicals and campaigns. The Council awards the European Diploma for protection of sites of European significance, supervises a network of biogenetic reserves, and co-ordinates conservation action for threatened animals and plants.

Regional disparities constitute a major obstacle to the process of European integration. Conferences of ministers of regional planning are held to discuss these issues. In 2000 they adopted guiding principles for sustainable development of the European continent and, in 2001, a resolution detailing a ten-point programme for greater cohesion among the Regions of Europe.

EXTERNAL RELATIONS

Agreements providing for co-operation and exchange of documents and observers have been concluded with the United Nations and its agencies, and with most of the European inter-governmental organizations and the Organization of American States. Particularly close relations exist with the EU, OECD, and the OSCE. Relations with non-member states, other organizations and non-governmental organizations are co-ordinated by the Directorate General of Political Affairs.

Israel, Canada and Mexico are represented in the Parliamentary Assembly by observer delegations, and certain European and other non-member countries participate in or send observers to certain meetings of technical committees and specialized conferences at intergovernmental level. Full observer status with the Council was granted to the USA in 1995, to Canada and Japan in 1996 and to Mexico in 1999. The Holy See has had a similar status since 1970.

The European Centre for Global Interdependence and Solidarity (the 'North–South Centre') was established in Lisbon, Portugal, in 1990, in order to provide a framework for European co-operation in this area and to promote pluralist democracy and respect for human rights. The Centre is co-managed by parliamentarians, governments, non-governmental organizations and local and regional authorities. Its activities are divided into three programmes: public information and media relations; education and training for global interdependence; and dialogue for global partnership. The Centre organizes workshops, seminars and training courses on global interdependence and convenes international colloquies on human rights.

During the early 1990s the Council of Europe established a structure of programmes to assist the process of democratic reform in central and eastern European countries that had formerly been under communist rule. In October 1997 the meeting of heads of state or of government of Council members agreed to extend the programmes as the means by which all states are assisted to meet their undertakings as members of the Council. These specific co-operation programmes were mainly concerned with the development of the rule of law; the protection and promotion of human rights; and strengthening local democracy. A scheme of Democratic Leadership Programmes has also been established for the training of political leaders. Within the framework of the co-operation programme 22 information and documentation centres/offices have been established in 17 countries of central and eastern Europe. A secretariat representation to co-ordinate the Council's contribution to the UN operation in Kosovo was established in Priština (the capital of Kosovo and Metohija), in mid-1999.

Finance

The budget is financed by contributions from members on a proportional scale of assessment (using population and gross domestic product as common indicators). The 2003 budget totalled €175.5m.

Publications

The Council of Europe: 800 million Europeans (introductory booklet).

Activities Report (in English and French).

The Bulletin (newsletter of the CLRAE, 3 a year).

The Europeans (electronic bulletin of the Parliamentary Assembly).

Naturopa (3 a year, in 15 languages).

Bulletin On Constitutional Case-Law (3–4 times a year, in English and French).
The Pompidou Group Newsletter (3 a year).

Penological Information Bulletin (annually, in English and French).
Human Rights Information Bulletin (monthly, in English and French).

EUROPEAN BANK FOR RECONSTRUCTION AND DEVELOPMENT—EBRD

Address: One Exchange Square, 175 Bishopsgate, London, EC2A 2EH, United Kingdom.
Telephone: (20) 7338-6000; **fax:** (20) 7338-6100; **e-mail:** generalenquiries@ebrd.com; **internet:** www.ebrd.com.

The EBRD was founded in May 1990 and inaugurated in April 1991. Its object is to contribute to the progress and the economic reconstruction of the countries of central and eastern Europe which undertake to respect and put into practice the principles of multiparty democracy, pluralism, the rule of law, respect for human rights and a market economy.

MEMBERS

Countries of Operations:

Albania	Lithuania
Armenia	Macedonia, former Yugoslav
Azerbaijan	republic
Belarus	Moldova
Bosnia and Herzegovina	Poland
Bulgaria	Romania
Croatia	Russia
Czech Republic	Serbia and Montenegro
Estonia	Slovakia
Georgia	Slovenia
Hungary	Tajikistan
Kazakhstan	Turkmenistan
Kyrgyzstan	Ukraine
Latvia	Uzbekistan

EU members*:

Austria	Italy
Belgium	Luxembourg
Denmark	Netherlands
Finland	Portugal
France	Spain
Germany	Sweden
Greece	United Kingdom
Ireland	

EFTA members:

Iceland	Norway
Liechtenstein	Switzerland

Other countries:

Australia	Malta
Canada	Mexico
Cyprus	Mongolia
Egypt	Morocco
Israel	New Zealand
Japan	Turkey
Republic of Korea	USA

* The European Community and the European Investment Bank are also shareholder members in their own right.

Organization

(July 2003)

BOARD OF GOVERNORS

The Board of Governors, to which each member appoints a Governor and an alternate, is the highest authority of the EBRD.

BOARD OF DIRECTORS

The Board is responsible for the organization and operations of the EBRD. The Governors elect 23 directors for a three-year term and a President for a term of four years. Vice-Presidents are appointed by the Board on the recommendation of the President.

ADMINISTRATION

The EBRD's operations are conducted by its Banking Department, headed by the First Vice-President. The other departments are: Finance; Human Resources and Administration; Evaluation, Operational and Environmental Support; Internal Audit; Communications; and Offices of the Secretary-General, the General Counsel and the Chief Economist. A structure of country teams, industry teams and operations support units oversee the implementation of projects. The EBRD has 32 local offices in all 27 of its countries of operations. At December 2002 there were 903 regular staff at the Bank's headquarters.

President: JEAN LEMIERRE (France).
First Vice-President: NOREEN DOYLE (USA).

Activities

In April 1996 EBRD shareholders, meeting in Sofia, Bulgaria, agreed to increase the Bank's capital from ECU 10,000m. to ECU 20,000m., to enable the Bank to continue, and to enhance, its lending programme (the ECU was replaced by the euro, with an equivalent value, from 1 January 1999). It was agreed that 22.5% of the new resources, was to be paid-up, with the remainder as 'callable' shares. Contributions were to be paid over a 13-year period from April 1998. By 31 December 2002 paid-up capital amounted to €5,197m.

The Bank aims to assist the transition of the economies of central Europe, southern and eastern Europe and the Caucasus, and central Asia and Russia towards a market economy system, and to encourage private enterprise. The Agreement establishing the EBRD specifies that 60% of its lending should be for the private sector, and that its operations do not displace commercial sources of finance. The Bank helps the beneficiaries to undertake structural and sectoral reforms, including the dismantling of monopolies, decentralization, and privatization of state enterprises, to enable these countries to become fully integrated in the international economy. To this end, the Bank promotes the establishment and improvement of activities of a productive, competitive and private nature, particularly small and medium-sized enterprises (SMEs), and works to strengthen financial institutions. It mobilizes national and foreign capital, together with experienced management teams, and helps to develop an appropriate legal framework to support a market-orientated economy. The Bank provides extensive financial services, including loans, equity and guarantees, and aims to develop new forms of financing and investment in accordance with the requirements of the transition process. The EBRD's founding Agreement specifies that all operations are to be undertaken in the context of promoting environmentally sound and sustainable development. It undertakes environmental audits and impact assessments in areas of particular concern, which enable the Bank to incorporate environmental action plans into any project approved for funding. An Environment Advisory Council assists with the development of policy and strategy in this area.

The economic crisis in Russia, in August 1998, undermined the viability of many proposed projects and adversely affected the Bank's large portfolio of Russian investments. In March 1999, partly in response to the region's economic difficulties, the Board of Directors approved a new medium-term strategy for 2000–03, which focused on advancing the process of transition. Key aspects of the strategy were to develop a sound financial sector and investment climate in its countries of operations; to provide leadership for the development of SMEs; to promote infrastructure development; and to ensure a balanced and focused project portfolio. In April 1999 the Bank and the European Commission launched a new EU/EBRD SME Finance Facility, with committed funds of €125m., to provide equity and loan financing for SMEs in countries seeking accession to the EU. During 2001 the Bank directed substantial investment to the so-called accession countries, and supported the development of institutions in areas including financial regulation, competition policy and telecommunications. During 2001 the Bank also further strengthened measures to improve institutional governance, in particular to combat money-laundering. A Trade Facilitation Programme, which extends bank guarantees in order to promote trading capabilities in the region, was expanded during 1999. By the end of 2002 74 issuing banks in 20 countries of operations, together with 400 confirming banks in countries world-wide, were participating in the Programme. During 1999 the Bank participated in international efforts to secure economic and political stability in the Balkans, following the conflict in Kosovo. Subsequently the Bank has promoted the objectives of the Stability Pact for South-Eastern Europe by expanding its commitments in the region and by taking a lead role among international financial institutions in promoting private sector development. In July 2000 a US/EBRD SME Financing Facility was established for South East Europe and other early transition countries, and by early 2003 this had leveraged loans across the region to the value of $114m. During 2001 the Bank committed €678m. to 46 new projects in the six Stability Pact countries. In October the Bank development an Action Plan for Central Asia in order to accelerate development and economic stability in the countries neighbouring Afghanistan, as part of a wider objective of securing peace in the region.

In the year ending 31 December 2002 the EBRD approved 102 operations, involving funds of €3,899m., compared with €3,656m. for 102 operations in the previous year. During 2002 29.95% of all project financing committed was allocated to the financial sector and 26.3% to infrastructure. Support to micro-, small and medium-sized enterprises through financial intermediaries totalled €509m., bringing the cumulative total committed since 1991 to more than €3,900m.

A high priority is given to attracting external finance for Bank-sponsored projects, in particular in countries at advanced stages of transition, from government agencies, international financial institutions, commercial banks and export credit agencies. The EBRD's Technical Co-operation Funds Programme (TCFP) aims to facilitate access to the Bank's capital resources for countries of operations by providing support for project preparation, project implementation and institutional development. During 1991–2002 technical co-operation funding from donor countries and institutions reached a cumulative total of €100m. In 2002 the EBRD committed €101.7m. to finance some 261 consultancy assignments under the TCFP. Resources for technical co-operation originate from regular TCFP contributions, specific agreements and contributions to Special Funds. The Baltic Investment Programme, which is administered by Nordic countries, consists of two special funds to co-finance investment and technical assistance projects in the private sectors of Baltic states. The Funds are open to contributions from all EBRD member states. The Russia Small Business Fund (RSBF) was established in 1994 to support local SMEs through similar investment and technical co-operation activities over a period of 10 years. Other financing mechanisms that the EBRD uses to address the needs of the region include Regional Venture Funds, which invest equity in privatized companies, in particular in Russia, and provide relevant management assistance, and the Central European Agency Lines, which disburse lines of credit to small-scale projects through local intermediaries. A TurnAround Management Programme (TAM) provides practical assistance to senior managers of industrial enterprises to facilitate the expansion of businesses in a market economy. A Business Advisory Services programme complements TAM by undertaking projects to improve competitiveness, strategic planning, marketing and financial management in SMEs. In 2001 the EBRD collaborated with other donor institutions and partners to initiate a Northern Dimension Environmental Partnership (NDEP) to strengthen and co-ordinate environmental projects in northern Europe; the Partnership, which became operational in November 2002, includes a 'nuclear window' to address the nuclear legacy of the Russian Northern Fleet. The Bank manages the NDEP Support Fund.

PROJECT FINANCING COMMITTED BY SECTOR

	2002	
	Number	Amount (€ million)
Financial institutions		
Bank equity	7	311
Bank lending	13	541
Equity funds	6	126
Non-bank financial institutions	7	166
Small business finance . .	3	24
Specialized industries		
Agribusiness	12	425
Property, tourism and shipping	1	95
Telecommunications, information technology and media	6	241
Infrastructure		
Municipal and environmental infrastructure . . .	11	482
Transport	9	543
Energy		
Energy Efficiency . . .	2	76
Natural Resources . . .	3	265
Power and Energy . . .	4	219
General industry		
General industry	17	385
Total	102	3,899

PROJECT FINANCING COMMITTED BY COUNTRY

	2002		Cumulative to 31 Dec. 2002	
	Number	Amount (€ million)	Number	Amount (€ million)
Albania	2	42	15	156
Armenia	1	4	7	122
Azerbaijan . . .	1	52	12	358
Belarus	0	8	6	164
Bosnia and Herzegovina	2	39	18	230
Bulgaria	6	182	39	667
Croatia	8	318	44	1,180
Czech Republic . .	2	69	37	902
Estonia	4	73	42	446
Georgia	2	16	17	205
Hungary	1	27	60	1,326
Kazakhstan . . .	6	175	25	818
Kyrgyzstan . . .	0	2	13	143
Latvia	0	9	24	321
Lithuania	1	5	25	407
Macedonia, former Yugoslav republic	2	20	16	258
Moldova	2	10	19	181
Poland	9	463	118	2,688
Romania	6	447	63	2,251
Russia	25	1,289	152	4,818
Slovakia	4	121	37	952
Slovenia	1	181	25	588
Tajikistan . . .	0	0	5	31
Turkmenistan . .	1	10	5	163
Ukraine	5	170	50	1,293
Uzbekistan . . .	1	34	18	612
Yugoslavia* . . .	10	135	15	366
Total	102	3,899	905	21,6467

Note: Operations may be counted as fractional numbers if multiple sub-loans are grouped under one framework agreement.
*Renamed Serbia and Montenegro in February 2003.

Source: EBRD, *Annual Report 2002*.

In 1997 the G-7, together with the European Community and Ukraine, endorsed the creation of the CSF-financed Chornobyl Unit 4 Shelter Implementation Plan (SIP) to assist Ukraine in stabilizing the protective sarcophagus covering the damaged Chornobyl (Chernobyl) reactor. The plan also provides for the construction of a new confinement structure to safely enclose the building, to be completed by 2007. In 1995 the G-7 requested that the Bank fund the completion of two new nuclear reactors in Ukraine, to provide alternative energy sources to the Chornobyl power-station. A study questioning the financial viability of the proposed reactors threatened funding in early 1997; asecond survey, however, carried out by the EBRD, pronounced the plan viable, although environmental groups continued to dispute the proposals. In July 2000 donor countries committed additional funds to the SIP, raising the total pledged to €766m.

The funds have enabled the closure of nuclear plants for safety reasons in countries where this would otherwise have been prohibitively costly. In December 2000 Chornobyl unit 3 was closed, and in 2002 two units were closed in Bulgaria. The closure of a further two units in Bulgaria and units in Lithuania and the Slovak Republic are expected in the next few years. The NSA is also financing the construction of two major pre-decommissioning facilities in Ukraine, scheduled to be completed in 2003.

Throughout 2002 the EBRD was involved in negotiations over financing for the Baku-Tbilisi-Ceyhan (BTC) oil pipeline; a decision on this was expected by the end of 2003. Construction of the pipeline commenced in April of that year.

Publications

Annual Report.
EBRD Report to the Donor and Co-financing Community (annually).
Environments in Transition (2 a year).
Law in Transition (2 a year).
Transition Report (annually).

THE EUROPEAN UNION—EU

The European Union (EU)'s permanent institutions are based in Brussels, Luxembourg and Strasbourg.

The European Coal and Steel Community (ECSC) was created by a treaty signed in Paris on 18 April 1951 (effective from 25 July 1952–25 July 2002) to pool the coal and steel production of the six original members (see below). It was seen as a first step towards a united Europe. The European Economic Community (EEC) and European Atomic Energy Community (Euratom) were established by separate treaties signed in Rome on 25 March 1957 (effective from 1 January 1958), the former to create a common market and to approximate economic policies, the latter to promote growth in nuclear industries. The common institutions of the three Communities were established by a treaty signed in Brussels on 8 April 1965 (effective from 1 July 1967).

The EEC was formally changed to the European Community (EC) under the Treaty on European Union (effective from 1 November 1993), although in practice the term EC had been used for several years to describe the three Communities together. The new Treaty established a European Union (EU), introducing citizenship thereof and aiming to increase intergovernmental co-operation in economic and monetary affairs; to establish a common foreign and security policy; and to introduce co-operation in justice and home affairs. The EU was placed under the supervision of the European Council (comprising Heads of State or Government of member countries), while the EC continued to exist, having competence in matters relating to the Treaty of Rome and its amendments.

MEMBERS

Austria	Germany	Netherlands
Belgium	Greece	Portugal
Denmark	Ireland	Spain
Finland	Italy	Sweden
France	Luxembourg	United Kingdom

*Original members. Denmark, Ireland and the United Kingdom joined on 1 January 1973, and Greece on 1 January 1981. In a referendum held in February 1982, the inhabitants of Greenland voted to end their membership of the Community, entered into when under full Danish rule. Greenland's withdrawal took effect from 1 February 1985. Portugal and Spain became members on 1 January 1986. Following the reunification of Germany in October 1990, the former German Democratic Republic immediately became part of the Community, although a transitional period was to be allowed before certain Community legislation took effect there. Austria, Finland and Sweden became members on 1 January 1995. In October 2002 the European Council confirmed that 10 candidate countries (Cyprus, Czech Republic, Estonia, Hungary, Latvia, Lithuania, Malta, Poland, Slovakia and Slovenia) fulfilled the political criteria and would be able to fulfil the economic criteria for membership from the beginning of 2004. The accession negotiations were concluded at the Copenhagen summit in December 2002, and the Accession Treaty was signed in Athens in April 2003.

PERMANENT REPRESENTATIVE OF MEMBER STATE IN CENTRAL AND SOUTH-EASTERN EUROPE

Greece: 25 rue Montoyer, 1000 Brussels; tel. (2) 551-56-11; fax (2) 551-56-51; e-mail mea.bruxelles@rp-grece.be ARISTIDE AGATHOCLES.

Regional Relations

ASSOCIATION COUNCILS

EC–HUNGARY (Europe Agreement entered into force 1 January 1994); EC–POLAND (Europe Agreement entered into force 1 February 1994); EC–CZECH REPUBLIC (Europe Agreement entered into force 1 February 1995); EC–ROMANIA (Europe Agreement entered into force 1 February 1995); EC–BULGARIA (Europe Agreement entered into force 1 February 1995); EC–SLOVAKIA (Europe Agreement entered into force 1 February 1995); EC–ESTONIA (Europe Agreement entered into force 1 February 1998); EC–LATVIA (Europe Agreement entered into force 1 February 1998); EC–LITHUANIA (Europe Agreement entered into force 1 February 1998); EC–SLOVENIA (Europe Agreement entered into force 1 February 1999).

Co-operation agreements seek to facilitate economic and, or, trade co-operation between the EU and both European and non-European countries. Prior to 1989 co-operation agreements were the EC's preferred form of relationship with eastern European countries. 'Association Agreements' were initially signed between the EC and other European countries for the purpose of customs union or possible accession. After the decline of Communism in Eastern Europe in 1989 it was decided that the new states, many of which expressed a desire to become full members of the EC, should be offered association status in the first instance. The resulting accords are known as 'Europe Agreements'. Association Agreements and Europe Agreements provide for the establishment of bilateral Association Councils. Within the framework of the Stabilization and Association Process the EU is negotiating Stabilization and Association Agreements (SAAs) with Balkans countries, with the long-term goal of admitting them as members. In addition several Euro-Mediterranean Association Agreements have been concluded.

The Treaty of Amsterdam, which entered into force on 1 May 1999, aimed to strengthen the concept of a common foreign and security policy within the Union and incorporated a process of common strategies to co-ordinate external relations with a third party. Accordingly, in October a High Representative was appointed to represent the EU at international meetings. In March of that year representatives of the Commission and NATO held a joint meeting, for the first time, to discuss the conflict in the southern Serbian republic of Kosovo and Metohija (see below). In April a meeting of NATO heads of state and of government determined that its equipment, personnel and infrastructure would be available to any future EU military operation. The Union is a party to various international conventions (in some of these to the exclusion of the individual member states).

ACCESSION PARTNERSHIPS

In the late 1980s the extensive political changes and reforms in Eastern Europe led to a strengthening of links with the EC. Agreements on trade and economic co-operation were concluded with Hungary (1988), Poland (1989), Czechoslovakia (1988—on trade only—and 1990), Bulgaria (1990), and Romania (1990). In December 1989 EC heads of government agreed to establish a European Bank for Reconstruction and Development (EBRD), to promote investment in Eastern Europe, with participation by member states of the Organisation for Economic Co-operation and Development (OECD) and the Council for Mutual Economic Assistance (CMEA, or Comecon), which provided economic co-operation and co-ordination in the Communist bloc between 1949 and 1991. The EBRD began operations in 1991. In the same year the EC established a programme providing technical assistance to the Commonwealth of Independent States (TACIS).

In July 1989 the EC was entrusted with the co-ordination of aid from member states of the OECD to Hungary and Poland, to support economic and political transition there. This programme, known as 'Operation PHARE'—Poland/Hungary Aid for the Restructuring of Economies, was extended to assist the following countries with preparations for membership of the EU: the Baltic states (Estonia, Latvia and Lithuania), Bulgaria, the Czech Republic, Romania, Slovakia and Slovenia. Albania, Bosnia and Herzegovina and the former Yugoslav republic of Macedonia (FYRM) were also admitted as PHARE partner countries. (Croatia was suspended in 1995.) In the case of these latter states, the PHARE programme aimed to support their transition to democracy and a market economy. In 2000 the EU's PHARE and other schemes for the then five countries with SAAs (see below) were streamlined into the CARDS (Community Assistance for Reconstruction, Democratization and Stabilization) programme, now the EU's main channel for financial and technical assistance to the countries of South-Eastern Europe. A total of €4,650m. was allocated under CARDS for 2000–06. During the period 2000–06 PHARE was to be allocated an annual budget amounting to €1,500m., of which some 70% was to finance activities in support of investment and the remaining 30% was to fund institution-building.

PHARE and TACIS Information Centre: 19 rue Montoyer, 1000 Brussels, Belgium; tel. (2) 545-90-10; fax (2) 545-90-11; e-mail phare-tacis@cec.eu.int; internet europa.eu.int/comm/dgla/index .htm.

The EC formally recognized the independence of the three Baltic republics in August 1991 and extended the PHARE programme to them in December. Trade and co-operation agreements with the three states were signed in May 1992. In July 1994 free-trade agreements with the republics were finalized by the EU, coming into effect on 1 January 1995. The EU concluded Europe Agreements with the Baltic states in June 1995. In October 1995 Latvia submitted a formal application for EU membership. Formal applications by Estonia and Lithuania were submitted in November and December, respectively. The EU's 'Northern Dimension' programme, covering the Baltic states, Scandinavia and northwest Russia, aims to address the specific challenges of these areas and to encourage co-operation with external states. The Northern Dimension programme operates within the framework of the TACIS programme, as well as other agreements and financial instruments. Europe Agreements between the EC and Czechoslovakia, Hungary and Poland were signed in December 1991, with the aim of establishing a free-trade area within 10 years and developing political co-operation. Hungary and Poland submitted formal applications for EU membership in March and April 1994, respectively. The Czech Republic applied formally in January 1996. In June 1991 the EC established diplo-matic relations with Albania, and in May 1992 an agreement on trade and co-operation was signed. Europe Agreements were initialled with Romania in October and with Bulgaria in March 1993. In June 1995 Romania formally applied for EU membership, followed by Bulgaria in December. In September 1993 a co-operation agreement with Slovenia came into force. A Europe Agreement was signed in 1996 and Slovenia then (in June) formally applied for EU membership. Slovakia's Europe Agreement came into force in February 1995, and the country applied for membership of the EU in June of that year. In June 1993 the European Council approved measures to accelerate the opening of EC markets to goods from Central and Eastern European countries, with customs duties on many industrial items to be removed by the end of 1994. An interim agreement came into force in January 1997, providing for the gradual establishment of a free-trade area over a transitional period of six years. In December 2000 a preferential trade regime with the EU entered into effect in the region.

In May 1994 a Conference on Stability in Europe was convened in Paris to discuss the prevention of ethnic and territorial conflicts in Central and Eastern Europe. In particular, the conference sought to secure bilateral 'good-neighbour' accords between nine European countries that were regarded as potential future members of the EU (Bulgaria, the Czech Republic, Estonia, Hungary, Latvia, Lithuania, Poland, Romania and Slovakia). These countries, together with EU member states and other European countries (including Belarus, Moldova, Russia and Ukraine), signed a 'Stability Pact' in Paris in March 1995.

In July 1997 the European Commission published a report entitled 'Agenda 2000', which presented the Commission's new 'reinforced pre-accession strategy', uniting all the existing forms of support, including PHARE, into a single 'Accession Partnership' (AP) programme for each candidate country. These APs, approved by the Commission in March 1998, were designed to support each country's preparations for accession by identifying priority areas and providing financial assistance. Each AP was complemented by a 'National Programme for the Adoption of the Acquis' (NPAA). (The

acquis communautaire is the entire body of legislation of the European Community.)

Concurrently with Agenda 2000 the Commission published 'Opinions' on the application for membership of each of the candidate countries. It proposed that accession negotiations should commence with the Czech Republic, Estonia, Hungary, Poland and Slovenia. It was recommended that discussions with Bulgaria, Latvia, Lithuania, Romania and Slovakia be deferred, owing to the need for further economic or democratic reform in those countries. The report acknowledged that it was necessary for the EU to be restructured in order to ensure its successful operation following expansion. Accession negotiations at ministerial level commenced in November 1998 with the first group of applicant countries. In February 2000 accession negotiations were initiated with Bulgaria, Latvia, Lithuania, Romania and Slovakia. At the Copenhagen summit in December 2002, an historic agreement was reached when the European Council agreed that 10 candidate countries, including the Czech Republic, Estonia, Hungary, Latvia, Lithuania, Poland, Slovakia and Slovenia, should join the EU in May 2004. By the time of the summit accession negotiations covering more than 30 issues, including free movement of goods, capital, persons and services; agriculture; fisheries; company law; energy; the environment; external relations; and so on had been completed with all of the candidate countries, thus allowing them to be formally accepted as members. Financing agreements were signed with each of the 10 countries concerned during 2002, with financial assistance set aside for projects such as cross-border co-operation, phasing out nuclear plants, agricultural development schemes, etc., in readiness for accession. At the Copenhagen summit the EU agreed to increase aid to the 10 states to €40,800m. for 2004–06. The largest share of the money was allocated to Poland; the Polish Government had been negotiating for extra assistance to compensate for the reduction in subsidies to its farmers, in the form of higher production quotas and extended tariff protection, but accepted a package of immediate direct budgetary assistance in place of longer-term regional aid. By July 2003 referendums held on EU membership in the Czech Republic, Hungary, Lithuania, Poland, Slovakia and Slovenia had resulted in each case in a vote in favour. In April 2003 the EU member states and the 10 accession countries signed a Treaty of Accession which, subject to its ratification by, at the latest, 30 April 2004, was to enter into force on 1 May 2004.

Two Eastern European programmes designed to aid candidate countries in their efforts towards accession began in 2000. The Special Accession Programme for Agriculture and Rural Development (SAPARD) aims to help candidate countries manage the problems of structural adjustment in their agricultural sectors. It has an annual budget of €250m. The Instrument for Structural Policies for Preaccession (ISPA) has a budget for 2000–06 of €1,040m. Funds are available for infrastructure projects in the environment and transport sectors of candidate countries.

GREEK–TURKISH RELATIONS

The EC Association Agreement signed with Greece in 1961 established free access to the Community market for most industrial products and tariff reductions for most agricultural products. Annexed were financial protocols under which the Community was to provide concessional finance. Greece joined the EC in 1972. An Association Agreement with Turkey, concluded in September 1963, entered into force in December 1964. In 1987 Turkey applied for membership of the Community. In 1989 the European Commission stated that, for formal negotiations on Turkish membership to take place, it would be necessary for Turkey, among other factors, to harmonize its relations with Greece. Negotiations in early 1995 to conclude a customs union agreement with Turkey were obstructed by the opposition of Greece. In early March, however, Greece removed its veto on the customs union, having received assurance on the accession of Cyprus to the EU. In 1996 and 1997 the EU, along with the USA, took part in extensive diplomatic activity to facilitate Cyprus' accession as a single entity. In March 1997 Turkey received assurances that its application for membership would be considered on equal terms with that of any other country. However, in July the commission published 'Agenda 2000' (see above), which recommended that accession negotiations should begin with the (Greek) Cypriot Government, while talks with Turkey were to be postponed indefinitely. In December ministers of foreign affairs, meeting in Luxembourg, endorsed the report's proposals. From August 1999, when a devastating earthquake struck north-western Turkey, a *rapprochement* began to take place between Greece and Turkey. Greece lifted its longstanding veto on disbursements of aid to Turkey and the EU made a loan of €600m. to the Turkish Government to assist reconstruction. This improvement in relations culminated, at the Helsinki summit meeting of EU leaders in December, in a formal invitation to Turkey to present its candidacy for EU membership. In December 2002 the Commission agreed on a programme of pre-accession financial assistance for Turkey, which had received financial assistance during the year of €142m., but at the same time refused to give the Turkish Government a firm date for accession talks as a candidate country, deciding instead to review Turkey's progress towards meeting membership terms in December 2004. In December 2002 the European Council agreed to admit Cyprus (alongside the nine other candidate countries) to the Union from May 2004. (Membership negotiations had commenced in February 2000.) However, the northern Turkish) part of Cyprus was to be excluded unless a reunification plan was agreed; peace talks between the Greek and Turkish Cypriot areas ended in failure in March 2003, with no further negotiations scheduled. In April Cyprus (and the nine other candidate countries) signed a Treaty of Accession with the EU member states that was to enter into force on 1 May 2004 (subject to its ratification by, at the latest, 30 April 2004).

THE FORMER YUGOSLAVIA

A co-operation agreement was signed with Yugoslavia in 1980 (but not ratified until April 1983), allowing tariff-free imports and Community loans. New financial protocols were signed in 1987 and 1991. However, EC aid was suspended in July 1991, following the declarations of independence by the Yugoslav republics of Croatia and Slovenia, and the subsequent outbreak of civil conflict. Efforts were made in the ensuing months by EC ministers of foreign affairs to negotiate a peaceful settlement between the Croatian and Serbian factions, and a team of EC observers was maintained in Yugoslavia from July onwards, to monitor successive cease-fire agreements. In October the EC proposed a plan for an association of independent states, to replace the Yugoslav federation: this was accepted by all the Yugoslav republics except Serbia, which demanded a redefinition of boundaries to accommodate within Serbia all predominantly Serbian areas. In November the application of the Community's co-operation agreements with Yugoslavia was suspended (with exemptions for the republics which co-operated in the peace negotiations). In January 1992 the Community granted diplomatic recognition to the former Yugoslav republics of Croatia and Slovenia, and in April it recognized Bosnia and Herzegovina, while withholding recognition from Macedonia (owing to pressure from the Greek Government, which feared that the existence of an independent Macedonia would imply a claim on the Greek province of the same name). In May EC ambassadors were withdrawn from Belgrade, in protest at Serbia's support for aggression by Bosnian Serbs against other ethnic groups in Bosnia and Herzegovina; in the same month the Community imposed a trade embargo on Serbia and Montenegro.

New proposals for a settlement of the Bosnian conflict, submitted by EC and UN mediators in 1993, were accepted by the Bosnian Croats and by the Bosnian Government in March, but rejected by the Bosnian Serbs. In June the European Council pledged more rigorous enforcement of sanctions against Serbia. In July, at UN/EC talks in Geneva, all three parties to the Bosnian war agreed on a plan to divide Bosnia and Herzegovina into three separate republics; however, the Bosnian Government rejected the proposals for the share of territory to be allotted to the Muslims.

In April 1994, following a request from EU ministers of foreign affairs, a Contact Group, consisting of France, Germany, the United Kingdom, the USA and Russia, was initiated to undertake peace negotiations. The following month ministers of foreign affairs of the USA, Russia and the EU (represented by five member states) jointly endorsed a proposal to divide Bosnia and Herzegovina in proportions of 49% to the Bosnian Serbs and 51% to the newly established Federation of Muslims and Croats. The proposal was rejected by the Bosnian Serb assembly in July and had to be abandoned after the Muslim-Croat Federation withdrew its support subsequent to the Bosnian Serb vote. In July the EU formally assumed political control of Mostar, a town in southern Bosnia and Herzegovina, in order to restore the city's administrative infrastructure and secure peace.

Despite some criticism of US policy towards the former Yugoslavia, in September 1994 the EU supported US-led negotiations in Geneva to devise a plan to end the conflict in Bosnia and Herzegovina. The plan closely resembled the previous proposals of the Contact Group: two self-governing entities were to be created within Bosnia and Herzegovina, with 51% of territory being allocated to the Muslim-Croat Federation, and 49% to Bosnian Serbs. The proposals were finally agreed after negotiations in Dayton, USA, in November 1995, and an accord was signed in Paris in December. In September 1998 EU observers criticized the management of a general election in Bosnia and Herzegovina. During 1991–2000 Bosnia and Herzegovina received a total of €1,032m. in assistance from the EU. The ECHO (European Community Humanitarian Office) programme for that country was phased out in the country in 2000; under the CARDS programme the country was allocated €105m. in 2001. In 2000 the EU published a 'road map' for Bosnia and Herzegovina, outlining measures that must be undertaken by the Government prior to the initiation of a feasibility study on the formulation of an SAA. In September 2002 the Commission reported that Bosnia and Herzegovina had essentially adhered to the terms of the road map. In January 2003 a new European Union Police Mission (EUPM) took over from the UN peace-keeping force in Bosnia and Herzegovina,

with a budget of €38m. for 2003. An EU consultative task force (CTF) is in operation in that country, with the aim of developing a legal and regulatory framework compatible with that of the EU.

Negotiations towards a trade and co-operation agreement with Croatia began in June 1995, but talks were suspended in early August, following Croatia's military offensive in the Krajina region, which was strongly criticized by the EU. The election of a new administration in Croatia in early 2000 prompted more rapid progress in co-operation with the EU. A CTF was set up in the country in February. Negotiations on an SAA began in November, and the agreement was adopted in October 2001. During 1991–2000 the EU extended €367.33m. to Croatia; €60m. was budgeted under the CARDS programme for 2001.

In January 1996 the EU announced its intention to recognize Yugoslavia (Serbia and Montenegro), despite the opposition of the USA. During 1996–99 the EU allocated ECU 1,000m. for the repatriation of refugees, restructuring the economy and technical assistance, in addition to ECU 1,000m. in humanitarian aid provided since the beginning of the conflict in the former Yugoslavia.

In December 1993 six member states of the EU formally recognized the former Yugoslav republic of Macedonia (FYRM) as an independent state, but in February 1994 Greece imposed a commercial embargo against the FYRM, on the grounds that the use of the name and symbols (e.g. on the state flag) of 'Macedonia' was a threat to Greek national security. In March, however, ministers of foreign affairs of the EU decided that the embargo was in contravention of EU law, and in April the Commission commenced legal proceedings in the European Court of Justice against Greece. In September 1995 Greece and the FYRM began a process of normalizing relations, after the FYRM agreed to change the design of its state flag. In October Greece ended its economic blockade of the FYRM, and in November the Council of the European Union authorized the Commission to begin negotiating a trade and co-operation agreement with the FYRM, which entered into force in January 1998. From March 2001 insecurity prevailed in the FYRM, owing to an insurgency by ethnic Albanian rebels. The EU undertook diplomatic efforts in pursuit of a settlement to the conflict,and committed funds for reconstruction and rehabilitation. In April an SAA was signed with the FYRM. At the same time, an interim agreement was adopted, allowing for trade-related matters of the SAA to enter into effect on 1 June, without the need for formal ratification by the national parliaments of the EU member states. (The SAA provided for the EU to open its markets to 95% of exports from the FYRM.) However, the Macedonian Government was informed that it would be required to deliver concessions to the ethnic Albanian minority population prior to entering into the agreement. In 2002 the remit of the European Agency for Reconstruction, which had been originally established to implement aid programmes in Kosovo, was extended to include the FYRM. The EU made humanitarian payments of €3m. to the FYRM in 2002.

In March 1997 the EU sent two advisory delegations to Albania to help restore order after violent unrest and political instability erupted in that country. A request by the Albanian Government for the deployment of EU peace-keeping troops was refused, but it was announced in early April that the EU was to provide humanitarian aid of some ECU 2m., to be used for emergency relief. In September 2002 the European Parliament voted in support of opening negotiations for an SAA with Albania, following satisfactory progress in that country, with regard to presidential elections and electoral reform.

In 1998 the escalation of violence in Kosovo and Metohija (Federal Republic of Yugoslavia—FRY, now Serbia and Montenegro) between Serbs and the ethnic Albanian majority, prompted the imposition of sanctions by EU ministers of foreign affairs. In March ministers agreed to impose an arms embargo, to halt export credit guarantees to Yugoslavia and to restrict visas for Serbian officials. A ban on new investment in the region was imposed in June. In the same month military observers from the EU, Russia and the USA were deployed to Kosovo. In September the EU agreed to deny JAT, the Yugoslav airline, landing rights in EU countries. During the following month the Yugoslav Government allowed a team of international experts to investigate atrocities in the region, under an EU mandate. Several EU countries participated in the NATO military offensive against Yugoslavia, which was initiated in March 1999 owing to the continued repression of ethnic Albanians in Kosovo by Serbian forces. Ministers approved a new series of punitive measures in April, including an embargo on the sale or supply of petroleum to the Yugoslav authorities and an extension of a travel ban on Serbian official and business executives. Humanitarian assistance was extended to provide relief for the substantial numbers of refugees who fled Kosovo amid the escalating violence, in particular to assist the Governments of Albania and the FYRM. In September 1999 EU foreign ministers agreed to ease the sanctions in force against Kosovo and Montenegro. In October the EU began to implement an 'energy for democracy' initiative, with the objective of supplying some €5m.-worth of heating oil to Serbian towns controlled by groups in opposition to the then Yugoslav president, Slobodan Milošević. In

February 2000 the EU suspended its ban on the Yugoslav national airline. However, the restrictions on visas for Serbian officials were reinforced. Kosovo received a total of €474.7m. under EU programmes in 2000 and the EU remained the largest financial contributor to the province in 2001.

In May 2000 the EU agreed an emergency aid package of €20m. to support Montenegro against destabilization by Serbia. Following the election of a new FRY administration in late 2000 the EU immediately withdrew all remaining sanctions, with the exception of those directed against Milošević and his associates, and pledged financial support of €200m. The FRY was welcomed as a full participant in the stabilization and association process (see Stability Pact, below). It was announced that a CTF would be set up when conditions permitted. The EU insisted that the FRY must co-operate fully with the International Criminal Tribunal for the Former Yugoslavia (ICTY). Following the arrest of Milošević by the FRY authorities in April 2001, the first part of the EU's aid package for that year (amounting to €240m.) was released. During 2002 EU humanitarian aid to Serbia totalled €37.5m., to assist the large numbers of refugees and displaced persons. The FRY was renamed Serbia and Montenegro in February 2003.

The European Agency for Reconstruction, established in February 2000 to assume the responsibilities of the European Commission's former Task Force for the Reconstruction of Kosovo (which had become operational in July 1999 following the end of hostilities in the province), is mandated to manage the EU's main assistance programmes in Kosovo and other parts of the FRY and (since December 2001) the FYRM.

European Agency for Reconstruction: POB 10177, 54626 Thessaloniki; Egnatia 4, 54626 Thessaloniki, Greece; tel. (31) 505120; fax (31) 5051172; e-mail info@ear.eu.int; internet www.ear.eu.int; Dir RICHARD ZINK.

At a Balkan summit convened in Zagreb, Croatia, in November 2000, the EU pledged €4,650m. for reconstruction aid to the region in 2000–06. The allocation of aid in 2002 for the Balkans was half that of 2001, owing to the return to relative normality in the region and the decline in humanitarian needs.

STABILITY PACT FOR SOUTH EASTERN EUROPE

On 10 June 1999, at a meeting in Cologne, Germany of foreign ministers and representatives of international organizations and regional institutions, an EU-initiated Stability Pact for South Eastern Europe was adopted. The Pact was officially launched in Sarajevo, Bosnia and Herzegovina, on 30 July 1999, under the auspices of the OSCE. Its objectives were: to secure lasting peace, prosperity and stability in the region; to foster effective regional co-operation through the observance of the Helsinki Final Act (see OSCE); and to improve the market economies of the countries of South-Eastern Europe. It was envisaged that the Pact would represent a new strategy of longer-term conflict prevention. Its eventual aim was to facilitate the integration of the South-East European countries into the EU. For its part, the EU proposed to offer customized SAAs (see above) to Albania, Bosnia and Herzegovina, Croatia, the FYRM and, eventually, the FRY, provided that they fulfilled certain conditions. (The FRY was to be excluded from the Pact until October 2000, following the staging there of democratic presidential elections.) Three Working Tables (on Democratization and Human Rights; Economic Reconstruction, Co-operation and Development; and Security Issues—which incorporated two sub-tables, on Military and Defence and Home Affairs) were established, each with key initiatives and projects. Since the Pact was founded, heads of state and government of the South-East European countries have met regularly in the framework of the South East Europe Co-operation Process (SEECP).

The Stability Pact's first regional funding conference was held in March 2000. The Special Co-ordinator promised a 'quick start package', comprising 244 projects from the three Working Tables. By June 2001 201 projects were under way.

Participant organizations: Council of Europe, EIB, EBRD, EU, NATO, OECD, OSCE, UN (including UNDP, UNHCR, UNICEF, WFP, WHO, the IMF and World Bank), WEU, and various regional organizations.

Participant countries: Albania, Austria, Belgium, Bosnia and Herzegovina, Bulgaria, Canada, Croatia, Czech Republic, Denmark, Finland, France, Germany, Greece, Hungary, Ireland, Italy, Japan, Luxembourg, the FYRM, Moldova, Netherlands, Norway, Poland, Portugal, Romania, Russia, Serbia and Montenegro, Slovakia, Slovenia, Spain, Sweden, Switzerland, Turkey, United Kingdom, USA; **Address:** 50 rue Wiertz, 1050 Brussels, Belgium; tel. (2) 401-87-00; fax (2) 401-87-12; e-mail scsp@stabilitypact.org; internet www.stabilitypact.org

Special co-ordinator: ERHARD BUSEK (Austria).

Deputy Co-ordinator: JOHN RIDDLE (USA).

Finance

STRUCTURAL FUNDS

The Community's 'structural funds' comprise the European Agricultural Guidance and Guarantee Fund, the European Regional Development Fund, the European Social Fund and the Cohesion Fund. There is also a financial instrument for fisheries guidance. 'Agenda 2000' (see above) provided for the reform of the structural funds to make available some €213,000m. for 2000–06.

Cohesion Fund

The Treaty on European Union and its protocol on economic and social cohesion provided for the establishment of a 'cohesion fund', which began operating on 1 April 1993. The Fund aimed to to subsidize projects in the fields of the environment and trans-European energy and communications networks in member states with a per-capita GNP of less than 90% of the Community average (in practice, Greece, Ireland, Portugal and Spain). The overall aim was to help the least prosperous states participate in economic and monetary union. Commitments for financing projects under the Cohesion Fund came to €2,789m. in 2002. The Fund's total budget for the period 2000–06 amounted to €18,000m.

European Agricultural Guidance and Guarantee Fund (EAGGF)—Guidance Section

Created in 1962, the European Agricultural Guidance and Guarantee Fund is administered by the Commission. The Guidance section covers expenditure on Community aid for projects to improve farming conditions in the member states. It includes aid for poor rural areas and the structural adjustment of rural areas, particularly in the context of the reform of the common agricultural policy (CAP). This aid is usually granted in the form of financial contributions to programmes supported by the member governments themselves.

European Regional Development Fund—ERDF

The ERDF is intended to compensate for the unequal rate of development in different regions of the Community, by encouraging investment and improving infrastructure in 'problem regions'. It covers all development areas, but is mostly used to co-finance investment relating to job-creation and local business and development initiatives. Payments began in 1975.

European Social Fund

The Fund (established in 1960) aims to combat long-term unemployment and facilitate the integration of young people and the socially disadvantaged into the labour market. It also supports schemes to help workers adapt to industrial changes and to combat discrimination. The budget for 2000–06 was set at €60,000m.

INTERNATIONAL ORGANIZATION FOR MIGRATION— IOM

Address: 17 route des Morillons, CP 71, 1211 Geneva 19, Switzerland.

Telephone: (22) 7179111; **fax:** (22) 7986150; **e-mail:** info@iom.int; **internet:** www.iom.int.

The Intergovernmental Committee for Migration (ICM) was founded in 1951 as a non-political and humanitarian organization with a predominantly operational mandate, including the handling of orderly and planned migration to meet specific needs of emigration and immigration countries; and the processing and movement of refugees, displaced persons and other individuals in need of international migration services to countries offering them resettlement opportunities. In 1989 ICM's name was changed to the International Organization for Migration (IOM). IOM was admitted as an observer to the UN General Assembly in October 1992.

MEMBERS

Albania	Finland	Panama
Algeria	France	Paraguay
Angola	Georgia	Peru
Argentina	Germany	Philippines
Armenia	Greece	Poland
Australia	Guatemala	Portugal
Austria	Guinea	Romania
Azerbaijan	Guinea-Bissau	Rwanda
Bangladesh	Haiti	Senegal
Belgium	Honduras	Serbia and
Belize	Hungary	Montenegro
Benin	Iran	Sierra Leone
Bolivia	Ireland	Slovakia
Bulgaria	Israel	Slovenia
Burkina Faso	Italy	Sri Lanka
Cambodia	Japan	Sudan
Canada	Jordan	Sweden
Cape Verde	Kazakhstan	Switzerland
Chile	Kenya	Tajikistan
Colombia	Korea, Republic	Tanzania
Congo, Democratic	Kyrgyzstan	Thailand
Republic	Latvia	Tunisia
Congo, Republic	Liberia	Uganda
Costa Rica	Lithuania	Ukraine
Côte d'Ivoire	Luxembourg	United Kingdom
Croatia	Madagascar	USA
Cyprus	Mali	Uruguay
Czech Republic	Mexico	Venezuela
Denmark	Morocco	Yemen
Dominican	Netherlands	Zambia
Republic	Nicaragua	Zimbabwe
Ecuador	Nigeria	
Egypt	Norway	
El Salvador	Pakistan	

Observers: Afghanistan, Belarus, Bhutan, Bosnia and Herzegovina, Brazil, Burundi, People's Republic of China, Cuba, Estonia, Ethiopia, Ghana, Holy See, India, Indonesia, Jamaica, Libya, former Yugoslav republic of Macedonia, Malta, Mozambique, Namibia, Nepal, Papua New Guinea, Russia, San Marino, São Tomé and Príncipe, Somalia, Sovereign Military Order of Malta, Spain, Turkey, Turkmenistan and Viet Nam. In addition, some 50 international governmental and non-governmental organizations hold observer status with IOM.

Organization

(July 2003)

IOM is governed by a Council which is composed of representatives of all member governments, and has the responsibility for making final decisions on policy, programmes and financing. An Executive Committee of nine member governments elected by the Council prepares the work of the Council and makes recommendations on the basis of reports from the Sub-Committee on Budget and Finance and the Sub-Committee on the Co-ordination of Transport.

Director General: BRUNSON MCKINLEY (USA).

Deputy Director General: NDIORO NDIAYE (Senegal).

COUNTRY AND REGIONAL OFFICES IN CENTRAL AND SOUTH-EASTERN EUROPE

Albania: Brigada e Tege, Villa 3, Tirana; tel. (42) 57836; fax (42) 57835; e-mail iomtirana@iomtirana.org.al.

Bosnia and Herzegovina: 33000 Sarajevo, Vilsonovo Setaliste 10; tel. (33) 648137; fax (33) 648202; e-mail missionsarajevo@iom.int.

Bulgaria: 1000 Sofia, Vassil Levski Blvd 66A; tel. (2) 9816365; fax (2) 9816741; e-mail iomsofia@iom.int.

Croatia: 10000 Zagreb, POB 299; tel. (1) 4816774; fax (1) 4816879; e-mail iomzagreb@iom.int.

Czech Republic: Dukelskysch hrdinu 692/35, 17000 Prague 7; tel. (2) 33370160; fax (2) 33382259; e-mail prague@iom.int; internet www.iom.cz.

Greece: POB 430, 174 02 Athens; tel. (10) 9919040; fax (10) 9910914; e-mail iomathens@iom.int.

Hungary: 1065 Budapest, Révay u. 12; tel. (1) 2690323; fax (1) 3740532; e-mail mrfbudapest@iom.int.

Kosovo: 38000 Priština, Nazim Hikmet 49, Dragodan 2; tel. (38) 549042; fax (38) 549039; e-mail iompristina@iom.ipko.org; internet www.iompristina.org.

Latvia: L. Pils iela 21, Rīga 1167; tel. 750-3626; fax 750-3603; e-mail ilmars@undp.riga.lv.

Lithuania: Jaksto St 12, Vilnius 2000; tel. and fax (2) 261-0115; e-mail iomvilnius@iom.elnet.lt.

Macedonia, former Yugoslav republic: 1000 Skopje, POB 43; tel. (2) 3082815; fax (2) 3082811; e-mail iomskopje@iom.skopje.org.mk.

Romania: 71222 Bucharest 1, Bd. Dacia 89/1; tel. (1) 2304702; fax (1) 2303614; e-mail iombucharest@iom.int.

Serbia and Montenegro: 11060 Belgrade, POB 27; tel. (11) 661450; fax (11) 3441009; e-mail iombeograd@iom.int.

Slovakia: Pribinova 25, POB 54, 810 11 Bratislava; tel. (2) 5063-3320; fax (2) 5063-3314; e-mail bratislava@iom.int.

Slovenia: 1000 Ljubljana, Trdinova 7; tel. (1) 4347351; fax (1) 2311119; e-mail iomljubljana@iom.int.

Activities

IOM aims to provide assistance to member governments in meeting the operational challenges of migration, to advance understanding of migration issues, to encourage social and economic development through migration and to work towards effective respect of the human dignity and well-being of migrants. It provides a full range of migration assistance to, and sometimes *de facto* protection of, migrants, refugees, displaced persons and other individuals in need of international migration services. This includes recruitment, selection, processing, medical examinations, and language and cultural orientation courses, placement, activities to facilitate reception and integration and other advisory services. IOM co-ordinates its refugee activities with the UN High Commissioner for Refugees (UNHCR) and with governmental and non-governmental partners. In May 1997 IOM and UNHCR signed a memorandum of understanding which aimed to facilitate co-operation between the two organizations. Since it commenced operations in February 1952 IOM has provided assistance to an estimated 11m. migrants.

IOM operates within the framework of the main service areas outlined below. It also administers special programmes. In June 2001 IOM established a Migration Policy and Research Programme to strengthen the capacity of governments to manage migration effectively, and to contribute to a better understanding of migration issues. IOM was designated as one of the implementing organizations of the settlement agreement concluded between survivors of the Nazi holocaust and Swiss banks. IOM established the Holocaust Victim Assets Programme (HVAP) to process claims made by certain target groups. A German Forced Labour Compensation Programme (GFLCP) was founded to process applications for claims of forced labour and personal injury and for property loss. The deadline for filing claims under both programmes was 31 December 2001.

MOVEMENTS

IOM's constitution mandates the organization to provide for the organized transfer of migrants, refugee displaced persons, and others to countries offering to receive them. Accordingly, IOM provides assistance to persons fleeing conflict situations, to refugees being resettled in third countries or repatriated, to stranded individuals, to internally and externally displaced persons, to other persons compelled to leave their homelands, to individuals seeking to reunite with other members of their families and to migrants involved in regular migration, including qualified migrants travelling under the Facilitated Passage Programme. IOM provides these individuals with secure, reliable, cost-effective services, including counselling, document processing, medical examination, transportation, language training, and cultural orientation and integration assistance. IOM offers discounted transport services and assistance during departure, transit and arrival.

IOM movements are undertaken by the Movement Management Department, which is also responsible for statistical recording of IOM activities and for the development of effective procedures and operational guide-lines. In a humanitarian emergency situation, the department assumes the focal point of IOM operations until field missions are prepared to co-ordinate activities. From April–June 1999 IOM co-operated with UNHCR and the OSCE to facilitate the evacuation of refugees from Kosovo and Metohija (Federal Republic of Yugoslavia, now Serbia and Montenegro), following an escalation of violence against the local Albanian population by Serbian forces and the initiation of a NATO military offensive. The joint Humanitarian Evacuation Programme included land transportation to move substantial numbers of refugees away from overcrowded camps in the border region of the former Yugoslav republic of Macedonia (FYRM), and the provision of charter flights to evacuate those refugees most at need to third countries. IOM was also involved in implementing a programme to register the refugees in Albania, the FYRM and Montenegro, and to reissue identification documents where necessary.

ASSISTED RETURNS SERVICE

IOM assists migrants to return home, on a voluntary basis. These people may include unsuccessful asylum seekers, stranded students, labour migrants, qualified nationals and refugees referred by UNHCR. IOM provides return services directly to the migrant, as well as in co-operation with other organizations to assist wider groups of people. As with its movements service, IOM provides assistance at each stage of the process, i.e. pre-departure, transportation, and post-arrival. It aims to act in a mediating role between the countries and governments of origin, transit and destination and often extends assistance through a period of rehabilitation, to longer-term reconstruction and development efforts.

Since its establishment IOM has been involved in the voluntary repatriation of refugees, displaced persons, and other vulnerable groups. Between 1996 and 1998 more than 160,000 Bosnians were assisted to return voluntarily under IOM auspices. In June 1999, following the end of the conflict in Kosovo and Metohija, IOM co-ordinated the return movement of refugees and worked with the UN mission and UNHCR to assist returnees to move to their final destination in Kosovo. From July 1999–December 2000 IOM assisted some 170,000 Kosovars to return to the province.

IOM aims to contribute towards alleviating economic and social problems through the recruitment and selection of high-level workers and professionals to fill positions in priority sectors of the economy in developing countries for which qualified persons are not available locally, taking into account national development priorities as well as the needs and concerns of receiving communities. IOM screens possible returnees, identifies employment opportunities and provides reintegration assistance. Selection Migration programmes help qualified professionals to migrate to countries in need of specific expertise when the country cannot find the required skills from within or through the return of nationals. Integrated Experts programmes provide temporary expatriate expertise to states for up to six years: these experts transfer their skills to their working partners and contribute directly to productive output. Programmes of Intraregional Co-operation in the field of qualified human resources encourage collective self-reliance among developing countries by fostering the exchange of governmental experts and the transfer of professionals and technicians within a given region. IOM maintains recruitment offices throughout the world. In November 1996 IOM established a Return of Qualified Nationals (RQN) programme to facilitate the employment of refugees returning to Bosnia and Herzegovina. By December 1999, when the programme was terminated, more than 750 professionals had been placed in jobs in that country. In 2001 IOM initiated a Programme for the Return of Judiciary and Prosecutors to Minority Areas in Bosnia and Herzegovina.

In recent years IOM has increasingly assisted in the return home and reintegration of demobilized soldiers, police officials, and their dependents. During 1997–99 IOM undertook a programme of assistance for demobilized soldiers and their families in Angola. IOM was also involved in the resettlement of demobilized forces in Guatemala in 1998. In mid-1999 IOM established an Information Counselling and Referral Service (ICRS) to undertake the registration of former combatants in Kosovo and assist their rehabilitation. From July–November 1999 the ICRS registered 25,723 demobilized soldiers from the Kosovo Liberation Army; during that period IOM helped 4,122 of the former combatants to start their own businesses or to find other permanent employment.

COUNTER TRAFFICKING

IOM aims to counter the growing problem of smuggling and trafficking in migrants, which has resulted in several million people being exploited by criminal agents and employers. IOM aims to provide shelter and assistance for victims of trafficking; to provide legal and medical assistance to migrants uncovered in transit or in the receiving country; and to offer voluntary return and reintegration assistance. IOM organizes mass information campaigns in countries of origin, in order to highlight the risks of smuggling and trafficking, and aims to raise general awareness of the problem. It also provides training to increase the capacity of governments and other organizations to counter irregular migration. Since 1996 IOM has worked in Cambodia and Thailand to help victims of trafficking to return home. A transit centre has been established on the border between the two countries, where assessments are carried out, advice is given, and the process of tracing families is undertaken. During 2001 IOM operated a pilot project for the return of trafficked migrants to Bosnia and Herzogovina.

TECHNICAL CO-OPERATION ON MIGRATION

Through its technical co-operation programmes IOM offers advisory services on migration to governments, intergovernmental agencies and non-governmental organizations. They aim to assist in the formation and implementation of effective and coherent migration policy, legislation and administration. IOM technical co-operation also focuses on capacity building projects such as training courses for government migration officials, and analysis of and suggestions for solving emerging migration problems. Throughout these activities IOM aims to maintain an emphasis on the rights and well-being of migrants, and in particular to ensure that the specific needs of migrant women are incorporated into programmes and policies.

MASS INFORMATION

IOM furthers the understanding of migration through mass information campaigns, in particular to provide migrants with enough knowledge to make informed decisions. In recent years information campaigns have addressed migrant rights, trafficking in women and children, migration and health, promoting the image of migrants, and amnesty programmes. Information campaigns may also inform refugees and displaced persons on the nature and extent of humanitarian aid during an emergency. Information programmes may be implemented to address a specific need, or as part of a wider strategy for migration management. Through its research IOM has developed mechanisms to gather information on potential migrants' attitudes and motivations, as well as on situations which could lead to irregular migration flows. Trends in international migration point to information as an essential resource for individuals making life-changing decisions about migrating; for governments setting migration policies; for international, regional or non-governmental organizations designing migration programmes; and for researchers, the media and individuals analyzing and reporting on migration.

MIGRATION HEALTH

IOM's migration health services aim to ensure that migrants are fit to travel, do not pose a danger to those travelling with them, and that they receive medical attention and care when necessary. IOM also undertakes research and other technical support and policy development activities in the field of health care. Medical screening of prospective migrants is routinely conducted, along with immunizations and specific counselling, e.g. for HIV/AIDS. IOM administers programmes for disabled refugees and undertakes medical evacuation of people affected by conflict. Under its programmes for health assistance and advice, IOM conducts health education programmes, training for health professionals in post-conflict regions, and assessments of availability and access to health care for migrant populations. IOM provides assistance for post-emergency returning populations, through the rehabilitation of health infrastructures, provision of medical supplies, mental health programmes, and training of personnel. In September 1999 IOM established a one-year Psychosocial and Trauma Response in Kosovo project, to enhance the local capacity to respond to problems arising from the conflict and mass displacement. Following the end of the project, during which 37 people graduated as counsellors, IOM developed a new programme to establish community psychosocial centres, to train a further 40 counsellors and to enhance access to psychosocial support for ethnic minorities.

IOM collaborates with government health authorities and relevant intergovernmental and non-governmental organizations. In September 1999 IOM and UNAIDS signed a co-operation framework to promote awareness on HIV/AIDS issues relating to displaced populations, and to ensure the needs of migrants are incorporated into national and regional AIDS strategies. In October IOM and WHO signed an agreement to strengthen collaborative efforts to improve the health care of migrants. IOM maintains a database of its tuberculosis diagnostic and treatment programmes, which facilitates the management of the disease. An information system on immigration medical screening data was being developed to help to analyse disease trends among migrants.

INTERNATIONAL CENTRE FOR MIGRATION AND HEALTH

11 route du Nant-d'Avril, 1214 Geneva, Vernier, Switzerland; tel. (22) 7831080; fax (22) 7831087; e-mail admin@icmh.ch; internet www.icmh.ch.

Established in March 1995, by IOM and the University of Geneva, with the support of WHO, to respond to the growing needs for information, documentation, research, training and policy development in migration health; designated a WHO collaborating centre, in August 1996, for health-related issues among people displaced by disasters.

Co-ordinator: Dr MANUEL CARBALLO.

Finance

The approved IOM budget for 2000 amounted to US $208.4m. for operations and 34.1m. Swiss francs for administration.

Publications

International Migration (quarterly).
IOM News (quarterly, in English, French and Spanish).
Migration and Health (quarterly).
Report by the Director General (in English, French and Spanish).
Trafficking in Migrants (quarterly).
World Migration Report (annually).
Research reports, *IOM Info Sheets* surveys and studies.

INTERNATIONAL RED CROSS AND RED CRESCENT MOVEMENT

The International Red Cross and Red Crescent Movement is a worldwide independent humanitarian organization, comprising three components: the International Committee of the Red Cross (ICRC), founded in 1863; the International Federation of Red Cross and Red Crescent Societies (the Federation), founded in 1919; and National Red Cross and Red Crescent Societies in 178 countries.

Organization

INTERNATIONAL CONFERENCE

The supreme deliberative body of the Movement, the Conference comprises delegations from the ICRC, the Federation and the National Societies, and of representatives of States Parties to the Geneva Conventions (see below). The Conference's function is to determine the general policy of the Movement and to ensure unity in the work of the various bodies. It usually meets every four to five years, and is hosted by the National Society of the country in which it is held. The 27th International Conference was held in Geneva, Switzerland, in October/November 1999.

STANDING COMMISSION

The Commission meets at least twice a year in ordinary session. It promotes harmony in the work of the Movement, and examines matters which concern the Movement as a whole. It is formed of two representatives of the ICRC, two of the Federation, and five members of National Societies elected by the Conference.

COUNCIL OF DELEGATES

The Council comprises delegations from the National Societies, from the ICRC and from the Federation. The Council is the body where the representatives of all the components of the Movement meet to discuss matters that concern the Movement as a whole.

In November 1997 the Council adopted an Agreement on the organization of the activities of the Movement's components. The Agreement aimed to promote increased co-operation and partnership between the Movement's bodies, clearly defining the distribution of tasks between agencies. In particular, the Agreement aimed to ensure continuity between international operations carried out in a crisis situation and those developed in its aftermath.

Fundamental Principles of the Movement

Humanity: The International Red Cross and Red Crescent Movement, born of a desire to bring assistance without discrimination to the wounded on the battlefield, endeavours, in its international and national capacity, to prevent and alleviate human suffering wherever it may be found. Its purpose is to protect life and health and to ensure respect for the human being. It promotes mutual understanding, friendship, co-operation and lasting peace amongst all peoples.

Impartiality: It makes no discrimination as to nationality, race, religious beliefs, class or political opinions. It endeavours to relieve the suffering of individuals, being guided solely by their needs, and to give priority to the most urgent cases of distress.

Neutrality: In order to continue to enjoy the confidence of all, the Movement may not take sides in hostilities or engage in controversies of a political, racial, religious or ideological nature.

Independence: The Movement is independent. The National Societies, while auxiliaries in the humanitarian services of their governments and subject to national laws, must retain their autonomy so that they may always be able to act in accordance with the principles of the Movement.

Voluntary Service: It is a voluntary relief movement not prompted by desire for gain.

Unity: There can be only one Red Cross or Red Crescent Society in any one country. It must be open to all. It must carry on its humanitarian work throughout the territory.

Universality: The International Red Cross and Red Crescent Movement, in which all National Societies have equal status and share equal responsibilities and duties in helping each other, is worldwide.

In 1997 all constituent parts of the Movement (National Societies, the ICRC and the International Federation of Red Cross and Red Crescent Societies) adopted the Seville Agreement on co-operation in the undertaking of international relief activities. The Agreement excludes activities that are entrusted to individual components by the statutes of the Movement or the Geneva Conventions.

International Committee of the Red Cross—ICRC

Address: 19 ave de la Paix, 1202 Geneva, Switzerland.

Telephone: (22) 7346001; **fax:** (22) 7332057; **e-mail:** press.gva@icrc.org; **internet:** www.icrc.org.

Founded in 1863, the ICRC is at the origin of the Red Cross and Red Crescent Movement, and co-ordinates all international humanitarian activities conducted by the Movement in situations of conflict. New statutes of the ICRC, incorporating a revised institutional structure, were adopted in June 1998 and came into effect in July.

Organization

(July 2003)

INTERNATIONAL COMMITTEE

The ICRC is an independent institution of a private character composed exclusively of Swiss nationals. Members are co-opted, and their total number may not exceed 25. The international character of the ICRC is based on its mission and not on its composition.

President: JAKOB KELLENBERGER.

Vice-Presidents: Prof. JACQUES FORSTER, ANNE PETITPIERRE.

ASSEMBLY

Under the new decision-making structures, approved in 1998, the Assembly was defined as the supreme governing body of the ICRC. It formulates policy, defines the Committee's general objectives and strategies, oversees its activities, and approves its budget and accounts. The Assembly is composed of the members of the ICRC, and is collegial in character. The President and Vice-Presidents of the ICRC hold the same offices in the Assembly.

ASSEMBLY COUNCIL

The Council (formerly the Executive Board) is a subsidiary body of the Assembly, to which the latter delegates certain of its responsibilities. It prepares the Assembly's activities and takes decisions on matters within its competence. The Council is composed of five members elected by the Assembly and is chaired by the President of the ICRC.

Members: JAKOB KELLENBERGER, Prof. JACQUES FORSTER, JEAN ABT, JEAN DE COURTEN, JACQUES MOREILLON.

DIRECTORATE

The Directorate is the executive body of the ICRC, overseeing the efficient running of the organization and responsible for the application of the general objectives and institutional strategies decided by the Assembly. Members are appointed by the Assembly to serve a four-year term.

Director-General: ANGELO GNAEDINGER.

Members: PIERRE KRAEHENBUEL (Director of Operations), JACQUES STROUN (Director of Human Resources), DORIS PFISTER (Director of Resources and Operational Support), YVES DACCORD (Director of Communication), FRANÇOIS BUGNION (Director for International Law and Co-operation within the Movement).

Activities

The International Committee of the Red Cross was founded in 1863 in Geneva, by Henry Dunant and four of his friends. The original purpose of the Committee was to promote the foundation, in every country, of a voluntary relief society to assist wounded soldiers on the battlefield (the origin of the National Societies of the Red Cross or Red Crescent), as well as the adoption of a treaty protecting wounded soldiers and all those who come to their rescue. The mission of the ICRC was progressively extended through the Geneva Conventions (see below). The present activities of the ICRC consist in giving legal protection and material assistance to military and civilian victims of wars (international wars, internal strife and disturbances) and in promoting and monitoring the application of international humanitarian law. The ICRC takes into account the legal standards and the specific cultural, ethical and religious features of the environment in which it operates. It aims to influence the conduct of all actual and potential perpetrators of violence by seeking direct dialogue with combatants. In 1990 the ICRC was granted observer status at the United Nations General Assembly. The ICRC overall programme of activities covers the following areas:

The protection of vulnerable individuals and groups under international humanitarian law, including activities related to ensuring respect for detainees (monitoring prison conditions), respect for civilians, reuniting relatives separated in conflict situations and restoring family links, and tracing missing persons.

The implementation of assistance activities, aimed at restoring a sufficient standard of living to victims of armed conflict, including the provision of medical aid and emergency food supplies, initiatives to improve water supply, basic infrastructure and access to health care, and physical rehabilitation assistance (for example to assist civilians injured by land-mines).

Preventive action, including the development and implementation of international humanitarian law and dissemination of humanitarian principles, with a view to protecting non-combatants from violence.

The use of humanitarian diplomacy to raise awareness of humanitarian issues among states and within international organizations.

Building private sector relations.

Co-operation with National Societies.

In January 1996 an ICRC Advisory Service became operational; this was intended to assist national authorities in their implementation of humanitarian law and to provide a basis for consultation, analysis and harmonization of legislative texts. A Documentation Centre has also been established for exchanging information on national measures and activities aimed at promoting humanitarian law in countries. The Centre is open to all states and National Societies, as well as to interested institutions and the general public.

In 1996 the ICRC launched the 'Avenir' project to define the organization's future role, in recognition of significant changes in the world situation and the consequent need for changes in humanitarian action. Four main priorities were identified: improving the status of international humanitarian action and knowledge of and respect for humanitarian law; carrying out humanitarian action in closer proximity to victims, with long-term plans and identified priorities; strengthening dialogue with all parties (including launching joint appeals with other organizations if necessary, and the establishment of a combined communication and information dissemination unit); and increasing the ICRC's efficiency. In April 1998 the Assembly endorsed a plan of action, based on these priorities. In November 1999 the 27th International Conference of the Red Cross and Red Crescent adopted a further plan of action for the movement, covering the four-year period 2000–03. The plan incorporated the following three main objectives: to strengthen respect for international humanitarian law, including the conformity of weapons with legal guide-lines, in order to protect victims of armed conflict; to improve national and international preparedness to respond effectively to disaster situations, as well as to improve mechanisms of co-operation and protection of humanitarian personnel working in the field; and strategic partnerships to improve the lives of vulnerable people through health initiatives, measures to reduce discrimination and violence, and strengthening National Societies' capacities and their co-operation with other humanitarian organizations.

The ICRC consistently reviews the 1980 UN Convention on prohibitions or restrictions on the use of certain conventional weapons which may be deemed to be excessively injurious or to have indiscriminate effects (ratified by 90 states at April 2003) and its protocols. In September 1997 the ICRC participated in an international conference, held in Oslo, Norway, at which a Convention was adopted, prohibiting 'the use, stockpiling, production and transfer of anti-personnel mines' and ensuring their destruction. The treaty was opened for signature in December and became legally binding on 1 March 1999 for the 66 states that had then ratified it. By April 2003 the treaty had been ratified by 132 states. In April 1998 the Swiss Government established a Geneva International Centre for Humanitarian Demining, in co-operation with the United Nations and the ICRC, to co-ordinate the destruction of landmines worldwide.

In 1995 the ICRC adopted a 'Plan of Action concerning Children in Armed Conflicts', to promote the principle of non-recruitment and non-participation in armed conflict of children under the age of 18 years. A co-ordinating group was established, with representatives of the individual National Societies and the International Federation of Red Cross and Red Crescent Societies. The ICRC participated in drafting the Optional Protocol to the Convention on the Rights of the Child, which was adopted by the UN General Assembly in May 2000 and entered into force in February 2002, raising from 15 to 18 years the minimum age for recruitment in armed conflict.

In February 2003 the ICRC launched 'The Missing', a major initiative that aimed to raise awareness of the issue of persons unaccounted for owing to armed conflict or internal violence.

The ICRC's presence in the field is organized under the following three categories: responsive action, aimed at addressing the immediate effects of crises; remedial action, with an emphasis on rehabilitation; and environment-building activities, aimed at creating political, institutional, humanitarian and economic situations that are suitable for generating respect for human rights. ICRC operational delegations focus on responsive action and remedial action, while environment-building is undertaken by ICRC regional delegations. The regional delegations undertake humanitarian diplomacy efforts (e.g. networking, promoting international humanitarian law and distributing information), logistical support to operational delegations, and their own operations; they also have an early warning function, alerting the ICRC to developing conflict situations. The ICRC targets its activities at the following groups: 'victims', comprising civilians affected by violent crises, people deprived of their freedom, and the wounded and sick; and institutions and individuals with influence, i.e. national and local authorities, security forces, representatives of civil society, and Red Cross or Red Crescent National Societies. Children, women and girls, internally displaced people and missing persons are of particular concern to the ICRC.

During 2002 ICRC representatives visited some 448,063 prisoners held in more than 75 countries. A total of 978,724 messages were collected from or distributed to family members separated by conflict, and more than 1,635 persons reported as missing were traced. Regular substantial assistance was provided to 67 hospitals in 18 countries world-wide.During the year the ICRC participated in orthopaedic projects in 21 countries, including the manufacturing and fitting of artificial limbs. In mid-2003 the ICRC was actively concerned with around 80 conflicts and was undertaking major operations in Afghanistan, the Caucasus, Colombia, the Democratic Republic of the Congo, Iraq, Israel and the Palestinian territories, Liberia, Rwanda and Sudan. In March, following the initiation of US-led military action against the Saddam Hussain regime in Iraq, the ICRC signed an agreement with UNHCR on co-operation in providing humanitarian relief in Iraq and neighbouring countries. In April, following the fall of the Iraqi regime, the ICRC urged the US-led coalition to protect Iraq's essential infrastructure, such as hospitals and water supply facilities, from damage by looters and rioters. In 2003 operations in Africa were allocated the highest proportion of the total field budget (some 40.9%), followed by Asia and the Pacific (21.2%) and Europe and North America (16.0%).

THE GENEVA CONVENTIONS

In 1864, one year after its foundation, the ICRC submitted to the states called to a Diplomatic Conference in Geneva a draft international treaty for 'the Amelioration of the Condition of the Wounded in Armies in the Field'. This treaty was adopted and signed by 12 states, which thereby bound themselves to respect as neutral wounded soldiers and those assisting them. This was the first Geneva Convention.

With the development of technology and weapons, the introduction of new means of waging war, and the manifestation of certain phenomena (the great number of prisoners of war during World War I; the enormous number of displaced persons and refugees during World War II; the internationalization of internal conflicts in recent years), the necessity was felt of having other international treaties to protect new categories of war victims. The ICRC, for more than 134 years, has been the leader of a movement to improve and complement international humanitarian law.

There are now four Geneva Conventions, adopted on 12 August 1949: I—to protect wounded and sick in armed forces on land, as well as medical personnel; II—to protect the same categories of people at sea, as well as the shipwrecked; III—concerning the treatment of prisoners of war; IV—for the protection of civilians in time of war; and there are two Additional Protocols of 8 June 1977, for the protection of victims in international armed conflicts (Protocol I) and in non-international armed conflicts (Protocol II).

By January 2003 189 states were parties to the Geneva Conventions; 161 were parties to Protocol I and 156 to Protocol II.

In April 2000 a joint working group on the emblems of the National Red Cross and Red Crescent Societies recommended the formulation of a Third Additional Protocol to the Geneva Conventions, designating a new official emblem so that National Societies could be recognized in countries that did not wish to be represented by either current symbol or did not wish to choose between the two.

Finance

The ICRC's work is financed by a voluntary annual grant from governments parties to the Geneva Conventions, voluntary contributions from National Red Cross and Red Crescent Societies and by gifts and legacies from private donors. The ICRC's total budget for 2003 amounted to some 938.7m. Swiss francs, of which 788.8m. Swiss francs were allocated to field operations.

Publications

Annual Report (editions in English, French and Spanish).

The Geneva Conventions (texts and commentaries).

ICRC News (weekly, English, French, German and Spanish editions).

International Review of the Red Cross (quarterly in English and French; annually in Arabic, Russian and Spanish).

The Additional Protocols (texts and commentaries).

FORUM series.

Various publications on subjects of Red Cross interest (medical studies, international humanitarian law, etc.), some in electronic form.

International Federation of Red Cross and Red Crescent Societies

Address: 17 chemin des Crêts, Petit-Saconnex, CP 372, 1211 Geneva 19, Switzerland.

Telephone: (22) 7304222; **fax:** (22) 7330395; **e-mail:** secretariat@ifrc.org; **internet:** www.ifrc.org.

The Federation was founded in 1919 (as the League of Red Cross Societies). It works on the basis of the Principles of the Red Cross and Red Crescent Movement to inspire, facilitate and promote all forms of humanitarian activities by the National Societies, with a view to the prevention and alleviation of human suffering, and thereby contribute to the maintenance and promotion of peace in the world. The Federation acts as the official representative of its member societies in the field. The Federation maintains close relations with many inter-governmental organizations, the United Nations and its Specialized Agencies, and with non-governmental organizations. It has permanent observer status with the United Nations.

MEMBERS

National Red Cross and Red Crescent Societies in 178 countries in July 2003, with a total of 97m. members and volunteers.

Organization

(July 2003)

GENERAL ASSEMBLY

The General Assembly is the highest authority of the Federation and meets every two years in commission sessions (for development, disaster relief, health and community services, and youth) and plenary sessions. It is composed of representatives from all National Societies that are members of the Federation.

GOVERNING BOARD

The Board (formerly the Executive Council) meets every six months and is composed of the President of the Federation, nine Vice-Presidents, representatives of 16 National Societies elected by the Assembly, and the Chairman of the Finance Commission. Its functions include the implementation of decisions of the General Assembly; it also has powers to act between meetings of the Assembly.

COMMISSIONS

Development Commission.
Disaster Relief Commission.
Finance Commission.
Health and Community Services Commission.
Youth Commision.

The Commissions meet, in principle, twice a year, just before the Governing Board. Members are elected by the Assembly under a system that ensures each Society a seat on one Commission.

SECRETARIAT

The Secretariat assumes the statutory responsibilities of the Federation in the field of relief to victims of natural disasters, refugees and civilian populations who may be displaced or exposed to abnormal hardship. In addition, the Secretariat promotes and co-ordinates assistance to National Societies in developing their basic structure and their services to the community. From 2000 the Secretariat underwent a process of restructuring. In 2003 there were some 230 staff at the Secretariat, employed in the following divisions: co-operation and development, disaster management and co-ordination, external relations, support services, monitoring and evaluation, and governance and planning.

Secretary-General: MARKKO NISKALA (acting).

Activities

In October 1999 the Assembly adopted Strategy 2010, outlining the Federation's objectives and strategies for the next 10 years, in order to address new demands placed on it, for example by the proliferation of other humanitarian groups, restricted finance, and pressure from donors for efficiency, transparency and results. The Strategy involved a significant restructuring of the organization.

DISASTER RESPONSE

The Federation supports the establishment of emergency response units, which aim to act effectively and independently to meet the needs of victims of natural or man-made disasters. The units cover basic health care provision, referral hospitals, water sanitation, logistics, telecommunications and information units. The Federation advises National Societies in relief health. In the event of a disaster the following areas are covered: communicable disease alleviation and vaccination; psychological support and stress management; health education; the provision of medicines; and the organization of mobile clinics and nursing care. The Societies also distribute food and clothing to those in need and assist in the provision of shelter and adequate sanitation facilities and in the management of refugee camps.

DEVELOPMENT

The Federation undertakes capacity-building activities with the National Societies to train and develop staff and volunteers and to improve management structures and processes, in particular in the area of disaster-preparedness. Blood donor programmes are often undertaken by National Societies, sometimes in conjunction with WHO. The Federation supports the promotion of these programmes and the implementation of quality standards. Other activities in the health sector aim to strengthen existing health services and promote community-based health care and first aid; the prevention of HIV/AIDS and substance abuse; and health education and family planning initiatives. The Federation also promotes the establishment and development of education and service programmes for children and for other more vulnerable members of society, including the elderly and disabled. Education projects support the promotion of humanitarian values.

Finance

The permanent Secretariat of the Federation is financed by the contributions of member Societies on a pro-rata basis. Each relief action is financed by separate, voluntary contributions, and development programme projects are also financed on a voluntary basis.

Publications

Annual Report.
Handbook of the International Red Cross and Red Crescent Movement (with the ICRC).
Red Cross, Red Crescent (quarterly, English, French and Spanish).
Weekly News.
World Disasters Report (annually).
Newsletters on several topics; various guides and manuals for Red Cross and Red Crescent activities.

NORTH ATLANTIC TREATY ORGANIZATION—NATO

Address: blvd Léopold III, 1110 Brussels, Belgium.

Telephone: (2) 707-41-11; **fax:** (2) 707-45-79; **e-mail:** natodoc@hq.nato.int; **internet:** www.nato.int.

The Atlantic Alliance was established on the basis of the 1949 North Atlantic Treaty as a defensive political and military alliance of a group of European states (then numbering 10) and the USA and Canada. The Alliance aims to provide common security for its members through co-operation and consultation in political, military and economic fields, as well as scientific, environmental, and other non-military aspects. The objectives of the Alliance are implemented by NATO. Following the collapse of the Ccommunist governments in Central and Eastern Europe, from 1989 onwards, and the dissolution of the Warsaw Pact (which had hitherto been regarded as the Alliance's principal adversary) in 1991, NATO has undertaken a fundamental transformation of its structures and policies to meet the new security challenges in Europe.

* Greece and Turkey acceded to the Treaty in 1952, and the Federal Republic of Germany in 1955. France withdrew from the integrated military structure of NATO in 1966, although remaining a member of the Atlantic Alliance; in 1996 France resumed participation in some, but not all, of the military organs of NATO. Spain acceded to the Treaty in 1982, but remained outside the Alliance's integrated military structure until 1999. The Czech Republic, Hungary and Poland were formally admitted as members of NATO in March 1999. In March 2003 protocols of accession, amending the North Atlantic Treaty, were adopted by the 19 NATO member states with a view to admitting Bulgaria, Estonia, Latvia, Lithuania, Romania, Slovakia and Slovenia to the Alliance in May 2004.

Organization

(July 2003)

NORTH ATLANTIC COUNCIL

The Council, the highest authority of the Alliance, is composed of representatives of the 16 member states. It meets at the level of Permanent Representatives, ministers of foreign affairs, or heads of state and government, and, at all levels, has effective political and decision-making authority. Ministerial meetings are held at least twice a year. Occasional meetings of defence ministers are also held. At the level of Permanent Representatives the Council meets at least once a week.

The Secretary-General of NATO is Chairman of the Council, and each year a minister of foreign affairs of a member state is nominated honorary President, following the English alphabetical order of countries.

MEMBERS*

Belgium	Hungary	Poland
Canada	Iceland	Portugal
Czech Republic	Italy	Spain
Denmark	Luxembourg	Turkey
France	Netherlands	United Kingdom
Germany	Norway	USA
Greece		

Decisions are taken by common consent and not by majority vote. The Council is a forum for wide consultation between member governments on major issues, including political, military, economic and other subjects, and is supported by the Senior or regular Political Committee, the Military Committee and other subordinate bodies.

DEFENCE PLANNING COMMITTEE

Most defence matters are dealt with in the Defence Planning Committee, composed of representatives of all member countries except France. The Committee provides guidance to NATO's military authorities and, within the field of its responsibilities, has the same functions and authority as the Council. Like the Council, it meets regularly at ambassadorial level and assembles twice a year in ministerial sessions, when member countries are represented by their ministers of defence.

NUCLEAR PLANNING GROUP

Defence ministers of countries participating in the Defence Planning Committee meet regularly in the Nuclear Planning Group (NPG) to discuss specific policy issues relating to nuclear forces, such as safety, deployment issues, nuclear arms control and proliferation. The NPG is supported by a Staff Group, composed of representatives of all members participating in the NPG, which meets at least once a week.

OTHER COMMITTEES

There are also committees for political affairs, economics, military medical services, armaments, defence review, science, infrastructure, logistics, communications, civil emergency planning, information and cultural relations, and civil and military budgets. In addition, other committees consider specialized subjects such as NATO pipelines, air traffic management, etc. Since 1992 most of these committees consult on a regular basis with representatives from central and eastern European countries.

INTERNATIONAL SECRETARIAT

The Secretary-General is Chairman of the North Atlantic Council, the Defence Planning Committee and the Nuclear Planning Group. He is the head of the International Secretariat, with staff drawn from the member countries. He proposes items for NATO consultation and is generally responsible for promoting consultation and co-operation in accordance with the provisions of the North Atlantic Treaty. He is empowered to offer his help informally in cases of disputes between member countries, to facilitate procedures for settlement.

Secretary-General: Lord ROBERTSON OF PORT ELLEN (United Kingdom).

Deputy Secretary-General: ALESSANDRO MINUTO RIZZO (Italy).

There is an Assistant Secretary-General for each of the operational divisions listed below.

PRINCIPAL DIVISIONS

Division of Defence Investment: responsible for enhancing NATO's defence capacity (including armaments planning, air defence and security investment) by developing and investing in the Alliance's assets and capabilities; Asst Sec. Gen. ROBERT BELL (USA).

Division of Defence Policy and Planning: responsible for defence planning, nuclear policy and defence against weapons of mass destruction; Asst Sec. Gen. EDGAR BUCKLEY (United Kingdom).

Division of Executive Management: ensures the efficient running of the International Secretariat and provides support to elements such as conference services, information management and human and financial resources; Asst Sec. Gen. JUAN MARTINEZ ESPARZA (Spain).

Division of Operations: responsible for the Alliance's crisis management and peacekeeping activities and civil emergency planning and exercises; Asst Sec. Gen. (vacant).

Division of Political Affairs and Security Policy: is concerned with regional, economic and security affairs and relations with other international organizations and partner countries; Asst Sec. Gen. GÜNTHER ALTENBURG (Germany).

Division of Public Diplomacy: responsible for dissemination of information on NATO's activities and policies through the media, the official web site and print publications as well as seminars and conferences; Asst Sec. Gen. JEAN FOURNET (France).

Military Organization

MILITARY COMMITTEE

Composed of the allied Chiefs-of-Staff, or their representatives, of all member countries: the highest military body in NATO under the authority of the Council. Meets at least twice a year at Chiefs-of-Staff level and remains in permanent session with Permanent Military Representatives. It is responsible for making recommendations to the Council and Defence Planning Committee and Nuclear Planning Group on military matters and for supplying guidance on military questions to Supreme Allied Commanders and subordinate military authorities. The Committee is supported by an International Military Staff.

In December 1995 France agreed to rejoin the Military Committee, which it formally left in 1966.

Chairman: Gen. HARALD KUJAT (Germany).

COMMANDS

Allied Command Operations: Casteau, Belgium—Supreme Headquarters Allied Powers Europe—SHAPE; Supreme Allied Commander Europe—SACEUR Gen. JAMES L. JONES (USA).

Activities

The common security policy of the members of the North Atlantic Alliance is to safeguard peace through the maintenance of political solidarity and adequate defence at the lowest level of military forces needed to deter all possible forms of aggression. Each year, member countries take part in a Defence Review, designed to assess their contribution to the common defence in relation to their respective capabilities and constraints. Allied defence policy is reviewed periodically by ministers of defence.

Since the 1980s the Alliance has been actively involved in co-ordinating policies with regard to arms control and disarmament issues designed to bring about negotiated reductions in conventional forces, intermediate and short-range nuclear forces and strategic nuclear forces. A Verification Co-ordinating Committee was established in 1990. In April 1999 the summit meeting determined to improve co-ordination on issues relating to weapons of mass destruction through the establishment of a separate centre at NATO headquarters.

Political consultations within the Alliance take place on a permanent basis, under the auspices of the North Atlantic Council (NAC), on all matters affecting the common security interests of the member countries, as well as events outside the North Atlantic Treaty area.

Co-operation in scientific and technological fields as well as co-operation on environmental challenges takes place in the NATO Science Committee and in its Committee on the Challenges of Modern Society. Both these bodies operate an expanding international programme of science fellowships, advance study institutes and research grants. NATO has also pursued co-operation in relation to civil emergency planning. These activities represent NATO's 'Third Dimension'.

At a summit meeting of the Conference on Security and Co-operation in Europe—CSCE, now renamed the Organization for Security and Co-operation in Europe—OSCE (see p. 762), in November 1990 the member countries of NATO and the Warsaw Pact signed an agreement limiting Conventional Armed Forces in Europe (CFE), whereby conventional arms would be reduced to within a common upper limit in each zone. The two groups also issued a Joint Declaration, stating that they were no longer adversaries and that none of their weapons would ever be used 'except in self-defence'. Following the dissolution of the USSR the eight former Soviet republics with territory in the area of application of the CFE Treaty committed themselves to honouring its obligations in June 1992. In March 1992, under the auspices of the CSCE, the ministers of foreign affairs of the NATO and of the former Warsaw Pact countries (with Russia, Belarus, Ukraine and Georgia taking the place of the USSR) signed the 'Open Skies' treaty. Under this treaty, aerial reconnaissance missions by one country over another were to be permitted, subject to regulation. At the summit meeting of the OSCE in December 1996 the signatories of the CFE Treaty agreed to begin negotiations on a revised treaty governing conventional weapons in Europe. In July 1997 the CFE signatories concluded an agreement on Certain Basic Elements for Treaty Adaptation, which provided for substantial reductions in the maximum levels of conventional military equipment at national and territorial level, replacing the previous bloc-to-bloc structure of the Treaty.

An extensive review of NATO's structures was initiated in June 1990, in response to the fundamental changes taking place in Central and Eastern Europe. In November 1991 NATO heads of government, convened in Rome, recommended a radical restructuring of the organization in order to meet the demands of the new security environment, which was to involve further reductions in military forces in Europe, active involvement in international peace-keeping operations, increased co-operation with other international institutions and close co-operation with its former adversaries, the USSR and the countries of Eastern Europe. The basis for NATO's new force structure was incorporated into a new Strategic Concept, which was adopted in the Rome Declaration issuing from the summit meeting. The concept provided for the maintenance of a collective defence capability, with a reduced dependence on nuclear weapons. Substantial reductions in the size and levels of readiness of NATO forces were undertaken, in order to reflect the Alliance's strictly defensive nature, and forces were reorganized within a streamlined integrated command structure. Forces were categorized into immediate and rapid reaction forces (including the ACE Rapid Reaction Corps—ARRC, which was inaugurated in October 1992), main defence forces and augmentation forces, which may be used to reinforce any NATO region or maritime areas for deterrence, crisis management or defence. In December the NAC, meeting at ministerial level, endorsed a new military structure, which envisaged a reduction in the number of NATO command headquarters from 65 to 20, and instructed the military authorities of the Alliance to formulate a plan for the transitional process. During 1998 work was undertaken on the formulation of a new Strategic Concept, reflecting the changing security environment and defining NATO's future role and objectives, which recognized a broader sphere of influence of NATO in the 21st century and confirmed NATO to be the principal generator of security in the Euro-Atlantic area. It emphasized NATO's role in crisis management and a renewed commitment to partnership and dialogue. The document was approved at a special summit meeting, convened in Washington, USA, in April 1999, to commemorate the 50th anniversary of the Alliance. A separate initiative was approved to assist member states to adapt their defence capabilities to meet changing security requirements, for example improving the means of troop deployment and equipping and protecting forces. A High-Level Steering Group was established to oversee implementation of the Defence Capabilities Initiative. The Washington meeting, which had been envisaged as a celebration of NATO's achievements since its foundation, was, however, dominated by consideration of the situation in the southern Serbian province of Kosovo and Metohija and the conduct of its military offensive against the Federal Republic of Yugoslavia, initiated in late March (see below).

In January 1994 NATO heads of state and government welcomed the entry into force of the Maastricht Treaty, establishing the European Union (EU, superseding the EC). The Treaty included an agreement on the development of a common foreign and security policy, which was intended to be a mechanism to strengthen the European pillar of the Alliance. NATO subsequently co-operated with Western European Union (WEU) in support of the development of a European Security and Defence Identity. In June 1996 NATO ministers of foreign affairs reached agreement on the implementation of the 'Combined Joint Task Force (CJTF) concept', which had been adopted in January 1994. Measures were to be taken to establish the 'nuclei' of these task forces at certain NATO headquarters, which would provide the basis for missions that could be activated at short notice for specific purposes such as crisis management and peace-keeping. It was also agreed to make CJTFs available for operations undertaken by WEU. In conjunction with this, WEU was to be permitted to make use of Alliance hardware and capabilities (in practice, mostly belonging to the USA) subject to the endorsement of the NAC. The summit meeting, held in April 1999, confirmed NATO's willingness to establish a direct NATO-EU relationship. In February 2000 the first joint NATO-WEU crisis management exercise was conducted. However, in accordance with decisions taken by the EU in late 1999 and 2000 to implement a common security and defence policy, it was agreed that routine NATO-WEU consultation mechanisms were to be suspended. The first formal meeting of the Military Committees of the EU and NATO took place in June 2001 to exchange information relating to the development of EU-NATO security co-operation. In order to support an integrated security structure in Europe, NATO also co-operates with the OSCE and has provided assistance for the development of the latter's conflict prevention and crisis management activities.

In January 2001 NATO established an *ad hoc* working committee in response to concerns expressed by several member governments regarding the health implications of the use of depleted uranium munitions during the Alliance's military intervention in the Balkans. The committee was to co-ordinate the compilation of information regarding the use of depleted uranium and to co-operate with the Yugoslav authorities in the rehabilitation of the local environment. An extraordinary meeting of chiefs of military medical services, including surgeons-general and medical experts, was also convened to consider the issue.

On 12 September 2001 the NAC agreed to invoke, for the first time, Article 5 of the North Atlantic Treaty, providing for collective self-defence, in response to the terrorist attacks against targets in the USA of the previous day. The measure was formally implemented in early October after the US authorities presented evidence substantiating claims that the attacks had been directed from abroad. The NAC endorsed eight specific US requests for logistical and military support in its efforts to counter terrorism, including enhanced sharing of intelligence and full access to airfields and ports in member states. It also agreed to dispatch five surveillance aircraft to help to patrol US airspace and directed the standing naval force to the Eastern Mediterranean. Accordingly, Operation Active Endeavour, conducting the surveillance and monitoring of maritime trade in the region, was subsequently launched. In December NATO ministers of defence initiated a review of military capabilities and defences with a view to strengthening its ability to counter international terrorism.

In February–early May 2003 NATO deployed surveillance aircraft and missile defences in Turkey, and provided assistance with civil emergency planning, to defend that country from possible repercussions of the US-led military action against neighbouring Iraq that was initiated in March.

On 7 April 2003 an agreement was signed by six member states—the Czech Republic, Denmark, Germany, the Netherlands, Norway and Poland—formally establishing the Civil-Military Co-operation Group North. . The group, which was conceived in 2000, was to be based at Budel, Netherlands, and was intended to provide NATO commanders with a co-ordinated approach to civil-military co-operation during crises and in post-conflict areas. In mid-June NATO defence ministers agreed an historic reform of the Alliance's command which was to reflect its new missions and enable the transition to smaller, more flexible forces. The number of commands was to be reduced from 20 to 11 and their responsibilites redefined. The restructuring woulod include a Response Force which, it was hoped, would become operational by the end of the year.

PARTNERSHIPS

In May 1997 a Euro-Atlantic Partnership Council (EAPC) was inaugurated as a successor to the North Atlantic Co-operation Council (NACC), that had been established in December 1991 to provide a forum for consultation on political and security matters with the countries of central and eastern Europe, including the former Soviet republics. An EAPC Council was to meet monthly at ambassadorial level and twice a year at ministerial level. It was to be supported in its work by a steering committee and a political committee. The EAPC was to pursue the NACC Work Plan for Dialogue, Partnership and Co-operation and incorporate it into a new Work Plan, which was to include an expanded political dimension of consultation and co-operation among participating states. The Partnership for Peace (PfP) programme, which was established in January 1994 within the framework of the NACC, was to remain an integral element of the new co-operative mechanism. The PfP incorporated practical military and defence-related co-operation activities that had originally been part of the NACC Work Plan. Participation in the PfP requires an initial signature of a framework agreement, establishing the common principles and objectives of the partnership, the submission of a presentation document, indicating the political and military aspects of the partnership and the nature of future co-operation activities, and thirdly, the development of individual partnership programmes establishing country-specific objectives. In June 1994 Russia, which had previously opposed the strategy as being the basis for future enlargement of NATO, signed the PfP framework document, which included a declaration envisaging an 'enhanced dialogue' between the two sides. Despite its continuing opposition to any enlargement of NATO, in May 1995 Russia agreed to sign a PfP Individual Partnership Programme, as well as a framework document for NATO-Russian dialogue and co-operation beyond the PfP. During 1994 a Partnership Co-ordination Cell (PCC), incorporating representatives of all partnership countries, became operational in Mons, Belgium. The PCC, under the authority of the NAC, aims to co-ordinate joint military activities and planning in order to implement PfP programmes. The first joint military exercises with countries of the former Warsaw Pact were conducted in September. NATO began formulating a PfP Status of Forces Agreement (SOFA) to define the legal status of Allies' and partners' forces when they are present on each other's territory; the PfP SOFA was opened for signature in June 1995. The new EAPC was to provide a framework for the development of an enhanced PfP programme, which NATO envisaged would become an essential element of the overall European security structure. Accordingly, the military activities of the PfP were to be expanded to include all Alliance missions and incorporate all NATO committees into the PfP process, thus providing for greater co-operation in crisis management, civil emergency planning and training activities. In addition, all PfP member countries were to participate in the CJTF concept through a structure of Partners Staff Elements, working at all levels of the Alliance military structure. Defence ministers of NATO and the 27 partner countries were to meet regularly to provide the political guidance for the enhanced Planning and Review Process of the PfP. In December 1997 NATO ministers of foreign affairs approved the establishment of a Euro-Atlantic Disaster Response Co-ordination Centre (EDRCC), and a non-permanent Euro-Atlantic Disaster Response Unit. The EDRCC was inaugurated in June 1998 and immediately commenced operations to provide relief to ethnic Albanian refugees fleeing the conflict in the Serbian province of Kosovo. In November the NAC approved the establishment of a network of PfP training centres, the first of which was inaugurated in Ankara, Turkey. The centres were a key element of a Training and Education Programme, which was endorsed at the summit meeting in April 1999. During 2000 *ad hoc* working groups were convened to consider EAPC involvement in global humanitarian action against mines, the challenge of small arms and light weapons, and prospects for regional co-operation in South-Eastern Europe and in the Caucasus. The EAPC Action Plan for 2002–04 aimed to promote new approaches to co-operation in the combating of international terrorism.

The enlargement of NATO, through the admission of new members from the former USSR and Central and Eastern European countries, was considered to be a progressive means of contributing to the enhanced stability and security of the Euro-Atlantic area. In December 1996 NATO ministers of foreign affairs announced that invitations to join the Alliance would be issued to some former eastern bloc countries during 1997. The NATO Secretary-General and member governments subsequently began intensive diplomatic efforts to secure Russia's tolerance of these developments. It was agreed that no nuclear weapons or large numbers of troops would be deployed on the territory of any new member country in the former Eastern bloc. In May 1997 NATO and Russia signed the Founding Act on Mutual Relations, Co-operation and Security, which provided for enhanced Russian participation in all NATO decision-making activities, equal status in peace-keeping operations and representation at the Alliance headquarters at ambassadorial level, as part of a recognized shared political commitment to maintaining stability and security throughout the Euro-Atlantic region. A NATO-Russian Permanent Joint Council (PJC) was established under the Founding Act, and met for the first time in July; the Council provided each side the opportunity for consultation and participation in the other's security decisions, but without a right of veto. In March 1999 Russia condemned NATO's military action against the Federal Republic of Yugoslavia and announced the suspension of all relations within the framework of the Founding Act, as well as negotiations on the establishment of a NATO mission in Moscow. The PJC convened once more in May 2000, and subsequent meetings were held in June and December. In February 2001 the NATO Secretary-General agreed with the then acting Russian President a joint statement of commitment to pursuing dialogue and co-operation. A NATO information office was opened in Moscow in that month. The PJC condemned major terrorist attacks perpetrated against the USA in September and pledged to strengthen Russia-NATO co-operation with a view to combating international terrorism. In December an agreement was concluded by NATO ministers of foreign affairs and their Russian counterpart to establish an eventual successor body to the PJC. The new NATO-Russia Council, in which NATO member states and Russia were to have equal status in decision-making, was inaugurated in May 2002. The Council aimed to strengthen co-operation in issues including counter-terrorism, crisis management, nuclear non-proliferation, and arms control.

In May 1997 NATO ministers of foreign affairs, meeting in Sintra, Portugal, concluded an agreement with Ukraine providing for enhanced co-operation between the two sides; the so-called Charter on a Distinctive Relationship was signed at the NATO summit meeting held in Madrid, Spain, in July. In May 1998 NATO agreed to appoint a permanent liaison officer in Ukraine to enhance co-operation between the two sides and assist Ukraine to formulate a programme of joint military exercises. The first NATO-Ukraine meeting at the level of heads of state took place in April 1999. A NATO-Ukraine Commission met for the first time in March 2000.

The Madrid summit meeting in July 1997 endorsed the establishment of a Mediterranean Co-operation Group to enhance NATO relations with Egypt, Israel, Jordan, Mauritania, Morocco and Tunisia. The Group was to provide a forum for regular political dialogue between the two groupings and to promote co-operation in training, scientific research and information exchange. In April 1999 NATO heads of state endorsed measures to strengthen the so-called Mediterranean Dialogue. Algeria joined the Mediterranean Dialogue in February 2000.

In July 1997 heads of state and government formally invited the Czech Republic, Hungary and Poland to begin accession negotiations, with the aim of extending membership to those countries in April 1999. During 1997 concern was expressed on the part of some member governments with regard to the cost of expanding the Alliance; however, in November the initial cost of incorporating the Czech Republic, Hungary and Poland into NATO was officially estimated at US $1,300m. over a 10-year period, which was widely deemed to be an acceptable figure. Accession Protocols for the admission of those countries were signed in December and required

ratification by all member states. The three countries formally became members of NATO in March 1999. In April the NATO summit meeting, held in Washington, DC, USA, initiated a new Membership Action Plan to extend practical support to aspirant member countries and to formalize a process of reviewing applications. Albania, Bulgaria, Estonia, Latvia, Lithuania, Romania, Slovakia, Slovenia and the former Yugoslav republic of Macedonia were participating in the Membership Action Plan in 2001. In March 2003 NATO membership accords were adopted by Bulgaria, Estonia, Latvia, Lithuania, Romania, Slovakia and Slovenia; these states were scheduled to join NATO in May 2004.

PEACE-KEEPING ACTIVITIES

During the 1990s NATO increasingly developed its role as a mechanism for peace-keeping and crisis management. In June 1992 NATO ministers of foreign affairs, meeting in Oslo, Norway, announced the Alliance's readiness to support peace-keeping operations under the aegis of the CSCE on a case-by-case basis: NATO would make both military resources and expertise available to such operations. In July NATO, in co-operation with WEU, undertook a maritime operation in the Adriatic Sea to monitor compliance with the UN Security Council's resolutions imposing sanctions against the Yugoslav republics of Serbia and Montenegro. In October NATO was requested to provide, staff and finance the military headquarters of the United Nations peace-keeping force in Bosnia and Herzegovina, the UN Protection Force in Yugoslavia (UNPROFOR). In December NATO ministers of foreign affairs expressed the Alliance's readiness to support peace-keeping operations under the authority of the UN Security Council. From April 1993 NATO fighter and reconnaissance aircraft began patrolling airspace over Bosnia and Herzegovina in order to enforce the UN prohibition of military aerial activity over the country. In addition, from July NATO aircraft provided protective cover for UNPROFOR troops operating in the 'safe areas' established by the UN Security Council. In February 1994 NATO conducted the first of several aerial strikes against artillery positions that were violating heavy-weapons exclusion zones imposed around 'safe areas' and threatening the civilian populations. Throughout the conflict the Alliance also provided transport, communications and logistics to support UN humanitarian assistance in the region.

The peace accord for the former Yugoslavia, which was initialled in Dayton, USA, in November 1995, and signed in Paris in December, provided for the establishment of a NATO-led Implementation Force (IFOR) to ensure compliance with the treaty, in accordance with a strictly defined timetable and under the authority of a UN Security Council mandate. In early December a joint meeting of allied foreign and defence ministers endorsed the military structure for the peace mission, entitled Operation Joint Endeavour, which was to involve approximately 60,000 troops from 31 NATO and non-NATO countries. The mission was to be under the overall authority of the Supreme Allied Commander Europe (ACE), with the Commander of the ACE Rapid Reaction Corps providing command on the ground. IFOR, which constituted NATO's largest military operation ever, formally assumed responsIbility for peace-keeping in Bosnia and Herzegovina from the UN on 20 December.

By mid-1996 the military aspects of the Dayton peace agreement had largely been implemented under IFOR supervision, including the withdrawal of former warring parties to behind agreed lines of separation and the release of prisoners of war. Substantial progress was achieved in the demobilization of soldiers and militia and in the cantonment of heavy weaponry. However, in August and September the Bosnian Serbs obstructed IFOR weapons inspections and the force was obliged to threaten the Serbs with strong military retaliation to secure access to the arms sites. During 1996 IFOR personnel undertook many activities relating to the civilian reconstruction of Bosnia and Herzegovina, including the repair of roads, railways and bridges; reconstruction of schools and hospitals; delivery of emergency food and water supplies; and emergency medical transportation. IFOR also co-operated with, and provided logistical support for, the Office of the High Representative of the International Community in Bosnia and Herzegovina, which was charged with overseeing implementation of the civilian aspects of the Bosnian peace accord. IFOR assisted the OSCE in preparing for and overseeing the all-Bosnia legislative elections that were held in September, and provided security for displaced Bosnians who crossed the inter-entity boundary in order to vote in their towns of origin. In December NATO ministers of foreign affairs approved a follow-on operation, with an 18-month mandate, to be known as the Stabilization Force (SFOR). SFOR was to be about one-half the size of IFOR, but was to retain 'the same unity of command and robust rules of engagement' as the previous force. SFOR became operational on 20 December. Its principal objective was to maintain a safe environment at a military level to ensure that the civil aspects of the Dayton peace accord could be fully implemented, including the completion of the de-mining process, the repatriation of refugees and preparations for municipal elections. In July 1997 NATO heads of government expressed their support for a more determined implementation of SFOR's mandate permitting the arrest of people sought by the International Criminal Tribunal for the Former Yugoslavia—ICTY if they were discovered within the normal course of duties. A few days later troops serving under SFOR seized two former Serb officials who had been indicted on charges of genocide. SFOR has subsequently undertaken this objective as part of its operational activities. From mid-1997 SFOR assisted efforts to maintain the security and territorial integrity of the Republika Srpska in the face of violent opposition from nationalist supporters of the former President, Radovan Karadžić, based in Pale. In August NATO authorized SFOR to use force to prevent the use of the local media to incite violence, following attacks on multinational forces by Serb nationalists during attempts to regain control of police buildings. In November SFOR provided the general security framework, as well as logistical and communications assistance, in support of the OSCE's supervision of legislative elections that were conducted in the Republika Srpska. In December NATO ministers of defence confirmed that SFOR would be maintained at its current strength of some 31,000 troops, subject to the periodic six-monthly reviews. In February 1998 NATO resolved to establish within SFOR a specialized unit to respond to civil unrest and uphold public security. At the same time the NAC initiated a series of security co-operation activities to promote the development of democratic practices and defence mechanisms in Bosnia and Herzegovina. In October 1999 the NAC formally agreed to implement a reduction in SFOR's strength to some 20,000 troops, as well as a revision of its command structure, in response to the improved security situation in Bosnia and Herzegovina. In 2001 some 35 countries contributed troops to SFOR. Its main activities continued to be in support of the peace process, assisting the collection and disposal of illegal weapons, distributing humanitarian aid, and rebuilding the country's infrastructure. In May 2002, in view of the improved security environment in Bosnia and Herzegovina, NATO determined to reduce SFOR to 12,000 troops by the end of the year.

In March 1998 an emergency session of the NAC was convened at the request of the Albanian Government, which was concerned at the deteriorating security of its border region with the Serbian province of Kosovo and Metohija, following intensified action by the Kosovo Liberation Army (KLA) and retaliatory attacks by Serbian security forces. In mid-June NATO defence ministers authorized the formulation of plans for airstrikes against Serbian targets. A few days later some 80 aircraft dispatched from 15 NATO bases flew close to Albania's border with Kosovo, in an attempt to demonstrate the Alliance's determination to prevent further reprisals against the ethnic Albanian population. In September NATO defence ministers urged a diplomatic solution to the conflict, but insisted that, with an estimated 50,000 refugees living without shelter in the mountainous region bordering Albania, their main objective was to avert a humanitarian disaster. In late September the UN Security Council issued a resolution (1199) demanding an immediate cease-fire in Kosovo, the withdrawal of the majority of Serbian military and police forces, co-operation by all sides with humanitarian agencies, and the initiation of political negotiations on some form of autonomy for the province. Plans for NATO airstrikes were finalized in early October. However, the Russian Government remained strongly opposed to the use of force and there was concern among some member states whether there was sufficient legal basis for NATO action without further UN authorization. Nevertheless, in mid-October, following Security Council condemnation of the humanitarian situation in Kosovo, the NAC agreed on limited airstrikes against Serbian targets, with a 96-hour delay on the 'activation order'. At the same time the US envoy to the region, Richard Holbrooke, concluded an agreement with President Milošević to implement the conditions of UN Resolution 1199. A 2,000-member international observer force, under the auspices of the OSCE, was to be established to monitor compliance with the agreement, supported by a NATO Co-ordination Unit, based in the former Yugoslav republic of Macedonia (FYRM), to assist with aerial surveillance. In mid-November NATO ambassadors approved the establishment of a 1,200–1,800 strong multinational force, under French command, to assist in any necessary evacuation of OSCE monitors. A NATO Kosovo Verification Command Centre was established in Kumanovo, north-east FYRM, in late November; however, President Milošević warned that the dispatch of foreign troops into Kosovo would be treated as an act of aggression.

In January 1999 NATO ambassadors convened in an emergency session following the discovery of the bodies of 45 ethnic Albanians in the Kosovan village of Racak. The meeting demanded that Serbia co-operate with an inquiry into the incident by the Prosecutor of the ICTY, guarantee the security and safety of all international personnel, withdraw security forces (which had continued to undertake offensives within Kosovo), and uphold the cease-fire. Intensive diplomatic efforts, co-ordinated by the six-country 'Contact Group' on the former Yugoslavia, succeeded in bringing both sides in the dispute to talks on the future of Kosovo. During the first stage of negotiations, held in Rambouillet, France, a provisional framework for a political settlement was formulated, based on a form of autonomy for Kosovo (to be reviewed after a three-year period), and incorporating a mandate for a NATO force of some 28,000 troops to monitor its implementation. The talks were suspended in late February with neither side having agreed to the accord. On the resumption of negotiations in mid-March representatives of the KLA confirmed that they would sign the peace settlement. President Milošević, however, continued to oppose the establishment of a NATO force in Kosovo and, despite further diplomatic efforts by Holbrooke, declined to endorse the agreement in accordance with a deadline imposed by the Contact Group. Amid reports of renewed Serbian violence against Albanian civilians in Kosovo, the NAC subsequently reconfirmed its support for NATO military intervention.

On 24 March 1999 an aerial offensive against the Federal Republic of Yugoslavia (now Serbia and Montenegro) was initiated by NATO, with the declared aim of reducing that country's capacity to commit attacks on the Albanian population. The first phase of the allied operation was directed against defence facilities, followed, a few days later, by the second phase which permitted direct attacks on artillery positions, command centres and other military targets in a declared exclusion zone south of the 44th parallel. The escalation of the conflict prompted thousands of Albanians to flee Kosovo, while others were reportedly forced from their homes by Serbian security personnel, creating massive refugee populations in neighbouring countries. In early April NATO ambassadors agreed to dispatch some 8,000 troops, as an ACE Mobile Force Land operation (entitled 'Operation Allied Harbour'), to provide humanitarian assistance to the estimated 300,000 refugees in Albania at that time and to provide transportation to relieve overcrowded camps, in particular in border areas. Refugees in the FYRM were to be assisted by the existing NATO contingent (numbering some 12,000 troops by early April), which was permitted by the authorities in that country to construct new camps for some 100,000 displaced Kosovans. An additional 1,000 troops were transferred from the FYRM to Albania in mid-May in order to construct a camp to provide for a further 65,000 refugees. In mid-April NATO ministers of foreign affairs, meeting in special session, expressed extreme concern at the refugee situation throughout the region. The ministers also clarified the conditions necessary to halt the offensive, which included Serbia's agreement to an international military presence in Kosovo, provision for the safe return of all refugees and an undertaking to work on the basis of the Rambouillet accord. Russia continued to pursue diplomatic efforts to secure a peaceful settlement to the conflict, however, Milošević's reported agreement to allow an unarmed international force in Kosovo, conditional on the immediate end to the NATO campaign, was dismissed by NATO governments. From early April there was increasing evidence of civilian casualties resulting from NATO's aerial bombing of transport, power and media infrastructure and suspected military targets. In mid-April NATO initiated an inquiry following the bombing of a convoy of lorries which resulted in the deaths of some 69 refugees. In the following month NATO was obliged to apologise to the authorities of the People's Republic of China after the accidental bombing of its embassy in Belgrade. At the same time there was widespread concern among governments at increasing evidence of systematic killings and ethnic violence being committed by Serbian forces within Kosovo, and at the estimated 100,000 Albanian men unaccounted for among the massive displaced population. NATO's 50th anniversary summit meeting, held in Washington, USA, in late April, was dominated by consideration of the conflict and of the future stability of the region. A joint statement declared the determination of all Alliance members to increase economic and military pressure on President Milošević to withdraw forces from Kosovo. In particular, the meeting agreed to prevent shipments of petroleum reaching Serbia through Montenegro, to complement the embargo imposed by the EU and a new focus of the bombing campaign which aimed to destroy the fuel supply within Serbia. However, there was concern on the part of several NATO governments on the legal and political aspects of implementing the embargo. The meeting failed to adopt a unified position on the use of ground forces, which many expert commentators insisted, throughout the campaign, were necessary to secure NATO's objectives. In May ministers of foreign affairs of the Group of Seven industrialized nations and Russia (the G-8) agreed on general principles for a political solution, which was to form the basis of UN Security Council resolution. Later in that month NATO estimated that a future Kosovo Peace Implementation Force (KFOR), installed to guarantee a settlement, would require at least 48,000 troops. Following further intensive diplomatic efforts to secure a cease-fire in Kosovo, on 9 June a Military Technical Agreement was signed between NATO and the Federal Republic of Yugoslavia, incorporating a timetable for the withdrawal of all Serbian security personnel. On the following day the UN Security Council adopted Resolution 1244, which authorized an international security presence in Kosovo, under NATO, and an international civilian presence, the UN Interim Administration Mission in Kosovo (UNMIK). The NAC subsequently suspended the airstrike campaign, which, by that time, had involved some 38,000 sorties. KFOR was organized into six brigades, under the leadership of France,

Germany, Italy, USA and the United Kingdom (with responsibility for two brigades). An initial force of 20,000 troops entered Kosovo on 12 June. A few days later an agreement was concluded with Russia, whose troops had also entered Kosovo and taken control of Pristina airport, which provided for the joint responsibility of the airstrip with a NATO contingent and for the participation of some 3,600 Russian troops in KFOR, reporting to the country command in each sector. On 20 June the withdrawal of Yugoslav troops from Kosovo was completed, providing for the formal ending of NATO's air campaign. The KLA undertook to demilitarize and transform the force, as required under Resolution 1244, which was reported to have been achieved in September. KFOR's immediate responsibility was to provide a secure environment to facilitate the safe return of refugees, and, pending the full deployment of UNMIK, to assist the reconstruction of infrastructure and civil and political institutions. In addition, NATO troops were to assist personnel of the international tribunal to investigate sites of alleged violations of human rights and mass graves. From August an escalation of ethnic violence and deterioration of law and order in some parts of the province was an outstanding concern. In January 2000 NATO agreed that the Eurocorps defence force (see under WEU) would assume command of KFOR headquarters in April. At that time KFOR's main concerns were to protect the minority populations, maintain security and reintegrate members of the KLA into civilian life. KFOR was also to continue to work closely with UNMIK in the provision of humanitarian aid, the rehabilitation of infrastructure and the development of civil administration. In February an emergency meeting of the NAC was convened to review the situation in the divided town of Titova Mitrovica, northern Kosovo, where violent clashes had occurred between the ethnic populations and five people had died during attempts by KFOR to impose order. The NAC expressed its determination to reinforce KFOR's troop levels. In September KFOR undertook to protect ethnic Serbians who were eligible to vote in a general election in the Federal Republic of Yugoslavia, and in the following month KFOR worked with OSCE and UN personnel to maintain a secure environment and provide logistical assistance for the holding of municipal elections in Kosovo. During the year KFOR attempted to prevent the movement and stockpiling of illegal armaments in the region. In November there was a marked deterioration in the security situation in Kosovo, and KFOR attempted to halt several outbreaks of cross-border violence. In February 2001 NATO conducted negotiations with the Yugoslav Government regarding new security arrangements to prevent further attacks on the local population in southern Serbia and to counter illegal arms-trafficking. A Weapons Destruction Programme was successfully conducted by KFOR between April 2000–December 2001; a second programme was initiated in March 2002, while an Ammunition Destruction Programme commenced in January.

In March 2001 Albanian separatists in the FYRM escalated their campaign in the north of that country. KFOR troops attempted to prevent Kosovo Albanians from supporting the rebels, fighting as the National Liberation Army (NLA), in order to avert further violence and instability. NATO dispatched military and political missions to meet with the Macedonian authorities, and agreed that Serbian troops were to be permitted to enter the ground safety zone in the Presevo valley (bordering on Kosovo and the FYRM) to strengthen security and prevent it becoming a safe haven for the rebel fighters. The Secretary-General also requested an additional 1,400 troops from member countries to reinforce border security. In mid-March the NLA seized strategic positions around Tetovo, in north-west FYRM. After several days of conflict Macedonian troops initiated an offensive against the rebel strongholds, prompting thousands of Albanians to flee into Kosovo. Nevertheless, hostilities intensified again from late April, resulting in further population displacements. In June NATO troops supervised the withdrawal of some 300 armed Albanian rebels who had been besieged in a town neighbouring Skopje, the Macedonian capital. A cease-fire agreement, mediated by NATO, was concluded by the Macedonian authorities and Albanian militants in early July, as a prelude to negotia-

tions on a political settlement. Meanwhile, NATO, at the request of the Macedonian Government, was drafting contingency plans to deploy troops in the FYRM with a mandate to supervise the voluntary disarmament of the Albanian militants and to collect and destroy their weapons, on condition that both sides showed commitment to maintaining the cease-fire and pursuing peace talks. In mid-July, however, ethnic Albanian insurgents in the Tetovo area were reportedly violating the cease-fire accord. An agreement regarding disarmament and conditions for ethnic minorities, as well as for the immediate withdrawal of troops, was concluded in August. Some 3,800 NATO troops were deployed at the end of that month, under so-called Operation Essential Harvest. At the end of the operation's 30-day mandate almost 4,300 guns had been surrendered, together with 400,000 mines, grenades and ammunition rounds. The NLA formally disbanded, in accordance with the peace agreement. The NAC approved a successor mission, comprising 700 troops, initially with a three-month mandate (subsequently suspended), to protect the civilian observers of the accord (to be deployed by the EU and OSCE). In June 2002 a team from NATO headquarters met with the Macedonian authorities to discuss measures to enhance the country's co-operation with the Alliance.

In April 2003 NATO determined to enhance its support to the International Security Assistance Force in Afghanistan, mandated by the United Nations Security Council in December 2001 to assist the Afghan Interim Authority in maintaining security; NATO was to assume responsibility for command, co-ordination and planning of the operation on 11 August 2003.

Finance

As NATO is an international, not a supra-national, organization, its member countries themselves decide the amount to be devoted to their defence effort and the form which the latter will assume. Thus, the aim of NATO's defence planning is to develop realistic military plans for the defence of the Alliance at reasonable cost. Under the annual defence planning process, political, military and economic factors are considered in relation to strategy, force requirements and available resources. The procedure for the co-ordination of military plans and defence expenditures rests on the detailed and comparative analysis of the capabilities of member countries. All installations for the use of international forces are financed under a common-funded infrastructure programme. In accordance with the terms of the Partnership for Peace strategy, partner countries undertake to make available the necessary personnel, assets, facilities and capabilities to participate in the programme. The countries also share the financial cost of military exercises in which they participate. The administrative (or 'civil') budget, which includes the NATO Science Programme, amounted to US $133m. in 2000. The total military budget approved for 2001 amounted to $716m. (including the operating costs of NATO command structures in the former Yugoslavia, but excluding the costs of assignment of military personnel, met by the contributing countries).

Publications

NATO publications (in English and French, with some editions in other languages) include:
NATO Basic Texts.
NATO Ministerial Communiqués.
NATO Handbook.
NATO in the 21st Century.
NATO Review (quarterly in 11 languages; annually in Icelandic).
NATO Update (weekly, electronic version only).
Economic and scientific publications

ORGANISATION FOR ECONOMIC CO-OPERATION AND DEVELOPMENT—OECD

Address: 2 rue André-Pascal, 75775 Paris Cédex 16, France.
Telephone: 1-45-24-82-00; **fax:** 1-45-24-85-00; **e-mail:** webmaster@oecd.org; **internet:** www.oecd.org.

OECD was founded in 1961, replacing the Organisation for European Economic Co-operation (OEEC) which had been established in 1948 in connection with the Marshall Plan. It constitutes a forum for governments to discuss, develop and attempt to co-ordinate their economic and social policies. The Organisation aims to promote policies designed to achieve the highest level of sustainable economic growth, employment and increase in the standard of living, while maintaining financial stability and democratic government, and to contribute to economic expansion in member and non-member states and to the expansion of world trade.

MEMBERS

Australia	Hungary	Norway
Austria	Iceland	Poland
Belgium	Ireland	Portugal
Canada	Italy	Slovakia
Czech Republic	Japan	Spain
Denmark	Republic of Korea	Sweden
Finland	Luxembourg	Switzerland
France	Mexico	Turkey
Germany	Netherlands	United Kingdom
Greece	New Zealand	USA

The European Commission also takes part in OECD's work.

Organization

(July 2003)

COUNCIL

The governing body of OECD is the Council, at which each member country is represented. The Council meets from time to time (usually once a year) at the level of government ministers, with the chairmanship rotated among member states. It also meets regularly at official level, when it comprises the Secretary-General and the Permanent Representatives of member states to OECD. It is responsible for all questions of general policy and may establish subsidiary bodies as required, to achieve the aims of the Organisation. Decisions and recommendations of the Council are adopted by mutual agreement of all its members.

Heads of Permanent Delegations
(with ambassadorial rank)

Czech Republic: Jiri Maceska.

Greece: George E. Krimpas.

Hungary: Béla Kádár.

Poland: Jan Bielawski.

Slovakia: Dusan Bella.

EXECUTIVE COMMITTEE

The Executive Committee prepares the work of the Council. It is also called upon to carry out specific tasks where necessary. In addition to its regular meetings, the Committee meets occasionally in special sessions attended by senior government officials.

SECRETARIAT

The Council, the committees and other bodies in OECD are assisted by an independent international secretariat headed by the Secretary-General. An Executive Director is responsible for the management of administrative support services.

Secretary-General: Donald J. Johnston (Canada).

Deputy Secretaries-General: Richard E. Hecklinger (USA), Herwig Schlögl (Germany), Seiichi Kondo (Japan), Berglind Asgeirsdóttir (Iceland).

Executive Director: Pierre-Dominique Schmidt (Belgium).

AUTONOMOUS AND SEMI-AUTONOMOUS BODIES

Centre for Educational Research and Innovation—CERI: f. 1968; includes all member countries; Dir John Martin.

Development Centre.
European Conference of Ministers of Transport.
Financial Action Task Force on Money Laundering.
International Energy Agency (see p. 760).
Nuclear Energy Agency (see p. 761).

Activities

The greater part of the work of OECD, which covers all aspects of economic and social policy, is prepared and carried out in about 200 specialized bodies (committees, working parties, etc.); all members are normally represented on these bodies, except on those of a restricted nature.

ECONOMIC POLICY

Through its work on economic policy, OECD aims to promote stable macroeconomic environments in member and non-member countries and the equitable distribution of income. The main organ for the consideration and direction of economic policy is the Economic Policy Committee, which comprises governments' chief economic advisers and central bankers, and meets two or three times a year. It has several working parties and groups, the most important of which are Working Party No. 1 on Macro-Economic and Structural Policy Analysis, Working Party No. 3 on Policies for the Promotion of Better International Payments Equilibrium, and the Working Party on Short-Term Economic Prospects. In 2002 the Committee's priority work areas included tax reform, environmentally sustainable economic growth, and improving the effectiveness of public spending.

The Economic and Development Review Committee, comprising all member countries, is responsible for the annual examination of the economic situation and macro economic and structural policies of each member country. A report, including specific policy recommendations, is issued every 12 to 18 months on each country, after an examination carried out by the Committee. This process of peer review has been extended to other branches of the Organisation's work (agriculture, environment, manpower and social affairs, scientific policy and development aid efforts).

STATISTICS

Statistical data and related methodological information are collected from member governments and, where possible, consolidated, or converted into an internationally comparable form. The Statistics Directorate maintains data required for macroeconomic forecasting, i.e. national accounts, the labour force, foreign trade, prices, output, and monetary, financial, industrial and other short-term statistics. Work is also undertaken to develop new statistics and new statistical standards and systems in areas of emerging policy interest (such as sustainable development). In addition, the Directorate passes on to non-member countries member states' experience in compiling statistics. In 2001 the Organisation launched OECD Statistics Strategy (OSS), identifying statistics reform as a priority for 2002-04. The aim of the OSS was to improve the quality of OECD statistics and the efficiency of the Organisation's statistical activities, and four priority areas were established in this connection: an 'internal policy dimension' aiming, *inter alia*, to optimize co-operation and co-ordination of various OECD Directorates active in statistics and related fields; a 'communication and dissemination dimension' targeting the visibility and accessibilty of OECD statistics; a 'technical infrastructure dimension' aiming to improve tools for collection, storage and management of data; and an 'external policy dimension' seeking to develop interrelationships with national data providers and other international organizations. In 2001 implementation of the OSS concerned itself mainly with the development of new infrastructure for improving internal co-ordination, dissemination and communication, data collection, dialogue between OECD statisticians and co-operation with National Statistical Offices and international organizations. In 2002 attention was focused on the consolidation of the previous year's achievements, on the development of a new OECD statistical information system (*OECD.stat*), and on the design of an 'OECD Quality Framework' (OQF) for statistics. In 2003 it was planned fully to implement *OECD.stat* and to adopt the OQF in respect of all new statistical activities.

DEVELOPMENT CO-OPERATION

The Development Assistance Committee (DAC) is the principal body through which the Organisation deals with issues relating to co-operation with developing countries and is one of the key forums in which the major bilateral donors work together to increase their effectiveness in support of sustainable development. The DAC holds an annual high-level meeting of ministers or heads of aid agencies. Work is supported by the Development Co-operation Directorate, which monitors aid programmes and resource flows, compiles statistics and seeks to establish codes of practice in aid. There are also working parties on statistics, on aid evaluation, on gender equality and on development co-operation and environment; and networks on poverty reduction, on good governance and capacity development, and on conflict, peace and development co-operation.

Guided by the Development Partnerships Strategy formulated in 1996, the DAC's mission is to foster co-ordinated, integrated, effective and adequately financed international efforts in support of sustainable economic and social development. Recognizing that developing countries themselves are ultimately responsible for their own development, the DAC concentrates on how international co-operation can contribute to the population's ability to overcome poverty and participate fully in society. Principal activities include: adopting authoritative policy guide-lines; conducting periodic critical reviews of members' programmes of development co-operation; providing a forum for dialogue, exchange of experience and the building of international consensus on policy and management issues; and publishing statistics and reports on aid and other resource flows to developing countries and countries in transition. A working set of indicators of development progress has been established by the DAC, in collaboration with experts from UN agencies (including the World Bank) and from developing countries.

The Development Partnerships Strategy was followed by a report entitled *Shaping the 21st Century—The Contribution Of Development Co-operation* , which outlined a series of poverty reduction and development objectives. In 2000 the Partnership for Poverty Reduction was launched, with the aim of establishing a partnership approach for bilateral co-operation with developing countries. In late 2000 the DAC established a Task Force on Donor Practices, which aimed to strengthen partner countries' ownership of development programmes by improving and co-ordinating donor practices. In April 2001 OECD adopted a Recommendation on Untying Official Development Assistance to the Least Developed Countries, in accordance with which recipient countries may use aid to purchase goods and services from any state, not just the donor country. The high-level meeting of the DAC held in April 2003 emphasized the need to make further progress towards improving policies, strategies, practices and performance linked to achieving the development goals of the Millennium Declaration signed in 2000, in particular at a time of uncertainties in the international economic and political environment. In an informal exchange of views, participants in the meeting expressed their concern to advance the emergence a self-governed Iraq with a functional economy; and agreed on the important role of the UN in the integration of urgent humanitarian needs with long-term development objectives in that country.

PUBLIC MANAGEMENT

The Public Governance and Territorial Development Directorate is concerned with identifying changing needs in society and in markets, and with helping countries to adapt their governmental systems and territorial policies. One of the Directorate's primary functions is to provide a forum for exchanging ideas on how to meet the challenges countries face in the area of governance. Within the Directorate there are two committees, the Public Management Committee (PUMA) and the Territorial Development Policy Committee (TDPC), complemented by specialist working groups, ad hoc expert groups and international symposia. PUMA serves as a forum for senior officials responsible for the central management systems of government, providing information, analysis and recommendations on public management and governing capacity. This is in line with the Directorate's support for improving public sector governance through comparative data and analysis, the setting and promotion of standards, and the facilitation of transparency and peer review. A joint initiative of OECD and the EU, operating within OECD, supports good governance in the countries of Central and Eastern Europe that are to accede or are candidates for either accession to or association with the European Union (EU). The so-called Support for Improvement in Governance and Management (SIGMA) programme assists in the reform and modernization of public institutions in those countries and assesses their progress in those areas.

CO-OPERATION WITH NON-MEMBER ECONOMIES

The Centre for Co-operation with Non-Members (CCNM) was established in January 1998, by merger of the Centre for Co-operation with Economies in Transition (founded in 1990) and the Liaison and Co-ordination Unit. It serves as the focal point for the development of policy dialogue with non-member economies, managing multi-

country, thematic, regional and country programmes. These include a Baltic Regional Programme, a Russia Programme, an Emerging Asian Economies Programme and the OECD Programme of Dialogue and Co-operation with China. The Centre also manages OECD's various Global Forums, which discuss a wide range of specific issues that defy resolution in a single country or region.

Non-member economies are invited by the CCNM, on a selective basis, to participate in or observe the work of certain OECD committees and working parties. The Centre also provides a limited range of training activities in support of policy implementation and institution building. Multilateral tax centres, for instance, provide workshops and seminars for senior officials in tax administration and policy. In 1994 the OECD Centre for Private Sector Development in Istanbul, Turkey, commenced operations as a joint project between the OECD and the Turkish Government to provide policy advice and training to administrators from transitional economies in Eastern Europe, Central Asia and Transcaucasus. Subsequently, the Centre has evolved into a regional forum for policy dialogue and co-operation with regard to issues of interest to transitional economies. The CCNM is also a sponsor of the Joint Vienna Institute, which offers a variety of administrative, economic and financial management courses to participants from transition economies. The Centre co-ordinates and maintains OECD's relations with other international organizations.

INTERNATIONAL TRADE

OECD's Trade Committee supports the continued liberalization and efficient operation of the multilateral trading system, with the aim of contributing to the expansion of world trade on a non-discriminatory basis. Its activities include examination of issues concerning trade relations among member countries as well as relations with non-member countries, and consideration and discussion of trade measures taken by a member country which adversely affect another's interests. Through its working parties, the Committee analyses trade issues relating to, for example, the environment and agriculture. It holds regular consultations with civil society organizations.

Through its export credit agreement, OECD maintains an export credit system, stipulating generous financial terms and conditions, and serves as a forum for the discussion and co-ordination of export credit policies. The Working Party on Export Credits and Credit Guarantees works to achieve a level playing field in this area.

The Trade Committee considers the challenges that are presented to the existing international trading system by financial or economic instability, the process of globalization of production and markets and the ensuing deeper integration of national economies. OECD provided support to the multilateral trade negotiations conducted under the General Agreement on Tariffs and Trade (GATT), assisting member countries to analyse the effects of the trade accords and promoting its global benefits. Following the entry into force of the World Trade Organization (WTO) agreements in 1995, OECD continued to study and assess aspects of the international trade agenda. In November 1999 OECD published a report on the impact of further trade liberalization on developing countries, in preparation for the next round of multilateral trade negotiations (which were launched by WTO in November 2001). In 2000 all OECD governments adopted a set of revised guide-lines for multinational enterprises.

FINANCIAL, FISCAL AND ENTERPRISE AFFAIRS

Promoting the efficient functioning of markets and enterprises and strengthening the multilateral framework for trade and investment is the responsibility of the six main OECD committees supported by the Directorate for Financial, Fiscal and Enterprise Affairs. The Directorate works to encourage policy convergence, provides policy guide-lines, gives examples of best practice and maintains benchmarks to measure progress.

The Committee on Capital Movements and Invisible Transactions monitors the implementation of the Codes of Liberalization of Invisible Transactions and of Current Invisible Operations as legally binding norms for all member countries. The Committee on International Investment and Multinational Enterprises monitors the OECD Guide-lines for Multinational Enterprises, a corporate Code of Conduct recommended by OECD member governments, business and labour units. A Declaration on International Investment and Multinational Enterprises, while non-binding, contains commitments on the conduct and treatment of foreign-owned enterprises established in member countries. A comprehensive review of the Declaration was completed in 2000. Negotiations on a Multilateral Agreement on Investment (MAI), initiated by OECD ministers in 1995 to provide a legal framework for international investment, broke down in October 1998, although 'informal consultation' on the issue was subsequently continued.

The Committee on Competition Law and Policy promotes the harmonization of national competition policies, co-operation in competition law enforcement, common merger reporting rules and pro-competitive regulatory reform, the development of competition laws and institutions, and efforts to change policies that restrain competition. The Committee on Financial Markets exercises surveillance over recent developments, reform measures and structural and regulatory conditions in financial markets. It aims to promote international trade in financial services, to encourage the integration of non-member countries into the global financial system, and to improve financial statistics. The Insurance Committee monitors structural changes and reform measures in insurance markets. In recent years its work has been focused on the liberalization of insurance markets, financial insolvency, co-operation on insurance and reinsurance policy, the monitoring and analysis of regulatory and structural developments, and private pensions and health insurance. A working party on private pensions meets twice a year. In 2002 OECD member governments approved guide-lines for the administration of private pension funds, the first initiative they had taken to set international standards for the governance and supervision of collective pension funds.

The Committee on Fiscal Affairs has recently focused its efforts on the tax implications of the globalization of national economies. Its activities include promoting the removal of tax barriers and monitoring the implementation and impact of major tax reforms, as well as developing a neutral tax framework for electronic commerce. Since 1998 OECD has promoted co-ordinated action for the elimination of so-called 'harmful' tax practices, designed to reduce the incidence of international money-laundering, and the level of potential tax revenue lost by OECD members. In mid-2000 it launched an initiative to abolish 'harmful tax systems', identifying a number of offshore jurisdictions as 'tax havens' lacking financial transparency, and inviting these to co-operate with the Organisation by amending national financial legislation. Several of the countries and territories named agreed to follow a timetable for reform, with the aim of eliminating such practices by the end of 2005. Others, however, were reluctant to participate. (The USA also strongly opposed the initiative.) In April 2002 OECD announced that co-ordinated defensive measures would be implemented against non-complying jurisdictions ('un-co-operative tax havens') from early 2003. The Organisation has also highlighted examples of preferential tax regimes in member countries. OECD provides the secretariat for the Financial Action Task Force on Money Laundering (FATF).

In May 1997 the OECD Council endorsed plans to introduce a global ban on the corporate bribery of public officials; the OECD Convention on Bribery of Foreign Public Officials in International Business Transactions entered into force in February 1999. By October 2002 the Convention had been ratified by 35 countries. In May 1999 ministers endorsed a set of OECD Principles for Corporate Governance, covering ownership and control of corporate entities, the rights of shareholders, the role of stakeholders, transparency, disclosure and the responsibilities of boards. In 2000 these became one of the 12 core standards of global financial stability, and they are used as a benchmark by other international financial institutions. OECD also collaborates with the World Bank and other organizations to promote good governance world-wide, for example through regional round tables and the Global Corporate Governance Forum.

FOOD, AGRICULTURE AND FISHERIES

The Committee for Agriculture reviews major developments in agricultural policies, deals with the adaptation of agriculture to changing economic conditions, elaborates forecasts of production and market prospects for the major commodities, manages a programme to develop product standards in agriculture, identifies best practices for limiting the impact of agricultural production on the environment, promotes the use of sustainable practices in the sector, considers questions of agricultural development in emerging and transition economies, and evaluates progress towards the integration of the agro-food sector into the multilateral trading system. OECD agriculture ministers have agreed on the long-term objective of seeking a substantial reduction in agricultural support. A separate Fisheries Committee carries out similar tasks in its sector, and, in particular, analyses the consequences of policy measures with a view to promoting responsible and sustainable fisheries. OECD is currently seeking to develop indicators measuring economic and social sustainability in the fisheries sector.

TERRITORIAL DEVELOPMENT

The Territorial Development Policy Committee assists central governments with the design and implementation of more effective, area-based strategies, encourages the emergence of locally driven initiatives for economic development, and promotes better integration of local and national approaches. A high-level meeting of the Committee that was convened in 2003 aimed to support and encourage a growing consensus among OECD countries on the need to shift territorial policies away from subsidies towards a more open policy stance promoting regional competitiveness through private and public investment, entrepreneurship and reliance on local

assets. Generally, the Committee's work programme emphasizes the need for innovative policy initiatives and exchange of knowledge in a wide range of policies, such as entrepreneurship and technology diffusion and issues of social exclusion and urban deprivation.

ENVIRONMENT

The OECD Environment Directorate works in support of the Environment Policy Committee (EPOC) on environmental issues. EPOC assesses performance; encourages co-operation on environmental policy; promotes the integration of environmental and economic policies; works to develop principles, guide-lines and strategies for effective environmental management; provides a forum for member states to address common problems and share data and experience; and promotes the sharing of information with non-member states. Working parties consider a range of issues, in some cases collaborating with other Directorates (for example, the Working Parties on Trade and Environment and on Agriculture and Environment). An Experts Group on Climate Change, based in the Environment Directorate, undertakes studies related to international agreements on climate change.

In April 1998 environment ministers of member countries agreed upon a set of 'Shared Goals for Action', with four principal aims: to promote strong national policies and effective regulatory structures for the protection of the natural environment and human health; to promote an integrated policy approach, encouraging coherence among economic, environmental and social policies; to strengthen international co-operation in meeting global and regional environmental commitments; and to support participation, transparency, the provision of information and accountability in environmental policy-making at all levels. In May 2001 ministers adopted an Environmental Strategy for the 21st Century, containing recommendations for future work. The Strategy, which was to be implemented by 2010, focused on fostering sustainable development, and strengthening co-operation with non-member countries and partnerships with the private sector and civil society. Fundamental objectives included the efficient use of renewable and non-renewable resources; the avoidance of irreversible damage; the maintenance of ecosystems; and separating environmental pressures from economic growth. The Strategy identified several issues requiring urgent action, such as the generation of municipal waste, increased car and air travel, greenhouse gas emissions, groundwater pollution, and the exploitation of marine fisheries. It aimed to ensure the implementation of agreed policies and the formulation of new ones.

The Environment Directorate also provides the secretariat for the Task Force for the Implementation of the Environmental Action Programme in Central and Eastern Europe, which encourages countries in Eastern Europe and the CIS to take environmental issues into consideration in the process of economic restructuring. A first cycle of 32 Environmental Performance Reviews of member and selected non-member countries was completed in 2000, and a second cycle commenced in 2001. The Directorate aims to improve understanding of past and future trends through the collection and dissemination of environmental data.

In a report to the Secretary-General in late 1997 an advisory group on the environment, comprising non-governmental experts, recommended that OECD should evolve into the principal intergovernmental organization providing the analytical and comparative framework of policy necessary for industrialized countries to make the transition to sustainable development. At a meeting in April 1998 ministers from member countries reiterated that the achievement of sustainable development was a priority, and recommended wide-ranging projects over the forthcoming three years in areas relating to technology, the effects of climate change, the environmental impact of subsidies, and the creation of indicators of sustainability, in order comprehensively to address the economic, social and environmental dimensions of sustainable development. In May 2001 OECD ministers of the environment, convened in Paris, France, adopted the OECD Environmental Strategy for the First Decade of the 21st Century, as well as the use of a set of key environmental indicators and guide-lines for the provision of environmentally sustainable transport.

SCIENCE, TECHNOLOGY AND INDUSTRY

The principal objective of the Directorate for Science, Technology and Industry is to assist member countries in formulating and implementing policies that optimize the contribution of science, technology, industrial development and structural change to economic growth, employment and social development. The Committee for Scientific and Technological Policy reviews national and international policy issues relating to science and technology. It provides indicators and analysis on emerging trends in these fields, identifies and promotes best practices, and offers a forum for dialogue. Important themes include: the management and reform of science systems; the development of policies to promote the innovative capacity of members' economies; and policy responses to the globalization of science and technology.

A working party on biotechnology was established in 1993 and its mandate was renewed in 1998. Among the priority topics it has addressed in recent work programmes were scientific and technological infrastructure, and the relation of biotechnology to sustainable industrial development. In 1992 a megascience forum was established to bring together senior science policy-makers for consultations regarding large scientific projects and programmes. It was succeeded, in 1999, by the Global Science Forum. In mid-2003 the Forum's activities included research into near earth objects, compact high-intensity short-pulse lasers, and radio astronomy and the radio spectrum. In 2000 multilateral negotiations on establishing a Global Biodiversity Information Facility (GBIF) were concluded. The GBIF was to connect global biodiversity databases in order to make available a wide range of online data.

The Committee for Information, Computer and Communications Policy monitors developments in telecommunications and information technology and their impact on competitiveness and productivity, with a new emphasis on technological and regulatory convergence. It also promotes the development of new rules (e.g. guidelines on information security) and analyses trade and liberalization issues. The Committee maintains a database of communications indicators and telecommunications tariffs. In December 1999 the OECD Council adopted a set of Guide-lines for Consumer Protection in the Context of Electronic Commerce. OECD supports the Digital Opportunities Task Force (Dot.force) which was established in June 2000 by the Group of Seven industrialized nations and Russia (the G-8) to recommend action with a view to eliminating the so-called 'digital divide' between developed and less developed countries and between different population sectors within nations. OECD's Global Conference on Telecommunications Policy for the Digital Environment, held in January 2002, stressed the importance of competition in the sector and the need for regulatory reform.

The Committee on Industry and the Business Environment focuses on industrial production; business performance; innovation and competitiveness in industrial and services sectors; and policies for private sector development in member and selected non-member economies. In recent years the Committee has addressed issues connected with globalization, regulatory reform, small and medium-sized enterprises (SMEs), and the role of industry in sustainable development. Business and industry policy fora explore a variety of issues with the private sector and develop recommendations. Issues addressed recently include environmental strategies for industry and new technologies. A working party on SMEs conducts an ongoing review of the contribution of SMEs to growth and employment and carries out a comparative assessment of best practice policies. OECD, in conjunction with the Italian Government, organized its first ministerial conference on SMEs in Bologna, Italy, in 2000. A second such conference is scheduled to take place in Turkey in 2004. Databases enabling internationally comparable monitoring of structural change in areas of science and technology, investment, production, employment and trade have been prepared by a working party on statistics.

The Transport Division of the Directorate for Science, Technology and Industry considers aviation, maritime, shipbuilding, road and intermodal transport issues. A road transport research programme covers all aspects of road transport, including its integration into overall transport systems and multimodal transport strategies. Two databases on road transport research and road safety are maintained. The Maritime Transport and Steel Committees aim to promote multilateral solutions to sectoral friction and instability based on the definition and monitoring of rules. The Working Party on Shipbuilding seeks to establish normal competitive conditions in that sector, especially through dialogue with non-OECD countries. In June 1994 negotiations between leading shipbuilding nations, conducted under OECD auspices, concluded a multilateral agreement to end state subsidies to the industry. However, continued failure by the US Congress to ratify the agreement disrupted its entry into force. The Tourism Committee promotes sustained growth in the tourism sector and encourages the integration of tourism issues into other policy areas.

EDUCATION, EMPLOYMENT, LABOUR AND SOCIAL AFFAIRS

The Employment, Labour and Social Affairs Committee is concerned with the development of the labour market and selective employment policies to ensure the utilization of human capital at the highest possible level and to improve the quality and flexibility of working life, as well as the effectiveness of social policies; it plays a central role in addressing OECD's concern to reduce high and persistent unemployment through the creation of high-quality jobs.

The Committee's work covers such issues as the role of women in the economy, industrial relations, international migration, measurements of unemployment, and the development of an extensive social database. The Committee also carries out single-country and thematic reviews of labour-market policies and social assistance systems. It has assigned a high priority to work on the policy implications of an ageing population and on indicators of human capital investment.

The Health Policy Unit of the Employment, Labour and Social Affairs Committee provides analysis to policymakers on health care and health expenditure issues, and analyses the organization and performance of health systems. In 2001 a new, three-year OECD Health Project was launched with the aim of evaluating and analysing the performance of health-care systems in member countries and the factors affecting their performance. The Non-Member Economies and International Migration Division works on social policy issues in emerging economies and economies in transition, especially relating to education and labour market reforms and to the economic and social aspects of migration. Policies for education and training at all levels, education and training policy reviews and the compilation of education data and indicators were formerly the responsibility of an Education Committee. In 2002 a new Directorate for Education was created in order to raise the profile of OECD's work, which is conducted in the context of its view of education as a lifelong activity. Together, the Employment, Labour and Social Affairs and Education Directorates seek to provide for the greater integration of labour market and educational policies and the prevention of social exclusion.

OECD's Centre for Educational Research and Innovation (CERI) promotes the development of research activities in education together with experiments of an advanced nature designed to test innovations in educational systems and to stimulate research and development.

Finance

In 2003 OECD's total consolidated budget amounted to €299.9m.

Publications

Activities of OECD (Secretary-General's Annual Report).

Agricultural Outlook (annually).

Energy Balances (quarterly).

Energy Prices and Taxes (quarterly).

Financial Market Trends (3 a year).

Financial Statistics (Part 1 (domestic markets): monthly; Part 2 (international markets): monthly; Part 3 (OECD member countries): 25 a year).

Foreign Trade Statistics (monthly).

Higher Education Management and Policy (3 a year).

Indicators of Industry and Services Activity (quarterly).

International Trade by Commodities Statistics (5 a year).

Joint BIS-IMF-OECD-World Bank Statistics on External Debt (quarterly).

Main Developments in Trade (annually).

Main Economic Indicators (monthly).

Monthly Statistics of International Trade.

National Accounts Quarterly.

OECD Economic Outlook (2 a year).

OECD Economic Studies (2 a year).

OECD Economic Surveys (every 12 to 18 months for each country).

OECD Employment Outlook (annually).

OECD Journal of Competition Law and Policy (quarterly).

The OECD Observer (every 2 months).

Oil and Gas Statistics (quarterly).

PEB Exchange (newsletter of the Programme on Educational Building, 3 a year).

Quarterly Labour Force Statistics.

Short-term Economic Indicators: Transition Economies (quarterly).

Numerous specialized reports, working papers, books and statistics on economic and social subjects (about 130 titles a year, both in English and French) are also published.

International Energy Agency—IEA

Address: 9 rue de la Fédération, 75739 Paris Cédex 15, France.
Telephone: 1-40-57-65-00; **fax:** 1-40-57-65-59; **e-mail:** info@iea.org; **internet:** www.iea.org.

The Agency was established by the OECD Council in 1974 to develop co-operation on energy questions among participating countries.

MEMBERS

Australia	Greece	Norway
Austria	Hungary	Portugal
Belgium	Ireland	Spain
Canada	Italy	Sweden
Czech Republic	Japan	Switzerland
Denmark	Republic of Korea	Turkey
Finland	Luxembourg	United Kingdom
France	Netherlands	USA
Germany	New Zealand	

The European Commission is also represented.

Organization

(July 2003)

GOVERNING BOARD

Composed of ministers or senior officials of the member governments. Meetings are held every two years at ministerial level and five times a year at senior official level. Decisions may be taken by a weighted majority on a number of specified subjects, particularly concerning emergency measures and the emergency reserve commitment; a simple weighted majority is required for procedural decisions and decisions implementing specific obligations in the agreement. Unanimity is required only if new obligations, not already specified in the agreement, are to be undertaken.

SECRETARIAT

The Secretariat comprises the following four divisions: Standing Group on Long-Term Co-operation; Standing Group on the Oil Market; Standing Group on Emergency Questions; Committee on Energy Research and Technology (with working parties); Committee on Non-Member Countries; Coal Industry Advisory Board; and Industry Advisory Board.

Executive Director: CLAUDE MANDIL (France).

Activities

The Agreement on an International Energy Programme was signed in November 1974 and formally entered into force in January 1976. The Programme commits the participating countries of the International Energy Agency to share petroleum in emergencies, to strengthen their long-term co-operation in order to reduce dependence on petroleum imports, to increase the availability of information on the petroleum market, to co-operate in the development and co-ordination of energy policies, and to develop relations with the petroleum-producing and other petroleum-consuming countries. The IEA issues energy statistics and publications and provides information and analysis on the energy sector. It sponsors conferences, symposia and workshops to enhance international co-operation among member and non-member states.

An emergency petroleum-sharing plan has been established, and the IEA ensures that the necessary technical information and facilities are in place so that it can be readily used in the event of a reduction in petroleum supplies. The IEA undertakes emergency response reviews and workshops, and publishes an Emergency Management Manual to facilitate a co-ordinated response to a severe disruption in petroleum supplies. A separate division monitors and reports on short-term developments in the petroleum market. It also considers other related issues, including international crude petroleum pricing, petroleum trade and stock developments and investments by major petroleum-producing countries.

The IEA Long-Term Co-operation Programme is designed to strengthen the security of energy supplies and promote stability in world energy markets. It provides for co-operative efforts to conserve energy, to accelerate the development of alternative energy sources by means of both specific and general measures, to strengthen research and development of new energy technologies and to remove legislative and administrative obstacles to increased energy supplies. Regular reviews of member countries' efforts in the fields of energy conservation and accelerated development of alternative energy sources assess the effectiveness of national programmes in relation to the objectives of the Agency.

The IEA also reviews the energy situation in non-member countries, in particular the petroleum-producing countries of the Middle East and Central and Eastern European countries. In the latter states the IEA has provided technical assistance for the development of national energy legislation, regulatory reform and energy efficiency projects.

The IEA aims to contribute to the energy security of member countries through energy technology and research and development projects, in particular those concerned with energy efficiency, conservation and protection of the environment. The IEA promotes international collaboration in this field and the participation of energy industries to facilitate the application of new technologies, through effective transfer of knowledge, technology innovation and training. Member states adopt Implementing Agreements, which provide mechanisms for collaboration and information exchange in specific areas, for example, electric vehicle technologies, electric demand-side management and photovoltaic power systems. Non-member states are encouraged to participate in these Agreements. The Agency sponsors conferences, symposia and workshops to further enhance international co-operation among member and non-member countries.

In recent years the IEA has increased its focus on issues related to the environment and sustainable development. In 2000 and 2001 it supported analysis of actions to mitigate climate change, studies of the implications of the Kyoto Protocol to the UN Framework Convention on Climate Change, and analysis of policies designed to reduce greenhouse gas emissions, including emissions trading. (In June/July 2000 it organized an emissions-trading simulation involving 17 countries.) In 2003 two new policy information websites were launched. The first, 'Dealing with Climate Change', provides data on energy-related policies and measures taken by IEA member countries to reduce greenhouse gas emissions. The second, 'Renewable Energy Policies and Measures in IEA Countries', contains details of legislation designed to encourage the development and market uptake of renewable energy sources. The Agency also analyses the regulation and reform of energy markets, especially for electricity and gas. The IEA Regulatory Forum held in February 2002 considered the implications for security of supply and public service of competition in energy markets.

Publications

Coal Information (annually).
Electricity Information (annually).
Natural Gas Information (annually).
Oil Information (annually).
Oil Market Report (monthly).
World Energy Outlook (annually).
Reports, studies, statistics, country reviews.

OECD Nuclear Energy Agency—NEA

Address: Le Seine Saint-Germain, 12 blvd des Îles, 92130 Issy-les-Moulineaux, France.

Telephone: 1-45-24-10-10; **fax:** 1-45-24-11-10; **e-mail:** nea@nea.fr; **internet:** www.nea.fr.

The NEA was established in 1958 to further the peaceful uses of nuclear energy. Originally a European agency, it has since admitted OECD members outside Europe.

MEMBERS

All members of OECD (except New Zealand and Poland).

Organization

(July 2003)

STEERING COMMITTEE FOR NUCLEAR ENERGY

Meets twice a year. Comprises senior representatives of member governments, presided over by a chairman.

SECRETARIAT

Director-General: Luis Enrique Echávarri (Spain).

Deputy Director-General: Carol Kessler (USA).

MAIN COMMITTEES

Committee on Nuclear Regulatory Activities.

Committee on Radiation Protection and Public Health.

Committee on the Safety of Nuclear Installations.

Committee for Technical and Economic Studies on Nuclear Energy Development and the Fuel Cycle.

Nuclear Law Committee.

Nuclear Science Committee.

Radioactive Waste Management Committee.

NEA DATA BANK

The Data Bank was established in 1978, as a successor to the Computer Programme Library and the Neutron Data Compilation Centre. The Data Bank develops and supplies data and computer programmes for nuclear technology applications to users in laboratories, industry, universities and other areas of interest. Under the supervision of the Nuclear Science Committee, the Data Bank collates integral experimental data, and functions as part of a network of data centres to provide direct data services. It was responsible for co-ordinating the development of the Joint Evaluation Fission and Fusion (JEFF) data reference library, and works with the Radioactive Waste Management Division of the NEA on the Thermonuclear Database project (see below).

Activities

The mission of the Agency is to assist its member countries in maintaining and further developing—through international co-operation—the scientific, technological and legal bases required for the safe, environmentally-friendly and economical use of nuclear energy for peaceful purposes. The Agency maintains a continual survey with the co-operation of other organizations, notably the International Atomic Energy Agency (IAEA), of world uranium resources, production and demand, and of economic and technical aspects of the nuclear fuel cycle.

A major part of the Agency's work is devoted to the safety and regulation of nuclear power, including co-operative studies and projects related to the prevention of nuclear accidents and the long-term safety of radioactive waste disposal systems. It is also concerned with the harmonization of nuclear legislation and the dissemination of information on nuclear law issues. A Nuclear Development Committee provides members with statistics and analysis on nuclear resources, economics, technology and prospects. The NEA also co-operates with non-member countries of Central and Eastern Europe and the CIS in areas such as nuclear safety, radiation protection and nuclear law.

JOINT PROJECTS

Nuclear Safety

OECD Fire Project: Covers the period 2002–05; aims to encourage multilateral co-operation in the collection and analysis of data relating to fire events; eight initial participants.

OECD Halden Reactor Project: Halden, Norway; experimental boiling heavy water reactor, which became an OECD project in 1958. From 1964, under successive agreements with participating countries, the reactor has been used for long-term testing of water reactor fuels and for research into automatic computer-based control of nuclear power stations. The main focus is on nuclear fuel safety and man-machine interface. Some 100 nuclear energy research institutions and authorities in 20 countries support the project.

OECD International Common Cause Failure Data Exchange—ICDE Project: initiated in 1994 and formally operated by the NEA since April 1998; encourages multilateral co-operation in the collection and analysis of data on common cause failure (CCF) events occurring at nuclear power plants, with the aim of enabling greater understanding and prevention of such events; 11 participating countries.

OECD-IPSN CABRI Water Loop Project: revised programme initiated in 2000; conducted at the Institute for Protection and Nuclear Safety (IPSN), based in France; investigates the capacity of high burn-up fuel to withstand sharp power peaks that may occur in power reactors owing to rapid reactivity insertion in the reactor core (i.e. reactivity-initiated accidents); 12 participating countries.

OECD MASCA Project: initiated in 2000 as a follow-up to the NEA-sponsored RASPLAV Project, which studied the behaviour of molten core material in a reactor pressure vessel during a severe accident; MASCA is undertaking additional tests in order to resolve remaining uncertainties related to the heat load that the reactor vessel can support during an accident involving core melt; scheduled for completion in July 2003; 17 participating countries.

OECD Melt Coolability and Concrete Interaction—MCCI Project: initiated 2002; conducted at the Argonne National Laboratory, USA; aims to provide experimental data on severe accident molten core coolability and interaction with containment concrete, contributing to improved accident management; 13 participating countries.

OECD Piping Failure Data Exchange Project—OPDE: OECD Piping Failure Data Exchange Project (OPDE) covering the period 2002-05; aims to collect and analyse piping failure event data with the aims of generating qualitative insights into the root causes of such events; 12 participating countries. OECD PSB-VVER Project covering the period 2003–06; conducted at a large-scale, thermal-hydraulics facility located at the Electrogorsk Research and Engineering Centre in Russia; is intended to provide the experimental data needed to allow full validation of the computer codes used in the thermal-hydraulic analysis of Russian-designed VVER-1000 reactors; six participating countries.

OECD SETH Project: Covers the period 2001–05; conducted at the Paul Scherrer Institute PANDA facility, based in Switzerland, and the Siemens Primär Kreislauf, Germany; researches important thermal-hydraulic phenomena in support of accident management; 15 participating countries.

Bubbler Condenser Project: initiated 2002; conducted at the Electrogorsk Research and Engineering Centre, Russia; performs thermal-hydraulic and structural experiments to resolve outstanding issues surrounding the bubbler condenser function for VVER-213 reactors; eight participating countries

Sandia Lower Head Failure Project: initiated in 1999; conducted at the Sandia National Laboratory, USA; researches the rupture behaviour of the reactor pressure vessel lower head and, consequently, provides information for the development of severe accident management strategies; eight participating countries

Radioactive Waste Management

Co-operative Programme for the Exchange of Scientific and Technical Information Concerning Nuclear Installation Decommissioning Projects Programme: initiated in 1985; promotes exchange of technical information and experience for ensuring that safe, economic and optimum environmental options for decommissioning are used; 12 participating countries

Sorption Project: phase II commenced in 2000; comprises benchmark exercises co-ordinated by the NEA; aims to evaluate various approaches used to model sorption phenomena in the context of performance assessments of geologic disposal concepts for the disposal of radioactive waste in deep geological formations; 10 participating countries and 16 participating organizations

Thermonuclear Database—TDB Project: phase II commenced in 1998; aims to develop a quality-assured, comprehensive thermodynamic database of selected chemical elements for use in the safety assessment of radioactive waste repositories; data are selected by review teams; 12 participating countries and 17 participating organizations

Radiation Protection

Information System on Occupational Exposure—ISOE: initiated in 1992 and co-sponsored by the IAEA; maintains largest database world-wide on occupational exposure to ionizing radiation at nuclear power plants; participants: 452 reactors in 28 countries; the system also contains information from 39 nuclear reactors which are either defunct or actively decommissioning

Finance

The Agency's annual budget amounts to some €11.8m.

Publications

Annual Report.

NEA News (2 a year).

Nuclear Energy Data (annually).

Nuclear Law Bulletin (2 a year).

Publications on a range of issues relating to nuclear energy, reports and proceedings.

ORGANIZATION FOR SECURITY AND CO-OPERATION IN EUROPE—OSCE

Address: 1010 Vienna, Kärntner Ring 5–7, Austria.

Telephone: (1) 514-36-180; **fax:** (1) 514-36-105; **e-mail:** info@osce .org; **internet:** www.osce.org.

The OSCE was established in 1972 as the Conference on Security and Co-operation in Europe (CSCE), providing a multilateral forum for dialogue and negotiation. It produced the Helsinki Final Act of 1975 on East–West relations (see below). The areas of competence of the CSCE were expanded by the Charter of Paris for a New Europe (1990), which transformed the CSCE from an *ad hoc* forum to an organization with permanent institutions, and the Helsinki Document 1992 (see 'Activities'). In December 1994 the summit conference adopted the new name of OSCE, in order to reflect the Organization's changing political role and strengthened secretariat.

PARTICIPATING STATES

Albania	Greece	Romania
Andorra	Hungary	Russia
Armenia	Iceland	Serbia and
Austria	Ireland	Montenegro
Azerbaijan	Italy	Slovakia
Belarus	Kazakhstan	Slovenia
Belgium	Kyrgyzstan	Spain
Bosnia and	Latvia	Sweden
Herzegovina	Liechtenstein	Switzerland
Bulgaria	Lithuania	Tajikistan
Canada	Luxembourg	Turkey
Croatia	Macedonia, former	Turkmenistan
Cyprus	Yugoslav republic	Ukraine
Czech Republic	Malta	United Kingdom
Denmark	Moldova	USA
Estonia	Monaco	Uzbekistan
Finland	Netherlands	Vatican City (Holy
France	Norway	See)
Georgia	Poland	
Germany	Portugal	

Organization

(July 2003)

SUMMIT CONFERENCES

Heads of state or government of OSCE participating states normally meet every two to three years to set priorities and political orientation of the Organization. The most recent conference was held in İstanbul, Turkey, in November 1999.

MINISTERIAL COUNCIL

The Ministerial Council (formerly the Council of Foreign Ministers) comprises ministers of foreign affairs of member states. It is the central decision-making and governing body of the OSCE and meets every year in which no summit conference is held.

SENIOR COUNCIL

The Senior Council (formerly the Council of Senior Officials—CSO) is responsible for the supervision, management and co-ordination of OSCE activities. Member states are represented by senior political officers, who convene at least twice a year in Prague, Czech Republic, and once a year as the Economic Forum.

PERMANENT COUNCIL

The Council, which is based in Vienna, is responsible for day-to-day operational tasks. Members of the Council, comprising the permanent representatives of member states to the OSCE, convene weekly. The Council is the regular body for political consultation and decision-making, and may be convened for emergency purposes.

FORUM FOR SECURITY CO-OPERATION—FSC

The FSC, comprising representatives of delegations of member states, meets weekly in Vienna to negotiate and consult on measures aimed at strengthening security and stability throughout Europe. Its main objectives are negotiations on arms control, disarmament, and confidence- and security-building; regular consultations and intensive co-operation on matters related to security; and the further reduction of the risks of conflict. The FSC is also responsible for the implementation of confidence- and security-building measures (CSBMs); the preparation of seminars on military doctrine; the holding of annual implementation assessment meetings; and the provision of a forum for the discussion and clarification of information exchanged under agreed CSBMs.

CHAIRMAN-IN-OFFICE—CIO

The CIO is vested with overall responsibility for executive action. The position is held by a minister of foreign affairs of a member state for a one-year term. The CIO may be assisted by a troika, consisting of the preceding, current and succeeding chairpersons; *ad hoc* steering groups; or personal representatives, who are appointed by the CIO with a clear and precise mandate to assist the CIO in dealing with a crisis or conflict.

Chairman-in-Office: JAAP DE HOOP SCHEFFER (Netherlands).

SECRETARIAT

The Secretariat comprises two principal departments: the Conflict Prevention Centre (including an Operations Centre), which focuses on the support of the CIO in the implementation of OSCE policies, in particular the monitoring of field activities and co-operation with other international bodies; and the Department of Management and Finance, responsible for technical and administrative support activities. The OSCE maintains an office in Prague, Czech Republic, which assists with documentation and information activities, and a centre in Tashkent, Uzbekistan.

The position of Secretary-General was established in December 1992 and the first appointment to the position was made in June 1993. The Secretary-General is appointed by the Ministerial Council for a three-year term of office. The Secretary-General is the representative of the CIO and is responsible for the management of OSCE structures and operations.

Secretary-General: JÁN KUBIŠ (Slovakia).

Co-ordinator of OSCE Economic and Environmental Activities: MARCIN SWIECICKI (Poland).

HIGH COMMISSIONER ON NATIONAL MINORITIES

POB 20062, 2500 EB The Hague, Netherlands; tel. (70) 3125500; fax (70) 3635910; e-mail hcnm@hcnm.org; internet www.osce.org/hcnm.

The establishment of the office of High Commissioner on National Minorities was proposed in the 1992 Helsinki Document, and endorsed by the Council of Foreign Ministers in Stockholm, Sweden in December 1992. The role of the High Commissioner is to identify ethnic tensions that might endanger peace, stability or relations between OSCE participating states, and to promote their early resolution. The High Commissioner may issue an 'early warning' for the attention of the Senior Council of an area of tension likely to degenerate into conflict. The High Commissioner is appointed by the Ministerial Council, on the recommendation of the Senior Council, for a three-year term.

High Commissioner: ROLF EKÉUS (Sweden).

OFFICE FOR DEMOCRATIC INSTITUTIONS AND HUMAN RIGHTS—ODIHR

Aleje Ujazdowskie 19, 00-557 Warsaw, Poland; tel. (22) 520-06-00; fax (22) 520-06-05; e-mail office@odihr.pl; internet www.osce.org .odihr.

Established in July 1999, the ODIHR has responsibility for promoting human rights, democracy and the rule of law. The Office provides a framework for the exchange of information on and the promotion of democracy-building, respect for human rights and elections within OSCE states. In addition, it co-ordinates the monitoring of elections and provides expertise and training on constitutional and legal matters.

Director: CHRISTIAN STROHAL (Switzerland).

OFFICE OF THE REPRESENTATIVE ON FREEDOM OF THE MEDIA

Kärntner Ring 5–7, 1010 Vienna, Austria; tel. (1) 512-21-450; fax (1) 512-21-459; e-mail pm-fom@osce.org; internet www.osce.org/fom.

The office was founded in 1998 to strengthen the implementation of OSCE commitments regarding free, independent and pluralistic media.

Representative: FREIMUT DUVE (Germany).

PARLIAMENTARY ASSEMBLY

Rådhusstraede 1, 1466 Copenhagen K, Denmark; tel. 33-37-80-40; fax 33-37-80-30; e-mail osce@oscepa.dk; internet www.osce.org/pa.

The OSCE Parliamentary Assembly, which is composed of 317 parliamentarians from 55 participating countries, was inaugurated in July 1992, and meets annually. The Assembly comprises a Standing Committee, a Bureau and three General Committees and is supported by a Secretariat in Copenhagen, Denmark.

President: BRUCE GEORGE (United Kingdom).

Secretary-General: R. SPENCER OLIVER (USA).

OSCE Related Bodies

COURT OF CONCILIATION AND ARBITRATION

266 route de Lausanne, 1292 Chambésy, Geneva, Switzerland; tel. (22) 7580025; fax (22) 7582510; e-mail cca.osce@bluewin.ch.

The establishment of the Court of Conciliation and Arbitration was agreed in 1992 and effected in 1994. OSCE states that have ratified the OSCE Convention on Conciliation and Arbitration may submit a dispute to the Court for settlement by the Arbitral Tribunal or the Conciliation Commission.

President: ROBERT BADINTER.

JOINT CONSULTATIVE GROUP—JCG

The states that are party to the Treaty on Conventional Armed Forces in Europe (CFE), which was concluded within the CSCE framework in 1990, established the Joint Consultative Group (JCG). The JCG, which meets in Vienna, addresses questions relating to compliance with the Treaty; enhancement of the effectiveness of the Treaty; technical aspects of the Treaty's implementation; and disputes arising out of its implementation. There are currently 30 states participating in the JCG.

OPEN SKIES CONSULTATIVE COMMISSION

The Commission represents all states parties to the 1992 Treaty on Open Skies, and promotes its implementation. Its regular meetings are serviced by the OSCE secretariat.

Activities

In July 1990 heads of government of the member countries of the North Atlantic Treaty Organization (NATO) proposed to increase the role of the CSCE 'to provide a forum for wider political dialogue in a more united Europe'. The Charter of Paris for a New Europe, which undertook to strengthen pluralist democracy and observance of human rights, and to settle disputes between participating states by peaceful means, was signed in November. At the summit meeting the Treaty on Conventional Armed Forces in Europe (CFE), which had been negotiated within the framework of the CSCE, was signed by the member states of NATO and of the Warsaw Pact. The Treaty limits non-nuclear air and ground armaments in the signatory countries. In April 1991 parliamentarians from the CSCE countries agreed on the creation of a pan-European parliamentary assembly. Its first session was held in Budapest, Hungary, in July 1992.

The Council of Foreign Ministers met for the first time in Berlin, Germany, in June 1991. The meeting adopted a mechanism for consultation and co-operation in the case of emergency situations, to be implemented by the Council of Senior Officials (CSO, which was subsequently renamed the Senior Council). A separate mechanism regarding the prevention of the outbreak of conflict was also adopted, whereby a country can demand an explanation of 'unusual military activity' in a neighbouring country. These mechanisms were utilized in July in relation to the armed conflict in Yugoslavia between the Republic of Croatia and the Yugoslav Government. In mid-August a meeting of the CSO resolved to reinforce considerably the CSCE's mission in Yugoslavia and in September the CSO agreed to impose an embargo on the export of armaments to Yugoslavia. In October the CSO resolved to establish an observer mission to monitor the observance of human rights in Yugoslavia.

In January 1992 the Council of Foreign Ministers agreed that the Conference's rule of decision-making by consensus was to be altered to allow the CSO to take appropriate action against a participating state 'in cases of clear and gross violation of CSCE commitments'. This development was precipitated by the conflict in Yugoslavia, where the Yugoslav Government was held responsible by the majority of CSCE states for the continuation of hostilities. It was also agreed at the meeting that the CSCE should undertake fact-finding and conciliation missions to areas of tension, with the first such mission to be sent to Nagornyi Karabakh, the largely Armenian-populated enclave in Azerbaijan.

In March 1992 CSCE participating states reached agreement on a number of confidence-building measures, including commitments to exchange technical data on new weapons systems; to report activation of military units; and to prohibit military activity involving very large numbers of troops or tanks. Later in that month at a meeting of the Council of Foreign Ministers, which opened the Helsinki Follow-up Conference, the members of NATO and the former members of the Warsaw Pact (with Russia, Belarus, Ukraine and Georgia taking the place of the USSR) signed the Open Skies Treaty. Under the treaty, aerial reconnaissance missions by one country over another were permitted, subject to regulation. An Open Skies Consultative Commission was subsequently established (see above).

The summit meeting of heads of state and government that took place in Helsinki, Finland, in July 1992 adopted the Helsinki Document 1992, in which participating states defined the terms of future CSCE peace-keeping activities. Conforming broadly to UN practice, peace-keeping operations would be undertaken only with the full consent of the parties involved in any conflict and only if an effective cease-fire were in place. The CSCE may request the use of the military resources of NATO, the CIS, the EU, Western European Union (WEU) or other international bodies. (NATO and WEU had recently changed their Constitutions to permit the use of their forces for CSCE purposes.) The Helsinki Document declared the CSCE a 'regional arrangement' in the sense of Chapter VIII of the UN's Charter, which states that such a regional grouping should attempt to resolve a conflict in the region before referring it to the Security Council. In 1993 the First Implementation Meeting on Human Dimension Issues (the CSCE term used with regard to issues concerning human rights and welfare) took place. The Meeting, for which the ODIHR serves as a secretariat, provides a now annual forum for the exchange of news regarding OSCE commitments in the fields of human rights and democracy.

In December 1993 a Permanent Committee (now renamed the Permanent Council) was established in Vienna, providing for greater political consultation and dialogue through its weekly meetings. In December 1994 the summit conference redesignated the CSCE as the Organization for Security and Co-operation in Europe—OSCE and endorsed the role of the Organization as the primary instrument for early warning, conflict prevention and crisis management in the region. The conference adopted a 'Code of Conduct on Politico-Military Aspects of Security', which set out principles to guide the role of the armed forces in democratic societies. The summit conference that was held in Lisbon, Portugal, in December 1996 agreed to adapt the CFE Treaty, in order to further arms-reduction negotiations on a national and territorial basis. The conference also adopted the 'Lisbon Declaration on a Common and Comprehensive Security Model for Europe for the 21st Century', committing all parties to pursuing measures to ensure regional security. A Security Model Committee was established and began to meet regularly during 1997 to consider aspects of the Declaration, including the identification of risks and challenges to future European security; enhancing means of joint co-operative action within the OSCE framework in the event of non-compliance with OSCE commitments by participating states; considering other new arrangements within the OSCE framework that could reinforce security and stability in Europe; and defining a basis of co-operation between the OSCE and other relevant organizations to co-ordinate security enforcement. In November 1997 the Office of the Representative on Freedom of the Media was established in Vienna, to support the OSCE's activities in this field. In the same month a new position of Co-ordinator of OSCE Economic and Environmental Activities was created.

In November 1999 OSCE heads of state and of government, convened in İstanbul, Turkey, signed a new Charter for European Security, which aimed to formalize existing norms regarding the observance of human rights and to strengthen co-operation with other organizations and institutions concerned with international security. The Charter focused on measures to improve the operational capabilities of the OSCE in early warning, conflict prevention, crisis management and post-conflict rehabilitation. Accordingly, Rapid Expert Assistance and Co-operation (REACT) teams were to be established to enable the Organization to respond rapidly to requests from participating states for assistance in crisis situations. The REACT programme became operational in April 2001. At the İstanbul meeting a revised CFE Treaty was also signed, providing for a stricter system of limitations and increased transparency, which was to be open to other OSCE states not currently signatories. The US and EU governments determined to delay ratification of the Agreement of the Adaptation of the Treaty until Russian troop levels in the Caucasus had been reduced.

In April 2000 the OSCE High Commissioner on National Minorities issued a report reviewing the problems confronting Roma and Sinti populations in OSCE member states. In April 2001 the ODIHR launched a programme of assistance for the Roma communities of south-eastern Europe. The OSCE and UN Office for Drug Control and Crime Prevention (ODCCP) jointly organized a conference in October 2000, supported by the Governments of Kazakhstan, Kyrgyzstan, Tajikistan, Turkmenistan and Uzbekistan and attended by representatives of 67 states and 44 international organizations, which aimed to promote co-operation, democratization, security and stability in Central Asia and to address the threat of drugs-trafficking, organized crime and terrorism in the sub-region. In November an OSCE Document on Small Arms and Light Weapons was adopted, aimed at curtailing the spread of armaments in member states. A workshop on implementation of the Document was held in February 2002. In mid-November 2000 the Office of the Representative on Freedom of the Media organized a conference, staged in Dushanbe, Tajikistan, of journalists from Kazakhstan, Kyrgyzstan, Tajikistan and Uzbekistan. In February 2001 the ODIHR established an Anti-Trafficking Project Fund to help to finance its efforts to combat trafficking in human beings. In July the OSCE Parliamentary Assembly adopted a resolution concerned with strengthening transparency and accountability within the Organization.

In September 2001 the Secretary-General condemned the major terrorist attacks perpetrated against targets in the USA, allegedly by militant Islamist fundamentalists. In early October OSCE member states unanimously adopted a statement in support of the developing US-led global coalition against international terrorism. Meanwhile, the Organization determined to establish a working group on terrorism to draft an action plan on counter-terrorism measures. In December the Ministerial Council, meeting in Romania, approved the 'Bucharest Action Plan' outlining the Organization's contribution to countering terrorism. A Personal Representative for Terrorism was appointed by the CIO in January 2002 to co-ordinate the implementation of the initiatives. Later in December 2001 the OSCE sponsored, with the ODCCP, an International Conference on Security and Stability in Central Asia, held in Bishek, Kyrgyzstan. The meeting, which was attended by representatives of more than 60 countries and organizations, was concerned with strengthening efforts to counter terrorism and providing effective support to the Central Asian states. In October 2002 the ODIHR and the Government of Azerbaijan organized an international conference on religious freedom and combating terrorism. At a Ministerial Council meeting held in Porto, Portugal in December the OSCE issued a Charter on Preventing Terrorism, which condemned terrorism 'in all its forms and manifestations' and called upon member states to work together to counter, investigate and prosecute terrorist acts. The charter also acknowledged the links between terrorism, organized crime and trafficking in human beings. At the same time, a political declaration entitled 'Responding

to Change' was adopted, in which member states pledged their commitment to mutual co-operation in combating threats to security. At the OSCE's first Annual Security Review Conference, held in Vienna, in July 2003, a range of practical options for addressing the new threats and challenges to security were set out. These included the introduction of common security features on travel documentation, stricter controls on manual portable air defence systems, and the improvement of border security and policing methods. Security issues were also the subject of the Rotterdam Declaration, adopted by some 300 members of the Parliamentary Assembly in July, which stated that it was imperative for the OSCE to maintain a strong field presence and for field missions to be provided with sufficient funding and highly trained staff. It also recommended that the OSCE assume a role in unarmed peace-keeping operations.

During July 2003 the first OCSE conference on the effects of globalization was convened in Vienna, attended by some 200 representatives from international organizations. Participants called for the advancement of good governance in the public and private sectors, the development of democratic institutions, and the creation of conditions that would enable populations to benefit from the global economy.

OSCE MISSIONS AND FIELD ACTIVITIES IN CENTRAL AND SOUTH-EASTERN EUROPE

At mid-2003 there were long-term OSCE missions in Bosnia and Herzegovina, Croatia, Georgia, the former Yugoslav republic of Macedonia, Moldova, Tajikistan, Serbia and Montenegro, and Kosovo. The OSCE was also undertaking field activities in Albania, Armenia, Azerbaijan, Belarus, Kazakhstan, Kyrgyzstan, Turkmenistan, and Uzbekistan.

In March 1997 the OSCE dispatched a fact-finding mission to Albania to help restore political and civil stability, which had been undermined by the collapse of national pyramid saving schemes at the start of the year. An agreement was negotiated between Albania's President Sali Berisha and opposition parties to hold elections in mid-1997 and to establish a government of national reconciliation. At the end of March the Permanent Council agreed to establish an OSCE Presence in Albania, and confirmed that the organization should provide the framework for co-ordinating other international efforts in the country. OSCE efforts focused on reaching a political consensus on new legislation for the conduct of the forthcoming elections to establish a government of national reconciliation. Voting took place in June–July, with 500 OSCE observers providing technical electoral assistance and helping to monitor the voting. In December the Permanent Council confirmed that the Presence should provide the framework for co-ordinating other international efforts in the country. In March 1998 the OSCE Presence was mandated to monitor the country's borders with the Kosovan region of southern Serbia and to prevent any spillover effects from the escalating crisis. This role was reduced following the political settlement for Kosovo and Metohija concluded in mid-1999. In June 1998 the OSCE observed local elections in Albania. It became the Co-Chair, with the EU, of the Friends of Albania group, which then brought together countries and international bodies concerned with the situation in Albania for the first time in September. (The sixth annual meeting of the group was held in April 2002.) In October 1998 the Permanent Council determined to enhance the Presence's role in border-monitoring activities. With other organizations, the OSCE was involved in the preparation of the country's draft constitution, finalized in October, and an ODIHR Election Observation Mission was established to observe the referendum on the constitution held in November. The OSCE Presence in Albania has subsequently provided advice and support to the Albanian Government regarding democratization, the rule of law, the media, human rights, election preparation and monitoring, and the development of civil society. It supports an Economics and Environment Unit and an Elections Unit, which since the parliamentary elections of 2001 has facilitated the process of electoral reform. The Presence also monitors the Government's weapons collection programme. In October 2002 the Victims Assistance Team, a one-year project funded by the ODIHR and implemented in close co-operation with Albanian government ministries, was established to offer legal advice and other assistance to vicitms of human trafficking returning to Albania.

The OSCE Spillover Monitor Mission to Skopje was established in September 1992 to help to prevent the conflict in the former Yugoslavia from destabilizing the former Yugoslav republic of Macedonia (FYRM). Its principal mandate is to monitor the border region, as well as monitoring human rights and promoting the development of democratic institutions, including an independent media. The Mission is also concerned with mediating between inter-ethnic groups in the country, and has provided support for implementation of a framework political agreement signed in August 2001 through the deployment of international confidence-building monitors and police advisers. In December OSCE monitors accompanied multi-ethnic police officers to areas of early conflict, as part of the August agreement. In March 2002 OSCE signed its first memorandum of understanding with the European Commission, in respect of policing operations in FYRM. In September 2002 the OSCE was involved with monitoring the parliamentary elections in FYRM, which were judged to have been free and fair.

The OSCE Mission to Bosnia and Herzegovina was established in December 1995 to achieve the objectives of the peace accords for the former Yugoslavia, in particular to oversee the process of democratization. The OSCE's efforts to organize and oversee the Bosnian national elections, which were held in September 1996, was the largest-ever electoral operation undertaken by the organization, with some 1,200 electoral observers deployed. The OSCE subsequently monitored Bosnian municipal elections, held in September 1997, and the elections to the National Assembly of the Serb Republic and to the Bosnian Serb presidency in November. In 1998 the mission was charged with organizing the second post-war general elections in Bosnia and Herzegovina (comprising elections to the legislature of Bosnia and Herzegovina, the Federation and the Serb Republic, and to the presidencies of Bosnia and Herzegovina and the Serb Republic). The mission assisted with the registration of voters and, in September, was responsible for the supervision of the elections at polling stations within and outside the country. The final results of the election to the Bosnian Serb presidency were delayed, owing to the unexpected victory of an extreme nationalist, Nikola Poplasen, which, it was feared, could jeopardize the peace process. The OSCE immediately emphasized the necessity of maintaining the process. It also insisted on the need to transfer responsibility for the electoral process to the national authorities for future elections. In March 1999 the OSCE initiated an educational campaign relating to new election laws. However, a permanent electoral legal framework had not been approved by the time of legislative elections held in November 2000; the OSCE was therefore active in both preparing and monitoring these. The Mission's responsibility for elections in the country ended in November 2001 when a new permanent Election Commission was inaugurated. However, it was to continue to provide support for the Commission's secretariat. Other key areas of Mission activity are the promotion of democratic values, monitoring and promoting respect for human rights, strengthening the legal system, assisting with the creation of a modernized, non-discriminatory education system and establishing democratic control over the armed forces. An Agreement on Regional Arms Control was signed in 1995, providing for confidence- and security-building measures and a reduction in excess armaments. The Mission has established consultative commissions to promote dialogue among military personnel from different entities within the country. An audit of the entities' defence budgets was conducted in 2001. In late 2002 an OSCE-sponsored audit of several public enterprises and government ministries in Bosnia and Herzegovina was initiated. The results of the audits of three utility companies and of the Ministry of Social Policy, Displace Persons and Refugees were published in March 2003.

The OSCE Mission to Croatia was established in April 1996 to provide assistance and expertise in the field of human and minority rights, and to assist in the implementation of legislation and the development of democratic institutions. The Mission's mandate was extended in June 1997 in order to enhance its capacity to protect human rights, in particular the rights of minorities, to monitor the return and treatment of refugees and displaced persons, and to make specific recommendations to the Croatian authorities. In March 1998, following the integration of the disputed region into Croatia, the OSCE criticized the conditions imposed by the Croatian Government for the return of Serb refugees, stating that the right to return to one's own country was inalienable and must not depend on the fulfilment of conditions. The Mission conducts extensive field monitoring to facilitate the return of refugees and displaced persons. In October 1998 the Mission assumed the responsibilities of the United Nations Police Support Group. The OSCE Police Monitoring Group, comprising a maximum of 120 unarmed OSCE civilian police monitors, was deployed in the region, representing the Organization's first police-monitoring role. The Group was terminated in October 2000, although the OSCE was to continue to advise on and monitor police activities in Croatia. The OSCE was also to be responsible for maintaining the border regions, with particular concern for customs activities. The OSCE/ODIHR monitored legislative and presidential elections held in Croatia in January 2000. Local government elections were held in May 2001.

In mid-1998 the OSCE was involved in the mediation effort to resolve the conflict between the Serbian authorities and ethnic Albanian separatists in the formerly autonomous Serbian province of Kosovo and Metohija. In October, following months of diplomatic effort and the threat of NATO air-strikes, Yugoslav President Slobodan Milošević agreed to comply with UN Security Council Resolution 1199, which required an immediate cease-fire, Serbian troop withdrawals, the commencement of meaningful peace negotiations, and unrestricted access for humanitarian aid. Under a peace plan proposed by the US special envoy, Richard Holbrooke, President Milošević agreed to the formation of a 2,000-member OSCE Kosovo

Verification Mission (KVM) to monitor compliance, in addition to surveillance flights by unarmed NATO aircraft. The KVM was to patrol the region to ensure the withdrawal of Serbian military and police units, and to oversee the safe return of refugees and the non-harassment of ethnic Albanian inhabitants. It was also to monitor border control activities and accompany police units in Kosovo, when necessary, to assist them to perform their normal policing roles. The Mission's mandate was formally established on 25 October 1998 for a period of one year. Upon achievement of a political settlement defining the area's self-government, and its subsequent implementation, the KVM was to be responsible for supervising elections in Kosovo, assisting in the establishment of democratic institutions and developing a Kosovo police force. The long-term mission was accepted in return for the eventual removal of Yugoslavia's suspension from the OSCE. However, sporadic fighting continued in the province, and the monitoring force began unofficially to assume a peace-keeping role. In January 1999, following the KVM's denunciation of the killing of some 45 ethnic Albanians by Serbian security forces in the village of Racak, President Milošević ordered the head of the Mission, William Walker, to leave the region. This was later revoked. Meanwhile, OSCE monitors were forced to withdraw from Racak under fire from Serbian troops. An emergency meeting of the OSCE in Vienna agreed to maintain the KVM. However, on 19 March, following the failure of negotiations to resolve the crisis, the CIO decided to evacuate the 1,380 unarmed monitors, owing to the deteriorating security situation in Kosovo. Five days later NATO commenced an aerial offensive against Yugoslavia. In early April the CIO condemned the mass expulsion of ethnic Albanians from Kosovo and other violations of human rights committed by Serbian forces. Later in the same month the CIO, at a meeting of a ministerial troika attended by the Secretary-General, announced that the OSCE was willing to assist in the implementation of a political settlement in Kosovo. The OSCE was also concerned with measures to prevent the crisis affecting the other Balkan states. Within the framework of a political settlement for Kosovo, which was formally concluded in June, the OSCE (whose Mission in Kosovo, mandated to comprise 1,400 personnel, was established on 1 July) was responsible for democracy- and institution-building under the auspices of the UN Interim Administration Mission for Kosovo (UNMIK). OSCE monitors were deployed to assess the human rights situation throughout the region, and in August a new OSCE-administered police training school was inaugurated. (By the end of 2001 5,700 police officers had trained under the OSCE police education programme.) In December 1999 the OSCE published a report on the situation in Kosovo, which confirmed that Serbian forces had conducted systematic abuses of human rights but also raised suspicion against the KLA for organizing retribution attacks against Serbian civilians later in the year. In February 2000 the OSCE Mission established an Institute for Civil Administration to train public officials in principles of democratic governance. A Kosovo Law Centre was established in June, to provide technical assistance to the legal community, with a view to promoting democratic principles and human rights. In the following month the Department for Democratic Governance and Civil Society was established by UNMIK, and was to be administered by the OSCE. In August an Ombudsperson, nominated by the OSCE, was appointed to a new Office of the Ombudsperson, which became operational in November. The role of the Ombudsperson was to investigate and mediate claims of human rights violations arising within Kosovo. The OSCE was responsible for registering about 1m. voters prior to municipal elections that were held in Kosovo in October. During 2001 the Mission assisted the registration process for voting in a general election, and supervised the polling which took place in November. In early 2002 the Mission initiated training sessions for members of the new Kosovo Assembly. At that time the Mission was restructured, consolidating the number of field offices from 21 to nine. Further municipal elections were held in October and were declared free and fair by local and international observers. In 2003 the Mission was to effect the handover of electoral responsibilities to local institutions.

In November 2000 the Federal Republic of Yugoslavia (FRY, now Serbia and Montenegro) was admitted into the OSCE. In March 2001 an OSCE Mission to the FRY was inaugurated. This was to assist in the areas of democracy and protection of human rights and in the restructuring and training of law enforcement agencies and the judiciary, to provide advice to government authorities with regard to reform of the media, and, in close co-operation with the United Nations High Commissioner for Refugees, to facilitate the return of refugees to and from neighbouring countries as well as within the FRY. In March 2002 members of the Mission were facilitating the census process in southern Serbia. In June 2003 the Mission announced the launch of a border-policing project in an effort to reduce human trafficking and organized crime in Serbia and Montenegro.

In March 2000 the OSCE adopted a Regional Strategy for South-Eastern Europe, aimed at enhancing co-operation amongst its presences in the region. The OSCE was actively involved in co-ordinating the Stability Pact for South-Eastern Europe, which was initiated, in June 1999, as a collaborative plan of action by the EU, the Group of Seven industrialized nations and Russia (the G-8), regional governments and other organizations concerned with the stability of the region. (This can be accessed at www.stabilitypact.org.) A meeting of participants in the Pact was convened to coincide with the OSCE summit meeting, held in November. In October 2001 the OSCE organized a Stability Pact regional conference, held in Bucharest, Romania. A memorandum of understanding between the OSCE Mission to the FRY and the Stability Pact was signed in December.

Prague Office of the OSCE Secretariat: Ryt‡rská 31, 110 11 Prague 1, Czech Republic; tel. (2) 21610217; fax (2) 21610227; e-mail quest@osceprag.cz.

OSCE Presence in Albania: Rruga Donika Kastrioti 6, Tirana; tel. (42) 35993; fax (42) 35994; e-mail post.albania@osce.org; Head of Presence OSMO LIPPONEN.

OSCE Mission to Bosnia and Herzegovina: 71000 Sarajevo, Fra Andjela Zvizdovica 1; tel. (33) 752100; fax (33) 752289; e-mail info@oscebih.org; Head of Mission ROBERT MASON BEECROFT.

OSCE Mission to Croatia: 10000 Zagreb, Florijana Andrašeca 14; tel. (1) 3096620; fax (1) 3096621; e-mail osce-croatia@oscecro.org; Head of Mission PETER SEMNEBY.

OSCE Mission in Kosovo: 38000 Priština, Beogradska 32; tel. (38) 500162; fax (38) 500188; e-mail press@omik.org; Head of Mission PASCAL FIESCHI.

OSCE Mission to the former Yugoslav Republic of Macedonia: 91000 Skopje, Marshal Tito 9-2, Makosped Building; tel. (2) 111143; fax (2) 111267; e-mail oscemsk@unet.com.mk; Head of Mission CRAIG JENNESS.

OSCE Mission to Serbia and Montenegro: 11000 Belgrade, Cakorska 1; tel. (11) 3606149; fax (11) 3672429; e-mail osce-portparol@omifry.org; Head of Mission MAURIZIO MASSARI.

Finance

All activities of the institutions, negotiations, *ad hoc* meetings and missions are financed by contributions from member states. The budget for 2003 amounted to €185.7m., of which some 84% was allocated to OSCE missions and field activities.

Publications

Annual Report of the Secretary-General.
The Caucasus: In Defence of the Future.
Decision Manual (annually).
OSCE Handbook (annually).
OSCE Newsletter (monthly).

ORGANIZATION OF THE BLACK SEA ECONOMIC CO-OPERATION—BSEC

Address: İstinye Cad. Müşir Fuad Paşa Yalısı, Eski Tersane 80860 İstinye-İstanbul, Turkey.

Telephone: (212) 229-63-30; **fax:** (212) 229-63-36; **e-mail:** bsec@turk.net; **internet:** www.bsec.gov.tr.

The Black Sea Economic Co-operation (BSEC) was established in 1992 to strengthen regional co-operation, particularly in the field of economic development. In June 1998, at a summit meeting held in Yalta, Ukraine, participating countries signed the BSEC Charter, thereby officially elevating BSEC to regional organization status. The Charter entered into force on 1 May 1999, at which time BSEC formally became the Organization of the Black Sea Economic Co-operation, retaining the same acronym.

MEMBERS

Albania	Georgia	Russia
Armenia	Greece	Turkey
Azerbaijan	Moldova	Ukraine
Bulgaria	Romania	

Note: Observer status has been granted to Egypt, France, Germany, Israel, Italy, Poland, Slovakia and Tunisia. The BSEC Business Council, International Black Sea Club, and the Energy Charter Conference also have observer status. Iran, the former Yugoslav republic of Macedonia, Serbia and Montenegro and Uzbekistan have applied for full membership.

Organization

(July 2003)

PRESIDENTIAL SUMMIT

The Presidential Summit, comprising heads of state or government of member states, represents the highest authority of the body.

COUNCIL

The Council of Ministers of Foreign Affairs is BSEC's principal decision-making organ. Ministers meet twice a year to review progress and to define new objectives. Chairmanship of the Council rotates among members; the Chairman-in-Office co-ordinates the activities undertaken by BSEC. The Council is supported by a Committee of Senior Officials.

PARLIAMENTARY ASSEMBLY

Address: 1 Hareket Kösku, Dolmabahçe Sarayi, Besiktas, 80680 İstanbul, Turkey.

Telephone: (212) 227-6070; **fax:** (212) 227-6080; **e-mail:** vdeiv@pabsec.org; **internet:** www.pabsec.org.

The Parliamentary Assembly, consisting of the representatives of the national parliaments of member states, was created in February 1993 to provide a legal basis for the implementation of decisions within the BSEC framework. It comprises three committees concerning economic, commercial, technological and environmental affairs; legal and political affairs; and cultural, educational and social affairs.

PERMANENT INTERNATIONAL SECRETARIAT

The Secretariat commenced operations in March 1994. Its tasks are, primarily, of an administrative and technical nature, and include the maintenance of archives, and the preparation and distribution of documentation. Much of the organization's activities are undertaken by 15 working groups, each headed by an Executive Manager, and by various *ad hoc* groups and meetings of experts.

Secretary-General: VALERI CHECHELASHVILI (Georgia).

Activities

In June 1992, at a summit meeting held in İstanbul, heads of state and of government signed the summit declaration on BSEC, and adopted the Bosphorus statement, which established a regional structure for economic co-operation. The grouping attained regional organization status in May 1999 (see above). The Organization's main areas of co-operation include transport; communications; trade and economic development; banking and finance; energy; tourism; agriculture and agro-industry; health care and pharmaceuticals; environmental protection; science and technology; the exchange of statistical data and economic information; collaboration between customs authorities; and combating organized crime, drugs-trafficking, trade in illegal weapons and radioactive materials, and terrorism. In order to promote regional co-operation, the organization also aims to strengthen the business environment by providing support for small and medium-sized enterprises; facilitating closer contacts between businesses in member countries; progressively eliminating obstacles to the expansion of trade; creating appropriate conditions for investment and industrial co-operation, in particular through the avoidance of double taxation and the promotion and protection of investments; encouraging the dissemination of information concerning international tenders organized by member states; and promoting economic co-operation in free-trade zones.

In recent years BSEC has undergone a process of reform aimed at developing a more project-based orientation. In April 2001 the Council adopted the so-called BSEC Economic Agenda for the Future Towards a More Consolidated, Effective and Viable BSEC Partnership, which provided a roadmap for charting the implementation of the Organization's goals. In 2002 a project development fund was established and a regional programme of governance and institutional renewal was launched. Under the new orientation the roles of BSEC's Committee of Senior Officials and network of country-co-ordinators were to be enhanced.

BSEC aims to foster relations with other international and regional organizations, and has been granted observer status at the UN General Assembly. In 1999 BSEC agreed upon a Platform of Co-operation for future structured relations with the European Union. The main areas in which BSEC determined to develop co-operation with the EU were transport, energy and telecommunications infrastructure; trade and the promotion of foreign direct investment; sustainable development and environmental protection, including nuclear safety; science and technology; and combating terrorism and organized crime. BSEC supports the Stability Pact for South-Eastern Europe, initiated in June 1999 as a collaborative plan of action by the EU, the Group of Seven industrialized nations and Russia (the G-8), regional governments and other organizations concerned with the stability of the region. The Declaration issued by

BSEC's decennial anniversary summit, held in Istanbul in June 2002, urged that collaboration with the EU should be enhanced.

A BSEC Business Council was established in Istanbul in December 1992 by the business communities of member states. It has observer status at the BSEC, and aims to identify private and public investment projects, maintain business contacts and develop programmes in various sectors. A Black Sea Trade and Development Bank has been established, in Thessaloníki, Greece, as the organization's main funding institution, to finance and implement joint regional projects. It began operations on 1 July 1999. The European Bank for Reconstruction and Development (EBRD) was entrusted as the depository for all capital payments made prior to its establishment. A BSEC Co-ordination Centre, located in Ankara, Turkey, aims to promote the exchange of statistical and economic information. In September 1998 a Black Sea International Studies Centre was inaugurated in Athens, Greece, in order to undertake research concerning the BSEC, in the fields of economics, industry and technology. The transport ministers of BSEC member states adopted a Transport Action Plan in March 2001, which envisaged reducing the disparities in regional transport systems and integrating the BSEC regional transport infrastructure with wider international networks and projects.

BSEC has supported implementation of the Bucharest Convention on the Protection of the Black Sea Against Pollution, adopted by Bulgaria, Georgia, Romania, Russia, Turkey and Ukraine in April 1992. In October 1996 those countries adopted the Strategic Action Plan for the Rehabilitation and Protection of the Black Sea (BSSAP), to be implemented by the Commission of the Bucharest Convention.

WESTERN EUROPEAN UNION—WEU

Address: 15 rue de l'Association, 1000 Brussels, Belgium.

Telephone: (2) 500-44-50; **fax:** (2) 500-44-70; **e-mail:** ueo .secretarygeneral@skynet.be; **internet:** www.weu.int.

Based on the Brussels Treaty of 1948, the Western European Union (WEU) was set up in 1955 as an intergovernmental organization for European co-operation in the field of security and defence. In the 1990s WEU was developed as the defence component of the European Union—EU, and as the means of strengthening the European pillar of the Atlantic Alliance under NATO. However, in June 1999 the European Council resolved to formulate a common European security and defence policy, incorporating the main crisis management responsibilities of WEU. Consequently, WEU relinquished these functions to the EU by July 2001.

MEMBERS*

Belgium	Luxembourg
France	Netherlands
Germany	Portugal
Greece	Spain
Italy	United Kingdom

* WEU has invited the other members of the EU to join the organization and has invited other European members of NATO to become Associate Members to enable them to participate fully in WEU activities. In November 1992 Denmark and Ireland took up observer status and on 1 January 1995 Austria, Finland and Sweden became Observers following their accession to the EU. Associate Member status was granted to Iceland, Norway and Turkey in November 1992. Associate Partner status was granted to Bulgaria, the Czech Republic, Estonia, Hungary, Latvia, Lithuania, Poland, Romania and Slovakia in May 1994 and to Slovenia in June 1996. The Czech Republic, Hungary and Poland became Associate Partners in March 1999.

Organization

(July 2003)

COUNCIL

The Council is the WEU's main body, responsible for addressing all security and defence matters within WEU's remit. It is organized so as to be able to function on a permanent basis and may be convened at any time at the request of a member state. The Permanent Council, chaired by the WEU Secretary-General, is the central body responsible for day-to-day management of the organization and for assigning tasks to and co-ordinating the activities of the various working groups. It is composed of permanent representatives, sup-

ported by military delegates, and meets as often as required. The presidency of the Council is rotated between member states on a six-monthly basis.

SECRETARIAT-GENERAL

Secretary-General: Dr JAVIER SOLANA MADARIAGA (Spain).

WEU's Secretariat also headquarters the secretariats of the Western European Armaments Group (WEAG), a forum for armaments co-operation, and the Western European Armaments Organization (WEAO), which operates as a research cell.

Activities

The Brussels Treaty was signed in 1948 by Belgium, France, Luxembourg, the Netherlands and the United Kingdom. It foresaw the potential for international co-operation in Western Europe and provided for collective defence and collaboration in economic, social and cultural activities. Within this framework, NATO and the Council of Europe (see chapters) were formed in 1949.

On the collapse in 1954 of plans for a European Defence Community, a nine-power conference was convened in London to try to reach a new agreement. This conference's decisions were embodied in a series of formal agreements drawn up by a ministerial conference held in Paris in October. The agreements entailed: arrangements for the Brussels Treaty to be strengthened and modified to include the Federal Republic of Germany and Italy, the ending of the occupation regime in the Federal Republic of Germany, and the invitation to the latter to join NATO. These agreements were ratified on 6 May 1955, on which date the seven-power Western European Union came into being. WEU was reactivated in October 1984 by restructuring its organization and by holding more frequent ministerial meetings, in order to harmonize members' views on defence questions, arms control and disarmament, developments in East-West relations, Europe's contribution to the Atlantic alliance, and European armaments co-operation.

In April 1990 ministers of foreign affairs and defence discussed the implications of recent political changes in central and eastern Europe, and mandated WEU to develop contacts with democratically elected governments there. In June 1992 an extraordinary meeting of WEU's Ministerial Council with the ministers of defence and foreign affairs of Hungary, Czechoslovakia, Poland, Romania, Bulgaria, Estonia, Latvia and Lithuania agreed on measures to enhance co-operation. The ministers were to meet annually, while a forum of consultation was to be established between the WEU Council and the ambassadors of the countries concerned, which was to meet at least twice a year. The focus of consultations was to be the security structure and political stability of Europe; the future development of the CSCE (now the OSCE); and arms control and disarmament, in particular the implementation of the Treaty on Conventional Armed Forces in Europe (the CFE Treaty) and the 'Open Skies' Treaty (see NATO for both). In May 1994 the Council of Ministers, meeting in Luxembourg, issued the Kirchberg Declaration, according the nine countries concerned (including the Czech Republic and Slovakia, which were the legal successors to Czechoslovakia) the status of Associate Partners of WEU, thereby suspending the forum of consultation.

The EC Treaty on European Union, which was agreed at Maastricht, in the Netherlands, in December 1991, and entered into force on 1 November 1993, referred to WEU as an 'integral part of the development of European Union' and requested WEU 'to elaborate and implement decisions and actions of the Union which have defence implications'. The Treaty also committed EU member countries to the 'eventual framing of a common defence policy which might in time lead to a common defence'. A separate declaration, adopted by WEU member states in Maastricht, defined WEU's role as being the defence component of the European Union but also as the instrument for strengthening the European pillar of the Atlantic Alliance, thus maintaining a role for NATO in Europe's defence and retaining WEU's identity as distinct from that of the EU. In January 1993 WEU's Council and Secretariat-General moved to Brussels (from Paris and London, respectively), in order to promote closer co-operation with both the EU and NATO, which have their headquarters there.

In June 1992 WEU ministers of defence and foreign affairs convened in Petersberg, Germany, to consider the implementation of the Maastricht decisions. In the resulting 'Petersberg Declaration' member states declared that they were prepared to make available military units from the whole spectrum of their conventional armed forces for military tasks conducted under the authority of WEU. In addition to contributing to the common defence in accordance with Article V of the modified Brussels Treaty, three categories of missions were identified for the possible employment of military units under the aegis of WEU: humanitarian and rescue tasks; peace-keeping tasks; and crisis management, including peace-making. (Missions of this kind are often described as 'Petersberg tasks'.) The Petersberg Declaration stated that the WEU was prepared to support peace-keeping activities of the CSCE and UN Security Council on a case-by-case basis. A WEU planning cell was established in Brussels in October, which was to be responsible for preparing contingency plans for the employment of forces under WEU auspices for humanitarian operations, peace-keeping and crisis-management activities. It was expected that the same military units identified by member states for deployment under NATO would be used for military operations under WEU: this arrangement was referred to as 'double-hatting'. In May 1995 WEU ministers, convened in Lisbon, Portugal, agreed to strengthen WEU's operational capabilities through new structures and mechanisms, including the establishment of a politico-military group to advise on crises and crisis management, a Situation Centre able to monitor WEU operations and support decisions taken by the Council, and an Intelligence Section within the planning cell. WEU rules of engagement, with a view to implementing the missions identified in the Petersberg Declaration, were to be formulated.

In January 1994 NATO heads of state gave their full support to the development of a European Security and Defence Identity (ESDI) and to the strengthening of WEU. They declared their readiness to make collective assets of the Alliance available for WEU operations, and endorsed the concept of Combined Joint Task Forces (CJTFs), which was to provide separable, but not separate, military capabilities that could be employed by either organization. In May 1996 NATO and WEU signed a security agreement, which provided for the protection and shared use of classified information. In June NATO ministers, meeting in Berlin, Germany, agreed on a framework of measures to enable the implementation of the CJTF concept and the development of an ESDI within the Alliance. WEU was to be permitted to request the use of a CJTF headquarters for an operation under its command and to use Alliance planning capabilities and military infrastructure. In May 1998 the Council of both organizations approved a set of consultation arrangements as a guide to co-operation in a crisis situation. A framework document on principles and guide-lines for detailed practicalities of cases where NATO assets and/or capabilities were loaned to WEU was subsequently prepared.

In November 1994 a WEU ministerial meeting in Noordwijk, the Netherlands, adopted a set of preliminary conclusions on the formulation of a common European defence policy. The role and place of WEU in further European institutional arrangements were addressed by the EU's Intergovernmental Conference, which commenced in March 1996. The process was concluded in June 1997 with agreement having been reached on the Treaty of Amsterdam. The Treaty, which was signed in October and entered into force on 1 May 1999, confirmed WEU as providing the EU with access to operational capability for undertaking the Petersberg tasks, which were incorporated into the revised Treaty. It advocated enhanced EU-WEU co-operation and referred to the possible integration of the WEU into the EU, should the European Council so decide (the United Kingdom being the main opponent). Following the entry into force of the Treaty of Amsterdam WEU and the EU approved a set of arrangements for enhanced co-operation. In June the EU determined to strengthen its common security and defence policy, and initiated a process of assuming direct responsibility for the Petersberg tasks. Javier Solana was appointed as the EU's first High Representative for foreign and security policy, and subsequently named as the new WEU Secretary-General, providing for the highest level of co-operation between the two organizations. In November WEU ministers adopted a series of recommendations, based on the results of an audit of assets, to enable European countries to respond rapidly to conduct crisis management operations, to enhance collective capabilities in strategic intelligence and planning, and to strengthen military air, sea and transport equipment and capabilities for use in humanitarian and peace-keeping operations. By July 2001 the transfer of WEU's crisis management functions to the EU had been finalized, leaving commitments relating to collective defence as WEU's key focus area. The EU assumed responsibility for two former subsidiary bodies of the WEU (a Satellite Centre and the Paris-based Institute for Strategic Studies) in January 2002. The remaining functions of the restructured WEU related to the provision of military and other aid and assistance should a member state become the object of an armed attack in Europe, as provided for under the Brussels Treaty; institutional dialogue within the Assembly, support to the Western European Armaments Group and the Western European Armaments Organization, and other administrative tasks.

In the early 1990s WEU's operational capabilities were substantially developed. From mid-July 1992 warships and aircraft of WEU members undertook a monitoring operation in the Adriatic Sea, in co-ordination with NATO, to ensure compliance with the UN Security Council's resolutions imposing a trade and armaments embargo on Serbia and Montenegro. In mid-November the UN Security Council gave the NATO/WEU operation the power to search vessels suspected of attempting to flout the embargo. In June 1993 the Councils of WEU and NATO agreed to establish a unified command for the operation, which was to implement a Security Council resolution to strengthen the embargo against Serbia and Montenegro. Under the agreement, the Councils were to exert joint political control, and military instructions were to be co-ordinated within a joint *ad hoc* headquarters. In April WEU ministers offered civil assistance to Bulgaria, Hungary and Romania in enforcing the UN embargo on the Danube, and a monitoring mission began operations in June. In June 1996 the NATO/WEU naval monitoring mission in the Adriatic Sea was suspended, following the decision of the UN Security Council to remove the embargo on the delivery of armaments to the former Yugoslavia. WEU provided assistance for the administration of Mostar, Bosnia and Herzegovina, for which the EU assumed responsibility in July 1994.

In May 1997 WEU dispatched a Multinational Advisory Police Element (MAPE) to Albania to provide training and advice on restructuring the police force in that country. By the end of 1999 a new State Police Law, formulated with MAPE's support, had been ratified by the Albanian legislature, while some 3,000 police officers had been trained at centres in Tirana and Dürres and through field programmes. In February the WEU Council approved plans for an enhanced MAPE, with greater geographical coverage and operational mobility, with an initial mandate until April 2000. MAPE was being conducted by WEU at the request of the EU, enabling a large part of the costs to be met from the EU budget. In response to the escalation of conflict in the Serbian province of Kosovo and Metohija in 1999, MAPE assisted the Albanian authorities to establish an Emergency Crisis Group to help to administer and to assist the massive refugee population which entered Albania in March and April. MAPE terminated its operational activities in Albania on 31 May 2001.

In April 1999 WEU and Croatia signed an agreement to establish a WEU De-mining Assistance Mission (WEUDAM) in that country, upon a request by the Council of the EU. WEUDAM, which commenced activities in May, provided advice, technical expertise and training to the Croatian Mine Action Centre. WEUDAM was terminated on 31 November 2001.

Publications

Account of the Session (WEU Assembly, 2 a year).

Annual Report of the Council.

Assembly of Western European Union: Texts adopted and Brief Account of the Session (2 a year).

Assembly documents and reports.

WORLD TRADE ORGANIZATION—WTO

Address: Centre William Rappard, rue de Lausanne 154, 1211 Geneva, Switzerland.
Telephone: (22) 7395111; **fax:** (22) 7314206; **e-mail:** enquiries@wto.org; **internet:** www.wto.org.

The WTO is the legal and institutional foundation of the multilateral trading system. It was established on 1 January 1995, as the successor to the General Agreement on Tariffs and Trade (GATT).

MEMBERS

In mid-2002 WTO had 144 members; a further 27 governments had requested to join the WTO, and their applications were under consideration by accession working parties.

MEMBERS IN CENTRAL AND SOUTH-EASTERN EUROPE

Albania
Bulgaria
Croatia
Czech Republic
Estonia
Greece
Hungary
Latvia
Lithuania
Poland
Romania
Slovakia
Slovenia

Organization

(July 2003)

MINISTERIAL CONFERENCE

The Ministerial Conference is the highest authority of the WTO. It is composed of representatives of all WTO members at ministerial level, and may take decisions on all matters under any of the multilateral trade agreements. The Conference is required to meet at least every two years. The fourth Conference was held in Doha, Qatar, in November 2001; the fifth Conference was scheduled to be convened in Mexico in September 2003.

GENERAL COUNCIL

The General Council, which is also composed of representatives of all WTO members, is required to report to the Ministerial Conference and conducts much of the day-to-day work of the WTO. The Council convenes as the Dispute Settlement Body, to oversee the trade dispute settlement procedures, and as the Trade Policy Review Body, to conduct regular reviews of the trade policies of WTO members. The Council delegates responsibility to three other major Councils: for trade-related aspects of intellectual property rights, for trade in goods and for trade in services.

TRADE NEGOTIATIONS COMMITTEE

The Committee was established in November 2001 by the Declaration of the fourth Ministerial Conference, held in Doha, Qatar, to supervise the agreed agenda of trade negotiations. It was to operate under the authority of the General Council and was mandated to establish negotiating mechanisms and subsidiary bodies for each subject under consideration. A structure of negotiating groups and a declaration of principles and practices for the negotiations were formulated by the Committee in February 2002

SECRETARIAT

The WTO Secretariat comprises some 550 staff. Its responsibilities include the servicing of WTO delegate bodies, with respect to negotiations and the implementation of agreements, undertaking accession negotiations for new members and providing technical support and expertise to developing countries. In July 1999 member states reached a compromise agreement on the appointment of a new Director-General, having postponed the decision several times after failing to achieve the required consensus. Two candidates were appointed to serve consecutive three-year terms-in-office. In December 2001 the Director-General announced that the Secretariat was to be reorganized, in order to provide greater support to developing countries.

In June 2001 a WTO Training Institute was established, at the Secretariat, to extend the provision of training activities previously undertaken. Courses were to be held on trade policy, WTO dispute settlement rules and procedures, and other specialized topics; other programmes included training-of-trainers programmes and distance-learning services.

Director-General: SUPACHAI PANITCHPAKDI (Thailand).
Deputy Directors-General: RODERICK ABBOT (United Kingdom), KIPKORIR ALY AZAD RANA (Kenya), FRANCISCO THOMPSON-FLORES (Brazil), RUFUS YERXA (USA).

Activities

The Final Act of the Uruguay Round of GATT multilateral trade negotiations, which were concluded in December 1993, provided for extensive trade liberalization measures and for the establishment of a permanent structure to oversee international trading procedures. The Final Act was signed in April 1994, in Marrakesh, Morocco. At the same time a separate accord, the Marrakesh Declaration, was signed by the majority of GATT contracting states, endorsing the establishment of the WTO. The essential functions of the WTO are: to administer and facilitate the implementation of the results of the Uruguay Round; to provide a forum for multilateral trade negotiations; to administer the trade dispute settlement procedures; to review national trade policies; and to co-operate with other international institutions, in particular the IMF and World Bank, in order to achieve greater coherence in global economic policy-making.

The WTO Agreement contains some 29 individual legal texts and more than 25 additional Ministerial declarations, decisions and understandings, which cover obligations and commitments for member states. All these instruments are based on a few fundamental principles, which form the basis of the WTO Agreement. An integral part of the Agreement is 'GATT 1994', an amended and updated version of the original GATT Agreement of 1947, which was formally concluded at the end of 1995. Under the 'most-favoured nation' (MFN) clause, members are bound to grant to each other's products treatment no less favourable than that accorded to the products of any third parties. A number of exceptions apply, principally for customs unions and free-trade areas and for measures in favour of and among developing countries. The principle of 'national treatment' requires goods, having entered a market, to be treated no less favourably than the equivalent domestically-produced goods. Secure and predictable market access, to encourage trade, investment and job creation, may be determined by 'binding' tariffs, or customs duties. Other WTO agreements also contribute to predictable trading conditions by demanding commitments from member countries and greater transparency of domestic laws and national trade policies. By permitting tariffs, whilst adhering to the guidelines of being non-discriminatory, the WTO aims to promote open, fair and undistorted competition.

The WTO aims to encourage development and economic reform among the increasing number of developing countries and countries with economies in transition participating in the international trading system. These countries, particularly the least-developed states, have been granted transition periods and greater flexibility to implement certain WTO provisions. Industrial member countries are encouraged to assist developing nations by their trading conditions and by not expecting reciprocity in trade concession negotiations. In addition, the WTO operates a limited number of technical assistance programmes, mostly relating to training and the provision of information technology. The final declaration issued from the Ministerial Conference in December 1996 incorporated a text on the contentious issue of core labour standards, although it was emphasized that the relationship between trade and labour standards was not part of the WTO agenda.

The WTO Agreement recognized the need to protect the environment and to promote sustainable development. A new Committee on Trade and Environment was established to identify the relationship between trade policies, environmental measures and sustainable development and to recommend any appropriate modifications of the multilateral trading provisions.

In late November 1999 the third Ministerial Conference, which was held in Seattle, USA, was severely disrupted by public demonstrations by a diverse range of interest groups concerned with the impact of WTO accords on the environment, workers' rights and developing countries. In addition, ongoing differences between member states with regard to a formal agenda failed to be resolved during extensive negotiations, and the Conference was suspended. In May 2000 the Council resolved to initiate a series of Special Sessions to consider implementation of existing trade agreements, and approved more flexible provisions for implementation of the agreement on Trade-Related Aspects of Intellectual Property Rights (TRIPS), as part of ongoing efforts to address the needs of developing member states and strengthen their confidence in the multilateral trading system. The fourth Ministerial Conference, held in Doha, Qatar, in November 2001, adopted a final declaration providing a mandate for a three-year agenda for negotiations on a range of subjects, commencing 1 January 2002. A new Trade Negotiations Committee was established to supervise the process, referred to as the Doha Development Round, which was scheduled to be concluded within three years. Several aspects of existing agreements were to be negotiated, while new issues included WTO rules, such as subsidies, regional trade agreements and anti-dumping measures, and market access. With regard to agriculture a compromise agreement was reached with the EU to commit to a reduction in export subsidies, with a view to phasing them out (without a firm deadline for their elimination). Member states agreed to aim for further reductions in market access restrictions and domestic support mechanisms, and to incorporate non-trade concerns, including environmental protection, food security and rural development, into the negotiations. The Conference approved a separate decision on implementation-related issues and concerns, to address the concerns of developing countries in meeting their WTO commitments. Specific reference was made in the Declaration to providing greater technical co-operation and capacity-building assistance to WTO developing country members. On assuming office in September 2002 the new WTO Director-General, Supachai Panitchpakdi, announced that the ongoing trade negotiations should be brought to a swift conclusion, and that this goal would be supported by the strengthening of the following four pillars of the Organization: beneficial use of the legal framework binding together the multilateral system; technical and capacity-building assistance to least-developed and developing countries; greater coherence in international economic policy-making; and the WTO's functioning as an institution.

SETTLEMENT OF DISPUTES

A separate annex to the WTO agreement determines a unified set of rules and procedures to govern the settlement of all WTO disputes, substantially reinforcing the GATT procedures. WTO members are committed not to undertake unilateral action against perceived violations of the trade rules, but to seek recourse in the dispute settlement mechanism and abide by its findings. The principal elements of the dispute procedure are the Dispute Settlement Body, dispute panels, and a seven-member Appellate Body.

The Doha Declaration, which was adopted in November 2001, mandated further negotiations to be conducted on a review of the WTO's understanding on dispute settlement, and on additional proposals to amending the dispute procedure. Negotiations were to be concluded by May 2003.

International Trade Centre UNCTAD/WTO: Palais des Nations, 1211 Geneva 10, Switzerland; tel. (22) 7300111; fax (22) 7334439; e-mail itcreg@intracen.org; internet www.intracen.org.

The ITC was founded by GATT in 1964, and has been jointly operated with the UN (through UNCTAD) since 1968. It works with developing countries in product and market development, the development of trade support services, trade information, human resource development, international purchasing and supply management, and needs assessment and programme design for trade promotion. Publs *International Trade Forum* (quarterly), market studies, handbooks, etc.

Executive Director: J. DENIS BÉLISLE.

Finance

The WTO's 2003 budget amounted to 155m. Swiss francs, financed mainly by contributions from members in proportion to their share of total trading conducted by WTO members.

Publications

Annual Report (2 volumes).
International Trade Statistics (annually).
World Trade Review (3 a year).
WTO Focus (monthly).

OTHER REGIONAL ORGANIZATIONS

Agriculture, Food, Forestry and Fisheries

(For organizations concerned with agricultural commodities, see Commodities)

European and Mediterranean Plant Protection Organization—EPPO: 1 rue Le Nôtre, 75016 Paris, France; tel. 1-45-20-77-94; fax 1-42-24-89-43; e-mail hq@eppo.fr; internet www.eppo.org; f. 1951, present name adopted in 1955; aims to promote international co-operation between government plant protection services to prevent the introduction and spread of pests and diseases of plants and plant products; mems: governments of 44 countries and territories; Chair. OLIVER FÉLIX; Dir-Gen. Dr IAN M. SMITH; publs *EPPO Bulletin, Data Sheets on Quarantine Organisms, Guidelines for the Efficacy Evaluation of Pesticides, Crop Growth Stage Keys, Summary of the Phytosanitary Regulations of EPPO Member Countries, Reporting Service.*

European Association for Animal Production—EAAP (Fédération européenne de zootechnie): Via Nomentana 134A, 00162 Rome, Italy; tel. (06) 86329141 ; fax (06) 86329263; e-mail eaap@eaap.org; internet www.eaap.org; f. 1949 to help improve the conditions of animal production and meet consumer demand; holds annual meetings; mems: asscns in 37 countries; Pres. A. AUMAITRE (France); publ. *Livestock Production Science* (16 a year).

European Confederation of Agriculture—CEA: 23 rue de la Science, bte 23, 1040 Brussels, Belgium; tel. (2) 230-43-80; fax (2) 230-46-77; e-mail cea@pophost.eunet.be; f. 1889 as International Confederation, re-formed in 1948 as European Confederation; represents the interests of European agriculture in the international field; provides social security for independent farmers and foresters in the member countries; mems: 300 mems. in 30 countries; Pres. BEN GILL (UK); Gen. Sec. CHRISTOPHE HÉMARD (France); publs *CEA Dialog, Annual Report.*

European Livestock and Meat Trading Union—UECBV: 81A rue de la Loi, 1040 Brussels, Belgium; tel. (2) 230-46-03; fax (2) 230-94-00; e-mail uecbv@pophost.eunet.be; internet uecbv.eunet.be; f. 1952 to study problems of the European livestock and meat trade and inform members of all relevant legislation; acts as an international arbitration commission; conducts research on agricultural markets, quality of livestock, and veterinary regulations; mems: national organizations in 23 countries, and the European Association of Livestock Markets; Pres. LAURENT SPANGHERO; Sec.-Gen. JEAN-LUC MERIAUX.

International Baltic Sea Fishery Commission: 00-528 Warsaw, 20 Hozastr., Poland; tel. (22) 6288647; fax (22) 6253372; e-mail ibsfc@polbox.pl; internet www.ibsfc.org; f. 1973 by the Convention on Fishing and Conservation of the Living Resources in the Baltic Sea and the Belts (the Gdansk Convention) to protect the living marine resources of the Baltic Sea and to make rational use of such resources; Mems: Estonia, the EU, Latvia, Lithuania, Poland and the Russian Federation; several international organizations have observer status; Chair. L. VAARJA (Estonia).

International Dairy Federation—IDF: Diamant Bldg, 80 blvd Auguste Reyers, 1030 Brussels, Belgium; tel. (2) 733-98-88; fax (2) 733-04-13; e-mail info@fil-idf.org; internet www.fil-idf.org; f. 1903 to link all dairy asscns, in order to encourage the solution of scientific, technical and economic problems affecting the dairy industry; mems: national cttees in 41 countries; Dir-Gen. EDWARD HOPKIN (UK); publs *Bulletin of IDF, IDF Standards.*

International Hop Growers' Convention: c/o Inštitut za hmeljarstvo in pivovarstvo, POB 51, 3310 Žalec, Slovenia; tel. (63) 712-16-18; fax (63) 712-16-20; e-mail martin.pavlovic@uni-lj.si; internet www.hmelj-giz.si/ihgc; f. 1950; acts as a centre for the collection of data and reports on hop production, beer exports and imports and sales, estimates the world crop and promotes scientific research; mems: national asscns in 19 countries; Pres. MARTIN JOLLY (UK); Gen. Sec. Dr MARTIN PAVLOVIČ.

International Sericultural Commission—ISC: 25 quai Jean-Jacques Rousseau, 69350 La Mulatière, France; tel. 4-78-50-41-98; fax 4-78-86-09-57; f. 1948 to encourage the development of silk production; mems: governments of Brazil, Egypt, France, India, Indonesia, Iran, Japan, Lebanon, Madagascar, Romania, Thailand, Tunisia, Turkey; Sec.-Gen. Dr GÉRARD CHAVANCY (France); publ. *Sericologia* (quarterly).

World Ploughing Organization—WPO: Søkildevej 17, 5270 Odense N, Denmark; tel. 65-97-80-06; fax 65-93-24-40; internet www.worldploughing.org; f. 1952 to promote the World Ploughing Contest in a different country each year, to improve techniques and promote better understanding of soil cultivation practices through research and practical demonstrations; arranges tillage clinics world-wide; mems: affiliates in 29 countries; Gen. Sec. CARL ALLESO; publ. *WPO Handbook* (annually).

Arts and Culture

Baltic Music Network: Willemoesgade 52.3, 2100 Copenhagen Ø, Denmark; tel. 35-26-49-07; fax 33-93-44-13; internet www.sjoki.uta .fi/&ub.nft;latvis/TBMN; f. 1991 to encourage the international exchange of culture, particularly music, in the Baltic Sea region; Mems: organizations and individuals in nine countries; Co-ordinator IB JENSON.

Europa Nostra—Pan-European Federation for Heritage: Lange Voorhout 35, 2514 EC The Hague, Netherlands; tel. (70) 302-4050; fax (70) 361-7865; e-mail office@europanostra.org; internet www.europanostra.org; f. 1963; groups organizations and individuals concerned with the protection and enhancement of the European architectural and natural heritage and of the European environment; has consultative status with the Council of Europe; mems: 225 mem. organizations, more than 150 associate mems, more than 40 supporting bodies, more than 1,200 individual mems; Pres. HRH The Prince Consort of Denmark; Exec. Pres. OTTO VON DER GABLENTZ (Germany); Sec.-Gen. SNESKA QUAEDVLIEG-MIHAILOVIĆ.

European Association of Conservatoires, Music Academies and Music High Schools: POB 805, 3500 AV Utrecht, Netherlands; tel. (30) 236-12-42; fax (30) 236-12-90; e-mail aecinfo@aecinfo .org; internet www.aecinfo.org; f. 1953; aims to establish and foster contacts and exchanges between and represent the interests of members; initiates and supports international collaboration through research projects, congresses and seminars; mems: 187 mems, 22 associate mems.; Pres. Dr IAN HORSBRUGH; Gen. Sec. JOHANNES JOHANSSON; publs *The European Cultural Heritage Review* (annually), *Europa Nostra Scientific Bulletin,* conference proceedings.

International Centre for the Study of the Preservation and Restoration of Cultural Property—ICCROM: Via di San Michele 13, 00153 Rome, Italy; tel. (06) 585-531; fax (06) 5855-3349; e-mail iccrom@iccrom.org; internet www.iccrom.org; f. 1959; assembles documents on the preservation and restoration of cultural property; stimulates research and proffers advice; organizes missions of experts; undertakes training of specialists; mems: 104 countries; Dir-Gen. Dr NICHOLAS STANLEY-PRICE (UK); publ *Newsletter* (annually, in English and French).

International Council of Museums—ICOM: Maison de l'UNESCO, 1 rue Miollis, 75732 Paris Cédex 15, France; tel. 1-47-34-05-00; fax 1-43-06-78-62; e-mail secretariat@icom.museum; internet www.icom.museum; f. 1946 to further international co-operation among museums and to advance museum interests; maintains with UNESCO the organization's documentation centre; mems: 17,000 individuals and institutions in 1409 countries; Pres. JACQUES PEROT (France); Sec.-Gen. MANUS BRINKMAN (Netherlands); publ *ICOM News—Nouvelles de l'ICOM—Noticias del ICOM* (quarterly).

International Council on Monuments and Sites—ICOMOS: 49-51 rue de la Fédération, 75015 Paris, France; tel. 1-45-67-67-70; fax 1-45-66-06-22; e-mail secretariat@icomos.org; internet www .icomos.org; f. 1965 to promote the study and preservation of monuments and sites and to arouse and cultivate the interest of public authorities and people of every country in their cultural heritage; disseminates the results of research into the technical, social and administrative problems connected with the conservation of the architectural heritage; holds triennial General Assembly and Symposium; mems: c. 7,000, 21 international committees, 105 national committees; Pres. Dr MICHAEL PETZET (Germany); Sec.-Gen. JEAN-LOUIS LUXEN (Belgium); publs *ICOMOS Newsletter* (quarterly), *Scientific Journal* (quarterly).

International Music Council—IM: Maison de l'UNESCO, 1 rue Miollis, 75732 Paris Cédex 15, France; tel. 1-45-68-48-50; fax 1-43-06-87-98; e-mail imc@unesco.org; internet www.unesco.org/imc; f.

1949 to foster the exchange of musicians, music (written and recorded), and information between countries and cultures; mems: 34 international non-governmental organizations, national committees in 74 countries; Pres. KIFAH FAKHOURI (Jordan); Exec. Dir SILJA FISCHER (Germany).

Members of IMC include:

European Festivals Association: Château de Coppet, BP 26, 1296 Coppet, Switzerland; tel. (22) 776-8673; fax (22) 776-4275; e-mail geneva@eurofestival.net; internet www.euro-festival.net; f. 1952 to maintain high artistic standards and the representative character of art festivals; holds annual General Assembly; mems: 92 regular international performing arts festivals in 30 European countries, Israel, Japan, Lebanon and Mexico; Pres. FRANS DE RUITER; publ *Festivals* (annually).

International Federation of Musicians: 21 bis rue Victor Massé, 75009 Paris, France; tel. 1-45-26-31-23; fax 1-45-26-31-57; e-mail fimparis@compuserve.com; internet www.fim-musicians.com/; f. 1948 to promote and protect the interests of musicians in affiliated unions; promotes international exchange of musicians; mems: 69 unions totalling 250,000 individuals in 57 countries; Pres. JOHN MORTON (UK); Gen. Sec. BENOÎT MACHUEL (France).

International Music Centre (Internationales Musikzentrum—IMZ): 1230 Vienna, Speisinger Str. 121–127, Austria; tel. (1) 889 03-15; fax (1) 889 03-1577; e-mail office@imz.at; internet www.imz.at; f. 1961 for the study and dissemination of music through technical media (film, television, radio, gramophone); organizes congresses, seminars and screenings on music in audio-visual media; holds courses and competitions designed to strengthen the relationship between performing artists and audio-visual media; mems: 110 ordinary mems and 30 associate mems in 33 countries, including 50 broadcasting organizations; Pres. HENK VAN DER MEULEN (Netherlands); Sec.-Gen. FRANZ A. PATAY (Austria); publ *IMZ-Magazine* (5 a year, in English).

International PEN (A World Association of Writers): 9–10 Charterhouse Bldgs, Goswell Rd, London, EC1M 7AT, United Kingdom; tel. (20) 7253-4308; fax (20) 7253-5711; e-mail intpen@dircon.co.uk; internet www.internatpen.org; f. 1921 to promote co-operation between writers; mems: c. 14,000, 134 centres world-wide. International; Pres. HOMERO ARIDJIS; International Sec. TERRY CARLBOM; publ *PEN International* (2 a year, in English, French and Spanish, with the assistance of UNESCO).

Organization of World Heritage Cities: 56 Saint-Pierre St, Suite 401, Quebec City, QC, G1K 4AI, Canada; tel. (418) 692-0000; fax (418) 692-5558; e-mail secretariat@ovpm.org; internet www.ovpm.org; f. 1993 to assist cities inscribed on the UNESCO World Heritage List to implement the Convention concerning the Protection of the World Cultural and Natural Heritage (1972); promotes co-operation between city authorities, in particular in the management and sustainable development of historic sites; holds a General Assembly, comprising the mayors of member cities, at least every two years; mems: 187 cities world-wide; Sec.-Gen. D. S. MYRVOLL (acting).

Commodities

Common Fund for Commodities: Postbus 74656, 1070 BR, Amsterdam, Netherlands; tel. (20) 575-4949; fax (20) 676-0231; e-mail managing.director@common-fund.org; internet www.common-fund.org; f. 1989 as the result of an UNCTAD negotiation conference; finances commodity development measures including research, marketing, productivity improvements and vertical diversification, with the aim of increasing the long-term competitiveness of particular commodities; paid-in capital US $165m; mems: 105 countries and the AU, EC and COMESA; Man. Dir (also Chief Exec. and Chair.) ROLF BOEHNKE.

European Aluminium Association—EEA: 12 ave de Broqueville, 1150 Brussels, Belgium; tel. (2) 775-63-63; fax (2) 779-05-31; e-mail eaa@eaa.be; internet www.eaa.net; f. 1981 to encourage studies, research and technical co-operation, to make representations to international bodies and to assist national asscns in dealing with national authorities; mems: individual producers of primary aluminium, 17 national groups for wrought producers, the Organization of European Aluminium Smelters, representing producers of recycled aluminium, and the European Aluminium Foil Association, representing foil rollers and converters; Chair. R. BELDA; Sec.-Gen. P. DE SCHRYNMAKERS; publs *Annual Report, EAA Quarterly Report.*

International Confederation of European Sugar Beet Growers (Confédération internationale des betteraviers européens—CIBE): 29 rue du Général Foy, 75008 Paris, France; tel. 1-44-69-39-00; fax 1-42-93-28-93; f. 1925 to act as a centre for the co-ordination and dissemination of information about beet sugar production and the industry to represent the interests of sugar beet growers at an international level; mems: asscns in Austria, Belgium, Czech Republic, Denmark, Finland, France, Germany, Greece, Hungary, Ireland, Italy, Lithuania, Netherlands, Poland, Portugal, Romania, Slovakia, Spain, Sweden, Switzerland, United Kingdom; Pres. J. KIRSCH (Germany); Sec.-Gen. H. CHAVANES (France).

International Cotton Advisory Committee—ICAC: 1629 K St, NW, Suite 702, Washington, DC 20006-1636, USA; tel. (202) 463-6660; fax (202) 463-6950; e-mail secretariat@icac.org; internet www.icac.org; f. 1939 to observe developments in world cotton to collect and disseminate statistics; to suggest measures for the furtherance of international collaboration in maintaining and developing a sound world cotton economy; and to provide a forum for international discussions on cotton prices; mems: 43 countries; Exec. Dir Dr TERRY TOWNSEND (USA); publs *Cotton This Month, Cotton: Review of the World Situation, Cotton: World Statistics, The ICAC Recorder.*

International Grains Council—IGC: 1 Canada Sq., Canary Wharf, London, E14 5AE, United Kingdom; tel. (20) 7513-1122; fax (20) 7513-0630; e-mail igc@igc.org.uk; internet www.igc.org.uk; f. 1949 as International Wheat Council, present name adopted in 1995; responsible for the administration of the Grains Trade Convention of the International Grains Agreement, 1995; aims to further international co-operation in all aspects of trade in grains and to promote the freest possible flow of this trade, in particular, to support developing countries; seeks to contribute to the stability of the international grain market; acts as a forum for consultations between members; provides comprehensive information on the international grain market; mems: 28 countries and the EU; Exec. Dir. G. DENIS; publs *World Grain Statistics* (annually), *Wheat and Coarse Grain Shipments* (annually), *Report for the Fiscal Year* (annually), *Grain Market Report* (monthly), *Grain Market Indicators* (weekly) *Food Aid Shipments.*

International Lead and Zinc Study Group—ILZSG: 2 King St, London, SW1Y 6QP, United Kingdom; tel. (20) 7484-3300; fax (20) 7930-4635; e-mail root@ilzsg.org; internet www.ilzsg.org; f. 1959 for intergovernmental consultation on world trade in lead and zinc; conducts studies and provides information on trends in supply and demand; mems: 28 countries; Chair. A. IGNATOW (Canada); Sec.-Gen. DON SMALE; publ *Lead and Zinc Statistics* (monthly).

International Olive Oil Council: Príncipe de Vergara 154, 28002 Madrid, Spain; tel. (91) 59033638; fax (91) 5631263; e-mail iooc@internationaloliveoil.org; internet www.internationaloliveoil.org; f. 1959 to administer the International Agreement on Olive Oil and Table Olives, which aims to promote international co-operation in connection with problems of the world economy for olive products; works to prevent unfair competition, to encourage the production and consumption of, and international trade in, olive products, and to reduce the disadvantages caused by fluctuations of supplies on the market; mems: of the 1986 Agreement (Fourth Agreement, amended and extended in 1993; last prolonged in 2002): nine mainly producing countries, five mainly importing country, and the European Commission; Dir a.i. AHMED TOUZANI; publs *Information Sheet of the IOOC* (fortnightly, in French and Spanish), *OLIVAE* (5 a year, in English, French, Italian and Spanish).

International Sugar Organization: 1 Canada Sq., Canary Wharf, London, E14 5AA, United Kingdom; tel. (20) 7513-1144; fax (20) 7513-1146; e-mail exdir@isosugar.org; internet www.isosugar.org; administers the International Sugar Agreement (1992), with the objectives of stimulating co-operation, facilitating trade and encouraging demand; aims to improve conditions in the sugar market through debate, analysis and studies; serves as a forum for discussion; holds annual seminars and workshops; sponsors projects from developing countries; mems: 63 countries producing some 80% of total world sugar; Exec. Dir Dr P. BARON; publs *Sugar Year Book, Monthly Statistical Bulletin, Market Report and Press Summary, Quarterly Market Review*, seminar proceedings.

International Tungsten Industry Association—ITIA: 2 Baron's Gate, 33 Rothschild Rd, London, W4 5HT, United Kingdom; tel. (20) 8742-2274; fax (20) 8742-7345; e-mail info@itia.info; internet www.itia.org.uk/; f. 1988 (fmrly Primary Tungsten Asscn, f. 1975); promotes use of tungsten; collates statistics; prepares market reports; monitors health and environmental issues in the tungsten industry; mems: 51; Pres. D. LANDSBERGER; Sec.-Gen. MICHAEL MABY.

International Vine and Wine Office (Office International de la Vigne et du Vin—OIV): 18 rue d'Aguesseau, 75008 Paris, France; tel. 1-44-94-80-80; fax 1-42-66-90-63; e-mail oiv@oiv.int; internet www.oiv.int; f. 1924 to study all the scientific, technical, economic and human problems concerning the vine and its products to spread knowledge and facilitate contacts between researchers; mems: 46 countries; Dir-Gen. GEORGES DUTRUC-ROSSET; France; publs *Bulletin de l'OIV* (every 2 months), *Lettre de l'OIV* (monthly), *Lexique de la Vigne et du Vin, Recueil des méthodes internationales d'analyse des vins, Code international des Pratiques oenologiques, Codex oenologique international*, numerous scientific publications.

International Zinc Association: 168 ave de Tervueren, Box 4, 1150 Brussels, Belgium; tel. (2) 776-00-70; fax (2) 776-00-89; e-mail email@iza.com; internet www.iza.com; f. 1990 to represent the world zinc industry; provide a forum for senior executives to address global issues requiring industry-wide action; consider new applications for zinc and zinc products; foster understanding of zinc's role in the environment; build a sustainable development policy; mems: 28 zinc-producing countries; Exec. Dir EDOUARD GERVAIS; publ. *Zinc Protects* (4 a year).

Lead Development Association International: 42 Weymouth St, London, W1G 6NP, United Kingdom; tel. (20) 7499-8422; fax (20) 7493-1555; e-mail enq@ldaint.org; internet www.ldaint.org; f. 1956; provides authoritative information on the use of lead and its compounds; Financed by lead producers and users in the United Kingdom, Europe and elsewhere; Dir Dr D. N. WILSON (UK).

Organization of the Petroleum Exporting Countries—OPEC: Obere Donaustrasse 93, 1020 Vienna, Austria; tel. (1) 211-12; fax (1) 214-98-27; e-mail prid@opec.org; internet www.opec.org; f. 1960 to link countries whose main source of export earnings is petroleum; aims to unify and co-ordinate members' petroleum policies and to safeguard their interests generally; Established the OPEC Fund for International Development, 1976, which assists developing countries with their economic and social development; Sec.-Gen. Dr ALÍ RODRÍGUEZ ARAQUE (Venezuela); Publs *Annual Report, Annual Statistical Bulletin, Monthly Oil Market Report, OPEC Bulletin* (monthly), *OPEC Review* (quarterly).

Development and Economic Co-operation

Caritas Internationalis (International Confederation of Catholic Organizations for charitable and social action): Palazzo San Calisto, 00120 Città del Vaticano; tel. (06) 6987-9799; fax (06) 6988-7237 ; e-mail caritas.internationalis@caritas.va; internet www.caritas.org; f. 1950 to study problems arising from poverty, their causes and possible solutions; national mem. organizations undertake assistance and development activities. The Confederation co-ordinates emergency relief and development projects, and represents mems at international level; mems: 154 national orgs; Pres. Mgr YOUHANNA-FOUAD EL-HAGE (Bishop of Imperatriz (Brazil)); Sec.-Gen. DUNCAN MACLAREN; publs *Caritas Matters* (quarterly), *Emergency Calling* (2 a year).

Central European Free Trade Association: internet www.ijs.si/cefta; f. 1992, entered into force 1993; free-trade agreement covering a number of sectors; Mems: Bulgaria, Czech Republic, Hungary, Poland, Romania, Slovakia, Slovenia.

European Free Trade Association—EFTA: 9–11 rue de Varembé, 1211 Geneva 20, Switzerland; tel. (22) 7491111; fax (22) 7339291; e-mail efta-mailbox@efta.int; internet www.efta.int; f. 1960 to bring about free trade in industrial goods and to contribute to the liberalization and expansion of world trade; EFTA states (except Switzerland) now participate in the European Economic Area (EEA) with the 15 member countries of the European Union; has concluded free-trade agreements with *inter alia* Bulgaria, Czech Republic, Estonia, Hungary, Latvia, Lithuania, Macedonia, Poland, Romania and Slovakia; Mems: Iceland, Liechtenstein, Norway, Switzerland; Sec.-Gen. WILLIAM ROSSIER (Switzerland); Publs *EFTA Annual Report, EFTA Traders' ABC*.

Economics and Finance

Association of European Institutes of Economic Research—AIECE (Association d'instituts européens de conjoncture économique): 3 place Montesquieu, 1348 Louvain-la-Neuve, Belgium; tel. (10) 47-34-26; fax (10) 47-39-45; e-mail olbrechts@ires.ucl.ac.be; internet www.aiece.org; f. 1957; provides a means of contact between member institutes; organizes two meetings annually, at which discussions are held on the economic situation and on a special theoretical subject; mems: 40 institutes in 20 European countries; Admin. Sec. PAUL OLBRECHTS.

Bank for International Settlements (BIS): Centralbahnplatz 2, 4002 Basel, Switzerland; tel. (61) 2808080; fax (61) 2809100; e-mail email@bis.org; internet www.bis.org; f. pursuant to the Hague Agreements of 1930 to promote co-operation among national central banks and to provide additional facilities for international financial operations; Mems: central banks in 50 countries, incl. the Russian Federation; Chair. and Pres. NOUT WELLINK (Netherlands); Publs *Annual Report, Quarterly Review: International Banking and Financial Market Developments, The BIS Consolidated International Banking Statistics* (every 6 months), *Joint BIS-IMF-OECD-World Bank Statistics on External Debt* (quarterly), *Regular OTC Derivatives Market Statistics* (every 6 months), *Central Bank Survey of Foreign Exchange and Derivatives Market Activity* (every 3 years).

Comité Européen des Assurances—CEA: 3 bis rue de la Chaussée d'Antin, F-75009 Paris, France; tel. 1-44-83-11-83; fax 1-47-70-03-75; internet www.cea.assur.org; f. 1953 to represent the interests of European insurers, to encourage co-operation between members, to allow the exchange of information and to conduct studies; mems: national insurance asscns of 30 countries; Pres. GIJSBERT J. SWALEF (Netherlands); Dir -Gen. DANIEL G. SCHANTÉ (France); publs *CEA INFO—Euro Brief* (every 2 months), *CEA Executive Update* (monthly newsletter), *European Insurance in Figures* (annually), *The European Life Insurance Market* (annually).

European Private Equity and Venture Capital Association—EVCA: 4 Minervastraat, 1930 Zaventem, Belgium; tel. (2) 715-00-20; fax (2) 725-07-04; e-mail evca@evca.com; internet www.evca.com; f. 1983 to link private equity and venture capital companies within Europe; provides information services; supports networking; organizes lobbies and campaigns; works to promote the asset class in Europe and worldwide; holds three conferences each year as well as seminars, organizes EVCA Institute training courses; mems: over 950; Chair.. MAX BURGER; Sec.-Gen. JAVIER ECHARRI; publs *Yearbook* (annually), research and special papers; legal documents, industry guide-lines.

Inter-American Development Bank (IDB): 1300 New York Ave, NW, Washington, DC 20577, USA; tel. (202) 623-1000; fax (202) 623-3096; internet www.iadb.org; f. 1959 to promote the individual and collective development of Latin American and Caribbean countries through the financing of economic and social development projects and the provision of technical assistance; Mems: 46 countries, incl. Croatia and Slovenia; Pres. ENRIQUE V. IGLESIAS (Uruguay); Publs *Annual Report* (in English, French, Spanish and Portuguese), *Equidad* (2 a year), *IDBAmérica* (monthly, in English and Spanish), other reports, newsletters, economic reviews.

International Bank for Economic Co-operation—IBEC: 107815 GSP Moscow B-78, ul. Masha Poryvaeva 11, Russia; tel. (095) 975-38-61; fax (095) 975-22-02; f. 1963 by members of the Council for Mutual Economic Assistance (dissolved in 1991), as a central institution for credit and settlements following the decision in 1989–91 of most member states to adopt a market economy, the IBEC abandoned its system of multilateral settlements in transferable roubles, and (from 1 January 1991) began to conduct all transactions in convertible currencies; The Bank provides credit and settlement facilities for member states, and also acts as an international commercial bank, offering services to commercial banks and enterprises; Capital ECU 143.5m., reserves ECU 164.8m. (Dec. 1998); Mems: 10 states, incl. Bulgaria, Czech Republic, Hungary, Poland, Romania and Slovakia; Chair. VITALII S. KHOKHLOV; Man. Dirs V. SYTNIKOV, A. ORASCU.

International Investment Bank: 107078 Moscow, ul. Masha Poryvaeva 7, Russia; tel. (095) 975-40-08; fax (095) 975-20-70; f. 1970 to grant credits for joint investment projects and the development of enterprises following the decision in 1989–91 of most member states to adopt a market economy, the Bank conducted its transactions (from 1 January 1991) in convertible currencies, rather than in transferable roubles; The Bank focuses on production and scientific and technical progress; By the end of 1996 the Bank had approved financing of some ECU 7,000m. for 159 projects; Authorized capital ECU 1,300m., paid-up capital ECU 214.5m., reserves ECU 835.4m. (Dec. 1997); Mems: 10 states, incl. Bulgaria, Czech Republic, Hungary, Poland, Romania and Slovakia.

Islamic Development Bank—IDB: POB 5925, Jeddah 21432, Saudi Arabia; tel. (2) 6361400; fax (2) 6366871; e-mail archives@isdb.org.sa; internet www.isdb.org; f. 1975 following a conference held in Jeddah in Dec. 1973; Aims to encourage the economic development and social progress of member countries and of Muslim communities in non-member countries, in accordance with the principles of the Islamic *Shari'a* (sacred law); The IDB was planning to establish Bosnia Bank International by mid-2000; The Bank would operate in both entities of Bosnia and Herzegovina, with headquarters in Sarajevo and branches in Banja Luka, Bihać, Mostar, Tuzla and Zenica; Mems: 53, incl. Albania; Pres. Dr AHMED MOHAMED ALI; Publ. *Annual Report*.

Education

Comparative Education Society in Europe—CESE: Institut für Augemeine Pädagogik, Humboldt-Universität zu Berlin, Unter den Linden 6, 10099 Berlin, Germany; tel. (30) 20934094; fax (30) 20931006; e-mail juergen.schriewer@educat.hu-berlin.de; internet www.ceseurope.org; f. 1961 to promote teaching and research in comparative and international education; organizes conferences and promotes literature; mems: in 49 countries; Pres. Prof. DONATELLA PALOMBA (Italy); Sec. and Treas. Prof. MIGUEL A. PEREYRA (Spain); publ *Newsletter* (quarterly).

European Association for the Education of Adults: rue Liedts 27, 1030 Brussels, Belgium; tel. (2) 513-5205; fax (2) 513-5734; e-mail eaea@eaea.org; internet www.eaea.org; f. 1953; aims to create a 'learning society' by encouraging demand for learning, particularly from women and excluded sectors of society; seeks to improve response of providers of learning opportunities and authorities and agencies; mems: 90 in 30 countries; Pres. János Tóth; Gen. Sec. Ellinor Haase; publs *EAEA Monograph Series*, newsletter.

European Cultural Foundation: Jan van Goyenkade 5, 1075 HN Amsterdam, Netherlands; tel. (20) 6760222; fax (20) 6752231; e-mail eurocult@eurocult.org; internet www.eurocult.org; f. 1954 as a non-governmental organization, supported by private sources, to promote activities of mutual interest to European countries on aspects of culture; maintains national committees in 23 countries and a transnational network of institutes and centres: European Institute of Education and Social Policy, Paris; Institute for European Environmental Policy, London, Madrid and Berlin; Association for Innovative Co-operation in Europe (AICE), Brussels; EURYDICE Central Unit (the Education Information Network of the European Community), Brussels; European Institute for the Media, Düsseldorf; European Foundation Centre, Brussels; Fund for Central and East European Book Projects, Amsterdam; Institute for Human Sciences, Vienna; East West Parliamentary Practice Project, Amsterdam; and Centre Européen de la Culture, Geneva. A grants programme, for European co-operation projects is also conducted; Pres. HRH Princess Margriet of the Netherlands; Sec.-Gen. Gottfried Wagner; publs *Annual Report*, *Newsletter* (3 a year).

European Foundation for Management Development—EFMD: 88 rue Gachard, 1050 Brussels, Belgium; tel. (2) 629-08-10; fax (2) 629-08-11; e-mail info@efmd.be; internet www.efmd.be; f. 1971 through merger of European Association of Management Training Centres and International University Contact for Management Education; aims to help improve the quality of management development, disseminate information within the economic, social and cultural context of Europe and promote international co-operation; mems: over 390 institutions in 41 countries world-wide (26 in Europe); Pres. Gerard Van Schaik; Dir-Gen. Eric Cornuel; publs *Forum* (3 a year), *The Bulletin* (3 a year), *Guide to European Business Schools and Management Centres* (annually).

European University Association—EUA: 42 rue de la Loi, 1040 Brussels, Belgium; tel. (2) 230-55-44; fax (2) 230-57-51; e-mail info@eua.unige.ch; internet www.unige.ch/eua/; f. 2001 by merger of the Association of European Universities and the Confederation of EU Rectors' Conferences; represents European universities and national rectors' conferences; promotes the development of a coherent system of European higher education and research; provides support and guidance to its mems; focuses policies and services on the creation of a European area for higher education and research. mems: 37 collective and 8 assoc. universities and rectors' conferences in 45 countries; Sec.-Gen. Lesley Wilson; publs *Thema*, *Directory*, *Annual Report*.

International Federation of Catholic Universities (Fédération internationale d'universités catholiques—FIUC): 21 rue d'Assas, 75270 Paris Cédex 06, France; tel. 1-44-39-52-26; fax 1-44-39-52-28; e-mail sgfiuc@bureau.fiuc.org; internet www.fiuc.org/; f. 1948; aims to ensure a strong bond of mutual assistance among all Catholic universities in the search for truth; to help to solve problems of growth and development, and to co-operate with other international organizations; mems: 191 in 41 countries; Pres. Rev. Jan Peters (Netherlands); Sec.-Gen. Guy-Réal Thivierge (Canada); publ *Monthly Newsletter*.

League of European Research Libraries (Ligue des bibliothèques européennes de recherche—LIBER): c/o Secretariat, Susan Vejlsgaard, Det Kongelige Bibliotek, POB 2149, 1016 Copenhagen K, Denmark; tel. 33-93-62-22; fax 33-91-95-96; e-mail sv@kb.dk ; internet www.kb.dk/liber; f. 1971 to encourage collaboration between the general research libraries of Europe, and national and university libraries in particular; gives assistance in finding practical ways of improving the quality of the services provided; mems: 310 libraries and individuals in 33 countries; Dir-Gen. Erland Kolding Nielsen; Sec. Peter K. Fox (UK); publ *LIBER Quarterly*.

Environmental Conservation

Coalition Clean Baltic—CCB: Asögatan 115, POB 4625, 116 91 Stockholm, Sweden; tel. and fax (8) 643-65-95; e-mail secretariat@ccb.se; f. 1990, network of 25 environmental non-governmental organizations from all countries bordering the Baltic Sea; Exec. Sec. Gunnar Norén.

Friends of the Earth International: Prins Hendrikkade 48, POB 19199, 1000 GD Amsterdam, Netherlands; tel. (20) 6221369; fax (20) 6392181; e-mail foei@foei.org; internet www.foei.org; f. 1971 to promote the conservation, restoration and rational use of the environ-ment and natural resources through public education and campaigning; mems: 68 national groups; Publs *Link* (quarterly), .

Greenpeace International: Keizersgracht 176, 1016 DW Amsterdam, Netherlands; tel. (20) 5236222; fax (20) 5236200; e-mail supporter.services@ams.greenpeace.org; internet www.greenpeace.org/; f. 1971 to campaign for the protection of the environment; aims to bear witness to environmental destruction, and to demonstrate solutions for positive change; mems: offices in 41 countries; Chair. Anne Summers (Australia); Exec. Dir Gerd Leipold (Germany).

Greenway—Central and East European Network of Environmental NGOs: POB 163, 814 99 Bratislava, Slovakia; tel. and fax (2) 5541-4674; e-mail greenway@isternet.sk; internet www.fns.uniba.sk/zp/greenway/; f. 1985 as Clean Up The World, an environmental educational project; runs seminars, workshops and training courses on energy and waste and co-ordinates activities of environmental non-governmental organizations in Central and Eastern Europe; 31 mem. organizations; Principal Officer Dr Elena Vartíková.

Helsinki Commission—HELCOM, Baltic Marine Environment Protection Commission: Katajanokanlaituri 6b, 00160 Helsinki, Finland; tel. (9) 6220220; fax (9) 62202239; e-mail helcom@helcom.fi; internet www.helcom.fi; governing body of the Convention on the Protection of the Marine Environment of the Baltic Sea Area; responsibilities include the prevention of airborne, sea and land-based pollution; Contracting parties: the nine states bordering the Baltic Sea area and the European Community; Exec. Sec. Mieczyslaw S. Ostojski.

International Seabed Authority: 14–20 Port Royal St, Kingston, Jamaica; tel. 922-9105; fax 922-0195; e-mail postmaster@isa.org.jm; internet www.isa.org.jm; f. Nov. 1994 upon the entry into force of the 1982 United Nations Convention on the Law of the Sea; The Authority is the institute through which states party to the Convention organize and control activities in the international seabed area beyond the limits of national jurisdiction, particularly with a view to administering the resources of that area; Publs *Annual Report*, *WWF News* (quarterly).

Regional Environmental Centre for Central and Eastern Europe: 2000 Szentendre, Ady Endre ut. 9–11, Hungary; tel. (26) 311–199; fax (26) 311–294; e-mail rec-info@rec.org; internet www.rec.org; f. 1990; aims to assist in the solution of environmental problems in Central and Eastern Europe through the promotion of co-operation between non-governmental organizations, governments and businesses, the free exchange of information and public participation in decision-making; provides grants and training and facilitates networking; 15 local offices; Exec. Dir Jernej Stritih.

Wetlands International: POB 471, 6700 AL Wageningen, Netherlands; tel. (317) 478854; fax (317) 478850; e-mail post@wetlands.agro.nl; internet www.wetlands.org; f. 1995 by merger of several regional wetlands organizations; aims to sustain and restore wetlands, their resources and biodiversity through research, information exchange and conservation activities; promotes implementation of the 1971 Ramsar Convention on Wetlands; Chair. Stew Morrison; CEO Simon Nash; publs *Wetlands* (2 a year), other studies, technical publications, manuals, proceedings of meetings.

World Conservation Union—IUCN: 28 rue Mauverney, 1196 Gland, Switzerland; tel. (22) 9990000; fax (22) 9990002; e-mail mail@hq.iucn.org; internet www.iucn.org; f. 1948, as the International Union for Conservation of Nature and Natural Resources; supports partnerships and practical field activities to promote the conservation of natural resources, to secure the conservation of nature, and especially of biological diversity, as an essential foundation for the future; to ensure wise use of the earth's natural resources in an equitable and sustainable way; and to guide the development of human communities towards ways of life in enduring harmony with other components of the biosphere, developing programmes to protect and sustain the most important and threatened species and eco-systems and assisting governments to devise and carry out national conservation strategies; maintains a conservation library and documentation centre and units for monitoring traffic in wildlife; mems: government agencies in 98 countries and national and international non-governmental organizations in 128 countries; 37 non-voting affiliate mems; Pres. Yolanda Kakabadse Navarro (Ecuador); Dir-Gen. Achim Steiner; publs *World Conservation Strategy*, *Caring for the Earth*, *Red List of Threatened Plants*, *Red List of Threatened Species*, *United Nations List of National Parks and Protected Areas*, *World Conservation* (quarterly) *IUCN Today*.

World Wide Fund for Nature—WWF: ave de Mont-Blanc, 1196 Gland, Switzerland; tel. (22) 3649111; fax (22) 3643239; e-mail kevans@wwfnet.org; internet www.panda.org; f. 1961 (as World Wildlife Fund); aims to stop the degradation of the natural environment, conserve bio-diversity, ensure the sustainable use of renewable resources, promote the reduction of pollution and wasteful consumption; mems: 27 national organizations, five associates, c. 5m. individual mems world-wide; Pres. Chief EMEKA ANYAOKU (Nigeria); Dir-Gen. Dr CLAUDE MARTIN.

Government and Politics

Atlantic Treaty Association: 10 rue Crevaux, 75116 Paris, France; tel. 1-45-53-28-80; fax 1-47-55-49-63; e-mail ata sg@noos .fr; internet www.atasec.org; f. 1954 to inform public opinion on the North Atlantic Alliance and to promote the solidarity of the peoples of the North Atlantic; holds annual assemblies, seminars, study conferences for teachers and young politicians; mems: national asscns in the 19 member countries of NATO; 19 assoc. mems from central and eastern Europe, two observer mems; Chair. ALAN LEE WILLIAMS (UK); Sec.-Gen. ANTÓNIO BORGES DE CARVALHO (Portugal).

Baltic Assembly: Rīga, Latvia; tel. 770-1795; fax 770-1796; internet www.baltsam.org; f. 1991 to develop co-operation among the parliaments of Estonia, Latvia and Lithuania; comprises 20 parliamentarians from each country, who participate in seven working committees: budget and audit; legal; social and economic affairs; environment and energy; communications and informatics; education, science and culture; and security and foreign affairs; holds twice-yearly sessions; in 1994 the Assembly and the Baltic Council of Ministers formed the Baltic Council, as an institution of co-operation; from 1996 also holds joint sessions with the Nordic Council (comprising Denmark, Finland, Iceland, Norway and Sweden) to promote co-operation in Northern Europe; Pres. LAIMA ANDRIKIENE (Lithuania); Sec.-Gen. ANCE KARNUPA (Latvia).

Baltic Battalion (BALTBAT): Adazi, Latvia; f. 1994 as an international peace-keeping unit by heads of government of Estonia, Latvia and Lithuania; overseen by international co-ordinating body; consists of 800 professional military personnel from the three countries, with command of the battalion undertaken on a rotating basis; has participated in UN and NATO peace-keeping operations; Cmmdr Lt-Col ALAR LANEMAN (Estonia).

Baltic Council: f. 1993 by the Baltic Assembly, comprising 60 parliamentarians from Estonia, Latvia and Lithuania; the Council of Ministers of the three Baltic countries co-ordinates policy in the areas of foreign policy, justice, the environment, education and science.

Central European Initiative—CEI: CEI Executive Secretariat, Via Genova 9, 34121 Trieste, Italy; tel. (040) 7786777; fax (040) 360640; e-mail cei-es@cei-es.org; internet www.ceinet.org; f. 1989 as 'Quadrilateral' co-operation between Austria, Italy, Hungary and Yugoslavia, became 'Pentagonal' in 1990 with the admission of Czechoslovakia, and 'Hexagonal' with the admission of Poland in 1991, present name adopted in 1992, when Bosnia and Herzegovina, Croatia and Slovenia were admitted; the Czech Republic and Slovakia became separate mems in January 1993, and Macedonia also joined in that year; Albania, Belarus, Bulgaria, Romania and Ukraine joined the CEI in 1995 and Moldova in 1996; Serbia and Montenegro (then the Federal Republic of Yugoslavia) was admitted in 2000; aims to encourage regional and bilateral political and economic co-operation, working within the OSCE; Dir-Gen. Dr HARALD KREID.

European Movement: 25 Square de Meeus, 1000 Brussels, Belgium; tel. (2) 508-30-88; fax (2) 508-30-89; e-mail secretariat@ europeanmovement.org; internet www.europeanmovement.org; f. 1947 by a liaison committee of representatives from European organizations, to study the political, economic and technical problems of a European Union and suggest how they could be solved and to inform and lead public opinion in the promotion of integration; Conferences have led to the creation of the Council of Europe, College of Europe, etc; mems: national councils and committees in 39 European countries, and several international social and economic organizations; Pres. JOSÉ MARIA GIL-ROBLES (Spain); Sec.-Gen. HENRIK H. KRÖNER.

International Democrat Union: c/o Queen Anne's Gate, London, SW1H 9AA, United Kingdom; tel. (20) 7222-0847; fax (20) 7222-5999; e-mail rnormington@idu.org; internet www.idu.org; f. 1983 as a group of centre and centre-right political parties; facilitates the exchange of information and views; promotes networking; organizes campaigning seminars for politicians and party workers; holds Party Leaders' meetings every three or four years, also executive meetings and a Young Leaders' Forum; mems: political parties in 41 countries, 46 assoc. mems in regions; Exec. Sec. RICHARD NORMINGTON.

International Federation of Resistance Movements—FIR: c/o R. Maria, 5 rue Rollin, 75005 Paris, France; tel. 1-43-26-84-29; f. 1951; supports the medical and social welfare of former victims of fascism; works for peace, disarmament and human rights, and against fascism and neo-fascism; mems: 82 national organizations in 29 countries; Pres. ALIX LHOTE (France); Sec.-Gen. OSKAR WIES-FLECKER (Austria); publs *Feuille d'information* (in French and

German), *Cahier d'informations médicales, sociales et juridiques* (in French and German).

International Institute for Peace: Möllwaldplatz 5, 1040 Vienna, Austria; tel. (1) 504-43-76; fax (1) 505-32-36; e-mail iip@aon.at; internet www.iip.at; f. 1957; non-governmental organization with consultative status at ECOSOC and UNESCO; studies conflict prevention; new structures in international law; security issues in Europe and world-wide; mems: individuals and corporate bodies invited by the executive board; Pres. ERWIN LANC (Austria); Dir PETER STANIA (Russia); publs *Peace and Security* (quarterly, in English), occasional papers (2 or 3 a year, in English and German).

International Institute for Strategic Studies—IISS: Arundel House, 13–15 Arundel St, London, WC2R 3DX, United Kingdom; tel. (20) 7379-7676; fax (20) 7836-3108; e-mail iiss@iiss.org; internet www.iiss.org; f. 1958; concerned with the study of the role of force in international relations, including problems of international strategy, the ethnic, political and social sources of conflict, disarmament and arms control, peace-keeping and intervention, defence economics, etc.; independent of any government; mems: c. 3,000; Dir Dr JOHN M. W. CHIPMAN; publs *Survival* (quarterly), *The Military Balance* (annually), *Strategic Survey* (annually), *Adelphi Papers* (10 a year), *Strategic Comments* (10 a year).

Liberal International: 1 Whitehall Place, London, SW1A 2HD, United Kingdom; tel. (20) 7839-5905; fax (20) 7925-2685; e-mail all@ liberal-international.org; internet www.liberal-international.org; f. 1947; world union of 83 liberal parties in 58 countries; co-ordinates foreign policy work of member parties, and promotes freedom, tolerance, democracy, international understanding, protection of human rights and market-based economics; has consultative status at ECOSOC of United Nations and the Council of Europe; Pres. ANNEMIE NEYTS-UYTTEBROECK; Sec.-Gen. FREDERICA SABBATI; publ. *London Aerogramme* (quarterly).

Multinational Peace Force South-Eastern Europe— MPFSEE: Plovdiv, Bulgaria; e-mail mpfsee@mbox.infotel.bg; internet www.seebrig.pims.org; f. 1999; also known as South-Eastern Europe Brigade (SEEBRIG); a regional co-operation structure to contribute to regional security and stability in the Euro-Atlantic area and to foster good relations among the countries of South-East Europe; units allocated to the force remain at their permanent locations, and committed under a task force principle for exercises and operations; rotation of the force headquarters (every four years), command of the force (every two years) and the presidency of the Politico-Military Steering Committee (every two years); Mems: 7 countries, incl. Albania, Bulgaria, Greece, Macedonia and Romania; Slovenia and Croatia have observer status; Pres. OVIDIU DRAHGA (Romania); Commdr of Force Brig. Gen. ANDREAS KOUZELIS (Greece).

Nato Parliamentary Assembly: 3 place du Petit Sablon, 1000 Brussels, Belgium; tel. (2) 513-28-65; fax (2) 514-18-47; e-mail secretariat@naa.be; internet www.nato-pa.int; f. 1955 as the NATO Parliamentarians' Conference; name changed 1966 to North Atlantic Assembly; renamed as above 1999; the inter-parliamentary assembly of the North Atlantic Alliance; holds two plenary sessions a year and meetings of committees (Political, Defence and Security, Economics and Security, Civil Dimension of Security, Science and Technology), where parliamentarians from North America, western Europe and eastern Europe (associate delegates) examine the problems confronting the Alliance and European security issues in general; Pres. DOUGLAS BEREUTER (USA); Sec.-Gen. SIMON LUNN (United Kingdom).

Nordic Council: Store Strandstraede 18, 1255 Copenhagen, Denmark; tel. 33-96-04-00; fax 33-11-18-70; internet www.norden.org; f. 1952 for co-operation between the Nordic parliaments and governments; the Nordic Council of Ministers co-ordinates the activities of the governments of the Nordic countries when decisions are to be implemented; co-operation with adjacent areas includes the Baltic States, where Nordic governments are committed to furthering democracy, security and sustainable development, to contribute to peace, security and stability in Europe; the Nordic–Baltic Scholarship Scheme awards grants to students, teachers, scientists, civil servants and parliamentarians; Sec.-Gen. SØREN CHRISTENSEN (Denmark); Publs *Norden the Top of Europe* (monthly newsletter in English, French and German), *Norden this week* (weekly newsletter).

Organization of the Islamic Conference (OIC): Kilo 6, Mecca Rd, POB 178, Jeddah 21411, Saudia Arabia; tel. (2) 680-0800; fax (2) 687-3568; e-mail info@oic-oci.org; internet www.oic-oci.org; f. 1971 following a summit meeting of Muslim heads of state at Rabat, Morocco, in Sept. 1969, and the Islamic Foreign Ministers' Conference in Jeddah in March 1970, and in Karachi, Pakistan, in Dec. 1970; Mems: 56 countries, incl. Albania; Bosnia and Herzegovina has been granted observer status; Sec.-Gen. Dr ABDELOUAHED BELKEZIZ (Morocco).

Socialist International: Maritime House, Clapham, London, SW4 0JW, United Kingdom; tel. (20) 7627-4449; fax (20) 7720-4448; e-mail secretariat@socialistinternational.org; internet www .socialistinternational.org; f. 1864; re-established in 1951; the world's oldest and largest asscn of political parties, grouping democratic socialist, labour and social democratic parties from every continent; provides a forum for political action, policy discussion and the exchange of ideas; works with many international organizations and trades unions (particularly members of ICFTU; holds Congress every three years. The Council meets twice a year, and regular conferences and meetings of party leaders are also held; committees and councils on a variety of subjects and in different regions meet frequently; mems: 89 full member, 25 consultative and 15 observer parties in 110 countries; There are three fraternal organizations and nine associated organizations, including: the Party of European Socialists (PES), the Group of the PES at the European Parliament and the International Federation of the Socialist and Democratic Press; Pres. ANTONIO GUTERRES (Portugal); Gen. Sec. LUIS AYALA (Chile); publ. *Socialist Affairs* (quarterly).

Stockholm International Peace Research Institute—SIPRI: Signalistgatan 9, 169 70 Solna, Sweden; tel. (8) 655-97-00; fax (8) 655-97-33; e-mail sipri@sipri.se; internet www.sipri.se; f. 1966; carries out studies on international security and arms control issues, including on conflict and crisis management, peace-keeping and regional security, and chemical and biological warfare; mems: about 50 staff mems, half of whom are researchers; Dir ALYSON J. K. BAILES (UK); Chair. ROLF EKÉUS (Sweden); publs *SIPRI Yearbook: Armaments, Disarmament and International Security*, monographs and research reports.

Union of Baltic Cities—UBC: 80-828 Gdańsk, Dlugi Targ 24, Poland; tel. (58) 3017637; fax (58) 3010917; e-mail info@ubc.net; internet www.ubc.net; f. to promote economic and political co-operation in the Baltic Sea region, and European integration, with the aim of facilitating the Baltic states' entry into the EU; comprises 10 commissions concerned with business co-operation, communication, culture, education, environment, social and health affairs, sport, tourism, transportation, and urban planning; Mems: 101 cities in 10 countries; Sec.-Gen. PAWEL ZABOKLICKI (Poland).

Unrepresented Nations' and Peoples' Organization—UNPO: Eisenhowelaan 136, 2517 KN The Hague, Netherlands; tel. (70) 360-3318; fax (70) 360-3346; e-mail unpo@unpo.nl; internet www.unpo .org; f. 1991 to provide an international forum for indigenous and other unrepresented peoples and minorities; provides training in human rights, law, diplomacy and public relations to UNPO members; provides conflict resolution services; mems: 52 organisations representing occupied nations, indigenous peoples and minorities; Gen. Sec. MICHAEL VAN WALT; publs *UNPO News, UNPO Yearbook*.

Industrial and Professional Relations

European Trade Union Confederation—ETUC (Confédération européenne des syndicats): 5 blvd du Roi Albert II, 1210 Brussels, Belgium; tel. (2) 224-04-11; fax (2) 224-04-54; e-mail etuc@etuc.org; internet www.etuc.org; f. 1973; comprises 78 national trade union confederations and 11 European industrial federations in 34 European countries, representing 60m. workers; holds congress every four years; Pres. FRITZ VERZETNITSCH (Austria); Gen. Sec. EMILIO GABAGLIO (Italy).

International Confederation of Free Trade Unions—ICFTU: 5 blvd Roi Albert II, 1210 Brussels, Belgium; tel. (2) 224-02-11; fax (2) 201-58-15; e-mail internetpo@icftu.org; internet www.icftu.org; f. 1949 by trade union federations which had withdrawn from the World Federation of Trade Unions; aims to promote the interests of working people and to secure recognition of workers' organizations as free bargaining agents; Mems: 225 organizations in 148 countries; Gen. Sec. GUY RYDER; Publs *Survey of Violations of Trade Union Rights* (annually, in English, French and Spanish), *Trade Union World* (monthly, in English, French and Spanish).

World Confederation of Labour—WCL: 33 rue de Trèves, 1040 Brussels, Belgium; tel. (2) 285-47-00; fax (2) 230-87-22; e-mail info@ cmt-wcl.org; internet www.cmt-wcl.org; f. 1920 as the International Federation of Christian Trade Unions (IFCTU); reconstituted under present title in 1968; Mems: about 26m. in 116 countries, incl. Czech Republic, Hungary, Lithuania, Poland, Romania and Slovakia; Sec.-Gen. WILLY THYS (Belgium); Publs *Tele-flash* (every 2 weeks), *Labor Magazine* (quarterly).

World Federation of Trade Unions (WFTU): Branická 112, 14701 Prague 4, Czech Republic; tel. (2) 44462140; fax (2) 44461378; e-mail wftu@login.cz; internet www.wftu.cz; f. 1945 on a world-wide basis; Mems: 132m. in 121 countries; Gen. Sec. ALEKSANDR ZHARIKOV (Russia); Publ. *Flashes from the Trade Unions* (every 2 weeks).

Law

Council of the Bars and Law Societies of the European Union—CCBE: 45 rue de Trèves, 1040 Brussels, Belgium; tel. (2) 234-65-10; fax (2) 234-65-11; e-mail ccbe@ccbe.org; internet www .ccbe.org; f. 1960; the officially recognized representative organization for the legal profession in the European Union and European Economic Area; liaises between the bars and law societies of member states and represents them before the European institutions; also maintains contact with other international organizations of lawyers; principal objective is to study all questions affecting the legal profession in member states and to harmonize professional practice; mems: 18 delegations (representing some 500,000 European lawyers), and observers from Bulgaria, Croatia, Cyprus, Czech Republic, Estonia, Hungary, Poland, Romania, Slovakia, Slovenia, Switzerland and Turkey; Pres. HELGE JAKOB KOLRUD; Sec.-Gen. JONATHAN GOLDSMITH.

International Commission on Civil Status: 3 place Arnold, 67000 Strasbourg, France; e-mail ciec-sg@ciec1.org; internet www .ciec1.org; f. 1950 for the establishment and presentation of legislative documentation relating to the rights of individuals; carries out research on means of simplifying the judicial and technical administration with respect to civil status; mems: governments of Austria, Belgium, Croatia, France, Germany, Greece, Hungary, Italy, Luxembourg, Netherlands, Poland, Portugal, Spain, Switzerland, Turkey, United Kingdom; Pres. H. G. KOUMANTOS (Greece); Sec.-Gen. P. LAGARDE (France); publs *Guide Pratique international de l'état civil* (available on-line), various studies on civil status.

International Council of Environmental Law: Adenauerallee 214, 53113 Bonn, Germany; tel. (228) 2692-240; fax (228) 2692-250; e-mail 100651.317@compuserve.com; internet www.law.pace.edu/ env/icelsite/icelhome.html; f. 1969 to exchange information and expertise on legal, administrative and policy aspects of environmental questions; Exec. Governors Dr WOLFGANG E. BURHENNE (Germany), Dr ABDULBAR AL-GAIN (Saudi Arabia); publs *Directory, References, Environmental Policy and Law, International Environmental Law—Multilateral Treaties*, etc.

International Criminal Police Organization—INTERPOL: 200 quai Charles de Gaulle, 69006 Lyon, France; tel. 4-72-44-70-00; fax 4-72-44-71-63; e-mail cp@interpol.int; internet www.interpol.int; f. 1923, reconstituted 1946; aims to promote and ensure mutual assistance between police forces in different countries; co-ordinates activities of police authorities of member states in international affairs; works to establish and develop institutions with the aim of preventing transnational crimes; centralizes records and information on international criminals; operates a telecommunications network of 179 stations; holds General Assembly annually; mems: official bodies of 179 countries; Sec.-Gen. RONALD K. NOBLE (USA); publs *International Criminal Police Review, International Crime Statistics, Stolen Works of Art* (CD Rom), *Interpol Guide to Vehicle Registration Documents* (annually).

International Development Law Institute—IDLI: Via di San Sebastianello 16, 00187 Rome, Italy; tel. (06) 6979261; fax (06) 6781946; e-mail idlo@idlo.int; internet www.idli.org; f. 1983; designs and conducts courses and seminars for lawyers, legal advisors and judges from developing countries, central and eastern Europe and the former USSR; also provides in-country training workshops; training programme addresses legal skills, international commercial law, economic law reform, governance and the role of the judiciary; Chair. JAMES HURLOCK; Dir-Gen. WILLIAM T. LORIS.

Medicine and Health

Association of National European and Mediterranean Societies of Gastroenterology—ASNEMGE: c/o Andrea Bauer, Vereinsmanagement Lassingleithnerplatz 2/3, 1020 Vienna, Austria; tel. 1-533-35-42; fax 1-535-10-45; e-mail info@asnemge.org; internet www.asnemge.org; f. 1947 to facilitate the exchange of ideas between gastroenterologists and to disseminate knowledge; organizes International Congress of Gastroenterology every four years; mems: in 37 countries, national societies and sections of national medical societies; Pres. Prof. PETER FERENCI (Austria); Sec. Prof. JØRGEN RASK-MADSEN (Denmark).

Balkan Medical Union (Uniunii Medicale Balcanice—UMB): POB 149, 1 rue G. Clémenceau, 70148 Bucharest, Romania; tel. (1) 3137857; fax (1) 3121570; f. 1932; studies medical problems, particularly ailments specific to the Balkan region; promotes a regional programme of public health; facilitates the exchange of information between doctors in the region; organizes research programmes and congresses; mems: doctors and specialists from Albania, Bulgaria, Cyprus, Greece, Moldova, Romania, Turkey and the former Yugoslav republics; Pres. Prof. H. CIOBANU (Moldova); publs *Archives de* *l'union médicale Balkanique* (quarterly), *Bulletin de l'union médicale Balkanique* (6 a year), *Annuaire*.

Cystic Fibrosis Worldwide: Bosbes 12, 5708 DA Helmond, Netherlands; tel. (492) 520-241; fax (492) 599-068; e-mail info@cfww.org; internet www.cfww.org; f. 2003 by merger of the International Association of Cystic Fibrosis Adults and International Cystic Fibrosis (Muscoviscidosis) Association (f. 1964); promotes the development of lay organizations and the advancement of knowledge among medical, scientific and health professionals in underdeveloped areas; convenes annual conference, 2003: Belfast, UK; 2004: Birmingham, UK; Pres. HERMAN WEGGEN (Netherlands); Sec. GINA STEEKAMER (Netherlands); publs: *Annual Report, CFW Newsletter* (quarterly), *Joseph Levy Lecture,* Physiotherapy booklet.

European Health Management Association—EHMA: Vergemount Hall, Clonskeagh, Dublin 6, Ireland; tel. (1) 2839299; fax (1) 2838653; e-mail pcberman@ehma.org; internet www.ehma.org; f. 1966; aims to improve health care in Europe by raising standards of managerial performance in the health sector; fosters co-operation between health service organizations and institutions in the field of health-care management education and training; mems: 225 in 30 countries; Pres. Prof. JOAN HIGGINS; Dir PHILIP C. BERMAN; publs *Newsletter, Eurobriefing* (quarterly).

Eurotransplant International Foundation: POB 2304, 2301 CH Leiden, Netherlands; tel. (71) 5795795; fax (71) 5790057; internet www.eurotransplant.nl; f. 1967; co-ordinates the exchange of organs for transplants in Austria, Belgium, Germany, Luxembourg, Netherlands and Slovenia; keeps register of c. 15,000 patients with all necessary information for matching with suitable donors in the shortest possible time; organizes transport of the organ and transplantation; collaborates with similar organizations in western and eastern Europe; Dirs Dr B. COHEN, Dr G. G. PERSIJN.

World Association for Disaster and Emergency Medicine—WADEM: 3330 University Ave, Room 352, Madison, WI 53705, USA; tel. (608) 263-2069; fax (608) 265-3037; e-mail mlb@medicine.wisc.edu; internet wadem.medicine.wisc.edu; f. 1976 to improve the world-wide delivery of emergency and humanitarian care in mass casualty and disaster situations, through training, symposia, and publications; mems: 600 in 62 countries; Pres. KNUT OLE SUNDNES (Norway); Sec. DEMETRIOS PYRROS (Greece); publ. *Prehospital and Disaster Medicine.*

World Self-Medication Industry—WSMI: Centre International de Bureaux, 13 chemin du Levant, 01210 Ferney-Voltaire, France; tel. 450-28-47-28; fax 450-28-40-24; e-mail dwebber@wsmi.org; internet www.wsmi.org; Dir-Gen. Dr DAVID E. WEBBER.

Posts and Telecommunications

European Conference of Postal and Telecommunications Administrations: Ministry of Transport and Communications, Odos Xenofontos 13, 10191 Athens, Greece; tel. (1) 9236494; fax (1) 9237133; internet www.cept.org; f. 1959 to strengthen relations between member administrations and to harmonize and improve their technical services; set up Eurodata Foundation, for research and publishing; mems: 26 countries; Sec. Z. PROTOPSALTI; publ. *Bulletin.*

European Telecommunications Satellite Organization—EUTELSAT: 70 rue Balard, 75015, Paris Cédex 15, France; tel. 1-53-98-47-47; fax 1-53-98-37-00; internet www.eutelsat.com; f. 1977 to operate satellites for fixed and mobile communications in Europe; EUTELSAT's in-orbit resource comprises 18 satellites; commercialises capacity in three satellites operated by other companies; mems: public and private telecommunications operations in 47 countries; Dir-Gen. GIULIANO BERRETTA.

Press, Radio and Television

Association of European Journalists—AEJ: Balistraat 46, Den Haag, 2585 Netherlands; tel. (70) 3635875; fax (70) 3107217; e-mail hhetzel@atglobal.net; internet www.aej.org; f. 1963 to participate actively in the development of a European consciousness to promote deeper knowledge of European problems and secure appreciation by the general public of the work of European institutions; and to facilitate members' access to sources of European information; mems: 2,100 individuals and national asscns in 23 countries; Pres. HELMUT HETZEL (Netherlands); Sec.-Gen. JURAJ ALNER (Slovakia); publ. *Newsletter.*

European Broadcasting Union—EBU: CP 45, Ancienne-Route 17A, 1218 Grand-Saconnex, Geneva, Switzerland; tel. (22) 7172111; fax (22) 74740003; e-mail ebu@ebu.ch; internet www.eurovision.net; f. 1950 in succession to the International Broadcasting Union; a professional asscn of broadcasting organizations, supporting the interests of members and assisting the development of broadcasting

in all its forms; activities include the Eurovision news and programme exchanges and the Euroradio music exchanges; mems: 71 active (European) in 52 countries, and 45 associate in 28 countries; Pres. ARNE WESSBERG (Finland); Sec.-Gen. JEAN STOCK (France); publs *EBU Technical Review* (annually), *Diffusion* (2 a year).

Religion

Christian Peace Conference: Prokopova 4, 130 00 Prague 3, Czech Republic; tel. (2) 22781800; fax (2) 22781801; e-mail christianpeace@volny.cz; internet www.volny.cz/christianpeace; f. 1958 as an international movement of theologians, clergy and laypeople, aiming to bring Christendom to recognize its share of guilt in both world wars and to dedicate itself to the service of friendship, reconciliation and peaceful co-operation of nations, to concentrate on united action for peace and justice, and to co-ordinate peace groups in individual churches and facilitate their effective participation in the peaceful development of society; works through five continental asscns, regional groups and member churches in many countries; Moderator Dr SERGIO ARCE MARTÍNEZ; Co-ordinator Rev. BRIAN G. COOPER; publs *CPC Information* (8 a year in English and German), occasional *Study Volume.*

Conference of European Churches—CEC: POB 2100, 150 route de Ferney, 1211 Geneva 2, Switzerland; tel. (22) 7916111; fax (22) 7916227; e-mail cec@cec-kek.org; internet www.cec-kek.org; f. 1959 as a regional ecumenical organization for Europe and a meeting-place for European churches, including members and non-members of the World Council of Churches; holds assemblies every six years; mems: 128 Protestant, Anglican, Orthodox and Old Catholic churches in all European countries; Gen. Sec. Rev. Dr KEITH CLEMENTS; publs *Monitor* (quarterly), CEC communiqués, reports.

Lutheran World Federation: 150 route de Ferney, POB 2100, 1211 Geneva 2, Switzerland; tel. (22) 7916111; fax (22) 7916111; e-mail info@lutheranworld.org; internet www.lutheranworld.org; f. 1947; groups 128 Lutheran Churches in 70 countries; provides inter-church aid and relief work in various areas of the globe; gives service to refugees, including resettlement; carries out theological research, conferences and exchanges; grants scholarship aid in various fields of church life; conducts inter-confessional dialogue with Roman Catholic, Seventh-day Adventist, Anglican and Orthodox churches; Pres. Rt Rev. Dr CHRISTIAN KRAUSE (Germany); Gen. Sec. Rev. Dr ISHMAEL NOKO (Zimbabwe); publs *Lutheran World Information* (English and German, daily e-mail news service and monthly print edition), *LWF Today* and *LWF Documentation* (both irregular).

World Council of Churches (WCC): Route de Ferney 150, Postfach 2100, 1211 Geneva 2, Switzerland; tel. (22) 7916111; fax (22) 7910361; e-mail info@wcc-coe.org; internet www.wcc-coe.org; f. 1948 to promote co-operation between Christian Churches and to prepare for a clearer manifestation of the unity of the Church; Activities are grouped into four 'clusters': Relationships, Issues and Themes, Communication, and Finance, Services and Administration; Mems: 342 Churches in more than 120 countries, incl. Armenia and Russia; Gen. Sec. Rev. Dr KONRAD RAISER (Germany); Publs *Current Dialogue* (2 a year), *Ecumenical News International* (weekly), *Ecumenical Review* (quarterly), *International Review of Mission* (quarterly), *WCC Yearbook.*

Science

Association of European Atomic Forums—FORATOM: 15–17 rue Belliard, 1040 Brussels, Belgium; tel. (2) 502-45-95; fax (2) 502-39-02; e-mail foratom@foratom.org; internet www.foratom.org; f. 1960; promotes the peaceful use of nuclear energy; provides information on nuclear energy issues to the EU, the media and the public; represents the nuclear industry within the EU institutions; holds periodical conferences; mems: atomic forums in 16 countries; Pres. FRANCIS TÉTREAU; Sec.-Gen. Dr PETER HAUG.

European Organization for Nuclear Research—CERN: European Laboratory for Particle Physics, 1211 Geneva 23, Switzerland; tel. (22) 7676111; fax (22) 7676555; internet www.cern.ch; f. 1954 to provide for collaboration among European states in nuclear research of a pure scientific and fundamental character, for peaceful purposes only; Council comprises two representatives of each member state; major experimental facilities: Proton Synchrotron (of 25–28 GeV), and Super Proton Synchrotron (of 450 GeV). Budget (1998) 875m. Swiss francs; mems: 20 European countries; observers: Israel, Japan, Russia, Turkey, USA, European Commission, UNESCO; Dir-Gen. LUCIANO MAIANI (Italy); publs *CERN Courier* (monthly), *Annual Report, Scientific Reports.*

European-Mediterranean Seismological Centre: c/o LDG, BP 12, 91680 Bruyères-le-Châtel, France; tel. 1-69-26-78-14; fax 1-69-26-70-00; e-mail csem@mail.csem.fr; internet www.emsc-csem.org; f. 1976 for rapid determination of seismic hypocentres in the region;

maintains data base; mems: institutions in 21 countries; Pres. C. BROWITT; Sec.-Gen. F. RIVIERE; publ. *Newsletter* (two a year).

European Space Agency (ESA): 8–10 rue Mario Nikis, 75738 Paris Cédex 15, France; tel. 1-53-69-76-54; fax 1-53-69-75-60; e-mail mailcom@esa.int; internet www.esa.int; f. 1975; fmrly the European Space Research Organisation and the European Launcher Development Organisation; provides for, and promotes, European co-operation in space research and technology, and their applications, for exclusively peaceful purposes; puts into effect a long-term European space policy of scientific research and technological development; Dir-Gen. ANTONIO RODOTÀ (Italy); Publs *ESA Annual Report, ECSL News* (quarterly), *ESA Bulleti* (quarterly), *Earth Observation Quarterly, Microgravity News* (3 a year), *Preparing for the Future* (quarterly), *Reaching for the Skies* (quarterly).

International Commission for the Scientific Exploration of the Mediterranean Sea (Commission internationale pour l'exploration scientifique de la mer Méditerranée—CIESM): 16 blvd de Suisse, 98000 Monaco; tel. 93-30-38-79; fax 92-16-11-95; e-mail fbriand@ciesm.org; internet www.ciesm.org; f. 1919 for scientific exploration of the Mediterranean Sea; organizes multilateral research investigations; includes 6 scientific committees; mems: 22 member countries, 2,500 scientists; Pres SAS Prince ALBERT OF MONACO; Sec.-Gen. Prof. F. DOUMENGE; Dir-Gen. Prof. F. BRIAND; publs Congress reports, science and workshop series.

International Council for Science—ICSU: 51 blvd de Montmorency, 75016 Paris, France; tel. 1-45-25-03-29; fax 1-42-88-94-31; e-mail secretariat@icsu.org; internet www.icsu.org; f. 1919 as International Research Council; present name adopted 1931; new statutes adopted 1996; to co-ordinate international co-operation in theoretical and applied sciences and to promote national scientific research through the intermediary of affiliated national organizations; General Assembly of representatives of national and scientific members meets every three years to formulate policy. The following committees have been established: Cttee on Science for Food Security, Scientific Cttee on Antarctic Research, Scientific Cttee on Oceanic Research, Cttee on Space Research, Scientific Cttee on Water Research, Scientific Cttee on Solar-Terrestrial Physics, Cttee on Science and Technology in Developing Countries, Cttee on Data for Science and Technology, Programme on Capacity Building in Science, Scientific Cttee on Problems of the Environment, Steering Cttee on Genetics and Biotechnology and Scientific Cttee on International Geosphere-Biosphere Programme. The following services and Inter-Union Committees and Commissions have been established: Federation of Astronomical and Geophysical Data Analysis Services, Inter-Union Commission on Frequency Allocations for Radio Astronomy and Space Science, Inter-Union Commission on Radio Meteorology, Inter-Union Commission on Spectroscopy, Inter-Union Commission on Lithosphere; National mems: academies or research councils in 98 countries; Scientific mems and assocs: 26 international unions (see below) and 28 scientific associates; Pres. W. ARBER; Sec.-Gen. H. A. MOONEY; publs *ICSU Yearbook, Science International* (quarterly), *Annual Report.*

International Council for the Exploration of the Sea—ICES: Palægade 2–4, 1261 Copenhagen K, Denmark; tel. 33-15-42-25; fax 33-93-42-15; e-mail ices.info@ices.dk; internet www.ices.dk; f. 1902 to encourage and facilitate research on the utilization and conservation of living resources and the environment in the North Atlantic Ocean and its adjacent seas; publishes and disseminate results of research; advises member countries and regulatory commissions; mems: 19 mem. countries and five countries or bodies with observer status; Gen. Sec. D. DE G. GRIFFITH; publs *ICES Journal of Marine Science, ICES Marine Science Symposia, ICES Fisheries Statistics, ICES Cooperative Research Reports, ICES Oceanographic Data Lists and Inventories, ICES Techniques in Marine Environmental Sciences, ICES Identification Leaflets for Plankton, ICES Identification Leaflets for Diseases and Parasites of Fish and Shellfish, ICES/CIEM Information.*

Social Sciences

Association for the Study of the World Refugee Problem—AWR: Piazzale di Porta Pia 121, 00198 Rome, Italy; tel. (06) 44250159; f. 1951 to promote and co-ordinate scholarly research on refugee problems; mems: 475 in 19 countries; Pres. FRANCO FOSCHI (Italy); Sec.-Gen. ALDO CLEMENTE (Italy); publs *AWR Bulletin* (quarterly, in English, French, Italian and German), treatises on refugee problems (17 vols).

European Association for Population Studies—EAPS: POB 11676, 2502 AR The Hague, Netherlands; tel. (70) 3565200; fax (70) 3647187; e-mail contact@eaps.nl; internet www.eaps.nl; f. 1983 to foster research and provide information on European population problems; organizes conferences, seminars and workshops; mems: demographers from 40 countries; Exec. Sec. GYS BEETS; publ. *Euro-*

pean Journal of Population/Revue Européenne de Démographie (quarterly).

European Co-ordination Centre for Research and Documentation in Social Sciences: 1010 Vienna, Grünangergasse 2, Austria; tel. (1) 512-43-33-0; fax (1) 512-53-66-16; f. 1963 for promotion of contacts between East and West European countries in all areas of social sciences; Activities include co-ordination of international comparative research projects; training of social scientists in problems of international research; organization of conferences; exchange of information and documentation; administered by a Board of Directors (23 social scientists from East and West) and a permanent secretariat in Vienna; Pres. ØRJAR ØYEN (Norway); Dir L. KIUZADJAN; Publs *Vienna Centre Newsletter, ECSSID Bulletin,* and books.

International Peace Academy—IPA: 777 United Nations Plaza, New York, NY 10017, USA; tel. (212) 687-4300; fax (212) 983-8246; e-mail ipa@ipacademy.org; internet www.ipacademy.org; f. 1970 to promote the prevention and settlement of armed conflicts between and within states through policy research and development; educates government officials in the procedures needed for conflict resolution, peace-keeping, mediation and negotiation, through international training seminars and publications; off-the-record meetings are also conducted to gain complete understanding of a specific conflict; Chair. RITA E. HAUSER; Pres. OLARA A. OTUNNU; publs *Annual Report, Newsletter* (2 a year).

International Peace Research Association—IPRA: c/o Copenhagen Peace Research Institute, University of Copenhagen, Fredericiagade 18, 1310 Copenhagen, Denmark; tel. 3345-5052; fax 3345-5060; e-mail bmoeller@copn.dk; internet www.copn.dk/ipra/ipra.html; f. 1964 to encourage interdisciplinary research on the conditions of peace and the causes of war; mems: 150 corporate, five regional branches, 1,000 individuals, in 93 countries; Pres. URSULA OSWALD (Mexico); Sec.-Gen. BJOERN MOELLER (Denmark); publ. *IPRA Newsletter* (quarterly).

International Social Science Council—ISSC: Maison de l'UNESCO, 1 rue Miollis, 75732 Paris Cédex 15, France; tel. 1-45-68-25-58; fax 1-45-66-76-03; e-mail issclak@unesco.org; internet www.unesco.org/ngo/issc; f. 1952; aims to promote the advancement of the social sciences throughout the world and their application to the major problems of the world; encourages co-operation at an international level between specialists in the social sciences. ISSC has a Senior Board; and programmes on International Human Dimensions of Global Environmental Change (IHDP) and Comparative Research on Poverty (CROP); mems: International Association of Legal Sciences, International Economic Association, International Federation of Social Science Organizations, International Geographical Union, International Institute of Administrative Sciences, International Law Association, International Peace Research Association, International Political Science Association, International Sociological Association, International Union for the Scientific Study of Population, International Union of Anthropological and Ethnological Sciences, International Union of Psychological Science, World Association for Public Opinion Research, World Federation for Mental Health;17 national organizations;, 16 associate member organizations; Pres. KURT PAWLIK (Germany); Sec.-Gen. LESZEK A. KOSINSKI (Canada).

World Society for Ekistics: c/o Athens Center of Ekistics, 24 Strat. Syndesmou St, 106 73 Athens, Greece; tel. (1) 3623216; fax (1) 3629337; e-mail ekistics@otenet.gr; internet www.ekistics.org; f. 1965; aims to promote knowledge and ideas concerning human settlements through research, publications and conferences; mems: 170 individuals; Pres. ALEXANDER B. LEMAN; Sec.-Gen. P. PSOMOPOULOS; publs *Ekistics, The Problems and Science of Human Settlements, Ekistic Index of Periodicals.*

Social Welfare and Human Rights

Aid to Displaced Persons and its European Villages: 35 rue du Marché, 4500 Huy, Belgium; tel. (85) 21-34-81; fax (85) 23-01-47; e-mail aidepersdepl.huy@proximedia.be; internet www.proximedia.com/aideperso.html; f. 1957 to carry on and develop work begun by the Belgian asscn Aid to Displaced Persons; aims to provide material and moral aid for refugees; European Villages established at Aachen, Bregenz, Augsburg, Berchem-Ste-Agathe, Spiesen, Euskirchen, Wuppertal as centres for refugees; Pres. LUC DENYS (Belgium).

Amnesty International: 1 Easton St, London, WC1X 0DW, United Kingdom; tel. (20) 7413-5500; fax (20) 7956-1157; e-mail amnestyis@amnesty.org; internet www.amnesty.org; f. 1961; an independent world-wide movement that campaigns impartially for the release of all prisoners of conscience, for fair and prompt trials for all political prisoners, for the abolition of torture and the death penalty and for an end to extrajudicial executions and 'disappearances'; also opposes abuses by opposition groups (hostage-taking, torture and arbitrary killings); financed by donations; mems: 1m. represented by 7,500 local, youth, student and other specialist groups, in more than 100 countries and territories; nationally organized sections in 56 countries; Sec.-Gen. IRENE KHAN (Bangladesh); publs *International Newsletter* (monthly), *Annual Report*, other country reports.

Aviation sans Frontières—ASF: Brussels National Airport, Brucargo 706, POB 7339, 1931 Brucargo, Belgium; tel. (2) 753-24-70; fax (2) 753-24-71; e-mail office@asfbelgium.org; internet www .asfbelgium.org; f. 1983 to make available the resources of the aviation industry to humanitarian organizations, for carrying supplies and equipment at minimum cost, both on long-distance flights and locally; Pres. PHILIPPE DEHENNIN; Gen. Man. XAVIER FLAMENT.

European Federation of Older Persons—EURAG: Wielandgasse 9, 1 Stock, 8010 Graz, Austria; tel. (316) 81-46-08; fax (316) 81-47-67; e-mail eurag.europe@aon.at; internet www.eurag-europe.org; f. 1962 as the European Federation for the Welfare of the Elderly (present name adopted 2002); serves as a forum for the exchange of experience and practical co-operation among member organizations; represents the interests of members before international organizations; promotes understanding and co-operation in matters of social welfare; draws attention to the problems of old age; mems: organizations in 33 countries; Pres. EDMÉE MANGERS-ANEN (Luxembourg); Sec.-Gen. Dr ULLA HERFORT-WÖRNDLE (Austria); publs (in English, French, German and Italian) *EURAG Newsletter* (quarterly), *EURAG Information* (monthly).

International Council of Voluntary Agencies—ICVA: 48 Chemin du Grand-Montfleury, 1290 Versoix, Switzerland; tel. (22) 9509600; fax (22) 9509609; e-mail secretariat@icva.ch; internet www .icva.ch; f. 1962 as a global network of human rights and humanitarian and development NGOs; focuses on information exchange and advocacy, primarily in the areas of humanitarian affairs and refugee issues; mems: 78 non-governmental organizations; Chair. ANDERS LADEKARL; Co-ordinator ED SCHENKENBERG VAN MIEROP; publ. *Talk Back* (newsletter; available on website).

International Federation of Human Rights Leagues—FIDH: 17 passage de la Main d'Or, 75011 Paris, France; tel. 1-43-55-25-28; fax 1-43-55-18-80; e-mail fidh@csi.com; internet www.fidh.imaginet .fr; f. 1922; promotes the implementation of the Universal Declaration of Human Rights and other instruments of human rights protection; aims to raise awareness and alert public opinion to issues of human rights violations; undertakes investigation and observation missions; carries out training; uses its consultative and observer status to lobby international authorities; mems: 105 national leagues in over 86 countries; Pres. PATRICK BAUDOUIN; publs *Lettre* (2 a month), mission reports.

International Federation of Persons with Physical Disability—FIMITIC: Plittersdorfer Str. 103, 53173 Bonn, Germany; tel. (228) 9359-191; fax (228) 9359-192; e-mail fimitic@t-online.de; internet www.fimitic.org; f. 1953; brings together representatives of the disabled and handicapped into an international, non-profit, politically and religiously neutral organization under the guidance of the disabled themselves; focuses on ensuring equalization of opportunities and full participation of persons with disabilities; combats discrimination; mems: national groups from 25 European countries, corresponding mems from eight countries; Pres. MARIJA-LIDIJA STIGLIC (Germany); Gen. Sec. MARIJA ŠTIGLIC (Germany); publs *Bulletin*, *Nouvelles*.

International League against Racism and Antisemitism: CP 1754, 1211 Geneva 1, Switzerland; tel. (22) 7310633; fax (22) 7370634; e-mail licra@mnet.ch; internet www.licra.ch; f. 1927; mems in 17 countries; Pres. PIERRE AIDENBAUM (France).

International League for Human Rights: 823 UN Plaza Suite 717, New York, NY 10017, USA; tel. (212) 661-0480; fax (212) 661-0416; e-mail info@ilhr.org; internet www.ilhr.org; f. 1942 to implement political, civil, social, economic and cultural rights contained in the Universal Declaration of Human Rights adopted by the United Nations and to support and protect defenders of human rights worldwide; mems: individuals, national affiliates and correspondents throughout the world; Exec. Dir CATHERINE A. FITZPATRICK; publs various human rights reports.

International Planned Parenthood Federation—IPPF: Regent's College, Inner Circle, Regent's Park, London, NW1 4NS, United Kingdom; tel. (20) 7487-7900; fax (20) 7487-7950; e-mail info@ippf.org; internet www.ippf.org; f. 1952; aims to promote and support sexual and reproductive health and family planning services throughout the world, with a particular focus on the needs of young people; works to bring relevant issues to the attention of the media, parliamentarians, academics, governmental and non-governmental organizations, and the general public; mobilizes financial resources to fund programmes and information materials; offers technical assistance and training; collaborates with other international organizations. The International Medical Panel of the IPPF formulates guide-lines and statements on current medical and sci-

entific advice and best practices; mems: independent family planning asscns in over 150 countries; Pres. ANGELA GÓMEZ; Dir-Gen. Dr STEVEN SINDING.

Médecins sans frontières—MSF: 39 rue de la Tourelle, 1040 Brussels, Belgium; tel. (2) 280-18-81; fax (2) 280-01-73; internet www.msf.org; f. 1971; independent medical humanitarian org composed of physicians and other members of the medical profession; aims to provide medical assistance to victims of war and natural disasters; operates longer-term programmes of nutrition, immunization, sanitation, public health, and rehabilitation of hospitals and dispensaries; awarded the Nobel peace prize in Oct. 1999; mems: national sections in 18 countries in Europe, Asia and North America; Pres. Dr NORTEN ROSTRUP; Sec.-Gen. RAFAEL VILASANJUAN; publ. *Activity Report* (annually).

World Veterans Federation: 17 rue Nicolo, 75116 Paris, France; tel. 1-40-72-61-00; fax 1-40-72-80-58; e-mail fmacwvf@noos.fr; f. 1950 to maintain international peace and security by the application of the San Francisco Charter and work to help implement the Universal Declaration of Human Rights and related international conventions; aims to defend the spiritual and material interests of war veterans and war victims; promotes practical international co-operation in disarmament, legislation concerning war veterans and war victims, and development of international humanitarian law, etc; in 1986 established International Socio-Medical Information Centre (United Kingdom) for psycho-medical problems resulting from stress. Regional committees for Africa, Asia and the Pacific, and Europe and Standing Committee on Women; mems: national organizations in 84 countries, representing about 27m. war veterans and war victims; Pres. ABDUL HAMID IBRAHIM; Sec.-Gen. MAREK HAGMAJER (Poland); publs special studies (disarmament, human rights, rehabilitation).

Sport and Recreations

International Amateur Athletic Federation—IAAF: 17 rue Princesse Florestine, BP 359, 98007 Monte Carlo Cédex, Monaco; tel. 93-10-88-88; fax 93-15-95-15; e-mail headquarters@iaaf.org; f. 1912 to ensure co-operation and fairness and to combat discrimination in athletics; compiles athletic competition rules and organizes championships at all levels; frames regulations for the establishment of World, Olympic and other athletic records; settles disputes between members; conducts a programme of development consisting of coaching, judging courses, etc.; and affiliates national governing bodies; mems: national asscns in 210 countries and territories; Gen. Sec. ISTVÁN GYULAI (Hungary); publs *IAAF Handbook* (every 2 years), *IAAF Review* (quarterly), *IAAF Directory* (annually), *New Studies in Athletics* (quarterly).

International Olympic Committee—IOC: Château de Vidy, 1007 Lausanne, Switzerland; tel. (21) 6216111; fax (21) 6216216; internet www.olympic.org; f. 1894 to ensure the regular celebration of the Olympic Games; The IOC is the final authority on all questions concerning the Olympic Games and the Olympic movement; Mems: representatives from 128 countries; Dir-Gen. FRANÇOIS CARRARD; Publ. *Olympic Review* (6 a year).

International Tennis Federation: Bank Lane, Roehampton, London, SW15 5XZ, United Kingdom; tel. (20) 8878-6464; fax (20) 8878-7799; e-mail communications@itftennis.com; internet www .itftennis.com; f. 1913 to govern the game of tennis throughout the world, promote its teaching and preserve its independence of outside authority; produces the Rules of Tennis; promotes the Davis Cup Competition for men, the Fed. Cup for women, the Olympic Games Tennis Event, wheelchair tennis, 16 cups for veterans, the ITF Sunshine Cup and the ITF Continental Connelly Cup for players of 18 years old and under, the World Youth Cup for players of 16 years old and under, and the World Junior Tennis Tournament for players of 14 years old and under; organizes tournaments; mems: 141 full and 57 associate; Pres. FRANCESCO RICCI BITTI; publs *World of Tennis* (annually), *Davis Cup Yearbook*, *ITF World* (quarterly), *ITF This Week* (weekly).

International Weightlifting Federation—IWF: PF 614, 1374 Budapest, Hungary; tel. (1) 3530530; fax (1) 3530199; e-mail iwf@iwf .net; internet www.iwf.net; f. 1905 to control international weightlifting; draws up technical rules; trains referees; supervises World Championships, Olympic Games, regional games and international contests of all kinds; registers world records; mems: 167 national organizations; Pres. Dr THOMÁS AJAN (Hungary); Gen. Sec. YANNIS SGOUROS (Greece); publs *IWF Constitution and Rules* (every 4 years), *World Weightlifting* (quarterly).

Union of European Football Associations—UEFA: route de Genève 46, 1260 Nyon 2, Switzerland; tel. (22) 9944444; fax (22) 9944488; internet www.uefa.com; f. 1954; works on behalf of Europe's national football asscns to promote football; aims to foster unity and solidarity between national asscns; mems: 51 national asscns; Pres. LENNART JOHANSSON; CEO GERHARD AIGNER; Publ *Magazine* (available online).

Technology

European Convention for Constructional Steelwork—ECCS: 32-36 ave des Ombrages, bte 20, 1200 Brussels, Belgium; tel. (2) 762-04-29; fax (2) 762-09-35; e-mail eccs@steelconstruct.com; internet www.steelconstruct.com; f. 1955 for the consideration of problems involved in metallic construction; mems: in 25 countries; Sec.-Gen. G. GENDEBEN; Publs Information sheets and documents, symposia reports, model codes.

European Organisation for the Exploitation of Meteorological Satellites—EUMETSAT: 64295 Darmstadt, Am Kavalleriesand 31, Germany; tel. (6151) 807377; fax (6151) 807304; e-mail ops@eumetsat.de; internet www.eumetsat.de; f. 1986; maintains and exploits European systems of meteorological satellites, including the Meteosat programme for gathering weather data; mems: 18 European countries and four co-operating states; Chair. Dr HENRI MALCORPS (Belgium); Dir Dr TILLMANN MOHR; Publs *Annual Report*, *IMAGE Newsletter*, brochures, conference and workshop proceedings.

International Federation for Information and Documentation: POB 90402, 2509 LK The Hague, Netherlands; tel. (70) 3140671; fax (70) 3140667; e-mail fid@fid.nl; internet www.fid.nl; f. 1895; aims to promote, and improve, through international co-operation, research in and development of information science, information management and documentation; maintains regional commissions for Latin America, North America and the Caribbean, Asia and Oceania, Western, Eastern and Southern Africa, North Africa and the Near East, and for Europe; mems: 62 national, five international, 330 institutional and individual mems; Pres. K. BRUNNSTEIN; Exec. Dir J. STEPHEN PARKER; Publs *FID Review* (every 2 months), *FID Directory* (every 2 years).

International Measurement Confederation—IMEKO: POB 457, 1371 Budapest 5, Hungary; tel. and fax (1) 353-1562; e-mail imeko.ime@mtesz.hu; internet www.imeko.org; f. 1958 as a federation of member organizations concerned with the advancement of measurement technology; aims to promote exchange of scientific and technical information in field of measurement and instrumentation and to enhance co-operation between scientists and engineers; holds World Congress every 3 years (2003: Dubrovnik; 2006: Rio de Janeiro); mems: 35 orgs; Pres. Prof. M. PETERS (Germany); Sec.-Gen. Dr TAMÁS KEMÉNY (Hungary); Publs *Acta IMEKO* (proccedings of World Congresses), *IMEKO TC Events Series*, *Measurement* (quarterly), *IMEKO Bulletin* (2 a year).

Regional Council of Co-ordination of Central and East European Engineering Organizations: c/o MTESZ, 1055 Budapest, Kossuth Lajos tér 6–8, Hungary; tel. (361) 353-4795; fax (361) 353-0317; e-mail mtesz@mtesz.hu; f. 1992; Hon. Pres. JÁNOS TÓTH.

Tourism

Baltic Sea Tourism Commission—BTC: Nya Redstugagatan 3, 602 24 Norrköping, Sweden; tel. (11) 12-35-80; fax (11) 10-31-03; e-mail info@baltic.com; internet www.balticsea.com; f. in 1984 as a non-profit organization to promote tourism to and within the Baltic Sea Region; Mems: more than 80 members in 15 countries, incl. Estonia, Latvia, Lithuania and Poland; Pres. KNUT HÄNSCHKE (Germany).

European Travel Commission: 61 rue du Marché aux Herbes, 1000 Brussels, Belgium; tel. (2) 504-03-03; fax (2) 514-18-43; e-mail etc@planetinternet.be; internet www.etc-europe-travel.org; f. 1948 to promote tourism in and to Europe, to foster co-operation and the exchange of information, and to organize research; mems: national tourist organizations in 31 European countries; Exec. Dir WALTER LEU (Switzerland).

Trade and Industry

Energy Charter Secretariat: blvd de la Woluwe 56, 1200 Brussels, Belgium; tel. (2) 775-98-00; fax (2) 775-98-01; e-mail info@encharter.org; internet www.encharter.org; f. 1995 under the provisions of the Energy Charter Treaty (1994); aims to promote trade and investment in the energy industries; mems: 51 signatory states; Sec.-Gen. RIA KEMPER (Germany); publs *Promoting Energy Efficiency*, *Trade in Energy*, *The Energy Charter Treaty - A Reader's Guide*, reports.

European Brewery Convention: POB 510, 2380 BB Zoeterwoude, Netherlands; tel. (71) 545-60-47; fax (71) 541-00-13; e-mail secretariat@ebc-nl.com; internet www.ebc-nl.com; f. 1947, present name adopted 1948; aims to promote scientific co-ordination in malting and brewing; mems: national asscns in 22 European countries; Pres. E. PAJUNEN (Finland); Sec.-Gen. M. VAN WIJNGAARDEN (Netherlands); publs *Analytica*, *Thesaurus*, *Dictionary of Brewing*, monographs, conference proceedings, manuals of good practice.

European Crop Protection Association: Ave E. van Nieuwenhuyse, 1160 Brussels, Belgium; tel. (2) 663-15-50; fax (2) 663-15-60; aims to harmonize national and international regulations concerning crop protection products, to support the development of the industry and to promote observation of the FAO Code of Conduct on the Distribution and Use of Pesticides, forms part of the Global Crop Protection Federation; European Dir-Gen. Dr PIERRE A. URECH.

European Federation of Tile and Brick Manufacturers: Obstgartenstrasse 28, 8035 Zürich, Switzerland; tel. (1) 3619650; fax (1) 3610205; e-mail office@tbe-euro.ch; internet www.tbe-euro .com; f. 1952 to co-ordinate research between members of the industry, improve technical knowledge and encourage professional training; mems: asscns in 23 European and east European countries; Chair. VITTORIO VITOLO; Dir Dr W. P. WELLER.

European General Galvanizers Association—EGGA: Maybrook House, Godstone Rd, Caterham, Surrey, CR3 6RE, United Kingdom; tel. (1883) 331277; fax (1883) 331287; e-mail mail@egga .com; internet www.egga.com; f. 1955 to promote co-operation between members of the industry, especially in improving processes and finding new uses for galvanized products; mems: asscns in 17 European countries; Pres. FRAN THIEL (Netherlands).

European Packaging Federation: c/o Institut Français de l'Emballage et du Conditionnement IFEC, 33 rue Louis Blanc, 93582 St-Ouen Cédex, France; tel. 1-40-11-22-12; fax 1-40-11-01-06; e-mail info@ifecpromotion.tm.fr; internet www.ifecpromotion.tm.fr/epf .htm; f. 1953 to encourage the exchange of information between national packaging institutes and to promote technical and economic progress; mems: organizations in 12 European countries; Pres. J. P. POTHET (France); Sec.-Gen. A. FREIDINGER-LEGAY (France).

International Chamber of Commerce (ICC): 38 cours Albert 1er, 75008 Paris, France; tel. 1-49-53-28-28; fax 1-49-53-29-42; e-mail icc@iccwbo.org; internet www.iccwbo.org; f. 1919 to promote free trade and private enterprise, provide practical services and represent business interests at governmental and intergovernmental levels; Mems: about 5,500 individual corporations and 1,700 organizations; National Committees or Groups in more than 60 countries and territories, incl. Czech Republic, Greece, Hungary, Lithuania, Poland, Romania, Slovakia, Slovenia and Yugoslavia; Sec.-Gen. MARIA LIVANOS CATTAUI; Publs *Annual Report*, *Business World* (electronic magazine), *Documentary Credits Insight* (quarterly), *ICC Contact* (newsletter), other reference works, and rules and guide-lines governing commercial and banking practices.

International Federation of Grocers' Associations—IFGA: Vakcentrum, Woerden, Netherlands; tel. (348) 419771; fax (348) 421801; f. 1927; initiates special studies and works to further the interests of members, with special regard to conditions resulting from European integration and developments in consuming and distribution; mems: 30 asscns representing 125,000 sales outlets.

Union of Industrial and Employers' Confederations of Europe—UNICE: 40 rue Joseph II, 1000 Brussels, Belgium; tel. (2) 237-65-11; fax (2) 231-14-45; e-mail main@unice.be; internet www .unice.org; f. 1958; aims to ensure that European Union policy-making takes account of the views of European business; committees and working groups develop joint positions in fields of interest to business and submit these to the Community institutions concerned; the Council of Presidents (of member federations) lays down general policy; the Executive Committee (of Directors-General of member federations) is the managing body; and the Committee of Permanent Delegates, consisting of federation representatives in Brussels, ensures permanent liaison with mems; mems: 20 industrial and employers' federations from the EU member states, and 15 federations from non-EU countries, four observer federations; Pres. JÜRGEN STRUBE; publ. *UNICE@News* (monthly, by e-mail).

Transport

Association of European Airlines: 350 ave Louise, bte 4, 1050 Brussels, Belgium; tel. (2) 639-89-89; fax (2) 639-89-90; e-mail aea .secretariat@aca.be; internet www.aea.be; f. 1954 to carry out research on political, commercial, economic and technical aspects of air transport; maintains statistical data bank; mems: 29 airlines; Chair. LEO M. VAN WIJK (Netherlands); Sec.-Gen. KARL-HEINZ NEUMEISTER (Germany).

Baltic and International Maritime Council—BIMCO: Bagsvaerdvej 161, 2880 Bagsvaerd, Denmark; tel. 44-36-68-00; fax 44-36-68-68; e-mail mailbox@bimco.dk; internet www.bimco.dk; f. 1905 to unite shipowners and other persons and organizations connected with the shipping industry; mems: in 122 countries, representing over 65% of world merchant tonnage; Pres. MICHAEL EVERARD (UK); Sec.-Gen. TRULS W. L'ORANGE; publs *BIMCO Review* (annually), *BIMCO Bulletin* (6 a year), *Vessel* (CD-ROM), manuals.

Danube Commission: Benczúr utca 25, 1068 Budapest, Hungary; tel. (1) 352-1835; fax (1) 352-1839; e-mail secretariat@ danubecom-intern.org; internet www.danubecom-intern.org; f. 1948; ; supervises implementation of the Belgrade Convention on the Regime of Navigation on the Danube; approves projects for river maintenance; supervises a uniform system of traffic regulations on the whole navigable portion of the Danube and on river inspection; mems: Austria, Bulgaria, Croatia, Germany, Hungary, Moldova, Romania, Russia, Serbia and Montenegro, Slovakia, Ukraine; Pres. Dr S. NICK; Dir-Gen. Capt. D. NEDIALKOV; publs *Basic Regulations for Navigation on the Danube, Hydrological Yearbook, Statistical Yearbook*, proceedings of sessions.

European Civil Aviation Conference—ECAC: 3 bis Villa Emile-Bergerat, 92522 Neuilly-sur-Seine Cédex, France; tel. 1-46-41-85-44; fax 1-46-24-18-18; e-mail ecac@compuserve.com; internet www .ecac-ceac.org; f. 1955; aims to promote the continued development of a safe, efficient and sustainable European air transport system; mems: 41 European states; Pres. ALFREDO ROMA; Exec. Sec. RAYMOND BENJAMIN.

European Conference of Ministers of Transport—ECMT: 2 rue André Pascal, 75775 Paris Cédex 16, France; tel. 1-45-24-82-00; fax 1-45-24-97-42; e-mail ecmt.contact@oecd.org; internet www.oecd .org/cem; f. 1953 to achieve the maximum use and most rational development of European transport; aims to create a safe, sustainable, efficient, integrated transport system; provides a forum for analysis and discussion; holds round tables, seminars and symposia; shares Secretariat staff with OECD; mems: 41 member countries, 6 associate mems, 2 observer countries; Sec.-Gen. JACK SHORT; publs *Activities of the Conference* (annually), *ECMT News* (2 a year), *Catalogue of Publications*, various statistical publications and surveys.

European Organisation for the Safety of Air Navigation—EUROCONTROL: 96 rue de la Fusée, 1130 Brussels, Belgium; tel. (2) 729-90-11; fax (2) 729-90-44; internet www.eurocontrol.int; f. 1960; aims to develop a coherent and co-ordinated air traffic control system in Europe. A revised Convention was signed in June 1997, incorporating the following institutional structure: a General Assembly (known as the Commission in the transitional period), a Council (known as the Provisional Council) and an Agency under the supervision of the Director General; there are directorates, covering human resources and finance matters and a general secretariat. A special organizational structure covers the management of the European Air Traffic Management Programme. EUROCONTROL also operates the Experimental Centre (at Brétigny-sur-Orge, France),

the Institute of Air Navigation Services (in Luxembourg), the Central Route Charges Office, the Central Flow Management Unit (both in Brussels) and the Upper Area Control Centre (in Maastricht, Netherlands); mems: 31 European countries; Dir-Gen. VÍCTOR M. AGUADO (Spain).

Organisation for the Collaboration of Railways: Hozà 63–67, 00681 Warsaw, Poland; tel. (22) 6573600; fax (22) 6573654; e-mail osjd@osjd.org.pl; f. 1956; aims to improve standards and co-operation in railway traffic between countries of Europe and Asia; promotes co-operation on issues relating to traffic policy and economic and environmental aspects of railway traffic; ensures enforcement of a number of rail agreements; aims to elaborate and standardize general principles for international transport law. Conference of Ministers of mem. countries meets annually; Conference of Gen. Dirs of Railways meets at least once a year; mems: ministries of transport of 27 countries world-wide; Chair. TADEUSZ SZOZDA; publ *OSShD Journal* (every 2 months, in Chinese, German and Russian).

Youth and Students

European Students' Forum (Association des états généraux des étudiants de l'Europe): 15 rue Nestor de Tiere, 1040 Brussels, Belgium; tel. (2) 245-23-00; fax (2) 245-62-60; e-mail info@aegee.org; internet www.aegee.org; promotes cross-border communication and integration between students; holds specialized conferences; mems: 17,000 students in 271 university cities in 40 countries.

European Youth Forum: 120 rue Joseph II, 1000 Brussels, Belgium; tel. (2) 286-94-12; fax (2) 233-37-09; e-mail youthforum@ youthforum.org; internet www.europeanyouthforum.com; f. 1996; promotes development of a coherent and integrated youth policy; promotes the rights of young people, as well as understanding and respect for human rights; consults with international organizations and governments on issues relevant to young people.

International Union of Students: POB 58, 17th November St, 110 01 Prague 01, Czech Republic; tel. (2) 312812; fax (2) 316100; internet www.stud.uni-hannover/delgruppen/ius; f. 1946 to defend the rights and interests of students and strive for peace, disarmament, the eradication of illiteracy and of all forms of discrimination; operates research centre, sports and cultural centre and student travel bureau; activities include conferences, meetings, solidarity campaigns, relief projects; awards 30–40 scholarships annually; mems: 140 organizations from 115 countries; Pres. JOSEF SKALA; Vice-Pres. MARTA HUBIČKOVÁ; Gen. Sec. GIORGOS MICHAELIDES (Cyprus); publs *World Student News* (quarterly), *IUS Newsletter*, *Student Life* (quarterly), *DE—Democratization of Education* (quarterly).

RESEARCH INSTITUTES

INSTITUTES STUDYING CENTRAL AND SOUTH-EASTERN EUROPE

ALBANIA

Institute of History: Rruga Naim Fransheri 7, Tirana; tel. and fax (4) 225869; attached to Albania Academy of Sciences; research history of Albanians in their own and neighbouring states and in wider diaspora; library of 70,000 vols; Dir Dr ANA LALAJ.

Institute of International and Strategic Studies: Rruga Barrikadave 8, Tirana; tel. (4) 22896; fax (4) 228388; e-mail elezi@albmail.com; f. 1994; research into problems of South-Eastern Europe, particularly economic transition and ethnic minorities; Dir Dr MEHMET ELEZI; publ. *Balkan Analyst* (in English, quarterly).

ARGENTINA

Centro de Estudios de Europa Central y Oriental (CEECO) (Centre for the Study of Central and Eastern Europe): Blanco Encalada 3225 D8, 1426 Buenos Aires; tel. (11) 4541-8676; fax (11) 4541-8676; e-mail ceeco@mail.fsoc.uba.ar; f. 1992; research into Central and Eastern European matters, especially the wars in the former Yugoslavia, problems of post-communism, organized crime and economic reforms; advises governments, state agencies and companies on matters related to the region; Dir Prof. JUAN BELIKOW; publ. *Cuadernos de Trabajo CARI-UBA.*

Centro de Estudios Internacionales para el Desarrollo (CEID) (International Development Research Centre): San José de Calasanz 537, Planta Baja, A, 1424 Buenos Aires; tel. (11) 4686-0212; fax (11) 4686-0212; e-mail admin@ceid.edu.ar; internet www.ceid.edu.ar; f. 1998; international relations in Central and South-Eastern Europe, Eastern Europe, the Russian Federation and the CIS; education, corruption, ecology; Pres. Lic. MARCELO JAVIER DE LOS REYES; publ. *Revista del CEID* (2 a year).

AUSTRALIA

Australian Institute of International Affairs (AIIA): Stephen House, 32 Thesiger Court, Deakin, ACT 2600; tel. (2) 6282-2133; fax (2) 6285-2334; e-mail ceo@aiia.asn.au; internet www.aiia.asn.au; f. 1933; promotes interest in and understanding of international affairs in Australia; library of approx. 5,000 vols; Pres. NEAL BLEWETT; Exec. Dir ROSS COTTRILL; publs *Australian Journal of International Affairs* (3 a year), *Australia in World Affairs* (every 5 years), *The Cambridge Asia-Pacific Studies, Regime Change and Regime Maintenance.*

Contemporary Europe Research Centre (CERC): University of Melbourne, 2nd Floor, 234 Queensberry St, Carlton, Vic 3052; tel. (3) 8344-9502; fax (3) 8344-9507; e-mail cerc@cerc.unimelb.edu.au; internet www.cerc.unimelb.edu.au; f. 1997; research (fundamental and applied) and provision of information on the CIS and Central and Eastern Europe for business, government and the media; database of social, political and economic developments in the former USSR and Eastern Europe; press, periodical and statistical materials in languages of the CIS and Central and Eastern Europe; Dir Dr PHILOMENA MURRAY; Dep. Dir Prof. LESLIE HOLMES; publs *Russian and Euro-Asian Bulletin* (monthly), CERC Working Paper series, occasional monographs and collections of articles.

AUSTRIA

Centre for the Study of Balkan Societies and Cultures (CSBSC): Dept for Southeast European History, University of Graz, 8010 Graz, Mozartgasse 3; tel. (316) 380-23-77; fax (316) 380-97-35; e-mail csbsc@gewi.kfunigraz.ac.at; internet www-gewi.kfunigraz.ac.at/csbsc/; sociocultural and historical research on the Balkans; investigation of current social, economic and political developments in the Balkans; library of 40,000 vols, 1,500 monographs; Dir Prof. Dr KARL KASER.

Forschungsstelle für Institutionellen Wandel und Europäische Integration (IWE) (Research Unit for Institutional Change and European Integration—ICE): 1040 Vienna, Prinz Eugen Str. 8–10; tel. (1) 515-81-75-65; fax (1) 515-81-75-66; e-mail iwe@oeaw.ac.at; f. 1998; attached to Austrian Acad. of Sciences; Dir Dr SONJA PUNTSCHER RIEKMANN.

Institut für den Donauraum und Mitteleuropa (IDM) (Institute for Danube and Central European Studies): 1090 Vienna, Hahngasse 6/1/24; tel. (1) 319-72-58; fax (1) 319-72-58-4; e-mail idm@idm.at; internet www.idm.at; f. 1953; research into the sciences, economics, social sciences, cultural studies and history of the Danube region and Central Europe; Dir Prof. Dr ERHARD BUSEK.

Institut für die Wissenschaften vom Menschen (IWM) (Institute for Human Sciences): 1090 Vienna, Spittelauer Lände 3; tel. (1) 313-58-0; fax (1) 313-58-30; e-mail iwm@iwm.at; internet www.iwm.at; f. 1982; attached to University of Vienna; research into political and social transformation in Central and Eastern Europe, social consequences of economic transformation in East Central Europe, the transformation of the national higher education and research systems of Central Europe; library of more than 30,000 vols, 252 periodicals; Man. Dirs SUSANNE FRÖSCHL, ANITA TRANINGER; publ. *IWM Newsletter* (quarterly, in English and German).

Institut für Osteuropäische Geschichte (Institute for Eastern European History): 1090 Vienna, Spitalgasse 2, Hof 3; tel. (1) 42-77-41-101; fax (1) 42-77-94-11; e-mail suedosteuropaforschung@univie.ac.at; internet www.univie.ac.at/iog; research into and education in Eastern and South-Eastern Europe; Dir Prof. Dr ARNOLD SUPPAN.

Internationales Institut für den Frieden (International Institute for Peace—IIP): 1040 Vienna, Möllwaldplatz 5; tel. (1) 504-64-37; fax (1) 505-32-36; e-mail iip@aon.at; internet www.iip.at; f. 1957; research into peace research and studies into interdependence as a strategy for peace, the security structure of Europe in the post-Cold War era, reconstruction of countries in Central and Eastern Europe, the prevention of conflicts; Pres. ERWIN LANC; Dir PETER STANIA; publs *IIP Occasional Papers, Peace and the Sciences* (quarterly).

Österreichische Gesellschaft für Aussenpolitik und Internationale Beziehungen (ÖGA) (Austrian Association for Foreign Policy and International Relations): 1010 Vienna, Hofburg/Schweizerhof/Brunnenstiege; tel. (1) 535-46-27; fax (1) 532-26-05; e-mail oega@utanet.at; internet www.start.at/oega; f. 1958; lectures, discussions; approx. 400 mems; Pres. Dr WOLFGANG SCHALLENBERG; publ. *Österreichisches Jahrbuch für Internationale Politik* (annually).

Österreichische Ost- und Südosteuropa-Institut (ÖSI) (Austrian Institute of East and South-East European Studies): 1010 Vienna, Josefsplatz 6; tel. (1) 512-18-95; fax (1) 512-18-95-53; e-mail sekretariat@osi.ac.at; internet www.osi.ac.at/; f. 1958; research into the geography, cartography, ecology, history, contemporary history, social sciences, nationality and minority studies of Eastern and South-Eastern European countries; library of 41,000 vols; Dir Dr PETER JORDAN; publs *Österreichische Osthefte* (quarterly), *Wiener Osteuropastudien, Schriftenreihe des Österreichischen Ost- und Südosteuropa-Instituts, Veröffentlichungen des Österreichischen Ost- und Südosteuropa-Instituts.*

Österreichisches Institut für Internationale Politik (ÖIIP) (Austrian Institute for International Affairs): 1040 Vienna, Operngasse 20B; tel. (1) 581-11-06; fax (1) 581-11-06-10; e-mail info@oiip.at; internet www.oiip.at; f. 1978; research studies on national and international security policy, European integration, Central and Eastern Europe and Russia, the Near East, the Balkans, Austrian foreign policy; organization of international conferences; approx. 8,000 vols; Dir Prof. Dr OTMAR HÖLL; publ. working paper series.

Universitätzentrum für Friedenforschung (UZF) (University Centre for Peace Research): 1010 Vienna, Universitätsstr. 7/III Stock; tel. (1) 42-77-28-201; fax (1) 42-77-47-439; internet www.frieden.univie.ac.at; f. 1973; attached to University of Vienna; research into international peace dialogue, East-West relations, development policy, arms control, disarmament and European security structure; undergraduate and postgraduate studies; conferences and workshops; Pres. Prof. Dr NORBERT LESER; Sec.-Gen. Dr SIGRID PÖLLINGER; publ. *Wiener Blätter zur Friedensforschung* (quarterly).

Wiener Institut für Internationale Wirtschaftsvergleiche (WIIW) (Vienna Institute for International Economic Studies): 1010 Vienna, Oppolzergasse 6; tel. (1) 533-66-10; fax (1) 533-66-10-50; e-mail wiiw@wiiw.at; internet www.wiiw.ac.at/; f. 1974; expertise on Central and Eastern Europe, CIS and the Balkans; research into economic developments in countries in transition; studies East-West integration and focuses on comparative aspects of global economic trends; 13,000 vols; Research Dir MICHAEL LANDESMANN; Exec. Dir INGRID GAZZARI; publ. *WIIW Monthly Database on Central and Eastern Europe* (on-line).

BELGIUM

Centre de Recherches Interdisciplinaires sur la Transition des Pays de l'Est vers l'Économie de Marché (CRITEME) (Centre for Interdisciplinary Research on the Transition of Eastern Countries to a Market Economy): 50 ave F. D. Roosevelt, CP 172, 1050 Brussels; tel. (2) 650-32-63; fax (2) 650-35-21; internet www.ulb.ac.be/rech/inventaire/unites/ULB424.html; attached to Institute of Sociology, Université Libre de Bruxelles; socioeconomic developments in Central and Eastern Europe and the former USSR; Dir Prof. MARIO TELO.

Centre for European Policy Studies (CEPS): 1 pl. du Congrès, 1000 Brussels; tel. (2) 229-39-11; fax (2) 219-41-51; e-mail info@ceps.be; internet www.ceps.be; f. 1983; independent policy research institute; research programmes on: macroeconomic policy, financial markets and institutions, trade developments and policy, energy for the 21st century, political institutions and society, wider Europe, European security, and justice and home affairs; conferences and seminars; Dir DANIEL GROS; Chief Exec. KAREL LANNOO; publs *CEPS Paperbacks*, research reports, working party reports, working documents, policy briefs, European Security Forum working papers.

Centre for the New Europe (CNE): 23 rue de Luxembourg, 1000 Brussels; tel. (2) 506-40-00; fax (2) 506-40-09; e-mail info@cne.be; internet www.centreforthenewurope.org; f. 1993; pan-European policy research; conducts research in order to develop and promote policy alternatives favouring a market-orientated economy and individual, rather than collectivist, values; Pres. TIM EVANS; Head of Academic Affairs Dr HARDY BOUILLON; publs *CNE Newsletter*, research papers.

Institut d'Etudes Européennes (Institute for European Studies): Université Libre de Bruxelles, 39 ave F. D. Roosevelt, 1050 Brussels; tel. (2) 650-30-67; fax (2) 650-30-68; e-mail iee@admin.ulb.ac.be; internet www.ulb.ac.be/iee/; f. 1963; research into European economics, law and politics; conferences, courses and seminars; directs the Centre de Documentation Européenne (CDE); Pres. Prof. GINETTE KURGAN-VAN HENTENRYK; Dir Prof. PAUL MAGNETTE; publ. *Les Collections de l'Institut d'Etudes Européennes.*

Institut Royal des Relations Internationales (IRRI) (Royal Institute of International Relations): 69 rue de Namur, 1000 Brussels; tel. (2) 223-41-14; fax (2) 223-41-16; e-mail info@irri-kiib.be; internet www.irri-kiib.be; f. 1947; research into international relations, international economics, international law and international politics; 16,000 vols and 600 periodicals; archives; Chair. ÉTIENNE DAVIGNON;

Dir-Gen. FRANÇOIS DE KERCHOVE D'EXAERDE; publs *Studia Diplomatica* (6 a year), *Internationale Spectator* (monthly).

BRAZIL

Instituto Brasileiro de Relações Internacionais (Brazilian Institute of International Relations): Multiuso 1, Bloc B, Campus Universitário, CP 4602, 70910-900 Brasília, DF; tel. (61) 348-2590; fax (61) 274-1448; f. 1954; 1,000 vols; Exec. Dir JOSÉ CARLOS B. ALEIXO; Sec. ALCIDES COSTA VAZ; publ. *Revista Brasileira de Política Internacional* (quarterly).

Instituto de Relações Internacionais (Institute of International Relations): Pontifícia Universidade Católica do Rio de Janeiro, rua Marquês de São Vicente 225, Casa 19, Gávea 22453-900, Rio de Janeiro, RJ; tel. (21) 3114-1557; fax (21) 3114-1560; e-mail iripuc@rdc.puc-rio.br; internet www.puc-rio.br/sobrepuc/depto/iri; f. 1979; research into international relations, integration, foreign policy and the environment; postgraduate courses; Dir Dr SONIA DE CAMARGO; publ. *Contexto Internacional* (2 a year).

BULGARIA

Institute for European Studies and Information: 1125 Sofia, POB 28, 6th Floor, Blvd Dr G. M. Dimitrov 52A; tel. and fax (2) 971-24-11; e-mail ces@mail.cesbg.org; internet www.cesbg.org; f. 1990 as Centre for European Studies, renamed 1999; European documentation centre; information on the political, legal, economic and social aspects of European integration and co-operation; 2,000 vols; Dir Dr INGRID SHIKOVA; publ. *Europa* (monthly).

Institute for International Relations: 1000 Sofia, Tcherkovna 39B; tel. (2) 943-15-12; e-mail iir@balcanica.org; f. 1997; non-profit, private research institute, involved in study of Balkan and European issues; Dir Dr YULIA ZAHARIEVA.

Institute of Balkan Studies: Bulgarian Academy of Sciences, Sofia 1000, Moskovska 45; tel. and fax (2) 980-62-97; e-mail balkani@cl.bas.bg; internet www.cl.bas.bg/Balkan-Studies; f. 1964; research into Balkan states, relations between Balkan states and other regions, including the Mediterranean, Western Europe and the Middle East; Dir Dr AGOP GARABEDYAN; Sec.-Gen Dr OGNYANA HRISIMOVA; publ. *Etudes balkaniques* (quarterly, in French, English and German).

Institute of Economics: Bulgarian Academy of Sciences, 1040 Sofia, Aksakov St 3; tel. (2) 989-05-95; fax (2) 988-21-08; e-mail ineco@iki.bas.bg; internet internet www.iki.bas.bg; f. 1949; research into regional economy, sectoral economy, international economics, macroeconomics, and corporate economics; Dir Dr MITKO DIMITROV; Deputy Dir Dr STOYAN TOTEV; publs *Economic Thought* (6 a year in Bulgarian, 1 a year in English), *Economic Studies* (3 a year), monographs.

CANADA

Canadian Institute of International Affairs: Glendon Hall, Glendon College, 2275 Bayview Ave, Toronto, ON M4N 3M5; tel. (416) 487-6830; fax (416) 487-6831; e-mail mailbox@ciia.org; internet www.ciia.org; f. 1928; 8,000 vols; Pres. and Chief Exec. BARBARA MCDOUGALL; Chair. ROY MACLAREN; publs *Behind the Headlines, International Journal* (quarterly), *Contemporary Affairs* (annually), *Annual Report.*

Centre for Russian and East European Studies (CREES): University of Toronto, Munk Centre for International Studies, 1 Devonshire Pl., Toronto, ON M5S 3K7; tel. (416) 946-8938; fax (416) 946-8939; internet www.utoronto.ca/crees/; f. 1963; research and graduate study of Russia and Central and South-Eastern Europe; Dir PETER H. SOLOMON, Jr; publs working papers of the Stalin-Era Research and Archives Project, *Tolstoy Studies Journal, Bulletin on Current Research in Soviet and East European Law, Rossiiane v Azii.*

Office for Central and Eastern Europe Initiatives (OCEEI): International Development Research Centre (IDRC), 250 Albert St, POB 8500, Ottawa, ON K1G 3H9; tel. (613) 236-6163; fax (613) 563-0815; e-mail sdavies@idrc.ca; internet www.idrc.ca/oceei; f. 1993 as unit within the IDRC; develops and manages IDRC activities in Central and Eastern Europe; Dir JEAN-H. GUILMETTE.

PEOPLE'S REPUBLIC OF CHINA

Eastern Europe and Central Asia Studies Institute: Renmin University, 39 Haidian Rd, Haidian District, Beijing 100872; tel. (10) 62563399; fax (10) 62566374; f. 1937 as Eastern Europe and Soviet Union Studies Institute, renamed 1991; research into history and current political and economic situation in Eastern Europe and the former USSR; Dir Prof. ZHOU XINCHENG; Deputy Dirs Prof. ZHONG YAPIN, GUAN XUELIN.

Institute of East European, Russian and Central Asian Studies (IEERCAS): Chinese Academy of Social Sciences, POB 1103, Beijing 10000; tel. (10) 64014006; fax (10) 64014008; f. 1965 as the Soviet and East European Studies Institute; present name adopted in 1992; over 60,000 vols; Dir Prof. ZHANG WENWU.

Institute of European Studies: Jianguomennei Dajie 5, Beijing 100732; tel. (10) 65138428; fax (10) 65125818; e-mail caes@ies.cass.net.cn; f. 1981; part of Institute of Chinese Academy of Social Sciences; incorporates the Chinese Asscn of European Studies; 45,000 vols; Chair. Prof. QIU YUANLUN; publ. *Europe* (2 a month).

CHINA (TAIWAN)

Graduate Institute of Slavic Studies: Tamkang University, Tamshui 25137, Taipei Hsein; tel. (2) 26215656; fax (2) 26209908; e-mail tisx@www2.tku.edu.tw; internet www2.tku .edu.tw/~tisx; f. 1990; studies in politics, society, economics, diplomacy and military issues of Russia and the states of the former USSR; 3,000 vols; Dir ALEXANDER PISAREV.

Institute of European and American Studies: Academia Sinica, No. 128, Sec. 2, Yen-Chiu-Yuan Rd, Taipei; tel. (2) 27899390; fax (2) 27851787; e-mail cylin@sinica.edu.tw; internet www.ea.sinica.edu.tw; f. 1973, renamed 1991; US and European studies, with emphasis on law, history, politics, economics, education, sociology, demography, literature, philosophy, anthropology and international relations; Sino-American and Sino-European relations; conferences; 87,738 vols in foreign languages, 20,340 vols in Chinese; Dir Dr CHENG-YI LIN; Deputy Dir Dr CHYONG-FANG KO; publ. *Eur-America* (quarterly).

Institute of International Relations: 64 Wan Shou Rd, Wen Shan 116, Taipei; tel. (2) 29394921; fax (2) 29378609; e-mail iir@nccu.edu.tw; f. 1953; concerned with international relations and mainland Chinese affairs, including Eastern Europe and the former USSR; Dir SZU-YIN HO; publ. *Issues and Studies* (quarterly).

COLOMBIA

Instituto de Estudios Politicos y Relaciones Internacionales (IEPRI) (Institute of Political Studies and International Relations): Universidad Nacional de Colombia, Edif. Manuel Ancízar, Of. 3026, Ciudad Universitaria, Santafé de Bogotá, DC; tel. (1) 316-5217; fax (1) 316-5246; e-mail iepri@ bacata.usc.unal.edu.co; internet www.unal.edu.co/iepri; research into international relations, including European studies; Dir WILLIAM RAMÍREZ TOBÓN.

CROATIA

Centre for International Studies: University of Zagreb, Faculty of Political Science, Zagreb, Lepušićeva 6; tel. (1) 4655294; fax (1) 4655316; e-mail radovanvukadinovic@ hotmail.com; international relations, European security and political instability in the Balkans; undergraduate and postgraduate studies in international relations; conferences and seminars; Dir Prof. RADOVAN VUKADINOVIĆ; publs *Međunarodne Studije* (quarterly), *International Studies* (in English, annually).

Institut za Međunarodne Odnose (Institute for International Relations): 10000 Zagreb, ul. Ljudevita Farkaša Vukotinovića 2, POB 303; tel. (1) 4826522; fax (1) 4828361; e-mail ured@irmo.hr; internet www.imo.hr/; f. 1963; study of economic development and transformation, international economic and cultural co-operation, international relations; analysis of Croatia's participation in world development and

trade; 9,000 vols, over 400 periodicals; Dir Prof. Dr MLADEN STANIČIĆ; publs *Culturelink* (in English, quarterly), *Euroscope Reports* (in English, quarterly), *Croatian International Relations Review* (in English, quarterly).

CUBA

Instituto de Política Internacional (Institute of International Politics): Ministry of Foreign Affairs, Calzada 360, Vedado, Havana; tel. (7) 32-3279; f. 1962; part of the Ministry of Foreign Affairs; Dir RENÉ ALVÁREZ RÍOS.

CZECH REPUBLIC

Evropské Studijní Centrum, Štiřín (European Studies Centre at Stirín): Národní 3, 110 00 Prague 1; tel. 22358435; fax 2228585; research into political, economic, cultural and security issues in Eastern and Central Europe; conferences; training and consultation services; Dir STEPHEN HEINTZ; Deputy Dir Prof. KRZYSZTOF NERS.

Mezinárodní politologicky ústav (International Institute for the Study of Politics): School of Law, Masaryk University, Veveri 70, 611 80 Brno; tel. 541214852; fax 541213162; e-mail bohanes@isildur.law.muni.cz; f. 1990; research and education programme; lectures and conferences; Dir Dr JAROSLAV BOHANES; Sec. VOJTECH SIMÍCEK; publs *Budování státu* (monthly), *Politologicky Casopis* (quarterly), *Report on the Czech and Slovak Republics* (monthly).

Stredisko mezinárodních studií Jana Masaryka (Jan Masaryk Centre for International Relations): Faculty of International Relations, University of Economics, nám. W. Churchilla 4, 130 67 Prague 3; tel. 224095232; fax 224095289; e-mail lehmann@vse.cz; internet fmv.vse.cz/depts/sms/index.html; f. 1991; research into international relations; training; conferences and consultancy; Dir Dr ZUZANA LEHMANNOVÁ.

Ústav mezinárodních vztahů (Institute of International Relations—IIR): Nerudova 3, Malá Strana, 118 50 Prague 1; tel. 251108111; fax 251108222; e-mail umv@iir.cz; internet www.iir.cz; f. 1957; research into international relations, the process of globalization and European integration, Czech foreign and security policy and bilateral relations with neighbouring countries; publishing, training, education, seminars, conferences; 70,000 vols; Dir JIŘÍ ŠEDIVÝ; Deputy Dir PETR DRULÁK; publs *Mezinárodní politika* (International Politics, monthly, in Czech), *Mezinárodní vztahy* (International Relations, quarterly, in Czech), *Perspectives* (2 a year, in English).

DENMARK

Centre for East European Studies (CEES): Copenhagen Business School, Howitzvej 60, 2000 Frederiksberg C; tel. 38-15-30-30; fax 38-15-25-00; e-mail mail.cees@cbs.dk; internet www.cbs.dk/centres/cees/; f. 1996; concerned with the transition in Eastern Europe, East and West education initiatives on business, economic and social conditions; Dir Prof KLAUS MEYER.

Dansk Udenrigspolitisk Institut (DUPI) (Danish Institute of International Affairs): Nytorv 5, 1450 Copenhagen K; tel. 33-36-65-65; fax 33-36-65-66; e-mail dupi@dupi.dk; internet www.dupi.dk/; f. 1995; research into the organization of Europe, Denmark in a regional and international context, and security and defence studies; approx. 10,000 vols, 200 periodicals, 6,000 documents; Dir PER CARLSEN; publs *DUPI News* (6 a year, on-line version available), *Danish Foreign Policy Yearbook*.

Institute of East European Studies: University of Copenhagen, Snorresgade 17-19, 2300 Copenhagen S; tel. 35-32-85-40; fax 35-32-85-32; e-mail osteuro@hum.ku.dk; internet www .hum.ku.dk.osteuro; f. 1992; research into linguistics, literature, history, social and political science of Russia, the CIS, the Baltic states, Central and Eastern Europe, Greece; 50,000 vols; Dir Assoc. Prof. LARS NØRGAARD.

Udenrigspolitiske Selskab (Foreign Policy Society): Amaliegade 40A, 1256 Copenhagen K; tel. 33-14-88-86; fax 33-14-85-20; e-mail udenrigs@udenrigs.dk; f. 1946; studies, debates, courses and conferences on international affairs; library of 150 periodicals and publs from various international orgs; Dir

Klaus Carsten Pedersen; Chair. Erling Olsen; publs *Udenrigs, Udenrigspolitiske Skirfter*.

ESTONIA

Eesti Konjunktuuriinstituut (EKI) (Estonian Institute of Economic Research): Rävala 6, Tallinn 19080; tel. 681-4650; fax 667-8399; e-mail eki@ki.ee; internet www.ki.ee; f. 1934; economic study of Estonia, Latvia, Lithuania; collection and analysis of current economic data for use by government institutions and private cos; Dir Marje Josing; publs *Konjunktuur* (quarterly, in English and Estonian), *Economic Survey of the Baltic States* (quarterly, in English), *Baltic Facts* (annually), *Economic Indicators of Estonia* (monthly).

Eurouuringute Instituut (Institute for European Studies—IES): Tallinn Pedagogical University, Estonia pst. 7, Tallinn 10143; tel. and fax 645-4926; internet www.ies.ee; f. 1998; Dir Aksel Kirch.

Institute of Baltic Studies: Kompanii 2, Tartu 51007; tel. (7) 300-329; fax (7) 441-722; e-mail webmaster@ibs.ee; internet www.ibs.ee; aims to develop effective and democratic public institutions in Estonia, Latvia and Lithuania.

Jaan Tõnissoni Instituut (Jaan Tõnisson Institute): Endla 4, Tallinn 10142; tel. 626-3151; fax 626-3152; e-mail jti@jti.ee; internet www.ngonet.ee/jti/contents.html; f. 1991; political issues and the development of democracy in Estonia, Russia and other Eastern European countries; also research into relations between Eastern European countries, national security and defence studies, human rights; Exec. Dir Agu Laius; publs educational guides and monographs.

FINLAND

Aleksanteri Institute: Finnish Centre for Russian and East European Studies (FCREES): University of Helsinki, 6th Floor, Yliopistonkatu 5, POB 4, 00014 Helsinki; tel. (9) 19124175; fax (9) 19123822; e-mail alekstanteri@helsinki.fi; internet www.helsinki.fi/aleksanteri; f. 1996; promotion of new significant research projects on the Baltic states and Eastern Europe; fund-raising, networking among academic and business communities; Dir Prof. Markku Kivinen.

Bank of Finland Institute for Economies in Transition (BOFIT): Kluuvikatu 7, 3rd Floor, POB 160, 00101, Helsinki; tel. (9) 1832268; fax (9) 1832294; e-mail bofit@bof.fi; internet www.bof.fi/bofit; f. 1991 as the Unit for Eastern European Economies, present name adopted in 1998; academic analysis of national economies in transition from command to market economy; focuses on Russia and the Baltics, but also covers rest of Eastern Europe; Dir Dr Pekka Sutela; publs *Russian and Baltic Economies: The Week in Review, Russian Economy: The Month in Review, Baltic Economies: Bimonthly Review, BOFIT Discussion Papers, BOFIT Online*.

Pan-European Institute: Turku School of Economics and Business Administration, Lemminkäisenkatu 14–18c, POB 110, 20521 Turku; tel. (2) 4814548; fax (2) 4814268; e-mail setunimi.sukunimi@tukkk.fi; internet www.tukkk.fi/pei; f. 1989 as Institute for European Studies, present name adopted in 1998, following merger with Institute for East-West Trade; issues of European Union and European integration; research and training in trade and economic development; information service; Dir Prof. Esa Stenberg.

Ulkopoliitinen Instituutti (UPI) (Finnish Institute of International Affairs): Mannerheimintie 15A, 00260 Helsinki; tel. (9) 4342070; fax (9) 43420769; e-mail firstname .lastname@upi-fiia.fi; internet www.upi-fiia.fi/index.html; f. 1961; research into peace, Russian foreign policy in the post-Cold War era and political and economic changes in Europe; research into the economic and political position of Central and Eastern Europe; Dir Tapani Vaahtoranta; publs *Ulkopolitiikka* (quarterly), *Northern Dimensions* (annually, in English).

Venäjän ja Itä-Euroopan Instituutti (Finnish Institute for Russian and East European Studies): Annankatu 44, 00100 Helsinki; tel. (9) 22854434; fax (9) 22854431; e-mail bibliotek@rusin.fi(library); internet www.rusin.fi; research into Russia and Eastern Europe; library, information and

documentation series; communications and publishing; more than 90,000 vols, 50 regular newspapers and 300 journals, maps and other materials; Chair. and Admin Dir Håkan Mattlin; publ. *Studia Slavica Finlandensia* (annually).

FRANCE

Association d'Etudes et d'Informations Politiques Internationales (Association for International Political Study and Information): 86 blvd Haussmann, 75008 Paris; f. 1949; Dir G. Albertini; publs *Est et Ouest* (Paris, 2 a month), *Documenti sul Comunismo* (Rome), *Este y Oeste* (Caracas).

Association Française pour l'Etude de la Méditerranée Orientale et du Monde Turco-Iranien (AFEMOTI) (French Association for the Study of the Eastern Mediterranean and the Turkish-Iranian World): 4 rue de Chevreuse, 76006, Paris; fax 1-44-10-84-50; e-mail vaner@ ceri-sciences-po.org; f. 1989; study of Balkan countries, the countries of the North-East Mediterranean (Greece, Turkey and Cyprus), particularly 'the Turkish factor' in South-Eastern Europe, and the Black Sea region; Pres. Semih Vaner; publ. *Cahiers d'Etudes sur la Méditerranée Orientale et le Monde Turco-Iranien* (2 a year).

Centre d'Etudes du Monde Russe, Soviétique et Post-soviétique (Centre of Russian, Soviet and Post-Soviet Studies): 54 blvd Raspail, 75006 Paris; tel. 1-49-54-25-58; fax 1-49-54-24-83; e-mail berelowi@ehess.fr; internet www.ehess .fr/centres/cemrsps; f. 1995; history of Russia, the USSR, and its successor states; social and demographic studies; diplomacy and cultural links; library contains 22,000 vols, 115 periodicals, 700 microfilms; Dir Wladimir Berelowitch; publs *Les Cahiers du Monde Russe, La Revue d'Études Comparatives Est-Oest*.

Centre d'Etudes Prospectives et d'Informations Internationales (CEPII) (Centre for International Prospective Studies and Information): 9 rue Georges Pitard, 75740 Paris Cédex 15; tel. 1-53-68-55-01; fax 1-53-68-55-03; e-mail hurion@cacepii.fr; internet www.cepii.fr; f. 1978; study of international economic development prospects and transition economies; 20,000 vols, 400 periodicals; Dir Lionel Fontagné; publs *Economie Internationale* (quarterly), *La Lettre du CEPII* (monthly), *CEPII Newsletter* (2 a year).

Centre d'Etudes sur l'Economie Internationale et Européenne (C3E) (Centre for Studies on International and European Economies): Nantes Economics Laboratory, University of Nantes, Chemin de la Censive du Tertre, BP 52231, 44322 Nantes Cédex 3; tel. and fax 2-40-14-17-32; e-mail feve@sc-eco.univ-nantes.fr; internet www.sc-eco.univ-nantes .fr/LEN/C3E/C3e.html; international economics; Dir Patrick Fève.

Institut d'Etudes de Sécurité de l'Union de l'Europe Occidentale (Institute for Security Studies of the Western European Union): 43 ave du Président-Wilson, 75775 Paris Cédex 16; tel. 1-53-67-22-00; fax 1-47-20-81-78; e-mail weu_iss@compuserve.com; internet www.weu.int; f. 1990; conceptual, political, economic and military aspects of security, concentrating on post-Cold War crisis management, regional security (the Baltics, Central Europe, South-Eastern Europe and the Black Sea); Dir Nicole Gnesotto; publs *Chaillot Papers*, Occasional Papers, *Newsletter*.

Institut Français des Relations Internationales (IFRI) (French Institute for International Relations): 27 rue de la Procession, 75740 Paris Cédex 15; tel. 1-40-61-60-00; fax 1-40-61-60-60; e-mail ifri@ifri.org; internet www.ifri.org; f. 1979; international politics and economy, security issues, regional studies; 31,000 vols, 450 periodicals; Dir-Gen. Prof. Thierry de Montbrial; publs *Politique étrangère* (quarterly), *Notes de l'Ifri, Cahiers de l'Ifri, Travaux et Recherches de l'Ifri, Rapport Annuel sur le Système Economique et les Stratégies—RAMSES*.

GEORGIA

Institut Ekonomiki I Prava (Economics and Law Institute): Georgian Academy of Sciences, 380007 Tbilisi, Markharadze 14; fax (32) 99-88-23; research in the fields of economics and law, in co-operation with researchers from institutes in other countries, particularly Eastern Europe; Dir AVTANDIL L. GUNIYA.

GERMANY

Centrum für Angewandte Politikforschung (CAP) (Centre for Applied Policy Research): Maria-Theresia-Str. 21, 81675 Munich; tel. (89) 21801300; fax (89) 21801329; e-mail cap.office@lrz.uni-muenchen.de; internet www.cap .uni-muenchen.de; f. 1995; research into South-Eastern Europe and the Baltic states; Dir Prof. Dr WERNER WEIDENFELD.

Deutsche Gesellschaft für Auswärtige Politik eV (German Council on Foreign Relations): Rauchstr. 17–18, 10787 Berlin; tel. (30) 2542310; fax (30) 25423116; e-mail info@.org; internet www.dgap.org; f. 1955; discusses and promotes research into problems of international politics; 52,000 vols; Pres. Prof. Dr KARL KAISER; publs *Die Internationale Politik* (annually), *Internationale Politik* (monthly).

Deutsche Gesellschaft für Osteuropakunde eV (German Society for Eastern European Studies): Schaperstr. 30, 10719 Berlin; tel. (30) 21478412; fax (30) 21478414; e-mail info@ dgo-online.org; internet dgo-online.org; f. 1913; conferences, seminars; Pres. Prof. Dr RITA SÜSSMUTH; Dir Dr HEIKE DÖRRENBÄCHER; publs *Osteuropa* (monthly), *Osteuropa-Recht* (6 a year), *Osteuropa-Wirtschaft* (quarterly).

Europa-Institut (Institute of European Studies): Law Dept, University of Saarland, POB 151150, 66041 Saarbrücken; tel. (681) 302-3653; fax (681) 302-4369; e-mail llm@europainstitut .de; internet europainstitut.de; f. 1951; international economics, political, economic and historical aspects of European integration; country-wide studies; approx. 37,000 vols, 200 journals; Dirs Prof. Dr TORSTEN STEIN, Prof. Dr WERNER MENG, Prof. Dr GEORG RESS; publ. *Zeitschrift für Europarechtliche Studien* (ZEuS, quarterly).

Forschungsstelle Osteuropa an der Universität Bremen (Research Centre for East European Studies, University of Bremen): Klagenfurter Str. 3, 28359 Bremen; tel. (421) 2183687; fax (421) 2183269; e-mail anlorenz@osteuropa .uni-bremen.de; internet www.forschungsstelle.uni-bremen .de; f. 1982; research into contemporary cultural and social developments in Central and Eastern Europe; cultural and political consultations in Germany and Eastern Europe; 25,000 vols; Dir Prof. Dr WOLFGANG EICHWEDE; publs *Veröffentlichungen zur Kultur und Gesellschaft im östlichen Europa*, *Dokumentationen zu Kultur und Gesellschaft im östlichen Europa*.

Frankfurter Institut für Transformationsstudien (FIT) (Frankfurt Institute for Transformation Studies): European University Viadrina, POB 1786, 15207 Frankfurt (Oder); tel. (335) 5534607; fax (335) 5534807; e-mail fritz@ euv-frankfurt-o.de; internet fit.euv-frankfurt-o.de/; research on cultural dimensions of political and economic systems in Central and Eastern Europe; transformation and capital markets and banking reform; Exec. Dir Prof. Dr HANS-JÜRGEN WAGENER; publs discussion papers, annual report.

Herder-Institut Marburg: Gisonenweg 5-7, 35037 Marburg/Lahn; tel. (6421) 1840; fax (6421) 184139; e-mail herder@mailer.uni-marburg.de; internet www.uni-marburg .de/herder-institut; f. 1950 as Johann Gottfried Herder Institute; historical research into countries and peoples of Eastern Central Europe; conferences; exhibitions; 340,000 vols, maps, documents, press archive; Dir Dr EDUARD MÜHLE; publ. *Zeitschrift für Ostmitteleuropa-Forschung* (Journal of East Central European Studies, quarterly).

Institut für Agrarentwicklung in Mittel- und Osteuropa (IAMO) (Institute of Agricultural Development in Central and Eastern Europe): Theodor-Lieser Str. 2, 06120 Halle/Saale; tel. (345) 29280; fax (345) 2928119; e-mail iamo@ iamo.de; internet www.iamo.de; Exec. Dir Prof. Dr PETER TILLACK.

Institut für Friedensforschung und Sicherheitspolitik (IFSH) (Institute for Peace Research and Security Policy): University of Hamburg, Falkenstein 1, 22587 Hamburg; tel.

(40) 8660770; fax (40) 8663615; e-mail ifsh@rrz.uni-hamburg .de; internet www.rrz.uni-hamburg.de/ifsh; f. 1971; collective European security policy, international security and conflict resolution; also research into Eastern European politics; Centre for OSCE Research (CORE) founded at the Institute; approx. 18,000 vols; Dir Prof. Dr DIETER S. LUTZ; publs *Hamburger Beiträge zur Friedensforschung und Sicherheitspolitik* (8–12 a year), *Hamburger Informationen zur Friedensforschung und Sicherheitspolitik* (quarterly), *IFSH aktuell*.

Institut für Ostseeforschung Warnemünde (IOW) (Baltic Sea Research Institute, Warnemünde): Seestr. 15, 18119 Rostock, Warnemünde; tel. (381) 5197; fax (381) 5197; e-mail webmaster@io-warnemuende.de; internet www .io-warnemuende.de; f. 1992, as successor to the Institute for Marine Research Warnemünde; scientific programme dedicated to the Baltic Sea ecosystem; depts of physical oceanography, marine chemistry, biological oceanography and marine geology; books, reports and dissertations, 750 periodicals; Dir Dr BODO V. BODUNGEN; publ. marine science reports.

Mannheimer Zentrum für Europäische Sozialforschung (MZES) (Mannheim Centre for European Social Research): MZES, Postfach, 68131 Mannheim; tel. (621) 1812868; fax (621) 1812866; e-mail direktorat@mzes .uni-mannheim.de; internet www.mzes.uni-mannheim.de; Head Prof. Dr WALTER MÜLLER; Man. Dir Dr REINHART SCHNEIDER.

Osteuropa-Institut (OEI) der Freien Universität Berlin (Institute for Eastern European Studies of Free University of Berlin): Garystr. 55, 14195 Berlin; tel. (30) 83853380; fax (30) 83853788; e-mail oei@zedat.fu-berlin.de; internet www.oei .fu-berlin.de; f. 1951; study of political science, sociology, philosophy, jurisprudence and economics, history and culture in Eastern, East Central and South-Eastern Europe; approx. 360,000 vols; Dir Prof. Dr HOLM SUNDHAUSSEN; publs *Berliner Osteuropa Info* (2 a year), *Balkanologische Veröffentlichungen* (irreg.), *Arbeitspapiere des Osteuropa-Instituts, Bereich Politik und Gesellschaft* (irreg.), *Arbeitspapiere des Osteuropa-Instituts, Bereich Geschichte und Kultur* (irreg.).

Osteuropa-Institut München (Institute for East European Studies, Munich): Scheinerstr. 11, 81679 Munich; tel. (89) 9983960; fax (89) 9810110; e-mail oeim@lrz.uni-muenchen.de; internet www.lrz-muenchen.de/~oeim; f. 1952; history and economics of Eastern Europe and the former USSR; 166,000 vols; Dir Prof. Dr L. HOFFMANN; publs *Jahrbücher für Geschichte Osteuropas* (quarterly), *Economic Systems* (quarterly).

Stiftung Wissenschaft und Politik (SWP): German Institute for International and Security Affairs, Ludwigkirchplatz 3–4, 10719 Berlin; tel. (30) 880070; fax (30) 88007100; e-mail swp@swp-berlin.org; internet www.swp-berlin.org; f. 1962; Dir Dr CHRISTOPH BERTRAM.

Südosteuropa-Gesellschaft (SOG) ((South-Eastern Europe Association)): Widenmayerstr. 49, 80538 Munich; tel. (89) 2121540; fax (89) 2289469; e-mail Suedosteuropa-Gesellshaft@t-online.de; internet www .suedosteuropa-gesellschaft.com; f. 1952; Pres. GERNOT ERLER; Exec. Dir Dr HANSJÖRG BREY.

Zentralinstitut für Mittel- und Osteuropastudien (ZIMOS) der Katholischen Universität Eichstätt (KUE) (Central Institute of Central and East European Studies of the Catholic University of Eichstätt): Ostenstr. 27, 85072 Eichstätt; tel. (421) 931717; fax (421) 931780; e-mail gga052@ ku-eichstaett.de; internet www1.ku-eichstaett.de/ZIMOS/ zimos.htm; f. 1994; history of former Eastern bloc countries, changes in science, culture and society in region; approx. 4.5m. vols; Dir Prof. Dr NIKOLAUS LOBKOWICZ; Deputy Dir Dr LEONID LUKS; publ. *Forum für Mittel- und Osteuropäische Zeit- und Ideengeschichte* (2 a year).

GREECE

Foundation for Mediterranean Studies (FMS): Lykavittou 2, 106 71 Athens; tel. (21) 03636026; fax (21) 03629352; e-mail imm@hol.gr; internet www.imm.gr; f. 1983; research and education in international relations, economics, sociology, political science and the Balkans; conferences; publs monographs.

Greek Institute for International and Strategic Studies: Odos Kriezotou 7, 106 71 Athens; tel. (21) 03627878; fax (21) 03629572; f. 1991; research into international relations, Greek defence and foreign policy; studies political change in Eastern Europe, European-Greek political co-operation, strategic issues and nuclear non-proliferation; Pres. COSTAS TSIRIS; Dir THEMIS STOFOROPOULOS; publs occasional papers, monographs.

Hellenic Centre for European Studies (EKEM): 1 Odos G. Prassa and Didotou, 106 80 Athens; tel. (21) 03636880; fax (21) 03631133; e-mail info@ekem.gr; internet www.ekem.gr; f. 1988; linked to the Ministry of Foreign Affairs; advises public administration on matters of European policy; interest in activities of European Union in areas of Central and Eastern Europe, as well as developments in the Balkans and Black Sea countries; maintains Depository Library of the European Community, with more than 7,000 vols, 300 periodicals; Pres. and Gen. Dir Prof. PANAYIOTIS C. IOAKIMIDIS; publs *Balkan Briefing* (monthly), *The Balkans* (2 a year).

Hellenic Foundation for European and Foreign Policy (ELIAMEP): Odos Xenophontos 4, 105 57 Athens; tel. (21) 033150225; fax (21) 03642139; e-mail eliamep@eliamep.gr; internet www.eliamep.gr; f. 1988; forum for the study and understanding of issues relating to foreign and security policy, European affairs and international relations; research into political, economic and military issues in South-Eastern Europe and the Black Sea area; Pres. Prof. LOUKAS TSOUKALIS; Dir-Gen. Prof. THEODORE COULOUMBIS; publs *Journal of Southeast European and Black Sea Studies*, *Greece and the World* (annually).

Institute for Balkan Studies (IMXA): Odos Meg. Alexandrou 31A, 546 41 Thessaloníki; tel. (231) 0832143; fax (231) 0831429; e-mail imxa@imxa.gr; internet www.imxa.gr; f. 1953; concerned with the historical, political, economic and social development of the Balkan peoples from the 17th century to the present day; conferences; 30,000 vols; Pres. Prof. Dr BASIL KONDIS; Dir Prof. Dr IANNIS MOURELOS; publs *Balkan Studies* (2 a year), *Balkanika Symmikta* (annually), monographic series (irreg.).

Institute of International Economic Relations (IIER): Odos Panepistimiou 16, 106 72 Athens; tel. (21) 03620274; fax (21) 03626610; e-mail sae@hol.gr; internet www.idec.gr/iier; f. 1993; research into the promotion of Greek business activity in the Balkans, Eastern/Central Europe and the Mediterranean, the analysis of Greek foreign trade structures, the promotion of Greek exports and foreign investment in Greece; Pres. PARIS KYRIAKOPOULOS; Dir Dr CHARALAMBOS TSARDANIDAS.

Institute of International Relations (IIR): 3-5 Hill St, 105 58 Athens; tel. (21) 03312325; fax (21) 03313575; e-mail idis@idis.gr; internet www.idis.gr/; f. 1989; research into international politics, security, business and economics, particularly in the Balkans and South-Eastern Europe; library of 2,000 vols; Dir Prof. DIMITRI CONSTAS; publs annual yearbook, occasional research papers, *Cosmos* (newsletter).

HUNGARY

Biztonságpolititkai és Honvédelmi Kutatások Központja Alapítvány (Centre for Security and Defence Studies—CSDS): 1062 Budapest, Andrássy u. 107; tel. (1) 322-8790; fax (1) 322-8790; e-mail bhkka@elender.hu; f. 1990; research and studies into international defence and security issues including Eastern Europe and the former USSR; conferences and debates; Research Dir Dr PÉTER DEÁK; publs *Newsletter* (quarterly), *Security and Defence Studies*.

Central European Research Centre (CERD): 1024 Budapest, Retek u. 26; tel. (1) 135-7857; fax (1) 115-0078; f. 1990; European foreign policy, political and economic changes in Poland, the Czech Republic, Slovakia and Hungary; Chair. Dr LÁSZLÓ LÁNG; publs *Central European Update and Investment Overview* (monthly), monographs.

Institute for Strategic and Defence Studies: Miklós Zrínyi National Defence University, 1241 Budapest, POB 181;

tel. (1) 432-9092; fax (1) 432-9058; e-mail svki@mltc.hu; f. 1992; affiliated to the Ministry of Defence; Central and Eastern European security, European-Atlantic security, conflict management and the transformation of the Hungarian Defence Forces; operates the NATO-WEU Office of Information; 3,000 vols; Dir Prof. FERENC GAZDAG; publ. *Defence Studies* (6 a year).

Teleki László Intézet (Teleki László Institute): 1125 Budapest, Szilágyi Erzsébet fasor 22/c; tel. (1) 275-2496; fax (1) 275-2497; internet www.tla.hu; f. 1999 by merger of Hungarian Institute of International Affairs (f. 1972) and Central Europe Institute; now operates Centre for Foreign Policy Studies and Centre for Central European Studies; prepares analytical material and information for foreign policy institutions; research into theoretical issue of international relations; conferences, seminars, lectures; Dir Dr Prof. GYÖRGY GRANASZTÓI; publs *Külügyi Szemle* (quarterly), *Régió* (quarterly).

Világgazdasági Kutató Intézet (Institute for World Economics): Hungarian Academy of Sciences, 1535 Budapest, POB 936; tel. (1) 224-6700; fax (1) 224-6761; e-mail vki@vki.hu; internet www.vki.hu; f. 1973; regional economic developments and their impact on Hungary, integration of Central and Eastern Europe into the global market economy; approx. 106,000 vols; Dir ANDRÁS INOTAI; publs *Trends in World Economy*, *Working Papers* (all irreg., in English), *Kihívások* (Challenges, irreg.), *Mühelytanulmányok* (Workshop Studies, irreg.).

INDIA

Centre for Defence Studies and Alalyses: Block No. 3, Old JNU Campus, New Delhi 110 67; tel. (11) 26170953; fax (11) 26189023; e-mail idsa@vsnl.com; internet www.idsa.india.org; f. 1965; Dir K. SANTHANAM; publs *Strategic Analysis* (quarterly), *Asian Strategic Review* (annually).

Centre for International Politics, Organization and Disarmament, Jawaharlal Nehru University: School of International Studies, New Mehrauli Rd, New Delhi 110 067; tel. (11) 2667676; research into international politics, organization and disarmament; Dir Dr K. D. BAJPAI.

IRELAND

Centre for European Studies: University of Limerick, Limerick, Ireland; tel. (61) 202202; fax (61) 202569; internet www.ul.ie/~ceuros; Dir Prof. EDWARD MOXON-BROWNE; publ. *CEUROS Newsletter* (6 a year).

ISRAEL

Cummings Center for Russian and Eastern European Studies: Tel Aviv University, Ramat Aviv, 69978 Tel Aviv; tel. 3-6424277; fax 3-6409721; e-mail crees@post.tau.ac.il; internet www.tau.ac.il/~russia; f. 1971 as the Russian and East European Research Center; research and documentation relating to history and current affairs of Eastern Europe; Dir Prof. YAACOV RO'I.

ITALY

European University Institute (EUI): Badia Fiesolana, Via dei Roccettini 9, 50016 S. Domenico di Fiesole, Florence; tel. (055) 4685283; fax (055) 4685206; e-mail euipress@iue.it; internet www.iue.it; f. 1972; research and postgraduate training in European affairs, including economics, human and social sciences; Robert Schuman Centre conducts research into political themes of contemporary European societies; 500,000 vols; Pres. Prof. YVES MÉNY; publs *Yearly Information Booklet, EUI Working Papers, European Journal of International Law, European Foreign Policy Bulletin, President's Annual Report, European Law Journal, EUI Review.*

Istituto Affari Internazionali (IAI) (Institute of International Affairs): Palazzo Rondinini, Via Angelo Brunetti 9, 00186 Rome; tel. (06) 3224360; fax (06) 3224363; e-mail iai@iai.it; internet www.iai.it; f. 1965; European integration, Eastern European transition, relations with Southern Mediterranean countries; 18,000 vols; Pres. STEFANO SILVESTRI; Dir GIANNI BONVICINI; publs *The International Spectator* (quarterly, in English), *L'Italia e la Politica Internazionale* (annually), working papers.

Istituto di Studi e Documentazione sull'Europa Comunitaria e l'Europa Orientale (ISDEE) (European Community and Eastern European Study and Documentation Centre): Corso Italia 27, 34122 Trieste; tel. (040) 639130; fax (040) 634248; e-mail isdee@spin.it; internet www.isdee.it; f. 1969; research, documentation and study relating to economic, political, institutional and social development in Europe and Western-Eastern European relations; Chair. FULVIO DEGRASSI; Dir TITO FAVARETTO; publ. *Est-Ovest* (6 a year).

Osservatorio sull'Evoluzione nei Paesi dell'Europa Orientale (Centre on Evolution in Eastern European Countries—EUROEST): University of Trento, Via Inama 5, 38100 Trento; tel. (0461) 882162; fax (0461) 882222; e-mail euroest@risc1.gelso.unitn.it; internet euroest.gelso.unitn.it/Euroest/euroest.htm; f. 1992; change in the countries of Central-Eastern Europe in the fields of economics, law, society and technology; organizes conferences and seminars; Scientific Dir Prof. GIOVANNI PEGORETTI; publs *Blue Series, Green Series*.

JAPAN

Association for East European Studies (AEES): University of Tokyo, Komaba 3-8-1, Meguro-ku, Tokyo 153-8902; f. 1975; publ. *Journal of East European Studies*.

Centre for European Studies: Nanzan University, 18 Yamazato-cho, Showa-ku, Nagoya 466-8673; tel. (52) 832-3111; fax (52) 831-2741; e-mail cfes@ic.nanzan-u.ac.jp; internet www.ic.nanzan-u.ac.jp/English/centers_european.htm; f. 1992; interdisciplinary study of European politics, economics and society covering Central and Eastern Europe; seminars and symposia; 3,500 vols, 155 periodicals; Dir Prof. TOSHIAKI TOMOOKA; publ. *Nanzan Daigaku yoroppa kenkyu senta-ho* (Bulletin of the Nanzan Centre for European Studies, annually).

Hokkaido Daigaku Suraby Kenkyu Senta (Hokkaido University Slavic Research Centre—SRC): Kita 9, Nishi 7, Kita-ku, Sapporo 060-0809; tel. (11) 706-2388; fax (11) 706-4952; e-mail src@slav.hokudai.ac.jp; internet src-h.slav.hokudai.ac.jp; f. 1955; research on Slavic countries in the fields of humanities, international relations, economics, political-social systems, geography/ethnology; 92,000 vols, 740 periodicals; Dir Prof. OSAMU IEDA; publs *Acta Slavica Iaponica* (annually), *Suravu Kenkyu* (Slavic Studies, annually), *SRC Occasional Paper Series, Bibliography of Japanese Slavic and East European Studies, Directory of Japanese Slavic and East European Scholars, SRC Newsletter*.

Nihon Kokusai Mondai Kenkyusho (Japanese Institute of International Affairs—JIIA): 11F Kasumigaseki Bldg, 3-2-5 Kasumigaseki, Chiyoda-ku, Tokyo 100-6011; tel. (3) 3503-7263; fax (3) 3503-7186; e-mail info@jiia.or.jp; internet www.jiia.or.jp; f. 1959; international studies; research into the former USSR and Central and Eastern Europe conducted at the Centre for Russian Studies; f. 1984; library of approx. 20,000 vols; Pres. YUKIO SATOH; Dir TOSHINORI SHIGEIE (acting); publs *Japan Review of International Affairs* (2 a year), *Kokusai Mondai* (monthly), *Roshia Kenkya* (2 a year), *JIIA Newsletter* (monthly).

REPUBLIC OF KOREA

Institute for Russian and East European Studies: Seoul National University, Sinlim-dong, Kwanak-gu, Seoul 151-742; tel. (2) 880-6014; fax (2) 871-5302; internet plaza1.snu.ac.kr/~rusins; attached to College of Humanities.

Institute of Foreign Affairs and National Security (IFANS): 1376-2 Socho 2-dong, Socho-ku, Seoul 137-072; tel. (2) 3497-7661; fax (2) 3497-7713; e-mail yjlee99@mofat.go.kr; internet www.ifans.go.kr; f. 1963; affiliated to the Japanese Institute of International Affairs; research and educational courses on major aspects of foreign affairs, including international economics; parent organization Ministry of Foreign Affairs and Trade; 33,000 vols, 520 periodicals; Chancellor CHOI YOUNG-JIN; publs *Analysis of Major International Affairs*

(weekly), *Outlook on the International Situation* (annually), various monographs.

Korean Institute of International Studies: POB 426, Seoul 110-604; tel. (2) 752-7727; fax (2) 752-7710; f. 1965; research, particularly on issues affecting communist or former communist countries; 3,000 vols; Pres. Prof. CHOI CHONG-KI; publ. *Korean Journal of International Studies* (quarterly).

LATVIA

Latvijas Arpolitikas instituts (LAI) (Latvian Institute of International Affairs): Elizabetes iela 57, Rīga 1050; tel. 728-6302; fax 782-8089; internet www.lai.lv; f. 1992; dissemination of information about international events and Baltic security issues; Baltic co-operation, Baltic-Russian relations and Baltic-European integration, issues relevant to Baltic security interests; library of 1,231 vols; Dir and Chair. ATIS LEJINS; publs *Baltic Security Studies Series, Pasaule kabata Series* (The World in Your Pocket), *PPA Series* (Topical Issues in World Politics).

LITHUANIA

Europos Integracijos Studiju Centras (EISC) (European Integration Studies Centre): J. Tumo-Vaizganto 2-216, 2600 Vilnius; tel. (5) 236-44-24; fax (5) 261-72-21; e-mail eisc@urm.lt; f. 1995; integration of Lithuania into the EU; conferences; seminars; Chair. of Sup. Council ROMUALDAS KALONAITIS; Dir GIEDRE BACEVICIUTE.

Institute of International Relations and Political Science: University of Vilnius, Vokiečių 10, 2001 Vilnius; tel. (5) 251-41-30; fax (5) 251-41-34; e-mail tspmi@tspmi.vu.lt; internet www.tspmi.vu.lt; f. 1992 as the Institute of International Relations; trains specialists of international relations in public administration, international law and political science; Central European research group; Dir Dr RAIMUNDAS LOPATA; publ. *Politologija* (quarterly).

LUXEMBOURG

Institut d'Etudes Européenes et Internationales du Luxembourg (Luxembourg Institute for European and International Studies): 21 rue Philippe II, 2340 Luxembourg; tel. 46-65-80; fax 46-65-79; e-mail armande.clesse@ieis.lu; internet www.ieis.lu; f. 1990; research into various European and international security and monetary issues, including the economies of Central and Eastern European countries, economic convergence and regional integration; Dir Dr ARMAND CLESSE.

FORMER YUGOSLAV REPUBLIC OF MACEDONIA

Ekonomski Institut na Univerzitetet 'Sveti Kiril I Metodij' (Economic Institute of SS Cyril and Methodius University): 1000 Skopje, POB 576, Krste Misirkov bb; tel. (2) 116323; fax (2) 116370; e-mail eis@ek-ins.ukim.edu.mk; f. 1952; research into the transition of the FYRM economy; library of 13,000 vols and 4,300 periodicals; Dir Dr ALEKSANDAR PETROSKI; publ. *Economic Development*.

MALAYSIA

Institute of Strategic and International Studies (ISIS): 1 Pesiaran Sultan Salahuddin, POB 12424, 50778 Kuala Lumpur; tel. (3) 26939366; fax (3) 26939475; e-mail webmaster@isis.po.my; internet www.jaring.my/isis; f. 1983; concerned with international economics, international relations, strategic studies and national economic policies; 16,250 vols; Dir-Gen. Dr NOORDIN SJOPIEE; publs *ISIS Focus* (monthly), *Negarawan* (6 a year), monograph series, seminar papers.

MALTA

European Documentation and Research Centre: University of Malta, Tal-Qroqq, Msida, MSD 06; tel. 32902001; fax 21337624; e-mail edrc@um.edu.mt; internet home.um.edu.mt/edrc; f. 1992; research and teaching centre in European policy studies; Chair. Prof. PETER G. XUEREB; publs *EDRC*

Information Paper Series, *EDRC Research Paper Series*, *The State of the European Union* (annually).

NETHERLANDS

Europese Culturele Stichting (ECS) (European Cultural Foundation): Jan van Goyenkade 5, 10575 HN Amsterdam; tel. (20) 5733868; fax (20) 6752231; e-mail eurocult@eurocult .org; internet www.eurocult.org; f. 1954 in Geneva, Switzerland; moved to Amsterdam in 1957; promoting cultural co-operation in European Union (EU) and non-EU Europe; from 2000 encouraged involvement in projects from, or taking place in, the Baltic region and South-Eastern Europe, as well as tackling issues concerning cultural aspects of EU enlargement; Pres. HRH Princess MARGRIET of the Netherlands; Sec.-Gen. GOTTFRIED WAGNER; publs newsletter, annual report, grants report, programmes booklet.

Nederlands Instituut voor Internationale Betrekkingen, Clingendael (Netherlands Institute of International Relations, Clingendael): Clingendael 7, POB 93080, 2509 The Hague; tel. (70) 3245384; fax (70) 3282002; e-mail info@clingendael.nl; internet www.clingendael.nl; f. 1983; research on international issues, including political science, economics, history, law, military security studies; lectures; training in international negotiation; information and documentation; 22,000 vols, 300 periodicals; Dir Prof. Dr ALFRED VAN STADEN; publ. *Internationale Spectator* (monthly).

Slavische Talen, Russisch, Midden- en Oost-Europakunde ((Dept of Slavic Languages)): University of Groningen, Onde Kijk in 't Jaststraat 26, POB 716, 9700 AS Groningen; tel. (50) 3636061; fax (50) 3635821; e-mail cet@let .rug.nl; internet www.let.rug.nl/slav; Slavic languages and literature; Middle and East European history, culture and economics; Chair. Prof. Dr J. J. VAN BAAK.

NEW ZEALAND

New Zealand Institute of International Affairs: Victoria University of Wellington, 6 Waiteata Rd, Kelburn, POB 600, Wellington; tel. (4) 463-5356; fax (4) 473-1261; e-mail nziia@ vuw.ac.nz; internet www.vuw.ac.nz/nziia/; f. 1934 to promote understanding of international questions and problems, particularly those relating to New Zealand; Pres. Sir KENNETH KEITH; Dir GERALD McGHIE; publ. *New Zealand International Review* (every 2 months).

NIGERIA

Nigerian Institute of International Affairs: 13-15 Kofo Abayomi Rd, Victoria Island, POB 1727, Lagos; tel. (1) 615606; fax (1) 2611360; f. 1961; non-political organization for the study of international affairs, to disseminate and maintain information on international questions through conferences, lectures and discussions; 67,553 vols, 19,918 pamphlets, 316,461 press clippings, 1,774 journals; Dir-Gen. Prof. U. JOY OGWU; publs *Nigerian Journal of International Affairs* (quarterly), *Nigerian Forum* (monthly), *Nigeria: Bulletin on Foreign Affairs* (2 a year).

NORWAY

Fridtjof Nansens Institutt (FNI) (Fridtjof Nansen Institute): Fridtjof Nansens vei 17, POB 326, 1326 Lysaker; tel. 67-11-19-00; fax 67-11-19-10; e-mail post@fni.no; internet www .fni.no/; f. 1958; social-science research on international issues concerning energy, resource management and the environment; research programmes on multilateral assistance, polar politics and law, Russia and Eastern Europe and European energy and environment; Dir ARILD MOE; publs *Energy, Environment and Development Reports*, *Yearbook of International Co-operation on Environment and Development*, *International Northern Sea Route Programme Working Papers*, *Nansen News*, research reports.

Norsk Utenrikspolitisk Institutt (NUPI) (Norwegian Institute of International Affairs): Grønlandsleiret 25, POB 8159 Dep, 0033 Oslo; tel. 22-05-65-00; fax 22-17-70-15; e-mail internet@nupi.no; internet www.nupi.no; f. 1959; research and information on political and economic issues, interna-

tional security policy, long-term political development of Europe and Russia, international economic and development issues, conflict resolution and peace operations; 25,000 vols, 400 journals; Dir SVERRE LODGAARD; publs *Internasjonal Politikk* (quarterly), *Forum for Development Studies* (2 a year), *Hvor Hender Det* (weekly), *Nordisk Østforum* (quarterly).

PAKISTAN

Pakistan Institute of International Affairs: Aiwan-e-Sadar Rd, POB 1447, Karachi 74200; tel. (21) 5682891; f. 1947 to study international affairs and to promote the scientific study of international politics, Pakistani foreign policy, economics and jurisprudence; 30,820 vols; Chair. FATEHYAB ALI KHAN; publs *Pakistan Horizon* (4 a year), *Aalami Ufaq* (*Urdu Quarterly*).

POLAND

Central and East European Economic Research Centre (CEEERC): Dept of Economics, University of Warsaw, 02-097 Warsaw, ul. Banacha 2B; tel. (22) 8227404; fax (22) 8227405; e-mail wisniewski@ceeerc.wne.uw.edu.pl; f. 1998; helps develop the skills of economists from Central and Eastern Europe by offering technical assistance and adequate financial remuneration; promotes research collaboration; Admin. Dir MARIAN WISNIEWSKI.

Centre for Eastern Studies: University of Warsaw, 00-564 Warsaw, ul. Nowy Świat 69; tel. (22) 6200381; fax (22) 267520; f. 1989; research in the transformational directions of political, economic, social and cultural, national and ethnic spheres in Estonia, Lithuania and Latvia; conferences; Dir Dr MICHAŁ DOBROCZYŃSKI; Deputy Dirs Dr MARIANNA LIPIEC-ZAJCHOWSKA, Dr LESZEK JUCHNIEWICZ; publs *Biuletyn Kalinigradzki* (monthly), *Biuletyn Ukrainski, Eurazja, Monitor, Przeglad Prasowy* (2 a week).

Foundation Natolin European Centre (College of Europe): 02-797 Warsaw 78, POB 120, ul. Nowoursynowska 84; tel. (22) 5459800; fax (22) 6491299; e-mail info@natolin .edu.pl; internet ww.natolin.edu.pl/; f. 1994; hosts the second campus of the College of Europe (based in Bruges, Belgium); research into the transition economies, on European Union politics and policy, security and economic problems; conferences and seminars; Vice-Rector of the College Dr PIOTR NOWINA-KONOPKA; Dir-Gen. of the Foundation ELŻBIETA GOGOLEWSKA; publs *Working Paper* (annually), conference and seminar proceedings.

Institute for Central and Eastern Europe: 20-080 Lublin, Plac Litewski 2; f. 1991; research into how other Central and Eastern European countries' histories are perceived in Poland; also concerned with national and religious minorities in Central and Eastern Europe and the historiography of the region.

Instytut Baltycki (Baltic Institute): 80-958 Gdańsk, POB 358, ul. Tkacka 11/13; tel. (58) 314786; f. 1925; research into the modern history of relations between Poland and Germany, Estonia, Latvia, Lithuania and Scandinavia; Dir Prof. Dr CZESŁAW CIESIELSKI; publ. *Komunikaty Instytutu Baltyckiego* (annually).

Instytut Gospodarki Światowej (World Economy Research Institute—WERI): Warsaw School of Economics, 02-521 Warsaw, Rakowiecka 24; tel. (22) 8489132; fax (22) 8489132; e-mail weri@sgh.waw.pl; internet www.sgh.waw.pl; f. 1985; research into Polish relations with the European Union, Polish economic relations and the evolution of a new political and economic order in Central and Eastern Europe, Polish-German economic relations, economic developments in the Baltic states, and the US economy; 9,500 vols, 62 periodicals; Dir Prof. JANUSZ GOŁĘBIOWSKI; publs *Poland—International Economic Report* (in English, annually), *Transforming the Polish Economy, Working Papers* (irreg.).

Instytut Slawistyki (Institute of Slavic Research): Polish Academy of Sciences, 00-478 Warsaw, Al. Ujazdowskie 18 m. 16; tel. (22) 6566256; fax (22) 8267688; e-mail ispan@ispan .waw.pl; internet www.ispan.waw.pl/; f. 1954; research and study of Slavonic history, literature and linguistics; 120,000 vols; Dir Dr Hab ZBIGNIEW GREŃ; publs *Acta Baltico-Slavica* (annually), *Studia z Filologii Polskiej I Slowianskiej* (annually), *Slavia Meridionalis* (annually), *Studia Litteraria Polono-Slavica* (annually), *Slavica* (in Polish).

Polski Instytut Spraw Międzynarodowych (Polish Institute of International Affairs—PIIA): 00-950 Warsaw, ul. Warecka 1A; tel. (22) 5568000; fax (22) 5568099; e-mail pism@pism.pl; internet www.pism.pl; f. 1999; research into international affairs; 150,000 vols; Dir RYSZARD STEMPLOWSKI; publs *Polski Przeglad Dyplomatyczny* (every two months, in Polish), *The Polish Foreign Affairs Digest* (quarterly, in English), *Evropa* (quarterly, in Russian).

ROMANIA

Institutul de Studii Sud-Est Europene (Institute for South-East European Studies): Romanian Academy, 70346 Bucharest, Calea 13 Septembrie 13, Casa Academiei Române, CP 22-159; tel. (21) 3144996; fax (21) 3124134; e-mail iesee@yahoo.com; f. 1963; research into South-Eastern European affairs and relations; 40,000 vols; Dir Prof. PAUL H. STAHL; publ. *Revue des études sud-est européennes* (quarterly).

Institutul Roman de Studii Internationale (IRSI) (Romanian Institute of International Studies): 72238 Bucharest, Aleea Alexandru 24; tel. (21) 3129865; fax (21) 3129866; f. 1991; political strategies and security and co-operation; international law and international institutions; the management of international relations; Dir IOAN MAXIM; publ. *Romanian Journal of International Affairs* (quarterly).

RUSSIA

Centre for National Security and International Relations: 121814 Moscow, per. Khlebnyi 2-3; tel. (095) 291-66-23; fax (095) 203-70-17; e-mail srogov@glas.apc.org; f. 1992; research into Russian civil-military relations, ethnic conflicts in Eastern Europe, peace-keeping; Dir SERGEI M. ROGOV; publ. bulletin on security issues in countries of the former USSR (monthly).

Institut Evropy (Institute of Europe): Russian Academy of Sciences, 125993 Moscow, ul. Mokhovaya 11-3; tel. (095) 203-41-87; fax (095) 200-42-98; e-mail europe@mline.msk.ru; internet isn.rsuh.ru/iu/engl/; f. 1988; research into European integration, international organizations, Russia's role in the CIS, European Union regional policy, and European economic and political problems; 3,000 vols; Dir VITALII V. ZHURKIN; publ. *Reports* (6 a year).

Institut Mezhdunarodnykh Ekonomicheskikh I Politicheskikh Issledovaniy (Institute for International Economic and Political Studies—IIEPS): Russian Academy of Sciences, 117418 Moscow, ul. Novocheryomushkinskaya 46; tel. (095) 120-82-00; fax (095) 310-70-61; e-mail imepi@transecon.ru; internet www.transecon.ru; f. 1961 as the Institute for the Economy of the World Socialist System; name changed in 1990; political and economic reform, and foreign and security policy; Central and Eastern European studies, especially on former Soviet Republics and their transition to democracy; Dir OLEG TIMOFEEVICH BOGOMOLOV; publs *Politekonom* (joint German-Russian journal), *Russia and the Contemporary World*, *The Bulletin of Research Information*, scholarly articles.

Institut Mirovoy Economiki I Mezhdunarodnykh Otnosheniy (IMEMO) (Institute of World Economics and International Relations): 117859 Moscow, ul. Profsoyuznaya 23; tel. (095) 128-33-33; fax (095) 310-70-27; e-mail imemoran@glasnet.ru; f. 1956; attached to the Russian Academy of Sciences; research into issues of global economy and international relations, including economic relations and the conversion of military economies; Dir V. A. MARTYNOV (acting); publs *Disarmament and Security Yearbook*, *Mirovaya Economika I Mezhdunarodnye Otnosheniya* (monthly), *Russia and Post-Soviet States Today* (monthly).

Institute for Contemporary International Studies (ICIS): 107078 Moscow, per. Bolshoi Kzlovskii 4; tel. (095) 208-94-61; fax (095) 208-94-66; e-mail icipu@glas.apc.org; f.

1994; research into international relations, diplomacy, political science, international law, world economy; also research into the transition to democracy and market economy in Eastern Europe; Dir YEVGENII BAZHANOV; publs *Diplomatic Yearbook*, *Eurasian Politics* (monthly), *Theory and Practice of Foreign Policy* (monthly).

Institute of Slavonic and Balkan Studies: Russian Academy of Sciences, 125040 Moscow, pr. Leninskii 32A; tel. (095) 938-17-80; fax (095) 938-22-88; f. 1946; major centre of Slavic and Balkan research in Russia; also study of the relationship of the Slavs and other neighbouring ethnic groups with the Russian people; Dir VLADIMIR K. VOLKOV; publs monographs and periodicals.

Moscow State Institute of International Relations (MGIMO): 11754 Moscow, pr. Vemadskogo 76; tel. (095) 434-00-89; e-mail nam@mgimo.ru; internet www.mgimo.ru; f. 1944; Rector Prof. ANATOLII V. TORKNNOV.

SERBIA AND MONTENEGRO

G17 Institute: 11000 Belgrade, Knez Mihailova 10; tel. (11) 3346086; fax (11) 3346172; internet www.g17institute.com/default.htm; f. 2001 to improve academic understanding of economic reform and its impact on the domestic market economy; Exec. Dir MILKO STIMAĆ; Publ. *Economic Review* (monthly).

Institut za Evropske Studije (Institute for European Studies): 11000 Belgrade, trg Nikole Pašića 11; tel. (11) 3234497; fax (11) 3232940; e-mail ies@eunet.yu; social and political sciences, economic and cultural relations; Dir DJURO KOVACEVIĆ.

Institute for Balkan Studies: Serbian Academy of Sciences and Arts (SANU), 11000 Belgrade, Knez Mihailova 35; tel. (11) 639830; e-mail BalkInst@eunet.yu; internet www.sanu.ac.yu/English/Institutes/balkan.htm; f. 1969; Dir Dr LJUBINKO RADENKOVIĆ.

Institute of International Politics and Economics: 11000 Belgrade, POB 750, Makedonska 25; tel. (11) 3373633; fax (11) 3373835; e-mail iipe@diplomacy.bg.ac.yu; internet www.diplomacy.bg.ac.yu; f. 1947; international relations, world economy, international law, social, economic and political development in all countries; 250,000 vols; Dir VATROSLAV VEKARIĆ; publs *Medjunarodni problemi* (International Problems, quarterly), *Pregled europskog zakonodavstva* (Survey of European Legislations, 6 a year).

Institute of Political Studies: 11000 Belgrade, Savski trg 7; tel. (11) 624042; fax (11) 659920; post-communist transition and Balkan studies.

SINGAPORE

Singapore Institute of International Affairs (SIIA): 6 Nassim Rd, Singapore 258373; tel. 65-7349600; fax 65-7336217; internet www.siiaonline.org; f. 1961; organizes talks, conferences, etc.; provides secretariat of Singapore National Cttee of Council for Security Co-operation in the Asia-Pacific Region; Chair. Dr SIMON TAY; Deputy Dir M. RAJARETNAM; publ. newsletter.

SLOVAKIA

Centrum pre Európsku Politiku (CEP) (Centre for European Policy): Panenská 30, 811 02 Bratislava; tel. (2) 54-43-13-89; fax (2) 54-62-68-62; e-mail cep@cpep.sk; internet www.cpep.sk; f. 1997; study of European Union and trans-Atlantic issues; Exec. Dir KAMIL SLÁDEK.

Slovensky Inštitút medzinárodných stúdií (Slovak Institute for International Studies): Drotárska cesta 46, 811 02 Bratislava; tel. (2) 59-35-41-19; fax (2) 62-80-25-17; research into international affairs, including economics, foreign policy and law; Dir ATTILA SZÉP; publs various monographs.

Výskumné centrum Slovenskej spolo nosti pre zahrani nú politiku (Research Center of the Slovak Foreign Policy Association—RC SFPA): Panenská 33, 811 03 Bratislava; tel. (2) 54-43-31-51; fax (2) 54-43-31-61; e-mail duleba@sfpa.sk; internet www.sfpa.sk; f. 1995; research into the foreign policy of Slovakia and Central European countries; European Union and NATO integration; security and defence policy; bilateral relations with Ukraine and Russia; 5,000 vols; Dir Dr ALEXANDER DULEBA; publs *Newsletter of the SFPA* (monthly), *Slovak Foreign Policy Affairs* (2 a year, in English).

SLOVENIA

Slavistino društvo Slovenije (Slovene Slavonic Studies Society): 1001 Ljubljana, Aškereva 2; tel. (1) 2411320; fax (1) 4257055; e-mail Zoltan.Jan@guest.neticom.si; internet www.neticom.si/kronika; f. 1935; promotion of Slovene language and literature and awareness of Slovene history; Pres. ZOLTAN JAN; publs *Slavistina revija* (Slavonic Studies Journal, quarterly), *Jezik in slovstvo* (Language and Literature, 10 a year).

SOUTH AFRICA

South African Institute of International Affairs (SAIIA): University of the Witwatersrand, Jan Smuts House, POB 31596, Braamfontein, Johannesburg 2017; tel. (11) 339-2021; fax (11) 339-2154; e-mail saiiagen@global.co.za; internet www.wits.ac.za/saiia; f. 1934 to facilitate the scientific study of international questions, particularly those affecting southern Africa; 10,000 books, 2,000 journals; Chair. FRED PHASWANA; Nat. Dir Dr GREG MILLS; publs *South African Journal of International Affairs* (2 a year), *South African Yearbook of International Affairs*.

SPAIN

Instituto de Cuestiones Internacionales y Política Exterior (INCIPE) (Institute of International Affairs and Foreign Policy): Rafael Calvo 42, 28010 Madrid; tel. (91) 3085550; fax (91) 3081906; e-mail incipe@mad.servicom.es; f. 1988; Dir ALONSO ALVAREZ DE TOLEDO; publ. *La Opinión Pública Española y la Política Exterior* (2 a year).

Instituto de Estudios Europeos (Institute of European Studies): Deusto University, Edif. Central, Campus Bilbao, Avda de las Universidades 24, Apdo 1, 48007 Bilbao; tel. and fax (94) 4139284; e-mail relint@relint.deusto.es; internet www.relint.deusto.es/rel/ingles/ECTS/catabilbo/ins4.asp; f. 1979; research in the field of European integration, particularly economic issues; sponsors postgraduate education; Dir BEATRIZ PÉREZ DE LAS HERAS; publ. *Cuadernos Europeos de Deusto* (2 a year).

SWEDEN

Centre for Russian and East European Studies (CREES): Centre for European Research at Göteborg University (CERGU), Pilgaten 19, 1st Floor, POB 720, 405 30 Göteborg; tel. (31) 773-43-16; fax (31) 773-44-61; e-mail crees@crees.gu.se; internet www.crees.gu.se; f. 1995 to stimulate multi-disciplinary research and education, focusing on European issues.

Östersjöinstitutet (Baltic Institute): Högabergsgatan 3, POB 544 371 34 Karlskrona; tel. (455) 335-180; fax (455) 14-468; e-mail info@balticinstitute.se; internet www.balticinstitute.se; f. 1992; research on economic and trade development and co-operation between Baltic countries; forum for the promotion of Baltic co-operation; Man. Dir YVONNE SANDBERG-FRIES.

Stockholm Institute of Transition Economics and East European Economies (SITE): Stockholm School of Economics, POB 6501, 113 83 Stockholm; tel. (8) 736-96-70; fax (8) 31-64-22; e-mail site@hhs.se; internet www.hhs.se/site; f. 1989; research into the economic development of Eastern Europe, particularly the transition from a planned to a market economy; Dir Assoc. Prof. ERIK BERGLÖF; publs *Baltic Economic Trends* (quarterly), newsletters, reports.

Stockholm International Peace Research Institute (SIPRI): Signalistgatan 9, 169 70 Solna; tel. (8) 655-97-00; fax (8) 655-97-33; e-mail sipri@sipri.org; internet www.sipri.se; f. 1966; research into problems of peace and conflict, particularly arms control and disarmament; 32,000 vols; Dir Dr ALYSON J. K. BAILES; Deputy Dir Dr CHRISTER AHLSTRÖM; publ. *SIPRI Yearbook*.

Utrikespolitiska Institutet (Swedish Institute of International Affairs—SIIA): POB 1253, 111 82 Stockholm; tel. (8) 696-05-00; fax (8) 20-10-49; e-mail info@ui.se; internet www.ui.se; f. 1938; research into current international affairs; 40,000 vols, 400 periodicals; Pres. LEIF LEIFLAND; Man. Dir Dr ANDERS MELLBOURN; publs *Världspolitikens dagsfrågor, Internationella studier, Länder I fickformat, Världens Fakta,* conference papers, research report, monograph series.

SWITZERLAND

Forschungstelle für Sicherheitspolitik ETH Zürich (Centre for Security Studies, Swiss Federal Institute of Technology Zurich): ETH Zentrum SE1, 8092 Zurich; tel. (1) 6324025; fax (1) 6321941; e-mail postmaster@sipo.gess.ethz.ch; internet fsk.ethz.ch; f. 1986; administers electronic International Relations and Security Network (ISN); Dir Prof. ANDREAS WENGER.

Institut Suisse de Recherche sur les Pays de l'Est (Swiss Eastern Research Institute): Jubiläumsstr. 41, 3000 Bern 6; tel. (31) 431212; fax (31) 433891; f. 1959; study and information on the development of former communist countries; Dir Dr GEORG J. DOBROVOLNY; Admin. Dir SIMON MAURER; publs *Zeit-bild* (2 a month), *Le Périscope* (monthly), *Swiss Press Review* (2 a month), *Schwejzarskij Vestnik* (monthly, in Russian), *SOI-Bilanz* (monthly).

Interfaculty Institute of East and Central Europe: University of Fribourg, 7 route d'Englisberg, 1763 Granges-Pascot; tel. (26) 3007913; fax (26) 3009796; e-mail eoc@unifr.ch; internet www.unifr.ch/ieo; f. 1889; researches East European philosophy and theory of cultural sciences; Dir CH. GIORDANO.

TAJIKISTAN

Institute of World Economics and International Relations: Tajik Academy of Sciences, 734000 Dushanbe, ul. Aini 44; tel. (372) 23-27-32; fax (372) 22-57-65; f. 1964; economic development, with particular attention to transitional economies and the process of integration into the global economy; Dir RASHID K. RAKHIMOV; publ. *Ekonomiko-Matematicheskie Metody v Planirovanii Narodnogo Khozyaistva*.

THAILAND

Centre for European Studies (CES): 3rd Floor, Vidyabhathna Bldg, Chulalongkorn University, Phyathai Rd, Patumwan, Bangkok 10330; tel. (2) 218-3923; fax (2) 215-3580; e-mail ces@chula.ac.th; internet www.ces.chula.ac.th; f. 1997; aims to create better understanding of European Union affairs and the interaction between Asia/Thailand and Europe; areas of interest include Central and South-Eastern Europe; European Documentation Centre; Dir Dr CHARIT TINGSABADH.

TURKEY

European Community Institute: Marmara University, Goztepe Campus, 81040 Kadýkoy, İstanbul; tel. (216) 3384196; fax (216) 3474543; e-mail eci@marun.edu.tr; research on European Union (EU) integration, relations between Turkey and the EU; publ. *Avrupa Arastýrmalarý Dergisi* (2 a year, in Turkish and English).

Karadeniz ve Orta Asya Ülkeri Arastirma Merkezi (Black Sea and Central Asian Countries Research Centre): Middle East Technical University, Ismet Inönü Bul., 06531 Ankara; tel. (312) 2102046; fax (312) 2103051; e-mail kora@metu.edu.tr; internet www.metu.edu.tr/home/wwwkora/; f. 1992; data analysis and economic and political forecasting; Dir Dr Prof. AYŞE AYATA.

UKRAINE

Centre for European Studies at the Ukrainian Institute of International Relations: Taras G. Shevchenko State University, 254119 Kiev 119, ul. Melnikov 36/1; tel. (44) 213-09-90; fax (44) 213-07-67; e-mail post@iir.kiev.ua; internet www.iir.kiev.ua.

Institute of Social and Economic Problems of Foreign Countries: Ukrainian Academy of Sciences, 252030 Kiev, vul. Leontovicha 5; tel. (44) 225-51-27; fax (44) 225-22-31; research and studies on European and national economic, political and social problems; also studies the transition of Eastern European countries to a market economy; Dir A. N. SHLEPAKOV.

UNITED KINGDOM

Baltic Research Unit (BRU): University of Bradford, Bradford BD7 1DP; tel. (1274) 232323; fax (1274) 305340; e-mail J .Hiden@bradford.ac.uk; internet www.brad.ac.uk/acad/ mod-lang/planning_units; research into the importance of the Baltic region in the process of European enlargement; Dir Prof. JOHN HIDEN.

Bosnian Institute: 14–16 St Mark's Rd, London W11 1RQ; tel. (20) 7243-2900; fax (20) 7243-8874; e-mail bosinst@ globalnet.co.uk; internet www.bosnia.org.uk; f. 1997; education and information on history and contemporary culture of Bosnia and Herzegovina; forums, seminars; approx. 2,000 vols; Dir QUINTIN HOARE; publs *Bosnia Report* (every 2 months, on-line), *Books on Bosnia* (bibliography of books published in Western European languages since 1990), seminar series, etc.

Centre for Economic Reform and Transformation (CERT): School of Management, Heriot-Watt University, Riccarton, Edinburgh EH14 4AS; tel. (131) 451-3485; fax (131) 451-3498; e-mail s.a.ashby@hw.ac.uk; internet www.som.hw .ac.uk/cert/; f. 1990; analysis of economic transformations in Central and Eastern Europe; Dir Prof. MARK E. SCHAFFER; publ. *The Economics of Transition.*

Centre for Russian and East European Studies (CREES): University of Birmingham, European Research Institute, Edgbaston, Birmingham B15 2TT; tel. (121) 414-6346; fax (121) 414-3423; e-mail crees@bham.ac.uk; internet www.crees.bham.ac.uk; f. 1963; teaching and research on Central and Eastern European politics and society, post-communist economic transformation, the history of Russia and the former USSR, and security studies; 90,000 vols; Dir Dr HILARY PILKINGTON.

Centre for the Study of Public Policy: University of Strathclyde, Livingstone Tower, 26 Richmond St, Glasgow G1 1XH; tel. (141) 548-3217; fax (141) 552-4711; e-mail o.j .robertson@strath.ac.uk; internet www.cspp.strath.ac.uk; f. 1976; research on politics and economics of Russia and post-communist countries of Central and South-Eastern Europe; Dir Prof. RICHARD ROSE.

Centre for the Study of South-Eastern Europe: University of Wales Lampeter, SA48 7ED; tel. (1570) 424-872; fax (1570) 423-885; e-mail cssee@lamp.ac.uk; internet www.swan .ac.uk/cssee/cssee.htm; f. 1999; Dir PATRICK FINNEY.

Institute for Slavonic Studies: University of Oxford, Rewley House, 1 Wellington Sq., Oxford OX1 2JA; internet users.ox.ac.uk/slavinfo/research/institute.html; f. 1988 as the Institute of Russian, Soviet and East European Studies, changed name in 1994; co-ordinates research, disseminates scholarly material and professional information, administers academic exchanges; Dir CHRISTOPHER DAVIS.

Institute of Central and East European Studies (ICEES): University of Glasgow, Rm S602, Bute Gardens, Glasgow G12 8RT; tel. (141) 330-8855; fax (141) 330-5594; e-mail k.mcwalter@socsci.gla.ac.uk; internet www.gla.ac.uk/ departments/icees; f. 1999; research and postgraduate teaching on Central and Eastern European studies, concentrating on history, politics, economics, culture and society; approx. 80,000 vols; Dir Prof. JOHN LÖWENHARDT; publ. *Europe-Asia Studies* (formerly *Soviet Studies*).

Institute of Russian, Soviet, Central and East European Studies: Dept of Russian and Slavonic Studies, University of Nottingham, University Park, Nottingham NG7 2RD; tel. (115) 951-5824; fax (115) 951-5834; e-mail slavonic-enquiries@nottingham.ac.uk; internet www .nottingham.ac.uk/slavonic/irscees; f. 1986; inter-disciplinary research activity in Russian, Soviet, Central and East Euro-

pean studies; seminars, workshops and conferences; Dir Prof. LESLEY MILNE.

Pan-European Institute (PEI): University of Essex, Wivenhoe Park, Colchester CO4 3SQ; tel. (1206) 873976; fax (1206) 873965; e-mail pei@essex.ac.uk; internet www.essex.ac .uk/centres/pei; f. 1997; research into European integration and post-communist studies; Dir ALASTAIR MCAULEY; Exec. Officer LYNN BAIRD.

Research Unit on South-East European Studies: University of Bradford, Bradford BD7 1DP; tel. (1274) 235193; fax (1274) 720494; internet www.brad.ac.uk/acad/ihs/ southeasteuropeanstudies; f. 1968; interdisciplinary social science research into Albania, Bulgaria, Greece, Romania and the states of the former Yugoslavia; Head of Research Unit Dr JOHN B. ALLCOCK; Deputy Head Prof. TOM GALLAGHER; publ. *Bradford Studies in South-Eastern Europe* (irreg.).

Royal Institute of International Affairs: Chatham House, 10 St James's Sq., London SW1Y 4LE; tel. (20) 7957-5700; fax (20) 7957-5710; e-mail contact@riia.org; internet www.riia .org; f. 1920; an independent body, which aims to promote the study and understanding of international affairs; approx. 140,000 vols; Dir VICTOR BULMER-THOMAS; publs *The World Today* (monthly), *International Affairs* (quarterly).

Russian and East European Centre: St Antony's College, University of Oxford, 62 Woodstock Rd, Oxford OX2 6JF; tel. (1865) 284728; fax (1865) 310518; e-mail jackie.willcox@sant .ox.ac.uk; internet www.sant.ox.ac.uk/russian; f. 1953; research into Russian, Soviet, Eastern and East-Central European politics, economics, history, literature and culture; approx. 24,000 vols; Dir Dr ALEX PRAVDA.

School of Slavonic and East European Studies (SSEES): University College London, Senate House, Malet St, London WC1E 7HU; tel. (20) 7862-8000; fax (20) 7862-8640; e-mail ssees@ssees.ac.uk; internet www.ssees.ac.uk/; f. 1915; study of language, literature, history, anthropology, economics, politics, sociology and international relations of Eastern Europe; incorporates the Centres for the Study of Central Europe and for South-Eastern European Studies; approx. 357,000 books, periodicals and pamphlets; Dir Prof. GEORGE KOLANKIEWICZ; publs *Slavonic and East European Review* (quarterly), *Slovo: An Inter-disciplinary Journal of Russian, East European and Eurasian Affairs* (2 a year), *Solanus: An International Journal for Russian and East. European Bibliographic, Library and Publishing Studies.*

USA

Brookings Institution: 1775 Massachusetts Ave, NW, Washington, DC 20036; tel. (202) 797-6000; fax (202) 797-6004; e-mail brookinfo@brookings.edu; internet www .brookings.edu; f. 1916; governmental, economic and foreign-policy studies programmes; provides information for policy-makers, the public and the news media; 80,000 vols; Pres. STROBE TALBOTT; publs *Brookings Review, Brookings Papers on Economic Activity, Brookings Papers on Education Policy, Brookings-Wharton Papers on Financial Services, Brookings-Wharton Papers on Urban Affairs, Brookings Trade Forum.*

Center for Eurasian, Russian and East European Studies (CERES): Edmund A. Walsh School of Foreign Service, Georgetown University, Intercultural Center 232, POB 571031, Washington, DC 20057; tel. (202) 687-6080; fax (202) 687-5829; e-mail guceres@georgetown.edu; internet www.georgetown.edu/sfs/ceres; f. 1959; interdisciplinary research on relevant regions; approx. 5,000 vols; Dir Dr ANGELA E. STENT; Assoc. Dir Dr JENNIFER E. LONG; publ. monthly newsletter.

Center for European and Eurasian Studies (CERS): University of California, Los Angeles (UCLA), 11367 Bunche Hall, POB 951446, Los Angeles, CA 90095-1446; tel. (310) 825-4060; fax (310) 206-3555; e-mail vwheeler@international .ucla.edu; internet www.isop.ucla.edu/euro/; f. 1957 as Center for Russian and East European Studies; part of UCLA International Institute; promotes and assists interdisciplinary teaching and research; over 250,000 vols and 1,000 periodicals relating to Russia and Eastern Europe; Dir IVAN BEREND.

Center for Nations in Transition (CNT): Hubert H. Humphrey Institute of Public Affairs, University of Minnesota, 230 Hubert H. Humphrey Center, 301 19th Ave S., Minneapolis, MN 55455; tel. (612) 625-3073; fax (612) 626-9860; e-mail thageman@hhh.umn.edu; internet www.hhh.umn.edu/centers/cnt/main.htm; research and institutional design for sustainable development, and educational activities in Poland and other Central and Eastern European Countries; Dir ZBIGNIEW BOCHNIARZ.

Center for Russian and East European Studies (CREES): University of Michigan, Suite 4668, 1080 S. University Ave, Ann Arbor, MI 48109-1106; tel. (734) 764-0351; fax (734) 763-4765; e-mail crees@umich.edu; internet www.umich.edu/~iinet/crees; f. 1959; part of University of Michigan International Institute; Dir BARBARA A. ANDERSON.

Center for Russian, East European and Eurasian Studies (CREEES): Stanford University, Bldg 40, Main Quad, Stanford, CA 94305-2006; tel. (650) 723-3562; fax (650) 725-6119; e-mail rschnoor@stanford.edu; internet www.stanford.edu/dept/CREES; f. 1969; the promotion and support of the interdisciplinary study of the region; scholarly connections with leading organizations and academic institutions in the region; Dir Prof. NANCY S. KOLLMANN; publs newsletter, conference papers.

Center for Russian and East European Studies (REES): University of Pittsburgh, University Center for International Studies, 4G15 Posvar Hall, Pittsburgh, PA 15260; tel. (412) 648-7407; fax (412) 648-7002; e-mail crees@ucis.pitt.edu; internet www.ucis.pitt.edu/crees; f. 1965; research into economic and political transition and international relations of the region, including Balkan and Slovak studies; 348,000 vols; Dir Prof ROBERT M. HAYDEN; publs *REES News, Carl Beck Papers, Pitt Series in Russian and East European Studies.*

Center for Russian and East European Studies: University of Kansas, 320 Bailey Hall, 1440 Jayhawk Blvd, Lawrence, KS 66045-7574; tel. (785) 864-4236; fax (785) 864-3800; e-mail crees@ku.edu; internet www.ukans.edu/~crees; f. 1960; offers programme for US army officers specializing in East and Central Europe; 350,000 vols, 3,000 periodicals; special collections; Dir Dr MARIA CARLSON.

Center for Russian, Central and East European Studies (CRCEES): Rutgers, the State University of New Jersey, 172 College Ave, New Brunswick, NJ 08901-8537; tel. (732) 932-8551; fax (732) 932-1144; e-mail crcees@rci.rutgers.edu; internet www.rci.rutgers.edu/~crcees/center.html; multidisciplinary and comparative study of Russia, Central and East Europe; research into the development of viable solutions for the economic and political challenges faced by the emerging democracies; Dir Dr JAN KUBIK.

Center for Slavic and East European Studies (CSEES): Ohio State University, 303 Oxley Hall, 1712 Neil Ave, Columbus, OH 43210-1219; tel. (614) 292-8770; fax (614) 292-4273; e-mail csees@osu.edu; internet www.cohums.ohio-state.edu/slavicctr; f. 1965; Dir HALINA STEPHAN.

Center for Slavic, Eurasian, and East European Studies: University of North Carolina at Chapel Hill, 223 E. Franklin St, Campus Box 5125, Chapel Hill, NC 27599-5125; tel. (919) 962-0901; fax (919) 962-2494; e-mail slavic@email.unc.edu; internet www.unc.edu/depts/slavic; f. 1991; conferences, seminars; Dir ROBERT JENKINS; publ. *Inflections* (quarterly).

Center for Strategic and International Studies (CSIS): 1800 K St, NW, Washington, DC 20006; tel. (202) 887-0200; fax (202) 775-3199; e-mail webmaster@csis.org; internet www.csis.org/; f. 1962; research into international finance, US trade and economic policy, national and international security issues, energy, and telecommunications; Pres. and Chief Exec. JOHN J. HAMRE; publ. *Washington Quarterly.*

Center of International Studies: Woodrow Wilson School of Public and International Affairs, Princeton University, Bendheim Hall, Princeton, NJ 08544-1022; tel. (609) 258-4851; fax (609) 258-3988; internet www.wws.princeton.edu/

~cis; f. 1951; research into international security and political economy, privatization, and the restructuring of economies and states in Eastern Europe; Dir AARON L. FRIEDBERG; publs *World Politics* (quarterly), books, occasional papers.

East Central Europe Center: Columbia University, 420 West 118th St, New York, NY 10027; tel. (212) 854-4008; fax (212) 854-8577; e-mail kph2@columbia.edu; internet www.columbia.edu/REGIONAL/ECE/homepage.html; regional institute of School of International and Public Affairs; Dir Dr JOHN S. MICGIEL; publ. *Intermarium* (on-line journal).

EastWest Institute: 700 Broadway, 2nd Floor, New York, NY 10003; tel. (212) 824-4100; fax (212) 824-4149; e-mail ny@iews.org; internet www.iews.org; f. 1981; research into East-West relations and economics; affiliated to the Institute of Europe, Russian Academy of Sciences; Pres. JOHN EDWIN MROZ; publs *Annual Report of the EastWest Institute, Rose Occasional Papers.*

Hudson Institute: Herman Kahn Center, 5395 Emerson Way, POB 26-919, Indianapolis, IN 46226-0919; tel. (317) 545-1000; fax (317) 545-9639; e-mail info@hudson.org; internet www.hudson.org; f. 1961; research into Central and Eastern European countries; 13,000 vols; Pres. HERBERT (HERB) I. LONDON; publs *American Outlook* (every two months), *Visions* (quarterly).

Institute of Slavic, East European and Eurasian Studies (ISEEES): University of California, Berkeley, 260 Stephens Hall 2304, Berkeley, CA 94720-2304; tel. (510) 642-3230; fax (510) 643-5045; e-mail iseees@uclink4.berkeley.edu; internet socrates.berkeley.edu/~iseees; f. 1957; research, graduate training and scholarly and public programmes on the region; 750,000 vols, 10,000 serial titles; Dir Prof. VICTORIA E. BONNELL.

Russian and East European Institute (REEI): Indiana University, 1020 E. Kirkwood Ave, Ballantine Hall 565, Bloomington, IN 47405-6615; tel. (812) 855-7309; fax (812) 855-6411; e-mail reei@indiana.edu; internet www.indiana.edu/~reeiweb/index.html; f. 1958; study of Russia and Eastern Europe; over 600,000 vols; Dir DAVID L. RANSEL; publ. *REEIfication* (quarterly).

Russian, East European and Central Asian Studies Center: University of Washington's Jackson School of International Studies, Thomson Hall, Room 203, POB 353650, Seattle, WA 98195-3650; tel. (206) 543-4852; fax (206) 685-0668; e-mail reecas@u.washington.edu; internet depts.washington.edu/reecas/intro.htm; resource centre for the study of Russia, Eastern Europe and Central Asia; business and organizational contacts with the region; Dir STEPHEN HANSON.

Henry L. Stimson Center: 9th Floor, 11 Dupont Circle, NW, Washington, DC 20036; tel. (202) 223-5956; fax (202) 785-9604; e-mail info@stimson.org; internet www.stimson.org; f. 1989; research on regional security, arms control and nuclear, chemical and biological weapons; also concerned with conflict in the former Yugoslavia; Pres.and CEO ELLEN LAIPSON; Vice-Pres. and COO CHERYL RAMP; publs *Stimson Centre Newsletter* (3 a year), occasional paper series, reports, numerous monographs.

Weatherhead Center for International Affairs: Harvard University, 1033 Massachusetts Ave, Cambridge, MA 02138; tel. (617) 495-4420; fax (617) 495-8292; internet www.wcfia.harvard.edu; f. 1957; US-European relations and US foreign policy; regional studies; international economics; Dir Prof. JAMES A. COONEY; publs *Centrepiece* (quarterly), books and monographs.

VIET NAM

Institute of International Relations (IIR): Lang Thuong, Dong Da, Hanoi; tel. (4) 8343543; fax (4) 8343543; f. 1959; research on international relations; library of 25,000 vols; publ. *International Studies* (6 a year in Vietnamese, 2 a year in English).

SELECT BIBLIOGRAPHY (PERIODICALS)

Adelphi Papers. International Institute of Strategic Studies—IISS, 23 Tavistock St, London WC2E 7NQ, United Kingdom; tel. (20) 7379-7676; fax (20) 7836-3108; e-mail iiss@iiss.org.uk; internet www3.oup.co.uk/adelph/; f. 1964; analysis of contemporary and future international security problems; English; 8-10 a year.

Agora. Provoli Publications, Leoforos Kifissias 178, Halandri, 152 31 Athens, Greece; tel. (21) 6473384; fax (21) 6477893; f. 1987; Greek business, financial, economic and political affairs; Greek; Editor A. KEFALAS; every 2 weeks.

American Bibliography of Slavic and Eastern European Studies (ABSEES). University of Illinois Library at Urbana-Champaign, 128 Observatory, 901 South Mathews Ave, Urbana, IL 61801, USA; tel. (217) 333-0284; fax (217) 333-7011; e-mail absees@uiuc.edu; internet www.library.uiuc.edu/absees/; f. 1956 under the auspices of the American Asscn for the Advancement of Slavic Studies; covers US and Canadian scholarship on Central and Eastern Europe and the former USSR; contains bibliographic records, book extracts and reviews, dissertations, online resources and selected government publs; available online; English; Exec. Editor AARON TREHUB.

Annual Report of the EastWest Institute. 700 Broadway, 2nd Floor, New York, NY 10003, USA; tel. (212) 824-4100; fax (212) 821-4149; e-mail iews@iews.org; internet www.iews.org; f. 1981; East-West relations and economics; Czech, English, Slovak and Ukrainian; Editor ELIZABETH BELFER.

Australian Journal of International Affairs. Australian Institute of International Affairs, 32 Thesiger Court, Deakin, ACT 2600, Australia; tel. (6) 282-2133; fax (6) 285-2334; internet www.aiia.asn.au; f. 1946; international political, social, economic and legal issues; English; Editor Prof. WILLIAM TOW; 3 a year.

Avrupa Arastýrmalarý. Marmara University European Community Institute, Goztepe Campus, 81040 Kadýkoy, İstanbul, Turkey; tel. (216) 3384196; fax (216) 3474543; e-mail eci@camarun.edu.tr; f. 1991; EU integration; Turkish, English; Editor Prof. ASLAN GUNDUZ; 2 a year.

Bailrigg Memoranda. Centre for Defence and International Security Studies—CDISS, University of Lancaster, Dept of Politics and International Relations, Lancaster LA1 4YR, United Kingdom; tel. (1524) 594254; fax (1524) 594258; e-mail cdiss@lancaster.ac.uk; internet www.cdiss.org; f. 1980; security, defence and change in Eastern Europe; English; Editor HUMPHRY CRUM EWING; irregular.

Bailrigg Papers on International Security. Centre for Defence and International Security Studies—CIDISS, University of Lancaster, Dept of Politics and International Relations, Lancaster LA1 4YR, United Kingdom; tel. (1524) 594254; fax (1524) 594258; e-mail cdiss@lancaster.ac.uk; f. 1980; international security, defence and arms control; English; Editor HUMPHRY CRUM EWING; irregular.

Balkan Analyst. Institute of International and Strategic Studies, Rruga e Barrikadave, P8 Apt 27, Tirana, Albania; tel. (42) 29393; English; quarterly.

Balkan Reconstruction Report. Chlumova 22, 130 00 Prague, Czech Republic; tel. 222780805; fax 2227808004; e-mail transitions@tol.cz; internet balkanreport.tol.cz; English.

Balkan Studies. Institute for Balkan Studies, Leoforous Megalou Alexandrou 31A, 546 41, Thessaloníki, Greece; tel. (31) 832143; fax (31) 831429; e-mail imxa@imxa.gr; internet www.imxa.gr; political, cultural and artistic trends in the Balkans from the 17th century; English and other languages; Editor-in-Chief Prof. B. KONDIS; 2 a year.

Balkanistica. University of Mississippi, Dept of Modern Languages, Mississippi, MS 38677, USA; tel. (662) 915-7298; fax (662) 915-1086; e-mail mldyer@olemiss.edu; internet olemiss.edu/~mldyer/balk; f. 1972; Balkan issues; English; Editor DONALD L. DYER; annual.

Balkanologie. Association Française d'Etudes sur les balkans, Maison des Sciences de l'Homme, Bureau 108, 54 blvd Raspail, 75006 Paris, France; e-mail patrick.michels@afebalk.org; internet www.afebalk.org; f. 1997; French; Dir PATRICK MICHELS; 2 a year.

Baltic Economies: Bimonthly Review. Bank of Finland Institute for Economies in Transition (BOFIT), POB 160, 00101 Helsinki, Finland; tel. (9) 1832268; fax (9) 1832294; e-mail bofit@bof.fi; internet www.bof.fi/bofit; f. 1999; economic policy developments in Estonia, Latvia and Lithuania; available on-line, and by e-mail; English; Editor IIKKA KORHONEN; every 2 months.

Baltic Facts. Estonian Institute of Economic Research, Rävala pst. 6, Tallinn 19080, Estonia; tel. (6) 814-650; fax (6) 678-399; e-mail eki@ki.ee; internet www.ki.ee; demographic, economic and social indicators; English; annual.

Baltic Review. 3rd Floor, Kinga 10, POB 90, Tallinn 0090, Estonia; tel. (6) 31-31-70; fax (6) 31-33-32; e-mail tbr@tbr.ee; internet www.tbr.ee; f. 1993; business and economic issues in the Baltic region; published in association with the Estonian Institute for Futures Studies; English; Editor-in-Chief Dr ERIK TERK; quarterly; circ. 8,500.

Baltic Times. Skunu 16, Rīga 1050, Latvia; tel. 722-9978; fax 722-6041; e-mail editorial@baltictimes.com; internet www.baltictimes.com/; f. 1996, fmrly *Baltic Observer* and *Baltic Independent*; newspaper covering the three Baltic countries; available on-line; English; Editor-in-Chief ILZE ARKLINA; weekly; circ. 11,500 (2000).

Banks in Yugoslavia. 11000 Belgrade, SJU Borba Ekonomska Politika, trg Nikole Pašić 7, POB 629, Serbia and Montenegro; tel. (11) 334531; f. 1972; finance and insurance issues; Serbian, English; Editor VLADIMIR GRLIČKOV; annual.

BBC Global Newsline. BBC Monitoring Marketing Unit, Caversham Park, Reading, RG4 8TZ, United Kingdom; tel. (118) 946-9289; fax (118) 946-3823; e-mail marketing@mon.bbc.co.uk; political and economic news covering eight regions, incl. Central Europe and the former USSR (Russia, the Baltic states, the Caucasus and the western former USSR); English; daily, by e-mail.

Berlin Contributions to Peace and Conflict Research. Institute for Peace and Conflict Research, Humboldt University of Berlin, 10117 Berlin, Ziegelstr. 13A, Germany; tel. (30) 2814148; fax (30) 20932770; peace and conflict issues, Eastern European politics; quarterly.

Bizness i Baltya. Balasta dambis 3, Rīga 1081, Latvia; tel. 703-3011; fax 703-3010; e-mail root@info.bb.neonet.lv; internet www.bb.lv; business information; Russian, with English summaries; Editor-in-Chief TATJANA FAST; daily.

Blueline. Dimitris Dimopoulos, Pericleous 28, Nea Halkidona 143 43, Athens, Greece; Greek and Mediterranean issues; English.

Bradford Studies in South Eastern Europe. Research Unit in South East European Studies, University of Bradford, Bradford BD7 1DP, United Kingdom; tel. (1274) 233993; fax (1274) 720494; internet www.brad.ac.uk/acad/rusees/Publications.htm; English; Editors Dr JOHN B. ALLCOCK, M. MILIVOJEVIĆ, J. J. HORTON; irregular.

Bulgarian Economic Review. 1000 Sofia, Blvd Tzarigradsko 47A, Bulgaria; tel. (2) 943-31-47; fax (2) 943-31-88; e-mail office@pari.bg; internet www.news.pari.bg; f. 1992; business and economic affairs; fortnightly edition of *Bulgarian Financial and Business News Daily* (available on-line); English; Editor CHAIKA CHISTOVA; every 2 weeks.

Bulgarisches Wirtschaftsblatt und Sudosteuropäischer Report (Bulgarian Economic Newspaper and South East European Report). 1000 Sofia, Tsar Assen St 31, Biznes za Vseki; Sofia, POB 594; f. 1992; business and financial, for firms in German-speaking countries; monthly (also available on-line); Editor IVAN GANEV; circ. 10,000 (2001).

Business and Politics. Russian Foreign Policy Foundation, 107078 Moscow, per. Bolshoi Kozlovsky 4, Russia; tel. (095) 924-72-70; fax (095) 208-08-06; Russian foreign policy, business and economic relations; English; monthly.

Business Eastern Europe. Economist Intelligence Unit, 111 West 57th St, New York, NY 10019, USA; tel. (212) 540-0600; fax (212) 586-1181; e-mail bee@eiu.com; internet www.eiu.com; commercial and business information; English; Man. Editor PAUL LEWIS; Editor JOHN REED; weekly.

Canadian American Slavic Studies. Charles Schlacks, Jr, POB 1256, Idyllwild, CA 92549-1256, USA; tel. (909) 659-4641; e-mail schslavic@tazland.net; humanities and social sciences articles and book reviews; quarterly.

Canadian Slavonic Papers. Canadian Asscn of Slavists, University of Alberta, Dept of Modern Languages and Cultural Studies, 200 Arts Bldg, Edmonton, Alberta T6G 2EG, Canada; tel. (780) 492-2566; fax (780) 492-9106; e-mail gust.olson@ualberta.ca; internet www.ualberta.ca/~csp/; f. 1956; research articles on Russia, Central and Eastern Europe; English and French; Man. Editor EDWARD MOZEJKO; quarterly.

CEMOTI (Cahiers d'études sur la Méditerranée Orientale et le Monde Turco-Iranien). AFEMOTI, 4 rue de Chevreuse, 75006 Paris, France; tel. 1-44-10-84-75; fax 1-58-71-70-90; e-mail vaner@ceri.sciences-po.fr; internet www.ceri-sciencespo.com/publica/cemoti/presente.htm; f. 1985; news relating to the region extending from the Balkan peninsula and the Eastern Mediterranean to Central Asia; French; Editor SEMIH VANER; 2 a year.

Central European Economic Review. Dow Jones and Co (Europe) Inc., 87 blvd Bland Whitlock, 1200 Brussels, Belgium; tel. (2) 741-12-11; fax (2) 732-11-02; f. 1993; business and transitional economics in Central Europe; English; Editor PHIL REZVIN; monthly.

Central Europe Review. Chlumova 22, 130 00 Prague 3, Czech Republic; tel. 222780805; fax 222780804; e-mail transitions@tol.cz; internet www.culture.tol.cz; f. 1999; on-line journal concerned with Central and Eastern European politics, society and culture; merged with Transitions Online in 2002; English; Senior Editor SUSAN ABBOTT; every 2 weeks.

CEPS Papers. Centre for European Policy Studies (CEPS), 1 pl. du Congrès, 1000 Brussels, Belgium; tel. (2) 218-22-47; fax (2) 219-41-51; e-mail info@ceps.be; internet www.ceps.be; f. 1983; EU strategy and business policy with regard to Central and Eastern Europe; English; Editor ANNE HARRINGTON.

CESTAT Statistical Bulletin. c/o Czech Statistical Office, Sokolovska 142, 186 04, Prague 8, Czech Republic; tel. (2) 84820092; fax (2) 74052457; e-mail chyleova@gw.czso.cz; f. 1991; statistical information on Czech Republic, Hungary, Poland, Romania, Slovakia and Slovenia; Czech, English; quarterly.

Chinese Communist Affairs Monthly. Institute of International Relations, 64 Wan Shou Rd, Mucha, Taipei 11625, China (Taiwan); tel. (2) 9394921; fax (2) 9378609; countries of the former USSR and East European issues, in addition to Chinese affairs; Chinese; monthly.

Cold War History. Frank Cass & Co Ltd, Crown House, 47 Chase Side, Southgate, London N14 5BP, United Kingdom; tel. (20) 8920-2100; fax (20) 8447-8548; e-mail info@frankcass.com; internet www.frankcass.com/jnls/cwh.htm; f. 2000; English; Editors ALEXANDER CHUBARIAN (et al).

Colloquia: A Journal of Central European History. Institute for Central European Studies, Babes-Bolyai University of Cluj-Napoca, 3400 Cluj, Str. M. Kogalniceanu 1, Romania; tel. (64) 431659; fax (64) 191906; e-mail isce@napocensis.ubbcluj.ro; f.

1994; Central European history and culture; English, French, German, Italian; Editor POMPILIU TEODOR; 2 a year.

COM Documents. Office for Official Publications of the European Communities—EUR-OP, 2 rue Mercier, 2985 Luxembourg, Luxembourg; tel. 49-92-81; fax 49-57-19; f. 1983; working papers detailing EU policy proposals and information on the implementation of EU policies; Danish, Dutch, English, French, German, Greek, Italian, Portuguese and Spanish; Editor LUCIEN EMRINGER; 2 a month.

Communist and Post-Communist Studies. Centre for European and Russian Studies, University of California, 11367 Bunche Hall, POB 951446, Los Angeles CA 90095-1446, USA; tel. (310) 825-4060; fax (310) 206-3555; e-mail lvwheeler@isop.ucla.edu; internet www.isop.ucla.edu/euro/; Editor ANDRZEJ LORBONSKI.

Contemporary Security Policy. Frank Cass & Co Ltd, Crown House, 47 Chase Side, Southgate, London N14 5BP, United Kingdom; tel. (20) 8920-2100; fax (20) 8447-8548; e-mail info@frankcass.com; internet www.frankcass.com/jnls/csp.htm; English; Editors STUART CROFT, TERRY TERRIFF; 3 a year.

Courrier des Pays de l'Est. Centre for Research and Documentation on the CIS, China and Eastern Europe (CEDUCEE), 29 quai Voltaire, 75344 Paris Cédex 07, France; tel. 1-40-15-71-47; fax 1-40-15-69-93; e-mail cpe@ladocumentationfrancaise.fr; internet www.ladocumentationfrancaise.fr; f. 1967; trade and economic trends and co-operation; French; Editor SOPHIE MOATI; 10 a year.

CTK Business News: Bulletin of Economic News from the Czech Republic and Slovakia. Czech News Agency, Opletalova 5, 111 44 Prague 1, Czech Republic; tel. 222098465; e-mail ctk@mail.ctk.cz; internet www.ctk.cz; f. 1990; English; Editor SYLVIA IRGLOV; 5 a week.

Current Digest of the Post-Soviet Press. 3857 N High St, Columbus, OH 43214, USA; tel. (614) 292-4234; fax (614) 267-6310; e-mail fowler.40@osu.edu; f. 1949; translations and abstracts from Russian-language press materials; English; Editor FRED SCHULZE; weekly.

Czech Weekly Market Report. Wood Co, Martinsk 4, 110 00 Prague 1; tel. 224227731; fax 224227759; internet www.wood.cz.

Defence Studies. Institute for Strategic and Defence Studies, 1241 Budapest, POB 181, Hungary; tel. (1) 262-1920; fax (1) 264-9623; e-mail h9315gaz@huella.bitnet; security, conflict resolution and the armed forces; English; 6 a year.

Defense Analysis. Centre for Defence and International Security Studies (CDISS), University of Lancaster, Dept of Politics and International Relations, Lancaster LA1 4YL, United Kingdom; tel. (1524) 594254; fax (1524) 594258; e-mail cdiss@lancaster.ac.uk; internet www.tandf.co.uk/journals/carfax/07430175.html; f. 1985; Russian and Eastern European military and defence issues; English; Editor-in-Chief Dr MARTIN EDMONDS; 4 a year.

Delovie Lyudi. Press Contact, 117342 Moscow, ul. Profsoyuznaya 73, Russia; tel. (095) 333-33-40; fax (095) 330-15-68; f. 1990; business, management and economics in Russia and Eastern Europe; Russian and English; Editor VADIM BIRYUKOV; monthly.

East Central Europe. Charles Schlacks, Jr, POB 1256, Idyllwild, CA 92549-1256, USA; tel. (909) 659-4641; e-mail schslavic@tazland.net; internet www.ece-journal.org; f. 1974; social sciences and humanities; Editor JULIA SZALAI; 2 a year.

East Europe Monographs. Park College, Kansas City, MO 64152, USA; tel. (816) 741-2000; f. 1969; English; Editors JERZY HAUPTMANN, GOTTHOLD RHODE.

East European Constitutional Review. NYU School of Law, 12th Floor, 161 Avenue of the Americas, New York, NY 10013, USA; fax (212) 995-4600; e-mail rosea@juris.law.nyu.edu; internet www.law.nyu.edu/eecr/; f. 1992; covers post-socialist law and politics; Russian language version available at www.ilpp.ru; English; Editor STEPHEN HOLMES; quarterly.

East European Jewish Affairs. Frank Cass & Co Ltd, Crown House, 47 Chase Side, Southgate, London N14 5BP, United Kingdom; tel. (20) 8920-2100; fax (20) 8447-8548; e-mail info@frankcass.com; internet www.frankcass.com/jnls/eej.htm; fmrly known as *Soviet Jewish Affairs*; published under the aegis of the

Dept of Hebrew and Jewish Studies of University College, London, and the Oxford Institute for Yiddish Studies; concerned with Jewish issues in the former USSR and East-Central Europe; English; Man. Editor HOWARD SPEER; Editors GENNADY ESTRAIKH, JOHN KLIER, MIKHAIL KRUTIKOV; 2 a year.

East European Politics and Societies. Dept of Government and Politics, University of Maryland, College Park, MD 20742-7215, USA; tel. (510) 642-6188; fax (510) 642-9917; e-mail journals@ucop.edu; internet www.ucpress.edu/journals/eeps; f. 1986; economic, social and political issues in Eastern Europe; English; Editor VLADIMIR TISMANEANU; 3 a year.

East European Quarterly. Box 29, University of Colorado, Regent Hall, Boulder, CO 80309, USA; tel. and fax (941) 753-4782; e-mail eeqeem@web.tv.net; f. 1967; history, politics, economics, culture and civilization of Eastern Europe; English; Editor STEPHEN FISCHER-GALATI; quarterly.

East-West Business and Trade. 62 SE 6th Ave, Delray Beach, FL 33483, USA; tel. (407) 279-0956; fax (407) 278-8845; f. 1972; investment, economic, political and business developments in Central and Eastern Europe and the former USSR; English; Editor JUSTIN FORD; 2 a week.

East-West Business and Trade. Welt Publishing LLC, Suite 1400, 1413 K St, NW, Washington, DC 2005, USA; tel. (407) 279-095; fax (407) 278-8845; f. 1972; business relations, economic development, political stability and international organizations; English; Editor JOHN JUSTIN FORD; every 2 weeks.

Eastern Europe Newsletter (Political Briefing). London, United Kingdom; tel. (20) 8743-2829; fax (20) 8743-8637; e-mail charles@easterneurope.fsnet.co.uk; English; Editor CHARLES MEYNELL; 6 a year.

Eastern European Analyst. World Reports Ltd, 108 Horseferry Rd, London SW1P 2EF, United Kingdom; tel. (020) 7222-3826; fax (020) 7233-0185; Eastern European economics, and international economic developments caused by Russian foreign policy; English; Editor CHRISTOPHER STORY; quarterly.

Eastern European Consensus Forecasts. Consensus Economics, Inc., 53 Upper Brook St, London W1K 2LT, United Kingdom; tel. (20) 7491-3211; fax (20) 7409-2331; e-mail editors@consensusforecasts.com; internet www.consensusforecasts.com; f. 1998; economic forecasts for the Eastern European region, including Turkey; English; Editor NICHOLAS BOUGHTON; monthly.

Eastern European Economics: A Journal of Translations. M. E. Sharpe Inc., Armonk, NY 10504, USA; tel. (914) 273-1800; fax (914) 273-2106; internet www.mesharpe.com; f. 1962; macroeconomic and microeconomic analysis of Eastern European transitional economies; English; Editor JOSEF C. BRADA; 6 a year.

Economic Review. Privredni Preglad, 10000, Belgrade, Maršala Birjuzova 3-5, Serbia and Montenegro; tel. (11) 182888; fax (11) 627591; f. 1955; Yugoslav economic and business issues; Editor VLADIMIR KACANSKI; monthly.

Economic Survey of Europe. Economic Commission for Europe, United Nations, Palais des Nations, 1211 Geneva 10, Switzerland; tel. (22) 9172606; fax (22) 9170027; e-mail unpubli@unog.ch; economic analysis and statistical information; English and Russian; 2 a year.

Economic Survey of the Baltic States. Estonian Institute of Economic Research, Rävala pst. 6, Tallinn 19080, Estonia; tel. (6) 814-650; fax (6) 678-399; e-mail eki@ki.ee; internet www.ki.ee; economic and trade relations; English; quarterly.

Economic Systems. East European Institute of Munich, Scheinerstr. 11, 81679 Munich, Germany; tel. (89) 9983960; fax (89) 9810110; e-mail rfrensch@lrz-muenchen.de; internet www.lrz-muenchen.de/~econsys; f. 1970; comparative economics, particularly in Eastern Europe; English, with German abstracts; Man. Editor RICHARD FRENSCH; quarterly.

Economics of Transition. Blackwell Publishers Ltd, 108 Cowley Rd, Oxford OX4 1JF, United Kingdom; tel. (1865) 791100; fax (1865) 791347; e-mail subscrip@blackwellpub.com; internet www.blackwellpublishers.co.uk; published for the European Bank for Reconstruction and Development (EBRD); transition economies; Editors PHILIPPE AGHION, WENDY CARLIN; English; 3 a year.

Ekonom. Prague, Czech Republic; internet www.ekonom.ihned.cz; national and international economic, political and development issues; Czech.

Ekonomist. Savez Economista Jugoslavije, 11000 Belgrade, Nusiceva 6-III, Serbia and Montenegro; tel. (11) 334417; f. 1948; journal of the Yugoslav Asscn of Economists; Serbo-Croat; Editor OTO NORCIĆ; quarterly.

Ekonomska Politika. SJU Borba Ekonomska Politika, 11000 Belgrade, trg Nikole Pašicaa 7, POB 629, Serbia and Montenegro; tel. (11) 3298263; fax (11) 3298300; Editor-in-Chief VERICA DUKANAČ; weekly.

Ekonomski Pregled. Institute of Economics, 10000, Zagreb, trg J. F. Kennedy 7, Croatia; tel. (1) 2335700; fax (1) 2335165; e-mail dragomir.vojnic@ekist.eizghr; f. 1935; Croatian, with summaries in English and Russian; Editor-in-Chief Dr DRAGOMIR VOJNIĆ; 2 a month.

Emerging Europe Monitor. 179 Queen Victoria St, London EC4V 4DU, United Kingdom; tel. (20) 7248-0468; fax (20) 7248-0467; e-mail subs@businessmonitor.com; internet www.businessmonitor.com; English; Editor ANN-LOUISE HAGGER; monthly.

ELIAMEP Newsletter. Hellenic Foundation for European and Foreign Policy (ELIAMEP), Odos Xenophontos 4, 105 57 Athens, Greece; tel. (21) 03315022; fax (21) 03642139; e-mail eliamep@eliamep.gr; internet www.eliamep.gr; international strategic issues; English; Editor Dr FOTINI BELLOU; quarterly.

Est-Ovest. Istituto di Studi e Documentazione sull'Europa Comunitaria e l'Europa Orientale—ISDEE, Corso Italia 27, 34122 Trieste, Italy; tel. (40) 639130; fax (40) 634248; e-mail isdee@spin.it; f. 1970; socio-economic, political and institutional aspects of Eastern Europe and of East-West relations; Italian, English and French; Man. Editor TITO FAVARETTO; 6 a year.

Etudes Balkaniques. Institute of Balkan Studies, Bulgarian Academy of Sciences, 1000 Sofia, 45 Moskovska, Bulgaria; tel. and fax (2) 980-62-97; e-mail balkani@cl.bas.bg; internet www.cl.bas.bg/Balkan-Studies; f. 1964; multidisciplinary articles on Balkan peoples and states; English, French, German, Italian, Russian; Editor-in-Chief Prof. AGOP GARABEDYAN; quarterly.

Eurasian Geography and Economics. Bellwether Publishing Ltd, 8640 Guilford Rd, Suite 200, Columbia, MD 21046, USA; tel. (410) 290-3870; fax (410) 290-8726; e-mail subs@bellpub.com; internet www.bellpub.com/psge/; f. 1960 as *Soviet Geography*, and subsequently renamed *Post-Soviet Geography and Economics*; economics and geography of the countries of the former USSR, Central and Eastern Europe, and former and existing, socialist countries of Asia; English; Editor RALPH S. CLEM; 8 a year.

Euro-Bulletin, The Newsletter of Article 19's Central and Eastern European Programme. Article 19, 33 Islington High St, London N1 9LH, United Kingdom; tel. (20) 7278-9292; fax (20) 7713-1356; e-mail info@article19.org; internet www.article19.org; f. 1996; English.

Euro-est. Europe Information Service, 66 ave Adolphe Lacombl, 1040 Brussels, Belgium; tel. (2) 737-77-06; fax (2) 732-67-57; e-mail compta@eis.be; internet www.eis.be; f. 1972; relations between the EU and European Economic Area, and Central and Eastern European countries, including major business developments; English and French; Editors MARC PAOLONI, PETER O'DONNELL; 11 a year.

Europäische Sicherheit. E. S. Mitter und Sohn GmbH, 32052 Herford, Steintorwall 17, Germany; tel. (5221) 59910; fax (5221) 599149; f. 1951; European security policies and issues; German; Editor FRANZ MENDEL; monthly.

European Journal of International Affairs. Erasmus Press, Via dei Giubbonari 30, 00186 Rome, Italy; tel. (6) 6873196; fax (6) 6872549; international affairs and international relations; English; Editor GIUSEPPE SACCO; quarterly.

European Journal of International Relations. Geschwister-Scholl-Institut für Politische, Wissenschaft Oettingenstrasse 67, G-80358 München, Germany; tel. (89) 21809050; fax (89) 21783052; e-mail friedrich.kratochwil@lrz.uni-muenchen.de; internet www.sagepub.co.uk/journals/details/j0148.html; published under auspices of Standing Group of International Relations; available on-line; English; Editor FRIEDRICH V. KRA-TOCHWIL; quarterly.

European Security. Frank Cass & Co Ltd, Crown House, 47 Chase Side, Southgate, London N14 5BP, United Kingdom; tel. (20) 8920-2100; fax (20) 8447-8548; e-mail info@frankcass.com; internet www.frankcass.com/jnls/es.htm; English; Editors PAUL D'ANIERI, CHRISTOPHER DONNELLY, ALVIN BERNSTEIN; quarterly.

European Social Policy. Foundation for European Studies—European Institute, University of Łódź, Łódź, ul. Piotrkowska 262-264, Poland; tel. (42) 370593; fax (42) 370586; e-mail obeul@plunlo51.bitnet; Polish relations with the rest of Europe, including the EU; Polish; quarterly.

Folia Oeconomica Cracoviensia. Komisja Nauk Ekonomicznych, Polska Academia Nauk, Oddzial w Krakowie, 30-018 Kraków, ul. Sw. Jana 28, Poland; tel. (12) 224853; fax (12) 222791; f. 1960; published by the Economic Science Commission of the Polish Academy of Sciences; Polish, with summaries in English and Russian; Editor JANUSZ MACIASZEK; annual.

Frontier. Keston Institute, 38 St Aldate's, Oxford OX1 1BN, United Kingdom; tel. (1865) 792929; fax (1865) 240042; e-mail keston.institute@keston.org; internet www.keston.org; religious issues affecting Eastern Europe and the former USSR; English; Editor Dr PHILIP WALTERS; 6 a year.

Gospodarska Gibanja. Economic Institute of the Law School, University of Ljubljana, 1001 Ljubljana, Prešernova 21, Slovenia; tel. (1) 2521688; fax (1) 4256870; e-mail eipf@guest.arnes .si; internet www2.armes.si/~ljeipf/eipf.htm; f. 1971; economic trends; Slovene; Editors JOŽE MENCINGER, FRANJO ŠTIBLAR; monthly.

Harriman Review. Harriman Institute, Columbia University, 420 West 188th St, New York, NY 10027, USA; tel. (212) 854-6218; fax (212) 666-3481; f. 1994; politics, culture and society of Eastern and Central Europe; English; Editor RONALD MEYER; monthly.

Hellenews. Hellenews Publications, Odos Halandriou 39, Marousi, 151 25 Athens, Greece; tel. (21) 6827582; fax (21) 6825858; internet www.kapatel.gr/express; f. 1958; economic, business and financial information; English; Editor J. M. GERMANOS; weekly.

Hellenic Review of International Relations. Institute of International Public Law and International Relations, Leoforos Megalou Alexandrou 15 and Hadji, 546 40 Thessaloníki, Greece; tel. (31) 841751; fax (31) 853427; Greek international relations; 2 a year.

Heti Világgazdaság. 1126 Budapest, 64 N,metvölgy u. 1, Hungary; tel. (1) 155-5411; f. 1979; international economics; Hungarian; Editor-in-Chief IVÁN LIPOVECZ; weekly.

Horizons Nouveaux. Asscn of International Political Studies, 4 ave BenoÔt-Frachon, 92023 Nanterre, France; tel. (1) 46-14-09-29; fax (1) 46-14-09-25; f. 1949; formerly *Est et Ouest*; international political development, focusing on Central and Eastern Europe; French; monthly.

Ikonomichesky Zhivot. 1009 Sofia, Moskovska St, Bulgaria; tel. (2) 87-95-06; fax (2) 88-21-40; f. 1966; finance, economy and foreign trade in Bulgaria; Bulgarian; Editor VASSIL ALEXIEV; weekly.

International Affairs. Royal Institute of International Affairs, Chatham House, 10 St James's Sq., London SW1Y 4LE, United Kingdom; tel. (20) 7957-5700; fax (20) 7957-5710; e-mail contact@riia.org; internet www.riia.org/publications/ia/iaffs .html; f. 1922; English; Editor CAROLINE SOPER; quarterly; circ. 6,000.

International Affairs. Russian Foreign Policy Foundation, 107078 Moscow, per. Bolshoi Kozlovsky 4, Russia; tel. (095) 924-72-70; fax (095) 208-08-06; internet www.mosinfo.ru/news/int-aff/subintaf.html; f. 1992; available on-line; English; 6 a year.

International Initiative. Multilateral International Initiative-Independent Asscn, 1421 Sofia, 78 Kroum Popov St, Bulgaria; tel. and fax (2) 66-44-58; Bulgarian foreign policy and international relations; English; quarterly.

International Peace-keeping. Frank Cass & Co Ltd, Crown House, 47 Chase Side, Southgate, London N14 5BP, United Kingdom; tel. (20) 8920-2100; fax (20) 8447-8548; e-mail info@frankcass.com; internet www.frankcass.com/jnls/ip.htm; English; Editor MICHAEL PUGH; quarterly.

International Spectator. Istituto Affari Internazionali—IAI, Palazzo Rondinini, Via Angelo Brunetti 9, 00186 Rome, Italy; tel. (06) 3224360; fax (06) 3224363; e-mail iai@iai.it; internet www .iai.it; European integration, particularly Eastern European transition and relations with the southern Mediterranean; English; Man. Editor ETTORE GRECO; quarterly.

IPIS Brochures. International Peace Information Service—IPIS, Italiëlie 98A, 2000, Antwerp, Belgium; tel. (3) 225-00-22; fax (3) 231-01-51; e-mail ipis@skynet.be; internet users.skynet .be/ipis/etstudy.htm; f. 1980; peace and security issues in Eastern Europe and developing countries; Dutch; 10 a year.

Journal Export. Exportpress, 11000 Belgrade, Ulica 27, Marta 39/1, POB 358, Serbia and Montenegro; tel. (11) 3222659; internet www.journal.co.yu; f. 1954; Yugoslav international economic relations; English, French, German and Russian; Editor-in-Chief NIKOLA VUCETIC; every 2 weeks.

Journal of Communist Studies and Transition Politics. Frank Cass & Co Ltd, Crown House, 47 Chase Side, Southgate, London N14 5BP, United Kingdom; tel. (20) 8920-2100; fax (20) 8447-8548; e-mail info@frankcass.com; internet www.frankcass.com/ jnls/cst.htm; f. 1985; English; Editors STEPHEN WHITE, RONALD J. HILL, PAUL G. LEWIS, MARGOT LIGHT, RICHARD SAKWA; quarterly.

Journal of East-West Business. Haworth Press, Inc., 10 Alice St, Binghamton, NY 13904-1580, USA; tel. (717) 566-3054; fax (717) 566-8589; e-mail k9x@psu.edu; internet www .haworthpressinc.com/; f. 1994; business studies, strategies, development and practice, focusing on Eastern and Central European countries and the CIS; English; Editor Dr ERDENER KAYNAK; quarterly.

Journal of European Integration. Dept of Government, University of Essex, Wivenhoe Park, Colchester, Essex CO4 3SQ, United Kingdom; tel. (1206) 872749; fax (1206) 873598; e-mail emil@essex.ac.uk; internet www.tandf.co.uk/journals/online/ 0703%2D6337.html; English; Exec. Editor EMIL KIRCHNER; quarterly.

Journal of European Social Policy. School of Social Sciences, University of Bath, Claverton Down, Bath BA2 7AY, United Kingdom; tel. (1225) 826826; fax (1225) 826381; e-mail jesp@ bath.ac.uk; f. 1991; European social policy; English; Editor IAN GOUGH; quarterly.

Journal of Slavic Military Studies. Frank Cass & Co Ltd, Crown House, 47 Chase Side, Southgate, London N14 5BP, United Kingdom; tel. (20) 8920-2100; fax (20) 8447-8548; e-mail info@ frankcass.com; internet www.frankcass.com/jnls/jsm.htm; security and military affairs in an historical and geopolitical context; English; Editors DAVID M. GLANTZ, CHRISTOPHER DONNELLY; English; quarterly.

Journal of Southeast European and Black Sea Studies. Frank Cass & Co Ltd, Crown House, 47 Chase Side, Southgate, London N14 5BP, United Kingdom; tel. (20) 8920-2100; fax (20) 8447-8548; e-mail info@frankcass.com; internet www.frankcass.com/ jnls/bss/; f. 2001; covers the politics, political economy, international relations and modern history of South-Eastern Europe and the Black Sea region; English; Editors FRANZ-LOTHAR ALTMAN, SHIREEN HUNTER, THEODORE COULOUMBIS, THANOS VEREMIS, JONATHAN EYAL; English; 3 a year.

Journal of Southern Europe and the Balkans. Taylor and Francis Group PLC, 11 New Fetter Lane, London EC4P 4EE, United Kingdom; tel. (20) 75839855; fax (20) 78422298; e-mail beverley.acreman@tandf.co.uk; internet www.tandf.co.uk/ journals/carfax/14613190.html; encourages comparative discussion; available on-line; English; Editor VASSILIS FOUSKAS; 2 a year.

Konfliktus Együttmuködès. Hungarian Academy of Sciences, 1364, Budapest, Egyetem tér 1-3, POB 109, Hungary; tel. and fax (1) 118-8055; European and international security issues; Hungarian; annual.

Konjunktuur. Estonian Institute of Economic Research (EKI), Ravala pst. 6, Tallinn 19080, Estonia; tel. (6) 814-650; fax (6) 678-399; e-mail eki@ki.ee; internet www.ki.ee/konjunktuur .htm; Estonian and English; Editor MARJE JOSING; quarterly.

Korean Journal of International Studies. POB 426, Seoul 110-604, Republic of Korea; tel. (2) 752-7727; fax (2) 752-7710; f. 1970; international issues affecting communist and former communist countries; English; Editor CHOI CHONG-KI; quarterly.

Külügyi Szemle. 1125 Budapest, Szilágyi Erszébet fasor 22C Hungary; tel. (1) 391-5700; f. 1974 as Külpolitika, name changed 1999; Hungarian, with summaries in English and Russian; Editor TAMÁS MAGYARICS; quarterly.

Lumea Magazin. Bucharest, Romania; tel. (1) 185081; e-mail lumea@fx.ro; internet www.lumeam.ro/nr5_2002/index.html; f. 1963; global politics and world events; Romanian, English, French, German, Russian and Spanish; Editor MAGDALENA BOIANGIU; monthly.

Masaryk Journal. School of Slavonic and East European Studies, University of London, Senate House, London WC1E 7HU, United Kingdom; tel. (20) 7636-8000; fax (20) 7862-8644; e-mail katerina.kocourek@st-antonys.ox.ac.uk; f. 1997; history, sociological and political theory, current political affairs; English, with articles in Czech; Editor KATYA A. M. KOCOUREK; annual.

Mediterranean Politics. Frank Cass & Co Ltd, Crown House, 47 Chase Side, Southgate, London N14 5BP, United Kingdom; tel. (20) 8920-2100; fax (20) 8447-8548; e-mail info@frankcass.com; internet www.frankcass.com/jnls/mp.htm; Editor RICHARD GILLESPIE; 3 a year.

Millennium: Journal of International Studies. London School of Economics, Houghton St, London WC2A 2AE, United Kingdom; tel. (20) 7955-6232; fax (20) 7955-7438; e-mail millennium@lse .ac.uk; internet www.lse.ac.uk/Depts/intrel/millenn/; f. 1971; English; Editors EVA GROSS, ALVARO MENDEZ.

Nations and Needs. Center for International Development and Conflict Management, University of Maryland, Dept of Government and Politics, 0145 Tidings Hall, College Park, MD 20742-7231, USA; tel. (301) 314-7703; fax (301) 314-9256; e-mail ewilson@dss2.und.edu; international peace and conflict issues, including Eastern Europe; English; 2 a year.

Nations in Transit. 1319 18th St NW, Washington, DC 20036, USA; tel. (202) 296-5101; fax (202) 296-5078; e-mail fh@ freedomhouse.org; internet www.freedomhouse.org/research/ nattransit.htm; comparative study of 27 former communist countries; English; annual.

New Zealand Slavonic Journal. Victoria University of Wellington, POB 600, Wellington, New Zealand; tel. (4) 463-5322; fax (4) 463-5419; e-mail slavonic-journal@vuw.ac.nz; internet www .vuw.ac.uz/nzsj; f. 1967; English, Russian; Editor IRENE ZOHRAB; annual.

Newsline: Central and Eastern Europe/Southeastern Europe. Radio Free Europe/Radio Liberty, 110 00 Prague 1, Vinohradská 1, Czech Republic; tel. 221122407; fax 221123013; e-mail sunkovskaj@rferl.org; internet www.rferl.org; f. 1949; analysis of major political events and trends across Eastern and South-Eastern Europe; all relevant languages, English; Editor ELIZABETH FULLER; daily.

RFE/RL Balkan Report. e-mail moorep@rferl.org; Editor PATRICK G. MOORE; weekly.

RFE/RL Baltic States Report. e-mail banionisa@rferl.org; Editor ASTA BANIONIS; weekly.

RFE/RL East European Perspectives. e-mail shafirm@referl .org; Editor Dr MICHAEL SHAFIR; weekly.

RFE/RL Poland, Belarus and Ukraine Report. e-mail maksymiukj@rferl.org; Editor JAN MAKSYMIUK; weekly.

RFE/RL South Slavic Report. e-mail moorep@rferl.org; Editor PATRICK MOORE; weekly.

News2biz.com. Northroup Newsletters, Bredgade 25 D, 1260 Copenhagen K, Denmark; tel. (33) 330720; fax (33) 330791; e-mail contact@news2biz.com; internet www.news2biz.com; online business newsletter for Poland, Lithuania, Latvia and Estonia; in English.

Novoye Vremya. 127994 Moscow, Malyi Putinkooskii per. 1/2, Russia; tel. (095) 209-98-18; fax (095) 200-42-23; e-mail contact@ newtimes.ru; internet www.newtimes.ru; f. 1943; foreign and Russian affairs; English (monthly) and Russian (monthly); Editor ALEKSANDR PUMPY.

Ost-Wirtschaftsreport. Verlagsgruppe Handelsblatt GmbH, 40213 Düsseldorf, Kasernenstr. 67, Germany; tel. (211) 8870; internet www.vhb.de; f. 1973; German; Editor JULIANE LANGE-NECKER; every 2 weeks.

Osteuropa. German Society for Eastern European Studies, 52062 Aachen, Grosskölnstr. 32-34, Germany; tel. (241) 32707; fax (241) 405879; e-mail oe@rwth-aachen.de; internet www .rwth-aachen.de/ipw/Ww/osteuropa/index.html; f. 1925; Central and Eastern European cultures, economies, nationalities, politics and society; German; Editor ALEXANDER STEININGER; monthly.

Osteuropa-Wirtschaft. German Society for East European Studies, 80336 Munich, Güllstr. 7, Germany; tel. (89) 74613321; fax (89) 74613333; e-mail u9511aa@mail.lrz-muenchen.de; f. 1956; economic issues in Central and Eastern Europe, particularly problems of transition, new trends and developments; German, with some articles in English and French; Editor Dr FRANZ-LOTHAR ALTMANN; quarterly.

Paneuropa Deutschland. Paneuropa-Verlag, 80222 Munich, Karlstr. 57, Germany; tel. (89) 554683; fax (89) 594768; f. 1977; democratization in Central and Eastern Europe; German; Editor W. STOCK; quarterly.

Political Crossroads. James Nicholas Publishers, POB 244, Albert Park, Vic 3206, Australia; tel. (3) 696-5545; fax (3) 699-2040; f. 1978; international relations, political theory, economic and administrative organizations, leadership and cultural ideology; English; Editors ILYA ZEMTSOV, GENADY OSIPOV; quarterly.

Politics and Policy. Dept of Political Science, Georgia Southern University, Statesboro, GA 30460-8101, USA; tel. (912) 681-0572; fax (912) 681-5348; e-mail journalp@gasou.edu; internet www2.gasou.edu/pap; f. 1973; fmrly *Southeastern Political Review*; political science; English; Editor Dr GEORGE COX; quarterly.

Politik Ekonomie. University of Economics, W. Churchill n m. 4, 130 67 Prague 3, Czech Republic; tel. and fax 224095819; e-mail papers@vse.cz; internet www.vse.cz/polek; f. 1953; economic theory and policy; Czech, with abstracts in English; Editor MILAN ŽÁK; every 2 months; circ. 4,000.

Politika Ndërkomëtare. Institute of International Relations, c/o Akademie Shkencave, Rruga Myslim Shryi 7, Tirana, Albania; tel. (42) 29521; fax (42) 32970; Albanian; quarterly.

Politologicky Caspopis. International Institute for the Study of Politics, School of Law, Masaryk University, Veveri 70, 611 80 Brno, Czech Republic; tel. 541214852; fax 541213162; e-mail bohanes@caisildur.law.muni.cz; Czech; quarterly.

Polityka Wschodnia. Centre for Eastern Studies, University of Warsaw, 00-046 Warsaw, ul. Nowy Swiat 69, Poland; internet www.uw.edu.pl; relations between the successor states of the former USSR; Polish; 2 a year.

Post-Communist Economies. Centre for Research into Communist Economies (CRCE), 2 Lord North St, London SW1P 3LB, United Kingdom; tel. (20) 7799-3745; fax (20) 7233-1050; e-mail beverley.acreman@tandf.co.uk; internet www.tandf.co.uk/ journals/carfax/14631377.html; f. 1989; transformation economics of communist and former communist countries, in particular in Eastern Europe; fmrly *Communist Economies and Economic Transformation*; English; Editor ROGER CLARKE; quarterly.

Post-Soviet Affairs. Bellwether Publishing Ltd, 8640 Guilford Rd, Suite 200, Columbia, MD 21046, USA; tel. (410) 290-3870; fax (410) 290-8726; e-mail subs@bellpub.com; internet www .bellpub.com/psa/; f. 1985; political science, foreign policy and nationality issues; English; Editor GEORGE W. BRESLAUER; quarterly.

Prague Economic Papers. University of Economics, W. Churchill n m. 4, 130 67 Prague 3, Czech Republic; tel. and fax 224095819; e-mail papers@vse.cz; internet www.vse.cz/pep; f. 1992; economic theory and policy; English; Editor Milan Žák; quarterly; circ. 1,000.

Problems of Economic Transition. M. E. Sharpe Inc., 80 Business Park Drive, Armonk, New York, NY 10504, USA; tel. (914) 273-1800; fax (914) 273-2106; internet www.mesharpe.com; f. 1958 as *Problems in Economics*; English; Editor Ben Slay; monthly.

Problems of Post-Communism. M. E. Sharpe Inc., 80 Business Park Drive, Armonk, New York, NY 10504, USA; tel. (914) 273-1800; fax (914) 273-2106; e-mail popc@gwu.edu; internet www .mesharpe.com; f. 1951; analysis of post-communist countries; English; Editor James R. Millar; 6 a year.

Przeglad Zachodni. Institute for Western Affairs, 61-854 Poznań, ul. Mostowa 27, Poland; tel. (61) 8527691; fax (61) 8524905; e-mail izpozpl@man.poznan.pl; internet www.iz .poznan.pl; f. 1945; European integration, Polish-German relations; Polish; Editor Dr Hanka Dmochowska; quarterly.

Reforma Monthly. International Foundation for Economic and Social Reforms—Reforma Foundation, 109240 Moscow, nab. Kotelnicheskaya 17, Russia; tel. (095) 915-96-57; fax (095) 915-40-25; Russian and English; Editor-in-Chief Viktor Kamyshanov; monthly.

Religion in Eastern Europe. AMBS, 3003 Benham Ave, Elkhart, IN 46517, USA; tel. (574) 296-6209; fax (574) 295-0092; e-mail waltersawatsky@cs.com; internet cis.georgefox.edu/ree; f. 1981 as Occasional Papers on Religion in Eastern Europe, adopted current name in 1993; published by the Princeton Theological Seminary; English; Editor Dr Walter Sawatsky; 6 a year.

Religion, State and Society. Keston Institute, 38 St Aldate's, Oxford OX1 1BN, United Kingdom; tel. (1865) 792929; fax (1865) 240042; e-mail keston.institute@keston.org; internet www.keston.org; f. 1973 as Religion in Communist Lands; present name adopted 1992; all aspects of religion and religion-state relations in communist and post-communist states; English; Editor Dr Philip Walters; 4 a year.

Revista de Estudios Europeos. Centre for European Studies, Avda 3ra, No 1805, entre 18 y 20, Miramar, Playa, Playa, Havana, Cuba; tel. (7) 22-6767; fax (7) 33-1435; e-mail cee@ tinored.cu; f. 1987; Spanish; Editor Jos, Eloy Valdes; quarterly.

Revue d'Intégration Européene. Canadian Council for European Affairs, University of Saskatchewan, Dept of Political Studies, 9 Campus Drive, Saskatoon SK S7N 0W0, Canada; tel. (306) 966-5231; fax (306) 966-5250; e-mail michelmann@sask.usask.ca; f. 1977; European integration; French and English; Editor H. J. Michelmann, P. Soldatos; 2 a year.

Revue des Etudes Comparatives Est Ouest. Centre National de la Recherche Scientifique, 44 rue de l'Amiral Mouchez, 75014, Paris, France; tel. 1-43-13-56-69; fax 1-43-13-56-68; e-mail receo@ivry.cnrs.fr; f. 1970 as *Revue de l'Est*; French, with English summaries; Editor Kathy Rousselet; quarterly.

Revue des Etudes Sud-Est Européenes. Institute for South-East European Studies, Romanian Academy, Bd. Republicii 13, CP 22-159, Romania; tel. (1) 6144996; quarterly.

Revue Roumaine d'Etudes / Revista Romna de Studii Internationale Internationales. Asscn of International Law and International Relations, 71268 Bucharest, 'Nicolae Titulescu' Memorial House, Sos. Kiseleff 47, Sector 1, Romania; tel. (21) 6185462; fax (21) 3124422; e-mail adiri@sunu.rnc.ro; f. 1967; French, Romanian and English; Editor A. Pop; 6 a year.

Rocznik Polskiej Polityki Zagranicznej (Yearbook of Polish Foreign Policy). Ministry of Foreign Affairs, 00-950 Warsaw, Warecka 1A, POB 1000, Poland; tel. (22) 5239035; fax (22) 5239027; e-mail warecka@qdnet.pl; internet www.qdnet.pl/ warecka/rocznik_polskiej_polityki_zagranicznej.html; f. 1991; Polish foreign policy; Polish, English; Editor Barbara Wizimirska; annual.

Romanian Journal of International Affairs. Centre for Romanian Studies, Oficiul Postal 1, Casuta Postala 108, 6600 Iasi, Romania; tel. (32) 219000; fax (32) 219010; e-mail csr@ romanianstudies.ro; internet www.romanianstudies.ro/rointaff .html; f. 1995; English, with articles in French and German; Editor-in-Chief Viorica Rusu; quarterly.

Russia Briefing. London, United Kingdom; tel. (20) 8743-2829; fax (20) 8743-8637; e-mail charles@easterneurope.fsnet.co.uk; English; Editor Charles Meynell; quarterly.

Russian and Baltic Economies: The Week in Review. Bank of Finland Institute for Economies in Transition (BOFIT), POB 160, 00101 Helsinki, Finland; tel. (9) 1832286; fax (9) 1832294; e-mail bofit@bof.fi; internet www.bof.fi/bofit; f. 1997; review of events in Estonia, Latvia, Lithuania and Russia; available online, and by e-mail; English; Editor Timo Harell; weekly.

Russian and East European Finance and Trade. M. E. Sharpe Inc., 80 Business Park Drive, Armonk, New York, NY 10504, USA; tel. (914) 273-1800; fax (914) 273-2106; internet www .me-sharpe.com; English; Editor Ali M. Kutan; 6 a year.

Schriftenreihe des Bundesinstituts für ostwissenschaftliche und internationale Studien. Federal Institute for Russian, Eastern European and International Studies, 50823 Cologne, Lindenbornstr. 22, Germany; tel. (221) 57470; fax (221) 5747110; e-mail e-mail@mail.rrz.uni-koeln.de; f. 1978; politics and international relations; German; 2 a year.

Slavia Orientalis. Instytut Filologii Wschodniosłowiańskiej, Uniwesytet Jagielloński, 31-123, Kraków, ul. Krupnicza 35, Poland; tel. and fax (12) 4214876; e-mail slavia@vela.filg.uj.edu .pl; f. 1952; culture, religion and sociopolitical issues of Slavonic nations; Belorusian, English, Polish, Russian, Ukrainian; Editor Prof. Lucjan Suchanek; quarterly.

Slavic and Eastern European Journal. American Asscn of Teachers of Slavic and Eastern European Languages, 1933 N Fountain Park Drive, Tucson, AZ 85715-5538, USA; tel. (520) 885-2663; e-mail aatseel@compuserve.com; internet clover .Slavic.pitt.edu/~aatseel/; all areas of Slavic languages and culture; English; Editor Dr Stephen L. Baehr.

Slavic Review: American Quarterly of Russian, Eurasian, and East European Studies. University of Illinois at Urbana-Champaign, 57 E Armory Ave, Champaign, IL 61820, USA; tel. (217) 333-3621; fax (217) 333-3872; e-mail slavrev@uiuc.edu; internet www.econ.uiuc.edu~/slavrev/; f. 1941 as *American Slavic and East European Review*, name changed 1961; English; Editor Diane P. Koenker; quarterly.

Slavistična revija. Slovene Slavonic Studies Society, Aškerčeva 2, pp. 580, Ljubljana, Slovenia; tel. (1) 2411320; fax (1) 4257055; e-mail center-slo@ff.uni-lj.si; internet www.ijs.si/lit/sr.html; f. 1948; Slovene; Exec. Editor Franc Zadravec; quarterly; circ. 1,300.

Slavonic and Eastern European Review. School of Slavonic and East European Studies, University College London, Senate House, Malet St, London WC1E 7HU, United Kingdom; tel. (20) 7862-8536; fax (20) 7862-8641; e-mail seer@ssees.ac.uk; internet www.ssees.ac.uk; available on-line; Editor Dr Martyn Rady; quarterly.

Slavonica. Sheffield Academic Press, Mansion House, 19 Kingfield Rd, Sheffield S11 9AS, United Kingdom; tel. (114) 255-4433; fax (114) 255-4626; e-mail katya.young@man.ac.uk; f. 1983; language, history and culture in Russia and Central and Eastern Europe; Editor Jekaterina Young; 2 a year.

Slovak Foreign Policy Affairs. Panenská, 811 03 Bratislava, Slovakia; tel. (2) 5443-3151; fax (2) 5443-3161; e-mail luka@sfpa .sk; f. 2000; journal of the Slovak Foreign Policy Asscn; English; Editor Pavol Luká; 2 a year.

Slovenia Weekly. 1000 Ljubljana, Vitrim d.o.o., Hradeckega 38, Slovenia; tel. (1) 4261412; fax (1) 1402027; e-mail marketing@ vitrum.si; internet www.vitrum.si; f. 1994; on-line version available; English; Editor Gerdina Toma; weekly.

Slovo. School of Slavonic and Eastern European Studies, University of London, Senate House, Malet St, London WC1E 7HU, United Kingdom; tel. (20) 7862-8619; fax (20) 7862-8641; e-mail slovo@ssees.co.uk; internet www.ssees.ac.uk/slovo.htm; interdisciplinary journal concerned with Central and East European, Russian and Eurasian affairs; English; Man. Editor Sergiu Troie; annual.

Social Science in Eastern Europe. Informationszentrum Sozialwissenschaften, Abteilung Informationstransfer Osteuropa in der Aussenstelle der GESIS, Schiffbauerdamm 19, 10117 Berlin, Germany; tel. (30) 30874246; fax (30) 2823692; e-mail oenews@berlin.iz-soz.de; internet www.gesis.org/en/publications/magazines/newsletter_eastern_europe/; discusses social science institutes and their areas of research, profiles important journals in the field of social science, and contains short essays on Eastern European social science issues; English; at least 4 a year.

Solanus. An International Journal for Russian and East European Bibliographic, Library and Publishing Studies. School of Slavonic and East European Studies, University of London, Senate House, Malet St, London WC1E 7HU, United Kingdom; tel. (20) 7412-7587; fax (20) 7412-7554; e-mail chris.thomas@bl.uk; Editor Dr CHRISTINE THOMAS; annual.

SouthEastern Europe. Charles Schlacks, Jr, POB 1256, Idyllwild, CA 92549-1256, USA; tel. (909) 659-4641; e-mail schslavic@tazland.net; Editor CODRIN CUTITARU; English, French, German; annual.

SouthEastern Europe Business Brief. CEEBIC, US Dept of Commerce, Ronald Reagan Bldg, 1401 Constitution Ave NW, Washington, DC 20230, USA; tel. (202) 482-5471; fax (202) 482-3898; e-mail ceebic@ita.doc.gov; internet www.mac.doc.gov/eebic/balkan/seebb.html; compiled by the Southeast Europe Task Force at the US Dept of Commerce; business information on Albania, Bosnia and Herzegovina, Bulgaria, Croatia, Kosovo (Yugoslavia), the former Yugoslav republic of Macedonia, Romania and Slovenia; weekly, by e-mail.

South European Society and Politics. Frank Cass & Co Ltd, Crown House, 47 Chase Side, Southgate, London N14 5BP, United Kingdom; tel. (20) 8920-2100; fax (20) 8447-8548; e-mail info@frankcass.com; internet www.frankcass.com/jnls/sesp.htm; Editors NANCY BERMEO, PAUL HEYWOOD, SUSANNAH VERNEY; 3 a year.

The South Slav Journal. South Slav Research and Study Centre, 4 Church Rd, London N6 4QT, United Kingdom; tel. (20) 8340-9713; fax (20) 8348-5659; e-mail nemar76@hotmail.com.

Soviet and Post-Soviet Review. Charles Schlacks, Jr, POB 1256, Idyllwild, CA 92549-1256, USA; tel. (909) 659-4641; e-mail schslavic@tazland.net.

Sprawy Miedzynarodowe (Polish Quarterly of International Affairs). Polish Foundation of International Affairs, 00-950 Warsaw, ul. Warecka 1A, POB 1000, Poland; tel. (22) 5239012; fax (22) 5239027; e-mail warecka@qdnet.pl; internet www.qdnet.pl/warecka; f. 1948, English version f. 1994; international policy; Polish, English; Editor HENRYK SZLAJFER; quarterly.

Stanford Slavic Studies. Berkeley Slavic Specialties, POB 30334, Oakland, CA 94609-0034, USA; tel. (510) 653-8048; fax (510) 653-6313; e-mail gfreidin@stanford.edu; internet www.stanford.edu/dept/slavic/ar/slavstudies.html; f. 1987; series of publications on Slavic language and literature; Editors LAZAR FLEISHMAN, JOSEPH FRANK, GREGORY FREIDIN, RICHARD SCHUPBACH.

Statistical Yearbook of the Republic of Poland. CSO Poland, (Statistical Publishing Establishment), 00-925 Warsaw, al. Niepodległości 208, Poland; tel. (22) 6083145; fax (22) 6083867; e-mail dissem@stat.gov.pl; internet www.stat.gov.pl; Polish, English.

Statistical Yearbook on Candidate and South-East European Countries. Office for Official Publications of the European Communities, 2 rue Mercier, 2985 Luxembourg; tel. 29291; fax 495719; e-mail europ@opoce.cec.be; internet eur-op.eu.int.

Stopanksi Preglad. Sojuzot na Drustvata na Ekonomisite na Makedonija, 91000 Skopje, Ekonomiski Fakulet, K. Misirkov bb., POB 489, former Yugoslav republic of Macedonia; tel. (2) 224311; fax (2) 224973; f. 1950; published by the Macedonian Union of Asscns of Economists; Macedonian; Editor NIKOLA KLJUSEK; 6 a year.

Stosunki Miydzynarodowe (International Relations). Institute of International Relations, University of Warsaw, Dept of Journalism and Political Sciences, 00-503 Warsaw, ul. Zurawia 4, Poland; tel. (22) 5531635; fax (22) 5531636; e-mail ismn@mercury.ci.uw.edu.pl; f. 1978; Polish; Editor Prof. STANISŁAW BIELEN; quarterly.

Suravu Kenkyu. Slavic Research Center, Hokkaido University, Kita 9, Nishi 7, Kita-ku, Sapporo 060-0809, Japan; tel. (11) 706-

2388; fax (11) 706-4952; e-mail src@slav.hokudai.ac.jp; internet src-h.slav.hokudai.ac.jp; Japanese; annual.

Theory and Practice of Foreign Policy. Institute for Current International Problems, 119021 Moscow, ul. Ostozhenka 53/2, Russia; tel. (095) 208-94-61; fax (095) 208-94-66; Russian foreign policy and international diplomacy; monthly.

TOL Annual Survey. Chlumova 22, 130 00 Prague, Czech Republic; tel. 222780805; fax 2227808004; e-mail transitions@tol.cz; internet www.tol.cz; English; available on CD-ROM.

Transitions Online (TOL). Chlumova 22, 130 00 Prague 3, Czech Republic; tel. 222780805; fax 222780804; e-mail transitions@tol.cz; internet www.tol.cz; f. 1999; culture, politics, economy and media in East Central Europe, the Balkans and the former USSR; English; Editor JEREMY DRUKER; updated daily.

Transnational Organized Crime. Frank Cass & Co Ltd, Crown House, 47 Chase Side, Southgate, London N14 5BP, United Kingdom; tel. (20) 8920-2100; fax (20) 8447-8548; e-mail info@frankcass.com; internet www.frankcass.com/jnls/index.htm; f. 1995; cross-border criminal activities and government responses to such crime; English; Man. Editor PHIL WILLIAMS; quarterly.

Tregtia e Jashtme Popullore. Rruga Konferenca e Pezës 6, Tirana, Albania; tel. (42) 22934; f. 1961; published by the Albanian Chamber of Commerce; English and French; Editor AGIM KORBI; 6 a year.

Trends in World Economy. Institute for World Economics, Hungarian Academy of Sciences, 1124 Budapest, Kálló esperes u. 15, Hungary; tel. (1) 166-8433; fax (1) 162-0661; e-mail hlll90vki@ella.hu; f. 1995; English; Editor GÁBOR FOTI; 3-4 a year.

Turkish Review of Balkan Studies. Foundation for Middle East and Balkan Studies, Salacak, Kasap Veli Sok 10, Uskudur, 81160 İstanbul, Turkey; f. 1993; Balkan studies, ethnic conflicts; English and French; annual.

Ukazetelu soci lniho a hospod Øského vývoje Ćeské, republiky EkonomickehoRozvoje Ceske Republiky. Czech Statistical Office Information Service, Sokolovsk 142, 186 04 Prague 8, Czech Republic; tel. 26832734; fax 266310429; e-mail bondyova@gw.czso.cz; f. 1994; statistical series; Czech and English; quarterly.

Ulkopolitiikka. Finnish Institute of International Affairs, Mannerheimintie 15A, 00260 Helsinki, Finland; tel. (9) 4342070; fax (9) 43420769; e-mail maarika.toivonen@upi-fiia.fi; internet www.upi-fiia.fi; f. 1972; foreign policy and democracy in Eastern Europe; Finnish; Editor-in-Chief Dr TUOMAS FORSBERG; quarterly.

The Week in Europe. European Commission Representation in the United Kingdom, Jean Monnet House, 8 Storey's Gate, London SW1P 3AT, United Kingdom; tel. (20) 7973-1992; fax (20) 7973-1907; e-mail ue-uk-press@cec.eu.int; internet www.cec.org.uk; summary of EU affairs; English; Editor JONATHAN HEWITT; weekly.

Yearbook of Foreign Policy: Greece and the World. Hellenic Foundation for European and Foreign Policy (ELIAMEP), Odos Xenophontos 4, 105 57 Athens, Greece; tel. (21) 03315022; fax (21) 03642139; e-mail eliamep@eliamep.gr; internet www.eliamep.gr; f. 1992; Greek foreign policy and international relations; Greek; Editors THANOS DOKOS, THEODORE COULOUMBIS; annual.

Zaranie Slaskie. Silesian Scientific Institute, 40-956 Katowice, ul. Graniczna 32, Poland; tel. (3) 1565873; Central European international relations; Polish; quarterly.

Zbiór Dokumentów. Polish Foundation of International Affairs, 00-950 Warsaw, ul. Warecka 1A, POB 1000, Poland; tel. (22) 5239087; fax (22) 5239027; e-mail warecka@qdnet.pl; internet www.qdnet.pl/warecka; f. 1937; Polish and international documents; Polish, English; Editor JERZY MENKES; quarterly.

Zbornik: Politicka Ekonomia. Institute of Marxism-Leninism, Comenius Institute of Bratislava, 818 06 Bratislava, Slovakia; tel. (2) 321-594; fax (2) 363-836; f. 1972; Slovak, with summaries in German and Russian; Editor JAN KUKEL; annual.

Zeitschrift für Ostmitteleuropa-Forschung. Herder-Institut Marburg, 35037 Marburg, Gisonenweg 5-7, Germany; tel. (6421) 184125; fax (6421) 184139; e-mail vertrieb@mailer.uni-marburg.de; internet www.uni-marburg.de/herder-institut; f. 1952; history of East Central Europe; German and English; Editor Dr WINIFRIED IRGANG; quarterly.

Zwischen Krise und Konsolidierung: Gefährdeter Systemwechsel im Osten Europas: Jahrbuch des BIOst. Federal Institute for Russian, East European and International Studies—BIOst, 50823 Cologne, Lindenbornstr. 22, Germany; tel. (221) 57470; fax (221) 5747110; e-mail e-mail@mail.rrz.uni_koeln.de; f. 1961; political, economic and social developments in Eastern Europe; German; every 2 years.

SELECT BIBLIOGRAPHY (BOOKS)

For books on individual countries see the Bibliography at the end of each Country Chapter in Part Two

Aage, Hans (Ed.). *Environmental Transition in Nordic and Baltic Countries*. Cheltenham, Edward Elgar, 1998.

Ádám, Magda. *The Little Entente and Europe (1920–1929)*. Budapest, Akadémiac Kiadó, 1989 (English translation, 1993).

Allcock, John B., Milivojević, Marko, and Horton, John J. (Eds). *Conflict in the former Yugoslavia: an Encyclopedia*. Santa Barbara, CA, ABC-Clio, 1998.

Ardittis, Solon (Ed.). *The Politics of East-West Migration*. London, Macmillan, 1994.

Asmus, Ronald D. *Opening NATO's Door*. New York, NY, Columbia University Press, 2002.

Auty, Phyllis, and Clogg, Richard (Eds). *British Policy Towards Wartime Resistance in Yugoslavia and Greece*. London, Macmillan (in association with the School of Slavonic and East European Studies, University of London), 1975.

Bátonyi, Gábor. *Britain and Central Europe 1918–1933*. Oxford, Oxford University Press, 1999.

Bauer, Yahuda (Ed.). *The Danger of Anti-Semitism in Central and Eastern Europe in the Wake of 1989–1990*. Jerusalem, Hebrew University of Jerusalem, 1991.

Bennett, Robert J. (Ed.). *Local Government and Market Decentralization: Experiences in Industrialised, Developing, and Former Eastern Bloc Countries*, Tokyo, United Nations University Press, 1994.

Berend, Ivan T. *Central and Eastern Europe 1944–1993: Detour from the Periphery to the Periphery*. Cambridge, Cambridge University Press, 1996.

Berglund, Sten, Tomas, Hellén, and Aarebrot, Frank H. *The Handbook of Political Change in Eastern Europe*. Cheltenham, Edward Elgar, 1998.

Bideleux, Robert, and Jeffries, Ian. *A History of Eastern Europe: Crisis and Change*. London, Routledge, 1998.

Bonin, John P., Mizsei, Kálmán, Szekely, István P., and Wachtel, Paul. *Banking in Transition Economies: Developing Market Oriented Banking Sectors in Eastern Europe*. Cheltenham, Edward Elgar, 1998.

Bougarel, Xavier, and Clayer, Nathalie (Eds). *Le Nouvel Islam Balkanique: les Musulmans, Acteurs du Postcommunisme, 1990-2000*. Paris, Editions Maisonneuve et Larose, 2001.

Bridger, Sue, and Pine, Frances (Eds). *Surviving Post-Socialism: Local Strategies and Regional Responses in Eastern Europe and the Former Soviet Union*. London, Routledge, 1998.

Brogan, Patrick. *Eastern Europe 1939–1989: The Fifty Years War*. London, Bloomsbury, 1990.

Brunner, Georg. *Nationality Problems and Minority Conflicts in Eastern Europe*. Gütersloh, Bertelsmann Foundation, 1996.

Bukowski, Charles, and Racz, Barnabus (Eds). *The Return of the Left in Post-Communist States: Current Trends and Future Prospects*. Cheltenham, Edward Elgar, 1999.

Carter, Francis W., and Turnock, David (Eds). *Environmental Problems in East-Central Europe*. London, Routledge, 2001 (second edn).

Carter, F. W., and Norris, H. T. (Eds). *The Changing Shape of the Balkans*. London, UCL Press, 1996.

Chamberlain, Lesley. *In the Communist Mirror: Journeys in Eastern Europe*. London, Faber and Faber, 1990.

Cheles, Luciano, Ferguson, Ronnie, and Vaughan, Michalina (Eds). *The Far Right in Western and Eastern Europe*. Harlow, Longman, 1995 (second edn).

Clark, Victoria. *Why Angels Fall: A Journey through Orthodox Europe from Byzantium to Kosovo*. London, Macmillan, 2000.

Clark, Wesley K. *Waging Modern War: Bosnia, Kosovo and the Future of Combat*. New York, NY, Public Affairs, 2001.

Cockerham, William C. *Health and Social Change in Russia and Eastern Europe*. London, Routledge, 1999.

Connelly, John. *Captive University: The Sovietization of East German, Czech and Polish Higher Education, 1945–1956*. Chapel Hill, NC, University of North Carolina Press, 2000.

Conquest, Robert, and Djordjevich, Dušan (Eds). *Political and Idiological Confrontations in Twentieth Century Europe. Essays in Honour of Miorad M. Drachkovitch*. New York, NY, St Martin's Press, 1996.

Corrin, Chris (Ed.). *Gender and Identity in Central and Eastern Europe*. London, Frank Cass, 1999.

Cottey, Andrew (Ed.). *Sub-regional Co-operation in the New Europe: Building Security, Prosperity and Solidarity from the Barents to the Black Sea*. London, Routledge (in association with the EastWest Institute), 1999.

Coulson, Andrew (Ed.). *Local Government in Eastern Europe: Establishing Democracy at the Grassroots*. Aldershot, Edward Elgar, 1995.

Crampton, Richard, and Crampton, Ben. *Atlas of Eastern Europe in the Twentieth Century*. London, Routledge, 1997.

Crampton, R. J. *Eastern Europe in the Twentieth Century and After*. London, Routledge, 1997 (second edn).

   The Balkans Since the Second World War. Harlow, Longman, 2002.

Crowe, David. *The Baltic States and the Great Powers: Foreign Relations, 1938-1940*. Boulder, CO, Westview Press, 1993.

Crowe, David, and Kolsti, John. *The Gypsies of Eastern Europe*. New York, NY, M. E. Sharpe, 1991.

Darst, R. G. *Smokestack Diplomacy: Co-operation and Conflict in East-West Environmental Politics (Global Environmental Accord: Strategies for Sustainability and Institutional Innovation*. Cambridge, MA, The MIT Press, 2001.

Dawisha, Karen, and Parrott, Bruce. *Politics, Power and the Struggle for Democracy in South-East Europe*. Cambridge, Cambridge University Press, 1997.

Deakin, William, Barker, Elisabeth, and Chadwick, Jonathan (Eds). *British Political and Military Strategy in Central, Eastern and Southern Europe in 1944*. London, Macmillan, 1988.

De Zayas, Alfred-Maurice, and Barber, Charles M. *A Terrible Revenge: The Ethnic Cleansing of the East European Germans 1944–1950*. New York, NY, St Martin's Press, 1994.

Dickinson, D. G. *et al. Financial and Monetary Integration in the New Europe: Convergence Between the EU and Central and Eastern Europe (Elgar Monographs)*. Cheltenham, Edward Elgar, 2002.

Dunay, Pál, Kardos, Gábor, and Williams, Andrew J. *New Forms of Security: Views from Central, Eastern and Western Europe*. Aldershot, Dartmouth, 1995.

Earle, John S., Frydman, Roman, Rapaczynski, Andrzej, and Turkewizt, Joel. *Small Privatization: The Transformation of Retail Trade and Consumer Services in the Czech Republic, Hungary and Poland*. Budapest, Central European University Press, 1994.

East, Roger, and Pontin, Jolyon. *Revolution and Change in Central and Eastern Europe*. London, Pinter, 1997 (revised edn).

Ekiert, Grzegorz. *The State Against Society: Political Crises and their Aftermath in East Central Europe*. Princeton, NJ, Princeton University Press, 1996.

Eksteins, Modris. *Walking Since Daybreak: A Story of Eastern Europe, World War II and the Heart of the Twentieth Century*. London, Papermac, 1999.

Elster, Jon (Ed.). *The Roundtable Talks and the Breakdown of Communism*. Chicago, IL, University of Chicago Press, 1996.

Estrin, Saul, Hughes, Kirsty, and Todd, Sarah. *Foreign Direct Investment in Central and Eastern Europe: Multinationals in Transition*. London, Pinter, 1997.

Estrin, Saul (Ed.). *Privatization in Central and Eastern Europe: Key Issues in the Realignment of Central and Eastern Europe*. Harlow, Longman, 1994.

Estrin, Saul, Brada, Josef C., Gelb, Alan, and Singh, Inderjit. *Restructuring and Privatization in Central and Eastern Europe: Case Studies of Firms in Transition*. Armonk, NY, M. E. Sharpe, 1995.

Eyal, Jonathan. *Vicious Circles: Security in the Balkans*. London, Royal United Services Institute for Defence Studies, Whitehall Paper Series, 1992.

Falk, Barbara J. *The Dilemmas of Dissidence in East-Central Europe*. Budapest, CEU Press, 2003.

Feldman, Robert A., Watson, C. Maxwell, *et al. Into the EU: Policy Frameworks in Central Europe*. Washington, DC, IMF, 2002.

Fings, Karola, Heuss, Herbert, and Sparing, Frank. *The Gypsies during the Second World War No 1: From 'Race Science' to the Camps*. Hatfield, University of Hertfordshire Press, 1997.

Fitzmaurice, John. *Politics and Government in the Visegrad Countries: Poland, Hungary, the Czech Republic and Slovakia*. London, Macmillan, 1998.

Fowkes, Ben. *Eastern Europe 1945–1969: From Stalinism to Stagnation*. Harlow, Pearson Education, 2000.

Frucht, Richard (Ed.). *Encyclopaedia of Eastern Europe: From the Congress of Vienna to the Fall of Communism*. New York, NY, Garland, 2000.

Frydman, Roman, Gray, Cheryl W., and Rapaczynski, Andrzej (Eds). *Corporate Governance in Central Europe and Russia*. Budapest, Central European University Press, 1996.

Frydman, Roman, Rapaczynski, Andrzej, and Earle, John S. *et al. The Privatization Process in Russia, Ukraine and the Baltic States*. London, Central European University Press, 1993.

Gabrisch, Hubert, and Pohl, Rüdiger (Eds). *EU Enlargement and its Macroeconomic Effects in Eastern Europe: Currencies, Prices, Investment and Competitiveness*. Studies in Economic Transition, London, Macmillan, 1999.

Gallagher, Tom. *Outcast Europe: The Balkans 1789 to 1989, from the Ottomans to Milošević*. London, Routledge, 2001.

The Balkans after Communism: From Tyranny to Tragedy. London, Routledge, 2003.

Gardner, Hall (Ed.). *Central and Southeast Europe in Transition: Perspectives on Success and Failure since 1989*. Westport, CT, Praeger, 2000.

Garton-Ash, Timothy. *We the People: The Revolution of '89 witnessed in Warsaw, Budapest, Berlin and Prague*. Cambridge, Granta, 1990.

History of the Present: Essays, Sketches and Despatches from Europe in the 1990s. London, Penguin, 1999.

Glenny, Misha. *The Rebirth of History: Eastern Europe in the Age of Democracy*. London, Penguin, 1990.

The Balkans 1804–1999: Nationalism, War and the Great Powers. London, Granta, 2000.

Grabbe, Heather, and Hughes, Kirsty. *Enlarging the EU Eastwards*. London, Chatham House Papers, Royal Institute of International Affairs, 2000 (reprint).

Granberg, Leo, and Kovách, Imre (Eds). *Actors on the Changing European Countryside*. Budapest, Institute for Political Science of the Hungarian Academy of Sciences, 1998.

Graute, Ulrich (Ed.). *Sustainable Development for Central and Eastern Europe: Spatial Development in the European Context*. Berlin, Springer, 1998.

Gros, Daniel, and Steinherr, Alfred. *Winds of Change: Economic Transition in Central and Eastern Europe*. Harlow, Longman, 1996.

Gruber, Ruth Ellen. *Upon the Doorposts of Thy House: Jewish Life in East-Central Europe, Yesterday and Today*. New York, NY, John Wiley, 1994.

Guy, Will (Ed.). *Between Past and Future: The Roma of Central and Eastern Europe*. Hatfield, University of Hertfordshire Press, 2001.

Haavisto, Tarmo (Ed.). *The Transition to a Market Economy: Transformation and Reform in the Baltic States*. Cheltenham, Edward Elgar, 1997.

Hall, Derek, and Darrick, Danuta (Eds). *Reconstructing the Balkans: a Geography of the New Southeast Europe*. Chichester, John Wiley, 1996.

Hawkesworth, Celia. *Voices in the Shadows: Women and Verbal Art in Serbia and Bosnia*. Budapest, Central European University Press, 2000.

Helme, Mehis. *Fortress Railways of the Baltic Shores*. London, Plateway Press, 1994.

Held, Joseph (Ed.). *Democracy and Right-wing Politics in Eastern Europe in the 1990s*. Boulder, CO, East European Monographs, 1993.

Henderson, Karen (Ed.). *Back to Europe: Central and Eastern Europe and the European Union*. London, UCL Press, 1999.

Hiden, John. *The Baltic States and Weimar Ostpolitik*. Cambridge, Cambridge University Press, 1987.

Hiden, John, and Lane, Thomas (Eds). *The Baltic and the Outbreak of the Second World War*. Cambridge, Cambridge University Press, 1992.

Holbrooke, Richard. *To End a War*. Random House, New York, NY, 1998.

Hosking, Geoffrey, and Schöpflin, George (Eds). *Myths and Nationhood*. London, C. Hurst (in association with the School of Slavonic and East European Studies, University of London), 1997.

Howard, Marc Morjé. *The Weakness of Civil Society in Post-Communist Europe*. College Park, MD, University of Maryland Press, 2003.

Hunya, Gábor (Ed.). *Integration through Foreign Direct Investment: Making Central European Industries Competitive*. Cheltenham, Edward Elgar (in association with the Vienna Institute for International Economic Studies), 2000.

Hupchick, Dennis P. *The Balkans: From Constantinople to Communism*. New York, NY, Palgrave Macmillan, 2002.

Iwaskiw, Walter R. (Ed.). *Estonia, Latvia, and Lithuania: Country Studies*. Washington, DC, Federal Research Division, Library of Congress, 1996.

Janos, Andrew C. *East Central Europe in the Modern World: The Politics of the Borderlands from Pre- to Post-Communism*. Stanford, CA, Stanford University Press, 2000.

Jelavich, Barbara. *History of the Balkans: Twentieth Century*. Cambridge, Cambridge University Press, 1983.

History of the Balkans: Eighteenth and Nineteenth Centuries. Cambridge, Cambridge University Press, 1997 (first edn, 1983).

Jha, Shashikant (Ed.). *Ethnicity and Nation-building in Eastern Europe*. London, Sangam, 1998.

Joenniemi, Pertti, and Prikulis, Juris (Eds). *The Foreign Policies of the Baltic Countries: Basic Issues*. Rīga, Centre of Baltic-Nordic History and Political Studies, 1994.

Katzenstein, Peter J. (Ed.). *Mitteleuropa: Between Europe and Germany*. Providence, RI, Berghahn, 1997.

Kaplan, Robert D. *Balkan Ghosts: A Journey Through History*. New York, NY, St Martin's Press, 1993.

Kemp, Walter A. *Nationalism and Communism in Eastern Europe and the Soviet Union: a Basic Contradiction?* London, Macmillan, 1999.

Kenny, Padraic. *A Carnival of Revolution: Central Europe 1989*. Princeton, NJ, Princeton University Press, 2002.

Kenrick, Donald (Ed.). *The Gypsies during the Second World War No. 2: In the Shadow of the Swastika*. Hatfield, University of Hertfordshire University Press, 1999.

Kirschbaum, Stanislav J. (Ed.). *Historical Reflections on Central Europe: Selected Papers from the Fifth World Congress of Central and Eastern European Studies, Warsaw 1995*. London, Macmillan, 1999.

Klarer, Jürg, and Moldan, Bedrich (Eds). *The Environmental Challenge for Central European Economies in Transition.* Chichester, John Wiley, 1997.

Klein, Patricia V., Helweg, Arthur W., and McCrea, Barbara P. (Eds). *Struggling with the Communist Legacy: Studies of Yugoslavia, Romania, Poland and Czechoslovakia.* Boulder, CO, East European Monographs, 1998.

Köhn, Jörg, and Schiewer, Ulrich (Eds). *The Future of the Baltic Sea: Ecology, Economics, Administration and Teaching.* Marburg, Metropolis-Verlag, 1995.

Kola, Paulin. *The Myth of Greater Albania.* London, C. Hurst, 2002.

Koslowski, Rey. *Migrants and Citizens: Demographic Change in the European State System.* New York, NY, Cornell University Press, 2000.

Kozminski, Andrzej K., and Yip, George S. (Eds). *Strategies for Central and Eastern Europe.* London, Macmillan, 2000.

Kupferberg, Feiwel. *The Break-up of Communism in East Germany and Eastern Europe.* London, Macmillan, 1999.

Lendavi, Paul. *Blacklisted: A Journalists Life in Central Europe.* London, I. B. Tauris, 1998.

Levin, Don. *Baltic Jews under the Soviets 1940–1946.* Jerusalem, Hebrew University of Jerusalem, 1994.

Lewis, David W. P., and Lepesant, Gilles (Eds). *What Security for Which Europe? Case Studies from the Baltic to the Black Sea.* New York, NY, Peter Lang, 1999.

Lieven, Anatol. *The Baltic Revolution: Estonia, Latvia, Lithuania and the Path to Independence.* New Haven, CT, Yale University Press, 1993.

Los, Marie (Ed.). *The Second Economy in Marxist States.* London, Macmillan, 1990.

Luxmoore, Jonathan, and Babiuch, Jolanta. *The Vatican and the Red Flag: The Struggle for the Souls of Eastern Europe.* London, Geoffrey Chapman, 1999.

Magocsi, Paul Robert. *Historical Atlas of East Central Europe.* Seattle, WA, and London, University of Washington Press, 1993.

Mayhew, Alan. *Recreating Europe: The European Union's Policy towards Central and Eastern Europe.* Cambridge, Cambridge University Press, 1998.

Mazower, Mark. *The Balkans: A Short History.* London, Weidenfeld and Nicholson, 2000.

Mendelsohn, Ezra. *The Jews of East Central Europe between the Two World Wars.* Bloomington, IN, Indiana University Press, 1983 and 1987.

Meurs, Mieke (Ed.). *Many Shades of Red: State Policy and Collective Agriculture.* Lanham, MD, Rowman and Littlefield, 1999.

Miall, Hugh (Ed.). *Redefining Europe: New Patterns of Conflict and Co-operation.* London, Pinter, 1994.

Michas, Takis. *Unholy Alliance: Greece and Milošević's Serbia in the Nineties.* College Station, TX, A&M University Press, 2002.

Milanovic, Branko. *Income, Inequality, and Poverty during the Transition from Planned to Market Economy.* Washington, DC, World Bank, 1998.

Miller, David. *The Cold War: A Military History.* London, John Murray, 1998.

Misiunas, Romuald, and Taagepera, Rein. *The Baltic States: Years of Dependence, 1940–1990.* London, C. Hurst, 1993.

Moore, Deborah Dash. *East European Jews in Two Worlds: Studies from the Yivo Annual.* Evanston, IL, Northwestern University Press, 1990 (first published 1946).

Moseley, Christopher (Ed.). *From Baltic Shores: Short Stories.* Norwich, Norvik Press, University of East Anglia, 1994.

Müller, Johannes, Beddies, Christian H., Burgess, Robert M., Kramarenko, Vitali, and Mongardini, Joannes F. *The Baltic Countries: Medium-term Fiscal Issues related to EU and NATO Accession.* Washington, DC, IMF, 2002.

Müller, Rolf-Dieter, and Ueberschär, Gerd R. *Hitler's War in the East 1941-1945: A Critical Assessment.* Providence, RI, Berghahn, 1997.

Nadeau, Remi. *Stalin, Churchill and Roosevelt divide Europe.* New York, NY, Praeger, 1990.

Naimark, Norman M. *Fires of Hatred: Ethnic Cleansing in Twentieth-Century Europe.* Cambridge, MA, and London, Harvard University Press, 2001.

Nelson, Daniel N. (Ed.). *Local Politics in Communist Countries.* Lexington, KY, University Press of Kentucky, 1980.

Nelson, Joan M., Tilly, Charles, and Walker, Lee (Eds). *Transforming Post-Communist Political Economies.* Washington, DC, National Academy Press, 1997.

Nonneman, Gerd, Niblock, Tim, and Szajkowski, Bogdan (Eds). *Muslim Communities in the New Europe.* Reading, Garnet, 1996.

Paquette, Laure. *NATO and Eastern Europe after 2000: Strategic Interactions with Poland, the Czech Republic, Romania and Bulgaria.* New York, NY, Nova Science, 2001.

Parry, Ken, Melling, David J., Brady, Dimitri, Griffith, Sidney H., and Healey, John F. (Eds). *The Blackwell Dictionary of Eastern Christianity.* Oxford, Blackwell, 1999.

Pavlowitch, Stevan K. *A History of the Balkans 1804–1945.* London, Longman, 1999.

Perica, Vjekoslav. *Balkan Idols: Religion and Nationalism in Yugoslav States.* New York, NY, Oxford University Press, 2002.

Pettai, V., and Zielonka, J. (Eds). *The Road to the European Union: Lithuania, Estonia and Latvia (Europe in Change).* Manchester, Manchester University Press, 2003.

Plasser, Fritz, and Pribersky Andreas (Eds). *Political Culture in East Central Europe.* Aldershot, Ashgate, 1996.

Pogany, István. *Europe in Change: Righting Wrongs in Eastern Europe.* Manchester, Manchester University Press, 1997.

Poulton, Hugh. *The Balkans: Minorities and States in Conflict.* London, Minority Rights Publications, 1994 (second edition).

Poulton, Hugh, and Taji-Farouki, Suha (Eds). *Muslim Identity and the Balkan State.* London, C. Hurst (in association with the Islamic Council), 1997.

Preston, Christopher. *Enlargement and Integration in the European Union.* London, Routledge, 1997.

Pridham, Geoffrey, and Lewis, Paul G. (Eds). *Stabilizing Fragile Democracies: Comparing New Party Systems in Southern and Eastern Europe.* London, Routledge, 1996.

Rak, Shirin, Pilkington, Hilary, and Phizacklea, Annie (Eds). *Women in the Face of Change: The Soviet Union, Eastern Europe and China.* London, Routledge, 1992.

Ramet, Sabrina Petra (Ed.). *Protestantism and Politics in Eastern Europe and Russia: The Communist and Post-Communist Eras.* Durham, NC, Duke University Press, 1992.

Ramet, Pedro (Ed.). *Eastern Christianity and Politics in the Twentieth Century.* Durham, NC, Duke University Press, 1988.

Catholicism and Politics in Communist Societies. Durham, NC, Duke University Press, 1990.

Ramet, Sabrina P. *Eastern Europe: Politics, Culture and Society since 1939.* Bloomington, IN, Indiana University Press, 1998.

Ramet, Sabrina P (Ed.). *The Radical Right in Central and Eastern Europe since 1989.* University Park, PA, Pennsylvania State University Press, 1999.

Riff, Michael. A. *The Face of Survival: Jewish life in Eastern Europe Past and Present.* London, Valentine Mitchell, 1992.

Rothschild, Joseph. *East Central Europe between the Two World Wars.* Seattle, WA, University of Washington Press, 1977.

Rothschild, Joseph, and Wingfield, Nancy M. *Return to Diversity.* New York, NY, Oxford University Press Inc., 1999 (third edition).

Saxonberg, Steven. *The Fall: A Comparative Study of the End of Communism in Czechoslovakia, East Germany, Hungary and Poland.* Amsterdam, Harwood Academic, 2001.

Seaton-Watson, Hugh. *Eastern Europe 1918–1941.* Cambridge, Cambridge University Press, 1945.

The Pattern of Communist Revolution: A Historical Analysis. London, Methuen, 1953.

The East European Revolution. Boulder, CO, Westview Press, 1985.

Schapiro, Leonard. *Political Opposition in One Party States.* London, Macmillan, 1972.

Schenk, Karl-Ernst, Kruse, Jörn, and Müller Jürgen (Eds). *Telecommunications Takeoff in Transition Countries.* Aldershot, Ashgate, 1997.

Schöpflin, George. *Nations, Identity, Power: The New Politics of Europe.* London, C. Hurst, 2000.

Schöpflin, George. *Politics in Eastern Europe.* Oxford, Blackwell, 1993.

Sfikas, Thanasis D., and Williams, Christopher (Eds). *Ethnicity and Nationalism in East Central Europe and the Balkans.* Aldershot, Ashgate, 1999.

Shea, John. *Macedonia and Greece: The Struggle to Define a New Balkan Nation.* Jefferson, NC, McFarland, 1997.

Shoup, Paul S. (Ed.), and Hoffman, George W. *Problems of Balkan Security: South-eastern Europe in the 1990s.* Washington, DC, Wilson Centre Press, 1990.

Sluga, Glenda. *Culture and Society in Eastern Europe since 1945.* Leicester, Continuum Int. Publishing Group-Leicester University Press, 2003.

Smith, Alan. *The Return to Europe: The Re-integration of Eastern Europe into the European Economy.* London, Macmillan, 2000.

Smith, Graham (Ed.). *The Baltic States: The National Self Determination of Estonia, Latvia and Lithuania.* London, Macmillan, 1996 (reprint).

Smith, D. G. *et al. The Baltic States: Estonia, Latvia and Lithuania (Postcommunist States and Nations).* London, Routledge, 2002.

Smith, Jane, and Teague, Elizabeth (Eds). *Democracy in the New Europe: The Politics of Post-Communism.* London, Greycoat Press, 1999.

Spinka, Matthew. *A History of Christianity in the Balkans: A Study of the Spread of Byzantine Culture among the Slavs.* Chicago, IL, American Society of Church History, 1933.

Stehle, Hans-Jakob. *Eastern Politics of the Vatican 1917–1979.* Athens, OH, Ohio University Press, 1981.

Stephan, Johannes. *Economic Transition in Hungary and East Germany: Gradualism and Shock Therapy in Catch-up Development.* Studies in Economic Transition, London, Macmillan, 1999.

Stephenson, Paul. *Byzantium's Balkan Frontier.* Cambridge, Cambridge University Press, 2000.

Stokes, Gale. *The Walls Came Tumbling Down: The Collapse of Communism in Eastern Europe.* Oxford, Oxford University Press, 1993.

From Stalinism to Pluralism. New York, NY, Oxford University Press Inc., 1996 (revised edn).

Swain, Geoffrey, and Swain, Nigel. *Eastern Europe since 1945.* Basingstoke, Palgrave, 1998 (second edn).

Swettenham, John Alexander. *The Tragedy of the Baltic States.* London, Hollis and Carter, 1952.

Szemerkényi, Réka. *Central European Civil-Military Reforms at Risk: Progress in Establishing Democratic Controls over the Military Has Not Been Sustained.* London, Oxford University Press (for the International Institute for Strategic Studies), 1996.

Tägil, Sven. *Regions in the History of Central Europe.* London, C. Hurst, 1999.

Taras, Ray (Ed.). *National Identities and Ethnic Minorities in Eastern Europe: Selected Papers from the Fifth World Congress of Central and Eastern European Studies, Warsaw 1995.* London, Macmillan, 1998.

Teichova, Alice (Ed.). *Central Europe in the Twentieth Century: an Economic History Perspective.* Aldershot, Scholar Press, 1997.

Thaden, Edward C. (Ed.). *Russification in the Baltic Provinces and Finland, 1855–1914.* Princeton, NJ, Princeton University Press, 1981.

Tickle, Andrew, and Welsh, Ian (Eds). *Environment and Society in Eastern Europe.* Harlow, Longman, 1998.

Timmins, Graham, and Smith, Martin (Eds). *Uncertain Europe: Building a New European Security Order?* London, Routledge, 2001.

Todorova, Maria. *Imagining the Balkans.* New York, NY, and Oxford, Oxford University Press, 1997.

Tőkés, Rudolf L. *Opposition in Eastern Europe.* London, Macmillan, 1979.

Tsipis, Kosta (Ed.). *Common Security Regimes in the Balkans.* Boulder, CO, East European Monographs, 1996.

Turner, Barry (Ed.). *Central Europe Profiled: Essential Facts on Society, Politics and Business in Central Europe.* London, Macmillan, 2000.

Turnock, David. *Eastern Europe: An Historical Geography 1815–1945.* London, Routledge, 1989.

Eastern Europe: Economic and Political Geography. London, Routledge, 1989.

The East European Economy in Context. London, Routledge, 1997.

The States of Eastern Europe (2 vols). London, Routledge, 1999.

East Central Europe and the Former Soviet Union. London, Routledge, 2001.

The Human Geography of Central and Eastern Europe. London, Routledge, 2002.

Turnock, David, and Carter, Francis W. (Eds). *The States of Eastern Europe, Vol. 1: North-Eastern Europe.* Aldershot, Ashgate, 1999.

The States of Eastern Europe Vol. 2: South-Eastern Europe. Aldershot, Ashgate, 1999.

Turnock, David (Ed.). *Privatization in Rural Eastern Europe: the Process of Restitution and Restructuring.* Cheltenham, Edward Elgar, 1998.

Vago, Bela, and Mosse, George (Eds). *Jews and Non-Jews in Eastern Europe, 1918–1945.* New York, NY, John Wiley, 1974.

Vaknin, Sam. *After the Rain: How the West lost the East.* Prague, Narcissus, 2000.

Van Brabant, Jozef M. *The Transformation of Eastern Europe: joining the European Integration Movement.* New York, NY, Nova Science, 1995.

Van Creveld, Martin. *Hitler's Strategy 1940–1941: The Balkan Clue.* Cambridge, Cambridge University Press, 1973.

Van Den Bempt, Paul, and Theelen, Greet. *From Europe Agreements to Accession: the Integration of the Central and East European Countries into the European Union.* Brussels, European Inter-University Press, 1996.

Van Oudenaren, John. *Uniting Europe: European Integration and the Post-Cold War World.* Lanham, MD, Rowman and Littlefield, 2000.

Vertovec, Steven, and Peach, Ceri (Eds). *Islam in Europe: the Politics of Religion and Community.* Basingstoke, Macmillan, 1997.

Volkan, Vamik D., and Itzkowitz, Norman. *Turks and Greeks: Neighbours in Conflict.* Huntingdon, Eothen Press, 1994.

Von Rauch, Georg. *The Baltic States: Years of Independence, 1917-1940.* London, C. Hurst, 1995.

Vukmanović, Svetozar. *Struggle for the Balkans.* London, Merlin, 1980 (English translation 1990).

Wädekin, Karl-Eugen (Ed.). *Communist Agriculture: Farming in the Soviet Union and Eastern Europe.* London, Routledge, 1990.

Wegren, Stephen K. *Land Reform in the former Soviet Union and Eastern Europe.* London, Routledge, 1998.

Westing, Arthur H. (Ed.). *Comprehensive Security for the Baltic: An Environmental Approach.* London, Sage, 1989.

White, George W. *Nationalism and Territory: Constructing Group Identity in South-Eastern Europe.* Lanham, MD, Rowman and Littlefield, 2000.

White, Stephen, Batt, Judy, and Lewis, Paul G. (Eds). *Developments in Central and East European Politics 2.* London, Macmillan, 1998.

Williams, Kieran, and Deletant, Dennis. *Security Intelligence Services in New Democracies: The Czech Republic, Slovakia and Romania*. Basingstoke, Palgrave, 2001.

Winchester, Simon. *The Fracture Zone: A Return to the Balkans*. London, Penguin, 1999.

Woodward, Susan. *Balkan Tragedy*. Washington, DC, Brookings Institution, 1995.

Socialist Unemployment. Princeton, NJ, Princeton University Press, 1995.

INDEX OF REGIONAL ORGANIZATIONS

(Main reference only)

THE EUROPA WORLD YEAR BOOK 2003

Globally respected as one of the world's leading reference resources, this 44th edition contains:

- Detailed surveys of over 250 countries and territories
- A comprehensive listing of over 1,650 international organizations
- Access to the very latest statistics, directory information and current analysis
- An in-depth and up-to-date focus on world-wide affairs

THE WORLD OF LEARNING 2004

An invaluable directory and reference resource covering over 30,000 academic institutions and 200,000 staff and officials. Includes universities and colleges as well as details on international cultural, scientific and educational organizations.

- Extensive coverage of over 3,000 universities and colleges
- Information on over 400 international cultural, scientific and educational organizations
- Completely revised and updated every year

THE INTERNATIONAL WHO'S WHO 2004

Outlines the lives and achievements of some 20,000 of the most influential men and women globally. From heads of state, politicians, religious leaders and ambassadors, to the eminent and successful in business, finance, technology, film, music, fashion, sport, literature and the performing arts.

- Entries are included on merit, achievement and for their continuing interest and importance
- Fully updated every year to ensure accuracy
- Provides invaluable information on the headline-makers
- Replaces numerous single-nation directories, saving time and money in research

THE INTERNATIONAL FOUNDATION DIRECTORY 2003

This newly revised directory of international foundations, trusts, charitable and grant-making NGOs and other similar non-profit institutions provides a comprehensive picture of foundation activity on a world scale.

- Introductory essays cover the history and development of the third sector; researching and applying to foundations; globalization and foundations
- Foundations are arranged by country
- Each entry contains the institution's name, postal, internet and e-mail addresses, telephone and fax numbers, together with full details about the foundation including, date of establishment and details of the organization's function, activities, restrictions on grants, geographical area of activity, finances, publications and key executives

THE EUROPA DIRECTORY OF INTERNATIONAL ORGANIZATIONS 2003

An extensive and unequalled one-volume guide to international organizations.

- Introductory essays define the changing role of international organizations in today's world
- A chronology charts the historical development of international organizations
- Texts of significant international charters, treaties and documents
- Lists of key UN Security Council and General Assembly resolutions, plus information about peace-keeping activities
- A who's who of leading officials within international organizations
- A directory and further information on each organization, including contact information, details of membership, leading officials, activities, finance, publications and subsidiary organizations

For further information on any of the above titles contact our marketing department on:
tel: + 44 (0) 20 7842 2110
fax: + 44 (0) 20 7842 2249
e-mail: info.europa@tandf.co.uk
web: www.europapublications.com

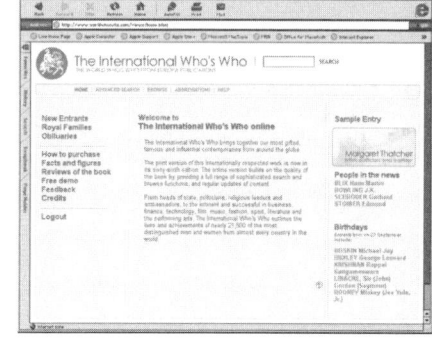

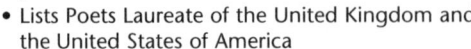